The TIME ALMANAC 1999

BORGNA BRUNNER
EDITOR

Information Please LLC
www.infoplease.com

The Time Almanac welcomes comments and suggestions from readers. Though the editors carefully consider each suggestion, because of the volume of correspondence we receive we cannot respond personally to each writer. The *Time Almanac* does not rule on bets or wagers.

Editorial Office
Information Please LLC
31 St. James Avenue
Boston, MA 02116-4101
Email: ipa@infoplease.com

Customer Service
Attention: Time Almanac
PO Box 11016
Des Moines, IA 50336-1016

ISBN: 1-883013-46-1 Paperback
ISBN: 1-883013-51-8 Hardcover
ISSN: 0073-7860

If you would like to order additional copies of any Time books, please call us at 1-800-327-6388 (Monday through Friday, 7:00 a.m.–8:00 p.m. or Saturday, 7:00 a.m.–6:00 p.m. Central Time).

Printed in the United States of America.
WP Pa BP Hbd 10 9 8 7 6 5 4 3 2 1

Keyword Index

Section Index

COMPREHENSIVE INDEX

Page numbers followed by "n" indicate information in footnotes.

A

D

E

H

J

K

N

O

Q

R

U

THE TIME ALMANAC 1999

Throughout 1998 computer programmers battled the Millennium Bug, a tiny glitch built into the machine, which threatened to crash the world's information infrastructure precisely at the turn of the century. It was an apt symbol for the year, when the virus of uncertainty proved contagious, and the buoyant optimism of the mid-1990s trailed off into a flurry of question marks: Would Bill Clinton's presidency survive a sex scandal—or end in impeachment or resignation? Could Boris Yeltsin's Russia survive an ongoing economic collapse? Would Wall Street's long-running bull market finally crash in the wake of Asia's fiscal crisis? To escape the uneasy sense of danger ahead, Americans flocked to the most successful movie in decades: Titanic.

CURRENT EVENTS

The News of 1998: Nation

High Crimes or Misdemeanors?

The Clinton sex scandal of course eclipsed all other news events in 1998. President Clinton's foreign policy triumphs—his significant contributions to the peace accords in Northern Ireland and the Middle East—shone dimly next to the glare generated by his affair with a young White House intern, Monica Lewinsky. In his Jan. 1998 testimony in the Paula Jones sexual harassment suit, Clinton denied that he had had a sexual relationship with the intern and had attempted to cover it up. When word of the alleged affair became public, he again adamantly denied it. The allegations gave new impetus to Independent Counsel Kenneth Starr's 41-month, $40-million investigation of the Whitewater real estate deal and other possible presidential wrongdoings. Finally, on Aug. 17, 1998, after relentless media attention, leaks, and news of Lewinsky's upcoming testimony, President Clinton admitted to having had an "inappropriate" relationship with the intern. The President's overall popularity among Americans, however, remained high. The country seemed willing to ignore Clinton's weaknesses in character as long as the economy was good, his policies were popular, and the United States remained strong abroad.

The "Starr Report" was released to the House of Representatives on Sept. 9. While the report outlined 11 possible grounds for impeachment stemming from the Lewinsky affair, it did not cite any impeachable offenses relating to the original subjects of the investigation, including Whitewater. Starr's accusations against Clinton included perjury, witness tampering, and obstruction of justice. Highly embarrassing to Clinton in its attention to sexual detail, the report was seen by the President's supporters as a gratuitously libidinous, politically inspired vendetta by Starr, a conservative Republican. A videotape of the President's testimony before the grand jury was released on Sept. 21, showing Clinton evading questions about his sexual relationship through legalistic hedging. As calls for the President's impeachment were raised, the definition of "high crimes and misdemeanors" was debated, with public opinion ranging from contentions that Clinton was morally unfit for the presidency to the belief that betraying his wife, however reprehensible, was not the same as betraying his country. Although polls clearly indicated that Americans had no stomach for impeachment hearings, on Oct. 8 the House of Representatives voted largely along party lines (258–178) to conduct a wide-ranging impeachment inquiry, slated to begin after November's Congressional elections.

Congress: Lewinsky or Legislation?

Not only the President, but Congress itself was in danger of having its reputation rest on the sex scandal. With the public's approval ratings of Congress only 43% in Sept. 1998, many Americans felt Congress's partisan exploitation of Clinton's troubles occurred at the expense of legislative achievement, preventing either side from keeping its promises. Democrats failed to raise the minimum wage, tackle the tobacco industry, follow through on a "patient's bill of rights," or reform the campaign finance system, while Republicans failed to produce a tax cut or override the veto of the "partial-birth" abortion bill. Neither party faced the social security issue. Congress's achievements included an overhaul of the I.R.S., increased educational funding, and the expansion of NATO. In its final act of the term, Congress hastily cobbled together a 4,000-page budget laden with pork—including a $1.1 million manure-handling project in Mississippi and $1 million for peanut research in Georgia—which only reinforced Americans' growing cynicism toward their government.

The Iraqi Albatross

U.S. foreign policy was dominated in 1998 by continued difficulties with Iraq. On Nov. 13, 1997, Iraq expelled the American members of the U.N. inspection team mandated to determine whether Iraq had destroyed its nuclear, biological, and ballistic weapons. Under the 1991 Gulf War cease-fire resolution, the U.N. had agreed not to lift sanctions until Iraq's full compliance had been verified. As the inspection standoff stretched over months, the U.S. began a military build-up in the Gulf. In Feb. 1998 U.N. Secretary-General Kofi Annan brokered a peaceful solution, but over the next months, Baghdad continued to impede inspections, finally putting a complete halt to them in Aug. 1998. A number of countries condemned the U.S.'s inflexibility on sanctions, which they saw as responsible for the appalling humanitarian crisis in Iraq. The United States, however, faulted President Saddam Hussein for his own people's misery—he had only to comply with the U.N. agreement to end their suffering. Although repeatedly frustrated with the U.N.'s seemingly oversolicitous attitude toward Iraq, after the August standoff the U.S. opted for diplomatic arm-twisting instead of a military solution. In September the U.N. Security Council unanimously affirmed that there would be no talk of lifting sanctions without U.N. inspections. Yet the brief solidarity the U.S. felt with the U.N. faded when no progress occurred and Hussein resumed his defiant shell game.

Playing Hardball with Terrorism

The Clinton Administration demonstrated an atypically aggressive response toward terrorism after an assault on two U.S. embassies in Africa. On Aug. 7, the U.S. embassies in Nairobi, Kenya, and Dar es Salaam, Tanzania, were bombed by terrorists, leaving 258 people dead and more than 5,000 injured. In response, the U.S. launched cruise missiles on Aug. 20, 1998, striking a terrorism training complex in Afghanistan and destroying a pharmaceutical manufacturing facility in Khartoum, Sudan, that reportedly produced nerve gas. Both targets were believed to have been financed by wealthy Islamic radical Osama bin Laden, who was allegedly behind the embassy bombings as well as an international terrorism network targeting the United States. Serious doubts have been raised about whether the pharmaceutical company was indeed involved in terrorist activities, or whether the U.S. made an ill-conceived, trigger-happy strike against a nation it has long considered a pariah state. Past U.S. foreign policy has opted for the use of sanctions or a U.N. resolution authorizing the use of force, but the U.N.'s flaccid dealings with Iraq, the lack of support from Muslim allies (most notably the Saudis' indifference to the 1996 truck bomb explosion that killed 19 U.S. service members), and the necessity of deterring attacks on other American embassies led to the U.S.'s more hawkish policy.

The News of 1998: World

South Asia's Nuclear States

India and Pakistan raised fears of a budding Asian nuclear arms race when each detonated nuclear tests in May 1998. Just two months after staunch Hindu nationalist Atal Bihari Vajpayee became prime minister, India unexpectedly set off an underground nuclear explosive near the Pakistani border. The May 11 test violated the Nuclear Proliferation Prevention Act of 1994, a worldwide ban on nuclear testing. International condemnation was immediate. Two days later, India defiantly conducted two more explosions. On May 29 and 30, Pakistan, bristling at what it saw as its enemy's deliberate provocation, responded with several nuclear tests of its own, despite international urgings of restraint.

At the basis of India and Pakistan's show of nuclear brinkmanship was the disputed territory of Kashmir, which had already caused two wars between the countries as well as a half-century of acrimony. Slapped with sanctions by the U.S. and other countries, Pakistan and India agreed in October (with major caveats) to sign the Comprehensive Test Ban Treaty.

The possibility of Asian nuclear proliferation resurfaced when North Korea launched a test missile over Japan in Sept. 1998. Although North Korea claimed it had simply launched a scientific satellite, Japan and much of the rest of the world remained apprehensive over North Korea's commitment to the 1994 non-proliferation treaty.

Asian Financial Crisis Trickles Down

When Thailand's economy, once one of the strongest in Asia, collapsed under the weight of foreign debt in 1997, its downfall set off a chain reaction in the region, sparking the Asian currency crisis. While far from completely recovered in 1998, Thailand appeared to be in better condition than many of its Asian neighbors, whose financial downturn provoked political upheaval.

When banks in Indonesia failed and the value of the country's currency plummeted, anti-government demonstrations and riots broke out in early 1998. As food shortages and unemployment overwhelmed the nation—the fourth most populous in the world—President Suharto's ouster was demanded. On May 21, 1998, Suharto stepped down after 32 years of authoritarian rule and crony capitalism and was replaced by his little-known protégé, B. J. Habibie.

South Korea's currency also underwent a massive devaluation in 1997, and the subsequent political instability brought Kim Dae Jung to power in Feb. 1998. Once imprisoned as a dissident, Kim became the first South Korean president ever elected from the political opposition.

In fall 1998, disagreement over how to rectify Malaysia's economic downturn led Prime Minister Mahathir bin Mohamad to denounce and jail his heir apparent, Anwar Ibrahim, inciting protests throughout the country.

But the international community was most alarmed when Japan's economy, the world's second-largest after the United States, began experiencing its worst recession since World War II, leading to the resignation of Prime Minister Ryutaro Hashimoto in July 1998. Japan's uncharacteristic vulnerability augured the development of the Asian crisis into a global one.

The Russian Market Collapse

The crippling economic epidemic spread to Russia when its currency began to plummet in Nov. 1997, finally collapsing the following year. In Aug. 1998, the ruble was devalued and by Aug. 25 had taken its worst fall in four years. In a futile attempt to stem the tide, President Boris Yeltsin dismissed his entire government twice over the course of 1998. Russia's financial emergency quickly spread through the Commonwealth of Independent States, particularly to the Ukraine and Belarus, whose Soviet-style planned economies are highly dependent on Russia. Farther afield, markets around the world dropped, and on Aug. 31 the Dow Jones Industrial Average fell 512 points, its second-greatest single-day fall ever.

Kosovo Bleeds

Since Feb. 1998 the Yugoslav army and Serbian police have fought against the separatist Kosovo Liberation Army, but their scorched-earth tactics have been concentrated on ethnic Albanian civilians—Muslims who make up 90% of Kosovo's population. More than 900 Kosovars have been killed in the fighting this year, and the hundreds of thousands forced to flee their homes are without adequate food and shelter. Although Serbs make up only 10% of Kosovo's population, the region figures strongly in Serbian nationalist mythology.

NATO was reluctant to intervene because Kosovo—unlike Bosnia in 1992—was legally a province of Yugoslavia. The proof of civilian massacres finally gave NATO the impetus to intervene for the first time ever in the dealings of a sovereign nation with its own people. In an agreement brokered by American diplomat Richard Holbrooke, and under the threat of a military air strike—for which there was little enthusiasm among several NATO countries—President Slobodan Milosevic agreed to the withdrawal of military forces and to future elections in Kosovo.

A Small Step for Middle East Peace . . .

An Oct. 1998 summit at Wye Mills, Md., generated the first real progress in the stymied Middle East peace talks in 19 months. With President Bill Clinton mediating—and a late assist from an ailing King Hussein of Jordan—Israeli Prime Minister Benjamin Netanyahu and Palestinian President Yasir Arafat settled several important interim issues called for by the 1993 Oslo Peace Accords. The Palestinians agreed to remove language from their founding charter that called for the dismantling of the Jewish state; Israelis agreed to cede an additional 13% percent of the West Bank.

But several highly sensitive issues—Palestinian statehood, the drawing of borders, and the status of Jerusalem—went unbroached, although only six months remained before the Oslo Accord deadline of May 4, 1999. If significant progress were not made by then, Arafat threatened to unilaterally declare a Palestinian state, which would inevitably lead to retaliation by Israel.

A Giant Step for Northern Ireland

A more definitive peace was achieved in Northern Ireland, where sectarian violence between Catholics and Protestants has resulted in more than 3,000 deaths since 1969. The landmark settlement, the Good Friday Accord of April 10, 1998, came after 22 months of intensive negotiations that involved eight of the ten Northern Irish political parties.

Chaired by former U.S. Senator George Mitchell, the talks were advanced by a high-profile set of mediators, including British Prime Minister Tony Blair, Irish Prime Minister Bertie Ahern, and President Bill Clinton. Two participating groups, the Protestant Ulster Democratic Party and Sinn Fein, were temporarily suspended from the talks because of continued paramilitary activities.

The accord called for Protestants to share political power with the minority Catholics, and gave the Republic of Ireland a voice in Northern Irish affairs. In turn, Catholics were to suspend the goal of a united Ireland—a territorial claim that was the raison d'être of the IRA and was written into the Irish Republic's constitution—unless the largely Protestant North voted in favor of such an arrangement, an unlikely occurrence.

The resounding commitment to the settlement was demonstrated in a dual referendum on May 22: the North approved the accord by a vote of 71% to 29%, and in the Irish Republic 94% favored it. But the deaths of three Catholic boys in July 1998 during the traditional Protestant marches through Catholic neighborhoods was an appalling reminder of the fragility of peace. In October, the Nobel Peace Prize was awarded to John Hume and David Trimble, leaders of the largest Catholic and Protestant political parties, an incentive for all sides to ensure that this time the peace would last. □

What Happened in 1998: Month by Month

Highlights of key events of the year, organized month by month, in three categories for easy reference. For the year's major Supreme Court decisions, *see* pp. 98–99, and for more 1998 business news, *see* pp. 822–824. Countries of the World covers specific international events, country by country. *See* Milestones for more people in the news and obituaries.

January 1998

WORLD

Netanyahu Survives Parliamentary Test (Jan. 4): Israeli Prime Minister's majority threatened by resignation of Foreign Minister David Levy. **(Jan. 5):** Netanyahu blocks challenge to government when Parliament approves 1998 budget by vote of 58 to 52.

Major Hong Kong Bank Shuts Down (Jan. 12): Peregrine Investments Holdings is first major casualty of Asia's economic and currency crisis.

Israel Sets Stringent Terms for Withdrawal (Jan. 13): Demands Palestinians accept new conditions before any further Israeli departure from West Bank.

Iraq Blocks Weapons Inspection (Jan. 13): Charges American in charge, William Scott Ritter Jr., is a spy. **(Jan. 17):** President Saddam Hussein threatens to expel United Nations arms inspectors in six months if Iraq is not cleared of suspicion of arms violations and U.N. sanctions are not lifted.

Drastic Economic Reforms for Indonesia (Jan. 15): President Suharto signs agreement with International Monetary Fund for economic bailout in exchange for curbs on spending and dismantling of monopolies that enriched family and friends.

Turkish Court Orders Islamic Party Disbanded (Jan. 16): Highest tribunal rules that nation's largest political party works to overthrow the secular government.

Clinton Signs Charter With 3 Baltic Nations (Jan. 16): Affirms partnership with presidents of Estonia, Latvia, and Lithuania and pledges United States support for their aspirations to join NATO.

Clinton Offers Netanyahu Withdrawal Plan (Jan. 20): In White House conference, President proposes phased pullout of Israel from West Bank. Netanyahu insists that redeployment depends on compliance with Israeli demands, including rights of settlers.

Pope Visits Cuba for Five Days (Jan. 21–25): John Paul II preaches against abortion and for improved education, calls for release of political prisoners, stresses human rights, and criticizes U.S. embargo.

U.S. and Japan Settle Major Trade Dispute (Jan. 30): Agree to remove most restrictions on air traffic between them, and to provide more service.

NATION

Clinton Proposes Expanding Medicare (Jan. 6): Offers plan for system to cover hundreds of thousands of early retirees, laid-off workers and uninsured Americans between ages of 55 and 65.

Clinton Proposes Funds for Child Care (Jan. 7): Seeks to spend $21 billion in grants and tax breaks over next five years. Republican opposition likely.

Asian Crisis Pushes U.S. Stocks Down (Jan. 9): Dow Jones average falls nearly 3 percent as fears over effect on U.S. economy spur selling wave.

President Questioned in Paula Jones Case (Jan. 17): In six-hour session, defends himself under oath against allegation of sexual misconduct when Governor.

White House Sex Scandal Charged (Jan. 21, et seq.): President Clinton denies allegations of sexual affair with intern, Monica S. Lewinsky. Whitewater Independent Counsel Ken Starr presses investigation of new charges. **(Jan. 27):** President's wife brands investigation part of a "vast right-wing conspiracy." **(Jan. 29):** U.S. judge in Arkansas forbids use of Lewinsky evidence in sexual harassment suit against President.

BUSINESS/SCIENCE/SOCIETY

U.S. Jury Blocks Death Penalty in Second Bombing Trial (Jan. 7): Jury divided on extent of Terry L. Nichols's role in Oklahoma City bombing. Panel had convicted him of conspiracy but not of committing terrorist act. Judge to decide on prison term.

Unabomber Pleads Guilty (Jan. 8): Case of Theodore J. Kaczynski thrown into turmoil with report that he had attempted suicide. **(Jan. 22):** In Sacramento Federal Court, he admits to having killed and maimed people with package bombs. With his request to represent himself denied by a judge, he agrees to plead guilty to all U.S. charges. Kaczynski accepts unconditional sentence of life in prison without parole and gives up right to appeal.

Storm Cripples Northeast (Jan. 9): Floods and freezing rain knock out power lines for more than a million people in upstate New York, New England, and Canada. **(Jan. 12):** Fifteen dead in Eastern Canada as dangerous cold spell adds to havoc.

Bombing Mastermind Gets Life (Jan. 9): U.S. judge sentences Ramzi Ahmed Yousef to solitary confinement for role in 1993 bombing of New York's World Trade Center.

Court Bars Dismissal of Gay Sailor (Jan. 26): U.S. judge accuses Navy of "search and outing" mission against chief petty officer who posted on-line computer message describing marital status as gay.

February 1998

WORLD

Cuba Responds to Pope's Appeal (Feb. 12): Havana announces it will free more than 200 prisoners held on political and other charges, in answer to appeal by John Paul II during his Jan. trip to Cuba.

Sinn Fein Expelled From Peace Talks (Feb. 20): Irish and British governments take temporary measures against political wing of Irish Republican Army.

Iraq Reported to Agree to Lift Arms Inspection Ban (Feb. 22): U.N. reveals agreement with President Saddam Hussein to permit access to presidential properties. **(Feb 25):** Clinton seeks British, French, and Russian support for Security Council resolution warning against violation of pact.

P. W. Botha Pleads Not Guilty to Contempt (Feb. 23): Former South African president denies charges. Accuses Truth and Reconciliation Commission of breaking agreement to let him testify in writing.

Israeli Intelligence Chief Resigns (Feb. 24): Danny Yatom, head of the Israeli intelligence agency the Mossad, resigns under heavy agency pressure to accept responsibility for bungled attack on a top Palestinian militant in Jordan in 1997.

Swiss Confirm Capture of Israeli Agents (Feb. 26): Acknowledge that five agents of the Mossad were trapped while trying to bug house in Bern thought by some to be Iranian diplomatic base.

NATION

F.D.A. Revises Rules on Financial Disclosure (Feb. 2): Requires physicians who try out new drugs and medical devices to reveal whether they received stock or other financial support from manufacturers.

First Balanced Budget in 30 Years (Feb. 3): President holds out possibility of surplus after five years of steady economic growth and cautious spending.

Clinton Friend Surrenders in Campaign Finance Inquiry (Feb. 3): Yah Lin Trie, Democratic fund-raiser, returns after fleeing U.S. when finance scandals broke out.

National Airport Named for Reagan (Feb. 4): Congress votes to honor former President for 87th birthday by renaming Washington National Airport.

"China Area" Linked to Campaign Donations (Feb. 10): Republican investigation finds illegal gifts to Democrats were linked to "greater China area" but cannot establish a role for Beijing Government.

New Surgeon General Confirmed (Feb. 10): Senate approves Dr. David Satcher, first in three years to fill post marked by disputes over abortion and family values.

Senate Rejects Ban on Human Cloning (Feb. 11): Defeats Republican measure that aroused concerns over effect of bill on scientific research.

Line-Item Veto Ruled Unconstitutional (Feb. 12): U.S. judge rebuffs Clinton and G.O.P. in Congress over measure to allow veto of individual items in a bill.

Executive Privilege Reported Invoked by Clinton (Feb. 24): Lawyers say President seeks to shield top assistants from testifying before grand jury about White House discussions on Monica Lewinsky inquiry.

Senate Blocks Campaign Spending Reform (Feb. 26): Delays revision for at least a year in face of Republican filibuster, after yearlong investigation of abuses in 1996 election. Close vote results in continued debate.

BUSINESS/SCIENCE/SOCIETY

Texas Execution Ends Controversy (Feb. 3): State puts to death its first woman to be executed since Civil War. Karla Faye Tucker, 38, killed two people with a pick ax 15 years earlier.

U.S. Plane Cuts Ski Cable in Italy; 20 Killed (Feb. 3): Low-flying Marine Corps craft on training flight over Dolomite mountains sends car plunging 260 feet.

Auto Makers Compromise on Emissions (Feb. 4): General Motors, Ford, and Chrysler agree to produce cleaner cars than government standards require.

Thousands Dead in Afghanistan Quake (Feb. 4, et seq.): Thousands more reported homeless and injured in remote northeastern area. New tremors destroy villages and split mountain roads, hindering relief.

Winter Olympic Games Open in Japan (Feb. 7): Final games of 20th century begin in Nagano with celebration of traditional Japanese culture.

Judge Backs Disabled Golfer on Cart (Feb. 11): Casey Martin wins suit under Americans With Disabilities Act for right to transportation in professional tournaments.

Cigarette Maker Altered Nicotine Content (Feb. 22): Industry documents suggest that R. J. Reynolds, one of largest producers, altered content in apparent belief that it increased effect on smokers.

Megan's Laws Allowed to Stand (Feb. 23): Justices reject constitutional challenges to statutes in New York and New Jersey providing for communities to be notified of presence of paroled sex offenders.

March 1998

WORLD

Russian Atomic Minister Ousted (March 2): Viktor N. Mikhailov, influential in nation's military and civilian nuclear establishment, dismissed to surprise of many.

Serbs Battle Ethnic Albanians (March 5, et seq.): Hundreds of police reported to fire mortar rounds, set homes on fire, and shoot men in villages in central Kosovo Province, in sweep to stamp out separatist movement. **(March 9):** U.S. and allies decide to impose modest diplomatic and economic sanctions on Yugoslavia for "unacceptable" use of force. Serbian police renew counter-insurgency action. More than 80 reported dead in Kosovo.

Russia Plans Nuclear Reactor Sales to Iran (March 6): In rebuff to U.S., Moscow's Atomic Energy Ministry reveals plan to supply additional equipment.

Rightist Leader Resigns in Chile (March 10): Gen. Augusto Pinochet quits as armed forces commander-in-chief to be sworn in as senator for life. His 17 years as dictator were marked by mass killings.

Financial Scandals Erupt in Japan (March 12): Prosecutors raid central bank and arrest official suspected of leaking secrets to nation's banks.

A Sweeping Amnesty in South Korea (March 13): President Kim Dae Jung frees scores of political prisoners and clears records of 5.5 million Koreans.

U.S. Drops Condemnation of China (March 13): Administration abandons sponsorship of U.N.'s annual resolution criticizing Beijing on human rights record.

Vatican Regrets Inaction in Holocaust (March 16): Document, an "act of repentance," admits failure of Roman Catholic Church to deter mass killing of Jews during World War II.

Major Reforms Pledged for China (March 19): Zhu Rongji, new Prime Minister, outlines sweeping 3-year program for changes to make state-owned industries solvent, overhaul banking system, and redesign Government.

India's Prime Minister Sworn In (March 19): Ascendancy of Hindu nationalist Atal Bihari Vajpayee alarms Muslims, moderate Hindus.

Yeltsin Dismisses Entire Cabinet (March 23): In display of power, he includes trusted Prime Minister Viktor S. Chernomyrdin among those on list. **(March 27):** President appoints Sergei Kiriyenko, 35, a reform-minded banker, to succeed Chernomyrdin.

Iraq Arrests Germ Weapons Specialist (March 23): Baghdad reports detention of Dr. Nassir al-Hindawi as he was preparing to flee country. Action is blow to U.N. arms inspectors, who had hoped to interview him.

Clinton Acclaimed on Visit to Africa (March 23, et seq.): Opens 12-day tour with speech in Ghana pledging more U.S. interest and aid. **(March 24):** In Uganda, President expresses regret for American role in African slavery. **(March 25):** In Uganda conference he gets commitment from six East African leaders to work for democracy. **(March 26):** In Cape Town, South Africa, Clinton says U.S. has "profound" stake in nation's new democracy.

Saudis End Inquiry Into U.S. Airmen's Deaths (March 30): Saudi Arabian government delays report on investigation into 1996 terrorist bombing that killed 19 Americans.

NATION

Top Army Soldier Cleared of Sex Charges (March 13): Court martial acquits Sergeant Major Gene C. McKinney of sexual misconduct, but convicts him on one count of obstructing justice. **(March 16):** Military jury metes mild sentence of reprimand and rules that Sgt. McKinney get one-step demotion to master sergeant.

Volunteer Recalls Approach by Clinton (March 15): In TV interview, Kathleen E. Willey, a 51-year-old former White House assistant, says President made unwanted sexual approach. **(March 16):** White House releases correspondence showing that Ms. Willey maintained cordial relationship with President in four years since alleged incident.

Democratic Fund-Raiser Pleads Guilty (March 16): Johnny Chung, California businessman, faces sentence on charges of bank fraud, tax evasion, and conspiracy in connection with $20,000 in illegal contributions to Clinton-Gore re-election campaign.

Clinton Invokes Executive Privilege (March 20): Also calls on attorney-client relationship privilege to block testimony by senior White House aides in grand jury investigation of alleged Monica Lewinsky affair.

House Defeats Election Reform Bill (March 30): Approves only two minor changes in campaign law. Bars floor debate on bipartisan plan for major overhaul.

Democrats Offer Patient Protection Bill (March 31): Leaders in Congress say legislation would regulate practices of health insurance companies and health maintenance organizations. Consumer groups, unions, and American Medical Association support plan.

BUSINESS/SCIENCE/SOCIETY

Princess Diana's Two Sons Share Bulk of Estate (March 2): Will allots total of $21.3 million to Princes William and Harry.

Austria to Return Confiscated Artworks (March 6): Owners to receive possessions seized by Nazis from Jews and kept in Vienna museums as national treasures.

Vitamin E Found to Cut Prostate Cancer Risk (March 17): Researchers in Finland say pills reduced incidence by a third and death rate by 41 percent in study of thousands of smokers. Vitamin A had no effect.

Presbyterians Keep Ban on Gay Clergy (March 18): Regional bodies of Presbyterian Church (USA) vote against replacing law with broader statute that would be open to individual interpretation.

Three Nations Announce Oil Production Cut (March 22): Saudi Arabia, Venezuela, and Mexico cooperate in move expected to reverse sharp drop in world prices. Other countries also expected to reduce output.

Two Boys Kill 5 at Arkansas School (March 24): Boy, 13, and cousin, 11, slay four girls and a teacher. Also wound 11 at Jonesboro middle school. Older boy said to have vowed to kill all girls who had broken up with him. Killers seized while fleeing.

F.D.A. Approves Male Impotence Pill (March 27): Prescription drug, sildenafil citrate, or Viagra, is made by Pfizer Inc. It acts on normal physiological system.

El Niño Loses Influence (March 29): Effects of Pacific Ocean high sea-surface temperature wane as spring relieves North America's harmful weather pattern.

April 1998

WORLD

Indonesia Reaches Third Pact With I.M.F. (April 7): Agreement offers new proposals for rescuing economy. It is new effort to get Indonesia to meet conditions allowing $43 billion in aid.

Experts Dispute Iraq's Germ Warfare Stand (April 9): After review, independent team rejects contention by Saddam Hussein that Baghdad has made progress in eliminating biological weapons.

Northern Ireland Accord Reached (April 10): Landmark settlement exacts concessions from both Protestants and Roman Catholics. Under plan, both groups will govern jointly. Britain retains Ulster, with Republic gaining voice in affairs. Two referendums scheduled.

Iraq Executes at Least 1,500 During Year (April 13): Most were for political reasons, according to report for United Nations Human Rights Commission.

Somali Gunmen Kidnap Nine Foreigners (April 15): Capture Red Cross workers in the capital, Mogadishu, even as main faction leaders reach agreement in Nairobi conference to set up a new government.

Israel Improves Human Rights Standards (April 15): Releases Ahmad Quatamesh, 46, longest-serving Palestinian prisoner held without trial. He was jailed on suspicion of being a leader of Popular Front for the Liberation of Palestine.

Free Trade Zone for Americas Planned (April 19): Leaders of 34 nations schedule talks and set goal of signing agreement in 2005.

China Releases a Top Dissident (April 19): Wang Dan, a leader in Tiananmen Square democracy movement, enters exile in United States. Move viewed as step to win favor with Clinton administration.

Irish Parliament Backs Peace Agreement (April 22): Gives nearly unanimous approval to accord for British Ulster reached by Protestants and Roman Catholics.

U.S. Bans Arms Exports to Britain (April 22): Revokes all pending licenses in first step to halt sales of weapons to all 15 nations of European Union.

Parliament Approves Yeltsin Appointee (April 24): Lower house votes 251–25, after long dispute, to confirm Sergei Kiriyenko, 35, as Russian Prime Minister.

Crowds View Rwanda Executions (April 24): Tens of thousands watch as police shoot 22 prisoners convicted of genocide crimes. Government had rejected international appeals for stay of executions.

NATION

Court Throws Out Paula Jones Case (April 1): In victory for President Clinton, Federal judge in Arkansas rules "there are no genuine issues for trial" in sexual misconduct case brought against the President by former state employee when he was Governor. **(April 16):** Jones announces she plans to appeal.

C.I.A. Accuses Dismissed Spy (April 3): Charges Douglas F. Groat, 50, sent two foreign nations secret U.S. information after failing in attempt to extort $500,000 from agency in exchange for loyalty.

Energy Secretary Resigns (April 6): Federico Peña, 51, former Transportation Secretary, will focus on his family.

U.S. Treasury Seeks Economic Reforms (April 14): Secretary outlines plan for updating world financial systems to prevent future economic convulsions.

U.S. Appeals Court Bars Hiring Plan (April 14): Voids government program that requires radio and television stations to seek minority job applicants. Ruling called setback to affirmative action.

U.S. Trade Deficit Biggest in Decade (April 17): Exports to Japan plunged in February, showing wide effects of Tokyo's stagnant economy.

Senate Votes for Tax Breaks for Education Savings (April 23): Passes Republican measure for modest concessions for parents who save for school expenses.

Hillary Rodham Clinton Questioned on Legal Work (April 25): Interrogated for five hours by Whitewater prosecutors about connection with failed Arkansas savings and loan institution. Session videotaped for legal use.

U.S. Court Rejects Campaign Spending Limits (April 27): Appeals bench in Cincinnati holds restrictions are an unconstitutional limit on free speech.

Senate Votes for NATO Expansion (April 30): Decides, 80–19, in ballot crossing party lines, to accept resolution to add Poland, Hungary, and Czech Republic. U.S. will become fifth of 16 existing members supporting change in treaty dating from 1949.

Clinton Confidant Indicted (April 30): Webster L. Hubbell, former law partner of Hillary Rodham Clinton, charged by Whitewater special prosecutor with tax evasion, including failure to pay taxes and penalties of more than $850,000 over previous four years.

BUSINESS/SCIENCE/SOCIETY

Dow Jones Average Exceeds 9,000 (April 6): Industrial index above level for first time. Increase spurred by news of biggest corporation merger in history, between Travelers and Citicorp.

Tornadoes in South Kill Dozens (April 9): Rescue workers frantically seek survivors after storms destroy whole communities in Mississippi, Alabama, and Georgia.

Paraguayan Executed in Virginia (April 14): Supreme Court denies clemency for Angel Francisco Breard, 32, for murder despite pleas from International Court of Justice and Paraguayan Government.

Student Kills Chaperoning Teacher (April 25): Shoots science teacher at Edinboro, Pa., school's graduation dance. Wounds another teacher and two students.

May 1998

WORLD

Former Premier Admits to Rwanda Massacres (May 1): Jean Kambanda pleads guilty to genocide charges before U.N. tribunal. He faces life in prison.

Europeans Agree on Single Currency (May 3): Monetary plan for all nations approved at Brussels conference after France and Germany resolve dispute over choice of candidate to head central bank.

Pope's Chief Guard Killed in Vatican (May 4): Bodies of Swiss Guards' new commandant, Col. Alois Estermann, his wife, and Vice Corporal were found shortly after the colonel's appointment. Authorities suspect murder-suicide by the subordinate.

Western Nations Move Against Serbia (May 9): Leading industrial states impose investment ban and freeze assets abroad in concern over violence in southern Serbian province of Kosovo. Ministers call for discussions between Belgrade and Albanian leadership.

India Sets Off Atomic Blasts (May 11): Conducts three underground tests in northwestern desert in defiance of worldwide rejection of nuclear testing. International condemnation is instantaneous. **(May 13):** India stages two more nuclear tests, defying plans by U.S. and other nations to impose severe sanctions.

Clinton Decides on Sanctions on India (May 12): Plans to invoke penalties called for in the Nuclear Proliferation Prevention Act of 1994.

Indonesian Students Stage Protests (May 13): Thousands rally to demand resignation of President Suharto. Police kill six students and wound others. **(May 23):** Army drives students from Parliament building. **(May 28):** Students resume protests, opposing new Government's timetable for holding elections next year.

Indonesian President Resigns (May 21): Suharto quits under pressure after economic crisis. In a television address, he apologizes for mistakes made during 32 years in power. He is succeeded by Vice President B. J. Habibie.

Irish Voters Approve Peace Agreement (May 22): Overwhelmingly support accord to end sectarian strife that has raged in Ireland for centuries. Accord approved in the North with 71 percent in favor, indicating that majority of Protestants support the agreement. "Yes" vote in the Irish Republic is 94 percent.

Russian Economy Threatened (May 27): Nation's financial markets near collapse. Moscow takes drastic steps to preserve value of currency and halt exodus of foreign investors. **(May 29):** International Monetary Fund pledges $670 million and sets conditions for stabilizing Russian financial markets.

Pakistan Stages Nuclear Tests (May 29): In response to India, announces that it has conducted five underground explosions. Clinton made prior futile appeal to prevent them. Afterward, he denounces them and imposes penalties that could cost billions. **(May 30):** Pakistan detonates another nuclear device.

NATION

Space Shuttle Returns Safely (May 3): *Columbia* lands at Kennedy Space center with live and dead animals after two weeks of laboratory work that advanced brain research.

Unabomber Sentenced to Four Life Terms (May 4): U.S. judge metes additional 30 years to Theodore J. Kaczynski, saying that "he committed unspeakable and monstrous crimes for which he shows utterly no remorse."

Susan H. McDougal Indicted (May 4): U.S. grand jury in Arkansas charges criminal contempt and obstruction of justice by former law partner of the Clintons in the Whitewater land venture for her refusal to answer questions about the President and Mrs. Clinton.

U.S. Judge Bars White House Move (May 5): Rebuffs President's effort to limit scope of independent counsel's investigation by ruling President cannot invoke executive privilege or attorney-client privilege to restrict a prosecutor's questioning of close advisers, lawyers, and other officials involved.

House Investigator Resigns Under Fire (May 6): David N. Bossie, top aide in campaign finance inquiry, quits after bipartisan criticism of his role in releasing tapes of Webster L. Hubbell's prison conversations.

Senate Retreats on Welfare Law Reform (May 12): Votes 92–8, to restore food stamps to a quarter of a million legal immigrants and refugees. **(May 22):** In House, 98 Republicans join Democrats to block conservative move to reform welfare law.

House Votes to Bar Satellite Exports to China (May 20): In bipartisan action, moves overwhelmingly to prevent the sending of sensitive technology that many in both parties fear could aid the accuracy of nuclear missiles.

Court Rejects Clinton "Privilege" Bid (May 22): U.S. judge rules Secret Service agents can be forced to testify about President's relationship with a former White House intern. Decision is a victory for Whitewater Independent Counsel, Kenneth W. Starr.

BUSINESS/SCIENCE/SOCIETY

Scores of 737's Grounded for Check (May 10): Federal Aviation Administration orders inspection of old aircraft after finding fuel-pump damage in some planes. Some flights around nation are canceled.

Public Television Upheld in Debates (May 18): Court rules 6–3 that stations have editorial discretion to exclude fringe or minority-party candidates who have little chance of election, providing that the decision is not based on the candidate's views.

Art Thieves Steal Treasures in Rome (May 20): Tie up guards in National Gallery of Modern Art and escape with two paintings by Van Gogh and one by Cézanne.

Student Held in Four Oregon Killings (May 21): Youth, 15, charged with fatal shooting of two students in school cafeteria and his parents at home in Springfield.

June 1998

WORLD

Serbs Renew Attack on Albanian Rebels (June 1): Yugoslav President launches major campaign against separatist movement in province of Kosovo.

Dictator of Nigeria Dies (June 8): Gen. Sani Abacha had been condemned around world for ruthless suppression of opponents, human rights and democracy. As successor, top military leaders select Gen. Abdulsalam Abubakar, averting drawn-out power struggle. **(June 9):** Abubakar says he will turn over power to elected civilian government by Oct. 1.

Serbs Warned to Halt Attacks (June 12): U.S., Russia, and six other major powers bolster NATO alliance's threat of military action to stem attacks on ethnic Albanians in province of Kosovo. **(June 15):** Nearly 100 NATO jets roam skies near Serbia to reinforce warning. **(June 16):** Yugoslav President Milosevic promises concessions. **(June 29):** Serb forces launch massive assault on rebel forces in Kosovo.

Chinese Use of U.S. Satellites Reported (June 12): U.S. files show that for two years China's military had relied on equipment sold for civilian purposes.

Poisoned Iraqi Weapons Reported (June 23): Laboratory tests find evidence of nerve gas on missile warheads. Case for U.N. oil embargo strengthened.

President Clinton Visits China (June 25, et seq.): Welcomed in Xian as first U.S. president to visit China in a decade. **(June 27):** Summit meeting ends after unusual live TV exchange between leaders on human rights, Tibet, and China's future.

NATION

Clinton Drops Executive Privilege Claim (June 1): Moves to avert quick Supreme Court review in Lewinsky investigation by independent counsel. President continues to press claim for lawyer–client privilege.

Full Testing of HIV Vaccine Approved (June 3): Federal Drug Administration authorizes California company to conduct world's first large-scale study.

School Prayer Motion Fails in House (June 4): Amendment for organized school prayer rejected, 224–203, after debate on conservatives' measure.

Starr Admits Leaks on Inquiry (June 13): Independent counsel investigating President Clinton says information he gave did not involve grand jury testimony or violate Justice Department code.

Administration Defends Satellite Exports (June 18): Top officials say China's military did not benefit from transfers of sensitive American technology and that there are safeguards against any such use.

Energy Secretary Appointed (June 19): President names William B. Richardson, veteran diplomat, congressman and Clinton's Chief Delegate to United Nations.

White House Broadens Medicare Rules (June 22): Requires sweeping protections for beneficiaries.

BUSINESS/SCIENCE/SOCIETY

Californians Reject Bilingual Education (June 3): In referendum, voters reject long-standing policy of public schools.

Life Sentence in Oklahoma Blast (June 4): U.S. judge in Denver orders prison without parole for Terry L. Nichols for conspiring to bomb Oklahoma City Federal building, where 168 persons were killed.

Earth's Temperature Sets High Record (June 8): White House announces analysis by government scientists shows warming trend in first five months of 1998.

Harassment Suit Settled for $34 Million (June 11): Mitsubishi subsidiary agrees to payment in Federal lawsuit charging sexual mistreatment of hundreds in automobile plant in Illinois. Settlement is the largest ever negotiated by Federal Government.

Shuttle Returns After Last Mission to *Mir* (June 12): Spacecraft *Discovery* safely brings back seventh and last American after his four-and-a-half months in orbit aboard Russian space station.

July 1998

WORLD

Clinton Ends Nine-Day Trip to China (July 1): In Shanghai, President speaks to nation in broadcast interview. He praises economic liberalization; says U.S. does not wish to dictate China's development. **(July 3):** President ends visit in Hong Kong. Tells banquet U.S. will do its best to boost Asia's economy. In news conference, he praises leaders, calling President Jiang Zemin a force for democracy.

Japan Announces Economic Program (July 3): Reveals plan to clear away huge debt in move to bolster global confidence in world's second-largest economy.

Palestinians Get Broader U.N. Role (July 7): Despite U.S. opposition, General Assembly votes to give them first step toward full U.N. membership.

Kosovo Rebels Blunt Serbian Drive (July 10): Ethnic Albanian separatists shift balance of power in province with stocks of anti-tank and anti-aircraft weapons. Serbian army and police forces fall back. **(July 26):** Yugoslav troops and police storm rebel positions held by ethnic Albanians; refugees endangered.

Japanese Voters Oust Ruling Party (July 12): Decisive election sets stage for resignation of Prime Minister Ryutaro Hashimoto and creates uncertainties about country's political and economic future. **(July 24):** Foreign Minister Keizo Obuchi elected president of governing party, in line to become Prime Minister despite hostility to him.

Protestants Parade Peacefully in Ulster (July 13): Thousands of Orange Order march in several hundred parades across Northern Ireland. Marches follow week of Protestant violence over issue of patriotic parades in Roman Catholic neighborhoods and deaths of three young Catholic brothers in arson attack.

I.M.F. Backs Emergency Aid for Russia (July 20): Board approves $17 billion rescue plan. Fund trims back first payment because of Russia's reform delays.

NATION

Congress Votes to Overhaul I.R.S. (July 9): Senate, 96–2, approves measure to make tax agency more helpful to citizens, with new rights and protections. Bill already approved by House, 402–8.

Clinton's Guards Testify in Inquiry (July 17): For first time in history, members of Secret Service become witnesses in a criminal case involving a U.S. President.

House Votes for Funding for Arts Agency (July 21): In sharp reversal it approves, 253–173, $98 million for National Endowment for the Arts, long a target of conservatives.

President Aids Drought-Stricken Area (July 23): Releases $100 million in emergency Federal funds for 11 states in South. After 2 months of high temperatures, scores are dead and many crops are killed.

House Overrides Abortion Bill Veto (July 23): Upholds measure to outlaw late-term procedure.

Clinton Subpoenaed in Inquiry (July 25): Independent counsel summons President to testify before U.S. grand jury investigating reported relationship with Monica S. Lewinsky. **(July 29):** Clinton agrees to testify by video.

BUSINESS/SCIENCE/SOCIETY

CNN Retracts Nerve Gas Report (July 2): Cable News Network apologizes for broadcast stating that U.S. military used lethal sarin in Laos in 1970 with intention of killing American defectors.

Suspect Convicted in Cosby Death (July 7): Los Angeles jury finds Mikail Markhasev guilty of murdering Ennis W. Cosby, son of entertainer Bill Cosby.

Accord Reached in Implant Damage Suits (July 8): Dow Corning Corporation agrees on $3.2 billion settlement for tens of thousands of women claiming injury from manufacturer's silicone breast implants.

Thalidomide Approved to Fight Leprosy (July 16): F.D.A. action foreshadows possibility of wide use of sedative drug banned in 1960 after causing deformities in thousands of babies.

Pacific Tidal Wave Kills Hundreds (July 17, et seq.): Ocean earthquake sends 23-foot wall of water over wide area of Papua New Guinea's northwest coast, killing at least 2,000. Most victims reported to be children. Villages leveled.

G.M. and Union Agree on Ending Strike (July 28): Company and union settle dispute that shut down two auto parts plants in Flint, Mich. and assembly factories across North America.

August 1998

WORLD

Arafat Reshuffles Cabinet (Aug. 5): Palestinian leader defies Legislative Council by retaining ministers it wanted ousted for alleged mismanagement.

Iraq Ends Cooperation with Inspectors (Aug. 5): Government demands removal of chief U.N. arms inspector, Richard Butler. **(Aug. 6):** Security Council rebukes Iraq and demands that Baghdad reverse decision.

Two U.S. Embassies in Africa Bombed (Aug. 7): Powerful weapons explode minutes apart in Kenya and Tanzania. 190 killed, including eight Americans. Officials believe attacks were coordinated. Thousands are injured over wide areas. Many people reported missing. **(Aug. 11):** U.S. temporarily halts operations at some foreign embassies and other diplomatic posts following threats.

Swiss Reach Agreement on Holocaust Payments (Aug. 12): Commercial banks and Holocaust survivors settle on $1.25 billion payment in reparations over three years. Deal hinges on ending plans for sanctions.

Serbian Troops Step Up Terror in Kosovo (Aug. 15): Drive tens of thousands of ethnic Albanians from their homes and loot and burn their villages.

Car Bomb Kills 28 in Northern Ireland (Aug. 15): Wounds 220 in town of Omagh, including pregnant women and infants. Attack is deadliest ever in Ulster, and raises doubts for survival of peace agreement. Roman Catholic splinter group, the Real I.R.A., takes responsibility.

Russia Fights to Avert Financial Collapse (Aug. 17): Government takes drastic steps, including delaying payments on foreign debts and restructuring bonds.

U.N. Renews Sanctions on Iraq (Aug. 20): Security Council acts after Baghdad insists it will not cooperate with arms inspectors until restrictions are lifted. William S. Ritter, longest-serving U.S. weapons inspector, has resigned, charging U.N. and U.S. had balked efforts to uncover Iraq's hidden program.

Canadian Court Limits Quebec Separation (Aug. 20): Supreme bench rules simple vote is insufficient for French-speaking province to secede legally. Approval of a clear majority of the people in Quebec and complex constitutional negotiations would be required.

U.S. Cruise Missiles Hit Suspected Terrorist Bases (Aug. 20): Dozens launched by ships strike targets in Afghanistan and the Sudan. President Clinton calls attack an act of self-defense against terrorist plots and retaliation for embassy bombings in Africa.

Yeltsin Shakes Up Government (Aug. 23): Brings back previously dismissed Viktor S. Chernomyrdin as Prime Minister, in move to bolster political support. **(Aug. 31):** Russian Parliament rejects appointment.

Suspect in African Bombings Arrested (Aug. 27): Federal agents bring prisoner to U.S. Man linked to attacks on embassies tells of training at terrorist camps.

North Korea Fires Missile Across Japan (Aug. 31): Firing of two-stage missile shows increased range. Japanese call firing "extremely dangerous." North Korea insists it launched satellite, not missile.

NATION

Chief Justice Rebuffs White House (Aug. 4): Rehnquist rejects motion to keep White House lawyers from testifying in special counsel's investigation of President Clinton's relationship with Monica Lewinsky.

Grand Jury Hears Former White House Intern (Aug. 6): Monica Lewinsky reported to testify that she and President carried on a sexual affair.

F.D.A. Authority on Tobacco Overruled (Aug. 14): Appeals Court decides agency does not have authority to regulate cigarettes or smokeless tobacco.

Clinton Admits to Extramarital Affair (Aug. 17): Testifies by closed circuit television to grand jury about relations with former White House intern, Monica S. Lewinsky. Later, in televised address to nation, he asks forgiveness of Americans and of his wife.

Starr Demands Clinton DNA Samples (Aug. 19): Whitewater counsel requests genetic material to establish forensic proof of sexual relationship with former intern.

Court Bars Sampling for 2000 Census (Aug. 24): U.S. judges rule that bureau's plan for statistical supplement to traditional head-counting violates Federal law.

Reno Orders Fund-Raising Inquiry (Aug. 26): In 90-day preliminary step, she seeks to determine whether to ask for special prosecutor to investigate role of Vice President Gore in 1996 campaign.

BUSINESS/SCIENCE/SOCIETY

Two Boys Accused of Killing Girl, 11 (Aug. 10): Chicago pair, aged 7 and 8, charged with murder in attempt to steal girl's bicycle.

Two Boys Punished in Arkansas Killings (Aug. 11): Judge sentences pair, aged 14 and 12, to juvenile detention center for March shooting of teacher and four girls at their Jonesboro school.

Former Klan Wizard Convicted in Killing (Aug. 21): Mississippi jury finds Sam H. Bowers guilty of ordering firebombing death in 1966 of Vernon Dahmer Sr., who registered fellow black voters at his store.

China Reports 3,004 Deaths in Floods (Aug. 26): Millions driven from homes during summer.

Stock Market Plunges 512 Points (Aug. 31): Wave of selling pushes prices 19 percent below peak reached six weeks previously. Wall Street slump tied to investors' anxiety over crises in Asia and Russia.

September 1998

WORLD

U.N. Tribunal Convicts Rwandan in Genocide (Sept. 2): In first such verdict, finds former small-town mayor guilty in mass killings.

More Iraqi Interference Charged (Sept. 3): Chief U.N. weapons inspector says Baghdad has gone beyond blocking surprise checks and is interfering with routine monitoring operations at installations.

Old Foes Meet in Northern Ireland (Sept. 7): Two rival leaders, Gerry Adams, Roman Catholic, and David Trimble, Protestant, meet to further peace efforts.

Yeltsin Names Compromise Official (Sept. 10): Appoints Foreign Minister Yevgeny Primakov as Prime Minister to avoid clash with emboldened opposition. **(Sept. 11):** Russian Parliament easily confirms Primakov.

Two New Suspects Linked to Bombings (Sept. 17): U.S. accuses Islamic extremist of being planner for terror attack on Kenya Embassy. Also arrests Texan described as former personal secretary to Osama bin Laden, Saudi exile at center of worldwide inquiry.

Japanese Parties Agree on Economy (Sept. 18): Governing party and opposition break deadlock to lay groundwork for revamping unstable financial system and resolving the nation's recessionary crisis.

Clinton Urges World War on Terrorism (Sept. 21): In U.N. address, President calls for better international cooperation to prevent and punish attacks.

Britain Seizes 7 in Terrorist Raid (Sept. 23): Arrests band of suspected associates of Osama bin Laden, exiled Saudi financier accused of carrying out bombings of American embassies in Kenya and Tanzania.

U.N. Warns Yugoslavian President (Sept. 23): Security Council tells Slobodan Milosevic to stop Serbian attacks on civilians in ethnically Albanian province of Kosovo or face international intervention. Only China does not support vote.

Pakistan Pledges A-Bomb Test Ban (Sept. 23): Pakistan agrees to end nuclear testing if sanctions are lifted. **(Sept. 24):** New Delhi announces that India agrees to end testing when details are settled.

Joint Force Formed in Southeast Europe (Sept. 26): Italy, Greece, Turkey, Albania, Bulgaria, Macedonia, and Romania form multinational peacekeeping operation.

Helmut Kohl Defeated in German Election (Sept. 27): 16–year Chancellor beaten by Gerhard Schröder, Social Democrat, as new era in Europe begins.

NATION

Senate Democrat Scolds Clinton (Sept. 3): In speech on floor, Joseph I. Lieberman of Connecticut denounces President's conduct in Lewinsky affair as "disgraceful" and "immoral." His words reflect growing Democratic discontent with President.

Rep. Dan Burton Admits Extramarital Affair (Sept. 4): Indiana Republican confirms reports that he fathered child in liaison early in the 1980s.

Reno Orders Campaign Spending Inquiry (Sept. 8): In 90–day proceeding, Attorney General seeks to determine whether President circumvented Federal election financing laws in 1996.

Starr Report on Clinton Made Public (Sept. 11): Independent counsel outlines case for possible impeachment proceedings. Report includes lurid details of President's affair with Monica S. Lewinsky. Clinton's lawyers charge report is designed to humiliate him and drive him out.

Clinton Counters Economic Threat (Sept. 17): Outlines strategy for U.S. to deter financial confusion affecting three continents.

Veto of Abortion Bill Sustained (Sept. 18): Senate, 64–36, fails for second time in two years to override Clinton's rejection of measure to outlaw late-term procedure, branded by foes as partial birth.

Tape of Clinton Testimony Broadcast (Sept. 21): Nation hears President's account to grand jury on charges of perjury in sex scandal. In four-hour testimony, he repeatedly rebuffs prosecutors' attempts to have him give sexual details of affair with White House intern.

Poll Shows Rebound by Clinton (Sept. 21): Standing with public has increased since release of testimony.

U.S. Surplus First in Three Decades (Sept. 30): Fiscal year ends with record of about $70 billion, largest surplus on record. President hails "a landmark achievement" and predicts era of balanced budgets ahead. Surplus raises disagreement between Administration and House Republicans on how to use funds.

BUSINESS/SCIENCE/SOCIETY

Atlantic Air Crash Kills 229 (Sept. 2): Swissair jet plunges into ocean off Nova Scotia. **(Sept. 8):** Flight data records show a series of vital operating systems were breaking down.

Breast-Cancer Drugs Recommended (Sept. 2): Panel recommends F.D.A. approval of tamoxifen to reduce risk and Herceptin for use in advanced cases.

Two Boys Cleared in Girl's Killing (Sept. 4): Children, aged 7 and 8, exonerated by new evidence in August murder of 11-year-old Chicago girl.

Manila Ferry Sinks; 23 Dead (Sept. 19): Many missing as *The Princess of the Orient* flounders in storm.

Hurricane Death Toll Nearly 300 (Sept. 24): Storm Georges rages across Caribbean, crosses Cuba and heads toward U.S. coast. **(Sept. 30):** Remnants of hurricane drench South with rain, sending rivers over banks as storm crosses Florida, Georgia, and South Carolina. Flood warnings in effect.

Iran Ends Salman Rushdie Death Threat (Sept. 24): Islamic Government lifts edict imposed on Indian-born British author of *The Satanic Verses,* a book viewed as heretical. Britain resumes diplomatic relations with Iran.

Major Emmy Awards for TV, 1997–1998

(Sept. 14, 1997)

Drama Series: *The Practice* (ABC)
Actress: Christine Lahti, *Chicago Hope*
Actor: Andre Braugher, *Homicide: Life on the Street*
Supporting actress: Camryn Manheim, *The Practice*
Supporting actor: Gordon Clapp, *NYPD Blue*
Comedy Series: *Frasier* (NBC)
Actress: Helen Hunt, *Mad About You*
Actor: Kelsey Grammer, *Frasier*
Supporting actress: Lisa Kudrow, *Friends*
Supporting actor: David Hyde Pierce, *Frasier*
Variety, Music or Comedy Series: *Late Show With David Letterman* (CBS)
Variety, Music or Comedy Special: *The 1997 Tony Awards* (CBS)
Miniseries or Special: *From the Earth to the Moon* (HBO)
Actress: Ellen Barkin, *Before Women Had Wings*
Actor: Gary Sinise, *George Wallace*
Supporting actress: Mare Winningham, *George Wallace*
Supporting actor: George C. Scott, *12 Angry Men*
Made for TV Movie: *Don King: Only in America* (HBO)
Individual Performance, Variety or Music Program: Billy Crystal, *The 70th Annual Academy Awards*

October 1998

WORLD

China to Improve Human Rights (Oct. 5): Signs major international agreement that includes ban on arbitrary arrest and torture, and protects freedom of thought, religion, and expression. Move seen as an important first step for China.

Italian Prime Minister Ousted in Vote of No-Confidence (Oct. 9): Romano Prodi loses power by one vote in Parliamentary decision. He will remain in post with weakened power until replacement is found.

Netanyahu Names Ariel Sharon Foreign Minister (Oct. 9): Palestinians upset by appointment of former general and defense minister fired after massacre of hundreds of Palestinian refugees in Lebanon in 1982. Israeli commitment to peace process questioned.

Pakistan Clears Way for Islamic Order (Oct. 9): National Assembly grants federal government power to rule based on interpretation of the Qu'ran. Bill consolidates power of Prime Minister Nawaz Sharif and poses threat to women and minorities.

NATO Reaches Agreement with Yugoslav Federation President (Oct. 12): On verge of ordering air strikes, NATO receives last-minute commitment from Milosevic to withdraw forces from Kosovo. Agreement keeps Kosovo with Serbia while granting more autonomy to majority Albanian population.

Japanese Government Plans to Bail Out Banks (Oct. 12): Parliament passes bank reform legislation to help recover economy. $513 billion in aid to banks sends stock markets up worldwide.

Pinochet Arrested in London (Oct. 16): Former Chilean ruler detained in London medical clinic at request of Spanish magistrate. Charged with murder of Spanish citizens in his 17-year rule, during which at least 3,000 political opponents vanished or died. Chilean reaction is divided, as rallies break out across nation.

Mideast Peace Talks Extended (Oct. 18): Key issues remain in dispute between Israeli Prime Minister Benjamin Netanyahu and Palestinian leader Yasir Arafat as talks carry into unplanned fifth day. **(Oct. 19):** Two hand grenades explode in crowd, injuring at least 60 people. After calling off part of talks, Netanyahu softens stance and agrees to discuss security issues and work toward an agreement with Arafat.

India and Pakistan End Talks With Little Progress (Oct. 18): First diplomatic meeting since nuclear testing by both countries in May comes to a close. Tensions remain high, as only agreement achieved is to meet again in February.

Hundreds Die in Nigerian Pipeline Explosion (Oct. 18): At least 700 die in blaze while scooping gasoline from a broken pipeline.

Rwanda to Free 10,000 Held on Genocide Charges (Oct. 19): Government to release portion of reported 120,000 accused of aiding in extremist Hutu government's slaughter of half a million people in 1994. Many had been imprisoned based simply on accusations.

NATION

Panel Votes in Favor of Impeachment Probe (Oct. 5): House Judiciary Committee votes 21–16 to recommend full-scale investigation of whether Clinton's alleged cover-up of affair with Monica Lewinsky is grounds for impeachment. **(Oct. 9):** In historic vote, House decides 258–176 to approve the inquiry.

Clinton Advisers Resign (Oct. 5): Chief of Staff Erskine B. Bowles and Senior Adviser Rahm Emanuel announce their departure, only three weeks after resignation of Press Secretary Michael D. McCurry.

Religious Freedom Bill Passed By Senate (Oct. 9): Unanimous vote approves legislation requiring president to impose sanctions against countries practicing religious persecution.

Black Farmers' Case Ruled Class Action (Oct. 9): Federal judge clears way for more farmers to join $3 billion lawsuit against government Agricultural Department, accused of denying Blacks farm loans, crop subsidies and other benefits from 1983 to 1997.

Congress Passes Digital Copyright Bill (Oct. 12): Legislation aims to punish those who circumvent high-technology security in order to copy software, movies, music, and other protected works.

Congress Approves Budget Proposal (Oct. 21): Package includes increased funding for education, the International Monetary Fund, and the environment. Clinton criticizes Republicans for drawing out 8-month, partisan battle over how to apportion $500 billion.

BUSINESS/SCIENCE/SOCIETY

Amnesty International Criticizes U.S. in Human Rights (Oct. 5): U.S. found to frequently violate the standards it demands of other countries. Practices include use of shock-emitting stun belts on prisoners, unprovoked beatings by police, and use of death penalty in many states.

Student, 21, Savagely Beaten in Suspected Hate Crime (Oct. 6): Gay University of Wyoming student, Matthew Shepard, burned, badly beaten, and left tied to a fence. Two young suspects charged with kidnapping, aggravated robbery, and attempted first-degree murder. **(Oct. 12):** Shepard dies in hospital after being in a coma for several days.

New Technique Similar to Cloning Stirs up Debate (Oct. 8): Scientists add genes of infertile woman's egg to another egg and fertilize with sperm, making genetically-related children possible for infertile women. Practice banned in California.

20-Year-Old Sentenced to Life in Las Vegas Murder Case (Oct. 14): Young man who molested and strangled 7-year-old girl in casino toilet in 1997 is given four life terms without parole. No charges brought against a friend of the man, who observed killing without intervening.

Severe Weather in Texas Kills 10 (Oct. 17, et seq.): Floods and tornadoes hit state. 1,500 people forced out of homes in emergency evacuations. **(Oct. 21):** Death toll climbs to 22 as rains continue.

U.S. Begins Antitrust Case Against Microsoft (Oct. 19): Department of Justice starts presentation of evidence that aims to prove Microsoft practices have been unfair to consumers and competition. Outcome could have profound implications on U.S. economy.

1998 Nobel Prize Winners

Peace: John Hume and David Trimble (both Northern Ireland), whose efforts made possible Northern Ireland's Good Friday peace accord in 1998 and have led to political progress in a deep-rooted conflict. Hume is the leader of the Catholic Social Democratic and Labor Party, and Trimble heads the predominant Protestant Ulster Unionist Party.

Literature: José Saramago (Portugal), who, according to the committee, "with parables sustained by imagination, compassion, and irony, continually enables us once again to apprehend an elusory reality." The first Portuguese writer to win the Nobel, his novels have been translated into more than 20 languages.

Physics: Robert B. Laughlin (U.S.), Horst L. Störmer (Germany), and Daniel C. Tsui (U.S.), "for their discovery of a new form of quantum fluid with fractionally charged excitations." The findings of the three scientists will have implications on our understanding of the destruction of Earth's ozone layer.

Chemistry: Walter Kohn (U.S.) and John A. Pople (U.K.) for their developments in the study of the properties of molecules and the chemical processes in which they are involved. Kohn's density-functional theory simplifies the mathematical explanation of the bonding between atoms within molecules, making it possible for scientists to study large, complex molecules. Pople was cited for his development of computer techniques that make it possible to create models of chemical reactions that cannot otherwise be recreated in the laboratory.

Medicine: Robert F. Furchgott, Louis J. Ignarro, and Ferid Murad (all U.S.) for discovering that nitric oxide acts as a signal in the cardiovascular system. Their findings are relevant to the function of the recently popular anti-impotence drug Viagra, and will also have implications for the treatment of heart disease, shock, and other medical conditions.

Economics: Amartya Sen (India), "for his contributions to welfare economics." His studies, including an examination of the Bangladesh famine of 1974, have contributed to the understanding of how complex economic factors relate to famine and poverty. The committee credited him for "restoring an ethical dimension to the discussion of vital economic problems."

CONGRESSIONAL ELECTION RESULTS NOV. 3, 1998

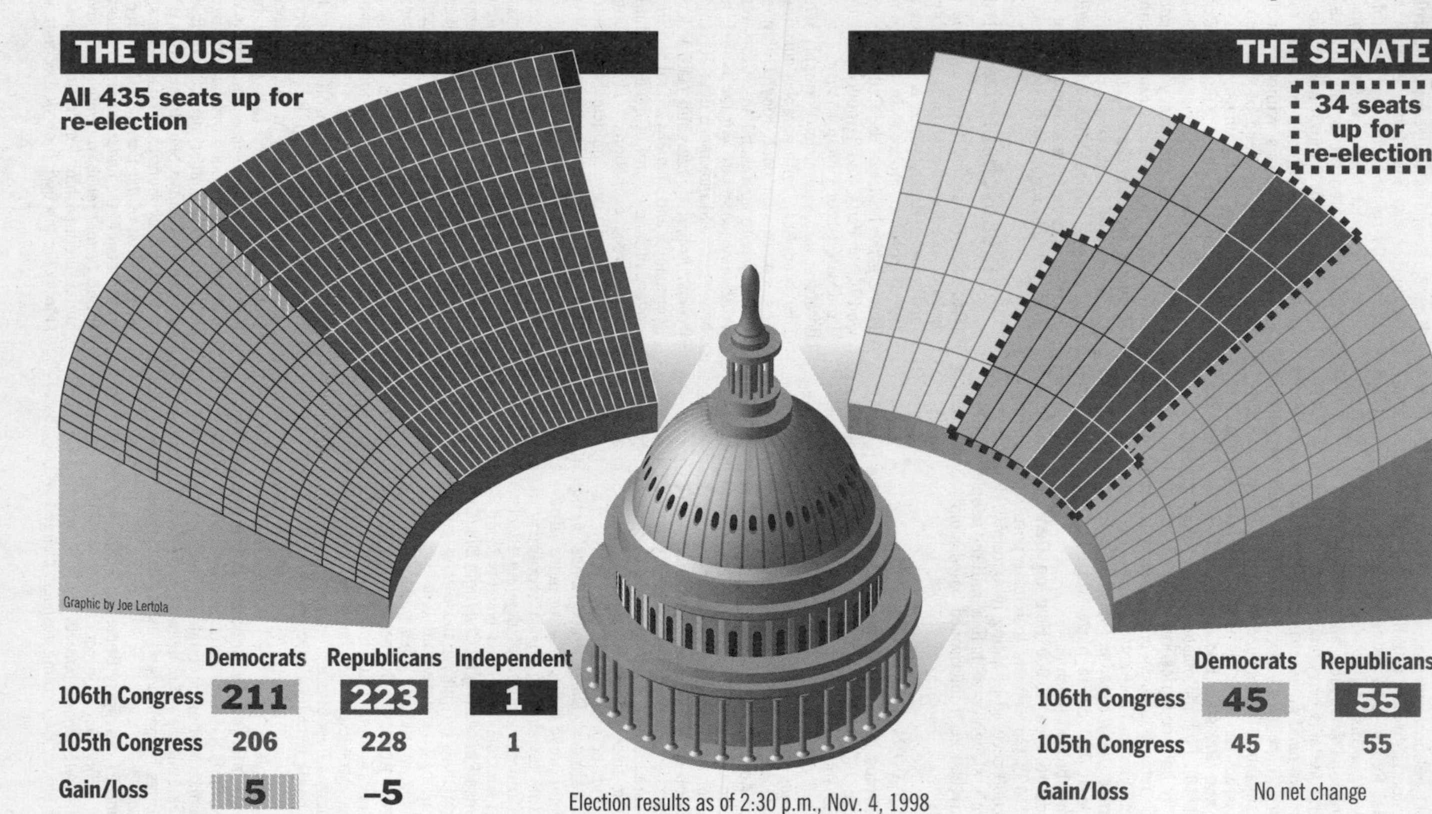

The Hundred and Sixth Congress

Composition of the 105th and 106th Congresses

106th Congress	Rep.	Dem.	Ind.	Male	Female
Senate	55	45	—	91	9
House	223	211	1	379	56

105th Congress	Rep.	Dem.	Ind.	Male	Female
Senate	55	45	—	91	9
House	228	206	1	380	55

The Senate

In the following list, the senior senator is listed first. Dates in left column indicate term in office; birthdates are given in parentheses after name and party affiliation. All terms are for six years and expire in January. Mailing address: The Senate, Washington, D.C. 20515. NOTE: Election results as of 2:30 p.m., Nov. 4, 1998.

Alabama
1987–2005 Richard C. Shelby (R) (1934)
1997–2003 Jeff Sessions (R) (1946)
Alaska
1969–2003 Ted Stevens (R) (1923)
1981–2005 Frank H. Murkowski (R) (1933)
Arizona
1987–2005 John McCain (R) (1936)
1995–2001 Jon Kyl (R) (1942)
Arkansas
1979–2003 Tim Hutchinson (R) (1949)
1999–2005 Blanche Lambert Lincoln (D) (1960)
California
1993–2001 Dianne Feinstein (D) (1933)
1993–2005 Barbara Boxer (D) (1940)
Colorado
1993–2005 Ben Nighthorse Campbell (R) (1933)
1997–2003 Wayne Allard (R) (1943)
Connecticut
1981–2005 Christopher J. Dodd (D) (1944)
1989–2001 Joseph I. Lieberman (D) (1942)
Delaware
1971–2001 William V. Roth, Jr. (R) (1921)
1973–2003 Joseph R. Biden, Jr. (D) (1942)
Florida
1987–2005 Bob Graham (D) (1936)
1989–2001 Connie Mack III (R) (1940)
Georgia
1993–2005 Paul Douglas Coverdell (R) (1939)
1997–2003 Max Cleland (D) (1942)
Hawaii
1963–2005 Daniel K. Inouye (D) (1924)
1990–2001 Daniel K. Akaka (D) (1924)
Idaho
1991–2003 Larry E. Craig (R) (1945)
1999–2005 Mike Crapo (R) (1951)
Illinois
1997–2003 Richard J. Durbin (D) (1944)
1999–2005 Peter G. Fitzgerald (R) (1960)
Indiana
1977–2001 Richard G. Lugar (R) (1932)
1999–2005 Evan Bayh (D) (1955)
Iowa
1981–2005 Charles E. Grassley (R) (1933)
1985–2003 Tom Harkin (D) (1939)
Kansas
1997–2005 Sam Brownback (R) (1956)
1997–2003 Pat Roberts (R) (1936)
Kentucky
1985–2003 Mitch McConnell (R) (1942)
1999–2005 Jim Bunning (R) (1931)
Louisiana
1987–2005 John B. Breaux (D) (1944)
1997–2003 Mary L. Landrieu (D) (1955)
Maine
1995–2001 Olympia J. Snowe (R) (1947)
1997–2003 Susan M. Collins (R) (1952)
Maryland
1977–2001 Paul Sarbanes (D) (1933)
1987–2005 Barbara A. Mikulski (D) (1936)
Massachusetts
1963–2001 Edward M. Kennedy (D) (1932)
1985–2003 John F. Kerry (D) (1943)
Michigan
1979–2003 Carl Levin (D) (1934)
1995–2001 Spencer Abraham (R) (1952)
Minnesota
1991–2003 Paul Wellstone (D) (1944)
1995–2001 Rod Grams (R) (1948)
Mississippi
1979–2003 Thad Cochran (R) (1937)
1989–2001 Trent Lott (R) (1941)
Missouri
1987–2005 Christopher S. "Kit" Bond (R) (1939)
1995–2001 John Ashcroft (R) (1942)
Montana
1978–2003 Max Baucus (D) (1941)
1989–2001 Conrad Burns (R) (1935)
Nebraska
1989–2001 Robert Kerrey (D) (1943)
1997–2003 Chuck Hagel (R) (1946)
Nevada
1987–2005 Harry Reid (D) (1939)
1989–2001 Dick Bryan (D) (1937)
New Hampshire
1991–2003 Robert C. Smith (R) (1941)
1993–2005 Judd Gregg (R) (1947)
New Jersey
1983–2001 Frank R. Lautenberg (D) (1924)
1997–2003 Robert G. Torricelli (D) (1951)
New Mexico
1973–2003 Pete V. Domenici (R) (1932)
1983–2001 Jeff Bingaman (D) (1943)
New York
1977–2001 Daniel P. Moynihan (D) (1927)
1999–2005 Charles E. Schumer (D) (1950)
North Carolina
1973–2003 Jesse Helms (R) (1921)
1999–2005 John Edwards (D) (1953)
North Dakota
1993–2001 Kent Conrad (D) (1948)
1987–2005 Byron L. Dorgan (D) (1942)
Ohio
1995–2001 Mike DeWine (R) (1947)
1999–2005 George V. Voinovich (R) (1936)
Oklahoma
1989–2005 Don Nickles (R) (1948)
1994–2003 James M. Inhofe (R) (1934)
Oregon
1996–2005 Ron Wyden (D) (1949)
1997–2003 Gordon Smith (R) (1952)
Pennsylvania
1981–2005 Arlen Specter (R) (1930)
1995–2001 Rick Santorum (R) (1958)

Rhode Island
1976–2001 John H. Chafee (R) (1922)
1997–2003 Jack Reed (D) (1949)
South Carolina
1957–2003 Strom Thurmond (R) (1902)
1966–2005 Ernest Hollings (D) (1922)
South Dakota
1987–2005 Thomas A. Daschle (D) (1947)
1997–2003 Tim Johnson (D) (1946)
Tennessee
1995–2003 Fred Thompson (R) (1942)
1995–2001 Bill Frist (R) (1952)
Texas
1985–2003 Phil Gramm (R) (1942)
1995–2001 Kay Bailey Hutchison (R) (1943)
Utah
1977–2001 Orrin G. Hatch (R) (1934)
1993–2005 Robert F. Bennett (R) (1933)
Vermont
1975–2005 Patrick Leahy (D) (1940)
1989–2001 James M. Jeffords (R) (1934)
Virginia
1979–2003 John H. Warner (R) (1927)
1989–2001 Charles Robb (D) (1939)
Washington
1989–2001 Slade Gorton (R) (1928)
1993–2005 Patty Murray (D) (1950)
West Virginia
1959–2001 Robert C. Byrd (D) (1917)
1985–2003 John D. "Jay" Rockefeller IV (D) (1937)
Wisconsin
1989–2001 Herbert Kohl (D) (1935)
1993–2005 Russ Feingold (D) (1953)
Wyoming
1995–2001 Craig Thomas (R) (1933)
1997–2003 Michael B. Enzi (R) (1944)

The House of Representatives

In the following lists, the numeral indicates the Congressional District represented; AL is for representatives At Large. All terms expire January 1999. Mailing address: House of Representatives, Washington, D.C. 20515. NOTE: Election results as of 2:30 p.m., Nov. 4, 1998.

Alabama
1. H. L. Sonny Callahan (R)
2. Terry Everett (R)
3. Bob Riley (R)
4. Robert Aderholt (R)
5. Robert E. "Bud" Cramer (D)
6. Spencer Bachus (R)
7. Earl F. Hilliard (D)

Alaska
AL Don Young (R)

Arizona
1. Matt Salmon (R)
2. Ed Pastor (D)
3. Bob Stump (R)
4. John Shadegg (R)
5. Jim Kolbe (R)
6. J. D. Hayworth (R)

Arkansas
1. Marion Berry (D)
2. Vic Snyder (D)
3. Asa Hutchinson (R)
4. Jay Dickey (R)

California
1. Mike Thompson (D)
2. Wally Herger (R)
3. Doug Ose (R)
4. John T. Doolittle (R)
5. Robert T. Matsui (D)
6. Lynn Woolsey (D)
7. George Miller (D)
8. Nancy Pelosi (D)
9. Barbara Lee (D)
10. Ellen O. Tauscher (D)
11. Richard W. Pombo (R)
12. Tom Lantos (D)
13. Fortney Pete Stark (D)
14. Anna G. Eshoo (D)
15. Tom Campbell (R)
16. Zoe Lofgren (D)
17. Sam Farr (D)
18. Gary A. Condit (D)
19. George Radanovich (R)
20. Cal Dooley (D)
21. Bill Thomas (R)
22. Lois Capps (D)
23. Elton W. Gallegly (R)
24. Brad Sherman (D)
25. Howard "Buck" McKeon (R)
26. Howard L. Berman (D)
27. James E. Rogan (R)
28. David Dreier (R)
29. Henry A. Waxman (D)
30. Xavier Becerra (D)
31. Matthew G. Martinez (D)
32. Julian C. Dixon (D)
33. Lucille Roybal-Allard (D)
34. Grace Flores Napolitano (D)
35. Maxine Waters (D)
36. Steven T. Kuykendall (R)
37. Juanita Millender-McDonald (D)
38. Steve Horn (R)
39. Ed Royce (R)
40. Jerry Lewis (R)
41. Gary G. Miller (R)
42. George E. Brown, Jr. (D)
43. Ken Calvert (R)
44. Mary Bono (R)
45. Dana Rohrabacher (R)
46. Loretta Sanchez (D)
47. Christopher Cox (R)
48. Ron Packard (R)
49. Brian P. Bilbray (R)
50. Bob Filner (D)
51. Randy "Duke" Cunningham (R)
52. Duncan Hunter (R)

Colorado
1. Diana DeGette (D)
2. Mark Udall (D)
3. Scott McInnis (R)
4. Bob Schaffer (R)
5. Joel Hefley (R)
6. Tom Tancredo (R)

Connecticut
1. John B. Larson (D)
2. Sam Gejdenson (D)
3. Rosa L. DeLauro (D)
4. Christopher Shays (R)
5. Jim Maloney (D)
6. Nancy L. Johnson (R)

Delaware
AL Michael N. Castle (R)

Florida
1. Joe Scarborough (R)
2. Allen Boyd (D)
3. Corrine Brown (D)
4. Tillie K. Fowler (R)
5. Karen L. Thurman (D)
6. Clifford "Cliff" Stearns (R)
7. John L. Mica (R)
8. Bill McCollum (R)
9. Michael Bilirakis (R)
10. C. W. Bill Young (R)
11. Jim Davis (D)
12. Charles T. Canady (R)
13. Dan Miller (R)
14. Porter Goss (R)
15. Dave Weldon (R)
16. Mark Foley (R)
17. Carrie P. Meek (D)
18. Ileana Ros-Lehtinen (R)
19. Robert Wexler (D)
20. Peter Deutsch (D)
21. Lincoln Diaz-Balart (R)
22. Clay Shaw, Jr. (R)
23. Alcee L. Hastings (D)

Georgia
1. Jack Kingston (R)
2. Sanford Dixon Bishop, Jr. (D)
3. Michael A. "Mac" Collins (R)
4. Cynthia McKinney (D)
5. John Lewis (D)
6. Newt Gingrich (R)
7. Bob Barr (R)
8. Saxby Chambliss (R)
9. Nathan Deal (R)
10. Charlie Norwood (R)
11. John Linder (R)

Hawaii
1. Neil Abercrombie (D)
2. Patsy Takemoto Mink (D)

Idaho
1. Helen Chenoweth (R)
2. Mike Simpson (R)

Illinois
1. Bobby L. Rush (D)
2. Jesse L. Jackson, Jr. (D)
3. William O. Lipinski (D)
4. Luis V. Gutierrez (D)
5. Rod R. Blagojevich (D)
6. Henry J. Hyde (R)
7. Danny K. Davis (D)
8. Philip M. Crane (R)
9. Janice D. "Jan" Schakowsky (D)
10. John E. Porter (R)
11. Gerald C. Weller (R)
12. Jerry F. Costello (D)

13. Judy Biggert (R)
14. J. Dennis Hastert (R)
15. Thomas W. Ewing (R)
16. Donald Manzullo (R)
17. Lane A. Evans (D)
18. Ray LaHood (R)
19. David D. Phelps (D)
20. John M. Shimkus (R)

Indiana

1. Peter J. Visclosky (D)
2. David M. McIntosh (R)
3. Tim Roemer (D)
4. Mark E. Souder (R)
5. Steve Buyer (R)
6. Dan Burton (R)
7. Edward A. Pease (R)
8. John N. Hostettler (R)
9. Baron Hill (D)
10. Julia M. Carson (D)

Iowa

1. Jim Leach (R)
2. Jim Nussle (R)
3. Leonard L. Boswell (D)
4. Greg Ganske (R)
5. Tom Latham (R)

Kansas

1. Jerry Moran (R)
2. Jim Ryun (R)
3. Dennis Moore (D)
4. Todd Tiahrt (R)

Kentucky

1. Edward Whitfield (R)
2. Ron Lewis (R)
3. Anne Meagher Northup (R)
4. Ken Lucas (D)
5. Harold "Hal" Rogers (R)
6. Ernest Fletcher (R)

Louisiana

1. Robert L. "Bob" Livingston (R)
2. William J. Jefferson (D)
3. W. J. "Billy" Tauzin (R)
4. Jim McCrery (R)
5. John Cooksey (R)
6. Richard Baker (R)
7. Chris John (D)

Maine

1. Thomas H. Allen (D)
2. John E. Baldacci (D)

Maryland

1. Wayne T. Gilchrest (R)
2. Robert L. Ehrlich, Jr. (R)
3. Benjamin L. Cardin (D)
4. Albert R. Wynn (D)
5. Steny H. Hoyer (D)
6. Roscoe Bartlett (R)
7. Elijah E. Cummings (D)
8. Constance A. Morella (R)

Massachusetts

1. John W. Olver (D)
2. Richard E. Neal (D)
3. James P. McGovern (D)
4. Barney Frank (D)
5. Martin T. Meehan (D)
6. John F. Tierney (D)
7. Edward J. Markey (D)
8. Michael E. Capuano (D)
9. John Joseph Moakley (D)
10. William D. Delahunt (D)

Michigan

1. Bart Stupak (D)
2. Peter Hoekstra (R)
3. Vernon Ehlers (R)
4. Dave Camp (R)
5. James A. Barcia (D)
6. Fred Upton (R)
7. Nick Smith (R)
8. Debbie Stabenow (D)
9. Dale E. Kildee (D)
10. David E. Bonior (D)
11. Joe Knollenberg (R)
12. Sander Levin (D)
13. Lynn Nancy Rivers (D)
14. John Conyers, Jr. (D)
15. Carolyn Cheeks Kilpatrick (D)
16. John D. Dingell (D)

Minnesota

1. Gil Gutknecht (R)
2. David Minge (D)
3. Jim Ramstad (R)
4. Bruce F. Vento (D)
5. Martin Olav Sabo (D)
6. Bill Luther (D)
7. Collin C. Peterson (D)
8. James L. Oberstar (D)

Mississippi

1. Roger F. Wicker (R)
2. Bennie G. Thompson (D)
3. Charles W. "Chip" Pickering, Jr. (R)
4. Ronnie Shows (D)
5. Gene Taylor (D)

Missouri

1. William "Bill" Clay, Sr. (D)
2. James M. Talent (R)
3. Richard A. Gephardt (D)
4. Ike Skelton (D)
5. Karen McCarthy (D)
6. Pat "Patsy Ann" Danner (D)
7. Roy Blunt (R)
8. Jo Ann Emerson (R)
9. Kenny Hulshof (R)

Montana

AL Rick Hill (R)

Nebraska

1. Doug Bereuter (R)
2. Lee Terry (R)
3. Bill Barrett (R)

Nevada

1. Shelley Berkley (D)
2. Jim Gibbons (R)

New Hampshire

1. John E. Sununu (R)
2. Charles Bass (R)

New Jersey

1. Robert E. Andrews (D)
2. Frank A. LoBiondo (R)
3. Jim Saxton (R)
4. Christopher H. Smith (R)
5. Marge Roukema (R)
6. Frank Pallone, Jr. (D)
7. Bob Franks (R)
8. Bill J. Pascrell, Jr. (D)
9. Steven R. Rothman (D)
10. Donald M. Payne (D)
11. Rodney P. Frelinghuysen (R)
12. Rush Holt (D)
13. Robert Menendez (D)

New Mexico

1. Heather A. Wilson (R)
2. Joe Skeen (R)
3. Tom Udall (D)

New York

1. Michael P. Forbes (R)
2. Rick A. Lazio (R)
3. Peter T. King (R)
4. Carolyn McCarthy (D)
5. Gary L. Ackerman (D)
6. Gregory W. Meeks (D)
7. Joseph Crowley (D)
8. Jerrold L. Nadler (D)
9. Anthony Weiner (D)
10. Edolphus Towns (D)
11. Major R. Owens (D)
12. Nydia M. Velazquez (D)
13. Vito J. Fossella (R)
14. Carolyn B. Maloney (D)
15. Charles B. Rangel (D)
16. Jose E. Serrano (D)
17. Eliot L. Engel (D)
18. Nita M. Lowey (D)
19. Sue W. Kelly (R)
20. Benjamin A. Gilman (R)
21. Michael R. McNulty (D)
22. John E. Sweeney (R)
23. Sherwood L. Boehlert (R)
24. John M. McHugh (R)
25. James T. Walsh (R)
26. Maurice D. Hinchey (D)
27. Thomas M. Reynolds (R)
28. Louise M. Slaughter (D)
29. John J. La Falce (D)
30. Jack Quinn (R)
31. Amory Houghton (R)

North Carolina

1. Eva M. Clayton (D)
2. Bob Etheridge (D)
3. Walter B. Jones (R)
4. David Price (D)
5. Richard Burr (R)
6. Howard Coble (R)
7. Mike McIntyre (D)
8. Robert C. "Robin" Hayes (R)
9. Sue Myrick (R)
10. T. Cass Ballenger (R)
11. Charles H. Taylor (R)
12. Mel Watt (D)

North Dakota

AL Earl Pomeroy (D)

Ohio

1. Steve Chabot (R)
2. Rob Portman (R)
3. Tony P. Hall (D)
4. Michael G. Oxley (R)
5. Paul E. Gillmor (R)
6. Ted Strickland (D)
7. Dave Hobson (R)
8. John A. Boehner (R)
9. Marcy Kaptur (D)
10. Dennis J. Kucinich (D)
11. Stephanie Tubbs Jones (D)
12. John R. Kasich (R)
13. Sherrod Brown (D)
14. Thomas C. Sawyer (D)
15. Deborah Pryce (R)
16. Ralph Regula (R)
17. James A. Traficant, Jr. (D)
18. Bob Ney (R)
19. Steven C. LaTourette (R)

Oklahoma

1. Steve Largent (R)
2. Tom A. Coburn (R)
3. Wes Watkins (R)
4. J. C. Watts, Jr. (R)
5. Ernest Istook (R)
6. Frank D. Lucas (R)

Oregon

1. David Wu (D)
2. Greg Walden (R)
3. Earl Blumenauer (D)
4. Peter A. DeFazio (D)
5. Darlene Hooley (D)

Pennsylvania
1. Robert A. Brady (D)
2. Chaka Fattah (D)
3. Robert A. Borski (D)
4. Ron Klink (D)
5. John E. Peterson (R)
6. Tim Holden (D)
7. Curt Weldon (R)
8. Jim Greenwood (R)
9. Bud Shuster (R)
10. Don Sherwood (R)
11. Paul E. Kanjorski (D)
12. John P. Murtha (D)
13. Joseph M. Hoeffel (D)
14. William J. Coyne (D)
15. Pat Toomey (R)
16. Joseph R. Pitts (R)
17. George W. Gekas (R)
18. Mike Doyle (D)
19. Bill Goodling (R)
20. Frank Mascara (D)
21. Phil English (R)

Rhode Island
1. Patrick J. Kennedy (D)
2. Robert A. Weygand (D)

South Carolina
1. Mark Sanford (R)
2. Floyd D. Spence (R)
3. Lindsey Graham (R)
4. Jim DeMint (R)
5. John Spratt (D)
6. James E. Clyburn (D)

South Dakota
AL John R. Thune (R)

Tennessee
1. William L. Jenkins (R)
2. John J. Duncan (R)
3. Zach Wamp (R)
4. William V. Hilleary (R)
5. Bob Clement (D)
6. Bart Gordon (D)
7. Ed Bryant (R)
8. John S. Tanner (D)
9. Harold E. Ford, Jr. (D)

Texas
1. Max Sandlin (D)
2. Jim Turner (D)
3. Sam Johnson (R)
4. Ralph M. Hall (D)
5. Pete Sessions (R)
6. Joe Barton (R)
7. Bill Archer (R)
8. Kevin Brady (R)
9. Nick Lampson (D)
10. Lloyd Doggett (D)
11. Chet Edwards (D)
12. Kay Granger (R)
13. Mac Thornberry (R)
14. Ron Paul (R)
15. Ruben Hinojosa (D)
16. Silvestre Reyes (D)
17. Charlie Stenholm (D)
18. Sheila Jackson Lee (D)
19. Larry Combest (R)
20. Charlie Gonzalez (D)
21. Lamar Smith (R)
22. Tom DeLay (R)
23. Henry Bonilla (R)
24. Martin Frost (D)
25. Ken Bentsen (D)
26. Dick Armey (R)
27. Solomon P. Ortiz (D)
28. Ciro D. Rodriguez (D)
29. Gene Green (D)
30. Eddie Bernice Johnson (D)

Utah
1. James V. Hansen (R)
2. Merrill Cook (R)
3. Chris Cannon (R)

Vermont
AL Bernie Sanders (I)

Virginia
1. Herbert H. "Herb" Bateman (R)
2. Owen B. Pickett (D)
3. Robert C. "Bobby" Scott (D)
4. Norman Sisisky (D)
5. Virgil H. Goode, Jr. (D)
6. Robert W. "Bob" Goodlatte (R)
7. Thomas J. "Tom" Bliley, Jr. (R)
8. James P. Moran, Jr. (D)
9. Frederick C. "Rick" Boucher (D)
10. Frank R. Wolf (R)
11. Thomas M. Davis III (R)

Washington
1. Jay Inslee (D)
2. Jack Metcalf (R)
3. Brian Baird (D)
4. Doc Hastings (R)
5. George Nethercutt (R)
6. Norm Dicks (D)
7. Jim McDermott (D)
8. Jennifer Dunn (R)
9. Adam Smith (D)

West Virginia
1. Alan B. Mollohan (D)
2. Bob Wise (D)
3. Nick Joe Rahall II (D)

Wisconsin
1. Paul Ryan (R)
2. Tammy Baldwin (D)
3. Ron Kind (D)
4. Jerry Kleczka (D)
5. Tom Barrett (D)
6. Thomas E. Petri (R)
7. David R. Obey (D)
8. Mark Green (R)
9. F. James Sensenbrenner, Jr. (R)

Wyoming
AL Barbara Cubin (R)

The Governors of the Fifty States

State	Governor	Current term[1]
Ala.	Don Siegelman (D)	1999–2003
Alaska	Tony Knowles (D)	1998–2002[2]
Ariz.	Jane Dee Hull (R)	1999–2003
Ark.	Mike Huckabee (R)	1999–2003
Calif.	Gray Davis (D)	1999–2003
Colo.	Bill Owens (R)	1999–2003
Conn.	John G. Rowland (R)	1999–2003
Del.	Thomas R. Carper (D)	1997–2001
Fla.	Jeb Bush (R)	1999–2003
Ga.	Roy E. Barnes (D)	1999–2003
Hawaii	Benjamin J. Cayetano (D)	1998–2002[2]
Idaho	Dirk Kempthorne (R)	1999–2003
Ill.	George H. Ryan (R)	1999–2003
Ind.	Frank O'Bannon (D)	1997–2001
Iowa	Tom Vilsack (D)	1999–2003
Kans.	Bill Graves (R)	1999–2003
Ky.	Paul E. Patton (D)	1995–1999[2]
La.	Mike Foster (D)	1996–2000
Maine	Angus S. King, Jr. (I)	1999–2003
Md.	Parris N. Glendening (D)	1999–2003
Mass.	Argeo Paul Cellucci (R)	1999–2003
Mich.	John Engler (R)	1999–2003
Minn.	Jesse Ventura (RF)[3]	1999–2003
Miss.	Kirk Fordice (R)	1996–2000
Mo.	Mel Carnahan (D)	1997–2001
Mont.	Marc Racicot (R)	1997–2001
Nebr.	Mike Johanns (R)	1999–2003
Nev.	Kenny Guinn (R)	1999–2003
N.H.	Jeanne Shaheen (D)	1999–2001
N.J.	Christine Todd Whitman (R)	1998–2002
N.M.	Gary E. Johnson (R)	1999–2003
N.Y.	George E. Pataki (R)	1999–2003
N.C.	James B. Hunt, Jr. (D)	1997–2001
N.D.	Edward T. Schafer (R)	1997–2001
Ohio	Bob Taft (R)	1999–2003
Okla.	Frank Keating (R)	1999–2003
Ore.	John Kitzhaber (D)	1999–2003
Pa.	Tom Ridge (R)	1999–2003
R.I.	Lincoln C. Almond (R)	1999–2003
S.C.	Jim Hodges (D)	1999–2003
S.D.	William J. Janklow (R)	1999–2003
Tenn.	Don Sundquist (R)	1999–2003
Tex.	George W. Bush (R)	1999–2003
Utah	Michael O. Leavitt (R)	1997–2001
Vt.	Howard Dean (D)	1999–2001
Va.	James S. Gilmore (R)	1998–2002
Wash.	Gary Locke (D)	1997–2001
W. Va.	Cecil H. Underwood (R)	1997–2001
Wis.	Tommy G. Thompson (R)	1999–2003
Wyo.	Jim Geringer (R)	1999–2003

1. Except where indicated, all terms begin and end in January. 2. Term begins and ends in December. 3. Reform Party.
NOTE: Election results as of 2:30 p.m., Nov. 4, 1998.

Senate and House Standing Committees, 105th Congress

Committees of the Senate

Aging (18 members)
Chairman: Charles E. Grassley (Iowa)
Ranking Dem.: John B. Breaux (La.)
Agriculture, Nutrition, and Forestry (18 members)
Chairman: Richard G. Lugar (Ind.)
Ranking Dem.: Tom Harkin (Iowa)
Appropriations (28 members)
Chairman: Ted Stevens (Alaska)
Ranking Dem.: Robert C. Byrd (W.Va.)
Armed Services (18 members)
Chairman: Strom Thurmond (S.C.)
Ranking Dem.: Carl Levin (Mich.)
Banking, Housing, and Urban Affairs (18 members)
Chairman: Alfonse D'Amato (N.Y.)
Ranking Dem.: Paul S. Sarbanes (Md.)
Budget (22 members)
Chairman: Pete V. Domenici (N.M.)
Ranking Dem.: Frank R. Lautenberg (N.J.)
Commerce, Science, and Transportation (20 members)
Chairman: John McCain (Ariz.)
Ranking Dem.: Ernest F. Hollings (S.C.)
Energy and Natural Resources (20 members)
Chairman: Frank H. Murkowski (Alaska)
Ranking Dem.: Dale Bumpers (Ark.)
Environment and Public Works (18 members)
Chairman: John H. Chafee (R.I.)
Ranking Dem.: Max Baucus (Mont.)
Ethics (6 members)
Chairman: Robert C. Smith (N.H)
Ranking Dem.: Harry Reid (Nev.)
Finance (20 members)
Chairman: William V. Roth, Jr. (Del.)
Ranking Dem.: Daniel Patrick Moynihan (N.Y.)
Foreign Relations (18 members)
Chairman: Jesse Helms (N.C.)
Ranking Dem.: Joseph R. Biden Jr. (Del.)
Governmental Affairs (16 members)
Chairman: Fred Thompson (Tenn.)
Ranking Dem.: John Glenn (Ohio)
Indian Affairs (14 members)
*Chairman:*Ben Nighthorse Campbell (Colo.)
Ranking Dem.: Daniel K. Inouye (Hawaii)
Intelligence (19 members)
Chairman: Richard C. Shelby (Ala.)
Ranking Dem.: Bob Kerrey (Neb.)
Judiciary (18 members)
Chairman: Orrin G. Hatch (Utah)
Ranking Dem.: Patrick J. Leahy (Vt.)
Labor and Human Resources (18 members)
Chairman: James M. Jeffords (Vt.)
Ranking Dem.: Edward M. Kennedy (Mass.)
Rules and Administration (16 members)
Chairman: John W. Warner (Va.)
Ranking Dem.: Wendell H. Ford (Ky.)
Small Business (18 members)
Chairman: Christopher S. Bond (Mo.)
Ranking Dem.: John Kerry (Mass.)
Veterans' Affairs (12 members)
Chairman: Arlen Specter (Pa.)
Ranking Dem: John D. Rockefeller IV (W.Va.)
Year 2000 Technology Problem (9 members)
Chairman: Robert F. Bennett (Utah)
Ranking Dem: Christopher J. Dodd (Conn.)

Committees of the House

Agriculture (50 members)
Chairman: Bob Smith (Ore.)
Ranking Dem.: Charles W. Stenholm (Tex.)
Appropriations (60 members)
Chairman: Robert L. Livingston (La.)
Ranking Dem.: David R. Obey (Wis.)
Banking and Financial Services (54 members)
Chairman: Jim Leach (Iowa)
Ranking Dem.: Henry B. Gonzalez (Texas)
Budget (43 members)
Chairman: John R. Kasich (Ohio)
Ranking Dem.: John M. Spratt Jr. (S.C.)
Commerce (51 members)
Chairman: Thomas J. Bliley, Jr. (Va.)
Ranking Dem.: John D. Dingell (Mich.)
Education and the Workforce (45 members)
Chairman: Bill Goodling (Pa.)
Ranking Dem.: William L. Clay (Mo.)
Government Reform and Oversight (44 members)
Chairman: Dan Burton (Ind.)
Ranking Dem.: Henry A. Waxman (Calif.)
House Oversight (9 members)
Chairman: Bill Thomas (Calif.)
Ranking Dem.: Sam Gejdenson (Conn.)
Intelligence (16 members)
Chairman: Porter J. Goss (Fla.)
Ranking Dem.: Norm Dicks (Wash.)
International Relations (47 members)
Chairman: Benjamin A. Gilman (N.Y.)
Ranking Dem.: Lee H. Hamilton (Ind.)
Judiciary (35 members)
Chairman: Henry J. Hyde (Ill.)
Ranking Dem.: John Conyers, Jr. (Mich.)
National Security (59 members)
Chairman: Floyd D. Spence (S.C.)
Ranking Dem.: Ike Skelton (Mo.)
Energy and Natural Resources (50 members)
Chairman: Don Young (Alaska)
Ranking Dem.: George Miller (Calif.)
Rules (13 members)
Chairman: Gerald B. H. Solomon (N.Y.)
Ranking Dem.: Joe Moakley (Mass.)
Science (46 members)
Chairman: F. James Sensenbrenner Jr. (Wis.)
Ranking Dem.: George E. Brown, Jr. (Calif.)
Small Business (35 members)
Chairman: James M. Talent (Mo.)
Ranking Dem.: John J. LaFalce (N.Y.)
Standards of Official Conduct (10 members)
Chairman: James V. Hansen (Utah)
Ranking Dem.: Howard L. Berman (Calif.)
Transportation and Infrastructure (75 members)
Chairman: Bud Shuster (Pa.)
Ranking Dem.: James L. Obestar (Minn.)
Veterans' Affairs (30 members)
Chairman: Bob Stump (Ariz.)
Ranking Dem.: Lane Evans (Ill.)
Ways and Means (39 members)
Chairman: Bill Archer (Texas)
Ranking Dem.: Charles B. Rangel (N.Y.)

Speakers of the House of Representatives

Dates served	Congress	Name and state	Dates served	Congress	Name and state
1789–1791	1	Frederick A. C. Muhlenberg (Pa.)	1869–1869	40	Theodore M. Pomeroy (N.Y.)[5]
1791–1793	2	Jonathan Trumbull (Conn.)	1869–1875	41–43	James G. Blaine (Maine)
1793–1795	3	Frederick A. C. Muhlenberg (Pa.)	1875–1876	44	Michael C. Kerr (Ind.)[6]
1795–1799	4–5	Jonathan Dayton (N.J.)[1]	1876–1881	44–46	Samuel J. Randall (Pa.)
1799–1801	6	Theodore Sedgwick (Mass.)	1881–1883	47	J. Warren Keifer (Ohio)
1801–1807	7–9	Nathaniel Macon (N.C.)	1883–1889	48–50	John G. Carlisle (Ky.)
1807–1811	10–11	Joseph B. Varnum (Mass.)	1889–1891	51	Thomas B. Reed (Maine)
1811–1814	12–13	Henry Clay (Ky.)[2]	1891–1895	52–53	Charles F. Crisp (Ga.)
1814–1815	13	Langdon Cheves (S.C.)	1895–1899	54–55	Thomas B. Reed (Maine)
1815–1820	14–16	Henry Clay (Ky.)[3]	1899–1903	56–57	David B. Henderson (Iowa)
1820–1821	16	John W. Taylor (N.Y.)	1903–1911	58–61	Joseph G. Cannon (Ill.)
1821–1823	17	Philip P. Barbour (Va.)	1911–1919	62–65	Champ Clark (Mo.)
1823–1825	18	Henry Clay (Ky.)	1919–1925	66–68	Frederick H. Gillett (Mass.)
1825–1827	19	John W. Taylor (N.Y.)	1925–1931	69–71	Nicholas Longworth (Ohio)
1827–1834	20–23	Andrew Stevenson (Va.)[4]	1931–1933	72	John N. Garner (Tex.)
1834–1835	23	John Bell (Tenn.)	1933–1934	73	Henry T. Rainey (Ill.)[7]
1835–1839	24–25	James K. Polk (Tenn.)	1935–1936	74	Joseph W. Byrns (Tenn.)[8]
1839–1841	26	Robert M. T. Hunter (Va.)	1936–1940	74–76	William B. Bankhead (Ala.)[9]
1841–1843	27	John White (Ky.)	1940–1947	76–79	Sam Rayburn (Tex.)
1843–1845	28	John W. Jones (Va.)	1947–1949	80	Joseph W. Martin, Jr. (Mass.)
1845–1847	29	John W. Davis (Ind.)	1949–1953	81–82	Sam Rayburn (Tex.)
1847–1849	30	Robert C. Winthrop (Mass.)	1953–1955	83	Joseph W. Martin, Jr. (Mass.)
1849–1851	31	Howell Cobb (Ga.)	1955–1961	84–87	Sam Rayburn (Tex.)[10]
1851–1855	32–33	Linn Boyd (Ky.)	1962–1971	87–91	John W. McCormack (Mass.)[11]
1855–1857	34	Nathaniel P. Banks (Mass.)	1971–1977	92–94	Carl Albert (Okla.)[12]
1857–1859	35	James L. Orr (S.C.)	1977–1987	95–99	Thomas P. O'Neill, Jr. (Mass.)[13]
1859–1861	36	Wm. Pennington (N.J.)	1987–1989	100–101	James C. Wright, Jr. (Tex.)[14]
1861–1863	37	Galusha A. Grow (Pa.)	1989–1994	101–103	Thomas S. Foley (Wash.)
1863–1869	38–40	Schuyler Colfax (Ind.)	1995–	104–	Newt Gingrich (Ga.)

1. George Dent (Md.) was elected Speaker pro tempore for April 20 and May 28, 1798. 2. Resigned during second session of 13th Congress. 3. Resigned between first and second sessions of 16th Congress. 4. Resigned during first session of 23rd Congress. 5. Elected Speaker and served the day of adjournment. 6. Died between first and second sessions of 44th Congress. During first session, there were two Speakers pro tempore: Samuel S. Cox (N.Y.), appointed for Feb. 17, May 12, and June 19, 1876, and Milton Sayler (Ohio), appointed for June 4, 1876. 7. Died in 1934 after adjournment of second session of 73rd Congress. 8. Died during second session of 74th Congress. 9. Died during third session of 76th Congress. 10. Died between first and second sessions of 87th Congress. 11. Not a candidate in 1970 election. 12. Not a candidate in 1976 election. 13. Not a candidate in 1986 election. 14. Resigned during first session of 101st Congress. *Source: Congressional Directory.*

Floor Leaders of the Senate

Democratic

Gilbert M. Hitchcock, Neb. (Min. 1919–20)
Oscar W. Underwood, Ala. (Min. 1920–23)
Joseph T. Robinson, Ark. (Min. 1923–33, Maj. 1933–37)
Alben W. Barkley, Ky. (Maj. 1937–46, Min. 1947–48)
Scott W. Lucas, Ill. (Maj. 1949–50)
Ernest W. McFarland, Ariz. (Maj. 1951–52)
Lyndon B. Johnson, Tex. (Min. 1953–54, Maj. 1955–60)
Mike Mansfield, Mont. (Maj. 1961–77)
Robert C. Byrd, W. Va. (Maj. 1977–81, Min. 1981–86, Maj. 1987–88)
George John Mitchell, Maine (Maj. 1989–1994)
Thomas A. Daschle, S.D. (Min. 1995–)

Republican

Charles Curtis, Kan. (Maj. 1925–29)
James E. Watson, Ind. (Maj. 1929–33)
Charles L. McNary, Ore. (Min. 1933–44)
Wallace H. White, Jr., Maine (Min. 1944–47, Maj. 1947–48)
Kenneth S. Wherry, Neb. (Min. 1949–51)
Styles Bridges, N.H. (Min. 1951–52)
Robert A. Taft, Ohio (Maj. 1953)
William F. Knowland, Calif. (Maj. 1953–54, Min. 1955–58)
Everett M. Dirksen, Ill. (Min. 1959–69)
Hugh Scott, Pa. (Min. 1969–1977)
Howard H. Baker, Jr., Tenn. (Min. 1977–81, Maj. 1981–84)
Robert J. Dole, Kan. (Maj. 1985–86, Min. 1987–94, Maj. 1995–96)
Trent Lott, Miss. (Maj. 1996–)

NOTE: Min. = Minority Leader; Maj. = Majority Leader. *Source:* United States Senate, Secretary for the Majority.

How a President Is Nominated and Elected

The Conventions

The National Conventions of both major parties are held during the summer of a presidential-election year. Earlier, each party selects delegates by primaries, conventions, committees, etc.

At each convention, a temporary chairman is chosen. After a credentials committee seats the delegates, a permanent chairman is elected. The convention then votes on a platform, drawn up by the platform committee.

By the third or fourth day, presidential nominations begin. The chairman calls the roll of states alphabetically. A state may place a candidate in nomination or yield to another state.

Voting, again alphabetically by roll call of states, begins after all nominations have been made and seconded. A simple majority is required in each party, although this may require many ballots.

Finally, the vice-presidential candidate is selected. Although there is no law saying that the candidates *must* come from different states, it is, practically, necessary for this to be the case. Otherwise, according to the Constitution (*see* the 12th Amendment), electors from that state could vote for only one of the candidates and would have to cast their other vote for some person of another state. This could result in a presidential candidate's receiving a majority electoral vote and his running mate's failing to.

The Electoral College

The next step in the process is the nomination of electors in each state, according to its laws. These electors must not be Federal office holders. In the November election, the voters cast their votes for electors, not for president. In some states, the ballots include only the names of the presidential and vice-presidential candidates; in others, they include only names of the electors. Nowadays, it is rare for electors to be split between parties. The last such occurrence was in North Carolina in 1968[1]; the last before that, in Tennessee in 1948. On three occasions (1824, 1876, and 1888), the presidential candidate with the largest popular vote failed to obtain an electoral-vote majority.

Each state has as many electors as it has Senators and Representatives. For the 1992 election, the total electors were 538, based on 100 Senators, 435 Representatives, plus 3 electoral votes from the District of Columbia as a result of the 23rd Amendment to the Constitution.

On the first Monday after the second Wednesday in December, the electors cast their votes in their respective state capitols. Constitutionally they may vote for someone other than the party candidate but usually they do not since they are pledged to one party and its candidate on the ballot. Should the presidential or vice-presidential candidate die between the November election and the December meetings, the electors pledged to vote for him could vote for whomever they pleased. However, it seems certain that the national committee would attempt to get an agreement among the state party leaders for a replacement candidate.

The votes of the electors, certified by the states, are sent to Congress, where the president of the Senate opens the certificates and has them counted in the presence of both Houses on January 6. The new president is inaugurated at noon on January 20.

Should no candidate receive a majority of the electoral vote for president, the House of Representatives chooses a president from among the three highest candidates, voting, not as individuals, but as states, with a majority (now 26) needed to elect. Should no vice-presidential candidate obtain the majority, the Senate, voting as individuals, chooses from the highest two.

1. In 1956, one of Alabama's 11 electoral votes was cast for Walter B. Jones. In 1960, six of Alabama's 11 electoral votes and one of Oklahoma's eight electoral votes were cast for Harry Flood Byrd. (Byrd also received all eight of Mississippi's electoral votes.)

Electoral College List of States and Votes, 1996 Presidential Election

(Total electoral votes: 538; majority needed to elect: 270)

State	Votes	State	Votes	State	Votes
Alabama	9	Kentucky	8	North Dakota	3
Alaska	3	Louisiana	9	Ohio	21
Arizona	8	Maine	4	Oklahoma	8
Arkansas	6	Maryland	10	Oregon	7
California	54	Massachusetts	12	Pennsylvania	23
Colorado	8	Michigan	18	Rhode Island	4
Connecticut	8	Minnesota	10	South Carolina	8
Delaware	3	Mississippi	7	South Dakota	3
District of Columbia	3	Missouri	11	Tennessee	11
Florida	25	Montana	3	Texas	32
Georgia	13	Nebraska	5	Utah	5
Hawaii	4	Nevada	4	Vermont	3
Idaho	4	New Hampshire	4	Virginia	13
Illinois	22	New Jersey	15	Washington	11
Indiana	12	New Mexico	5	West Virginia	5
Iowa	7	New York	33	Wisconsin	11
Kansas	6	North Carolina	14	Wyoming	3

Presidential Election of 1996, Electoral and Popular Vote Summary

Principal Candidates for President and Vice President:
Democratic—William J. Clinton; Albert A. Gore, Jr.
Republican—Robert J. Dole; Jack F. Kemp
Independent—H. Ross Perot; Pat Choate

	William J. Clinton		Robert J. Dole		H. Ross Perot		Electoral votes		
	Popular vote	%	Popular vote	%	Popular vote	%	D	R	I
Alabama	662,165	43%	769,044	50%	92,149	6%		9	
Alaska	80,380	33	122,746	51	26,333	11		3	
Arizona	653,288	46	622,073	44	112,072	8	8		
Arkansas	475,171	54	325,416	37	69,884	8	6		
California	5,119,835	51	3,828,380	38	697,847	7	54		
Colorado	671,152	44	691,848	46	99,629	7		8	
Connecticut	735,740	52	483,109	35	139,523	10	8		
Delaware	140,355	52	99,062	37	28,719	11	3		
D.C.	158,220	85	17,339	9	3,611	2	3		
Florida	2,546,870	48	2,244,536	42	483,870	9	25		
Georgia	1,053,849	46	1,080,843	47	146,337	6		13	
Hawaii	205,012	57	113,943	32	27,358	7	4		
Idaho	165,443	34	256,595	52	62,518	13		4	
Illinois	2,341,744	54	1,587,021	37	346,408	8	22		
Indiana	887,424	42	1,006,693	47	224,299	10		12	
Iowa	620,258	50	492,644	40	105,159	8	7		
Kansas	387,659	36	583,245	54	92,639	9		6	
Kentucky	636,614	46	623,283	45	120,396	9	8		
Louisiana	927,837	52	712,586	40	123,293	7	9		
Maine	312,788	52	186,378	31	85,970	14	4		
Maryland	966,207	54	681,530	38	115,812	6	10		
Massachusetts	1,571,763	61	718,107	28	227,217	9	12		
Michigan	1,989,653	52	1,481,212	38	336,670	9	18		
Minnesota	1,120,438	51	766,476	35	257,704	12	10		
Mississippi	394,022	44	439,838	49	52,222	6		7	
Missouri	1,025,935	47	890,016	41	217,188	10	11		
Montana	167,922	41	179,652	44	55,229	13		3	
Nebraska	236,761	35	363,467	54	71,278	10		5	
Nevada	203,974	44	199,244	43	43,986	9	4		
New Hampshire	246,214	49	196,532	39	48,390	10	4		
New Jersey	1,652,329	54	1,103,078	36	262,134	8	15		
New Mexico	273,495	49	232,751	42	32,257	6	5		
New York	3,756,177	59	1,933,492	31	503,458	8	33		
North Carolina	1,107,849	44	1,225,938	49	168,059	7		14	
North Dakota	106,905	40	125,050	47	32,515	12		3	
Ohio	2,148,222	47	1,859,883	40	483,207	11	21		
Oklahoma	488,105	40	582,315	48	130,788	11		8	
Oregon	649,641	47	538,152	39	121,221	9	7		
Pennsylvania	2,215,819	49	1,801,169	40	430,984	10	23		
Rhode Island	233,050	60	104,683	27	43,723	11	4		
South Carolina	506,283	44	573,458	50	64,386	5		8	
South Dakota	139,333	43	150,543	46	31,250	10		3	
Tennessee	909,146	48	863,530	46	105,918	5	11		
Texas	2,459,683	44	2,736,167	49	378,537	7		32	
Utah	221,633	33	361,911	54	66,461	10		5	
Vermont	137,894	53	80,352	31	31,024	12	3		
Virginia	1,091,060	45	1,138,350	47	159,861	7		13	
Washington	1,123,323	50	840,712	37	201,003	9	11		
West Virginia	327,812	51	233,946	37	71,639	11	5		
Wisconsin	1,071,971	49	845,029	39	227,339	10	11		
Wyoming	77,934	37	105,388	50	25,928	12		3	
Total	**47,402,357**	**49%**	**39,198,755**	**41%**	**8,085,402**	**8%**	**379**	**159**	

NOTE: Total electoral votes = 538. Total electoral votes needed to win = 270. *Source:* Federal Election Commission.

National Political Conventions Since 1856

Opening date	Party	Where held
June 17, 1856	Republican	Philadelphia
June 2, 1856	Democratic	Cincinnati
May 16, 1860	Republican	Chicago
April 23, 1860	Democratic	Charleston and Baltimore
June 7, 1864	Republican[1]	Baltimore
Aug. 29, 1864	Democratic	Chicago
May 20, 1868	Republican	Chicago
July 4, 1868	Democratic	New York City
June 5, 1872	Republican	Philadelphia
June 9, 1872	Democratic	Baltimore
June 14, 1876	Republican	Cincinnati
June 28, 1876	Democratic	St. Louis
June 2, 1880	Republican	Chicago
June 23, 1880	Democratic	Cincinnati
June 3, 1884	Republican	Chicago
July 11, 1884	Democratic	Chicago
June 19, 1888	Republican	Chicago
June 6, 1888	Democratic	St. Louis
June 7, 1892	Republican	Minneapolis
June 21, 1892	Democratic	Chicago
June 16, 1896	Republican	St. Louis
July 7, 1896	Democratic	Chicago
June 19, 1900	Republican	Philadelphia
July 4, 1900	Democratic	Kansas City
June 21, 1904	Republican	Chicago
July 6, 1904	Democratic	St. Louis
June 16, 1908	Republican	Chicago
July 7, 1908	Democratic	Denver
June 18, 1912	Republican	Chicago
June 25, 1912	Democratic	Baltimore
June 7, 1916	Republican	Chicago
June 14, 1916	Democratic	St. Louis
June 8, 1920	Republican	Chicago
June 28, 1920	Democratic	San Francisco
June 10, 1924	Republican	Cleveland
June 24, 1924[2]	Democratic	New York City
June 12, 1928	Republican	Kansas City
June 26, 1928	Democratic	Houston
June 14, 1932	Republican	Chicago
June 27, 1932	Democratic	Chicago
June 9, 1936	Republican	Cleveland
June 23, 1936	Democratic	Philadelphia
June 24, 1940	Republican	Philadelphia
July 15, 1940	Democratic	Chicago
June 26, 1944	Republican	Chicago
July 19, 1944	Democratic	Chicago
June 21, 1948	Republican	Philadelphia
July 12, 1948	Democratic	Philadelphia
July 17, 1948	(3)	Birmingham
July 22, 1948	Progressive	Philadelphia
July 7, 1952	Republican	Chicago
July 21, 1952	Democratic	Chicago
Aug. 20, 1956	Republican	San Francisco
Aug. 13, 1956	Democratic	Chicago
July 25, 1960	Republican	Chicago
July 11, 1960	Democratic	Los Angeles
July 13, 1964	Republican	San Francisco
Aug. 24, 1964	Democratic	Atlantic City
Aug. 5, 1968	Republican	Miami Beach
Aug. 26, 1968	Democratic	Chicago
July 10, 1972	Democratic	Miami Beach
Aug. 21, 1972	Republican	Miami Beach
July 12, 1976	Democratic	New York City
Aug. 16, 1976	Republican	Kansas City, Mo.
Aug. 11, 1980	Democratic	New York City
July 14, 1980	Republican	Detroit
Aug. 20, 1984	Republican	Dallas
July 16, 1984	Democratic	San Francisco
July 18, 1988	Democratic	Atlanta
Aug. 15, 1988	Republican	New Orleans
July 13, 1992	Democratic	New York City
Aug. 17, 1992	Republican	Houston
Aug. 10, 1996	Republican	San Diego
Aug. 26, 1996	Democratic	Chicago

1. The Convention adopted name Union party to attract War Democrats and others favoring prosecution of war. 2. In session until July 10, 1924. 3. States' Rights delegates from 13 southern states.

National Committee Chairmen Since 1944

Chairman and (state)	Term
Republican	
Herbert Brownell, Jr. (N.Y.)	1944–1946
Carroll Reece (Tenn.)	1946–1948
Hugh D. Scott, Jr. (Pa.)	1948–1949
Guy G. Gabrielson (N.J.)	1949–1952
Arthur E. Summerfield (Mich.)	1952–1953
Wesley Roberts (Kan.)	1953
Leonard W. Hall (N.Y.)	1953–1957
Meade Alcorn (Conn.)	1957–1959
Thruston B. Morton (Ky.)	1959–1961
William E. Miller (N.Y.)	1961–1964
Dean Burch (Ariz.)	1964–1965
Ray C. Bliss (Ohio)	1965–1969
Rogers C. B. Morton (Md.)	1969–1971
Robert Dole (Kan.)	1971–1973
George H. Bush (Tex.)	1973–1974
Mary Louise Smith (Iowa)	1974–1977
William E. Brock III (Tenn.)	1977–1981
Richard Richards (Utah)	1981–1983
Frank J. Fahrenkopf, Jr. (Nevada)	1983–1989
Lee Atwater (S.C.)	1989–1991
Clayton K. Yeutter (Neb.)	1991–1992
Richard Bond (N.Y.)	1992–1993
Haley Barbour (Miss.)	1993–1997
Jim Nicholson (Colo.)	1997–
Democratic	
Robert E. Hannegan (Mo.)	1944–1947
J. Howard McGrath (R.I.)	1947–1949
William M. Boyle, Jr. (Mo.)	1949–1951
Frank E. McKinney (Ind.)	1951–1952
Stephen A. Mitchell (Ill.)	1952–1954
Paul M. Butler (Ind.)	1955–1960
Henry M. Jackson (Wash.)	1960–1961
John M. Bailey (Conn.)	1961–1968
Lawrence F. O'Brien (Mass.)	1968–1969
Fred R. Harris (Okla.)	1969–1970
Lawrence F. O'Brien (Mass.)	1970–1972
Jean Westwood (Utah)	1972
Robert S. Strauss (Tex.)	1972–1977
Kenneth M. Curtis (Me.)	1977
John C. White (Tex.)	1977–1981
Charles T. Manatt (Calif.)	1981–1985
Paul G. Kirk, Jr. (Mass.)	1985–1989
Ronald H. Brown (D.C.)	1989–1993
David Wilhelm (Ill.)	1993–1994
Christopher J. Dodd (Conn.)	1995–1996
Steven Grossman (Mass.)	1996–

Republican National Committee: 310 First St., S.E., Washington, D. C. 20003. *Democratic National Committee:* 430 South Capitol St., S.E., Washington, D.C. 20003.

Presidential Elections, 1789–1996

For the original method of electing the president and the vice president (elections of 1789, 1792, 1796, and 1800), *see* Article II, Section 1, of the Constitution. The election of 1804 was the first one in which the electors voted for president and vice president on separate ballots. (See Amendment XII to the Constitution.)

Year	Presidential candidate	Party	Electoral votes
1789[1]	George Washington	(no party)	69
	John Adams	(no party)	34
	Scattering	(no party)	35
	Votes not cast		8
1792	George Washington	Federalist	132
	John Adams	Federalist	77
	George Clinton	Anti-Federalist	50
	Thomas Jefferson	Anti-Federalist	4
	Aaron Burr	Anti-Federalist	1
	Votes not cast		6
1796	John Adams	Federalist	71
	Thomas Jefferson	Dem.-Rep.	68
	Thomas Pinckney	Federalist	59
	Aaron Burr	Dem.-Rep.	30
	Scattering		48
1800[2]	Thomas Jefferson	Dem.-Rep.	73
	Aaron Burr	Dem.-Rep.	73
	John Adams	Federalist	65
	Charles C. Pinckney	Federalist	64
	John Jay	Federalist	1

Year	Presidential candidate	Party	Electoral votes	Vice-presidential candidate	Party	Electoral votes
1804	Thomas Jefferson	Dem.-Rep.	162	George Clinton	Dem.-Rep.	162
	Charles C. Pinckney	Federalist	14	Rufus King	Federalist	14
1808	James Madison	Dem.-Rep.	122	George Clinton	Dem.-Rep.	113
	Charles C. Pinckney	Federalist	47	Rufus King	Federalist	47
	George Clinton	Dem.-Rep.	6	John Langdon	Ind. (no party)	9
	Votes not cast		1	James Madison	Dem.-Rep.	3
				James Monroe	Dem.-Rep.	3
				Votes not cast		1
1812	James Madison	Dem.-Rep.	128	Elbridge Gerry	Dem.-Rep.	131
	De Witt Clinton	Federalist	89	Jared Ingersoll	Federalist	86
	Votes not cast		1	Votes not cast		1
1816	James Monroe	Dem.-Rep.	183	Daniel D. Tompkins	Dem.-Rep.	183
	Rufus King	Federalist	34	John E. Howard	Federalist	22
	Votes not cast		4	James Ross	Ind. (no party)	5
				John Marshall	Federalist	4
				Robert G. Harper	Ind. (no party)	3
				Votes not cast		4
1820	James Monroe	Dem-Rep	231	Daniel D. Tompkins	Dem.-Rep.	218
	John Quincy Adams	Ind. (no party)	1	Richard Stockton	Ind. (no party)	8
	Votes not cast		3	Daniel Rodney	Ind. (no party)	4
				Richard Rush	Ind. (no party)	1
				Robert G. Harper	Ind. (no party)	1
				Votes not cast		3
1824[3]	John Quincy Adams	(no party)	84	John C. Calhoun	(no party)	182
	Andrew Jackson	(no party)	99	Nathan Sanford	(no party)	30
	William H. Crawford	(no party)	41	Nathaniel Macon	(no party)	24
	Henry Clay	(no party)	37	Andrew Jackson	(no party)	13
				Martin Van Buren	(no party)	9
				Henry Clay	(no party)	2
				Votes not cast		1
1828	Andrew Jackson	Democratic	178	John C. Calhoun	Democratic	171
	John Quincy Adams	Natl. Rep.	83	Richard Rush	Natl. Rep.	83
				William Smith	Democratic	7
1832	Andrew Jackson	Democratic	219	Martin Van Buren	Democratic	189
	Henry Clay	Natl. Rep.	49	John Sergeant	Natl. Rep.	49
	John Floyd	Ind. (no party)	11	Henry Lee	Ind. (no party)	11
	William Wirt	Antimasonic[4]	7	Amos Ellmaker	Antimasonic	7
	Votes not cast		2	William Wilkins	Ind. (no party)	30
				Votes not cast		2
1836	Martin Van Buren	Democratic	170	Richard M. Johnson[5]	Democratic	147
	William H. Harrison	Whig	73	Francis Granger	Whig	77
	Hugh L. White	Whig	26	John Tyler	Whig	47
	Daniel Webster	Whig	14	William Smith	Ind. (no party)	23
	W. P. Mangum	Ind. (no party)	11			

Year	Presidential candidate	Party	Electoral votes	Vice-presidential candidate	Party	Electoral votes
1840	William H. Harrison[6]	Whig	234	John Tyler	Whig	234
	Martin Van Buren	Democratic	60	Richard M. Johnson	Democratic	48
				L. W. Tazewell	Ind. (no party)	11
				James K. Polk	Democratic	1
1844	James K. Polk	Democratic	170	George M. Dallas	Democratic	170
	Henry Clay	Whig	105	Theo. Frelinghuysen	Whig	105
1848	Zachary Taylor[7]	Whig	163	Millard Fillmore	Whig	163
	Lewis Cass	Democratic	127	William O. Butler	Democratic	127
1852	Franklin Pierce	Democratic	254	William R. King	Democratic	254
	Winfield Scott	Whig	42	William A. Graham	Whig	42
1856	James Buchanan	Democratic	174	John C.	Democratic	174
	John C. Fremont	Republican	114	Breckinridge	Republican	114
	Millard Fillmore	American[8]	8	William L. Dayton	American[8]	8
				A. J. Donelson		
1860	Abraham Lincoln	Republican	180	Hannibal Hamlin	Republican	180
	John C.	Democratic	72	Joseph Lane	Democratic	72
	Breckinridge	Const. Union	39	Edward Everett	Const. Union	39
	John Bell	Democratic	12	H. V. Johnson	Democratic	12
	Stephen A. Douglas					
1864	Abraham Lincoln[9]	Union[10]	212	Andrew Johnson	Union[15]	212
	George B. McClellan	Democratic	21	G. H. Pendleton	Democratic	21
1868	Ulysses S. Grant	Republican	214	Schuyler Colfax	Republican	214
	Horatio Seymour	Democratic	80	Francis P. Blair, Jr.	Democratic	80
	Votes not counted[11]		23	Votes not counted[11]		23

Year	Presidential candidate	Party	Electoral votes	Popular votes	Vice-presidential candidate and party
1872	Ulysses S. Grant	Republican	286	3,597,132	Henry Wilson—R
	Horace Greeley	Dem , Liberal Rep.	([12])	2,834,125	B. Gratz Brown—D, LR—(47)
	Thomas A. Hendricks	Democratic	42		Scattering—(19)
	B. Gratz Brown	Dem., Liberal Rep.	18		Votes not counted—(14)
	Charles J. Jenkins	Democratic	2		
	David Davis	Democratic	1		
	Votes not counted		17		
1876[13]	Rutherford B. Hayes	Republican	185	4,033,768	William A. Wheeler—R
	Samuel J. Tilden	Democratic	184	4,285,992	Thomas A. Hendricks—D
	Peter Cooper	Greenback	0	81,737	Samuel F. Cary—G
1880	James A. Garfield[14]	Republican	214	4,449,053	Chester A. Arthur—R
	Winfield S. Hancock	Democratic	155	4,442,035	William H. English—D
	James B. Weaver	Greenback	0	308,578	B. J. Chambers—G
1884	Grover Cleveland	Democratic	219	4,911,017	Thomas A. Hendricks—D
	James G. Blaine	Republican	182	4,848,334	John A. Logan—R
	Benjamin F. Butler	Greenback	0	175,370	A. M. West—G
	John P. St. John	Prohibition	0	150,369	William Daniel—P
1888	Benjamin Harrison	Republican	233	5,440,216	Levi P. Morton—R
	Grover Cleveland	Democratic	168	5,538,233	A. G. Thurman—D
	Clinton B. Fisk	Prohibition	0	249,506	John A. Brooks—P
	Alson J. Streeter	Union Labor	0	146,935	Charles E. Cunningham—UL
1892	Grover Cleveland	Democratic	277	5,556,918	Adlai E. Stevenson—D
	Benjamin Harrison	Republican	145	5,176,108	Whitelaw Reid—R
	James B. Weaver	People's[15]	22	1,041,028	James G. Field—Peo
	John Bidwell	Prohibition	0	264,133	James B. Cranfill—P
1896	William McKinley	Republican	271	7,035,638	Garret A. Hobart—R
	William J. Bryan	Dem., People's[15]	176	6,467,946	Arthur Sewall—D—(149)
					Thomas E. Watson—Peo—(27)
	John M. Palmer	Natl. Dem.	0	133,148	Simon B. Buckner—ND
	Joshua Levering	Prohibition	0	132,007	Hale Johnson—P
1900	William McKinley[16]	Republican	292	7,219,530	Theodore Roosevelt—R
	William J. Bryan	Dem., People's[15]	155	6,358,071	Adlai E. Stevenson—D, Peo
	Eugene V. Debs	Social Democratic	0	94,768	Job Harriman—SD

Year	Presidential candidate	Party	Electoral votes	Popular votes	Vice-presidential candidate and party
1904	Theodore Roosevelt	Republican	336	7,628,834	Charles W. Fairbanks—R
	Alton B. Parker	Democratic	140	5,084,491	Henry G. Davis—D
	Eugene V. Debs	Socialist	0	402,400	Benjamin Hanford—S
1908	William H. Taft	Republican	321	7,679,006	James S. Sherman—R
	William J. Bryan	Democratic	162	6,409,106	John W. Kern—D
	Eugene V. Debs	Socialist	0	402,820	Benjamin Hanford—S
1912	Woodrow Wilson	Democratic	435	6,286,214	Thomas R. Marshall—D
	Theodore Roosevelt	Progressive	88	4,126,020	Hiram Johnson—Prog
	William H. Taft	Republican	8	3,483,922	Nicholas M. Butler—R[17]
	Eugene V. Debs	Socialist	0	897,011	Emil Seidel—S
1916	Woodrow Wilson	Democratic	277	9,129,606	Thomas R. Marshall—D
	Charles E. Hughes	Republican	254	8,538,221	Charles W. Fairbanks—R
	A. L. Benson	Socialist	0	585,113	G. R. Kirkpatrick—S
1920	Warren G. Harding[18]	Republican	404	16,152,200	Calvin Coolidge—R
	James M. Cox	Democratic	127	9,147,353	Franklin D. Roosevelt—D
	Eugene V. Debs	Socialist	0	917,799	Seymour Stedman—S
1924	Calvin Coolidge	Republican	382	15,725,016	Charles G. Dawes—R
	John W. Davis	Democratic	136	8,385,586	Charles W. Bryan—D
	Robert M. LaFollette	Progressive, Socialist	13	4,822,856	Burton K. Wheeler—Prog S
1928	Herbert Hoover	Republican	444	21,392,190	Charles Curtis—R
	Alfred E. Smith	Democratic	87	15,016,443	Joseph T. Robinson—D
	Norman Thomas	Socialist	0	267,420	James H. Maurer—S
1932	Franklin D. Roosevelt	Democratic	472	22,821,857	John N. Garner—D
	Herbert Hoover	Republican	59	15,761,841	Charles Curtis—R
	Norman Thomas	Socialist	0	884,781	James H. Maurer—S
1936	Franklin D. Roosevelt	Democratic	523	27,751,597	John N. Garner—D
	Alfred M. Landon	Republican	8	16,679,583	Frank Knox—R
	Norman Thomas	Socialist	0	187,720	George Nelson—S
1940	Franklin D. Roosevelt	Democratic	449	27,244,160	Henry A. Wallace—D
	Wendell L. Willkie	Republican	82	22,305,198	Charles L. McNary—R
	Norman Thomas	Socialist	0	99,557	Maynard C. Krueger—S
1944	Franklin D. Roosevelt[19]	Democratic	432	25,602,504	Harry S. Truman—D
	Thomas E. Dewey	Republican	99	22,006,285	John W. Bricker—R
	Norman Thomas	Socialist	0	80,518	Darlington Hoopes—S
1948	Harry S. Truman	Democratic	303	24,179,345	Alben W. Barkley—D
	Thomas E. Dewey	Republican	189	21,991,291	Earl Warren—R
	J. Strom Thurmond	States' Rights Dem.	39	1,176,125	Fielding L. Wright—SR
	Henry A. Wallace	Progressive	0	1,157,326	Glen Taylor—Prog
	Norman Thomas	Socialist	0	139,572	Tucker P. Smith—S
1952	Dwight D. Eisenhower	Republican	442	33,936,234	Richard M. Nixon—R
	Adlai E. Stevenson	Democratic	89	27,314,992	John J. Sparkman—D
1956	Dwight D. Eisenhower	Republican	457	35,590,472	Richard M. Nixon—R
	Adlai E. Stevenson	Democratic	73[20]	26,022,752	Estes Kefauver—D
1960	John F. Kennedy[22]	Democratic	303	34,226,731	Lyndon B. Johnson—D
	Richard M. Nixon	Republican	219[21]	34,108,157	Henry Cabot Lodge—R
1964	Lyndon B. Johnson	Democratic	486	43,129,484	Hubert H. Humphrey—D
	Barry M. Goldwater	Republican	52	27,178,188	William E. Miller—R
1968	Richard M. Nixon	Republican	301	31,785,480	Spiro T. Agnew—R
	Hubert H. Humphrey	Democratic	191	31,275,166	Edmund S. Muskie—D
	George C. Wallace	American Independent	46	9,906,473	Curtis F. LeMay—AI

Year	Presidential candidate	Party	Electoral votes	Popular votes	Vice-presidential candidate and party
1972	Richard M. Nixon[23]	Republican	520[24]	47,169,911	Spiro T. Agnew—R
	George McGovern	Democratic	17	29,170,383	Sargent Shriver—D
	John G. Schmitz	American	0	1,099,482	Thomas J. Anderson—A
1976	Jimmy Carter	Democratic	297	40,830,763	Walter F. Mondale—D
	Gerald R. Ford	Republican	240[25]	39,147,973	Robert J. Dole—R
	Eugene J. McCarthy	Independent	0	756,631	None
1980	Ronald Reagan	Republican	489	43,899,248	George Bush—R
	Jimmy Carter	Democratic	49	36,481,435	Walter F. Mondale—D
	John B. Anderson	Independent	0	5,719,437	Patrick J. Lucey—I
1984	Ronald Reagan	Republican	525	54,455,075	George Bush—R
	Walter F. Mondale	Democratic	13	37,577,185	Geraldine A. Ferraro—D
1988	George H. Bush	Republican	426	48,886,097	J. Danforth Quayle—R
	Michael S. Dukakis	Democratic	111[26]	41,809,074	Lloyd Bentsen—D
1992	William J. Clinton	Democratic	370	44,909,889	Albert A. Gore, Jr.—D
	George H. Bush	Republican	168	39,104,545	J. Danforth Quayle—R
	H. Ross Perot	Independent	0	19,742,267	James B. Stockdale—I
1996	William J. Clinton	Democratic	379	47,402,357	Albert A. Gore, Jr.—D
	Robert J. Dole	Republican	159	39,198,755	Jack F. Kemp—R
	H. Ross Perot	Independent	0	8,085,402	Pat Choate—I

1. Only 10 states participated in the election. The New York legislature chose no electors, and North Carolina and Rhode Island had not yet ratified the Constitution. 2. As Jefferson and Burr were tied, the House of Representatives chose the president. In a vote by states, 10 votes were cast for Jefferson, 4 for Burr; 2 votes were not cast. 3. As no candidate had an electoral-vote majority, the House of Representatives chose the president from the first three. In a vote by states, 13 votes were cast for Adams, 7 for Jackson, and 4 for Crawford. 4. The Antimasonic Party on Sept. 26, 1831, was the first party to hold a nominating convention to choose candidates for president and vice president. 5. As Johnson did not have an electoral-vote majority, the Senate chose him 33–14 over Granger, the others being legally out of the race. 6. Harrison died April 4, 1841, and Tyler succeeded him April 6. 7. Taylor died July 9, 1850, and Fillmore succeeded him July 10. 8. Also known as the Know-Nothing Party. 9. Lincoln died April 15, 1865, and Johnson succeeded him the same day. 10. Name adopted by the Republican National Convention of 1864. Johnson was a War Democrat. 11. 23 Southern electoral votes were excluded. 12. *See* Election of 1872 in Unusual Voting Results. 13. *See* Election of 1876 in Unusual Voting Results. 14. Garfield died Sept. 19, 1881, and Arthur succeeded him Sept. 20. 15. Members of People's Party were called Populists. 16. McKinley died Sept. 14, 1901, and Roosevelt succeeded him the same day. 17. James S. Sherman, Republican candidate for vice president, died Oct. 30, 1912, and the Republican electoral votes were cast for Butler.18. Harding died Aug. 2, 1923, and Coolidge succeeded him Aug. 3. 19. Roosevelt died April 12, 1945, and Truman succeeded him the same day. 20. One electoral vote from Alabama was cast for Walter B. Jones. 21. Sen. Harry F. Byrd received 15 electoral votes. 22. Kennedy died Nov. 22, 1963, and Johnson succeeded him the same day. 23. Nixon resigned Aug. 9, 1974, and Gerald R. Ford succeeded him the same day. 24. One electoral vote from Virginia was cast for John Hospers, Libertarian Party. 25. One electoral vote from Washington was cast for Ronald Reagan. 26. One electoral vote from West Virginia was cast for Lloyd Bentsen.

Gerrymander

Source: The Reader's Companion to American History, Houghton Mifflin Company.

Gerrymander refers to the drawing of boundaries of legislative districts to benefit one party or group and handicap another. Although the practice dates back to the colonial period, its name is derived from Elbridge Gerry, a signer of the Declaration of Independence, a nonsigning delegate to the Federal Convention of 1787, and a leader of the Jeffersonian Republican party.

In 1812, while Gerry was governor of Massachusetts, the Republican-dominated legislature redrew district lines to weigh representation in favor of Republicans and against Federalists. The Federalists attacked the redistricting, specifically blaming Gerry although he had nothing to do with the project and, in private, opposed it. A Federalist newspaper published a political cartoon depicting the oddly shaped district covering Essex County as a salamander; the cartoonist dubbed his creation a "Gerry-mander." The word quickly passed into common parlance.

Since the 1950s, the federal courts have been increasingly willing to examine states' defining of representative districts to determine their adherence to the principle of "one man, one vote," as enunciated in *Baker v. Carr* (1962). Ironically, in light of the term's New England origins, most gerrymanders examined by the Supreme Court have come from southern states, where local legislatures sought to dilute the representation of urban residents and blacks.

Facts About Elections

Candidate with highest popular vote: Reagan (1984), 54,455,075.

Candidate with highest electoral vote: Reagan (1984), 525

Candidate carrying most states: Nixon (1972) and Reagan (1984), 49.

Candidate running most times: Norman Thomas, six (1928, 1932, 1936, 1940, 1944, 1948).

Candidate elected, defeated, then reelected: Cleveland (1884, 1888, 1892).

Qualifications for Voting

The Supreme Court decision of March 21, 1972, declared lengthy requirements for voting in state and local elections unconstitutional and suggested that 30 days was an ample period. Most of the states have changed or eliminated their durational residency requirements to comply with the ruling, as shown.

NO DURATIONAL RESIDENCY REQUIREMENT

Alabama[1], Arkansas, Connecticut[2], Delaware[3], District of Columbia[4], Florida[5], Georgia[6], Hawaii[6], Iowa[1], Louisiana[7], Maine, Maryland, Massachusetts[8], Missouri[9], Nebraska[10], New Hampshire[11], New Mexico[12], Oklahoma, South Carolina[13], South Dakota[14], Texas[6], Virginia, West Virginia[6], Wyoming[6]

30-DAY RESIDENCY REQUIREMENT

Alaska[15], Arizona[16], Idaho[17], Illinois, Indiana, Michigan, Mississippi[18], Montana, Nevada, New Jersey, New York, North Carolina, North Dakota, Ohio, Pennsylvania[6], Rhode Island, Tennessee[6], Utah, Washington[6]

OTHER

California[19], Colorado[20], Minnesota[21], and Oregon[22], 20 days; Kentucky, 28 days; Kansas, 14 days; Vermont, 10–12 days[23]; Wisconsin, 10 days

1. 10-day registration requirement. In-person registration by 5 PM, eleven days before election date. 2. Registration deadline 14th day before election; registration and party enrollment deadline by 12 noon the day before primary. 3. Must reside in Delaware and register by the last day that the books are open for registration. 4. Registration stops 30 days before any election. Voters must inform Board of Elections of change of address within 30 days of moving. 5. 29-day registration requirement before national election; 29-day registration requirement before first and second state primary. 6. 30-day registration requirement. 7. Register 24 days prior to any election. 8. No residency required to register to vote. 9. Must be registered by the fourth Wednesday prior to election. 10. Registration requirement, 2nd Friday prior to elections. 11. Registration requirement, 10 days prior to elections. Same day registrations for federal and state elections. 12. Must register 28 days before election. 13. Registration certificate not valid for 30 days but if you move within the state you can vote in old precinct during the 30 days. 14. 15-day registration requirement. 15. If otherwise qualified but has not been a resident of the election district for at least 30 days preceding the date of a presidential election, is entitled to register and vote for presidential and vice-presidential candidates. 16. Residency in the state 29 days preceding the election. 17. May register 25 days prior to any election with County Clerk. If eligible to vote, an individual may register in person at the polling place on election day at the resident precinct and complete a registration card, make an oath and provide proof of residence. 18. 30 days registration required, 60 days if registration is by mail. 19. Must be a registered voter 29 days before an election. 20. 25 days immediately preceding the election. 21. Permits registration and voting on election day with approved ID. 22. By close of business day registering agencies (which varies) 21st day before the election. 23. Administrative cut-off date for processing applications 2nd Saturday before the election by 12 noon. *Source:* questionnaires to the states.

Plurality and Majority

In order to win a plurality, a candidate must receive a greater number of votes than anyone running against him. If he receives 50 votes, for example, and two other candidates receive 49 and 2, he will have a plurality of one vote over his closest opponent.

However, a candidate does not have a majority unless he receives more than 50% of the total votes cast. In the example above, the candidate does not have a majority, because his 50 votes are less than 50% of the 101 votes cast.

Unusual Voting Results

Election of 1872

The presidential and vice-presidential candidates of the Liberal Republicans and the northern Democrats in 1872 were Horace Greeley and B. Gratz Brown. Greeley died Nov. 29, 1872, before his 66 electors voted. In the electoral balloting for President, 63 of Greeley's votes were scattered among four other men, including Brown.

Election of 1876

In the election of 1876 Samuel J. Tilden, the Democratic candidate, received a popular majority but lacked one undisputed electoral vote to carry a clear majority of the electoral college. The crux of the problem was in the 22 electoral votes which were in dispute because Florida, Louisiana, South Carolina, and Oregon each sent in two sets of election returns. In the three southern states, Republican election boards threw out enough Democratic votes to certify the Republican candidate, Hayes. In Oregon, the Democratic governor disqualified a Republican elector, replacing him with a Democrat. Since the Senate was Republican and the House of Representatives Democratic, it seemed useless to refer the disputed returns to the two houses for solution. Instead Congress appointed an Electoral Commission with five representatives each from the Senate, the House, and the Supreme Court. All but one Justice was named, giving the Commission seven Republican and seven Democratic members. The naming of the fifth Justice was left to the other four. He was a Republican who first favored Tilden but, under pressure from his party, switched to Hayes, ensuring his election by the Commission voting 8 to 7 on party lines.

Minority Presidents

Sixteen candidates have become president of the United States with a popular vote less than 50% of the total cast. It should be noted, however, that in elections before 1872, presidential electors were not chosen by popular vote in all states. Adams's election in 1824 was by the House of Representatives, which chose him over Jackson, who had a plurality of both electoral and popular votes, but not a majority in the electoral college.

The "minority" presidents are listed below.

Votes Received by Minority Presidents

Year	President	Electoral percent	Popular percent
1824	John Q. Adams	31.8%	29.8%
1844	James K. Polk (D)	61.8	49.3
1848	Zachary Taylor (W)	56.2	47.3
1856	James Buchanan (D)	58.7	45.3
1860	Abraham Lincoln (R)	59.4	39.9
1876	Rutherford B. Hayes (R)	50.1	47.9
1880	James A. Garfield (R)	57.9	48.3
1884	Grover Cleveland (D)	54.6	48.8
1888	Benjamin Harrison (R)	58.1	47.8
1892	Grover Cleveland (D)	62.4%	46.0%
1912	Woodrow Wilson (D)	81.9	41.8
1916	Woodrow Wilson (D)	52.1	49.3
1948	Harry S. Truman (D)	57.1	49.5
1960	John F. Kennedy (D)	56.4	49.7
1968	Richard M. Nixon (R)	56.1	43.4
1992	William J. Clinton (D)	68.8	43.0
1996	William J. Clinton (D)	70.4	49.0

National Voter Turnout in Federal Elections: 1960–1996

Year	Voting age population	Voter registration	Voter turnout	Turnout of voting-age popuation (percent)
1996	196,511,000	146,211,960	96,456,345	49.1%
1994	193,650,000	130,292,822	75,105,860	38.8
1992	189,529,000	133,821,178	104,405,155	55.1
1990	185,812,000	121,105,630	67,859,189	36.5
1988	182,778,000	126,379,628	91,594,693	50.1
1986	178,566,000	118,399,984	64,991,128	36.4
1984	174,466,000	124,150,614	92,652,680	53.1
1982	169,938,000	110,671,225	67,615,576	39.8
1980	164,597,000	113,043,734	86,515,221	52.6
1978	158,373,000	103,291,265	58,917,938	37.2
1976	152,309,190	105,037,986	81,555,789	53.6
1974	146,336,000	96,199,020[1]	55,943,834	30.2
1972	140,776,000	97,328,541	77,718,554	55.2
1970	124,498,000	82,496,747[2]	58,014,338	46.6
1968	120,328,186	81,658,180	73,211,875	60.8
1966	116,132,000	76,288,283[3]	56,188,046	48.4
1964	114,090,000	73,715,818	70,644,592	61.9
1962	112,423,000	65,393,751[4]	53,141,227	47.3
1960	109,159,000	64,833,096[5]	68,838,204	63.1

1. Registrations from Iowa not included. 2. Registrations from Iowa and Mo. not included. 3. Registrations from Iowa, Kans., Miss., Mo., Nebr., and Wyo. not included. D.C. did not have independent status. 4. Registrations from Ala., Alaska, D.C., Iowa, Kans., Ky., Miss., Mo., Nebr., N.C., N.D., Okla., S.D., Wis., and Wyo. not included. 5. Registrations from Ala., Alaska, D.C., Iowa, Kans., Ky., Miss., Mo., Nebr., N.M., N.C., N.D., Okla., S.D., Wis., and Wyo. not included. *Source:* Federal Election Commission. Data drawn from Congressional Research Service reports, Election Data Services Inc., and State Election Offices.

The Declaration of Independence

On April 12, 1776, the legislature of North Carolina authorized its delegates to the Continental Congress to join with others in a declaration of separation from Great Britain; the first colony to instruct its delegates to take the actual initiative was Virginia on May 15. On June 7, 1776, Richard Henry Lee of Virginia offered a resolution to the Congress to the effect "that these United Colonies are, and of right ought to be, free and independent States. . . ." A committee consisting of Thomas Jefferson, John Adams, Benjamin Franklin, Robert R. Livingston, and Roger Sherman, was organized to "prepare a declaration to the effect of the said first resolution." The Declaration of Independence was adopted on July 4, 1776. Most delegates signed the Declaration August 2, but George Wythe (Va.) signed August 27; Richard Henry Lee (Va.), Elbridge Gerry (Mass.), and Oliver Wolcott (Conn.) in September; Matthew Thornton (N.H.), not a delegate until September, in November; and Thomas McKean (Del.), although present on July 4, not until 1781 by special permission, having served in the army in the interim.

In Congress, July 4, 1776

The unanimous Declaration of the thirteen United States of America

When in the Course of human events it becomes necessary for one people to dissolve the political bands which have connected them with another, and to assume among the powers of the earth, the separate and equal station to which the Laws of Nature and of Nature's God entitle them, a decent respect to the opinions of mankind requires that they should declare the causes which impel them to the separation.

We hold these truths to be self-evident, that all men are created equal, that they are endowed by their Creator with certain unalienable Rights, that among these are Life, Liberty and the pursuit of Happiness.—That to secure these rights, Governments are instituted among Men, deriving their just powers from the consent of the governed.—That whenever any Form of Government becomes destructive of these ends, it is the Right of the People to alter or to abolish it, and to institute new Government, laying its foundation on such principles and organizing its powers in such form, as to them shall seem most likely to effect their Safety and Happiness. Prudence, indeed, will dictate that Governments long established should not be changed for light and transient causes; and accordingly all experience hath shewn that mankind are more disposed to suffer, while evils are sufferable, than to right themselves by abolishing the forms to which they are accustomed. But when a long train of abuses and usurpations, pursuing invariably the same Object evinces a design to reduce them under absolute Despotism, it is their right, it is their duty, to throw off such Government, and to provide new Guards for their future security.—Such has been the patient sufferance of these Colonies; and such is now the necessity which constrains them to alter their former Systems of Government. The history of the present King of Great Britain is a history of repeated injuries and usurpations, all having in direct object the establishment of an absolute Tyranny over these States. To prove this, let Facts be submitted to a candid world.

He has refused his Assent to Laws, the most wholesome and necessary for the public good.

He has forbidden his Governors to pass Laws of immediate and pressing importance, unless suspended in their operation till his Assent should be obtained; and when so suspended, he has utterly neglected to attend to them.

He has refused to pass other Laws for the accommodation of large districts of people, unless those people would relinquish the right of Representation in the Legislature, a right inestimable to them and formidable to tyrants only.

He has called together legislative bodies at places unusual, uncomfortable, and distant from the depository of their Public Records, for the sole purpose of fatiguing them into compliance with his measures.

He has dissolved Representative Houses repeatedly, for opposing with manly firmness his invasions on the rights of the people.

He has refused for a long time, after such dissolutions, to cause others to be elected; whereby the Legislative Powers, incapable of Annihilation, have returned to the People at large for their exercise; the State remaining in the mean time exposed to all the dangers of invasion from without, and convulsions within.

He has endeavoured to prevent the population of these States; for that purpose obstructing the Laws for Naturalization of Foreigners; refusing to pass others to encourage their migrations hither, and raising the conditions of new Appropriations of Lands.

He has obstructed the Administration of Justice, by refusing his Assent to Laws for establishing Judiciary Powers.

He has made Judges dependent on his Will alone, for the tenure of their offices, and the amount and payment of their salaries.

He has erected a multitude of New Offices, and sent hither swarms of Officers to harass our people, and eat out their substance.

He has kept among us, in times of peace, Standing Armies without the Consent of our legislatures.

He has affected to render the Military independent of and superior to the Civil Power.

He has combined with others to subject us to a jurisdiction foreign to our constitution, and unacknowledged by our laws; giving his Assent to their Acts of pretended Legislation:

For quartering large bodies of armed troops among us:

For protecting them, by a mock Trial, from punishment for any Murders which they should commit on the Inhabitants of these States:

For cutting off our Trade with all parts of the world:

For imposing Taxes on us without our Consent:

For depriving us in many cases, of the benefits of Trial by Jury:

For transporting us beyond Seas to be tried for pretended offences:

For abolishing the free System of English Laws in a neighbouring Province, establishing therein an Arbitrary government, and enlarging its Boundaries so as to render it at once an example and fit instrument for introducing the same absolute rule into these Colonies:

For taking away our Charters, abolishing our most valuable Laws and altering fundamentally the Forms of our Governments:

For suspending our own Legislatures, and declaring themselves invested with power to legislate for us in all cases whatsoever.

He has abdicated Government here, by declaring us out of his Protection and waging War against us.

He has plundered our seas, ravaged our Coasts, burnt our towns, and destroyed the lives of our people.

He is at this time transporting large Armies of foreign Mercenaries to compleat the works of death, desolation, and tyranny, already begun with circumstances of Cruelty & Perfidy scarcely paralleled in the most barbarous ages, and totally unworthy the Head of a civilized nation.

He has constrained our fellow Citizens taken Captive on the high Seas to bear Arms against their Country, to become the executioners of their friends and Brethren, or to fall themselves by their Hands.

He has excited domestic insurrections amongst us, and has endeavoured to bring on the inhabitants of our frontiers, the merciless Indian Savages, whose known rule of warfare, is an undistinguished destruction of all ages, sexes and conditions.

In every stage of these Oppressions We have Petitioned for Redress in the most humble terms: Our repeated Petitions have been answered only by repeated injury. A Prince, whose character is thus marked by every act which may define a Tyrant, is unfit to be the ruler of a free people.

Nor have We been wanting in attentions to our Brittish brethren. We have warned them from time to time of attempts by their legislature to extend an unwarrantable jurisdiction over us. We have reminded them of the circumstances of our emigration and settlement here. We have appealed to their native justice and magnanimity, and we have conjured them by the ties of our common kindred to disavow these usurpations, which would inevitably interrupt our connections and correspondence. They too have been deaf to the voice of justice and of consanguinity. We must, therefore, acquiesce in the necessity, which denounces our Separation, and hold them, as we hold the rest of mankind, Enemies in War, in Peace Friends.

We, therefore, the Representatives of the United States of America, in General Congress, Assembled, appealing to the Supreme Judge of the world for the rectitude of our intentions, do, in the Name, and by Authority of the good People of these Colonies, solemnly publish and declare, That these United Colonies are, and of Right ought to be Free and Independent States; that they are Absolved from all Allegiance to the British Crown, and that all political connection between them and the State of Great Britain, is and ought to be totally dissolved; and that as Free and Independent States, they have full Power to levy War, conclude Peace, contract Alliances, establish Commerce, and to do all other Acts and Things which Independent States may of right do.—And for the support of this Declaration, with a firm reliance on the protection of Divine Providence, we mutually pledge to each other our Lives, our Fortunes and our sacred Honor.

—John Hancock

New Hampshire
Josiah Bartlett
Wm. Whipple
Matthew Thornton

Rhode Island
Step. Hopkins
William Ellery

Connecticut
Roger Sherman
Sam'el Huntington
Wm. Williams
Oliver Wolcott

New York
Wm. Floyd
Phil. Livingston
Frans. Lewis
Lewis Morris

New Jersey
Richd. Stockton
Jno. Witherspoon
Fras. Hopkinson
John Hart
Abra. Clark

Pennsylvania
Robt. Morris
Benjamin Rush
Benj. Franklin
John Morton
Geo. Clymer
Jas. Smith
Geo. Taylor
James Wilson
Geo. Ross

Massachusetts-Bay
Saml. Adams
John Adams
Robt. Treat Paine
Elbridge Gerry

Delaware
Caesar Rodney
Geo. Read
Tho. M'Kean

Maryland
Samuel Chase
Wm. Paca
Thos. Stone
Charles Carroll of Carrollton

Virginia
George Wythe
Richard Henry Lee
Th. Jefferson
Benj. Harrison
Ths. Nelson, Jr.
Francis Lightfoot Lee
Carter Braxton

North Carolina
Wm. Hooper
Joseph Hewes
John Penn

South Carolina
Edward Rutledge
Thos. Heyward, Junr.
Thomas Lynch, Junr.
Arthur Middleton

Georgia
Button Gwinnett
Lyman Hall
Geo. Walton

Constitution of the United States of America

(Historical text has been edited to conform to contemporary American usage. The bracketed words are designations for your convenience; they are not part of the Constitution.)

The oldest federal constitution in existence was framed by a convention of delegates from twelve of the thirteen original states in Philadelphia in May, 1787, Rhode Island failing to send a delegate. George Washington presided over the session, which lasted until September 17, 1787. The draft (originally a preamble and seven Articles) was submitted to all thirteen states and was to become effective when ratified by nine states. It went into effect on the first Wednesday in March, 1789, having been ratified by New Hampshire, the ninth state to approve, on June 21, 1788. The states ratified the Constitution in the following order:

Delaware	December 7, 1787
Pennsylvania	December 12, 1787
New Jersey	December 18, 1787
Georgia	January 2, 1788
Connecticut	January 9, 1788
Massachusetts	February 6, 1788
Maryland	April 28, 1788
South Carolina	May 23, 1788
New Hampshire	June 21, 1788
Virginia	June 25, 1788
New York	July 26, 1788
North Carolina	November 21, 1789
Rhode Island	May 29, 1790

[Preamble]

We the people of the United States, in order to form a more perfect Union, establish justice, insure domestic tranquility, provide for the common defence, promote the general welfare, and secure the blessings of liberty to ourselves and our posterity, do ordain and establish this Constitution for the United States of America.

Article I

Section 1

[Legislative powers vested in Congress.] All legislative powers herein granted shall be vested in a Congress of the United States, which shall consist of a Senate and House of Representatives.

Section 2

[Composition of the House of Representatives.—1.] The House of Representatives shall be composed of members chosen every second year by the people of the several States, and the electors in each State shall have the qualifications requisite for electors of the most numerous branch of the State Legislature.

[Qualifications of Representatives.—2.] No Person shall be a Representative who shall not have attained to the age of twenty-five years, and been seven years a citizen of the United States, and who shall not, when elected, be an inhabitant of that State in which he shall be chosen.

[Apportionment of Representatives and direct taxes—census.[1]—3.] (Representatives and direct taxes shall be apportioned among the several States which may be included within this Union, according to their respective numbers, which shall be determined by adding to the whole number of free persons, including those bound to service for a term of years, and excluding Indians not taxed, three fifths of all other persons.) The actual enumeration shall be made within three years after the first meeting of the Congress of the United States, and within every subsequent term of ten years, in such manner as they shall by law direct. The number of Representatives shall not exceed one for every thirty thousand, but each State shall have at least one Representative; and until such enumeration shall be made, the State of New Hampshire shall be entitled to choose three, Massachusetts eight, Rhode-Island and Providence Plantations one, Connecticut five, New York six, New Jersey four, Pennsylvania eight, Delaware one, Maryland six, Virginia ten, North Carolina five, South Carolina five, and Georgia three.

[Filling of vacancies in representation.—4.] When vacancies happen in the representation from any State, the Executive Authority thereof shall issue writs of election to fill such vacancies.

[Selection of officers; power of impeachment.—5.] The House of Representatives shall choose their Speaker and other officers; and shall have the sole power of impeachment.

Section 3[2]

[The Senate.—1.] The Senate of the United States shall be composed of two Senators from each State, chosen by the Legislature thereof, for six years; and each Senator shall have one vote.

[Classification of Senators; filling of vacancies.—2.] Immediately after they shall be assembled in consequence of the first election, they shall be divided as equally as may be into three classes. The seats of the Senators of the first class shall be vacated at the expiration of the second year, of the second class at the expiration of the fourth year, and of the third class at the expiration of the sixth year, so that one-third may be chosen every second year; and if vacancies happen by resignation, or otherwise, during the recess of the Legislature of any State, the Executive thereof may make temporary appointments (until the next meeting of the Legislature, which shall then fill such vacancies).

[Qualification of Senators.—3.] No person shall be a Senator who shall not have attained to the age of thirty years, and been nine years a citizen of the United States, and who shall not, when elected, be an inhabitant of that State for which he shall be chosen.

[Vice President to be President of Senate.—4.] The Vice President of the United States shall be President of the Senate, but shall have no vote, unless they be equally divided.

1. The clause included in parentheses is amended by the 14th Amendment, Section 2. 2. The first paragraph of this section and the part of the second paragraph included in parentheses are amended by the 17th Amendment.

[Selection of Senate officers; President pro tempore.—5.] The Senate shall choose their other officers, and also a President pro tempore, in the absence of the Vice President, or when he shall exercise the office of President of the United States.

[Senate to try impeachments.—6.] The Senate shall have the sole power to try all impeachments. When sitting for that purpose, they shall be on oath or affirmation. When the President of the United States is tried, the Chief Justice shall preside: and no person shall be convicted without the concurrence of two thirds of the members present.

[Judgment in cases of Impeachment.—7.] Judgment in cases of impeachment shall not extend further than to removal from office, and disqualification to hold and enjoy any office of honor, trust, or profit under the United States: but the party convicted shall nevertheless be liable and subject to indictment, trial, judgment and punishment, according to Law.

Section 4

[Control of congressional elections.—1.] The times, places, and manner of holding elections for Senators and Representatives, shall be prescribed in each State by the Legislature thereof; but the Congress may at any time by law make or alter such regulations, except as to the places of choosing Senators.

[Time for assembling of Congress[3]—2.] The Congress shall assemble at least once in every year, and such meeting shall be on the first Monday in December, unless they shall by law appoint a different day.

Section 5

[Each house to be the judge of the election and qualifications of its members; regulations as to quorum.—1.] Each House shall be the judge of the elections, returns, and qualifications of its own members, and a majority of each shall constitute a quorum to do business; but a smaller number may adjourn from day to day, and may be authorized to compel the attendance of absent members, in such manner, and under such penalties as each House may provide.

[Each house to determine its own rules.—2.] Each House may determine the rules of its proceedings, punish its members for disorderly behavior, and, with the concurrence of two thirds, expel a member.

[Journals and yeas and nays.—3.] Each House shall keep a journal of its proceedings, and from time to time publish the same, excepting such parts as may in their judgment require secrecy; and the yeas and nays of the members of either House on any question shall, at the desire of one fifth of those present, be entered on the journal.

[Adjournment.—4.] Neither House, during the session of Congress, shall, without the consent of the other, adjourn for more than three days, nor to any other place than that in which the two Houses shall be sitting.

Section 6

[Compensation and privileges of members of Congress.—1.] The Senators and Representatives shall receive a compensation for their services, to be ascertained by law, and paid out of the Treasury of the United States. They shall in all cases, except treason, felony, and breach of the peace, be privileged from arrest during their attendance at the session of their respective Houses, and in going to and returning from the same; and for any speech or debate in either House, they shall not be questioned in any other place.

[Incompatible offices; exclusions.—2.] No Senator or Representative shall, during the time for which he was elected, be appointed to any civil office under the authority of the United States, which shall have been created, or the emoluments whereof shall have been increased during such time; and no person holding any office under the United States shall be a member of either House during his continuance in office.

Section 7

[Revenue bills to originate in House.—1.] All bills for raising revenue shall originate in the House of Representatives; but the Senate may propose or concur with amendments as on other bills.

[Manner of passing bills; veto power of President.—2.] Every bill which shall have passed the House of Representatives and the Senate, shall, before it becomes a law, be presented to the President of the United States; if he approve he shall sign it, but if not he shall return it, with his objections to that House in which it shall have originated, who shall enter the objections at large on their journal, and proceed to reconsider it. If after such reconsideration two thirds of that House shall agree to pass the bill, it shall be sent, together with the objections, to the other House, by which it shall likewise be reconsidered, and if approved by two thirds of that House, it shall become a law. But in all such cases the votes of both Houses shall be determined by yeas and nays, and the names of the persons voting for and against the bill shall be entered on the journal of each house, respectively. If any bill shall not be returned by the President within ten days (Sundays excepted) after it shall have been presented to him, the same shall be a law, in like manner as if he had signed it, unless the Congress by their adjournment prevent its return, in which case it shall not be a law.

[Concurrent orders or resolutions, to be passed by President.—3.] Every order, resolution, or vote to which the concurrence of the Senate and House of Representatives may be necessary (except on a question of adjournment) shall be presented to the President of the United States; and before the same shall take effect, shall be approved by him, or being disapproved by him, shall be repassed by two thirds of the Senate and House of Representatives, according to the rules and limitations prescribed in the case of a bill.

3. Amended by the 20th Amendment, Section 2.

Section 8

[General powers of Congress.[4]]

[Taxes, duties, imposts, and excises.—1.] The Congress shall have power to lay and collect taxes, duties, imposts and excises, to pay the debts and provide for the common defense and general welfare of the United States; but all duties, imposts and excises shall be uniform throughout the United States;

[Borrowing of money.—2.] To borrow money on the credit of the United States;

[Regulation of commerce.—3.] To regulate commerce with foreign nations, and among the several States, and with the Indian tribes;

[Naturalization and bankruptcy.—4.] To establish a uniform rule of naturalization, and uniform laws on the subject of bankruptcies throughout the United States;

[Money, weights and measures.—5.] To coin money, regulate the value thereof, and of foreign coin, and fix the standard of weights and measures;

[Counterfeiting.—6.] To provide for the punishment of counterfeiting the securities and current coin of the United States;

[Post offices.—7.] To establish post offices and post roads;

[Patents and copyrights.—8.] To promote the progress of science and useful arts, by securing for limited times to authors and inventors the exclusive right to their respective writings and discoveries;

[Inferior courts.—9.] To constitute tribunals inferior to the Supreme Court;

[Piracies and felonies.—10.] To define and punish piracies and felonies committed on the high seas, and offences against the law of nations;

[War; marque and reprisal.—11.] To declare war, grant letters of marque and reprisal, and make rules concerning captures on land and water;

[Armies.—12.] To raise and support armies, but no appropriation of money to that use shall be for a longer term than two years;

[Navy.—13.] To provide and maintain a navy;

[Land and naval forces.—14.] To make rules for the government and regulation of the land and naval forces;

[Calling out militia.—15.] To provide for calling forth the militia to execute the laws of the Union, suppress insurrections, and repel invasions;

[Organizing, arming, and disciplining militia.—16.] To provide for organizing, arming, and disciplining, the militia, and for governing such part of them as may be employed in the service of the United States, reserving to the States, respectively, the appointment of the officers, and the authority of training the militia according to the discipline prescribed by Congress;

[Exclusive legislation over District of Columbia.—17.] To exercise exclusive legislation in all cases whatsoever, over such district (not exceeding ten miles square) as may, by cession of particular States, and the acceptance of Congress, become the seat of the Government of the United States, and to exercise like authority over all places purchased by the consent of the Legislature of the State in which the same shall be, for the erection of forts, magazines, arsenals, dock-yards, and other needful buildings;—And

[To enact laws necessary to enforce Constitution.—18.] To make all laws which shall be necessary and proper for carrying into execution the foregoing powers, and all other powers vested by this Constitution in the Government of the United States, or in any department or officer thereof.

Section 9

[Migration or importation of certain persons not to be prohibited before 1808.—1.] The migration or importation of such persons as any of the States now existing shall think proper to admit, shall not be prohibited by the Congress prior to the year one thousand eight hundred and eight, but a tax or duty may be imposed on such importation, not exceeding ten dollars for each person.

[Writ of habeas corpus not to be suspended; exception.—2.] The privilege of the writ of habeas corpus shall not be suspended, unless when in cases of rebellion or invasion the public safety may require it.

[Bills of attainder and ex post facto laws prohibited.—3.] No bill of attainder or ex post facto law shall be passed.

[Capitation and other direct taxes.—4.] No capitation, or other direct, tax shall be laid, unless in proportion to the census or enumeration herein before directed to be taken.[5]

[Exports not to be taxed.—5.] No tax or duty shall be laid on articles exported from any State.

[No preference to be given to ports of any States; interstate shipping.—6.] No preference shall be given by any regulation of commerce or revenue to the ports of one State over those of another: nor shall vessels bound to, or from, one State, be obliged to enter, clear, or pay duties in another.

[Money, how drawn from treasury; financial statements to be published.—7.] No money shall be drawn from the Treasury, but in consequence of appropriations made by law; and a regular statement and account of the receipts and expenditures of all public money shall be published from time to time.

[Titles of nobility not to be granted; acceptance by government officers of favors from foreign powers.—8.] No title of nobility shall be granted by the United States: and no person holding any office of profit or trust under them, shall, without the consent of the Congress, accept of any present, emolument, office, or title, of any kind whatever, from any king, prince, or foreign state.

Section 10

[Limitations of the powers of the several States.—1.] No State shall enter into any treaty, alliance, or confederation; grant letters of marque and reprisal; coin money; emit bills of credit; make any thing but gold and silver coin a tender in payment of debts; pass any bill of attainder, ex post facto law, or law impairing the obligation of contracts, or grant any title of nobility.

4. By the 16th Amendment, Congress is given the power to lay and collect taxes on income. 5. *See* the 16th Amendment.

[State imposts and duties.—2.] No State shall, without the consent of the Congress, lay any imposts or duties on imports or exports, except what may be absolutely necessary for executing its inspection laws; and the net produce of all duties and imposts, laid by any State on imports or exports, shall be for the use of the Treasury of the United States; and all such laws shall be subject to the revision and control of the Congress.

[Further restrictions on powers of States.—3.] No State shall, without the consent of Congress, lay any duty of tonnage, keep troops, or ships of war in time of peace, enter into any agreement or compact with another state, or with a foreign power, or engage in war, unless actually invaded, or in such imminent danger as will not admit of delay.

Article II

Section 1

[The President; the executive power.—1.] The executive power shall be vested in a President of the United States of America. He shall hold his office during the term of four years, and, together with the Vice President, chosen for the same term, be elected, as follows

[Appointment and qualifications of presidential electors.—2.] Each State shall appoint, in such manner as the Legislature thereof may direct, a number of electors, equal to the whole number of Senators and Representatives to which the State may be entitled in the Congress: but no Senator or Representative, or person holding an office of trust or profit under the United States, shall be appointed an elector.

[Original method of electing the Presidentand Vice President.[6]] (The electors shall meet in their respective States, and vote by ballot for two persons, of whom one at least shall not be an inhabitant of the same State with themselves. And they shall make a list of all the persons voted for, and of the number of votes for each; which list they shall sign and certify, and transmit sealed to the seat of the Government of the United States, directed to the President of the Senate. The President of the Senate shall, in the presence of the Senate and House of Representatives, open all the certificates, and the votes shall then be counted. The person having the greatest number of votes shall be the President, if such number be a majority of the whole number of electors appointed; and if there be more than one who have such majority, and have an equal number of votes, then the House of Representatives shall immediately choose by ballot one of them for President; and if no person have a majority, then from the five highest on the list the said House shall in like manner choose the President. But in choosing the President, the votes shall be taken by States, the representation from each State having one vote; A quorum for this purpose shall consist of a member or members from two thirds of the States, and a majority of all the states shall be necessary to a choice. In every case, after the choice of the President, the person having the greatest number of votes of the electors shall be the Vice President. But if there should remain two or more who have equal votes, the Senate should choose from them by ballot the Vice President.)

[Congress may determine time of choosing electors and day for casting their votes.—3.] The Congress may determine the time of choosing the electors, and the day on which they shall give their votes; which day shall be the same throughout the United States.

[Qualifications for the office of President.[7]—4.] No person except a natural born citizen, or a citizen of the United States, at the time of the adoption of this Constitution, shall be eligible to the office of President; neither shall any person be eligible to that office who shall not have attained to the age of thirty-five years, and been fourteen years a resident within the United States.

[Filling vacancy in the office of President.[8]—5.] In case of the removal of the President from office, or of his death, resignation, or inability to discharge the powers and duties of the said office, the same shall devolve on the Vice President, and the Congress may by law provide for the case of removal, death, resignation or inability, both of the President and Vice President, declaring what officer shall then act as President, and such officer shall act accordingly, until the disability be removed, or a President shall be elected.

[Compensation of the President.—6.] The President shall, at stated times, receive for his services, a compensation, which shall neither be increased nor diminished during the period for which he shall have been elected, and he shall not receive within that period any other emolument from the United States, or any of them.

[Oath to be taken by the President.—7.] Before he enter on the execution of his office, he shall take the following oath or affirmation:—"I do solemnly swear (or affirm) that I will faithfully execute the office of President of the United States, and will to the best of my ability, preserve, protect, and defend the Constitution of the United States."

Section 2

[The President to be commander in chief of army and navy and head of executive departments; may grant reprieves and pardons.—1.] The President shall be Commander in Chief of the Army and Navy of the United States, and of the militia of the several States, when called into the actual service of the United States; he may require the opinion, in writing, of the principal officer in each of the executive departments, upon any subject relating to the duties of their respective offices, and he shall have power to grant reprieves and pardons for offences against the United States, except in cases of impeachment.

[President may, with concurrence of Senate, make treaties, appoint ambassadors, etc.; appointment of inferior officers, authority of Congress over.—2.] He shall have power, by and with the advice and consent of the Senate, to make treaties, provided two thirds of the Senators present concur; and he shall nominate, and by and with the advice and consent of the Senate, shall appoint ambassadors, other public ministers and consuls,

6. This clause has been superseded by the 12th Amendment. 7. For qualifications of the Vice President, *see* the 12th Amendment. 8. Amended by the 20th Amendment, Sections 3 and 4.

judges of the Supreme Court, and all other officers of the United States, whose appointments are not herein otherwise provided for, and which shall be established by law: but the Congress may by law vest the appointment of such inferior officers, as they think proper, in the President alone, in the courts of law, or in the heads of departments.

[President may fill vacancies in office during recess of Senate.—3.] The President shall have power to fill up all vacancies that may happen during the recess of the Senate, by granting commissions which shall expire at the end of their session.

Section 3

[President to give advice to Congress; may convene or adjourn it on certain occasions; to receive ambassadors, etc.; have laws executed and commission all officers.] He shall from time to time give to the Congress information of the state of the Union, and recommend to their consideration such measures as he shall judge necessary and expedient; he may, on extraordinary occasions, convene both Houses, or either of them, and in case of disagreement between them, with respect to the time of adjournment, he may adjourn them to such time as he shall think proper; he shall receive ambassadors and other public ministers: he shall take care that the laws be faithfully executed, and shall commission all the officers of the United States.

Section 4

[All civil officers removable by impeachment.] The President, Vice President, and all civil officers of the United States shall be removed from office on impeachment for, and conviction of, treason, bribery, or other high crimes and misdemeanors.

Article III

Section 1

[Judicial powers; how vested; term of office and compensation of judges.] The judicial Power of the United States, shall be vested in one Supreme Court, and in such inferior courts as the Congress may from time to time ordain and establish. The judges, both of the supreme and inferior courts, shall hold their offices during good behavior, and shall, at stated times, receive for their services, a compensation, which shall not be diminished during their continuance in office.

Section 2

[Jurisdiction of Federal courts[9]—1.] The judicial power shall extend to all cases, in law and equity, arising under this Constitution, the laws of the United States, and treaties made, or which shall be made, under their authority; to all cases affecting ambassadors, other public ministers and consuls; to all cases of admiralty and maritime jurisdiction; to controversies to which the United States, shall be a party; to controversies between two or more States; between a State and citizens of another State; between citizens of different States; between citizens of the same State claiming lands under grants of different states, and between a State, or the citizens thereof, and foreign states, citizens, or subjects.

[Original and appellate jurisdiction of Supreme Court.—2.] In all cases affecting ambassadors, other public ministers and consuls, and those in which a State shall be party, the Supreme Court shall have original jurisdiction. In all the other cases before mentioned, the Supreme Court shall have appellate jurisdiction, both as to law and fact, with such exceptions, and under such regulations, as the Congress shall make.

[Trial of all crimes, except impeachment, to be by jury.—3.] The trial of all crimes, except in cases of impeachment, shall be by jury; and such trial shall be held in the State where the said crimes shall have been committed; but when not committed within any State, the trial shall be at such place or places as the Congress may by law have directed.

Section 3

[Treason defined; conviction of.—1.] Treason against the United States, shall consist only in levying war against them, or, in adhering to their enemies, giving them aid and comfort. No person shall be convicted of treason unless on the testimony of two witnesses to the same overt act, or on confession in open court.

[Congress to declare punishment for treason; proviso.—2.] The Congress shall have power to declare the punishment of treason, but no attainder of treason shall work corruption of blood, or forfeiture except during the life of the person attained.

Article IV

Section 1

[Each State to give full faith and credit to the public acts and records of other States.] Full faith and credit shall be given in each State to the public acts, records, and judicial proceedings of every other State. And the Congress may by general laws prescribe the manner in which such acts, records, and proceedings shall be proved, and the effect thereof.

Section 2

[Privileges of citizens.—1.] The citizens of each State shall be entitled to all privileges and immunities of citizens in the several States.

[Extradition between the several States.—2.] A person charged in any State with treason, felony, or other crime, who shall flee from justice, and be found in another State, shall on demand of the Executive authority of the State from which he fled, be delivered up, to be removed to the State having jurisdiction of the crime.

[Persons held to labor or service in one State, fleeing to another, to be returned.—3.] No person held to service or labor in one State, under the laws thereof, escaping into another, shall, in consequence of any law or regulation therein, be discharged from such service or labor, but shall be delivered up on claim of the party to whom such service or labor may be due.

9. This section is abridged by the 11th Amendment.

Section 3

[New States.—1.] New States may be admitted by the Congress into this Union; but no new State shall be formed or erected within the jurisdiction of any other State; nor any State be formed by the junction of two or more States, or parts of States, without the consent of the Legislatures of the States concerned as well as of the Congress.

[Regulations concerning territory.—2.] The Congress shall have power to dispose of and make all needful rules and regulations respecting the territory or other property belonging to the United States; and nothing in this Constitution shall be so construed as to prejudice any claims of the United States, or of any particular State.

Section 4

[Republican form of government and protection guaranteed the several States.] The United States shall guarantee to every State in this Union a Republican form of government, and shall protect each of them against invasion; and on application of the Legislature, or of the Executive (when the Legislature cannot be convened) against domestic violence.

Article V

[Ways in which the Constitution can be amended.] The Congress, whenever two thirds of both Houses shall deem it necessary, shall propose amendments to this Constitution, or, on the application of the Legislatures of two thirds of the several States shall call a convention for proposing amendments, which, in either case, shall be valid to all intents and purposes, as part of this Constitution, when ratified by the Legislatures of three fourths of the several States, or by conventions in three fourths thereof, as the one or the other mode of ratification may be proposed by the Congress; provided that no amendment which may be made prior to the year one thousand eight hundred and eight shall in any manner affect the first and fourth clauses in the ninth Section of the first Article; and that no State, without its consent, shall be deprived of its equal suffrage in the Senate.

Article VI

[Debts contracted under the confederation secured.—1.] All debts contracted and engagements entered into, before the adoption of this Constitution, shall be as valid against the United States under this Constitution, as under the Confederation.

[Constitution, laws, and treaties of the United States to be supreme.—2.] This Constitution, and the laws of the United States which shall be made in pursuance thereof; and all treaties made, or which shall be made, under the authority of the United States, shall be the supreme law of the land; and the judges in every State shall be bound thereby, any thing in the Constitution or laws of any State to the contrary notwithstanding.

[Who shall take constitutional oath; no religious test as to official qualification.—3.] The Senators and Representatives before mentioned, and the members of the several State Legislatures, and all executive and judicial officers, both of the United States and of the several States, shall be bound by oath or affirmation, to support this Constitution; but no religious test shall ever be required as a qualification to any office or public trust under the United States.

Article VII

[Constitution to be considered adopted when ratified by nine States.] The ratification of the conventions of nine States shall be sufficient for the establishment of this Constitution between the States so ratifying the same.

Done in convention by the unanimous consent of the States present the seventeenth day of September in the year of our Lord one thousand seven hundred and eighty seven and of the independence of the United States of America the Twelfth. In witness whereof we have hereunto subscribed our names.

George Washington
President and Deputy from Virginia

New Hampshire
John Langdon
Nicholas Gilman

Massachusetts
Nathaniel Gorham
Rufus King

Connecticut
Wm. Saml. Johnson
Roger Sherman

New York
Alexander Hamilton

New Jersey
Wil. Livingston
Wm. Paterson
David Brearley
Jona. Dayton

Pennsylvania
B. Franklin
Thomas Mifflin
Robt. Morris
Geo. Clymer
Thos. FitzSimons
Jared Ingersoll
James Wilson
Gouv. Morris

Delaware
Geo. Read
Gunning Bedford Jun.
John Dickinson
Richard Bassett
Jaco. Broom

Maryland
James McHenry
Dan. of St. Thos. Jenifer
Danl. Carroll

Virginia
John Blair
James Madison, Jr.

North Carolina
Wm. Blount
Richd Dobbs Spaight
Hu. Williamson

South Carolina
J. Rutledge
Charles Cotesworth Pinckney
Charles Pinckney
Pierce Butler

Georgia
William Few
Abr. Baldwin

Attest: William Jackson, Secretary

Amendments to the Constitution of the United States

(Amendments I to X inclusive, popularly known as the Bill of Rights, were proposed and sent to the states by the first session of the First Congress. They were ratified Dec. 15, 1791.)

Amendment I

[Freedom of religion, speech, of the press, and right of petition.] Congress shall make no law respecting an establishment of religion, or prohibiting the free exercise thereof; or abridging the freedom of speech, or of the press; or the right of the people peaceably to assemble, and to petition the Government for a redress of grievances.

Amendment II

[Right of people to bear arms not to be infringed.] A well regulated militia, being necessary to the security of a free State, the right of the people to keep and bear arms, shall not be infringed.

Amendment III

[Quartering of troops.] No soldier shall, in time of peace be quartered in any house, without the consent of the owner, nor in time of war, but in a manner to be prescribed by law.

Amendment IV

[Persons and houses to be secure from unreasonable searches and seizures.] The right of the people to be secure in their persons, houses, papers, and effects, against unreasonable searches and seizures, shall not be violated, and no warrants shall issue, but upon probable cause, supported by oath or affirmation, and particularly describing the place to be searched, and the persons or things to be seized.

Amendment V

[Trials for crimes; just compensation for private property taken for public use.] No person shall be held to answer for a capital, or otherwise infamous crime, unless on a presentment or indictment of a Grand Jury, except in cases arising in the land or naval forces, or in the militia, when in actual service in time of war or public danger; nor shall any person be subject for the same offence to be twice put in jeopardy of life or limb; nor shall be compelled in any criminal case to be a witness, against himself, nor be deprived of life, liberty, or property, without due process of law; nor shall private property be taken for public use, without just compensation.

Amendment VI

[Civil rights in trials for crimes enumerated.] In all criminal prosecutions, the accused shall enjoy the right to a speedy and public trial, by an impartial jury of the State and district wherein the crime shall have been committed, which district shall have been previously ascertained by law, and to be informed of the nature and cause of the accusation; to be confronted with the witnesses against him; to have compulsory process for obtaining witnesses in his favor, and to have the assistance of counsel for his defense.

Amendment VII

[Civil rights in civil suits.] In suits at common law, where the value in controversy shall exceed twenty dollars, the right of trial by jury shall be preserved, and no fact tried by a jury, shall be otherwise re-examined in any court of the United States, than according to the rules of the common law.

Amendment VIII

[Excessive bail, fines, and punishments prohibited.] Excessive bail shall not be required, nor excessive fines imposed, nor cruel and unusual punishments inflicted.

Amendment IX

[Reserved rights of people.] The enumeration in the Constitution, of certain rights, shall not be construed to deny or disparage others retained by the people.

Amendment X

[Powers not delegated, reserved to states and people respectively.] The powers not delegated to the United States by the Constitution, nor prohibited by it to the States, are reserved to the States, respectively, or to the people.

Amendment XI

(The proposed amendment was sent to the states Mar. 5, 1794, by the Third Congress. It was ratified Feb. 7, 1795.)

[Judicial power of United States not to extend to suits against a State.] The judicial power of the United States shall not be construed to extend to any suit in law or equity, commenced or prosecuted against one of the United States by citizens of another State, or by citizens or subjects of any foreign state.

Amendment XII

(The proposed amendment was sent to the states Dec. 12, 1803, by the Eighth Congress. It was ratified July 27, 1804.)

[Present mode of electing President and Vice-President by electors.[1]]

The electors shall meet in their respective states, and vote by ballot for President and Vice President, one of whom, at least, shall not be an inhabitant of the same state with themselves; they shall name in their ballots the person voted for as President, and in distinct ballots the person voted for as Vice President, and they shall make distinct lists of all persons voted for as President, and of all persons voted for as Vice President, and of the number of votes for each, which lists they shall sign and certify, and transmit sealed to the seat of the government of the United States, directed to the President of the Senate; the President of the Senate shall, in the presence

1. Amended by the 20th Amendment, Sections 3 and 4.

of the Senate and House of Representatives, open all the certificates and the votes shall then be counted; the person having the greatest number of votes for President, shall be the President, if such number be a majority of the whole number of electors appointed; and if no person have such majority, then from the persons having the highest numbers not exceeding three on the list of those voted for as President, the House of Representatives shall choose immediately, by ballot, the President. But in choosing the President, the votes shall be taken by states, the representation from each State having one vote; a quorum for this purpose shall consist of a member or members from two thirds of the states, and a majority of all the states shall be necessary to a choice. And if the House of Representatives shall not choose a President whenever the right of choice shall devolve upon them, before the fourth day of March next following, then the Vice President shall act as President, as in the case of the death or other constitutional disability of the President. The person having the greatest number of votes as Vice President, shall be the Vice President, if such number be a majority of the whole number of electors appointed, and if no person have a majority, then from the two highest numbers on the list, the Senate shall choose the Vice President; a quorum for the purpose shall consist of two thirds of the whole number of Senators, and a majority of the whole number shall be necessary to a choice. But no person constitutionally ineligible to the office of President shall be eligible to that of Vice President of the United States.

Amendment XIII

(The proposed amendment was sent to the states Feb. 1, 1865, by the Thirty-eighth Congress. It was ratified Dec. 6, 1865.)

Section 1

[Slavery prohibited.] Neither slavery nor involuntary servitude, except as a punishment for crime whereof the party shall have been duly convicted, shall exist within the United States, or any place subject to their jurisdiction.

Section 2

[Congress given power to enforce this article.] Congress shall have power to enforce this article by appropriate legislation.

Amendment XIV

(The proposed amendment was sent to the states June 16, 1866, by the Thirty-ninth Congress. It was ratified July 9, 1868.)

Section 1

[Citizenship defined; privileges of citizens.] All persons born or naturalized in the United States, and subject to the jurisdiction thereof, are citizens of the United States and of the State wherein they reside. No State shall make or enforce any law which shall abridge the privileges or immunities of citizens of the United States; nor shall any State deprive any person of life, liberty, or property, without due process of law; nor deny to any person within its jurisdiction the equal protection of the laws.

Section 2

[Apportionment of Representatives.] Representatives shall be apportioned among the several States according to their respective numbers, counting the whole number of persons in each State, excluding Indians not taxed. But when the right to vote at any election for the choice of electors for President and Vice President of the United States, Representatives in Congress, the executive and judicial officers of a State, or the members of the Legislature thereof, is denied to any of the male inhabitants of such State, being twenty-one years of age, and citizens of the United States, or in any way abridged, except for participation in rebellion, or other crime, the basis of representation therein shall be reduced in the proportion which the number of such male citizens shall bear to the whole number of male citizens twenty-one years of age in such State.

Section 3

[Disqualification for office; removal of disability.] No person shall be a Senator or Representative in Congress, or elector of President and Vice President, or hold any office, civil or military, under the United States, or under any State, who, having previously taken an oath, as a member of Congress, or as an officer of the United States, or as a member of any State Legislature, or as an executive or judicial officer of any State, to support the Constitution of the United States, shall have engaged in insurrection or rebellion against the same, or given aid or comfort to the enemies thereof. But Congress may, by a vote of two thirds of each House, remove such disability.

Section 4

[Public debt not to be questioned; payment of debts and claims incurred in aid of rebellion forbidden.] The validity of the public debt of the United States, authorized by law, including debts incurred for payment of pensions and bounties for services in suppressing insurrection or rebellion, shall not be questioned. But neither the United States nor any State shall assume or pay any debt or obligation incurred in aid of insurrection or rebellion against the United States, or any claim for the loss or emancipation of any slave; but all such debts, obligations, and claims shall be held illegal and void.

Section 5

[Congress given power to enforce this article.] The Congress shall have power to enforce, by appropriate legislation, the provisions of this article.

Amendment XV

(The proposed amendment was sent to the states Feb. 27, 1869, by the Fortieth Congress. It was ratified Feb. 3, 1870.)

Section 1

[Right of certain citizens to vote established.] The right of citizens of the United States to vote shall not be denied or abridged by the United States or by any State on account of race, color, or previous condition of servitude.

Section 2

[Congress given power to enforce this article.] The Congress shall have power to enforce this article by appropriate legislation.

Amendment XVI

(The proposed amendment was sent to the states July 12, 1909, by the Sixty-first Congress. It was ratified Feb. 3, 1913.)

[Taxes on income; Congress given power to lay and collect.] The Congress shall have power to lay and collect taxes on incomes, from whatever source derived, without apportionment among the several States, and without regard to any census or enumeration.

Amendment XVII

(The proposed amendment was sent to the states May 16, 1912, by the Sixty-second Congress. It was ratified April 8, 1913.)

[Election of United States Senators; filling of vacancies; qualifications of electors.] The Senate of the United States shall be composed of two Senators from each State, elected by the people thereof, for six years; and each Senator shall have one vote. The electors in each State shall have the qualifications requisite for electors of the most numerous branch of the State Legislatures.

When vacancies happen in the representation of any State in the Senate, the executive authority of such State shall issue writs of election to fill such vacancies: Provided, that the legislature of any State may empower the executive thereof to make temporary appointment until the people fill the vacancies by election as the legislature may direct.

This amendment shall not be so construed as to affect the election or term of any Senator chosen before it becomes valid as part of the Constitution.

Amendment XVIII[2]

(The proposed amendment was sent to the states Dec. 18, 1917, by the Sixty-fifth Congress. It was ratified by three quarters of the states by Jan. 16, 1919, and became effective Jan. 16, 1920.)

Section 1

[Manufacture, sale, or transportation of intoxicating liquors, for beverage purposes, prohibited.] After one year from the ratification of this article the manufacture, sale, or transportation of intoxicating liquors within, the importation thereof into, or the exportation thereof from the United States and all territory subject to the jurisdiction thereof for beverage purposes is hereby prohibited.

Section 2

[Congress and the several States given concurrent power to pass appropriate legislation to enforce this article.] The Congress and the several States shall have concurrent power to enforce this article by appropriate legislation.

Section 3

[Provisions of article to become operative, when adopted by three fourths of the States.] This article shall be inoperative unless it shall have been ratified as an amendment to the Constitution by the legislatures of the several States, as provided in the Constitution, within seven years from the date of the submission hereof to the States by Congress.

Amendment XIX

(The proposed amendment was sent to the states June 4, 1919, by the Sixty-sixth Congress. It was ratified Aug. 18, 1920.)

[The right of citizens to vote shall not be denied because of sex.] The right of citizens of the United States to vote shall not be denied or abridged by the United States or by any State on account of sex.

[Congress given power to enforce this article.] Congress shall have power to enforce this article by appropriate legislation.

Amendment XX

(The proposed amendment, sometimes called the "Lame Duck Amendment," was sent to the states Mar. 3, 1932, by the Seventy-second Congress. It was ratified Jan. 23, 1933; but, in accordance with Section 5, Sections 1 and 2 did not go into effect until Oct. 15, 1933.)

Section 1

[Terms of President, Vice President, Senators, and Representatives.] The terms of the President and Vice President shall end at noon on the twentieth day of January, and the terms of Senators and Representatives at noon on the third day of January, of the years in which such terms would have ended if this article had not been ratified; and the terms of their successors shall then begin.

Section 2

[Time of assembling Congress.] The Congress shall assemble at least once in every year, and such meeting shall begin at noon on the third day of January, unless they shall by law appoint a different day.

Section 3

[Filling vacancy in office of President.] If, at the time fixed for the beginning of the term of the President, the President-elect shall have died, the Vice President-elect shall become President. If a President shall not have been chosen before the time fixed for the beginning of his term, or if the President-elect shall have failed to qualify, then the Vice President shall have qualified; and the Congress may by law provide for the case wherein neither a President-elect nor a Vice President-elect shall have qualified, declaring who shall then act as President, or the manner in which one who is to act shall be selected, and such person shall act accordingly until a President or Vice President shall have qualified.

Section 4

[Power of Congress in Presidential succession.] The Congress may by law provide for the case of the death of any of the persons from whom the House of Representatives may choose a President whenever the right of choice shall have devolved

2. Repealed by the 21st Amendment.

upon them, and for the case of the death of any of the persons from whom the Senate may choose a Vice President whenever the right of choice shall have devolved upon them.

Section 5

[Time of taking effect.] Sections 1 and 2 shall take effect on the 15th day of October following the ratification of this article.

Section 6

[Ratification.] This article shall be inoperative unless it shall have been ratified as an amendment to the Constitution by the legislatures of three fourths of the several States within seven years from the date of its submission.

Amendment XXI

(The proposed amendment was sent to the states Feb. 20, 1933, by the Seventy-second Congress. It was ratified Dec. 5, 1933.)

Section 1

[Repeal of Prohibition Amendment.] The eighteenth article of amendment to the Constitution of the United States is hereby repealed.

Section 2

[Transportation of intoxicating liquors.] The transportation or importation into any State, territory, or possession of the United States for delivery or use therein of intoxicating liquors, in violation of the laws thereof, is hereby prohibited.

Section 3

[Ratification.] This article shall be inoperative unless it shall have been ratified as an amendment to the Constitution by convention in the several States, as provided in the Constitution, within seven years from the date of the submission thereof to the States by the Congress.

Amendment XXII

(The proposed amendment was sent to the states Mar. 21, 1947, by the Eightieth Congress. It was ratified Feb. 27, 1951.)

Section 1

[Limit to number of terms a President may serve.] No person shall be elected to the office of the President more than twice, and no person who has held the office of President, or acted as President, for more than two years of a term to which some other person was elected President shall be elected to the office of the President more than once. But this article shall not apply to any person holding the office of President when this article was proposed by the Congress, and shall not prevent any person who may be holding the office of President, or acting as President, during the term within which this article becomes operative from holding the office of President or acting as President during the remainder of such term.

Section 2

[Ratification.] This article shall be inoperative unless it shall have been ratified as an amendment to the Constitution by the legislatures of three fourths of the several States within seven years from the date of its submission to the States by the Congress.

Amendment XXIII

(The proposed amendment was sent to the states June 16, 1960, by the Eighty-sixth Congress. It was ratified March 29, 1961.)

Section 1

[Electors for the District of Columbia.] The District constituting the seat of Government of the United States shall appoint in such manner as the Congress may direct: A number of electors of President and Vice President equal to the whole number of Senators and Representatives in Congress to which the District would be entitled if it were a State, but in no event more than the least populous State; they shall be in addition to those appointed by the States, but they shall be considered, for the purposes of the election of President and Vice President, to be electors appointed by a State; and they shall meet in the District and perform such duties as provided by the twelfth article of amendment.

Section 2

[Congress given power to enforce this article.] The Congress shall have the power to enforce this article by appropriate legislation.

Amendment XXIV

(The proposed amendment was sent to the states Aug. 27, 1962, by the Eighty-seventh Congress. It was ratified Jan. 23, 1964.)

Section 1

[Payment of poll tax or other taxes not to be prerequisite for voting in federal elections.] The right of citizens of the United States to vote in any primary or other election for President or Vice President, for electors for President or Vice President, or for Senator or Representative in Congress, shall not be denied or abridged by the United States or any State by reasons of failure to pay any poll tax or other tax.

Section 2

[Congress given power to enforce this article.] The Congress shall have the power to enforce this article by appropriate legislation.

Amendment XXV

(The proposed amendment was sent to the states July 6, 1965, by the Eighty-ninth Congress. It was ratified Feb. 10, 1967.)

Section 1

[Succession of Vice President to Presidency.] In case of the removal of the President from office or of his death or resignation, the Vice President shall become President.

Section 2

[Vacancy in office of Vice President.] Whenever there is a vacancy in the office of the Vice President, the President shall nominate a Vice President who shall take office upon confirmation by a majority vote of both Houses of Congress.

Section 3

[Vice President as Acting President.] Whenever the President transmits to the President pro tempore of the Senate and the Speaker of the House of Representatives his written declaration that he is unable to discharge the powers and duties of his office, and until he transmits to them a written declaration to the contrary, such powers and duties shall be discharged by the Vice President as Acting President.

Section 4

[Vice President as Acting President.] Whenever the Vice President and a majority of either the principal officers of the executive departments or of such other body as Congress may by law provide, transmit to the President pro tempore of the Senate and the Speaker of the House of Representatives their written declaration that the President is unable to discharge the powers and duties of his office, the Vice President shall immediately assume the powers and duties of the office as Acting President.

Thereafter, when the President transmits to the President pro tempore of the Senate and the Speaker of the House of Representatives his written declaration that no inability exists, he shall resume the powers and duties of his office unless the Vice President and a majority of either the principal officers of the executive department or of such other body as Congress may by law provide, transmit within four days to the President pro tempore of the Senate and the Speaker of the House of Representatives their written declaration that the President is unable to discharge the powers and duties of his office. Thereupon Congress shall decide the issue, assembling within forty-eight hours for that purpose if not in session. If the Congress, within twenty-one days after receipt of the latter written declaration, or, if Congress is not in session, within twenty-one days after Congress is required to assemble, determines by two thirds vote of both Houses that the President is unable to discharge the powers and duties of his office, the Vice President shall continue to discharge the same as Acting President; otherwise, the President shall resume the powers and duties of his office.

Amendment XXVI

(The proposed amendment was sent to the states Mar. 23, 1971, by the Ninety-second Congress. It was ratified July 1, 1971.)

Section 1

[Voting for 18-year-olds.] The right of citizens of the United States, who are 18 years of age or older, to vote shall not be denied or abridged by the United States or by any state on account of age.

Section 2

[Congress given power to enforce this article.] The Congress shall have power to enforce this article by appropriate legislation.

Amendment XXVII

(Ratified May 7, 1992.)

[Congressional raises.] No law, varying the compensation for the services of the Senators and Representatives, shall take effect, until an election of Representatives shall have intervened.

Order of Presidential Succession

1. The Vice President
2. Speaker of the House
3. President pro tempore of the Senate
4. Secretary of State
5. Secretary of the Treasury
6. Secretary of Defense
7. Attorney General
8. Secretary of the Interior
9. Secretary of Agriculture
10. Secretary of Commerce
11. Secretary of Labor
12. Secretary of Health and Human Services
13. Secretary of Housing and Urban Development
14. Secretary of Transportation
15. Secretary of Energy
16. Secretary of Education
17. Secretary of Veterans Affairs

NOTE: An official cannot succeed to the Presidency unless that person meets the Constitutional requirements.

History of the Flag

Source: Encyclopaedia Britannica.

The first official American flag, the Continental or Grand Union flag, was displayed on Prospect Hill, Jan. 1, 1776, in the American lines besieging Boston. It had 13 alternate red and white stripes, with the British Union Jack in the upper left corner.

On June 14, 1777, the Continental Congress adopted the design for a new flag, which actually was the Continental flag with the red cross of St. George and the white cross of St. Andrew replaced on the blue field by 13 stars, one for each state. No rule was made as to the arrangement of the stars, and while they were usually shown in a circle, there were various other designs. It is uncertain when the new flag was first flown, but its first official announcement is believed to have been on Sept. 3, 1777.

The first public assertion that Betsy Ross made the first Stars and Stripes appeared in a paper read before the Historical Society of Pennsylvania on March 14, 1870, by William J. Canby, a grandson. However, Mr. Canby on later investigation found no official documents of any action by Congress on the flag before June 14, 1777. Betsy Ross's own story, according to her daughter, was that Washington, Robert Morris, and George Ross, as representatives of Congress, visited her in Philadelphia in June 1776, showing her a rough draft of the flag and asking her if she could make one. However, the only actual record of the manufacture of flags by Betsy Ross is a voucher in Harrisburg, Pa., for 14 pounds and some shillings for flags for the Pennsylvania navy.

On Jan. 13, 1794, Congress voted to add two stars and two stripes to the flag in recognition of the admission of Vermont and Kentucky to the Union. By 1818, there were 20 states in the Union, and as it was obvious that the flag would soon become unwieldy, Congress voted April 18 to return to the original 13 stripes and to indicate the admission of a new state simply by the addition of a star the following July 4. The 49th star, for Alaska, was added July 4, 1959; and the 50th star, for Hawaii, was added July 4, 1960.

The first Confederate flag, adopted in 1861 by the Confederate convention in Montgomery, Ala., was called the Stars and Bars; but because of its similarity in colors to the American flag, there was much confusion in the Battle of Bull Run. To remedy this situation, Gen. G. T. Beauregard suggested a battle flag, which was used by the Southern armies throughout the war. The flag consisted of a red field on which was placed a blue cross of St. Andrew separated from the field by a white fillet and adorned with 13 white stars for the Confederate states.[1] In May 1863, at Richmond, an official flag was adopted by the Confederate Congress. This flag was white and twice as long as wide; the union, two-thirds the width of the flag, contained the battle flag designed for Gen. Beauregard. A broad transverse stripe of red was added Feb. 4, 1865, so that the flag might not be mistaken for a signal of truce.

1. 11 states formally seceded, and unofficial groups in Kentucky and Missouri adopted ordinances of secession. On this basis, these two states were admitted to the Confederacy, although the official state governments remained in the Union.

The Pledge of Allegiance to the Flag[1]

I pledge allegiance to the Flag of the United States of America, and to the Republic for which it stands, one Nation under God,[2] indivisible, with liberty and justice for all.

1. The original pledge was published in the Sept. 8, 1892, issue of *The Youth's Companion* in Boston. For years, the authorship was in dispute between James B. Upham and Francis Bellamy of the magazine's staff. In 1939, after a study of the controversy, the United States Flag Association decided that authorship be credited to Bellamy. 2. The phrase "under God" was added to the pledge on June 14, 1954.

The Statue of Liberty

The Statue of Liberty ("Liberty Enlightening the World") is a 225-ton, steel-reinforced copper female figure, 152 ft. in height, facing the ocean from Liberty Island[1] in New York Harbor. The right hand holds aloft a torch, and the left hand carries a tablet upon which is inscribed: "July IV MDCCLXXVI."

The statue was designed by Fredéric Auguste Bartholdi of Alsace as a gift to the United States from the people of France to memorialize the alliance of the two countries in the American Revolution and their abiding friendship. The French people contributed the $250,000 cost.

The 150-foot pedestal was designed by Richard M. Hunt and built by Gen. Charles P. Stone, both Americans. It contains steel underpinnings designed by Alexander Eiffel of France to support the statue. The $270,000 cost was borne by popular subscription in this country. President Grover Cleveland accepted the statue for the United States on Oct. 28, 1886.

On Sept. 26, 1972, President Richard M. Nixon dedicated the American Museum of Immigration, housed in structural additions to the base of the statue. In 1984 scaffolding went up for a major restoration and the torch was extinguished on July 4. It was relit with much ceremony July 4, 1986 to mark its centennial.

On a tablet inside the pedestal is engraved the following sonnet, written by Emma Lazarus (1849–1887):

The New Colossus

Not like the brazen giant of Greek fame.
With conquering limbs astride from land to land;
Here at our sea-washed, sunset gates shall stand
A mighty woman with a torch, whose flame
Is the imprisoned lightning, and her name
Mother of Exiles. From her beacon-hand
Glows world-wide welcome; her mild eyes command
The air-bridged harbor that twin cities frame.
"Keep, ancient lands, your storied pomp!" cries she
With silent lips. "Give me your tired, your poor,
Your huddled masses yearning to breathe free,
The wretched refuse of your teeming shore.
Send these, the homeless, tempest-tost to me,
I lift my lamp beside the golden door!"

1. Called Bedloe's Island prior to 1956.

The Mayflower Compact

On Sept. 6, 1620, the *Mayflower,* a sailing vessel of about 180 tons, started her memorable voyage from Plymouth, England, with about 100[1] pilgrims aboard, bound for Virginia to establish a private permanent colony in North America. Arriving at what is now Provincetown, Mass., on Nov. 11 (Nov. 21, new style calendar), 41 of the passengers signed the famous "Mayflower Compact" as the boat lay at anchor in that Cape Cod harbor. A small detail of the pilgrims, led by William Bradford, assigned to select a place for permanent settlement landed at what is now Plymouth, Mass., on Dec. 21 (n.s.).

The text of the compact follows:

In the name of God, Amen. We, whose names are underwritten, the Loyal Subjects of our dread Sovereign Lord, King *James,* by the Grace of God, of *Great Britain, France* and *Ireland,* King, *Defender of the Faith,* &c.

Having undertaken for the Glory of God, and Advancement of the Christian Faith, and the Honour of our King and Country, a voyage to plant the first colony in the northern Parts of Virginia; do by these Presents, solemnly and mutually in the Presence of God and one of another, covenant and combine ourselves together into a civil Body Politick, for our better Ordering and Preservation, and Furtherance of the Ends aforesaid; And by Virtue hereof to enact, constitute, and frame, such just and equal Laws, Ordinances, Acts, Constitutions and Offices, from time to time, as shall be thought most meet and convenient for the General good of the Colony; unto which we promise all due Submission and Obedience.

In Witness whereof we have hereunto subscribed our names at *Cape Cod* the eleventh of *November,* in the Reign of our Sovereign Lord, King *James* of *England, France* and *Ireland,* the eighteenth, and of *Scotland* the fifty-fourth. *Anno Domini,* 1620

John Carver
Digery Priest
William Brewster
Edmund Margesson
John Alden
George Soule
James Chilton
Francis Cooke
Moses Fletcher
John Ridgate
Christopher Martin
William Mullins
Thomas English
John Howland
Stephen Hopkins
Edward Winslow
Gilbert Winslow
Miles Standish
Richard Bitteridge
Francis Eaton
John Tilly
John Billington
Thomas Tinker
Samuel Fuller
Richard Clark
John Allerton
Richard Warren
Edward Liester
William Bradford
Thomas Williams
Isaac Allerton
Peter Brown
John Turner
Edward Tilly
John Craxton
Thomas Rogers
John Goodman
Edward Fuller
Richard Gardiner
William White
Edward Doten

1. Historians differ as to whether 100, 101, or 102 passengers were aboard.

The Monroe Doctrine

The Monroe Doctrine was announced in President James Monroe's message to Congress, during his second term on Dec. 2, 1823, in part as follows:

"In the discussions to which this interest has given rise, and in the arrangements by which they may terminate, the occasion has been deemed proper for asserting as a principle in which rights and interests of the United States are involved, that the American continents, by the free and independent condition which they have assumed and maintain, are henceforth not to be considered as subjects for future colonization by any European power. . . We owe it, therefore, to candor and to the amicable relations existing between the United States and those powers to declare that we should consider any attempt on their part to extend their system to any portion of this hemisphere as dangerous to our peace and safety. With the existing colonies or dependencies of any European power we have not interfered and shall not interfere. But with the governments who have declared their independence and maintain it, and whose independence we have, on great consideration and on just principles, acknowledged, we could not view any interposition for the purpose of oppressing them or controlling in any other manner their destiny by any European power in any other light than as the manifestation of an unfriendly disposition toward the United States."

Territorial Expansion

Accession	Date	Area[1]
United States	—	3,536,278
Territory in 1790	—	891,364
Louisiana Purchase	1803	831,321
Florida	1819	69,866
Texas	1845	384,958
Oregon	1846	283,439
Mexican Cession	1848	530,706
Gadsden Purchase	1853	29,640
Alaska	1867	591,004
Hawaii	1898	6,471
Other territory	—	4,664
Philippines	1898	115,600[2]
Puerto Rico	1899	3,426
Guam	1899	209
American Samoa	1900	77
Canal Zone[3]	1904	553
Virgin Islands of U.S.	1917	134
Trust Territory of Pacific Islands	1947	177[4]
All other	—	14
Total, 1990	—	**3,540,315**

1. Total land and water area in square miles. 2. Became independent in 1946. 3. Reverted to Panama. 4. Land area only; Palau only Trust Territory remaining. *Source:* U.S. Bureau of the Census, web: www.census.gov.

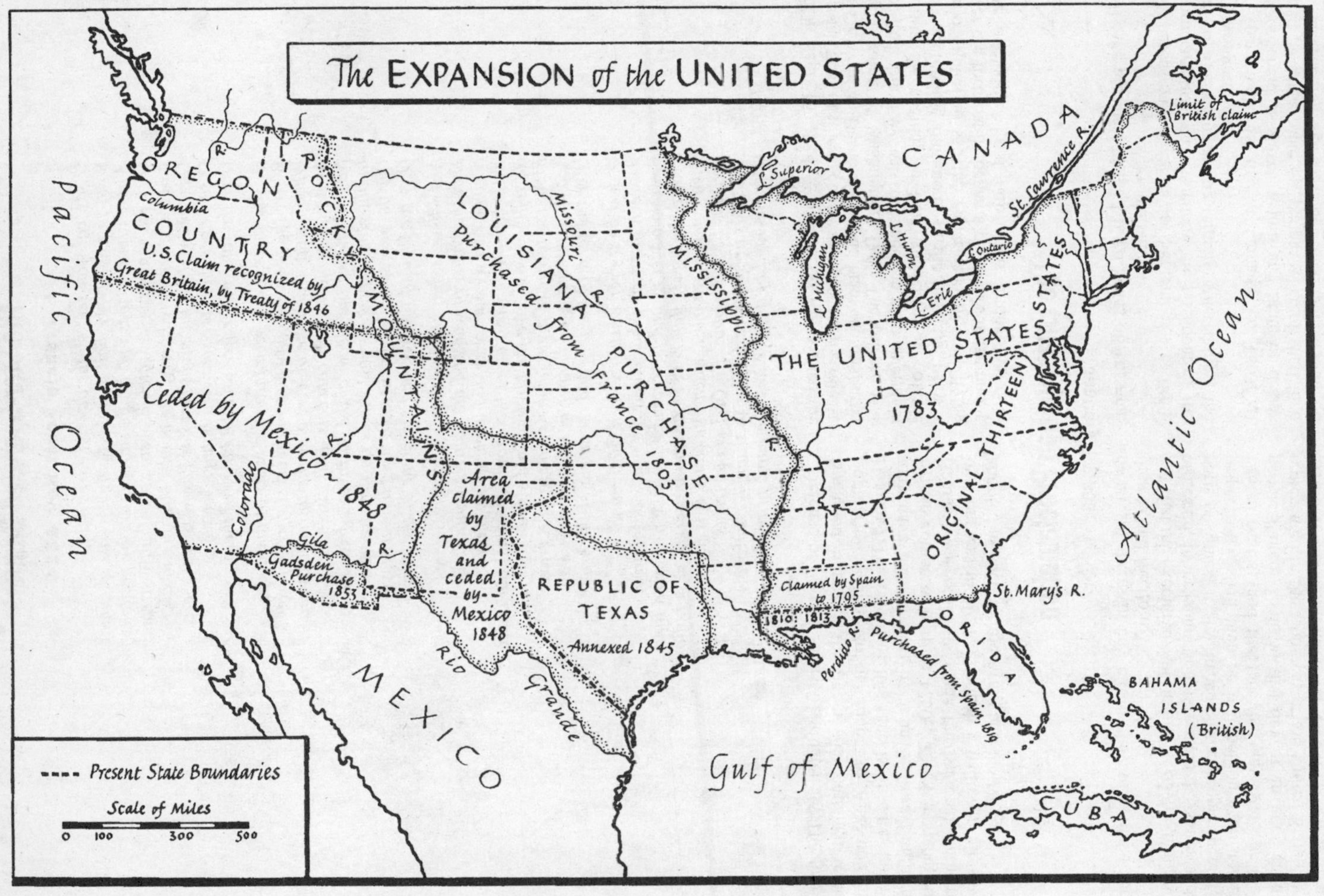
The EXPANSION of the UNITED STATES
Pacific Ocean
Atlantic Ocean
Gulf of Mexico
MEXICO
CANADA
OREGON COUNTRY
Columbia R.
U.S. Claim recognized by Great Britain, by Treaty of 1846
ROCKY MOUNTAINS
Ceded by Mexico 1848
Colorado R.
Gila R.
Gadsden Purchase 1853
Rio Grande
Area claimed by Texas and ceded by Mexico 1848
REPUBLIC OF TEXAS
Annexed 1845
LOUISIANA PURCHASE
Purchased from France 1803
Missouri R.
Mississippi R.
THE UNITED STATES 1783
ORIGINAL THIRTEEN STATES
L. Superior
L. Michigan
L. Huron
L. Erie
L. Ontario
St. Lawrence R.
Limit of British claim
Claimed by Spain to 1795
1810
1813
Perdido R.
FLORIDA
Purchased from Spain, 1819
St. Mary's R.
BAHAMA ISLANDS (British)
CUBA
Present State Boundaries
Scale of Miles
0 100 300 500

The Star-Spangled Banner

Francis Scott Key, 1814

O say, can you see, by the dawn's early light,
What so proudly we hail'd at the twilight's last gleaming?
Whose broad stripes and bright stars, thro' the perilous fight,
O'er the ramparts we watch'd, were so gallantly streaming?
And the rockets' red glare, the bombs bursting in air,
Gave proof thro' the night that our flag was still there.
O say, does that star-spangled banner yet wave
O'er the land of the free and the home of the brave?

On the shore dimly seen thro' the mists of the deep,
Where the foe's haughty host in dread silence reposes,
What is that which the breeze, o'er the towering steep,
As it fitfully blows, half conceals, half discloses?
Now it catches the gleam of the morning's first beam,
In full glory reflected, now shines on the stream:
'Tis the star-spangled banner: O, long may it wave
O'er the land of the free and the home of the brave!

And where is that band who so vauntingly swore
That the havoc of war and the battle's confusion,
A home and a country should leave us no more?
Their blood has wash'd out their foul footsteps' pollution.
No refuge could save the hireling and slave
From the terror of flight or the gloom of the grave:
And the star-spangled banner in triumph doth wave
O'er the land of the free and the home of the brave.

O thus be it ever when free-men shall stand
Between their lov'd home and the war's desolation;
Blest with vict'ry and peace, may the heav'n-rescued land
Praise the Pow'r that hath made and preserv'd us a nation!
Then conquer we must, when our cause it is just,
And this be our motto: "In God is our trust!"
And the star-spangled banner in triumph shall wave
O'er the land of the free and the home of the brave!

On Sept. 13, 1814, Francis Scott Key visited the British fleet in Chesapeake Bay to secure the release of Dr. William Beanes, who had been captured after the burning of Washington, D.C. The release was secured, but Key was detained on ship overnight during the shelling of Fort McHenry, one of the forts defending Baltimore. In the morning, he was so delighted to see the American flag still flying over the fort that he began a poem to commemorate the occasion. First published under the title "Defense of Fort M'Henry," and later as "The Star-Spangled Banner," the poem soon attained wide popularity as sung to the tune "To Anacreon in Heaven." The origin of this tune is obscure, but it may have been written by John Stafford Smith, a British composer born in 1750. "The Star-Spangled Banner" was officially made the National Anthem by Congress in 1931, although it had been already adopted as such by the Army and the Navy.

The Emancipation Proclamation

January 1, 1863

By the president of the United States of America:

A Proclamation.

Whereas on the 22d day of September, A.D. 1862, a proclamation was issued by the president of the United States, containing, among other things, the following, to wit:

"That on the 1st day of January, A.D. 1863, all persons held as slaves within any State or designated part of a State the people whereof shall then be in rebellion against the United States shall be then, thenceforward, and forever free; and the executive government of the United States, including the military and naval authority thereof, will recognize and maintain the freedom of such persons and will do not act or acts to repress such persons, or any of them, in any efforts they may make for their actual freedom."

"That the executive will on the 1st day of January aforesaid, by proclamation, designate the States and parts of States, if any, in which the people thereof, respectively, shall then be in rebellion against the United States; and the fact that any State or the people thereof shall on that day be in good faith represented in the Congress of the United States by members chosen thereto at elections wherein a majority of the qualified voters of such States shall have participated shall, in the absence of strong countervailing testimony, be deemed conclusive evidence that such State and the people thereof are not then in rebellion against the United States."

Now, therefore, I, Abraham Lincoln, president of the United States, by virtue of the power in me vested as Commander-in-Chief of the Army and Navy of the United States in time of actual armed rebellion against the authority and government of the United States, and as a fit and necessary war measure for suppressing said rebellion, do, on this 1st day of January, A.D. 1863, and in accordance with my purpose so to do, publicly proclaimed for the full period of one hundred days from the first day above mentioned, order and designate as the States and parts of States wherein the people thereof, respectively, are this day in rebellion against the United States the following, to wit:

Arkansas, Texas, Louisiana (except the parishes of St. Bernard, Plaquemines, Jefferson, St. John, St. Charles, St. James, Ascension, Assumption, Terrebonne, Lafourche, St. Mary, St. Martin, and Orleans, including the city of New Orleans), Mississippi, Alabama, Florida, Georgia, South Carolina, North Carolina, and Virginia (except the forty-eight counties designated as West Virginia, and also the counties of Berkeley, Accomac, Northhampton, Elizabeth City, York, Princess Anne, and Norfolk, including the cities of Norfolk and Portsmouth), and which excepted parts are for the present left precisely as if this proclamation were not issued.

And by virtue of the power and for the purpose aforesaid, I do order and declare that all persons held as slaves within said designated States and parts of States are, and henceforward shall be, free; and that the Executive Government of the United States, including the military and naval authorities thereof, will recognize and maintain the freedom of said persons.

And I hereby enjoin upon the people so declared to be free to abstain from all violence, unless in necessary self-defense; and I recommend to them that, in all cases when allowed, they labor faithfully for reasonable wages.

And I further declare and make known that such persons of suitable condition will be received into the armed service of the United States to garrison forts, positions, stations, and other places, and to man vessels of all sorts in said service.

And upon this act, sincerely believed to be an act of justice, warranted by the Constitution upon military necessity, I invoke the considerate judgment of mankind and the gracious favor of Almighty God.

The Confederate States of America

	State	Seceded from Union	Readmitted to Union[1]
1.	South Carolina	Dec. 20, 1860	July 9, 1868
2.	Mississippi	Jan. 9, 1861	Feb. 23, 1870
3.	Florida	Jan. 10, 1861	June 25, 1868
4.	Alabama	Jan. 11, 1861	July 13, 1868
5.	Georgia	Jan. 19, 1861	July 15, 1870[2]
6.	Louisiana	Jan. 26, 1861	July 9, 1868
7.	Texas	March 2, 1861	March 30, 1870
8.	Virginia	April 17, 1861	Jan. 26, 1870
9.	Arkansas	May 6, 1861	June 22, 1868
10.	North Carolina	May 20, 1861	July 4, 1868
11.	Tennessee	June 8, 1861	July 24, 1866

1. Date of readmission to representation in U.S. House of Representatives. 2. Second readmission date. First date was July 21, 1868, but the representatives were unseated March 5, 1869. NOTE: Four other slave states—Delaware, Kentucky, Maryland, and Missouri—remained in the Union.

Lincoln's Gettysburg Address

The Battle of Gettysburg, one of the most noted battles of the Civil War, was fought on July 1–3, 1863. On Nov. 19, 1863, the field was dedicated as a national cemetery by President Lincoln in a two-minute speech that was to become immortal. At the time of its delivery the speech was relegated to the inside pages of the papers, while a two-hour address by Edward Everett, the leading orator of the time, caught the headlines.

The following is the text of the address revised by President Lincoln from his own notes:

> Fourscore and seven years ago our fathers brought forth on this continent a new nation conceived in liberty and dedicated to the proposition that all men are created equal. Now we are engaged in a great civil war testing whether that nation, or any nation so conceived and so dedicated, can long endure. We are met on a great battlefield of that war. We have come to dedicate a portion of that field as a final resting-place for those who here gave their lives that that nation might live. It is altogether fitting and proper that we should do this. But, in a larger sense, we cannot dedicate, we cannot consecrate, we cannot hallow this ground. The brave men, living and dead, who struggled here have consecrated it far above our poor power to add or detract. The world will little note nor long remember what we say here, but it can never forget what they did here. It is for us the living rather to be dedicated here to the unfinished work which they who fought here have thus far so nobly advanced. It is rather for us to be here dedicated to the great task remaining before us—that from these honored dead we take increased devotion to that cause for which they gave the last full measure of devotion—that we here highly resolve that these dead shall not have died in vain, that this nation under God shall have a new birth of freedom, and that government of the people, by the people, for the people shall not perish from the earth.

The Early Congresses

At the urging of Massachusetts and Virginia, the First Continental Congress met in Philadelphia on Sept. 5, 1774, and was attended by representatives of all the colonies except Georgia. Patrick Henry of Virginia declared: "The distinctions between Pennsylvanians, New Yorkers, and New Englanders are no more. I am not a Virginian but an American." This Congress, which adjourned Oct. 26, 1774, passed intercolonial resolutions calling for extensive boycott by the colonies against British trade.

The following year, most of the delegates from the colonies were chosen by popular election to attend the Second Continental Congress, which assembled in Philadelphia on May 10. As war had already begun between the colonies and England, the chief problems before the Congress were the procuring of military supplies, the establishment of an army and proper defenses, the issuing of continental bills of credit, etc. On June 15, 1775, George Washington was elected to command the Continental army. Congress adjourned Dec. 12, 1776.

Other Continental Congresses were held in Baltimore (1776–1777), Philadelphia (1777), Lancaster, Pa. (1777), York, Pa. (1777–1778), and Philadelphia (1778–1781).

In 1781, the Articles of Confederation, although establishing a league of the thirteen states rather than a strong central government, provided for the continuance of Congress. Known thereafter as the Congress of the Confederation, it held sessions in Philadelphia (1781–1783), Princeton, N.J. (1783), Annapolis, Md. (1783–1784), and Trenton, N.J. (1784). Five sessions were held in New York City between the years 1785 and 1789.

The Congress of the United States, established by the ratification of the Constitution, held its first meeting on March 4, 1789, in New York City. Several sessions of Congress were held in Philadelphia, and the first meeting in Washington, D.C., was on Nov. 17, 1800.

Presidents of the Continental Congresses

Name	Elected	Birth and Death Dates
Peyton Randolph, Va.	9/5/1774	c.1721–1775
Henry Middleton, S.C.	10/22/1774	1717–1784
Peyton Randolph, Va.	5/10/1775	c.1721–1775
John Hancock, Mass.	5/24/1775	1737–1793
Henry Laurens, S.C.	11/1/1777	1724–1792
John Jay, N.Y.	12/10/1778	1745–1829
Samuel Huntington, Conn.	9/28/1779	1731–1796
Thomas McKean, Del.	7/10/1781	1734–1817
John Hanson, Md.	11/5/1781	1715–1783
Elias Boudinot, N.J.	11/4/1782	1740–1821
Thomas Mifflin, Pa.	11/3/1783	1744–1800
Richard Henry Lee, Va.	11/30/1784	1732–1794
John Hancock, Mass.[1]	11/23/1785	1737–1793
Nathaniel Gorham, Mass.	6/6/1786	1738–1796
Arthur St. Clair, Pa.	2/2/1787	1734–1818
Cyrus Griffin, Va.	1/22/1788	1748–1810

1. Resigned May 29, 1786, never having served, because of continued illness.

"In God We Trust"

"In God We Trust" first appeared on U.S. coins after April 22, 1864, when Congress passed an act authorizing the coinage of a 2-cent piece bearing this motto. Thereafter, Congress extended its use to other coins. On July 30, 1956, it became the national motto.

The Great Seal of the U.S.

On July 4, 1776, the Continental Congress appointed a committee consisting of Benjamin Franklin, John Adams, and Thomas Jefferson "to bring in a device for a seal of the United States of America." After many delays, a verbal description of a design by William Barton was finally approved by Congress on June 20, 1782. The seal shows an American bald eagle with a ribbon in its mouth bearing the device *E pluribus unum* (One out of many). In its talons are the arrows of war and an olive branch of peace. On the reverse side it shows an unfinished pyramid with an eye (the eye of Providence) above it. Although this description was adopted in 1782, the first drawing was not made until four years later, and no die has ever been cut.

Assassinations and Attempts in U.S. Since 1865

Lincoln, Abraham (President of U.S.): Shot April 14, 1865, in Washington, D.C., by John Wilkes Booth; died April 15.

Seward, William H. (Secretary of State): Escaped assassination (though injured) April 14, 1865, in Washington, D.C., by Lewis Powell (or Paine), accomplice of John Wilkes Booth.

Garfield, James A. (President of U.S.): Shot July 2, 1881, in Washington, D.C., by Charles J. Guiteau; died Sept. 19.

McKinley, William (President of U.S.): Shot Sept. 6, 1901, in Buffalo by Leon Czolgosz; died Sept. 14.

Roosevelt, Theodore (ex-President of U.S.): Escaped assassination (though shot) Oct. 14, 1912, in Milwaukee while campaigning for President.

Cermak, Anton J. (Mayor of Chicago): Shot Feb. 15, 1933, in Miami by Giuseppe Zangara, who attempted to assassinate Franklin D. Roosevelt; Cermak died March 6.

Roosevelt, Franklin D. (President-elect of U.S.): Escaped assassination unhurt Feb. 15, 1933, in Miami.

Long, Huey P. (U.S. Senator from Louisiana): Shot Sept. 8, 1935, in Baton Rouge by Dr. Carl A. Weiss; died Sept. 10.

Truman, Harry S. (President of U.S.): Escaped assassination unhurt Nov. 1, 1950, in Washington, D.C., as 2 Puerto Rican nationalists attempted to shoot their way into Blair House.

Kennedy, John F. (President of U.S.): Shot Nov. 22, 1963, in Dallas, Tex., allegedly by Lee Harvey Oswald; died same day. Injured was Gov. John B. Connally of Texas. Oswald was shot and killed two days later by Jack Ruby.

King, Martin Luther, Jr. (civil rights leader): Shot April 4, 1968, in Memphis by James Earl Ray; died same day.

Kennedy, Robert F. (U.S. Senator from New York): Shot June 5, 1968, in Los Angeles by Sirhan Bishara Sirhan; died June 6.

Wallace, George C. (Governor of Alabama): Shot and critically wounded in assassination attempt May 15, 1972, at Laurel, Md., by Arthur Herman Bremer. Wallace paralyzed from waist down.

Ford, Gerald R. (President of U.S.): Escaped assassination attempt Sept. 5, 1975, in Sacramento, Calif., by Lynette Alice (Squeaky) Fromm, who pointed but did not fire .45-caliber pistol. Escaped assassination attempt in San Francisco, Calif., Sept. 22, 1975, by Sara Jane Moore, who fired one shot from a .38-caliber pistol that was deflected.

Jordan, Vernon E., Jr. (civil rights leader): Shot and critically wounded in assassination attempt May 29, 1980, in Fort Wayne, Ind.

Reagan, Ronald (President of U.S.): Shot in left lung in Washington by John W. Hinckley, Jr., on March 30, 1981; three others also wounded.

"High Crimes and Misdemeanors:" A Short History of Impeachment

The Mechanics of Impeachment

The right to impeach public officials is secured by the U.S. Constitution in Article I, Sections 2 and 3, which discuss the procedure, and in Article II, Section 4, which indicates the grounds for impeachment: "the President, Vice President, and all civil officers of the United States shall be removed from office on impeachment for, and conviction of, treason, bribery, or other high crimes and misdemeanors."

Removing an official from office requires two steps: (1) a formal accusation, or impeachment, by the House of Representatives, and (2) a trial and conviction by the Senate. Impeachment requires a majority vote of the House; conviction is more difficult, requiring a two-thirds vote by the Senate. The vice president presides over the Senate proceedings in the case of all officials except the president, whose trial is presided over by the Chief Justice of the Supreme Court. This is because the vice president can hardly be considered a disinterested party—if his boss is forced out of office he is next in line for the top job!

What are "High Crimes and Misdemeanors?"

Bribery, perjury, and treason are among the least ambiguous reasons meriting impeachment, but the ocean of wrongdoing encompassed by the Constitution's stipulation of "high crimes and misdemeanors" is vast. Abuse of power and serious misconduct in office fit this category, but one act that is definitely not grounds for impeachment is partisan discord. Several impeachment cases have confused political animosity with genuine crimes. Since Congress, the vortex of partisanship, is responsible for indicting, trying, and convicting public officials, it is necessary for legislative branch to temporarily cast aside its factional nature and adopt a judicial role.

The Infamous Fifteen

Since 1797 the House of Representatives has impeached fifteen federal officials. These include a president, a cabinet member, a senator, a justice of the Supreme Court, and eleven federal judges. Of those, the Senate has convicted and removed seven, all of them judges. Not included in this list are the office holders who have resigned rather than face impeachment, most notably, President Richard M. Nixon.

The Small Fry

The first official impeached in this country was Senator William Blount of Tennessee for a plot to help the British seize Louisiana and Florida from Spain in 1797. The Senate dismissed the charges on Jan. 14, 1799, determining that it had no jurisdiction over its own members. The Senate and the House do, however, have the right to discipline their members, and the Senate expelled Blount the day after his impeachment.

Judge John Pickering of New Hampshire was the first impeached official actually convicted. He was found guilty of drunkenness and unlawful rulings, on March 12, 1804, and was believed to have been insane.

Associate Justice Samuel Chase, a strong Federalist, was impeached but acquitted of judicial bias against anti-Federalists. The acquittal on March 1, 1805, established that political differences were not grounds for impeachment.

Other officials impeached were implicated in bribery, cheating on income tax, perjury, and treason.

The Big Fish

Only one president has been impeached: Andrew Johnson, the seventeenth chief executive. Johnson, a Southern Democrat who became president after Lincoln's assassination, supported a mild policy of Reconstruction after the Civil War. The Radical Republicans in Congress were furious at his leniency toward ex-Confederates and obvious lack of concern for ex-slaves, demonstrated by his veto of civil rights bills and opposition to the Fourteenth Amendment. To protect Radical Republicans in Johnson's administration and diminish the strength of the president, Congress passed the Tenure of Office Act in 1867, which prohibited the president from dismissing office holders without the Senate's approval. A defiant Johnson tested the constitutionality of the Act by attempting to oust Secretary of War Edwin M. Stanton. His violation of the Act became the basis for impeachment in 1868. But the Senate was one vote short of the two-thirds majority needed to convict, and Johnson was acquitted May 26, 1868.

Senator Charles Sumner, witness to the proceedings, defined them as "political in character." Historians today generally agree with his assessment and consider the grounds for Johnson's impeachment flimsy—the Tenure of Office Act was partially repealed in 1887, and then declared unconstitutional in 1926.

The One That Got Away

Of thirty-four attempts at impeachment in the nineteenth century only seven came to trial. Because it cripples Congress with a lengthy trial, impeachment is infrequent. Many officials, seeing the writing on the wall, resign rather than face the ignominy of a public trial.

The most famous of these cases is of course that of President Richard Nixon. After five men hired by Nixon's reelection committee were caught burglarizing Democratic party headquarters at the Watergate Complex on June 17, 1972, President Nixon's subsequent behavior—his cover-up of the burglary and refusal to turn over evidence—led the House Judiciary Committee to issue three articles of impeachment on July 30, 1974. The document also indicted Nixon for illegal wire tapping, misuse of the CIA, perjury, bribery, obstruction of justice, and other abuses of executive power. "In all of this," the Articles of Impeachment summarize, "Richard M. Nixon has acted in a manner contrary to his trust as president and subversive of constitutional government, to the great prejudice of the cause of law and justice, and to the manifest injury of the people of the United States." Impeachment appeared inevitable, and Nixon resigned on Aug. 9, 1974.

Impeachments of Federal Officials

Source: Congressional Directory.

The procedure for the impeachment of Federal officials is detailed in Article I, Section 3, of the Constitution. The Senate has sat as a court of impeachment in the following cases:

William Blount, Senator from Tennessee; charges dismissed for want of jurisdiction, Jan. 14, 1799.

John Pickering, Judge of the U.S. District Court for New Hampshire; removed from office March 12, 1804.

Samuel Chase, Associate Justice of the Supreme Court; acquitted March 1, 1805.

James H. Peck, Judge of the U.S. District Court for Missouri; acquitted Jan. 31, 1831.

West H. Humphreys, Judge of the U.S. District Court for the middle, eastern, and western districts of Tennessee; removed from office June 26, 1862.

Andrew Johnson, President of the United States; acquitted May 26, 1868.

William W. Belknap, Secretary of War; acquitted Aug. 1, 1876.

Charles Swayne, Judge of the U.S. District Court for the northern district of Florida; acquitted Feb. 27, 1905.

Robert W. Archbald, Associate Judge, U.S. Commerce Court; removed Jan. 13, 1913.

George W. English, Judge of the U.S. District Court for eastern district of Illinois; resigned Nov. 4, 1926; proceedings dismissed.

Harold Louderback, Judge of the U.S. District Court for the northern district of California; acquitted May 24, 1933.

Halsted L. Ritter, Judge of the U.S. District Court for the southern district of Florida; removed from office April 17, 1936.

Harry E. Claiborne, Judge of the U.S. District Court for the district of Nevada; removed from office Oct. 9, 1986.

Alcee L. Hastings, Judge of the U.S. District Court for the southern district of Florida; removed from office Oct. 20, 1988.

Walter L. Nixon, Judge of the U.S. District Court for Mississippi; removed from office Nov. 3, 1989.

The American's Creed

William Tyler Page

"I believe in the United States of America as a government of the people, by the people, for the people; whose just powers are derived from the consent of the governed; a democracy in a republic; a sovereign Nation of many sovereign States; a perfect union, one and inseparable; established upon those principles of freedom, equality, justice, and humanity for which American patriots sacrificed their lives and fortunes.

"I therefore believe it is my duty to my country to love it, to support its Constitution, to obey its laws, to respect its flag, and to defend it against all enemies."

NOTE: William Tyler Page, Clerk of the U.S. House of Representatives, wrote "The American's Creed" in 1917. It was accepted by the House on behalf of the American people on April 3, 1918.

How a Bill Becomes a Law

When a Senator or a Representative introduces a bill, he sends it to the clerk of his house, who gives it a number and title. This is the *first reading,* and the bill is referred to the proper committee.

The committee may decide the bill is unwise or unnecessary and *table* it, thus killing it at once. Or it may decide the bill is worthwhile and hold hearings to listen to facts and opinions presented by experts and other interested persons. After members of the committee have debated the bill and perhaps offered amendments, a vote is taken; and if the vote is favorable, the bill is sent back to the floor of the house.

The clerk reads the bill sentence by sentence to the house, and this is known as the *second reading.* Members may then debate the bill and offer amendments. In the House of Representatives, the time for debate is limited by a *cloture rule,* but there is no such restriction in the Senate for cloture, where 60 votes are required. This makes possible a *filibuster,* in which one or more opponents hold the floor to defeat the bill.

The *third reading* is by title only, and the bill is put to a vote, which may be by voice or roll call, depending on the circumstances and parliamentary rules. Members who must be absent at the time but who wish to record their vote may be paired if each negative vote has a balancing affirmative one.

The bill then goes to the other house of Congress, where it may be defeated, or passed with or without amendments. If the bill is defeated, it dies. If it is passed with amendments, a joint Congressional committee must be appointed by both houses to iron out the differences.

After its final passage by both houses, the bill is sent to the president. If he approves, he signs it, and the bill becomes a law. However, if he disapproves, he *vetoes* the bill by refusing to sign it and sending it back to the house of origin with his reasons for the veto. The objections are read and debated, and a roll-call vote is taken. If the bill receives less than a two-thirds vote, it is defeated and goes no farther. But if it receives a two-thirds vote or greater, it is sent to the other house for a vote. If that house also passes it by a two-thirds vote, the president's veto is *overridden,* and the bill becomes a law.

Should the president desire neither to sign nor to veto the bill, he may retain it for ten days, Sundays excepted, after which time it automatically becomes a law without signature. However, if Congress has adjourned within those ten days, the bill is automatically killed, that process of indirect rejection being known as a *pocket veto.*

The White House

Source: Department of the Interior, U.S. National Park Service.

The White House, the official residence of the president, is at 1600 Pennsylvania Avenue in Washington, D.C. 20500. The site, covering about 18 acres, was selected by President Washington and Pierre Charles L'Enfant, and the architect was James Hoban. The design appears to have been influenced by Leinster House, Dublin, and James Gibb's *Book of Architecture.* The cornerstone was laid Oct. 13, 1792, and the first residents were President and Mrs. John Adams in November 1800. The building was burned by the British in 1814.

From December 1948 to March 1952, the interior of the White House was rebuilt, and the outer walls were strengthened.

The rooms for public functions are on the first floor; the second and third floors are used as the residence of the president and first family. The most celebrated public room is the East Room, where formal receptions take place. Other public rooms are the Red Room, the Green Room, and the Blue Room. The State Dining Room is used for formal dinners. There are 132 rooms.

U.S. Capitol

When the French architect and engineer Maj. Pierre L'Enfant first began to lay out the plans for a new Federal city (now Washington, D.C.), he noted that Jenkins' Hill, overlooking the area, seemed to be "a pedestal waiting for a monument." It was here that the U.S. Capitol would be built. The basic structure as we know it today evolved over a period of more than 150 years. In 1792 a competition was held for the design of a capitol building. Dr. William Thornton, a physician and amateur architect, submitted the winning plan, a simple, low-lying structure of classical proportions with a shallow dome.

Later, internal modifications were made by Benjamin Henry Latrobe. After the building was burned by the British in 1814, Latrobe and architect Charles Bulfinch were responsible for its reconstruction. Finally, under Thomas Walter, who was Architect of the Capitol from 1851 to 1865, the House and Senate wings and the imposing cast iron dome topped with the Statue of Freedom were added, and the Capitol assumed the form we see today. It was in the old Senate chamber that Daniel Webster cried out, "Liberty and Union, now and forever, one and inseparable!" In Statuary Hall, which used to be the old House chamber, a small disk on the floor marks the spot where John Quincy Adams was fatally stricken after more than 50 years of service to his country. A whisper from one side of this room can be heard across the vast space of the hall. Visitors can see the original Supreme Court chamber a floor below the Rotunda.

In addition to its historical association, the Capitol Building is also a vast artistic treasure house. The works of such famous artists as Gilbert Stuart, Rembrandt Peale, and John Trumbull are displayed on the walls. The Great Rotunda, with its 180-foot-(54.9-m-) high dome, is decorated with a massive fresco by Constantino Brumidi, which extends some 300 feet (90 m) in circumference. Throughout the building are many paintings of events in U.S. history and sculptures of outstanding Americans. The Capitol itself is situated on a 68-acre (27.5-ha) park designed by the 19th-century landscape architect Frederick Law Olmsted. There are free guided tours of the Capitol, which include admission to the House and Senate galleries. Those who wish to visit the visitors' gallery in either wing without taking the tour may obtain passes from their Senators or Congressmen. Visitors may ride on the monorail subway that joins the House and Senate wings of the Capitol with the Congressional office buildings.

Washington Monument

Construction of this magnificent Washington, D.C., monument, which draws some two million visitors a year, took nearly a century of planning, building, and controversy. Provision for a large equestrian statue of George Washington was made in the original city plan, but the project was soon dropped. After Washington's death it was taken up again, and a number of false starts and changes of design were made. Finally, in 1848, work was begun on the monument that stands today. The design, by architect Robert Mills, then featured an ornate base. In 1854, however, political squabbling and a lack of money brought construction to a halt. Work was resumed in 1880, and the monument was completed in 1884 and opened to the public in 1888. The tapered shaft, faced with white marble and rising from walls 15 feet thick (4.6 m) at the base was modeled after the obelisks of ancient Egypt. The monument, one of the tallest masonry constructions in the world, stands just over 555 feet (169 m). Memorial stones from the 50 States, foreign countries, and organizations line the interior walls. The top, reached only by elevator, commands a panoramic view of the city.

The Liberty Bell

The Liberty Bell was cast in England in 1752 for the Pennsylvania Statehouse (now named Independence Hall) in Philadelphia. It was recast in Philadelphia in 1753. It is inscribed with the words, "Proclaim liberty throughout all the land unto all the inhabitants thereof" (Lev. 25:10). The bell was rung on July 8, 1776, for the first public reading of the Declaration of Independence. Hidden in Allentown during the British occupation of Philadelphia, it was replaced in Independence Hall in 1778. The bell cracked on July 8, 1835, while tolling the death of Chief Justice John Marshall. In 1976 the Liberty Bell was moved to a special exhibition building near Independence Hall.

Arlington National Cemetery

Arlington National Cemetery occupies 612 acres in Virginia on the Potomac River, directly opposite Washington. This land was part of the estate of John Parke Custis, Martha Washington's son. His son, George Washington Parke Custis, built the mansion which later became the home of Robert E. Lee. In 1864, Arlington became a military cemetery. More than 240,000 service members and their dependents are buried there. Expansion of the cemetery began in 1966, using a 180-acre tract of land directly east of the present site.

In 1921, an Unknown American Soldier of World War I was buried in the cemetery; the monument at the Tomb of the Unknown Soldier was opened to the public without ceremony in 1932. Two additional Unknowns, one from World War II and one from the Korean War, were buried May 30, 1958. The Unknown Serviceman of Vietnam was buried on May 28, 1984. In June 1998 his body was disinterred and recent DNA-testing technology was used to identify him as First Lt. Michael Blassie, an Air Force pilot from St. Louis. It is possible that technology will prevent there from ever being another "unknown" buried in the tomb.

The inscription carved on the Tomb of the Unknowns reads:

HERE RESTS IN
HONORED GLORY
AN AMERICAN
SOLDIER
KNOWN BUT TO GOD

Milestones in the Gay Rights Movement

Source: Excerpted from *The Reader's Companion to American History.* Copyright © 1991 by Houghton Mifflin Company.

Late in the [19th] century, as large cities allowed for greater anonymity, as wage labor apart from family became common, and as more women were drawn out of the home, evidence of a new pattern of homosexual expression surfaced. . . .

At first, these individuals developed ways of meeting one another and institutions to foster a sense of identity. . . . By 1915, one participant in this new gay world was referring to it as "a community distinctly organized." For the most part hidden from view because of social hostility, an urban gay subculture had come into existence by the 1920s and 1930s.

World War II served as a critical divide in the social history of homosexuality. Large numbers of the young left families, small towns, and closely knit ethnic neighborhoods to enter a sex-segregated military or to migrate to larger cities for wartime employment. . . .

After the war, many of them made choices designed to support their gay identities. Pat Bond, a woman from Iowa who first met other lesbians while in the military, decided to stay in San Francisco after her discharge. [Donald] Vining remained in New York City rather than return to his small hometown in New Jersey. They, along with countless others, sustained a vibrant gay subculture that revolved around bars and friendship networks. Many cities saw their first gay bars during the 1940s. . . .

This new visibility provoked latent cultural prejudices....Firings from government jobs and purges from the military intensified in the 1950s. President Dwight D. Eisenhower issued an executive order in 1953 barring gay men and lesbians from all federal jobs. Many state and local governments and private corporations followed suit. The FBI began a surveillance program against homosexuals.

The lead taken by the federal government encouraged local police forces to harass gay citizens. Vice officers regularly raided gay bars, sometimes arresting dozens of men and women on a single night. . . . Under these conditions, some gays began to organize politically. In November 1950 in Los Angeles, a small group of men led by Harry Hay and Chuck Rowland met to form what would become the Mattachine Society. Mostly male in membership, it was joined in 1955 by a lesbian organization in San Francisco, the Daughters of Bilitis, founded by Del Martin and Phyllis Lyon. In the 1950s these organizations remained small, but they established chapters in several cities and published magazines that were a beacon of hope to the readers.

In the 1960s, influenced by the model of a militant black civil rights movement, the "homophile movement," as the participants dubbed it, became more visible. Activists, such as Franklin Kameny and Barbara Gittings, picketed government agencies in Washington to protest discriminatory employment policies. In San Francisco, Martin, Lyon, and others targeted police harassment. By 1969, perhaps fifty homophile organizations existed in the United States, with memberships of a few thousand.

Then, on Friday evening, June 27, 1969, the police in New York City raided a Greenwich Village gay bar, the Stonewall Inn. Contrary to expectations, the patrons fought back, provoking three nights of rioting in the area accompanied by the appearance of "gay power" slogans on the buildings. Almost overnight, a massive grassroots gay liberations movement was born. Owing much to the radical protest of blacks, women, and college students in the 1960s, gays challenged all forms of hostility and punishment meted out by society. Choosing to "come out of the closet" and publicly proclaim their identity, they ushered in a social change movement that has grown substantially. By 1973, there were almost eight hundred gay and lesbian organizations in the United States; by 1990, the number was several thousand. By 1970, 5,000 gay men and lesbians marched in New York City to commemorate the first anniversary of the Stonewall Riots; in October 1987, over 600,000 marched in Washington, to demand equality.

The changes were far-reaching. Over the next two decades, half the states decriminalized homosexual behavior, and police harassment was sharply contained. Many large cities included sexual orientation in their civil rights statutes, as did Wisconsin and Massachusetts, first among the states to do so....[In 1975] the Civil Service Commission eliminated the ban on the employment of homosexuals in most federal jobs. Many of the nation's religious denominations engaged in spirited debates about the morality of homosexuality, and some, like Unitarianism and Reformed Judaism, opened their doors to gay and lesbian ministers and rabbis. The lesbian and gay world was no longer an underground subculture but, in larger cities especially, a well-organized community, with businesses, political clubs, social service agencies, community centers, and religious congregations bringing people together. In a number of places, openly gay candidates ran for elective office and won.

These changes spawned opposition. In 1977 the singer Anita Bryant led a campaign to repeal a gay rights ordinance in Dade County, Florida. Her success encouraged others, and by the early 1980s, a well-organized conservative force had materialized to target the gay rights movement. Politicians, such as Senator Jesse Helms of North Carolina, and fundamentalist ministers, such as Jerry Falwell of Lynchburg, Virginia, who formed Moral Majority, Inc., joined forces to slow the progress of the gay movement.

The onset of the AIDS epidemic in the 1980s, although it intensified the antigay rhetoric of the New Right, also stimulated further organizing within the gay community. AIDS made political mobilization a matter of life and death. With a large majority of the cases striking male homosexuals, the gay community in short order created a host of organizations, such as the Gay Men's Health Crisis in New York City, to provide services and assistance to those infected. Local and national gay civil rights groups also grew in size and number, as the community sought to increase funding for research and education and to win protection against discrimination. A personal and social tragedy of immense proportions, AIDS paradoxically strengthened the political arm of the gay movement. □

Populations of the Ten Largest Reservations

(1990 Census figures)

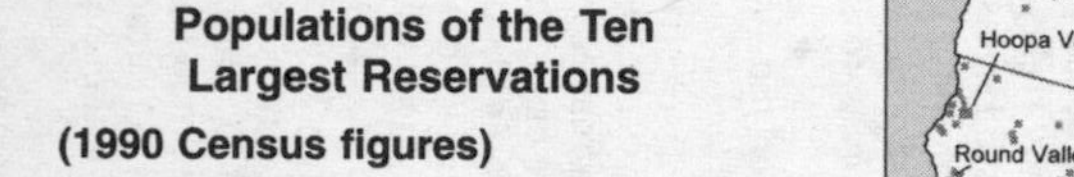

Name	Population
Navajo (Ariz., N.M., Utah)	143,405
Pine Ridge (Neb., S.D.)	11,182
Fort Apache (Ariz.)	9,825
Gila River (Ariz.)	9,116
Papago (Ariz.)	8,480
Rosebud (S.D.)	8,043
San Carlos (Ariz.)	7,110
Zuni Pueblo (Ariz., N.M.)	7,073
Hopi (Ariz.)	7,061
Blackfeet (Mont.)	7,025

The 218,320 American Indians living on these 10 reservations account for about half of all American Indians living on reservations and trust lands. *Source:* 1990 Census. *Map source:* Frederick E. Hoxie, ed., *Encyclopedia of North American Indians* (Boston: Houghton Mifflin, 1996). Reprinted with permission.

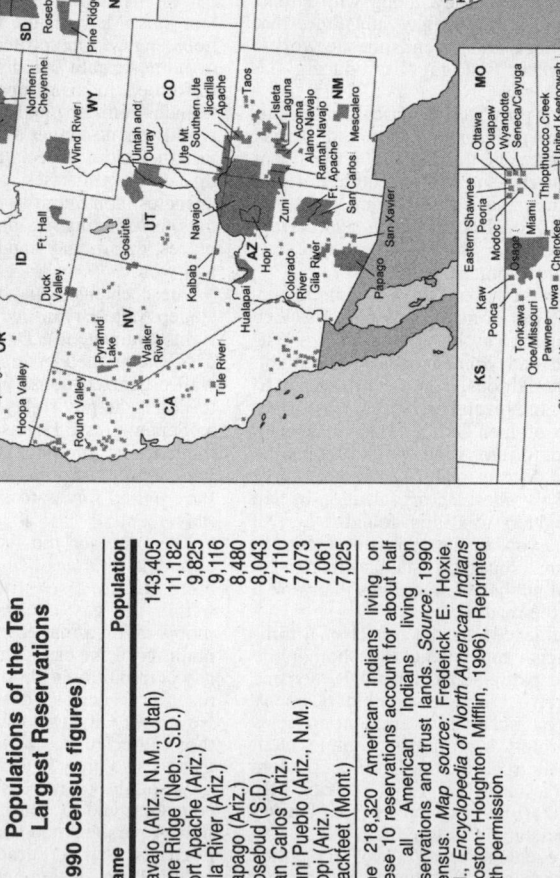

U.S. Federal and State Reservations

Firsts in America

This selection is based on our editorial judgment. Other sources may list different firsts.

Admiral in U.S. Navy: David Glasgow Farragut, 1866.

Airmail route, first transcontinental: Between New York City and San Francisco, 1920.

Assembly, representative: House of Burgesses, founded in Virginia, 1619.

Bank established: Bank of North America, Philadelphia, 1781.

Birth in America to English parents: Virginia Dare, born Roanoke Island, N.C., 1587.

Black newspaper: *Freedom's Journal,* 1827, edited by John B. Russworm.

Black U.S. diplomat: Ebenezer D. Bassett, 1869, minister-resident to Haiti.

Black elected governor of a state: L. Douglas Wilder, Virginia, 1990.

Black elected to U.S. Senate: Hiram Revels, 1870, Mississippi.

Black elected to U.S. House of Representatives: Jefferson Long, Georgia, 1870.

Black associate justice of U.S. Supreme Court: Thurgood Marshall, Oct. 2, 1967.

Black U.S. cabinet minister: Robert C. Weaver, 1966, Secretary of the Department of Housing and Urban Development.

Botanic garden: Established by John Bartram in Philadelphia, 1728 and is still in existence in its original location.

Cartoon, colored: "The Yellow Kid," by Richard Outcault, in *New York World,* 1895.

College: Harvard, founded 1636.

College to confer degrees on women: Oberlin (Ohio) College, 1841.

College to establish coeducation: Oberlin (Ohio) College, 1833.

Electrocution of a criminal: William Kemmler in Auburn Prison, Auburn, N.Y., Aug. 6, 1890.

Five and Dime Store: Founded by Frank Woolworth, Utica, N.Y., 1879 (moved to Lancaster, Pa., same year).

Fraternity, Greek-letter: Phi Beta Kappa; founded Dec. 5, 1776, at College of William and Mary.

Gay and lesbian civil rights advocacy organization: National Gay and Lesbian Task Force, founded in New York City, 1973.

Gay Power: Rioting following police raid on N.Y.C. gay bar, the Stonewall Inn, mobilizes gay community and leads to birth of gay liberation movement, June 27, 1969.

Homosexual, acknowledged, elected to high local office: Harvey Milk, 1977, San Francisco Board of Supervisors.

Law to be declared unconstitutional by U.S. Supreme Court: Judiciary Act of 1789. Case: *Marbury* v. *Madison,* 1803.

Library, circulating: Philadelphia, 1731.

Newspaper, illustrated daily: *New York Daily Graphic,* 1873.

Newspaper published daily: *Pennsylvania Packet and General Advertiser,* Philadelphia, Sept., 1784.

Newspaper published over a continuous period: *The Boston News-Letter,* April, 1704.

Newsreel: Pathé Frères of Paris, in 1910, circulated a weekly issue of their *Pathé Journal.*

Oil well, commercial: Titusville, Pa., 1859.

Panel quiz show on radio: *Information Please,* May 17, 1938.

Postage stamps issued: 1847.

Public School: Boston Latin School, Boston, 1635.

Radio station licensed: KDKA, Pittsburgh, Pa., Oct. 27, 1920.

Railroad, transcontinental: Central Pacific and Union Pacific railroads, joined at Promontory, Utah, May 10, 1869.

Savings bank: The Provident Institute for Savings, Boston, 1816.

Science museum: Founded by Charleston (S.C.) Library Society, 1773.

Skyscraper: Home Insurance Co., Chicago, 1885 (10 floors, 2 added later).

Slaves brought into America: At Jamestown, Va., 1619, from a Dutch ship.

Sorority: Kappa Alpha Theta, at De Pauw University, 1870.

State to abolish capital punishment: Michigan, 1847.

State to enter Union after original 13: Vermont, 1791.

Steam-heated building: Eastern Hotel, Boston, 1845.

Steam railroad (carried passengers and freight): Baltimore & Ohio, 1830.

Strike on record by union: Journeymen Printers, New York City, 1776.

Subway: Opened in Boston, 1897.

"Tabloid" picture newspaper: *The Illustrated Daily News* (now *The Daily News*), New York City, 1919.

Vaudeville theater: Gaiety Museum, Boston, 1883.

Woman astronaut appointed shuttle commander: Lt. Col. Eileen Collins, *Columbia,* Dec. 1998.

Woman astronaut to ride in space: Dr. Sally K. Ride, 1983.

Woman astronaut to walk in space: Dr. Kathryn D. Sullivan, 1984.

Woman cabinet member: Frances Perkins, Secretary of Labor, 1933.

Woman candidate for President: Victoria Claflin Woodhull, nominated by National Woman's Suffrage Assn. on ticket of Nation Radical Reformers, 1872.

Woman candidate for Vice President: Geraldine A. Ferraro, nominated on a major party ticket, Democratic Party, 1984.

Woman doctor of medicine: Elizabeth Blackwell; M.D. from Geneva Medical College of Western New York, 1849.

Woman elected governor of a state: Nellie Tayloe Ross, Wyoming, 1925.

Woman elected to U.S. Senate: Hattie Caraway, Arkansas; elected Nov., 1932.

Woman graduate of law school: Ada H. Kepley, Union College of Law, Chicago, 1870.

Woman member of U.S. House of Representatives: Jeannette Rankin; elected Nov., 1916.

Woman member of U.S. Senate: Rebecca Latimer Felton of Georgia; appointed Oct. 3, 1922.

Woman member of U.S. Supreme Court: Sandra Day O'Connor; appointed July 1981.

Woman Secretary of State: Madeleine Albright, appointed Dec. 1996.

Woman suffrage granted: Wyoming Territory, 1869.

Written constitution: *Fundamental Orders of Connecticut,* 1639.

States by Order of Entry into Union

State	Entered Union	Year Settled	Representatives in Congress[1]
1. Delaware	Dec. 7, 1787	1638	1
2. Pennsylvania	Dec. 12, 1787	1682	21
3. New Jersey	Dec. 18, 1787	1660	13
4. Georgia	Jan. 2, 1788	1733	11
5. Connecticut	Jan. 9, 1788	1634	6
6. Massachusetts	Feb. 6, 1788	1620	10
7. Maryland	Apr. 28, 1788	1634	8
8. South Carolina	May 23, 1788	1670	6
9. New Hampshire	June 21, 1788	1623	2
10. Virginia	June 25, 1788	1607	11
11. New York	July 26, 1788	1614	31
12. North Carolina	Nov. 21, 1789	1660	12
13. Rhode Island	May 29, 1790	1636	2
14. Vermont	Mar. 4, 1791	1724	1
15. Kentucky	June 1, 1792	1774	6
16. Tennessee	June 1, 1796	1769	9
17. Ohio	Mar. 1, 1803	1788	19
18. Louisiana	Apr. 30, 1812	1699	7
19. Indiana	Dec. 11, 1816	1733	10
20. Mississippi	Dec. 10, 1817	1699	5
21. Illinois	Dec. 3, 1818	1720	20
22. Alabama	Dec. 14, 1819	1702	7
23. Maine	Mar. 15, 1820	1624	2
24. Missouri	Aug. 10, 1821	1735	9
25. Arkansas	June 15, 1836	1686	4
26. Michigan	Jan. 26, 1837	1668	16
27. Florida	Mar. 3, 1845	1565	23
28. Texas	Dec. 29, 1845	1682	30
29. Iowa	Dec. 28, 1846	1788	5
30. Wisconsin	May 29, 1848	1766	9
31. California	Sept. 9, 1850	1769	52
32. Minnesota	May 11, 1858	1805	8
33. Oregon	Feb. 14, 1859	1811	5
34. Kansas	Jan. 29, 1861	1727	4
35. West Virginia	June 20, 1863	1727	3
36. Nevada	Oct. 31, 1864	1849	2
37. Nebraska	Mar. 1, 1867	1823	3
38. Colorado	Aug. 1, 1876	1858	6
39. North Dakota	Nov. 2, 1889	1812	1
40. South Dakota	Nov. 2, 1889	1859	1
41. Montana	Nov. 8, 1889	1809	1
42. Washington	Nov. 11, 1889	1811	9
43. Idaho	July 3, 1890	1842	2
44. Wyoming	July 10, 1890	1834	1
45. Utah	Jan. 4, 1896	1847	3
46. Oklahoma	Nov. 16, 1907	1889	6
47. New Mexico	Jan. 6, 1912	1610	3
48. Arizona	Feb. 14, 1912	1776	6
49. Alaska	Jan. 3, 1959	1784	1
50. Hawaii	Aug. 21, 1959	1820	2

1. Does not include Senators. *Source:* Compiled from various sources by the editors.

Figures and Legends in American Folklore

Appleseed, Johnny (John Chapman, 1774–1847): Massachusetts-born nurseryman; reputed to have spread seeds and seedlings out of which grew the apple orchards of the Midwest.

Billy the Kid (William H. Bonney, 1859–1881): Desperado who killed his first man before he reached his teens; after short life of crime in Wild West was gunned down by Sheriff Pat Garrett; symbol of lawless West.

Boone, Daniel (1734–1820): Frontiersman and Indian fighter, about whom legends of early America have been built; figured in Byron's *Don Juan.*

Buffalo Bill (William F. Cody, 1846–1917): Buffalo hunter and Indian scout; many of legends about him stem from his own Wild West show, which he operated in late 19th century.

Bunyan, Paul: Mythical lumberjack; subject of tall tales throughout timber country (that he dug Grand Canyon, for example).

Crockett, David (1786–1836): Frontiersman, Congressman, and defender of the Alamo, his backwoods humor and larger-than-life adventures made him synonymous with the Wild West.

James, Jesse (1847–1882): Bank and train robber; often portrayed as the American Robin Hood.

Jones, Casey (John Luther Jones, 1863–1900): Example of heroic locomotive engineer given to feats of prowess; died in wreck when his Illinois Central "Cannonball" express hit a freight train at Vaughan, Miss.

Ross, Betsy (1752–1836): Member of Philadelphia flag-making family; reported to have designed and sewn first American flag. (Report is without confirmation.)

Uncle Sam: Personification of U.S. and its people; origin uncertain; may be based on inspector of government supplies in Revolutionary War and War of 1812.

Presidents

	Name and (party)[1]	Term	State of birth	Born	Died	Religion	Age at inaug.	Age at death
1.	Washington (F)[2]	1789–1797	Va.	2/22/1732	12/14/1799	Episcopalian	57	67
2.	J. Adams (F)	1797–1801	Mass.	10/30/1735	7/4/1826	Unitarian	61	90
3.	Jefferson (DR)	1801–1809	Va.	4/13/1743	7/4/1826	Deist	57	83
4.	Madison (DR)	1809–1817	Va.	3/16/1751	6/28/1836	Episcopalian	57	85
5.	Monroe (DR)	1817–1825	Va.	4/28/1758	7/4/1831	Episcopalian	58	73
6.	J. Q. Adams (DR)	1825–1829	Mass.	7/11/1767	2/23/1848	Unitarian	57	80
7.	Jackson (D)	1829–1837	S.C.	3/15/1767	6/8/1845	Presbyterian	61	78
8.	Van Buren (D)	1837–1841	N.Y.	12/5/1782	7/24/1862	Reformed Dutch	54	79
9.	W. H. Harrison (W)[3]	1841	Va.	2/9/1773	4/4/1841	Episcopalian	68	68
10.	Tyler (W)	1841–1845	Va.	3/29/1790	1/18/1862	Episcopalian	51	71
11.	Polk (D)	1845–1849	N.C.	11/2/1795	6/15/1849	Methodist	49	53
12.	Taylor (W)[3]	1849–1850	Va.	11/24/1784	7/9/1850	Episcopalian	64	65
13.	Fillmore (W)	1850–1853	N.Y.	1/7/1800	3/8/1874	Unitarian	50	74
14.	Pierce (D)	1853–1857	N.H.	11/23/1804	10/8/1869	Episcopalian	48	64
15.	Buchanan (D)	1857–1861	Pa.	4/23/1791	6/1/1868	Presbyterian	65	77
16.	Lincoln (R)[4]	1861–1865	Ky.	2/12/1809	4/15/1865	Liberal	52	56
17.	A. Johnson (U)[5]	1865–1869	N.C.	12/29/1808	7/31/1875	([6])	56	66
18.	Grant (R)	1869–1877	Ohio	4/27/1822	7/23/1885	Methodist	46	63
19.	Hayes (R)	1877–1881	Ohio	10/4/1822	1/17/1893	Methodist	54	70
20.	Garfield (R)[4]	1881	Ohio	11/19/1831	9/19/1881	Disciples of Christ	49	49
21.	Arthur (R)	1881–1885	Vt.	10/5/1830	11/18/1886	Episcopalian	50	56
22.	Cleveland (D)	1885–1889	N.J.	3/18/1837	6/24/1908	Presbyterian	47	71
23.	B. Harrison (R)	1889–1893	Ohio	8/20/1833	3/13/1901	Presbyterian	55	67
24.	Cleveland (D)[7]	1893–1897	—	—	—	—	55	—
25.	McKinley (R)[4]	1897–1901	Ohio	1/29/1843	9/14/1901	Methodist	54	58
26.	T. Roosevelt (R)	1901–1909	N.Y.	10/27/1858	1/6/1919	Reformed Dutch	42	60
27.	Taft (R)	1909–1913	Ohio	9/15/1857	3/8/1930	Unitarian	51	72
28.	Wilson (D)	1913–1921	Va.	12/28/1856	2/3/1924	Presbyterian	56	67
29.	Harding (R)[3]	1921–1923	Ohio	11/2/1865	8/2/1923	Baptist	55	57
30.	Coolidge (R)	1923–1929	Vt.	7/4/1872	1/5/1933	Congregationalist	51	60
31.	Hoover (R)	1929–1933	Iowa	8/10/1874	10/20/1964	Quaker	54	90
32.	F. D. Roosevelt (D)[3]	1933–1945	N.Y.	1/30/1882	4/12/1945	Episcopalian	51	63
33.	Truman (D)	1945–1953	Mo.	5/8/1884	12/26/1972	Baptist	60	88
34.	Eisenhower (R)	1953–1961	Tex.	10/14/1890	3/28/1969	Presbyterian	62	78
35.	Kennedy (D)[4]	1961–1963	Mass.	5/29/1917	11/22/1963	Roman Catholic	43	46
36.	L. B. Johnson (D)	1963–1969	Tex.	8/27/1908	1/22/1973	Disciples of Christ	55	64
37.	Nixon (R)[8]	1969–1974	Calif.	1/9/1913	4/22/1994	Quaker	56	81
38.	Ford (R)	1974–1977	Neb.	7/14/1913	—	Episcopalian	61	—
39.	Carter (D)	1977–1981	Ga.	10/1/1924	—	Southern Baptist	52	—
40.	Reagan (R)	1981–1989	Ill.	2/6/1911	—	Disciples of Christ	69	—
41.	Bush (R)	1989–1993	Mass.	6/12/24	—	Episcopalian	64	—
42.	Clinton (D)	1993–	Ark.	8/19/46	—	Baptist	46	—

1. F—Federalist; DR—Democratic-Republican; D—Democratic; W—Whig; R—Republican; U—Union. 2. No party for first election. The party system in the U.S. made its appearance during Washington's first term. 3. Died in office. 4. Assassinated in office. 5. The Republican National Convention of 1864 adopted the name Union Party. It renominated Lincoln for president; for vice president it nominated Johnson, a War Democrat. Although frequently listed as a Republican vice president and president, Johnson undoubtedly considered himself strictly a member of the Union Party. When that party broke apart after 1868, he returned to the Democratic Party. 6. Johnson was not a professed church member; however, he admired the Baptist principles of church government. 7. Second nonconsecutive term. 8. Resigned Aug. 9, 1974.

Vice Presidents

	Name and (party)[1]	Term	State of birth	Birth and death dates	President served under
1.	John Adams (F)[2]	1789–1797	Massachusetts	1735–1826	Washington
2.	Thomas Jefferson (DR)	1797–1801	Virginia	1743–1826	J. Adams
3.	Aaron Burr (DR)	1801–1805	New Jersey	1756–1836	Jefferson
4.	George Clinton (DR)[3]	1805–1812	New York	1739–1812	Jefferson and Madison
5.	Elbridge Gerry (DR)[3]	1813–1814	Massachusetts	1744–1814	Madison
6.	Daniel D. Tompkins (DR)	1817–1825	New York	1774–1825	Monroe
7.	John C. Calhoun[4]	1825–1832	South Carolina	1782–1850	J. Q. Adams and Jackson
8.	Martin Van Buren (D)	1833–1837	New York	1782–1862	Jackson
9.	Richard M. Johnson (D)	1837–1841	Kentucky	1780–1850	Van Buren
10.	John Tyler (W)[5]	1841	Virginia	1790–1862	W. H. Harrison
11.	George M. Dallas (D)	1845–1849	Pennsylvania	1792–1864	Polk
12.	Millard Fillmore (W)[5]	1849–1850	New York	1800–1874	Taylor
13.	William R. King (D)[3]	1853	North Carolina	1786–1853	Pierce
14.	John C. Breckinridge (D)	1857–1861	Kentucky	1821–1875	Buchanan
15.	Hannibal Hamlin (R)	1861–1865	Maine	1809–1891	Lincoln
16.	Andrew Johnson (U)[5]	1865	North Carolina	1808–1875	Lincoln
17.	Schuyler Colfax (R)	1869–1873	New York	1823–1885	Grant
18.	Henry Wilson (R)[3]	1873–1875	New Hampshire	1812–1875	Grant
19.	William A. Wheeler (R)	1877–1881	New York	1819–1887	Hayes
20.	Chester A. Arthur (R)[5]	1881	Vermont	1830–1886	Garfield
21.	Thomas A. Hendricks (D)[3]	1885	Ohio	1819–1885	Cleveland
22.	Levi P. Morton (R)	1889–1893	Vermont	1824–1920	B. Harrison
23.	Adlai E. Stevenson (D)	1893–1897	Kentucky	1835–1914	Cleveland
24.	Garrett A. Hobart (R)[3]	1897–1899	New Jersey	1844–1899	McKinley
25.	Theodore Roosevelt (R)[5]	1901	New York	1858–1919	McKinley
26.	Charles W. Fairbanks (R)	1905–1909	Ohio	1852–1918	T. Roosevelt
27.	James S. Sherman (R)[3]	1909–1912	New York	1855–1912	Taft
28.	Thomas R. Marshall (D)	1913–1921	Indiana	1854–1925	Wilson
29.	Calvin Coolidge (R)[5]	1921–1923	Vermont	1872–1933	Harding
30.	Charles G. Dawes (R)	1925–1929	Ohio	1865–1951	Coolidge
31.	Charles Curtis (R)	1929–1933	Kansas	1860–1936	Hoover
32.	John N. Garner (D)	1933–1941	Texas	1868–1967	F. D. Roosevelt
33.	Henry A. Wallace (D)	1941–1945	Iowa	1888–1965	F. D. Roosevelt
34.	Harry S. Truman (D)[5]	1945	Missouri	1884–1972	F. D. Roosevelt
35.	Alben W. Barkley (D)	1949–1953	Kentucky	1877–1956	Truman
36.	Richard M. Nixon (R)	1953-1961	California	1913–1994	Eisenhower
37.	Lyndon B. Johnson (D)[5]	1961–1963	Texas	1908–1973	Kennedy
38.	Hubert H. Humphrey (D)	1965–1969	South Dakota	1911–1978	Johnson
39.	Spiro T. Agnew (R)[6]	1969–1973	Maryland	1918–1996	Nixon
40.	Gerald R. Ford (R)[7]	1973–1974	Nebraska	1913–	Nixon
41.	Nelson A. Rockefeller (R)[8]	1974–1977	Maine	1908–1979	Ford
42.	Walter F. Mondale (D)	1977–1981	Minnesota	1928–	Carter
43.	George Bush (R)	1981–1989	Massachusetts	1924–	Reagan
44.	J. Danforth Quayle (R)	1989–1993	Indiana	1947–	Bush
45.	Albert A. Gore, Jr. (D)	1993–	Washington, D.C.	1948—	Clinton

1. F—Federalist; DR—Democratic-Republican; D—Democratic; W—Whig; R—Republican; U—Union. 2. No party for first election. The party system in the U.S. made its appearance during Washington's first term as president. 3. Died in office. 4. Democratic-Republican with J. Q. Adams; Democratic with Jackson. Calhoun resigned in 1832 to become a U.S. Senator. 5. Succeeded to presidency on death of president. 6. Resigned Oct. 10, 1973, after pleading no contest to Federal income tax evasion charges. 7. Nominated by Nixon on Oct. 12, 1973, under provisions of 25th Amendment. Confirmed by Congress on Dec. 6, 1973, and was sworn in same day. He became president Aug. 9, 1974, upon Nixon's resignation. 8. Nominated by Ford Aug. 20, 1974; confirmed by Congress on Dec. 19, 1974, and was sworn in same day.

Burial Places of the Presidents

President	Burial place	President	Burial place
Washington	Mt. Vernon, Va.	Hayes	Fremont, Ohio
J. Adams	Quincy, Mass.	Garfield	Cleveland, Ohio
Jefferson	Charlottesville, Va.	Arthur	Albany, N.Y.
Madison	Montpelier Station, Va.	Cleveland	Princeton, N.J.
Monroe	Richmond, Va.	B. Harrison	Indianapolis
J. Q. Adams	Quincy, Mass.	McKinley	Canton, Ohio
Jackson	The Hermitage, nr. Nashville, Tenn.	T. Roosevelt	Oyster Bay, N.Y.
		Taft	Arlington National Cemetery
Van Buren	Kinderhook, N.Y.	Wilson	Washington National Cathedral
W. H. Harrison	North Bend, Ohio	Harding	Marion, Ohio
Tyler	Richmond, Va.	Coolidge	Plymouth, Vt.
Polk	Nashville, Tenn.	Hoover	West Branch, Iowa
Taylor	Louisville, Ky.	F. D. Roosevelt	Hyde Park, N.Y.
Fillmore	Buffalo, N.Y.	Truman	Independence, Mo.
Pierce	Concord, N.H.	Eisenhower	Abilene, Kan.
Buchanan	Lancaster, Pa.	Kennedy	Arlington National Cemetery
Lincoln	Springfield, Ill.	L. B. Johnson	Stonewall, Tex.
A. Johnson	Greeneville, Tenn.	Nixon	Yorba Linda, Calif.
Grant	New York City		

Wives and Children of the Presidents

President	Wife's name	Year and place of wife's birth	Married	Wife died	Children[1] Sons	Daughters
Washington	Martha Dandridge Custis	1732, Va.	1759	1802	—	—
John Adams	Abigail Smith	1744, Mass.	1764	1818	3	2
Jefferson	Martha Wayles Skelton	1748, Va.	1772	1782	1	5
Madison	Dorothy "Dolley" Payne Todd	1768, N.C.	1794	1849	—	—
Monroe	Elizabeth "Eliza" Kortright	1768, N.Y.	1786	1830	—	2
J. Q. Adams	Louisa Catherine Johnson	1775, England	1797	1852	3	1
Jackson	Mrs. Rachel Donelson Robards	1767, Va.	1791	1828	—	—
Van Buren	Hannah Hoes	1788, N.Y.	1807	1819	4	—
W. H. Harrison	Anna Symmes	1775, N.J.	1795	1864	6	4
Tyler	Letitia Christian	1790, Va.	1813	1842	3	4
	Julia Gardiner	1820, N.Y.	1844	1889	5	2
Polk	Sarah Childress	1803, Tenn.	1824	1891	—	—
Taylor	Margaret Smith	1788, Md.	1810	1852	1	5
Fillmore	Abigail Powers	1798, N.Y.	1826	1853	1	1
	Caroline Carmichael McIntosh	1813, N.J.	1858	1881	—	—
Pierce	Jane Means Appleton	1806, N.H.	1834	1863	3	—
Buchanan	(Unmarried)	—	—	—	—	—
Lincoln	Mary Todd	1818, Ky.	1842	1882	4	—
A. Johnson	Eliza McCardle	1810, Tenn.	1827	1876	3	2
Grant	Julia Dent	1826, Mo.	1848	1902	3	1
Hayes	Lucy Ware Webb	1831, Ohio	1852	1889	7	1
Garfield	Lucretia Rudolph	1832, Ohio	1858	1918	5	2
Arthur	Ellen Lewis Herndon	1837, Va.	1859	1880	2	1
Cleveland	Frances Folsom	1864, N.Y.	1886	1947	2	3
B. Harrison	Caroline Lavinia Scott	1832, Ohio	1853	1892	1	1
	Mary Scott Lord Dimmick	1858, Pa.	1896	1948	—	1
McKinley	Ida Saxton	1847, Ohio	1871	1907	—	2
T. Roosevelt	Alice Hathaway Lee	1861, Mass.	1880	1884	—	1
	Edith Kermit Carow	1861, Conn.	1886	1948	4	1
Taft	Helen Herron	1861, Ohio	1886	1943	2	1
Wilson	Ellen Louise Axson	1860, Ga.	1885	1914	—	3
	Edith Bolling Galt	1872, Va.	1915	1961	—	—
Harding	Florence Kling DeWolfe	1860, Ohio	1891	1924	—	—
Coolidge	Grace Anna Goodhue	1879, Vt.	1905	1957	2	—
Hoover	Lou Henry	1875, Iowa	1899	1944	2	—
F. D. Roosevelt	Anna Eleanor Roosevelt	1884, N.Y.	1905	1962	5	1
Truman	Bess Wallace	1885, Mo.	1919	1982	—	1
Eisenhower	Mamie Geneva Doud	1896, Iowa	1916	1979	2	—

President	Wife's name	Year and place of wife's birth	Married	Wife died	Children[1] Sons	Daughters
Kennedy	Jacqueline Lee Bouvier	1929, N.Y.	1953	1994	2	1
L. B. Johnson	Claudia Alta "Lady Bird" Taylor	1912, Tex.	1934	—	—	2
Nixon	Thelma Catherine "Pat" Ryan	1912, Nev.	1940	1993	—	2
Ford	Elizabeth "Betty" Bloomer Warren	1918, Ill.	1948	—	3	1
Carter	Rosalynn Smith	1928, Ga.	1946	—	3	1
Reagan	Jane Wyman	1914, Mo.	1940[2]	—	1[3]	1
	Nancy Davis	1921 (?)[4], N.Y.	1952	—	1	1
Bush	Barbara Pierce	1925, N.Y.	1945	—	4	2
Clinton	Hillary Rodham	1946, Ill.	1975	—	—	1

1. Includes children who died in infancy. 2. Divorced in 1948. 3. Adopted. 4. Birthday officially given as 1923 but her high school and college records show 1921 for year of birth.

Presidential Libraries

The presidential library system is made up of ten presidential libraries and one presidential project. These are not traditional libraries, but rather repositories for preserving and making available the papers, records, and other historical materials of the presidents since Herbert Hoover. The presidential library system formally began in 1939, when President Franklin Roosevelt donated his personal and presidential papers to the federal government. Roosevelt's decision stemmed from a firm belief that presidential papers are an important part of the national heritage and should be accessible to the public. Below is a list of the presidential libraries and their locations.

Hoover Library
Herbert Hoover National Historic Site
211 Parkside Drive
P.O. Box 488
West Branch, IA 52358-0488

Roosevelt Library
511 Albany Post Road
Hyde Park, NY 12538-1999

Truman Library
500 West U.S. Highway 24
Independence, MO 64050-1798

Eisenhower Library
200 SE 4th Street
Abilene, KS 67410-2900

Kennedy Library
Columbia Point
Boston, MA 02125-3398

Johnson Library
2313 Red River Street
Austin, TX 78705-5702

Nixon Presidential Materials Staff (the Nixon Project)[1]
National Archives at College Park
8601 Adelphi Road
College Park, MD 20740-6001

Ford Library
1000 Beal Avenue
Ann Arbor, MI 48109-2114

Carter Library
1 Copenhill Avenue, NE
Atlanta, GA 30307-1406

Reagan Library
40 Presidential Drive
Simi Valley, CA 93065-0666

Bush Library
701 University Drive East, Suite 300
College Station, TX 77840-9554

1. The Nixon Project is not affiliated with the Richard Nixon Library and Birthplace in Yorba Linda, Calif., a private institution that was established by Nixon in 1990. *Source:* National Archives and Records Administration. Web: www.nara.gov/nara/president.

Government Officials

Cabinet Members With Dates of Appointment

Although the Constitution made no provision for a president's advisory group, the heads of the three executive departments (State, Treasury, and War) and the Attorney General were organized by Washington into such a group; and by about 1793, the name "Cabinet" was applied to it. With the exception of the Attorney General up to 1870 and the Postmaster General from 1829 to 1872, Cabinet members have been heads of executive departments.

Cabinet members are appointed by the president, subject to the confirmation of the Senate; and as their terms are not fixed, they may be replaced at any time by the president. At a change in Administration, it is customary for Cabinet members to tender their resignations, but they remain in office until successors are appointed.

The table of Cabinet members lists only those members who actually served after being duly commissioned.

The dates shown are those of appointment. "Cont." indicates that the term continued from the previous Administration for a substantial amount of time.

With the creation of the Department of Transportation in 1966, the Cabinet consisted of 12 members. This figure was reduced to 11 when the Post Office Department became an independent agency in 1970 but, with the establishment in 1977 of a Department of Energy, became 12 again. Creation of the Department of Education in 1980 raised the number to 13. Creation of the Department of Veterans' Affairs in 1989 raised the number to 14.

Washington

Secretary of State	Thomas Jefferson, 1789
	Edmund Randolph, 1794
	Timothy Pickering, 1795
Secretary of the Treasury	Alexander Hamilton, 1789
	Oliver Wolcott, Jr., 1795
Secretary of War	Henry Knox, 1789
	Timothy Pickering, 1795
	James McHenry, 1796
Attorney General	Edmund Randolph, 1789
	William Bradford, 1794
	Charles Lee, 1795

J. Adams

Secretary of State	Timothy Pickering (Cont.)
	John Marshall, 1800
Secretary of the Treasury	Oliver Wolcott, Jr. (Cont.)
	Samuel Dexter, 1801
Secretary of War	James McHenry (Cont.)
	Samuel Dexter, 1800
Attorney General	Charles Lee (Cont.)
Secretary of the Navy	Benjamin Stoddert, 1798

Jefferson

Secretary of State	James Madison, 1801
Secretary of the Treasury	Samuel Dexter (Cont.)
	Albert Gallatin, 1801
Secretary of War	Henry Dearborn, 1801
Attorney General	Levi Lincoln, 1801
	Robert Smith, 1805
	John Breckinridge, 1805
	Caesar A. Rodney, 1807
Secretary of the Navy	Benjamin Stoddert (Cont.)
	Robert Smith, 1801

Madison

Secretary of State	Robert Smith, 1809
	James Monroe, 1811
Secretary of the Treasury	Albert Gallatin (Cont.)
	George W. Campbell, 1814
	Alexander J. Dallas, 1814
	William H. Crawford, 1816
Secretary of War	William Eustis, 1809
	John Armstrong, 1813
	James Monroe, 1814
	William H. Crawford, 1815
Attorney General	Caesar A. Rodney (Cont.)
	William Pinckney, 1811
	Richard Rush, 1814
Secretary of the Navy	Paul Hamilton, 1809
	William Jones, 1813
	B. W. Crowninshield, 1814

Monroe

Secretary of State	John Quincy Adams, 1817
Secretary of the Treasury	William H. Crawford (Cont.)
Secretary of War	John C. Calhoun, 1817
Attorney General	Richard Rush (Cont.)
	William Wirt, 1817
Secretary of the Navy	B. W. Crowninshield (Cont.)
	Smith Thompson, 1818
	Samuel L. Southard, 1823

J. Q. Adams

Secretary of State	Henry Clay, 1825
Secretary of the Treasury	Richard Rush, 1825
Secretary of War	James Barbour, 1825
	Peter B. Porter, 1828
Attorney General	William Wirt (Cont.)
Secretary of the Navy	Samuel L. Southard (Cont.)

Jackson

Secretary of State	Martin Van Buren, 1829
	Edward Livingston, 1831
	Louis McLane, 1833
	John Forsyth, 1834
Secretary of the Treasury	Samuel D. Ingham, 1829
	Louis McLane, 1831
	William J. Duane, 1833
	Roger B. Taney[1], 1833
	Levi Woodbury, 1834
Secretary of War	John H. Eaton, 1829
	Lewis Cass, 1831
Attorney General	John M. Berrien, 1829
	Roger B. Taney, 1831
	Benjamin F. Butler, 1833
Postmaster General[2]	William T. Barry, 1829
	Amos Kendall, 1835
Secretary of the Navy	John Branch, 1829
	Levi Woodbury, 1831
	Mahlon Dickerson, 1834

1. Not confirmed by the Senate. 2. The Postmaster General did not become a Cabinet member until, 1829. Earlier Postmasters General were: Samuel Osgood (1789), Timothy Pickering (1791), Joseph Habersham (1795), Gideon Granger (1801), Return J. Meigs, Jr. (1814), and John McLean (1823).

Van Buren

Secretary of State	John Forsyth (Cont.)
Secretary of the Treasury	Levi Woodbury (Cont.)
Secretary of War	Joel R. Poinsett, 1837
Attorney General	Benjamin F. Butler (Cont.)
	Felix Grundy, 1838
	Henry D. Gilpin, 1840
Postmaster General	Amos Kendall (Cont.)
	John M. Niles, 1840
Secretary of the Navy	Mahlon Dickerson (Cont.)
	James K. Paulding, 1838

W. H. Harrison

Secretary of State	Daniel Webster, 1841
Secretary of the Treasury	Thomas Ewing, 1841
Secretary of War	John Bell, 1841
Attorney General	John J. Crittenden, 1841
Postmaster General	Francis Granger, 1841
Secretary of the Navy	George E. Badger, 1841

Tyler

Secretary of State	Daniel Webster (Cont.)
	Abel P. Upshur, 1843
	John C. Calhoun, 1844
Secretary of the Treasury	Thomas Ewing (Cont.)
	Walter Forward, 1841
	John C. Spencer[1], 1843
	George M. Bibb, 1844
Secretary of War	John Bell (Cont.)
	John C. Spencer, 1841
	James M. Porter[1], 1843
	William Wilkins, 1844
Attorney General	John J. Crittenden (Cont.)
	Hugh S. Legaré, 1841
	John Nelson, 1843
Postmaster General	Francis Granger (Cont.)
	Charles A. Wickliffe, 1841
Secretary of the Navy	George E. Badger (Cont.)
	Abel P. Upshur, 1841
	David Henshaw[1], 1843
	Thomas W. Gilmer, 1844
	John Y. Mason, 1844

1. Not confirmed by the Senate.

Polk

Secretary of State	James Buchanan, 1845
Secretary of the Treasury	Robert J. Walker, 1845
Secretary of War	William L. Marcy, 1845
Attorney General	John Y. Mason, 1845
	Nathan Clifford, 1846
	Isaac Toucey, 1848
Postmaster General	Cave Johnson, 1845
Secretary of the Navy	George Bancroft, 1845
	John Y. Mason, 1846

Taylor

Secretary of State	John M. Clayton, 1849
Secretary of the Treasury	William M. Meredith, 1849
Secretary of War	George W. Crawford, 1849
Attorney General	Reverdy Johnson, 1849
Postmaster General	Jacob Collamer, 1849
Secretary of the Navy	William B. Preston, 1849
Secretary of the Interior	Thomas Ewing, 1849

Fillmore

Secretary of State	Daniel Webster, 1850
	Edward Everett, 1852
Secretary of the Treasury	Thomas Corwin, 1850
Secretary of War	Charles M. Conrad, 1850
Attorney General	John J. Crittenden, 1850
Postmaster General	Nathan K. Hall, 1850
	Samuel D. Hubbard, 1852
Secretary of the Navy	William A. Graham, 1850
	John P. Kennedy, 1852
Secretary of the Interior	Thos. M. T. McKennan, 1850
	Alex. H. H. Stuart, 1850

Pierce

Secretary of State	William L. Marcy, 1853
Secretary of the Treasury	James Guthrie, 1853
Secretary of War	Jefferson Davis, 1853
Attorney General	Caleb Cushing, 1853
Postmaster General	James Campbell, 1853
Secretary of the Navy	James C. Dobbin, 1853
Secretary of the Interior	Robert McClelland, 1853

Buchanan

Secretary of State	Lewis Cass, 1857
	Jeremiah S. Black, 1860
Secretary of the Treasury	Howell Cobb, 1857
	Philip F. Thomas, 1860
	John A. Dix, 1861
Secretary of War	John B. Floyd, 1857
	Joseph Holt, 1861
Attorney General	Jeremiah S. Black, 1857
	Edwin M. Stanton, 1860
Postmaster General	Aaron V. Brown, 1857
	Joseph Holt, 1859
	Horatio King, 1861
Secretary of the Navy	Isaac Toucey, 1857
Secretary of the Interior	Jacob Thompson, 1857

Lincoln

Secretary of State	William H. Seward, 1861
Secretary of the Treasury	Salmon P. Chase, 1861
	William P. Fessenden, 1864
	Hugh McCulloch, 1865
Secretary of War	Simon Cameron, 1861
	Edwin M. Stanton, 1862
Attorney General	Edward Bates, 1861
	James Speed, 1864
Postmaster General	Montgomery Blair, 1861
	William Dennison, 1864
Secretary of the Navy	Gideon Welles, 1861
Secretary of the Interior	Caleb B. Smith, 1861
	John P. Usher, 1863

A. Johnson

Secretary of State	William H. Seward (Cont.)
Secretary of the Treasury	Hugh McCulloch (Cont.)
Secretary of War	Edwin M. Stanton (Cont.)
	John M. Schofield, 1868
Attorney General	James Speed (Cont.)
	Henry Stanbery, 1866
	William M. Evarts, 1868
Postmaster General	William Dennison (Cont.)
	Alexander W. Randall, 1866
Secretary of the Navy	Gideon Welles (Cont.)
Secretary of the Interior	John P. Usher (Cont.)
	James Harlan, 1865
	Orville H. Browning, 1866

Grant

Secretary of State	Elihu B. Washburne, 1869
	Hamilton Fish, 1869
	George S. Boutwell, 1869
	William A. Richardson, 1873
	Benjamin H. Bristow, 1874
	Lot M. Morrill, 1876
Secretary of War	John A. Rawlins, 1869
	William W. Belknap, 1869
	Alphonso Taft, 1876
	James D. Cameron, 1876
Attorney General	Ebenezer R. Hoar, 1869
	Amos T. Akerman, 1870
	George H. Williams, 1871
	Edwards Pierrepont, 1875
	Alphonso Taft, 1876
Postmaster General	John A. J. Creswell, 1869
	Marshall Jewell, 1874
	James N. Tyner, 1876
Secretary of the Navy	Adolph E. Borie, 1869
	George M. Robeson, 1869
Secretary of the Interior	Jacob D. Cox, 1869
	Columbus Delano, 1870
	Zachariah Chandler, 1875

Hayes

Secretary of State	William M. Evarts, 1877
Secretary of the Treasury	John Sherman, 1877
Secretary of War	George W. McCrary, 1877
	Alexander Ramsey, 1879
Attorney General	Charles Devens, 1877
Postmaster General	David M. Key, 1877
	Horace Maynard, 1880
	Richard W. Thompson, 1877
	Nathan Goff, Jr., 1881
Secretary of the Interior	Carl Schurz, 1877

Garfield

Secretary of State	James G. Blaine, 1881
Secretary of the Treasury	William Windom, 1881
Secretary of War	Robert T. Lincoln, 1881
Attorney General	Wayne MacVeagh, 1881
Postmaster General	Thomas L. James, 1881
Secretary of the Navy	William H. Hunt, 1881
Secretary of the Interior	Samuel J. Kirkwood, 1881

Arthur

Secretary of State	James G. Blaine (Cont.)
	F. T. Frelinghuysen, 1881
Secretary of the Treasury	William Windom (Cont.)
	Charles J. Folger, 1881
	Walter Q. Gresham, 1884
	Hugh McCulloch, 1884
Secretary of War	Robert T. Lincoln (Cont.)
Attorney General	Wayne MacVeagh (Cont.)
	Benjamin H. Brewster, 1881
Postmaster General	Thomas L. James (Cont.)
	Timothy O. Howe, 1881
	Walter Q. Gresham, 1883
	Frank Hatton, 1884

Secretary of the Navy	William H. Hunt (Cont.) William E. Chandler, 1882
Secretary of the Interior	Samuel J. Kirkwood (Cont.) Henry M. Teller, 1882

Cleveland

Secretary of State	Thomas F. Bayard, 1885
Secretary of the Treasury	Daniel Manning, 1885 Charles S. Fairchild, 1887
Secretary of War	William C. Endicott, 1885
Attorney General	Augustus H. Garland, 1885
Postmaster General	William F. Vilas, 1885 Don M. Dickinson, 1888
Secretary of the Navy	William C. Whitney, 1885
Secretary of the Interior	Lucius Q. C. Lamar, 1885 William F. Vilas, 1888
Secretary of Agriculture	Norman J. Colman, 1889

B. Harrison

Secretary of State	James G. Blaine, 1889 John W. Foster, 1892
Secretary of the Treasury	William Windom, 1889 Charles Foster, 1891
Secretary of War	Redfield Proctor, 1889 Stephen B. Elkins, 1891
Attorney General	William H. H. Miller, 1889
Postmaster General	John Wanamaker, 1889
Secretary of the Navy	Benjamin F. Tracy, 1889
Secretary of the Interior	John W. Noble, 1889
Secretary of Agriculture	Jeremiah M. Rusk, 1889

Cleveland

Secretary of State	Walter Q. Gresham, 1893 Richard Olney, 1895
Secretary of the Treasury	John G. Carlisle, 1893
Secretary of War	Daniel S. Lamont, 1893
Attorney General	Richard Olney, 1893 Judson Harmon, 1895
Postmaster General	Wilson S. Bissell, 1893 William L. Wilson, 1895
Secretary of the Navy	Hilary A. Herbert, 1893
Secretary of the Interior	Hoke Smith, 1893 David R. Francis, 1896
Secretary of Agriculture	Julius Sterling Morton, 1893

McKinley

Secretary of State	John Sherman, 1897 William R. Day, 1898 John Hay, 1898
Secretary of the Treasury	Lyman J. Gage, 1897
Secretary of War	Russell A. Alger, 1897 Elihu Root, 1899
Attorney General	Joseph McKenna, 1897 John W. Griggs, 1898 Philander C. Knox, 1901
Postmaster General	James A. Gary, 1897 Charles E. Smith, 1898
Secretary of the Navy	John D. Long, 1897
Secretary of the Interior	Cornelius N. Bliss, 1897 Ethan A. Hitchcock, 1898
Secretary of Agriculture	James Wilson, 1897

T. Roosevelt

Secretary of State	John Hay (Cont.) Elihu Root, 1905 Robert Bacon, 1909
Secretary of the Treasury	Lyman J. Gage (Cont.) Leslie M. Shaw, 1902 George B. Cortelyou, 1907
Secretary of War	Elihu Root (Cont.) William H. Taft, 1904 Luke E. Wright, 1908
Attorney General	Philander C. Knox (Cont.) William H. Moody, 1904 Charles J. Bonaparte, 1906
Postmaster General	Charles E. Smith (Cont.) Henry C. Payne, 1902 Robert J. Wynne, 1904 George B. Cortelyou, 1905 George von L. Meyer, 1907
Secretary of the Navy	John D. Long (Cont.) William H. Moody, 1902 Paul Morton, 1904 Charles J. Bonaparte, 1905 Victor H. Metcalf, 1906 Truman H. Newberry, 1908
Secretary of the Interior	Ethan A. Hitchcock (Cont.) James R. Garfield, 1907
Secretary of Agriculture	James Wilson (Cont.)
Secretary of Commerce and Labor	George B. Cortelyou, 1903 Victor H. Metcalf, 1904 Oscar S. Straus, 1906

Taft

Secretary of State	Philander C. Knox, 1909
Secretary of the Treasury	Franklin MacVeagh, 1909
Secretary of War	Jacob M. Dickinson, 1909 Henry L. Stimson, 1911
Attorney General	George W. Wickersham, 1909
Postmaster General	Frank H. Hitchcock, 1909
Secretary of the Navy	George von L. Meyer, 1909
Secretary of the Interior	Richard A. Ballinger, 1909 Walter L. Fisher, 1911
Secretary of Agriculture	James Wilson (Cont.)
Secretary of Commerce and Labor	Charles Nagel, 1909

Wilson

Secretary of State	William J. Bryan, 1913 Robert Lansing, 1915 Bainbridge Colby, 1920
Secretary of the Treasury	William G. McAdoo, 1913 Carter Glass, 1918 David F. Houston, 1920
Secretary of War	Lindley M. Garrison, 1913 Newton D. Baker, 1916
Attorney General	James C. McReynolds, 1913 Thomas W. Gregory, 1914 A. Mitchell Palmer, 1919
Postmaster General	Albert S. Burleson, 1913
Secretary of the Navy	Josephus Daniels, 1913
Secretary of the Interior	Franklin K. Lane, 1913 John B. Payne, 1920
Secretary of Agriculture	David F. Houston, 1913 Edwin T. Meredith, 1920
Secretary of Commerce	William C. Redfield, 1913 Joshua W. Alexander, 1919
Secretary of Labor	William B. Wilson, 1913

Harding

Secretary of State	Charles E. Hughes, 1921
Secretary of the Treasury	Andrew W. Mellon, 1921
Secretary of War	John W. Weeks, 1921
Attorney General	Harry M. Daugherty, 1921
Postmaster General	Will H. Hays, 1921 Hubert Work, 1922 Harry S. New, 1923
Secretary of the Navy	Edwin Denby, 1921
Secretary of the Interior	Albert B. Fall, 1921 Hubert Work, 1923
Secretary of Agriculture	Henry C. Wallace, 1921
Secretary of Commerce	Herbert Hoover, 1921
Secretary of Labor	James J. Davis, 1921

Coolidge

Secretary of State	Charles E. Hughes (Cont.) Frank B. Kellogg, 1925
Secretary of the Treasury	Andrew W. Mellon (Cont.)
Secretary of War	John W. Weeks (Cont.) Dwight F. Davis, 1925

Attorney General	Harry M. Daughtery (Cont.)
	Harlan F. Stone, 1924
	John G. Sargent, 1925
Postmaster General	Harry S. New (Cont.)
Secretary of the Navy	Edwin Denby (Cont.)
	Curtis D. Wilbur, 1924
Secretary of the Interior	Hubert Work (Cont.)
	Roy O. West, 1928
Secretary of Agriculture	Henry C. Wallace (Cont.)
	Howard M. Gore, 1924
	William M. Jardine, 1925
Secretary of Commerce	Herbert Hoover (Cont.)
	William F. Whiting, 1928
Secretary of Labor	James J. Davis (Cont.)

Hoover

Secretary of State	Frank B. Kellogg (Cont.)
	Henry L. Stimson, 1929
Secretary of the Treasury	Andrew W. Mellon (Cont.)
	Ogden L. Mills, 1932
Secretary of War	James W. Good, 1929
	Patrick J. Hurley, 1929
Attorney General	William D. Mitchell, 1929
Postmaster General	Walter F. Brown, 1929
Secretary of the Navy	Charles F. Adams, 1929
Secretary of the Interior	Ray Lyman Wilbur, 1929
Secretary of Agriculture	Arthur M. Hyde, 1929
Secretary of Commerce	Robert P. Lamont, 1929
	Roy D. Chapin, 1932
Secretary of Labor	James J. Davis (Cont.)
	William N. Doak, 1930

F. D. Roosevelt

Secretary of State	Cordell Hull, 1933
	E. R. Stettinius, Jr., 1944
Secretary of the Treasury	William H. Woodin, 1933
	Henry Morgenthau, Jr., 1934
Secretary of War	George H. Dern, 1933
	Harry H. Woodring, 1936
	Henry L. Stimson, 1940
Attorney General	Homer S. Cummings, 1933
	Frank Murphy, 1939
	Robert H. Jackson, 1940
	Francis Biddle, 1941
Postmaster General	James A. Farley, 1933
	Frank C. Walker, 1940
Secretary of the Navy	Claude A. Swanson, 1933
	Charles Edison, 1940
	Frank Knox, 1940
	James Forrestal, 1944
Secretary of the Interior	Harold L. Ickes, 1933
Secretary of Agriculture	Henry A. Wallace, 1933
	Claude R. Wickard, 1940
Secretary of Commerce	Daniel C. Roper, 1933
	Harry L. Hopkins, 1938
	Jesse H. Jones, 1940
	Henry A. Wallace, 1945
Secretary of Labor	Frances Perkins, 1933

Truman

Secretary of State	E. R. Stettinius, Jr. (Cont.)
	James F. Byrnes, 1945
	George C. Marshall, 1947
	Dean Acheson, 1949
Secretary of the Treasury	Henry Morgenthau, Jr. (Cont.)
	Frederick M. Vinson, 1945
	John W. Snyder, 1946
Secretary of Defense	James Forrestal, 1947
	Louis A. Johnson, 1949
	George C. Marshall, 1950
	Robert A. Lovett, 1951
Attorney General	Francis Biddle (Cont.)
	Tom C. Clark, 1945
	J. Howard McGrath, 1949
	James P. McGranery, 1952
Postmaster General	Frank C. Walker (Cont.)
	Robert E. Hannegan, 1945
	Jesse M. Donaldson, 1947
Secretary of the Interior	Harold L. Ickes (Cont.)
	Julius A. Krug, 1946
	Oscar L. Chapman, 1949
Secretary of Agriculture	Claude R. Wickard (Cont.)
	Clinton P. Anderson, 1945
	Charles F. Brannan, 1948
Secretary of Commerce	Henry A. Wallace (Cont.)
	W. Averell Harriman, 1946
	Charles Sawyer, 1948
Secretary of Labor	Frances Perkins (Cont.)
	Lewis B. Schwellenbach, 1945
	Maurice J. Tobin, 1948
Secretary of War[1]	Henry L. Stimson (Cont.)
	Robert P. Patterson, 1945
	Kenneth C. Royall, 1947
Secretary of the Navy[1]	James Forrestal (Cont.)

1. On July 26, 1947, the Departments of War and of the Navy were incorporated into the Department of Defense.

Eisenhower

Secretary of State	John Foster Dulles, 1953
	Christian A. Herter, 1959
Secretary of the Treasury	George M. Humphrey, 1953
	Robert B. Anderson, 1957
Secretary of Defense	Charles E. Wilson, 1953
	Neil H. McElroy, 1957
	Thomas S. Gates, Jr., 1959
Attorney General	Herbert Brownell, Jr., 1953
	William P. Rogers, 1958
Postmaster General	Arthur E. Summerfield, 1953
Secretary of the Interior	Douglas McKay, 1953
	Frederick A. Seaton, 1956
Secretary of Agriculture	Ezra Taft Benson, 1953
Secretary of Commerce	Sinclair Weeks, 1953
	Lewis L. Strauss[1], 1958
	Frederick H. Mueller, 1959
Secretary of Labor	Martin P. Durkin, 1953
	James P. Mitchell, 1953
Secretary of Health, Education, and Welfare	Oveta Culp Hobby, 1953
	Marion B. Folsom, 1955
	Arthur S. Flemming, 1958

1. Not confirmed by the Senate.

Kennedy

Secretary of State	Dean Rusk, 1961
Secretary of the Treasury	C. Douglas Dillon, 1961
Secretary of Defense	Robert S. McNamara, 1961
Attorney General	Robert F. Kennedy, 1961
Postmaster General	J. Edward Day, 1961
	John A. Gronouski, 1963
Secretary of the Interior	Stewart L. Udall, 1961
Secretary of Agriculture	Orville L. Freeman, 1961
Secretary of Commerce	Luther H. Hodges, 1961
Secretary of Labor	Arthur J. Goldberg, 1961
	W. Willard Wirtz, 1962
Secretary of Health, Education, and Welfare	Abraham A. Ribicoff, 1961
	Anthony J. Celebrezze, 1962

L. B. Johnson

Secretary of State	Dean Rusk (Cont.)
Secretary of the Treasury	C. Douglas Dillon (Cont.)
	Henry H. Fowler, 1965
	Joseph W. Barr[1], 1968
Secretary of Defense	Robert S. McNamara (Cont.)
	Clark M. Clifford, 1968
Attorney General	Robert F. Kennedy (Cont.)
	N. de B. Katzenbach, 1965
	Ramsey Clark, 1967
Postmaster General	John A. Gronouski (Cont.)
	Lawrence F. O'Brien, 1965
	W. Marvin Watson, 1968
Secretary of the Interior	Stewart L. Udall (Cont.)

Secretary of Agriculture	Orville L. Freeman (Cont.)
Secretary of Commerce	Luther H. Hodges (Cont.)
	John T. Connor, 1964
	A. B. Trowbridge, 1967
	C. R. Smith, 1968
Secretary of Labor	W. Willard Wirtz (Cont.)
Secretary of Health, Education, and Welfare	Anthony J. Celebrezze (Cont.)
	John W. Gardner, 1965
	Wilbur J. Cohen, 1968
Secretary of Housing and Urban Development	Robert C. Weaver, 1966
	Robert C. Wood[1], 1969
Secretary of Transportation	Alan S. Boyd, 1966

1. Recess appointment.

Nixon

Secretary of State	William P. Rogers, 1969
	Henry A. Kissinger, 1973
Secretary of the Treasury	David M. Kennedy, 1969
	John B. Connally, 1971
	George P. Shultz, 1972
	William E. Simon, 1974
Secretary of Defense	Melvin R. Laird, 1969
	Elliot L. Richardson, 1973
	James R. Schlesinger, 1973
Attorney General	John N. Mitchell, 1969
	Richard G. Kleindienst, 1972
	Elliot L. Richardson, 1973
	William B. Saxbe, 1974
Postmaster General[1]	William M. Blount, 1969
Secretary of the Interior	Walter J. Hickel, 1969
	Rogers C. B. Morton, 1971
Secretary of Agriculture	Clifford M. Hardin, 1969
	Earl L. Butz, 1971
Secretary of Commerce	Maurice H. Stans, 1969
	Peter G. Peterson, 1972
	Frederick B. Dent, 1973
Secretary of Labor	George P. Shultz, 1969
	James D. Hodgson, 1970
	Peter J. Brennan, 1973
Secretary of Health, Education, and Welfare	Robert H. Finch, 1969
	Elliot L. Richardson, 1970
	Caspar W. Weinberger, 1973
Secretary of Housing and Urban Development	George Romney, 1969
	James T. Lynn, 1973
Secretary of Transportation	John A. Volpe, 1969
	Claude S. Brinegar, 1973

1. The Postmaster General is no longer a Cabinet member.

Ford

Secretary of State	Henry A. Kissinger (Cont.)
Secretary of the Treasury	William E. Simon (Cont.)
Secretary of Defense	James R. Schlesinger (Cont.)
	Donald H. Rumsfeld, 1975
Attorney General	William B. Saxbe (Cont.)
	Edward H. Levi, 1975
Secretary of the Interior	Rogers C. B. Morton (Cont.)
	Stanley K. Hathaway, 1975
	Thomas S. Kleppe, 1975
Secretary of Agriculture	Earl L. Butz (Cont.)
	John Knebel, 1976
Secretary of Commerce	Frederick B. Dent (Cont.)
	Rogers C. B. Morton, 1975
	Elliot L. Richardson, 1976
Secretary of Labor	Peter J. Brennan (Cont.)
	John T. Dunlop, 1975
	William J. Usery, Jr., 1976
Secretary of Health, Education, and Welfare	Caspar W. Weinberger (Cont.)
	F. David Mathews, 1975
Secretary of Housing and Urban Development	James T. Lynn (Cont.)
	Carla A. Hills, 1975
Secretary of Transportation	Claude S. Brinegar (Cont.)
	William T. Coleman, Jr., 1975

Carter

Secretary of State	Cyrus R. Vance, 1977
	Edmund S. Muskie, 1980
Secretary of the Treasury	W. Michael Blumenthal, 1977
	G. William Miller, 1979
Secretary of Defense	Harold Brown, 1977
Attorney General	Griffin B. Bell, 1977
	Benjamin R. Civiletti, 1979
Secretary of the Interior	Cecil D. Andrus, 1977
Secretary of Agriculture	Bob S. Bergland, 1977
Secretary of Commerce	Juanita M. Kreps, 1977
	Philip M. Klutznick, 1979
Secretary of Labor	F. Ray Marshall, 1977
Secretary of Health and Human Services[1]	Joseph A. Califano, Jr., 1977
	Patricia Roberts Harris, 1979
Secretary of Housing and Urban Development	Patricia Roberts Harris, 1977
	Moon Landrieu, 1979
Secretary of Transportation	Brock Adams, 1977
	Neil E. Goldschmidt, 1979
Secretary of Energy	James R. Schlesinger, 1977
	Charles W. Duncan, Jr., 1979
Secretary of Education	Shirley Mount Hufstedler, 1979

1. Known as Department of Health, Education, and Welfare until May, 1980.

Reagan

Secretary of State	Alexander M. Haig, Jr., 1981
	George P. Shultz, 1982
Secretary of the Treasury	Donald T. Regan, 1981
	James A. Baker 3rd, 1985
	Nicholas F. Brady, 1988
Secretary of Defense	Caspar W. Weinberger, 1981
	Frank C. Carlucci, 1987
Attorney General	William French Smith, 1981
	Edwin Meese 3rd, 1985
	Richard L. Thornburgh, 1988
Secretary of the Interior	James G. Watt, 1981
	William P. Clark, 1983
	Donald P. Hodel, 1985
Secretary of Agriculture	John R. Block, 1981
	Richard E. Lyng, 1986
Secretary of Commerce	Malcolm Baldrige, 1981
	C. William Verity, Jr., 1987
Secretary of Labor	Raymond J. Donovan, 1981
	William E. Brock, 1985
	Ann Dore McLaughlin, 1987
Secretary of Health and Human Services	Richard S. Schweiker, 1981
	Margaret M. Heckler, 1983
	Otis R. Bowen, 1985
Secretary of Housing and Urban Development	Samuel R. Pierce, Jr., 1981
Secretary of Transportation	Andrew L. Lewis, Jr., 1981
	Elizabeth H. Dole, 1983
	James H. Burnley 4th, 1987
Secretary of Energy	James B. Edwards, 1981
	Donald P. Hodel, 1983
	John S. Herrington, 1985
Secretary of Education	T. H. Bell, 1981
	William J. Bennett, 1985
	Lauro F. Cavazos, 1988

Bush

Secretary of State	James A. Baker 3d, 1989
	Lawrence S. Eagleburger, 1992
Secretary of the Treasury	Nicholas F. Brady (Cont.)
Secretary of Defense	Richard Cheney, 1989
Attorney General	Richard L. Thornburgh (Cont.)
	William P. Barr, 1992
Secretary of the Interior	Manuel Lujan Jr., 1989
Secretary of Agriculture	Clayton K. Yeutter, 1989
	Edward Madigan, 1991
Secretary of Commerce	Robert A. Mosbacher Sr., 1989
	Barbara H. Franklin, 1992
Secretary of Labor	Elizabeth H. Dole, 1989
	Lynn Martin, 1991

Secretary of Health and Human Services	Louis W. Sullivan, 1989
Secretary of Housing and Urban Development	Jack F. Kemp, 1989
Secretary of Transportation	Samuel K. Skinner, 1989 Andrew Card, 1992
Secretary of Energy	James D. Watkins, 1989
Secretary of Education	Lauro F. Cavazos (Cont.) Lamar Alexander, 1991
Secretary of Veterans Affairs	Edward J. Derwinski, 1989

Clinton

Secretary of State	Warren M. Christopher, 1993–96 Madeleine Albright, 1996
Secretary of the Treasury	Lloyd Bentsen, 1993–95 Robert E. Rubin, 1995
Secretary of Defense	Les Aspin, 1993–94 William J. Perry, 1994–96 William S. Cohen, 1997
Attorney General	Janet Reno, 1993
Secretary of the Interior	Bruce Babbitt, 1993
Secretary of Agriculture	Mike Espy, 1993–95 Dan Glickman, 1995
Secretary of Commerce	Ronald H. Brown, 1993–96 Mickey Kantor, 1996-97 William M. Daley, 1997
Secretary of Labor	Robert B. Reich, 1993–97 Alexis Herman, 1997
Secretary of Health and Human Services	Donna E. Shalala, 1993
Secretary of Housing and Urban Development	Henry G. Cisneros, 1993–97 Andrew M. Cuomo, 1997
Secretary of Transportation	Federico F. Pena, 1993–97 Rodney Slater, 1997
Secretary of Energy	Hazel R. O'Leary, 1993–97 Frederico F. Pena, 1997–1998 Bill Richardson, 1998
Secretary of Education	Richard W. Riley, 1993
Secretary of Veterans Affairs	Jesse Brown, 1993–98 Togo D. West, Jr., 1998

Members of the Supreme Court of the United States

Mailing address for the Supreme Court: U.S. Supreme Court Building, 1 First Street NE, Washington, D.C. 20543.

	Service		Birth			
Name; appointed from	**Term**	**Yrs**	**Place**	**Date**	**Died**	**Religion**
Chief Justices						
John Jay, N.Y.	1789–1795	5	N.Y.	1745	1829	Episcopal
John Rutledge, S.C.	1795	0	S.C.	1739	1800	Church of England
Oliver Ellsworth, Conn.	1796–1800	4	Conn.	1745	1807	Congregational
John Marshall, Va.	1801–1835	34	Va.	1755	1835	Episcopal
Roger B. Taney, Md.	1836–1864	28	Md.	1777	1864	Roman Catholic
Salmon P. Chase, Ohio	1864–1873	8	N.H.	1808	1873	Episcopal
Morrison R. Waite, Ohio	1874–1888	14	Conn.	1816	1888	Episcopal
Melville W. Fuller, Ill.	1888–1910	21	Maine	1833	1910	Episcopal
Edward D. White, La.	1910–1921	10	La.	1845	1921	Roman Catholic
William H. Taft, Conn.	1921–1930	8	Ohio	1857	1930	Unitarian
Charles E. Hughes, N.Y.	1930–1941	11	N.Y.	1862	1948	Baptist
Harlan F. Stone, N.Y.	1941–1946	4	N.H.	1872	1946	Episcopal
Frederick M. Vinson, Ky.	1946–1953	7	Ky.	1890	1953	Methodist
Earl Warren, Calif.	1953–1969	15	Calif.	1891	1974	Protestant
Warren E. Burger, Va.	1969–1986	17	Minn.	1907	1995	Presbyterian
William H. Rehnquist, Ariz.	1986–		Wis.	1924	—	Lutheran
Associate Justices						
James Wilson, Pa.	1789–1798	8	Scotland	1742	1798	Episcopal
John Rutledge, S.C.	1790–1791	1	S.C.	1739	1800	Church of England
William Cushing, Mass.	1790–1810	20	Mass.	1732	1810	Unitarian
John Blair, Va.	1790–1796	5	Va.	1732	1800	Presbyterian
James Iredell, N.C.	1790–1799	9	England	1751	1799	Episcopal
Thomas Johnson, Md.	1792–1793	0	Md.	1732	1819	Episcopal
William Paterson, N.J.	1793–1806	13	Ireland	1745	1806	Protestant
Samuel Chase, Md.	1796–1811	15	Md.	1741	1811	Episcopal
Bushrod Washington, Va.	1799–1829	30	Va.	1762	1829	Episcopal
Alfred Moore, N.C.	1800–1804	3	N.C.	1755	1810	Episcopal
William Johnson, S.C.	1804–1834	30	S.C.	1771	1834	Presbyterian
Brockholst Livingston, N.Y.	1807–1823	16	N.Y.	1757	1823	Presbyterian
Thomas Todd, Ky.	1807–1826	18	Va.	1765	1826	Presbyterian
Gabriel Duval, Md.	1811–1835	23	Md.	1752	1844	French Protestant
Joseph Story, Mass.	1812–1845	33	Mass.	1779	1845	Unitarian
Smith Thompson, N.Y.	1823–1843	20	N.Y.	1768	1843	Presbyterian
Robert Trimble, Ky.	1826–1828	2	Va.	1777	1828	Protestant
John McLean, Ohio	1830–1861	31	N.J.	1785	1861	Methodist-Epis.
Henry Baldwin, Pa.	1830–1844	14	Conn.	1780	1844	Trinity Church
James M. Wayne, Ga.	1835–1867	32	Ga.	1790	1867	Protestant
Philip P. Barbour, Va.	1836–1841	4	Va.	1783	1841	Episcopal
John Catron, Tenn.	1837–1865	28	Pa.	1786	1865	Presbyterian

Name; appointed from	Service		Birth		Died	Religion
	Term	Yrs	Place	Date		
John McKinley, Ala.	1837–1852	14	Va.	1780	1852	Protestant
Peter V. Daniel, Va.	1841–1860	18	Va.	1784	1860	Episcopal
Samuel Nelson, N.Y.	1845–1872	27	N.Y.	1792	1873	Protestant
Levi Woodbury, N.H.	1845–1851	5	N.H.	1789	1851	Protestant
Robert C. Grier, Pa.	1846–1870	23	Pa.	1794	1870	Presbyterian
Benjamin R. Curtis, Mass.	1851–1857	5	Mass.	1809	1874	(2)
John A. Campbell, Ala.	1853–1861	8	Ga.	1811	1889	Episcopal
Nathan Clifford, Maine	1858–1881	23	N.H.	1803	1881	(1)
Noah H. Swayne, Ohio	1862–1881	18	Va.	1804	1884	Quaker
Samuel F. Miller, Iowa	1862–1890	28	Ky.	1816	1890	Unitarian
David Davis, Ill.	1862–1877	14	Md.	1815	1886	(4)
Stephen J. Field, Calif.	1863–1897	34	Conn.	1816	1899	Episcopal
William Strong, Pa.	1870–1880	10	Conn.	1808	1895	Presbyterian
Joseph P. Bradley, N.J.	1870–1892	21	N.Y.	1813	1892	Presbyterian
Ward Hunt, N.Y.	1872–1882	9	N.Y.	1810	1886	Episcopal
John M. Harlan, Ky.	1877–1911	33	Ky.	1833	1911	Presbyterian
William B. Woods, Ga.	1880–1887	6	Ohio	1824	1887	Protestant
Stanley Matthews, Ohio	1881–1889	7	Ohio	1824	1889	Presbyterian
Horace Gray, Mass.	1882–1902	20	Mass.	1828	1902	(3)
Samuel Blatchford, N.Y.	1882–1893	11	N.Y.	1820	1893	Presbyterian
Lucius Q. C. Lamar, Miss.	1888–1893	5	Ga.	1825	1893	Methodist
David J. Brewer, Kan.	1889–1910	20	Asia Minor	1837	1910	Protestant
Henry B. Brown, Mich.	1890–1906	15	Mass.	1836	1913	Protestant
George Shiras, Jr., Pa.	1892–1903	10	Pa.	1832	1924	Presbyterian
Howell E. Jackson, Tenn.	1893–1895	2	Tenn.	1832	1895	Baptist
Edward D. White, La.*	1894–1910	16	La.	1845	1921	Roman Catholic
Rufus W. Peckham, N.Y.	1895–1909	13	N.Y.	1838	1909	Episcopal
Joseph McKenna, Calif.	1898–1925	26	Pa.	1843	1926	Roman Catholic
Oliver W. Holmes, Mass.	1902–1932	29	Mass.	1841	1935	Unitarian
William R. Day, Ohio	1903–1922	19	Ohio	1849	1923	Protestant
William H. Moody, Mass.	1906–1910	3	Mass.	1853	1917	Episcopal
Horace H. Lurton, Tenn.	1909–1914	4	Ky.	1844	1914	Episcopal
Charles E. Hughes, N.Y.*	1910–1916	5	N.Y.	1862	1948	Baptist
Willis Van Devanter, Wyo.	1910–1937	26	Ind.	1859	1941	Episcopal
Joseph R. Lamar, Ga.	1910–1916	4	Ga.	1857	1916	Ch. of Disciples
Mahlon Pitney, N.J.	1912–1922	10	N.J.	1858	1924	Presbyterian
James C. McReynolds, Tenn.	1914–1941	26	Ky.	1862	1946	Disciples of Christ
Louis D. Brandeis, Mass.	1916–1939	22	Ky.	1856	1941	Jewish
John H. Clarke, Ohio	1916–1922	5	Ohio	1857	1945	Protestant
George Sutherland, Utah	1922–1938	15	England	1862	1942	Episcopal
Pierce Butler, Minn.	1923–1939	16	Minn.	1866	1939	Roman Catholic
Edward T. Sanford, Tenn.	1923–1930	7	Tenn.	1865	1930	Episcopal
Harlan F. Stone, N.Y.*	1925–1941	16	N.H.	1872	1946	Episcopal
Owen J. Roberts, Pa.	1930–1945	15	Pa.	1875	1955	Episcopal
Benjamin N. Cardozo, N.Y.	1932–1938	6	N.Y.	1870	1938	Jewish
Hugo L. Black, Ala.	1937–1971	34	Ala.	1886	1971	Baptist
Stanley F. Reed, Ky.	1938–1957	19	Ky.	1884	1980	Protestant
Felix Frankfurter, Mass.	1939–1962	23	Austria	1882	1965	Jewish
William O. Douglas, Conn.	1939–1975	36	Minn.	1898	1980	Presbyterian
Frank Murphy, Mich.	1940–1949	9	Mich.	1890	1949	Roman Catholic
James F. Byrnes, S.C.	1941–1942	1	S.C.	1879	1972	Episcopal
Robert H. Jackson, Pa.	1941–1954	13	N.Y.	1892	1954	Episcopal
Wiley B. Rutledge, Iowa	1943–1949	6	Ky.	1894	1949	Unitarian
Harold H. Burton, Ohio	1945–1958	13	Mass.	1888	1964	Unitarian
Tom C. Clark, Tex.	1949–1967	17	Tex.	1899	1977	Presbyterian
Sherman Minton, Ind.	1949–1956	7	Ind.	1890	1965	Roman Catholic
John M. Harlan, N.Y.	1955–1971	16	Ill.	1899	1971	Presbyterian
William J. Brennan, Jr., N.J.	1956–1990	33	N.J.	1906	1997	Roman Catholic
Charles E. Whittaker, Mo.	1957–1962	5	Kan.	1901	1973	Methodist
Potter Stewart, Ohio	1958–1981	23	Mich.	1915	1985	Episcopal
Byron R. White, Colo.	1962–1993	31	Colo.	1917	—	Episcopal
Arthur J. Goldberg, Ill.	1962–1965	2	Ill.	1908	1990	Jewish
Abe Fortas, Tenn.	1965–1969	3	Tenn.	1910	1982	Jewish
Thurgood Marshall, N.Y.	1967–1991	24	Md.	1908	1993	Episcopal
Harry A. Blackmun, Minn.	1970–1994	24	Ill.	1908	—	Methodist
Lewis F. Powell, Jr., Va.	1972–1987	15	Va.	1907	1998	Presbyterian
William H. Rehnquist, Ariz.*	1972–1986	14	Wis.	1924	—	Lutheran

Name; appointed from	Service Term	Service Yrs	Birth Place	Birth Date	Died	Religion
John Paul Stevens, Ill.	1975–	—	Ill.	1920	—	Protestant
Sandra Day O'Connor, Ariz.	1981–	—	Tex.	1930	—	Episcopal
Antonin Scalia, D.C.	1986–	—	N.J.	1936	—	Roman Catholic
Anthony M. Kennedy, Calif.	1988–	—	Calif.	1936	—	Roman Catholic
David H. Souter, N.H.	1990–	—	Mass.	1939	—	Episcopal
Clarence Thomas, D.C.	1991–	—	Ga.	1948	—	Roman Catholic
Ruth Bader Ginsburg, D.C.	1993–	—	N.Y.	1933	—	Jewish
Stephen G. Breyer, Mass.	1994–	—	Calif.	1938	—	n.a.

*Served as both Chief Justice and Associate Justice. 1. Congregational; later Unitarian. 2. Unitarian; then Episcopal. 3. Unitarian or Congregational. 4. Not a member of any church. NOTE: n.a. = not available.

Milestone Cases in Supreme Court History

1803 ***Marbury v. Madison*** was the first instance in which a law passed by Congress was declared unconstitutional. The decision greatly expanded the power of the Court by establishing its right to overturn acts of Congress, a power not explicitly granted by the Constitution.

1819 ***McCulloch v. Maryland*** upheld the right of Congress to create a Bank of the United States, ruling that it was a power implied but not enumerated by the Constitution. The case is significant because it advanced the doctrine of implied powers, or a loose construction of the Constitution. The Court, Chief Justice John Marshall wrote, would sanction laws reflecting "the letter and spirit" of the Constitution.

1857 ***Dred Scott v. Sanford*** was a highly controversial case that intensified the national debate over slavery. The case involved Dred Scott, a slave, who was taken from a slave state to a free territory. Scott filed a lawsuit claiming that because he had lived on free soil he was entitled to his freedom. Chief Justice Roger B. Taney disagreed, ruling that blacks were not citizens and therefore could not sue in Federal Court. Taney further inflamed anti-slavery forces by declaring that Congress had no right to ban slavery from U.S. territories.

1896 ***Plessy v. Fergusson*** was the infamous case that asserted that "equal but separate accommodations" for blacks on railroad cars did not violate the "equal protection under the laws" clause of the 14th Amendment. By defending the constitutionality of racial segregation, the Court paved the way for the repressive Jim Crow laws of the south. The lone dissenter on the Court, Justice John Marshall Harlan, protested, "The thin disguise of 'equal' accommodations . . . will not mislead anyone."

1954 ***Brown v. Board of Education of Topeka*** invalidated racial segregation in schools, and led to the unraveling of de jure segregation in all areas of public life. In the unanimous decision spearheaded by Chief Justice Earl Warren, the Court invalidated the Plessy ruling, declaring "in the field of public education, the doctrine of 'separate but equal' has no place," and contending that "separate educational facilities are inherently unequal." Future Supreme Court Justice Thurgood Marshall was one of the NAACP lawyers who successfully argued the case.

1973 ***Roe v. Wade*** legalized abortion and is at the center of the current controversy between "Pro-Life" and "Pro-Choice" advocates. The Court ruled that a woman has the right to an abortion without interference from the government in the first trimester of pregnancy, contending that it is part of her "right to privacy." The Court maintained that right to privacy is not absolute, however, and granted states the right to intervene in the second and third trimesters of pregnancy.

Major Decisions of the U.S. Supreme Court, 1997–1998 Term

Banks Upheld Over Credit Unions (Feb. 25, 1998): Court voids federal regulation allowing millions to join credit unions as alternatives to banks.

Immunity for Local Officials Upheld (March 3, 1998): Justices rule unanimously that members of local and county governments have absolute exemption from suits for damages for legislative actions. Verdict confers same immunity already held by members of Congress and state and regional bodies.

Sex Harassment Claims in Workplace Widened (March 4, 1998): Court rules unanimously in important discrimination case that federal law protects employees from being harassed by members of the same sex.

"Gray Market" in U.S. Products Supported (March 9, 1998): Court holds unanimously that manufacturers cannot use copyright law to block domestic sale of goods they originally sold abroad at discounted prices.

Bankruptcy Law Protection Limited (March 24, 1998): Court rules unanimously that federal statute does not excuse obligation to pay damage judgments resulting from fraudulent action.

Justices Hear Disabilities Act Case (March 30, 1998): In a 5-4 split, the Court decided that the Americans with Disabilities Act of 1990 includes protection against discrimination for people infected with HIV, whether they show symptoms of the disease or not.

Right to Lie-Test Overruled (March 31, 1998): Justices, 8–1, rule that since polygraph results have not been scientifically approved, a criminal defendant has no constitutional right to present evidence at a trial of having passed such a test.

Paraguayan Executed in Virginia (April 14, 1998): Supreme Court denies clemency for Angel Francisco Breard, 32, for murder despite pleas from International Court of Justice and Paraguayan government.

Ruling Affects Grand Juries' Makeup (April 21, 1998): Justices decide, 9–0, that white criminal defendants can challenge indictments by grand juries from which black people have been excluded.

Environmental Agency Upheld in Suit (June 9, 1998): Court rules unanimously that a parent company can be held responsible for costs of cleaning up a subsidiary's toxic waste site if the parent company had unusual responsibility for operation of the site.

Use of Funds for Legal Services Questioned (June 15, 1998): Divided, 5–4, justices cast constitutional doubt on state programs that raise $100 million yearly on interest from funds deposited with lawyers by their clients and used to help the needy.

School Districts Get Harassment Shield (June 22, 1998): In a 5–4 ruling, highly restrictive standard is set for determining when they can be found liable for a teacher's sexual harassment of a student.

Line-Item Veto Outlawed (June 25, 1998): In a 6–3 decision, justices rule Constitution prohibits president from rewriting legislation by striking out single items of spending or specific tax breaks passed by Congress.

Decency Test in Arts Awards Upheld (June 25, 1998): By 8–1, justices uphold disputed provision of 1990 law that requires National Endowment for the Arts to take "general standards" into account in its awards.

Rules on Sexual Harassment Clarified (June 26, 1998): Two 7–2 decisions make some lawsuits easier to win, and provide employers with a new protection.

Executive Departments and Agencies

Source: United States Government Manual, 1997–1998.

Unless otherwise indicated, addresses shown are in Washington, D.C.

White House Offices and Agencies

Office of Administration
Old Executive Office Bldg. (20503)
Established: Dec. 12, 1977
Director: Patsy L. Thomasson

Office of National Drug Control Policy
Executive Office of the President (20502)
Established: March 13, 1989
Director: Barry R. McCaffrey

Council of Economic Advisers (CEA)
Room 314, Old Executive Office Bldg. (20503)
Members: 3
Established: Feb. 20, 1946
Chair: Janet L. Yellen

Council on Environmental Quality
Old Executive Office Bldg. (20503)
Members: 3
Established: 1969
Chair: Kathleen A. McGinty

Office of Management and Budget
Old Executive Office Bldg. (20503)
Established: July 1, 1970
Director: Jacob J. Lew

Office of Science and Technology Policy
Executive Office Building (20500)
Established: May 11, 1976
Director: Kerri-Ann Jones

National Security Council (NSC)
Old Executive Office Bldg. (20503)
Members: 4
Established: July 26, 1947
Chair: The President

National Security Adviser: Samuel R. (Sandy) Berger
Other members: Vice President; Secretary of State; Secretary of Defense

Office of the United States Trade Representative
600 17th St. (20506)
Established: Jan. 15, 1963
Trade Representative: Charlene Barshefsky

Executive Departments

Department of Agriculture
Independence Ave.,14th St., S.W. (20250).
Established: May 15, 1862. Administered by Commissioner of Agriculture until 1889, when it was made executive department.
Secretary: Dan Glickman
Deputy Secretary: Richard Rominger

Department of Commerce
14th St. between Constitution Ave. & Constitution Ave., N.W. (20230)
Established: Department of Commerce and Labor was created Feb. 14, 1903. On March 4, 1913, all labor activities were transferred out of Department of Commerce and Labor and it was renamed Department of Commerce.
Secretary: William M. Daley

Department of Defense
The Pentagon (20301)
Established: July 26, 1947, as National Department Establishment; name changed to Department of Defense on Aug. 10, 1949. Subordinate to Secretary of Defense are Secretaries of Army, Navy, Air Force.
Secretary: William S. Cohen
Deputy Secretary: John Hamre
Secretary of Army: Louis Caldera
Secretary of Navy: John H. Dalton
Secretary of Air Force: Sheila E. Widnall
Commandant of Marine Corps: Gen. Charles C. Krulak
Joint Chiefs of Staff: Gen. Harry Sheltoni, Chairman; Gen. Joseph W. Ralston, Vice Chairman; Gen. Dennis J. Reimer, Army; Adm. Jay L. Johnson, Navy (acting chief); Gen. Michael Ryan, Air Force; Gen. Richard D. Hearney, Marine Corps.

Department of Education
600 Independence Ave., S.W. (20202)
Established: Oct. 17, 1979
Secretary: Richard Riley
Deputy Secretary: Marshall Smith (acting)

Department of Energy
1000 Independence Ave., S.W. (20585)
Established: Aug. 1977
Secretary: Bill Richardson
Deputy Secretary: Elizabeth Anne Moler

Department of Health and Human Services[1]
200 Independence Ave., S.W. (20201)
Established: April 11, 1953, replacing Federal Security Agency created in 1939
Secretary: Donna Shalala
Surgeon General: David Satcher

Department of Housing and Urban Development
451 7th St., S.W. (20410)
Established: 1965, replacing Housing and Home Finance Agency created in 1947
Secretary: Andrew M. Cuomo
Under Secretary: Saul Ramirez

Department of the Interior
1849 C St. (20240)
Established: March 3, 1849

---

1. Originally Department of Health, Education and Welfare. Name changed in May 1980 when Department of Education was activated.

Secretary: Bruce Babbitt
Deputy Secretary: John Garamendi

Department of Justice
950 Pennsylvania Ave., N.W. (20530)
Established: Office of Attorney General was created Sept. 24, 1789. Although he was one of original Cabinet members, he was not executive department head until June 22, 1870, when Department of Justice was established.
Attorney General: Janet Reno
Deputy Attorney General: Eric Holder Jr.
Solicitor General: Seth P. Waxman
Director of FBI: Louis Joseph Freeh

Department of Labor
Third Street and Constitution Ave., N.W. (20210)
Established: Bureau of Labor was created in 1884 under Department of the Interior; later became independent department without executive rank. Returned to bureau status in Department of Commerce and Labor, but on March 4, 1913, became independent executive department under its present name.
Secretary: Alexis Herman
Deputy Secretary: Cynthia A. Metzler (acting)

Department of State
2201 C St., N.W. (20520)
Established: 1781 as Department of Foreign Affairs; reconstituted, 1789, following adoption of Constitution; name changed to Department of State Sept. 15, 1789.
Secretary: Madeleine Albright
Chief Delegate to U.N.: Richard Holbrooke

Department of Transportation
400 7th St., S.W. (20590)
Established: Oct. 15, 1966, as result of Department of Transportation Act, which became effective April 1, 1967.
Secretary: Rodney Slater
Deputy Secretary: Mort Downey

Department of the Treasury
15th St. & Pennsylvania Ave., N.W. (20220)
Established: Sept. 2, 1789
Secretary: Robert E. Rubin
Deputy Secretary: Lawrence H. Summers
Treasurer of the U.S.: Mary Ellen Withrow

Department of Veterans' Affairs
810 Vermont Avenue, N.W. (20420)
Established: March 15, 1989, replacing Veterans Administration created in 1930
Secretary: Togo D. West Jr.
Deputy Secretary: Hershel Gober

Major Independent Agencies

U.S. Arms Control and Disarmament Agency
320 21st St., N.W., (20451)
Established: Sept. 26, 1961
Director: John Holum

Central Intelligence Agency (CIA)
Washington, D.C. (20505)
Established: 1947
Director: George J. Tenet

U.S. Commission on Civil Rights
624 9th St. (20425)
Members: 8
Established: 1957
Chair: Mary Frances Berry

Consumer Product Safety Commission
4330 East West HIghway, Bethesda, Md. (20814)
Members: 5
Established: Oct. 27, 1972
Chairperson: Ann Brown

Corporation for National Service
1201 New York Ave., N.W. (20525)
Established: April 9, 1994
CEO: Harris Wofford

Environmental Protection Agency (EPA)
401 M St., S.W. (20460)
Established: Dec. 2, 1970
Administrator: Carol M. Browner

Equal Employment Opportunity Commission (EEOC)
1801 L St. (20507)
Members: 5
Established: July 2, 1965
Chair: Paul M. Igasaki

Farm Credit Administration (FCA)
1501 Farm Credit Dr., McLean, Va. (22102)
Members: 13
Established: July 17, 1916
Chair: Marsha Pyle Martin

Federal Deposit Insurance Corporation (FDIC)
550 17th St., N.W. (20429)
Members: 3
Established: June 16, 1933
Chair: Donna Tanoue

Federal Election Commission (FEC)
999 E St., N.W. (20463)
Members: 6
Established: 1974
Chair: Joan D. Aikens

Federal Maritime Commission
800 North Capitol St., N.W. (20573–0001)
Members: 5
Established: Aug. 12, 1961
Chair: Richard Barnes

Federal Mediation and Conciliation Service (FMCS)
2100 K St., N.W. (20427)
Established: 1947
Director: John Calhoun Wells

Federal Reserve System (FRS), Board of Governors of
20th St. & Constitution Ave., N.W. (20551)
Members: 7
Established: Dec. 23, 1913
Chair: Alan Greenspan

Federal Trade Commission (FTC)
Pennsylvania Ave. at 6th St., N.W. (20580)
Members: 5
Established: Sept. 26, 1914
Chair: Robert Pitofsky

General Services Administration (GSA)
18th and F Sts., N.W. (20405)
Established: July 1, 1949
Acting Administrator: David L. Barram

U.S. Information Agency
301 Fourth St., S.W. (20547)
Established: Aug. 1, 1953. Reorganized April 1, 1978.
Director: Dr. Joseph Duffey.

National Aeronautics and Space Administration (NASA)
300 E St., S.W. (20546)
Established: 1958
Administrator: Daniel S. Goldin

National Foundation on the Arts and the Humanities
1100 Pennsylvania Ave., N.W., (20506)
Established: 1965
Chairs: National Endowment for the Arts, Chair, William Ivey; National Endowment for the Humanities, Chair, Sheldon Hackney.

National Labor Relations Board (NLRB)
1099 14th St., N.W. (20570)
Members: 5
Established: July 5, 1935
Chair: William Gould IV

National Mediation Board
Suite 250 East, 1301 K St. (20572)
Members: 3
Established: June 21, 1934
Chair: Magdalena G. Jacobsen

National Science Foundation (NSF)
4201 Wilson Blvd., Arlington, Va. (22230)
Established: 1950
Director: Neal F. Lane

National Transportation Safety Board
490 L'Enfant Plaza, S.W. (20594)
Members: 5
Established: April 1, 1975
Chair: James Hall

Nuclear Regulatory Commission (NRC)
Rockville, Md. (20852)
Members: 5
Established: Jan. 19, 1975
Chair: Shirley Jackson

Office of Personnel Management (OPM)
1900 E St., N.W. (20415)
Members: 3
Established: Jan. 1, 1979
Director: Janice R. Lachance

U.S. Postal Service
475 L'Enfant Plaza West, S.W. (20260)
Established: In 1775 with the appointment of Benjamin Franklin as the first Postmaster General under the Continental Congress. In 1970 became independent agency headed by 11-member board of governors.
Postmaster General: Marvin T. Runyon
Deputy Postmaster General: William J. Henderson

Securities and Exchange Commission (SEC)
450 5th St., N.W. (20549)
Members: 5
Established: July 2, 1934
Chair: Arthur Levitt

Selective Service System (SSS)
National Headquarters 1515 Wilson Blvd., Arlington, Va. 22209
Established: Sept. 16, 1940
Director: Gil Coronado

Small Business Administration (SBA)
409 3rd St., S.W. (20416)
Established: July 30, 1953
Administrator: Aida Alvarez

U.S. International Trade Commission
500 E St., S.W. (20436)
Members: 6
Established: Sept. 8, 1916
Chair: Lynn Bragg

Tennessee Valley Authority (TVA)
400 West Summit Hill Drive, Knoxville, Tenn. (37902). Washington office: One Massachusetts Ave. (20444–0001).
Members of Board of Directors: 3
Established: May 18, 1933
Chairman: Craven H. Crowell, Jr.

Other Independent Agencies

Administrative Conference of the United States—Suite 500, 2120 L St., N.W. (20037)
American Battle Monuments Commission—Room 5127 Pulaski Bldg. 20 Massachusetts Ave., N.W. (20314)
Appalachian Regional Commission—1666 Connecticut Ave., N.W. (20235)
Commission of Fine Arts—Pension Bldg. 441 F St., N.W. (20001)
Commodity Futures Trading Commission—1155 21 St., N.W. (20581)
Export-Import Bank of the United States—811 Vermont Ave., N.W. (20571)
Federal Emergency Management Agency—500 C St., S.W. (20472)
Federal Housing Finance Board—1777 F St., N.W. (20006)
Federal Labor Relations Authority—607 14th St., N.W. (20424)
Inter-American Foundation901 N. Stuart St., Arlington, Va. (22203)
National Commission on Libraries and Information Science—Suite 820, 1110 Vermont Ave., N.W. (20005)
National Credit Union Administration—1775 Duke St., Alexandria, Va. (22314–3428)
Occupational Safety and Health Review Commission—1120 20th St., N.W. (20036–3419)
Panama Canal Commission—Suite 1050, 1825 I St., N.W. (20006)
Peace Corps—1990 K St., N.W. (20526)
Pension Benefit Guaranty Corporation—1200 K St.(20006)
Postal Rate Commission—Suite 300, 1333 H St., N.W. (20268–0001)
President's Committee on Employment of People With Disabilities—Suite 300, 1331 F St., N.W. (20004)
President's Council on Physical Fitness and Sports—701 Pennsylvania Ave., N.W., Suite 250 (20004)
U.S. Railroad Retirement Board (RRB)—844 Rush St., Chicago, Ill. (60611); Office of Legislative Affairs: Suite 500, 1310 G St., N.W. (20005–3004).
U.S. Parole Commission—5550 Friendship Blvd., Chevy Chase, Md. (20815)

Legislative Department

Architect of the Capitol—Room SB-15 U.S. Capitol Building (20515)
General Accounting Office (GAO)—441 G St., N.W. (20548)
Government Printing Office (GPO)—North Capitol & H Sts., N.W. (20401)
Library of Congress—101 Independence Ave., S.E. (20540)
Office of Technology Assessment—600 Pennsylvania Ave., S.E. (20510)
United States Botanic Garden—Office of Director, 245 First St., S.W. (20024)

Quasi-Official Agencies

American National Red Cross—430 Seventeenth St., N.W.(20006)
Legal Services Corporation—750 First St., N.E. (20002–4250)
National Academy of Sciences, National Academy of Engineering, National Research Council, Institute of Medicine—2101 Constitution Ave., N.W. (20418)
National Railroad Passenger Corporation (Amtrak)—60 Massachusetts Ave., N.E. (20002)
Smithsonian Institution—1000 Jefferson Dr., S.W. (20560)

Biographies of the Presidents

GEORGE WASHINGTON was born on Feb. 22, 1732 (Feb. 11, 1731/2, old style) in Westmoreland County, Va. While in his teens, he trained as a surveyor, and at the age of 20 he was appointed adjutant in the Virginia militia. For the next three years, he fought in the wars against the French and Indians, serving as Gen. Edward Braddock's aide in the disastrous campaign against Fort Duquesne. In 1759, he resigned from the militia, married Martha Dandridge Custis, a widow, and settled down as a gentleman farmer at Mount Vernon, Va.

As a militiaman, Washington had been exposed to the arrogance of the British officers, and his experience as a planter with British commercial restrictions increased his anti-British sentiment. He opposed the Stamp Act of 1765 and after 1770 became increasingly prominent in organizing resistance. A delegate to the Continental Congress, Washington was selected as commander in chief of the Continental Army and took command at Cambridge, Mass., on July 3, 1775.

Inadequately supported and sometimes covertly sabotaged by the Congress, in charge of troops who were inexperienced, badly equipped, and impatient of discipline, Washington conducted the war on the policy of avoiding major engagements with the British and wearing them down by harassing tactics. His able generalship, along with the French alliance and the growing weariness within Britain, brought the war to a conclusion with the surrender of Cornwallis at Yorktown, Va., on Oct. 19, 1781.

The chaotic years under the Articles of Confederation led Washington to return to public life in the hope of promoting the formation of a strong central government. He presided over the Constitutional Convention and yielded to the universal demand that he serve as first president. He was inaugurated on April 30, 1789, in New York, the first national capital. In office, he sought to unite the nation and establish the authority of the new government at home and abroad. Greatly distressed by the emergence of the Hamilton-Jefferson rivalry, Washington worked to maintain neutrality but actually sympathized more with Hamilton. Following his unanimous re-election in 1792, his second term was dominated by the Federalists. His Farewell Address on Sept. 17, 1796 (published but never delivered) rebuked party spirit and warned against "permanent alliances" with foreign powers.

He died at Mount Vernon on Dec. 14, 1799.

JOHN ADAMS born on Oct. 30 (Oct. 19, old style), 1735, at Braintree (now Quincy), Mass. A Harvard graduate, he considered teaching and the ministry but finally turned to law and was admitted to the bar in 1758. Six years later, he married Abigail Smith. He opposed the Stamp Act, served as lawyer for patriots indicted by the British, and by the time of the Continental Congresses, was in the vanguard of the movement for independence. In 1778, he went to France as commissioner. Subsequently he helped negotiate the peace treaty with Britain, and in 1785 became envoy to London. Resigning in 1788, he was elected vice president under Washington and was re-elected in 1792.

Though a Federalist, Adams did not get along with Hamilton, who sought to prevent his election to the presidency in 1796 and thereafter intrigued against his administration. In 1798, Adam's independent policy averted a war with France but completed the break with Hamilton and the right-wing Federalists; at the same time, the enactment of the Alien and Sedition Acts, directed against foreigners and against critics of the government, exasperated the Jeffersonian opposition. The split between Adams and Hamilton resulted in Jefferson's becoming the next president. Adams retired to his home in Quincy. He and Jefferson died on the same day, July 4, 1826, the 50th anniversary of the signing of the Declaration of Independence.

His *Defence of the Constitutions of Government of the United States* (1787) contains original and striking, if conservative, political ideas.

THOMAS JEFFERSON was born on April 13 (April 2, old style), 1743, at Shadwell in Goochland (now Albemarle) County, Va. A William and Mary graduate, he studied law, but from the start showed an interest in science and philosophy. His literary skill and political clarity brought him to the forefront of the revolutionary movement in Virginia. As delegate to the Continental Congress, he drafted the Declaration of Independence. In 1776, he entered the Virginia House of Delegates and initiated a comprehensive reform program for the abolition of feudal survivals in land tenure and the separation of church and state.

In 1779, he became governor, but constitutional limitations on his power, combined with his own lack of executive energy, caused an unsatisfactory administration, culminating in Jefferson's virtual abdication when the British invaded Virginia in 1781. He retired to his beautiful home at Monticello, Va., to his family. His wife, Martha Wayles Skelton, whom he married in 1772, died in 1782.

Jefferson's *Notes on Virginia* (1784–85) illustrate his many-faceted interests, his limitless intellectual curiosity, his deep faith in agrarian democracy. Sent to Congress in 1783, he helped lay down the decimal system and drafted basic reports on the organization of the western lands. In 1785 he was appointed minister to France, where the Anglo-Saxon liberalism he had drawn from John Locke, the British philosopher, was stimulated by contact with the thought that would soon ferment in the French Revolution. In 1789, Washington appointed him Secretary of State. While favoring the Constitution and a strengthened central government, Jefferson came to believe that Hamilton contemplated the establishment of a monarchy. Growing differences resulted in Jefferson's resignation on Dec. 31, 1793.

Elected vice president in 1796, Jefferson continued to serve as spiritual leader of the opposition to Federalism, particularly to the repressive Alien and Sedition Acts. He was elected president in 1801 by the House of Representatives as a result of Hamilton's decision to throw the Federalist votes to him rather than to Aaron Burr, who had tied him in electoral votes. He was the first president to be inaugurated in Washington, which he had helped to design.

The purchase of Louisiana from France in 1803, though in violation of Jefferson's earlier constitutional scruples, was the most notable act of his administration. Re-elected in 1804, with the Federalist Charles C. Pinckney opposing him, Jefferson tried desperately to keep the United States out of the Napoleonic Wars in Europe, employing to this end the unpopular embargo policy.

After his retirement to Monticello in 1809, he developed his interest in education, founding the University of Virginia and watching its development with never-flagging interest. He died at Monticello on July 4, 1826. Jefferson had an enormous variety of interests and skills, ranging from education and science to architecture and music.

JAMES MADISON was born in Port Conway, Va., on March 16, 1751 (March 5, 1750/1, old style). A Princeton graduate, he joined the struggle for independence on his return to Virginia in 1771. In the 1770s and 1780s he was active in state politics, where he championed the Jefferson reform program, and in the Continental Congress. Madison was influential in the Constitutional Convention as leader of the group favoring a strong central government and as recorder of the debates; and he subsequently wrote, in collaboration with Alexander Hamilton and John Jay, the *Federalist* papers to aid the campaign for the adoption of the Constitution.

Serving in the new Congress, Madison soon emerged as the leader in the House of the men who opposed Hamilton's financial program and his pro-British leanings in foreign policy. Retiring from Congress in 1797, he continued to be active in Virginia and drafted the Virginia Resolution protesting the Alien and Sedition Acts. His intimacy with Jefferson made him the natural choice for Secretary of State in 1801.

In 1809, Madison succeeded Jefferson as president, defeating Charles C. Pinckney. His attractive wife, Dolley Payne Todd, whom he married in 1794, brought a new social sparkle to the executive mansion. In the meantime, increasing tension with Britain culminated in the War of 1812—a war for which the United States was unprepared and for which Madison lacked the executive talent to clear out incompetence and mobilize the nation's energies. Madison was re-elected in 1812, running against the Federalist De Witt Clinton. In 1814, the British actually captured Washington and forced Madison to flee to Virginia.

Madison's domestic program capitulated to the Hamiltonian policies that he had resisted 20 years before and he now signed bills to establish a United States Bank and a higher tariff.

After his presidency, he remained in retirement in Virginia until his death on June 28, 1836.

JAMES MONROE was born on April 28, 1758, in Westmoreland County, Va. A William and Mary graduate, he served in the army during the first years of the Revolution and was wounded at Trenton. He then entered Virginia politics and later national politics under the sponsorship of Jefferson. In 1786, he married Elizabeth (Eliza) Kortright.

Fearing centralization, Monroe opposed the adoption of the Constitution and, as senator from Virginia, was highly critical of the Hamiltonian program. In 1794, he was appointed minister to France, where his ardent sympathies with the Revolution exceeded the wishes of the State Department. His troubled diplomatic career ended with his recall in 1796. From 1799 to 1802, he was governor of Virginia. In 1803, Jefferson sent him to France to help negotiate the Louisiana Purchase and for the next few years he was active in various negotiations on the Continent.

In 1808, Monroe flirted with the radical wing of the Republican Party, which opposed Madison's candidacy; but the presidential boom came to naught and, after a brief term as governor of Virginia in 1811, Monroe accepted Madison's offer to become Secretary of State. During the War of 1812, he vainly sought a field command and instead served as Secretary of War from September 1814 to March 1815.

Elected president in 1816 over the Federalist Rufus King, and re-elected without opposition in 1820, Monroe, the last of the Virginia dynasty, pursued the course of systematic tranquilization that won for his administrations the name "the era of good feeling." He continued Madison's surrender to the Hamiltonian domestic program, signed the Missouri Compromise, acquired Florida, and with the able assistance of his Secretary of State, John Quincy Adams, promulgated the Monroe Doctrine in 1823, declaring against foreign colonization or intervention in the Americas. He died in New York City on July 4, 1831, the third president to die on the anniversary of Independence.

JOHN QUINCY ADAMS was born on July 11, 1767, at Braintree (now Quincy), Mass., the son of John Adams, the second president. He spent his early years in Europe with his father, graduated from Harvard, and entered law practice. His anti-Paine newspaper articles won him political attention. In 1794, he became minister to the Netherlands, the first of several diplomatic posts that occupied him until his return to Boston in 1801. In 1797, he married Louisa Catherine Johnson.

In 1803, Adams was elected to the Senate, nominally as a Federalist, but his repeated displays of independence on such issues as the Louisiana Purchase and the embargo caused his party to demand his resignation and ostracize him socially. In 1809, Madison rewarded him for his support of Jefferson by appointing him minister to St. Petersburg. He helped negotiate the Treaty of Ghent in 1814, and in 1815 became minister to London. In 1817 Monroe appointed him Secretary of State where he served with great distinction, gaining Florida from Spain without hostilities and playing an equal part with Monroe in formulating the Monroe Doctrine.

When no presidential candidate received a majority of electoral votes in 1824, Adams, with the support of Henry Clay, was elected by the House in 1825 over Andrew Jackson, who had the original plurality. Adams had ambitious plans of government activity to foster internal improvements and promote the arts and sciences, but congressional obstructionism, combined with his own unwillingness or inability to play the role of a politician, resulted in little being accomplished. After being defeated for re-election by Jackson in 1828, he successfully ran for the House of Representatives in 1830. There though nominally a Whig, he pursued as ever an independent course. He led the fight to force Congress to receive antislavery petitions and fathered the Smithsonian Institution.

Adams had a stroke while on the floor of the House, and died two days later on Feb. 23, 1848. His long and detailed *Diary* gives a unique picture of the personalities and politics of the times.

ANDREW JACKSON was born on March 15, 1767, in what is now generally agreed to be Waxhaw, S.C. After a turbulent boyhood as an orphan and a British prisoner, he moved west to Tennessee, where he soon qualified for law practice but found time for such frontier pleasures as horse racing, cockfighting, and dueling. His marriage to Rachel Donelson Robards in 1791 was complicated by subsequent legal uncertainties about the status of her divorce. During the 1790s, Jackson served in the Tennessee Constitutional Convention, the United States House of Representatives and Senate, and on the Tennessee Supreme Court.

After some years as a country gentleman, living at the Hermitage near Nashville, Jackson in 1812 was given command of Tennessee troops sent against the Creeks. He defeated the Indians at Horseshoe Bend in 1814; subsequently he became a major general and won the Battle of New Orleans over veteran British troops, though after the treaty of peace had been signed at Ghent. In 1818, Jackson invaded Florida, captured Pensacola, and hanged two

Englishmen named Arbuthnot and Ambrister, creating an international incident. A presidential boom began for him in 1821, and to foster it, he returned to the Senate (1823–25). Though he won a plurality of electoral votes in 1824, he lost in the House when Clay threw his strength to Adams. Four years later, he easily defeated Adams.

As president, Jackson greatly expanded the power and prestige of the presidential office and carried through an unprecedented program of domestic reform, vetoing the bill to extend the United States Bank, moving toward a hard-money currency policy, and checking the program of federal internal improvements. He also vindicated federal authority against South Carolina with its doctrine of nullification and against France on the question of debts. The support given his policies by the workingmen of the East as well as by the farmers of the East, West, and South resulted in his triumphant re-election in 1832 over Clay.

After watching the inauguration of his handpicked successor, Martin Van Buren, Jackson retired to the Hermitage, where he maintained a lively interest in national affairs until his death on June 8, 1845.

MARTIN VAN BUREN was born on Dec. 5, 1782, at Kinderhook, N.Y. After graduating from the village school, he became a law clerk, entered practice in 1803, and soon became active in state politics as state senator and attorney general. In 1820, he was elected to the United States Senate. He threw the support of his efficient political organization, known as the Albany Regency, to William H. Crawford in 1824 and to Jackson in 1828. After leading the opposition to Adams's administration in the Senate, he served briefly as governor of New York (1828–29) and resigned to become Jackson's Secretary of State. He was soon on close personal terms with Jackson and played an important part in the Jacksonian program.

In 1832, Van Buren became vice president; in 1836, president. The Panic of 1837 overshadowed his term. He attributed it to the overexpansion of the credit and favored the establishment of an independent treasury as repository for the federal funds. In 1840, he established a 10-hour day on public works. Defeated by Harrison in 1840, he was the leading contender for the Democratic nomination in 1844 until he publicly opposed immediate annexation of Texas, and was subsequently beaten by the Southern delegations at the Baltimore convention. This incident increased his growing misgivings about the slave power.

After working behind the scenes among the antislavery Democrats, Van Buren joined in the movement that led to the Free-Soil Party and became its candidate for president in 1848. He subsequently returned to the Democratic Party while continuing to object to its pro-Southern policy. He died in Kinderhook on July 24, 1862. His *Autobiography* throws valuable sidelights on the political history of the times.

His wife, Hannah Hoes, whom he married in 1807, died in 1819.

WILLIAM HENRY HARRISON was born in Charles City County, Va., on Feb. 9, 1773. Joining the army in 1791, he was active in Indian fighting in the Northwest, became secretary of the Northwest Territory in 1798 and governor of Indiana in 1800. He married Anna Symmes in 1795. Growing discontent over white encroachments on Indian lands led to the formation of an Indian alliance under Tecumseh to resist further aggressions. In 1811, Harrison won a nominal victory over the Indians at Tippecanoe and in 1813 a more decisive one at the Battle of the Thames, where Tecumseh was killed.

After resigning from the army in 1814, Harrison had an obscure career in politics and diplomacy, ending up 20 years later as a county recorder in Ohio. Nominated for president in 1835 as a military hero whom the conservative politicians hoped to be able to control, he ran surprisingly well against Van Buren in 1836. Four years later, he defeated Van Buren but caught pneumonia and died in Washington on April 4, 1841, a month after his inauguration. Harrison was the first president to die in office.

JOHN TYLER born in Charles City County, Va., on March 29, 1790. A William and Mary graduate, he entered law practice and politics, serving in the House of Representatives (1817–21), as governor of Virginia (1825–27), and as senator (1827–36). A strict constructionist, he supported Crawford in 1824 and Jackson in 1828, but broke with Jackson over his United States Bank policy and became a member of the Southern state-rights group that cooperated with the Whigs. In 1836, he resigned from the Senate rather than follow instructions from the Virginia legislature to vote for a resolution expunging censure of Jackson from the Senate record.

Elected vice president on the Whig ticket in 1840, Tyler succeeded to the presidency on Harrison's death. His strict-constructionist views soon caused a split with the Henry Clay wing of the Whig party and a stalemate on domestic questions. Tyler's more considerable achievements were his support of the Webster-Ashburton Treaty with Britain and his success in bringing about the annexation of Texas.

After his presidency he lived in retirement in Virginia until the outbreak of the Civil War, when he emerged briefly as chairman of a peace convention and then as delegate to the provisional Congress of the Confederacy. He died on Jan. 18, 1862. He married Letitia Christian in 1813 and, two years after her death in 1842, Julia Gardiner.

JAMES KNOX POLK was born in Mecklenburg County, N.C., on Nov. 2, 1795. A graduate of the University of North Carolina, he moved west to Tennessee, was admitted to the bar, and soon became prominent in state politics. In 1825, he was elected to the House of Representatives, where he opposed Adams and, after 1829, became Jackson's floor leader in the fight against the Bank. In 1835, he became Speaker of the House. Four years later, he was elected governor of Tennessee, but was beaten in tries for re-election in 1841 and 1843.

The supporters of Van Buren for the Democratic nomination in 1844 counted on Polk as his running mate; but, when Van Buren's stand on Texas alienated Southern support, the convention swung to Polk on the ninth ballot. He was elected over Henry Clay, the Whig candidate. Rapidly disillusioning those who thought that he would not run his own administration, Polk proceeded steadily and precisely to achieve four major objectives—the acquisition of California, the settlement of the Oregon question, the reduction of the tariff, and the establishment of the independent treasury. He also enlarged the Monroe Doctrine to exclude all non-American intervention in American affairs, whether forcible or not, and he forced Mexico into a war that he waged to a successful conclusion.

His wife, Sarah Childress, whom he married in 1824, was a woman of charm and ability. Polk died in Nashville, Tenn., on June 15, 1849.

ZACHARY TAYLOR was born at Montebello, Orange County, Va., on Nov. 24, 1784. Embarking on a military career in 1808, Taylor fought in the War of 1812, the Black Hawk War, and the Seminole War, meanwhile holding garrison jobs on the frontier or desk jobs in Washington. A brigadier general as a result of his victory over the Seminoles at Lake Okeechobee (1837), Taylor held a succession of Southwestern commands and in 1846 established a base on the Rio Grande, where his forces engaged in hostilities that precipitated the war with Mexico. He captured Monterrey in September 1846 and, disregarding Polk's orders to stay on the defensive, defeated Santa Anna at Buena Vista in February 1847, ending the war in the northern provinces.

Though Taylor had never cast a vote for president, his party affiliations were Whiggish and his availability was increased by his difficulties with Polk. He was elected president over the Democrat Lewis Cass. During the revival of the slavery controversy, which was to result in the Compromise of 1850, Taylor began to take an increasingly firm stand against appeasing the South; but he died in Washington on July 9, 1850, during the fight over the Compromise. He married Margaret Mackall Smith in 1810. His bluff and simple soldierly qualities won him the name Old Rough and Ready.

MILLARD FILLMORE was born at Locke, Cayuga County, N.Y., on Jan. 7, 1800. A lawyer, he entered politics with the Anti-Masonic Party under the sponsorship of Thurlow Weed, editor and party boss, and subsequently followed Weed into the Whig Party. He served in the House of Representatives (1833–35 and 1837–43) and played a leading role in writing the tariff of 1842. Defeated for governor of New York in 1844, he became State comptroller in 1848, was put on the Whig ticket with Taylor as a concession to the Clay wing of the party, and became president upon Taylor's death in 1850.

As president, Fillmore broke with Weed and William H. Seward and associated himself with the pro-Southern Whigs, supporting the Compromise of 1850. Defeated for the Whig nomination in 1852, he ran for president in 1856 as candidate of the American, or Know-Nothing Party, which sought to unite the country against foreigners in the alleged hope of diverting it from the explosive slavery issue. Fillmore opposed Lincoln during the Civil War. He died in Buffalo on March 8, 1874.

He was married in 1826 to Abigail Powers, who died in 1853, and in 1858 to Caroline Carmichael McIntosh.

FRANKLIN PIERCE was born at Hillsboro, N.H., on Nov. 23, 1804. A Bowdoin graduate, lawyer, and Jacksonian Democrat, he won rapid political advancement in the party, in part because of the prestige of his father, Gov. Benjamin Pierce. By 1831 he was Speaker of the New Hampshire House of Representatives; from 1833 to 1837, he served in the federal House and from 1837 to 1842 in the Senate. His wife, Jane Means Appleton, whom he married in 1834, disliked Washington and the somewhat dissipated life led by Pierce; in 1842 Pierce resigned from the Senate and began a successful law practice in Concord, N.H. During the Mexican War, he was a brigadier general.

Thereafter Pierce continued to oppose antislavery tendencies within the Democratic Party. As a result, he was the Southern choice to break the deadlock at the Democratic convention of 1852 and was nominated on the 49th ballot. In the election, Pierce overwhelmed Gen. Winfield Scott, the Whig candidate.

As president, Pierce followed a course of appeasing the South at home and of playing with schemes of territorial expansion abroad. The failure of his foreign and domestic policies prevented his renomination. He died in Concord on Oct. 8, 1869, in relative obscurity.

JAMES BUCHANAN was born near Mercersburg, Pa., on April 23, 1791. A Dickinson graduate and a lawyer, he entered Pennsylvania politics as a Federalist. With the disappearance of the Federalist Party, he became a Jacksonian Democrat. He served with ability in the House (1821–31), as minister to St. Petersburg (1832–33), and in the Senate (1834–45), and in 1845 became Polk's Secretary of State. In 1853, Pierce appointed Buchanan minister to Britain, where he participated with other American diplomats in Europe in drafting the expansionist Ostend Manifesto.

He was elected president in 1856, defeating John C. Frémont, the Republican candidate, and former President Millard Fillmore of the American Party. The growing crisis over slavery presented Buchanan with problems he lacked the will to tackle. His appeasement of the South alienated the Stephen Douglas wing of the Democratic Party without reducing Southern militancy on slavery issues. While denying the right of secession, Buchanan also denied that the federal government could do anything about it. He supported the administration during the Civil War and died in Lancaster, Pa., on June 1, 1868.

The only president to remain a bachelor throughout his term, Buchanan used his charming niece, Harriet Lane, as White House hostess.

ABRAHAM LINCOLN was born in Hardin (now Larue) County, Ky., on Feb. 12, 1809. His family moved to Indiana and then to Illinois, and Lincoln gained what education he could along the way. While reading law, he worked in a store, managed a mill, surveyed, and split rails. In 1834, he went to the Illinois legislature as a Whig and became the party's floor leader. For the next 20 years he practiced law in Springfield, except for a single term (1847–49) in Congress, where he denounced the Mexican War. In 1855, he was a candidate for senator and the next year he joined the new Republican Party.

A leading but unsuccessful candidate for the vice-presidential nomination with Frémont, Lincoln gained national attention in 1858 when, as Republican candidate for senator from Illinois, he engaged in a series of debates with Stephen A. Douglas, the Democratic candidate. He lost the election, but continued to prepare the way for the 1860 Republican convention and was rewarded with the presidential nomination on the third ballot. He won the election over three opponents.

From the start, Lincoln made clear that, unlike Buchanan, he believed the national government had the power to crush the rebellion. Not an abolitionist, he held the slavery issue subordinate to that of preserving the Union, but soon perceived that the war could not be brought to a successful conclusion without freeing the slaves. His administration was hampered by the incompetence of many Union generals, the inexperience of the troops, and the harassing political tactics both of the Republican Radicals, who favored a hard policy toward the South, and the Democratic Copperheads, who desired a negotiated peace. The Gettysburg Address of Nov. 19, 1863, marks the high point in the record of American eloquence. Lincoln's long search for a winning combination finally brought Generals Ulysses S. Grant and William T. Sherman on the top; and their series of victories in 1864 dispelled the mutterings from both Radicals and Peace Democrats that at one time seemed to threaten Lincoln's re-election. He was re-elected in 1864, defeating Gen. George B. McClellan, the Democratic candidate. His inaugural address urged leniency toward the South: "With malice toward none, with charity for all . . . let us strive on to finish the work we are in; to bind up the nation's wounds . . ." This policy aroused growing opposition on the part of the Republican Radicals, but before the matter could be put to the test, Lincoln was shot by the actor John Wilkes Booth at Ford's Theater, Washington, on April 14, 1865. He died the next morning.

Lincoln's marriage to Mary Todd in 1842 was often unhappy and turbulent, in part because of his wife's pronounced instability.

ANDREW JOHNSON was born at Raleigh, N.C., on Dec. 29, 1808. Self-educated, he became a tailor in Greeneville, Tenn., but soon went into politics, where he rose steadily. He served in the House of Representatives (1843–54), as governor of Tennessee (1853–57), and as a senator (1857–62). Politically he was a Jacksonian Democrat and his specialty was the fight for a more equitable land policy. Alone among the Southern Senators, he stood by the Union during the Civil War. In 1862, he became war governor of Tennessee and carried out a thankless and difficult job with great courage. Johnson became Lincoln's running mate in 1864 as a result of an attempt to give the ticket a nonpartisan and nonsectional character. Succeeding to the presidency on Lincoln's death, Johnson sought to carry out Lincoln's policy, but without his political skill. The result was a hopeless conflict with the Radical Republicans who dominated Congress, passed measures over Johnson's vetoes, and attempted to limit the power of the executive concerning appointments and removals. The conflict culminated with Johnson's impeachment for attempting to remove his disloyal Secretary of War in defiance of the Tenure of Office Act which required senatorial concurrence for such dismissals. The opposition failed by one vote to get the two thirds necessary for conviction.

After his presidency, Johnson maintained an interest in politics and in 1875 was again elected to the Senate. He died near Carter Station, Tenn., on July 31, 1875. He married Eliza McCardle in 1827.

ULYSSES SIMPSON GRANT was born (as Hiram Ulysses Grant) at Point Pleasant, Ohio, on April 27, 1822. He graduated from West Point in 1843 and served without particular distinction in the Mexican War. In 1848 he married Julia Dent. He resigned from the army in 1854, after warnings from his commanding officer about his drinking habits, and for the next six years held a wide variety of jobs in the Middle West. With the outbreak of the Civil War, he sought a command and soon, to his surprise, was made a brigadier general. His continuing successes in the western theaters, culminating in the capture of Vicksburg, Miss., in 1863, brought him national fame and soon the command of all the Union armies. Grant's dogged, implacable policy of concentrating on dividing and destroying the Confederate armies brought the war to an end in 1865. The next year, he was made full general.

In 1868, as Republican candidate for president, Grant was elected over the Democrat, Horatio Seymour. From the start, Grant showed his unfitness for the office. His Cabinet was weak, his domestic policy was confused, many of his intimate associates were corrupt. The notable achievement in foreign affairs was the settlement of controversies with Great Britain in the Treaty of London (1871), negotiated by his able Secretary of State, Hamilton Fish.

Running for re-election in 1872, he defeated Horace Greeley, the Democratic and Liberal Republican candidate. The Panic of 1873 graft scandals close to the presidency created difficulties for his second term.

After retiring from office, Grant toured Europe for two years and returned in time to accede to a third-term boom, but was beaten in the convention of 1880. Illness and bad business judgment darkened his last years, but he worked steadily at the *Personal Memoirs,* which were to be so successful when published after his death at Mount McGregor, near Saratoga, N.Y., on July 23, 1885.

RUTHERFORD BIRCHARD HAYES was born in Delaware, Ohio, on Oct. 4, 1822. A graduate of Kenyon College and the Harvard Law School, he practiced law in Lower Sandusky (now Fremont) and then in Cincinnati. In 1852 he married Lucy Webb. A Whig, he joined the Republican party in 1855. During the Civil War he rose to major general. He served in the House of Representatives from 1865 to 1867 and then confirmed a reputation for honesty and efficiency in two terms as Governor of Ohio (1868–72). His election to a third term in 1875 made him the logical candidate for those Republicans who wished to stop James G. Blaine in 1876, and he was nominated.

The result of the election was in doubt for some time and hinged upon disputed returns from South Carolina, Louisiana, Florida, and Oregon. Samuel J. Tilden, the Democrat, had the larger popular vote but was adjudged by the strictly partisan decisions of the Electoral Commission to have one fewer electoral vote, 185 to 184. The national acceptance of this result was due in part to the general understanding that Hayes would pursue a conciliatory policy toward the South. He withdrew the troops from the South, took a conservative position on financial and labor issues, and urged civil service reform.

Hayes served only one term by his own wish and spent the rest of his life in various humanitarian endeavors. He died in Fremont on Jan. 17, 1893.

JAMES ABRAM GARFIELD the last president to be born in a log cabin, was born in Cuyahoga

County, Ohio, on Nov. 19, 1831. A Williams graduate, he taught school for a time and entered Republican politics in Ohio. In 1858, he married Lucretia Rudolph. During the Civil War, he had a promising career, rising to major general of volunteers; but he resigned in 1863, having been elected to the House of Representatives, where he served until 1880. His oratorical and parliamentary abilities soon made him the leading Republican in the House, though his record was marred by his unorthodox acceptance of a fee in the DeGolyer paving contract case and by suspicions of his complicity in the Crédit Mobilier scandal.

In 1880, Garfield was elected to the Senate, but instead became the presidential candidate on the 36th ballot as a result of a deadlock in the Republican convention. In the election, he defeated Gen. Winfield Scott Hancock, the Democratic candidate. Garfield's administration was barely under way when he was shot by Charles J. Guiteau, a disappointed office seeker, in Washington on July 2, 1881. He died in Elberton, N.J., on Sept. 19.

CHESTER ALAN ARTHUR was born at Fairfield, Vt., on Oct. 5, 1830. A graduate of Union College, he became a successful New York lawyer. In 1859, he married Ellen Herndon. During the Civil War, he held administrative jobs in the Republican state administration and in 1871 was appointed collector of the Port of New York by Grant. This post gave him control over considerable patronage. Though not personally corrupt, Arthur managed his power in the interests of the New York machine so openly that President Hayes in 1877 called for an investigation and the next year Arthur was suspended.

In 1880 Arthur was nominated for vice president in the hope of conciliating the followers of Grant and the powerful New York machine. As president upon Garfield's death, Arthur, stepping out of his familiar role as spoilsman, backed civil service reform, reorganized the Cabinet, and prosecuted political associates accused of post office graft. Losing machine support and failing to gain the reformers, he was not nominated for a full term in 1884. He died in New York City on Nov. 18, 1886.

STEPHEN GROVER CLEVELAND was born at Caldwell, N.J., on March 18, 1837. He was admitted to the bar in Buffalo, N.Y., in 1859 and lived there as a lawyer, with occasional incursions into Democratic politics, for more than 20 years. He did not participate in the Civil War. As mayor of Buffalo in 1881, he carried through a reform program so ably that the Democrats ran him successfully for governor in 1882. In 1884 he won the Democratic nomination for president. The campaign contrasted Cleveland's spotless public career with the uncertain record of James G. Blaine, the Republican candidate, and Cleveland received enough Mugwump (independent Republican) support to win.

As president, Cleveland pushed civil service reform, opposed the pension grab and attacked the high tariff rates. While in the White House, he married Frances Folsom in 1886. Renominated in 1888, Cleveland was defeated by Benjamin Harrison, polling more popular but fewer electoral votes. In 1892, he was elected over Harrison. When the Panic of 1893 burst upon the country, Cleveland's attempts to solve it by sound-money measures alienated the free-silver wing of the party, while his tariff policy alienated the protectionists. In 1894, he sent troops to break the Pullman strike. In foreign affairs, his firmness caused Great Britain to back down in the Venezuela border dispute.

In his last years Cleveland was an active and much-respected public figure. He died in Princeton, N.J., on June 24, 1908.

BENJAMIN HARRISON was born in North Bend, Ohio, on Aug. 20, 1833, the grandson of William Henry Harrison, the ninth president. A graduate of Miami University in Ohio, he took up the law in Indiana and became active in Republican politics. In 1853, he married Caroline Lavinia Scott. During the Civil War, he rose to brigadier general. A sound-money Republican, he was elected senator from Indiana in 1880. In 1888, he received the Republican nomination for president on the eighth ballot. Though behind on the popular vote, he won over Grover Cleveland in the electoral college by 233 to 168.

As president, Harrison failed to please either the bosses or the reform element in the party. In foreign affairs he backed Secretary of State Blaine, whose policy foreshadowed later American imperialism. Harrison was renominated in 1892 but lost to Cleveland. His wife died in the White House in 1892 and Harrison married her niece, Mary Scott (Lord) Dimmick, in 1896. After his presidency, he resumed law practice. He died in Indianapolis on March 13, 1901.

WILLIAM MCKINLEY was born in Niles, Ohio, on Jan. 29, 1843. He taught school, then served in the Civil War, rising from the ranks to become a major. Subsequently he opened a law office in Canton, Ohio, and in 1871 married Ida Saxton. Elected to Congress in 1876, he served there until 1891, except for 1883–85. His faithful advocacy of business interests culminated in the passage of the highly protective McKinley Tariff of 1890. With the support of Mark Hanna, a shrewd Cleveland businessman interested in safeguarding tariff protection, McKinley became governor of Ohio in 1892 and Republican presidential candidate in 1896. The business community, alarmed by the progressivism of William Jennings Bryan, the Democratic candidate, spent considerable money to assure McKinley's victory.

The chief event of McKinley's administration was the war with Spain, which resulted in our acquisition of the Philippines and other islands. With imperialism an issue, McKinley defeated Bryan again in 1900. On Sept. 6, 1901, he was shot at Buffalo, N.Y., by Leon F. Czolgosz, an anarchist, and he died there eight days later.

THEODORE ROOSEVELT was born in New York City on Oct. 27, 1858. A Harvard graduate, he was early interested in ranching, in politics, and in writing picturesque historical narratives. He was a Republican member of the New York Assembly in 1882–84, an unsuccessful candidate for mayor of New York in 1886, a U.S. Civil Service Commissioner under Benjamin Harrison, Police Commissioner of New York City in 1895, and Assistant Secretary of the Navy under McKinley in 1897. He resigned in 1898 to help organize a volunteer regiment, the Rough Riders, and take a more direct part in the war with Spain. He was elected governor of New York in 1898 and vice president in 1900, in spite of lack of enthusiasm on the part of the bosses.

Assuming the presidency of the assassinated McKinley in 1901, Roosevelt embarked on a wide-ranging program of government reform and conservation of natural resources. He ordered antitrust suits against several large corporations, threatened to intervene in the anthracite coal strike of 1902, which prompted the operators to accept arbitration, and, in general, championed the rights of the "little man" and fought the "malefactors of great wealth." He was also responsible for such progressive legislation as the Elkins Act of 1901, which outlawed freight rebates by railroads; the bill establishing the Department of Commerce and Labor; the Hepburn Act, which gave the I.C.C. greater control over the railroads; the Meat Inspection Act; and the Pure Food and Drug Act.

In foreign affairs, Roosevelt pursued a strong policy, permitting the instigation of a revolt in Panama to dispose of Colombian objections to the Panama Canal and helping to maintain the balance of power in the East by bringing the Russo-Japanese War to an end, for which he won the Nobel Peace Prize, the first American to achieve a Nobel prize in any category. In 1904, he decisively defeated Alton B. Parker, his conservative Democratic opponent.

Roosevelt's increasing coldness toward his successor, William Howard Taft, led him to overlook his earlier disclaimer of third-term ambitions and to re-enter politics. Defeated by the machine in the Republican convention of 1912, he organized the Progressive Party (Bull Moose) and polled more votes than Taft, though the split brought about the election of Woodrow Wilson. From 1915 on, Roosevelt strongly favored intervention in the European war. He became deeply embittered at Wilson's refusal to allow him to raise a volunteer division. He died in Oyster Bay, N.Y., on Jan. 6, 1919. He was married twice: in 1880 to Alice Hathaway Lee, who died in 1884, and in 1886 to Edith Kermit Carow.

WILLIAM HOWARD TAFT was born in Cincinnati on Sept. 15, 1857. A Yale graduate, he entered Ohio Republican politics in the 1880s. In 1886 he married Helen Herron. From 1887 to 1890, he served on the Ohio Superior Court; 1890–92, as solicitor general of the United States; 1892–1900, on the federal circuit court. In 1900 McKinley appointed him president of the Philippine Commission and in 1901 governor general. Taft had great success in pacifying the Filipinos, solving the problem of the church lands, improving economic conditions, and establishing limited self-government. His period as Secretary of War (1904–08) further demonstrated his capacity as administrator and conciliator, and he was Roosevelt's hand-picked successor in 1908. In the election, he polled 321 electoral votes to 162 for William Jennings Bryan, who was running for the presidency for the third time.

Though he carried on many of Roosevelt's policies, Taft got into increasing trouble with the progressive wing of the party and displayed mounting irritability and indecision. After his defeat in 1912, he became professor of constitutional law at Yale. In 1921 he was appointed Chief Justice of the United States Supreme Court. He died in Washington on March 8, 1930.

THOMAS WOODROW WILSON was born in Staunton, Va., on Dec. 28, 1856. A Princeton graduate, he turned from law practice to post-graduate work in political science at Johns Hopkins University, receiving his Ph.D. in 1886. He taught at Bryn Mawr, Wesleyan, and Princeton, and in 1902 was made president of Princeton. After an unsuccessful attempt to democratize the social life of the university, he welcomed an invitation in 1910 to be the Democratic gubernatorial candidate in New Jersey, and was elected. His success in fighting the machine and putting through a reform program attracted national attention.

In 1912, at the Democratic convention in Baltimore, Wilson won the nomination on the 46th ballot and went on to defeat Roosevelt and Taft in the election. Wilson proceeded under the standard of the New Freedom to enact a program of domestic reform, including the Federal Reserve Act, the Clayton Antitrust Act, the establishment of the Federal Trade Commission, and other measures designed to restore competition in the face of the great monopolies. In foreign affairs, while privately sympathetic with the Allies, he strove to maintain neutrality in the European war and warned both sides against encroachments on American interests.

Re-elected in 1916 as a peace candidate, he tried to mediate between the warring nations; but when the Germans resumed unrestricted submarine warfare in 1917, Wilson brought the United States into what he now believed was a war to make the world safe for democracy. He supplied the classic formulations of Allied war aims and the armistice of Nov. 11, 1918 was negotiated on the basis of Wilson's Fourteen Points. In 1919 he strove at Versailles to lay the foundations for enduring peace. He accepted the imperfections of the Versailles Treaty in the expectation that they could be remedied by action within the League of Nations. He probably could have secured ratification of the treaty by the Senate if he had adopted a more conciliatory attitude toward the mild reservationists; but his insistence on all or nothing eventually caused the diehard isolationists and diehard Wilsonites to unite in rejecting a compromise.

In September 1919 Wilson suffered a paralytic stroke that limited his activity. After leaving the presidency he lived on in retirement in Washington, dying on Feb. 3, 1924. He was married twice—in 1885 to Ellen Louise Axson, who died in 1914, and in 1915 to Edith Bolling Galt.

WARREN GAMALIEL HARDING was born in Morrow County, Ohio, on Nov. 2, 1865. After attending Ohio Central College, Harding became interested in journalism and in 1884 bought the *Marion* (Ohio) *Star*. In 1891 he married a wealthy widow, Florence Kling De Wolfe. As his paper prospered, he entered Republican politics, serving as state senator (1899–1903) and as lieutenant governor (1904–06). In 1910, he was defeated for governor, but in 1914 was elected to the Senate. His reputation as an orator made him the keynoter at the 1916 Republican convention.

When the 1920 convention was deadlocked between Leonard Wood and Frank O. Lowden, Harding became the dark-horse nominee on his solemn affirmation that there was no reason in his past that he should not be. Straddling the League question, Harding was easily elected over James M. Cox, his Democratic opponent. His Cabinet contained some able men, but also some manifestly unfit for public office. Harding's own intimates were mediocre when they were not corrupt. The impending disclosure of the Teapot Dome scandal in the Interior Department and illegal practices in the Justice Department and Veterans' Bureau, as well as political setbacks, profoundly worried him. On his return from Alaska in 1923, he died unexpectedly in San Francisco on Aug. 2.

JOHN CALVIN COOLIDGE was born in Plymouth, Vt., on July 4, 1872. An Amherst graduate, he went into law practice at Northampton, Mass., in 1897. He married Grace Anna Goodhue in 1905. He entered Republican state politics, becoming successively mayor of Northampton, state senator, lieutenant governor and, in 1919, governor. His use of the state militia to end the Boston police strike in 1919 won him a somewhat undeserved reputation for decisive action and brought him the Republican vice-presidential nomination in 1920. After Harding's death Coolidge handled the Washington scandals with care and finally managed to save the Republican Party from public blame for the widespread corruption.

In 1924, Coolidge was elected without difficulty, defeating the Democrat, John W. Davis, and Robert M. La Follette running on the Progressive ticket. His second term, like his first, was characterized by a general satisfaction with the existing economic order. He stated that he did not choose to run in 1928.

After his presidency, Coolidge lived quietly in Northampton, writing an unilluminating autobiography and conducting a syndicated column. He died there on Jan. 5, 1933.

HERBERT CLARK HOOVER was born at West Branch, Iowa, on Aug. 10, 1874, the first president to be born west of the Mississippi. A Stanford graduate, he worked from 1895 to 1913 as a mining engineer and consultant throughout the world. In 1899, he married Lou Henry. During World War I, he served with distinction as chairman of the American Relief Committee in London, as chairman of the Commission for Relief in Belgium, and as U.S. Food Administrator. His political affiliations were still too indeterminate for him to be mentioned as a possibility for either the Republican or Democratic nomination in 1920, but after the election he served Harding and Coolidge as Secretary of Commerce.

In the election of 1928, Hoover overwhelmed Gov. Alfred E. Smith of New York, the Democratic candidate and the first Roman Catholic to run for the presidency. He soon faced the worst depression in the nation's history, but his attacks upon it were hampered by his devotion to the theory that the forces that brought the crisis would soon bring the revival and then by his belief that there were too many areas in which the federal government had no power to act. In a succession of vetoes, he struck down measures proposing a national employment system or national relief, he reduced income tax rates, and only at the end of his term did he yield to popular pressure and set up agencies such as the Reconstruction Finance Corporation to make emergency loans to assist business.

After his 1932 defeat, Hoover returned to private business. In 1946, President Truman charged him with various world food missions; and from 1947 to 1949 and 1953 to 1955, he was head of the Commission on Organization of the Executive Branch of the Government. He died in New York City on Oct. 20, 1964.

FRANKLIN DELANO ROOSEVELT was born in Hyde Park, N.Y., on Jan. 30, 1882. A Harvard graduate, he attended Columbia Law School and was admitted to the New York bar. In 1910, he was elected to the New York State Senate as a Democrat. Reelected in 1912, he was appointed Assistant Secretary of the Navy by Woodrow Wilson the next year. In 1920, his radiant personality and his war service resulted in his nomination for vice president as James M. Cox's running mate. After his defeat, he returned to law practice in New York. In August 1921, Roosevelt was stricken with infantile paralysis while on vacation at Campobello, New Brunswick. After a long and gallant fight, he recovered partial use of his legs. In 1924 and 1928, he led the fight at the Democratic national conventions for the nomination of Gov. Alfred E. Smith of New York, and in 1928 Roosevelt was himself induced to run for governor of New York. He was elected, and was reelected in 1930.

In 1932, Roosevelt received the Democratic nomination for president and immediately launched a campaign that brought new spirit to a weary and discouraged nation. He defeated Hoover by a wide margin. His first term was characterized by an unfolding of the New Deal program, with greater benefits for labor, the farmers, and the unemployed, and the progressive estrangement of most of the business community.

At an early stage, Roosevelt became aware of the menace to world peace posed by totalitarian fascism, and from 1937 on he tried to focus public attention on the trend of events in Europe and Asia. As a result, he was widely denounced as a warmonger. He was re-elected in 1936 over Gov. Alfred M. Landon of Kansas by the overwhelming electoral margin of 523 to 8, and the gathering international crisis prompted him to run for an unprecedented third term in 1940. He defeated Wendell L. Willkie.

Roosevelt's program to bring maximum aid to Britain and, after June 1941, to Russia was opposed, until the Japanese attack on Pearl Harbor restored national unity. During the war, Roosevelt shelved the New Deal in the interests of conciliating the business community, both in order to get full production during the war and to prepare the way for a united acceptance of the peace settlements after the war. A series of conferences with Winston Churchill and Joseph Stalin laid down the bases for the postwar world. In 1944 he was elected to a fourth term, running against Gov. Thomas E. Dewey of New York.

On April 12, 1945, Roosevelt died of a cerebral hemorrhage at Warm Springs, Ga., shortly after his return from the Yalta Conference. His wife, Anna Eleanor Roosevelt, whom he married in 1905, was a woman of great ability who made significant contributions to her husband's policies.

HARRY S. TRUMAN was born on a farm near Lamar, Mo., on May 8, 1884. During World War I, he served in France as a captain with the 129th Field Artillery. He married Bess Wallace in 1919. After engaging briefly and unsuccessfully in the haberdashery business in Kansas City, Mo., Truman entered local politics. Under the sponsorship of Thomas Pendergast, Democratic boss of Missouri, he held a number of local offices, preserving his personal honesty in the midst of a notoriously corrupt political machine. In 1934, he was elected to the Senate and was re-elected in 1940. During his first term he was a loyal but quiet supporter of the New Deal, but in his second term, an appointment as head of a Senate committee to investigate war production brought out his special qualities of honesty, common sense, and hard work, and he won widespread respect.

Elected vice president in 1944, Truman became president upon Roosevelt's sudden death in April 1945 and was immediately faced with the problems of winding down the war against the Axis and preparing the nation for postwar adjustment.

The years 1947–48 were distinguished by civil-rights proposals, the Truman Doctrine to contain the spread of Communism, and the Marshall Plan to aid in the economic reconstruction of war-ravaged nations. Truman's general record, highlighted by a vigorous Fair Deal campaign, brought about his unexpected election in 1948 over the heavily favored Thomas E. Dewey.

Truman's second term was primarily concerned with the Cold War with the Soviet Union, the implementing of the North Atlantic Pact, the United Nations police action in Korea, and the vast rearmament program with its accompanying problems of economic stabilization.

On March 29, 1952, Truman announced that he would not run again for the presidency. After leaving the White House, he returned to his home in Independence, Mo., to write his memoirs. He further busied himself with the Harry S. Truman Library there. He died in Kansas City, Mo., on Dec. 26, 1972.

DWIGHT DAVID EISENHOWER was born in Denison, Tex., on Oct. 14, 1890. His ancestors lived in Germany and emigrated to America, settling in Pennsylvania, early in the 18th century. His father, David, had a general store in Hope, Kans., which failed. After a brief time in Texas, the family moved to Abilene, Kan.

After graduating from Abilene High School in 1909, Eisenhower did odd jobs for almost two years. He won an appointment to the Naval Academy at Annapolis, but was too old for admittance. Then he received an appointment in 1910 to West Point, from which he graduated as a second lieutenant in 1915.

He did not see service in World War I, having been stationed at Fort Sam Houston, Tex. There he met Mamie Geneva Doud, whom he married in Denver on July 1, 1916, and by whom he had two sons: Doud Dwight (died in infancy) and John Sheldon Doud.

Eisenhower served in the Philippines from 1935 to 1939 with Gen. Douglas MacArthur. Afterward, Gen. George C. Marshall, the Army Chief of Staff, brought him into the War Department's General Staff and in 1942 placed him in command of the invasion of North Africa. In 1944, he was made Supreme Allied Commander for the invasion of Europe.

After the war, Eisenhower served as Army Chief of Staff from November 1945 until February 1948, when he was appointed president of Columbia University.

In December 1950, President Truman recalled Eisenhower to active duty to command the North Atlantic Treaty Organization forces in Europe. He held his post until the end of May 1952.

At the Republican convention of 1952 in Chicago, Eisenhower won the presidential nomination on the first ballot in a close race with Senator Robert A. Taft of Ohio. In the election, he defeated Gov. Adlai E. Stevenson of Illinois.

Through two terms, Eisenhower hewed to moderate domestic policies. He sought peace through Free World strength in an era of new nationalisms, nuclear missiles, and space exploration. He fostered alliances pledging the United States to resist Red aggression in Europe, Asia, and Latin America. The Eisenhower Doctrine of 1957 extended commitments to the Middle East.

At home, the popular president lacked Republican Congressional majorities after 1954, but he was re-elected in 1956 by 457 electoral votes to 73 for Stevenson.

While retaining most Fair Deal programs, he stressed "fiscal responsibility" in domestic affairs. A moderate in civil rights, he sent troops to Little Rock, Ark., to enforce court-ordered school integration.

With his wartime rank restored by Congress, Eisenhower returned to private life and the role of elder statesman, with his vigor hardly impaired by a heart attack, an ileitis operation, and a mild stroke suffered while in office. He died in Washington on March 28, 1969.

JOHN FITZGERALD KENNEDY was born in Brookline, Mass., on May 29, 1917. His father, Joseph P. Kennedy, was Ambassador to Great Britain from 1937 to 1940.

Kennedy was graduated from Harvard University in 1940 and joined the Navy the next year. He became skipper of a PT boat that was sunk in the Pacific by a Japanese destroyer. Although given up for lost, he swam to a safe island, towing an injured enlisted man.

After recovering from a war-aggravated spinal injury, Kennedy entered politics in 1946 and was elected to Congress. In 1952, he ran against Senator Henry Cabot Lodge, Jr., of Massachusetts, and won.

Kennedy was married on Sept. 12, 1953, to Jacqueline Lee Bouvier, by whom he had three children: Caroline, John Fitzgerald, Jr., and Patrick Bouvier (died in infancy).

In 1957 Kennedy won the Pulitzer Prize for a book he had written earlier, *Profiles in Courage.*

After strenuous primary battles, Kennedy won the Democratic presidential nomination on the first ballot at the 1960 Los Angeles convention. With a plurality of only 118,574 votes, he carried the election over Vice President Richard M. Nixon and became the first Roman Catholic president.

Kennedy brought to the White House the dynamic idea of a "New Frontier" approach in dealing with problems at home, abroad, and in the dimensions of space. Out of his leadership in his first few months in office came the 10-year Alliance for Progress to aid Latin America, the Peace Corps, and accelerated programs that brought the first Americans into orbit in the race in space.

Failure of the U.S.-supported Cuban invasion in April 1961 led to the entrenchment of the Communist-backed Castro regime, only 90 miles from United States soil. When it became known that Soviet offensive missiles were being installed in

Cuba in 1962, Kennedy ordered a naval "quarantine" of the island and moved troops into position to eliminate this threat to U.S. security. The world seemed on the brink of a nuclear war until Soviet Premier Khrushchev ordered the removal of the missiles.

A sudden "thaw," or the appearance of one, in the cold war came with the agreement with the Soviet Union on a limited test-ban treaty signed in Moscow on Aug. 6, 1963.

In his domestic policies, Kennedy's proposals for medical care for the aged, expanded area redevelopment, and aid to education were defeated, but on minimum wage, trade legislation, and other measures he won important victories.

Widespread racial disorders and demonstrations led to Kennedy's proposing sweeping civil rights legislation. As his third year in office drew to a close, he also recommended an $11-billion tax cut to bolster the economy. Both measures were pending in Congress when Kennedy, looking forward to a second term, journeyed to Texas for a series of speeches.

While riding in a procession in Dallas on Nov. 22, 1963, he was shot to death by an assassin firing from an upper floor of a building. The alleged assassin, Lee Harvey Oswald, was killed two days later in the Dallas city jail by Jack Ruby, owner of a strip-tease place.

At 46 years of age, Kennedy became the fourth president to be assassinated and the eighth to die in office.

LYNDON BAINES JOHNSON was born in Stonewall, Tex., on Aug. 27, 1908. On both sides of his family he had a political heritage mingled with a Baptist background of preachers and teachers. Both his father and his paternal grandfather served in the Texas House of Representatives.

After his graduation from Southwest Texas State Teachers College, Johnson taught school for two years. He went to Washington in 1932 as secretary to Rep. Richard M. Kleberg. During this time, he married Claudia Alta Taylor, known as "Lady Bird." They had two children: Lynda Bird and Luci Baines.

In 1935, Johnson became Texas administrator for the National Youth Administration. Two years later, he was elected to Congress as an all-out supporter of Franklin D. Roosevelt, and served until 1949. He was the first member of Congress to enlist in the armed forces after the attack on Pearl Harbor. He served in the Navy in the Pacific and won a Silver Star.

Johnson was elected to the Senate in 1948 after he had captured the Democratic nomination by only 87 votes. He was 40 years old. He became the Senate Democratic leader in 1953. A heart attack in 1955 threatened to end his political career, but he recovered fully and resumed his duties.

At the height of his power as Senate leader, Johnson sought the Democratic nomination for president in 1960. When he lost to John F. Kennedy, he surprised even some of his closest associates by accepting second place on the ticket.

Johnson was riding in another car in the motorcade when Kennedy was assassinated in Dallas on Nov. 22, 1963. He took the oath of office in the presidential jet on the Dallas airfield.

With Johnson's insistent backing, Congress finally adopted a far-reaching civil-rights bill, a voting-rights bill, a Medicare program for the aged, and measures to improve education and conservation. Congress also began what Johnson described as "an all-out war" on poverty.

Amassing a record-breaking majority of nearly 16 million votes, Johnson was elected president in his own right in 1964, defeating Senator Barry Goldwater of Arizona.

The double tragedy of a war in Southeast Asia and urban riots at home marked Johnson's last two years in office. Faced with disunity in the nation and challenges within his own party, Johnson surprised the country on March 31, 1968, with the announcement that he would not be a candidate for re-election. He died of a heart attack suffered at his LBJ Ranch on Jan. 22, 1973.

RICHARD MILHOUS NIXON was born in Yorba Linda, Calif., on Jan. 9, 1913, to Midwestern-bred parents, Francis A. and Hannah Milhous Nixon, who raised their five sons as Quakers.

Nixon was a high school debater and was undergraduate president at Whittier College in California, where he was graduated in 1934. As a scholarship student at Duke University Law School in North Carolina, he graduated third in his class in 1937.

After five years as a lawyer, Nixon joined the Navy in August 1942. He was an air transport officer in the South Pacific and a legal officer stateside before his discharge in 1946 as a lieutenant commander.

Running for Congress in California as a Republican in 1946, Nixon defeated Rep. Jerry Voorhis. As a member of the House Un-American Activities Committee, he made a name as an investigator of Alger Hiss, a former high State Department official, who was later jailed for perjury. In 1950, Nixon defeated Rep. Helen Gahagan Douglas, a Democrat, for the Senate. He was criticized for portraying her as a Communist dupe.

Nixon's anti-Communism, his Western base, and his youth figured in his selection in 1952 to run for vice president on the ticket headed by Dwight D. Eisenhower. Demands for Nixon's withdrawal followed disclosure that California businessmen had paid some of his Senate office expenses. He televised rebuttal, known as "the Checkers speech" (named for a cocker spaniel given to the Nixons), brought him support from the public and from Eisenhower. The ticket won easily in 1952 and again in 1956.

Eisenhower gave Nixon substantive assignments, including missions to 56 countries. In Moscow in 1959, Nixon won acclaim for his defense of U.S. interests in an impromptu "kitchen debate" with Soviet Premier Nikita S. Khrushchev.

Nixon lost the 1960 race for the presidency to John F. Kennedy.

In 1962, Nixon failed in a bid for California's governorship and seemed to be finished as a national candidate. He became a Wall Street lawyer, but kept his old party ties and developed new ones through constant travels to speak for Republicans.

Nixon won the 1968 Republican presidential nomination after a shrewd primary campaign, then made Gov. Spiro T. Agnew of Maryland his surprise choice for vice president. In the election, they edged out the Democratic ticket headed by Vice President Hubert H. Humphrey by 510,314 votes out of 73,212,065 cast.

Committed to winding down the U.S. role in the Vietnamese War, Nixon pursued "Vietnamization"—training and equipping South Vietnamese to do their own fighting. American ground combat forces in Vietnam fell steadily from 540,000 when Nixon took office to none in 1973 when the military draft was ended. But there was heavy continuing use of U.S. air power.

Nixon improved relations with Moscow and reopened the long-closed door to mainland China with a good-will trip there in February 1972. In May of that year, he visited Moscow and signed agreements on arms limitation and trade expansion and approved plans for a joint U.S.-Soviet space mission in 1975.

Inflation was a campaign issue for Nixon, but he failed to master it as president. On Aug. 15, 1971, with unemployment edging up, Nixon abruptly announced a new economic policy: a 90-day wage-price freeze, stimulative tax cuts, a temporary 10% tariff, and spending cuts. A second phase, imposing guidelines on wage, price and rent boosts, was announced October 7.

The economy responded in time for the 1972 campaign, in which Nixon played up his foreign-policy achievements. Played down was the burglary on June 17, 1972, of Democratic national headquarters in the Watergate apartment complex in Washington. The Nixon-Agnew re-election campaign cost a record $60 million and swamped the Democratic ticket headed by Senator George McGovern of South Dakota with a plurality of 17,999,528 out of 77,718,554 votes. Only Massachusetts, with 14 electoral votes, and the District of Columbia, with 3, went for McGovern.

In January 1973, hints of a cover-up emerged at the trial of six men found guilty of the Watergate burglary. With a Senate investigation under way, Nixon announced on April 30 the resignations of his top aides, H. R. Haldeman and John D. Ehrlichman, and the dismissal of White House counsel John Dean III. Dean was the star witness at televised Senate hearings that exposed both a White House cover-up of Watergate and massive illegalities in Republican fund-raising in 1972.

The hearings also disclosed that Nixon had routinely tape-recorded his office meetings and telephone conversations.

On Oct. 10, 1973, Agnew resigned as vice president, then pleaded no-contest to a negotiated federal charge of evading income taxes on alleged bribes. Two days later, Nixon nominated the House minority leader, Rep. Gerald R. Ford of Michigan, as the new vice president. Congress confirmed Ford on Dec. 6, 1973.

In June 1974, Nixon visited Israel and four Arab nations. Then he met in Moscow with Soviet leader Leonid I. Brezhnev and reached preliminary nuclear arms limitation agreements.

But, in the month after his return, Watergate ended the Nixon regime. On July 24 the Supreme Court ordered Nixon to surrender subpoenaed tapes. On July 30, the Judiciary Committee referred three impeachment articles to the full membership. On August 5, Nixon bowed to the Supreme Court and released tapes showing he halted an FBI probe of the Watergate burglary six days after it occurred. It was in effect an admission of obstruction of justice, and impeachment appeared inevitable.

Nixon resigned on Aug. 9, 1974, the first president ever to do so. A month later, President Ford issued an unconditional pardon for any offenses Nixon might have committed as president, thus forestalling possible prosecution.

In 1940, Nixon married Thelma Catherine (Pat) Ryan. They had two daughters, Patricia (Tricia) Cox and Julie, who married Dwight David Eisenhower II, grandson of the former president.

He died on April 22, 1994, in New York City of a massive stroke.

GERALD RUDOLPH FORD was born in Omaha, Neb., on July 14, 1913, the only child of Leslie and Dorothy Gardner King. His parents were divorced in 1915. His mother moved to Grand Rapids, Mich., and married Gerald R. Ford. The boy was renamed for his stepfather.

Ford captained his high school football team in Grand Rapids, and a football scholarship took him to the University of Michigan, where he starred as varsity center before his graduation in 1935. A job as assistant football coach at Yale gave him an opportunity to attend Yale Law School, from which he graduated in the top third of his class in 1941.

He returned to Grand Rapids to practice law, but entered the Navy in April 1942. He saw wartime service in the Pacific on the light aircraft carrier *Monterey* and was a lieutenant commander when he returned to Grand Rapids early in 1946 to resume law practice and dabble in politics.

Ford was elected to Congress in 1948 for the first of his 13 terms in the House. He was soon assigned to the influential Appropriations Committee and rose to become the ranking Republican on the subcommittee on Defense Department appropriations and an expert in the field.

As a legislator, Ford described himself as "a moderate on domestic issues, a conservative in fiscal affairs, and a dyed-in-the-wool internationalist." He carried the ball for Pentagon appropriations, was a hawk on the war in Vietnam, and kept a low profile on civil-rights issues.

He was also dependable and hard-working and popular with his colleagues. In 1963, he was elected chairman of the House Republican Conference. He served in 1963-64 as a member of the Warren Commission that investigated the assassination of John F. Kennedy. A revolt by dissatisfied younger Republicans in 1965 made him minority leader.

Ford shelved his hopes for the speakership on Oct. 12, 1973, when Nixon nominated him to fill the vice presidency left vacant by Agnew's resignation under fire. It was the first use of the procedures for filling vacancies in the vice presidency laid down in the 25th Amendment to the Constitution, which Ford had helped enact.

Congress confirmed Ford as vice president on Dec. 6, 1973. Once in office, he said he did not believe Nixon had been involved in the Watergate scandals, but criticized his stubborn court battle against releasing tape recordings of Watergate-related conversations for use as evidence.

The scandals led to Nixon's unprecedented resignation on Aug. 9, 1974, and Ford was sworn in immediately as the 38th president, the first to enter the White House without winning a national election.

Ford assured the nation when he took office that "our long national nightmare is over" and pledged "openness and candor" in all his actions. He won a warm response from the Democratic 93rd Congress when he said he wanted "a good marriage" rather than a honeymoon with his former colleagues. In December 1974 Congressional majorities backed his choice of former New York Gov. Nelson A. Rockefeller as his successor in the again-vacant vice presidency.

The cordiality was chilled by Ford's announcement on Sept. 8, 1974, that he had granted an unconditional pardon to Nixon for any crimes he might have committed as president. Although no formal charges were pending, Ford said he feared "ugly passions" would be aroused if Nixon were brought to trial. The pardon was widely criticized.

To fight inflation, the new president first proposed fiscal restraints and spending curbs and a 5% tax surcharge that got nowhere in the Senate and House. Congress again rebuffed Ford in the spring of 1975 when he appealed for emergency military aid to help the governments of South Vietnam and Cambodia resist massive Communist offensives.

In November 1974, Ford visited Japan, South Korea, and the Soviet Union, where he and Soviet leader Leonid I. Brezhnev conferred in Vladivostok and reached a tentative agreement to limit the number of strategic offensive nuclear weapons. It was Ford's first meeting as president with Brezhnev, who planned a return visit to Washington in the fall of 1975.

Politically, Ford's fortunes improved steadily in the first half of 1975. Badly divided Democrats in Congress were unable to muster votes to override his vetoes of spending bills that exceeded his budget. He faced some right-wing opposition in his own party, but moved to pre-empt it with an early announcement—on July 8, 1975—of his intention to be a candidate in 1976.

Early state primaries in 1976 suggested an easy victory for Ford despite Ronald Reagan's bitter attacks on administration foreign policy and defense programs. But later Reagan primary successes threatened the President's lead. At the Kansas City convention, Ford was nominated by the narrow margin of 1,187 to 1,070. But Reagan had moved the party to the right, and Ford himself was regarded as a caretaker president lacking in strength and vision. He was defeated in November by Jimmy Carter.

In 1948, Ford married Elizabeth Anne (Betty) Bloomer. They had four children, Michael Gerald, John Gardner, Steven Meigs, and Susan Elizabeth.

JAMES EARL CARTER, JR., was born in the tiny village of Plains, Ga., Oct. 1, 1924, and grew up on the family farm at nearby Archery. Both parents were fifth-generation Georgians. His father, James Earl Carter, was known as a segregationist, but treated his black and white workers equally. Carter's mother, Lillian Gordy, was a matriarchal presence in home and community and opposed the then-prevailing code of racial inequality. The future president was baptized in 1935 in the conservative Southern Baptist Church and spoke often of being a "born again" Christian, although committed to the separation of church and state.

Carter married Rosalynn Smith, a neighbor, in 1946. Their first child, John William, was born a year later in Portsmouth, Va. Their other children are James Earl III, born in Honolulu in 1950; Donnel Jeffrey, born in New London, Conn., in 1952, and Amy Lynn, born in Plains in 1967.

In 1946 Carter was graduated from the U.S. Naval Academy at Annapolis and served in the nuclear-submarine program under Adm. Hyman G. Rickover. In 1954, after his father's death, he resigned from the Navy to take over the family's flourishing warehouse and cotton gin, with several thousand acres for growing seed peanuts.

Carter was elected to the Georgia Senate in 1962. In 1966 he lost the race for Governor, but was elected in 1970. His term brought a state government reorganization, sharply reduced agencies, increased economy and efficiency, and new social programs, all with no general tax increase. In 1972 the peanut farmer-politician set his sights on the presidency and in 1974 built a base for himself as he criss-crossed the country as chairman of the Democratic Campaign Committee, appealing for revival and reform. In 1975 his image as a typical Southern white was erased when he won support of most of the old Southern civil-rights coalition after endorsement by Rep. Andrew Young, black Democrat from Atlanta, who had been the closest aide to the Rev. Martin Luther King, Jr. At Carter's 1971 inauguration as Governor he had called for an end to all forms of racial discrimination.

In the 1976 spring primaries, he won 19 out of 31 with a broad appeal to conservatives and liberals, black and white, poor and well-to-do. Throughout his campaigning Carter set forth his policies in his soft Southern voice, and with his electric-blue stare faced down skeptics who joked about "Jimmy Who?" His toothy smile became his trademark. He was nominated on the first roll-call vote of the 1976 Bicentennial Democratic National Convention in New York, and defeated Gerald R. Ford in November. Likewise, in 1980 he was renominated on the first ballot after vanquishing Senator Edward M. Kennedy of Massachusetts in the primaries. At the convention he defeated the Kennedy forces in their attempt to block a party rule that bound a large majority of pledged delegates to vote for Carter. In the election campaign, Carter attacked his rivals, Ronald Reagan and John B. Anderson, independent, with the warning that a Reagan Republican victory would heighten the risk of war and impede civil rights and economic opportunity. In November Carter lost to Reagan, who won 489 Electoral College votes and 51% of the popular tally, to 49 electoral votes and 41% for Carter.

In his one term, Carter fought hard for his programs against resistance from an independent-minded Democratic Congress that frustrated many pet projects although it overrode only two vetoes. Many of his difficulties were traced to his aides' brusqueness in dealing with Capitol Hill and insensitivity to Congressional feelings and tradition. Observers generally viewed public dissatisfaction with the "stagflation" economy as a principal factor in his defeat. Others included his jittery performance in the debate Oct. 28 with Reagan and the final uncertainties in the negotiations for freeing the Iranians' hostages, along with earlier staff problems, friction with Congress, long gasoline lines, and the months-long Iranian crisis, including the abortive sally in April 1980 to free the hostages. The president, however, did deflect criticism resulting from the activities of his brother, Billy. Yet, assessments of his record noted many positive elements. There was, for one thing, peace throughout his term, with no American combat deaths and with a brake on the advocates of force. Regarded as perhaps his greatest personal achievements were the Camp David accords between Israel and Egypt and the resulting treaty—the first between Israel and an Arab neighbor. The treaty with China and the Panama Canal treaties were also major achievements. Carter worked for nuclear-arms control. His concern for international human rights was credited with saving lives and reducing torture, and he supported the British policy that ended internecine warfare in Rhodesia, now Zimbabwe. Domestically, his environmental record was a major accomplishment. His judicial appointments won acclaim; the Southerner who had forsworn racism made 265 choices for the Federal bench that included minority members and women. On energy, he ended by price decontrols the practice of holding U.S. petroleum prices far below world levels.

—*Arthur P. Reed, Jr.*

RONALD WILSON REAGAN rode to the presidency in 1980 on a tide of resurgent right-wing sentiment among an electorate battered by winds of unwanted change, longing for a distant, simpler era.

He left office in January 1989 with two-thirds of the American people approving his performance during his two terms. It was the highest rating for any retiring president since World War II. In his farewell speech, Reagan exhorted the nation to cling to the revival of patriotism that he had fostered. And he spoke proudly of the economic recovery during his Administrations, although regretting the huge budget deficit, for which, in part, many blamed his policies.

Reagan had retained the public's affection as he applied his political magic to policy goals. His place in history will rest, perhaps, on the short- and intermediate-range missile treaty consummated on a cordial visit to the Soviet Union that he had once reviled as an "evil empire." Its provisions, including a ground-breaking agreement on verification inspection, were formulated in four days of summit talks in Moscow in May 1988 with the Soviet leader, Mikhail S. Gorbachev.

And Reagan can point to numerous domestic achievements: sharp cuts in income tax rates, sweeping tax reform; creating economic growth without inflation, reducing the unemployment rate, among others. He failed, however, to win the "Reagan Revolution" on such issues as abortion and school prayer, and he seemed aloof from "sleazy" conduct by some top officials.

In his final months Reagan campaigned aggressively to win election as president for his two-term Vice President, George Bush.

Reagan's popularity with the public dipped sharply in 1986 when the Iran-Contra scandal broke, shortly after the Democrats gained control of the Senate. Observers agreed that Reagan's presidency had been weakened, if temporarily, by the two unrelated events. Then the weeks-long Congressional hearings in the summer of 1987 heard an array of Administration officials, present and former, tell their tales of a White House riven by deceit and undercover maneuvering. Yet no breath of illegality touched the President's personal reputation; on Aug. 12, 1987, he told the nation that he had not known of questionable activities but agreed that he was "ultimately accountable."

Ronald Reagan, actor turned politician, New Dealer turned conservative, came to the films and politics from a thoroughly Middle-American background—middle class, Middle West and small town. He was born in Tampico, Ill., Feb. 6, 1911, the second son of John Edward Reagan and Nelle Wilson Reagan, and the family later moved to Dixon, Ill. The father, of Irish descent, was a shop clerk and merchant with Democratic sympathies. It was an impoverished family; young Ronald sold homemade popcorn at high school games and worked as a lifeguard to earn money for his college tuition. When the father got a New Deal WPA job, the future president became an ardent Roosevelt Democrat.

Reagan won a B.A. degree in 1932 from Eureka (Ill.) College, where a photographic memory aided in his studies and in debating and college theatricals. In a Depression year, he was making $100 a week as a sports announcer for radio station WHO in Des Moines, Iowa, from 1932 to 1937. His career as a film and TV actor stretched from 1937 to 1966, and his salary climbed to $3,500 a week. As a World War II captain in Army film studios, Reagan recoiled from what he saw as the laziness of Civil Service workers, and moved to the Right. As president of the Screen Actors Guild, he resisted what he considered a Communist plot to subvert the film industry. With advancing age, Reagan left leading-man roles and became a television spokesman for the General Electric Company at $150,000.

With oratorical skill his trademark, Reagan became an active Republican. At the behest of a small group of conservative Southern California businessmen, he ran for governor with a pledge to cut spending, and was elected by almost a million votes over the political veteran, Democratic Gov. Edmund G. Brown, father of the later governor.

In the 1980 election battle against Jimmy Carter, Reagan broadened his appeal by espousing moderate policies, gaining much of his support from disaffected Democrats and blue-collar workers. The incoming Administration immediately set out to "turn the government around" with a new economic program. Over strenuous Congressional opposition, Reagan triumphed on his "supply side" theory to stimulate production and control inflation through tax cuts and sharp reductions in government spending.

The president won high acclaim for his nomination of Sandra Day O'Connor as the first woman on the Supreme Court. His later nominations met increasing opposition but did much to tilt the Court's orientation to the Right.

In 1982, the President's popularity had slipped as the economy declined into the worst recession in 40 years, with persistent high unemployment and interest rates. Initial support for "supply side" economics faded but the President won crucial battles in Congress.

Internationally, Reagan confronted numerous critical problems in his first term. The successful invasion of Grenada accomplished much diplomatically. But the intervention in Lebanon and the withdrawal of Marines after a disastrous terrorist attack were regarded as military failures.

The popular president won reelection in the 1984 landslide, with the economy improving and inflation under control. Domestically, a tax reform bill that

Reagan backed became law. But the constantly growing budget deficit remained a constant irritant, with the President and Congress persistently at odds over priorities in spending for defense and domestic programs. His foreign policy met stiffening opposition, with Congress increasingly reluctant to increase spending for the Nicarguan "Contras" and the Pentagon and to expand the development of the MX missile. But even severe critics praised Reagan's restrained but decisive handling of the crisis following the hijacking of an American plane in Beirut by Muslim extremists. The attack on Libya in April 1986 galvanized the nation, although it drew scathing disapproval from the NATO alliance.

Barely three months into his first term, Reagan was the target of an assassin's bullet; his courageous comeback won public admiration.

Reagan is devoted to his wife, Nancy, whom he married after his divorce from the screen actress Jane Wyman. The children from his first marriage are Maureen, his daughter by Wyman, and Michael, an adopted son. He had two children by Nancy: Patricia and Ron. Reagan continues to struggle with Alzheimer's disease, which he developed in the years following his presidency.

—*Arthur P. Reed, Jr.*

GEORGE HERBERT WALKER BUSH became president on January 20, 1989, with his theme harmony and conciliation after the often-turbulent Reagan years. With his calm and unassuming manner, he emerged from his subordinate vice-presidential role with an air of quiet authority. His Inaugural address emphasized "A new breeze is blowing, and the old bipartisanship must be made new again."

In his first months, the President, the nation's 41st, established himself as his own man and all but erased memories of what many had regarded as his fiercely abrasive presidential election campaign of 1988 and questionable tactics against his Democratic opponent. People liked his easy style and readiness to compromise even as he remained a staunch conservative, although that readiness had disconcerted some conservatives.

Bush's early Cabinet choices reflected a pragmatic desire for an efficient nonideological Government. And with his usual cautious instinct, in 1990 he nominated to the Supreme Court the scholarly David H. Souter, with broadly conservative views. Souter was confirmed without a bruising battle.

In his first year, Bush, a World War II hero, had won plaudits at home and abroad for his confident, competent conduct at the NATO 40th anniversary summit meeting in Brussels, the Paris economic conference, on his tour of Eastern Europe, and at the Malta conference with Gorbachev. Grave challenges in that year were the Lebanese hostage crisis and the ongoing war on the drug traffic.

Domestically, Bush had to cope with such issues as the *Exxon Valdez* oil spill in Alaska and the dispute over flag-burning restrictions, which was resolved, if only for a time, in mid-1990.

But in his second year, 1990, the President confronted a mounting array of problems, the most critical being on the domestic side. Chief among them were the staggering and mushrooming budget deficit and the savings and loan crisis. Other vexing issues were the question of cutting defense expenditures with consequent economic dislocation, the war on drugs and environmental matters.

At home, the President's popularity dipped sharply from its near-record public approval following the invasion of Panama in late 1989. This plunge followed Bush's recantation of his campaign "no new taxes" pledge as he sat down with Congressional leaders to tame the budget deficit and deal with a faltering economy.

In 1991, the 67-year-old president emerged as the leader of an international coalition of Western democracies, Japan, and even some Arab states that freed invaded Kuwait and vanquished, at least for a time, Iraq's President Saddam Hussein and his armies.

A nation grateful at feeling the end of the "Vietnam syndrome" gave the President an overall rating of 89 percent in a Gallup poll in March after the end of the war. The approval rate fell as the year went on, but a solid majority continued to approve the President's performance, although with growing concern about the faltering economy and other domestic problems. And there were nagging doubts about the Persian Gulf war, its motives and conduct, and about the ensuing refugee crisis.

A major Bush accomplishment in 1991 was the Strategic Arms Reduction Treaty (Start), signed in July with Soviet president Mikhail S. Gorbachev at their fourth summit conference, marking the end of the long weapons buildup. Succeeding events in the Soviet Union and the apparent disintegration of the Communist empire could only enhance his status.

The year also saw the President undergoing treatment for Graves' disease, a thyroid disorder, from which he suffered serious side effects.

Bush, scion of an aristocratic New England family, came to the White House after a long career in public service, in which he held top positions in national and international organizations. As vice president, he avoided the appearance of direct involvement in the Iran-Contra affair while not seeming to shy away from the President.

Earlier, in the 1960s, Bush won two contests for a Texas Republican seat in the House of Representatives, but lost two bids for a Senate seat and one for the presidency. After his second race for the Senate, President Nixon appointed him U.S. delegate to the United Nations with the rank of Ambassador and he later became Republican National Chairman. He headed the United States liaison office in Beijing before becoming Director of Central Intelligence.

In 1980 Bush became Reagan's running mate despite earlier criticism of Reagan "voodoo economics" and by the 1984 election had won acclaim for devotion to Reagan's conservative agenda despite his own reputation as somewhat more liberally inclined. Nevertheless, die-hard right-wingers could find satisfaction in Bush's war record and his Government service, particularly with the C.I.A. Throughout he remained influential in White House decisions, particularly in foreign affairs.

In the 1988 campaign, Bush's choice of Senator Dan Quayle of Indiana for vice president surprised his friends and provoked criticism and ridicule that continued even after the Administration was established in office. Nonetheless Bush strongly defended his choice.

In the 1992 presidential election, Bush was defeated by Gov. Bill Clinton of Arkansas.

The future president joined the Navy after war broke out and at 18 became the Navy's youngest commissioned pilot, serving from 1942 to 1945. The man later derided by some as a "wimp" fought the Japanese on 58 missions and was shot down once. He won the Distinguished Flying Cross.

Throughout his whole career, Bush had the backing of an established family, headed by his father, the autocratic and wealthy Prescott Bush, who was elected to the Senate from Connecticut in 1952. And his family helped the young patrician became established in his early business ventures, a rich uncle raising most of the capital required for founding a new oil company in Texas.

George Herbert Walker Bush was born June 12, 1924, in Milton, Mass., to Prescott and Dorothy Bush. The family later moved to Connecticut. The youth studied at the elite Phillips Academy in Andover, Mass., before entering the Navy.

After the war, Bush earned an economics degree and a Phi Beta Kappa key in two and a half years at Yale University. While there he captained the baseball team and was initiated into "Skull and Bones," the prestigious Yale secret society.

In 1945 Bush married Barbara Pierce of Rye, N.Y., daughter of a magazine publisher. With his bride, Bush moved to Texas instead of entering his father's investment banking business. There he founded his oil company and in 1980 reported an estimated wealth of $1.4 million.

The Bushes have lived in 17 cities and more than a score of homes and have traveled in as many countries. In her husband's frequent absences during the early years, Mrs. Bush was often matriarch of a family of four boys and a girl. Bush is close to his immediate family and to 10 grandchildren, a sister, and three brothers.

After the Clinton inauguration in January, the Bushes returned to Houston, Texas.

—*Arthur P. Reed, Jr.*

WILLIAM JEFFERSON CLINTON was born William Jefferson Blythe III in Hope, Ark., on August 19, 1946. He was named for his father, who was killed in an automobile accident before Clinton's birth. Virginia Kelley, his mother, set an example of hard work and perseverance. She eventually married Roger Clinton, a car dealer, whose name the future president later adopted.

In high school in Hot Springs, Ark., Clinton considered becoming a doctor, but politics beckoned after a meeting with President John F. Kennedy in Washington on a Boys' Nation trip. He earned a B.S. in international affairs in 1968 at Georgetown University, having spent his junior year working for Arkansas Senator J. William Fulbright. He was a Rhodes scholar at Oxford between 1968 and 1970. He then attended Yale Law School, where he met his future wife, Hillary Rodham, a Wellesley graduate. The couple has one child, Chelsea.

Clinton taught at the University of Arkansas (1974–1976), was elected state attorney general (1976), and in 1979 became the nation's youngest governor. But he was defeated for reelection by voters irate at a rise in the state's automobile license fees. In 1982 he was elected again. This time he reined in liberal tendencies to accommodate the conservative bent of the voters.

Clinton became the 42nd U.S. president following a turbulent political campaign. He overcame vigorous personal attacks on his character and on his actions during the Vietnam War, which he actively opposed. The "character issue" stemmed from allegations of infidelity, which Clinton refuted in a television interview in which he and Hillary avowed their relationship was solid. Throughout his term in office, Clinton was dogged by allegations in connection with the Whitewater real estate deal in which he and Hillary were involved prior to the 1992 election. Though the Clintons were never accused of any wrongdoing, their partners in the venture, including the governor of Arkansas, Jim Guy Tucker, were convicted of fraud and conspiracy in a trial in 1996.

The problems faced by the new president were as daunting as they were varied. Almost immediately after his inauguration in January 1993 he became embroiled with the military leadership over a politically sensitive issue—his campaign pledge to allow homosexuals to serve openly in the armed services. He ultimately agreed to a compromise, dubbed the "don't ask, don't tell" policy. This controversy was soon supplanted by a series of blunders in appointments to fill positions in his administration.

Early in his tenure, the new president encountered a major defeat when Congress rejected his proposed economic stimulus package. He later won approval for his budget despite criticisms by conservatives in Congress, including Democrats, who demanded more spending cuts, fewer taxes, and caps on entitlement programs. In his second year, Clinton faced persistent troubles on the domestic front, with acrimonious battles raging over health care, welfare reform, crime prevention, and White House personnel problems. Clinton appointed his wife to craft a health care reform package, but after months of effort the plan failed to gain sufficient support. Clinton had to reduce his objectives from massive overhaul to incremental reform. Though the health care reform was defeated, Clinton won a major victory with the passage of the North American Free Trade Agreement (NAFTA) and the Global Agreement on Tariffs and Trade (GATT). Congress also approved a deficit reduction bill, rules allowing abortion counseling in federally funded clinics, a waiting period for handgun purchases (the Brady Bill), and a national service program.

As his tenure wore on, Clinton came under increasing pressure from Kenneth Starr, the independent counsel who in 1994 took over the investigation of the Clintons' involvement in the Whitewater land deal. Over time, Starr's brief was expanded to include other matters, such as the death of White House lawyer Vincent Foster, the handling of firings in the White House travel office, and allegations of sexual misconduct and cover-ups by the White House.

Foreign affairs, once a weak point for a man elected on a domestic economic agenda, became a proving ground for Clinton. With issues erupting around the world, in places as disparate as Bosnia, Somalia, Rwanda, Haiti, and Cuba, Clinton was able to capitalize on several opportunities to improve his international image. The Israel-Jordan peace agreement was signed at the White House in the summer of 1994 by Israeli prime minister Yitzhak Rabin and Jordan's King Hussein. In the fall of that year, the administration succeeded in restoring Haiti's ousted president, Jean-Bertrand Aristide, to power. Clinton scored again by bolstering Russian president Boris Yeltsin's popularity with promises of economic aid.

But the problems in Eastern Europe put an end to his winning streak. Though Clinton wanted desperately to end the brutal "ethnic cleansing" in Bosnia and offer security to the 2 million refugees scrambling from one U.N. safe haven to another, he did not want to commit American ground troops to do so. A peace accord, which included provisions for American troops in a peacekeeping role, was ultimately constructed by Richard Holbrook and signed in Dayton, Ohio, in November 1995. The peace accord, however tenuous, greatly improved Clinton's standing in the eyes of the international community.

Foreign affairs continued to plague Clinton's presidency in 1996. In Russia, Clinton's support for Yeltsin drew criticism as the war for Chechen independence erupted. In the Middle East, Israeli-Palestinian disputes continued and Iraq invaded Kurdish territory. Clinton responded to the Iraqi aggression by ordering missile attacks on Iraqi planes and ground forces.

The Republican sweep of the 1994 elections resulted in a Republican-controlled Congress, and 1995 was largely a tug-of-war between the White House and Capitol Hill over budget-balancing and other key points of the G.O.P.'s "Contract with America," crafted by Speaker of the House Newt Gingrich.

In 1996, anticipating the fall election, Clinton moved to the political center by approving several major and widely popular legislative measures, including a welfare-reform bill that reversed several decades of federal policy, for which he was sharply criticized by liberals. He also enacted measures to improve access to health care, to raise the minimum wage by 90 cents per hour to $5.15, and to impose sanctions on companies that do business with Iran and Libya. In a move to discourage teenage smoking, Clinton approved a series of curbs on cigarette advertising and introduced plans for the FDA to regulate nicotine as a controlled substance.

Clinton's second term saw a shift away from the budget battlefield, as a soaring economy facilitated an agreement on balanced-budget legislation in 1997. But the character issues that had dogged Clinton since he first emerged on the national scene soon came to dominate his second term. In 1997 a series of investigations aimed to uncover irregularities in Democratic fund-raising for the 1996 election. Though Clinton and Vice President Gore insisted their actions were within the letter of the law and no charges were brought, the ensuing controversy highlighted the need for campaign-finance reform. Ironically, Clinton had called for such reforms during his first term, but could not get the Republican-controlled Congress to cooperate.

Clinton was able to strengthen his place on the world stage in 1998. Just before Easter, former Senate majority leader George Mitchell, Clinton's hand-picked envoy, helped broker a historic peace agreement that promised to end decades of fighting between Protestants and Catholics in Northern Ireland. In May–June Clinton made a controversial diplomatic visit to China. Critics balked at Clinton's decision to visit a country linked to questionable Democratic Party campaign contributions and at his decision to visit Tiananmen Square, the site of the notorious June 1989 massacre in which the Chinese government killed hundreds of pro-democracy demonstrators. Despite pre-trip criticism, Clinton was generally praised for making advancements in U.S. relations with the most populous country in the world while taking a clear stance against Chinese human rights practices.

But Clinton's foreign policy gains were far overshadowed by Independent Counsel Ken Starr's investigation of Clinton's conduct in two sexually-charged cases. The President seemed to win a point in April when a federal judge in Arkansas threw out a long-pending sexual harassment suit brought by Paula Corbin Jones, a former Arkansas state employee. But Starr had already begun investigating the possibility that Clinton had perjured himself in his testimony in the Jones case over an alleged affair with a young White House intern, Monica S. Lewinsky. On Jan. 17, Clinton adamantly denied ever having engaged in sexual relations with Lewinsky, or of asking anyone to lie to cover up the affair.

Despite the explosive charges, Clinton's overall popularity among Americans remained high. The country seemed willing to ignore Clinton's alleged weaknesses in character as long as the economy was good, his policies were popular, and the United States remained strong abroad. On August 17, 1998, Clinton made history by becoming the first U.S. president to testify in front of a grand jury, in an investigation of his own possibly criminal conduct. In an address to the nation that evening, he now admitted to having had an "inappropriate" relationship with Lewinsky, but reaffirmed that he did not ask anyone to lie about or cover up the affair.

By August, the Lewinsky scandal so dominated Clinton's agenda that when he responded to the bombing of two American embassies in Africa by sending U.S. cruise missiles to strike alleged terrorist sites in Sudan and Afghanistan, many questioned whether the strike was a ploy to draw attention away from his domestic plight.

Independent Counsel Starr—a conservative Republican whose investigation was seen by Clinton supporters as a politically-inspired vendetta—delivered his report on the presidential investigation to the House of Representatives on Sept. 9. While the report outlined 11 possible grounds for impeachment stemming from the president's relationship with Monica Lewinsky, it did not cite any impeachable offenses relating to the initial subjects of the investigation, including the Whitewater real estate deal. Included among Starr's accusations against President Clinton were perjury, witness tampering, and obstruction of justice. The president's decision to testify before the grand jury by video transmission rather than in person led to the controversial public release of the videotapes, in which Clinton was shown trying to avoid discussing the details of his sexual relationship. Public and political reactions to Clinton's testimony varied greatly, even within the Democratic party.

Clinton's future in the presidency was uncertain in the fall of 1998, as the possibility of impeachment, congressional censure, or resignation hung over the White House.

In any broad overview of history, arbitrary compartmentalization of facts is self-defeating (and makes locating interrelated people, places, and things that much harder). Therefore, Headline History is designed as a "timeline"—a chronology that highlights both the march of time and interesting, sometimes surprising, juxtapositions. *See also* related sections of the almanac, particularly Inventions and Discoveries and Countries of the World.

B.C.E.

Before the Common Era (B.C.E.) or Before Christ (B.C.)

Ra, Sun God (3000–2000 B.C.E.)

4.5 billion B.C.E. Planet Earth formed.

3 billion B.C.E. First signs of primeval life (bacteria and blue-green algae) appear in oceans.

600 million B.C.E. Earliest date to which fossils can be traced.

4.4 million B.C.E. Earliest known hominid fossils (*Australopithecus ramidis*) found in Aramis, Ethiopia, 1994.

4.2 million B.C.E. *Australopithecus anamensis* found in Lake Turkana, Kenya, 1995.

3.2 million B.C.E. *Australopithecus afarenis* (nicknamed "*Lucy*") found in Ethiopia, 1974.

2.5 million B.C.E. *Homo habilis* ("Handy Man"), first brain expansion and first chipped stones.

1.8 million B.C.E. *Homo erectus* ("Upright Man"). Brain size twice that of *Australopithecine* species.

1.7 million B.C.E. *Homo erectus* leaves Africa.

100,000 B.C.E. First modern *Homo sapiens* in South Africa.

70,000 B.C.E. Neanderthal man (use of fire and advanced tools).

35,000 B.C.E. Neanderthal man replaced by later groups of *Homo sapiens* (i.e. Cro-Magnon man, etc.).

18,000 B.C.E. Cro-Magnons replaced by later cultures.

15,000 B.C.E. Migrations across Bering Straits into the Americas.

10,000 B.C.E. Semi-permanent agricultural settlements in Old World.

10,000–4,000 B.C.E. Development of settlements into cities and development of skills such as the wheel, pottery and improved methods of cultivation in Mesopotamia and elsewhere.

4500–3000 B.C.E. Sumerians in the Tigris and Euphrates valleys develop a city-state civilization; first phonetic writing (c. 3500 B.C.E.). Egyptian agriculture develops. Western Europe is neolithic, without metals or written records. Earliest recorded date in Egyptian calendar (4241 B.C.E.). First year of Jewish calendar (3760 B.C.E.). Copper used by Egyptians and Sumerians.

The Great Pyramid at Giza (c. 2680 B.C.E.)

3000–2000 B.C.E. Pharaonic rule begins in Egypt. King Khufu (Cheops), 4th dynasty (2700–2675 B.C.E.) completes construction of the Great Pyramid at Giza (c. 2680 B.C.E.). The Great Sphinx of Giza (c. 2540 B.C.E.) is built by King Khafre. Earliest Egyptian mummies. Papyrus. Phoenician settlements on coast of what is now Syria and Lebanon. Semitic tribes settle in Assyria. Sargon, first Akkadian king, builds Mesopotamian empire. The Gilgamesh epic (c. 3000 B.C.E.). Abraham leaves Ur (c. 2000 B.C.E.). Systematic astronomy in Egypt, Babylon, India, China.

Stonehenge (c. 3000–1500 B.C.E.)

3000–1500 B.C.E. The most ancient civilization on the Indian subcontinent, the sophisticated and extensive Indus Valley civilization, flourishes in what is today Pakistan. In Britain, Stonehenge erected according to some unknown astronomical rationale. Its three main phases of construction are thought to span c. 3000–1500 B.C.E.

2000–1500 B.C.E. Hyksos invaders drive Egyptians from Lower Egypt (17th century B.C.E.). Amosis I frees Egypt from Hyksos (c. 1600 B.C.E.). Assyrians rise to power—cities of Ashur and Nineveh. Twenty-four-character alphabet in Egypt. Israelites enslaved in Egypt. Cuneiform inscriptions used by Hittites. Peak of Minoan culture on Isle of Crete—earliest form of written Greek. Hammurabi, king of Babylon, develops oldest existing code of laws (18th century B.C.E.).

1500–1000 B.C.E. Ikhnaton develops monotheistic religion in Egypt (c. 1375 B.C.E.). His successor, Tutankhamen, returns to earlier gods. Moses leads Israelites out of Egypt into Canaan—Ten Commandments. Greeks destroy Troy (c. 1193 B.C.E.). End of Greek civilization in Mycenae with invasion of Dorians. Chinese civilization develops under Shang Dynasty. Olmec civilization in Mexico—stone monuments; picture writing.

1000–900 B.C.E. Solomon succeeds King David, builds Jerusalem temple. After Solomon's death, kingdom divided into Israel and Judah. Hebrew elders begin to write Old Testament books of Bible. Phoenicians colonize Spain with settlement at Cadiz.

900–800 B.C.E. Phoenicians establish Carthage (c. 810 B.C.E.). The *Iliad* and the *Odyssey,* perhaps composed by Greek poet Homer.

800–700 B.C.E. Prophets Amos, Hosea, Isaiah. First recorded Olympic games (776 B.C.E.). Legendary founding of Rome by Romulus (753 B.C.E.). Assyrian king Sargon II conquers Hittites, Chaldeans, Samaria (end of Kingdom of Israel). Earliest written music. Chariots introduced into Italy by Etruscans.

700–600 B.C.E. End of Assyrian Empire (616 B.C.E.).—Nineveh destroyed by Chaldeans (Neo-Babylonians) and Medes (612 B.C.E.). Founding of Byzantium by Greeks (c. 660 B.C.E.). Building of the Acropolis in Athens. Solon, Greek lawgiver (640-560 B.C.E.). Sappho of Lesbos, Greek poetess, Lao-tse, Chinese philosopher and founder of Taoism (born c. 604 B.C.E.).

600–500 B.C.E. Babylonian King Nebuchadnezzar builds empire, destroys Jerusalem (586 B.C.E.). Babylonian Captivity of the Jews (starting 587 B.C.E.). Hanging Gardens of Babylon. Cyrus the Great of Persia creates great empire, conquers Babylon (539 B.C.E.), frees the Jews. Athenian democracy develops. Aeschylus, Greek dramatist (525-465 B.C.E.). Pythagoras (c. 582– c. 507 B.C.E.), Greek philosopher and mathematician. Confucius (551-479 B.C.E.) develops ethical and social philosophy in China. The *Analects* or Lun-yü ("collected sayings") were compiled by the second generation of Confucian disciples. Buddha (563-483 B.C.E.) founds Buddhism in India.

Pythagoras (c. 582–c. 507 B.C.E.)

Buddha (563–483 B.C.E.)

SOME ANCIENT CIVILIZATIONS

Name	Approximate dates	Location	Major cities
Akkadian	2350-2230 B.C.E.	Mesopotamia, parts of Syria, Asia Minor, Iran	Akkad, Ur, Erich
Assyrian	1800-889 B.C.E.	Mesopotamia, Syria	Assur, Nineveh, Calah
Babylonian	1728-1686 B.C.E. (old) 625-539 B.C.E. (new)	Mesopotamia, Syria, Palestine	Babylon
Cimmerian	750-500 B.C.E.	Caucasus, northern Asia Minor	—
Egyptian	2850-715 B.C.E.	Nile valley	Thebes, Memphis, Tanis
Etruscan	900-396 B.C.E.	Northern Italy	—
Greek	900-200 B.C.E.	Greece	Athens, Sparta, Thebes, Mycenae, Corinth
Hittite	1640-1200 B.C.E.	Asia Minor, Syria	Hattusas, Nesa
Indus Valley	3000-1500 B.C.E.	Pakistan, Northwestern India	—
Lydian	700-547 B.C.E.	Western Asia Minor	Sardis, Miletus
Mede	835-550 B.C.E.	Iran	Media
Minoan	3000-1100 B.C.E.	Crete	Knossos
Persian	559-330 B.C.E.	Iran, Asia Minor, Syria	Persepolis, Pasargadae
Phoenician	1100-332 B.C.E.	Palestine (colonies: Gibraltar, Carthage, Sardinia)	Tyre, Sidon, Byblos
Phrygian	1000-547 B.C.E.	Central Asia Minor	Gordion
Roman	500 B.C.E.-C.E. 300	Italy, Mediterranean region, Asia Minor, western Europe	Rome, Byzantium
Scythian	800-300 B.C.E.	Caucasus	—
Sumerian	3200-2360 B.C.E.	Mesopotamia	Ur, Nippur

Confucius
(551–479 B.C.E.)

Parthenon
(447–432 B.C.E.)

Plato
(427?–347 B.C.E.)

500–400 B.C.E. Greeks defeat Persians: battles of Marathon (490 B.C.E.), Thermopylae (480 B.C.E.), Salamis (480 B.C.E.). Peloponnesian Wars between Athens and Sparta (431-404 B.C.E.)—Sparta victorious. Pericles comes to power in Athens (462 B.C.E.). Flowering of Greek culture during the Age of Pericles (450-400 B.C.E.). The Parthenon is built in Athens as a temple of the goddess Athena (447–432 B.C.E.). Ictinus and Callicrates were the architects and Phidias was responsible for the sculpture. Sophocles, Greek dramatist (496-c.406 B.C.E.). Hippocrates, Greek "Father of Medicine" (born 460 B.C.E.). Xerxes I, king of Persia (rules 485-465 B.C.E.).

400–300 B.C.E. Pentateuch—first five books of the Old Testament evolve in final form. Philip of Macedon assassinated (336 B.C.E.) after conquering Greece; succeeded by son, Alexander the Great (356-323 B.C.E.) who destroys Thebes (335 B.C.E.), conquers Tyre and Jerusalem (332 B.C.E.), occupies Babylon (330 B.C.E.), invades India, and dies in Babylon. His empire is divided among his generals; one of them, Seleucis I, establishes Middle East empire with capitals at Antioch (Syria) and Seleucia (in Iraq). Trial and execution of Greek philosopher Socrates (399 B.C.E.). Dialogues recorded by his student, Plato. Euclid's work on geometry (323 B.C.E.). Aristotle, Greek philosopher (384-322 B.C.E.). Demosthenes, Greek orator (384-322 B.C.E.). Praxiteles, Greek sculptor (400-330 B.C.E.).

300–251 B.C.E. First Punic War (264-241 B.C.E.): Rome defeats the Carthaginians and begins its domination of the Mediterranean. Temple of the Sun at Teotihuacan, Mexico (c. 300 B.C.E.). Invention of Mayan calendar in Yucatán—more exact than older calendars. First Roman gladiatorial games (264 B.C.E.). Archimedes, Greek mathematician (287-212 B.C.E.).

250–201 B.C.E. Second Punic War (219-201 B.C.E.): Hannibal, Carthaginian general (246-142 B.C.E.), crosses the Alps (218 B.C.E.), reaches gates of Rome (211 B.C.E.), retreats, and is defeated by Scipio Africanus at Zama (202 B.C.E.). Great Wall of China built (c. 215 B.C.E.).

200-151 B.C.E. Romans defeat Seleucid King Antiochus III at Thermopylae (191 B.C.E.)— beginning of Roman world domination. Maccabean revolt against Seleucids (167 B.C.E.).

150–101 B.C.E. Third Punic War (149-146 B.C.E.): Rome destroys Carthage, killing 450,000 and enslaving the remaining 50,000 inhabitants. Roman armies conquer Macedonia, Greece, Anatolia, Balearic Islands, and southern France. Venus de Milo (c. 140 B.C.E.). Cicero, Roman orator (106-43 B.C.E.).

100–51 B.C.E. Julius Caesar (100-44 B.C.E.) invades Britain (55 B.C.E.) and conquers Gaul (France) (c. 50 B.C.E.). Spartacus leads slave revolt against Rome (71 B.C.E.). Romans conquer Seleucid empire. Roman general Pompey conquers Jerusalem (63 B.C.E.). Cleopatra on Egyptian throne (51-31 B.C.E.). Chinese develop use of paper (c. 100 B.C.E.). Virgil, Roman poet (70-19 B.C.E.). Horace, Roman poet (65-8 B.C.E.).

50–1 B.C.E. Caesar crosses Rubicon to fight Pompey (50 B.C.E.). Herod made Roman governor of Judea (47 B.C.E.). Caesar murdered (44 B.C.E.). Caesar's nephew, Octavian, defeats Mark Antony and Cleopatra at Battle of Actium (31 B.C.E.), and establishes Roman empire as Emperor Augustus—rules 27 B.C.E.-C.E. 14. Pantheon built for the first time under Agrippa, 27 B.C.E. Ovid, Roman poet (43 B.C.E.-C.E. 18).

C.E.

The Common Era (C.E.) or Christian Era (A.D.)

Roman Aqueduct
Montpellier, France

1–49 Birth of Jesus Christ (variously given from 4 B.C.E. to C.E. 7). After Augustus, Tiberius becomes emperor (dies, 37), succeeded by Caligula (assassinated, 41), who is followed by Claudius. Crucifixion of Jesus (probably 30). Han dynasty in China founded by Emperor Kuang Wu Ti. Buddhism introduced to China.

50–99 Claudius poisoned (54), succeeded by Nero (commits suicide, 68). Missionary journeys of Paul the Apostle 34-60). Jews revolt against Rome; Jerusalem destroyed (70). Roman persecutions of Christians begin (64). Colosseum built in Rome (71-80). Trajan (rules 98-116); Roman empire extends to Mesopotamia, Arabia, Balkans. First Gospels of St. Mark, St. John, St. Matthew.

100–149 Hadrian rules Rome (117-138); codifies Roman law, rebuilds Pantheon, establishes postal system, builds wall between England and Scotland. Jews revolt under Bar Kokhba (122-135); final *Diaspora* (dispersion) of Jews begins.

150–199 Marcus Aurelius (rules Rome 161-180). Oldest Mayan temples in Central America (c. 200).

200-249 Goths invade Asia Minor (c. 220). Roman persecutions of Christians increase. Persian (Sassanid) empire re-established. End of Chinese Han dynasty.

250–299 Increasing invasions of the Roman empire by Franks and Goths. Buddhism spreads in China. Classic period of Mayan civilization (250–900); develop hieroglyphic writing, advances in art, architecture, science.

300–349 Constantine the Great (rules 312-337) reunites eastern and western Roman empires, with new capital (Constantinople) on site of Byzantium (330); issues Edict of Milan legalizing Christianity (313); becomes a Christian on his deathbed (337). Council of Nicaea (325) defines orthodox Christian doctrine. First Gupta dynasty in India (c. 320).

350–399 Huns (Mongols) invade Europe (c. 360). Theodosius the Great (rules 392-395)—last emperor of a united Roman empire. Roman empire permanently divided in 395: western empire ruled from Rome; eastern empire ruled from Constantinople.

400–449 Western Roman empire disintegrates under weak emperors. Alaric, king of the Visigoths, sacks Rome (410). Attila, Hun chieftain, attacks Roman provinces (433). St. Patrick returns to Ireland (432) and brings Christianity to the island. St. Augustine's *City of God* (411).

450–499 Vandals destroy Rome (455). Western Roman empire ends as Odoacer, German chieftain, overthrows last Roman emperor, Romulus Augustulus, and becomes king of Italy (476). Ostrogothic kingdom of Italy established by Theodoric the Great (493). Clovis, ruler of the Franks, is converted to Christianity (496). First schism between western and eastern churches (484).

500–549 Eastern and western churches reconciled (519). Justinian I, the Great (483-565), becomes Byzantine emperor (527), issues his first code of civil laws (529), conquers North Africa, Italy, and part of Spain. Plague spreads through Europe (from 542). Arthur, semi-legendary king of the Britons (killed, c. 537). Boëthius, Roman scholar (executed, 524).

550–599 Beginnings of European silk industry after Justinian's missionaries smuggle silkworms out of China (553). Mohammed, founder of Islam (570-632). Buddhism in Japan (c. 560). St. Augustine of Canterbury brings Christianity to Britain (597). After killing about half the population, plague in Europe subsides (594).

600–649 Mohammed flees from Mecca to Medina (the *Hegira*); first year of the Muslim calendar (622). Muslim empire grows (634). Arabs conquer Jerusalem (637), destroy Alexandrian library (641), conquer Persians (641). Fatima, Mohammed's daughter (606-632).

650–699 Arabs attack North Africa (670), destroy Carthage (697). Venerable Bede, English monk (672-735).

700–749 Arab empire extends from Lisbon to China (by 716). Charles Martel, Frankish leader, defeats Arabs at Tours/Poitiers, halting Arab advance in Europe (732). Charlemagne (742-814). Introduction of pagodas in Japan from China.

750–799 Caliph Harun al-Rashid rules Arab empire (786-809): the "golden age" of Arab culture. Vikings begin attacks on Britain (790), land in Ireland (795). Charlemagne becomes king of the Franks (771). City of Machu Picchu flourishes in Peru.

800–849 Charlemagne crowned first Holy Roman Emperor in Rome (800). Arabs conquer Crete, Sicily, and Sardinia (826-827). Charlemagne dies (814), succeeded by his son, Louis the Pious, who divides France among his sons (817).

850–899 Norsemen attack as far south as the Mediterranean but are thwarted (859), discover Iceland (861). Alfred the Great becomes king of Britain (871), defeats Danish invaders (878). Russian nation founded by Vikings under Prince Rurik, establishing capital at Novgorod (855-879).

900–949 Vikings discover Greenland (c. 900). Arab Spain under Abd ar-Rahman III becomes center of learning (912-961). Beginning of Mayan Post-Classical period (900–1519).

950–999 Eric the Red establishes first Viking colony in Greenland (982). Mieczyslaw I becomes first ruler of Poland (960). Hugh Capet elected King of France in 987; Capetian dynasty to rule until 1328. Musical notation systematized (c. 990).

Mayan Pyramid at Chichén Itzá

Celtic Cross

Japanese Pagoda

Viking Ship (c. 900)

Mesa Verde Cliff Dwellings (c. 1000–1300)

Cathedral and Tower at Pisa

Chartres Cathedral

King John (1167–1216)

Thomas Aquinas (1225–74)

Vikings and Danes attack Britain (988-999). Holy Roman Empire founded by Otto I, King of Germany since 936, crowned by Pope John XII in 962.

1000–1099 (C.E.)

c.1000 Hungary and Scandinavia converted to Christianity. Viking raider Leif Ericson discovers North America, calls it *Vinland.* Chinese invent gunpowder. *Beowulf,* Old English epic.

1000–1300 Classic Pueblo period of Anasazi culture; cliff dwellings.

1009 Muslims destroy Holy Sepulchre in Jerusalem.

1013 Danes control England. Canute takes throne (1016), conquers Norway (1028), dies (1035); kingdom divided among his sons: Harold Harefoot (England), Sweyn (Norway), Hardecanute (Denmark).

1040 Macbeth murders Duncan, king of Scotland.

1053 Robert Guiscard, Norman invader, establishes kingdom in Italy, conquers Sicily (1072).

1054 Final separation between Eastern (Orthodox) and Western (Roman) churches.

1055 Seljuk Turks, Asian nomads, move west, capture Baghdad, Armenia (1064), Syria, and Palestine (1075).

1066 William of Normandy invades England, defeats last Saxon king, Harold II, at Battle of Hastings, crowned William I of England ("the Conqueror").

1068 Construction on the Cathedral in Pisa, Italy, begins.

1073 Emergence of strong papacy when Gregory VII is elected. Conflict with English and French kings and German emperors will continue throughout medieval period.

1095 At Council of Clermont, Pope Urban II calls for a holy war to wrest control of Jerusalem from Muslims, which launches the First Crusade (1096), one of at least 8 European military campaigns between 1095 and 1291 to regain the Holy Land.

1100–1199 (C.E.)

1100–1300 Construction of Cathedral at Chartres, France.

1150–67 Universities of Paris and Oxford founded in France and England.

1162 Thomas á Becket named Archbishop of Canterbury, murdered by Henry II's men (1170). Troubadours (wandering minstrels) glorify romantic concepts of feudalism.

1189 Richard I ("the Lionhearted") succeeds Henry II in England, killed in France (1199), succeeded by King John.

1200–1299 (C.E.)

1211 Genghis Khan invades China, captures Peking (1214), conquers Persia (1218), invades Russia (1223), dies (1227).

1215 King John forced by barons to sign Magna Carta at Runneymede, limiting royal power.

1233 The Inquisition begins as Pope Gregory IX assigns Dominicans responsibility for combating heresy. Torture used (1252). Ferdinand and Isabella establish Spanish Inquisition (1478). Tourquemada, Grand Inquisitor, forces conversion or expulsion of Spanish Jews (1492). Forced conversion of Moors (1499). Inquisition in Portugal (1531). First Protestants burned at the stake in Spain (1543). Spanish Inquisition abolished (1734).

1241 Mongols defeat Germans in Silesia, invade Poland and Hungary, withdraw from Europe after Ughetai, Mongol leader, dies.

THE CRUSADES (1096–1291)

In 1095 at Council of Clermont, Pope Urban II calls for war to rescue Holy Land from Muslim infidels. The *First Crusade* (1096) was assembled in response to Emperor Alexius I. The Christians captured Antioch (1098) and Jerusalem (1099). They established the Crusader States, ruled by Europeans. It was the only crusade to be successful. The *Second Crusade* begins after the Seljuk Turks recapture Edessa, one of the Crusader States, in 1144. It is led by King Louis VIII of France and Holy Roman Emperor Conrad III. Crusaders perish in Asia Minor (1147).

Saladin controls Egypt (1171), unites Islam in Holy War *(Jihad)* against Christians, recaptures Jerusalem (1187). *Third Crusade* (1189) under kings of France, England, and Germany fails to reduce Saladin's power. *Fourth Crusade* (1200-1204)—French knights sack Greek Christian Constantinople, establish Latin empire in Byzantium. Greeks re-establish Orthodox faith (1262).

Children's Crusade (1212)—Only 1 of 30,000 French children and about 200 of 20,000 German children survive to return home. Other Crusades—against Egypt (1217), *Sixth* (1228), *Seventh* (1248), *Eighth* (1270). Mamelukes conquer Acre; end of the Crusades (1291).

1251 Kublai Khan governs China, becomes ruler of Mongols (1259), establishes Yuan dynasty in China (1280), invades Burma (1287), dies (1294).
1271 Marco Polo of Venice travels to China, in court of Kublai Khan (1275-1292), returns to Genoa (1295) and writes *Travels.*
1273 Thomas Aquinas stops work on *Summa Theologica,* the basis of all Catholic theological teaching.
1295 English King Edward I summons the Model Parliament.

1300–1399 (C.E.)

1312–37 Mali Empire reaches its height in Africa under King Mansa Musa.
1337–1453 Hundred Years' War—English and French kings fight for control of France.
c.1325 The beginning of the Renaissance in Italy: writers Dante, Petrarch, Boccaccio; painter Giotto. Development of *No* drama in Japan. Aztecs establish capital on site of modern Mexico City. Peak of Muslim culture in Spain. Small cannon in use.
1347–1351 At least 25 million people die in Europe's "Black Death" (bubonic plague).
1368 Ming Dynasty begins in China.
1376–82 John Wycliffe, pre-Reformation religious reformer and followers translate Latin Bible into English.
1378 The Great Schism (to 1417)—rival popes in Rome and Avignon, France, fight for control of Roman Catholic Church.
c.1387 Chaucer's *Canterbury Tales.*

1400–1499 (C.E.)

1415 Henry V defeats French at Agincourt. Jan Hus, Bohemian preacher and follower of Wycliffe, burned at stake in Constance as heretic.
1418–60 Portugal's Prince Henry the Navigator sponsors exploration of Africa's coast. Brunelleschi begins work on the duomo in Florence (1420).
1428 Joan of Arc leads French against English, captured by Burgundians (1430) and turned over to the English, burned at the stake as a witch after ecclesiastical trial (1431).
1438 Inca rule in Peru.
1450 Florence becomes center of Renaissance arts and learning under the Medicis.
1453 Turks conquer Constantinople, end of the Byzantine empire. Hundred Years' War between France and England ends.
1455 The Wars of the Roses, civil wars between rival noble factions, begin in England (to 1485). Having invented printing with movable type at Mainz, Germany, Johann Gutenberg completes first Bible.
1462 Ivan the Great rules Russia until 1505 as first czar; ends payment of tribute to Mongols.
1492 Moors conquered in Spain by troops of Ferdinand and Isabella. Columbus becomes first European to encounter Caribbean islands, returns to Spain (1493). Second voyage to Dominica, Jamaica, Puerto Rico (1493–1496). Third voyage to Orinoco (1498). Fourth voyage to Honduras and Panama (1502–1504).
1497 Vasco da Gama sails around Africa and discovers sea route to India (1498). Establishes Portuguese colony in India (1502). John Cabot, employed by England, reaches and explores Canadian coast. Michelangelo's *Bacchus* sculpture.

1500–1599 (C.E.)

1501 First black slaves in America brought to Spanish colony of Santo Domingo.
c.1503 Leonardo da Vinci paints the *Mona Lisa.* Michelangelo sculpts the *David* (1504).
1506 St. Peter's Church started in Rome; designed and decorated by such artists and architects as Bramante, Michelangelo, da Vinci, Raphael, and Bernini before its completion in 1626.
1509 Henry VIII ascends English throne. Michelangelo paints the ceiling of the Sistine Chapel.
1513 Balboa becomes the first European to encounter the Pacific ocean.
1517 Turks conquer Egypt, control Arabia. Martin Luther posts his 95 theses denouncing church abuses on church door in Wittenberg—start of the Reformation in Germany.
1519 Ulrich Zwingli begins Reformation in Switzerland. Hernando Cortes conquers Mexico for Spain. Charles I of Spain is chosen Holy Roman Emperor Charles V. Portuguese explorer Ferdinand Magellan sets out to circumnavigate the globe.

The Duomo in Florence

Joan of Arc (1412–1431)

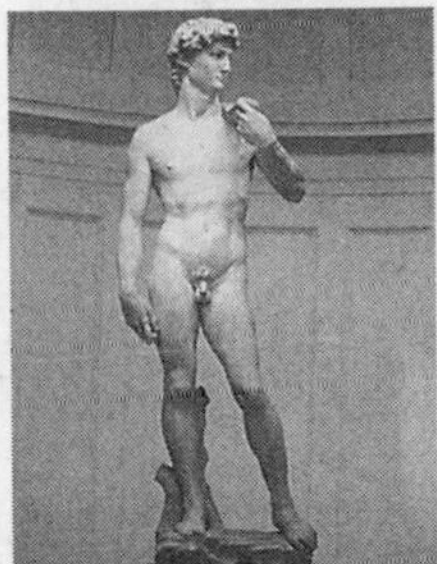
Michelangelo's David (1504)

Martin Luther (1483–1546)

Henry VIII (1491–1547)

Queen Elizabeth I (1533–1603)

William Shakespeare (1564–1616)

Pocahontas (c. 1595–1617)

Marie de Medici (1573–1642)

Galileo (1564–1642)

1520 Luther excommunicated by Pope Leo X. Suleiman I ("the Magnificent") becomes Sultan of Turkey, invades Hungary (1521), Rhodes (1522), attacks Austria (1529), annexes Hungary (1541), Tripoli (1551), makes peace with Persia (1553), destroys Spanish fleet (1560), dies (1566). Magellan reaches the Pacific, is killed by Philippine natives (1521). One of his ships under Juan Sebastián del Cano continues around the world, reaches Spain (1522).

1524 Verrazano, sailing under the French flag, explores the New England coast and New York Bay.

1527 Troops of the Holy Roman Empire attack Rome, imprison Pope Clement VII—the end of the Italian Renaissance. Castiglione writes *The Courtier.* The Medici expelled from Florence.

1532 Pizarro marches from Panama to Peru, kills the Inca chieftain, Atahualpa, of Peru (1533). Machiavelli's *Prince* published posthumously.

1535 Reformation begins as Henry VIII makes himself head of English Church after being excommunicated by Pope. Sir Thomas More executed as traitor for refusal to acknowledge king's religious authority. Jacques Cartier sails up the St. Lawrence River, basis of French claims to Canada.

1536 Henry VIII executes second wife, Anne Boleyn. John Calvin establishes Presbyterian form of Protestantism in Switzerland, writes *Institutes of the Christian Religion.* Danish and Norwegian Reformations. Michelangelo's *Last Judgment.*

1541 John Knox leads Reformation in Scotland, establishes Presbyterian church (1560).

1543 Publication of *On the Revolution of Heavenly Bodies* by Polish scholar Nicolaus Copernicus—giving his theory that the earth revolves around the sun.

1545 Council of Trent to meet intermittently until 1563 to define Catholic dogma and doctrine, reiterate papal authority.

1547 Ivan IV ("the Terrible") crowned as Czar of Russia, begins conquest of Astrakhan and Kazan (1552), battles nobles (boyars) for power (1564), kills his son (1580), dies, and is succeeded by his weak and feeble-minded son, Fydor I.

1553 Roman Catholicism restored in England by Queen Mary I.

1556 Akbar the Great becomes Mogul emperor of India, conquers Afghanistan (1581), continues wars of conquest (until 1605).

1558 Queen Elizabeth I ascends the throne (rules to 1603). Restores Protestantism, establishes state Church of England (Anglicanism). Renaissance will reach height in England—Shakespeare, Marlowe, Spenser.

1561 Persecution of Huguenots in France stopped by Edict of Orleans. French religious wars begin again with massacre of Huguenots at Vassy. St. Bartholomew's Day Massacre—thousands of Huguenots murdered (1572). Amnesty granted (1573). Persecution continues periodically until Edict of Nantes (1598) gives Huguenots religious freedom (until 1685).

1568 Protestant Netherlands revolts against Catholic Spain; independence will be acknowledged by Spain in 1648. High point of Dutch Renaissance—painters Rubens, Van Dyck, Hals, and Rembrandt.

1570 Japan permits visits of foreign ships. Queen Elizabeth I excommunicated by Pope. Turks attack Cyprus and war on Venice. Turkish fleet defeated at Battle of Lepanto by Spanish and Italian fleets (1571). Peace of Constantinople (1572) ends Turkish attacks on Europe.

1580 Francis Drake returns to England after circumnavigating the globe. Knighted by Queen Elizabeth I (1581). Montaigne's *Essays* published.

1583 William of Orange rules The Netherlands; assassinated on orders of Philip II of Spain (1584).

1587 Mary, Queen of Scots, executed for treason by order of Queen Elizabeth I. Monteverdi's *First Book of Madrigals.*

1588 Defeat of the Spanish Armada by English. Henry, King of Navarre and Protestant leader, recognized as Henry IV, first Bourbon king of France. Converts to Roman Catholicism in 1593 in attempt to end religious wars.

1590 Henry IV enters Paris, wars on Spain (1595), marries Marie de Medici (1600), assassinated (1610). Spenser's *The Faerie Queen,* El Greco's *St. Jerome.* Galileo's experiments with falling objects.

1598 Boris Godunov becomes Russian Czar. Tycho Brahe describes his astronomical experiments.

1600–1699 (C.E.)

1600 Giordano Bruno burned as a heretic. Ieyasu rules Japan, moves capital to Edo (Tokyo). Shakespeare's *Hamlet* begins his most productive decade. English East India Company established to develop overseas trade.

1607 Jamestown, Virginia, established—first permanent English colony on American mainland. Pocahontas, daughter of Chief Powhatan, saves life of John Smith.

1609 Samuel de Champlain establishes French colony of Quebec.

1611 Gustavus Adolphus elected King of Sweden. King James Version of the Bible published in England. Rubens paints his *Descent from the Cross.*

1614 John Napier discovers logarithms.

1618 Start of the Thirty Years' War (to 1648)—Protestant revolt against Catholic oppression; Denmark, Sweden, and France will invade Germany in later phases of war. Kepler proposes last of 3 laws of planetary motion.

1619 A Dutch ship brings the first African slaves to British North America.

1620 Pilgrims, after three-month voyage in *Mayflower,* land at Plymouth Rock. Francis Bacon's *Novum Organum.*

1633 Inquisition forces Galileo to recant his belief in Copernican theory.

1642 English Civil War. Cavaliers, supporters of Charles I, against Roundheads, parliamentary forces. Oliver Cromwell defeats Royalists (1646). Parliament demands reforms. Charles I offers concessions, brought to trial (1648), beheaded (1649). Cromwell becomes Lord Protector (1653). Rembrandt paints his *Night Watch.*

1643 Taj Mahal completed.

1644 End of Ming Dynasty in China—Manchus come to power. Descartes' *Principles of Philosophy.*

1648 End of the Thirty Years' War. German population about half of what it was in 1618 because of war and pestilence.

1658 Cromwell dies; son Richard resigns and Puritan government collapses.

1660 English Parliament calls for the restoration of the monarchy; invites Charles II to return from France.

1661 Charles II is crowned King of England. Louis XIV begins personal rule as absolute monarch; starts to build Versailles.

1664 British take New Amsterdam from the Dutch. English limit "Nonconformity" with re-established Anglican Church. Isaac Newton's experiments with gravity.

1665 Great Plague in London kills 75,000.

1666 Great Fire of London. Molière's *Misanthrope.*

1667 Milton's *Paradise Lost,* widely considered the greatest epic poem in English.

1683 War of European powers against the Turks (to 1699). Vienna withstands three-month Turkish siege; high point of Turkish advance in Europe.

1685 James II succeeds Charles II in England, calls for freedom of conscience (1687). Protestants fear restoration of Catholicism and demand "Glorious Revolution." William of Orange invited to England and James II escapes to France (1688). William III and his wife, Mary, crowned. In France, Edict of Nantes of 1598, granting freedom of worship to Huguenots is revoked by Louis XIV; thousands of Protestants flee.

1689 Peter the Great becomes Czar of Russia—attempts to westernize nation and build Russia as a military power. Defeats Charles XII of Sweden at Poltava (1709). Beginning of the French and Indian Wars (to 1763), campaigns in America linked to a series of wars between France and England for domination of Europe.

1690 William III of England defeats former King James II and Irish rebels at Battle of the Boyne in Ireland. John Locke's *Human Understanding.*

1700–1799 (C.E.)

1701 War of the Spanish Succession begins—the last of Louis XIV's wars for domination of the continent. The Peace of Utrecht (1714) will end the conflict and mark the rise of the British Empire. Called Queen Anne's War in America, it ends with the British taking New Foundland, Acadia, and Hudson's Bay Territory from France, and Gibraltar and Minorca from Spain.

1704 Deerfield (Mass.) Massacre of English colonists by French and Indians. Bach's first cantata. Jonathan Swift's *Tale of a Tub. Boston News Letter*—first newspaper in America.

Johannes Kepler (1571–1630)

Rembrandt van Rijn (1606–1669)

Taj Mahal

John Milton (1608–1674)

Benjamin Franklin (1706–1790)

Frederick the Great (1712–1786)

Samuel Johnson (1709–1784)

George Washington (1732–1799)

1707 United Kingdom of Great Britain formed—England, Wales, and Scotland joined by parliamentary Act of Union.

1729 J. S. Bach's *St. Matthew Passion.* Isaac Newton's *Principia* translated from Latin into English.

1732 Benjamin Franklin begins publishing *Poor Richard's Almanack.*

1735 John Peter Zenger, New York editor, acquitted of libel in New York, establishing press freedom.

1740 Capt. Vitus Bering, Dane employed by Russia, discovers Alaska. Frederick II "the Great" crowned King of Prussia.

1746 British defeat Scots under Stuart Pretender Prince Charles at Culloden Moor. Last battle fought on British soil.

1751 Publication of the *Encyclopédie* begins in France, the "bible" of the Enlightenment.

1755 Samuel Johnson's *Dictionary* first published. Great earthquake in Lisbon, Portugal—over 60,000 die. U.S. postal service established.

1756 Seven Years' War (French and Indian War in America) (to 1763), in which Britain and Prussia defeat France, Spain, Austria, and Russia. France loses North American colonies; Spain cedes Florida to Britain in exchange for Cuba. In India, over 100 British prisoners die in "Black Hole of Calcutta."

1757 Beginning of British Empire in India as Robert Clive, British commander, defeats Nawab of Bengal at Plassey.

1759 British capture Quebec from French. Voltaire's *Candide.* Haydn's *Symphony No. 1.*

1762 Catherine II ("the Great") becomes Czarina of Russia. J. J. Rousseau's *Social Contract.* Mozart tours Europe as six-year-old prodigy.

1765 James Watt invents the steam engine.

1769 Sir William Arkwright patents a spinning machine—an early step in the Industrial Revolution.

1772 Joseph Priestley and Daniel Rutherford independently discover nitrogen. Partition of Poland—in 1772, 1793, and 1795, Austria, Prussia, and Russia divide land and people of Poland, end its independence.

1775 The American Revolution begins. Priestley discovers hydrochloric and sulfuric acids.

1776 Adam Smith's *Wealth of Nations.* Edward Gibbon's *Decline and Fall of the Roman Empire.* Thomas Paine's *Common Sense.* Fragonard's *Washerwoman.* Mozart's *Haffner Serenade.* Gen. Washington crosses the Delaware Christmas night (*see* The Founding of the American Nation).

1778 Capt. James Cook discovers Hawaii. Franz Mesmer uses hypnotism.

1781 Immanuel Kant's *Critique of Pure Reason.* Herschel discovers Uranus.

1783 End of Revolutionary War. William Blake's poems. Beethoven's first printed works.

THE FOUNDING OF THE AMERICAN NATION

Colonization of America begins: Jamestown, Va. (1607); Pilgrims in Plymouth (1620); Massachusetts Bay Colony (1630); New Netherland founded by Dutch West India Company (1623), captured by English (1664). Delaware established by Swedish trading company (1638), absorbed later by Penn family. Proprietorships by royal grants to Lord Baltimore (Maryland,1632); Captain John Mason (New Hampshire, 1635); Sir William Berkeley and Sir George Carteret (New Jersey,1663); friends of Charles II (the Carolinas, 1663); William Penn (Pennsylvania,1682); James Oglethorpe and others (Georgia,1732).

Increasing conflict between colonists and Britain on western frontier because of royal edict limiting western expansion (1763) and regulation of colonial trade and increased taxation of colonies (Writs of Assistance allow search for illegal shipments, 1761; Sugar Act, 1764; Currency Act, 1764; Stamp Act, 1765; Quartering Act, 1765; Duty Act, 1767.) Boston Massacre (1770). Lord North attempts conciliation (1770). Boston Tea Party (1773), followed by punitive measures passed by Parliament—the "Intolerable Acts."

First Continental Congress (1774) sends "Declaration of Rights and Grievances" to king, urges colonies to form Continental Association. Paul Revere's ride and Lexington and Concord battle between Massachusetts Minutemen and British (1775).

Second Continental Congress (1775), while sending "olive branch" to the king, begins to raise army, appoints Washington commander-in-chief, and seeks alliance with France. Some colonial legislatures urge their delegates to vote for independence. Declaration of Independence **(July 4, 1776).**

Major Battles of the Revolutionary War: *Long Island:* Howe defeats Putnam's division of Washington's Army in Brooklyn Heights, but Americans escape across East River (1776). *Trenton and Princeton:* Washington defeats Hessians at Trenton, British at Princeton. Winters at Morristown (1776-77). Howe winters in Philadelphia; Washington at Valley Forge (1777-78). Burgoyne surrenders British army to General Gates at *Saratoga* (1777).

France recognizes American independence (1778). The War moves south: Savannah captured by British (1778); Charleston occupied (1780); Americans fight successful guerrilla actions under Marion, Pickens, and Sumter. In the West, George Rogers Clark attacks Forts Kaskaskia and Vincennes (1778-1779), defeating British in the region. Cornwallis surrenders at *Yorktown,* Virginia **(Oct. 19, 1781).** By 1782, Britain is eager for peace because of conflicts with European nations. *Peace of Paris* (1783): Britain recognizes American independence.

1784 Crimea annexed by Russia. John Wesley's *Deed of Declaration,* the basic work of Methodism.

1785 Russians settle Aleutian Islands.

1787 The Constitution of the United States signed. Lavoisier's work on chemical nomenclature. Mozart's *Don Giovanni.*

1788 French *Parlement* presents grievances to Louis XVI who agrees to convening of Estates-General in 1789—not called since 1613. Goethe's *Egmont.* Laplace's *Laws of the Planetary System.*

1789 French Revolution. In U.S., George Washington elected President with all 69 votes of the Electoral College, takes oath of office in New York City. Vice President: John Adams. Secretary of State: Thomas Jefferson. Secretary of Treasury: Alexander Hamilton.

1790 H.M.S. *Bounty* mutineers settle on Pitcairn Island. Aloisio Galvani experiments on electrical stimulation of the muscles. Philadelphia temporary capital of U.S. as Congress votes to establish new capital on Potomac. U.S. population about 3,929,000, including 698,000 slaves. Lavoisier formulates *Table of 31 chemical elements.*

1791 U.S. Bill of Rights ratified. Boswell's *Life of Johnson.*

1794 Kosciusko's uprising in Poland quelled by the Russians. In U.S., Whiskey Rebellion in Pennsylvania as farmers object to liquor taxes.

1796 Napoleon Bonaparte, French general, defeats Austrians. In the U.S., Washington's Farewell Address **(Sept. 17);** John Adams elected President; Thomas Jefferson, vice president. Edward Jenner introduces smallpox vaccination.

1798 Napoleon extends French conquests to Rome and Egypt. U.S. Navy Department established.

1799 Napoleon leads coup that overthrows Directory, becomes First Consul—one of three who rule France.

1800–1899 (C.E.)

1800 Napoleon conquers Italy, firmly establishes himself as First Consul in France. In the U.S., federal government moves to Washington. Robert Owen's social reforms in England. William Herschel discovers infrared rays. Alessandro Volta produces electricity.

1801 Austria makes temporary peace with France. United Kingdom of Great Britain and Ireland established with one monarch and one parliament; Catholics excluded from voting.

1803 U.S. negotiates Louisiana Purchase from France: for $15 million, U.S. doubles its domain, increasing its territory by 827,000 sq. mi. (2,144,500 sq km), from Mississippi River to Rockies and from Gulf of Mexico to British North America.

1804 Haiti declares independence from France; first black nation to gain freedom from European colonial rule. Napoleon proclaims himself emperor of France, systematizes French law under *Code Napoleon.* In the U.S., Alexander Hamilton is mortally wounded in duel with Aaron Burr. Lewis and Clark expedition begins exploration of what is now northwestern U.S.

1805 Lord Nelson defeats the French-Spanish fleets in the Battle of Trafalgar. Napoleon victorious over Austrian and Russian forces at the Battle of Austerlitz.

1807 Robert Fulton makes first successful steamboat trip on *Clermont* between New York City and Albany.

1808 French armies occupy Rome and Spain, extending Napoleon's empire. Britain begins aiding Spanish guerrillas against Napoleon in Peninsular War. In the U.S., Congress bars importation of slaves. Beethoven's *Fifth* and *Sixth Symphonies* performed.

Alexander Hamilton (1755–1804)

Napoleon Bonaparte (1769–1821)

Ludwig van Beethoven (1770–1827)

Edgar Allen Poe (1809–1849)

FRENCH REVOLUTION (1789–1799)

Revolution begins when Third Estate (Commons) delegates swear not to disband until France has a constitution. Paris mob storms Bastille, symbol of royal power **(July 14, 1789).** National Assembly votes for Constitution, Declaration of the Rights of Man, a limited monarchy, and other reforms (1789-90). Legislative Assembly elected, Revolutionary Commune formed, and French Republic proclaimed (1792). War of the First Coalition—Austria, Prussia, Britain, Netherlands, and Spain fight to restore French nobility (1792-97). Start of series of wars between France and European powers that will last, almost without interruption, for 23 years. Louis XVI and Marie Antoinette executed. Committee of Public Safety begins Reign of Terror as political control measure. Interfactional rivalry leads to mass killings. Danton and Robespierre executed. Third French Constitution sets up Directory government (1795).

Richard Wagner (1813–1883)

Frederick Douglass (c. 1817–1895)

Harriet Tubman (c. 1820–1913)

Harriet Beecher Stowe (1811–1896)

Walt Whitman (1819–1892)

1812 Napoleon's Grand Army invades Russia in June. Forced to retreat in winter, most of Napoleon's 600,000 men are lost. In the U.S., war with Britain declared over freedom of the seas for U.S. vessels. U.S.S. *Constitution* sinks British frigate.

1814 French defeated by allies (Britain, Austria, Russia, Prussia, Sweden, and Portugal) in War of Liberation. Napoleon exiled to Elba, off Italian coast. Bourbon King Louis XVIII takes French throne. George Stephenson builds first practical steam locomotive.

1815 Napoleon returns: "Hundred Days" begin. Napoleon defeated by Wellington at Waterloo, banished again to St. Helena in South Atlantic. Congress of Vienna: victorious allies change the map of Europe.

1817 Simón Bolívar establishes independent Venezuela, as Spain loses hold on South American countries. Bolívar named President of Colombia (1819). Peru, Guatemala, Panama, and Santo Domingo proclaim independence from Spain (1821).

1820 Missouri Compromise—Missouri admitted as slave state but slavery barred in rest of Louisiana Purchase north of 36°30′ N.

1822 Greeks proclaim a republic and independence from Turkey. Turks invade Greece. Russia declares war on Turkey (1828). Greece also aided by France and Britain. War ends and Turks recognize Greek independence (1829). Brazil becomes independent of Portugal. Schubert's *Eighth Symphony* ("The Unfinished").

1823 U.S. Monroe Doctrine warns European nations not to interfere in Western Hemisphere.

1824 Mexico becomes a republic, three years after declaring independence from Spain. Beethoven's *Ninth Symphony.*

1825 First passenger-carrying railroad in England.

1830 French invade Algeria. Louis Philippe becomes "Citizen King" as revolution forces Charles X to abdicate. Mormon church formed in U.S. by Joseph Smith.

1831 Polish revolt against Russia fails. Belgium separates from the Netherlands. In U.S., Nat Turner leads unsuccessful slave rebellion.

1833 Slavery abolished in British Empire.

1834 Charles Babbage invents "analytical engine," precursor of computer. McCormick patents reaper.

1836 Boer farmers start "Great Trek"—Natal, Transvaal, and Orange Free State founded in South Africa. Mexican army besieges Texans in Alamo. Entire garrison, including Davy Crockett and Jim Bowie, wiped out. Texans gain independence from Mexico after winning Battle of San Jacinto. Dickens's *Pickwick Papers.*

1837 Victoria becomes Queen of Great Britain. Mob kills Elijah P. Lovejoy, Illinois abolitionist publisher.

1839 First Opium War (to 1842) between Britain and China, over importation of drug into China.

1840 Lower and Upper Canada united.

1841 U.S. President Harrison dies (April 4) one month after inauguration; John Tyler becomes first vice president to succeed to Presidency.

1843 Wagner's opera *The Flying Dutchman.*

1844 Democratic convention calls for annexation of Texas and acquisition of Oregon ("Fifty-four-forty-or-fight"). Five Chinese ports opened to U.S. ships. Samuel F. B. Morse patents telegraph.

1845 Congress adopts joint resolution for annexation of Texas. Edgar Allan Poe publishes *The Raven and Other Poems.*

1846 Failure of potato crop causes famine in Ireland. U.S. declares war on Mexico. California and New Mexico annexed by U.S. Brigham Young leads Mormons to Great Salt Lake. W. T. Morton uses ether as anesthetic. Sewing machine patented by Elias Howe. Frederick Douglass launches abolitionist newspaper *The North Star.*

1848 Revolt in Paris: Louis Philippe abdicates; Louis Napoleon elected President of French Republic. Revolutions in Vienna, Venice, Berlin, Milan, Rome, and Warsaw. Put down by royal troops in 1848-49. U.S.-Mexico War ends; Mexico cedes claims to Texas, California, Arizona, New

WAR OF 1812

British interference with American trade, impressment of American seamen, and "War Hawks" drive for western expansion lead to war. American attacks on Canada foiled; U.S. Commodore Perry wins battle of Lake Erie (1813). British capture and burn Washington (1814) but fail to take Fort McHenry at Baltimore. Andrew Jackson repulses assault on New Orleans after treaty of Ghent ends war (1815). War settles little but strengthens U.S. as independent nation.

Mexico, Utah, Nevada. U.S. treaty with Britain sets Oregon Territory boundary at 49th parallel. Karl Marx and Friedrich Engels's *Communist Manifesto*. Harriet Tubman escapes from slavery and joins the Underground Railroad.

1849 California gold rush begins.

1850 Henry Clay opens great debate on slavery, warns South against secession.

1851 Herman Melville's *Moby Dick*.

1852 South African Republic established. Louis Napoleon proclaims himself Napoleon III ("Second Empire"). Harriet Beecher Stowe's *Uncle Tom's Cabin*.

1853 Crimean War begins as Turkey declares war on Russia. Commodore Perry reaches Tokyo.

1854 Britain and France join Turkey in war on Russia. In U.S., Kansas-Nebraska Act permits local option on slavery; rioting and bloodshed. Japanese allow American trade. Antislavery men in Michigan form Republican Party. Tennyson's *Charge of the Light Brigade*. Thoreau's *Walden*.

1855 Armed clashes in Kansas between pro- and anti-slavery forces. Florence Nightingale nurses wounded in Crimea. Walt Whitman's *Leaves of Grass*.

1856 Flaubert's *Madame Bovary*.

1857 Supreme Court, in Dred Scott decision, rules that a slave is not a citizen. Financial crisis in Europe and U.S. Great Mutiny (Sepoy Rebellion) begins in India. India placed under crown rule as a result.

1858 Pro-slavery constitution rejected in Kansas. Abraham Lincoln makes strong antislavery speech in Springfield, Ill.: "...this Government cannot endure permanently half slave and half free." Lincoln-Douglas debates. First trans-atlantic telegraph cable completed by Cyrus W. Field.

1859 John Brown raids Harpers Ferry; is captured and hanged. Work begins on Suez Canal. Unification of Italy starts under leadership of Count Cavour, Sardinian premier. Joined by France in war against Austria. Edward Fitzgerald's *Rubaiyat of Omar Khayyam*. Charles Darwin's *Origin of Species*. J. S. Mill's *On Liberty*.

1861 U.S. Civil War begins as attempts at compromise fail. Congress creates Colorado, Dakota, and Nevada territories; adopts income tax; Lincoln inaugurated. Serfs emancipated in Russia. Pasteur's theory of germs. Independent Kingdom of Italy proclaimed under Sardinian King Victor Emmanuel II.

1863 French capture Mexico City; proclaim Archduke Maximilian of Austria emperor.

Dred Scott
(1795?–1858)

Abraham Lincoln
(1809–1865)

Charles Darwin
(1809–1882)

THE CIVIL WAR

Apart from the matter of slavery, the Civil War arose out of both the economic and political rivalry between an agrarian South and an industrial North and the issue of the right of states to secede from the Union.

1861 After South Carolina secedes **(Dec. 20, 1860)**, Mississippi, Florida, Alabama, Georgia, Louisiana, and Texas follow, forming the Confederate States of America, with Jefferson Davis as president **(Jan.-March)**. War begins as Confederates fire on Fort Sumter **(April 12)**. Lincoln calls for 75,000 volunteers. Southern ports blockaded by superior Union naval forces. Virginia, Arkansas, Tennessee, and North Carolina secede to complete 11-state Confederacy. Union army advancing on Richmond repulsed at first Battle of Bull Run **(July)**.

1862 Edwin M. Stanton named Secretary of War **(Jan.)**. Grantwins first important Union victory in West, at Fort Donelson; Nashville falls **(Feb.)**. Ironclads, Union's *Monitor* and Confederate's *Virginia (Merrimac)* duel at Hampton Roads **(March)**. New Orleans falls to Union fleet under Farragut; city occupied **(April)**. Grant's army escapes defeat at Shiloh. Memphis falls as Union gunboats control upper Mississippi **(June)**. Confederate General Robert E. Lee victorious at second Battle of Bull Run **(Aug.)**. Union army under McClellan halts Lee's attack on Washington in the Battle of Antietam **(Sept.)**. Lincoln removes McClellan for lack of aggressiveness. Burnside's drive on Richmond fails at Fredericksburg **(Dec.)**. Union forces under Rosecrans chase Bragg through Tennessee; battle of Murfreesboro **(Oct.-Jan. 1863)**.

1863 Lee defeats Hooker at Chancellorsville; "Stonewall" Jackson, Confederate general, dies **(May)**. Confederate invasion of Pennsylvania stopped at Gettysburg by George Meade—Lee loses 20,000 men—the greatest battle of the War **(July)**. It and the Union victory at Vicksburg mark the war's turning point. Union general George H. Thomas, the "Rock of Chickamauga," holds Bragg's forces on Georgia-Tennessee border **(Sept.)**. Sherman, Hooker, and Thomas drive Bragg back to Georgia. Tennessee restored to the Union **(Nov.)**.

1864 Ulysses S. Grant named commander-in-chief of Union forces **(March)**. In the Wilderness campaign, Grant forces Lee's Army of Northern Virginia back toward Richmond **(May-June)**. Sherman's Atlanta campaign and "march to the sea" **(May-Sept.)**. Farragut's victory at Mobile Bay **(Aug.)**. Hood's Confederate army defeated at Nashville. Sherman takes Savannah **(Dec.)**.

1865 Sheridan defeats Confederates at Five Forks; Confederates evacuate Richmond **(April)**. On **April 9**, Lee surrenders to Grant at Appomattox.

Robert E. Lee (1807–1870)

William Tecumseh Sherman (1820–1891)

Chief Joseph (c. 1840–1904)

Statue of Liberty

Samuel Clemens (Mark Twain) (1835–1910)

1865 Lincoln fatally shot at Ford's Theater by John Wilkes Booth. Vice President Johnson sworn as successor. Booth caught and dies of gunshot wounds; four conspirators are hanged. Joseph Lister begins antiseptic surgery. Gregor Mendel's *Law of Heredity.* Lewis Carroll's *Alice's Adventures in Wonderland.*

1866 Alfred Nobel invents dynamite (patented in Britain 1867). Seven Weeks' War: Austria defeated by Prussia and Italy.

1867 Austria-Hungary Dual Monarchy established. French leave Mexico; Maximilian executed. Dominion of Canada established. U.S. buys Alaska from Russia for $7,200,000. South African diamond field discovered. Volume I of Marx's *Das Kapital.* Strauss's *Blue Danube.*

1868 Revolution in Spain; Queen Isabella deposed, flees to France. In U.S., Fourteenth Amendment giving civil rights to blacks is ratified. Georgia under military government after legislature expels blacks.

1869 First U.S. transcontinental rail route completed. James Fisk and Jay Gould attempt to control gold market causes Black Friday panic. Suez Canal opened. Mendeleev's periodic table of elements.

1870 Franco-Prussian War (to 1871): Napoleon III capitulates at Sedan. Revolt in Paris; Third Republic proclaimed.

1871 France surrenders Alsace-Lorraine to Germany; war ends. German Empire proclaimed with Prussian King as Kaiser Wilhelm I. Fighting with Apaches begins in American West. Boss Tweed corruption exposed in New York. The Chicago Fire, with 250 deaths and $196-million damage. Stanley meets Livingston in Africa.

1872 Congress gives amnesty to most Confederates. Jules Verne's *Around the World in 80 Days.*

1873 Economic crisis in Europe. U.S. establishes gold standard.

1875 First Kentucky Derby.

1876 Sioux kill Gen. George A. Custer and 264 troopers at Little Big Horn River. Alexander Graham Bell patents the telephone.

1877 After Presidential election of 1876, Electoral Commission gives disputed Electoral College votes to Rutherford B. Hayes despite Tilden's popular majority. Russo-Turkish war (ends in 1878 with power of Turkey in Europe broken). Reconstruction ends in the American South. Thomas Edison patents phonograph. The Nez Perce leader Chief Joseph is forced to surrender. Tchaikovsky's *Swan Lake.*

1878 Congress of Berlin revises Treaty of San Stefano ending Russo-Turkish War; makes extensive redivision of southeastern Europe. First commercial telephone exchange opened in New Haven, Conn.

1880 U.S.-China treaty allows U.S. to restrict immigration of Chinese labor.

1881 President Garfield fatally shot by assassin; Vice President Arthur succeeds him. Charles J. Guiteau convicted and executed (in 1882).

1882 Terrorism in Ireland after land evictions. Britain invades and conquers Egypt. Germany, Austria, and Italy form Triple Alliance. In U.S., Congress adopts Chinese Exclusion Act. Rockefeller's Standard Oil Trust is first industrial monopoly. In Berlin, Robert Koch announces discovery of tuberculosis germ.

1883 Congress creates Civil Service Commission. Brooklyn Bridge and Metropolitan Opera House completed.

1885 British Gen. Charles G. "Chinese" Gordon killed at Khartoum in Egyptian Sudan.

1886 Bombing at Haymarket Square, Chicago, kills seven policemen and injures many others. Eight alleged anarchists accused—three imprisoned, one commits suicide, four hanged. (In 1893, Illinois Governor Altgeld, critical of trial, pardons three survivors.) Statue of Liberty dedicated. Geronimo, Apache Indian chief, surrenders.

1887 Queen Victoria's Golden Jubilee. Sir Arthur Conan Doyle's first Sherlock Holmes story, *A Study in Scarlet.*

1888 Historic March blizzard in Northeast U.S.—many perish, property damage exceeds $25 million. George Eastman's box camera (the Kodak). J. B. Dunlop invents pneumatic tire. Jack the Ripper murders in London.

1889 Second (Socialist) International founded in Paris. Indian Territory in Oklahoma opened to settlement. Thousands die in Johnstown, Pa., flood. Mark Twain's *A Connecticut Yankee in King Arthur's Court.* Eiffel Tower built for the Paris exposition.

1890 Congress votes Sherman Antitrust Act. Sitting Bull killed in Sioux uprising.

1892 Battle between steel strikers and Pinkerton guards at Homestead, Pa.; union defeated after militia intervenes. Silver mine strikers in Idaho fight non-union workers; U.S. troops dispatched. Diesel engine patented.

1894 Sino-Japanese War begins (ends in 1895 with China's defeat). In France, Capt. Alfred Dreyfus convicted on false treason charge (pardoned in 1906). In U.S., Jacob S. Coxey of Ohio leads "Coxey's Army" of unemployed on Washington. Eugene V. Debs calls general strike of rail workers to support Pullman Company strikers; strike broken, Debs jailed for six months. Thomas A. Edison's kinetoscope given first public showing in New York City.

1895 X-rays discovered by German physicist, Wilhelm Roentgen.

1896 Supreme Court's *Plessy v. Ferguson* decision—"separate but equal" doctrine. Alfred Nobel's will establishes prizes for peace, science, and literature. Marconi receives first wireless patent in Britain. William Jennings Bryan delivers "Cross of Gold" speech at Democratic Convention in Chicago. First modern Olympic games held in Athens, Greece.

1898 Chinese "Boxers," anti-foreign organization, established. They stage uprisings against Europeans in 1900; U.S. and other Western troops relieve Peking legations. Spanish-American War. Pierre and Marie Curie discover radium and polonium.

1899 Boer War (or South African War). Conflict between British and Boers (descendants of Dutch settlers of South Africa). Causes rooted in long-standing territorial disputes and in friction over political rights for English and other "uitlanders" following 1886 discovery of vast gold deposits in Transvaal. (British victorious as war ends in 1902.) Casualties: 5,774 British dead, about 4,000 Boers. Union of South Africa established in 1908 as confederation of colonies; becomes British dominion in 1910.

Marie Curie (1867–1934)

Sigmund Freud (1856–1939)

1900–1999 (C.E.)

1900 Hurricane ravages Galveston, Tex.; 6,000 drown. Fauvist movement in painting begins, led by Henri Matisse. Sigmund Freud's *The Interpretation of Dreams.*

1901 Queen Victoria dies, and is succeeded by her son, Edward VII. As President McKinley begins second term, he is shot fatally by anarchist Leon Czolgosz. Theodore Roosevelt sworn in as successor.

1902 Enrico Caruso's first gramophone recording.

1903 Wright brothers, Orville and Wilbur, fly first powered, controlled, heavier-than-air plane at Kitty Hawk, N.C. Henry Ford organizes Ford Motor Company.

1904 Russo-Japanese War—competition for Korea and Manchuria: In 1905, Port Arthur surrenders to Japanese and Russia suffers other defeats; President Roosevelt mediates Treaty of Portsmouth, N.H., ending war with concessions for Japan. *Entente Cordiale:* Britain and France settle their international differences. General theory of radioactivity by Rutherford and Soddy. New York City subway opened.

1905 General strike in Russia; first workers' soviet set up in St. Petersburg. Sailors on battleship *Potemkin* mutiny; reforms including first Duma (parliament) established by Czar's "October Manifesto." Albert Einstein's special theory of relativity and other key theories in physics. Franz Lehar's *Merry Widow.*

1906 San Francisco earthquake and three-day fire; 500 dead. Roald Amundsen, Norwegian explorer, fixes magnetic North Pole.

1907 Second Hague Peace Conference, of 46 nations, adopts 10 conventions on rules of war. Financial panic of 1907 in U.S. Mahler begins work on "Song of the Earth."

1908 Earthquake kills 150,000 in southern Italy and Sicily. U.S. Supreme Court, in Danbury Hatters' case, outlaws secondary union boycotts.

Henri Matisse (1869–1954)

Albert Einstein (1879–1955)

SPANISH-AMERICAN WAR (1898–1899)

War fires stoked by "jingo journalism" as American people support Cuban rebels against Spain. American business sees economic gain in Cuban trade and resources and American power zones in Latin America. Outstanding events: Submarine mine sinks U.S. battleship *Maine* in Havana Harbor **(Feb. 15)**; 260 killed; responsibility never fixed. Congress declares independence of Cuba **(Apr. 19)**. Spain declares war on U.S. **(Apr. 24)**; Congress **(Apr. 25)** formally declares nation has been at war with Spain since Apr. 21. Commodore George Dewey wins seven-hour battle of Manila Bay **(May 1)**. Spanish fleet destroyed off Santiago, Cuba **(July 3)**; city surrenders **(July 17)**. Treaty of Paris (ratified by Senate 1899) ends war. U.S. given Guam and Puerto Rico and agrees to pay Spain $20 million for Philippines. Cuba independent of Spain; under U.S. military control for three years until **May 20, 1902.** Yellow fever is eradicated and political reforms achieved.

W. E. B. Du Bois (1868–1963)

Woodrow Wilson (1856–1924)

Vladimir Lenin (1870–1924)

1909 North Pole reached by American explorers Robert E. Peary and Matthew Henson. The National Association for the Advancement of Colored People is founded in New York by prominent black and white intellectuals and led by W. E. B. Du Bois.

1910 Boy Scouts of America incorporated.

1911 First use of aircraft as offensive weapon in Turkish-Italian War. Italy defeats Turks and annexes Tripoli and Libya. Chinese Republic proclaimed after revolution overthrows Manchu dynasty. Sun Yat-sen named president. Mexican Revolution: Porfirio Diaz, president since 1877, replaced by Francisco Madero. Triangle Shirtwaist Company fire in New York; 145 killed. Richard Strauss's *Der Rosenkavalier.* Irving Berlin's *Alexander's Ragtime Band.* Amundsen reaches South Pole.

1912 Balkan Wars (1912–13) resulting from territorial disputes: Turkey defeated by alliance of Bulgaria, Serbia, Greece, and Montenegro; London peace treaty (1913) partitions most of European Turkey among the victors. In second war (1913), Bulgaria attacks Serbia and Greece and is defeated after Romania intervenes and Turks recapture Adrianople. *Titanic* sinks on maiden voyage; over 1,500 drown.

1913 Suffragettes demonstrate in London. Garment workers strike in New York and Boston; win pay raise and shorter hours. Sixteenth Amendment (income tax) and 17th (popular election of U.S. senators) adopted. Bill creating U.S. Federal Reserve System becomes law. Stravinsky's *The Rite of Spring.* Woodrow Wilson becomes 28th U.S. President.

1914 World War I begins. Panama Canal officially opened. Congress sets up Federal Trade Commission, passes Clayton Antitrust Act. U.S. Marines occupy Veracruz, Mexico, intervening in civil war to protect American interests.

1915 U.S. protests German submarine actions and British blockade of Germany. U.S. banks lend $500 million to France and Britain. D. W. Griffith's film *Birth of a Nation.* Albert Einstein's *General Theory of Relativity.* Genocide of estimated 600,000 Armenians by Turkish soldiers.

1916 Congress expands armed forces. Tom Mooney arrested for San Francisco bombing (pardoned in1939). Pershing fails in raid into Mexico in quest of rebel Pancho Villa. U.S. buys Virgin Islands from Denmark for $25 million. President Wilson re-elected with "he kept us out of war" slogan. "Black Tom" explosion at munitions dock in Jersey City, N.J., $40,000,000 damages; traced to German saboteurs. Margaret Sanger opens first birth control clinic. Easter Rebellion in Ireland put down by British troops.

WORLD WAR I (1914–1918)

Imperial, territorial, and economic rivalries lead to the "Great War" between the Central Powers (Austria-Hungary, Germany, Bulgaria, and Turkey) and the Allies (U.S., Britain, France, Russia, Belgium, Serbia, Greece, Romania, Montenegro, Portugal, Italy, Japan). About 10 million combatants killed, 20 million wounded.

1914 Austrian Archduke Francis Ferdinand and wife assassinated in Sarajevo by Serbian nationalist, Gavrilo Princip **(June 28).** Austria declares war on Serbia **(July 28).** Germany declares war on Russia **(Aug. 1),** on France **(Aug. 3),** invades Belgium **(Aug. 4).** Britain declares war on Germany **(Aug. 4).** Germans defeat Russians in Battle of Tannenberg on Eastern Front **(Aug.).** First Battle of the Marne **(Sept.).** German drive stopped 25 miles from Paris. By end of year, war on the Western Front is "positional" in the trenches.

1915 German submarine blockade of Great Britain begins **(Feb.).** Dardanelles Campaign—British land in Turkey **(April),** withdraw from Gallipoli **(Dec. to Jan. 1916).** Germans use gas at second Battle of Ypres **(April–May).** ***Lusitania*** sunk by German submarine—1,198 lost, including 128 Americans **(May 7).** On Eastern Front, German and Austrian "great offensive" conquers all of Poland and Lithuania; Russians lose 1 million men (by **Sept. 6**) "Great Fall Offensive" by Allies results in little change from 1914 **(Sept.–Oct.).** Britain and France declare war on Bulgaria **(Oct. 14).**

1916 Battle of Verdun—Germans and French each lose about 350,000 men **(Feb.).** Extended submarine warfare begins **(March).** British-German sea battle of Jutland **(May);** British lose more ships, but German fleet never ventures forth again. On Eastern front, the Brusilov offensive demoralizes Russians, costs them 1 million men **(June–Sept.).** Battle of the Somme—British lose over 400,000; French, 200,000; Germans, about 450,000; all with no strategic results **(July–Nov.).** Romania declares war on Austria-Hungary **(Aug. 27).** Bucharest captured **(Dec.).**

1917 U.S. declares war on Germany **(April 6).** Submarine warfare at peak **(April).** On Italian Front, Battle of Caporetto—Italians retreat, losing 600,000 prisoners and deserters **(Oct.-Dec.).** On Western Front, Battles of Arras, Champagne, Ypres (third battle), etc. First large British tank attack **(Nov.).** U.S. declares war on Austria-Hungary **(Dec. 7).** Armistice between new Russian Bolshevik government and Germans **(Dec. 15).**

1918 Great offensive by Germans **(March-June).** Americans' first important battle role at Château-Thierry—as they and French stop German advance **(June).** Second Battle of the Marne **(July-Aug.)**—start of Allied offensive at Amiens, St. Mihiel, etc. Battles of the Argonne and Ypres panic German leadership **(Sept.-Oct.).** British offensive in Palestine **(Sept.).** Germans ask for armistice **(Oct. 4).** British armistice with Turkey **(Oct.).** German Kaiser abdicates **(Nov.).** Hostilities cease on Western Front **(Nov. 11).**

1917 First U.S. combat troops in France as U.S. declares war **(April 6).** Russian Revolution—climax of long unrest under czars. February Revolution—Czar forced to abdicate, liberal government created. Kerensky becomes prime minister and forms provisional government **(July).** In October Revolution, Bolsheviks seize power in armed coup d'état led by Lenin and Trotsky. Kerensky flees. Revolutionaries execute the czar and his family (1918). Reds set up Third International in Moscow (1919). Balfour Declaration promises Jewish homeland in Palestine. Sigmund Freud's *Introduction to Psychoanalysis.*

1918 Russian Civil War between Reds (Bolsheviks) and Whites (anti-Bolsheviks); Reds win in 1920. Allied troops (U.S., British, French) intervene (**March);** leave in 1919. Japanese hold Vladivostok until 1922. World-wide influenza epidemic strikes; by 1920, nearly 20 million are dead. In U.S. alone, 500,000 perish.

1919 Third International (Comintern) establishes Soviet control over international Communist movements. Paris peace conference. Versailles Treaty, incorporating Woodrow Wilson's draft Covenant of League of Nations, signed by Allies and Germany; rejected by U.S. Senate. Congress formally ends war in 1921. Eighteenth (Prohibition) Amendment adopted. Alcock and Brown make first trans-Atlantic non-stop flight. Mahatma Gandhi initiates satyagraha ("truth force") campaigns, beginning his nonviolent resistance movement against British rule in India.

1920 League of Nations holds first meeting at Geneva, Switzerland. U.S. Dept. of Justice "red hunt" nets thousands of radicals; aliens deported. Women's suffrage (19th) amendment ratified. First Agatha Christie mystery. Sinclair Lewis's *Main Street.*

1921 Reparations Commission fixes German liability at 132 billion gold marks. German inflation begins. Major treaties signed at Washington Disarmament Conference limit naval tonnage and pledge to respect territorial integrity of China. Irish Free State formed in southern Ireland as self-governing dominion of British Empire. In U.S., Nicola Sacco and Bartolomeo Vanzetti, Italian-born anarchists, convicted of armed robbery murder; case stirs world-wide protests; they are executed in 1927.

1922 Mussolini marches on Rome; forms Fascist government. Irish Free State officially proclaimed.

1923 Adolf Hitler's "Beer Hall Putsch" in Munich fails; in 1924 he is sentenced to five years in prison where he writes *Mein Kampf;* released after eight months. Occupation of Ruhr by French and Belgian troops to enforce reparations payments. Widespread Ku Klux Klan violence in U.S. George Gershwin's *Rhapsody in Blue.* Bessie Smith, known as "the Empress of the Blues," makes her first record. Irish poet William Butler Yeats, considered one of the greatest literary figures of the 20th century, wins Nobel Prize in Literature.

1924 Death of Lenin; Stalin wins power struggle, rules as Soviet dictator until death in 1953. Italian Fascists murder Socialist leader Giacomo Matteotti. Interior Secretary Albert B. Fall and oilmen Harry Sinclair and Edward L. Doheny are charged with conspiracy and bribery in the Teapot Dome scandal, involving fraudulent leases of naval oil reserves. In 1931, Fall is sentenced to year in prison; Doheny and Sinclair acquitted of bribery. Nathan Leopold and Richard Loeb convicted in "thrill killing" of Bobby Franks in Chicago; defended by Clarence Darrow; sentenced to life imprisonment. (Loeb killed by fellow convict in 1936; Leopold paroled in 1958, dies in 1971.) Robert Frost wins first of four Pulitzers.

1925 Nellie Tayloe Ross elected governor of Wyoming; first woman governor elected in U.S. Locarno conferences seek to secure European peace by mutual guarantees. John T. Scopes convicted and fined for teaching evolution in a public school in Tennessee "Monkey Trial"; sentence set aside. John Logie Baird, Scottish inventor, transmits human features by television. Adolf Hitler publishes Volume I of *Mein Kampf.*

1926 General strike in Britain brings nation's activities to standstill. U.S. marines dispatched to Nicaragua during revolt; they remain until 1933. Gertrude Ederle of U.S. is first woman to swim English Channel. Ernest Hemingway's *The Sun Also Rises.*

1927 German economy collapses. Socialists riot in Vienna; general strike follows acquittal of Nazis for political murder. Trotsky expelled from Russian Communist Party. Charles A. Lindbergh flies first successful solo non-stop flight from New York to Paris. Ruth Snyder and Judd Gray convicted of murder of Albert Snyder; they are executed at Sing Sing

Mahatma Gandhi (1869–1948)

Benito Mussolini (1883–1945)

Joseph Stalin (1879–1953)

Bessie Smith (1894–1937)

William Butler Yeats (1865–1939)

Dorothea Lange's photo "Migrant Mother" (1936) documented the Great Depression (1929–1940)

Franklin Delano Roosevelt (1882–1945)

Adolf Hitler (1889–1945)

prison in 1928. *The Jazz Singer,* with Al Jolson, first part-talking motion picture.

1928 Kellogg-Briand Pact, outlawing war, signed in Paris by 65 nations. Alexander Fleming discovers penicillin. Richard E. Byrd starts expedition to Antarctic; returns in 1930.

1929 Trotsky expelled from U.S.S.R. Lateran Treaty establishes independent Vatican City. In U.S., stock market prices collapse, with U.S. securities losing $26 billion—first phase of Depression and world economic crisis. St. Valentine's Day gangland massacre in Chicago.

1930 Britain, U.S., Japan, France, and Italy sign naval disarmament treaty. Nazis gain in German elections. Cyclotron developed by Ernest O. Lawrence, U.S. physicist.

1931 Spain becomes a republic with overthrow of King Alfonso XIII. German industrialists finance 800,000-strong Nazi party. British parliament enacts statute of Westminster, legalizing dominion equality with Britain. Mukden Incident begins Japanese occupation of Manchuria. In U.S., Hoover proposes one-year moratorium of war debts. Harold C. Urey discovers heavy hydrogen. Gangster Al Capone sentenced to 11 years in prison for tax evasion (freed in 1939; dies in 1947).

1932 Nazis lead in German elections with 230 Reichstag seats. Famine in U.S.S.R. In U.S., Congress sets up Reconstruction Finance Corporation to stimulate economy. Veterans march on Washington—most leave after Senate rejects payment of cash bonuses; others removed by troops under Douglas MacArthur. U.S. protests Japanese aggression in Manchuria. Amelia Earhart is first woman to fly Atlantic solo. Charles A. Lindbergh's baby son kidnapped, killed. (Bruno Richard Hauptmann arrested in 1934, convicted in 1935, executed in 1936.)

1933 Hitler appointed German chancellor, gets dictatorial powers. Reichstag fire in Berlin; Nazi terror begins. Germany and Japan withdraw from League of Nations. Giuseppe Zangara executed for attempted assassination of President-elect Roosevelt in which Chicago Mayor Cermak is fatally shot. Roosevelt inaugurated ("the only thing we have to fear is fear itself"); launches New Deal. Prohibition repealed. U.S.S.R. recognized by U.S.

1934 Chancellor Dollfuss of Austria assassinated by Nazis. Hitler becomes Führer. U.S.S.R. admitted to League of Nations. Dionne sisters, first quintuplets to survive beyond infancy, born in Canada.

1935 Saar incorporated into Germany after plebiscite. Nazis repudiate Versailles Treaty, introduce compulsory military service. Mussolini invades Ethiopia; League of Nations invokes sanctions. Roosevelt opens second phase of New Deal in U.S., calling for social security, better housing, equitable taxation, and farm assistance. Huey Long assassinated in Louisiana.

THE HOLOCAUST (1933–1945)

"Holocaust" is the term describing the Nazi annihilation of about 6 million Jews (two thirds of the pre-World War II European Jewish population), including 4,500,000 from Russia, Poland, and the Baltic; 750,000 from Hungary and Romania; 290,000 from Germany and Austria; 105,000 from The Netherlands; 90,000 from France; 54,000 from Greece.

The Holocaust was unique in its being *genocide*—the systematic destruction of a people solely because of religion, race, ethnicity, nationality, or sexual preference—on an unmatched scale. Along with the Jews, another 9 to 10 million people—Gypsies, Slavs (Poles, Ukrainians, and Belarussians), homosexuals, and the disabled—were exterminated.

1933 Hitler named German Chancellor **(Jan.)**. Dachau, first concentration camp, established **(March)**. Boycotts against Jews begin **(April)**.

1935 Anti-Semitic Nuremberg Laws passed by Reichstag; Jews lose citizenship and civil rights **(Sept.)**.

1937 Buchenwald concentration camp opens **(July)**.

1938 Extension of anti-Semitic laws to Austria after annexation **(March)**. *Kristallnacht* (Night of Broken Glass)—anti-Semitic riots and destruction of Jewish institutions in Germany and Austria **(Nov. 9)**. 26,000 Jews sent to concentration camps; Jewish children expelled from schools **(Nov. 9-10)**. Expropriation of Jewish property and businesses **(Dec.)**.

1940 As war continues, Einsatzgruppen (mobile killing squads) follow German army into conquered lands, rounding up and massacring Jews and other "undesirables."

1941 Goering instructs Heydrich to carry out the "final solution to the Jewish question" **(July 31)**. Deportation of German Jews begins; massacres of Jews in Odessa and Kiev **(Nov.)**; and in Riga and Vilna **(Dec.)**.

1942 Mass killings using Zyklon-B begin at Auschwitz-Birkenau **(Jan.)**. Nazi leaders attend Wannsee Conference to coordinate the "final solution." **(Jan. 20)**. 100,000 Jews from Warsaw Ghetto deported to Treblinka death camp **(July)**.

1943 Warsaw Ghetto uprisings **(Jan.** and **April)**; Ghetto exterminated **(May)**.

1944 476,000 Hungarian Jews sent to Auschwitz **(May-June)**. D-day **(June 6)**. Soviet Army liberates Maidanek death camp **(July)**. Nazis try to hide evidence of death camps **(Nov.)**.

1945 As Allies advance, Nazis force concentration camp inmates on death marches. Americans liberate Buchenwald and British liberate Bergen-Belsen camps **(April)**. Nuremberg War Crimes Trial **(Nov. 1945** to **Oct. 1946)**.

1936 Germans occupy Rhineland. Italy annexes Ethiopia. Rome-Berlin Axis proclaimed (Japan to join in 1940). Trotsky exiled to Mexico. King George V dies; succeeded by son, Edward VIII, who soon abdicated to marry American-born divorcée, and is succeeded by brother, George VI. Spanish civil war begins. (Franco's fascist forces defeat Loyalist forces by 1939, when Madrid falls.) War between China and Japan begins, to continue through World War II. Japan and Germany sign anti-Comintern pact; joined by Italy in 1937.

1937 Hitler repudiates war guilt clause of Versailles Treaty; continues to build German power. Italy withdraws from League of Nations. U.S. gunboat *Panay* sunk by Japanese in Yangtze River. Japan invades China, conquers most of coastal area. Amelia Earhart lost somewhere in Pacific on round-the-world flight. Picasso's *Guernica* mural.

1938 Hitler marches into Austria; political and geographical union of Germany and Austria proclaimed. Munich Pact—Britain, France, and Italy agree to let Germany partition Czechoslovakia. Douglas "Wrong-Way" Corrigan flies from New York to Dublin.

1939 Germany occupies Bohemia and Moravia; renounces pacts with Poland and England and concludes 10-year non-aggression pact with U.S.S.R. Russo-Finnish War begins; Finns to lose one-tenth of territory in 1940 peace treaty. World War II begins. In U.S., Roosevelt submits $1,319-million defense budget, proclaims U.S. neutrality, and declares limited emergency. Einstein writes FDR about feasibility of atomic bomb. New York World's Fair opens.

1940 Churchill becomes Britain's Prime Minister. Trotsky assassinated in Mexico. Estonia, Latvia, and Lithuania annexed by U.S.S.R. U.S. trades 50 destroyers for leases on British bases in Western Hemisphere. Selective Service Act signed.

Pablo Picasso (1881–1973)

Amelia Earhart (1897–1937)

WORLD WAR II (1939–1945)

Axis powers (Germany, Italy, Japan, Hungary, Romania, Bulgaria) *vs.* Allies (U.S., Britain, France, U.S.S.R., Australia, Belgium, Brazil, Canada, China, Denmark, Greece, Netherlands, New Zealand, Norway, Poland, South Africa, Yugoslavia).

1939 Germany invades Poland and annexes Danzig; Britain and France give Hitler ultimatum **(Sept. 1)**, declare war **(Sept. 3)**. Disabled German pocket battleship *Admiral Graf Spee* blown up off Montevideo, Uruguay, on Hitler's orders **(Dec. 17)**. Limited activity ("Sitzkrieg") on Western Front.

1940 Nazis invade Netherlands, Belgium, and Luxembourg **(May 10)**. Chamberlain resigns as Britain's prime minister; Churchill takes over **(May 10)**. Germans cross French frontier **(May 12)** using air/tank/infantry "Blitzkrieg" tactics. Dunkerque evacuation—about 335,000 out of 400,000 Allied soldiers rescued from Belgium by British civilian and naval craft **(May 26-June 3)**. Italy declares war on France and Britain; invades France **(June 10)**. Germans enter Paris; city undefended **(June 14)**. France and Germany sign armistice at Compiègne **(June 22)**. Nazis bomb Coventry, England **(Nov. 14)**.

1941 Germans launch attacks in Balkans. Yugoslavia surrenders—General Mihajlovic continues guerrilla warfare; Tito leads left-wing guerrillas **(April 17)**. Nazi tanks enter Athens; remnants of British Army quit Greece **(April 27)**. Hitler attacks Russia **(June 22)**. Atlantic Charter—FDR and Churchill agree on war aims **(Aug. 14)**. Japanese attacks on Pearl Harbor, Philippines, Guam force U.S. into war; U.S. Pacific fleet crippled **(Dec. 7)**. U.S. and Britain declare war on Japan. Germany and Italy declare war on U.S.; Congress declares war on those countries **(Dec. 11)**.

1942 British surrender Singapore to Japanese **(Feb. 15)**. Roosevelt orders Japanese and Japanese Americans in western U.S. to be exiled to "relocation centers," many for the remainder of the war **(Feb. 19)**. U.S. forces on Bataan peninsula in Philippines surrender **(April 9)**. U.S. and Filipino troops on Corregidor island in Manila Bay surrender to Japanese **(May 6)**. Village of Lidice in Czechoslovakia razed by Nazis **(June 10)**. U.S. and Britain land in French North Africa **(Nov. 8)**.

1943 Casablanca Conference—Churchill and FDR agree on unconditional surrender goal **(Jan. 14-24)**. German 6th Army surrenders at Stalingrad—turning point of war in Russia **(Feb. 1-2)**. Remnants of Nazis trapped on Cape Bon, ending war in Africa **(May 12)**. Mussolini deposed; Badoglio named premier **(July 25)**. Allied troops land on Italian mainland after conquest of Sicily **(Sept. 3)**. Italy surrenders **(Sept. 8)**. Nazis seize Rome **(Sept. 10)**. Cairo Conference: FDR, Churchill, Chiang Kai-shek pledge defeat of Japan, free Korea **(Nov. 22-26)**. Teheran Conference: FDR, Churchill, Stalin agree on invasion plans **(Nov. 28-Dec. 1)**.

1944 U.S. and British troops land at Anzio on west Italian coast and hold beachhead **(Jan. 22)**. U.S. and British troops enter Rome **(June 4)**. D-Day—Allies launch Normandy invasion **(June 6)**. Hitler wounded in bomb plot **(July 20)**. Paris liberated **(Aug. 25)**. Athens freed by Allies **(Oct. 13)**. Americans invade Philippines **(Oct. 20)**. Germans launch counteroffensive in Belgium—Battle of Bulge **(Dec. 16)**.

1945 Yalta Agreement signed by FDR, Churchill, Stalin—establishes basis for occupation of Germany, returns to Soviet Union lands taken by Germany and Japan; U.S.S.R. agrees to friendship pact with China **(Feb. 11)**. Mussolini killed at Lake Como **(April 28)**. Admiral Doenitz takes command in Germany; suicide of Hitler announced **(May 1)**. Berlin falls **(May 2)**. V-E Day—Germany signs unconditional surrender terms at Rheims **(May 7)**. Potsdam Conference—Truman, Churchill, Atlee (after **July 28**), Stalin establish council of foreign ministers to prepare peace treaties; plan German postwar government and reparations **(July 17-Aug. 2)**. A-bomb dropped on Hiroshima by U.S. **(Aug. 6)**. U.S.S.R. declares war on Japan **(Aug. 8)**. Nagasaki hit by A-bomb **(Aug. 9)**. Japan surrenders **(Aug. 14)**. V-J Day—Japanese sign surrender terms aboard battleship *Missouri* **(Sept. 2)**.

Winston Churchill (1874–1965)

Yalta Conference

Anne Frank (1929–1945)

Chuck Yeager (1923–)

Harry S. Truman (1884–1972)

1941 Japanese surprise attack on U.S. fleet at Pearl Harbor brings U.S. into World War II. Manhattan Project (atomic bomb research) begins. Roosevelt enunciates "four freedoms," signs Lend-Lease Act, declares national emergency, promises aid to U.S.S.R.

1942 Nazi leaders attend Wannsee Conference to coordinate the "final solution to the Jewish question," the systematic genocide of Jews known as the Holocaust. Declaration of United Nations signed in Washington. Women's military services established. Enrico Fermi achieves nuclear chain reaction. More than 120,000 Japanese and persons of Japanese ancestry living in western U.S. moved to "relocation centers," some for the duration of the war. Coconut Grove nightclub fire in Boston kills 491.

1943 President freezes prices, salaries, and wages to prevent inflation. Income tax withholding introduced.

1944 G.I. Bill of Rights enacted. Bretton Woods Conference creates International Monetary Fund and World Bank. Dumbarton Oaks Conference—U.S., British Commonwealth, and U.S.S.R. propose establishment of United Nations.

1945 Yalta Conference (Roosevelt, Churchill, Stalin) plans final defeat of Germany **(Feb.)**. Germany surrenders **(May 7)**. San Francisco Conference establishes U.N. **(April–June)**. FDR dies (April 12). Potsdam Conference (Truman, Churchill, Stalin) establishes basis of German reconstruction **(July–Aug.)**. Atomic bombs dropped on Japanese cities of Hiroshima **(Aug. 6)** and Nagasaki **(Aug. 8)** by U.S. Japan signs surrender **(Sept. 2)**.

1946 First meeting of U.N. General Assembly opens in London **(Jan. 10)**. League of Nations dissolved **(April)**. Italy abolishes monarchy **(June)**. Verdict in Nuremberg war trial: 12 Nazi leaders (including 1 tried in absentia) sentenced to hang; 7 imprisoned; 3 acquitted **(Oct. 1)**. Goering commits suicide a few hours before 10 other Nazis are executed **(Oct. 15)**. Winston Churchill's "Iron Curtain" speech warns of Soviet expansion.

1947 Britain nationalizes coal mines **(Jan. 1)**. Peace treaties for Italy, Romania, Bulgaria, Hungary, Finland signed in Paris **(Feb. 10)**. Soviet Union rejects U.S. plan for U.N. atomic-energy control **(March 4)**. Truman Doctrine proposed—the first significant U.S. attempt to "contain" communist expansion **(March 12)**. Marshall Plan for European recovery proposed—a coordinated program to help European nations recover from ravages of war **(June)**. (By 1951, this "European Recovery Program" had cost $11 billion.) India and Pakistan gain independence from Britain **(Aug. 15)**. U.S. Air Force pilot Chuck Yeager becomes first person to break the sound barrier **(Oct. 14)**. Anne Frank's *The Diary of a Young Girl* published.

1948 Gandhi assassinated in New Delhi by Hindu fanatic **(Jan. 30)**. Communists seize power in Czechoslovakia **(Feb. 23-25)**. Burma and Ceylon granted independence by Britain. Organization of American States (OAS) Charter signed at Bogotá, Colombia **(April 30)**. Nation of Israel proclaimed; British end Mandate at midnight; Arab armies attack **(May 14)**. Berlin airlift begins **(June 21)**; ends **May 12, 1949.** Stalin and Tito break **(June 28)**. Independent Republic of Korea is proclaimed, following election supervised by U.N. **(Aug. 15)**. Verdict in Japanese war trial: Tojo and six others hanged **(Dec. 23)**; 18 imprisoned **(Nov. 12)**. United States of Indonesia established as Dutch and Indonesians settled conflict **(Dec. 27)**. Alger Hiss, former U.S. State Department official, indicted on perjury charges after denying passing secret documents to communist spy ring. Convicted in second trial (1950) and sentenced to five-year prison term. Tennessee Williams' *A Streetcar Named Desire* wins Pulitzer.

1949 Cease-fire in Palestine **(Jan. 7)**. Truman proposes Point Four Program to help world's less developed areas **(Jan. 20)**. Israel signs armistice with Egypt **(Feb. 24)**. Start of North Atlantic Treaty Organization (NATO)—treaty signed by 12 nations **(April 4)**. German Federal Republic (West Germany) established **(Sept. 21)**. Truman discloses Soviet Union has set off atomic explosion **(Sept. 23)**. Communist People's Republic of China formally proclaimed by Chairman Mao Zedong. **(Oct. 1)**.

1950 Truman orders development of hydrogen bomb **(Jan. 31)**. Korean War. Assassination attempt on President Truman by Puerto Rican nationalists **(Nov. 1)**. Brink's robbery in Boston; almost $3 million stolen **(Jan. 17)**.

1951 Six nations agree to Schuman Plan to pool European coal and steel **(March 19)**—in effect **Feb. 10, 1953.** Julius and Ethel Rosenberg sentenced to death for passing atomic secrets to Russians **(March)**. Japanese peace treaty signed in San Francisco by 49 nations **(Sept. 8).** Color television introduced in U.S.

1952 George VI dies; his daughter becomes Elizabeth II **(Feb. 6).** NATO conference approves European army **(Feb.).** AEC announces "satisfactory" experiments in hydrogen-weapons research; eyewitnesses tell of blasts near Enewetak **(Nov.).**

1953 Gen. Dwight D. Eisenhower inaugurated President of United States **(Jan. 20).** Stalin dies **(March 5).** Malenkov becomes Soviet Premier; Beria, Minister of Interior; Molotov, Foreign Minister **(March 6).** Dag Hammarskjöld begins term as U.N. Secretary-General **(April 10).** Edmund Hillary of New Zealand and Tenzing Norgay of Nepal reach top of Mt. Everest **(May 29).** East Berliners rise against Communist rule; quelled by tanks **(June 17).** Egypt becomes republic ruled by military junta **(June 18).** Julius and Ethel Rosenberg executed in Sing Sing prison **(June 19).** Korean armistice signed **(July 27).** Moscow announces explosion of hydrogen bomb **(Aug. 20).** Ernest Hemingway wins Pulitzer for *The Old Man and The Sea.*

1954 First atomic submarine *Nautilus,* launched **(Jan. 21).** Five U.S. Congressmen shot on floor of House as Puerto Rican nationalists fire from spectators' gallery; all five recover **(March 1).** *Army* v. *McCarthy* inquiry—Senate subcommittee report blames both sides **(Apr. 22-June 17).** Dien Bien Phu, French military outpost in Vietnam, falls to Vietminh army **(May 7).** U.S. Supreme Court (in *Brown* v. *Board of Education of Topeka*) unanimously bans racial segregation in public schools **(May 17).** Eisenhower launches world atomic pool without Soviet Union **(Sept. 6).** Eight-nation Southeast Asia defense treaty (SEATO) signed at Manila **(Sept. 8).** West Germany is granted sovereignty, admitted to NATO and Western European Union **(Oct. 23).** Dr. Jonas Salk starts inoculating children against polio. Algerian War of Independence against France begins **(Nov.);** France struggles to maintain colonial rule until 1962 when it agrees to Algeria's independence. William Faulkner's *A Fable* wins Pulitzer.

1955 Nikolai A. Bulganin becomes Soviet Premier, replacing Malenkov **(Feb. 8).** Churchill resigns; Anthony Eden succeeds him **(April 6).** Federal Republic of West Germany becomes a sovereign state **(May 5).** Warsaw Pact, east European mutual defense agreement, signed **(May 14).** Argentina ousts Perón **(Sept. 19).** President Eisenhower suffers coronary thrombosis in Denver **(Sept. 24).** Martin Luther King, Jr., leads black boycott of Montgomery, Ala., bus system **(Dec. 1);** desegregated service begun **(Dec. 21).** AFL and CIO become one organization—AFL-CIO **(Dec. 5).** Tennessee Williams's *Cat on a Hot Tin Roof* wins Pulitzer.

1956 Nikita Khrushchev, First Secretary of U.S.S.R. Communist Party, denounces Stalin's excesses **(Feb. 24).** First aerial H-bomb tested over Namu islet, Bikini Atoll—10 million tons TNT equivalent **(May 21).** Workers' uprising against Communist rule in Poznan, Poland, is crushed **(June 28-30).** Egypt takes control of Suez Canal **(July 26).** Israel launches attack on Egypt's Sinai peninsula and drives toward Suez Canal **(Oct. 29).** British and French invade Egypt at Port Said **(Nov. 5).** Cease-fire forced by U.S. pressure stops British, French, and Israeli advance **(Nov. 6).** Revolt starts in Hungary—Soviet troops and tanks crush anti-Communist rebellion **(Nov.).** Ingmar Bergman's *The Seventh Seal.* Woody Guthrie composes "This Land is Your Land."

1957 Eisenhower Doctrine calls for aid to Mideast countries which resist armed aggression from Communist-controlled nations **(Jan. 5).** Eisenhower sends troops to Little Rock, Ark., to quell mob and protect school integration **(Sept. 24).** Russians launch *Sputnik I,* first earth-orbiting satellite—the Space Age begins **(Oct. 4).**

Atomic Bomb

Dwight D. Eisenhower (1890–1969)

Woody Guthrie (1912–1967)

Martin Luther King, Jr. (1929–1968)

KOREAN WAR (1950–1953)

1950 North Korean Communist forces invade South Korea **(June 25).** U.N. calls for cease-fire and asks U.N. members to assist South Korea **(June 27).** Truman orders U.S. forces into Korea **(June 27).** North Koreans capture Seoul **(June 28).** Gen. Douglas MacArthur designated commander of unified U.N. forces **(July 8).** Pusan Beachhead—U.N. forces counterattack and capture Seoul **(Aug.-Sept.),** capture Pyongyang, North Korean capital **(Oct.).** Chinese Communists enter war **(Oct. 26),** force U.N. retreat toward 39th parallel **(Dec.).**

1951 Gen. Matthew B. Ridgeway replaces MacArthur after he threatens Chinese with massive retaliation **(April 11).** Armistice negotiations **(July)** continue with interruptions until **June 1953.**

1953 Armistice signed **(July 27).** Chinese troops withdraw from North Korea **(Oct. 26, 1958),** but over 200 violations of armistice noted to **1959.**

Fidel Castro
(1926–)

Robert Frost
(1874–1963)

1958 Army's Jupiter-C rocket fires first U.S. earth satellite, *Explorer I,* into orbit **(Jan. 31).** Egypt and Syria merge into United Arab Republic **(Feb. 1).** European Economic Community (Common Market) established by Rome Treaty becomes effective **Jan. 1, 1958.** Khrushchev becomes Premier of Soviet Union as Bulganin resigns **(Mar. 27).** Gen. Charles de Gaulle becomes French premier **(June 1),** remaining in power until 1969. New French constitution adopted **(Sept. 28),** de Gaulle elected president of 5th Republic **(Dec. 21).** Eisenhower orders U.S. Marines into Lebanon at request of President Chamoun, who fears overthrow **(July 15).**

1959 Cuban President Batista resigns and flees—Castro takes over **(Jan. 1).** Tibet's Dalai Lama escapes to India **(Mar. 31).** St. Lawrence Seaway opens, allowing ocean ships to reach Midwest **(April 25).**

1960 American U-2 spy plane, piloted by Francis Gary Powers, shot down over Russia **(May 1).** Khrushchev kills Paris summit conference because of U-2 **(May 16).** Powers sentenced to prison for 10 years **(Aug. 19)**—freed in **February 1962** in exchange for Soviet spy. Top Nazi murderer of Jews, Adolf Eichmann, captured by Israelis in Argentina **(May 23)**—executed in Israel in 1962. Communist China and Soviet Union split in conflict over Communist ideology. Belgium starts to break up its African colonial empire, gives independence to Belgian Congo (Zaire) on **June 30.** Cuba begins confiscation of $770 million of U.S. property **(Aug. 7).**

1961 U.S. breaks diplomatic relations with Cuba **(Jan. 3).** Robert Frost recites "The Gift Outright" at John F. Kennedy's inauguration as President of U.S. **(Jan. 20).** Kennedy proposes Alliance for Progress—10-year plan to raise Latin American living standards **(Mar. 13).** Moscow announces putting first man in orbit around earth, Maj. Yuri A. Gagarin **(April 12).** Cuba invaded at Bay of Pigs by an estimated 1,200 anti-Castro exiles aided by U.S.; invasion crushed **(April 17).** First U.S. spaceman, Navy

VIETNAM WAR (1950–1975)

U.S., South Vietnam, and Allies versus North Vietnam and National Liberation Front (Viet Cong). Outstanding events:

1950 President Truman sends 35-man military advisory group to aid French fighting to maintain colonial power in Vietnam.

1954 After defeat of French at Dien Bien Phu, Geneva Agreements **(July)** provide for withdrawal of French and Vietminh to either side of demarcation zone (DMZ) pending reunification elections, which are never held. Presidents Eisenhower and Kennedy (from 1954 onward) send civilian advisors and, later, military personnel to train South Vietnamese.

1960 Communists from National Liberation Front in South.

1963 Ngo Dinh Diem, South Vietnam's premier, slain in coup **(Nov. 1).**

1961-1963 U.S. military advisors rise from 2,000 to 15,000.

1964 North Vietnamese torpedo boats reportedly attack U.S. destroyers in Gulf of Tonkin **(Aug. 2).** President Johnson orders retaliatory air strikes. Congress approves Gulf of Tonkin resolution **(Aug. 7)** authorizing President to take necessary steps to "maintain peace."

1965 U.S. planes begin combat missions over South Vietnam. In **June,** 23,000 American advisors committed to combat. By end of year over 184,000 U.S. troops in area.

1966 B-52s bomb DMZ, reportedly used by North Vietnam for entry into South **(July 31).**

1967 South Vietnam National Assembly approves election of Nguyen Van Thieu as President **(Oct. 21).**

1968 U.S. has almost 525,000 men in Vietnam. In Tet offensive **(Jan.-Feb.),** Viet Cong guerrillas attack Saigon, Hue, and some provincial capitals. President Johnson orders halt to U.S. bombardment of North Vietnam **(Oct. 31).** Saigon and N.L.F. join U.S. and North Vietnam in Paris peace talks.

1969 President Nixon announces Vietnam peace offer **(May 14)**—begins troop withdrawals **(June).** Viet Cong forms Provisional Revolutionary Government. U.S. Senate calls for curb on commitments **(June 25).** Ho Chi Minh, 79, North Vietnam president, dies **(Sept. 3);** collective leadership chosen. Some 6,000 U.S. troops pulled back from Thailand and 1,000 marines from Vietnam (announced **Sept. 30**). Massive demonstrations in U.S. protest or support war policies **(Oct. 15).**

1970 Nixon announces sending of troops to Cambodia **(April 30).** Last U.S. troops removed from Cambodia **(June 29).**

1971 Congress bars use of combat troops, but not air power, in Laos and Cambodia **(Jan. 1).** South Vietnamese troops, with U.S. air cover, fail in Laos thrust. Many American ground forces withdrawn from Vietnam combat. *New York Times* publishes Pentagon papers, classified material on expansion of war **(June).**

1972 Nixon responds to North Vietnamese drive across DMZ by ordering mining of North Vietnam ports and heavy bombing of Hanoi-Haiphong area **(April 1).** Nixon orders "Christmas bombing" of north to get North Vietnamese back to conference table **(Dec.).**

1973 President orders halt to offensive operations in North Vietnam **(Jan. 15).** Representatives of North and South Vietnam, U.S., and N.L.F. sign peace pacts in Paris, ending longest war in U.S. history **(Jan. 27).** Last American troops departed in their entirety **(March 29).**

1974 Both sides accuse each other of frequent violations of cease-fire agreement.

1975 Full-scale warfare resumes. Communists victorious **(April 30).** South Vietnam Premier Nguyen Van Thieu resigns **(April 21).** U.S. Marine Embassy guards and U.S. civilians and dependents evacuated **(April 30).** More than 140,000 Vietnamese refugees leave by air and sea, many to settle in U.S. Provisional Revolutionary Government takes control **(June 6).**

1976 Election of National Assembly paves way for reunification of North and South.

Cmdr. Alan B. Shepard, Jr., rockets 116.5 miles up in 302-mile trip **(May 5).** Virgil Grissom becomes second American astronaut, making 118-mile-high, 303-mile-long rocket flight over Atlantic **(July 21).** Gherman Stepanovich Titov is launched in Soviet spaceship *Vostok II:* makes 17 1/2 orbits in 25 hours, covering 434,960 miles before landing safely **(Aug. 6).** East Germans erect Berlin Wall between East and West Berlin to halt flood of refugees **(Aug. 13).** U.S.S.R. fires 50-megaton hydrogen bomb, biggest explosion in history **(Oct. 29).**

John H. Glenn, Jr. (1921–)

1962 Lt. Col. John H. Glenn, Jr., is first American to orbit earth—three times in 4 hr 55 min **(Feb. 20).** Adolf Eichmann hanged in Israel for his part in Nazi extermination of six million Jews **(May 31).** France transfers sovereignty to new republic of Algeria **(July 3).** Cuban missile crisis—U.S.S.R. to build missile bases in Cuba; Kennedy orders Cuban blockade, lifts blockade after Russians back down **(Aug.-Nov.).** James H. Meredith, escorted by federal marshals, registers in University of Mississippi **(Oct. 1).** Pope John XXIII opens Second Vatican Council (Oct. 11)—Council holds four sessions, finally closing **Dec. 8, 1965.** Cuba releases 1,113 prisoners of 1961 invasion attempt **(Dec. 24).** William Faulkner wins Pulitzer for *The Reivers.*

Malcolm X (1925–1965)

1963 France and West Germany sign treaty of cooperation ending four centuries of conflict **(Jan. 22).** Pope John XXIII dies **(June 3)**—succeeded June 21 by Cardinal Montini, who becomes Paul VI. U.S. Supreme Court rules no locality may require recitation of Lord's Prayer or Bible verses in public schools **(June 17).** Civil rights rally held by 200,000 blacks and whites in Washington, D.C. **(Aug. 28).** Washington-to-Moscow "hot line" communications link opens, designed to reduce risk of accidental war **(Aug. 30).** President Kennedy shot and killed by sniper in Dallas, Tex. Lyndon B. Johnson becomes President same day **(Nov. 22).** Lee Harvey Oswald, accused assassin of President Kennedy, is shot and killed by Jack Ruby, Dallas nightclub owner **(Nov. 24).**

1964 U.S. Supreme Court rules that Congressional districts should be roughly equal in population **(Feb. 17).** Jack Ruby convicted of murder in slaying of Lee Harvey Oswald; sentenced to death by Dallas jury **(March 14)**—conviction reversed **Oct. 5, 1966;** Ruby dies **Jan. 3, 1967,** before second trial can be held. Three civil rights workers—Schwerner, Goodman, and Cheney—murdered in Mississippi **(June).** Twenty-one arrests result in trial and conviction of seven by federal jury. President's Commission on the Assassination of President Kennedy issues Warren Report concluding that Lee Harvey Oswald acted alone. The Beatles appear on *The Ed Sullivan Show.*

John F. Kennedy (1917–1963)

1965 Rev. Dr. Martin Luther King, Jr., and more than 2,600 other blacks arrested in Selma, Ala., during three-day demonstrations against voter-registration rules **(Feb. 1).** Malcolm X, black-nationalist leader, shot to death at Harlem rally in New York City **(Feb. 21).** U.S. Marines land in Dominican Republic as fighting persists between rebels and Dominican army **(April 28).** Medicare, senior citizens' government medical assistance program, begins **(July 1).** Blacks riot for six days in Watts section of Los Angeles: 34 dead, over 1,000 injured, nearly 4,000 arrested, fire damage put at $175 million **(Aug. 11-16).** Power failure in Ontario plant blacks out parts of eight northeastern states of U.S. and two provinces of southeastern Canada **(Nov. 9).**

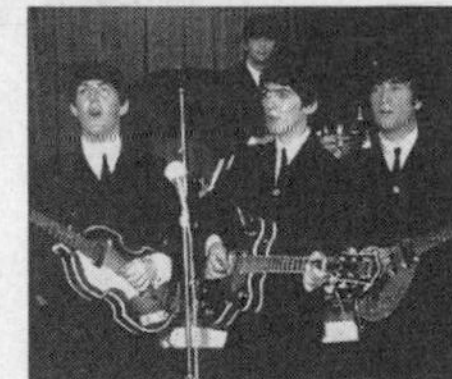

The Beatles

1966 Black teen-agers riot in Watts, Los Angeles; two men killed and at least 25 injured **(March 15).** Michael E. De Bakey implants artificial heart in human for first time at Houston hospital; plastic device functions and patient lives **(April 21).**

Thurgood Marshall (1908–1993)

1967 Three Apollo astronauts—Col. Virgil I. Grissom, Col. Edward White II, and Lt. Cmdr. Roger B. Chaffee—killed in spacecraft fire during simulated launch **(Jan. 27).** Israeli and Arab forces battle; six-day war ends with Israel occupying Sinai Peninsula, Golan Heights, Gaza Strip, and east bank of Suez Canal **(June 5).** Red China announces explosion of its first hydrogen bomb **(June 17).** Racial violence in Detroit; 7,000 National Guardsmen aid police after night of rioting. Similar outbreaks occur in New York City's Spanish Harlem, Rochester, N.Y., Birmingham, Ala., and New Britain, Conn. **(July 23).** Thurgood Marshall sworn in as first black U.S. Supreme Court justice **(Oct. 2).** Dr. Christiaan N. Barnard and team of South African surgeons perform world's first successful human heart transplant **(Dec. 3)**—patient dies 18 days later.

Richard Nixon
(1913–1994)

1968 North Korea seizes U.S. Navy ship *Pueblo;* holds 83 on board as spies **(Jan. 23).** President Johnson announces he will not seek or accept presidential renomination **(March 31).** Martin Luther King, Jr., civil rights leader, is slain in Memphis **(April 4)**—James Earl Ray, indicted in murder, captured in London on **June 8.** In 1969 Ray pleads guilty and is sentenced to 99 years. Sen. Robert F. Kennedy is shot and critically wounded in Los Angeles hotel after winning California primary **(June 5)**—dies **June 6.** Sirhan B. Sirhan convicted 1969. Czechoslovakia is invaded by Russians and Warsaw Pact forces to crush liberal regime **(Aug. 20).**

1969 Richard M. Nixon is inaugurated 37th President of the U.S. **(Jan. 20).** Apollo 11 astronauts—Neil A. Armstrong, Edwin E. Aldrin, Jr., and Michael Collins—take man's first walk on moon **(July 20).** Sen. Edward M. Kennedy pleads guilty to leaving scene of fatal accident at Chappaquiddick, Mass. **(July 18)** in which Mary Jo Kopechne was drowned—gets two-month suspended sentence **(July 25).**

Mao Zedong
(1893–1976)

1970 Biafra surrenders after 32-month fight for independence from Nigeria **(Jan. 12).** Rhodesia severs last tie with British Crown and declares itself a racially segregated republic **(March 1).** Four students at Kent State University in Ohio slain by National Guardsmen at demonstration protesting April 30 incursion into Cambodia **(May 4).** Senate repeals Gulf of Tonkin resolution **(June 24).**

1971 Supreme Court rules unanimously that busing of students may be ordered to achieve racial desegregation **(April 20).** Anti-war militants attempt to disrupt government business in Washington **(May 3)**—police and military units arrest as many as 12,000; most are later released. Twenty-sixth Amendment to U.S. Constitution lowers voting age to 18. U.N. seats Communist China and expels Nationalist China **(Oct. 25).**

Lyndon B. Johnson
(1908–1973)

1972 President Nixon makes unprecedented eight-day visit to Communist China and meets with Mao Zedong **(Feb.).** Britain takes over direct rule of Northern Ireland in bid for peace **(March 24).** Gov. George C. Wallace of Alabama is shot by Arthur H. Bremer at Laurel, Md., political rally **(May 15).** Five men are apprehended by police in attempt to bug Democratic National Committee headquarters in Washington D.C.'s Watergate complex—start of the Watergate scandal **(June 17).** Supreme Court rules that death penalty is unconstitutional **(June 29).** Eleven Israeli athletes at Olympic Games in Munich are killed after eight members of an Arab terrorist group invade Olympic Village; five guerrillas and one policeman are also killed **(Sept. 5).** Ingmar Bergman's *Cries and Whispers.*

Duke Ellington
(1899–1974)

1973 Great Britain, Ireland, and Denmark enter European Common Market **(Jan. 1).** Nixon, on national TV, accepts responsibility, but not blame, for Watergate; accepts resignations of advisers H. R. Haldeman and John D. Ehrlichman, fires John W. Dean III as counsel. **(April 30).** Greek military junta abolishes monarchy and proclaims republic **(June 1).** U.S. bombing of Cambodia ends, marking official halt to 12 years of combat activity in Southeast Asia **(Aug. 15).** Fourth and biggest Arab-Israeli conflict begins as Egyptian and Syrian forces attack Israel as Jews mark Yom Kippur, holiest day in their calendar. **(Oct. 6).** Spiro T. Agnew resigns as Vice President and then, in federal court in Baltimore, pleads no contest to charges of evasion of income taxes on $29,500 he received in 1967, while Governor of Maryland. He is fined $10,000 and put on three years' probation **(Oct. 10).** In the "Saturday Night Massacre," Nixon fires special Watergate prosecutor Archibald Cox and Deputy Attorney General William D. Ruckelshaus; Attorney General Elliot L. Richardson resigns **(Oct. 20).** Egypt and Israel sign U.S.-sponsored cease-fire accord **(Nov. 11).** Duke Ellington's autobiography, *Music is My Mistress,* is published.

1974 Patricia Hearst, 19-year-old daughter of publisher Randolph Hearst, kidnapped by Symbionese Liberation Army. **(Feb. 5).** House Judiciary Committee adopts three articles of impeachment charging President Nixon with obstruction of justice, failure to uphold laws, and refusal to produce material subpoenaed by the committee **(July 30).** Richard M. Nixon announces he will resign the next day, the first President to do so **(Aug. 8).** Vice President Gerald R. Ford of Michigan is sworn in as 38th President of the U.S. **(Aug. 9).** Ford grants "full, free, and absolute pardon" to ex-President Nixon **(Sept. 8).**

1975 John N. Mitchell, H. R. Haldeman, John D. Ehrlichman found guilty of Watergate cover-up and are sentenced on Feb. 21 to 30 months to 8 years in jail **(Jan. 1).** American merchant ship *Mayaguez,* seized by Cambodian forces, is rescued in operation by U.S. Navy and Marines, 38 of whom are killed **(May 15).** *Apollo* and *Soyuz* spacecraft take off for U.S.-Soviet link-up in space **(July 15).** President Ford escapes assassination attempt in Sacramento, Calif., **(Sept. 5).** President Ford escapes second assassination attempt in 17 days. **(Sept. 22).**

1976 Supreme Court rules that blacks and other minorities are entitled to retroactive job seniority **(March 24).** Ford signs Federal Election Campaign Act **(May 11).** Supreme Court rules that death penalty is not inherently cruel or unusual and is a constitutionally acceptable form of punishment **(July 3).** Nation celebrates Bicentennial **(July 4).** Israeli airborne commandos attack Uganda's Entebbe Airport and free 103 hostages held by pro-Palestinian hijackers of Air France plane; one Israeli and several Ugandan soldiers killed in raid **(July 4).** Mysterious disease that eventually claims 29 lives strikes American Legion convention in Philadelphia **(Aug. 4).** Jimmy Carter elected U.S. President **(Nov. 2).**

1977 First woman Episcopal priest ordained **(Jan. 1).** Scientists identify previously unknown bacterium as cause of mysterious "legionnaire's disease" **(Jan. 18).** Carter pardons Vietnam draft evaders **(Jan. 21).** Scientists report using bacteria in lab to make insulin **(May 23).** Supreme Court rules that states are not required to spend Medicaid funds on elective abortions **(June 20).** Deng Xiaoping, purged Chinese leader, restored to power as "Gang of Four" is expelled from Communist Party **(July 22).** Nuclear-proliferation pact, curbing spread of nuclear weapons, signed by 15 countries, including U.S. and U.S.S.R. **(Sept. 21).**

1978 President chooses federal Appeals court Judge William H. Webster as F.B.I. Director **(Jan. 19).** Rhodesia's Prime Minister Ian D. Smith and three black leaders agree on transfer to black majority rule **(Feb. 15).** Former Italian Premier Aldo Moro kidnapped by left wing terrorists, who kill five bodyguards **(March 16);** he is found slain **(May 9).** U.S. Senate approves Panama Canal neutrality treaty **(March 16);** votes treaty to turn canal over to Panama by year 2000 **(April 18).** Californians in referendum approve Proposition 13 for nearly 60% slash in property tax revenues **(June 6).** Supreme Court, in Bakke case, bars quota systems in college admissions but affirms constitutionality of programs giving advantage to minorities **(June 28).** Pope Paul VI, dead at 80, mourned **(Aug. 6);** new Pope, John Paul I, 65, dies unexpectedly after 34 days in office **(Sept. 28);** succeeded by Karol Cardinal Wojtyla of Poland as John Paul II **(Oct. 16).** "Framework for Peace" in Middle East signed by Egypt's President Anwar el-Sadat and Israel Premier Menachem Begin after 13-day conference at Camp David led by President Carter **(Sept. 17).**

1979 Oil spills pollute ocean waters in Atlantic and Gulf of Mexico **(Jan. 1, June 8, July 21).** Ohio agrees to pay $675,000 to families of dead and injured in Kent State University shootings **(Jan. 4).** Vietnam and Cambodian insurgents it backs announce fall of Phnom Penh, Cambodian capital, and collapse of Pol Pot regime **(Jan. 7).** Shah leaves Iran after year of turmoil **(Jan. 16);** revolutionary forces under Muslim leader, Ayatollah Ruhollah Khomeini, take over **(Feb. 1** et seq.). Conservatives win British election; Margaret Thatcher new Prime Minister **(March 28).** Nuclear power plant accident at Three Mile Island, Pa., releases radiation **(March 28).** Carter and Brezhnev sign SALT II agreement **(June 14).** Nicaraguan President Gen. Anastasio Somoza Debayle resigns and flees to Miami **(July 17);** Sandinistas form government **(July 19).** Earl Mountbatten of Burma, 79, British World War II hero, and three others killed by blast on fishing boat off Irish coast **(Aug. 27);** two I.R.A. members accused **(Aug. 30).** Iranian militants seize U.S. Embassy in Teheran and hold hostages **(Nov. 4).** Soviet invasion of Afghanistan stirs world protests **(Dec. 27).** Tennessee Williams receives Kennedy Center Honor.

1980 Six U.S. Embassy aides escape from Iran with Canadian help **(Jan. 29).** F.B.I.'s undercover operation "Abscam" (for Arab scam) implicates public officials **(Feb. 2).** U.S. breaks diplomatic ties with Iran **(April 7).** Eight U.S. servicemen are killed and five are injured as helicopter and cargo plane collide in abortive desert raid to rescue American hostages in Teheran **(April 25).** Supreme Court upholds limits on federal aid for abortions **(June 30).** Shah of Iran dies at 60 **(July 27).** Anastasio

Anwar Sadat
(1918–1981)

Pope John Paul II
(1920–)

Ayatollah Ruhollah Khomeini
(1900–1989)

Tennessee Williams
(1911–1983)

Ronald Reagan
(1911–)

Sandra Day O'Connor
(1930–)

Indira Gandhi
(1917–1984)

Somoza Debayle, ousted Nicaragua ruler, and two aides assassinated in Asunción, Paraguay capital **(Sept. 17)**. Iraq troops hold 90 square miles of Iran after invasion **(Sept. 19)**. Ronald Reagan elected President in Republican sweep **(Nov. 4)**. Three U.S. nuns and lay worker found shot in El Salvador **(Dec. 4)**. John Lennon of Beatles shot dead in New York City **(Dec. 8)**. Martin Scorsese's *Raging Bull.*

1981 U.S.-Iran agreement frees 52 hostages held in Teheran since Nov. 4, 1979 **(Jan. 20);** hostages welcomed back in U.S. **(Jan. 25)**. Ronald Reagan takes oath as 40th President **(Jan. 20)**. President Reagan wounded by gunman, with press secretary and two law-enforcement officers **(March 30)**. Pope John Paul II wounded by gunman **(May 14)**. Supreme Court rules, 4-4, that former President Nixon and three top aides may be required to pay monetary damages for unconstitutional wiretap of home telephone of former national security aide **(June 22)**. Reagan nominates Judge Sandra Day O'Connor, 51, of Arizona, as first woman on Supreme Court **(July 7)**. More than 110 die in collapse of aerial walkways in lobby of Hyatt Regency Hotel in Kansas City; 188 injured **(July 18)**. Air controllers strike, disrupting flights **(Aug. 3);** Government dismisses strikers **(Aug. 11)**.

1982 British overcome Argentina in Falklands war **(April 2-June 15)**. Israel invades Lebanon in attack on P.L.O. **(June 4)**. John W. Hinckley, Jr. found not guilty because of insanity in shooting of President Reagan **(June 21)**. Alexander M. Haig, Jr., resigns as Secretary of State **(June 25)**. Equal rights amendment fails ratification **(June 30)**. Lebanese Christian Phalangists kill hundreds of people in two Palestinian refugee camps in West Beirut **(Sept. 15)**. Princess Grace, 52, dies of injuries when car plunges off mountain road; daughter, Stephanie, 17, suffers serious injuries **(Sept. 14)**. Leonid I. Brezhnev, Soviet leader, dies at 75 **(Nov. 10)**. Yuri V. Andropov, 68, chosen as successor **(Nov. 15)**. Artificial heart implanted for first time in Dr. Barney B. Clark, 61, at University of Utah Medical Center in Salt Lake City **(Dec. 2);** Barney Clark dies **(March 23, 1983)**.

1983 Pope John Paul II signs new Roman Catholic code incorporating changes brought about by Second Vatican Council **(Jan. 25)**. Second space shuttle, *Challenger,* makes successful maiden voyage, which includes the first U.S. space walk in nine years **(April 4)**. U.S. Supreme Court declares many local abortion restrictions unconstitutional **(June 15)**. Sally K. Ride, 32, first U.S. woman astronaut in space as a crew member aboard space shuttle *Challenger* **(June 18)**. U.S. admits shielding former Nazi Gestapo chief, Klaus Barbie, 69, the "butcher of Lyon," wanted in France for war crimes **(Aug. 15)**. Benigno S. Aquino, Jr., 50, political rival of Philippines President Marcos, slain in Manila **(Aug. 21)**. South Korean Boeing 747 jetliner bound for Seoul apparently strays into Soviet airspace and is shot down by a Soviet SU-15 fighter after it had tracked the airliner for two hours; all 269 aboard are killed, including 61 Americans **(Aug. 30)**. Terrorist explosion kills 237 U.S. Marines in Beirut **(Oct. 23)**. U.S. and Caribbean allies invade Grenada **(Oct. 25)**.

1984 Bell System broken up **(Jan. 1)**. France gets first deliveries of Soviet natural gas **(Jan. 1)**. Syria frees captured U.S. Navy pilot, Lieut. Robert C. Goodman, Jr. **(Jan. 3)**. U.S. and Vatican exchange diplomats after 116-year hiatus **(Jan. 10)**. Reagan orders U.S. Marines withdrawn from Beirut international peacekeeping force **(Feb. 7)**. Yuri V. Andropov dies at 69; Konstantin U. Chernenko, 72, named Soviet Union leader **(Feb. 9)**. Italy and Vatican agree to end Roman Catholicism as state religion **(Feb. 18)**. Reagan ends U.S. role in Beirut by relieving Sixth Fleet from peacekeeping force **(March 30)**. Congress rebukes President Reagan on use of federal funds for mining Nicaraguan harbors **(April 10)**. Soviet Union withdraws from summer Olympic games in U.S., and other bloc nations follow (**May 7** et seq.). José Napoleón Duarte, moderate, elected president of El Salvador **(May 11)**. Three hundred slain as Indian Army occupies Sikh Golden Temple in Amritsar **(June 6)**. Thirty-ninth Democratic National Convention, in San Francisco, nominates Walter F. Mondale and Geraldine A. Ferraro **(July 16-19)**. Thirty-third Republican National Convention, at Dallas, renominates President Reagan and Vice President Bush **(Aug. 20-25)**. Brian Mulroney and Conservative party win Canadian election in landslide **(Sept. 4)**. Indian Prime Minister Indira Gandhi assassinated by two Sikh bodyguards; 1,000 killed in anti-Sikh riots; son Rajiv succeeds her **(Oct. 31)**. President Reagan re-elected in landslide with 59% o[illegible]f vote (**Nov. 7**). Toxic gas leaks from Union Carbide plant in Bhopal, India, killing 2,000 and injuring 150,000 (**Dec. 3**).

1985 Ronald Reagan, 73, [illegible] takes oath for second term as 40th President (**Jan. 20**). General Westmoreland settles libel action against CBS (**Feb. 18**). Prime Minister Margaret Thatcher addresses Congress, endorsing [illegible] policies (**Feb. 20**). U.S.S.R. leader Chernenko dies at 73 and [illegible] replaced by Mikhail Gorbachev, 54 (**March 11**). Two Shi'ite Muslim gunmen capture TWA airliner with 133 aboard, 104 of them Americans (**June 14**); 39 remaining hostages freed in Beirut (**June 30**). Supreme Court, 5-4, bars public school teachers from parochial schools (**July 1**). Arthur James Walker, 50, retired naval officer, convicted by federal judge of participating in Soviet spy ring (**Aug. 9**). P.L.O. terrorists hijack *Achille Lauro,* Italian cruise ship, with 80 passengers, plus crew (**Oct. 7**); American, Leon Klinghoffer, killed (**Oct. 8**). Italian government toppled by political crisis over hijacking of *Achille Lauro* (**Oct. 16**). John A. Walker and son, Michael I. Walker, 22, sentenced in Navy espionage case (**Oct. 28**). Reagan and Gorbachev meet at summit (**Nov. 19**); agree to step up arms control talks and renew cultural contacts (**Nov. 21**). Terrorists seize Egyptian Boeing 737 airliner after takeoff from Athens (**Nov. 23**); 59 dead as Egyptian forces storm plane on Malta (**Nov. 24**). U.S. budget-balancing bill enacted (**Dec. 12**).

Corazon Aquino (1933–)

Margaret Thatcher (1925–)

1986 Spain and Portugal join Common Market (**Jan. 1**). President freezes Libyan assets in U.S. (**Jan. 8**). Supreme Court bars racial bias in trial jury selection (**Jan. 14**). *Voyager 2* spacecraft reports secrets of Uranus (**Jan. 26**). Space shuttle *Challenger* explodes after launch at Cape Canaveral, Fla., killing all seven aboard (**Jan. 28**). Haiti President Jean-Claude Duvalier flees to France (**Feb. 7**). President Marcos flees Philippines after ruling 20 years, as newly elected Corazon Aquino succeeds him (**Feb. 26**). Prime Minister Olaf Palme of Sweden shot dead (**Feb. 28**). Kurt Waldheim's service as Nazi army officer revealed (**March 3**). Union Carbide agrees to settlement with victims of Bhopal gas leak in India (**March 22**). Halley's Comet yields information on return visit (**April 10**). U.S. planes attack Libyan "terrorist centers" (**April 14**). Desmond Tutu elected Archbishop in South Africa (**April 14**). Major nuclear accident at Soviet Union's Chernobyl power station alarms world (**April 26** et seq.). Ex-Navy analyst, Jonathan Jay Pollard, 31, guilty as spy for Israel (**June 4**). Supreme Court reaffirms abortion rights (**June 11**). World Court rules U.S. broke international law in mining Nicaraguan waters (**June 27**). Supreme Court voids automatic provisions of budget-balancing law (**July 7**). Jerry A. Whitworth, ex-Navy radioman, convicted as spy (**July 24**). Muslim captors release Rev. Lawrence Martin Jenco (**July 26**). Senate Judiciary Committee approves William H. Rehnquist to be Chief Justice of U.S. (**Aug. 14**). House votes arms appropriations bill rejecting Administration's "star wars" policy (**Aug. 15**). Three Lutheran church groups in U.S. set to merge (**Aug. 29**). Congress overrides Reagan veto of stiff sanctions against South Africa (**Sept. 29** and **Oct. 2**). Congress approves immigration bill barring hiring of illegal aliens, with amnesty provision (**Oct. 17**). Reagan signs $11.7-billion budget reduction measure (**Oct. 21**). He approves sweeping revision of U.S. tax code (**Oct. 22**). Democrats triumph in elections, gaining eight seats to win Senate majority (**Nov. 4**). Secret initiative to send arms to Iran revealed (**Nov. 6** et seq.); Reagan denies exchanging arms for hostages and halts arms sales (**Nov. 19**); diversion of funds from arms sales to Nicaraguan Contras revealed (**Nov. 25**). Walkers, father and son, sentenced in naval spy ring (**Nov. 6**). Soviet lifts ban on Andrei D. Sakharov, rights activist (**Dec. 19**).

Mikhail S. Gorbachev (1931–)

William Rehnquist (1924–)

1987 William Buckley, U.S. hostage in Lebanon, reported slain (**Jan. 20**). U.S. puts Austrian President Kurt Waldheim on list of those banned from country (**April 27**). Quebec accepts Canadian Constitution as "distinct society" (**May 1**). Supreme Court rules Rotary Clubs must admit women (**May 4**). Iraqi missiles kill 37 in attack on U.S. frigate *Stark* in Persian Gulf (**May 17**); Iraqi president apologizes (**May 18**). Prime Minister Thatcher wins rare third term in Britain (**June 11**). Supreme Court Justice Lewis F. Powell, Jr., retires (**June 26**). Klaus Barbie, 73, Gestapo wartime chief in Lyon, sentenced to life by French court for war crimes (**July 4**). Marine Lieut. Col. Oliver North, Jr., tells Congressional inquiry higher officials approved his secret Iran-Contra operations (**July 7-10**).

François Mitterrand (1916–1996)

Dalai Lama (1935–)

Hubble Space Telescope

General Colin Powell (1937–)

Admiral John M. Poindexter, former Nat[illegible]onal Security Adviser, testifies he authorized use of Iran arms sale profit[illegible]s to aid Contras (**July 15-22**). George P. Shultz testifies he was deceive[illegible]ed repeatedly on Iran-Co[illegible] affair (**July 23-24**). Defense Secretary C[illegible]aspar W. Weinber[illegible] inquiry of official deception and intrigue (**Ju[illegible]y 31, Aug. 3**) [illegible] Iran arms-Contra policy went astray and accep[illegible]ts resp[illegible] Severe earthquake strikes Los Angeles, leaving [illegible] and six dead (**Oct. 1**). Senate, 58-42, rejects Robert H. Bork as Supreme Court Justice (**Oct. 23**).

1988 U.S. and Canada reach free trade agreement (**Jan. 2**). Supreme Court, 5-3, backs public school officials' power to censor student activities (**Jan. 13**). Robert C. McFarlane, former National Security Adviser, pleads guilty in Iran-Contra case (**March 11**). Supreme Court rules against private-club membership restrictions (**June 20**). U.S. Navy ship shoots down Iranian airliner in Persian Gulf, mistaking it for jet fighter; 290 killed (**July 3**). Terrorists kill nine tourists on Aegean cruise (**July 11**). Democratic convention nominates Gov. Michael Dukakis of Massachusetts for President and Texas Senator Lloyd Bentsen for Vice President (**July 17** et seq.). Republicans nominate George Bush for President and Indiana Senator Dan Quayle for Vice President (**Aug. 15** et seq.). Plane blast kills Pakistani President Mohammad Zia ul-Haq (**Aug. 17**). Republicans sweep 40 states in election. Vice President Bush beats Gov. Dukakis (**Nov. 8**). Soviet legislature approves political restructuring and new national legislature (**Dec. 1**). Benazir Bhutto, first Islamic woman prime minister, chosen to lead Pakistan's government (**Dec. 1**). Pan-Am 747 explodes from terrorist bomb and crashes in Lockerbie, Scotland, killing all 259 aboard and 11 on ground (**Dec. 21**). François Mitterrand wins second term as France's first Socialist president.

1989 U.S. planes shoot down two Libyan fighters over international waters in Mediterranean (**Jan. 4**). Emperor Hirohito of Japan dead at 87 (**Jan. 7**). George Herbert Walker Bush inaugurated as 41st U.S. President (**Jan. 20**). Iran's Ayatollah Khomeini declares author Salman Rushdie's book *The Satanic Verses* offensive and sentences him and his publishers to death (**Feb. 14**). Ruptured tanker *Exxon Valdez* sends 11 million gallons of crude oil into Alaska's Prince William Sound (**March 24**). Tens of thousands of Chinese students take over Beijing's central square in rally for democracy (**April 19** et seq.). More than one million in Beijing demonstrate for democracy; chaos spreads across nation (**mid-May** et seq.). Mikhail S. Gorbachev named Soviet President (**May 25**). U.S. jury convicts Oliver L. North in Iran-Contra affair (**May 4**). Thousands killed as Chinese leaders take hard line toward demonstrators (**June 4** et seq.). Army Gen. Colin R. Powell is first black to become Chairman of Joint Chiefs of Staff (**Aug. 9**). P.W. Botha quits as South Africa's President (**Aug. 14**). *Voyager 2* spacecraft speeds by Neptune after making startling discoveries about the planet and its moons (**Aug. 29**). L. Douglas Wilder, Democrat, is elected as first black governor of Virginia (**Nov. 7**). Deng Xiaoping resigns from China's leadership (**Nov. 9**). After 28 years, Berlin Wall is open to West (**Nov. 11**). Czech Parliament ends Communists' dominant role (**Nov. 30**). Romanian uprising overthrows Communist government (**Dec. 15** et seq.); President Ceausescu and wife executed (**Dec. 25**). U.S. troops invade Panama, seeking capture of Gen. Manuel Noriega (**Dec. 20**); resistance to U.S. collapses (**Dec. 24**). Dalai Lama wins Nobel Peace Prize.

1990 Gen. Manuel Noriega surrenders in Panama (**Jan. 3**). Yugoslav Communists end 45-year monopoly of power (**Jan. 22**). Soviet Communists relinquish sole power (**Feb. 7**). South Africa frees Nelson Mandela, imprisoned 27½ years (**Feb. 11**). Violeta Barrios de Chamorro inaugurated as Nicaraguan President; Hubble Space Telescope launched (**April 25**). U.S.-Soviet summit reaches accord on armaments (**June 1**). Supreme Court upsets law banning flag burning (**June 11**). Western Alliance ends cold war and proposes joint action with Soviet Union and Eastern Europe (**July 6**). U.S. Appeals court overturns Oliver North's Iran-Contra conviction (**July 20**). Iraqi troops invade Kuwait and seize petroleum reserves, setting off Persian Gulf War (**Aug. 2** et seq.). East and West Germany reunited (**Aug. 31** et seq.). Republicans set back in midterm elections (**Nov. 8**). Gorbachev assumes emergency powers (**Nov. 17**). Leaders of 34 nations in Europe and North America proclaim a united Europe (**Nov. 21**). Margaret Thatcher resigns as British Prime Minister (**Nov. 22**); John Major succeeds her (**Nov. 28**).

Lech Walesa wins Poland's runoff Presidential election **(Dec. 9).** Haiti elects leftist priest as President in first democratic election **(Dec. 17).**

1991 Lithuania Government resigns **(Jan. 8).** U.S. and Allies at war with Iraq **(Jan. 15).** U.N. forces win Persian Gulf war **(Feb. 4** et seq.). Liberal priest becomes Haiti president **(Feb. 7).** Warsaw Pact dissolves military alliance **(Feb. 25).** Supreme Court limits race in trial jury selection **(April 1).** Cease-fire ends Persian Gulf war **(April 3).** Europeans end sanctions on South Africa **(April 15).** Supreme Court limits death row appeals **(April 16).** Winnie Mandela sentenced in kidnapping **(May 13).** William H. Webster retires as Director of Central Intelligence; Robert H. Gates succeeds him **(May 14).** France agrees to sign 1968 treaty banning spread of atomic weapons **(June 3).** Communist Government of Albania resigns **(June 4).** Jiang Qing, widow of Mao, commits suicide **(June 4).** South African Parliament repeals apartheid laws **(June 5).** Warsaw Pact dissolved **(July 1).** Boris N. Yeltsin inaugurated as first freely elected president of Russian Republic **(July 10).** Bush-Gorbachev summit negotiates strategic arms reduction treaty **(July 31).** China accepts nuclear nonproliferation treaty **(Aug. 10).** Coup fails to unseat Gorbachev after Soviet hardliners seize him; he credits Yeltsin for rescue **(Aug. 18** et seq.). Gorbachev seals Communist Party doom, resigns as secretary-general **(Aug. 24).** Three Baltic republics win independence **(Aug. 25);** Bush recognizes them **(Sept. 2).** New Soviet ruling council recognizes independence of Lithuania, Estonia, and Latvia **(Sept. 6).** Charges against Oliver North dropped **(Sept. 15).** Haitian troops seize president in uprising **(Sept. 30).** U.S. suspends assistance to Haiti **(Oct. 1).** Professor Anita Hill accuses Judge Clarence Thomas of sexual harassment **(Oct. 6);** Senate, 52-48, confirms Thomas for Supreme Court after stormy hearings **(Oct. 15).** Israel and Soviet Union resume relations after 24 years **(Oct. 18).** First photo ever taken of an asteroid in space, *Gaspara* **(Oct. 29).** U.S. indicts two Libyans in 1988 bombing of Pan Am Flight 103 over Lockerbie, Scotland **(Nov. 15).** Anglican envoy Terry Waite and U.S. Prof. Thomas M. Sutherland freed by Lebanese **(Nov. 18).** Last three U.S. hostages freed in Lebanon **(Dec. 2-4).** Soviet Union breaks up after President Gorbachev's resignation; constituent republics form Commonwealth of Independent States, which U.S. and other nations move to recognize **(Dec. 25).**

1992 Yugoslav Federation broken up **(Jan. 15).** Bush and Yeltsin proclaim formal end to Cold War **(Feb. 1).** U.S. lifts trade sanctions against China **(Feb. 21).** U.S. recognizes three former Yugoslav republics **(April 7).** Gen. Noriega, former Panama leader, convicted in U.S. court **(April 9).** Small new Yugoslavia proclaimed **(April 27).** Four officers acquitted in Los Angeles beating; violence erupts in Los Angeles **(April 29** et seq.). Caspar W. Weinberger indicted in Iran-Contra affair **(June 16).** Last Western hostages freed in Lebanon **(June 17).** Supreme Court reaffirms

Lech Walesa (1943–)

George Bush (1924–)

Saddam Hussein (1937–)

THE PERSIAN GULF WAR (Aug. 2, 1990–April 6, 1991)

1990: Iraq invades its tiny neighbor, Kuwait, after talks break down over oil production and debt repayment. Iraqi Pres. Saddam Hussein later annexes Kuwait and declares it a 19th province of Iraq **(Aug. 2).** President Bush believes that Iraq intends to invade Saudi Arabia and take control of the region's oil supplies. He begins organizing a multi-national coalition to seek Kuwait's freedom and restoration of its legitimate government. The U.N. Security Council authorizes economic sanctions against Iraq. Pres. Bush orders U.S. troops to protect Saudi Arabia at the Saudis' request and "Operation Desert Shield" begins **(Aug. 6).** 230,000 American troops arrive in Saudi Arabia to take defensive action, but when Iraq continues a huge military buildup in Kuwait, the President orders an additional 200,000 troops deployed to prepare for a possible offensive action by the U.S.-led coalition forces. He subsequently obtains a U.N. Security Council resolution setting a Jan. 15, 1991, deadline for Iraq to withdraw unconditionally from Kuwait **(Nov. 8).**

1991: Pres. Bush wins Congressional approval for his position with the most devastating air assault in history against military targets in Iraq and Kuwait **(Jan. 16).** He rejects a Soviet-Iraq peace plan for a gradual withdrawal that does not comply with all the U.N. resolutions and gives Iraq an ultimatum to withdraw from Kuwait by noon February 23 **(Feb. 22).** The President orders the ground war to begin **(Feb. 24).** In a brilliant and lightning-fast campaign, U.S. and coalition forces smash through Iraq's defenses and defeat Saddam Hussein's troops in only four days of combat. Allies enter Kuwait City **(Feb. 26).** Iraqi army sets fire to over 500 of Kuwait's oil wells as final act of destruction to Kuwait's infrastructure. Pres. Bush orders a unilateral cease-fire 100 hours after the ground offensive started **(Feb. 27).** Allied and Iraq military leaders meet on battlefield to discuss terms for a formal cease-fire to end the Gulf War. Iraq agrees to abide by all of the U.N. resolutions **(Mar. 3).** The first Allied prisoners of war are released **(Mar. 4).** Official cease-fire accepted and signed **(April 6).** 532,000 U.S. forces served in Operation Desert Storm. There were a total of 148 battle deaths during the Gulf War, 145 nonbattle deaths, and 467 wounded in action. Battle deaths by branch of service were: Army, 98; Navy, 6; Marines, 24; Air Force, 20. Nonbattle deaths: Army, 105; Navy, 8; Marines, 26; and Air Force, 6. The United States estimated that Iraqi military casualties were 100,000 killed, 300,000 wounded, and over 88,000 captured.

Boris Yeltsin (1931–)

Benazir Bhutto (1953–)

Nelson Mandela (1918–)

Toni Morrison (1931–)

right to abortion (**June 29**). Gen. Noriega sentenced to 40 years on drug charges (**July 10**). Court clears *Exxon Valdez* skipper (**July 10**). Democrats nominate Bill Clinton and Al Gore (**July 1**). Israeli Parliament approves Yitzhak Rabin's coalition government, dominated by Labor Party (**July 13**). Supreme Court upholds return of Haitians (**Aug. 1**). U.S. indicts four police officers in Los Angeles beating (**Aug. 5**). North American trade compact announced (**Aug. 12**). Republicans renominate Bush and Quayle (**Aug. 20**). U.N. expels Serbian-dominated Yugoslavia (**Sept. 22**). Senate ratifies second Strategic Arms Limitation Treaty (**Oct. 1**). Top Japanese leader, Shin Kanemaru, resigns in scandal (**Oct. 14**). Bill Clinton elected President, Al Gore Vice President; Democrats keep control of Congress (**Nov. 3**). Russian Parliament approves START treaty (**Nov. 4**). U.S. forces leave Philippines, ending nearly a century of American military presence (**Nov. 24**). Czechoslovak Parliament approves separation into two nations (**Nov. 25**). U.N. approves U.S.-led force to guard food for Somalia (**Dec. 3**). Prince and Princess of Wales agree to separate (**Dec. 9**). Bush pardons former Reagan Administration officials involved in Iran-Contra affair (**Dec. 24**).

1993 Vaclav Havel elected as Czech President (**Jan. 26**). Clinton agrees to compromise on military's ban on homosexuals (**Jan. 29**). U.S. begins airlift of supplies to besieged Bosnia towns (**Feb. 28**). Federal agents besiege Texas Branch Davidian religious cult after six are killed in raid (**March 1** *et seq.*). Five arrested, sixth sought in bombing of World Trade Center in New York (**March 29**). Two police officers convicted in Los Angeles on civil rights charges in Rodney King beating (**April 17**). Fire kills 72 as cult standoff in Texas ends with federal assault (**April 19**). President of Sri Lanka assassinated (**May 1**). British Commons approves European unity pact (**May 20**). Twenty-two U.N. troops killed in Somalia (**June 5**). Ruth Bader Ginsburg, rights advocate, appointed to Supreme Court (**June 14**). Iraq accepts U.N. weapons monitoring (**July 19**). Vincent W. Foster, Jr., senior White House lawyer, commits suicide (**July 22**). Midwest flood damage expected to exceed $10 billion (**July 24**). Two Los Angeles police officers sentenced in Rodney King beating (**Aug. 4**). Israeli-Palestinian accord reached (**Aug. 28**). South Africa agrees to share transition powers (**Sept. 7**). Yeltsin dissolves Russian Parliament (**Sept. 21**). Benazir Bhutto wins second term as Prime Minister of Pakistan (**Oct.**) U.S. agents blamed in Waco, Tex., siege (**Oct. 1**). Yeltsin's forces crush revolt in Russian Parliament (**Oct. 4** et seq.). China breaks nuclear test moratorium (**Oct. 5**). NATO offers "peace partnership" to Eastern European nations (**Oct. 20-21**). Canada's opposition Liberal Party regains power in landslide (**Oct. 25**). Europe's Maastricht Treaty takes effect, creating European Union (**Nov. 1**). Jean Chretien sworn in as Canada's 20th Prime Minister (**Nov. 4**). Yeltsin approves new draft constitution for Russia (**Nov. 8**). House of Representatives approves North American Free Trade Agreement (**Nov. 17**); Senate follows (**Nov. 21**). South Africa adopts majority rule constitution (**Nov. 18**). Clinton signs Brady bill regulating firearms purchases (**Nov. 30**). Toni Morrison wins Nobel prize for literature.

1994 Serbs heavy weapons pound Sarajevo (**Jan. 5-6**). Olympic figure skater Nancy Kerrigan attacked (**Jan. 6**); three arrested in attack (**Jan. 13**). Major earthquake jolts Los Angeles; 51 dead (**Jan. 17** et seq.). Clinton ends trade embargo on Vietnam (**Feb. 9**). Aldrich Ames, high C.I.A. official, charged with spying for Soviets (**Feb. 22**). Four convicted in World Trade Center bombing (**March 4**). Mexican Presidential candidate assassinated (**March 23**). Nelson Mandela elected President of South Africa (**April**). Thousands dead in Rwanda massacre (**April 6**). Strike halts major trucking companies (**April 6**); accord reached to end tie-up (**April 29**). South Africa holds first interracial national election (**April 29**). Israel and Palestinians sign accord (**May 4**). Clinton accused of sexual harassment while Governor (**May 6**). Congress votes protection for women's health clinics (**May 12**). Jacqueline Kennedy Onassis dies of cancer (**May 20**). O. J. Simpson arrested in killings of wife, Nicole Brown Simpson, and friend, Ronald Goldman (**June 18**). Russia and NATO agree on close military ties (**June 22**). Supreme Court approves limit on abortion protests (**June 30**). Senate confirms Stephen G. Breyer for Supreme Court (**July 29**). Women's health clinic doctor shot dead outside Florida clinic (**July 29**); U.S. indicts accused killer (**Aug. 12**). Major league baseball players strike (**Aug. 13**). Carlos "the Jackal," international terrorist, captured (**Aug. 15**). I.R.A. declares cease-fire in

Northern Ireland (**Aug. 31**). Small plane crashes against White House (**Sept. 12**). Baseball owners end season and cancel World Series (**Sept. 14**). Powerful earthquake strikes Japan (**Oct. 4**). Aristide returns to joyous Haiti (**Oct. 4**). U.S. sends forces to Persian Gulf (**Oct. 7**). Ulster Protestants declare cease-fire (**Oct. 13**). Israel and Jordan sign peace treaty (**Oct. 17**). Reagan, 83, reveals Alzheimer's disease (**Nov. 6**). G.O.P. wins control of House and Senate (**Nov. 8**). Aristide forms Haitian Government with Prime Minister and full Cabinet (**Nov. 9**). Clinton orders Bosnian arms embargo ended (**Nov. 10**). Killer of women's health doctor sentenced twice (**Dec. 2**). Newt Gingrich named House Speaker (**Dec. 5**). Bentsen resigns as Treasury Secretary (**Dec. 6**). Russians attack secessionist Republic of Chechnya (**Dec. 11** *et seq.*). James Woolsey, Jr., resigns as Director of Central Intelligence (**Dec. 28**). John Salvi kills two at Massachusetts Planned Parenthood clinic (**Dec. 30**).

Jean-Bertrand Aristide (1953–)

1995 Republicans take control of Congress (**Jan. 4**). More than 5,000 dead in Japanese earthquake (**Jan. 17 et seq.**). Criminal trial of O. J. Simpson opens in California (**Jan. 24**). Clinton offers $20 billion aid to Mexico (**Jan. 31**). U.S. rescues Mexico's economy with $20-billion aid program (**Feb. 21**). Senate rejects balanced-budget amendment (**March 2**). Russian space station greets first Americans (**March 14**). Nerve gas attack in Tokyo subway kills eight and injures thousands. The Aum Shinrikyo ("Supreme Truth") cult is to blame (**March 20**). Selena, 23, popular Spanish-language singer, slain in Texas (**March 31**). Major league baseball strike ends (**April 2**). Appeals court upholds woman's plea to enter Citadel military academy (**April 13**). U.N. Council votes easier sanctions for Iraq (**April 14**). Scores killed as terrorist's car bomb blows up block-long Oklahoma City federal building (**April 19**); Timothy McVeigh, 27, Army veteran, arrested as suspect (**April 21**); authorities seek second suspect, link right-wing paramilitary groups to bombing (**April 22**). Death toll 2,000 in Rwanda massacre (**April 22**). Fighting escalates in Bosnia and Croatia (**May 1**). Japanese police seize cult leader in subway nerve gas attack (**May 18**). Supreme Court rejects term-limit laws (**May 22**). Colombia seizes a top drug-ring leader (**June 9**). U.S. shuttle docks with Russian space station (**June 27**). F.B.I. suspends four in Idaho siege inquiry (**Aug. 11**). France explodes nuclear device in Pacific; wide protests ensue (**Sept. 5**). Senator Bob Packwood of Oregon resigns under pressure for sexual and official misconduct (**Sept. 6**). Israelis and Palestinians agree on transferring West Bank to Arabs (**Sept. 24**). Los Angeles jury finds O. J. Simpson not guilty of murder charges (**Oct. 3**). Pope John Paul II visits U.S. on whirlwind tour (**Oct. 4-8**). Warring parties agree on cease-fire in Bosnia (**Oct. 5**). Million Man March draws hundreds of thousands of black men to capital (**Oct. 16**). Quebec narrowly rejects independence from Canada (**Oct. 30**). Israel Prime Minister Yitzhak Rabin slain by Jewish extremist at peace rally (**Nov. 4**). U.S. servicemen admit rape of Japanese schoolgirl in Okinawa (**Nov. 7**). Nigeria hangs writer and eight other minority rights advocates (**Nov. 10**). Irish voters approve end to constitutional ban on divorce (**Nov. 24**). Combatants sign Bosnia peace treaty (**Dec. 14**). House move stalls Congress-White House negotiations to avert Government shutdown (**Dec. 20**). Seamus Heaney wins Nobel prize for literature.

Seamus Heaney (1939–)

William J. Clinton (1946–)

1996 U.S. budget crisis in fourth month (**Jan 3**). Global warming climbs to record (**Jan. 3**). Clinton approves resumption of many government operations (**Jan. 6**). Chechens capture 2,000 Russians (**Jan. 9**). Sheik sentenced to life in U.S. bomb plot (**Jan. 17**). Senate ratifies major arms reduction treaty (**Jan. 26**). France announces end to nuclear tests (**Jan. 29**). At least 73 dead in Sri Lankan suicide bombing (**Feb. 1**). Suicide bombers kill 59 in Israel (**March 4**). Bob Dole sweeps primaries (**March 5**). Disco fire kills at least 150 in Manila (**March 19**). Britain alarmed by deadly cow disease (**March 20 et seq.**). U.N. tribunal charges war crimes by Bosnian Muslims and Croats (**March 22**). Commerce Secretary Ronald H. Brown, 54, killed in plane crash (**April 3**). F.B.I. arrests suspected Unabomber (**April 3**). Clinton signs line-item veto bill (**April 9**). President blocks ban on late-term abortions (**April 10**). Nations pledge $1.23 billion in aid to rebuild Bosnia (**April 22**). South Africa gets new constitution (**May 8**). Valujet crashes in Everglades; all 110 aboard killed (**May 11**). Chechnya peace treaty signed (**May 27**). Israel elects Benjamin Netanyahu as prime minister (**May 31**). China agrees to world ban on atomic testing (**June 6**). Leaders in Balkans sign accord on arms limits (**June 14**). Jazz great Ella Fitzgerald dies (**June 15**). Truck

Yitzhak Rabin (1922–1995)

Ella Fitzgerald (1918–1996)

Kofi Annan (1938–)

Madeleine Albright (1937–)

Hale-Bopp Comet

bomb kills 19 at U.S. base in Saudi Arabia (**June 25**). Boris Yeltsin is reelected in Russian election (**July 3**). Prince Charles and Princess Diana agree on divorce (**July 12**). 747 airliner crashes in Atlantic off Long Island; all 230 aboard perish (**July 17**). Bomb mars Summer Olympic games in Atlanta (**July 25**). Congress passes welfare reform bill (**Aug. 2**). Republican convention opens in San Diego (**Aug. 12**); Bob Dole and Jack Kemp nominated (**Aug. 14**). Clinton signs bill to raise minimum wage (**Aug. 2**); approves welfare reform bill (**Aug. 22**). Democrats convene in Chicago (**Aug. 26**). Iraqis strike at Kurdish enclave (**Aug. 31**); after warning, U.S. attacks Iraq's southern air defenses (**Sept. 2–3**); Iraq halts attacks on U.S. planes enforcing flight exclusion zones in north and south (**Sept. 13**). Bosnians re-elect existing ethnic leaders in three-person presidency (**Sept. 10**). Virginia Military Institute agrees to admit women (**Sept. 21**). Violence flares in Jerusalem over Israel opening tourist tunnel (**Sept. 24**). Taliban Muslim fundamentalists capture Afghan capital (**Sept. 27**). Ethnic violence breaks out in Zairian refugee camps (**Oct. 13**); thousands of refugees from Rwanda and Burundi abandon camps (**Oct. 21**). Clinton-Gore ticket wins national election; Republicans retain control of Congress (**Nov. 5**). Bomb kills 13 in Russian cemetery (**Nov. 10**). Mid-air collision in India kills 342 (**Nov. 12**). Clinton approves Canadian plan for U.N.-backed relief mission for 1.2 million Hutu refugees starving in eastern Zaire (**Nov. 13**). Texaco settles racial bias suit (**Nov. 15**). Hundreds of thousands of Hutu refugees return to Rwanda (**Nov. 15–18**). Clinton appoints Madeleine Albright as first female secretary of state (**Dec. 5**). Kofi Annan, 58, a Ghanian, named U.N. Secretary-General (**Dec. 13**). F.B.I. agent charged with spying for Moscow (**Dec. 18**). Thousands march in Belgrade in continuing protest against president's annulment of election results (**Dec. 26**).

1997 Two Hutu sentenced to death in Rwanda genocide (**Jan. 3**). Death toll above 200 in European cold wave (**Jan. 3**). Floods cause wide damage in U.S. west (**Jan. 5**). Newt Gingrich re-elected as House Speaker (**Jan. 7**). Hebron agreement signed: Israel gives up large part of West Bank city of Hebron (**Jan. 16**). U.S. shuttle joins Russian space station (**Jan. 17**). Gingrich found guilty of ethics violations (**Jan. 17**). President Clinton starts second term (**Jan. 20**). Madeleine Albright sworn in as first woman U.S. Secretary of State. (**Jan. 23**). U.S., U.K., and France agree to freeze Nazis' gold loot (**Feb. 3**). O. J. Simpson found liable in civil suit (**Feb. 5**). Deng Xiaoping, Chinese leader, dead at 92 (**Feb. 19**). Cloning of sheep stirs ethical controversy (**Feb. 23**). Israeli government approves establishment of Jewish settlement in East Jerusalem, a setback in Middle East peace process (**Feb. 26**). Tornadoes wreak havoc in Arkansas, Ohio, and Kentucky (**March 3**). Senate dooms balanced-budget amendment (**March 4**). State of anarchy in Albania when third of population loses savings because of pyramid schemes (**March 13**). Heaven's Gate cult members commit mass suicide in California (**March 27**). U.S. Appeals Court upholds California ban on affirmative action (**April 8**). U.S. judge upholds California marijuana law (**April 11**). Tiger Woods breaks multiple records in Masters golf tournament (**April 13**). Fire kills 300 pilgrims outside Mecca (**April 15**). Peruvian government soldiers free 72 hostages held for 4 months by Túpac Amaru rebels (**April 22**). Senate, 74–26, approves chemical weapons treaty (**April 24**). Thousands flee North Dakota flood (**April 27**). Thousands of Rwandan refugees trapped in Zaire (**April 30**). U.N. tribunal convicts Bosnian Serb for killings and tortures (**May 7**). Sergeant Major of the Army, Gene C. McKinney, charged in sex cases (**May 7**). Russia's President Yeltsin signs Chechnya peace treaty (**May 12**). Senate, 64–36, approves ban on late-term abortions (**May 20**). U.S.–Russian spaceship linkup in orbit ends (**May 21**). French vote for Leftist coalition in rejection of economic austerity (**June 1**). U.S. jobless rate for May reported 4.8 percent, lowest since 1973 (**June 6**). Mary Robinson resigns as President of Ireland to take top U.N. human rights post (**June 12**). European Union bolsters currency merger (**June 16**). Fugitive Pakistani seized in C.I.A. killings (**June 17**). Historic tobacco settlement proposed (**June 20**). Congress votes major tax cuts (**June 26**). Hong Kong returns to Chinese rule (**June 30**). U.S. spacecraft begins exploration of Mars (**July 4**). U.N. tribunal sentences Bosnian Serb for atrocities (**July 14**). Andrew Cunanan murders fashion designer Gianni Versace at end of a killing spree (**July 15**). Khmer Rouge hold trial of longtime leader Pol Pot; world opinion considers it a mere public relations stunt (**July 25**). White House and

G.O.P. agree on measure to balance budget (**July 28**). Strike cripples United Parcel Service (**Aug. 3**); company and union reach tentative agreement to end 15–day tie-up (**Aug. 18**). U.S. spacecraft transmits thousands of pictures from Mars (**Aug. 8**). Clinton exercises new line-item veto (**Aug. 11**). Timothy J. McVeigh sentenced to death in Oklahoma City bombing (**Aug. 14**). Former East German leader Egon Krenz sentenced to prison (**Aug. 25**). F. W. de Klerk retires from politics in South Africa (**Aug. 26**). Princess Diana, 36, killed with two others in Paris car crash (**Aug. 31**). Vice President Gore is target of campaign finance inquiry (**Sept. 3**). Three Islamic suicide bombers kill four persons in Jerusalem (**Sept. 4**). Mother Teresa, Nobel Peace Prize winner, dead at 87 (**Sept. 5**). World-wide public mourning marks Princess Diana's funeral (**Sept. 6**). Swiss plan first payment to Holocaust victims (**Sept. 17**). Israel pledges 300 new houses on West Bank (**Sept. 24**). Plane crash on Sumatra kills 234 (**Sept. 26**). U.S. space shuttle docks with Russian *Mir*, bringing new astronaut (**Sept. 27**). Militant Taliban leaders seize Kabul, capital of Afghanistan (**Sept. 27**). Tyrannosaurus remains auctioned for $8.36 million (**Oct. 4**). Israeli Prime Minister center of controversy over failed attempt to assassinate militant Islamic leader (**Oct. 6**). NASA launches plutonium-powered space probe (**Oct. 15**). Iraq expels all U.S. members of U.N. arms-inspection team (**Oct. 29**). Terry L. Nichols goes on trial in Oklahoma City bombing (**Nov. 3**). G.O.P. victorious in off-year elections (**Nov. 4**). Pakistani convicted in 1993 C.I.A. killings (**Nov. 10**). Two convicted in New York Trade Center bombing (**Nov. 12**). Egyptian Islamic militants kill 62 at Luxor tourist site (**Nov. 17**). F.B.I. ends 16-month investigation of crash of Flight 800 off Long Island, which killed 230; denies sabotage (**Nov. 18**). Woman in Iowa gives birth to seven (**Nov. 19**). Attorney General exonerates Clinton and Gore on fund-raising calls (**Dec. 2**). South Korea and I.M.F. agree on $57 billion loan (**Dec. 3**). World Islamic Conference scorns terrorism (**Dec. 11**). European Union plans to admit six nations (**Dec. 13**). Opposition figure elected President of South Korea (**Dec. 18**). Airliner crash on Sumatra kills 104 (**Dec. 19**). Gunmen kill 45 in raid on Indian village in Mexico (**Dec. 22**). U.S. company launches first commercial spy satellite (**Dec. 24**). Paris court convicts "Carlos the Jackal" of murder (**Dec. 24**). U.S. warns Iraq of military action over U.N. arms inspection (**Dec. 30**). Riots over unemployment erupt across France (**Dec. 31**).

Mother Teresa (1910–1997)

Princess Diana (1961–1997)

PICTURE CREDITS

The editors wish to thank the following organizations and individuals who have contributed illustrations to Headline History. The sources are listed alphabetically, with the name of the illustrations in the order in which they appear in the book.

Agence France Press/Archive Photos: **Mao Tse-tung;** AIP Niels Bohr Library: **Marie Curie, Albert Einstein;** AMW Pressedienst/Archive Photos: **Nelson Mandela;** Archive Photos: **Richard Wagner, William Butler Yeats, Pablo Picasso, Anne Frank, Woody Guthrie, Robert Frost, William Faulkner, The Beatles, Mahatma Gandhi, Duke Ellington, Tennessee Williams, Toni Morrison, Seamus Heaney, Ella Fitzgerald, Lech Walesa, Princess Diana, Pope John Paul, Mother Teresa, Yitzak Rabin, Malcolm X, William Rehnquist; Anwar Sadat;** Linda J. Barnes: **the Duomo in Florence;** British Information Services: **Margaret Thatcher;** Consolidated News/Archive Photos: **Jean-Bertrand Aristide;** Tina Diodati: **Aqueduct, Parthenon;** Embassy of the Philippines: **Corazon Aquino;** The French Consulate, Boston: **François Mitterrand;** Peter F. Harrington: **Stonehenge;** Erik Hjortshoj: **Pagoda;** Imapress/Archive Photos: **Boris Yeltsin;** INA/Reuters/Archive Photos: **Saddam Hussein;** John Fitzgerald Kennedy Library, Boston: **John F. Kennedy;** Priscilla Lee: **Dalai Lama;** Leo Baeck Inst./Archive Photos: **Sigmund Freud;** The Library of Congress Picture Collection: **Pocahontas, Taj Mahal, Edgar Allen Poe, Harriet Tubman, Walt Whitman, Dred Scott, Samuel Clemens (Mark Twain), Henri Matisse, W. E. B. DuBois, Woodrow Wilson, Bessie Smith, Dorothea Lange photo, Amelia Earhart, Harry S. Truman, John H. Glenn, Jr., Richard Nixon, Lyndon B. Johnson;** Pete Maio: **Mesa Verde;** Muzammil Paha/Reuters/Archive Photos: **Benazir Bhutto;** National Archives and Records Admin.: **Frederick Douglass, Harriet Beecher Stowe, Abraham Lincoln, Robert E. Lee, William Tecumseh Sherman, Chief Joseph, Benito Mussolini, Franklin Delano Roosevelt, Adolf Hitler, Winston Churchill, Atomic Bomb, Dwight D. Eisenhower, Rev. Martin Luther King, Jr.;** NASA: **Hubble Space Telescope;** Novosti Photos: **Vladimir Lenin, Mikhail S. Gorbachev;** Elaine Ouellette: **Pantheon in Rome;** The Permanent Mission of India to the U.N.: **Indira Gandhi;** Permanent Mission of Islamic Republic of Iran to the U.N.: **Ayatollah Ruhollah Khomeini;** Renée Scott: **Celtic Cross, Mayan Pyramid;** The Republican National Committee: **Ronald Reagan, George Bush;** Kim Storm: **Egyptian Pyramid;** United Nations: **Fidel Castro, Kofi Annan;** U.S. Army Photos: **Joseph Stalin, Yalta Conference, General Colin Powell;** U.S. State Department: **Madeleine Albright;** U.S. Supreme Court: **Thurgood Marshall, Sandra Day O'Connor;** Tasha Vincent: **Cathedral and Tower at Pisa, Chartres Cathedral, Michelangelo's David, Statue of Liberty;** The White House: **William J. Clinton.**

A Profile of the World

Source: The World Factbook, 1997.

Geography

Total area: 510.072 million sq km (196.93 million sq mi.). **Land area:** 148.94 million sq km (57.50 sq mi.). **Water area:** 361.132 million sq km (139.43 sq mi.). **Comparative area:** Land area about 15 times the size of the United States. **Note:** 70.8% of the world is water, 29.2% is land.

Land boundaries: The land boundaries in the world total 251,480.24 km (157,175.15 mi.) (not counting shared boundaries twice).

Maritime claims: *Contiguous zone:* 24 nm (nautical miles) claimed by most but can vary. *Continental shelf:* 200-m (656 ft.) depth claimed by most or to the depth of exploration, others claim 200 nm or to the edge of the continental margin. *Exclusive fishing zone:* 200 nm claimed by most but can vary. *Exclusive economic zone:* 200 nm claimed by most but can vary. *Territorial sea:* 12 nm claimed by most but can vary.

Note: Boundary situations with neighboring states prevent many countries from extending their fishing or economic zones to a full 200 nm; 43 nations and other areas that are landlocked include Afghanistan, Andorra, Armenia, Austria, Azerbaijan, Belarus, Bhutan, Bolivia, Botswana, Burkina Faso, Burundi, Central African Republic, Chad, Czech Republic, Ethiopia, Holy See (Vatican City), Hungary, Kazakhstan, Kyrgyzstan, Laos, Lesotho, Liechtenstein, Luxembourg, Malawi, Mali, Moldova, Mongolia, Nepal, Niger, Paraguay, Rwanda, San Marino, Slovakia, Swaziland, Switzerland, Tajikistan, The Former Yugoslav Republic of Macedonia, Turkmenistan, Uganda, Uzbekistan, West Bank, Zambia, Zimbabwe.

Climate: Two large areas of polar climates are separated by two rather narrow temperate zones from a wide equatorial band of tropical to subtropical climates.

Terrain: Highest elevation is Mt. Everest at 8,848 meters (29,028 ft.) and lowest land depression is the Dead Sea at –408 meters (–1,286 ft.) below sea level. An ice covered portion of Antarctica is –8,327 ft (–2,538 m) below sea level.

Natural resources: The rapid consumption of nonrenewable mineral resources, the depletion of forest areas and wetlands, the extinction of animal and plant species, and the deterioration in air and water quality (especially in Eastern Europe and the former U.S.S.R.) pose serious long-term problems that governments and peoples are only beginning to address.

Land use: *Arable land:* 10%. *Permanent crops:* 1%. *Meadows and pastures:* 26%. *Forests and woodlands:* 32%. *Other:* 31% (1993 est.).

Environment: Large areas are subject to severe weather (tropical cyclones), natural disasters (earthquakes, landslides, tsunamis, volcanic eruptions), overpopulation, industrial disasters, pollution (air, water, acid rain, toxic substances), loss of vegetation (overgrazing, deforestation, desertification), loss of wildlife, soil degradation, soil depletion, erosion.

People

Population: 5,930,695,974 (July 20, 1998, est. from U.S. Census Bureau).

Growth rate: 1.4% (1997 est.).

Birth rate: 23 births/1,000 population (1997 est.).

Death rate: 9 deaths/1,000 live births (1997 est.).

Sex ratio: 1.01 male(s)/female (1997 est.)

Infant mortality rate: 59 deaths/1,000 live births (1997 est.).

Life expectancy at birth: *Total population:* 63 years. *Male:* 61 years. *Female:* 64 years (1997 est.).

Total fertility rate: 2.9 children born/woman (1997 est.).

Literacy: Age 15 and over can read and write (1994 est.) *Combined:* 82%. *Male:* 68%. *Female:* 75%.

Government

Administrative divisions: 266 sovereign nations, dependent areas, other, and miscellaneous entries.

Legal system: Varies by individual country; 186 (not including Yugoslavia) are parties to the United Nations International Court of Justice (ICJ or World Court).

Economy

Overview: Real global output—gross world product (GWP)—rose an estimated 3.6% in 1996, with the newly industrializing Third World countries setting the pace. Results varied widely among regions and countries. Average growth of 2.3% in the GDP of industrialized countries (55% of GWP in 1996) and average growth of 6.5% in the GDP of less developed countries (39% of GWP) were partly offset by a 2% drop in the GDP of the former U.S.S.R./Eastern Europe area (only 6% of GWP). With the notable exception of Japan at 3%, unemployment was typically 6%–12% in the industrial world. The U.S. accounted for 21% of GWP in 1996; Western Europe accounted for 20%; and Japan accounted for 8%. These are the three "economic superpowers" presumably destined to compete for mastery in international markets on into the 21st century. As for the less developed countries: China, India, and the Four Dragons—South Korea, Taiwan, Hong Kong, and Singapore—once again posted records of 5% growth or better; however, many other countries, especially in Africa, continued to suffer from drought, rapid population growth, inflation, and civil strife. Central Europe and the 15 successor states to the USSR generally made progress in moving toward "market-friendly" economies, but output in Russia and Ukraine continued to fall. Externally, the nation-state, as a bedrock economic-political institution, is steadily losing control over international flows of people, goods, funds, and technology. Internally, the central government in a number of cases is losing control over resources as separatist regional movements—typically based on ethnicity—gain momentum, e.g., in the successor states of the former Soviet Union, in the former Yugoslavia, in India, and in Canada. In Western Europe, governments face the difficult political problem of channeling resources away from welfare programs in order to increase investment and strengthen incentives to seek employment. The addition of nearly 100 million people each year to an already overcrowded globe is exacerbating the problems of pollution, desertification, underemployment, epidemics, and famine. Because of their own internal problems, the industrialized countries have inadequate resources to deal effectively with the poorer areas of the world, which, at least from the economic point of view, are becoming further marginalized.

GDP: GWP (gross world product)—purchasing power parity—$35.8 trillion (1996 est.).

GDP—real growth rate: 3.6% (1996 est.).

GDP—per capita: $6,200 (1996 est.)

Inflation rate (consumer price index): *All countries:* 25% *Developed countries:* 2%–6% typically (1996 est.). *Developing countries:* 10%–60% typically (1996 est.).

Note: *National inflation rates vary widely individual cases.*

Labor force: 2.24 billion (1992).

Unemployment rate: 30% combined unemployment and underemployment in many nonindustrialized countries; developed countries, typically 6%–12% unemployment (1996 est.).

Exports: $4.6 trillion (f.o.b. 1996 est.) from the developed countries.

Imports: $4.4 trillion (c.i.f., 1996 est.).

External debt: $2 trillion for less developed countries (1996 est.).

Industrial production growth rate: 5% (1996 est.).

Electricity: 4 billion kW capacity; 12.34268 trillion kWh produced, 1,996 kWh per capita (1995).

Industries: Industry worldwide is dominated by the onrush of technology, especially in computers, robotics, telecommunications, and medicines and medical equipment; most of these advances take place in Organization for Economic Cooperation and Development (OECD)[1] nations; only a small portion of non-OECD countries have succeeded in rapidly adjusting to these technological forces; the accelerated development of new industrial (and agricultural) technology is complicating already grim environmental problems.

Agriculture: World agriculture runs the gamut of crops, livestock, forest products, and fish.

1. 24 full members: Australia, Austria, Belgium, Canada, Denmark, Finland, France, Germany, Greece, Iceland, Ireland, Italy, Japan, Luxembourg, Netherlands, New Zealand, Norway, Portugal, Spain, Sweden, Switzerland, Turkey, U.K., U.S.

Transportation

Railroads: 148,775 mi. (239,430 km) of narrow gauge track; 441,642 mi. (710,754 km) of standard gauge track; 156,059 mi. (251,153 km) of broad gauge track; includes about 118,060 to 121,167 mi. (190,000 to 195,000 km) of electrical routes of which 91,814 mi. (147,760 km) are in Europe, 15,229 mi. (24,509 km) in the Far East, 6,866 mi. (11,050 km) in Africa, 2,624 mi. (4,223 km) in South America, and only 2,585 mi. (4,160 km) in North America; fastest speed in daily service is 186 mph (300 kph) attained by France's SNCF TGV-Atlantique line.

Largest Ports and Harbors: Chiba, Houston, Kawasaki, Kobe, Marseille, Mina' al Ahmadi (Kuwait), New Orleans, New York, Rotterdam, Yokohama.

Merchant marine: 25,521 ships (1,000 GRT [gross register ton] or over) totaling 442,276,527 GRT/701,647,274 DWT (dead weight ton) (1996 est.).

Dependent Areas

Source: The World Factbook, 1997.

Dependent areas refer to a broad category of political entities associated in some way with a nation.

Australian Dependencies (6)

Ashmore and Cartier Islands
Christmas Island
Cocos (Keeling) Islands
Coral Sea Islands
Heard Island and McDonald Islands
Norfolk Island

Danish Dependencies (2)

Faroe Islands
Greenland

Dutch Dependencies (2)

Aruba
Netherlands Antilles

French Dependencies (16)

Bassas da India
Clipperton Island
Europa Island
French Guiana
French Polynesia
French Southern and Antarctic Lands
Glorioso Islands
Guadeloupe
Juan de Nova Island
Martinique
Mayotte
New Caledonia
Reunion
Saint Pierre and Miquelon
Tromelin Island
Wallis and Futuna

New Zealand Dependencies (3)

Cook Islands
Niue
Tokelau

Norwegian Dependencies (3)

Bouvet Island
Jan Mayen
Svalbard

Portuguese dependency (1)

Macau

UK Dependencies (15)

Anguilla
Bermuda
British Indian Ocean Territory
British Virgin Islands
Cayman Islands
Falkland Islands
Gibraltar
Guernsey
Jersey
Isle of Man
Montserrat
Pitcairn Islands
Saint Helena
South Georgia and the South Sandwich Islands
Turks and Caicos Islands

U.S. Dependencies (14)

American Samoa
Baker Island
Guam
Howland Island
Jarvis Island
Johnston Atoll
Kingman Reef
Midway Islands
Navassa Island
Northern Mariana Islands
Palmyra Atoll
Puerto Rico
Virgin Islands
Wake Island

Nothing is Rotten in the State of Denmark

Corruption survey labels Scandinavian country the world's least corrupt

The same, however, cannot be said for Cameroon, which was considered to be the most corrupt country in 1998, according to the annual survey by Transparency International, a Berlin-based organization that ranks countries according to their governments' propensity to accept bribes. Because of the absence of reliable data, only 85—roughly half—of the countries of the world could be surveyed.

In descending order after Denmark, the least corrupt countries were Finland, Sweden, New Zealand, Iceland, Canada, Singapore, the Netherlands, Norway, and Switzerland. Starting from the bottom of the corruption scale with Cameroon and ascending upward were Paraguay, Honduras, Tanzania, Nigeria, Indonesia, Colombia, Venezuela, Ecuador, and Russia. The United States ranked 17th from the top.

Country Statistics at a Glance

Country rankings of the type presented below cannot pretend to be definitive; instead they aspire only to provide the reader with a general approximation of the high and low ends on a particular scale. Country data vary enormously depending on the sources, and the absence of reliable data on some countries requires their omission, which further skews the results.

LARGEST COUNTRIES[1] (in sq mi.): 1998

(1)	Russia	6,592,800
(2)	Canada	3,851,809
(3)	China	3,691,521
(4)	United States	3,536,341
(5)	Brazil	3,286,470
(6)	Australia	2,966,150
(7)	India	1,229,737
(8)	Argentina	1,072,067
(9)	Kazakhstan	1,049,000
(10)	Sudan	967,491

HIGHEST POPULATION DENSITY[2] (per sq mi.): 1998

(1)	Monaco	43,844
(2)	Singapore	14,148
(3)	Malta	3,111
(4)	Bahrain	2,568
(5)	Maldives	2,524
(6)	Bangladesh	2,295
(7)	Taiwan	1,577
(8)	Barbados	1,560
(9)	Mauritius	1,484
(10)	Nauru	1,281

LOWEST POPULATION DENSITY[2] (per sq mi.): 1998

(1)	Western Sahara	1.4
(2)	Mongolia	4.3
(3)	Namibia	5.1
(4)	Botswana	6.2
(5)	Australia	6.3
	Mauritania	6.3
(7)	Iceland	6.8
	Suriname	6.8
(9)	Canada	8.0
(10)	Libya	8.4

HIGHEST GDP PER CAPITA[3] (PPP in US dollars): 1996

(1)	United States	$28,600
(2)	Norway	26,200
(3)	Canada	25,000
	Monaco	25,000
(5)	Luxembourg[4]	24,500
(6)	United Arab Emirates	23,800
(7)	Australia	23,600
(8)	Liechtenstein	23,000
(9)	Denmark	22,700
	Japan	22,700

LOWEST GDP PER CAPITA[3] (PPP in US dollars): 1995

(1)	Congo, Democratic Republic of the	$400
	Rwanda	400
(3)	Ethiopia	430
(4)	Somalia	500
(5)	Eritrea	570
(6)	Bosnia and Herzegovina	600
	Burundi	600
	Chad	600
	Mali	600
(10)	Niger[5]	640

LOWEST LITERACY RATES[2]: 1990

(1)	Burkina Faso	18%
(2)	Eritrea[1]	20
(3)	Sierra Leone	21
(4)	Benin	23
(5)	Somalia	24
	Guinea	24
(7)	Nepal	26
(8)	Sudan	27
	Gambia	27
(10)	Ethiopia	28
	Niger	28

HIGHEST INFLATION[3]: 1996

(1)	Angola	1,700%
(2)	Turkmenistan	600
(3)	Democratic Republic of the Congo[4]	542
(4)	Bulgaria	311
(5)	Afghanistan	240
(6)	Sudan	133
(7)	Venezuela	103
(8)	Yemen	85
(9)	Malawi[4]	83
(10)	Turkey	80

LOWEST INFLATION[3]: 1996

(1)	Nauru[6]	–3.6%
(2)	St. Kitts and Nevis[4]	–0.9
(3)	Seychelles[4]	–0.3
(4)	Bahrain	0
	Suriname	0
(6)	Japan	0.3
(7)	Oman	0.5
(8)	Finland	0.7
(9)	Liechtenstein	0.8
	Switzerland	0.8

HIGHEST INFANT MORTALITY RATE[2]: 1998 (deaths per 1,000 births)

(1)	Afghanistan	143.65
(2)	Western Sahara	139.74
(3)	Malawi	133.77
(4)	Angola	132.44
(5)	Sierra Leone	129.38
(6)	Guinea	128.92
(7)	Somalia	125.77
(8)	Ethiopia	125.65
(9)	Mali	121.72
(10)	Mozambique	120.26

HIGHEST LIFE EXPECTANCY[2] (in years): 1998

(1)	Andorra	83.45
(2)	San Marino	81.42
(3)	Japan	80.00
(4)	Australia	79.89
(5)	Sweden	79.19
(6)	Canada	79.16
(7)	Switzerland	78.88
(8)	Iceland	78.84
(9)	France	78.51
(10)	Singapore	78.49

LOWEST LIFE EXPECTANCY[2] (in years): 1998

(1)	Malawi	36.59
(2)	Zambia	37.07
(3)	Swaziland	38.53
(4)	Zimbabwe	39.16
(5)	Botswana	40.09
(6)	Ethiopia	40.85
(7)	Namibia	41.48
(8)	Niger	41.52
(9)	Rwanda	41.93
(10)	Uganda	42.60

LOWEST INFANT MORTALITY RATE[2]: 1998 (deaths per 1,000 births)

(1)	Finland	3.82
(2)	Singapore	3.87
(3)	Sweden	3.93
(4)	Andorra	4.09
(5)	Japan	4.10
(6)	Switzerland	4.92
(7)	Norway	5.01
(8)	Luxembourg	5.04
(9)	Austria	5.16
(10)	Denmark	5.17
	Netherlands	5.17

Sources: 1. Information Please Data Base 2. Bureau of the Census, International Data Base 3. *The World Factbook, 1997.* 4. Figure is for 1995. 5. Figure is for 1996. 6. Figure is for 1993. Note: Only countries for which statistics were available in sources 1, 2, or 3 figure in these lists.

World's 20 Most Populous Countries: 1998 and 2028

	1998			2028 (projected)	
Rank	Country	Population	Rank	Country	Population
1.	China	1,236,914,658	1.	India	1,457,646,922
2.	India	984,003,683	2.	China	1,408,192,504
3.	United States	270,311,758	3.	United States	342,517,584
4.	Indonesia	212,941,810	4.	Indonesia	294,788,383
5.	Brazil	169,806,557	5.	Pakistan	218,998,936
6.	Russia	146,861,022	6.	Nigeria	216,484,300
7.	Pakistan	135,135,195	7.	Brazil	212,569,857
8.	Bangladesh	127,567,002	8.	Bangladesh	185,447,506
9.	Japan	125,931,533	9.	Mexico	145,667,585
10.	Nigeria	110,532,242	10.	Russia	137,345,872
11.	Mexico	98,552,776	11.	Philippines	124,833,544
12.	Germany	82,079,454	12.	Japan	117,841,591
13.	Philippines	77,725,862	13.	Iran	116,223,642
14.	Vietnam	76,236,259	14.	Dem. Rep. of the Congo (formerly Zaire)	114,038,130
15.	Iran	68,959,931	15.	Vietnam	106,497,842
16.	Egypt	66,050,004	16.	Ethiopia	104,682,836
17.	Turkey	64,566,511	17.	Egypt	100,352,231
18.	Thailand	60,037,366	18.	Turkey	92,018,402
19.	United Kingdom	58,970,119	19.	Germany	73,614,282
20.	France	58,804,944	20.	Thailand	70,759,563

Source: U.S. Department of Commerce, Bureau of the Census, International Database.

World's 25 Most Populous Cities

		City proper				Metropolitan area	
Rank	City and country	Population	Year	Rank	City and country	Population	Year
1.	Seoul, South Korea	10,776,201	1995 est.	1.	Tokyo, Japan	27,242,000	1996 est.
2.	Bombay (Mumbai), India	9,925,891	1991 cen.	2.	Mexico City, Mexico	16,908,000	1996 est.
3.	Mexico City, Mexico	9,815,795	1990 cen.	3.	São Paulo, Brazil	16,792,000	1996 est.
4.	São Paulo, Brazil	9,393,753	1995 est.	4.	New York City, U.S.	16,390,000	1996 est.
5.	Jakarta, Indonesia	9,160,500	1995 est.	5.	Bombay (Mumbai), India	15,725,000	1996 est.
6.	Shanghai, China	8,930,000	1993 est.	6.	Shanghai, China	13,659,000	1996 est.
7.	Moscow, Russia	8,436,447	1996 est.	7.	Los Angeles, U.S.	12,576,000	1996 est.
8.	Tokyo, Japan	7,966,195	1995 cen.	8.	Calcutta, India	12,118,000	1996 est.
9.	Istanbul, Turkey	7,774,169	1995 est.	9.	Buenos Aires, Argentina	11,931,000	1996 est.
10.	New York City, U.S.	7,380,906	1996 est.	10.	Seoul, South Korea	11,768,000	1996 est.
11.	Delhi, India	7,206,704	1991 cen.	11.	Jakarta, Indonesia	11,500,000	1995 est.
12.	Cairo, Egypt	6,849,000	1994 est.	12.	Beijing, China	11,414,000	1996 est.
13.	Beijing, China	6,690,000	1993 est.	13.	Lagos, Nigeria	10,878,000	1996 est.
14.	Lima, Peru	5,706,127	1993 est.	14.	Tianjin, China	10,687,000	1995 est.
15.	Rio de Janeiro, Brazil	5,473,033	1995 est.	15.	Osaka, Japan	10,618,000	1996 est.
16.	Karachi, Pakistan	5,208,132	1981 cen.	16.	Delhi, India	10,298,000	1996 est.
17.	Tianjin, China	5,000,000	1993 est.	17.	Rio de Janeiro, Brazil	10,264,000	1996 est.
18.	Calcutta, India	4,339,819	1991 cen.	18.	Karachi, Pakistan	10,119,000	1996 est.
19.	Dhaka, Bangladesh	3,839,000	1991 cen.	19.	Cairo, Egypt	9,900,000	1996 est.
20.	Los Angeles, U.S.	3,553,638	1996 est.	20.	Paris, France	9,469,000	1995 est.
21.	Buenos Aires, Argentina	2,988,006	1995 est.	21.	Manila, Philippines	9,280,000	1995 est.
22.	Osaka, Japan	2,602,352	1995 cen.	22.	Moscow, Russia	9,233,000	1995 est.
23.	Paris, France	2,156,766	1991 cen.	23.	Dhaka, Bangladesh	8,500,000	1996 est.
24.	Manila, Philippines	1,654,761	1995 est.	24.	Istanbul, Turkey	7,817,000	1995 est.
25.	Lagos, Nigeria	1,518,000	1996 est.	25.	Lima, Peru	7,452,000	1995 est.

Source: 1998 Britannica Book of the Year. ©1998 by Encyclopedia Britannica, Inc. Reprinted with permission.

Total Population of the World by Decade, 1950–2050

(historical and projected)

Year	Total world population (mid-year figures)	Ten-year growth rate (%)	Year	Total world population (mid-year figures)	Ten-year growth rate (%)
1950	2,556,000,053	18.9%	2010	6,848,932,929	10.7%
1960	3,039,451,023	22.0	2020	7,584,821,144	8.7
1970	3,706,618,163	20.2	2030	8,246,619,341	7.3
1980	4,453,831,714	18.5	2040	8,850,045,889	5.6
1990	5,278,639,789	15.2	2050	9,346,399,468	—
2000	6,082,966,429	12.6			

Source: U.S. Bureau of the Census, International Data Base.

Area and Population of Countries

Mid-1998 Estimates

Country	Area (in sq km)	Population
Afghanistan	647,500	24,792,375
Albania	28,750	3,330,754
Algeria	2,381,740	30,480,793
Andorra	450	64,716
Angola	1,246,700	10,864,512
Antigua and Barbuda	440	64,006
Argentina	2,766,890	36,265,463
Armenia	29,800	3,421,775
Australia	7,686,850	18,613,087
Austria	83,850	8,133,087
Azerbaijan	86,600	7,855,576
The Bahamas	13,940	279,833
Bahrain	620	616,342
Bangladesh	144,000	127,567,002
Barbados	430	259,025
Belarus	207,600	10,409,050
Belgium	30,510	10,174,922
Belize	22,960	230,160
Benin	112,620	6,100,799
Bhutan	47,000	1,908,307
Bolivia	1,098,580	7,826,352
Bosnia and Herzegovina	51,233	3,365,727
Botswana	600,370	1,448,454
Brazil	8,511,965	169,806,557
Brunei	5,770	315,292
Bulgaria	110,910	8,240,426
Burkina Faso	274,200	11,266,393
Burma (Myanmar)	676,560	47,305,319
Burundi	27,830	5,537,387
Cambodia	181,040	11,339,562
Cameroon	475,440	15,029,433
Canada	9,976,140	30,675,398
Cape Verde	4,030	399,857
Central African Republic	622,980	3,375,771
Chad	1,284,000	7,359,512
Chile	756,950	14,787,781
China, People's Republic of	9,596,960	1,236,914,658
Colombia	1,138,910	38,580,949
Comoros	2,170	545,528
Republic of Congo	342,000	2,658,123
Democratic Republic of the Congo (formerly Zaire)	2,345,410	49,000,511
Costa Rica	51,100	3,604,642
Côte d'Ivoire	322,460	15,446,231
Croatia	56,538	4,671,584
Cuba	110,860	11,050,729
Cyprus	9,250	748,982
Czech Republic	78,703	10,286,470
Denmark	43,070	5,333,617
Djibouti	22,000	440,727
Dominica	750	65,777
Dominican Republic	48,730	7,998,766
Ecuador	283,560	12,336,572
Egypt	1,001,450	66,050,004
El Salvador	21,040	5,752,067
Equatorial Guinea	28,050	454,001
Eritrea	121,320	3,842,436
Estonia	45,100	1,421,335
Ethiopia	1,127,127	58,390,351
Fiji	18,270	802,611
Finland	337,030	5,149,242
France	547,030	58,804,944
Gabon	267,670	1,207,844
The Gambia	11,300	1,291,858
Georgia	69,700	5,108,527
Germany	356,910	82,079,454
Ghana	238,540	18,497,206
Greece	131,940	10,662,138
Grenada	340	96,217
Guatemala	108,890	12,007,580
Guinea	245,860	7,477,110
Guinea-Bissau	36,120	1,206,311
Guyana	214,970	707,954
Haiti	27,750	6,780,501
Honduras	112,090	5,861,955
Hungary	93,030	10,208,127
Iceland	103,000	271,033
India	3,287,590	984,003,683
Indonesia	1,919,440	212,941,810
Iran	1,648,000	68,959,931
Iraq	437,072	21,722,287
Ireland	70,280	3,619,480
Israel	20,770	5,643,966
Italy	301,230	56,782,748
Jamaica	10,990	2,634,678
Japan	377,835	125,931,533
Jordan	89,213	4,434,978
Kazakhstan	2,717,300	16,846,808
Kenya	582,650	28,337,071
Kiribati	717	83,976
North Korea	120,540	21,234,387
South Korea	98,480	46,416,796
Kuwait	17,820	1,913,285
Kyrgyzstan	198,500	4,522,281
Laos	236,800	5,260,842
Latvia	64,100	2,385,396
Lebanon	10,400	3,505,794
Lesotho	30,350	2,089,829
Liberia	111,370	2,771,901
Libya	1,759,540	5,690,727
Liechtenstein	160	31,717
Lithuania	65,200	3,600,158
Luxembourg	2,586	425,017
Macedonia	25,333	2,009,387
Madagascar	587,040	14,462,509
Malawi	118,480	9,840,474

Country	Area (in sq km)	Population
Malaysia	329,750	20,932,901
Maldives	300	290,211
Mali	1,240,000	10,108,569
Malta	320	379,563
Marshall Islands	181.3	63,031
Mauritania	1,030,700	2,511,473
Mauritius	1,860	1,168,256
Mexico	1,972,550	98,552,776
Micronesia	702	129,658
Moldova	33,700	4,457,729
Monaco	(acres) 465	32,035
Mongolia	1,565,000	2,578,530
Morocco	446,550	29,114,497
Mozambique	801,590	18,641,469
Namibia	825,418	1,622,328
Nauru	21	10,501
Nepal	140,800	23,698,421
Netherlands	37,330	15,731,112
New Zealand	268,680	3,625,388
Nicaragua	129,494	4,583,379
Niger	1,267,000	9,671,848
Nigeria	923,770	110,532,242
Norway	324,220	4,419,955
Oman	212,460	2,363,591
Pakistan	803,940	135,135,195
Palau	458	18,110
Panama	78,200	2,735,943
Papua New Guinea	461,690	4,599,785
Paraguay	406,750	5,291,020
Peru	1,285,220	26,111,110
Philippines	300,000	77,725,862
Poland	312,683	38,606,922
Portugal	92,080	9,927,556
Qatar	11,000	697,126
Romania	237,500	22,395,848
Russia	17,075,200	146,861,022
Rwanda	26,340	7,956,172
Saint Kitts and Nevis	269	42,291
Saint Lucia	620	152,335
Saint Vincent and the Grenadines	340	119,818
Samoa	2,860	224,713
San Marino	62	24,894
Sao Tome and Principe	960	150,123
Saudi Arabia	1,960,582	20,785,955
Senegal	196,190	9,723,149
Seychelles	455	78,641
Sierra Leone	71,740	5,080,004
Singapore	632.6	3,490,356
Slovakia	48,845	5,392,982
Slovenia	20,256	1,971,739
Solomon Islands	28,450	441,039
Somalia	637,660	6,841,695
South Africa	1,219,912	42,834,520
Spain	504,750	39,133,996
Sri Lanka	65,610	18,933,558
Sudan	2,505,810	33,550,552
Suriname	163,270	427,980
Swaziland	17,360	966,462
Sweden	449,964	8,886,738
Switzerland	41,290	7,260,357
Syria	185,180	16,673,282
Taiwan	35,980	21,908,135
Tajikistan	143,100	6,020,095
Tanzania	945,090	30,608,769
Thailand	514,000	60,037,366
Togo	56,790	4,905,827
Tonga	748	108,207
Trinidad and Tobago	5,130	1,116,595
Tunisia	163,610	9,380,404
Turkey	780,580	64,566,511
Turkmenistan	488,100	4,297,629
Tuvalu	26	10,444
Uganda	236,040	22,167,195
Ukraine	603,700	50,125,108
United Arab Emirates	75,581	2,303,088
United Kingdom	244,820	58,970,119
United States	9,372,610	270,311,758
Uruguay	176,220	3,284,841
Uzbekistan	447,400	23,784,321
Vatican City	.44	850
Vanuatu	14,760	185,204
Venezuela	912,050	22,803,409
Vietnam	329,560	76,236,259
Yemen	527,970	16,387,963
Yugoslavia[1]	102,350	10,526,135
Zambia	752,610	9,460,736
Zimbabwe	390,580	11,044,147

1. On April 27, 1992, Serbia and Montenegro formed a new state, the Federal Republic of Yugoslavia. *Source:* U.S. Bureau of the Census, International Data Base and *The World Factbook, 1997*.

Estimates of World Population by Regions

	Estimated population in millions							
Year	North America[1]	Latin America[2]	Europe[3]	Former U.S.S.R.	Asia[4]	Africa	Oceania	World total
1650	1	7	103	(5)	257	100	2	470
1750	1	10	144	(5)	437	100	2	694
1850	26	33	274	(5)	656	100	2	1,091
1900	81	63	423	(5)	857	141	6	1,571
1950	166	164	392	180	1,380	219	13	2,513
1960	199	215	425	214	1,683	275	16	3,027
1970	226	283	460	244	2,091	354	19	3,678
1980	252	365	484	266	2,618	472	23	4,478
1990	276	442	501	298	3,130	625	26	5,292
1995	292	481	509	297	3,403	721	28	5,734
1996	295	488	507	293	3,428	731	29	5,772
1997	297	496	508	293	3,477	750	29	5,852

1. U.S. (including Alaska and Hawaii), Bermuda, Canada, Greenland, and St. Pierre and Miquelon. 2. Mexico, Central and South America, and Caribbean Islands. 3. Includes Russia 1650–1900. 4. Excludes Russia (U.S.S.R.). 5. Included in Europe. NOTE: From 1930 on European Turkey included in Asia not Europe. *Sources:* W.F. Willcox, 1650–1900; United Nations, 1930–70. United States Department of Commerce, Bureau of the Census, International Database, 1980–97.

Infant Mortality Rates and Life Expectancy at Birth, by Sex, for Selected Countries, 1998

Country	Infant deaths per 1,000 live births			Life expectancy at birth (years)		
	Both sexes	Male	Female	Both sexes	Male	Female
North America						
Canada	5.59	6.08	5.06	79.16	75.86	82.63
Mexico	25.82	29.06	22.41	71.63	68.62	74.79
United States	6.44	7.43	5.40	76.13	72.85	79.58
Central and South America						
Brazil	36.96	40.86	32.88	64.36	59.39	69.59
Chile	10.39	11.07	9.68	75.16	72.01	78.48
Costa Rica	13.10	13.79	12.38	75.93	73.50	78.48
Ecuador	32.07	36.55	27.35	71.80	69.19	74.54
Guatemala	47.68	51.48	43.68	66.04	63.40	68.81
Panama	24.00	26.33	21.58	74.47	71.73	77.31
Peru	43.42	46.67	40.01	69.97	67.78	72.25
Trinidad and Tobago	18.84	21.52	16.09	70.51	68.06	73.03
Uruguay	14.11	15.59	12.56	75.53	72.39	78.84
Venezuela	27.52	31.06	23.72	72.66	69.68	75.87
Europe						
Albania	45.01	47.52	42.30	68.64	65.58	71.94
Austria	5.16	5.64	4.66	77.31	74.13	80.67
Belgium	6.27	6.93	5.58	77.35	74.13	80.74
Cyprus	7.97	9.93	5.92	76.79	74.62	79.07
Czech Republic	6.79	7.82	5.71	74.11	70.75	77.65
Denmark	5.17	5.80	4.50	76.31	73.64	79.12
Finland	3.82	4.16	3.46	77.15	73.61	80.83
France	5.69	6.45	4.89	78.51	74.60	82.62
Germany	5.20	5.76	4.61	76.99	73.83	80.33
Greece	7.26	7.65	6.84	78.31	75.76	81.04
Hungary	9.70	10.90	8.43	70.83	66.46	75.44
Ireland	6.04	6.46	5.59	76.19	73.44	79.11
Italy	6.40	6.93	5.83	78.38	75.26	81.70
Netherlands	5.17	5.88	4.41	78.01	75.14	81.03
Norway	5.01	5.55	4.44	78.23	75.42	81.21
Poland	13.18	14.57	11.72	72.77	68.60	77.16
Portugal	6.87	7.59	6.10	75.66	72.27	79.25
Russia	23.26	25.13	21.29	64.97	58.61	71.64
Slovakia	9.73	10.88	8.52	73.19	69.41	77.15
Spain	6.51	7.33	5.64	77.56	73.78	81.59
Sweden	3.93	4.45	3.37	79.19	76.52	82.00
Switzerland	4.92	5.47	4.33	78.88	75.71	82.22
United Kingdom	5.87	6.51	5.19	77.19	74.57	79.96
Asia						
Bangladesh	97.67	105.45	89.51	56.66	56.69	56.63
China	45.46	36.46	55.82	69.69	68.32	71.06
India	63.14	64.47	61.74	62.90	62.11	63.73
Iran	48.95	49.89	47.95	68.25	66.83	69.74
Israel	8.02	8.65	7.37	78.41	76.52	80.39
Japan	4.10	4.53	3.64	80.00	76.91	83.25
Pakistan	93.48	95.02	91.88	59.07	58.23	59.96
South Korea	7.79	8.07	7.48	73.95	70.37	78.00
Sri Lanka	16.33	18.00	14.57	72.55	69.82	75.41
Syria	37.60	38.65	36.51	67.76	66.48	69.11
Africa						
Egypt	69.23	71.10	67.28	62.07	60.09	64.14
Kenya	59.38	62.16	56.52	47.57	47.02	48.13
South Africa	52.04	56.65	47.29	55.65	53.56	57.80
Oceania						
Australia	5.26	5.80	4.68	79.89	76.95	82.98
New Zealand	6.37	7.42	5.26	77.55	74.35	80.91

Source: U.S. Bureau of the Census, International Data Base.

Crude Birth and Death Rates for Selected Countries

(per 1,000 population)

	Birth rate						Death rate					
Country	1998	1994	1990	1985	1980	1975	1998	1994	1990	1985	1980	1975
Australia	13.47	14.5	15.4	15.7	15.3	16.9	6.89	7.1	7.0	7.5	7.4	7.9
Austria	9.89	11.5	11.6	11.6	12.0	12.5	10.05	10.0	10.6	11.9	12.2	12.8
Belgium	10.21	11.6	12.6	11.5	12.7	12.2	10.41	10.4	10.6	11.2	11.6	12.2
Czech Republic[1]	8.96	10.3	13.4	14.5	16.4	19.6	10.92	11.3	11.7	11.8	12.1	11.5
Denmark	12.18	13.4	12.4	10.6	11.2	14.2	11.08	11.8	11.9	11.4	10.9	10.1
France	11.68	12.3	13.5	13.9	14.8	14.1	9.12	9.0	9.3	10.1	10.2	10.6
Germany[2]	8.84	9.5	11.4	9.6	10.0	9.7	10.77	10.9	11.2	11.5	11.6	12.1
Greece	9.65	9.9	10.2	11.7	15.4	15.7	9.37	9.4	9.3	9.4	9.1	8.9
Ireland	13.49	13.4	15.1	17.6	21.9	21.5	8.51	8.6	9.1	9.4	9.7	10.6
Israel	19.99	21.2	22.2	23.5	24.1	28.2	6.19	6.3	6.2	6.6	6.7	7.1
Italy	9.13	9.2	9.8	10.1	11.2	14.8	10.18	9.6	9.4	9.5	9.7	9.9
Japan	10.26	9.9	9.9	11.9	13.7	17.2	7.94	7.0	6.7	6.2	6.2	6.4
Luxembourg	11.12	13.6	13.3	11.2	11.5	11.2	9.29	9.5	10.1	11.0	11.5	12.2
Mauritius	18.64	19.6	21.0	18.8	27.0	25.1	6.69	6.7	6.5	6.8	7.2	8.1
Netherlands	11.62	12.7	13.3	12.3	12.8	13.0	8.69	8.7	8.6	8.5	8.1	8.3
New Zealand	14.89	16.3	18.0	15.6	n.a.	18.4	7.60	7.8	7.9	8.4	n.a.	8.1
Norway	12.90	13.6	14.3	12.3	12.5	14.1	10.17	10.1	10.7	10.7	10.1	9.9
Panama	21.99	21.7	23.9	26.6	26.8	32.3	5.14	n.a.	n.a.	n.a.	n.a.	n.a.
Poland	9.79	12.5	14.3	18.2	19.5	18.9	9.76	10.1	10.2	10.3	9.8	8.7
Portugal	10.63	10.7	11.8	12.8	16.4	19.1	10.26	9.9	10.4	9.6	9.9	10.4
Romania	9.33	11.0	13.6	15.8	n.a.	n.a.	11.62	11.6	10.6	10.9	n.a.	n.a.
Switzerland	10.81	11.9	12.5	11.6	11.3	12.3	9.03	8.9	9.5	9.2	9.2	8.7
Tunisia	20.07	22.7	25.8	31.3	35.2	36.6	5.06	n.a.	n.a.	n.a.	n.a.	n.a.
United Kingdom	12.01	12.9	13.9	13.3	13.5	12.5	10.72	10.7	11.2	11.8	11.8	11.9
United States	14.40	15.2	16.7	15.7	16.2	14.0	8.80	8.8	8.6	8.7	8.9	8.9

1. Data prior to 1994 pertain to the former Czechoslovakia. 2. All data pertaining to Germany prior to 1990 are for West Germany. NOTE: n.a. = not available. *Source:* United Nations, *Monthly Bulletin of Statistics, June 1997*. Data for 1998 from the U.S. Bureau of the Census, International Database.

Crude Marriage Rates for Selected Countries

(per 1,000 population)

Country	1997	1996	1995	1994	1993	1992	1991	1990
Australia	5.8	5.8	6.1	6.2	6.4	6.6	6.6	6.9
Austria	5.1	5.2	5.3	5.4	5.6	5.8	5.6	5.8
Belgium	n.a.	5.0	5.1	5.2	5.4	5.8	6.2	6.6
Bulgaria	n.a.	n.a.	4.0	4.5	4.9	5.0	5.4	6.7
Czech Republic[1]	5.6	5.2	5.3	5.6	6.4	n.a.	6.7	8.4
Denmark	6.4	6.8	6.6	6.8	6.1	6.2	6.0	6.1
Finland	4.6	4.6	4.7	4.7	4.9	4.6	4.7	4.8
France	n.a.	4.8	4.4	4.4	4.4	4.7	4.9	5.1
Germany[2]	5.1	5.2	5.3	5.4	5.4	5.7	6.3	6.5
Greece	n.a.	4.3	6.1	5.4	5.9	4.7	6.0	5.8
Hungary	4.6	4.9	5.2	5.3	5.3	5.5	5.9	6.4
Ireland	n.a.	4.6	4.4	4.6	4.5	4.5	4.8	5.0
Israel	n.a.	6.1	6.1	n.a.	6.2	6.5	6.5	7.0
Italy	4.8	4.7	4.9	5.0	4.8	5.4	5.5	5.4
Japan	6.3	6.4	6.3	6.3	6.4	6.1	6.0	5.8
Luxembourg	n.a.	5.1	5.1	5.9	6.0	6.4	6.7	6.2
Netherlands	5.5	5.4	5.2	5.4	5.8	6.4	6.3	6.4
New Zealand	5.8	6.0	6.2	6.3	6.4	6.5	6.8	7.0
Norway	n.a.	n.a.	n.a.	4.6	n.a.	4.5	4.7	5.2
Poland	5.3	5.3	5.4	5.4	5.4	5.7	6.0	6.7
Portugal	6.5	6.5	n.a.	n.a.	6.9	7.1	6.8	7.3
Romania	6.5	6.7	6.8	6.7	7.1	7.7	7.9	8.3
Russia	n.a.	5.9	7.3	7.3	n.a.	7.1	8.5	8.9
Sweden	n.a.	3.8	3.8	3.9	3.9	4.3	4.6	4.7
Switzerland	5.3	5.7	5.6	6.1	6.2	6.6	7.0	6.9
United Kingdom	n.a.	5.6	6.4	5.7	5.9	6.0	6.1	6.8
United States	n.a.	8.8	8.9	9.1	9.0	9.2	9.4	9.8
Yugoslavia[3]	5.3	5.3	5.7	5.7	5.8	6.0	n.a.	6.2

1. Data prior to 1993 pertain to the former Czechoslovakia. 2. All data pertaining to Germany prior to 1990 are for West Germany. 3. Beginning January 1992, data refer to the Federal Republic of Yugoslavia. Prior to that date, data refer to the Socialist Federal Republic of Yugoslavia. NOTE: n.a. = not available. *Source:* United Nations, *Monthly Bulletin of Statistics, June 1998.*

Divorce Rate per 1,000 Married Women

Selected Countries, 1970–1994

Country	1970	1980	1990	1992	1993	1994
Canada	6	10	11	11	11	11
Denmark	8	11	13	13	13	13
France	3	6	8	n.a.	n.a.	n.a.
Germany[1]	5	6	8	7	7	n.a.
Italy	1	1	2	2	n.a.	n.a.
Japan	4	5	5	6	6	n.a.
Netherlands	3	8	8	9	9	n.a.
Sweden	7	11	12	13	13	n.a.
United Kingdom	5[2]	12[2]	13	13	13	n.a.
United States	15	23	21	21	21	21

NOTE: n.a. = not available. 1. Data prior to 1991 are for the former West Germany. 2. England and Wales only. *Source: Statistical Abstract of the United States, 1996.*

Prevalence of Contraceptive Use by Region

Region	Year(s)	No method	All methods	Pill	IUD	Condom	Sterilization			Other modern	Tradi- tional
							Total	Male	Female		
Asia	1972–1994	47.7%	52.3%	8.7%	7.3%	5.4%	18.6%	3.3%	16.1%	4.0%	9.1%
Commonwealth of Independent States	1990	71.0	29.0	5.4	31.1	4.8	0.8	n.a.	n.a.	6.2	13.3
Eastern Europe	1976–1993	39.8	60.2	12.8	11.1	9.4	2.1	0.5	2.3	1.6	37.4
Latin America and the Caribbean	1975–1994	47.4	52.6	15.0	6.3	5.1	16.8	0.7	16.0	4.3	7.2
North Africa	1988–1992	52.7	47.3	22.2	12.6	1.2	1.1	0.0	4.2	0.8	6.4
North America	1984–1988	26.3	73.7	13.1	3.7	9.3	39.9	12.9	27.0	3.6	4.5
Near East	1971–1993	66.1	34.0	9.4	7.0	2.9	2.9	0.2	3.2	0.5	11.7
Oceania	1976–1986	68.7	31.3	15.9	6.0	7.2	21.2	6.5	15.3	1.4	10.4
Sub-Saharan Africa	1982–1994	79.9	20.1	5.9	1.7	1.1	2.7	0.2	1.9	2.9	7.0
Western Europe	1973–1993	27.1	72.9	29.2	11.0	12.4	8.2	3.6	5.8	1.8	12.5

NOTE: n.a. = not available. *Source:* U.S. Bureau of the Census, International Data Base.

Legal Abortions in Selected Countries, 1985–1994

Country	1985	1987	1988	1989	1990	1991	1992	1993	1994
Bulgaria	132,041	133,815	—	132,021	144,644	—	132,891	107,416	—
Canada	60,956	63,585	—	70,705	71,092	70,277	59,694	—	—
Cuba	138,671	152,704	155,325	151,146	147,530	124,059	—	—	—
Denmark	19,919	20,830	21,199	21,456	20,589	19,729	18,833	18,607	17,598
Finland	13,832	13,000[1]	12,995	12,658	12,232	—	—	—	10,013
France	173,335	161,036	163,000	165,199	161,646	162,902	—	—	—
Germany[1]	—	—	—	—	—	124,377	118,609	111,236	103,586
Greece	180	—	—	—	—	11,109	11,977	—	—
Hungary	81,970	84,547	87,106	90,508	90,394	89,931	87,065	75,258	74,491
Iceland	705	691	673	670	714	658	743	—	—
India	583,704	—	534,870	582,161	596,345	581,215	—	—	—
Israel	18,406	15,290	16,181	15,216	18,000	15,767	18,444	17,164	—
Italy	210,192	187,618	175,541	166,290	161,285	157,173	149,824	144,761	124,334
Japan	550,127	497,756	486,146	466,876	456,797	436,299	413,032	386,807	364,350
Netherlands	17,300	17,760	18,014	17,996	18,384	19,568	19,422	19,804	20,811
New Zealand	7,130	8,789	10,000	10,200	—	11,594	11,460	—	—
Norway	14,599	15,422	15,852	16,208	15,551	15,528	15,164	14,909	—
Poland	135,564	122,536	105,333	80,127	59,417	30,878	11,640	1,208	874
Russia	—	4,385,627	4,608,953	4,427,713	4,103,425	3,608,412	3,436,695	3,243,957	2,481,493
Singapore	23,512	21,226	20,135	20,619	18,654	17,798	17,073	16,476	15,690
Sweden	30,838	34,707	37,585	37,920	37,489	35,788	34,849	34,169	32,293
United Kingdom	180,983	165,542	178,426	180,622	184,092	178,416	171,260	173,686	169,964
United States	1,588,600	1,353,671	1,371,285	1,396,658	1,429,577	1,388,937	—	—	—

1. Figures for Germany represent those available after the unification of the Federal Republic of Germany and the German Democratic Republic in October 1990. NOTE: Data latest available. *Source:* United Nations, *Demographic Yearbook, 1996.*

Gross Domestic Product Per Capita, 1996 (in 1996 U.S. Dollars)

More Than $15,000
Andorra
Aruba
Australia
Austria
Bahamas, The
Belgium
Bermuda
Brunei
Canada
Cayman Islands
Denmark
Faroe Islands
Finland
France
Germany
Greenland
Iceland
Ireland
Israel
Italy
Japan
Kuwait
Liechtenstein
Luxembourg
Monaco
Netherlands
Norway
Qatar
San Marino
Singapore
Spain
Sweden
Switzerland
United Arab Emirates
United Kingdom
United States

$10,001 to $15,000
Bahrain
Barbados
British Virgin Islands
Chile
Cyprus
Czech Republic
Guam
Macau
Malaysia
Malta
Man, Isle of
Mauritius
Northern Mariana Islands
Portugal
Saudi Arabia
St. Pierre and Miquelon
Slovenia
South Korea
Taiwan
Trinidad and Tobago
Virgin Islands (U.S.)

$3,001 to $10,000
Algeria
Anguilla
Antigua and Barbuda
Argentina
Belarus
Botswana
Brazil
Bulgaria
Columbia
Costa Rica
Croatia
Dominican Republic
Ecuador
Egypt
Estonia
Fiji
French Guiana
French Polynesia
Gabon
Gibraltar
Greece
Grenada
Guadeloupe
Guatemala
Hungary
Indonesia
Iran
Jamaica
Jordan
Latvia
Lebanon
Libya
Lithuania
Martinique
Mexico
Montserrat
Morocco
Namibia
Nauru
Netherlands Antilles
New Caledonia
Oman
Palau
Panama
Paraguay
Peru
Poland
Puerto Rico
Reunion
Romania
Russia
St. Kitts and Nevis
St. Lucia
Seychelles
Slovakia
South Africa
Sri Lanka
Suriname
Swaziland
Syria
Thailand
Tunisia
Turkey
Turks and Caicos Islands
Ukraine
Uruguay
Venezuela

$1,000 to $3,000
Albania
American Samoa
Armenia
Azerbaijan
Bangladesh
Belize
Benin
Bolivia
Burma
Cameroon
Cape Verde
China
Congo, Republic of
Cook Islands
Côte d'Ivoire
Cuba
Djibouti
Dominica
El Salvador
Gambia, The
Gaza Strip
Georgia
Ghana
Guyana
Haiti
Honduras
India
Iraq
Kazakhstan
Kenya
Kyrgyzstan
Laos
Lesotho
Liberia
Maldives
Marshall Islands
Mauritania
Micronesia, Federated States of
Moldova
Mongolia
Nepal
Nicaragua
Nigeria
Pakistan
Papua New Guinea
Philippines
St. Vincent and the Grenadines
São Tomé and Príncipe
Senegal
Serbia and Montenegro
Solomon Islands
Tokelau Islands
Tonga
Turkmenistan
Uzbekistan
Vanuatu
Vietnam
Wallis and Futuna Islands
West Bank
Western Samoa
Yemen
Zimbabwe

Less than $1,000
Afghanistan
Angola
Bhutan
Bosnia and Herzegovina
Burkina Faso
Burundi
Cambodia
Central African Republic
Chad
Comoros
Congo, Dem. Republic of the
Equatorial Guinea
Eritrea
Ethiopia
Guinea
Guinea-Bissau
Kiribati
Madagascar
Malawi
Mali
Mayotte
Mozambique
Niger
Rwanda
Sierra Leone
Somalia
Sudan
Tajikistan
Tanzania
The Former Yugoslav Republic of Macedonia
Togo
Tuvalu
Uganda
Zambia

Source: CIA Handbook of International Economic Statistics.

Consumer Price Indexes for All Items for Selected Countries, 1997

(1990 = 100)

Country	Index	Country	Index	Country	Index
Australia	116.4	Indonesia	176.4	Singapore	117.3
Austria	121.0	Italy	135.4	Slovakia[1, 3]	178.6
Canada	115.3	Japan	109.0	South Africa	198.9
Chile	217.8	Jordan	135.1	Spain	135.9
Czech Republic	297.9	South Korea	148.1	Sri Lanka	207.1
Denmark	115.1	Mexico[2]	364.0	Sweden	123.9
Egypt	200.4	Morocco[1]	139.5	Turkey[3]	3,359.1
Finland	114.0	Netherlands	119.5	United Kingdom	124.9
France	115.2	Norway	116.8	United States	122.8
Germany[1]	118.6	Philippines	186.7	Uruguay	1,660.7
Greece	218.5	Russia[1,3]	284,429.0		

1. Base: 1991 = 100. 2. Base: 1994 = 100. 3. Data is for 1996 *Source:* International Labour Office from *U.N. Monthly Bulletin of Statistics, June 1998.*

Wheat, Rice, and Corn Exports and Imports, 1990–1994

	Exports				Imports		
Leading exporters	1990	1993	1994	Leading importers	1990	1993	1994
Wheat				**Wheat**			
United States	28,749	37,141	32,110	China	13,487	7,368	8,120
France	19,337	20,954	15,033	Japan	5,474	5,814	6,353
Canada	18,166	18,415	21,683	Russia	n.a.	5,774	2,285
Australia	11,629	9,582	12,823	Brazil	1,962	5,671	6,322
Argentina	6,041	6,019	5,572	Italy	4,705	5,066	4,904
Germany	2,829	4,640	6,148	Egypt	6,439	5,038	7,125
United Kingdom	4,561	4,014	3,616	South Korea	2,516	4,939	6,057
Italy	1,777	1,902	1,823	Algeria	3,604	4,244	5,585
Belgium-Luxembourg	1,367	1,797	1,888	Uzbekistan	n.a.	4,100	—
Saudi Arabia	1,267	1,569	895	Pakistan	2,047	2,890	1,902
Rice				**Rice**			
Thailand	4,017	4,989	4,859	Iran	620	1,159	475
United States	2,474	2,680	2,822	Brazil	414	701	987
Vietnam	1,624	1,765	1,970	Iraq	380	655	200
China	405	1,507	1,630	Saudi Arabia	280	577	434
Pakistan	744	1,032	984	Malaysia	330	389	341
India	505	768	891	South Africa	306	385	431
Italy	577	574	619	Hong Kong	374	373	358
Uruguay	290	505	408	Cuba	235	370	255
Australia	424	482	585	United Arab Emirates	309	370	350
Indonesia	2	351	169	Senegal	392	363	348
Corn				**Corn**			
United States	52,172	40,365	35,877	Japan	16,008	16,863	15,930
China	3,405	11,098	8,740	South Korea	6,158	6,207	5,749
France	7,195	7,758	8,013	China	5,440	5,466	5,601
Argentina	2,998	4,871	4,154	Russia	n.a.	4,391	901
Belgium-Luxembourg	20	414	489	Spain	1,810	2,401	2,339
Canada	122	357	381	Egypt	1,900	2,148	2,021
Germany	226	219	308	Malaysia	1,480	2,058	1,969
South Africa	2,001	216	4,000	United Kingdom	1,627	1,508	1,602
Zimbabwe	742	216	150	Brazil	699	1,323	1,409
Italy	80	213	16	Belgium-Luxembourg	1,035	1,284	1,557

In thousands of metric tons. Countries listed are the 10 leading exporters or importers in 1993. — Represents or rounds to zero. n.a. = not available. *Source:* Food and Agriculture Organization of the United Nations, Rome, Italy, FAO AGRISTAT database. From *Statistical Abstract of the United States 1996.* NOTE: Data are most recent available.

Exchange Rates For Selected Currencies, 1996

Country	Currency	1996	Country	Currency	1996
Afghanistan	Afghani	50.600	Kuwait	Dinar	0.299
Albania	Lek	104.500	Laos	Kip	921.135
Algeria	Algerian Dinar	54.749	Latvia	Lats	0.551
Argentina	Peso	1.000	Lebanon	Lebanese Pound	1,571.440
Armenia	Dram	414.040	Lesotho	Loti	4.299
Aruba	Aruban Florin	1.790	Liberia	Liberian Dollar	1.000
Australia	Australian Dollar	1.278	Libya	Libyan Dollar	0.362
Austria	Schilling	10.587	Lithuania	Litas	4.000
Bahamas, The	Bahamanian Dollar	1.000	Luxembourg	Franc	30.962
Bangladesh	Taka	41.794	Madagascar	Malagasy Franc	4,061.250
Barbados	Barbados Dollar	2.011	Mali	Cfa Franc	511.550
Belgium	Franc	30.962	Mauritius	Rupee	17.948
Belize	Belize Dollar	2.000	Mexico	New Peso	7.601
Benin	Cfa Franc	511.550	Moldova	Leu	4.603
Bhutan	Ngultrum	35.433	Mongolia	Tugrik	548.400
Botswana	Pula	3.324	Morocco	Dirham	8.716
Brazil	Real	1.005	Mozambique	Metical	11,293.800
Bulgaria	Lev	177.890	Namibia	Namibia Dollar	4.299
Burkina Faso	Cfa Franc	511.550	Nepal	Rupee	56.692
Burma	Kyat	5.918	Netherlands	Guilder	1.686
Cambodia	Riels	2,624.100	New Zealand	New Zealand Dollar	1.455
Canada	Canadian Dollar	1.363	Nicaragua	Cordoba	8.436
Cape Verde	Escudo	82.592	Niger	Cfa Franc	511.550
Chile	Peso	412.268	Norway	Krone	6.450
China	Yuan	8.314	Pakistan	Rupee	36.079
Congo, Republic of	Cfa Franc	511.550	Panama	Balboa	1.000
Costa Rica	Colon	207.689	Papua New Guinea	Kina	1.319
Croatia	Kuna	5.430	Paraguay	Guarani	2,063.800
Cyprus	Cyprus Pound	0.466	Philippines	Peso	26.216
Czech Republic	Koruna	27.140	Poland	Zloty	2.696
Denmark	Krone	5.799	Portugal	Escudo	154.244
Dominica	E. Caribbean Dollar	2.700	Russia	Ruble	5,121.000
Dominican Republic	Peso	13.775	Rwanda	Rwanda Franc	306.820
Ecuador	Sucre	3,189.470	Saudi Arabia	Riyal	3.745
Egypt	Egyptian Pound	3.391	Senegal	Cfa Franc	511.550
El Salvador	Colon	8.755	Sierra Leone	Leone	920.732
Estonia	Kroon	12.034	Singapore	Singapore Dollar	1.410
Ethiopia	Birr	6.352	Slovakia	Koruna	30.650
Finland	Markka	4.594	Slovenia	Tolar	135.360
France	Franc	5.116	South Africa	Rand	4.299
Gabon	Cfa Franc	511.550	Spain	Peseta	126.662
Germany	Deutsche Mark	1.505	Sri Lanka	Rupee	55.271
Greece	Drachma	240.712	Suriname	Guilder	401.260
Guatemala	Quetzal	6.050	Sweden	Krona	6.706
Haiti	Gourde	15.701	Switzerland	Swiss Franc	1.236
Honduras	Lempira	11.705	Syria	Syrian Pound	11.225
Hungary	Forint	152.647	Tanzania	Tanzania Shilling	579.977
Iceland	Krona	66.500	Thailand	Baht	25.343
India	Rupee	35.433	Togo	Cfa Franc	511.550
Indonesia	Rupiah	2,342.300	Tonga	Pa'Anga	1.232
Iran	Rial	1,750.760	Trinidad and Tobago	Tt Dollar	6.005
Iraq	Dinar	0.311	Tunisia	Dinar	0.973
Ireland	Irish Pound	0.625	Turkey	Lira	81,405.000
Israel	Shekel	3.192	Uganda	Uganda Shilling	1,046.080
Italy	Lira	1,542.950	Ukraine	Karbovanet	1.830
Jamaica	Jamaica Dollar	37.120	United Arad Emirates	Dirham	3.671
Japan	Yen	108.780	United Kingdom	Pound Sterling	0.641
Jordan	Dinar	0.709	Uruguay	Peso	7.972
Kazakhstan	Tenge	67.300	Yemen	Rial	50.040
Kenya	Kenya Shilling	57.115	Zambia	Kwacha	1,203.710
Korea, South	Won	804.450			

National currency units per dollar, except as noted. Data are averages of certified noon buying rates for cable transfers. *Source: Statistical Abstract of the United States, 1997,* based on data from the Board of Governors of the Federal Reserve System, *Federal Reserve Bulletin,* monthly.

Worldwide Unemployment Figures

	Year	Percentage unemployed: Both sexes	Male	Female
Albania	1991	9.1%	n.a.%	n.a%
Algeria	1992	23.8	24.2	20.3
Argentina	1995	18.8	16.5	22.3
Australia	1995	8.5	8.8	8.0
Austria	1996	4.1	3.9	4.5
Bahamas	1994	13.3	12.6	14.0
Barbados	1995	19.7	16.5	22.9
Belarus	1995	2.7	2.2	3.3
Belgium	1995	9.3	7.3	12.2
Belize	1994	11.1	9.0	15.1
Bolivia	1996	4.2	3.7	4.5
Brazil	1993	6.2	5.4	7.4
Bulgaria	1995	11.1	n.a.	n.a.
Canada	1995	9.5	9.8	9.2
Chile	1995	4.7	4.4	5.3
China	1994	2.8	0.8	1.1
Hong Kong	1996	2.8	3.1	2.3
Costa Rica	1995	5.2	4.6	6.5
Croatia	1993	16.8	14.0	20.1
Cyprus	1995	2.6	1.9	3.7
Czech Republic	1996	3.9	3.3	4.6
Denmark	1995	7.0	5.6	8.6
Dominican Republic	1996	16.7	10.2	28.7
Ecuador	1994	7.1	5.8	9.3
Egypt	1994	11.0	7.4	22.8
El Salvador	1995	7.7	8.7	5.9
Estonia	1995	8.7	9.6	7.7
Fiji	1995	5.4	n.a.	n.a.
Finland	1995	17.4	17.3	16.7
France	1995	11.6	9.8	13.9
French Guiana	1991	9.7	8.2	11.6
Germany	1996	8.8	8.2	9.6
Greece	1995	10.0	6.7	15.4
Guadeloupe	1991	19.9	n.a.	n.a.
Guam	1993	5.5	n.a.	n.a.
Honduras	1995	3.2	3.1	3.4
Hungary	1996	9.9	10.7	8.8
Iceland	1996	3.7	3.4	4.1
Ireland	1996	11.9	11.9	11.9
Israel	!995	6.9	5.6	8.6
Italy	1994	11.1	8.5	15.8
Jamaica	1992	15.9	9.7	22.9
Japan	1995	3.2	3.1	3.2
Kazakstan	1993	1.0	n.a.	n.a.
Korea, Republic of	1996	2.0	2.3	1.6
Latvia	1995	6.6	6.0	7.2
Lithuania	1995	7.3	6.6	8.0
Luxembourg	1994	2.7	n.a.	n.a.
Macau	1995	3.6	4.1	3.0
Malaysia	1995	2.8%	n.a.%	n.a.%
Malta	1993	4.5	5.2	2.5
Mauritius	1995	9.8	7.8	13.9
Mexico	1995	4.7	4.6	5.0
Morocco	1992	16.0	13.0	25.3
Netherlands	1995	7.1	5.9	8.8
Netherlands Antilles	1994	12.8	n.a.	n.a.
New Zealand	1996	6.1	6.2	6.1
Nicaragua	1991	14.0	11.3	19.4
Norway	1995	4.9	5.2	4.6
Pakistan	1994	4.8	3.9	10.0
Panama	1996	13.9	11.0	19.4
Paraguay	1994	4.4	4.9	3.7
Peru	1995	7.1	6.0	8.7
Philippines	1995	8.4	7.7	9.4
Poland	1996	12.3	11.0	13.9
Portugal	1996	7.2	6.4	8.2
Puerto Rico	1995	13.7	16.6	10.8
Republic of Moldova	1995	1.0	n.a.	n.a
Reunion	1993	34.4	n.a.	n.a.
Romania	1996	6.7	6.3	7.4
Russian Federation	1996	9.3	9.6	9.0
San Marino	1995	3.9	1.5	7.0
Singapore	1996	3.0	2.9	3.1
Slovakia	1995	13.1	13.8	12.6
Slovenia	1996	7.3	7.5	7.0
South Africa	1995	4.5	n.a.	n.a.
Spain	1995	22.9	18.2	30.6
Sri Lanka	1995	12.5	8.8	19.7
Suriname	1994	12.7	11.4	15.0
Sweden	1996	8.0	8.5	7.5
Switzerland	1996	3.7	3.4	4.1
Syrian Arab Republic	1991	6.8	5.2	14.0
Thailand	1993	1.5	1.2	1.8
The FYR of Macedonia	1995	35.6	31.9	41.7
Trinidad and Tobago	1995	17.2	15.1	20.6
Turkey	1995	6.6	6.6	6.8
United Kingdom	1996	8.2	9.7	6.3
United States	1995	5.6	5.6	5.6
U.S. Virgin Islands	1995	5.7	n.a	n.a.
Uruguay	1995	10.2	8.0	13.2
Uzbekistan	1995	0.4	0.3	0.5
Venezuela	1995	10.3	9.0	12.8

Source: International Labour Office, *Year Book of Labour Statistics 1997* (Geneva, 1997). Unless otherwise indicated, data are from labor force sample surveys or general household sample surveys.

Countries with Nuclear Weapons Capability

Acknowledged Nuclear Weapons Capability:

Britain
China
France
India
Pakistan
Russia
United States

Unacknowledged Nuclear Weapons Capability:

Israel

Seeking Nuclear Weapons Capability:

Iran
Iraq

Abandoned Nuclear Weapons Development:

North Korea[1]

1. An accord was reached with the North Korean government in 1994 to freeze and dismantle nuclear weapons development. *Source:* U.S. State Department.

Worldwide Armed Conflicts

(1990–1996)

An armed conflict is defined as "major" when at least 1,000 battle-related deaths have occurred since the beginning of the conflict. Major armed conflicts are divided into two categories: war (more than 1,000 battle-related deaths during the year in question); and, intermediate (less than 1,000 battle-related deaths in a given year).

All regions of the world have witnessed at least one major armed conflict during the 1990s. Not unexpectedly, Asia and Africa—the largest regions in population and territory respectively—consistently had the greatest number of wars, although the number has declined in both regions over the period in question. In Southeast Asia and Southern Africa, especially, there are fewer conflicts, of less intensity.

In Europe, after reaching a peak in 1993 and 1994, the number of major armed conflicts continued to fall from six in 1993 to two in 1996 (Chechnya and Northern Ireland). By the end of the year, however, the fighting in Chechnya had ceased.

In the Americas, a reduction in the intensity of conflicts meant a considerable shift from wars to intermediate armed conflicts, although the total numbers declined only slightly. Unlike the other regions, the Middle East showed no significant decline in either the number or the intensity of the armed conflicts recorded for the period.

	1990	1991	1992	1993	1994	1995	1996
Europe / Total	**1**	**2**	**4**	**6**	**5**	**3**	**2**
War	0	1	2	4	1	2	1
Intermediate	1	1	2	2	4	1	1
Middle East / Total	**5**	**7**	**5**	**6**	**6**	**6**	**6**
War	1	3	1	1	2	1	1
Intermediate	4	4	4	5	4	5	5
Asia / Total	**15**	**12**	**13**	**11**	**11**	**12**	**11**
War	6	7	7	4	2	2	2
Intermediate	2	2	0	3	5	4	3
Africa / Total	**11**	**11**	**7**	**7**	**7**	**6**	**6**
War	9	9	7	4	2	2	3
Intermediate	2	2	0	3	5	4	3
Americas / Total	**4**	**4**	**3**	**3**	**3**	**3**	**3**
War	3	1	3	2	0	0	0
Intermediate	1	3	0	1	3	3	3

Source: International Federation of Red Cross and Red Crescent Societies and the Department of Peace and Conflict Research, Uppsala University, Sweden. Reprinted with permission.

Refugees and Asylum Seekers by Country of Origin, 1996

Area	Refugees
Africa	**3,526,000**
Angola	190,000
Burundi	285,000
Chad	16,000
Djibouti	10,000
Eritrea	340,000
Ethiopia	75,000
Liberia	730,000
Mali	85,000
Mauritania	80,000
Niger	20,000
Rwanda	250,000
Senegal	15,000
Sierra Leone	345,000
Somalia	440,000
Sudan	430,000
Togo	30,000
Uganda	15,000
Western Sahara	80,000
Congo, Democratic Republic of the	90,000
East Asia and Pacific	**613,100**
Burma (Myanmar)	136,500
Cambodia	34,400
China (Tibet)	141,000
Indonesia	9,500
Laos	3,500
Vietnam	288,200
South and Central Asia	**3,112,400**
Afghanistan	2,552,800
Bangladesh	48,000
Bhutan	119,000
Sri Lanka	101,000
Tajikistan	240,000
Uzbekistan	51,600
Middle East	**4,374,900**
Iran	45,800
Iraq	639,600
Palestine	3,689,600
Europe	**1,895,800**
Armenia	198,800
Azerbaijan	325,000
Bosnia and Herzegovina	944,000
Croatia	300,000
Georgia	108,000
Turkey	15,000
Yugoslavia	5,000
Americas and the Caribbean	**81,700**
Columbia	700
Cuba	4,000
El Salvador	12,000
Guatemala	34,000
Haiti	15,000
Nicaragua	16,000
World Total	**13,603,900**

Note: Global refugee figures continue to decrease. In Africa, figures are down by nearly two million reflecting the return home of people to Rwanda and Angola. The figures also clearly show the intractable nature of many refugee problems with the numbers of refugees and asylum seekers failing to return home remaining constant over the years for many countries.
Source: U.S. Committee for Refugees. Reprinted with permission.

Major sources: Questionnaires to the individual countries, C.I.A. *World Factbook,* and Center for International Research, Bureau of the Census. (Information as of Sept. 15, 1998.)

Definitions: Gross domestic product (GDP): The value of all goods and services produced domestically; Purchasing power parity (PPP): The PPP method involves the use of standardized international dollar price weights, which are applied to the GDP produced in a given economy. The data derived from the PPP method provide a better comparison of economic well-being between countries than conversions at official currency exchange rates. Gross national product (GNP): the value of all goods and services produced domestically plus income earned abroad, minus income earned by foreigners from domestic production; c.i.f.: cost, insurance, and freight; f.o.b.: free on board; inflation based on consumer prices; literacy rates are supplied by the U.S. Census Bureau.

Afghanistan

ISLAMIC EMIRATE OF AFGHANISTAN

National name: Dowlat-e Eslami-ye Afghanestan
Head of State: Mullah Mohammad Omar (1996)
Area: 250,000 sq mi. (647,500 sq km)
Population (1998 est.): 24,792,375 (average annual rate of natural increase: 4.21%); birth rate: 42.4/1000; infant mortality rate: 143.6/1000; density per sq mi.: 99
Capital: Kabul. **Largest cities (1993 est.):** Kabul, 1,424,400; Kandahar, 225,500; Herat, 177,300; Mazare-Sharif, 131,000. **Monetary unit:** Afghani. **Languages:** Pushtu, Dari Persian, other Turkic and minor languages. **Ethnicity/Race:** Pashtun 38%, Tajik 25%, Uzbek 6%, Hazara 19%, minor ethnic groups (Chahar Aimaks, Turkmen, Baloch, and others). **Religion:** Islam (Sunni, 84%; Shi'ite, 15%; other 1%). **Literacy rate:** 29%
Economic summary: GDP/PPP (1996): $18.1 billion; $800 per capita. **Real growth rate:** n.a. **Inflation:** 240% (1996 est.). **Arable land:** 12%. **Products:** wheat, corn, barley, rice, cotton, fruit, nuts, karakul pelts, wool. **Labor force:** 7.1 million; labor force in industry, 10.2%; agriculture and animal husbandry, 67.8%; construction, 6.3%; services and other, 10.7%. **Unemployment:** 8% (1995 est.) **Industry:** carpets, rugs, textiles, furniture, shoes, fertilizer, cement, soap. **Natural resources:** natural gas, oil, coal, copper, sulfur, lead, zinc, iron, salt, precious and semi-precious stones. **Exports:** $80 million (1996 est.): fresh and dried fruits, nuts, natural gas, carpets, karakul. **Imports:** $150 million (1996 est.): petroleum products, sugar, manufactured goods, tea. **Major trading partners:** Europe, Central Asian republics, Japan, Singapore, Malaysia, India, and Pakistan.

Geography Afghanistan, approximately the size of Texas, is bordered on the north by Turkmenistan, Uzbekistan, and Tajikistan, on the extreme northeast by China, on the east and south by Pakistan, and by Iran in the west. The country is split east to west by the Hindu Kush mountain range, rising in the east to heights of 24,000 feet (7,315 m). With the exception of the southwest, most of the country is covered by high snow-capped mountains and is traversed by deep valleys.

Government On Sept. 27, 1996, the ruling members of the Afghan Government were displaced by members of the Islamic Taliban movement, who have declared themselves the legitimate government of Afghanistan. The U.N. has deferred a decision on the question of legitimacy. Mullah Mohammad Omar, known as the Emir al-Momineen (Leader of the Faithful) has served as the de facto leader since the Taliban came to power in 1996.

History Darius I and Alexander the Great were first to use Afghanistan as the gateway to India. Islamic conquerors arrived in the 7th century, and Genghis Khan and Tamerlane followed in the 13th and 14th centuries.

In the 19th century, Afghanistan became a battleground in the rivalry of imperial Britain and Czarist Russia for control of Central Asia. Three Anglo-Afghan Wars (1839–42, 1878–80, and 1919) ended inconclusively. In 1893 Britain established an unofficial border, the Durand Line, separating Afghanistan from British India, and London granted full independence in 1919. Emir Amanullah founded an Afghan monarchy in 1926.

During the cold war, King Mohammed Zahir Shah developed close ties with the Soviet Union, accepting extensive economic assistance from Moscow. He was overthrown in 1973 by his cousin Mohammed Daoud, who was himself was ousted in a 1978 coup by Noor Taraki. Taraki and his successor, Babrak Karmal, attempted to create a Marxist state. However, the new leadership was criticized by armed insurgents who bitterly opposed communism and hoped to create an Islamic state in Afghanistan. Fearing his government was on the verge of collapse, Karmal called for Soviet troops. Moscow responded with a full-scale invasion of the country in December of 1979. The Soviets were met with fierce resistance from groups already energized by opposition to the Karmal government. The guerrilla forces, calling themselves mujahedeen, pledged a jihad, or holy war, to expel the invaders. Initially armed with outdated weapons, the mujahedeen became a focus of U.S. cold war strategy against the Soviet Union, and with Pakistan's help, Washington began funneling sophisticated arms to the resistance. Moscow's troops were soon bogged down in a no-win conflict with determined Afghan fighters. In April 1988 the U.S.S.R., U.S., Afghanistan, and Pakistan signed accords calling for an end to outside aid to the warring factions. In return, a Soviet withdrawal took place in Feb. 1989, but the pro-Soviet government of President Najibullah was left in the capital Kabul.

By mid-April 1992 Najibullah was ousted as Islamic rebels advanced on the capital. Almost immediately, the various rebel groups began fighting each other for control. Amid the chaos of competing factions, a group calling itself the Taliban—or Islamic students—seized control of Kabul in Sept. 1996. It imposed strict religious law, particularly on women, prohibiting them from working outside the home and requiring them to be covered from head to toe in traditional Islamic Afghan dress. By fall 1998 the Taliban controlled about 90% of the country, with the remainder in the hands of an opposition alliance headed by former President Burhanuddin Rabbani, whose government is still recognized by the United Nations. In May 1998, U.N.-sponsored peace talks among the warring factions broke down and fighting in the mountainous north of the country resumed.

On Aug. 20, 1998, U.S. cruise missiles struck a terrorism training complex in Afghanistan believed to have been financed by Osama bin Laden, a wealthy Islamic radical sheltered by the Taliban. The U.S. asked for the deportation of bin Laden, whom they believed was involved in the bombing of the U.S. embassies in Kenya and Tanzania on Aug. 7, 1998. The Taliban refused. In Sept. 1998 Iran dispatched thousands of troops on its border with Afghanistan after the Taliban admitted killing eight Iranian diplomats and a journalist.

Albania

THE REPUBLIC OF ALBANIA

National name: Republika E Shqiperise
President: Rexhep Mejdani (1997)
Prime Minister: Fatos Nano (1997)
Area: 11,100 sq mi. (28,750 sq km)
Population (1998 est.): 3,330,754 (average annual rate of natural increase: 0.97%); birth rate: 21.4/1000; infant mortality rate: 45.0/1000; density per sq mi.: 300
Capital and largest city (1991 est.): Tiranë, 300,000. **Monetary unit:** Lek. **Language:** Albanian, Greek. **Ethnicity/Race:** Albanian 95%, Greeks 3%, other 2%: Vlachs, Gypsies, Serbs, and Bulgarians (1989 est.).. **Religions (1980):** Muslim, 70%; Albanian Orthodox, 20%; Roman Catholic, 10%. **Literacy rate** 72%
Economic summary: GDP/PPP (1996 est.): $4.4 billion; $1,290 per capita (1996 est.). **Real growth rate** (1996 est.) 5%. **Inflation:** 17.4% (1996 est.). **Unemployment:** 13% (1996 est.). **Arable land:** 21%. **Agriculture:** wheat, corn, potatoes, sugar beets, cotton, tobacco. **Labor force** (1994 est.), 1.692 million; by occupation: agriculture, 49.5%; private sector, 22.2%; state sector, 28.3%. **Products:** textiles, timber, construction materials, fuels, semi-processed minerals. **Exports:** $205 million (f.o.b., 1995): asphalt, petroleum products, metals and metallic ores, electricity, crude oil, vegetables, fruits, and tobacco. **Imports:** $680 million (f.o.b., 1995): machinery, consumer goods, grains. **Major trading partners:** Italy, Macedonia, Turkey, Bulgaria, Greece, U.S.

Geography Albania is situated on the eastern shore of the Adriatic Sea, with Montenegro and Serbia to the north, Macedonia to the east, and Greece to the south. Slightly larger than Maryland, Albania may be divided into two major physiographic regions: a mountainous highland region (north, east, and south) constituting 70 percent of the land area, and a western coastal lowland region that contains nearly all of the country's agricultural lands and is the most densely populated part of Albania.

Government A multiparty system was installed in March 1991. The unicameral 140-member People's Assembly elects the president, who in turn appoints the prime minister and Council of Ministers (the cabinet).

History A part of Illyria in ancient times, and later of the Roman Empire, Albania was ruled by the Byzantine Empire from C.E. 535 to 1204. An alliance (1444–1466) of Albanian chiefs failed to halt the advance of the Turks and the country remained under at least nominal Turkish rule for more than four centuries, until it proclaimed its independence on Nov. 28, 1912.

Largely agricultural, Albania is one of the poorest countries in Europe. A battlefield in World War I, after the war it became a republic in which a conservative Muslim landlord, Ahmed Zogu, proclaimed himself president in 1925, and king (Zog I) in 1928. He ruled until Italy annexed Albania in 1939. Communist guerrillas under Enver Hoxha seized power in 1944, near the end of World War II. Hoxha was a devotee of Stalin, emulating the Soviet leader's repressive tactics, imprisoning or executing landowners and others who did not conform to the socialist ideal. Hoxha eventually broke with Soviet communism in 1961 because of differences with Khrushchev, and then aligned himself with Chinese communism, which he also abandoned in 1978 after the death of Mao. From then on Albania went its own way to forge its individual version of the socialist state, and became one of the most isolated countries in the world. Hoxha was succeeded by Ramiz Alia in 1982.

The elections in March 1991 gave the Communists a decisive majority. But a general strike and street demonstrations soon forced the all-Communist cabinet to resign. In June 1991 the Communist Party of Labor renamed itself the Socialist Party and renounced its past ideology. The opposition Democratic Party won a landslide victory in 1992 elections. Albania's experiment with democratic reform and a free-market economy went disastrously awry in March 1997, when large numbers of its citizens invested in shady, get-rich-quick pyramid schemes. When five of these schemes collapsed in the beginning of the year, robbing Albanians of an estimated $1.2 billion in savings, their rage turned against the government, which appeared to have sanctioned the nationwide swindle. Rioting broke out, the country's fragile infrastructure collapsed, and gangsters and rebels overran the country, resulting in more than 1,500 deaths. A multinational protection force eventually restored order and set up the elections that formally ousted President Sali Berisha. In Sept. 1998 former Prime Minister Berisha provoked violent clashes with government troops after the death of one of his aides, demanding that Prime Minister Fatos Nano resign.

Algeria

DEMOCRATIC AND POPULAR REPUBLIC OF ALGERIA

National name: Al Jumhuriyah al Jaza'iriyah ad Dimuqratiyah ash Shabiyah
President: Liamine Zeroual (1994)
Prime Minister: Ahmed Ouyahia (1995)
Area: 919,595 sq mi. (2,381,740 sq km)
Population (1998 est.): 30,480,793 (average annual rate of natural increase: 2.14%); birth rate: 27.5/1000; infant mortality rate: 45.4/1000; density per sq mi.: 33
Capital: Algiers. **Largest cities (1987):** Algiers, 1,507,241; Oran, 628,558; Constantine, 440,842; Annaba, 305,526. **Monetary unit:** Dinar. **Languages:** Arabic (official), French, Berber dialects. **Ethnicity/**

Race: Arab-Berber 99%, European less than 1%. **Religion:** 99% Islam (Sunni). **Literacy rate** 57%.

Economic summary: GDP/PPP (1996 est.): $115.9 billion; $4,000 per capita. **Real growth rate:** 4%. **Inflation:** 19.8%. **Unemployment:** 28%. **Arable land:** 3%. **Agriculture:** wheat, barley, oats, wine, citrus fruits, olives, livestock. **Labor force:** 7.8 million (1996 est.); by occupation: government, 29.5%; agriculture, 22%; construction and public works, 16.2%; industry, 13.6%; commerce and services, 13.5%; transportation and communication, 5.2% (1989). **Industry:** petroleum, gas, petrochemicals, fertilizers, iron and steel, textiles, transport equipment. **Natural resources:** petroleum, natural gas, iron ore, phosphates, lead, zinc, mercury, uranium. **Exports:** $11 billion (f.o.b., 1996 est.): petroleum and natural gas, 97%. **Imports:** $10.5 billion (f.o.b., 1996 est.): capital goods, 39.7%; food and beverages, 21.7%; consumer goods, 11.8% (1990). **Major trading partners:** France, Germany, Italy, Spain, U.S., Japan.

Geography Nearly four times the size of Texas, Algeria is bordered on the west by Morocco and Western Sahara and on the east by Tunisia and Libya. To the south are Mauritania, Mali, and Niger. The Saharan region, which is 85% of the country, is almost completely uninhabited. The highest point is Mount Tahat in the Sahara, which rises 9,850 feet (3,000 m).

Government Parliamentary republic.

History As ancient Numidia, Algeria became a Roman colony, part of what was called Mauretania Caesariensis, at the close of the Punic Wars (145 B.C.E.). Conquered by the Vandals about C.E. 440, it fell from a high state of civilization to virtual barbarism, from which it partly recovered after invasion by the Muslims about 650.

In 1492 the Moors and Jews, who had been expelled from Spain, settled in Algeria. Falling under control of the Ottoman Empire by 1536, Algiers served for three centuries as the headquarters of the Barbary pirates. The French took Algeria in 1830 and made it a part of France in 1848.

Algerian independence movements led to the uprisings of 1954–55, which developed into full-scale war. In 1962, French President Charles de Gaulle began the peace negotiations, and on July 5, 1962, Algeria was proclaimed independent.

In Oct. 1963, Ahmed Ben Bella was elected president. He began to nationalize foreign holdings and aroused opposition. He was overthrown in a military coup on June 19, 1965, by Col. Houari Boumediène, who suspended the constitution and sought to restore financial stability.

In Dec. 1991 in the first parliamentary elections ever held in Algeria, the fundamentalist Islamic Salvation Front (Front Islamique du Salut; FIS) won the largest number of votes. To thwart the electoral results, the army cancelled the general election. As a result, the country was plunged into a bloody civil war. An estimated 75,000 civilians have been massacred by Islamic terrorists since war began in Jan. 1992.

The undeclared civil war escalated in 1997–98 in its brutality and senselessness. Islamic extremists, who had originally focused their attacks on government officials and then shifted to intellectuals and journalists, abandoned political motivations entirely and targeted defenseless villagers. The mass slaughters have been as savage as they have been random. The government has been markedly ineffectual in stemming the violence, and there is some evidence that the army has looked the other way. Algeria has refused international mediation, and the outside world remains in the dark about much of what occurs within its borders. In Sept. 1998 President Zeroual announced his desire to retire early and his intention to hold elections in Feb. 1999 instead of 2000.

Andorra

PRINCIPALITY OF ANDORRA

National name: Valls d'Andorra
Head of Government: Marc Forné Molné (1994)
Area: 175 sq mi. (450 sq km)
Population (1998 est.): 64,716 (average annual growth rate: 1.50%); birth rate: 10.5/1000; infant mortality rate: 4.1/1000; density per sq mi.: 370
Capital and largest city (1993 est.): Andorra la Vella, 22,390. **Monetary units:** French franc and Spanish peseta. **Languages:** Catalán (official); French, Spanish. **Ethnicity/Race:** Spanish 61%, Andorran 30%, French 6%, other 3%. **Religion:** Roman Catholic. **Literacy rate** 100%
Economic summary: GDP/PPP (1995 est.): $1.2 billion; $18,000 per capita. **Real growth rate:** n.a. **Inflation:** n.a. **Unemployment:** 0%. **Arable land:** 2%. **Agriculture:** oats, barley, cattle, sheep. **Labor force:** n.a. **Industry:** tobacco products, electric power, tourism. **Natural resources:** water power, mineral water. **Exports:** $47 million (f.o.b., 1995): electricity, tobacco products, furniture. **Imports:** $1 billion (1995): consumer goods, food. **Major trading partners:** Spain, France, and U.S.

Geography Andorra is nestled high in the Pyrenees Mountains on the French-Spanish border.

Government A parliamentary democracy. Their first constitution was approved on March 14, 1993, which redefined Andorra as a parliamentary co-principality and sharply differentiated the three branches of government. The 28-seat General Council and its cabinet became the legislative branch, headed by a chief executive. This reduced the co-princes (the bishop of Urgel and the president of France) to constitutional heads of state, largely in name only.

History An autonomous and semi-independent co-principality, Andorra has been under the joint suzerainty of the French state and the Spanish bishops of Urgel since 1278. In the late 20th century, Andorra has become a popular tourist destination and an important international retail center because of its opportunities for various winter sports, low taxes, and lack of customs duties. In 1990 Andorra approved a customs union treaty with the E.U. permitting free movement of industrial goods between the two, but Andorra would apply the E.U.'s external tariffs to third countries. This treaty went into effect on July 1, 1991. Andorra became a member of the U.N. in 1993 and a member of the Council of Europe in 1994.

Angola

REPUBLIC OF ANGOLA

President: José Eduardo dos Santos (1979)
Prime Minister: Fernando José de Franca Dias van Dunen (1996)
Area: 481,350 sq mi. (1,246,700 sq km)
Population (1998 est.): 10,864,512 (average annual rate of natural increase: 2.8%); birth rate: 43.6/1000; infant mortality rate: 132.4/1000; density per sq mi.: 23

Capital and largest city (1993): Luanda, 2,000,000. **Other large cities (1993 est.):** Huambo, 400,000; Lubango, 105,000. **Monetary unit:** Kwanza. **Languages:** Bantu, Portuguese (official). **Ethnicity/Race:** Ovimbundu 37%, Kimbundu 25%, Bakongo 13%, mestico (mixed European and Native African) 2%, European 1%, other 22%. **Religions:** Roman Catholic, 47%; Protestant, 38%; Indigenous, 15%. **Literacy rate:** 42%

Economic summary: GDP/PPP (1996 est.): $8.3 billion; $800 per capita. **Real growth rate:** 9%. **Inflation:** 1,700% (1996 est.). **Unemployment** extensive. **Arable land:** 2%. **Agriculture:** coffee, sisal, corn, cotton, sugar, tobacco, bananas, cassava. **Labor force:** 2.783 million; by occupation: agriculture, 85%; industry, 15% (1985 est.). **Industry:** oil, diamonds, processed fish, tobacco, textiles, cement, processed food and sugar, brewing. **Natural resources:** diamonds, gold, iron, oil. **Exports:** $4 billion (f.o.b., 1996 est.): oil, coffee, diamonds, fish and fish products, iron ore, timber, corn. **Imports:** $1.7 billion (f.o.b., 1995 est.): machinery and electrical equipment, bulk iron, steel and metals, textiles, clothing, food, substantial military deliveries. **Major trading partners:** U.S., France, Germany, Netherlands, Brazil, Portugal, Spain.

Geography Angola, more than three times the size of California, extends for more than 1,000 miles (1,609 km) along the South Atlantic in southwestern Africa. The Democratic Republic of the Congo and the Republic of Congo are to the north and east, Zambia is to the east, and Namibia is to the south. A plateau averaging 6,000 feet (1,829 m) above sea level rises abruptly from the coastal lowlands. Nearly all the land is desert or savanna, with hardwood forests in the northeast.

Government Angola underwent a transition from a one-party socialist state to a multiparty democracy in 1992.

History The original inhabitants of Angola are thought to have been Khoisan speakers. After C.E. 1000, large numbers of Bantu speakers migrated to the region and became the dominant group. Angola derives its name from the Bantu kingdom of Ndongo, whose name for its king is ngola.

Explored by the Portuguese navigator Diego Cao in 1482, Angola became a link in trade with India and Southeast Asia. Later it was a major source of slaves for Portugal's New World colony of Brazil. Development of the interior began after the Berlin Conference in 1885 fixed the colony's borders, and British and Portuguese investment pushed mining, railways, and agriculture.

Following World War II, independence movements began but were sternly suppressed by Portuguese military force. The major nationalist organizations were the Popular Movement for the Liberation of Angola (MPLA), a Marxist party, National Front for the Liberation of Angola (FNLA), and the National Union for the Total Independence of Angola (UNITA). In 1975, Portugal granted independence to Angola, and the MPLA, which had led the independence movement, has controlled the government ever since. UNITA disputed the MPLA's ascendancy, and civil war broke out almost immediately. With the Soviet Union and Cuba supporting the Marxist MPLA, and the United States and South Africa supporting the anti-communist UNITA, the country became a cold war battleground.

With the waning of the cold war and the withdrawal of Cuban troops in 1989, the MPLA began to make the transition to a multiparty democracy. Despite shifting ideologies, the civil war continued for more than 30 years, with UNITA's charismatic rebel leader, Jonas Savimbi, armed and sustained by his control of approximately 80% of the country's diamond trade. Free elections took place in 1992, with incumbent president José Eduardo dos Santos and the MPLA winning the U.N.-certified election over Savimbi and UNITA. Savimbi then withdrew, charging election fraud, and the civil war resumed.

In 1997 Angola played a crucial role in the civil wars of both the Republic of Congo and the Democratic Republic of the Congo. By aiding in the overthrow of these countries' leaders, Pascal Lissouba and Mobutu Sese Seko, the Angolan government was also able to destroy the UNITA strongholds within the borders of these countries. Angola again came to the aid of the Democratic Republic of the Congo's new leader, Laurent Kabila, in 1998, helping to quash the rebellion against his shaky year-old administration.

Current peace efforts have been underway for four years, and in 1997 it was agreed that a coalition government with UNITA would be implemented, though Savimbi remains in hiding, fearing for his safety. But since then Savimbi has refused to give up his strongholds and failed to demobilize his army. As a result, the government suspended coalition rule in Sept. 1998. The country seems poised once again at the edge of civil war, which analysts say neither side has the military power to win.

Antigua and Barbuda

Sovereign: Queen Elizabeth II (1952)
Governor-General: Sir James Beethoven Carlisle (1993)
Prime Minister: Hon. Lester Bryant Bird (1994)
Land area: 171 sq mi. (440 sq km)
Population (1998 est.): 64,006 (average annual growth rate: 0.39%); birth rate: 16.7/1000; infant mortality rate: 21.4/1000; density per sq mi.: 374
Capital and largest city (1991): St. John's, 21,514; Codrington (capital of Barbuda), est. pop. 1,000. **Monetary unit:** East Caribbean dollar. **Language:** English. **Ethnicity/Race:** black, British, Portuguese, Lebanese, Syrian. **Religions:** Anglican and Roman Catholic. **Literacy rate:** 90%
Economic summary: GDP/PPP (1996 est.): $446 million; per capita $6,800. **Real growth rate:** 4.7%. **Inflation:** 4%. **Unemployment:** (1995 est.), 5%–10%. **Arable land:** 18%. **Products:** cotton, bananas, coconuts, cucumbers, mangoes. **Labor force:** 30,000; by occupation: industry, 7%; commerce and services, 82%; agriculture, 11%. **Industry:** tourism, transport and communications, trade, and public utilities. **Exports:** $45 million (f.o.b., 1996 est.): petroleum products, manufactured goods, machinery and transport equipment. **Imports:** $350.8 million (f.o.b., 1996 est.): fuel, food, machinery. **Major trading partners:** U.K., U.S., Canada, Caribbean community and Common Market members. **Member of Commonwealth of Nations**

Geography Antigua, the larger of the two main islands located 295 miles (420 km) south-southeast of San Juan, P.R., is low-lying except for a range of hills in the south that rise to their highest point at Boggy Peak (1,330 ft.; 405 m). Because of its relative flatness, Antigua suffers from cyclical drought, despite a mean annual rainfall of 44 inches. Well-wooded Antigua is 108 sq miles (280 sq km); the island dependencies of Redonda (an uninhabited rocky islet) and Barbuda (a coral island formerly known as Dulcina) are 0.5 sq miles (1.30 sq km) and 62 sq miles (161 sq km), respectively.

Government Executive power is held by the cabinet, presided over by Prime Minister Lester B. Bird. A 17-member parliament is elected by universal suffrage. The Antigua Labour Party, led by Prime Minister Bird, holds 11 seats.

History Antigua was visited by Christopher Columbus in 1493 and named for the Church of Santa Maria de la Antigua in Seville. Antigua was colonized by Britain in 1632; Barbuda was first colonized in 1678. The country joined the West Indies Federation in 1958. With the breakup of the federation, it became one of the West Indies Associated States in 1967, self-governing its internal affairs. Full independence was granted Nov. 1, 1981. The Bird family has controlled the islands since Vere C. Bird founded the Antigua Labor Party in the mid-1940s. Bird, the former prime minister, and his sons, one of whom is the current prime minister, have a history of corruption that includes money laundering, arms sales, drug trafficking, and extortion.

In 1995, protests against new taxes yielded a government concession not to add any in the 1995 budget, while September's Hurricane Luis caused major damage to the country's infrastructure. The offshore banking sector created major problems for Antigua and Barbuda in 1997, forcing the government to close certain banks and refrain from issuing any new offshore banking licenses.

Argentina

ARGENTINE REPUBLIC

National name: República Argentina.
President: Carlos S. Menem (1989)
Area: 1,072,067 sq mi. (2,766,890 sq km)
Population (1998 est.): 36,265,463 (average annual rate of natural increase: 1.30%); birth rate: 20/1000; infant mortality rate: 19/1000; density per sq mi.: 34
Capital and largest city: Buenos Aires: city proper (1995 est.) 2,988,006; metro. area (1996 est.) 11,931,000 . **Other large cities (1991 est.):** Córdoba, 1,180,000; La Matanza, 1,121,164; General Sarmiento, 646,900; Morón, 641,540 (1983); Rosario, 950,000 (1983). **Monetary unit:** Peso. **Language:** Spanish, English, Italian, German, French. **Ethnicity/ Race:** white 85%, mestizo, Indian, or other nonwhite groups 15%. **Religion:** Predominantly Roman Catholic (nominally). **Literacy rate:** 96% (1990)
Economic summary: GDP/PPP (1996 est.): $296.9 billion; $8,610 per capita. **Real growth rate:** 4.4%. **Inflation:** 0.1%. **Unemployment:** 17.3% (Oct. 1996). **Arable land:** 9%. **Products:** grains, oilseeds, livestock products. **Labor force** (1995 est.), 14.5 million; industry: 31%, agriculture, 12%, services, 57% (1985 est.). **Products:** processed foods, motor vehicles, consumer durables, textiles, chemicals. **Natural resources:** minerals, lead, zinc, tin, copper, iron, manganese, oil, uranium. **Exports:** $23.8 billion (f.o.b., 1996): meat, wheat, corn, oilseed, manufactures. **Imports:** $23.7 billion (c.i.f., 1996): machinery and equipment, chemicals, metals, agricultural products. **Major trading partners:** U.S., Brazil, Bolivia, Germany, Japan, Italy, Netherlands, Bolivia.

Geography Second in South America only to Brazil in size and population, Argentina is a plain, rising from the Atlantic to the Chilean border and the towering Andes peaks. Aconcagua (23,034 ft.; 7,021 m) is the highest peak in the world outside Asia. Argentina is also bordered by Bolivia and Paraguay on the north, and by Uruguay and Brazil on the east. The northern area is the swampy and partly wooded Gran Chaco, bordering on Bolivia and Paraguay. South of that are the rolling, fertile Pampas, which are rich in agriculture and sheep and cattle grazing and support most of the population. Next southward is Patagonia, a region of cool, arid steppes with some wooded and fertile sections.

Government Argentina is a federal union of 23 provinces and the federal district. Under the constitution of 1853, the president and vice president are elected every six years by popular vote through an electoral college. The president appoints his cabinet. The vice president presides over the Senate but has no other powers. The Congress consists of two houses: a 46-member Senate and a 254-member Chamber of Deputies.

History Discovered in 1516 by Juan Díaz de Solis, Argentina developed slowly under Spanish colonial rule. Buenos Aires was settled in 1580; the cattle industry was thriving as early as 1600. Invading British forces were expelled in 1806–07, and after Napoleon conquered Spain (1808), the Argentinians set up their own government in 1810. On July 9, 1816, independence was formally declared.

As it had in World War I, Argentina proclaimed neutrality at the outbreak of World War II, but in the closing phase declared war on the Axis powers on March 27, 1945. Juan D. Perón, an army colonel, emerged as the strongman of the postwar era, winning the presidential elections of 1946 and 1951. Perón's political strength was reinforced by his second wife—Eva Duarte de Perón (Evita)—and his popularity with the working classes. Although she never held any government post, Evita acted as de facto minister of health and labor, establishing a national charitable organization, and awarding generous wage increases to the unions, who responded with political support for Perón. Opposition to Perón's increasing authoritarianism led to a coup by the armed forces that sent Perón into exile in 1955, three years after Evita's death. Argentina entered a long period of military dictatorships with brief intervals of constitutional government.

The former dictator returned to power in 1973 and his third wife, Isabel Martínez de Perón, was elected vice president. After Perón's death in 1974, she became the hemisphere's first woman chief of state, but was deposed in 1976 by a military junta. On April 2, 1982, Lt. Gen. Leopoldo Galtieri, commander of the army and the new president, landed thousands of troops on the Falkland Islands and reclaimed Las Malvinas, their Spanish name, as national territory. By May 21, more than 5,000 British marines and paratroops landed and regained control of the islands. Galtieri resigned three days after the surrender of the island garrison on June 14. Maj. Gen. Reynaldo Bignone took office as president on July 1, 1982.

In the presidential election of Oct. 1983, Raúl Alfonsín, leader of the middle-class Radical Civic Union, handed the Peronist Party its first defeat since its founding. However, the twin economic problems of growing unemployment and quadruple-digit inflation led to a Peronist victory in the elections of May 1989. Inflation of food prices led to riots that induced Alfonsín to step down in June 1989, six months early, in favor of the new Peronist president, Carlos Menem. A group of army leaders and their followers attempted an uprising on Dec. 3, 1990. Most commanders, however, stood by the legitimate government, and the insurrection was suppressed in less than 24 hours.

In 1991 President Menem hammered out a vast deregulation of the economy designed to reverse decades of state intervention and protectionism. During the first half of 1997 the president and his ruling Peronist Party saw their popularity dramatically fall as a result of increasing social disturbances and a scandal over presidential links to an alleged mobster. Argentina closed out 1997 with a strong gross domestic product but a high unemployment rate, which further damaged Peronist Party popularity. Menem had the constitution changed in 1994 to allow him to serve for a second term; in 1998 he planned to change it again to allow for a third term. Amid opposition threats of civil disobedience and dissatisfaction in his own party, however, he abandoned his bid for a third term.

Armenia

President: Robert Kocharyan (1998)
Prime Minister: Armen Darbinyan (1998)
Area: 11,500 sq mi. (29,800 sq km)
Population (1998 est.): 3,421,775 (average annual rate of increase: –0.36%) (Armenian, 93%; others, Kurds, Ukrainians, and Russians); birth rate: 13.5/1000; infant mortality rate: 40.8/1000, density per sq mi.: 298
Capital and largest city (1994 est.): Yerevan, 1,226,000; other large cities (1994 est.): Gyumri (Leninakan), 120,000. **Monetary unit:** Dram. **Language:** Armenian. **Ethnicity/Race:** Armenian 93%, Azeri 3%, Russian 2%, other (mostly Yezidi Kurds) 2% (1989) Note: as of the end of 1993, virtually all Azeris had emigrated from Armenia.. **Religion:** Armenian Orthodox, 94%. **Literacy rate:** 100% (1970)
Economic summary: GDP/PPP (1996 estimate as extrapolated from the World Bank estimate for 1994): $9.7 billion; $2,800 per capita. **Real growth rate:** (1996 est.) 4%. **Inflation:** 5.7% (1996 est.). **Unemployment:** 7.4% officially unemployed, with large numbers underemployed. **Labor force** (1996), 1.6 million; industry and construction, 23%; agriculture, 38%; services 37%; other, 2% (1996). **Agriculture:** 35% of gross domestic product; **Arable land:** 17%; fruit, vegetables, vineyards. **Exports:** $273 million (f.o.b., 1996): gold and jewelry, aluminum, transport equipment, scrap metal. **Imports:** $830 million (c.i.f., 1996): from countries outside the successor states of the former U.S.S.R.: machinery, energy, consumer goods. **Major trading partners:** Iran, Russia, Turkmenistan, Georgia, U.S., E.U.

Geography Armenia is located in the southern Caucasus and is the smallest of the former Soviet republics. It is bounded by Georgia on the north, Azerbaijan on the east, Iran on the south, and Turkey on the west. It is a land of rugged mountains and extinct volcanoes. Mt. Aragats, 13,435 ft. (4,095 m), is the highest point.

Government According to the constitution of 1995, the president, who is directly elected by popular vote, appoints the Council of Ministers (Cabinet) and its head, who serves as prime minister.

History Armenia has been the scene of struggle throughout its long history with the Greeks, Romans, Persians, Mongols, and Turks. Russia acquired present-day Armenia from Persia in 1828. However, the Ottoman Empire continued to rival Russia for dominance in Armenia. Following a Russian conquest in 1916, Armenia, with Georgia and Azerbaijan, formed an anti-Bolshevik Transcaucasian Federation, but it was dissolved in 1918. Armenia's independence was short-lived and it was annexed by the Red Army in 1920. On March 12, 1922, the Soviets joined Georgia, Armenia, and Azerbaijan to form the Transcaucasian Soviet Socialist Republic, which became part of the U.S.S.R. In 1936, after a reorganization, Armenia became a separate constituent republic of the U.S.S.R.

Since 1983, Armenia has been involved in a territorial dispute with Azerbaijan over the enclave of Nagorno-Karabakh, to which both republics lay claim. The autonomous region of Nagorno-Karabakh lies entirely within Azerbaijan. The majority population of the enclave are Armenian Christians who want to secede from Azerbaijan and join with Armenia. Armenia declared its independence from the collapsing Soviet Union on Aug. 23, 1990. In the years that followed, Armenia successfully fought Azerbaijan for control of Nagorno-Karabakh. The political disruption in Azerbaijan in June 1993 led to significant military advances for the Armenian forces, leaving them in control of much of the disputed region as well as a corridor to Armenia proper. A cease-fire agreement was reached between the two countries in 1994. Azerbaijan has offered broad autonomy to the enclave in exchange for the withdrawal of Armenian troops from Azeri lands. But the enclave wants either full independence or annexation to Armenia.

In March 1995 a treaty was signed with Russia permitting the latter to maintain two military bases in the country for 25 years.

Australia

COMMONWEALTH OF AUSTRALIA

Sovereign: Queen Elizabeth II (1952)
Governor-General: Sir William Deane (1996)
Prime Minister: John Howard (1996)
Area: 2,966,150 sq mi. (7,686,850 sq km)
Population (1998 est.): 18,613,087 (average annual rate of natural increase: 0.93%); birth rate: 13.5/1000; infant mortality rate: 5.3/1000; density per sq mi.: 6
Capital (1994 est.): Canberra, 278,904. **Largest cities (1994 est.):** Sydney, 3,738,500; Melbourne, 3,198,200; Adelaide, 1,076,400; Perth, 1,239,100; Brisbane, 786,442. **Monetary unit:** Australian dollar. **Language:** English. **Ethnicity/Race:** Caucasian 95%, Asian 4%, aboriginal and other 1%. **Religions:** Anglican 26.1%, Roman Catholic 26.0%, Other Christian 24.3%. **Literacy rate:** 100%
Economic summary: GDP/PPP (1996 est.): $430.5 billion. $23,600 per capita. **Real growth rate:** 3.6%. **Inflation:** 3.1%. **Unemployment:** 8.5%. **Arable land:** 6%. **Agriculture:** wool, meat, cereals, sugar, sheep, cattle, dairy products. **Labor force:** 8.4 million (Dec. 1996); finance and services, 34%; public and

community services, 23%; wholesale and retail trade, 20%; manufacturing, 17%. **Natural resources:** iron ore, bauxite, zinc, lead, tin, coal, oil, gas, copper, nickel, uranium. **Exports:** $59.5 billion (f.o.b, 1996): coal, gold, meat, wool, aluminum, wheat, machinery, and transport equipment. **Imports:** $59.7 billion (f.o.b, 1996): machinery and transport equipment, computers and office machines, crude oil and petroleum products. **Major trading partners:** Japan, U.S., U.K., New Zealand, Germany, South Korea, Singapore. **Member of Commonwealth of Nations**

Geography The continent of Australia, with the island state of Tasmania, is approximately equal in area to the United States (excluding Alaska and Hawaii). Mountain ranges run from north to south along the east coast, reaching their highest point in Mount Kosciusko (7,308 ft.; 2,228 m). The western half of the continent is occupied by a desert plateau that rises into barren, rolling hills near the west coast. It includes the Great Victoria Desert to the south and the Great Sandy Desert to the north. The Great Barrier Reef, extending about 1,245 miles (2,000 km), lies along the northeast coast. The island of Tasmania (26,178 sq mi.; 67,800 sq km) is off the southeastern coast.

Government The federal parliament consists of a bicameral legislature. The House of Representatives has 147 members elected for three years by popular vote. The Senate has 76 members elected by popular vote for six years. One-half of the Senate is elected every three years. Voting is compulsory at 18. Symbolic executive power is vested in the British monarch, who is represented throughout Australia by the governor-general.

History Australia has been inhabited by Aborigines for at least 40,000—and perhaps as many as 60,000—years. They emigrated from Southeast Asia. Estimates of the size of the Aboriginal population at the time of European settlement in 1788 range from 300,000 to more than 1,000,000. Dutch, Portuguese, and Spanish ships sighted Australia in the 17th century; the Dutch landed at the Gulf of Carpentaria in 1606. Australia was called New Holland, Botany Bay, and New South Wales until about 1820. Captain James Cook, in 1770, claimed possession for Great Britain. A British penal colony was set up at what is now Sydney, then Port Jackson, in 1788, and about 161,000 transported English convicts were settled there until the system was suspended in 1839.

Free settlers established six colonies: New South Wales (1786), Tasmania (then Van Diemen's Land) (1825), Western Australia (1829), South Australia (1834), Victoria (1851), and Queensland (1859). The six colonies became states and in 1901 federated into the Commonwealth of Australia with a constitution that incorporated British parliamentary tradition and U.S. federal experience. Australia became known for its liberal legislation: free compulsory education, protected trade unionism with industrial conciliation and arbitration, the "Australian" ballot facilitating selection, the secret ballot, women's suffrage, maternity allowances, and sickness and old-age pensions.

Australia fought alongside Britain in World War I, notably with the Australia and New Zealand Army Corps (ANZAC) in the Dardanelles campaign (1915). Participation in World War II brought Australia closer to the United States; ties with Britain diminished, and, after 1942, the British Royal Navy ceased defending Australia. Parliamentary power in the second half of the 20th century shifted between three political parties: the Australian Labour Party, the Liberal Party, and the National Party.

Since World War II, Australia has assumed a leading role in Asian and Pacific affairs. Although it experienced some setbacks, the Aboriginal movement grew in strength from the 1960s, and Aborigines succeeded in obtaining rights to some tribal lands. In March 1996 the opposition Liberal Party–National Party coalition easily won the national elections, removing the Labour Party after 13 years in power. Pressure from the new, conservative One Nation Party threatened to reduce the gains made by Aborigines and to limit immigration.

In 1999, all Australians will vote in a constitutional referendum to decide whether or not Australia will become a republic, thereby replacing the British monarch–appointed governor-general with an Australian president as head of state and eliminating all formal allegiance to the British Crown.

Australian External Territories

Norfolk Island (13 sq mi.; 36.3 sq km) was placed under Australian administration in 1914. Population 2,285 (1996 census). A former penal colony, Norfolk Island became home to the entire population of Pitcairn Island in 1856. The 194 residents of tiny Pitcairn embarked on the 3,700-mile journey to Norfolk because of overpopulation. Pitcairn—and then Norfolk Island residents—were descendants of the mutineers from the H.M.S. *Bounty* and their Tahitian wives. Many Norfolk residents today can trace their genealogy directly to the *Bounty*.

The Ashmore and Cartier Islands (0.8 sq mi.), situated in the Indian Ocean off the northwest coast of Australia, came under Australian administration in 1934. In 1938 the islands were annexed to the Northern Territory. On the attainment of self-government by the Northern Territory in 1978, these uninhabited islands were retained as Commonwealth Territory.

The Australian Antarctic Territory (2,360,000 sq mi.; 6,112,400 sq km) is made up of all the islands and territories, other than Adélie Land, situated south of lat. 60°S and lying between long. 160° to 45°E. It came under Australian administration in 1936.

Heard Island and the McDonald Islands (158 sq mi.; 409.2 sq km), lying in the sub-Antarctic, were placed under Australian administration in 1947. The islands are uninhabited.

Christmas Island (52 sq mi.; 134.7 sq km) is situated in the Indian Ocean. It came under Australian administration in 1958. Most of the island's residents traditionally have been employees of the Phosphate Mining Company of Christmas Island, Ltd., which is owned by the Australian government. It has a population of 889 (July 1995).

Coral Sea Islands (400,000 sq mi.; 1,036,000 sq km, but only a few sq mi. of land) became a territory of Australia in 1969. There is no permanent population on the islands.

Cocos (Keeling) Islands are made up of a group of 27 small coral islands in two separate atolls in the Indian Ocean, 1,721 miles (2,768 kilometers) northwest of Perth. West Island is the largest, about 6.2 miles (10 kilometers) long. The islands became an Australian territory in 1955. In April 1984 the residents voted to merge with Australia. The population of the Cocos is 604 (July 1995).

Austria

REPUBLIC OF AUSTRIA

National name: Republik Österreich
President: Thomas Klestil (1992)
Chancellor: Viktor Klima (1997)
Area: 32,375 sq mi. (83,850 sq km)
Population (1998 est.): 8,133,611 (average annual rate of natural increase: 0.05%); birth rate 9.9/1000; infant mortality rate: 5.2/1000; density per sq mi.: 251
Capital and largest city (1991 est.): Vienna, 1,600,000. **Other large cities (1995 est.):** Graz, 237,150; Linz, 203,000; Salzburg, 144,000; Innsbruck, 118,000. **Monetary unit:** Schilling. **Languages:** German 98% (small Slovene, Croatian, and Hungarian-speaking minorities). **Religion:** Roman Catholic 85%, Protestant 6%, other 9%. **Ethnicity/Race:** German 99.4%, Croatian 0.3%, Slovene 0.2%. **Literacy rate:** 99%
Economic summary: GDP/PPP (1996): $157.6 billion; $19,700 per capita. **Real growth rate:** 1.1%. **Inflation:** 1.8%. **Unemployment:** 6.2%. **Arable land:** 17%. **Agriculture:** livestock, forest products, grains, sugar beets, potatoes. **Labor force** (1996), 3.648 million; 56.4% in services. **Products:** iron and steel, textiles, chemicals, machinery, paper, and pulp. **Natural resources:** iron ore, petroleum, timber, magnesite, aluminum, coal, lignite, cement, copper, hydropower. **Exports:** $55.5 billion (1996 est.): iron and steel products, timber, paper, textiles, chemical products. **Imports:** $65.8 billion (1996 est.): machinery, chemicals, foodstuffs, textiles and clothing, petroleum. **Major trading partners:** European Union (mostly Germany and Italy), Eastern Europe, U.S., Japan.

Geography Slightly smaller than Maine, Austria includes much of the mountainous territory of the eastern Alps (about 75% of the area). The country contains many snowfields, glaciers, and snowcapped peaks, the highest being the Grossglockner (12,530 ft.; 3,819 m). The Danube is the principal river. Forests and woodlands cover about 40% of the land.

Government Austria is a federal republic composed of nine provinces (Bundesländer), including Vienna. The president is elected by the people for a term of six years. The bicameral legislature consists of the Bundesrat, with 58 members chosen by the provincial assemblies, and the Nationalrat, with 183 members popularly elected for four years.

History Settled in prehistoric times, the central European land that is now Austria was overrun in pre-Roman times by various tribes, including the Celts. After the fall of the Roman Empire, of which Austria was part, the area was invaded by Bavarians and Slavic Avars. Charlemagne conquered the area in C.E. 788 and encouraged colonization and Christianity. In 1252, Ottokar, King of Bohemia, gained possession, only to lose the territories to Rudolf of Hapsburg in 1278. Thereafter, until World War I, Austria's history was largely that of its ruling house, the Hapsburgs. Austria emerged from the Congress of Vienna in 1815 as the continent's dominant power. The *Ausgleich* of 1867 provided for a dual sovereignty, the empire of Austria and the kingdom of Hungary, under Franz Joseph I, who ruled until his death on Nov. 21, 1916. The Austrian-Hungarian minority rule of this immensely diverse empire became increasingly difficult in an age of emerging nationalist movements. When the archduke Ferdinand was assassinated by a Serbian nationalist in Sarajevo in 1914, World War I, as well as the destruction of the Austro-Hungarian Empire, began.

During World War I, Austria-Hungary was one of the Central powers with Germany, Bulgaria, and Turkey, and the conflict left the country in political chaos and economic ruin. Austria, shorn of Hungary, was proclaimed a republic in 1918, and the monarchy was dissolved in 1919. A parliamentary democracy was set up by the constitution of Nov. 10, 1920. To check the power of Nazis advocating union with Germany, Chancellor Engelbert Dolfuss in 1933 established a dictatorship, but was assassinated by the Nazis on July 25, 1934. Kurt von Schuschnigg, his successor, struggled to keep Austria independent, but on March 12, 1938, German troops occupied the country, and Hitler proclaimed its *Anschluss* (union) with Germany, annexing it to the Third Reich.

After World War II, the U.S. and Britain declared the Austrians a "liberated" people. But the Russians prolonged the occupation. Finally Austria concluded a state treaty with the U.S.S.R. and the other occupying powers and regained its independence on May 15, 1955. The second Austrian republic, established Dec. 19, 1945, on the basis of the 1920 constitution (amended in 1929), was declared by the federal parliament to be permanently neutral.

On June 8, 1986, former U.N. Secretary-General Kurt Waldheim was elected to the ceremonial office of president in a campaign marked by controversy over his alleged links to Nazi war crimes in Yugoslavia (he was replaced by diplomat Thomas Klestil in 1992). On Jan. 1, 1995, Austria became a member of the European Union. Despite the membership, it retained its strict constitutional neutrality and forbade the stationing of foreign troops on its soil.

In 1998, Austria discussed the return of hundreds of art objects now owned by Austria that had been confiscated by the Nazi regime from their former, primarily Jewish, owners.

Azerbaijan

REPUBLIC OF AZERBAIJAN

President: Heydar Aliyev (1993)
Prime Minister: Artur Rasizade (1996)
Area: 33,400 sq mi. (86,600 sq km)
Population (1998 est.): 7,855,576 (average annual rate of natural increase: 0.70%). Birth rate: 22.2/1000; infant mortality rate: 81.6/1000; density per sq mi.: 235
Capital and largest city (1991): Baku, 1,713,300, a port on the Caspian Sea. Other large cities: Ganja (1989), 278,000; Sumgait, 231,000. **Monetary unit:** Manat. **Languages:** Azerbaijani Turkic, 82%; Russian, 7%; Armenian, 2%. **Ethnicity/Race:** Azeri 90%, Dagestani Peoples 3.2%, Russian 2.5%, Armenian 2.3%, other 2% (1995 est.) note: almost all Armenians live in the separatist Nagorno-Karabakh region. **Religion:** Muslim, 87%; Russian Orthodox, 5.6%; Armenian Orthodox, 2%.
Economic summary: GDP/PPP (1996 estimate as extrapolated from World Bank estimate for 1994):

$11.9 billion; $1,550 per capita (1996 est.). **Real growth rate:** (1995 est.) 1.2%. **Inflation:** 20% (1996 est.). **Unemployment:** 1.1%. Azerbaijan's Apsheron peninsula is an oil-rich area and is now being developed under a $7.4 billion contract with western oil companies. **Industry:** petroleum and natural gas, petroleum products, oilfield equipment, steel, iron ore, cement, chemicals, petrochemicals, and textiles. **Agriculture:** cotton, wheat, tobacco, fruit, wine grapes, potatoes, sheep and other livestock. **Labor force:** 2.789 million (1990); agriculture and forestry, 32%; industry and construction, 26%; other, 42%. **Exports:** $700 million (f.o.b., 1996) to outside the successor states of the former U.S.S.R: oil and gas, chemicals, textiles, cotton. **Imports:** $900 million (c.i.f., 1996) from outside the successor states of the former U.S.S.R.: machinery and parts, consumer durables, foodstuffs, textiles. **Major trading partners:** Mostly C.I.S. and European countries.

Geography Azerbaijan is located on the western shore of the Caspian Sea at the southeastern extremity of the Caucasus. The region is a mountainous country. About 7% of it is arable land. The Kura River valley is the area's major agricultural zone.

Government A constitutional republic with a 125-seat parliament.

History Azerbaijan was known in ancient times as Albania. The area was the site of many conflicts involving Arabs, Kazars, and the Turks. After the 11th century, the territory became dominated by the Turks and eventually became a stronghold of the Shi'ite Muslim religion and Islamic culture. The territory of Soviet Azerbaijan was acquired by Russia from Persia through the Treaty of Gulistan in 1813 and the Treaty of Turkamanchai in 1828.

After the Bolshevik Revolution, Azerbaijan declared its independence from Russia in May 1918. The republic was reconquered by the Red Army in 1920, and was annexed into the Transcaucasian Soviet Socialist Republic in 1922. It was later reestablished as a separate Soviet Republic on Dec. 5, 1936.

Since 1983, the rival republics of Azerbaijan and Armenia have been feuding over the enclave of Nagorno-Karabakh, located within Azerbaijan. Both nations claim this autonomous region. The majority of the enclave's residents are Armenian Christians agitating to secede from the predominantly Muslim Azerbaijan and join with Armenia. War broke out in 1988 when Nagorno-Karabakh tried to break away and annex itself to Armenia. An estimated 35,000 have been killed since the beginning of the conflict.

Azerbaijan declared independence from the collapsing Soviet Union on Aug. 30, 1991. In the years that followed, Armenia successfully fought Azerbaijan for control of Nagorno-Karabakh. A political power struggle erupted in Azerbaijan in 1993 when rebel forces advanced on the capital. These events were set against a worsening of the economy and major reverses in the war with Armenia. A cease-fire agreement was reached between the two countries in 1994, with Armenia retaining its hold over the disputed enclave. Azerbaijan has offered broad autonomy to the enclave in exchange for the withdrawal of Armenian troops from Azeri lands. But the enclave wants either full independence or annexation to Armenia.

The country's continued economic decline may be stemmed by Western investment in Azerbaijan's oil resources, but difficult negotiations over the route of the pipelines and political instability have stalled Azerbaijan's potential oil boom.

Bahamas

COMMONWEALTH OF THE BAHAMAS

Sovereign: Queen Elizabeth II (1952)
Governor-General: Sir Orville Alton Turnquest (1995)
Prime Minister: Hubert Ingraham (1992)
Area: 5,380 sq mi. (13,940 sq km)
Population (1998 est.): 279,833 (average annual rate of natural increase: 1.39%); birth rate: 21/1000; infant mortality rate: 19/1000; density per sq mi.: 52
Capital and largest city (1991 census): Nassau, 171,542. **Monetary unit:** Bahamian dollar. **Language:** English. **Ethnicity/Race:** black 85%, white 15%. **Religions:** Baptist, 29%; Anglican, 23%; Roman Catholic, 22%, others. **Literacy rate:** 95%
Economic summary: GDP/PPP (1995 est.): $4.8 billion; $18,700 per capita. **Real growth rate:** 2% (1995 est.). **Inflation:** 1.5% (1996). **Unemployment** 15% (1995 est.). **Labor force:** 136,900 (1993); government, 30%; tourism, 40%; business services, 10%; agriculture, 5%. **Agriculture:** fruits, vegetables. **Industry:** fish, refined petroleum, pharmaceutical products, tourism, banking, rum, cement, salt production, spiral welded steel pipe. **Natural resources:** salt, aragonite, timber. **Exports:** $267.5 million (f.o.b., 1995): rum, crawfish, pharmaceuticals, cement. **Imports:** $1.17 billion (c.i.f., 1995): foodstuffs, manufactured goods, fuels. **Major trading partners:** U.S., U.K., Nigeria, Japan, Norway, France, Denmark. **Member of Commonwealth of Nations**

Geography The Bahamas are an archipelago of about 700 islands and 2,400 uninhabited islets and cays lying 50 miles off the east coast of Florida. They extend for about 760 miles (1,223 km). Only about 30 of the islands and cays are inhabited; the most important is New Providence (80 sq mi.; 207 sq km), on which Nassau is situated. Other islands include Grand Bahama, Abaco, Eleuthera, Andros, Cat Island, and San Salvador (or Watling's Island). All the islands of the archipelago are composed of coraline limestone, mostly lie only a few feet above sea level, and are generally flat.

Government The House of Assembly, a legislative body consisting of members elected by popular vote for maximum five-year terms, appoints a prime minister, who wields the country's executive power. The other, less important legislative body is the Senate, with most of its members appointed by the prime minister and the leader of the largest opposition party in the House of Assembly.

History The islands were reached by Columbus in Oct. 1492, and were a favorite pirate area in the early 18th century. The Bahamas were a Crown colony from 1717 until they were granted internal self-government in 1964. The Bahamas moved toward greater autonomy in 1968 after the overwhelming victory in general elections of the Progressive Liberal Party, led by Prime Minister Lynden O. Pindling, over the predominately white United Bahamians Party. With its new mandate from the 85% black population, Pindling's government negotiated a new constitution with Britain under which the colony became the Commonwealth of the Bahama Islands in 1969. On July 10, 1973, the Bahamas became an independent nation as the Commonwealth of the Bahamas.

Hubert A. Ingraham, of the Free National Movement Party, was sworn in as prime minister on Aug. 20, 1992, ending 25 years of rule by the Progressive Liberal Party. The government was elected to a second term as a result of March 1997 elections, which saw the further decline of the progressive liberals.

Bahrain

STATE OF BAHRAIN

Emir: Sheik Isa ibn-Sulman al-Khalifah (1961)
Prime Minister: Sheik Khalifah ibn Sulman al-Khalifa (1970)
Area: 240 sq mi. (620 sq km)
Population (1998 est.): 616,342 (average annual rate of natural increase: 2.09%); birth rate: 22.4/1000; infant mortality rate: 15.5/1000; density per sq mi.: 2,568
Capital (1992 est.): Al-Manámah, 140,401. **Monetary unit:** Bahrain dinar. **Languages:** Arabic (official), English, Farsi, Urdu. **Ethnicity/Race:** Bahraini 63%, Asian 13%, other Arab 10%, Iranian 8%, other 6%. **Religion:** Islam. **Literacy rate:** 77%
Economic summary: GDP/PPP (1996 est.): $7.7 billion, $13,000 per capita. **Real growth rate:** 3%. **Inflation:** 0%. **Unemployment:** 15% (1996 est.). **Labor force:** 140,000; industry, 85%; agriculture, 5%; services, 5%; government, 3% (1982). **Agriculture:** eggs, vegetables, fruits, shrimp. **Industry:** petroleum processing and refining, aluminum smelting, offshore banking, ship repairing. **Natural resources:** oil, fish. **Exports:** $4.2 billion (f.o.b., 1996 est.): petroleum and petroleum products, 80%; aluminum, 7%. **Imports:** $3.5 billion (c.i.f., 1996 est.): machinery, oil-industry equipment, motor vehicles, foodstuffs. **Major trading partners:** Saudi Arabia, U.S., U.K., Japan, India, Germany, U.A.E.

Geography Bahrain is an archipelago in the Persian Gulf off the coast of Saudi Arabia. The islands for the most part are level expanses of sand and rock. A causeway connects Bahrain to Saudi Arabia.

Government Traditional monarchy. Political parties are prohibited.

History At the time of the Muslim conquest in the 7th century, Bahrain was governed by a Christian Arab in the rule of Persia. The 'Abbasids took the land in the 8th century, and it remained under Arab control until 1521, when Portugal seized it. In 1602, after 80 years of unrest, the Persians took Bahrain. In 1783 Ahmad ibn al-Khalifah ousted the Persians, and his family has ruled Bahrain ever since. Bahrain became, by treaty, a British protectorate in 1820. It has become a major Middle Eastern oil center and, through use of oil revenues, is one of the most developed of the Persian Gulf sheikdoms. Sheik Isa ibn Sulman al-Khalifa, who became emir in 1961, is a member of the original ruling family. Bahrain announced its independence on Aug. 14, 1971.

After independence, tensions between the Shi'ite and Sunni communities increased, and Shi'ite Muslims, emboldened by Iran's revolution in 1979, continued to press for greater participation in government. In 1996, the government arrested 29 Shi'ites on charges of plotting to overthrow the ruling family and establish an Iranian-style Muslim regime. In an effort to increase trade and investment, an economic agreement aimed at furthering joint projects was signed between Jordan and Bahrain in June 1997.

Bangladesh

PEOPLE'S REPUBLIC OF BANGLADESH

President: Shahabuddin Ahmed (1996)
Prime Minister: Sheik Hasina Wazed (1996)
Area: 55,598 sq mi. (144,000 sq km)
Population (1998 est.): 127,567,002 (average annual rate of natural increase: 1.76%); birth rate: 28.9/1000; infant mortality rate: 97.7/1000; density per sq mi.: 2,295
Capital and largest city : Dhaka: city proper (1991 census) 3,839,000; metro. area (1996 est.) 8,500,000. **Other large cities (est. mid-1994):** Chittagong, 3,000,000; Khulna, 2,000,000. **Monetary unit:** Taka. **Principal languages:** Bangla (official), English. **Ethnicity/Race:** Bengali 98%, Biharis 250,000, tribals less than 1 million. **Religions:** Muslim 83%, Hindu 16%, Buddhist, Christian, other. **Literacy rate:** 35%
Economic summary: GDP/PPP (1996 est.): $155.1 billion; $1,260 per capita. **Real growth rate:** 4.7%. **Inflation:** 4.0% (FY 95/96). **Unemployment:** 35.9% (1996)**Arable land:** 73%. **Agriculture:** rice, jute, tea, wheat, sugar, potatoes, beef. Agriculture accounts for 40% of gross domestic and 70% of employment. **Labor force:** 50.1 million; agriculture, 65%; services, 21%; industry and mining, 14% (1989). **Industry:** jute goods, textiles, sugar, fertilizer, paper, processed foods. **Natural resources:** natural gas, uranium, timber. **Exports:** $3.9 billion (1996 est.): garments, jute and jute goods, leather and leather goods, seafood, tea, paper, fertilizer. **Imports:** $6.8 billion (1996 est.): capital goods, petroleum, food, textiles. **Major trading partners:** U.S., E.U., Japan, China, Hong Kong, Singapore. **Member of Commonwealth of Nations**

Geography Bangladesh, on the northern coast of the Bay of Bengal, is surrounded by India, with a small common border with Burma in the southeast. It is approximately the size of Wisconsin. The country is low-lying riverine land traversed by the many branches and tributaries of the Ganges and Brahmaputra rivers. Elevations average less than 600 feet (183 m) above sea level. Tropical monsoons and frequent floods and cyclones inflict heavy damage in the delta region.

Government Bangladesh is an independent republic within the British Commonwealth.

History What is now called Bangladesh is part of the historic region of Bengal, the northeastern portion of the Indian subcontinent. The earliest reference to the region was to a kingdom called Vanga, or Banga (c.1000 B.C.E.). Buddhists ruled for centuries, but by the 10th century Bengal was primarily Hindu. In 1576, Bengal became part of the Mogul Empire, and the majority of East Bengalis converted to Islam. Bengal was ruled by British India from 1757 until Britain withdrew in 1947, and Pakistan was founded out of the two predominantly Muslim regions of the Indian subcontinent. West Pakistan and East Pakistan were united by religion (Islam), but their peoples were separated by culture, physical features, and 1,000 miles of Indian territory. Bangladesh consists primarily of East Bengal (West Bengal is part of India and its people are primarily Hindu) plus the Sylhet district of the Indian state of Assam. For almost 25 years after independence from Britain, its history was part of Pakistan's (*see* Pakistan).

Tension between East and West Pakistan developed from the outset because of their vast geographic, economic, and cultural differences. East

Pakistan's Awami League, a political party founded by the Bengali nationalist Sheik Mujibur Rahman in 1949, sought independence from West Pakistan. Although 56 percent of the population resided in East Pakistan, the West held the lion's share of political and economic power. In 1970 East Pakistanis secured a majority of the seats in the National Assembly. President Yahya Khan postponed the opening of the National Assembly in an attempt to circumvent East Pakistan's demand for greater autonomy. As a consequence East Pakistan seceded, and the independent state of Bangladesh, or Bengali nation, was proclaimed March 26, 1971. Civil war broke out, and with the help of Indian troops in the last few weeks of the war, East Pakistan defeated West Pakistan on Dec. 16, 1971. An estimated one million Bengalis were killed in the fighting or later slaughtered. Ten million more took refuge in India. In Feb. 1974, Pakistan agreed to recognize the independence of Bangladesh.

Founding president Sheikh Mujibur was assassinated in 1975, as was the next president, Zia ur-Rahman. On March 24, 1982, Gen. Hossain Mohammad Ershad, army chief of staff, took control in a bloodless coup but was forced to resign on Dec. 6, 1990, amidst violent protests and numerous allegations of corruption. A succession of prime ministers governed in the 1990s, including Khaleda Zia, wife of the assassinated president Zia ur-Rahman, and the current prime minister and leader of the liberal Awami League, Hasina Wazed, the daughter of Sheik Mujibur. Disastrous floods in 1998 stranded nearly 8 million people and damaged crops and structures.

Barbados

Sovereign: Queen Elizabeth II (1952)
Governor-General: Sir Clifford Husbands (June 1996)
Prime Minister: Owen Arthur (1994)
Area: 166 sq mi. (430 sq km)
Population (1998 est.): 259,025; (growth rate: 0.09%); birth rate: 14.9/1000; infant mortality rate: 17.3/1000; density per sq mi.: 1,560
Capital and largest city (1990): Bridgetown, 6,700. **Monetary unit:** Barbados dollar. **Language:** English. **Ethnicity/Race:** African 80%, European 4%, other 16%. **Religions:** Anglican, 40%; Methodist, 7%; Pentecostal, 8%; Roman Catholic, 4%. **Literacy rate:** 99%
Economic summary: GDP/PPP (1996 est.): $2.65 billion; $10,300 per capita. **Real growth rate:** 3.5%. **Inflation:** 1.8% (1996 est.). **Unemployment:** 16.2% (1996). **Arable land:** 37%. **Products:** sugar cane, cotton, subsistence foods. **Industry:** light manufactures, sugar milling, tourism. **Labor force:** (1993), 126,000 services and government 41%; commerce 15%; manufacturing and construction 18%; transportation (1992 est.). **Exports:** $235 million (f.o.b., 1995): sugar and molasses, chemicals, electrical components, clothing, rum, machinery and transport equipment. **Imports:** $763 million (c.i.f., 1995): foodstuffs, consumer durables, raw materials, machinery, crude oil, construction materials, chemicals. **Major trading partners:** U.S., Caribbean nations, U.K., Japan. **Member of Commonwealth of Nations**

Geography An island in the Atlantic about 300 miles (483 km) north of Venezuela, Barbados is only 21 miles long (34 km) and 14 miles across (23 km) at its widest point. It is circled by fine beaches and narrow coastal plains. The highest point is Mount Hillaby (1,105 ft.; 337 m) in the north central area.

Government The Barbados legislature dates from 1627. It is bicameral, with a Senate of 21 members appointed by the governor-general and an Assembly of 28 elected members. The major political parties are the Barbados Labour Party (led by Prime Minister Owen Arthur) and the Democratic Labour Party.

History Barbados is thought to have been originally inhabited by Arawak Indians from South America. By 1536, however, no Indians survived.

Barbados, with a population that is 90% black, was settled by the British in 1627. Slaves were brought in from Africa to work sugar plantations. Slavery was abolished in the British Empire in 1834, and in 1838 slaves on the island achieved freedom.

Barbados became a Crown colony in 1885 and was a member of the Federation of the West Indies from 1958 to 1962. Britain granted the colony independence on Nov. 30, 1966, and it became a parliamentary democracy within the Commonwealth.

Since independence, Barbados has been politically stable. However, local anger over rulings by the final appeals court, appointed by Queen Elizabeth, led to the creation in 1997 of a constitutional commission to consider abandoning all ties to Great Britain.

Belarus

REPUBLIC OF BELARUS

President: Alyaksandr Lukashenka (1994)
Prime Minister: Syarhei Linh (1996)
Area: 80,200 sq mi. (207,600 sq km)
Population (1998 est.): 10,409,050 (average annual rate of natural increase: –0.05%) (In 1989: Belarussian, 77.9%; Russian, 13.2%; Polish, 4.1%; Ukrainian, 2.9%; Jewish, 1.1%); birth rate: 9.7/1000; infant mortality rate: 14.2/1000; density per sq mi.: 130
Capital (1992 est.): Mensk (Minsk), 1,666,000. **Other large cities (1992 est.):** Gomel, 517,300; Vitebsk, 373,000; Mogilyov, 364,000; Grodno, 291,800; Brest, 284,000; Bobruysk, 224,000. **Monetary unit:** Belarussian ruble. **Language:** Belarussian (White Russian). **Ethnicity/Race:** Belarussian 77.9%, Russian 13.2%, Polish 4.1%, Ukrainian 2.9%, other 1.9%. **Religion:** Orthodoxy is predominant. **Literacy rate:** 100%
Economic summary: GDP/PPP (1995 estimate as extrapolated from the World Bank estimate for 1996): $51.9 billion; $5,000 per capita. **Real growth rate:** (1996 est.) 3% . **Inflation:** 33%. **Unemployment:** 3.1%. **Labor force:** 4.731 million; industry and construction, 36%; agriculture and forestry, 19%; services, 45%. Industry accounts for about two-thirds of the country's income. **Industry:** tractors, trucks, agricultural machinery, textiles, timber, chemical products including fertilizers, light manufacturing including TV sets, refrigerators, and food processing. Belarus's land is not well suited for farming. One-quarter of the republic's work force is employed in agriculture. High-yield agricultural crops are potatoes and vegetables, flax, rye, oats, other grains, sugar beets, fruit, and considerable quantities of meat, milk, and eggs. **Exports:** $5.2 billion (f.o.b., 1996): machinery and transport equipment, chemicals, foodstuffs; to outside of the successor states of the former U.S.S.R. **Imports:** $6.8 billion (c.i.f., 1996):

fuel, natural gas, industrial raw materials, textiles, sugar; from outside of the successor states of the former U.S.S.R. **Major trading partners:** Russia, Ukraine, Poland, Germany.

Geography Much of Belarus (formerly the Belarussian Soviet Socialist Republic of the U.S.S.R., and then Byelorussia) is a hilly lowland with forests, swamps, and numerous rivers and lakes. There are wide rivers emptying into the Baltic and Black seas. Its forests cover over one-third of the land and its peat marshes are a valuable natural resource. The largest lake is Narach, 31 sq mi. (79.6 sq km).

Government Under the 1994 constitution, the president, directly elected for a term of five years, is the head of state and of the executive branch. The 260-member unicameral parliament, called the Supreme Soviet, is also directly elected and sits for five years.

History In the 5th century, Belarus (also known as White Russia) was colonized by east Slavic tribes and was dominated by Kiev from the 9th to 12th centuries. After the destruction of Kiev by the Mongols in the 13th century, the territory was conquered by the dukes of Lithuania, although it retained substantial autonomy. Belarus became part of the Grand Duchy of Lithuania, which merged with Poland in 1569. Following the partitions of Poland in 1772, 1793, and the final partition which divided Poland between Russia, Prussia, and Austria, Belarus became part of the Russian empire.

The peace treaty of Riga in March 1921 ending the Polish-Soviet War ceded west Belarus to Poland. The eastern part of the country was joined to the U.S.S.R. in 1922. In 1939, the Soviet Union took back West Belarus under the secret protocol of the Nazi-Soviet Nonaggression Pact and incorporated it into the Belarussian Soviet Socialist Republic. Belarus was one of the most devastated areas in World War II. At the end of the war, Belarus was given membership in the United Nations in 1945. Belarus declared its sovereignty in July 1990 and its independence in Aug. 1991.

The Chernobyl nuclear power plant in Ukraine exploded in 1986, and 70% of its radioactivity fell on Belarus. Cancer and other illnesses have multiplied as a result.

The Belarus president, Nikolai Dementei, a communist hard-liner, was forced to resign under pressure following the Aug. 1991 attempted coup, and Stanislav S. Shushkevich, first deputy chairman of the parliament, assumed leadership of the country. Belarus became a co-founder of the Commonwealth of Independent States (C.I.S.) in Dec. 1991. In Jan. 1994, the country's parliament ousted its reform-minded leader in protest against his support for market economics. In March 1994, parliament adopted a new constitution, creating a presidency, and reconstructed the 260-seat parliament.

With much fanfare, Belarus and Russia signed a treaty in April 1997 aimed at significantly increasing cooperation between the two states, stopping just short of union. Many of the details remain ambiguous, however, as do their implications. Critics continue to denounce the increasingly oppressive political atmosphere and human rights violations in Belarus.

The Russian financial crisis in fall 1998 was expected to severely affect Belarus's Soviet-style planned economy. Belarus is almost completely dependent on Russia, which buys 70% of its exports.

Belgium

KINGDOM OF BELGIUM

National name: Royaume de Belgique—Koningrijk van België
Sovereign: King Albert II (1993)
Prime Minister: Jean-Luc Dehaene (1992)
Area: 11,781 sq mi. (30,510 sq km)
Population (1998 est.): 10,174,922 (average annual rate of natural increase: 0.09%); birth rate: 10.2/1000; infant mortality rate: 6.3/1000; density per sq mi.: 864
Capital and largest city (1994): Brussels, 949,070 (metro area). **Other large cities (1994):** Antwerp, 476,044; Ghent, 229,900; Liège, 207,496; Charleroi, 206,898; Bruges, 116,724. **Monetary Unit:** Belgian franc. **Languages:** Flemish, 57%; French, 32%; bilingual (Brussels), 10%; German, 0.7%. **Ethnicity/ Race:** Fleming 55%, Walloon 33%, mixed or other 12%. **Religion:** Roman Catholic, 75%. **Literacy rate:** 99%
Economic summary: GDP/PPP (1996 est.): $204.8 billion; $20,300 per capita. **Real growth rate:** 1.4% (1996 est.). **Inflation:** 2.1% (1996 est.). **Unemployment:** 14% (1996 est.). **Arable land:** 24%. **Agriculture:** pork, beef, milk, fruits and vegetables, meals, sugar beets, eggs, dairy products. **Labor force:** 4.126 million; services, 69.7%, industry, 27.7%; agriculture, 2.6% (1992). **Products:** chemicals, mechanical, electrical and plastic equipment, textiles, nonferrous metals, iron and steel, glass. **Exports:** $108 billion (f.o.b., 1994): machinery, transportation equipment, iron and steel, tractors, diamonds, mineral products. **Imports:** $140 billion (c.i.f., 1994): pharmaceuticals and chemicals, plastics, fuels, grains, and foodstuffs. **Major trading partners:** Germany, France, Netherlands, U.S.

Geography Located in western Europe, Belgium has about 40 miles of seacoast on the North Sea, at the Strait of Dover, and is approximately the size of Maryland. The Meuse and the Schelde, Belgium's principal rivers, are important commercial arteries.

Government Belgium, a parliamentary democracy under a constitutional monarch, consists of ten provinces. Its bicameral legislature has a Senate, with 71 members elected for four years. The 150 members of the Chamber of Representatives are directly elected for four years by proportional representation. There is universal suffrage, and those who do not vote are fined. NATO and the European Union have their headquarters in Brussels.

Under the 1994 constitution, autonomy was granted to the Walloon region (Wallonia), the Flemish region (Flanders), and the bilingual Brussels-Capital region; autonomy was also guaranteed for the Flemish-, French-, and German-speaking "communities." The central government retains responsibility for foreign policy, defense, taxation, and social security; the regional governments are responsible for transport, the environment, and trade promotion; the "community" governments oversee cultural and personal matters, including education.

History Belgium occupies part of the Roman province of Belgica, named after the Belgae, a people of ancient Gaul. The area was conquered by Julius

Caesar in 57–50 B.C.E., then was overrun by the Franks in the 5th century. It was part of Charlemagne's empire in the 8th century, then in the next century was absorbed into Lotharingia and later into the Duchy of Lower Lorraine. In the 12th century it was partitioned into the Duchies of Brabant and Luxembourg, the Bishopric of Liège, and the domain of the Count of Hainaut, which included Flanders. In the 16th century, Belgium, with most of the area of the Low Countries, passed to the Duchy of Burgundy and was inherited by Charles V, who incorporated it into his Holy Roman Empire. Then, in 1555, they were united with Spain. By the treaty of Utrecht in 1713, the country's sovereignty passed to Austria. During the wars that followed the French Revolution, Belgium was occupied and later annexed to France. But with the downfall of Napoleon, the Congress of Vienna in 1815 gave the country to the Netherlands. The Belgians revolted in 1830 and declared their independence.

Germany's invasion of Belgium in 1914 set off World War I. The Treaty of Versailles (1919) gave the areas of Eupen, Malmédy, and Moresnet to Belgium. Leopold III succeeded Albert, king during World War I, in 1934. In World War II, Belgium was overwhelmed by Nazi Germany, and Leopold III was held prisoner. When he attempted to return in 1950, socialists and liberals revolted. He abdicated July 16, 1951, and his son, Baudouin, became king. Because of growing opposition to Belgian rule in its African colonies, Belgium granted independence to Congo (now Democratic Republic of the Congo) in 1960 and to Ruanda-Urundi (now the nations of Rwanda and Burundi) in 1962.

Divisions between Flemings and Walloons grew, and linguistic regionalization increased, culminating in the revised constitution of 1994, which granted more autonomy to Belgium's three regions and language "communities." The discovery of a child sex and murder ring in 1996 led to national outrage that was compounded by disclosures that official negligence and corruption had resulted in even more children's deaths. As the scandal continued into 1997, it fueled pressure for reform of the political, judicial, and police systems.

Belize

Sovereign: Queen Elizabeth II (1952)
Governor-General: Colville Young (1993)
Prime Minister: Manuel Esquivel (1993)
Area: 8,867 sq mi. (22,960 sq km)
Population (1998 est.): 230,160 (average annual rate of natural increase: 2.42%); birth rate: 31.1/1000; infant mortality rate: 32.4/1000.; density per square mi.: 26
Capital (1993 est.): Belmopan, 3,852. **Largest city (1993):** Belize City, 47,724. **Monetary unit:** Belize dollar. **Languages:** English (official) and Spanish, Maya, Carib. **Ethnicity/Race:** mestizo 44%, Creole 30%, Maya 11%, Garifuna 7%, other 8%. **Religions:** Roman Catholic, 62%; Protestant, 30%. **Literacy rate:** 91%
Economic summary: GDP/PPP (1996 est.): $649 million; $2,960 per capita. **Real growth rate:** 3%. **Inflation:** 6.4%. **Unemployment:** 15% (1996 est.). **Agriculture:** sugar cane, corn, cocoa, citrus, bananas, livestock, fish. **Labor force:** 51,500; agriculture, 30%; services, 16%; government, 15.4%; commerce, 11.2%; manufacturing, 10.3%. **Industry:** timber, processed foods, furniture, rum, soap. **Natural resources:** timber, fish. **Exports:** $204 million (f.o.b., 1996): sugar, molasses, clothing, lumber, citrus concentrates, fish. **Imports:** $264 million (c.i.f., 1996): fuels, transportation equipment, foodstuffs, machinery, chemicals, pharmaceuticals, manufactured goods. **Major trading partners:** European Union, Mexico, CARICOM, U.S. **Member of Commonwealth of Nations**

Geography Belize is situated on the Caribbean Sea south of Mexico and east and north of Guatemala in Central America. In area, it is about the size of New Hampshire. Most of the country is heavily forested with various hardwoods. Mangrove swamps and cays along the coast give way to hills and mountains in the interior. The highest point is Victoria Peak, 3,681 feet (1,122 m).

Government Formerly the colony of British Honduras, Belize's executive power is nominally wielded by Queen Elizabeth II through an appointed governor-general but effective power is held by the prime minister, who is responsible to a 29-member parliament elected by universal suffrage.

History Once a part of the Mayan empire, the area was deserted until British timber cutters began exploiting valuable hardwoods in the 17th century. Efforts by Spain to dislodge British settlers, including a major naval attack in 1798, were defeated. The territory was formally named a British colony in 1862 but administered by the governor of Jamaica until 1884.

Guatemala has long made claims to the territory. Although the dispute between Guatemala and Great Britain remained unresolved, Belize became independent on Sept. 21, 1981, after having been self-governing since 1964. Guatemala recognized Belize's sovereignty in Sept. 1991 and abandoned its territorial claim, although unease remains.

The general election of June 1993 saw a victory for the United Democratic Party, which won 16 of the 29 seats in the House of Representatives. Although of increasing importance to drug trafficking, Belize received a national-security waiver from the U.S., permitting the continuation of official aid. In early 1997 Belizean-U.S. anti-drug forces staged two raids off the coast.

Benin

REPUBLIC OF BENIN

National name: Republique du Benin
President: Mathieu Kerekou (1996)
Prime Minister: Adrien Houngbédji (1996)
Area: 43,483 sq mi. (112,620 sq km)
Population (1998 est.): 6,100,799 (average annual rate of natural increase: 3.31%); birth rate: 45.8/1000; infant mortality rate: 100.2/1000; density per sq mi.: 140
Capital and largest city (1996): Porto-Novo (official), 177,660; Cotonou (de facto capital) 33,212. **Other large city (1992):** Djougou, 132,192. **Monetary unit:** Franc CFA. **Ethnic groups:** Fons and Adjas, Baribas, Yorubas, Mahis. **Languages:** French, African languages. **Ethnicity/Race:** African 99% (42 ethnic groups, most important being Fon, Adja, Yoruba, Bariba), Europeans 5,500. **Religions:** indigenous, 70%; Christian, 15%; Islam, 15%. **Literacy rate:** 23%
Economic summary: GDP/PPP (1996 est.): $8.2 billion; $1,440 per capita. **Real growth rate:** 5.5%. **Inflation:** 14.5% (1995 est.). **Unemployment:** n.a. **Arable land:** 13%. **Agriculture:** palm oils, peanuts, cotton, coffee, sorghum, corn, rice, livestock. **Labor force:** 1.9 million (1987); agriculture, 60%; transport, commerce, and public services, 38%; industry, less than 2%. **Industry:**

processed palm oil, palm kernel oil, textiles, beverages, textiles. **Natural resources:** limestone, some offshore oil, marble, timber. **Exports:** $300 million (f.o.b., 1995): crude oil, cotton, palm products, cocoa. **Imports:** $380 million (c.i.f., 1995): foodstuffs, beverages, tobacco, petroleum products, intermediate goods, capital goods, light consumer goods. **Major trading partners:** France and other Western European countries, Japan, U.S.

Geography This West African nation on the Gulf of Guinea, between Togo on the west and Nigeria on the east, is about the size of Tennessee. It is bounded also by Burkina Faso and Niger on the north. The land consists of a narrow coastal strip that rises to a swampy, forested plateau and then to highlands in the north. A hot and humid climate blankets the entire country.

Government The change in name from Dahomey to Benin was announced by President Mathieu Kerekou on Nov. 30, 1975. The name Benin commemorates an African kingdom that flourished from the 15th to the 17th century in what is now southwestern Nigeria. Benin is a republic under a multiparty democratic rule with a unicameral legislature, the National Assembly.

History The Abomey kingdom of the Dahomey, or Fon, peoples was established in 1625. One of the smallest and most densely populated states in Africa, Benin was annexed by the French in 1893, and incorporated into French West Africa in 1904. It became an autonomous republic within the French Community in 1958, and on Aug. 1, 1960, Dahomey was granted its independence within the community.

Gen. Christophe Soglo deposed the first president, Hubert Maga, in an army coup in 1963. He dismissed the civilian government in 1965, proclaiming himself chief of state. A group of young army officers seized power in Dec. 1967, deposing Soglo. They promulgated a new constitution in 1968. In Dec. 1969, Benin had its fifth coup of the decade, with the army again taking power. In May 1970, a three-man presidential commission was created to take over the government. The commission had a six-year term. In May 1972, yet another army coup ousted the triumvirate and installed Lt. Col. Mathieu Kerekou as president. Between 1974 and 1989 Dahomey embraced socialism, and changed its name to the People's Republic of Benin. In 1990 it abandoned Marxist ideology, began moving toward multiparty democracy, and changed its name again, to the Republic of Benin.

Since 1990 the government has embarked on a vast privatization drive. The sale of SONICOG (a producer of butter, soap, and edible oils) in 1997 was contingent on the retention of the entire labor force. Presidential elections in March 1996 resulted in a victory for former president and Marxist military ruler Kerekou, with 52.49% of the vote, over the incumbent Soglo.

Bhutan

KINGDOM OF BHUTAN

National name: Druk-yul
Ruler: King Jigme Singye Wangchuck (1972)
Area: 18,000 sq mi. (47,000 sq km)
Population (1998 est.): 1,908,307 (average annual rate of natural increase: 2.27%); birth rate: 37.3/1000; infant mortality rate: 111.7/1000; density per sq mi.: 107
Capital and largest city (1993): Thimphu (official), 30,340. **Monetary unit:** Ngultrum. **Language:** Dzongkha (official). **Ethnicity/Race:** Bhote 50%, ethnic Nepali 35%, indigenous or migrant tribes 15%. **Religions:** Buddhist, 75%; Hindu, 25%. **Literacy rate:** n.a.
Economic summary: GDP/PPP (1995 est.): $1.3 billion; $730 per capita. **Real growth rate:** 6.9% (1995 est.). **Inflation:** 8.6% (FY 94/95 est.). **Unemployment:** n.a. **Arable land:** 2%. **Labor force:** n.a.; agriculture: 93%; services: 5%; industry and commerce: 2%. Principal products: wood, wood products, rice, barley, wheat, potatoes, fruit, cardamom, coal, limestone, gypsum, dolomite, graphite. **Industry:** hydroelectricity, wood, wood products, cement, calcium carbide, ferro silicon, fruit processing, alcoholic beverages. **Natural resources:** hydroelectric power, timber, minerals. **Exports:** $70.9 million (f.o.b., FY 94/95 est.): cardamom, gypsum, timber, handicrafts, cement, fruit, electricity (to India), precious stones, spices. **Imports:** $113.6 million (c.i.f., FY 94/95 est.): equipment for telecommunications, machinery, rice, fuel, vehicles, grains, consumer merchandise. **Major trading partners:** India, Bangladesh.

Geography Mountainous Bhutan, half the size of Indiana, is situated on the southeast slope of the Himalayas, bordered on the north and east by Tibet and on the south and west and east by India. The landscape consists of a succession of lofty and rugged mountains running generally from north to south and separated by deep valleys. In the north, towering peaks reach a height of 24,000 feet (7,315 m).

Government Bhutan is a monarchy. The king rules with a cabinet and a Royal Advisory Council. There is a National Assembly (parliament), which meets semiannually, but no political parties.

History Although archeological exploration of Bhutan has been limited, evidence of civilization in the region dates back to at least 2,000 B.C.E. Aboriginal Bhutanese, known as Monpa, are believed to have migrated from Tibet. The traditional name of the country since the 17th century has been Drukyul, Land of the Drokpa (Dragon People), a reference to the dominant branch of Tibetan Buddhism that is still practiced in the Himalayan kingdom.

British troops invaded the region in 1865, and negotiated an agreement under which Britain agreed to pay an annual allowance to the Bhutanese monarchy on condition of good behavior. A treaty between India and the seat of government, Thimphu, in 1949 increased this subsidy and placed Bhutan's foreign affairs under Indian control. In the 1960s Bhutan undertook modernization, abolishing slavery and the caste system, emancipating women, and enacting land reform. In 1985, Bhutan made its first diplomatic links with non-Asian countries.

A pro-democracy campaign emerged in 1991 that the government claimed was composed largely of Nepali immigrants. As a result of the campaign, some 100,000 Nepali civil servants were either evicted or encouraged to emigrate. Most of them crossed the border back into Nepal, where they were housed in U.N.-administered refugee camps. The mass exodus prompted the International Red Cross to investigate charges of human rights violations in

1993. By 1995, discussions with Nepal over the problem had born little fruit, with Thimphu insisting that the refugees had left of their own free will or were Nepali nationals wanting to immigrate to Bhutan.

In 1998, King Jigme Singye Wangchuck voluntarily curtailed his powerful monarchy by yielding to the formerly rubber-stamp legislature, giving it the right to remove him from leadership and appoint his Cabinet. The move was the largest step to date in a gradual program to dilute the monarchy after nearly a century of absolute rule.

Bolivia

REPUBLIC OF BOLIVIA

National name: República de Bolivia
President: Hugo Banzer Suárez (1997)
Area: 424,162 sq mi. (1,098,580 sq km)
Population (1998 est.): 7,826,352 (average annual rate of natural increase: 2%); birth rate: 31.41000; infant mortality rate: 63.9/1000; density per sq mi.: 18
Historic and Judicial capital (1992): Sucre, 130,952
Administrative capital (1992): La Paz, 711,036.
Largest cities (1992 est.): Santa Cruz, 694,616; El Alto, 404,367; Cochabamba, 404,102; Oruro, 183,194. **Monetary unit:** Boliviano. **Languages:** Spanish, Quechua, Aymara. **Ethnicity/Race:** Quechua 30%, Aymara 25%, mestizo (mixed European and Indian ancestry) 25%–30%, European 5%–15%. **Religion:** Roman Catholic, 85%. **Literacy rate:** 82%
Economic summary: GDP/PPP (1996 est.): $21.5 billion; $3,000 per capita. **Real growth rate:** 3.9%. **Inflation:** 8%. **Unemployment:** 18.8%. **Arable land:** 2%. **Agriculture:** (1994): soybeans, timber, sugar, cotton, coca, corn, coffee. **Industry:** refined petroleum, processed foods, tin, textiles, clothing. **Labor force** (1995): 2.3 million; agriculture: n.a.; services and utilities: n.a.; manufacturing, mining, and construction: n.a. **Natural resources:** petroleum, natural gas, tin, lead, zinc, copper, tungsten, bismuth, antimony, gold, sulfur, silver, iron ore. **Exports:** $1.1 billion (f.o.b., 1995 est.): metals 39%, natural gas 9%, soybeans 11%, jewelry 11%, wood 8%. **Imports:** $1.4 billion (c.i.f., 1995 est.): food, petroleum, consumer goods, capital goods. **Major trading partners:** U.S., Argentina, U.K., Peru, Chile, Brazil, Japan, Germany.

Geography Landlocked Bolivia is equal in size to California and Texas combined. Brazil forms its eastern border; its other neighbors are Peru and Chile on the west and Argentina and Paraguay on the south. The western part, enclosed by two chains of the Andes, is a great plateau—the Altiplano, with an average altitude of 12,000 ft. (3,658 m). Almost half the population lives on the plateau, which contains Oruru, Potosí, and La Paz. At an altitude of 11,910 feet (3,630 m), La Paz is the highest administrative capital city in the world. The Oriente, a lowland region ranging from rain forests to grasslands, comprises the northern and eastern two-thirds of the country. Lake Titicaca, at an altitude of 12,507 ft. (3,812 m), is the highest commercially navigable body of water in the world.

Government The 1947 Bolivian constitution provides for a democratic, representative, unitary republic. Executive power is exercised by the president, who is elected by a direct vote for a five-year term; the president may not be immediately reelected. Legislative power is vested in the 157-member National Congress, consisting of the Chamber of Deputies and the Senate. Judicial power is in the hands of the Supreme Court of Justice, made up of twelve members.

History Famous since Spanish colonial days for its mineral wealth, modern Bolivia was once a part of the ancient Incan Empire. After the Spaniards defeated the Incas in the 16th century, Bolivia's predominantly Indian population was reduced to slavery. By the end of the 17th century the mineral wealth had begun to dry up. The country won its independence in 1825 and was named after Simón Bolívar, the famed liberator. Hampered by internal strife, Bolivia lost great slices of territory to three neighbor nations. Several thousand square miles and its outlet to the Pacific were taken by Chile after the War of the Pacific (1879–84). In 1903 a piece of Bolivia's Acre province, rich in rubber, was ceded to Brazil. And in 1938, after losing the Chaco War of 1932–35 to Paraguay, Bolivia gave up its claim to nearly 100,000 square miles of the Gran Chaco. Political instability ensued.

In 1965, a guerrilla movement mounted from Cuba and headed by Maj. Ernesto (Ché) Guevara began a revolutionary war. With the aid of U.S. military advisers, the Bolivian army smashed the guerrilla movement, capturing and killing Guevara on Oct. 8, 1967. Faltering steps toward restoration of civilian government were halted abruptly on July 17, 1980, when Gen. Luis Garcia Meza Tejada seized power. A series of military leaders followed before the military returned the government to civilian rule in 1982. Hernán Siles Zuazo was inaugurated president on Oct. 10, 1982. Under Siles's left-of-center government, the country was regularly shut down by work stoppages, and the bulk of Bolivia's natural resources—natural gas, gold, lithium, potassium, and tungsten—were either sold on the black market or left in the ground. The country also had the lowest per capita income in South America, and inflation approached 3,000 percent. In 1985, Siles decided he was unable to carry on and quit a year early.

As in 1985 the inconclusive presidential election of 1989 was decided in Congress, when Bánzer, in second place, threw his support to Paz Zamora, who finished third, in exchange for naming a majority of the new cabinet. The presidential elections of June 1993 gave the post to Gonzalo Sánchez de Lozada, who ran on a platform calling for free-market policies and privatization. A presidential proposal to privatize six state companies was passed by Congress in March 1994. Former General Bánzer was elected president for the second time in Aug. 1997.

Bosnia and Herzegovina

THE FEDERATION OF BOSNIA AND HERZEGOVINA

President: Alija Izetbegovic (1990)
Co-Prime Ministers: Haris Silajdzic and Boro Bosic (1997)
Area: 19,741 sq mi. (51,233 sq km)
Population (1998 est.): 3,365,727 (all data dealing with population is subject to considerable error because of the dislocations caused by military action and ethnic cleansing); (average annual rate of natural increase: 3.63%); Birth rate: 8.7/1000; infant mortality rate: 30.8/1000; density per sq mi.: 171
Capital and largest city (1994 est.): Sarajevo (Bosnia), 300,000 (unofficial). Mostar, 126,067 (1991), is capital

of Herzegovina. **Other large city (1991, prewar est.):** Banja Luka (Bosnia), 195,139. **Monetary unit:** Dinar. **Language:** The language that used to be known as Serbo-Croatian but is now known as Serbian, Croatian, or Bosnian, depending on the speaker's ethnic and political affiliation. It is written in Latin and Cyrillic.. **Ethnicity/Race:** Serb 40%, Muslim 38%, Croat 22% (est.). **Religions:** Slavic Muslim, 44%; Orthodox, 31%; Catholic, 15%; Protestant, 4%, other, 6%.

Economic summary: (Reliable economic statistics not available) **GDP/PPP** (1995 est.): $1.9 billion, **Real growth rate:** n.a. **Inflation:** n.a. **Unemployment:** 40–70% **Labor force:** 1,026,254. **Industry:** steel production, mining (coal, iron ore, lead, zinc, manganese, and bauxite, vehicle assembly, textiles, tobacco products, wooden furniture, domestic appliances, oil refining. **Agriculture:** orchards, vineyards, livestock, some wheat and corn. **Exports:** $152 million (1995 est.) **Imports:** $1.1 billion (1995 est.) **Major trading partners:** principally the other former Yugoslav republics.

Geography Bosnia and Herzegovina make up a triangular-shaped republic, about half the size of Kentucky, on the Balkan peninsula. The Bosnian region in the north is mountainous and covered with thick forests. The Herzegovina region in the south is largely a rugged and flat farm land. It has a narrow coastline without natural harbors stretching 13 miles (20 km) along the Adriatic Sea.

Government Democratic republic with bicameral legislature. Following the post-war general elections in 1996, a three-person multi-ethnic collective presidency was formed.

History Bosnia and Herzegovina were once part of the Roman provinces of Illyricum, named after the original Illyrian inhabitants, and Pannonia. Serbs first settled in the land during the 7th century C.E., and by the end of the 10th century Bosnia became an independent state. Later Bosnia came under Hungarian rule in the middle of the 12th century. Medieval Bosnia reached the height of its power and prestige during the 14th century, when it controlled many of the surrounding territories including Herzegovina. During this period, religious strife arose among Roman Catholics, Orthodox, and Muslims, weakening the country. In 1463, Ottoman Turks conquered the nation.

At the Congress of Berlin in 1878 following the end of the Russo-Turkish War (1877–78), Austria-Hungary was given a mandate to occupy and govern Bosnia and Herzegovina. Although the provinces were still officially part of the Ottoman Empire, they were annexed by the Austro-Hungarian Empire on Oct. 7, 1908. As a result, relations with Serbia, which had claims on Bosnia and Herzegovina, became embittered. The hostility between the two countries climaxed in the assassination of Austrian Archduke Franz Ferdinand in Sarajevo on June 28, 1914, by a Serbian nationalist. This event precipitated the start of World War I (1914–1918). Bosnia and Herzegovina were annexed to Serbia as part of the newly formed Kingdom of Serbs, Croats, and Slovenes on Oct. 26, 1918. The name was later changed to Yugoslavia in 1929.

When Germany invaded Yugoslavia in 1941, Bosnia and Herzegovina were made part of a Croatian state that was controlled by a fascist dictatorship. During the German and Italian occupation of their land, Bosnian and Herzegovinian resistance fighters fought a fierce guerrilla war against the fascist troops. At the end of World War II in 1945, Bosnia and Herzegovina were reunited into a single state as one of the six republics of the newly reestablished Yugoslavia, under Marshall Tito, who died in 1980.

In Dec. 1991, Bosnia and Herzegovina declared their independence from Yugoslavia and asked for recognition by the European Union (E.U.). In a March 1992 referendum, Bosnian voters chose independence, and President Izetbegovic declared the nation an independent state. Attempting to carve out enclaves for themselves, the Serbian minority, with the help of the largely Serbian Yugoslav army, took the offensive and laid siege, particularly on Sarajevo, resulting in countless deaths. By the end of August, rebel Bosnian Serbs had conquered over 60% of Bosnia. The Serbs formally halted their siege of Sarajevo in Feb. 1994 at the request of Russia. In March, the government signed an agreement with Bosnian Croats linking their territories into a single federation.

U.S.-sponsored peace talks in Dayton, Ohio, led to an agreement in 1995 that called for a Muslim-Croat federation and a Serb entity. 60,000 NATO troops were to supervise its implementation. Fighting abated and orderly elections were held in Sept. 1996. President Alija Izetbegovic won the majority of votes to become the leader of the three-member presidency. The other two presidents of the rotating chair are Momcilo Krajisnik (Serb) and Kresimir Zubak (Croat).

The terms of the Dec. 1995 Dayton Peace Accord were largely ignored by Bosnian Serbs, with the former president, arch-nationalist Radovan Karadzic, still in de facto control of the Serbian enclave. Many indicted war criminals, including Karadzic, remain at large. Despite NATO's pledge in Oct. 1997 to remain in Bosnia beyond the 1998 mandate, the force remains mired in chronic ambivalence, unable to decide whether to jump into the fray or stand by and hope its presence is enough to spawn peace.

Two crucial priorities faced Bosnian leaders in 1998: the estimated one million refugees still displaced and the necessity of establishing a working government. Much of the administrative power in Bosnia and Herzegovina lies with the local authorities, the Muslim-Croat Federation and the Bosnian Serb Republic, whose president for a time was Biljana Plavsic (1996–98), the former Serb hard-liner who had been viewed by the West as the best hope for Bosnian Serb moderation. That hope was dashed, however, in the Sept. 1998 elections, when Nikola Poplasen, the leader of Bosnia's ultranationalist Radical party, defeated Plavsic.

Botswana

REPUBLIC OF BOTSWANA

President: Festus Mogae (1998)

Area: 231,800 sq mi. (600,370 sq km)

Population (1998 est.): 1,448,454 (average annual rate of natural increase: 1.11%); birth rate: 32/1000; infant mortality rate: 59.3/1000; density per sq mi.: 6

Capital and largest city (1992 est.): Gaborone, 138,000. **Monetary unit:** Pula. **Languages:** English, Setswana. **Ethnicity/Race:** Batswana 95%, Kalanga, Basarwa, and Kgalagadi 4%, white 1%. **Religions:** indigenous beliefs, 50%; Christian, 50%. **Literacy rate:** 74%

Economic summary: GDP/PPP (1996 est.): $4.6 billion, $3,100 per capita. **Real growth rate:** 5%. **Inflation:** 9.8% (1996 est.). **Unemployment:** 21%. **Arable land:** 1%. **Agriculture:** livestock, sorghum, corn, millet, cowpeas, beans. **Labor force:** (1992), 428,000; 220,000 formal sector employees, most others involved in cattle raising and subsistence agriculture; 14,300 employed in South African mines. **Industry:** diamonds, copper, nickel, salt, soda ash, potash, coal, frozen beef, tourism. **Natural resources:** diamonds, copper, nickel, salt, soda ash, potash, coal, natural gas. **Exports:** $2.1 billion (f.o.b., 1995): diamonds, 71%; copper and nickel, 5%; meat, 3%. **Imports:** $1.5 billion (c.i.f., 1995): foodstuffs, vehicles, textiles, petroleum products. **Major trading partners:** Switzerland, U.K., Southern African Customs Union (SACU), U.S. **Member of Commonwealth of Nations**

Geography Twice the size of Arizona, Botswana is in south-central Africa, bounded by Namibia, Zambia, Zimbabwe, and South Africa. Most of the country is near-desert, with the Kalahari occupying the western part of the country. The eastern part is hilly, with salt lakes in the north.

Government A parliamentary republic. The Botswana constitution provides, in addition to the unicameral National Assembly, for a House of Chiefs, which has a voice on bills affecting tribal affairs. There is universal suffrage.

History The earliest inhabitants of the region were the San, who were followed by the Tswana. About half the country today is ethnic Tswana. The term for the country's people, *Batswana,* refers to national rather than ethnic origin.

Encroachment by the Zulu in the 1820s and by Boers from Transvaal in the 1870s and 1880s threatened the peace of the region. In 1885 Britain established the area as a protectorate, then known as Bechuanaland. In 1961, Britain granted a constitution to the country. Self-government began in 1965, and on Sept. 30, 1966, the country became independent.

After independence, Botswana maintained good relations with its white-ruled neighbors, but gradually changed its policies, harboring rebel groups from South Rhodesia as well as some from South Africa.

Botswana, along with Namibia and Zimbabwe, received permission in June 1997 from a U.N. wildlife panel to sell 5.9 tons of stockpiled ivory to Japan.

After 17 years in power, 72-year-old President Ketumile Masire retired in 1997, and Festus Mogae became the new president.

Brazil

FEDERATIVE REPUBLIC OF BRAZIL

National name: República Federativa do Brasil
President: Fernando Henrique Cardoso (1994)
Area: 3,286,470 sq mi. (8,511,965 sq km)
Population (1998 est.): 169,806,557 (average annual rate of natural increase: 1.24%); birth rate: 20.9/1000; infant mortality rate: 37/1000; density per sq mi.: 52
Capital (1995 est.): Brasilia, 2,500,000. **Largest cities:** São Paulo: city proper (1995 est.) 9,393,753; metro. area (1996 est.) 16,792,000; Rio de Janeiro: city proper (1995 est.) 5,473,033; metro. area (1996 est.) 10,264,000; Porto Alegre, 3,000,000; Recife, 2,900,999; Salvador, 2,600,000; Belo Horizonte, 2,600,000. **Monetary unit:** Real. **Language:** Portuguese. **Ethnicity/Race:** white (includes Portuguese, German, Italian, Spanish, Polish) 55%, mixed white and African 38%, African 6%, other (includes Japanese, Arab, Amerindian) 1%. **Religion:** Roman Catholic, 90% (nominal). **Literacy rate:** 81%
Economic summary: GDP/PPP (1995 est.): $1.022 trillion; $6,300 per capita. **Real growth rate:** 2.9%. **Inflation:** 10% (1996). **Unemployment:** 5.2%. **Arable land:** 5%. **Agriculture:** world's largest producer of coffee; sugar cane, oranges, cocoa, soybeans, tobacco, cattle. **Labor force** (1989 est.), 57 million; services, 42%; agriculture, 31%; industry, 27%. **Industry:** steel, chemicals, petrochemicals, machinery, motor vehicles, cement, lumber. **Natural resources:** iron ore, manganese, bauxite, nickel, other industrial metals, hydropower, timber. **Exports:** $47.7 billion (f.o.b., 1996): coffee, iron ore, soybeans, sugar, beef, transport equipment, footwear, orange juice. **Imports:** $53.3 billion (f.o.b., 1996): crude oil, capital goods, chemical products, foodstuffs, coal. **Major trading partners:** U.S., European Union, Japan, Latin America, Middle East.

Geography Brazil covers nearly half of South America and is the continent's largest nation. It extends 2,965 miles (4,772 km) north-south, 2,691 miles (4,331 km) east-west, and borders every nation on the continent except Chile and Ecuador. Brazil may be divided physiographically into the Brazilian Highlands, or plateau, in the south and the Amazon River basin in the north. More than a third of Brazil is drained by the Amazon and its more than 200 tributaries. The Amazon is navigable for ocean steamers to Iquitos, Peru, 2,300 miles (3,700 km) upstream. Southern Brazil is drained by the Plata system—the Paraguay, Uruguay, and Paraná rivers. The most important stream entirely within Brazil is the São Francisco, navigable for 1,000 miles (1,903 km), but broken near its mouth by the 275-foot (84 m) Paulo Afonso Falls.

Government A federal republic under the 1988 constitution. The president and vice president are elected for a 4-year term. A 1997 amendment to the constitution allows them to run for consecutive terms. The National Congress maintains a bicameral structure—a Senate, whose members serve eight-year terms, and a Chamber of Deputies, elected for four-year terms.

History Brazil is the only Latin American nation deriving its language and culture from Portugal. The native inhabitants mostly consisted of the nomadic Tupí-Guaraní Indians. Adm. Pedro Alvares Cabral claimed the territory for Portugal in 1500 and brought back a type of wood containing valuable red dye, pau-brasil, from which the land received its name. Portugal began colonization in 1532 and made the area a royal colony in 1549.

During the Napoleonic wars, King João VI, fearing the advancing French armies, fled the country in 1808 and set up his court in Rio de Janeiro. João was drawn home in 1820 by a revolution, leaving his son as regent. When Portugal sought to again reduce Brazil to colonial status, the prince declared Brazil's independence on Sept. 7, 1822, and became Pedro I, emperor of Brazil. Harassed by his parliament, Pedro I abdicated in 1831 in favor of his five-year-old son, who became emperor in 1840 as Pedro II. The son was a popular monarch, but discontent built up and, in 1889, following a military revolt, he had to abdicate. Although a republic was proclaimed, Brazil was under military dictatorships until a revolt permitted a gradual return to stability under civilian presidents.

President Wenceslau Braz cooperated with the Allies and declared war on Germany during World War I. In World War II, Brazil again cooperated with the Allies, welcoming Allied air bases, patrolling the South Atlantic, and joining the invasion of Italy after declaring war on the Axis powers.

In the last in a long series of military coups, Gen. João Baptista de Oliveira Figueiredo became president in 1979 and pledged a return to democracy in 1985. The election of Tancredo Neves on Jan. 15, 1985, as the first civilian president since 1964 brought a nationwide wave of optimism, but when Neves died on April 21, Vice President Sarney became president. Sarncy was widely distrusted because he had previously been a member of the military regime's political party. Collor de Mello won the election of late 1989 pledging to lower the chronic hyperinflation by following the path of free-market economics. When Collor faced impeachment by Congress because of a corruption scandal in Dec. 1992 and resigned, Vice President Itamar Franco assumed the presidency.

A former finance minister, Fernando Cordoso won the presidency in the Oct. 1994 election with 54% of the vote even though his party's coalition failed to win a congressional majority. In light of graphic revelations of police brutality, a new law was passed in April 1997 making torture a crime. Preparations are underway for the disposal of government-owned assets in the telecommunications and electrical power industries.

Brunei Darussalam

STATE OF BRUNEI DARUSSALAM

Sultan: Haji Hassanal Bolkiah (1967)
Area: 2,226 sq mi. (5,770 sq km)
Population (1998 est.): 315,292 (annual rate of natural increase: 2.44%); birth rate: 24.9/1000; infant mortality rate: 23.3/1000; density per sq mi.: 142
Capital and largest city (1991 est.): Bandar Seri Begawan, 52,300. **Other large cities:** Seria 23,511, Kuala Belait 19,335. **Monetary unit:** Brunei Dollar. **Languages:** Malay (official), Chinese, English. **Ethnicity/Race:** Malay 64%, Chinese 20%, other 16%. **Religions:** Islam (official religion), 67%; Buddhist, 12%; Christian, 9%; indigenous beliefs and other, 12%. **Literacy rate:** 80%
Economic summary: GDP/PPP (1995 est.): $4.6 billion; $15,800 per capita. **Real growth rate:** 2%. **Inflation:** 2.5% (1996 est.). **Unemployment:** 4.8% (1996 est.). **Arable land:** 1%. **Agriculture:** fruit, rice, pepper, buffaloes. **Labor force:** 119,000 (1993); government, 48%; oil, natural gas, services, and construction, 42%; agriculture, forestry, and fishing, 4%; other, 6%. **Industry:** crude petroleum, liquefied natural gas, timber. **Natural resources:** petroleum, natural gas, timber. **Exports:** $2.7 billion (f.o.b., 1995 est.): crude petroleum, liquefied natural gas. **Imports:** $2 billion (c.i.f., 1995 est.): machinery, transport equipment, manufactured goods, foodstuffs, chemicals. **Major trading partners:** Japan, Thailand, U.S., U.K., Singapore, South Korea; regional group trading partners: ASEAN, APEC, and E.U.

Geography About the size of Delaware, Brunei is an independent sultanate on the northwest coast of the island of Borneo in the South China Sea, wedged between the Malaysian states of Sabah and Sarawak. Three-quarters of the thinly populated country is covered with tropical rain forest; there are rich oil and gas deposits.

Government Sultan Hassanal Bolkiah is ruler of the state, a former British protectorate.

History Brunei (pronounced broon-eye) was trading with China during the 6th century C.E., and, through allegiance to the Javanese Majapahit kingdom (13th to 15th century), it came under Hindu influence. In the early 15th century, with the decline of the Majapahit kingdom and widespread conversion to Islam, Brunei became an independent sultanate. Brunei was a powerful state from the 16th to the 19th century, ruling over the northern part of Borneo and adjacent island chains. But it fell into decay and lost Sarawak in 1841, becoming a British protectorate in 1888 and a British dependency in 1905. Japan occupied Brunei during World War II; it was liberated by Australia in 1945.

The Sultan regained control over internal affairs in 1959, but Britain retained responsibility for the state's defense and foreign affairs until 1984, when the sultanate became fully independent. Sultan Bolkiah was crowned in 1968 at the age of 22, succeeding his father, Sir Omar Ali Saifuddin, who had abdicated. During his reign, exploitation of the rich Seria oilfield had made the sultanate wealthy. It has one of the highest per capita incomes, and the sultan is believed to be the richest man in the world after Microsoft's Bill Gates. In recent years scandal rocked the nation: the sultan punished his younger brother, Prince Jefri, for squandering billions of dollars, and a former Miss U.S.A. accused the sultan and his brother of attempting to turn her into a sex slave. In Aug. 1998, Oxford-educated Prince Al-Muhtadee Billah was inaugurated as heir to the 500-year-old monarchy.

Bulgaria

REPUBLIC OF BULGARIA

National name: Narodna Republika Bulgariya
President: Petar Stoyanov (1997)
Prime Minister: Ivan Kostov (1997)
Area: 42,823 sq mi. (110,910 sq km)
Population (1998 est.): 8,240,426 (average annual rate of natural increase: 2.44%); birth rate: 8.1/1000; infant mortality rate: 12.8/1000; density per sq mi.: 192
Capital and largest city (1994 est.): Sofia, 1,113,674. **Largest cities (1994 est.):** Plovdiv, 345,205; Varna, 307,200; Burgas, 198,439; Ruse, 170,209. **Monetary unit:** Lev. **Language:** Bulgarian. **Ethnicity/Race:** Bulgarian 85.3%, Turk 8.5%, Gypsy 2.6%, Macedonian 2.5%, Armenian 0.3%, Russian 0.2%, other 0.6%. **Religions:** Bulgarian Orthodox 85%, Muslim 13%, Jewish 0.8%, Roman Catholic 0.5%, Uniate Catholic 0.2%, Protestant, Gregorian-Armenian, and other 0.5%. **Literacy rate:** 98%
Economic summary: GDP/PPP (1996 est.): $39.9 billion, $4,630 per capita. **Real growth rate:** -10%. **Inflation:** 311%. **Unemployment:** 12.5%. **Arable land:** 37%. **Agriculture:** grains, tobacco, fruits, vegetables. **Labor force:** 3.57 million; industry, 41%; agriculture, 18%; other, 41%. **Industry:** processed agricultural products, machinery, electronics, chemicals. **Natural resources:** metals, minerals, timber. **Exports:** $4.2 billion (f.o.b., 1996 est.): machinery and transport equipment, fuels, minerals, raw materials, agricultural products. **Imports:** $4.1 billion (c.i.f., 1996 est.): machinery and transportation equipment, fuels, raw materials, metals, agricultural raw products. **Major trading partners:** Russia, Eastern European countries, E.U.

Geography Two mountain ranges and two great valleys mark the topography of Bulgaria, a country the size of Tennessee and situated on the Black Sea. The Balkan Mountains cross the center of the country, rising to a height of 6,888 feet (2,100 m). The Rhodope, Rila, and Pirin mountains are to the west and south. The Maritsa is Bulgaria's principal river, and the Danube also flows through it, forming most of the northern boundary with Romania.

Government According to the constitution of 1991, Bulgaria is a democratic republic with a president elected directly for a five-year term and a unicameral National Assembly whose 240 members are elected to four-year terms.

History The Thracians lived in what is now known as Bulgaria from about 3500 B.C.E.; they were absorbed by the Roman Empire in the first century C.E. The Bulgars crossed the Danube from the north in C.E. 679 and took control of the region. They adopted a Slav dialect and Slavic customs and twice conquered most of the Balkan peninsula between 893 and 1280. The Bulgars gradually fell prey to the Turks, and from 1396 to 1878 Bulgaria was a Turkish province. In 1878, Russia forced Turkey to give the country its independence; but the European powers, fearing that Bulgaria might become a Russian dependency, intervened. By the Treaty of San Stefano in 1878, Bulgaria became autonomous under Turkish sovereignty.

In 1887, Prince Ferdinand of Saxe-Coburg-Gotha was elected ruler of Bulgaria; on Oct. 5, 1908, he declared the country independent and took the title of tsar. Bulgaria joined Germany in World War I and lost. On Oct. 3, 1918, Tsar Ferdinand abdicated in favor of his son, Tsar Boris III. Boris assumed dictatorial powers in 1934–35. When Hitler awarded Bulgaria southern Dobruja, taken from Romania in 1940, Boris joined the Nazis in war the next year and occupied parts of Yugoslavia and Greece. Later the Germans tried to force Boris to send his troops against the Russians. Boris resisted and died under mysterious circumstances on Aug. 28, 1943. Simeon II, infant son of Boris, became nominal ruler under a regency. Russia declared war on Bulgaria on Sept. 5, 1944. An armistice was agreed to three days later, after Bulgaria had declared war on Germany. Russian troops streamed in the next day and under an informal armistice a coalition "Fatherland Front" cabinet was set up under Kimon Georgiev.

A Soviet-style People's Republic was established in 1947 and Bulgaria acquired the reputation of being the most slavishly loyal to Moscow of all the East European Communist countries. The general secretary of the Bulgarian Communist Party, Todor Zhikov, resigned in 1989 after 35 years in power. His successor, Peter Mladenov, purged the Politburo, ended the Communist monopoly on power, and held free elections in May 1990 that led to a surprising victory for the Communists, renamed the Bulgarian Socialist Party (BSP). Mladenov was forced to resign in July 1990. Power shifted back and forth between the pro–Western Union of Democratic Forces (UDF) and the BSP during the 1990s. The economy continued to deteriorate amid growing concern over the spread of organized crime. The new UDF government, elected in 1997, pledged to work toward qualifying for membership in the European Union and NATO.

Burkina Faso

National name: Burkina Faso
President: Blaise Compaore (1991)
Prime Minister: Kadre Desire Ouedraogo (1996)
Area: 105,870 sq mi. (274,200 sq km)
Population (1998 est.): 11,266,393 (average annual rate of natural increase: 2.72%); birth rate: 46.2/1000; infant mortality rate: 109.2/1000; density per sq mi.: 106
Capital and largest city (1994 est.): Ouagadougou, 500,000. **Monetary unit:** Franc CFA. **Languages:** French, tribal languages. **Ethnicity/Race:** Mossi (about 24%), Gurunsi, Senufo, Lobi, Bobo, Mande, Fulani. **Religions:** Muslim, 50%; Christian (mainly Roman Catholic), 10%; indigenous beliefs, 40%. **Literacy rate:** 18%
Economic summary: GDP/PPP (1996 est.): $8 billion; $740 per capita. **Real growth rate:** 5.4%. **Inflation:** 7.8%. **Unemployment:** n.a. **Arable land:** 13%. **Agriculture:** millet, sorghum, corn, rice, livestock, peanuts, sugar cane, cotton. **Labor force:** n.a.; in agriculture, 80%; industry, 15%; commerce, services, and government, 5%. **Industry:** processed agricultural products, light industrial items, brick, brewed products. **Natural resources:** manganese, limestone, marble, gold, uranium, bauxite, copper. **Exports:** $298 million (f.o.b., 1995 est.): oilseeds, cotton, live animals, gold. **Imports:** $500 million (f.o.b., 1995 est.): grain, dairy products, petroleum, machinery. **Major trading partners:** E.U., Côte d'Ivoire, Africa, Taiwan, Japan, Thailand.

Geography Slightly larger than Colorado, Burkina Faso, formerly known as Upper Volta, is a landlocked country in West Africa. Its neighbors are Côte d'Ivoire, Mali, Niger, Benin, Togo, and Ghana. The country consists of extensive plains, low hills, high savannas, and a desert area in the north.

Government Military rule since independence.

History Burkina Faso was originally inhabited by the Bobo, Lobi, and Gurunsi peoples, with the Mossi and Gurma peoples immigrating to the region in the 14th century. The lands of the Mossi empire became a French protectorate in 1897, and by 1903 France had subjugated the other ethnic groups. Called Upper Volta by the French, it became a separate colony in 1919, was partitioned among Niger, the Sudan, and Côte d'Ivoire in 1932, and was reconstituted in 1947. An autonomous republic within the French Community, Upper Volta became independent on Aug. 5, 1960.

President Maurice Yameogo was deposed on Jan. 3, 1966, by a military coup led by Col. Sangoulé Lamizana, who dissolved the National Assembly and suspended the constitution. Constitutional rule returned in 1978 with the election of an Assembly and a presidential vote in June in which Gen. Lamizana won by a narrow margin over three other candidates.

On Nov. 25, 1980, a bloodless coup took place that put Gen. Lamizana under house arrest. Col. Sayé Zerbo took charge as the president of the Military Committee of Reform for National Progress. Maj. Jean-Baptiste Ouedraogo toppled Zerbo in another coup on Nov. 7, 1982. Captain Thomas Sankara, in turn, deposed Ouedraogo a year later. His government changed the country's name on Aug. 3, 1984, to Burkina Faso ("the land of upright men") to sever ties with its colonial past. In Feb. 1996 a little-known economist, Kadre Desire Ouedraogo, became prime minister.

Burma (Myanmar)

UNION OF BURMA OR UNION OF MYANMAR

National name: Pyidaungsu Myanmar Naingngandau
Head of State (Chairman): Senior Gen. Than Shwe (1992)
Area: 261,220 sq mi. (676,560 sq km)
Population (1998 est.): 47,305,319 (average annual rate of natural increase: 1.65%); birth rate: 29/1000; infant mortality rate: 78.4/1000; density per sq mi.: 181
Capital: Rangoon (Yangon). **Largest cities (est. 1983):** Rangoon (Yangon), 2,458,712; Mandalay, 532,895. **Monetary unit:** Kyat. **Language:** Burmese, minority languages. **Ethnicity/Race:** Burman 68%, Shan 9%, Karen 7%, Rakhine 4%, Chinese 3%, Mon 2%, Indian 2%, other 5%. **Religions:** Buddhist 89.5%, Christian 4.9%, Muslim 3.8%, Hindu 0.05%, Animist 1.3%. **Literacy rate:** 81%
Economic summary: GDP/PPP (1996 est.): $51.5 billion; $1,120 per capita. **Real growth rate:** 7%. **Inflation:** 30–40% (1996 est.). **Arable land:** 15%. **Agriculture:** oilseed, pulses, sugar cane, corn, rice. **Labor force** (FY89 est.), 16,007,000; agriculture, 65.2%; industry; 14.3%. **Industry:** textiles, footwear, processed agricultural products, wood and wood products, refined petroleum. **Natural resources:** timber, tin, antimony, zinc, copper, precious stones, crude oil and natural gas. **Exports** (1996 est.): $1.1 billion: rice, teak, oilseeds, metals, rubber, gems. **Imports** (1996 est.): $2 billion: machinery, transportation equipment, chemicals, food products. **Major trading partners:** Japan, E.U., China, Singapore, Thailand, India, Hong Kong, Malaysia.

Geography Slightly smaller than Texas, Burma occupies the northwest portion of the Indochinese peninsula. India lies to the northwest and China to the northeast. Bangladesh, Laos, and Thailand are also neighbors. The Bay of Bengal touches the southwestern coast. The fertile delta of the Irrawaddy in the south contains a network of intercommunicating canals and nine principal river mouths.

Government A military regime. In 1989, the military government changed the name of Burma to Myanmar. The U.S. State Department does not recognize the name Myanmar or the military regime that represents it.

History The ethnic origins of modern Burma (also known as Myanmar) are a mixture of Indo-Aryans, who began pushing into the area around 700 B.C.E., and the Mongolian invaders under Kublai Khan who penetrated the region in the 13th century. Anawrahta (1044–77) was the first great unifier of Burma.

In 1612 the British East India Company sent agents to Burma, but the Burmese doggedly resisted efforts of British, Dutch, and Portuguese traders to establish posts on the Bay of Bengal. Through the Anglo-Burmese War in 1824–26 and two subsequent wars, the British East India Company expanded to the whole of Burma by 1886. Burma was annexed to India, then became a separate colony in 1937.

During World War II, Burma was a key battleground; the 800-mile Burma Road was the Allies' vital supply line to China. The Japanese invaded the country in Dec. 1941, and by May 1942 had occupied most of it, cutting off the Burma Road. After one of the most difficult campaigns of the war, Allied forces liberated most of Burma prior to the Japanese surrender in Aug. 1945.

Burma became independent on Jan. 4, 1948. In 1951 and 1952, the socialists achieved power. In 1968, after the government had made headway against communist and separatist rebels, the military regime adopted a policy of strict nonalignment and set out to follow "the Burmese Way" to socialism. But the insurgents continued to be active.

The civilian government was overthrown in Sept. 1988 by a military junta led by General Saw Maung, an associate of U Ne Win. Virtually the entire country protested the takeover, but demonstrations were brutally quashed. When the new government held elections in May 1990, the opposition National League for Democracy won in a landslide. But the military, or SLORC (State Law and Order Restoration Council), refused to recognize the election results. The leader of the opposition, Aung San Suu Kyi, was awarded the Nobel Peace Prize in 1991, which focused world attention on SLORC's repressive policies. Daughter of the assassinated general Aung San, who was revered as the father of Burmese independence, Suu Kyi remained under house arrest from 1989 until July 10, 1995. A new constitution was drafted in 1994 that called for an elected executive branch but appeared designed specifically to forbid Suu Kyi from becoming president. Suu Kyi continued to protest against the government, but almost every move she made was answered with a counterblow from SLORC.

Although the ruling junta has maintained a tight grip on Burma since 1988, it has not been able to subdue an insurgency in the country's south that has gone on for decades. The ethnic Karen movement has sought an independent homeland along Burma's southern border with Thailand.

In April 1997 the U.S. government imposed sanctions intended to prevent U.S. private investment in Burma. In 1998, Suu Kyi's party set a deadline of Aug. 21 for the convening of the 1990 parliament, which was never allowed to meet after its election. Suu Kyi also challenged the unofficial ban on her leaving the capital, a move that brought retaliation against many of her supporters. In the boldest protests since 1998, opposition politicians, headed by Suu Kyi, declared in Sept. 1998 that they would act as the country's parliament and announced that the ruling junta was illegitimate.

Burundi

REPUBLIC OF BURUNDI

National name: Republika Y'Uburundi
President: Pierre Buyoya (1996)
Prime Minister: Pascal Firmin Ndmira (1996)
Area: 10,747 sq mi. (27,830 sq km)
Population (1998 est.): 5,537,387 (average annual rate of natural increase: 3.51%); birth rate: 41.6/1000; infant mortality rate: 101.2/1000; density per sq mi.: 515
Capital and largest city (1994 est.): Bujumbura, 300,000. **Other large city (est. 1982):** Gitega, 101,827. **Monetary unit:** Burundi franc. **Languages:** Kirundi and French (official), Swahili. **Ethnicity/Race:** Hutu (Bantu) 85%, Tutsi (Hamitic) 14%, Twa (Pygmy) 1%;. **Religions:** Roman Catholic, 62%; Protestant, 5%; indigenous, 32%. **Literacy rate:** 41%
Economic summary: GDP/PPP (1995 est.): $4 billion; $600 per capita. **Real growth rate:** –3.7%. **Inflation:** 40% (1996 est.). **Arable land:** 44%. **Agriculture:** coffee, tea, cotton, bananas, sorghum. **Labor force:** 1.9 million (1983 est.); 93% in agriculture. **Industry:** light consumer goods. **Natural resources:** nickel,

uranium, rare earth oxide, peat, cobalt, copper, unexploited platinum, vanadium. **Exports:** $117 million (f.o.b., 1995): coffee, tea, cotton, hides and skins. **Imports:** $234 million (c.i.f., 1995): food, petroleum products, capital goods, consumer goods. **Major trading partners:** U.S., Western Europe, Asia.

Geography Wedged between Tanzania, the Democratic Republic of the Congo, and Rwanda in east central Africa, Burundi occupies a high plateau divided by several deep valleys. It is equal in size to Maryland.

Government A republic. Legislative and executive power is vested in the president. A new constitution adopted by referendum on March 9, 1992, established a multiparty system.

History The original inhabitants of Rwanda were the Twa, a Pygmy people who now make up only 1% of the population. It is not certain when the Hutu migrated to the region, except that they were well established by the time the Tutsi migrated there in the 14th century. The military skills of the Tutsi led to their dominance over the Hutu, a dominance that remained unchanged over centuries, despite their minority status.

Burundi was once part of German East Africa. Belgium won a League of Nations mandate in 1923, and subsequently Burundi, with Rwanda, was transferred to the status of a United Nations trust territory. In 1962, Burundi gained independence and became a kingdom under Mwami Mwambutsa IV, a Tutsi. A Hutu rebellion took place in 1965, leading to brutal Tutsi retaliations. Mwambutsa was deposed by his son, Ntaré V, in 1966. Ntaré in turn was overthrown the same year in a military coup by Premier Michel Micombero, also a Tutsi. In 1970–71, a civil war erupted, leaving more than 100,000 Hutu dead.

On Nov. 1, 1976, Lt. Col. Jean-Baptiste Bagaza led a coup and assumed the presidency. He suspended the constitution and announced that a 30-member Supreme Revolutionary Council would be the governing body. In Sept. 1987 Bagaza was overthrown by Major Pierre Buyoya, who became president. Ethnic hatred again flared in Aug. 1988, and about 20,000 Hutu were slaughtered. Buyoya, however, began reforms to heal the country's ethnic rift. The Burundi Democracy Front's candidate, Melchior Ndadaye, won the country's first democratic presidential elections, held on June 2, 1993. Ndadaye, the first Hutu to assume power in Burundi, was killed within months during a coup. The second Hutu president, Cyprien Ntaryamira, was killed on April 6, 1994, when a plane carrying him and the Rwandan president was shot down. As a result, Hutu youth gangs began massacring Tutsi; the Tutsi-controlled army retaliated by killing Hutus.

The frequency of ethnic clashes increased, developing into a low-intensity civil war. A six-nation regional proposal to send troops into Burundi to maintain peace and order was devised in July 1996. Distrustful of the scheme, the Tutsi-dominated army led a coup deposing the Hutu president and installed Tutsi major Pierre Buyoya that month. Ethnic violence continued in 1998.

Cambodia

King: Norodom Sihanouk (1991)
Prime Minister: Hun Sen (1993)
Area: 69,884 sq mi. (181,040 sq km)
Population (1998 est.): 11,339,562 (average annual rate of natural increase: 2.51%); birth rate: 41.6/1000; infant mortality rate: 106.8/1000; density per sq mi.: 162
Capital and largest city (1991 est.): Phnom Penh, 900,000. **Monetary unit:** Riel. **Ethnic groups:** Khmer, 90%; Chinese, 5%; other minorities 5%. **Languages:** Khmer (official), French, English. **Ethnicity/Race:** Khmer 90%, Vietnamese 5%, Chinese 1%, other 4%. **Religion:** 95% Theravada Buddhist, 5% others. **Literacy rate:** 69%
Economic summary: GDP/PPP (1996 est.): $7.7 billion; $710 per capita. **Real growth rate:** 7.4%. **Inflation:** 5%. **Arable land:** 13%. **Agriculture:** rice, rubber, corn. **Labor force:** 2.5–3.0 million; 80% in agriculture. **Industry:** fish, wood and wood products, milled rice, rubber, cement. **Natural resources:** timber, gemstones, iron ore, manganese, phosphate. **Exports:** $464 million (1996 est.): natural rubber, rice, pepper, wood. **Imports:** $1.4 billion (1995 est.): foodstuffs, fuel, machinery, consumer goods. **Major trading partners:** Vietnam, Japan, India, Singapore, Malaysia, China, Thailand.

Geography Situated on the Indochinese peninsula, Cambodia is bordered by Thailand and Laos on the north and Vietnam on the east and south. The Gulf of Siam is off the western coast. The country, the size of Missouri, consists chiefly of a large alluvial plain ringed in by mountains and on the east by the Mekong River. The plain is centered on Lake Tonle Sap, which is a natural storage basin of the Mekong.

Government Constitutional monarchy.

History The area that is present-day Cambodia came under Khmer rule about C.E. 600, when the region was at the center of a vast empire that stretched over most of Southeast Asia. Under the Khmers, who were Hindus, a magnificent temple complex was constructed at Angkor. Buddhism was introduced in the 12th century during the rule of Jayavaram VII. However, the kingdom, then known as Kambuja, fell into decline after Jayavaram's reign and was nearly annihilated by Thai and Vietnamese invaders. Its power steadily diminished until 1863, when France colonized the region, joining Cambodia, Laos, and Vietnam into a single protectorate known as French Indochina.

The French quickly usurped all but ceremonial powers from the monarch, Norodom. When he died in 1904, the French passed over his sons and handed the throne to his brother, Sisowath. Sisowath and his son ruled until 1941, when Norodom Sihanouk was elevated to power. Sihanouk's coronation, along with the Japanese occupation during the war, worked to reinforce a sentiment among Cambodians that the region should be free from outside control. After World War II, Cambodians sought independence, but France was reluctant to part with its colony. Cambodia was granted independence within the French Union in 1949. But the French-Indochinese War provided an opportunity for Sihanouk to gain full military control of the country. He abdicated in 1955 in favor of his parents, remaining head of the government, and when his father died in 1960, became chief of state without returning to the throne. In 1963, he sought a guarantee of Cambodia's neutrality from all parties to the Vietnam War.

However, North Vietnamese and Vietcong troops had begun using eastern Cambodia as a safe haven from which to launch attacks into South Vietnam, making it increasingly difficult to stay out of the war. An indigenous communist guerrilla movement known as the Khmer Rouge also began to put pressure on the government in Phnom Penh. On March 18, 1970, while Sihanouk was abroad, anti-Vietnamese riots broke out and Sihanouk was overthrown by Gen. Lon Nol. The Vietnam peace agreement of 1973 stipulated withdrawal of foreign forces from Cambodia, but fighting continued between Hanoi-backed insurgents and U.S.-supplied government troops.

Combat climaxed in April 1975 when the Lon Nol regime was overthrown by Pol Pot, leader of the Khmer Rouge forces. The four years of nightmarish Khmer Rouge rule led to the state-sponsored extermination of citizens by its own government. Between 1 million and 2 million people were massacred on the "killing fields" of Cambodia or worked to death through forced labor. Pol Pot's radical vision of transforming the country into a Marxist agrarian society led to the virtual extermination of the country's professional and technical class.

Pol Pot was ousted by Vietnamese forces on Jan. 8, 1979, and a new pro-Hanoi government led by Heng Samrin was installed. Pol Pot and 35,000 Khmer Rouge fighters fled into the hills of western Cambodia, where they were joined by forces loyal to the ousted Sihanouk in a guerrilla movement aimed at overthrowing the Heng Samrin government. The Vietnamese plan originally called for a withdraw by early 1990 and a negotiated political settlement. The talks became protracted, however, and a U.N. agreement was not signed until 1992, when Sihanouk was appointed leader of an interim Supreme National Council to run the country until elections could be held in 1993.

Free elections in May 1993 saw the defeat of Heng Samrin's successor, Hun Sen, who refused to accept the outcome of the vote and insisted instead on a power-sharing agreement. Under the arrangement, Hun Sen and Sihanouk's son, Prince Norodom Ranariddh, would act as co–prime ministers.

The Khmer Rouge stronghold in the western jungles splintered in 1997, with factions either battling each other or defecting. Ranariddh and Hun Sen both courted Khmer Rouge factions in an effort to shore up their power. In early July, Hun Sen took advantage of the charged political atmosphere to depose Ranariddh, officially the First Prime Minister and the country's only popularly elected leader. Hun Sen later launched a brutal purge, executing more than 40 political opponents. Skirmishes between Ranariddh's forces and Hun Sen's troops continued through the fall. Meanwhile, King Norodom Sihanouk, a beloved but ineffectual figurehead, was unable to broker peace between Hun Sen and his son, Prince Ranariddh.

Shortly after the July coup, the Khmer Rouge organized a show trial of their notorious leader, Pol Pot, in an apparent bid to distance themselves from the bloody history of his regime. Visibly enfeebled from reported bouts with malaria, Pol Pot had not been seen by the West in more than two decades. He was sentenced to house arrest for his crimes against humanity. On April 15, 1998, Pol Pot died and his body was quickly cremated by former Khmer Rouge comrades.

In the July 1998 election, Hun Sen was victorious over opposition leaders Sam Rainsy and Prince Ranariddh, but the opposition parties accused him of voter fraud. Rainsy organized protests that turned into violent riots. Although Hun Sen's party won the most seats, it needed to form a coalition with Ranariddh's party to reach the two-thirds majority needed to form a government. The coalition would return Cambodia to its untenable political balance in 1997, the antagonistic partnership between Hun Sen and Prince Ranariddh.

Cameroon

REPUBLIC OF CAMEROON

National name: République du Cameroun
President: Paul Biya (1988)
Prime Minister: Peter Musonge Mafani (1996)
Area: 183,569 sq mi. (475,440 sq km)
Population (1998 est.): 15,029,433 (average annual rate of natural increase: 2.81%); birth rate: 42.1/1000; infant mortality rate: 76.9/1000; density per sq mi.: 82
Capital: Yaoundé. **Largest cities (1991 est.):** Douala, 908,000; Yaoundé, 730,000. **Monetary unit:** Franc CFA. **Languages:** French and English (both official); 24 major African language groups. **Ethnicity/Race:** Cameroon Highlanders 31%, Equatorial Bantu 19%, Kirdi 11%, Fulani 10%, Northwestern Bantu 8%, Eastern Nigritic 7%, other African 13%, non-African less than 1%. **Religions:** 51% indigenous beliefs, 33% Christian, 16% Muslim. **Literacy rate:** 54%
Economic summary: GDP/PPP (1996 est.): $17.5 billion; $1,230 per capita. **Real growth rate:** 3.4%. **Inflation:** 6% (FY96/97 est.). **Unemployment:** n.a. **Arable land:** 13%. **Agriculture:** coffee, cocoa, timber, peanuts, cotton, rubber, bananas, oilseed, grains, livestock, root starches. **Labor force** in agriculture, 74.4%; industry and transport, 11.4%; other services, 14.2% (1983). **Industry:** crude oil products, food processing, light consumer goods, textiles, sawmills. **Natural resources:** timber, some oil, bauxite, hydropower potential. **Exports:** $1.9 billion (f.o.b., 1995): cocoa, coffee, timber, petroleum, aluminum products. **Imports:** $1.3 billion (f.o.b., 1995): machines and electrical equipment, transport equipment, consumer goods. **Major trading partners:** France, U.S., Western European nations, African countries, Japan.

Geography Cameroon is a Central African nation on the Gulf of Guinea, bordered by Nigeria, Chad, the Central African Republic, the Republic of Congo, Equatorial Guinea, and Gabon. It is nearly twice the size of Oregon. Mount Cameroon (13,350 ft.; 4,069 m), near the coast, is the highest elevation in the country. The main rivers are the Benue, Nyong, and Sanaga.

Government After a 1972 plebiscite, a unitary nation was formed out of East and West Cameroon to replace the former federal republic. At present the country is a multiparty democracy with a one-house legislative body, the National Assembly, holding 180 seats.

History Bantu speakers were among the first groups to settle Cameroon, followed by the Muslim Fulani in the 18th and 19th centuries. The land escaped colonial rule until 1884, when treaties with tribal chiefs brought the area under German domination. After World War I, the League of Nations gave the French a mandate over 80% of the area, and the British 20% adjacent to Nigeria. After World War II, when the country came under a U.N. trusteeship in 1946, self-government was granted, and the Cameroon People's Union emerged as the dominant party by campaigning for reunification of French and British Cameroon and for independence. Accused of being under Communist control, it waged a campaign of revolutionary terror from 1955 to 1958, when it was crushed. In British Cameroon, unification was also promoted by the leading party, the Kamerun National Democratic Party, led by John Foncha.

France set up Cameroon as an autonomous state in 1957, and the next year its legislative assembly voted for independence by 1960. In 1959 a fully autonomous government of Cameroon was formed under Ahmadou Ahidjo. Cameroon became an independent republic on Jan. 1, 1960. In 1961 the southern part of the British territory joined the new Federal Republic of Cameroon and the northern section voted for unification with Nigeria. The president of Cameroon since independence, Ahmadou Ahidjo, was replaced in 1982 by the prime minister, Paul Biya. Both administrations were characterized by authoritarian rule. Calls for reform led to constitutional amendments in 1993 providing for a democratic form of government.

Canada

Sovereign: Queen Elizabeth II (1952)
Governor-General: Roméo LeBlanc (1995)
Prime Minister: Jean Chrétien (1993)
Area: 3,851,809 sq mi. (9,976,140 sq km)
Population (1998 est.): 30,675,398. Average annual rate of natural increase: 1.09%; birth rate: 12.1/1000; infant mortality rate: 5.6/1000; density per sq mi.: 8
Capital: Ottawa, Ontario. **Largest cities (1996 census; metropolitan areas):** Toronto, 4,263,757; Montreal, 3,326,510; Vancouver, 1,831,665; Ottawa/Hull, 1,010,498; Edmonton, 862,597; Calgary, 821,628; Quebec, 671,889; Winnipeg, 667,209; Hamilton, 624,360; London, 398,616; . **Monetary Unit:** Canadian dollar. **Languages:** English, French (both official). **Ethnicity/Race:** British Isles origin 40%, French origin 27%, other European 20%, indigenous Indian and Inuit 1.5%, other, mostly Asian 11.5%. **Religions:** 46% Roman Catholic, 16% United Church, 10% Anglican. **Literacy rate:** 99%
Economic Summary: GDP/PPP (1996 est.): $721 billion; $25,000 per capita. **Real growth rate:** 1.4%. **Inflation:** 1.4% (1996 est.). **Unemployment:** 9.7%. **Arable land:** 5%. **Agriculture:** wheat, barley, oats, livestock. **Labor force:** 15.1 million; 74% in services. **Industry:** transportation equipment, petroleum, chemicals, wood products. **Exports:** $195.4 billion (f.o.b., 1996 est.): newsprint, wood pulp, timber, crude petroleum, machinery, natural gas, aluminum, motor vehicles and parts, telecommunications equipment. **Imports:** $169.5 billion (c.i.f., 1996 est.): crude petroleum, chemicals, motor vehicles and parts, durable consumer goods, computers, telecommunications equipment and parts. **Major trading partners:** U.S., Japan, E.U., Mexico, South Korea, Taiwan, China.

Geography Covering most of the northern part of the North American continent and with an area larger than that of the United States, Canada has an extremely varied topography. In the east the mountainous maritime provinces have an irregular coastline on the Gulf of St. Lawrence and the Atlantic. The St. Lawrence plain, covering most of southern Quebec and Ontario, and the interior continental plain, covering southern Manitoba and Saskatchewan and most of Alberta, are the principal cultivable areas. They are separated by a forested plateau rising from lakes Superior and Huron.

Westward toward the Pacific, most of British Columbia, Yukon, and part of western Alberta are covered by parallel mountain ranges, including the Rockies. The Pacific border of the coast range is ragged with fiords and channels. The highest point in Canada is Mount Logan (19,850 ft.; 6,050 m), which is in the Yukon. The two principal river systems are the Mackenzie and the St. Lawrence. The St. Lawrence, with its tributaries, is navigable for over 1,900 miles (3,058 km).

Government Canada is a federation of 10 provinces (Alberta, British Columbia, Manitoba, New Brunswick, Newfoundland, Nova Scotia, Ontario, Prince Edward Island, Quebec, and Saskatchewan) and two territories (Northwest Territories and Yukon) whose powers were spelled out in the British North America Act of 1867. With the passing of the Constitutional Act of 1982, the act and the constitutional amending power were transferred from the British parliament to Canada so that the Canadian constitution is now entirely in the hands of Canadians.

While the governor-general is officially the representative of Queen Elizabeth II as the head of state, in reality the governor-general acts only upon the advice of the Canadian prime minister and the cabinet, who also sit in the federal parliament. Parliament has two houses: a Senate of 104 members appointed for a term ending on their 75th birthday, and a House of Commons of 301 members apportioned according to provincial population. Elections are held at least every five years or whenever the party in power is voted down in the House of Commons or considers it expedient to appeal to the people. The prime minister is the leader of the majority party in the House of Commons—or, if no single party holds a majority, the leader of the party able to command the support of a majority of members of the House. Laws must be passed by both

Population by Provinces and Territories

Province	1997	1996
	(in thousands)	
Alberta	2,847.0	2,793.3
British Columbia	3,933.3	3,857.6
Manitoba	1,145.2	1,140.4
New Brunswick	762.0	762.0
Newfoundland	563.6	571.7
Nova Scotia	947.9	943.2
Ontario	11,407.7	11,258.4
Prince Edward Island	137.2	136.7
Quebec	7,419.9	7,388.0
Saskatchewan	1,023.5	1,019.6
Northwest Territories	67.5	66.8
Yukon Territory	31.6	31.4
Total	**30,286.6**	**29,969.2**

Source: Statistics Canada.

Canadian Governors General and Prime Ministers Since 1867

Term of Office	Governor General	Term	Prime Minister	Party
1867–1868	Viscount Monck[1]	1867–1873	Sir John A. Macdonald	Conservative
1869–1872	Baron Lisgar	1873–1878	Alexander Mackenzie	Liberal
1872–1878	Earl of Dufferin	1878–1891	Sir John A. Macdonald	Conservative
1878–1883	Marquess of Lorne	1891–1892	Sir John J. C. Abbott	Conservative
1883–1888	Marquess of Lansdowne	1892–1894	Sir John S. D. Thompson	Conservative
1888–1893	Baron Stanley of Preston	1894–1896	Sir Mackenzie Bowell	Conservative
1893–1898	Earl of Aberdeen	1896	Sir Charles Tupper	Conservative
1898–1904	Earl of Minto	1896–1911	Sir Wilfrid Laurier	Liberal
1904–1911	Earl Grey	1911–1917	Sir Robert L. Borden	Conservative
1911–1916	Duke of Connaught	1917–1920	Sir Robert L. Borden	Unionist
1916–1921	Duke of Devonshire	1920–1921	Arthur Meighen	Unionist
1921–1926	Baron Byng of Vimy	1921–1926	W. L. Mackenzie King	Liberal
1926–1931	Viscount Willingdon	1926	Arthur Meighen	Conservative
1931–1935	Earl of Bessborough	1926–1930	W. L. Mackenzie King	Liberal
1935–1940	Baron Tweedsmuir	1930–1935	Richard B. Bennett	Conservative
1940–1946	Earl of Athlone	1935–1948	W. L. Mackenzie King	Liberal
1946–1952	Viscount Alexander	1948–1957	Louis S. St. Laurent	Liberal
1952–1959	Vincent Massey	1957–1963	John G. Diefenbaker	Conservative
1959–1967	George P. Vanier	1963–1968	Lester B. Pearson	Liberal
1967–1973	Roland Michener	1968–1979	Pierre Elliott Trudeau	Liberal
1974–1979	Jules Léger	1979–1980	Charles Joseph Clark	Conservative
1979–1984	Edward R. Schreyer	1980–1984	Pierre Elliott Trudeau	Liberal
1984–1990	Jeanne Sauvé	1984–1984	John Turner	Liberal
1990–1995	Raymond John Hnatyshyn	1984–1993	Brian Mulroney	Conservative
1995–	Roméo LeBlanc	1993–1993	Kim Campbell	Conservative
		1993–	Jean Chrétien	Liberal

1. Became governor-general of British North America in 1861.

houses of parliament and signed by the governor-general in the queen's name.

The 10 provincial governments are nominally headed by lieutenant governors appointed by the federal government, but the executive power in each actually is vested in a cabinet headed by a premier, who is leader of the majority party. The provincial legislatures are composed of one-house assemblies whose members are elected for four-year terms. They are known as Legislative Assemblies, except in Newfoundland, where it is the House of Assembly, and in Quebec, where it is the National Assembly.

History Native Indian peoples, including Inuit (Eskimo), inhabited Canada in antiquity. The Norse explorer Leif Ericson probably reached the shores of Canada (Labrador or Nova Scotia) in C.E. 1000, but the history of the white man in the country actually began in 1497, when John Cabot, an Italian in the service of Henry VII of England, reached Newfoundland or Nova Scotia. Canada was taken for France in 1534 by Jacques Cartier. The actual settlement of New France, as it was then called, began in 1604 at Port Royal in what is now Nova Scotia; in 1608, Quebec was founded. France's colonization efforts were not very successful, but French explorers by the end of the 17th century had penetrated beyond the Great Lakes to the western prairies and south along the Mississippi to the Gulf of Mexico. Meanwhile, the English Hudson's Bay Company had been established in 1670. Because of the valuable fisheries and fur trade, a conflict developed between the French and English; in 1713, Newfoundland, Hudson Bay, and Nova Scotia (Acadia) were lost to England. During the Seven Years' War (1756–63), England extended its conquest, and the British Maj. Gen. James Wolfe won his famous victory over Gen. Louis Montcalm outside Quebec on Sept. 13, 1759. The Treaty of Paris in 1763 gave England control.

At that time the population of Canada was almost entirely French, but in the next few decades, thousands of British colonists emigrated to Canada from the British Isles and from the American colonies. In 1849, the right of Canada to self-government was recognized. By the British North America Act of 1867, the dominion of Canada was created through the confederation of Upper and Lower Canada, Nova Scotia, and New Brunswick. Prince Edward Island joined the dominion in 1873. In 1869, Canada purchased from the Hudson's Bay Company the vast middle west (Rupert's Land) from which the provinces of Manitoba (1870), Alberta (1905), and Saskatchewan (1905) were later formed. In 1871, British Columbia joined the dominion. The country was linked from coast to coast in 1885 by the Canadian Pacific Railway.

During the formative years between 1866 and 1896, the Conservative Party, led by Sir John A. Macdonald, governed the country, except during the years 1873–78. In 1896, the Liberal Party took over and, under Sir Wilfrid Laurier, an eminent French Canadian, ruled until 1911. By the Statute of Westminster in 1931 the British dominions, including Canada, were formally declared to be partner nations with Britain, "equal in status, in no way subordinate to each other," and bound together only by allegiance to a common Crown.

Newfoundland became Canada's 10th governor-generalince on March 31, 1949, following a plebiscite. Canada also includes two territories—the Yukon Territory, and the Northwest Territories, including all of Canada north of 60° north latitude except Yukon and the northernmost sections of Quebec and Newfoundland. This area includes all of the Arctic north of the mainland, Norway having recognized Canadian sovereignty over the Svendrup Islands in the Arctic in 1931.

The Liberal Party, led by William Lyon Mackenzie King, dominated Canadian politics from 1921 until 1957, when it was succeeded by the Progressive Conservatives. The Liberals, under the leadership of Lester B. Pearson, returned to power in 1963. Pearson remained prime minister until 1968, when he retired and was replaced by a former law professor, Pierre Elliott Trudeau. Trudeau maintained Canada's defensive alliance with the United States, but began moving toward a more independent policy in world affairs. Trudeau's election was considered in part a response to the most serious problem confronting the country, the division between French- and English-speaking Canadians, which had led to a separatist movement in the predominantly French governor-generalince of Quebec. In 1974, the governor-generalincial government voted to make French the official language of Quebec. In Dec. 1979, the Quebec law making French the exclusive official language of the province was voided by the Canadian Supreme Court. Resolving a dispute that had occupied Trudeau since the beginning of his tenure, Queen Elizabeth II, in Ottawa on April 17, 1982, signed the Constitution Act, cutting the last legal tie between Canada and Britain. The constitution retains Queen Elizabeth as queen of Canada and keeps Canada's membership in the Commonwealth.

In the national election on Sept. 4, 1984, the Progressive Conservative Party scored an overwhelming victory, fundamentally changing the country's political landscape. The Conservatives, led by Brian Mulroney, a 45-year-old corporate lawyer, won the highest political majority in Canadian history. The dominant foreign issue was a free-trade pact with the U.S., a treaty bitterly opposed by the Liberal and New Democratic parties. The conflict led to elections in Nov. 1988 that solidly re-elected Mulroney and gave him a mandate to proceed with the agreement.

The issue of separatist sentiments in French-speaking Quebec flared up again in 1990 with the failure of the Meech Lake Accord. The accord was designed to ease the Quebecers' fear of losing their identity within the English-speaking majority by giving Quebec constitutional status as a "distinct society." In an attempt to keep Canada united, the three major political parties came to an agreement in Feb. 1992 on constitutional reforms. Voters in the Northwest Territories authorized the division of their region in two, creating a homeland for Canadian Eskimos, the Inuits. Also in 1992, Canada announced its decision to withdraw its combat units from NATO command. The economy continued to be mired in a long recession that many blamed on the free trade agreement. A national referendum was held in Oct. 1992 on the proposal to change the constitution to insure greater representation in parliament for the more populous regions and thereby the French-speaking Quebecers. The referendum, however was defeated.

Brian Mulroney's popularity continued to slump in 1992 and early 1993, leading to his decision to retire prior to the required November election. The governing Progressive Conservative Party chose Defense Minister Kim Campbell as its leader in June, making her the first female prime minister in Canadian history.

The national election in Oct. 1993 resulted in the reemergence of the Liberal Party and the installation of Jean Chrétien as prime minister. The Quebec referendum on secession in Oct. 1995 yielded a narrow rejection of the proposal. But the separatists vowed to try again. Early parliamentary elections in June 1997 gave a reduced majority to the ruling Liberals. The Reform Party, based largely in the West, replaced the Bloc Quebecois as the official opposition.

Cape Verde

REPUBLIC OF CAPE VERDE

National name: República de Cabo Verde
President: Antonio Mascarenhas Monteiro (1991)
Prime Minister: Carlos Wahnon Veiga (1991)
Area: 1,557 sq mi. (4,030 sq km)
Population: (1998 est.): 399,857 (average annual rate of natural increase: 1.49%); birth rate: 34.5/1000; infant mortality rate: 47.5/1000; density per sq mi.: 257
Capital (1990): Praia, 61,797. **Other large city (est. 1982):** Mindelo, 50,000. **Monetary unit:** Cape Verdean escudo. **Language:** Portuguese, Criuolo. **Ethnicity/Race:** Creole (mulatto) 71%, African 28%, European 1%. **Religion:** Roman Catholic fused with indigenous beliefs. **Literacy rate:** 67%
Economic summary: GDP/PPP (1995 est.): $472 million; $1,000 per capita. **Real growth rate:** 4.7% (1995). **Inflation:** 7.8%. **Unemployment:** n.a. **Arable land:** 11%. **Agriculture:** bananas, corn, sugar cane, beans, fish. **Labor force** n.a. **Industry:** fishing, salt mining. **Natural resources:** salt, siliceous rock. **Exports:** $10 million (f.o.b., 1995 est.): fish, bananas, fuels. **Imports:** $211.8 million (f.o.b., 1995 est.): foodstuffs, consumer goods, industrial products, fuels. **Major trading partners:** Portugal, Angola, Algeria, Italy, Netherlands, Spain, France, U.S., Germany, Sweden.

Geography Cape Verde, only slightly larger than Rhode Island, is an archipelago in the Atlantic 385 miles (500 km) west of Senegal.

The islands are divided into two groups: Barlavento in the north, composed of Santo Antão (291 sq mi.; 754 sq km), Boa Vista (240 sq mi.; 622 sq km), São Nicolau (132 sq mi.; 342 sq km), São Vicente (88 sq mi.; 246 sq km), Sal (83 sq mi.; 298 sq km), and Santa Luzia (13 sq mi.; 34 sq km); and Sotavento in the south, consisting of São Tiago (383 sq mi.; 992 sq km), Fogo (184 sq mi.; 477 sq km), Maio (103 sq mi.; 267 sq km), and Brava (25 sq mi.; 65 sq km). The islands are mostly mountainous, with the land deeply scarred by erosion. There is an active volcano on Fogo.

Government A republic.

History Uninhabited upon their discovery in 1456, the Cape Verde islands became part of the Portuguese empire in 1495. A majority of their modern inhabitants are of mixed Portuguese and African ancestry.

Positioned on the great trade routes between Africa, Europe, and the New World, the islands became a prosperous center for the slave trade, but suffered economic decline after the slave trade was abolished in 1876. In the 20th century Cape Verde has served as a shipping port.

In 1951 Cape Verde's status changed from a Portuguese colony to an overseas province, and in 1961 the inhabitants became full Portuguese citizens. An independence movement led by the African Party for the Independence of Guinea-Bissau (another former Portuguese colony) and Cape Verde (PAIGC) was founded in 1956, and on July 5, 1975, the islands became independent.

Elections of Jan. 13, 1991, resulted in the ruling African Party for the Independence of Cape Verde losing its majority in the 79-seat parliament. The big winner was the Movement for Democracy, whose candidate, Antonio Monteiro, won the subsequent presidential election on Feb. 17. These were the first free elections since independence in 1975. In the presidential ballot of Feb. 1996 Monteiro handily won reelection. The government announced in October that although economic figures were favorable, the level of imports was unacceptably widening.

Central African Republic

National name: République Centrafricaine
Head of Government: Gen. André Kolingba (1986)
President: Ange-Félix Patassé (1993)
Prime Minister: Michel Gbezera-Bria (1997)
Area: 241,313 sq mi. (622,980 sq km)
Population (1998 est.): 3,375,771 (average annual rate of natural increase: 2.02%); birth rate: 38.7/1000; infant mortality rate: 105.7/1000; density per sq mi.: 14
Capital and largest city (1990 est.): Bangui, 706,000. **Monetary unit:** Franc CFA. **Languages:** French (official), Sangho, Arabic, Hansa, Swahili. **Ethnicity/Race:** Baya 34%, Banda 27%, Sara 10%, Mandjia 21%, Mboum 4%, M'Baka 4%, Europeans 6,500 (including 3,600 French). **Religions:** 24% indigenous beliefs, 50% Protestant and Roman Catholic with animist influence, 15% Muslim, 11% other. **Literacy rate:** 38%
Economic summary: GDP/PPP (1995 est.): $2.5 billion; $800 per capita. **Real growth rate:** 4.8%. **Inflation:** 19.4% (1995 est.). **Unemployment:** n.a. **Arable land:** 3%. **Agriculture:** cotton, coffee, peanuts, food crops, livestock. **Labor force** n.a. **Industry:** timber, textiles, soap, cigarettes, diamonds, processed food, brewed beverages. **Natural resources:** diamonds, uranium, timber. **Exports:** $181 million (f.o.b., 1995): diamonds, cotton, timber, coffee, tobacco. **Imports:** $176 million (f.o.b., 1995): machinery and electrical equipment, petroleum products, textiles, food, motor vehicles, chemicals, pharmaceuticals, consumer goods, industrial products. **Major trading partners:** France, Belgium, Italy, Japan, U.S., Western Europe, Algeria, Yugoslavia.

Geography Situated about 500 miles (805 km) north of the equator, the Central African Republic is a landlocked nation bordered by Cameroon, Chad, the Sudan, the Democratic Republic of the Congo, and the Republic of Congo.

Twice the size of New Mexico, it is covered by tropical forests in the south and semidesert land in the east. The Ubangi and the Shari are the largest of many rivers.

Government A multiparty republic since 1991.

History From the 16th to 19th centuries, the people of this region were ravaged by slave traders. In the 18th and 19th centuries, other African peoples migrated to the area to escape slave traders raiding their original homelands. The Banda, Baya, Ngbandi, and Azande make up the largest ethnic groups.

The French occupied the region in 1894. As the colony of Ubangi-Shari, what is now the Central African Republic was united with Chad in 1905. In 1910 it was joined with Gabon and the Middle Congo to become French Equatorial Africa. After World War II a rebellion in 1946 forced the French to grant self-government. In 1958 the territory voted to become an autonomous republic within the French Community, and on Aug. 13, 1960, President David Dacko proclaimed the republic's independence from France. Dacko moved the country into Beijing's orbit, but was overthrown in a coup on Dec. 31, 1965, by Col. Jean-Bédel Bokassa, army chief of staff.

On Dec. 4, 1976, the Central African Republic became the Central African Empire. Marshal Jean-Bédel Bokassa, who had ruled the republic since he took power in 1965, was declared Emperor Bokassa I. Brutality and excess characterized his regime. He was overthrown in a coup on Sept. 20, 1979. Former President David Dacko returned to power and changed the country's name back to the Central African Republic. An army coup on Sept. 1, 1981, deposed President Dacko again.

In 1991, President Kolingba, under pressure, announced a move toward multiparty democracy. Elections in Aug. 1993 saw the defeat of Kolingba and the victory of Prime Minister Patassé as president. A military revolt was crushed with the aid of French soldiers in Jan. 1997. Later that month the president appointed Gbezera-Bria to replace the prime minister, who was thought to side with the rebellion.

Chad

REPUBLIC OF CHAD

National name: République du Tchad
President: Lieut. Gen. Idriss Deby (1990)
Prime Minister: Nassour Guelengdoussia Ouaido (1997)
Area: 495,752 sq mi. (1,284,000 sq km)
Population (1998 est.): 7,359,512 (average annual rate of natural increase, 2.66%); birth rate: 43.5/1000; infant mortality rate: 117/1000; density per sq mi.: 15
Capital and largest city (1993): N'Djamena, 529,555. **Monetary unit:** Franc CFA. **Languages:** French and Arabic (official), more than 100 tribal languages. **Ethnicity/Race:** North and center: Muslims (Arabs, Toubou, Hadjerai, Fulbe, Kotoko, Kanembou, Baguirmi, Boulala, Zaghawa, and Maba); South: non-Muslims (Sara [the largest ethnic group, 25% of the population], Ngambaye, Mbaye, Goulaye, Moundang, Moussei, Massa). **Religions:** Islam, 44%; Christian, 33%; traditional, 23%. **Literacy rate:** 30%
Economic summary: GDP/PPP (1995 est.): $3.3 billion; $600 per capita. **Real growth rate:** 2.6%. **Inflation:** 9% (1995 est.). **Arable land:** 3%. **Agriculture:** cotton, cattle, rice, subsistence crops. **Labor force:** n.a.; in agriculture, 85%. **Products:** livestock and livestock products, beer, food processing, textiles, cigarettes. **Natural resources:** petroleum, unexploited uranium, kaolin. **Exports:** $226 million (f.o.b., 1995): cotton, livestock and animal products, fish, textiles. **Imports:** $225 million (f.o.b., 1995): machinery and transportation equipment, industrial goods, petroleum products, foodstuffs. **Major trading partners:** France, Nigeria, U.S., Cameroon, Portugal.

Geography A landlocked country in north central Africa, Chad is about 85% the size of Alaska. Its neighbors are Niger, Libya, the Sudan, the Central

African Republic, Cameroon, and Nigeria. Lake Chad, from which the country gets its name, lies on the western border with Niger and Nigeria. In the north is a desert that runs into the Sahara.

Government Hissen Habré was overthrown by Lieut. Gen. Idriss Deby in Dec. 1990. A transitional government mandate expired in April 1996 and parliamentary elections were scheduled in anticipation of complete democracy.

History The area around Lake Chad has been inhabited since at least 500 B.C.E. In the 8th century C.E. Berbers began migrating to the area. Islam arrived in 1085, and by the 16th century a trio of rival kingdoms flourished: the Kanem-Bornu, the Baguirmi, and Ouaddaï. In 1883–93, all three kingdoms came under the rule of the Sudanese conqueror Rabih al-Zubayr. In 1900, Rabih was overthrown by the French, who absorbed it into the colony of French Equatorial Africa, as part of Ubangi-Shari, in 1910.

France began the country's development after 1920, when it became a separate colony. In 1946, French Equatorial Africa was admitted to the French Union, and in 1958 the Chad territory became an autonomous republic within the French Union. An independence movement led by the first premier and president, François (later Ngarta) Tombalbaye, achieved complete independence on Aug. 11, 1960. Tombalbaye was killed in the 1975 coup and succeeded by Gen. Félix Malloum, who faced a Libyan-financed civil war throughout his tenure in office. In 1977 Libya seized a strip of Chadian land and launched an invasion two years later.

Nine rival groups meeting in Lagos, Nigeria, in March 1979 agreed to form a provisional government headed by Goukouni Oueddei, a former rebel leader. Fighting broke out again in Chad in March 1980, when Defense Minister Hissen Habré challenged Goukouni and seized the capital. Libyan President Muammar al-Qaddafi, in Jan. 1981 proposed a merger of Chad with Libya. The Libyan proposal was rejected and Libyan troops withdrew from Chad that year, but in 1983 poured back into the northern part of the country in support of Goukouni. France, in turn, sent troops into southern Chad in support of Habré. Government troops then launched an offensive in early 1987 that drove the Libyans out of most of the country.

After the overthrow of Habré's government, Idriss Deby, a former defense minister and head of a rebel group (Patriotic Salvation Movement), declared himself president, dissolved the legislature (elected the previous July), and suspended the constitution.

Chile

REPUBLIC OF CHILE

National name: República de Chile
President: Eduardo Frei Ruiz-Tagle (1994)
Area: 292,132 sq mi. (756,950 sq km)
Population (1998 est.): 14,787,781 (average annual rate of natural increase: 1.27%); birth rate: 18.3/1000; infant mortality rate: 10.4/1000; density per sq mi.: 51
Capital and largest city (1993 est.): Santiago, 4,628,320. **Other large cities (1993 est.):** Valparaíso, 301,677; Concepción, 318,140; Viña del Mar, 319,440; Temuco, 262,624; Talcahuano, 257,767. **Monetary unit:** Peso. **Language:** Spanish. **Ethnicity/Race:** European and European-Indian 95%, Indian 3%, other 2%. **Religion:** Roman Catholic, 89%; Protestant, 11%; small Jewish and Muslim populations. **Literacy rate:** 95%
Economic summary: GDP/PPP (1996 est.): $120.6 billion; $8,400 per capita. **Real growth rate:** 6.5%. **Inflation:** 6.7%. **Unemployment:** 6.5%. **Arable land:** 5%. **Agriculture:** wheat, corn, sugar beets, vegetables, fish, livestock. **Labor force:** 5.5 million. 38.3% in services; 33.8% in industry and commerce; 19.2% in agriculture, forestry and fishing. **Industry:** processed fish, iron and steel, pulp, paper, furniture, apparel, processed food. **Natural resources:** copper, gold, timber, fruits and vegetables, nitrates, iron. **Exports:** $15.2 billion (f.o.b., 1996 est.): copper, bleached pulp, fishmeal, fresh fruit, timber, seafood, frozen and canned fruits, wine. **Imports:** $16.5 billion (f.o.b., 1996): oil, vehicles, computers, industrial machinery, electric and electronic equipment, chemicals. **Major trading partners:** U.S., European Union, Asia, Latin America.

Geography Situated south of Peru and west of Bolivia and Argentina, Chile fills a narrow 1,800-mile (2,897 km) strip between the Andes and the Pacific. Its area is nearly twice that of Montana. One-third of Chile is covered by the towering ranges of the Andes. In the north is the mineral-rich Atacama Desert, and in the center is a 700-mile-long (1,127 km) thickly populated valley with most of Chile's arable land. At the southern tip of Chile's mainland is Punta Arenas, the southernmost city in the world, and beyond that lies the Strait of Magellan and Tierra del Fuego, an island divided between Chile and Argentina. The southernmost point of South America is Cape Horn, a 1,390-foot (424-m) rock on Horn Island in the Wollaston group, which belongs to Chile. Chile also claims sovereignty over 482,628 sq mi. (1,250,000 sq km) of Antarctic territory, the Juan Fernández Islands, about 400 miles (644 km) west of the mainland, and Easter Island, about 2,000 miles (3,219 km) west.

Government The president serves a six-year term (with the exception of the 1990–1994 term). There is a bicameral legislature, the National Congress, which has a lower house of 120 members and an upper house of 47 members.

History Chile was originally under the control of the Incas in the north and the nomadic Araucanos in the south. In 1541, a Spaniard, Pedro de Valdivia, founded Santiago. Chile won its independence from Spain in 1818 under Bernardo O'Higgins and an Argentinian, José de San Martin. O'Higgins, dictator until 1823, laid the foundations of the modern state with a two-party system and a centralized government.

The dictator from 1830 to 1837, Diego Portales, fought a war with Peru in 1836–39 that expanded Chilean territory. Until 1861 Chile was ruled by a constitutionally supported oligarchy of landholders. Then the Liberals, winning a share of power for the next 30 years, disestablished the church and limited presidential power. Chile fought the War of the Pacific with Peru and Bolivia from 1879 to 1883, winning Antofagasta, Bolivia's only outlet to the sea, and extensive areas from Peru. A revolt in 1890 led by Pedro Montt overthrew, in 1891, José Balmaceda and established a parliamentary dictatorship that existed until a new constitution was adopted in 1925. Industrialization began before World War I and led to the formation of Marxist groups. Juan Antonio Ríos, president during World War II, was originally pro-Nazi but in 1944 led his country into the war on the side of the Allies.

A small abortive army uprising in 1969 raised the fear of military intervention in preventing a Marxist, Salvador Allende Gossens, from taking office after his election to the presidency on Sept. 4, 1970. Dr. Allende was the first president in a non-Communist country freely elected on a Marxist-Leninist program. Allende quickly established relations with Cuba and the People's Republic of China and nationalized several American companies. Allende's overthrow and death in an army assault on the presidential palace in Sept. 1973 ended a 46-year era of constitutional government in Chile.

The takeover was led by a four-man junta headed by Army Chief of Staff Augusto Pinochet Ugarte, who assumed the office of president. Committed to "exterminat[ing] Marxism," the junta embarked on a right-wing dictatorship. It suspended Parliament, banned political activity, and broke relations with Cuba. In 1977, Pinochet, in a speech marking his fourth year in power, promised elections by 1985 if conditions warranted. Earlier, he had abolished DINA, the secret police, and decreed an amnesty for political prisoners. Pinochet was inaugurated on March 11, 1981, for an eight-year term as president, at the end of which, according to the constitution adopted six months earlier, the junta would nominate a civilian as successor. He stepped down in Jan. 1990 in favor of Patricio Aylwin, who was elected Dec. 1989 as the head of a 17-party coalition. The election of Dec. 1993 saw the reemergence of a member of the Frei family, with Eduardo Frei Ruiz-Tagle, the candidate of a center-left coalition, winning the presidency. His father had been president from 1964 to 1970.

China

PEOPLE'S REPUBLIC OF CHINA

National name: Zhonghua Renmin Gongheguo
President: Jiang Zemin (1993)
Premier: Zhu Rongji (1989)
Area: 3,691,521 sq mi. (9,596,960 sq km)[1]
Population (1998 est.): 1,236,914,658 (average rate of natural increase: 0.83%); birth rate: 15.7/1000; infant mortality rate: 45.5/1000; density per sq mi.: 335. China has 56 ethnic groups. In 1991, the Han people accounted for 92% of the population
Capital: Beijing. **Largest cities :** Chongqing, 30,000,000; Shanghai: city proper (1993 est.) 8,930,000; metro. area (1996 est.) 13,659,000; Beijing (Peking): city proper (1993 est.) 6,690,000; metro. area (1996 est.) 11,414,000; Tianjin (Tientsin): city proper (1993 est.) 5,000,000; metro. area. (1995 est.) 10,687,000; Canton, 2,914,000; Wuhan, 3,284,200; Shenyang (Mukden), 3,604,000; Nanjing (Nanking), 2,100,000; Harbin, 2,443,400. **Monetary unit:** Yuan. **Languages:** Chinese, Mandarin, also local dialects. **Ethnicity/Race:** Han Chinese 91.9%, Zhuang, Uygur, Hui, Yi, Tibetan, Miao, Manchu, Mongol, Buyi, Korean, and other nationalities 8.1%. **Religions:** Officially atheist but traditional religion contains elements of Confucianism, Taoism, Buddhism. **Literacy rate:** 84%
Economic summary: GDP/PPP (1995): $3.39 trillion (may be overstated by as much as 25%); $2,800 per capita. **Real growth rate:** 9.7%. **Inflation** 10.1% (1996 est.). **Unemployment:** in urban areas, 3%; substantial in rural areas. **Arable land:** 10%. **Agriculture:** rice, wheat, grains, cotton. **Labor force:** 614.7 million; agriculture and forestry, 54%; industry and commerce, 26%; construction and mining, 7%. **Industry:** iron and steel, textiles, armaments, petroleum. **Natural resources:** coal, natural gas, limestone, marble, metals, hydropower potential. **Exports:** $151.07 billion (f.o.b., 1996): textiles, garments, footwear, toys, machinery and equipment, weapon systems. **Imports:** $138.83 billion (c.i.f., 1996): rolled steel, motor vehicles, textile machinery, oil products, aircraft. **Major trading partners:** Japan, Hong Kong, U.S., Germany, Taiwan and Macau, Russia.

1. Including Manchuria and Tibet.

Geography China is slightly larger in area than the U.S. The greater part of the country is mountainous. Its principal ranges are the Tien Shan, the Kunlun chain, and the Trans-Himalaya. In the southwest is Tibet, which China annexed in 1950. The Gobi Desert lies to the north. China proper consists of three great river systems: the Yellow River (Huang Ho), 2,109 miles (5,464 km) long; the Chang Jiang (Yangtze Kiang), the third-longest river in the world at 2,432 miles (6,300 km); and the Zhujiang (Si Kiang), 848 miles (2,197 km) long.

Government With 2,978 deputies, elected for four-year terms by universal suffrage, the National People's Congress is the chief legislative organ. A State Council has the executive authority. All ministries are under the State Council, headed by the premier. The Communist Party controls the government.

History The earliest recorded human settlements in what is today called China were discovered in the Huang Ho basin and date from about 5000 B.C.E. During the Shang Dynasty (1500–1000 B.C.E.), the precursor of modern China's ideographic writing system developed, allowing the emerging feudal states of the era to achieve an advanced stage of civilization, rivaling in sophistication anything found at the time in Europe, the Middle East, or the Americas. It was following this initial flourishing of civilization, in a period known as the Chou Dynasty (1122–249 B.C.E.), that Lao-tse, Confucius, Mo Ti, and Mencius contributed the foundation of Chinese philosophical thought.

The feudal states, often at war with one another, were first united under Emperor Ch'in Shih Huang Ti, during whose reign (246–210 B.C.E.) work was begun on the Great Wall of China, a monumental bulwark against invasion from the West. Although the Great Wall symbolized China's desire to protect itself from outside world, under the Han Dynasty (206 B.C.E.–C.E. 220), the civilization opened extensive commercial trading with the West.

In the T'ang Dynasty (618–907), often called the golden age of Chinese history, painting, sculpture, and poetry flourished, and wood-block printing, which enabled the mass production of books, made its earliest known appearance. The Mings, last of the native rulers (1368–1644), overthrew the Mongol, or Yuan, Dynasty (1271–1368) established by Kublai Khan. The Mings in turn were overthrown in 1644 by invaders from the north, the Manchus.

China remained largely isolated from the rest of the world's civilizations, closely restricting foreign activities. By the end of the 18th century only Canton (location of modern-day Hong Kong) and the

Provinces and Regions of China

Name	Area (sq mi.)	Area (sq km)	Capital
Provinces			
Anhui (Anhwei)	54,015	139,900	Hefei (Hofei)
Fujian (Fukien)	47,529	123,100	Fuzhou (Fukien)
Gansu (Kansu)	137,104	355,100	Lanzhou (Lanchow)
Guangdong (Kwangtung)	76,100	197,100	Canton
Guizhou (Kweichow)	67,181	174,000	Guiyang (Kweiyang)
Hainan	13,200	34,300	Haikou
Hebei (Hopei)	81,479	211,030	Shijiazhuang (Shitikiachwang)
Heilongjiang (Heilungkiang)[1]	178,996	463,600	Harbin
Henan (Honan)	64,479	167,000	Zhengzhou (Chengchow)
Hubei (Hupeh)	72,394	187,500	Wuhan
Hunan	81,274	210,500	Changsha
Jiangsu (Kiangsu)	40,927	106,000	Nanjing (Nanking)
Jiangxi (Kiangsi)	63,629	164,800	Nanchang
Jilin (Kirin)[1]	72,201	187,000	Changchun
Liaoning[1]	53,301	138,050	Shenyang
Quinghai (Chinghai)	278,378	721,000	Xining (Sining)
Shaanxi (Shensi)	75,598	195,800	Xian (Sian)
Shandong (Shantung)	59,189	153,300	Jinan (Tsinan)
Shanxi (Shansi)	60,656	157,100	Taiyuan
Sichuan (Szechwan)	219,691	569,000	Chengdu (Chengtu)
Yunnan	168,417	436,200	Kunming
Zhejiang (Chekiang)	39,305	101,800	Hangzhou (Hangchow)
Autonomous Regions			
Guangxi Zhuang (Kwangsi Chuang)	85,096	220,400	Nanning
Nei Monggol (Inner Mongolia)[1]	454,633	1,177,500	Hohhot (Huhehot)
Ningxia Hui	30,039	77,800	Yinchuan (Yinchwan)
Xinjiang Uygur (Sinkiang Uighur)[1]	635,829	1,646,800	Urumqi (Urumchi)
Xizang (Tibet)	471,660	1,221,600	Lhasa

1. Together constitute (with Taiwan) what has been traditionally known as Outer China, the remaining territory forming the historical China Proper. NOTE: Names are in Pinyin, with conventional spelling in parentheses.

Portuguese port of Macao were open to European merchants. But with the first Anglo-Chinese War in 1839–42, a long period of instability and concessions to Western colonial powers began. Following the war, several ports were opened up for trading, and Hong Kong was ceded to Britain. Treaties signed after further hostilities (1856–60) weakened Chinese sovereignty and gave foreigners immunity from Chinese jurisdiction. European powers took advantage of the disastrous Chinese-Japanese War of 1894–95 to gain further trading concessions from China. Peking's response, the Boxer Rebellion (1900), was suppressed by an international force.

The death of the Empress Dowager Tzu Hsi in 1908 and the accession of the infant Emperor Hsüan T'ung (Pu-Yi) were followed by a nationwide rebellion led by Dr. Sun Yat-sen, who overthrew the Manchus and became the first president of the Provisional Chinese Republic in 1911. Dr. Sun resigned in favor of Yuan Shih-k'ai, who suppressed the Republicans in a bid to consolidate his power. Yuan's death in June 1916 was followed by years of civil war between rival militarists and Dr. Sun's Republicans. Nationalist forces, led by General Chiang Kai-shek and with the advice of Communist experts, soon occupied most of China, setting up a Kuomintang regime in 1928. Internal strife continued, however, and Chiang eventually broke with the Communists.

On Sept. 18, 1931, Japan launched an invasion of Manchuria, capturing the province. Tokyo set up a puppet state dubbed Manchukuo and installed the last Manchu emperor, Henry Pu-Yi (Hsüan Tung), as its nominal leader. Japanese troops moved to seize China's northern provinces in July 1937, but were resisted by Chiang, who had been able to use the Japanese invasion to unite most of China behind him. Within two years, however, Japan had seized most of the nation's eastern ports and railways. The Kuomintang government retreated first to Hankow and then to Chungking, while the Japanese set up a puppet government at Nanking, headed by Wang Jingwei.

Japan's surrender in 1945 touched off civil war between the Kuomintang forces under Chiang and Communists led by Mao Zedong, who had been battling since the 1930s for control of China. Despite U.S. aid, the Kuomintang were overcome by the Soviet-supported Communists, and Chiang and his followers were forced to flee the mainland, establishing a government-in-exile on the island of Formosa (Taiwan). The Mao regime proclaimed the People's Republic of China on Oct. 1, 1949, with Beijing as the new capital and Zhou Enlai as premier.

After the Korean War began in June 1950, China led the Communist bloc in supporting North Korea, and on Nov. 26, 1950, the Mao regime sent troops to assist the North in its efforts to capture the South.

In an attempt to restructure China's primarily agrarian economy, Mao undertook the "Great Leap Forward" campaign in 1958, a disastrous program that aimed to combine the establishment of rural communes with a crash program of village industrialization. The Great Leap forced the abandonment of farming activities, leading to widespread famine in which more than 20 million people died of malnutrition.

In 1959, a failed uprising against China's invasion and occupation of Tibet forced Tibetan Buddhism's spiritual leader, the Dalai Lama, and 100,000 of his followers to flee to India. The invasion of Tibet, as well as border disputes between China and India—with whom Moscow had warm relations—and a perceived rivalry for the leadership of the world Communist movement caused a serious souring of relations between China and the U.S.S.R., former allies.

The failure of the Great Leap Forward touched off a power struggle within the Chinese Communist Party between Mao and his supporters, and a reformist faction, including future premier Deng Xiaoping. Mao moved to Shanghai, and from that base he and his supporters waged what they called the Cultural Revolution. Beginning in the spring of 1966, Mao ordered the closing of schools and the formation of ideologically pure Red Guard units, dominated by youths and students. The Red Guards campaigned against "old ideas, old culture, old habits, and old customs." Millions died as a series of violent purges were carried out. By early 1967, the Cultural Revolution had succeeded in bolstering Mao's position as China's paramount leader.

Anxious to exploit the Sino-Soviet rift, the Nixon Administration made a dramatic announcement in July 1971 that National Security Adviser Henry Kissinger had secretly visited Beijing and reached an agreement whereby Nixon would visit China. The movement toward reconciliation, which signaled the end of the U.S. containment policy toward China, provided momentum for China's admission to the U.N. Despite U.S. opposition to expelling Taiwan (Nationalist China), the world body overwhelmingly voted to oust Taiwan in favor of Beijing's Communist government.

President Nixon went to Beijing for a week early in 1972, meeting Mao as well as Zhou. The summit ended with a historic communiqué on Feb. 28, in which both nations promised to work toward improved relations. Full diplomatic relations were barred by China as long as the U.S. continued to recognize the legitimacy of Nationalist China.

Following Zhou's death on Jan. 8, 1976, his successor, Vice Premier Deng Xiaoping, was supplanted within a month by Hua Guofeng, former minister of public security. Hua became permanent premier in April. In October he was named successor to Mao as chairman of the Communist Party. But Mao's death on Sept. 10 unleashed the bitter intra-party rivalries that had been suppressed since the Cultural Revolution. Old opponents of Mao launched a campaign against his widow, Jiang Qing, and three of her "radical" colleagues. The so-called "Gang of Four" was denounced for having undermined the party, the government, and the economy. They were tried and convicted in 1981. Meanwhile, in 1977 Deng Xiaoping was reinstated as deputy premier, chief of staff of the army, and member of the central committee of the politburo.

Beijing and Washington announced full diplomatic relations on Jan. 1, 1979, and the Carter Administration abrogated the Taiwan defense treaty. Deputy Premier Deng sealed the agreement with a visit to the U.S. that coincided with the opening of embassies in both capitals on March 1. On Deng's return from the U.S., Chinese troops invaded and briefly occupied an area along Vietnam's northern border. The action was seen as a response to Vietnam's invasion of Cambodia and ouster of the Khmer Rouge government, which China had supported.

In 1981, Deng protége Hu Yaobang replaced Hua Guofeng as party chairman. Deng became chairman of the committee's military commission, giving him control over the army. The body's 215 members concluded the session with a statement holding Mao Zedong responsible for the "grave blunder" of the Cultural Revolution.

Under Deng Xiaoping's leadership, meanwhile, China's Communist ideology went through a massive reinterpretation, and sweeping economic changes were set in motion in the early 1980s. The Chinese scrapped the personality cult that idolized Mao Zedong, muted Mao's old call for class struggle and exportation of the Communist revolution, and imported Western technology and management techniques to replace the Marxist tenets that had slowed modernization. Deng concluded an agreement for the return of Hong Kong following the expiration of Britain's 99-year lease on the territory on July 1, 1997.

The removal of Hu Yaobang as party chairman in Jan. 1987 signaled a hard-line resurgence within the party. Hu—who had become a hero to many reform-minded Chinese—was replaced by former Premier Zhao Ziyang. With the death of Hu in April, 1989, the ideological struggle spilled into the streets of the capital, as student demonstrators occupied Beijing's Tiananmen Square in May, calling for democratic reforms. Less than a month later, the demonstrations were crushed in a bloody crackdown as troops and tanks moved into the square and fired on protesters, killing several hundred.

In annual sessions of the rubber-stamp National People's Congress in 1992 and 1993, the government called for accelerating the drive for economic reform, but were widely seen as an effort to maintain China's moves toward a market economy while retaining political authoritarianism. At the session in 1993, Communist Party leader Jiang Zemin was elected president, while hard-liner Li Peng was re-elected to another five-year term as prime minister. Since 1993, the Chinese economy has continued to grow rapidly. In November the Central Committee adopted a resolution envisaging the conversion of state-owned enterprises into joint-stock companies, and the creation of a central bank and modern tax system.

Deng Xiaoping's death in Feb. 1997 left a younger generation in charge of managing the enormous country. Hong Kong's reversion to Chinese rule on July 1 was watched with studied concern by the international community for signs of future developments within other parts of China. In 1998, Prime Minister Zhu Rongji introduced a sweeping program to privatize state-run businesses and further liberalize the nation's economy, a move lauded by Western economists.

Hong Kong

Status: Special Administrative Region of the People's Republic of China
Chief Executive: Tung Chee Hwa (1997)
Area: 416 sq mi. (1,077 sq km)
Population (1998 est.): 6,706,965 (average annual rate of natural increase: 2.24%); birth rate: 12.9/1000;

infant mortality rate: 5.2/1000; density per sq mi.: 16,123
Capital (1995 est.): Victoria (Hong Kong Island), 6,205,300. **Monetary unit:** Hong Kong dollar. **Literacy rate:** 81%
Economic summary: GDP/PPP (1996 est.): $163.6 billion; $26,000 per capita. **Real growth rate:** 4.7%. **Inflation:** 6.5%. **Unemployment:** 3.1%. **Arable land:** 6%. **Agriculture:** vegetables, rice, dairy products. **Labor force** (1994), 3.251 million; wholesale, retail, hotels, restaurants, 34.4%; services, 19.8%; manufacturing, 14.2%. **Industry:** textiles, clothing, toys, transistor radios, watches, electronic components. **Exports:** $197.2 billion (including re-exports) (f.o.b., 1996 est.): clothing, textiles, toys, watches, electrical appliances, footwear. **Imports:** $217.2 billion (c.i.f., 1996): raw materials, transport equipment, food. **Major trading partners:** U.S., U.K., Japan, Germany, China, Taiwan.

The territory of Hong Kong consists of the island of Hong Kong (32 sq mi.; 83 sq km), Stonecutters' Island, Kowloon Peninsula, and the New Territories on the adjoining mainland. The island of Hong Kong, located at the mouth of the Pearl River about 90 miles (145 km) southeast of Canton, was ceded to Britain in 1841. Stonecutters' Island and Kowloon were annexed in 1860, and the New Territories, which are mainly agricultural lands, were leased from China in 1898 for 99 years. Hong Kong was attacked by Japanese troops on Dec. 7, 1941, and surrendered the following Christmas. It remained under Japanese occupation until Aug. 1945.

After two years of painstaking negotiation, authorities of Britain and the People's Republic of China agreed in 1984 that Hong Kong would return to Chinese sovereignty on July 1, 1997, when Britain's lease on the New Territories expired. They also agreed that the vibrant capitalist enclave on China's coast would retain its status as a free port, with its laws remaining unchanged for 50 years.

The chief executive under the new government, Tung Chee Hwa, formulated a policy agenda based upon the concept of "one country, two systems," thus preserving Hong Kong's economic freedom. Hong Kong will continue to have its own finances and issue its own travel documents, and Beijing will not levy taxes. As the British lease on Hong Kong expired on July 1, 1997, the international community anxiously eyed the Chinese takeover for signs of its commitment to upholding the region's free-market economy.

Colombia

REPUBLIC OF COLOMBIA

National name: República de Colombia
President: Andrés Pastrana Arango (1998)
Area: 439,735 sq mi. (1,138,910 sq km)
Population (1998 est.): 38,580,949 (average annual rate of natural increase, 1.89%); birth rate: 24.9/1000; infant mortality rate: 25.4/1000; density per sq mi.: 88
Capital and largest city (1995 est.): Santafé de Bogotá 5,025,989. **Largest cities (1995 est.):** Cali, 1,718,871; Medellín, 1,621,356; Barranquilla, 1,064,255; Cartagena, 745,689. **Monetary unit:** Peso. **Language:** Spanish. **Ethnicity/Race:** mestizo 58%, white 20%, mulatto 14%, black 4%, mixed black-Indian 3%, Indian 1%. **Religion:** 95% Roman Catholic. **Literacy rate:** 87%
Economic summary: GDP/PPP (1996 est.): $201.4 billion; $5,400 per capita. **Real growth rate:** 2.1%. **Inflation:** 21.6%. **Unemployment:** 11.5%. **Arable land:** 4%. **Agriculture:** coffee, bananas, rice, corn, sugar cane, cocoa beans, cotton, tobacco, oilseeds, fresh cut flowers. **Labor force:** 12 million (1990); services, 46% ; agriculture, 30%; industry, 24%. **Industry:** textiles, processed food, beverages, chemicals, cement. **Natural resources:** petroleum, natural gas, coal, iron ore, nickel, gold, copper, emeralds. **Exports:** $10.3 billion (f.o.b., 1996 est.): coffee, fuel oil, coal, bananas, fresh cut flowers, nickel, chemicals, emeralds. **Imports:** $12.4 billion (c.i.f., 1996 est.): machinery, paper products, aircraft, telecommunications equipment, vehicles, gasoline, wheat. **Major trading partners:** U.S., E.U., Japan, Venezuela, Brazil.

Geography Colombia, in the northwestern part of South America, is the only country on that continent that borders both the Atlantic and Pacific oceans. It is nearly equal in size to the combined areas of California and Texas. Colombia is bordered by Panama on the northwest, on the east by Venezuela and Brazil, and on the southwest by Peru and Ecuador. Through the western half of the country, three Andean ranges run north and south, merging into one at the Ecuadorean border. The eastern half is a low, jungle-covered plain, drained by spurs of the Amazon and Orinoco, inhabited mostly by isolated, tropical-forest Indian tribes. The fertile plateau and valley of the eastern range are the most densely populated parts of the country.

Government Colombia's president, who appoints his own cabinet, serves a four-year term. The Senate, the upper house of Congress, has 102 members elected for four years by direct vote. The House of Representatives of 165 members is directly elected for four years. Mayor and state governors are also elected by direct vote for three-year terms.

History Spaniards in 1510 founded Darien, the first permanent European settlement on the American mainland. In 1538 the Spaniards established the colony of New Granada, the area's name until 1861. After a 14-year struggle, in which Simón Bolívar's Venezuelan troops won the battle of Boyacá in Colombia on Aug. 7, 1819, independence was attained in 1824. Bolívar united Colombia, Venezuela, Panama, and Ecuador in the Republic of Greater Colombia (1819–30), but lost Venezuela and Ecuador to separatists. Bolívar's Vice President Francisco de Paula Santander founded the Liberal Party as the Federalists while Bolívar established the Conservatives as the Centralists.

Santander's presidency (1832–36) re-established order, but later periods of Liberal dominance (1849–57 and 1861–80), when the Liberals sought to disestablish the Roman Catholic Church, were marked by insurrection and even civil war. Rafael Nuñez, in a 15-year presidency, restored the power of the central government and the church, which led in 1899 to a bloody civil war and the loss in 1903 of Panama over ratification of a lease to the U.S. of the Canal Zone. For 21 years, until 1930, the Conservatives held power as revolutionary pressures built up. The Liberal administrations of Enrique Olaya Herrera and Alfonso López (1930–38) were marked by social reforms that failed to solve the country's problems, and in 1946, insurrection and banditry broke out, claiming hundreds of thousands of lives by 1958. Laureano Gómez (1950–53); the army chief of staff, Gen. Gustavo Rojas Pinilla (1953–56), and a military junta (1956–57) sought to curb disorder by repression.

The Liberals won a solid majority in 1982, but a party split enabled Belisario Betancur Cuartas, the Conservative candidate, to win the presidency on May 31. After his inauguration, he ended the state of siege that had existed almost continuously for 34 years. In an official war against drug trafficking, Colombia became a public battleground with bombs, killings, and kidnapping. In 1989 a leading presidential candidate, Luis Carlos Galán, was murdered. In an effort to quell the terror President Gaviria proposed lenient punishment in exchange for surrender by the leading drug dealers. In addition, in 1991 the constitutional convention voted to ban extradition. In July 1992 Pablo Escobar of the Medellín drug cartel escaped from prison in an operation that left six dead. He died the next year, but the Medellín drug cartel continues to operate.

In the country's closest presidential contest in 24 years, Ernesto Samper, the candidate of the Liberal Party, won 50% of the vote in June 1994. Amid allegations of having accepted campaign contributions from drug traffickers, Samper in May 1996 ordered emergency security measures in southern Columbia to fight leftist rebels, but the House of Representatives absolved him of the charges by a 111–43 vote. In 1997 a constitutional amendment that allowed for nonretroactive extradition was passed while civil unrest and intermittent guerrilla warfare and drug wars continued throughout the country

Comoros

FEDERAL ISLAMIC REPUBLIC OF THE COMOROS

National name: République Fédéral Islamique des Comores
President: Mohamed Taki Abdoulkarim (1996)
Area: 690 sq mi. (2,170 sq km)
Population (1998 est.): 545,528 (average annual rate of natural increase: 3.1%); birth rate: 40.5/1000; infant mortality rate: 84.5/1000; density per sq mi.: 7918
Capital and largest city (1990 est.): Moroni (on Grande Comoro), 23,432. **Monetary unit:** Franc CFA. **Languages:** Shaafi Islam (Swahili dialect), Malagasu, French, Arabic. **Ethnicity/Race:** Antalote, Cafre, Makoa, Oimatsaha, Sakalava. **Religions:** Sunni Muslim, 86%; Roman Catholic, 14%. **Literacy rate:** 48%
Economic summary: GDP/PPP (1995 est.): $370 million; $650 per capita. **Real growth rate:** –2.3%. **Inflation:** 7.1% (1995 est.). **Unemployment** n.a. **Arable land:** 35%. **Agriculture:** perfume essences, copra, coconuts, cloves, vanilla, cassava, bananas. **Labor force:** 140,000 (1982); 80% in agriculture. **Industry:** perfume distillations. **Exports:** $11.2 million (f.o.b., 1995 est.): perfume essences, vanilla, copra, cloves. **Imports:** $40.9 million (f.o.b., 1993 est.): foodstuffs, cement, petroleum products, consumer goods. **Major trading partners:** France, Germany, U.S., Africa, Pakistan, China.

Geography The Comoros Islands—Grande Comoro, Anjouan, Mohéli, and Mayotte (which is not part of the country and retains ties to France)—are an archipelago of volcanic origin in the Indian Ocean between Mozambique and Madagascar.

Government Democratic elections were held in March 1990. The interim President Said Djohar won from among a field of eight candidates. The constitution dates from Oct. 1, 1978, and the country is an Islamic republic with a 42-member unicameral legislature.

History Comoros had been visited by travellers from Africa, Madagascar, Indonesia, and Arabia before the first Europeans encountered the islands. Arabic influence has been the strongest.

Under French rule since 1886, the Comoros declared themselves independent on July 6, 1975. However, Mayotte, with a Christian majority, voted against joining the other, mainly Islamic, islands, in the move to independence. It remains a French overseas territory.

A month after independence, Justice Minister Ali Soilih staged a coup with the help of mercenaries, overthrowing the new nation's first president, Ahmed Abdallah. He was himself overthrown on May 13, 1978.

Anjouan declared independence on August 3, 1997, after months of protests and clashes with security forces. The secessionists want a return to French rule, contending that independence from France has brought economic disaster and political chaos. Mohéli, the smallest island, also seceded. France has refused to support the secession of either island. A failed assault by President Taki's forces in Sept. 1997 attempted to retake Anjouan. Taki then declared a state of emergency, which is still in effect. Since he took office in 1996, he has dismissed his government three times. There has been no prime minister since May 1998.

Congo

REPUBLIC OF CONGO

National name: République Populaire du Congo
President: Denis Sassou-Nguesso (1997)
Prime Minister: Bernard Kolelas (1997)
Area: 132,046 sq mi. (342,000 sq km)
Population (1998 est.): 2,658,123 (average annual rate of natural increase: 2.21%); birth rate: 38.5/1000; infant mortality rate: 102.7/1000; density per sq mi.: 20
Capital and largest city (1992 est.): Brazzaville, 937,580. **Other large city (1992 est.):** Pointe-Noire, 576,206. **Monetary unit:** Franc CFA. **Languages:** French, Lingala, Kikongo, others. **Ethnicity/Race:** south: Kongo 48%; north: Sangha 20%, M'Bochi 12%; center: Teke 17%, Europeans 8,500 (mostly French). **Religions:** 50% Christian, 48% animist, 2% Muslim. **Literacy rate:** 57%
Economic summary: GDP/PPP (1995 est.): $4.9 billion; $1,960 per capita. **Real growth rate:** 0.9%. **Inflation:** 3% (1996 est.). **Arable land:** 0%. **Agriculture:** cassava, rice, corn, peanuts, coffee, cocoa. **Labor force:** n.a. **Industry:** crude oil, cigarettes, cement, beverages, milled sugar. **Natural resources:** wood, potash, petroleum, natural gas. **Exports:** $952 million (f.o.b., 1994 est.): oil, lumber, coffee, cocoa, sugar, diamonds. **Imports:** $559 million (c.i.f., 1994 est.): foodstuffs, consumer goods, intermediate manufactures, capital equipment. **Major trading partners:** France, Italy, Spain, Germany, other E.U. countries, Brazil, Japan, U.S.

Geography The Congo is situated in west Central Africa astride the Equator. It borders Gabon, Cameroon, the Central African Republic, the Democratic Republic of the Congo, and the Angola exclave of

Cabinda, with a short stretch of coast on the South Atlantic. Its area is nearly three times that of Pennsylvania. Most of the inland is tropical rain forest, drained by tributaries of the Congo River, which flows south along the eastern border with the Democratic Republic of the Congo to Stanley Pool. The narrow coastal plain rises to highlands separated from the inland plateaus by the 200-mile-wide Niari River valley, which gives passage to the coast.

History In precolonial times, the region now called the Republic of Congo was dominated by three kingdoms: Kongo (originating c. C.E. 1000), the Loango (flourishing in the 17th century), and Tio. After the Portuguese located the Congo River in 1482, commerce was carried on with the tribes, especially the slave trade.

The Frenchman Pierre Savorgnan de Brazza signed a treaty with Makoko, ruler of the Bateke people, in 1880, thus establishing French control. It was first called French Congo, and after 1905 Middle Congo. With Gabon and Ubangi-Shari, it became the colony of French Equatorial Africa in 1910. Abuse of laborers led to public outcry against the French colonialists as well as rebellions among the Congolese, but the exploitation of the native workers continued until 1930. During World War II the colony joined Chad in supporting the Free French cause against the Vichy government. The Congo proclaimed its independence without leaving the French Community in 1960, calling itself the Republic of Congo.

Congo's second president, Alphonse Massemba-Débat, instituted a Marxist-Leninist government. In 1968, Maj. Marien Ngouabi overthrew him but kept Congo on a socialist course. He was sworn in for a second five-year term in 1975. A four-man commando squad assassinated Ngouabi on March 18, 1977. Col. Joachim Yhombi-Opango, army chief of staff, assumed the presidency on April 4. Yhombi-Opango resigned on Feb. 4, 1979, and was replaced by Col. Denis Sassou-Nguesso.

In July 1990 the leaders of the ruling party voted to end the one-party system. A national political conference, hailed as a model for Sub-Saharan Africa, renounced Marxism in 1991, and scheduled the country's first free elections for 1992. The national conference ending in June 1991 rewrote the constitution.

Political and ethnic tensions intensified in 1993 after legislative elections in May and runoffs in June. The opposition's rejection of the results developed into violence. A peacc agreement was achieved between the government and the opposition in August 1994. A four-month civil war (June 5–Oct. 15, 1997) devastated Brazzaville, the capital. Buttressed by military aid from Angola, former Marxist dictator Denis Sassou-Nguesso overthrew President Pascal Lissouba, the country's first democratically elected president.

Congo, Democratic Republic of the

DEMOCRATIC REPUBLIC OF THE CONGO

President: Laurent Kabila (1997)
Area: 905,365 sq mi. (2,345,410 sq km)
Population (1998 est.): 49,000,051 (average annual rate of natural increase: 3%); birth rate: 46.8/1000; infant mortality rate: 101.6/1000; density per sq mi.: 54
Capital and largest city (1994 est.): Kinshasa, 4,655,313. **Other large cities:** Lubumbashi, 851,381; Mbuji-Mayi, 806,475; Kisangani, 417,517; Kolwezi, 417,810. **Monetary unit:** Zaire. **Languages:** French (official), English, Bantu dialects, mainly Swahili, Lingala, Ishiluba, and Kikongo. **Ethnicity/Race:** over 200 African ethnic groups, the majority are Bantu; the four largest tribes—Mongo, Luba, Kongo (all Bantu), and the Mangbetu-Azande (Hamitic)—make up about 45% of the population. **Religions:** Roman Catholic 50%, Protestant 20%, Kimbanguist 10%, Islam 10%; syncretic and traditional, 10%. **Literacy rate:** 72%
Economic summary: GDP/PPP (1995 est.): $16.5 billion; $400 per capita. **Real growth rate:** –.07%. **Inflation:** 542% (1995). **Unemployment:** n.a. **Arable land:** 3%. **Agriculture:** coffee, palm oil, rubber, quinine, cassava, bananas, plantains, vegetables, fruits. **Labor force:** 14.51 million; 16% in industry. **Industry:** processed and unprocessed minerals, consumer goods, diamonds. **Natural resources:** copper, cobalt, zinc, industrial diamonds, manganese, tin, gold, silver, bauxite, iron, coal, crude oil, hydroelectric potential. **Exports:** $1.47 billion (f.o.b., 1995 est.): copper, cobalt, diamonds, petroleum, coffee. **Imports:** $1.25 billion (f.o.b., 1995 est.): consumer goods, foodstuffs, mining and other machinery, transport equipment, and fuels. **Major trading partners:** Belgium, France, U.S., Germany, South Africa, Italy, Japan, U.K.

Geography Congo, in west central Africa, is bordered by the Congo Republic, the Central African Republic, the Sudan, Uganda, Rwanda, Burundi, Tanzania, Zambia, Angola, and the Atlantic Ocean. It is one quarter the size of the U.S. The principal rivers are the Ubangi and Bomu in the north and the Congo in the west, which flows into the Atlantic. The entire length of Lake Tanganyika lies along the eastern border with Tanzania and Burundi.

Government A republic with a single-party system.

History Formerly the Belgian Congo, this territory was inhabited by ancient Negrito peoples (Pygmies), who were pushed into the mountains by Bantu and Nilotic invaders. The American correspondent Henry M. Stanley navigated the Congo River in 1877 and opened the interior to exploration. Commissioned by King Leopold II of the Belgians, Stanley made treaties with native chiefs that enabled the king to obtain personal title to the territory at the Berlin Conference of 1885.

Criticism of forced labor under royal exploitation prompted Belgium to take over administration of the Congo, which remained a colony until agitation for independence forced Brussels to grant freedom on June 30, 1960. Moise Tshombe, premier of the then Katanga Province seceded from the new republic on July 11, and another mining province, South Kasai, followed. Belgium sent paratroopers to quell the civil war, and with President Joseph Kasavubu and Premier Patrice Lumumba of the national government in conflict, the United Nations flew in a peacekeeping force.

Kasavubu staged an army coup in 1960 and handed Lumumba over to the Katangan forces. A U.N. investigating commission found that Lumumba had been killed by a Belgian mercenary in the presence of Tshombe. Dag Hammarskjold, U.N. secretary-general, died in a plane crash en route to a peace conference with Tshombe on Sept. 17, 1961.

U.N. Secretary-General U Thant submitted a national reconciliation plan in 1962 that Tshombe rejected. Tshombe's troops fired on the U.N. force in December, and in the ensuing conflict Tshombe capitulated on Jan. 14, 1963. The peacekeeping force withdrew, and, in a complete about-face, Kasavubu named Tshombe premier in order to fight a spreading rebellion. Tshombe used foreign mercenaries, and with the help of Belgian paratroops airlifted by U.S. planes, defeated the most serious opposition, a Communist-backed regime in the northeast.

Kasavubu abruptly dismissed Tshombe in 1965 and was himself ousted by Gen. Joseph-Desiré Mobutu, Army Chief of Staff. The new president nationalized the Union Minière, the Belgian copper mining enterprise that had been a dominant force in the Congo since colonial days. The plane carrying the exiled Tshombe was hijacked in 1967 and he was held prisoner in Algeria until his death from a heart attack was announced June 29, 1969.

Mobutu eliminated opposition to win the election in 1970. In 1975, he nationalized much of the economy, barred religious instruction in schools, and decreed the adoption of African names. On March 8, 1977, invaders from Angola calling themselves the Congolese National Liberation Front pushed into Shaba and threatened the important mining center of Kolwezi. France and Belgium responded to Mobutu's pleas for help with weapons, but the U.S. gave only nonmilitary supplies. In April, France flew 1,500 Moroccan troops to Shaba to defeat the invaders, who were, Mobutu charged, Soviet-inspired and Cuban-led. U.S. intelligence sources, however, confirmed Soviet and Cuban denials of any participation and identified the rebels as former Katanga gendarmes who had fled to Angola after their 1963 defeat.

In April 1990 Mobutu announced he intended to introduce multiparty democracy, but that elections in Jan. 1991 would reduce the number of political parties to two besides his own. Opposition leaders denounced the scheme as giving Mobutu's party an unfair advantage.

In early 1993 Mobutu rejected Western demands that he yield power and announced plans to regroup his one-party parliament, dismissing the main opposition leader, Prime Minister Tshisekedi. In Jan. 1994 Mobutu dissolved parliament and dismissed his prime minister, which led to a general strike in the capital.

Mobutu Sese Seko was overthrown in May 1997, ending one of the world's most corrupt and megalomaniacal regimes. The last of the CIA-nurtured cold war despots, Mobutu deftly courted France and the U.S., which used Zaire as a launching pad for covert operations against bordering countries, particularly Marxist Angola. Mobutu's disastrous policies drove his country to economic collapse while he siphoned off millions of dollars for himself.

Laurent Kabila and his long-standing but little-known guerrilla movement launched a seven-month campaign that ousted Mobutu. The country was renamed the Democratic Republic of the Congo, its name before Mobutu changed it to Zaire in 1971. Mobutu's downfall began in Oct. 1996, when he planned to banish the Zairian Tutsi who had lived for centuries in eastern Zaire. Neighboring Rwanda's Tutsi-led government came to their aid, as did other rebel groups, one of which was led by Kabila. After conquering eastern Zaire, Kabila earned the support of a host of Mobutu's enemies, including Uganda, Burundi, Tanzania, Zambia, Zimbabwe, and Angola. His troops swept through the country, encountering little resistance. Mobutu fled in exile to Morocco on May 16, where he died of cancer in September.

Elation over Mobutu's downfall faded as Kabila's own autocratic style emerged and he seemed devoid of a clear plan for reconstructing the country. He stymied U.N. human rights investigations into the alleged massacres of Hutu refugees and continued to depend on foreign troops for border skirmishes rather than establish a strong national army. Many Congolese dismissed him as a puppet ruler who allowed his country to be overrun by outsiders, particularly the Rwandans. At the same time he has alienated many of his former supporters, including Rwanda and Uganda.

In August 1998, Congolese rebel forces, led by ethnic Tutsi in eastern Congo who are believed to be backed by Rwanda and Uganda, launched an attack. The rebels gained control of a large portion of the country until Angolan, Namibian, and Zimbabwean troops came to Kabila's aid and pushed the rebels back.

Costa Rica

REPUBLIC OF COSTA RICA

National name: República de Costa Rica
President: Miguel Angel Rodríguez (1998)
Area: 19,652 sq mi. (51,100 sq km)
Population (1998 est.): 3,604,642 (average annual rate of natural increase: 1.95%); birth rate: 22.9/1000; infant mortality rate: 13.1/1000; density per sq mi.: 183
Capital and largest city (1994 est.): San José, 315,909. **Monetary unit:** Colón. **Language:** Spanish. **Ethnicity/Race:** white (including mestizo) 96%, black 2%, Indian 1%, Chinese 1%. **Religion:** 95% Roman Catholic. **Literacy rate:** 93%
Economic summary: GDP/PPP (1996 est.): $19 billion; $5,500 per capita. **Real growth rate:** -0.9%. **Inflation:** 13.9% (1996 est.). **Unemployment:** 5.5%. **Arable land:** 6%. **Agriculture:** bananas, coffee, sugar cane, rice, corn, livestock. **Labor force:** 868,300; industry and commerce, 35.1%; government and services, 33%; agriculture, 27% (1985 est.). **Industry:** processed foods, textiles and clothing, construction materials, fertilizer. **Natural resource:** hydropower potential. **Exports:** $3.82 billion (f.o.b., 1996 est.): coffee, bananas, textiles, sugar. **Imports:** $3.857 billion (c.i.f., 1996 est.): raw materials, consumer goods, capital equipment, petroleum. **Major trading partners:** U.S., Central American countries, Germany, Japan, United Kingdom, France, Netherlands.

Geography This Central American country lies between Nicaragua to the north and Panama to the south. Its area slightly exceeds that of Vermont and New Hampshire combined. Most of Costa Rica is tableland, from 3,000 to 6,000 feet (914 to 1,829 m) above sea level. Costa Rica has a narrow Pacific coastal region that rises abruptly into central highlands. The highlands, forming the rugged backbone of the country, descend much more gradually toward the generally wider Caribbean (Atlantic) Plain. Cocos Island (10 sq mi.; 26 sq km), about 300 miles (483 km) off the Pacific Coast, is under Costa Rican sovereignty.

Government Under the 1949 constitution, the president and the one-house Legislative Assembly of 57 members are elected for terms of four years.

The army was abolished in 1949, but there is a civil guard and a rural guard.

History Costa Rica was inhabited by 25,000 Indians when Columbus landed on it and probably named it in 1502. Few of the Indians survived the Spanish conquest, which began in 1563. The region grew slowly and was administered as a Spanish province. Costa Rica achieved independence in 1821 but was absorbed for two years by Agustín de Iturbide in his Mexican Empire. It was established as a republic in 1848. Except for the military dictatorship of Tomás Guardia from 1870 to 1882, Costa Rica has enjoyed one of the most democratic governments in Latin America.

Rodrigo Carazo Odio, leader of a four-party coalition called the Unity Party, won the presidency in Feb. 1978. His tenure was marked by a disastrous decline in the economy. On Feb. 2, 1986, Oscar Arias Sanchez won the national elections on a neutralist platform. Arias initiated a policy of preventing the Nicaraguan Contra rebels from using Costa Rican territory to train and hide from Nicaraguan government forces. Rafael Calderón won the presidential election of Feb. 4, 1990 with 51% of the vote.

The presidential election in Feb. 1994 was won by José Maria Figueres Olsen, of the National Liberation Party, although the tone of the campaign shocked many Costa Ricans. Mr. Figueres proposed more government intervention in the economy. As a result of IMF displeasure with the government's economic programs, the World Bank withheld $100 million of financing. In 1998 Miguel Angel Rodríguez of the Social Christian Unity Party became president.

Côte d'Ivoire

REPUBLIC OF CÔTE D'IVOIRE

National name: République de la Côte d'Ivoire
President: Henri Konan Bédié (1993)
Prime Minister: Daniel Kablan Duncan (1993)
Area: 124,502 sq mi. (322,460 sq km)
Population (1998 est.): 15,446,231 (average annual rate of natural increase: 2.41%); birth rate: 42.2/1000; infant mortality rate: 96/1000; density per sq mi.: 124
Capital (1988): Yamoussoukro (official); Abidjan (administrative) (since March 1983), 106,786. **Largest city (est. 1988):** Abidjan, 2,797,000. **Monetary unit:** Franc CFA. **Languages:** French and African languages (Diaula esp.). **Ethnicity/Race:** Baoule 23%, Bete 18%, Senoufou 15%, Malinke 11%, Agni, foreign Africans (mostly Burkinabe and Malians, about 3 million). **Religions:** 60% indigenous, 23% Islam, 17% Christian. **Literacy rate:** 54%
Economic summary: GDP/PPP (1996 est.): $23.9 billion; $1,620 per capita. **Real growth rate:** 6.5%. **Inflation:** (1996 est.): 8%. **Unemployment:** n.a. **Arable land:** 8%. **Agriculture:** coffee, cocoa, corn, beans, timber. **Labor force:** n.a. **Industry:** food, wood, refined oil, textiles, fertilizer. **Natural resources:** diamonds, iron ore, crude oil, manganese, cobalt, bauxite, copper. **Exports:** $3.7 billion (f.o.b., 1995): cocoa 36% (world's largest exporter), coffee 22%, tropical woods 4%, petroleum, cotton, bananas, pineapples, palm oil. **Imports:** $2.4 billion (f.o.b., 1995 est.): food, capital goods, consumer goods, fuel. **Major trading partners:** France, Germany, Netherlands, Belgium, Spain, other E.U. countries, U.S., Nigeria, Japan.

Geography Côte d'Ivoire (also known as the Ivory Coast), in western Africa on the Gulf of Guinea, is a little larger than New Mexico. Its neighbors are Liberia, Guinea, Mali, Burkina Faso, and Ghana. The country consists of a coastal strip in the south, dense forests in the interior, and savannas in the north. Rainfall is heavy, especially along the coast.

Government The government is headed by a president who is elected every five years by popular vote, together with a National Assembly of 175 members.

History Côte d'Ivoire was originally made up of numerous isolated settlements; today it represents more than sixty distinct tribes, including the Beti, Senufo, Baule, Anyi, Malinke, Dan, and Lobi. Côte d'Ivoire attracted both French and Portuguese merchants in the 15th century who were in search of ivory and slaves. French traders set up establishments early in the 19th century, and in 1842, the French obtained territorial concessions from local tribes, gradually extending their influence along the coast and inland. The area was organized as a territory in 1893, became an autonomous republic in the French Union after World War II, and achieved independence on Aug. 7, 1960. The Côte d'Ivoire formed a customs union in 1959 with Dahomey (Benin), Niger, and Burkina Faso. The nation's economy is one of the most developed in sub-Saharan Africa. It is the world's largest exporter of cocoa and one of the largest exporters of coffee.

From independence until his death in 1993, Felix Houphouët-Boigny served as president. Massive protests by students, farmers, and professionals forced the president to legalize opposition parties and hold the first contested presidential election in Oct. 1990, which Houphouët-Boigny won with 81% of the vote. In Sept. 1998, thousands of demonstrators protested a constitutional revision that granted President Henri Konan Bedie greatly enhanced powers.

Croatia

REPUBLIC OF CROATIA

President: Franjo Tudjman (1990)
Prime Minister: Zlatko Matesa (1995)
Area: 21,829 sq mi. (56,538 sq km)
Population (1998 est.): 4,671,584 (average annual rate of natural increase: 0.13%), Birth rate: 10.5/1000; infant mortality rate: 8/1000; density per sq mi.: 214
Capital (1991): Zagreb, 930,753. **Other large cities (1991):** Split, 189,444; Rijeka, 167,757; Osijek, 129,792. **Monetary unit:** Kuna (May 1994). **Languages:** Croatian. **Ethnicity/Race:** Croat 78%, Serb 12%, Muslim 0.9%, Hungarian 0.5%, Slovenian 0.5%, others 8.1% (1991). **Literacy rate:** 97%. **Religions:** Catholic 76.5%, Orthodox 11.1%, Slavic Muslim 1.2%, Protestant 0.4%, others and unknown 10.8%
Economic summary: GDP/PPP (1996 est.): $21.4 billion; $4,300 per capita. **Real growth rate:** 4%. **Inflation:** 4%. **Unemployment:** 13% (year end 1996). **Industry:** chemicals, plastics, machine tools, fabricated metals, electronics, rolled steel products, aluminum processing, wood products, building materials, petroleum and petroleum refining, food processing, beverages, pharmaceuticals, and shipbuilding. **Agriculture:** wheat, corn, oats, sugar beets, potatoes, livestock breeding, dairy farming, vineyards, and fishing. **Exports:** $4.6 billion (f.o.b., 1995): machinery and transport equipment, chemicals, food and live animals, raw materials, fuels and

lubricants, and beverages and tobacco. **Imports:** $7.6 billion (c.i.f.,1995): machinery and transport equipment, fuels, manufactured articles, raw materials, tobacco. **Major Trading Partners:** Germany, Italy, Slovenia

Geography Croatia is a former Yugoslav republic on the Adriatic Sea; it is about the size of West Virginia. Part of Croatia is a barren, rocky region lying in the Dinaric Alps. The Zagorje region north of the capital, Zagreb, is a land of rolling hills, and the fertile agricultural region of the Pannonian Plain is bordered by the Drava, Danube, and Sava Rivers in the east. Over one-third of Croatia is forested.

Government A parliamentary democracy with a bicameral legislative body, the Sabor, with 124 members.

History The original home of the Slavic Croats was in an area that was part of the Republic of Ukraine. During the 6th century C.E., other tribes arrived in the region which was then part of the Roman province of Pannonia. The Croats converted to Christianity between the 7th and 9th centuries and adopted the Roman alphabet under the suzerainty of Charlemagne. In C.E. 925, the Croats defeated Byzantine and Frankish invaders and established their own independent kingdom, which reached its peak during the 11th century. A civil war ensued in 1089 which later led to the country being conquered by the Hungarians in 1091. The signing of the *Pacta Conventa* by Croatian tribal chiefs and the Hungarian king in 1102 united the two nations politically under the Hungarian monarch, but Croatia retained its autonomy.

When the Hungarians were defeated by the Turks in 1526, most of Croatia fell under Ottoman rule until the end of the 17th century. The rest of Croatia elected Ferdinand of Austria as their king and became associated with the Hapsburgs of Austria. After the establishment of the Austro-Hungarian kingdom in 1867, Croatia and Slovenia became part of Hungary until the collapse of Austria-Hungary in 1918 following their defeat in World War I. On Oct. 29, 1918, Croatia proclaimed its independence and joined in union with Montenegro, Serbia, and Slovenia to form the kingdom of Serbs, Croats, and Slovenes. The name was changed to Yugoslavia in 1929.

When Germany invaded Yugoslavia in 1941, an independent Croatian state was created that was controlled by a fascist dictatorship sympathetic to the Nazis. After Germany was defeated in 1945, Croatia was made into a republic of the newly reestablished communist nation of Yugoslavia. In June 1991, the Croatian parliament passed a declaration of independence from Yugoslavia. A six-month civil war followed with the Serbian-dominated Yugoslavian army. The war claimed thousands of lives and wrought mass destruction.

A U.N. cease-fire was arranged on Jan. 2, 1992. The Security Council in Feb. approved sending a 14,000-member peacekeeping force to monitor the cease-fire and protect the minority Serbs in Croatia. In a 1993 referendum the Serb-occupied portion of Croatia (Krajina) resoundingly voted for integration with Serbs in Bosnia and Serbia proper. Although the Zagreb government and representatives of Krajina signed a cease-fire in March 1994, further negotiations broke down shortly afterward over the political status of the latter region. In a lightning operation the Croatian army retook western Slavonia in May 1995. Similarly, in August the central Croatian region of Krajina, held by Serbs, was returned to Zagreb's control. Since then, Croatia has worked on reintegrating eastern Slavonia and rebuilding its shattered economy.

Cuba

REPUBLIC OF CUBA

National name: República de Cuba
President: Fidel Castro Ruz (1976)
Area: 42,843 sq mi. (110,860 sq km)
Population (1998 est.): 11,050,729 (average annual rate of natural increase: 0.43%); birth rate: 13.1/1000; infant mortality rate: 7.9/1000; density per sq mi.: 258
Capital and largest city (1994 est.): Havana, 2,241,000. **Other large cities (1994 est.):** Santiago de Cuba, 440,084; Camaguëy, 293,961; Holguin, 242,085; Guantánamo, 207,796; Santa Clara, 205,400. **Monetary unit:** Peso. **Language:** Spanish. **Ethnicity/Race:** mulatto 51%, white 37%, black 11%, Chinese 1%. **Religion:** at least 85% nominally Roman Catholic before Castro assumed power. **Literacy rate:** 94%
Economic summary: GDP/PPP (1996 est.): $16.2 billion; $1,480 per capita. **Real growth rate:** 7.8%, **Inflation:** n.a. **Unemployment:** n.a. **Arable land:** 24%. **Agriculture:** sugar and sugar by-products, tobacco, coffee, rice, fruits. **Labor force** (1989), 4.71 million; services and government, 30%; industry, 22%; agriculture, 20%; commerce, 11%. **Industry:** processed sugar and tobacco, refined oil products, textiles, chemicals, paper and wood products, metals, consumer products. **Natural resources:** metals (primarily nickel), timber. **Exports:** $2.1 billion (f.o.b., 1996 est.): coffee, sugar (world's largest sugar exporter), nickel, shellfish, tobacco, medical products, citrus. **Imports:** $3.5 billion (c.i.f., 1996 est.). petroleum, food, machinery, chemicals. Trading partners: China, Canada, Mexico, Spain, Russia.

Geography The largest island of the West Indies group (equal in area to Pennsylvania), Cuba is also the westernmost—just west of Hispaniola (Haiti and the Dominican Republic), and 90 miles (145 km) south of Key West, Florida, at the entrance to the Gulf of Mexico. The island is mountainous in the southeast and south central area (Sierra Maestra). It is flat or rolling elsewhere. Cuba also includes numerous smaller islands, islets, and cays.

Government Since 1976, elections have been held every five years to elect the 510–member National Assembly, which in turn elects the 31-member Council of States, its president, and Secretary. Fidel Castro is president of the Council of States and of the government and First Secretary of the Communist Party of Cuba, the only legal political party.

History Arawak (or Taino) Indians inhabiting Cuba when Columbus landed on the island in 1492 died off from diseases brought by sailors and settlers. By 1511, Spaniards under Diego Velásquez were founding settlements that served as bases for Spanish exploration. Cuba also became an assembly point for treasure looted by the conquistadores, attracting French and English pirates.

Black slaves and free laborers were imported to work sugar and tobacco plantations, and waves of chiefly Spanish immigrants maintained a European character in the island's culture. Early slave rebellions and conflicts between colonials and Spanish rulers laid the foundation for an independence movement that turned into open warfare from 1867 to 1878. Slavery was abolished in 1886. In 1895, the poet José Marti led the struggle that finally ended Spanish rule, thanks largely to U.S. intervention in 1898 after the sinking of the battleship *Maine* in Havana harbor.

A treaty in 1899 made Cuba an independent republic under U.S. protection. The U.S. occupation, which ended in 1902, suppressed yellow fever and brought large American investment. From 1906 to 1909, Washington invoked the Platt Amendment to the treaty, which gave it the right to intervene in order to suppress any revolt. U.S. troops came back in 1912 and again in 1917 to restore order. The Platt Amendment was abrogated in 1934.

Fulgencio Batista, an army sergeant, led a revolt in 1933 that overthrew the regime of President Gerado Machado. Batista's Cuba was a police state. Corrupt officials used intimidation and took payoffs from American gamblers who operated casinos, demanded bribes from Cubans for various public services, and enriched themselves with raids on the public treasury.

Fidel Castro Ruz, a tall, bearded attorney in his thirties who had been in exile in Mexico, landed in Cuba on Christmas Day 1956 with a band of 12 fellow revolutionaries, evaded Batista's soldiers, and set up headquarters in the jungled hills of the Sierra Maestra range. By 1958 his force had grown to about 2,000 guerrillas, for the most part young and middle class. Castro's brother Raul, and Ernesto (Ché) Guevara, an Argentine physician, were his top lieutenants. Businessmen and landowners who opposed the Batista regime gave financial support to the rebels. The United States, meanwhile, cut off arms shipments to Batista's army. The beginning of the end for Batista came when the rebels routed 3,000 government troops and captured Santa Clara, capital of Las Villas province 150 miles from Havana, and a trainload of Batista reinforcements refused to get out of their railroad cars. On New Year's Day 1959, Batista flew to exile in the Dominican Republic and Castro took over the government. Crowds cheered the revolutionaries on their seven-day march to the capital.

The United States initially welcomed what looked like the prospect for a democratic Cuba, but a rude awakening came within a few months when Castro established military tribunals for political opponents, jailed hundreds, and began to veer leftward. Castro disavowed Cuba's 1952 military pact with the United States. He confiscated U.S. investments in banks and industries and seized large U.S. landholdings, turning them first into collective farms and then into Soviet-type state farms. The United States broke relations with Cuba on Jan. 3, 1961. Castro forged an alliance with the Soviet Union.

From the ranks of the Cuban exiles who had fled to the United States, the Central Intelligence Agency recruited and trained an expeditionary force, numbering less than 2,000 men, to invade Cuba, with the expectation that the invasion would spark an uprising of the Cuban populace against Castro. Planned under the Eisenhower administration, President John F. Kennedy gave the go-ahead for the invasion in early 1961, but rejected a CIA proposal for U.S. planes to provide air support. The landing at the Bay of Pigs on April 17, 1961, was a fiasco. Not only did the invaders fail to receive any support from the populace, but Castro's tanks and artillery made short work of the small force.

A Soviet attempt to change the global power balance by installing medium-range missiles in Cuba—capable of striking targets in the United States with nuclear warheads—provoked a crisis between the superpowers in 1962 that had the potential of touching off World War III. Denouncing the Soviets for "deliberate deception," President Kennedy on Oct. 22 announced that the U.S. Navy would enforce a "quarantine" of shipping to Cuba and search Soviet bloc ships to prevent the missiles themselves from reaching the island. After six days of tough public statements on both sides and secret diplomacy, Soviet Premier Nikita Khrushchev on Oct. 28 ordered the missile sites dismantled, and shipped back to the Soviet Union, in return for a U.S. pledge not to attack Cuba.

During the 1960s and 1970s Cuba became a stalwart Soviet satellite and surrogate for spreading communist revolution in developing nations. The U.S. established limited diplomatic ties with Cuba on Sept. 1, 1977. Emigration increased dramatically after April 1, 1980, when Castro, irritated by the granting of asylum to would-be refugees by the Peruvian embassy in Havana, removed guards and allowed 10,000 Cubans to swarm into the embassy grounds.

As an airlift began taking the refugees to Costa Rica, Castro opened the port of Mariel to a "freedom flotilla" of ships and yachts from the United States, many of them owned or chartered by Cuban-Americans to bring out relatives. It wasn't until after they had reached the United States that it was discovered that the regime had opened prisons and mental hospitals to permit criminals, homosexuals, and others unwanted by the Cuban government to join the refugees.

For most of President Ronald Reagan's first term, U.S.-Cuban relations were frozen. But late in 1984, an agreement was reached between the two countries. Cuba would take back more than 2,700 Cubans who had come to the United States in the Mariel exodus but were not eligible to stay in the country under U.S. immigration law because of criminal or psychiatric disqualification. Castro cancelled it when the U.S. began the Radio Marti broadcasts in May 1985 to bring a non-Communist view to the Cuban people.

With the collapse of communism in Eastern Europe, Cuba's foreign trade plummeted as did aid from Russia, producing the worst economic crisis in the island's history. The government moved slightly toward a mixed economy in 1993 by permitting limited private enterprise in a number of trades and services and allowing Cubans to possess convertible currencies. Christmas was declared an official holiday in Cuba in 1997, for the first time since the revolution, in preparation for Pope John Paul II's historic visit to Cuba in Jan. 1998. By Castro allowing the pope's visit, he raised hopes that the gesture signalled a new openness, easing of restrictions, and increased religious freedom for Cubans.

In March 1996, the U.S. passed the Helms-Burton Act, which further extended the U.S. trade embargo on Cuba by penalizing non-U.S. companies doing business with Cuba. Reaction to the measure was widespread international condemnation that included the U.S.'s North American neighbors, Canada, Mexico, and the Caribbean nations.

Cyprus

REPUBLIC OF CYPRUS

National name: Kypriaki Dimokratia—Kibris Cumhuriyeti
President: Glafcos Clerides (1993)
Area: 3,572 sq mi (9,250 sq km)
Population (1998 est.): 748,982; (average annual rate of natural increase: 0.69%[1]; birth rate: 13.9/1000[1]; infant mortality rate: 8/1000[1]; density per sq mi.: 210
Capital and largest city (1993): Lefkosia (Nicosia) (in government controlled area), 186,400. **Monetary unit:** Cyprus pound. **Languages:** Greek, Turkish (official), English is widely spoken. **Ethnicity/Race:** total: Greek 78% (99.5% of the Greeks live in the Greek area; 0.5% of the Greeks live in the Turkish area), Turkish 18% (1.3% of the Turks live in the Greek area; 98.7% of the Turks live in the Turkish area), other 4% (99.2% of the other ethnic groups live in the Greek area; 0.8% of the other ethnic groups live in the Turkish area). **Religions (1993 est.):** Greek Orthodox, 78%; Sunni Muslim, 18%; Maronite, Armenian, Apostolic, Latin and others, 4%. **Literacy rate:** 94%
Economic summary: GDP/PPP (1996[1]): $8.8 billion; $11,800 per capita. **Real growth rate:** 4%. **Inflation:** (1996 est.): 3.3%. **Unemployment:** 2.3%. **Arable land:** 12%. **Agriculture:** vine products, citrus, potatoes, vegetables, olives, barley. **Labor force:** 299,700; industry, 25% ; services, 62% ; agriculture, 13%. **Industry:** food, beverages, footwear, clothing, metal products, pharmaceuticals, furniture. Hotels and restaurants contributed 8.6% to the gross domestic product in 1996. **Natural resources:** copper, asbestos, gypsum, timber, marble, clay, amber, ochre. **Exports:** $1.4 billion (f.o.b., 1996): citrus, potatoes, grapes, wine, cement, clothing, footwear, chemical products, paper products. **Imports:** $4 billion (c.i.f., 1996): consumer goods, petroleum and lubricants, food and feed grains, machinery. **Major trading partners:** U.K., Greece, Lebanon, Germany, Saudi Arabia. **Member of Commonwealth of Nations**

1. Government-controlled area only.

Geography The third largest island in the Mediterranean (one and one-half times the size of Delaware), Cyprus lies off the southern coast of Turkey and the western shore of Syria. Most of the country consists of a wide plain lying between two mountain ranges that cross the island. The highest peak is Mount Olympus at 6,406 feet (1,953 m).

Government Mediation efforts by the U.N. seek to achieve reunification of the island under one federated system of government. The president is elected for a five-year term and exercises executive power through an appointed Council of Ministers. Since Turkish-Cypriot ministers and other officials withdrew from their posts in 1963, the 24 seats in the House of Representatives allotted to the Turkish Cypriots remain vacant.

History Cyprus was the site of early Phoenician and Greek colonies. For centuries its rule passed through many hands. It fell to the Turks in 1571, and a large Turkish colony settled on the island.

In World War I, on the outbreak of hostilities with Turkey, Britain annexed the island. It was declared a Crown colony in 1925.

For centuries the Greek population, regarding Greece as its mother country, has sought self-determination and reunion with it *(enosis)*. The resulting quarrel with Turkey threatened NATO. Cyprus became an independent nation on Aug. 16, 1960, with Britain, Greece, and Turkey as guarantor powers.

Archbishop Makarios, president since 1959, was overthrown July 15, 1974, by a military coup led by the Cypriot National Guard. The new regime named Nikos Giorgiades Sampson as president and Bishop Gennadios as head of the Cypriot Church to replace Makarios. Diplomacy failed to resolve the crisis. Turkey invaded Cyprus by sea and air July 20, 1974, asserting its right to protect the Turkish Cypriote minority.

Geneva talks involving Greece, Turkey, Britain, and the two Cypriote factions failed in mid-August, and the Turks subsequently gained control of 40% of the island. Greece made no armed response to the superior Turkish force, but bitterly suspended military participation in the NATO alliance.

The tension continued after Makarios returned to become president on Dec. 7, 1974. He offered self-government to the Turkish minority, but rejected any solution "involving transfer of populations and amounting to partition of Cyprus."

Turkish Cypriots proclaimed a separate state under Rauf Denktas in the northern part of the island in Nov. 1983, and proposed a "biregional federation."

Makarios died on Aug. 3, 1977, and Spyros Kyprianou was elected to serve the remainder of his term. Kyprianou was subsequently re-elected in 1978, 1983, and 1985. In 1988, George Vassiliou defeated Kyprianou.

Then-President Vassiliou won a plurality in the presidential election of Feb. 1993 but fell short of a majority. A 73-year-old conservative and critic of U.N. proposals to reunify Cyprus narrowly won the second round of elections to become president

Parliamentary elections in May 1996 resulted in the ruling conservative-center coalition retaining a seat majority ahead of the Communists. The purchase of missiles capable of reaching the Turkish coast evoked threats of retaliation from Turkey in Jan. 1997.

Northern Cyprus— In 1974, Turkey invaded Cyprus and has since occupied 37% of the island in the north. Some 180,000 Greek Cypriots (about 40% of the Greek Cypriot population) were forced by the Turkish troops to flee to the Government-controlled area in the south and are still prevented by the occupying forces from returning to their homes and properties.

On Nov. 15, 1993, Turkish Cypriot leader Rauf Denktas unilaterally declared the occupied area independent, naming it the "Turkish Republic of Northern Cyprus." The U.N. Security Council, in its Resolution 541 of Nov. 18, 1983, declared this action legally invalid and called for withdrawal. No country except Turkey has recognized this illegal entity. The government of the Republic of Cyprus is the only internationally recognized Government on the island.

Czech Republic

President: Vaclav Havel (1993)
Prime Minister: Milos Zeman (1998)
Area: 30,464 sq mi. (78,703 sq km)
Population (1998 est.): 10,286,470 (average annual rate of natural increase: –0.11%); birth rate: 9/1000; infant mortality rate: 6.8/1000; density per sq mi.: 338
Capital and largest city (Jan. 1, 1994): Prague, 1,215,771. **Other large cities:** Brno, 389,727; Ostrava, 326,396; Plzen, 172,402; Olomouc, 106,003. **Monetary unit:** Koruna. **Language:** Czech; Slovak minority. **Ethnicity/Race:** Czech 94.4%, Slovak 3%, Polish 0.6%, German 0.5%, Roma (Gypsy) 0.3%, Hungarian 0.2%, other 1%. **Religions:** atheist 39.8%, Roman Catholic 39.2%, Protestant 4.6%, Orthodox 3%, other 13.4%. **Literacy rate:** 99%
Economic summary: GDP: (1996 est.): $114.3 billion; $11,100 per capita. **Real growth rate:** 5%. **Inflation:** 8.7%. **Unemployment:** 3.3%. The Czech Republic has a developed but deteriorating industrialized economy, much of its plant equipment is among the oldest in Europe. **Natural resources:** hard coal, kaolin, clay, graphite. **Industry:** fuels, ferrous metallurgy, machinery and equipment, coal, motor vehicles, glass, armaments. **Agriculture:** diversified crops including grains, potatoes, sugar beets, hops, fruit, hogs, cattle and poultry. **Labor force** (1996), 5.107 million; industry, 33.1%; agriculture, 6.9%; construction, 9.1%; services 43.7%. **Exports:** $21.9 billion (f.o.b., 1996 est.): manufactured goods, machinery and transport equipment, chemicals, fuels, minerals, and metals. **Imports:** $27.8 billion (f.o.b., 1996 est.): machinery and transport equipment, fuels and lubricants, manufactured goods, raw materials, chemicals, agricultural products. **Major trading partners:** E.U., former Soviet republics, Eastern Europe, Slovakia.

Geography The Czech Republic's central European landscape is dominated by the Bohemian Massif, which rises to heights of 3,000 feet (900 m) above sea level. This ring of mountains encircles a large elevated basin, the Bohemian Plateau. The principal rivers are the Elbe and the Vltava.

Government A parliamentary democracy headed by the president. The Parliament consists of two chambers—the 200-member Chamber of Deputies, elected for four-year terms, and the 81-member Senate, elected for six-year terms. The president is elected for a five-year term by both chambers of Parliament.

History Probably about the 5th century C.E., Slavic tribes from the Vistula basin settled in the region of the traditional Czech lands of Bohemia, Moravia, and Silesia. The Czechs founded the kingdom of Bohemia, the Premyslide Dynasty, which ruled Bohemia and Moravia from the 10th to the 16th century. One of the Bohemian kings, Charles IV, Holy Roman Emperor, made Prague an imperial capital and a center of Latin scholarship. The Hussite movement founded by Jan Hus (1369?–1415) linked the Slavs to the Reformation and revived Czech nationalism, previously under German domination. A Hapsburg, Ferdinand I, ascended the throne in 1526. The Czechs rebelled in 1618, precipitating the Thirty Years' War (1618–48). Defeated in 1620, they were ruled for the next 300 years as part of the Austrian Empire. Full independence from the Hapsburgs was not achieved until the end of World War I following the collapse of the Austrian-Hungarian Empire.

A union of the Czech lands and Slovakia was proclaimed in Prague on Nov. 14, 1918, and the Czech nation became one of the two component parts of the newly formed Czechoslovakian state. In March 1939, German troops occupied Czechoslovakia, and Czech Bohemia and Moravia became German protectorates for the duration of World War II. The former government returned in April 1945 when the war ended and the country's pre-1938 boundaries were restored. When elections were held in 1946, Communists became the dominant political party and gained control of the Czechoslovakian government in 1948. Thereafter, the former democracy was turned into a Soviet-style state.

Nearly 42 years of Communist rule ended when Vaclav Havel was elected president of Czechoslovakia in 1989. The return of democratic political reform saw a strong Slovak nationalist movement emerge by the end of 1991, which sought independence for Slovakia as a sovereign nation and the breakup of the two Czechoslovakian republics. When the general elections of June 1992 failed to resolve the continuing coexistence of the two republics within the Federation, Czech and Slovak political leaders agreed to separate their states into two fully independent nations. On Jan. 1, 1993 the Czechoslovakian federation was dissolved and two separate independent countries were established—the Czech Republic and Slovakia.

In 1997, the Czech Republic was offered membership in NATO and invited on to start membership talks with the European Union (E.U.). Economic problems overshadowed these long-awaited developments.

Denmark

KINGDOM OF DENMARK

National name: Kongeriget Danmark
Sovereign: Queen Margrethe II (1972)
Prime Minister: Poul Nyrup Rasmussen (1993)
Area: 16,631 sq mi. (43,070 sq km)[1]
Population (1998 est.): 5,333,617 (average annual rate of natural increase: 0.49%); birth rate: 12.2/1000; infant mortality rate: 5.2/1000; density per sq mi.: 321
Capital and largest city (1992): Copenhagen, 1,339,395. **Other large cities (1992):** Århus, 204,139; Odense, 140,886; Ålborg, 114,970. **Monetary unit:** Krone. **Language:** Danish, Faeroese, Greenlandic (an Inuit dialect), small German-speaking minority. **Ethnicity/Race:** Scandinavian, Eskimo, Faroese, German. **Religions:** Evangelical Lutheran 91%, other Protestant and Roman Catholic 2%, other 7%. **Literacy rate:** 99%
Economic summary: GDP/PPP (1996 est.): $118.2 billion; $22,700 per capita. **Real growth rate:** 2%. **Inflation:** 2.1%. **Unemployment:** 8.2%. **Arable land:** 60%. **Agriculture:** meat, dairy products, fish, grains. **Labor force:** 2,895,950; private services, 40%; government services, 30%; manufacturing and mining, 19%. **Industry:** processed foods, machinery and equipment, textiles. **Natural resources:** crude oil, natural gas, fish, salt, limestone. **Exports:** $47.6 billion (f.o.b., 1996): meat and dairy products, fish, industrial machinery, chemical products, transportation equipment. **Imports:** $42.4 billion (c.i.f., 1996 est.): machinery and equipment, transport equipment, petroleum, chemicals, grains and foodstuffs, textiles, paper. **Major trading partners:** Germany, Sweden, France, U.K., U.S., Norway, Japan.

1. Excluding Faeroe Islands and Greenland.

Geography Smallest of the Scandinavian countries (half the size of Maine), Denmark occupies the Jutland peninsula, a lowland area. The country also consists of several islands in the Baltic Sea; the two largest are Sjælland, the site of Copenhagen, and Fyn.

Government Denmark has been a constitutional monarchy since 1849. Legislative power is held jointly by the sovereign and parliament. The constitution of 1953 provides for a unicameral parliament called the Folketing, consisting of 179 popularly elected members (including two from the Faeroe Islands and two from Greenland) who serve for four years. The cabinet is presided over by the sovereign, who formally appoints the prime minister, who is responsible to parliament. The sovereign, Queen Margrethe II, became queen on Jan. 15, 1972. The nation's constitution was amended in 1953 to permit her to succeed her father in the absence of a male heir to the throne. (Denmark was ruled six centuries ago by Margrethe I, but she was never crowned queen since there was no female right of succession.)

History From 10,000 to 1500 B.C.E., the population of present-day Denmark progressed from an existence as hunters and fishers to a more settled lifestyle as agriculturists. Denmark emerged as a nation with establishment of the Norwegian dynasty of the Ynglinger in Jutland at the end of the 8th century. Danish mariners played a major role in the raids of the Vikings, or Norsemen, on Western Europe and particularly England. The country was Christianized by St. Ansgar and Harald Blaatand (Bluetooth)—the first Christian king—in the 10th century. Harald's son, Sweyn, conquered England in 1013. His son, Canute the Great, who reigned from 1014 to 1035, united Denmark, England, and Norway under his rule; the southern tip of Sweden was part of Denmark until the 17th century. On Canute's death, civil war tore the country until Waldemar I (1157–82) re-established Danish hegemony over the north.

In 1282, the nobles won the Great Charter, and Eric V was forced to share power with parliament and a Council of Nobles. Waldemar IV (1340–75) restored Danish power, checked only by the Hanseatic League of north German cities allied with ports from Holland to Poland. His daughter, Margrethe, in 1397 united under her rule Denmark, Norway, and Sweden. But Sweden later achieved autonomy and in 1523, under Gustavus I, independence. Denmark supported Napoleon, for which it was punished at the Congress of Vienna in 1815 by the loss of Norway to Sweden. In 1864, the Prussians, under Bismarck, and the Austrians made war on Denmark as an initial step in the unification of Germany. Denmark was neutral in World War I.

In 1940, Denmark was invaded by the Nazis. King Christian X reluctantly cautioned his fellow Danes to accept the occupation, but there was widespread resistance against the Nazis. In 1944, Iceland declared its independence from Denmark, ending a union that had existed since 1380. Liberated by British troops in May 1945, the country staged a fast recovery in both agriculture and manufacturing and was a leader in liberalizing trade. It joined the United Nations in 1945 and NATO in 1949. In 1948, Denmark granted home rule to the Faroe Islands, which had been part of Denmark since 1380. Greenland was officially incorporated into Denmark in 1953 and was granted home rule in 1979. Denmark became a member of the European Community (now the European Union) in 1973.

A referendum on the Maastricht accord, which paved the way for greater E.U. economic integration, in May 1993 passed with 56.8 percent of the vote but confidence in European monetary and political unity was on the wane. A Danish court in June 1997 upheld the constitutionality of the Maastricht treaty. Critics had charged that the treaty would surrender Denmark's sovereignty.

Outlying Territories of Denmark

Faeroe Islands

Status: Autonomous part of Denmark
Chief of State: Queen Margrethe II (1972)
High Commissioner: Bent Klinte (1992)
Prime Minister: Anfinn Kallsberg (1998)
Area: 540 sq mi. (1,399 sq km)
Population (1998 est.): 41,834 (average annual growth rate: –1.72%); birth rate: 13.1/1000; infant mortality rate: 10.5/1000; density per sq mi.: 78
Capital and largest city (1993 est.): Tórshavn, 16,100. **Monetary unit:** Faeroese krone. **Language:** Faeroese, Danish (both official). **Ethnicity/Race:** Scandinavian. **Literacy rate:** 99%
Economic summary: GDP/PPP (1996 est.): $800 million; $16,300 per capita. **Real growth rate.** 6%. **Inflation:** (1996 est.) 2.8%. **Unemployment:** (1996 est.) 11%. **Arable land:** 6%. **Agriculture:** sheep, vegetables. **Labor force:** (1995 est.) 20,345; largely engaged in fishing manufacturing, transportation and commerce. **Industry:** fish, ships, handicrafts. **Exports:** $362 million (f.o.b., 1995 est.): fish and fish products. **Imports:** $315.6 million (c.i.f., 1995 est.): machinery and transport equipment, foodstuffs, petroleum and petroleum products. **Major trading partners:** Denmark, U.S., U.K., Germany, Sweden, France, Norway.

This group of 18 islands, of which 17 are inhabited, are located in the North Atlantic about 200 miles (322 km) northwest of the Shetland Islands. They were settled by the Vikings, the ancestors of the modern-day Faeroese, in the 8th century. The Faeroese language is derived from Old Norse. The islands joined Denmark in 1386 and have been part of the Danish kingdom ever since. The islands were occupied by British troops during World War II, because of Germany's occupation of Denmark. The Faeroes have had home rule, under Danish authority, since 1948.

Greenland

Status: Autonomous part of Denmark
Chief of State: Queen Margrethe II (1972)
High Commissioner: Torben Hede Pedersen (1993)
Premier: Jonathan Motzfeldt (1997)
Area: 840,000 sq mi. (incl. 708,069 sq mi. covered by icecap) (2,175,600 sq km)
Population (1997 est.): 59,309 (growth rate: 0.90%); birth rate: 15.8/1000; infant mortality rate: 21.3/1000; density per sq mi.: 0.1.
Capital and largest city (1995 est.): Godthaab, 12,723. **Monetary unit:** Krone. **Ethnicity/Race:** Greenlander 87% (Eskimos and Greenland-born whites), Danish and other 13%. **Literacy rate:** 99%

Economic summary: GNP: (purchasing power parity, 1996 est.): $892 million; $15,500 per capita. **Real growth rate:** n.a. **Inflation:** (1995 est.) 1.8%. **Unemployment:** (1995 est.) 10.5%. **Arable land:** 0%. **Agriculture:** hay, sheep, garden produce. **Labor force:** 22,800; largely engaged in fishing, hunting, sheep breeding. **Industry:** fish processing, lead and zinc processing, handicrafts. **Natural resources:** metals, cryolite, iron ore, coal, uranium, fish. **Exports:** $363.4 million (f.o.b., 1995): fish and fish products, metallic ores and concentrates. **Imports:** $421 million (c.i.f., 1995 est.): petroleum and petroleum products, machinery and transport equipment, foodstuffs, manufactured goods. **Major trading partners:** Denmark, U.S., Germany, Sweden, Japan, Norway.

The Inuit are believed to have crossed from North America to northwest Greenland, the world's largest island, using the islands of the Canadian Arctic as stepping stones in a series of migrations that stretched from 4000 B.C.E. to C.E. 1000. Several distinct cultures are known, including the Sarqaq (c. 1400–700 B.C.E.), Dorset (c. 800 B.C.E.–C.E. 1300), and such others as the Dundas (Thule) and Inugsuk. Greenland was colonized in C.E. 985–86 by Eric the Red. The Norse settlements declined in the 14th century, however, mainly as a result of a cooling in Greenland's climate, and in the 15th century they became extinct. In 1721, Greenland was re-colonized by the Royal Greenland Trading Company of Denmark and the coast was closed to foreign trade until 1950.

Greenland was under U.S. protection during World War II, but maintained Danish sovereignty. A definitive agreement for the joint defense of Greenland within the framework of NATO was signed in 1951. A large U.S. air base at Thule in the far north was completed in 1953. Under 1953 amendments to the Danish constitution, Greenland became part of Denmark, with two representatives in the Danish Folketing. On May 1, 1979, Greenland gained home rule, with its own local parliament (Landsting). In Feb. 1982, Greenlanders voted to withdraw from the European Union, which they had joined as part of Denmark in 1973. Danish Premier Anker Jørgensen said he would support the request, but with reluctance.

Djibouti

REPUBLIC OF DJIBOUTI

National name: Jumhouriyya Djibouti
President: Hassan Gouled Aptidon (1977)
Prime Minister: Barkat Gourad Hamadou (1978)
Area: 8,878 sq mi. (22,000 sq km)
Population (1998 est.): 440,727 (average annual rate of natural increase: 1.51%); birth rate: 41.8/1000; infant mortality rate: 102.4/1000; density per sq mi.: 50
Capital (1992 est.): Djibouti, 395,000. **Monetary unit:** Djibouti franc. **Languages:** Arabic, French, Afar, Somali. **Ethnicity/Race:** Somali 60%, Afar 35%, French, Arab, Ethiopian, and Italian 5%. **Religions:** Muslim, 94%; Christian, 6%. **Literacy rate:** 48%
Economic summary: GDP/PPP (1995 est.): $500 million; $1,200 per capita. **Real growth rate:** –3.1%. **Inflation:** 4.9% (1995 est.). **Unemployment:** 40–50% (1996 est.). **Arable land:** 0%. **Agriculture:** goats, sheep, camels. **Labor force:** 282,000; agriculture, 75%; industry, 11%; services, 14% (1991 est.). **Industry:** small-scale enterprises such as dairy products and mineral-water bottling. Djibouti is a free port. **Natural resources:** salt, limestone, gypsum, perlite, diatoms, geothermal energy. **Exports:** $184 million (f.o.b., est. 1994): hides, skins, livestock. **Imports:** $384 million (f.o.b., 1994 est.): foodstuffs, machinery, transport equipment, consumer goods. **Major trading partners:** Ethiopia, Somalia, the Republic of Yemen, Saudi Arabia.

Geography Djibouti lies in northeastern Africa on the Gulf of Aden at the southern entrance to the Red Sea. It borders on Ethiopia, Eritrea, and Somalia. The country, the size of Massachusetts, is mainly a stony desert, with scattered plateaus and highlands.

Government A republic with a unicameral legislature.

History Ablé immigrants from Arabia migrated to what is now Djibouti in about the 3rd century B.C.E. Their descendants are the Afars, one of the two main ethnic groups that make up Djibouti today. Somali Issas arrived thereafter. Islam came to the region in C.E. 825.

Djibouti was acquired by France between 1843 and 1886 by treaties with the Somali sultans. Small, arid, and sparsely populated, it is important chiefly because of the capital city's port, the terminal of the Djibouti–Addis Ababa railway that carries 60% of Ethiopia's foreign trade. Originally known as French Somaliland, the colony voted in 1958 and 1967 to remain under French rule. It was renamed the Territory of the Afars and Issas in 1967 and took the name of its capital city on attaining independence. On June 27, 1977, France transferred sovereignty to the new nation of Djibouti. On Sept. 4, 1992, voters approved in referendum a new multiparty constitution. The last presidential election took place May 7, 1993, and President Aptidon was re-elected for another six-year term

In 1991 conflict between the Afars and the Issa-dominated government erupted and the continued warfare has ravaged the country.

Dominica

COMMONWEALTH OF DOMINICA

President: Crispin Sorhaindo (1993)
Prime Minister: Edison James (1995)
Area: 290 sq mi. (750 sq km)
Population: (1998 est.): 65,777 (average annual rate of natural increase: –1.33%); birth rate: 17.4/1000; infant mortality rate: 9/1000; density per sq mi.: 227
Capital and largest city (1991): Roseau, 15,853. **Monetary unit:** East Caribbean dollar. **Languages:** English and French patois. **Ethnicity/Race:** black, Carib Indians. **Religions:** Roman Catholic, 77%; Protestant, 15%. **Literacy rate:** 94%
Economic summary: GDP/PPP (1995 est.): $208 million; $2,500 per capita. **Real growth rate:** 1.7%. **Inflation:** 1.2%. **Unemployment:** 15% (1992 est.). **Arable land:** 9%. **Agriculture:** bananas, citrus fruits, coconuts, plantains. **Labor force:** 25,000; agriculture, 40%; industry and commerce. 32%; services, 28% (1984 est.). **Industry:** agricultural processing; tourism. **Exports:** $40 million (f.o.b., 1996): bananas, soap, bay oil, vegetables, grapefruit, oranges. **Imports:** $122 million (f.o.b., 1996): manufactured goods, machinery and equipment, food, chemicals. **Major trading partners:** U.K., Caribbean countries, U.S., Italy, Canada. **Member of Commonwealth of Nations**

Geography Dominica is a mountainous island of volcanic origin of the Lesser Antilles in the Caribbean south of Guadeloupe and north of Martinique.

Government Dominica is a republic governed in accordance with the 1978 constitution, with a president elected by the House of Assembly as head of state and a prime minister appointed by the president on the advice of the Assembly. The United Workers Party is led by Prime Minister Edison James, other major parties include The Freedom Party and the United Dominica Labor Party.

History Visited by Columbus in 1493, Dominica was claimed by Britain and France until 1763, when it was formally ceded to Britain. Dominica, along with other Windward Isles, became a self-governing member of the West Indies Associated States in free association with Britain in 1967.

Dissatisfaction over the slow pace of reconstruction after Hurricane David devastated the island in Sept. 1979 brought a landslide victory for the Freedom Party in July 1980. The vote gave the prime ministership to Mary Eugenia Charles, a strong advocate of free enterprise. The Freedom Party won again in 1985 elections, giving Charles a second five-year term as prime minister. She and her party won a third term in elections on May 28, 1990, and the government pursued a policy of divesting itself of state enterprises.

The opposition United Workers' Party captured the general election of June 1995. The new government planned to privatize numerous enterprises. Prime Minister James reshuffled his cabinet in June 1996, taking on in addition to his other duties those of the Ministry of Finance. In 1997 Dominica became the first Caribbean country to participate in the work of Green Globe, aiming to make it a model eco-tourism destination.

Dominican Republic

National name: República Dominicana
President: Leonel Fernández Reyna (1996)
Area: 18,704 sq mi. (48,730 sq km)
Population (1998 est.): 7,998,766 (average annual rate of natural increase: 1.63%); birth rate: 26.4/1000; infant mortality rate: 44.3/1000; density per sq mi.: 428
Capital and largest city (1993): Santo Domingo, 2,100,000. **Other large city (1993):** Santiago de los Caballeros, 690,000. **Monetary unit:** Peso. **Language:** Spanish, English widely spoken. **Ethnicity/Race:** white 16%, black 11%, mixed 73%. **Religion:** 90% Roman Catholic. **Literacy rate:** 84%
Economic summary: GDP/PPP (1996 est.): $29.8 billion; $3,670 per capita. **Real growth rate:** 7.3%. **Inflation:** 12.5% (1996 est.). **Unemployment:** 30%. **Arable land:** 21%. **Agriculture:** sugar cane, coffee, cotton, cocoa, tobacco, beef, fruit and vegetables. Agriculture accounts for 13% of gross domestic product. **Labor force** (1991 est.), 2.3–2.6 million; agriculture, 50%; services and government, 32%; industry, 18%. **Industry:** tourism, sugar processing, ferronickel and gold mining, textiles, cement, tobacco. **Natural resources:** nickel, bauxite, gold, silver. **Exports:** $3.1 billion (f.o.b., 1996): sugar, coffee, cocoa, gold, ferronickel, silver, meats, fruits and vegetables. **Imports:** $5.3 billion (f.o.b., 1996 est.): foodstuffs, petroleum, cotton and fabrics, chemicals and pharmaceuticals. **Major trading partners:** U.S., including Puerto Rico, E.U.

Geography The Dominican Republic in the West Indies occupies the eastern two-thirds of the island of Hispaniola, which it shares with Haiti. Its area equals that of Vermont and New Hampshire combined. It is crossed from northwest to southeast by a mountain range called the Cordillera Central which includes Duarte Peak, which at 10,417 feet (3,175 m) is the highest point in the West Indies. The country has fertile, well-watered land in the north and east, where nearly two thirds of the population lives. The southwest part is arid and has poor soil, except around Santo Domingo.

Government The president is elected by direct vote every four years. Legislative powers rest with a Senate and a Chamber of Deputies, both elected by direct vote, also for four years. The Senate has 30 members, one representing each province and the national district, while the Chamber of Deputies has 120 members chosen on the basis of population. All citizens must vote when they reach 18 years of age, or even earlier if they are married.

History The Dominican Republic was visited by Columbus in 1492. He named it La Española, and his son, Diego, was its first viceroy. The capital, Santo Domingo, founded in 1496, is the oldest European settlement in the Western Hemisphere. Spain ceded the colony to France in 1795, and Haitian blacks under Toussaint L'Ouverture conquered it in 1801. In 1808 the people revolted and captured Santo Domingo the next year, setting up the first republic. Spain regained title to the colony in 1814. In 1821 the people overthrew Spanish rule, but in 1822 they were reconquered by the Haitians. They revolted again in 1844, threw out the Haitians, and established the Dominican Republic, headed by Pedro Santana. Uprisings and Haitian attacks led Santana to make the country a province of Spain from 1861 to 1865. The U.S. Senate refused to ratify a treaty of annexation. Disorder continued until the dictatorship of Ulíses Heureaux; in 1916, when disorder broke out again, the U.S. sent in a contingent of marines, who remained until 1934.

A sergeant in the Dominican army trained by the marines, Rafaél Leonides Trujillo Molina, overthrew Horacio Vásquez in 1930 and established a dictatorship that lasted until his assassination 31 years later. Leftists rebelled April 24, 1965, and U.S. President Lyndon Johnson sent in marines and troops. After a cease-fire on May 6, a compromise installed Hector Garcia-Godoy as provisional president. Joaquin Balaguer won in free elections in 1966 against Bosch, and a peacekeeping force of 9,000 U.S. troops and 2,000 from other countries withdrew. Balaguer restored political and economic stability.

In 1978, the army suspended the counting of ballots when Balaguer trailed in a fourth-term bid. After a warning from President Jimmy Carter, however, Balaguer accepted the victory of Antonio Guzmán of the opposition Dominican Revolutionary Party. Salvador Jorge Blanco of the Dominican Revolutionary Party was elected president on May 16, 1982, defeating Balaguer and Bosch. Balaguer was elected president in May 1986 and aimed economic policy at diversifying the economy.

In a bitter presidential contest Balaguer maintained a slim lead over his opponent in the May 1994 election before election officials stopped releasing tallies. The opposition charged widespread fraud, but the crisis eased when a constitutional amendment gave the current president a two-year term with new elections scheduled for May 1996. In the June runoff, U.S.-raised Leonel Fernandez secured more than 51% of the vote through an alliance with Balaguer. The first item on the president's agenda in August 1996 was the partial sale of a number of state-owned enterprises. As of 1997, investors are allowed to own a maximum of 50% of the stock in the companies. Increased employment of Haitian sugarcane cutters led to a wave of anti-Haitian feeling, and more than 15,000 Haitians were deported in 1996 and 1997 before the two countries reached an agreement to halt large-scale repatriations and respect human rights.

Ecuador

REPUBLIC OF ECUADOR

National name: República del Ecuador
President: Jamil Mahuad (1998)
Area: 106,822[1] sq mi (283,560 sq km)
Population (1998 est.): 12,336,572 (average annual rate of natural increase: 1.86%); birth rate: 23.2/1000; infant mortality rate: 32.1/1000; density per sq mi.: 116
Capital: Quito. **Largest cities (1992):** Guayaquil, 1,475,118; Quito, 1,094,318; Cuenca, 195,738. **Monetary unit:** Sucre. **Languages:** Spanish (by 90% of population), Quéchua. **Ethnicity/Race:** mestizo (mixed Indian and Spanish) 55%, Indian 25%, Spanish 10%, black 10%. **Religion:** Roman Catholic, 95%. **Literacy rate:** 90%
Economic summary: GDP/PPP (1996 est.): $47 billion; $4,100 per capita. **Real growth rate:** 2%. **Inflation:** 26%. **Unemployment:** 8.5% (1996 est.). **Arable land:** 6%. **Agriculture:** bananas, cocoa, coffee, sugar cane, shrimp, manioc, plantains, potatoes, rice. **Labor force** (1996 est.), 3.4 million; agriculture, 29%; manufacturing, 18%; services, 38%. **Industry:** food processing, textiles, chemicals, fishing, timber, petroleum. **Exports:** $4.9 billion (f.o.b., 1996): petroleum, coffee, bananas, cocoa products, shrimp, fish products. **Imports:** $3.7 billion (c.i.f., 1995): transport equipment, vehicles, machinery, chemicals. **Major trading partners:** U.S., Latin America, E.U., Caribbean, Japan.

1. Does not include area under dispute with Peru.

Geography Ecuador, about equal in area to Nevada, is in the northwest part of South America fronting on the Pacific. To the north is Colombia and to the east and south is Peru. Two high and parallel ranges of the Andes, traversing the country from north to south, are topped by tall volcanic peaks. The highest is Chimborazo at 20,577 feet (6,272 m). The Galápagos Islands (or Colón Archipelago; 3,029 sq mi.; 7,845 sq km), in the Pacific Ocean about 600 miles (966 km) west of the South American mainland, became part of Ecuador in 1832.

Government A 1979 constitution returned Ecuador to civilian government after eight years of military rule. The president is elected to a single term of four years and the 71-member unicameral National Congress' members are elected for either two or four-year terms.

History The tribes in the northern highlands of Ecuador formed the kingdom of Quito around C.E. 1000. It was absorbed, by conquest and marriage, into the Inca Empire. Pizarro conquered the land in 1532, and through the 17th century a thriving colony was built by exploitation of the Indians. The first revolt against Spain occurred in 1809. Ecuador then joined Venezuela, Colombia, and Panama in a confederacy known as Greater Colombia.

On the collapse of this union in 1830, Ecuador became independent. Revolts and dictatorships followed; it had 48 presidents during the first 131 years of the republic. Conservatives ruled until the revolution of 1895 ushered in nearly a half century of Radical Liberal rule, during which the church was disestablished and freedom of worship, speech, and press was introduced. Peru invaded Ecuador in 1941 and was able to seize a large tract of Ecuadorian territory in the disputed Amazonian area; the uneasy situation flared up again in 1981.

José María Velasco Ibarra was elected president five times between 1944 and 1972 but completed only one term; little progress in social and economic affairs were made during this tumultuous period. In 1988, Rodrigo Borja was elected president, confirming a leftward shift in the government and promising smoother executive-legislative relations. Blamed for economic conditions, the governing Social Democrats were defeated in elections of May 1992 by right-wing parties promising free-market reforms. On charges of mental incapacity, Congress voted in Feb. 1997 to remove President Bucaram, who refused to yield, and declared its leader Fabián Alarcón president. In May a national referendum overwhelmingly approved the interim presidency and constitution reform is imminent.

Egypt

ARAB REPUBLIC OF EGYPT

President: Hosni Mubarak (1981)
Prime Minister: Kamal Ganzouri (1996)
Area: 386,900 sq. mi. (1,001,450 sq km)
Population (1998 est.): 66,050,004 (average annual rate of natural increase: 1.86%); birth rate: 27.3/1000; infant mortality rate: 69.2/1000; density per sq mi.: 171
Capital and largest city : Cairo: city proper (1994 est.) 6,849,000; metro. area (1996 est.) 9,900,000. **Other large cities (1992 est.):** Alexandria, 3,382,000; Giza, 2,144,000; Shubra el Khema, 834,000; El Mahalla el Kubra, 408,000. **Monetary unit:** Egyptian pound. **Language:** Arabic. **Ethnicity/Race:** Eastern Hamitic stock (Egyptians, Bedouins, and Berbers) 99%, Greek, Nubian, Armenian, other European (primarily Italian and French) 1%. **Religions:** Islam, 94%; Christian (mostly Coptic), 6%. **Literacy rate:** 48%
Economic summary: GDP/PPP (1996 est.): $183.9 billion; $2,900 per capita. **Real growth rate** 4.9%. **Inflation:** 7.3%. **Unemployment:** 9.4% (FY95/96 official estimate). **Arable land:** 2%. **Agriculture:** cotton, wheat, rice, corn, beans. **Labor force:** 17.4 million; agriculture, 40%; government, public sector enterprises, and armed forces. 38%; privately owned services and manufacturing, 22%. **Industry:** textiles, food processing, tourism, chemicals, petroleum, construction, cement, metals. **Natural resources:** crude oil, natural gas, iron ore, phosphates, manganese, limestone, gypsum, talc, asbestos, lead, zinc. **Exports:** $4.6 billion (f.o.b., FY95/96 est.): cotton, petroleum, yarn, textiles, metal products, chemicals. **Imports:** $13.8 billion (c.i.f., FY95/96 est.): foodstuffs, machinery, fertilizers, woods, durable consumer goods, capital goods. **Major trading partners:** U.S., E.U., Japan, Eastern Europe.

Geography Egypt, at the northeast corner of Africa on the Mediterranean Sea, is bordered on the west by Libya, on the south by the Sudan, and on the east by the Red Sea and Israel. It is nearly one and one-half times the size of Texas. Egypt is divided into two unequal, extremely arid regions by the landscape's dominant feature, the northward-flowing Nile River. The Nile starts 100 miles (161 km) south of the Mediterranean and fans out to a sea front of 155 miles between the cities of Alexandria and Port Said.

Government Executive power is held by the president, who is elected every six years and appoints one or more vice presidents, the prime minister, the Cabinet, and 10 members of the 454-member unicameral legislature, the People's Assembly. The National Democratic Party, led by President Hosni Mubarak, is the dominant political party. Elections in Nov. 1990 confirmed its huge majority. There are also 14 opposition parties and some independents in the Parliament.

History Egyptian history dates back to about 4000 B.C.E., when the kingdoms of upper and lower Egypt, already highly civilized, were united. Egypt's "Golden Age" coincided with the 18th and 19th dynasties (16th to 13th centuries B.C.E.), during which the empire was established. Persia conquered Egypt in 525 B.C.E., Alexander the Great subdued it in 332 B.C.E., and then the dynasty of the Ptolemies ruled the land until 30 B.C.E., when Cleopatra, last of the line, committed suicide and Egypt became a Roman, then Byzantine, province. Arab caliphs ruled Egypt from 641 until 1517, when the Turks took it for their Ottoman Empire.

Napoleon's armies occupied the country from 1798 to 1801. In 1805, Mohammed Ali, leader of a band of Albanian soldiers, became Pasha of Egypt. After completion of the Suez Canal in 1869, the French and British took increasing interest in Egypt. British troops occupied Egypt in 1882, and British resident agents became its actual administrators, though it remained under nominal Turkish sovereignty. In 1914, this fiction was ended, and Egypt became a protectorate of Britain.

Egyptian nationalism forced Britain to declare Egypt an independent, sovereign state on Feb. 28, 1922, although the British reserved rights for the protection of the Suez Canal and the defense of Egypt. In 1936, by an Anglo-Egyptian treaty of alliance, all British troops and officials were to be withdrawn, except from the Suez Canal Zone. When World War II started, Egypt remained neutral. British imperial troops finally ended the Nazi threat to Suez in 1942 in the battle of El Alamein, west of Alexandria. In 1951, Egypt abrogated the 1936 treaty and the 1899 Anglo-Egyptian condominium of the Sudan. Rioting and attacks on British troops in the Suez Canal Zone followed, reaching a climax in Jan. 1952. The army, led by Gen. Mohammed Naguib, seized power on July 23, 1952. Three days later, King Farouk abdicated in favor of his infant son. The monarchy was abolished and a republic proclaimed on June 18, 1953, with Naguib holding the posts of provisional president and premier. He relinquished the latter in 1954 to Gamal Abdel Nasser, leader of the ruling military junta. Naguib was deposed seven months later and Nasser confirmed as president in a referendum on June 23, 1956.

Nasser's policies embroiled his country in continual conflict. In 1956, the U.S. and Britain withdrew their pledges of financial aid for the building of the Aswan High Dam. In response, Nasser nationalized the Suez Canal and expelled British oil and embassy officials. Israel, barred from the canal and exasperated by terrorist raids, invaded the Gaza Strip and the Sinai Peninsula. Britain and France, after demanding Egyptian evacuation of the canal zone, attacked Egypt on Oct. 31, 1956. Worldwide pressure forced Britain, France, and Israel to halt the hostilities. A U.N. emergency force occupied the canal zone, and all troops were evacuated in the spring of 1957.

On June 5, 1967, Israel invaded the Sinai Peninsula, the East Bank of the Jordan River, and the zone around the Gulf of Aqaba. A U.N. ceasefire on June 10 saved the Arabs from complete rout. Nasser declared the 1967 cease-fire void along the canal in April 1969 and began a war of attrition. The U.S. peace plan of June 19, 1970, resulted in Egypt's agreement to reinstate the cease-fire for at least three months, (from August) and to accept Israel's existence within "recognized and secure" frontiers that might emerge from U.N.-mediated talks. In return, Israel accepted the principle of withdrawing from occupied territories. On Sept. 28, 1970, Nasser died at 52 of a heart attack. The new president was Anwar el-Sadat, an associate of Nasser and a former newspaper editor.

In July 1972, Sadat ordered the expulsion of Soviet "advisers and experts" from Egypt because the Russians had not provided the sophisticated weapons he felt were needed to retake territory lost to Israel in 1967. The fourth Arab-Israeli war broke out Oct. 6, 1973, while Israelis were commemorating Yom Kippur, the Jewish high holy day. Egypt swept deep into the Sinai, while Syria strove to throw Israel off the Golan Heights. A U.N.-sponsored truce was accepted on Oct. 22. In Jan. 1974, both sides agreed to a settlement negotiated by U.S. Secretary of State Henry A. Kissinger that gave Egypt a narrow strip along the entire Sinai bank of the Suez Canal. In June, President Nixon made the first visit by a U.S. President to Egypt and full diplomatic relations were established. The Suez Canal was cleared and reopened on June 5, 1975.

In the most audacious act of his career, Sadat flew to Jerusalem at the invitation of Prime Minister Menachem Begin and pleaded before Israel's Knesset on Nov. 20, 1977, for a permanent peace settlement. The Arab world reacted with fury—only Morocco, Tunisia, Sudan, and Oman approved. Egypt and Israel signed a formal peace treaty on March 26, 1979. The pact ended 30 years of war and established diplomatic and commercial relations.

Egyptian and Israeli officials met in the Sinai desert on April 26, 1979, to implement the peace treaty calling for the phased withdrawal of occupation forces from the peninsula. By mid-1980, two thirds of the Sinai was transferred, but progress here was not matched elsewhere—the negotiation of Arab autonomy in the Gaza Strip and the West Bank remained stymied. Sadat halted further talks in August 1980 because of continued Israeli settlement of the West Bank. On Oct. 6, 1981, Sadat was assassinated by extremist Muslim soldiers at a parade in Cairo. Vice President Hosni Mubarak, a former Air Force chief of staff, succeeded him. Although feared unrest in Egypt did not occur in the wake of the assassination, and Israel completed the return of the Sinai to Egyptian control on April 25, 1982, Mubarak was unable to revive the autonomy talks. Israel's invasion of Lebanon in June imposed a new strain on him, and brought a marked cooling in Egyptian-Israeli relations, but not a disavowal of the peace treaty.

While President Mubarak's stand during the Persian Gulf War won wide praise in the West, domestically this position proved far less popular. A presidential referendum in Oct. 1993 supported Mubarak's bid for a third term although only a third of the population registered to vote. The government has concentrated much of its time and attention in recent years combating Islamic extremism, particularly attacks against Copts (Egyptian Christians). In Nov. 1995's elections, the ruling National Democratic Party won 416 seats and the opposition 13, with independents taking the remaining seats. The People's Assembly in Feb. 1997 assented to the president's decree extending the state of emergency, introduced with the assassination of Anwar Sadat, into the year 2000.

Suez Canal. The Suez Canal, in Egyptian territory between the Arabian desert and the Sinai Peninsula, is an artificial waterway about 100 miles (161 km) long between Port Said on the Mediterranean and Suez on the Red Sea. Construction work, directed by the French engineer Ferdinand de Lesseps, was begun April 25, 1859, and the Canal was opened Nov. 17, 1869. The cost was 432,807,882 francs. The concession was held by an Egyptian joint stock company, Compagnie Universelle du Canal Maritime de Suez, in which the British government held 353,504 out of a total of 800,000 shares. The concession was to expire Nov. 17, 1968, but the company was nationalized July 26, 1956, by unilateral action of the Egyptian government. The Canal was closed in June 1967 after the Arab-Israeli conflict. With the help of the U.S. Navy, work was begun on clearing the Canal in 1974, after the cease-fire ending the Arab-Israeli war. It was reopened to traffic June 5, 1975 and an average of 55 ships use it daily.

El Salvador

REPUBLIC OF EL SALVADOR

National name: República de El Salvador
President: Armando Calderón Sol (1994)
Area: 8,260 sq mi. (21,040 sq km)
Population (1998 est.): 5,752,067 (average annual rate of natural increase: 1.57%); birth rate: 26.7/1000; infant mortality rate: 29.1/1000; density per sq mi.: 696
Capital and largest city (1993 est.): San Salvador, 972,810. **Other large cities (1993 est.):** Santa Ana, 208,322; San Miguel, 161,156; Zacatecoluca, 81,035. **Monetary unit:** Colón. **Language:** Spanish. **Ethnicity/Race:** mestizo 94%, Indian 5%, white 1%. **Religion:** Roman Catholic. **Literacy rate:** 73%
Economic summary: GDP/PPP (1996 est.): $12.2 billion; $2,080 per capita. **Real growth rate:** 3%. **Inflation:** 7.4%. **Unemployment:** 7.6% (1993). **Arable land:** 27%. **Agriculture:** coffee, cotton, corn, sugar, rice, sorghum. **Labor force:** 2.2 million (1996 est.); agriculture, 40%; commerce, 16%; manufacturing, 15%; government, 13%; financial services, 9%. **Industry:** processed foods, clothing and textiles, petroleum products. **Natural resources:** hydro- and geothermal power, crude oil. **Exports:** $1.8 billion (f.o.b., 1996 est.): coffee, cotton, sugar, shrimp. **Imports:** $3.2 billion (c.i.f., 1996 est.): raw materials, consumer goods, capital goods. **Major trading partners:** U.S., Guatemala, Germany, Mexico, Venezuela, Costa Rica.

Geography Situated on the Pacific coast of Central America, El Salvador has Guatemala to the west and Honduras to the north and east. It is the smallest of the Central American countries, its area equal to that of Massachusetts, and the only one without an Atlantic coastline.

Most of the country is a fertile volcanic plateau about 2,000 feet (607 m) high. Much of the previously forested lowland area has been cleared for agriculture and pasture. There are some active volcanoes and many scenic crater lakes.

Government In accordance with the 1983 constitution, the president is elected for a nonrenewable, five-year term, and legislative power is in a unicameral 84-member National Assembly elected for three-year terms by universal suffrage and proportional representation.

History When the Spaniards reached El Salvador in 1524, they found the Pipil Indians and their kingdom of Cuzcatlán situated in the western half of the country. Pedro de Alvarado, a lieutenant of Cortés, conquered El Salvador in 1525.

El Salvador, with the other countries of Central America, declared its independence from Spain on Sept. 15, 1821, and was part of a federation of Central American states until that union was dissolved in 1838. Its independent career for decades thereafter was marked by numerous revolutions and wars against other Central American republics. From 1931 to 1979 El Salvador was ruled by a series of military dictatorships.

On Oct. 15, 1979, a junta deposed the president, Gen. Carlos Humberto Romero, seeking to halt increasingly violent clashes between leftist and rightist forces. On Dec. 4, 1980, three American nuns and an American lay worker were killed in an ambush near San Salvador, causing the Carter administration to suspend all aid pending an investigation.

By that time, leftist anti-government guerrilla units had merged into a single organization, the Farabundo Martí National Liberation Front (FMLN), and announced the opening of a "final offensive" in Jan. 1981. The offensive was by no means final, however, and the fortunes of the guerrilla army would ebb and flow throughout the balance of the country's civil war.

The naming of José Napoleón Duarte, a moderate civilian, as head of the governing junta brought a resumption of U.S. aid. In an election closely monitored by U.S. and other foreign observers, Duarte was elected president in May 1984.

Duarte's Christian Democratic Party scored an unexpected electoral triumph in national legislative and municipal elections held in March 1985, a winning majority in the new National Assembly. The civil war against anti-government guerrillas continued to be waged mainly in the countryside. The decisive victory of Alfredo Cristiani, the ARENA candidate for president, gave the right-wing party effective control of the country, given its political control of most of the municipalities.

On Jan. 16, 1992, the government signed a peace treaty with the guerrilla forces formally ending the 12-year civil war that had claimed 75,000 lives. The candidate of the right-wing ARENA party, Calderón Sol, won the presidential election of March 1994 on a pledge to continue the peace process. Elections for the National Assembly in March 1997 denied a majority to either of the two major parties with ARENA and the National Liberation effectively splitting the Assembly.

Equatorial Guinea

REPUBLIC OF EQUATORIAL GUINEA

National name: Républica de Guinea Ecuatorial
President: Col. Teodoro Obiang Nguema Mbasogo (1979)
Prime Minister: Angel Serafin Seriche Dougan (1996)
Area: 10,830 sq mi. (28,050 sq km)
Population (1998 est.): 454,001 (average annual rate of natural increase: 2.56%); birth rate: 38.9/1000; infant mortality rate: 93.5/1000; density per sq mi.: 42
Capital and largest city (1983): Malabo, 30,418. **Monetary unit:** CFA Franc. **Languages:** Spanish (official), French (2nd official) pidgin English, Fang, Bubi, Creole. **Ethnicity/Race:** Bioko (primarily Bubi, some Fernandinos), Rio Muni (primarily Fang), Europeans less than 1,000, mostly Spanish. **Religions:** Roman Catholic, Protestant, traditional. **Literacy rate:** 50%
Economic summary: GDP/PPP (1996 est.): $328 million; $800 per capita. **Real growth rate:** 11.2% (1995 est.). **Inflation:** 10.9%. **Unemployment:** n.a. **Arable land:** 5%. **Products:** cocoa, wood, coffee, rice, yams. **Labor force:** 4.228 million (1993 est.); agriculture, 70%; transport and services, 22%; industry, 8%. **Natural resources:** wood, crude oil. **Exports:** $83.5 million (f.o.b., 1995 est.): cocoa, wood, coffee. **Imports:** $52.3 million (f.o.b., 1995 est.): petroleum, foodstuffs, textiles, machinery. **Major trading partners:** South Africa, U.K., Germany, and Japan.

Geography Equatorial Guinea, formerly Spanish Guinea, consists of Rio Muni (10,045 sq mi.; 26,117 sq km), on the western coast of Africa, and several islands in the Gulf of Guinea, the largest of which is Bioko (formerly Fernando Po) (785 sq mi.; 2,033 sq km). The other islands are Annobón, Corisco, Elobey Grande, and Elobey Chico. The total area is twice that of Connecticut.

Government A president with a 17-member Supreme Military Council following a 1979 coup.

History The mainland was originally inhabited by Pygmies. The Fang and Bubi migrated there in the 17th century and to the main island of Fernando Po (now called Bioko) in the 19th century. In the eighteenth century, the Portuguese ceded land to the Spanish that included Equatorial Guinea. From 1827 to 1844, Britain administered Fernando Po, but it was then reclaimed by Spain. Río Muni, the mainland, was not occupied by the Spanish until 1926. Spanish Guinea, as it was then called, gained independence from Spain on Oct. 12, 1968. It is Africa's only Spanish-speaking country.

From the outset, President Francisco Macías Nguema, considered the father of independence, began a brutal reign, destroying the economy of the fledgling country and abusing human rights. Calling himself the "Unique Miracle," Nguema is considered one of the worst despots in African history. In 1971, the U.S. State Department reported that his regime was "characterized by abandonment of all government functions except internal security, which was accomplished by terror; this led to the death or exile of up to one-third of the population."

On Aug. 3, 1979, Nguema was overthrown and executed by his nephew, Lieut. Col. Teodoro Obiang Nguema Mbasogo. Obiang has been gradually modernizing the country, but has retained many of his uncle's dictatorial practices, including the amassing of personal wealth by siphoning it from the public coffers. A recent petroleum bonanza promises to boost the country's standard of living, but the president's family is believed to control the industry.

Eritrea

President: Isaias Afwerki (1993)
Area: 45,754 sq mi. (121,320 sq km)
Population (1998 est.): 3,842,436 (of which 0.5 million are refugees awaiting repatriation). Average annual rate of natural increase: 3.39%; birth rate: 42.5/1000; infant mortality rate: 78.5/1000; density per sq mi.: 84
Capital and largest city (1993): Asmara, 400,000. Other major cities: the ports of Massawa and Assab. **Monetary unit:** Birr. **Languages:** Afar, Bilen, Kunama, Nara, Arabic, Tobedawi, Saho, Tigre, Tigrinya. **Ethnicity/Race:** ethnic Tigrinya 50%, Tigre and Kunama 40%, Afar 4%, Saho (Red Sea coast dwellers) 3%. **Religions:** Islam and Eritrean Orthodox Christianity. **Literacy rate:** 20%
Economic summary: GDP/PPP (1995 est.): $2 billion; $570 per capita. **Real growth rate:** 3.9%. **Inflation:** 8%. **Unemployment:** n.a. **Labor force:** n.a. The economy and infrastructure were severely damaged by the war for independence and natural disasters. Eritrea has inherited the entire coastline of Ethiopia and has long-term prospects for revenues from the development of offshore oil, offshore fishing, and tourism. Major manufacturing industries are textiles, leather, food products, beverages. Most Eritreans are employed in agriculture and important crops are cotton, wheat, and coffee. Major mineral resources are salt and copper. **Exports:** $81 million (1995 est.): livestock, sorghum, textiles. **Imports:** $404 million (1995 est.): processed goods, machinery, petroleum products. Important trading partners: Ethiopia, Saudi Arabia, Yemen, Italy, Germany, U.K.

Geography Eritrea was formerly the northernmost province of Ethiopia and is about the size of Indiana. Much of the country is mountainous. Its narrow Red Sea coastal plain is one of the hottest and driest places in Africa. The cooler central highlands have fertile valleys that support agriculture. Eritrea is bordered by the Sudan on the north and west, the Red Sea on the north and east, and Ethiopia and Djibouti on the south.

Government A transitional government committed to a democratic system.

History Eritrea was part of the first Ethiopian kingdom of Askum until its decline in the 8th century C.E. It came under control of the Ottoman Empire in the 16th century, and later the Egyptians. The Italians captured the coastal areas in 1885, and the Treaty of Uccialli (May 2, 1889) gave Italy sovereignty over part of Eritrea. The Italians named their colony after the Roman name for the Red Sea—*Mare Erythraeum*—and ruled it up until World War II.

The British captured Eritrea in 1941 and later administered it as a U.N. Trust Territory until it became federated with Ethiopia on Sept. 15, 1952. It was made an Ethiopian province on Nov. 14, 1962.

A civil war broke out against the Ethiopian government led by rebel groups who opposed the union and wanted independence for Eritrea. The bitter conflict raged on for 17 years against the hard-line

Communist regime of the Ethiopian dictator, Mengistu Haile Mariam until he was overthrown in May 1991.

The Eritrean People's Liberation Front (EPLF) took control of Eritrea and shared power in a multiparty government in Addis Ababa with the Ethiopian People's Revolutionary Democratic Front (EPRDF). They agreed to hold a referendum on Eritrean independence within two years and on April 23–25, 1993, Eritrean voters almost unanimously opted for an independent republic. Ethiopia recognized Eritrea's sovereignty on May 3, 1993, and sought a new era of cooperation between the two countries.

While relations with Ethiopia remained good in 1995, those with the Sudan deteriorated. In Nov. 1996 Eritrea accused the Sudan of plotting to assassinate the president. The mission was thwarted by a Sudanese anti-government group. Sudan denied the charge, although Eritrea provided specific names and dates of those allegedly involved.

Since Eritrea's independence, Eritrea and Ethiopia had disagreed about the exact demarcation of their borders, and in May 1998 border clashes broke out between them.

Estonia

REPUBLIC OF ESTONIA

National name: Eesti
President: Lennart Meri (1992)
Prime Minister: Mart Siiman (1997)
Area: 18,370 sq mi. (45,100 sq km)
Population (1998 est.): 1,421,335 (average annual rate of natural increase: –0.99%); birth rate: 9/1000; infant mortality rate: 14/1000; density per sq mi.: 77
Capital and largest city (1992 est.): Tallinn, 471,608. Other large city (1992 est.): Tartu, 113,400. **Monetary unit:** Kroon. **Languages:** Estonian (official), Russian, Finnish, English. **Ethnicity/Race:** Estonian 61.5%, Russian 30.3%, Ukrainian 3.2%, Belarussian 1.8%, Finn 1.1%, other 2.1% (1989). **Religions:** Lutheran, 78%; Orthodox, 19%. **Literacy:** 100%
Economic summary: GDP/PPP (1996 est. as extrapolated from World Bank estimate for 1994): $8.1 billion; $5,560 per capita. **Real growth rate:** 3%. **Inflation:** 23%. **Unemployment** (1996 official est.), 3%. **Labor force** (1992), 750,000; industry and construction, 42%; agriculture and forestry, 20%. The Estonian government has pursued a program of market reforms and rough stabilization measures, which is rapidly transforming the economy. There is low inflation, living standards are rising, and the private sector is growing rapidly. **Exports:** $2 billion (f.o.b., 1996): textiles 16%, food products 16%, machinery and equipment 16%, metals 9%. **Imports:** $3.1 billion (c.i.f., 1996): machinery and equipment 29%, foodstuffs 14%, minerals 13%, textiles 13%, metals 12%.**Major trading partners:** Finland, Russia, Sweden, Germany, Holland, Latvia.

Geography Estonia is mainly a lowland country that borders on the Baltic Sea. It has numerous lakes and forests and many rivers, most draining northward into the Gulf of Finland or eastward into Lake Peipus. Lake Peipus is Estonia's largest lake and is important to the fishing and shipping industries.

Government Estonia's government centers on the single-chamber Riigikogu (Parliament), the 101 members of which are elected through proportional representation to four-year terms. The Riigikogu selects both the president and the prime minister.

History Born out of World War I, this small Baltic state enjoyed a mere two short decades of independence before it was absorbed again by its powerful neighbor, the Soviet Union. Estonians were able to resist assaults by Vikings, Danes, Swedes and Russians before the 13th century. In 1346 the Danish crown, which possessed northern Estonia and the islands, sold its sovereignty to the Teutonic Knights of Germany, who already possessed Livonia (southern Estonia and Latvia). The Teutonic Knights reduced the Estonians to serfdom. In 1526, the Swedes took over, and the power of the German (Balt) landowning class was reduced. But after 1721, when Russia succeeded Sweden as the ruling power under the Peace of Nystad, the Estonians were subject to a double bondage—the Balts and the tsarist officials. The oppression lasted until the closing months of World War I, when Estonia finally achieved independence after a victorious war of independence (1918–20).

Shortly after the start of World War II, the nation was occupied by Russian troops and was incorporated as the 16th republic of the U.S.S.R. in 1940. Germany occupied the nation from 1941 to 1944, when it was retaken by the Russians.

Soon after Lithuania's declaration of independence from the Soviet Union in March 1990, the Estonian congress cautiously promoted national autonomy. After the attempted Soviet coup to remove President Gorbachev failed, Estonia formally declared its independence from the U.S.S.R. on August 20, 1991. Recognition by European and other countries followed. The Soviet Union recognized Estonia's independence on Sept. 6 and it received U.N. membership on Sept. 17, 1991. The newly independent nation embraced free-market reforms. Fueled by foreign investments, economic advances continued unabated in 1997. This prompted the European Commission (EC) to recommend that Estonia begin accession talks for membership in the European Union.

Ethiopia

FEDERAL DEMOCRATIC REPUBLIC OF ETHIOPIA

President: Negasso Gidada (1995)
Prime Minister: Meles Zenawi (1995)
Area: 446,952 sq mi. (1,127,127 sq km)
Population (1998 est.): 58,390,351 (average annual rate of natural increase: 2.21%); birth rate: 44.7/1000; infant mortality rate: 125.7/1000; density per sq mi.: 131
Capital and largest city (1993 est.): Addis Ababa, 2,200,186. **Monetary unit:** Birr. **Languages:** Amharic (official), English, Orominga, Tigrigna, over 70 languages spoken. **Ethnicity/Race:** Oromo 40%, Amhara and Tigrean 32%, Sidamo 9%, Shankella 6%, Somali 6%, Afar 4%, Gurage 2%, other 1%. **Religions:** Ethiopian Orthodox, 35–40%; Islam, 40–45%; animist, 15–20%; other, 5%. **Literacy rate:** 28%
Economic summary: GDP/PPP (1996 est.): $24.8 billion; $430 per capita. **Real growth rate:** 7.7%. **Inflation:** (1995 est.): 10%. **Unemployment:** n.a. **Arable land:** 12%. **Agriculture:** coffee, barley, wheat, pulses, sugar cane, cotton, oilseeds, livestock. **Industry:** cement, textiles, processed foods, refined oil, beverages, footwear, furniture. **Natural resources:** potash, gold, platinum, copper. **Labor force:** 18 million; agriculture and animal husbandry, 80%; government and services, 12%; industry and

construction, 8% (1985 est.). **Exports:** $423 million (f.o.b., 1995 est.): coffee, leather products, gold. **Imports:** $1.15 billion (f.o.b., 1995 est.): food and live anomals, petroleum and petroleum products, chemicals. **Major trading partners:** Japan, U.S., Djibouti, Saudi Arabia, Germany, Italy, France, Eritrea.

Geography Ethiopia is in east central Africa, bordered on the west by the Sudan, the east by Somalia and Djibouti, the south by Kenya, and northeast by Eritrea. It is nearly three times the size of California. Over its main plateau land, Ethiopia has several high mountains, the highest of which is Ras Dashan at 15,158 feet (4,620 m). The Blue Nile, or Abbai, rises in the northwest and flows in a great semicircle east, south, and northwest before entering the Sudan. Its chief reservoir, Lake Tana, lies in the northwestern part of the plateau.

Government A constitution was ratified by a constituent assembly elected in June 1994. The bicameral parliament has 548 seats (House of People's Representatives, and the federal council has one seat for each nationality plus one seat for each additional one million of the nationality).

History Black Africa's oldest state, Ethiopia can trace 2,000 years of recorded history. Its now deposed royal line claimed descent from King Menelik I, traditionally believed to have been the son of the queen of Sheba and King Solomon. The present nation is a consolidation of smaller kingdoms that owed feudal allegiance to the Ethiopian emperor.

Hamitic peoples migrated to Ethiopia from Asia Minor in prehistoric times. Semitic traders from Arabia penetrated the region in the 7th century B.C.E. Its Red Sea ports were important to the Roman and Byzantine Empires. Coptic Christianity came to the country in C.E. 341, and a variant of that communion became Ethiopia's state religion.

Ancient Ethiopia reached its peak in the 5th century, then was isolated by the rise of Islam and weakened by feudal wars. Modern Ethiopia emerged under Emperor Menelik II, who established its independence by routing an Italian invasion in 1896. He expanded Ethiopia by conquest.

Disorders that followed Menelik's death brought his daughter to the throne in 1917, with his cousin, Tafari Makonnen, as Regent, heir presumptive, and strongman. When the Empress died in 1930, Tafari was crowned Emperor Haile Selassie I.

As regent, Haile Selassie outlawed slavery. As Emperor, he worked for centralization of his diffuse realm, in which 70 languages are spoken, and for moderate reform. In 1931, he granted a constitution, revised in 1955, that created a parliament with an appointed Senate and an elected Chamber of Deputies, and a system of courts. But basic power remained with the Emperor.

Bent on colonial empire, fascist Italy invaded Ethiopia on Oct. 3, 1935, forcing Haile Selassie into exile in May 1936. Ethiopia was annexed to Eritrea, then an Italian colony, and Italian Somaliland to form Italian East Africa, losing its independence for the first time in recorded history. In 1941, British troops routed the Italians, and Haile Selassie returned to Addis Ababa.

In August 1974, the armed forces committee nationalized Haile Selassie's palace and estates and directed him not to leave Addis Ababa. On Sept. 12, 1974, he was deposed after nearly 58 years as Regent and Emperor. The 82-year-old "Lion of Judah" was placed under guard. Parliament was dissolved, the constitution suspended and Ethiopia was proclaimed a socialist state.

Lt. Col. Mengistu Haile Mariam was named head of state, Feb. 2, 1977, and when a communist regime was established on Sept. 10, 1984, Mengistu became party leader. A cut-off of Soviet aid led to mass animosity, and a rebel offensive began in Feb. 1991. Mengistu resigned and fled the country in May. A group called the Ethiopian People's Revolutionary Democratic Front seized the capital. Also in May a separatist guerrilla organization, the Eritrean People's Liberation Front, took control of the province of Eritrea. The two groups agreed in early July that Eritrea would have an internationally supervised referendum on independence. This election took place in April 1993 with an almost unanimous support for Eritrean independence. Ethiopia accepted and recognized Eritrea as an independent state within a few days.

Sixty-eight leaders of the former military government were put on trial in April 1996 on charges including genocide and crimes against humanity. Since Eritrea's independence, Eritrea and Ethiopia had disagreed about the exact demarcation of their borders, and in May 1998 border clashes broke out between them.

Fiji

REPUBLIC OF FIJI

President: Ratu Sir Kamisese Mara (1994)
Prime Minister: Maj. Gen. Sitiveni Rabuka (1992)
Area: 7,078 sq mi. (18,270 sq km)
Population (1998 est.): 802,611 (average annual rate of natural increase: 1.28%); birth rate: 22.9/1000; infant mortality rate: 16.7/1000; density per sq mi.: 113
Capital (1990 est.): Suva (on Viti Levu), 200,000. **Monetary unit:** Fiji dollar. **Languages:** Fijian, Hindustani, English (official). **Ethnicity/Race:** Fijian 49%, Indian 46%, European, other Pacific Islanders, overseas Chinese, and other 5%. **Religions:** Christian, 52%; Hindu, 38%; Islam, 8%; other, 2%. **Literacy rate:** 79%
Economic summary: GDP/PPP (1996 est.): $5.1 billion; $6,500 per capita. **Real growth rate:** 5%. **Inflation:** 3% (1997 est.). **Unemployment** (1997 est.), 6%. **Arable land:** 10%. **Products:** sugar, coconuts, fish. **Labor force** 287,000; subsistence agriculture, 67%; wage earners, 18%; salary earners, 15% (1987). **Industry:** refined sugar, gold, lumber, copra. **Natural resources:** timber, fish, gold, copper. **Exports:** $607 million (f.o.b., 1995): sugar, copra, processed fish, lumber, gold, clothing. **Imports:** $864 million (c.i.f., 1995): machinery and transport equipment, food, petroleum products, consumer goods, chemicals. **Major trading partners:** E.U., Australia, Japan, U.S., New Zealand, other Pacific Islands.

Geography Fiji consists of 332 islands in the southwestern Pacific Ocean about 1,960 miles (3,152 km) from Sydney, Australia. About 110 of these islands are inhabited. The two largest are Viti Levu (4,109 sq mi.; 10,642 sq km) and Vanua Levu (2,242 sq mi.; 5,807 sq km). The island of Rotuma (18 sq mi.; 47 sq km), about 400 miles (644 km) to the north, is a province of Fiji. The largest islands in the group are mountainous and volcanic, with the tallest peak being Mount Victoria (4,341 ft.; 1,323 m) on Viti Levu.

Government Military coup leader Major General Sitiveni Rabuka formerly declared Fiji a republic on Oct. 6, 1987. The Sept. 23, 1988 constitution provided for a bicameral parliament consisting of a 342-member Senate and a 70-member House of Representatives. The new constitution, which took effect in 1998, provides for a multiracial Cabinet.

History Fiji, which had been inhabited since the second millennium B.C.E., was explored by the Dutch and the British in the 17th and 18th centuries. In 1874, an offer of cession by the Fijian chiefs was accepted, and Fiji was proclaimed a possession and dependency of the British Crown. In the 1880s large-scale cultivation of sugarcane began. During World War II, the archipelago was an important air and naval station on the route from the U.S. and Hawaii to Australia and New Zealand.

Fiji became independent on Oct. 10, 1970. The next year it joined the five-island South Pacific Forum, which intends to become a permanent regional group to promote collective diplomacy of the newly independent members. In Oct. 1987, then Brig. Gen. Sitiveni Rabuka, the coup leader, declared Fiji a republic and removed it from the British Commonwealth. The military coup caused an exodus of thousands of Fijians of Indian origin who suffered ethnic discrimination at the hands of the government.

In July 1997, the parliament unanimously approved a new constitution for Fiji. The new constitution, which took effect in July 1998, provided for a multiracial cabinet and raised the prospect of a coalition government. The previous constitution, from 1990, guaranteed the political dominance to ethnic Fijians over ethnic Indians. Following the approval of the new constitution, Fiji was readmitted to the Commonwealth of Nations.

Finland

REPUBLIC OF FINLAND

National name: Suomen Tasavalta—Republiken Finland
President: Martti Ahtisaari (1994)
Prime Minister: Paavo Lipponen (1995)
Area: 130,558 sq mi. (337,030 sq km)
Population (1998 est.): 5,149,242 (average annual rate of natural increase: 0.20%); birth rate: 11.2/1000; infant mortality rate: 3.8/1000; density per sq mi.: 39
Capital and largest city (1995 est.): Helsinki, 515,765. **Other large cities (1995 est.):** Espoo, 186,507; Tampere, 179,251; Vantaa, 164,376; Turku, 162,370. **Monetary unit:** Markka. **Languages:** Finnish, Swedish (both official); small Lapp- and Russian-speaking minorities. **Ethnicity/Race:** Finn 93%, Swede 6%, Sami (Lapp) 0.11%, Romany (Gypsy) 0.12%, Tatar 0.02%. **Religions:** Evangelical Lutheran, 90%; Greek Orthodox, 1.2%; none, 9%; other, 1%. **Literacy rate:** 100%
Economic summary: GDP/PPP (1996 est.): $97.1 billion; $19,000 per capita. **Real growth rate:** 2.5%. **Inflation:** 0.7%. **Unemployment:** 16.6%. **Arable land:** 8%. **Agriculture:** dairy and meat products, cereals, sugar beets, potatoes. **Labor force:** 2.533 million; public services, 30.4%; industry, 20.9%; commerce, 15%; finance, insurance, and business services, 10.2%. **Products:** metal manufactures, forestry and wood products, refined copper, ships, machinery, chemicals, clothing, footwear. Natural resource: timber. **Exports:** $29.7 billion (f.o.b., 1994): timber, paper and pulp, ships, machinery, clothing, footwear, chemicals. **Imports:** $23.2 billion (c.i.f., 1994): petroleum and petroleum products, chemicals, transportation equipment, machinery, textile yarns, foodstuffs, fodder grain, iron and steel. **Major trading partners:** E.U., U.S., Russia, Norway.

Geography Finland is three times the size of Ohio. It is heavily forested and contains thousands of lakes, numerous rivers, and extensive areas of marshland. Except for a small highland region in the extreme northwest, the country is a lowland less than 600 feet (180 m) above sea level. Off the southwest coast are the Swedish-populated Åland Islands (581 sq mi.; 1,505 sq km), which have had an autonomous status since 1921.

Government The president, chosen for six years by popular vote, appoints the cabinet. The unicameral parliament, the Eduskunta, consists of 200 members elected for four-year terms by proportional representation. Coalition governments are usually created from among Finland's four major political parties.

History Human habitation in Finland dates back to at least 7200 B.C.E. and includes the ancestors of the present-day Sami (Lapp) people.

The Finns migrated to Finland in the first millennium B.C.E., taking the country from the Sami, who retreated northward. The Finns' repeated raids on the Scandinavian coast impelled Eric IX, the Swedish king, to conquer the country in 1157 and bring it into contact with Western Christendom. Finland was made part of the kingdom of Sweden.

By 1809 the whole of Finland was conquered by Alexander I of Russia, who set up Finland as a Grand Duchy. The period of Russification (1809–1914) resulted in a lessening of the powers of the Finnish Diet, the Russian language being made official, and the Finnish military system being superseded by the Russian. When Russian control was weakened as a consequence of the March Revolution of 1917, the Diet proclaimed Finland's independence on July 20, 1917.

Finland rejected Soviet territorial demands, and the U.S.S.R. attacked on Nov. 30, 1939. The Finns made an amazing stand of three months and finally capitulated, ceding 16,000 square miles (41,440 sq km) to the U.S.S.R. Under German pressure, the Finns joined the Nazis against Russia in 1941, but were defeated again and ceded the Petsamo area to the U.S.S.R. In 1948, a treaty of friendship and mutual assistance was signed by the two nations. Finland continued to pursue a foreign policy of non-alignment throughout the cold war era.

Running on a platform calling to invigorate the economy, Ahtisaari, a Social Democrat, won the country's first direct presidential election in a runoff in Feb. 1994. Previously the president had been chosen by electors. Finland became a member of the European Union in Jan. 1995, but made clear it would not become a full member of the Western European Union. Showing concern over NATO expansion eastward, Russian President Yeltsin in March 1997 iterated his view that Finnish membership in the military alliance was unacceptable, due to Finland's policy of non-alignment.

France

FRENCH REPUBLIC

National name: République Française
President: Jacques Chirac (1995)
Prime Minister: Lionel Jospin (1997)
Area: 211,208 sq mi. (547,030 sq km)
Population (1998 est.): 58,804,944 (average annual rate of natural increase: 0.31%); birth rate: 11.7/1000; infant mortality rate: 5.7/1000; density per sq mi.: 278
Capital and largest city: Paris. **Other large cities :** Paris: city proper (1991 census) 2,156,766; metro. area (1995 est.) 9,469,000; Marseille, 801,000; Lyon, 415,000; Toulouse, 359,000; Nice, 342,000; Strasbourg, 252,000; Nantes, 245,000; Bordeaux, 201,000. **Monetary unit:** French Franc. **Language:** French, declining regional dialects (Provençal, Breton, Alsatian, Corsican). **Ethnicity/Race:** Celtic and Latin with Teutonic, Slavic, North African, Southeast Asian, and Basque minorities. **Religion:** Roman Catholic, 81%; Protestant, 1.7%; Muslim, 6.9%; Jewish, 1.3%. **Literacy rate:** 99%
Economic summary: GDP/PPP (1996 est.): $1.22 trillion; $20,900 per capita. **Real growth rate:** 1.3%. **Inflation:** 1.7%. **Unemployment:** 12.7% (1966). **Arable land:** 33%. **Agriculture:** cereals, feed grains, livestock and dairy products, wine, fruits, vegetables, potatoes. **Labor force:** 25.5 million, services, 69%; industry, 26%; agriculture, 5%. **Products:** chemicals, automobiles, processed foods, iron and steel, aircraft, textiles, clothing. **Natural resources:** coal, iron ore, bauxite, fish, forests. **Exports:** $275 billion (f.o.b., 1996): textiles and clothing, chemicals, machinery and transport equipment, agricultural products, foodstuffs. **Imports:** $255.5 billion (f.o.b., 1996): machinery, crude petroleum, chemicals, agricultural products, iron and steel products. **Major trading partners:** Germany, Italy, U.S., Belgium-Luxembourg, U.K., Netherlands, Spain, Japan.

Geography France is about 80% the size of Texas. In the Alps near the Italian and Swiss borders is Western Europe's highest point—Mont Blanc (15,781 ft.; 4,810 m). The forest-covered Vosges Mountains are in the northeast, and the Pyrenees are along the Spanish border. Except for extreme northern France, the country may be described as four river basins and a plateau. Three of the streams flow west—the Seine into the English Channel, the Loire into the Atlantic, and the Garonne into the Bay of Biscay. The Rhône flows south into the Mediterranean. For about 100 miles (161 km), the Rhine is France's eastern border. In the Mediterranean, about 115 miles (185 km) east-southeast of Nice, is the island of Corsica (3,367 sq mi.; 8,721 sq km).

Government The constitution of the Fifth Republic, adopted in 1958, vests executive authority in the president, who is elected to a seven-year term by popular vote. The president appoints the premier, and the cabinet is responsible to parliament. The parliament consists of two houses: the 577-member National Assembly and the 321-member Senate.

History Archaeological excavations have uncovered artifacts more than 100,000 years old in France, which with the long ensuing record indicate continuous settlement of the region from Paleolithic times. About 1200 B.C.E. the Gauls, a predominantly Celtic people, began a southward and westward migration from the Rhine valley into what is now France and northern Italy. In about 600 B.C.E. Ionian Greeks established a trading colony at Massilia (now Marseille), the best known of a number of Ionian settlements that flourished for centuries in what is now southern France. Julius Caesar conquered part of Gaul in 57–52 B.C.E., and it remained Roman until Franks invaded it in the 5th century.

The Treaty of Verdun (C.E. 843), divided the territories corresponding roughly to France, Germany, and Italy among the three grandsons of Charlemagne. Charles the Bald, inherited *Francia Occidentalis,* which became an increasingly feudalized kingdom. By C.E. 987, the Crown passed to Hugh Capet, a princeling who controlled only the Ile-de-France, the region surrounding Paris. For 350 years, an unbroken Capetian line added to its domain and consolidated royal authority until the accession in 1328 of Philip VI, first of the Valois line. France was then the most powerful nation in Europe, with a population of 15 million.

The missing pieces in Philip Valois' domain were the French provinces still held by the Plantagenet kings of England, who also claimed the French Crown. Beginning in 1338, the Hundred Years' War eventually settled the contest. After France's victory in the final battle, Castillon (1453), the Valois were firmly established as France's ruling family, and the English had lost all their French holdings except Calais. Protestantism spread throughout France in the 16th century and led to civil wars. Henry IV, of the Bourbon dynasty, issued the Edict of Nantes (1598), granting religious tolerance to the Huguenots (French Protestants). Absolute monarchy reached its apogee in the reign of Louis XIV (1643–1715), the Sun King, whose brilliant court was the center of the Western world.

After a series of costly foreign wars that weakened the government, the French Revolution plunged France into a blood bath beginning in 1789 with the establishment of the First Republic and ending with a new authoritarianism under Napoleon Bonaparte, who had successfully defended the infant republic from foreign attack and then made himself First Consul in 1799 and Emperor in 1804. The Congress of Vienna (1815) sought to restore the pre-Napoleonic order in the person of Louis XVIII, but industrialization and the middle class, both fostered under Napoleon, built pressure for change, and a revolution in 1848 drove Louis Phillipe, last of the Bourbons, into exile. Prince Louis Napoleon, a nephew of Napoleon I, declared the Second Empire in 1852 and took the throne as Napoleon III. His opposition to the rising power of Prussia ignited the Franco-Prussian War (1870–71), ending in his defeat, his abdication, and the creation of the Third Republic.

A new France emerged from World War I as the continent's dominant power. But four years of hostile occupation had reduced northeast France to ruins. Beginning in 1919, French foreign policy aimed at keeping Germany weak through a system of alliances, but it failed to halt the rise of Adolf Hitler and the Nazi war machine. On May 10, 1940, Nazi troops attacked, and, as they approached Paris, Italy joined with Germany. The Germans marched into an undefended Paris and Marshal Henri Philippe Pétain signed an armistice June 22. France was split into an occupied north and an unoccupied south, Vichy France, the latter becoming a totalitarian, German puppet state with Pétain as its chief. Allied armies liberated France in August 1944, and

Rulers of France

Name	Born	Ruled[1]
Carolingian Dynasty		
Pepin the Short	c. 714	751–768
Charlemagne[2]	742	768–814
Louis I the Debonair[3]	778	814–840
Charles I the Bald[4]	823	840–877
Louis II the Stammerer	846	877–879
Louis III[5]	c. 863	879–882
Carloman[5]	?	879–884
Charles II the Fat[6]	839	884–887[7]
Eudes (Odo), Count of Paris	?	888–898
Charles III the Simple[8]	879	893–923[9]
Robert I[10]	c. 865	922–923
Rudolf (Raoul), Duke of Burgundy	?	923–936
Louis IV d'Outremer	c. 921	936–954
Lothair	941	954–986
Louis V the Sluggard	c. 967	986–987
Capetian Dynasty		
Hugh Capet	c. 940	987–996
Robert II the Pious[11]	c. 970	996–1031
Henry I	1008	1031–1060
Philip I	1052	1060–1108
Louis VI the Fat	1081	1108–1137
Louis VII the Young	c.1121	1137–1180
Philip II (Philip Augustus)	1165	1180–1223
Louis VIII the Lion	1187	1223–1226
Louis IX (St. Louis)	1214	1226–1270
Philip III the Bold	1245	1270–1285
Philip IV the Fair	1268	1285–1314
Louis X the Quarreler	1289	1314–1316
John I[12]	1316	1316
Philip V the Tall	1294	1316–1322
Charles IV the Fair	1294	1322–1328
House of Valois		
Philip VI	1293	1328–1350
John II the Good	1319	1350–1364
Charles V the Wise	1337	1364–1380
Charles VI the Well-Beloved	1368	1380–1422
Charles VII	1403	1422–1461
Louis XI	1423	1461–1483
Charles VIII	1470	1483–1498
Louis XII the Father of the People	1462	1498–1515
Francis I	1494	1515–1547
Henry II	1519	1547–1559
Francis II	1544	1559–1560
Charles IX	1550	1560–1574
Henry III	1551	1574–1589
House of Bourbon		
Henry IV of Navarre	1553	1589–1610
Louis XIII	1601	1610–1643
Louis XIV the Great	1638	1643–1715
Louis XV the Well-Beloved	1710	1715–1774
Louis XVI	1754	1774–1792[13]
Louis XVII (Louis Charles de France)[14]	1785	1793–1795
First Republic		
National Convention	—	1792–1795
Directory (Directoire)	—	1795–1799
Consulate		
Napoleon Bonaparte[15]	1769	1799–1804
First Empire		
Napoleon I	1769	1804–1815[16]
Restoration of House of Bourbon		
Louis XVIII le Désiré	1755	1814–1824
Charles X	1757	1824–1830[17]
Bourbon-Orleans Line		
Louis Philippe ("Citizen King")	1773	1830–1848[18]
Second Republic		
Louis Napoleon[19]	1808	1848–1852
Second Empire		
Napoleon III (Louis Napoleon)	1808	1852–1870[20]
Third Republic (Presidents)		
Louis Adolphe Thiers	1797	1871–1873
Marie E. P. M. de MacMahon	1808	1873–1879
François P. J. Grévy	1807	1879–1887
Sadi Carnot	1837	1887–1894
Jean Casimir-Périer	1847	1894–1895
François Félix Faure	1841	1895–1899
Émile Loubet	1838	1899–1906
Clement Armand Fallières	1841	1906–1913
Raymond Poincaré	1860	1913–1920
Paul E. L. Deschanel	1856	1920–1920
Alexandre Millerand	1859	1920–1924
Gaston Doumergue	1863	1924–1931
Paul Doumer	1857	1931–1932
Albert Lebrun	1871	1932–1940
Vichy Government (Chief of State)		
Henri Philippe Pétain	1856	1940–1944
Provisional Government (Presidents)		
Charles de Gaulle	1890	1944–1946
Félix Gouin	1884	1946–1946
Georges Bidault	1899	1946–1947
Fourth Republic (Presidents)		
Vincent Auriol	1884	1947–1954
René Coty	1882	1954–1959
Fifth Republic (Presidents)		
Charles de Gaulle	1890	1959–1969
Georges Pompidou	1911	1969–1974
Valéry Giscard d'Estaing	1926	1974–1981
François Mitterrand	1916	1981–1995
Jacques Chirac	1932	1995–

1. For kings and emperors through the Second Empire, year of end of rule is also that of death, unless otherwise indicated. 2. Crowned Emperor of the West in 800. His brother, Carloman, ruled as king of the Eastern Franks from 768 until his death in 771. 3. Holy Roman Emperor 814–840. 4. Holy Roman Emperor 875–877 as Charles II. 5. Ruled jointly 879–882. 6. Holy Roman Emperor 881–887 as Charles III. 7. Died 888. 8. King 893–898 in opposition to Eudes. 9. Died 929. 10. Not counted in regular line of kings of France by some authorities. Elected by nobles but killed in Battle of Soissons. 11. Sometimes called Robert I. 12. Posthumous son of Louis X; lived for only five days. 13. Executed 1793. 14. Titular king only. He died in prison according to official reports, but many pretenders appeared during the Bourbon restoration. 15. As First Consul, Napoleon held the power of government. In 1804, he became Emperor. 16. Abdicated first time June 1814. Re-entered Paris March 1815, after escape from Elba; Louis XVIII fled to Ghent. Abdicated second time June 1815. He named as his successor his son, Napoleon II, who was not acceptable to the Allies. He died 1821. 17. Died 1836. 18. Died 1850. 19. President; became Emperor in 1852. 20. Died 1873.

a provisional government in Paris headed by Gen. Charles de Gaulle was established. The Fourth Republic was born on Dec. 24, 1946. The Empire became the French Union; the National Assembly was strengthened and the presidency weakened; and France joined NATO. A war against Communist insurgents in French Indochina, now Vietnam, was abandoned after the defeat of French forces at Dien Bien Phu in 1954. A new rebellion in Algeria threatened a military coup, and on June 1, 1958, the Assembly invited de Gaulle to return as premier with extraordinary powers. He drafted a new constitution for a Fifth Republic, adopted Sept. 28, which strengthened the presidency and reduced legislative power. He was elected president Dec. 21, 1958.

France next turned its attention to decolonialization in Africa; the French protectorates of Morocco and Tunisia had received independence in 1956. French West Africa was partitioned and the new nations were granted independence in 1960. Algeria, after a long civil war, finally became independent in 1962. Relations with most of the former colonies remained amicable. De Gaulle took France out of the NATO military command in 1967 and expelled all foreign-controlled troops from the country. De Gaulle's government was weakened by massive protests in May 1968 when student rallies became violent and millions of factory workers engaged in wildcat strikes across France. After normalcy was reestablished by 1969, de Gaulle's successor Georges Pompidou modified Gaullist policies to include a classical laissez-faire attitude toward domestic economic affairs. The conservative, probusiness climate contributed to the election of Valéry Giscard d'Estaing as president in 1974.

Socialist François Mitterrand attained a stunning victory in the May 10, 1981, presidential election. The victors immediately moved to carry out campaign pledges to nationalize major industries, halt nuclear testing, suspend nuclear power plant construction, and impose new taxes on the rich. The Socialists' policies during Mitterrand's first two years created a 12% inflation rate, a huge trade deficit, and devaluations of the franc. In March 1986, a center-right coalition led by Jacques Chirac won a slim majority in legislative elections. Chirac became prime minister, initiating a period of "cohabitation" between him and the socialist president, Mitterrand. Mitterrand's decisive reelection in 1988 led to Chirac being replaced as premier by Michel Rocard, a socialist. Relations, however, cooled with Rocard, and in May 1991 he was replaced with Edith Cresson, France's first female prime minister and, like Mitterrand, a socialist. But Cresson's unpopularity forced Mitterand to replace Cresson with a more well-liked socialist, Pierre Bérégovoy, who eventually was embroiled in a scandal and committed suicide. Mitterrand did succeed in helping draft the Maastricht Treaty and, after winning a slim victory in a referendum, confirming close economic and security ties between France and the European Union (E.U.).

On his third try Chirac won the presidency in May 1995, campaigning vigorously on a platform to reduce unemployment. He moved quickly to cement ties with Germany and the rest of the E.U. Elections for the National Assembly in 1997 gave the socialist coalition a majority. Shortly after becoming president, Chirac resumed France's nuclear testing in the South Pacific, despite widespread international protests as well as rioting in the countries affected by it. Socialist leader Lionel Jospin became prime minister in 1997.

Overseas Departments

Overseas Departments elect representatives to the National Assembly, and the same administrative organization as that of continental France applies to them.

French Guiana (including Inini)

Status: Overseas Department
Prefect: Pierre Dartout (1995)
Area: 32,253 sq mi. (83,534 sq km)
Population (1998 est.): 162,547; growth rate: 3.4%; birth rate 23.7/1000; infant mortality rate 13.5/1000; density per sq mi.: 5
Capital and largest city (1995 est.): Cayenne, 41,659. **Monetary unit:** Franc. **Language:** French. **Ethnicity/Race:** black or mulatto 66%, white 12%, East Indian, Chinese, Amerindian 12%, other 10%. **Religion:** Roman Catholic. **Literacy rate:** 80%
Economic summary: GDP/PPP (1993 est.): $800 million; $6,000 per capita. **Inflation:** (1992) 2.5%. **Unemployment:** 24.1%. **Arable land:** 0% **Agriculture:** rice, corn, bananas, sugar cane. **Labor force** (1993): 46,300; services, government and commerce, 60.6%; industry, 21.2%; agriculture, 18.2% (1980). **Industry:** timber, rum, rosewood essence, gold mining, processed shrimp. **Natural resources:** bauxite, timber, cinnabar, kaolin. **Exports:** $80 million (f.o.b., 1994): shrimp, timber, rum, rosewood essence. **Imports:** $610 million (c.i.f., 1994): food, consumer and producer goods, petroleum. **Major trading partners:** U.S., France, Japan.

French Guiana, lying north of Brazil and east of Suriname on the northeast coast of South America, was first settled in 1637. Penal settlements, embracing the area around the mouth of the Maroni River and the Iles du Salut (including Devil's Island), were founded in 1852; they were closed in 1945. During World War II, French Guiana at first adhered to the Vichy government, but the Free French took over in 1943. French Guiana accepted the new constitution of the French Fifth Republic in 1958 and has remained an Overseas Department of the French Republic which sends two elected representatives to France's National Assembly and one to the Senate.

Guadeloupe

Status: Overseas Department
Prefect: Michel Diefenbacher
Area: 327 sq mi. (1,848 sq km)
Population (1998 est.): 416,439 (average annual growth rate: 1.1%); birth rate: 16.7/1000; infant mortality rate: 8.8/1000; density per sq mi.: 1,274
Capital (1990): Basse-Terre, 14,000. **Largest city (1990):** Pointe-à-Pitre, over 26,029. **Monetary unit:** Franc. **Language:** French, Creole patois. **Ethnicity/Race:** black or mulatto 90%, white 5%, East Indian, Lebanese, Chinese less than 5%. **Religions:** Roman Catholic. **Literacy rate:** 91%
Economic summary: GDP/PPP (1995 est.): $3.7 billion; $9,200 per capita. **Real growth rate:** n.a. **Inflation:** (1990), 3.7%. **Unemployment:** (1995), 33.3%. **Arable land:** 14%. **Agriculture:** sugar cane, bananas, cattle, flowers. **Labor force:** (1993), 128,000; agriculture, 15%; industry, 20%; services, 65%. **Industry:** construction, public works, sugar, rum, tourism. **Exports:** $145 million (f.o.b., 1994): sugar, rum, bananas. **Imports:** $1.6 billion (c.i.f., 1994): foodstuffs, clothing, consumer goods, construction materials, petroleum products, vehicles. **Major trading partners:** France, Martinique, Italy, Germany, U.S.

Guadeloupe, in the West Indies about 300 miles (483 km) southeast of Puerto Rico, was explored by Columbus in 1493. It consists of the twin islands of Basse-Terre and Grande-Terre and five dependencies—Marie-Galante, Les Saintes, La Désirade, St. Barthélemy, and the northern half of St. Martin. The volcano Soufrière (4,813 ft.; 1,467 m), also called La Grande Soufrière, is the highest point on Guadeloupe. Violent activity in 1976 and 1977 caused thousands to flee their homes. French colonization began in 1635, and in 1674 Guadeloupe became part of the domain of France. In 1958, Guadeloupe voted in favor of the new constitution of the French Fifth Republic and remained an Overseas Department of the French Republic. It is represented in the French National Assembly by four deputies and in the French Senate by two senators.

Martinique

Status: Overseas Department
Prefect: Jean-Francois Cordet
Area: 436 sq mi. (1,128 sq km)
Population (1998 est.): 407,284 (average annual growth rate: 1.05%); birth rate: 16.5/1000; infant mortality rate: 6.9/1000; density per sq mi.: 934
Capital and largest city (1990): Fort-de-France, 100,072; Other cities (1990): Le Lamentin, 30,026; Schoelcher, 19,683; Sainte-Marie, 19,683. **Monetary unit:** Franc. **Languages:** French, Creole patois. **Ethnicity/Race:** African and African-white-Indian mixture 90%, white 5%, East Indian, Lebanese, Chinese less than 5%. **Religion:** Roman Catholic. **Literacy rate:** 100%
Economic summary: GDP/PPP (1995 est.): $3.95 billion, $10,000 per capita. **Inflation** (1990), 3.9%. **Unemployment** (1994), 23.5%. **Real growth rate:** n.a. **Arable land:** 8%. **Agriculture:** sugar cane, bananas, rum, pineapples. **Labor force:** (1994), 160,000; service industry, 73%. **Industry:** sugar, rum, refined oil, cement, tourism. **Natural resources:** coastal scenery and beaches. **Exports:** $220 million (f.o.b., 1994): bananas, refined petroleum products, rum, sugar, pineapples. **Imports:** $1.6 billion (c.i.f., 1994): foodstuffs, clothing and other consumer goods, petroleum products, construction materials. **Major trading partners:** France, U.S., Guadeloupe, Germany, U.K., Italy, Japan.

Martinique, a mountainous island lying in the Lesser Antilles about 300 miles (483 km) northeast of Venezuela, was probably explored by Columbus in 1502 and was taken for France in 1635. Martinique became a domain of the French crown in 1674. In 1958, Martinique voted in favor of the new constitution of the French Fifth Republic and remained an Overseas Department of the French Republic, sending four deputies to the French National Assembly and two senators to the French Senate. The area is administered by a Prefect assisted by an elected council. Martinique's young people continue to emigrate heavily, mostly to France.

Réunion

Status: Overseas Department
Prefect: Pierre Steinmetz (1995)
Area: 970 sq mi. (2,512 sq km)
Population (1998 est.): 705,053 (average annual growth rate: 1.81%); birth rate: 22.8/1000; infant mortality rate: 7.1/1000; density per sq mi.: 727
Capital and largest city (1993): Saint-Denis, 121,999. Other cities (est. 1993): Saint-Paul, 71,667; Saint-Pierre, 58,846; Le Tampon, 47,598. **Monetary unit:** Franc. **Languages:** French, Creole. **Ethnicity/Race:** French, African, Malagasy, Chinese, Pakistani, Indian. **Religion:** Roman Catholic, 70%
Economic summary: GDP/PPP (1995 est.): $2.9 billion, $4,300 per capita. **Real growth rate:** 2.7%; **Inflation:** n.a. **Unemployment:** (1994), 35%. **Arable land:** 17%. **Agriculture:** rum, vanilla, bananas, perfume plants. **Industry:** rum, cigarettes, processed sugar. **Labor force:** 242,169; agriculture, 30%; industry, 21%; services, 49%. **Exports:** $171.776 million (f.o.b., 1994): sugar, perfume essences, rum, molasses. **Imports:** $2.354 billion (c.i.f., 1994): manufactured goods, foodstuffs, beverages, machinery and transportation equipment, petroleum products. **Major trading partners:** France, Mauritius, Bahrain, South Africa, Italy.

Of volcanic origin, Réunion consists mostly of rugged mountains in an advanced state of dissection by short torrential rivers. It is located about 450 miles (724 km) east of Madagascar, in the Indian Ocean. First explored by Portuguese navigators in the 16th century, the island of Réunion, then uninhabited, was taken as a French possession in 1642. African slaves were imported first to work coffee and then sugar plantations; with the abolition of slavery in 1848, indentured laborers from Indochina, India, and East Africa were brought in. In 1958, Réunion approved the constitution of the Fifth French Republic and remained an Overseas Department of the French Republic. Réunion elects five deputies to the French National Assembly and three to the Senate. The island is administered by an appointed prefect and a general council composed of 44 elected members.

Overseas Territories

Overseas Territories are comparable to Departments, except that their administrative organization includes a locally elected government.

French Polynesia

Status: Overseas Territory
High Commissioner: Paul Ronciere (1994)
Area: 1,609 sq mi. (4,167 sq km)
Population (1998 est.): 237,844 (average annual growth rate: 1.81%); birth rate: 22.7/1000; infant mortality rate: 13.7/1000; density per sq mi.: 148
Capital (1988): Papeete (on Tahiti), 23,555. **Monetary unit:** Pacific financial community franc. **Language:** French. **Ethnicity/Race:** Polynesian 78%, Chinese 12%, local French 6%, metropolitan French 4%. **Religions:** Protestant, 55%; Roman Catholic, 30%; Other, 16%. **Literacy rate:** 98%
Economic summary: GDP/PPP (1995 est.): $1.76 billion, $8,000 per capita. **Inflation:** (1994) 1.5%. **Unemployment:** (1992 est.) 15%. **Principal agricultural product:** coconuts, vanilla, fruits, poultry. **Industry:** tourism, maintenance of French nuclear test base. **Exports:** $245 million (f.o.b., 1994): coconut products, mother of pearl, vanilla, shark meat. **Imports:** $967 million (c.i.f., 1994): fuels, foodstuffs, equipment. **Major trading partners:** France, U.S.

The term French Polynesia is applied to the scattered French possessions in the South Pacific—Mangareva (Gambier), Makatea, the Marquesas Islands, Rapa, Rurutu, Rimatara, the Society Islands, the Tuamotu Archipelago, Tubuai, Raivavae, and the island of Clipperton—which were organized into a single colony in 1903. There are 120 islands, of which 25 are uninhabited.

The president of the Territorial Government is assisted by a Council of Government and a popularly elected Territorial Assembly. The principal and most populous island—Tahiti, in the Society group—was claimed as French in 1768. In 1958, French Polynesia voted in favor of the new constitution of the French Fifth Republic and remained an

Overseas Territory of the French Republic. The indigenous people are mostly Maoris.

The Pacific Nuclear Test Center on the atoll of Mururoa, 744 miles (1,200 km) from Tahiti, was completed in 1966. In 1975 worldwide opposition forced the French to move the testing underground on Fangataufa. To compensate the residents for the nuclear weapons tests in 1995–96 France offered a 10-year $194 million annual compensation package. An independence movement continues to flourish in French Polynesia.

New Caledonia and Dependencies

Status: Overseas Territory
High Commissioner: Dominique Bur (1995)
Area: 7,374 sq mi. (19,103 sq km)[1]
Population (1998 est.): 194,197 (average annual growth rate: 1.64%); birth rate: 21.1/1000; infant mortality rate: 12.7/1000; density per sq mi.: 26
Capital (1989): Nouméa, 65,110. **Monetary unit:** Pacific financial community franc. **Languages:** French, Melanesian and Polynesian dialects. **Ethnicity/Race:** Kanak (Melanesian) 42.5%, European 37.1%, Wallisian 8.4%, Polynesian 3.8%, Indonesian 3.6%, Vietnamese 1.6%, other 3%. **Religion:** Roman Catholic, 60%; Protestant, 30%. **Literacy rate:** 91%
Economic summary: GDP/PPP (1995 est.): $1.5 billion, $8,000 per capita income; **Real growth rate:** n.a. **Inflation:** (1990) 1.4%. **Unemployment:** (1994) 15%. **Agriculture:** coffee, beef, wheat, vegetables. **Industry:** nickel. **Natural resources:** nickel, chromite, iron ore. **Labor force:** 70,044: 32% in agriculture; 20% in industry; 40% in services; 8% in mining **Exports:** $528 million (f.o.b., 1995): nickel metal and ore. **Imports:** $926 million (c.i.f., 1992): mineral fuels, machinery, electrical equipment, foodstuffs. **Major trading partners:** France, Japan, U.S., Australia.

1. Including dependencies.

New Caledonia (6,466 sq mi.; 16,747 sq km), about 1,070 miles (1,722 km) northeast of Sydney, Australia, was explored by Capt. James Cook in 1774 and annexed by France in 1853. The government also administers the Isle of Pines, the Loyalty Islands (Uvéa, Lifu, and Maré), the Belep Islands, the Huon Island group, and Chesterfield Islands. The native people are Melanesians called the Kanak. In 1984, the French National Assembly passed a law that granted internal autonomy to New Caledonia, and in May 1998 reached an agreement with New Caledonia to end its status as an overseas territory by the end of this year, and to work toward complete independence within 20 years.

Southern and Antarctic Lands

Status: Overseas Territory
Administrator: Christian Dors
Area: 3,004 sq mi. (7,781 sq km, excluding Adélie Land)
Capital: Port-au-Français

This territory is uninhabited except for the personnel of scientific bases. It consists of Adélie Land (166,752 sq mi.; 431,888 sq km) on the Antarctic mainland (which the U.S. does not recognize) and the following islands in the southern Indian Ocean: the Kerguelen and Crozet archipelagos and the islands of Saint-Paul and New Amsterdam.

Wallis and Futuna Islands

Status: Overseas Territory
Administrator: Léon-Alexandre Legrand (1997)
Area: 106 sq mi. (274 sq km)
Population (1998 est.): 14,974; growth rate 1.06%; birth rate 23/1000; infant mortality rate 20.9/1000; density per sq mi.: 141
Capital (1983): Mata-Utu. **Languages:** French, Wallisian. **Ethnicity/Race:** Polynesian. **Religion:** Roman Catholic. **Literacy rate:** 50%
Economic summary: GDP/PPP (1995 est.): $28.7 million, $2,000 per capita. **Exports:** $370,000 (f.o.b., 1995 est.). **Imports:** $13.5 million (c.i.f., 1995 est.): foodstuffs, manufactured goods, transport equipment, fuel.

The two islands groups in the South Pacific between Fiji and Samoa were settled by French missionaries at the beginning of the 19th century. A protectorate was established in the 1880s. There is a French-appointed High Administrator, a 20-member Territorial Assembly, and a deputy and a senator to the French national parliament. The three traditional Polynesian kings also help decide internal policy matters. Following a referendum by the Polynesian inhabitants, the status was changed to that of an Overseas Territory in 1961.

Territorial Collectivities

The Territorial Collectivity status was created in 1976 for Mayotte; it was conceived as being midway between an Overseas Territory and an Overseas Department. A Territorial Collectivity is represented in the French National Assembly by a deputy and in the French Senate by a senator. The head of government, the Prefect, is appointed by the French government.

St. Pierre and Miquelon

Status: Territorial Collectivity
Prefect: René Maurice
Area: 93 sq mi. (242 sq km)
Population (1998 est.): 6,914; growth rate 0.76%; birth rate 12.5/1000; infant mortality rate 8.6/1000; density per sq mi.: 74
Capital (1990): Saint Pierre, 5,683. **Ethnicity/Race:** Basques and Bretons (French fishermen). **Literacy rate:** 99%
Economic summary: GDP/PPP (1995 est.): $74 million, $11,000 per capita. **Unemployment:** 9.3%. **Industry:** fishing, canneries. **Labor force:** 2,980. **Exports:** $5 million (f.o.b., 1995): fish, pelts. **Imports:** $70.2 million (c.i.f., 1995): meat, clothing, fuel, electrical equipment, machinery, building materials. **Major trading partners:** Canada, France, U.S., U.K., the Netherlands.

The sole remnant of the French colonial empire in North America, these islands were first occupied by the French in 1604. Their only importance arises from proximity to the Grand Banks, located 10 miles south of Newfoundland, making them the center of the French Atlantic cod fisheries. On July 19, 1976, the islands became an Overseas Department of the French Republic. In May 1985, the archipelago was given a new status with a new name, Territorial Collectivity, because the former departmental arrangement conflicted with the tariff structure of the European Economic Community (now European Union), to which France belongs.

Mayotte

Status: Territorial Collectivity
Prefect: Alain Weil
Area: 146 sq mi. (378 sq km)
Population (1998 est.): 141,944; average annual rate of natural increase 5.16%; birth rate 47/1000; infant

mortality rate 71.1/1000; density per sq mi.: 972
Capital and largest city (1991): Mamoudzou (Dzaoudzi), 20,450
Economic summary: GDP/PPP (1993 est.): $54 million, $600 per capita. **Exports:** $3.64 million (f.o.b., 1996). **Imports:** $131.5 million (f.o.b., 1996). **Products:** vanilla, ylang-ylang, coffee, copra. **Exports:** ylang-ylang, vanilla. **Imports:** building materials, transportation equipment, rice, clothing, flour. **Major trading partners:** France, Comoros, Réunion, Kenya, South Africa, Pakistan.

France gained colonial control over Mayotte in 1843. The most populous of the Comoro Islands in the Indian Ocean with a Christian majority, Mayotte voted in 1974 and 1976 against joining the other predominantly Muslim islands in declaring themselves independent. Comoros laid claim to Mayotte shortly after independence and continues to do so. In 1979, the United Nations passed a resolution affirming the sovereignty of Comoros over Mayotte; France, however, retains de facto control of Mayotte.

Gabon

GABONESE REPUBLIC

National name: République Gabonaise
President: Omar Bongo (1967)
Premier: Paulin Obame-Nguema (1994)
Area: 103,346 sq mi. (267,670 sq km)
Population (1998 est.): 1,207,844 (average annual rate of natural increase: 1.48%); birth rate: 28/1000; infant mortality rate: 85.4/1000; density per sq mi.: 12
Capital and largest city (1994): Libreville, 419,596. Other cities (1994): Port-Gentil, 80,000; Franceville, 42,000. **Monetary unit:** Franc CFA. **Languages:** French (official). **Ethnicity/Race:** (1993) Bantu tribes, including six major tribal groupings: Fang 25%, Punu 23%, Nzeiby 13%, Mbede (Obamba/Bateke) 9%, Kota 7%, and Myene 5%; Pygmies 0.7%, naturalized population 0.3%, foreigners 15%. **Religions:** Catholic 75%, Protestant 20%, Animist 4%. **Literacy rate:** 61%
Economic summary: GDP/PPP (1996 est.): $6.3 billion; $5,400 per capita. **Real growth rate:** 2.6%. **Inflation:** 6.2%. **Unemployment:** 20% (1995). **Arable land:** 1%. **Agriculture:** cocoa, coffee, wood, palm oil. **Labor force:** 120,000; agriculture, 65%; industry and commerce, services, government. **Industry:** petroleum, natural gas, processed wood, manganese, uranium. **Natural resources:** wood, petroleum, iron ore, manganese, uranium. **Exports:** $2.7 billion (f.o.b., 1995 est.): crude oil, 78%; manganese, 4%; uranium. **Imports:** $700 million (f.o.b., 1995 est.): foodstuffs, chemical products, petroleum products, construction materials, manufactures, machinery. **Major trading partners:** France, U.S., Germany, Japan, Cameroon. **Member of French Community**

Geography This West African country with the Atlantic as its western border is also bounded by Equatorial Guinea, Cameroon, and the Congo. Its area is slightly less than Colorado's. From mangrove swamps on the coast, the land becomes divided plateaus in the north and east and mountains in the north. Most of the country is covered by a dense tropical forest.

Government A republic, with a multiparty presidential regime (opposition parties legalized 1990). The president is elected for a five-year term. Legislative powers are exercised by a 120-seat National Assembly, which is elected for a five-year term.

History The earliest humans in Gabon were believed to be the Babinga, or Pygmies, dating back to 7000 B.C.E., who were later followed by Bantu groups from southern and eastern Africa. Now there are many tribal groups in the country, the largest being the Fang peoples, who constitute 25% of the population.

Gabon was first explored by the Portuguese navigator Diego Cam in the 15th century. In 1472 the Portuguese explorers encountered the mouth of the Como river, and because its shape looks like a coat, they named it "Rio de Gabao," river of Gabon, which later became the name of the country. The Dutch began arriving in 1593, and the French in 1630. In 1839, the French founded their first settlement on the left bank of the Gabon Estuary and gradually occupied the hinterland during the second half of the 19th century. It was organized as a French territory in 1888 and became an autonomous republic within the French Union after World War II and an independent republic on Aug. 17, 1960.

After his conversion to Islam in 1973, President Bongo changed his given name, Albert Bernard, to Omar. He has been reelected every five years since 1967. Following strikes and riots the president called a national conference in March 1990. In May it adopted a transitional constitution legalizing political parties and calling for free elections. In its first multiparty election in Dec. 1993 the incumbent president received just over 51% of the vote while the opposition candidate refused to accept defeat; he alleged fraud and tried to establish a rival government.

Rioting in the capital led the president to declare a state of siege in Feb. 1994. A university strike by students in May caused the government to close the institution for a period. Growing dissension within the army also led the president to call for a peace conference in September. As a result a coalition government was formed that November.

Gambia, The

REPUBLIC OF THE GAMBIA

President: Colonel Yahya A. J. J. Jammeh (1997)
Area: 4,093 sq mi. (11,300 sq km)
Population (1998 est.): 1,291,858 (average annual rate of natural increase: 3.42%); birth rate: 43.3/1000; infant mortality rate: 77.1/1000; density per sq mi.: 316
Capital (1986): Banjul, 44,188. **Monetary unit:** Dalasi. **Languages:** Native tongues, English (official). **Ethnicity/Race:** African 99% (Mandinka 42%, Fula 18%, Wolof 16%, Jola 10%, Serahuli 9%, other 4%), non-Gambian 1%. **Religions:** Islam, 90%; Christian, 9%; traditional, 1%. **Literacy rate:** 27%
Economic summary: GDP/PPP (1995 est.): $1.1 billion; $1,100 per capita. **Real growth rate:** 2%. **Inflation:** 7%. **Arable land:** 18%. **Products:** peanuts, rice, palm kernels. **Labor force:** 400,000 (1986 est.); agriculture, 75.0%; industry, commerce and services, 18.9%; government, 6.1%. **Industry:** processed peanuts, fish, and hides. **Natural resources:** fish. **Exports:** $127 million (f.o.b., 1995 est.): peanuts and peanut products, 70%; fish, cotton, lint, palm kernels. **Imports:** $201 million (c.i.f., 1995 est.): foodstuffs, fuel, machinery, transport equipment, manufactures, raw materials. **Major trading partners:** U.S., E.U., Asia. **Member of Commonwealth of Nations**

Geography Situated on the Atlantic coast in westernmost Africa and surrounded on three sides by Senegal, Gambia is twice the size of Delaware. The

Gambia River flows for 200 miles (322 km) through Gambia on its way to the Atlantic. The country, the smallest on the continent, averages only 20 miles (32 km) in width.

Government A civilian government, following presidential and legislative elections in Sept. 1996 and Jan. 1997 respectively.

History Since the 13th century, the Wolof, Malinke, and Fulani peoples settled in what is now The Gambia. The Portuguese were the first European explorers, encountering the Gambia River in 1455, and in 1681 the French founded an enclave at Albredabut. During the 17th century, Gambia was settled by various companies of English merchants. Slavery was the chief source of revenue before it was abolished in 1807. Gambia became a Crown colony in 1843 and an independent nation within the Commonwealth of Nations on Feb. 18, 1965. Full independence was approved in a 1970 referendum, and on April 24 of that year Gambia proclaimed itself a republic.

Elections of April 29, 1992, returned President Jawara for a fifth term. His People's Progressive Party won 25 of the 36 seats in the House of Representatives. A military coup led by Capt. Yahya Jammeh deposed the president in July 1994, suspended the constitution, and banned political parties. Jammeh promised new elections, which were held in Sept. 1996. Incumbent President Jammeh won 55% of the vote against his nearest rival, Ousseynou Darboe, who received 36%. The next month Jammeh was sworn in as president, and in April 1997 he completed the promised return to civilian rule. Censorship of the press and a ban on some opposition parties, however, continue to mar the country's transition to democracy.

Georgia

GEORGIA

Sakartvelo

President: Eduard Shevardnadze (1992)
Secretary of State: Niko Lekishvili (1995)
Area: 26,900 sq mi. (69,700 sq km)
Population (1998 est.): 5,108,527; average annual rate of natural increase: –0.92%; birth rate: 11.7/1000; infant mortality rate: 51.1/1000; density per sq mi.: 190
Capital and largest city (1991): Tbilisi, 1,279,000. Other cities (1989): Kutaisi, 235,000; Batoumi, 136,000; and Sokhumi, 121,000. **Monetary unit:** Lari. **Language:** Georgian (official), 71%; Russian, 9%; Armenian, 7%; Azerbaijani, 6%. **Ethnicity/Race:** Georgian 70.1%, Armenian 8.1%, Russian 6.3%, Azeri 5.7%, Ossetian 3%, Abkhaz 1.8%, other 5%. **Religion:** Georgian Orthodox, 65%; Russian Orthodox, 10%; Armenian Orthodox, 8%; Muslim, 11%
Economic summary: GDP/PPP (1996 estimate as extrapolated from the World Bank estimate for 1994): $7.1 billion; $1,350 per capita. **Real growth rate:** 11%. **Inflation:** 13.3% (1996 est.). **Unemployment:** 21%. **Labor force:** 2.2 million: industry and construction, 31%; agriculture and forestry, 25%. **Industry:** heavy industrial products include raw steel, rolled steel, cement, lumber, machine tools, foundry equipment, electric locomotives, tower cranes, welding equipment, meat packing, dairy and fishing, farm machinery. **Agriculture:** citrus fruits, grapes, sugar, vegetables, grains, cattle, sheep, goats, pigs, and poultry. **Exports:** $356 million (f.o.b., 1995): citrus fruits, tea, other agricultural products, diverse types of machinery, ferrous and nonferrous metals, textiles. **Imports:** $647 million (c.i.f., 1995): machinery and parts, fuel, transport equipment, textiles. **Major trading partners:** Russia, Turkey, Azerbaijan, Ukraine, Germany, U.S.

Geography Georgia is bordered by the Black Sea in the west, by Turkey and Armenia in the south, by Azerbaijan in the east, and Russia in the north. The republic also includes the Abkhaz and Adzhar autonomous republics and the Yugo-Ossetian Autonomous Oblast. Mt. Elbrus (Lalbuzi in Georgian) at 18,841 is the highest peak in Europe. Georgia's principal rivers, Mtkvari and the Rioni, provide an abundance of hydroelectric power for the country.

Government A republic with a unicameral parliament. The president and 246-member parliament were elected on Nov. 5, 1995.

History Georgia became a kingdom about 4 B.C.E. and Christianity was introduced in C.E. 337. It reached its greatest period of expansion during the reign of Queen Tamara (1184–1213) when its territory included the whole of Transcaucasia. During the 13th century, the population of five million was reduced catastrophically by Mongol and other invasions. The country was the scene of a struggle between Persia and Turkey from the 16th century on, and in the 18th century became a vassal to Russia in exchange for protection from the Turks and Persians.

Georgia joined Azerbaijan and Armenia in 1917 to establish the anti-Bolshevik Transcaucasian Federation, and upon its dissolution, proclaimed its independence in 1918. In 1922, Georgia, Armenia, and Azerbaijan were annexed and formed into the Transcaucasian Soviet Socialist Republic affiliated with the U.S.S.R. In 1936, it became a separate Soviet republic. Under Soviet rule Georgia was transformed from an agrarian country to a largely industrial, urban society.

Zviad Gamsakhurdia won the first directly elected Soviet presidency in 1990, pledging to lead Georgia toward independence. Georgia proclaimed its independence on April 6, 1991. Gamsakhurdia was later accused of dictatorial policies, the jailing of opposition leaders, human rights abuses, and clamping down on the media. A two-week civil war centered in the capital of Tbilisi ensued and Gamsakhurdia was forced to flee to Azerbaijan and later to Armenia. A ruling military council was established by the opposition until a civilian authority could be restored. In 1992–93, the government engaged in armed conflict with separatists in the breakaway province of Abkhazia. In 1994, Russia and Georgia signed a cooperation treaty that authorized Russia to keep three military bases in Georgia and allowed Russians to train and equip the Georgian army. In 1996, Georgia and its breakaway region of South Ossetia agreed to a cessation of hostilities in their six-year conflict. With little progress in resolving the Abkhazia situation, however, parliament in April 1997 voted overwhelmingly to threaten Russia with loss of its military bases should it fail to extend Russian military control of the separatist region.

Germany

FEDERAL REPUBLIC OF GERMANY

National name: Bundesrepublik Deutschland
President: Roman Herzog (1994)
Chancellor: Gerhard Schröder (1998)
Area: 137,826 sq mi. (356,910 sq km)
Population (1998 est.): 82,079,454 (average annual growth rate: 0.02%); birth rate: 8.8/1000; infant mortality rate: 5.2/1000; density per sq mi.: 596
Capital and largest city (1997): Berlin (capital since Oct. 3, 1990), 3,477,900; Bonn (administrative seat of government), 295,300. **Other large cities (1997):** Hamburg, 1,703,800; Munich, 1,251,100; Cologne, 963,300; Frankfurt, 656,200; Essen, 619,600; Dortmund, 601,500; Stuttgart, 592,000; Duesseldorf, 573,100; Bremen, 551,000; Hanover, 526,400; Duisberg, 536,500. **Monetary unit:** Deutsche Mark. **Language:** German. **Ethnicity/Race:** German 91.5%, Turkish 2.4%, Italians 0.7%, Greeks 0.4%, Poles 0.4%, Other 4.6%. **Religions:** Protestant 38%, Roman Catholic 34%, Muslim 1.7%, Unaffiliated or other 26.3%. **Literacy rate:** 99%
Economic summary (1996): GDP/PPP (1996 est.): $1.7 trillion; $20,400 per capita. **Real growth rate:** 1.4%. **Inflation (1996):** 1.5%. **Unemployment (1997):** 11.2%. **Labor force:** 38.7 million; industry, 41%; agriculture, 3%. **Exports:** $501.3 billion (f.o.b., 1996 est.): manufactures 88.2% (including machines and precision tools, chemicals, motor vehicles, iron and steel products), agricultural products 5.0%, raw materials 2.3%, fuels 1.0%. **Imports:** $430.7 billion (f.o.b., 1996 est.): manufactures 74.2%, agricultural products 9.9%, fuels 6.4%, raw materials 2.3%. **Industry:** Among the world's largest producers of iron, steel, coal, cement, chemicals, machinery, vehicles, machine tools, electronics, food and beverages. Other industries include: metal fabrication, shipbuilding, machine building, petroleum refining, fishing and forestry. **Agriculture:** potatoes, wheat, rye, barley, sugar beets, fruit, cabbage, poultry, pork, beef, chicken, milk, hides, and skins. **Natural resources:** iron ore, coal, potash, timber, lignite, uranium, copper, natural gas, salt, nickel. **Major trading partners:** E.U., other western European nations, U.S., eastern Europe, Japan.

Geography Located in central Europe, Germany comprises three major physiographic regions from north to south: the North German Plain, the Central German Uplands (Mittelgebirge), and the Southern German Highlands. The Bavarian plateau in the southwest averages 1,600 feet (488 m) above sea level, but it reaches 9,721 feet (2,962 m) in the Zugspitze Mountains, the highest point in the country. Germany's major rivers are the Danube, the Elbe, the Oder, the Weser, and the Rhine. It is about the size of Montana.

Government Under the constitution (Basic Law) of May 23, 1949, the Federal Republic of Germany was established as a parliamentary democracy. The parliament consists of the Bundesrat, an upper chamber representing and appointed by the Länder, or states, and the Bundestag, a lower house elected for four years by universal suffrage. A federal assembly composed of Bundestag deputies as well as deputies from the state parliaments elects the president of the Republic for a five-year term; the Bundestag alone chooses the Chancellor, or prime minister. Each of the 16 Länder have a legislature popularly elected for a four-year or five-year term.

The major political parties are the Christian Democratic Union-Christian Social Union (CDU-CSU), led by Chancellor Helmut Kohl; the Social Democratic Party (SPD); the Free Democratic Party (FDP); the Alliance '90/Greens; and the Party of Democratic Socialism (PDS). Kohl's government is a coalition with the Free Democrats.

History By the end of the 2nd century B.C.E., Germanic tribes had advanced into southern and central Germany, displacing the Celts and coming into contact with the Romans in Gaul. One of those tribes, the Franks, attained supremacy in western Europe under Charlemagne, who was crowned Holy Roman Emperor in C.E. 800. By the Treaty of Verdun (843), Charlemagne's lands east of the Rhine were ceded to the German Prince Louis. Additional territory acquired by the Treaty of Mersen (870) gave Germany approximately the area it maintained throughout the Middle Ages. For several centuries after Otto the Great was crowned king in 936, German rulers were also usually heads of the Holy Roman Empire.

By the 14th century, the Holy Roman Empire was little more than a loose federation of the German princes who elected the Holy Roman Emperor. In 1438, Albert of Hapsburg became emperor; thereafter the Hapsburgs held the throne almost continuously until the dissolution of the Holy Roman Empire in 1806. Relations between state and church were changed by the Reformation, which began with Martin Luther's 95 theses, and came to a head in 1547, when Charles V scattered the forces of the Protestant League at Mühlberg. Freedom of worship was guaranteed by the Peace of Augsburg (1555), but a Counter Reformation took place later, and a dispute over the succession to the Bohemian throne brought on the Thirty Years' War (1618–48), which devastated Germany and left the empire divided into hundreds of small principalities virtually independent of the Emperor.

Meanwhile, Prussia was developing into a state of considerable strength. Frederick the Great (1740–86) reorganized the Prussian army and defeated Maria Theresa of Austria in a struggle over Silesia. After the defeat of Napoleon at Waterloo (1815), the struggle between Austria and Prussia for supremacy in Germany continued, reaching its climax in the defeat of Austria in the Seven Weeks' War (1866) and the formation of the Prussian-dominated North German Confederation (1867). The architect of this new German unity was Otto von Bismarck, a conservative, monarchist, and militaristic Prussian prime minister. He unified all Germany in a series of three wars against Denmark (1864), Austria (1866), and France (1870–71). On Jan. 18, 1871, King Wilhelm I of Prussia was proclaimed German Emperor in the Hall of Mirrors at Versailles. The North German Confederation, created in 1867, was abolished, and the Second German Reich, consisting of the North and South German states, was born. With a powerful army, an efficient bureaucracy, and a loyal bourgeoisie, Chancellor Bismarck consolidated a powerful centralized state.

Wilhelm II dismissed Bismarck in 1890 and embarked upon a "New Course," stressing an intensified colonialism and a powerful navy. His chaotic foreign policy culminated in the diplomatic isolation of Germany and the disastrous defeat in World War I (1914–18). The Second German Empire collapsed following the defeat of the German armies in 1918, the naval mutiny at Kiel, and the flight of the Kaiser

Rulers of Germany and Prussia

Name	Born	Ruled[1]
Kings of Prussia		
Frederick I[2]	1657	1701–1713
Frederick William I	1688	1713–1740
Frederick II the Great	1712	1740–1786
Frederick William II	1744	1786–1797
Frederick William III	1770	1797–1840
Frederick William IV	1795	1840–1861
William I	1797	1861–1871[3]
Emperors Of Germany		
William I	1797	1871–1888
Frederick III	1831	1888–1888
William II	1859	1888–1918[4]
Weimar Republic		
Friedrich Ebert[5]	1871	1919–1925
Paul von Hindenburg[5]	1847	1925–1934
Third Reich		
Adolf Hitler[6, 7]	1889	1934–1945
Karl Doenitz[6]	1891	1945–1945
German Federal Republic (West) Chancellors		
Konrad Adenauer	1876	1949–1963
Ludwig Erhard	1897	1963–1966
Kurt Georg Kiesinger	1904	1966–1969
Willy Brandt	1913	1969–1974
Helmut Schmidt	1918	1974–1982
Helmut Kohl	1930	1982–1990
German Democratic Republic (East)		
Wilhelm Pieck[5]	1876	1949–1960
Walter Ulbricht[8]	1893	1960–1973
Willi Stoph[9]	1914	1973–1976
Erich Honecker[9]	1912	1976–1989
Egon Krenz[9]	1937	1989–1989
Manfred Gerlach[9]	1928	1989–1990
Sabine Bergman-Pohl[9]	1946	1990–1990
German Federal Republic Chancellors		
Helmut Kohl	1930	1991–1998
Gerhard Schröder	1944	1998–

1. Year of end of rule is also that of death, unless otherwise indicated. 2. Was Elector of Brandenburg (1688–1701) as Frederick III. 3. Became Emperor of Germany in 1871. 4. Died 1941. 5. President. 6. Führer. 7. Named Chancellor by President von Hindenburg in 1933. 8. Chairman of Council of State. Died 1973. 9. Chairman of Council of State.

to the Netherlands. The Social Democrats, led by Friedrich Ebert and Philipp Scheidemann, crushed the Communists and established a moderate state, known as the Weimar Republic, with Ebert as president. The Weimar constitution of 1919 provided for a president to be elected for seven years by universal suffrage and a bicameral legislature, consisting of the Reichsrat, representing the states, and the Reichstag, representing the people. It contained a model Bill of Rights. It was weakened, however, by a provision that enabled the president to rule by decree. President Ebert died Feb. 28, 1925, and on April 26, Field Marshal Paul von Hindenburg was elected president. The mass of Germans regarded the Weimar Republic as a child of defeat, imposed upon a Germany whose legitimate aspirations to world leadership had been thwarted by a world conspiracy. Added to this were a crippling currency debacle, a tremendous burden of reparations, and acute economic distress.

Adolf Hitler, an Austrian war veteran and a fanatical nationalist, fanned discontent by promising a Greater Germany, abrogation of the Treaty of Versailles, restoration of Germany's lost colonies, and the destruction of the Jews, whom he scapegoated as the reason for Germany's downfall and depressed economy. When the Social Democrats and the Communists refused to combine against the Nazi threat, President von Hindenburg made Hitler the chancellor on Jan. 30, 1933. With the death of von Hindenburg on Aug. 2, 1934, Hitler repudiated the Treaty of Versailles and began full-scale rearmament. In 1935 he withdrew Germany from the League of Nations, and the next year he reoccupied the Rhineland and signed the anti-Comintern pact with Japan, at the same time strengthening relations with Italy. Austria was annexed in March 1938. By the Munich agreement in Sept. 1938 he gained the Czech Sudetenland, and in violation of this agreement he completed the dismemberment of Czechoslovakia in March 1939. His invasion of Poland on Sept. 1, 1939, precipitated World War II.

Hitler established the death camps to carry out "the final solution to the Jewish question." By the end of the war, Hitler's holocaust had killed 6 million Jews, as well as Gypsies, homosexuals, Communists, the handicapped, and others not fitting the Aryan ideal. After some dazzling initial successes in 1939–42, Germany surrendered unconditionally to Allied and Soviet military commanders on May 8, 1945. On June 5 the four-nation Allied Control Council became the de facto government of Germany.

(For details of World War II and the Holocaust, *see* Headline History, World War II.)

At the Berlin (or Potsdam) Conference (July 17–Aug. 2, 1945) President Truman, Premier Stalin, and Prime Minister Clement Attlee of Britain set forth the guiding principles of the Allied Control Council. They were Germany's complete disarmament and demilitarization, destruction of its war potential, rigid control of industry, and decentralization of the political and economic structure. Pending final determination of territorial questions at a peace conference, the three victors agreed to the ultimate transfer of the city of Königsberg (now Kaliningrad) and its adjacent area to the U.S.S.R. and to the administration by Poland of former German territories lying generally east of the Oder-Neisse Line. For purposes of control, Germany was divided into four national occupation zones, each headed by a Military Governor.

The Western powers were unable to agree with the U.S.S.R. on any fundamental issue. Work of the Allied Control Council was hamstrung by repeated Soviet vetoes; and finally, on March 20, 1948, Russia walked out of the Council. Meanwhile, the U.S. and Britain had taken steps to merge their zones economically (Bizone); and on May 31, 1948, the U.S., Britain, France, and the Benelux countries agreed to set up a German state comprising the three Western Zones. The U.S.S.R. reacted by clamping a blockade on all ground communications between the Western Zones and West Berlin, an enclave in the

The Berlin Wall (1961–1990)

Major anti-Communist riots broke out in East Berlin in June 1953 and, on Aug. 13, 1961, the Soviet Sector was sealed off by a Communist-built wall, 26½ miles (43 km) long, running through the city. It was built to stem the flood of refugees seeking freedom in the West, 200,000 having fled in 1961 before the wall was erected.

On Nov. 9, 1989, several weeks after the resignation of East Germany's long-time Communist leader, Erich Honecker, the wall's designer and chief proponent, the East German government opened its borders to the West and allowed thousands of its citizens to pass freely through the Berlin Wall. They were cheered and greeted by thousands of West Berliners, and many of the jubilant newcomers celebrated their new freedom by climbing on top of the hated wall.

The following day, East German troops began dismantling parts of the wall. It was ironic that this wall was built to keep the citizens from leaving and, 28 years later, it was being dismantled for the same reason. On Nov. 22, new passages were opened at the north and south of the Brandenburg Gate in an emotional ceremony attended by Chancellor Helmut Kohl of West Germany and Chancellor Hans Modrow of East Germany. The opening of the Brandenburg Gate climaxed the ending of the barriers that had divided the German people since the end of World War II. By the end of 1990, the entire wall had been removed.

Soviet Zone. The Western Allies countered by organizing a gigantic airlift to fly supplies into the beleaguered city, assigning 60,000 men to it. The U.S.S.R. was finally forced to lift the blockade on May 12, 1949.

The Federal Republic of Germany was proclaimed on May 23, 1949, with its capital at Bonn. In free elections, West German voters gave a majority in the Constituent Assembly to the Christian Democrats, with the Social Democrats largely making up the opposition. Konrad Adenauer became chancellor, and Theodor Heuss of the Free Democrats was elected first president.

When the Federal Republic of Germany was established in West Germany, the East German states adopted a more centralized constitution for the Democratic Republic of Germany, and it was put into effect on Oct. 7, 1949. The U.S.S.R. thereupon dissolved its occupation zone but Soviet troops remained. The Western Allies declared that the East German Republic was a Soviet creation undertaken without self-determination and refused to recognize it. It was recognized only within the Soviet bloc. Soviet forces created a state controlled by the secret police with a single party, the Socialist Unity (Communist) Party. The 25-year diplomatic hiatus between East Germany and the U.S. ended Sept. 4, 1974, with the establishment of formal relations.

Agreements in Paris in 1954 giving the Federal Republic full independence and complete sovereignty came into force on May 5, 1955. Under it, West Germany and Italy became members of the Brussels treaty organization created in 1948 and renamed the Western European Union. West Germany also became a member of NATO. In 1955 the U.S.S.R. recognized the Federal Republic. The Saar territory, under an agreement between France and West Germany, held a plebiscite and despite economic links to France, voted to rejoin West Germany. It became a state of West Germany on Jan. 1, 1957.

The division between West Germany and East Germany was intensified when the Communists erected the Berlin Wall in 1961. In 1968, the East German Communist leader, Walter Ulbricht, imposed restrictions on West German movements into West Berlin. The Soviet-bloc invasion of Czechoslovakia in August 1968 added to the tension. West Germany in 1970 signed a treaty with Poland, renouncing force and setting Poland's western border as the Oder-Neisse Line. It subsequently resumed formal relations with Czechoslovakia in a pact that "voided" the Munich treaty that gave Nazi Germany the Sudetenland. By 1973, normal relations were established between East and West Germany and the two states entered the United Nations.

Willy Brandt, winner of a Nobel Peace Prize for his foreign policies, was forced to resign in 1974 when an East German spy was discovered to be one of his top staff members. Succeeding him was a moderate Social Democrat, Helmut Schmidt. Schmidt staunchly backed U.S. military strategy in Europe, staking his political fate on the strategy of placing U.S. nuclear missiles in Germany unless the Soviet Union reduced its arsenal of intermediate missiles. The chancellor also strongly opposed nuclear freeze proposals and won 2–1 support for his stand at the convention of Social Democrats in April. The Free Democrats then deserted the Socialists after losing ground in local elections and joined with the Christian Democrats to unseat Schmidt and install Helmut Kohl as chancellor in 1982. An economic upswing in 1986 led to Kohl's reelection.

The fall of the Communist government in East Germany left only Soviet objections to German reunification to be dealt with. This was resolved in July 1990. Soviet objections to a reunified Germany belonging to NATO were dropped in return for German promises to reduce its military and engage in wide-ranging economic cooperation with the Soviet Union. In ceremonies beginning the evening of Tuesday, Oct. 2, 1990, and continuing throughout the next day, the German Democratic Republic acceded to the Federal Republic and Germany became a united and sovereign state for the first time since 1945. Some one million people gathered at midnight Oct. 2 at the Reichstag in Berlin. At midnight, a replica of the Liberty Bell, a gift from the United States, rang, and unity was officially proclaimed.

Following unification, the Federal Republic became the second largest country in Europe, after the Soviet Union. A reunited Berlin serves as the official capital, although the government would continue to have administrative functions in Bonn during the 12-year transition period. The issue of the cost of reunification and the modernization of the former East Germany were serious issues facing the reunified nation. Germany ratified the Maastricht Treaty in Oct. 1993, being the last of the 12 E.U. members to do so. Voters in the relatively new state of Brandenburg in the east rejected in May 1996 a proposal to merge with Berlin, dramatizing a lingering psychological division between eastern and western Germany.

Owing to a budget deficit that threatened the country's eligibility for introducing the future common European currency, the government in June 1997 proposed to revalue its foreign exchange holdings. Germany's other main challenge was to render Germany competitively attractive as an industrial location by radically reducing taxes so as to attract investment capital, foreign and domestic, within the E.U., and thus lower the high rate of unemployment.

In its most important election in decades, on Sept. 27, 1998, Germans chose Social Democrat Gerhard Schröder as chancellor over Christian Democrat incumbent Helmut Kohl, ending a 16-year-long rule that oversaw the reunification of East and West Germany and symbolized the end of the cold war in Europe. A centrist in the style of Clinton and Blair, Schröder campaigned for "the new middle" and promised to rectify Germany's high unemployement rate of 10.6%.

Ghana

REPUBLIC OF GHANA

President: Jerry John Rawlings
Area: 92,100 sq mi. (238,540 sq km)
Population (1998 est.): 18,497,206 (average annual rate of natural increase: 2.13%); birth rate: 32.8/1000; infant mortality rate: 77.5/1000; density per sq mi.: 201
Capital: Accra. **Largest cities (est. 1988):** Accra, 949,100; Kumasi, 385,200; Tamale, 151,100. **Monetary unit:** Cedi. **Languages:** English (official), Native tongues (Brong Ahafo, Twi, Fanti, Ga, Ewe, Dagbani). **Ethnicity/Race:** black African 99.8% (major tribes: Akan 44%, Moshi-Dagomba 16%, Ewe 13%, Ga 8%), European and other 0.2%. **Religions:** indigenous beliefs, 38%; Islam, 30%; Christian, 24%. **Literacy rate:** 60%
Economic summary: GDP/PPP (1996 est.): $27 billion; $1,530 per capita. **Real growth rate:** 5%. **Inflation:** 36%. **Unemployment** (1993 est.), 10%. **Arable land:** 12%. **Agriculture:** cocoa, coconuts, coffee, cassava, yams, rice, rubber. **Labor force:** (1983), 3.7 million; agriculture and fishing, 54.7%; industry, 18.7%. **Industry:** mining products, cocoa products, aluminum. **Natural resources:** gold, 39%; cocoa, 31%; timber, 6%, industrial diamonds, bauxite, manganese, timber, fish. **Exports:** $1.43 billion (f.o.b., 1995 est.): cocoa beans and products, gold, timber, tuna, bauxite, and aluminum. **Imports:** $1.84 billion (c.i.f., 1995 est.): petroleum, consumer goods, foods, intermediate goods, capital equipment. **Major trading partners:** U.K., U.S., Germany, France, Japan, South Korea. **Member of Commonwealth of Nations**

Geography A West African country bordering on the Gulf of Guinea, Ghana is bounded by Côte d'Ivoire to the west, Burkina Faso to the north, Togo to the east and the Atlantic Ocean to the south. It compares in size to Oregon, and its largest river is the Volta.

Government A republic. After a period of military rule, presidential and parliamentary elections were held Nov. 3, 1992 and ushered in the Fourth Republic on Jan. 7, 1993.

History Several major civilizations flourished in the general region of what is now Ghana. The ancient empire of Ghana (located 500 miles northwest of the contemporary state) reigned until the 13th century. The Akan peoples established the next major civilization, beginning in the 13th century, and then Ashanti empire flourished in the 18th and 19th centuries.

Called the Gold Coast, the area was first seen by Portuguese traders in 1470. They were followed by the English (1553), the Dutch (1595), and the Swedes (1640). British rule over the Gold Coast began in 1820, but it was not until after quelling the severe resistance of the Ashanti in 1901 that it was firmly established. British Togoland, formerly a colony of Germany, was incorporated into Ghana by referendum in 1956. Created as an independent country on March 6, 1957, Ghana, as the result of a plebiscite, became a republic on July 1, 1960.

Premier Kwame Nkrumah attempted to take leadership of the Pan-African Movement, holding the All-African People's Congress in his capital, Accra, in 1958 and organizing the Union of African States with Guinea and Mali in 1961. But he oriented his country toward the Soviet Union and China and built an autocratic rule over all aspects of Ghanaian life. In Feb. 1966, while Nkrumah was visiting Beijing and Hanoi, he was deposed by a military coup led by Gen. Emmanuel K. Kotoka.

A series of military coups followed and on June 4, 1979, Flight Lieutenant Jerry Rawlings overthrew Lt. Gen. Frederick Akuffo's military rule. Rawlings permitted the election of a civilian president to go ahead as scheduled the following month, and Hilla Limann, candidate of the People's National Party, took office. Charging the civilian government with corruption and repression, Rawlings staged another coup on Dec. 31, 1981. As chairman of the Provisional National Defense Council, Rawlings instituted an austerity program and reduced budget deficits. In the elections of late 1992 Rawlings won a majority of the votes for president.

Despite consistent economic growth, almost daily demonstrations occurred largely in protest against the introduction of a 17.5% value-added tax in March 1995. In June it was removed, and the finance minister resigned in July. Elections in Dec. 1996 saw the reelection of Rawlings as president with 57% of the vote. His party also secured 133 of the 200 seats in parliament. The opposition New Patriotic Party won 60 seats.

Greece

HELLENIC REPUBLIC

National name: Elliniki Dimokratia
President: Kostis Stephanopoulos (1995)
Prime Minister: Kostas Simitis (1996)
Area: 50,961 sq mi. (131,940 sq km)
Population (1998 est.): 10,662,138 (average annual rate of natural increase: 0.43%); birth rate: 9.7/1000; infant mortality rate: 7.3/1000; density per sq mi.: 209
Capital: Athens. **Largest cities (1991 est.):** Athens, 3,000,000; Thessaloníki, 720,000; Piraeus, 170,000; Patras, 155,000. **Monetary unit:** Drachma. **Language:** Greek. **Ethnicity/Race:** Greek 98%, other 2% note: the Greek government states there are no ethnic divisions in Greece. **Religions:** Greek Orthodox, 98%; Muslim, 1.3%; Other, 0.7%. **Literacy rate:** 93%
Economic summary: GDP/PPP (1996 est.): $106.9 billion; $10,000 per capita. **Real growth rate:** 2.2%. **Inflation:** 8.6%. **Unemployment:** 10%. **Arable land:**

19%; **Agriculture:** grains, fruits, vegetables, olives, olive oil, tobacco, cotton, livestock, dairy products. **Labor force:** (1995), 4.21 million; services, 52% ; agriculture, 23%; industry, 25%. **Industry:** textiles, chemicals, food processing. **Natural resources:** bauxite, lignite, magnesite, crude oil, marble. **Exports:** $5.9 billion (f.o.b., 1995): manufactured goods, food and live animals, fuels and lubricants, raw materials. **Imports:** $20.3 billion (f.o.b., 1995): machinery and automotive equipment, petroleum, consumer goods, chemicals, foodstuffs. **Major trading partners:** Germany, Italy, France, U.S., U.K.

Geography Located in southern Europe, Greece forms an irregular-shaped peninsula in the Mediterranean with two additional large peninsulas projecting from it: the Chalcidice and the Peloponnese. The Greek Islands are generally subdivided into two groups, according to location: the Ionian Islands (including Corfu, Cephalonia, and Leucas) west of the mainland and the Aegean Islands (including Euboea, Samos, Chios, Lesbos, and Crete) to the east and south. North-central Greece, Epirus, and western Macedonia all are mountainous. The main chain of the Pindus Mountains extend from northwestern Greece to the Peloponnese. Mt. Olympus, rising to 9,570 feet (2,909 m), is the highest point in the country.

Government A referendum in Dec. 1974, five months after the collapse of a military dictatorship, ended the Greek monarchy and established a republic. Ceremonial executive power is held by the president; the prime minister heads the government and is responsible to a 300-member unicameral parliament.

History Indo-European peoples, including the Mycenaeans, began entering Greece about 2000 B.C.E. and set up sophisticated civilizations. About 1200 B.C.E. the Dorians, another Indo-European people, invaded Greece, and a dark age followed, known mostly through the Homeric epics. At the end of this time, classical Greece began to emerge (c. 750 B.C.E.) as a loose composite of city-states with a heavy involvement in maritime trade and a devotion to art, literature, politics, and philosophy. Greece reached the peak of its glory in the 5th century B.C.E., but the Peloponnesian War (431–404 B.C.E.) weakened the nation and it was conquered by the Macedonians. By the middle of the 2nd century B.C.E. it had declined to the status of a Roman province. It remained within the Eastern Roman Empire until Constantinople fell to the Crusaders in 1204. In 1453, the Turks took Constantinople and by 1460, Greece was a Turkish province with its Orthodox Church intact. The insurrection made famous by the poet Lord Byron broke out in 1821, and in 1827 Greece won independence with sovereignty guaranteed by Britain, France, and Russia.

The protecting powers chose Prince Otto of Bavaria as the first king of modern Greece in 1832 to reign over an area only slightly larger than the Peloponnese peninsula. Chiefly under the next king, George I, chosen by the protecting powers in 1863, Greece acquired much of its present territory. During his 57-year reign, a period in which he encouraged parliamentary democracy, Thessaly, Epirus, Macedonia, Crete, and most of the Aegean islands were added from the disintegrating Turkish empire. Unfavorable economic conditions forced about one-sixth of the entire Greek population to emigrate (mostly to the U.S.) in the late 19th and early 20th centuries. An unsuccessful war against Turkey after World War I brought down the monarchy, to be replaced by a republic in 1923.

Two military dictatorships and a financial crisis brought George II back from exile, but only until 1941, when Italian and German invaders defeated tough Greek resistance. After British and Greek troops liberated the country in Oct. 1944, Communist guerrillas staged a long military campaign against the government. The Greek government received U.S. aid under the Truman Doctrine, the predecessor of the Marshall Plan, and eliminated the Communist guerilla threat. A military junta seized power in April 1967, sending young King Constantine II into exile. Col. George Papadopoulos, as prime minister, converted the government to republican form in 1973 and as president, ended martial law. He was moving to restore democracy when he was ousted in November of that year by his military colleagues. The regime of the "colonels," which had tortured its opponents and scoffed at human rights, resigned in 1974, after having bungled an attempt to seize Cyprus. Former Premier Karamanlis returned from exile to become premier of Greece's first civilian government since 1967. Greece has continued to be ruled by freely elected civilian governments ever since and on Jan. 1, 1981, Greece became the 10th member of the European Union.

Greece continues to experience tensions with Turkey over a disputed unpopulated 10-acre island and over Cyprus, which is divided into Greek and Turkish sectors. The collapse of neighboring Albania's government in 1997 posed questions of safety and security for the Greek minority living in southern Albania.

Grenada

STATE OF GRENADA

Sovereign: Queen Elizabeth II (1952)
Governor General: Daniel Williams (1996)
Prime Minister: Keith C. Mitchell (June 1995)
Area: 133 sq mi. (340 sq km)
Population (1998 est.): 96,217 (average annual growth rate 0.77%); birth rate: 28.1/1000; infant mortality rate: 11.4/1000; density per sq mi.: 723
Capital and largest city (1991): St. George's, 4,439. **Monetary unit:** East Caribbean dollar. **Ethnic groups (1991):** black African descent 85%, mixed 11%, white, other 0.3%. **Language:** English. **Ethnicity/Race:** black African. **Religions:** Roman Catholic, 64%; Anglican, 21%. **Literacy rate:** 98%
Economic summary: GDP/PPP (1996 est.): $300 million; $3,160 per capita. **Real growth rate:** 3%. **Inflation:** 2.6%. **Unemployment:** 20% (Oct. 1996). **Arable land:** 15%. **Agriculture:** spices, cocoa, bananas. **Labor force:** 36,000; services, 31%; agriculture, 24%; construction, 8%; manufacturing, 5%. Tourism is the leading foreign exchange earner followed by agricultural exports. **Exports:** $24 million (f.o.b., 1996 est.): nutmeg, cocoa beans, bananas, mace, textiles. **Imports:** $128 million (f.o.b., 1996 est.): foodstuffs, machinery, manufactured goods, petroleum, chemicals, fuel. **Major trading partners:** U.K., Trinidad and Tobago, U.S., Japan, Canada. **Member of Commonwealth of Nations**

Geography Grenada (the first "a" is a long vowel) is the most southerly of the Windward Islands, about 100 miles (161 km) from the Venezuelan coast. It is a volcanic island traversed by a mountain range, the highest peak of which is Mount St. Catherine (2,756 ft.; 840 m).

Government A governor-general represents the sovereign, Elizabeth II. In accordance with the 1974 independence constitution, the prime minister is the head of government. There is a bicameral parliament with a 15–member House of Representatives elected by universal suffrage every five years and a Senate whose 13 members are appointed.

History Grenada, also known as the isle of spice, was explored by Columbus in 1498, where he encountered the warlike Caribs who continued to rule the island for another 150 years. In 1672 the island became subject to the French crown and remained so until 1762, when British forces captured it. After more than 200 years of British rule, most recently as part of the West Indies Associated States, it became independent Feb. 7, 1974, with Eric M. Gairy as prime minister.

In 1979 the left-wing New Jewel Movement staged a bloodless coup, proclaimed the People's Revolutionary Government (PRG), and named its leader, Maurice Bishop, as prime minister. Bishop, a protégé of Cuba's President Castro, was killed in a military coup on Oct. 19, 1983.

In an effort to establish order on the island and eliminate the Cuban military presence, U.S. President Ronald Reagan ordered an invasion of Grenada on Oct. 25 involving over 1,900 U.S. troops and a small military force from Barbados, Dominica, Jamaica, St. Lucia, and St. Vincent. The troops met strong resistance from Cuban military personnel on the island but soon occupied it. After a gradual withdrawal of peacekeeping forces, a centrist coalition led by Herbert A. Blaize, a 66-year-old lawyer, won a parliamentary majority in 1984. Parliamentary elections in June 1995 gave the opposition New National Party a majority of seats and allowed its leader, Dr. Keith C. Mitchell, to form a new government. Mitchell flew to Cuba in April 1997 to meet with Castro and signed an economic cooperation agreement. In 1998 Castro made his first official state visit to the island.

Guatemala

REPUBLIC OF GUATEMALA

National name: República de Guatemala
President: Alvaro Arzú Irigoyen (1996)
Area: 42,042 sq mi. (108,890 sq km)
Population (1998 est.): 12,007,580 (average annual rate of natural increase: 2.71%); birth rate: 36/1000; infant mortality rate: 47.7/1000; density per sq mi.: 286
Capital and largest city (1994 est.): Guatemala City, 1,150,452. **Other large cities (1994 est.):** Mixco, 413,002; Villa Nueva, 154,508. **Monetary unit:** Quetzal. **Languages:** Spanish, Indian languages. **Ethnicity/Race:** Mestizo—mixed Amerindian-Spanish ancestry (in local Spanish called Ladino) 56%, Amerindian or predominantly Amerindian 44%. **Religion:** Roman Catholic, Protestant, Mayan. **Literacy rate:** 55%
Economic summary: GDP/PPP (1996 est.): $39 billion; $3,460 per capita. **Real growth rate:** 3%. **Inflation:** 10.9%. **Unemployment:** 4.9%, underemployment, 30–40%. **Arable land:** 12%. **Agriculture:** corn, beans, coffee, cotton, cattle, sugar, bananas, fruits and vegetables. **Labor force:** 3.1 million (1995 est.); agriculture. 58%; services, 14%; manufacturing, 14%; commerce, 7%; construction, 4%. **Industry:** sugar, textiles and clothing, furniture, chemicals, petroleum, metals, rubber. **Natural resources:** nickel, crude oil, rare woods, fish, chicle. **Exports:** $1.81 billion (f.o.b., 1996): coffee, sugar, bananas, beef. **Imports:** $3.11 billion (f.o.b., 1996): fuel and petroleum products, machinery, grain, fertilizers, motor vehicles. **Major trading partners:** U.S., Central American nations, Caribbean, Mexico, Germany.

Geography The northernmost of the Central American nations, Guatemala is the size of Tennessee. Its neighbors are Mexico on the north and west, and Belize, Honduras, and El Salvador on the east. The country consists of three main regions—the cool highlands with the heaviest population, the tropical area along the Pacific and Caribbean coasts, and the tropical jungle in the northern lowlands (known as the Petén). The principal mountain range rises to the highest elevation in Central America and contains many volcanic peaks. Volcanic eruptions are frequent.

Government A republic governed under a constitution that was approved in 1985, effective in 1986. It has a president elected to five-year terms and a unicameral legislative branch, the Congress of the Republic, whose members also serve five-year terms.

History Once the site of the impressive ancient Mayan civilization, Guatemala was conquered by Spanish conquistador Pedro de Alvarado in 1524 and set itself up as a republic in 1839 after the United Provinces of Central America collapsed. From 1898 to 1920, the dictator Manuel Estrada Cabrera ran the country and welcomed U.S. investment, and from 1931 to 1944, Gen. Jorge Ubico Castaneda was the strong man.

After Ubico's overthrow in 1944, liberal-democratic coalitions led by Juan José Arévalo (1945–51) and Jacobo Arbenz Guzmán (1951–54) instituted sweeping social and political reforms that strengthened the peasantry and urban workers at the expense of the military and big landowners like the United Fruit Company. With covert U.S. backing, a revolt was led by Col. Carlos Castillo Armas, and Arbenz took refuge in Mexico.

A succession of center-right governments led by the military and backed by the upper and middle classes tried unsuccessfully to cope with economic disparity in Guatemala. Violence accelerated as the government periodically tried to rid the country of left-wing extremists through terrorist measures of its own. The administration of Gen. Romeo Lucas Garcia was charged by Amnesty International with responsibility for at least 5,000 political murders in a reign of brutality and corruption that brought a cutoff of U.S. military aid in 1978.

More military leaders followed until civilian Jorge Serrano Elias took office in 1986. In 1993 Serrano moved to dissolve Congress and the Supreme Court and suspend constitutional rights, but the military deposed Serrano and allowed the inauguration of de Leon Carpio, the former Attorney General of Human Rights. A peace agreement was signed in Dec. 1996 ending the 36-year civil war. In June 1997 new President Arzu and the guerrilla movement leader Ricardo Ramirez were awarded the UNESCO Houphouet–Boigny peace prize.

Guinea

REPUBLIC OF GUINEA

National name: République de Guinée
President: Brig. Gen. Lansana Conté (1984)
Premier: Sidia Touré (1996)
Area: 94,925 sq mi. (245,860 sq km)
Population (1998 est.): 7,477,110 (average annual rate of natural increase: 0.83%); birth rate: 41.3/1000; infant mortality rate: 128.9/1000; density per sq mi.: 79
Capital and largest city (1995 est.): Conakry, 1,508,000. **Monetary unit:** Guinean franc. **Languages:** French (official), native tongues (Malinké, Susu, Fulani). **Ethnicity/Race:** Peuhl 40%, Malinke 30%, Soussou 20%, smaller tribes 10%. **Religions:** Islam, 85%; 7% indigenous, 8% Christian. **Literacy rate:** 24% in French; 48% in local languages
Economic summary: GDP/PPP (1996 est.): $7.1 billion; $950 per capita. **Real growth rate:** 6%. **Inflation:** 5.1% (1995 est.). **Arable land:** 2%. **Agriculture:** rice, cassava, millet, corn, coffee, bananas, pineapples. **Labor force:** 2.4 million (1983); agriculture, 80%; industry and commerce, 11%; services, 5.4%; civil service, 3.6%. **Industry:** bauxite, aluminum, light manufactured and processed goods, diamonds. **Natural resources:** bauxite, iron ore, diamonds, gold, water power. **Exports:** $725 million (1995 est.): bauxite, aluminum, diamonds, pineapples, bananas, coffee. **Imports:** $775 million (1995 est.): petroleum, machinery, transport equipment, foodstuffs, textiles. **Major trading partners:** U.S., France, Brazil, Germany, Belgium, Ireland, Spain, Côte d'Ivoire, Hong Kong.

Geography Guinea, in West Africa on the Atlantic, is also bordered by Guinea-Bissau, Senegal, Mali, Côte d'Ivoire, Liberia, and Sierra Leone. Slightly smaller than Oregon, the country consists of a coastal plain, a mountainous region, a savanna interior, and a forest area in the Guinea Highlands. The highest peak is Mount Nimba at 5,748 ft. (1,752 m).

Government Military government headed by President Lansana Conté after a 1984 coup. In 1989, President Conté announced that Guinea would move to a multiparty democracy. A new constitution approved in a nationwide referendum, Dec. 1990, provided for the establishment of a directly elected multiparty parliament (five-year terms) and a popularly elected president for a maximum of two five-year terms, and a judiciary to be independent of either the presidency or the legislature. A transitional Committee for National Recovery (CTRN) replaced the military committee to guide implementation of the new constitution.

History Beginning in C.E. 900, the Susu, a group related to the Malinke peoples (from whom Mali gets its name), migrated from the north and began settling the area, achieved its height in the 13th century. From the 16th–19th centuries, the Fulani empire dominated the area. In 1849, the French claimed the area as a protectorate. First called Rivières du Sud, it was rechristened French Guinea, and finally, in 1895, it became part of French West Africa.

Guinea achieved independence on Oct. 2, 1958, became an independent state with Sékou Touré as president. Touré led the country into being the first avowedly Marxist state in Africa. Diplomatic relations with France were suspended in 1965, with the Soviet Union replacing France as the country's chief source of economic and technical assistance.

Prosperity came in 1960 after the start of exploitation of bauxite deposits. Touré was re-elected to a seven-year term in 1974 and again in 1981. Touré died after 26 years as president in March 1984. A week later, a military regime headed by Col. Lansana Conté took power. Conté became president and his co-conspirator in the coup, Col. Diara Traoré, became prime minister, but Conté later demoted Traoré to Education Minister. Traoré tried to seize power on July 4, 1985, while Conté was out of the country, but his attempted coup was crushed by troops loyal to Conté.

In 1991 voters approved a new constitution that would lead the country to democracy. Under mounting popular pressure Conté declared in April 1992 that constitutional rule would begin. In Dec. 1993 elections the president's Unity and Progress Party took almost 51% of the vote cast. In Feb. 1996 rebellious soldiers demanding pay in arrears besieged the presidential palace. Loyal troops repulsed the attacks.

The president appointed Sidia Touré to the newly created position of premier in July 1996.

Guinea-Bissau

REPUBLIC OF GUINEA-BISSAU

National name: Républica da Guiné-Bissau
President: João Bernardo Vieira (1980)
Prime Minister: Carlos Correia (1997)
Area: 13,948 sq mi. (36,120 sq km)
Population (1998 est.): 1,206,311 (average annual rate of natural increase: 2.32%); birth rate: 38.7/1000; infant mortality rate: 111.6/1000; density per sq mi.: 87
Capital and largest city (1991 est.): Bissau, 200,000. **Monetary unit:** Guinea-Bissau peso. **Language:** Portuguese Criolo, African languages. **Ethnicity/Race:** African 99% (Balanta 30%, Fula 20%, Manjaca 14%, Mandinga 13%, Papel 7%), European and mulatto less than 1%. **Religions:** traditional, 65%; Islam, 30%; Christian, 5%. **Literacy rate:** 37% (1991 est.)
Economic summary: GDP/PPP (1996 est.): $1.1 billion; $950 per capita. **Real growth rate:** 4% **Inflation:** 45.4%. **Unemployment:** n.a. **Arable land:** 11%. **Agriculture:** palm kernels, cotton, cashew nuts, peanuts. **Labor force:** n.a. **Industry:** food processing, beer, soft drinks. **Natural resources:** unexploited deposits of bauxite, petroleum, phosphates; fish and timber. **Exports:** $33 million (f.o.b., 1994): peanuts, cashews, fish, palm kernels. **Imports:** $52.4 million (f.o.b., 1994): capital equipment, consumer goods, semiprocessed goods, foods, petroleum. **Major trading partners:** Portugal, Spain, and other European countries, Senegal, U.S., China, India, Nigeria.

Geography A neighbor of Senegal and Guinea in West Africa, on the Atlantic coast, Guinea-Bissau is about half the size of South Carolina. The country is a low-lying coastal region of swamps, rain forests, and mangrove-covered wetlands, with about 25 islands off the coast. The Bijagos archipelago extends 30 miles (48 km) out to sea.

Government After the overthrow of Louis Cabral in Nov. 1980, the nine-member Council of the Revolution formed an interim government. Constitutional government was restored in 1984. At present the government consists of a president and a single 100-member legislative body.

History The land now known as Guinea-Bissau was once the kingdom of Gabú, which was part of the larger Mali empire. After 1546 Gabú became more autonomous, and at least portions of the kingdom existed until 1867. Guinea-Bissau was explored by the Portuguese Nuno Tristao in 1446; colonists in the Cape Verde Islands obtained trading rights in the territory, and it became a center of the Portuguese slave trade. In 1879 the connection with the islands was broken.

The African Party for the Independence of Guinea-Bissau and Cape Verde (another Portuguese colony) was founded in 1956 and guerrilla warfare by nationalists grew increasingly effective. By 1974 the rebels controlled most of the countryside, where they formed a government that was soon recognized by scores of countries. The military coup in Portugal in April 1974 brightened the prospects for freedom, and in August the Lisbon government signed an agreement granting independence to the province. The new republic took the name Guinea-Bissau.

In Nov. 1980, Prémier João Bernardo Vieira headed a military coup that deposed Luis Cabral, president since 1974. A Revolutionary Council assumed the powers of government, with Vieira as its head, until a new constitution was adopted in 1984.

July 1994 multiparty presidential and legislative elections gave the president's party 64 seats in the Assembly although Vieira himself received less than a majority. In the runoff election Vieira officially received 52% of the vote.

Citing continuing economic problems, President Vieira dissolved the government of Prime Minister Manuel Saturnino Costa in May 1997, and in June named Carlos Correia the new prime minister.

Guyana

COOPERATIVE REPUBLIC OF GUYANA

President: Samuel Hinds (1997)
Prime Minister: Janet Jagan (1997)
Area: 83,000 sq mi. (214,970 sq km)
Population (1998 est.): 707,954 (average annual rate of natural increase: –0.47%); birth rate: 18.5/1000; infant mortality rate: 48.7/1000; density per sq mi.: 9
Capital and largest city (1992 est.): Georgetown, 248,500. **Monetary unit:** Guyana dollar. **Languages:** English (official), Amerindian dialects. **Ethnicity/Race:** East Indian 51%, black and mixed 43%, Amerindian 4%, European and Chinese 2%. **Religions:** Hindu, 34%; Protestant, 18%; Islam, 9%; Roman Catholic, 18%; Anglican, 16%. **Literacy rate:** 96%
Economic summary: GDP/PPP (1996 est.): $1.8 billion; $2,490 per capita. **Real growth rate:** 7.9%. **Inflation:** 4.5%. **Unemployment:** (1994 est.), 8–10%. **Arable land:** 2%. **Agriculture:** sugar, rice. **Labor force:** (1995), 300,000; industry and commerce, 44.5%. **Products:** bauxite, aluminum. **Natural resources:** bauxite, gold, diamonds, hardwood timber, shrimp. **Exports:** $565 million (f.o.b., 1996 est.): sugar, bauxite, rice, timber, shrimp, gold, molasses, rum. **Imports:** $589 million (c.i.f., 1996 est.): petroleum, food, machinery, manufactured goods. **Major trading partners:** U.K., U.S., Canada, Japan, Trinidad and Tobago, Germany. **Member of Commonwealth of Nations**

Geography Guyana is the size of Idaho and is situated on the northern coast of South America east of Venezuela, west of Suriname, and north of Brazil. The country consists of a low coastal area and the Guyana Highlands, a tropical forest zone covering more than 80 percent of the country, in the south. There is an extensive north-south network of rivers.

Government Guyana, formerly British Guiana, proclaimed itself a republic on Feb. 23, 1970, ending its tie with Britain while remaining in the Commonwealth. Guyana has a unicameral legislature, the National Assembly, with 53 members directly elected for five-year terms and 12 elected by local councils. A 13-member cabinet is headed by the president.

History By the early 17th century Dutch settlements dominated the territory, but the colonies were taken over by the British during the Napoleonic Wars. Starting in the 1840s, East Indian and Chinese indentured servants were brought to work the plantations, as the freed slaves bought their own land and refused to work on the sugar estates. British Guiana was made a Crown colony in 1928, and in 1953 it was granted a constitution providing for parliamentary home rule.

The People's Progressive Party, headed by Cheddi B. Jagan, won the first elections and Jagan became prime minister. A coalition ousted Jagan in 1964, installing a moderate socialist, Forbes Burnham, as prime minister. On May 26, 1966, the country became an independent member of the Commonwealth and resumed its traditional name, Guyana. After ruling Guyana for 21 years, Burnham died in 1985, and in 1992 Jagan's People's Progressive Party won a majority in the general election. Upon President Jagan's death in March 1997, Prime Minister Samuel Hinds assumed the presidency. Nine days later the American-born Janet Jagan, the late president's widow, became prime minister.

Haiti

REPUBLIC OF HAITI

National name: République d'Haïti
President: René García Préval (1996)
Prime Minister: Position empty (1997)
Area: 10,714 sq mi. (27,750 sq km)
Population (1998 est.): 6,780,501 (average annual rate of natural increase: 1.51%); birth rate: 32.8/1000; infant mortality rate: 99/1000; density per sq mi.: 633
Capital and largest city (1993 est.): Port-au-Prince, 1.5 million. **Monetary unit:** Gourde. **Languages:** Creole, French. **Ethnicity/Race:** black 95%, mulatto and European 5%. **Religion:** Roman Catholic, 80%; Protestant, 16%; Vaudou, 95%. **Literacy rate:** 53%
Economic summary: GDP/PPP (1996 est.): $6.8 billion; $1,000 per capita. **Real growth rate:** 2%. **Inflation:** 18% (1996). **Unemployment:** 60%. **Arable land:** 20%. **Agriculture:** coffee, sugar cane, rice, corn, sorghum. **Labor force:** 2.3 million; agriculture, 66%; services, 25%; industry, 9%. **Industry:** refined sugar, textiles, flour, cement, light assembly products. Natural resource: bauxite. **Exports:** $123 million (f.o.b., 1996): coffee, light industrial products, agricultural products. **Imports:** $666 million (f.o.b., 1996): machines and manufactures, food and beverages, petroleum products, fats and oils, chemicals. **Major trading partners:** U.S., Europe, Latin America.

Geography Haiti, in the West Indies, occupies the western third of the island of Hispaniola, which it shares with the Dominican Republic. About the size of Maryland, Haiti is two-thirds mountainous, with the rest of the country marked by great valleys, extensive plateaus, and small plains.

Government A republic with a bicameral assembly consisting of an upper house or Senate and a lower house, the House of Deputies. The National Assembly consists of 27 senate seats and 83 deputies. In 1987 a new constitution was approved by popular referendum which prohibited the president from serving consecutive terms.

History Visited by Columbus on Dec. 6, 1492, Haiti's native Arawaks fell victim to Spanish rule. In 1697 Haiti became a French possession known as Saint-Dominique. An insurrection among a slave population of 480,000 in 1791 ended with a declaration of independence by Pierre-Dominique Toussaint l'Ouverture in 1801. Napoleon Bonaparte suppressed the independence movement, but it eventually triumphed in 1804 under Jean-Jacques Dessalines, who gave the new nation the Arawak name Haiti.

Its prosperity was hampered by internal strife as well as disputes with neighboring Santo Domingo during a succession of 19th-century dictatorships; a bankrupt Haiti accepted a U.S. customs receivership from 1905 to 1941. Occupation by U.S. Marines from 1915 to 1934 brought a measure of stability and a population growth that made Haiti the most densely populated nation in the hemisphere.

In 1949, after four years of democratic rule by President Dumarsais Estimé, dictatorship returned under Gen. Paul Magloire, who was succeeded by François Duvalier, nicknamed "Papa Doc," in 1957. Duvalier established a dictatorship based on secret police, known as the "Tontons Macoutes," who gunned down opponents of the regime. Duvalier's son, Jean-Claude, or "Baby Doc," succeeded his father in 1971 as ruler of the poorest nation in the Western Hemisphere. His infamous dictatorship, marked by pervasive corruption and repression, rivaled that of his father's. Duvalier fled the country in 1986 amid strong protests and the country remained under military rule.

Jean-Bertrand Aristide, a Roman Catholic priest, was sworn in as president on Feb. 7, 1991—the country's first democratically elected chief executive. President Aristide was replaced by a de facto regime in Oct. 1991 following a military coup on Sept. 30, 1991. He was reinstated in Oct. 1993 by a U.S.-led multinational force appointed by U.N. Resolution 940. A U.S. peace mission in Sept. 1994 reached a compromise with the military leaders, avoiding a U.S. invasion. Acting as peacekeepers, U.S. troops landed in Haiti, allowing Aristide to return in mid-October. Freely elected President René Préval was inaugurated in Feb. 1996. Former President Aristide's new opposition Lavalas Family Party scored well in the legislative elections of April 1997, but voter turnout was minuscule amid charges of fraud. In early June 1997 Prime Minister Rosny Smarth, with a deteriorating economy, announced his resignation and has not yet been replaced.

Honduras

REPUBLIC OF HONDURAS

National name: República de Honduras
President: Carlos Roberto Flores Facusse (1998)
Area: 43,872 sq mi. (112,090 sq km)
Population (1998 est.): 5,861,955 (average annual rate of natural increase: 2.33%); birth rate: 31.8/1000; infant mortality rate: 41.9/1000; density per sq mi.: 134
Capital and largest city (1995): Tegucigalpa, 1,500,000. **Monetary unit:** Lempira. **Languages:** Spanish (official), English widely spoken in business. **Ethnicity/Race:** mestizo (mixed Indian and European) 90%, Indian 7%, black 2%, white 1%. **Religion:** Roman Catholic, 94%, Protestant minority. **Literacy rate:** 73%
Economic summary: GDP/PPP (1996 est.): $11.5 billion; $2,000 per capita. **Real growth rate:** 3%. **Inflation:** 25.4%. **Unemployment:** 15%; underemployed 40% (1996). **Arable land:** 15%. **Agriculture:** bananas, coffee, timber, beef, shrimp, citrus. **Labor force:** (1985), 1.3 million; agriculture, 62%; services, 20%; manufacturing, 9%; construction, 3%. **Industry:** processed agricultural products, textiles and clothing, wood products. **Natural resources:** timber, gold, silver, copper, lead, zinc, iron ore, antimony. **Exports:** $2.401 billion (f.o.b., 1996): bananas, coffee, lumber, shrimp and lobster, minerals. **Imports:** $3.133 billion (c.i.f., 1996): manufactured goods, machinery, transportation equipment, chemicals, petroleum. **Major trading partners:** U.S., Caribbean countries, Western Europe, Japan, Latin America.

Geography Honduras, in the north central part of Central America, has a 400-mile (644-km) Caribbean coastline and a 40-mile (64-km) Pacific frontage. Its neighbors are Guatemala to the west, El Salvador to the south, and Nicaragua to the east. The second largest country in Central America, Honduras is slightly larger than Tennessee. Generally mountainous, the country is marked by fertile plateaus, river valleys, and narrow coastal plains.

Government Under the 1982 constitution, the president serves an unrenewable four-year term and there is a 128-member National Congress. Honduras's two major political parties are the Liberal Party, a moderately conservative organization advocating social reform, and the National Party, a right-wing group with close ties to the military.

History Honduras was part of the Mayan civilization during the first millennium, and its cultural vortex was Copàn. Columbus explored the country on his last voyage in 1502. Honduras, with four other countries of Central America, declared its independence from Spain in 1821 and was part of a federation of Central American states until 1838. In that year it seceded from the federation and became a completely independent country. Political unrest rocked the country in the early twentieth century, including an occupation by U.S. Marines, until it was quelled by the dictatorship of General Tiburcio Carias Andino in 1932.

In July 1969, El Salvador invaded Honduras after Honduran landowners had deported several thousand Salvadorans. By threatening economic sanctions and military intervention, the OAS induced El Salvador to withdraw. Although parliamentary democracy returned with the election of Roberto Suazo Córdova as president in 1982 after a decade of military rule, Honduras faced severe economic problems and tensions along its border with Nicaragua. "Contra" rebels, waging a guerrilla war against the Sandinista regime in Nicaragua, used Honduras as a training and staging area. At the same time, the United States used Honduras as a site for military exercises and built bases to train both Honduran and Salvadoran troops.

The lack of a final resolution of a maritime border dispute with Nicaragua led to incidents in 1997 in which Nicaraguan and Honduran gunboats exchanged fire in the disputed waters. In Nov. 1997 Carlos Flores Facussé of the Liberal Party was elected president. Honduras continues to suffer from rapid population growth, high unemployment, inflation, a lack of basic services, and economic dependence on coffee and bananas, which are subject to sharp price fluctuations.

Hungary

REPUBLIC OF HUNGARY

National name: Magyar Köztársaság
President: Árpád Göncz (1990)
Premier: Viktor Orbán (1998)
Area: 35,919 sq mi. (93,030 sq km)
Population (1998 est.): 10,208,127 (average annual rate of natural increase: –0.23%); birth rate: 10.7/1000; infant mortality rate: 9.7/1000; density per sq mi.: 284
Capital and largest city (1995 est.): Budapest, 2,008,546. **Other large cities (1995 est.):** Debrecen, 210,000; Miskolc, 182,000; Szeged, 169,000; Pécs, 163,000. **Monetary unit:** Forint. **Languages:** Magyar (Hungarian), 98.2%; Other, 1.8%. **Ethnicity/Race:** Hungarian 89.9%, Gypsy 4%, German 2.6%, Serb 2%, Slovak 0.8%, Romanian 0.7%. **Religions:** Roman Catholic, 67.5%; Protestant, 25%; atheist and others, 7.5%. **Literacy rate:** 98%
Economic summary: GDP/PPP (1996 est.): $74.7 billion; $7,500 per capita. **Real growth rate:** 0.5%. **Inflation:** 20%. **Unemployment:** 11% (1996 est.). **Arable land:** 51%. **Agriculture:** corn, wheat, potatoes, sugar beets, sun flowers, livestock, dairy products. **Labor force:** (1996) 6.2 million; services, trade and government, 58.7%; industry, 34.7%; agriculture, 6.6%. **Industry:** steel, chemicals, pharmaceuticals, textiles, transport equipment. **Natural resources:** bauxite, coal, natural gas. **Exports:** $14.2 billion (f.o.b., 1996 est.): raw materials, semi-finished goods, chemicals, machinery, light industry, food and agricultural, fuels and energy. **Imports:** $16.8 billion (f.o.b., 1996 est.): fuels and energy, raw materials, semi-finished goods, chemicals, machinery, light industry, food and agriculture. **Major trading partners:** E.U., Eastern Europe, Russia.

Geography This central European country is the size of Indiana. Most of Hungary is a fertile, rolling plain lying east of the Danube River, and drained by the Danube and Tisza rivers. In the extreme northwest is the Little Hungarian Plain. South of that area is Lake Balaton (250 sq mi.; 648 sq km).

Government Hungary is a Republic with legislative power vested in the unicameral National Assembly, whose 386 members are elected directly for four-year terms. The National Assembly elects the president. The premier is usually that party leader who commands a voting majority in the National Assembly. The major political parties are the Socialist Party, the Hungarian Democratic Forum, the Alliance of Free Democrats, the Independent Socialist Party, the Independent Smallholder's Party, and the Young Democrats (FIDESZ).

History By 14 B.C.E., western Hungary was part of the Roman Empire's provinces of Pannonia and Dacia. The area east of the Danube was never a part of the Roman Empire and was largely occupied by various Germanic and Asiatic peoples. In C.E. 896 all of Hungary was invaded by the Magyars, who founded a kingdom. Christianity was accepted during the reign of Stephen I (St. Stephen) (997–1038). A devastating invasion by the Mongols killed half of Hungary's population in 1241. The peak of Hungary's great period of medieval power came during the reign of Louis I the Great (1342–82), whose dominions touched the Baltic, Black, and Mediterranean Seas. War with the Turks broke out in 1389, and for more than 100 years the Turks advanced through the Balkans. When the Turks smashed a Hungarian army in 1526, western and northern Hungary accepted Hapsburg rule to escape Turkish occupation. Transylvania became independent under Hungarian princes. Intermittent war with the Turks was waged until a peace treaty was signed in 1699.

After the suppression of the 1848 revolt against Hapsburg rule, led by Louis Kossuth, the dual monarchy of Austria-Hungary was set up in 1867. The dual monarchy was defeated with the other Central Powers in World War I. After a short-lived republic in 1918, the chaotic Communist rule of 1919 under Béla Kun ended with the Romanians occupying Budapest on Aug. 4, 1919. When the Romanians left, Adm. Nicholas Horthy entered the capital with a national army. The Treaty of Trianon of June 4, 1920, cost Hungary 68% of its land and 58% of its population. Meanwhile, the National Assembly had restored the legal continuity of the old monarchy; and, on March 1, 1920, Horthy was elected Regent. Following the German invasion of Russia on June 22, 1941, Hungary joined the attack against the Soviet Union, but the war was not popular and Hungarian troops were almost entirely withdrawn from the eastern front by May 1943. German occupation troops set up a puppet government after Horthy's appeal for an armistice with advancing Soviet troops on Oct. 15, 1944 had resulted in his overthrow. The German regime soon fled the capital, however, and on Dec. 23 a provisional government was formed in Soviet-occupied eastern Hungary. On Jan. 20, 1945, it signed an armistice in Moscow. Early the next year, the National Assembly approved a constitutional law abolishing the thousand-year-old monarchy and establishing a republic.

By the Treaty of Paris (1947), Hungary had to give up all territory it had acquired since 1937 and to pay $300 million reparations to the U.S.S.R., Czechoslovakia, and Yugoslavia. In 1948 the Communist Party, with the support of Soviet troops seized control. Hungary was proclaimed a People's Republic and one-party state in 1949. Industry was nationalized, the land collectivized into state farms, and the opposition terrorized by the secret police. The terror, modeled after that of the U.S.S.R., reached its height with the trial and life imprisonment of József Cardinal Mindszenty, the leader of Hungary's Roman Catholics, in 1948. On Oct. 23, 1956, an anti-Communist revolution broke out in Budapest. To cope with it, the Communists set up a coalition government and called former Premier

Imre Nagy back to head it. But he and most of his ministers were swept by the logic of events into the anti-Communist opposition, and he declared Hungary a neutral power, withdrawing from the Warsaw Treaty and appealing to the United Nations for help. One of his ministers, János Kádár, established a counter-regime and asked the U.S.S.R. to send in military power. Soviet troops and tanks suppressed the revolution in bloody fighting after 190,000 people had fled the country. Under Kádár (1956–88), communist Hungary henceforth maintained more liberal policies in the economic and cultural spheres, and Hungary became the most liberal of the Soviet-bloc nations of eastern Europe. Continuing his program of national reconciliation, Kádár emptied prisons, reformed the secret police, and eased travel restrictions.

Hungary's Communists abandoned their monopoly on power in 1989 voluntarily and the constitution was amended in Oct. 1989 to allow a multiparty state. The last Soviet troops left Hungary in June 1991, thereby ending almost 47 years of military presence. The transition to a market economy proved difficult. Hungary strengthened its ties with Poland and Czechoslovakia but grew concerned about the fate of ethnic Hungarians in neighboring countries. Hungary normalized relations with the Catholic Church in 1997 by signing an agreement concerning restitution or compensation for property seized during the Communist era. Also in 1997, Hungary experienced continued growth of the economy, significant changes in the electorate's party preferences, and increasing public debate over joining NATO and the E.U.

Iceland

REPUBLIC OF ICELAND

National name: Lydveldid Island
President: Ólafur Ragnar Grimsson (1996)
Prime Minister: David Oddsson (1991)
Area: 39,709 sq mi. (103,000 sq km)[1]
Population (1998 est.): 271,033 (average annual rate of natural increase: 0.52%); birth rate: 15.1/1000; infant mortality rate: 5.3/1000; density per sq mi.: 7
Capital and largest city (1994 est.): Reykjavik, 103,036. **Monetary unit:** Icelandic króna. **Language:** Icelandic. **Ethnicity/Race:** homogeneous mixture of descendants of Norwegians and Celts. **Religion:** Church of Iceland (Evangelical Lutheran) 96%, other Protestant and Roman Catholic 3%, none 1%.. **Literacy rate:** 100%
Economic summary: GDP/PPP (1996 est.): $5.3 billion; $19,800 per capita. **Real growth rate:** 3.3%. **Inflation:** 2.5%. **Unemployment:** 5%. **Arable land:** 0%. **Agriculture:** livestock, potatoes and turnips. **Labor force:** 145,000; commerce, transportation, and services, 60%; manufacturing, 12.5%; fishing and fish processing, 11.8%. **Products:** processed aluminum, fish. **Natural resources:** fish, diatomite, hydroelectric and geothermal power. **Exports:** $1.67 billion (f.o.b., 1995): fish, animal products, aluminum, diatomite, ferrosilicon. **Imports:** $1.62 billion (f.o.b., 1994): petroleum products, machinery and transportation equipment, food, textiles. **Major trading partners:** E.U., European Free Trade Association (EFTA) countries, U.S., and Japan.

1. Including some offshore islands.

Geography Iceland, an island about the size of Kentucky, lies in the north Atlantic Ocean east of Greenland and just touches the Arctic Circle. It is one of the most volcanic regions in the world. The island is dotted with small fresh-water lakes, and there are many natural phenomena, including hot springs, geysers, sulfur beds, canyons, waterfalls, and swift rivers. More than 13% of the area is covered by snowfields and glaciers, and most of the people live in the 7% of the island that comprises fertile coastland.

Government The president is elected for four years by popular vote. Executive power resides in the prime minister, and his cabinet, who is elected by the Althing (the unicameral parliament), which is composed of 63 members.

History The earliest inhabitants of Iceland were Irish hermits, who fled the island upon the arrival of the pagan Norse people in the late 9th century C.E. A constitution drawn up c. 930 created a form of democracy and provided for an Althing, the world's oldest practicing legislative assembly. In 1262–64, Iceland came under Norwegian rule and passed to ultimate Danish control through the unification of the kingdoms of Norway, Sweden, and Denmark (the Kalmar Union) in 1397. In 1874, Icelanders obtained their own constitution. In 1918, Denmark recognized Iceland, via the Act of Union, as a separate state with unlimited sovereignty but still nominally under the Danish monarchy.

During the German occupation of Denmark during World War II, British, then American, troops occupied Iceland and used it for a strategic air base. While officially neutral, Iceland cooperated with the Allies throughout the conflict. On June 17, 1944, after a popular referendum, the Althing proclaimed Iceland an independent republic. Iceland joined the North Atlantic Treaty Organization in 1949, and subsequently received an American air force base in 1951. Iceland was admitted to the European Free Trade Association in 1970. Iceland unilaterally extended its territorial fishing limit from 3 to 200 nautical miles in 1972, precipitating a dispute with the U.K. known as the "cod wars," which ended in 1976, when the U.K. recognized the new limits. In 1980, the Icelanders elected a woman to the office of the presidency, the first elected female chief of state (i.e., president as distinct from prime minister) in the world.

After the recession of the early 1990s, Iceland began strengthening its economy. Government projections in mid-1997 showed that the country would have a large budget surplus for the year owing to fiscal management and a healthy economy. The government hoped to cut public spending further and boost the surplus.

India

REPUBLIC OF INDIA

National name: Bharat
President: K. R. Narayanan (1997)
Prime Minister: Atal Bihari Vajpayee (1998)
Area: 1,229,737 sq mi. (3,287,590 sq km)
Population (1998 est.): 984,003,683 (average annual rate of natural increase: 1.71%); birth rate: 25.9/1000; infant mortality rate: 63.1/1000; density per sq mi.: 800
Capital (1991): New Delhi, 294,149. **Largest cities:** Bombay (Mumbai): city proper (1991 census) 9,925,891; metro. area (1996 est.) 15,725,000; Delhi: city proper (1991 census) 7,206,704; metro. area

(1996 est.) 10,298,000; Calcutta: city proper (1991 census) 4,339,819; metro. area (1996 est.) 12,118,000; Madras (Chennai), 5,361,468; Ahmedabad, 4,775,670; Bangalore, 4,807,019; Kanpur, 2,284,000. **Monetary unit:** Rupee. **Principal languages:** Hindi (official), English (official), Bengali, Gujarati, Kashmiri, Malayalam, Marathi, Oriya, Punjabi, Tamil, Telugu, Urdu, Kannada, Assamese, Sanskrit, Sindhi (all recognized by the constitution). Dialects, 1,652. **Ethnicity/Race:** Indo-Aryan 72%, Dravidian 25%, Mongoloid and other 3%. **Religions:** Hindu, 82.6%; Islam, 11.3%; Christian, 2.4%; Sikh, 2%; Buddhists, 0.71%; Jains, 0.48%. **Literacy rate:** 52%

Economic summary: GDP/PPP (1996 est.): $1.538 trillion; $1,600 per capita. **Real growth rate:** 6.5%. **Inflation:** 10.3% (1995). **Unemployment:** n.a. **Arable land:** 56%. **Agriculture:** rice, wheat, oilseeds, cotton, tea, opium poppy (for pharmaceuticals). **Labor force:** (1995 est.), 370 million; agriculture 65% or more. **Industry:** jute, processed food, steel, machinery, transport machinery, cement. **Natural resources:** iron ore, coal, manganese, mica, bauxite, limestone, textiles. **Exports:** $30.5 billion (f.o.b., 1995): gems and jewelry, clothing, engineering goods, leather manufactures, cotton yarn and fabric. **Imports:** $34.5 billion (c.i.f., 1995): crude oil and petroleum products, gems, fertilizer, chemicals, machinery. **Major trading partners:** C.I.S. nations, Germany, Italy, Belgium. **Member of Commonwealth of Nations**

Geography One-third the area of the United States, the Republic of India occupies most of the subcontinent of India in south Asia. It borders on China in the northeast. Other neighbors are Pakistan on the west, Nepal and Bhutan on the north, and Burma and Bangladesh on the east.

The country can be divided into three distinct geographic regions: the Himalayan region in the north, which contains some of the highest mountains in the world, the Gangetic Plain, and the plateau region in the south and central part. Its three great river systems have extensive deltas and all rising in the Himalayas: the Ganges, 1,540 miles (2,478 km), the Indus, and the Brahmaputra..

India includes several groups of islands—the Laccadives (14 islands) in the Arabian Sea and the Andamans (204 islands) and the Nicobars (19 islands) in the Bay of Bengal.

Government India is a federal republic. It is also a member of the Commonwealth of Nations, a status defined at the 1949 London Conference of Prime Ministers, by which India recognizes the queen as head of the Commonwealth. Under the constitution effective Jan. 26, 1950, India has a parliamentary type of government.

The constitutional head of the state is the president, who is elected every five years. He or she is advised by the prime minister and a cabinet based on a majority of the bicameral parliament, which consists of a Council of States (Rajya Sabha), representing the constituent units of the republic and a House of the People (Lok Sabha), elected every five years by universal suffrage.

History One of the earliest civilizations, the Indus Valley Civilization, flourished on the Indian subcontinent from c. 2600 B.C.E. to c. 2000 B.C.E. The Aryans who invaded India c. 1500 B.C.E. from the northwest found a land that was already home to an advanced civilization. They introduced Sanskrit and the Vedic religion, a forerunner of Hinduism, to the area. Buddhism was founded in the 6th century B.C.E. and spread throughout northern India, most notably by one of the great ancient kings of the Mauryan dynasty, Asoka (c. 269–232 B.C.E.), who also unified most of the Indian subcontinent for the first time.

In 1526, Muslim invaders founded the great Mogul empire, centered on Delhi, which lasted, at least in name, until 1857. Akbar the Great (1542–1605) strengthened and consolidated this empire. The long reign of his great-grandson, Aurangzeb (1618–1707), represents both the greatest extent of the Mogul empire and the beginning of its decay.

Vasco da Gama, the Portuguese explorer, visited India first in 1498, and for the next 100 years the Portuguese had a virtual monopoly on trade with the subcontinent. Meanwhile, the English founded the East India Company, which set up its first factory at Surat in 1612 and began expanding its influence, fighting the Indian rulers and the French, Dutch, and Portuguese traders simultaneously.

Bombay, taken from the Portuguese, became the seat of English rule in 1687. The defeat of French and Mogul armies by Lord Clive in 1757 laid the foundation of the British Empire in India. The East India Company continued to suppress native uprisings and extend British rule until 1858, when the administration of India was formally transferred to the British Crown following the Sepoy Mutiny of native troops in 1857–58.

After World War I, in which the Indian states sent more than 6 million troops to fight beside the Allies, Indian nationalist unrest rose to new heights under the leadership of a Hindu lawyer, Mohandas K. Gandhi, called Mahatma Gandhi. His philosophy of civil disobedience called for nonviolent noncooperation against British authority. He soon became the leading spirit of the Indian National Congress Party, which was the spearhead of revolt. In 1919 the British gave added responsibility to Indian officials, and in 1935 India was given a federal form of government and a measure of self-rule.

In 1942, with the Japanese pressing hard on the eastern borders of India, the British War Cabinet tried and failed to reach a political settlement with nationalist leaders. The Congress Party took the position that the British must quit India. In 1942, fearing mass civil disobedience, the government of India carried out widespread arrests of Congress leaders, including Gandhi.

Gandhi was released in 1944 and negotiations for a settlement were resumed. Finally, in August 1947, India gained full independence. The victory was soured, however, by the partitioning of the predominantly Muslim regions of the north into the separate nation of Pakistan. The Muslim League, led by Mohammed Ali Jinnah, demanded a separate nation for the Muslim minority to prevent Hindu political and social domination. Indian Hindus, however, had hoped for a unified rather than balkanized Indian subcontinent. Lord Mountbatten as Viceroy partitioned India along religious lines and split the provinces of Bengal and the Punjab, which both nations claimed. The partition of Pakistan and India led to the largest migration in human history, with 17 million people fleeing across the borders in both directions to escape the bloody riots occurring among sectarian groups. Armed conflict also broke out over rival claims to the princely states of Jammu and Kashmir.

Jawaharlal Nehru, nationalist leader and head of the Congress Party, was made prime minister. In 1949 a constitution, along the lines of the U.S. Constitution, was approved making India a sovereign republic. Under a federal structure the states were organized on linguistic lines. The dominance of the Congress Party contributed to stability. In 1956 the republic absorbed the former French settlements. Five years later, it forcibly annexed the Portuguese enclaves of Goa, Damao, and Diu.

Nehru died in 1964. His successor, Lal Bahadur Shastri, died on Jan. 10, 1966. Nehru's daughter, Indira Gandhi, became prime minister, and she continued his policy of nonalignment.

In 1971 the Pakistani army moved in to quash the independence movement in East Pakistan that was supported by India, and some 10 million Bengali refugees poured across the border into India, creating social, economic, and health problems. After numerous border incidents, India invaded East Pakistan and in two weeks forced the surrender of the Pakistani army. East Pakistan was established as an independent state and renamed Bangladesh.

In the summer of 1975, the world's largest democracy veered suddenly toward authoritarianism when a judge in Allahabad, Mrs. Gandhi's home constituency, found her landslide victory in the 1971 elections invalid because civil servants had illegally aided her campaign. Amid demands for her resignation, Mrs. Gandhi decreed a state of emergency on June 26 and ordered mass arrests of her critics, including all opposition party leaders except the Communists.

Despite strong opposition to her repressive measures, particularly resentment against compulsory birth control programs, Mrs. Gandhi in 1977 announced parliamentary elections for March. At the same time, she freed most political prisoners. The landslide victory of Morarji R. Desai unseated Mrs. Gandhi. Mrs. Gandhi, however, staged a spectacular comeback in the elections of Jan. 1980.

In 1984, she ordered the Indian army to root out a band of Sikh holy men and gunmen who were using the most sacred shrine of the Sikh religion, the Golden Temple in Amritsar, as a base for terrorist raids in a violent campaign for greater political autonomy in the strategic Punjab border state. The perceived sacrilege to the Golden Temple kindled outrage among many of India's 14 million Sikhs and brought a spasm of mutinies and desertions by Sikh officers and soldiers in the army.

On Oct. 31, 1984, Mrs. Gandhi was assassinated by two men identified by police as Sikh members of her bodyguard. The ruling Congress Party chose her older son, Rajiv Gandhi, to succeed her as prime minister for four years. While running for reelection, former Prime Minister Rajiv Gandhi was assassinated on May 22, 1991 by Tamil militants who objected to India's mediation of the civil war in Sri Lanka. Final phases of the election were postponed a month. When they were resumed the Congress Party and its allies won 236 seats in the lower house, 20 short of a majority. P. V. Narasimha Rao was chosen to form a new government.

The ruling Congress Party lost the parliamentary elections of May 1996, and its waning has resulted in a period of political instability. The Hindu nationalist Bharatiya Janata Party's leader, Atal Bihari Vajpayee, became prime minister in May 1996, but his government lasted only 13 days. H. D. Deve Gowda of the United Front coalition became the next prime minister. Losing the support of the Congress party, Prime Minister Deve Gowda lost a confidence vote in April 1997. Foreign Minister Inder Gujral was sworn in later that month, only to be replaced by Atal Vajpayee in March 1998, his second time as prime minister (his first term lasting less than two weeks). Vajpayee is the first Hindu nationalist to become prime minister, and the chauvinistic ideology of his party has made a number of Muslims and moderate Hindus uneasy. In May 1998 India set off five nuclear tests, surprising the international community, which widely condemned India's pro-nuclear stance. Despite international urgings for restraint, Pakistan responded by conducting several nuclear tests of its own two weeks later. India has resisted signing the Comprehensive Test Ban Treaty for nuclear weapons and has been slapped with sanctions by the U.S. and other countries. India and Pakistan began talks about the disputed territory of Kashmir, which is the issue at the basis of their chronic antagonism as well as their recent displays of nuclear strength.

Native States. Most of the 560-odd native states and subdivisions of pre-1947 India acceded to the new nation, and the central government pursued a vigorous policy of integration. This took three forms: merger into adjacent provinces, conversion into centrally administered areas, and grouping into unions of states. Finally, under a controversial reorganization plan effective Nov. 1, 1956, the unions of states were abolished and merged into adjacent states, and India became a union of 15 states and 8 centrally administered areas. A 16th state was added in 1962, and in 1966, the Punjab was partitioned into two states. Today India consists of 25 states and 7 Union Territories.

The territorial dispute over Kashmir led to war between India and Pakistan in 1949, again in 1965 and 1971, and remains unresolved.

In April 1975, the Indian parliament voted to make the 300-year-old kingdom of Sikkim a full-fledged Indian state, and the annexation took effect May 16. Situated in the Himalayas, Sikkim was a virtual dependency of Tibet until the early 19th century. Under an 1890 treaty between China and Great Britain, it became a British protectorate, and was made an Indian protectorate after Britain quit the subcontinent.

Indonesia

REPUBLIC OF INDONESIA

National name: Republik Indonesia
President: Bacharuddin Jusuf Habibie (1998)
Area: 735,268 sq mi. (1,919,440 sq km)[1]
Population (1998 est.): 212,941,810 (average annual rate of natural increase: 1.49%); birth rate: 23.1/1000; infant mortality rate: 59.2/1000; density per sq mi.: 290
Capital and largest city: Jakarta: city proper (1995 est.) 9,160,500; metro. area (1995 est.) 11,500,000. **Other large cities (1990):** Surabaya, 2,421,000; Medan, 1,685,972; Bandung, 2,026,893; Semarang, 1,005,316. **Monetary unit:** Rupiah. **Languages:** Bahasa Indonesia (official), Dutch, English, and more than 583 languages, and dialects. **Ethnicity/Race:** Javanese 45%, Sundanese 14%, Madurese 7.5%, coastal Malays 7.5%, other 26%. **Religions:** Islam, 87%; Christian, 9%; Hindu, 2%; other, 2%. **Literacy rate:** 84%

Economic summary: GDP/PPP (1996 est.): $779.7 billion; $3,770 per capita. **Real growth rate:** 7%. **Inflation:** 7%. **Unemployment:** (1994 est.) 3% official, with vast underemployment. **Arable land:** 10%. **Agriculture:** rice, cassava, peanuts, rubber, coffee. **Labor force:** 67 million; agriculture, 55%; manufacturing, 10%; construction, 4%; transport and communications, 3% (1985 est.). **Industry:** petroleum, timber, textiles, cement, fertilizer, rubber. **Natural resources:** oil, timber, nickel, natural gas, tin, bauxite, copper. **Exports:** $49.8 billion (f.o.b., 1996): petroleum and liquid natural gas, timber, rubber, coffee, textiles. **Imports:** $42.9 billion (f.o.b., 1996): chemicals, machinery, manufactured goods. **Major trading partners:** Japan, U.S., Singapore, Germany.

1. Includes West Irian (former Netherlands New Guinea), renamed Irian Jaya in March 1973 (159,355 sq mi.; 421,981 sq km), and former Portuguese Timor (5,763 sq mi.; 14,874 sq km), annexed in 1976.

Geography Indonesia is an archipelago in Southeast Asia with an area nearly three times that of Texas. It consists of 17,000 islands (6,000 inhabited) and straddles the equator. The largest islands are Sumatra, Java (the most populous), Bali, Kalimantan (Indonesia's part of Borneo), Sulawesi (Celebes), the Nusa Tenggara islands, the Maluku Islands, and Irian Jaya (eastern part of New Guinea). Its neighbor to the north is Malaysia and to the east is Papua New Guinea.

A backbone of mountain ranges extends throughout the main islands of the archipelago. Indonesia, part of the "ring of fire," has the largest number of active volcanoes in the world. Earthquakes are frequent. The "Wallace Line," a zoological demarcation between Asian and Australian flora and fauna, divides Indonesia.

Government The president is elected by the People's Consultative Assembly, whose 1,000 members include the functioning legislative arm, the 500-member House of Representatives. Meeting at least once every five years, the Assembly has broad policy functions. The House, 100 of whose members are appointed from the armed forces, meets at least once annually. General Suharto was elected unopposed to a sixth five-year term in 1993, though he stepped down in 1998 in favor of Vice President B. J. Habibie.

History The 13,000 islands that make up Indonesia were home to a diversity of cultures and indigenous beliefs when they came under the influence of Hindu priests and traders in the first and second centuries C.E. Muslim invasions began in the 13th century, and most of the archipelago had converted to Islam by the 15th. Portuguese traders arrived early in the next century but were ousted by the Dutch around 1595. The Dutch United East India Company established posts on the island of Java, in an effort to control the spice trade.

After Napoleon subjugated the Netherlands in 1811, the British seized the islands but returned them to the Dutch in 1816. In 1922 Indonesia was made an integral part of the Dutch kingdom. During World War II, Japan seized the islands. Tokyo was primarily interested in Indonesia's oil, which was vital to the war effort, and tolerated fledgling nationalists such as Sukarno and Mohammed Hatta. After Japan's surrender, Sukarno and Hatta proclaimed Indonesian independence on Aug. 17, 1945. Allied troops, mostly British Indian forces, fought nationalist militia to reassert the pre-war status quo until the arrival of Dutch troops.

In Nov. 1946, a draft agreement on forming a Netherlands-Indonesian Union was reached, but differences in interpretation resulted in more fighting between Dutch and nationalist forces. Following a bitter war for independence, leaders on both sides agreed to terms of a union on Nov. 2, 1949. The transfer of sovereignty took place at Amsterdam on Dec. 27, 1949. In Feb. of 1956 Indonesia abrogated the Union, and began seizing Dutch property in the islands.

In 1963, Netherlands New Guinea (the Dutch portion of the island of New Guinea) was transferred to Indonesia and renamed West Irian, which became Irian Jaya in 1973. Hatta and Sukarno, the co-fathers of Indonesian independence, split over Sukarno's concept of "guided democracy," and under Sukarno's rule the Indonesian Communist Party (PKI) steadily increased its influence.

Three years later, Sukarno was named president for life. Sukarno enjoyed mass support for his policies, but a growing power struggle between the military and the PKI loomed over his government. After an attempted military coup was put down by army Chief of Staff General Suharto and officers loyal to him, Suharto's forces killed hundreds of thousands of suspected Communists in a massive purge aimed at undermining Sukarno's rule.

Suharto took over the reins of government and gradually eased Sukarno out of office, completing his consolidation of power in 1967. Under Suharto the military assumed an overarching role in national affairs, and relations with the West were enhanced. Indonesia's economy improved dramatically and national elections were permitted, although the opposition was so tightly controlled as to virtually choke off dissent.

In 1975, Indonesia invaded the former Portuguese half of the island of Timor and annexed the territory in 1976. More than 100,000 Timorese, a sixth of the mostly Catholic population, are reported to have died from famine, disease, and fighting since the annexation.

In the summer of 1997, Indonesia suffered a major economic setback along with most other Asian economies. Banks failed and the value of Indonesia's currency, the rupiah, plummeted. Anti-government demonstrations took to the streets and riots broke out, directed mainly at the country's prosperous ethnic Chinese. As the economic crisis deepened, student demonstrators occupied the national parliament, demanding Suharto's ouster. On May 21, 1998, Suharto stepped down, ending 32 years of rule and handing over power to Vice President B. J. Habibie.

Iran

ISLAMIC REPUBLIC OF IRAN

Chief of State: Ayatollah Khamenei (1989)
President: Mohammad Khatami (1997)
Area: 636,293 sq mi. (1,648,000 sq km)
Population (1998 est.): 68,959,931 (average annual rate of natural increase: 2.04%); birth rate: 31.4/1000; infant mortality rate: 49/1000; density per sq mi.: 108
Capital: Teheran. **Largest cities (1991 est.):** Teheran, 6,450,500; Mashad, 1,500,000; Isfahan, 1,100,000; Tabriz, 1,090,000. **Monetary unit:** Rial. **Languages:** Farsi (Persian), Azari, Kurdish, Arabic. **Ethnicity/Race:** Persian 51%, Azerbaijani 24%, Gilaki and Mazandarani 8%, Kurd 7%, Arab 3%, Lur 2%, Baloch 2%, Turkmen

2%, other 1%. **Religions:** Shi'ite Muslim, 95%; Sunni Muslim, 4%. **Literacy rate:** 54% (1996)

Economic summary: GDP/PPP (1996 est.): $343.5 billion; $5,200 per capita. **Real growth rate:** 3.6% (1995 est.). **Inflation:** 23%. **Unemployment:** over 30%. **Arable land:** 10%. **Agriculture:** wheat, barley, rice, sugar beets, cotton, dates, raisins, sheep, goats. **Labor force:** 15.4 million; agriculture, 33%; manufacturing, 21%. **Industry:** crude and refined oil, textiles, petrochemicals, cement, processed foods, steel and copper fabrication. **Natural resources:** oil, gas, iron, copper. **Exports:** $21.3 billion (f.o.b., 1996 est.): petroleum 85%, carpets, fruits, nuts, hides. **Imports:** $13.3 billion (f.o.b., 1996 est.): machinery, military supplies, foodstuffs, pharmaceuticals, metal works, technical services. **Major trading partners:** Japan, Germany, Netherlands, U.K., Italy, Spain, Turkey, France.

Geography Iran, a Middle Eastern country south of the Caspian Sea and north of the Persian Gulf, is three times the size of Arizona. It shares borders with Iraq, Turkey, Azerbaijan, Turkmenistan, Armenia, Afghanistan, and Pakistan.

In general, the country is a plateau averaging 4,000 feet (1,219 m) in elevation. There are also maritime lowlands along the Persian Gulf and the Caspian Sea. The Elburz Mountains in the north rise to 18,603 feet (5,670 m) at Mt. Damavend. From northwest to southeast, the country is crossed by a desert 800 miles (1,287 km) long.

Government Iran has been a theocracy since the Pahlavi monarchy regime was overthrown on Feb. 11, 1979. The constitution grants ultimate power to the country's religious leader (formerly the Ayatollah Khomeini, and upon his death in 1989, the Ayatollah Khamenei). The president, elected for a four-year term, nominally heads the executive branch. The religious leader, called the supreme leader (rahbar-e moazam), rules for life and has control over the judiciary, military, and the state-run radio and television stations.

History The region now called Iran was occupied by the Medes and the Persians in the 1500s B.C.E., until the Persian King Cyrus the Great overthrew the Medes and became ruler of the Achaemenid (Persian) Empire, which reached from the Indus to the Nile at its zenith in 525 B.C.E. Persia fell to Alexander in 331–330 B.C.E., and a succession of other rulers: the Seleucids (312–302 B.C.E.), the Greek-speaking Parthians (247 B.C.E.–C.E. 226), the Sasanians, and the Arab Muslims (in 641). By the mid-800s Persia had become an international scientific and cultural center. In the 12th century it was invaded by the Mongols. The Safavid Dynasty (1501–1722), under whom the dominant religion became Shi'ite Islam, followed, and was then replaced by the Qajar Dynasty (1794–1925).

During the Qajar Dynasty, the Russians and the British fought for economic control of the area, and during World War I its neutrality did not stop it from becoming a battlefield for Russian and British troops. A coup in 1921 brought Reza Kahn to power. In 1925 he became Shah and changed his name to Reza Shah Pahlavi. He subsequently did much to modernize the country and abolished all foreign extraterritorial rights.

The country's pro-Axis allegiance in World War II led to Anglo-Russian occupation of Iran in 1941 and deposition of the Shah in favor of his son, Mohammed Reza Pahlavi. Pahlavi's Westernization programs alienated the clergy, and his authoritarian rule led to massive demonstrations during the 1970s, to which the Shah responded with the imposition of martial law in Sept. 1978. The Shah and his family fled Iran on Jan. 16, 1979, and the exiled cleric Ayatollah Ruhollah Khomeini returned to establish an Islamic theocracy. Khomeini proceeded with his plans for revitalizing Islamic traditions. He urged women to return to the veil, banned alcohol, western music, and mixed bathing, shut down the media, closed universities, and eliminated political parties.

Revolutionary militants invaded the U.S. embassy in Teheran on Nov. 4, 1979, seized staff members as hostages, and precipitated an international crisis. Khomeini refused all appeals, even a unanimous vote by the U.N. Security Council demanding immediate release of the hostages. Iranian hostility toward Washington was reinforced by the Carter administration's economic boycott and deportation order against Iranian students in the U.S., the break in diplomatic relations, and ultimately an aborted U.S. raid in April aimed at rescuing the hostages.

As the first anniversary of the embassy seizure neared, Khomeini and his followers insisted on their original conditions: guarantee by the U.S. not to interfere in Iran's affairs, cancellation of U.S. damage claims against Iran, release of $8 billion in frozen Iranian assets, an apology, and the return of the assets held by the former imperial family. These conditions were largely met and the 52 American hostages were released on Jan. 20, 1980 ending 444 days in captivity.

The sporadic war with Iraq regained momentum in 1982, as Iran launched an offensive in March and regained much of the border area occupied by Iraq in late 1980. The stalemated war with Iraq dragged on well into 1988. Although Iraq expressed its willingness to cease fighting, Iran stated that it would not stop the war until Iraq agreed to make payment for war damages to Iran, and to punish the Iraqi government leaders involved in the conflict. On July 20, 1988, Khomeini, after a series of Iranian military reverses, agreed to cease-fire negotiations with Iraq. A cease-fire went into effect Aug. 20, 1988. Khomeini died in June 1989 and Ayotollah Khamenei succeeded him as the supreme leader.

By early 1991 the Islamic Revolution appeared to have lost much of its militancy. Attempting to revive a stagnant economy, President Rafsanjani took measures to decentralize the command system and introduce free-market mechanisms.

Mohammad Khatami, a moderate cleric and former culture minister, won the presidential election in a stunning victory over the conservative ruling elite in May 1997. Khatami has supported greater social and political freedoms, and has made overtures for friendlier relations with the U.S. His steps at liberalizing the strict clerical rule governing the country has put him at odds with the supreme leader, Ayatollah Khamenei. In 1998, Tehran mayor Gholam-Hossein Karbaschi, a strong supporter of Khatami's liberalization process, was sentenced to prison for embezzlement. Many saw this as a politically motivated attack aimed at Khatami.

In Sept. 1998 Iran deployed thousands of troops on its border with Afghanistan after the Taliban admitted killing eight Iranian diplomats and a journalist. Iran, mainly Shi'ite, supports the rebels fighting against the extremist Sunni Taliban.

Iraq

REPUBLIC OF IRAQ

National name: Jumhouriyat Al Iraq
President: Saddam Hussein (1979)
Area: 167,920 sq mi. (437,072 sq km)
Population (1998 est.): 21,722,287 (average annual rate of natural increase: 3.2%); birth rate: 38.6/1000; infant mortality rate: 62.4/1000; density per sq mi.: 129
Capital: Baghdad. **Largest cities (est. 1987):** Baghdad (1995), 4,478,000; Mosul, 664,221 Irbil 485,968; Karkuk (Kirkuk) 418,624; Basra, 406,296. **Monetary unit:** Iraqi dinar. **Languages:** Arabic (official) and Kurdish. **Ethnicity/Race:** Arab 75%–80%, Kurdish 15%–20%, Turkoman, Assyrian or other 5%. **Religions:** Muslim 97% (Shi'ite 60%–65%, Sunni 32%–37%), Christian or other 3%. **Literacy rate:** 60%
Economic summary: GDP/PPP (1996 est.): $42 billion, $2,000 per capita. **Real growth rate:** 0%. **Inflation:** n.a. **Unemployment:** n.a. **Arable land:** 12%. **Agriculture:** dates, livestock, wheat, barley, cotton, rice. **Labor force:** 4.4 million (1989); services, 48%; agriculture, 30%; industry, 22%. **Industry:** petroleum, chemicals, textiles, construction materials. **Natural resources:** oil, natural gas, phosphates, sulfur. **Exports:** n.a.; crude oil. **Imports:** n.a.; manufactured goods, food. **Major trading partners:** France, Jordan, Turkey, Australia, Vietnam.

Geography Iraq, a triangle of mountains, desert, and fertile river valley, is bounded on the east by Iran, on the north by Turkey, the west by Syria and Jordan, and the south by Saudi Arabia and Kuwait. It is twice the size of Idaho. The country has arid desertland west of the Euphrates, a broad central valley between the Euphrates and Tigris, and mountains in the northeast.

Government One-party republic.

History From earliest times Iraq was known as Mesopotamia—the land between the rivers—for it embraces a large part of the alluvial plains of the Tigris and Euphrates.

An advanced civilization existed by 4000 B.C.E. Sometime after 2000 B.C.E. the land became the center of the ancient Babylonian and Assyrian empires. Mesopotamia was conquered by Cyrus the Great of Persia in 538 B.C.E., and by Alexander in 331 B.C.E. After an Arab conquest in C.E. 637–40, Baghdad became capital of the ruling caliphate. The country was cruelly pillaged by the Mongols in 1258, and during the 16th, 17th, and 18th centuries was the object of repeated Turkish-Persian competition.

Nominal Turkish suzerainty imposed in 1638 was replaced by direct Turkish rule in 1831. In World War I, Britain occupied most Mesopotamia and was given a mandate over the area in 1920. The British renamed the area Iraq and recognized it as a kingdom in 1922. In 1932 the monarchy achieved full independence. Britain again occupied Iraq during World War II because of its pro-Axis stance in the initial years of the war.

Iraq became a charter member of the Arab League in 1945, and Iraqi troops took part in the Arab invasion of Palestine in 1948.

King Faisal II, born on May 2, 1935, succeeded his father, Ghazi I, who was killed in an automobile accident on April 4, 1939. Faisal and his uncle, Crown Prince Abdul-Illah, were assassinated in July 1958 in a swift revolutionary coup that ended the monarchy and brought to power a military junta headed by Abdul Karem Kassim. Kassim reversed the monarchy's pro-Western policies, attempted to rectify the economic disparities between rich and poor, and began to form alliances with Communist countries. Kassim was overthrown and killed in a coup staged March 8, 1963, by the Ba'ath Socialist Party. Abdel Salam Arif, a leader in the 1958 coup, staged another coup in Nov. 1963, driving the Ba'ath members of the revolutionary council from power. He adopted a new constitution in 1964. In 1966, he, two cabinet members, and other supporters died in a helicopter crash. His brother, Gen. Abdel Rahman Arif, assumed the presidency, crushed the opposition, and won an indefinite extension of his term in 1967. His regime was ousted in July 1968 by a junta led by Maj. Gen. Ahmed Hassan al-Bakr of the Ba'ath Party. Bakr and his second-in-command, Saddam Hussein, imposed authoritarian rule in an effort to end the decades of political instability that followed World War II. One of the world's leading producers of oil, Iraq's oil revenues were used to develop one of the strongest military forces in the region. On July 16, 1979, President Bakr was succeeded by Saddam Hussein, whose regime developed an international reputation for repression, human rights abuses, and terrorism.

A long-standing territorial dispute over control of the Shatt-al-Arab waterway between Iraq and Iran broke into full-scale war on Sept. 20, 1980. Iraqi planes attacked Iranian airfields and the Abadan refinery, and Iraqi ground forces moved into Iran. Despite the smaller size of its armed forces, Iraq took and held the initiative by seizing Abadan and Khurramshahr together with substantial Iranian territory by December, and beating back Iranian counterattacks in January.

In 1982, the Iraqis fell back to their own country and dug themselves in behind sandbagged defensive fortifications. From the beginning of the war in Sept. 1980 to Sept. 1984, foreign military analysts estimated that more than 150,000 Iraqis had been killed. The Iraqis clearly wanted to end the war, but the Iranians refused. In Feb. 1986, Iranian forces gained on two fronts; but Iraq retook most of the lost ground in 1988 and a ceasefire took effect that August.

In July 1990, President Hussein claimed that Kuwait was flooding world markets with oil and forcing down prices. A mediation attempt by Arab leaders failed, and on Aug. 2, 1990, over this and territorial claims, Iraqi troops invaded Kuwait and set up a puppet government. On Jan. 18, 1991, U.N. forces, under the leadership of U.S. General Norman Schwarzkopf, launched Operation Desert Storm, liberating Kuwait in less than a week.

Despite rebellions by both Shi'ites and Kurds following Iraq's crushing defeat in the Gulf War, Saddam Hussein maintained his draconian grip on Iraq. The U.N. Security Council has barred Iraq from selling oil except in exchange for food and medicine. Despite the debilitating effects of U.N. sanctions, Hussein continued to defy the terms of the cease-fire agreement, waging a propaganda campaign that blamed the U.S. for the starvation and poverty suffered by the Iraqi people rather than his own refusal to meet the terms required to remove sanctions. Several minor military skirmishes between Iraqi and U.S. forces have resulted.

On Nov. 13, 1997, Iraq expelled the American members of the U.N. inspection team mandated to ascertain that Iraq has destroyed all its nuclear, chemical, biological, and ballistic arms. Under the 1991 cease-fire resolution, the U.N. will not lift sanctions until Iraq fully complies. The standoff stretched on over months and as tensions rose the U.S. began a military build-up in the Gulf. In Feb. 1998 U.N. secretary-general Kofi Annan brokered a peaceful solution to the stand-off. Over the next months Baghdad continued to impede the U.N. inspection team, demanding that sanctions be lifted. In Aug. 1998 Hussein put a complete halt to the inspections once again. This time, the U.S. opted for diplomatic arm-twisting rather than military threats, and in September the U.N. Security Council voted unanimously that the lifting of sanctions would not be discussed until cooperation with U.N. arms inspectors resumes.

Ireland

National name: Ireland, or Eire in the Irish language
President: Mary McAleese (1997)
Taoiseach (Prime Minister): Bertie Ahern (1997)
Area: 27,136 sq mi. (70,280 sq km)
Population (1998 est.): 3,619,480 (average annual rate of natural increase: 0.36%); birth rate: 13.5/1000; infant mortality rate: 6/1000; density per sq mi.: 133
Capital: Dublin. **Largest cities (1991):** Dublin, 1,056,666; Cork, 293,254; Galway, 131,503; Limerick, 112,975. **Monetary unit:** Irish pound (punt). **Languages:** English, Irish Gaelic. **Ethnicity/Race:** Celtic, English. **Religions:** Roman Catholic 93%, Anglican 3%, none 1%, unknown 2%, other 1%. **Literacy rate:** 98%
Economic summary: GDP/PPP (1996 est.): $59.9 billion; $16,800 per capita. **Real growth rate:** 7%. **Inflation:** 1.8%. **Unemployment:** 11.9%. **Arable land:** 13%. **Agriculture:** cattle and dairy products, pigs, poultry and eggs, sheep and wool, horses, barley, sugar beets. **Labor force:** (1996 est.), 1.474 million; services, 62.3% manufacturing and construction, 26%. **Products:** processed foods, brews, textiles, clothing, chemicals, pharmaceuticals, machinery, transportation equipment, glass and crystal. **Natural resources:** zinc, lead, natural gas, crude oil, barite, copper, gypsum, limestone, dolomite, peat, silver. **Exports:** $43.4 billion (f.o.b., 1995): livestock, dairy products, machinery, chemicals, data processing equipment. **Imports:** $32.7 billion (c.i.f., 1995): food, animal feed, chemicals, petroleum products, machinery, textile clothing. **Major trading partners:** E.U., U.S.

Geography Ireland is situated in the Atlantic Ocean and separated from Great Britain by the Irish Sea. Half the size of Arkansas, it occupies the entire island except for the six counties which make up Northern Ireland. Ireland resembles a basin—a central plain rimmed with mountains, except in the Dublin region. The mountains are low, with the highest peak, Carrantuohill in County Kerry, rising to 3,415 feet (1,041 m). The principal river is the Shannon, which begins in the north central area, flows south and southwest for about 240 miles (386 km), and empties into the Atlantic.

Government According to the country's constitution, which was adopted by plebiscite in 1937, Ireland is a parliamentary democracy. The national parliament (Oireachtas) consists of the president and two Houses, the House of Representatives (Dáil Eireann) and the Senate (Seanad Eireann), whose members serve for a maximum term of five years. The House of Representatives has 166 members elected by proportional representation; the Senate has 60 members, 11 of whom are nominated by the prime minister, 6 by the universities and the remaining 43 from five vocational panels. The prime minister (Taoiseach), who is the head of government, is appointed by the president on the nomination of the House of Representatives, to which he or she is responsible. The president is elected by direct vote of the people for a term of seven years and is eligible for reelection for a second term.

History In the Stone and Bronze Ages, Ireland was inhabited by Picts in the north and a people called the Erainn in the south, the same stock, apparently, as in all the isles before the Anglo-Saxon invasion of Britain. About the 4th century B.C.E., tall, red-haired Celts arrived from Gaul or Galicia. They subdued and assimilated the inhabitants and established a Gaelic civilization. By the beginning of the Christian Era, Ireland was divided into five kingdoms—Ulster, Connacht, Leinster, Meath, and Munster. St. Patrick introduced Christianity in C.E. 432 and the country developed into a center of Gaelic and Latin learning. Irish monasteries, the equivalent of universities, attracted intellectuals as well as the pious and sent out missionaries to many parts of Europe and, some believe, to North America.

Norse depredations along the coasts, starting in 795, ended in 1014 with Norse defeat at the Battle of Clontarf by forces under Brian Boru. In the 12th century, the Pope gave all Ireland to the English Crown as a papal fief. In 1171, Henry II of England was acknowledged "Lord of Ireland," but local sectional rule continued for centuries, and English control over the whole island was not reasonably absolute until the 17th century. By the Act of Union (1801), England and Ireland became the "United Kingdom of Great Britain and Ireland."

A steady decline in the Irish economy followed in the next decades. The population had reached 8.25 million when the great potato famine of 1846–48 took many lives and drove more than 2 million people to emigrate to North America. In the meantime, anti-British agitation continued along with demands for Irish home rule. The advent of World War I delayed the institution of home rule and resulted in the Easter Rebellion in Dublin (April 24–29, 1916), in which Irish nationalists unsuccessfully attempted to throw off British rule. Guerrilla warfare against British forces followed proclamation of a republic by the rebels in 1919. The Irish Free State was established as a dominion on Dec. 6, 1922, with the six northern counties remaining as part of the United Kingdom. The constitution of 1937 changed the nation's name to Éire. Ireland was neutral in World War II.

In 1948, Eamon de Valera, American-born leader of the Sinn Fein, who had won establishment of the Free State in 1921 in negotiations with Britain's David Lloyd George, was defeated by John A. Costello, who demanded final independence from Britain. The Republic of Ireland was proclaimed on April 18, 1949. It withdrew from the Commonwealth, but in 1955 Ireland entered the United Nations. Through the 1960s, two antagonistic currents dominated Irish politics. One sought to bind the wounds of the rebellion and civil war. The other was the effort of the outlawed Irish Republican Army to bring Northern Ireland into the republic.

Under the First Programme for Economic Expansion (1958–63), economic protection was dismantled and foreign investment was encouraged. This prosperity brought profound social and cultural changes to what had been one of the poorest and least technologically advanced countries in Europe. Ireland joined the European Economic Community (now the E.U.) in 1973. In the 1990 presidential election, Mary Robinson was elected the republic's first woman president. The election of a candidate with socialist and feminist sympathies was regarded as a watershed in Irish political life, reflecting the changes taking place in Irish society. Irish voters approved the Maastricht Treaty, which paved the way for the establishment of the E.U., by a large majority in a referendum held in 1992. In 1993, the Irish and British governments signed a joint peace initiative (the Downing Street Declaration), in which they pledged to seek mutually agreeable political structures in Northern Ireland and between the two islands. A referendum on allowing divorce under certain conditions—hitherto had been constitutionally forbidden—was held in Nov. 1995 and narrowly passed.

In 1998 hope for a solution to the troubles in Northern Ireland seemed palpable. An agreement, brokered by former U.S. Senator George Mitchell and bolstered by British Prime Minister Tony Blair and U.S. President Bill Clinton, holds out promise of a more peaceful and just coexistence between Catholics and Protestants.

Israel

STATE OF ISRAEL

National name: Medinat Yisra'el
President: Ezer Weizman (1993)
Prime Minister: Benjamin Netanyahu (1996)
Area: 8,020 sq mi. (20,770 sq km)
Population (1998 est.): 5,643,966[1] (average annual rate of natural increase: 1.91%); birth rate: 20/1000; infant mortality rate: 8/1000; density per sq mi.: 704
Capital and largest city (1993 est.): Jerusalem[2], 550,500. **Other large cities (1993 est.):** Tel Aviv, 355,900; Haifa, 250,000. **Monetary unit:** Shekel. **Languages:** Hebrew, Arabic, English. **Ethnicity/Race:** Jewish 82% (Israel-born 50%, Europe/Americas/Oceania-born 20%, Africa-born 7%, Asia-born 5%), non-Jewish 18% (mostly Arab) (1993 est.). **Religions:** Judaism, 82%; Islam, 14%; Christian, 2%; others, 2%. **Literacy rate:** 92%
Economic summary: GDP/PPP (1996 est.): $85.7 billion; $16,400 per capita. **Real growth rate:** 4.6%. **Inflation:** 11.3%. **Unemployment:** 6.5%. **Arable land:** 17%. **Agriculture:** citrus and other fruits, vegetables, beef, dairy and poultry products. **Labor force:** (1996), 2.2 million; public services, 29.3%; industry, 22.1%; commerce, 13.9%; finance and business, 10.4%. **Industry:** processed foods, cut diamonds, clothing and textiles, chemicals, metal products, transport and electrical equipment, high-technology electronics. **Natural resources:** sulfur, copper, phosphates, potash, bromine. **Exports:** $20.3 billion (f.o.b., 1996 est.): polished diamonds, citrus and other fruits, clothing and textiles, processed foods, electronics, military hardware, fertilizer and chemical products. **Imports:** $28.3 billion (c.i.f., 1996 est.): rough diamonds, chemicals, oil, machinery, iron and steel, cereals, textiles, vehicles, ships, aircraft. **Major trading partners:** U.S., E.U., Japan.

1. Includes West Bank, Gaza Strip, East Jerusalem. 2. Not recognized by U.S., which recognizes Tel Aviv.

Geography Israel, slightly larger than Massachusetts, lies at the eastern end of the Mediterranean Sea. It is bordered by Egypt on the west, Syria and Jordan on the east, and Lebanon on the north. Northern Israel is largely a plateau traversed from north to south by mountains and broken by great depressions, also running from north to south.

The maritime plain of Israel is remarkably fertile. The southern Negev region, which comprises almost half the total area, is largely a wide desert steppe area. Parts of it have been irrigated and cultivated. The Jordan, the only important river, flows from the north through Lake Hule (Waters of Merom) and Lake Kinneret (Sea of Galilee or Sea of Tiberias), finally entering the Dead Sea, 1,290 feet (393 m) below sea level. This "sea," which is actually a salt lake (394 sq mi.; 1,020 sq km), has no outlet, its water balance being maintained by evaporation.

Government Israel, which does not have a written constitution, has a republican form of government headed by a president elected for a five-year term by the Knesset. The president may serve no more than two terms. The Knesset has 120 members elected by universal suffrage under proportional representation for four years.

The government is administered by the cabinet, which is headed by the prime minister. Since 1996, the prime minister has been directly elected by the people; previously the president appointed the prime minister. Though Israel has numerous political parties, the two strongest are the Likud ("Unity") Party, a staunchly nationalist, security-conscious group, and the Labor Party, which favors a compromise among ethnic and religious groups to achieve a lasting peace. Israel grants automatic citizenship to every Jew who desires to settle within its borders.

History Palestine, considered a holy land by Jews, Muslims, and Christians, and homeland of the modern state of Israel, was known as Canaan to the ancient Hebrews. Palestine's name derives from the Philistines, a people who occupied the southern coastal part of the country in the 12th century B.C.E.

A Hebrew kingdom established in 1000 B.C.E. was later split into the kingdoms of Judah and Israel; they were subsequently invaded by Assyrians, Babylonians, Egyptians, Persians, Macedonians, and Romans. By C.E. 135, few Jews were left in Palestine; most lived in the scattered and tenacious communities of the Diaspora. Palestine became a center of Christian pilgrimage after the emperor Constantine converted to that faith. The Arabs took Palestine from the Byzantine empire in C.E. 634–40. Interrupted only by Christian crusaders, Muslims ruled Palestine until the 20th century (Turkish rule from 1516). During World War I, British forces defeated the Turks in Palestine and governed the area under a League of Nations mandate from 1923.

As part of the 19th-century Zionist movement, Jews had begun settling in Palestine as early as 1820. This effort to establish a Jewish homeland had received British approval in the Balfour Declaration of 1917. During the 1930s, Jews persecuted by the Hitler regime poured into Palestine. The postwar acknowledgment of the Holocaust—Hitler's genocide of six million Jews—increased international interest in and sympathy for the cause of Zionism. However, Arabs in Palestine and surrounding countries bitterly opposed pre-war and postwar proposals to partition Palestine into Arab and Jewish sectors. The British mandate to govern Palestine ended after the war, and in 1947 the U.N. voted to partition Palestine. When the British officially withdrew on May 14, 1948, the Jewish National Council proclaimed the state of Israel

U.S. recognition came within hours. The next day, Arab forces from Egypt, Jordan, Syria, Lebanon, and Iraq invaded the new nation. By the cease-fire on Jan. 7, 1949, Israel had increased its original territory by 50%, taking western Galilee, a broad corridor through central Palestine to Jerusalem, and part of modern Jerusalem. Chaim Weizmann and David Ben-Gurion became Israel's first president and prime minister. The new government was admitted to the U.N. on May 11, 1949.

The next clash with Arab neighbors came when Egypt nationalized the Suez Canal in 1956 and barred Israeli shipping. Coordinating with an Anglo-French force, Israeli troops seized the Gaza Strip and drove through the Sinai to the east bank of the Suez Canal, but withdrew under U.S. and U.N. pressure. In the Six-Day War of 1967, Israel made simultaneous air attacks against Syrian, Jordanian, and Egyptian air bases, totally defeating the Arabs. Expanding its territory by 200%, Israel at the cease-fire held the Golan Heights, the West Bank of the Jordan River, Jerusalem's Old City, and all of the Sinai and the east bank of the Suez Canal.

In the face of Israeli reluctance even to discuss the return of occupied territories, the fourth Arab-Israeli war erupted on Oct. 6, 1973, with a surprise Egyptian and Syrian assault on the Jewish high holy day of Yom Kippur. Initial Arab gains were reversed when a cease-fire took effect two weeks later, but Israel suffered heavy losses.

A dramatic breakthrough in the tortuous history of Mideast peace efforts occurred on Nov. 9, 1977, when Egypt's president Anwar Sadat declared his willingness to go anywhere to talk peace. Prime Minister Menachem Begin on Nov. 15 extended an invitation to the Egyptian leader to address the Knesset. Sadat's arrival in Israel four days later raised worldwide hopes, but a peace agreement between Egypt and Israel was long in coming. On March 14, 1979, the Knesset approved a final peace treaty, and 12 days later Begin and Sadat signed the document, together with President Jimmy Carter, in a White House ceremony. Israel began its withdrawal from the Sinai, which it had annexed from Egypt, on May 25, and the two countries opened their border on May 29.

Although Israel withdrew its last settlers from the Sinai in April 1982, the fragile Mideast peace was shattered on June 9 by a massive Israeli assault on southern Lebanon, where the Palestinian Liberation Organization was entrenched. The PLO had long plagued Israelis with terrorist actions. Israel destroyed PLO strongholds in Tyre and Sidon and reached the suburbs of Beirut on June 10. A U.S.-mediated accord between Lebanon and Israel, signed on May 17, 1983, provided for Israeli withdrawal from Lebanon. Israel eventually withdrew its troops from the Beirut area, but kept them in southern Lebanon, where occasional skirmishes would continue. Lebanon, under pressure from Syria, canceled the accord in March 1984.

A continual source of tension has been the relationship between the Jews and the Palestinians living within Israeli territories. Most Arabs fled the region when the state of Israel was declared, but those who remain now make up almost one-fifth of the population of Israel. They are about two-thirds Muslim, as well as Christian and Druze. Palestinians living on the West Bank and the Gaza Strip fomented the riots begun in 1987, known as the Intifadeh. Violence heightened as Israeli police cracked down and Palestinians retaliated. Continuing Jewish settlement of lands designated for Palestinians has added to the unrest.

In 1989 the leader of the PLO, Yasir Arafat, reversed decades of PLO polemic by acknowledging Israel's right to exist. He stated his willingness to enter negotiations to create a Palestinian political entity that would coexist with the Israeli state.

In 1991 Israel was struck by Iraqi missiles during the Persian Gulf War. The Israelis did not retaliate in order to preserve the international coalition against Iraq. In 1992 Yitzhak Rabin became prime minister. He halted the disputed Israeli settlement of the occupied territories. Highly secretive talks in Norway resulted in an agreement between the PLO and the Israeli government (the Oslo agreement, 1993). The accord stipulated a five-year plan in which Palestinians of the West Bank and the Gaza Strip would gradually become self-governing. In 1994 Israel signed a peace treaty with Jordan. Israel has no formal peace with Syria or Lebanon.

On Nov. 4, 1995, Prime Minister Rabin was slain by a Jewish extremist, jeopardizing the tenuous progress toward peace. Shimon Peres succeeded him until May 1996 elections for the Knesset gave Israel a new hard-line prime minister, Benjamin Netanyahu, by a razor-thin margin. Netanyahu has reversed or stymied much of the Oslo agreement, contending it offered too many concessions too fast and jeopardized Israeli's safety. Elections for seats on the Palestinian Council and for its president took place in Jan. 1996. Yasir Arafat obtained an easy victory as president.

Israeli-Palestinian peace negotiations in 1997 were repeatedly undermined by both sides. Although the Hebron accord was signed in January, calling for the withdrawal of Israeli troops from the city, the construction of new Jewish settlements on the West Bank in March profoundly upset progress toward peace. Some Jews cited the influx of immigration from Russia (since the collapse of the Soviet Union, more than 700,000 Russian Jews arrived in Israel) as necessitating the additional settlements. Others believe that Netanyahu wishes to curb Palestinian expectations raised by the Oslo agreement.

Terrorism erupted again in 1997 when radical Hamas suicide bombers claimed the lives of more than 20 Israeli civilians. Netanyahu, accusing Palestinian Authority President Arafat of lax security, retaliated with draconian sanctions against Palestinians working in Israel, including the withholding of millions of dollars in tax revenue, a blatant violation of the Oslo agreements. Netanyahu persisted in authorizing right-wing Israelis to build new settlements in mostly Arab East Jerusalem. Arafat, meanwhile, seemed unwilling or unable to curb the violence of extremist Arabs.

Though progress under the Oslo agreement seems stalled, negotiations continue, and the fact remains that much of Gaza and most West Bank towns are controlled by Palestinians. They have the right to vote and may yet attain a peaceful coexistence with the Israeli Jews. Other challenges that face the

50-year-old country involve the relationship between church and state and between Jews of differing cultural and geographic origins.

Italy

ITALIAN REPUBLIC

National name: Repubblica Italiana
President: Oscar Luigi Scalfaro (1992)
Prime Minister: Romano Prodi (1996)
Area: 116,500 sq mi. (301,230 sq km)
Population (1998 est.): 56,782,748 (average annual rate of natural increase: –0.08%); birth rate: 9.1/1000; infant mortality rate: 6.4/1000; density per sq mi.: 487
Capital and largest city (1994 est.): Rome, 2,693,383. **Other large cities:** Milan, 1,561,438; Naples, 1,204,149; Turin, 952,736; Genoa, 706,754; Palermo, 694,749; Florence, 460,924; Bologna, 394,969; Catania, 372,212; Bari, 355,352; Venice, 306,439. **Monetary unit:** Lira. **Languages:** Italian; small German-, French-, and Slovene-speaking minorities. **Ethnicity/Race:** Italian (includes small clusters of German-, French-, and Slovene-Italians in the north and Albanian-Italians and Greek-Italians in the south), Sicilians, Sardinians. **Religion:** Roman Catholic 98%, other 2%. **Literacy rate:** 97%
Economic summary: GDP/PPP (1996 est.): $1.12 trillion, $19,600 per capita. **Real growth rate:** 0.8%. **Inflation:** 4%. **Unemployment:** 12% (1996 est.). **Arable land:** 31%. **Agriculture:** grapes, olives, citrus fruits, vegetables, wheat, corn. **Labor force:** 22.851 million; services, 61%; industry, 32%; agriculture, 7%. **Industry:** machinery, iron and steel, autos, textiles, shoes, chemicals. **Natural resources:** mercury, potash, sulfur, fish, gas, marble. **Exports:** $250 billion (f.o.b., 1996 est.): textiles, apparel, metals, transport equipment, chemicals. **Imports:** $205 billion (c.i.f., 1996 est.): petroleum, industrial machinery, chemicals, food, metals. **Major trading partners:** E.U., U.S., OPEC.

Geography Italy, slightly larger than Arizona, is a long peninsula shaped like a boot bounded on the west by the Tyrrhenian Sea and on the east by the Adriatic. Approximately 600 of Italy's 708 miles (1,139 km) of length are in the long peninsula that projects into the Mediterranean from the fertile basin of the Po River. The Apennine Mountains, branching off from the Alps between Nice and Genoa, form the peninsula's backbone, and rise to a maximum height of 9,560 feet (2,912 m) at the Gran Sasso d'Italia (Corno). The Alps form Italy's northern boundary.

Italy has many northern lakes, lying below the snow-covered peaks of the Alps. The largest are Garda (143 sq mi.; 370 sq km), Maggiore (83 sq mi.; 215 sq km), and Como (55 sq mi.; 142 sq km). The Po, the principal river, flows from the Alps on Italy's western border and crosses the Lombard plain to the Adriatic Sea.

Several islands form part of Italy. Sicily (9,926 sq mi.; 25,708 sq km) lies off the toe of the boot, across the Strait of Messina, with a steep and rock-bound northern coast and gentler slopes to the sea in the west and south. Mount Etna, an active volcano, rises to 10,741 feet (3,274 m), and most of Sicily is more than 500 feet (3,274 m) in elevation. Sixty-two miles (100 km) southwest of Sicily lies Pantelleria (45 sq mi.; 117 sq km), and south of that are Lampedusa and Linosa. Sardinia (9,301 sq mi.; 24,090 sq km), which is just south of Corsica and about 125 miles (200 km) west of the mainland, is mountainous, stony, and unproductive.

Government The president is elected for a term of seven years by parliament in joint session with regional representatives. The president nominates the prime minister and, upon the prime minister's recommendations, the members of the cabinet. Parliament is composed of two houses: a Senate with 315 elective members (and 11 members-for-life) and a Chamber of Deputies of 630 members elected by the people for a five-year term.

History The migrations of Indo-European peoples into Italy probably began about 2000 B.C.E. and continued down to 1000 B.C.E. From about the 9th century B.C.E. until it was overthrown by the Romans in the 3rd century B.C.E., the Etruscan civilization dominated the area. By 264 B.C.E. all Italy south of Cisalpine Gaul was under the leadership of Rome. For the next seven centuries, until the Barbarian invasions destroyed the western Roman Empire in the 4th and 5th centuries C.E., the history of Italy was largely the history of Rome. From C.E. 800 on, the Holy Roman Emperors, Roman Catholic Popes, Normans, and Saracens all vied for control over various segments of the Italian peninsula. Numerous city states, such as Venice and Genoa, whose political and commercial rivalries were intense, and many small principalities flourished in the late Middle Ages. Although Italy remained politically fragmented for centuries, it became the cultural center of the Western world from the 13th to the 16th century.

In 1713, after the War of the Spanish Succession, Milan, Naples, and Sardinia were handed over to the Hapsburgs of Austria, which lost some of its Italian territories in 1735. After 1800, Italy was unified by Napoleon, who crowned himself king of Italy in 1805; but with the Congress of Vienna in 1815, Austria once again became the dominant power in a disunited Italy. Austrian armies crushed Italian uprisings in 1820–1821, and 1831. In the 1830s Giuseppe Mazzini, brilliant liberal nationalist, organized the Risorgimento (Resurrection), which laid the foundation for Italian unity. Disappointed Italian patriots looked to the House of Savoy for leadership. Count Camille di Cavour (1810–61), premier of Sardinia in 1852 and the architect of a united Italy, joined England and France in the Crimean War (1853–56), and in 1859, helped France in a war against Austria, thereby obtaining Lombardy. By plebiscite in 1860, Modena, Parma, Tuscany, and the Romagna voted to join Sardinia. In 1860, Giuseppe Garibaldi conquered Sicily and Naples and turned them over to Sardinia. Victor Emmanuel II, King of Sardinia, was proclaimed king of Italy in 1861. The annexation of Venetia in 1866 and of papal Rome in 1870 marked the complete unification of peninsular Italy into one nation under a constitutional monarchy.

Italy declared its neutrality upon the outbreak of World War I on the ground that Germany had embarked upon an offensive war. In 1915, Italy entered the war on the side of the Allies but obtained less territory than it expected in the postwar settlement. Benito ("Il Duce") Mussolini, a former socialist, organized discontented Italians in 1919 into the Fascist Party to "rescue Italy from Bolshevism." He led his Black Shirts in a march on

Rome and, on Oct. 28, 1922, became premier. He transformed Italy into a dictatorship, embarking on an expansionist foreign policy with the invasion and annexation of Ethiopia in 1935 and allying himself with Adolf Hitler in the Rome-Berlin Axis in 1936. When the Allies invaded Italy in 1943, Mussolini's dictatorship collapsed; he was executed by Partisans on April 28, 1945 at Dongo on Lake Como. Following the armistice with the Allies (Sept. 3, 1943), Italy joined the war against Germany as a co-belligerent. A June 1946 plebiscite rejected monarchy and a republic was proclaimed. The peace treaty of Sept. 15, 1947, required Italian renunciation of all claims in Ethiopia and Greece and the cession of the Dodecanese to Greece and of five small Alpine areas to France. The Trieste area west of the new Yugoslav territory was made a free territory (until 1954, when the city and a 90-square-mile zone were transferred to Italy and the rest to Yugoslavia).

Italy became an integral member of NATO and the European Economic Community (later the E.U.) as it successfully rebuilt its postwar economy. A prolonged outbreak of terrorist activities by the left-wing Red Brigades threatened domestic stability in the 1970s, but by the early 1980s the terrorist groups had been suppressed. Scandal brought the long reign of the Christian Democrats to an end when Italy's 40th premier since World War II, Arnaldo Forlani, was forced to resign in the wake of disclosure that many high-ranking Christian Democrats and civil servants belonged to a secret Masonic lodge known as "P-2." During 1993, the nation was riveted by a political scandal of a seemingly ever-growing size involving the Mafia and many government leaders. In a referendum, voters approved changing the proportional system of representation in the Senate for one utilizing majority voting. This series of scandals led to the collapse of the post-World War II party system and new parties filled the political vacuum. In 1996, Italians elected a government dominated by a center-left coalition for the first time since the proclamation of the Italian Republic. In 1997, Italian forces assumed leadership of a military mission to protect international aid reaching strife-torn Albania. The Communists, Italy's single largest party, refused to support the operation but refrained from withdrawing support from the government.

Jamaica

Sovereign: Queen Elizabeth II (1952)
Governor-General: H. E. The Most Hon. Sir Howard F. H. Cooke (1991)
Prime Minister: The Rt. Hon. Percival J. Patterson (1992)
Area: 4,411 sq mi. (10,990 sq km)
Population (1998 est.): 2,634,678 (average annual rate of natural increase: 0.7%); birth rate: 20.9/1000; infant mortality rate: 14.5/1000; density per sq mi.: 597
Capital and largest city (1991 est.): Kingston, 104,000. **Monetary unit:** Jamaican dollar. **Languages:** English, Jamaican Creole. **Ethnicity/Race:** African 76.3%, Afro-European 15.1%, East Indian and Afro-East Indian 3%, white 3.2%, Chinese and Afro-Chinese 1.2%, other 1.2%. **Religions:** Protestant, 55.9%; Roman Catholic, 5%; other, 39.1%. **Literacy rate:** 98%
Economic summary: GDP/PPP (1996 est.): $8.4 billion; $3,260 per capita. **Real growth rate:** 0.5%. **Inflation:** 17%. **Unemployment:** 15.4% (1994 est.). **Arable land:** 14%. **Agriculture:** sugar cane, citrus fruits, bananas, coffee, potatoes, livestock. **Labor force:** 1,062,100; services, 41%; agriculture, 22.5%; industry, 19% (1989). **Industry:** tourism, bauxite mining, textiles, processed foods, light manufactures. **Natural resources:** bauxite, gypsum. **Exports:** $1.4 billion (f.o.b., 1996 est.): alumina, bauxite, sugar, bananas. **Imports:** $2.8 billion (f.o.b., 1996 est.): fuels, machinery, consumer goods, construction goods, food. **Major trading partners:** U.S., U.K., Canada, Norway, Trinidad and Tobago, Venezuela, Japan. **Member of Commonwealth of Nations**

Geography Jamaica is an island in the West Indies, 90 miles (145 km) south of Cuba and 100 miles (161 km) west of Haiti. It is a little smaller than Connecticut. The island is made up of coastal lowlands, a limestone plateau, and the Blue Mountains, a group of volcanic hills, in the east. Blue Mountain (7,402 ft.; 2,256 m) is the tallest peak.

Government Under Jamaica's 1962 constitution, the bicameral parliament consists of a 60-member House of Representatives elected by universal suffrage and an appointed Senate of 21 members. The governor-general 's role is largely ceremonial, however, and executive power is exercised by the Cabinet under the leadership of the prime minister, who is the leader of the majority party in parliament. The Jamaica Labour Party and the People's National Party are the main political parties.

History Jamaica was inhabited by Arawak Indians when Columbus visited it in 1494 and named it St. Iago. It remained under Spanish rule until 1655, when it became a British possession. The island prospered from wealth brought by buccaneers to their base, Port Royal, the capital, until the city disappeared into the sea in 1692 after an earthquake. The Arawaks died off from disease and exploitation, and slaves, mostly black, were imported to work sugar plantations. During the 17th and 18th centuries the British were consistently harassed and attacked by the Maroons, armed and organized freed slaves who operated from rural Jamaica. Abolition of the slave trade (1807), emancipation of the slaves (1833), and a gradual drop in sugar prices led to depressed economic conditions that resulted in an uprising in 1865. The following year Jamaica's status was changed to that of a Crown colony, and conditions improved considerably. Introduction of banana cultivation made the island less dependent on the sugar crop for its well-being.

On May 5, 1953, Jamaica attained internal autonomy, and in 1958 it led in organizing the West Indies Federation. This effort at Caribbean unification failed. A nationalist labor leader, Sir Alexander Bustamente, led a campaign for withdrawal from the Federation. As the result of a popular referendum in 1961, Jamaica became independent on Aug. 6, 1962. Michael Manley, of the People's National Party, became prime minister in 1972 and initiated a socialist program.

The Labour Party defeated Manley's People's National Party in 1980 and its capitalist-oriented leader, Edward P. G. Seaga, became prime minister. He instituted measures to encourage private investment. Like other Caribbean countries, Jamaica was hard-hit by the 1981–82 recession. By 1984, austerity measures that Seaga instituted in the hope of bringing the economy back into balance included elimination of government subsidies. Devaluation of the Jamaican dollar made Jamaican products more competitive on the world market and Jamaica achieved record growth in tourism and agriculture. While manufacturing also grew, the cost of many foods went up 50% to 75% and thousands of Jamaicans fell deeper into poverty.

In 1989, Manley swept back into power with a clear-cut victory. He indicated that he would pursue more centrist policies than he did in his previous administration. Manley stepped down in 1992 for reasons of health, and was replaced by P. J. Patterson. In May 1997 the government signed a "Shiprider Agreement" allowing U.S. authorities, in an effort to curb drug trafficking, to enter Jamaican waters and search vessels with the Jamaican government's permission.

Japan

National name: Nippon
Emperor: Akihito (1989)
Prime Minister: Keizo Obuchi (1998)
Area: 145,874 sq mi. (377,835 sq km)
Population (1998 est.): 125,931,533 (average annual rate of natural increase: 0.20%); birth rate: 10.3/1000; infant mortality rate: 4.1/1000; density per sq mi.: 863
Capital and largest city: Tokyo: city proper (1995 census) 7,966,195; metro. area (1996 est.) 27,242,000. **Other large cities:** Osaka: city proper (1995 census) 2,602,352; metro area (1996 est.) 10,618,000; Yokohama, 3,276,000; Nagoya, 2,162,000; Sapporo, 1,719,000; Kobe, 1,501,000; Kyoto, 1,456,000; Fukuoka, 1,263,000; Kawasaki, 1,196,000; Hiroshima, 1,099,000. **Monetary unit:** Yen. **Language:** Japanese. **Ethnicity/Race:** Japanese 99.4%, other 0.6% (mostly Korean). **Religions:** Shintoist, 111.8 million; Buddhist, 93.1 million; Christian, 1.4 million; other, 11.4 million. **Literacy rate:** 99%
Economic summary: GDP/PPP (1996 est.): $2.85 trillion; $22,700 per capita. **Real growth rate:** 3.6%. **Inflation:** 0.3%. **Unemployment:** 3.4%. **Arable land:** 11%. **Agriculture:** rice, vegetables, fruits, meat and dairy products. **Labor force:** (March 1997): 67.23 million; trade and services, 50%; manufacturing, mining, and construction, 33%; agriculture, forestry, and fishing, 6% (1994). **Industry:** machinery and equipment, metals and metal products, autos, consumer electronics, chemicals, electrical and electronic equipment. **Natural resource:** fish. **Exports:** $385 billion (f.o.b, 1996 est.): machinery and equipment, automobiles, metals and metal products, consumer electronics, semiconductors. **Imports:** $329 billion (c.i.f., 1996 est.): fossil fuels, raw materials, foodstuffs, machinery and equipment. **Major trading partners:** U.S., Southeast Asia, E.U.

Geography An archipelago extending in an arc more than 1,744 miles (2,790 km) from northeast to southwest in the Pacific, Japan is separated from the east coast of Asia by the Sea of Japan. It is approximately the size of Montana.

Japan's four main islands are Honshu, Hokkaido, Kyushu, and Shikoku. The Ryukyu chain to the southwest was U.S.-occupied from 1945 to 1972, when it reverted to Japanese control, and the Kurils to the northeast are Russian-occupied. The surface of the main islands consists largely of mountains separated by narrow valleys.

Located within a geologically active region, Japan sustains approximately 1,000 earthquakes per year, though most are minor. Offshore earthquakes can produce tsunamis, massive ocean waves that can wreak destruction along the Pacific shore. Several of Japan's mountains are active volcanoes.

Government Japan's constitution, promulgated on Nov. 3, 1946, replaced the Meiji constitution of 1889. The 1946 constitution, sponsored by the U.S. during its occupation of Japan, brought fundamental changes to the Japanese political system, including a public statement from the emperor that he was no longer to be considered divine. The Diet (parliament) consists of a House of Representatives of 500 members, elected for four years, and a House of Councilors of 252 members, half of whom are elected every three years for six-year terms. Executive power is vested in the cabinet, which is headed by a prime minister, nominated by the Diet from its members.

On Jan. 7, 1989, Emperor Hirohito, Japan's longest-reigning monarch, died and was succeeded by his son, Akihito (born 1933). He was married in 1959 to Michiko Shoda (the first time a Crown Prince married a commoner).

History Legend attributes creation of Japan to the sun goddess, from whom the emperors were descended. The first of them was Jimmu, supposed to have ascended the throne in 660 B.C.E., a tradition that constituted official doctrine until 1945.

Recorded Japanese history begins in approximately C.E. 400, when the Yamato clan, eventually based in Kyoto, managed to exact a loose control of the other family groups of central and western Japan. Contact with Korea introduced Buddhism to Japan at about this time. Through the 700s Japan was much influenced by China, and the Yamato clan set up an imperial court similar to that of China. In the ensuing centuries, the authority of the imperial court was undermined as powerful gentry families vied for control.

At the same time, warrior clans were rising to prominence as a distinct class known as samurai. In 1192 the Minamoto clan set up a military government under their leader, Yoritomo. He was designated shogun (military dictator). For the following 700 years, shoguns from a succession of clans ruled in Japan, while the imperial court existed in relative obscurity.

First contact with the West came in about 1542, when a Portuguese ship off course arrived in Japanese waters. Portuguese traders, Jesuit missionaries, and Spanish, Dutch, and English traders followed. Suspicious of Christianity and of Portuguese support of a local Japanese revolt, the shoguns of the Tokugawa period (1603–1867) prohibited all trade with foreign countries; only a Dutch trading post at Nagasaki was permitted. Western attempts to renew trading relations failed until 1853, when Commodore Matthew Perry sailed an American fleet into Tokyo Bay. Trade with the West was forced upon Japan under terms less than favorable to the Japanese. Strife caused by these actions brought down the feudal world of the shoguns. In 1868 the emperor Meiji came to the throne, and the shogun system was abolished.

Japan quickly made the transition from a medieval to a modern power. An imperial army was established with conscription, and parliamentary government was formed in 1889. The Japanese began to take steps to extend their empire. After a brief war with China in 1894–95, Japan acquired Formosa (Taiwan), the Pescadores Islands, and part of southern Manchuria. China also recognized the independence of Korea (Chosen), which Japan later annexed (1910).

In 1904–05, Japan defeated Russia in the Russo-Japanese War, gaining the territory of southern Sakhalin (Karafuto) and Russia's port and rail rights in Manchuria. In World War I Japan seized Germany's Pacific islands and leased areas in China. The Treaty of Versailles then awarded it a mandate over the islands.

At the Washington Conference of 1921–22, Japan agreed to respect Chinese national integrity, but in 1931 invaded Manchuria. The following year, Japan set up this area as a puppet state, "Manchukuo," under Emperor Henry Pu-Yi, the last of China's Manchu Dynasty. On Nov. 25, 1936, Japan joined the Axis. The invasion of China came the next year followed by the Pearl Harbor attack on the U.S. on Dec. 7, 1941. Japan won its first military engagements during the war, extending its power over a vast area of the Pacific. Yet after 1942 the Japanese were forced to retreat, island by island, to their own country. The dropping of atomic bombs on the cities of Hiroshima and Nagasaki in 1945 by the United States finally brought the government to admit defeat. Japan surrendered formally on Sept. 2, 1945, aboard the battleship *Missouri* in Tokyo Bay. Southern Sakhalin and the Kuril Islands reverted to the U.S.S.R., and Formosa (Taiwan) and Manchuria to China. The Pacific islands remained under U.S. occupation.

Gen. Douglas MacArthur was appointed supreme commander of the U.S. occupation of postwar Japan (1945–52). In 1947 a new constitution took affect. The emperor became largely a symbolic head of state. The U.S. and Japan signed a security treaty in 1951, allowing for U.S. troops to be stationed in Japan. In 1952 Japan regained full sovereignty, and in 1972 the U.S. returned to Japan the Ryuku Islands, including Okinawa.

Japan's postwar economic recovery was nothing short of remarkable. New technologies and manufacturing were undertaken with great success. A shrewd trade policy gave Japan larger shares in many Western markets, an imbalance that caused some tensions with the U.S. The close involvement of Japanese government in the country's banking and industry produced accusations of protectionism. Yet economic growth continued through the 1970s and 1980s, eventually making Japan the world's second-largest economy (after the U.S.).

Japan has also been criticized for hesitation to take an active role in world affairs. Its failure to join the international coalition in the Persian Gulf War in 1991 was a case in point. Japanese prime minister Toshiki Kaifu pledged to provide $9 billion to the U.S. to help defray the expense of the latter's operations in the Persian Gulf. The government attempted to push legislation that would have permitted Japan to send a military contingent to the Gulf in noncombat roles. This was defeated amid public outcry against it.

During the 1990s, Japan has suffered an economic downturn marked by scandals involving government officials, bankers, and leaders of industry. Banks have closed under the weight of bad loans, unemployment has risen, real estate values have dropped, and many businesses have failed. These setbacks led Prime Minister Ryutaro Hashimoto to resign in July 1998, to be replaced by Keizo Obuchi.

In Sept. 1998 North Korea launched a test missile over Japan, claiming it was simply a scientific satellite, and alarming Japan and much of the rest of the world about its intentions to reenter the nuclear arms race.

Jordan

THE HASHEMITE KINGDOM OF JORDAN

National name: Al Mamlaka al Urduniya al Hashemiyah
Ruler: King Hussein I (1952)
Prime Minister: Fayez Tarawneh (1998)
Area: 34,573 sq mi (89,213 sq km) excludes West Bank
Population (1998 est.): 4,434,978 (average annual rate of natural increase: 2.54%); birth rate: 35.2/1000; infant mortality rate: 33.3/1000; density per sq mi.: 128
Capital and largest city (1994 est.): Amman, 963,490. **Largest cities (1994 est.):** Zarka, 420,900 (1990); Irbid, 208,201; As-Salt, 187,014. **Monetary unit:** Jordanian dinar. **Languages:** Arabic (official), English. **Ethnicity/Race:** Arab 98%, Circassian 1%, Armenian 1%. **Religions:** Islam, 92%; Christian, 6%; Other, 2%. **Literacy rate:** 80%
Economic summary: GDP/PPP (1996 est.): $20.9 billion; $5,000 per capita. **Real growth rate:** 5.9%. **Inflation:** 4.5%. **Unemployment:** 16% (1994 est.). **Arable land:** 4%. **Agriculture:** wheat, fruits, vegetables, olive oil. **Labor force:** (1992), 600,000: industry, 11.4%; commerce, restaurants, and hotels, 10.5%; construction, 10%; transport and communications, 8.7%; agriculture, 7.4%. **Products:** phosphate, refined petroleum products, cement. **Natural resources:** phosphate, potash. **Exports:** $1.9 billion (f.o.b., 1996): phosphates, fruits, and vegetables, shale oil, fertilizer, manufactures. **Imports:** $4.1 billion (c.i.f., 1996): petroleum products, textiles, capital goods, motor vehicles, foodstuffs. **Major trading partners:** U.S., Japan, Saudi Arabia, Iraq, E.U., China, India

Geography The Middle East kingdom of Jordan is bordered on the west by Israel and the Dead Sea, on the north by Syria, on the east by Iraq, and on the south Saudi Arabia. It is comparable in size to Indiana. Arid hills and mountains make up most of the country. The southern section of the Jordan River flows through the country.

Government Jordan is a constitutional hereditary monarchy with a bicameral parliament. The upper house consists of 40 members appointed by the king and the lower house is composed of 80 members elected by popular vote. The constitution guarantees freedom of religion, speech, press, association, and private property. Political parties were legalized in 1991.

History In biblical times, the country that is now Jordan contained the lands of Edom, Moab, Ammon, and Bashan. Together with other Middle Eastern territories, Jordan passed in turn to the Assyrians, the Babylonians, the Persians, and, about 330 B.C.E., the Seleucids. Conflict between the Seleucids and the Ptolemies enabled the Arabic-speaking Nabataeans to create a kingdom in southeastern Jordan. In C.E. 106 it became part of the

Roman province of Arabia and in 633–36 was conquered by the Arabs. In the 16th century, Jordan submitted to Ottoman Turkish rule and was administered from Damascus. Taken from the Turks by the British in World War I, Jordan (formerly known as Transjordan) was separated from the Palestine mandate in 1920, and in 1921, placed under the rule of Abdullah ibn Hussein.

In 1923, Britain recognized Jordan's independence, subject to the mandate. In 1946, grateful for Jordan's loyalty in World War II, Britain abolished the mandate. That part of Palestine occupied by Jordanian troops was formally incorporated by action of the Jordanian parliament in 1950. King Abdullah was assassinated in 1951. His son Talal was deposed as mentally ill the next year. Talal's son Hussein, born Nov. 14, 1935, succeeded him.

From the beginning of his reign, Hussein had to steer a careful course between his powerful neighbor to the west, Israel, and rising Arab nationalism, frequently a direct threat to his throne. Riots erupted when he joined the Central Treaty Organization (the Baghdad Pact) in 1955, and he incurred further unpopularity when Britain, France, and Israel attacked the Suez Canal in 1956, forcing him to place his army under nominal command of the United Arab Republic of Egypt and Syria. The 1961 breakup of the UAR eased Arab national pressure on Hussein, who was the first to recognize Syria after it reclaimed its independence. Jordan was swept into the 1967 Arab-Israeli war, however, and lost the old city of Jerusalem and all of its territory west of the Jordan river, the West Bank. Embittered Palestinian guerrilla forces virtually took over sections of Jordan in the aftermath of defeat, and open warfare broke out between the Palestinians and government forces in 1970.

Despite intervention of Syrian tanks, Hussein's Bedouin army defeated the Palestinians. The Jordanians drove out the Syrians and 12,000 Iraqi troops who had been in the country since the 1967 war. Ignoring protests from other Arab states, Hussein, by mid-1971, crushed Palestinian strength in Jordan and shifted the problem to Lebanon, where many of the guerrillas had fled. As Egypt and Israel neared final agreement on a peace treaty early in 1979, Hussein met with Yasir Arafat, the PLO leader, on March 17 and issued a joint statement of opposition. Although the U.S. pressed Jordan to break Arab ranks on the issue, Hussein elected to side with the great majority, cutting ties with Cairo and joining the boycott against Egypt.

Jordan's stance during the Persian Gulf War strained relations with the U.S. and led to the termination of U.S. aid. The signing of a national charter by King Hussein and leaders of the main political groups in June 1991 meant political parties were permitted in exchange for acceptance of the constitution and the monarchy. King Hussein's decision to join the Middle East peace talks in mid-1991 helped restore his country's relations with the U.S.

In July 1994 King Hussein and the Israeli prime minister signed a declaration ending the state of belligerency between the two countries. A peace between the two countries was signed on Oct. 26, 1994, although a clause in it calling the king the "custodian" of Islamic holy shrines in Jerusalem angered the PLO. In the wake of the agreement Jordan's relations with the U.S. and with the moderate Arab states, including Saudi Arabia, warmed. In 1997, Jordan began negotiating with the United States about membership in the World Trade Organization, determined to attract foreign investment. In 1998 King Hussein was treated for cancer, and after 46 years on Jordan's throne, his illness threatens not only the stability of his country but of the entire Middle East, where he has played an influential role as a statesman and voice of moderation.

Kazakhstan

REPUBLIC OF KAZAKHSTAN

President: Nursultan A. Nazarbaev (1990)
Prime Minister: Nurlan Balgimbayev (1997)
Area: 1,049,000 sq mi. (2,717,300 sq km)
Population (1998 est.): 16,846,808; average annual rate of natural increase: -0.17%; birth rate: 17.2/1000; infant mortality rate, 58.3/1000; density per sq mi.: 16
Capital and largest city (1991 est.): Almaty, 1,200,000. **Other large cities (1991):** Karaganda, 608,600; Shymkent, 438,000; Ust-Kamenogorsk, 332,900; Taraz, 312,300; Aqmola, 287,000; Aqtöbe, 266,600. **Monetary unit:** Tenge. **Languages:** Kazak (Qazaq), official language spoken by over 40% of population; Russian, official language spoken by two-thirds of population and used in everyday business. **Ethnicity/ Race:** Kazak (Qazaq) 46%, Russian 34.7%, Ukrainian 4.9%, German 3.1%, Uzbek 2.3%, Tatar 1.9%, other 7.1% (1996). **Religion:** Muslim, 47%; Russian Orthodox 44%, Protestant 2%, other 7%. **Literacy rate:** 98%
Economic summary: GDP/PPP (1996 estimate as extrapolated from the World Bank estimate for 1994): $48.6 billion; $2,880 per capita. **Real growth rate:** 1.1%. **Inflation:** 28.7% (1996 est.). **Unemployment:** 2.6% (official figure, but large numbers of underemployed). **Labor force:** 6.9 million; industry 27%; agriculture and forestry, 23% (1996). **Industry:** extractive industries (oil, coal, iron ore, manganese, bauxite, gold, silver, phosphates, sulfur), iron and steel, nonferrous metals, tractors and other agricultural machinery, electric motors, construction materials. **Agriculture:** grains, meat, cotton, and wool. **Exports:** $5.7 (1996 est.): oil, ferrous and nonferrous metals, chemicals, wool, grain, meat. **Imports:** $6 billion (1996 est.): from outside the successor states of the former U.S.S.R.: machinery and parts, industrial materials. **Trading partners:** Russia, Ukraine, Uzbekistan, other former Soviet republics, China

Geography Kazakhstan lies in the north of the central Asian republics and is bounded by Russia in the north, China in the east, the Kyrgyzstan and Uzbekistan in the south, and the Caspian Sea and part of Turkmenistan in the west. It has almost 15,000 miles (24,000 km) of coastline on the Caspian Sea. Kazakhstan is slightly more than twice the size of Texas. The territory is mostly steppe land with hilly plains and plateaus.

Government Under the constitution approved in 1995, Kazakstan is a republic with the president as chief of state. The president, who is directly elected to a five-year term, governs in conjunction with a Cabinet headed by the prime minister and other ministers appointed by the president. The country's bicameral legislature consists of a Senate and an Assembly (Mazhilis), whose members serve five-year terms.

History The indigenous Kazakhs were a nomadic Turkic people who belonged to several divisions of Kazakh hordes. They grouped together in settlements and lived in dome-shaped tents made of felt called "yurts." Their tribes migrated seasonally to find pastures for their herds of sheep, horses, and goats. Although they had chiefs, the Kazakhs were rarely united as a single nation under one great leader. Their tribes fell under Mongol rule in the 13th century and they were dominated by Tartar Khanates until the area was conquered by Russia in the 18th century.

The area became part of the Kirgiz Autonomous Republic formed by the Soviet authorities in 1920, and in 1925 this entity's name was changed to the Kazakh Autonomous Soviet Socialist Republic (Kazakh A.S.S.R.). After 1927, the Soviet government began forcing the nomadic Kazaks to settle on collective and state farms, and the Soviets continued the tsarist policy of encouraging large numbers of Russians and other Slavs to settle in the region.

Owing to the region's intensive agricultural development and its use as a testing ground for nuclear weapons by the Soviet government, serious environmental problems developed by the late 20th century. Along with the other Central Asian republics, Kazakstan obtained its independence from the collapsing Soviet Union in 1991. Kazakhstan proclaimed its membership in the Commonwealth of Independent States on Dec. 21, 1991, along with ten other former Soviet republics. In 1993, the country overwhelmingly approved the Nuclear Non-Proliferation Treaty. In 1994, the Kazak government resolved to transfer the national capital from Almaty to Aqmola by 2000. In a referendum held on April 29, 1995, the electorate voted in support of extending the president's term to Dec. 2000. The president restructured and consolidated many operations of the government in 1997, eliminating a third of the government ministries and agencies.

Kazakstan has the potential for becoming one of central Asia's richest countries because of its huge mineral resources and its liberalized economy, which encourages Western investment.

Kenya

REPUBLIC OF KENYA

National name: Jamhuri ya Kenya
President: H. E. Daniel Toroitch arap Moi (1978)
Area: 224,960 sq mi. (582,650 sq km)
Population (1998 est.): 28,337,071 (average annual rate of natural increase: 1.71%); birth rate: 31.7/1000; infant mortality rate: 59.4/1000; density per sq mi.: 126
Capital and largest city (1991 est.): Nairobi, 2,000,000. **Other large city:** Mombasa, 600,000. **Monetary unit:** Kenyan shilling. **Languages:** English (official), Swahili (national), and several other languages spoken by 25 ethnic groups. **Ethnicity/Race:** Kikuyu 22%, Luhya 14%, Luo 13%, Kalenjin 12%, Kamba 11%, Kisii 6%, Meru 6%, Asian, European, and Arab 1%, other 15%. **Religions:** Protestant, 40%; Roman Catholic, 36%; traditional, 6%; Islam, 16%, others, 2%. **Literacy rate:** 69%
Economic summary: GDP/PPP (1996 est.): $39.2 billion; $1,400 per capita. **Real growth rate:** 4%. **Inflation:** 1.6%. **Unemployment:** 35% urban (1994 est.). **Arable land:** 7%. **Agriculture:** coffee, sisal, tea, pineapples, livestock. **Labor force:** 8.78 million; agriculture, 75–80% (1993 est.). **Industry:** textiles, processed foods, consumer goods, refined oil. **Natural resources:** gold, limestone, minerals, wildlife. **Exports:** $1.9 billion (f.o.b., 1995 est.): tourism, tea, coffee, horticulture, petroleum products, cement, soda ash, and pyrethrum extracts. **Imports:** $2.6 billion (f.o.b., 1995 est.): crude oil, pharmaceuticals, industrial supplies, machinery, other capital equipment. **Major trading partners:** Uganda, U.K., Tanzania, Germany, Netherlands, France, Italy, Saudi Arabia, United Arab Emirates, U.S., Japan, India.
Member of Commonwealth of Nations

Geography Kenya lies across the equator in east central Africa on the coast of the Indian Ocean. It is twice the size of Nevada. Kenya borders Somalia to the east, Ethiopia to the north, Tanzania to the south, Uganda to the west, and Sudan to the northwest. In the north, the land is arid; the southwestern corner is in the fertile Lake Victoria Basin; and a length of the eastern depression of Great Rift Valley separates western highlands from those that rise from the lowland coastal strip. Large game reserves have been developed.

Government Under its constitution Kenya has a one-house National Assembly of 188 members elected for five years by universal suffrage and 12 nominated and 2 ex-officio, for a total of 202. Since 1992, the president has been elected in a presidential and parliamentary election.

History Paleontologists believe people may first have inhabited Kenya about 2 million years ago. In the 700s Arab seafarers established settlements along the coast, and the Portuguese took control of the area in the early 1500s. More than 40 ethnic groups reside in Kenya. Its largest group, the Kikuyu, migrated to the region at the beginning of the 18th century.

The land became a British protectorate in 1890 and a Crown colony in 1920, when it went by the name British East Africa. Nationalist stirrings began in 1940s, and in 1952 the Mau Mau movement, made up of Kikuyu militants, rebelled against the government. The fighting lasted until 1956.

On Dec. 12, 1963, Kenya became fully independent. Jomo Kenyatta, a nationalist leader during the independence struggle who had been jailed by the British, became its first president. From 1964 to 1992 the country was ruled as a one-party state by the Kenya African National Union (KANU), first under Kenyatta and then under Daniel arap Moi. Demonstrations and riots pressured Moi to allow for multiparty elections in 1992.

The economy has not flourished under Daniel arap Moi's rule. In the 1990s Kenya's infrastructure began disintegrating and official graft was rampant, contributing to the withdrawal of much foreign aid. In early 1995 President Moi moved against the opposition, and ordered the arrest of anyone who insulted him. In June the renowned paleontologist Richard Leakey registered a new political party in protest of the government's policies.

A series of disasters plagued Kenya in 1997 and 1998: severe flooding destroyed roads, bridges, and crops; epidemics of malaria and cholera overwhelmed the ineffectual health care system; and ethnic clashes erupted between the Kikuyu and Kalenjin ethnic groups in the Rift Valley. President Moi won his fifth five-year term in Jan. 1998.

On Aug. 7, 1998, the U.S. embassy in Nairobi was bombed by terrorists, killing 243 and injuring more than 1,000. The embassy in neighboring Tanzania was bombed the same day, killing 10.

Kiribati

REPUBLIC OF KIRIBATI

President: Teburoro Tito (1994)
Area: 280 sq mi. (717 sq km)
Population (1998 est.): 83,976 (average annual growth rate: 1.82%); birth rate: 26.5/1000; infant mortality rate: 49.7/1000; density per sq mi.: 300
Capital (1990): Tarawa, 25,154. **Monetary unit:** Australian dollar. **Languages:** English (official), I-Kiribati (Gilbertese). **Ethnicity/Race:** Micronesian. **Religions:** Roman Catholic, 52.6%; Protestant, 40.9%. **Literacy rate:** 90%
Economic summary: GDP/PPP (1996 est.): $62 million; $800 per capita. **Real growth rate:** 2.6% (1995 est.). **Inflation:** 5.1% (1994 est.). **Unemployment:** 2%, underemployment, 70% (1992 est.). **Arable land:** n.a. **Agriculture:** copra, vegetables. **Exports:** $6.3 million (f.o.b., 1995 est.): fish, copra. **Imports:** $38.6 million (c.i.f., 1995 est.): foodstuffs, fuel, transportation equipment. **Major trading partners:** New Zealand, Australia, Japan, American Samoa, U.K., U.S., Fiji. **Member of Commonwealth of Nations**

Geography Kiribati, formerly the Gilbert Islands, consists of three widely separated main groups of southwest Pacific islands, the Gilberts on the equator, the Phoenix Islands to the east, and the Line Islands farther east. Ocean Island, producer of phosphates until it was mined out in 1981, is also included in the two million square miles of ocean. Most of the islands of Kiribati are low-lying coral atolls built on a submerged volcanic chain and encircled by reefs.

Government The president holds executive power. The legislature consists of a House Assembly with 39 members.

History Kiribati was first settled by early Austronesian-speaking peoples long before the 1st century C.E.. Fijians and Tongans arrived about the 14th century and subsequently merged with the older groups to form the traditional I-Kiribati Micronesian society and culture. The islands were first sighted by British and American ships in the late 18th and early 19th centuries and the first British settlers arrived in 1837. A British protectorate since 1892, the Gilbert and Ellice Islands became a Crown colony in 1915–16. Kiritimati (Christmas) Atoll became a part of the colony in 1919, the Phoenix Islands in 1937.

Tarawa and others of the Gilbert group were occupied by Japan during World War II. Tarawa was the site of one of the bloodiest battles in U.S. Marine Corps history when Marines landed in Nov. 1943 to dislodge the Japanese defenders. The Gilbert Islands and Ellice Islands (now Tuvalu) were separated in 1975 and granted internal self-government by Britain. Kiribati became independent on July 12, 1979.

Kiribati's 1995 act of moving the international date line far to the east, so that it encompassed Kiribati's Line Islands group, courted controversy. The move, which fulfilled one of President Tito's campaign promises, was intended to enable Kiribati to become the first country to reach midnight on Dec. 31, 1999 and welcome the new millennium—an event of significance for tourism.

Korea, North

DEMOCRATIC PEOPLE'S REPUBLIC OF KOREA

National name: Choson Minjujuui Inmin Konghwaguk
Head of State: Kim Jong Il (1994)
Premier: Hong Song Nam (1997)
Area: 46,768 sq mi. (120,540 sq km)
Population (1998 est.): 21,234,387 (average annual rate of natural increase: –0.03%); birth rate: 15.3/1000; infant mortality rate: 87.8/1000; density per sq mi.: 454
Capital and largest city (est. 1987): Pyongyang, 2,355,000. **Monetary unit:** Won. **Language:** Korean. **Ethnicity/Race:** racially homogeneous. **Religions:** Buddhism and Confucianism, religious activities almost nonexistent. **Literacy rate:** 100%
Economic summary: GDP/PPP (1996 est.): $20.9 billion; $900 per capita. **Real growth rate:** –5%. **Unemployment:** n.a. **Arable land:** 14%. **Agriculture:** corn, rice, vegetables. **Labor force:** 9.615 million; agricultural, 36%; nonagricultural, 64%. **Industry:** machines, electric power, chemicals, textiles, processed food, metallurgical products. **Natural resources:** coal, iron ore, hydroelectric power. **Exports:** $805 million (f.o.b., 1995 est.): minerals, metallurgical products, agricultural products, manufactures (including armaments). **Imports:** $1.24 billion (c.i.f., 1995 est.): machinery and equipment, petroleum, grain, coking coal. **Major trading partners:** C.I.S. countries, China, Japan, Hong Kong, Germany, Singapore

Geography Korea is a 600-mile (966 km) peninsula jutting from Manchuria and China (and a small portion of the U.S.S.R.) into the Sea of Japan and the Yellow Sea off eastern Asia. North Korea occupies an area slightly smaller than Pennsylvania north of the 38th parallel.

The country is almost completely covered by a series of north-south mountain ranges separated by narrow valleys. The Yalu River forms part of the northern border with Manchuria.

Government The elected Supreme People's Assembly, as the chief organ of government, chooses a Presidium and a cabinet. The cabinet, which exercises executive authority, is subject to approval by the Assembly and the Presidium.

The Korean Workers (Communist) Party is the only political party.

History The ancient history of the Korean peninsula can be traced to the Neolithic Age, when Turkic-Manchurian-Mongol peoples migrated into the region from China. The first agriculturally based settlements appeared around 6000 B.C.E. Some of the larger communities of this era were established along the Han-gang River near modern-day Seoul, others near Pyongyang and Pusan. According to ancient lore, Korea's earliest civilization, known as Choson, was founded in 2333 B.C.E. by Tan-gun.

In the 17th century, Korea became a vassal state of China and was cut off from outside contact until the Sino-Japanese war of 1894–95. Following Japan's victory, Korea was granted independence. By 1910 Korea had been annexed by Japan, which developed the country but never won over the Korean nationalists who continued to agitate for independence.

After Japan's surrender at the conclusion of World War II, the Korean peninsula was partitioned into two occupation zones, divided at the 38th parallel. The U.S.S.R. controlled the north, with the

U.S. taking charge of the south. In 1948, the division was made permanent with the establishment of the separate regimes of North and South Korea. The Democratic People's Republic of Korea (North Korea) was established on May 1, 1948, with Kim Il Sung as president.

Hoping to unify the Koreas under a single Communist government, the North launched a surprise invasion of South Korea on June 25, 1950. In the following days, the U.N. Security Council condemned the attack and demanded an immediate withdrawal.

President Harry S. Truman ordered U.S. air and naval units into action to enforce the U.N. order. The British government followed suit, and soon a U.N. multinational command was set up to aid the South Koreans.

The North Korean invaders swiftly seized Seoul and surrounded the allied forces in the peninsula's southeast corner near Pusan. In a desperate bid to reverse the military situation, U.N. Commander Gen. Douglas MacArthur ordered an amphibious landing at Inchon on Sept. 15 and routed the North Korean army. MacArthur's forces pushed north across the 38th parallel, approaching the Yalu River.

Prompted by this successful counter-offensive, Communist China entered the war, forcing the U.N. troops into a headlong retreat. Seoul was lost again, then regained; ultimately the war stabilized near the 38th parallel but dragged on for two years while negotiations took place. An armistice was agreed to on July 27, 1953.

By early 1994 tensions had mounted over international inspection of North Korea's nuclear sites. Kim Il Sung's death on July 8, 1994 introduced a period of uncertainty, as his son, Kim Jong-Il assumed the leadership mantle. Negotiations over the country's suspected atomic weapons dragged on, but an agreement was reached in June 1995 which included a provision for providing the North with a South Korean nuclear reactor.

The nuclear crises that characterized the mid-1990s were overshadowed when famine struck the nation's 24 million inhabitants. Two years of floods were followed by severe droughts in 1997 and 1998, causing devastating crop failures. Although international relief programs saved many people, the situation was still considered serious in 1998, with aid agencies warning that North Korea's nationalized food distribution program had virtually shut down, forcing many people to rely on bark and wild plants to sustain themselves. Despite the staggering food crisis, hermetic North Korea remains one of the world's few remaining hard-line communist regimes.

In Sept. 1998 North Korea launched a test missile over Japan, claiming it was simply a scientific satellite. This launch alarmed Japan and much of the rest of the world about North Korea's intentions regarding reentry into the nuclear arms race.

Korea, South

REPUBLIC OF KOREA

National name: Taehan Min'guk
President: Kim Dae Jung (1998)
Prime Minister: Kim Jong Pil (1998)
Area: 38,031 sq mi. (98,480 sq km)
Population (1998 est.): 46,416,796 (average annual rate of natural increase: 1.01%); birth rate: 16.1/1000; infant mortality rate: 7.8/1000; density per sq mi.: 1,221
Capital and largest city: Seoul: city proper (1995 est.) 10,776,201; metro. area (1996 est.) 11,768,000. **Other large cities:** Pusan, 3,814,000; Taegu, 2,449,000; Inchon, 2,308,000. **Monetary unit:** Won. **Language:** Korean. **Ethnicity/Race:** homogeneous (except for about 20,000 Chinese). **Religions (est. mid-1996):** Christian, 48.2%; Buddhist, 48.8%; Confucianist, 0.8%; Chondogyo (religion of the Heavenly Way), 0.2%; Other, 2%. **Literacy rate:** 98%
Economic summary: GDP/PPP (1996 est.): $647.2 billion; $14,200 per capita. **Real growth rate:** 6.9%. **Inflation:** 5% (1996). **Unemployment:** 1.9% (1996). **Arable land:** 19%. **Agriculture:** rice, soybeans, corn, barley. **Labor force:** (1991), 20 million; services and other, 52%; mining and manufacturing, 27%. **Products:** clothing, textiles, automobiles, steel, electronics equipment. **Natural resources:** coal, iron, zinc, lead, tungsten, hydropower. **Exports:** $130.9 billion (f.o.b., 1996): agricultural products, electronics, machinery, textiles, steel and metal products, chemicals. **Imports:** $150.2 billion (c.i.f., 1996): machinery, mineral fuels, electronic parts, agricultural products, iron and steel products, raw materials. **Major trading partners:** U.S., Japan.

Geography Slightly larger than Indiana, South Korea lies below the 38th parallel on the Korean peninsula, bordering the East Sea and the Yellow Sea. It is mountainous in the east; in the west and south are many harbors on the mainland and offshore islands.

Government Constitutional amendments enacted in Sept. 1987 called for direct election of a president, who would be limited to a single five-year term, and increased the powers of the National Assembly vis à vis the president.

History South Korea came into being after World War II, the result of a 1945 agreement reached by the Allies at the Potsdam Conference, making the 38th parallel the boundary between a northern zone of the Korean peninsula to be occupied by the U.S.S.R. and southern zone to be controlled by U.S. forces. (For details, *see* Korea, North.)

Elections were held in the U.S. zone in 1948 for a national assembly, which adopted a republican constitution and elected Syngman Rhee as the nation's president. The new republic was proclaimed on August 15 and was recognized as the legal government of Korea by the U.N. on Dec. 12, 1948.

On June 25, 1950, North Korean Communist forces launched a massive surprise attack on South Korea, quickly overrunning the capital, Seoul. U.S. armed intervention was ordered on June 27 by President Harry S. Truman, and on the same day the U.N. invoked military sanctions against North Korea. Gen. Douglas MacArthur was named commander of the U.N. forces. U.S. and South Korean troops fought a heroic holding action, but by the first week of August were forced back to a 4,000-square-mile beachhead in southeast Korea. There they stood off superior North Korean forces until Sept. 15, when a major U.N. amphibious assault was launched deep behind Communist lines at Inchon, the port of Seoul.

By Sept. 30, U.N. forces were in complete control of South Korea. They then crossed the 38th parallel and pursued retreating Communist forces into North

Korea. In late October, as U.N. forces neared the Sino-Korean border, several hundred thousand Chinese Communist troops entered the conflict, pushing MacArthur's forces back to the border between North and South Korea. By the time truce talks began on July 10, 1951, U.N. forces had crossed over the parallel again and were driving back into North Korea. Cease-fire negotiations dragged on for two years before an armistice was finally signed at Panmunjom on July 27, 1953, leaving a devastated Korea in need of large-scale rehabilitation. No official peace treaty has ever been signed between the former combatants.

Rhee, after 12 years in office, was forced to resign in 1960 amid rising discontent with his autocratic leadership. Po Sun Yun was elected to succeed him, but political instability continued. In 1961, Gen. Park Chung Hee seized power and subsequently began a program of economic reforms designed to stimulate the nation's economy. The U.S. stepped up military aid, strengthening South Korea's armed forces to 600,000 men. Park's assassination on Oct. 26, 1979, by Kim Jae Kyu, head of the Korean Central Intelligence Agency, brought a liberalizing trend as new president Choi Kyu Hah freed imprisoned dissidents.

The release of opposition leader Kim Dae Jung in Feb. 1980 sparked anti-government demonstrations that turned into riots, which were brutally suppressed by authorities. Kim, the most visible leader of the opposition, was imprisoned again. Choi resigned on Aug. 16. Chun Doo Hwan, head of a military Special Committee for National Security Measures, was the sole candidate as the electoral college confirmed him as president on Aug. 27. In 1986–87, South Korea's opposition demanded the president be selected by direct popular vote. After weeks of protest and rioting, Chun agreed to the demand. A split in the opposition led to Roh Tae Woo's election on Dec. 16, 1987.

In August of 1996 Roh was convicted on bribery charges and Chun was convicted for bribery as well as his role in the 1979 coup and the 1980 crackdown on rioters. In 1997, an accumulation of corrupt business practices and bad loans led to a series of bankruptcies and a massive devaluation of South Korea's currency. The political instability that followed helped former dissident Kim Dae Jung become the first South Korean president ever to be elected from the political opposition.

Kuwait

STATE OF KUWAIT

National name: Dawlat al Kuwayt
Emir: Sheik Jaber al-Ahmad al-Sabah (1977)
Prime Minister: Sheik Saad al-Abdullah Al-Sabah. (1978)
Area: 6,880 sq mi. (17,820 sq km)
Population (1998 est.): 1,913,285 (average annual rate of natural increase: 4.10%); birth rate: 21/1000; infant mortality rate: 10.7/1000; density per sq mi.: 281
Capital (1990 est.): Kuwait, 151,060. **Other large city (1993 est.):** as-Salimiyah, 116,104. **Monetary unit:** Kuwaiti dinar. **Languages:** Arabic and English. **Ethnicity/Race:** Kuwaiti 45%, other Arab 35%, South Asian 9%, Iranian 4%, other 7%. **Religions:** Islam 85% (Shi'ite 30%, Sunni 45%, other 10%); Christian, Hindu, Parsi, and other 15%. **Literacy rate:** 73%
Economic summary: GDP/PPP (1996 est.): $32.5 billion; $16,700 per capita. **Real growth rate:** 3%. **Inflation:** 4.5% (1996 est.). **Labor force:** 1 million (1994 est.); industry and agriculture, 25%; services, 25%; government and social services, 50%. **Products:** crude and refined oil, petrochemicals, building materials, salt. **Natural resources:** petroleum, fish, shrimp. **Exports:** $13.6 billion (f.o.b., 1996 est.): oil. **Imports:** $8.4 billion (f.o.b., 1996 est.): foodstuffs, automobiles, building materials, machinery, textiles. **Major trading partners:** U.S., Japan, E.U., Canada

Geography Kuwait is situated northeast of Saudi Arabia at the northern end of the Persian Gulf, south of Iraq. It is slightly larger than Hawaii. The low-lying land is mainly sandy and barren.

Government Kuwait is a constitutional monarchy, governed by the Sabah family (al-Sabah). Sheik Jaber al-Ahmad al-Sabah rules as Emir of Kuwait and appoints the prime minister, who appoints his cabinet (Council of Ministers). National elections were held in 1992 and the National Assembly (legislative branch), dissolved in 1986 was reinstated. There are no political parties in Kuwait.

History At the beginning of the 18th century C.E., the 'Anizah tribe of central Arabia began an eastward search for better pasture and water and founded Kuwait city. (The traditional date of founding is 1710.) The foundation of the autonomous sheikdom dates from 1756, when 'Abd Rahim of the Al Sabah became sheik. The Sabah family continues to rule Kuwait. In the late 18th and early 19th century the sheikdom belonged to the fringes of the Ottoman empire. Kuwait obtained British protection in 1897 when the sheik feared that the Turks would expand their hold over the area. In 1961, Britain ended the protectorate, giving Kuwait independence, but agreed to give military aid on request. Iraq immediately threatened to occupy the area, and the British sent troops to defend Kuwait. Soon afterward the Arab League sent in troops, replacing the British. Iraq's claim was dropped when the Arab League recognized Kuwait's independence on July 20, 1961. Kuwait typically followed a neutral and mediatory policy among Arab states.

Oil was discovered in the 1930s. Kuwait proved to have 20% of the world's known oil resources. Since 1946 it has been the world's second largest oil exporter. The sheik, who receives half the profits, devotes most of them to the education, welfare, and modernization of his kingdom. In 1966, Sheik Sabah designated a relative, Jaber al-Ahmad al-Sabah, as his successor. By 1968, the sheikdom had established a model welfare state, and it sought to establish dominance among the sheikdoms and Emirates of the Persian Gulf.

In July 1990, Iraq President Hussein blamed Kuwait for falling oil prices. After a failed Arab mediation attempt to solve the dispute peacefully, Iraq invaded Kuwait on Aug. 2, 1990, set up a pro-Iraqi provisional government, and drained Kuwait of its economic resources. A coalition of Arab and Western military forces drove Iraqi troops from Kuwait in a mere four days, from Feb. 23–27, ending the Persian Gulf War. The Emir returned to his country from Saudi Arabia in mid-March. Martial law, in effect since the end of the Gulf War, ended in late June. The U.S. sent 2,400 troops to the country in August 1992 as part of a training exercise but this was widely interpreted as a show of strength to Saddam Hussein.

The general election of Oct. 1992 was a success for supporters of a return to Islamic law. A political independent was named speaker of the parliament, and the opposition held 31 of the 50 seats. Iraqi "training" maneuvers near the Kuwaiti border in Oct. 1994 renewed fears of aggression in the country. A Kuwaiti appeal brought the quick deployment of U.S. and British troops and equipment. In the wake of Oct. 1996 parliamentary elections the Emir reappointed the prime minister. The results of the election are seen as producing a plurality of pro-government MPs.

Kyrgyzstan

THE KYRGYZ REPUBLIC

President: Askar Akaev (1990)
Prime Minister: Kubanychbek Jumaliyev (1998)
Area: 76,000 sq mi. (198,500 sq km)
Population (1998 est.): 4,522,281; (Kyrgyz, 52%; Russian, 21%; Uzbek, 13%, other, 14%); average annual rate of natural increase: 0.37%; birth rate: 22/1000; infant mortality rate: 74.8/1000; density per sq mi.: 58
Capital and largest city (1994): Bishkek (formerly Frunze), 631,000. **Other Large City (1994):** Osh 213,000. **Monetary unit:** Som. **Language:** Kyrgyz (official); Russian is de facto second language of communication. **Ethnicity/Race:** Kirghiz 52.4%, Russian 18%, Uzbek 12.9%, Ukrainian 2.5%, German 2.4%, other 11.8%. **Religion:** Muslim 75%, Russian Orthodox 20%, other 5%. **Literacy rate:** 100%
Economic summary: GDP/PPP (1996 estimate as extrapolated from the World Bank estimate for 1994): $5.8 billion, $1,290 per capita. **Real growth rate:** 5.6%. **Inflation:** 32%. **Unemployment:** 4.8%, includes registered unemployed; 7.8% by ILO methodology (Dec. 1995). **Natural resources:** rare earth metals, gold, coal. Industrial production: electrical engineering, hydroelectric power, agricultural machine building, washing machines, furniture, cement, paper, and brick. Agricultural products are food crops: vegetables, grains, fruit. Also cotton, hemp, tobacco, livestock: cattle, sheep, goats. **Labor force:** 1.7 million; agriculture and forestry, 40%; industry and construction, 19% (1995 est.). **Exports:** $506 million (1996): wool, chemicals, cotton, ferrous and nonferrous metals, shoes, machinery, tobacco. **Imports:** $890 million (1996): grain, lumber, industrial products, ferrous metals, fuel, machinery, textiles, footwear. **Trading Partners:** Russia, Ukraine, Uzbekistan, Kazakhstan

Geography Kyrgyzstan (formerly Kirghizia) is a rugged country with the Tien Shan mountain range covering approximately 95 percent of the whole territory. The mountain tops are covered with perennial snow and glaciers. Kyrgyzstan borders Kazakhstan on the north and northwest, Uzbekistan in the southwest, Tajikistan in the south, and China in the southeast. The republic is the same size in area as the state of Nebraska.

Government Kyrgyzstan is a constitutional republic. The president, who is head of state and has extensive executive powers, appoints the prime minister. There is a bicameral parliament.

History The native Kyrgyz are a Turkic people who in ancient times first settled in the Tien Shan mountains. They were traditionally pastoral nomads. There was extensive Russian colonization in the 1900s and Russian settlers were given much of the best agricultural land. This led to an unsuccessful and disastrous revolt by the Kyrgyz people in 1916. Kyrgyzstan became part of the Soviet Federated Socialist Republic in 1924, and was made an autonomous republic in 1926. Kyrgyzstan became a constituent republic of the U.S.S.R. in 1936. The Soviets forced the Kyrgyz to abandon their nomadic culture and brought modern farming and industrial production techniques into their society. It has greatly changed their traditional way of life.

Kyrgyzstan proclaimed its independence from the Soviet Union on Aug. 31, 1991. On Dec. 21, 1991, Kyrgyzstan joined the Commonwealth of Independent States. The country joined the U.N. and the IMF in 1992 and adopted a shock-therapy economic program. Voters formally overwhelmingly endorsed market reforms in a referendum held in Jan. 1994. In 1996, referendum voters overwhelmingly endorsed proposed constitutional changes that enhanced the power of the president. Representatives of the country along with those of Russia, China, Kazakhstan, and Tajikistan signed a non-aggression agreement in April 1996. In March 1997, Russian border control was extended until the end of the year as authorities in Kyrgyzstan grew increasingly concerned about the growth of the illegal narcotics trade in the country.

Laos

LAO PEOPLE'S DEMOCRATIC REPUBLIC

President: Khamtai Siphandon (1998)
Prime Minister: Sisavat Keobounphan (1998)
Area: 91,429 sq mi. (236,800 sq km)
Population (1998 est.): 5,260,842 (average annual rate of natural increase: 2.76%); birth rate: 40.6/1000; infant mortality rate: 91.8/1000; density per sq mi.: 58
Capital and largest city (1990): Vientiane, 442,000. **Monetary unit:** Kip. **Languages:** Lao (official), French, English. **Ethnicity/Race:** Lao Loum (lowland) 68%, Lao Theung (upland) 22%, Lao Soung (highland) including the Hmong ("Meo") and the Yao (Mien) 9%, ethnic Vietnamese/Chinese 1%. **Religions:** Buddhist, 85%; animist and other, 15%. **Literacy rate:** 45%
Economic summary: GDP/PPP (1996 est.): $5.7 billion; $1,150 per capita. **Real growth rate:** 7.5%. **Inflation:** 15%. **Unemployment:** (1994 est.), 5.6% in urban areas. **Arable land:** 3%. **Agriculture:** rice, corn, vegetables. **Labor force:** 1–1.5 million; agriculture, 80% (1992 est.). **Industry:** tin, timber, electric power, gypsum. **Natural resources:** tin, timber, hydroelectric power. **Exports:** $240 million (f.o.b., 1996 est.): electric power, forest products, tin concentrates, coffee, gypsum, cardamon, rattan, clothing and textiles. **Imports:** $570 million (c.i.f., 1996 est.): rice, foodstuffs, petroleum products, machinery, transport equipment. **Major trading partners:** Thailand, Malaysia, Vietnam, C.I.S. countries, Japan, France, U.S., Hong Kong, Singapore

Geography A landlocked nation in Southeast Asia occupying the northwestern portion of the Indochinese peninsula, Laos is surrounded by China, Vietnam, Cambodia, Thailand, and Burma. It is twice the size of Pennsylvania.

Laos is a mountainous country, especially in the north, where peaks rise above 9,000 feet (2,800 m). Dense forests cover the northern and eastern areas. The Mekong River, which forms the boundary with Burma and Thailand, flows entirely through the country for 932 miles (1,500 km) of its course.

Government Communist state. The Lao People's Revolutionary Party (Pathet Lao) is the only political party. The monarchy was abolished Dec. 2, 1975, when the Pathet Lao ousted a coalition government and King Sisavang Vatthana abdicated.

History The Lao people migrated into Laos from southern China from the 8th century C.E. onward. In the 14th century the first Laotian state was founded, the Lan Xang kingdom, which ruled Laos until it split into three separate kingdoms in 1713. During the 18th century the three kingdoms came under Siamese (Thai) rule, and in 1893 became a French protectorate. Its territory was incorporated into the union of Indochina. A strong nationalist movement developed during World War II, but France reestablished control in 1946 and made the King of Luang Prabang constitutional monarch of all Laos. France granted semiautonomy in 1949 and then, spurred by the Viet Minh rebellion in Vietnam, full independence within the French Union in 1950.

In 1951, Prince Souphanouvong organized the Pathet Lao, a Communist independence movement, in North Vietnam. Viet Minh and Pathet Lao forces invaded central Laos, and civil war resulted. By the Geneva agreements of 1954 and an armistice of 1955, two northern provinces were given the Pathet Lao: the rest went to the royal regime. Full sovereignty was given the kingdom by the Paris agreements of Dec. 29, 1954. In 1957, Prince Souvanna Phouma, the royal premier, and the Pathet Lao leader, Prince Souphanouvong, the premier's half-brother, agreed to reestablishment of a unified government, with Pathet Lao participation and integration of Pathet Lao forces into the royal army. The agreement broke down in 1959, and armed conflict broke out again.

In 1960, the struggle became three-way as Gen. Phoumi Nosavan, controlling the bulk of the royal army, set up in the south a pro-Western revolutionary government headed by Prince Boun Gum. General Phoumi took Vientiane in December, driving Souvanna Phouma into exile in Cambodia. The Soviet bloc supported Souvanna Phouma. In 1961, a cease-fire was arranged and the three princes agreed to a coalition government headed by Souvanna Phouma.

But North Vietnam, the U.S. (in the form of Central Intelligence Agency personnel), and China remained active in Laos after the settlement. North Vietnam used a supply line (Ho Chi Minh trail) running down the mountain valleys of eastern Laos into Cambodia and South Vietnam, particularly after the U.S.–South Vietnamese incursion into Cambodia in 1970 stopped supplies via Cambodian seaports.

An agreement, reached in 1973 revived coalition government. The Communist Pathet Lao seized complete power in 1975, installing Souphanouvong as president and Kaysone Phomvihane as premier. Since then other parties and political groups have been moribund and most of their leaders have fled the country.

The Supreme People's Assembly in August 1991 adopted a new constitution that dropped all references to socialism but retained the one-party state. In addition to implementing market-oriented policies, the country has passed laws governing property, inheritance and contracts. Laos agreed to trade with Moscow and Hanoi in hard currency.

During 1995 the country continued to relax tensions with its neighbors. Economic agreements were reached with Burma, and the U.S. announced a lifting of its ban on aid. The sixth congress of the ruling People's Revolutionary Party took place in March 1996. Later that month Laos formally applied for full leadership in ASEAN.

By most international estimates, Laos is one of the ten poorest countries in the world. The subsistence farmers who make up more than 80 percent of the population have been plagued with poor agricultural conditions—alternately flood or drought—since 1993.

Latvia

THE REPUBLIC OF LATVIA

National name: Latvija
President: Guntis Ulmanis (1993)
Prime Minister: Guntars Krasts (1997)
Area: 25,400 sq mi. (64,100 sq km)
Population (1998 est.): 2,385,396; average annual rate of natural increase: –1.41%; birth rate: 8.1/1000; infant mortality rate: 17.4/1000; density per sq mi.: 94
Capital and largest city (1993 est.): Riga, 874,000. **Other large cities:** Daugavpils, 125,000; Liepaja, 108,000. **Monetary unit:** Lats. **Language:** Latvian. **Ethnicity/Race:** Latvian 51.8%, Russian 33.8%, Belarussian 4.5%, Ukrainian 3.4%, Polish 2.3%, other 4.2%. **Religions:** Lutheran, Catholic, and Baptist. **Literacy:** 100%
Economic summary: Most industrialized of the Baltic states. **GDP/PPP** (1996 est.): $9.4 billion; (1996 estimate as extrapolated from World Bank estimate for 1994) $3,800 per capita. **Real growth rate:** 2.5%. **Inflation:** 13.2%. **Unemployment:** (1996 official est.), 7.5%. **Labor force:** 1.268 million; industry and construction, 41%; agriculture and forestry, 16% (1990). Latvia's major industries are: forestry, wood products, building materials, and metals. Agriculture is principally dairy farming and livestock raising. **Natural resources:** peat, sapropel, timber, limestone, dolomite, and clay. **Exports:** $1.6 billion (f.o.b., 1996): timber and wood products, ferrous metals and products, electrical machinery and equipment, fish, furniture, apparel, pharmaceuticals, appliances, buses. **Imports:** $2.4 billion (c.i.f., 1996): machinery and appliances, electrical equipment, natural gas, fuels, pharmaceuticals, electricity, cars, apparel. **Major trading partners:** E.U., C.I.S. countries, Lithuania, Poland, Estonia, U.S., Czech Republic, Australia, Hungary, Japan

Geography Latvia borders Estonia on the north, Lithuania in the south, the Baltic Sea with the Gulf of Riga in the west, Russia in the east, and Belarus in the southeast. Latvia is largely a fertile lowland with numerous lakes and hills to the east.

Government Latvia is a parliamentary democracy. The Supreme Council of Latvia appoints the Council of Ministers, which is responsible for government administration.

History Latvia was originally settled by the ancient people known as Balts. In the 9th century the Balts came under the overlordship of the Vikings, but a more lasting dominance was established over them by their German-speaking neighbors to the west, who Christianized Latvia in the 12th and 13th centuries. The German Knights of the Teutonic Order conquered all of Latvia by 1230, and German overlordship of the area continued for three centuries, with a German landowning class ruling over an enserfed Latvian peasantry. Poland conquered the territory in 1562 and ruled until 1795 in Courland; control of Livonia was disputed between Sweden and Poland from 1562 to 1629. Sweden controlled Livonia from 1629 to 1721. Russia took over Livonia in the latter year and Courland after the third partition of Poland in 1795.

From that time until 1918, the Latvians remained Russian subjects, although they preserved their language, customs, and folklore. The Russian Revolution of 1917 gave them their opportunity for freedom, and the Latvian republic was proclaimed on Nov. 18, 1918. The republic lasted little more than 20 years. It was occupied by Russian troops in 1939 and incorporated into the Soviet Union in 1940. German armies occupied the nation from 1941 to 1943–44, when they were driven out by the Russians. Most countries, including the United States, refused to recognize the Soviet annexation of Latvia. Latvia's farms were forcibly collectivized in 1949, and its flourishing economy was integrated into that of the Soviet Union. Latvia remained one of the most prosperous and highly industrialized parts of the Soviet Union until 1991.

When the coup against Soviet President Mikhail Gorbachev failed, the Baltic nations saw a historic opportunity to free themselves from Soviet domination and, following the actions of Lithuania and Estonia, Latvia declared its independence on Aug. 21, 1991. European and most other nations quickly recognized their independence, and on Sept. 2, 1991, President Bush announced full diplomatic recognition for Latvia, Estonia, and Lithuania. The Soviet Union recognized Latvia's independence on Sept. 6, and U.N. membership followed on Sept. 17, 1991.

In the first post-Soviet parliamentary elections in June 1993 an alliance of former Communists and emigres made a strong showing. The franchise, however, was by and large not extended to the non-ethnic-Latvian minority. In 1994, Latvia celebrated the official withdrawal of Russian troops from the country and its citizenship law was amended in accordance with the wishes of the Council of Europe. Latvia's bid to join the European Union was not accepted in talks that began in 1997. In addition to improving its administrative systems, Latvia was told that it had to speed up naturalization of minorities, in particular its large number of Russians. Also in 1997, Latvia received support from a number of Western countries in its quest to become a member of NATO, but all three Baltic states were turned down.

Lebanon

REPUBLIC OF LEBANON

National name: Al-Joumhouriya al-Lubnaniya
President: Elias Hrawi (1989)
Premier: Rafiq al-Hariri (1992)
Area: 4,015 sq mi. (10,400 sq km)
Population (1998 est.): 3,505,794 (average annual rate of natural increase: 1.62%); birth rate: 22.7/1000; infant mortality rate: 31.6/1000; density per sq mi.: 873
Capital and largest city (1991 est.): Beirut, 1,100,000. **Other large cities:** Tripoli, 240,000; Sidon, 100,000. **Monetary unit:** Lebanese pound. **Languages:** Arabic (official), French, English. **Ethnicity/Race:** Arab 95%, Armenian 4%, other 1%. **Religions:** Islam, 60%; Christian, 40% (17 recognized sects); Judaism negl. (1 sect). **Literacy rate:** 80%
Economic summary: GDP/PPP (1996 est.): $13 billion; $3,400 per capita. **Real growth rate:** 3.5%. **Inflation:** 10%. **Unemployment:** 20%. **Arable land:** 21%. **Agriculture:** citrus fruits, vegetables, potatoes, tobacco, olives, shrimp. **Labor force:** 1 million, plus as many as 1 million foreign workers; services, 59%; industry, 28%; agriculture, 13% (1990 est.). **Industry:** processed foods, textiles, cement, chemicals, refined oil. **Exports:** $1 billion (f.o.b., 1996 est.): fruits, vegetables, textiles, chemicals, semiprecious metals and jewelry, metals and metal products. **Imports:** $7 billion (c.i.f., 1996 est.): consumer goods, machinery and transport equipment, petroleum products. **Major trading partners:** U.S., Western European and Arab countries

Geography Lebanon lies at the eastern end of the Mediterranean Sea north of Israel and west of Syria. It is four-fifths the size of Connecticut.

The Lebanon Mountains, which parallel the coast on the west, cover most of the country, while on the eastern border is the Anti-Lebanon range. Between the two lies the Bekaa Valley, the principal agricultural area.

Government Lebanon is governed by a president, elected by parliament for a six-year term, and a cabinet of ministers appointed by the president but responsible to parliament.

The unicameral parliament has 108 members elected for a four-year term by universal suffrage and chosen by proportional division of religious groups.

History After World War I, France was given a League of Nations mandate over Lebanon and its neighbor Syria, which together had previously been a single political unit in the Ottoman Empire. France divided them in 1920 into separate colonial administrations, drawing a border that separated predominantly Muslim Syria from the kaleidoscope of religious communities in Lebanon where Maronite Christians were then dominant. After 20 years of the French mandate regime, Lebanon's independence was proclaimed on Nov. 26, 1941, but full independence came in stages. Under an agreement between representatives of Lebanon and the French National Committee of Liberation, most of the powers exercised by France were transferred to the Lebanese government on Jan. 1, 1944. The evacuation of French troops was completed in 1946.

According to the National Pact, different religious communities are represented in the government by having a Maronite Christian president, a Sunni Muslim prime minister, and a Shi'ite National Assembly speaker. The arrangement worked for two decades. Civil war broke out in 1958, with Muslim factions led by Kamal Jumblat and Saeb Salam rising in insurrection against the Lebanese government headed by President Camille Chamoun, a Maronite Christian favoring close ties to the West. At Chamoun's request, President Eisenhower on July 15 sent U.S. troops to reestablish the government's authority.

Clan warfare between various religious factions in Lebanon goes back centuries. The hodgepodge includes Maronite Christians, who since independence have dominated the government; Sunni Muslims, who have prospered in business and shared political power; the Druze, who hold a faith incorporating aspects of Islam and Gnosticism; and Shi'ite Muslims.

A new—and bloodier—Lebanese civil war that broke out in 1975 resulted in the addition of still another ingredient in the brew—the Syrians. In the fighting between Lebanese factions, 40,000 Lebanese were estimated to have been killed and 100,000 wounded between March 1975 and Nov. 1976. At that point, a Syrian-dominated Arab Deterrent Force intervened and brought large-scale fighting to a halt.

Palestinian guerrillas staging raids on Israel from Lebanese territory drew punitive Israeli raids on Lebanon, and two large-scale Israeli invasions. The Israelis withdrew in June after the U.N. Security Council created a 6,000-man peacekeeping force for the area, called UNIFIL. As they departed, the Israelis turned their strong points over to a Christian militia that they had organized, instead of to the U.N. force.

The second Israeli invasion came on June 6, 1982, and this time it was total. It was in response to an assassination attempt by Palestinian terrorists on the Israeli ambassador in London. As a stronghold of the PLO, Lebanon became the Israelis' target. Israel's government had complained that Lebanon had countenanced the presence of these militant Palestinians.

A U.S. envoy negotiated the dispersal of most of the PLO to other Arab nations and Israel pulled back some of its forces. The violence seemed to have come to an end when, on Sept. 14, Bashir Gemayel, the 34-year-old president-elect, was killed by a bomb that destroyed the headquarters of his Christian Phalangist Party.

The day after Gemayel's assassination, Israeli troops moved into west Beirut in force. On Sept. 17 it was revealed that Christian militiamen had massacred hundreds of Palestinians in two refugee camps, but Israel denied responsibility. On Sept. 20, Amin Gemayel, older brother of Bashir Gemayel, was elected president by the parliament.

The massacre in the refugee camps prompted the return of a multinational peacekeeping force composed of U.S. Marines and British, French, and Italian soldiers. Their mandate was to support the central Lebanese government, but they soon found themselves drawn into the struggle for power between different Lebanese factions. During their stay in Lebanon, 260 U.S. Marines and about 60 French soldiers were killed, most of them in suicide bombings of the Marine and French army compounds on Oct. 23, 1983. The multinational force left in the spring of 1984.

In July 1986, Syrian observers took position in Beirut to monitor a peacekeeping agreement. The agreement broke down and fighting between Shi'ite and Druze militia in West Beirut became so intense that Syrian troops moved in force in Feb. 1987, suppressing militia resistance.

Amin Gemayel's presidency expired on Sept. 23, 1988. The impossibility of setting up elections led Gemayel to designate a government under army chief Gen. Michael Aoun. Aoun's government was rejected by Prime Minister Selim al-Hoss, who established a rival government in Muslim West Beirut.

In Oct. 1989, Lebanese Christian and Muslim deputies approved a tentative peace accord and the new National Assembly selected a president.

In early 1991 the Lebanese government, backed by Syria, attempted to regain control over the south and disband all private militias, thereby ending the 16-year civil war. These conflicts destroyed much of the infrastructure and industry of Lebanon.

In the general elections of August 1992 most Christians abstained from voting, demanding that Syrian forces first leave the country. The new legislature consisted of mostly pro-Syrian members. The largest Christian party was further weakened when in Jan. 1993 it appeared to split into two factions.

In May 1995 the prime minister asked for a constitutional amendment to allow the presidential term to be extended by three years in the interests of stability. Despite some opposition, the amendment was passed in October. In the multi-round parliamentary elections in Sept. 1996, pro-Syrian candidates and those favored by the government won a major victory.

Lesotho

KINGDOM OF LESOTHO

Sovereign: King Letsie III (1990)
Prime Minister: Pakalitha Mosisili (1998)
Area: 11,720 sq mi. (30,350 sq km)
Population (1998 est.): 2,089,829 (average annual rate of natural increase: 1.91%); birth rate: 31.8/1000; infant mortality rate: 78.3/1000; density per sq mi.: 178
Capital and largest city (1992): Maseru (1992), 170,000. **Monetary unit:** Loti. **Languages:** English and Sesotho (official); also Zulu and Xhosa. **Ethnicity/Race:** Sotho 99.7%, Europeans 1,600, Asians 800. **Religions:** Christian, 80%; indigenous beliefs; Muslim; and Bahai. **Literacy rate:** 56% (1989)
Economic summary: GDP/PPP (1996 est.): $3.7 billion; $1,860 per capita. **Real growth rate:** 10%. **Inflation:** 8.7% (1996 est.). **Unemployment:** substantial unemployment and underemployment effecting more than half of the labor force (1996 est.). **Arable land:** 11%. **Agriculture:** corn, wheat, sorghum, barley. **Labor force:** 689,000; subsistence agriculture, 86%. **Natural resources:** diamonds. **Exports:** $218 million (f.o.b., 1996 est.): wool, mohair, wheat, cattle, hides and skins, peas, beans, corn, baskets. **Imports:** $1.1 billion (c.i.f., 1996 est.): foodstuffs, building materials, clothing, vehicles, machinery, corn, medicines. **Major trading partners:** Asia, South Africa, E.U., North and South America. **Member of Commonwealth of Nations**

Geography Mountainous Lesotho, the size of Maryland, is surrounded by the Republic of South Africa in the east central part of that country except for short borders on the east and south with two discontinuous units of the Republic of Transkei. The Drakensberg Mountains in the east are Lesotho's principal chain. Elsewhere the region consists of rocky tableland.

Government A constitutional monarchy. The executive power is with the prime minister and the cabinet (Council of Ministers).

History Lesotho (formerly Basutoland) was constituted a native state under British protection by a treaty signed with the native chief Moshesh in 1843. It was annexed to Cape Colony in 1871, but in 1884 it was restored to direct control by the Crown. The colony of Basutoland became the independent nation of Lesotho on Oct. 4, 1966, with King Moshoeshoe II as sovereign.

In the 1970 elections, Ntsu Mokhehle, head of the Basutoland Congress Party, claimed a victory, but Prime Minister Leabua Jonathan declared a state of emergency, suspended the constitution, and arrested Mokhehle. King Moshoeshoe returned after a compromise with Jonathan in which the new constitution would name him head of state but forbid his participation in politics.

After the king refused to approve the replacements in Feb. 1990 of individuals dismissed by Justin Metsino Lekhanya, the chairman of the Military Council, the latter stripped the king of his executive power. Then in early March Lekhanya sent the king into exile. In November the king was dethroned, and his son was sworn in as King Letsie III.

Lekhanya was himself forced to resign in April 1991 and Col. Ramaema became the new chairman in May. In Jan. 1995 the crown reverted to the father of Letsie III, Moshoeshoe II. Letsie again became Crown Prince. In 1996, however, King Moshoeshoe died in an automobile accident and Letsie again assumed the throne.

In fall 1998, hundreds of demonstrators protested for weeks in front of the king's palace, claiming voting fraud in the May elections that put Prime Minister Pakalitha Mosisili in power. They demanded that the government step down and hold new elections.

Liberia

REPUBLIC OF LIBERIA

President: Charles Taylor (1997)
Area: 43,000 sq mi. (111,370 sq km)
Population (1998 est.): 2,771,901 (average annual rate of natural increase: 5.76%); birth rate: 41.9/1000; infant mortality rate: 103.1/1000; density per sq mi.: 65
Capital and largest city (1993 est.): Monrovia, 1,000,000. **Monetary unit:** Liberian dollar. **Languages:** English (official) and tribal dialects. **Ethnicity/Race:** indigenous African tribes 95% (including Kpelle, Bassa, Gio, Kru, Grebo, Mano, Krahn, Gola, Gbandi, Loma, Kissi, Vai, and Bella), Americo-Liberians 5% (descendants of former slaves). **Religions:** traditional, 70%; Christian, 10%; Islam, 20%. **Literacy rate:** 40%
Economic summary: Civil war since 1990 has destroyed much of Liberia's economy. **GDP/PPP** (1995 est.): $2.4 billion; $1,100 per capita. **Real growth rate:** 0%. **Inflation:** 50% (1994 est.). **Unemployment:** n.a. **Arable land:** 1%. **Agriculture:** rubber, rice, palm oil, cassava, coffee, cocoa. **Labor force:** 510,000; agriculture, 70.5%; services, 10.8%; industry and commerce, 4.5%. **Industry:** iron ore, diamonds, processed rubber, processed food, construction materials. **Natural resources:** iron ore, gold, timber, diamonds. **Exports:** $667 million (f.o.b., 1995 est.): iron ore, rubber, timber, coffee. **Imports:** $5.8 billion (f.o.b., 1995 est.) machinery, petroleum products, transport equipment, foodstuffs. **Major trading partners:** U.S., E.U., Netherlands, Japan, China

Geography Lying on the Atlantic in the southern part of West Africa, Liberia is bordered by Sierra Leone, Guinea, and Côte d'Ivoire. It is comparable in size to Tennessee.

Most of the country is a plateau covered by dense tropical forests, which thrive under an annual rainfall of about 160 inches a year.

Government A dual system of statutory law based on Anglo-American common law for the modern sector and customary law based on tribal practice for the indigenous sector.

History Africa's first republic, Liberia was founded in 1822 as a result of the efforts of the American Colonization Society to settle freed American slaves in West Africa. In 1847, it became the Free and Independent Republic of Liberia. The English-speaking Americo-Liberians, descendants of former American slaves, make up only 5% of the population, but have historically dominated the intellectual and ruling class. Liberia's indigenous population is primarily composed of Mande, Kwa, and Mel peoples.

The government of Africa's first republic was modeled after that of the United States, and Joseph J. Roberts of Virginia was elected the first president. After 1920, considerable progress was made toward opening up the interior, a process that was spurred in 1951 by the establishment of a 43-mile (69-km) railroad to the Bomi Hills from Monrovia. In July 1971, while serving his sixth term as president, William V. S. Tubman died following surgery and was succeeded by his long-time associate, Vice President William R. Tolbert, Jr. Tolbert was ousted in a military coup carried out April 12, 1980, by Master Sgt. Samuel K. Doe, who was backed by the U.S. government. A rebellion led by Charles Taylor, a former Doe aide, started in Dec. 1989 and, with the help of Côte d'Ivoire and Burkina Faso, took control of Liberia's key population and economic centers by mid-July 1990. His three attempts to take the capital failed, however, and the bloody civil war continued. By mid-April 1996 factional fighting by the country's warlords had destroyed any last vestige of normality and civil society.

In what was considered by international observers a free election, Charles Taylor won 75.3% of the presidential vote in July 1997, and since then has been in the process of reconstructing the country after its seven-year civil war.

Libya

SOCIALIST PEOPLE'S LIBYAN ARAB JAMAHIRIYA

National name: Socialist People's Libyan Arab Jamahiriya
Head of State: Col. Muammar al-Qaddafi (1969)
Secretary of the General People's Committee: Muhammad Ahmad al-Mangoush (1997)
Area: 679,536 sq mi. (1,759,540 sq km)
Population (1998 est.): 5,690,727; (average annual rate of natural increase: 3.68%); birth rate: 44/1000; infant mortality rate: 55.8/1000; density per sq mi.: 8
Capital: Tripoli. **Largest cities (est. 1988):** Tripoli, 591,062; Benghazi, 446,250. **Monetary unit:** Libyan dinar. **Language:** Arabic, Italian and English widely understood in major cities. **Ethnicity/Race:** Berber and Arab 97%, Greeks, Maltese, Italians, Egyptians, Pakistanis, Turks, Indians, Tunisians. **Religion:** Islam. **Literacy rate:** 64%
Economic summary: GDP/PPP (1995 est.): $34.5 billion; $6,570 per capita. **Real growth rate:** 2.2%. **Inflation:** 25% (1995 est.). **Unemployment:** n.a. **Arable land:** 1%. **Agriculture:** wheat, barley, olives, dates, citrus fruits, peanuts. **Labor force:** 1 million (includes about 280,000 resident foreigners); industry, 31%; services, 27%; government, 24%; agriculture, 18% (July 1997 est.). **Products:** petroleum, processed

foods, textiles, handicrafts, cement. **Natural resources:** petroleum, natural gas. **Exports:** $8.4 billion (f.o.b., 1995 est.): petroleum, peanuts, hides, natural gas. **Imports:** $7.3 billion (f.o.b., 1995 est.): machinery, foodstuffs, manufactured goods. **Major trading partners:** Italy, Germany, U.K., France, Spain, Japan, Turkey, former U.S.S.R., Korea, Belgium/Luxembourg

Geography Libya stretches along the northeastern coast of Africa between Tunisia and Algeria on the west and Egypt on the east; to the south are the Sudan, Chad, and Niger. It is one-sixth larger than Alaska. A greater part of the country lies within the Sahara. Along the Mediterranean coast and farther inland is arable plateau land.

Government In a bloodless coup d'état on Sept. 1, 1969, the military seized power in Libya. King Idris I, who had ruled since 1951, was deposed and the Libyan Arab Republic proclaimed. The official name was changed in 1977 to the Socialist People's Libyan Arab Jamahiriya (a state of the masses): in theory, governed by the populace through local councils; in fact, a military dictatorship. The Revolutionary Council that had governed since the coup was renamed the General Secretariat of the General People's Congress. The Arab Socialist Union Organization is the only political party.

History In the 7th century B.C.E., Phoenicians settled in Tripolitania, which later became the eastern province of the Carthaginian state. When the Romans conquered the region (1st century B.C.E.), Tripolitania became part of the Africa Nova province, and Cyrenaica became a province combined with Crete. The Byzantine Empire gained control of the territory after the decline of Rome, and in the 7th century C.E. Muslim Arabs began their long domination. Libya was a part of the Turkish dominions from the 16th century until 1911. Following the outbreak of hostilities between Italy and Turkey in that year, Italian troops occupied Tripoli; Italian sovereignty was recognized in 1912.

Libya was the scene of much desert fighting during World War II. After the fall of Tripoli on Jan. 23, 1943, it came under Allied administration. In 1949, the U.N. voted that Libya should become independent by 1952. The discovery of oil in 1959 transformed Libya into an oil-rich monarchy, and a decade later a group of army officers led by Colonel Muammar al-Qaddâfi deposed the king and made the country a Pan-Arab and puritanically Muslim republic.

On Aug. 19, 1981, two U.S. Navy F-14s shot down two Soviet-made SU-22s of the Libyan air force that had attacked them in air space above the Gulf of Sidra, claimed by Libya but held to be international by the U.S. In December, Washington asserted that Libyan "hit squads" had been dispatched to the U.S. and security was drastically tightened around President Reagan and other officials. When the Mobil Oil Company abandoned its operations in April 1982, only four U.S. firms were still in Libya, using Libyan or third-country personnel. On March 24, 1986, U.S. and Libyan forces skirmished in the Gulf of Sidra, with two Libyan patrol boats being sunk. Qaddafi's troops also supported rebels in Chad but suffered major military reverses in 1987. A two-year-old U.S. covert policy to destabilize the Libyan government with U.S.-trained Libyan ex-P.O.W.s ended in failure in Dec. 1990 when a Libyan-supplied guerrilla force assumed power in Chad, where the commandos were based, and asked the band to leave.

Libya's aid to terrorists and various military ventures continued to bring protests from many countries. The U.N. approved trade and air traffic embargoes in April 1992, seriously affecting the Libyan economy. Against the wishes of the United States, the Vatican in March 1997 established diplomatic ties with Libya in the hope of protecting its small Catholic population and to promote peace in the region.

Negotiations with Libya over handing over the suspects in the bombing of Pan Am Flight 103 were agreed to in principle in Sept. 1998. A firm agreement would lead to the lifting of U.N.-imposed sanctions.

Liechtenstein

PRINCIPALITY OF LIECHTENSTEIN

Ruler: Prince Hans Adam II (1989)
Prime Minister: Mario Frick (1993)
Area: 61 sq mi. (160 sq km)
Population (1998 est.): 31,717 (average annual growth rate: 1.05%); birth rate: 12.6/1000; infant mortality rate: 5.3/1000; density per sq mi.: 520
Capital and largest city (1994): Vaduz, 5,067. **Monetary unit:** Swiss franc. **Languages:** German (official), Alemmanic dialect. **Ethnicity/Race:** Alemannic 87.5%; Italian, Turkish, and other 12.5% . **Religions:** Roman Catholic 80%, Protestant 6.9%, unknown 5.6%, other 7.5%. **Literacy rate:** 100%
Economic summary: GDP/PPP (1996 est.): $713 million; $23,000 per capita. **Real growth rate:** n.a. **Inflation:** 0.8%. **Unemployment:** 1.1% (1996). **Arable land:** 25%. **Agriculture:** livestock, vegetables, corn, wheat, potatoes, grapes. **Labor force:** (1994), 212,187 (including 13,576 foreigners); industry, trade and building, 45%; service, 53%. **Industry:** electronics, metal products, textiles, ceramics, pharmaceuticals, food products, precision instruments. Natural resource: hydroelectric power. **Exports:** $2.14 billion (1994): small specialty machinery, dental products, stamps, hardware, pottery. **Imports:** $852.3 million (1994): machinery, processed foods, metal goods, textiles, motor vehicles. **Major trading partners:** Switzerland and E.U.

Geography Tiny Liechtenstein, not quite as large as Washington, D.C., lies on the east bank of the Rhine River south of Lake Constance between Austria and Switzerland. It consists of low valley land and Alpine peaks. Falknis (8,401 ft.; 2,561 m) and Naafkopf (8,432 ft.; 2,570 m) are the tallest.

Government Liechtenstein is a constitutional monarchy in which governmental power derives from both the prince and the populace. The constitution of 1921 provides for a legislature, the Landtag, of 15 members elected for four-year terms.

History The Liechtensteiners are descended from the Alemanni tribe that came into the region after C.E. 500. Founded in 1719, Liechtenstein was a member of the German Confederation from 1815 to 1866, when it became an independent principality. It abolished its army in 1868 and has managed to stay neutral and undamaged in all European wars since then. Liechtenstein still claims 1,600 sq km of Czech territory (the royal family's ancestral home) confiscated in 1918; the Czech Republic insists that restitution does not go back before Feb. 1948, when the communists seized power. In a referendum on

July 1, 1984, male voters granted women the right to vote in national (but not local) elections—a victory for Prince Hans Adam. A treaty negotiated between EFTA and the European Union linking the two as the European Economic Area was ratified in a Dec. 1993 vote, but Switzerland rejected it. After renegotiation the treaty was again subjected to a referendum in April 1995 and approved. Liechtenstein won a special concession limiting immigration.

Lithuania

REPUBLIC OF LITHUANIA

National name: Lietuva
President: Valdas Adamkus (1998)
Prime Minister: Gediminas Vagnorius (1996)
Area: 25,212 sq mi. (65,200 sq km)
Population (1998 est.): 3,600,158; (average annual rate of natural increase: –0.45%); birth rate: 10.6/1000; infant mortality rate: 14.8/1000; density per square mi: 143
Capital and largest city (1993 est.): Vilnius, 590,100. **Other large cities:** Kaunas, 429,000; Klaipéda, 206,400. **Monetary unit:** Litas. **Languages:** Lithuanian (official), Polish, Russian. **Ethnicity/Race:** Lithuanian 80.1%, Russian 8.6%, Polish 7.7%, Belarussian 1.5%, other 2.1%. **Religion:** Catholic, 85%; others include Lutheran, Russian Orthodox, Protestant, evangelical Christian Baptist, Islam, Judaism. **Literacy:** 98%
Economic summary: GDP/PPP (1996 estimate as extrapolated from the World Bank estimate for 1994): $14.1 billion; $3,870 per capita. **Real growth rate:** 3.4% (1996 est.). **Inflation:** 13.1% (1996 official est.). **Labor force:** 1.836 million; industry and construction, 42%; agriculture and forestry, 18% (1990). **Natural resources:** peat, sand and gravel, quartz, gypsum, dolomite, clay, limestone, mineral water. Amber found on Baltic Sea coast. **Industry:** metal cutting, electric motors, TV sets, refrigerators and freezers, petroleum refining, shipbuilding, furniture, textiles, food processing, electronic components, computers. Agriculture (36% of Labor force): Most developed are the livestock and dairy branches. Lithuania is a net exporter of meat, milk, and eggs. **Exports:** $3.3 billion (1996 est.): textiles, chemical products and related industries, mineral products, mechanical goods and electrical equipment. **Imports:** $4.56 billion (1996 est.): mineral products (incl. oil and gas), machinery, electrical equipment, metals, transport equipment. **Major trading partners:** C.I.S. nations, E.U. (including Germany, the Netherlands, and Italy)

Geography Lithuania is situated on the eastern shore of the Baltic Sea and borders Latvia on the north, Belarus on the east and south, Poland and the Kaliningrad region of Russia on the southwest. It is a country of gently rolling hills, many forests, rivers and streams, and lakes. Its principal natural resource is agricultural land.

Government Lithuania is a parliamentary democracy. The head of state is the directly elected president. The president nominates the prime minister who is then approved by the parliament (Seimas).

History The Lithuanian tribes united in the mid-13th century under the leadership of Mindaugas. His successors ruled the united Lithuania as grand dukes, and one of them, Gediminas, expanded Lithuania into an empire that dominated much of eastern Europe from the 14th to the 16th century. In 1386, the reigning Lithuanian grand duke also became the king of Poland, and the two countries remained closely associated for the next 400 years. Lithuania became in effect the subordinate member of the Polish-Lithuanian state, and it remained so until the Third Partition of Poland (1795) placed Lithuania under Russian rule. Lithuania did not regain its independence until 1918, toward the end of World War I.

The republic was occupied and annexed by the Soviet Union in 1940. From June 1941 to 1944 it was occupied by German troops and then was retaken by Russia. Western countries, including the United States, never recognized the Russian annexation of Lithuania.

1988 saw a re-emergence of the Lithuanian independence movement. Elections were held on Feb. 24, 1990, and Vytautas Landsbergis, the non-Communist head of the largest Lithuanian popular movement (Sajudis) was elected to parliament that day, and on March 11, 1990, the parliament elected him as its president. On the same day, the Supreme Council rejected Soviet rule and declared the restoration of Lithuania's independence, the first Baltic republic to take this action. Confrontation with the Soviet Union ensued along with economic sanctions, but they were lifted after both sides agreed to a face-saving compromise. Lithuania's independence was quickly recognized by major European and other nations, including the United States. The Soviet Union finally recognized the independence of the Baltic states on Sept. 6. U.N. admittance followed on Sept. 17, 1991. Successful implementation of structural and legislative reforms in Lithuania attracted greater foreign direct investments by the mid-1990s. The European Commission (E.C.) in 1997 decided to exclude Lithuania from the Eastern European states recommended to begin formal negotiations in 1998 for European Union (E.U.) membership.

Luxembourg

GRAND DUCHY OF LUXEMBOURG

National name: Grand-Duché de Luxembourg
Ruler: Grand Duke Jean (1964)
Premier: Jean-Claude Juncker (1995)
Area: 999 sq mi. (2,586 sq km)
Population (1998 est.): 425,017 (average annual rate of natural increase: 1.02%); birth rate: 11.1/1000; infant mortality rate: 5/1000; density per sq mi.: 425
Capital and largest city (1991): Luxembourg, 75,622. **Monetary unit:** Luxembourg franc. **Languages:** Luxermbourgish, French, German. **Ethnicity/Race:** Celtic base (with French and German blend), Portuguese, Italian, and European (guest and worker residents). **Religion:** Roman Catholic 97%, Protestant and Jewish 3%. **Literacy rate:** 100%
Economic summary: GDP/PPP (1995 est.): $10 billion; $24,500 per capita. **Real growth rate:** 3.7%. **Inflation:** 2.3% (1995). **Unemployment:** 3% (1995). **Arable land:** 24%. **Agriculture:** livestock, dairy products, wine. **Labor force:** (1994), 213,100; one-third are foreign workers; trade, restaurants, hotels, 20%; mining, quarrying, manufacturing, 16%; other services, 32%. **Industry:** banking, steel, processed food, chemicals, metal products, tires, glass. Natural resource: Iron ore. **Exports:** $7.3 billion (f.o.b., 1995 est.): steel, chemicals, rubber products, glass, aluminum. **Imports:** $9.1 million (c.i.f., 1995 est.): minerals, metals, foodstuffs, consumer goods. **Major trading partners:** European Union

Geography Luxembourg is about half the size of Delaware. The Ardennes Mountains extend from Belgium into the northern section of Luxembourg. The rolling plateau of the fertile Bon Pays is in the south.

Government Luxembourg's unicameral legislature, the Chamber of Deputies, consists of 60 members elected for five years. A Council of State is appointed by the grand duke and functions as a second legislative chamber whose powers are mainly advisory. Executive power is vested in the grand duke but is exercised by a prime minister and his ministerial council, who are responsible to the Chamber of Deputies.

History Luxembourg, once part of Charlemagne's empire, became an independent state in C.E. 963, when Siegfried, Count of Ardennes, became sovereign of Lucilinburhuc ("Little Fortress"). In 1060, Conrad, a descendant of Siegfried, took the title Count of Luxembourg. From the 15th to the 18th century, Spain, France, and Austria held it in turn. The Congress of Vienna in 1815 made it a Grand Duchy and gave it to William I, king of the Netherlands. In 1839 the Treaty of London ceded the western part of Luxembourg to Belgium. The eastern part, continuing in personal union with the Netherlands and a member of the German Confederation, became autonomous in 1848 and a neutral territory by decision of the London Conference of 1867, governed by its Grand Duke. Germany occupied the duchy in World Wars I and II. Allied troops liberated the enclave in 1944.

Luxembourg joined NATO in 1949, the Benelux Economic Union (with Belgium and the Netherlands) in 1948, and the European Economic Community (later the E.U.) in 1957. In 1961, Prince Jean, son and heir of Grand Duchess Charlotte, was made head of state, acting for his mother. She abdicated in 1964, and Prince Jean became Grand Duke. Grand Duchess Charlotte died in 1985. Luxembourg's parliament approved the "Maastricht Accord," paving the way for the economic unity of the E.U., in July 1992, with the proviso that the country negotiate an exemption to the clause granting foreigners the vote. In July 1997 Luxembourg assumed the rotating presidency of the European Union for the second time.

Macedonia

REPUBLIC OF MACEDONIA[1]

National Name: Republica Makedonija
President: Kiro Gilgorov (1991)
Prime Minister: Branko Crvenkovski (1992)
Area: 9,928 sq mi. (25,333 sq km)
Population (1998 est.): 2,009,387 (average annual rate of natural increase: 0.68%); birth rate: 15.7/1000; infant mortality rate: 19.5/1000; density per sq mi.: 202
Capital and largest city (1994 est.): Skopje, 444,229. Other large cities: Bitola, 84,002; Prelep, 70,152; Kumanovo, 68,148. **Monetary unit:** Denar. **Languages:** Macedonian, which uses the Cyrillic alphabet, 70%; Albanian, 21%; Turkish, 3%; other, 6%. **Ethnicity/Race:** Macedonian 65%, Albanian 22%, Turkish 4%, Serb 2%, Rom (Gypsy) 3%, other 4%. **Religions (1994):** Eastern Orthodox, 67%; Muslim, 30%
Economic summary: GDP/PPP (1996 est.): $2 billion; $960 per capita. **Real growth rate:** 1.1%. **Inflation:** 5%. **Unemployment:** 38%. **Labor force:** 591,773 (June 1994); manufacturing and mining, 40% (1992). **Industry:** low-level technology (basic fuels) mining, basic textiles, wood products, and tobacco. **Agriculture:** rice, tobacco, wheat, corn, millet, cotton, citrus fruits, and vegetables. **Exports:** $900 million (1996 est.): manufactured goods, machinery and transport equipment, miscellaneous manufactured articles, beverages and tobacco. **Imports:** $1.4 billion (1996 est.): fuel and lubricants, manufactured goods, machinery and transport equipment. **Major trading partners:** Germany, Albania, Bulgaria, other former Yugoslav republics, Greece.

1. The U.N. recognized the Republic of Macedonia on April 8, 1993, under the temporary name the Former Yugoslav Republic of Macedonia. The U.S. recognized Macedonia as a state in Feb. 1994.

Geography Macedonia is a landlocked state in the heart of the Balkans and is slightly smaller than the state of Vermont. It is a mountainous country with small basins of agricultural land linked by rivers. The three major rivers are the Aliakmon, the Vardar, and the Strymon. The Vardar is the largest and most important river.

Government A democratic republic with a legislative house consisting of 120 deputies, each elected for a four-year term. The Assembly's president and vice presidents are elected from among its members.

History The Republic of Macedonia occupies the western half of the ancient Kingdom of Macedonia. Historic Macedonia was defeated by Rome and became a Roman province in 148 B.C.E. After the Roman Empire was divided in C.E. 395, Macedonia was intermittently ruled by the Byzantine Empire until Turkey took possession of the land in 1389. The Ottoman Turks dominated Macedonia for the next five centuries, up until 1913. During the 19th and 20th centuries, there was a constant struggle by the Balkan powers to possess Macedonia for its economic and strategic military corridors. The Treaty of San Stefano in 1878 ending the Russo-Turkish War gave the largest part of Macedonia to Bulgaria. Bulgaria lost much of its Macedonian territory when it was defeated by the Greeks and Serbs in the Second Balkan War of 1913. Most of Macedonia went to Serbia and the remainder was divided among Greece and Bulgaria.

In 1914, Serbia, which included Macedonia, joined in union with Croatia, Slovenia, and Montenegro to form the kingdom of Serbs, Croats, and Slovenes, which was renamed Yugoslavia in 1929. Bulgaria joined the Axis powers in World War II and occupied parts of Yugoslavia including Macedonia in 1941. During the occupation of their country, Macedonian resistance fighters fought a guerrilla war against the invading troops. The Yugoslavian Republic was reestablished after the defeat of Germany in 1945, and in 1946, the government removed Macedonia from Serbian control and made it an autonomous Yugoslavian republic. Later, when President Tito recognized the Macedonian people as a separate nation, the Macedonians strove to develop their own culture and language separate from Bulgaria and Serbia.

In Jan. 1992, Macedonia declared its independence from Yugoslavia and asked for recognition from the European Union nations. In Dec. 1993, six European nations recognized Macedonia; it was later recognized by the U.N. and the U.S. In Oct.

1995, Greece lifted its trade embargo as a result of an agreement recognizing Macedonia's right to its national title. Also in 1995, Macedonia was admitted into the Council of Europe. The Macedonian government, in 1997, urged NATO to extend its peacekeeping role in the Balkans beyond its mid-1998 mandate, saying NATO troops provided a stabilizing role. Ethnic tensions between ethnic Albanians and ethnic Macedonians continue to rise.

Madagascar

REPUBLIC OF MADAGASCAR

National name: Repoblikan'i Madagasikara
President and Head of State: Didier Ratsiraka (1997)
Prime Minister: Tantely Andrianarivo (1998)
Area: 226,660 sq mi. (587,040 sq km)
Population (1998 est.): 14,462,509 (average annual rate of natural increase: 2.81%); birth rate: 41.9/1000; infant mortality rate: 90.6/1000; density per sq mi.: 64
Capital and largest city (1993 est.): Antananarivo, 1,000,000. **Monetary unit:** Malagasy franc. **Languages:** Malagasy, French. **Ethnicity/Race:** Malayo-Indonesian (Merina and related Betsileo), Cotiers (mixed African, Malayo-Indonesian, and Arab ancestry—Betsimisaraka, Tsimihety, Antaisaka, Sakalava), French, Indian, Creole, Comoran. **Religions:** traditional, 52%; Christian, 41%; Islam, 7%. **Literacy rate:** 80%
Economic summary: GDP/PPP (1996 est.): $12.1 billion; $880 per capita. **Real growth rate:** 3.5%. **Inflation:** 47% (1995 est.). **Arable land:** 4%. **Agriculture:** rice, livestock, coffee, vanilla, sugar, cloves, cardamom, beans, bananas. **Labor force:** 4.9 million in subsistence agriculture (96% of total labor force not receiving money wages). **Industry:** processed food, textiles, assembled automobiles, soap, cement. **Natural resources:** graphite, chromium, bauxite, semiprecious stones. **Exports:** $493 million (f.o.b., 1996 est.): coffee, cloves, vanilla, sugar, petroleum products. **Imports:** $612 million (f.o.b., 1996 est.): consumer goods, foodstuffs, crude petroleum. **Major trading partners:** France, U.S., Japan, Italy, Germany, U.K., and other E.U.

Geography Madagascar lies in the Indian Ocean off the southeast coast of Africa opposite Mozambique. The world's fourth-largest island, it is twice the size of Arizona. The country's low-lying coastal area gives way to a central plateau. The once densely wooded interior has largely been cut down.

Government A multiparty republic.

History The Malagasy are of mixed Malayo-Indonesian and African-Arab ancestry. Indonesians are believed to have migrated about C.E. 700. King Andrianampoinimerina (1787–1810) ruled the major kingdom on the island, and his son, Radama I (1810–28) unified much of the island. The French made the island a protectorate in 1885, and then in 1894–95 ended the monarchy, exiling Queen Rànavàlona III to Algiers. A colonial administration was set up, to which the Comoro Islands were attached in 1908, and other territories later. In World War II, the British occupied Madagascar, which retained ties to Vichy France.

An autonomous republic within the French Community since 1958, Madagascar became an independent member of the community in 1960. In May 1973, an army coup led by Maj. Gen. Gabriel Ramanantsoa ousted Philibert Tsiranana, president since 1959. Comdr. Didier Ratsiraka, named president on June 15, 1975, announced that he would follow a socialist course and, after nationalizing banks and insurance companies, declared all mineral resources nationalized. Repression and censorship characterized his regime. Ratsiraka was reelected in 1989 in a suspicious election that led to riots as well as the formation of a multiparty system in 1990. In 1991 Ratsiraka agreed to share power with democratically minded opposition leader, Albert Zafy, who then overwhelmingly won the presidential elections in Feb. 1993. But Zafy was impeached by parliament for abusing his constitutional powers during an economic crisis and lost the 1996 presidential election to Ratsiraka, who became president in Feb. 1997.

Malawi

REPUBLIC OF MALAWI

President: Bakili Muluzi (1994)
Area: 45,747 sq mi. (118,480 sq km)
Population (1998 est.): 9,840,474 (average annual rate of natural increase: 1.66%); birth rate: 40.2/1000; infant mortality rate: 133.8/1000; density per sq mi.: 215
Capital (1993 est.): Lilongwe, 260,000. **Largest city (1993 est.):** Blantyre, 399,000. **Monetary unit:** Kwacha. **Languages:** English and Chichewa (National). **Ethnicity/Race:** Chewa, Nyanja, Tumbuko, Yao, Lomwe, Sena, Tonga, Ngoni, Ngonde, Asian, European. **Religions:** Christian, 75%; Islam, 20%. **Literacy rate:** 49%
Economic summary: GDP/PPP (1996 est.): $7.5 billion; $800 per capita. **Real growth rate:** 6%. **Inflation:** 83.3% (1995 est.). **Arable land:** 18%. **Agriculture:** tobacco, tea, sugar, corn, cotton. Agriculture accounts for 40% of GDP and 90% of export revenues. **Labor force:** 3.5 million; agriculture, 86%; wage earners, 14%. **Industry:** food, tobacco, cement, processed wood, consumer goods. **Natural resources:** limestone, uranium, coal, bauxite. **Exports:** $431 million (f.o.b., 1995 est.): tobacco, sugar, tea, coffee, peanuts. **Imports:** $348 million (f.o.b., 1995 est.): transport equipment, food, petroleum, consumer goods. **Major trading partners:** U.K., U.S., Japan, Germany, South Africa, Zambia, Zimbabwe. **Member of Commonwealth of Nations**

Geography Malawi is a landlocked country the size of Pennsylvania in southeastern Africa, surrounded by Mozambique, Zambia, and Tanzania. Lake Malawi, formerly Lake Nyasa, occupies most of the country's eastern border. The north-south Rift Valley is flanked by mountain ranges and high plateau areas.

Government Under a provisional constitution which came into effect on May 17, 1994, the president is the head of state and government. The National Assembly (parliament) is composed of 177 members. There are eight registered parties and the ruling party since May 17, 1994, is the United Democratic Front (UDF) of President Bakili Muluzi.

History Early human inhabitants of what is now Malawi date back to between 8000 and 2000 B.C.E. Bantu-speaking peoples migrated there between the 1st and 4th centuries C.E. A large slave trade took place in the 18th and 19th centuries, and brought Islam to the region. At the same time, missionaries introduced Christianity. Several major kingdoms were established in the pre-colonial period: the Maravi in 1480, the Ngonde in 1600, and in the Chikulamayembe in the 18th century.

The first European to make extensive explorations in the area was David Livingstone in the 1850s and 1860s. In 1884, Cecil Rhodes's British South African Company received a charter to develop the country. The company came into conflict with the Arab slavers in 1887–89. Britain annexed what was then called the Nyasaland territory in 1891 and made it a protectorate in 1892. Sir Harry Johnstone, the first high commissioner, used Royal Navy gunboats to wipe out the slavers.

Between 1951 and 1953 Britain combined Nyasaland with the colonies of Northern and Southern Rhodesia to form a federation, a move protested by black Africans who were wary of alignment with the ultra conservative white-minority rule in South Rhodesia. On July 6, 1964, Nyasaland became the independent nation of Malawi. Two years later, it became a republic within the Commonwealth of Nations. Dr. Hastings K. Banda, Malawi's first prime minister, became its first president. In 1971 he became president for life, further consolidating his authoritarian rule. In addition to allowing former colonialists to retain considerable power in the country, he maintained warm relations with the white-minority government of South Africa. These policies drew heavy criticism from Malawian citizens and other African nations. In 1992 Banda faced violent protests.

Bakili Muluzi won the country's first free election in May 1994, ending Banda's 30-year rule. He was sworn in a few days later and quickly released the remaining political prisoners. Budget trimming was the order of the day in 1995, which received commendation from the IMF.

Malaysia

Paramount Ruler: His Majesty Tuanku Ja'afar ibni Al-Marhum Tuanku Abdul Rahman (1994)
Prime Minister: Dato' Seri Dr. Mahathir bin Mohamad (1981)
Area: 128,328 sq mi. (339,750 sq km)
Population (1998 est.): 20,932,901 (average annual rate of natural increase: 2.11%); birth rate: 26.5/1000; infant mortality rate: 22.5/1000; density per sq mi.: 163
Capital and largest city (1991 est.): Kuala Lumpur, 1,145,000. **Largest cities (1991 est.):** Georgetown (Pinang), 220,000; Ipoh, 382,600. **Monetary unit:** Ringgit. **Languages:** Malay (official), Chinese, Tamil, English. **Ethnicity/Race:** Malay and other indigenous 59%, Chinese 32%, Indian 9%. **Ethnic divisions:** 59% Malay and other indigenous; 32% Chinese; 9% Indian. **Religions:** Malays (all Muslims), Chinese (predominantly Buddhists), Indians (predominantly Hindus). **Literacy rate:** 78%
Economic summary: GDP/PPP (1996 est.): $214.7 billion; $10,750 per capita. **Real growth rate:** 8.2%. **Inflation:** 3.5% (1996). **Unemployment:** 2.6%. **Arable land:** 3%. **Agriculture:** rice, rubber, palm products. **Labor force:** (1996 est.), 8.398 million. **Industry:** processed rubber, timber, and palm oil, tin, petroleum, light manufactures, electronics equipment. **Natural resources:** tin, oil, copper, timber. **Exports:** $84.6 billion (1996): natural rubber, palm oil, tin, timber, petroleum, electronics, textiles. **Imports:** $83.2 billion (1996): food, crude oil, capital equipment, chemicals, consumer goods. **Major trading partners:** Japan, Singapore, U.S., Western European countries, Taiwan. **Member of Commonwealth of Nations**

Geography Malaysia is on the Malay Peninsula in southeast Asia. The nation also includes Sabah and Sarawak on the island of Borneo to the east. Its area slightly exceeds that of New Mexico.

Most of Malaysia is covered by forest, with a mountain range running the length of the peninsula. Extensive forests provide ebony, sandalwood, teak, and other woods.

Government Malaysia is a sovereign constitutional monarchy practicing parliamentary democracy based on universal suffrage. The paramount ruler is elected for a five-year term by the hereditary rulers of the states from among themselves. He is advised by the prime minister and his cabinet. There is a bicameral legislature. The Senate, whose role is comparable more to that of the British House of Lords than to the U.S. Senate, has 69 members, partly appointed by the paramount ruler to represent minority and special interests, and partly elected by the legislative assemblies of the various states.

The House of Representatives, is made up of 192 members, who are elected for five-year terms.

History The ancestors of the people that now inhabit the Malaysian peninsula first migrated to the area between 2500 and 1500 B.C.E. Those living in the coastal regions had early contact with Chinese and Indians; seafaring traders from India brought with them Hinduism, which was blended with the local animist beliefs. As Muslims conquered India, they spread the religion of Islam to Malaysia. In the 15th century C.E., Islam acquired a firm hold on the region when the Hindu ruler of the powerful city-state of Malacca, Parameswara Dewa Shah, was overthrown by his Muslim half-brother, Mudzaffar Shah.

British and Dutch interest in the region grew in the 1800s, with the British East India Company establishing a trading settlement on the island of Singapore. Trade soared, with Singapore's population growing from only 5,000 in 1820 to nearly 100,000 in just 50 years. In the 1880s, Britain formally established protectorates in Malaysia. At about the same time, rubber trees were introduced from Brazil. With the mass production of automobiles rubber became a valuable export, and laborers were brought in from India to work the rubber plantations.

Following the Japanese occupation of Malaysia during World War II, a growing nationalist movement prompted the British to establish the semi-autonomous Federation of Malaya in 1948. But Communist guerrillas took to the jungles to begin a war of national liberation against the British, who declared a state of emergency to quell the insurgency, which lasted until 1960.

The independent state of Malaysia came into existence on Sept. 16, 1963, as a federation of Malaya, Singapore, Sabah (North Borneo), and Sarawak. In 1965, Singapore withdrew from the federation to become a separate nation. Since 1966, the 11 states of former Malaya have been known as West Malaysia, and Sabah and Sarawak have been known as East Malaysia.

By the late 1960s Malaysia was torn by communal rioting directed against Chinese and Indians, who controlled a disproportionate share of the country's wealth. Beginning in 1968, the government moved to achieve greater economic balance through a national economic policy.

Malaysia was significantly affected in 1978 by the "boat people" fleeing Vietnam. Because the refugees were mostly ethnic Chinese, the government was apprehensive about any increase of a minority that previously had been the source of internal conflict in the country. In April 1988, it announced that within the year it would cease accepting refugees.

In the 1980s, Dr. Mohamed Mahathir succeeded Datuk Hussein as prime minister. Mahathir instituted economic reforms that would transform Malaysia into one of the so-called Asian Tigers. Through the 1990s, Mahathir embarked on a massive project to build a new capital from scratch in an attempt to bypass congested Kuala Lumpur.

Beginning in 1997 and continuing through the next year, Malaysia suffered from the Asian currency crisis, with the Malaysian ringgit plummeting. Mahathir blamed market speculators for the crisis, and many of his ambitious building projects had to be placed on hold as a result of the economic downturn.

Maldives

REPUBLIC OF MALDIVES

President: Maumoon Abdul Gayoom (1978)
Area: 115 sq mi. (300 sq km)
Population (1998 est.): 290,211 (average annual rate of natural increase: 3.42%); birth rate: 40.1/1000; infant mortality rate: 41.1/1000; density per sq mi.: 2,524
Capital and largest city (1995 census): Malé, 62,973. **Monetary unit:** Maldivian Rufiyaa. **Languages:** Dhivehi (official); Arabic, Hindi, and English are also spoken. **Ethnicity/Race:** Sinhalese, Dravidian, Arab, African. **Religion:** Islam (Sunni Muslim). **Literacy rate:** 91%
Economic summary: GDP: (1995 est.): $423 million; $1,620 per capita. **Real growth rate:** 5.8%. **Inflation:** 7.7%. **Unemployment:** negl. **Arable land:** 10%. **Agriculture:** maize, sorghum, finger millet, alocasia, cassava, sweet potato, onion, coconuts. **Labor force:** 56,435 (1990 est.); fishing and agriculture, 25%. **Products:** fish, processed coconut, handicraft. Natural resource: fish. Tourism is also an important sector of the economy. **Exports:** $50 million (f.o.b., 1995 est.): fish, clothing. **Imports:** $268 million (f.o.b., 1995 est.): intermediate and capital goods, consumer goods, petroleum products. **Major trading partners:** Thailand, U.S., Singapore, U.K., Germany, India

Geography The Republic of Maldives is a group of atolls in the Indian Ocean about 417 miles (671 km) southwest of Sri Lanka. Its 1,190 coral islets stretch over an area of 35,200 square miles (90,000 sq km). With concerns over global warming and the shrinking of the polar ice caps, Maldives feels directly threatened, as none of its islands rises more than six feet above sea level.

Government The 15-member cabinet is headed by the president, who is elected to a renewable five-year term. The Majlis (parliament) is a unicameral legislature consisting of 48 members. Eight of these are appointed by the president. The others are elected for five-year terms, 2 from the capital island of Malé and 2 from each of the 19 administrative atolls. There are no political parties in the Maldives.

History The Maldives (formerly called the Maldive Islands) were first settled in the 5th century B.C.E. by Buddhist seafarers from India and Sri Lanka. According to tradition, Islam was adopted in C.E. 1153. Originally the islands were under the suzerainty of Ceylon (now Sri Lanka). They came under British protection in 1887 and were a dependency of the then-colony of Ceylon until 1948. The independence agreement with Britain was signed July 26, 1965. For centuries a Sultanate, the islands adopted a republican form of government in 1952, but the Sultanate was restored in 1954. In 1968, however, as the result of a referendum, a republic was again established in the recently independent country. Ibrahim Nasir, president since 1968, was removed from office by the Majlis in Nov. 1978 and replaced by Maumoon Abdul Gayoom. President Gayoom was elected to a fourth five-year term in Oct. 1993. Ever concerned with the possibility of rising sea levels, the Maldives, one of the world's poorest nations, has constructed, with Japanese aid, a line of concrete breakwaters along the capital's southern coast.

Mali

REPUBLIC OF MALI

National name: République de Mali
President of the Republic: Alpha Oumar Konaré (1992)
Prime Minister: Ibrahima Boubacar Keita (1994)
Area: 478,819 sq mi. (1,240,000 sq km)
Population (1998 est.): 10,108,569 (average annual rate of natural increase: 3.24%); birth rate: 49.9/1000; infant mortality rate: 121.7/1000; density per sq mi.: 21
Capital and largest city (1992 est.): Bamako, 746,000. **Monetary unit:** Franc CFA. **Ethnic groups:** Bambara, Peul, Soninke, Malinke, Songhai, Dogon, Senoufo, Minianka, Berbers, and Moors. **Languages:** French (official), African languages. **Ethnicity/Race:** Mande 50% (Bambara, Malinke, Sarakole), Peul 17%, Voltaic 12%, Songhai 6%, Tuareg and Moor 10%, other 5%. **Religions:** Islam, 90%; traditional, 9%; Christian, 1%. **Literacy rate:** 32%
Economic summary: GDP/PPP (1995 est.): $5.8 billion; $600 per capita. **Real growth rate:** 5.2%. **Inflation:** 12.7% (1995 est.). **Unemployment:** n.a. **Arable land:** 2%. **Agriculture:** millet, corn, rice, cotton, peanuts, livestock. **Labor force:** 2.666 million (1986 est.); agriculture, 80%; services, 19%; industry and commerce, 1% (1981). **Industry:** consumer goods, phosphates, gold, fish. **Natural resources:** bauxite, iron ore, manganese, phosphate, salt, limestone, gold. **Exports:** $320 million (f.o.b., 1994): cotton, livestock, gold. **Imports:** $422 million (f.o.b., 1994): machinery and equipment, foodstuffs, construction materials, petroleum, textiles. **Major trading partners:** Western Europe

Geography Most of Mali, in West Africa, lies in the Sahara. A landlocked country four-fifths the size of Alaska, it is bordered by Guinea, Senegal, Mauritania, Algeria, Niger, Burkina Faso, and the Côte d'Ivoire. The only fertile area is in the south, where the Niger and Senegal Rivers provide irrigation.

Government The military dictatorship of General Traoré was overthrown in March 1991. The present government is a multiparty democracy with one parliamentary house of 129 seats, 13 of which are designated for Malians abroad.

History Caravan routes have passed through Mali since C.E. 300. The Malinke empire ruled regions of Mali from the 12th to 16th centuries, and the Songhai empire reigned over the Timbuktu-Gao region in the 15th century. Morocco conquered Timbuktu in 1591, and ruled over it for two centuries. Subjugated by France by the end of the 19th century, the land became a colony in 1904 (named French Sudan in 1920) and in 1946 became part of the French Union. On June 20, 1960, it became independent and, under the name of Sudanese Republic, was federated with the Republic of Senegal in the Mali Federation. However, Senegal seceded from the Federation on Aug. 20, 1960, and the Sudanese Republic then changed its name to the Republic of Mali on Sept. 22.

In the 1960s, Mali concentrated on economic development, continuing to accept aid from both Soviet bloc and Western nations, as well as international agencies. In the late 1960s, it began retreating from close ties with China. But a purge of conservative opponents brought greater power to President Modibo Keita, and in 1968 the influence of the Chinese and their Malian sympathizers increased. The army overthrew the government on Nov. 19, 1968, and until 1991, Mali was under a military dictatorship. Mali and Burkina Faso fought a brief border war from Dec. 25 to 29, 1985. Mali's second multiparty national elections took place in May 1997, with President Konaré winning reelection.

Malta

MALTA

President: Ugo Mifsud Bonnicí (1994)
Prime Minister: Eddie Fenech Adami (1998)
Area: 122 sq mi. (320 sq km)
Population (1998 est.): 379,563 (average annual rate of natural increase: 0.58%); birth rate: 11.7/1000; infant mortality rate: 7.6/1000; density per sq mi.: 3,111
Capital (1992 est.): Valletta, 9,183. **Largest city (est. 1990):** Sliema, 13,541. **Monetary unit:** Maltese lira. **Languages:** Maltese and English (both official). **Ethnicity/Race:** Maltese (descendants of ancient Carthaginians and Phoenicians, with strong elements of Italian and other Mediterranean stock), Spanish, English, Arab. **Religion:** Roman Catholic, 98%. **Literacy rate:** 88%
Economic summary: GDP/PPP (1996 est.): $4.7 billion; $12,600 per capita. **Real growth rate:** 4%. **Inflation:** 3% (1996). **Unemployment:** 3.7% (Sept. 1996). **Arable land:** 38%. **Agriculture:** potatoes, wheat, barley, citrus, vegetables, hogs, poultry. **Labor force:** 145,085; government services, 37%; other services, 28%; manufacturing and construction, 25%. Major manufacturing products are high-tech semiconductors, electrical switch gear, gold and silver items, rubber products, and textiles. The same products are exported. Tourism is also important to the economy. **Exports:** $1.9 billion (f.o.b., 1995): clothing, textiles, footwear, ships. **Imports:** $3 billion (c.i.f., 1995): food, petroleum, machinery, and semi-manufactured goods. **Major trading partners:** Germany, Italy, U.K., U.S. **Member of Commonwealth of Nations**

Geography The five Maltese islands—Malta, Gozo, Comino, Comminotto, and Filflawith—have a combined land area smaller than Philadelphia. Malta is located in the Mediterranean Sea, about 60 miles (97 km) south of the southeastern tip of Sicily.

Government The government is headed by a prime minister, responsible to a 65-member House of Representatives elected by universal suffrage. The president, the constitutional head of state, is elected by the parliament to a five-year term.

History The strategic importance of Malta was recognized by the Phoenicians, who occupied it, as did, in turn, the Greeks, Carthaginians, and Romans. The apostle Paul was shipwrecked there in C.E. 60. With the division of the Roman Empire in C.E. 395, Malta was assigned to the eastern portion dominated by Constantinople. Later, in 870, the Arabs made themselves the island's masters. In 1091 the Norman noble Roger I, then master of Sicily, came to Malta with a small retinue and defeated the Arabs. The Knights of St. John (Malta), who obtained the three habitable Maltese islands of Malta, Gozo, and Comino from Charles V in 1530, reached their highest fame when they withstood an attack by superior Turkish forces in 1565. Napoleon seized Malta in 1798, but the French forces were ousted by British troops the next year, and British rule was confirmed by the Treaty of Paris in 1814.

Malta was heavily attacked by German and Italian aircraft during World War II, but was never invaded by the Axis powers. Malta became an independent nation on Sept. 21, 1964, and a republic Dec. 13, 1974, but remained in the British Commonwealth. In 1979, when its alliance with Great Britain ended, Malta sought to guarantee its neutrality through agreements with other countries. The European Council indicated in 1994 that Malta's application for membership in the European Union would probably be accepted in the next expansion phase. However, immediately after the election of Oct. 1996, the new Labour Party government froze Malta's application to join the E.U. The new government also withdrew Malta from the NATO Partnership for Peace program in an effort to maintain its neutrality.

Marshall Islands

REPUBLIC OF THE MARSHALL ISLANDS

President: Imata Kabua (1997)
Total land area: 70 sq mi (181.3 sq km), includes the atolls of Bikini, Eniwetok, and Kwajalein
Population (1998 est.): 63,031; average annual rate of natural increase 3.85%; birth rate 45.4/1000; infant mortality rate 44.5/1000; density per sq mi.: 900
Capital and largest city (1990 est.): Majuro, 20,000. **Ethnicity/Race:** Micronesian. **Religion:** predominantly Christian, mostly Protestant. **Literacy rate:** 91%. **Language:** Both Marshallese and English are official languages. Marshallese is a language in the Malayo-Polynesian family.
Economic summary: GDP/PPP (1995 est.): $94 million; per capita, $1,680. **Real growth rate:** 1.5%. **Inflation:** 4%. **Unemployment:** 16% (1991 est.). **Labor force:** (1986), 4,800. **Exports:** $21.3 million (f.o.b., 1995 est.): coconut oil, fish, live animals, trichus shells. **Imports:** $69.9 million (c.i.f., 1995 est.): foodstuffs, machinery and equipment, beverages and tobacco, fuels. Agriculture, marine resources, and tourism are the top development priorities for the Republic of the Marshall Islands (RMI). The government of the RMI is the largest employer with some 2,000 workers. Direct U.S. aid under the Compact of Free Association, the U.S. is to provide approximately $40 million annually in aid. **Major trading partners:** U.S., Japan, Australia

Geography The Marshall Islands, east of the Carolines, are divided into two chains: the western, or Ralik, group, including the atolls Jaluit, Kwajalein, Wotho, Bikini, and Eniwetok; and the eastern, or Ratak, group, including the atolls Mili, Majuro, Maloelap, Wotje, and Likiep. The islands are of the coral-reef type and rise only a few feet above sea level. The Marshall Islands comprise an area slightly larger than Washington, D.C.

Government The Marshallese government consists of a president elected by a 33-member parliament known as the Nitijela. The 12-member Council of Iroij ("Chiefs") has mainly a consultative function, concerned with traditional laws and customs.

History Sighted in 1529 by the Spanish navigator Alvaro Saavedra, the Marshall Islands, inhabited by Micronesians for centuries, lacked the wealth to encourage exploitation. In 1885, Germany declared the islands a protectorate. Japan seized them in 1914 and later (after 1919) administered them as a League of Nations mandate. Occupied by the United States in World War II, after heavy fighting at Kwajalein and Enewetak, the Marshall Islands were made part of the United Nations Trust Territory of the Pacific Islands under U.S. jurisdiction in 1947. U.S. nuclear testing began in 1946 and ceased in 1958, and clean-up efforts were completed; but Bikini and Enewetak remained too badly contaminated for the return of their indigenous populations. The United States and the Marshall Islands signed a Compact of Free Association which became effective on Oct. 21, 1986. The Republic of the Marshall Islands became fully self-governing in free association with the United States after the termination of the Trusteeship Agreement became effective on Nov. 3, 1986. The Marshall Islands were admitted to the U.N. on Sept. 17, 1991.

In 1997, President Kabua deferred plans for a feasibility study of a controversial proposal to develop Bikini as a commercial nuclear-waste dump for radioactive material produced by Asian power plants. The Compact of Free Association with the U.S. and the associated economic aid are scheduled to expire in 2001. Consequently, the government began a reform of the public service that was designed to reduce the number of jobs by 25% in the late 1990s.

Mauritania

ISLAMIC REPUBLIC OF MAURITANIA

National name: République Islamique de Mauritanie
Chief of State and Head of Government: Col. Maaouye Ould Sidi Ahmed Taya (1984)
Prime MInister: Cheikh El Afia Ould Mohamed Khouna (1996)
Area: 397,953 sq mi. (1,030,700 sq km)
Population (1998 est.): 2,511,473 (average annual rate of natural increase: 2.52%); birth rate: 44.5/1000; infant mortality rate: 78.2/1000; density per sq mi.: 6
Capital and largest city (1992 est.): Nouakchott, 480,000. **Monetary unit:** Ouguyia. **Languages:** Arabic (official) and French. **Ethnicity/Race:** mixed Maur/black 40%, Maur 30%, black 30%. **Religion:** Islam. **Literacy rate:** 34%
Economic summary: GDP/PPP (1995 est.): $2.8 billion; $1,200 per capita. **Real growth rate:** 6% (1995). **Inflation:** 6.5% (1995). **Unemployment** (1991 est.), 20%. **Arable land:** 0%. **Agriculture:** livestock, millet, maize, wheat, dates, rice. **Labor force:** 465,000 (1981 est.); wage earners, 45,000; agriculture, 47%; services, 29%; industry and commerce, 14%; government, 10%. **Industry:** iron ore, processed fish. **Natural resources:** copper, iron ore, gypsum, fish. **Exports:** $483 million (f.o.b., 1995 est.): iron ore, fish, gum arabic, gypsum. **Imports:** $365 million (c.i.f., 1995 est.): foodstuffs, petroleum, capital goods. **Major trading partners:** E.U., Japan, Côte d'Ivoire, Algeria, China, U.S.

Geography Mauritania, three times the size of Arizona, is situated in northwest Africa with about 350 miles (592 km) of coastline on the Atlantic Ocean. It is bordered by Morocco on the north, Algeria and Mali on the east, and Senegal on the south. The country is mostly desert, with the exception of the fertile Senegal River valley in the south and grazing land in the north.

Government One-party military government since 1978. The legal system is based on the Islamic religion.

History Mauritania was first inhabited by blacks and Berbers, and it became a center for the Berber Almoravid movement, which sought to spread Islam through western Africa. It was first explored by the Portuguese in the 15th century, but by the 19th century the French gained control. They organized the area into a territory in 1904, and made it part of French West Africa.

Mauritania became an independent nation on Nov. 28, 1960, and was admitted to the United Nations in 1961 over the strenuous opposition of Morocco, which claimed the territory. With Moors, Arabs, Berbers, and blacks frequently in conflict, the government in the late 1960s sought to make Arab culture dominant to unify the country.

Mauritania acquired administrative control of the southern part of the former Spanish Sahara when the colonial administration withdrew in 1975, under an agreement with Morocco and Spain. Increased military spending and rising casualties in Western Sahara helped bring down the civilian government of Ould Daddah in 1978. A succession of military rulers followed.

In 1989 Mauritania fought a border war with Senegal. Although the country voted in the U.N. to support the embargo against Iraq, the government actually leaned the other way.

Although slavery was officially outlawed in 1980, it is believed that approximately 100,000 blacks are still enslaved.

Mauritius

President: Cassam Uteem (1992)
Prime Minister: Navinchandra Ramgoolam (1995)
Area: 787 sq mi. (1,860 sq km)
Population (1998 est.): 1,168,256 (average annual rate of natural increase: 1.20%); birth rate: 18.6/1000; infant mortality rate: 16.5/1000; density per sq mi.: 1,484
Capital and largest city (1993 est.): Port Louis, 134,516. **Monetary unit:** Mauritian rupee. **Languages:** English (official), French, Creole, Hindi, Urdu, Hakka, Bojpoori. **Ethnicity/Race:** Indo-Mauritian 68%, Creole 27%, Sino-Mauritian 3%, Franco-Mauritian 2%. **Religions:** Hindu, 52%, Christian, 28.3%; Islam, 16.6%; other, 3.1%. **Literacy rate:** 81%
Economic summary: GDP/PPP (1996 est.): $11.7 billion; $10,300 per capita. **Real growth rate:** 5%. **Inflation:** 6% (1995). **Unemployment:** 2.4% (1991 est.). **Arable land:** 49%. **Agriculture:** sugar cane, tea. **Labor force:** 479,500 (1993 est.); construction and

industry, 37%; services, 24%. **Products:** processed sugar, wearing apparel, chemical products, textiles. **Natural resources:** fish. **Exports:** $1.57 billion (f.o.b., 1995): sugar, light manufactures, textiles. **Imports:** $1.98 billion (c.i.f., 1995): foodstuffs, manufactured goods. **Major trading partners:** E.U., South Africa, U.S. **Member of Commonwealth of Nations**

Geography Mauritius is a mountainous island in the Indian Ocean east of Madagascar.

Government Mauritius is a republic within the British Commonwealth. The unicameral Legislative Assembly has 70 members, 62 of whom are elected by direct suffrage. The remaining 8 are chosen from among the unsuccessful candidates.

History After a brief Dutch settlement, French immigrants who came in 1715 named the island Île de France and established the first road and harbor infrastructure, as well as the sugar industry, under the leadership of Gov. Mahe de Labourdonnais. Blacks from Africa and Madagascar came as slaves to work in the cane fields. In 1810, the British captured the island and in 1814, by the Treaty of Paris, it was ceded to Great Britain along with its dependencies.

Indian immigration, which followed the abolition of slavery in 1835, rapidly changed the fabric of Mauritian society, and the country flourished with the increased cultivation of sugar cane. The opening of the Suez Canal in 1869 heralded the decline of Mauritius as a port-of-call for ships rounding the southern tip of Africa, bound for South and East Asia. The economic instability of the price of sugar, the main crop, in the first half of the 20th century brought civil unrest, then economic, administrative, and political reforms. Mauritius became independent on March 12, 1968.

The effects of Cyclone Claudette in 1979, and of falling world sugar prices in the early 1980s, led the government to initiate a vigorous program of agricultural diversification and to develop the processing of imported goods for the export market. The country formally broke ties with the British Crown in March 1992, becoming a republic within the Commonwealth.

Mexico

UNITED MEXICAN STATES

Official name: Estados Unidos Mexicanos
President: Ernesto Zedillo Ponce de Léon (1994)
Area: 761,600 sq mi. (1,972,550 sq km)
Population (1998 est.): 98,552,776 (average annual rate of natural increase: 1.77%); birth rate: 25.5/1000; infant mortality rate: 25.8/1000; density per sq mi.: 129
Capital and largest city: Mexico City: city proper (1990 census) 9,815,795; metro. area (1996 est.) 16,908,000. **Other large cities (1995):** Guadalajara, 2,178,000; Monterrey, 1,702,000; Ecatepec, 1,456,438 (part of Mexico City metropolitan area); Nezahualcóyotl, 1,259,543; Puebla, 1,222,177. **Monetary unit:** Peso. **Languages:** Spanish, Indian languages. **Ethnicity/Race:** mestizo (Indian-Spanish) 60%, Amerindian or predominantly Amerindian 30%, Caucasian or predominantly Caucasian 9%, other 1%. **Religion:** nominally Roman Catholic, 97%; Protestant, 3%. **Literacy rate:** 87%
Economic summary: GDP/PPP (1996 est.): $777.3 billion; $8,100 per capita. **Real growth rate:** 5.1%. **Inflation:** 28%. **Unemployment:** 10%, plus considerable underemployment. **Arable land:** 12%. **Agriculture:** corn, cotton, fruits, wheat, beans, coffee, tomatoes, rice. **Labor force** (1994), 36.3 million (Nov. 1996); commerce, 14.6%; manufacturing, 11.1%; agriculture, forestry, hunting and fishing, 28%; services, 31.7%. **Products:** processed foods, chemicals, basic metals and metal products, petroleum. **Natural resources:** petroleum, silver, copper, gold, lead, zinc, natural gas, timber. **Exports:** $95 billion (f.o.b., 1996 est.): motor vehicles, consumer electronics, cotton, shrimp, coffee, petroleum, petroleum products, engines. **Imports:** $88.5 billion (f.o.b., 1996 est.): grain, metal manufactures, agricultural machinery, electrical equipment, car parts for assembly, motor vehicle repair parts, aircraft and aircraft parts. **Major trading partners:** U.S., Japan, Western European countries

Geography Mexico is bordered by the United States to the north, Belize and Guatemala to the southeast; Mexico is about one-fifth the size of the Unite States. Baja California in the west is an 800-mile (1,287-km) peninsula and forms the Gulf of California. In the east are the Gulf of Mexico and the Bay of Campeche, which is formed by Mexico's other peninsula, the Yucatán. The center of Mexico is a great, high plateau, open to the north, with mountain chains on east and west and with ocean-front lowlands lying outside of them.

Government Mexico is a federal republic. The Constitution of 1917 provides for the separation of powers among the executive, legislative, and judicial branches. The president, who is popularly elected for six years and is ineligible to succeed himself, governs with a cabinet of secretaries. Congress has two houses—a 500-member Chamber of Deputies, elected for three years, and a 128-member Senate, elected for six years, half of which is renewed every three years. Popularly elected officials (president, members of Congress, mayors, etc.) cannot seek reelection. Each of the 31 states has considerable autonomy, with a popularly elected governor, a legislature, and a local judiciary.

History At least three great civilizations—the Mayas, the Olmecs, and later the Toltecs—preceded the wealthy Aztec empire, conquered in 1519–21 by the Spanish under Hernando Cortés. Spain ruled Mexico as part of the viceroyalty of New Spain for the next 300 years until Sept. 16, 1810, when the Mexicans first revolted. They continued the struggle and finally won independence in 1821.

From 1821 to 1877, there were two emperors, several dictators, and enough presidents and provisional executives to make a new government on the average of every nine months. Mexico lost Texas (1836), and after defeat in the war with the U.S. (1846–48) it lost the area made up of the present states of California, Nevada, and Utah, most of Arizona and New Mexico, and parts of Wyoming and Colorado under the Treaty of Guadalupe Hidalgo. In 1855, the Indian patriot Benito Juárez began a series of liberal reforms, including the disestablishment of the Catholic Church, which had acquired vast property. A subsequent civil war was interrupted by the French invasion of Mexico (1861), the crowning of Maximilian of Austria as Emperor (1864), and then his overthrow and execution by forces under Juárez, who again became president in 1867.

The years after the fall of the Dictator Porfirio Diaz (1877–80 and 1884–1911) were marked by bloody political-military strife and trouble with the U.S., culminating in the punitive U.S. expedition into northern Mexico (1916–17) in unsuccessful pursuit of the revolutionary Pancho Villa. Since a brief period of civil war in 1920, Mexico has enjoyed a period of gradual agricultural, political, and social reforms. The Partido Nacional Revolucionario (PNR; National Revolutionary Party), dominated by revolutionary and reformist politicians from northern Mexico, was established in 1929; it continued to control Mexico through the 20th century and was renamed the Partido Revolucionario Institucional (PRI; Institutional Revolutionary Party) in 1946. Relations with the U.S. were again disturbed in 1938 when all foreign oil wells were expropriated, but an agreement on compensation was finally reached in 1941.

Following World War II, the government placed heavy emphasis on economic growth. During the mid-1970s, under the leadership of President José López Portillo, Mexico emerged as one of the world's major petroleum-producing countries. By the end of Portillo's term, however, Mexico had accumulated a huge external debt because of the government's unrestrained borrowing on the strength of its petroleum revenues. The collapse of oil prices in 1986 cut into Mexico's export earnings and worsened the situation.

In 1994 the leading presidential candidate was shot and killed in Tijuana. The campaign manager was then selected to be the party's presidential candidate. Zedillo won the election by more than 20% and the PRI party retained its majority in both legislative houses. In Feb. 1995 agreement was reached with the U.S. to prevent the collapse of Mexico's private banks. The strict provisions, however, gave the U.S. virtual veto power over key elements in Mexico's economic policy. Elections in July 1997 brought a stunning upset for the long ruling PRI, which lost control of the lower legislative house and the mayoralty of Mexico City, in what observers called the freest election in the country's history.

Micronesia

FEDERATED STATES OF MICRONESIA

President: Jacob Nena (1997)
Total area: 271 sq mi (702 sq km). Land area, same (includes islands of Pohnpei, Yap, Chuuk, and Kosrae)
Population (1998 est.): 129,658 (average annual rate of natural increase: 3.31%); birth rate: 27.6/1000; infant mortality rate: 34.5/1000; density per sq mi.: 478
Capital: Palikir. **Language:** English is the official and common language; major indigenous languages are Chukese, Pohnpeian, Yapase, and Kosrean.. **Ethnicity/Race:** nine ethnic Micronesian and Polynesian groups. **Literacy rate:** 85%
Economic summary: GDP/PPP (1994 est.): $205 million (note: GDP is supplemented by grant aid, averaging perhaps $100 million annually); $1,700 per capita. **Real growth rate:** 1.4%. **Inflation:** 4% (1994 est.). **Labor force:** n.a. **Unemployment:** 27% (1989). **Exports:** $29.1 million (f.o.b., 1994 est.): fish, garments, bananas, black pepper. **Imports:** $141.1 million (c.i.f., 1994 est.): food, manufactured goods, machinery and equipment, beverages. Financial assistance from the U.S. is the primary source of revenue, with the U.S. pledged to spend $1 billion in the islands in the 1990s. Micronesia also earns about $4 million a year in fees from foreign fishing concerns. Economic activity consists primarily of subsistence farming and fishing. **Unemployment:** 80% **Aid:** Under the terms of the Compact of Free Association, the U.S. will provide $1.3 billion in grand aid during the period 1986–2001.

Geography The Federated States of Micronesia is composed of the island states of Yap, Chuuk (Truk), Pohnpei (Ponape), and Kosrae, all in the Caroline Islands. The islands vary geologically from high mountainous islands to low, coral atolls, with volcanic outcroppings on Pohnpei, Kosrae, and Chuuk. They are located 3,200 miles (5,150 km) west-southwest of Hawaii, in the north Pacific Ocean.

Government The president and vice president are elected by the unicameral National Congress, which is made up of one at-large senator from each state, with four-year terms, and single-district senators, with two-year terms, elected on the basis of population. The Federated States of Micronesia has been in free association with the United States since Nov. 1986.

History The islands that make up the Federated States of Micronesia (FMA) were probably settled by people from eastern Melanesia some 3,500 years ago. The islands were colonized by Spain in the 17th century and eventually came under Japanese rule after World War I. They were taken by American forces during World War II. On April 2, 1947, the United Nations Security Council created the Trust Territory of the Pacific Islands under which the Northern Mariana, Caroline, and Marshall Islands were placed under the administration of the United States. Under the new constitution of the Federated States of Micronesia, the country became an internally self-governing federation in 1979. In 1983, the F.M.A. voted to accept a Compact of Free Association with the U.S., and in Nov. 1986, the U.S. government declared the Trust Territory agreements no longer in effect—thereby granting the Federated States of Micronesia full independence. The F.M.A. was admitted to the United Nations on Sept. 17, 1991. In July 1993, the country became a member of the International Monetary Fund. Economic difficulties continued through the mid-1990s as the government tried to plan for the end, in 2001, of the Compact of Free Association with the United States, and the accompanying guaranteed economic aid.

Moldova

REPUBLIC OF MOLDOVA

President: Petru Lucinschi (1997)
Prime Minister: Ion Ciubuc (1997)
Area: 13,000 sq mi. (33,700 sq km)
Population (1998 est.): 4,457,729 (average annual rate of natural increase: 0.04%); birth rate: 14.4/1000; infant mortality rate: 43.7/1000, density per sq mi.: 343
Capital and largest city (1991): Chisinau, 676,700. **Other large cities (1991 est.):** Tiraspol, 186,000; Beltsy, 165,000; Bendery (Tighina), 141,500. **Monetary unit:** Moldovan Lem. **Language:** Moldovan (official, virtually the same as Romanian), Russian, Gagauz (a Turkish dialect). **Religions (1991):** Eastern Orthodox 98.5%, Jewish 1.5%, Baptist (only about 1,000 members). **Ethnicity/Race:** Moldavian/Romanian 64.5%, Ukrainian 13.8%, Russian 13%, Gagauz 3.5%, Jewish 1.5%, Bulgarian 2%, other 1.7% (1989 figures)
Economic summary: GDP/PPP (1996 estimate extrapolated from the World Bank estimate for 1994):

$10.8 billion; $2,400 per capita. **Real growth rate:** 1.5%. **Inflation:** 15%. **Unemployment:** 1.4% (includes only officially registered unemployed; large numbers of underemployed workers). **Arable land:** 53%. **Labor force:** 2.03 million (Jan. 1994); agriculture, 39.5%; industry, 12.0%; other, 48.5%. Others include power engineering, textiles, metalworking, building materials, machine-building, TV sets, washing machines and other consumer goods, and manufacturing of electrical equipment. Agricultural products are wheat, corn, barley, sugar beets, fruits, and wine grapes, soybeans, tobacco, and animal husbandry. Eighty-five percent of all the land is cultivated. **Exports:** $775 million (1996): foodstuffs, wine, tobacco, textiles and footwear, machinery, chemicals. **Imports:** $1.048 billion (1996): oil, gas, coal, steel machinery, foodstuffs, automobiles and other consumer durables. **Major trading partners:** Russia, Kazakhstan, Ukraine, Uzbekistan, Romania, Germany

Geography Moldova (formerly Moldavia) is a landlocked republic of hilly plains lying west of the Carpathian Mountains between the Prut and Dnestr (Dneister) Rivers. The country is sandwiched between Romania and Ukraine. The area is a very fertile region with rich black soil (chernozem) covering three-quarters of the territory.

Government A democratic republic with a parliament (presidium) made up of 101 deputies. Executive power is divided between a president and a Council of Ministers, which is headed by a prime minister. The president is elected to a four-year term and designates the prime minister, who must be approved by parliament.

History Most of Moldova was an independent principality in the 14th century. In the 16th century it came under Ottoman Turkish rule. Russia acquired Moldovan territory in 1791, and in 1812 (The Treaty of Bucharest) when Turkey gave up the province of Bessarabia[1] to Russia. Turkey held the rest of Moldova but it was passed to Romania in 1918. Russia did not recognize the cession of this territory.

In 1924, the U.S.S.R. established Moldova as an Autonomous Soviet Socialist Republic of the Ukraine. As a result of the Nazi-Soviet Nonaggression Pact of 1939, Romania was forced to cede all of Bessarabia to the Soviet Union in 1940 and the Moldovan A.S.S.R. was merged with the Romanian-speaking districts of Bessarabia to form the Moldovan Soviet Socialist Republic. During World War II, Romania joined Germany in the attack on the Soviet Union and reconquered Bessarabia. Soviet troops retook the territory in 1944 and reestablished the Moldovan S.S.R.

For many years, a controversy existed between Romania and the U.S.S.R. over Bessarabia. Following the aborted coup against Soviet President Mikhail Gorbachev, Moldova proclaimed its independence in Sept. 1991. Conflict between ethnic Romanians and Slavs in Trans-Dniester erupted upon independence. The prime minister and most of his cabinet resigned in early June 1992 because of the continued strife. Russia and Moldova agreed in July 1992 to send a joint peacekeeping force to the region and outlined guarantees for its future. The first parliamentary elections in Feb. 1994 saw a victory for the former Communist establishment. A new government formed in Jan. 1997, received parliamentary approval a week later. In May, Moldova and Trans-Dniester signed a document in Moscow agreeing to the integrity of the country and calling for the removal of Russian troops upon the conclusion of a definite peace settlement. The Russian financial crisis in fall 1998 was expected to severely affect Moldova, which relies on Russia for 60% of its foreign trade.

1. The area between the Prut and Dnestr Rivers.

Monaco

PRINCIPALITY OF MONACO

National name: Principauté de Monaco
Ruler: Prince Rainier III (1949)
Minister of State: Michel Lévêque (1997)
Area: 0.73 sq mi. (465 acres)
Population (1998 est.): 32,035 (average annual growth rate: 0.40%); birth rate 10.7/1000; infant mortality rate: 6.6/1000; density per sq mi.: 43,884
Capital and largest city (1995 est.): Monaco, 30,400. **Monetary unit:** French franc. **Languages:** French (official), English, Italian, Monégasque. **Ethnicity/Race:** French 47%, Monegasque 16%, Italian 16%, other 21%. **Religion:** Roman Catholic, 95%. **Literacy rate:** 99%
Economic summary: GDP/PPP (1996 est.): $800 million; $25,000 per capita. **Real growth rate:** n.a. **Labor force:** 30,540 (1 Jan. 1994). **Unemployment:** 3.1% 1994). About 50% of Monaco's revenues come from value-added taxes on hotels, banks, and industrial sector. About 25% of revenues comes from tourism. **Exports:** n.a. **Imports:** n.a. Full customs integration with France, which collects and rebates Monacan trade duties; also participates in E.U.

Geography Monaco is a tiny, hilly wedge driven into the French Mediterranean coast; it is nine miles east of Nice, France.

Government Prince Albert of Monaco gave the principality a constitution in 1911, creating a National Council of 18 members popularly elected for five years. Legislative power is shared by the prince and the National Council. The head of government is the Minister of State (who must be a French citizen) and three state councillors acting under the authority of the prince, who is the official chief of state.

History The Phoenicians, and after them the Greeks, had a temple on the Monacan headland honoring Hercules. From *Monoikos,* the Greek surname for this mythological strong man, the principality took its name. After being independent for 800 years, Monaco was annexed to France in 1793 and was placed under Sardinia's protection in 1815. By the Franco-Monegasque treaty of 1861, Monaco went under French guardianship but continued to be independent. In 1865, a customs union was established between the two countries. Another treaty that was made with France, in 1918, contained a clause providing that, in the event that the male Grimaldi dynasty should become extinct, Monaco would become an autonomous state under French protection.

Monaco is a little land of pleasure with a tourist business that runs as high as 1.5 million visitors a year. It had popular gaming tables as early as 1856. Five years later, a 50-year concession to operate the games was granted to François Blanc, of Bad Homburg. This concession passed into the hands of a private company in 1898. Prince Rainier III, born

May 31, 1923, succeeded his grandfather, Louis II, on the latter's death, May 9, 1949. Rainier was married, in 1956, to U.S. actress Grace Kelly and they subsequently had three children. Their son, Prince Albert Louis Pierre (b. 1958) is eligible to assume control of the principality upon his father's death or abdication. Immensely popular, Princess Grace died Sept. 14, 1982, of injuries received in a car accident near Monte Carlo. She was 52.

Monaco's practice of providing a tax shelter for French businessmen resulted in a 1962 dispute between the countries. A compromise was reached by which French citizens with less than five years residence in Monaco were taxed at French rates and taxes were imposed on Monegasque companies doing more than 25 percent of their business outside the principality. In 1967, Rainier took control of the Société des Bains de Mer, operator of the famous Monte Carlo gambling casino, in a program to increase hotel and convention space. The country was admitted to the U.N. in May 1993, making it the smallest country represented there. The country celebrated the 700th anniversary of the Grimaldi reign during 1997, as it saw its revenue from the state-controlled Société des Bains de Mer continue to decline. These losses were offset, however, by a relatively diverse underlying economy.

Mongolia

MONGOLIA

President: Ntsaagiyn Bagabandi (1997)
Prime Minister: Tsakhiagiyn Elbegdorj (1998)
Area: 604,250 sq mi. (1,565,000 sq km)
Population (1998 est.): 2,578,530 (average annual rate of natural increase: 1.54%); birth rate: 23.6/1000; infant mortality rate: 66.3/1000; density per sq mi.: 4
Capital and largest city (1993 est.): Ulan Bator, 619,000. **Monetary unit:** Tugrik. **Language:** Mongolian, 90%; also Turkic, Russian, and Chinese. **Ethnicity/Race:** Mongol 90%, Kazak 4%, Chinese 2%, Russian 2%, other 2%. **Religion:** predominantly Tibetan Buddhist; Islam about 4%. **Literacy rate:** 97% (est.)
Economic summary: GDP/PPP (1996 est.): $5.1 billion; $2,060 per capita. **Real growth rate:** 3%. **Inflation:** 53%. **Unemployment:** 6% (1995 est.). **Labor force:** 1.115 million (mid-1993 est.); involved in primarily herding and agricultural work. **Arable land:** 1%. **Agriculture:** livestock, wheat, potatoes, forage, barley. Mongolia has the highest number of livestock per person in the world. **Industry:** coal, copper and molybdenum concentrate. **Natural resources:** coal, copper, molybdenum, iron, oil, lead, gold, and tungsten. **Exports:** $400 million (f.o.b., 1995 est.): copper, cashmere, livestock, animal products, wool, nonferrous metals. **Imports:** $473 million (f.o.b., 1995 est.): fuels, food products, industrial consumer goods, chemicals, building materials, machinery and equipment. **Major trading partners:** C.I.S. nations, China, Japan, Austria

Geography Mongolia lies in central Asia between Siberia on the north and China on the south. It is slightly larger than Alaska.

The productive regions of Mongolia—a tableland ranging from 3,000 to 5,000 feet (914 to 1,524 m) in elevation—are in the north, which is well drained by numerous rivers, including the Hovd, Onon, Selenga, and Tula. Much of the Gobi Desert falls within Mongolia.

Government In Jan. 1992, the Great People's Hural (parliament) approved a new constitution that became effective Feb. 12, 1992, and changed the name of the former communist state to Mongolia. Mongolia became an independent sovereign republic now in transition from communism. The highest organ of state power is the State Great Hural (SGH). The SGH has one chamber consisting of 76 members. Its chairman and vice-chairman are elected for a term of four years.

History Nomadic tribes that periodically plundered agriculturally based China from the west are recorded in Chinese history dating back more than 2,000 years. It was to protect China from these marauding peoples that the Great Wall was constructed around 200 B.C.E. The name Mongol comes from a small tribe whose leader, Ghengis Khan, began a conquest that would eventually encompass an enormous empire stretching from Asia to Europe, as far west as the Black Sea and as far south as India and the Himalayas. However, by the 14th century, the kingdom was in serious decline, with invasions from a resurgent China and internecine warfare.

The State of Mongolia was formerly known as Outer Mongolia. It contains the original homeland of the historic Mongols, whose power reached its zenith during the 13th century under Kublai Khan. The area accepted Manchu rule in 1689, but after the Chinese Revolution of 1911 and the fall of the Manchus in 1912, the northern Mongol princes expelled the Chinese officials and declared independence under the Khutukhtu, or "Living Buddha."

In 1921 Soviet troops entered the country, and facilitated the establishment of a republic by Mongolian revolutionaries in 1924. China also made a claim to the region, but was too weak to assert it. Under the 1945 Chinese-Russian Treaty, China agreed to give up Outer Mongolia, which, after a plebiscite, became a nominally independent country.

Allied with the U.S.S.R. in its dispute with China, Mongolia began mobilizing troops along its borders in 1968 when the two powers became involved in border clashes on the Kazakh-Sinkiang frontier to the west and at the Amur and Ussuri Rivers. A 20-year treaty of friendship and cooperation, signed in 1966, entitled Mongolia to call upon the U.S.S.R. for military aid in the event of invasion.

Free elections held in August 1990 produced a multiparty government, though it was still largely Communist. As a result, Mongolia has moved gradually toward a market economy. With the collapse of the U.S.S.R., however, Mongolia was deprived of Soviet aid. Many of the country's factories were forced to shut down, and unemployment rose to 30 percent. Primarily in reaction to the economic turmoil, the former Communist Party won a significant majority in parliamentary elections in 1992. In 1997, a former communist and chairman of the People's Revolutionary Party was elected president, further strengthening the hand of the anti-reformers.

Disagreement within Mongolia's ruling coalition over the pace and direction of market reforms in April 1998 caused a shake-up that thrust Tsakhiagiyn Elbegdorj, a pro-reform politician, into the prime minister's position. Elbegdorj has promised to accelerate the reform process and speed up the inflow of foreign investment.

Morocco

KINGDOM OF MOROCCO

National name: al-Mamlaka al-Maghrebia
Ruler: King Hassan II (1961)
Prime Minister: Abderrahmane El Youssoufi (1998)
Area: 172,413 sq mi. (446,550 sq km)
Population (1998 est.): 29,114,497 (average annual rate of natural increase: 1.89%); birth rate: 26.4/1000; infant mortality rate: 66.3/1000; density per sq mi.: 169
Capital (1993 est.): Rabat, 1,220,000. **Largest cities:** Casablanca, 2,943,000; Marrakech, 602,000; Fez, 564,000; Salé, 521,000. **Monetary unit:** Dirham. **Languages:** Arabic, French, Berber dialects, Spanish. **Ethnicity/Race:** Arab-Berber 99.1%, other 0.7%, Jewish 0.2%. **Religions:** Islam, 98.7%, Christian, 1.1%; Jewish, 0.2%. **Literacy rate:** 50%
Economic summary: GDP/PPP (1996 est.): $97.6 billion; $3,260 per capita. **Real growth rate:** 9%. **Inflation:** 5%. **Unemployment:** 20% (1995 est.). **Arable land:** 21%. **Agriculture:** barley, wheat, citrus fruits, vegetables. **Labor force:** 7.4 million; agriculture, 50%; services, 26%; industry, 15% (1985). **Industry:** textiles, processed food, phosphates, leather goods. **Natural resources:** phosphates, lead, manganese, fisheries. **Exports:** $7.7 billion (f.o.b., 1996 est.): food and beverages, semiprocessed goods, consumer goods, phosphates. **Imports:** $9.8 billion (c.i.f., 1996 est.): capital goods, fuels, foodstuffs, raw materials, consumer goods. **Major trading partners:** E.U., C.I.S. nations, Japan, U.S., India, Iraq.

Geography Morocco, about one-tenth larger than California, is just south of Spain across the Strait of Gibraltar and looks out on the Atlantic from the northwest shoulder of Africa. Algeria is to the east and Mauritania to the south. On the Atlantic coast there is a fertile plain. The Mediterranean coast is mountainous. The Atlas Mountains, running northeastward from the south to the Algerian frontier, average 11,000 feet (3,353 m) in elevation.

Government A constitutional monarchy. The king, after suspending parliament in 1965, promulgated a new constitution in 1972. He continued to rule by decree until June 3, 1977, when the first free elections since 1962 took place. The constitution was revised and approved by referendum in 1992, and again in 1996. The king appoints the prime minister. The National Assembly has 306 members who serve six year terms. Morocco has 14 political parties.

History Morocco was historically the home of the Berbers. In C.E. 46, Morocco was annexed by Rome as part of the province of Mauritania, and it is thought that the province was almost entirely Christianized during the latter part of Roman rule. The Berbers helped the Arabs invade Spain in C.E. 711 and then revolted against them and gradually won control of large areas of Spain for a time after 739.

The country was ruled successively by various native dynasties and maintained regular commercial relations with Europe, even during the 17th and 18th centuries when it was the headquarters of the famous Salé pirates. In the 19th century, there were frequent clashes with the French and Spanish. Finally, in 1904, France and Spain divided Morocco into zones of French and Spanish influence, and these were established as protectorates in 1912. Meanwhile, Morocco had become the object of big-power rivalry, which almost led to a European war in 1905 when Germany attempted to gain a foothold in the rich mineral country. By terms of the Algeciras Conference (1906), Morocco was internationalized economically, and France's privileges were limited.

The Tangier Statute, concluded by Britain, France, and Spain in 1923, created an international zone at the port of Tangier, permanently neutralized and demilitarized. In World War II, Spain occupied the zone, ostensibly to ensure order, but was forced to withdraw in 1945. Sultan Mohammed V was deposed by the French in 1953 and replaced by his uncle, but nationalist agitation forced his return in 1955. On his death on Feb. 26, 1961, his son, Hassan, became king. France and Spain recognized the independence and sovereignty of Morocco in 1956.

In 1975, tens of thousands of Moroccans crossed the border into Spanish Sahara to back their government's contention that the northern part of the territory was historically part of Morocco. At the same time, Mauritania occupied the southern half of the territory in defiance of Spanish threats to resist such a takeover. Abandoning its commitment to self-determination for the territory, Spain withdrew, and only Algeria protested. When Mauritania signed a peace treaty with the Algerian-backed Polisario Front in August 1979, Morocco occupied the southern part of the Western Sahara in addition to the northern part, which it already occupied. Under pressure from other African leaders, Hassan agreed in mid-1981 to a cease-fire with a referendum under international supervision to decide the fate of the Sahara territory, but the referendum was never carried out. Armed conflict over the region continued into the 1990s, though on a reduced scale.

King Hassan became the second Arab leader to meet with an Israeli leader when, on July 21, 1986, Israeli Prime Minister Shimon Peres came to Morocco. Morocco became the first Arab state to condemn the 1990 Iraqi invasion of Kuwait and promised to send an 1,100-men contingent to Saudi Arabia. Public opinion, however, as evidenced by sanctioned marches in Rabat, mounted against Moroccan involvement and demanded withdrawal from the U.S.-led alliance. In May 1995, the U.N. Security Council extended the mandate for U.N. forces in the Western Sahara by one month. In late June the Polisario rebels pulled out of a U.N.-sponsored voter registration program. Representatives of the government and of the Polisario discussed the status of Western Sahara in the presence of U.N. mediators for the first time in June 1997.

Mozambique

REPUBLIC OF MOZAMBIQUE

National name: República de Moçambique
President: Joaquim Chissanó (1986)
Prime Minister: Pascoal Mocumbi (1994)
Area: 303,073 sq mi. (801,590 sq km)
Population (1998 est.): 18,641,469 (average annual rate of natural increase: 2.57%); birth rate: 43.5/1000; infant mortality rate: 120/1000; density per sq mi.: 62
Capital and largest city (1996 est.): Maputo, 1,095,300. **Monetary unit:** Metical. **Languages:** Portuguese (official), Bantu languages. **Ethnicity/Race:** indigenous tribal groups 99.6% (Shangaan, Chokwe, Manyika, Sena, Makua, and others), Europeans 0.06%, Euro-Africans 0.2%, Indians 0.08%. **Religions:** traditional, 60%; Christian, 30%; Islam, 10%. **Literacy rate:** 33%

Economic summary: GDP/PPP (1995 est.): $12.2 billion; $670 per capita. **Real growth rate:** 3%. **Inflation:** 22% (1996 est.). **Unemployment:** (1989 est.) 50%. **Arable land:** 4%. **Agriculture:** cotton, cashew nuts, sugar, tea, shrimp. **Labor force:** n.a.; agriculture, 80% (1993). **Industry:** processed foods, petroleum products, beverages, textiles, tobacco. **Natural resources:** coal, titanium. **Exports:** $169 million (f.o.b., 1995): cashew nuts, sugar, shrimp, copra, citrus. **Imports:** $784 million (c.i.f., 1995) incl. aid: food, clothing, farm equipment, petroleum. **Major trading partners:** Spain, South Africa, Portugal, U.S., France, U.K., Japan.

Geography Mozambique stretches for 1,535 miles (2,470 km) along Africa's southeast coast. It is nearly twice the size of California. Tanzania is to the north; Malawi, Zambia, and Zimbabwe to the west; and South Africa and Swaziland to the south.

The country is generally a low-lying plateau broken up by 25 sizable rivers that flow into the Indian Ocean. The largest is the Zambezi, which provides access to central Africa. The principal ports are Maputo, Beira, and Nacala.

Government A multiparty republic.

History Bantu-speakers migrated to Mozambique in the first millennium, and Arab and Swahili traders settled the region thereafter. It was explored by Vasco da Gama in 1498, and first colonized by Portugal in 1505. By 1510, the Portuguese had control of all the former Arab Sultanates on the east African coast. Mozambique was administered as part of Goa, in India, until 1752, when it received its own captain-general. Portuguese colonial rule was repressive.

Guerrilla activity began in 1963 and became so effective by 1973 that Portugal was forced to dispatch 40,000 troops to fight the rebels. A cease-fire was signed in Sept. 1974, and after having been under Portuguese colonial rule for 470 years, Mozambique became independent on June 25, 1975. The first president, Samora Moises Machel, had been the head of the National Front for the Liberation of Mozambique (FRELIMO) in its 10-year guerrilla war for independence. He died in a plane crash on Oct. 19, 1986, and was succeeded by his Foreign Minister, Joaquim Chissano.

On Jan. 25, 1985, after a decade of independence, the government was locked in a five-year-old paralyzing war with anti-government guerrillas, known as the MNR, backed by the white minority government in South Africa. The guerrilla movement weakened President Chissano's attempts to institute socialism, which he then decided to abandon in 1989. A new constitution was drafted calling for three branches of government and granting civil liberties. A cease-fire agreement was signed in Oct. 1992 between the government and the MNR to end 16 years of civil war.

In April 1994 the president announced that a multiparty general election would be held in late October. The incumbent won. In Nov. 1995 the country became the first non-former-British colony to become a member of the British Commonwealth. The president's disciplined economic plan has been extremely successful, winning the country foreign confidence and aid.

Myanmar

SEE BURMA.

Namibia

REPUBLIC OF NAMIBIA

President: Sam Nujoma (1990)
Prime Minister: Hage Geingob (1990)
Status: Independent Country
Area: 318,261 sq mi. (825,418 sq km)
Population (1998 est.): 1,622,328 (average annual growth rate: 1.6%); birth rate: 35.8/1000; infant mortality rate: 66.8/1000; density per sq mi.: 5
Capital and largest city (1992 est.): Windhoek, 161,000
Summer capital (est. 1980): Swakopmund, 17,500. **Monetary unit:** Namibian dollars. **Languages:** Afrikaans, German, English (official), several indigenous. **Ethnicity/Race:** black 86%, white 6.6%, mixed 7.4%. Note: about 50% of the population belong to the Ovambo tribe and 9% to the Kavangos tribe; other ethnic groups are: Herero 7%, Damara 7%, Nama 5%, Caprivian 4%, Bushmen 3%, Baster 2%, Tswana 0.5%. **Religion:** Predominantly Christian. **Literacy rate:** 38%
Economic summary: GDP/PPP (1996 est.): $6.2 billion; $3,700 per capita. **Real growth rate:** 1.5%. **Inflation:** 8%. **Unemployment:** 21.8% (1993). **Arable land:** 1%. **Agriculture:** corn, millet, sorghum, livestock. **Labor force:** 500,000; agriculture, 49%; industry and commerce, 25%; services, 5%; government, 18%; mining, 3% (1994 est.). **Products:** canned meat, dairy products, tanned leather, textiles, clothing. **Natural resources:** diamonds, copper, lead, zinc, uranium, fish. **Exports:** $1.45 billion (f.o.b., 1996 est.): diamonds, copper, lead, zinc, beef cattle, karakul pelts, marble, semi-precious stones, uranium, beef, gold. **Imports:** $1.55 billion (f.o.b., 1996 est.): construction materials, fertilizer, grain, foodstuffs, petroleum products and fuel. **Major trading partners:** Australia, U.K., South Africa, France, Germany, Switzerland, U.S., Japan.

Geography Namibia, bounded on the north by Angola and Zambia and on the east by Botswana and South Africa in the south. It is for the most part a portion of the high plateau of southern Africa with a general elevation of from 3,000 to 4,000 feet.

Government Namibia became independent in 1990 after its new constitution was ratified. A multiparty democracy with an independent judiciary was established. There is a bicameral legislature consisting of a 26 seat National Council and a 72-seat National Assembly.

History The San peoples may have inhabited what is now Namibia more than 2000 years ago. The Bantu-speaking Herero migrated there in the 1600s. The Ovambo, the largest ethnic group today, migrated there in the 1800s.

In the late 15th century, the Portuguese explorer Bartholomius Diaz became the first European to visit Namibia. Formerly called South West Africa, the territory became a German colony in 1884. In 1908 German troops massacred the majority of the Herero population. The land was taken by South African forces in 1915, becoming a South African mandate by the terms of the Treaty of Versailles in 1920.

South Africa's application for incorporation of the territory was rejected by the U.N. General Assembly in 1946 and South Africa was invited to prepare a trusteeship agreement instead. By a law passed in 1949, however, the territory was brought into much closer association with South Africa—including representation in its parliament.

In 1969, South Africa extended its laws to the mandate over the objection of the U.N., particularly its black African members. When South Africa refused to withdraw them, the Security Council condemned it. Under a 1974 Security Council resolution, South Africa was required to begin the transfer of power to the Namibians by May 30, 1975, or face U.N. action. Prime Minister Balthazar J. Vorster rejected U.N. supervision claiming that his government was prepared to negotiate Namibian independence, but not with the South West African People's Organization, the principal black separatist group. Meanwhile, the all-white legislature of South West Africa eased several laws on apartheid in public places.

Despite international opposition, the Turnhalle Conference in Windhoek drafted a constitution to organize an interim government based on racial divisions, a proposal overwhelmingly endorsed by white voters in the territory in 1977. At the urging of ambassadors of the five Western members of the Security Council, South Africa on June 11 announced rejection of the Turnhalle constitution and acceptance of the Western proposal to include the South West Africa People's Organization (SWAPO) in negotiations.

As policemen wielding riot sticks charged demonstrators in a black, South West Africa township, South Africa handed over limited powers to a new, multiracial administration in the former German colony on June 17, 1985. Installation of the new government ended South Africa's direct rule, but South Africa retained an effective veto over the new government's decisions along with responsibility for the territory's defense and foreign policy.

An agreement between South Africa, Angola, and Cuba arranged for elections for a constituent assembly in Nov. 1989 to establish a new government. SWAPO won 57% of the vote, a majority but not enough to dictate a constitution unilaterally. In Feb. 1990, SWAPO leader Sam Nujoma was elected president and took office when Namibia became independent on March 21, 1990.

In Dec. 1994 elections SWAPO obtained an overwhelming mandate winning not only the presidency again for the incumbent but also absolute control of the parliament.

Nauru

REPUBLIC OF NAURU

President: Bernard Dowiyogo (1998)
Area: 8.2 sq mi. (21 sq km)
Population (1998 est.): 10,501; average annual growth rate: 1.33%; birth rate 18/1000; infant mortality rate 40.6/1000; density per sq mi.: 1,281
Capital (1983): Yaren, 559. **Monetary unit:** Australian dollar. **Languages:** Nauruan and English. **Ethnicity/Race:** Nauruan 58%, other Pacific Islander 26%, Chinese 8%, European 8%. **Religions:** Protestant, 58%; Roman Catholic, 24%; Confucian and Taoist, 8%. **Literacy rate:** 99%
Economic summary: GDP/PPP (1993 est.): $100 million; $10,000 per capita. **Real growth rate:** n.a. **Inflation:** –3.6%, (1993). **Unemployment:** 0%. **Industry:** phosphates. **Natural resources:** phosphates. **Exports:** $25.3 million (f.o.b., 1991): phosphates. **Imports:** $21.1 million (c.i.f., 1991): foodstuffs, fuel, machinery. **Major trading partners:** Australia, New Zealand, U.K., Japan. **Special relationship within the Commonwealth of Nations**

Geography Nauru (pronounced NAH-oo-roo) is an island in the Pacific just south of the equator, about 2,500 miles (4,023 km) southwest of Honolulu.

Government Legislative power is invested in a popularly elected 18-member parliament, which elects the president from among its members. Executive power rests with the president, who is assisted by a five-member cabinet.

History As suggested by its unique, blended language, Nauru probably was settled at differing periods by drift voyages from other Pacific islands. In 1798, a British navigator, John Fearn of the ship *Hunter*, was the first European to visit the island. European-supplied firearms helped promote incessant interclan warfare between 1878 and 1888. Nauru was annexed by Germany in 1888. After the discovery of phosphate on the island in 1899, a British company began in 1906 to exploit the deposits, dividing the profits with a German firm. It was placed under joint Australian, New Zealand, and British mandate after World War I. During World War II, the Japanese occupied the island (1942–45) and forcibly deported 1,200 Nauruans. In 1947, it became a U.N. trusteeship administered by Australia. Nauruans gained control of the phosphate mining by agreement and sale in 1967. On Jan. 31, 1968, Nauru became an independent republic.

In 1993, Australia offered an out-of-court settlement for damages Nauru presented to the International Court of Justice because of phosphate mining. Australia agreed to pay $2.5 million Australian dollars for 20 years, and New Zealand and the U.K. additionally agreed to pay a one-time settlement of $12 million each. Declining phosphate prices, the high cost of maintaining an international airline, and investments that did not perform well combined to make the economy flounder in the late 1990s.

Nepal

KINGDOM OF NEPAL

Ruler: King Birendra Bir Bikram Shah Dev (1972)
Prime Minister: Girija Prasad Koirala (1998)
Area: 54,463 sq mi. (140,800 sq km)
Population (1998 est.): 23,698,421 (average annual rate of natural growth: 2.52%); birth rate: 35.7/1000; infant mortality rate: 76/1000; density per sq mi.: 435
Capital and largest city (1993): Kathmandu, 535,000. **Other large cities:** Lalitpur, 190,000; Biratnagar, 132,000. **Monetary unit:** Nepalese rupee. **Languages:** Nepali (official), Newari, Bhutia, Maithali. **Ethnicity/Race:** Newars, Indians, Tibetans, Gurungs, Magars, Tamangs, Bhotias, Rais, Limbus, Sherpas. **Religions:** Hindu, 90%; Buddhist, 5%; Islam, 3%. **Literacy rate:** 26%
Economic summary: GDP/PPP (1996 est.): $26.5 billion; $1,200 per capita. **Real growth rate:** 2.9% (FY95/96 est.). **Inflation:** 9.2%. **Unemployment:** n.a.; substantial underemployment (1996).**Arable land:** 17%. **Agriculture:** rice, maize, wheat, millet, jute, sugar cane, oilseed, potatoes. **Labor force:** 9.2 million; agriculture, 90%; services, 7%; industry, 3% (note: severe lack of skilled labor). Agriculture is the mainstay of the economy accounting for 42% of the GDP and 90% of the work force. **Products:** sugar, textiles, jute, cigarettes, cement. **Natural resources:** water, timber, hydroelectric potential. **Exports:** $343 million (f.o.b., 1996 est., does not include unrecorded border trade with India): clothing, carpets, leather

goods, grain. **Imports:** $1.3 billion (c.i.f., 1996 est.): petroleum products, fertilizer, machinery. **Major trading partners:** India, U.S., Germany, Singapore, U.K., Japan.

Geography A landlocked country the size of Arkansas, lying between India and the Tibetan Autonomous Region of China, Nepal contains Mount Everest (29,108 ft.; 8,872 m), the tallest mountain in the world. Along its southern border, Nepal has a strip of level land that is partly forested, partly cultivated. North of that is the slope of the main section of the Himalayan range, including Everest and many other peaks higher than 8,000 m.

Government In Nov. 1990, King Birendra promulgated a new constitution and introduced a multiparty democracy in Nepal. In the general elections held in Nov. 1994, the Nepal Communist Party (NML) emerged as the single largest party with 88 seats and formed a minority government headed by Prime Minister Man Mohan Adhikari on Nov. 30, 1994. Parliament consists of two houses: the higher with 60 members and a lower house with 205.

History The first civilizations in Nepal, which flourished around the 6th century B.C.E., were confined to the fertile Kathmandu Valley where the present-day capital of the same name is located today. It was in this region that Prince Siddhartha Gautama was born circa 563 B.C.E. Gautama achieved enlightenment as Buddha, and spawned Buddhist belief.

Nepali rulers' early patronage of Buddhism largely gave way to Hinduism, reflecting the increased influence of India, around the 12th century C.E. Though the successive dynasties of the Gopalas, the Kiratis, and the Licchavis expanded their rule, it was not until the reign of the Malla kings from C.E. 1200–1769 that Nepal assumed the approximate dimensions of the modern state.

The kingdom of Nepal was unified in 1768 by King Prithvi Narayan Shah, who had fled India following the Moghul conquests of the subcontinent. Under Shah and his successors Nepal's borders expanded as far west as Kashmir and as far east as Sikkim (now part of India). A commercial treaty was signed with Britain in 1792, and again in 1816 after more than a year of hostilities with the British East India Company.

In 1923, Britain recognized the absolute independence of Nepal. Between 1846 and 1951, the country was ruled by the Rana family, which always held the office of prime minister. In 1951, however, the king took over all power and proclaimed a constitutional monarchy. Mahendra Bir Bikram Shah became king in 1955. After Mahendra died of a heart attack in 1972, Prince Birendra, at 26, succeeded to the throne.

In 1990, a pro-democracy movement forced King Birendra to lift the ban on political parties and appoint an opposition leader to head an interim government as prime minister. The first free election in three decades provided a victory for the liberal Nepali Congress Party in 1991, although the communists made a strong showing. Parliamentary elections held in Nov. 1994 placed the communists in control of 88 seats in the House of Representatives. The communist leader became prime minister later that month. In June 1995 the king dissolved parliament and ordered new elections. Two opposition parties contested that decision, and the Supreme Court agreed. The leader of the Congress Party became prime minister, forming a coalition government with the National Democratic Party.

Prime Minister Sher Bahadur Deuba narrowly lost a vote of confidence in March 1997. The communists, despite previous efforts to diminish the power of the monarchy, supported royalist Lokendra Bahadur Chand for prime minister in return for his support for their coalition. A chaotic year followed, in which Chand's coalition narrowly held onto power during elections in May, only to be replaced months later by shifting political alliances. Surya Bahadur Thapa assumed the post, but resigned after only six months in office. Thapa was replaced by Girija Prasad Koirala who had already served a two-year stint as prime minister in 1991, following the restoration of democracy.

The Netherlands

KINGDOM OF THE NETHERLANDS

National name: Koninkrijk der Nederlanden
Sovereign: Queen Beatrix (1980)
Premier: Wim Kok (1994)
Area: 16,033 sq mi. (37,330 sq km)
Population (1998 est.): 15,731,112 (average annual rate of natural increase: 0.5%); birth rate: 11.6/1000; infant mortality rate: 5.2/1000; density per sq mi.: 981
Capital and largest city (1994 est.): Amsterdam, 724,096. **Other large cities (1994 est.):** Rotterdam, 598,521; The Hague (seat of government), 445,279; Utrecht, 234,106; Eindhoven, 196,130. **Monetary unit:** Guilder. **Language:** Dutch. **Ethnicity/Race:** Dutch 96%, Moroccans, Turks, and other 4% (1988). **Religions:** Roman Catholic 34%, Protestant 25%, Muslim 3%, other 2%, unaffiliated 36%. **Literacy rate:** 99%
Economic summary: GDP/PPP (1996 est.): $317.8 billion; $20,500 per capita. **Real growth rate:** 2.7%. **Inflation:** 2%. **Unemployment:** 6.5% (Nov. 1996). **Arable land:** 27%. **Agriculture:** wheat, barley, sugar beets, potatoes, meat and dairy products. **Labor force:** 6.4 million (1993); services, 73%; manufacturing and construction, 23%; agriculture, 4% (1994). **Products:** metal fabrication, electrical machinery and equipment, chemicals, electronic equipment, petroleum, fishing. **Exports:** $176.2 billion (f.o.b., 1996): foodstuffs, natural gas, chemicals, metal products, textiles, tobacco, agricultural products. **Imports:** $159.7 billion (c.i.f., 1996): raw materials, consumer goods, transportation equipment, food products, crude petroleum. **Major trading partners:** Germany, Belgium-Luxembourg, France, U.K., U.S.

Geography The Netherlands, on the coast of the North Sea, is twice the size of New Jersey. Part of the great plain of north and west Europe, the Netherlands has maximum dimensions of 190 by 160 miles (360 by 257 km) and is low and flat except in Limburg in the southeast, where some hills rise to 300 feet (92 m). About half the country's area is below sea level, making the famous Dutch dikes a requisite to the use of much land. Reclamation of land from the sea through dikes has continued through recent times. All drainage reaches the North Sea, and the principal rivers—Rhine, Maas (Meuse), and Schelde—have their sources outside the country.

Government The Netherlands and its former colonies, the Netherlands Antilles and the self-governing island of Aruba, form the kingdom of the

Netherlands. The country is a constitutional monarchy with a bicameral parliament. The Upper Chamber has 75 members elected for six years by representative bodies of the provinces, half of the members retiring every three years. The Lower Chamber has 150 members elected by universal suffrage for four years. The two Chambers have the right of investigation and interpolation; the Lower Chamber can initiate legislation and amend bills.

History Julius Caesar found the low-lying Netherlands inhabited by Germanic tribes—the Nervii, Frisii, and Batavi. The Batavi on the Roman frontier did not submit to Rome's rule until 13 B.C.E., and then only as allies. A part of Charlemagne's empire in the 8th and 9th centuries C.E., the area later passed into the hands of Burgundy and the Austrian Hapsburgs, and finally in the 16th century came under Spanish rule. When Philip II of Spain suppressed political liberties and the growing Protestant movement in the Netherlands, a revolt led by William of Orange broke out in 1568. Under the Union of Utrecht (1579), the seven northern provinces became the United Provinces of the Netherlands. War between the United Provinces and Spain continued into the 17th century, but in 1648 Spain finally recognized Dutch independence. The Dutch East India Company was established in 1602, and by the end of the 17th century Holland was one of the great sea and colonial powers of Europe.

The nation's independence was not completely established until after the Thirty Years' War (1618–48), after which the country's rise as a commercial and maritime power began. In 1688, the English parliament invited William of Orange, stadtholder, and his wife, Mary Stuart, to rule England as William III and Mary II. William then used the combined resources of England and the Netherlands to wage war on Louis XIV's France. In 1814, all the provinces of Holland and Belgium were merged into one kingdom, but in 1830 the southern provinces broke away to form the kingdom of Belgium. A liberal constitution was adopted by the Netherlands in 1848. The country remained neutral during World War I.

In spite of its neutrality in World War II, the Netherlands was invaded by the Nazis in May 1940, and the Dutch East Indies were later taken by the Japanese. The nation was liberated in May 1945. In 1948, after a reign of 50 years, Queen Wilhelmina abdicated and was succeeded by her daughter Juliana. In 1949, after a four-year war, the Netherlands granted independence to the Dutch East Indies, which became the Republic of Indonesia. The Netherlands also joined NATO that year. The Netherlands joined the European Economic Community (later, the E.U.) in 1958. In 1963, it turned over the western half of New Guinea to Indonesia, ending 300 years of Dutch presence in Asia. Attainment of independence by Suriname on Nov. 25, 1975, left the Netherlands Antilles and Aruba as the country's only overseas territories. Although prostitution is legal, the government moved in July 1997 to permit the operation of brothels as a means of regulating the former. Only those with a valid resident's permit would be permitted to be employed in the brothels.

The Sovereign, Queen Beatrix Wilhelmina Armgard, born Jan. 31, 1938, assumed the throne in 1980. In 1967, Beatrix gave birth to a son, Willem-Alexander Claus George Ferdinand, the first male heir to the throne since 1884.

Netherlands Autonomous Countries

Netherlands Antilles

Status: Part of the Kingdom of the Netherlands
Governor: J. M. Saleh (1990)
Premier: Mingull A. Pourier (1994)
Area: 313 sq mi. (800 sq km)
Population (1998 est.): 205,693 (average annual growth rate: 1.06%); birth rate: 17.6/1000; infant mortality rate: 13/1000; density per sq mi.: 657. **Ethnicity/Race:** mixed African 85%, Carib Indian, European, Latin, Asian
Capital and largest city (1993 est.): Willemstad, 197,019.. **Literacy rate:** 94%
Economic summary: GDP/PPP (1996 est.): $2.04 billion; $9,800 per capita. **Real growth rate:** 0%. **Inflation:** 3% (1996). **Unemployment:** 13.4% (1993 est.). **Arable land:** 10%. **Agriculture:** aloes, sorghum, peanuts. **Labor force:** 89,000; industry and commerce, 28%; government, 65% (1983). **Industry:** oil refining, tourism. Natural resource: phosphate. **Exports:** $1.3 billion (f.o.b., 1993): petroleum products. **Imports:** $1.8 billion (f.o.b., 1993): crude petroleum, food. **Major trading partners:** U.S., Venezuela, Netherlands, U.K., Guadeloupe.

Geography Two groups of Caribbean islands 500 miles (805 km) apart: one, about 40 miles (64 km) off the Venezuelan coast, consists of Curaçao (173 sq mi.; 448 sq km) and Bonaire (95 sq mi.; 246 sq km), the other, lying to the northeast, consists of Sint Eustatius, the southern part of Saint Martin (Dutch: Sint Maarten), and Saba, with a total area of 34 square miles (88 sq km) comprise the Netherlands Antilles.

Government There is a constitutional government formed by the governor and cabinet and a legislative assembly, called the Staten, which has 22 members elected to four-year terms by popular vote. In 1954 the islands became an integral part of The Netherlands, with full autonomy in domestic affairs. There are also local governments for Curaçao, Bonaire, and the northeastern group of islands. In 1994 the Netherlands Antilles voted to preserve their federation with the Netherlands.

Aruba

Status: Part of the Kingdom of the Netherlands
Governor: Olindo Koolman (1992)
Prime Minister: Henny Eman (1994)
Area: 75 sq mi. (193 sq km)
Population (1998 est.): 68,325; growth rate 0.47%; birth rate: 13.7/1000; infant mortality rate: 8/1000; density per sq mi.: 911
Capital and largest city (1991 est.): Oranjestad, 20,050. **Ethnicity/Race:** mixed European/Caribbean Indian 80%. **Literacy rate:** 95%
Economic summary: GDP/PPP (1996 est.): $1.4 billion; $21,000 per capita. **Real growth rate:** 5%. **Inflation:** 3.5% (1996). **Unemployment:** 0.5% (1994). Little agriculture. **Industry:** tourism, light manufacturing (tobacco, beverages, consumer goods). **Exports:** $1.3 billion (f.o.b., 1995, including oil re-exports): mostly petroleum products. **Imports:** $1.8 billion (f.o.b., 1995): food, consumer goods, manufacturers. **Major trading partners:** U.S., E.U.

Geography Aruba, an island slightly larger than Washington D.C., lies 18 miles (28.9 km) off the coast of Venezuela in the southern Caribbean.

Government The Netherlands controls Aruba's defense and foreign affairs, but all internal affairs are handled by an island government directing its own civil service, judiciary, revenue, and currency. The governmental structure is composed of the governor, appointed by the queen for a term of six years; the Legislature consisting of 21 members elected by universal suffrage for terms not exceeding four years; and the council of ministers, presided over by the prime minister, who holds executive power. On Jan. 1, 1986, Aruba seceded from the federation of the Netherlands Antilles. But in 1994 the Aruban government, in conjunction with the governments of The Netherlands and the Netherlands Antilles, decided to postpone indefinitely the transition to full independence.

New Zealand

Sovereign: Queen Elizabeth II (1952)
Governor-General: Sir Michael Hardie Boys (1996)
Prime Minister: Jenny Shipley (1997)
Area: 103,884 sq mi. (268,680 sq km) (excluding dependencies)
Population (1998 est.): 3,625,388 (average annual growth rate: 1.04%); birth rate: 14.9/1000; infant mortality rate: 6.4/1000; density per sq mi.: 35
Capital: Wellington. **Largest cities (est. 1995):** Auckland, 952,600; Wellington, 331,100; Christchurch, 324,400. **Monetary unit:** New Zealand dollar. **Languages:** English, Maori. **Ethnicity/Race:** European 88%, Maori 8.9%, Pacific Islander 2.9%, other 0.2%. **Religions:** Christian, 81%; none or unspecified, 18%; Hindu, Confucian, and other, 1%. **Literacy rate:** 99%
Economic summary: GDP/PPP (1996 est.): $65.6 billion; $18,500 per capita. **Real growth rate:** 2.8%. **Inflation:** 2.8%. **Unemployment:** 5.9% (Dec. 1996). **Arable land:** 9%. **Agriculture:** wool, meat, dairy products, livestock. **Labor force:** 1,634,500 (Sept. 1995); services, 64.6%; industry, 25%; agriculture, 10.4% (1994). **Products:** processed foods, textiles, machinery, transport equipment, wood and paper products, financial services. **Natural resources:** forests, natural gas, iron ore, coal, gold. **Exports:** $13.7 billion (1995): meat, dairy products, wool. **Imports:** $14 billion (1995): consumer goods, petroleum, motor vehicles, industrial equipment. **Major trading partners:** Japan, Australia, E.U., U.S., China, South Korea, Taiwan. **Member of Commonwealth of Nations**

Geography New Zealand, about 1,250 miles (2,012 km) southeast of Australia, consists of two main islands and a number of smaller, outlying islands so scattered that they range from the tropical to the antarctic. The country is the size of Colorado. New Zealand's two main components are North Island and South Island, separated by Cook Strait, which varies from 16 to 190 miles (26 to 396 km) in width. North Island (44,281 sq mi.; 115,777 sq km) is 515 miles (829 km) long and volcanic in its south-central part. This area contains many hot springs and beautiful geysers. South Island (58,093 sq mi.; 151,215 sq km) has the Southern Alps along its west coast, with Mount Cook (12,283.3 ft.; 3,754 m) the highest point. The largest of the outlying islands are the Auckland Islands (234 sq mi.; 606 sq km), Campbell Island (44 sq mi.; 114 sq km), the Antipodes Islands (24 sq mi.; 62 sq km), and the Kermadec Islands (13 sq mi.; 34 sq km).

Government New Zealand was granted self-government in 1852, a full parliamentary system and ministries in 1856, and dominion status in 1907. The queen is represented by a governor-general, and the cabinet is responsible to a unicameral parliament of 99 members, who are elected by popular vote for three years. New Zealand has no written constitution. New Zealand voted in a referendum (1993) for the mixed member system of proportional representation which replaced the former system in the 1996 general election.

History Polynesian occupation of New Zealand dates to at least C.E. 1000 and probably two or three centuries earlier. During the late Polynesian period of the 18th century, an estimated 100,000 to 200,000 Maori inhabited the main islands. New Zealand was visited and named in 1642 by Abel Tasman, a Dutch navigator. Captain James Cook explored the islands in 1769. In 1840, Britain formally annexed them. Relations between settlers and the Maori deteriorated when the Maori became reluctant to sell prime land. In 1860 troops were used to dislodge Maori from land sold under questionable circumstances; war broke out and continued for most of the decade. Eventually British forces, militia, and Maori allied to the government defeated the tribes opposed to selling land.

In the early 1880s the development of refrigerated ships made it possible for farmers to ship butter, cheese, and meat to Great Britain, thus inaugurating an agriculturally based economy. From the first, the country has been in the forefront in instituting social welfare legislation. It adopted old age pensions (1898); a national child welfare program (1907); social security for the aged, widows, and orphans, along with family benefit payments; minimum wages; a 40-hour week and unemployment and health insurance (1938); and socialized medicine (1941). The country's participation in World War I was a boon to its export trade but was costly in lives. New Zealand's entrance into World War II began with the sending of troops to Europe in 1939. After 1941, however, New Zealand was threatened directly by Japan and became involved in the war in the Pacific.

In the general election of Oct. 1996, the first under the new system of proportional representation, the National Party received 34% of the vote and Labour received 28%.

Cook Islands and Overseas Territories

The Cook Islands (93 sq mi.; 241 sq km) were placed under New Zealand administration in 1901. They achieved self-governing status in association with New Zealand in 1965. **Population (1998 est.):** 19,989; growth rate 1.06%; birth rate: 22.5/1000; infant mortality rate: 24.7/1000; density per square mile: 215. The seat of government is on Rarotonga Island. **Economic summary: GDP/PPP** (1993 est.): $57 million; $3,000 per capita. **Exports:** $3.9 million (f.o.b., 1993): citrus juice, clothing, canned fruit, and pineapple juice. **Imports:** $67 million (c.i.f., 1993): foodstuffs, textiles, fuels, timber.

Nearly all of the trade is with New Zealand; some with Japan, Australia, and U.S.

Niue (100 sq mi.; 259 sq km) was formerly administered as part of the Cook Islands. It was placed under separate New Zealand administration in 1901 and achieved self-governing status in association with New Zealand in 1974. The capital is Alofi. **Population (July 1995 est.):** 1,837; growth rate –3.66%. **Economic summary: GDP/PPP** (1993 est.): $2.4 million; per capita, $1,200. **Exports:** $117,500 (f.o.b., 1989): canned coconut cream, copra, honey, passion fruit products, pawpaw, root crops, limes, footballs, stamps, handicrafts. **Imports:** $4.1 million (c.i.f., 1989): food, live animals, manufactured goods, machinery, fuels, chemicals, lubricants, drugs. **Major trading partners:** New Zealand, Fiji, Japan.

The Ross Dependency (160,000 sq mi.; 414,400 sq km), an Antarctic region, was placed under New Zealand administration in 1923.

Tokelau (4 sq mi.; 10 sq km) was formerly administered as part of the Gilbert and Ellice Islands colony. It was placed under New Zealand administration in 1925. Its population is about 1,503 (July 1995 est.).

Nicaragua

REPUBLIC OF NICARAGUA

National name: República de Nicaragua
President: Arnoldo Alemán (1997)
Area: 50,180 sq mi. (129,494 sq km)
Population (1998 est.): 4,583,379 (average annual rate of natural increase: 2.92%); birth rate: 36/1000; infant mortality rate: 42.3/1000; density per sq mi.: 91
Capital and largest city (1992 est.): Managua, 974,000. **Monetary unit:** Cordoba. **Language:** Spanish. **Ethnicity/Race:** mestizo (mixed Amerindian and white) 69%, white 17%, black 9%, Indian 5%. **Religion:** Roman Catholic, 95%; Protestant, 5%. **Literacy rate:** 57%
Economic summary: GDP/PPP (1996 est.): $7.7 billion; $1,800 per capita. **Real growth rate:** 5.5%. **Inflation:** 11% (1996). **Unemployment:** 16%; underemployment, 36%. **Arable land:** 9%. **Agriculture:** coffee, sugar cane, corn, beans, cattle. **Labor force:** 1.086 million; industry, 13%; services, 43%; agriculture, 44% (1986). **Products:** processed foods, chemicals, metal products, clothing and textiles, beverages, footwear. **Natural resources:** timber, fisheries, gold, silver, copper, tungsten, lead, zinc. **Exports:** $607 million (f.o.b., 1996): coffee, cotton, seafood, bananas, sugar, meat, chemicals. **Imports:** $1.188 billion (c.i.f., 1996): machinery, chemicals, food, clothing, petroleum. **Major trading partners:** E.U., U.S., Japan, Costa Rica, El Salvador, Mexico, Venezuela, Guatemala.

Geography Largest but most sparsely populated of the Central American nations, Nicaragua borders on Honduras to the north and Costa Rica to the south. It is slightly larger than New York State. Nicaragua is mountainous in the west, with fertile valleys. A plateau slopes eastward toward the Caribbean. Two big lakes—Nicaragua, about 100 miles long (161 km), and Managua, about 38 miles long (61 km)—are connected by the Tipitapa River. The Pacific coast is volcanic and very fertile. The Caribbean coast, swampy and indented, is aptly called the "Mosquito Coast."

Government A republic. The president is chief of state and head of government and serves for a five year term. The 93-seat unicameral National Assembly forms the legislative branch.

History Nicaragua, which derives its name from the chief of the area's leading Indian tribe during the Spanish Conquest, was first settled by the Spanish in 1522. The country achieved independence from Spain in 1838. For the next century, Nicaragua's politics were dominated by the competition for power between the Liberals, who were centered in the city of León, and the Conservatives, centered in Granada.

To back up its support of the new Conservative government in 1909, the U.S. sent a small detachment of Marines to Nicaragua and kept them there from 1912 to 1925. The Bryan-Chamorro Treaty of 1916 (terminated in 1970) gave the U.S. an option on a canal route through Nicaragua, and naval bases. Disorder after the 1924 elections brought in the U.S. Marines again. A guerrilla leader, Gen. César Augusto Sandino, began fighting the occupation force in 1927. He fought the U.S. troops until their withdrawal in 1933.

Gen. Anastasio Somoza García emerged, after ordering the assassination of Sandino, and ruled as dictator from 1936 until his assassination in 1956. He was succeeded by his son Luis, who alternated with trusted family friends in the presidency until his death in 1967. Another son, Maj. Gen. Anastasio Somoza Debayle, became president in 1967. The Somozas ruled Nicaragua with an iron fist, making Nicaragua less dependent on banana income, exiling political foes, and amassing a great family fortune.

Sandinista guerrillas, leftists who took their name from Gen. Sandino, launched an offensive in May 1979. After seven weeks of fighting, Somoza fled the country on July 17, 1979. The Sandinistas assumed power on July 19, promising to maintain a mixed economy, a non-aligned foreign policy, and a pluralist political system. On Jan. 23, 1981, the Reagan Administration suspended U.S. aid, charging that Nicaragua, with the aid of Cuba and the Soviet Union, was supplying arms to rebels in El Salvador. The Sandinistas denied the charges. Later that year, Nicaraguan guerrillas known as "Contras," began a war to overthrow the Sandinistas. The elections were finally held on Nov. 4, 1984, with Daniel Ortega Saavedra, the Sandinista junta coordinator, winning the presidency. The war intensified in 1986–87, with the resupplied Contras establishing themselves inside the country. Negotiations sponsored by the Contadora (neutral Latin American) nations foundered, but a peace plan sponsored by Arias, the Costa Rican president, led to a treaty signed by the Central American leaders in August 1987, that called for an end to outside aid to guerrillas and negotiations between hostile parties.

Violetta Barrios de Chamorro, owner of the opposition paper *La Prensa,* led a broad anti-Sandinista coalition to victory in the presidential and legislative elections of 1990, ending 11 years of Sandinista rule. After a year in office President Chamorro found herself besieged. Business groups were dissatisfied with the pace of reforms; Sandinistas, upset with what they regarded as the dismantling of their earlier achievements, and threatened to take up arms again. In Feb. 1991 the president brought the military under her direct command. By early 1993 relations between the president and the coalition that backed her had soured over charges of corruption and the continuing influence of the Sandinistas in the government and the army. Former Managua mayor and Conservative candidate Arnoldo Aleman won the 1996 election. His closest rival was former President Daniel Ortega. In April 1997 Aleman ordered an investigation of possible frauds during the previous government's privatization programs.

Niger

REPUBLIC OF NIGER

National name: République du Niger
President: Col. Ibrahim Bare Mainassara (1996)
Prime Minister: Ibrahim Hassane Mayaki (1997)
Area: 489,206 sq mi. (1,267,000 sq km)
Population (1998 est.): 9,671,848 (average annual rate of natural increase: 2.96%); birth rate: 53/1000; infant mortality rate: 114.4/1000; density per sq mi.: 20
Capital and largest city (1988): Niamey, 398,265. **Other large cities:** Zinder, 120,900; Maradi, 112,970. **Monetary unit:** Franc CFA. **Ethnicity/Race:** Hausa 56%, Djerma 22%, Fula 8.5%, Tuareg 8%, Beri Beri (Kanouri) 4.3%, Arab, Toubou, and Gourmantche 1.2%, about 4,000 French expatriates. **Languages:** French (official); Hausa, Songhai; Arabic. **Religions:** Islam, 80%; Animist and Christian, 20%. **Literacy rate:** 28%
Economic summary: GDP/PPP (1996 est.): $5.9 billion; $640 per capita. **Real growth rate:** 4%. **Inflation:** 10.6% (1995 est.). **Arable land:** 3%. **Agriculture:** peanuts, cotton, livestock, millet, sorghum, cassava, rice. **Labor force:** 2.5 million (1982); agriculture, 90%; industry and commerce, 6%; government, 4%. **Industry:** uranium, cement, bricks, light industrial products. **Natural resources:** uranium, coal, iron ore, tin, phosphates. **Exports:** $247 million (f.o.b., 1995 est.): uranium (among the top uranium producers in the world), cowpeas, livestock, hides, skins. **Imports:** $307 million (c.i.f., 1995 est.): fuels, machinery, transport equipment, foodstuffs, consumer goods, pharmaceuticals, chemical products. **Major trading partners:** France, Nigeria, Algeria, U.S., Italy, Côte d'Ivoire, Germany.

Geography Niger, in West Africa's Sahara region, is four-fifths the size of Alaska. It is surrounded by Mali, Algeria, Libya, Chad, Nigeria, Benin, and Burkina Faso.

The Niger River in the southwest flows through the country's only fertile area. Elsewhere the land is semiarid.

Government Niger held its first democratic elections in April 1993, but a coup on Jan. 27, 1996, led by Col. Mainassara, replaced Niger's brief episode of democracy with military rule.

History The nomadic Tuaregs were the first inhabitants in the Sahara region. The Hausa (14th century), the Zerma (17th century), the Gobir (18th century), and Fulani also established themselves in the region now called Niger.

Niger was incorporated into French West Africa in 1896. There were frequent rebellions, but when order was restored in 1922, the French made the area a colony. In 1958, the voters approved the French constitution and voted to make the territory an autonomous republic within the French community. The republic adopted a constitution in 1959 and the next year withdrew from the community, proclaiming its independence.

The 1974 army coup ousted President Hamani Diori, who had held office since 1960. An estimated 2 million people were starving in Niger, but 200,000 tons of imported food, half U.S.-supplied, substantially ended famine conditions by the year's end. The new president, Lt. Col. Seyni Kountché, Chief of Staff of the army, installed a 12-man military government. A predominantly civilian government was formed by Kountché in 1976.

In 1993 the country's first multiparty election resulted in the presidency of Ousmane Mahamane, who was then deposed in a Jan. 1996 coup. The constitution was suspended and the president arrested. In July the military leader of the coup was declared the winner of a presidential election by a commission he established after removing the independent commission during the balloting.

A cease-fire between the government and Tuareg rebels (Revolutionary Armed Forces of the Sahara) went into effect in 1995, and in June 1997, the Democratic Renewal Front, a hold-out Tuareg rebel group, also agreed to sign a peace accord.

Nigeria

FEDERAL REPUBLIC OF NIGERIA

Head of State: Gen. Abdulsalam Abubakar (1998)
Area: 356,700 sq mi. (923,770 sq km)
Population (1998 est.): 110,532,242; average annual rate of natural increase: 2.96%; birth rate: 42.2/1000; infant mortality rate: 70.7/1000; density per sq mi.: 310
Capital (1995 est.): Abuja, 339,000. **Largest cities:** Lagos: city proper (1996 est.) 1,518,000; metro. area (1996 est.) 10,878, 000. **Other large cities:** Ibadan, 1,365,000; Ogbomosho, 711,900; Kano, 657,300. **Monetary unit:** Naira. **Languages:** English (official) Hausa, Yoruba, Ibo, and more than 200 others. **Ethnicity/Race:** Hausa, Fulani, Yoruba, Ibo, Kanuri, Ibibio, Tiv, Ijaw. **Religions:** Islam, 50%; Christian, 40%; indigenous, 10%. **Literacy rate:** 51%
Economic summary: GDP/PPP (1996 est.): $143.5 billion; $1,380 per capita. **Real growth rate:** 3%. **Inflation:** 57% (1996 est.). **Unemployment:** 28% (1992 est.). **Arable land:** 33%. **Agriculture:** peanuts, rubber, cocoa, grains, fish, yams, cassava, livestock. **Labor force:** 42.844 million; agriculture, 54%; government, 15%; industry, commerce and services, 19%. **Products:** crude oil, natural gas, coal, tin, processed rubber, cotton, petroleum, hides, textiles, cement, chemicals. **Natural resources:** petroleum, tin, columbite, iron ore, coal, limestone, lead. **Exports:** $11.6 billion (f.o.b., 1995): oil, cocoa, palm products, rubber. **Imports:** $10 billion (c.i.f., 1995): consumer goods, capital equipment, raw materials, chemicals. **Major trading partners:** Western European countries, U.S., Japan. **Member of Commonwealth of Nations**

Geography Nigeria, one-third larger than Texas and the largest country in Africa, is situated on the Gulf of Guinea in West Africa. Its neighbors are Benin, Niger, Cameroon, and Chad. The lower course of the Niger River flows south through the western part of the country into the Gulf of Guinea. Swamps and mangrove forests border the southern coast; inland are hardwood forests.

Government A military government since Dec. 31, 1983.

History The first inhabitants of what is now Nigeria were thought to have been the Nok people (500 B.C.E.–circa C.E. 200). The Kanuri, Hausa, and Fulani peoples subsequently migrated there. Islam was introduced in the 13th century, and the empire of Kanem controlled the area from the end of the 11th century to the 14th.

The Fulani empire ruled the region from the beginning in the 19th century until the British annexed Lagos in 1851 and seized control of the rest of the region by 1886. It formally became the Colony and Protectorate of Nigeria in 1914. During World War I, native troops of the West African frontier force joined with French forces to defeat the German garrison in the Cameroons.

On Oct. 1, 1960, Nigeria gained independence, becoming a member of the Commonwealth of Nations and joining the United Nations. Organized as a loose federation of self-governing states, the independent nation faced an overwhelming task of unifying a country with 250 ethnic and linguistic groups.

Rioting broke out in 1966, and military leaders, primarily of Ibo ethnicity, seized control. In July, a second military coup put Col. Yakubu Gowon in power, a choice unacceptable to the Ibos. Also in that year, the Muslim Hausas in the north massacred the predominantly Christian Ibos in the east, many of whom had been driven from the north. Thousands of Ibos took refuge in the eastern region, which declared its independence as the Republic of Biafra on May 30, 1967. Civil war broke out. In Jan. 1970, after 31 months of civil war, Biafra surrendered to the federal government.

Gowon's nine-year rule was ended in 1975 by a bloodless coup that made Army Brigadier Muritala Rufai Mohammed the new chief of state. The return of civilian leadership was established with the election of Alhaji Shehu Shagari as president in 1979. An oil boom in the 1970s buoyed the economy and by the 1980s Nigeria was considered an exemplar of African democracy and economic well-being.

The military again seized power in 1984, only to be followed by another military coup the following year. Maj. Gen. Ibrahim Babangida announced that the country would be returned to civilian rule, but after the presidential election of June 12, 1993, he voided the results. Nevertheless, Babangida resigned as president in August. In November the military, headed by defense minister Sani Abacha, seized power again.

Corruption and notorious governmental inefficiency as well as a harshly repressive military regime characterized Abacha's reign over this oil-rich country. A U.N. fact-finding mission in 1996 reported that Nigeria's "problems of human rights are terrible and the political problems are terrifying." During the 1970s Nigeria had the 33rd highest per-capita income in the world, but by 1997 it had dropped to the 13th poorest.

Nigeria has established itself as West Africa's superpower through its military interventions in the civil wars of Liberia and Sierra Leone. Although Nigeria was unsuccessful in its attempt to defeat Charles Taylor's invasion of Liberia, in Sierra Leone Nigerian troops played a major role in overthrowing the military junta in 1998 and restoring its democratically elected president to power.

Under military rule for all but ten years since independence from Britain, the military has reneged on its promises to give up power eight times. Nigeria again promised free elections in August 1998 in response to international pressure to institute democratic rule, though few believed the notoriously authoritarian Gen. Sani Abacha, whose formidable security forces kept a tight reign over the country, would give up power.

Abacha died of a heart attack on June 8, 1998, and was succeeded by another military ruler, Gen. Abdulsalam Abubakar, who also pledged to step aside for an elected leader by May 1999. Abubakar's freeing of political prisoners and other gestures of easing the military's iron-clad rule have shown some signs of hope for Nigeria. However, the sudden and some believe suspicious death of opposition leader Mashood Abiola, who had been imprisoned by the military ever since he legally won the 1993 presidential election, was a crushing blow to democratic proponents.

Norway

KINGDOM OF NORWAY

National name: Kongeriket Norge
Sovereign: King Harald V (1991)
Prime Minister: Kjell Magne Bondevik (1997)
Area: 125,049 sq mi. (324,220 sq km)
Population (19978 est.): 4,419,955 (average annual growth rate: 0.44%); birth rate: 12.9/1000; infant mortality rate: 5/1000; density per sq mi.: 35
Capital and largest city (1995): Oslo, 483,401. **Other large cities:** Bergen, 221,717; Trondheim, 142,927; Stavanger, 103,496. **Monetary unit:** Krone. **Languages:** Norwegian (official); small Lapp (Sami)- and Finnish-speaking minorities. **Ethnicity/Race:** Germanic (Nordic, Alpine, Baltic), Lapps (Sami) 20,000. **Religion:** Evangelical Lutheran 87.8% (state church), other Protestant and Roman Catholic 3.8%, none 3.2%, unknown 5.2%. **Literacy rate:** 99%
Economic summary: GDP/PPP (1996 est.): $114.1 billion; $26,200 per capita. **Real growth rate:** 4.8%. **Inflation:** 1.2%. **Unemployment:** 4.5%. **Arable land:** 3%. **Agriculture:** dairy products, livestock, grain, potatoes, furs, wool. **Labor force:** 2.13 million; services, 71%; industry, 23%; agriculture, forestry and fishing, 6% (1993). **Industry:** oil and gas, fish, pulp and paper, ships, aluminum, iron, steel, nickel, fertilizers, transportation equipment, hydroelectric power, petrochemicals. **Natural resources:** fish, timber, hydroelectric power, ores, oil, gas. **Exports:** $41.7 billion (f.o.b., 1995): oil, natural gas, fish products, ships, pulp and paper, aluminum. **Imports:** $32.7 billion (c.i.f., 1995): machinery, fuels and lubricants, transportation equipment, chemicals foodstuffs, and clothing. **Major trading partners:** E.U., U.S., Japan

Geography Norway is situated in the western part of the Scandinavian peninsula. It extends about 1,100 miles (1,770 km) from the North Sea along the Norwegian Sea to more than 300 miles (483 km) above the Arctic Circle, the farthest north of any European country. It is slightly larger than New Mexico. Nearly 70% of Norway is uninhabitable and covered by mountains, glaciers, moors, and rivers. The hundreds of deep fiords that cut into the coastline give Norway an overall oceanfront of more than 12,000 miles (19,312 km). Galdhø Peak, at 8,100 feet (2,469 m), is Norway's highest point and the Glåma (Glomma) is the principal river, at 372 miles (598 km) long.

Government Norway is a constitutional hereditary monarchy. Legislative power, according to the 1814 constitution, is vested in the Storting, the unicameral parliament composed of 165 members who are popularly elected under proportional representation. The Storting discusses and votes on political and financial questions, but divides itself into two sections (Lagting and Odelsting) to discuss and pass on legislative matters. Executive power is held nominally by the monarch; the Council of State, consisting of a prime minister and at least seven other members, exercises executive authority.

History Norwegians, like the Danes and Swedes, are of Teutonic origin. The Norsemen, also known as Vikings, ravaged the coasts of northwestern Europe from the 8th to the 11th century and were ruled by local chieftains. Olaf II Haraldsson became the first effective king of all Norway in 1015 and began converting the Norwegians to Christianity. After 1442, Norway was ruled by Danish kings until 1814, when it was united with Sweden, although retaining a degree of independence and receiving new constitution, in an uneasy partnership. In 1905, the Norwegian parliament arranged a peaceful separation and invited a Danish prince to the Norwegian throne—King Haakon VII. A treaty with Sweden provided that all disputes be settled by arbitration and that no fortifications be erected on the common frontier.

When World War I broke out, Norway joined with Sweden and Denmark in a decision to remain neutral and to cooperate in the joint interest of the three countries. In World War II, Norway was invaded by the Germans on April 9, 1940. It resisted for two months before the Nazis took over complete control. King Haakon and his government fled to London, where they established a government-in-exile. Maj. Vidkun Quisling, whose name is now synonymous with traitor. He was executed by the Norwegians on Oct. 24, 1945.

Despite severe losses in the war, Norway recovered quickly as its economy expanded. The country led the world in social experimentation. It entered the North Atlantic Treaty Organization in 1949. The Labor Party and the Conservative Party see-sawed for control, each sometimes having to lead minority governments, in the late 20th century. An important debate has been over Norway's membership in the European Union. In an advisory referendum held in Nov. 1994, voters rejected seeking membership for their nation in the E.U. The country became the second largest net oil exporter after Saudi Arabia in 1995. Norway continued to experience rapid economic growth in the late 1990s.

Dependencies of Norway

Svalbard (24,208 sq mi.; 62,700 sq km), in the Arctic Ocean about 360 miles north of Norway, consists of the Spitsbergen group and several smaller islands, including Bear Island, Hope Island, King Charles Land, and White Island (or Gillis Land). The capital is Longyearbyen. It came under Norwegian administration in 1925. Population (1997 est.): 2,624; growth rate: –3.81%. Coal mining is major economic activity. There is also some trapping of seal, polar bear, fox, and walrus. **Bouvet Island** (23 sq mi.; 60 sq km), an island nature reserve in the South Atlantic about 1,600 miles south-southwest of the Cape of Good Hope, came under Norwegian administration in 1928. It is uninhabited.

Jan Mayen Island (147 sq mi.; 380 sq km), in the Arctic Ocean between Norway and Greenland, came under Norwegian administration in 1929. There are no permanent inhabitants, just workers at the navigation base and weather/radio station. **Peter I Island** (96 sq mi.; 249 sq km), lying off Antarctica in the Bellinghausen Sea, came under Norwegian administration in 1931. **Queen Maud Land,** a section of Antarctica, came under Norwegian administration in 1939.

Oman

SULTANATE OF OMAN

National name: Saltonat Uman
Sultan: Qabus ibn Sa'id (1970)
Area: 82,030 sq mi. (212,460 sq km)[1]
Population (1998 est.): 2,363,591 (average annual rate of natural increase: 3.45%); birth rate: 37.8/1000; infant mortality rate: 25.6/1000; density per sq mi.: 29
Capital and largest city (1991 est.): Muscat, 350,000. **Monetary unit:** Omani Rial. **Language:** Arabic (official); also English and Indian languages. **Ethnicity/Race:** Arab, Baluchi, South Asian (Indian, Pakistani, Sri Lankan, Bangladeshi), African. **Religion:** Islam, 95%. **Literacy rate:** 65.8%
Economic summary: GDP/PPP (1996 est.): $20.8 billion; $9,500 per capita. **Real growth rate:** 6.5%. **Inflation:** 0.5%. **Unemployment:** n.a. **Agriculture:** dates, fruit, cereal, livestock. **Labor force:** 454,000; agriculture, 37% (1993 est.). **Industry:** petroleum drilling, fishing, construction. **Natural resources:** oil, marble, copper, limestone. **Exports:** $7.2 billion (f.o.b., 1996 est.): oil, 85%; reexports: fish, processed copper, textiles. **Imports:** $5.5 billion (c.i.f., 1996 est.): machinery and transport equipment, food, manufactured goods, livestock, lubricants. **Major trading partners:** U.K., U.S., Japan, U.A.E., South Korea, France.

1. Excluding the Kuria Muria Islands.

Geography Oman is a 1,000-mile-long (1,700-km) coastal plain at the southeastern tip of the Arabian peninsula lying on the Arabian Sea and the Gulf of Oman. The interior is a plateau. The country is the size of Kansas.

Government Oman is an independent sultanate ruled by an absolute monarch with the aid of a handpicked cabinet and, since 1981, with a consultative assembly appointed by the sultan. The country is ruled without a constitution, elected legislature, or legal political parties.

History Arab migration to Oman began in the 9th century B.C.E. and conversion to Islam occurred in the 7th century C.E.. Muscat, the capital of the geographical area known as Oman, was occupied by the Portuguese from 1508 to 1648. Then it fell to Persian princes and later was regained by the sultan. After 1744, the sultans created a substantial empire in Oman and East Africa, and for a time the Omani capital was in Zanzibar. After 1861, however, Oman and Zanzibar were ruled separately.

The tribes of the Omani interior frequently clashed with the ruling dynasty by continuing to support the elected Ibadi imam rather than the sultan. Peace was not restored in the interior until 1959, when the last Ibadi imam was evicted from

Oman. In a palace coup on July 23, 1970, the sultan, Sa'id bin Taimur, who had ruled since 1932, was overthrown by his son, who promised to establish a modern government and use new-found wealth to aid the people of this very isolated state. Oman joined the Arab League and the United Nations in 1971.

A long border dispute with Yemen ended in late Oct. 1992 when the sultan signed an agreement with the Yemeni president. In 1997, Oman and Yemen signed maps defining the border between the two countries. Sultan Qabus in June 1997 granted women the right to be elected to the country's consultative body the Shura Council.

Pakistan

ISLAMIC REPUBLIC OF PAKISTAN

President: Mohammad Rafiq Tarar (1998)
Prime Minister: Nawaz Sharif (1997)
Area: 310,400 sq mi. (803,940 sq km)[1]
Population (1998 est.): 135,135,195 (average annual growth rate: 2.20%); birth rate: 34.4/1000; infant mortality rate: 93.5/1000; density per sq mi.: 435
Capital (1981 census): Islamabad, 201,000. **Largest cities:** Karachi: city proper (1981 census) 5,208,132; metro. area (1996 est.) 10,119,000; Lahore, 2,952,700; Faisalabad, (Lyallpur) 1,920,000; Rawalpindi, 920,000; Hyderabad, 795,000. **Monetary unit:** Pakistan rupee. **Principal languages:** Punjabi 48%, Sindhi 12%, Siraiki (a Punjabi variant) 10%, Pashtu 8%, Urdu (official) 8%, Balochi 3%, Hindko 2%, Brahui 1%, English, Burushaski, and others . **Ethnicity/Race:** Punjabi, Sindhi, Pashtun (Pathan), Baloch, Muhajir (immigrants from India and their descendants). **Religions:** Islam, 97%; Hindu, Christian, Buddhist, Parsi. **Literacy rate:** 35%
Economic summary: GNP: (purchasing power parity, 1996 est.): $296.5 billion; $2,300 per capita. **Real growth rate:** 5.5%. **Inflation:** 10.8% (FY95/96). **Unemployment:** n.a. **Arable land:** 27%. **Agriculture:** wheat, rice, cotton, sugarcane. **Labor force:** 36.7 million (1997); agriculture, 47%; mining and manufacturing, 17%; services, 17%; other, 19%. **Industry:** cotton textiles, processed foods, petroleum products, construction materials. **Natural resources:** natural gas, limited petroleum, iron ore. **Exports:** $8.3 billion (FY95/96): cotton, rice, textiles, clothing. **Imports:** $12 billion (FY95/96): edible oil, crude oil, machinery, chemicals, transport equipment. **Major trading partners:** E.U., Hong Kong, Saudi Arabia.

1. Excluding Kashmir and Jammu.

Geography Pakistan is situated in the western part of the Indian subcontinent, with Afghanistan and Iran on the west, India on the east, and the Arabian Sea on the south. The name "Pakistan" is derived from the Urdu words "Pak" (meaning pure) and "stan" (meaning country). It is nearly twice the size of California.

The northern and western highlands of Pakistan contain the towering Karakoram and Pamir mountain ranges, which include some of the world's highest peaks: K2 (28,250 feet [8,611 m]) and Nanga Parbat (26,660 feet [8,126 m]). The Baluchistan Plateau lies to the west, and the Thar Desert and an expanse of alluvial plains, the Punjab and Sind, lie to the east. The 1,000-mile-long (1,609 km) Indus River and its tributaries flow through the country from the Kashmir region to the Arabian Sea.

Government Pakistan is a federal republic with a bicameral legislature—a 217-member National Assembly and an 87-member Senate.

History Pakistan was one of the two original successor states to British India, which was partitioned along religious lines in 1947. For almost 25 years following independence, it consisted of two separate regions, East and West Pakistan, but now is made up only of the western sector. Both India and Pakistan have laid claim to the Kashmir region, and this territorial dispute led to war in 1949, again in 1965 and 1971, and remains unresolved.

What is now Pakistan was in prehistoric times the Indus Valley civilization (c. 2500–1700 B.C.E.). A series of invaders—Aryans, Persians, Greeks, Arabs, Turks, and others—controlled the region for the next several thousand years. Islam, the dominant religion, was introduced in C.E. 711. In 1526, the land became part of the Mogul Empire, which ruled most of the Indian subcontinent from the 16th to the mid-18th centuries. By 1857 the British became the dominant power in the region. With Hindus holding most of the economic, social, and political advantages, the Muslim minority's dissatisfaction grew, leading to the formation of the nationalist Muslim League in 1906 by Mohammed Ali Jinnah (1876–1949). The League supported Britain in the Second World War while the Hindu nationalist leaders, Nehru and Gandhi, refused. In return for the League's support of Britain, Jinnah expected British backing for Muslim autonomy. Britain agreed to the formation of Pakistan as a separate dominion within the Commonwealth in August 1947, a bitter disappointment to India's dream of a unified subcontinent. Jinnah became governor-general. The partition of Pakistan and India along religious lines resulted in the largest migration in human history, with 17 million people fleeing across the borders in both directions to escape the sectarian violence accompanying the partition.

Pakistan became a republic on March 3, 1956, with Major General Iskander Mirza becoming the first president. Military rule prevailed for the next two decades. Tensions between East and West Pakistan existed from the outset. Separated by more than a thousand miles, the two regions shared few cultural and social traditions other than religion. To the growing resentment of East Pakistan, the West monopolized the country's political and economic power. In 1970, East Pakistan's Awami League, led by the Bengali leader Sheik Mujibur Rahman, secured a majority of the seats in the National Assembly. President Yahya Khan postponed the opening of the National Assembly to skirt East Pakistan's demand for greater autonomy, provoking civil war. The independent state of Bangladesh, or Bengali nation, was proclaimed March 26, 1971. Indian troops entered the war in its last weeks fighting on the side of the new state. Pakistan was defeated on Dec. 16, 1971, and President Yahya Khan stepped down. Zulfikar Ali Bhutto took over Pakistan and accepted Bangladesh as an independent entity. In 1976 formal relations between India and Pakistan resumed.

Pakistan's first elections under civilian rule took place in March 1977, and the overwhelming victory of Bhutto's Pakistan People's Party (PPP) was denounced as fraudulent. A rising tide of violent protest and political deadlock led to a military takeover on July 5 by Gen. Mohammed Zia ul-Haq. Bhutto was tried and convicted for the 1974 murder of a political opponent, and despite worldwide protests was executed on April 4, 1979, touching off riots by his supporters. Zia declared himself president on Sept. 16, 1978, and ruled by martial law until Dec. 30, 1985. A measure of representative government was restored with the election of a new National Assembly in Feb. 1985, although leaders of opposition parties were banned from the election. On Aug. 19, 1988, President Zia was killed in a mid-air explosion of a Pakistani Air Force plane. Elections at the end of 1988 brought longtime Zia opponent Benazir Bhutto, daughter of Zulfikar Bhutto, into office as prime minister.

In the 1990s, Pakistan saw a shaky succession of governments. Benazir Bhutto was prime minister twice and dismissed each time by the president for incompetence or corruption. Nawaz Sharif's government is now in power for the third time. In April 1997 parliament amended the constitution to prevent a president from dismissing a government.

India's detonation of five nuclear tests in May 1998 near Pakistan's borders further deteriorated relations between the two countries, and in an act of nuclear brinksmanship, Pakistan evened the score by conducting nuclear tests of its own on May 28th and May 30th. In the fall of 1998 Pakistan indicated a willingness to sign a nuclear test ban treaty to rid itself of Western sanctions, which had been imposed since the nuclear testing. Pakistan began talks about the disputed territory of Kashmir, a major factor in its antagonistic relationship with India.

Palau

REPUBLIC OF PALAU

President: Kuniwo Nakamura (1993)
Total area: 177 sq mi. (458 sq km)
Population (1998 est.): 18,110 (average rate of natural increase: 1.96%); birth rate: 21.3/1000; infant mortality rate: 18.8/1000; density per sq mi.: 102
Capital and largest city (1995): Koror, 12,299. **Monetary unit:** U.S. dollar used. **Language:** Palauan is the official language, though English is commonplace. **Ethnicity/Race:** Palauans are a composite of Polynesian, Malayan, and Melanesian races. **Religion:** Christian. About one-third of the islanders observe Modekngei religion, indigenous to Palau. **Literacy rate:** 86%
Economic summary: GDP: (1994 est.): $81.8 million (note: GDP numbers reflect U.S. spending), $5,000 per capita. **Unemployment:** n.a. **Industry:** tourism, craft items (shell, wood, pearl), some commercial fishing, and agriculture (subsistence-level production of coconut, copra, cassava, sweet potatoes). **Exports:** $600,000 (f.o.b., 1989) trochus (a shellfish), tuna, copra, handicrafts. **Imports:** $24.6 million (c.i.f., 1989). **Major trading partners:** U.S., Japan.

Geography The Palau island chain consists of about 200 islands located in the western Pacific Ocean 528 mi. (650 km) southeast of the Philippines. The islands vary geologically from the high mountainous largest island, Babelthuap, to low, coral islands usually fringed by large barrier reefs.

Government A republic with a bicameral parliament. There is a 14-member Senate and a 16-member House of Delegates. Palau became a sovereign nation on Oct. 1, 1994.

History The Palau islands' position on the western threshold of Oceania and their proximity to Southeast Asia have led to the population being a mixture of Malay, Melanesian, Filipino, and Polynesian ancestry. Visited by the Spanish navigator Ruy López de Villalobos in 1543, the islands remained under nominal Spanish ownership for more than 300 years before Spain sold them to Germany in 1899. Japan occupied Palau during World War I and received a mandate over them from the League of Nations in 1920. It remained in Japanese control and served as an important naval base until the U.S. seized it during World War II. After the war it became a U.N. trusteeship (1947), administered by the U.S. Palau signed a compact of free association with the U.S. in 1992 requiring the U.S. to provide economic aid in exchange for the right to build and maintain U.S. military facilities in Palau. Palau became a sovereign state in 1994.

Panama

REPUBLIC OF PANAMA

National name: República de Panamá
President: Ernesto Pérez Balladares (1994)
Area: 29,761 sq mi. (78,200 sq km)
Population (1998 est.): 2,735,943 (average annual rate of natural increase: 1.56%); birth rate: 22/1000; infant mortality rate: 24/1000; density per sq mi.: 92
Capital and largest city (1993 est.): Panama City, 450,668. **Other large cities:** San Miguelito, 293,564; Colón, 137,825. **Monetary unit:** Balboa. **Language:** Spanish (official); many bilingual in English. **Ethnicity/Race:** mestizo (mixed Indian and European ancestry) 70%, West Indian 14%, white 10%, Indian 6%. **Religions:** Roman Catholic, over 93%; Protestant, 6%. **Literacy rate:** 89%
Economic summary: GDP/PPP (1996 est.): $14 billion; $5,300 per capita. **Real growth rate:** 1.5%. **Inflation:** 1.3%. **Unemployment:** 14%. **Arable land:** 7%. **Agriculture:** bananas, corn, sugar, rice, coffee. **Labor force:** 1.015 million (1996 est.); government and community services, 31.8%; agriculture, hunting, fishing, 26.8%; commerce, restaurants, hotels, 16.4%; manufacturing and mining, 9.4%; construction, 3.2%; transportation and communications, 6.2%; finance, insurance, and real estate, 4.3%. **Industry:** refined petroleum, sugar, cement, paper products. **Natural resources:** copper, mahogany, shrimp. **Exports:** $570 million (f.o.b., 1996 est.): bananas, sugar, shrimp, coffee, clothing. **Imports:** $2.512 billion (c.i.f., 1996 est.): petroleum, manufactured goods, machinery and transportation equipment, food, chemicals. **Major trading partners:** U.S., E.U., Central America and Caribbean, Japan.

Geography The southernmost of the Central American nations, Panama is south of Costa Rica and north of Colombia. The Panama Canal bisects the isthmus at its narrowest and lowest point, allowing passage from the Caribbean Sea to the Pacific Ocean. Panama is slightly smaller than South Carolina. It is marked by a chain of mountains in the west, moderate hills in the interior, and a low range on the east coast. There are extensive forests in the fertile Caribbean area.

Government Panama is a civilian republic, governed principally by the constitution of 1972, with major reforms adopted in 1983. The executive power is vested in the president and two vice presidents who exercise power jointly with a cabinet of

12 ministers of state appointed by the president. Presidents and vice presidents are elected for five-year terms and may not succeed themselves. The legislative function is exercised through the 72–member unicameral National Assembly. The legislators are elected for five-year terms by direct vote and can be re-elected.

History Visited by Columbus in 1502 on his fourth voyage and explored by Balboa in 1513, Panama was the principal transshipment point for Spanish treasure and supplies to and from South and Central America in colonial days. In 1821, when Central America revolted against Spain, Panama joined Colombia, which had already declared its independence. For the next 82 years, Panama attempted unsuccessfully to break away from Colombia. Between 1850 and 1900 Panama had 40 administrations, 50 riots, 5 attempted secessions, and 13 U.S. interventions. After U.S. proposals for canal rights over the narrow isthmus had been rejected by Colombia, Panama proclaimed its independence from Colombia with U.S. backing in 1903.

For canal rights in perpetuity, the U.S. paid Panama $10 million and agreed to pay $250,000 each year, which was increased to $430,000 in 1933. It was further increased under a revised treaty signed in 1955. In exchange, the U.S. got the Canal Zone—a 10-mile-wide strip across the isthmus—and a considerable degree of influence in Panama's affairs. Panama and the U.S. agreed in 1974 to negotiate the eventual reversion of the canal to Panama, despite strongly expressed opposition in the U.S. Congress. The texts of two treaties—one governing the transfer of the canal and the other guaranteeing its neutrality after transfer—were signed by President Omar Torrijos Herara and President Carter in Washington on Sept. 7. The new basic treaties provided for gradual transfer of the operations of the canal to Panamanians, the phasing out of U.S. military bases, and reversion of lands and waters used in the management of the canal. Similarly, Panama was to assume jurisdiction over the zone by degrees. A second pact promised an open and neutral canal in peace and war for all nations. The transfer was to be completed by Dec. 31, 1999. A Panamanian referendum approved the treaties in October, but further changes were insisted upon by the U.S. Senate. The principal change was a reservation specifying that despite the neutrality treaty's specification that only Panama shall maintain forces in its territory after transfer of the canal Dec. 31, 1999, the U.S. should have the right to use military force to keep the canal operating if it should become obstructed. The U.S. Senate approved the treaties in March–April 1978.

Nicolas Ardito Barletta, Panama's first directly elected President in 16 years, was inaugurated on Oct. 11, 1984, for a five-year term. He was a puppet of behind-the-scenes strong man Gen. Manuel Noriega and was replaced by Vice president Eric Arturo Delvalle, another Noriega supporter, a year later. In 1988, Noriega was indicted in the U.S. for drug trafficking, but when Delvalle attempted to fire him he forced the National Assembly to replace Delvalle with Manuel Solis Palma. In Dec. 1989, the Assembly named Noriega the "maximum leader" and declared the U.S. and Panama to be in a state of war. In Dec. 1989, 24,000 U.S. troops seized control of Panama City in an attempt to capture Noriega after a U.S. soldier was killed in Panama. On Jan. 3, 1990, Noriega surrendered himself to U.S. custody and was transported to Miami to stand trial for drug trafficking (he was subsequently convicted). Guillermo Endara, who probably would have won the election suppressed by Noriega, was installed as president.

Ernesto Pérez Balladares of the Democratic Revolutionary Party, whose campaign invoked memories of the party's founder, Omar Torrijos, won the May 1994 elections. In June 1997, a new law created an autonomous Canal Authority to administer the Panama Canal after the U.S. relinquishes its last controls over the waterway.

Panama Canal. First conceived by the Spaniards in 1524, when King Charles V of Spain ordered a survey of a waterway across the Isthmus, a construction concession was granted by the Colombian government in 1878 to St. Lucien N. B. Wyse, representing a French company. Two years later, the French Canal Company, inspired by Ferdinand de Lesseps, began construction of what was to have been a sea-level canal. The effort ended in bankruptcy nine years later and the United States ultimately paid the French $40 million for their rights and assets.

The U.S. project, built on territory controlled by the United States, and calling for the creation of an interior lake connected to both oceans by locks, got under way in 1904. Completed in 1914, the Canal is 50.7 miles long and lifts ships 85 feet above sea level through a series of three locks on the Pacific and Atlantic sides. Enlarged in later years, each lock now measures 1,000 feet in length, 110 feet in width, and 40 feet in depth of water. With waiting time, most ships require about 15 to 20 hours to negotiate passage.

Papua New Guinea

Sovereign: Queen Elizabeth II (1952)
Governor General: Silas Atopare (1997)
Prime Minister: Bill Skate (1997)
Area: 178,704 sq mi. (461,690 sq km)
Population (1998 est.): 4,599,785 (average annual rate of natural increase: 2.27%); birth rate: 32.4/1000; infant mortality rate: 57.1/1000; density per sq mi.: 26
Capital and largest city (1994 est.): Port Moresby, 250,000. **Monetary unit:** Kina. **Languages:** English, Tok Pisin (a Melanesian Creole English), Hiri Motu, and 717 distinct native languages. **Ethnicity/Race:** Papuan, Melanesian, Negrito, Micronesian, Polynesian. **Religions:** over half are Christian, remainder indigenous. **Literacy rate:** 50%
Economic summary: GDP/PPP (1996 est.): $10.7 billion; $2,400 per capita. **Real growth rate:** 2.3%. **Inflation:** 6%. **Unemployment:** n.a. **Labor force:** 1.941 million; agriculture, 64% (1993 est.). **Agriculture:** coffee, copra, palm oil, cocoa, tea, coconuts. **Industry:** coconut oil, plywood, wood chips, gold, silver. **Natural resources:** copper, gold, silver, timber, natural gas. **Exports:** $2.7 billion (f.o.b., 1995 est.): gold, copper, coffee, palm oil, copra, timber, lobster. **Imports:** $1.3 billion (c.i.f., 1995 est.): food, machinery, transport equipment, fuels, chemicals, consumer goods. **Major trading partners:** Australia, U.K., Japan, Singapore, New Zealand, U.S., South Korea, Germany. **Member of Commonwealth of Nations**

Geography Papua New Guinea occupies the eastern half of the island of New Guinea, just north of Australia, and many outlying islands. The Indonesian province of Irian Jaya is to the west. To the north and east are the islands of Manus, New Britain, New Ireland, and Bougainville, all part of Papua New Guinea. About one-tenth larger than California, its mountainous interior has only recently been explored. Two major rivers, the Sepik and the Fly, are navigable for shallow-draft vessels.

Government The 1975 constitution vests executive power in the national executive council, headed by the prime minister. The prime minister is the leader of the majority party in the single-chamber national parliament. The British monarch continues to be the nominal head of state and is represented by a governor-general who is a citizen of Papua New Guinea.

History It is believed that migrations from Southeast Asia via Indonesia to New Guinea occurred about 50,000 years ago. The earliest people on the island were hunter-gatherers; agriculture was introduced through later migratory movements. The eastern half of New Guinea was first visited by Spanish and Portuguese explorers in the 16th century, but a permanent European presence was not established until 1884, when Germany declared a protectorate over the northern coast and Britain took similar action in the south. Both nations formally annexed their protectorates and, in 1906, Britain transferred its rights to a newly independent Australia. Australian troops invaded German New Guinea in World War I and retained control under a League of Nations mandate. Papua New Guinea was invaded by Japanese forces in 1942. After being liberated by the Australians in 1945, it became a United Nations trusteeship, administered by Australia.

Australia granted limited home rule in 1951. Autonomy in internal affairs came nine years later. In Dec. 1973, Papua New Guinea became self-governing; it achieved complete independence from Britain in Sept. 1975, becoming, at that time, a full member of the Commonwealth. In 1989, guerrillas of the Bougainville Revolutionary Army (BRA) closed the island's copper mine, a major source of revenue for the country. In 1990, the BRA declared Bougainville's independence, whereupon the government blockaded the island until Jan. 1991, when a peace treaty was signed. In 1997, Papua New Guinea's government hired South African mercenary soldiers to fight on the island of Bougainville in order to end the long-running secessionist crisis. On July 17, 1998, an earthquake-triggered tsunami (tidal wave) off the northern coast of Papua New Guinea killed at least 1,500 people and left thousands more injured and homeless.

Paraguay

REPUBLIC OF PARAGUAY

National name: República del Paraguay
President: Raúl Cubas Grau (1998)
Area: 157,047 sq mi. (406,750 sq km)
Population (1998 est.): 5,291,020 (average annual rate of natural increase: 2.27%); birth rate: 32.2/1000; infant mortality rate: 37.4/1000; density per sq mi.: 34
Capital and largest city (1992): Asunción, 502,426. **Other large cities (1992):** Ciudad del Este, 133,893; San Lorenzo, 133,311. **Monetary unit:** Guaraní. **Languages:** Spanish (official), Guaraní. **Ethnicity/Race:** mestizo (mixed Spanish and Indian) 95%, whites plus Amerindians 5%. **Religion:** Roman Catholic, 90%. **Literacy rate:** 90%
Economic summary: GDP/PPP (1996 est.): $17.7 billion; $3,200 per capita. **Real growth rate:** 1.5%. **Inflation:** 8.2% (Dec. 1996). **Unemployment:** 5.3% (urban 1995). **Arable land:** 6%. **Agriculture:** soybeans, cotton, timber, cassava, tobacco, corn, rice, sugar cane. **Labor force** (1995 est.), 1.8 million; agriculture, 45%. **Industry:** packed meats, crushed oilseeds, beverages, textiles, light consumer goods, cement. **Natural resources:** iron ore, timber, manganese, limestone, hydropower. **Exports:** $819.5 million (f.o.b., 1995): cotton, soybeans, meat products, timber, coffee, tung oil, vegetable oils. **Imports:** $2.871 billion (c.i.f., 1995): fuels and lubricants, beverages, tobacco, foodstuffs, capital goods, consumer goods, fuels and lubricants. **Major trading partners:** Argentina, Brazil, U.S., E.U., Japan.

Geography California-size Paraguay is surrounded by Brazil, Bolivia, and Argentina in south central South America. Eastern Paraguay, between the Paraná and Paraguay Rivers, is upland country with the thickest population settled on the grassy slope that inclines toward the Paraguay River. The greater part of the Chaco region to the west is covered with marshes, lagoons, dense forests, and jungles.

Government The president is elected by popular vote for five-year terms and is barred from seeking reelection. The legislature is bicameral, consisting of a Senate of 45 members and a Chamber of Representatives of 80 members who all serve five-year terms concurrent with the president. There is also a Council of State, whose members are nominated by the government.

History Indian tribes speaking the Guaraní language occupied Paraguay long before the arrival of the Europeans. In 1526 and again in 1529, Sebastian Cabot explored Paraguay when he sailed up the Paraná and Paraguay Rivers. From 1608 until their expulsion from the Spanish dominions in 1767, the Jesuits maintained an extensive establishment in the south and east of Paraguay. In 1811, Paraguay revolted against Spanish rule and became a nominal republic under two consuls.

Paraguay was governed by three dictators during the first 60 years of independence. The third, Francisco López, waged war against Brazil and Argentina in 1865–70, a conflict in which the male population was almost wiped out. A new constitution in 1870, designed to prevent dictatorships and internal strife, failed to do so, and not until 1912 did a period of comparative economic and political stability begin. The Chaco War (1932–35) with Bolivia won Paraguay more western territory.

After World War II, politics became particularly unstable. Alfredo Stroessner ruled under a state of siege from 1954 until 1965, when the dictatorship was relaxed and exiles returned. The constitution was revised in 1967 to permit Stroessner to be re-elected. The Stroessner regime was criticized by the U.S. during the Carter administration as a violator of human rights, but unlike Argentina and Uruguay, Paraguay did not suffer cuts in U.S. military aid. Stroessner was overthrown by an army leader, Gen. Andres Rodriguez, in 1989. Rodriguez won in

Paraguay's first multi-candidate election in decades. Paraguay's new constitution went into effect in 1992. In 1993, Juan Carlos Wasmosy, a wealthy businessman and the candidate of the governing Colorado Party won a five-year term in freely held elections. In June 1997, a banking crisis struck Paraguay, involving the president, his entire government, and the central bank president. Raúl Cubas Grau was elected president in May 1998.

Peru

REPUBLIC OF PERU

National name: República del Perú
President: Alberto Fujimori (1990)
Prime Minister: Alberto Pandolfi (1998)
Area: 496,222 sq mi. (1,285,220 sq km)
Population (1998 est.): 26,111,110 (average annual rate of natural increase: 1.97%); birth rate: 26.7/1000; infant mortality rate: 43.4/1000; density per sq mi.: 53
Capital and largest city : Lima: city proper (1993 est.) 5,706,127; metro. area (1995 est.) 7,452,000. **Other large cities:** Arequipa, 939,800; Callao, 648,000; Trujillo, 1,287,000; Chiclayo, 951,000. **Monetary unit:** Nuevo Sol (1991). **Languages:** Spanish, Québchua, Aymara, and other native languages. **Ethnicity/Race:** Indian 45%, mestizo (mixed Indian and European ancestry) 37%, white 15%, black, Japanese, Chinese, and other 3%. **Religion:** Roman Catholic. **Literacy rate:** 85%
Economic summary: GDP/PPP (1996 est.): $92 billion; $3,800 (est.) per capita. **Real growth rate:** 2.8%. **Inflation:** 11.5% (1996). **Unemployment:** 8.2%, extensive underemployed (1996). **Arable land:** 3%. **Agriculture:** wheat, potatoes, beans, rice, sugar, cotton, coffee. **Labor force:** 7.6 million (1996 est.); government and other services, agriculture, industry. **Products:** processed minerals, fish meal, refined petroleum, textiles. **Natural resources:** silver, gold, iron, copper, fish, petroleum, timber. **Exports:** $6 billion (f.o.b., 1996): copper, fish products, cotton, sugar, coffee, lead, silver, zinc, oil. **Imports:** $7.5 billion (f.o.b., 1996): machinery, foodstuffs, chemicals, pharmaceuticals, transport equipment. **Major trading partners:** U.S., Japan, Western European, and Latin American countries.

Geography Peru, in western South America, extends for nearly 1,500 miles (2,414 km) along the Pacific Ocean. Colombia and Ecuador are to the north, Brazil and Bolivia to the east, and Chile to the south. Five-sixths the size of Alaska, Peru is divided by the Andes Mountains into three sharply differentiated zones. To the west is the coastline, much of it arid, extending 50 to 100 miles (80 to 160 km) inland. The mountain area, with peaks over 20,000 feet (6,096 m), lofty plateaus, and deep valleys, lies centrally. Beyond the mountains to the east is the heavily forested slope leading to the Amazonian plains.

Government A republic. A presidential emergency declaration in April 1992 suspended the constitution, imposed censorship and political restrictions, and instituted rule by decree. A new constitution, promulgated in 1993, grants enhanced executive power to the president, who is directly elected to a five-year term and is permitted to seek immediate reelection. The president governs with the assistance of a Council of Ministers, appointed by the president. A unicameral 120-member congress is also elected by universal suffrage for five-year terms.

History Peru was once part of the great Incan empire and later the major vice-royalty of Spanish South America. It was conquered in 1531–33 by Francisco Pizarro. On July 28, 1821, Peru proclaimed its independence, but the Spanish were not finally defeated until 1824. For a hundred years thereafter, revolutions were frequent; a new war was fought with Spain in 1864–66, and unsuccessful war was fought with Chile from 1879 to 1883 (the War of the Pacific).

Peru emerged from 20 years of dictatorship in 1945 with the inauguration of President José Luis Bustamente y Rivero after the first free election in many decades. But he served for only three years and was succeeded in turn by Gen. Manual A. Odria, Manuel Prado y Ugarteche, and Fernando Belaúnde Terry. On Oct. 3, 1968, Belaúnde was overthrown by Gen. Juan Velasco Alvarado. Velasco nationalized the nation's second biggest bank and turned two large newspapers over to Marxists in 1970, but he also allowed a new agreement with a copper-mining consortium of four American firms. In 1975, Velasco was replaced in a bloodless coup by his premier, Gen. Francisco Morales Bermudez, who promised to restore civilian government. In elections held on May 18, 1980, Belaunde Terry, the last previous civilian president and the candidate of the conservative parties that have traditionally ruled Peru, was elected president again.

Peru's fragile democracy survived this period of stress. In 1985, Belaunde Terry was the first elected president to turn over power to a constitutionally elected successor since 1945. Alberto Fujimori won the 1990 elections. Citing continuing terrorism, drug trafficking, and corruption, Fujimori in April 1992 dissolved Congress, suspended the constitution, and imposed censorship. A new constitution was approved in 1993. In Jan. 1995 fighting flared once again along part of the poorly defined border with Ecuador. In April, President Fujimori was re-elected, and his party (Change 90–New Majority) obtained a majority in the legislature.

In Dec. 1996, Tupac Amaru rebels seized control of the diplomatic compound of the Japanese ambassador's residence in Lima, holding 72 hostages. The standoff continued until April when government forces successfully stormed the residence, freeing the hostages. In the months that followed Fujimori came under fire for his increasingly authoritarian style. The disastrous El Niño of 1997 caused the failure of the fish harvest and a severe drought in Peru.

The Philippines

REPUBLIC OF THE PHILIPPINES

National name: Republika ng Pilipinas
President: Joseph Estrada (1998)
Area: 115,830 sq mi. (300,000 sq km)
Population (1998 est.): 77,725,862 (average annual rate of natural increase: 2.09%); birth rate: 28.4/1000; infant mortality rate: 34.6/1000; density per sq mi.: 671
Capital and largest city : Manila: city proper (1995 est.) 1,654,761; metro. area (1995 est.) 9,280,000. **Other large cities:** Quezon City, 1,669,776; Cebu, 610,415. **Monetary unit:** Peso. **Languages:** Filipino (based on Tagalog), English; regional languages: Tagalog, Ilocano, Cebuano, others. **Ethnicity/Race:** Christian Malay 91.5%, Muslim Malay 4%, Chinese 1.5%, other 3%. **Religions:** Roman Catholic, 84%; Protestant,

10%; Islam, 5%; Buddhist and other, 3%. **Literacy rate:** 94%

Economic summary: GDP/PPP (1996 est.): $194.2 billion; $2,600 per capita. **Real growth rate:** 5.5%. **Inflation:** 8.4% (1996). **Unemployment:** 8.6% (1996). **Arable land:** 19%. **Agriculture:** rice, corn, coconuts, sugar cane, bananas, pineapple. **Labor force:** 29.13 million; agriculture, 43.4%; services, 22.6%; industry and commerce, 16.1% (1995). **Products:** textiles, pharmaceuticals, chemicals, food processing, electronics assembly. **Natural resources:** forests, crude oil, metallic and non-metallic minerals. **Exports:** $20.5 billion (f.o.b., 1996): electrical equipment, coconut products, chemicals, logs and lumber, copper concentrates, nickel. **Imports:** $33.3 billion (f.o.b., 1996): petroleum, industrial equipment, raw materials. **Major trading partners:** U.S., Japan, E.U., Taiwan, Saudi Arabia.

Geography The Philippine Islands are an archipelago of over 7,000 islands lying about 500 miles (805 km) off the southeast coast of Asia. The overall land area is comparable to that of Arizona. Only about 7% of the islands are larger than one square mile, and only one-third have names. The largest are Luzon in the north (40,420 sq mi.; 104,687 sq km), Mindanao in the south (36,537 sq mi.; 94,631 sq km), Samar (5,124 sq mi.; 13,271 sq km). The islands are of volcanic origin, with the larger ones crossed by mountain ranges. The highest peak is Mount Apo (9,690 ft.; 2,954 m) on Mindanao.

Government On Feb. 2, 1987, the Filipino people voted for a new constitution that established a 24-seat Senate and a 250-seat House of Representatives and gave the president a six-year term. It limits the powers of the president, who cannot be reelected.

History Ferdinand Magellan, the Portuguese navigator in the service of Spain, explored the Philippines in 1521. Twenty-one years later, a Spanish exploration party named the group of islands in honor of Prince Philip, who was later to become Philip II of Spain. Spain retained possession of the islands for the next 350 years.

The Philippines were ceded to the U.S. in 1899 by the Treaty of Paris after the Spanish-American War. Meanwhile, the Filipinos, led by Emilio Aguinaldo, had declared their independence. They initiated guerrilla warfare against U.S. troops which persisted until the capture of Aguinaldo in 1901. By 1902, peace was established except among the Islamic Moros on the southern island of Mindanao.

The first U.S. civilian governor-general was William Howard Taft (1901–04). The Jones Law (1916) provided for the establishment of a Philippine Legislature composed of an elective Senate and House of Representatives. The Tydings-McDuffie Act (1934) provided for a transitional period until 1946, at which time the Philippines would become completely independent. Under a constitution approved by the people of the Philippines in 1935, the Commonwealth of the Philippines came into being with Manuel Quezon y Molina as president.

On Dec. 8, 1941, the islands were invaded by Japanese troops. Following the fall of Gen. Douglas MacArthur's forces at Bataan and Corregidor, Quezon established a government-in-exile which he headed until his death in 1944. He was succeeded by Vice President Sergio Osmeña. U.S. forces under MacArthur reinvaded the Philippines in Oct. 1944 and, after the liberation of Manila in Feb. 1945, Osmeña reestablished the government.

The Philippines achieved full independence on July 4, 1946. Manual A. Roxas y Acuña was elected its first president, succeeded by Elpidio Quirino (1948–53), Ramón Magsaysay (1953–57). Carlos P. García (1957–61), Diosdado Macapagal (1961–65), Ferdinand E. Marcos (1965–86).

Under Marcos, civil unrest broke out in opposition to the leader's despotic rule. Martial law was declared on Sept. 21, 1972, and Marcos proclaimed a new constitution that ensconced himself as president. Martial law was officially lifted on Jan. 17, 1981, but Marcos and his wife Imelda retained broad powers.

Despite warnings that his life would be endangered, opposition leader Benigno S. Aquino returned to the Philippines from self-exile on Aug. 21, 1983. He was shot to death as he was being escorted from his plane by military police at Manila International Airport. There was widespread suspicion that Marcos had ordered Aquino's assassination. The event became a watershed in modern Philippines political history, acting as a catalyst for opposition groups and the "People Power" movement, led by the late leader's widow, Corazon Aquino.

In an attempt to re-secure American support, Marcos set presidential elections for Feb. 7, 1986. With the support of the Catholic church, Corazon Aquino declared her candidacy. Marcos was declared the official winner, but independent observers reported widespread election fraud and vote-rigging. Anti-Marcos protests exploded in the capital Manila, Defense Minister Juan Enrile and Lt. Gen. Fidel Ramos defected to the opposition, and Marcos lost virtually all support; he was forced to flee into exile and entered the U.S. on Feb. 25, 1986.

The Aquino government survived coup attempts by Marcos supporters and other right-wing elements, including one in November by Enrile. Legislative elections on May 11, 1987, gave pro-Aquino candidates a large majority. Negotiations on renewal of leases for U.S. military bases threatened to sour relations between the two countries. Volcanic eruptions from Mount Pinatubo, however, severely damaged Clark Air Base, and in July 1991 the U.S. decided simply to abandon it.

In elections of May 1992 Gen. Fidel Ramos, who had the support of outgoing Aquino, won the presidency in a seven-way race. In September of that year, the U.S. Navy turned over the Subic Bay naval base to the Philippincs, ending a long-standing U.S. military presence. Meanwhile, the separatist Moro National Liberation Front was fighting a protracted war for an Islamic homeland on Mindinao, the southernmost of the two main islands. In 1996, the group agreed to a government plan designed to grant it a greater degree of political autonomy. An administrative body, headed by the former rebel chief, was established to oversee development on the southern islands. Although frequent and violent clashes continue between the army and another rebel group, the Moro Islamic Liberation Front, separate peace talks were ongoing in 1998.

Even as the Philippines experienced a somewhat lower rate of growth than many of its Asian neighbors throughout the 1990s, it was also spared the brunt of the region's financial crisis following a wave of currency devaluations sparked in July 1997.

In May 1998, 61-year-old former action film star Joseph Estrada was elected president of the Philippines, succeeding Fidel Ramos, who declined to contest elections.

Poland

REPUBLIC OF POLAND

National name: Rzeczpospolita Polska
President: Aleksander Kwasniewski (1995)
Prime Minister: Jerzy Buzek (1997)
Area: 120,727 sq mi. (312,683 sq km)
Population (1998 est.): 38,606,922 (average annual rate of natural increase: –0.04%); birth rate: 9.8/1000; infant mortality rate: 13.2/1000; density per sq mi.: 320
Capital and largest city (1994 est.): Warsaw, 1,642,700. **Other large cities:** Lodz, 833,700; Krakow, 745,100; Wroclaw, 642,300; Poznan, 582,800; Gdansk, 463,100; Szczecin, 417,700. **Monetary unit:** Zloty. **Language:** Polish. **Ethnicity/Race:** Polish 97.6%, German 1.3%, Ukrainian 0.6%, Belarussian 0.5% (1990 est.). **Religions:** Roman Catholic, 95% (about 75% practicing); Russian Orthodox, Protestant, and other, 5%. **Literacy rate:** 98%
Economic summary: GDP/PPP (1996 est.): $246.3 billion; $6,400 per capita. **Real growth rate:** 6%. **Inflation:** 18.8%. **Unemployment:** 13.3% (year end 1996). **Arable land:** 47%. **Agriculture:** rye, rapeseed, potatoes, hogs and other livestock. **Labor force:** 17.662 million (1996 est.); industry and construction, 32%, agriculture, 27.6%; trade, transport and communications, 14.7% (1992). **Products:** iron and steel, chemicals, textiles, processed foods, machine building. **Natural resources:** coal, sulfur, copper, natural gas. **Exports:** $30.9 billion (f.o.b., 1995): coal, machinery and equipment, industrial products, chemicals, metals. **Imports:** $34.6 billion (f.o.b., 1995): machinery and equipment, fuels, agricultural and food products, chemicals. **Major trading partners:** E.U., Russia, former Soviet republics, other eastern European countries

Geography Poland, a country the size of New Mexico, is in north central Europe. Most of the country is a plain with no natural boundaries except the Carpathian Mountains in the south and the Oder and Neisse Rivers in the west. Other major rivers, which are important to commerce, are the Vistula, Warta, and Bug.

Government Voters approved a new constitution in May 1997 that upholds a market economy, private ownership of land, personal freedoms, and clear divisions of power within the branches of the government. The supreme organ of state authority is the Sejm (parliament), which is composed of 460 members elected for four years and a 100–member senate (Senat).

History The year C.E. 966 is accepted as the founding date of Poland, when the Piast ruler of Great (northern) Poland, Mieszko I, adopted Christianity. A few decades later, the tribes of southern Poland united into Little Poland. In C.E. 1047 both Great Poland and Little Poland recognized Casimir I the Restorer as their monarch. Poland was united with Lithuania by royal marriage in 1386. The Polish-Lithuanian state reached the peak of its power between the 14th and 16th centuries, scoring military successes against the (Germanic) Knights of the Teutonic Order, the Russians, and the Ottoman Turks. Swedish and Russian invasions of Poland in 1655 began a period of continuing conflicts between the Commonwealth and those nations. Internally, the Polish-Lithuanian state succumbed to economic stagnation and social conflicts between Roman Catholic and Orthodox Poles.

Lack of a strong monarchy enabled Russia, Prussia, and Austria to carry out a first partition of the country in 1772, a second in 1792, and a third in 1795. For more than a century thereafter, there was no Polish state, just Austrian, Prussian, and Russian sectors, but the Poles never ceased their efforts to regain their independence. The Polish people revolted against Russian, Prussian, and Austrian dominance throughout the 19th century. Poland was formally reconstituted in Nov. 1918, with Marshal Josef Pilsudski as Chief of State. In 1919, Ignace Paderewski, the famous pianist and patriot, became the first premier. In 1926, Pilsudski seized complete power in a coup and ruled dictatorially until his death on May 12, 1935.

Despite a 10-year nonaggression pact signed in 1934, Hitler attacked Poland on Sept. 1, 1939. Soviet troops invaded from the east on Sept. 17, and on Sept. 28 a German-Soviet agreement divided Poland between the U.S.S.R. and Germany. Wladyslaw Raczkiewicz formed a government-in-exile in France, which moved to London after France's defeat in 1940. All of Poland was occupied by Germany after the Nazi attack on the U.S.S.R. in June 1941. Nazi Germany's occupation policy in Poland was designed to eradicate Polish culture through mass executions and to exterminate the country's large Jewish minority.

The Polish government-in-exile was replaced with the Communist-dominated Polish Committee of National Liberation by the Soviet Union in 1944. Moving to Lublin after that city's liberation, it proclaimed itself the Provisional Government of Poland. Some former members of the Polish government in London joined with the Lublin government to form the Polish Government of National Unity, which Britain and the U.S. recognized. On Aug. 2, 1945, in Berlin, President Harry S. Truman, Joseph Stalin, and Prime Minister Clement Attlee of Britain established a new de facto western frontier for Poland along the Oder and Neisse Rivers. (The border was finally agreed to by West Germany in a nonaggression pact signed Dec. 7, 1970.) On Aug. 16, 1945, the U.S.S.R. and Poland signed a treaty delimiting the Soviet-Polish frontier. Under these agreements, Poland was shifted westward. In the east it lost 69,860 square miles (180,934 sq km); in the west it gained (subject to final peace-conference approval) 38,986 square miles (100,973 sq km).

A new constitution in 1952 made Poland a "people's democracy" of the Soviet type. In 1955, Poland became a member of the Warsaw Treaty Organization, and its foreign policy became identical to that of the U.S.S.R. The government undertook persecution of the Roman Catholic Church as a remaining source of opposition. Wladyslaw Gomulka was elected leader of the United Workers (Communist) Party in 1956. He denounced the Stalinist terror, ousted many Stalinists, and improved relations with the church. Most collective farms were dissolved, and the press became freer. A strike that began in shipyards and spread to other industries in August 1980 produced a stunning victory for workers when the economically hard-pressed government accepted for the first time in a Marxist state the right of workers to organize in independent unions.

Led by Solidarity, a free union founded by Lech Walesa, workers launched a drive for liberty and improved conditions. A national strike for a five-day week in Jan. 1981 led to the dismissal of Premier Pinkowski and the naming of the fourth premier in less than a year, Gen. Wojciech Jaruzelski. Martial law was declared on Dec. 13, when Walesa and other Solidarity leaders were arrested. It formally ended in 1984 but the government retained emergency powers. Increasing opposition to the government because of the failing economy led to a new wave of strikes in 1988. Unable to totally quell the dissent, the government relegalized Solidarity and allowed it to compete in elections.

Solidarity members won a stunning victory in 1989, taking almost all the seats in the Senate and all of the 169 seats they were allowed to contest in the Sejm. This gave them substantial influence in the new government. Taduesz Mazowiecki was appointed prime minister. Solidarity leader Lech Walesa won the presidential election of 1990 with 74% of the vote. In 1991, the first fully free parliamentary election since World War II resulted in representation for 29 political parties. In the second democratic parliamentary election of Sept. 1993 voters returned power to ex-Communists and their allies. In 1995, Aleksander Kwasniewski, leader of the successor to the Communist Party, won the presidency over Walesa, despite strong support for Walesa from the church. In 1997, the Solidarity Electoral Action (AWS), a loose coalition of some 30 right-wing groups dominated by the Solidarity trade union, handily defeated the former communists. Also in 1997, the Polish parliament voted to abolish the death penalty.

Portugal

REPUBLIC OF PORTUGAL

National name: República Portuguesa
President: Jorge Sampaio (1996)
Prime Minister: Antonio Guterres (1995)
Area: 35,550 sq mi. (92,080 sq km)
Population (1998 est.): 9,927,556 (average annual rate of natural increase: –0.07%); birth rate: 10.6/1000; infant mortality rate: 6.9/1000; density per sq mi.: 279
Capital and largest city (1991): Lisbon, 677,790. **Other large city (1991):** Oporto, 350,000. **Monetary unit:** Escudo. **Language:** Portuguese. **Ethnicity/Race:** Homogeneous Mediterranean stock in mainland, Azores, Madeira Islands; citizens of black African descent who immigrated to mainland during decolonization number less than 100,000. **Religions:** Roman Catholic 97%, 1% Protestant, 2% other. **Literacy rate:** 85%
Economic summary: GDP/PPP (1996 est.): $122.1 billion; $12,400 per capita. **Real growth rate:** 2.5%. **Inflation:** 3.4%. **Unemployment:** 7%. **Arable land:** 26%. **Agriculture:** grains, potatoes, olives, wine grapes. **Labor force** (1996 est.), 4.53 million; services, 54.5%; manufacturing, 24.4%; agriculture, forestry and fisheries, 11.2%; construction, 8.3%; utilities, 1.0%; mining, 0.5% (1992). **Products:** textiles, footwear, wood pulp, paper, cork, metal products, refined oil, chemicals, canned fish, wine. **Natural resources:** fish, cork, tungsten, iron ore. **Exports:** $25.8 billion (f.o.b., 1996): cotton, textiles, cork and cork products, canned fish, wine, timber and timber products, resin, machinery, appliances. **Imports:** $34.2 billion (c.i.f., 1996): machinery and transport equipment, agricultural products, chemicals, petroleum, textiles. **Major trading partners:** E.U., U.S.

Geography Portugal occupies the western part of the Iberian Peninsula and is slightly smaller than Indiana. The country is crossed by three large rivers that rise in Spain, flow into the Atlantic, and divide the country into three geographic areas. The Minho River, part of the northern boundary, cuts through a mountainous area that extends south to the vicinity of the Douro River. South of the Douro, the mountains slope to the plains about the Tejo River. The remaining division is the southern one of Alentejo. The Azores, stretching over 340 miles (547 km) in the Atlantic, consist of nine islands divided into three groups, with a total area of 902 square miles (2,335 sq km). The Azores are an important station on Atlantic air routes, and Britain and the U.S. established airbases there during World War II. Madeira, consisting of two inhabited islands, Madeira and Porto Santo, and two groups of uninhabited islands, lie in the Atlantic about 535 miles (861 km) southwest of Lisbon. The Madeiras are 307 square miles (796 sq km) in area.

Government A republic. The president is elected for a five-year term; the unicameral legislature (the Assembly of the Republic) comprises 250 members who are elected for four years. The president names the prime minister, who must have the support of the majority of the Assembly.

History In the 1st millennium B.C.E., Celtic peoples settled the peninsula, frequently intermarrying with the indigenous population to form the Celtiberians. Despite their fierce resistance, the Roman Empire subdued them in about 140 B.C.E. Portugal was a part of Moorish Spain until it won its independence in the middle of the 12th century. King John I (1385–1433) unified his country at the expense of the Castilians and the Moors of Morocco. The expansion of Portugal was brilliantly coordinated by John's son, Prince Henry the Navigator. In 1488, Bartolomew Diaz reached the Cape of Good Hope, proving that Asia was accessible by sea. In 1498, Vasco da Gama reached the west coast of India. By the middle of the 16th century, the Portuguese Empire extended to West and East Africa, Brazil, Persia, Indochina, and Malaya.

In 1581, Philip II of Spain invaded Portugal and held it for 60 years, precipitating a catastrophic decline of Portuguese commerce. Courageous and shrewd explorers, the Portuguese proved to be inefficient and corrupt colonizers. By the time the Portuguese monarchy was restored in 1640, Dutch, English, and French competitors began to seize the lion's share of the world's colonies and commerce. Portugal retained Angola and Mozambique in Africa, and Brazil (until 1822).

The corrupt King Carlos, who ascended the throne in 1889, made Joao Franco the premier with dictatorial power in 1906. In 1908, Carlos and his heir were shot dead on the streets of Lisbon. The new king, Manoel II, was driven from the throne in the revolution of 1910 and Portugal became a

French-style republic. Traditionally friendly to Britain, Portugal fought in World War I on the Allied side in Africa as well as on the Western Front. Weak postwar governments and a revolution in 1926 brought Antonio Oliveira Salazar to power. As minister of finance (1928–40) and premier (1932–68), Salazar ruled Portugal as a virtual dictator. He kept Portugal neutral in World War II but gave the Allies naval and air bases after 1943. Portugal joined NATO as a founding member in 1949 but did not gain admission to the United Nations until 1955.

Portugal's foreign and colonial policies met with increasing difficulty both at home and abroad beginning in the 1950s—the bloodiest and most protracted wars against colonialism in Africa were fought against the Portuguese. Portugal lost the tiny remnants of its Indian empire—Goa, Daman, and Diu—to Indian military occupation in 1961, the year an insurrection broke out in Angola. For the next 13 years, Salazar, who died in 1970, and his successor, Marcello Caetano, fought independence movements amid growing world criticism. Leftists in the armed forces, weary of a losing battle, launched a successful revolution on April 25, 1974. After the 1974 revolution, the new military junta gave up its territories, beginning with Portuguese Guinea in Sept. 1974, which became the Republic of Guinea-Bissau. The decolonization of the Cape Verde Islands and Mozambique was effected in July 1975. Angola achieved independence later that same year, thus ending a colonial involvement in that continent that had begun in 1415. Full-scale, internationalized civil war, however, followed Portugal's departure from Angola, and Indonesia forcibly annexed briefly independent East Timor. Also in that year, the government nationalized banking, transport, heavy industries, and the media. Portugal continued to experience social, economic, and political upheavals for the next decade.

Portugal was admitted to the European Economic Community (now European Union) on Jan. 1, 1986, and on Feb. 16, Mario Soares became the country's first civilian president in 60 years. Aníbal Cavaço Silva, an advocate of free-market economics and the Social Democratic candidate, was elected as prime minister in 1985, signalling a more politically stable era. General elections in Oct. 1995 went to the Socialist Party, which fell just short of an absolute majority in the Assembly. Lisbon mayor Jorge Sampaio, a socialist, won the race for president in Jan. 1996. Portugal's socialist government continued to take advantage of rosy economic conditions in 1997 as it appeared increasingly likely that the country would become a founding member of the European economic and monetary union (EMU) at the scheduled Jan. 1, 1999, start date.

Portuguese Overseas Territory

Macau

Status: Territory
Governor: Vasco Rocha Vieira (1991)
Area: 6 sq mi. (15.5 sq km)
Population (1998 est.): 429,152 (average annual growth rate: 1.91%); birth rate: 12.8/1000; infant mortality rate: 4.4/1000; density per sq mi.: 71,525
Capital (1991): Macao, 326,460. **Monetary unit:** Patacá. **Languages:** Portuguese and Chinese (Cantonese) are both official languages. **Ethnicity/Race:** Chinese 95%, Portuguese 3%, other 2%. **Religions:** Buddhist 45%, Roman Catholic 7%, Protestant 1%, none 45.8%, other 1.2%. **Literacy rate (1981):** 90%
Economic summary: GDP/PPP (1996 est.): $6.8 billion; $13,600 per capita. **Real growth rate:** 4%. **Inflation:** 5.5% (first half 1996). **Industry:** clothing, textiles, plastics, furniture. **Exports:** $1.99 billion (f.o.b., 1996 est.): textiles, clothing, toys. **Imports:** $1.99 billion (c.i.f., 1996 est.): raw materials, foodstuffs, capital goods. **Major trading partners:** Hong Kong, China, U.S., E.U., Japan.

Macau comprises the peninsula of Macau and the two small islands of Taipa and Colôane on the South China coast, about 35 miles (53 km) from Hong Kong. Established by the Portuguese in 1557, it is the oldest European outpost in China, but Portugal's sovereign rights to the port were not recognized by China until 1887. The port has been eclipsed in importance by Hong Kong, but it is still a busy distribution center and also has an important fishing industry. Tourism is an extremely important factor in Macau's economy, and the colony in effect serves as the playground of nearby Hong Kong. Chinese culture predominates, overlaid by a veneer of Portuguese architecture and customs. In 1987, Portugal and China reached an agreement to return Macau to Chinese rule on Dec. 20, 1999. They agreed upon provisions to insure the autonomy of Macau, including its right to elect local leaders, the right of its residents to travel freely, and the right to maintain its way of life for 50 years after the start of Chinese rule.

Qatar

STATE OF QATAR

Emir: Sheikh Hamad bin Khalifa al-Thani (1995)
Prime Minister: Abdullah bin Khalifa al-Thani (1996)
Area: 4,000 sq mi. (11,000 sq km)
Population (1998 est.): 697,126 (average annual rate of natural increase: 3.82%); birth rate: 17/1000; infant mortality rate: 18.1/1000; density per sq mi.: 174
Capital (1990 est.): Doha, 300,000. **Monetary unit:** Qatari riyal. **Language:** Arabic; English is also widely spoken. **Ethnicity/Race:** Arab 40%, Pakistani 18%, Indian 18%, Iranian 10%, other 14%. **Religion:** Islam, 95%. **Literacy rate:** 76%
Economic summary: GDP/PPP (1996 est.): $11.7 billion; $21,300 per capita. **Real growth rate:** 2.5%. **Inflation:** 1.2% (1995). **Unemployment:** n.a. **Labor force:** 233,000 (1993 est.) 83.49% of the population is non-national. **Industry:** oil. While Qatar depends on oil for much of its revenue, the government is increasing the development of its natural gas production. Qatar is one of the five leading gas producers in the world. **Natural resources:** oil, gas. **Exports:** $4 billion (f.o.b., 1996 est.): petroleum products 85%; steel, fertilizers. **Imports:** $4.4 billion (f.o.b., 1996 est.): machinery and equipment, consumer goods, food, chemicals. **Major trading partners:** France, U.K., U.S., Germany, Japan, Brazil, South Korea, U.A.E.

Geography Qatar occupies a small peninsula that extends into the Persian Gulf from the east side of the Arabian Peninsula. Saudi Arabia is to the west and the United Arab Emirates to the south. The country is mainly barren.

Government Qatar is a traditional monarchy. The constitution promulgated in April 1970 and revised since declared Qatar an independent and sovereign state with executive power vested in the emir, who holds the post of prime minister.

History The rift between the sheikhs of Bahrain and their nominal subjects on Qatar grew, and in 1867 full-scale war broke out. Bahrain routed the Qataris and in the following year the British, concerned about the unrest in the area and the frequent outbreaks of piracy, installed Muhammad ibn Thani Al Thani, scion of the leading family in Qatar, as ruling sheikh. After the decline of the Turkish Ottoman Empire's influence in the Persian Gulf in 1916, the Emir accepted British protection. After the discovery of oil in the 1940s and its exploitation in the 1950s and 1960s, political unrest spread to the sheikhdoms. The State of Qatar declared independence in 1971, when the British protectorate was terminated. The Emir agreed to the deployment of Arab and Western forces in Qatar following the Iraqi invasion of Kuwait in 1991.

A border dispute erupted with Saudi Arabia that was settled in Dec. 1992. A territorial dispute with Bahrain over the Hawar Islands remains unresolved, however. In 1994, Qatar signed a defense pact with the U.S., becoming the third Gulf state to do so. In June 1995 Crown Prince Hamad bin Khalifa al-Thani asked his father, the Emir, to leave the country. The Emir was not stripped of his title, and much of the power was already in the son's hands. The dispute between Qatar and Bahrain over control of a number of islands in the Persian Gulf cooled off in 1997 after both sides agreed to let the International Court of Justice decide the issue.

Romania

REPUBLIC OF ROMANIA

President: Emil Constantinescu (1996)
Prime Minister: Radu Vasile (1998)
Area: 91,700 sq mi. (237,500 sq km)
Population (1998 est.): 22,395,848 (average annual rate of natural increase: –0.32%); birth rate: 9.33/1000; infant mortality rate: 18.8/1000; density per sq mi.: 244
Capital and largest city (1992): Bucharest, 2,351,000. **Largest cities (1992):** Constanta, 350,476; Iasi, 342,994; Timisoara, 334,278; Cluj-Napoca, 328,008; Galati, 325,788; Brasov, 323,835. **Monetary unit:** Leu. **Languages:** Romanian (official); Hungarian- and German-speaking minorities. **Ethnicity/Race:** Romanian 89.1%, Hungarian 8.9%, German 0.4%, Ukrainian, Serb, Croat, Russian, Turk, and Gypsy 1.6%. **Religions:** Greek Orthodox 70%, Roman Catholic 6% (of which 3% are Uniate), Protestant 6%, unaffiliated 18%. **Literacy rate:** 96%
Economic summary: GDP/PPP (1996 est.): $113.2 billion; $5,200 per capita. **Real growth rate:** 4.1%. **Inflation:** 56.9%. **Unemployment:** 6.1%. **Arable land:** 41%. **Agriculture:** corn, wheat, livestock, sunflowers, potatoes. **Labor force:** 10.1 million (1996 est.): industry, 28.8%, agriculture, 36.4%, other, 34.8% (1994). **Products:** timber, metal production and processing, chemicals, food processing, petroleum. **Natural resources:** oil, timber, natural gas, coal, iron ore. **Exports:** $7.7 billion (f.o.b., 1996 est.): machinery, metals, chemicals, timber, furniture, textiles, foodstuffs. **Imports:** $93.8 billion (f.o.b., 1996 est.): minerals, fuel, machinery, consumer goods. **Major trading partners:** E.U., Russia, Turkey, China, U.S., Egypt.

Geography Romania is in southeastern Europe, and is slightly smaller than Oregon. The Carpathian Mountains divide Romania's upper half from north to south and connect near the center of the country with the Transylvanian Alps, running east and west. North and west of these ranges lies the Transylvanian plateau, and to the south and east are the plains of Moldavia and Walachia. In its last 190 miles (306 km), the Danube River flows through Romania only. It enters the Black Sea in northern Dobruja, just south of the border with the Ukraine.

Government A multiparty republic with a bicameral parliament consisting of an upper house or Senate and a lower house, the Chamber of Deputies.

History Most of Romania was the Roman province of Dacia from about C.E. 100 to 271. From the 3rd to the 12th century, wave after wave of barbarian conquerors overran the native Daco-Roman population. Subjection to the first Bulgarian empire (8th–10th century) brought Eastern Orthodox Christianity to the Romanians. In the 11th century, Transylvania was absorbed into the Hungarian empire. By the 16th century, the main Romanian principalities of Moldavia and Walachia had become satellites within the Ottoman Empire, although they retained much independence. After the Russo-Turkish War of 1828–29, they became Russian protectorates. The nation became a kingdom in 1881 after the Congress of Berlin.

At the start of World War I, Romania proclaimed its neutrality, but later joined the Allied side and in 1916 declared war on the Central Powers. The armistice of Nov. 11, 1918, gave Romania vast territories from Russia and the Austro-Hungarian Empire, doubling its size. The areas acquired included Bessarabia, Transylvania, and Bukovina. The Banat, a Hungarian area, was divided with Yugoslavia. King Carol II was crowned in 1930 and gradually became a powerful political force in the country. In 1938, he abolished the democratic constitution of 1923. In 1940, the country was reorganized along Fascist lines, and the Fascist Iron Guard became the nucleus of the new totalitarian party. On June 27, the Soviet Union occupied Bessarabia and northern Bukovina. King Carol II dissolved parliament, granted the new premier, Ion Antonescu, full power, abdicated his throne, and went into exile.

Romania subsequently signed the Axis Pact on Nov. 23, 1940, and the following June joined in Germany's attack on the Soviet Union, reoccupying Bessarabia. Following the invasion of Romania by the Red Army in August 1944, King Michael led a coup that ousted the Antonescu government. An armistice with the Soviet Union was signed in Moscow on Sept. 12, 1944. A Communist-dominated government bloc won elections in 1946, Michael abdicated on Dec. 30, 1947, and in 1955 Romania joined the Warsaw Treaty Organization and the United Nations.

Nikolae Ceausescu, famous for his secret police's brutality, ruled from 1965 to 1989, when he was overthrown by a coup rising from opposition to his repressive domestic policies. Ceausescu instituted a rigorous austerity program in the 1980s to pay for the huge foreign debt Romania accumulated in the 1970s; as a result, the Romanians saw their standard of living plummet. An army-assisted rebellion in Dec. 1989 led to Ceausescu's overthrow, trial, and execution. The May 1990 elections were won by the

National Salvation Front, whose formerly communist leaders called for a gradual and controlled transition to a free-market economy in Romania.

The country applied for membership in the E.U. in June 1995 and much legislation that year was crafted in hopes of meeting that objective. Nevertheless, the reform process proceeded slowly. Growing dissatisfaction with the government's inefficiencies and economic policies led to a wave of protests by workers, students, and others that peaked in Oct. 1997. Romania's chances for inclusion in the E.U. and NATO (another goal) continue to look slim.

Russia

RUSSIAN FEDERATION

President: Boris N. Yeltsin (1991)
Prime Minister: Yevgeny Primakov (1998)
Area: 6,592,800 sq mi. (17,075,200 sq km)
Population (1998 est.): 146,861,022 (average annual rate of natural increase: –0.31%); birth rate: 9.6/1000; infant mortality rate: 23.3/1000; density per sq mi.: 22
Capital and largest city : Moscow: city proper (1996 est.) 8,436,447; metro. area (1995 est.) 9,233,000. **Other large cities:** St. Petersburg, 4,882,600; Novosibirsk, 1,418,200; Samara, 1,222,500; Chelyabinsk, 1,124,500; Yekaterinburg, 1,347,000; Nizhny Novgorod, 1,424,600; Kazau, 1,092,300; Perm, 1,086,100; Ufa, 1,091,800; Volgograd, 1,000,400. **Monetary unit:** Ruble. **Religions:** Russian Orthodox, Muslim, others. **Ethnicity/Race:** Russian 81.5%, Tatar 3.8%, Ukrainian 3%, Chuvash 1.2%, Bashkir 0.9%, Byelorussian 0.8%, Moldavian 0.7%, other 8.1%. **Languages:** Russian, others. **Literacy rate:** 98%
Economic summary: Russia is a highly industrialized-agrarian republic. Its vast mineral resources include oil and natural gas, coal, iron, zinc, lead, nickel, aluminum, molybdenum, gold, platinum, and other nonferrous metals. Russia has the world's largest oil and natural gas reserves. Three-quarters of the republic's mineral wealth is concentrated in Siberia and the Far East. Approximately ten million people are engaged in agriculture and they produce half of the region's grain, meat, milk, and other dairy products. The largest granaries are located in the North Caucasus and the Volga and Amur regions. **GDP/PPP** (1996 estimate as extrapolated from the World Bank estimate for 1994): $767 billion; $5,200 per capita (1996 est.). **Real growth rate:** –6%. **Inflation:** 22% (1996). **Unemployment:** 9.3% (Dec. 9), considerable underemployment. **Labor force** (1996), 73 million. **Exports:** $88.3 billion (1996): petroleum and petroleum products, natural gas, wood and wood products, coal, nonferrous metals, chemicals, civilian and military manufacturers. **Imports:** $59.8 billion (1996): machinery and equipment, chemicals, consumer goods, grain, meat, semifinished metal products. **Major trading partners:** Europe, N. America, Japan, Cuba.

Geography The Russian Federation is the largest republic of the Commonwealth of Independent States. It occupies an area about one- and four-fifths of the size of the United States and occupies most of eastern Europe and north Asia. Russia stretches from the Baltic Sea in the west to the Pacific Ocean in the east and from the Arctic Ocean in the north to the Black Sea and the Caucasus, the Altai, and Sayan Mountains, and the Amur and Ussuri Rivers in the south. It is bordered by Norway and Finland in the northwest, Estonia, Latvia, Belarus and Ukraine in the west, Georgia and Azerbaijan in the southwest, and Kazakhstan, Mongolia, and China along the southern border. The federation is composed of 21 republics.

Government A constitutional republic. A new constitution, adopted Dec. 12, 1993, gave the president considerable power to rule independently of the parliament. The upper house or Federation Council has 176 elected members, two from each of Russia's 88 constituent regions. The State Duma or lower house has 450 elected members. The president and the parliament are elected for four-year terms.

History Tradition says the Viking Rurik came to Russia in C.E. 862 and founded the first Russian dynasty in Novgorod. The various tribes were united by the spread of Christianity in the 10th and 11th centuries; Vladimir "the Saint" was converted in 988. During the 11th century, the grand dukes of Kiev held such centralizing power as existed. In 1240, Kiev was destroyed by the Mongols, and the Russian territory was split into numerous smaller dukedoms. Early dukes of Moscow extended their dominion over other Russian cities through their office of tribute collector for the Mongols and because of Moscow's role as an administrative and trade center.

In the late 15th century, Duke Ivan III acquired Novgorod and Tver and threw off the Mongol yoke. Ivan IV, the Terrible (1533–84), first Muscovite tsar, is considered to have founded the Russian state. He crushed the power of rival princes and boyars (great landowners), but Russia remained largely medieval until the reign of Peter the Great (1689–1725), grandson of the first Romanov tsar, Michael (1613–45). Peter made extensive reforms aimed at westernization and, through his defeat of Charles XII of Sweden at the Battle of Poltava in 1709, he extended Russia's boundaries to the west. Catherine the Great (1762–96) continued Peter's westernization program and also expanded Russian territory, acquiring the Crimea, Ukraine, and part of Poland. During the reign of Alexander I (1801–25), Napoleon's attempt to subdue Russia was defeated (1812–13), and new territory was gained, including Finland (1809) and Bessarabia (1812). Alexander originated the Holy Alliance, which for a time crushed Europe's rising liberal movement.

Alexander II (1855–81) pushed Russia's borders to the Pacific and into central Asia. Serfdom was abolished in 1861, but heavy restrictions were imposed on the emancipated class. Revolutionary strikes, following Russia's defeat in the war with Japan, forced Nicholas II (1894–1917) to grant a representative national body (Duma), elected by narrowly limited suffrage. It met for the first time in 1906, little influencing Nicholas in his reactionary course.

World War I demonstrated tsarist corruption and inefficiency and only patriotism held the poorly equipped army together for a time. Disorders broke out in Petrograd (renamed Leningrad and now St. Petersburg) in March 1917, and defection of the Petrograd garrison launched the revolution. Nicholas II was forced to abdicate on March 15, 1917, and he and his family were killed by revolutionists on July 16, 1918. A provisional government under the successive premierships of Prince Lvov and a moderate, Alexander Kerensky, lost ground to the radical, or Bolshevik, wing of the Socialist Democratic

Labor Party. On Nov. 7, 1917, the Bolshevik revolution, engineered by N. Lenin[1] and Leon Trotsky, overthrew the Kerensky government and authority was vested in a Council of People's Commissars, with Lenin as premier.

The humiliating Treaty of Brest-Litovsk (March 3, 1918) concluded the war with Germany, but civil war and foreign intervention delayed Communist control of all Russia until 1920. A brief war with Poland in 1920 resulted in Russian defeat.

Emergence of the U.S.S.R. The Union of Soviet Socialist Republics was established as a federation on Dec. 30, 1922. The death of Lenin on Jan. 21, 1924, precipitated an intraparty struggle between Joseph Stalin, general secretary of the party, and Trotsky, who favored swifter socialization at home and fomentation of revolution abroad. Trotsky was dismissed as commissar of war in 1925 and banished from the Soviet Union in 1929. He was murdered in Mexico City on Aug. 21, 1940, by a political agent. Stalin further consolidated his power by a series of purges in the late 1930s, liquidating prominent party leaders and military officers. Stalin assumed the premiership May 6, 1941.

Soviet foreign policy, at first friendly toward Germany and antagonistic toward Britain and France and then, after Hitler's rise to power in 1933, becoming anti-Fascist and pro-League of Nations, took an abrupt turn on Aug. 24, 1939, with the signing of a nonaggression pact with Nazi Germany. The next month, Moscow joined in the German attack on Poland, seizing territory later incorporated into the Ukrainian and Belarussian S.S.R.'s. The war with Finland (1939–40) added territory to the Karelian S.S.R. set up March 31, 1940; the annexation of Bessarabia and Bukovina from Romania became part of the new Moldavian S.S.R. on Aug. 2, 1940; and the annexation of the Baltic republics of Estonia, Latvia, and Lithuania in June 1940 created the 14th, 15th, and 16th Soviet Republics. The illegal annexation of the Baltic republics was never recognized by the U.S. for the 51 years leading up to Soviet recognition of Estonia, Latvia, and Lithuania's independence on Sept. 6, 1991. The Soviet-German collaboration ended abruptly with a lightning attack by Hitler on June 22, 1941, which seized 500,000 square miles of Russian territory before Soviet defenses, aided by U.S. and British arms, could halt it. The Soviet resurgence at Stalingrad from Nov. 1942 to Feb. 1943 marked the turning point in a long battle, ending in the final offensive of Jan. 1945. Then, after denouncing a 1941 nonaggression pact with Japan in April 1945, when Allied forces were nearing victory in the Pacific, the Soviet Union declared war on Japan on Aug. 8, 1945, and quickly occupied Manchuria, Karafuto, and the Kuril islands.

The U.S.S.R. built a cordon of Communist states running from Poland in the north to Albania and Bulgaria in the south, including East Germany, Czechoslovakia, Hungary, and Romania, composed of the territories Soviet troops occupied at the war's end. With its Eastern front solidified, the Soviet Union launched a political offensive against the non-Communist West, moving first to block the Western access to Berlin. The Western powers countered with an airlift, completed unification of West Germany, and organized the defense of Western Europe in the North Atlantic Treaty Organization (NATO). Stalin died on March 6, 1953, and was succeeded the next day by G. M. Malenkov as premier.

The new power in the Kremlin was Nikita S. Khrushchev, first secretary of the party. Khrushchev formalized the Eastern European system into a Council for Mutual Economic Assistance (Comecon) and a Warsaw Pact Treaty Organization as a counterweight to NATO. The Soviet Union exploded a hydrogen bomb in 1953, developed an intercontinental ballistic missile by 1957, sent the first satellite into space (Sputnik I) in 1957, and put Yuri Gagarin in the first orbital flight around the earth in 1961. Khrushchev's downfall stemmed from his decision to place Soviet nuclear missiles in Cuba and then, when challenged by the U.S., backing down and removing the weapons. He was also blamed for the ideological break with China after 1963. Khrushchev was forced into retirement on Oct. 15, 1964, and was replaced by Leonid I. Brezhnev as first secretary of the party and Aleksei N. Kosygin as premier.

U.S. President Jimmy Carter and the ailing Brezhnev signed the SALT II treaty in Vienna on June 18, 1979, setting ceilings on each nation's arsenal of intercontinental ballistic missiles. The U.S. Senate refused to ratify the treaty because of the invasion of Afghanistan by Soviet troops on Dec. 27, 1979. On Nov. 10, 1982, Soviet radio and television announced the death of Leonid Brezhnev. Yuri V. Andropov, who had formerly headed the K.G.B., was chosen to succeed Brezhnev as general secretary. By mid-June 1983, Andropov had assumed all of Brezhnev's three titles.

After months of illness, Andropov died in Feb. 1984. Konstantin U. Chernenko, a 72-year-old party stalwart who had been close to Brezhnev, succeeded him as general secretary and, by mid-April, had also assumed the title of president. In the months following Chernenko's assumption of power, the Kremlin took on a hostile mood toward the West of a kind rarely seen since the height of the cold war 30 years before. Led by Moscow, all the Soviet bloc countries except Romania boycotted the 1984 Summer Olympic Games in Los Angeles—tit-for-tat for the U.S.-led boycott of the 1980 Moscow Games, in the view of most observers. After 13 months in office, Chernenko died on March 10, 1985. He had been ill much of the time and left only a minor imprint on Soviet history.

Chosen to succeed him as Soviet leader was Mikhail S. Gorbachev, at 54 the youngest man to take charge of the Soviet Union since Stalin. Under Gorbachev, the Soviet Union began its long-awaited shift to a new generation of leadership. Unlike his immediate predecessors, Gorbachev did not also assume the title of president but wielded power from the post of party general secretary. In a surprise move, Gorbachev elevated Andrei Gromyko, 75, for 28 years the Soviet Union's stony-faced foreign minister, to the largely ceremonial post of president. He installed a younger man with no experience in foreign affairs, Eduard Shevardnadze, 57, as foreign minister. The Soviet Union took much criticism in early 1986 over the April 24 meltdown

1. N. Lenin was the pseudonym taken by Vladimir Ilich Ulyanov. It is sometimes given as Nikolai Lenin or V. Lenin.

Rulers of Russia Since 1533

Name	Born	Ruled [1]	Name	Born	Ruled [1]
Ivan IV the Terrible	1530	1533–1584	Nicholas I	1796	1825–1855
Theodore I	1557	1584–1598	Alexander II	1818	1855–1881
Boris Godunov	c.1551	1598–1605	Alexander III	1845	1881–1894
Theodore II	1589	1605–1605	Nicholas II	1868	1894–1917[7]
Demetrius I[2]	?	1605–1606	**PROVISIONAL GOVERNMENT (PREMIERS)**		
Basil IV Shuiski	?	1606–1610[3]	Prince Georgi Lvov	1861	1917–1917
"Time of Troubles"	—	1610–1613	Alexander Kerensky	1881	1917–1917
Michael Romanov	1596	1613–1645	**POLITICAL LEADERS OF U.S.S.R.**		
Alexis I	1629	1645–1676	N. Lenin	1870	1917–1924
Theodore III	1656	1676–1682	Aleksei Rykov	1881	1924–1930
Ivan V[4]	1666	1682–1689[5]	Vyacheslav Molotov	1890	1930–1941
Peter I the Great[4]	1672	1682–1725	Joseph Stalin[8]	1879	1941–1953
Catherine I	c.1684	1725–1727	Georgi M. Malenkov	1902	1953–1955
Peter II	1715	1727–1730	Nikolai A. Bulganin	1895	1955–1958
Anna	1693	1730–1740	Nikita S. Khrushchev	1894	1958–1964
Ivan VI	1740	1740–1741[6]	Leonid I. Brezhnev	1906	1964–1982
Elizabeth	1709	1741–1762	Yuri V. Andropov	1914	1982–1984
Peter III	1728	1762–1762	Konstantin U. Chernenko	1912	1984–1985
Catherine II the Great	1729	1762–1796	Mikhail S. Gorbachev	1931	1985–1991
Paul I	1754	1796–1801	**PRESIDENT OF RUSSIA**		
Alexander I	1777	1801–1825	Boris Yeltsin	1931	1991–

1. For tsars through Nicholas II, year of end of rule is also that of death, unless otherwise indicated. 2. Also known as Pseudo-Demetrius. 3. Died 1612. 4. Ruled jointly until 1689, when Ivan was deposed. 5. Died 1696. 6. Died 1764. 7. Killed 1918. 8. general secretary of Communist Party, 1924–53.

at the Chernobyl nuclear plant and its reluctance to give out any information on the accident.

In June 1987, Gorbachev obtained the support of the Central Committee for proposals that would loosen some government controls over the economy and in June 1988, an unusually open party conference approved several resolutions for changes in the structure of the Soviet system. These included a shift of some power from the party to local soviets, and a ten-year limit on the terms of elected government and party officials. Gorbachev was elected president in 1989. The elections to the Congress were the first competitive elections in the Soviet Union since 1917. Dissident candidates won a surprisingly large minority although pro-Government deputies maintained a strong lock on the Supreme Soviet.

Dissolution of the U.S.S.R. The possible beginning of the fragmentation of the Communist Party took place when Boris Yeltsin, leader of the Russian S.S.R. who urged faster reform, left the Communist Party along with other radicals. In March 1991, the Soviet people were asked to vote on a referendum on national unity engineered by President Gorbachev. The resultant victory for the federal government was tempered by the separate approval in Russia for the creation of a popularly elected presidency of the Russian republics. The bitter election contest for the Russian presidency, principally between Yeltsin and a Communist loyalist, resulted in a major victory for Yeltsin. He took the oath of office for the new position on July 10, 1991.

Reversing his relative hard-line position, Gorbachev together with leaders of nine Soviet republics signed an accord called the Union Treaty, which was meant to preserve the unity of the nation. In exchange the federal government would have turned over control of industrial and natural resources to the individual republics. An attempted coup d'état took place on August 19, 1991, orchestrated by a group of eight senior officials calling itself the State Committee on the State of Emergency. Boris Yeltsin, barricaded in the Russian parliament building, defiantly called for a general strike. The next day huge crowds demonstrated in Leningrad, and Yeltsin supporters fortified barricades surrounding the parliament building. On August 21 the coup committee disbanded, and at least some of its members attempted to flee Moscow. The Soviet parliament formally reinstated Gorbachev as president. Two days later he resigned from his position as General-Secretary of the Communist Party and recommended that its Central Committee be disbanded. On August 29 the parliament approved the suspension of all Communist Party activities pending an investigation of its role in the failed coup. At the time of the attempted coup, the republic's President Boris Yeltsin was the most popular political figure in the lands comprising the former Soviet Union. A leading reformer, he became the first directly elected leader in Russian history and received 60% of the vote for president of the Russian Republic.

Yeltsin championed the cause for national reconstruction and the adoption of a Union Treaty with the other republics to create a free-market economic association. On Dec. 12, 1991, the Russian parliament ratified Yeltsin's plea to establish a new commonwealth of independent nations open to all former members of the Soviet Union. The new union was created with the governments of Ukraine and Belarus who along with Russia were the three original cofounders of the Soviet Union in 1922. After the end of the Soviet Union, Russia and ten other Soviet republics joined in a Commonwealth of Independent States on Dec. 21, 1991.

At the start of 1992, Russia embarked on a series of dramatic economic reforms, including the freeing of prices on most goods, which led to an immediate downturn. A national referendum on confidence in Yeltsin and his economic program took place in April 1993. To the surprise of many, the president and his shock-therapy program won by a resounding margin. Yeltsin convened a constitutional conference in June, which adopted a draft constitution in July. In September, Yeltsin dissolved the legislative bodies left over from the Soviet era. The impasse between the executive and the legislature resulted in an armed conflict on Oct. 3. Yeltsin prevailed largely through the support of the military and other forces. The constitutional referendum on Dec. 12 was a victory for Yeltsin, but the parliamentary election on the same day saw the rise of the extreme nationalist Vladimir Zhirinovsky, with Western-oriented parties performing relatively poorly.

The southern republic of Chechnya's president accelerated his region's drive for independence in 1994. In December, Russian troops closed the borders and sought to squelch the independence drive. The Russian military forces met firm and costly resistance. Shortly before the scheduled presidential election of June 1996, a ceasefire was arranged in Chechnya. Yeltsin started the year with slim chances for reelection. But bolstered by favorable media attention, fear of a Communist resurgence, and vigorous campaigning he won the second round of voting in July against a Communist opponent. In May 1997, the two-year war formally ended with the signing of a peace treaty that adroitly avoided the issue of Chechen independence.

Yeltsin bounded back into the political fray in March 1997 after eight months' absence caused by sickness. His first action was to reshuffle the Cabinet to include new ministers with strong reform credentials. The "young reformers" announced plans to overhaul taxation, housing, and welfare; restore central control over headstrong regional leaders; and curb the power of Russia's monopolies (natural gas, electricity, and railways). These plans for reform, however, went awry.

In March 1998 Yeltsin dismissed his entire government and replaced Prime Minister Viktor Chernomyrdin with the young and little known fuel and energy minister Sergey Kiriyenko. On August 28, 1998, amid the Russian stock market's free fall, the Russian government halted trading of the ruble on international currency markets. This financial crisis led to a long-term economic downturn and to political upheaval. President Boris Yeltsin then sacked Prime Minister Kiriyenko and reappointed Chernomyrdin. The Duma rejected Chernomyrdin, and on Sept. 11 elected foreign minister Yevgeny Primakov as prime minister. The repercussions of Russia's financial emergency were felt throughout the commonwealth of independent nations.

Rwanda

RWANDESE REPUBLIC

National name: Repubulika y'u Rwanda
President: Pasteur Bizimungu (1994)
Prime Minister: Pierre-Célestin Rwigema (1995)
Area: 10,169 sq mi. (26,340 sq km)
Population (1998 est.): 7,956,172 (average annual rate of natural increase: 2.5%); birth rate: 39/1000; infant mortality rate: 113.3/1000; density per sq mi.: 782
Capital and largest city (1991): Kigali, 232,733. **Monetary unit:** Rwanda franc. **Languages:** Kinyarwanda, French, Swahili, English. **Ethnicity/Race:** Hutu 80%, Tutsi 19%, Twa (Pygmoid) 1%. **Religions:** Roman Catholic, 56%; Protestant, 18%; Islam, 1%; Animist, 25%. **Literacy rate:** 50%
Economic summary: GDP/PPP (1995 est.): $3.8 billion; $400 per capita. **Real growth rate:** n.a.%. **Inflation:** 22% (1995 est.). **Unemployment:** n.a. **Arable land:** 35%. **Agriculture:** coffee, tea, bananas, yams, beans. **Labor force:** 3.6 million; agriculture, 93%; government and services, 5%; industry and commerce, 2%. **Products:** processed foods, light consumer goods, minerals. **Natural resources:** gold, cassiterite, wolfram. **Exports:** $51.2 million (f.o.b., 1995 est.): coffee, tea, tungsten, tin, pyrethrum. **Imports:** $237.3 million (f.o.b., 1995 est.): textiles, foodstuffs, machinery, and equipment, capital goods, steel. **Major trading partners:** Belgium, Germany, Kenya, Japan, France, U.S., Italy, U.K.

Geography Rwanda, in east central Africa, is surrounded by Congo, Uganda, Tanzania, and Burundi. It is slightly smaller than Maryland. Steep mountains and deep valleys cover most of the country. Lake Kivu in the northwest, at an altitude of 4,829 feet (1,472 m) is the highest lake in Africa. Extending north of it are the Virunga Mountains, which include the volcano Karisimbi (14,187 ft.; 4,324 m), Rwanda's highest point.

Government A republic. A National Unity government was installed by the Rwandan Patriotic Front on July 19, 1994. Maj. Gen. Paul Kagame, the victorious Tutsi rebel leader, is both vice president and defense minister.

History The original inhabitants of Rwanda were the Twa, a Pygmy people who now make up only 1% of the population. It is not certain when the Hutu migrated to the region, except that they were well established by the time the Tutsi arrived in the 14th century. The military skills of the Tutsi led to their dominance over the Hutu, a dominance that remained unchanged over centuries, despite their minority status.

Rwanda, which became a part of German East Africa in 1890, was first visited by European explorers in 1854. During World War I, it was occupied in 1916 by Belgian troops. After the war, it became a Belgian League of Nations mandate, along with Burundi, under the name of Ruanda-Urundi. The mandate was made a U.N. trust territory in 1946. Until the Belgian Congo achieved independence in 1960, Ruanda-Urundi was administered as part of that colony. Belgium at first maintained Tutsi dominance but eventually encouraged power-sharing between Hutu and Tutsi. Ethnic tensions led to civil war, forcing many Tutsi into exile. When Ruanda became the independent nation of Rwanda on July 1, 1962, it was under Hutu rule.

In Oct. 1990 rebel Tutsi (RPF) in exile in Uganda invaded. Peace accords were signed in August 1993, calling for a coalition government. After the downing of an aircraft in April 1994 carrying the presidents of Rwanda and Burundi, both of whom died in the crash, deep-seated ethnic hatred erupted and Hutus slaughtered an estimated 800,000 Tutsi civilians. It is believed that the plane was shot down by Hutu extremists who rejected the Hutu-Tutsi power-sharing plan proposed by President Juvénal Habyarimana, a Hutu moderate. Although the genocidal slaughter seemed a spontaneous eruption of hatred, it has in fact been shown to have been carefully orchestrated. In response, Tutsi rebels swept across the country in a 14-week civil war, routing the largely Hutu government. In the immediate aftermath an estimated 1.7 million Hutu fled across the border into neighboring Zaire (now the Democratic Republic of the Congo), creating an international humanitarian problem.

Amid the legitimate refugees were Hutu militiamen who began waging guerrilla warfare from Zaire. The Hutu guerrillas in Zaire, as well as Zaire's threat to exile their own ethnic Tutsi, led to Rwanda's support of rebel forces bent on overthrowing Mobutu Sese Seko's Zaire. But Rwanda's support for the new regime of Laurent Kabila in the Democratic Republic of the Congo soon turned to disenchantment. The new government was not able to prevent the raids from Hutu guerrillas that continued to traumatize the country and destabilize the region. In August 1998, a little more than a year after Kabila took over, a rebellion began against his reign. Despite their denials, it is believed to have been instigated by Rwanda and Uganda.

Refugee problems, continued massacres, and the scars of genocide continued to haunt the national psyche. In Sept. 1998, a U.N. tribunal sentenced Jean Kambanda, a former prime minister of Rwanda, to life in prison for his part in the 1994 genocide. He became the first person in history to be convicted for the crime of genocide, first defined in the 1948 Genocide Convention after World War II.

St. Kitts and Nevis

FEDERATION OF ST. KITTS AND NEVIS

Sovereign: Queen Elizabeth II (1952)
Governor General: Sir Cuthbert Montroville Sebastian (1996)
Prime Minister: Denzil Douglas (1995)
Area: St. Kitts 65 sq mi. (169 sq km); Nevis 35 sq mi. (100 sq km)
Population (1998 est.): 42,291 (average annual rate of natural increase: 1.23%); birth rate: 22.9/1000; infant mortality rate: 17.9/1000; density per sq mi.: 423
Capital: Basseterre (on St. Kitts), 19,000. **Largest town on Nevis:** Charlestown, 1,771. **Monetary unit:** East Caribbean dollar. **Ethnicity/Race:** black African. **Literacy rate:** 98%
Economic summary: GDP/PPP (1996 est.): $235 million; $5,700 per capita. **Real growth rate:** 4%. **Inflation:** –0.9% (1995). **Unemployment:** 4.3% (May 1995). **Arable land:** 22%. **Agriculture:** sugar, rice, yams. **Labor force:** 18,172 (June 1995); services, 69%; manufacturing, 31%. **Industry:** tourism, sugar processing, salt extraction. **Exports:** $35.4 million (f.o.b., 1994 est.): sugar, manufactures, postage stamps. **Imports:** $112.4 million (f.o.b., 1994 est.): foodstuffs, manufactured goods, machinery, fuels. **Major trading partners:** U.S., U.K., Japan, Trinidad and Tobago, Canada.

Geography St. Kitts and Nevis are related physiographically by a volcanic mountain chain that dominates the central core of both islands. St. Kitts is roughly oval in shape except for a long, narrow peninsula to the southeast. St. Kitts' highest point is Mount Liamuiga (3,792 feet [1,156 m]), which has a lake in its forested crater. The Narrows, a 2-mile-(3-kilometer-) wide channel, separates the two islands. The circularly shaped Nevis is surrounded by coral reefs and the island is almost entirely a single mountain, Nevis Peak (3,232 feet [985 m]).

Government The Monarch and the National Assembly constitute the parliament, some of whose members are appointed. Nevis is entitled to no less than one-third of the seats in the National Assembly. Nevis, while represented in the National Assembly, also has its own legislature and enjoys a certain amount of autonomy within the federal structure. The national constitution includes provisions for Nevis to secede from the Federation.

History When Christopher Columbus visited the islands in 1493, they were inhabited by the Carib people. St. Kitts, formerly St. Christopher, was settled by the British in 1623; Nevis in 1628. The French settled on St. Kitts in 1627, and an Anglo-French rivalry lasted for more than 100 years. After a decisive British victory over the French at Brimstone Hill in 1782, the islands came under permanent British control. The islands, including nearby Anguilla, were united in 1882. They joined the West Indies federation in 1958 and remained in that association until its dissolution in 1962. St. Kitts-Nevis-Anguilla became an associated state of the United Kingdom in 1967. Anguilla seceded in 1980, and St. Kitts and Nevis became independent on Sept. 19, 1983.

A drop in world sugar prices hurt the nation's economy through the mid-1980s, and the government sought to reduce the islands' dependence on sugar production and to diversify the economy. In 1990, the premier of Nevis announced that he intended to seek an end to the federation with St. Kitts by 1992, but a local election in June 1992 put the idea on hold. In August 1998, 62% of Nevis voters favored a referendum permitting Nevis to secede, but the vote fell short of the two-thirds majority required.

St. Lucia

Sovereign: Queen Elizabeth II (1952)
Governor-General: H. E. William George Mallet (1996)
Prime Minister: Kenny D. Anthony (1997)
Area: 238 sq mi. (620 sq km)
Population (1998 est.): 152,335 (average annual rate of natural increase: 1.11%); birth rate: 22.5/1000; infant mortality rate: 17/1000; density per sq mi.: 640
Capital and largest city (1992 est.): Castries, 13,600. **Monetary unit:** East Caribbean dollar. **Languages:** English and patois. **Ethnicity/Race:** African descent 90.3%, mixed 5.5%, East Indian 3.2%, white 0.8%. **Religions:** Roman Catholic, 90%; Protestant, 7%; Anglican, 3%. **Literacy rate:** 67%
Economic summary: GDP/PPP (1996 est.): $695 million; $4,400 per capita. **Real growth rate:** 4.3%. **Inflation:** 3%. **Unemployment** (1995 est.), 25%. **Labor force:** 43,800; agriculture, 43.4%; services, 38.9%; industry and commerce, 17.7% (1983 est.). **Arable land:** 8%. **Agriculture:** bananas, coconuts, cocoa, citrus fruit. **Industry:** clothing, assembled electronics, beverages. **Exports:** $104.1 million (f.o.b., 1995): bananas, cocoa, clothing, vegetables, fruits, coconut oil. **Imports:** $270.5 million (f.o.b., 1995): foodstuffs, machinery and equipment, fertilizers, petroleum products. **Major trading partners:** U.K., U.S., Caribbean countries, Japan, Canada. **Member of Commonwealth of Nations**

Geography One of the Windward Islands of the eastern Caribbean, St. Lucia lies just south of Martinique. It is of volcanic origin. A chain of wooded mountains runs from north to south, and from them flow many streams into fertile valleys.

Government A governor-general represents the sovereign, Queen Elizabeth II. A prime minister is head of government, chosen by a 17-member House of Assembly elected by universal suffrage for a maximum term of five years. The Senate's members are appointed.

History Explored by Spain in 1503, and ruled by Spain and then France, St. Lucia became a British territory in 1814 and one of the Windward Islands in 1871. Representative government was granted by the constitution of 1924, and the constitution of 1936 provided for an unofficial majority of elected representatives in the legislative council. With other Windward Islands, St. Lucia was granted home rule in 1967 as one of the West Indies Associated States. On Feb. 22, 1979, St. Lucia achieved full independence in ceremonies boycotted by the opposition St. Lucia Labour Party, which had advocated a referendum before cutting ties with Britain. The United Workers Party (UWP), then in power, called for new elections and was defeated by the St. Lucia Labour Party (SLP). The UWP was returned to power in the elections of 1982, 1987, and 1992.

Parliamentary elections in May 1997 gave the opposition St. Lucia Labour Party 16 of the 17 seats. The SLP had stressed economic issues and corruption, but the United Workers Party denied the corruption charges.

St. Vincent and The Grenadines

Sovereign: Queen Elizabeth II (1952)
Governor-General: Sir Charles Antrobus (1996)
Prime Minister: Sir James Fitz-Allen Mitchell (1984)
Area: 150 sq mi. (340 sq km)
Population (1998 est.): 119,818 (average annual rate of natural increase: 0.60%); birth rate: 18.7/1000; infant mortality rate: 15.7/1000; density per sq mi.: 799
Capital and largest city (1992 est.): Kingstown, 15,466. **Monetary unit:** East Caribbean dollar. **Language:** English (official), French patois. **Ethnicity/Race:** African descent, white, East Indian, Carib Indian. **Religions:** Anglican, 47%; Methodist, 28%; Roman Catholic, 13%. **Literacy rate:** 96%
Economic summary: GDP/PPP (1996 est.): $259 million; $2,190 per capita. **Real growth rate:** 3%. **Inflation:** 3%. **Unemployment:** 35–40% (1994 est.). **Arable land:** 10%; **Agriculture:** bananas, arrowroot, coconuts. **Labor force:** 67,000 (1984 est.); in agriculture 26%, industry 17%, services 57% (1980 est.). **Major industry:** food processing. **Exports:** $55 million (f.o.b., 1996 est.): bananas, arrowroot, eddos and dasheen (taro), tennis racquets. **Imports:** $122 million (f.o.b., 1996 est.): foodstuffs, machinery and equipment, chemicals, fuels, minerals. **Major trading partners:** U.K., U.S., Caribbean nations. **Member of Commonwealth of Nations**

Geography St. Vincent, chief island of the chain, is 18 miles (29 km) long and 11 miles (18 km) wide, and is located 100 miles (161 km) west of Barbados. The island is mountainous and well forested. St. Vincent is dominated by the volcano Mount Soufrière, which rises to 4,048 feet (1,234 m). The Grenadines, a chain of nearly 600 islets with a total area of only 17 square miles (27 sq km), extend for 60 miles (96 km) between St. Vincent and Grenada. The main islands in the Grenadines are Bequia, Balliceau, Canouan, Mayreau, Mustique, Isle D'Quatre, Petit Saint Vincent, and Union Island.

Government The unicameral House of Assembly consists of 15 members elected for five-year terms and six Senators appointed by the governor-general. The prime minister, who is the leader of the House of Assembly's majority party and is appointed by the governor-general, holds executive power.

History The Carib people were firmly entrenched on St. Vincent before the Europeans arrived and the island still sports a sizable number of Carib artifacts. Explored by Columbus in 1498, and alternately claimed by Britain and France, St. Vincent became a British colony by the Treaty of Paris in 1763. In 1773 the Caribs, by treaty, recognized British sovereignty and permitted the island to be divided between themselves and the British, but tensions remained. After the Caribs revolted and were subdued in 1796, the British deported most of them to islands in the Gulf of Honduras. Sugarcane cultivation brought thousands of African slaves and, later, Portuguese and East Indian laborers.

The islands won home rule in 1969 as part of the West Indies Associated States, after being part of the federation of the West Indies from 1958 until its dissolution in 1962, and achieved full independence Oct. 26, 1979. Prime Minister Milton Cato's government quelled a brief rebellion on Dec. 8, 1979, attributed to economic problems following the eruption of La Soufrière in April 1979 (which had caused the evacuation of the northern two-thirds of the island). The eruption, followed by Hurricane Allen in 1980, seriously damaged the nation's economy, particularly the important banana crop, in the 1980s. But by the 1990s the economy had begun to rebound and the small tourism industry began to grow. In 1996, St. Vincent and the Grenadines signed agreements with the U.S. that allowed U.S. Coast Guard personnel to pursue suspected drug smugglers into their territorial waters and provided for extradition of criminals. In 1997, the country's permanent representative to the Organization of American States assumed the chairmanship of that body's Permanent Council.

Samoa

INDEPENDENT STATE OF SAMOA

Head of State: Malietoa Tanumafili II (1962)
Prime Minister: Tofilau Eti Alesana (1988)
Area: 1,093 sq mi. (2,860 sq km)
Population (1998 est.): 224,713 (average annual growth rate: 2.33%); birth rate: 29.6/1000; infant mortality rate: 31.8/1000; density per sq mi.: 205
Capital and largest city (1991): Apia, 32,859. **Monetary unit:** Tala. **Languages:** Samoan and English. **Ethnicity/Race:** Samoan 92.6%, Euronesians 7% (persons of European and Polynesian blood), Europeans 0.4%. **Religions:** Christian, 99.7%. **Literacy rate:** 98.3%
Economic summary: GDP: (1995 est.): $415 million; $1,900 per capita. **Real growth rate:** 6.7%. **Inflation:** 1% (1995). **Arable land:** 19%. **Agriculture:** copra, coconuts, cocoa, bananas, taro, yams. **Labor force** 45,635 (1986 est.); 65% employed in agriculture, 30% in services. Agriculture accounts for 50% of GDP. **Industry:** timber, processed food, fish. Natural resource: timber. **Exports:** $8.7 million (f.o.b., 1995): copra, cocoa, coconut oil and cream, timber. **Imports:** $91 million (c.i.f., 1995): food, manufactured goods, machinery. **Major trading partners:** New Zealand, E.U., Australia, U.S., Fiji, Japan. **Member of Commonwealth of Nations.**

Geography Samoa, formerly Western Samoa, is in the South Pacific Ocean about 2,200 miles (3,540 km) south of Hawaii. The larger islands in the Samoan chain, Upolu and Savai'i, are mountainous and of volcanic origin. There is little level land except in the coastal areas, where most cultivation takes place.

Government Samoa has a 49-member legislature, consisting mainly of the titleholders (chiefs) of family groups, with two non-title members. All members are elected by universal suffrage. When the present head of state dies, successors will be elected by the legislature for five-year terms.

History Polynesians, possibly from Tonga, first settled in the Samoan group about 1000 B.C.E.. A short time before European arrival, stratified society with paramount chiefs and fortified settlements developed. Samoa was explored by Dutch and French traders in the 18th century. Toward the end of the 19th century, conflicting interests of the U.S., Britain, and Germany resulted in a treaty signed in 1899. It recognized the paramount interests of the U.S. in those islands east of 171° west longitude (American Samoa) and Germany's interests in the other islands (Western Samoa).

Chafing under German rule, Samoans formed the Savai'i-based Mau a Pule resistance movement in 1908. New Zealand occupied Western Samoa in 1914, and was granted a League of Nations mandate in 1920. In 1947, the islands became a U.N. trust territory administered by New Zealand. Western Samoa became independent on Jan. 1, 1962. Later that year, a Treaty of Friendship was signed with New Zealand, authorizing New Zealand to act as an agent for Western Samoa in foreign relations when requested to do so. A referendum in 1990 gave most women the right to vote for the first time. In 1997, a new constitutional amendment changed the country's name to Samoa.

San Marino

MOST SERENE REPUBLIC OF SAN MARINO

National name: Repubblica di San Marino
Captains Regent: Loris Francini and Edda Ceccoli (1998)
Area: 23.6 sq mi. (62 sq km)
Population (1998 est.): 24,894 (average annual growth rate 0.7%); birth rate: 10.5/1000; infant mortality rate: 5.4/1000; density per sq mi.: 1,055
Capital and largest city (1992 est.): San Marino, 2,397. **Monetary unit:** Italian lira. **Language:** Italian. **Ethnicity/Race:** Sammarinese, Italian. **Religion:** Roman Catholic. **Literacy rate:** 96%
Economic summary: GDP/PPP (1994 est.): $408 million; $16,900 per capita. **Real growth rate:** 4.8%. **Inflation:** 5.3% (1995). **Unemployment:** 3.6% (April 1996). **Arable land:** 17%. **Agriculture:** wheat and other grains, grapes, olives, cheese. **Labor force:** 15,600 (1995); industry, 40%; agriculture, 2% (1993). The tourist sector contributed over 50% of GDP. **Industry:** apparel, electronics, and ceramics. Other industrial products: textiles, leather, cement, wine, olive oil. **Exports:** (trade data are included with the statistics for Italy) building stone, lime, chestnuts, wheat, hides, baked goods. **Imports:** (trade data are included with the statistics for Italy) manufactured consumer goods, food. Major trading partner: Italy.

Geography One-tenth the size of New York City, San Marino is surrounded by Italy. It is situated in the Apennines, a little inland from the Adriatic Sea near Rimini.

Government The San Marino constitution, originating from the Statutes of 1600, provides for a parliamentary form of government. The Great and General Council (parliament) has 60 members, elected every five years. It has legislative and administrative powers and nominates every six months the two Captains Regent. Executive power is exercised by ten ministers (the Congress of State). In 1959, the parliament granted women the vote. San Marino is a member of the Conference on Security and Cooperation in Europe.

History According to tradition, San Marino was founded about C.E. 350 and had the good luck for centuries to stay out of the many wars and feuds on the Italian peninsula. It is the oldest republic in the world. San Marino has survived attacks by other self-governing Italian city-states, the Napoleonic Wars, the unification of Italy, and two world wars completely intact. Those born in San Marino remain citizens and can vote no matter where they live. Throughout the 1990s San Marino has taken a more active role in international diplomacy, establishing strong diplomatic and economic ties to a host of other countries.

São Tomé and Príncipe

DEMOCRATIC REPUBLIC OF SÃO TOMÉ AND PRÍNCIPE

President: Miguel Trovoada (1991)
Prime Minister: Raul Neto (1997)
Area: 370 sq mi. (960 sq km)
Population (1998 est.): 150,123 (average annual growth rate: 3.1%); birth rate: 43.5/1000; infant mortality rate: 54.6/1000; density per sq mi.: 406
Capital and largest city (1990 est.): São Tomé, 43,420. **Monetary unit:** Dobra. **Language:** Portuguese. **Ethnicity/Race:** mestico, angolares (descendants of Angolan slaves), forros (descendants of freed slaves), servicais (contract laborers from Angola, Mozambique, and Cape Verde), tongas (children of servicais born on the islands), Europeans (primarily Portuguese). **Religions:** Roman Catholic, Evangelical Protestant, Seventh-Day Adventist. **Literacy rate:** 57%
Economic summary: GDP/PPP (1995 est.): $149 million; $1,000 per capita. **Real growth rate:** 2.6%. **Inflation:** 38% (1994 est.). **Unemployment:** n.a. **Arable land:** 2%. **Agriculture:** cocoa, copra, coconuts, palm oil, coffee, bananas. **Labor force:** Most engaged in subsistence agriculture and fishing. Shortages of plantation labor and of skilled workers. **Industry:** shirts, soap, beer, processed fish and shrimp. **Exports:** $7.8 million (f.o.b., 1995 est.): cocoa, coffee, copra, palm oil. **Imports:** $26.2 million (c.i.f., 1995 est.): textiles, machinery, electrical equipment, fuels, food products. **Major trading partners:** Netherlands, Portugal, Germany, China, Angola.

Geography The tiny volcanic islands of São Tomé and Príncipe lie in the Gulf of Guinea about 150 miles (240 km) off West Africa. São Tomé (about 330 sq mi.; 859 sq km) is covered by a dense mountainous jungle, out of which have been carved large plantations. Príncipe (about 40 sq mi.; 142 sq km) consists of jagged mountains. Other islands in the republic are Pedras Tinhosas and Rolas. About 95% of the population lives on São Tomé.

Government The constitution grants supreme power to a 55-seat People's Assembly composed of members elected for four years. In 1990 a referendum approved a new constitution paving the way for a multiparty democracy.

History São Tomé and Príncipe, believed to have been originally uninhabited, were explored by Portuguese navigators in 1471 and settled by the end of the century. Intensive cultivation by slave labor made the islands a major producer of sugar during the 17th century but output declined until the introduction of coffee and cacao in the 19th century brought new prosperity. The island of São Tomé was the world's largest producer of cacao in 1908 and the crop is still the most important. Working conditions for laborers, however, were horrendous, and in 1909 British and German chocolate manufacturers boycotted São Tomé cocoa in protest. An exile liberation movement was formed in 1953 after Portuguese landowners quelled labor riots by killing several hundred African workers.

The Portuguese revolution of 1974 brought the end of the overseas empire and the new Lisbon government transferred power to the liberation movement on July 12, 1975. A former prime minister and dissident, Miguel Trovoada, was elected president in March 1991 after the withdrawal of the two other candidates.

In April 1995 Príncipe became autonomous. In August a bloodless military coup was reversed through Angolan mediation. In December an agreement was struck on forming a coalition government. President Trovoada won reelection in July 1996 against challenger and former President Pinto da Costa. Protests erupted in April 1997 when the government, in response to its inability to pay for imported oil, raised gasoline prices 140% in order to stem demand.

Saudi Arabia

KINGDOM OF SAUDI ARABIA

National name: Al-Mamlaka al-'Arabiya as-Sa'udiya
King and Prime Minister: King Fahd bin 'Abdulaziz (1982)
Area: 865,000 sq mi. (1,960,582 sq km)
Population (1998 est.): 20,785,955 (average annual rate of natural increase: 3.41%); birth rate: 37.6/1000; infant mortality rate: 41.3/1000; density per sq mi.: 24
Capital: Riyadh. **Largest cities (1993):** Riyadh, 3,000,000; Jeddah, 2,500,000; Makkah (Mecca) (1994 est.) 550,000. **Monetary unit:** Riyal. **Language:** Arabic, English widely spoken. **Ethnicity/Race:** Arab 90%, Afro-Asian 10%. **Religion:** Islam, 100%. **Literacy rate:** 62%
Economic summary: GDP/PPP (1996 est.): $205.6 billion; $10,600 per capita. **Real growth rate:** 6%. **Inflation:** 1%. **Unemployment:** 6.5% (1992 est.). **Arable land:** 2%. **Agriculture:** dates, grains, livestock, wheat, fish, flowers. **Labor force:** 6–7 million; government, 40%; industry and oil, 25%; services, 30%; agriculture, 5%. **Industry:** petroleum, cement, plastic products, steel, packaged goods. **Natural resources:** oil, natural gas, iron ore. **Exports:** $53.1 billion (f.o.b., 1996 est.): petroleum and petroleum products 90%. **Imports:** $25.5 billion (f.o.b., 1996 est.): manufactured goods, transport equipment, construction materials, processed food. **Major trading partners:** U.S., Germany, U.K. and other Western European countries, South Korea, Taiwan, Japan.

Geography Saudi Arabia occupies most of the Arabian Peninsula, with the Red Sea and the Gulf of Aqaba to the west, the Arabian Gulf to the east. Neighboring countries are Jordan, Iraq, Kuwait, Qatar, the United Arab Emirates, the Sultanate of Oman, Yemen, and Bahrain, connected to the Saudi mainland by a causeway. A narrow coastal plain on the Red Sea rims a mountain range that spans the length of the western coastline. East of these mountains is a massive plateau that slopes gently downward toward the Arabian Gulf. Part of this plateau is covered by the world's largest continuous sand desert, the Rub Al-Khali, or Empty Quarter. Saudi Arabia's oil region lies primarily in the eastern province along the Arabian Gulf, but significant recent discoveries have also been made in the interior south of Riyadh.

Government Saudi Arabia was an absolute monarchy until 1992, at which time the Sa'ud royal family introduced the country's first constitution. The legal system is based on the Sharia (Islamic law), as revealed in the Qur'an (the holy book) and the Hadith (teachings and sayings of the prophet Mohammed). The Council of Ministers, composed of 21 members (four are members of the Saudi royal family) and introduced in 1953, passes laws. The Consultative Council, introduced by the 1992 constitution, proposes and reviews laws. Royal and ministerial decrees account for most of the promulgated legislation, treaties, and conventions. There are no political parties.

History Mohammed united the Arabs in the 7th century, and his followers, led by the caliphs, founded a great empire, with its capital at Medina. Later, the caliphate capital was transferred to Damascus and then Baghdad, but Arabia retained its importance because of the holy cities of Mecca and Medina. In the 16th and 17th centuries, the Turks established at least nominal rule over much of Arabia, and in the middle of the 18th century, it was divided into separate principalities.

The kingdom of Saudi Arabia is almost entirely the creation of King Ibn Saud (1882–1953). A descendant of earlier Wahabi rulers, he seized Riyadh, the capital of Nejd, in 1901 and set himself up as leader of the Arab nationalist movement. By 1906 he had established Wahabi dominance in Nejd and conquered Hejaz in 1924–25. In 1927, the British, who had held Saudi lands as a protectorate since 1915, acknowledged the independence and sovereignty of the kingdom of the Hejaz and Najd. The two kingdoms were unified under the name Kingdom of Saudi Arabia in 1932. A year later the region of Asir was incorporated into the kingdom.

Oil was discovered in 1936, and commercial production began during World War II. Saudi Arabia was neutral until nearly the end of the war, but it was permitted to be a charter member of the United Nations. The country joined the Arab League in 1945 and took part in the 1948–49 war against Israel. On Ibn Saud's death in 1953, his eldest son, Saud, began an 11-year reign marked by an increasing hostility toward the radical Arabism of Egypt's Gamal Abdel Nasser. In 1964, the ailing Saud was deposed and replaced by the premier, Crown Prince Faisal, who gave vocal support but no military help to Egypt in the 1967 Mideast War.

Faisal's assassination by a deranged kinsman in 1975 shook the Middle East, but failed to alter his kingdom's course. His successor was his brother, Prince Khalid. Khalid gave influential support to Egypt during negotiations on Israeli withdrawal from the Sinai desert. King Khalid died of a heart attack in 1982, and was succeeded by his half-brother, Prince Fahd bin 'Abdulaziz, 60, who had exercised the real power throughout Khalid's reign. King Fahd, a pro-Western modernist, chose his 58-year-old half-brother, Abdullah, as Crown Prince.

Saudi Arabia and the smaller, oil-rich Arab states on the Persian Gulf, fearful that they might become Ayatollah Ruhollah Khomeini's next targets if Iran conquered Iraq, made large financial contributions to the Iraqi war effort during the 1980s. At the same time, cheating by other members of the Organization of Petroleum Exporting Countries, competition from nonmember oil producers, and conservation efforts by consuming nations combined to drive down the world price of oil. Saudi Arabia has one-third of all known oil reserves, but falling demand and rising production outside OPEC combined to reduce its oil revenues from $120 billion in 1980 to less the $25 billion in 1985, threatening the country with domestic unrest and undermining its influence in the Gulf area.

At the start of 1996 King Faud passed authority to Crown Prince Abdullah, saying he needed rest. Although not an abdication, it was unclear how long the king would be absent. Strong oil prices, accounting for 80% of Saudi revenues, were responsible for a government surplus of 700 million rials at the end of 1996, the first officially recorded annual surplus since 1983.

Senegal

REPUBLIC OF SENEGAL

National name: République du Sénegal
President: Abdou Diouf (1981)
Prime Minister: Mamadou Lamine Loum (1998)
Area: 75,954 sq mi. (196,190 sq km)
Population (1998 est.): 9,723,149 (average annual rate of natural increase: 3.33%); birth rate: 44.4/1000; infant mortality rate: 61.2/1000; density per sq mi.: 128
Capital and largest city (1994 est.): Dakar, 1,729,823. **Monetary unit:** Franc CFA. **Ethnicity/Race:** Wolof 36%, Fulani 17%, Serer 17%, Toucouleur 9%, Diola 9%, Mandingo 9%, European and Lebanese 1%, other 2%. **Languages:** French (official); Wolof, Serer, other ethnic dialects. **Religions:** Islam, 92%; indigenous, 6%; Christian, 2%. **Literacy rate:** 38%
Economic summary: GDP/PPP (1996 est.): $15.6 billion; $1,700 per capita. **Real growth rate:** 5%. **Inflation:** 7.8% (1995). **Unemployment:** n.a. **Arable land:** 12%. **Agriculture:** peanuts, millet, corn, rice, sorghum. **Labor force:** 2.509 million; 77% subsistence-level agriculture workers; less than 1% wage earners (private sector, 40%; government and parapublic, 60%). **Industry:** processed food, phosphates, refined petroleum, cement, and fish. **Natural resources:** fish, phosphate, iron ore. **Exports:** $968 million (f.o.b., 1995): peanuts, phosphate rock, canned fish, petroleum products. **Imports:** $1.22 billion (f.o.b., 1995): foodstuffs, consumer goods, machinery, transport equipment, petroleum. **Major trading partners:** U.S., Western European countries, African neighbors, Japan, China, India.

Geography The capital of Senegal, Dakar, is the westernmost point in Africa. The country, slightly smaller than South Dakota, surrounds Gambia on three sides and is bordered on the north by Mauritania, on the east by Mali, and on the south by Guinea and Guinea-Bissau.

Senegal is mainly a low-lying country, with a semidesert area in the north and northeast and forests in the southwest. The largest rivers include the Senegal in the north and the Casamance in the south tropical climate region.

Government A parliamentary democracy with socialist leanings. There is a National Assembly of 120 members, elected every five years. There is universal suffrage and a constitutional guarantee of equality before the law.

History The Toucouleur people, among the early inhabitants of Senegal, converted to Islam in the 11th century, although their religious beliefs retained strong elements of animism. The Portuguese had some stations on the banks of the Senegal River in the 15th century, and the first French settlement was made at Saint-Louis in 1659. Gorée Island became a major center for the Atlantic slave trade through the 1700s, and millions of Africans were shipped from there to the New World. The British took parts of Senegal at various times, but the French gained possession in 1840 and made it part of French West Africa in 1895. In 1946, together with other parts of French West Africa, Senegal became an overseas territory of France. On June 20, 1960, it became an independent republic federated with Mali.

In 1973, Senegal joined with six other states to create the West African Economic Community. In elections of Feb. 21, 1993, President Diouf was reelected. In June 1997 the government announced its intended sale of 49% of the state-owned, highly profitable electric company SENELEC to a private firm. The government would retain the majority share. Clashes in the Casamance region between separatists and government troops took place throughout 1997.

Seychelles

REPUBLIC OF SEYCHELLES

President: France-Albert René (1977)
Area: 175 sq mi. (455 sq km)
Population (1998 est.): 78,641 (average annual rate of natural increase: 0.67%); birth rate: 19.7/1000; infant mortality rate: 17/1000; density per sq mi.: 449
Capital and largest city (1993 est.): Victoria, 25,000. **Monetary unit:** Seychelles rupee. **Languages:** English, French, and Seselwa (a creole). **Ethnicity/Race:** Seychellois (mixture of Asians, Africans, Europeans). **Religions:** Roman Catholic, 90%; Anglican, 8%. **Literacy rate:** 58%
Economic summary: GDP/PPP (1995 est.): $450 million; $6,000 per capita. **Real growth rate:** 1.1%. **Inflation:** –0.3%. **Unemployment** n.a. **Arable land:** 2%. **Agriculture:** vanilla, coconuts, cinnamon. **Labor force:** 26,600 (1996); industry and commerce, 31%; services, 21%; government, 20%; agriculture, forestry, and fishing, 12% (1985). **Industry:** processed coconut and vanilla, coir rope. **Exports:** $56.1 million (f.o.b., 1995): fish, canned tuna, copra, cinnamon bark. **Imports:** $238 million (c.i.f., 1995): food, tobacco, manufactured goods, machinery, petroleum products, transport equipment. **Major trading partners:** E.U., Japan, Pakistan, Réunion, South Africa. **Member of Commonwealth of Nations**

Geography Seychelles consists of an archipelago of about 100 islands in the Indian Ocean northeast of Madagascar. The principal islands are Mahé (55 sq mi.; 142 sq km), Praslin (15 sq mi.; 38 sq km), and La Digue (4 sq mi.; 10 sq km). The Aldabra, Farquhar, and Desroches groups are included in the territory of the republic.

Government Seychelles is a socialist multiparty state whose 1979 constitution provides for a president as head of state and commander in chief and a unicameral People's Assembly. The political party that dominates the republic is the Seychelles People's Progressive Front (FPPS), which nominates the president, who is then subject to approval by popular vote.

History The first recorded landing on the uninhabited Seychelles was made in 1609 by an expedition of the British East India Company. The archipelago was formally annexed to France in 1756. France surrendered the archipelago to the British in 1810, and it was formally ceded to Great Britain by the Treaty of Paris in 1814. The abolition of slavery in the 1830s deprived the islands' European colonists of their labor force and compelled them to switch from raising cotton and grains to less labor-intensive crops such as coconut, vanilla, and cinnamon. In 1903, the Seychelles became a British Crown colony. Self-government was granted in 1975, and independence on June 29, 1976 (within the Commonwealth of Nations). In 1975, a coalition government, with James R. Mancham as president and France-Albert René as prime minister, was formed. In 1977, René became president in a coup d'état. In 1979, René revised the constitution and created a one-party socialist state. In June 1993, a new constitution reintroduced a multiparty system, but the presidential election later that year affirmed René's position and that of his party, the FPPS.

To increase revenue the government in 1996 quietly initiated an Economic Citizenship Program that provides foreigners with the opportunity to obtain a Seychelles passport upon payment of $25,000. A new law in late 1995 granted immunity from criminal prosecution to anyone investing $10 million in the country. In elections held in March 1998, President France-Albert René was reelected with 66.6% of the vote.

Sierra Leone

REPUBLIC OF SIERRA LEONE

President: (vacant) (1998)
Area: 27,925 sq mi (71,740 sq km)
Population (1998 est.): 5,080,004 (average annual rate of natural increase: 4.01%); birth rate: 46.2/1000; infant mortality rate: 129.4/1000; density per sq mi.: 182
Capital and largest city (1994 est.): Freetown, 1,300,000. **Monetary unit:** Leone. **Languages:** English (official), Mende, Temne, Krio. **Ethnicity/Race:** 18 native African tribes 99% (Temne 30%, Mende 30%, other 39%), Creole, European, Lebanese, and Asian 1%. **Religions:** Islam, 40%, Christian, 35%; Indigenous, 20%. **Literacy rate:** 21%
Economic summary: GDP/PPP (1996 est.): $4.7 billion; $980 per capita. **Real growth rate:** 5%. **Inflation:** 5.6% (1996). **Unemployment:** n.a. **Arable land:** 7%. **Agriculture:** coffee, cocoa, palm kernels, rice. **Labor force:** 1.369 million (1981 est.); agriculture, 49%; industry, 21%; services, 30% (1995). **Industry:** diamonds, bauxite, rutile, beverages, cigarettes, textiles, footwear. **Natural resources:** diamonds, bauxite, iron ore. **Exports:** $39.3 million (f.o.b., 1995): diamonds, rutile, bauxite, cocoa, coffee. **Imports:** $140 million (c.i.f., 1995): food, petroleum, products, capital goods. **Major trading partners:** U.K., U.S., Western European countries, Japan, China, Nigeria.
Member of Commonwealth of Nations

Geography Sierra Leone, on the Atlantic Ocean in West Africa, is half the size of Illinois. Guinea, in the north and east, and Liberia, in the south, are its neighbors. Mangrove swamps lie along the coast, with wooded hills and a plateau in the interior. The eastern region is mountainous.

Government A military government came into power in April 1992 but was replaced by a democratically elected president and an independent parliament in March 1996.

History The Bulom people were thought to have been the earliest inhabitants of Sierra Leone, followed by the Mende and Temne peoples in the 15th century, and thereafter the Fulani. The Portuguese were the first Europeans to explore the land, and gave Sierra Leone its name, which means "lion mountains." Freetown, on the coast, was ceded to English settlers in 1787 as a home for blacks discharged from the British armed forces and also for runaway slaves who had found asylum in London. In 1808 the coastal area became a British colony, and in 1896 a British protectorate was proclaimed over the hinterland.

Sierra Leone became an independent nation on April 27, 1961. A military coup overthrew the civilian government in 1967, which was in turn replaced by civilian rule a year later. The country declared itself a republic on April 19, 1971.

A coup attempt early in 1971 led to then Prime Minister Stevens calling in troops from neighboring Guinea's army who remained for two years. Stevens turned the government into a one-party state under the aegis of the All People's Congress Party in April 1978. In 1992 rebel soldiers overthrew Stevens's successor, Joseph Momoh, calling for a return to a multiparty system. In 1996, another military coup ousted the country's military leader and president. Nevertheless, a multiparty presidential election proceeded in 1996, and People's Party candidate Ahmed Tejan Kabbah won with 59.4% of the vote, becoming Sierra Leone's first democratically elected president. But a violent military coup ousted President Kabbah's civilian government in May 1997, and in June the leader of the coup, Lieut. Col. Johnny Paul Koroma, assumed the title, "Head of the Armed Forces Revolutionary Council." Koroma began a reign of terror, destroying the economy and murdering enemies. The Commonwealth of Nations demanded the reinstatement of Kabbah and Nigerian troops intervened to this end. After ten months in exile, Kabbah resumed his rule over Sierra Leone on March 10, 1998, although the ousted junta and other rebel forces continued to wage attacks, many of which include the maiming of civilians. Liberia's Charles Taylor, intent on punishing Sierra Leone for supporting Nigeria in the drive against him, has harbored anti-Kabbah guerrillas behind his borders. One of Kabbah's tasks will be demobilizing the 2,500 child soldiers who fought on his side during the civil war.

Singapore

REPUBLIC OF SINGAPORE

President: Ong Teng Cheong (1993)
Prime Minister: Goh Chok Tong (1990)
Area: 246.7 sq mi. (632.6 sq km)
Population (19978 est.): 3,490,356 (average annual rate of natural increase: 1.20%); birth rate: 13.8/1000; infant mortality rate: 3.9/1000; density per sq mi.: 14,148
Capital (1992 est.): Singapore, 2,792,000. **Monetary unit:** Singapore dollar. **Languages:** Malay, Chinese (Mandarin), Tamil, English. **Ethnicity/Race:** Chinese 76.4%, Malay 14.9%, Indian 6.4%, other 2.3%. **Religions:** Islam, Christian, Buddhist, Hindu, Taoist. **Literacy rate:** 90%
Economic summary: GDP/PPP (1996 est.): $72.2 billion; $21,200 per capita. **Real growth rate:** 6.5% (1996). **Inflation:** 1.3% (1996). **Unemployment:** 2.7%. **Arable land:** 2%. **Agriculture:** poultry, rubber, copra, vegetables, fruits. **Labor force** (1996 est.), 1.801 million; manufacturing, 25.6%; commerce, 22.9%; financial and business services, 33.5% (1994). **Industry:** petroleum refining, ship repair, electronics, financial and business services, biotechnology. **Exports:** $144.8 billion (1996 est.): petroleum products, rubber, manufactured goods, electrical and electronics, computers and computer peripherals. **Imports:** $151.1 billion (1996 est.): aircraft, petroleum, chemicals, foodstuffs. **Major trading partners:** U.S., E.U., Hong Kong, Japan, Malaysia. **Member of Commonwealth of Nations**

Geography The Republic of Singapore consists of the main island of Singapore, off the southern tip of the Malay Peninsula between the South China Sea and the Indian Ocean, and 58 nearby islands.

Government A republic with a cabinet, headed by the prime minister, and a parliament of 81 members elected by universal suffrage.

History Inhabitants of the Malaysian peninsula and the island of Singapore first migrated to the area between 2500 and 1500 B.C.E. (*see* Malaysia). British and Dutch interest in the region grew with the spice trade, and the trading post of Singapore was founded in 1819 by Sir Stamford Raffles. It was made a separate Crown colony of Britain in 1946, when the former colony of the Straits Settlements was dissolved. The other two settlements on the peninsula—Penang and Malacca—became part of the Union of Malaya, and the small island of Labuan was transferred to North Borneo. The Cocos (or Keeling) Islands and Christmas Island were transferred to Australia in 1955 and in 1958, respectively.

Singapore attained full internal self-government in 1959, and Lee Kwan Yew, an economic visionary with an authoritarian streak, took the helm as prime minister. On Sept. 16, 1963, Singapore joined Malaya, Sabah (North Borneo), and Sarawak in the Federation of Malaysia. It withdrew from the Federation on Aug. 9, 1965, and a month later proclaimed itself a republic.

Under Lee, Singapore developed into one of the cleanest, safest, and most economically prosperous cities in Asia. However, Singapore's strict rules of civil obedience also drew criticism from those who said the nation's prosperity was achieved at the expense of individual freedoms. In 1990, Lee stepped down as prime minister but remained "senior minister" with considerable influence over his successor, Goh Chok Tong, who continued to preside over Singapore through difficult economic times in 1998.

The first direct presidential election took place in August 1993. Ong Teng Cheong faced what initially appeared to be only token opposition but which ultimately took 40% of the vote. Parliamentary elections on New Year's Day, 1997, gave the ruling People's Action Party 34 of the 36 contested seats. For the other 47 seats the PAP ran unopposed.

In 1998, Singapore and Malaysia's often-strained relations soured again against the backdrop of the Asian financial crisis, which was taking a heavy toll on both economies. Singaporean leaders accused Malaysia of using a newly built $2.3 billion international airport at Kuala Lumpur to supplant the island nation as a regional air hub.

Slovakia

REPUBLIC OF SLOVAKIA

President: Michal Kovác (1993)
Prime Minister: Vladimir Meciar (1994)
Area: 18,917 sq mi. (48,845 sq km)
Population (1998 est.): 5,392,982 (Average annual rate of natural increase: 0.08%); birth rate: 10/1000; infant mortality rate: 9.7/1000; density per sq mi.: 285
Capital and largest city (1993 est.): Bratislava, 446,600. **Other large city (1993 est.):** Kosice, 237,300. **Monetary unit:** Koruna (SKK). **Language:** Slovak (official), Hungarian. **Ethnicity/Race:** Slovak 85.7%, Hungarian 10.7%, Gypsy 1.5%, Czech 1%, Ruthenian 0.3%, Ukrainian 0.3%, German 0.1%, Polish 0.1%. **Religions:** Roman Catholic 60.3%, atheist 9.7%, Protestant 8.4%, Orthodox 4.1%, other 17.5%. **Literacy rate:** 99%
Economic summary: GDP/PPP (1996 est.): $42.8 billion; $8,000 per capita. **Real growth rate:** 7%. **Inflation:** 5.5%. **Unemployment:** 12%. **Arable land:** 31%. **Industry:** iron and nonferrous mining, metal processing, shipbuilding, construction materials, consumer appliances, and leather goods. **Labor force:** 2.538 million; industry, 29.3%; agriculture, 8.9%; services, 45.6% (1994). **Agriculture:** grains, potatoes, sugar beets, fruit, vegetables, forestry. Livestock: pigs, cattle, poultry, sheep. **Exports:** $8.1 billion (Jan.–Nov.1996): machinery and transport equipment, chemicals, fuels, minerals, metals, agricultural products. **Imports:** $9.6 billion (Jan.–Nov. 1996): machinery, transport equipment, fuels and lubricants, manufactured goods, raw materials, chemicals, agricultural products. **Major trading partners:** Czech Republic, E.U., former Soviet republics, U.S., central and eastern European countries.

Geography Slovakia is located in central Europe. The land has rugged mountains, rich in mineral resources, with vast forests and pastures. The Carpathian Mountains dominate the topography of Slovakia, with lowland areas in the southern region. Slovakia is about twice the size of the state of Maryland.

Government A parliamentary democracy. The president is elected to a five-year term by the unicameral National Council (legislative branch). The 150 members of the National Council are elected for a four-year term. The president appoints the prime minister, who administers the government.

History Present-day Slovakia was settled by Slavic Slovaks about the 6th century C.E. They were politically united in the Moravian empire in the 9th century. In 907, the Germans and the Magyars conquered the Moravian state and the Slovaks fell under Hungarian control from the 10th century up until 1918. When the Hapsburg-ruled empire collapsed in 1918 following World War I, the Slovaks joined the Czech lands of Bohemia, Moravia, and part of Silesia to form the new joint state of Czechoslovakia. In March 1939, Germany occupied Czechoslovakia, established a German "protectorate," and created a puppet state out of Slovakia with Monsignor Josef Tiso as premier. The country was liberated from the Germans by the Soviet army in the spring of 1945, and Slovakia was restored to its pre-war status and rejoined to a new Czechoslovakian state.

After the Communist party took power in Feb. 1948, Slovakia was again subjected to a centralized Czech-dominated government and antagonism between the two republics developed. On Jan. 1969, the nation became the Slovak Socialist Republic of Czechoslovakia. Nearly 42 years of Communist rule for Slovakia ended when Vaclav Havel became president of Czechoslovakia in 1989 and democratic political reform began. However, with the demise of Communist power, a strong Slovak nationalist movement resurfaced and the rival relationship between the two states increased. By the end of 1991, tensions heightened between Slovak and Czech political leaders following a debate over a Declaration of Slovak Sovereignty that had been proclaimed by the Slovak parliament. Various attempts to resolve the issue by both parties failed. A crisis developed over whether the Czech and Slovak republics should continue to coexist within the federal structure or divide into two independent states.

The results of the general election in June 1992 failed to affirm the continuing coexistence of the Czech and Slovak Republics within a federal state and resulted in the Czech and Slovak political leaders agreeing to separate their nations into two fully independent republics. The Republic of Slovakia came into existence on Jan. 1, 1993. The parliament in Feb. elected Michael Kovac as president. Although Prime Minister Meciar signed a bilateral treaty with Hungary in March 1995, it failed to end concern for ethnic minorities in Slovakia. A referendum in May 1997 on whether the country should join NATO was boycotted by 90% of the electorate after it turned into a showdown between the prime minister and the president, who wanted a question about direct election of the president placed on the ballot. Also in 1997, Slovakia quarrelled with the Czech Republic over disposition of remaining common Czechoslovak government property.

Slovenia

REPUBLIC OF SLOVENIA

President: Milan Kucan (1990)
Prime Minister: Janez Drnovsek (1992)
Area: 7,819 sq mi. (20,256 sq km)
Population (1998 est.): 1,971,739 (average annual rate of natural increase: –0.08%); birth rate: 8.6/1000; infant mortality rate: 5.3/1000; density per sq mi.: 252
Capital and largest city (1996 est.): Ljubljana, 330,000. **Other large city:** Maribor, 103,512. **Monetary unit:** Slovenian Tolar. **Languages:** Slovenian; most can also speak Serbo-Croatian. **Ethnicity/Race:** Slovene 91%, Serbo-Croation, 6%; other, 3%. **Religions:** Roman Catholic 70.8% (including 2% Uniate), Lutheran 1%, Muslim 1%, other 27.2%. **Literacy rate:** 99%
Economic summary: GDP/PPP (1996 est.): $24 billion; $12,300 per capita. **Real growth rate:** 3%. **Inflation:** 8.8%. **Unemployment:** 13%. **Arable land:** 12%. **Labor force:** 857,400. **Agriculture:** corn, rye, oats, potatoes, fruit, livestock raising, and forestry. Mineral resources include coal, timber, and natural gas. **Manufactured products:** automobiles, iron and steel, cement, chemicals, textiles, furniture, shoes, electrical machinery, pharmaceuticals. **Exports:** $8.3 billion (f.o.b., 1996): machinery and transport equipment, 38%; other manufactured goods, 44%; chemicals, 9%; food and live animals, 4.6%; raw materials, 3%. **Imports:** $9.5 billion (f.o.b., 1996): machinery and transport equipment, 35%; other manufactured goods, 26.7%; chemicals, 14.5%; raw materials, 9.4%; fuels and lubricants, 7%. **Major Trading Partners:** E.U., former Yugoslav republics, U.S.

Geography Slovenia occupies an area about the size of the state of Massachusetts. It is largely a mountainous republic and almost half of the land is forested, with hilly plains spread across the central and eastern regions. Mount Triglav, the highest peak, rises to 9,393 ft. (2,864 m).

Government A parliamentary democracy with two legislative houses consisting of an 90-member National Assembly and 40-member State Council. The prime minister and cabinet are appointed by the president with the support of the legislature.

History The Slovenes were a south-Slavic group that settled in the region during the 6th century C.E. During the 7th century, they established the Slavic state of Samu, which owed its allegiance to the Avars, who dominated the Hungarian plain until Charlemagne defeated them in the late 8th century. In the 11th century, Slovenia was a separate province of the kingdom of Hungary. When the Hungarians were defeated by the Turks in 1526, Hungary accepted Austrian Hapsburg rule in order to escape Turkish domination. Thus, Slovenia and Croatia became part of the Austro-Hungarian kingdom when the dual-monarchy was established in 1857. Following the defeat and collapse of Austria-Hungary in World War I, Slovenia declared its independence. It formally joined with Montenegro, Serbia, and Croatia on Dec. 4, 1918, to form the new nation called the kingdom of the Serbs, Croats, and Slovenes. The name was later changed to Yugoslavia in 1929.

During World War II, Germany occupied Yugoslavia and Slovenia was divided among Germany, Italy, and Hungary. For the duration of the war many Slovenes fought a guerrilla war against the Nazis under the leadership of the Croatian-born communist resistance leader, Marshal Tito. After the final defeat of the Axis powers in 1945, Slovenia was again made into a republic of the newly established nation of Yugoslavia. In the late 1980s, Slovenia's communist leaders began moving to create a multiparty system in their republic, thus putting them at odds with Yugoslavia's Serbian-dominated communist party. Slovenia declared its independence from Yugoslavia on June 25, 1991. The Serbian-dominated Yugoslavian army tried to keep Slovenia in line and some brief fighting took place, but the Yugoslavian army withdrew its forces and, unlike neighboring Croatia, Slovenia was able to maintain a peaceful status. With recognition of its independence granted by the European Community in 1992, the country began realigning its economy and society toward western Europe. In April 1997, all of the country's political parties declared their support for membership in NATO.

Solomon Islands

Sovereign: Queen Elizabeth II (1952)
Governor-General: Sir Moses Pitakaka (1994)
Prime Minister: Bartholomew Ulufa'alu (1997)
Area: 11,500 sq mi. (28,450 sq km)
Population (1998 est.): 441,039 (average annual rate of natural increase: 3.24%); birth rate: 36.6/1000; infant mortality rate: 23.9/1000; density per sq mi.: 38
Capital and largest city (1990 est.): Honiara (on Guadalcanal), 35,288. **Monetary unit:** Solomon Islands dollar. **Languages:** English, Solomon Pijin (an English pidgin), over 60 indigenous Melanesian languages. **Ethnicity/Race:** Melanesian 93%, Polynesian 4%, Micronesian 1.5%, European 0.8%, Chinese 0.3%, other 0.4%. **Religions:** Anglican; Roman Catholic; South Seas Evangelical; Seventh-Day Adventist, United (Methodist) Church, other Protestant. **Literacy rate:** 30%
Economic summary: GDP/PPP (1996 est.): $1.2 billion; $3,000 per capita. **Real growth rate:** 4.5%. **Inflation:** 10.4% (1996). **Unemployment:** n.a. **Arable land:** 1%. **Agriculture:** coconuts, palm oil, rice, cocoa, yams, pigs. **Labor force:** 26,842; agriculture, forestry, fishing, 23.7%; services, 41.5%; commerce, transport and finance, 21.7%; construction, manufacturing and mining, 13.1% (1992 est.). **Industry:** processed fish, copra. **Natural resources:** fish, timber, gold, bauxite. **Exports:** $170 million (f.o.b., 1995 est.): fish, timber, copra, palm oil. **Imports:** $152 million (c.i.f., 1995 est.): machinery and transport equipment, foodstuffs, fuel. **Major trading partners:** Japan, E.U., Australia, Thailand, Singapore, Hong Kong, China. **Member of British Commonwealth**

Geography A scattered archipelago of mountainous islands and low-lying coral atolls, the Solomon Islands lie east of Papua New Guinea and northeast of Australia in the south Pacific. The islands include: Guadalcanal, Malaita, Santa Isabel, San Cristóbal, Choiseul, New Georgia, Santa Cruz group, and numerous smaller islands.

Government Solomon Islands is a constitutional monarchy with the British monarch, represented by a governor-general, as head of state. Legislative power is vested in a unicameral legislature of 47 members, led by the prime minister.

History The Solomon Islands were initially settled by at least 2000 B.C.E., probably by people of the Austronesian language group. Explored in 1568 by Alvaro de Mendana, the Solomons were not visited again for about 200 years. In 1886, Great Britain and Germany divided the islands between them. German claims to the Northern Solomons were transferred to the British in 1898–99. The British evacuated the islands shortly before the Japanese, in 1942, invaded them, and fighting in the Solomons in the next three years was among the most bitter in the Pacific, particularly on Guadalcanal. British rule was restored in 1945.

From 1946 to 1950, an independence movement, known as Marching Rule, developed, and in 1970 Britain granted a new constitution that provided a governing council with some local representation. In 1975 the protectorate was granted internal self-government, and it attained full independence on July 7, 1978. Despite progress in talks on border management and defense cooperation, the border with Papua New Guinea (PNG) remained a source of tension. Incursions into Solomon Islands territory by PNG forces countering secessionist action in Bougainville gave rise to formal protests in mid-1997.

Somalia

SOMALI DEMOCRATIC REPUBLIC

National name: Al Jumhouriya As-Somalya al-Dimocradia
President: Vacant, no functioning government in place
Prime Minister: Vacant
Area: 246,199 sq mi. (637,660 sq km)
Population (1998 est.): 6,841,695 (average annual rate of natural increase: 4.43%); birth rate: 46.8/1000; infant mortality rate: 125.8/1000; density per sq mi.: 28
Capital and largest city (1990 est.): Mogadishu, 900,000. **Monetary unit:** Somali shilling. **Language:** Somali (official), Arabic, English, Italian. **Ethnicity/Race:** Somali 85%, Bantu, Arabs. **Religion:** Islam (Sunni). **Literacy rate:** 24%
Economic summary: Political turmoil in 1991–92 resulted in widespread famine and a substantial drop in economic output. Much of the economy has been devastated by the civil war. Agriculture is most important sector with livestock accounting for about 40% of GDP and about 65% of export earnings. **GDP/PPP** (1995 est.): $3.6 billion; $500 per capita. **Real growth rate:** 2%. **Inflation:** n.a. **Unemployment:** n.a. **Arable land:** 2%. **Agriculture:** livestock, bananas, sorghum, cereals, sugar cane, maize. **Labor force:** 3.7 million (1993 est.); very few are skilled laborers. A few small industries: sugar refining, textiles, petroleum refining. **Natural resources:** uranium. **Exports:** $130 million (1994 est.): livestock, skins and hides, bananas. **Imports:** $269 million (1994 est.): textiles, foodstuffs, construction materials and equipment, petroleum products. **Major trading partners:** Saudi Arabia, Italy, U.S., U.K., Germany.

Geography Somalia, situated in the Horn of Africa, lies along the Gulf of Aden and the Indian Ocean. It is bounded by Djibouti in the northwest, Ethiopia in the west, and Kenya in the southwest. In area it is slightly smaller than Texas. Generally arid and barren, Somalia has two chief rivers, the Shebelle and the Juba.

Government None. Last president was overthrown in Jan. 1991; since then Somalia has been plunged into anarchy.

History From the 7th to the 10th century, Arab and Persian trading posts were established along the coast of present-day Somalia. Nomadic tribes occupied the interior, occasionally pushing into Ethiopian territory. In the 16th century, Turkish rule extended to the northern coast and the Sultans of Zanzibar gained control in the south.

After British occupation of Aden in 1839, the Somali coast became its source of food. The French established a coaling station in 1862 at the site of Djibouti and the Italians planted a settlement in Eritrea. Egypt, which for a time claimed Turkish rights in the area, was succeeded by Britain. By 1920, a British protectorate and an Italian protectorate occupied what is now Somalia. The British ruled the entire area after 1941, with Italy returning in 1950 to serve as United Nations trustee for its former territory.

By 1960, Britain and Italy granted independence to their respective sectors, enabling the two to join as the Republic of Somalia on July 1, 1960. Somalia broke diplomatic relations with Britain in 1963 when the British granted the Somali-populated Northern Frontier District of Kenya to the Republic of Kenya.

On Oct. 15, 1969, President Abdi Rashid Ali Shermarke was assassinated and the army seized power, dissolving the legislature and arresting all government leaders. Maj. Gen. Mohamed Siad Barre, as president of a renamed Somali Democratic Republic, leaned heavily toward the U.S.S.R. In 1977, Somalia openly backed rebels in the easternmost area of Ethiopia, the Ogaden desert, which had been seized by Ethiopia at the turn of the century. Somalia acknowledged defeat in an eight-month war against the Ethiopians that year, having lost much of its 32,000-man army and most of its tanks and planes.

President Siad Barre fled the country in late Jan. 1991. His departure left Somalia in the hands of a number of clan-based guerrilla groups, none of which trusted each other.

Africa's worst drought occurred in 1992, and coupled with the devastation of civil war, Somalia was plunged into a severe famine—an estimated one-third of the population was in danger of dying from starvation. U.S. troops were sent in to protect the delivery of food in Dec. 1992. In May the U.N. took control of the relief efforts from the U.S. The warlord Mohammed Farah Aidid ambushed U.N. troops and dragged American bodies through the streets, causing an about-face in America's willingness to involve itself in the fate of this anarchic country. Peace talks in Kenya appeared to be moving slowly but steadily toward an agreement on an interim government, at least in principle, when on March 23, 1994, they collapsed. The last of the U.S. troops left in late March, leaving 19,000 U.N. troops behind.

Since 1991 Somalia has been engulfed in anarchy. Over the past seven years peace negotiations between the various factions have been fruitless, and no attempt has been made to rebuild the government. In 1991, a breakaway nation, the Somaliland Republic, proclaimed its independence. Since then several warlords have begun to set up their own mini-states—Colonel Abdullahi Yussuf Ahmed is president of breakaway Puntland and Mohamed "General Morgan" Said Hersi began setting up Jubaland in the fall of 1998.

South Africa

REPUBLIC OF SOUTH AFRICA

National name: Republic of South Africa
President: Nelson Mandela (1994)
Deputy President: Thabo Mbeki
Area: 471,440 sq mi. (1,219,912 sq km)
Population (1998 est.): 42,834,520 (average annual rate of natural increase: 1.42%); birth rate: 26.4/1000; infant mortality rate: 52/1000; density per sq mi.: 91
Administrative capital: Pretoria
Legislative capital: Cape Town
Judicial capital: Bloemfontein. No decision has been made to relocate the seat of government. South Africa is demarcated into nine provinces, consisting of the Gauteng, Northern Province, Mpumalanga, North West, KwaZulu/Natal, Eastern Cape, Western Cape, Northern Cape, and Free State. Each province has its own capital. **Largest metropolitan areas (1995):** Cape Peninsula, 2,350,157; Johannesburg 1,916,063; East Rand, 1,378,792; Durban/Pinetown, 1,137,378; Pretoria, 1,080,187. **Monetary unit:** Rand. **Languages:** English, Afrikaans, Ndebele, Sesotho sa Leboa, Sesotho, Swati, Xitsonga, Setswana, Tshivenda, Xhosa and Zulu are the official languages of the interim period. **Ethnicity/Race:** black 75.2%, white 13.6%, Colored 8.6%, Indian 2.6%. **Religions:** Christian; Hindu; Islam. **Literacy rate:** 76%
Economic summary: GDP/PPP (1996 est.): $227 billion; $5,400 per capita. **Real growth rate:** 3%. **Inflation:** 9%. **Unemployment:** 34%, plus 11% underemployed. **Arable land:** 10%. **Agriculture:** corn, wool, wheat, sugar cane, fruits, vegetables. **Labor force:** 14.2 million economically active (1996); by occupation: services, 35%, agriculture, 30%, industry, 20%, mining, 9%, other, 6%. **Industry:** gold, chromium, diamonds, assembled automobiles, machinery, textiles, iron and steel, chemicals, fertilizer. **Natural resources:** gold, diamonds, platinum, uranium, coal, iron ore, phosphates, manganese. **Exports:** $29.2 billion (f.o.b 1996): gold, diamonds, minerals and metals, food, chemicals. **Imports:** $26.9 billion (f.o.b., 1996): motor vehicle parts, machinery, metals, chemicals, textiles, scientific instruments. **Major trading partners:** Germany, U.S., other E.U., Japan, U.K., Hong Kong, Italy, Taiwan.

Geography South Africa, on the continent's southern tip, is washed by the Atlantic Ocean on the west and by the Indian Ocean on the south and east. Its neighbors are Namibia in the northwest, Zimbabwe and Botswana in the north, and Mozambique and Swaziland in the northeast. The kingdom of Lesotho forms an enclave within the southeastern part of South Africa. Bophuthatswana, Transkei, Ciskei, and Venda are independent states within South Africa, which occupies an area nearly three times that of California.

The southernmost point of Africa is Cape Agulhas, located in the Western Cape Province about 100 miles (161 km) southeast of the Cape of Good Hope.

Government South Africa is a constitutional state with three tiers of government, and a chapter for fundamental human rights. Parliament consists of a 400-member National Assembly and a 90-person Council of Provinces. The National Assembly consists of 200 members from the provincial ballot. Election to these bodies takes place on the basis of proportional representation. A new constitution was adopted in May 1996 guaranteeing equal rights for everyone. The constitution came into effect over a three-year period.

History The San people were the first settlers. The Dutch East India Company landed the first European settlers on the Cape of Good Hope in 1652, launching a colony that by the end of the 18th century numbered only about 15,000. Known as Boers or Afrikaners, speaking a Dutch dialect known as Afrikaans, the settlers as early as 1795 tried to establish an independent republic.

After occupying the Cape Colony in that year, Britain took permanent possession in 1814 at the end of the Napoleonic wars, bringing in 5,000 settlers. Anglicization of government and the freeing of slaves in 1833 drove about 12,000 Afrikaners to make the "great trek" north and east into African tribal territory, where they established the republics of the Transvaal and the Orange Free State.

The discovery of diamonds in 1867 and gold nine years later brought an influx of "outlanders" into the republics and spurred Cecil Rhodes to plot annexation. Rhodes's scheme of sparking an "outlander" rebellion to which an armed party under Leander Starr Jameson would ride to the rescue misfired in 1895, forcing Rhodes to resign as prime minister of the Cape colony. What British expansionists called the "inevitable" war with the Boers eventually broke out on Oct. 11, 1899. The defeat of the Boers in 1902 led in 1910 to the Union of South Africa, composed of four provinces, the two former republics and the old Cape and Natal colonies. Louis Botha, a Boer, became the first prime minister. Organized political activity among Africans started with the establishment of the African National Congress in 1912.

Jan Christiaan Smuts brought the nation into World War II on the Allied side against Nationalist opposition, and South Africa became a charter member of the United Nations in 1945, but refused to sign the Universal Declaration of Human Rights. Apartheid—racial separation—dominated domestic politics as the Nationalists gained power and imposed greater restrictions on Bantus, Asians, and Coloreds (in South Africa the term meant any nonwhite person). African voters were removed from the voter rolls in 1936.

Afrikaner hostility to Britain triumphed in 1961 with the declaration on May 31 of the Republic of South Africa and the severing of ties with the Commonwealth. Nationalist Prime Minister H. F. Verwoerd's government in 1963 asserted the power to restrict freedom of those who opposed rigid racial laws. Three years later, amid increasing racial tension and criticism from the outside world, Verwoerd was assassinated. His Nationalist successor, Balthazar J. Vorster, launched a campaign of conciliation toward conservative black African states, offering development loans and trade concessions.

Elections on May 7, 1987, increased the power of President Botha's Nationalist party while enabling the far-right Conservative Party to replace the liberal Progressives as the official opposition. The results of the whites-only vote indicated a strong conservative reaction against Botha's policy of limited reform.

A stroke led Botha to step down as leader of his party in 1989 in favor of F. W. de Klerk. De Klerk accelerated the pace of reform. He unbanned the African National Congress, the principal anti-apartheid organization, and released Nelson Mandela, the ANC deputy president and all other anti-apartheid movements/organizations after 27 years of imprisonment. Negotiations between the government and the ANC commenced.

On June 5, 1991, the parliament scrapped the country's apartheid laws concerning property ownership. On June 17 the parliament did the same for the Population Registration Act of 1950, which classified all South Africans at birth by race. In Feb. 1993 the ANC approved a plan that would allow minority parties to participate in the government for five years after the end of white rule. Also in Feb., the first nonwhites entered the cabinet in an apparent bid to broaden the base of the ruling National Party.

The 1994 election, as expected, resulted in a massive victory for Mandela and his ANC. The new government included six ministers from the National Party and three from the Inkatha Freedom Party.

In 1997 the Truth and Reconciliation Commission, chaired by Desmond Tutu, began hearings regarding human rights violations between 1960 and 1993. The commission promised amnesty to those who confessed their crimes under the Apartheid system. In 1998 F. W. de Klerk, P. W. Botha, and leaders of the ANC appeared before the commission, and the nation continued to grapple with its enlightened but often painful and divisive process of national recovery.

Spain

KINGDOM OF SPAIN

National name: Reino de España
Ruler: King Juan Carlos I (1975)
Prime Minister: Joeé María Aznar (1996)
Area: 195,364.5 sq mi. (504,750 sq km)[1]
Population (1998 est.): 39,133,996 (average annual growth rate: 0.08%); birth rate: 9.7/1000; infant mortality rate: 6.5/1000; density per sq mi.: 200
Capital and largest city (1994 est.): Madrid, 3,041,101. **Other large cities:** Barcelona, 1,630,867; Valencia, 764,293; Seville, 714,148. **Monetary unit:** Peseta. **Languages:** Castilian Spanish 74%, Catalan 17%, Galician 7%, Basque 2%. **Ethnicity/Race:** composite of Mediterranean and Nordic types. **Religion:** Roman Catholic, 99%. **Literacy rate:** 96%
Economic summary: GDP/PPP (1996 est.): $593 billion; $15,300 per capita. **Real growth rate:** 2.4%. **Inflation:** 3.7%. **Unemployment** (1996 est.), 22%. **Arable land:** 30%. **Agriculture:** cereals, vegetables, citrus fruits, wine, olives and olive oil, livestock. **Labor force:** 12.475 million; services, 62%; manufacturing, mining, and construction, 29%; agriculture, 9% (1996). **Industry:** processed foods, textiles, footwear, petro-chemicals, steel, automobiles, ships. **Natural resources:** coal, lignite, water power, uranium, mercury, pyrites, fluorospar, gypsum, iron ore, zinc, lead, tungsten, copper. **Exports:** $94.5 billion (f.o.b., 1995): cars and trucks, semifinished manufactured goods, foodstuffs, machinery and electrical equipment. **Imports:** $118.3 billion (c.i.f., 1995): machinery and transportation equipment, chemicals, petroleum, semifinished goods, consumer goods, machines and electrical equipment. **Major trading partners:** E.U., U.S.

1. Including the Balearic and Canary Islands.

Geography Spain occupies 85% of the Iberian Peninsula in southwestern Europe, which it shares with Portugal. Africa is less than 10 miles (16 km) south at the Strait of Gibraltar. A broad central plateau slopes to the south and east, crossed by a series of mountain ranges and river valleys. Principal rivers are the Ebro in the northeast, the Tajo in the central region, and the Guadalquivir in the south. Off Spain's east coast in the Mediterranean are the Balearic Islands (1,936 sq mi.; 5,014 sq km), the largest of which is Majorca. Sixty miles (97 km) west of Africa are the Canary Islands (2,808 sq mi.; 7,273 sq km).

Government A parliamentary monarchy. The Cortes, or parliament, consists of a Chamber of Deputies of 350 members and a Senate of 208, all elected by universal suffrage. Executive power rests in the prime minister, who is named by the king upon the recommendation of the majority party.

History Spain, originally inhabited by Celts, Iberians, and Basques, became a part of the Roman Empire in 206 B.C.E., when it was conquered by Scipio Africanus. In C.E. 412, the barbarian Visigothic leader Ataulf crossed the Pyrenees and ruled Spain, first in the name of the Roman emperor and then independently. In 711, the Muslims under Tariq entered Spain from Africa and within a few years completed the subjugation of the country. In 732, the Franks, led by Charles Martel, defeated the Muslims near Poitiers, thus preventing the further expansion of Islam in southern Europe. Internal dissension of Spanish Islam invited a steady Christian conquest from the north.

Aragon and Castile were the most important Spanish states from the 12th to the 15th century, consolidated by the marriage of Ferdinand II and Isabella I in 1469. The last Muslim stronghold, Granada, was captured in 1492. Roman Catholicism was established as the official state religion and most Jews (1492) and Muslims (1502) were expelled. In the era of exploration, discovery, and colonization, Spain amassed tremendous wealth and a vast colonial empire through the conquest of Peru by Pizarro (1532–33) and of Mexico by Cortés (1519–21). The Spanish Hapsburg monarchy became for a time the most powerful in the world. In 1588, Philip II sent his invincible Armada to invade England, but its destruction cost Spain its supremacy on the seas and paved the way for England's colonization of America. Spain then sank rapidly to the status of a second-rate power, under the rule of weak Hapsburg kings, and never again played a major role in European politics. The War of the Spanish Succession (1701–14) resulted in Spain's loss of Belgium, Luxembourg, Milan, Sardinia, and Naples. Its colonial empire in the Americas and the Philippines vanished in wars and revolutions during the 18th and 19th centuries.

In World War I, Spain maintained a position of neutrality. In 1923, Gen. Miguel Primo de Rivera became dictator. In 1930, King Alfonso XIII revoked the dictatorship, but a strong antimonarchist and republican movement led to his leaving Spain in 1931. The new constitution declared Spain a workers' republic, broke up the large estates, separated church and state, and secularized the schools. The elections held in 1936 returned a strong Popular Front majority, with Manuel Azaña as president.

On July 18, 1936, a conservative army officer in Morocco, Francisco Franco Bahamonde, led a mutiny against the government. The civil war that followed lasted three years and cost the lives of nearly a million people. Franco was aided by Fascist Italy and Nazi Germany, while Soviet Russia helped the Loyalist side. Several hundred leftist Americans served in the Abraham Lincoln Brigade on the side of the republic. The war ended when Franco took Madrid on March 28, 1939. Franco became head of the state, national chief of the Falange Party (the governing party), and premier and caudillo (leader). In a referendum in 1947, the Spanish people approved a Franco-drafted succession law declaring Spain a monarchy again. Franco, however, continued as chief of state.

In 1969, Franco and the Cortes-designated Prince Juan Carlos Alfonso Victor María de Borbón (who married Princess Sophia of Greece on May 14, 1962) to become king of Spain when the provisional government headed by Franco came to an end. Franco died of a heart attack on Nov. 20, 1975, after more than a year of ill health, and Juan Carlos was proclaimed king seven days later. Under pressure from Catalonian and Basque nationalists, Premier Adolfo Suárez granted home rule to these regions in 1979. Basque separatists (ETA) committed hundreds of terrorist bombings and kidnappings that continue through the present. With the overwhelming election of Prime Minister Felipe González Márquez and his Spanish Socialist Workers Party in the Oct. 20, 1982, parliamentary elections, the Franco past was finally buried.

Spain entered NATO in 1982. A treaty admitting Spain, along with Portugal, to the European Economic Community, now the European Union, took effect on Jan. 1, 1986. Later that year, Spain voted to remain in NATO, but outside of its military command. For the 1992 quincentennial of Christopher Columbus' first voyage from Spain to the Americas, Spain celebrated with a fair in Seville and the Olympic Games in Barcelona. General elections in March 1996 produced a victory for the conservative Popular Party, which, although lacking an absolute majority in the Cortes, received the backing of regional parties for a coalition government with Aznar as prime minister.

Sri Lanka

DEMOCRATIC SOCIALIST REPUBLIC OF SRI LANKA

President: Chandrika B. Kumaratunga (1994)
Prime Minister: Sirimavo Bandaranaike (1994)
Area: 25,332 sq mi. (65,610 sq km)
Population (1998 est.): 18,933,558 (average annual rate of natural increase: 1.12%); birth rate: 18.4/1000; infant mortality rate: 16.3/1000; density per sq mi.: 747
Capital and largest city (1992 est.): Sri Jayewardenepura Kotte (Colombo), 1,994,000. **Other large cities (1992 est.):** Gampaha, 1,543,000; Kurunegala, 1,445,000; Kandy, 1,257,000. **Monetary unit:** Sri Lanka rupee. **Languages:** Sinhala, Tamil, English. **Ethnicity/Race:** Sinhalese 74%, Tamil 18%, Moor 7%, Burgher, Malay, and Vedda 1%. **Religions:** Buddhist, 69%; Hindu, 15%; Islam, 8%; Christian, 8%. **Literacy rate:** 88%
Economic summary: GDP/PPP (1996 est.): $69.7 billion; $3,760 per capita. **Real growth rate:** 3.7%. **Inflation** (1996), 15.9%. **Unemployment** (1994), 13.1%. **Arable land:** 14%. **Agriculture:** tea, coconuts, rubber, rice, spices. **Labor force:** 6.2 million (1994); agriculture. 42%; services, 40%; industry, 18% (1994). **Products:** processed rubber, tea, coconuts, textiles, cement, refined petroleum. **Natural resources:** limestone, graphite, gems. **Exports:** $4 billion (f.o.b., 1996 est.): textiles, tea, rubber, petroleum products, gems and jewelry. **Imports:** $5 billion (c.i.f., 1996 est.): petroleum, machinery, transport equipment, sugar. **Major trading partners:** U.S., U.K., Germany, Japan, Singapore, India, Iran, Taiwan, Belgium, Hong Kong, China. **Member of Commonwealth of Nations**

Geography An island in the Indian Ocean off the southeast tip of India, Sri Lanka is about half the size of Alabama. Most of the land is flat and rolling; mountains in the south central region rise to over 8,000 feet (2,438 m).

Government Ceylon became an independent country in 1948 after British rule and reverted to the traditional name ("resplendent island") on May 22, 1972. A new constitution adopted in 1978 set up the National State Assembly, a 225-member unicameral legislature that serves for six years unless dissolved earlier.

History Indo-Aryan emigration from India in the 5th century B.C.E. came to form the largest ethnic group on Sri Lanka today, the Sinhalese. Tamils, the second-largest ethnic group on the island, were originally from the Tamil region of India, and emigrated between the 3rd century B.C.E. and C.E. 1200. Until colonial powers controlled Ceylon (the country's name until 1972), Sinhalese and Tamil rulers fought for dominance over the island. The Tamils, primarily Hindus, claimed the northern section of the island and the Sinhalese, who are predominantly Buddhist, controlled the south. In 1505 the Portuguese took possession of Ceylon until the Dutch India Company usurped control (1658–1796). The British took over in 1796, and Ceylon became an English Crown colony in 1802. The British developed coffee, tea, and rubber plantations. On Feb. 4, 1948, after pressure from Ceylonese nationalist leaders (which briefly unified the Tamil and Sinhalese) Ceylon became a self-governing dominion of the Commonwealth of Nations.

S. W. R. D. Bandaranaike became prime minister in 1956 and championed Sinhalese nationalism, making Sinhala the country's only official language and including state support of Buddhism, further marginalizing the Tamil minority. He was assassinated in 1959 by a Buddhist monk. His widow, Sirimavo Bandaranaike, became the world's first female prime minister in 1960.

The Tamil minority's mounting resentment toward the Sinhalese majority's monopoly on political and economic power, exacerbated by cultural and religious differences, erupted in bloody violence in 1983. The civil war continues today. Tamils make up about 18% of the population in Sri Lanka, whereas approximately three-quarters of Sri Lanka's 18-million people are Sinhalese. Tamil rebel groups, the strongest of which are the Liberation Tigers of Tamil Eelam, or Tamil Tigers, are fighting for a separate nation.

India had sent a peace-keeping force in July 1987 to help maintain an accord granting the Tamil minority limited autonomy. The agreement failed, and Indian troops withdrew at the end of 1989.

President Ranasinghe Premadasa was assassinated at a May Day political rally in 1993 when a Tamil rebel detonated explosives strapped to himself. Tamil extremists have frequently resorted to terrorist attacks against civilians. The civil war continues unabated and the president has extended the state of emergency to the entire country.

Sudan

REPUBLIC OF THE SUDAN

National name: Jamhuryat es-Sudan
President: Lt. Gen. Omar Hassan Ahmad al-Bashir (1993)
Area: 967,491 sq mi. (2,505,810 sq km)
Population (1998 est.): 33,550,552 (average annual rate of natural increase: 2.73%); birth rate: 39.9/1000; infant mortality rate: 72.6/1000; density per sq mi.: 35
Capital (1993 est.): Khartoum, 924,505. **Largest cities:** Omdurman, 1,267,077; Port Sudan, 305,385.
Monetary unit: Sudanese pound. **Languages:** Arabic, English, tribal dialects. **Ethnicity/Race:** black 52%, Arab 39%, Beja 6%, foreigners 2%, other 1%. **Religions:** Islam, 70% (Sunni); indigenous, 20%; Christian, 5%. **Literacy rate:** 27%
Economic summary: GDP/PPP (1996 est.): $26.6 billion; $860 per capita. **Real growth rate:** 4%. **Inflation:** 133%. **Unemployment:** 30% (FY 92/93 est.). **Arable land:** 5%. **Agriculture:** cotton, oil seeds, gum arabic, sorghum, wheat, millet, sheep. **Labor force:** 11 million; agriculture, 80%; industry and commerce, 10%; government, 6% (note: labor shortages for almost all categories of skilled employment) (1983 est.). **Industry:** cement, textiles, pharmaceuticals, shoes, soap, refined petroleum, gold. **Natural resources:** crude oil, some iron ore, copper, chrome, industrial metals. **Exports:** $500 million (f.o.b., 1996 est.): cotton, peanuts, gum arabic, sesame. **Imports:** $1 billion (1996 est.): petroleum products, machinery and equipment, medicines and chemicals. **Major trading partners:** Western Europe, Saudi Arabia, Eastern Europe, Japan.

Geography The Sudan, in northeast Africa, is the largest country on the continent, measuring about one-fourth the size of the United States. Its neighbors are Chad and the Central African Republic on the west, Egypt and Libya on the north, Ethiopia and Eritrea on the east, and Kenya, Uganda, and Congo on the south. The Red Sea washes about 500 miles of the eastern coast. The country extends from north to south about 1,200 miles (1,931 km) and west to east about 1,000 miles (1,609 km). The northern region is a continuation of the Libyan Desert. The southern region is fertile, abundantly watered, and, in places, heavily forested. It is traversed from north to south by the Nile, all of whose great tributaries are partly or entirely within its borders.

Government A military government headed by President Omar Hassan Ahmad al-Bashir, who outlawed political parties and suspended the constitution.

History What is now northern Sudan was in ancient times the kingdom of Nubia, which came under Egyptian rule after 2600 B.C.E. An Egyptian and Nubian civilization called Kush flourished until C.E. 350. Missionaries converted the region to Christianity in the 6th century, but an influx of Muslim Arabs, who had already conquered Egypt, eventually controlled the area and replaced Christianity with Islam. During the 1500s a people called the Funj conquered much of Sudan, and several other black African groups settled in the south, including the Dinka, Shilluk, Nuer, and Azande. Egyptians again conquered the Sudan in 1874, and after Britain occupied Egypt in 1882, it took over Sudan in 1898, ruling the country in conjunction with Egypt. It was known as the Anglo-Egyptian Sudan between 1898 and 1955.

The 20th century saw the growth of Sudanese nationalism, and in 1953 Egypt and Britain granted the Sudan self-government. Independence was proclaimed on Jan. 1, 1956. Since independence, the Sudan has been ruled by a series of unstable parliamentary governments and military regimes. Under Maj. Gen. Gaafar Mohamed Nimeiri, the Sudan instituted fundamentalist Islamic law in 1983. This exacerbated the rift between the Arab North, the seat of the government, and the black African animists and Christians in the South. Differences in language, religion, ethnicity, and political power erupted in an unending civil war between government forces, strongly influenced by the National Islamic Front (NIF), and the southern rebels, whose most influential faction is the Sudanese People's Liberation Army. Neither side has gained the upper hand, and more than an estimated 1 million people have died in battle or from famines and disease resulting from war. Human rights violations, religious persecution, and allegations that the Sudan has been a safe haven for terrorists have isolated the country from most of the international community.

On Aug. 20, 1998, the United States launched cruise missiles that destroyed a pharmaceutical manufacturing facility in Khartoum that allegedly manufactured chemical weapons. Sudan has close ties with Iraq, which has thwarted the U.N. inspections of its weapons stockpiles that are thought to include biological weapons. The U.S. contended that the Sudanese factory was financed by the wealthy Islamic militant, Osama bin Laden.

Suriname

REPUBLIC OF SURINAME

President: Jules Wijdenbosch (1996)
Prime Minister: Pretaapnarian Radhakishun (1996)
Area: 63,251 sq mi. (163,270 sq km)
Population (1998 est.): 427,980 (average annual rate of natural increase: 0.77%); birth rate: 22.5/1000; infant mortality rate: 27.4/1000; density per sq mi.: 7
Capital and largest city (1993 est.): Paramaribo, 200,970. **Monetary unit:** Suriname guilder. **Languages:** Dutch, Surinamese (lingua franca), English widely spoken. **Ethnicity/Race:** Hindustani (also known locally as "East" Indians; their ancestors emigrated from northern India in the latter part of the 19th century) 37%, Creole (mixed European and African ancestry) 31%, Javanese 15.3%, "Bush Black" (also known as "Bush Creole" whose ancestors were brought to the country in the 17th and 18th centuries as slaves) 10.3%, Amerindian 2.6%, Chinese 1.7%, Europeans 1%, other 1.1%. **Religions:** Protestant, 25.2%; Roman Catholic, 22.8%; Hindu, 27.4%; Islam, 19.6%; indigenous, about 5%. **Literacy rate:** 95%
Economic summary: GDP/PPP (1996 est.): $1.4 billion; $3,150 per capita. **Real growth rate:** 3%. **Inflation:** 0%. **Unemployment:** n.a. **Arable land:** 0%. **Agriculture:** rice. **Labor force:** n.a. **Products:** aluminum, alumina, processed foods, lumber. **Natural resources:** bauxite, iron ore, timber, fish, shrimp. **Exports:** $432 million (f.o.b, 1995 est.): bauxite, alumina, aluminum, rice, shrimp and fish, bananas. **Imports:** $418 million (f.o.b., 1995 est.): capital equipment, petroleum, cotton, foodstuffs, consumer goods. **Major trading partners:** U.S., Trinidad, Netherlands, Norway, Germany, Brazil, U.K., Japan, Netherlands Antilles.

Geography Suriname lies on the northeast coast of South America, with Guyana to the west, French Guiana to the east, and Brazil to the south. It is about one-tenth larger than Michigan. The principal rivers are the Corantijn on the Guyana border, the Marowijne in the east, and the Suriname, on which the capital city of Paramaribo is situated.

Government Suriname, formerly known as Dutch Guiana, returned to civilian rule in 1987, after having been ruled for seven years by a military council, and adopted a new constitution. The executive branch consists of the president and prime minister, Cabinet of Ministers, and Council of State. The legislative branch consists of a unicameral National Assembly with 51 members. The military maintains a continuing role in government by means of an executive Council of State, which can annul laws passed by the National Assembly.

History Suriname's earliest inhabitants were the Surinen Indians, after whom the country is named. By the 16th century they had been supplanted by other South American Indians. Spain explored it in 1593, but by 1602 the Dutch began to settle the land, followed by the English. The English transferred sovereignty to the Dutch in 1667 (the Treaty of Breda) in exchange for New Amsterdam (New York). Colonization was confined to a narrow coastal strip, and until the abolition of slavery in 1863, African slaves furnished the labor for the coffee and sugarcane plantation economy. Escaped African slaves fled into the interior and reconstituted their western African culture and government and came to be called "Bush Negroes" by the Dutch. After 1870, laborers were imported from British India and the Dutch East Indies.

In 1948, the colony was integrated into the kingdom of the Netherlands and two years later was granted full home rule in matters other than foreign affairs and defense. After race rioting over unemployment and inflation, The Netherlands granted Suriname complete independence on Nov. 25, 1975. A coup d'état in 1980 brought military rule. During much of the 1980s Suriname was under the control of Lieut. Col. Dési Bouterse, who in late Dec. 1990 resigned as commander of the armed forces. A guerrilla insurgency by the Jungle Commando (a Bush Negro guerilla group) furthered disruption in the country, and the instability in the region caused some foreign governments to withhold economic aid. Free elections were held on May 25, 1991, depriving the military of much of its political power. In 1992 a peace treaty was signed between the government and several guerrilla groups. In March 1997 the president announced new economic measures including eliminating import tariffs on most basic goods coupled with strict price controls. Later that year, The Netherlands declared that it would prosecute the former military dictator of Suriname, Dési Bouterse, for large-scale cocaine trafficking.

Swaziland

KINGDOM OF SWAZILAND

Ruler: King Mswati III (1986)
Prime Minister: Barnabas Sibusiso Dlamini (July 1996)
Area: 6,704 sq mi. (17,360 sq km)
Population (1998 est.): 966,462 (average annual rate of natural increase: 1.96%); birth rate: 41/1000; infant mortality rate: 103.4/1000; density per sq mi.: 144
Capital and largest city (1990 est.): Mbabane 47,020. **Monetary unit:** Lilangeni. **Languages:** English and Swazi (official). **Ethnicity/Race:** African 97%, European 3%. **Religions:** Christian, 60%; indigenous, 40%. **Literacy rate:** 70%
Economic summary: GDP/PPP (1996 est.): $3.8 billion; $3,800 per capita. **Real growth rate:** 2.9%. **Inflation:** 14.7% (1995). **Unemployment:** 15% (1992 est.). **Arable land:** 11%. **Agriculture:** corn, livestock, sugar cane, citrus fruits, cotton, sorghum, peanuts. The economy is based on subsistence agriculture, which

occupies more than 60% of the population and contributes nearly 25% to GDP. Manufacturing, which includes a number of agroprocessing factories, accounts for another quarter of GDP. **Labor force:** 160,355 (1986 est.); 65% in the private sector; 35% in the public sector. **Industry:** milled sugar, ginned cotton, processed meat and wood. **Natural resources:** asbestos, diamonds. **Exports:** $700 million (f.o.b., 1996): sugar, wood pulp, asbestos, citrus fruits. **Imports:** $831 million (f.o.b., 1996): motor vehicles, transport equipment, petroleum products, foodstuffs, chemicals. **Major trading partners:** South Africa, U.K., U.S. **Member of Commonwealth of Nations**

Geography Swaziland, 85% the size of New Jersey, is surrounded by South Africa and Mozambique. The country consists of a high veld in the west and a series of plateaus descending from 6,000 feet (1,829 m) to a low veld of 1,500 feet (457 m).

Government In 1967, a new constitution established King Sobhuza II as head of state and provided for an Assembly of 24 members elected by universal suffrage, together with a Senate of 12 members—half appointed by the Assembly and half by the king. In 1973, the king renounced the constitution, suspended political parties, and took total power for himself. In 1977, he replaced the parliament with an assembly of tribal leaders. The parliament reconvened in 1979.

History Bantu peoples migrated southwest to the area of Mozambique in the 16th century. A number of clans broke away from the main body in the 18th century and settled in Swaziland. In the 19th century they organized as a tribe, partly because they were in constant conflict with the Zulu. Their ruler, Mswazi, applied to the British in the 1840s for help against the Zulu. The British and the Transvaal governments guaranteed the independence of Swaziland in 1881.

South Africa held Swaziland as a protectorate from 1894 to 1899, but after the Boer War, in 1902, Swaziland was transferred to British administration. The Paramount Chief was recognized as the native authority in 1941.

In 1963, the territory was constituted a protectorate, and on Sept. 6, 1968, it became the independent nation of Swaziland.

The king in Oct. 1992 dissolved parliament and announced plans for a new constitution allowing a multiparty democracy. The first democratic elections took place in Sept. 1993.

The government presented a tax reform plan in June 1997 intended to broaden the tax base and thereby increase revenues by at least 38%. Since 1992 the budget has gone from a surplus to a considerable deficit.

Sweden

KINGDOM OF SWEDEN

National name: Konungariket Sverige
Sovereign: King Carl XVI Gustaf (1973)
Prime Minister: Göran Persson (1996)
Area: 173,800 sq mi. (449,964 sq km)
Population (1998 est.): 8,886,738 (average annual rate of natural increase 0.26%); birth rate: 11.7/1000; infant mortality rate: 3.9/1000; density per sq mi.: 51
Capital and largest city (1994): Stockholm, 703,627. **Largest cities:** Göteborg, 444,553; Malmö, 242,706; Uppsala, 181,191. **Monetary unit:** Krona. **Language:** Swedish. **Ethnicity/Race:** white, Lapp (Sami), foreign-born or first-generation immigrants 12% (Finns, Yugoslavs, Danes, Norwegians, Greeks, Turks). **Religions:** Evangelical Lutheran 94%, Roman Catholic 1.5%, Pentecostal 1%, other 3.5%. **Literacy rate:** 99%
Economic summary: GDP/PPP (1996 est.): $184.3 billion; $20,800 per capita. **Real growth rate:** 1.4%. **Inflation:** 0.2% (Sept. 1996). **Unemployment:** 8%, plus 6% in training programs (Sept. 1996). **Arable land:** 7%. **Agriculture:** dairy products, grains, sugar beets, potatoes. **Labor force:** 4.552 million (84% unionized, 1992); community, social, and personal services, 38.3%; mining and manufacturing, 21.2%; commerce, hotels and restaurants, 14.1%; banking and insurance, 9% (1991). **Industry:** iron and steel, precision equipment, wood pulp and paper products, automobiles. **Natural resources:** forests, iron ore, hydroelectric power, zinc, uranium. **Exports:** $79.9 billion (f.o.b., 1995): machinery, motor vehicles, wood pulp, paper products, chemicals, petroleum and petroleum products, iron and steel products. **Imports:** $64.4 billion (c.i.f., 1995): machinery, clothing, petroleum and petroleum products, foodstuffs, iron and steel, chemicals. **Major trading partners:** E.U., Finland, Norway, U.S.

Geography Sweden, which occupies the eastern part of the Scandinavian peninsula, is the fourth largest country in Europe, and is one-tenth larger than California. The country slopes eastward and southward from the Kjólen Mountains along the Norwegian border, where the peak elevation is Kebnekaise at 6,965 feet (2,123 m) in Lapland. In the north are mountains and many lakes. To the south and east are central lowlands and south of them are fertile areas of forest, valley, and plain. Along Sweden's rocky coast, chopped up by bays and inlets, are many islands, the largest of which are Gotland and Öland.

Government Sweden is a constitutional monarchy. Under the 1975 constitution, the unicameral Riksdag is the sole governing body and the prime minister is the political chief executive. Of the Riksdag's 349 total seats, 310 are directly elected and the remainder are apportioned to contending parties on the basis of votes received nationally. The members are popularly elected for three years. The king, Carl XVI Gustaf, was born April 30, 1946, and succeeded to the throne Sept. 19, 1973. Under the new Act of Succession, effective Jan. 1, 1980, the first child of the reigning monarch, regardless of sex, is heir to the throne. This makes Princess Victoria, born July 14, 1977, the heir apparent.

History The earliest historical mention of Sweden is found in Tacitus's *Germania,* where reference is made to the powerful king and strong fleet of the Sviones. In the 11th century, Olaf Sköttkonung became the first Swedish king to be baptized as a Christian. Around 1400, an attempt was made to unite Sweden, Norway, and Denmark into one kingdom, but this led to bitter strife between the Danes and the Swedes. In 1520, the Danish king, Christian II, conquered Sweden and in the "Stockholm Bloodbath" put leading Swedish personages to death. Gustavus Vasa (1523–60) broke away from Denmark and fashioned the modern Swedish state.

Sweden played a leading role in the second phase (1630–35) of the Thirty Years' War (1618–48). By the Treaty of Westphalia (1648), Sweden obtained western Pomerania and some neighboring territory on the Baltic. In 1700, a coalition of Russia, Poland, and Denmark united against Sweden and by the Peace of Nystad (1721) forced it to relinquish Livonia, Ingria, Estonia, and parts of Finland. Around this time, the Reformation reached the nation and Lutheranism became the state religion. Sweden emerged from the Napoleonic Wars with the acquisition of Norway from Denmark and with a new royal dynasty stemming from Marshal Jean Bernadotte of France, who became king Charles XIV (1818–44). The artificial union between Sweden and Norway led to an uneasy relationship, and the union was finally dissolved in 1905. Sweden maintained a position of neutrality in both World Wars.

An elaborate structure of welfare legislation, imitated by many larger nations, began with the establishment of old-age pensions in 1911. Economic prosperity based on its neutralist policy enabled Sweden, together with Norway, to pioneer in public health, housing, and job security programs. Forty-four years of socialist government were ended in 1976 with the election of a conservative coalition headed by Thorbjörn Fälldin. The Socialists were returned to power in the election of 1982. Elections in Sept. 1991 ousted the Social Democrats (Socialists) from power. The new coalition of four conservative parties pledged to cut taxes and cut back on the welfare state but not alter Sweden's traditional neutrality. General elections in Sept. 1994 saw the emergence again of the Social Democrats after three years of being in opposition. Short of a majority by 13 seats in the Riksdag, they decided to establish a minority government. In a referendum held in Nov. 1994 voters approved joining the European Union. Although supportive of a European monetary union, Sweden announced in 1997 that it would not adopt the European single currency when it debuted in 1999 owing to public opinion against such a move.

Switzerland

SWISS CONFEDERATION

National name: Schweiz/Suisse/Svizzera/Svizra
President: Flavio Cotti (1998)
Vice President: Delamuraz Jean-Pascal (1995)
Area: 15,941 sq mi. (41,290 sq km)
Population (1998 est.): 7,260,357 (average annual rate of natural increase: 0.22%); birth rate: 10.8/1000; infant mortality rate: 4.9/1000; density per sq mi.: 456
Capital (1994 est.): Bern, 129,423. **Largest cities:** Zurich, 343,045; Basel, 176,220; Geneva, 171,744; Lausanne, 117,153. **Monetary unit:** Swiss franc. **Languages:** German, French, Italian, Romansch. **Ethnicity/Race:** total population: German 65%, French 18%, Italian 10%, Romansch 1%, other 6%. Swiss nationals: German 74%, French 20%, Italian 4%, Romansch 1%, other 1%. **Religions:** Roman Catholic 49%, Protestant 40%, other 5%, no religion 8.3%. **Literacy rate:** 99%
Economic summary: GDP/PPP (1996 est.): $161.3 billion; $22,600 per capita. **Real growth rate:** –0.75%. **Inflation:** 0.8% (1996). **Unemployment:** 5.3% (Dec. 1996). **Arable land:** 10%. **Agriculture:** cheese and other dairy products, livestock. **Labor force:** 3.776 million (939,000 foreign workers); services, 67%; manufacturing and construction, 29%; agriculture and forestry, 4% (1992). **Industry:** watches and clocks, precision instruments, machinery, chemicals, pharmaceuticals, textiles. **Natural resources:** water power, timber, salt. **Exports:** $81.35 billion (f.o.b., 1995): machinery and equipment, precision instruments, textiles, foodstuffs, metal products. **Imports:** $80.05 billion (c.i.f., 1995): transport equipment, foodstuffs, chemicals, textiles, construction material. **Major trading partners:** E.U., U.S., Japan.

Geography Switzerland, in central Europe, is the land of the Alps. Its tallest peak is the Dufourspitze at 15,203 feet (4,634 m) on the Swiss side of the Italian border, one of 10 summits of the Monte Rose massif in the Apennines. The tallest peak in all of the Alps, Mont Blanc (15,771 ft.; 4,807 m), is actually in France. Most of Switzerland is composed of a mountainous plateau bordered by the great bulk of the Alps on the south and by the Jura Mountains on the northwest. About one-fourth of the total area is covered by mountains and glaciers. The country's largest lakes—Geneva, Constance (Bodensee), and Maggiore—straddle the French, German-Austrian, and Italian borders, respectively. The Rhine, navigable from Basel to the North Sea, is the principal inland waterway. Other rivers are the Aare and the Rhône. Switzerland is twice the size of New Jersey.

Government The Swiss Confederation consists of 23 sovereign cantons, of which three are divided into six half-cantons. Federal authority is vested in a bicameral legislature. The Ständerat, or State Council, consists of 46 members, two from each canton. The lower house, the Nationalrat, or National Council, has 200 deputies, elected for four-year terms. Executive authority rests with the Bundesrat, or federal council, consisting of seven members chosen by parliament. The parliament elects the president, who serves for one year and is succeeded by the vice president. The federal government regulates foreign policy, railroads, postal service, and the national mint. Each canton reserves for itself important local powers.

History Called Helvetia in ancient times, Switzerland in 1291 was an anti-Hapsburg league of cantons of the Holy Roman Empire. Fashioned around the nucleus of three German forest districts of Schwyz, Uri, and Unterwalden, the Swiss Confederation slowly added new cantons. In 1648 the Treaty of Westphalia gave Switzerland its independence from the Holy Roman Empire. French revolutionary troops occupied the country in 1798 and named it the Helvetic Republic, but Napoleon in 1803 restored its federal government. By 1815, the French- and Italian- speaking peoples of Switzerland had been granted political equality.

In 1815, the Congress of Vienna guaranteed the neutrality and recognized the independence of Switzerland. In the revolutionary period of 1847, the Catholic cantons seceded and organized a separate union called the *Sonderbund*, but were defeated and rejoined the federation. In 1848, the new Swiss constitution established a union modeled upon that of the U.S. The federal constitution of 1874 established a strong central government while maintaining large powers of control in each canton. National unity and political conservatism grew as the country prospered from its neutrality. Its banking system became the world's leading repository for international accounts. Strict neutrality was its policy in World Wars I and II. Geneva was the seat of the League of

Nations (later the European headquarters of the United Nations) and of a number of international organizations.

In 1959, Switzerland became a member of the European Free Trade Association, and in 1972, it signed a free-trade agreement with the European Community. In 1986, Swiss voters rejected a parliamentary proposal to join the United Nations in the belief that such an act would subvert the country's policy of neutrality. Allegations in the 1990s concerning secret assets of Jewish Holocaust victims deposited in Swiss banks led to international criticism and the establishment of a fund to reimburse them and their families.

Syria

SYRIAN ARAB REPUBLIC

National name: Al-Jamhouriya al Arabiya As-Souriya
President: Hafez al-Assad (1971)
Prime Minister: Mahmoud al-Zubi (1987)
Area: 71,498 sq mi. (185,180 sq km)
Population (1998 est.): 16,673,282 (average annual rate of natural increase: 3.23%); birth rate: 37.8/1000; infant mortality rate: 37.6/1000; density per sq mi.: 233
Capital (1994 est.): Damascus, 1,549,932. **Largest cities:** Aleppo, 1,591,400; Homs, 644,204; Latakia, 306,535; Hama, 229,000. **Monetary unit:** Syrian pound. **Language:** Arabic (official), French and English widely understood. **Ethnicity/Race:** Arab 90.3%, Kurds, Armenians, and other 9.7%. **Religions:** Islam, 90%; Christian, 10%. **Literacy rate:** 65%
Economic summary: GDP/PPP (1996 est.): $98.3 billion; $6,300 per capita. **Real growth rate:** 5.2%. **Inflation:** 20%. **Unemployment:** 9% (1994 est.). **Arable land:** 28%. **Agriculture:** cotton, wheat, barley, lentils, sheep, goats. **Labor force:** 4.7 million (1995 est.): services, 40%; industry, 20%; agriculture, 40% (1996 est.). **Industry:** textiles, phosphate, petroleum, processed food. **Natural resources:** chrome, manganese, asphalt, iron ore, rock salt, phosphate, oil, gypsum. **Exports:** $4.4 billion (f.o.b., 1996 est.): petroleum, textiles, cotton, fruits and vegetables, phosphates. **Imports:** $5.2 billion (c.i.f., 1996 est.): petroleum, machinery, base metals, foodstuffs and beverages. **Major trading partners:** E.U. countries, U.S., Canada, Arab countries, former U.S.S.R. nations.

Geography Slightly larger than North Dakota, Syria lies at the eastern end of the Mediterranean Sea. It is bordered by Lebanon and Israel on the west, Turkey on the north, Iraq on the east, and Jordan on the south. Coastal Syria is a narrow plain, in back of which is a range of coastal mountains, and still farther inland a steppe area. In the east is the Syrian Desert, and in the south is the Jebel Druze Range. The highest point in Syria is Mount Hermon (9,232 ft.; 2,814 m) on the Lebanese border.

Government A republic under a military regime since March 1963. The ruling party is the Arab Socialist Resurrectionist (Ba'th) Party. Legislative power resides in a unicameral People's Council, an administrative body of the Ba'th Party that is composed of 250 members who are directly elected to four-year terms. Syria's constitution, which was adopted in 1973, vests executive power in the president, who is directly elected to a seven-year term. The president governs with the assistance of an appointed Council of Ministers, headed by a prime minister.

History Ancient Syria was conquered by Egypt about 1500 B.C.E., and after that by Hebrews, Assyrians, Chaldeans, Persians, and Greeks. From 64 B.C.E. until the Arab conquest in C.E. 636, it was part of the Roman Empire except during brief periods. The Arabs made it a trade center for their extensive empire, but it suffered severely from the Mongol invasion in 1260 and fell to the Ottoman Turks in 1516. Syria remained a Turkish province until World War I.

A secret Anglo-French pact of 1916 put Syria in the French zone of influence. The League of Nations gave France a mandate over Syria after World War I, but the French were forced to put down several nationalist uprisings. In 1930, France recognized Syria as an independent republic, but still subject to the mandate. After nationalist demonstrations in 1939, the French High Commissioner suspended the Syrian constitution. In 1941, British and Free French forces invaded Syria to eliminate Vichy control. During the rest of World War II, Syria was an Allied base. Again in 1945, nationalist demonstrations broke into actual fighting, and British troops had to restore order. Syrian forces met a series of reverses while participating in the Arab invasion of Palestine in 1948. In 1958, Egypt and Syria formed the United Arab Republic, with Gamal Abdel Nasser of Egypt as president. However, Syria became independent again on Sept. 29, 1961, following a revolution.

In the war of 1967, Israel quickly vanquished the Syrian army. Before acceding to the U.N. cease-fire, the Israeli forces took over control of the fortified Golan Heights. Syria joined Egypt in attacking Israel in Oct. 1973 in the fourth Arab-Israeli war, but was pushed back from initial successes on the Golan Heights to end up losing more land. However, in the settlement worked out by U.S. Secretary of State Henry A. Kissinger in 1974, the Syrians recovered all the territory lost in 1973 and a token amount of territory, including the deserted town of Quneitra, lost in 1967.

In the mid-1970s Syria sent some 20,000 troops to support Muslim Lebanese in their armed conflict with Christian militants supported by Israel during the civil war in Lebanon. Syrian troops frequently clashed with Israeli troops during Israel's 1982 invasion of Lebanon and remained thereafter as occupiers of large portions of Lebanon.

The first Arab country to condemn Iraq's invasion of Kuwait, Syria sent troops to help defend Saudi Arabia from possible Iraqi attack. After the Gulf War, hope for peace negotiations between Israel and Arab states, particularly Syria, rose but then foundered. In 1990, President Assad ruled out any possibility of legalizing opposition political parties. According to official sources, voters in Dec. 1991 approved Assad staying on for a fourth term in office, giving him 99.98% of the vote.

The slowdown in the Israeli-Palestinian peace process brought with it no progress or improvement in Israeli-Syrian relations during the late 1990s. Confronted with a steadily strengthening strategic partnership between Israel and Turkey, Syria took steps to construct a countervailing alliance by improving relations with Iraq, strengthening ties with Iran, and collaborating more closely with Saudi Arabia.

Taiwan

REPUBLIC OF CHINA

President: Lee Teng-hui (1988)

Premier: Lien Chan (1993)
Area: 13,895 sq mi. (35,980 sq km)
Population (1998 est.): 21,908,135 (average annual rate of natural increase: 0.94%); birth rate: 14.8/1000; infant mortality rate: 6.3/1000; density per sq mi.: 1,577

Capital and largest city (1995): Taipei, 2,643,439. **Largest cities:** Kaohsiung, 1,423,163; Tai Chung, 848,320; Tainan, 705,565; Keelung, 367,668. **Monetary unit:** New Taiwan dollar. **Languages:** Chinese (Mandarin). **Ethnicity/Race:** Taiwanese 84%, mainland Chinese 14%, aborigine 2%. **Religions:** Buddhist, 4.86 million; Taoist, 3.3 million; Protestant, 422,000; Catholic, 304,000. **Literacy rate:** 92%

Economic summary: GNP (purchasing power parity, 1996 est.): $315 billion; $14,700 per capita income. **Real growth rate:** 5.7% (1996). **Inflation:** 3.1%. **Unemployment:** 2.6% (1996). **Arable land:** 24%. **Agriculture:** rice, yams, sugar cane, bananas, pineapples, citrus fruits. **Labor force:** 9.31 million: industry, 38%; agriculture, 10%; services, 52%. **Industry:** textiles, clothing, chemicals, processed foods, electronic equipment, cement, ships, plywood. **Natural resources:** coal, natural gas, limestone, marble. **Exports:** $116 billion (f.o.b., 1996): textiles, electronic products, information and commercial products, plywood. **Imports:** $102.4 billion (c.i.f., 1996): machinery, basic metals, crude oil, chemicals. **Major trading partners:** U.S., Hong Kong, Japan, Germany.

Geography The Republic of China today consists of the island of Taiwan, an island 100 miles (161 km) off the Asian mainland in the Pacific; two offshore islands, Kinmen (Quemoy) and Matsu; and the nearby islets of the Pescadores chain. It is slightly larger than the combined areas of Massachusetts and Connecticut. Taiwan is divided by a central mountain range that runs from north to south, rising sharply on the east coast and descending gradually to a broad western plain, where cultivation is concentrated.

Government The central government consists of five major branches called Yuans: Executive, Legislative, Judicial, Control, and Examination. The president and vice president are popularly elected for a term of four years. The role of parliament is jointly filled by the National Assembly, the members of which are elected for four-year terms, and the Legislative Yuan, to which members are elected for three-year terms. The majority and ruling party is the Kuomintang (KMT; Nationalist Party) led by President Lee Teng-hui. The main opposition parties are the Democratic Progressive Party (DPP) and the New Party.

History Taiwan was inhabited by aborigines of Malayan descent when Chinese from the areas now designated as Fukien and Kwangtung began settling it in the 7th century, becoming the majority. The Portuguese explored the area in 1590, naming it "the Beautiful" (Formosa). In 1624 the Dutch set up forts in the south, the Spanish in the north. The Dutch forced out the Spanish in 1641 and controlled the island until 1661, when Chinese General Koxinga took it over and established an independent kingdom. The Manchus seized the island in 1683 and held it until 1895, when it passed to Japan after the first Sino-Japanese War. Japan developed and exploited Formosa. It was the target of heavy American bombing during World War II, and at the close of the war the island was restored to China.

After the defeat of its armies on the mainland, the Nationalist Government of Generalissimo Chiang Kai-shek retreated to Taiwan in Dec. 1949. Chiang dominated the island, even though only 15% of the population consisted of the 1949 immigrants, the Kuomintang. He maintained a 600,000-man army in the hope of eventually recovering the mainland. Beijing viewed the Taiwanese government with suspicion and anger, referring to Taiwan as a breakaway province of China.

The U.N. seat representing all of China was held by the Nationalists for over two decades before being lost in Oct. 1971, when the People's Republic of China was admitted and Taiwan was forced to abdicate its seat to Beijing.

Chiang died at 87 of a heart attack on April 5, 1975. His son, Chiang Ching-kuo, continued as premier and was a dominant figure in the Taipei regime. In April 1991, President Lee Teng-hui formally declared an end to emergency rule, which had existed since Chiang's forces originally occupied the island. In the first full election in many decades, the governing Kuomintang in Dec. 1991 won 71% of the vote, affirming the island's opposition to reunification with China. In Feb. 1993 the president, himself a native Taiwanese, nominated Lien Chan, another native, to be prime minister, marking a further generational shift away from the mainland exiles.

In the island's first free presidential election voters defied mainland intimidation and gave 54% of the vote to incumbent President Lee Teng-hui. The second-place finisher, with 21%, advocated complete independence from China. The ruling Nationalists successfully defeated numerous no-confidence motions raised in response to a crime wave in May 1997. The president made a public apology and promised a new Cabinet would be formed. In 1998, Taiwan renewed its push for a separate U.N. seat—its sixth attempt in recent years. The move has been blocked each time by the Beijing government.

Tajikistan

REPUBLIC OF TAJIKISTAN

President: Imomali Rakhmonov (1992)
Prime Minister: Yakhyo Azimov (1996)
Area: 55,300 sq mi. (143,100 sq km)
Population (1997 est.): 6,020,095 (average annual rate of natural increase: 1.3%); birth rate, 27.7/1000; infant mortality rate: 112.1/1000; density per sq mi.: 109

Capital and largest city (1994 est.): Dushanbe, 524,000;. **Other large city:** Khodzhent (Leninabad), 164,500. **Monetary unit:** Tajik ruble. **Religion:** Sunni Muslim, 80%. **Ethnicity/Race:** Tajik 64.9%, Uzbek 25%, Russian 3.5% (declining because of emigration), other 6.6%. **Language:** Tajik. **Literacy rate:** 98% (1989)

Economic summary: GNP (purchasing power parity, 1996 estimate as extrapolated from the World Bank estimate for 1994): $5.4 billion; $920 per capita. **Real growth rate:** –17%. **Inflation:** 65% (1996). **Unemployment:** 2.4%, also includes large numbers of underemployed, and unregistered unemployed (Dec. 1996). **Arable land:** 6%. **Labor force:** 1.9 million (1996); agriculture and forestry, 52%, services, 31%, manufacturing, mining, and construction, 14% (1995).

Industry: aluminum, zinc, lead, cement, vegetable oil, metal cutting machine tools, refrigerators and freezers. **Agriculture:** cotton, grain, fruits, and grapes. **Exports:** $768 million (1996 est.): aluminum, cotton, fruits, vegetable oil, textiles. **Imports:** $657 million (1996 est.): chemicals, machinery and transport equipment, textiles, foodstuffs. **Major trading partners:** Russia, Kazakhstan, Ukraine, Uzbekistan, Turkmenistan.

Geography Ninety-three percent of Tajikistan's territory is mountainous and the mountain glaciers are the source of its rivers. Tajikistan is an earthquake-prone area. The republic is bounded by China in the east, Afghanistan to the south, Uzbekistan and Kirghizia to the west and north. The central Asian republic also includes the Gorno-Badakh Shan Autonomous region. Tajikistan is slightly larger than the state of Illinois.

Government A new constitution that established a strong, unicameral elected parliament (Majlis), a directly elected president, and a judiciary including several high courts was adopted in 1994.

History The Tajiks are descended from the nomadic Persian-speaking people that once predominated in Central Asia. They were part of the empires of the Persians and of Alexander the Great and his successors, and in the 7th–8th centuries they were conquered by the Arabs and Islamicized. They were successively ruled by Uzbeks and then Afghans until claimed by Russia in the 1860s. In 1924, Tajikistan was consolidated into a newly formed Tajik Autonomous Soviet Socialist Republic, which was administratively a part of the Uzbek S.S.R. until the Tajik A.S.S.R. gained full-fledged republic status in 1929.

Tajikistan declared its sovereignty in August 1990. In 1991, the republic's Communist leadership supported the attempted coup against Soviet President Mikhail Gorbachev. Tajikistan joined with ten other former Soviet republics in the Commonwealth of Independent States on Dec. 21, 1991. A parliamentary republic was proclaimed and presidential rule abolished on Nov. 1992. After independence, Tajikistan experienced sporadic conflict as the Communist-dominated government struggled to combat an insurgency by Islamic and democratic opposition forces. Despite continued international efforts to end the civil war, periodic fighting continued. Tajikistan's civil war ended officially on June 27, 1997, with the signing in Moscow of peace accords between the government of President Imomali Rakhmonov and the United Tajik Opposition (UTO), a coalition of largely Islamic groups. Since then, however, peace has been tenuous, marred regularly by killing sprees.

Tanzania

UNITED REPUBLIC OF TANZANIA

President: Benjamin William Mkapa (1995)
Prime Minister: Frederick Tluway Sumaye (1995)
Area: 364,879 sq mi. (945,090 sq km)[1]
Population (1998 est.): 30,608,769 (average annual rate of natural increase: 2.14%); birth rate: 40.8/1000; infant mortality rate: 96.9/1000; density per sq mi.: 84
Capital and largest city (1988): Dar es Salaam, 1,360,850[2]. **Monetary unit:** Tanzanian shilling. **Languages:** Swahili, English, local languages. **Ethnicity/Race:** mainland: native African (95% Bantu, consisting of well over 100 tribes) 99%, Asian, European, and Arab 1%. Zanzibar: Arab, mixed Arab and native African, native African. **Religions:** Christian, 40%; Muslim, 33%. **Literacy rate:** 52%
Economic summary: GDP/PPP (1995 est.): $18.9 billion; $650 per capita. **Real growth rate:** 3.5%. **Inflation:** 30%. **Unemployment:** n.a. **Arable land:** 3%. **Agriculture:** tobacco, corn, cassava, wheat, cotton, coffee, sisal, cashew nuts, pyrethrum, cloves. **Labor force:** 13.495 million; agriculture, 90%; industry and commerce, 10% (1995 est.). **Industry:** textiles, wood products, refined oil, processed agricultural products, diamonds, cement, fertilizer. **Natural resources:** hydroelectric potential, phosphates, iron and coal. **Exports:** $679 million (f.o.b., 1995): coffee, cotton, sisal, cloves, cashew nuts, tobacco, tea. **Imports:** $1.69 billion (c.i.f., 1995): manufactured goods, machinery and transport equipment, crude oil, foodstuffs, cotton piece goods. **Major trading partners:** Germany, U.K., U.S., Japan, Italy, Denmark, Kenya, Netherlands, Hong Kong. **Member of Commonwealth of Nations**

1. Including Zanzibar. 2. Some government offices have been transferred to Dodoma, which is planned as the new national capital by the end of the 1990s.

Geography Tanzania is in East Africa on the Indian Ocean. To the north are Uganda and Kenya; to the west, Burundi, Rwanda, and Congo; and to the south, Mozambique, Zambia, and Malawi. Its area is three times that of New Mexico. Tanzania contains three of Africa's best-known lakes—Victoria in the north, Tanganyika in the west, and Nyasa in the south. Mount Kilimanjaro in the north, 19,340 feet (5,895 m), is the highest point on the continent. The island of Zanzibar is separated from the mainland by a 22–mile channel.

Government Under the republican form of government, Tanzania has a president elected by universal suffrage who appoints the cabinet ministers, and a 275-member National Assembly.

History Arab traders first began to colonize the area in C.E. 700. Portuguese explorers reached the coastal regions in 1500 and held some control until the 17th century, when the Sultan of Oman took power. With what are now Burundi and Rwanda, Tanganyika became the colony of German East Africa in 1885. After World War I, it was administered by Britain under a League of Nations mandate and later as a U.N. trust territory.

Although not mentioned in old histories until the 12th century, Zanzibar was believed always to have had connections with southern Arabia. The Portuguese made it one of their tributaries in 1503 and later established a trading post, but they were driven out by Arabs from Oman in 1698. Zanzibar was declared independent of Oman in 1861 and, in 1890, it became a British protectorate.

Tanganyika became independent on Dec. 9, 1961; Zanzibar on Dec. 10, 1963. On April 26, 1964, the two nations merged into the United Republic of Tanganyika and Zanzibar. The name was changed to Tanzania six months later.

An invasion by Ugandan troops in Nov. 1978 was followed by a counterattack in Jan. 1979, in which 5,000 Tanzanian troops were joined by 3,000 Ugandan exiles opposed to President Idi Amin. Within a month, full-scale war developed. Tanzanian President Julius Nyerere kept troops in Uganda in open support of former Ugandan President Milton Obote, despite protests from opposition groups, until the national elections in Dec. 1980.

In Nov. 1985, Nyerere stepped down as president. Ali Hassan Mwinyi, his vice-president, succeeded him. Running unopposed, Mwinyi was elected president in October. Shortly thereafter plans were announced to study the benefits of instituting a multiparty democracy.

The crisis in Rwanda in 1994 sent hundreds of thousands of refugees fleeing into Tanzania, taxing the already-meager resources of the country. The government immediately appealed for international aid. In Oct. 1995 the country's first multiparty elections since independence took place.

On August 7, 1998, the U.S. Embassy in Dar es Salaam was bombed by terrorists, killing 10. The same day an even more devastating explosion destroyed the U.S. embassy in neighboring Kenya.

Thailand

KINGDOM OF THAILAND

Ruler: King Bhumibol Adulyadej (1946)
Prime Minister: Chuan Leekpai (1997)
Area: 198,455 sq mi. (514,000 sq km)
Population (1998 est.): 60,037,366 (average annual rate of natural increase 0.97%); birth rate: 16.8/1000; infant mortality rate: 30.8/1000; density per sq mi.: 303
Capital and largest city (1993 est.): Bangkok, 5,572,712. **Other large cities:** Nonthanburi, 261,335; Chiang Mai, 170,397. **Monetary unit:** Baht. **Languages:** Thai (Siamese), Chinese, English. **Ethnicity/Race:** Thai 75%, Chinese 14%, other 11%. **Religions:** Buddhist, 94.4%; Islam, 4%; Hinduism, 1.1%; Christian, 0.5%. **Literacy rate:** 93%
Economic summary: GDP/PPP (1996 est.): $455.7 billion; $7,700 per capita. **Real growth rate:** 6.7%. **Inflation:** 5.9%. **Unemployment:** 2.6%. **Arable land:** 34%. **Agriculture:** rice, rubber, corn, tapioca, sugar, coconuts. **Labor force:** 34.03 million; agriculture, 57%; industry, 17%; commerce, 11%; services, including government, 15% (1993 est.). **Industry:** tourism (largest source of foreign exchange), textiles and garments, agricultural processing, beverages, tobacco, cement, light manufacturing, electric appliances and components, integrated circuits, furniture, plastics, tungsten and tin. **Natural resources:** fish, natural gas, forests, fluorite, tin, tungsten. **Exports:** $57.3 billion (f.o.b., 1996): machinery and manufactures, 76.9%; agricultural products, 14.9%; fisheries products, 5.9%. **Imports:** $72.4 billion (c.i.f., 1996): capital goods, 41.4%; intermediate goods and raw materials, 32.8%; consumer goods, 10.4%; oil, 8.2%. **Major trading partners:** Japan, U.S., Singapore, Germany, Taiwan, Malaysia, Hong Kong, South Korea, U.K., France.

Geography Thailand occupies the western half of the Indochinese peninsula and the northern two-thirds of the Malay peninsula in southeast Asia. Its neighbors are Burma (Myanmar) on the north and west, Laos on the north and northeast, Cambodia on the east, and Malaysia on the south. Thailand is about the size of France.

Government A constitutional monarchy. The government is run by an elected civilian coalition of political parties. King Bhumibol Adulyadej, who was born Dec. 5, 1927, second son of Prince Mahidol of Songkhla, succeeded to the throne on June 9, 1946. He was married on April 28, 1950, to Queen Sirikit; their son, Vajiralongkorn, born July 28, 1952, is the Crown Prince.

History The Thais first began settling their present homeland from the Asian continent in the 6th century C.E., and by the end of the 13th century ruled most of the western portion. During the next 400 years, they fought sporadically with the Cambodians to the east and Burmese to the west. The British gained a colonial foothold in the region in 1824, but by 1896 an Anglo-French accord guaranteed the independence of Thailand. A coup in 1932 demoted the monarchy to titular status and established representative government with universal suffrage.

At the outbreak of World War II, Japanese forces attacked Thailand. After five hours of token resistance Thailand yielded to Japan on Dec. 8, 1941, subsequently becoming a staging area for the Japanese campaign against Malaya. Following the demise of a pro-Japanese puppet government in July 1944, Thailand repudiated the declaration of war it had been forced to make in 1942 against Britain and the U.S.

By the late 1960s the nation's problems largely stemmed from conflicts brewing in neighboring Cambodia and Vietnam. Although Thailand had received $2 billion in U.S. economic and military aid since 1950, and had sent troops (paid by the U.S.) to Vietnam while permitting U.S. bomber bases on its territory, the collapse of South Vietnam and Cambodia in the spring of 1975 brought rapid changes in the country's diplomatic posture. At the Thai government's insistence, the U.S. agreed to withdraw all 23,000 U.S. military personnel remaining in Thailand by March 1976.

Three years of civilian government ended with a military coup on Oct. 6, 1976. Political parties, banned after the coup, gained limited freedom in 1980. The same year, the National Assembly elected Gen. Prem Tinsulanonda as prime minister. General elections held on April 18, 1983, and July 27, 1986, resulted in Prem continuing as prime minister over a coalition government.

Fleeing from Laos, Vietnam, and the genocidal regime of Cambodia's Pol Pot, refugees flooded into Thailand in 1978 and 1979. Despite efforts by the United States and other Western countries to resettle them, a total of 130,000 Laotians and Vietnamese were living in camps along the Cambodian border in mid-1980. A drive by troops of the Vietnamese occupation against forces loyal to Pol Pot culminated in invasions of Thai territory in late June, driving an additional 100,000 Cambodian refugees into Thailand.

On April 3, 1981, a military coup against the Prem government failed. Another coup attempt on Sept. 9, 1985 was crushed by loyal troops after 10 hours of fighting in Bangkok. In Feb. 1991 a bloodless putsch led by Gen. Suchinda Kraprayoon overthrew the democratic government on charges of corruption. The new junta declared a state of emergency; under martial law, the houses of parliament were dismissed and the constitution abolished. Parliamentary elections in March 1992 gave more than half the seats at stake to pro-military parties. In April, the top military commander was appointed prime minister. A scandal over a land-reform program caused the fall of the government in May 1995. The prime minister dissolved parliament and set a date for new elections. Voters in early July gave the largest number of seats in parliament to the Thai Nation Party, whose leader moved quickly to form a coalition government. A new draft constitution, calling for cabinet ministers to relinquish their parliamentary seats, came under fire in the early months of 1997 from a number of politicians.

Following several years of unprecedented economic growth, Thailand's economy, once one of the strongest in the region, collapsed under the weight of foreign debt in 1997. The Thai economy's downfall set off a chain reaction in the region, sparking the Asian currency crisis. Although one of the first Asian economies to be ravaged by the currency crisis, the Thai government quickly accepted restructuring guidelines as a condition of the International Monetary Fund's $17 billion bailout. By 1998, Thailand's economy, while far from completely recovered, appeared to be in better condition than that of many of its Asian neighbors.

Togo

REPUBLIC OF TOGO

National name: République Togolaise
President: Gen. Gnassingbe Eyadema (1967)
Prime Minister: Kwassi Klutse (1996)
Area: 21,925 sq mi. (56,790 sq km)
Population (1998 est.): 4,905,827 (average annual rate of natural increase: 3.52%); birth rate: 45.2/1000; infant mortality rate: 79.8/1000; density per sq mi.: 224
Capital and largest city (1983): Lomé, 366,476. **Monetary unit:** Franc CFA. **Languages:** Ewé, Mina (south), Kabyé, Cotocoli (north), French (official), and many dialects. **Ethnicity/Race:** native African (37 tribes; largest and most important are Ewe, Mina, and Kabre) 99%, European and Syrian-Lebanese less than 1%. **Religions:** Indigenous beliefs, 70%; Christian, 20%; Islam, 10%. **Literacy rate:** 43%
Economic summary: GDP/PPP (1996 est.): $4.45 billion; $970 per capita. **Real growth rate:** 6%. **Inflation:** 7.2% (1995 est.). **Unemployment:** n.a. **Arable land:** 38%. **Agriculture:** yams, cotton, millet, sorghum, cocoa, coffee, rice. **Labor force** (1993 est.), 1.538 million; agriculture, 64%; industry, 9%; services, 21% (1981 est.). **Industry:** phosphate, textiles, processed food. **Natural resources:** marble, phosphate, limestone. **Exports:** $265 million (f.o.b., 1996 est.): phosphate, cocoa, coffee, cotton. **Imports:** $350 million (c.i.f., 1996 est.): consumer goods, fuels, machinery, foodstuffs, chemical products. **Major trading partners:** E.U., Japan, U.S., Africa.

Geography Togo, twice the size of Maryland, is on the south coast of West Africa bordering on Ghana to the west, Burkina Faso to the north and Benin to the east. The Gulf of Guinea coastline, only 32 miles long (51 km), is low and sandy. The only port is at Lomé. The Togo hills traverse the central section.

Government Republic. The Assembly of the Togolese People is currently the only political party.

History The Voltaic peoples and the Kwa were the earliest-known inhabitants. The Ewe followed in the 14th century, and the Ane in the 18th century. The Danish claimed the land in the 18th century, but by 1884 it was established as a German colony (Togoland). The area was split between the British and the French as League of Nations mandates after World War I and subsequently administered as U.N. trusteeships. The British portion voted for incorporation with Ghana. The French portion became Togo, which declared its independence on April 27, 1960.

The government of Nicolas Grunitzky was overthrown in a bloodless coup on Jan. 13, 1967, led by Lt. Col. Etienne Eyadema (now Gen. Gnassingbé Eyadema). A National Reconciliation Committee was set up to rule the country. In April, however, Eyadema dissolved the Committee and took over as president. The presidential election held in August 1993 gave Eyadema more than 96% of the vote, but only 36% of the electorate went to the polls. Many of the major opposition candidates withdrew prior to the election. In August 1996 Prime Minister Edem Kodjo resigned. The Planning Minister, Kwassi Klutse, was then appointed prime minister.

Tonga

KINGDOM OF TONGA

Sovereign: King Taufa'ahau Tupou IV (1965)
Prime Minister: Baron Vaea (1991)
Area: 290 sq mi. (748 sq km)
Population (1998 est.): 108,207 (average annual growth rate: 0.81%); birth rate: 26.4/1000; infant mortality rate: 38.6/1000; density per sq mi.: 373
Capital and largest city (1990 est.): Nuku'alofa, 34,000. **Monetary unit:** Pa'anga. **Languages:** Tongan (an Austronesian language), English. **Ethnicity/Race:** Polynesian, European (about 300). **Religions:** Christian; Free Wesleyan Church claims over 30,000 adherents. **Literacy rate:** 47%
Economic summary: GDP/PPP (FY 95/96 est.): $228 million; $2,140 per capita. **Real growth rate:** -1.9%. **Inflation (1995):** 1.4% **Arable land:** 24%. **principal agricultural products:** vanilla, coffee, ginger, black pepper, coconuts, bananas, copra. **Labor force (1990 est.):** 32,013; agriculture, 70% (1995 est.). **Natural resources:** fish, copra. **Exports:** $15.25 million (f.o.b., 1995): copra, coconut products, bananas, fruits, vegetables, fish, vanilla. **Imports:** $80.3 million (c.i.f., 1995): foodstuffs, machinery and transport equipment, fuels, chemicals, building materials. **Major trading partners:** New Zealand, Australia, Fiji, U.S., Japan, E.U. **Member of Commonwealth of Nations**

Geography Situated east of the Fiji Islands in the South Pacific, Tonga (also called the Friendly Islands) consists of some 150 islands, of which 36 are inhabited. Most of the islands contain active volcanic craters; others are coral atolls.

Government Tonga is a constitutional monarchy. Executive authority is vested in the sovereign, a privy council, and a cabinet headed by the prime minister. Legislative authority is vested in the Legislative Assembly. Nine seats are reserved for commoners; the others filled by appointees of the king.

History Tonga was inhabited at least 3,000 years ago by Austronesian-speaking peoples who developed a stratified social system headed by a paramount ruler whose dominion, in the 13th century, extended as far as the Hawaiian Islands. The first European to visit Tonga was the Dutch navigator Jakob Le Maire, who sighted Tafahi in 1616. The present dynasty of Tonga was founded in 1831 by Taufa'ahau Tupou, who took the name George I. He consolidated the kingdom by conquest and in 1875 granted a constitution. In 1900, his great-grandson, George II, signed a treaty of friendship with Britain, and the country became a British protected state.

The treaty was revised in 1959. Tonga became independent on June 4, 1970.

The continuing challenge to the government—largely controlled by the king, his nominees, and a small group of hereditary nobles—posed by the pro-democracy movement was institutionalized in Sept. 1994 with the formation of the Tonga Democratic Party. In March 1997, Cyclone Hina caused damage to crops and buildings, mostly on Tongatapu; one person was reported killed.

Trinidad and Tobago

REPUBLIC OF TRINIDAD AND TOBAGO

President: A.N.R. Robinson (1997)
Prime Minister: Basdeo Panday (1995)
Area: 1,980 sq mi. (5,130 sq km)
Population (1998 est.): 1,116,595 (average annual rate of natural increase: –1.27%); birth rate: 14.9/1000; infant mortality rate: 18.8/1000; density per sq mi.: 564
Capital and largest city (1995): Port-of-Spain, 52,451.
Monetary unit: Trinidad and Tobago dollar.
Languages: English (official); Hindi, French, Spanish.
Ethnicity/Race: black 43%, East Indian (a local term–primarily immigrants from northern India) 40%, mixed 14%, white 1%, Chinese 1%, other 1%.
Religions: Roman Catholic, 33%; Hindu, 25%; Anglican, 15%; other Christian, 14%; Muslim, 6%.
Literacy rate: 95%
Economic summary: GDP/PPP (1996 est.): $17.1 billion; $13,500 per capita. **Real growth rate:** 3.1%. **Inflation:** 5.3% (1995). **Unemployment:** 16.1% (Dec. 1996). **Arable land:** 15%. **Agriculture:** sugar cane, cocoa, coffee, citrus. **Labor force:** 404,500; manufacturing, mining, and quarrying, 14%; construction and utilities, 13%; agriculture, 11%; services, 62% (1993 est.). **Industry:** petroleum, processed food, cement; tourism. **Natural resources:** petroleum, natural gas, asphalt. **Exports:** $2.3 billion (f.o.b., 1996): including reexports—petroleum and petroleum products, steel products, fertilizer, sugar, cocoa, coffee, citrus fruits (1988). **Imports:** $1.8 billion (c.i.f., 1996): raw materials, capital goods, consumer goods. **Major trading partners:** U.S., Caribbean, Latin America, Western Europe, U.K., Canada.
Member of Commonwealth of Nations

Geography Trinidad and Tobago lie in the Caribbean Sea off the northeast coast of Venezuela. The area of the two islands is slightly less than that of Delaware. Trinidad, the larger at 1,864 sq mi. (4,828 sq km), is mainly flat and rolling, with mountains in the north that reach a height of 3,085 feet (940 m) at Mount Aripo. Tobago, at just 116 sq mi. (300 sq km), is heavily forested with hardwood trees.

Government Trinidad and Tobago is a parliamentary democracy under its 1976 Constitution. The bicameral legislature consists of a 31-member Senate and a 36-member House of Representatives. Legislation passed in 1980 gave Tobago considerable autonomy and established a separate Tobago House of Assembly of 15 members, and in 1987 Tobago was granted full internal self-government.

History When Trinidad was explored by Columbus in 1498 it was inhabited by the Arawaks; the Carib people inhabited Tobago. Trinidad remained in Spanish possession, despite raids by other European nations, until it capitulated to the British in 1797 during a war between Britain and Spain. Trinidad was officially ceded to Britain in 1802. The British first attempted to settle Tobago in 1721, but the French captured the island in 1781 and transformed it into a sugar-producing colony. Tobago passed between Britain and France several times before it was ultimately ceded to Britain in 1814. In 1845, the immigration of indentured workers from India for the sugarcane plantations began; it continued until 1917. In 1889 Tobago was administratively combined with Trinidad.

Partial self-government was begun in 1925 and from 1958 to 1962, the nation was a part of the West Indies Federation. On Aug, 31, 1962, it became independent and on Aug. 1, 1976, Trinidad and Tobago became a republic, remaining within the Commonwealth. The People's National Movement (PNM) won six consecutive elections and held power from 1956 to 1986. In Dec. 1986 the National Alliance for Reconstruction (NAR), a coalition party, won the majority of parliamentary seats, promising divestment of most state-owned companies, reorganization of the civil service, and structural readjustment of the economy in the light of shrinking oil revenues. In July 1990 a small, radical Muslim group attempted a coup in which several ministers, including the prime minister, were held hostage for six days. The NAR was defeated in elections in Dec. 1991, and the PNM returned to power. In the 1995 elections, the United National Congress (UNC), led by Basdeo Panday, teamed up with the NAR and formed a coalition government.

Tunisia

REPUBLIC OF TUNISIA

National name: Al-Joumhouria Attunisia
President: Zine El Abidine Ben Ali (1987)
Prime Minister: Hamed Karoui (1989)
Area: 63,170 sq mi. (163,610 sq km)
Population (1998 est.): 9,380,404 (average annual rate of natural increase: 1.43%); birth rate: 20.1/1000; infant mortality rate: 32.6/1000; density per sq mi.: 149
Capital and largest city (1994): Tunis, 887,800.
Monetary unit: Tunisian dinar. **Languages:** Arabic, French. **Ethnicity/Race:** Arab-Berber 98%, European 1%, Jewish less than 1%. **Religion:** Islam (Sunni), 98%; Christian, 1%; Jewish, less than 1%. **Literacy rate:** 65%
Economic summary: GDP/PPP (1996 est.): $43.3 billion; $4,800 per capita. **Real growth rate:** 7.1%. **Inflation:** 6%. **Unemployment:** 16% (1995 est.). **Arable land:** 19%. **Agriculture:** wheat, olives, oranges, grapes, dates. **Labor force:** 2.917 million (1993 est.); services, 55%; industry, 23%; agriculture, 22% (1995 est.). **Industry:** textiles and leather, chemical fertilizers, petroleum, phosphate, iron ore. Tourism is an important industry. **Natural resources:** oil, phosphates, iron ore, lead, zinc. **Exports:** $5.7 billion (f.o.b., 1996 est.): textiles, crude oil, olive oil, phosphoric acid, chemical fertilizers, triple superphosphate, fish, dates. **Imports:** $7.7 billion (c.i.f., 1996 est.): raw materials, consumer goods, machinery and equipment, foodstuffs. **Major trading partners:** France, Italy, Germany, U.S., Belgium and Luxemburg, Spain, the Netherlands.

Geography Tunisia, at the northernmost bulge of Africa, thrusts out toward Sicily to mark the division between the eastern and western Mediterranean Sea. Twice the size of South Carolina, it is bordered on the west by Algeria and by Libya on the south. Coastal plains on the east rise to a north-south escarpment which slopes gently to the west. Saharan in the south, Tunisia is more mountainous in the north, where the Atlas range continues from Algeria.

Government Executive power is vested by the constitution in the president, elected for five years and eligible for reelection to two additional terms. Legislative power is vested in a Chamber of Deputies elected by universal suffrage.

History Tunisia was settled by the Phoenicians in the twelfth century B.C.E. By the sixth century B.C.E., the Carthaginian kingdom encompassed most of present-day Tunisia. Except for an interval of Vandal conquest in C.E. 439–533, it was part of the Roman Empire until the Arab conquest of 648–69. It was ruled by various Arab and Berber dynasties until the Turks took it in 1570–74 and held it until the nineteenth century. French troops occupied the country in 1881, and the Bey, the local Tunisian ruler, signed a treaty acknowledging a French protectorate.

Nationalist agitation forced France to recognize Tunisian independence and sovereignty in 1956. The Constituent Assembly deposed the Bey on July 25, 1957, declared Tunisia a republic, and elected Habib Bourguiba as president. Bourguiba maintained a pro-Western foreign policy that earned him enemies. Tunisia refused to break relations with the U.S. during the Israeli-Arab war in June 1967. Concerned with Islamic fundamentalist plots against the state, the government stepped up efforts to eradicate the movement including censorship and frequent detention of suspects.

Amid widespread unrest in 1987, the aged Bourguiba was declared mentally unfit to rule and was removed from office. He was succeeded as president by General Zine al-Abidine Ben Ali, whose tenure was marked by a rise in Islamic fundamentalism and growing anti-Western sentiments among the populace. However, an Association Agreement was signed in July 1995 with the E.U. that after 12 years would make the country a part of a free-trade area around the Mediterranean, called the European Economic Area.

Turkey

REPUBLIC OF TURKEY

National name: Türkiye Cumhuriyeti
President: Süleyman Demirel (1993)
Prime Minister: Mesut Yilmaz (1997)
Area: 300,947 sq mi. (incl. 9,121 in Europe) (780,580 sq km)
Population (1997 est.): 64,566,511; average annual rate of natural increase 1.60%; birth rate: 21.4/1000; infant mortality rate: 38.3/1000; density per sq mi.: 215
Capital: Ankara (2,719,981). **Largest cities :** Istanbul: city proper (1995 est.) 7,774,169; metro. area (1995 est.) 7,817,000; Izmir, 1,920,807; Adana, 1,010,363; Bursa, 949,810; Gaziantep, 683,557. **Monetary unit:** Turkish Lira. **Language:** Turkish. **Ethnicity/Race:** Turkish 80%, Kurdish 20%. **Religion:** Islam (mostly Sunni), 98%. **Literacy rate:** 81%
Economic summary: GDP/PPP (1996 est.): $379.1 billion; $6,100 per capita. **Real growth rate:** 7%. **Inflation:** 80% (1996). **Unemployment:** 6.3%, plus another 6.3% underemployed. **Arable land:** 32%. **Agriculture:** cotton, tobacco, cereals, sugar beets, fruits, olives. **Labor force:** 21.3 million; agriculture, 47%; services, 33%; industry, 20% (1995), (note: in 1994 about 1.5 million Turks worked abroad). **Industry:** textiles, coal, minerals, processed foods, steel, petroleum. **Natural resources:** coal, chromite, copper, borate, sulfur, petroleum. **Exports:** $22 billion (f.o.b., 1996 est.): agricultural products, textiles, leather, glass. **Imports:** $42 billion (f.o.b., 1996 est.): crude oil, machinery, motor vehicles, metals, mineral fuels, fertilizer, chemicals. **Major trading partners:** E.U., U.S., Iran, Japan, Russia.

Geography Turkey is at the northeastern end of the Mediterranean Sea in southeast Europe and southwest Asia. To the north is the Black Sea and to the west is the Aegean Sea. Its neighbors are Greece and Bulgaria to the west, Russia and Ukraine to the north (through the Black Sea), Georgia, Armenia, Azerbaijain, and Iran to the east, and Syria and Iraq to the south. The Dardanelles, the Sea of Marmara, and the Bosporus divide the country. Turkey in Europe comprises an area about equal to the state of Massachusetts. It is hilly country drained by the Maritsa River and its tributaries. Turkey in Asia, or Anatolia, is about the size of Texas. Its center is a treeless plateau rimmed by mountains.

Government Under the 1982 Constitution, the president is elected by the 550–member Grand National Assembly for a nonrenewable seven-year term. The prime minister and the Council of Ministers hold the executive power although the president has the right to veto legislation.

History Anatolia (Turkey in Asia) was occupied in about 1900 B.C.E. by the Indo-European Hittites and after the Hittite Empire's collapse in 1200 B.C.E., by Phrygians and Lydians. The Persian empire occupied the area in the 6th century B.C.E., giving way to the Roman Empire, then later the Byzantine Empire. The Ottoman Turks first appeared in the early 13th century, subjugating Turkish and Mongol bands pressing against the eastern borders of Byzantium and making the Christian Balkan states their vassals. They gradually spread through the Near East and Balkans, capturing Constantinople in 1453 and storming the gates of Vienna two centuries later. At its height, the Ottoman Empire stretched from the Persian Gulf to western Algeria.

After the reign of Sultan Süleyman I the Magnificent (1494–1566), the Ottoman Empire began to decline politically, administratively, and economically. By the 18th century, Russia was seeking to establish itself as the protector of Christians in Turkey's Balkan territories. Russian ambitions were checked by Britain and France in the Crimean War (1854–56), but the Russo-Turkish War (1877–78) gave Bulgaria virtual independence and Romania and Serbia liberation from their nominal allegiance to the Sultan. Turkish weakness stimulated a revolt of young liberals known as the Young Turks in 1909. They forced Sultan Abdul Hamid to grant a constitution and install a liberal government. Reforms were no barrier to further defeats, however, in a war with Italy (1911–12) and the Balkan Wars (1912–13). Under the influence of German military advisers, Turkey signed a secret alliance with Germany on Aug. 2, 1914, that led to a declaration of war by the Allied powers and the ultimate humiliation of the occupation of Turkish territory by Greek and other Allied troops.

Turkey's present boundaries were drawn in 1923 at the Conference of Lausanne, and Turkey became a republic with Kemal Atatürk as the first president.

The Ottoman sultanate and caliphate were abolished, and modernization, reform, and industrialization began under Atatürk's direction. He secularized Turkish society, reducing Islam's dominant role and replacing Arabic with the Latin alphabet for writing the Turkish language. After Atatürk's death in 1938, parliamentary government and a multiparty system gradually took root in Turkey, despite periods of instability and brief intervals of military rule. Neutral during most of World War II, Turkey, on Feb. 23, 1945, declared war on Germany and Japan, but took no active part in the conflict. Turkey became a full member of NATO in 1952, was a signatory in the Balkan Entente (1953), joined the Baghdad Pact (1955; later CENTO), joined the Organization for European Economic Co-operation (OEEC) and the Council of Europe, and became an associate member of the European Common Market in 1963.

Turkey invaded Cyprus by sea and air July 20, 1974, following the failure of diplomatic efforts to resolve conflicts between Turkish and Greek Cypriots. Turkey unilaterally announced a cease-fire August 16, after having gained control of 40% of the island. Turkish Cypriots established their own state in the north on Feb. 13, 1975. In July 1975, after a 30-day warning, Turkey took over control of all the U.S. installations except the big joint defense base at Incirlik, which it reserved for "NATO tasks alone."

The establishment of military government in Sept. 1980 stopped the slide toward anarchy and brought some improvement in the economy. A Constituent Assembly, consisting of the six-member National Security Council and members appointed by them, drafted a new constitution that was approved by an overwhelming (91.5%) majority of the voters in a Nov. 6, 1982, referendum. Martial law was gradually lifted. The emergence of a militant Kurdish separatist campaign in 1983 was a source of ongoing conflict during the 1980s and '90s. In March 1995, as many as 35,000 Turkish troops moved into northern Iraq seeking to root out Kurdish rebels, who had used Iraq as a base. The army, alarmed at the government's failures to rein in radical Islamic groups and practices, warned in Feb. 1997 of the possibility of military intervention. In May, the prime minister pledged not to follow the path of Iran.

Turkmenistan

TURKMENISTAN

President: Saparmurad A. Niyazov (1990)
Area: 188,500 sq mi. (488,100 sq km)
Population (1998 est.): 4,297,629 (average annual rate of natural increase: 1.6%); birth rate: 26.2/1000; infant mortality rate: 72.9/1000; density per sq mi.: 23
Capital and largest city (1994 est.): Ashgabat, 518,000. **Other large cities:** Chardzhou, 166,400; Tashauz, 117,000. **Monetary unit:** Manat. **Languages:** Turkmen, 72%; Russian, 12%; Uzbek, 9%. **Ethnicity/Race (1995):** Turkmen 77%, Uzbek 9.2%, Russian 6.7%, Kazak 2%, other 5.1%. **Religions:** Muslim 89%, Eastern Orthodox 9%, unknown 2%. **Literacy rate:** 98%
Economic summary: GDP/PPP (1996 estimate as extrapolated form the World Bank estimate for 1994): $11.8 billion; $2,840 per capita. **Real growth rate:** 0.1%. **Inflation:** 600%. **Unemployment:** n.a. **Arable land:** 3%. **Labor force:** 1.68 million (1995); agriculture and forestry, 43%; industry and construction, 20%; other, 37% (1992). **Industry:** oil and gas, petrochemicals, fertilizers, food processing, textiles. **Agriculture:** cotton, fruits, vegetables. **Exports:** $1.8 billion to outside former U.S.S.R. countries (1996 est.): natural gas, oil, chemicals, cotton, textiles, carpets. **Imports:** $1.3 billion from outside the former U.S.S.R. countries (1996 est.): machinery and parts, plastics and rubber, consumer durables, textiles, grain, foodstuffs. **Major trading partners:** C.I.S. countries, Russia, Eastern European countries, Turkey, Argentina.

Geography Turkmenistan (formerly Turkmenia) is bounded by the Caspian Sea in the west, Kazakhstan in the north, Uzbekistan in the east, and Iran and Afghanistan in the south. About nine-tenths of Turkmenistan is desert, chiefly the Kara-Kum; this is one of the world's largest sand deserts at approximately 138,966 sq mi. (360,000 sq km) in area. Many irrigation canals and reservoirs have been built, including the Kara-Kum Canal, which runs from the Amu Darya River westward to the Caspian Sea for a distance of 870 miles (1,400 km).

Government A republic. The constitution allows for a strong presidential rule. The president heads the Cabinet of Ministers, whose members he appoints with the consent of the Meglis (parliament). There are two parliamentary bodies, the unicameral People's Council (Halk Maslahaty) with over 100 members and the 50-member unicameral Assembly (Majlis).

History Turkmenistan was once part of the ancient Persian empire. The Turkmen people were originally pastoral nomads and some of them continued this way of life up into the 20th century, living in transportable dome-shaped felt tents. The territory was ruled by the Seljuk Turks in the 11th century. The Mongols of Ghenghis Khan conquered the land in the 13th century and dominated the area for the next two centuries until they were deposed in the late 15th century by invading Uzbeks. Prior to the 19th century, Turkmenia was divided into two lands, one belonging to the Khanate of Khiva and the other belonging to the Khanate of Bukhara. In 1868, the Khanate of Khiva was made part of the Russian empire and Turkmenia became known as the Transcaspia Region of Russian Turkistan. Turkmenistan was later formed out of the Turkistan Autonomous Soviet Socialist Republic, founded in 1922, and was made an independent Soviet Socialist Republic on May 13, 1925.

Turkmenistan declared its sovereignty in August 1990 and became a member of the Commonwealth of Independent States on Dec. 21, 1991, together with ten other former Soviet republics. Turkmenistan established a government more authoritarian than those functioning in the other newly independent Central Asian republics. The country left the ruble zone in Nov. 1993, introducing its own currency emblazoned with the president's image. Protests both domestic and foreign against his authoritarian rule and practices notwithstanding, the president extended his term into the next century. The government signed a cooperation agreement with Iran and Armenia in April 1997 concerning trade, transport, banking, energy, and tourism. Later that year, an agreement was reached with Pakistan and the Unocal oil company, a U.S. firm, on the construction of a pipeline through Iran to transport natural gas.

Tuvalu

Sovereign: Queen Elizabeth II (1952)
Governor-General: Tulaga Manuella (1994)
Prime Minister: Bikenibeu Paeniu (1996)
Area: 10 sq mi. (26 sq km)
Population (1998 est.): 10,444; growth rate: 1.4%; birth rate: 22.6/1000; infant mortality rate: 26.2/1000; density per sq mi.: 1,044
Capital and largest city (1991): Funafuti, 3,839. **Monetary unit:** Tuvaluan dollar, Australian dollar. **Languages:** Tuvaluan, English. **Ethnicity/Race:** Polynesian 96%. **Religion:** Church of Tuvalu (Congregationalist), 97%. **Literacy rate:** less than 50%
Economic summary: GDP/PPP (1995 est.): $7.8 million; per capita income: $800; **Real growth rate:** 8.7% (1995) **Inflation:** 2.9% (1989). **Unemployment:** n.a. **Arable land:** 0%. **Agriculture:** copra and coconuts. **Exports:** $165,000 (f.o.b., 1989): copra. **Imports:** $4.4 million (c.i.f., 1989) food, fuels, machinery, animals, manufactured goods. **Major trading partners:** Australia, Fiji, New Zealand. **Member of Commonwealth of Nations**

Geography Tuvalu consists of nine small islands scattered over 500,000 square miles of the western Pacific, just south of the equator. The islands include Niulakita, Nukulaelae, Funafuti, Nukufetau, Vaitupu, Nui, Niutao, Nanumaga (Nanumanga), and Nanumea.

Government According to its revised constitution of 1986, the British monarch is the head of state in Tuvalu, represented by a Tuvaluan chosen as governor-general by the Tuvaluan prime minister. The unicameral parliament has 12 members elected to four-year terms; the parliament in turn elects the prime minister, who is assisted by a Cabinet of ministers.

History Formerly the Ellice Islands, Tuvalu's first Polynesian settlers were probably Samoans or Tongans. The Spanish explorer Alvaro de Mendaña de Neira sighted Nui in 1568 and Niulakita in 1595. In 1865, London Missionary Society pastors established themselves and rapidly converted the islanders to Christianity. The Ellice Islands became a British protectorate in 1892 and were annexed by Britain in 1915–16 as part of the Gilbert and Ellice Islands Colony. The Ellice Islands were separated in 1975, given home rule, and renamed Tuvalu. Full independence was granted on Sept. 30, 1978. Early in 1979, the U.S. signed a treaty of friendship with Tuvalu and relinquished its claims to the four southern islands. Tuvalu faced land shortages and the prospect of growing unemployment in the 1990s. In 1997, the government adopted a strong stance on the need to control emissions of greenhouse gases in order to ensure the survival of low-lying island nations.

Uganda

REPUBLIC OF UGANDA

President: Yoweri Museveni (1986)
Prime Minister: Kintu Musoke (1994)
Area: 91,459 sq mi. (236,040 sq km)
Population (1998 est.): 22,167,195 (average annual rate of natural increase: 2.85%); birth rate: 49.2/1000; infant mortality rate: 92.9/1000; density per sq mi.: 242
Capital and largest city (1991 est.): Kampala, 773,463. **Monetary unit:** Ugandan shilling. **Languages:** English (official), Swahili, Luganda, Ateso, Luo. **Ethnicity/Race:** Baganda 17%, Karamojong 12%, Basogo 8%, Iteso 8%, Langi 6%, Rwanda 6%, Bagisu 5%, Acholi 4%, Lugbara 4%, Bunyoro 3%, Batobo 3%, European, Asian, Arab 1%, other 23%. **Religions:** Christian, 66%; Islam, 16%. **Literacy rate:** 54%
Economic summary: GDP/PPP (1995 est.): $16.8 billion; $900 per capita. **Real growth rate:** 7.1%. **Inflation:** 7.3% (1996 est.). **Arable land:** 25%. **Agriculture:** coffee, tea, cotton, sugar. **Labor force:** 8.361 million (1993 est.); agriculture, 86%; industry, 4%; services, 10% (1980 est.). **Industry:** refined sugar, beer, tobacco, cotton textiles, cement. **Natural resources:** copper, cobalt, limestone, salt. **Exports:** $555 million (f.o.b., FY 94/95): coffee 97%, cotton, tea. **Imports:** $1.18 billion (c.i.f., FY 94/95): petroleum products, machinery, transport equipment, metals, food. **Major trading partners:** U.S., U.K., Kenya, Italy, France, Spain, South Africa. **Member of the Commonwealth of Nations**

Geography Uganda, twice the size of Pennsylvania, is in East Africa. It is bordered on the west by Congo, on the north by the Sudan, on the east by Kenya, and on the south by Tanzania and Rwanda. The country, which lies across the equator, is divided into three main areas—swampy lowlands, a fertile plateau with wooded hills, and a desert region. Lake Victoria forms part of the southern border.

Government Since 1996, a multiparty democracy.

History About 500 B.C.E. Bantu-speaking peoples migrated to the area now called Uganda. By the 14th century, three kingdoms dominated, Buganda (meaning "state of the Gandas"), Bunyoro, and Ankole. Uganda was first explored by Europeans as well as Arab traders in 1844. An Anglo-German agreement of 1890 declared it to be in the British sphere of influence in Africa, and the Imperial British East Africa Company was chartered to develop the area. The company did not prosper financially, and in 1894 a British protectorate was proclaimed. Few Europeans permanently settled in Uganda, but it attracted Indians, Pakistanis, and Goans, who became important players in Ugandan commerce.

Uganda became independent on Oct. 9, 1962, and Sir Edward Mutesa, the king of Buganda (Mutesa II), was elected the first president and Milton Obote the first prime minister of the newly independent country. With the help of a young army officer, Col. Idi Amin, Prime Minister Obote seized control of the government from President Mutesa four years later.

On Jan. 25, 1971, Col. Amin deposed President Obote. Obote went into exile in Tanzania. Amin expelled Asian residents and launched a reign of terror against Ugandan opponents, torturing and killing tens of thousands. In 1976, he had himself proclaimed "President for Life." In 1977, Amnesty International estimated that 300,000 may have died under his rule, including church leaders and recalcitrant cabinet ministers.

After Amin held military exercises on the Tanzanian border, angering Tanzania's President Julius Nyerere, a combined force of Tanzanian troops and Ugandan exiles loyal to former President Obote invaded Uganda and chased Amin into exile in

Saudi Arabia. After a series of interim administrations, President Obote led his People's Congress Party to victory in 1980 elections that opponents charged were rigged. On July, 27, 1985, army troops staged a coup and took over the government. Obote fled into exile. The military regime installed Gen. Tito Okello as Chief of State.

The National Resistance Army (NRA), an anti-Obote group led by Yoweri Museveni, kept fighting after it had been excluded from the new regime. They seized Kampala on Jan. 29, 1986, and Museveni was declared president. Museveni has transformed the ruins of Idi Amin and Milton Obote's Uganda into an economic miracle, preaching a philosophy of self-sufficiency and anti-corruption. Western countries have flocked to assist him in the country's transformation. Nevertheless, it remains one of Africa's poorest countries. A ban on political parties was lifted in 1996, and the incumbent Museveni won 72% of the vote, reflecting his popularity due to the country's economic recovery.

Close ties with Rwanda (many Rwandan Tutsi exiles helped Museveni come to power) led to Uganda and Rwanda assisting in the ousting of Zaire's Mobutu Sese Seko in 1997, and a year later, in efforts to unseat his successor, Laurent Kabila, whom both countries originally supported but from whom they grew estranged. Uganda continues to battle the extremist Lord's Resistance Army based in Sudan.

Ukraine

UKRAINE

President: Leonid D. Kuchma (1994)
Prime Minister: Valery Pustovoitenko (1997)
Area: 233,000 sq mi. (603,700 sq km)
Population (1998 est.): 50,125,108 (average annual rate of natural increase: –0.64%): birth rate: 9.5/1000; infant mortality rate: 21.8/1000; density per sq mi.: 215
Capital: Kyiv (Kiev), 2,637,000. **Other large cities:** Kharkiv, 1,622,000; Donetske, 1,121,000; Odessa, 1,104,000; Lviv, 803,000. **Monetary unit:** Hryvnia (since Sept. 2, 1996). **Language:** Ukrainian. **Ethnicity/Race:** Ukrainian 73%, Russian 22%, Jewish 1%, other 4%. **Religion:** Orthodox, 76%; Ukrainian Catholic (Uniate), 13.5%; Jewish, 2.3%; Baptist, Mennonite, Protestant, and Muslim, 8.2%. **Literacy rate:** 100%
Economic summary: GDP/PPP (1996 estimate as extrapolated from the World Bank estimate for 1994): $161.1 billion; $3,170 per capita. **Real growth rate:** -10% (1996 est.). **Inflation:** 40% (yearend, 1996). **Unemployment:** 1%, plus large numbers of underemployed (Dec. 1996). **Arable land:** 58%. **Labor force** (Jan. 1996), 23 million; industry and construction, 33%; agriculture and forestry, 21%; health, education, and culture, 16%, other, 30% (1992). **Natural resources:** iron ore, coal, manganese, natural gas, oil, salt, sulfur, graphite, titanium, magnesium, kaolin, nickel, mercury, and timber. **Agriculture:** grain, vegetables, meat, and milk. **Exports:** $18.6 billion (1996 est.): coal, electric power, ferrous and nonferrous metals, chemicals, machinery and transportation equipment, grain and meat. **Imports:** $19.4 billion (1996 est.): machinery and parts, transportation equipment, chemicals, and textiles. **Major trading partners:** C.I.S. countries, E.U., Poland, Czech Republic, China, Switzerland.

Geography Located in southeastern Europe, the country consists largely of fertile black soil steppes. Mountainous areas include the Carpathians in the southwest and the Crimean chain in the south. There are forest lakes in the north. Ukraine is bordered by Belarus on the north, by Russia on the north, northeast, and east, by the Sea of Azov and the Black Sea on the south, by Moldova and Romania on the southwest, and by Hungary, Slovakia, and Poland on the west.

Government Ukraine is a constitutional republic with a unicameral parliament, or Supreme Council, with 450 members who are elected to four-year terms. The prime minister, who heads the Cabinet of Ministers, is chosen by the president with parliamentary approval.

History Ukraine was known as "Kievan Rus" (from which Russia is a derivative) up until the 16th century. In the 9th century, Kiev was the major political and cultural center in eastern Europe. Kievan Rus reached the height of its power in the 10th century and adopted Byzantine Christianity, the Church Slavonic written language, and the Cyrillic alphabet during that period. The Mongol conquest in 1240 ended Kievan power. From the 13th to the 16th century, Kiev was under the influence of Poland and western Europe. The negotiation of the Union of Brest-Litovsk in 1596 divided the Ukrainians into Orthodox and Ukrainian Catholic faithful. In 1654, Ukraine asked the czar of Moscovy for protection against Poland and the Treaty of Pereyasav signed that year recognized the suzerainty of Moscow. The agreement was interpreted by Moscow as an invitation to take over Kiev and the Ukrainian state was eventually absorbed into the Russian empire.

After the Russian revolution, Ukraine declared its independence from Russia on Jan. 28, 1918, and several years of warfare ensued with several groups. The Red Army finally was victorious over Kiev and in 1920, Ukraine became a Soviet republic. In 1922, Ukraine became one of the founders of the United Soviet Socialist Republics. In the 1930s, the Soviet government's enforcement of collectivization met with peasant resistance, which in turn prompted the confiscation of grain from Ukrainian farmers by Soviet authorities; the resulting famine took an estimated five million lives. Ukraine was one of the most devastated Soviet republics during World War II. (For details on World War II, *see* Headline History, World War II.) On April 15, 1986, the nation's nuclear power plant at Chernobyl was the site of the world's worst nuclear accident. On Oct. 29, 1991, the Ukrainian parliament voted to shut down the reactor within two years' time and asked for international assistance in dismantling it.

When President Leonid Kravchuk was elected by the Ukrainian parliament in 1990, he vowed to seek Ukrainian sovereignty. Ukraine declared its independence on Aug. 24, 1991. In Dec. 1991, Ukrainian, Russian, and Belarus leaders cofounded a new Commonwealth of Independent States with the new capital to be situated in Minsk, Belarus. The new country's government was slow to reform the Soviet-era state-run economy, which was plagued by declining production, rising inflation, and widespread unemployment in the years following independence. The U.S. announced in Jan. 1994 that an agreement had been reached with Russia and Ukraine for the destruction of Ukraine's entire nuclear arsenal. In Oct. 1994, Ukraine began a program of economic liberalization and moved to re-establish central authority over Crimea. In 1995, Crimea's separatist leader was removed and the Crimean constitution revoked.

In June 1996, the last strategic nuclear warhead was removed to Russia. Also that month parliament approved a new constitution that allows for private ownership of land. An agreement was signed in May 1997 on the future of the Black Sea fleet, by which Ukrainian and Russian ships will share the port of Sevastopol for 20 years. Ukraine and Russia also signed a 10-year political treaty three days later, by which, among other provisions, Russia recognized the political and territorial integrity of Ukraine, including the Crimean Peninsula.

The Russian financial crisis in fall 1998 led to severe problems for the Ukranian economy, which is dependent on Russia for 40% of its foreign trade.

United Arab Emirates

President: Sheikh Zayed Bin Sultan Al-Nahyan (1971)
Prime Minister: Sheikh Maktoum Bin Rashid Al-Maktoum (1990)
Area: 32,000 sq mi. (75,581 sq km)
Population (1998 est.): 2,303,088 (average annual rate of natural increase: 1.78%); birth rate: 18.6/1000; infant mortality rate: 14.8/1000; density per sq mi.: 72
Capital and largest city (1989 est.): Abu Dhabi, 363,432. **Monetary unit:** U.A.E. Dirham. **Language:** Arabic. English as a second language. **Ethnicity/Race:** Emiri 19%, other Arab and Iranian 23%, South Asian 50%, other expatriates (includes Westerners and East Asians) 8% (1982). **Religions:** Islam (Sunni 80%, Shi'ite 16%), others 4%. **Literacy rate:** 68%
Economic summary: GDP/PPP (1996 est.): $72.9 billion; $23,800 per capita. **Real growth rate:** 1.4%. **Inflation:** 5.2%. **Arable land:** 0%. **Agriculture:** vegetables, dates, poultry, fish. **Labor force:** 794,400 (1993 est.); industry and commerce, 56%; services, 38%; agriculture, 6% (note: 75% of the labor force is foreign, July 1997 est.). **Industry:** light manufactures, petroleum, construction materials. Natural resource: oil. **Exports:** $31.3 billion (f.o.b., 1996 est.): oil and gas exports, re-exports, dried fish, dates. **Imports:** $22.3 billion (c.i.f., 1996 est.): consumer goods, food, capital goods. **Major trading partners:** Japan, Western Europe, U.S., Singapore, Korea, India, Iran, China, Taiwan.

Geography The United Arab Emirates, in the eastern part of the Arabian Peninsula, extends along part of the Gulf of Oman and the southern coast of the Persian Gulf. The nation is the size of Maine. Its neighbors are Saudi Arabia to the west and south, Qatar to the north, and Oman to the east. Most of the land is barren and sandy.

Government The United Arab Emirates was formed in 1971 by seven Emirates known as the Trucial States—Abu Dhabi (the largest), Dubai, Sharjah, Ajman, Fujairah, Ras al Khaimah and Umm al-Qaiwain. The loose federation allows joint policies in foreign relations, defense, and development, with each member state keeping its internal local system of government headed by its own ruler. A 40-member legislature consists of eight seats each for Abu Dhabi and Dubai, six seats each for Ras al Khaimah and Sharjah, and four each for the others. It is a member of the Arab League.

History Originally the area was inhabited by a seafaring people who were converted to Islam in the 7th century. Later, a dissident sect, the Carmathians, established a powerful sheikdom, and its army conquered Mecca. After the sheikdom disintegrated, its people became pirates. Threatening the Sultanate of Muscat and Oman early in the 19th century, the pirates provoked the intervention of the British, who in 1820 enforced a partial truce and in 1853 a permanent truce. Thus what had been called the Pirate Coast was renamed the Trucial Coast. From 1873 to 1947 the Trucial Coast was administered by British India and after 1947 by the London Foreign Office, but the British never assumed sovereignty. Each state maintained full internal control.

When the British vacated the Persian Gulf in 1971, the Trucial States federated and became known as the United Arab Emirates. Ra's al-Khaymah joined the federation in 1972, while Bahrain and Qatar opted for separate independence. The country signed a military defense agreement with the U.S. in 1994 and one with France in 1995. In 1997, U.A.E. officials protested Iranian military activities in the Persian Gulf, especially in regard to the ownership of three Gulf islands, which had been the subjects of disputes for many years.

United Kingdom

UNITED KINGDOM OF GREAT BRITAIN AND NORTHERN IRELAND

Sovereign: Queen Elizabeth II (1952)
Prime Minister: Tony Blair (1997)
Area: 94,247 sq mi. (244,820 sq km)
Population (1998 est.): 58,970,119 (average annual rate of natural increase: 0.25%); birth rate: 12/1000; infant mortality rate: 5.9/1000; density per sq mi.: 626
Capital and largest city (1992 est.): London, 6,679,699. **Other large cities:** Birmingham, 1,009,100; Leeds, 721,800; Glasgow, 681,470; Liverpool, 479,000; Bradford, 477,500; Edinburgh, 439,880; Manchester, 434,600; Bristol, 396,600. **Monetary unit:** Pound sterling (£). **Languages:** English, Welsh, Scots Gaelic. **Ethnicity/Race:** English 81.5%; Scottish 9.6%; Irish 2.4%; Welsh 1.9%; Ulster 1.8%; West Indian, Indian, Pakistani, and other 2.8%. **Religions:** Church of England (established church); Church of Wales (disestablished); Church of Scotland (established church—Presbyterian); Church of Ireland (disestablished); Roman Catholic; Methodist; Congregational; Baptist; Jewish. **Literacy rate:** 99%
Economic summary: GDP/PPP (1996 est.): $1.19 trillion; $20,400 per capita. **Real growth rate:** 2.4%. **Inflation:** 2.6%. **Unemployment:** 6.7% (Dec. 1996). **Arable land:** 25%. **Agriculture:** wheat, barley, potatoes, sugar beets, livestock, dairy products. **Labor force:** 28.1 million (Sept. 1996); services, 62.8%; manufacturing and construction, 25.0%; government, 9.1% (June 1992). **Industry:** machinery and transport equipment, metals, processed food, paper, textiles, chemicals, clothing, aircraft, shipbuilding, electronics and communications. **Natural resources:** coal, oil, gas. **Exports:** $240.4 billion (f.o.b., 1995): machinery, transport equipment, chemicals, petroleum, manufactured goods, semifinished goods. **Imports:** $258.8 billion (f.o.b., 1995): foodstuffs, machinery, manufactured goods, semifinished goods, consumer goods. **Major trading partners:** E.U., U.S.

Geography The United Kingdom, consisting of England, Wales, Scotland, and Northern Ireland, is twice the size of New York State. England, in the southeast part of the British Isles, is separated from Scotland on the north by the granite Cheviot Hills; from them the Pennine chain of uplands extends south through the center of England, reaching its highest point in the Lake District in the northwest. To the west along the border of Wales—a land of steep hills and valleys—are the Cambrian Mountains, while the Cotswolds, a range of hills in Gloucestershire, extend into the surrounding shires.

The remainder of England is plain land, though not necessarily flat, with the rocky sand-topped moors in the southwest, the rolling downs in the south and southeast, and the reclaimed marshes of the low-lying fens in the east-central districts.

Scotland is divided into three physical regions—the Highlands; the Central Lowlands, containing two-thirds of the population; and the Southern Uplands. The western Highland coast is intersected throughout by long, narrow sea-lochs, or fiords. Scotland also includes the Outer and Inner Hebrides and other islands off the west coast and the Orkney and Shetland Islands off the north coast. Wales is generally hilly; the Snowdon range in the northern part culminates in Mount Snowdon (3,560 ft., 1,085 m), highest in both England and Wales.

Important rivers flowing into the North Sea are the Thames, Humber, Tees, and Tyne. In the west are the Severn and Wye, which empty into the Bristol Channel and are navigable, as are the Mersey and Ribble.

Government The United Kingdom is a constitutional monarchy and parliamentary democracy, with a queen and a parliament that has two houses: the House of Lords with about 830 hereditary peers, 26 spiritual peers, about 270 life peers and peeresses, and 9 law-lords, who are hereditary peers, and the House of Commons, which has 651 popularly elected members. Supreme legislative power is vested in parliament, which sits for five years unless sooner dissolved. The House of Lords was stripped of most of its power in 1911, and now its main function is to revise legislation.

The executive power of the Crown is exercised by the cabinet, headed by the prime minister. The latter, normally the head of the party commanding a majority in the House of Commons, is appointed by the Sovereign, with whose consent he or she in turn appoints the rest of the cabinet. All ministers must be members of one or the other house of parliament; they are individually and collectively responsible to the Crown and parliament. The cabinet proposes bills and arranges the business of parliament, but it depends entirely on the votes in the House of Commons. The House of Lords cannot hold up "money" bills, but it can delay other bills for a maximum of one year. By the Act of Union (1707), the Scottish parliament was assimilated with that of England, and Scotland is now represented in Commons by 71 members. The Secretary of State for Scotland, a member of the cabinet, is responsible for the administration of Scottish affairs.

Ruler Queen Elizabeth II, born April 21, 1926, elder daughter of King George VI and Queen Elizabeth, succeeded to the throne on the death of her father on Feb. 6, 1952. On Nov. 20, 1947, she married Prince Philip, Duke of Edinburgh, born June 10, 1921. Their children are Prince Charles[1] (heir presumptive), born Nov. 14, 1948; Princess Anne, born Aug. 15, 1950; Prince Andrew, born Feb. 19, 1960; and Prince Edward, born March 10, 1964. Prince William Arthur Philip Louis, son of Prince Charles and the late Princess of Wales and second in line to the throne, was born June 21, 1982. A second son, Prince Henry Charles Albert David, was born Sept. 15, 1984, and is third in line.

History The early pre-Roman inhabitants of Britain were Celtic-speaking peoples, including the Brythonic people of Wales, the Picts of Scotland, and the Britons of Britain. Roman invasions of the 1st century B.C.E. brought Britain into contact with continental Europe. When the Roman legions withdrew in the 5th century C.E., Britain fell easy prey to the invading hordes of Angles, Saxons, and Jutes from Scandinavia and the Low Countries. The invasions had little effect on the Celtic peoples of Wales and Scotland. Seven large Anglo-Saxon kingdoms were established, and the original Britons were forced into Wales and Scotland. It was not until the 10th century that the country finally became united under the kings of Wessex. Following the death of Edward the Confessor (1066), a dispute about the succession arose, and William, Duke of Normandy, invaded England, defeating the Saxon king, Harold II, at the Battle of Hastings (1066). The Norman conquest introduced Norman French law and feudalism.

The reign of Henry II (1154–89), first of the Plantagenets, saw an increasing centralization of royal power at the expense of the nobles, but in 1215 John (1199–1216) was forced to sign the Magna Carta, which awarded the people, especially the nobles, certain basic rights. Edward I (1272–1307) continued the conquest of Ireland, reduced Wales to subjection, and made some gains in Scotland. In 1314, however, English forces led by Edward II were ousted from Scotland after the Battle of Bannockburn. The late 13th and early 14th centuries saw the development of a separate House of Commons with tax-raising powers. Edward III's claim to the throne of France led to the Hundred Years' War (1338–1453) and the loss of almost all the large English territory in France. In England, the great poverty and discontent caused by the war were intensified by the Black Death, a plague that reduced the population by about one-third. The Wars of the Roses (1455–85), a struggle for the throne between the House of York and the House of Lancaster, ended in the victory of Henry Tudor (Henry VII) at Bosworth Field (1485).

During the reign of Henry VIII (1509–47), the Church in England asserted its independence from the Roman Catholic Church. Under Edward VI and Mary, the two extremes of religious fanaticism were reached, and it remained for Henry's daughter, Elizabeth I (1558–1603), to set up the Church of England on a moderate basis. In 1588, the Spanish Armada, a fleet sent out by Catholic King Philip II of Spain, was defeated by the English and destroyed during a storm. During Elizabeth's reign, England

1. The title Prince of Wales, which is not inherited, was conferred on Prince Charles by his mother on July 26, 1958. The investiture ceremony took place on July 1, 1969. The previous Prince of Wales was Prince Edward Albert, who held the title from 1911 to 1936 before he became Edward VIII.

Rulers of England and Great Britain

Name	Born	Ruled [1]
SAXONS[2]		
Egbert[3]	c.775	828–839
Ethelwulf	?	839–858
Ethelbald	?	858–860
Ethelbert	?	860–866
Ethelred I	?	866–871
Alfred the Great	849	871–899
Edward the Elder	c.870	899–924
Athelstan	895	924–939
Edmund I the Deed-doer	921	939–946
Edred	c.925	946–955
Edwy the Fair	c.943	955–959
Edgar the Peaceful	943	959–975
Edward the Martyr	c.962	75–979
Ethelred II the Unready	968	979–1016
Edmund II Ironside	c.993	1016–1016
DANES		
Canute	995	1016–1035
Harold I Harefoot	c.1016	1035–1040
Hardecanute	c.1018	1040–1042
SAXONS		
Edward the Confessor	c.1004	1042–1066
Harold II	c.1020	1066–1066
HOUSE OF NORMANDY		
William I the Conqueror	1027	1066–1087
William II Rufus	c.1056	1087–1100
Henry I Beauclerc	1068	1100–1135
Stephen of Boulogne	c.1100	1135–1154
HOUSE OF PLANTAGENET		
Henry II	1133	1154–1189
Richard I Coeur de Lion	1157	1189–1199
John Lackland	1167	1199–1216
Henry III	1207	1216–1272
Edward I Longshanks	1239	1272–1307
Edward II	1284	1307–1327
Edward III	1312	1327–1377
Richard II	1367	1377–1399[4]
HOUSE OF LANCASTER		
Henry IV Bolingbroke	1367	1399–1413
Henry V	1387	1413–1422
Henry VI	1421	1422–1461[5]
HOUSE OF YORK		
Edward IV	1442	1461–1483[5]
Edward V	1470	1483–1483
Richard III	1452	1483–1485
HOUSE OF TUDOR		
Henry VII	1457	1485–1509
Henry VIII	1491	1509–1547
Edward VI	1537	1547–1553
Jane (Lady Jane Grey)[6]	1537	1553–1553
Mary I ("Bloody Mary")	1516	1553–1558
Elizabeth I	1533	1558–1603
HOUSE OF STUART		
James I[7]	1566	1603–1625
Charles I	1600	1625–1649
COMMONWEALTH		
Council of State	—	1649–1653
Oliver Cromwell[8]	1599	1653–1658
Richard Cromwell[8]	1626	1658–1659[9]
RESTORATION OF HOUSE OF STUART		
Charles II	1630	1660–1685
James II	1633	1685–1688[10]
William III[11]	1650	1689–1702
Mary II[11]	1662	1689–1694
Anne	1665	1702–1714
HOUSE OF HANOVER		
George I	1660	1714–1727
George II	1683	1727–1760
George III	1738	1760–1820
George IV	1762	1820–1830
William IV	1765	1830–1837
Victoria	1819	1837–1901
HOUSE OF SAXE-COBURG[12]		
Edward VII	1841	1901–1910
HOUSE OF WINDSOR[12]		
George V	1865	1910–1936
Edward VIII	1894	1936–1936[13]
George VI	1895	1936–1952
Elizabeth II	1926	1952–

1. Year of end of rule is also that of death, unless otherwise indicated. 2. Dates for Saxon kings are still subject of controversy. 3. Became king of West Saxons in 802; considered (from 828) first king of all England. 4. Died 1400. 5. Henry VI reigned again briefly 1470–71. 6. Nominal queen for 9 days; not counted as queen by some authorities. She was beheaded in 1554. 7. Ruled in Scotland as James VI (1567–1625). 8. Lord Protector. 9. Died 1712. 10. Died 1701. 11. Joint rulers (1689–1694). 12. Name changed from Saxe-Coburg to Windsor in 1917. 13. Was known after his abdication as the Duke of Windsor, died 1972.

became a world power. Elizabeth's heir was a Stuart—James VI of Scotland—who joined the two crowns as James I (1603–25). The Stuart kings incurred large debts and were forced either to depend on parliament for taxes or to raise money by illegal means. In 1642, war broke out between Charles I and a large segment of the parliament; Charles was defeated and executed in 1649, and the monarchy was then abolished. After the death in 1658 of Oliver Cromwell, the Lord Protector, the Puritan Commonwealth fell to pieces and Charles II was placed on the throne in 1660. The struggle between the king and parliament continued, but Charles II knew when to compromise. His brother, James II (1685–88), possessed none of his ability and was ousted by the Revolution of 1688, which confirmed the primacy of parliament. James's daughter, Mary, and her husband, William of Orange, then became the rulers.

Queen Anne's reign (1702–14) was marked by the Duke of Marlborough's victories over France at Blenheim, Oudenarde, and Malplaquet in the War of the Spanish Succession. England and Scotland meanwhile were joined by the Act of Union (1707). Upon the death of Anne, the distant claims of the elector of Hanover were recognized, and he became king of Great Britain and Ireland as George I. The unwillingness of the Hanoverian kings to rule resulted in the formation by the royal ministers of a cabinet, headed by a prime minister, which directed all public business. Abroad, the constant wars with France expanded the British Empire all over the globe, particularly in North America and India. This imperial growth was checked by the revolt of the American colonies (1775–81). Struggles with France broke out again in 1793 and during the Napoleonic Wars, which ended at Waterloo in (1815).

British Prime Ministers Since 1770

Name	Term	Name	Term
Lord North (Tory)	1770–1782	William E. Gladstone (Liberal)	1886–1886
Marquis of Rockingham (Whig)	1782–1782	Marquis of Salisbury (Conservative)	1886–1892
Earl of Shelburne (Whig)	1782–1783	William E. Gladstone (Liberal)	1892–1894
Duke of Portland (Coalition)	1783–1783	Earl of Rosebery (Liberal)	1894–1895
William Pitt, the Younger (Tory)	1783–1801	Marquis of Salisbury (Conservative)	1895–1902
Henry Addington (Tory)	1801–1804	Arthur James Balfour (Conservative)	1902–1905
William Pitt, the Younger (Tory)	1804–1806	Sir H. Campbell-Bannerman (Liberal)	1905–1908
Baron Grenville (Whig)	1806–1807	Herbert H. Asquith (Liberal)	1908–1915
Duke of Portland (Tory)	1807–1809	Herbert H. Asquith (Coalition)	1915–1916
Spencer Perceval (Tory)	1809–1812	David Lloyd George (Coalition)	1916–1922
Earl of Liverpool (Tory)	1812–1827	Andrew Bonar Law (Conservative)	1922–1923
George Canning (Tory)	1827–1827	Stanley Baldwin (Conservative)	1923–1924
Viscount Goderich (Tory)	1827–1828	James Ramsay MacDonald (Labor)	1924–1924
Duke of Wellington (Tory)	1828–1830	Stanley Baldwin (Conservative)	1924–1929
Earl Grey (Whig)	1830–1834	James Ramsay MacDonald (Labor)	1929–1931
Viscount Melbourne (Whig)	1834–1834	James Ramsay MacDonald (Coalition)	1931–1935
Sir Robert Peel (Tory)	1834–1835	Stanley Baldwin (Coalition)	1935–1937
Viscount Melbourne (Whig)	1835–1841	Neville Chamberlain (Coalition)	1937–1940
Sir Robert Peel (Tory)	1841–1846	Winston Churchill (Coalition)	1940–1945
Earl Russell (Whig)	1846–1852	Clement R. Attlee (Labor)	1945–1951
Earl of Derby (Tory)	1852–1852	Sir Winston Churchill (Conservative)	1951–1955
Earl of Aberdeen (Coalition)	1852–1855	Sir Anthony Eden (Conservative)	1955–1957
Viscount Palmerston (Liberal)	1855–1858	Harold Macmillan (Conservative)	1957–1963
Earl of Derby (Conservative)	1858–1859	Sir Alec Frederick Douglas-Home (Conservative)	1963–1964
Viscount Palmerston (Liberal)	1859–1865	Harold Wilson (Labor)	1964–1970
Earl Russell (Liberal)	1865–1866	Edward Heath (Conservative)	1970–1974
Earl of Derby (Conservative)	1866–1868	Harold Wilson (Labor)	1974–1976
Benjamin Disraeli (Conservative)	1868–1868	James Callaghan (Labor)	1976–1979
William E. Gladstone (Liberal)	1868–1874	Margaret Thatcher (Conservative)	1979–1990
Benjamin Disraeli (Conservative)	1874–1880	John Major (Conservative)	1990–1997
William E. Gladstone (Liberal)	1880–1885	Tony Blair (Labor)	1997–
Marquis of Salisbury (Conservative)	1885–1886		

The Victorian era, named after Queen Victoria (1837–1901), saw the growth of a democratic system of government that had begun with the Reform Bill of 1832. The two important wars in Victoria's reign were the Crimean War against Russia (1853–56) and the Boer War (1899–1902), the latter enormously extending Britain's influence in Africa. Increasing uneasiness at home and abroad marked the reign of Edward VII (1901–10). Within four years after the accession of George V in 1910, Britain entered World War I when Germany invaded Belgium. The nation was led by coalition Cabinets, headed first by Herbert Asquith and then, starting in 1916, by the Welsh statesman David Lloyd George. Postwar labor unrest culminated in the general strike of 1926.

King Edward VIII succeeded to the throne on Jan. 20, 1936, at his father's death, but abdicated on Dec. 11, 1936 (in order to marry an American divorcee, Wallis Warfield Simpson) in favor of his brother, who became George VI.

The efforts of Prime Minister Neville Chamberlain to stem the rising threat of Nazism in Germany failed with the German invasion of Poland on Sept. 1, 1939, which was followed by Britain's entry into World War II on Sept. 3. Allied reverses in the spring of 1940 led to Chamberlain's resignation and the formation of another coalition war cabinet by the Conservative leader, Winston Churchill, who led Britain through most of World War II. Churchill resigned shortly after V-E Day, May 7, 1945, but then formed a "caretaker" government that remained in office until after the parliamentary elections in July, which the Labor Party won overwhelmingly. The new government, formed by Clement R. Attlee, began a moderate socialist program.

(For details of World War II [1939–45], *see* Headline History World War II.)

In 1951, Churchill again became prime minister at the head of a Conservative government. George VI died Feb. 6, 1952, and was succeeded by his daughter Elizabeth II. Churchill stepped down in 1955 in favor of Sir Anthony Eden, who resigned on grounds of ill health in 1957, and was succeeded by Harold Macmillan and Sir Alec Douglas-Home. In 1964, Harold Wilson led the Labor Party to victory. A lagging economy brought the Conservatives back to power in 1970. Prime Minister Edward Heath won Britain's admission to the European Community. Margaret Thatcher became Britain's first woman prime minister as the Conservatives won 339 seats on May 3, 1979.

An Argentine invasion of the Falkland Islands on April 2, 1982, involved Britain in a war 8,000 miles from the home islands. Although Argentina had long claimed the Falklands, known as the Malvinas in Spanish, negotiations were in progress until a month before the invasion. When more than 11,000 Argentine troops on the Falklands surrendered on June 14, 1982, Thatcher declared her intention to garrison the islands indefinitely, together with a naval presence. Although there were continuing economic problems and foreign policy disputes, an upswing in the economy in 1986–87 led Thatcher to call elections for June 11 in which she won a near-unprecedented third consecutive term. Through much, if not all, of

1990 the Conservatives were losing the confidence of the electorate. The unpopularity of her poll tax together with an uncompromising position toward further European integration eroded support within her own party. When John Major won the Conservative Party leadership in November, Mrs. Thatcher resigned, paving the way for the queen to ask Mr. Major to form a government.

In the middle of a long recession John Major called a national election for April 1992. Confounding many political observers the Conservatives won but by a far narrower margin than previously. After months of political maneuvering the U.K. ratified the Maastrict treaty in August 1993. Eighteen years of Conservative rule ended in May 1997 when Tony Blair and the Labour Party triumphed in the British elections. Blair has been compared to U.S. President Bill Clinton for his youthful, telegenic personality and centrist views. He has embarked upon constitutional reform aimed at decentralizing the U.K.; Scotland and Wales elected in 1997 to form their own parliaments. Britain turned over its colony Hong Kong to China in July 1997. Blair's controversial meeting in October with Sinn Fein's political leader, Gerry Adams, was the first meeting in 76 years between a British prime minister and a Sinn Fein leader. It infuriated numerous factions but was a symbolic gesture in support of the nascent peace talks in Northern Ireland. In 1998 an agreement, brokered by former U.S. Senator George Mitchell and bolstered by Tony Blair and Bill Clinton, holds out promise of a more peaceful and just coexistence between Catholics and Protestants.

Northern Ireland

Status: Part of United Kingdom
Secretary of State: Sir Patrick Mayhew (1992)
Area: 5,452 sq mi. (14,121 sq km)
Population (1993 est.): 1,631,800; density per sq mi.: 300
Capital and largest city (June 30, 1992): Belfast, 287,500. **Monetary unit:** British pound sterling. **Languages:** English, Gaelic. **Religions:** Roman Catholic, Presbyterian, Church of Ireland, Methodist.

Geography Northern Ireland is composed of 26 districts, derived from the boroughs of Belfast and Londonderry and the counties of Antrim, Armagh, Down, Fermanagh, Londonderry, and Tyrone. Together they are commonly called Ulster, though the territory does not include the entire ancient province of Ulster. Predominantly Protestant, it forms the northern part of the island of Ireland, westernmost of the British Isles. It is slightly larger than Connecticut.

Government Northern Ireland is an integral part of the United Kingdom (it has 12 representatives in the British House of Commons), but under the terms of the government of Ireland Act in 1920, it had a semiautonomous government. In 1972, however, after three years of sectarian violence between Protestants and Catholics that resulted in more than 400 dead and thousands injured, Britain suspended the Ulster parliament. The Ulster counties became governed directly from London after an attempt to return certain powers to an elected assembly in Belfast.

The Northern Ireland Assembly was dissolved in 1975 and a Constitutional Convention was elected to write a constitution acceptable to Protestants and Catholics. The convention failed to reach agreement and closed down the next year.

The Good Friday Agreement of 1998, widely approved by referendum in both Northern Ireland and the Republic of Ireland, laid the groundwork for a new form of government. A 108-member assembly, with proportional representation of Catholics and Protestants and safeguards to prevent domination by the Protestant majority, was elected in June 1998. A 12-member executive committee will lead the government. A cross-border council will oversee joint projects between North and South, and the republic of Ireland will rescind its territorial claim to the North. Also, a British-Irish council is to be created, with representation from the Republic of Ireland, London, and the future assemblies of Northern Ireland, Wales, and Scotland. Though rejected by Catholic and Protestant hard-liners, the plan represents the most comprehensive effort to achieve peace in the conflict-riven North. The newly-elected assembly first met in July 1998.

History Ulster was part of Catholic Ireland until the reign of Elizabeth I (1558–1603) when, after crushing three Irish rebellions, the Crown confiscated lands in Ireland and settled the Scots Presbyterians in Ulster. Another rebellion in 1641–51, crushed as brutally by Oliver Cromwell, resulted in the settlement of Anglican Englishmen in Ulster. Subsequent political policy favoring Protestants and disadvantaging Catholics encouraged further Protestant settlement in Northern Ireland.

But the North did not separate from the South until William Gladstone presented in 1886 his proposal for home rule in Ireland. The Protestants in the North feared domination by the Catholic majority. Industry, moreover, was concentrated in the North and dependent on the British market.

When World War I began, civil war threatened between the regions. Northern Ireland, however, did not become a political entity until the six counties accepted the Home Rule Bill of 1920. This set up a semiautonomous parliament in Belfast and a crown-appointed governor advised by a cabinet of the prime minister and eight ministers, as well as a 12-member representation in the House of Commons in London.

When the Republic of Ireland gained sovereignty, relations improved between North and South, although the Irish Republican Army, outlawed in recent years, continued the struggle to end the partition of Ireland. In 1966–69, rioting and street fighting between Protestants and Catholics occurred in Londonderry, fomented by extremist nationalist Protestants, who feared the Catholics might attain a local majority, and by Catholics demonstrating for civil rights. These confrontations became known as "the Troubles."

The religious communities, Catholic and Protestant, became hostile armed camps. British troops were brought in to separate them but themselves became a target of Catholics, particularly the terrorist wing of the I.R.A. Their goal was to eject the British and unify Northern Ireland with the Irish Republic to the south. The Protestants remained tenaciously loyal to the United Kingdom.

Various attempts at representational government and power-sharing foundered during the 1970s.

Extremists from both sides further polarized the Protestants and Catholics. Direct rule from London and the presence of British troops failed to stop the violence.

In Oct. 1977, the 1976 Nobel Prize for Peace was awarded to Mairead Corrigan and Betty Williams for their campaign for peace in Northern Ireland. Intermittent violence continued, however, and on Aug. 27, 1979, an I.R.A. bomb killed Lord Mountbatten as he was sailing off southern Ireland, heightening tensions. Catholic protests over the death of I.R.A. hunger striker Bobby Sands in 1981 fueled more violence. Riots, sniper fire, and terrorist attacks killed more than 3,200 people between 1969 and 1998.

In Nov. 1995, a new agreement was reached that established a 3-member international commission. The British and Irish governments in Feb. 1995 announced an approved framework within which a settlement of the status of Northern Ireland could eventually be reached.

In 1997, Northern Ireland made a significant step in the direction of stemming sectarian strife. The first formal peace talks began on Oct. 6 with representatives of eight major Northern Irish political parties participating, a feat that in itself required three years of negotiations. Two smaller Protestant parties, including Ian Paisley's Democratic Unionists, boycotted the talks. For the first time, Sinn Fein won two seats in the British parliament, which went to Sinn Fein president Gerry Adams and second-in-command Martin McGuinness. Although the election strengthened the I.R.A.'s political legitimacy, it was their resumption of the 17-month cease-fire, which had collapsed in Feb. 1996, that gained the I.R.A. a place at the negotiating table.

In 1998 an agreement, brokered by former U.S. Senator George Mitchell and bolstered by British Prime Minister Tony Blair and U.S. President Bill Clinton, holds out promise of a more peaceful and just coexistence between Catholics and Protestants. Though supported by two thirds of Irish voters in May 1998, its implementation will be difficult. Hard-line members of each group protest the agreement, and violence continues—epitomized by the deaths of three Catholic boys in July 1998. A firebomb was tossed into their home during altercations concerning traditional Protestant triumphal marches through Catholic neighborhoods.

Dependencies of the United Kingdom

Anguilla

Status: Dependency
Governor: Robert Harris (1997)
Chief Minister: Hubert Hughes (1994)
Area: 35 sq mi. (91 sq km)
Population (1998 est.): 11,147; average annual rate of natural increase: 3.25%; birth rate: 17/1000; infant mortality rate: 20.2/1000; density per sq mi.: 319
Capital (1992): The Valley, 1,400. **Monetary unit:** East Caribbean dollar. **Ethnicity/Race:** black African. **Literacy:** 95%
Economic summary: GDP/PPP (1995 est.): $52 million; $7,400 per capita. **Real growth rate:** -4.3%. **Inflation:** 1.6%. **Unemployment** 7% (1992) . **Industry:** tourism, boat building, salt, lobster fishing. **Labor force** (1992): 4,400; commerce, 36%; services, 29%; construction, 18%; transportation and utilities, 10%. **Exports:** $1.3 million (f.o.b., 1995). **Imports:** $39.8 million (f.o.b., 1995).

Anguilla was first colonized in 1650 by English settlers from St. Christopher (St. Kitts) and has since remained a British territory. It was originally part of the West Indies Associated States as a component of the St. Kitts-Nevis-Anguilla Federation. In 1967, Anguilla declared its independence from the Federation but Britain did not recognize this action. In Feb. 1969, Anguilla voted to cut all ties with Britain and become an independent republic. In March, Britain landed troops on the island and, on March 30, a truce was signed. In July 1971, Anguilla became a dependency of Britain and two months later Britain ordered the withdrawal of all its troops. A new constitution for Anguilla, effective in Feb. 1976, provides for separate administration and a government of elected representatives. The Associated State of St. Kitts-Nevis-Anguilla ended in 1980 and in 1982 a new Anguillan constitution took effect.

Bermuda

Status: Self-governing dependency
Governor: Thorold Masefield (1997)
Premier: Pamela Gordon (1997)
Area: 20 sq mi. (52 sq km)
Population (1998 est.): 62,009; average annual rate of natural increase: 0.77%; birth rate: 12.2/1000; infant mortality rate: 9.6/1000; density per sq mi.: 3,101
Capital (1994 est.): Hamilton, 1,100. **Monetary unit:** Bermuda dollar. **Literacy rate:** 98%
Economic summary: GDP/PPP (1996 est.): $1.8 billion; $29,000 per capita. **Real growth rate:** 2.4%. **Unemployment:** negl. (1995). **Arable land:** n.a. **Agriculture:** bananas, vegetables, citrus fruits, dairy products. **Labor force:** 34,133; clerical, 23% ; services, 23%; laborers, 17%; technical and professional, 16%; administrative and managerial, 12%. **Industry:** structural concrete, paints, pharmaceuticals. **Natural resources:** limestone, sandy beaches and clear water. **Exports:** $54 million (f.o.b., 1995): semi-tropical produce, light manufactures. **Imports:** $550 million (f.o.b., 1995): foodstuffs, fuel, machinery. **Major trading partners:** U.S., U.K., Canada, Venezuela, Japan.

Bermuda is an archipelago of about 360 small islands, 580 miles (934 km) east of North Carolina. The largest is (Great) Bermuda, or Main Island. Explored by Juan de Bermúdez, a Spaniard, early in the 16th century, the islands were settled in 1612 by an offshoot of the Virginia Company. Bermuda became a Crown colony in 1684.

In 1968, Bermuda was granted a new constitution, its first prime minister, and autonomy, except for foreign relations, defense, and internal security. The predominantly white United Bermuda Party has retained power in four elections against the opposition—the black-led Progressive Labor Party—although Bermuda's population is 60% black. U.S. air and navy bases, which had been leased in 1941 for 99-year terms, closed in 1995, along with Canadian, British Army, and Royal Navy. In a referendum held in August 1995 nearly three-fourths of those voting opposed independence. The prime minister's unexpected resignation in March 1997 led the ruling United Bermuda Party to name Pamela Gordon the country's first female and youngest premier.

British Antarctic Territory

Status: Dependency
Commissioner: Peter M. Newton (1992)
Area: 500,000 sq mi. (1,395,000 sq km)
Population: no permanent residents

The British Antarctic Territory consists of the South Shetland Islands, South Orkney Islands, and nearby Graham Land on the Antarctic continent, largely uninhabited. They are dependencies of the British Crown colony of the Falkland Islands but received a separate administration in 1962, being governed by a British-appointed High Commissioner who is governor of the Falklands.

British Indian Ocean Territory

Status: Dependency
Commissioner: David Ross MacLennan (1994)
Administrative headquarters: Victoria, Seychelles
Area: 85 sq mi. (220 sq km)

This dependency, consisting of the Chagos Archipelago and other small island groups, was formed in 1965 by agreement with Mauritius and the Seychelles. There is no permanent civilian population in the territory. One of its islands, Diego Garcia (17 sq mi.), is a joint U.S.-U.K. refueling and support station that was used during the Persian Gulf War (1991).

British Virgin Islands

VIRGIN ISLANDS
Status: Dependency
Governor: David Mackilligin (1995)
Chief Minister: Ralph O'Neal (1995)
Area: 59 sq mi. (153 sq km)
Population (1998 est.): 18,705; average annual rate of natural increase: 2.41%; birth rate: 16.2/1000; infant mortality rate: 23/1000; density per sq mi.: 317
Capital (1991 census): Road Town (on Tortola): 3,983. **Monetary unit:** U.S. dollar. **Literacy rate:** 98%
Economic summary: GDP/PPP (1995 est.): $135 million; $10,200 per capita. **Real growth rate:** 4%. **Inflation:** 2.5% (1990 est.) . **Unemployment:** 3% (1995)**Labor force:** 4,911 (1980). **Exports** (f.o.b., 1990): $3.4 million: rum, fresh fish, gravel, sand, fruits, animals. **Imports** (c.i.f., 1988): $11.5 million: building materials, automobiles, foodstuffs, machinery.

Some 36 islands (more than 20 are uninhabited) in the Caribbean Sea northeast of Puerto Rico and west of the Leeward Islands, the British Virgin Islands are economically interdependent with the U.S. Virgin Islands to the south. The principal islands are Tortola, Virgin Gorda, Anegada, and Jost Van Dyke. When Christopher Columbus visited the islands in 1493, he found the Carib people living there. By 1596 most of the Caribs had fled or been killed.

The British Virgin Islands were formerly part of the administration of the Leeward Islands, having been annexed in 1672. The English planters' slave-based sugar plantations declined after slavery was abolished in the first half of the 19th century. The islands received a separate administration in 1956 as a Crown colony. In 1967 a new constitution was promulgated that provided for a ministerial system of government headed by the governor, which was continued under the new constitution of 1977. Tourism is the islands' economic mainstay.

Cayman Islands

Status: Dependency
Governor: John Wynne Owen (1995)
Area: 100 sq mi. (259 sq km)
Population (1998 est.): 37,716; average annual rate of natural increase: 4.22%; birth rate: 14/1000; infant mortality rate: 8.4/1000; density per sq mi.: 377
Capital (1992 est.): George Town (on Grand Cayman), 15,000. **Monetary unit:** Cayman Islands dollar. **Literacy rate:** 98%
Economic Summary: GDP: (1996 est.): $860 million; $23,800 per capita. **Inflation:** 4.5%. **Unemployment:** 7% (1992). **Exports:** $10 million (f.o.b., 1993 est.): turtle products, manufactured goods. **Imports:** $329 million (c.i.f., 1995 est.): foodstuffs, manufactured goods. **Major trading partners:** U.S., Trinidad and Tobago, U.K., Netherland Antilles, Japan.

This dependency consists of three islands—Grand Cayman (76 sq mi.; 197 sq km), Cayman Brac (22 sq mi.; 57 sq km), and Little Cayman (20 sq mi.; 52 sq km)—situated about 180 miles (290 km) northwest of Jamaica. They were dependencies of Jamaica until 1959, when they became a unit territory within the Federation of the West Indies. In 1962, upon the dissolution of the Federation, the Cayman Islands became a British dependency, and a new constitution approved in 1972 provided for a greater degree of autonomy. The government of the Cayman Islands is administered according to the revised constitution of 1994. It provides for a Legislative Assembly composed of the governor, 3 official members, and 15 elected members; there are no political parties. An Executive Council, composed of three official and five elected members, advises the governor. Tourism and finance are the Cayman Islands' major industries; tourism increased eightfold between the mid-1970s and the early 1990s and there are more than 500 licensed banks and trust companies on the islands.

Channel Islands

Status: Crown dependencies
Lieutenant Governor of Jersey: Sir Michael Wilkes (1995)
Lieutenant Governor of Guernsey: Vice Adm. Sir John Coward (1994)
Area: 120 sq mi. (311 sq km)
Populations (1997 est.): Jersey, 89,136; Guernsey, 64,555
Capital of Jersey (1991): St. Helier, 28,123
Capital of Guernsey (1991): St. Peter Port, 16,648. **Monetary units:** Guernsey pound; Jersey pound

This group of islands, lying in the English Channel off the northwest coast of France, is the only portion of the Duchy of Normandy belonging to the English Crown, to which it has been attached since the conquest of 1066. It was the only British possession occupied by Germany during World War II. English and French are commonly spoken (though use of the latter is declining), and a Norman-French patois survives.

For purposes of government, the islands are divided into the Bailiwick of Jersey (45 sq mi.; 117 sq km), including the Ecrehous rocks and Les Minquiers, and the Bailiwick of Guernsey (30 sq mi.; 78 sq km), including Alderney (3 sq mi.; 7.8 sq km); Sark (2 sq mi.; 5.2 sq km), Herm, Jethou, etc. The islands are administered according to their own laws and customs by local governments. Acts of Parliament in London are not binding on the islands unless they are specifically mentioned. The queen is represented in each bailiwick by a lieutenant-governor. The Channel Islands also enjoy tax sovereignty, and their exports are protected by British tariff barriers. Financial services, tourism, market gardening, and dairy farming are important industries.

Falkland Islands and Dependencies

Status: Dependency
Governor: Richard Ralph (1996)
Chief Executive: R. Sampson
Area: 4,700 sq mi. (12,173 sq km)
Population (1997 est.): 2,432; density per sq mi.: 0.5
Capital (1991): Stanley (on East Falkland), 1,643. **Monetary unit:** Falkland Island pound
Exports: $7.6 million (f.o.b., 1995): wool, hides, meat. **Imports:** $24.7 million (1995): food, clothing, timber, and machinery. **Major trading partners:** U.K., Netherlands, Netherland Antilles, Japan.

This sparsely inhabited dependency consists of a group of islands in the South Atlantic, about 250 miles (402 km) east of the South American mainland. The largest islands are East Falkland and West Falkland. The English captain John Strong made the first recorded landing in the Falklands in 1690. The islands passed between the French, Spanish, and British until 1820, when the Argentine government proclaimed its sovereignty. In 1833 a British force expelled the few remaining Argentine officials from the island without firing a shot, and in 1841 a British civilian lieutenant-governor was appointed for the Falklands. Colonial status was granted to the Falklands in 1892. Argentina, calling the islands *Las Islas Malvinas*, regularly protested Britain's occupation of the islands. On April 2, 1982, Argentina's military government invaded the Falklands. The Falkland Islands War ended 10 weeks later with the surrender of the Argentine forces at Stanley to British troops, who had forcibly reoccupied the islands. Argentina still claims the islands. But an agreement between Argentina and the United Kingdom in 1995 sought to defuse licensing and sovereignty conflicts that would dampen foreign interest in exploiting the Falkland Islands' potential oil reserves.

The Falkland Islands' dependencies are South Georgia Island (1,450 sq mi.; 3,756 sq km), the South Sandwich Islands, and other islets. Three former dependencies—Graham Land, the South Shetland Islands, and the South Orkney Islands—were established as a new British dependency, the British Antarctic Territory, in 1962.

The islands' chief industry is sheep raising and, apart from the production of wool (the chief export), hides and skins, and tallow, there are no known resources. The whaling industry is carried on from South Georgia Island.

Gibraltar

Status: Self-governing dependency
Governor: Sir Richard Luce (1997)
Chief Minister: Peter Caruana (1996)
Area: 2.25 sq mi. (5.8 sq km)
Population (1998 est.): 29,045; average annual rate of natural increase: 0.43%; birth rate: 13/1000; infant mortality rate: 6.6/1000; density per sq mi.: 12,909. **Monetary unit:** Gibraltar pound. **Literacy rate:** 99% (est.)
Economic summary: GNP: (purchasing power parity, 1993 est.): $205 million; $6,600 per capita. **Exports:** $57 million (f.o.b., 1993): re-exports of tobacco, petroleum, wine. **Imports:** $708 million (c.i.f., 1993): manufactured goods, fuels, foodstuffs. **Major trading partners:** U.K, Morocco, Portugal, Netherlands, Spain, U.S.

Gibraltar, at the south end of the Iberian Peninsula, is a rocky promontory commanding the western entrance to the Mediterranean. Aside from its strategic importance, it is also a free port, naval base, and coaling station. It was captured by the Arabs crossing from Africa into Spain in C.E. 711. In the 15th century, it passed to the Moorish ruler of Granada and later became Spanish. It was captured by an Anglo-Dutch force in 1704 during the War of the Spanish Succession and passed to Great Britain by the Treaty of Utrecht in 1713. Most of the inhabitants of Gibraltar are of Spanish, Italian, and Maltese descent.

Spanish efforts to recover Gibraltar culminated in a referendum in 1967 in which the residents voted overwhelmingly to retain their link with Britain. Spain sealed Gibraltar's land border in 1969 and did not open communications until April 1980, after the two governments had agreed to resolve their dispute in keeping with a United Nations resolution calling for restoration of the "Rock" to Spain. The last British military battalion on the "Rock" was withdrawn in March 1991. Spain suggested a form of joint control, but the U.K. refused.

Isle of Man

Status: Self-Governing Crown Dependency
Lieutenant Governor: Sir Timothy Daunt (1995)
Chief Minister: Miles Walker (1986)
Area: 221 sq mi. (572 sq km)
Population (1998 est.): 75,121; average annual rate of natural increase: 0.79%; birth rate: 12.5/1000; infant mortality rate: 2.4/1000; density per sq mi.: 340
Capital (1991): Douglas, 22,214. **Monetary unit:** Isle of Man pound

The Isle of Man is situated in the Irish Sea, equidistant from Scotland, Ireland, and England. Among its earliest inhabitants were Celts, and their language, Manx, which is closely related to Gaelic, remained the everyday speech of the people until the first half of the 19th century. Manx now has no native speakers. Norse (Viking) invasions began about C.E. 800, and the island was a dependency of Norway until 1266. During this period the Isle of Man came under a Scandinavian system of government that has remained practically unchanged ever since. The island came under the control of England in 1341. After allowing a succession of feudal lords rule the island, the British parliament purchased sovereignty over the island in 1765. The Isle of Man continues to be administered according to its own laws by a government composed of the lieutenant-governor, a legislative council, and a House of Keys, one of the most ancient legislative assemblies in the world. The chief exports are beef and lamb, fish, and livestock; the Isle of Man levies its own taxes.

Leeward Islands

SEE BRITISH VIRGIN ISLANDS; MONTSERRAT.

Montserrat

Status: Dependency
Governor: Tony Abbot (1997)
Chief Minister: David Brandt (1997)
Area: 38 sq mi. (98 sq km)
Population (1998 est.): 12,828; average annual rate of natural increase: 0.23%; birth rate: 14.3/1000; infant mortality rate: 11.9/1000; density per sq mi.: 338
Capital (1991 est.): Plymouth, 2,500. **Monetary unit:** East Caribbean dollar
Economic summary: GDP/PPP (1995 est.): $55.3 million; $4,360 per capita. **Real growth rate:** -2.9%. **Inflation:** 4%. **Labor force:** 4,521 (1992). **Exports:** $12.1 million (f.o.b., 1995 est.): electric parts, plastic bags, apparel, hot peppers, live plants, cattle. **Imports:** $29.9 million (f.o.b., 19924 est.): machinery and transportation equipment, foodstuffs, cattle, potatoes, cotton, lint, recapped tires, mangoes, tomatoes, manufactured goods, fuels, lubricants and related materials.

The island of Montserrat is in the Lesser Antilles of the West Indies. Until 1956, it was a division of the Leeward Islands. In 1958 Montserrat joined the Federation of the West Indies, remaining a member until that organization's dissolution in 1962. Unlike most other British West Indies possessions, Montserrat, with its weak economy, has not vigorously sought independence. The Soufrière Hills volcano began erupting in 1995 and the situation continued to worsen through 1998, with the capital, Plymouth, destroyed and the southern and central parts of the British colony having been evacuated. Only about 4,000 people were left in the northern "safe zone" in 1998 after thousands had moved to nearby Antigua, Britain, or other parts of the Caribbean.

Pitcairn Island

Status: Dependency
Governor: Robert John Alston (nonresident) (1994)
Island Magistrate: Jay Warren
Area: 1.75 sq mi. (4.5 sq km)
Population (July 1997 est.): 54; density per sq mi.: 30
Capital: Adamstown

Pitcairn Island, in the South Pacific about midway between Australia and South America, consists of the island of Pitcairn and the three uninhabited islands of Henderson, Duicie, and Oeno. The island of Pitcairn was settled in 1790 by British mutineers from the ship *Bounty,* commanded by Capt. William Bligh. It was annexed as a British colony in 1838. Overpopulation forced removal of the settlement to Norfolk Island in 1856, but about 40 persons soon returned.

The descendants of First Mate Fletcher Christian, the 8 other mutineers, and the dozen or so Tahitians who accompanied them still inhabit the island, and, in addition to English, they speak a dialect that is a mixture of Tahitian and 18th-century English.

St. Helena

Status: Dependency
Governor: David Smallman (1995)
Area: 120 sq mi. (310 sq km)
Population (1998 est.): 7,091; average annual rate of natural increase: 0.76%; birth rate: 14.1/1000; infant mortality rate: 28.8/1000; density per sq mi.: 59
Capital (1987): Jamestown, 1,332. **Monetary unit:** Pound sterling. **Literacy rate:** 97%

St. Helena is a volcanic island in the South Atlantic about 1,100 miles (1,770 km) from the west coast of Africa. It is famous as the place of exile of Napoleon (1815–21). The island was discovered in 1502 by João da Nova, a Spanish navigator in the service of Portugal. It was taken for England in 1659 by the East India Company and was brought under the direct government of the Crown in 1834. After the opening of the Suez Canal, in 1870, St. Helena's importance as a port of call diminished. About two-thirds of the colony's budget is provided by the United Kingdom in the form of a subsidy; the remainder is raised from the sale of postage stamps and from customs duties and wharf fees.

St. Helena has two dependencies: Ascension (34 sq mi.; 88 sq km), an island about 700 miles (1,127 km) northwest of St. Helena; and Tristan da Cunha (40 sq mi.; 104 sq km), a group of six islands about 1,500 miles (2,414 km) south-southwest of St. Helena.

Turks and Caicos Islands

Status: Dependency
Governor: John Kelly (1996)
Chief Minister: Derek H. Taylor (1995)
Area: 193 sq mi. (500 sq km)
Population (1998 est.): 16,249; average annual rate of natural increase: 3.77%; birth rate: 27.1/1000; infant mortality rate: 21.7/1000; density per sq mi.: 84
Capital (1990): Cockburn Town, 3,720. **Monetary unit:** U.S. dollar. **Literacy rate:** 98%
Economic summary: GDP/PPP (1993 est.): $84.5 million; $6,400 per capita. **Real growth rate:** 2%. **Labor force:** 4,848 (1990 est.); majority engaged in fishing and tourist industries. **Exports:** $6.8 million (f.o.b., 1993): lobster, dried and fresh conch, conch shells. **Imports:** $42.8 million (1993): food and beverages, tobacco, clothing, manufactures, construction materials. **Major trading partners:** U.S., U.K.

These two groups of islands are situated at the southeast end of the Bahamas, about 90 miles north of the Dominican Republic. The principal islands in the Turks group are Grand Turk and Salt Cay; the principal islands in the Caicos group are South Caicos, East Caicos, Middle (or Grand) Caicos, North Caicos, Providenciales, and West Caicos. The governor is president of the Executive Council, which includes the various ministers, under the 1976 Constitution. The islands were not settled by Europeans until 1678, when British settlers from Bermuda established a salt-panning industry. The islands were at first placed under The Bahamas government, but in 1874 they were annexed to the colony of Jamaica. They were dependencies of Jamaica until 1959, when they became a unit territory within the Federation of the West Indies. In 1962, when Jamaica became independent, the Turks and Caicos became a British Crown colony. The salt production industry, the islands' economic mainstay, ceased in 1964 and gave way to tourism, offshore financial services, and fishing. Some efforts toward independence were made in the early 1980s, but these ceased in 1986 when scandals forced the governor to dissolve the Executive Council and assume administrative control. In 1988, representative rule was restored.

United States

THE UNITED STATES OF AMERICA

President: William J. Clinton (1993)

Vice President: Albert A. Gore, Jr. (1993)
Land area: 3,536,341 sq mi. (9,372,610 sq km)
Resident population (1998 est.): 269,816,000;
(1990 census): 248,709,873 (change 1980–1990: 9.8%). White: 199,686,070 (80.3%); Black: 29,986,060 (12.1%); American Indian, Eskimo, or Aleut: 1,959,234 (0.8%); Asian or Pacific Islander: 7,273,662 (2.9%); Other Race: 9,804,847 (3.9%); Hispanic Origin[1]: 22,354,059 (9.0%); (average annual rate of natural increase: 0.87%); birth rate: 14.4/1000; infant mortality rate: 6.4/1000; density per sq mi.: 76
Capital (1990 census.): Washington, D.C., 606,900. **Largest cities:** New York: city proper (1996 est.) 7,380,906; metro. area (1996 est.) 16,390,000; Los Angeles: city proper (1996 est.) 3,553,638; metro. area (1996 est.) 12,576, 000; Chicago, 2,721,547; Houston, 1,744,058; Philadelphia, 1,478,002; San Diego, 1,171,121; Phoenix, 1,159,014; San Antonio, 1,067,816; Dallas, 1,052,292; Detroit, 1,000,272. **Monetary unit:** Dollar. **Languages:** predominantly English, sizable Spanish-speaking minority. **Ethnicity/ Race:** white 83.4%, black 12.4%, Asian 3.3%, Native American 0.8% (1992). **Religions:** Protestant, 61%; Roman Catholic, 25%; Jewish, 2%; other, 5%; none, 7%. **Literacy rate:** 97%
Economic summary: GDP/PPP (1996 est.): $7.61 trillion; $28,600 per capita. **Real growth rate:** 2.4%. **Inflation:** 3%. **Unemployment:** 5.4% (1996). **Arable land:** 19%. **Agriculture:** corn, wheat, barley, oats, sugar, potatoes, soybeans, fruits, beef, veal, pork. **Labor force:** 133.943 million (includes unemployed, 1996); managerial and professional, 28.8%; technical, sales and administrative support, 29.7%; services; 13.6; manufacturing, mining, transportation and crafts, 25.1%. **Industry:** petroleum products, fertilizers, cement, pig iron and steel, plastics and resins, newsprint, motor vehicles, machinery, natural gas, electricity. **Natural resources:** coal, oil, copper, gold, silver, minerals, timber. **Exports:** $584.7 billion (f.o.b., 1995): machinery, chemicals, aircraft, military equipment, cereals, motor vehicles, grains. Illicit drugs: illicit producer of cannabis for domestic consumption. Ongoing eradication program aimed at small plots and greenhouses unsuccessful. **Imports:** $771 billion (c.i.f., 1995): crude and partly refined petroleum, machinery, automobiles. **Major trading partners:** Canada, Japan, Western Europe.

1. Persons of Hispanic origin can be of any race.

Government The president is elected for a four-year term and may be re-elected only once. The bicameral Congress consists of the 100-member Senate, elected to a six-year term with one-third of the seats becoming vacant every two years, and the 435-member House of Representatives, elected every two years. The minimum voting age is 18.

(*See also* Profile of the United States, U.S. States (and territories), U.S. Cities, U.S. Statistics, and U.S. Government and History.)

Uruguay

ORIENTAL REPUBLIC OF URUGUAY

National name: Republica Oriental del Uruguay
President: Julio María Sanguinetti Cairolo (1995)
Area: 68,040 sq mi. (176,220 sq km)
Population (1998 est.): 3,284,841 (average annual rate of natural increase: 0.71%); birth rate: 16.9/1000; infant mortality rate: 14.1/1000; density per sq mi.: 48
Capital and largest city (1992 est.): Montevideo, 1,500,000. **Monetary unit:** Peso. **Languages:** Spanish. **Ethnicity/Race:** white 88%, mestizo 8%, black 4%. **Religion:** Roman Catholic, 66%; Protestant, 2%; Jewish, 2%. **Literacy rate:** 96%
Economic summary: GDP/PPP (1996 est.): $26 billion: $8,000 per capita. **Real growth rate:** 4.9% (1996). **Inflation:** 24.4% (Dec. 1996). **Unemployment:** 12%. **Arable land:** 7%. **Agriculture:** livestock, grains. **Labor force** 1.436 million; government, 25%; manufacturing, 19%; commerce, 12%; agriculture, 11% (1988 est.). **Products:** processed meats, wool and hides, textiles, shoes, handbags and leather wearing apparel, cement, refined petroleum. **Natural resources:** hydroelectric power potential. **Exports:** $2.4 billion (f.o.b., 1996): meat, hides, wool, fish. **Imports:** $3.3 billion (c.i.f., 1996): transportation equipment, chemicals, machinery, plastics, minerals. **Major trading partners:** U.S., Brazil, Argentina, Germany, China, Italy, Nigeria.

Geography Uruguay, on the east coast of South America south of Brazil and east of Argentina, is comparable in size to Oklahoma. The country consists of a low, rolling plain in the south and a low plateau in the north. It has a 120-mile (193 km) Atlantic shore line, a 235-mile (378 km) frontage on the Rio de la Plata, and 270 miles (435 km) on the Uruguay River, its western boundary.

Government A republic. Presidents serve a single five-year term. The bicameral Congress, the General Assembly, consists of the 31-member Chamber of Senators and the 99-member Chamber of Deputies.

History Prior to European settlement, Uruguay was inhabited by groups of indigenous peoples collectively known as the Charrúas. Juan Díaz de Solis, a Spaniard, visited Uruguay in 1516, but the Portuguese were first to settle it when they founded the town of Colonia del Sacramento in 1680. After a long struggle, Spain wrested the country from Portugal in 1778, by which time almost all of the indigenous people had been exterminated. Uruguay revolted against Spain in 1811, only to be conquered in 1817 by the Portuguese from Brazil. Independence was reasserted with Argentine help in 1825, and the republic was set up in 1828.

Independence, however, did not restore order, and a revolt in 1836 touched off nearly 50 years of factional strife, including an inconclusive civil war (1839–51) and a war with Paraguay (1865–70), accompanied by occasional armed intervention by Argentina and Brazil. Uruguay, made prosperous by meat and wool exports, founded a welfare state early in the 20th century under President José Batlle y Ordóñez, who ruled from 1903 to 1929. A decline began in the 1950s as successive governments struggled to maintain a large bureaucracy and costly social benefits. Economic stagnation and left-wing terrorist activity followed.

A military coup ousted the civilian government in 1973. The military dictatorship that followed used fear and terror to demoralize the population, taking thousands of political prisoners. After ruling for 12 years, the brutal military regime permitted election of a civilian government in Nov. 1984 and relinquished rule in March 1985; full political and civil rights were then restored.

Subsequent leaders contended with high inflation and a mammoth national debt. Presidential and legislative elections in Nov. 1994 resulted in a narrow victory for the center-right Colorado Party and its presidential candidate Julio Sanguinetti Cairolo, who had been president in 1985–90. The new president pushed for constitutional and economic reforms aimed at reducing inflation and the size of the public sector, partially through tax increases and privatization.

Uzbekistan

REPUBLIC OF UZBEKISTAN

National Name: Uzbekiston Respublikasi
President: Islam A. Karimov (1990)
Prime Minister: Otkir Sultonov (1995)
Area: 172,700 sq mi. (447,400 sq km)
Population (1998 est.): 23,784,321; (average annual rate of natural increase: 1.33%); birth rate: 23.7/1000; infant mortality rate: 71/1000; density per sq mi.: 138
Capital and largest city (1992 est.): Tashkent, 2,106,000. **Other large cities:** Samarkand, 372,000; Andijon, 302,000. **Languages:** Uzbek 74.3%, Russian 14.2%, Tajik 4.4%, other 7.1%. **Ethnicity/Race (1996 est.):** Uzbek 80%, Russian 5.5%, Tajik 5%, Kazak 3%, Karakalpak 2.5%, Tatar 1.5%, other 2.5%. **Religion:** Muslim (mostly Sunnis), 88%; Eastern Orthodox, 9%; other, 3%. **Literacy rate:** 97%
Economic summary: GDP/PPP (1996 est. as extrapolated from World Bank est. for 1994)): $57 billion; $2,430 per capita. **Real growth rate** 1.6% (1996 est.). **Inflation:** 55%. **Unemployment:** 0.3% officially, plus large numbers of underemployed Dec. 1996). **Arable land:** 9%. **Labor force** 8.2 million; agriculture and forestry, 44%; industry and construction, 20% (1995). **Natural resources:** natural gas, petroleum, coal, gold, uranium, silver, copper, lead and zinc, tungsten, molybdenum. **Agriculture:** major crop is cotton. **Exports:** $3.2 billion (1996): cotton, gold, textiles, chemicals, mineral fertilizers, vegetable oil. **Imports:** $3.2 billion (1996): machinery and parts, consumer durables, grain, and other food. **Major Trading Partners:** Russia, Ukraine, Eastern Europe, U.S., Czech Republic.

Geography Uzbekistan is situated in Central Asia between the Amu Darya and Syr Darya Rivers, the Aral Sea, and the slopes of the Tien Shan Mountains. It is bounded by Kazakhstan in the north and northwest, Kyrgyzstan and Tajikistan in the east and southeast, and Turkmenistan in the southwest. The republic also includes the Karakalpakstan Autonomous Republic with its capital, Nukus (1992 est. pop., 182,000). The land is made up of deserts, oases, and mountains with valleys. Two-thirds of the territory are occupied by deserts and semi-deserts. The country is about one-tenth larger in area than the state of California.

Government Under the 1992 constitution, the chief executive is the president and the legislative body of the republic is its Supreme Assembly. The People's Democratic Party (formerly the Communist Party of Uzbekistan) holds power and has suppressed all opposition parties.

History The Uzbekistan land was once part of the ancient Persian empire and was later conquered by Alexander the Great in 4 B.C.E. During the 8th century, the nomadic Turkic tribes living there were converted to Islam by invading Arab forces who dominated the area. The Mongols under Ghengis Khan took over the region from the Seljuk Turks in the 13th century and it later became part of Tamerlane the Great's empire and his successors until the 16th century. The Uzbeks invaded the territory in the early 16th century and merged with the other inhabitants in the area. Their empire broke up into separate Uzbek principalities, the khanates of Khiva, Bukhara, and Kokand. These city-states resisted Russian expansion into the area, but were conquered by the Russian forces in the mid-19th century.

The territory was made into the Uzbek Republic in 1924 and became the independent Uzbekistan Soviet Socialist Republic in 1925. Under Soviet rule, Uzbekistan concentrated on growing cotton with the help of irrigation, mechanization, and chemical fertilizers and pesticides, causing serious environmental damage.

In June 1990, Uzbekistan became the first Central Asian republic to declare that its own laws had sovereignty over those of the central Soviet government. Uzbekistan became fully independent and joined with ten other former Soviet republics on Dec. 21, 1991, in the Commonwealth of Independent States. In February 1992, President Karimov, a former Communist Party boss, affirmed his commitment to democracy and human rights, but effectively suppressed opposition parties in mid-1993. The criminal code was amended to impose stricter penalties for antigovernment activity. Opposition groups were largely excluded in future elections while the ruling party continued to post decisive victories. Uzbekistan's main foreign policy concerns in 1997 were its eastern and southern neighbors. The Uzbek leadership sought international support to help end the fighting in Afghanistan and signed onto the peace accords that formally ended the civil war in Tajikistan.

Vanuatu

REPUBLIC OF VANUATU

President: Jean-Marie Leye (1994)
Prime Minister: Donald Kalpokas (1998)
Area: 5,700 sq mi. (14,760 sq km)
Population (1998 est.): 185,204 (average annual rate of natural increase: 2.07%); birth rate: 29.2/1000; infant mortality rate: 61.3/1000; density per sq mi.: 33
Capital and largest city (1993 est.): Port Vila, 26,100. **Monetary unit:** Vatu. **Languages:** Bislama (a Melanesian pidgin English), English, French (all 3 official). **Ethnicity/Race:** indigenous Melanesian 94%, French 4%, Vietnamese, Chinese, other Pacific Islanders. **Religions:** Presbyterian, 36.7%; Roman Catholic, 15%; Anglican, 15%; other Christian, 10%; indigenous beliefs, 7.6%; other, 15.7%. **Literacy rate:** 55%
Economic Summary: GDP/PPP (1995 est.): $219 million, $1,230 per capita. **Real growth rate:** 2% (1995). **Inflation:** 4% (1995). **Labor force:** 66,597 (1989 est.); by occupation: agriculture, 65%; services, 32%; industry, 5%. **Arable land:** 2%. **Agriculture:** copra, cocoa, coffee. Agriculture accounts for 40% of GDP. **Exports:** $28 million (f.o.b., 1995): copra, cocoa, coffee, frozen fish, timber, beef. **Imports:** $93 million (f.o.b., 1995 est.): machines and vehicles, food, raw materials, fuel, chemicals. **Major trading partners:** E.U., New Zealand, Japan, Australia.

Geography Vanuatu is an archipelago of some 80 islands lying between New Caledonia and Fiji in the South Pacific. Largest of the islands is Espiritu Santo (875 sq mi.; 2,266 sq km); others are Efate, Malekula, Malo, Pentecost, and Tanna.

Government The constitution by which Vanuatu achieved independence on July 30, 1980, vests executive authority in a president, elected by an electoral college for a five-year term. A unicameral legislature of 46 members exercises legislative power.

History Many of the northern islands that now compose Vanuatu, formerly known as the New Hebrides, have been inhabited by Melanesian peoples for at least 3,000 years. The islands were sighted by Pedro Fernandes de Queiros of Portugal in 1606 and were charted and named by the British navigator James Cook in 1774. Conflicting British and French interests were resolved by a joint naval commission that administered the islands from 1887. A condominium government was established in 1906. The islands' plantation economy, based on imported Vietnamese labor, was prosperous until the 1920s, when markets for its products declined. The islands escaped Japanese invasion during World War II and became a major Allied base. After World War II, the indigenous Melanesian's concern over landownership—more than one-third of the New Hebrides was owned by foreigners—increased.

Independence was agreed upon at a 1977 conference in Paris attended by British, French, and New Hebrides representatives. Elections were held and a constitution drawn up in 1979. A brief rebellion by French settlers and plantation workers on Espiritu Santo in May 1980 threatened the scheduled independence of the islands. Britain sent a company of Royal Marines and France a contingent of 50 policemen to quell the revolt, which the new government said was financed by the Phoenix Foundation, a right-wing U.S. group. With the British and French forces replaced by soldiers from Papua New Guinea, independence ceremonies took place on July 30 and revolt was quelled the following month. When French nuclear testing resumed in 1995, Vanuatu refused to join the other members of the South Pacific Forum in their condemnation, on the grounds that it was France's domestic matter.

Vatican City (Holy See)

National name: Stato della Città del Vaticano
Ruler: Pope John Paul II (1978)
Area: 0.17 sq mi. (0.44 sq km)
Population (1997 est.): 850; population growth rate: 1.15%; density per sq mi.: 5,000. **Monetary unit:** Lira. **Languages:** Latin, Italian, and various other languages. **Ethnicity/Race:** Italians, Swiss. **Religion:** Roman Catholic.
Labor force: High dignitaries, priests, nuns, guards, and 3,000 lay workers who live outside the Vatican.
Budget (1994): Revenues: $175.5 million; Expenditures: $175.5 million, including capital expenditures.

Geography The Vatican City State is situated on the Vatican hill, on the right bank of the Tiber River, within the city of Rome.

Government The Pope has full legal, executive, and judicial powers. Executive power over the area is in the hands of a commission of Cardinals appointed by the Pope. The college of Cardinals is the Pope's chief advisory body, and upon his death the cardinals elect his successor for life. The cardinals themselves are created for life by the Pope. In the Vatican the central administration of the Roman Catholic Church throughout the world (Holy See) is carried on by the Secretariat of State, nine Congregations, six commissions, three tribunals, eleven councils, and five offices. In its diplomatic relations, the Holy See is represented by the Papal Secretary of State.

History The Vatican City State, sovereign and independent, is the survivor of the papal states that in 1859 comprised an area of some 17,000 square miles (44,030 sq km). During the struggle for Italian unification, from 1860 to 1870, most of this area became part of Italy. By an Italian law of May 13, 1871, the temporal power of the Pope was abrogated, and the territory of the Papacy was confined to the Vatican and Lateran palaces and the villa of Castel Gandolfo. The Popes consistently refused to recognize this arrangement and, by the Lateran Treaty of Feb. 11, 1929, between the Vatican and the kingdom of Italy, the exclusive dominion and sovereign jurisdiction of the Holy See over the city of the Vatican was again recognized, thus restoring the Pope's temporal authority over the area.

The first session of Ecumenical Council Vatican II was opened by John XXIII on Oct. 11, 1962, to plan and set policies for the modernization of the Roman Catholic Church. Pope Paul VI continued the Council, opening the second session on Sept. 29, 1963.

On Aug. 26, 1978, Cardinal Albino Luciani was chosen by the College of Cardinals to succeed Paul VI, who had died of a heart attack on Aug. 6. The new Pope took the name John Paul I. (For a listing of all the Popes, *see* the table in Religion.) Only 34 days after his election, John Paul I died of a heart attack, ending the shortest reign in 373 years. On Oct. 16, Cardinal Karol Wojtyla, 58, was chosen Pope and took the name John Paul II.

On May 13, 1981, a Turkish terrorist shot the Pope in St. Peter's Square, the first assassination attempt against the Pontiff in modern times. On June 3, 1985, the Vatican and Italy ratified a new church-state treaty, known as a concordat, replacing the Lateran Pact of 1929. The new accord affirmed the independence of Vatican City but ended a number of privileges the Catholic Church had in Italy, including its status as the state religion. The treaty ended Rome's status as a "sacred city." Relations, diplomatic and ecclesiastical, with Eastern Europe have improved dramatically with the fall of communism. Relations with Russia, while improving, have not yet reached the ambassadorial level. Diplomatic ties were established in March 1994 with Jordan and full relations established with Israel in June. Six months earlier the two nations had accorded each other mutual recognition. The Holy See, calling for closer relations with Orthodoxy, was scheduled to meet with Russian Patriarch Alexy II in June 1997, but differences prevented the encounter from taking place. In Jan. 1998, Pope John Paul II made an historic visit to Cuba, hoping to promote religious freedom in that communist nation.

Venezuela

REPUBLIC OF VENEZUELA

National name: Republica de Venezuela
President: Rafael Caldera (1994)
Area: 352,143 sq mi. (912,050 sq km)
Population (1998 est.): 22,803,409 (average annual rate of natural increase: 1.77%); birth rate: 23/1000;

infant mortality rate: 27.5/1000; density per sq mile: 65
Capital: Caracas. **Largest cities (1990 est.):** Caracas, city, 1,824,892, metro area, 2,784,042; Maracaibo, 1,206,726; Valencia, 616,000; Barquisimento, 723,587. **Monetary unit:** bolivar. **Language:** Spanish, various indigenous languages in the remote interior. **Ethnicity/Race:** mestizo 67%, white 21%, black 10%, Amerindian 2%. **Religion:** Roman Catholic, 96%; Protestant, 2%. **Literacy rate:** 91.1%
Economic summary: GDP: (1996 est.): $197 billion, $9,000 per capita. **Real growth rate:** -1.6% (1996). **Inflation:** 103% (1996). **Unemployment:** 13%. **Arable land:** 4%. **Agriculture:** rice, coffee, corn, cacao, sugar, bananas, dairy and meat products. **Labor force:** 8.8 million; services, 64%; industry, 23%. **Industry:** refined petroleum products, aluminum, iron and steel, cement, textiles, transport equipment. **Natural resources:** petroleum, natural gas, iron ore, hydroelectric power. **Exports:** $22.8 billion (f.o.b., 1996 est.): petroleum, iron ore, bauxite. **Imports:** $10.2 billion (f.o.b., 1996 est.): industrial machinery and equipment, manufactures, chemicals, foodstuffs. **Major trading partners:** U.S., Japan, Germany, Italy, Netherlands, Canada.

Geography Venezuela, a third larger than Texas, occupies most of the northern coast of South America on the Caribbean Sea. It is bordered by Colombia to the west, Guyana to the east, and Brazil to the south. Mountain systems break Venezuela into four distinct areas: (1) the Maracaibo lowlands; (2) the mountainous region in the north and northwest; (3) the Orinoco basin, with the llanos (vast grass-covered plains) on its northern border and great forest areas in the south and southeast, (4) the Guiana Highlands, south of the Orinoco, accounting for nearly half the national territory. About 80% of Venezuela is drained by the Orinoco and its tributaries.

Government Venezuela is a federal republic. There is a bicameral Congress, the 50 members of the Senate and the 199 members of the Chamber of Deputies being elected by popular vote to five-year terms. The president is also elected for five years, and is not eligible for reelection until 10 years after the end of his or her term.

History Isolated indigenous groups settled extensively throughout the coastal and Llanos regions before the arrival of European colonists in the 16th century. Columbus explored Venezuela on his third voyage in 1498. A subsequent Spanish explorer gave the country its name, meaning "Little Venice." There were no important settlements until Caracas was founded in 1567. Simón Bolívar, who led the liberation of much of the continent from Spain, was born in Caracas in 1783. With Bolívar taking part, Venezuela was one of the first South American colonies to revolt against Spain, in 1810, but it was not until 1821 that independence was won. Federated at first with Colombia and Ecuador as the Republic of Greater Colombia, the country set up a republic in 1830 and then sank for many decades into a condition of revolt, dictatorship, and corruption.

From 1908 to 1935, Gen. Juan Vicente Gómez was an absolute dictator. A military junta ruled after his death in 1935. Dr. Rómulo Betancourt and the liberal Acción Democrática Party won a majority of seats in a constituent assembly to draft a new Constitution in 1946. A well-known writer, Rómulo Gallegos, candidate of Betancourt's party, easily won the presidential election of 1947. But the army ousted Gallegos the following year and instituted a military junta. The country overthrew the dictatorship of Marcos Peréz Jiménez in 1958 and thereafter enjoyed a series of mostly left-of-center democratically elected governments beginning with that of Rómulo Betancourt who served from 1959–64. His programs led to social and economic advancement and the beginnings of political and economic stability. Rafael Caldera Rodríguez, president from 1969 to 1974, legalized the Communist Party and established diplomatic relations with Moscow.

In 1974, President Carlos Andrés Pérez took office and, in 1976, Venezuela nationalized 21 oil companies, mostly subsidiaries of U.S. firms, offering compensation of $1.28 billion. Venezuela's developing market economy (Venezuela has the highest GNP per capita of any country in South America) continues to be supported mainly by the exploitation of petroleum, natural gas, and mineral reserves. President Pérez, after being reelected to a non-consecutive term in 1988, surrendered his powers in May 1993 in order to defend himself in impeachment proceedings arising out of corruption charges. After a partial recount, Rafael Caldera, a former president, was elected president in 1994. In June 1994 approximately half of the country's banking sector collapsed and the government dealt with falling oil prices, foreign debt repayment, and high inflation in the mid-1990s. In 1997, the government announced it planned to permit large-scale gold and diamond mining in the Imataca reserve in order to reap large tax revenues and create new, badly needed jobs.

Vietnam

SOCIALIST REPUBLIC OF VIETNAM

National name: Công Hòa Xa Hôi Chú Nghia Viêt Nam
President: Tran Duc Luong (1997)
Prime Minister: Phan Van Khai (1997)
Area: 127,246 sq mi. (329,560 sq km)
Population (1998 est.): 76,236,259 (average annual rate of natural increase: 1.43%); birth rate: 21.6/1000; infant mortality rate: 36/1000; density per sq mi.: 599
Capital: Hanoi. **Largest cities (1992):** Ho Chi Minh City (Saigon),[1] 4,000,000; Hanoi, 2,961,000. Other large cities (1989): Haiphong, 456,049; Da Nang, 370,670; Nha Trang, 213,687; Qui Nho'n, 160,091; Hué 211,085. **Monetary unit:** Dong. **Languages:** Vietnamese (official), French, English, Khmer, Chinese. **Ethnicity/Race:** Vietnamese 85%–90%, Chinese 3%, Muong, Thai, Meo, Khmer, Man, Cham. **Religions:** Buddhist, Roman Catholic, Islam, Taoist, Confucian, Animist. **Literacy rate:** 94%
Economic summary: GDP/PPP (1996 est.): $108.7 billion; $1,470 per capita. **Real growth rate:** 9.4%. **Inflation:** 4.5% (1996). **Unemployment:** 25% (1995 est.). **Arable land:** 17%. **Agriculture:** rice, rubber, fruits and vegetables, corn, sugar cane, fish. **Labor force:** 32.7 million; agriculture, 65%, industry and services, 35%. **Industry:** processed foods, textiles, cement, chemical fertilizers, glass, tires. **Natural resources:** phosphates, forests, coal. **Exports:** $7.1 billion (f.o.b., 1996 est.): agricultural products, minerals, marine products, coffee, petroleum, rice. **Imports:** $11.1 billion (f.o.b., 1996 est.): petroleum, steel products, railroad equipment, chemicals, medicines, raw cotton, fertilizer, grain. **Major trading partners:** Singapore, Japan, Hong Kong, Thailand, Germany, Indonesia, South Korea, Taiwan.

1. Includes suburb of Cholon.

Geography Vietnam occupies the eastern and southern part of the Indochinese peninsula in Southeast Asia, with the South China Sea along its entire coast. China is to the north and Laos and Cambodia to the west. Long and narrow on a north-south axis, Vietnam is about twice the size of Arizona. The Mekong River delta lies in the south and the Red River delta in the north. Heavily forested mountain and plateau regions make up most of the country.

Government July 2, 1976, was the official reunification date of North and South Vietnam. Hanoi became the capital. A new constitution was adopted in April 1992 that affirmed the free-market economy and the role of the Communist Party as limited to that of guidance. Foreign assets are guaranteed against nationalization.

History The Vietnamese are descendants of nomadic Mongols from China and migrants from Indonesia. According to mythology, the first ruler of Vietnam was Hung Vuong, who founded the nation in 2879 B.C.E. From 111 B.C.E. China ruled the nation then known as Nam Viet as a vassal state until the 15th century, an era of nationalistic expansion, when Cambodians were pushed out of the southern area of what is now Vietnam.

A century later, the Portuguese were the first Europeans to enter the area. France established its influence early in the 19th century, and within 80 years conquered the three regions into which the country was then divided—Cochin-China in the south, Annam in the central region, and Tonkin in the north.

France first unified Vietnam in 1887, when a single governor-generalship was created, followed by the first physical links between north and south—a rail and road system. Even at the beginning of World War II, however, there were internal differences among the three regions. Japan took over military bases in Vietnam in 1940 and a pro-Vichy French administration remained until 1945. Veteran Communist leader Ho Chi Minh organized an independence movement known as the Vietminh to exploit the confusion surrounding France's weakened influence in the region. At the end of the war, Ho's followers seized Hanoi and declared a short-lived republic, which ended with the arrival of French forces in 1946.

Paris proposed a unified government within the French Union under the former Annamite emperor, Bao Dai. Cochin-China and Annam accepted the proposal, and Bao Dai was proclaimed emperor of all Vietnam in 1949. Ho and the Vietminh withheld support, and the revolution in China gave them the outside help needed for a war of resistance against French and Vietnamese troops armed largely by a United States worried about cold war communist expansion.

A bitter defeat at Dien Bien Phu in northwest Vietnam on May 5, 1954, broke the French military campaign and resulted in the division of Vietnam at the conference of Geneva that year. In the new South, Ngo Dinh Diem, premier under Bao Dai, deposed the monarch in 1955 and established a republic with himself as president. Diem used strong U.S. backing to create an authoritarian regime that suppressed all opposition but could not eradicate the Northern-supplied Communist Viet Cong.

Skirmishing grew into a full-scale war, with escalating U.S. involvement. A military coup, U.S.-inspired in the view of many, ousted Diem on Nov. 1, 1963, and a kaleidoscope of military governments followed. The most savage fighting of the war occurred in early 1968 during the Vietnamese New Year, known as Tet. Although the so-called Tet Offensive ended in a military defeat for the North, its psychological impact changed the course of the war.

U.S. public reaction to the seemingly endless conflict made it impossible to commit more than the existing 550,000 U.S. troops, and there was a new emphasis on shifting the burden of combat to South Vietnam's own forces. Ho Chi Minh's death on Sept. 3, 1969, brought a ruling committee to replace him, but no flagging in the Northern will to fight.

U.S. bombing and an invasion of Cambodia in the summer of 1970—an effort to destroy Viet Cong bases in the neighboring state—marked the end of major U.S. participation in the fighting. Most American ground troops were withdrawn from combat by mid-1971 when the U.S. conducted heavy bombing raids on the Ho Chi Minh trail—a crucial North Vietnamese supply line that ran through neighboring Laos and Cambodia, infiltrating men and material into the South.

In 1972, heavy U.S. attacks on Hanoi and Haiphong Harbor forced North Vietnam to the table in secret peace negotiations led by Secretary of State Henry A. Kissinger. When the talks deadlocked President Richard Nixon ordered the "Christmas bombing" of the North, in an effort to step up pressure on Hanoi's leadership to conclude a deal. The discourse resumed and a peace settlement was signed in Paris on Jan. 27, 1973. It called for the release of all U.S. prisoners, withdrawal of U.S. forces, limitation of both U.S. and North Vietnamese forces inside the South, and a commitment to peaceful reunification of the nation.

An armored charge across the border in Jan. 1975 panicked the South Vietnamese army and brought Hanoi's troops within 40 miles of Saigon, the South's capital, by April 9. South Vietnam's President Thieu resigned on April 21 and fled. Vice President Tran Van Huong assumed the post but quit a week later, turning over the office to Gen. Duong Van Minh. Duong surrendered Saigon on April 30, ending a war that claimed the lives of 1.3 million Vietnamese and 58,000 Americans, at a cost of $141 billion in U.S. aid.

On May 3, 1977, the U.S. and Vietnam opened negotiations in Paris to normalize relations. Two major issues remained to be settled, however: the return of the bodies of some 2,500 U.S. servicemen registered as missing in the war, and the claim by Hanoi that former President Nixon had promised reconstruction aid under the 1973 agreement. Negotiators failed to resolve these issues. With the new year also came an intensification of border clashes between Vietnam and Cambodia, as well as accusations by Beijing that Chinese residents of Vietnam were being subjected to persecution. Beijing cut off all aid and withdrew 800 technicians.

Hanoi was also preoccupied with a continuing war in Cambodia, where 60,000 Vietnamese troops had invaded and overthrown the country's communist leader Pol Pot and his pro-Chinese regime. In early 1979, Vietnam was conducting a two-front war: defending its northern border against a Chinese invasion, and supporting its army in Cambodia which was still fighting Pol Pot's Khmer Rouge guerrillas. Hanoi's Marxist policies combined with the destruction of the country's infrastructure during the decades of fighting devastated Vietnam's economy. However, it started to pick up in 1986 under *do Maui* (economic renovation), an effort at limited privatization. Vietnamese troops began limited withdrawals from Laos and Cambodia in 1988, and Vietnam supported the Cambodian peace agreement signed in Oct. 1991.

The U.S. lifted a Vietnamese trade embargo in Feb. of 1994 that had been in place since its involvement in the war. Full diplomatic relations were announced between the two countries in July 1995. In April 1997, a pact was signed with the U.S. concerning repayment of the $146 million wartime debt incurred by the South Vietnamese government, and the following year the nation began a drive to eliminate inefficient bureaucrats and streamline the approval process for direct foreign investment. Although reform-minded officials have in recent years won key roles in government, Vietnam's ruling Communist Party has adamantly resisted political changes, even as major economic restructuring has been set in motion

(For a Vietnam War chronology, *see* Headline History.)

Western Sahara

WESTERN SAHARA

Head of State: none
Area: 165,185 sq mi. (266,000 sq km)
Population (1998): 228,730; growth rate: 2.4%; birth rate: 45.8/1000; infant mortality rate: 139.7/1000; density per sq mi.: 1
Largest cities (1991): El Aaiun (20,010). **Monetary unit:** Moroccan dirham (DH). **Languages:** Hassaniya Arabic, Moroccan Arabic. **Ethnicity/Race:** Saharawi, Arab, Berber. **Religions:** Muslim. **Literacy rate:** n.a.
Economic summary: GDP: n.a.; **Labor force:** 12,000; pastoral nomadism, fishing, and phosphate mining are the principal sources of income.**Industry:** phosphates, handicrafts; **Major Trading Partners:** Morocco claims and administers Western Sahara, so trade partners are included in overall Moroccan accounts.

Geography Located in Northern Africa and bordering the North Atlantic Ocean, Western Sahara is surrounded by Algeria to the east, Morocco to the north, and Mauritania to the south. About the size of Colorado, it is mostly low, flat desert with some small mountains in the south and northeast.

Government Legal status of the territory is disputed and sovereignty unresolved; a U.N. referendum on the issue is planned. The territory is contested by Morocco and the Polisario Front, which in Feb. 1976 formerly proclaimed a government-in-exile of the Saharawi Arab Democratic Republic, now officially recognized by about 70 countries.

History Little is known about Western Sahara until the 4th century B.C.E. when trade with Europe began. During the Middle Ages it was occupied first by Berbers, and then by the Arabic-speaking Muslim Bedouins. In the 19th century the Spanish lay claim to the southern coastal region, called Rio de Oro, and later occupied the northern interior region, Saguia el Hamra, in 1934. The Spanish formally united the two regions, and it became known as Spanish Sahara in 1958. Both Morocco and Mauritania sought to control the territory, and when the Spanish departed in 1976 they divided the territory between them. In the meantime, the indigenous Saharawis began fighting for independence. In 1976, the insurgents, called the Polisario Front, declared a government-in-exile (the Saharawi Arab Democratic Republic) from their base in Algeria. Mauritania reached a peace agreement with the Polisario in 1979, but Morocco then seized the land given up by Mauritania, and now exerts administrative control over the entire region. The U.N. is attempting to hold a referendum on the issue, and a U.N.-administered cease-fire has been in effect since Sept. 1991.

Republic Of Yemen

National name: Al Jumhuriyahal Yamaniyah
President: Ali Abdullah Saleh
Prime Minister: Abdul Karim al-Iryani (1998)
Area: 203,850 sq mi. (527,970 sq km)
Population (1998 est.): 16,387,963 (average annual rate of natural increase: 3.31%); birth rate: 43.4/1000; infant mortality rate: 72.2/1000; density per sq mi.: 80
Capital (1995): Sanaá 972,011. **Largest cities (1995):** Tiaz, 2,205,947; Hodiedah, 1,749,944; Aden, 562,162. **Monetary unit:** Rial. **Language:** Arabic. **Ethnicity/Race:** predominantly Arab; Afro-Arab concentrations in western coastal locations; South Asians in southern regions; small European communities in major metropolitan areas. **Religion:** Islam (Sunni and Shi'ite). **Literacy rate:** 39%
Economic summary: GDP: (1996 est.): $39.1 billion; $2,900 per capita. **Real growth rate:** 2.8%. **Inflation:** 85%. **Unemployment:** 30% (1995 est.). **Arable land:** 3%. **Argriculture:** wheat, sorghum, cattle, sheep, cotton, fruits, coffee, dates. **Industry:** crude and refined oil, textiles, leather goods, handicrafts, fish. **Exports:** $2.5 billion (f.o.b., 1996 est.): cotton, coffee, hides, vegetables, dried fish. **Imports:** $2.2 billion (f.o.b., 1996 est.): textiles, manufactured consumer goods, foodstuffs, sugar, grain, flour. **Major trading partners:** U.K., Japan, Saudi Arabia, Australia, U.S.

Geography Formerly known as the states of People's Democratic Republic of Yemen and the Yemen Arab Republic, the Republic of Yemen occupies the southwestern tip of the Arabian Peninsula on the Red Sea opposite Ethiopia, and extends along the southern part of the Arabian Peninsula on the Gulf of Aden and the Indian Ocean. Saudi Arabia is to the north and Oman is to the east. The country is about the size of France. A 700-mile (1,130-km) narrow coastal plain in the south gives way to a mountainous region and then a plateau area. Some of the interior highlands in the west attain a height of 12,000 feet (3,660 m).

Government Parliamentary. The Presidential Council was abolished by a new constitution approved in Sept. 1994.

History The history of Yemen dates back to the Minaean (1200–650 B.C.E.) and Sabaean (750–115 B.C.E.) kingdoms. It accepted Islam in C.E. 628, and in the 10th century came under the control of the Rassite dynasty of the Zaidi sect, who remained involved in Yemeni politics until 1962. The Ottoman Turks occupied the area from 1538 to 1630 and from 1849 to 1918. The sovereign status of Yemen was confirmed by treaties signed with Saudi Arabia and Britain in 1934.

In 1962, a military revolt of elements favoring President Gamal Abdel Nasser of Egypt broke out. A ruling junta proclaimed a republic, and Yemen became an international battleground, with Egypt and the U.S.S.R. supporting the revolutionaries, and King Saud of Saudi Arabia and King Hussein of Jordan the royalists. The civil war continued until the war between the Arab states and Israel broke out in June 1967. Nasser had to pull out many of his troops and agree to a cease-fire and withdrawal of foreign forces. The war finally ended with the defeat of the royalists in mid-1969.

The People's Republic of Southern Yemen was established Nov. 30, 1967, when Britain granted independence to the Federation of South Arabia. This Federation consisted of the state (once the colony) of Aden and 16 of the 20 states of the protectorate of South Arabia (once the Aden protectorate). The four states of the protectorate that did not join the Federation later became part of Southern Yemen.

The Republic of Yemen was established on May 22, 1990, when pro-western Yemen and Marxist Yemen Arab Republic merged after 300 years of separation to form the new nation. The union had been approved by both governments in Nov. 1989. The new president, Ali Abdullah Saleh of Yemen, was elected by the parliaments of both countries.

In the Gulf War, Yemen favored Iraq, and border clashes have occurred periodically with Saudi Arabia since 1995 despite ongoing talks. A constitution was approved by a landslide referendum in May 1992.

Differences over power-sharing and the pace of integration between the north and the south came to a head in 1994, resulting in a civil war. The north's superior forces quickly overwhelmed the south in May and early June despite the south's brief declaration of succession. The victorious north presented a reconciliation plan providing for a general amnesty and pledges to protect political democracy.

The president's party, the General People's Congress, won an enormous victory in the April 1997 parliamentary elections, the first since the civil war. One of the poorest countries in the Middle East, Yemen began an economic reform program in 1995 with the assistance of the World Bank and the IMF.

Yugoslavia

FEDERAL REPUBLIC OF YUGOSLAVIA

National name: Federativna Republika Jugoslavijá
President: Slobodan Milosevic (1997)
Prime Minister: Momir Bulatovic (1998)
Area: 39,449 sq mi. (102,350 sq km)
Population (1998 est.): 10,526,135 (average annual rate of natural increase: –0.02%); birth rate: 12.6/1000; infant mortality rate: 17.1/1000; density per sq mi.: 266
Capital and largest city (1994 est.): Belgrade, 1,168,454. **Other large cities:** Novi Sad, 179,626; Nis, 175,391; Pristina, 155,499. **Monetary unit:** Yugoslav new Dinar. **Languages:** Serbo-Croatian 95%, Albanian 5%. **Ethnicity/Race:** Serbs 63%, Albanians 14%, Montenegrins 6%, Hungarians 4%, other 13%. **Religions:** Orthodox 65%, Muslim 19%, Roman Catholic 4%, Protestant 1%, other 11%. **Literacy rate:** 90.5%
Economic summaryGDP/PPP (1995 est.): $21 billion; per capita $1,900; **Growth rate** 6%. **Inflation** 79%. **Unemployment:** more than 35%. **Arable land:** n.a. **Labor force** 2.178 million; industry, 41%; services, 35%; agriculture, 5%. **Industry:** machine building (incl. aircraft, trucks, automobiles), nonferrous metallurgy, consumer goods, electronics, chemicals, petroleum products, pharmaceuticals. **Exports:** $1.4 billion (1995 est.): machinery and transportation equipment, manufactured goods and articles, chemicals, food, and live animals. **Imports:** $2.4 billion (1995 est.): machinery and transport equipment, fuels and lubricants, other manufacturers, chemicals, raw materials, food, and animals. **Major Trading Partners:** former Soviet republics, Russia, E.U., Eastern European countries.

Geography Yugoslavia consists of the two states of Serbia and Montenegro. The nation is about the size of the state of Kentucky. Yugoslavia is largely a mountainous country. The northeastern section of Serbia is part of the rich, fertile Danubian Plain drained by the Danube, Tisa, Sava, and Morava River systems. Montenegro is a jumbled mass of mountains, containing also some grassy slopes and fertile river valleys.

Government Yugoslavia (Serbia and Montenegro) is a federal republic. The bicameral Federal Assembly consists of a 40-seat upper house, or Chamber of Republics, and a 138-seat lower house, or Chamber of Deputies. The current Federation is the third state to be referred to by the name Yugoslavia.

History Yugoslavia was formed Dec. 4, 1918, from the patchwork of Balkan states and territories. World War I began there with the assassination of Archduke Ferdinand of Austria at Sarajevo on June 28, 1914. The new kingdom of Serbs, Croats, and Slovenes included the former kingdoms of Serbia and Montenegro; Bosnia-Herzegovina, previously administered jointly by Austria and Hungary; Croatia-Slavonia, a semi-autonomous region of Hungary; and Dalmatia, formerly administered by Austria. King Peter I of Serbia became the first monarch, his son, Alexander I, succeeded him on Aug. 16, 1921. Croatian demands for a federal state forced Alexander to assume dictatorial powers in 1929 and to change the country's name to Yugoslavia. Serbian dominance continued despite his efforts, amid the resentment of other regions. A Macedonian associated with Croatian dissidents assassinated Alexander in Marseilles, France, on Oct. 9, 1934, and his cousin, Prince Paul, became Regent for the king's son, Prince Peter.

Paul's pro-Axis policy brought Yugoslavia to sign the Axis Pact on March 25, 1941, and opponents overthrew the government two days later. On April 6 the Nazis occupied the country, and the young king and his government fled. Two guerrilla armies—the Chetniks under Draza Mihajlovic supporting the monarchy, and the Partisans under Tito (Josip Broz) leaning toward the U.S.S.R.—fought the Nazis for the duration of the war. In 1943, Tito established an Executive National Committee of Liberation to function as a provisional government. Tito won the election held in the fall of 1945, as monarchists boycotted the vote. A new Assembly abolished the monarchy and proclaimed the Federal People's Republic of Yugoslavia, with Tito as prime minister. Tito ruthlessly eliminated the opposition and broke with the Soviet bloc in 1948. Yugoslavia followed a middle road, combining orthodox Communist control of politics and general overall economic policy with a varying degree of freedom in the arts, travel, and individual enterprise. Tito became president in 1953 and president-for-life under a revised Constitution adopted in 1963.

After Tito's death on May 4, 1980, a rotating presidency designed to avoid internal dissension was put into effect immediately, and the feared clash of Yugoslavia's multiple nationalities and regions appeared to have been averted. In May 1991 Croatian voters supported a referendum calling for their republic to become an independent nation. A similar referendum passed in December in Slovenia. In June the respective parliaments in both republics passed declarations of independence. Ethnic violence flared almost immediately. The largely Serbian-led Yugoslav military pounded break-away Bosnia and Herzegovina, leading the U.N. Security Council in May 1992 to impose economic sanctions on the Belgrade government.

Despite rampant inflation reaching approximately 3000% per month in Dec. 1993, the Serbian government of Slobodan Milosevic maintained its effective control over the rump Yugoslavia. Trade sanctions were lifted in Dec. 1995 following the signing of the Dayton Accords. In June 1996, the U.N. Security Council lifted its heavy weapons embargo. Large groups of demonstrators in 1996–97 engaged in several months of daily protests after Slobodan Milosevic refused to recognize opposition victories in local elections and in elections in Montenegro. Constitutionally barred from another term as president of Serbia, Milosevic became president of the Federal Republic of Yugoslavia (Serbia and Montenegro) in July 1997.

The situation in Serbia's provinces of Montenegro and Kosovo grew divisive in 1997 and 1998. In May 1998, Montenegro elected the reform-minded Milo Djukanovic as president. Not only is he an outspoken critic of Yugoslav President Slobodan Milosevic but he has openly contemplated secession. The predominately ethnic Albanian province of Kosovo has been torn apart by violence. Less than a year after Milosevic and Ibrahim Rugova, head of the shadow government of the "Republic of Kosovo," signed an agreement calling for the reintegration of Kosovo schools and the return of some 300,000 Albanian-speaking children to classes, clashes between Serbian security forces and ethnic Albanians intensified. The agreement, which had been pushed by Western countries and was hailed as the first major breakthrough in normalizing relations between Serbs and Albanians, was never implemented. Rugova appealed for Western mediation, but Milosevic was unenthusiastic. Several European countries and the U.S. advocated a special status for Kosovo to guarantee local autonomy but emphasized that secession was not an option. The federal Yugoslav economy, devastated by international trade sanctions, years of mismanagement, failure to push privatization, half-hearted reforms, and lack of interest by foreign investors, showed little signs of improvement in the late 1990s.

Zaire

SEE CONGO, DEMOCRATIC REBUBLIC OF.

Zambia

REPUBLIC OF ZAMBIA

President: Frederick T. J. Chiluba (1991)
Area: 290,586 sq mi. (752,610 sq km)
Population (1998 est.): 9,460,736 (average annual rate of natural increase: 2.13%); birth rate: 44.6/1000; infant mortality rate: 92.6/1000; density per sq mi.: 33
Capital: Lusaka. **Largest cities (1997):** Lusaka, 1.6 million; (1990 est.) Kitwe, 338,207; Ndola, 376,311; Chingola, 167,954. **Monetary unit:** Kwacha. **Languages:** English and local dialects. **Ethnicity/Race:** African 98.7%, European 1.1%, other 0.2%. **Religions:** Christian, 50–75%; Islam and Hindu, 24–49%; remainder indigenous beliefs. **Literacy rate:** 73%
Economic summary: GDP/PPP (1996 est.): $9.7 billion; $1,060 per capita. **Real growth rate:** 6.4%. **Inflation:** 34% (1995 est.). **Unemployment:** 22% (1991). **Arable land:** 7%. **Agriculture:** corn, tobacco, rice, sugar cane. **Labor force:** 3.4 million; agriculture 85%. **Industry:** copper, textiles, chemicals, zinc, fertilizers. **Natural resources:** copper, zinc, lead, cobalt, coal. **Exports:** $975 million (f.o.b., 1996 est.): copper, zinc, lead, cobalt, tobacco. **Imports:** $990 million (f.o.b., 1996 est.): manufactured goods, machinery and transport equipment, foodstuffs, fuels. **Major trading partners:** Western Europe, Japan, South Africa, U.S., Saudi Arabia, India. **Member of Commonwealth of Nations.**

Geography Zambia, a landlocked country in south central Africa, is about one-tenth larger than Texas. It is surrounded by Angola, Zaire, Tanzania, Malawi, Mozambique, Zimbabwe, Botswana, and Namibia. The country is mostly a plateau that rises to 8,000 feet (2,434 m) in the east.

Government A multiparty system. Zambia (formerly Northern Rhodesia) is governed by a president, elected by universal suffrage, and a unicameral Legislative Assembly, consisting of 150 members elected by universal suffrage every five years.

History Early humans inhabited present-day Zambia between one and two million years ago. Today the country is made up almost entirely of Bantu-speaking peoples.

Empire builder Cecil Rhodes obtained mining concessions in 1889 from King Lewanika of the Barotse and sent settlers to the area soon thereafter. The region was ruled by the British South Africa Company, which he established, until 1924, when the British government took over the administration.

From 1953 to 1964, Northern Rhodesia was federated with Southern Rhodesia and Nyasaland (now Malawi) in the Federation of Rhodesia and Nyasaland. On Oct. 24, 1964, Northern Rhodesia became the independent nation of Zambia.

Kenneth Kaunda, the first president, kept Zambia within the Commonwealth of Nations. The country's economy, dependent on copper exports, was threatened when Rhodesia declared its independence from British rule in 1965 and defied U.N. sanctions, which Zambia supported, an action that deprived Zambia of its trade route through Rhodesia. The U.S., Britain, and Canada organized an airlift in 1966 to ship gasoline into Zambia. In 1967, Britain agreed to finance new trade routes for Zambia.

Kaunda visited China in 1967, and China later agreed to finance a 1,000-mile railroad from the copper fields to Dar es Salaam in Tanzania. A pipeline was opened in 1968 from Ndola in Zambia's copper belt to the Indian Ocean at Dar es Salaam, ending the three-year oil drought. In 1969, Kaunda announced the nationalization of the foreign copper-mining industry, with Zambia to take 51% (over $1 billion, estimated). He then announced a similar takeover of foreign oil producers.

With a soaring debt and inflation rate in 1991, riots took place in Lusaka, resulting in a number of killings. Mounting domestic pressure forced Kaunda to move Zambia toward multiparty democracy.

National elections on Oct. 31, 1991 brought a stunning defeat to the long-serving President Kaunda and a repudiation of his long belief in a one-party state. The newly elected chief executive, Frederick Chiluba, called for sweeping economic reforms including privatization and the establishment of a stock market. Parliament passed a bill in May 1996 that stated a president may serve only two terms, thus preventing any possible political return of Kenneth Kaunda, a measure criticized by opposition parties. General elections in Nov. 1996 saw the reelection of President Chiluba with 70% of the vote.

Zimbabwe

REPUBLIC OF ZIMBABWE

Executive President: Robert Mugabe (1987)
Area: 150,698 sq mi. (390,580 sq km)
Population (1998 est.): 11,044,147 (average annual rate of natural increase: 1.12%); birth rate: 31.3/1000; infant mortality rate: 61.8/1000; density per sq mi.: 73
Capital and largest city (1992): Harare, 1,184,169. **Other large cities:** Bulawayo, 621,000; Chitungwiza, 274,035. **Monetary unit:** Zimbabwean dollar. **Languages:** English (official), Ndebele, Shona (85%). **Ethnicity/Race:** African 98% (Shona 71%, Ndebele 16%, other 11%), white 1%, mixed and Asian 1%. **Religions:** Christian, 25%; Animist, 24%; Syncretic, 50%. **Literacy rate:** 85%
Economic summary: GDP/PPP (1996 est.): $26.4 billion; $2,340 per capita. **Real growth rate:** 5.5%. **Inflation:** 21.7%. **Unemployment:** at least 45% (1994 est.). **Arable land:** 7%. **Agriculture:** tobacco, corn, sugar, cotton, livestock. **Labor force:** 4.228 million (1993 est.); agriculture, 70%; transport and services, 22%. **Industry:** steel, textiles, chemicals, vehicles, gold, copper. **Natural resources:** gold, copper, chrome, nickel, tin, asbestos. **Exports:** $2.4 billion (f.o.b., 1996 est.): gold, tobacco, asbestos, copper, meat, chrome, nickel, corn, sugar. **Imports:** $2.2 billion (f.o.b., 1996 est.): machinery, petroleum products, transport equipment. **Major trading partners:** U.K., South Africa, Germany, Japan, U.S.

Geography Zimbabwe, a landlocked country in south central Africa, is slightly smaller than California. It is bordered by Botswana on the west, Zambia on the north, Mozambique on the east, and South Africa on the south.

Government A parliamentary democracy with a 150-seat unicameral legislature, the House of Assembly. The executive president is chief of state and head of government. There are two co-vice presidents.

History The remains of early humans, dating back 500,000 years have been discovered in present-day Zimbabwe. The land's earliest settlers, the Khoisan, date back to 200 B.C.E. After a period of Bantu domination, the Shona people ruled, followed by the Nguni and Zulu peoples. By the mid-19th century the descendents of the Nguni and Zulu, the Ndebele, had established a powerful warrior kingdom.

The first British explorers, colonists, and missionaries arrived in the 1850s, and the massive influx of foreigners led to the establishment of the territory Rhodesia, named after Cecil Rhodes of the British South Africa Company. In 1923, European settlers voted to become the self-governing British colony of Southern Rhodesia. After a brief federation with Northern Rhodesia and Nyasaland (now Malawi) in the post-World War II period, Southern Rhodesia (also known as Rhodesia) chose to remain a colony when its two partners voted for independence in 1963.

On Nov. 11, 1965, the conservative white-minority government of Rhodesia declared its independence from Britain. The country resisted the demands of black Africans, and Prime Minister Ian Smith withstood British pressure, economic sanctions, and guerrilla attacks to uphold white supremacy. On March 1, 1970, Rhodesia formally proclaimed itself a republic. Heightened guerrilla war and a withdrawal of South African military aid in 1976 marked the beginning of the collapse of Smith's 11 years of resistance.

Black nationalist movements were led by Bishop Abel Muzorewa of the African National Congress and Ndabaningi Sithole, who were moderates, and guerrilla leaders Robert Mugabe of the Zimbabwe African National Union (ZANU) and Joshua Nkomo of the Zimbabwe African People's Union (ZAPU), who advocated revolution.

On March 3, 1978, Smith, Muzorewa, Sithole, and Chief Jeremiah Chirau signed an agreement to transfer power to the black majority by Dec. 31, 1978. They constituted themselves an Executive Council, with chairmanship rotating but Smith retaining the title of prime minister. Blacks were named to each cabinet ministry, serving as co-ministers with the whites already holding these posts. African nations and rebel leaders immediately denounced the action, but western governments were more reserved, although none granted recognition to the new regime.

The white minority finally consented to hold multiracial elections in 1980, and Robert Mugabe won a landslide victory. The country achieved independence on April 17, 1980, under the name Zimbabwe. Mugabe eventually established a one-party socialist state, but by 1990 he instituted multiparty elections and in 1991 deleted all references to Marxism-Leninism and scientific socialism from the constitution. Parliamentary elections in April 1995 gave Mugabe's party a stunning victory with 63 of the 65 contested seats, and in 1996 Mugabe won another six-year term as president.

Preamble of the United Nations Charter

The Charter of the United Nations was adopted at the San Francisco Conference of 1945. The complete text may be obtained by writing to the United Nations Sales Section, United Nations, New York, N.Y. 10017, and enclosing $1.

We the peoples of the United Nations determined to save succeeding generations from the scourge of war, which twice in our lifetime has brought untold sorrow to mankind, and

To reaffirm faith in fundamental human rights, in the dignity and worth of the human person, in the equal rights of men and women and of nations large and small, and

To establish conditions under which justice and respect for the obligations arising from treaties and other sources of international law can be maintained, and

To promote social progress and better standards of life in larger freedom, and for these ends

To practice tolerance and live together in peace with one another as good neighbors, and

To unite our strength to maintain international peace and security, and

To insure, by the acceptance of principles and the institution of methods, that armed force shall not be used, save in the common interest, and

To employ international machinery for the promotion of the economic and social advancement of all peoples, have resolved to combine our efforts to accomplish these aims.

Accordingly, our respective Governments, through representatives assembled in the city of San Francisco, who have exhibited their full powers found to be in good and due form, have agreed to the present Charter of the United Nations and do hereby establish an international organization to be known as the United Nations.

Principal Organs of the United Nations

Secretariat

This is the directorate on UN operations, apart from political decisions. All members contribute to its upkeep. Its headquarters staff of about 4,730 specialists is recruited from member nations on the basis of as wide a geographical distribution as possible. The staff works under the Secretary-General, whom it assists and advises.

Secretaries-General

Kofi Annan, Ghana, Jan. 1, 1997.

Boutros Boutros-Ghali, Egypt, Jan. 1, 1992–Dec. 31, 1996.

Javier Pérez de Cuéllar, Peru, Jan. 1, 1982–Dec. 31, 1991.

Kurt Waldheim, Austria, Jan. 1, 1972–Dec. 31, 1981.

U Thant, Burma (Myanmar), Nov. 3, 1961–Dec. 31, 1971.

Dag Hammarskjöld, Sweden, April 11, 1953–Sept. 17, 1961.

Trygve Lie, Norway, Feb. 1, 1946–April 10, 1953.

General Assembly

The General Assembly is the world's forum for discussing matters affecting world peace and security, and for making recommendations concerning them. It has no power of its own to enforce decisions. It is composed of the 51 original member nations and those admitted since, a total of 185. Each nation has one vote. On important questions including international peace and security, a two-thirds majority of those present and voting is required. Decisions on other questions are made by a simple majority. The assembly's agenda can be as broad as the charter. It can make recommendations to member nations, the Security Council, or both. Emphasis is given on questions relating to international peace and security brought before it by any member, the Security Council, or nonmembers. It also maintains a broad program of international cooperation in economic, social, cultural, educational, and health fields, and for assisting in human rights and freedoms. Among other duties, the assembly has functions relating to the trusteeship system, and considers and approves the UN budget. Every member contributes to operating expenses according to its means.

Security Council

The Security Council is the primary instrument for establishing and maintaining international peace. Its main purpose is to prevent war by settling disputes between nations. Under the charter, the council is permitted to dispatch a UN force to stop aggression. All member nations undertake to make available armed forces, assistance, and facilities to maintain international peace and security. Any member may bring a dispute before the Security Council or the General Assembly. Any nonmember may do so if it accepts the charter obligations of pacific settlement. The Security Council has 15 members. There are five permanent members: the United States, the Russian Federation, Britain, France, and China; and 10 temporary members elected by the General Assembly for two-year terms, from five different regions of the world. Voting on procedural matters requires a nine-vote majority to carry. However, on questions of substance, the vote of each of the five permanent members is required. The ten non-permanent members of the Council in 1998 are Costa Rica (1998), Japan (1998), Kenya (1998), Portugal (1998), Sweden (1998), Gabon (1999), The Gambia (1999), Slovenia (1999), Bahrain (1999), and Brazil (1999).

Economic and Social Council

This council is composed of 54 members elected by the General Assembly to 3-year terms. It works closely with the General Assembly as a link with groups formed within the UN to help peoples in such fields as education, health, and human rights.

It insures that there is no overlapping and sets up commissions to deal with economic conditions and collect facts and figures on conditions over the world. It issues studies and reports and may make recommendations to the assembly and specialized agencies.

Functional Commissions

Commission on Population and Development; Commission for Social Development; Commission on Human Rights; Commission on the Status of Women; Statistical Commission; Commission on Narcotic Drugs; Commission on Sustainable Development; Commission on Crime Prevention and Criminal Justice; Commission on Science and Technology for Development.

Regional Commissions

Economic Commission for Europe (ECE); Economic and Social Commission for Asia and the Pacific (ESCAP); Economic Commission for Latin America and the Caribbean (ECLAC); Economic Commission for Africa (ECA); Economic and Social Commission for Western Asia (ESCWA).

Trusteeship Council

The Trusteeship Council has five members: China, France, the Russian Federation, the United Kingdom, and the United States. With the independence of Palau, the last remaining United Nations trust territory, the council formally suspended operation on November 1, 1994. By a resolution adopted on that day, the council amended its rules of procedure to drop the obligation to meet annually and agreed to meet as occasion required—by its decision or the decision of its president, or at the request of a majority of its members or the General Assembly or the Security Council.

International Court of Justice

The International Court of Justice sits at The Hague, the Netherlands. Its 15-judge bench was established to hear disputes among states, which must agree to accept its verdicts. Its judges, charged with administering justice under international law, deal with cases ranging from disputes over territory to those concerning rights of passage.

Following are the members of the court and the years in which their terms expire on Feb. 5:

President: Stephen M. Schwebel, United States (2000 as president, 2006 term)
Vice President: Christopher Gregory Weeramantry, Sri Lanka (2000)
Mohammed Bedjaoui, Algeria (2006)
Carl-August Fleischauer, Germany (2003)
Gilbert Guillaume, France (2000)
Géza Herczegh, Hungary (2003)
Rosalyn Higgins, United Kingdom (2000)
Jiuyong Shi, China (2003)
Pieter H. Kooijmans, Netherlands (2006)
Abdul G. Koroma, Sierra Leone (2003)
Shigeru Oda, Japan (2003)
Gonzalo Parra-Aranguren, Venezuela (2000)
Raymond Ranjeva, Madagascar (2000)
José Francisco Rezek, Brazil (2006)
Vladlen S. Vereshchetin, Russian Federation (2006)

Agencies of the United Nations

Linked to the United Nations through special agreements, the separate, autonomous specialized agencies of the UN family set standards and guidelines, help formulate policies, provide technical assistance, and other forms of practical help in virtually all areas of economic and social endeavor.

The International Labor Organization (ILO) formulates policies and programs to improve working conditions and employment opportunities, and defines international labor standards as guidelines for governments.

The Food and Agriculture Organization of the UN (FAO) works to raise levels of nutrition and standards of living, to improve agricultural productivity and food security, and to better the conditions of rural populations.

The UN Educational, Scientific and Cultural Organization (UNESCO) promotes education for all, cultural development, protection of the world's natural and cultural heritage, press freedom, and communication.

The World Health Organization (WHO) coordinates programs aimed at solving health problems and the attainment by all people of the highest possible level of health; it works in areas such as immunization, health education, and the provision of essential drugs.

The World Bank group provides loans and technical assistance to developing countries to reduce poverty and advance sustainable economic growth.

The International Monetary Fund (IMF) facilitates international monetary cooperation and financial stability, and provides a permanent forum for consultation, advice, and assistance on financial issues.

The International Civil Aviation Organization (ICAO) sets international standards necessary for the safety, security, efficiency, and regularity of air transport, and serves as the medium for cooperation in all areas of civil aviation.

The Universal Postal Union (UPU) establishes international regulations for the organization and improvement of postal services, provides technical assistance, and promotes cooperation in postal matters.

The International Telecommunication Union (ITU) fosters international cooperation for the improvement and use of telecommunications of all kinds, coordinates usage of radio and TV frequencies, promotes safety measures, and conducts research.

The World Meteorological Organization (WMO) promotes scientific research on the atmosphere and on climate change, and facilitates the global exchange of meteorological data and information.

The International Maritime Organization (IMO) works to improve international shipping procedures, encourages the highest standards in marine safety, and seeks to prevent marine pollution from ships.

The World Intellectual Property Organization (WIPO) promotes international protection of intellectual property and fosters cooperation on copyrights, trademarks, industrial designs, and patents.

The International Fund for Agricultural Development (IFAD) mobilizes financial resources for better food production and nutrition among the poor in developing countries.

The UN Industrial Development Organization (UNIDO) promotes the industrial advancement of developing countries through technical assistance, advisory services, and training.

The International Atomic Energy Agency (IAEA), an autonomous intergovernmental organization under the aegis of the UN, works for the safe and peaceful uses of atomic energy.

The UN and the World Trade Organization (WTO), the major entity overseeing international trade, cooperate in assisting developing countries' exports through the Geneva-based International Trade Center.

U.S. Representatives to the United Nations

Year	Ambassador	Year	Ambassador
1946	Edward R. Stettinius, Jr.	1975–76	Daniel P. Moynihan
1946–47	Herschel V. Johnson (acting)	1976–77	William W. Scranton
1947–53	Warren R. Austin	1977–79	Andrew Young
1953–60	Henry Cabot Lodge, Jr.	1979–81	Donald McHenry
1960–61	James J. Wadsworth	1981–85	Jeane J. Kirkpatrick
1961–65	Adlai E. Stevenson	1985–89	Vernon A. Walters
1965–68	Arthur J. Goldberg	1989–92	Thomas J. Pickering
1968	George W. Ball	1992–93	Edward J. Perkins
1968–69	James Russell Wiggins	1993–96	Madeleine K. Albright
1969–71	Charles W. Yost	1997–98	Bill Richardson
1971–73	George Bush	1998–	Richard Holbrooke
1973–75	John A. Scali		

The 185 Members of the United Nations

Country	Joined UN[1]
Afghanistan	1946
Albania	1955
Algeria	1962
Andorra	1993
Angola	1976
Antigua and Barbuda	1981
Argentina	1945
Armenia	1992
Australia	1945
Austria	1955
Azerbaijan	1992
Bahamas	1973
Bahrain	1971
Bangladesh	1974
Barbados	1966
Belarus	1945
Belgium	1945
Belize	1981
Benin	1960
Bhutan	1971
Bolivia	1945
Bosnia and Herzegovina	1992
Botswana	1966
Brazil	1945
Brunei Darussalam	1984
Bulgaria	1955
Burkina Faso	1960
Burma (Myanmar)	1948
Burundi	1962
Cambodia	1955
Cameroon	1960
Canada	1945
Cape Verde	1975
Central African Republic	1960
Chad	1960
Chile	1945
China[2]	1945
Colombia	1945
Comoros	1975
Congo	1960
Congo, Democratic Republic of the (formerly Zaire)	1960
Costa Rica	1945
Côte d'Ivoire	1960
Croatia	1992
Cuba	1945
Cyprus	1960
Czech Republic[3]	1993
Denmark	1945
Djibouti	1977
Dominica	1978
Dominican Republic	1945
Ecuador	1945
Egypt	1945
El Salvador	1945
Equatorial Guinea	1968
Eritrea	1993
Estonia	1991
Ethiopia	1945
Fiji	1970
Finland	1955
France	1945
Gabon	1960
Gambia	1965
Georgia	1992
Germany	1973
Ghana	1957
Greece	1945
Grenada	1974
Guatemala	1945
Guinea	1958
Guinea-Bissau	1974
Guyana	1966
Haiti	1945
Honduras	1945
Hungary	1955
Iceland	1946
India	1945
Indonesia	1950
Iran	1945
Iraq	1945
Ireland	1955
Israel	1949
Italy	1955
Jamaica	1962
Japan	1956
Jordan	1955
Kazakhstan	1992
Kenya	1963
North Korea (Democratic People's Republic of Korea)	1991
South Korea (Republic of Korea)	1991
Kuwait	1963
Kyrgyzstan	1992
Laos	1955
Latvia	1991
Lebanon	1945
Lesotho	1966
Liberia	1945
Libya	1955
Liechtenstein	1990
Lithuania	1991
Luxembourg	1945
Macedonia[3]	1993
Madagascar	1960
Malawi	1964
Malaysia	1957
Maldives	1965
Mali	1960
Malta	1964
Marshall Islands	1991
Mauritania	1961

Country	Joined UN[1]	Country	Joined UN[1]	Country	Joined UN[1]
Mauritius	1968	Qatar	1971	Sweden	1946
Mexico	1945	Romania	1955	Syria	1945
Micronesia	1991	Russian Federation	1945	Tajikistan	1992
Moldova	1992	Rwanda	1962	Tanzania	1961
Monaco	1993	St. Kitts and Nevis	1983	Thailand	1946
Mongolia	1961	St. Lucia	1979	Togo	1960
Morocco	1956	St. Vincent and the Grenadines	1980	Trinidad and Tobago	1962
Mozambique	1975	Samoa, Western	1976	Tunisia	1956
Namibia	1990	San Marino	1992	Turkey	1945
Nepal	1955	São Tomé and Príncipe	1975	Turkmenistan	1992
Netherlands	1945	Saudi Arabia	1945	Uganda	1962
New Zealand	1945	Senegal	1960	Ukraine	1945
Nicaragua	1945	Seychelles	1976	United Arab Emirates	1971
Niger	1960	Sierra Leone	1961	United Kingdom	1945
Nigeria	1960	Singapore	1965	United States	1945
Norway	1945	Slovakia[4]	1993	Uruguay	1945
Oman	1971	Slovenia	1992	Uzbekistan	1992
Pakistan	1947	Solomon Islands	1978	Vanuatu	1981
Palau	1994	Somalia	1960	Venezuela	1945
Panama	1945	South Africa	1945	Viet Nam	1977
Papua New Guinea	1975	Spain	1955	Yemen, Republic of	1947
Paraguay	1945	Sri Lanka	1955	Yugoslavia	1945
Peru	1945	Sudan	1956	Zambia	1964
Philippines	1945	Suriname	1975	Zimbabwe	1980
Poland	1945	Swaziland	1968		
Portugal	1955				

1. The UN officially came into existence on Oct. 24, 1945. 2. On Oct. 25, 1971, the UN voted membership to the People's Republic of China, which replaced the Republic of China (Taiwan) in the world body. 3. The General Assembly on April 8, 1993 decided to admit the state provisionally being referred to as "The Former Yugoslav Republic of Macedonia" pending settlement of the difference that has arisen over its name. 4. Czechoslovakia was an original member of the United Nations from Oct. 24, 1945. As of December 31, 1992 it ceased to exist and the Czech Republic and Slovakia as successor states were admitted January 19, 1993.

Foreign Embassies in the United States

Source: U.S. Department of State.

Embassy of the Republic of Albania, 2100 S. St., N.W., Washington, D.C. Phone: 202-223-4942, 8187. Fax: 202-628-7342.

Embassy of the Democratic & Popular Republic of Algeria, 2118 Kalorama Rd., N.W., Washington, D.C. 20008. Phone: 202-265-2800. Fax: 202-667-2174.

Embassy of Andorra, 2 United Nations Plaza, 25th flr. New York, N.Y. 10017. Phone: 212-750-8064. Fax: 202-750-6650.

Embassy of the Republic of Angola, 1615 M. St., N.W., Suite 900, Washington D.C. 20036. Phone: 202-785-1156. Fax: 202-785-1258.

Embassy of Antigua & Barbuda, 3216 New Mexico Ave., N.W., Washington, D.C. 20016. Phone: 202-362-5211, 5166, 5122. Fax: 202-362-5225.

Embassy of the Argentine Republic, 1600 New Hampshire Ave., N.W., Washington, D.C. 20009. Phone: 202-939-6400 to 6403, inclusive. Fax: 202-332-3171.

Embassy of the Republic of Armenia, 2225 R Street, N.W., Washington, D.C. 20008. Phone: 202-319-1976. Fax: 202-319-2982.

Embassy of Australia, 1601 Massachusetts Ave., N.W., Washington, D.C. 20036. Phone: 202-797-3000. Fax: 202-797-3168.

Embassy of Austria, 3524 International Court, N.W., Washington, D.C. 20008. Phone: 202-895-6700. Fax: 202-895-6750.

Embassy of the Republic of Azerbaijan, 927-15th St., N.W., Suite 700, P.O. Box 27839, Washington, D.C. 20038-7839. Phone: 202-842-0001. Fax: 202-842-0004.

Embassy of The Commonwealth of The Bahamas, 2220 Massachusetts Ave., N.W., Washington, D.C. 20008. Phone: 202-319-2660. Fax: 202-319-2668.

Embassy of the State of Bahrain, 3502 International Dr., N.W., Washington, D.C. 20008. Phone: 202-342-0741, 0742. Fax: 202-362-2192.

Embassy of the People's Republic of Bangladesh, 2201 Wisconsin Ave., N.W., Washington, D.C. 20007. Phone: 202-342-8372 to 8376.

Embassy of Barbados, 2144 Wyoming Ave., N.W., Washington, D.C. 20008. Phone: 202-939-9200 to 9202.

Embassy of the Republic of Belarus, 1619 New Hampshire Ave., N.W., Washington, D.C. 20009. Phone: 202-986-1640. Fax: 202-986-1805.

Embassy of Belgium, 3330 Garfield St., N.W., Washington, D.C. 20008. Phone: 202-333-6900. Fax: 202-333-3079.

Embassy of Belize, 2535 Massachusetts Ave., N.W., Washington, D.C. 20008. Phone: 202-332-9636. Fax: 202-332-6888.

Embassy of the Republic of Benin, 2737 Cathedral Ave., N.W., Washington, D.C. 20008. Phone: 202-232-6656 to 6658. Fax: 202-265-1996.

Embassy of the Republic of Bolivia, 3014 Massachusetts Ave., N.W., Washington, D.C. 20008. Phone: 202-483-4410 to 4412. Fax: 202-328-3712.

Embassy of the Republic of Bosnia and Herzegovina, 2109 E St. N.W., Washington, D.C. 20037. Phone: 202-337-1500. Fax: 202-337-1502.

Embassy of the Republic of Botswana, 3400 International Dr., N.W., Suite 7M, Washington, D.C. 20008. Phone: 202-244-4990, 4991. Fax: 202-244-4164.

Brazilian Embassy, 3006 Massachusetts Ave., N.W., Washington, D.C. 20008. Phone: 202-745-2700. Fax: 202-745-2827.

Embassy of the State of Brunei Darussalam, Watergate, 2600 Virginia Ave., N.W., Suite 300, 3rd floor, Washington, D.C. 20037. Phone: 202-342-0159. Fax: 202-342-0158.

Embassy of the Republic of Bulgaria, 1621-22nd St., N.W., Washington, D.C. 20008. Phone: 202-387-7969. Fax: 202-234-7973.

Embassy of Burkina Faso, 2340 Massachusetts Ave., N.W., Washington, D.C. 20008. Phone: 202-332-5577, 6895.

Embassy of the Union of Burma, 2300 S. St., N.W., Washington, D.C. 20008. Phone: 202-332-9044, 9045. Fax: 202-332-9046.

Embassy of the Republic of Burundi, 2233 Wisconsin Ave., N.W., Suite 212, Washington, D.C. 20007. Phone: 202-342-2574.

Embassy of the Republic of Cambodia, 4500 16th St., N.W., Washington, D.C. 20011. Phone: 202-726-7742. Fax: 202-726-8381.

Embassy of the Republic of Cameroon, 2349 Massachusetts Ave., N.W., Washington, D.C. 20008. Phone: 202-265-8790 to 8794.

Embassy of Canada, 501 Pennsylvania Ave., N.W., Washington, D.C. 20001. Phone: 202-682-1740. Fax: 202-682-7726.

Embassy of the Republic of Cape Verde, 3415 Massachusetts Ave., N.W., Washington, D.C. 20007. Phone: 202-965-6820. Fax: 202-965 1207.

Embassy of Central African Republic, 1618-22nd St. N.W., Washington, D.C. 20008. Phone: 202-483-7800, 7801. Fax: 202-332-9893.

Embassy of the Republic of Chad, 2002 R St., N.W., Washington, D.C. 20009. Phone: 202-462-4009. Fax: 202-265-1937.

Embassy of Chile, 1732 Massachusetts Ave., N.W., Washington, D.C. 20036. Phone: 202-785-1746. Fax: 202-887-5579.

Embassy of the People's Republic of China, 2300 Connecticut Ave., N.W., Washington, D.C. 20008. Phone: 202-328-2500 to 2502.

Embassy of Colombia, 2118 Leroy Pl., N.W., Washington, D.C. 20008. Phone: 202-387-8338. Fax: 202-232-8643.

Embassy of the Federal and Islamic Republic of Comoros, c/o Permanent Mission of the Federal and Islamic Republic of Comoros to the United Nations, 336 E. 45th St., 2nd floor, New York, N.Y. 10017. Phone: 212-972-8010.

Embassy of the Democratic Republic of Congo, 1800 New Hampshire Ave., N.W., Washington, D.C. 20009. Phone: 202-234-7690, 7691. Fax: 202-6863631.

Embassy of the Republic of Congo, 4891 Colorado Ave., N.W., Washington, D.C. 20011. Phone: 202-726-5500. Fax: 202-726-1860.

Embassy of Costa Rica, 2114 S St., N.W., Washington, D.C. 20008. Phone: 202-234-2945. Fax: 202-265-4795.

Embassy of the Republic of Côte d'Ivoire, 2424 Massachusetts Ave., N.W., Washington, D.C. 20008. Phone: 202-797-0300.

Embassy of the Republic of Croatia, 2343 Massachusetts Ave., N.W., Washington, D.C. 20008. Phone: 202-588-5899. Fax: 202-588-8936.

Cuban Interests Section, 2630 16th St., N.W., Washington, D.C. 20009. Phone: 202-797-8518 to 8520.

Embassy of the Republic of Cyprus, 2211 R St. N.W., Washington, D.C. 20008. Phone: 202-462-5772. Fax: 202-483-6710.

Embassy of the Czech Republic, 3900 Spring of Freedom St., N.W., Washington, D.C. 20008. Phone: 202-363-6315. Fax: 202-966-8540.

Royal Danish Embassy, 3200 Whitehaven St., N.W., Washington, D.C. 20008. Phone: 202-234-4300. Fax: 202-328-1470.

Embassy of the Republic of Djibouti, 1156-15th St., N.W., Suite 515, Washington, D.C. 20005. Phone: 202-331-0270. Fax: 202-331-0302.

Embassy of the Commonwealth of Dominica, 3216 New Mexico Ave., N.W., Washington, D.C. 20016. Phone: 202-364-6781. Fax: 202-364-6791.

Embassy of the Dominican Republic, 1715-22nd St., N.W., Washington, D.C. 20008. Phone: 202-332-6280, 6281. Fax: 202-265-8057.

Embassy of Ecuador, 2535-15th St., N.W., Washington, D.C. 20009. Phone: 202-234-7200. Fax: 202-393-0525.

Embassy of the Arab Republic of Egypt, 3521 International Court, N.W., Washington, D.C. 20008. Phone: 202-895-5400. Fax: 202-244-4319/5131.

Embassy of El Salvador, 2308 California St., N.W., Washington, D.C. 20008. Phone: 202-265-9671, 9672.

Embassy of Equatorial Guinea, 1511 K St., N.W., Suite 405, Washington, D.C. 20005. Phone: 202-393-0525. Fax: 202-393-0348.

Embassy of the State of Eritrea, 1708 New Hampshire Ave., N.W., Washington, D.C., 20009. Phone: 202-319-1991. Fax: 202-319-1304.

Embassy of Estonia, 2131 Massachusetts Ave., Washington, D.C. 20008. Phone: 202-588-0101. Fax: 202-588-0108.

Embassy of Ethiopia, 2134 Kalorama Rd., N.W., Washington, D.C. 20008. Phone: 202-234-2281, 2282. Fax: 202-328-7950.

Embassy of The Republic of Fiji, 2233 Wisconsin Ave., N.W., Suite 240, Washington, D.C. 20007. Phone: 202-337-8320. Fax: 202-337-1996.

Embassy of Finland, 3301 Massachusetts Ave., N.W., Washington, D.C. 20008. Phone: 202-298-5800. Fax: 202-298-6030.

Embassy of France, 4101 Reservoir Rd., N.W., Washington, D.C. 20007. Phone: 202-944-6000. Fax: 202-944-6166.

Embassy of the Gabonese Republic, 2034-20th St., N.W., Washington, D.C. 20009. Phone: 202-797-1000. Fax: 202-332-0668.

Embassy of The Gambia, 1155-15th St., N.W., Suite 1000, Washington, D.C. 20005. Phone: 202-785-1399, 1379, 1425. Fax: 202-785-1430.

Embassy of the Republic of Georgia, 1511 K St., N.W., Suite 424, Washington, D.C. 20005. Phone: 202-393-5959. Fax: 202-393-4537.

Embassy of the Federal Republic of Germany, 4645 Reservoir Rd., N.W., Washington, D.C. 20007. Phone: 202-298-4000. Fax: 202-298-4249.

Embassy of Ghana, 3512 International Dr., N.W., Washington, D.C. 20008. Phone: 202-686-4520. Fax: 202-686-4527.

Embassy of Greece, 2221 Massachusetts Ave., N.W., Washington, D.C. 20008. Phone: 202-939-5800. Fax: 202-939-5824.

Embassy of Grenada, 1701 New Hampshire Ave., N.W., Washington, D.C. 20009. Phone: 202-265-2561.

Embassy of Guatemala, 2220 R St., N.W., Washington, D.C. 20008. Phone: 202-745-4952 to 4954. Fax: 202-745-1908.

Embassy of the Republic of Guinea, 2112 Leroy Pl., N.W., Washington, D.C. 20008. Phone: 202-483-9420. Fax: 202-483-8688.

Embassy of the Republic of Guinea-Bissau, 1511 K. St., N.W., Suite 519, Washington, D.C. 20005. Phone: 202-347-3950. Fax: 202-347-3954.

Embassy of Guyana, 2490 Tracy Pl., N.W., Washington, D.C. 20008. Phone: 202-265-6900, 6901.

Embassy of the Republic of Haiti, 2311 Massachusetts Ave., N.W., Washington, D.C. 20008. Phone: 202-332-4090 to 4092. Fax: 202-745-7215.

Apostolic Nunciature of the Holy See, 3339 Massachusetts Ave., N.W., Washington, D.C. 20008. Phone: 202-333-7121.

Embassy of Honduras, 3007 Tilden St., N.W., Suite 100, Washington, D.C. 20008. Phone: 202-966-7702, 2604, 5008, 4596. Fax: 202-966-9751.

Embassy of the Republic of Hungary, 3910 Shoemaker St., N.W., Washington, D.C. 20008. Phone: 202-362-6730. Fax: 202-966-8135.

Embassy of Iceland, 1156-15th St., N.W., Suite 1200, Washington, D.C. 20005. Phone: 202-265-6653 to 6655. Fax: 202-265-6656.

Embassy of India, 2107 Massachusetts Ave., N.W., Washington, D.C. 20008. Phone: 202-939-7000. Fax: 202-483-3972.

Embassy of the Republic of Indonesia, 2020 Massachusetts Ave., N.W., Washington, D.C. 20036. Phone: 202-775-5200. Fax: 202-775-5365.

Iranian Interests Section, 2209 Wisconsin Ave., N.W., Washington, D.C. 20007. Phone: 202-965-4990.

Iraqi Interests Section, 1801 P St., N.W., Washington, D.C. 20036. Phone: 202-483-7500.

Embassy of Ireland, 2234 Massachusetts Ave., N.W., Washington, D.C. 20008. Phone: 202-462-3939. Fax: 202-232-5993.

Embassy of Israel, 3514 International Dr., N.W., Washington, D.C. 20008. Phone: 202-364-5500. Fax: 202-364-5610.

Embassy of Italy, 1601 Fuller St., N.W., Washington, D.C. 20009. Phone: 202-328-5500. Fax: 202-483-2187.

Embassy of Jamaica, 1520 New Hampshire Ave., N.W., Washington, D.C. 20036. Phone: 202-452-0660. Fax: 202-452-0081.

Embassy of Japan, 2520 Massachusetts Ave., N.W., Washington, D.C. 20008. Phone: 202-238-6700. Fax: 202-328-2187.

Embassy of the Hashemite Kingdom of Jordan, 3504 International Dr., N.W., Washington, D.C. 20008. Phone: 202-966-2664. Fax: 202-966-3110.

Embassy of the Republic of Kazakhstan, (temporary) 3421 Massachusetts Ave., N.W., Washington, D.C. 20008. Phone: 202-333-4504. Fax: 202-333-4509.

Embassy of the Republic of Kenya, 2249 R St., N.W., Washington, D.C. 20008. Phone: 202-387-6101. Fax: 202-462-3829.

Embassy of the Republic of Korea, 2450 Massachusetts Ave., N.W., Washington, D.C. 20008. Phone: 202-939-5600. Fax: 202-387-0205.

Embassy of the State of Kuwait, 2940 Tilden St., N.W., Washington, D.C. 20008. Phone: 202-966-0702. Fax: 202-966-0517.

Embassy of the Kyrgyz Republic, 1732 Wisconsin Ave., Washington, D.C. 20007. Phone: 202-338–5141. Fax: 202-338-5139.

Embassy of the Lao People's Democratic Republic, 2222 S St., N.W., Washington, D.C. 20008. Phone: 202-332-6416. Fax: 202-332-4923.

Embassy of Latvia, 4325-17th St., N.W., Washington, D.C. 20011. Phone: 202-726-8213, 8214. Fax: 202-726-6785.

Embassy of Lebanon, 2560-28th St., N.W., Washington, D.C. 20008. Phone: 202-939-6300. Fax: 202-939-6324.

Embassy of the Kingdom of Lesotho, 2511 Massachusetts Ave., N.W., Washington, D.C. 20008. Phone: 202-797-5533 to 5536. Fax: 202-234-6815.

Embassy of the Republic of Liberia, 5201 16th St., N.W., Washington, D.C. 20011. Phone: 202-723-0437. Fax: 202-723-0436.

Embassy of the Republic of Lithuania, 2622 16th St., N.W., Washington, D.C. 20009. Phone: 202-234-5860. Fax: 202-328-0466.

Embassy of the Grand Duchy of Luxembourg, 2200 Massachusetts Ave., N.W., Washington, D.C. 20008. Phone: 202-265-4171. Fax: 202-328-8270.

Embassy of the Former Yugoslav Republic of Macedonia, 3050 K St., N.W., Suite 210, Washington, D.C. 20007. Phone: 202-337-3063. (202) 337-3093.

Embassy of the Republic of Madagascar, 2374 Massachusetts Ave., N.W., Washington, D.C. 20008. Phone: 202-265-5525, 5526.

Embassy of Malawi , 2408 Massachusetts Ave., N.W., Washington, D.C. 20008. Phone: 202-797-1007.

Embassy of Malaysia, 2401 Massachusetts Ave., N.W., Washington, D.C. 20008. Phone: 202-328-2700. Fax: 202-483-7661.

Embassy of the Republic of Mali, 2130 R St., N.W., Washington, D.C. 20008. Phone: 202-332-2249; 202-939-8950. Fax: 202-332-6603.

Embassy of Malta, 2017 Connecticut Ave., N.W., Washington, D.C. 20008. Phone: 202-462-3611, 3612. Fax: 202-387-5470.

Embassy of the Republic of the Marshall Islands, 2433 Massachusetts Ave., N.W., Washington, D.C. 20008. Phone: 202-234-5414. Fax: 202-232-3236.

Embassy of the Islamic Republic of Mauritania, 2129 Leroy Pl., N.W., Washington, D.C. 20008. Phone: 202-232-5700. (202) 319-2623.

Embassy of the Republic of Mauritius, 4301 Connecticut Ave., N.W., Suite 441, Washington, D.C. 20008. Phone: 202-244-1491, 1492. Fax: 202-966-0983.

Embassy of Mexico, 1911 Pennsylvania Ave., N.W., Washington, D.C. 20006. Phone: 202-728-1600. 202-728-1698.

Embassy of the Federated States of Micronesia, 1725 N St., N.W., Washington, D.C. 20036. Phone: 202-223-4383. Fax: 202-223-4391.

Embassy of the Republic of Moldova, 2101 S St., N.W., Washington, D.C. 20008. Phone: 202-667-1130. Fax: 202-667-1204.

Embassy of Mongolia, 2833 M St., N.W., Washington, D.C. 20007. Phone: 202-333-7117. Fax: 202-298-9227.

Embassy of the Kingdom of Morocco, 1601 21st St., N.W., Washington, D.C. 20009. Phone: 202-462-7979 to 7982, inclusive. Fax: 202-265-0161.

Embassy of the Republic of Mozambique, 1990 M St., N.W., Suite 570, Washington, D.C. 20036. Phone: 202-293-7146. Fax: 202-835-0245.

Embassy of the Union of Myanmar, 2300 S St., N.W., Washington, D.C. 20008. Phone: 202-332-9044, 9045.

Embassy of the Republic of Namibia, 1605 New Hampshire Ave., N.W., Washington, D.C. 20009. Phone: 202-986-0540. Fax: 202-986-0443.

Royal Nepalese Embassy, 2131 Leroy Pl., N.W., Washington, D.C. 20008. Phone: 202-667-4550. Fax: 202-667-5534.

Royal Netherlands Embassy, 4200 Linnean Ave., N.W., Washington, D.C. 20008. Phone: 202-244-5300; after 6 p.m. 202-494-8594. Fax: 202-362-3430.

Embassy of New Zealand, 37 Observatory Circle, N.W., Washington, D.C. 20008. Phone: 202-328-4800.

Embassy of Nicaragua, 1627 New Hampshire Ave., N.W., Washington, D.C. 20009. Phone: 202-939-6570.

Embassy of the Republic of Niger, 2204 R St., N.W., Washington, D.C. 20008. Phone: 202-483-4224 to 4227, inclusive.

Embassy of the Federal Republic of Nigeria, 1333 16th St., N.W., Washington, D.C. 20036. Phone: 202-986-8400. (202) 775-1385.

Royal Norwegian Embassy, 2720 34th St., N.W., Washington, D.C. 20008. Phone: 202-333-6000. Fax: 202-337-0870.

Embassy of the Sultanate of Oman, 2535 Belmont Rd., N.W., Washington, D.C. 20008. Phone: 202-387-1980 to 1982. Fax: 202-745-4933.

Embassy of Pakistan, 2315 Massachusetts Ave., N.W., Washington, D.C. 20008. Phone: 202-939-6200. Fax: 202-387-0484.

Embassy of the Republic of Palau, 1150 18th St., N.W., Suite 750, Washington, D.C. 20036. Phone: 202-452-6814. Fax: 202-452-6281.

Embassy of the Republic of Panama, 2862 McGill Terrace, N.W., Washington, D.C. 20008. Phone: 202-483-1407.

Embassy of Papua New Guinea, 1615 New Hampshire Ave., N.W., 3rd floor, Washington, D.C. 20009. Phone: 202-745-3680. Fax: 202-745-3679.

Embassy of Paraguay, 2400 Massachusetts Ave., N.W., Washington, D.C. 20008. Phone: 202-483-6960 to 6962. Fax: 202-234-4508.

Embassy of Peru, 1700 Massachusetts Ave., N.W., Washington, D.C. 20036. Phone: 202-833-9860 to 9869. Fax: 202-659-8124.

Embassy of the Philippines, 1600 Massachusetts Ave., N.W., Washington, D.C. 20036. Phone: 202-467-9300. Fax: 202-328-7614.

Embassy of the Republic of Poland, 2640 16th St., N.W., Washington, D.C. 20009. Phone: 202-234-3800 to 3802. Fax: 202-328-6271.

Embassy of Portugal, 2125 Kalorama Rd., N.W., Washington, D.C. 20008. Phone: 202-328-8610. Fax: 202-462-3726.

Embassy of the State of Qatar, 4200 Wisconsin Ave., N.W., Washington, D.C. 20016. Phone: 202-274-1600.

Embassy of Romania, 1607 23rd St., N.W., Washington, D.C. 20008. Phone: 202-332-4846, 4848, 4851; after hours 332-4846. Fax: 202-232-4748.

Embassy of the Russian Federation, 2650 Wisconsin Ave., N.W., Washington, D.C. 20007. Phone: 202-298-5700 to 5704 inclusive. Fax: 202-298-5735.

Embassy of the Republic of Rwanda, 1714 New Hampshire Ave., N.W., Washington, D.C. 20009. Phone: 202-232-2882. Fax: 202-232-4544.

Embassy of Saint Kitts and Nevis, 3216 New Mexico Ave., N.W., Washington, D.C. 20016. Phone: 202-686-2636. Fax: 202-686-5740.

Embassy of Saint Lucia, 3216 New Mexico Ave., N.W., Washington, D.C. 20016. Phone: 202-364-6792 to 6795. Fax: 202-364-6728.

Embassy of Saint Vincent and the Grenadines, 3216 New Mexico Ave., N.W., Washington, D.C. 20016. Phone: 202-364-6730. Fax: 202-364-6736.

Embassy of Saudi Arabia, 601 New Hampshire Ave., N.W., Washington, D.C. 20037. Phone: 202-342-3800.

Embassy of the Republic of Senegal, 2112 Wyoming Ave., N.W., Washington, D.C. 20008. Phone: 202-234-0540, 0541.

Embassy of the Republic of Seychelles, c/o Permanent Mission of Seychelles to the United Nations, 820 Second Ave., Suite 900F, New York, N.Y. 10017. Phone: 212-972-1785. Fax: 202-972-1786.

Embassy of Sierra Leone, 1701 19th St., N.W., Washington, D.C. 20009. Phone: 202-939-9261/63. Fax: 202-483-1793.

Embassy of the Republic of Singapore, 3501 International Pl., N.W., Washington, D.C. 20008. Phone: 202-537-3100. Fax: 202-537-0876.

Embassy of the Slovak Republic, 2201 Wisconsin Ave., N.W., Suite 250, Washington, D.C. 20007. Phone: 202-965-5161. Fax: 202-965-5166.

Embassy of the Republic of Slovenia, 1525 New Hampshire Ave., N.W., Washington, D.C. 20036. Phone: 202-667-5363. Fax: 202-667-4563.

Embassy of the Republic of South Africa, 3051 Massachusetts Ave., N.W., Washington, D.C. 20008. Phone: 202-232-4400. Fax: 202-265-1607.

Embassy of Spain, 2375 Pennsylvania Ave., N.W., Washington, D.C. 20037. Phone: 202-452-0100 and 728-2340. Fax: 202-833-5670.

Embassy of the Democratic Socialist Republic of Sri Lanka, 2148 Wyoming Ave., N.W., Washington, D.C. 20008. Phone: 202-483-4025 to 4028. Fax: 202-232-7181.

Embassy of the Republic of the Sudan, 2210 Massachusetts Ave., N.W., Washington, D.C. 20008. Phone: 202-338-8565 to 8570. Fax: 202-667-2406.

Embassy of the Republic of Suriname, 4301 Connecticut Ave., N.W., Suite 108, Washington, D.C. 20008. Phone: 202-244-7488, 7590 to 7592. Fax: 202-244-5878.

Embassy of the Kingdom of Swaziland, 3400 International Drive, N.W., Washington, D.C. 20008. Phone: 202-362-6683, 6685. Fax: 202-244-8059.

Embassy of Sweden, 1501 M St., N.W., Washington, D.C. 20005. Phone: 202-467-2600. Fax: 202-467-2699.

Embassy of Switzerland, 2900 Cathedral Ave., N.W., Washington, D.C. 20008. Phone: 202-745-7900. Fax: 202-387-2564.

Embassy of the Syrian Arab Republic, 2215 Wyoming Ave., N.W., Washington, D.C. 20008. Phone: 202-232-6313. Fax: 202-234-9548.

Embassy of the United Republic of Tanzania, 2139 R St., N.W., Washington, D.C. 20008. Phone: 202-939-6125. Fax: 202-797-7408.

Royal Thai Embassy, 1024 Wisconsin Ave., N.W., Washington, D.C. 20007. Phone: 202-944-3600. Fax: 202-944-3611.

Embassy of the Republic of Togo, 2208 Massachusetts Ave., N.W., Washington, D.C. 20008. Phone: 202-234-4212, 4213. Fax: 202-232-3190.

Embassy of Trinidad and Tobago, 1708 Massachusetts Ave., N.W., Washington, D.C. 20036. Phone: 202-467-6490. Fax: 202-785-3130.

Embassy of Tunisia, 1515 Massachusetts Ave., N.W., Washington, D.C. 20005. Phone: 202-862-1850.

Embassy of the Republic of Turkey, 1714 Massachusetts Ave., N.W., Washington, D.C. 20036. Phone: 202-659-8200.

Embassy of Turkmenistan, 2207 Massachusetts Ave., N.W., Washington, D.C. 20008. Phone: 202-588-1500. Fax: 202-588-0697.

Embassy of the Republic of Uganda, 5911-16th St., N.W., Washington, D.C. 20011. Phone: 202-726-7100 to 7102, 0416. Fax: 202-726-1727.

Embassy of Ukraine, 3350 M St., N.W., Washington, D.C. 20007. Phone: 202-333-0606. Fax: 202-333-0817.

Embassy of the United Arab Emirates, 1255, 22nd St., N.W., Suite 700, Washington, D.C. 20007. Phone: 202-955-7999.

United Kingdom of Great Britain & Northern Ireland—British Embassy, 3100 Massachusetts Ave., N.W., Washington, D.C. 20008. Phone: 202-588-6500. Fax: 202-588-7870.

Embassy of Uruguay, 2715 M St., N.W., Washington, D.C. 20007. Phone: 202-331-1313 to 1316. Fax: 202-331-8142.

Embassy of the Republic of Uzbekistan, 1746 Massachusetts Ave., N.W., Washington, D.C. 20036. Phone: 202-887-5300. Fax: 202-293-6804.

Embassy of the Republic of Venezuela, 1099 30th St., N.W., Washington D.C. 20007. Phone: 202-342-2214. Fax: 202-342-6820.

Embassy of Vietnam, 1233 20th St., N.W., Washington, D.C. 20036. Phone: 202-861-0737. Fax: 202-861-0917.

Embassy of the Independent State of Western Samoa, 820 Second Ave., Suite 800D, New York, N.Y. 10017. Phone: 212-599-6196, 6197. Fax: 212-599-0797.

Embassy of the Republic of Yemen, 2600 Virginia Ave., N.W., Suite 705, Washington, D.C. 20037. Phone: 202-965-4760, 4761. (202) 337–2017.

Embassy of the former Socialist Federal Republic of Yugoslavia, 2410 California St., N.W., Washington, D.C. 20008. Phone: 202-462-6566.

Embassy of the Republic of Zambia, 2419 Massachusetts Ave., N.W., Washington, D.C. 20008. Phone: 202-265-9717 to 9719. Fax: 202-332-0826.

Embassy of the Republic of Zimbabwe, 1608 New Hampshire Ave., N.W., Washington, D.C. 20009. Phone: 202-332-7100. Fax: 202-483-9326.

Diplomatic Personnel To and From the U.S.

Country	U.S. Representative to[1]	Rank	Representative from[2]	Rank
Albania	Marisa R. Lino	Amb.	Lublin Dilja	Amb.
Algeria	Cameron R. Hume	Amb.	Ramtane Lamamra	Amb.
Angola	Donald K. Steinberg	Amb.	Antonio dos Santos Franca	Amb.
Antigua and Barbuda [3]	—	—	Lionel A. Hurst	Amb.
Argentina	James R. Cheek	Amb.	Raul Enrique Granillo Ocampo	Amb.
Armenia	Michael Craig Lemmon	Amb.	Rouben Robert Shugarian	Amb.
Australia	Genta Hawkins Holmes	Amb.	Andrew Sharp Peacock	Amb.
Austria	Kathryn Walt Hall	Amb.	Helmut Tuerk	Amb.
Azerbaijan	Stanley T. Escudero	Amb.	Hafiz Mir Jalal Pashayev	Amb.
Bahamas	Arthur Schechter	Amb.	Sir Arlington Griffith Butler	Amb.
Bahrain	Johnny Young	Amb.	Muhammad Abdul Ghaffar Abdulla	Amb.
Bangladesh	John C. Holzman	Amb.	K. M. Shehabuddin	Amb.
Barbados [3]	William Crotty	Cd'A	Dr. Courtney N. Blackman	Amb.
Belarus	Daniel V. Speckhard	Amb.	Serguei Martynov	Amb.
Belgium	Paul L. Cejas	Amb.	Andre Adam	Amb.
Belize	Carolyn Curiel	Amb.	James S. Murphy	Amb.
Benin	John M. Yates	Amb.	Lucien Edgar Tonoukouin	Amb.
Bermuda	Robert A. Farmer	Cons. Gen.	—	—
Bolivia	Donna Hrinak	Amb.	Fernando Cossio	Amb.
Bosnia-Herzegovina	Richard Kazlarich	Amb.	Sven Alkalaj	Amb.
Botswana	Robert Krueger	Amb.	Archibald Mooketsa Mogwe	Cd'A.
Brazil	Melvyn Levitsky	Amb.	Paulo-Tarso Flecha de Lima	Amb.
Brunei	Glen R. Rase	Amb.	Shofry Abdul Ghafor	Amb.
Bulgaria	Avis T. Bohlen	Amb.	Snejana Damianova Botoucharova	Amb.
Burkina Faso	Sharon P. Wilkinson	Amb.	Gaetan R. Ouedrao	Amb.
Burma (Myanmar)	Kent M. Wiedemann	Ch'd	Tin Winn	Amb.
Burundi	Morris N. Hughes, Jr.	Amb.	Severin Ntahomvukiye	Amb.
Cambodia	Kenneth M. Quinn	Amb.	Huoth Var	Amb.
Cameroon	Charles H. Twining	Amb.	Jerome Mendouga	Amb.
Canada	Gordon D. Giffin	Amb.	Raymond A. J. Chretien	Amb.
Cape Verde	Lawrence N. Benedict	Amb.	Corentino Virgilio Santos	Amb.
Central African Republic	Mosina H. Jordan	Amb.	Henry Koba	Amb.
Chad	David C. Halsted	Amb.	Ahmat Mahamat-Saleh	Amb.
Chile	John O'Leary	Amb.	John Biehl	Amb.
China	James R. Sasser	Amb.	Li Dauyu	Amb.
Colombia	Curtis W. Kamman	Amb.	Juan Carlos Esguerra	Amb.
Comoros	(Closed)	—	—	—
Congo, Democratic Republic of	(suspended)	—	Serge Mombouli	Cd'A
Congo, Rep. of	(suspended)	—	Dieudonne Antoine Ganga	Min.-Consl.
Costa Rica	Thomas Dodd	Amb.	Sonia Picado	Amb.
Côte d'Ivoire	Lannon Walker	Amb.	Koffi Moise Koumoue	Amb.
Croatia	William Montgomery	Amb.	Miomir Zuzul	Amb.
Cyprus	Kenneth C. Brill	Amb.	Andros A. Nicolaides	Amb.
Czech Republic	Jenonne R. Walker	Amb.	Petr Vancura	Amb.
Denmark	(vacant)	—	K. Erik Tygesen	Amb.
Djibouti	Lange Schermerhorn	Amb.	Roble Olhaye	Amb.
Dominica [3]	—	—	Edward I. Watty	Amb.
Dominican Republic	Mari Carmen Aponte	Cd'A	Bernardo Vega	Amb.
Ecuador	Leslie Alexander	Amb.	Fernando Flores	Amb.

Country	U.S. Representative to[1]	Rank	Representative from[2]	Rank
Egypt	Daniel Kurtzer	Amb.	Ahmed Maher El Sayed	Amb.
El Salvador	Anne W. Patterson	Amb.	Ana Cristina Sol	Amb.
Equatorial Guinea	John E. Bennett	Amb.	Pastor Micha Ondo Bile	Amb.
Eritrea	William David Clarke	Amb.	Amdemicael Kahsai	Amb.
Estonia	Melissa F. Wells	Amb.	Lauri Lepik	Cd'A
Ethiopia	David H. Shinn	Amb.	Berhane Gebre-Christos	Amb.
Fiji	Don L. Gevirtz [4]	Amb.	Napolioni Masirewa	Amb.
Finland	Eric S. Edelman	Amb.	Jaakko Tapani Laajava	Amb.
France	Felix Rohatyn	Amb.	François V. Bujon	Amb.
Gabon	Elizabeth Raspolic	Amb.	Paul Boundoukou-Latha	Amb.
Gambia, The	George Williford Boyce Haley	Amb.	Malamin K. Juwara	Cd'A
Georgia	Kenneth Spencer Yalowitz	Amb.	Tedo Japaridze	Amb.
Germany	John Christian Kornblum	Amb.	Juergen Chrobog	Amb.
Ghana	Kathryn Dee Robinson	Amb.	Ekwow Spio-Garbrah	Amb.
Greece	R. Nicholas Burns	Amb.	Loucas Tsilas	Amb.
Grenada [3]	—	—	Denis G. Antoine	Amb.
Guatemala	Donald Planty	Amb.	Pedro Miguel Lamport	Amb.
Guinea	Tibor P. Nagy, Jr.	Amb.	Mohamed Aly Thiam	Amb.
Guinea-Bissau	(suspended)	—	Rufino Jose Mendes	Amb.
Guyana	James F. Mack	Amb.	Mohammed Ali Odeen Ishmael	Amb.
Haiti	Timothy Carney	Amb.	Jean Casimir	Amb.
Holy See	Lindy Boggs	Amb.	Most Rev. Agostino Cacciavillan	Pro-Nuncio
Honduras	James F. Creagan	Amb.	Roberto Bermudez	Amb.
Hungary	Peter Tufo	Amb.	Gyorgy Banlaki	Amb.
Iceland	Day O. Mount	Amb.	Einar Benediktsson	Amb.
India	Richard F. Celeste	Amb.	Naresh Chandra	Amb.
Indonesia	J. Stapleton Roy	Amb.	Arifin Siregar	Amb.
Ireland	Michael J. Sullivan	Amb.	Dermot A. Gallagher	Amb.
Israel	Edward S. Walker, Jr.	Amb.	Eliahu Ben-Elissar	Amb.
Italy	Thomas M. Foglietta	Amb.	Ferdinando Salleo	Amb.
Jamaica	Stanley L. McLelland	Amb.	Richard Leighton Bernal	Amb.
Japan	Thomas S. Foley	Amb.	Kunihiko Saito	Amb.
Jordan	Wesley W. Egan, Jr.	Amb.	Fayez A. Tarawneh	Amb.
Kazakhstan	Richard Henry Jones	Amb.	Bolat K. Nurgaliyev	Amb.
Kenya	Prudence Bushnell	Amb.	Benjamin Kipkorir	Amb.
South Korea	Stephen W. Bosworth	Amb.	Kun Woo Park	Amb.
Kuwait	James A. Larocco	Amb.	Mohammed Sabah Al-Salim Al-Sabah	Amb.
Kyrgyzstan	Eileen A. Malloy	Amb.	Baktybek Abdrissaev	Amb.
Laos	Wendy J. Chamberlin	Amb.	Hiem Phommachanh	Amb.
Latvia	Larry C. Napper	Amb.	Ojars Eriks Kalnins	Amb.
Lebanon	Richard H. Jones	Amb.	Victor El-Zmeter	Amb.
Lesotho	Katherine Hubay Peterson	Amb.	Dr. Eunice M. Bulane	Amb.
Liberia	William Milan	Cm.	T. H. Konah Blackett	Cd'A
Lithuania	Keith C. Smith	Amb.	Alfonsas Eidintas	Amb.
Luxembourg	Clay Constantinou	Amb.	Alphonse Berns	Amb.
Macedonia	Christopher R. Hill	Amb.	Lubica Z. Acevska	Amb.
Madagascar	Shirley Elizabeth Barnes	Amb.	Pierrot Rajaonarivelo	Amb.
Malawi	Peter R. Chaveas	Amb.	Willie Chokani	Amb.
Malaysia	John R. Malott	Amb.	Dato Dali Mahmud Hashim	Amb.
Mali	David P. Rawson	Amb.	Cheick Oumar Diarrah	Amb.
Malta	Kathryn Proffitt	Amb.	Albert Borg Olivier de Puget	Amb.
Marshall Islands	Joan M. Plaisted	Amb.	Banny De Brum	Amb.
Mauritania	Dorothy Myers Sanpas	Amb.	Bilal Ould Werzeg	Amb.
Mauritius	Harold W. Geisel	Amb.	Chitmansing Jesseramsing	Amb.
Mexico	Jeffrey Davidow	Amb.	Jesus Silva Herzog	Amb.
Micronesia	(vacant)	—	Jesse B. Marehalau	Amb.
Moldova	Rudolf Vilemk Perina	Amb.	Nicolae Tau	Amb.
Mongolia	Alphonso F. La Porta	—	Jalbuu Choinhor	Amb.
Morocco	Edward M. Gabriel	Amb.	Mohamed Benaissa	Amb.
Mozambique	B. Dean Curran	Amb.	Marcus Geraldo Namashulua	Amb.
Namibia	George F. Ward, Jr.	Amb.	Veiccoh Nghiwete	Amb.
Nepal	Ralph Frank	Amb.	Damodar Prasad Gautam	Amb.
Netherlands	Cynthia Perrin Schneider	Amb.	Adriaan Jacobovits de Szeged	Amb.
New Zealand	Josiah Horton Beeman	Amb.	L. John Wood	Amb.
Nicaragua	Lino Gutierrez	Amb.	Roberto Mayor-Cortes	Amb.
Niger	Charles O. Cecil	Amb.	Amadou Seydou	Amb.
Nigeria	William H. Twaddell	Amb.	Walkili Hassan Adamu	Amb.
Norway	David B. Hermelin	Amb.	Tom Eric Vraalsen	Amb.

Country	U.S. Representative to[1]	Rank	Representative from[2]	Rank
Oman	Frances D. Cook	Amb.	Abdulla Moh'd Aqueel Al-Dhahab	Amb.
Pakistan	Thomas W. Simmons	Amb.	Zamir Akram	Amb.
Palau	Thomas C. Hubbard	Amb.	David Orrukem	Cd'A
Panama	Simon Ferro	Amb.	Eduardo Gonzalez Morgan	Amb.
Papua New Guinea	Arma Jane Karaer	Amb.	Nagora Y. Bogan	Amb.
Paraguay	Maura Harty	Amb.	Jorge G. Prieto	Amb.
Peru	Dennis C. Jett	Amb.	Ricardo V. Luna	Amb.
Philippines	Thomas C. Hubbard	Amb.	Raul Chaves Rabe	Amb.
Poland	Daniel Fried	Amb.	Jerzy Kozminski	Amb.
Portugal	Gerald S. McGowan	Amb.	Fernando Andresen Guimaraes	Amb.
Qatar	Patrick N. Theros	Amb.	Sultan Al-Moraiki	Cd'A
Romania	Jim Rosapepe	Amb.	Mircea Dan Geoana	Amb.
Russia	James Collins	Amb.	Yuli M. Vorontsov	Amb.
Rwanda	Robert Gribbin III	Amb.	Theogene N. Rudasingwa	Amb.
Saint Kitts and Nevis [3]	—	—	Kutayba Y. Alghanim	Consl.
Saint Lucia [3]	—	—	Juliet Elaine Mallet Phillip	Cd'A
Saint Vincent and the Grenadines [3]	—	—	Kingsley C.A. Layne	Amb.
Samoa, Western	Josiah Horton Beeman	Amb.	Tuiloma Neroni Slade	Amb.
Saudi Arabia	Wyche Fowler, Jr.	Amb.	Prince Bandar Bin Sultan	Amb.
Senegal	Dane F. Smith, Jr.	Amb.	Mamadou Mansour Seck	Amb.
Seychelles	Carl Burton Stokes	Amb.	Claude Morel	Cd'A.
Sierra Leone	John L. Hirsch	Amb.	John Ernest Leigh	Amb.
Singapore	Steven J. Green	Amb.	Heng-Chee Chan	Amb.
Slovakia	Ralph Johnson	Amb.	Branislav Lichardus	Amb.
Slovenia	Nancy Halliday Ely-Raphel	Amb.	Ernest Petric	Amb.
Somalia	(suspended)	—	(suspended)	—
South Africa	James A. Joseph	Amb.	Franklin Sonn	Amb.
Spain	Edward L. Romero	Amb.	Antonio Oyarzabal	Amb.
Sri Lanka	Shaun E. Donnelly	Amb.	Jayantha Dhanapala	Amb.
Sudan	(suspended)	—	Mahdi Ibrahim Mohamed	Amb.
Suriname	Dennis Hays	Amb.	Cicyl Alwart	Cd'A
Swaziland	Alan R. McKee	Amb.	Mary M. Kanya	Amb.
Sweden	Lyndon L. Olson, Jr.	Amb.	Sihver Liljegren	Amb.
Switzerland	Madeleine May Kunin	Amb.	Carlo Jagmeti	Amb.
Syria	Christopher W.S. Ross	Amb.	Walid Al-Moualem	Amb.
Tajikistan	R. Grant Smith	Amb.	—	—
Tanzania	Richard Stith	Amb.	Mustafa Salim Nyang'anyi	Amb.
Thailand	William H. Itoh	Amb.	Nitya Pibulsonggram	Amb.
Togo	Johnny Young	Amb.	Kossivi Osseyi	Amb.
Trinidad and Tobago	Sally G. Cowal	Amb.	Corinne Averille McKnight	Amb.
Tunisia	Robin Raphel	Amb.	Azouz Ennifar	Amb.
Turkey	Mark R. Parris	Amb.	Nuzhet Kandemir	Amb.
Turkmenistan	Michael W. Cotter	Amb.	Halil Ugur	Amb.
Uganda	E. Michael Southwick	Amb.	Edith Ssempala	Amb.
Ukraine	Steven Carl Pifer	Amb.	Yuriy Mikolayevych Shcherbak	Amb.
United Arab Emirates	David C. Litt	Amb.	Mohammad bin Hussein Al-Shaali	Amb.
United Kingdom	Philip Lader	Amb.	John Olav Kerr	Amb.
Uruguay	Christopher Ashby	Amb.	Alvaro Diez de Medina	Amb.
Uzbekistan	Joe Presel	Amb.	Sodiq Safaev	Amb.
Venezuela	John F. Maisto	Amb.	Pedro Luis Echeverria	Amb.
Vietnam	Douglass B. Peterson	Amb.	Bang Van Le	Cd'A.
Yemen	Barbara K. Bodine	Amb.	Mohsin A. Alaini	Amb.
Yugoslavia (former)	(vacant)	—	Nebojsa Vujovic	Cd'A.
Zambia	Arlene Render	Amb.	Dunstan Weston Kamana	Amb.
Zimbabwe	Johnnie Carson	Amb.	Amos Bernard Muvengwa Midzi	Amb.

1. As of Sept. 1998. 2. As of Sept. 1998. 3. The U.S. Embassy in Barbados currently serves seven independent nations of the Eastern Caribbean (Barbados, Antigua and Barbuda, Dominica, Grenada, St. Kitts and Nevis, St. Lucia, and St. Vincent and the Grenadines) and provides consular services to American citizens in the nearby European dependent territories. 4. Ambassador to Fiji, Nauru, Tonga, and Tuvalu. NOTE: Amb.=Ambassador; Cd'A.=Charge d'Affaires; Secy.=Secretary; Cons. Gen.=Consul General; Consl.=Counselor; Min.=Minister; P.O.=Principal Officer; Dir.=Director; USLO=U.S. Liaison Office. *Source:* U.S. Department of State.

Current Travel Warnings

(for U.S. citizens; as of 7/13/98)

Country	Most recent warning issued	Country	Most recent warning issued
Afghanistan	8/21/98	Iraq	2/21/98
Albania	8/18/98	Lebanon	5/11/98
Algeria	5/1/98	Liberia	2/6/98
Angola	7/15/98	Libya	6/3/97
Bosnia and Herzegovina	7/13/98	Montserrat	8/27/97
Burundi	5/21/98	Nigeria	5/27/98
Cambodia	7/29/98	Pakistan	8/16/98
Central African Republic	3/28/97	Rwanda	5/1/98
Colombia	3/26/98	Serbia and Montenegro	7/1/98
Congo (Brazzaville)	6/17/97	Sierra Leone	7/14/98
Dem. Rep. of Congo (formerly Zaire)	8/14/98	Somalia	7/14/98
Eritrea	6/4/98	Sudan	8/21/98
Guinea-Bissau	6/14/98	Tajikistan	3/13/98
Iran	4/2/98		

Source: U.S. Department of State (http://travel.state.gov).

Tips on Tipping

Source: American Society of Travel Agents, Alexandria, Va.

Who do you tip? When? How much?

These are the questions that have nagged at consumers since the first service transaction. The practice of tipping is meant as a form of thank-you for services rendered, or beforehand as a subtle bribe for special treatment.

Tipping need not be considered mandatory or automatic. Too often, tips are taken for granted or expected regardless of the quality of service. Tipping should be done at your discretion and as a reward for good or superlative service.

Below are some tipping suggestions for travelers. At nearly every step of the traveling process, there are professionals waiting to "lighten your load" or provide assistance. So remember to carry a lot of change and small bills for tips.

1. **Taxi/Limo Drivers:** A $2 to $3 tip is usually satisfactory; more if he helps you with your bags and/or takes special steps to get you to your destination on time.
2. **Porters:** A standard tip for airport and train porters is $1 per bag; more if your luggage is very heavy.
3. **Hotel Bellman:** Again, $1 per bag is standard. Tip when he shows you to your room and again if he assists you upon checkout. Tip more if he provides any additional service. Note: A $5 tip upon arrival can usually guarantee you special attention should you require it.
4. **Doorman:** Typically, a $1 tip for hailing a taxi is appropriate. However, you may want to tip more for special service, such as carrying your bags or shielding you with an umbrella.
5. **Concierge:** Tip for special services such as making restaurant or theater reservations, arranging sightseeing tours, etc. The amount of the tip is generally dependent on the type and complexity of service(s) provided— $2 to $10 is a standard range. You may elect to tip for each service, or in one sum upon departure. If you want to ensure special treatment from the concierge, you might consider a $10–$20 tip upon arrival.
6. **Hotel Maid:** Maids are often forgotten about when it comes to tipping because they typically do their work when you are not around. For stays of more than one night, $1 per night is standard. The tip should be left in the hotel room in a marked envelope.
7. **Parking Attendants:** Tip $1 to $2 when your car is delivered.
8. **Waiters:** 15–20% of your pre-tax check is considered standard. The same applies for room service waiters. Some restaurants will automatically add a 15% gratuity to your bill, especially for large parties—look for it before tipping. If the 15% is added, you need only tip up to another 5% for superlative service.
9. **Cloakroom Attendants:** If there is a charge for the service, a tip is not necessary. However, if there is no charge, or extra care is taken with your coat and/or bags, a $1 to $2 tip is appropriate.
10. **Tour Guides/Charter Bus Drivers:** If a tip is not automatically included, tip $1 for a half-day tour, $2 for full-day tour, and anywhere from $5 to $10 for a week-long tour. Tip a private guide more.

These are some of the people you are most likely to encounter while traveling in the U.S. Undoubtedly there will be others. If there is one standard rule in tipping it is this: If someone renders special service to you along the way, show your appreciation with a tip.

NOTE: International travelers should be aware that tipping customs outside the U.S. are often very different. Consult travel guides for the country you are visiting.

The World's Top 40 Tourism Destinations, 1997

International Tourist Arrivals (excluding same-day visitors)

Rank 1990	1997	Country	Arrivals 1997	Rank 1990	1997	Country	Arrivals 1997
1	1	France	66,864,000	23	22	Singapore	6,542,000
2	2	United States	48,409,000	15	23	Malaysia	6,211,000
3	3	Spain	43,378,000	22	24	Belgium	5,875,000
4	4	Italy	34,087,000	26	25	Ireland	5,540,000
7	5	United Kingdom	25,960,000	55	26	South Africa	5,530,000
12	6	China	23,770,000	38	27	Indonesia	5,036,000
27	7	Poland	19,514,000	34	28	Macau	4,915,000
8	8	Mexico	19,351,000	32	29	Argentina	4,540,000
10	9	Canada	17,610,000	36	30	Australia	4,286,000
16	10	Czech Republic	17,400,000	29	31	Tunisia	4,263,000
5	11	Hungary	17,248,000	28	32	Japan	4,223,000
6	12	Austria	16,646,000	31	33	Korea Republic	3,908,000
9	13	Germany	15,837,000	18	34	Croatia	3,834,000
17[1]	14	Russian Federation	15,350,000	35	35	Egypt	3,657,000
11	15	Switzerland	11,077,000	37	36	Saudi Arabia	3,594,000
19	16	China, Hong Kong SAR	10,406,000	33	37	Puerto Rico	3,332,000
13	17	Greece	10,246,000	25	38	Morocco	3,115,000
14	18	Portugal	10,100,000	53	39	Brazil	2,995,000
24	19	Turkey	9,040,000	30	40	Romania	2,741,000
21	20	Thailand	7,263,000			**Total 1–40**	530,367,000
20	21	Netherlands	6,674,000			**World Total**	611,964,000

1. Former USSR. *Source:* World Tourism Organization (WTO). Reprinted with permission.

U.S. Passport Information

Source: Department of State, Bureau of Consular Affairs and Department of the Treasury, Customs Service.

With a few exceptions, a passport is required for all U.S. citizens to depart and enter the United States and to enter most foreign countries. A valid U.S. passport is the best documentation of U.S. citizenship available. Persons who travel to a country where a U.S. passport is not required should be in possession of documentary evidence of their U.S. citizenship and identity to facilitate reentry into the United States. Travelers should check passport and visa requirements with consular officials of the countries to be visited well in advance of their departure date.

Application for a passport may be made at a passport agency; to a clerk of any federal court or state court of record; to a judge or clerk of any probate court accepting applications; or at a post office selected to accept passport applications. Passport agencies are located in Boston, Chicago, Honolulu, Houston, Los Angeles, Miami, New Orleans, New York, Philadelphia, San Francisco, Seattle, Stamford, Conn., and Washington, D.C.

All persons are required to obtain individual passports in their own names. Neither spouses nor children may be included in each others' passports. Applicants age 13 years and older must appear in person before the clerk or agent executing the application. For children under the age of 13, a parent or legal guardian may execute an application for them.

First-time passport applicants must apply in person. Applicants must present evidence of citizenship (e.g., a certified copy of birth certificate), personal identification (e.g., a valid driver's license), two identical black-and-white or color photographs taken within six months (2×2 inches, with the image size measured from the bottom of the chin to the top of the head [including hair] not less than 1 inch nor more than 1 3/8 inches on a plain white or off-white background), plus a completed passport application (DSP-11). If you were born abroad, you may also use as proof of citizenship: a Certificate of Naturalization, a Certificate of Citizenship, a Report of Birth Abroad of a Citizen of the United States of America, or a Certification of Birth. A fee of $45 plus a $15 execution fee is charged for adults 16 years and older for a passport valid for ten years from the date of issue. The fee for minor children under 16 years of age is $25 for a five-year passport plus $15 for the execution of the application. Persons of all ages born outside the U.S. are required to pay an additional $100 complex case fee.

You may apply for a passport by mail if you have been the bearer of a passport issued within 12 years prior to the date of a new application, are able to submit your most recent U.S. passport with your new application, and your previous passport was not issued before your 16th birthday. If you are eligible to apply by mail, include your previous passport; a completed, signed, and dated DSP-82 "Application for Passport by Mail"; new photographs; and the passport fee of $40. The $15 execution fee is not required when renewing your passport. Mail the application and attachments in accordance with the instructions on the form.

Passports may be presented for amendment to show a married name or legal change of name or to correct descriptive data. Any alterations to the passport by the bearer other than in the spaces provided for change of address and next-of-kin data are forbidden.

If you *must* have your passport within 14 days, you will need to pay an additional $35 expedite fee and provide proof of the need for this service.

Loss, theft, or destruction of a passport should be reported to Passport Services, 1111 19th Street, N.W., Washington, D.C. 20522-1705 immediately, or to the nearest passport agency. If you are overseas, report loss to the nearest U.S. embassy or consulate and to local police authorities. Your passport is a valuable citizenship and identity document. It should be carefully safeguarded. Its loss could cause you unnecessary travel complications as well as significant expense. It is advisable to photocopy the data page of your passport and keep it in a place separate from your passport to facilitate the issuance of a replacement passport, should one be necessary.

To renew a passport by mail, applicants must:

1. Obtain an "Application for Passport by Mail" (Form DSP-82) from a passport acceptance facility (post office, court house, passport agency), or from the World Wide Web (http://travel.state.gov).
2. Complete and sign the application and attach the most recent passport issued not more than 12 years ago but after the applicant's 16th birthday, two identical 2″ × 2″ passport photographs, and a check or money order for $40 payable to Passport Services.
3. Mail the above items to the National Passport Center, Post Office Box 371971, Pittsburgh, Pa. 15250-7971.

Consumer Complaints against U.S. Airlines: 1988 to 1996

Complaint Category	1988	1989	1990	1991	1992	1993	1994	1995	1996
TOTAL	**21,493**	**10,553**	**7,703**	**6,106**	**5,639**	**4,438**	**5,179**	**4,629**	**5,778**
Flight problems[1]	8,831	4,111	3,034	1,877	1,624	1,211	1,586	1,133	1,626
Customer service[2]	2,120	1,002	758	714	695	599	805	667	1,000
Baggage	3,938	1,702	1,329	883	752	627	761	628	881
Ticketing/boarding[3]	1,445	821	624	659	680	577	598	666	857
Refunds	1,667	1,023	701	783	721	482	393	576	521
Oversales[4]	1,353	607	399	301	265	257	301	263	353
Fares[5]	455	341	312	388	573	398	267	185	180
Advertising	141	89	96	96	54	51	94	66	61
Tours	37	22	29	23	12	16	127	18	16
Smoking	546	232	74	30	25	30	20	15	13
Credit	35	19	5	10	10	4	2	4	3
Other	925	584	342	342	228	186	225	408	267

1. Cancellations, delays, etc. from schedule. 2. Unhelpful employees, inadequate meals or cabin service, treatment of delayed passengers. 3. Errors in reservations and ticketing; problems in making reservations and obtaining tickets. 4. All bumping problems, whether or not airline complied with DOT regulations. 5. Incorrect or incomplete information about fares, discount fare conditions, and availability, etc. *Source:* U.S. Dept. of Transportation, Office of Consumer Affairs, *Air Travel Consumer Report.*

Top 20 U.S. States & Territories Visited by Overseas Travelers[1]

State/Territory	1997 Market share (percent)	1997 Visitation (thousands)	State/Territory	1997 Market share (percent)	1997 Visitation (thousands)
California	26.6%	6,436	Arizona	4.0%	968
Florida	25.1	6,073	New Jersey	3.0	726
New York	21.8	5,274	Georgia	2.7	653
Hawaiian Islands	12.7	3,073	Pennsylvania	2.6	629
Nevada	9.1	2,202	Washington	2.4	581
District of Columbia	5.9	1,427	Colorado	2.2	532
Guam	5.6	1,355	North Carolina	2.0	484
Massachusetts	5.0	1,210	Ohio	1.8	436
Illinois	4.7	1,137	Utah	1.7	411
Texas	4.3	1,040	Louisiana	1.5	363

1. Excludes visitors from Canada and Mexico. *Source:* U.S. Dept. of Commerce, International Trade Administration, Tourism Industries Office.

State Tourism Offices

The following is a selected list of state tourism offices. Where a toll-free 800 or 888 number is available, it is given. However, the numbers are subject to change.

Alabama
Bureau of Tourism & Travel
P.O. Box 4927
Montgomery, AL 36103-4927
334-242-4169 or
1-800-ALABAMA

Alaska
Alaska Division of Tourism
P.O. Box 110801
Juneau, AK 99811-0801
907-465-2010

Arizona
Arizona Office of Tourism
2702 N. 3rd St., Ste. 4015
Phoenix, AZ 85004
602-230-7733 or
1-800-842-8257

Arkansas

Arkansas Department of Parks and Tourism
1 Capitol Mall
Little Rock, AR 72201
501-682-7777 or
1-800-NATURAL (from anywhere in the U.S.)

California

California Division of Tourism
P.O. Box 1499
Sacramento, CA 95812-1499
1-800-862-2543

Colorado

Colorado Travel and Tourism Authority
P.O. Box 3524
Englewood, CO 80155
1-800-COLORADO

Connecticut

Department of Tourism
505 Hudson St.
Hartford, CT 06106
860-270-8081 or
1–800-CT-BOUND (from anywhere in the U.S.)

Delaware

Delaware Tourism Office
Delaware Economic Development Office
99 Kings Highway
P.O. Box 1401
Dover, DE 19903
302-739-4271 or
1-800-441-8846 (from anywhere in the U.S.)

District of Columbia (Washington, D.C.)

Washington Convention and Visitors Association
717 14th St., NW
Washington, D.C. 20005-3992
202-789-7000

Florida

Visitor Services
Florida Tourism Industry Marketing Corp.
P.O. Box 1100
Tallahassee, FL 32302-1100
850-488-5607

Georgia

Tourist Division
P.O. Box 1776
Atlanta, GA 30301-1776
404-656-3590,
1-800-VISIT-GA

Hawaii

Hawaii Visitors Bureau
2270 Kalakaua Ave., Ste. 801
Honolulu, HI 96815
808-923-1811 or
1-800-GO-HAWAII

Idaho

Department of Commerce, Tourism Development
700 W. State St.
P.O. Box 83720
Boise, ID 83720-0093
208-334-2470 or
1-800-635-7820

Illinois

Illinois Bureau of Tourism
100 W. Randolph, Ste. 3-400
Chicago, IL 60601
1-800-2-CONNECT

Indiana

Indiana Department of Commerce
Department of Tourism
1 North Capitol, Ste. 700
Indianapolis, IN 46204-2288
1-800-291-8844

Iowa

Iowa Department of Economic Development
Division of Tourism
200 East Grand Ave.
Des Moines, IA 50309
515-242-4705 or
1-800-345-IOWA

Kansas

Dept. of Commerce & Housing
Travel & Tourism Development Division
700 SW Harrison St., Ste. 1300
Topeka, KS 66603-3712
785-296-2009 or
1-800-2-KANSAS

Kentucky

Department of Travel Development
Dept. MR
500 Mero St. Ste. 2200
P.O. Box 2011
Frankfort, KY 40601
1-800-225-TRIP Ext. 67 (from the U.S. and Canada)

Louisiana

Office of Tourism
P.O. Box 94291
Baton Rouge, LA 70804-9291
504-342-8100 or
1-800-33-GUMBO

Maine

Maine Publicity Bureau
P.O. Box 2300
Hallowell, ME 04347-2300
207-623-0363 or
1-888-MAINE-45

Maryland

Office of Tourism Development
217 E. Redwood St., 9th Floor
Baltimore, MD 21202
410-767-3400 (business office) or 1-800-543-1036

Massachusetts

Office of Travel and Tourism
State Transportation Building
10 Park Plaza, 4th Fl.
Boston, MA 02116
617-727-3201 or
1-800-227-MASS

Michigan

Michigan Jobs Commission
Travel Michigan
P.O. Box 3393
Livonia, MI 48151
1-888-78-GREAT

Minnesota

Minnesota Office of Tourism
500 Metro Square
121 7th Place E
St. Paul, MN 55101-2146
651-296-5029 or
1-800-657-3700

Mississippi

Department of Economic and Community Development
Tourism Development
P.O. Box 1705
Ocean Springs, MS 39566-1705
601-875-0079 or
1-800-927-6378

Missouri

Missouri Division of Tourism
Truman State Office Bldg.
301 W. High St.
P.O. Box 1055
Jefferson City, MO 65102
573-751-4133 or
1-800-877-1234

Montana

Department of Commerce
Travel Montana
P.O. Box 200533
Helena, MT 59620-0533
406-444-2654 or
1-800-VISIT-MT

Nebraska

Department of Economic Development
Tourism Office
P.O. Box 94666
Dept. 97 INT
Lincoln, NE 68509-4666
402-471-3796 or
1-800-228-4307 (from anywhere in the U.S.)

Nevada

Commission on Tourism
5151 S. Carson St.
Carson City, NV 89701
1-800-NEVADA-8

New Hampshire

Office of Travel and Tourism
P.O. Box 1856
Concord, NH 03302-1856
603-271-2343 or
1-800-FUN-IN-NH; for recorded weekly events, ski conditions, foliage reports
1-800-258-3608

New Jersey

Division of Travel and Tourism
CN 826
Trenton, NJ 08625
1-800-JERSEY-7

Average Daily Temperatures (°F) in Tourist Cities

(For U.S. Cities, *see* Climate of Selected U.S. Cities.)

Location	January		April		July		October	
	High	Low	High	Low	High	Low	High	Low
Acapulco (Mexico)	87	72	87	73	90	76	89	76
Amsterdam (Netherlands)	40	34	52	43	68	59	56	48
Athens (Greece)	54	42	67	52	90	72	74	60
Auckland (New Zealand)	73	60	67	56	56	46	63	52
Bangkok (Thailand)	89	69	94	78	91	77	89	76
Beijing (China)	35	15	68	44	87	71	67	44
Belgrade (Yugoslavia)	38	28	62	43	81	60	64	46
Berlin (Germany)	35	26	55	38	74	55	55	41
Bombay (India)	83	67	89	76	85	77	89	76
Cairo (Egypt)	65	47	83	57	96	70	86	65
Calcutta (India)	80	55	97	75	89	79	89	74
Cape Town (South Africa)	69	56	66	54	60	50	65	53
Caracas (Venezuela)	75	56	81	60	78	61	79	61
Copenhagen (Denmark)	36	29	50	37	72	55	53	42
Dublin (Ireland)	47	35	54	38	67	51	57	43
Glasgow (Scotland)	43	34	53	38	66	52	54	43
Hamilton (Bermuda)	68	58	71	59	85	73	79	69
Helsinki (Finland)	27	17	43	31	71	57	45	37
Hong Kong (China)	67	51	79	67	90	78	84	70
Istanbul (Turkey)	48	36	59	45	78	64	66	53
Jerusalem (Israel)	55	41	73	50	87	63	81	59
Kingston (Jamaica)	86	67	87	70	90	73	88	73
Lagos (Nigeria)	88	74	89	77	82	74	85	74
Lisbon (Portugal)	56	46	64	52	79	63	69	57
London (United Kingdom)	44	35	56	40	73	55	58	44
Madrid (Spain)	50	34	63	43	89	61	67	48
Mexico City (Mexico)	66	42	77	51	73	53	70	50
Montreal (Canada)	22	6	51	33	79	60	56	39
Moscow (Russia)	21	9	47	31	76	55	46	34
Nairobi (Kenya)	77	53	75	57	69	51	77	54
Nassau (Bahamas)	77	65	81	69	88	75	85	73
Oslo (Norway)	30	20	50	34	73	56	49	37
Paris (France)	42	32	60	41	76	55	59	44
Prague (Czech Republic)	34	25	55	40	74	58	54	44
Quebec (Canada)	19	3	45	30	77	58	51	37
Rio de Janeiro (Brazil)	84	73	80	69	75	63	77	66
Rome (Italy)	54	39	68	46	88	64	73	53
San José (Costa Rica)	75	58	79	62	77	62	77	60
San Juan (Puerto Rico)	81	70	83	72	86	76	86	75
Seoul (Korea)	33	17	62	42	84	70	67	47
Singapore	86	73	89	75	87	75	88	74
Stockholm (Sweden)	31	23	45	32	70	55	48	39
Sydney (Australia)	79	65	73	57	62	44	72	55
Taipei (Taiwan)	66	54	77	63	92	76	81	67
Tokyo (Japan)	48	31	64	48	84	71	70	56
Toronto (Canada)	30	17	51	35	79	60	57	42
Vancouver (Canada)	42	32	55	41	71	55	57	44
Vienna (Austria)	34	26	57	41	75	59	55	44
Zurich (Switzerland)	36	26	60	41	77	56	57	43

New Mexico

New Mexico Department of Tourism
491 Old Santa Fe Trail
Lamy Bldg.
Santa Fe, NM 87503
505-827-7400 or
1-800-SEE-NEWMEX

New York

Division of Tourism
1 Commerce Plaza
Albany, NY 12245
1-800-225-5697 (from anywhere in the U.S.);
518-474-4116 (from Canada)

North Carolina

Travel and Tourism Division
Department of Commerce
301 N. Wilmington St.
Raleigh, NC 27601-2825
919-733-4171 or
1-800-VISIT-NC

North Dakota

North Dakota Tourism Department
604 E. Boulevard
Bismarck, ND 58505
701-328-2525 or
1-800-HELLO-ND

Ohio

Ohio Division of Travel and Tourism
P.O. Box 1001
Columbus, OH 43266-1010
614-466-8844 (business office)
1-800-BUCKEYE (in U.S. and Canada)

Oklahoma

Oklahoma Tourism and Recreation Department
Literature Distribution Center
P.O. Box 60789
Oklahoma City, OK 73146-9910
405-521-2409 (in Oklahoma City area) or nationwide at 1-800-652-6552

Oregon

Tourism Commission
775 Summer St., NE
Salem, OR 97310
503-986-0000
1-800-547-7842 (travel information)

Pennsylvania

Office of Travel, Tourism, and Film Promotion
Room 456, Forum Building
Harrisburg, PA 17120
717-787-5453 (business office) or 1-800-VISIT-PA, ext. 257 (To order single free copy of Pa. Travel Guide)

Puerto Rico

Puerto Rico Tourism Company
2 La Princessa Drive
P.O. Box 4435
Old San Juan Station
San Juan, Puerto Rico 00902
1-800-223-6530

Rhode Island

Rhode Island Economic Development Corporation
1 West Exchange St.
Providence, RI 02903
401-222-2601 or 1-800-556-2484 (in U.S. and Canada)

South Carolina

South Carolina Division of Tourism
Department of Parks, Recreation, and Tourism
Box 71
Columbia, SC 29202
803-734-0122

South Dakota

Department of Tourism
Capitol Lake Plaza
711 E. Wells Ave.
Pierre, SD 57501-5070
605-773-3301 or 1-800-S-DAKOTA

Tennessee

Department of Tourist Development
320 Sixth Avenue N.
5th fl., Rachel Jackson Bldg.
Nashville, TN 37243
1-800-491-TENN

Texas

Travel Information Division
Texas Department of Transportation
P.O. Box 5064
Austin, TX 78763-5064
1-800-452-9292

Utah

Utah Travel Council
Council Hall, Capitol Hill
Salt Lake City, UT 84114
801-538-1030 or 1-800-200-1160
801-538-1399 (fax)

Vermont

Department of Tourism and Marketing
134 State St.
P.O. Box 1471
Montpelier, VT 05601-1471
1-800-VERMONT

Virginia

Virginia Tourism Corporation
901 East Byrd St.
Richmond, VA 23219
804-786-4484 or 1-800-932-5827

Washington

Washington State Department of Community, Trade and Economic Development
906 Columbia St., SW
P.O. Box 48300
Olympia, WA 98504-8300
360-753-7426

Washington, D.C.

See District of Columbia

West Virginia

Division of Tourism
P.O. Box 50312
2101 Washington St., E.
Charleston, WV 25305-0312
304-558-2200 or 1-800-CALL-WVA

Wisconsin

Travel Information
Wisconsin Travel Info Centers-Madison
201 West Washington Ave.
Madison, WI 53707
Toll free in WI and neighboring states: 1-800-372-2737; others: 608-266-2161; nationally: 1-800-432-TRIP

Wyoming

Wyoming Division of Tourism
I-25 at College Dr.
Cheyenne, WY 82002
307-777-7777 or 1-800-225-5996

International Visitors, (Inbound) and U.S. Residents (Outbound), 1988–1996

	International visitors inbound								
	1988	1989	1990	1991	1992	1993	1994	1995	1996[1]
From overseas[2]	**12,512**	**13,999**	**15,059**	**16,155**	**17,791**	**18,662**	**18,458**	**20,639**	**22,658**
% Change	18.80%	11.90%	7.60%	7.30%	10.10%	4.90%	–1.10%	11.80%	9.80%
From Canada[2]	**13,700**	**15,325**	**17,263**	**19,113**	**18,598**	**17,293**	**14,974**	**14,663**	**15,301**
% Change	11.80%	11.90%	12.60%	10.70%	–2.70%	–7.00%	–13.40%	–2.10%	4.40%
From Mexico[2]	**7,730**	**7,041**	**7,041**	**7,406**	**10,872**	**9,824**	**11,321**	**8,016**	**8,530**
% Change	53.20%	–8.90%	0.00%	5.20%	46.80%	–9.60%	15.20%	–29.20%	6.40%
Inbound totals[2]	**33,942**	**36,365**	**39,363**	**42,674**	**47,261**	**45,779**	**44,753**	**43,318**	**46,489**
% Change	21.90%	7.10%	8.20%	8.40%	10.70%	–3.10%	–2.20%	–3.20%	7.30%

	U.S. residents outbound								
	1988	1989	1990	1991	1992	1993	1994	1995	1996[1]
To overseas[2]	**14,443**	**14,791**	**15,990**	**14,521**	**15,965**	**17,102**	**18,149**	**19,059**	**19,786**
% Change	6.10%	2.40%	8.10%	–9.20%	9.90%	7.10%	6.10%	5.00%	3.80%
To Canada[2]	**12,763**	**12,184**	**12,252**	**12,003**	**11,819**	**12,024**	**12,542**	**12,933**	**12,909**
% Change	0.30%	–4.50%	0.60%	–2.00%	–1.50%	1.70%	4.30%	3.10%	–0.20%
To Mexico[2]	**13,463**	**14,163**	**16,381**	**15,042**	**16,114**	**15,285**	**15,759**	**18,771**	**19,616**
% Change	3.00%	5.20%	15.70%	–8.20%	7.10%	–5.10%	3.10%	19.10%	4.50%
Outbound totals[2]	**40,669**	**41,138**	**44,623**	**41,566**	**43,898**	**44,411**	**46,450**	**50,763**	**52,311**
% Change	3.20%	1.20%	8.50%	–6.90%	5.60%	1.20%	4.60%	9.30%	3.00%

1. Revised figures. 2. Figures are given in thousands. *Source:* U.S. Dept. of Commerce, International Trade Administration, Tourism Industries Office.

U.S. Household and Family Characteristics, 1997

Reports of the continuing rapid decline of the traditional American family are greatly exaggerated. From 1970 to 1990, married-couple households with children did decline sharply from 40% to 26% of all households. But, since 1990, decline has been slower—only a small decline to 25% in 1997.

Growth in the number of households has slowed dramatically in the 1990s. In 1997, the number of U.S. households reached 101 million, up from 93.3 million in 1990.[1] The rate of growth in the number of households has slowed during the past 27 years. Between 1970 and 1980, the number of households increased by an average of 1.7 million per year. During the 1980s, growth slowed to 1.3 million per year. Thus far in the 1990s, growth has been 1.1 million per year.

Growth in the number of households depends on population growth, changes in the age composition of the population, and decisions that individuals make about their living arrangements. Changes in the median age at first marriage, divorce rates, the condition of the economy, and improvements in the health of the elderly over time are also among the factors that can influence rate of growth and the composition of households.

The average household size has remained relatively unchanged since 1990. In 1997, the average number of people per household was 2.64, down from 3.14 in 1970. Between 1970 and 1990, the share of households with five or more people decreased from 21% to 10%. During the same period, the share of households with only one or two people increased from 46% to 58%. Since 1990, the distribution of households by number of members has remained unchanged.

In 1997, only 34% of all households contained "own" (birth, adopted, or step-) children of the householder—unchanged since 1990. By definition, nonfamily households contain no own children, although they may include other people under 18 who are not relatives of the householder.

In 1997, 76% of the 70.2 million American families were maintained by married couples. The remaining 24% were maintained by women or men with no spouse present. More than three-fourths of the latter group were maintained by women.

The number of families maintained by people with no spouse present is increasing rapidly. Since 1970, the number of female-householder families has increased by 133% (from 5.5 million to 12.8 million). The number of male-householder families grew by 213% (from 1.2 million to 3.8 million). In contrast, married-couple families grew only 20% (from 44.7 million to 53.6 million). However, most of this change occurred before 1990. From 1990 to 1997, growth was only 17% for female-householder families, 33% for male-householder families, and 2% for married-couple families.

Nowadays fewer families contain children under 18. In 1997, 51% of all families contained no own children under 18 at home. This figure is seven percentage points more than in 1970, when only 44% of families had no own children under 18 at home, but none of this change occurred since 1990.

Families without own children under 18 at home are not necessarily "childless." Some contain other related children, for example, nieces, nephews, or grandchildren. They also may include unrelated foster children. Other families may include adult sons and daughters who are still living at home. Still other families have adult children who are living away from home. These families are in the "empty nest" stage of their life cycle.

Younger families are more likely to be without own children under 18 now than in 1970. Among married-couple families with a householder under age 35, 29% had no own children under 18 in 1997, compared with 23% in 1970.

More adult sons and daughters are living at home. Nearly 22 million adult sons and daughters were living in a household maintained by one or both parents in 1997 compared with 15 million in 1970. Fifteen percent of all families included one or more own children age 18 or older in 1997, an increase of four percentage points since 1970. The increasing age at first marriage means that fewer young adults in the 1990s are setting up their own households than was the case a generation ago. Increases in the cost of setting up and maintaining a household in the 1990s may also mean that young adults today are not as well equipped financially to maintain a residence separate from their parents as they were in the 1970s.

Families are smaller than a generation ago. The average number of people in a family was 3.19 in 1997, up from 3.17 in 1990 but down from 3.58 in 1970. Only two people were present in 42% of all families. Fully 40% of married-couple families consisted of the husband and wife alone.

Families with a white householder were smaller than those with black or Hispanic householders: 3.13 people for whites, 3.41 for blacks, and 3.94 for Hispanics.[2] White married-couple families had an average size of 3.20, compared with blacks at 3.59, and Hispanics at 4.17. Female-householder families, with no spouse present, followed a similar pattern: for whites 2.86, for blacks 3.31, and for Hispanics 3.43 people. □

1. The Bureau of the Census produces several different estimation methods. The Current Population Survey, on which this report is based, is the best source for estimates of the demographic characteristics of U.S. households; housing estimates, derived from decennial census and administrative data, are the best source of the actual number of households.
2. People of Hispanic origin may be of any race. *Source:* U.S. Bureau of the Census, Current Population Reports, Series P20–509, *Household and Family Characteristics: March 1997.*

Families by Type and Selected Characteristics, 1997

Characteristics	All families	Married-couple families	Other families: Female householder	Other families: Male householder
All families	70,241	53,604	12,790	3,847
Size of family[1]				
2 people	29,780	21,504	6,080	2,196
3 people	16,239	11,456	3,777	1,006
4 people	14,602	12,442	1,776	383
5 people	6,326	5,479	692	156
6 people	2,108	1,803	245	60
7 people or more	1,186	920	220	46
Average size	3.19	3.25	3.02	2.85
Own children under 18				
Without own children under 18	35,575	28,521	4,916	2,138
With own children under 18	34,665	25,083	7,874	1,709
Average per family with own children under 18	1.84	1.89	1.75	1.55
Householder's age				
Under 25 years	2,964	1,333	1,245	386
25 to 34 years	13,737	9,902	2,803	1,034
35 to 44 years	19,026	14,254	3,769	1,001
45 to 54 years	14,383	11,484	2,198	701
55 to 64 years	8,997	7,536	1,127	334
65 to 74 years	7,120	5,949	933	238
75 years or more	4,014	3,146	716	152
Median age	44.7	46.1	41.2	39.8
Householder's marital status				
Married, spouse present	53,604	53,604	—	—
Married, spouse absent (incl. separated couples)	2,691	—	2,159	532
Widowed	2,677	—	2,264	413
Divorced	6,032	—	4,648	1,384
Never married	5,238	—	3,720	1,518

1. Note that "size of family" and "size of household" are different. Household members include all people living in the household, whereas family members include only the householder and his/her relatives. NOTE: Numbers are in thousands, except averages and medians. Data applies to U.S. families only. *Source:* U.S. Bureau of the Census, Current Population Survey.

Family Structure

(Under age 18, by race and Hispanic origin, for selected years 1970–1996.)

Family type	1970	1980	1990	1991	1992	1993	1994	1995	1996
Total									
Two parents	85%	77%	73%	72%	71%	71%	69%	69%	68%
Mother only	11	18	22	22	23	23	23	23	24
Father only	1	2	3	3	3	3	3	4	4
No parent	3	4	3	3	3	3	4	4	4
White									
Two parents	90	83	79	78	77	77	76	76	75
Mother only	8	14	16	17	18	17	18	18	18
Father only	1	2	3	3	3	3	3	3	4
No parent	2	2	2	2	2	2	3	3	3
Black									
Two parents	58	42	38	36	36	36	33	33	33
Mother only	30	44	51	54	54	54	53	52	53
Father only	2	2	4	4	3	3	4	4	4
No parent	10	12	8	6	7	7	10	11	9
Hispanic									
Two parents	78	75	67	66	65	65	63	63	62
Mother only	—	20	27	27	28	28	28	28	29
Father only	—	2	3	3	4	4	4	4	4
No parent	—	3	3	4	3	4	5	4	5

NOTE: Data applies to the U.S. *Source:* U.S. Bureau of the Census, Current Population Reports.

Marital Status

Declining proportions of adults are married. Although the number of currently married people has grown 23% since 1970 (from 95 million in 1970 to 116 million in 1996), the number of unmarried adults has grown significantly faster, doubling from 38 million to 77 million. These increases resulted in a decline in the proportion of adults age 18 and over who are married, from 72% in 1970 to 60% in 1996.

Declines in the proportion of adults currently married have occurred for whites, blacks, and Hispanics,[1] but the changes have been most pronounced for blacks. In 1996, 63% of white adults were currently married, down from 73% in 1970. Similarly, the proportion of Hispanics who were currently married declined from 72% to 58% between 1970 and 1996. Among black adults, 42% were currently married in 1996, a considerable decrease from 64% in 1970.

Divorced population growing fastest. The currently divorced population is the fastest growing marital status category. The number of divorced people has more than quadrupled, from 4.3 million in 1970 to 18.3 million in 1996. They represented 10% of adults age 18 and over in 1996, up from 3% in 1970.

Never-married adults more than doubled since 1970. In 1996, 44.9 million adults age 18 and older had never been married, more than twice the number in 1970 (21.4 million). Never-married adults accounted for 23% of all adults, and made up the largest share (59%) of the unmarried population in 1996, followed by those who were divorced (24%) and those who were widowed (18%).

Sharp increases in the proportion never married have been primarily seen among men and women in their late 20s and early 30s. Between 1970 and 1996, the proportion of 25- to 29-year-olds who had never married more than tripled for women from 11% to 38% and more than doubled for men, from 19% to 52%. Among 30- to 34-year-olds, the proportions never married tripled from 6% to 21% for women and from 9% to 30% for men.

The proportion who never married has increased for whites, blacks, and Hispanics. Among whites, the proportion increased from 16% to 21% between 1970 and 1996. Thirty-nine percent of black adults in 1996 had never been married, up from 21% in 1970. For Hispanics, the proportion rose from 19% to 30% during this period.

Postponement of marriage continues. The median age at first marriage has been rising since the mid-1950s and has increased quite rapidly during the past two decades. In the 20 years spanning 1955 to 1975, the estimated median age at first marriage increased about one full year (from 22.6 years to 23.5 years for men and from 20.2 to 21.1 for women). Since 1975, the median age has increased more than three full years for men and women, climbing to 27.1 years for men and 24.8 years for women in 1996.

1. Hispanics may be of any race. NOTE: Data applies to the U.S. *Source:* U.S. Bureau of the Census, Current Population Reports, Series P20-496, *Marital Status and Living Arrangements: March 1996.*

Percent Never Married: 1970 and 1996

Age	1970	1996	Age	1970	1996
Women:			Men:		
20 to 24 years	35.8%	68.5%	20 to 24 years	54.7%	81.0%
25 to 29 years	10.5	37.6	25 to 29 years	19.1	52.0
30 to 34 years	6.2	20.5	30 to 34 years	9.4	29.6
35 to 39 years	5.4	13.1	35 to 39 years	7.2	20.8
40 to 44 years	4.9	9.7	40 to 44 years	6.3	14.2

NOTE: Data applies to the U.S. *Source:* U.S. Bureau of the Census, Current Population Reports.

Who Receives Child Support?

Not only do women have better chances of being awarded child support . . .

In spring 1992, about one-half (6.2 million) of the 11.5 million custodial parents were awarded child support; award rates were higher for mothers than for fathers (56% compared with 41%).

. . . they are more likely to actually receive payments.

Fewer than half of the custodial parents (5.3 million, or 46%) were supposed to receive child support payments in 1991. Of the 4.9 million women due payments, 76% received at least a portion of the amount they were owed. The corresponding rate for the 400,000 men owed money was 63%.

More than 5 million custodial parents were without awards of financial support from their child(ren)'s other parent. About one-third of those without awards had chosen not to pursue them. Two other common reasons they did not have awards were that they did not want an award and that the noncustodial parent was unable to pay.

Much of the child support due goes unpaid.

A total of $11.9 billion was paid in child support in 1991, $5.8 billion less than the amount due. Nearly all of the money paid ($11.2 billion) went to women.

Although women receive more child support than men . . .

Women who received child support in 1991 were paid an average of $3,011 that year, about one-third more than their male counterparts ($2,292). On average, these support payments constituted 17% of 1991 money income for the women, but only 7% for the men.

. . . they still have lower incomes.

The mothers who received child support had lower average 1991 money income than the fathers who received it ($18,144 compared with $33,579). Income was lower for custodial parents who did not receive payments.

Visitation and joint custody help.

About 6.9 million of the 11.5 million parents who did not live with their children (noncustodial parents) had joint custody and/or visitation privileges to contact their children. It was more likely for the 5.3 million noncustodial parents who owed child support in 1991 to have made payments if they had one or both of these contact privileges than if they had neither (79% compared with 56%).

Fewer than half of awards include health care benefits.

About four in ten parents with child support awards as of 1992 had health-insurance benefits included in their award. However, about one-third (31%) of the noncustodial parents who were required to provide these benefits in 1991 as part of the award failed to do so. On the other hand, some noncustodial parents (18%) not required to provide these benefits as part of the award did so anyway.

Custodial fathers and mothers differ demographically.

Race and Hispanic origin: Custodial fathers were more likely than custodial mothers to be white (85% versus 70%) and less apt to be black (12% compared with 27%). They were about as likely to be Hispanic (approximately 10% each).

Marital Status: Custodial fathers were less likely than custodial mothers to have never been married (8% versus 26%), more apt to be currently married (46% compared with 27%), and just as likely to be divorced or separated (about 47% each). Custodial fathers were as likely to be currently married as they were to be divorced or separated. Also, custodial mothers were as likely to be currently married as they were to be never married.

Age: Custodial fathers were generally older than custodial mothers. About half (46%) of custodial fathers were at least 40 years old, while only 11% were under age 30. The corresponding percentages for custodial mothers were 24% and 31%, respectively. One percent each of custodial fathers and mothers were under age 18.

Education: Custodial fathers were better educated than custodial mothers. They were twice as likely to have at least a bachelor's degree (19% compared with 10%) and less apt to have only attained a high school diploma or less (56% versus 64%).

NOTE: Data applies to the U.S. *Source:* Economics and Statistics Administration, U.S. Department of Commerce.

Births to Unmarried Women, by Race

Excludes births to nonresidents of United States. Marital status is inferred from a comparison of the child's and parents' surnames on the birth certificate for those states that do not report on marital status. No estimates included for misstatements on birth records or failures to register births.

Race of child and age of mother	1980	1990	1992	1993	1994
Number (thousands)					
Total live births[1]	666	1,165	1,225	1,240	1,290
White	320	647	722	742	794
Black	326	473	459	452	448
Under 15 years old	9	11	11	11	12
15 to 19 years old	263	350	354	357	381
20 to 24 years old	237	404	436	439	449
25 to 29 years old	100	230	233	234	238
30 to 34 years old	41	118	128	132	137
35 years old and over	16	53	63	67	72
Percent distribution					
Total[1]	100.0%	100.0%	100.0%	100.0%	100.0%
White	48.1	55.6	58.9	59.8	61.6
Black	48.9	40.6	37.5	36.5	34.8
Under 15 years	1.4	0.9	0.9	0.9	0.9
15 to 19 years	39.5	30.0	28.9	28.8	29.6
20 to 24 years	35.6	34.7	35.6	35.4	34.8
25 to 29 years	15.0	19.7	19.1	18.9	18.4
30 to 34 years	6.2	10.1	10.4	10.7	10.6
35 years and over	2.4	4.5	5.1	5.4	5.6
As percent of all births in racial groups					
Total[1]	18.4%	28.0%	30.1%	31.0%	32.6%
White	11.0	20.1	22.6	23.6	25.4
Black	55.2	65.2	68.1	68.7	70.4

Race of child and age of mother	1980	1990	1992	1993	1994
Birth rate[2]					
Total[1,3]	29.4	43.8	45.2	45.3	46.9
White[3]	17.6	31.8	35.2	35.9	38.3
Black[3]	82.9	93.9	86.5	84.0	82.1
15 to 19 years	27.6	42.5	44.6	44.5	46.4
20 to 24 years	40.9	65.1	68.5	69.2	72.2
25 to 29 years	34.0	56.0	56.5	57.1	59.0
30 to 34 years	21.1	37.6	37.9	38.5	40.1

1. Includes other races not shown separately. 2. Rate per 1,000 unmarried women (never-married, widowed, and divorced) estimated as of July 1. 3. Covers women aged 15 to 44 years. *Source:* U.S. National Center for Health Statistics, *Vital Statistics of the United States*, annual; *Monthly Vital Statistics Report*; and unpublished data. From *Statistical Abstract of the United States 1997.*

Teen Birth Rates by Age, Race, and Hispanic Origin, Selected Years

(Births per 1,000 females in each age group.)

Age	1980	1985	1990	1993	1994	1995	1996[1]
All races							
10–14 years	1.1	1.2	1.4	1.4	1.4	1.3	1.2
15–19 years	53.0	51.0	59.9	59.6	58.9	56.8	54.7
White, non-Hispanic							
10–14 years	0.4	—	0.5	0.5	0.5	0.4	—
15–19 years	41.2	—	42.5	40.7	40.4	39.3	—
Black							
10–14 years	4.3	4.5	4.9	4.6	4.6	4.2	3.7
15–19 years	97.8	95.4	112.8	108.6	104.5	96.1	91.7
American Indian/Alaskan Native							
10–14 years	1.9	1.7	1.6	1.4	1.9	1.8	1.8
15–19 years	82.2	70.2	81.9	83.1	80.8	78.0	75.1
Asian/Pacific Islander							
10–14 years	0.3	0.4	0.7	0.6	0.7	0.7	0.6
15–19 years	26.2	23.8	26.4	27.0	27.1	26.1	25.4
Hispanic[2]							
10–14 years	1.7	—	2.4	2.7	2.7	2.7	2.6
15–19 years	82.2	—	100.3	106.8	107.7	106.7	101.6

1. Data for 1996 are preliminary. 2. Persons of Hispanic origin may be of any race. NOTE: Data applies to the U.S. *Source:* Centers for Disease Control and Prevention, National Center for Health Statistics, National Vital Statistics System.

Birth Rates by Educational Attainment and Age of Mother, 1994[1]

		Years of schooling completed by mother					
		0–11 years					
Age of mother	Total	Total	0–8 years	9–11 years	12 years	13–15 years	16 years or more
15–44 years[2]	66.7	72.7	88.9	67.9	78.0	48.4	70.9
15–17 years	37.6	35.0	31.2	35.8	—	—	—
18–19 years	91.5	114.4	281.4	103.8	140.3	20.2	—
20–24 years	111.1	216.1	247.9	207.0	174.6	55.7	45.0
25–29 years	113.9	133.4	166.1	120.2	125.7	97.7	108.5
30–34 years	81.5	68.7	107.0	54.2	69.7	66.4	124.1
35–39 years	33.7	31.4	44.9	23.8	26.2	25.4	56.0
40–44 years[3]	6.6	8.8	14.7	5.3	4.6	5.0	10.0

1. Rates are live births per 1,000 women in a specified group. Figures for educational attainment not stated are distributed. 2. Includes births to women under 15 years, not shown separately. 3. Rates computed by relating births to mothers aged 40 years and over to women aged 40–44 years. NOTE: Data applies to the U.S. *Source:* U.S. Bureau of the Census, *Monthly Vital Statistics Report*, April 1997.

Child Abuse and Neglect

Based on reports alleging child abuse and neglect that were referred for investigation by the respective child-protective services agency in each state. The reporting period may be either calendar year or fiscal year. The majority of states provided duplicated counts. Also, varying number of states reported the various characteristics presented below. A substantial case represents a type of investigation disposition that determines that there is sufficient evidence under state law to conclude that maltreatment occurred or that the child is at risk of maltreatment. An indicated case represents a type of disposition that concludes that there was a reason to suspect maltreatment had occurred.

Item	1990		1993		1994		1995	
	Number	Percent	Number	Percent	Number	Percent	Number	Percent
Types of substantiated maltreatment								
Victims, total[1]	690,658	—	966,163	—	1,011,595	—	1,000,502	—
Neglect	338,770	49.1%	472,170	48.9%	520,550	51.5%	523,049	52.3%
Physical abuse	186,801	27.0	231,111	23.9	241,338	23.9	244,903	24.5
Sexual abuse	119,506	17.3	137,265	14.2	136,362	13.5	126,095	12.6
Emotional maltreatment	45,621	6.6	47,643	4.9	47,337	4.7	44,648	4.5
Medical neglect	—	—	23,009	2.4	24,593	2.4	29,454	2.9
Other and unknown	61,477	8.9	145,096	15.0	153,894	15.2	144,733	14.5
Sex of victim								
Victims, total	794,101	100.0	926,322	100.0	903,195	100.0	834,174	100.0
Male	357,367	45.0	413,277	44.6	420,817	46.6	393,227	47.1
Female	405,409	51.1	470,658	50.8	472,535	52.3	437,407	52.4
Unknown	31,325	3.9	42,387	4.6	9,843	1.1	3,540	0.4
Age of victim								
Victims, total	807,965	100.0	926,674	100.0	901,573	100.0	833,115	100.0
1 year and younger	106,507	13.2	121,700	13.1	119,203	13.2	105,375	12.6
2 to 5 years old	192,018	23.8	236,997	25.6	240,925	26.7	222,243	26.7
6 to 9 years old	175,609	21.7	209,292	22.6	210,334	23.3	202,315	24.3
10 to 13 years old	150,507	18.6	177,581	19.2	172,800	19.2	160,107	19.2
14 to 17 years old	116,015	14.4	133,866	14.4	132,566	14.7	125,221	15.0
18 years and over	5,464	0.7	6,799	0.7	6,821	0.8	8,029	1.0
Unknown	61,845	7.7	40,439	4.4	18,924	2.1	9,825	1.2
Race/ethnic group of victim[2]								
Victims, total	793,773	100.0	926,924	100.0	895,831	100.0	822,609	100.0
White	428,506	54.0	497,924	53.7	499,485	55.8	456,163	55.5
Black	198,365	25.0	229,724	24.8	239,798	26.8	222,638	27.1
Asian and Pacific Islander	6,479	0.8	7,775	0.8	7,981	0.9	8,098	1.0
American Indian, Eskimo, and Aleut	10,323	1.3	13,657	1.5	15,098	1.7	14,819	1.8
Other races	11,088	1.4	13,659	1.5	13,678	1.5	15,412	1.9
Hispanic origin	73,590	9.3	85,067	9.2	85,332	9.5	84,754	10.3
Unknown	65,422	8.2	79,118	8.5	34,459	3.8	20,725	2.5

1. More than one type of maltreatment may be substantiated per child. Therefore, totals for this category will add up to be more than 100%. Victim totals and maltreatment types are based on subset of states that reported both the number of child victims and maltreatment incidences by type for that year. 2. Some states were unable to report on the number of Hispanic victims, thus it is probable that nationwide the percentage of Hispanic victims is higher. *Source:* U.S. Department of Health and Human Services, National Center on Child Abuse and Neglect Data System, *Child Maltreatment—1995;* and previous reports. From *Statistical Abstract of the United States 1997.*

Child Poverty and Family Income

Childhood poverty has both immediate and lasting negative effects. Children in low-income families fare more poorly than children in more affluent families in the areas of economic security, health, and education. Children living in families that are poor are more likely than children living in other families to have difficulty in school, to become teen parents, and, as adults, to earn less and be unemployed more. The child poverty rate provides important information about the percentage of U.S. children whose current life circumstances are hard and whose futures are potentially limited as a result of their family's low income.

• In 1996, 20% of American children lived in families with cash incomes below the poverty line.

• The percentage of children in poverty has stayed near or slightly above 20% since 1981.[1]

• Children under age 6 are more often found in families with incomes below the poverty line than children ages 6 to 17. In 1996, 23% of children under age 6 lived in poverty, compared to 18% of older children.

• Children with two married parents are much less likely to be living in poverty than children living only with their mothers. In 1996, 10% of children in two-parent families were living in poverty, compared to 49% in female-householder families.

• This contrast by family structure is especially pronounced among certain racial and ethnic minorities. For example, in 1996, 14% of black children in married-couple families lived in poverty, compared to 58% of black children in female-householder families. Twenty-nine percent of Hispanic children in married-couple families lived in poverty, compared to 67% in female-householder families.

• Most children in poverty are white and non-Hispanic. However, the proportion of black or Hispanic children in poverty is much higher than the proportion for white, non-Hispanic children. In

1996, 10% of white, non-Hispanic children lived in poverty, compared to 40% of black children and 40% of Hispanic children.

• In 1996, 8% of all children lived in families with incomes less than half the poverty level, or $8,018 a year for a family of four, while 31% of children lived in families with incomes less than 150% of the poverty level, or $24,054 a year for a family of four.

The full distribution of the income of children's families is important, not just the percentage in poverty. Knowing that more and more children live in affluent families tells us that a growing proportion of America's children enjoy economic well-being. The growing gap between rich and poor children suggests that poor children may experience more relative deprivation even if the percentage of poor children is holding steady.

• In 1996, children living in families with medium income made up the largest share of children by income group (34%). There were similar percentages of children living with low income and with high income, 23% and 24%, respectively.

• Since 1980, the percentage of children living in families with medium income has fallen from 41% to 34% in 1996, while the percentage of children living in families with high income and the percentage of children in extreme poverty have risen, from 17% to 24% and from 7% to 8%, respectively. The data indicate that there has been an increase in income disparity among children.

1. The child poverty rate for 1981 was 19.5%. *Source:* Federal Interagency Forum on Child and Family Statistics (www.childstats.gov), *America's Children 1998.*

Participation in Selected Government Assistance Programs

Year and selected characteristics	All major assistance programs[1]	Percent of population participating: AFDC or General Assistance	Food stamps	Medicaid	Housing assistance
1992, total	**13.4%**	**4.7%**	**8.2%**	**9.4%**	**4.3%**
Under 18 years old	22.5	10.8	15.9	17.6	6.4
18 to 64 years old	9.5	2.9	5.6	6.0	3.1
65 years old and over	13.0	0.3	3.9	8.6	5.7
White	10.3	3.0	6.0	7.1	2.9
Black	33.0	14.8	22.2	24.2	12.9
Hispanic origin[2]	26.9	10.2	17.7	19.4	7.1
Poverty status:					
Below the poverty level	56.5	26.2	44.9	43.2	17.1
At or above the poverty level	6.4	1.2	2.2	3.9	2.2
Family status:					
In married-couple families	7.5	1.7	4.2	4.8	1.7
With related children under 18 years old	10.0	2.7	6.1	6.5	2.3
In families with female householder, no spouse present	40.7	22.4	29.7	32.5	13.9
With related children under 18 years old	49.0	29.2	37.3	39.4	17.1
Unrelated individuals	13.5	0.8	5.1	7.9	7.2

1. Covers AFDC, General Assistance, SSI, food stamps, Medicaid, and housing assistance. 2. Persons of Hispanic origin may be of any race. NOTE: Data applies to the U.S. *Source:* U.S. Bureau of the Census, *Current Population Reports,* P70–46 and unpublished data. From *Statistical Abstract of the United States 1997.*

Family Reading

	Percentage of 3- to 5-year-olds[1] who were read to daily by a family member: 1993	1995	1996
Overall	53%	58%	57%
Gender			
Male	51	57	56
Female	54	59	57
Race and Hispanic origin[2]			
White, non-Hispanic	59	65	64
Black, non-Hispanic	39	43	44
Hispanic	37	38	39
Poverty status			
Above poverty threshold	56	62	61
At or below poverty threshold	44	48	46
Family type			
Two parents	55	61	61
One or no parent	46%	49%	46%
Mother's education[3]			
Less than high school	37	40	37
High school/GED	48	48	49
Vocational/technical or some college	57	64	62
College graduate	71	76	77
Mother's employment status[3]			
35 hours or more per week	52	55	54
Less than 35 hours per week	56	63	59
Not in labor force	55	60	59

1. Estimates based on children who have yet to enter kindergarten. 2. Persons of Hispanic origin may be of any race. 3. Children without mothers in the home are not included. *Source:* U.S. Department of Education, National Center for Education Statistics.

Sexual Harassment and the Law

In today's amorphous legal environment, sexual offenses can range from firing victims who don't give in to merely telling a dirty joke

By JOHN CLOUD TIME

Just 25 years ago, sexual harassment was considered a radical-fringe byproduct of feminist theory. Today it's embedded in multiple Supreme Court decisions, thousands of corporate policies, and a host of lower-court cases that have spread like kudzu across the legal landscape. The result is a thicket of rulings. Since 1991, juries have returned well over 500 verdicts on sexual harassment—decisions that often contradict one another and send mixed signals about how we should behave anytime we meet a coworker we'd like to see after five.

Because of the twin trends of long hours (10% more than we worked in 1969) and more women working (18 million more today than in 1980, or about 50% of the labor force), more Americans than ever are flirting, dating, and propositioning at work. Actually, only a tiny proportion of office come-ons result in harassment complaints; of those that do, just 9% end up in formal proceedings, whereas 38% of relationships that start on the job survive into the long term. The huge surge in sexual-harassment cases that took place in the early '90s has slowed. Such cases are still being filed at the rate of 15,500 a year—some 60 new cases every working day—compared with 6,900 in 1991, but the number hasn't changed much for three years. A recent survey of human-resources managers found that 7 out of 10 handled at least one sexual-harassment complaint last year, down from 9 out of 10 in 1995.

Meanwhile, employers fearing lawsuits are stopping harassment before it starts. Some, like General Motors and Wal-Mart, have instituted zero-tolerance policies banning just about any speech or conduct with sexual undertones, like sending email with a naughty Web address to a coworker, which not so long ago would have been deemed not just harmless but constitutionally protected. While it's rare for nonthreatening behavior to be ruled harassment, it happens. In 1993 the University of Nebraska forced a grad student to remove from his desk a picture of his bikini-clad wife after two fellow students complained that the photo violated the school's sexual-harassment policy.

Now, the Backlash

The legal principle of harassment hinges on impossibly squishy terms like "unwelcome" and "pervasive," words that a thousand lawyers can define in a thousand ways. As a consequence, some despicable harassers get off easy, just as some men

Sexual Harassment: A TIME/CNN Poll

■ Do you think sexual harassment of women in the workplace is a big problem?

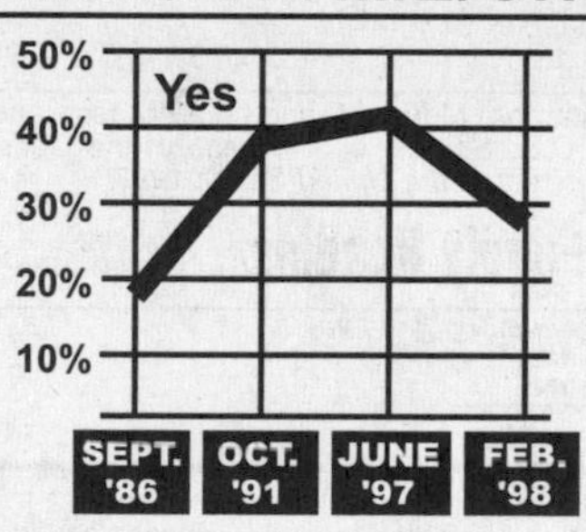

■ Are there circumstances when it is acceptable for a boss and an employee to become sexually involved, or is that always unacceptable?

Acceptable in some circumstances	43%
Always unacceptable	51%

■ Does sexual harassment occur when a man who is a woman's boss or supervisor:

	Yes
Asks the woman to have sex with him?	81%
Insists on telling the woman sexual jokes?	67%
Frequently puts his arm around the woman's shoulders?	53%
Flirts with the woman?	43%

From a telephone poll of 1,023 Americans taken for TIME/CNN on Feb.4-5, 1998, by Yankelovich Partners Inc. Margin of error is ±3.1. "Not sures" omitted (and, increasingly, women) with innocent intentions can have their lives ruined. That's because intent seldom defines harassment; reception and perception do.

The confusion and excessive rulemaking may already be sowing the seeds of backlash. In a recent TIME/CNN poll, just 26% of those surveyed called sexual harassment of women "a big problem," down from 37% in 1991. What's more, 57% of men—and 52% of women—agree that "we have gone too far in making common interactions between employees into cases of sexual harassment."

Two Kinds of Sexual Harassment

What exactly is the law on sexual harassment, and how did it evolve into such a beast? Legally speaking, there are two kinds of sexual harassment. The first is called "quid pro quo" harassment, and it's the easier to grasp. If your boss docks your pay or fires you or otherwise punishes you for rebuffing an advance, he's flat-out guilty. A generation ago, not even blatant quid pro quo harassment was illegal; many judges simply deemed such matters "personal." When they were allowed to bring lawsuits, plaintiffs—nearly all women at the time, and still nearly 90% women today—had no right to jury trials, leaving their fate up to a mostly male stable of judges.

Things began to change, albeit slowly, in the '60s. In 1964 southern members of Congress tacked "sex" onto the list of protections in the pending Civil Rights Act, not because they cared about harassment but because they thought the idea so laughable that it would kill the entire bill. It wasn't until the 1970s that courts started taking the antidiscrimination provisions on sex seriously, and not until 1977 that a federal court of any stature—the U.S. Court of Appeals for the District of Columbia—said quid pro quo harassment violated the act. After the 1991 furor between Anita Hill and Clarence Thomas raised public consciousness, George Bush signed a law granting sexual-harassment plaintiffs the right to jury trials and big-money damages.

In 1986 the Supreme Court, in its first ruling ever on sexual harassment, held that speech or conduct in itself can create a "hostile environment," and that such an environment violates the Civil Rights Act. According to the justices, unwelcome verbal or physical behavior, if "severe or pervasive" enough, is discriminatory even when there is no quid pro quo. Today quid pro quo cases remain hard to win, and most sexual-harassment cases are based on the looser principle of "hostile environment."

Even Lawyers Are Tied in Knots

Given the expansive terminology, just about anything can count as a hostile environment, depending on who's defining the terms. Companies have responded to the legal morass with wildly varying policies. Some ignore the issue, and others, particularly those burned with lawsuits, even ban interoffice dating. Nearly 9 out of 10 companies have procedures for dealing with sexual harassment, according to a recent survey, but many of those procedures are weak—"a paragraph in the company handbook," says Ellen Bravo, co-director of the National Association of Working Women.

The next big legal battle on sexual harassment will probably center on free-speech concerns. UCLA's Eugene Volokh says liberal court rulings have had a "chilling effect" on free speech at work. He says many employers are scared to write anything other than zero-tolerance policies that prohibit any potentially offensive speech. "Something like 'Women don't belong here,' that's sexist, but it should be protected speech," Volokh says. Few defendants have used the First Amendment as a defense. ("Lawyers just don't think about it," Volokh adds.) As sexual-harassment laws strike further and further into what we are allowed to say to our co-workers, look for that to change. Even after the court rules on these matters, there's likely to be confusion about sexual harassment.

The end of the old patriarchal system, in which male bosses behaved as they pleased with female subordinates, has necessarily complicated gender relations in American offices. To sort out who is misbehaving now, the law must rely on subjective notions of power and courtship, sex and sensitivity. The best company policy would allow co-workers their freedom and privacy but punish truly unwanted, harmful behavior. But no one has figured out exactly what that policy should be—least of all the lawyers and judges who keep adding new loops and threads to the complex web of sexual-harassment law. □

Gender of Sexual Partners in the United States

(Sexually Active Only)

	Same Gender		Both Genders		Opposite Genders	
	Men	Women	Men	Women	Men	Women
1988	2.3%	0.2%	0.3%	0.0%	97.4%	99.8%
1989	1.4	1.2	0.3	0.4	98.3	98.4
1990	1.1	0.5	0.9	0.0	98.0	99.5
1991	2.0	0.3	0.7	0.1	97.3	99.6
1993	1.8	1.8	0.3	0.4	97.9	97.8
1994	2.1	2.1	0.5	0.4	97.5	97.5
1996	3.5	2.1	0.6	0.9	96.0	97.0

Source: General Social Survey (GSS), National Opinion Research Center, University of Chicago, 1996.

My Daddy Takes Care of Me! Fathers as Care Providers

By LYNNE M. CASPER, U.S. Census Bureau

Over the past five years, there has been increasing interest in the roles fathers play in shaping their children's lives. It is undisputed among researchers that fathers' involvement is extremely important for children's proper social and emotional development. Furthermore, fathers interact differently with their children than do mothers, and it is fathers' unique interaction that is said to help specifically children's emotional development.

One aspect of fathers' involvement is their care for their children during mothers' working hours. In 1993, about one in four fathers took care of their preschoolers during the time mothers were working. In fact, fathers provided care for their children during more of the mother's working hours than did any other single care provider.

The increase in care by fathers between 1988 and 1991 may have been a response to the economic recession that occurred during the same period (the recession began in July 1990 and reached its lowest point in March 1991). Increases in the proportions of people who were not employed and working at part-time jobs may have meant that more fathers were available to serve as childcare providers. The increase in care by fathers may have also reflected the desire of parents to cut down on childcare costs by switching to more parental supervision of their children whenever possible. That the decline in care by fathers between 1991 and 1993 occurred at the same time as the economy was expanding also supports this notion.

Other findings about married fathers with preschoolers whose mothers were employed in 1993 include:

• Fathers who don't work and those whose jobs are at night or part-time are more likely to care for their preschoolers.

A married father's employment status makes a big difference in whether or not he provides care for his preschool-age children—those who are not employed are much more likely to be providing care. For example, in 1993, 58% of fathers who were not employed provided care for their preschoolers during their wives' working hours compared with only 23% of fathers who were employed. Non-employed fathers—those who were either unemployed or not in the labor force—were also much more likely to be primary care providers than employed fathers (50% compared with 16%).

• Care by fathers is most common in poor families.

Childcare costs constitute an especially large proportion of a poor family's budget, so it comes as no surprise that fathers in poor families are more likely to take care of their children than fathers in nonpoor families—43% compared with 24% in 1993, for example.

• Fathers in service occupations are more likely than fathers in other occupations to provide care for their preschoolers while their mothers are at work.

Fathers who work in service occupations such as maintenance, police, fire fighting, and security positions are about twice as likely as fathers in any other occupation to be taking care of the preschoolers while the mothers are working. For example, in 1993, 42% of fathers in service occupations cared for their preschool-age children compared with about 20% of fathers who were in managerial/professional or technical/sales occupations. Both patterns may be due to the fact that fathers in service occupations are more likely to work nontraditional schedules than other fathers and therefore may be more likely to be available for care.

• Veteran status makes a difference in whether or not a father cares for his preschoolers.

Fathers who had served in the armed forces were more likely to care for their children and to be primary care providers than fathers who did not serve.

Fathers Providing Care for Children While Mothers Are Working: 1998–1993

(Numbers in thousands)

Fathers Providing Care	1993 Number	1993 Percent	1991 Number	1991 Percent	1988 Number	1988 Percent
Caring for Children 0–14						
Total number of fathers[1]	14,849	100.0%	14,620	100.0%	14,278	100.0%
Providing some care	2,914	19.6	3,331	22.8	2,698	18.9
Primary provider of care	1,915	12.9	2,032	13.9	1,688	11.8
Caring for Children Under 5						
Total number of fathers	6,274	100.0	6,274	100.0	6,536	100.0
Providing some care	1,554	24.8	1,901	30.3	1,523	23.3
Primary provider of care	1,164	18.5	1,407	22.4	1,107	16.9
Caring for Children 5–14						
Total number of fathers	11,412	100.0	11,256	100.0	10,720	100.0
Providing some care	1,780	15.6	1,975	17.5	1,660	15.5
Primary provider of care	1,034	9.1	1,015	9.0	941	8.8

NOTE: Limited to married fathers whose wives are employed. 1. The number of fathers of children under 5 combined with the number of fathers of children ages 5–14 does not sum to the total number of fathers of children ages 0–14 because some fathers have children in both age groups. *Source:* Current Population Reports, P70–59, Sept. 1997.

In 1993, for example, 30% of fathers who were veterans took care of the children while their mothers were working compared with only 24% of fathers who were not veterans. Fathers who are nonveterans are more likely to be in managerial or professional occupations and to have higher family incomes; fathers with these characteristics are less likely to be caring for their preschoolers.

• **Care by fathers is most common in the Northeast and least common in the South.**

Care by fathers is more common in some areas of the country than in others. In 1993, fathers in the Northeast were the most likely to be taking care of their children and to be providing primary care, while those in the South were the least likely to be doing so. About 33% of fathers in the Northeast provided care for their preschoolers during the mothers' working hours, compared with 27% of fathers in the Midwest and West and only 18% in the South. Care by fathers was especially prevalent in New England, where 4 out of 10 fathers cared for their children in 1993.

Geographical differences in the frequency of fathers caring for their children may relate to regional variations in employment rates, and in costs of childcare and amounts of family income available to purchase alternative childcare services. Childcare costs are indeed more expensive in the Northeast than in either the Midwest or the South. And in 1993, fathers were more likely to be unemployed in the Northeast than in the Midwest or the South. It could also be that childcare facilities may be farther away in some areas than in others; this might cause more people to choose neighbors and relatives (including fathers) over childcare facilities that may be less accessible.

• **Care by fathers is the least common in the suburbs.**

In 1993, fathers in the suburbs were the least likely to care for their preschoolers when compared with fathers residing in the central cities and those in nonmetropolitan areas—22% of suburban fathers compared with 27% of the other two groups. One reason for this pattern is that fathers living in suburban areas are more likely to have higher incomes and be better able to purchase alternative care services.□

Source: Current Population Reports, P70-59, Sept. 1997.

The Wage Gap

The wage gap is a statistical indicator often used as an index of the status of women's earnings relative to men's. It is also used to compare the earnings of other races and ethnicities to those of white males, a group generally not subject to race- or sex-based discrimination. The wage gap is expressed as a percentage (e.g., in 1996, women earned 74% as much as men) and is calculated by dividing the median annual earnings for women by median annual earnings for men. Since 1963, when the Equal Pay Act was signed, the closing of the wage gap between men and women has been at a rate of less than half a penny a year.

1996 Median Annual Earnings by Race and Sex

Race/gender	Earnings	Wage ratio
White Men	$32,966	100.0%
White Women	$24,160	73.3
Black Men	$26,404	80.0
Black Women	$21,473	65.1
Hispanic Men	$21,056	63.9
Hispanic Women	$18,655	56.6

1996 Median Annual Earnings Year-Round, Full-Time Workers

Men	$32,144
Women	$23,710
Wage gap:	73.8%

Women's Earnings as a Percent of Men's, 1979–1997

Year	Hourly	Weekly	Annual
1979	64.1%	62.5%	59.7%
1980	64.8	64.4	60.2
1981	65.1	64.6	59.2
1982	67.3	65.4	61.7
1983	69.4	66.7	63.6
1984	69.8	67.8	63.7
1985	70.0	68.2	64.6
1986	70.2	69.2	64.3
1987	72.1	70.0	65.2
1988	73.8	70.2	66.0
1989	75.4%	70.1%	68.7%
1990	77.9	71.9	71.6
1991	78.6	74.2	69.9
1992	80.3	75.8	70.8
1993	80.4	77.1	71.5
1994	80.6	76.4	72.0
1995	80.8	75.5	71.4
1996	81.2	75.0	73.8
1997	80.8	74.4	—

Source: U.S. Women's Bureau.

What Do Kids Really Think About Race?

A TIME/CNN poll shows that teenagers, black and white, have moved beyond their parents' views of the color barrier

By CHRISTOPHER JOHN FARLEY TIME

What do most of today's children really think about the racial chasm that has divided this country since its inception? The days of Bull Connor, police dogs, and fire hoses are long gone, and many would find it comforting to believe that skin color is no longer an issue for kids. Has the newest generation of Americans finally arrived at that melanin-friendly Promised Land? No. But a TIME/CNN poll of 1,282 adults and 601 teens (ages 12 to 17) has found a startling number of youngsters, black and white, who seem to have moved beyond their parents' views of race. These kids say race is less important to them, both on a personal level and as a social divide, than it is for adults. It must be noted that more than half of both white kids and black still consider racism "a big problem" in America—however, more than a third classify it as "a small problem." Asked about the impact of racism in their own lives, a startling 89% of black teens call it "a small problem" or "not a problem at all." In fact, white adults and white teens are more convinced than black teens that racism in America remains a dominant issue.

Furthermore, black teens are more reluctant than others to blame racism for problems. Indeed, nearly twice as many black kids as white believe "failure to take advantage of available opportunities" is more of a problem for blacks than discrimination. That's especially extraordinary given the fact that 40% of the black teens surveyed believe SATS are loaded against them, and that blacks have to be better qualified than whites to get a job. These responses seem to indicate that black teens believe color barriers exist, but, despite that, they retain an admirably dogged belief in self-determination.

Optimism or Innocence?

Is this surprising portrait a sign of hope? Or is it just an example of youthful naiveté? Probably both. "One word explains it—experience," speculates sociologist Joe R. Feagin. "You have to be out looking for jobs and housing to know how much discrimination is out there. People doing that are usually over 19." Sure enough, only a quarter of black teens surveyed said they had been victims of discrimination, whereas half of black adults say they have. For all that, these kids remain astonishingly optimistic: 95% of the black youngsters think they're going on to college, as do 93% of the whites.

But is that gullibility? Or gutsiness? Today's teens have respect for the past, faith in the future—and a distaste for scapegoating that outstrips that of their parents. One of the survey's more notable findings: even though neither black teens nor white tend to blame racism as a cause of problems facing blacks, they nonetheless support gender- and race-based scholarships in greater numbers than adults.

Two Different Worlds

People don't always level with pollsters; they're notorious in fact for giving answers they believe to be socially acceptable at the expense of revealing their true feelings. But teens are less likely to do that than adults. Sociologist Howard Pinderhughes, author of the new book *Race in the Hood: Conflict and Violence Among Urban Youth,* says, "Teenagers are a mirror of our souls. They speak plainly about things that adults would like to hide. Political correctness isn't an issue to them. You're more likely to get what they think unfiltered."

Extensive interviews with children, parents, educators, researchers, and law-enforcement officials make clear that the new optimism takes place against a backdrop of a number of new challenges, such as the growing presence of hate groups on the Internet, and old ones, such as interracial dating and ethnic turf wars.

A disinclination to blame problems on racism does not mean a reduced sense of racial identity. Psychologist Beverly Tatum, author of the recently published *Why Are All the Black Kids Sitting Together in the Cafeteria?,* says she often asks her psychology students to complete this sentence: "I am _____. " White students tend to answer with personality traits: "I am friendly," "I am shy," etc. Students of color tend to fill in the blank with their ethnicity: "I am black" or "I am Puerto Rican." The foundation for racial identity, Tatum argues, is constructed in adolescence by peer pressure, societal influences, and self-reflection; it is a time when children make choices about who they are.

The attitudes expressed by respondents to the TIME/CNN poll are all the more remarkable given that outside of school, black teens and white teens most often live in separate neighborhoods and sometimes, it seems, on separate planets. Danny, 17, a white Chicago youngster interviewed by TIME professed to having "more black friends than I do white friends" but also admitted that "we just talk in school" and that he never visits the homes of his black buddies, who tend to live in crime-plagued housing projects.

Danny's situation is not uncommon. While few teens view their neighborhoods as dangerous, 40% of black teens reported that they knew someone their age who had been murdered, in contrast to only 15% of white teens. Black teens also feel they don't get a fair shake from the police: one-third of them feel that they are at risk of being treated unfairly by cops, while only one out of five white teens shares that fear. Real improvement in communication, says historian John Hope Franklin, head of President Clinton's task force on race, won't come until "you have improvement in the home conditions of kids of all kinds."

But growing up in a comparatively deprived environment doesn't necessarily lead to bad choices. In a direct counter to long-held stereotypes, the poll found that it is white kids, not black, who are most likely to have experimented with drugs and alcohol—by roughly 2 to 1.

America's schools are becoming increasingly diverse. But where kids live can lead to a separation that even a diverse school cannot bridge. For example, at Teaneck High School, a racially diverse school in New Jersey, the doors of opportunity are literal. There are three main entrances at the school, and the kids refer to them as "the black door," "the Latino door," and "the white door." Originally, the nicknames came from the fact that those were the doors the various groups entered when the buses dropped them off; even though Teaneck has become more integrated, the terms have stuck, and each group continues to hang out by its respective door.

Kris DeBlasio, 20, a graduate of Teaneck High School who is white and works as a lifeguard at the school pool, says when he was a student, he entered through the "black door" and a black student grabbed him by the throat until another black classmate said DeBlasio was "cool" and should be left alone. Still, DeBlasio, who says his best friend is black, believes there has been progress. "When my father was growing up in Brooklyn, I don't think he had a single black friend," he says. "[Racism] still exists, but it isn't as blatant as it used to be."

Gap Between Adults and Kids

The teenagers polled by TIME/CNN retain a bracing sense of optimism; three-fourths of the white youngsters believe race relations will get better, as do more than half the black teens (adults of both races were more skeptical). What we're seeing here is a hidden aspect of the black survival process, says Michael Eric Dyson, author of *Race Rules: Navigating the Color Line* and a visiting professor at Columbia University's Institute for Research in African-American Studies. "You imagine a reality better than the one in which you presently live. I wouldn't call it optimism; it goes too deep. It's hope. Hope goes against everything you can see."

That hope sometimes flies in the face of the pessimism and racial intolerance teenagers hear expressed by their elders. Thecla Hoeberechts, 13, who is of Dutch and Greek ancestry, often plays in Ridgefield Park, N.J., with friends of different races. Thecla says

Teens and Adults on Race: A Time/CNN Poll

■ Which of the following is more of a problem for blacks today?

	TEENS	ADULTS
Failure to take advantage of available opportunities		
Whites	31%	52%
Blacks	58%	51%
Discrimination by whites		
Whites	47%	22%
Blacks	26%	26%

■ Is racism a big problem or a small problem?

	TEENS	ADULTS
Big problem		
Whites	58%	64%
Blacks	62%	78%
Small problem		
Whites	34%	27%
Blacks	34%	17%

■ Are the problems that most blacks face today caused primarily by whites, or don't you think this is the case?

	TEENS	ADULTS
Yes		
Whites	32%	14%
Blacks	18%	29%
Not the case		
Whites	55%	72%
Blacks	74%	61%

■ Have you ever been a victim of discrimination because you are black?

	BLACK TEENS	BLACK ADULTS
Yes	23%	53%
No	77%	45%

■ Have you ever been a victim of discrimination because you are white?

	WHITE TEENS	WHITE ADULTS
Yes	16%	20%
No	83%	79%

■ Will race relations in this country ever get better?

	TEENS	ADULTS
Yes		
Whites	76%	60%
Blacks	55%	43%

■ Do you favor or oppose colleges reserving a certain number of scholarships exclusively for minorities and women?

	TEENS	ADULTS
Favor		
Whites	55%	46%
Blacks	64%	60%
Oppose		
Whites	33%	47%
Blacks	26%	34%

■ Do standardized tests, such as the SATs, give an unbiased measure of all applicants' qualifications, or are they biased against minority applicants?

	TEENS	ADULTS
Unbiased		
Whites	59%	53%
Blacks	45%	28%
Biased		
Whites	17%	25%
Blacks	40%	53%

	WHITE TEENS	BLACK TEENS
■ Are you likely to go to college?	Yes: 93%	Yes: 95%
■ Have you used illegal drugs?	Yes: 13%	Yes: 6%
■ Have you drunk alcohol?	Yes: 32%	Yes: 19%
■ Have you had sex?	Yes: 15%	Yes: 28%

From a telephone poll of 816 white adults, 374 black adults, 301 white teens and 300 black teens taken for TIME/CNN from Sept. 23 to Oct. 2, 1997, by Yankelovich Partners Inc. Margins of error are ±3.4%, 5.1%, 5.6% and 5.6%, respectively.

an older friend recently asked her why she hangs out with black people all the time: "She said, 'Look how loud and rude they are.' " Children of color face similar pressures. Cynthia Bou, 13, a Dominican-American friend of Thecla's, says an older cousin asked her why some of her friends are white. "White people are whack," she warned Cynthia. "You're going to change when they treat you wrong."

Parents too can serve as regressive influences, though perhaps less so than in the past. One out of eight white teens and one out of nine black youngsters say they've heard their parents say something negative about another race. In an interview, one white father in Chicago's Bridgeport neighborhood went on at length about his capacity for racial tolerance (he helps send holiday turkeys to poor black families), but when he was asked about the subject of interracial dating, he declared, "Listen, if Jesus himself stepped down off the cross asking to date my daughter, and he was black? I'd tell the guy to go to hell."

Some observers see trouble ahead because of the continued deprivation of so many black families in wrecked city neighborhoods. (Less than half the black teens polled live with a father or stepfather.) "This generation of kids we're raising now in these urban centers has no conscience, no values," says Rev. B. Herbert Martin, minister of Chicago's People's Church. "They are growing up in isolation."

That in itself can breed bigotry. One black Newark, N.J., teen interviewed by TIME launched into an ugly tirade about Jews—but many more expressed a sense of catharsis simply to be talking about the racial difficulties they face. On the other hand, white teens interviewed seemed to have more trouble discussing racial issues, and were often unable to even find the words to describe their feelings about ethnicity. Part of the problem, according to psychologist Tatum, is that some parents, particularly white ones, silence their children when racial issues are raised. This is done, sometimes, as part of a well-meaning effort to teach children that such distinctions don't matter. But as a result of such silencing, children are left without answers to their questions and without the social skills to deal with racial issues. □

Population of the United States by Race and Hispanic Origin

(as of May 1998)

	Total population	% of population
All races	269,612,000	100.0%
White	222,654,000	82.6
Black	34,298,000	12.7
American Indian, Eskimo, and Aleut	2,351,000	0.9
Asian and Pacific Islander	10,309,000	3.8%
Hispanic origin (of any race)	30,217,000	11.2

NOTE: Percentages add up to more than 100% because Hispanics may be of any race and are therefore counted under more than one category. *Source:* U.S. Bureau of the Census; Web: www.census.gov.

Race of U.S. Couples, 1990

	Total	White	Black	American Indian	Asian	Other race
Same-race couples	97.1%	97.0%	92.8%	26.4%	70.0%	74.7%
Interracial couples:						
Specified group and white race group	2.7	NA	5.8	70.6	28.7	23.2
Specified race group and other race groups [1]	0.2	3.0	1.5	3.1	1.3	2.1

1. Includes all other race groups except whites and the specified group, classified by the race of the male partner. *Source: 1990 Census of Population and Housing,* Public Use Microdata Samples.

Preference for Racial or Ethnic Terminology

Preferred term[1]	Percent
Hispanic	
Hispanic	57.88%
Of Spanish origin	12.34
Latino	11.74
Some other term	7.85
No preference	10.18
White	
White	61.66%
Caucasian	16.53
European American	2.35
Some other term	1.97
Anglo	.96
No preference	16.53

Preferred term[1]	Percent
Black	
Black	44.15%
African American	28.07
Afro-American	12.12
Negro	3.28
Some other term	2.19
Colored	1.09
No preference	9.11
American Indian	
American Indian	49.76%
Native American	37.35
Some other term	3.66
Alaska Native	3.51
No preference	5.72

1. Preferred term by group of people the term is meant to represent. *Source:* U.S. Census Bureau Survey, May 1995.

American Indian Tribes with Populations Greater than 10,000

(1990 U.S. Census figures)

American Indian tribe	Number	Percent distribution	American Indian tribe	Number	Percent distribution
American Indian population, total[1]	**1,878,285**	**100.0%**	Canadian and Latin American tribes	22,379	1.2%
Cherokee	308,132	16.4	Chickasaw	20,631	1.1
Navajo	219,198	11.7	Potawatomi	16,763	0.9
Chippewa	103,826	5.5	Tohono O'Odham	16,041	0.9
Sioux	103,255	5.5	Pima	14,431	0.8
Choctaw	82,299	4.4	Tlingit	13,925	0.7
Pueblo	52,939	2.8	Seminole	13,797	0.7
Apache	50,051	2.7	Alaskan Athabaskans	13,738	0.7
Iroquois	49,038	2.6	Cheyenne	11,456	0.6
Lumbee	48,444	2.6	Comanche	11,322	0.6
Creek	43,550	2.3	Paiute	11,142	0.6
Blackfoot	32,234	1.7	Puget Sound Salish	10,246	0.5

1. Includes other American Indian tribes not shown separately. *Source:* U.S. Bureau of the Census, *1990 Census of Population, General Population Characteristics, American Indian and Alaska Native Areas* (CP-1-1A); and press releases CB91-232 and CB92-244.

Social and Economic Characteristics of the American Indian Population

(1990 U.S. Census figures)

Characteristic	American Indian, total[1]	Cherokee	Navajo	Sioux	Chippewa	Choctaw	Pueblo	Apache	Iroquois	Lumbee
Total persons	**1,937,391**	**369,035**	**225,298**	**107,321**	**105,988**	**86,231**	**55,330**	**53,330**	**52,557**	**50,888**
Percent under 5 years old	9.7	6.3	13.6	12.3	10.3	8.2	10.3	10.2	8.1	8.3
Percent 18 years old and over	65.8	73.3	57.7	60.0	64.0	68.8	64.2	64.7	71.1	66.2
Percent 65 years old and over	5.9	7.2	4.6	4.4	4.7	8.0	5.8	3.4	6.7	5.6
Educational attainment										
Persons 25 years old and over	1,040,955	229,231	100,594	51,014	54,804	49,128	28,597	27,717	30.882	27,343
Percent high-school graduates or higher	65.6	68.2	51.0	69.7	69.7	70.3	71.5	63.8	71.9	51.6
Percent bachelor's degree or higher	9.4	11.1	4.5	8.9	8.2	13.3	7.3	6.9	11.3	9.4
Family type										
Total families	449,281	98,610	44,845	22,669	25,077	21,856	11,825	12,314	12,988	12,650
Percent distribution:										
Married couple	65.8	73.1	61.1	54.2	58.4	75.2	61.2	66.9	67.5	68.5
Female householder, no spouse present	26.2	20.8	28.6	36.0	33.1	20.0	29.2	24.7	25.5	23.9
Male householder, no spouse present	8.0	6.1	10.3	9.8	8.5	4.8	9.6	8.4	7.0	7.6
Income in 1989										
Median family (dol.)	$21,619	$24,907	$13,940	$16,525	$20,249	$24,467	$19,845	$19,690	$27,025	$23,934
Median household (dol.)	$19,900	$21,922	$12,817	$15,611	$18,801	$21,640	$19,097	$18,484	$23,460	$21,708
Per capita (dol.)	$8,284	$10,469	$4,788	$6,508	$7,777	$9,463	$6,679	$7,271	$10,568	$8,625
Families below poverty level	122,237	19,100	21,204	8,939	7,814	4,347	3,691	3,913	2,249	2,554
Percent below poverty level	27.2	19.4	47.3	39.4	31.2	19.9	31.2	31.8	17.3	20.2
Persons below poverty level	585,273	79,271	107,526	45,658	35,231	19,453	17,981	19,246	10,253	10,966
Percent below poverty level	31.2	22.0	48.8	44.4	34.3	23.0	33.2	37.5	20.1	22.1

1. Includes other American Indian tribes not shown separately. *Source:* U.S. Bureau of the Census, *1990 Census of Population, Characteristics of American Indians by Tribe and Language,* 1990 CP-3-7.

Persons Speaking a Language Other than English at Home

Language	Persons five years old and over who speak language	Language	Persons five years old and over who speak language
Speak only English	198,601,000	Hindi (Urdu)	331,000
Spanish	17,339,000	Russian	242,000
French	1,702,000	Yiddish	213,000
German	1,547,000	Thai (Laotian)	206,000
Italian	1,309,000	Persian	202,000
Chinese	1,249,000	French Creole	188,000
Tagalog	843,000	Armenian	150,000
Polish	723,000	Navajo	149,000
Korean	626,000	Hungarian	148,000
Vietnamese	507,000	Hebrew	144,000
Portuguese	430,000	Dutch	143,000
Japanese	428,000	Mon-Khmer (Cambodian)	127,000
Greek	388,000	Gujarathi	102,000
Arabic	355,000		

Source: U.S. Bureau of the Census, 1990 Census of Population and Housing Data Paper Listing (CPH-L-133).

Reversal of the American Dream: Hispanic Population Is Now the Poorest

Census Bureau data indicate that Hispanics in the United States are growing poorer. Between 1989 and 1998, annual income for Hispanics dropped 14%, from approximately $26,000 to less than $22,900. Furthermore, Hispanics now make up almost 24% of the poor in this country, a figure that has grown 8% since 1985. Hispanics now exceed the poverty rate of blacks, the racial and ethnic group that has traditionally been the poorest.

In presenting these statistics, the Census Bureau warns of the problems inherent in generalizing about Hispanic households. The term *Hispanic* is amorphously broad, encompassing people from 24 countries that are in themselves diverse—racially Hispanics can be either black or white. An umbrella term used by statisticians out of practical necessity, *Hispanic* applies to groups as diverse as the generally affluent Cuban Americans of Miami and the Puerto Ricans of New York, the country's poorest ethnic group.

Despite the vagueness and inclusivity of the term, it has not skewed the disheartening statistical outcome—across the board, Hispanics are experiencing a downward economic slide. Even the increasing number of illegal Hispanic immigrants in the country, who tend to have little education, lack English-language skills, and hold service-sector jobs, have not distorted these results. American-born Hispanics are experiencing an equal decline in their standard of living.

A number of researchers believe lack of education is responsible for the downward trend. Hispanics have the highest high school dropout rate in the nation: according to the 1990 Census, only 78% finish high school, compared with 91% of whites and 84% of blacks. A majority of Hispanics receive less schooling than their parents did. In 1994, only 9% of Hispanics over age 24 had college degrees, compared with 24% of non-Hispanics.

Ancestry of U.S. Population by Rank, 1990 Census

(Groups with populations exceeding one million)

1990 Rank	Ancestry group	Number	Percent	1990 Rank	Ancestry group	Number	Percent
	Total population	**248,709,873**	**100.0%**	17	French Canadian	2,167,127	0.9%
1	German	57,947,873	23.2	18	Welsh	2,033,893	0.8
2	Irish	38,735,539	15.6	19	Spanish	2,024,004	0.8
3	English	32,651,788	13.1	20	Puerto Rican	1,955,323	0.8
4	African American	23,777,098	9.6	21	Slovak	1,882,897	0.8
5	Italian	14,664,550	5.9	22	White	1,799,711	0.7
6	American	12,395,999	5.0	23	Danish	1,634,669	0.7
7	Mexican	11,586,983	4.7	24	Hungarian	1,582,302	0.6
8	French	10,320,935	4.1	25	Chinese	1,505,245	0.6
9	Polish	9,366,106	3.8	26	Filipino	1,450,512	0.6
10	American Indian	8,708,220	3.5	27	Czech	1,296,411	0.5
11	Dutch	6,227,089	2.5	28	Portuguese	1,153,351	0.5
12	Scotch-Irish	5,617,773	2.3	29	British	1,119,154	0.4
13	Scottish	5,393,581	2.2	30	Hispanic	1,113,259	0.4
14	Swedish	4,680,863	1.9	31	Greek	1,110,373	0.4
15	Norwegian	3,869,395	1.6	32	Swiss	1,045,495	0.4
16	Russian	2,952,987	1.2	33	Japanese	1,004,645	0.4

Note: Data are based on a sample and subject to sampling variability. Since persons who reported multiple ancestries were included in more than one group, the sum of the persons reporting the ancestry is greater than the total; for example, a person reporting "English-French" was tabulated in both the "English" and "French" categories. Ancestry groups with fewer than 2,000 persons were not included in this report. *Source:* U.S. Bureau of the Census, 1993.

Ethnic Concentrations in the United States

According to the 1990 U.S. Census, ancestry groups show striking differences in where they choose to settle in the United States. These differences often reflect initial settlement patterns, especially for the newer immigrant groups. Of the largest European ancestries, French, Scottish, and Welsh are distributed fairly evenly throughout the country. Other large European groups are more concentrated. For example, more than half of the nation's Italians live in the Northeast, and over half of the Norwegians and Czechs are clustered in the Midwest. About 47% of the Scotch-Irish are concentrated in the South, while 45% of the Danish live in the West.

The regional concentration of persons of Hispanic ancestry depended on their specific country of origin. For instance, the Northeast contained 86% of the country's Dominicans, 66% of Puerto Ricans, and 63% of Ecuadorians. The South was home to 69% of Cubans and 51% of Nicaraguans. About 62% of Salvadorans and Guatemalans and 57% of Mexicans lived in the West.

Persons of West Indian ancestry are concentrated in the Northeast: 59% of the nation's Jamaicans and 55% of Haitians live there.

Among the larger Southwest Asian ancestry groups, over half of the Armenians and Iranians reside in the West, and 43% of the Syrians live in the Northeast.

People of Asian and Pacific Islander ancestry are found largely in the West. The West is home to 87% of the country's Hawaiians, 72% of Japanese, 59% of Cambodians, and 54% of Chinese and Vietnamese.

California—the perennial destination of many migrants—has the largest number of persons of German, Irish, English, African American, Mexican, French, American Indian, Dutch, Scotch-Irish, Scottish, and Swedish ancestry of any state, according to the 1990 Census. New York—the traditional port of entry for large numbers of immigrants—has more Italians and Polish than any other state, and Minnesota ranks first for Norwegians.

About 5% of respondents to the 1990 Census reported their ancestry as "American." Texas has the largest number of persons who considered this to be their ethnic identity.

Population, by Selected Ancestry Group and Region: 1990

Ancestry group	Total	Percent distribution by region			
		North-east	Mid-west	South	West
Europe:					
Austrian	865,000	38%	21%	19%	22%
British	1,119,000	17	18	39	26
Croatian	544,000	21	43	20	16
Czech	1,296,000	10	52	22	16
Danish	1,635,000	9	34	12	45
Dutch	6,227,000	16	34	29	21
English	32,652,000	18	22	35	25
European	467,000	14	17	31	39
Finnish	659,000	14	47	11	27
French	10,321,000	26	26	29	20
German	57,947,000	17	39	25	19
Greek	1,110,000	37	23	21	19
Hungarian	1,582,000	36	32	17	16
Irish	38,736,000	24	25	33	17
Italian	14,665,000	51	17	17	15
Lithuanian	812,000	43	28	16	13
Norwegian	3,869,000	6	52	10	33
Polish	9,366,000	37	37	15	11
Portuguese	1,153,000	49	3	8	41
Russian	2,953,000	44	16	18	22
Scandinavian	679,000	8	33	15	45
Scotch-Irish	5,618,000	14	19	47	20
Scottish	5,394,000	20	21	33	26
Slovak	1,883,000	40	34	14	11
Swedish	4,681,000	14	40	14	32
Swiss	1,045,000	16	36	17	30
Ukrainian	741,000	51	22	14	13
Welsh	2,034,000	22%	24%	27%	27%
Yugoslavian	258,000	23	28	12	37
Central and South America and Spain:					
Cuban	860,000	18	3	69	9
Dominican	506,000	86	1	10	2
Hispanic	1,113,000	13	6	31	50
Mexican	11,587,000	1	9	33	57
Puerto Rican	1,955,000	66	11	15	8
Salvadoran	499,000	13	2	23	62
Spanish	2,024,000	16	8	30	45
West Indies:					
Jamaican	435,000	59	5	31	6
Asia:					
Asian Indian	570,000	32	19	26	24
Chinese	1,505,000	25	8	12	55
Filipino	1,451,000	10	9	13	68
Japanese	1,005,000	9	8	11	72
Korean	837,000	22	14	20	44
Vietnamese	536,000	9	8	28	54
North America:					
Acadian/Cajun	668,000	1	2	91	5
African American	23,777,000	15	21	54	10
American Indian	8,708,000	9	22	47	23
American	12,396,000	10	18	61	11
Canadian	550,000	34	18	21	28
French Canadian	2,167,000	45	20	20	15
United States	644,000	16	18	53	13
White	1,800,000	7	13	53	28

Source: U.S. Bureau of the Census, 1990. (As of April 1. Covers persons who reported single and multiple ancestry groups. Persons who reported multiple ancestry groups may be included in more than one category. Major classifications of ancestry groups do not represent strict geographic or cultural definitions.)

For more information on race and ethnicity, *see* U.S. Statistics.

Life-Saving Skills Summary

Skill	Adult (9 years and older)	Child (1 to 8 years)	Infant (birth to 1 year)
Rescue breathing (used when victim is not breathing)	Give 1 slow breath about every 5 seconds; about 1½ seconds per breath; 1 minute = about 10 to 12 breaths	Give 1 slow breath about every 3 seconds; about 1½ seconds per breath; 1 minute = about 20 breaths	Give 1 slow breath about every 3 seconds; about 1½ seconds per breath; 1 minute = about 20 breaths
CPR (used if victim is not breathing *and* does not have a heartbeat)	Depth of compression is about 2 inches; compressions are performed with both hands; complete 15 compressions in about 10 seconds; do cycles of 15 compressions and 2 breaths	Depth of compression is about 1½ inches; compressions are performed with 1 hand; complete 5 compressions in about 3 seconds; do cycles of 5 compressions and 1 breath	Depth of compression is about 1 inch; compressions are performed with 2 fingers; complete 5 compressions in about 3 seconds; do cycles of 5 compressions and 1 breath
Choking (conscious)	Determine if person is choking; stand behind person and deliver abdominal thrusts; repeat until object is expelled or victim loses consciousness	Determine if child is choking; stand or kneel behind child and deliver abdominal thrusts; repeat until object is expelled or child loses consciousness	Determine if infant is choking; give 5 back blows; give 5 chest thrusts; repeat until object is expelled or infant loses consciousness
Choking (unconscious)	Give 2 slow breaths; retilt head and give 2 slow breaths; give up to 5 abdominal thrusts; do finger sweep; give 2 slow breaths; repeat abdominal thrusts, finger sweep, and 2 slow breaths	Give 2 slow breaths; retilt head and give 2 slow breaths; give up to 5 abdominal thrusts; check for object in throat; do finger sweep if object is visible; give 2 slow breaths; repeat abdominal thrusts, foreign-body check/finger sweep, and 2 slow breaths	Give 2 slow breaths; retilt head and give 2 slow breaths; give 5 back blows; give 5 chest thrusts; check for object in throat; do finger sweep if object is visible; repeat back blows, chest thrusts, foreign-body check/finger sweep, and 2 slow breaths

Rescue Breathing

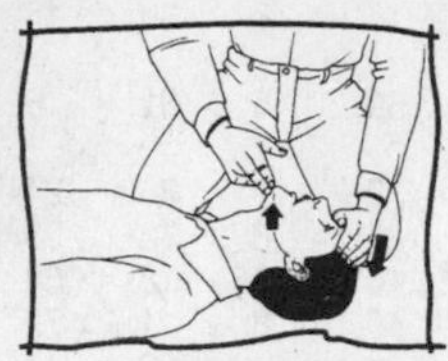

1. With head tilted back, pinch nose shut.

2. ADULT: Give 1 slow breath about every 5 seconds.

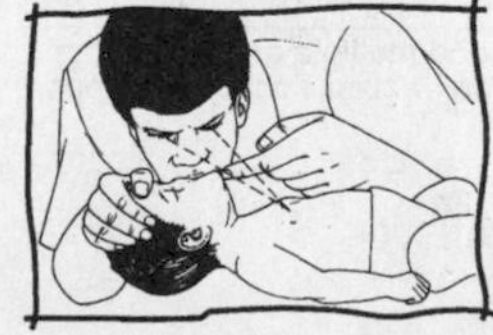

CHILD/INFANT: Give 1 slow breath about every 3 seconds.

CPR (Adult)

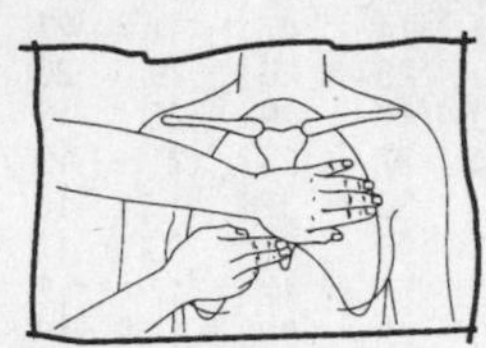

1. Find hand position.

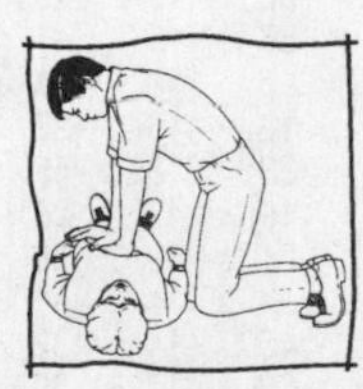

2. Position shoulders over hands. Compress chest 15 times.

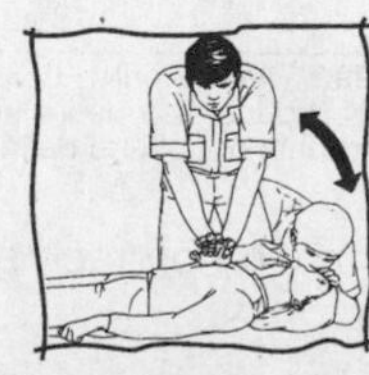

3. Give 2 slow breaths. Recheck pulse and breathing. If no pulse, continue sets of 15 compressions and 2 breaths.

Choking

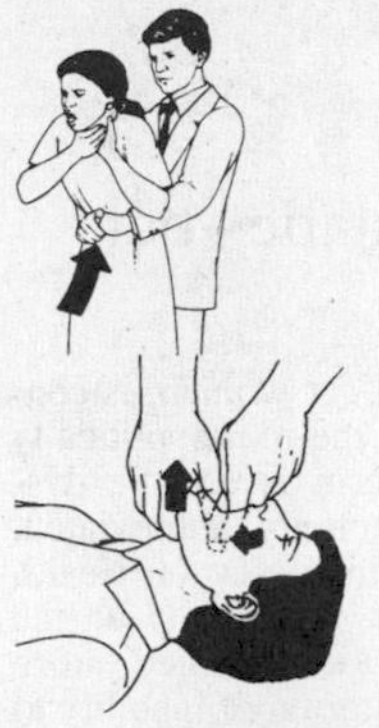

If conscious but choking, give abdominal thrusts until object comes out.

If a person becomes unconscious:

Step 1. Clear any object from mouth.

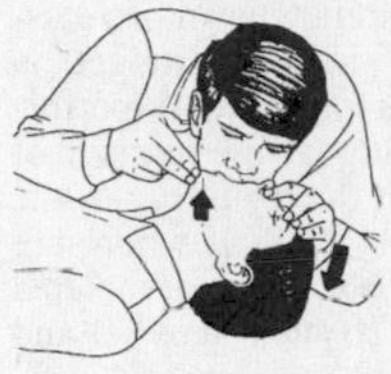

Step 2. Give 2 slow breaths.

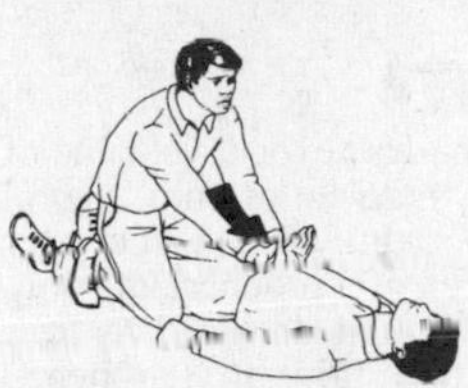

If air won't go in, give up to 5 abdominal thrusts.

Other Emergencies

Burns

First Degree: Signs/Symptoms—reddened skin. **Treatment**—Immerse quickly in cold water or apply ice until pain stops.

Second Degree: Signs/Symptoms—reddened skin, blisters. **Treatment**—(1) Cut away loose clothing. (2) Cover with several layers of cold moist dressings or, if limb is involved, immerse in cold water for relief of pain. (3) Treat for shock.

Third Degree: Signs/Symptoms—skin destroyed, tissues damaged, charring. **Treatment**—(1) Cut away loose clothing (do not remove clothing adhered to skin). (2) Cover with several layers of sterile, cold, moist dressings for relief of pain and to stop burning action. (3) Treat for shock.

Poisons

Treatment—(1) Dilute by drinking large quantities of water. (2) Induce vomiting except when poison is corrosive or a petroleum product. (3) Call the poison-control center or a doctor.

Shock

Shock may accompany any serious injury: blood loss, breathing impairment, heart failure, burns. Shock can kill—treat as soon as possible and continue until medical aid is available.

Signs/Symptoms—(1) Shallow breathing. (2) Rapid and weak pulse. (3) Nausea, collapse, vomiting. (4) Shivering. (5) Pale, moist skin. (6) Mental confusion. (7) Drooping eyelids, dilated pupils.

Treatment—(1) Establish and maintain an open airway. (2) Control bleeding. (3) Keep victim lying down. Exception: Head and chest injuries, heart attack, stroke, sun stroke. If no spine injury, victim may be more comfortable and breathe better in a semi-reclining position. If in doubt, keep the victim flat. Elevate the feet unless injury would be aggravated. Maintain normal body temperature. Place blankets under and over victim.

Frostbite

Most frequently frostbitten: toes, fingers, nose, and ears. It is caused by exposure to cold.

Signs/Symptoms—(1) Skin becomes pale or a grayish-yellow color. (2) Parts feel cold and numb. (3) Frozen parts feel doughy.

Treatment—(1) Victim should be wrapped in woolen cloth and kept dry. (2) Do not rub, chafe, or manipulate frostbitten parts. (3) Bring victim indoors. (4) Place affected parts in warm water (102° to 105°) and make sure water remains warm. Never thaw if the victim has to go back out into the cold, which may cause the affected area to be refrozen. (5) Do not use hot water bottles or a heat lamp, and do not place victim near a hot stove. (6) For serious frostbite, seek medical aid for thawing because pain will be intense and tissue damage extensive.

Heat Cramps

Affects people who work or do strenuous exercises in a hot environment. To prevent it, such people should drink large amounts of cool water and add a pinch of salt to each glass of water.

Signs/Symptoms—(1) Painful muscle cramps in legs and abdomen. (2) Faintness. (3) Profuse perspiration.

Treatment—(1) Move victim to a cool place. (2) Give victim sips of salted drinking water (one teaspoon of salt to one quart of water). (3) Apply manual pressure to the cramped muscle.

Heat Exhaustion

Signs/Symptoms—(1) Pale and clammy skin. (2) Profuse perspiration. (3) Rapid and shallow breathing. (4) Weakness, dizziness, and headache.

Treatment—(1) Care for victim as if he or she were in shock. (2) Remove victim to a cool area, do not allow chilling. (3) If body gets too cold, cover victim.

Heat Stroke

Signs/Symptoms—(1) Face is red and flushed. (2) Victim becomes rapidly unconscious. (3) Skin is hot and dry with no perspiration.

Treatment—(1) Lay victim down with head and shoulders raised. (2) Reduce the high body temperature as quickly as possible. (3) Apply cold applications to the body and head. (4) Use ice and fan if available. (5) Watch for signs of shock and treat accordingly. (6) Get medical aid as soon as possible.

NOTE: The almanac is not responsible for actions undertaken by anyone using these first-aid procedures. This information cannot substitute for a CPR or first-aid course. Contact your local Red Cross to find out about a variety of community programs that teach life-saving skills and safety information. *Sources:* "Life-saving Skills Summary" table and graphics from First Aid First © 1995 by the American Red Cross. "Other Emergencies" courtesy of First Aid, Mining Enforcement and Safety Administration, U.S. Dept. of the Interior.

The New Age of Pharmaceutical Sex

Viagra, a pill that cures impotence, leaves the afflicted ecstatic—but raises questions about the future of sexuality

By BRUCE HANDY TIME

Besides its phony name, funny shape, and unappetizing color, what's not to like about Viagra, the impotence-conquering pill introduced in April 1998 by Pfizer? Could there be a product more tailored to the easy-solution-loving, sexually insecure American psyche than this one? Within days of its release, Pfizer stock was skyrocketing and Viagra was (metaphorically speaking) on everyone's lips—fresh fodder for TV talk-shows, water-cooler gossip, and marital pillow-talks.

"We've always been waiting for the magic bullet," says Dr. Fernando Borges of the Florida Impotency Center in St. Petersburg, where he has been working with sexually dysfunctional patients for 21 years. "This," he says, "is pretty close to the magic bullet." Michael Podgurski, director of pharmacy at the 4,000-outlet Rite Aid drugstore chain, agrees: "It's the fastest takeoff of a new drug that I've ever seen, and I've been in this business for 27 years." Viagra is now being prescribed at the rate of at least 10,000 scripts a day, outpacing such popular drugs as the antidepressant Prozac and the baldness remedy Rogaine. More than 3.6 million prescriptions for Viagra were dispensed between late March and July of 1998.

In the past decade there have been great advances in the treatment of impotence, which is now seen by most therapists, in most cases, as a physiological rather than a psychological problem, rejecting the medical establishment's long-held view. The word impotence itself, like "frigidity" for women, is considered suspect in many circles; the more politically correct—or at least clinical—term is erectile dysfunction, or ED, as it is commonly abbreviated. Inspired by a 1992 National Institutes of Health (NIH) conference and landmark 1994 study on the problem, the diagnosis has been defined more broadly, from the rather strict criterion of inability to get an erection, period, to the somewhat more elastic and subjective criterion of inability to get an erection adequate for "satisfactory sexual performance." This has led to a tripling of the number of men estimated to be impotent in this country—some 30 million according to the NIH, half of whom are thought to be under the age of 65. ED is associated with age; it affects about 1 in 20 men ages 40 and up, 1 in 4 over 65.

The Science of Viagra

Known to chemists by the less evocative name of sildenafil (the word Viagra, redolent of both "vigor" and "Niagara," had been kicking around Pfizer for years, a brand name in search of a product), the drug began life as a heart medication designed to treat angina by increasing blood flow to the heart. Sildenafil, it turned out, wasn't so good at opening coronary arteries, but happy test subjects did notice increased blood flow to their penises, a side effect brought to Pfizer's attention when the test subjects were reluctant to return their leftover pills.

The medication works by suppressing the effect of the naturally occurring enzyme phosphodiesterase

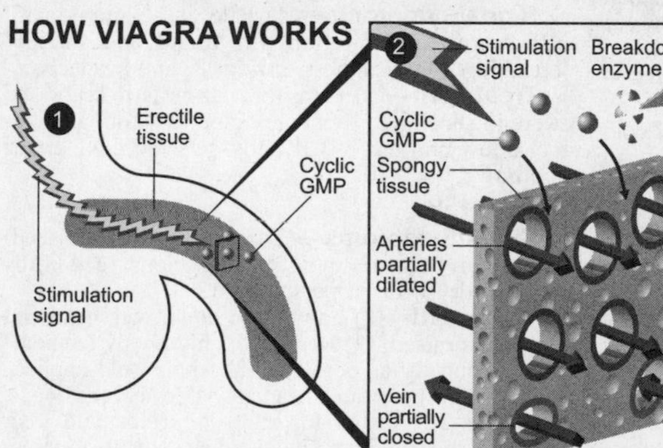

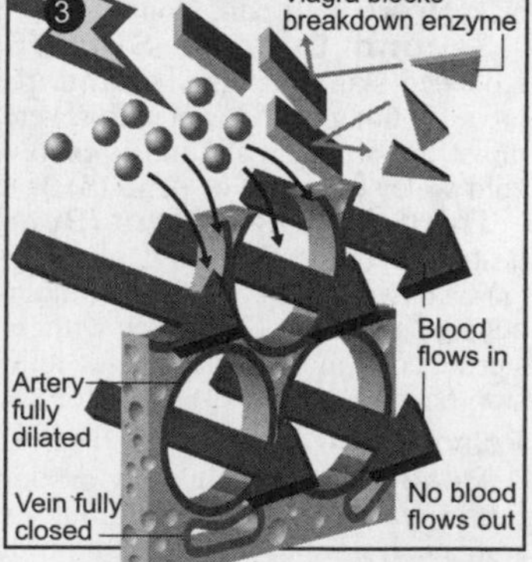

1 When things are working right, sexy signals from the brain stimulate the release of a chemical in the penis, cyclic GMP, that causes muscles in the spongy erectile tissue to relax and the arteries to expand.

2 Blood rushes into the newly opened spaces and the penis begins to stiffen. A full erection occurs, however, only after the veins that normally drain blood away have been squeezed shut.

In impotent men, the erectile tissue doesn't expand far enough to plug the veins, due to a shortage of cyclic GMP. Blood flows out of the penis as fast as it flows in, and the erection flags.

3 Viagra works by prolonging the effects of cyclic GMP (by blocking an enzyme that breaks it down), so that even a little chemistry can go a long way.

TIME Diagram by Joe Lertola

type 5 (PDE5), which causes an erection to subside after orgasm by breaking down the body chemical known as cyclic GMP. It is cyclic GMP that initiates the muscular and vascular changes that lead to an erection in the first place. While PDE5 is always present in the penis, cyclic GMP is produced only during arousal. The catch in impotent men is that they may not produce enough cyclic GMP to temporarily "win out" over the PDE5. Thus the efficacy of Viagra: by strong-arming PDE5, it allows a little bit of one's cyclic GMP to go a long way. So far, Viagra's side effects seem comparatively slight and manageable: chiefly headache, flushed skin, upset stomach, and curious vision distortions involving the color blue. But concern over use of the drug was heightened in late August 1998, when the Food and Drug Administration confirmed that 69 men had died while using Viagra, the majority of them victims of cardiac arrest.

Can Romance Survive Viagra?

There are other unnerving questions about Viagra, too, not so much on the face of it (the drug's merits appear to be manifold; doctors think it might even improve the sexual response of postmenopausal women) but in the broader philosophical implications. Is sexuality, like the state of happiness or male-pattern baldness, just one more hitherto mysterious and profound area of human-beingness that can be pharmaceutically manipulated, like any other fathomable construct of enzymes and receptors?

Viagra raises compelling social questions as well. Since it is taken—at prices ranging from $8 to $12 a pop—not on a day-in, day-out basis but only when one actually wants to have sex, will HMOs and other insurers soon be telling us how much sex is reimbursable? Sufficient? Normal? Necessary? Another tough one: if HMOs reimburse men for Viagra, shouldn't they reimburse women for birth control? And though Pfizer claims there is no evidence that overeager users could develop a physical addiction to Viagra, the notion of a psychological addiction to the drug is uncharted territory.

The promise of Viagra is its discretion and ease of use. Doctors recommend taking the pill an hour before sex, which might lead to some wastage among overly optimistic users but shouldn't otherwise interfere too greatly with the normal course of coital events. An even greater advantage, or at least a more naturalistic one: unlike an earlier treatment, injectable drugs, which when efficacious produced an erection regardless of context (famously proved by Dr. Giles Brindley, a leading British impotence researcher, who once demonstrated a successful experimental treatment by dropping his trousers in front of hundreds of astonished colleagues at a conference), Viagra merely paves the way for the possibility of arousal. Erections must still be achieved the old-fashioned way, whether through desire, attraction, physical stimulation, the guilty thrill of an illicit affair, page 27 of *The Godfather,* or what have you.

Dr. Domeena Renshaw, a psychiatrist who directs the Loyola Sex Therapy Clinic outside of Chicago, offers the instructive example of a couple who came to see her the day after the man had taken Viagra for the first time: "They went to bed to wait for something to happen and fell asleep while they were waiting. They forgot to have foreplay. They expected an instant erection." The next night, after Renshaw gently reminded them about the importance of stimulation, they had intercourse for the first time in three years.

As with the debate in psychiatry between traditional talk therapists and their more pharmacologically minded colleagues, controversy over Viagra and its cousins may well provoke a rift among sex researchers. Raymond Rosen, a professor of psychiatry at the Robert Wood Johnson Medical School in Piscataway, N.J., makes the obvious but necessary point that Viagra will not be the final word on sexual dysfunction or dissatisfaction: "There's a danger that we could lose sight of the fact that a lot of sexual problems relate to poor relationships or poor self-esteem or anxiety, depression, or other factors." Or as James R. Petersen, who writes the *Playboy* Adviser column, puts it, "You can take an angry couple and give them Viagra, and then you have an angry couple with an erection." Oddly, that's reassuring. □

Striking at Cancer's Roots

A new generation of drugs takes aim at the very heart of cancer—the abnormal genes that make cells malignant in the first place

By CLAUDIA WALLIS TIME

There's no doubt in the minds of cancer researchers today that a new era is dawning in the treatment of the U.S.'s No. 2 killer. Three decades ago, the federal government's "War on Cancer" underwrote basic discoveries about the ways broken-down genes lead to malignancies. Now that work is beginning to pay off. "The black box that was the cancer cell has been opened," says Dr. Bert Vogelstein, a world-renowned investigator of cancer genes at the Johns Hopkins University in Baltimore, Md. "As researchers, we feel a tremendous amount of hope, probably for the first time in the history of cancer treatment."

In pharmaceutical-company research departments and academic labs around the country, scientists are feverishly at work on drugs that target the products of specific genes—the very genes that make a cell cancerous. The hope is that these treatments will be more effective, longer lasting, and far less toxic than traditional chemotherapy and radiation—treatments that inspire dread so deep that they are almost as feared as cancer itself.

"Because of the early success with chemotherapy in some forms of leukemias and lymphomas," says Dr. Dennis Slamon, of the Revlon/UCLA Women's Cancer Research Program, "we have been slugging at cancer that way for 25 years. We didn't make any significant inroads, and in some cases, we ended up killing people. Now we are beginning to look specifically at what's broken in a cancer cell and trying to target that."

Broken Genes

What's broken in cancer cells is genes, usually genes that control some aspect of cell growth and division. Hundreds of genes play a role in this process, and more than three dozen have been identified as playing a role in cancer. Some are like accelerators, telling cells to grow, grow, grow. Others put the brakes on growth. Some regulate steps in cell division to make sure that DNA is copied correctly from mother to daughter cell. Some play executioner, killing mutant cells in which the copying has gone awry. Cancer is caused by errors in these genes, usually multiple errors. Though some of these errors may be inherited, most are acquired during years of living. Sunlight, cigarette smoke, environmental toxins, and aging itself help these errors accumulate.

Since every gene holds the recipe for a vital protein, corrupt genes mean corrupt proteins: too much of one protein, too little of another, or a misshapen protein that doesn't function properly. The new generation of cancer drugs takes aim at these defective proteins, blocking them, disrupting them in myriad ways. Unlike old-fashioned chemotherapy drugs, the new substances don't poison the tumor—an approach that usually causes collateral damage to healthy cells. Instead, they aim to halt the processes that make a cancer cell act like a cancer cell in the first place.

Manufactured by Genentech under the name Herceptin, the drug, if approved by the FDA, will join the lymphoma drug Rituxan, also an antibody, as the first of the new gene-based therapies to make it to market. Rituxan, made by IDEC Pharmaceuticals, was approved in late 1997.

Targeting Other Genes

Other substances in the works may be further from the market, but they are in some ways even more exciting. Several of them take aim at a growth-signaling protein made by a gene called RAS (for rat sarcoma, the cancer in which it was first discovered). In about 30% of cancers, the RAS protein is stuck in an "on" position, mindlessly ordering the cell to divide again and again. It plays a role in 90% of pancreatic cancers, 50% of colon cancers, and 25% of lung cancers.

Other drug companies are targeting another common cancer gene: one that codes for a protein called the EGF (epidermal growth factor) receptor. This receptor, which takes in growth signals and relays them to the RAS protein, is found in abnormally high numbers on the surface of about 40% of tumor cells, including about 90% of lung-cancer tumors, some prostate tumors, and other malignancies.

At the Memorial Sloan-Kettering Cancer Center in New York City, Dr. Mark Malkin is working with a substance that targets a receptor for another growth factor called PDGF (platelet-derived growth factor). This receptor studs the surfaces of cells in certain ovarian, prostate, lung, and brain tumors. Malkin has been testing the drug, SU101, on patients with an extraordinarily deadly brain tumor called glioblastoma. Median survival for a patient found to have this cancer is 14 months.

So far, the drug, manufactured by Sugen, appears to slow or arrest tumor growth in about a third of glioblastoma patients, but it's too soon to say how long the benefits will last. Side effects appear to be mild. "We have one patient who's been on it for two years and three months," says Malkin. "His tumor is still there, but it's stable. He's alive; he's at work. For someone with recurrent glioblastoma, that's remarkable."

Malkin is quick to point out that one growth-factor inhibitor isn't going to cure cancer. Cancer is a complicated disease. Tumors usually are made up of different types of cells, expressing different genes, sensitive to different growth factors and therefore responding to different drugs. "When you are trying to kill cancer cells, you're always likely to need combination treatment," says Dr. Edward Scolnick of Merck Research Laboratories. Like AIDS treatments, the new generation of cancer drugs will need to be combined with older drugs and possibly with one another to be most effective.

Stopping Cancer, Not Curing It

If the promise of these drugs holds up, however, cancer treatment in the 21st century will bear little resemblance to today's chemotherapy. Drugs will be precisely tailored to the individual tumor, and the cancers themselves will be described not by the site they attack—breast cancers, lung cancers, etc.—but by the genes they express.

It's also possible that the new generation of drugs emerging from the labs won't work very well, or that the much vaunted lack of major side effects will prove to be an illusion. All the enzymes and growth-factor receptors blocked by the new drugs play a role in normal cell division as well as in cancer. So disrupting them could cause harm.

Though patients long desperately for a "cure," extending life is the more realistic goal in treating cancer. The newer drugs, unlike chemotherapy agents, are "cancer stoppers," not "cancer killers," says Malkin. Chances are that they will have to be taken for many years, or even for the rest of a patient's life. But if such drugs can slow or stop the growth and spread of malignant cells, then cancer can be transformed from an acute and deadly disease into a chronic and manageable one. That doesn't make as sexy a headline as a cancer cure, but it's still the difference between life and death.□

Check Your Healthy Heart I.Q.

Source: The National Heart, Lung and Blood Institute

Answer true or false to the following questions to test your knowledge of heart disease and its risk factors.

1. The risk factors for heart disease that you can do something about are: high blood pressure, high blood cholesterol, smoking, obesity, and physical inactivity.
2. A stroke is often the first symptom of high blood pressure, and a heart attack is often the first symptom of high blood cholesterol.
3. A blood pressure greater than or equal to 140/90 mm Hg is generally considered to be high.
4. High blood pressure affects the same number of blacks as it does whites.
5. The best ways to treat and control high blood pressure are to control your weight, exercise, eat less salt (sodium), restrict your intake of alcohol, and take your high-blood-pressure medicine, if prescribed by your doctor.
6. A blood cholesterol of 240 mg/dL is desirable for adults.
7. The most effective dietary way to lower the level of your blood cholesterol is to eat foods low in cholesterol.
8. Lowering blood cholesterol levels can help people who have already had a heart attack.
9. Only children from families at high risk of heart disease need to have their blood cholesterol levels checked.
10. Smoking is a major risk factor for four of the five leading causes of death including heart attack, stroke, cancer, and lung diseases such as emphysema and bronchitis.
11. If you have had a heart attack, quitting smoking can help reduce your chances of having a second attack.
12. Someone who has smoked for 30 to 40 years probably will not be able to quit smoking.
13. The best way to lose weight is to increase physical activity and eat fewer calories.
14. Heart disease is the leading killer of men and women in the United States.

Healthy Heart I.Q.—Answers

1. **True.** High blood pressure, smoking, and high blood cholesterol are the three most important risk factors for heart disease. On the average, each one doubles your chance of developing heart disease. So, a person who has all three of the risk factors is eight times more likely to develop heart disease than someone who has none. Obesity increases the likelihood of developing high blood cholesterol and high blood pressure, which increase your risk of heart disease. Physical inactivity increases your risk for heart attack. Regular exercise and good nutrition are essential to reducing high blood pressure, high blood cholesterol, and weight. People who exercise are also more likely to cut down on or stop smoking.
2. **True.** A person with high blood pressure or high blood cholesterol may feel fine and look great; there are often no signs that anything is wrong until a stroke or heart attack occurs. To find out if you have high blood pressure or high blood cholesterol, you should be tested by a doctor, nurse, or other health professional.
3. **True.** A blood pressure of 140/90 mm Hg or greater is generally classified as high blood pressure. However, blood pressures that fall below 140/90 mm Hg can sometimes be a problem. If the diastolic pressure, the second or lower number, is between 85–89, a person is at an increased risk for heart disease or stroke and should have his/her blood pressure checked at least once a year by a health professional. The higher your blood pressure, the greater your risk of developing heart disease or stroke. Controlling high blood pressure reduces your risk.
4. **False.** High blood pressure is more common in blacks than whites. It affects 29 out of every 100 black adults compared to 26 out of every 100 white adults. Also, with aging, high blood pressure is generally more severe among blacks then among whites, and therefore causes more strokes, heart disease, and kidney failure.
5. **True.** Recent studies show that lifestyle changes can help keep blood pressure levels normal even into advanced age and are important in treating and preventing high blood pressure. Limit high-salt foods, which include many snack foods, such as potato chips, salted pretzels, and salted crackers; processed foods, such as canned soups; and condiments, such as ketchup and soy sauce. Also, it is extremely important to take blood pressure medication, if prescribed by your doctor, to make sure your blood pressure stays under control.
6. **False.** A total blood cholesterol of under 200 mg/dL is desirable and usually puts you at a lower risk for heart disease. A blood cholesterol level of 240 mg/dL or above is high and increases your risk of heart disease. If your cholesterol level is high, your doctor will want to check your levels of LDL-cholesterol ("bad" cholesterol) and HDL-cholesterol ("good" cholesterol). A HIGH level of LDL-cholesterol increases your risk for heart disease, as does a LOW level of HDL-cholesterol. A cholesterol level of 200–239 mg/dL is considered borderline-high and usually increases your risk for heart disease. If your cholesterol is borderline-high, you should speak to your doctor to see if additional cholesterol tests are needed. All adults 20 years of age or older should have their blood cholesterol level checked at least once every five years.

7. **False.** Reducing the amount of cholesterol in your diet is important; however, eating foods low in saturated fat is the most effective dietary way to lower blood cholesterol levels, along with eating less total fat and cholesterol. Choose low-saturated fat foods, such as grains, fruits, and vegetables; low-fat or skim milk and milk products; lean cuts of meat, fish, and chicken. Trim fat from meat before cooking; bake or broil meat rather than fry; use less fat and oil; and take the skin off chicken and turkey. Reducing weight will also help lower your level of LDL-cholesterol as well as increase your level of HDL-cholesterol.
8. **True.** People who have had one heart attack are at much higher risk for a second attack. Reducing blood cholesterol levels can greatly slow down (and, in some people, even reverse) the buildup of cholesterol and fat in the walls of the arteries and significantly reduce the chances of a second heart attack.
9. **True.** Children from "high risk" families, in which a parent has high blood cholesterol (240 mg/dL or above) or in which a parent or grandparent has had heart disease at an early age (at 55 years of age or younger), should have their cholesterol levels tested. If a child from such a family has a cholesterol level that is high, it should be lowered under medical supervision, primarily with diet, to reduce the risk of developing heart disease as an adult. For most children who are not from high-risk families, the best way to reduce the risk of adult heart disease is to follow a low-saturated-fat, low-cholesterol eating pattern. All children over the age of two years and all adults should adopt a heart-healthy eating pattern as a principal way of reducing coronary heart disease.
10. **True.** Heavy smokers are 2 to 4 times more likely to have a heart attack than nonsmokers, and the heart attack death rate among all smokers is 70% greater than that of nonsmokers. Older male smokers are also nearly twice as likely to die from stroke than older men who do not smoke, and these odds are nearly as high for older female smokers. Further, the risk of dying from lung cancer is 22 times higher for male smokers than male nonsmokers and 12 times higher for female smokers than female nonsmokers. Finally, 80% of all deaths from emphysema and bronchitis are directly due to smoking.
11. **True.** One year after quitting, ex-smokers cut their extra risk for heart attack by about half or more, and eventually the risk will return to normal in healthy ex-smokers. Even if you have already had a heart attack, you can reduce your chances of a second attack if you quit smoking. Ex-smokers can also reduce their risk of stroke and cancer, improve blood flow and lung function, and help stop diseases like emphysema and bronchitis from getting worse.
12. **False.** Older smokers are more likely to succeed at quitting smoking than younger smokers. Quitting helps relieve smoking-related symptoms like shortness of breath, coughing, and chest pain. Many quit to avoid further health problems and take control of their lives.
13. **True.** Weight control is a question of balance. You get calories from the foods you eat. You burn off calories by exercising. Cutting down on calories, especially calories from fat, is key to losing weight. Combining this with a regular physical activity, like walking, cycling, jogging, or swimming, not only can help in losing weight but also in maintaining weight loss. A steady weight loss of a half to one pound a week is safe for most adults, and the weight is more likely to stay off over the long run. Losing weight, if you are overweight, may also reduce your blood pressure, lower your LDL-cholesterol, and raise your HDL-cholesterol. Being physically active and eating fewer calories will also help you control your weight if you quit smoking.
14. **True.** Coronary heart disease is the No. 1 killer in the United States. Approximately 489,000 Americans died of coronary heart disease in 1990, and approximately half of the deaths were women.

Understanding AIDS

Acquired Immune Deficiency Syndrome, or AIDS, was first reported in mid-1981 in the United States; it is believed to have originated in Sub-Saharan Africa. The human immunodeficiency virus (HIV) that causes AIDS was identified in 1983, and by 1985 tests to detect the virus were available. The credit for discovering the AIDS virus is jointly shared by Dr. Robert Gallo, a researcher at the National Cancer Institute, and Luc Montagnier of the Pasteur Institute, France.

Although the first reported cases involved homosexual men in Los Angeles who were infected through sexual contact, the principal mode of transmission throughout the world is through the exchange of bodily fluids during heterosexual intercourse. According to the World Health Organization, extensive spread of HIV appears to have begun in the late 1970s and early 1980s among men and women with multiple sexual partners in East and Central Africa and among homosexual and bisexual men in certain urban areas of the Americas, Australasia, and Western Europe.

In addition to sexual contact, AIDS has been spread by intravenous drug users sharing infected hypodermic needles. The virus can also be passed on through transfused blood or its components. It may also be transmitted from infected mother to infant before, during, or shortly after birth.

Global Estimates of the HIV/AIDS Epidemic as of End 1997

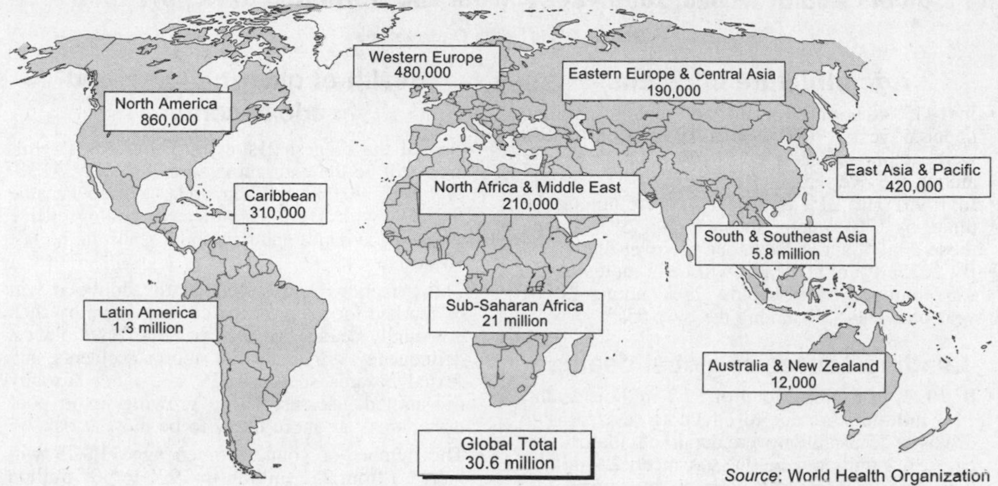

Source: World Health Organization

Two major types of HIV have been recognized, HIV-1 and HIV-2. HIV-1 is the dominant type worldwide. HIV-2 is found principally in West Africa but cases have been reported from East Africa, Europe, Asia, and Latin America. There are at least ten different genetic subtypes of HIV-1, but their biological and epidemiological significance is unclear at present. Both HIV-1 and HIV-2 are transmitted in the same ways.

A fatal and incurable disease caused by the human immunodeficiency virus (HIV), AIDS attacks and destroys the immune system, gradually leaving the individual defenseless against illnesses that lead to death. These illnesses are referred to as "opportunistic" infections or diseases: in AIDS patients the most common of these are *Pneumocystis carinii* pneumonia (PCP), a parasitic infection of the lungs; and a type of cancer known as Kaposi's sarcoma (KS). Other opportunistic infections include unusually severe infections with yeast, cytomegalovirus, herpes virus, and parasites such as Toxoplasma or Cryptosporidia. Milder infections with these organisms do not suggest immune deficiencies. Symptoms of full-blown AIDS include a persistent cough, fever, and difficulty in breathing. Multiple purplish blotches and bumps on the skin may indicate Kaposi's sarcoma. The virus can also cause brain damage.

People infected with the virus can have a wide range of symptoms—from none to mild to severe. At least a fourth to a half of those infected will develop AIDS within four to ten years. Many experts think the percentage will be much higher.

With no cure at present, prudence could save thousands of people who have yet to be exposed to the virus. Use of condoms lessens the possibility of transmission as does the elimination of sharing hypodermic needles. The fate of many will depend less on science than on the ability of large numbers of human beings to change their behavior in the face of growing danger.

New drugs and tests have given researchers renewed optimism in treating AIDS. As of July 1996, three dozen preventative HIV vaccines were being tested in small-scale clinical trials around the world. In the summer of 1998, the first AIDS vaccine trials took place in the United States. And for those already infected, powerful drug combinations are able to decrease the amount of HIV virus in the blood to undetectable levels.

Status of the AIDS Epidemic, End of 1997

	Total	Adults	Women	Children under 15 yrs
People newly infected with HIV in 1997	5.8 million	5.2 million	2.1 million	590,000
Number of people living with HIV/AIDS	30.6 million	29.4 million	12.2 million	1.1 million
AIDS deaths in 1997	2.3 million	1.8 million	800,000	460,000
Total number of AIDS deaths since beginning of epidemic	11.7 million	9.0 million	3.9 million	2.7 million

Source: World Health Organization

Global Health Trends, 1955–2025, from The World Health Report 1998

Source: World Health Organization.

Age structure of deaths

- In 1955, 40% of all deaths were among children under 5 years, 10% were 5–19 year-olds, 28% were among adults aged 20–64, and 21% were among the over-65s.
- In 1995, only 21% of all deaths were among the under-5s, 7% among those 5–19, 29% among those 20–64, and 43% among the over-65s.
- By 2025, 8% of all deaths will be in the under-5s, 3% among 5–19 year-olds, 27% among 20–64 year-olds and 63% among the over-65s.

Leading causes of global deaths

- In 1997, of a global total of 52.2 million deaths, 17.3 million were due to infectious and parasitic diseases; 15.3 million were due to circulatory diseases; 6.2 million were due to cancer; 2.9 million were due to respiratory diseases, mainly chronic obstructive pulmonary disease; and 3.6 million were due to perinatal conditions.
- Leading causes of death from infectious diseases were acute lower respiratory infections (3.7 million), tuberculosis (2.9 million), diarrhea (2.5 million), HIV/AIDS (2.3 million), and malaria (1.5–2.7 million).
- Most deaths from circulatory diseases were coronary heart disease (7.2 million), cerebrovascular disease (4.6 million), and other heart diseases (3 million).
- Leading causes of death from cancers were those of the lung (1.1 million), stomach (765,000), colon and rectum (525,000), liver, (505,000), and breast (385,000).

Health of infants and small children

- Spectacular progress in reducing under 5 mortality achieved in the last few decades is projected to continue. There were about 10 million such deaths in 1997 compared to 21 million in 1955.
- The infant mortality rate per 1,000 live births was 148 in 1955; 59 in 1995; and is projected to be 29 in 2025. The under-5 mortality rates per 1,000 live births for the same years are 210, 78, and 37 respectively.
- By 2025 there will still be 5 million deaths among children under five—97% of them in the developing world, and most of them due to infectious diseases such as pneumonia and diarrhea, combined with malnutrition.
- There are still 24 million low-birthweight babies born every year. They are more likely to die early, and those who survive may suffer illness, stunted growth, or even problems into adult life.
- In 1995, 27% (168 million) of all children under 5 were underweight. Mortality rates are 5 times higher among severely underweight children than those of normal weight.
- About 50% of deaths among children under 5 are associated with malnutrition.
- At least 2 million a year of the under-5 deaths could be prevented by existing vaccines. Most of the rest are preventable by other means.

Health of older children and adolescents

- One of the biggest 21st-century hazards to children will be the continuing spread of HIV/AIDS. In 1997, 590,000 children under age 15 became infected with HIV. The disease could reverse some of the major gains in child health in the last 50 years.
- The transition from childhood to adulthood will be marked for many in the coming years by such potentially deadly "rites of passage" as violence, delinquency, drugs, alcohol, motor accidents, and sexual hazards such as HIV and other sexually transmitted diseases. Those growing up in poor urban areas are more likely to be most at risk.
- The number of young women aged 15–19 will increase from 251 million in 1995 to 307 million in 2025.
- In 1995, young women aged 15–19 gave birth to 17 million babies. Because of population increase, that number is expected to drop only to 16 million in 2025. Pregnancy and childbirth in adolescence pose higher risks for both mother and child.

Health of adults

- Infectious diseases will still dominate in developing countries. As the economies of these countries grow, noncommunicable diseases will become more prevalent. This will be due largely to the adoption of "western" lifestyles and their accompanying risk factors—smoking, high-fat diet, obesity, and lack of exercise.
- In developed countries, non-communicable diseases will remain dominant. Heart disease and stroke have declined as causes of death in recent decades, while death rates from some cancers have risen.
- About 1.8 million adults died of AIDS in 1997 and the annual death toll is likely to continue to rise for some years.
- Diabetes cases in adults will more than double globally from 143 million in 1997 to 300 million by 2025 largely because of dietary and other lifestyle factors.
- Cancer will remain one of the leading causes of death worldwide. Only one-third of all cancers can be cured by earlier detection combined with effective treatment.
- By 2025 the risk of cancer will continue to increase in developing countries, with stable if not declining rates in industrialized countries.
- Cases and deaths of lung cancer and colorectal cancer will increase, largely due to smoking and unhealthy diet respectively. Lung cancer deaths among women will rise in virtually all industrialized countries, but stomach cancer will become less common generally, mainly because of improved food conservation, dietary changes, and declining related infection.

- Cervical cancer is expected to decrease further in industrialized countries due to screening. The incidence is almost four times greater in the developing world. The possible advent of a vaccine would greatly benefit both developed and developing countries.
- Liver cancer will decrease because of the results of current and future immunization against the hepatitis B virus in many countries.
- In general, more than 15 million adults aged 20–64 are dying every year. Most of these deaths are premature and preventable.
- Among the premature deaths are those of 585,000 young women who die each year in pregnancy or childbirth. Most of these deaths are preventable. Where women have many pregnancies the risk of related death over the course of a lifetime is compounded. While the risk in Europe is just 1 in 1,400, in Asia it is 1 in 65, and in Africa, 1 in 16.

Health of older people

- Cancer and heart disease are more prevalent in the 70–75 age group than any other; people over 75 become more prone to impairments of hearing, vision, mobility, and mental function.
- Over 80% of circulatory disease deaths occur in people over 65. Worldwide, circulatory disease is the leading cause of death and disability in people over 65 years.
- Data from France and the U.S. show breast cancer on average deprives women of at least 10 years of life expectancy, while prostate cancer reduces male average life expectancy by only 1 year.
- The risk of developing dementia rises steeply with age in people over 60 years. Women are more likely to suffer than men because of their greater longevity.

Bacteria That Cause Food-borne Illness

What is a food-borne illness?

Food-borne illness often shows itself as flu-like symptoms such as nausea, vomiting, diarrhea, or fever, so many people may not recognize the illness is caused by bacteria or other pathogens on food.

Thousands of types of bacteria are naturally present in our environment. Not all bacteria cause disease in humans. For example, some bacteria are used beneficially in making cheese and yogurt.

Bacteria that cause disease are called "pathogens." When certain pathogens enter the food supply, they can cause food-borne illness. Only a few types cause millions of cases of food-borne illness each year. Ironically, most cases of food-borne illness can be prevented. Proper cooking or processing of food destroys bacteria. They can grow in just about any food, but are fond of protein foods, such as meat, poultry, seafood, eggs, and dairy products in particular, as well as high-protein vegetables such as beans and grains.

How bacteria get in food

1. Bacteria may be present on products when you purchase them. Raw meat, poultry, seafood, and eggs are not sterile. Neither is produce such as lettuce, tomatoes, sprouts, and melons.
2. Foods, including safely cooked, ready-to-eat foods, can become cross-contaminated with bacteria introduced on raw products, meat juices, or other contaminated products, or by poor personal hygiene.

The "danger zone"

Bacteria multiply rapidly between 40° and 140° F. To keep food out of this "danger zone," keep cold food cold and hot food hot.

- Store food in the refrigerator (40° F or below) or freezer (0° F or below).
- Cook food to 160° F (145° F for roasts, steaks, and chops of beef, veal, and lamb).
- Maintain hot cooked food at 140° F.
- Reheat cooked food to 165° F.

Which Bacteria are Responsible for Food-borne Illness?

Some bacteria cause more serious illness than others, but only a few are responsible for the majority of cases. Below is information regarding nine prominent bacteria.

Campylobacter jejuni

Found: intestinal tracts of animals and birds, raw milk, untreated water, and sewage sludge.

Transmission: contaminated water, raw milk, and raw or under-cooked meat, poultry, or shellfish.

Symptoms: fever, headache, and muscle pain followed by diarrhea (sometimes bloody), abdominal pain and nausea that appear 2 to 5 days after eating; may last 7 to 10 days.

Clostridium botulinum

Found: widely distributed in nature: in soil and water, on plants, and in intestinal tracts of animals and fish. Grows only in little or no oxygen.

Transmission: bacteria produce a toxin that causes illness. Improperly canned foods, garlic in oil, and vacuum-packaged and tightly wrapped food.

Symptoms: toxin affects the nervous system. Symptoms usually appear within 18 to 36 hours, but can sometimes appear within as few as 4 hours or as many as 8 days after eating; double vision, droopy eyelids, trouble speaking and swallowing, and difficulty breathing. Fatal in 3 to 10 days if not treated.

Clostridium perfringens

Found: soil, dust, sewage, and intestinal tracts of animals and humans. Grows only in little or no oxygen.

Transmission: called "the cafeteria germ" because many outbreaks result from food left for long periods in steam tables or at room temperature. Bacteria destroyed by cooking, but some toxin-producing spores may survive.

Symptoms: diarrhea and gas pains may appear 8 to 24 hours after eating; usually last about 1 day, but less severe symptoms may persist for 1 to 2 weeks.

Escherichia coli O157:H7

Found: intestinal tracts of some mammals, raw milk, unchlorinated water; one of several strains of *E. coli* that can cause human illness.

Transmission: contaminated water, raw milk, raw or rare ground beef, unpasteurized apple juice or cider, uncooked fruits and vegetables; person-to-person.

Symptoms: diarrhea or bloody diarrhea, abdominal cramps, nausea, and malaise; can begin 2 to 5 days after food is eaten, lasting about 8 days. Some, especially the very young, have developed Hemolytic Uremic Syndrome (HUS) that causes acute kidney failure. A similar illness, thrombotic thrombocytopenic purpura (TTP), may occur in older adults.

Salmonella (over 1600 types)

Found: intestinal tract and feces of animals; *Salmonella enteritidis* in raw eggs.

Transmission: raw or undercooked eggs, poultry, and meat; raw milk and dairy products; seafood.

Symptoms: stomach pain, diarrhea, nausea, chills, fever, and headache usually appear 6 to 48 hours after eating; may last 1 to 2 days.

Streptococcus A

Found: noses, throats, pus, sputum, blood, and stools of humans.

Transmission: people-to-food from poor hygiene, ill food handlers, or improper food handling; outbreaks from raw milk, ice cream, eggs, lobster, salads, custard, and pudding allowed to stand at room temperature for several hours between preparation and eating.

Symptoms: sore throat, painful swallowing, tonsillitis, high fever, headache, nausea, vomiting, malaise; occurs 1 to 3 days after eating, lasting a few days to about a week.

Listeria monocytogenes

Found: intestinal tracts of humans and animals, milk, soil, leaf vegetables, and processed foods; can grow slowly at refrigerator temperatures.

Transmission: soft cheese, raw milk, improperly processed ice cream, raw leafy vegetables, meat, and poultry. Illness caused by bacteria that do not produce toxin.

Symptoms: fever, chills, headache, backache, sometimes abdominal pain and diarrhea; 12 hours to 3 weeks after ingestion; may later develop more serious illness (meningitis or spontaneous abortion in pregnant women); sometimes just fatigue.

Shigella (over 30 types)

Found: human intestinal tract; rarely found in other animals.

Transmission: person-to-person by fecal-oral route; fecal contamination of food and water. Most outbreaks result from food, especially salads, prepared and handled by workers using poor personal hygiene.

Symptoms: disease referred to as "shigellosis" or bacillary dysentery. Diarrhea containing blood and mucus, fever, abdominal cramps, chills, vomiting; 12 to 50 hours from ingestion of bacteria; can last a few days to 2 weeks. Sometimes, no symptoms seen.

Staphylococcus aureus

Found: on humans (skin, infected cuts, pimples, noses, and throats).

Transmission: people-to-food through improper handling. Multiply rapidly at room temperature to produce a toxin that causes illness.

Symptoms: severe nausea, abdominal cramps, vomiting, and diarrhea occur 1 to 6 hours after eating; recovery within 2 to 3 days—longer if severe dehydration occurs.

Source: Food Safety and Inspection Service, USDA.

Can Your Kitchen Pass the Food Safety Test?

By Paula Kurtzweil, Federal Drug Administration

Food safety concerns revolve around three main functions: food storage, food handling, and cooking. To see how well you're doing in each, take this quiz, and then read on to learn how you can make the meals and snacks from your kitchen the safest possible.

Quiz

1. The temperature of the refrigerator in my home is:
   a. 50° Fahrenheit (10° Celsius)
   b. 41° F (5° C)
   c. I don't know; I've never measured it
2. The last time we had leftover cooked stew or other food with meat, chicken, or fish, the food was:
   a. cooled to room temperature, then put in the refrigerator
   b. put in the refrigerator immediately after the food was served
   c. left at room temperature overnight or longer
3. The last time the kitchen sink drain, disposal, and connecting pipe in my home were sanitized was:
   a. last night
   b. several weeks ago
   c. can't remember
4. If a cutting board is used in my home to cut raw meat, poultry, or fish and it is going to be used to chop another food, the board is:
   a. reused as is
   b. wiped with a damp cloth
   c. washed with soap and hot water and sanitized with a mild chlorine bleach solution

5. The last time we had hamburgers in my home, I ate mine:
   a. rare
   b. medium
   c. well-done
6. I clean my kitchen counters and other surfaces that come in contact with food with:
   a. water
   b. hot water and soap
   c. hot water and soap, then bleach solution
   d. hot water and soap, then commercial sanitizing agent
7. When dishes are washed in my home, they are:
   a. cleaned by an automatic dishwasher and then air-dried
   b. left to soak in the sink for several hours and then washed with soap in the same water
   c. washed right away with hot water and soap in the sink and then air-dried
   d. washed right away with hot water and soap in the sink and immediately towel-dried
8. The last time I handled raw meat, poultry, or fish, I cleaned my hands afterwards by:
   a. wiping them on a towel
   b. rinsing them under hot, cold, or warm tap water
   c. washing with soap and water
9. Meat, poultry, and fish products are defrosted in my home by:
   a. setting them on the counter
   b. placing them in the refrigerator
   c. microwaving
10. The last time there was cookie dough in my home, the dough was:
   a. made with raw eggs, and I sampled some of it
   b. store-bought, and I sampled some of it
   c. not sampled until baked

Answers

1. (b) Refrigerators should stay at 41° F (5° C) or less. According to Joseph Madden, Ph.D., strategic manager for microbiology in the Food and Drug Administration's Center for Food Safety and Applied Nutrition, many people overlook the importance of maintaining an appropriate refrigerator temperature. "According to surveys, in many households, the refrigerator temperature is above 50° (10° C)," he said. His advice: Measure the temperature with a thermometer and, if needed, adjust the refrigerator's temperature control dial. A temperature of 41° F (5° C) or less is important because it slows the growth of most bacteria. The temperature won't kill the bacteria, but it will keep them from multiplying, and the fewer there are, the less likely you are to get sick from them. Freezing at zero F (–18° C) or less stops bacterial growth (although it won't kill all bacteria already present).
2. (b) Hot foods should be refrigerated as soon as possible—within two hours after cooking. But don't keep the food if it's been standing out for more than two hours. Don't taste test it, either. Even a small amount of contaminated food can cause illness. Date leftovers so they can be used within a safe time. Generally, they remain safe when refrigerated for three to five days. If in doubt, throw it out, says former FDA microbiologist Jeffery Rhodehamel, now with W. R. Grace and Co. "It's not worth a food-borne illness for the small amount of food usually involved."
3. (a) is the best answer; (b) is also acceptable. According to FDA's Madden, the kitchen sink drain, disposal, and connecting pipe are often overlooked, but they should be sanitized periodically by pouring down the sink a solution of 1 teaspoon (5 milliliters) of chlorine bleach in 1 quart (about 1 liter) of water or a solution of commercial kitchen-cleaning agent made according to product directions. Food particles get trapped in the drain and disposal and, when combined with the moistness, create an ideal environment for bacterial growth.
4. (c) Washing with soap and hot water and then sanitizing with a mild bleach solution is the safest practice, said Dhirendra Shah, director of the division of microbiological studies in FDA's Center for Food Safety and Applied Nutrition. If you picked (a), you're violating an important food safety rule: Never allow raw meat, poultry, and fish to come in contact with other foods. Answer (b) isn't good, either. Improper washing, such as with a damp cloth, will not remove bacteria.
5. (c) The safest way to eat hamburgers is to cook them until they are no longer red in the middle and the juices run clear. That doesn't happen with rare-cooked meats, and it may not happen with medium-cooked ones. Cooking food, including ground-meat patties, to an internal temperature of at least 160° F (71° F) usually protects against food-borne illness. Well-done meats reach that temperature. To be on the safe side, check cooked meat, fish, and poultry with a meat thermometer to ensure that they have reached a safe internal temperature. For microwaved food, follow directions, including the standing time, either in or out of the microwave, after cooking. Microwave cooking creates pockets of heat in the food, but allowing the food to stand before eating allows the heat to spread to the rest of the food.
6. Answers (c) or (d) are acceptable; answer (b) is partially acceptable. According to FDA's Madden, bleach and commercial kitchen-cleaning agents are the best sanitizers—provided they're diluted according to product directions. They're the most effective at getting rid of bacteria. Hot water and soap does a good job, too, but may not kill all strains of bacteria. Water may get rid of visible dirt, but not bacteria. Also, be sure to keep dishcloths and sponges clean because, when wet, these materials harbor bacteria and may promote their growth.
7. Answers (a) and (c) are acceptable; there are potential problems with (b) and (d). When you let dishes sit in water for a long time, it "creates a soup," FDA's Madden said. "The food left on the dish contributes nutrients for bacteria, so the bacteria will multiply." When washing dishes by hand, he said, it's best to wash them all within two hours. Also, it's best to air-dry them so you don't handle them while they're wet.

8. The only correct practice is answer (c). Wash hands with warm water and soap for at least 20 seconds before and after handling food, especially raw meat, poultry, and fish. If you have an infection or cut on your hands, wear rubber or plastic gloves. Wash gloved hands just as often as bare hands because the gloves can pick up bacteria. (However, when washing gloved hands, you don't need to take off your gloves and wash your bare hands, too.)
9. (b) or (c). Food safety experts recommend thawing foods in the refrigerator or the microwave oven or putting the package in a watertight plastic bag submerged in cold water and changing the water every 30 minutes. Changing the water ensures that the food is kept cold, an important factor for slowing bacterial growth that may occur on the outer thawed portions while inner areas are still thawing. Leave about 2 inches (about 5 centimeters) between the food and the inside surface of the microwave to allow heat to circulate. Smaller items will defrost more evenly than larger pieces of food. Foods defrosted in the microwave oven should be cooked immediately after thawing. Do not thaw meat, poultry, and fish products on the counter or in the sink without cold water; bacteria can multiply rapidly at room temperature.
10. If you answered (a) you may be putting yourself at risk for infection with *Salmonella enteritidis,* a bacterium that can be found in eggs. Cooking the egg or egg-containing food product to at least 140° F (60° C) kills the bacteria. So answer (c)—eating the baked product—is your best bet. Answer (b), however, is acceptable as well. Foods containing raw eggs, such as homemade ice cream, cake batter, mayonnaise, and eggnog, carry a Salmonella risk, but their commercial counterparts don't. Commercial products are made with pasteurized eggs; that is, eggs that have been heated sufficiently to kill bacteria, and also may contain an acidifying agent that kills the bacteria. Commercial preparations of cookie dough are not a food hazard. If you want to sample homemade dough or batter or eat other foods with raw-egg-containing products, consider substituting pasteurized eggs for raw eggs. Pasteurized eggs are usually sold in the grocer's refrigerated dairy case.

First Federal Obesity Guidelines: More than Half of All Americans are Too Fat

Source: National Heart, Lung, and Blood Institute

Overweight and obesity continue to be an alarming public-health problem in the United States, affecting 97 million American adults—an astonishing 55% of the population. Between 1960 and 1994, the prevalence of obesity in adults increased from nearly 13% to 22.5% of the U.S. population, with most of the increase occurring in the 1990s. These findings are recorded in the first federal guidelines on the identification, evaluation, and treatment of overweight and obesity in adults, which was released by the National Heart, Lung, and Blood Institute (NHLBI) in June 1998.

"There are several possible reasons for the increase," asserted Karen Donato, coordinator of the Obesity Education Initiative. "When people read labels, they're more likely to notice what's 'low fat and healthy' but may not be looking at calories. Also, more people are eating out and portion sizes have increased. Another issue is decreased physical activity. So people are consuming more calories and are less active. It doesn't take much to tip the energy balance," she said.

According to the guidelines, assessment of overweight involves evaluation of three key measures—body mass index (BMI), waist circumference, and a patient's risk factors for diseases and conditions associated with obesity. Overweight is defined as having a BMI of 25 to 29.9 and obesity as a BMI of 30 and above, which is consistent with the definitions used in many other countries. BMI describes body weight relative to height and is strongly correlated with total body-fat content in adults. According to the guidelines, a BMI of 30 is about 30 pounds overweight and is equivalent to 221 pounds in a 6′ person and to 186 pounds in someone who is 5′6. The BMI numbers apply to both men and women. Some very muscular people may have a high BMI without health risks.

Waist circumference, which is strongly associated with abdominal fat, is another measure of overweight—excess abdominal fat is an independent predictor of disease risk. A waist circumference of over 40 inches in men and over 35 inches in women signifies increased risk in those who have a BMI of 25 to 34.9.

According to the guidelines, the most successful strategies for weight loss include calorie reduction, increased physical activity, and behavior therapy designed to improve eating and physical activity habits. Other recommendations include:

- Engaging in moderate physical activity, progressing to 30 minutes or more on most or preferably all days of the week.
- Reducing dietary fat alone—without reducing calories—will not produce weight loss. Cutting back on dietary fat can help reduce calories and is heart-healthy.
- The initial goal should be to reduce body weight by about 10% from baseline, an amount that reduces obesity-related risk factors. With success, and if warranted, further weight loss can be attempted.
- A reasonable time-line for a 10% reduction in body weight is six months of treatment, with a weight loss of 1 to 2 pounds per week.

The guidelines have been reviewed by 115 health experts at major medical and professional societies, and have been endorsed by 54 professional societies, government agencies, and consumer organizations. The published report is available on the NHLBI Website: http://www.nhlbi.nih.gov/nhlbi/cardio/obes/prof/guidelns/ob_home.htm. Single free copies of the consumer tips referred to above are available by writing to the NHLBI Information Center, P.O. Box 30105, Bethesda, MD 20824–0105.

Measuring Body Mass

The new body mass index (BMI) applies to both men and women. To determine BMI, weight in kilograms is divided by height in meters, squared. To calculate your body mass index from the table below, locate your height in inches in the left-hand column, then follow it across until you locate your weight; the number at the very top is your body mass index. A BMI of 25 to 29.9 is considered overweight and one of 30 or above is considered obese.

Body Mass Index Chart

	19	20	21	22	23	24	25	26	27	28	29	30	31	32	33	34	35
Height (inches)	Body Weight (pounds)																
58	91	96	100	105	110	115	119	124	129	134	138	143	148	153	158	162	167
59	94	99	104	109	114	119	124	128	133	138	143	148	153	158	163	168	173
60	97	102	107	112	118	123	128	133	138	143	148	153	158	163	168	174	179
61	100	106	111	116	122	127	132	137	143	148	153	158	164	169	174	180	185
62	104	109	115	120	126	131	136	142	147	153	158	164	169	175	180	185	191
63	107	113	118	124	130	135	141	146	152	158	163	169	175	180	186	191	197
64	110	116	122	128	134	140	145	151	157	163	169	174	180	186	192	197	204
65	114	120	126	132	138	144	150	156	162	168	174	180	186	192	198	204	210
66	118	124	130	136	142	148	155	161	167	173	179	186	192	198	204	210	216
67	121	127	134	140	146	153	159	166	172	178	185	191	198	204	211	217	223
68	125	131	138	144	151	158	164	171	177	184	190	197	203	210	216	223	230
69	128	135	142	149	155	162	169	176	182	189	196	203	209	216	223	230	236
70	132	139	146	153	160	167	174	181	188	195	202	209	216	222	229	236	243
71	136	143	150	157	165	172	179	186	193	200	208	215	222	229	236	243	250
72	140	147	154	162	169	177	184	191	199	206	213	221	228	235	242	250	258
73	144	151	159	166	174	182	189	197	204	212	219	227	235	242	250	257	265
74	148	155	163	171	179	186	194	202	210	218	225	233	241	249	256	264	272
75	152	160	168	176	184	192	200	208	216	224	232	240	248	256	264	272	279
76	156	164	172	180	189	197	205	213	221	230	238	246	254	263	271	279	287

Source: National Heart, Lung, and Blood Institute

Nationwide Trends in Drug Abuse

Source: National Institute on Drug Abuse

According to the results of the 1996 National Household Survey on Drug Abuse, the number of current illicit-drug users did not change significantly from 1995 (12.8 million) to 1996 (13 million). Below are the report's findings on the extent of drug abuse for 1996, the most recent year for which figures are available.

Cocaine

Crack cocaine continues to dominate the nation's illicit-drug problem. The overall number of current cocaine users did not change significantly between 1995 and 1996 (1.45 million in 1995 and 1.75 million in 1996). This is down from a peak of 5.7 million in 1985. Nevertheless, there were still an estimated 652,000 Americans who used cocaine for the first time in 1995. Supplies remain abundant in nearly every city. Data indicate a leveling-off in many urban areas: cocaine-related deaths were stable or up slightly in nine of the ten areas where such information was reported; the percentage of treatment admissions for primary cocaine problems declined slightly or remained stable in 12 of the 14 areas where data were available; and prices of cocaine remained stable in most areas. Although demographic data continue to show most cocaine users as older, inner-city crack addicts, isolated field reports indicate new groups of users: teenagers smoking crack with marijuana in "blunts" (cigars emptied of tobacco and refilled with marijuana, often in combination with another drug) in some cities, Hispanic crack users in Texas, and in the Atlanta area, middle-class suburban users of cocaine hydrochloride, and female crack users in their 30s with no prior drug history.

Heroin

There has been an increasing trend in new heroin use since 1992, with an estimated 141,000 new heroin users in 1995. The estimated number of heroin users increased from 68,000 in 1993 to 216,000 in 1996. A large portion of these recent new users were smoking, snorting, or sniffing heroin, and most were under age 26. There is increasing incidence of new users (snorters) in the younger age groups, often among women. In some areas, such as San Francisco, the recent initiates increasingly include members of the middle class. In Boston and Newark, heroin users are also found in suburban populations. One concern is that young heroin snorters may shift to needle injecting, because of increased tolerance, nasal soreness, or declining or unreliable purity. Injection use would place them at increased risk for HIV/AIDS. Purity has, indeed, been declining or is inconsistent in some cities, such as Atlanta, Boston, and New York. Nevertheless, purity remains high, as does intranasal use, in the East and in some Midwestern cities, notably Chicago and Detroit. Supplies remain abundant. Aggressive marketing and price cutting has intensified in some cities, such as Boston, Detroit, and New York; heroin dealers often sell other drugs, too, as in Miami, Minneapolis/St. Paul, St. Louis, and some Atlanta neighborhoods.

Marijuana

There were an estimated 2.4 million people who started using marijuana in 1995. The resurgence in marijuana use continues, especially among adolescents. Two factors may be contributing to a dramatic leap in adverse consequences resulting from marijuana use: higher potency and the use of marijuana mixed with or in combination with other dangerous drugs. Marijuana cigarettes or "blunts" often include crack, a combination known by various street names, such as "3750s," "diablitos," "primos," "oolies," and "woolies." Joints and blunts are also frequently dipped in PCP and go by street names such as "happy sticks," "wicky sticks," "illies," "love boat," "wet," or "tical." Both types of combinations are reported in Boston, Chicago, and New York; the marijuana-crack combinations are also sold in St. Louis; and the marijuana-PCP combinations are reported in Philadelphia and parts of Texas. Marijuana cigarettes are also sometimes dipped in embalming fluid, as reported in Boston (where they are known as "shermans") and areas of Texas.

Methamphetamine

In several western and midwestern cities, methamphetamine indicators, which had been steadily increasing for several years, appear mixed. All indicators suggest increases in San Francisco and Seattle, while San Diego and Los Angeles indicators show stable or slightly declining trends. However, it is too soon to predict that the indicators in those areas have peaked. Increased methamphetamine availability and use is sporadically reported in diverse areas of the country, particularly rural areas, prompting some concern about its spread outside of the areas of endemic use (the West Coast). Most methamphetamine comes from large-scale Mexican operations. Recent seizures in Florida have included powder cocaine, heroin, and flunitrazepam in the same shipment with methamphetamine. Additionally, local labs remain common, with seizures increasing in areas such as Seattle, Arizona, and rural Georgia, Michigan, and Missouri. All four routes of administration—injecting, snorting, smoking (including "chasing the dragon" in San Francisco), and oral ingestion—are used but vary from city to city. Reports of violence related to methamphetamine persist in Honolulu and are now also occurring in Seattle.

Stimulants

Methylphenidate (Ritalin) abuse continues among heroin users in Chicago and adolescents in Detroit. Methcathinone ("cat" or "goobs") has been reported in several indicators in Detroit and Michigan's Upper Peninsula. Ephedrine-based products sold at convenience stores, truck stops, and health-food stores are common among adolescents in Atlanta, Detroit, Minneapolis/St. Paul, and Texas. New York state recently banned the sale of such products in an attempt to curb escalating abuse among adolescents. Methylenedioxymethamphetamine (MDMA or "ecstasy") use was reported most often among young adults and adolescents at clubs, raves, and rock concerts in Atlanta, Miami, St. Louis, Seattle, and areas of Texas.

Depressants

Use of gamma hydroxybutrate (GHB) in the club scene is becoming more widespread throughout the country, notably in Atlanta, Detroit, Honolulu, Miami, New York City (where it is also reportedly used by fashion models), Phoenix, and Texas. Ketamine ("Special K") use in nightclubs has also been reported in several cities. A mixture of GHB, ketamine, and alcohol, called "Special K-lude" because of the similar effects produced by methaqualone (Quaalude), is reported in New York City. Flunitrazepam (Rohypnol) use continues in many areas of the country (with the exception of the Northeast), most notably in Texas and Florida. Its widespread availability has declined, however, since the federal ban on its importation. Other medications from the same manufacturer are now being sold and abused as "roofies" in Miami, Minnesota, and Texas. These drugs include clonazepam (another pharmaceutical benzodiazepine, marketed in Mexico as Rivotril), which has the same distinguishing manufacturer's imprint as flunitrazepam. Clonazepam (marketed in the United States as Klonopin) is also used by addicts in Minneapolis/St. Paul and Atlanta to enhance the effects of methadone and other opiates.

Hallucinogens

According to field reports in numerous areas, such as Texas, Boston, Chicago, New York, Philadelphia, St. Louis, and Washington, D.C., phencyclidine (PCP) is often used in combination with other drugs. A frequently reported combination is joints or blunts containing marijuana mixed with or dipped into PCP. In other cities, such as Los Angeles and New Orleans, PCP is commonly purchased as a predipped cigarette. In New York City, PCP is combined with crack in "spaceballs." Lysergic acid diethylamide (LSD) remains widely available, especially in suburban and rural areas. Use of psilocybin mushrooms has also been reported among adolescents and young adults in Boston, Minneapolis/St. Paul, and Philadelphia.

Perceived Risk and Availability of Drugs

More than half of youths age 12–17 reported that marijuana was easy to obtain in 1996, and about one-quarter reported that heroin was easy to obtain. Fifteen percent of youths reported being approached by someone selling drugs in the month prior to being surveyed. In addition to demonstrating the accessibility of illicit drugs, youths showed a decrease in their perception of the risk in using illicit drugs. The percentage of youths who perceived great risk in using cocaine once a month decreased from 63% in 1994 to 54% in 1996. The percentage of youths age 12–17 that perceived great risk in using marijuana once a month decreased from 1990 (40%) to 1994 (33%), but remained level from 1994 to 1996.

Drug Use, by Type of Drug and Age Group: 1974 to 1994

Age and type of drug	Ever used 1974	Ever used 1985	Ever used 1994	Current user 1974	Current user 1985	Current user 1994
12 to 17 years old						
Marijuana	23.0%	23.2%	16.0%	12.0%	11.9%	7.3%
Cocaine	3.6	4.8	1.3	1.0	1.4	0.4
Hallucinogens	6.0	3.2	4.0	1.3	1.2	1.2
Heroin	.0	0.4	0.4	(B)	0.1	(B)
Alcohol	54.0	55.4	41.2	34.0	31.0	16.3
Cigarettes	52.0	45.3	33.5	25.0	15.3	9.8
18 to 25 years old						
Marijuana	52.7	59.4	43.4	25.2	21.9	12.2
Cocaine	12.7	24.4	9.6	3.1	7.5	1.0
Hallucinogens	16.6	11.6	11.7	2.5	1.8	1.5
Heroin	4.5	1.3	0.2	(B)	0.3	0.1
Alcohol	81.6	92.0	86.8	69.3	70.7	63.8
Cigarettes	68.8	75.2	68.6	48.8	36.6	26.5
26 years old and over						
Marijuana	9.9	26.6	35.0	2.0	6.0	3.0
Cocaine	0.9	9.2	10.9	(B)	1.9	0.6
Hallucinogens	1.3	6.0	8.0	(B)	(B)	—
Heroin	0.5	1.1	1.3	(B)	(B)	(B)
Alcohol	73.2	89.2	91.0	54.5	59.8	55.6
Cigarettes	65.4	80.6	76.8	39.1	32.7	24.7

B = Base too small to meet statistical standards for reliability of a derived figure. *Source:* U.S. Substance Abuse and Mental Health Services Administration, *National Household Survey on Drug Abuse.*

Smoking-Related Mortality

Cigarette smoking is the single most preventable cause of premature death in the United States. Each year, more than 400,000 Americans die from cigarette smoking. In fact, one in every five deaths in the United States is smoking related.

- About 10 million people in the United States have died from causes attributed to smoking (including heart disease, emphysema, and other respiratory diseases) since the first Surgeon General's report on smoking and health in 1964—2 million of these deaths were the result of lung cancer alone.
- Between 1960 and 1990, deaths from lung cancer among women have increased by more than 400%—exceeding breast cancer deaths in the mid-1980s. The American Cancer Society estimated that in 1994, 64,300 women died from lung cancer and 44,300 died from breast cancer. Men who smoke increase their risk of death from lung cancer by more than 22 times and from bronchitis and emphysema by nearly 10 times. Women who smoke increase their risk of dying from lung cancer by nearly 12 times and the risk of dying from bronchitis and emphysema by more than 10 times. Smoking triples the risk of dying from heart disease among middle-aged men and women.
- On average, smokers die nearly seven years earlier than nonsmokers.
- Annually, exposure to secondhand smoke (or environmental tobacco smoke) causes an estimated 3,000 deaths from lung cancer among American adults. Scientific studies also link secondhand smoke with heart disease.
- Approximately 80% of adult smokers started smoking before the age of 18. Every day, nearly 3,000 young people under the age of 18 become regular smokers.

Smoking Prevalence Among U.S. Adults, 1955–1994
(As a percent of population, 18 years of age and older)

Year	Overall population	Males	Females	Whites	Blacks
1955	—	56.9%	28.4%	—	—
1965	42.4%	51.9	33.9	42.1%	45.8%
1970	37.4	44.1	31.5	37.0	41.4
1974	37.1	43.1	32.1	36.4	44.0
1978	34.1	38.1	30.7	33.9	37.7
1980	33.2	37.6	29.3	32.9	36.9
1983	32.1	35.1	29.5	31.8	35.9
1985	30.1	32.6	27.9	29.6	34.9
1987	28.8	31.2	26.5	28.5	32.9
1988	28.1	30.8	25.7	27.8	31.7
1990	25.5	28.4	22.8	25.6	26.2
1991	25.7	28.1	23.5	25.5	29.1
1992	26.5	28.6	24.6	26.6	27.8
1993	25.0	27.7	22.5	24.9	26.1
1994	25.5	28.2	23.1	26.3	27.2

Source: Office on Smoking and Health, Centers for Disease Control and Prevention.

Heavy Alcohol Use, by Age Group, Race/Ethnicity, and Sex: 1985–1996

Demographic characteristics	1985	1988	1990	1991	1992	1993	1994	1995	1996
Total	8.3%	5.8%	6.3%	6.8%	6.2%	6.7%	6.2%	5.5%	5.4%
Age group									
12–17	9.5	4.0	4.4	6.0	3.4	3.4	2.5	2.8	2.9
18–25	13.8	12.0	14.9	15.2	15.1	14.0	13.2	12.0	12.9
26–34	11.5	7.1	8.2	7.9	8.5	8.5	8.0	7.9	7.1
≥35	5.2	4.0	3.7	4.4	3.9	5.0	4.8	3.9	3.8
Race/Ethnicity									
White	9.1	6.3	6.7	7.2	6.8	7.5	6.4	5.7	5.5
Black	3.5	2.8	4.1	4.3	3.5	3.3	4.8	4.6	5.3
Hispanic	7.1	5.3	5.9	6.8	6.3	6.0	7.3	6.3	7.2
Other	—	3.9	—	3.3	2.2	1.9	4.7	2.4	2.1
Sex									
Male	13.8	10.2	10.8	10.8	10.1	11.9	10.3	9.4	13.8
Female	3.2	1.8	2.1	3.1	2.7	1.9	2.5	2.0	1.9

NOTE: Heavy alcohol use is defined as drinking five or more drinks on the same occasion on each of five or more days in the past 30 days. *Source:* U.S. Substance Abuse and Mental Health Services Administration, Office of Applied Studies, *National Household Survey on Drug Abuse.*

Organ Transplantation Reform

Source: Department of Health and Human Services.

The nation's organ transplantation system is to be reformed, ensuring that allocation of scarce organs will be based on common medical criteria, not accidents of geography. Under the current system, organs are first offered to the region in which they become available. If no match is found there, the organ is offered nationwide. But the emphasis on treating local transplant patients means that less ill patients may receive a transplant while patients with more urgent medical need in other locations continue to wait. Today there is a wide variation in waiting times, with patients in some areas waiting five times longer or more for an organ than in other areas. The new criteria would provide for wider sharing to ensure organs are made available to patients with greatest medical need.

The scarcity of transplant organs has remained a chronic problem in the United States. In 1996, some 20,000 Americans—about 55 each day—were able to live healthier lives through transplantation. However, more than 55,000 people are on the transplant waiting list nationwide, and some 4,000 people—10 every day—die in the U.S. while awaiting a donated organ. For further information on organ donation, contact the U.S. Department of Health and Human Services' organ donation site: www.organdonor.gov.

Organ Transplants and Grafts: 1985–1996

(Based on reports of procurement programs and transplant centers in the U.S., except as noted.)

	Number of procedures							Number of centers		Number of people waiting, 1996	1-year patient survival rates, 1995 (percent)
Procedure	**1985**	**1990**	**1991**	**1992**	**1993**	**1994**	**1995**	**1990**	**1996**		
Transplant: [1]											
Heart	719	2,108	2,125	2,171	2,297	2,340	2,361	148	166	3,698	84.3%
Liver	602	2,690	2,953	3,064	3,441	3,652	3,924	85	120	7,467	83.8
Kidney	7,695	9,878	10,122	10,230	11,020	11,390	11,816	232	253	34,550	97.5
Heart-lung	30	52	51	48	60	71	68	79	99	237	NA
Lung	2	203	405	535	667	723	871	70	93	2,309	76.2
Pancreas/Islet cell	130	528	531	557	774	842	1,027	84	121	323	94.7
Cornea grafts [2]	26,300	40,631	41,393	42,337	40,215	43,743	44,652	107[3]	NA	NA	NA
Bone grafts	NA	350,000	350,000	350,000	NA	NA	450,000	30	NA	NA	NA
Skin grafts	NA	5,500	5,500	5,500	NA	NA	5,500	25	NA	NA	NA

1. Simultaneous kidney-pancreas transplants are counted twice, both in kidney transplants and in pancreas transplants. Double kidney, double lung, and heart-lung transplants are counted as one transplant. 2. 1985 through 1992, number of procedures and eye banks include Canada. 3. Eye banks. *Source:* Transplants: through 1992, U.S. Department of Health and Human Services, Public Health Service, Division of Organ Transplantation; beginning 1993, United Network for Organ Sharing, Richmond, Va.; American Association of Tissue Banks, McLean, Va; and Eye Bank Association of America, Washington, D.C.; and unpublished data.

The Common Cold

Source: National Institute of Allergy and Infectious Diseases, National Institutes of Health.

The Problem

In the course of a year, individuals in the United States suffer an estimated 1 billion colds. Colds are most prevalent among children, and seem to be related to youngsters' relative lack of resistance to infection and to contacts with other children in day-care centers and schools. Children have about six to ten colds a year. In families with children in school, the number of colds per child can be as high as 12 a year. Adults average about two to four colds a year, although the range varies widely. Women, especially those aged 20 to 30 years, have more colds than men, possibly because of their closer contact with children. On average, individuals older than 60 have fewer than one cold a year.

The Causes

The Viruses. More than 200 different viruses are known to cause the symptoms of the common cold. Some, such as the rhinoviruses, seldom produce serious illnesses. Others, such as parainfluenza and respiratory syncytial virus, produce mild infections in adults but can precipitate severe lower respiratory infections in young children.

Rhinoviruses (from the Greek *rhin,* meaning nose) cause an estimated 30 to 35 percent of all adult colds, and are most active in early fall, spring, and summer. More than 110 distinct rhinovirus types have been identified. These agents grow best at temperatures of 33° Celsius (about 91° Fahrenheit), the temperature of the human nasal mucosa.

Coronaviruses are believed to cause a large percentage of all adult colds. They induce colds primarily in the winter and early spring. Of the more than 30 isolated strains, three or four infect humans. The importance of coronaviruses as causative agents is hard to assess because, unlike rhinoviruses, they are difficult to grow in the laboratory.

The causes of 30% to 50% of adult colds, presumed to be viral, remain unidentified. The same viruses that produce colds in adults appear to cause colds in children. The relative importance of various viruses in pediatric colds, however, is unclear because of the difficulty in isolating the precise cause of symptoms in studies of children with colds.

Does cold weather cause a cold? Although many people are convinced that a cold results from exposure to cold weather, or from getting chilled or overheated, these conditions in fact have little or no effect on the development or severity of a cold. Nor is susceptibility apparently related to factors such as exercise, diet, or enlarged tonsils or adenoids. On the other hand, research suggests that psychological stress, allergic disorders affecting the nasal passages or pharynx (throat), and menstrual cycles may have an impact on a person's susceptibility to colds.

Cold Symptoms

Symptoms of the common cold usually begin two to three days after infection and often include nasal discharge, obstruction of nasal breathing, swelling of the sinus membranes, sneezing, sore throat, cough, and headache. Fever is usually slight but can climb to 102° F in infants and young children. Cold symptoms can last from two to 14 days, but two-thirds of people recover in a week. If symptoms occur often or last much longer than two weeks, they may be the result of an allergy rather than a cold.

Colds occasionally can lead to secondary bacterial infections of the middle ear or sinuses, requiring treatment with antibiotics. High fever, significantly swollen glands, severe facial pain in the sinuses, and a cough that produces mucus may indicate a complication or more serious illness requiring a doctor's attention.

How Cold Viruses Cause Disease

Viruses cause infection by overcoming the body's complex defense system. The body's first line of defense is mucus, produced by the membranes in the nose and throat. Mucus traps the material we inhale: pollen, dust, bacteria, and viruses. When a virus penetrates the mucus and enters a cell, it commandeers the protein-making machinery to manufacture new viruses which, in turn, attack surrounding cells.

Cold symptoms: the body fights back. Cold symptoms are probably the result of the body's immune response to the viral invasion. Virus-infected cells in the nose send out signals that recruit specialized white blood cells to the site of the infection. In turn, these cells emit a range of immune system chemicals such as kinins. These chemicals probably lead to the symptoms of the common cold by causing swelling and inflammation of the nasal membranes, leakage of proteins and fluid from capillaries and lymph vessels, and the increased production of mucus.

How Colds are Spread

Depending on the virus type, any or all of the following routes of transmission may be common:

- Touching infectious respiratory secretions on skin and on environmental surfaces and then touching the eyes or nose.
- Inhaling relatively large particles of respiratory secretions transported briefly in the air.
- Inhaling droplet nuclei, smaller infectious particles suspended in the air for long periods of time.

Prevention

Handwashing is the simplest and most effective way to keep from getting rhinovirus colds. Not touching the nose or eyes is another. Individuals with colds should always sneeze or cough into a facial tissue, and promptly throw it away. If possible, one should avoid close, prolonged exposure to persons who have colds.

Because rhinoviruses can survive up to three hours outside the nasal passages on inanimate objects and skin, cleaning environmental surfaces with a virus-killing disinfectant might help prevent spread of infection.

Treatment

Only symptomatic treatment is available for uncomplicated cases of the common cold: bed rest, plenty of fluids, gargling with warm salt water, petroleum jelly for a raw nose, and aspirin or acetaminophen to relieve headache or fever.

Nonprescription cold remedies, including decongestants and cough suppressants, may relieve some cold symptoms but will not prevent, cure, or even shorten the duration of illness. Nonprescription antihistamines may have some effect in relieving inflammatory responses such as runny nose and watery eyes.

Antibiotics do not kill viruses. These prescription drugs should be used only for rare bacterial complications, such as sinusitis or ear infections, that can develop as secondary infections. The use of antibiotic "just in case" will not prevent secondary bacterial infections.

Does vitamin C have a role? Many people are convinced that taking large quantities of vitamin C will prevent colds or relieve symptoms. To test this theory, several large-scale, controlled studies involving children and adults have been conducted. To date, no conclusive data has shown that large doses of vitamin C prevent colds. The vitamin may reduce the severity or duration of symptoms, but there is no definitive evidence.

Inhaling steam also has been proposed as a treatment of colds on the assumption that increasing the temperature inside the nose inhibits rhinovirus replication. Recent studies found that this approach had no effect on the symptoms or amount of viral shedding in individuals with rhinovirus colds. But steam may temporarily relieve symptoms of congestion associated with colds.

1-800-Toll-Free Numbers for Health Information

AL-ANON World Service Headquarters, 356-9996
Alcohol and Drug Helpline, 821-4357
Allergy Information Referral Line, 822-2762
Alzheimer's Disease Education and Referral Center, 438-4380
American Association of Kidney Patients, 749-2257
American Cancer Society Response Line, 227-2345
American Council of the Blind, 424-8666
American Council on Alcoholism, 527-5344
American Diabetes Association, 232-3472
American Foundation for Urologic Disease, 242-2383
American Heart Association Stroke Connection, 553-6321
American Institute for Cancer Research, 843-8114
American Kidney Fund, 638-8299
American Paralysis Association, 225-0292
American Parkinson's Disease Association, 223-2732
APA Spinal Cord Injury Hotline, 526-3456
Arthritis Foundation Information Hotline, 283-7800
Asthma and Allergy Foundation of America, 727-8462
Better Hearing Institute, 327-9355
Brain Injury Association, Family Helpline, 444-6443
Cancer Information Service, 4-CANCER; 422-6237
CDC National STD Hotline, 227-8922
Crohn's and Colitis Foundation of America, Inc., 932-2423
Cystic Fibrosis Foundation, 344-4823
Deafness Research Foundation, 535-3323
Endometriosis Association, 992-3636
Epilepsy Foundation of America, 332-1000
Huntington's Disease Society of America, 345-4372
International Childbirth Education Association, 624-4934
Juvenile Diabetes Foundation International Hotline, 223-1138
La Leche League International, LA-LECHE or 525-3243
Lupus Foundation of America, 558-0121
National Clearinghouse for Alcohol and Drug Information, 729-6686; 487-4889 (TTY/TDD)
National Cocaine Hotline, 262-2463
National Council on Alcoholism and Drug Dependence Hopeline Inc., 622-2255
National Down Syndrome Society Hotline, 221-4602
National Eye Research Foundation, 621-2258
National Headache Foundation, 843-2256
National Health Information Center, 336-4797
National Information Center for Children and Youth with Disabilities, 695-0285
National Institute of Mental Health, 647-2642 or 421-4211
National Kidney Foundation, 622-9010
National Marrow Donor Program, MARROW-2 or 627-7692
National Mental Health Association Information Center, 969-6642
National Multiple Sclerosis Society, LEARN-MS or 532-7667
National Neurofibromatosis Foundation, 323-7938
National Parkinson's Foundation, Inc., 327-4545
National Pesticide Telecommunications Network, 858-7378
National Spinal Cord Injury Association, 962-9629
National Stroke Association, STROKES or 787-6537
National Tuberous Sclerosis Association, 225-6872
Planned Parenthood, 230-PLAN or 230-7526
Project Inform HIV/AIDS Treatment Hotline, 822-7422
Safe Drinking Water Hotline, 426-4791
Sickle Cell Disease Association of America, 421-8453
Spina Bifida Association of America, 621-3141
Stuttering Foundation of America, 992-9392
Tourette Syndrome Association, 237-0717
United Cerebral Palsy Association, 872-5827
United Network for Organ Sharing, 243-6667
United Scleroderma Foundation, 722-HOPE or 722-4673
Y-ME National Organization for Breast Cancer Information Support Program, 221-2141

Health and Nutrition Web Sites

Centers for Disease Control www.cdc.gov
National Center for Infectious Diseases www.cdc.gov/ncidod/ncid.htm
National Institutes of Health www.nih.gov
National Cancer Institute www.nci.nih.gov
HIVNet www.hivnet.org
World Health Organization www.who.org
American Cancer Society www.cancer.org
American Heart Association www.amhrt.org
American Medical Association www.ama-assn.org
Alzheimers Association www.alz.org
American Psychological Association www.apa.org
Department of Health and Human Services www.dhhs.gov
American Academy of Pediatrics www.aap.org
Food and Drug Administration www.fda.gov
American Council on Science and Health www.acsh.org

Boot Camp Goes Soft

Attention! . . . *please?* Empathetic drill sergeants make basic training easier. But will the recruits be ready for war?

By MARK THOMPSON TIME

For most of this century, basic training was a deliberately harsh introduction to military life, a daily dose of screaming drill instructors dishing out vulgarity and physical intimidation to mortify—and motivate—trainees. These days drill sergeants spend more time mentoring than menacing. "We're no longer the charge-the-beach, stogie-in-the-mouth, cussing, hard-drinking, woman-chasing, World War II guy," says Senior Master Sergeant Paula Byrnes, who supervises basic training at Lackland Air Force Base in San Antonio, Texas. As the military's technology has grown more sophisticated, she says, the need for traditional warriors, trained in traditional ways, has waned. "The more technologically advanced we get," says Byrnes, "the less overtly brutal we need to be." And it's not just the Army. Complaints are ricocheting in all branches of the service that "basic" has lost its edge—the rigors aren't all that rigorous, there's more silliness than saluting at shape-ups, and there's altogether too much flirting between men and women.

Basic Training without the Basics

The services are under increasing pressure to stem a high dropout rate among trainees, and one way to do that is to make basic training easier for everyone to complete. The number of recruits who wash out after fewer than six months—which is how long it takes most members of the service to complete basic plus some advanced training—has climbed by a third over the past decade. "What we're ending up with is a kinder, gentler drill sergeant who is trying to keep attrition down," says Charles Moskos, a leading military sociologist at Northwestern University. "And kinder, gentler drill instructors are not necessarily creating the kind of force you want to go to war." Although the military denies it, many male soldiers and outside experts also believe that mingling men and women in boot camp—as the Air Force has done since 1977, the Navy since 1992, and the Army since 1994—leads to relaxed standards of physical performance and sexual tensions that diminish boot camp's effectiveness.

No one who went through boot camp in the 1950s or '60s would recognize the place today. Soldiers-in-training have swapped combat boots for sneakers (easier on the feet), fatigues for gym shorts and T shirts. Instead of running in formation, they run at their own pace, to challenge the speedy and avoid injuring the slower ones. On military obstacle courses they can run around, instead of over, some walls. In some quarters the very phrase "obstacle course" is frowned upon as too harsh. For the Navy, "confidence course" is now the preferred term.

To discourage physical abuse, which was once tolerated though never sanctioned, drill sergeants are forbidden to so much as touch recalcitrant recruits in an effort to get them to perform. "Stress created by physical or verbal abuse is non-productive and prohibited," says the Army's training manual. "Drill sergeants used to be able to discipline soldiers on the spot when they misbehaved," McQueen says. "But now you can't even touch them to check their ammunition."

Pampered Recruits

The nine weeks of Navy basic training begin on a luxury bus that takes recruits from O'Hare airport to the Navy's lone boot camp, Great Lakes Recruit Training Command, just north of Chicago. Onboard they watch an 18-minute orientation video with a rock-music soundtrack in which recent boot-camp grads tell the new arrivals that "physically, anybody can get through boot camp," and that it's O.K. to cry. Recruits get a "Blue Card," which helps them deal with stress. The card instructs a recruit to hand it over to a Navy trainer if he or she feels blue. "Thinking about running away?" it asks. "Help is less painful!"

On arrival recruits face a "moment of truth" during which they are told to divulge every secret in their past, such as drug use, arrests, and even traffic tickets. For years, that debriefing was a bit like a police interrogation, with signs threatening $10,000 fines and jail time for liars. Those signs have been replaced by posters of naval vessels and slides exhorting the kids to embrace "honor, courage, commitment." "When they see all these nice pictures, that gives them a warmer welcome than I got," says Senior Chief Petty Officer Norman Pretlow, a recruit-division commander.

The Navy has dropped other basic-training practices that old-timers say fostered cohesion and discipline. Since sailors don't usually salute other sailors below the rank of officer, recruits no longer salute their drill instructors, who are petty officers. Since few will ever use firearms in the line of duty, marching with rifles went out last year. The Navy says it's trying to instill standards that the recruits will understand and embrace, not just follow. "If I just say, 'At attention! Fall in!' I may get the behavior I want—80 recruits standing at attention—but what are they thinking about?" asks Master Chief Petty Officer Alan McCue. "But if you tell them that we're going to have this personnel inspection to instill pride in the unit, you will get pumped recruits who want to do it."

A Few Good Men

The Navy also says that approach gets results with young recruits who crave strict standards they may not be finding at home or in school. "The old method of getting right in your face and screaming and hollering sends them running," says Captain Cory Whitehead, commander of the Great Lakes boot camp. "They're hungry for standards, and if they're given one, they embrace it." Some officers outside of boot camp still think the whole enterprise has gone squishy. "When these kids get to the fleet," one commander says privately, "you can see it isn't working."

Lighter physical training, which many recruits get just three times a week, is another sore point. "They want us to put the Navy into our heart, not our muscles," complains recruit Michael Evans. Captain Whitehead counters that the old system overworked recruits, leading to stress fractures and other medical problems that delayed, or ended, fledgling Navy careers. "We had recruits piling up, waiting for them to get better so we could do it to them again," she says. "Now we rarely break them."

You're in the Army Now

As it happens, basic has become more congenial at the very moment when instructors face more recruits who, as products of an unbridled youth culture, have no instinctive respect for authority. "The resistance to leadership exhibited by this 'generation that was never spanked' undermines discipline and the rank-authority system," concludes a draft report prepared for the Pentagon by the Rand Corp., a California think tank. Older officers also complain that the new generation is more motivated than their predecessors by the financial incentives of the all-volunteer Army. "People used to come here for the 'duty, honor, country' aspect," says Sergeant Shawn Brown, an Army Reserve drill sergeant. "Now they're here for the Army College Fund." Retired Admiral Stan Arthur, who commanded Navy forces in the Persian Gulf War, sums it up this way: "It is almost as if the services are becoming unionized."

Mixing men and women in basic training has also caused some problems. Fresh from the sex scandal at the Army's Aberdeen Proving Ground in Maryland, the services are determined to make drill instructors understand that sexual exploitation of female recruits will not be tolerated. At the same time, military brass wants to discourage trainees from becoming distracted by the opposite sex. A recent Army study of mixed-gender training two years ago concluded: "Drill sergeants felt they had to keep the soldiers focused on the training, while the soldiers were focused on one another."

Forward, March!

Misgivings about the sturdiness of basic have gone all the way up the ranks. In 1997 Defense Secretary William Cohen ordered an outside panel, headed by former Sen. Nancy Kassebaum Baker, to assess training in all four branches of the service. The panel unanimously recommended tougher standards for recruits and their trainers. It also called for the segregation of men and women during basic training. Cohen supported the panel's recommendations except for its most controversial—the resegregation of troops. Reflecting the views of the Army, Navy, and Air Force chiefs, Cohen maintained that the military "cannot meet its obligations without the continued strong contribution of men and women working together."

The issue of gender segregation was a particularly sensitive one for the Army, having suspended mixed-gender training in 1982 after a five-year attempt—too many women were injured and too many men complained that training with women wasn't tough enough—then reinstating it in 1994. And of course the sex scandals at the Army's Aberdeen Proving Ground haven't helped its case. But Army officials insist integration is going well this time, and its top trainer, General William Hartzog, plans to lengthen basic training to include more human-relations instruction designed to curb sexual harassment. The issue of mixed-gender training has had no effect on the Marine Corp., which, unlike the three other branches, has never allowed men and women to train together in the first place.

Cohen's decision has infuriated some conservatives, and the controversy over mixed-gender training shows no signs of dying down soon. What few would debate, however, is the necessity of beefing up the rigors of basic training and improving recruits' physical fitness and combat skills. The draft of the Rand Corp. study that circulated around the Pentagon says only 42.9% of the troops surveyed believe their unit is ready for a crisis. "That number is unsettling," the study notes, "given that the military's job is to be prepared for what is essentially a sustained crisis." A lot of recruits agree. "If basic training was tougher, we'd end up with better soldiers," says Private Tony Steinhart at Fort Leonard Wood in Missouri. "I want somebody with me in my foxhole who can help me fight, and doesn't expect me to do it all." □

Highest Ranking Officers in U.S. History

General and Commander-in-Chief[1]

George Washington (1732–1799), b. Westmoreland County, Va., unanimously voted by Congress on June 15, 1775, to the rank of general and commander-in-chief (of the Continental Army).

General of the Armies[2]

John Joseph Pershing (1860–1948), b. Linn County, Mo., made permanent general of the armies 1919.

General of the Army, General of the Air Force (Five-Stars)

George Catlett Marshall (1880–1959), b. Uniontown, Pa., promoted December 1944.

Douglas MacArthur (1880–1964), b. Little Rock, Ark., promoted December 1944.

Dwight David Eisenhower (1890–1969), b. Denison, Texas, promoted December 1944.

Henry Harley Arnold (1866–1950), b. Gladwyne, Pa. Arnold had the unique distinction of being a five-star general twice—in 1944 as general of the army, and in June 1949 as general of the air force. He is the only air force general to have held the five-star rank.

Omar Nelson Bradley (1893–1981), b. Clark, Mo., promoted September 1950.

Fleet Admiral (Five-Star)

William Daniel Leahy (1875–1959), b. Hampton, Iowa, promoted December 1944.

Ernest Joseph King (1878–1956), b. Lorain, Ohio, promoted December 1944.

Chester William Nimitz (1885–1966), b. Fredericksburg, Texas, promoted December 1944.

William Frederick Halsey (1882–1959), b. Elizabeth, N.J., promoted December 1945.

1. On March 15, 1978, George Washington was promoted posthumously to the newly created rank of General of the Armies of the United States. Congress authorized this title to make it clear that Washington was the army's senior general. 2. General Pershing was given the option of five stars but he declined. *Source:* Department of Defense and U.S. Army Historian, Research and Analysis Center.

The Joint Chiefs of Staff (JCS)

The Joint Chiefs of Staff consist of the chairman, the vice chairman, the chief of staff of the army, the chief of naval operations, the chief of staff of the air force, and the commandant of the Marine Corps.

The collective body of the JCS is headed by the chairman (or vice chairman in the chairman's absence), who sets the agenda and presides over JCS meetings. Their responsibilities take precedence over their duties as the Chiefs of Military Services. The chairman is the principal military advisor to the president, the secretary of defense, and the National Security Council (NSC); however, all JCS members are by law military advisors, and they may respond to a request or voluntarily submit, through the chairman, advice or opinions to the president, the secretary of state, or the NSC. The Joint Chiefs of Staff have no executive authority to commit combatant forces.

In addition to their responsibilities on the JCS, the military service chiefs are responsible to the secretaries of their military departments for management of the services. The service chiefs serve for four years. By custom the vice chiefs of the services act for their chiefs in most matters having to do with day-to-day operation of the services.

Joint Chiefs of Staff, Mid-1998

Chairman of the Joint Chiefs of Staff, General Henry H. Shelton, U.S. Army; vice chairman of the Joint Chiefs of Staff, General Joseph W. Ralston, U.S. Air Force; General Dennis J. Reimer, chief of staff of the army; Admiral Jay L. Johnson, chief of naval operations; General Michael E. Ryan, chief of staff of the U.S. Air Force; and General Charles C. Krulak, commandant of the Marine Corps.

Past Chairmen of the JCS

General of the Army, Omar N. Bradley, 1949–1953
Adm. Arthur W. Radford, U.S. Navy, 1953–1957;
Gen. Nathan F. Twining, U.S. Air Force, 1957–1960
Gen. Lyman L. Lemnitzer, U.S. Army, 1960–1962
Gen. Maxwell D. Taylor, U.S. Army, 1962–1964
Gen. Earle G. Wheeler, U.S. Air Force, 1964–1970
Adm. Thomas H. Moorer, U.S. Navy, 1970–1974
Gen. George S. Brown, U.S. Air Force, 1974–1978
Gen. David C. Jones, U.S. Air Force, 1978–1982;
Gen. John W. Vessey, Jr., U.S. Army, 1982–1985
Adm. William J. Crowe, U.S. Navy, 1985–1989
Gen. Colin L. Powell, U.S. Army, 1989–1993
Gen. John M. Shalikashvili, U.S. Army, 1993–1997

U.S. Military Pay Grades

Source: U.S. Department of Defense.

Pay Grade	Army	Navy	Marines	Air Force
Commissioned Officers				
0-1	Second Lieutenant	Ensign	Second Lieutenant	Second Lieutenant
0-2	First Lieutenant	Lieutenant Junior Grade	First Lieutenant	First Lieutenant
0-3	Captain	Lieutenant	Captain	Captain
0-4	Major	Lieutenant Commander	Major	Major
0-5	Lieutenant Colonel	Commander	Lieutenant Colonel	Lieutenant Colonel
0-6	Colonel	Captain	Colonel	Colonel
0-7	Brigadier General	Rear Admiral (L)	Brigadier General	Brigadier General
0-8	Major General	Rear Admiral	Major General	Major General
0-9	Lieutenant General	Vice Admiral	Lieutenant General	Lieutenant General
0-10	General	Admiral	General	General
Special Grades[1]				
(5 stars)	General of the Army	Fleet Admiral	(none)	General of the Air Force
Warrant Officers				
W-1	Warrant Officer. Grades W-2 to W-5 Chief Warrant Officer			

Pay Grade	Army	Navy	Marines	Air Force
Enlisted Personnel				
E-1	Private	Seaman Recruit	Private	Airman Basic
E-2	Private	Seaman Apprentice	Private First Class	Airman
E-3	Private First Class	Seaman	Lance Corporal	Airman First Class
E-4	Corporal Specialist 4	Petty Officer, Third Class	Corporal	Sergeant Senior Airman
E-5	Sergeant Specialist 5	Petty Officer, Second Class	Sergeant	Staff Sergeant
E-6	Staff Sergeant Specialist 6	Petty Officer, First Class	Staff Sergeant	Technical Sergeant
E-7	Sergeant First Class Specialist 7	Chief Petty Officer	Gunnery Sergeant	Master Sergeant
E-8	First Sergeant Master Sergeant	Senior Chief Petty Officer	First Sergeant Master Sergeant	Senior Master Sergeant
E-9	Command Sergeant Major Sergeant Major	Master Chief Petty Officer	Sergeant Major Master Gunnery Sergeant	Chief Master Sergeant
Special Grades[2]				
	Sergeant Major of the Army	Master Chief Petty Officer of the Navy	Sergeant Major of the Marine Corps	Chief Master Sergeant of the Air Force

1. There are no living five-star commissioned officers. 2. Senior enlisted advisers. There is only one for each branch of service.

Monthly Basic Pay Rates by Grade, Effective 1998

Grade	Years of Service <2	2	4	6	10	14	16	18	20	26
Commissioned Officers										
0-10	7,566.30	7,832.40	7,832.40	7,832.40	8,133.00	8,583.60	9,197.70	9,197.70	9,813.60	10,424.70
0-9	6,705.60	6,881.40	7,028.10	7,028.10	7,206.60	7,506.60	8,133.00	8,133.00	8,583.60	9,197.70
0-8	6,073.50	6,255.90	6,404.10	6,404.10	6,881.40	7,206.60	7,506.60	7,832.40	8,133.00	8,333.70
0-7	5,046.60	5,389.80	5,389.80	5,631.60	5,958.00	6,255.90	6,881.40	7,354.80	7,354.80	7,354.80
0-6	3,740.40	4,109.40	4,379.10	4,379.10	4,379.10	4,527.90	5,243.70	5,511.30	5,631.60	6,461.70
0-5	2,991.90	3,512.70	3,755.70	3,755.70	3,868.80	4,350.90	4,676.70	4,944.30	5,094.60	5,272.50
0-4	2,521.50	3,070.80	3,275.40	3,336.30	3,721.20	4,109.40	4,290.30	4,407.90	4,407.90	4,407.90
0-3	2,343.30	2,619.90	3,099.00	3,247.50	3,546.00	3,812.40	3,812.40	3,812.40	3,812.40	3,812.40
0-2	2,043.60	2,231.70	2,771.40	2,828.70	2,828.70	2,828.70	2,828.70	2,828.70	2,828.70	2,828.70
0-1	1,774.20	1,846.50	2,231.70	2,231.70	2,231.70	2,231.70	2,231.70	2,231.70	2,231.70	2,231.70
Warrant Officers										
W-5	0.00	0.00	0.00	0.00	0.00	0.00	0.00	0.00	4,074.60	4,534.50
W-4	2,387.40	2,561.70	2,619.90	2,739.30	2,979.90	3,336.30	3,453.60	3,546.00	3,660.30	4,077.60
W-3	2,169.90	2,353.80	2,384.10	2,412.00	2,739.30	2,918.40	3,005.70	3,099.00	3,219.90	3,453.60
W-2	1,900.50	2,056.20	2,115.90	2,231.70	2,443.20	2,619.90	2,712.00	2,801.10	2,889.00	3,005.70
W-1	1,583.40	1,815.30	1,967.10	2,056.20	2,231.70	2,412.00	2,501.70	2,588.40	2,681.10	2,681.10
Enlisted Members										
E-9	0.00	0.00	0.00	0.00	2,777.40	2,904.00	2,970.90	3,037.50	3,096.00	3,576.00
E-8	0.00	0.00	0.00	0.00	2,396.10	2,522.70	2,589.60	2,648.40	2,713.50	3,193.50
E-7	1,626.30	1,755.60	1,884.30	1,948.50	2,074.80	2,236.20	2,299.80	2,363.40	2,394.30	2,873.10
E-6	1,398.90	1,524.90	1,655.70	1,718.10	1,845.30	2,001.30	2,065.80	2,097.00	2,097.00	2,097.00
E-5	1,227.60	1,336.20	1,462.20	1,558.20	1,685.70	1,779.90	1,779.90	1,779.90	1,779.90	1,779.90
E-4	1,144.80	1,209.30	1,379.10	1,433.70	1,433.70	1,433.70	1,433.70	1,433.70	1,433.70	1,433.70
E-3	1,079.10	1,137.90	1,230.30	1,230.30	1,230.30	1,230.30	1,230.30	1,230.30	1,230.30	1,230.30
E-2	1,038.30	1,038.30	1,038.30	1,038.30	1,038.30	1,038.30	1,038.30	1,038.30	1,038.30	1,038.30
E-1>4	926.10	926.10	926.10	926.10	926.10	926.10	926.10	926.10	926.10	926.10

NOTE: E-1 with less than 4 months: $856.80.

Service Academies

U.S. Military Academy

Source: U.S. Military Academy.

Established in 1802 by an act of Congress, the U.S. Military Academy is located on the west bank of the Hudson River some 50 miles north of New York City. To gain admission a candidate must first secure a nomination from an authorized source. These sources are:

Congressional Sources

Representatives
Senators
Other: Vice Presidential
District of Columbia
Puerto Rico
Am. Samoa, Guam, Virgin Is.

Military-Service-Connected Sources

Presidential—Sons or daughters of active-duty or retired service members
Enlisted members of Army
Enlisted members of Army Reserve/National Guard
Sons or daughters of deceased and disabled veterans
Honor military, naval schools, and ROTC
Sons or daughters of persons awarded the Medal of Honor

Any number of applicants can meet the requirements for a *nomination* in these categories. *Appointments* (offers of admission), however, can only be made to a much smaller number, about 1,150 to 1,200 each year.

Candidates may be nominated for vacancies during the year preceding the day of admission, which occurs in late June or early July. The best time to apply is during the spring of the junior year in high school.

Candidates must be citizens of the U.S. at time of enrollment (except foreign students admitted by agreement between the U.S. and another country), be unmarried, not be pregnant or have a legal obligation to support a child or children, be at least 17 but not yet 23 years old on July 1 of the year admitted, have a secondary-school education or its equivalent, and be able to meet the academic, medical, and physical aptitude requirements. Academic qualification is determined by an analysis of the entire scholastic record, and performance on either the American College Testing (ACT) Assessment Program Test or the College Entrance Examination Board Scholastic Assessment Tests (SAT). Entrance requirements and procedures for appointment are described in the Admissions Bulletin and the Admissions Prospectus, available without charge from Admissions, U.S. Military Academy, West Point, NY 10996-1797. Phone: 914-938-4041.

Cadets are members of the U.S. Army. As such they receive annual salaries of more than $6,500 from which they pay for their uniforms, textbooks, and incidental expenses. There is no tuition and room and board are provided. Upon successful completion of the four-year course, the graduate receives the degree of bachelor of science and is commissioned a second lieutenant in the U.S. Army with a requirement to serve as an officer on active duty for a minimum of five years.

U.S. Naval Academy

Source: U.S. Naval Academy.

The Naval School, established in 1845 at Fort Severn, Annapolis, Md., was renamed the U.S. Naval Academy in 1850. A four-year course was adopted a year later. The "Yard," as the campus is referred to, blends French Renaissance and modern architecture with many new academic, athletic, and laboratory facilities.

The superintendent is a navy admiral. A civilian academic dean heads the academic program. A captain heads the 4,000 members of the Brigade of Midshipmen and military, professional, and physical training. The 600-member faculty at the academy is about half military and half civilian professors. All courses are taught by these faculty members. The student-faculty ratio is low, with most class sizes ranging from 10 to 22 students.

Eighteen majors are offered in engineering, science, mathematics, social sciences, and the humanities. Graduates are awarded the bachelor of science or bachelor of science in engineering and are commissioned as officers in the U.S. Navy or Marine Corps.

To have basic eligibility for admission, candidates must be citizens of the U.S., of good moral character, at least 17 and not more than 23 years of age on July 1 of their entering year, unmarried, not pregnant, and without legal obligation to dependents.

The Admissions Board at the Naval Academy examines each candidate's school record, College Board or ACT scores, recommendations from school officials, extracurricular activities, and evidence from other sources concerning his or her character, leadership potential, academic preparation, and physical fitness. Qualification for admission is based on all of the above factors.

Tuition, board, lodging, and medical and dental care are provided. Midshipmen receive $543.90 a month for books, uniforms, and personal needs. In return, graduates agree to serve at least five years on active duty as an officer after graduation.

For general information or answers to specific questions, write: Director of Candidate Guidance, U.S. Naval Academy, Annapolis, MD 21402-5018, or call 1-800-638-9156.

U.S. Air Force Academy

Source: U.S. Air Force Academy.

The bill establishing the U.S. Air Force Academy was signed by President Eisenhower on April 1, 1954. The first class of 306 cadets was sworn in on July 11, 1955, at Lowry Air Force Base, Denver, Colo., the academy's temporary location. The Cadet Wing moved into the academy's permanent home north of Colorado Springs, Colo., in 1958.

Service Academy Web Sites

U.S. Military Academy: www.usma.edu
U.S. Air Force Academy: www.usafa.af.mil
U.S. Naval Academy: www.nadn.navy.mil
U.S. Coast Guard Academy: www.cga.edu
U.S. Merchant Marine Academy: www.usmma.edu

Military & Veterans Web Sites

U.S. Air Force: www.af.mil
U.S. Army: www.army.mil
U.S. Navy: www.navy.mil
MarineLINK: www.usmc.mil
U.S. Coast Guard: www.uscg.mil
DefenseLink (DOD): www.dtic.mil/defenselink
Military Woman:
www.wimsa.org (not a DOD or armed forces site)
Selective Service System: www.sss.gov
Department of Veterans Affairs (VA):
www.va.gov
BosniaLINK: www.dtic.mil/bosnia/index.html
Gulf War Veterans: www.gulfweb.org
Vietnam Veterans:
grunt.space.swri.edu/index.htm
WWII U.S. Veterans: ww2.vet.org
Korea War Veterans Memorial:
www.nps.gov/kwvm/index2.htm
Medal of Honor Museum:
www.ngeorgia.com/history/sites/mohm.htm
American Legion: www.legion.org
Air America: www.air-america.org
North Atlantic Treaty Organization (NATO):
www.nato.int

Cadets receive four years of academic, military, and physical education to prepare them for leadership as officers in the air force. The academy is authorized a total of 4,000 cadets. Each new class averages 1,200. The candidates for the academy must be at least 17 and not have passed their 23rd birthday on July 1 of the year for which they enter the academy, must be a U.S. citizen, be unmarried, have no dependents, be of good moral character, and be able to meet the mental and physical requirements. International students authorized admission are exempt from the U.S. citizenship requirement. A candidate is required to take the following examinations and tests: (1) the Service Academies' Qualifying Medical Examination; (2) either the American College Testing (ACT) Assessment Program test or the College Entrance Examination Board Scholastic Assessment Test (SAT); and (3) a candidate fitness test.

Cadets receive their entire education at government expense and, in addition, receive a monthly salary to pay for supplies, clothing, and personal expenses. Prior to admission, appointees deposit $2,500 to help defray the initial cost of uniforms and supplies. Upon completion of the four-year program, leading to a bachelor of science degree, a cadet who meets the qualifications is commissioned a second lieutenant in the U.S. Air Force. For details on admissions, call 1-800-443-9266, or write: HQ USAFA/RRS, 2304 Cadet Drive, Suite 200, USAF Academy, CO 80840-5025.

U.S. Coast Guard Academy

Source: U.S. Coast Guard Academy.

The U.S. Coast Guard Academy is the only one of the four armed forces service academies that offers appointments based solely on the basis of an annual nationwide competition, with no congressional appointments or geographical quotas. Competition is open to all U.S. citizens who have reached their 17th but not their 22nd birthday by July 1 of the entering year. Cadets receive a full scholarship including room and board. In addition, they receive a monthly allowance of approximately $560.

In selecting students for admission, the Academy prohibits discrimination based on gender, race, color, national origin, or religion. Factors considered in the competition include SAT or ACT scores, high-school standing, and leadership potential as demonstrated by participation in high-school extracurricular activities, community affairs, or part-time employment. All candidates must pass a strict medical and physical fitness examination.

A viewbook or video can be obtained by writing to Director of Admission, U.S. Coast Guard Academy, 15 Mohegan Avenue, New London, CT 06320, or by calling 1-800-883-8724 or 860-444-8500.

U.S. Merchant Marine Academy

Source: U.S. Merchant Marine Academy.

The U.S. Merchant Marine Academy, situated at Kings Point, N.Y., on the north shore of Long Island, was dedicated September 30, 1943. It is maintained by the Department of Transportation under direction of the Maritime Administration.

The academy has a complement of approximately 950 men and women representing every state, D.C., the Canal Zone, Puerto Rico, Guam, American Samoa, and the Virgin Islands. It is also authorized to admit up to 12 candidates from the Western Hemisphere and 30 other foreign students at any one time.

Candidates are nominated by senators and members of the House of Representatives. Nominations to the academy are governed by a state and territory quota system based on population and the results of the College Entrance Examination Board tests.

A candidate must be a citizen not less than 17 and not yet 25 years of age by July 1 of the year in which admission is sought. Candidates must have acceptable SAT or ACT test scores and have successfully completed at least 15 high-school credits, including 3 units in mathematics (from algebra, geometry, and/or trigonometry), 1 unit in science (physics or chemistry), and 3 in English.

The course is four years and includes one year of practical training aboard a merchant ship. Study includes marine engineering, navigation, satellite navigation and communications, electricity, ship construction, naval science and tactics, economics, business, languages, history, etc.

Upon completion of the course of study, a graduate receives a bachelor of science degree, a license as a merchant marine deck or engineering officer, and a commission as an ensign in the Naval Reserve.

For additional information, write to Admissions Office, U.S. Merchant Marine Academy, Kings Point, NY, 11024, or call 516-482-3933.

The National Guard

Source: Departments of the Army and the Air Force, National Guard Bureau.

Dual Role

The National Guard is unique among the U.S. reserve military forces, filling both federal and state missions. In peacetime, the National Guard is commanded by the governors of the states and territories and may be called to active state duty by the governor in response to natural disasters, civil disturbances, or other state emergencies. During a war or national emergency, the National Guard may be called to active duty by the president or Congress, and serves as the primary source of augmentation for the active army and active air force.

As a reserve component of the U.S. military, the National Guard makes up a significant part of what is called the Total Force—active-duty service members, the reserve components, and the civilians who are employed by the Department of Defense. The other federal reserve components include the Army Reserve, Naval Reserve, Marine Corps Reserve, Air Force Reserve, and Coast Guard Reserve. Members in all of these organizations are trained and equipped in units that are available for full-time duty in case of war or national emergency. However, the other federal reserve components of the military services, unlike the National Guard, are legally and operationally linked only to the active-duty services, not the states. This distinction of having both federal and state missions makes the National Guard unique.

Geographically Diverse

Today, the National Guard is composed of the Army National Guard and the Air National Guard. The Army National Guard is made up of more than 3,000 units located in 2,200 communities throughout the 50 states, Puerto Rico, Guam, the Virgin Islands, and the District of Columbia. The U.S. Army's largest reserve force, the Army National Guard provides roughly 55% of the army's total combat capability, and approximately 35% of its combat support and 35% of its combat service support units. Units are provided modern military equipment including M-1 tanks, Bradley Fighting Vehicles, and Blackhawk helicopters.

The Air National Guard has 89 flying units and 1,500 support units at 177 locations. This represents approximately one-third of the U.S. Air Force's fighter and air-transport assets. Air National Guard units fly F-16 fighters, KC-135 tankers, B-1B bombers, and C-130 transports, among other aircraft.

Same Benefits and Training as Active Duty

As part of the nation's total military force, Army and Air National Guard units are trained and equipped to mesh with active duty and other federal reserve component forces. Typically, members of the National Guard report for training duty one weekend per month, along with a minimum of 15 days of continuous unit training each year. Weekend training usually is performed at the unit's community armory or nearby military training facility. The annual training usually is performed at a large military training base or overseas location, frequently in cooperation with active duty and other reserve units.

National Guard members receive a full day's pay at their military rank for each unit training assembly they attend, for the 15 days of annual training, and for any military school or special assignment they may complete. All such training counts toward retirement. A member who has 20 or more years of qualifying military service begins to collect retired pay at age 60.

For 1997 the mission strength of the Army National Guard was 370,000, and the Air National Guard 110,000. The 1997 federal budget for both components was approximately $10 billion. States and territories provide additional funds to support state missions, recruiting and training administration, armory construction, and funding for state-salaried employees.

Additional information about the National Guard may be obtained from local units or from the National Guard Bureau, 2500 Army Pentagon, Washington, DC 20310-2500.

Veterans and Dependents on the Compensation and Pension Rolls (July 1, 1997)

	Veterans	Children	Parents	Surviving Spouses
Civil War	—	17	—	2
Indian Wars	—	1	—	2
Spanish-American War	—	356	—	810
Mexican Border	18	26	—	386
World War I	1,269	7,419	2	56,267
World War II	855,049	20,792	3,943	308,675
Korean Conflict	279,544	4,867	2,881	68,867
Vietnam Era	799,313	17,951	8,290	98,533
Persian Gulf War	192,929	5,805	319	3,766
Total	**2,554,214**[1]	**67,445**[2]	**18,772**[3]	**575,462**[4]

1. Includes 536,089 peacetime veterans with service between January 31, 1955, and August 5, 1964; peacetime veterans with service beginning after May 7, 1975, and all other peacetime periods; and 3 World War I Retired Emergency Officers. 2. Includes 10,211 children of deceased peacetime veterans. 3. Includes 3,337 parents of deceased peacetime veterans. 4. Includes 38,154 surviving spouses of deceased peacetime veterans. *Source:* Department of Veterans Affairs.

Active Military Duty Personnel, 1940–1997[1]

As of September 30, 1997, there were 1,438,562 active duty military personnel. This is a decrease of 33,160 from the FY 1996 figure.

Year	Army[2]	Air Force[2, 3]	Navy	Marine Corps	Total
1940	269,023		160,997	28,345	458,365
1945	8,266,373		3,319,586	469,925	12,055,884
1950	593,167	411,277	380,739	74,279	1,459,462
1955	1,109,296	959,946	660,695	205,170	2,935,107
1960	873,078	814,752	616,987	170,621	2,475,438
1965	969,066	824,662	669,985	190,213	2,653,926
1970	1,322,548	791,349	691,126	259,737	3,064,760
1975	784,333	612,751	535,085	195,951	2,128,120
1980	777,036	557,969	527,153	188,469	2,050,627
1985	780,787	601,515	570,705	198,025	2,151,032
1990	732,403	535,233	579,417	196,652	2,043,705
1991	710,821	510,432	570,262	194,040	1,985,555
1992	610,450	470,315	541,883	184,529	1,807,177
1993	572,423	444,351	509,950	178,379	1,705,103
1994	541,343	426,327	468,662	174,158	1,610,490
1995	508,559	400,409	434,617	174,639	1,518,224
1996	491,103	389,001	416,735	174,883	1,471,722
1997	491,707	377,385	395,564	173,906	1,438,562

1. Military personnel on extended or continuous active duty. Excludes reserves on active duty for training. Prior year totals have been corrected. 2. Represents "Command Strength" prior to June 30, 1956. 3. Army Air Forces and its predecessors for period prior to September 18, 1947. *Source:* Department of Defense.

The Medal of Honor

Often called the Congressional Medal of Honor, it is the nation's highest military award for "uncommon valor" by men and women in the armed forces. It is given for actions that are above and beyond the call of duty in combat against an armed enemy. The medal was first awarded by the army on March 25, 1863.

Recipients of the medal receive $400 per month for life, a right to burial at Arlington National Cemetery, admission for them or their children to a service academy (if they qualify and quotas permit), and free travel on government aircraft to almost anywhere in the world, on a space-available basis.

Medal of Honor Recipients

	Total[1]	Army	Navy	Marines	Air Force	Coast Guard
Civil War	1,520	1,195	308	17	—	—
Indian Wars (1861–1898)	428	428	—	—	—	—
Korea (1871)	15	—	9	6	—	—
Spanish-American War	109	30	64	15	—	—
Philippines/Samoa	91	70	12	9	—	—
Boxer Rebellion	59	4	22	33	—	—
Veracruz (1914)	55	—	46	9	—	—
Haiti (1915)	6	—	—	6	—	—
Dominican Republic	3	—	—	3	—	—
Haiti (1919–1920)	2	—	—	2	—	—
Nicaragua (1927–1933)	2	—	—	2	—	—
Peacetime (1865–1870)	12	—	12	—	—	—
Peacetime (1871–1898)	103	—	101	2	—	—
Peacetime (1899–1911)	51	1	48	2	—	—
Peacetime (1915–1916)	8	—	8	—	—	—
Peacetime (1920–1940)	18	2	15	1	—	—
World War I	124	96	21	7	—	—
World War II	440	301	57	81	—	1
Korean War	131	78	7	42	4	—
Vietnam War	239	155	15	57	12	—
Somalia (1993)	2	2	—	—	—	—
Unknown Soldiers	9	—	—	—	—	—
Total	**3,427**	**2,362**	**745**	**294**	**16**	**1**

1. These totals reflect the total number of Medals of Honor awarded. Nineteen (19) men received a second award. The total number of Medal of Honor recipients is 3,408. As of May 13, 1997, there are 169 living Medal of Honor recipients. *Source:* The Congressional Medal of Honor Society, Mt. Pleasant, S.C.

Female Military Personnel on Active Duty by Grade

Rank/Grade	Army	Air Force	Navy	Marine Corps	Total
Total officers	10,389	12,008	7,796	788	30,981
Total enlisted	61,849	53,167	44,142	8,498	167,656
Cadets & midshipmen	589	660	640	—	1,889
Grand total	72,827	65,835	52,578	9,286	200,526

U.S. Casualties in the Major Wars

War	Branch of service	Numbers engaged	Battle deaths	Other deaths	Total deaths	Wounds not mortal	Total casualties[1]
Revolutionary War (1775 to 1783)	Army	n.a.	4,044	n.a.	n.a.	6,004	n.a.
	Navy	n.a.	342	n.a.	n.a.	114	n.a.
	Marines	n.a.	49	n.a.	n.a.	70	n.a.
	Total	**n.a.**	**4,435**	**n.a.**	**n.a.**	**6,188**	**n.a.**
War of 1812 (1812 to 1815)	Army	n.a.	1,950	n.a.	n.a.	4,000	n.a.
	Navy	n.a.	265	n.a.	n.a.	439	n.a.
	Marines	n.a.	45	n.a.	n.a.	66	n.a.
	Total	**286,730**	**2,260**	**n.a.**	**n.a.**	**4,505**	**n.a.**
Mexican War (1846 to 1848)	Army	n.a.	1,721	11,550	13,271	4,102	17,373
	Navy	n.a.	1	n.a.	n.a.	3	n.a.
	Marines	n.a.	11	n.a.	n.a.	47	n.a.
	Total	**78,718**	**1,733**	**n.a.**	**n.a.**	**4,152**	**n.a.**
Civil War (1861 to 1865)[2]	Army	2,128,948	138,154	221,374	359,528	280,040	639,568
	Navy	84,415	2,112	2,411	4,523	1,710	6,233
	Marines		148	312	460	131	591
	Total	**2,213,363**	**140,414**	**224,097**	**364,511**	**281,881**	**646,392**
Spanish-American War (1898)	Army	280,564	369	2,061	2,430	1,594	4,024
	Navy	22,875	10	0	10	47	57
	Marines	3,321	6	0	6	21	27
	Total	**306,760**	**385**	**2,061**	**2,446**	**1,662**	**4,108**
World War I (1917 to 1918)	Army	4,057,101	50,510	55,868	106,378	193,663	300,041
	Navy	599,051	431	6,856	7,287	819	8,106
	Marines	78,839	2,461	390	2,851	9,520	12,371
	Total	**4,734,991**	**53,402**	**63,114**	**116,516**	**204,002**	**320,518**
World War II (1941 to 1946)	Army[3]	11,260,000	234,874	83,400	318,274	565,861	884,135
	Navy	4,183,466	36,950	25,664	62,614	37,778	100,392
	Marines	669,100	19,733	4,778	24,511	67,207	91,718
	Total	**16,112,566**	**291,557**	**113,842**	**405,399**	**670,846**	**1,076,245**
Korean War (1950 to 1953)	Army	2,834,000	27,709	2,452	30,161	77,596	107,757
	Navy	1,177,000	475	173	648	1,576	2,224
	Marines	424,000	4,270	339	4,609	23,744	28,353
	Air Force	1,285,000	1,198	298	1,496	368	1,864
	Total	**5,720,000**	**33,652**	**3,262**	**36,914**	**103,284**	**140,198**
War in Southeast Asia[4]	Army	4,368,000	30,914	7,275	38,189	96,802	134,991
	Navy	1,842,000	1,631	928	2,559	4,178	6,737
	Marines	794,000	13,082	1,754	14,836	51,392	66,228
	Air Force	1,740,000	1,739	844	2,583	931	3,514
	Total	**8,744,000**	**47,366**	**10,801**	**58,167**	**153,303**	**211,470**

1. Excludes captured or interned and missing in action who were subsequently returned to military control. 2. Union forces only. Totals should probably be somewhat larger as data or disposition of prisoners are far from complete. Final Confederate deaths, based on incomplete returns, were 133,821, to which should be added 26,000–31,000 personnel who died in Union prisons. 178,975 blacks served in the Union Army. 2,894 were killed in battle or mortally wounded, 33,953 died from other causes including 29,658 deaths from disease. 3. Army data include air force. 4. Vietnam figures provided by the U.S. Center of Military History, Reference Division, Washington, D.C., February 1994. Navy figures exclude coast guard, in which there were 5 battle deaths. NOTE: All data are subject to revision. For wars before World War I, information represents best data from available records. However, due to incomplete records and possible difference in usage of terminology, reporting systems, etc., figures should be considered estimates. n.a. = not available. *Source:* Department of Defense.

Casualties in World War I

Country	Total mobilized forces	Killed or died[1]	Wounded	Prisoners or missing	Total casualties
Austria-Hungary	7,800,000	1,200,000	3,620,000	2,200,000	7,020,000
Belgium	267,000	13,716	44,686	34,659	93,061
British Empire[2]	8,904,467	908,371	2,090,212	191,652	3,190,235
Bulgaria	1,200,000	87,500	152,390	27,029	266,919
France[2]	8,410,000	1,357,800	4,266,000	537,000	6,160,800
Germany	11,000,000	1,773,700	4,216,058	1,152,800	7,142,558
Greece	230,000	5,000	21,000	1,000	27,000
Italy	5,615,000	650,000	947,000	600,000	2,197,000
Japan	800,000	300	907	3	1,210
Montenegro	50,000	3,000	10,000	7,000	20,000
Portugal	100,000	7,222	13,751	12,318	33,291
Romania	750,000	335,706	120,000	80,000	535,706
Russia	12,000,000	1,700,000	4,950,000	2,500,000	9,150,000
Serbia	707,343	45,000	133,148	152,958	331,106
Turkey	2,850,000	325,000	400,000	250,000	975,000
United States	4,734,991	116,516	204,002	—	320,518

1. Includes deaths from all causes. 2. Official figures. NOTE: For additional U.S. figures, *see* the table U.S. Casualties in the Major Wars. *Source:* Department of Defense.

Casualties in World War II

Country	Men in war	Battle deaths	Wounded
Australia	1,000,000	26,976	180,864
Austria	800,000	280,000	350,117
Belgium	625,000	8,460	55,513[1]
Brazil[2]	40,334	943	4,222
Bulgaria	339,760	6,671	21,878
Canada	1,086,343[7]	42,042[7]	53,145
China[3]	17,250,521	1,324,516	1,762,006
Czechoslovakia	—	6,683[4]	8,017
Denmark	—	4,339	—
Finland	500,000	79,047	50,000
France	—	201,568	400,000
Germany	20,000,000	3,250,000[4]	7,250,000
Greece	—	17,024	47,290
Hungary	—	147,435	89,313
India	2,393,891	32,121	64,354
Italy	3,100,000	149,496[4]	66,716
Japan	9,700,000	1,270,000	140,000
Netherlands	280,000	6,500	2,860
New Zealand	194,000	11,625[4]	17,000
Norway	75,000	2,000	—
Poland	—	664,000	530,000
Romania	650,000[5]	350,000[6]	—
South Africa	410,056	2,473	—
U.S.S.R.	—	6,115,000[4]	14,012,000
United Kingdom	5,896,000	357,116[4]	369,267
United States	16,112,566	291,557	670,846
Yugoslavia	3,741,000	305,000	425,000

1. Civilians only. 2. Army and navy figures. 3. Figures cover period July 7, 1937–Sept. 2, 1945, and concern only Chinese regular troops. They do not include casualties suffered by guerrillas and local military corps. 4. Deaths from all causes. 5. Against Soviet Russia; 385,847 against Nazi Germany. 6. Against Soviet Russia; 169,822 against Nazi Germany. 7. National Defense Ctr., Canadian Forces Hq., Director of History. NOTE: The figures in this table are unofficial estimates obtained from various sources.

Merchant Marine Casualties in World War II

In 1988, the U.S. government conferred official veteran status on those who served aboard oceangoing merchant ships in World War II. The officers and crews played a key role in transporting the troops and war material that enabled the United States and its allies to defeat the Axis powers.

During the war, merchant seamen died as a result of enemy attacks at a rate that proportionately exceeded all branches of the armed services, with the exception of the U.S. Marine Corps.

Enemy action sank more than 700 U.S.-flag merchant ships and claimed the lives of over 6,000 civilian seafarers. Untold thousands of additional seamen were wounded or injured during these attacks, and nearly 600 were made prisoners of war.

U.S. Postal Rates and Fees

Domestic Rates as of Jan. 10, 1999

First-Class Mail

Single-Piece Letter/Flat Rates

1st ounce	$0.33
Each additional ounce	0.22

Weight not over (oz.)	Rate	Weight not over (oz.)	Rate
1*	$0.33	9	$2.09
2	0.55	10	2.31
3	0.77	11	2.53
4	0.99	12	2.75
5	1.21	13	2.97
6	1.43	Over 13 ounces, *see* Priority Mail.	
7	1.65		
8	1.87		

*Nonstandard surcharge may apply to pieces weighing 1 ounce or less based on size.

Card Rates

Single postal card sold by United States Postal Service	$0.20
Double postal card sold by USPS	0.40
Single postcard (commercial)	0.20

Postcard Dimensions: Not larger than 4¼ by 6 inches by 0.016 inch thick. Not smaller than 3½ by 5 inches by 0.007 inch thick.

Periodicals

Only publishers and registered news agents approved for periodicals mailing privileges may mail at periodicals rates. Publications mailed by the public are charged at the applicable Express Mail, Priority Mail, single-piece First-Class, standard "A," or standard "B" rates.

Standard "A"

Used primarily by retailers, catalogers, and other advertisers to promote products and services. See postmaster for details. **Use**—For mailing certain items—circulars, books, catalogs, other printed matter, merchandise, seeds, cuttings, bulbs, and plants—weighing less than 16 ounces.

Express Mail

Express Mail is the postal service's fastest service. Next-day delivery by 12 noon to most destinations. Delivered 365 days a year with no extra charge for Saturday, Sunday, or holiday delivery. All packages must use an Express Mail label. Items may weigh up to 70 pounds and measure up to 108 inches in combined length and girth. Call 1-800-222-1811 for delivery information between ZIP codes.

Features—Express Mail envelopes, labels, and boxes are available, at no additional charge, at post offices or by calling 1-800-222-1811.

Post Office to Addressee Service

Up to 8 ounces	$11.75
Over 8 ounces, up to 2 pounds	15.75
Up to 3 pounds	17.25
Up to 4 pounds	19.40
Up to 5 pounds	21.55
Up to 6 pounds	25.40
Up to 7 pounds	26.45
Over 7 pounds, see postmaster.	

Flat-Rate Envelope—Post Office to Addressee Service

$15.00, regardless of weight or destination for matter sent in a flat-rate envelope provided by the Postal Service.

Priority Mail

Priority Mail offers two-day service to most domestic destinations. Items may weigh up to 70 pounds and measure up to 108 inches in combined length and girth.

Delivery confirmation for Priority Mail has been introduced. For mailers who apply their own barcodes and access postal information systems for electronic confirmation, the service is free. Manual service is $0.35.

Features—Priority Mail envelopes, labels, and boxes are available, at no additional charge, at post offices or by calling 1-800-222-1811.

Single-Piece Rates[1]

Up to 2 pounds	$3.20
Up to 3 pounds	4.00
Up to 4 pounds	5.00
Up to 5 pounds	6.00
Over 5 pounds, see postmaster.	

1 A parcel weighing less than 15 pounds but measuring more than 84 inches in length and girth combined is chargeable with a minimum rate equal to that for a 15-pound parcel for the zone to which it is addressed.

Flat-Rate Envelope

$3.00, regardless of weight or destination, for matter sent in a flat-rate envelope provided by the Postal Service.

Standard "B"

For mailing circulars, books, catalogs, other printed matter, and packages weighing 16 ounces or more. Enclosed or attached First-Class Mail is charged at First-Class rates. Packages may weigh up to 70 pounds and measure up to 108 inches in combined length and girth.

Parcel Post Zone Rates

For rates priced by distance and weight, see postmaster.

Special Services (Domestic Mail)

Certificate of Mailing

Proves that an item was mailed. Must be purchased at time of mailing. No record kept at the post office.

Fee, in addition to postage—$0.60

Certified Mail

Provides a mailing receipt, and a record is kept at the recipient's post office. A return receipt can also be purchased for an additional fee. Available only with First-Class and Priority Mail.

Fee, in addition to postage—$1.40

Insurance

Provides coverage against loss or damage. Coverage up to $600.00 for standard "A" and standard "B" mail as well as standard "A" and standard "B" matter mailed at Priority Mail or First-Class Mail rate. Insurance up to $25,000 can be purchased by using Registered Mail. Do not insure a package for more than its value.

Liability	Fee, in addition to postage
$.01 to $50.00	$0.75
$50.01 to $100.00	1.60
$100.01 to $200.00	2.50
$200.01 to $300.00	3.40
$300.01 to $400.00	4.30
$400.01 to $500.00	5.20
$500.01 to $600.00	6.10

Money Orders

Provides safe transmission of money. Available in amounts up to $700.00.

Fee, in addition to postage—$0.80

Registered Mail

Provides maximum protection and security for valuables. Available only for Priority Mail and First-Class Mail. May be combined with COD, Restricted Delivery, or Return Receipt. Additional postal insurance available.

	Declared Value	Fee, in addition to postage
Without Insurance	$0.00	$6.00
With Insurance	$0.01 to $100	6.20
	$100.01 to $500.00	6.75
	$500.01 to $1,000.00	7.30
	$1,000.01 to $2,000.00	7.85

For higher values, consult your postmaster.

Restricted Delivery

Available only for Certified Mail, COD, Insured Mail for more than $50.00, or Registered Mail.

Fee, in addition to postage—$2.75

Return Receipt

Available only for Express Mail, Certified Mail, COD, Insured Mail for more than $50.00, or Registered Mail.

Requested at time of mailing:

Showing to whom (signature) and date delivered	$1.25
Showing to whom (signature), date, and addressee's address	1.50

Requested after mailing:

Showing to whom (signature) and date delivered	7.00

Special Delivery

Available for all classes except Express Mail. Provides preferential handling to the extent practicable in dispatch, transportation, and expedited delivery at the destination.

	Fee, in addition to postage		
Class of mail	2 lb. or less	Over 2 lb., but not over 10 lb.	Over 10 lb.
First-Class & Priority Mail	$ 9.95	$10.35	$11.15
Other classes	10.45	11.25	12.10

Collect on Delivery (COD)

Allows mailers to collect the price of goods and/or postage on merchandise ordered by addressee when it is delivered. Fees include insurance. Maximum amount $600.00; see postmaster for details.

Sizes for Domestic Mail

Mail must meet these standards:

• Thickness—No less than 0.007 inch thick. Pieces that are ¼ inch thick or less must be at least 3½ inches high, 5 inches long, and rectangular in shape.

• Combined length and girth—No more than 108 inches.

• Weight—No more than 70 pounds.

Keys and identification devices are exempted from these requirements.

Additional standards apply to bulk mail and mail addressed to APOs and FPOs.

The Mail-Order Merchandise Rule

The mail-order rule adopted by the Federal Trade Commission in October 1975 provides that when you order by mail:

• You must receive the merchandise when the seller says you will.

• If you are not promised delivery within a certain time period, the seller must ship the merchandise to you no later than 30 days after your order comes in.

• If you don't receive it shortly after that 30-day period, you can cancel your order and get your money back.

How the Rule Works

The seller must notify you if the promised delivery date (or the 30-day limit) cannot be met. The seller must also tell you what the new shipping date will be and give you the option to cancel the order and receive a full refund or agree to the new shipping date. The seller must also give you a free way to send back your answer, such as a stamped envelope or a postage-paid postcard. *If you don't answer, it means that you agree to the shipping delay.*

The seller must tell you if the shipping delay is going to be more than 30 days. You then can agree to the delay or, if you do not agree, the seller must return your money by the end of the first 30 days of the delay.

If you cancel a prepaid order, the seller must mail you the refund within seven business days. Where there is a credit sale, the seller must adjust your account within one billing cycle.

It would be impossible, however, for one rule to apply uniformly to such a varied field as mail-order merchandising. For example, the rule does not apply to mail-order photofinishing, magazine subscriptions, and other serial deliveries (except for the initial shipment); to mail-order seeds and growing plants; to COD orders; or to credit orders where the buyer's account is not charged prior to shipment of the merchandise.

International Postal Rates

As of July 1997

Letters and Letter Packages—Airmail Rates

All countries except Canada and Mexico

Weight not over (oz.)		Weight not over (oz.)	
0.5	$0.60	9.0	$ 7.40
1.0	1.00	9.5	7.80
1.5	1.40	10.0	8.20
2.0	1.80	10.5	8.60
2.5	2.20	11.0	9.00
3.0	2.60	11.5	9.40
3.5	3.00	12.0	9.80
4.0	3.40	12.5	10.20
4.5	3.80	13.0	10.60
5.0	4.20	13.5	11.00
5.5	4.60	14.0	11.40
6.0	5.00	14.5	11.80
6.5	5.40	15.0	12.20
7.0	5.80	15.5	12.60
7.5	6.20	16.0	13.00
8.0	6.60	16.5	13.40
8.5	7.00		

See postmaster for weights up to 4 lb. Maximum weight: 64 ounces.

Aerogrammes: All countries—$0.50

Letters and Letter Packages—Canada and Mexico

Weight not over (lb.)	(oz.)	Canada[1]	Mexico	Weight not over (lb.)	(oz.)	Canada[1]	Mexico
0	0.5	$0.46	$0.40	0	10	$2.28	$ 4.06
0	1	0.52	0.46	0	11	2.47	4.46
0	1.5	0.64	0.66	0	12	2.66	4.86
0	2	0.72	0.86	1	0	3.42	6.46
0	3	0.95	1.26	1	8	4.30	9.66
0	4	1.14	1.66	2	0	5.18	12.86
0	5	1.33	2.06	2	8	6.06	16.06
0	6	1.52	2.46	3	0	6.94	19.26
0	7	1.71	2.86	3	8	7.82	22.46
0	8	1.90	3.26	4	0	8.70	25.66
0	9	2.09	3.66				

1. A 4-pound maximum applies except for registered items sent to Canada. Canada-bound registered items may weigh up to 66 pounds. For registered items weighing over 4 pounds, the rate is $1.76 for each additional pound up to the 66-pound limit.

Postcards and Postal Rates: Canada—$0.40; Mexico—$0.35; all others—$0.50

All-Time Top 10 Most Popular Commemorative Stamps

Issue	Number of stamps saved (millions)	Issue	Number of stamps saved (millions)
Elvis '93	124.0	Legends of the West '94	46.5
Wildflowers '92	76.2	Marilyn Monroe '95	46.3
Rock and Roll '93	75.8	Bugs Bunny '97	45.3
Moon Landing '94	47.9	Summer Olympics '92	39.6
Civil War '95	46.6	Centennial Olympic Games '96	38.1

State Abbreviations

Since the Postal Service instituted ZIP codes and their accompanying state postal codes in 1963, the two-letter abbreviations have steadily gained popularity. Though it is usually preferable to write out the full name, space constraints often require use of an abbreviation; when this is the case, the standard abbreviation is strongly preferred. The postal code abbreviation should be used only in mailing addresses.

State	Preferred abbreviation	Postal code	State	Preferred abbreviation	Postal code	State	Preferred abbreviation	Postal code
Alabama	Ala.	AL	Kentucky	Ky.	KY	Ohio	Ohio	OH
Alaska	Alaska	AK	Louisiana	La.	LA	Oklahoma	Okla.	OK
Arizona	Ariz.	AZ	Maine	Maine	ME	Oregon	Ore.	OR
Arkansas	Ark.	AR	Maryland	Md.	MD	Pennsylvania	Pa.	PA
California	Calif.	CA	Massachusetts	Mass.	MA	Puerto Rico	P.R.	PR
Colorado	Colo.	CO	Michigan	Mich.	MI	Rhode Island	R.I.	RI
Connecticut	Conn.	CT	Minnesota	Minn.	MN	South Carolina	S.C.	SC
Delaware	Del.	DE	Mississippi	Miss.	MS	South Dakota	S.D.	SD
Dist. of Columbia	D.C.	DC	Missouri	Mo.	MO	Tennessee	Tenn.	TN
Florida	Fla.	FL	Montana	Mont.	MT	Texas	Tex.	TX
Georgia	Ga.	GA	Nebraska	Nebr.	NE	Utah	Utah	UT
Guam	Guam	GU	Nevada	Nev.	NV	Vermont	Vt.	VT
Hawaii	Hawaii	HI	New Hampshire	N.H.	NH	Virginia	Va.	VA
Idaho	Idaho	ID	New Jersey	N.J.	NJ	Virgin Islands	V.I.	VI
Illinois	Ill.	IL	New Mexico	N.M.	NM	Washington	Wash.	WA
Indiana	Ind.	IN	New York	N.Y.	NY	West Virginia	W.Va.	WV
Iowa	Iowa	IA	North Carolina	N.C.	NC	Wisconsin	Wis.	WI
Kansas	Kans.	KS	North Dakota	N.D.	ND	Wyoming	Wyo.	WY

Social Security Reform

Taxpayers say they'll take some risks to rescue Social Security

By KAREN TUMULTY TIME

The stock-market boom has, it seems, turned Americans into a nation of risk takers—even when it means tampering with the largest, most popular, and most politically treacherous social program ever devised. In a TIME/CNN poll, 60% of those surveyed said they would like to play the market with some of their Social Security taxes; and if they could, 80% said they and not Washington should control where the money goes. Support was strongest among people under age 35, the group that stands to get the least under the current system. The radical—and to Democratic traditionalists, heretical—idea of "privatizing" at least part of the system is being discussed seriously for the first time outside libertarian and conservative think tanks.

In the end, any fix in Social Security will involve adjusting the current system, changing the nature of the program—or, most likely, a little of both. Those who want to keep the existing system on life support can buy time the same way they have before: by raising taxes and reducing benefits. But even the most obvious measures will not be so easy to put in place. Many Americans already pay more in Social Security taxes than they do in income taxes. Further raising the retirement age (now slated to go to age 67) as a way of acknowledging that people are living longer would seem to make sense. But an increasing number of Americans are retiring earlier, not later. In fact, 60% of today's Social Security beneficiaries are beginning to collect at 62, accepting reduced benefits to get more years off the job. Only 10% took that option in 1960.

So the existing system may have been stretched about as far as it will go. Critics of the idea of privitization have warned that investors expecting big returns may be sobered by enormous administrative costs and turnover fees. And even Americans woozy from the stock market's climb still cling to their traditional concept of Social Security as a safety net, not an alternative to Merrill Lynch. More than two-thirds of those surveyed in the TIME/CNN poll said they regard Social Security primarily as a benefit program designed to assure the elderly a minimum income during retirement.

Fixing what's wrong with the system is no trickier than preserving the parts that work. But first the country has to understand which is which. Everyone from the libertarian Cato Institute to the American Association of Retired Persons is ready to offer a different answer, but for now all agree that the main thing is to get people thinking about the issue. □

Social Security: A TIME/CNN Poll

Is there a crisis in the financial condition of the Social Security system?

Crisis	31%
Problem	55%
No problem	10%

Will the Social Security system go bankrupt before you retire?*

Yes	54%
No	42%

Do you favor or oppose:	Favor	Oppose
Raising the taxes that higher-income retirees pay on their Social Security benefits?	41%	55%
Reducing payments for people receiving benefits?	20%	75%
Raising the retirement age to receive full benefits?	24%	73%
Raising taxes on all Americans receiving benefits?	11%	86%

From a telephone poll of 1,011 adult Americans taken for TIME/CNN on April 8 – 9, 1998, by Yankelovich Partners, Inc. Sampling error is ±3.1%. "Not Sures" omitted.

* Asked 853 people under 65. Sampling error is ±3.3.

Should the government allow Americans to invest a portion of their Social Security taxes in investments such as the stock market?

Should	60%
Should not	35%

If these investments were allowed, who should control them, the government or individuals?

Government	14%
Individuals	80%

Should the government compensate those who invest part of their Social Security taxes on their own and make less money than they would have in the Social Security system?

Yes	21%	**No**	72%

Have you saved for your retirement in any of these ways?*	Yes
Pension plan paid for by employer	50%
401(k) plan	45%
Tax-deferred IRA	34%
Taxable account	29%
None of the above	25%

Social Security

The original Social Security Act was passed in 1935 and is administered by the Social Security Administration and other agencies within the Department of Health and Human Services.

What Does Social Security Offer?

The Social Security contribution you pay gives you four different kinds of protection: (1) retirement benefits, (2) survivors' benefits, (3) disability benefits, and (4) Medicare hospital insurance benefits.

Retirement and Dependents' Benefits

Currently, a worker becomes eligible for the full amount of his retirement benefits at age 65, if he has retired under the definition in the law. A worker may retire at age 62 and get 80% of his full benefit. The closer he is to age 65, when he starts collecting his benefit, the larger is the fraction of his full benefit that he will get. Once the worker receives a reduced benefit, the reduction continues after age 65.

The amount of the retirement benefit you are entitled to at age 65 is the key to all other benefits under the program. The retirement benefit is based on covered earnings, which will be updated (indexed) to the second year before you reach age 62, become disabled, or die, and will reflect the increases in average wages that have occurred since the earnings were paid. The largest 35 years of adjusted earnings are averaged together and a formula is applied to the adjusted average to figure the benefit rate.

A worker who delays his retirement past age 65, or who does not receive a benefit for some months after age 65 because of high earnings, will get a special credit that can mean a larger benefit. The credit adds to a worker's benefits 1% (3% for workers age 62 from 1979–1986) for each year (1/12 of 1% for each month) from age 65 to age 70 for which he did not get benefits.

The law provides a special minimum benefit at retirement for people who had low incomes under Social Security during their working years. The amount of the special minimum depends on the number of years above a specific earnings level called "years of coverage." For a worker retiring at age 65 in January 1997 with 30 or more years of coverage, the special minimum benefit would be $548.30. These benefits are reduced if a worker is under 65 and are increased automatically for increases in the cost of living.

If you retired at age 65 in January 1997 with average earnings, you would get a benefit of $933. If your spouse is also 65, then he or she will get a spouse's benefit that is equal to half your benefit. So if your benefit is $933, your spouse gets $466.

If your spouse is between ages 62 and 65, he or she can draw a reduced benefit; the amount depends on the number of months before 65 that he or she starts getting checks. If he or she draws his or her benefit when he or she is 62, he or she will get about 3/8 of your basic benefit, or $349. (He or she will get this amount for the rest of his or her life, unless you should die first; then he or she can start getting widow's or widower's benefits, described below.)

If the spouse is entitled to a worker's retirement benefit on his or her own earnings, he or she can draw whichever amount is larger. If the spouse is entitled to a retirement benefit that is less than the spouse's benefit, he or she will receive his or her own retirement benefit plus the difference between the retirement benefit and the spouse's benefit.

If you have children under age 19 attending a primary or secondary school, or a son or daughter who became totally disabled prior to reaching age 22, they will receive a benefit equal to half your full retirement benefits (subject to maximum monthly payment that can be made to a family). Children who can qualify for benefits include your biological or legally adopted child, or dependent stepchild or grandchild. If your spouse is caring for your child, and the child is under 16 or disabled (and under the age of 22), he or she is eligible for benefits.

In general, the highest retirement check that can be paid to a worker who retired at 65 in January 1997 is about $1,327.60 a month. Maximum payment to the family of this retired worker is about $2,324.40 in January 1997. When your children reach age 18, their benefits will stop except for children age 19 and under attending an elementary or secondary school full time and except for a benefit that is going to a son or daughter who became totally disabled before attaining age 22. Such a person can continue to get his benefits as long as his disability meets the definition in the law.

If you are divorced, you can get Social Security benefits (the same as a former spouse, widow, or widower), based on your former spouse's earnings record if you were married at least 10 years and if your former spouse has retired or become disabled. If a divorced spouse has been divorced for at least 2 years, the spouse may be eligible for benefits even if the worker is not receiving benefits. However, both the worker and spouse must be age 62 or over and the worker must be fully insured. In either case, the divorced spouse must be unmarried.

Survivor Benefits

This feature of the Social Security program gives your family valuable life-insurance protection—in some cases benefits to a family could amount to $100,000 or more over a period of years. The amount of protection is again geared to what the worker would be entitled to if he had been age 65 when he died. Total family survivor benefits were estimated to be as high as $2,534.00 a month if the worker died in 1995. Your survivors could get:

1. A one-time cash payment. [NOTE: There is no restriction on the use of the lump-sum death payment.]

2. A benefit for each child until he reaches 18, or 19 if the child is in full-time attendance at an elementary or secondary school, or at any age if disabled before 22. "Child" includes biological or legally adopted child, or dependent stepchild or grandchild. Each eligible child receives 75% of the basic benefit (subject to reduction for the family maximum). A disabled child can continue to collect benefits after age 22.

3. A benefit for your widow(er), including your surviving divorced spouse, at any age, if she/he has your entitled children under 16 or disabled in care. These are called mother/father benefits. "Your children" includes your biological or

legally adopted children, dependent stepchildren, or grandchildren. In the case of a surviving divorced spouse, the child must also be the divorced spouse's biological or legally adopted child. Her/his benefit is also 75% of the basic benefit. She/he can collect this as long as she/he has an entitled child under 16 or disabled now "in care." If payments terminate they will start again upon application when she/he is 60 at a slightly lower amount.

4. Your spouse or divorced spouse can get a widow's, widower's, or surviving divorced spouse's benefit starting at age 60. This benefit equals 71½% of the basic amount at age 60. A widow, or widower, who first becomes entitled at 65 or later will get 100% of his or her deceased spouse's basic amount (or the amount of the deceased spouse's reduced benefits). A widow(er) or surviving divorced spouse, including those who are disabled, must be unmarried. However, a marriage occurring after age 60, or after age 50 if disabled at the time of the remarriage, is disregarded.
5. Dependent parents can sometimes collect survivors' benefits. They are usually eligible if: (a) they were getting at least half their support from the deceased worker at (1) the time of the worker's death if the worker did not qualify for disability benefits before death, or (2) if the worker had been entitled to disability benefits, which had not been terminated before death either at the beginning of the period of disability or at the time of death; (b) they have reached 62; (c) they are not eligible for a greater retirement benefit based on their own earnings; and (d) they have not married since the worker's death. One surviving parent can then get 82½% of the basic benefit. If two parents are eligible, each would get 75%.

If in addition to your Social Security benefit as a wife, husband, divorced spouse, widow, widower, or surviving divorced spouse you receive a pension based on your work in employment not covered by Social Security, your benefit as a spouse or survivor will be reduced by two-thirds of the amount of that pension. Under an exception in the law, your government pension will not affect your spouse's or survivor's benefit if you became eligible for that pension before December 1982 and if, at the time you apply or become entitled to your Social Security benefit as a spouse or survivor, you could have qualified for that benefit if the law in effect in January 1977 had remained in effect (e.g., at that time, men had to prove they were dependent upon their wives for half of their support to be eligible for benefits as a spouse or survivor.) There are also several other exceptions in the law. Your government pension may also affect Social Security benefits based on your own work covered by Social Security. (*See* Retirement and Dependents' Benefits).

Disability Benefits

Disability benefits can be paid to several groups of people:

• Disabled workers under age 65 and their families.

• Persons disabled before age 22 who continue to be disabled. These benefits are payable as early as age 18 when a parent (or step-parent or grandparent under certain circumstances) receives Social Security retirement or disability benefits or when an insured parent dies.

• Disabled widows and widowers and (under certain conditions) disabled, surviving, divorced spouses of workers who were insured at death. These benefits are payable as early as 50. Consult your local Social Security office for the latest disability information.

Medicare Program

The Medicare program is a federal health-insurance program for persons 65 and over, and certain disabled people under 65. Enacted under the Social Security Amendments of 1965, Medicare's official name is Title XVIII of the Social Security Act. These amendments also carried Title XIX, providing federal assistance to state medical-aid programs, which has come to be known as Medicaid.

Medicare Facts

• The federal health insurance program does not offer medical services. It helps pay hospital, doctor, and other medical bills. You should always make sure that healthcare facilities or persons who provide you with treatment or services are participating in Medicare. Usually, Medicare cannot pay for care from non-participating health care organizations.

• If you live in an area served by a managed care plan, you can get your Medicare benefits either through the fee-for-service system or through a managed care plan such as a health maintenance organization (HMO). Under fee-for-service, you can choose your doctor, hospital, or other health care provider. A fee is generally charged for each service and Medicare pays its share of the bill. Under managed care, you usually must get all of your care from the doctors, hospitals, and other health care providers that are part of the plan. Medicare pays the HMO for your care. Depending on the plan, you may have to pay a monthly premium and a co-payment each time you go to the doctor or use other services.

• There are two parts of the program: (1) the hospital insurance part for the payment of most of the cost of covered care provided by participating hospitals, skilled nursing facilities, home health agencies, and hospices; and (2) the medical insurance part that helps pay doctors' bills and certain other expenses.

• While Medicare pays the major share of the costs of many illnesses requiring hospitalization, it does not offer adequate protection for long-term illness or mental illness and Medicare does not pay for custodial care, so you may wish to consider supplemental insurance.

• For help in deciding whether to buy private supplemental insurance, ask at any Social Security office for the pamphlet *Guide to Health Insurance for People with Medicare.* This free pamphlet describes the various types of supplemental insurance available.

Do You Qualify for Hospital Insurance?

If you're entitled to monthly Social Security or railroad retirement checks (as a worker, dependent, or survivor), you have hospital insurance protection automatically when you're 65. People age 65 or older who are not entitled to monthly benefits must have worked long enough under Social Security or the railroad retirement system or in covered federal, state, and local employment to get hospital insurance without paying a monthly premium. If they do not have enough work, they can get hospital insurance by paying a monthly premium. Disabled people under 65 will receive hospital insurance automatically after they have been entitled to Social Security disability benefits for 24 months. Effective July 1, 1990, former disability beneficiaries are able to purchase hospital insurance if their premium-free coverage stops due to work activity. Federal, state, or local employees who are disabled before 65 may be eligible on the basis of their government employment. People are eligible at any age if they need maintenance dialysis or a kidney transplant for permanent kidney failure and are getting monthly Social Security or railroad retirement benefits, or have worked long enough.

To be sure your protection will start the month you reach 65, apply for Medicare insurance three months before reaching 65, even if you don't plan to retire.

Do You Qualify for Medicare Medical Insurance?

The medical insurance plan is a vital supplement to the hospital plan. It helps pay for doctors' and other medical services. Many people have not been able to obtain such insurance from private companies because they could not afford it or because of their medical histories.

Any person who can get premium-free hospital insurance benefits based on work as described above can enroll in the medical insurance plan and get medical insurance benefits. In addition, most United States residents age 65 or over can enroll in the medical insurance plan.

People who get Social Security benefits or retirement benefits under the railroad retirement system will be enrolled automatically for medical insurance when they become entitled to hospital insurance. Automatic enrollment does not apply to people who have not applied for Social Security or railroad retirement benefits, who have permanent kidney failure, who are eligible for Medicare on the basis of government employment, or people who have not worked long enough to be eligible for hospital insurance. These people have to apply for medical insurance if they want it. People who have medical insurance pay a monthly premium covering part of the cost of this protection. They should enroll for Part B as soon as they are eligible, to avoid paying premium surcharges for delayed enrollment. The basic premium for enrollees was $43.50 a month in 1997.

Is Other Insurance Necessary?

As already indicated, Medicare provides only partial reimbursement. Therefore, you should know how much medical cost you can bear and perhaps arrange for other insurance.

In 1997, for the first 60 days of in-patient hospital care in each benefit period, hospital insurance pays for all covered services except for the first $760. For the 61st through 90th day of a covered in-patient hospital stay, hospital insurance pays for all covered services except for $190 per day. People who need to be in a hospital for more than 90 days in a benefit period can use some or all of their 60 lifetime reserve days. Hospital insurance pays for all covered services except for $380 per day for each reserve day used. Hospital insurance pays the full cost of the first 20 days of an in-patient stay in a skilled nursing facility per benefit period.

Under medical insurance, the patient must meet an annual deductible. In 1996, the annual deductible was $100. After the patient has met the deductible, each year, medical insurance generally pays 80% of the approved amounts for any additional covered services the patient receives during the rest of the year.

How You Obtain Coverage

If you are receiving Social Security or railroad retirement monthly benefits, you will receive from the government information concerning Medicare about three months before you become eligible for hospital insurance.

All other eligible people have to file an application for Medicare. They should contact a Social Security office to apply for Medicare.

Medicare Benefits

Breast Cancer Screening (Mammography): Medicare medical insurance now helps pay for X-ray screenings to detect breast cancer. Women 65 or older can use the benefit every other year. Younger disabled women covered by Medicare can use it more frequently.

Physician Payment Reforms: As of 1996, physicians may not charge you more than 115% of the Medicare approved amount. Physicians who knowingly charge more than these amounts are subject to sanctions.

You no longer have to file claims to Medicare for covered medical insurance services. Doctors, suppliers, and other providers of services must submit the claims to Medicare within one year of providing the service to you or be subject to certain penalties. □

Spiriting Prayer into School

Prayer clubs are bringing religion back to school—legally

By DAVID VAN BIEMA TIME

A growing number of after-school prayer clubs have brought worship back to American public school campuses. In 1963 the Supreme Court issued a landmark ruling banning compulsory prayer in public schools. After that, any worship on public premises, let alone a prayer club, was widely understood as forbidden. But for the past few years, thanks to a subsequent court case, such groups not only have been legal but have become legion.

Available statistics are approximate, but they suggest that there are clubs in as many as one out of every four public schools in the country. In some areas the tally is much higher: evangelicals in Minneapolis–St. Paul claim that the vast majority of high schools in the Twin Cities region have a Christian group. Says Benny Proffitt, a Southern Baptist youth-club planter: "We had no idea in the early '90s that the response would be so great. We believe that if we are to see America's young people come to Christ and America turn around, it's going to happen through our schools, not our churches."

Legal Groundwork

The clubs' explosive spread coincides with a more radical but largely unsuccessful movement for a complete overturn of the 1963 ruling. The Religious Freedom Amendment, a constitutional revision proposed by House Republican Ernest Istook of Oklahoma that would have reinstated full-scale school prayer, failed to gain the support of the House. On one of many local battlefields, Alabama Governor Fob James signed a 1998 state bill mandating a daily moment of silence, which was proposed in response to a 1997 federal ruling voiding an earlier state pro–school prayer law. The law is likely to trigger court challenges, as have a number of past controversial church-state issues championed by the governor.

The new tolerance for religion in the schoolyard culminates a quarter-century of legislative and legal maneuvering. The 1963 Supreme Court decision and its broad-brush enforcement by school administrators infuriated conservative Christians, who gradually developed enough clout to force Congress to make a change. The resulting Equal Access Act of 1984 required any federally funded secondary school to permit religious meetings if the schools allowed other clubs not related to curriculum, such as public-service Key Clubs. The crucial rule was that the prayer clubs had to be voluntary, student-run, and not convened during class time.

Early drafts of the act were specifically pro-Christian. Ultimately, however, its argument was stated in pure civil-libertarian terms: prayers that would be coercive if required of all students during class are protected free speech if they are just one more after-school activity. Nevertheless, recalls Marc Stern, a staff lawyer with the American Jewish Congress, "there was great fear that this would serve as the base for very intrusive and aggressive proselytizing." Accordingly, Stern's group and other organizations challenged the law—only to see it sustained, 8 to 1, by the Supreme Court in 1990. Bill Clinton apparently agreed with the court. The President remains opposed to compulsory school prayer, but in a July 1995 speech he announced that "nothing in the First Amendment converts our public schools into religion-free zones or requires all religious expression to be left at the schoolhouse door."

Free Speech or Proselytizing?

Reaction to the prayer clubs may depend on which besieged minority one feels part of. In the many areas where Conservative Christians feel looked down on, they welcome the emotional support for their children's faith. Similarly, non-Christians in the Bible Belt may be put off by the clubs' evangelical fervor; members of the chess society, after all, do not inform peers that they must push pawns or risk eternal damnation. Not everyone shares the enthusiasm Proffitt expressed at a youth rally in Niagara Falls, N.Y.: "When an awakening takes place, we see 50, 100, 1,000, 10,000 come to Christ. Can you imagine 100, or 300, come to Christ in your school? We want to see our campuses come to Christ." Watchdog organizations like Americans United for the Separation of Church and State report cases in which such zeal has approached harassment of students and teachers, student prayer leaders have seemed mere puppets for adult evangelists, and activists have tried to establish prayer clubs in elementary schools, where the description "student-run" seems disingenuous. Nevertheless, the Jewish Congress's Stern concedes that "there's been much less controversy than one might have expected from the hysterical predictions we made."

For now, the prospects for prayer clubs seem unlimited. In fact, the tragic shooting of eight prayer-club members in December 1997 in West Paducah, Ky., by 14-year-old Michael Carneal provided the cause with martyrs and produced a hero in prayer-club president Ben Strong, who persuaded Carneal to lay down his gun. Strong recalls that the club's daily meetings used to draw only 35 to 60 students. "People didn't really look down on us, but I don't know if it was cool to be a Christian," he says. Now 100 to 150 teens attend. Strong has since toured three states extolling the value of Christian clubs. "It woke a lot of kids up," he says. "That's true everywhere I've spoken. This is a national thing." □

Non-Christian Religious Adherents in the United States

Adherents	Year 1900	% of total pop.	Mid-1970	% of total pop.	Mid-1990	% of total pop.	Mid-1995	% of total pop.	(Projected) mid-2000	% of total pop.
Total	**2,724,800**	**3.6**	**20,789,000**	**9.9**	**37,079,000**	**14.6**	**39,077,000**	**14.6**	**41,054,000**	**14.8**
Atheists	1,000	0.0	200,000	0.1	770,000	0.3	874,000	0.3	925,000	0.3
Baha'ists	2,800	0.0	138,000	0.1	600,000	0.2	683,000	0.3	750,000	0.3
Buddhists	30,000	0.0	200,000	0.1	1,680,000	0.7	1,864,000	0.7	2,000,000	0.7
Chinese folk religionists	70,000	0.1	90,000	0.0	76,000	0.0	74,000	0.0	70,000	0.0
Hindus	1,000	0.0	100,000	0.0	650,000	0.3	795,000	0.3	950,000	0.3
Jews	1,500,000	2.0	6,700,000	3.2	5,535,000	2.2	5,518,000	2.1	5,500,000	2.0
Muslims	10,000	0.0	800,000	0.4	3,600,000	1.4	3,767,000	1.4	3,950,000	1.4
Black Muslims	0	0.0	200,000	0.1	1,250,000	0.5	1,400,000	0.5	1,650,000	0.6
New-Religionists	0	0.0	110,000	0.1	575,000	0.2	603,000	0.2	675,000	0.2
Nonreligious	1,000,000	1.3	11,730,000	5.6	22,233,000	8.7	23,394,000	8.8	24,554,000	8.8
Sikhs	0	0.0	1,000	0.0	160,000	0.1	190,000	0.1	220,000	0.1
Tribal religionists	100,000	0.1	70,000	0.0	280,000	0.1	305,000	0.1	350,000	0.1
Other religionists	10,000	0.0	650,000	0.3	920,000	0.4	1,010,000	0.4	1,110,000	0.4

Non-Christians: Followers of non-Christian religions or of no religion; the 12 largest such varieties are listed. Jews: Core Jewish population relating to Judaism, excluding Jewish persons professing a different religion but including immigrants from the former U.S.S.R., Eastern Europe, Israel, and other areas. Figures for C.E. 2000 are projections based on current long-term trends. *Source:* Reprinted with permission from *1998 Britannica Book of the Year.* © 1998 Encyclopedia Britannica, Inc.

Religious Population of the World, 1996
(in thousands)

Statistics of the world's religions are only very rough approximations. Aside from Christianity, few religions, if any, attempt to keep statistical records; and even Protestants and Catholics employ different methods of counting members. All persons of whatever age who have received baptism in the Catholic Church are counted as members, while in most Protestant Churches only those who "join" the church are numbered. The compiling of statistics is further complicated by the fact that in China one may be at the same time a Confucian, a Taoist, and a Buddhist. In Japan, one may be both a Buddhist and a Shintoist.

Religion	Total	Percent distribution	Africa	Asia[1]	Latin America	Northern America	Europe[2]	Oceania
Total Religious Population[3]	**5,804,120**	**100.0%**	**748,130**	**3,513,218**	**490,444**	**295,677**	**727,678**	**28,973**
Christians (total)	1,955,229	33.7%	360,874	303,127	455,819	255,542	555,614	24,253
Roman Catholics	981,465	16.9%	125,376	94,250	408,968	75,398	269,021	8,452
Protestants	404,020	7.0%	114,726	45,326	34,816	121,361	79,534	8,257
Orthodox	218,350	3.8%	25,215	13,970	460	6,390	171,665	650
Anglicans	69,136	1.2%	27,200	650	1,089	6,300	28,357	5,540
Other Christians	282,258	4.9%	68,357	148,931	10,486	46,093	7,037	1,354
Muslims[4]	1,126,325	19.4%	308,660	778,362	1,356	5,530	32,032	385
Nonreligious[5]	886,929	15.3%	3,567	752,759	16,053	21,315	90,390	2,845
Hindus[6]	793,076	13.7%	1,986	786,991	760	1,365	1,650	323
Buddhists[7]	325,275	5.6%	38	321,985	569	920	1,563	200
Athiests[8]	222,195	3.8%	440	175,450	3,010	1,850	40,845	600
Chinese folk religionists[9]	220,971	3.8%	13	220,653	68	100	120	17
New-Religionists[10]	106,016	1.8%	21	103,361	919	900	803	11
Ethnic Religions	102,945	1.8%	70,250	30,350	1,042	45	1,150	108
Sikhs	19,508	0.3%	37	18,465	9	496	494	7
Jews	13,866	0.2%	165	4,257	1,084	5,836	2,432	92
Spiritists	10,293	0.2%	5	1,120	8,834	315	18	1
Baha'is	6,404	0.1%	1,923	3,230	722	357	95	77
Confucians	5,086	0.1%	1	5,050	3	27	5	1
Jains	4,920	0.1%	59	4,835	5	5	16	1
Shintoists	2,898	—	—	2,893	1	2	1	1
Other Religionists[11]	1,952	—	90	100	190	1,072	450	50
Parsees	191	—	2	185	1	1	1	1
Mandeans	45	—	—	45	—	—	—	—

1. Asia includes the former U.S.S.R. Central Asian republics. 2. Europe includes the Russian Federation, extending to its easternmost boundaries. 3. Total population figures are the U.N. medium variant figures for mid-1996. 4. Muslims: 83% Sunnis, 16% Shi'ites, 1% other. 5. Persons professing no religion, nonbelievers, agnostics, freethinkers, and formerly religious secularists. 6. Hindus: including 70% Vaishnavites, 25% Shaivites, 2% neo-Hindus and reform Hindus. 7. Buddhists: 56% Mahayana, 38% Theravada (Hinayana), and 6% Tantrayana (Lamaism). 8. Persons professing atheism, skepticism, disbelief, or antireligion (opposed to all religion). 9. Followers of the traditional Chinese religion (local deities, ancestor veneration, Confucian ethics, Taoism, universism, divination, some Buddhist elements). 10. Followers of Asian 20th-century New Religions, New Religious movements, radical new crisis religions, and non-Christian syncretistic mass religions, all founded since 1800 and most since 1945. 11. Including 70 minor world religions and a large number of spiritist religions, New Age religions, quasi-religions, and religious or mystic belief systems. Reprinted with permission from *1997 Britannica Book of the Year.* © 1997 Encyclopedia Britannica, Inc.

Major Religions of the World

Judaism

Judaism is the oldest of the monotheistic faiths. It affirms the existence of one God, Yahweh, who entered into covenant with the descendants of Abraham, God's chosen people. Judaism's holy writings reveal how God has been present with them throughout their history. These writings are known as the Torah, specifically the five books of Moses, but most broadly conceived as the Hebrew Scriptures (traditionally called the Old Testament by Christians) and the compilation of oral tradition known as the Talmud (which includes the Mishnah, the oral law).

According to Scripture, the Hebrew patriarch Abraham (20th century? B.C.E.) founded Judaism. He obeyed the call of God to depart northern Mesopotamia and travel to Canaan. God promised to bless his descendants if they remained faithful in worship. Abraham's line descended through Isaac, then Jacob (also called Israel; his descendants came to be called Israelites). The 12 families that descended from Jacob migrated to Egypt, where they were enslaved. They were led out of bondage (13th century? B.C.E.) by Moses, who united them in the worship of Yahweh. The Hebrews returned to Canaan after a 40-year sojourn in the desert, conquering from the local peoples the "promised land" that God had provided for them.

The 12 tribes of Israel lived in a covenant association during the period of the judges (1200?–1000? B.C.E.), leaders known for wisdom and heroism. Saul first established a monarchy (r. 1025?–1005? B.C.E.); his successor, David (r. 1005?–965? B.C.E.), unified the land of Israel and made Jerusalem its religious and political center. Under his son, Solomon (r. 968?–928? B.C.E.), a golden era culminated in the building of a temple, replacing the portable sanctuary in use until that time. Following Solomon's death, the kingdom was split into Israel in the north and Judah in the south. Political conflicts resulted in the conquest of Israel by Assyria (724 B.C.E.) and the defeat of Judah by Babylon (586 B.C.E.). Jerusalem and its temple were destroyed, and many Judeans were exiled to Babylon.

During the era of the kings, the prophets were active in Israel and Judah. Their writings emphasize faith in Yahweh as God of Israel and of the entire universe, and they warn of the dangers of idol worship. They also cry out for social justice.

The Judeans were permitted to return in 539 B.C.E. to Judea, where they were ruled as a Persian province. Though temple and cult were restored in Jerusalem, during the exile a new class of religious leaders had emerged—the scribes. They became rivals to the temple hierarchy and would eventually evolve into the party known as the Pharisees.

Persian rule ended when Alexander the Great conquered Palestine in 332 B.C.E. After his death, rule of Judea alternated between Egypt and Syria. When the Syrian ruler Antiochus IV Epiphanes tried to prevent the practice of Judaism, a revolt was led by the Maccabees (a Jewish family), winning Jewish independence in 128 B.C.E. The Romans conquered Jerusalem in 63 B.C.E.

During this period the Sadducees (temple priests) and the Pharisees (teachers of the law in the synagogues) offered different interpretations of Judaism. Smaller groups that emerged were the Essenes, a religious order; the Apocalyptists, who expected divine deliverance led by the Messiah; and the Zealots, who were prepared to fight for national independence. Hellenism also influenced Judaism at this time.

When the Zealots revolted, the Roman armies destroyed Jerusalem and its temple (C.E. 70). The Jews were scattered in the Diaspora (dispersion) and underwent much persecution. Rabbinic Judaism, developed according to Pharisaic practice and centered on Torah and synagogue, became the primary expression of faith. The Scriptures became codified, and the Talmud took shape. In the 12th century Maimonides formulated the influential 13 Articles of Faith, including belief in God, God's oneness and lack of physical or other form, the changelessness of Torah, restoration of the monarchy under the Messiah, and resurrection of the dead.

Two branches of European Judaism developed during the Middle Ages: the Sephardic, based in Spain and with an affinity to Babylonian Jews; and the Ashkenazic, based in Franco-German lands and affiliated with Rome and Palestine. Two forms of Jewish mysticism also arose at this time: medieval Hasidism and attention to the Kabbalah (a mystical interpretation of Scripture).

After a respite during the 18th-century Enlightenment, anti-Semitism again plagued European Jews in the 19th century, sparking the Zionist movement that culminated in the founding of the state of Israel in 1948. The Holocaust of World War II took the lives of more than 6 million Jews.

Jews today continue synagogue worship, which includes readings from the Law and the Prophets and prayers, such as the Shema (Hear, O Israel) and the Amidah (the 18 Benedictions). Religious life is guided by the commandments of the Torah, such as circumcision and Sabbath observance.

Present-day Judaism has three main expressions: Orthodox, Conservative, and Reform. Reform movements, resulting from the Haskala (Jewish Enlightenment) of the 18th century, began in western Europe but took root in North America. Reform Jews do not hold the oral law (Talmud) to be a divine revelation, and they emphasize ethical and moral teachings. Orthodox Jews follow the traditional faith and practice with great seriousness. They follow a strict kosher diet and keep the Sabbath with great care. Conservative Judaism, which developed in the mid–18th century, holds the Talmud to be authoritative and follows most traditional practices, yet tries to make Judaism relevant for each generation, believing that change and tradition can complement each other. Because the Torah assumes belief in God but does not require it, a strong secular movement also exists within Judaism, including atheist and agnostic elements.

In general, Jews do not proselytize, but they do welcome newcomers to their faith.

Christianity

Christianity is founded upon Jesus Christ, to whose life the New Testament and other writings testify. Jesus, a Jew, was born in about 7 B.C.E. and assumed his public life, probably after his 30th year, in Galilee. The Gospels tell of many extraordinary deeds that accompanied his ministry. He proclaimed the kingdom of God, a future reality that is at the same time already present. Nationalistic-Jewish expectations of the Messiah he rejected. Rather, he referred to himself as the Son of Man. Jesus set forth the religio-ethical demands for participation in the kingdom of God as a change of heart and repentance for sins, love of God and neighbor, and concern for justice.

At the Last Supper he signified his death as a sacrifice, which would inaugurate the New Covenant. Circa C.E. 30 he was executed on a cross in Jerusalem, a brutal form of punishment for those considered a political threat to the Roman Empire.

After his death his followers came to believe in him as the Christ, the Messiah. The Gospels report his resurrection, and the risen Jesus was witnessed by many of his followers. The apostle Paul helped spread the new faith in his missionary travels. His letters, contained in the New Testament, further develop the meaning of Jesus's life, death, and resurrection and state that Jesus will come again in glory.

Historically, Christianity arose out of Judaism and claims that Jesus fulfilled many of the promises of the Hebrew Scripture (referred to as the Old Testament). The early church designated itself "the true Israel," which expected the speedy return of Jesus.

The new religion spread rapidly throughout the Roman Empire. In its first two centuries, Christianity began to take shape as an organization, developing distinctive doctrine, liturgy, and ministry. By the fourth century the Catholic church had taken root in countries stretching from Spain in the West to Persia and India in the East. Christians had been repeatedly subject to persecution by the Roman state, but finally gained tolerance under Constantine the Great (C.E. 313). The church became favored under his successors, and in 380 the emperor Theodosius proclaimed Christianity the state religion. Paganism was suppressed.

Because differences in doctrine threatened to divide the Catholic church, a standard Christian creed was formulated by bishops at successive ecumenical councils, the first of which was held in C.E. 325 (Nicaea). Important doctrines were defined concerning the Trinity, in other words, that there is one God in three persons: Father, Son, and Holy Spirit (Constantinople, C.E. 381), and the nature of Christ as both divine and human (Chalcedon, C.E. 541).

Through differences and rivalry between Christians of the East and West, the unity of the church was broken by schism in 1054. The religious center for the Eastern Orthodox Church was Constantinople, and the Roman Catholic Church defined doctrine and practice for Christians in the West. In 1517 began the Reformation, which ultimately caused a schism in the Western church. Reformers wished to correct certain practices within the Roman church, but also came to view the Christian faith in a distinctly new way. The major Protestant denominations (Lutheran, Presbyterian, Reformed, and Anglican [Episcopalian]) thus came into being. Over the centuries, numerous denominations have broken with these major traditions, resulting in a spectrum of Christian expression.

In the 20th century, many Christians hope to regain a sense of unity through dialogue and cooperation among different traditions. The ecumenical movement led to the formation of the World Council of Churches in 1948 (Amsterdam), which has since been joined by many denominations.

Through its missionary activity Christianity has spread to most parts of the globe.

Eastern Orthodoxy

Eastern Orthodoxy comprises the faith and practices stemming from ancient churches in the eastern part of the Roman Empire. It encompasses Orthodox churches in communion with the see of Constantinople.

The Orthodox, Catholic, Apostolic Church is the direct descendant of the Byzantine state church and consists of independent national churches that are united by doctrine, liturgy, and hierarchical organization (church leaders include deacons and priests, who may either be married or be monks before ordination, and bishops, who must be celibates). The heads of these churches are called patriarchs or metropolitans. Rivalry between the pope of Rome and the patriarch of Constantinople, as well as differences that existed for centuries between the eastern and western parts of the empire, led to a schism in 1054. Repeated attempts at reunion have failed. The mutual excommunication pronounced in that year was lifted in 1965, however, and a climate of better understanding has been created in the 20th century. Orthodox churches belong to the World Council of Churches.

U.S. Religious Bodies with Members Over 1,000,000

Religious body	Members
Roman Catholic Church	61,207,914
Southern Baptist Convention	15,691,964
United Methodist Church	8,495,378
National Baptist Convention, U.S.A., Inc.	8,200,000
Church of God in Christ	5,499,875
Evangelical Lutheran Church in America	5,180,910
Church of Jesus Christ of Latter-day Saints	4,800,000
Presbyterian Church (U.S.A.)	3,637,375
National Baptist Convention of America, Inc.	3,500,000
African Methodist Episcopal Church	3,500,000
Lutheran Church—Missouri Synod	2,601,144
Episcopal Church	2,536,550
Progressive National Baptist Convention, Inc.	2,500,000
National Missionary Baptist Convention of America	2,500,000
Assemblies of God	2,467,588
Churches of Christ	2,250,000
Orthodox Church in America	2,000,000
Greek Orthodox Archdiocese of North and South America	1,950,000
American Baptist Churches in the U.S.A.	1,503,267
Baptist Bible Fellowship International	1,500,000
United Church of Christ	1,452,565
African Methodist Episcopal Zion Church	1,252,369
Christian Churches and Churches of Christ	1,071,616
Pentecostal Assemblies of the World	1,000,000

Source: Yearbook of American & Canadian Churches, 1998.

The Eastern Orthodox churches recognize only the canons of the seven ecumenical councils (325–787) as binding for faith, and they reject doctrines that have been added in the West.

The central worship service is called the Liturgy, which is understood as representation of God's acts of salvation. Its center is the celebration of the Eucharist, or Lord's Supper. Icons (sacred pictures) have a special place in Orthodox worship. The Mother of Christ, angels, and saints are highly venerated. The Orthodox Church and the Western Catholic Church recognize the same number of sacraments.

Orthodox Churches are found in Greece, Turkey, Russia, the Balkans, and other parts of the former Soviet Union. In this century Orthodox faith has spread to western Europe and other parts of the world, particularly America.

Eastern Rite Churches

These include the Uniate Churches that recognize the authority of the pope but keep their own traditional liturgies and those churches dating back to the fifth century that emancipated themselves from the Byzantine state church. They include the Melchites, Syrian Catholics, Maronites (Arab Christians in Lebanon), Catholic Copts and Ethiopians, the autonomous Nestorian Church, and others.

Roman Catholicism

Roman Catholicism comprises the belief and practice of the Roman Catholic Church. It stands under the authority of the bishop of Rome, the pope, and is ruled by him and bishops who are held to be, through ordination, successors of Peter and the apostles. Doctrine and sacraments are bound to the jurisdiction and consecration of the hierarchy. The pope, as the head of the hierarchy of archbishops, bishops, priests, and deacons, has full ecclesiastical power, granted him by Christ, through Peter. As successor to Peter, he is the Vicar of Christ. The powers that others in the hierarchy possess are delegated.

Roman Catholics believe their church to be the one, holy, catholic, and apostolic church, possessing all the properties of the one, true church of Christ.

The faith of the church is understood to be identical with that taught by Christ and his apostles and contained in the Bible and tradition. New definitions of doctrines, such as the Immaculate Conception of Mary (1854) and the bodily Assumption of Mary (1950), have been declared by popes, however. At Vatican Council I (1870) the pope was proclaimed "endowed with infallibility, *ex cathedra,* in other words, when exercising the office of Pastor and Teacher of all Christians."

The center of Roman Catholic worship is the celebration of the Mass, the Eucharist, which is the commemoration of Christ's sacrificial death and resurrection. Other sacraments are baptism, confirmation, penance, matrimony, anointing of the sick (formerly known as extreme unction), and holy orders. The Virgin Mary and the other saints, and their relics, are highly venerated and prayers are made to them to intercede with God, in whose presence they are believed to dwell.

The Roman Catholic Church is the largest Christian organization in the world, found in most countries.

Vatican Council II (1962–65) sought to "update" the church, bringing about changes in practice and more deeply involving the laity. The immensely popular Pope John Paul II (1978–) has taken a more conservative course and has reached out to Catholics worldwide through his extensive travels.

Protestantism

Protestantism encompasses the Christian churches that separated from Rome during the Reformation in the 16th century, initiated by an Augustinian monk, Martin Luther. "Protestant" was originally applied to followers of Luther, who protested at the Diet of Spires (1529) against the decree that prohibited all further ecclesiastical reforms. Other influential reformers included John Calvin, Ulrich Zwingli, and John Knox. Protestantism rejected attempts to tie God's revelation to earthly institutions and strictly adhered to the Word of God as sole authority in matters of faith and practice *(sola scriptura)*. Central in the reformers' understanding of the biblical message is the justification of the sinner by faith alone. The church is understood as a fellowship, and the priesthood of all believers is stressed.

The Augsburg Confession (1530) was the principal statement of Lutheran faith and practice. It became a model for other Protestant confessions of faith. Major Protestant denominations include the Lutheran, Reformed (Calvinist), Presbyterian, and Anglican (Episcopalian). Innumerable sects and denominations sprung from these roots, including Quakers, Baptists, Pentecostals, Congregationalists, Methodists, and nondenominational assemblies. Sects that base their faith on additional revelations or insights gained in the modern period include Mormons, Christian Scientists, and Jehovah's Witnesses.

Since the latter part of the 19th century, national councils of churches have been established in many countries, for example, the Federal Council of Churches of Christ in America in 1908. Churches of a particular denomination have joined in federations and world alliances, beginning with the Anglican Lambeth Conference in 1867.

Protestant missionary activity, particularly strong in the last century, resulted in the founding of many churches in Asia and Africa. The ecumenical movement, which originated with Protestant missions, aims at unity among Christians and churches.

Islam

Islam is the religion founded in Arabia by Muhammed between 610 and 632. There are an estimated 5.4 million Muslims in Northern America and 1 billion Muslims worldwide.

Muhammed was born in C.E. 570 at Mecca and belonged to the Quraysh tribe that was active in caravan trade. At the age of 25 he joined the caravan trade from Mecca to Syria in the employment of a rich widow, Khadiji, whom he married. Critical of the idolatry of the inhabitants of Mecca, he began to lead a contemplative life in the desert. There he received a series of revelations. Encouraged by Khadiji, he gradually became convinced that he was given a God-appointed task to devote himself to the reform of religion and society. Idolatry was to be abandoned.

The Hegira *(Hijra)* (emigration) of Muhammed from Mecca, where he was not honored, to Medina, where he was well received, occurred in 622 and marks the beginning of the Muslim era. In 630 he marched on Mecca and conquered it. He died at Medina in 632. His grave there has since been a place of pilgrimage.

Muhammed's followers, called Muslims, revered him as the prophet of Allah (God), beside whom there is no other God. Although he had no close knowledge of Judaism and Christianity, he considered himself succeeding and completing them as the seal of the Prophets. Sources of the Islamic faith are the Qur'an, regarded as the uncreated, eternal Word of God, and tradition *(hadith)* regarding sayings and deeds of the prophet.

Islam means surrender to the will of Allah. He is the all-powerful, whose will is supreme and determines humanity's fate. Good deeds will be rewarded at the Last Judgment in paradise and evil deeds will be punished in hell.

The Five Pillars, or primary duties, of Islam are: profession of faith; prayer, to be performed five times a day; almsgiving to the poor and the mosque (house of worship); fasting during daylight hours in the month of Ramadan; and pilgrimage to Mecca at least once in a Muslim's lifetime.

Islam, upholding the law of brotherhood, succeeded in uniting an Arab world that had disintegrated into tribes and castes. Disagreements concerning the succession of the prophet caused a great division in Islam between Sunnis and Shi'ites. The Shi'ites rejected the first three successors to Muhammed as usurpers, claiming the fourth, Muhammed's son-in-law Ali, as the rightful leader. The Sunnis (from the word *tradition)*, the largest division of Islam (today more than 80%), believe in the legitimacy of the first three successors. Among these, other sects arose (such as Wahhabi). Doctrinal issues also led to the rise of different schools of thought in theology. Nevertheless, since Arab armies turned against Syria and Palestine in 635, Islam has expanded greatly under Muhammed's successors. Islam is the principal religion of the Middle East, Asia, and of the northern half of Africa.

Hinduism

Hinduism is the major religion of India, practiced by more than 80% of the population. In contrast to other religions, it has no founder. Considered the oldest religion in the world, it dates back, perhaps, to prehistoric times.

No single creed or doctrine binds Hindus together. Intellectually there is complete freedom of belief, and one can be monotheist, polytheist, or atheist. Hinduism is a syncretic religion, welcoming and incorporating a variety of outside influences.

The most ancient sacred texts of the Hindu religion are written in Sanskrit and called the *Vedas* (*vedah* means "knowledge"). There are four Vedic books, of which the Rig-Veda is the oldest. It discusses multiple gods, the universe, and creation. The dates of these works are unknown (1000 B.C.E.?). Present-day Hindus rarely refer to these texts but do venerate them.

The Upanishads (dated 1000–300 B.C.E.), commentaries on the Vedic texts, speculate on the origin of the universe and the nature of deity, and atman (the individual soul) and its relationship to Brahman (the universal soul). They introduce the doctrine of karma and recommend meditation and the practice of yoga.

According to Hindu beliefs, Brahman is the principle and source of the universe. This divine intelligence pervades all beings, including the individual soul. Thus the many Hindu deities are manifestations of the one Brahman. Hinduism is based on the concept of reincarnation, in which all living beings, from plants below to gods above, are caught in a cosmic cycle of becoming and perishing.

Life is determined by the law of karma, according to which rebirth is dependent on moral behavior in a previous phase of existence. In this view, life on earth is regarded as transient and a burden. The goal of existence is liberation from the cycle of rebirth and death and entrance into the indescribable state of what in Hindu texts is called *moksha* (liberation).

Further important sacred writings include the Epics, which contain legendary stories about gods and humans. They are the Mahabharata (composed between 200 B.C.E. and C.E. 200) and the Ramayana. The former includes the Bhagavad-Gita (Song of the Lord), an influential text that describes the three paths to salvation. The Puranas (stories in verse, probably written between the 6th and 13th centuries) detail myths of Hindu gods and heroes and also comment on religious practice and cosmology. Of the many Hindu deities, the most popular are the cults of Vishnu, Shiva, and Shakti, and their various incarnations. Also important is Brahma, the creator god. Hindus also venerate human saints.

The practice of Hinduism consists of rites and ceremonies centering on the main socioreligious occasions of birth, marriage, and death. There are many Hindu temples, which are dwelling places of the deities and to which people bring offerings. There are also places of pilgrimage, the chief one being Benares on the Ganges, most sacred among the rivers in India.

Orthodox Hindu society in India was divided into four major hereditary classes: (1) the Brahmin (priestly and learned class); (2) the Kshatriya (military, professional, ruling, and governing occupations); (3) the Vaishya (landowners, merchants, and business occupations); and (4) the Sudra (artisans, laborers, and peasants). Below the Sudra was a fifth group, the Untouchables (lowest menial occupations and no social standing). The Indian government banned discrimination against the Untouchables in the constitution of India in 1950. Observance of class and caste distinctions varies throughout India.

In modern times work has been done to reform and revive Hinduism. One of the outstanding reformers was Ramakrishna (1836–86), who inspired many followers, one of whom founded the Ramakrishna mission. The mission is active both in India and in other countries and is known for its scholarly and humanitarian works.

Buddhism

Buddhism was founded in the fourth or fifth century B.C.E. in northern India by a man known traditionally as Siddhartha (meaning "he who has reached the goal") Gautama, the son of a warrior prince. Some scholars believe that he lived from 563 to 483 B.C.E., though his exact life span is uncertain. Troubled by the inevitability of suffering in human life, he left home and a pampered life at the age of

29 to wander as an ascetic, seeking religious insight and a solution to the struggles of human existence. He passed through many trials and practiced extreme self-denial. Finally, while meditating under the bodhi tree ("tree of perfect knowledge") he reached enlightenment and taught his followers about his new spiritual understanding.

Gautama's teachings differed from the Hindu faith prevalent in India at the time. Whereas in Hinduism the Brahmin caste alone performed religious functions and attained the highest spiritual understanding, Gautama's beliefs were more egalitarian, accessible to all who wished to be enlightened. At the core of his understanding were the Four Noble Truths: (1) all living beings suffer; (2) the origin of this suffering is desire—for material possessions, power, and so on; (3) desire can be overcome; and (4) there is a path that leads to release from desire. This way is called the Noble Eightfold Path: right views, right intention, right speech, right action, right livelihood, right effort, right concentration, and right ecstasy.

Gautama promoted the concept of anatman (that a person has no actual self) and the idea that existence is characterized by impermanence. This realization helps one let go of desire for transient things. Still, Gautama did not recommend extreme self-denial, but rather a disciplined life called the Middle Way. Like the Hindus, he believed that existence consisted of reincarnation, a cycle of birth and death. He held that it could be broken only by reaching complete detachment from worldly cares. Then the soul could be released into nirvana (literally "blowing out")—an indescribable state of total transcendence. Gautama traveled to preach the dharma (sacred truth) and was recognized as the Buddha (enlightened one). After his death his followers continued to develop doctrine and practice, which came to center on the Three Jewels: the dharma (the sacred teachings of Buddhism), the sangha (the community of followers, which now includes nuns, monks, and laity), and the Buddha. Under the patronage of the Mauryan emperor Ashoka (third century B.C.E.), Buddhism spread throughout India and to other parts of Asia. Monasteries were established, as well as temples dedicated to Buddha; at shrines his relics were venerated. Though by the fourth century C.E. Buddhist presence in India had dwindled, it flourished in other parts of Asia.

Numerous Buddhist sects have emerged. The oldest, called the Theravada (Way of the Elders) tradition, interprets Buddha as a great sage but not a deity. It emphasizes meditation and ritual practices that help the individual become an arhat, an enlightened being. Its followers emphasize the authority of the earliest Buddhist scriptures, the Tripitaka (Three Baskets), a compilation of sermons, rules for celibates, and doctrine. This sect is prevalent in Southeast Asia and Sri Lanka. It is sometimes called the Hinayana (Lesser Vehicle) tradition (once considered a pejorative term).

Between the second century B.C.E. and the second century C.E., the Mahayana (Greater Vehicle) tradition refocused Buddhism to concentrate less on individual attainment of enlightenment and more on concern for humanity. It promotes the ideal of the bodhisattva (enlightened being), who shuns entering nirvana until all sentient beings can do so as well, willingly remaining in the painful cycle of birth and death to perform works of compassion. Members of this tradition conceive of Buddha as an eternal being to whom prayers can be made; other Buddhas are revered as well, adding a polytheistic dimension to the religion. Numerous sects have developed from the Mahayana tradition, which has been influential in China, Korea, and Japan.

A third broad tradition, variously called Vajrayana (Diamond Vehicle), Mantrayana (Vehicle of the Mantra), or Tantric Buddhism, offers a quicker, more demanding way to achieve nirvana. Because of its level of challenge—enabling one to reach enlightenment in one lifetime—it requires the guidance of a spiritual leader. It is most prominent in Tibet and Mongolia. Zen Buddhism encourages individuals to seek the Buddha nature within themselves and to practice a disciplined form of sitting meditation in order to reach satori—spiritual enlightenment.

Confucianism

Confucius (K'ung Fu-tzu), born in the state of Lu (northern China), lived from 551 to 479 B.C.E. He was a brilliant teacher, viewing education not merely as the accumulation of knowledge but as a character-building experience leading to a ceaseless process of self-transformation. His legacy was not an organized religion, but a world view that combined philosophy, social ethics, scholarship, and political ideology.

Anthologies of ancient Chinese classics, along with Confucius's own Analects (Lun Yu), became the basis of Confucianism. These Analects were transmitted as a collection of his sayings as recorded by his students, with whom he discussed ethical and social problems.

In his teachings, Confucius emphasized the importance of an old Chinese concept *(li),* which has the connotation of proper conduct. There is some disagreement as to the religious ideas of Confucius, but he held high the concepts handed down from centuries before him. Thus he believed in heaven *(t'ien)* and encouraged ancestor worship as an expression of filial piety, which he considered the loftiest of virtues.

Piety to Confucius was the foundation of the family as well as the state. The family is the nucleus of the state, and the "five relations," between king and subject, father and son, man and wife, older and younger brother, and friend and friend, are determined by the virtues of love of fellow beings, righteousness, and respect.

Attaining humanity *(jen)* was the cardinal virtue and required liberation from "opinionatedness, dogmatism, obstinancy, and egoism," and cultivation of the golden rule: "do not do unto others what you would not want others to do unto you!"

Mencius (Meng Tse), who lived around 400 B.C.E., did much to propagate and elaborate Confucianism in its concern with ordering society. Thus, for two millennia, Confucius's doctrine of state, with its emphasis on ethics and social morality, rooted in ancient Chinese tradition and developed and continued by his disciples, has been standard in China and other parts of Asia.

Shintoism

Shinto, the Chinese term for the Japanese Kami no Michi (Way of the Gods), is made up of the religious ideas and cults indigenous to Japan. Kami, or gods, considered divine forces of nature that are worshipped, may reside in rivers, trees, rocks, mountains, certain animals, and particularly in the sun and moon. The worship of ancestors, heroes, and deceased emperors was incorporated later.

It is difficult to date the origins of Shinto, but it predated Buddhism, which was introduced to Japan in the sixth century from Korea. Shintoism gradually enfolded Buddhist beliefs and ceremonies into its own traditions, resulting in a syncretistic religion, a Twofold Shinto. Buddhist deities came to be regarded as manifestations of Japanese deities and Buddhist priests took over most of the Shinto shrines.

Under the reign of the Emperor Meiji (1868–1912) Shinto became the official state religion, in which loyalty to the emperor was emphasized. The line of succession of emperors is traced back to the first Emperor Jimmu (660 B.C.E.) and beyond him to the sun goddess Amaterasuomikami.

The centers of worship are the shrines and temples in which the deities are believed to dwell, and believers approach them through *torii* (gateways). Most important among the shrines is the imperial shrine of the sun goddess at Ise, where state ceremonies were once held in June and December. The Yasukuni shrine of the war dead in Tokyo is also well known.

Acts of worship consist of prayers, clapping of hands, acts of purification, and offerings. On feast days processions and performances of music and dancing take place and priests read prayers before the gods in the shrines. In Japanese homes there is a god-shelf, a small wooden shrine that contains the tablets bearing the names of ancestors. Offerings are made and candles lit before it.

After World War II the Allied Command ordered the disestablishment of state Shinto. To be distinguished from state Shinto is sect Shinto, consisting of 13 recognized sects. These have arisen in modern times. Most important among them is Tenrikyo in Tenri City (Nara), in which healing by faith plays a central role.

Taoism

Taoism, a religion of China, was, according to tradition, founded by Lao-tzu, a Chinese philosopher, long considered one of the prominent religious leaders from the sixth century B.C.E.

Information about him is for the most part legendary, however, and the Tao Te Ching (the classic of the Way and of its Power), traditionally ascribed to him, is now believed by many scholars to have originated in the third century B.C.E. The book is composed in short chapters, written in aphoristic rhymes. Central are the word *tao,* which means way or path and, in a deeper sense, signifies the principle that underlies the reality of this world and manifests itself in nature and in the lives of men, and the word *te* (power).

The virtuous man draws power from being absorbed in tao, the ultimate reality within an ever-changing world. By non-action and keeping away from human striving, it is possible for man to live in harmony with the principles that underlie and govern the universe. Tao cannot be comprehended by reason and knowledge, but only by inward quiet.

Besides the Tao Te Ching, dating from approximately the same period, there are two other Taoist works, written by Chuang Tzu and Lieh Tzu.

Theoretical Taoism of this classical philosophical movement of the fourth and third centuries B.C.E. in China differed from popular Taoism, into which it gradually degenerated. The standard of theoretical Taoism was maintained in the classics, of course, and among the upper classes it continued to be alive until modern times.

Religious Taoism is a form of religion dealing with deities and spirits, magic and soothsaying. In the second century C.E. it was organized with temples, cult, priests, and monasteries and was able to hold its own in the competition with Buddhism that came up at the same time.

After the seventh century C.E., however, Taoist religion further declined. Split into numerous sects, which often operate like secret societies, it has become a syncretic folk religion in which some of the old deities and saints live on.

Roman Catholic Pontiffs

St. Peter, of Bethsaida in Galilee, Prince of the Apostles, was the first pope. He lived first in Antioch and then in Rome for 25 years. In C.E. 64 or 67, he was martyred. St. Linus became the second pope.

Name	Birthplace	Reigned From	To
St. Linus	Tuscia	67	76
St. Anacletus (Cletus)	Rome	76	88
St. Clement	Rome	88	97
St. Evaristus	Greece	97	105
St. Alexander I	Rome	105	115
St. Sixtus I	Rome	115	125
St. Telesphorus	Greece	125	136
St. Hyginus	Greece	136	140
St. Pius I	Aquileia	140	155
St. Anicetus	Syria	155	166
St. Soter	Campania	166	175
St. Eleutherius	Epirus	175	189
St. Victor I	Africa	189	199
St. Zephyrinus	Rome	199	217
St. Callistus I	Rome	217	222
St. Urban I	Rome	222	230
St. Pontian	Rome	230	235
St. Anterus	Greece	235	236
St. Fabian	Rome	236	250
St. Cornelius	Rome	251	253
St. Lucius I	Rome	253	254
St. Stephen I	Rome	254	257
St. Sixtus II	Greece	257	258
St. Dionysius	Unknown	259	268
St. Felix I	Rome	269	274
St. Eutychian	Luni	275	283
St. Caius	Dalmatia	283	296

Name	Birthplace	Reigned From	To
St. Marcellinus	Rome	296	304
St. Marcellus I	Rome	308	309
St. Eusebius	Greece	309[1]	309[1]
St. Meltiades	Africa	311	314
St. Sylvester I	Rome	314	335
St. Marcus	Rome	336	336
St. Julius I	Rome	337	352
Liberius	Rome	352	366
St. Damasus I	Spain	366	384
St. Siricius	Rome	384	399
St. Anastasius I	Rome	399	401
St. Innocent I	Albano	401	417
St. Zozimus	Greece	417	418
St. Boniface I	Rome	418	422
St. Celestine I	Campania	422	432
St. Sixtus III	Rome	432	440
St. Leo I (the Great)	Tuscany	440	461
St. Hilary	Sardinia	461	468
St. Simplicius	Tivoli	468	483
St. Felix III (II)[2]	Rome	483	492
St. Gelasius I	Africa	492	496
Anastasius II	Rome	496	498
St. Symmachus	Sardinia	498	514
St. Hormisdas	Frosinone	514	523
St. John I	Tuscany	523	526
St. Felix IV (III)	Samnium	526	530
Boniface II	Rome	530	532
John II	Rome	533	535
St. Agapitus I	Rome	535	536
St. Silverius	Campania	536	537
Vigilius	Rome	537	555
Pelagius I	Rome	556	561
John III	Rome	561	574
Benedict I	Rome	575	579
Pelagius II	Rome	579	590
St. Gregory I (the Great)	Rome	590	604
Sabinianus	Tuscany	604	606
Boniface III	Rome	607	607
St. Boniface IV	Marsi	608	615
St. Deusdedit (Adeodatus I)	Rome	615	618
Boniface V	Naples	619	625
Honorius I	Campania	625	638
Severinus	Rome	640	640
John IV	Dalmatia	640	642
Theodore I	Greece	642	649
St. Martin I	Todi	649	655
St. Eugene I[3]	Rome	654	657
St. Vitalian	Segni	657	672
Adeodatus II	Rome	672	676
Donus	Rome	676	678
St. Agatho	Sicily	678	681
St. Leo II	Sicily	682	683
St. Benedict II	Rome	684	685
John V	Syria	685	686
Conon	Unknown	686	687
St. Sergius I	Syria	687	701
John VI	Greece	701	705
John VII	Greece	705	707
Sisinnius	Syria	708	708
Constantine	Syria	708	715
St. Gregory II	Rome	715	731
St. Gregory III	Syria	731	741
St. Zachary	Greece	741	752
Stephen II (III)[4]	Rome	752	757
St. Paul I	Rome	757	767
Stephen III (IV)	Sicily	768	772
Adrian I	Rome	772	795
St. Leo III	Rome	795	816
Stephen IV (V)	Rome	816	817
St. Paschal I	Rome	817	824
Eugene II	Rome	824	827
Valentine	Rome	827	827
Gregory IV	Rome	827	844
Sergius II	Rome	844	847
St. Leo IV	Rome	847	855
Benedict III	Rome	855	858
St. Nicholas I (the Great)	Rome	858	867
Adrian II	Rome	867	872
John VIII	Rome	872	882
Marinus I	Gallese	882	884
St. Adrian III	Rome	884	885
Stephen V (VI)	Rome	885	891
Formosus	Portus	891	896
Boniface VI	Rome	896	896
Stephen VI (VII)	Rome	896	897
Romanus	Gallese	897	897
Theodore II	Rome	897	897
John IX	Tivoli	898	900
Benedict IV	Rome	900	903
Leo V	Ardea	903	903
Sergius III	Rome	904	911
Anastasius III	Rome	911	913
Landus	Sabina	913	914
John X	Tossignano	914	928
Leo VI	Rome	928	928
Stephen VII (VIII)	Rome	928	931
John XI	Rome	931	935
Leo VII	Rome	936	939
Stephen VIII (IX)	Rome	939	942
Marinus II	Rome	942	946
Agapitus II	Rome	946	955
John XII	Tusculum	955	964
Leo VIII[5]	Rome	963	965
Benedict V[5]	Rome	964	966
John XIII	Rome	965	972
Benedict VI	Rome	973	974
Benedict VII	Rome	974	983
John XIV	Pavia	983	984
John XV	Rome	985	996
Gregory V	Saxony	996	999
Sylvester II	Auvergne	999	1003
John XVII	Rome	1003	1003
John XVIII	Rome	1004	1009
Sergius IV	Rome	1009	1012
Benedict VIII	Tusculum	1012	1024
John XIX	Tusculum	1024	1032
Benedict IX[6]	Tusculum	1032	1044
Sylvester III	Rome	1045	1045
Benedict IX (2nd time)	Tusculum	1045	1045
Gregory VI	Rome	1045	1046
Clement II	Saxony	1046	1047
Benedict IX (3rd time)	Tusculum	1047	1048
Damasus II	Bavaria	1048	1048
St. Leo IX	Alsace	1049	1054
Victor II	Germany	1055	1057
Stephen IX (X)	Lorraine	1057	1058
Nicholas II	Burgundy	1059	1061
Alexander II	Milan	1061	1073
St. Gregory VII	Tuscany	1073	1085
Bl. Victor III	Benevento	1086	1087

Name	Birthplace	Reigned From	Reigned To
Bl. Urban II	France	1088	1099
Paschal II	Ravenna	1099	1118
Gelasius II	Gaeta	1118	1119
Callistus II	Burgundy	1119	1124
Honorius II	Flagnano	1124	1130
Innocent II	Rome	1130	1143
Celestine II	Città di Castello	1143	1144
Lucius II	Bologna	1144	1145
Bl. Eugene III	Pisa	1145	1153
Anastasius IV	Rome	1153	1154
Adrian IV	England	1154	1159
Alexander III	Siena	1159	1181
Lucius III	Lucca	1181	1185
Urban III	Milan	1185	1187
Gregory VIII	Benevento	1187	1187
Clement III	Rome	1187	1191
Celestine III	Rome	1191	1198
Innocent III	Anagni	1198	1216
Honorius III	Rome	1216	1227
Gregory IX	Anagni	1227	1241
Celestine IV	Milan	1241	1241
Innocent IV	Genoa	1243	1254
Alexander IV	Anagni	1254	1261
Urban IV	Troyes	1261	1264
Clement IV	France	1265	1268
Bl. Gregory X	Piacenza	1271	1276
Bl. Innocent V	Savoy	1276	1276
Adrian V	Genoa	1276	1276
John XXI[7]	Portugal	1276	1277
Nicholas III	Rome	1277	1280
Martin IV[8]	France	1281	1285
Honorius IV	Rome	1285	1287
Nicholas IV	Ascoli	1288	1292
St. Celestine V	Isernia	1294	1294
Boniface VIII	Anagni	1294	1303
Bl. Benedict XI	Treviso	1303	1304
Clement V	France	1305	1314
John XXII	Cahors	1316	1334
Benedict XII	France	1334	1342
Clement VI	France	1342	1352
Innocent VI	France	1352	1362
Bl. Urban V	France	1362	1370
Gregory XI	France	1370	1378
Urban VI	Naples	1378	1389
Boniface IX	Naples	1389	1404
Innocent VII	Sul mona	1404	1406
Gregory XII	Venice	1406	1415
Martin V	Rome	1417	1431
Eugene IV	Venice	1431	1447
Nicholas V	Sarzana	1447	1455
Callistus III	Jativa	1455	1458
Pius II	Siena	1458	1464
Paul II	Venice	1464	1471
Sixtus IV	Savona	1471	1484
Innocent VIII	Genoa	1484	1492
Alexander VI	Jativa	1492	1503
Pius III	Siena	1503	1503
Julius II	Savona	1503	1513
Leo X	Florence	1513	1521
Adrian VI	Utrecht	1522	1523
Clement VII	Florence	1523	1534
Paul III	Rome	1534	1549
Julius III	Rome	1550	1555
Marcellus II	Montepulciano	1555	1555
Paul IV	Naples	1555	1559
Pius IV	Milan	1559	1565
St. Pius V	Bosco	1566	1572
Gregory XIII	Bologna	1572	1585
Sixtus V	Grottammare	1585	1590
Urban VII	Rome	1590	1590
Gregory XIV	Cremona	1590	1591
Innocent IX	Bologna	1591	1591
Clement VIII	Florence	1592	1605
Leo XI	Florence	1605	1605
Paul V	Rome	1605	1621
Gregory XV	Bologna	1621	1623
Urban VIII	Florence	1623	1644
Innocent X	Rome	1644	1655
Alexander VII	Siena	1655	1667
Clement IX	Pistoia	1667	1669
Clement X	Rome	1670	1676
Bl. Innocent XI	Como	1676	1689
Alexander VIII	Venice	1689	1691
Innocent XII	Spinazzola	1691	1700
Clement XI	Urbino	1700	1721
Innocent XIII	Rome	1721	1724
Benedict XIII	Gravina	1724	1730
Clement XII	Florence	1730	1740
Benedict XIV	Bologna	1740	1758
Clement XIII	Venice	1758	1769
Clement XIV	Rimini	1769	1774
Pius VI	Cesena	1775	1799
Pius VII	Cesena	1800	1823
Leo XII	Genga	1823	1829
Pius VIII	Cingoli	1829	1830
Gregory XVI	Belluno	1831	1846
Pius IX	Senegallia	1846	1878
Leo XIII	Carpineto	1878	1903
St. Pius X	Riese	1903	1914
Benedict XV	Genoa	1914	1922
Pius XI	Desio	1922	1939
Pius XII	Rome	1939	1958
John XXIII	Sotto il Monte	1958	1963
Paul VI	Concesio	1963	1978
John Paul I	Forno di Canale	1978	1978
John Paul II	Wadowice, Poland	1978	

1. Or 310. 2. He should be called Felix II, and his successors of the same name should be numbered accordingly. The discrepancy was caused by the erroneous insertion in some lists of the name of St. Felix of Rome, Martyr. 3. He was elected during the exile of St. Martin I, who endorsed him as pope. 4. After St. Zachary died, a Roman priest named Stephen was elected but died before his consecration as bishop of Rome. His name is not included in all lists for this reason. In view of this historical confusion, the *National Catholic Almanac* lists the true Stephen II as Stephen II (III), the true Stephen III as Stephen III (IV), etc. 5. Confusion exists concerning the legitimacy of claims. If the deposition of John was invalid, Leo was an antipope until after the end of Benedict's reign. If the deposition of John was valid, Leo was the legitimate pope and Benedict an antipope. 6. If the triple removal of Benedict IX was not valid, Sylvester III, Gregory VI, and Clement II were antipopes. 7. Elimination was made of the name of John XX in an effort to rectify the numerical designation of popes named John. The error dates back to the time of John XV. 8. The names of Marinus I and Marinus II were construed as Martin. In view of these two pontificates and the earlier reign of St. Martin I, this pontiff was called Martin IV. *Source: National Catholic Almanac,* from *Annuarto Pontificio*.

The Books of the Bible

Below is the Protestant canon of the Bible (New Revised Standard Version). The Roman Catholic canon also includes the Deuterocanonical books as part of the Old Testament (these are considered apocryphal by most Protestants). The Hebrew Bible recognizes the books referred to as the Old Testament in the Protestant Bible, but not the Apocryphal/Deuterocanonical books or the New Testament.

The Old Testament with the Apocryphal/ Deuterocanonical Books

The Hebrew Scriptures

Genesis
Exodus
Leviticus
Numbers
Deuteronomy
Joshua
Judges
Ruth
1 Samuel
2 Samuel
1 Kings
2 Kings
1 Chronicles
2 Chronicles
Ezra
Nehemiah
Esther
Job
Psalms
Proverbs
Ecclesiastes
Song of Solomon
Isaiah
Jeremiah
Lamentations
Ezekiel
Daniel
Hosea
Joel
Amos
Obadiah
Jonah
Micah
Nahum
Habakkuk
Zephaniah
Haggai
Zechariah
Malachi

The Apocryphal/ Deuterocanonical Books

Tobit
Judith
Additions to the Book of Esther
Wisdom of Solomon
Ecclesiasticus, or the Wisdom of Jesus Son of Sirach
Baruch
The Letter of Jeremiah
The Prayer of Azariah and the Song of the Three Jews
Susanna
Bel and the Dragon
1 Maccabees
2 Maccabees
1 Esdras
Prayer of Manasseh
Psalm 151
3 Maccabees
2 Esdras
4 Maccabees

The New Testament

Matthew
Mark
Luke
John
Acts of the Apostles
Romans
1 Corinthians
2 Corinthians
Galatians
Ephesians
Philippians
Colossians
1 Thessalonians
2 Thessalonians
1 Timothy
2 Timothy
Titus
Philemon
Hebrews
James
1 Peter
2 Peter
1 John
2 John
3 John
Jude
Revelation

The Ten Commandments

The Ten Commandments, also called the Decalogue (Greek, "ten words"), were divine laws revealed to Moses by God on Mt. Sinai. Appearing in both Exodus (Ex. 20: 2–17) and Deuteronomy (Deut. 5:6–21), the commandments are numbered differently depending on whether they appear in a Catholic, Protestant, or Hebrew Bible. The following is the version given in the Revised Standard Version of the Bible.

You shall have no other gods before me.

You shall not make for yourself a graven image, or any likeness of anything that is in heaven above, or that is in the earth beneath, or that is in the water under the earth; you shall not bow down to them or serve them; for I the Lord your God am a jealous God, visiting the iniquity of the fathers upon the children to the third and the fourth generation of those who hate me, but showing steadfast love to thousands of those who love me and keep my commandments.

You shall not take the name of the Lord your God in vain; for the Lord will not hold him guiltless who takes his name in vain.

Remember the Sabbath day, to keep it holy. Six days you shall labor, and do all your work; but the seventh day is a Sabbath to the Lord your God; in it you shall not do any work, you, or your son, or your daughter, your manservant, or your maidservant, or your cattle, or the sojourner who is within your gates; for in six days the Lord made heaven and earth, the sea, and all that is in them, and rested the seventh day; therefore the Lord blessed the Sabbath day and hallowed it.

Honor your father and your mother, that your days may be long in the land which the Lord your God gives you.

You shall not kill.

You shall not commit adultery.

You shall not steal.

You shall not bear false witness against your neighbor.

You shall not covet your neighbor's wife, or his manservant, or his maidservant, or his ox, or his ass, or anything that is your neighbor's.

Source: Revised Standard Version of the Bible (Ex.20: 2–17)

See Calendar and Holidays for listings of religious holidays.

Millennial Questions

When does the next millennium officially begin?

Although January 1, 2000, has a millennial ring to it, the new age actually begins on a less resounding date: January 1, 2001. Common sense might suggest that the year 2000 is the dawning of the third millennium, but it is in fact the waning of the second.

The first millennium began in C.E. 1. There is no year zero in our calendar: the sequence of years passes directly from 1 B.C.E. to C.E. 1. Adding a thousand years to the year 1 equals the year 1001, marking the start of the second millennium. Add another thousand to reach the beginning of the third millennium: January 1, 2001.

There is no doubt that both New Year's 2000 and 2001 will spark huge celebrations—one because it is the true millennial milestone, and the other because there is nothing quite like the numerical elegance of January 1, 2000. Popular opinion, however, overwhelmingly favors the 2000 celebration: all the Times Square hotels are booked for December 31, 1999, and the various millennium tours arranging for you to celebrate on top of Mount Kilimanjaro or at the base of the pyramids are scheduled for the end of 1999, not 2000.

Where will the Sun first rise on January 1, 2000?

Whether the millennium begins in 2000 or 2001 is not the only debate surrounding the New Year's Eve party of the century. Just exactly where the dawn of the new age will take place has become an international argument, with several places claiming to be the first to greet the millennium. Below are several of the more credible candidates.

Caroline Island, Kiribati: Caroline Island, one of the 33 South Pacific coral atolls that make up the nation of Kiribati (pronounced "Kirabas"), will be the first land to see the dawn as it crosses the International Date Line, signifying the change-over from December 31, 1999, to January 1, 2000. Kiribati owes this distinction to a relatively recent change in its timekeeping. Made up of three island groups—the Gilbert, Phoenix, and Line islands—Kiribati straddles the International Date Line. To the west of the International Date Line lie the Gilberts, to the east stretch the Phoenix and Line islands. This once meant that it could be Monday in the Gilberts but Sunday in the Phoenix Islands—not an easy way to run a country. So in 1993 Kiribati decided to consolidate all three island groups under a single time zone, and selected the Gilbert Islands, west of the Date Line, as the standard (the capital, Tarawa, is located in the Gilberts).

In 1996 Kiribati's time change suddenly caught the attention of its neighbors, as various South Pacific islands began making preparations for a big bash on New Year's 2000. At issue were tourist dollars—revelers would no doubt flock to the place where the New Year's bells would toll first. Kiribati, it seemed, had scooped its island neighbors on the first dawn: its easternmost point, Caroline Island, is the first place the Sun crosses the International Date Line, since the demarcation line had been moved to accommodate Kiribati's time change—even though its longitude is 150°15′ west, almost 30 degrees from the 180° meridian.[1] Tonga had considered itself the first country that would greet the New Year—and the king of Tonga is reportedly not pleased. The Chatham Islands, part of New Zealand, had also counted on being first. Kiribati, however, will see the first rays of the year 2000 a full 80 minutes before Tonga and 22 minutes before the Chathams.

Gisborne, New Zealand: This town on the East Cape of New Zealand's North Island has also claimed to be the right place at the right time for New Year's 2000. In strictly geographic terms, Gisborne has a point. At 178°35′ east longitude, it is less than two degrees from the International Date Line, but since the Date Line bends east and west rather than sticking to the 180° meridian, Gisborne has to forfeit its position to the various countries who have tailored the time zones to conform to their political borders. Gisborne still claims some distinction in spite of the Kiribati affair—according to the London *Times,* it is the first place west of the Date Line with good bars.

Balleny Islands, Antarctica: If the first sunrise is taken to mean the first piece of land to see the dawn on the year 2000, the answer would be the uninhabited islands of Balleny, Antarctica. On January 1, 2000, the Sun will rise over the island at 13:41 UT, whereas Caroline Island, Kiribati, will not see its rays until 15:43 UT. Because of the short rotation of the earth at the poles, the Sun is below the horizon for less than one hour per day in January. But it is an inhospitable place for a New Year's celebration.

Greenwich, England: If time rather than the sunrise is the determining factor, then Greenwich, England, where each day begins at the prime meridian at 00:00 UT, will mark the official start of the year 2000.

---

1. The International Date Line, which generally follows the 180° meridian, diverges east or west in certain locations to ensure that most of a country's territory is grouped in the same time zone. The 180° meridian, for example, cuts through the easternmost portion of Russia. Rather than have the country span two different calendar days, the International Date Line diverges from the meridian to approximately 175° west longitude, thereby encompassing all of Russia. In the case of Kiribati, the Date Line loops to 150°15′ west longitude to encompass the Phoenix and Line islands.

1999

January

S	M	T	W	T	F	S
					1	2
3	4	5	6	7	8	9
10	11	12	13	14	15	16
17	18	19	20	21	22	23
24	25	26	27	28	29	30
31						

February

S	M	T	W	T	F	S
	1	2	3	4	5	6
7	8	9	10	11	12	13
14	15	16	17	18	19	20
21	22	23	24	25	26	27
28						

March

S	M	T	W	T	F	S
	1	2	3	4	5	6
7	8	9	10	11	12	13
14	15	16	17	18	19	20
21	22	23	24	25	26	27
28	29	30	31			

April

S	M	T	W	T	F	S
				1	2	3
4	5	6	7	8	9	10
11	12	13	14	15	16	17
18	19	20	21	22	23	24
25	26	27	28	29	30	

1—New Year's Day
6—Epiphany
18—Martin Luther King, Jr.'s Birthday observed
19—Ramadan ends

2—Groundhog Day
12—Lincoln's Birthday
14—Valentine's Day
15—Washington's Birthday observed, or Presidents' Day
17—Ash Wednesday

2—Purim
17—St. Patrick's Day
28—Palm Sunday

1—1st Day of Passover
2—Good Friday
4—Easter Sunday
4—Daylight Saving Time begins

May

S	M	T	W	T	F	S
						1
2	3	4	5	6	7	8
9	10	11	12	13	14	15
16	17	18	19	20	21	22
23	24	25	26	27	28	29
30	31					

June

S	M	T	W	T	F	S
		1	2	3	4	5
6	7	8	9	10	11	12
13	14	15	16	17	18	19
20	21	22	23	24	25	26
27	28	29	30			

July

S	M	T	W	T	F	S
				1	2	3
4	5	6	7	8	9	10
11	12	13	14	15	16	17
18	19	20	21	22	23	24
25	26	27	28	29	30	31

August

S	M	T	W	T	F	S
1	2	3	4	5	6	7
8	9	10	11	12	13	14
15	16	17	18	19	20	21
22	23	24	25	26	27	28
29	30	31				

9—Mother's Day
13—Ascension Day
21—1st Day of Shavuot
23—Pentecost
31—Memorial Day observed

14—Flag Day
20—Father's Day

1—Canada Day
4—Independence Day

September

S	M	T	W	T	F	S
			1	2	3	4
5	6	7	8	9	10	11
12	13	14	15	16	17	18
19	20	21	22	23	24	25
26	27	28	29	30		

October

S	M	T	W	T	F	S
					1	2
3	4	5	6	7	8	9
10	11	12	13	14	15	16
17	18	19	20	21	22	23
24	25	26	27	28	29	30
31						

November

S	M	T	W	T	F	S
	1	2	3	4	5	6
7	8	9	10	11	12	13
14	15	16	17	18	19	20
21	22	23	24	25	26	27
28	29	30				

December

S	M	T	W	T	F	S
			1	2	3	4
5	6	7	8	9	10	11
12	13	14	15	16	17	18
19	20	21	22	23	24	25
26	27	28	29	30	31	

6—Labor Day
11—Rosh Hashanah
20—Yom Kippur

11—Columbus Day Observed
11—Thanksgiving Day (Canada)
31—Halloween
31—Daylight Saving Time ends

1—All Saints' Day
2—Election Day
11—Veterans Day
25—Thanksgiving Day
28—1st Sunday of Advent

4—1st Day of Hanukkah
10—Ramadan begins
25—Christmas Day

Seasons for the Northern Hemisphere, 1999

Mar. 20, 8:46 P.M. EST (Mar. 21, 01:46 UT*), sun enters sign of Aries; spring begins

June 21, 3:49 P.M. EDT (19:49 UT), sun enters sign of Cancer; summer begins

Sept. 23, 7:31 A.M. EDT (11:31 UT), sun enters sign of Libra; fall begins

Dec. 22, 2:44 A.M. EST (07:44 UT), sun enters sign of Capricorn; winter begins

*Universal Time (UT), also known as Greenwich Mean Time (GMT). *See* p. 451 for a conversion table of Universal Time.

1998

January

S	M	T	W	T	F	S
				1	2	3
4	5	6	7	8	9	10
11	12	13	14	15	16	17
18	19	20	21	22	23	24
25	26	27	28	29	30	31

February

S	M	T	W	T	F	S
1	2	3	4	5	6	7
8	9	10	11	12	13	14
15	16	17	18	19	20	21
22	23	24	25	26	27	28

March

S	M	T	W	T	F	S
1	2	3	4	5	6	7
8	9	10	11	12	13	14
15	16	17	18	19	20	21
22	23	24	25	26	27	28
29	30	31				

April

S	M	T	W	T	F	S
			1	2	3	4
5	6	7	8	9	10	11
12	13	14	15	16	17	18
19	20	21	22	23	24	25
26	27	28	29	30		

May

S	M	T	W	T	F	S
					1	2
3	4	5	6	7	8	9
10	11	12	13	14	15	16
17	18	19	20	21	22	23
24	25	26	27	28	29	30
31						

June

S	M	T	W	T	F	S
	1	2	3	4	5	6
7	8	9	10	11	12	13
14	15	16	17	18	19	20
21	22	23	24	25	26	27
28	29	30				

July

S	M	T	W	T	F	S
			1	2	3	4
5	6	7	8	9	10	11
12	13	14	15	16	17	18
19	20	21	22	23	24	25
26	27	28	29	30	31	

August

S	M	T	W	T	F	S
						1
2	3	4	5	6	7	8
9	10	11	12	13	14	15
16	17	18	19	20	21	22
23	24	25	26	27	28	29
30	31					

September

S	M	T	W	T	F	S
		1	2	3	4	5
6	7	8	9	10	11	12
13	14	15	16	17	18	19
20	21	22	23	24	25	26
27	28	29	30			

October

S	M	T	W	T	F	S
				1	2	3
4	5	6	7	8	9	10
11	12	13	14	15	16	17
18	19	20	21	22	23	24
25	26	27	28	29	30	31

November

S	M	T	W	T	F	S
1	2	3	4	5	6	7
8	9	10	11	12	13	14
15	16	17	18	19	20	21
22	23	24	25	26	27	28
29	30					

December

S	M	T	W	T	F	S
		1	2	3	4	5
6	7	8	9	10	11	12
13	14	15	16	17	18	19
20	21	22	23	24	25	26
27	28	29	30	31		

2000

January

S	M	T	W	T	F	S
						1
2	3	4	5	6	7	8
9	10	11	12	13	14	15
16	17	18	19	20	21	22
23	24	25	26	27	28	29
30	31					

February

S	M	T	W	T	F	S
		1	2	3	4	5
6	7	8	9	10	11	12
13	14	15	16	17	18	19
20	21	22	23	24	25	26
27	28	29				

March

S	M	T	W	T	F	S
			1	2	3	4
5	6	7	8	9	10	11
12	13	14	15	16	17	18
19	20	21	22	23	24	25
26	27	28	29	30	31	

April

S	M	T	W	T	F	S
						1
2	3	4	5	6	7	8
9	10	11	12	13	14	15
16	17	18	19	20	21	22
23	24	25	26	27	28	29
30						

May

S	M	T	W	T	F	S
	1	2	3	4	5	6
7	8	9	10	11	12	13
14	15	16	17	18	19	20
21	22	23	24	25	26	27
28	29	30	31			

June

S	M	T	W	T	F	S
				1	2	3
4	5	6	7	8	9	10
11	12	13	14	15	16	17
18	19	20	21	22	23	24
25	26	27	28	29	30	

July

S	M	T	W	T	F	S
						1
2	3	4	5	6	7	8
9	10	11	12	13	14	15
16	17	18	19	20	21	22
23	24	25	26	27	28	29
30	31					

August

S	M	T	W	T	F	S
		1	2	3	4	5
6	7	8	9	10	11	12
13	14	15	16	17	18	19
20	21	22	23	24	25	26
27	28	29	30	31		

September

S	M	T	W	T	F	S
					1	2
3	4	5	6	7	8	9
10	11	12	13	14	15	16
17	18	19	20	21	22	23
24	25	26	27	28	29	30

October

S	M	T	W	T	F	S
1	2	3	4	5	6	7
8	9	10	11	12	13	14
15	16	17	18	19	20	21
22	23	24	25	26	27	28
29	30	31				

November

S	M	T	W	T	F	S
			1	2	3	4
5	6	7	8	9	10	11
12	13	14	15	16	17	18
19	20	21	22	23	24	25
26	27	28	29	30		

December

S	M	T	W	T	F	S
					1	2
3	4	5	6	7	8	9
10	11	12	13	14	15	16
17	18	19	20	21	22	23
24	25	26	27	28	29	30
31						

Astrological Signs

♈ **Aries (Ram):** March 21–April 19

♉ **Taurus (Bull):** April 20–May 20

♊ **Gemini (Twins):** May 21–June 20

♋ **Cancer (Crab):** June 21–July 22

♌ **Leo (Lion):** July 23–Aug. 22

♍ **Virgo (Virgin):** Aug. 23–Sept. 22

♎ **Libra (Scales):** Sept. 23–Oct. 22

♏ **Scorpio (Scorpion):** Oct. 23–Nov. 21

♐ **Sagittarius (Archer):** Nov. 22–Dec. 21

♑ **Capricorn (Goat):** Dec. 22–Jan. 19

♒ **Aquarius (Water Bearer):** Jan. 20–Feb. 18

♓ **Pisces (Fish):** Feb. 19–March 20

PERPETUAL CALENDAR

1800...4	1844...9	1888...8	1932.13	1976.12	2020.11
1801...5	1845...4	1889...3	1933...1	1977...7	2021...6
1802...6	1846...5	1890...4	1934...2	1978...1	2022...7
1803...7	1847...6	1891...5	1935...3	1979...2	2023...1
1804...8	1848.14	1892.13	1936.11	1980.10	2024...9
1805...3	1849...2	1893...1	1937...6	1981...5	2025...4
1806...4	1850...3	1894...2	1938...7	1982...6	2026...5
1807...5	1851...4	1895...3	1939...1	1983...7	2027...6
1808.13	1852.12	1896.11	1940...9	1984...8	2028.14
1809...1	1853...7	1897...6	1941...4	1985...3	2029...2
1810...2	1854...1	1898...7	1942...5	1986...4	2030...3
1811...3	1855...2	1899...1	1943...6	1987...5	2031...4
1812.11	1856.10	1900...2	1944.14	1988.13	2032.12
1813...6	1857...5	1901...3	1945...2	1989...1	2033...7
1814...7	1858...6	1902...4	1946...3	1990...2	2034...1
1815...1	1859...7	1903...5	1947...4	1991...3	2035...2
1816...9	1860...8	1904.13	1948.12	1992.11	2036.10
1817...4	1861...3	1905...1	1949...7	1993...6	2037...5
1818...5	1862...4	1906...2	1950...1	1994...7	2038...6
1819...6	1863...5	1907...3	1951...2	1995...1	2039...7
1820.14	1864.13	1908.11	1952.10	1996...9	2040...8
1821...2	1865...1	1909...6	1953...5	1997...4	2041...3
1822...3	1866...2	1910...7	1954...6	1998...5	2042...4
1823...4	1867...3	1911...1	1955...7	1999...6	2043...5
1824.12	1868.11	1912...9	1956...8	2000.14	2044.13
1825...7	1869...6	1913...4	1957...3	2001...2	2045...1
1826...1	1870...7	1914...5	1958...4	2002...3	2046...2
1827...2	1871...1	1915...6	1959...5	2003...4	2047...3
1828.10	1872...9	1916.14	1960.13	2004.12	2048.11
1829...5	1873...4	1917...2	1961...1	2005...7	2049...6
1830...6	1874...5	1918...3	1962...2	2006...1	2050...7
1831...7	1875...6	1919...4	1963...3	2007...2	2051...1
1832...8	1876.14	1920.12	1964.11	2008.10	2052...9
1833...3	1877...2	1921...7	1965...6	2009...5	2053...4
1834...4	1878...3	1922...1	1966...7	2010...6	2054...5
1835...5	1879...4	1923...2	1967...1	2011...7	2055...6
1836.13	1880.12	1924.10	1968...9	2012...8	2056.14
1837...1	1881...7	1925...5	1969...4	2013...3	2057...2
1838...2	1882...1	1926...6	1970...5	2014...4	2058...3
1839...3	1883...2	1927...7	1971...6	2015...5	2059...4
1840.11	1884.10	1928...8	1972.14	2016.13	2060.12
1841...6	1885...5	1929...3	1973...2	2017...1	2061...7
1842...7	1886...6	1930...4	1974...3	2018...2	2062...1
1843...1	1887...7	1931...5	1975...4	2019...3	2063...2

DIRECTIONS: The number given with each year in the key above is the number of the calendar to use for that year.

1

JANUARY
S M T W T F S
1 2 3 4 5 6 7
8 9 10 11 12 13 14
15 16 17 18 19 20 21
22 23 24 25 26 27 28
29 30 31

FEBRUARY
S M T W T F S
1 2 3 4
5 6 7 8 9 10 11
12 13 14 15 16 17 18
19 20 21 22 23 24 25
26 27 28

MARCH
S M T W T F S
1 2 3 4
5 6 7 8 9 10 11
12 13 14 15 16 17 18
19 20 21 22 23 24 25
26 27 28 29 30 31

APRIL
S M T W T F S
1
2 3 4 5 6 7 8
9 10 11 12 13 14 15
16 17 18 19 20 21 22
23 24 25 26 27 28 29
30

MAY
S M T W T F S
1 2 3 4 5 6
7 8 9 10 11 12 13
14 15 16 17 18 19 20
21 22 23 24 25 26 27
28 29 30 31

JUNE
S M T W T F S
1 2 3
4 5 6 7 8 9 10
11 12 13 14 15 16 17
18 19 20 21 22 23 24
25 26 27 28 29 30

JULY
S M T W T F S
1
2 3 4 5 6 7 8
9 10 11 12 13 14 15
16 17 18 19 20 21 22
23 24 25 26 27 28 29
30 31

AUGUST
S M T W T F S
1 2 3 4 5
6 7 8 9 10 11 12
13 14 15 16 17 18 19
20 21 22 23 24 25 26
27 28 29 30 31

SEPTEMBER
S M T W T F S
1 2
3 4 5 6 7 8 9
10 11 12 13 14 15 16
17 18 19 20 21 22 23
24 25 26 27 28 29 30

OCTOBER
S M T W T F S
1 2 3 4 5 6 7
8 9 10 11 12 13 14
15 16 17 18 19 20 21
22 23 24 25 26 27 28
29 30 31

NOVEMBER
S M T W T F S
1 2 3 4
5 6 7 8 9 10 11
12 13 14 15 16 17 18
19 20 21 22 23 24 25
26 27 28 29 30

DECEMBER
S M T W T F S
1 2
3 4 5 6 7 8 9
10 11 12 13 14 15 16
17 18 19 20 21 22 23
24 25 26 27 28 29 30
31

2

JANUARY
S M T W T F S
1 2 3 4 5 6
7 8 9 10 11 12 13
14 15 16 17 18 19 20
21 22 23 24 25 26 27
28 29 30 31

FEBRUARY
S M T W T F S
1 2 3
4 5 6 7 8 9 10
11 12 13 14 15 16 17
18 19 20 21 22 23 24
25 26 27 28

MARCH
S M T W T F S
1 2 3
4 5 6 7 8 9 10
11 12 13 14 15 16 17
18 19 20 21 22 23 24
25 26 27 28 29 30 31

APRIL
S M T W T F S
1 2 3 4 5 6 7
8 9 10 11 12 13 14
15 16 17 18 19 20 21
22 23 24 25 26 27 28
29 30

MAY
S M T W T F S
1 2 3 4 5
6 7 8 9 10 11 12
13 14 15 16 17 18 19
20 21 22 23 24 25 26
27 28 29 30 31

JUNE
S M T W T F S
1 2
3 4 5 6 7 8 9
10 11 12 13 14 15 16
17 18 19 20 21 22 23
24 25 26 27 28 29 30

JULY
S M T W T F S
1 2 3 4 5 6 7
8 9 10 11 12 13 14
15 16 17 18 19 20 21
22 23 24 25 26 27 28
29 30 31

AUGUST
S M T W T F S
1 2 3 4
5 6 7 8 9 10 11
12 13 14 15 16 17 18
19 20 21 22 23 24 25
26 27 28 29 30 31

SEPTEMBER
S M T W T F S
1
2 3 4 5 6 7 8
9 10 11 12 13 14 15
16 17 18 19 20 21 22
23 24 25 26 27 28 29
30

OCTOBER
S M T W T F S
1 2 3 4 5 6
7 8 9 10 11 12 13
14 15 16 17 18 19 20
21 22 23 24 25 26 27
28 29 30 31

NOVEMBER
S M T W T F S
1 2 3
4 5 6 7 8 9 10
11 12 13 14 15 16 17
18 19 20 21 22 23 24
25 26 27 28 29 30

DECEMBER
S M T W T F S
1
2 3 4 5 6 7 8
9 10 11 12 13 14 15
16 17 18 19 20 21 22
23 24 25 26 27 28 29
30 31

3

JANUARY
S M T W T F S
1 2 3 4 5
6 7 8 9 10 11 12
13 14 15 16 17 18 19
20 21 22 23 24 25 26
27 28 29 30 31

FEBRUARY
S M T W T F S
1 2
3 4 5 6 7 8 9
10 11 12 13 14 15 16
17 18 19 20 21 22 23
24 25 26 27 28

MARCH
S M T W T F S
1 2
3 4 5 6 7 8 9
10 11 12 13 14 15 16
17 18 19 20 21 22 23
24 25 26 27 28 29 30
31

APRIL
S M T W T F S
1 2 3 4 5 6
7 8 9 10 11 12 13
14 15 16 17 18 19 20
21 22 23 24 25 26 27
28 29 30

MAY
S M T W T F S
1 2 3 4
5 6 7 8 9 10 11
12 13 14 15 16 17 18
19 20 21 22 23 24 25
26 27 28 29 30 31

JUNE
S M T W T F S
1
2 3 4 5 6 7 8
9 10 11 12 13 14 15
16 17 18 19 20 21 22
23 24 25 26 27 28 29
30

JULY
S M T W T F S
1 2 3 4 5 6
7 8 9 10 11 12 13
14 15 16 17 18 19 20
21 22 23 24 25 26 27
28 29 30 31

AUGUST
S M T W T F S
1 2 3
4 5 6 7 8 9 10
11 12 13 14 15 16 17
18 19 20 21 22 23 24
25 26 27 28 29 30 31

SEPTEMBER
S M T W T F S
1 2 3 4 5 6 7
8 9 10 11 12 13 14
15 16 17 18 19 20 21
22 23 24 25 26 27 28
29 30

OCTOBER
S M T W T F S
1 2 3 4 5
6 7 8 9 10 11 12
13 14 15 16 17 18 19
20 21 22 23 24 25 26
27 28 29 30 31

NOVEMBER
S M T W T F S
1 2
3 4 5 6 7 8 9
10 11 12 13 14 15 16
17 18 19 20 21 22 23
24 25 26 27 28 29 30

DECEMBER
S M T W T F S
1 2 3 4 5 6 7
8 9 10 11 12 13 14
15 16 17 18 19 20 21
22 23 24 25 26 27 28
29 30 31

4

JANUARY
S M T W T F S
1 2 3 4
5 6 7 8 9 10 11
12 13 14 15 16 17 18
19 20 21 22 23 24 25
26 27 28 29 30 31

FEBRUARY
S M T W T F S
1
2 3 4 5 6 7 8
9 10 11 12 13 14 15
16 17 18 19 20 21 22
23 24 25 26 27 28

MARCH
S M T W T F S
1
2 3 4 5 6 7 8
9 10 11 12 13 14 15
16 17 18 19 20 21 22
23 24 25 26 27 28 29
30 31

APRIL
S M T W T F S
1 2 3 4 5
6 7 8 9 10 11 12
13 14 15 16 17 18 19
20 21 22 23 24 25 26
27 28 29 30

MAY
S M T W T F S
1 2 3
4 5 6 7 8 9 10
11 12 13 14 15 16 17
18 19 20 21 22 23 24
25 26 27 28 29 30 31

JUNE
S M T W T F S
1 2 3 4 5 6 7
8 9 10 11 12 13 14
15 16 17 18 19 20 21
22 23 24 25 26 27 28
29 30

JULY
S M T W T F S
1 2 3 4 5
6 7 8 9 10 11 12
13 14 15 16 17 18 19
20 21 22 23 24 25 26
27 28 29 30 31

AUGUST
S M T W T F S
1 2
3 4 5 6 7 8 9
10 11 12 13 14 15 16
17 18 19 20 21 22 23
24 25 26 27 28 29 30
31

SEPTEMBER
S M T W T F S
1 2 3 4 5 6
7 8 9 10 11 12 13
14 15 16 17 18 19 20
21 22 23 24 25 26 27
28 29 30

OCTOBER
S M T W T F S
1 2 3 4
5 6 7 8 9 10 11
12 13 14 15 16 17 18
19 20 21 22 23 24 25
26 27 28 29 30 31

NOVEMBER
S M T W T F S
1
2 3 4 5 6 7 8
9 10 11 12 13 14 15
16 17 18 19 20 21 22
23 24 25 26 27 28 29
30

DECEMBER
S M T W T F S
1 2 3 4 5 6
7 8 9 10 11 12 13
14 15 16 17 18 19 20
21 22 23 24 25 26 27
28 29 30 31

5

JANUARY
S M T W T F S
1 2 3
4 5 6 7 8 9 10
11 12 13 14 15 16 17
18 19 20 21 22 23 24
25 26 27 28 29 30 31

FEBRUARY
S M T W T F S
1 2 3 4 5 6 7
8 9 10 11 12 13 14
15 16 17 18 19 20 21
22 23 24 25 26 27 28

MARCH
S M T W T F S
1 2 3 4 5 6 7
8 9 10 11 12 13 14
15 16 17 18 19 20 21
22 23 24 25 26 27 28
29 30 31

APRIL
S M T W T F S
1 2 3 4
5 6 7 8 9 10 11
12 13 14 15 16 17 18
19 20 21 22 23 24 25
26 27 28 29 30

MAY
S M T W T F S
1 2
3 4 5 6 7 8 9
10 11 12 13 14 15 16
17 18 19 20 21 22 23
24 25 26 27 28 29 30
31

JUNE
S M T W T F S
1 2 3 4 5 6
7 8 9 10 11 12 13
14 15 16 17 18 19 20
21 22 23 24 25 26 27
28 29 30

JULY
S M T W T F S
1 2 3 4
5 6 7 8 9 10 11
12 13 14 15 16 17 18
19 20 21 22 23 24 25
26 27 28 29 30 31

AUGUST
S M T W T F S
1
2 3 4 5 6 7 8
9 10 11 12 13 14 15
16 17 18 19 20 21 22
23 24 25 26 27 28 29
30 31

SEPTEMBER
S M T W T F S
1 2 3 4 5
6 7 8 9 10 11 12
13 14 15 16 17 18 19
20 21 22 23 24 25 26
27 28 29 30

OCTOBER
S M T W T F S
1 2 3
4 5 6 7 8 9 10
11 12 13 14 15 16 17
18 19 20 21 22 23 24
25 26 27 28 29 30 31

NOVEMBER
S M T W T F S
1 2 3 4 5 6 7
8 9 10 11 12 13 14
15 16 17 18 19 20 21
22 23 24 25 26 27 28
29 30

DECEMBER
S M T W T F S
1 2 3 4 5
6 7 8 9 10 11 12
13 14 15 16 17 18 19
20 21 22 23 24 25 26
27 28 29 30 31

6

JANUARY
S M T W T F S
1 2
3 4 5 6 7 8 9
10 11 12 13 14 15 16
17 18 19 20 21 22 23
24 25 26 27 28 29 30
31

FEBRUARY
S M T W T F S
1 2 3 4 5 6
7 8 9 10 11 12 13
14 15 16 17 18 19 20
21 22 23 24 25 26 27
28

MARCH
S M T W T F S
1 2 3 4 5 6
7 8 9 10 11 12 13
14 15 16 17 18 19 20
21 22 23 24 25 26 27
28 29 30 31

APRIL
S M T W T F S
1 2 3
4 5 6 7 8 9 10
11 12 13 14 15 16 17
18 19 20 21 22 23 24
25 26 27 28 29 30

MAY
S M T W T F S
1
2 3 4 5 6 7 8
9 10 11 12 13 14 15
16 17 18 19 20 21 22
23 24 25 26 27 28 29
30 31

JUNE
S M T W T F S
1 2 3 4 5
6 7 8 9 10 11 12
13 14 15 16 17 18 19
20 21 22 23 24 25 26
27 28 29 30

JULY
S M T W T F S
1 2 3
4 5 6 7 8 9 10
11 12 13 14 15 16 17
18 19 20 21 22 23 24
25 26 27 28 29 30 31

AUGUST
S M T W T F S
1 2 3 4 5 6 7
8 9 10 11 12 13 14
15 16 17 18 19 20 21
22 23 24 25 26 27 28
29 30 31

SEPTEMBER
S M T W T F S
1 2 3 4
5 6 7 8 9 10 11
12 13 14 15 16 17 18
19 20 21 22 23 24 25
26 27 28 29 30

OCTOBER
S M T W T F S
1 2
3 4 5 6 7 8 9
10 11 12 13 14 15 16
17 18 19 20 21 22 23
24 25 26 27 28 29 30
31

NOVEMBER
S M T W T F S
1 2 3 4 5 6
7 8 9 10 11 12 13
14 15 16 17 18 19 20
21 22 23 24 25 26 27
28 29 30

DECEMBER
S M T W T F S
1 2 3 4
5 6 7 8 9 10 11
12 13 14 15 16 17 18
19 20 21 22 23 24 25
26 27 28 29 30 31

7

JANUARY

S	M	T	W	T	F	S
						1
2	3	4	5	6	7	8
9	10	11	12	13	14	15
16	17	18	19	20	21	22
23	24	25	26	27	28	29
30	31					

FEBRUARY

S	M	T	W	T	F	S
		1	2	3	4	5
6	7	8	9	10	11	12
13	14	15	16	17	18	19
20	21	22	23	24	25	26
27	28					

MARCH

S	M	T	W	T	F	S
		1	2	3	4	5
6	7	8	9	10	11	12
13	14	15	16	17	18	19
20	21	22	23	24	25	26
27	28	29	30	31		

APRIL

S	M	T	W	T	F	S
					1	2
3	4	5	6	7	8	9
10	11	12	13	14	15	16
17	18	19	20	21	22	23
24	25	26	27	28	29	30

MAY

S	M	T	W	T	F	S
1	2	3	4	5	6	7
8	9	10	11	12	13	14
15	16	17	18	19	20	21
22	23	24	25	26	27	28
29	30	31				

JUNE

S	M	T	W	T	F	S
			1	2	3	4
5	6	7	8	9	10	11
12	13	14	15	16	17	18
19	20	21	22	23	24	25
26	27	28	29	30		

JULY

S	M	T	W	T	F	S
					1	2
3	4	5	6	7	8	9
10	11	12	13	14	15	16
17	18	19	20	21	22	23
24	25	26	27	28	29	30
31						

AUGUST

S	M	T	W	T	F	S
	1	2	3	4	5	6
7	8	9	10	11	12	13
14	15	16	17	18	19	20
21	22	23	24	25	26	27
28	29	30	31			

SEPTEMBER

S	M	T	W	T	F	S
				1	2	3
4	5	6	7	8	9	10
11	12	13	14	15	16	17
18	19	20	21	22	23	24
25	26	27	28	29	30	

OCTOBER

S	M	T	W	T	F	S
						1
2	3	4	5	6	7	8
9	10	11	12	13	14	15
16	17	18	19	20	21	22
23	24	25	26	27	28	29
30	31					

NOVEMBER

S	M	T	W	T	F	S
		1	2	3	4	5
6	7	8	9	10	11	12
13	14	15	16	17	18	19
20	21	22	23	24	25	26
27	28	29	30			

DECEMBER

S	M	T	W	T	F	S
				1	2	3
4	5	6	7	8	9	10
11	12	13	14	15	16	17
18	19	20	21	22	23	24
25	26	27	28	29	30	31

8

JANUARY

S	M	T	W	T	F	S
1	2	3	4	5	6	7
8	9	10	11	12	13	14
15	16	17	18	19	20	21
22	23	24	25	26	27	28
29	30	31				

FEBRUARY

S	M	T	W	T	F	S
			1	2	3	4
5	6	7	8	9	10	11
12	13	14	15	16	17	18
19	20	21	22	23	24	25
26	27	28	29			

MARCH

S	M	T	W	T	F	S
				1	2	3
4	5	6	7	8	9	10
11	12	13	14	15	16	17
18	19	20	21	22	23	24
25	26	27	28	29	30	31

APRIL

S	M	T	W	T	F	S
1	2	3	4	5	6	7
8	9	10	11	12	13	14
15	16	17	18	19	20	21
22	23	24	25	26	27	28
29	30					

MAY

S	M	T	W	T	F	S
		1	2	3	4	5
6	7	8	9	10	11	12
13	14	15	16	17	18	19
20	21	22	23	24	25	26
27	28	29	30	31		

JUNE

S	M	T	W	T	F	S
					1	2
3	4	5	6	7	8	9
10	11	12	13	14	15	16
17	18	19	20	21	22	23
24	25	26	27	28	29	30

JULY

S	M	T	W	T	F	S
1	2	3	4	5	6	7
8	9	10	11	12	13	14
15	16	17	18	19	20	21
22	23	24	25	26	27	28
29	30	31				

AUGUST

S	M	T	W	T	F	S
			1	2	3	4
5	6	7	8	9	10	11
12	13	14	15	16	17	18
19	20	21	22	23	24	25
26	27	28	29	30	31	

SEPTEMBER

S	M	T	W	T	F	S
						1
2	3	4	5	6	7	8
9	10	11	12	13	14	15
16	17	18	19	20	21	22
23	24	25	26	27	28	29
30						

OCTOBER

S	M	T	W	T	F	S
	1	2	3	4	5	6
7	8	9	10	11	12	13
14	15	16	17	18	19	20
21	22	23	24	25	26	27
28	29	30	31			

NOVEMBER

S	M	T	W	T	F	S
				1	2	3
4	5	6	7	8	9	10
11	12	13	14	15	16	17
18	19	20	21	22	23	24
25	26	27	28	29	30	

DECEMBER

S	M	T	W	T	F	S
						1
2	3	4	5	6	7	8
9	10	11	12	13	14	15
16	17	18	19	20	21	22
23	24	25	26	27	28	29
30	31					

9

JANUARY

S	M	T	W	T	F	S
	1	2	3	4	5	6
7	8	9	10	11	12	13
14	15	16	17	18	19	20
21	22	23	24	25	26	27
28	29	30	31			

FEBRUARY

S	M	T	W	T	F	S
				1	2	3
4	5	6	7	8	9	10
11	12	13	14	15	16	17
18	19	20	21	22	23	24
25	26	27	28	29		

MARCH

S	M	T	W	T	F	S
					1	2
3	4	5	6	7	8	9
10	11	12	13	14	15	16
17	18	19	20	21	22	23
24	25	26	27	28	29	30
31						

APRIL

S	M	T	W	T	F	S
	1	2	3	4	5	6
7	8	9	10	11	12	13
14	15	16	17	18	19	20
21	22	23	24	25	26	27
28	29	30				

MAY

S	M	T	W	T	F	S
			1	2	3	4
5	6	7	8	9	10	11
12	13	14	15	16	17	18
19	20	21	22	23	24	25
26	27	28	29	30	31	

JUNE

S	M	T	W	T	F	S
						1
2	3	4	5	6	7	8
9	10	11	12	13	14	15
16	17	18	19	20	21	22
23	24	25	26	27	28	29
30						

JULY

S	M	T	W	T	F	S
	1	2	3	4	5	6
7	8	9	10	11	12	13
14	15	16	17	18	19	20
21	22	23	24	25	26	27
28	29	30	31			

AUGUST

S	M	T	W	T	F	S
				1	2	3
4	5	6	7	8	9	10
11	12	13	14	15	16	17
18	19	20	21	22	23	24
25	26	27	28	29	30	31

SEPTEMBER

S	M	T	W	T	F	S
1	2	3	4	5	6	7
8	9	10	11	12	13	14
15	16	17	18	19	20	21
22	23	24	25	26	27	28
29	30					

OCTOBER

S	M	T	W	T	F	S
		1	2	3	4	5
6	7	8	9	10	11	12
13	14	15	16	17	18	19
20	21	22	23	24	25	26
27	28	29	30	31		

NOVEMBER

S	M	T	W	T	F	S
					1	2
3	4	5	6	7	8	9
10	11	12	13	14	15	16
17	18	19	20	21	22	23
24	25	26	27	28	29	30

DECEMBER

S	M	T	W	T	F	S
1	2	3	4	5	6	7
8	9	10	11	12	13	14
15	16	17	18	19	20	21
22	23	24	25	26	27	28
29	30	31				

10

JANUARY

S	M	T	W	T	F	S
		1	2	3	4	5
6	7	8	9	10	11	12
13	14	15	16	17	18	19
20	21	22	23	24	25	26
27	28	29	30	31		

FEBRUARY

S	M	T	W	T	F	S
					1	2
3	4	5	6	7	8	9
10	11	12	13	14	15	16
17	18	19	20	21	22	23
24	25	26	27	28	29	

MARCH

S	M	T	W	T	F	S
						1
2	3	4	5	6	7	8
9	10	11	12	13	14	15
16	17	18	19	20	21	22
23	24	25	26	27	28	29
30	31					

APRIL

S	M	T	W	T	F	S
		1	2	3	4	5
6	7	8	9	10	11	12
13	14	15	16	17	18	19
20	21	22	23	24	25	26
27	28	29	30			

MAY

S	M	T	W	T	F	S
				1	2	3
4	5	6	7	8	9	10
11	12	13	14	15	16	17
18	19	20	21	22	23	24
25	26	27	28	29	30	31

JUNE

S	M	T	W	T	F	S
1	2	3	4	5	6	7
8	9	10	11	12	13	14
15	16	17	18	19	20	21
22	23	24	25	26	27	28
29	30					

JULY

S	M	T	W	T	F	S
		1	2	3	4	5
6	7	8	9	10	11	12
13	14	15	16	17	18	19
20	21	22	23	24	25	26
27	28	29	30	31		

AUGUST

S	M	T	W	T	F	S
					1	2
3	4	5	6	7	8	9
10	11	12	13	14	15	16
17	18	19	20	21	22	23
24	25	26	27	28	29	30
31						

SEPTEMBER

S	M	T	W	T	F	S
	1	2	3	4	5	6
7	8	9	10	11	12	13
14	15	16	17	18	19	20
21	22	23	24	25	26	27
28	29	30				

OCTOBER

S	M	T	W	T	F	S
			1	2	3	4
5	6	7	8	9	10	11
12	13	14	15	16	17	18
19	20	21	22	23	24	25
26	27	28	29	30	31	

NOVEMBER

S	M	T	W	T	F	S
						1
2	3	4	5	6	7	8
9	10	11	12	13	14	15
16	17	18	19	20	21	22
23	24	25	26	27	28	29
30						

DECEMBER

S	M	T	W	T	F	S
	1	2	3	4	5	6
7	8	9	10	11	12	13
14	15	16	17	18	19	20
21	22	23	24	25	26	27
28	29	30	31			

11

JANUARY

S	M	T	W	T	F	S
			1	2	3	4
5	6	7	8	9	10	11
12	13	14	15	16	17	18
19	20	21	22	23	24	25
26	27	28	29	30	31	

FEBRUARY

S	M	T	W	T	F	S
						1
2	3	4	5	6	7	8
9	10	11	12	13	14	15
16	17	18	19	20	21	22
23	24	25	26	27	28	29

MARCH

S	M	T	W	T	F	S
1	2	3	4	5	6	7
8	9	10	11	12	13	14
15	16	17	18	19	20	21
22	23	24	25	26	27	28
29	30	31				

APRIL

S	M	T	W	T	F	S
			1	2	3	4
5	6	7	8	9	10	11
12	13	14	15	16	17	18
19	20	21	22	23	24	25
26	27	28	29	30		

MAY

S	M	T	W	T	F	S
					1	2
3	4	5	6	7	8	9
10	11	12	13	14	15	16
17	18	19	20	21	22	23
24	25	26	27	28	29	30
31						

JUNE

S	M	T	W	T	F	S
	1	2	3	4	5	6
7	8	9	10	11	12	13
14	15	16	17	18	19	20
21	22	23	24	25	26	27
28	29	30				

JULY

S	M	T	W	T	F	S
			1	2	3	4
5	6	7	8	9	10	11
12	13	14	15	16	17	18
19	20	21	22	23	24	25
26	27	28	29	30	31	

AUGUST

S	M	T	W	T	F	S
						1
2	3	4	5	6	7	8
9	10	11	12	13	14	15
16	17	18	19	20	21	22
23	24	25	26	27	28	29
30	31					

SEPTEMBER

S	M	T	W	T	F	S
		1	2	3	4	5
6	7	8	9	10	11	12
13	14	15	16	17	18	19
20	21	22	23	24	25	26
27	28	29	30			

OCTOBER

S	M	T	W	T	F	S
				1	2	3
4	5	6	7	8	9	10
11	12	13	14	15	16	17
18	19	20	21	22	23	24
25	26	27	28	29	30	31

NOVEMBER

S	M	T	W	T	F	S
1	2	3	4	5	6	7
8	9	10	11	12	13	14
15	16	17	18	19	20	21
22	23	24	25	26	27	28
29	30					

DECEMBER

S	M	T	W	T	F	S
		1	2	3	4	5
6	7	8	9	10	11	12
13	14	15	16	17	18	19
20	21	22	23	24	25	26
27	28	29	30	31		

12

JANUARY

S	M	T	W	T	F	S
				1	2	3
4	5	6	7	8	9	10
11	12	13	14	15	16	17
18	19	20	21	22	23	24
25	26	27	28	29	30	31

FEBRUARY

S	M	T	W	T	F	S
1	2	3	4	5	6	7
8	9	10	11	12	13	14
15	16	17	18	19	20	21
22	23	24	25	26	27	28
29						

MARCH

S	M	T	W	T	F	S
	1	2	3	4	5	6
7	8	9	10	11	12	13
14	15	16	17	18	19	20
21	22	23	24	25	26	27
28	29	30	31			

APRIL

S	M	T	W	T	F	S
				1	2	3
4	5	6	7	8	9	10
11	12	13	14	15	16	17
18	19	20	21	22	23	24
25	26	27	28	29	30	

MAY

S	M	T	W	T	F	S
						1
2	3	4	5	6	7	8
9	10	11	12	13	14	15
16	17	18	19	20	21	22
23	24	25	26	27	28	29
30	31					

JUNE

S	M	T	W	T	F	S
		1	2	3	4	5
6	7	8	9	10	11	12
13	14	15	16	17	18	19
20	21	22	23	24	25	26
27	28	29	30			

JULY

S	M	T	W	T	F	S
				1	2	3
4	5	6	7	8	9	10
11	12	13	14	15	16	17
18	19	20	21	22	23	24
25	26	27	28	29	30	31

AUGUST

S	M	T	W	T	F	S
1	2	3	4	5	6	7
8	9	10	11	12	13	14
15	16	17	18	19	20	21
22	23	24	25	26	27	28
29	30	31				

SEPTEMBER

S	M	T	W	T	F	S
			1	2	3	4
5	6	7	8	9	10	11
12	13	14	15	16	17	18
19	20	21	22	23	24	25
26	27	28	29	30		

OCTOBER

S	M	T	W	T	F	S
					1	2
3	4	5	6	7	8	9
10	11	12	13	14	15	16
17	18	19	20	21	22	23
24	25	26	27	28	29	30
31						

NOVEMBER

S	M	T	W	T	F	S
	1	2	3	4	5	6
7	8	9	10	11	12	13
14	15	16	17	18	19	20
21	22	23	24	25	26	27
28	29	30				

DECEMBER

S	M	T	W	T	F	S
			1	2	3	4
5	6	7	8	9	10	11
12	13	14	15	16	17	18
19	20	21	22	23	24	25
26	27	28	29	30	31	

13

JANUARY

S	M	T	W	T	F	S
					1	2
3	4	5	6	7	8	9
10	11	12	13	14	15	16
17	18	19	20	21	22	23
24	25	26	27	28	29	30
31						

FEBRUARY

S	M	T	W	T	F	S
	1	2	3	4	5	6
7	8	9	10	11	12	13
14	15	16	17	18	19	20
21	22	23	24	25	26	27
28	29					

MARCH

S	M	T	W	T	F	S
		1	2	3	4	5
6	7	8	9	10	11	12
13	14	15	16	17	18	19
20	21	22	23	24	25	26
27	28	29	30	31		

APRIL

S	M	T	W	T	F	S
					1	2
3	4	5	6	7	8	9
10	11	12	13	14	15	16
17	18	19	20	21	22	23
24	25	26	27	28	29	30

MAY

S	M	T	W	T	F	S
1	2	3	4	5	6	7
8	9	10	11	12	13	14
15	16	17	18	19	20	21
22	23	24	25	26	27	28
29	30	31				

JUNE

S	M	T	W	T	F	S
			1	2	3	4
5	6	7	8	9	10	11
12	13	14	15	16	17	18
19	20	21	22	23	24	25
26	27	28	29	30		

JULY

S	M	T	W	T	F	S
					1	2
3	4	5	6	7	8	9
10	11	12	13	14	15	16
17	18	19	20	21	22	23
24	25	26	27	28	29	30
31						

AUGUST

S	M	T	W	T	F	S
	1	2	3	4	5	6
7	8	9	10	11	12	13
14	15	16	17	18	19	20
21	22	23	24	25	26	27
28	29	30	31			

SEPTEMBER

S	M	T	W	T	F	S
				1	2	3
4	5	6	7	8	9	10
11	12	13	14	15	16	17
18	19	20	21	22	23	24
25	26	27	28	29	30	

OCTOBER

S	M	T	W	T	F	S
						1
2	3	4	5	6	7	8
9	10	11	12	13	14	15
16	17	18	19	20	21	22
23	24	25	26	27	28	29
30	31					

NOVEMBER

S	M	T	W	T	F	S
		1	2	3	4	5
6	7	8	9	10	11	12
13	14	15	16	17	18	19
20	21	22	23	24	25	26
27	28	29	30			

DECEMBER

S	M	T	W	T	F	S
				1	2	3
4	5	6	7	8	9	10
11	12	13	14	15	16	17
18	19	20	21	22	23	24
25	26	27	28	29	30	31

14

JANUARY

S	M	T	W	T	F	S
						1
2	3	4	5	6	7	8
9	10	11	12	13	14	15
16	17	18	19	20	21	22
23	24	25	26	27	28	29
30	31					

FEBRUARY

S	M	T	W	T	F	S
		1	2	3	4	5
6	7	8	9	10	11	12
13	14	15	16	17	18	19
20	21	22	23	24	25	26
27	28	29				

MARCH

S	M	T	W	T	F	S
			1	2	3	4
5	6	7	8	9	10	11
12	13	14	15	16	17	18
19	20	21	22	23	24	25
26	27	28	29	30	31	

APRIL

S	M	T	W	T	F	S
						1
2	3	4	5	6	7	8
9	10	11	12	13	14	15
16	17	18	19	20	21	22
23	24	25	26	27	28	29
30						

MAY

S	M	T	W	T	F	S
	1	2	3	4	5	6
7	8	9	10	11	12	13
14	15	16	17	18	19	20
21	22	23	24	25	26	27
28	29	30	31			

JUNE

S	M	T	W	T	F	S
				1	2	3
4	5	6	7	8	9	10
11	12	13	14	15	16	17
18	19	20	21	22	23	24
25	26	27	28	29	30	

JULY

S	M	T	W	T	F	S
						1
2	3	4	5	6	7	8
9	10	11	12	13	14	15
16	17	18	19	20	21	22
23	24	25	26	27	28	29
30	31					

AUGUST

S	M	T	W	T	F	S
		1	2	3	4	5
6	7	8	9	10	11	12
13	14	15	16	17	18	19
20	21	22	23	24	25	26
27	28	29	30	31		

SEPTEMBER

S	M	T	W	T	F	S
					1	2
3	4	5	6	7	8	9
10	11	12	13	14	15	16
17	18	19	20	21	22	23
24	25	26	27	28	29	30

OCTOBER

S	M	T	W	T	F	S
1	2	3	4	5	6	7
8	9	10	11	12	13	14
15	16	17	18	19	20	21
22	23	24	25	26	27	28
29	30	31				

NOVEMBER

S	M	T	W	T	F	S
			1	2	3	4
5	6	7	8	9	10	11
12	13	14	15	16	17	18
19	20	21	22	23	24	25
26	27	28	29	30		

DECEMBER

S	M	T	W	T	F	S
					1	2
3	4	5	6	7	8	9
10	11	12	13	14	15	16
17	18	19	20	21	22	23
24	25	26	27	28	29	30
31						

The Calendar

History of the Calendar

The purpose of a calendar is to reckon time in advance, to show how many days have to elapse until a certain event takes place—the harvest, a religious festival, or whatever. The earliest calendars, naturally, were crude, and they must have been strongly influenced by the geographical location of the people who made them. In the Scandinavian countries, for example, where the seasons are pronounced, the concept of the year was determined by the seasons, specifically by the end of winter. The Norsemen, before becoming Christians, are said to have had a calendar consisting of 10 months of 30 days each.

But in warmer countries, where the seasons are less pronounced, the Moon became the basic unit for time reckoning; an old Jewish book actually makes the statement that "the Moon was created for the counting of the days." All the oldest calendars for which we have reliable information were lunar calendars, based on the time interval from one new moon to the next—a so-called "lunation." But even in a warm climate there are annual events that pay no attention to the phases of the Moon. In some areas it was a rainy season; in Egypt it was the annual flooding of the Nile. It was, therefore, necessary to regulate daily life and religious festivals by lunations, but to take care of the annual event in some other manner.

The calendar of the Assyrians was based on the phases of the Moon. The month began with the first appearance of the lunar crescent, and since this can best be observed in the evening, the day began with sunset. They knew that a lunation was 29½ days long, so their lunar year had a duration of 354 days, falling 11 days short of the solar year.[1] After three years such a lunar calendar would be off by 33 days, or more than one lunation. We know that the Assyrians added an extra month from time to time, but we do not know whether they had developed a special rule for doing so or whether the priests proclaimed the necessity for an extra month from observation. If they made every third year a year of 13 lunations, their three-year period would cover 1,091½ days (using their value of 29½ days for one lunation), or just about 4 days too short. In one century this mistake would add up to 133 days by their reckoning (in reality closer to 134 days), requiring four extra lunations per century.

We now know that an eight-year period, consisting of five years with 12 months and three years with 13 months, would lead to a difference of only 20 days per century, but we do not know whether such a calendar was actually used.

The best approximation that was possible in antiquity was a 19-year period, with 7 of these 19 years having 13 months. This means that the period contained 235 months. This, still using the old value for a lunation, made a total of 6,932½ days, while 19 solar years added up to 6,939.7 days, a difference of just one week per period and about five weeks per century. Even the 19-year period required constant adjustment, but it was the period that became the basis of the religious calendar of the Jews. The Arabs used the same calendar at first, but Muhammed forbade shifting from 12 months to 13 months, so that the Islamic religious calendar, even today, has a lunar year of 354 days. As a result the Islamic religious festivals run through all the seasons of the year three times per century.

The Egyptians had a traditional calendar with 12 months of 30 days each. At one time they added 5 extra days at the end of every year. These turned into a 5-day festival because it was thought to be unlucky to work during that time.

When Rome emerged as a world power, the difficulties of making a calendar were well known, but the Romans complicated their lives because of their superstition that even numbers were unlucky. Hence their months were 29 or 31 days long, with the exception of February, which had 28 days. However, 4 months of 31 days, 7 months of 29 days, and 1 month of 28 days added up to only 355 days. Therefore, the Romans invented an extra month called Mercedonius of 22 or 23 days. It was added every second year.

Even with Mercedonius, the Roman calendar was so far off that Caesar, advised by the astronomer Sosigenes, ordered a sweeping reform in 45 B.C.E. One year, made 445 days long by imperial decree, brought the calendar back in step with the seasons. Then the solar year (with the value of 365 days and 6 hours) was made the basis of the calendar. The months were 30 or 31 days in length, and to take care of the 6 hours, every fourth year was made a 366-day year. Moreover, Caesar decreed the year began with the first of January, not with the vernal equinox in late March.

This was the Julian calendar, named after Julius Caesar. It is still the calendar of the Eastern Orthodox churches. However, the year is 11½ minutes shorter than the figure written into Caesar's calendar by Sosigenes, and after a number of centuries, even 11½ minutes add up.

While Caesar could decree that the vernal equinox should not be used as the first day of the new year, the vernal equinox is still a fact of nature that could not be disregarded. One of the first (as far as we know) to become alarmed about this was Roger Bacon. He sent a memorandum to Pope Clement IV, who apparently was not impressed. But Pope Sixtus IV (who reigned from 1471 to 1484) decided that another reform was needed and called the German astronomer Regiomontanus to Rome to advise him. Regiomontanus arrived in 1475, but one year later he died in an epidemic, one of the recurrent outbreaks of the plague. The pope himself survived, but his reform plans died with Regiomontanus.

Less than a hundred years later, in 1545, the Council of Trent authorized the then pope, Paul III, to reform the calendar once more. Most of the mathematical and astronomical work was done by Father Christopher Clavius, S.J. The immediate correction, advised by Father Clavius and ordered by Pope Gregory XIII, was that Thursday, Oct. 4, 1582, was to be the last day of the Julian calendar. The next day was Friday, with the date of October 15. For

1. The correct figures are lunation: 29 d, 12 h, 44 min, 2.8 sec (29.530585 d); solar year: 365 d, 5 h, 48 min, 46 sec (365.242216 d); 12 lunations: 354 d, 8 h, 48 min, 34 sec (354.3671 d).

Drift of the Vernal Equinox in the Julian Calendar

Date	Julian year	Date	Julian year	Date	Julian year
March 21	C.E. 325	March 17	C.E. 837	March 13	C.E. 1349
March 20	C.E. 453	March 16	C.E. 965	March 12	C.E. 1477
March 19	C.E. 581	March 15	C.E. 1093	March 11	C.E. 1605
March 18	C.E. 709	March 14	C.E. 1221		

long-range accuracy, a formula suggested by the Vatican librarian Aloysius Giglio (latinized into Lilius) was adopted: every fourth year is a leap year *unless* it is a century year like 1700 or 1800. Century years can be leap years *only* when they are divisible by 400 (e.g., 1600). This rule eliminates three leap years in four centuries, making the calendar sufficiently correct for all ordinary purposes.

Unfortunately, all the Protestant princes in 1582 chose to ignore the papal bull; they continued with the Julian calendar. It was not until 1698 that the German professor Erhard Weigel persuaded the Protestant rulers of Germany and of the Netherlands to change to the new calendar. In England the shift took place in 1752, and in Russia it needed the revolution to introduce the Gregorian calendar in 1918.

The average year of the Gregorian calendar, in spite of the leap year rule, is about 26 seconds longer than the earth's orbital period. But this discrepancy will need 3,323 years to build up to a single day.

Modern proposals for calendar reform do not aim at a "better" calendar, but at one that is more convenient to use, especially for commercial purposes. A 365-day year cannot be divided into equal halves or quarters; the number of days per month is haphazard; the months begin or end in the middle of a week; a holiday fixed by date (e.g., the Fourth of July) will wander through a week; a holiday fixed in another manner (e.g., Easter) can fall on 35 possible dates. The Gregorian calendar, admittedly, keeps the calendar dates in reasonable unison with astronomical events, but it still is full of minor annoyances. Moreover, you need a calendar every year to look up dates; an ideal calendar should be one that you can memorize for one year and that is valid for all other years, too.

Time and Calendar

The two natural cycles on which time measurements are based are the year and the day. The year is defined as the time required for Earth to complete one revolution around the Sun, while the day is the time required for Earth to complete one turn upon its axis. Unfortunately Earth needs 365 days plus about six hours to go around the Sun once, so that the year does not consist of so and so many days; the fractional day has to be taken care of by an extra day every fourth year.

But because Earth, while turning upon its axis, also moves around the Sun, there are two kinds of days. A day may be defined as the interval between the highest point of the Sun in the sky on two successive days. This, averaged out over the year, produces the customary 24-hour day. But one might also define a day as the time interval between the moments when a certain point in the sky, say a conveniently located star, is directly overhead. This is called:

Sidereal time. Astronomers use a point which they call the "vernal equinox" for the actual determination. Such a sidereal day is somewhat shorter than the "solar day," namely by about three minutes and 56 seconds of so-called "mean solar time."

Apparent solar time is the time based directly on the Sun's position in the sky. In ordinary life the day runs from midnight to midnight. It begins when the Sun is invisible by being 12 hours from its zenith. Astronomers use the so-called "Julian Day," which runs from noon to noon; the concept was invented by the astronomer Joseph Scaliger, who named it after his father, Julius. To avoid the problems caused by leap-year days and so forth, Scaliger picked a conveniently remote date in the past (4713 B.C.E.) and suggested just counting days without regard to weeks, months, and years. The reason for having the Julian Day run from noon to noon is the practical one that astronomical observations usually extend across the midnight hour, which would require a change in date (or in the Julian Day number) if the astronomical day, like the civil day, ran from midnight to midnight.

Mean solar time, rather than apparent solar time, is what is actually used most of the time. The mean solar time is based on the position of a fictitious "mean sun." The reason why this fictitious sun has to be introduced is the following: Earth turns on its axis regularly; it needs the same number of seconds regardless of the season. But the movement of Earth around the Sun is not regular because Earth's orbit is an ellipse. This has the result (as explained in the section The Seasons) that Earth moves faster in January and slower in July. Though it is Earth that changes velocity, it looks to us as if the Sun does. In January, when Earth moves faster, the *apparent* movement of the Sun looks faster. The mean sun of time measurements, then, is a sun that moves regularly all year round; the real Sun will be either ahead of or behind the mean sun. The difference between the real Sun and the fictitious mean sun is called the *equation of time.*

When the real Sun is west of the mean sun we have the "sun fast" condition, with the real Sun crossing the meridian ahead of the mean sun. The opposite is the "sun slow" situation, when the real Sun crosses the meridian after the mean sun. Of course, what is observed is the real Sun. The equation of time is needed to establish mean solar time, kept by the reference clocks.

But if all clocks were actually set by mean solar time we would be plagued by a welter of time differences that would be "correct" but a major nuisance. A clock on Long Island, correctly showing mean solar time for its location (this would be *local civil time*), would be slightly ahead of a clock in Newark, N.J. The Newark clock would be slightly ahead of a clock in Trenton, N.J., which, in turn, would be ahead of a clock in Philadelphia. This

The Names of the Days of the Week

Latin	Old English	English	German	French	Italian	Spanish
Dies Solis	Sun's Day	Sunday	Sonntag	dimanche	domenica	domingo
Dies Lunae	Moon's Day	Monday	Montag	lundi	lunedì	lunes
Dies Martis	Tiw's Day	Tuesday	Dienstag	mardi	martedì	martes
Dies Mercurii	Woden's Day	Wednesday	Mittwoch	mercredi	mercoledì	miércoles
Dies Jovis	Thor's Day	Thursday	Donnerstag	jeudi	giovedì	jueves
Dies Veneris	Frigg's Day	Friday	Freitag	vendredi	venerdì	viernes
Dies Saturni	Seterne's Day	Saturday	Samstag	samedi	sabato	sábado

NOTE: The seven-day week originated in ancient Mesopotamia and became part of the Roman calendar in C.E. 321. The names of the days are based on the seven celestial bodies (the Sun, the Moon, Mars, Mercury, Jupiter, Venus, and Saturn), believed at that time to revolve around Earth and influence its events. Most of Western Europe adopted the Roman nomenclature. The Germanic languages substituted Germanic equivalents for the names of four of the Roman gods: Tiw, the god of war, replaced Mars; Woden, the god of wisdom, replaced Mercury; Thor, the god of thunder, replaced Jupiter; and Frigg, the goddess of love, replaced Venus.

condition prevailed until 1884, when a system of standard time was adopted by the International Meridian Conference. Earth's surface was divided into 24 zones. The standard time of each zone is the mean astronomical time of one of 24 meridians, 15 degrees apart, beginning at the Greenwich, England, meridian and extending east and west around the globe to the International Date Line. (This system was actually put into use a year earlier by the railroad companies of the U.S. and Canada who, until then, had to contend with some 100 conflicting local sun times observed in terminals across the land.)

For practical purposes, this convention is sometimes altered. For example, Alaska, for a time, consisted of four of the eight U.S. time zones: the Pacific standard time zone (east of Juneau) and the 6th (Juneau), 7th (Anchorage), and 8th (Nome) zones, encompassing the 135°, 150°, and 165° meridians, respectively. In 1983, by act of Congress, the entire state (except the westernmost Aleutians) was united into the 6th zone, Alaska standard time.

The eight U.S. standard time zones are: Atlantic (includes Puerto Rico and the Virgin Islands), eastern, central, mountain, Pacific, Alaska, Hawaii-Aleutian (includes all of Hawaii and those Aleutians west of the Fox Islands), and Samoa standard time.

The Date Line. While the time zones are based on the natural event of the Sun crossing a meridian, the date must be an arbitrary decision. The meridians are traditionally counted from the meridian of the observatory of Greenwich, in England, which is called the zero meridian. The logical place for changing the date is 12 hours, or 180°, from Greenwich. Fortunately, the 180th meridian runs mostly through the open Pacific. The Date Line makes a zigzag in the north to incorporate the eastern tip of Siberia into the Siberian time system and then another one to incorporate a number of islands into the Hawaii-Aleutian time zone. In the south there is a similar zigzag for the purpose of tying a number of British-owned islands to the New Zealand time system. Otherwise, the Date Line is the same as 180° from Greenwich. At points to the east of the Date Line the calendar is one day earlier than at points to the west of it. A traveler going eastward across the Date Line from one island to another would not have to reset his watch because he would stay inside the time zone (provided he does so where the Date Line does *not* coincide with the 180° meridian), but it would be the same time of the *previous* day.

The Seasons

The seasons are caused by the tilt of Earth's axis (23.4°) and not by the fact that Earth's orbit around the Sun is an ellipse. The average distance of Earth from the Sun is 93 million miles; the difference between aphelion (farthest away from the Sun) and perihelion (closest to the Sun) is 3 million miles, so that perihelion is about 91.4 million miles from the Sun. Earth goes through the perihelion point a few days after New Year's Day, just when the Northern Hemisphere has winter. Aphelion is passed during the first days of July. This by itself shows that the distance from the Sun is not important within these limits. What is important is that when Earth passes through perihelion, the northern end of Earth's axis happens to tilt away from the Sun, so that the areas beyond the Tropic of Cancer receive only slanting rays from a Sun low in the sky.

The tilt of Earth's axis is responsible for four lines you find on every globe. When, say, the North Pole is tilted away from the Sun as much as possible, the farthest points in the North which can still be reached by the Sun's rays are 23.5° from the pole. This is the Arctic Circle. The Antarctic Circle is the corresponding limit 23.4° from the South Pole; the Sun's rays cannot reach beyond this point when we have midsummer in the North.

When the Sun is vertically above the equator, the day is of equal length all over Earth. This happens twice a year, and these are the "equinoxes" in March and in September. After having been over the equator in March, the Sun will seem to move northward. The northernmost point where the Sun can be straight overhead is 23.4° north of the equator. This is the Tropic of Cancer; the Sun can never be vertically overhead to the north of this line. Similarly the Sun cannot be vertically overhead to the south of a line 23.4° south of the equator—the Tropic of Capricorn.

This explains the climatic zones. In the belt (the Greek word *zone* means "belt") between the Tropic of Cancer and the Tropic of Capricorn, the Sun can be straight overhead; this is the tropical zone. The two zones where the Sun cannot be overhead but will be above the horizon every day of the year are the two temperate zones; the two areas where the Sun will not rise at all for varying lengths of time are the two polar areas, Arctic and Antarctic. □

The Names of the Months

January: named after Janus, protector of the gateway to heaven
February: named after Februalia, a time period when sacrifices were made to atone for sins
March: named after Mars, the god of war, presumably signifying that the campaigns interrupted by the winter could be resumed
April: from *aperire,* Latin for "to open" (buds)
May: named after Maia, the goddess of growth of plants
June: from *junius,* Latin for the goddess Juno
July: named after Julius Caesar
August: named after Augustus, the first Roman Emperor
September: from *septem,* Latin for "seven"
October: from *octo,* Latin for "eight"
November: from *novem,* Latin for "nine"
December: from *decem,* Latin for "ten"

NOTE: The earliest Latin calendar was a 10-month one; thus September was the seventh month, October, the eighth, etc. July was originally called Quintilis, as the fifth month; August was originally called Sextilis, as the sixth month.

Holidays

Religious and Secular, 1999

Since 1971, by federal law, Washington's Birthday, Memorial Day, Columbus Day, and Veterans Day have been celebrated on Mondays to create three-day weekends for federal employees.

First Day of Ramadan, Sunday, Dec. 20, 1998. This day marks the beginning of a month-long fast, which all Muslims must keep during the daylight hours. It commemorates the first revelation of the Qu'ran. The last day of Ramadan, Eid al-Fitr, is celebrated on Tuesday, Jan. 19, 1999. The next Ramadan (for the year A.H. 1420) will begin on Dec. 10, 1999.

New Year's Day, Friday, Jan. 1. A federal holiday in the United States, New Year's Day has its origin in Roman times, when sacrifices were offered to Janus, the two-faced Roman deity who looked back on the past and forward to the future.

Epiphany, Wednesday, Jan. 6. Falls on the 12th day after Christmas and commemorates the manifestation of Jesus as the Son of God, as represented by the adoration of the Magi, the baptism of Jesus, and the miracle of the wine at the marriage feast at Cana. Epiphany originally marked the beginning of the carnival season preceding Lent, and the evening (sometimes the eve) is known as Twelfth Night.

Martin Luther King, Jr.'s Birthday, Monday, Jan. 18. A federal holiday observed the third Monday in January. It honors the late civil rights leader. It became a public holiday in 1986.

Groundhog Day, Tuesday, Feb. 2. Legend has it that if the groundhog sees his shadow, he'll return to his hole, and winter will last another six weeks.

Lincoln's Birthday, Friday, Feb. 12. A federal holiday in many states, this day was first formally observed in Washington, D.C., in 1866, when both houses of Congress gathered for a memorial address in tribute to the assassinated president.

St. Valentine's Day, Sunday, Feb. 14. This day is the festival of two third-century martyrs, both named St. Valentine. It is not known why this day is associated with lovers. It may derive from an old pagan festival about this time of year, or it may have been inspired by the belief that birds mate on this day.

Washington's Birthday, Monday, Feb. 15. A federal holiday observed the third Monday in February. It is also known as Presidents' Day.

Shrove Tuesday, Feb. 16. Falls the day before Ash Wednesday and marks the end of the carnival season, which once began on Epiphany but is now usually celebrated the last three days before Lent. In France, the day is known as Mardi Gras (Fat Tuesday), and Mardi Gras celebrations are also held in several American cities, particularly in New Orleans. The day is sometimes called Pancake Tuesday by the English because fats, which were prohibited during Lent, had to be used up.

Ash Wednesday, Feb. 17. The seventh Wednesday before Easter and the first day of Lent, which lasts 40 days. Having its origin sometime before C.E. 1000, it is a day of public penance and is marked in the Roman Catholic Church by the burning of the palms blessed on the previous year's Palm Sunday. With the ashes from the palms the priest then marks a cross with his thumb upon the forehead of each worshipper. The Anglican Church and a few Protestant groups in the United States also observe the day, but generally without the use of ashes.

Purim (Feast of Lots), Tuesday, March 2. A day of joy and feasting celebrating the deliverance of the Jews from a massacre planned by the Persian minister Haman. The Jewish queen Esther interceded with her husband, King Ahasuerus, to spare the life of her uncle, Mordecai, and Haman was hanged on the same gallows he had built for Mordecai. The holiday is marked by the reading of the Book of Esther (megillah), and by the exchange of gifts, donations to the poor, and the presentation of Purim plays.

St. Patrick's Day, Wednesday, March 17. St. Patrick, patron saint of Ireland, has been honored in America since the first days of the nation. Perhaps the most notable part of the observance is the annual St. Patrick's Day parade on Fifth Avenue in New York City.

Palm Sunday, March 28. Observed the Sunday before Easter to commemorate the entry of Jesus into Jerusalem. The procession and the ceremonies introducing the benediction of palms probably had their origins in Jerusalem.

First Day of Passover (Pesach), Thursday, April 1. The Feast of the Passover, also called the Feast of Unleavened Bread, commemorates the escape of the Jews from Egypt. As the Jews fled they ate unleavened bread, and from that time the Jews have allowed no leavening in their houses during Passover, bread being replaced by matzoh.

Good Friday, April 2. The Friday before Easter, it commemorates the Crucifixion, which is retold during services from the Gospel according to St. John. A feature in Roman Catholic churches is the Liturgy of the Passion; there is no Consecration, the Host having been consecrated the previous day. The eating of hot-cross buns on this day is said to have started in England.

Easter Sunday, April 4. Observed in all Christian churches, Easter commemorates the Resurrection of Jesus. It is celebrated on the first Sunday after the full moon that occurs on or next after March 21 and is therefore celebrated between March 22 and April 25 inclusive. This date was fixed by the Council of Nicaea in C.E. 325. The Orthodox Church celebrates Easter (Paschal) on April 11.

Mother's Day, Sunday, May 9. Observed the second Sunday in May, as proposed by Anna Jarvis of Philadelphia in 1907.

Ascension Day, Thursday, May 13. The Ascension of Jesus took place in the presence of His apostles 40 days after the Resurrection. It is traditionally held to have occurred on Mount Olivet in Bethany.

First Day of Shavuot (Hebrew Pentecost), Friday, May 21. This festival, sometimes called the Feast of Weeks, or of Harvest, or of the First Fruits, falls 50 days after Passover and originally celebrated the end of the seven-week grain-harvesting season. In later tradition, it also celebrated the giving of the Law to Moses on Mount Sinai.

Pentecost (Whitsunday), Sunday, May 23. This day commemorates the descent of the Holy Ghost upon the apostles 50 days after the Resurrection. The sermon by the Apostle Peter, which led to the baptism of 3,000 who professed belief, originated the ceremonies that have since been followed. "Whitsunday" is believed to have come from "white Sunday" when, among the English, white robes were worn by those baptized on the day.

Memorial Day, Monday, May 31. Observed the last Monday in May. Also known as Decoration Day, Memorial Day is a federal holiday. In 1868, Gen. John A. Logan (Retired), commander in chief of the Grand Army of the Republic, issued an order designating the day as one on which the graves of soldiers would be decorated. The holiday was originally devoted to honoring the memory of those who fell in the Civil War, but is now also dedicated to the memory of all war dead.

Flag Day, Monday, June 14. This day commemorates the adoption by the Continental Congress on June 14, 1777, of the Stars and Stripes as the U.S. flag. Although it is a legal holiday only in Pennsylvania, President Truman, on Aug. 3, 1949, signed a bill requesting the president to call for its observance each year by proclamation.

Father's Day, Sunday, June 20. Observed the third Sunday in June. First celebrated June 19, 1910.

Independence Day, Sunday, July 4. The day of the adoption of the Declaration of Independence in 1776, celebrated in all states and territories. The observance began the next year in Philadelphia.

Labor Day, Monday, Sept. 6. A federal holiday observed the first Monday in September. Labor Day was first celebrated in New York in 1882 under the sponsorship of the Central Labor Union, following the suggestion of Peter J. McGuire, of the Knights of Labor, that the day be set aside in honor of labor.

First Day of Rosh Hashanah (Jewish New Year), Saturday, Sept. 11. This day marks the beginning of the Jewish year 5760 and opens the Ten Days of Penitence, which close with Yom Kippur.

Yom Kippur (Day of Atonement), Monday, Sept. 20. This day marks the end of the Ten Days of Penitence that began with Rosh Hashanah. It is described in Leviticus as a "Sabbath of rest," and synagogue services begin the preceding sundown, resume the following morning, and continue to sundown.

First Day of Sukkot (Feast of Tabernacles) Saturday, Sept. 25. This festival, also known as the Feast of the Ingathering, originally celebrated the fruit harvest, and the name comes from the booths or tabernacles in which the Jews lived during the harvest, although one tradition traces it to the shelters used by the Jews in their wandering through the wilderness. During the festival many Jews build small huts in their backyards or on the roofs of their houses.

Simhat Torah (Rejoicing of the Law), Saturday, Oct. 2. This joyous holiday falls on the eighth day of Sukkot. It marks the end of the year's reading of the Torah (Five Books of Moses) in the synagogue every Saturday and the beginning of the new cycle of reading.

Columbus Day, Monday, Oct. 11. A federal holiday, observed the second Monday in October, that commemorates Christopher Columbus's landing in the New World in 1492. Quite likely the first celebration of Columbus Day was that organized in 1792 by the Society of St. Tammany, or the Columbian Order, widely known as Tammany Hall.

Halloween, Sunday, Oct. 31. Eve of All Saints' Day, formerly called All Hallows and Hallowmass. Halloween is traditionally associated in some countries with old customs such as bonfires, masquerading, and the telling of ghost stories. These are old Celtic practices marking the beginning of winter.

All Saints' Day, Monday, Nov. 1. A Roman Catholic and Anglican holiday celebrating all saints, known and unknown.

Election Day, (legal holiday in certain states), Tuesday, Nov. 2. Since 1845, by act of Congress, the first Tuesday after the first Monday in November is the date for choosing presidential electors. State elections are also generally held on this day.

Veterans Day, Thursday, Nov. 11. Armistice Day, a federal holiday, was established in 1926 to commemorate the signing in 1918 of the armistice ending World War I. On June 1, 1954, the name was changed to Veterans Day to honor all men and women who have served America in its armed forces.

Thanksgiving, Thursday, Nov. 25. A federal holiday observed the fourth Thursday in November by act of Congress (1941), it was the first such national proclamation issued by President Lincoln in 1863, on the urging of Mrs. Sarah J. Hale, editor of *Godey's Lady's Book.* Most Americans believe that the holiday dates back to the day of thanks ordered by Governor Bradford of Plymouth Colony in New England in 1621, but scholars point out that days of thanks stem from ancient times.

First Sunday of Advent, Nov. 28. Advent is the season in which the faithful must prepare themselves for the advent of the Savior on Christmas. The four Sundays before Christmas are marked by special church services.

First Day of Hanukkah (Festival of Lights), Saturday, Dec. 4. This festival was instituted by Judas Maccabaeus in 165 B.C.E. to celebrate the purification of the Temple of Jerusalem, which had been desecrated three years earlier by Antiochus Epiphanes, who set up a pagan altar and offered sacrifices to Zeus Olympius. In Jewish homes, a light is lighted on each night of the eight-day festival.

Christmas (Feast of the Nativity), Saturday, Dec. 25. The most widely celebrated holiday of the Christian year, Christmas is observed as the anniversary of the birth of Jesus. Christmas customs are centuries old. The mistletoe, for example, comes from the Druids, who, in hanging the mistletoe, hoped for peace and good fortune. Use of such plants as holly comes from the ancient belief that such plants blossomed at Christmas.

Comparatively recent is the Christmas tree, first set up in Germany in the 17th century. The use of candles on trees developed from the belief that candles appeared by miracle on the trees at Christmas. Colonial Manhattan Islanders introduced the name Santa Claus, a corruption of the Dutch name St. Nicholas, who lived in fourth-century Asia Minor.

The Problem of Two Easters

The Orthodox church uses the same formula to calculate Easter as the Western church, but bases its date on a slightly different calendar—the traditional Julian calendar instead of the more contemporary Gregorian one. As a consequence, both churches rarely celebrate Easter on the same day. The theological inconsistency of two Easters has led the World Council of Churches to lament that "it has long been recognized that to celebrate this fundamental aspect of the Christian faith on different dates gives a divided witness and compromises the churches' credibility and effectiveness in bringing the Gospel to the world."

A meeting organized by the council (in Aleppo, Syria, March 5–10, 1997) proposed a solution: rather than opting for one method of calculating Easter over another, both methods would be replaced with the most advanced astronomically accurate calculations available. The proposed reform would begin in 2001—the year in which the Julian and Gregorian Easters next coincide.

Another proposal that has been offered is changing Easter from a movable to a fixed feast—the second Sunday in April has been suggested as the most likely date. Thus, this most movable of feasts may be moved in 2001 to a date that will satisfy both religious traditions and simplify a confusing calendrical morass.

Movable Holidays

Christian and Secular, 1999–2001

Year	Ash Wednesday	Easter	Pentecost	Labor Day	Election Day	Thanksgiving	1st Sun. Advent
1999	Feb. 17	April 4	May 23	Sept. 6	Nov. 2	Nov. 25	Nov. 28
2000	March 8	April 23	June 11	Sept. 4	Nov. 7	Nov. 23	Dec. 3
2001	Feb. 28	April 15	June 3	Sept. 3	Nov. 6	Nov. 22	Dec. 2

Shrove Tuesday: 1 day before Ash Wednesday. Palm Sunday: 7 days before Easter. Maundy Thursday: 3 days before Easter. Good Friday: 2 days before Easter. Holy Saturday: 1 day before Easter. Ascension Day: 10 days before Pentecost. Trinity Sunday: 7 days after Pentecost. Corpus Christi: 11 days after Pentecost. NOTE: Easter is celebrated on April 11, 1999, by the Orthodox church.

Jewish Holidays, 1999–2002

Year	Purim[1]	1st day Passover[2]	1st day Shavuot[3]	1st day Rosh Hashanah[4]	Yom Kippur[5]	1st day Sukkot[6]	Simhat Torah[7]	1st day Hanukkah[8]
1999	March 2	April 1	May 21	Sept. 11	Sept. 20	Sept. 25	Oct. 2	Dec. 4
2000	March 21	April 20	June 9	Sept. 30	Oct. 9	Oct. 14	Oct. 21	Dec. 22
2001	March 9	April 8	May 28	Sept. 18	Sept. 27	Oct. 2	Oct. 9	Dec. 10
2002	Feb. 26	March 28	May 17	Sept. 7	Sept. 16	Sept. 21	Sept. 28	Nov. 30

1. Feast of Lots. 2. Feast of Unleavened Bread. 3. Hebrew Pentecost; or Feast of Weeks, or of Harvest, or of First Fruits. 4. Jewish New Year. 5. Day of Atonement. 6. Feast of Tabernacles, or of the Ingathering. 7. Rejoicing of the Law. 8. Festival of Lights. Length of Jewish holidays (O=Orthodox, C=Conservative, R=Reform): Passover: O & C, 8 days (holy days: first 2 and last 2); R, 7 days (holy days: first and last). Shavuot: O & C, 2 days; R, 1 day. Rosh Hashana: O & C, 2 days; R, 1 day. Yom Kippur: All groups, 1 day. Sukkot: All groups, 7 days (holy days: O & C, first 2; R, first only); O & C observe two additional days: Shemini Atseret (Eighth Day of the Feast) and Simhat Torah; R observes Shemini Atseret but not Simhat Torah. Hanukkah: All groups, 8 days. NOTE: All holidays begin at sundown on the evening before the date given.

Islamic Holidays, 1998–2000 (A.H. 1419–1420)

In the Year of the Hegira	Muharram (Islamic New Year)	Mawlid al-Nabi (Muhammed's Birthday)	Ramadan begins	Eid al-Fitr (Ramadan ends)	Eid al-Adha (Festival of Sacrifice)
A.H. 1419	April 28, 1998	July 7, 1998	Dec. 20, 1998	Jan. 19, 1999	March 28, 1999
A.H. 1420	April 17, 1999	June 26, 1999	December 10, 1999	Jan. 8, 2000	March 17, 2000

NOTE: All holidays begin at sundown on the evening before the date given. Islamic holidays are based on the lunar calendar and thus may vary by one or two days. Dates apply to North America.

Hindu Festival Dates, 1999

Source: Jantri 500, by Pal Singh Purewal.

Jan. 14	Makar Sankranti	Aug. 26	Raksha Bandhan
Jan. 22	Vasant Panchami	Sept. 2	Sri Krishna Jayanti
Feb. 14	Maha Shivaratri Vrat (fast)	Sept.13	Ganesh Chaturathi
March 2	Holi (last day)	Sept. 25	Saradhas begin
March 18	Chetra Navratras begin	Oct. 10	Asuj Navratras begin
March 18	Bikarami Samvat begins	Oct. 19	Dassehra
March 25	Rama Navmi	Oct. 27	Karva Chauth Vrat (fast)
April 14	Vaisakhi (solar new year)	Nov. 7	Diwali (Festival of Lights)

Sikh Festival Dates, 1999

Source: Jantri 500, by Pal Singh Purewal. According to new Nanakshalhi Calendar.

Jan. 5	Birthday of Guru Gobind Singh Ji	Nov. 7	Bandichhor Day
Jan. 13	Maghi	Oct. 20	Installation of Holy Scriptures as Guru Granth Sahibi Ji
March 14	Hola Muhalla		
April 14	Vaisakhi (Khalsa era begins)	Nov. 23	Birthday of Guru Nanak Dev Ji
June 16	Martyrdom of Guru Arjan Dev Ji	Nov. 24	Martyrdom of Guru Tegh Bahadur Ji
Sept. 1	First Parkash Granth Sahib Ji		

NOTE: Dates for Sikh and Hindu holidays are determined according to the date of their observance in India. There has been, however, a gradual change in opinion, especially for Hindu festivals, that the dates should be calculated according to a North American location. If this is done, then some holidays will differ by one day.

Chinese New Year

1999	Feb. 16	**2002**	Feb. 12	**2005**	Feb. 9	**2008**	Feb. 7
2000	Feb. 5	**2003**	Feb. 1	**2006**	Jan. 29	**2009**	Jan. 26
2001	Jan. 24	**2004**	Jan. 22	**2007**	Feb. 18	**2010**	Feb. 14

Chinese Calendar

The Chinese lunar year is divided into 12 months of 29 or 30 days. The calendar is adjusted to the length of the solar year by the addition of extra months at regular intervals. The years are arranged in major cycles of 60 years. Each successive year is named after one of 12 animals. These 12-year cycles are continuously repeated. The Chinese New Year is celebrated at the second new moon after the winter solstice and falls between January 21 and February 19 on the Gregorian calendar.

Rat	Ox	Tiger	Cat (Rabbit)	Dragon	Snake	Horse	Sheep (Goat)	Monkey	Rooster	Dog	Pig
1900	1901	1902	1903	1904	1905	1906	1907	1908	1909	1910	1911
1912	1913	1914	1915	1916	1917	1918	1919	1920	1921	1922	1923
1924	1925	1926	1927	1928	1929	1930	1931	1932	1933	1934	1935
1936	1937	1938	1939	1940	1941	1942	1943	1944	1945	1946	1947
1948	1949	1950	1951	1952	1953	1954	1955	1956	1957	1958	1959
1960	1961	1962	1963	1964	1965	1966	1967	1968	1969	1970	1971
1972	1973	1974	1975	1976	1977	1978	1979	1980	1981	1982	1983
1984	1985	1986	1987	1988	1989	1990	1991	1992	1993	1994	1995
1996	1997	1998	1999	2000	2001	2002	2003	2004	2005	2006	2007

State Holidays

Jan. 6, Three Kings' Day: P.R.
Jan. 8, Battle of New Orleans Day: La.
Jan. 11, De Hostos's Birthday: P.R.
Jan. 19, Robert E. Lee's Birthday: Ark., Fla., Ky., La., S.C.; **(third Mon.):** Ala., Miss.
Jan. 19, Confederate Heroes Day: Tex.
Jan. (third Mon.), Lee-Jackson-King Day: Va.
Jan. 30, F. D. Roosevelt's Birthday: Ky.
Feb. 15, Susan B. Anthony's Birthday: Fla., Minn.
March (first Tues.), Town Meeting Day: Vt.
March 2, Texas Independence Day: Tex.
March (first Mon.), Casimir Pulaski's Birthday: Ill.
March 17, Evacuation Day: Mass. (in Suffolk County)
March 20 (first day of spring), Youth Day: Okla.
March 22, Abolition Day: P.R.
March 25, Maryland Day: Md.
March 26, Prince Jonah Kuhio Kalanianaole Day: Hawaii
March (last Mon.), Seward's Day: Alaska
April 2, Pascua Florida Day: Fla.
April 13, Thomas Jefferson's Birthday: Ala., Okla.
April 16, De Diego's Birthday: P.R.
April (third Mon.), Patriots' Day: Maine, Mass.
April 21, San Jacinto Day: Tex.
April 22, Arbor Day: Nebr.
April 22, Oklahoma Day: Okla.
April 26, Confederate Memorial Day: Fla., Ga.
April (fourth Mon.), Fast Day: N.H.
April (last Mon.), Confederate Memorial Day: Ala., Miss.
May 1, Bird Day: Okla.
May 8, Truman Day: Mo.
May 11, Minnesota Day: Minn.
May 20, Mecklenburg Independence Day: N.C.
June (first Mon.), Jefferson Davis's Birthday: Ala., Miss.
June 3, Jefferson Davis's Birthday: Fla., S.C.
June 3, Confederate Memorial Day: Ky., La.
June 9, Senior Citizens Day: Okla.
June 11, King Kamehameha I Day: Hawaii
June 15, Separation Day: Del.
June 17, Bunker Hill Day: Mass. (in Suffolk County)
June 19, Emancipation Day: Tex.
June 20, West Virginia Day: W.Va.
July 17, Muñoz Rivera's Birthday: P.R.
July 24, Pioneer Day: Utah
July 25, Constitution Day: P.R.
July 27, Barbosa's Birthday: P.R.
Aug. (first Sun.), American Family Day: Ariz.
Aug. (first Mon.), Colorado Day: Colo.
Aug. (second Mon.), Victory Day: R.I.
Aug. 16, Bennington Battle Day: Vt.
Aug. (third Friday), Admission Day: Hawaii
Aug. 27, Lyndon B. Johnson's Birthday: Tex.
Aug. 30, Huey P. Long Day: La.
Sept. 9, Admission Day: Calif.
Sept. 12, Defenders' Day: Md.
Sept. 16, Cherokee Strip Day: Okla.
Sept. (first Sat. after full moon), Indian Day: Okla.
Oct. 10, Leif Eriksson Day: Minn.
Oct. 10, Oklahoma Historical Day: Okla.
Oct. 18, Alaska Day: Ala.
Oct. 31, Nevada Day: Nev.
Nov. 4, Will Rogers Day: Okla.
Nov. (week of the 16th), Oklahoma Heritage Week: Okla.
Nov. 19, Discovery Day: P.R.
Dec. 7, Delaware Day: Del.

Birthstones

Month	Stone	Month	Stone	Month	Stone
January	Garnet	June	Pearl, Alexandrite, or Moonstone	October	Opal or Tourmaline
February	Amethyst	July	Ruby or Star Ruby	November	Topaz or Citrine
March	Aquamarine or Bloodstone	August	Peridot or Sardonyx	December	Turquoise, Lapis Lazuli, Blue Zircon, or Blue Topaz
April	Diamond	September	Sapphire or Star Sapphire		
May	Emerald				

Source: Jewelry Industry Council.

Traditional Wedding Anniversary Gift List

Anniv.	Gift	Anniv.	Gift	Anniv.	Gift	Anniv.	Gift
1st	Paper	7th	Copper, wool	13th	Lace	35th	Coral
2nd	Cotton	8th	Bronze, pottery	14th	Ivory	40th	Ruby
3rd	Leather	9th	Pottery, willow	15th	Crystal	45th	Sapphire
4th	Fruit, flowers	10th	Tin	20th	China	50th	Gold
5th	Wood	11th	Steel	25th	Silver	55th	Emerald
6th	Sugar	12th	Silk, linen	30th	Pearl	60th	Diamond

Modern Wedding Anniversary Gift List

Anniv.	Gift	Anniv.	Gift	Anniv.	Gift	Anniv.	Gift
1st	Gold jewelry	8th	Tourmaline	15th	Ruby	30th	Pearl jubilee
2nd	Garnet	9th	Lapis	16th	Peridot	35th	Emerald
3rd	Pearls	10th	Diamond jewelry	17th	Watch	40th	Ruby
4th	Blue topaz	11th	Turquoise	18th	Cat's-eye	45th	Sapphire
5th	Sapphire	12th	Jade	19th	Aquamarine	50th	Golden jubilee
6th	Amethyst	13th	Citrine	20th	Emerald	60th	Diamond jubilee
7th	Onyx	14th	Opal	25th	Silver jubilee		

Source: Jewelry Industry Council.

National Holidays Around the World, 1999

Afghanistan	Aug. 19
Albania	Nov. 28
Algeria	Nov. 1
Andorra	Sept. 8
Angola	Nov. 11
Antigua and Barbuda	Nov. 1
Argentina	May 25
Armenia	Sept. 21
Australia	Jan. 26
Austria	Oct. 26
Azerbaijan	May 28
Bahamas	July 10
Bahrain	Dec. 16
Bangladesh	March 26
Barbados	Nov. 30
Belarus	July 27
Belgium	July 21
Belize	Sept. 21
Benin	Aug. 1
Bhutan	Dec. 17
Bolivia	Aug. 6
Botswana	Sept. 30
Brazil	Sept. 7
Brunei Darussalam	Feb. 23
Bulgaria	March 3
Burkina Faso	Aug. 4
Burma (Myanmar)	Jan. 4
Burundi	July 1
Cambodia	Nov. 9
Cameroon	May 20
Canada	July 1
Cape Verde	Sept. 12
Central African Republic	Dec. 1
Chad	Aug. 11
Chile	Sept. 18
China	Oct. 1
Colombia	July 20
Comoros	July 6
Congo	Aug. 15
Costa Rica	Sept. 15
Côte d'Ivoire	Dec. 7
Croatia	May 30
Cuba	Jan. 1
Cyprus	Oct. 1
Czech Republic	Oct. 28
Denmark	April 16
Djibouti	June 27
Dominica	Nov. 3
Dominican Republic	Feb. 27
Ecuador	Aug. 10
Egypt	July 23
El Salvador	Sept. 15
Equatorial Guinea	Oct. 12
Eritrea	May 24
Estonia	Feb. 24
Ethiopia	May 28
Fiji	Oct. 10
Finland	Dec. 6
France	July 14
Gabon	Aug. 17
Gambia	Feb. 18
Georgia	May 26
Germany	Oct. 3
Ghana	March 6
Greece	March 25
Grenada	Feb. 7
Guatemala	Sept. 15
Guinea	Oct. 2
Guinea-Bissau	Sept. 24
Guyana	Feb. 23
Haiti	Jan. 1
Honduras	Sept. 15
Hungary	Aug. 20
Iceland	June 17
India	Jan. 26
Indonesia	Aug. 17
Iran	Feb. 11
Iraq	July 17
Ireland	March 17
Israel	April 21[1]
Italy	June 2
Jamaica	Aug. 2[2]
Japan	Dec. 23
Jordan	May 25
Kazakhstan	Oct. 25
Kenya	Dec. 12
North Korea (Democratic People's Rep. of Korea)	Sept. 9
South Korea (Rep. of Korea)	Aug. 15
Kuwait	Feb. 25
Kyrgyzstan	Aug. 31
Laos	Dec. 2
Latvia	Nov. 18
Lebanon	Nov. 22
Lesotho	Oct. 4
Liberia	July 26
Libya	Sept. 1
Liechtenstein	Aug. 15
Lithuania	Feb. 16
Luxembourg	June 23
Macedonia	Aug. 2
Madagascar	June 26
Malawi	July 6
Malaysia	Aug. 31
Maldives	July 26
Mali	Sept. 22
Malta	Sept. 21
Marshall Islands	May 1
Mauritania	Nov. 28
Mauritius	March 12
Mexico	Sept. 16
Micronesia	Nov. 3
Moldova	Aug. 27
Monaco	Nov. 19
Mongolia	July 11
Morocco	March 3
Mozambique	June 25
Namibia	March 21
Nepal	Dec. 28
Netherlands	April 30
New Zealand	Feb. 6
Nicaragua	Sept. 15
Niger	Dec. 18
Nigeria	Oct. 1
Norway	May 17
Oman	Nov. 18
Pakistan	March 23
Panama	Nov. 3
Papua New Guinea	Sept. 16
Paraguay	May 15
Peru	July 28
Philippines	June 12
Poland	May 3
Portugal	June 10
Qatar	Sept. 3
Romania	Dec. 1
Rwanda	July 1
St. Kitts and Nevis	Sept. 19
St. Lucia	Feb. 22
St. Vincent and the Grenadines	Oct. 27
San Marino	Sept. 3
São Tomé and Príncipe	July 12
Saudi Arabia	Sept. 23
Senegal	April 4
Seychelles	June 18
Sierra Leone	April 27
Singapore	Aug. 9
Slovakia	Sept. 1
Slovenia	June 25
Solomon Islands	July 7
Somalia	Oct. 21
South Africa	May 31
Spain	Oct. 12
Sri Lanka	Feb. 4
Sudan	Jan. 1
Suriname	Nov. 25
Swaziland	Sept. 6
Sweden	June 6
Switzerland	Aug. 1
Syria	April 17
Tajikistan	Sept. 9
Tanzania	April 26
Thailand	Dec. 5
Togo	Jan. 13
Tonga	June 4
Trinidad and Tobago	Aug. 31
Tunisia	March 20
Turkey	Oct. 29
Turkmenistan	Oct. 27
Uganda	Oct. 9
Ukraine	Aug. 24
United Arab Emirates	Dec. 2
United Kingdom	June 12[3]
United States	July 4
Uruguay	Aug. 25
Uzbekistan	Sept. 1
Vanuatu	July 30
Venezuela	July 5
Vietnam	Sept. 2
Western Samoa	June 1
Yemen, Republic of	May 22
Zambia	Oct. 24
Zimbabwe	April 18

1. Changes yearly according to Hebrew calendar. 2. Celebrated on first Monday in August. 3. Celebrated the second Saturday in June.

Save the Earth!

Mass extinctions of the past may have been caused by comets or asteroids crashing into Earth. Can we prevent a future calamity?

By LEON JAROFF TIME

It is a stunning concept. From the time that terrestrial life emerged nearly 4 billion years ago, it has been assailed time and again by global catastrophes that have caused the wholesale extinction of species. But now, for the first time, one species, *Homo sapiens,* has evolved the intelligence and capability to defend itself against the next such calamity—if it has the will to do so.

The great extinctions of the past, many scientists believe, were caused not by volcanism, disease, or long-term climactic changes, but by giant asteroids or comets smashing into Earth. These impacts, according to prevailing theory, not only destroyed life for hundreds and even thousands of miles around, but also blasted enough dust into the atmosphere to shroud the entire globe for months. In the ensuing darkness and plummeting temperatures, animal and plant life around the world perished.

Celestial Target Practice

Despite weathering and tectonic plate movement, the evidence for these ancient impacts is abundant in the form of 150-odd giant craters littering Earth's surface; some clearly visible, some evident only from the air, others long buried or on the bottom of the sea. By far the most notorious is the over 195-km-diameter crater discovered under the northern tip of Mexico's Yucatan Peninsula. It is the likely impact site of the 10-km-wide comet or asteroid that wiped out the dinosaurs and around 70% of the other co-existing species 65 million years ago. While that horrendous event seems to be safely tucked away in the past, there are more recent impacts—and near misses—to remind the world that the solar system is still swarming with mountain-size chunks and that it is only a matter of time before another one targets Earth.

Arizona's sharply defined Meteor Crater, for example, is only about 50,000 years old, and were the asteroid that gouged it to hit today, it would raise havoc over a large populated region. In 1908, a small asteroid or chunk of a comet, about 60 m across, rapidly heated as it encountered the atmosphere and exploded some eight km above the largely uninhabited Tunguska region of Siberia. It felled trees, started fires, and killed reindeer over an area of over 1,000 sq. km. If the blast, estimated at tens of megatons, had occurred over a large metropolitan area, say London or New York, hundreds of thousands of people might have died.

As recently as 1989, an asteroid 800 m across, undetected until after it passed, missed Earth by only a million km or so, a hairbreadth by astronomical standards. Had it arrived only six hours later, it would have struck Earth with catastrophic and probably global results. An even closer call occurred in 1997, when two astronomers at a University of Arizona observatory spotted an asteroid perhaps 500 m wide just four days before it whipped past, missing Earth by barely 450,000 km. It was the largest object ever observed to pass that close to Earth, and Duncan Steel, an Australian astronomer, calculated that if it had been on target it would have ripped through the atmosphere and hit the surface at 93,000 km/h. The resulting explosion, scientists estimate, would have been in the 3,000 to 12,000 megaton range. That, observed the late Eugene Shoemaker, the renowned U.S. Geological Survey astronomer/geologist, "is like taking all of the U.S. and Soviet nuclear weapons, putting them in one pile, and blowing them all up."

Shoemaker was chiefly responsible for alerting the world to the dangers of asteroid and comet impacts. In 1973, with geologist Eleanor Helin and on his own initiative, he began the world's first systematic watch for Near Earth Objects (NEOS)—asteroids or comets that cross or come close to Earth's orbit. Using a small wide-angled telescope at the Mt. Palomar Observatory in California, Helin and Shoemaker photographed one region of the sky after another, scanning photographic plates to seek out undiscovered objects in motion against the background of "fixed" stars. Shoemaker knew that once a new asteroid or comet was spotted and its orbit determined, astronomers could calculate, often decades in advance, if it presented a threat—if, on one of its future passes, it would cross Earth's orbit when the planet was at the same point. This might give the world enough time, he hoped, to take the necessary preventive measures.

Deadly Debris

Astronomers estimate that as many as 2,000 "Earth-crossing" asteroids wider than a kilometer are out there, with potential impact energies ranging from 100,000 to many millions of megatons. Any of them has the potential of causing worldwide, civilization-threatening catastrophes. But only 7% have been identified. "We simply don't know where the other objects are," says Eleanor Helin. "That should be enough to get the attention of [the U.S.] Congress and the public, yet it doesn't seem to. We're just barely eking by with this detection program, because we can't convince people that it's worthy of funding."

Equally disconcerting, an estimated 300,000 asteroids larger than 100 m wide are on paths that cross Earth's orbit, each one capable of devastating a large metropolitan area. And Tom Gehrels, a University of Arizona astronomer, thinks that the population of Earth-crossing asteroids larger than 20 m—one of which could destroy London—is as high as 100 million. "There is no way in the foreseeable future that you could detect all of these objects," he says.

There is yet another threat, one that would be terrifyingly visible before impact: a comet. Indeed, Gene Shoemaker believed that comets caused not only the Tunguska and dinosaur-dooming events, but also blasted out some of the other large terrestrial craters. "I'm considered a little far out by my colleagues," he said last year, "because I think that long-period comets may account for about half of the total hazard." Astronomers define long-period comets as those either making their first appearance or returning at intervals of greater than 200 years. Appearing without warning as they streak in from the outer reaches of the solar system, these comets usually flare and become visible only a few months to two years before passing Earth. Should one suddenly appear on a collision course, travelling as fast as 217,000 km/h relative to Earth, the world would not have the luxury of having many years to prepare defensive measures.

To get an early lead on a threatening comet, Shoemaker suggested, "I'd put my bucks into a couple of large telescopes with state-of-the-art infrared imaging systems." That would enable astronomers to spot comets before they begin volatilizing and reflecting sunlight. "Then we'd be able to find all the long-period comets all the way to the edge of the main planetary region," Shoemaker explained. "You'd have 20 years advance notice. Then if you see something that looked really serious, you'd get down to business and design a system to deal with it."

Star Wars

Scientists generally agree on the strategy for warding off disaster: detect the threatening object and dispatch a warhead-tipped rocket to intercept it and, at the very least, change its orbit. For a small asteroid detected years and many orbits before its predicted collision, the solution would be straightforward. "You apply some modest impulse to it at its perihelion, or its closest approach to the Sun," explains Greg Canavan, a senior scientist at Los Alamos National Laboratory in New Mexico. "The slight deflection that results will amplify during each orbit, ensuring that the asteroid misses Earth by a wide margin." That "modest impulse," he notes, could be provided by conventional high explosives.

However, nuclear explosives may be necessary for objects with diameters of 100 m or more that are spotted late in the game and intercepted at a distance any closer than about 150 million kilometers. At that distance, the energy needed to deflect a two-km-wide object enough to spare Earth is about equivalent to a one megaton nuclear explosion. If the same object gets to about a tenth of that distance, the energy required is 100 megatons, more powerful than any nuclear device yet exploded. More likely than not, a threatening asteroid of that size would be spotted earlier and farther away. But long-period comets are another matter. Given that defenders would have little time to prepare, a quick and most powerful nuclear bang would be all that stood between Earth and disaster. In attacking a large comet or rocky asteroid, however, the interceptors would have to take care not to blast their quarry into many large chunks, each of which would be a potential city-killer.

But at least one faction of astronomers has been adamantly opposed to the notion of having still more nuclear missiles at the ready, either on Earth or in orbit, poised to meet a space emergency. They fear that the missiles might someday be turned against Earthlings rather than cosmic interlopers—or the remote possibility that some madman might seize control of the defensive system and use it to divert some otherwise harmless asteroid into a collision with Earth. They also have not-too-subtly suggested that pro-nuclear Star Wars scientists, looking for new projects after the Cold War, are using the comet and asteroid threat to generate business. Some of the opposition to nukes weakened in 1994, however, when huge chunks of Comet Shoemaker-Levy put on a spectacular display, creating Earth-sized explosions as they plunged, one after another, into the atmosphere of Jupiter. That, even better than Earth's scars, demonstrated a planet's vulnerability to the solar system's deadly debris. "Nothing so clears the mind as the sight of the gallows," quips Canavan.

Still, before they decide what weaponry to use against an incoming threat, Earth's defenders should be aware of the nature of the intruder. Is it a rocky or iron asteroid? Is it solid and dense, or a loose conglomerate? "Once you know," says physicist Edward Tagliaferri, a U.S. space program consultant, "it becomes easier to decide if you want a standoff explosion, a surface explosion, or a subsurface explosion." If the asteroid or comet is small, a subsurface explosion will vaporize it. But for larger bodies, says Tagliaferri, "you'll probably have to nudge them into a new orbit." And while a surface explosion could safely deflect an iron asteroid, it might well shatter a rock asteroid into large city-destroying chunks.

Collision with Congress

Hopes that Congress might supply modest funding to set up a worldwide detection network may have been dashed by the refusal by most of the budget-conscious Congress to take the danger seriously. But wiser heads at the U.S. Air Force may yet prevail. They are mulling over plans to allow NEO hunters time on satellite tracking telescopes in three locations. This would involve equipping the telescopes with charged-coupled devices (C.C.D.S), which are extremely sensitive cameras that electronically record the images of celestial objects, as well as detection software, which would also improve the Air Force's satellite tracking ability. "They could do double duty," Gene Shoemaker explained, "tracking the satellites at twilight and surveying for NEOS in the middle of the night. They could become major players in this program." If they did, Shoemaker predicted, as many as 90% of the kilometer-or-larger NEOS could be detected within a decade. But even without full Air Force cooperation, he said, "if there's a reasonable but modest level of support, we're going to get to a 90% completeness in 20 years." □

Astronomical Terms

Planet is the term used for a body in orbit around the Sun. Its origin is Greek; even in antiquity it was known that a number of "stars" did not stay in the same relative positions to the others. There were five such restless "stars" known—Mercury, Venus, Mars, Jupiter, and Saturn—and the Greeks referred to them as *planetes,* a word which means "wanderers." That Earth is one of the planets was realized later. The additional planets were discovered after the invention of the telescope.

In 1994, Dr. Alexander Wolszcan, an astronomer at Pennsylvania State University, presented convincing evidence of the first known planets to exist outside our solar system. They circle a pulsar or exploded star in the constellation *Virgo.* Two of the planets are two to three times the size of Earth and a third is about the size of our Moon.

In 1995, several of these *extrasolar planets* were discovered orbiting ordinary stars similar to our Sun as a result of observing gravitational variations of the stars. Swiss astronomers found a planet orbiting star 57 in the constellation *Pegasus,* about 40 light-years away. It is the first planet ever discovered to circle a normal sunlike star. Over the last several years, at least ten more planets have been discovered.

Satellite (or *moon*) is the term for a body in orbit around a planet. As long as our own Moon was the only moon known, there was no need for a general term for the moons of planets. But when Galileo Galilei discovered the four main moons of the planet Jupiter, Johannes Kepler (in a letter to Galileo) suggested "satellite" (from the Latin *satelles,* which means attendant) as a general term for such bodies. The word is used interchangeably with "moons": astronomers speak and write about the moons of Neptune, Saturn, etc. A satellite may be any size.

Orbit is the term for the path traveled by a body in space. It comes from the Latin *orbis,* which means circle, circuit, etc., and *orbita,* which means a rut or a wheel track. Theoretically, four mathematical figures are possible orbits: two are open (hyperbola and parabola) and two are closed (ellipse and circle), but in reality all closed orbits are ellipses. These ellipses can be nearly circular, as are the orbits of most planets, or very elongated, as are the orbits of most comets. In these orbits, the Sun is in one focal point of the ellipse, and the other focal point is empty. In the orbits of satellites, the planet stands in one focal point of the orbit. The *primary* of an orbit is the body in the focal point. For planets, the point of the orbit closest to the Sun is the *perihelion,* and the point farthest from the Sun is the *aphelion.* For orbits around Earth, the corresponding terms are *perigee* and *apogee;* for orbits around other planets, corresponding terms are coined when necessary.

Two heavenly bodies are in *inferior* or *superior conjunction* when they have the same *right ascension,* or are in the same meridian; that is, when one is due north or south of the other. If the bodies appear near each other as seen from Earth, they will rise and set at the same time. They are in *opposition* when they are opposite each other in the heavens: when one rises as the other is setting. *Greatest elongation* is the greatest apparent angular distance from the Sun, when a planet is most favorably suited for observation. Mercury can be seen with the naked eye only at about this time. An *occultation* of a planet or star is an eclipse of it by some other body, usually the Moon.

The Milky Way, the galaxy containing our solar system, is about 100,000 light-years in diameter and about 10,000 light-years thick.

Stars are the basic units of population in the universe. Our Sun is the nearest star. Stars are very large (our Sun has a diameter of 865,400 miles—a comparatively small star). Stars are composed of intensely hot gasses, deriving their energy from nuclear reactions going on in their interiors.

Galaxies are immense systems containing billions of stars. All that you can see in the sky (with a very few exceptions) belongs to our galaxy—a system of roughly 200 billion stars. The few exceptions are other galaxies. Our own galaxy, the rim of which we see as the "Milky Way," is about 100,000 light-years in diameter and about 10,000 light-years in thickness. Its shape is roughly that of a thick lens; more precisely it is a "spiral nebula," a term first used for other galaxies when they were discovered and before it was realized that these were separate and distinct galaxies. The spiral galaxy nearest to ours is in the constellation *Andromeda.* It is somewhat larger than our own galaxy and is visible to the naked eye. Astronomers have estimated that the universe could contain 40 to 50 billion galaxies.

A *black hole* is the theoretical end-product of the total gravitational collapse of a massive star or group of stars. Crushed even smaller than an incredibly dense neutron star, such a body may become so dense that not even light can escape its gravitational field. It has been suggested that black holes may be detectable in proximity to normal stars when they draw matter away from their visible neighbors. Strong sources of X-rays in our galaxy and beyond may also indicate the presence of black holes.

Quasars ("quasi-stellar" objects), originally thought to be peculiar stars in our own galaxy, are now believed to be the most remote objects in the universe. Quasars emit tremendous amounts of light and microwave radiation. Recent Hubble Space Telescope images suggest that there may be a variety of mechanisms for "turning on" quasars. Although a number of images show collisions between pairs of galaxies, which could trigger the birth of quasars, some pictures reveal apparently normal, undisturbed galaxies possessing quasars.

Quasars are among the most baffling objects in the universe because of their small size and prodigious energy output. Quasars are not much bigger than Earth's solar system but pour out 100 to 1,000 times as much light as an entire galaxy containing a hundred billion stars.

A super massive black hole, gobbling up stars, gas, and dust, is theorized to be the "engine" powering a quasar. Most astronomers agree that an active black hole is the only credible possibility that explains how quasars can be so compact, variable, and powerful. However, no conclusive evidence supports this assumption.

Pulsars are believed to be rapidly spinning neutron stars, so crushed by their own gravity that a million tons of their matter would hardly fill a thimble. Pulsars are so named because they emit bursts of radio waves at regular intervals.

In 1996, astronomers found strong evidence for a massive black hole at the center of the Milky Way. Recent evidence suggests that black holes are so common that they probably exist at the core of nearly all galaxies.

The existence of brown dwarfs, also called failed stars, was confirmed in November 1995 when astronomers at Palomar Observatory in California took the first photograph of this mysterious object. Brown dwarfs lack the mass to generate nuclear fission like true stars but are also too massive and hot to be a planet.

Origin of the Universe

Evidence tends to confirm that the universe began its existence about 15 billion years ago as a dense, hot globule of gas expanding rapidly outward. At that time, the universe contained nothing but hydrogen and a small amount of helium. There were no stars and no planets. The first stars probably began to condense out of the primordial hydrogen when the universe was about 100 million years old and continued to form as the universe aged. The Sun arose in this way 4.6 billion years ago. Many stars came into being before the Sun was formed; many others formed after the Sun appeared. This process continues, and through telescopes we can now see stars forming out of compressed pockets of hydrogen in outer space.

In 1992, instruments aboard the Cosmic Background Explorer (COBE) satellite, launched in 1989, showed that 99.97% of the radiant energy of the universe was released within the first year of the primeval explosion. This evidence seems to confirm the Big Bang theory, which holds that the universe originated from a single violent explosion (a *big bang)* of a very small agglomeration of matter of extremely high density and temperatures. Astronomers also theorize that 99% of the matter in the universe is invisible or *dark matter* composed of some kind of matter that they cannot yet detect.

In March 1995, astronomers found supporting evidence for the Big Bang when they concluded that data obtained from the space shuttle's *Astro 2* observatory showed that helium was widespread in the early universe. The theory holds that hydrogen and helium were the first elements created when the universe was formed.

Birth and Death of a Star

When a star begins to form as a dense cloud of gas, the individual hydrogen atoms fall toward the center of the cloud under the force of the star's gravity. As it falls, it picks up speed, and its energy increases. The increase in energy heats the gas. When this process has continued for some millions of years, the temperature reaches about 20 million degrees Fahrenheit. At this temperature, the hydrogen within the star ignites and burns in a continuing series of nuclear reactions in which all the elements in the universe are manufactured from hydrogen and helium. The onset of these reactions marks the birth of a star. When a star begins to exhaust its hydrogen supply, its life nears an end. The first sign of old age is a swelling and reddening of its outer regions. Such an aging, swollen star is called a red giant. The Sun, a middle-aged star, will probably swell to a red giant in 5 billion years, vaporizing Earth and any creatures that may be left on its surface. When all its fuel has been exhausted, a star cannot generate sufficient pressure at its center to balance the crushing force of gravity. The star collapses under the force of its own weight; if it is a small star, it collapses gently and remains collapsed. Such a collapsed star, at its life's end, is called a white dwarf. The Sun will probably end its life in this way. A different fate awaits a large star. Its final collapse generates a violent explosion, blowing the innards of the star out into space. There, the materials of the exploded star mix with the primeval hydrogen of the universe. Later in the history of the galaxy, other stars are formed out of this mixture. The Sun is one of these stars. It contains the debris of countless other stars that exploded before the Sun was born.

Supernovas

On Feb. 24, 1987, Canadian astronomer Ian Shelter at the Las Campanas Observatory in Chile discovered a supernova—an exploding star—from a photograph taken on Feb. 23 of the Large Magellanic Cloud, a galaxy some 160,000 light-years away from Earth. Astronomers believe that the dying star was Sanduleak –69°202, a 10-million-year-old blue supergiant.

Supernova 1987A was the closest and best-studied supernova in almost 400 years. One was previously observed by Johannes Kepler in 1604, four years before the telescope was invented.

Formation of the Solar System

The Sun's age was calculated in 1989 to be 4.49 billion years old, less than the 4.7 billion years previously believed. It was formed from a cloud of hydrogen mixed with small amounts of other substances that had been manufactured in the bodies of other stars before the Sun was born. This was the parent cloud of the solar system. The dense hot gas at the center of the cloud gave rise to the Sun; the outer regions of the cloud—cooler and less dense—gave birth to the planets.

Our solar system consists of one star (the Sun), nine planets and all their moons, several thousand minor planets called asteroids or planetoids, and an equally large number of comets.

The Sun

All the stars, including our Sun, are gigantic balls of superheated gas, kept hot by atomic reactions in their centers. In our Sun, this atomic reaction is hydrogen fusion: four hydrogen atoms are combined

Astronomical Constants

Light-year (distance traveled by light in one year)	5,880,000,000,000 mi.
Parsec (parallax of one second, or stellar distances)	3.259 light-yrs.
Velocity of light	186,281.7 mi./sec.
Astronomical unit (A.U.), or mean distance Earth to Sun	ca. 93,000,000 mi.[1]
Mean distance, Earth to Moon	238,860 mi.
General precession	50′,.26
Obliquity of the ecliptic	23° 27′8′.26-0′.4684(t-1900)[2]
Equatorial radius of Earth	3963.34 statute mi.
Polar radius of Earth	3949.99 statute mi.
Earth's mean radius	3958.89 statute mi.
Oblateness of Earth	1/297
Equatorial horizontal parallax of the moon	57′2′.70
Earth's mean velocity in orbit	18.5 mi./sec.
Sidereal year	365d.2564
Tropical year	365d.2422
Sidereal month	27d.3217
Synodic month	29d.5306
Mean sidereal day	23h56m4s.091 of mean solar time
Mean solar day	24h3m56s.555 of sidereal time

1. Actual mean distance derived from radar bounces: 92,935,700 mi. The value of 92,897,400 mi. (based on parallax of 8″.80) is used in calculations. 2. *t* refers to the year in question, for example, 1999.

to form one helium atom. The temperature at the core of our Sun must be 20 million degrees centigrade, and the surface temperature averages 6,000° C, or about 11,000° F. The diameter of the Sun is 865,400 miles, and its surface area is approximately 12,000 times that of Earth. Compared with other stars, our Sun is just a bit below average in size and temperature, and is a yellow dwarf star. Its fuel supply (hydrogen) is estimated to be sufficient for another 5 billion years.

Our Sun is not motionless in space; in fact it has two proper motions. One is a seemingly straight-line motion in the direction of the constellation Hercules at the rate of about 12 miles per second. But since the Sun is a part of the Milky Way system and since the whole system rotates slowly around its own center, the Sun also moves at the rate of 175 miles per second as part of the rotating Milky Way system.

In addition to this motion, the Sun rotates on its axis. Observing the motion of sunspots (darkish areas that look like enormous whirling storms) and solar flares, which are usually associated with sunspots, has shown that the rotational period of the Sun is just short of 25 days. But this figure is valid for the Sun's equator only; the sections near the Sun's poles seem to have a rotational period of 34 days. Naturally, since the Sun generates its own heat and light, there is no temperature difference between poles and equator.

In 1998, scientists saw for the first time that solar flares produce seismic waves in the Sun's interior that resemble those created by earthquakes. They observed a flare-generated solar quake equivalent to a 11.3 magnitude earthquake. It contained about 40,000 times the energy released in the great 1906 San Francisco earthquake.

What we call the Sun's "surface" is technically known as the photosphere. Since the whole Sun is a ball of very hot gas, there is really no such thing as a surface; it is a question of visual impression. The next layer outside the photosphere is known as the chromosphere, which extends several thousand miles beyond the photosphere. It is in steady motion, and often enormous prominences can be seen to burst from it, extending as much as 100,000 miles into space. Outside the chromosphere is the corona. The corona consists of very tenuous gases (essentially hydrogen) and makes a magnificent sight when the Sun is eclipsed.

As the Sun ages, it gradually expands and heats. In 1994, American astrophysicists studying the eventual fate of the Sun estimated that its brilliancy will increase by 10% over the next 1.1 billion years or more and, in about 6.5 billion years hence, our aging star will have doubled its present luminosity. The extreme heat generated will cause a catastrophic greenhouse effect on Earth and our oceans will boil away, and life on Earth as we know it will end.

The Sun will eventually expand enormously to 166 times its present size and become over 2,000 times as bright. Eight billion years from now, the Sun's radius will engulf the planet Mercury and extend beyond the present orbit of Venus.

However, as the Sun expands, it will also lose considerable mass (as much as one-half) and weaken its gravitational pull on Venus and the other lifeless planets, causing them to orbit further away from the Sun and escape total destruction.

The Moon

Mercury and Venus do not have any moons. Therefore, Earth is the planet nearest the Sun to be orbited by a moon.

The next planet farther out, Mars, has two very small moons. Jupiter has four major moons and twelve minor ones. Saturn, the ringed planet, has 19 known moons (and possibly more), of which one (Titan) is larger than the planet Mercury. Uranus has 17 moons (four of them large) as well as rings, while Neptune has one large and seven small moons. Pluto has one moon, discovered in 1978. Some astronomers still consider Pluto to be a "runaway moon" of Neptune.

Our Moon, with a diameter of 2,160 miles, is one of the larger moons in our solar system and is especially large when compared with the planet that it orbits. In fact, the common center of gravity of the

The Brightest Stars

Star	Constellation	Mag.	Dist (l.-y.)
Sirius	Canis Major	-1.6	8
Canopus	Carina	-0.9	650
Alpha Centauri	Centaurus	+0.1	4
Vega	Lyra	0.1	23
Capella	Auriga	0.2	42
Arcturus	Boötes	0.2	32
Rigel	Orion	0.3	545
Procyon	Canis Minor	0.5	10
Achernar	Eridanus	0.6	70
Beta Centauri	Centaurus	0.9	130
Altair	Aquila	0.9	18
Betelgeuse	Orion	0.9	600
Aldebaran	Taurus	1.1	54
Spica	Virgo	1.2	190
Pollux	Gemini	1.2	31
Antares	Scorpius	1.2	170
Fomalhaut	Piscis Austrinus	1.3	27
Deneb	Cygnus	1.3	465
Regulus	Leo	1.3	70
Beta Crucis	Crux	1.5	465
Eta Carinae	Carina	1-7	—
Alpha-one Crucis	Crux	1.6	150
Castor	Gemini	1.6	44
Gamma Crucis	Crux	1.6	—
Epsilon Canis Majoris	Canis Major	1.6	325
Epsilon Ursae Majoris	Ursa Major	1.7	50
Bellatrix	Orion	1.7	215
Lambda Scorpii	Scorpius	1.7	205
Epsilon Carinae	Carina	1.7	325
Mira	Cetus	2-10	250

Earth-Moon system is only about 1,000 miles below Earth's surface. The closest the Moon can come to us (its perigee) is 221,463 miles; the farthest it can go away (its apogee) is 252,710 miles. The period of rotation of the Moon is equal to its period of revolution around Earth. Hence from Earth we can see only one hemisphere of the Moon. Both periods are 27 days, 7 hours, 43 minutes and 11.47 seconds. But while the rotation of the Moon is constant, its velocity in its orbit is not, since it moves more slowly in apogee than in perigee. Consequently, some portions near the rim that are not normally visible will appear briefly. This phenomenon is called "libration," and by taking advantage of the librations, astronomers have succeeded in mapping approximately 59% of the lunar surface. The other 41% can never be seen from Earth but has been mapped by American and Russian Moon-orbiting spacecraft.

Though the Moon goes around Earth in the time mentioned, the interval from new moon to new moon is 29 days, 12 hours, 44 minutes, and 2.78 seconds. This delay of nearly two days is due to the fact that Earth is moving around the Sun, so that the Moon needs two extra days to reach a spot in its orbit where no part is illuminated by the Sun, as seen from Earth.

If the plane of Earth's orbit around the Sun (the ecliptic) and the plane of the Moon's orbit around Earth were the same, the Moon would be eclipsed by Earth every time it is full, and the Sun would be eclipsed by the Moon every time the Moon is "new" (it would be better to call it the "black moon" when it is in this position). But because the two orbits do not coincide, the Moon's shadow normally misses Earth and Earth's shadow misses the Moon. The inclination of the two orbital planes to each other is 5°. The tides are, of course, caused by the Moon with the help of the Sun, but in the open ocean they are surprisingly low, amounting to about one yard. The very high tides that can be observed near the shore in some places are due to funnelling effects of the shorelines. At new moon and at full moon the tides raised by the Moon are reinforced by the Sun; these are the "spring tides." If the Sun's tidal power acts at right angles to that of the Moon (quarter moons) we get the low "neap tides."

The Pentagon announced in December 1994 that analysis of radio signals from the *Clementine* spacecraft sent to orbit the Moon in 1994 suggests that there is probably ice in a dark basin near the Moon's south pole. The *Lunar Prospector* spacecraft, to be launched in September 1997, will be able to confirm the presence of lunar ice if it exists

Earth

Earth, circling the Sun at an average distance of 93 million miles, is the fifth-largest planet and the third from the Sun. It orbits the Sun at a speed of 67,000 miles per hour, making one revolution in 365 days, 5 hours, 48 minutes, and 45.51 seconds. Earth completes one rotation on its axis every 23 hours, 56 minutes, and 4.09 seconds. Actually a bit pear-shaped rather than a true sphere, Earth has a diameter of 7,927 miles at the equator and a few miles less at the poles. It has an estimated mass of about 6.6 sextillion tons, with an average density of 5.52 grams per cubic centimeter. Earth's surface area encompasses 196,949,970 square miles of which about three-fourths is water.

Origin of Earth

Earth, along with the other planets, is believed to have been born 4.5 billion years ago as a solidified cloud of dust and gases left over from the creation of the Sun. For perhaps 500 million years, the interior of Earth stayed solid and relatively cool, perhaps 2000° F. The main ingredients, according to the best available evidence, were iron and silicates, with small amounts of other elements, some of them radioactive. As millions of years passed, energy released by radioactive decay—mostly of uranium, thorium, and potassium—gradually heated Earth, melting some of its constituents. The iron melted before the silicates, and, being heavier, sank toward the center. This forced up the silicates that it found there. After many years, the iron reached the center, almost 4,000 miles deep, and began to accumulate. No eyes were around at that time to view the turmoil that must have taken place on the face of Earth—gigantic heaves and bubblings on the surface, exploding volcanoes, and flowing lava covering everything in sight. Finally, the iron in the center accumulated as the core. Around it, a thin but fairly stable crust of solid rock formed as Earth cooled. Depressions in the crust were natural basins in which water, rising from the interior of the planet through volcanoes and fissures, collected to form the oceans. Slowly, Earth acquired its present appearance.

Earth Today

As a result of radioactive heating over millions of years, Earth's molten *core* is probably fairly hot today, around 11,000° F. By comparison, lead melts at around 800° F. Most of Earth's 2,100-mile-thick core is liquid, but there is evidence that the center of the core is solid. The liquid outer portion, about 95% of the core, is constantly in motion, causing Earth to have a magnetic field that makes compass needles point north and south. The details are not known, but the latest evidence suggests that planets that have a magnetic field probably have a solid core or a partially liquid one.

Outside the core is Earth's *mantle,* 1,800 miles thick and extending nearly to the surface. The mantle is composed of heavy silicate rock, similar to that brought up by volcanic eruptions. It is somewhere between liquid and solid, slightly yielding, and therefore contributing to an active, moving Earth. Most of Earth's radioactive material is in the thin *crust* that covers the mantle, but some is in the mantle and continues to give off heat. The crust's thickness ranges from 5 to 25 miles.

Scientists recently discovered that Earth's core is not a perfect sphere. X-ray-like images of inside Earth show that there are vast mountains six to seven miles high and deep valleys on the core. These features are in an upside-down relationship to Earth's surface.

In 1996, geophysicists discovered that Earth's solid-iron inner core rotates slightly faster than the rest of the planet and gains a quarter-turn every century. The finding may help explain how Earth's magnetic field periodically reverses its polarity.

Continental Drift

A great deal of recent evidence confirms the theory that the continents of Earth, made mostly of relatively light granite, float in the slightly yielding mantle, like logs in a pond. For many years it had been noticed that if North and South America could be pushed toward western and southern Europe and western Africa, they would fit like pieces in a jigsaw puzzle. Today, there is little question—the continents have drifted widely and continue to do so.

In 10 million years, the world as we know it may be unrecognizable, with California drifting out to sea, Florida joining South America, and Africa moving farther away from Europe and Asia.

Earth's Atmosphere

The thin blanket of atmosphere that envelops Earth extends several hundred miles into space. From sea level—the very bottom of the ocean of air—to a height of about 60 miles, the air in the atmosphere is made up of the same gases in the same ratio: about 78% nitrogen, 21% oxygen, and the remaining 1% being a mixture of argon, carbon dioxide, and tiny amounts of neon, helium, krypton, xenon, and other gases. The atmosphere becomes less dense with increasing altitude: more than three-fourths of Earth's huge envelope is concentrated in the first 5 to 10 miles above the surface. At sea level, a cubic foot of atmosphere weighs about an ounce and a quarter. The entire atmosphere weighs 5,700 trillion tons, and the force with which gravity holds it in place causes it to exert a pressure of nearly 15 pounds per square inch. Going out from Earth's surface, the atmosphere is divided into five regions. The regions, and the heights to which they extend, are: *troposphere,* 0 to 7 miles (at middle latitudes); *stratosphere,* 7 to 30 miles; *mesosphere,* 30 to 50 miles; *thermosphere,* 50 to 400 miles; and *exosphere,* above 400 miles. The boundaries between each of the regions are known respectively as the *tropopause, stratopause, mesopause,* and *thermopause.* Alternative terms often used for the layers above the troposphere are *ozonosphere* (for stratosphere) and *ionosphere* for the remaining upper layers.

The Seasons

Seasons are caused by the 23.4-degree tilt of Earth's axis, which alternately turns the North and South Poles toward the Sun. Times when the Sun's apparent path crosses the equator are known as *equinoxes.* Times when the Sun's apparent path is at the greatest distance from the equator are known as *solstices.* The lengths of the days are most extreme at each solstice. If Earth's axis were perpendicular to the plane of Earth's orbit around the Sun, there would be no seasons, and the days always would be equal in length. Since Earth's axis is at an angle, the Sun strikes Earth directly at the equator only twice a year: in March (vernal equinox) and September (autumnal equinox). In the Northern Hemisphere, spring begins at the vernal equinox, summer at the summer solstice, fall at the autumnal equinox, and winter at the winter solstice. The situation is reversed in the Southern Hemisphere.

Mercury

Mercury is the planet nearest the Sun. Appropriately named for the wing-footed Roman messenger of the gods, Mercury whizzes around the Sun at a speed of 30 miles per second, completing one circuit in 88 days. The days and nights are long on Mercury. It takes 59 Earth days for Mercury to make a single rotation. It spins at a rate of about 10 kilometers (about 6 miles) per hour, measured at the equator, as compared to Earth's spin of about 1,600 kilometers (about 1,000 miles) per hour at the equator.

The photographs *Mariner 10* (1974–75) radioed back to Earth revealed an ancient, heavily cratered surface on Mercury, closely resembling our own Moon. The pictures showed huge cliffs, or scarps, crisscrossing the planet. These apparently were created when Mercury's interior cooled and shrank, compressing the planet's crust. The cliffs are as high as two kilometers (1.2 miles) and as long as 1,500 kilometers (932 miles). Another unique feature is the Caloris Basin, a large impact crater about 1,300 kilometers (808 miles) in diameter.

Mercury, like Earth, appears to have a crust of light silicate rock. Scientists believe it has a heavy iron-rich core that makes up about half of its volume.

Instruments onboard *Mariner 10* discovered that the planet has a weak magnetic field and a trace of atmosphere—a trillionth the density of Earth's and composed chiefly of argon, neon, and helium. The spacecraft reported temperatures ranging from 510° C (950° F) on Mercury's sunlit side to –210° C (–346° F) on the dark side. Mercury literally bakes in daylight and freezes at night.

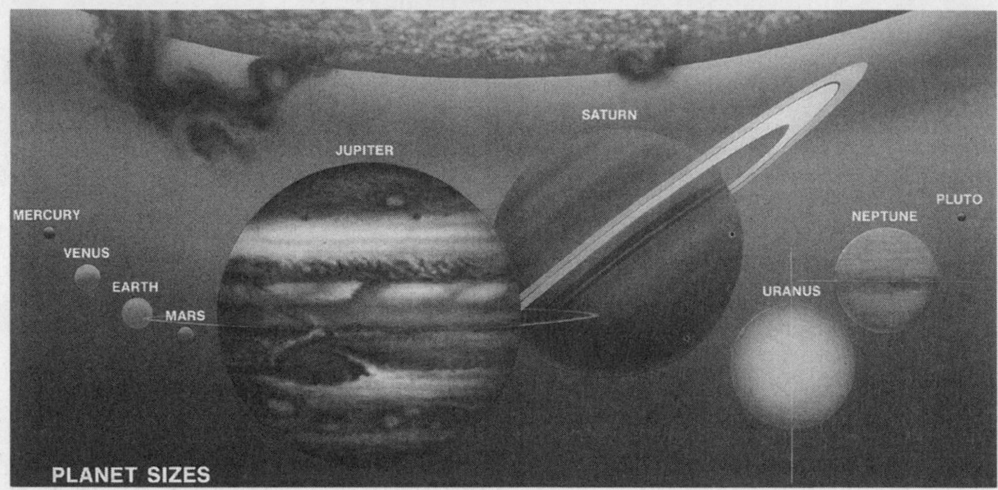

PLANET SIZES. Shown from left to right: Mercury, Venus, Earth, Mars, Jupiter, Saturn, Uranus, Neptune, and Pluto. *Copyright 1990 Hansen Planetarium, Salt Lake City, Utah. Reproduced with permission.*

Basic Planetary Data

	Mercury	Venus	Earth	Mars	Jupiter
Mean distance from sun (millions of kilometers)	57.9	108.2	149.6	227.9	778.3
Mean distance from sun (millions of miles)	36.0	67.24	92.9	141.71	483.88
Period of revolution	88 days	224.7 days	365.2 days	687 days	11.86 yrs
Rotation period	59 days	243 days retrograde	23 hr 56 min 4 sec	24 hr 37 min	9 hr 55 min 30 sec
Inclination of axis	Near 0°	3°	23°27′	25° 12′	3° 5′
Inclination of orbit to ecliptic	7°	3.4°	0°	1.9°	1.3°
Eccentricity of orbit	.206	.007	.017	.093	.048
Equatorial diameter (kilometers)	4,880	12,100	12,756	6,794	142,800
(miles)	3,032.4	7,519	7,926.2	4,194	88,736
Atmosphere (main components)	Virtually none	Carbon dioxide	Nitrogen oxygen	Carbon dioxide	Hydrogen helium
Satellites	0	0	1	2	16
Rings	0	0	0	0	1

	Saturn	Uranus	Neptune	Pluto
Mean distance from sun (millions of kilometers)	1,427	2,870	4,497	5,900
Mean distance from sun (millions of miles)	887.14	1,783.98	2,796.46	3,666
Period of revolution	29.46 yrs	84 yrs	165 yrs	248 yrs
Rotation period	10 hr 40 min 24 sec	16.8 hr(?) retrograde	16 hr 11 min(?)	6 days 9 hr 18 mins retrograde
Inclination of axis	26°44′	97°55′	28°48′	60° (?)
Inclination of orbit to ecliptic	2.5°	0.8°	1.8°	17.2°
Eccentricity of orbit	.056	.047	.009	.254
Equatorial diameter (kilometers)	120,660	51,810	49,528	2,290 (?)
(miles)	74,978	32,193	30,775	1,423 (?)
Atmosphere (main components)	Hydrogen helium	Helium hydrogen methane	Hydrogen helium methane	None detected
Satellites	19	17	8	1
Rings	1,000 (?)	11	4	?

Source: Basic NASA data and other sources.

Until the *Mariner 10* probe, little was known about the planet. Even the best telescopic views from Earth showed Mercury as an indistinct object lacking any surface detail. The planet is so close to the Sun that it is usually lost in the Sun's glare.

Radar images taken by astronomers at Jet Propulsion Laboratories and California Institute of Technology during the summer of 1991 suggest that the polar regions of Mercury may be covered with patches of water ice. Although this seems impossible due to the planet's sizzling heat, the polar regions receive very little sunlight and may get as cold as –235° F. The radar images showed bright patterns at the poles that are characteristic of ice reflecting radar signals. Other explanations may be offered for this unexpected discovery.

Mercury is a naked-eye object at morning or evening twilight when it is at greatest elongation.

Venus

Although Venus is Earth's closest neighbor, very little is known about the planet because it is permanently covered by thick clouds. In 1962, Soviet and American space probes, coupled with Earth-based radar and infrared spectroscopy, began slowly unraveling some of the mystery surrounding Venus. Twenty-eight years later, the *Magellan* spacecraft, sent by the United States, arrived at Venus in August 1990 and began radar-mapping the planet's surface in greater detail.

According to the latest results, Venus's atmosphere exerts a pressure at the surface 94.5 times greater than Earth's. Walking on Venus would be as difficult as walking a half-mile beneath the ocean. Because of a thick blanket of carbon dioxide, a "greenhouse effect" exists on Venus. Venus intercepts twice as much of the Sun's light as does Earth. The light enters freely through the carbon dioxide gas and is changed to heat radiation in molecular collisions. But carbon dioxide prevents the heat from escaping. Consequently, the temperature of the surface of Venus is over 800° F, hot enough to melt lead.

The atmospheric composition of Venus is about 96% carbon dioxide, 4% nitrogen, and minor amounts of water, oxygen, and sulfur compounds. There are at least four distinct cloud and haze layers that exist at different altitudes above the planet's surface. The haze layers contain small aerosol particles, possibly droplets of sulfuric acid. A concentration of sulfur dioxide above the cloud tops has been observed to be decreasing since 1978. The source of sulfur dioxide at this altitude is unknown; it may be injected by volcanic explosions or atmospheric overturning.

Measurements of the Venusian atmosphere and its cloud patterns reveal nearly constant high-speed zonal winds, about 100 meters per second (220 miles per hour) at the equator. The winds decrease toward the poles so that the atmosphere at cloud-top level rotates almost like a solid body. The wind speeds at the equator correspond to Venus's rotation period of four to five days at most latitudes. The circulation is always in the same direction—east to west—as Venus's slow retrograde motion. Earth's winds blow from west to east, the same direction as its rotation.

Venus is quite round, very different from the other planets and from the Moon. Venus has neither polar flattening nor an equatorial bulge. The diameter of Venus is 12,100 kilometers (7,519 miles). Venus has a retrograde axial rotation period of 243.1 Earth days. The surface atmospheric pressure is 1,396 pounds per square inch (95 Earth atmospheres). The planet's mean distance from the Sun is 108.2 million kilometers (67.2 million miles). The period of its revolution around the Sun is 224.7 days.

The highest point on Venus is the summit of Maxwell Montes, 10.8 kilometers (6.71 miles) above the mean level, more than a mile higher than Mount Everest. There is some evidence that this huge mountain is an active volcano. The lowest point is in the rift valley, Diana Chasma, 2.9 kilometers (1.8 miles) below the mean level. This point is about one-fifth the greatest depth on Earth in the Marianas Trench.

Venus has an extreme lowland basin, Atalanta Planitia, which is about the size of Earth's North Atlantic Ocean basin. The smooth surface of the Atalanta Planitia resembles the mare basins of the Moon.

There are only two highland or continental masses on Venus: Ishtar Terra and Aphrodite Terra. Ishtar Terra is 11 kilometers (6.8 miles) at its highest points (the highest peaks on Venus) and those of Aphrodite Terra rise to about 5 kilometers (3.10 miles) above the planet. Ishtar Terra is about the size of the continental United States and Aphrodite Terra is about the size of Africa.

The unmanned NASA spacecraft *Magellan* was launched on May 4, 1989, from the shuttle *Atlantis* and arrived at Venus August 10, 1990, to map most of the planet. Despite some problems with its radio transmissions, the results of the radar mapping delighted scientists and provided them with the sharpest images ever taken of the planet's surface. Images taken from *Magellan* show ten times more detail than ever seen before.

The radar images provided scientists with compelling evidence that the planet has been dominated by volcanism on a global scale. The photos also showed that the planet's second-highest mountain, Maat Mons, rising five miles (eight kilometers) above the Venusian plains, appears to be covered with fresh lava and is possibly an active volcano.

Magellan discovered the longest known channel in the solar system on Venus. It is 4,200 miles (6,800 kilometers) long and averages slightly over a mile (1.8 kilometers) wide. Its origin is puzzling to scientists because high-temperature lava is unlikely to have caused such a long-distance flow on the surface and there are no known substances that could remain liquid long enough under the planet's atmospheric pressure and temperature to have carved out this snake-like feature. The channel is slightly longer than the Nile River, the longest river on Earth. *Magellan* ended its radar and emissions mapping in September 1992 after covering 98% of the planet's surface.

Venus is the brightest of all the planets and is often visible in the morning or evening, when it is frequently referred to as the Morning Star or Evening Star. At its brightest, it can sometimes be seen in full daylight with the naked eye, if one knows where to look.

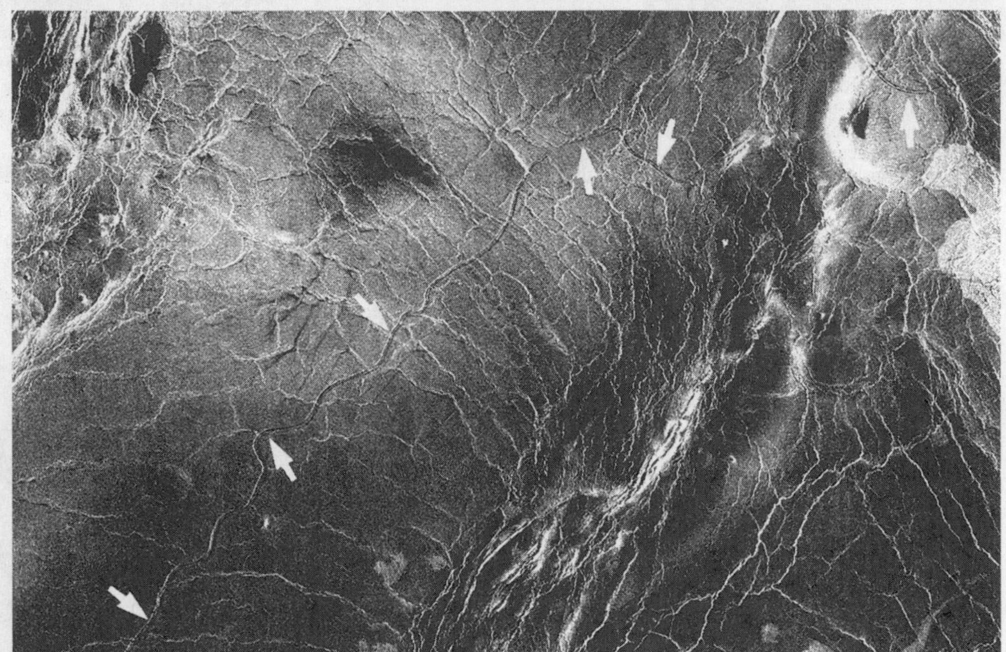

Largest Channel in Solar System. *Magellan* took the above image of the largest known channel on Venus. At 4,200 miles (6,800 kilometers) long and an average of 1.1 miles (1.8 kilometers) wide, it is longer than the Nile River, Earth's longest river, making it the longest known channel in the solar system. The channel was originally discovered by the Soviet *Venery 15* and *16* spacecraft orbiters. *Source:* NASA.

Mars

Mars, on the other side of Earth from Venus, is Venus's direct opposite in terms of physical properties. Its atmosphere is cold, thin, and transparent, and readily permits observation of the planet's features. We know more about Mars than any other planet except Earth. Mars is a forbidding, rugged planet with huge volcanoes and deep chasms. The largest volcano, Olympus Mons (Olympic Mountain) rises 78,000 feet above the surface, higher than Mount Everest. The plains of Mars are pockmarked by the hits of thousands of meteors over the years.

Until the arrival of *Mars Pathfinder* and *Mars Global Surveyor* in 1997, most of our information about Mars came from the *Mariner* and *Viking* spacecrafts. *Mariner 9* orbited the planet in 1971 and photographed 100% of the planet, uncovered spectacular geological formations, including a Martian "Grand Canyon" that dwarfs the one on Earth. Called Valles Marineris (Mariner Valley), it stretches more than 3,000 miles along the equatorial region of Mars and is over 4 kilometers (2.5 miles) deep in places and 80 to 100 kilometers (50–62 miles) wide. The spacecraft's cameras also recorded what appeared to be dried riverbeds, suggesting the one-time presence of water on the planet. The latter idea gave encouragement to scientists looking for life on Mars, for where there is water, there may be life. However, to date, no evidence of life has been found. Temperatures near the equator range from –17° F in the daytime to –130° F at night.

Mars rotates upon its axis in nearly the same period as Earth—24 hours, 37 minutes—so that a Mars day is almost identical to an Earth day. Mars takes 687 days to make one trip around the Sun. Because of its eccentric orbit, Mars's distance from the Sun can vary by about 36 million miles. Its distance from Earth can vary by as much as 200 million miles. The atmosphere of Mars is much thinner than Earth's; atmospheric pressure is about 1% that of our planet. Its gravity is one-third of Earth's. Major constituents are carbon dioxide and nitrogen. Water vapor and oxygen are minor constituents. Mars's polar caps, composed mostly of frozen carbon dioxide (dry ice), recede and advance according to the Martian seasons.

Mars has four seasons like Earth, but they are much longer. For example, in the northern hemisphere, the Martian spring is 198 days, and the winter season lasts 158 days.

The *Mars Pathfinder* lander and its rover, *Sojourner*, set down on the edge of a boulder-strewn outflow channel known as *Ares Vallis* on July 4, 1997, and provided scientists with a wealth of information on the rocks, soils, and atmosphere of Mars. The lander sent back the first live pictures of the planet's topography and its tiny rover explored a variety of rocks and analyzed their mineral composition with its cameras and on-board X-ray spectrometer.

Analysis of the reddish surface soil pointed to the presence of oxidized iron, indicating that the planet's surface is rusting. *Sojourner* samples of soil taken from several sites found their composition similar to those analyzed by the two *Viking* landers in 1976, indicating that the Martian winds have distributed the soil evenly over the planet.

Scientists were surprised to learn how rapidly the Martian temperature fluctuates due to atmospheric turbulence. It can change by as much as 30°–40° F

(17°–22° C) in a matter of minutes, possibly due to strong, gusty winds bringing warm air from one region or cold air from another.

Pictures and subsequent data from *Pathfinder* give the strongest evidence that Mars had an abundance of water millions of years ago. Scientists have inferred from the variety of rocks and sediments found in the *Ares* basin that the spacecraft landed in a channel that was once awash with torrential floods greater than any known on Earth. The diversity of rocks deposited there suggest their different origins, and it appears that they were washed down from the highlands at a time when great floods moved over the surface of Mars. (*See* Space section for additional details.)

Before *Pathfinder*, knowledge of the kinds of rocks present on Mars was based mostly on the Martian meteorites found on Earth. Chemical analysis of the Martian rocks and studies of different regions of soil found at *Ares Vallis* confirmed that these rocks have compositions distinct from those of the Martian meteorites found on Earth.

In its three months of operation, the mission returned more than 16,000 images of the Martian landscape from the lander's camera and 550 images from the rover.

The *Sojourner* rover traveled a total of about 328 feet (100 meters) and performed more than 16 chemical analyses of rocks and soil, and explored 820 square feet (250 square meters) of the planet's surface. Communications were lost with the lander on Sept. 27, 1997, after 83 days of commanding and data return.

NASA launched the *Mars Global Surveyor* spacecraft on Nov. 7, 1997, to provide detailed maps of the planet's surface, its distribution of minerals, and to monitor its weather. The spacecraft entered Mars's orbit on Sept. 11, 1997, and began mapping operations on March 27, 1998. The spacecraft will orbit Mars for 687 days, the length of one Martian year.

Surveyor discovered the first clear evidence of an ancient hydrothermal system near the equator. This implies that water was stable at or near the surface and that a thicker atmosphere existed in Mars's early history.

Most surprising to mission scientists was finding that the planet's northern hemisphere was exceptionally flat—like the Bonneville salt flats in Utah—with slopes and surface roughness increasing towards the equator.

Surveyor's three-dimensional views of the planet's northern polar ice cap showed often striking canyons and spiral troughs in the water and carbon dioxide ice that can reach depths as great as 3,600 feet below the surface. Its data also showed that large areas of the ice cap were extremely smooth, with elevations varying only a few feet over many miles.

Measurements from the spacecraft also revealed that Mars has traces of a global magnetic field that may have been as strong as Earth's is today.

Mars was named for the Roman god of war, because when seen from Earth its distinct red color reminded the ancient people of blood. We know now that the reddish hue reflects the oxidized (rusted) iron in the surface material.

The Martian Moons

Mars has two very small elliptical-shaped moons, Deimos and Phobos—the Greek names for the companions of the God Mars: Deimos (Terror) and Phobos (Fear). They were discovered in August 1877 by the American astronomer Asaph Hall (1829–1907) of the U.S. Naval Observatory in Washington, D.C.

The inner satellite, Phobos, is 27 kilometers (16.78 miles) long and it revolves around the planet in 7.6 hours. The outer moon, Deimos, is 15 kilometers (9.32 miles) long and it circles the planet in 30.35 hours. The short orbital period of Phobos means that the satellite travels around Mars twice in a Martian day. If an observer were suitably situated on the planet, he would see Phobos rise and set twice in a day.

Recent studies of Phobos indicate that its orbit is slowly decreasing downward and that in approximately 40 million years, it will crash into the planet's surface.

Meteorites from Mars

Research has shown that a group of eight meteorites, labeled SNC[1] (named for towns where they were found: Shergotty, India, in 1865; Nakhla, Egypt, in 1911; and Chassigny, France, in 1815), are probably samples of Mars. This hypothesis was based largely on the composition of noble gases (particularly argon and xenon) trapped in the meteorites, and the shergottites in particular, which resemble measurements of the Martian atmosphere made by the *Viking* spacecraft. Major element compositions of the SNCs are also similar to Martian soil analyses made by *Viking*.

The relatively young isotopic ages of the SNC meteorites (1.3 billion years or less) suggest that Mars has been volcanically active during its recent past.

In 1991, a ninth meteorite, LEW 88516, was identified as having reached Earth from Mars some 180 million years ago. It was discovered in December 1988 near Lewis Cliff in Antarctica. The meteorite is very small with a dark pitted surface and weighs 13.2 grams (less than half an ounce).

A 4-pound, 7-ounce (1.9 kilograms) meteorite, ALH 84001, found in the Allen Hills of Antarctica in 1984 was reclassified in 1993 as coming from the Red Planet, making it the tenth meteorite known to have originated from Mars. In 1996, NASA announced that meteorite ALH 84001 contained fossils of ancient Martian life forms.

A 40-pound meteorite that crashed to Earth in Nigeria in 1962 has been classified as coming from Mars. It was named Zagami for the region it was found in.

A 0.38-ounce (12-gram) meteorite (QUE 94201) found in Antarctica in 1995 became the 12th meteorite identified as having a Martian origin.

Scientists do not know how the meteorites were thrown off the Martian surface.

Jupiter

Jupiter is the largest planet in the solar system—a gaseous world as large as 1,300 Earths. Its equatorial diameter is 142,800 kilometers (88,736 miles), while from pole to pole, Jupiter measures only 133,500 kilometers (84,201 miles). For comparison,

1. Pronounced "snick."

the diameter of Earth is 12,756 kilometers (7,926.2 miles). The massive planet rotates at a dizzying speed—once every 9 hours and 55 minutes. It takes Jupiter almost 12 Earth years to complete a journey around the Sun.

The giant planet appears as a banded disk of turbulent clouds with all of its stripes running parallel to its bulging equator. Large dusky gray regions surround each pole. Darker gray or brown stripes called belts intermingle with lighter, yellow-white stripes called zones. The belts are regions of descending air masses and the zones are rising cloudy air masses. The strongest winds—up to 400 kilometers (250 miles) per hour—are found at boundaries between the belts and zones.

This uniquely colorful atmosphere is mainly 89% molecular hydrogen and 11% helium. It contains small amounts of methane, ammonia, ethane, and water.

Cloud-type lightning bolts similar to those on Earth have been found in the Jovian atmosphere. At the polar regions, auroras have been observed. A very thin ring of material less than one kilometer (0.6 mile) in thickness and about 6,000 kilometers (4,000 miles) in radial extent has been observed circling the planet about 55,000 kilometers (35,000 miles) above the cloud tops.

The most prominent feature on Jupiter is its "Great Red Spot," an oval larger than the planet Earth. It is a tremendous atmospheric storm that rotates counter-clockwise with one revolution every six days at the outer edge, while at the center almost no motion can be seen. The spot is about 25,000 kilometers (16,000 miles) on its long axis, and would cover three Earths. The outer rim shows streamline shapes of 360-kilometer (225-mile) winds. Jupiter also has several faint rings like Saturn.

Jupiter emits 67% more heat than it absorbs from the Sun. This heat is thought to have been accumulated during the planet's formation several billion years ago.

Twenty-one fragments of comet Shoemaker-Levy 9 bombarded the cloud-covered surface of Jupiter, July 16–22, 1994. It was the most violent event in the recorded history of our solar system. The cometary explosions caused towering plumes of debris and hot gas to rise from the darkened impact sites.

On Dec. 7, 1995, the *Galileo* spacecraft released a probe into Jupiter's atmosphere to study the planet's physical and chemical properties. The probe lasted 57 minutes and early results indicated a lower abundance of water than was expected.

Galileo data has shown that Jupiter has both wet and dry regions, just as Earth has tropics and deserts. This could explain why the probe found less water than anticipated. These dry spots cover less than 1% of the Jovian atmosphere.

Jovian Moons

The four great moons of Jupiter were discovered by Galileo Galilei (1564–1642) in January 1610, and are called the Galilean satellites after their discoverer. Their names are Io, Europa, Ganymede, and Callisto. Like our Moon, the satellites always keep the same face turned toward Earth. Jupiter has 16 known satellites.

Ganymede

Ganymede, 5,270 kilometers (3,275 miles) in diameter, is Jupiter's largest moon, and it is also the largest satellite in the solar system. Ganymede is about one and one-half times the size of our Moon. It is heavily cratered and probably has the greatest variety of geologic process recorded on its surface. Ganymede is half water and half rock, resulting in a density about two-thirds that of Europa, an ice-coated satellite. No atmosphere has been detected on it.

The first close-up photos of Ganymede taken by the *Galileo* spacecraft, during its June 1996 fly-by, revealed a surface pockmarked with ancient craters and a landscape wrinkled and torn by the same forces that make mountains and move continents on Earth. *Galileo*'s findings also indicated that Ganymede is enveloped in its own magnetic field, possibly created by a molten iron core or even a thin layer of conducting salty water underneath its icy crust.

Ganymede is the first known moon with its own magnetosphere.

Europa

Europa, the brightest of Jupiter's satellites, is about 1,950 miles (3,160 kilometers) in diameter or about the size of Earth's Moon. Its density is about three times that of water. The moon is covered with a thin ice crust and is crisscrossed with an amazingly complex network of ridges. Some of the fractures on its crust are more than 1,850 miles (3,000 kilometers) long. Very few impact craters are visible on the surface.

Galileo spacecraft photos taken at its closest fly-by on Feb. 20, 1997, at a distance of 363 miles (586 kilometers), showed the existence of ice flows on the surface that strongly suggest that the moon has a hidden subsurface ocean of water or ice-slush. The photos revealed chunky ice rafts that appear to be floating, comparable to icebergs on Earth. The presence of water and enough heat to keep water in a liquid state on Europa enhances the possibility that it could provide an environment for some form of extraterrestrial ocean life. Some researchers think that Europa may have active subsurface volcanoes. Oceanographers have found life near volcanic vents on Earth's sea floors.

NASA scientists have proposed to send a spacecraft called the *Europa Ice Clipper* to the moon in 2001 to determine if it has a global ocean and active volcanoes below its frozen crust. The spacecraft could send an impactor into Europa's surface with such a force that fragments of the moon would be injected into space, to be collected by the *Clipper* and returned to Earth for study.

Callisto

Callisto, 2,400 miles (4,800 kilometers) in diameter, is the outermost and, apparently, the least geologically active of Jupiter's four major satellites. Its density is less than twice that of water. Callisto has the oldest body and most cratered face of any body yet observed in the solar system. Like Ganymede, it seems to have a rocky core surrounded by ice. Unlike Ganymede, the surface of Callisto is completely covered with scars left by tens of thousands of meteoric impacts. Scientist estimate that it would take several billion years to accumulate the number of craters found there. So Callisto is believed to be

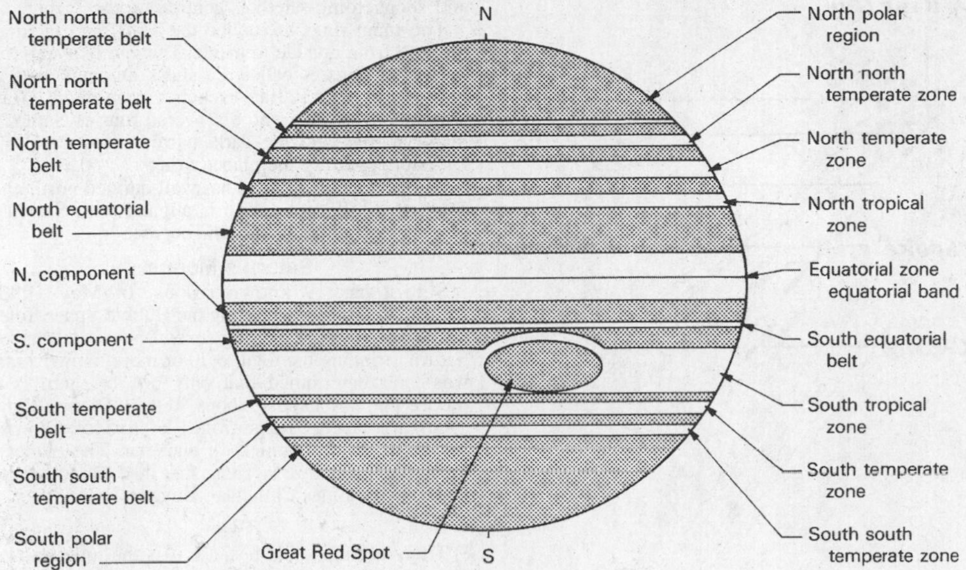

Schematic diagram of Jupiter's major features. *Source:* NASA.

inactive for at least that long. Although it is the darkest of the Galilean satellites, it is twice as bright as Earth's Moon.

Io

Io, 3,640 kilometers (2,262 miles) in diameter, is the most spectacular of the Galilean moons. Its brilliant colors of red, orange, and yellow set it apart from any other planet. Active volcanoes have been detected on Io, with some plumes extending up to 320 kilometers (200 miles) above the surface. The relative smoothness of Io's surface and its volcanic activity suggest that it has the youngest surface of Jupiter's moons. Its surface is composed of large amounts of sulfur and sulfur-dioxide frost, which account for the primarily yellow-orange surface color.

The volcanoes seem to eject a sufficient amount of sulfur dioxide to form a doughnut-shaped ring (torus) of ionized sulfur and oxygen atoms around Jupiter near Io's orbit. *Galileo* images taken in June 1996 revealed that Io's landscape undergoes constant change due to the numerous sulfur volcanoes that continuously erupt on its surface.

New observations by *Galileo* during 1998 revealed dozens of volcanic vents on Io where lava is hotter than any surface temperatures recorded on any planetary body in our solar system. At one such volcanic vent, known as Pillan Patera, two of the spacecraft's instruments indicated that the lava temperature may have been 3,140 degrees Fahrenheit.

In 1996, the *Galileo* spacecraft detected a huge iron core within Io that occupies half the moon's diameter. *Galileo* also discovered evidence that Io has its own magnetic field.

Amalthea

Amalthea, Jupiter's innermost satellite, was discovered in 1892. It is so small—265 kilometers (165 miles) long and 150 kilometers (90 miles) wide—that it is extremely difficult to observe from Earth. Amalthea is an elongated, irregularly shaped satellite of reddish color. It orbits the planet every 12 hours and is in synchronous rotation, with its long axis always oriented toward Jupiter.

Jupiter's other moons are named Adrasta, Metis, Thebe, Leda, Himalia, Lysithea, Elara, Ananke, Carne, Pasiphae, and Sinope.

The Magnetosphere

Perhaps the largest structure in the solar system is the magnetosphere of Jupiter. This is the region of space that is filled with Jupiter's magnetic field and is bounded by the interaction of that magnetic field with the solar wind, which is the Sun's outward flow of charged particles. The plasma of electrically charged particles that exists in the magnetosphere is flattened into a large disk more than 4.8 million kilometers (3 million miles) in diameter, is coupled to the magnetic field, and rotates around Jupiter. The Galilean satellites are located in the inner regions of the magnetosphere and are subjected to intense radiation bombardment.

The intense radiation field that surrounds Jupiter is fatal to humans. If astronauts were one day able to approach the planet as close as the *Voyager 1* spacecraft did, they would receive a dose of 400,000 rads or roughly 1,000 times the lethal dose for humans.

Even when nearest Earth, Jupiter is still almost 400 million miles away. However, because of its size, it may rival Venus in brilliance when near. Jupiter's four large moons may be seen through field glasses, moving rapidly around Jupiter and changing their positions from night to night.

Saturn

Saturn, the second-largest planet in the solar system, is the least dense. Its mass is 95 times the mass of Earth and its density is 0.70 gram per cubic centimeter, so that it would float in an ocean if there were one big enough to hold it.

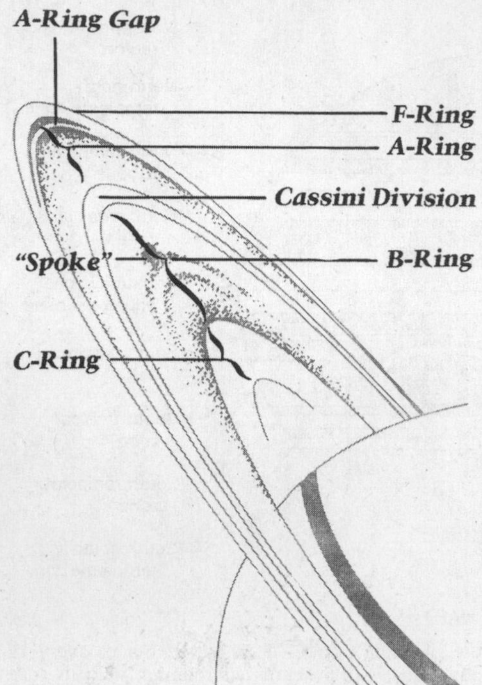

NASA illustration of the divisions in Saturn's ring system.

Saturn radiates about 80% more energy than it receives from the Sun. However, the excess thermal energy cannot be primarily attributed to Saturn's primordial heat loss, as is speculated for Jupiter.

Saturn's diameter is 120,660 kilometers (74,978 miles) but 10% less at the poles, a consequence of its rapid rotation. Its axis of rotation is tilted by 27 degrees and the length of its day is 10 hours, 39 minutes, and 24 seconds.

Saturn is composed primarily of liquid metallic hydrogen (about 80%) and the second most common element is believed to be helium.

Saturn's atmospheric appearance is very similar to Jupiter's with dark and light cloud markings and swirls, eddies, and curling ribbons; the belts and zones are more numerous and a thick haze mutes the markings. The temperature ranges from 80° K to 90° K (176° F to –203° F).

Winds blow at extremely high speeds on Saturn. Near the equator, the *Voyagers* measured winds of about 500 meters per second (1,100 miles per hour). The winds blow primarily in an eastward direction.

Saturn's Rings

Saturn's spectacular ring system is unique in the solar system, with uncountable billions of tiny particles of water ice (with traces of other material) in orbit around the planet. The ring particles range in size from smaller than grains of sugar to as large as a house. The main rings stretch out from about 7,000 kilometers (4,350 miles) to above the atmosphere of the planet out to the F ring, a total span of 74,000 kilometers (45,984 miles). Saturn's rings can be likened to a phonograph, rings within rings numbering in the hundreds, and spokes in the B rings, and shepherding satellites controlling the F ring.

The main rings are called the A, B, and C rings moving from outside to inside. The gap between the A and B rings is called Cassini's Division and is named for the Italian-French astronomer, Gian Domenico Cassini, who discovered four of Saturn's major moons and the dark, narrow gap, Cassini's Division, splitting the planet's rings.

Saturn's magnetic field has well-defined north and south magnetic poles, and is aligned with Saturn's axis of rotation to within one degree.

Saturn's Moons

Saturn has 19 known moons. In May 1995, American astronomers using the Hubble Space Telescope reported discovering several new satellites of Saturn, bringing the total to 20 or more. However, it was later determined that only one of them is a moon. The five largest moons, Tethys, Dione, Rhea, Titan, and Iapetus, range from 1060 to 5150 kilometers (650 to 3,200 miles) in diameter. The planet's outstanding satellite is Titan, first discovered by the Dutch astronomer Christiaan Huygens in 1656.

Titan

Titan is remarkable because it is the only known moon in the solar system that has a substantial atmosphere—largely nitrogen with a minor amount of methane and a rich variety of other hydrocarbons. Its surface is completely hidden from view (except at infrared and radio wavelengths) by a dense, hazy atmosphere.

The diameter of Titan is 5,150 kilometers (3,200 miles) and it is the second-largest satellite in the solar system after Jupiter's Ganymede. Titan is larger than the planet Mercury.

Titan's surface temperature is about –175° C (–280° F) and its surface pressure is about 50% greater than the surface pressure of Earth. After the *Voyager I* fly-by in 1980, scientists hypothesized that Titan may have an ocean of liquid hydrogen covering its surface. However, in 1990 it was shown that Titan's surface reflects and scatters radio waves, suggesting that the satellite has a solid surface with the possibility of small hydrocarbon lakes or ponds on the surface.

The data were obtained by using NASA's 70-meter antenna in California to transmit powerful radio waves to Titan, and the Very Large Array in New Mexico as the receiver of the reflected waves.

NASA plans to send a scientific probe to the surface of Titan in the summer of 2004 as part of its Cassini Mission. The probe will be provided by the European Space Agency (ESA).

Other Notable Saturnian Moons

The other four largest moons of Saturn are: Tethys, Dione, Rhea, and Iapetus.

Tethys is 1,060 kilometers (650 miles) in diameter. Its surface is heavily cratered and it has a huge, globe-girdling canyon, Ithaca Chasma. Part of the canyon stretches over three-quarters of the satellite's surface. Ithaca Chasma is about 2,500 kilometers (1,550 miles) long. It has an average width of about 100 kilometers (62 miles) and a depth of 3 to 5 kilometers (1.8 to 3.1 miles).

Tethys also has a huge impact crater named Odysseus, 4,400 kilometers (244 miles) in diameter, or more than one-third of the moon's diameter.

Dione is slightly larger than Tethys, 1,120 kilometers (696 miles) in diameter, and is more than half composed of water ice. It has bright, wispy markings resembling thin veils covering its features.

Rhea, the largest of the inner satellites, is 1,530 kilometers (951 miles) in diameter. It is composed mainly of water ice, causing its reflective surface to present an almost uniform white appearance.

Iapetus is the outermost of Saturn's icy satellites. Its appearance is unique because it has one dark and one bright hemisphere. The origin of the black coating of its dark face is unknown. Iapetus has a diameter of 1,460 kilometers (907 miles).

Other notable moons of Saturn are Mimas, Enceladus, Hyperion, Phoebe, and Pan.

Mimas is small, only 329 kilometers (244 miles) in diameter. It has a huge impact crater, Herschel, nearly one-third of its diameter. The crater is about 130 kilometers (81 miles) wide and its icy peak rises almost 10 kilometers (6.2 miles) above the floor.

Mimas is believed to be composed mainly of water and ice and to contain between 20% and 50% rock.

Enceladus is remarkable in that its surface shows signs of extensive and recent geological activity. There may be active water volcanism. The surface is extremely bright, reflecting more than 90% of incident sunlight. This suggests that its surface is composed of extremely pure ice without dust or rocks to contaminate it. Enceladus has a diameter of 500 kilometers (310 miles).

Hyperion orbits between Iapetus and Titan. It is irregular in shape, measuring about 400 by 250 by 200 kilometers (248 by 155 by 124 miles). It may be a remnant of a much larger object that was shattered by impact with another space body. It appears that Hyperion is composed primarily of water ice.

Hyperion orbits Saturn in a randomlike motion ("chaotic tumbling").

Phoebe is Saturn's outermost satellite. It travels in a retrograde orbit at a distance of over 10 million kilometers (6.2 million miles) away from the planet. It is the darkest moon of Saturn and is the planet's only known satellite that does not keep the same face always turned to Saturn. It has been speculated that it is an asteroid that was captured by the planet. Phoebe rotates in about nine hours and orbits Saturn in 406 days. It has a diameter of 200 kilometers (124 miles).

Pan was discovered in 1990 from *Voyager 2* photos taken in 1981. An official name, Pan, is to be approved by the International Astronomical Union. The satellite is estimated to be about 20 kilometers (12.43 miles) in diameter, which makes it the planet's smallest known moon. It orbits within the Encke Gap, a 325-kilometer (202-mile) division in Saturn's A ring. It was identified by Johann Franz Encke (1791–1865) in 1837.

The remaining eight moons range from 25 to 190 kilometers (15–120 miles) in diameter. They are all non-spherical in shape. Their names are Atlas, Prometheus, Pandora, Epimetheus, Janus, Telesto, Calypso, and Helene.

NASA's Cassini Mission to Saturn, launched in October 1997, will shed more light on the planet's mysteries when it arrives there in June 2004.

Saturn is the last of the planets visible to the naked eye. Saturn is never an object of overwhelming brilliance, but it looks like a bright star. The rings can be seen with a small telescope.

Uranus

Uranus, the first planet discovered in modern times by Sir William Herschel in 1781, is the seventh planet from the Sun, twice as far out as Saturn. Its mean distance from the Sun is 2,869 million kilometers (1,783 million miles). Uranus's equatorial diameter is 51,810 kilometers (32,200 miles). The axis of Uranus is tilted at 97 degrees, so it goes around the Sun nearly lying on its side.

Due to Uranus's unusual inclination, the polar regions receive more sunlight during a Uranus year of 84 Earth years. Scientists had thought that the temperature of its poles would be warmer than that at its equator, but *Voyager 2* discovered that the equatorial temperatures were similar to the temperatures at the poles, –209° C (–344° F), implying that some redistribution of heat toward the equatorial region must occur within the atmosphere. The wind patterns are much like Saturn's, flowing parallel to the equator in the direction of the planet's rotation.

Ninety-eight percent of the upper atmosphere is composed of hydrogen and helium; the remaining two percent is methane. Scientists speculate that the bulk of the lower atmosphere is composed of water (perhaps as much as 50%), methane, and ammonia. Methane is responsible for Uranus's blue-green color because it selectively absorbs red sunlight and condenses to form clouds of ice crystals in the cooler, higher regions of Uranus's atmosphere.

It was also discovered that the planet's magnetic field was 60 degrees tilted from the planet's axis of rotation and offset from the planet's center by one-third of Uranus's radius. It may be generated at a depth where water is under sufficient pressure to be electrically conductive.

The Uranian Rings

Voyager 2 also expanded the body of information pertaining to the rings and moons of Uranus. *Voyager*'s cameras obtained the first images of 9 previously known narrow rings and discovered at least 2 new rings, one narrow and one broadly diffused, bringing the total known rings to 11. It was found that a highly structured distribution of fine dust exists throughout the ring system.

The outermost (epsilon) ring contains nothing smaller than fist-sized particles. It is flanked by two small moons discovered interior to the orbit of the Uranian moon Miranda. The moons exert a shepherding influence on the epsilon ring and on the outer edges of the gamma and delta rings.

All of the rings lie within one planetary radius[1] of Uranus's cloud tops. Most of Uranus's rings are narrow, ranging in width from 1 to 93 kilometers (0.6 to 58 miles), and are only a few kilometers thick. The Uranian rings are colorless and extremely dark. The dark material may be either irradiated methane ice or organic-rich minerals mixed with water-impregnated, silicon-based compounds. There is evidence that incomplete rings, or "ring arcs," exist at Uranus.

1. The equatorial radius of Uranus is 25,560 kilometers (15,880 miles) at a pressure of 1 bar.

The Uranian Moons

There are 17 known moons of Uranus. In order of decreasing distance from the planet, the moons are Oberon, Titania, Umbriel, Ariel, Miranda, Puck, Belinda, Cressida, Portia, Rosalind, Desdemona, Juliet, Bianca, Ophelia, Cordelia, and two additional satellites that were discovered in late 1997 (*see* page 453). Nine of the moons range in size from 26 to 108 kilometers (16–67 miles) in diameter and, being closer to the planet, have faster periods of revolution (8–15 hours) than their more distant relatives.

Oberon and Titania

The two largest moons, Oberon, 1,516 kilometers (942 miles) in diameter, and Titania, 1,580 kilometers (982 miles) in diameter, are less than half the diameter of Earth's moon. Titania, the reddest of Uranus's moons, may have endured global tectonics as evidenced by complex valleys and fault lines etched into its surface. Smooth sections indicate that volcanic resurfacing has taken place.

Umbriel and Ariel

Umbriel and Ariel are roughly three-fourths the size of Oberon and Titania. Umbriel is the darkest of the large moons, with huge craters peppering its surface. Umbriel has a paucity of what are known as bright ray craters, which are formed on an older darker surface when bright submerged ice is excavated and sprayed by meteoroid impacts.

In contrast, the surface of Ariel, the brightest of the Uranian moons, is relatively free of pockmarks due to volcanism that periodically erases the damage done by foreign projectiles. However, there are several extremely deep cuts on Ariel's surface.

Miranda

The smallest of Uranus's large moons, Miranda, 472 kilometers (293 miles) in diameter, has been described as "the most bizarre body in the solar system," with the most geologically complex surface. Miranda's remarkable terrain consists of rolling, heavily cratered plains (the oldest known in the Uranian system) adjoined by three huge, 200- to 300-kilometer (120–180 mile) oval-to-trapezoidal regions known as coronae, which are characterized by networks of concentric canyons.

Puck

Puck was the first new moon discovered by *Voyager,* and is 154 kilometers (96 miles) in diameter and makes a trip around Uranus every 18 hours. Puck is shaped somewhat like a potato with a huge impact crater marring roughly one-fourth of its surface.

Uranus can—on rare occasions—become bright enough to be seen with the naked eye, if one knows exactly where to look; normally, a good set of field glasses or a small portable telescope is required.

Neptune

Little was known about Neptune until August 1989, when NASA's *Voyager 2* became the first spacecraft to observe the planet. Passing about 4,950 kilometers (3,000 miles) above Neptune's north pole, *Voyager 2* made its closest approach to any planet since leaving Earth 12 years prior. The spacecraft passed about 40,000 kilometers (25,000 miles) from Neptune's largest moon, Triton, the last solid body that *Voyager 2* will have studied.

Nearly 4.5 billion kilometers (3 billion miles) from the Sun, Neptune orbits the Sun once in 165 years, and therefore has made not quite a full circle around the Sun since it was discovered.[1]

With an equatorial diameter of 49,528 kilometers (30,775 miles), Neptune is the smallest of our solar system's four gas giants.[2] Even so, its volume could hold nearly 60 Earths. Neptune is also denser than the other gas giants (Jupiter, Saturn, and Uranus), and about 64% heavier than if it were composed entirely of water.

Neptune has a blue color as a result of methane in its atmosphere. Methane preferentially absorbs the longer wavelengths of sunlight (those near the red end of the spectrum). What are left to be reflected are colors at the blue end of the spectrum. The atmosphere of Neptune is mainly composed of hydrogen, with helium and traces of methane and ammonia.

Neptune is a dynamic planet even though it receives only 3% as much sunlight as Jupiter does. *Voyager 2* discovered several large, dark spots that were prominent features on the planet. The largest spot was about the size of Earth and was designated the "Great Dark Spot" by its discoverers. It appeared to be an anticyclone similar to Jupiter's Great Red Spot. While Neptune's Great Dark Spot is comparable in size, relative to the planet, and at the same latitude (22°S latitude) as Jupiter's Great Red Spot, it was far more variable in size and shape than its Jovian counterpart. Bright, wispy "cirrus-type" clouds overlaid the Great Dark Spot at its southern and northeastern boundaries.

At about 42° south, a bright, irregularly shaped, eastward-moving cloud circles much faster than did the Great Dark Spot, "scooting" around Neptune in about 16 hours. This "scooter" may have been a cloud plume rising between cloud decks.

Another spot, designated "D2," was located far to the south of the Great Dark Spot, at 55°S latitude. It is almond-shaped, with a bright central core, and moves eastward around the planet in about 16 hours.

In 1995, images taken by the Hubble Space Telescope showed that the Great Dark Spot has vanished. The great storm center has either dissipated or is obscured by other atmospheric conditions.

The atmosphere above Neptune's clouds is hotter near the equator, cooler in the mid-latitudes, and warm again at the south pole. Temperatures in the stratosphere were measured to be 750° K (900° F), while at the 100 millibar pressure level they were measured to be 55° K (–360° F).

Long, bright clouds, reminiscent of cirrus clouds on Earth, were seen high in Neptune's atmosphere. They appear to form above most of the methane, and consequently are not blue.

1. Astronomers have studied Neptune since Sept. 23, 1846, when Johann Gottfried Galle, of the Berlin Observatory, and Louis d'Arrest, an astronomy student, discovered the eighth planet on the basis of mathematical predictions by Urbain Jean Joseph Le Verrier. Similar predictions were made independently by John Couch Adams. Galileo Galilei had seen Neptune during several nights of observing Jupiter, in January 1613, but didn't realize he was seeing a new planet.
2. These four planets are about 4 to 12 times greater in diameter than Earth. They have no solid surfaces, but possess massive atmospheres that contain substantial amounts of hydrogen and helium with traces of other gases.

At northern low latitudes (27°N), *Voyager* captured images of cloud streaks casting their shadows on cloud decks estimated to be about 50 to 100 kilometers (30–60 miles) below. The widths of these cloud streaks range from 50 to 200 kilometers (30–125 miles). Cloud streaks were also seen in the southern polar regions (71°S) where the cloud heights were about 50 kilometers (30 miles).

Most of the winds on Neptune blow in a westward direction, which is retrograde, or opposite to the rotation of the planet. Near the Great Dark Spot, there are retrograde winds blowing up to 1,500 miles an hour—the strongest winds measured on any planet.

The Magnetic Field

Neptune's magnetic field is tilted 47 degrees from the planet's rotation axis, and is offset at least 0.55 radii (about 13,500 kilometers or 8,500 miles) from the physical center. The dynamo electric currents produced within the planet, therefore, must be relatively closer to the surface than for Earth, Jupiter, or Saturn. Because of its unusual orientation, and the tilt of the planet's rotation axis, Neptune's magnetic field goes through dramatic changes as the planet rotates in the solar wind.

Voyager's planetary radio astronomy instrument measured the periodic radio waves generated by the magnetic field and determined that the rotation rate of the interior of Neptune is 16 hours 7 minutes.

Voyager also detected auroras, similar to the northern and southern lights on Earth, in Neptune's atmosphere. Unlike those on Earth, due to Neptune's complex magnetic field, the auroras are extremely complicated processes that occur over wide regions of the planet, not just near the planet's magnetic poles.

Neptune's Moons

Triton

The largest of Neptune's eight known satellites, Triton is different from all other icy moons that *Voyager* has studied. Triton circles Neptune in a tilted, circular, retrograde orbit, completing an orbit in 5.875 days at an average distance of 330,000 kilometers (205,000 miles) above the planet's cloud tops.

Triton shows evidence of a remarkable geologic history, and *Voyager 2* images show active geyser-like eruptions spewing invisible nitrogen gas and dark dust particles 2 to 8 kilometers (1–5 miles) into space.

Triton is about three-quarters the size of Earth's Moon and has a diameter of about 2,705 kilometers (1,680 miles), and a mean density of about 2.066 grams per cubic centimeter. (The density of water is 1.0 grams per cubic centimeter.) This means that Triton contains more rock in its interior than the icy satellites of Saturn and Uranus.

The relatively high density and the retrograde orbit offer strong evidence that Triton did not originate near Neptune, but is a captured object.

An extremely thin atmosphere extends as much as 800 kilometers (500 miles) above the satellite's surface. Tiny nitrogen ice particles may form thin clouds a few kilometers above the surface. Triton is very bright, reflecting 60% to 95% of the sunlight that strikes it. (By comparison, Earth's Moon reflects only 11%.)

The atmospheric pressure at Triton's surface is about 14 microbars, a mere 1/70,000th the surface pressure on Earth. Temperature at the surface is about 38° K (–391° F), making it the coldest surface of any body yet visited in the solar system.

Nereid

Nereid was discovered in 1948 through Earth-based telescopes. Little is known about Nereid, which is slightly smaller than Proteus, having a diameter of 340 kilometers (211 miles). The satellite's surface reflects about 14% of the sunlight that strikes it. Nereid's orbit is the most eccentric in the solar system, ranging from about 1,353,600 kilometers (841,100 miles) to 9,623,700 kilometers (5,980,200 miles).

The Smaller Satellites

In addition to the previously known moons, Triton and Nereid, *Voyager 2* found six more satellites, making the total eight.

Proteus

Like all six of Neptune's recently discovered small satellites, it is one of the darkest objects in the solar system—"as dark as soot" is a good description. It reflects only 6% of the sunlight that strikes it. Proteus is an ellipsoid about 416 kilometers (258 miles) in diameter, larger than Nereid. It circles Neptune at a distance of about 92,800 kilometers (57,700 miles) above the cloud tops, and completes one orbit in 26 hours 54 minutes. Scientists say that it is about as large as a satellite can be without being pulled into a spherical shape by its own gravity.

Proteus and its tiny companions are cratered and irregularly shaped—they are not round—and show no signs of any geologic modifications. All circle the planet in the same direction as Neptune rotates, and remain close to Neptune's equatorial plane.

Larissa

This object is only about 48,800 kilometers (30,300 miles) from Neptune and circles the planet in 13 hours 18 minutes. Its diameter is 190 kilometers (120 miles).

Despina

The satellite is 27,700 kilometers (17,200 miles) from Neptune's clouds and makes one orbit every 8 hours. Its diameter is about 150 kilometers (90 miles).

Galatea

It lies 37,200 kilometers (23,100 miles) from Neptune. Its diameter is 180 kilometers (110 miles) and it completes an orbit in 10 hours 18 minutes.

Thalassa

The satellite appears to be about 80 kilometers (50 miles) in diameter. It orbits Neptune in 7 hours 30 minutes some 25,200 kilometers (15,700 miles) above the cloud tops.

Naiad

The last satellite discovered, it is about 60 kilometers (37 miles) in diameter and orbits Neptune about 23,200 kilometers (14,400 miles) above the clouds in 7 hours 6 minutes.

Neptune's Rings

Voyager found four rings and evidence of ring *arcs* or incomplete rings. The "Main Ring" orbits

Neptune at about 38,100 kilometers (23,700 miles) above the cloud tops. The "Inner Ring" is about 28,400 kilometers (17,700 miles) from Neptune's cloud tops. An "Inside Diffuse Ring"—a complete ring—is located about 17,100 kilometers (10,600 miles) from the planet's cloud tops. Some scientists suspect that this ring may extend all the way down to Neptune's cloud tops. An area called "the Plateau" is a broad, diffuse sheet of fine material just outside the so-called "Inner Ring." The fine material is approximately the size of smoke particles. All other rings contain a greater proportion of larger material.

Pluto

Pluto, the outermost and smallest planet in the solar system, is the only planet not visited by an exploring spacecraft. So little is known about it, that it is difficult to classify. Its distance is so great that the Hubble Space Telescope cannot reveal its surface features. Appropriately named for the Roman god of the underworld, it must be frozen, dark, and dead. Pluto's mean distance from the Sun is 5,900 million kilometers (3,666 million miles).

In 1978, light-curve studies gave evidence of a moon revolving around Pluto within the same period as Pluto's rotation. Therefore, it stays over the same point on Pluto's surface. In addition, it keeps the same face toward the planet. The satellite was later named Charon and is estimated to be about 789 miles (1,270 kilometers) in diameter. Recent estimates indicate Pluto's diameter is about 1,441.6 miles (2,220 kilometers), making the pair more like a double planet than any other in the solar system. Previously, the Earth-Moon system held this distinction. The density of Pluto is slightly greater than that of water.

There is evidence that Pluto has an atmosphere containing methane and polar ice caps that increase and decrease in size with the planet's seasons. It is not known to have water. The Hubble Space Telescope's faint-object camera revealed light and dark regions on Pluto indicating an ice cap at the planet's north pole. It is not known if there is an ice cap at Pluto's south pole.

Pluto was predicted by calculation when Percival Lowell (1855–1916) noticed irregularities in the orbits of Uranus and Neptune. Clyde Tombaugh (1906–1997) discovered the planet in 1930, precisely where Lowell predicted it would be. The name Pluto was chosen because the first two letters represent the initials of Percival Lowell.

Pluto has the most eccentric orbit in the solar system, bringing it at times closer to the Sun than Neptune. Pluto approached the perihelion of its orbit on Sept. 5, 1989, and for the rest of this century will be closer to the Sun than Neptune. Even then, it can be seen only with a large telescope.

The Asteroids

Between the orbits of Mars and Jupiter are an estimated 30,000 pieces of rocky debris, known collectively as the asteroids, or planetoids. The first and, incidentally, the largest (Ceres) was discovered during the New Year's night of 1801 by the Italian astronomer Father Piazzi (1746–1826), and its orbit was calculated by the German mathematician Karl Friedrich Gauss (1777–1855). Gauss invented a new method of calculating orbits on that occasion. A German amateur astronomer, the physician Olbers (1748–1840), discovered the second asteroid, Pallas. The number now known, catalogued, and named is over 6,000 and could reach 10,000 by the end of the 20th century. A few asteroids do not move in orbits beyond the orbit of Mars, but in orbits that cross the orbit of Mars. The first of them was named Eros because of this peculiar orbit. It had become the rule to bestow female names on the asteroids, but when it was found that Eros crossed the orbit of a major planet, it received a male name. Since then around two dozen orbit-crossers have been discovered, and they are often referred to as the "male asteroids." A few of them—Albert, Adonis, Apollo, Amor, and Icarus—cross the orbit of Earth, and two of them may come closer than our Moon; but the crossing is like a bridge crossing a highway, not like two highways intersecting. Hence there is very little danger of collision from these bodies. They are all small, 3 to 5 miles in diameter, and therefore very difficult objects to identify, even when quite close. Some scientists believe the asteroids represent the remains of an exploded planet.

On Oct. 29, 1991, the *Galileo* spacecraft took a historic photograph of asteroid 951 Gaspra from a distance of 10,000 miles (16,200 kilometers) away. It was the first close-up photo ever taken of an asteroid in space.

Gaspra is an irregular, potato-shaped object about 12.5 miles (20 kilometers) by 7.5 miles (12 kilometers) by 7 miles (11 kilometers) in size. Its surface is covered with a layer of loose rubble and its terrain is covered with several dozen small craters.

Close-up photos of Asteroid 243 Ida taken by the *Galileo* spacecraft on Aug. 28, 1993, revealed that Ida had a tiny egg-shaped moon measuring 0.9 miles by 0.7 miles (1.6 by 1.2 kilometers). The moon has been named Dactyl.

NASA's *Near-Earth Asteroid Rendezvous* spacecraft was launched on Feb. 17, 1996. It flew within 750 miles (282 kilometers) of minor planet 253 Mathilde on June 27, 1997, and took spectacular images of the dark, crater-battered world. The asteroid's mean diameter was found to be 33 miles (52 kilometers). The *NEAR* spacecraft discovered that the carbon-rich Mathilde is one of the darkest objects in the solar system, only reflecting about 3% of the Sun's light, making it twice as dark as a chunk of charcoal. The asteroid is almost completely cratered, and at least five of its craters just on the lighted side are larger than 12 miles (20 kilometers). The spacecraft will reach asteroid 433 Eros in February 1999 and orbit it for almost one year.

Comets

Comets, according to the noted astronomer Fred L. Whipple (1906–) are enormous "snowballs" of frozen gases (mostly carbon dioxide, methane, and water vapor) and contain very little solid material. The whole behavior of comets can then be explained as the behavior of frozen gas being heated by the Sun. When the comet Kohoutek made its first appearance to man in 1973, its behavior seemed to confirm this theory and later, the international study by five spacecraft that encountered Halley's comet in March 1986 confirmed Whipple's idea of the make-up of comets.

The First Ten Minor Planets (Asteroids)

Name	Year of discovery	Mean distance from sun (millions of miles)	Orbital period (years)	Diameter (miles)	Magnitude
1. Ceres	1801	257.0	4.60	485	7.4
2. Pallas	1802	257.4	4.61	304	8.0
3. Juno	1804	247.8	4.36	118	8.7
4. Vesta	1807	219.3	3.63	243	6.5
5. Astraea	1845	239.3	4.14	50	9.9
6. Hebe	1847	225.2	3.78	121	8.5
7. Iris	1847	221.4	3.68	121	8.4
8. Flora	1847	204.4	3.27	56	8.9
9. Metis	1848	221.7	3.69	78	8.9
10. Hygeia	1849	222.6	5.59	40(?)	9.5

Since comets appear in the sky without any warning, people in classical times and especially during the Middle Ages believed that they had a special meaning, which, of course, was bad. Since a natural catastrophe of some sort of a military conflict occurs every year, it was quite simple to blame the comet that happened to be visible. But even in the past, there were some people who used logical reasoning. When, in Roman times, a comet was blamed for the loss of a battle and hence was called a "bad omen," a Roman writer observed that the victors in the battle probably did not think so.

Up until the middle of the 16th century, comets were believed to be phenomena of the upper atmosphere; they were usually "explained" as "burning vapors" which had risen from "distant swamps." That nobody had ever actually seen burning vapors rise from a swamp did not matter.

But a large comet which appeared in 1577 was carefully observed by Tycho Brahe (1546–1601), a Danish astronomer who is often, and with the best of reasons, called "eccentric," but who insisted on precise measurements for everything. It was Tycho Brahe's accumulation of literally thousands of precise measurements that later enabled his younger collaborator, Johannes Kepler (1571–1630), to discover the laws of planetary motion. Measuring the motion of the comet of 1577, Tycho Brahe could show that it had been far beyond the atmosphere, even though he could not give figures for the distance. Tycho Brahe's work proved that comets were astronomical and not meteorological phenomena.

In 1682, the second Astronomer Royal of Great Britain, Dr. Edmond Halley (1656–1742), checked the orbit of a bright comet that was in the sky then and compared it with earlier comet orbits that were known in part. Halley found that the comet of 1682 was the third to move through what appeared to be the same orbit, and that the three appearances were roughly 76 years apart. Halley concluded that this was the same comet, moving around the Sun in a closed orbit, like the planets. He predicted that it would reappear in 1758 or 1759. Halley himself died in 1742, but a large comet appeared 16 years after his death as predicted and was immediately referred to as "Halley's comet."

Halley's comet appeared again in 1986, sparking a worldwide effort to study it up close. Five satellites in all took readings from the comet at various distances. Two Soviet craft, *Vega 1* and *Vega 2,* went in close to provide detailed pictures of the comet, including the first of the comet's core. The European Space Agency's craft, *Giotto,* entered the comet itself, coming to within 450 miles of the comet's center and successfully passing through its tail. In addition, two Japanese craft, the *Suisei* and the *Sakigake,* passed at a longer distance and analyzed the cloud and tail of the comet and the effect of solar radiation upon it.

Astronomers refer to comets as "periodic" or as "non-periodic" comets, but the latter term does not mean that these comets have no period; it merely means that their period is not known. The actual periods of comets run from 3.3 years (the shortest known) to many thousands of years. Their orbits are elliptical, like those of the planets, but they are very eccentric, long, and narrow ellipses. Only comet Schwassmann-Wachmann has an orbit that has such a low eccentricity (for a cometary orbit) that it could be the orbit of a minor planet.

When a comet, coming from deep space, approaches the Sun, it is at first indistinguishable from a minor planet. Somewhere between the orbits of Mars and Jupiter, its outline becomes fuzzy; it is said to develop a "coma" (the word used here is the Latin word *coma,* which means "hair," not the phonetically identical Greek word that means "deep sleep"). Then, near the orbit of Mars, the comet develops its tail, which at first trails behind. This grows steadily as the comet comes closer and closer to the Sun. As it rounds the Sun (as first noticed by Girolamo Fracastoro, 1483–1553) the tail always points away from the Sun so that the comet, when moving away from the Sun, points its tail ahead like the landing lights of an airplane.

The reason for this behavior is that the tail is pushed in these directions by the radiation pressure of the Sun. It sometimes happens that a comet loses its tail at perihelion; it then grows another one. Although the tail is clearly visible against the black of the sky, it is very tenuous. It has been said that if the tail of Halley's comet could be compressed to the density of iron, it would fit into a small suitcase.

Although very low in mass, comets are among the largest members of the solar system. The nucleus of a comet may be up to 10,000 miles in diameter; its coma between 10,000 and 50,000 miles in diameter; and its tail as long as 28 million miles.

Comet Shoemaker-Levy 9 broke up into 21 fragments in July 1992 and crashed into the surface of Jupiter, July 16–22, 1994, in the most violent event in the recorded history of the solar system.

In 1951, Dutch astronomer Gerard Kuiper first suggested the existence of a disk-shaped swarm of short-period comets that begin beyond the orbit of Neptune and extend past Pluto. In 1995, the Hubble

Space Telescope detected the long-sought Kuiper Belt and an estimated 200 million comets were discovered orbiting it.

Meteors and Meteorites

The term *meteor* for what is usually called a *shooting star* bears an unfortunate resemblance to the term *meteorology,* the science of weather and weather forecasting. This resemblance is due to an ancient misunderstanding that wrongly considered meteors an atmospheric phenomenon. Actually, the streak of light in the sky that scientists call a meteor is essentially an astronomical phenomenon: the entry of a small piece of cosmic matter into our atmosphere.

The distinction between *meteors* and *fireballs* (formerly also called *bolides*) is merely one of convenience; a fireball is an unusually bright meteor. Incidentally, it also means that a fireball is larger than a faint meteor.

Bodies that enter our atmosphere become visible when they are about 60 miles above the ground. The fact that they grow hot enough to emit light is not due to the "friction" of the atmosphere, as one can often read. The phenomenon responsible for the heating is one of compression. Unconfined air cannot move faster than the speed of sound. Since the entering meteorite moves with 30 to 60 times the speed of sound, the air simply cannot get out of the way. Therefore, it is compressed like the air in the cylinder of a diesel engine and is heated by compression. This heat—or part of it—is transferred to the moving body. The details of this process are now fairly well understood as a result of re-entry tests with ballistic-missile nose cones.

The average weight of a body producing a faint *shooting star* is only a small fraction of an ounce. Even a bright fireball may not weigh more than 2 or 3 pounds. Naturally, the smaller bodies are worn to dust by the passage through the atmosphere; only rather large ones reach the ground. Those that are found are called meteorites. (The *meteor,* to repeat, is the term for the light streak in the sky.) About 1,000 meteorites fall to the Earth each year.

The largest meteorite known is still imbedded in the ground near Grootfontein in southwest Africa and is estimated to weigh 70 tons. The second-largest known is the 34-ton Anighito (on exhibit in the Hayden Planetarium, New York), which was found by Admiral Peary in 1892 at Cape York in Greenland. The largest meteorite found in the United States is the Willamette meteorite (found in Oregon, weight ca. 15 tons), but large portions of this meteorite weathered away before it was found. Its weight as it struck the ground may have been 20 tons.

All these are iron meteorites (an iron meteorite normally contains about 7% nickel), which form one class of meteorites. The other class consists of the stony meteorites, and between them there are the so-called "stony irons." The so-called "tektites" consist of glass similar to our volcanic glass obsidian, and because of the similarity, there is doubt in a number of cases whether the glass is of terrestrial or of extraterrestrial origin.

Though no meteorite larger than the Grootfontein is actually known, we do know that Earth has, on occasion, been struck by much larger bodies. Evidence for such hits are the meteorite craters, of which an especially good example is located near the Cañon Diablo in Arizona. Another meteor crater in the United States is a rather old crater near Odessa, Texas. A large number of others are known, especially in eastern Canada; and for many "probables," meteoric origin has now been proved.

The 13th known lunar meteorite was found in December 1993 by a team from the Antarctic Search for Meteorites project. It is approximately 2 inches long and weighs 0.75 of an ounce.

Some scientists theorize that the mass extermination of dinosaurs from the face of Earth 65 million years ago was due to a large meteor that struck our planet at that time.

Meteor showers are caused by multitudes of very small bodies travelling in swarms. Earth travels in its orbit through these swarms like a car driving through falling snow. The point from which the meteors seem to emanate is called the *radiant* and is named for the constellation in that area. The Perseid meteor shower in August is the most spectacular of the year, boasting, at peak, roughly 60 meteors per hour under good atmospheric conditions. The presence of a bright moon diminishes the number of visible meteors.

The Constellations

Constellations are groupings of stars that form easily recognized and remembered patterns, such as Orion and the Big Dipper. The Big Dipper is actually an asterism, not a constellation, because it is only part of the constellation Ursa Major (the Big Bear). Actually, the stars in the majority of all constellations do not "belong together." Usually they are at greatly varying distances from Earth and just happen to lie more or less in the same line of sight as seen from our solar system. But in a few cases, the stars of a constellation are actually associated; most of the bright stars of the Big Dipper travel together and form what astronomers call an *open cluster*.

If you observe a planet, say Mars, for one complete revolution, you will see that it passes successively through 12 constellations. All planets (except Pluto at certain times) can be observed only in these 12 constellations, which form the so-called zodiac, and the Sun also moves through the zodiacal signs, though the Sun's apparent movement is actually caused by the movement of Earth.

Although the constellations are duc mainly to the optical accident of line of sight and have no real significance, astronomers have retained them as reference areas. It is much easier to speak of a star in Orion than to give its geometrical position in the sky. During the Astronomical Congress of 1928, it was decided to recognize 88 constellations. A description of their agreed-upon boundaries was published at Cambridge, England, in 1930, under the title *Atlas Céleste*.

The Auroras

The "northern lights" *(Aurora borealis)* as well as the "southern lights" *(Aurora australis)* are upper-atmosphere phenomena of astronomical origin. The auroras center around the magnetic (not the geographical) poles of Earth, which explains why, in the Western Hemisphere, they have been seen as far to the south as New Orleans and Florida, while the

The 88 Recognized Constellations

In astronomical works, the Latin names of the constellations are used. The letter N or S following the Latin name indicates whether the constellation is located to the north or south of the Zodiac. The letter Z indicates that the constellation is within the Zodiac.

Latin name	Letter	English version
Andromeda	N	Andromeda
Antlia	S	Airpump
Apus	S	Bird of Paradise
Aquarius	Z	Water Bearer
Aquila	N	Eagle
Ara	S	Altar
Aries	Z	Ram
Auriga	N	Charioteer
Boötes	N	Herdsmen
Caelum	S	Sculptor's Tool
Camelopardalis	N	Giraffe
Cancer	Z	Crab
Canes Venatici	N	Hunting Dogs
Canis Major	S	Great Dog
Canis Minor	S	Little Dog
Capricornus	Z	Goat (or Sea-Goat)
Carina	S	Keel (of Argo)[1]
Cassiopeia	N	Cassiopeia
Centaurus	S	Centaur
Cepheus	N	Cepheus
Cetus	S	Whale
Chameleon	S	Chameleon
Circinus	S	Compasses
Columba	S	Dove
Coma Berenices	N	Berenice's Hair
Corona Australis	S	Southern Crown
Corona Borealis	N	Northern Crown
Corvus	S	Crow (Raven)
Crater	S	Cup
Crux	S	Southern Cross
Cygnus	N	Swan
Delphinus	N	Dolphin
Dorado	S	Swordfish (Goldfish)
Draco	N	Dragon
Equuleus	N	Filly
Eridanus	S	Eridanus (river)
Fornax	S	Furnace
Gemini	Z	Twins
Grus	S	Crane
Hercules	N	Hercules
Horologium	S	Clock
Hydra	N	Sea Serpent
Hydrus	S	Water Snake
Indus	S	Indian
Lacerta	N	Lizard
Leo	Z	Lion
Leo Minor	N	Little Lion
Lepus	S	Hare
Libra	Z	Scales
Lupus	S	Wolf
Lynx	N	Lynx
Lyra	N	Lyre (Harp)
Mensa	S	Table (mountain)
Microscopium	S	Microscope
Monoceros	S	Unicorn
Musca	S	Southern Fly
Norma	S	Rule (straightedge)
Octans	S	Octant
Ophiuchus	N	Serpent-Bearer
Orion	S	Orion
Pavo	S	Peacock
Pegasus	N	Pegasus
Perseus	N	Perseus
Phoenix	S	Phoenix
Pictor	S	Painter (or his Easel)
Pisces	Z	Fishes
Piscis Austrinus	S	Southern Fish
Puppis	S	Poop (of Argo)[1]
Pyxis	S	Mariner's Compass
Reticulum	S	Net
Sagitta	N	Arrow
Sagittarius	Z	Archer
Scorpius	Z	Scorpion
Sculptor	S	Sculptor
Scutum	N	Shield
Serpens	N	Serpent
Sextans	S	Sextant
Taurus	Z	Bull
Telescopium	S	Telescope
Triangulum	N	Triangle
Triangulum Australe	S	Southern Triangle
Tucana	S	Toucan
Ursa Major	N	Big Dipper
Ursa Minor	N	Little Dipper
Vela	S	Sail (of Argo)[1]
Virgo	Z	Virgin
Volans	S	Flying Fish
Vulpecula	N	Fox

1. The original constellation Argo Navis (the Ship Argo) has been divided into Carina, Puppis, and Vela. Normally the brightest star in each constellation is designated by alpha, the first letter of the Greek alphabet, the second brightest by beta, the second letter of the Greek alphabet, and so forth. But the Greek letters run through Carina, Puppis, and Vela as if it were still one constellation.

equivalent latitude in the Eastern Hemisphere never sees an aurora. The northern magnetic pole happens to be in the Western Hemisphere.

The lower limit of an aurora is at about 50 miles. Upper limits have been estimated to be as high as 400 miles. Since about 1880, a connection between the auroras on Earth and sunspots has been suspected and has gradually come to be accepted. It was said that the sunspots probably eject "particles" (later the word *electrons* was substituted), which on striking Earth's atmosphere cause the auroras. But this explanation suffered from certain difficulties. Sometimes a very large sunspot group on the Sun, with individual spots bigger than Earth itself, would not cause an aurora. Moreover, even if a sunspot caused an aurora, the time that passed between the appearance of the one and the occurrence of the other was highly unpredictable.

This problem of the time lag is, in all probability, solved by the discovery of the Van Allen layer by artificial satellite *Explorer I.* The Van Allen layer[1] is a double layer of charged subatomic particles around Earth. The inner layer, with its center some 1,500 miles from the ground, reaches from about 40°N to about 40°S and does not touch the atmosphere. The outer layer, much larger and with its center several thousand miles from the ground, does touch the atmosphere in the vicinity of the magnetic poles.

It seems probable that the "leakage" of electrons from the outer Van Allen layer causes the auroras. A new burst of electrons from the Sun seems to be caught in the outer layer first. Under the assumption that all electrons are first caught in the outer layer, the time lag can be understood. There has to be an "overflow" from the outer layer to produce an aurora.

1. Named after the American physicist, James Alfred Van Allen (1914–) who discovered the broad bands of intense radiation surrounding Earth in 1958.

The Atmosphere

Though reasonably transparent to visible light, the atmosphere may absorb as much as 60% of the visible and near-visible light. It is opaque to most other wavelengths, except certain fairly short radio waves. In addition to absorbing much light, our atmosphere bends light rays entering at a slant (for a given observer) so that the true position of a star close to the horizon is not what it seems to be. One effect is that we see the Sun above the horizon before it actually is. And the unsteady movement of the atmosphere causes the "twinkling" of the stars, which may be romantic, but is a nuisance when it comes to observing.

The composition of our atmosphere near the ground is 78% nitrogen and 21% oxygen, the remaining 1% consisting of other gases, most of it argon. The composition stays the same to an altitude of at least 70 miles (except that higher up two impurities, carbon dioxide and water vapor, are missing), but the pressure drops very fast. At 18,000 feet, half of the total mass of the atmosphere is below, and at 100,000 feet, 99% of the mass of the atmosphere is below. The upper limit of the atmosphere is usually given as 120 miles; no definitive figure is possible, since there is no boundary line between the incredibly attenuated gases 120 miles up and space.

Astronomy Web Sites

Astronomical Society of the Pacific: www.aspsky.org
Asteroid and Comet Impact Hazards: impact.arc.nasa.gov/index.html
Space Telescope Science Institute (home of Hubble): www.stsci.edu
U.S. Naval Observatory: www.usno.navy.mil/
NASA Home Page: www.nasa.gov

Some Giant Telescopes

• The world's largest fixed-dish radio telescope (1963) is located near Arecibo, Puerto Rico. It is 1,000 ft. (35 m) in diameter and spans some 25 acres.

• The Very Large Array (VLA) telescope (1980) near Socorro, N.M., is the world's most powerful radio telescope. It is Y-shaped and has 27 separate mobile antennas (each 82 ft. in diameter) and is spread out over about a 25-mile area.

• The world's largest fully steerable radio telescope (1972), located at Effelsberg, Germany, has 100-meter (328-ft.) antenna.

• The 200-inch (5-meter) Hale telescope at Mount Palomar, Calif. (1948), is the second largest reflector in use.

• The 236-inch Special Astrophysical Observatory (1976) at Zelenchukskaya, on the northern slopes of the Caucasus Mountains in the Russian Federation, is the world's largest reflector telescope in use. However, problems with it make it less useful than the 200-inch Hale.

• The W. M. Keck Telescope (1991) at Mauna Kea, Hawaii, is the world's most powerful reflector telescope. It has a primary mirror composed of 36 hexagonal segments, each 1.8 meters in size. The Keck Telescope has a light gathering power four times greater than the 200-inch Hale.

• The 40-inch (1.01 meter) telescope at Yerkes Observatory (1897) at Williams Bay, Wis., is the world's largest refracting telescope.

Hubble Space Telescope

The $2 billion Edwin P. Hubble Space Telescope (HST) is the most complex and sensitive space observatory ever constructed. Over three times larger and heavier than any unmanned satellite launched before by NASA, it was placed into orbit by the space shuttle *Discovery* on April 25, 1990. It has a primary mirror of 94 inches (2.4 m) in diameter. HST is 43.3 ft. (13 m) long and 14 ft. (4 m) wide, about the size of a bus or truck. Standing upright, it looks like a five-story building. Hubble weighs 25,500 pounds (11,000 kg) and orbits 335 nautical miles (620 km) above Earth.

Since being lifted into orbit, HST has become the principal tool for exploring the universe through this decade and the next.

Astronomers discovered in June 1990 that there was a spherical aberration in one of the telescope's mirrors. In 1991, two of the craft's six gyroscopes failed, and a third failed on Nov. 18, 1993, causing additional problems. NASA successfully repaired the space telescope during the Dec. 2–13, 1993, mission of the *Endeavour*.

Crew members of the space shuttle *Discovery* made fresh repairs to the telescope during an upgrade mission in February 1997, and installed two powerful new scientific instruments—the Near Infrared Camera (NICMOS) and Multi-Object Spectrometer—giving HST still sharper and more distant views of the universe.

The Near Infrared Camera can see the universe at near infrared wavelengths more sensitively that any other existing or planned telescope. Developed at the University of Arizona, NICMOS is both a camera and a spectrometer.

Hubble's new Space Telescope Imagery Spectrograph (STIS) is sensitive to light in ultraviolet wavelengths and employs two-dimensional detectors that allow the instrument to gather 30 times more spectral data than the first-generation Hubble spectrographs. STIS is considered to be the most complex scientific instrument built for space science.

Although the Hubble Space Telescope's planned mission is scheduled to end in 2005, some NASA officials would like to extend its life for several more years until it can be replaced. Astronomers are debating what will be needed to replace Hubble when it is deactivated. □

Twice in a Blue Moon

The second time the Moon is full within a particular month, it is called a "blue moon". This condition occurs once every few years when the date of the first full moon is at or near the beginning of the month so that the following full moon comes before the end of the month. The expression "once in a blue moon," meaning "very seldom," stems from this phenomenon. Over the years a "blue moon" appears to have meant any rarely occurring kind of moon. A "blue moon" can also refer to a moon that appears to be blue in color, which is caused by unusual atmospheric conditions.

Full moons occur about once every 29.53 days, or 12.3683 times a year. Therefore, months containing two full moons occur on the average every 2.72 years. Approximately once every 19 years, one year will have two months with two full moons because February will have no full moon at all. February can never have two new or full moons because the shortest time between them is 29.27 days.

The rare phenomena of two "blue moons" occurring in the same year will take place in 1999. The first happens on January 31 and the second occurs on March 31.

Phenomena, 1999

Configurations of Sun, Moon, and Planets

NOTE: The hour listings are in Universal Time. For conversion to United States time zones, *see* Conversion of Universal Time to Civil Time, p. 451.

JANUARY

d	hr.	
2	03	FULL MOON
3	13	Earth at perihelion
5	08	Venus 1°7 S of Neptune
5	15	Regulus 0°2 S of Moon (Occn.)
8	22	Mars 4° N of Spica
9	14	LAST QUARTER
9	20	Mars 3° S of Moon
11	12	Moon at apogee
13	19	Venus 0°9 S of Uranus
17	16	NEW MOON
18	13	Ceres stationary
19	08	Venus 2° S of Moon
21	23	Jupiter 1°8 N of Moon
22	08	Neptune in conjunction with Sun
24	06	Saturn 2° N of Moon
24	19	FIRST QUARTER
26	21	Moon at perigee
27	07	Aldebaran 0°5 S of Moon (Occn.)
31	16	FULL MOON (Penumbral Eclipse)

FEBRUARY

d	hr.	
2	01	Regulus 0°3 S of Moon (Occn.)
2	02	Uranus in conjunction with Sun
4	05	Mercury in superior conjunction
4	08	Vesta at opposition
7	04	Mars 3° S of Moon
8	09	Moon at apogee
8	12	LAST QUARTER
14	12	Neptune 1°5 S of Moon
16	07	NEW MOON (Eclipse)
18	06	Venus 1°8 N of Moon
18	16	Jupiter 2° N of Moon
20	15	Moon at perigee
20	15	Saturn 3° N of Moon
23	03	FIRST QUARTER
23	13	Aldebaran 0°4 S of Moon (Occn.)
23	21	Venus 0°1 N of Jupiter

MARCH

d	hr.	
1	10	Regulus 0°2 S of Moon (Occn.)
2	07	FULL MOON
3	13	Mercury greatest elong. E (18°)
7	02	Mars 3° S of Moon
8	05	Moon at apogee
9	22	Mercury stationary
10	09	LAST QUARTER
13	23	Neptune 1°4 S of Moon
14	20	Uranus 1°3 S of Moon
15	02	Pluto stationary
17	19	NEW MOON
18	10	Mars stationary
18	11	Jupiter 3° N of Moon
19	19	Mercury in inferior conjunction
20	00	Moon at perigee
20	01	Venus 5° N of Moon
20	03	Saturn 3° N of Moon
20	21	Venus 3° N of Saturn
21	02	Equinox
22	18	Aldebaran 0°6 S of Moon (Occn.)
24	10	FIRST QUARTER
24	11	Vesta stationary
28	16	Regulus 0°3 S of Moon (Occn.)
31	23	FULL MOON

APRIL

d	hr.	
1	06	Jupiter in conjunction with Sun
1	06	Mercury stationary
1	19	Juno stationary
3	08	Mars 3° S of Moon
4	22	Moon at apogee
9	03	LAST QUARTER
10	09	Neptune 1°1 S of Moon (Occn.)
11	07	Uranus 1°0 S of Moon (Occn.)
14	04	Mercury 1°1 N of Moon (Occn.)
16	04	NEW MOON
16	16	Mercury greatest elong. W (28°)
17	05	Moon at perigee
18	21	Venus 7° N of Moon
19	02	Aldebaran 0°7 S of Moon (Occn.)
20	23	Pallas in conjunction with Sun
21	20	Venus 7° N of Aldebaran
22	19	FIRST QUARTER
24	18	Mars at oposition
24	21	Regulus 0°5 S of Moon (Occn.)
27	11	Saturn in conjunction with Sun
29	21	Mars 4° S of Moon
30	15	FULL MOON

MAY

d	hr.	
1	10	Mercury 1°7 S of Jupiter
1	17	Mars closest approach
2	06	Moon at apogee
7	01	Neptune stationary
7	17	Neptune 0°9 S of Moon (Occn.)
8	16	Uranus 0°7 S of Moon (Occn.)
8	17	LAST QUARTER
13	05	Jupiter 4° N of Moon
13	18	Mercury 0°7 N of Saturn
15	12	NEW MOON
15	15	Moon at perigee
16	13	Aldebaran 0°9 S of Moon (Occn.)
18	15	Venus 6° N of Moon
22	03	Regulus 0°7 S of Moon (Occn.)
22	04	Uranus stationary
22	06	FIRST QUARTER
25	18	Mercury in superior conjunction
25	19	Juno at opposition
26	11	Mars 5° S of Moon
29	08	Moon at apogee
30	07	FULL MOON
30	22	Venus 4° S of Pollux
31	00	Pluto at opposition

JUNE

d	hr.	
3	22	Neptune 0°7 S of Moon (Occn.)
4	22	Uranus 0°5 S of Moon
5	07	Mars stationary
7	04	LAST QUARTER
10	00	Jupiter 4° N of Moon
11	02	Saturn 3° N of Moon
11	12	Venus greatest elong. E (45°)
13	01	Moon at perigee
15	08	Mercury 4° N of Moon
17	03	Venus 2° N of Moon
18	11	Regulus 1°0 S of Moon (Occn.)
20	18	FIRST QUARTER
21	18	Mercury 5° S of Pollux
21	20	Solstice
22	20	Mars 6° S of Moon
25	16	Moon at apogee
28	22	FULL MOON
28	23	Mercury greatest elong. E (26°)

JULY

d	hr.	
1	03	Neptune 0°6 S of Moon (Occn.)
2	03	Uranus 0°4 S of Moon (Occn.)
6	12	LAST QUARTER
6	22	Earth at aphelion
7	15	Jupiter 4° N of Moon
8	15	Saturn 3° N of Moon
10	09	Aldebaran 0°8 S of Moon (Occn.)
11	06	Moon at perigee

d	hr.	
12	03	Mercury stationary
13	02	NEW MOON
13	07	Venus 1°5 S of Regulus
14	09	Mercury 3° S of Moon
14	19	Venus greatest brilliancy
15	21	Regulus 1°1 S of Moon (Occn.)
15	23	Venus 3° S of Moon
20	09	FIRST QUARTER
20	22	Mars 7° S of Moon
23	06	Moon at apogee
24	05	Ceres in conjunction with Sun
25	05	Juno stationary
26	10	Neptune at opposition
26	16	Mercury in inferior conjunction
27	20	Venus stationary
28	08	Neptune 0°6 S of Moon (Occn.)
28	11	FULL MOON (Eclipse)
29	07	Uranus 0°5 S of Moon (Occn.)

AUGUST

d	hr.	
4	02	Jupiter 4° N of Moon
4	17	LAST QUARTER
5	00	Saturn 3° N of Moon
5	16	Mercury stationary
6	16	Aldebaran 0°8 S of Moon (Occn.)
7	19	Uranus at opposition
8	00	Moon at perigee
10	03	Mercury 1°2 S of Moon (Occn.)
10	16	Venus 8° S of Regulus
11	11	NEW MOON (Eclipse)
14	14	Mercury greatest elong. W (19°)
18	12	Mars 7° S of Moon
19	02	FIRST QUARTER
19	23	Moon at apogee
20	12	Venus in inferior conjunction
21	07	Pluto stationary
24	14	Neptune 0°7 S of Moon (Occn.)
25	12	Jupiter stationary
25	13	Uranus 0°6 S of Moon (Occn.)
26	12	Mercury 10° N of Venus
27	00	FULL MOON
30	16	Saturn stationary
31	09	Jupiter 4° N of Moon

SEPTEMBER

d	hr.	
1	06	Saturn 3° N of Moon
2	18	Moon at perigee
2	22	Aldebaran 0°8 S of Moon (Occn.)
2	22	LAST QUARTER
7	16	Venus 8° S of Moon
8	15	Mercury in superior conjunction
8	15	Regulus 1°1 S of Moon (Occn.)
9	20	Venus stationary
9	22	NEW MOON
11	12	Vesta 0°9 N of Moon (Occn.)
16	10	Mars 7° S of Moon
17	07	Mars 3° N of Antares
17	20	FIRST QUARTER
20	22	Neptune 0°7 S of Moon (Occn.)
21	20	Uranus 0°6 S of Moon (Occn.)
23	12	Equinox
25	11	FULL MOON
26	15	Venus greatest brilliancy
27	13	Jupiter 4° N of Moon
28	12	Saturn 3° N of Moon
28	17	Moon at perigee
30	04	Aldebaran 1°0 S of Moon (Occn.)
30	16	Mercury 1°7 N of Spica

OCTOBER

d	hr.	
2	04	LAST QUARTER
5	17	Venus 5° S of Moon
5	22	Regulus 1°2 S of Moon (Occn.)
8	22	Venus 3° S of Regulus
9	12	NEW MOON
11	03	Mercury 7° S of Moon
13	22	Neptune stationary
14	14	Moon at apogee
15	13	Mars 5° S of Moon
17	15	FIRST QUARTER
18	07	Neptune 0°5 S of Moon (Occn.)
19	05	Uranus 0°4 S of Moon (Occn.)
22	03	Vesta in conjunction with Sun
23	11	Uranus stationary
23	19	Jupiter at opposition
24	17	Jupiter 4° N of Moon
24	21	FULL MOON
24	22	Mercury greatest elong. E (24°)
25	18	Saturn 2° N of Moon
26	13	Moon at perigee
27	12	Aldebaran 1°2 S of Moon (Occn.)
31	00	Venus greatest elong. W (46°)
31	12	LAST QUARTER

NOVEMBER

d	hr.	
3	23	Venus 3° S of Moon
5	08	Mercury stationary
6	14	Saturn at opposition
8	04	NEW MOON
11	06	Moon at apogee
13	16	Mars 3° S of Moon
14	15	Neptune 0°2 S of Moon (Occn.)
15	13	Uranus 0°1 S of Moon (Occn.)
15	22	Mercury in inferior conjunction, transit over Sun
16	09	FIRST QUARTER
20	22	Jupiter 4° N of Moon
22	01	Saturn 3° N of Moon
23	07	FULL MOON
23	22	Aldebaran 1°3 S of Moon (Occn.)
23	22	Moon at perigee
25	01	Mercury stationary
28	14	Mars 1°7 S of Neptune
29	04	Venus 4° N of Spica
29	23	LAST QUARTER

DECEMBER

d	hr.	
3	00	Pluto in conjunction with Sun
3	01	Mercury in greatest elong. W (20°)
3	21	Venus 3° S of Moon
5	23	Vesta 0°4 S of Moon (Occn.)
6	01	Mercury 3° S of Moon
7	23	NEW MOON
8	11	Moon at apogee
10	07	Pallas stationary
11	22	Neptune 0°07 N of Moon (Occn.)
12	19	Mars 0°6 S of Moon (Occn.)
12	21	Uranus 0°2 N of Moon (Occn.)
14	05	Mars 0°7 S of Uranus
16	01	FIRST QUARTER
17	08	Mercury 5° N of Antares
18	06	Jupiter 4° N of Moon
19	09	Saturn 3° N of Moon
21	05	Jupiter stationary
21	09	Aldebaran 1°3 S of Moon (Occn.)
22	08	Solstice
22	11	Moon at perigee
22	18	FULL MOON
28	20	Juno in conjunction with Sun
29	14	LAST QUARTER

Conversion of Universal Time (U.T.) to Civil Time

U.T.	E.D.T.[1]	E.S.T.[2]	C.S.T.[3]	M.S.T.[4]	P.S.T.[5]
00	*8P	*7P	*6P	*5P	*4P
01	*9P	*8P	*7P	*6P	*5P
02	*10P	*9P	*8P	*7P	*6P
03	*11P	*10P	*9P	*8P	*7P
04	M	*11P	*10P	*9P	*8P
05	1A	M	*11P	*10P	*9P
06	2A	1A	M	*11P	*10P
07	3A	2A	1A	M	*11P
08	4A	3A	2A	1A	M
09	5A	4A	3A	2A	1A
10	6A	5A	4A	3A	2A
11	7A	6A	5A	4A	3A
12	8A	7A	6A	5A	4A
13	9A	8A	7A	6A	5A
14	10A	9A	8A	7A	6A
15	11A	10A	9A	8A	7A
16	N	11A	10A	9A	8A
17	1P	N	11A	10A	9A
18	2P	1P	N	11A	10A
19	3P	2P	1P	N	11A
20	4P	3P	2P	1P	N
21	5P	4P	3P	2P	1P
22	6P	5P	4P	3P	2P
23	7P	6P	5P	4P	3P

1. Eastern Daylight Time. 2. Eastern Standard Time, same as Central Daylight Time. 3. Central Standard Time, same as Mountain Daylight Time. 4. Mountain Standard Time, same as Pacific Daylight Time. 5. Pacific Standard Time. NOTES: * denotes previous day. N = noon. M = midnight.

Eclipses of the Sun and Moon, 1999

Note: The day of an eclipse is given in Universal Time (U.T.) and may start a day earlier or later depending on your time zone. (*See* Phenomena, 1999 table to find time of eclipse in your area.)

January 31. Penumbral eclipse of the Moon. The beginning phase is visible in most of Asia, Australia, New Zealand, part of Antarctica (Wilkes Land), Hawaii, western United States, western Canada, the Arctic region, the Indian Ocean, except the extreme western part, most of the North Pacific Ocean, the western South Pacific Ocean, and the Arctic Ocean; the end is visible in Africa, except the northwestern coast, Europe, Greenland, except the extreme southern part, Asia, Australia, Alaska, except the southeastern part, the Arctic region, Antarctica (Wilkes Land), the extreme eastern Atlantic Ocean, the Indian Ocean, the western North Pacific Ocean, the extreme western South Pacific Ocean, and the Arctic Ocean.

February 16. Annular eclipse of the Sun. Visible in the South Atlantic Ocean, south of Africa, Indian Ocean, Indonesia, Malaysia, south of the Philippines, Antarctica, and Australasia.

July 28. Partial eclipse of the Moon. The beginning of the Umbral phase is visible along the northeastern coast of Asia, and in Japan, Australia, New Zealand, Hawaii, North America, except the northeastern part, western South America, Central America, most of Antarctica, the southeastern Indian Ocean, and the Pacific Ocean; the end is visible in extreme eastern Asia, Australia, New Zealand, Hawaii, extreme western North America, Antarctica, the eastern Indian Ocean, the North Pacific Ocean, and the South Pacific Ocean, except the extreme eastern part.

August 11. Total eclipse of the Sun. Visible in the northeastern part of the United States and eastern Canada, the North Atlantic Ocean, Europe, including the British Isles, North Africa, Asia, except the eastern part, and the North Indian Ocean.

Orbiting Infrared Telescope Planned

Work began in spring 1998 on the design and development phase of NASA's new Space Infrared Telescope Facility (SIRTF), an advanced orbiting observatory that will give astronomers unprecedented views of phenomena in the universe that are invisible to other types of telescopes.

Conventional optical telescopes can study stars and other objects that glow brightly enough to emit light in the visible portion of the electromagnetic spectrum. However, many objects, such as planets and unignited stars, do not "shine" in visible or ultraviolet light. Others that may burn brightly are veiled from Earth's view behind vast clouds of dust and gas that populate the universe. Most of these concealed attractions are detectable only with infrared telescopes whose unique capability lies in their ability to sense the heat of dark, faint, or hidden objects.

SIRTF is expected to do for infrared astronomy what the Hubble Space Telescope has done in its unveiling of the visible universe. It is scheduled for launch on a Delta rocket from Cape Canaveral in December 2001.

DECLINATION OF SUN AND PLANETS, 1999

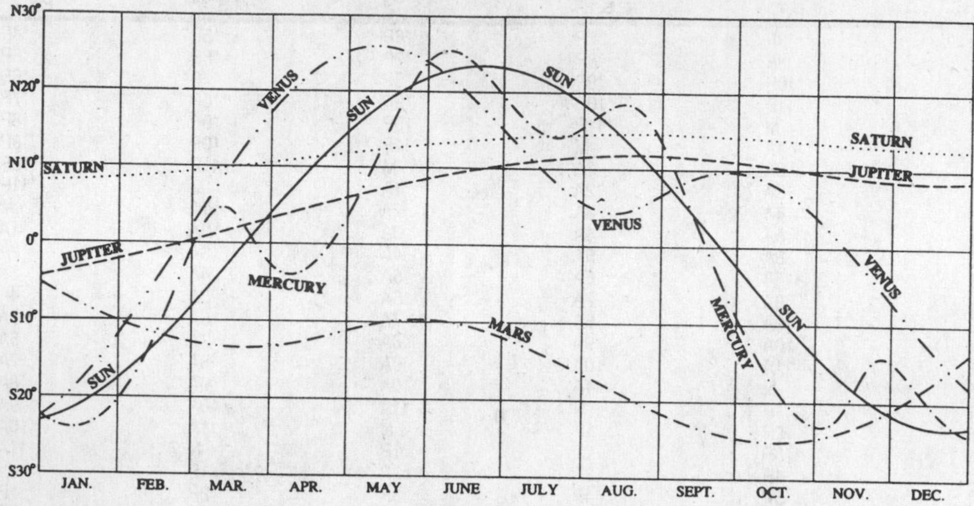

The Visibility of the Planets, 1999

Mercury can only be seen low in the east before sunrise, or low in the west after sunset (about the time of the beginning or end of civil twilight). It is visible in the mornings between the following approximate dates: January 1 to January 21, March 27 to May 18, August 4 to August 31, and November 22 to December 30. The planet is brighter at the end of each period (the best conditions in northern latitudes occur during late November and early December, and in southern latitudes from early April to early May). It is visible in the evenings between the following approximate dates: February 16 to March 12, June 2 to July 18, and September 20 to November 10. The planet is brighter at the beginning of each period (the best conditions in northern latitudes occur during late February and early March, and in southern latitudes in the second half of October). Mercury transits the Sun's disk on November 15 from 21 hr., 15 min., to 22 hr., 07 min.; the event is visible from South America except the extreme east, North America except the northeast of Canada, the extreme eastern part of Asia, Pacific Ocean, Hawaii, North Island of New Zealand, north Australia, Papua New Guinea, and east Indonesia.

Venus is a brilliant object in the evening sky from the beginning of the year until mid-August when it becomes too close to the Sun for observation. During the last week of August it reappears in the morning sky where it stays until the end of the year. Venus is in conjunction with Jupiter on February 23, with Saturn on March 20, and with Mercury on August 26.

Mars rises around midnight at the beginning of the year, in Virgo (passing 4° N of *Spica* on January 8), moving into Libra in mid-February and into Virgo again after mid-April. It is at opposition on April 24 when it is visible throughout the night. Its eastward elongation gradually decreases, moving into Libra in late July, Scorpius in early September, and Ophiucus in mid-September (passing 3° N of *Antares* on September 17). It then continues into Sagittarius after mid-October and into Capricornus from late November.

Jupiter can be seen at the beginning of the year in the evening sky in Aquarius, moving into Pisces during the second half of January and into Cetus for a few days from mid-March after which it becomes too close to the Sun for observation. It reappears in the morning sky from mid-April in Pisces and moves into Aries in early July. Its westward elongation gradually increases and from late July it can be seen for more than half the night. It is at opposition on October 23 when it is visible throughout the night. Its eastward elongation gradually decreases and after mid-October it passes into Pisces, in which constellation it remains for the rest of the year. Jupiter is in conjunction with Venus on February 23 and with Mercury on May 1.

Saturn is in Pisces, and can be seen in the evening sky from mid-January. It moves into Cetus in late March and into Aries from early April, in which constellation it remains for the rest of the year. It becomes too close to the Sun for observation during the second week of April, reappearing in the morning sky from mid-May. Its westward elongation gradually increases and is at opposition on November 6 when it is visible throughout the night. Its eastward elongation then gradually decreases and for the rest of the year it can be seen for more than half the night. Saturn is in conjunction with Venus on March 20 and with Mercury on May 13.

Uranus is visible as an evening star for the first half of January in Capricornus and remains in this constellation throughout the year. It then becomes too close to the Sun for observation until late February, when it reappears in the morning sky. It is at opposition on August 7 and from early November it can only be seen in the evening sky.

Neptune is visible as an evening star for the first half of January in Capricornus and remains in this constellation throughout the year. It then becomes too close to the Sun for observation until mid-February, when it reappears in the morning sky. It is at opposition on July 26 and from late October it can only be seen in the evening sky.

Do not confuse (1) Venus with Jupiter during the second half of February and with Saturn around mid-March when Venus is the brighter object. (2) Jupiter with Mercury in the first half of March and late April to early May when Jupiter is the brighter object. (3) Saturn with Mercury in mid-May when Mercury is the brighter object. □

Visibility of Planets in Morning and Evening Twilight

Morning		Evening	
Venus	August 25–December 31	Venus	January 1–August 16
Mars	January 1–April 24	Mars	April 24–December 31
Jupiter	April 15–October 23	Jupiter	January 1–March 18 October 23–December 31
Saturn	May 16–November 6	Saturn	January 1–April 10 November 6–December 31

The New Uranian Moons

In April 1998, astronomers confirmed their findings of two new small icy moons orbiting the planet Uranus, raising the total of Uranus's satellites from 15 to 17. Their proposed names, Caliban and Sycorax, need final approval by the International Astronomical Union (IAU). Until the IAU gives their approval sometime in August 2000, the official designations are Uranus XVI for Caliban and Uranus XVII for Sycorax. The objects were first detected in September 1997, and announced October 31, 1997.

The 15 previously known moons of Uranus traveled along on fairly evenly spaced and nearly circular equatorial orbits that lie close to the planet. Caliban and Sycorax are the first Uranian satellites discovered to have irregular or non-circular orbits around the planet.

Caliban, the smaller of the two moons, has a diameter of 37 miles (60 kilometers) and is orbiting the planet at an average distance of about 4.5 million miles (7.2 million kilometers), taking 1.6 years to complete one revolution.

Sycorax has an estimated diameter of 74.5 miles (120 kilometers) and takes 3.5 years to complete one orbit of Uranus at a mean distance of about 7.5 million miles (12.2 kilometers). Sycorax has a much more elliptical orbit that Caliban, bringing it as close as 3.7 million miles (6 million kilometers) to the planet.

The composition of both moons is probably a "plum-pudding" mixture of rocks and ice. The two moons are unusually red in color. This suggests a connection to recently discovered populations of comet-like bodies called trans-Neptunian objects, which orbit the Sun beyond the orbit of Neptune, and Centaurs, which cross the orbits of outer planets.

Both trans-Neptunians and Centaurs have a wide range of reddish colors, perhaps resulting from the bombardment of their organic-rich icy surfaces. This bombardment could come from cosmic rays or from the Sun's ultraviolet radiation. The methane on the moon's surfaces would be "cooked" by the radiation into hydrocarbons, showing up as a dark red through a telescope's filters. The newly discovered moons are presumed to have been captured by Uranus early in the history of the solar system.

Moons of Uranus are traditionally named after characters in the works of Shakespeare and Alexander Pope. Caliban is a character from Shakespeare's play *The Tempest,* a savage and deformed slave who is the son of the witch Sycorax. One of the larger Uranian planets is already named after a character from *The Tempest*—the fairy sprite Ariel.

The Search for Life on Europa

NASA's Galileo spacecraft is quietly studying one of the most interesting objects in the solar system, Jupiter's fourth moon, Europa. Slightly smaller than Earth's Moon, Europa is one of only four moons in the solar system with an atmosphere. More importantly, scientific data suggest an ocean of slush and water—as deep as 50 km—lies below Europa's icy surface. If such an ocean exists, Europa is one of the few places in the solar system where life may be possible.

Large portions of Europa's surface appear very similar to ice floes near the North Pole of Earth. Thousands of dark lines that resemble fault lines on Earth criss-cross the entire surface of Europa, separating the crust into plates. Scientists believe these lines result because water from below fills the fractures when the surface crust separates and then freezes into place.

If there is water there is a chance for life, however small, to exist. Most likely these would only be primitive forms of life, but discovery of living organisms in any form would cause a universal change in human understanding in the evolution and creation of life. The importance of such a discovery is why NASA is now concentrating its efforts into probing potential spots for life in the solar system.

Major Space Explorations

Ongoing Missions

Galileo (U.S.)

Destination: Jupiter. **Launch:** Oct. 18, 1989. **Achieved Orbit:** Dec. 7, 1995. **Mission:** To study the chemical composition and physical state of the largest planet in the solar system, its atmosphere, and four of its moons, for almost two years. The spacecraft encountered the asteroid 951 Gaspera on Oct. 29, 1991, and took the first close-up photographs ever of an asteroid in space. On Aug. 28, 1993, it passed by asteroid 243 Ida and took close-up photographs, which revealed that Ida has a tiny moon. Upon arrival at Jupiter, *Galileo* released a probe into the planet's atmosphere that descended for 57 minutes before it was destroyed by the planet's extreme temperature and pressure. In 1996, *Galileo* visited and photographed Jupiter's large moons Io, Callisto, and Europa and made fly-bys of Io, Ganymede, Europa, and Callisto in 1997. *Galileo* was named for the Italian astronomer Galileo Galilei, who discovered the four great moons of Jupiter that were the major targets of this mission.

Galileo Europa Mission (GEM): A two-year continuation of the original Galileo Mission, which was completed at the end of 1997. GEM will include eight more fly-bys of Europa through February 1999 and one or two fly-bys of Io in late 1999, as long as the spacecraft remains healthy.

Ulysses (U.S. and European Space Agency)

Destination: The Sun. **Launch:** Oct. 6, 1990. **Flew by Jupiter, released probe:** Feb. 8, 1992. **Achieved Orbit at South Pole:** September 1994. **Achieved Orbit at North Pole:** October 1995. **Mission:** An international project to study the Sun and interstellar space above and below its poles. The spacecraft was put into orbit at right angles to the solar system's ecliptic plane. This special orbit enabled *Ulysses* to examine for the first time the Sun's north and south polar regions. Besides investigating the Sun, the spacecraft is also studying phenomena from the Milky Way and beyond. The spacecraft completed its first full orbit around the Sun on April 17, 1998. *Ulysses* will continue to orbit the Sun and will pass over the north and south poles again in 2000 and 2001.

Near-Earth Asteroid Rendezvous (NEAR) (U.S.):

Destination: Asteroid 433 Eros. **Launched:** Feb. 17, 1996. **Arrival:** February 1999. **Mission:** To rendezvous with Eros and orbit the asteroid for almost one year. It will take comprehensive measurements of its surface, size, volume, mass, spin, and magnetic field. *NEAR* passed by and photographed minor planet 253 Mathilde on June 27, 1997.

Mars Global Surveyor (U.S.)

Launch: Nov. 7, 1996. **Arrival:** Sept. 11, 1997. **Mission:** An orbiting spacecraft designed to provide detailed maps of the planet's surface and distribution of minerals, and to monitor the Martian weather. Six instruments will study Martian surface, atmosphere, and gravitational and magnetic fields. *Surveyor*'s cameras will be able to distinguish features as small as 10 feet across.

Mapping operations began on March 27, 1998, and will continue until January 2000. The spacecraft will orbit Mars for 687 days, the length of one Martian year.

Lunar Prospector (U.S.)

Destination: Earth's moon. **Launch:** Jan. 6, 1998. **Arrival:** Jan 11, 1998. **Mission:** To fly in a low-polar orbit around the Moon for at least one year and map the chemical composition of the lunar surface, possible polar ice deposits, and its global magnetic and gravitational fields. The spacecraft detected signs of large amounts of frozen water at the Moon's north pole. *Prospector's* mission may be extended six months to obtain more detailed images at a lower altitude.

Cassini (U.S. and the European Space Agency)

Destination: Saturn. **Launch:** Oct. 6, 1997. **Arrival:** June 2004. **Mission:** Will orbit Saturn for four years. Before reaching Saturn, *Cassini* will encounter Jupiter and fly down the giant planet's magnetotail, performing studies complementing the Galileo Mission. While orbiting Saturn, *Cassini* will send a small probe named *Huygens* (after the Dutch astronomer Christiaan Huygens, who discovered Titan) to the surface of Saturn's largest moon, Titan, to learn more about its dense atmosphere and its surface state and composition. After relaying data to Earth from Titan, *Cassini* will continue with orbits of Saturn and fly-bys of the planet's 16 or more moons. The spacecraft will also examine Saturn's equatorial zone and study the planet's polar regions. The Cassini mission is named for the Italian-French astronomer Gian Domenico Cassini who discovered four of Saturn's major moons.

Planet-B (Japan)

Launch: July 4, 1998, from Kagoshima Space Center. **Arrival:** October 1999. **Mission:** To send an orbiter around Mars to study the effect of the solar wind on the planet's atmosphere for one Martian year (687 days). Its cameras will provide photographic data on cloud distribution, polar haze, dust storms, polar ice, and the planet's surface. After its successful launch, the spacecraft was renamed *Nazomi* (hope). Japan's new effort made it the third nation after the United States and Russia to conduct a mission to another planet.

Future Missions

(Note: Dates are tentative)

Mars Surveyor '98 (U.S.)

Launch: *Orbiter*—Dec. 10, 1998; *Lander*—January 1999. Two spacecraft will be launched separately but will compose a single mission. **Arrival:** *(Mars Surveyor Orbiter)*—Sept. 24, 1999; *(Mars Surveyor Lander)*—Dec. 3, 1999. **Mission:** Dual spacecraft will study the planet's weather-related changes in the atmosphere and on the surface. The *Mars Surveyor Lander* will be the first probe to land in the polar region of Mars. It will photograph the surface of the south polar region as it descends. After landing, it will deploy a package of stereo cameras, and analyze soil samples with a robotic arm. The lander will carry a microphone, funded by the Planetary Society, to detect sounds on Mars.

The lander will also carry two microprobes that will plunge into the Martian surface prior to the spacecraft's entry into the planet's atmosphere. The probes can detect subsurface water.

Stardust (U.S.) Comet Wild 2

Launch: February 6, 1999. **Mission:** To fly through coma of Comet Wild 2 in 2004, capture particles spewing out of comet, and return comet dust samples to Earth in 2006. Will be the first sample return mission. Enroute to comet, the spacecraft will also collect particles from the interstellar dust stream.

Deep Space 1 (U.S.)

Launch: October 1999. **Mission:** First launch of NASA's New Millennium program, a series of missions to test new technologies so they can be used on science missions of the 21st century. Will fly past near-Earth asteroid 1992 KD and take close-up pictures and other measurements. Mission may be upgraded to obtaining images and data from further targets such as another asteroid or a planet.

Genesis (U.S.)

Launch: January 2001. **Mission:** Gather and return samples of charged particles of the solar wind and return them to Earth in August 2003 for detailed analysis. Reentry vehicle will separate from spacecraft and parachute its sample return capsule to a location in the Utah desert. The data to be obtained are crucial for improving theories about the origin of the Sun and planets that formed from the same primordial dust cloud.

Mars Surveyor 2001 (U.S.)

Launch: *Orbiter*—March 2001; *Lander*—April 2001. **Arrival:** *(Mars Surveyor Orbiter)*—December 2001; *(Mars Lander)*—January 2002. **Mission:** The *Mars Surveyor 2001 Orbiter* will conduct mineralogical mapping of the entire planet and characterize its orbital radiation environment. The mission was to include a rover, but it was cancelled due to prohibitive costs. New plans call for placing a lander on the surface to conduct scientific experiments.

Future Mars Surveyors

Launch: 2003, 2005. **Missions**: Small orbiters will capitalize on the experience of the Mars *Pathfinder* lander mission and will serve as relay stations for international missions of the future. A hi-tech rover that will be capable of traveling long distances is under construction for use in the 2003 mission.

A search for water is being considered in 2001, and another planned mission will have a rover investigate an ancient highland bed to study the climate history of the planet. The *Mars Surveyor 2005* mission will be an attempt to bring back a sample of Martian rocks and soil.

Contour (U.S.) Comet Nucleus Tour

Launch: July 2002. **Mission:** To fly by Comet Encke at 60 miles (100 kilometers), followed by encounters with Comet Schwassmann-Wachmann-3 in June 2006, and Comet d'Arrest in August 2008. The spacecraft will take images and spectral maps of nuclei and analyze dust flowing from them. The mission will help scientists to learn more about the composition and structure of comets, which are believed to be quite individual in their properties.

Selene (Japan) SELenological and Engineering Explorer

Launch: 2003. **Mission:** An orbiting spacecraft to study the origin and evolution of the Moon for one year. It will map the entire surface and gather data on chemical and mineralogical composition, magnetic fields, and interior structure. After a year, the propulsion module of the orbiter will separate from the spacecraft and soft land on the lunar surface to continue the mission for two more months.

U.S. Unstaffed Planetary and Lunar Programs

Lunar Orbiter. Series of spacecraft designed to orbit the Moon, taking pictures and obtaining data in support of the subsequent staffed *Apollo* landings. The U.S. launched five *Lunar Orbiters* between Aug. 10, 1966 and Aug. 2, 1967.

Mariner. Designation for a series of spacecraft designed to fly past or orbit the planets, particularly Mercury, Venus, and Mars. *Mariners* provided the early information on Venus and Mars. *Mariner 9*, orbiting Mars in 1971, returned the most startling photographs of that planet and helped pave the way for a *Viking* landing in 1976. *Mariner 10* explored Venus and Mercury in 1973 and was the first probe to use a planet's gravity to propel it toward another.

Space Web Sites

NASA homepage: www.nasa.gov
Space Shuttle homepage: shuttle.nasa.gov/
International Space Station: station.nasa.gov
Mir Space Station: www.hq.nasa.gov/osf/mir
National Space Society: www.nss.org/
The Planetary Society: planetary.org
European Space Agency (ESA): www.esrin.esa.it/
SETI Institute: www.seti-inst.edu/
Project Galileo: galileo.ivv.nasa.gov
Lunar Prospector: lunar.arc.nasa.gov
Mars Global Surveyor: mars.jpl.nasa.gov

Pioneer. Designation for the United States' first series of sophisticated interplanetary spacecraft. *Pioneers 10* and *11* reached Jupiter in 1973 and 1974 and continued on to explore Saturn and the other outer planets. *Pioneer 11,* renamed *Pioneer Saturn,* examined the Saturn system in September 1979. Significant discoveries were the finding of a small new moon and a narrow new ring. In 1986, *Pioneer 10* was the first man-made object to escape the solar system. *Pioneer Venus 1* and *2* reached Venus in 1978 and provided detailed information about that planet's surface and atmosphere.

Ranger. NASA's earliest Moon-exploration program. Spacecraft were designed for a crash landing on the Moon, taking pictures and returning scientific data up to the moment of impact. Provided the first close-up views of the lunar surface. The *Rangers* provided more than 17,000 close-up pictures, giving us more information about the Moon in a few years than in all the time that had gone before.

Surveyor. Series of unstaffed spacecraft designed to land gently on the Moon and provide information on the surface in preparation for the staffed lunar landings. Their legs were instrumented to return data on the surface hardness of the Moon. *Surveyor* dispelled the fear that *Apollo* spacecraft might sink several feet or more into the lunar dust.

Viking. Designation for two spacecraft designed to conduct detailed scientific examination of the planet Mars, including a search for life. *Viking 1* landed on July 20, 1976; *Viking 2,* Sept. 3, 1976. More was learned about the red planet in a few short months than in all previous missions, but the question of whether there is life on Mars remains unresolved.

Voyager. Designation for two spacecraft designed to explore Jupiter and the other outer planets. *Voyager 1* and *Voyager 2* passed Jupiter in 1979 and sent back surprising color TV images of that planet and its moons. They took a total of about 33,000 pictures. *Voyager 1* passed Saturn in November 1980. *Voyager 2* passed Saturn in August 1981 and Uranus in January 1986.

It encountered Neptune on Aug. 29, 1989, and made many discoveries. It found four rings around the planet, six new moons, a giant spot, and evidence of volcanic-like activity on its largest moon, Triton. The spacecraft sent back over 9,000 pictures of the planet and its system.

On Feb. 13, 1990, at a distance of 3.7 billion miles, *Voyager 1* took its final pictures—the Sun and six of its planets as seen from deep space. NASA released the extraordinary images to the public on June 6, 1990. Only Mercury, Mars, and Pluto were not seen.

Notable Unstaffed Lunar and Interplanetary Probes

Spacecraft	Launch date	Destination	Remarks
Pioneer 3 (U.S.)	Dec. 6, 1958	Moon	Max. alt.: 66,654 mi. Discovered outer Van Allen layer.
Luna 2 (U.S.S.R.)	Sept. 12, 1959	Moon	Impacted on Sept. 14. First space vehicle to reach Moon.
Luna 3 (U.S.S.R.)	Oct. 4, 1959	Moon	Flew around Moon and transmitted first pictures of lunar far side, Oct. 7.
Mariner 2 (U.S.)	Aug. 27, 1962	Venus	Venus probe. Successful mid-course correction. Passed 21,648 mi. from Venus Dec. 14, 1962. Reported 800°F. surface temp. Contact lost Jan. 3, 1963, at 54 million mi.
Mariner 4 (U.S.)	Nov. 28, 1964	Mars	Transmitted first close-up pictures on June 14, 1965, from altitude of 6,000 mi.
Ranger 7 (U.S.)	July 28, 1964	Moon	Impacted near Crater Guericke 68.5 hr. after launch. Sent 4,316 pictures during last 15 min. of flight as close as 1,000 ft. above lunar surface.
Luna 9 (U.S.S.R.)	Jan. 31, 1966	Moon	3,428 lb. Instrument capsule of 220 lb. soft-landed Feb. 3, 1966. Sent back about 30 pictures.
Surveyor 1 (U.S.)	May 30, 1966	Moon	Landed June 2, 1966. Sent almost 10,400 pictures, a number after surviving the 14-day lunar night.
Lunar Orbiter 1 (U.S.)	Aug. 10, 1966	Moon	Orbited moon Aug. 14. 21 pictures sent.
Surveyor 3 (U.S.)	April 17, 1967	Moon	Soft-landed 65 hr. after launch on Oceanus Procellarum. Scooped and tested lunar soil.
Venera 4 (U.S.S.R.)	June 12, 1967	Venus	Arrived Oct. 17. Instrument capsule sent temperature and chemical data.
Surveyor 5 (U.S.)	Sept. 8, 1967	Moon	Landed near lunar equator Sept. 10. Radiological analysis of lunar soil. Mechanical claw for digging soil.
Surveyor 7 (U.S.)	Jan. 6, 1968	Moon	Landed near Crater Tycho Jan. 10. Soil analysis. Sent 3,343 pictures.
Pioneer 9 (U.S.)	Nov. 8, 1968	Sun orbit	Achieved orbit. Six experiments returned solar radiation data.
Venera 5 (U.S.S.R.)	Jan. 5, 1969	Venus	Landed May 16, 1969. Returned atmospheric data.
Mariner 6 (U.S.)	Feb. 24, 1969	Mars	Came within 2000 mi. of Mars July 31, 1969. Sent back data & TV pictures.
Luna 16 (U.S.S.R.)	Sept. 12, 1970	Moon	Soft-landed Sept. 20, scooped up rock, returned to Earth Sept. 24.
Luna 17 (U.S.S.R.)	Nov. 10, 1970	Moon	Soft-landed on Sea of Rains Nov. 17. *Lunokhod 1,* self-propelled vehicle, used for first time. Sent TV photos, made soil analysis, etc.

Spacecraft	Launch date	Destination	Remarks
Mariner 9 (U.S.)	May 30, 1971	Mars	First craft to orbit Mars, Nov. 13. 7,300 pictures, 1st close-ups of one of Mars' moons. Transmission ended Oct. 27, 1972.
Luna 20 (U.S.S.R.)	Feb. 14, 1972	Moon	Soft-landed Feb. 21 in Sea of Fertility. Returned Feb. 25 with rock samples.
Pioneer 10 (U.S.)	March 3, 1972	Jupiter	620-million-mile flight path through asteroid belt passed Jupiter Dec. 3, 1973, to give man first close-up of planet. In 1986, it became first man-made object to escape solar system.
Luna 21 (U.S.S.R.)	Jan. 8, 1973	Moon	Soft-landed Jan. 16. *Lunokhod 2* (moon-car) scooped up soil samples, returned them to Earth Jan. 27.
Mariner 10 (U.S.)	Nov. 3, 1973	Venus, Mercury	Passed Venus Feb. 5, 1974. Arrived Mercury March 29, 1974, for man's first close-up look at planet. First time gravity of one planet (Venus) used to propel spacecraft toward another (Mercury).
Viking 1 (U.S.)	Aug. 20, 1975	Mars	Carrying life-detection labs. Landed July 20, 1976, for detailed scientific research, including pictures. Designed to work for only 90 days, it operated for almost 6½ years before it went silent in November 1982.
Viking 2 (U.S.)	Sept. 9, 1975	Mars	Like Viking 1. Landed Sept. 3, 1976. Functioned 3½ years.
Luna 24 (U.S.S.R.)	Aug. 9, 1976	Moon	Soft-landed Aug. 18, 1976. Returned soil samples Aug. 22, 1976.
Voyager 1 (U.S.)	Sept. 5, 1977	Jupiter, Saturn	Fly-by mission. Reached Jupiter in March 1979; passed Saturn November 1980; passed Uranus 1986.
Voyager 2 (U.S.)	Aug. 20, 1977	Jupiter, Saturn, Uranus	Launched before *Voyager 1*. Encountered Jupiter in July 1979; flew by Saturn August 1981; passed Uranus January 1986; and passed Neptune in August 1989.
Pioneer Venus 1 (U.S.)	May 20, 1978	Venus	Arrived Dec. 4 and orbited Venus, photographing surface and atmosphere. Crashed into planet's surface mid-October 1992 after circling Venus for 14 years.
Pioneer Venus 2 (U.S.)	Aug. 8, 1978	Venus	Four part multiprobe, landed Dec. 9.
Venera 13 (U.S.S.R.)	Oct. 30, 1981	Venus	Landed March 1, 1982. Took first X-ray fluorescence analysis of the planet's surface. Transmitted data 2 hours 7 minutes.
VEGA 1 (U.S.S.R.)	Deployed on Venus, June 10, 1985	Halley's Comet	In fly-by over Venus while en route to encounter Halley's Comet, *VEGA 1* and *2* dropped scientific capsules onto Venus to study atmosphere and surface material. Encountered Halley's Comet on March 6 and March 9, 1986. Took TV pictures and studied comet's dust particles.
VEGA 2 (U.S.S.R.)	Deployed on Venus, June 14, 1985	Halley's Comet	See *VEGA 1* above.
Suisei (Japan)	Encountered Halley's Comet March 8, 1986	Halley's Comet	Spacecraft made fly-by of comet and studied atmosphere with ultraviolet camera. Observed rotation nucleus.
Sakigake (Japan)	Encountered Halley's Comet March 10, 1986	Halley's Comet	Spacecraft made fly-by to study solar wind and magnetic fields. Detected plasma waves.
Giotto (E.S.A.)	Encountered Halley's Comet March 13, 1986	Halley's Comet	European Space Agency spacecraft made closest approach to comet. Studied atmosphere and magnetic fields. Sent back best pictures of nucleus. Flew by comet Grigg-Skjellerup July 10, 1992. Unable to send pictures.
Phobos Mission (U.S.S.R.)	July 7 and July 12, 1988	Mars and Phobos	Two spacecraft to probe Martian moon Phobos starting April 1989. Were to study orbit, soil chemistry, send TV pictures and data of planet. Contact was lost with *Phobos 1* in August 1988 and later with *Phobos 2* in March 1989 after it reached the Martian moon.
Magellan (U.S.)	May 4, 1989	Venus	Arrived at Venus on Aug. 10, 1990 and made a geologic map of planet with a powerful radar. Crashed into Venus Oct. 12, 1994.
Galileo (U.S.)	Oct. 18, 1989	Jupiter	To study Jupiter's atmosphere and its moons during 22-month mission.

Spacecraft	Launch date	Destination	Remarks
Hubble Space Telescope (U.S., E.S.A.)	April 25, 1990	Earth orbit	Studies distant stars and galaxies and searches for evidence of planets in other solar systems. The telescope was repaired by space-shuttle crews in December 1993 and February 1997.
Ulysses (U.S., E.S.A.)	Oct. 6, 1990	Sun	To study the poles of the sun and interstellar space above and below the poles. First solar encounter was in 1994, second encounter in 1995.
Gamma-Ray Observatory (U.S.)	April 7, 1991	Earth orbit	To make first survey of gamma-ray sources across the whole sky, studying explosive energic sources such as supernovae, quasars, neutron stars, pulsars, and black holes.
Mars *Observer* (U.S.)	Sept. 25, 1992	Mars	Spacecraft was to arrive at Mars August 1993 and orbit the planet for one full Martian year to study atmosphere and surface change during the planet's seasons. Mission failed after communications with *Observer* lost Aug. 21, 1993.
Clementine (U.S.)	Jan. 25, 1994	Moon and asteroid Geographos 1620	Entered lunar orbit February 21 and took close-up photos of lunar surface for two months. Computer malfunction prevented planned rendezvous with *Geographos.*
Mars Pathfinder (U.S.)	Dec. 5, 1996	Ares Vallis, Mars	Landed July 4, 1997. The spacecraft lander and its rover, *Sojourner,* provided a wealth of information on the Martian rocks, soil, and atmosphere. Sent back the first live pictures. All *Pathfinder's* objectives were fulfilled and communications failed on Sept. 27, 1997.

U.S. Staffed Space Flights

Mercury. *Project Mercury,* initiated in 1958 and completed in 1963, was the United States' first human-in-space program. It was designed to further knowledge about humanity's capabilities in space.

In April 1959, seven military-jet test pilots were introduced to the public as America's first astronauts. They were: Lt. M. Scott Carpenter, USN; Capt. L. Gordon Cooper, Jr., USAF; Lt. Col. John H. Glenn, Jr., USMC; Cap. Virgil I. Grissom, USAF; Lt. Cdr. Walter M. Schirra, Jr., USN; Lt. Cdr. Alan B. Shepard, Jr., USN; and Capt. Donald K. Slayton, USAF. Six of the original seven would make a Mercury flight. Slayton was grounded for medical reasons, but remained a director of the astronaut office. He returned to flight status in 1975 as Docking Module Pilot on the *Apollo-Soyuz* flight.

Flight Summary

Each astronaut named his capsule and added the numeral 7 to denote the teamwork of the original astronauts.

May 5, 1961. Alan B. Shepard, Jr., made a suborbital flight in *Freedom 7* and became the first American in space. Time: 15 minutes, 22 seconds.

July 21, 1961. Virgil I. Grissom made the second successful suborbital flight in *Liberty Bell 7,* but spacecraft sank shortly after splashdown. Time: 15 minutes, 37 seconds. Grissom was later killed in *Apollo 1* fire, Jan. 27, 1967.

February 20, 1962. John H. Glenn, Jr., made a three-orbit flight and became the first American in orbit. Time: 4 hours, 55 minutes.

May 24, 1962. M. Scott Carpenter duplicated Glenn's flight in *Aurora 7.* Time: 4 hours, 56 minutes.

October 3, 1962. Walter M. Schirra, Jr., made a six-orbit engineering test flight in *Sigma 7.* Time: 9 hours, 13 minutes.

May 15–16, 1963. L. Gordon Cooper, Jr., performed the last *Mercury* mission and completed 22 orbits in *Faith 7* to evaluate effects of one day in space. Time: 34 hours, 19 minutes.

Gemini. *Gemini* was an extension of *Project Mercury,* to determine the effects of prolonged space flight on humans for two weeks or longer—the time it would take to reach the Moon and return. "Walks in space" provided invaluable information for astronauts' later walks on the Moon. The *Gemini* spacecraft, twice as large as the *Mercury* capsule, accommodated two astronauts. Its crew named the project *Gemini* for the third constellation of the Zodiac and its twin stars, Castor and Pollux. The capsule differed from the *Mercury* spacecrafts in that it had hatches above the capsules so that the astronauts could leave the spacecraft and perform spacewalks or extra-vehicular activities (EVAs).

There were 10 staffed flights in the *Gemini* program, starting with *Gemini 3* on March 23, 1965, and ending with the *Gemini 12* mission on Nov. 15, 1966. *Gemini 1* and *2* were unstaffed test flights of the equipment.

When the *Gemini* program ended, U.S. astronauts had perfected rendezvous and docking maneuvers with other orbiting vehicles.

Apollo. *Apollo* was the designation for the United States' effort to land a person on the Moon and return him safely to Earth. The goal was successfully accomplished with *Apollo 11* on July 20, 1969, culminating eight years of rehearsal and centuries of dreaming. Astronauts Neil A. Armstrong and Col. Edwin E. Aldrin, Jr., scooped up and brought back the first lunar rocks ever seen on Earth—about 47 pounds.

Tragedy struck Jan. 27, 1967, on the launch pad during a preflight test of what would have become *Apollo 1,* the first staffed mission. Astronauts Lt. Col. Virgil "Gus" Grissom, Lt. Col. Edward H.

White, and Lt. Cdr. Roger Chafee lost their lives when a fire swept through the command module.

Six *Apollo* flights followed, ending with *Apollo 17* in December 1972. The last three *Apollos* carried mechanized vehicles called lunar rovers for wide-ranging surface exploration of the Moon by astronauts. The rendezvous and docking of an *Apollo* spacecraft with a Russian *Soyuz* craft in Earth orbit on July 18, 1975, closed out the *Apollo* program.

During the Apollo project, the following 12 astronauts explored the lunar terrain: Col. Edwin E. "Buzz" Aldrin, Jr., and Neil A. Armstrong, *Apollo 11;* Cdr. Alan L. Bean and Cdr. Charles Conrad, Jr., *Apollo 12;* Edgar D. Mitchell and Alan B. Shepard (1923–1998), *Apollo 14;* Lt. Col. James B. Irwin (1930–1991) and Col. David R. Scott, *Apollo 15;* Col. Charles M. Duke, Jr., and Capt. John W. Young, *Apollo 16;* and Capt. Eugene A. Cernan and Dr. Harrison H. Schmitt, *Apollo 17*.

Apollo was a three-part spacecraft: the command module (CM), the crew's quarters and flight control section; the service modules (SM) for the propulsion and spacecraft support systems (when together, the two modules were called CSM); and the lunar module (LM) that took two of the crew to the lunar surface, supported them on the Moon, and returned them to the CSM in orbit. The crews that made the lunar flights where both command modules and lunar modules were involved selected call names for the vehicles. The call names for the spacecraft in the six lunar landing missions with the command module and lunar module designations respectively were:

Apollo 11, Columbia and *Eagle; Apollo 12, Yankee Clipper* and *Intrepid; Apollo 13**, *Odyssey* (CM) and *Aquarius* (LM); *Apollo 14, Kitty Hawk* and *Antares; Apollo 15, Endeavour* and *Falcon; Apollo 16, Casper* and *Orion;* and *Apollo 17, America* and *Challenger.*

*NOTE: The third lunar attempt, *Apollo 13,* April 11–17, 1970, 5 days, 22.9 hours, was aborted after the service module oxygen tank ruptured. The *Apollo 13* crew members were James A. Lovell, Jr., John L. Swigert, Jr., and Fred W. Haise, Jr. The mission was classified as a "successful failure," because the crew was rescued.

Skylab. America's first Earth-orbiting space station. *Project Skylab* was designed to demonstrate that men can work and live in space for prolonged periods without ill effects. Originally the spent third stage of a *Saturn 5* Moon rocket, *Skylab* measured 118 feet from stem to stern, and carried the most varied assortment of experimental equipment ever assembled in a single spacecraft. Three three-man crews visited the space stations, spending more than 740 hours observing the Sun and bringing home more than 175,000 solar pictures. These were the first recordings of solar activity above Earth's obscuring atmosphere. *Skylab* also evaluated systems designed to gather information on Earth's resources and environmental conditions. *Skylab*'s biomedical findings indicated that humans adapt well to space for at least a period of three months, provided they have a proper diet and adequately programmed exercise, sleep, work, and recreation periods. *Skylab* orbited Earth at a distance of about 300 miles. Five years after the last *Skylab* mission, the 77-ton space station's orbit began to deteriorate faster than expected, owing to unexpectedly high sunspot activity. On July 11, 1979, the parts of *Skylab* that did not burn up in the atmosphere came crashing down on parts of Australia and the Indian Ocean. No one was hurt.

Space Shuttle. The space shuttle *Columbia* was successfully launched on April 12, 1981. It made five flights (the first four were test runs), the last completed on Nov. 16, 1982. The second shuttle, *Challenger,* made its maiden flight on April 4, 1983. In April 1984, crew members of the *Challenger* captured, repaired, and returned the *Solar Max* satellite to orbit, making it the first time a disabled satellite had been repaired in space. The third shuttle, *Discovery,* made its first flight on Aug. 30, 1984. The fourth space shuttle, *Atlantis,* made its maiden flight on Oct. 3, 1985.

A tragedy occurred on Jan. 28, 1986, when the shuttle *Challenger* exploded, killing the crew of seven 73 seconds after takeoff. It was the world's worst space flight disaster.

The crew members who were killed were: Francis R. Scobee, shuttle commander; Cdr. Michael J. Smith, pilot; mission specialists Judith A. Resnik, Lt. Col. Ellison S. Onizuka, and Ronald E. McNair; and payload specialists Gregory B. Jarvis and Christa McAuliffe (who was to be the first civilian schoolteacher in space).

The cause of the explosion was a rupture in a seal on one of the booster rockets that let a jet of flame escape, igniting the fuel. The weakness in the seal was caused by the cold air temperature when the shuttle was launched.

NASA has estimated that the risk of a catastrophic failure is about 1 in 145 for each shuttle flight. Eventually, another disaster could occur.

The first U.S. space mission since the *Challenger* disaster was launched 32 months later, on Sept. 29, 1988, with the flight of *Discovery.* It had a crew of five and deployed a communications satellite.

The fifth and last orbiter, *Endeavour,* was built as a replacement for *Challenger.* It was named after the 16th-century British explorer James Cook's first ship. *Endeavour* was launched on its maiden voyage on May 7, 1992, with a crew of seven astronauts. They made four spacewalks and retrieved a disabled *Intelsat-6* communications satellite. During the mission, Dr. Kathryn Thornton became the second American woman to walk in space.

The shuttle *Columbia* spent a record 17 days, 15 hours in space, Nov. 19–Dec. 7, 1996.

The crew of the 50th mission aboard the *Endeavour,* launched Sept. 12, 1992, included the first black woman astronaut, Dr. Mae C. Jemison, and the first married couple to fly together in space, Air Force Lt. Col. Mark C. Lee and Dr. N. Jan Davis.

Lt. Col. Eileen M. Collins became the first woman to pilot a shuttle, *Discovery,* during the spacecraft's historic rendezvous with the Russian space station *Mir* on Feb. 6, 1995. The shuttle *Atlantis* made the first link-up with the *Mir* on June 29, 1995.

In March 1998, Lt. Col. Collins will become the first woman to command a space shuttle when *Columbia* is launched in January 1999 on a mission to deploy the Advanced X-ray Astrophysics Facility Imaging System (AXAF).

Senator John Glenn, 76, the first American in space, was selected by NASA in January 1998 to fly as a payload specialist on the October 1998 *Discovery* mission. He will study the effects of aging and microgravity on the human body.

Elementary schoolteacher Barbara Morgan, the woman who was the backup for Christa McAuliffe on the ill-fated *Challenger* mission, joined the astronaut candidate class of 1998 as an Educator Mission Specialist to prepare for a future shuttle mission in 2000.

Soviet Staffed Space Flight Programs

Vostok. The Soviets' first staffed capsule, roughly spherical, used to place the first six cosmonauts in Earth orbit (1961–65).

Voskhod. Adaptation of the *Vostok* capsule to accommodate two and three cosmonauts. *Voskhod 1* orbited three persons, and *Voskhod 2* orbited two persons, performing the world's first manned extravehicular activity.

Soyuz. Late-model manned spacecraft with provisions for three cosmonauts and a "working compartment" accessible through a hatch. Soyuz is the Russian word for "union." The *Soyuz* spacecraft can carry three cosmonauts, and routinely brings cosmonauts and their foreign "guests" to the *Mir* space station. *Soyuz 19,* launched July 15, 1975, docked with the American *Apollo* spacecraft.

Salyut. Earth-orbiting space station intended for prolonged occupancy and re-visitation by cosmonauts. They are usually launched by Soviet Proton rockets. *Salyut 1* was launched April 19, 1971. *Salyut 2,* launched April 3, 1973, malfunctioned in orbit and was never occupied. *Salyut 3* was launched June 25, 1974. *Salyut 4* was launched Dec. 26, 1974. *Salyut 5* was launched June 22, 1976. *Salyut 6* was launched on Sept. 29, 1977. *Salyut 7* was launched on April 19, 1982. A record breaking Russian endurance flight was set (Feb. 8, 1984–Oct. 2, 1985) when Soviet astronauts spent 237 days in orbit aboard *Salyut 7. Salyut 7* re-entered the atmosphere and crashed into the Atlantic Ocean on Feb. 6, 1991.

Mir. The former Soviet Union's space station was launched into orbit on Feb. 20, 1986. Since that time, several space endurance records have been set in the *Mir.* On Dec. 29, 1987, Col. Yuri Romanenko set a single-mission record of 326.5 days in space. On Dec. 21, 1989, Col. Vladimir Titov and Musa Manarov returned to Earth after spending 366 days aboard the orbiting space station. On March 22, 1995, Russian cosmonaut Valeriy Polyakov set a new record for the longest human flight in space—439 days. U.S. astronaut, Dr. Shannon W. Lucid set the American and women's space endurance records of 188 days and five hours aboard the *Mir* before returning to Earth on Sept. 26, 1996.

Over the past two years, the aging *Mir* has had a series of mishaps. The worst occurred on June 25, 1997, when an unmanned cargo ship collided with the station during docking tests. A solar array was damaged and the *Spektr* research module was punctured and lost its pressure. The *Spektr*'s electric cables prevented the module's hatch from closing and they were disconnected in order to close the hatch and seal off the depressurized *Spektr* from the rest of the station. This action caused the *Mir* to lose almost half its power.

During July 1998, the Russian government decided to make two final flights to the 12-year-old *Mir* before it is closed down, tentatively scheduled to be deorbited in July 1999. The aging space station will be given a slow, controlled reentry into Earth's lower atmosphere, where it will break-up harmlessly over the Pacific Ocean. In the meantime, the Russians are very gradually modifying the *Mir's* orbit so that it can be precisely guided into its final reentry phase by summer 1999. □

Notable Staffed Space Flights

Designation and country	Date	Astronauts	Flight time (hr./min)	Remarks
Vostok 1 (U.S.S.R.)	April 12, 1961	Yuri A. Gagarin	1/48	First manned orbital flight.
MR III (U.S.)	May 5, 1961	Alan B. Shepard, Jr.	0/15	Range 486 km (302 mi.), peak 187 km (116.5 mi); capsule recovered. First American in space.
Vostok 2 (U.S.S.R.)	Aug. 6–7, 1961	Gherman S. Titov	25/18	First long-duration flight.
MA VI (U.S.)	Feb. 20, 1962	John H. Glenn, Jr.	4/55	First American in orbit.
MA IX (U.S.)	May 15–16, 1963	L. Gordon Cooper, Jr.	34/20	Longest *Mercury* flight.
Vostok 6 (U.S.S.R.)	June 16–19, 1963	Valentina V. Tereshkova	70/50	First orbital flight by female cosmonaut.
Voskhod 1 (U.S.S.R.)	Oct. 12, 1964	Vladimir M. Komarov, Konstantin P. Feoktistov, Boris G. Yegorov	24/17	First 3-man orbital flight; also first flight without space suits.
Voskhod 2 (U.S.S.R.)	March 18, 1965	Alexei A. Leonov, Pavel I. Belyayev	26/2	First "space walk" (by Leonov), 10 min.
GT III (U.S.)	March 23, 1965	Virgil I. Grissom, John W. Young	4/53	First manned test of *Gemini* spacecraft.
GT IV (U.S.)	June 3–7, 1965	James A. McDivitt, Edward H. White, 2d	97/48	First American "space walk" (by White), lasting slightly over 20 min.
GT VIII (U.S.)	March 16–17, 1966	Neil A. Armstrong, David R. Scott	10/42	First docking between manned spacecraft and an unmanned space vehicle (an orbiting *Agena* rocket).

Designation and country	Date	Astronauts	Flight time (hr./min)	Remarks
Apollo 7 (U.S.)	Oct. 11–22, 1968	Walter M. Schirra, Jr., Donn F. Eisele, R. Walter Cunningham	260/9	First manned test of *Apollo* command module; first live TV transmissions from orbit.
Soyuz 3 (U.S.S.R.)	Oct. 26–30, 1968	Georgi T. Bergeovoi	94/51	First manned rendezvous and possible docking by Soviet cosmonaut.
Apollo 8 (U.S.)	Dec. 21–27, 1968	Frank Borman, James A. Lovell, Jr., William A. Anders	147/00	First spacecraft in circumlunar orbit; TV transmissions from this orbit. The three astronauts were also the first men to view the whole Earth.
Apollo 9 (U.S.)	Mar. 3–13, 1969	James A. McDivitt, David R. Scott, Russell L. Schweikart	241/1	First manned flight of Lunar Module.
Apollo 10 (U.S.)	May 18–26, 1969	Thomas P. Stafford, Eugene A. Cernan, John W. Young	192/3	First descent to within nine miles of Moon's surface by manned craft.
Apollo 11 (U.S.)	July 16–24, 1969	Neil A. Armstrong, Edwin E. Aldrin, Jr., Michael Collins	195/18	First staffed landing and EVA on Moon; soil and rock samples collected; experiments left on lunar surface.
Soyuz 6 (U.S.S.R.)	Oct. 11–16, 1969	Gorgiy Shonin, Valriy Kabasov	118/42	Three spacecraft and seven men put into Earth orbit simultaneously for first time.
Apollo 12 (U.S.)	Nov. 14–24, 1969	Charles Conrad, Jr., Richard F. Gordon, Jr., Alan Bean	244/36	Staffed lunar landing mission; investigated *Surveyor 3* spacecraft; collected lunar samples. EVA time: 15 hr. 30 min.
Apollo 13 (U.S.)	April 11–17, 1970	James A. Lovell, Jr., Fred W. Haise, Jr., John L. Swigert, Jr.	142/54	Third staffed lunar landing attempt; aborted due to pressure loss in liquid oxygen in service module and failure of fuel cells.
Apollo 14 (U.S.)	Jan. 31–Feb. 9, 1971	Alan B. Shepard, Stuart A. Roosa, Edgar D. Mitchell	216/42	Third staffed lunar landing: returned largest amount of lunar material.
Soyuz 11 (U.S.S.R.)	June 6–30, 1971	Georgiy Tomofeyevich Dobrovolskiy, Vladislav Nikolayevich Volkov, Viktor Ivanovich Patsyev	569/40	Linked up with first space station, *Salyut 1*. Astronauts died just before reentry due to loss of pressurization in spacecraft.
Apollo 15 (U.S.)	July 26–Aug. 7, 1971	David R. Scott, James B. Irwin, Alfred M. Worden	295/12	Fourth staffed lunar landing; first use of lunar rover propelled by Scott and Irwin; first live pictures of LM lift-off from Moon; exploration time: 18 hours.
Apollo 16 (U.S.)	April 16–27, 1972	John W. Young, Thomas K. Mattingly, Charles M. Duke, Jr.	265/51	Fifth staffed lunar landing; second use of lunar rover vehicle, propelled by Young and Duke. Total exploration time on the Moon was 20 hr. 14 min, setting new record. Mattingly's in-flight "walk in space" was 1 hr. 23 min. Approximately 213 lb of lunar rock returned.
Apollo 17 (U.S.)	Dec. 7–19, 1972	Eugene A. Cernan, Ronald E. Evans, Harrison H. Schmitt	301/51	Sixth and last staffed lunar landing; third to carry lunar rover. Cernan and Schmitt, during three EVA's, completed total of 22 hr. 05 min 3 sec. USS *Ticonderoga* recovered crew and about 250 lbs of lunar samples.
Skylab SL-2 (U.S.)	May 25–June 22, 1973	Charles Conrad, Jr., Joseph P. Kerwin, Paul J. Weitz	672/50	First staffed *Skylab* launch. Established Skylab Orbital Assembly and conducted scientific and medical experiments.
Skylab SL-3 (U.S.)	July 28–Sept. 25, 1973	Alan L. Bean, Jr., Jack R. Lousma, Owen K. Garriott	1427/9	Second staffed *Skylab* launch. New crew remained in space for 59 days continuing scientific and medical experiments and Earth observations from orbit.
Skylab SL-4 (U.S.)	Nov. 16, 1973–Feb. 8, 1974	Gerald Carr, Edward Gibson, William Pogue	2017/16	Third staffed *Skylab* launch; obtained medical data on crew for use in extending the duration of staffed space flight; crews "walked in space" 4 times, totaling 44 hr. 40 min. Longest space mission yet: 84 d 1 hr. 16 min. Splashdown in Pacific, Feb. 9, 1974.
Apollo/Soyuz Test Project (U.S. and U.S.S.R.)	July 15–24, 1975 (U.S.)	U.S.: Brig. Gen. Thomas P. Stafford, Vance D. Brand, Donald K. Slayton	216/05	World's first international staffed rendezvous and docking in space; aimed at developing a space rescue capability.
Apollo/Soyuz Test Project (U.S. and U.S.S.R.)	July 15–21, 1975 (U.S.S.R.)	U.S.S.R.: Col. A. A. Leonov, V. N.Kubasov	223/35	*Apollo* and *Soyuz* docked and crewmen exchanged visits on July 17, 1975. Mission duration for *Soyuz:* 142 hr. 31 min. For *Apollo:* 217 hr., 28 min.
Columbia (U.S.)	April 12–14, 1981	Capt. Robert L. Crippen, John W. Young	54/20	Maiden voyage of Space Shuttle, the first spacecraft designed specifically for re-use up to 100 times.

Designation and country	Date	Astronauts	Flight time (hr./min)	Remarks
Salyut 7 (U.S.S.R.)	Feb. 8, 1984–Oct. 2, 1985	Leonid Kizim, Vladimir Solovyov, Oleg Atkov	237 days	Set a record for Soviet team endurance flight in orbiting space station.
Mir (U.S.S.R.)	Feb. 8, 1987–Dec. 29, 1987	Yuri V. Romanenko[1]	326.5 days	Set a record for Soviet single endurance flight in orbiting space station.
Mir (U.S.S.R.)	Dec. 21, 1987–Dec. 21, 1988	Col. Vladimir Titov, Musa Manarov	366 days	Set current record for Soviet team endurance flight in orbiting space station.
Endeavour (U.S.)	May 7–16, 1992	Richard J. Hieb, Maj. Thomas D. Akers, Cdr. Pierre J. Thugt	8 days, 23 hr., 17 min	The three mission specialists remained free of the *Endeavour* for 8 hours and 20 minutes on May 13 during the repair of communications satellite, setting an absolute record for extravehicular duration in space. First capture of a satellite using hands only.
Endeavour (U.S.)	Dec. 2–13, 1993	Col. Richard O. Covey, Cdr. Kenneth D. Bowersox, Lt. Col. Tom Akers,* Dr. Jeffrey A. Hoffman,** Dr. Story Musgrave,** Claude Nicollier, Dr. Kathryn C. Thornton* (*two space walks; **three space walks)	10 days, 19 hr., 59 min	Repaired Hubble Space Telescope. Replaced gyroscopes, solar arrays, camera, electronics, and hardware. Installed COSTAR corrective optics to compensate for flaw in Hubble's primary mirror. Record five space walks in a single mission.
Discovery (U.S.)	Feb. 3–11, 1994	Col. Charles F. Bolden, Capt. Kenneth S. Reightier, Jr., Dr. N. Jan Davis, Dr. Frankling R. Chang-Diaz, Dr. Ronald M. Sega, Russian cosmonaut Sergei K. Krikalev	8 days 7 hr., 22 sec.	Test flight of Wake Shield Facility, an experimental, retrievable, free-flying satellite for use in developing exotic materials. Cargo bay carried a private, commercial pressurized-laboratory, *Spacehab*, for experimental use, leased by NASA. Crew member Sergei K. Krikalev was first Russian cosmonaut to be launched in an American spacecraft.
Columbia (U.S.)	July 8–23, 1994	Col. Robert D. Cabana, Lieut. Col. James D. Halsell, Jr., Richard J. Heib, Lieut. Col. Carl E. Walz, Dr. Leroy Chlao, Dr. Donald A. Thomas, Dr. Chiaki Naito-Mukai (the first Japanese woman astronaut)	14 days 17 hr., 55 min	Studied the effects of limited gravity of orbital flight on materials and living things including goldfish, killifish, jellyfish, sea urchins, and Japanese red-bellied newts.
Mir-17 (Russia)	Jan. 8, 1994–Mar. 22, 1995	Dr. Valery Polyakov	439[2] days	Record single endurance flight in orbiting space station. Returned to earth with crewmates cosmonaut Helena Kondakova and commander Alexander Viktorenko, who spent 169 days each in the *Mir.*
Discovery (U.S.)	Feb. 3–11, 1995	Cdr. James D. Wetherbee, Lt. Col. Eileen M. Collins, Dr. Janice Voss, Dr. Bernard A. Harris, Jr.,* Dr. C. Michael Foale,* Russian cosmonaut Co. Vladimir G. Titov *performed spacewalks.	8 days 6 hr., 29 min	First rendezvous of U.S. spacecraft with a Russian space station *(Mir),* Feb. 6. Lt. Col. Collins was first female shuttle pilot. Deployed and retrieved solar observatory satellite. Extra-vehicular activity to test new space suit modifications and practice space station assembly techniques. EVA time: 4 hr., 35 min.
Soyuz TM-21 (Russia)	March 14–22, 1995	Russian cosmonauts Lieut. Col. Vladimir N. Dezhurov and Gennady M. Strekalov, and U.S. astronaut Dr. Norman E. Thagard	—	Dr. Thagard became the first American astronaut to fly aboard a *Soyuz* spacecraft with a Russian crew launched from Baikonur Space Center in Kazakhstan. He also became the first American to enter the *Mir* space station on March 16.
Atlantis (U.S.)	June 27–July 7, 1995	Lt. Col. Charles J. Prescourt, Capt. Robert L. (Hoot) Gibson, Dr. Eileen S. Baker, Gregory J. Harbaugh, Dr. Bonnie Dunbar, Russian cosmonauts: *Mir-19* commander Anatoly Y. Solovyev, Nikolai M. Budarin	10 days	Marked 100th human mission in U.S. space program and first shuttle link-up with the *Mir:* docked June 29, undocked July 4. Joined spacecraft held a record 10 people: 6 Americans and 4 Russians. Three *Mir* crew (*Mir-18* commander, Lieut. Col. Vladimir N. Dezhurov, cosmonaut Grennady M. Strekalov, and U.S. astronaut Dr. Norman E. Thagard) returned to earth aboard the *Atlantis.* Dr. Thagard set a U.S. space record of 112 days in space aboard *Mir.* Cosmonauts Solovyev and Budarin remained aboard the *Mir.*

Designation and country	Date	Astronauts	Flight time (hr./min)	Remarks
Atlantis (U.S.)	Nov. 12–20, 1995	Col. Kenneth D. Cameron, Lieut. Col. James D. Halsell, Jr., Col. Jerry L. Ross, Lieut. Col. William S. McArthur, Jr., Canadian Major Chris A. Hadfield, who operated the robot arm	8 days, 4 hr., 31 min	Second docking with *Mir.* Carried 15-foot-long Russian-made docking module and attached it to the *Mir.* Brought 2 new solar-powered panels for *Mir* and also supplies and scientific equipment. U.S. and Russian astronauts spent 3 days together on *Mir* conducting experiments.
Endeavour (U.S.)	Jan. 11–20, 1996	Col. Brian Duffy, Brent Jett, Dr. Leroy Chiao,** Capt. Winston E. Scott,* Dr. Daniel T. Berry,* and Japanese astronaut Koichi Wakata, who operated robot arm (*one spacewalk; **two spacewalks)	8 days, 22 hr., 01 min	Deployed and retrieved NASA satellite, retrieved Japanese satellite. Two spacewalks performed to test spacesuit components and practice space station construction, tools, and techniques. Total EVA time: 13 hours.
Columbia (U.S.)	Feb. 22–March 9, 1996	Lieut. Col. Andrew M. Allen, Lt. Col. Scott J. Horowitz, Dr. Franklin R. Chang-Diaz, Dr. Jeffrey A. Hoffman, Italian astronauts Maurizio Cheli and Dr. Umberto Guidoni, Swiss astronaut Nicollier Claude	15 days, 17 hr., 40 min	Microgravity research flight. Second attempt to deploy Italian-built electricity-conducting satellite failed when metallic debris punctured insulation and broke tether after it was unreeled to almost its full 12.5 mile length.
Atlantis (U.S.)	March 22–31, 1996	Col. Kevin P. Chilton, Lieut. Col. Richard A. Searfoss, Dr. Ronald M. Sega, Dr. Linda M. Goodwin, Lieut. Col. Michael R. Clifford, Shannon W. Lucid	9 days, 5 hr., 15 min	Third linkup with *Mir.* (March 22–27). Clifford and Goodwin conducted 6-hour spacewalk in shuttle cargo bay while docked with *Mir.* Lucid remained on board *Mir* for scheduled 140-day tour to conduct biomedical and material science experiments. Booster problems delayed her return until mid-September. Lucid is first American woman to live on *Mir.* On July 15, 1996, she broke the previous record for the longest U.S. manned space flight.
Endeavour (U.S.)	May 19–29, 1996	Col. John H. Casper, Lieut. Col. Curtis L. Brown, Jr., Cdr. Daniel W. Bursch, Mario Runco, Jr., Dr. Andrew S.W. Thomas, Canadian astronaut Dr. Marc Garneau	10 days, 0 hr., 40 min	Made record four satellite rendezvous, including three with small PAMS satellite to test the concept of a self-stabilizing satellite in orbit. Deployed and retrieved a Spartan satellite that carried an experimental inflatable antenna.
Columbia (U.S.)	June 20–July 7, 1996	Col. Terence T. Henricks, Kevin R. Kregel, Lieut. Col. Susan J. Helms, Richard M. Linnehan, Cdr. Charles E. Brady, Jr., French astronaut Dr. Jean-Jacques Favler, Canadian astronaut Dr. Robert Brent Thirsk	16 days, 21 hr., 48 min	Second-longest mission to date. Studied the effects of weightlessness on people, plants, and animals, and material manufacturing in near-zero gravity.
Atlantis (U.S.)	Sept. 16–26, 1996	William F. Readdy, Terrence W. Wilcutt, Thomas D. Akers, John E. Blaha, Jerome Apt, Carl E. Waltz. Download: Shannon W. Lucid	10 days, 3hr., 19 min	Fourth *Mir* docking. Carried a Spacelab module. Transferred supplies and equipment to *Mir.* After breaking all American and women's space endurance records (188 days, 5 hr., 0 min), Lucid returned with *Atlantis* crew. John E. Blaha remained on *Mir* for a four-month stay.
Columbia (U.S.)	Nov. 19–Dec. 7, 1996	Kenneth D. Cockrell, Cdr. Kent V. Romingel, Tamara E. Jernigan, Thomas D. Jones, Dr. F. Story Musgrave	17 days, 15 hr., 53 min	Deployed and recovered two free-flying satellites during mission: an ultraviolet telescope and Wake Shield (semiconductor processing) Facility. A jammed airlock hatch canceled two scheduled spacewalks. Is longest mission to date. Dr. Musgrave, 61, became oldest person ever in space and first to fly on all five space shuttles.
Atlantis (U.S.)	Jan. 12–22, 1997	Capt. Michael A. Baker, Cdr. Brent W. Jett, Jr., John M. Grunsfeld, Marsha S. Ivins, Peter J.K. Wiscoff, Dr. Jerry L. Linenger. Download: John E. Blaha	10 days, 04 hr., 56 min	Fifth *Mir* docking (Jan.14–19). Carried Spacehab double module. Transferred supplies to *Mir.* Conducted experiments in Spacehab and *Mir.* John E. Blaha returned with *Atlantis* crew after 128 days in space, 118 aboard the *Mir.* Jerry Linenger remained aboard *Mir* for 4.5-month stay.

Designation and country	Date	Astronauts	Flight time (hr./min)	Remarks
Discovery (U.S.)	Feb. 11–21, 1997	Cdr. Kenneth Bowersox, Lt. Col. Scott J. Harowitz, Col. Mark C. Lee,* Steven A. Hawley, Gregory J. Harbaugh,* Steven L. Smith,* Joseph R. Tanner* (*spacewalks)	9 days, 23 hr., 38 min	Second space telescope servicing mission. Installed new imaging spectrograph and infrared camera. Also patched torn telescope insulating cover. Deployed telescope at higher altitude: 335 x 321 nautical mile orbit. Mission required five spacewalks totaling 33 hr., 11 min.
Columbia (U.S.)	April 4–8, 1997	Lt. Col. James D. Halsell, Jr., Lt. Cdr. Susan L. Still, Janice E.Voss, Michael L. Gernhardt, Donald A. Thomas, Roger K. Crouch, Gregory T. Linteris	3 days, 23 hr., 13 min	Planned 12-day mission to study behavior of metals, materials, and fluids in the absence of gravity and microgravity effects on fires. Was cut short due to a fuel-cell generator problem. Susan Still is second female shuttle pilot.
Atlantis (U.S.)	May 15–24,1997	Col. Charles J. Precourt, Lt. Col. Eileen M. Collins, Edward T. Lu, Maj. Carlos I. Noriega, Jean-Francois Clervoy (France), Elena V. Kondakova (Russia), C. Michael Foale. Download: Dr. Jerry M. Linenger	9 days, 5 hr., 20 min	Sixth *Mir* docking (May 16–21). Carried a Spacehab double module. Transferred supplies and equipment. Jerry M. Linenger returned with *Atlantis* after 132 days in space. Michael Foale remained on *Mir* for a 4.5-month stay.
Columbia (U.S.)	July 1–17, 1997	Lt. Col. James D. Halsell, Jr., Lt. Cdr. Susan L. Still, Janice E.Voss, Donald A. Thomas, Michael L. Gernhard, Roger K. Crouch, Gregory T. Linteris	15 days, 16 hr., 45 min	Successful reflight of the uncompleted Microgravity Science Mission (*Columbia,* April 4–8, 1997). Is first time the same crew flies together again to complete a previous mission.
Discovery (U.S.)	Aug. 7–19, 1997	Lt. Col. Curtis L. Brown, Jr., Cdr. Kent V. Rominger, N. Jan Davis, Lt. Cdr. Robert L. Curbeam, Jr., Stephen K. Robinson, Bjarni Tryggvason (Canada)	11 days, 20 hr., 28 min	Deployed Shuttle Pallet satellite with scientific instruments to study changes in Earth's atmosphere. Also conducted experiments with shuttle's robot arm for possible applications in Japanese experimental module of space station.
Atlantis (U.S.)	Sept. 25–Oct. 6, 1997	James T. Wetherbee, Michael J. Boomfield, Col. Vladimir G Titov,* Scott E. Parazynski,* Jean-Loup J.M. Chretien (France), Wendy B. Lawrence. Up: Dr. David Wolf. Down: C. Michael Foale after 145 days in space, 134 days on *Mir* (*spacewalks)	10 days, 19 hr., 22 min	7th Mir docking (Sept. 27–Oct. 3). 5 hr. spacewalks (Oct.1) retrieved U.S. experimental packages from *Mir* for return to Earth. Transferred supplies. Tested emergency jet packs for space station workers. Dr. David Wolf replaced Michael Foale on *Mir* for 4-month stay.
Columbia (U.S.)	Nov. 19–Dec. 5, 1997	Kevin R. Kregel, Maj. Steven W. Lindsey, Takao Doi* (Japan), Winston E. Scott,* Kalpana Chawla, Col. Leonid K. Kadenyuk* (Ukraine) (*spacewalks)	15 days, 6 hr., 35 min	Deployed (Nov. 21) and retrieved (Nov. 24 spacewalk) malfunctioning Spartan solar-observation satellite. A second spacewalk (Dec. 3) tested space station assembly tools and techniques. Total EVA by Doi and Scott: 12 hr., 44 min.
Endeavour (U.S.)	Jan. 22–31, 1998	Lt. Col. Terrence W. Wilcutt, Joe F. Edwards, Bonnie J. Dunbar, Maj. Michael P. Anderson, James F. Reilly, II, Salizhan S. Sharipov (Kirghizia), Andrew S.W. Thomas. Down: Dr. David Wolf	8 days, 19 hr., 48 min	8th *Mir* docking (Jan. 24–29). Thomas replaced David Wolf after 128 days in orbit. Thomas is the seventh and last American to live aboard the Mir.
Columbia (U.S.)	April 17–May 3, 1998	Lt. Col. Richard A. Searfoss, Lt. Cmdr. Scott D. Altman, Richard M. Linnehan, Dr. Dafydd Rhys Williams (Canada), Kathryn P. Hire, Dr. Jay C. Buckey Jr., James A. Pawelczyk	15 days, 21 hr., 15 min	Neurolab mission carried over 2,000 mice, rats, crickets, and fish for neurological research. Also studied effects of microgravity on nervous system of crew members.
Discovery (U.S.)	June 2–12, 1998	Col. Charles J. Precourt, Cmdr. Dominic L. Gorie, Cmdr. Wendy B. Lawrence, Franklin R. Chang-Diaz, Janet Kavandi, Valeriy Ruymin (Russia) Down: Andrew S.W. Thomas	9 days, 19 hr., 54 min	Ninth and final *Mir* docking mission concluded the joint U.S.–Russian program as a precursor to the International Space Station partnership. Thomas returned to Earth after a 4.5-month stay.

Designation and country	Date	Astronauts	Flight time (hr./min)	Remarks
Discovery (U.S.)	Tentatively Oct. 29–Nov. 7, 1998	Lt. Col. Curt Brown, Maj. Steven W. Lindsey, Stephen K. Robinson, Dr. Scott E. Parazynski, Pedro Duque (Spain), Dr. Chiaki Mukai (Japan), Senator John H. Glenn, Jr.	9 days	Deploy and retrieve Spartan solar observing satellite. Research with Hubble Telescope Optical Systems Test Platform (HOST). Study the effects of aging and microgravity in space.
Endeavour (U.S.)	Tentatively Dec. 3–14 1998	Capt. Robert D. Cabana, Capt. Frederick W. Sturckow, Lt. Col. Nancy Currie, Col. Jerry L. Ross, Jim H. Newman	10 days	First mission to carry hardware for International Space Station assembly (Node 1 named "Unity").
Columbia (U.S.)	Tentatively Jan. 21–26, 1999	Lt. Col., Eileen M. Collins, Cmdr. Jeffrey S. Ashby, Steven A. Hawley, Maj. Catherine G. Coleman, Col. Michel Tognini (France)	5 days	Deploy Advanced X-ray Astrophysics Facility (AXAF). Eileen Collins will become first female shuttle commander.

1. Returned to Earth with two fellow cosmonauts, Aleksandr P. Aleksandrov and Anatoly Levchenko, who had spent a shorter stay aboard the *Mir.* 2. From launch to landing. NOTE: The letters MR stand for Mercury (capsule) and Redstone (rocket); MA, for Mercury and Atlas (rocket); GT, for Gemini (capsule) and Titan-II (rocket). The first astronaut listed in the Gemini and Apollo flights is the command pilot. The Mercury capsules had names: MR-III was *Freedom 7,* MR-IV was *Liberty Bell 7,* MA-VI was *Friendship 7,* MA-VII was *Aurora 7,* MA-VIII was *Sigma 7,* and MA-IX was *Faith 7.* The figure 7 referred to the fact that the first group of U.S. astronauts numbered seven men. Only one Gemini capsule had a name: GT-III was called *Molly Brown* (after the Broadway musical *The Unsinkable Molly Brown*); thereafter the practice of naming the capsules was discontinued.

The International Space Station

Led by the U.S., the International Space Station will be the largest and most complex international science and engineering program ever attempted. Partners in the program are Russia, Japan, Canada, and participating countries of the European Space Agency (ESA): Belgium, Denmark, France, Germany, Italy, the Netherlands, Norway, Spain, Sweden, Switzerland, and the United Kingdom.

Beginning in late 1998, with the launch of the first space station element, more than 100 components will ultimately be assembled in low Earth orbit over the next five years, using approximately 45 assembly flights. As currently envisioned, the International Space Station will support a crew of up to seven and include five complete pressurized laboratories and attached external sites for research.

The NASA-financed core module, the functional cargo block, is to be launched on a proton rocket from the Baikonur Cosmodrome in Kazakhstan, and placed into orbit. This component will supply early power and propulsion systems for the station. A few weeks later, plans call for a space shuttle to carry aloft a six-port docking module called Node 1 (named "Unity") and join it to one end of the cargo block. After the two components are linked, three spacewalks will be performed from the shuttle to connect power, data, and utility lines, and install exterior equipment.

In 1999, plans call for the first crew to spend five months aboard the station. When they arrive, the station will consist of three modules: the Russian service module, which will serve as living quarters and onboard control center for the early station; the Russian-built control module or functional cargo block (FCB), and the U.S.-built Node 1, a connecting module that provides the attachment points for future U.S. segments.

The crew's mission will be a flight test of the new station as it assists with critical assembly activities from on board. In the first five months, three space shuttle assembly missions will dock, expanding the station by delivering the first truss-based U.S. solar arrays, the U.S. laboratory module, and the station's primary robotic arm, built by Canada.

The *Soyuz* spacecraft that the first crew rides to orbit will remain docked with the station, providing emergency return to Earth for crew members if needed. The *Soyuz* spacecraft attached to the station will be replaced with a fresh spacecraft about every six months to maintain the emergency crew return capability.

The inaugural crew will be composed of two Russians and one American. NASA astronaut William Shepherd (Capt. USN) will be the space station commander, Russian cosmonaut Yuri Gidzenko (Col. Russian Air Force) the *Soyuz* commander, and Russian cosmonaut Sergei Krikalev, the flight engineer.

When completed, the space station will be 356 feet across and 290 feet long. It will weigh about 940,000 pounds (470 tons). In orbit 220 miles above Earth, the space station will circle the globe at an inclination of 51.6 degrees to the equator. This orbit can be reached by the launch vehicles of all international partners and will provide an excellent Earth-observation of 85% of the globe.

Heading into Thick Air

Airlines look for better ways to spot life-threatening turbulence

By JEFFREY KLUGER TIME

The first thing you notice when your plane suddenly begins to drop is that you're becoming weightless. For those who like roller coasters, the sensation may not be too bad. Quickly, however, zero-G can become negative-G, meaning anything not fastened or seat-belted down will slam into the ceiling. Food trays get tossed, cutlery gets flung, carry-ons fly up as tray tables bang down. After a few seconds the plane stabilizes, and anything—or anyone—stuck to the ceiling crashes to the floor. Another case of midair turbulence is quickly over.

In January 1998, United Airlines Flight 826 from Tokyo experienced this special brand of aviation hell, leading to 83 injuries and one death. Though life-threatening turbulence happens far less often than the mild rumbles most flyers experience, it is still all too common. On average, 17 U.S.-based planes get slapped around enough to cause injuries each year; between 1980 and 1995, 129 people were seriously hurt, two fatally.

Things might have been different in January's disaster if the pilots had had some warning of what was coming. About half the time, turbulence is a side effect of storms. When pilots see roiling clouds ahead, they can take evasive action or at least warn passengers to belt up.

But what struck Flight 826 was so-called clear-air turbulence (CAT), which occurs when there is scarcely a puff of cloud in a pilot's path. CAT can be caused by a lot of things, including a change in direction of the jet stream, a clash of opposing air masses, or a swirl of wind rising off a mountain. Not only is the phenomenon invisible, both to the eye and to radar, but it can also be highly localized, lurking in a patch of sky as small as 1,000 ft. across. When CAT hits, says retired United Airlines captain Andy D. Yates Jr., it is "like an anvil in the sky."

Currently, the best defense pilots have against such sky skids is an alert by other pilots up ahead who have just traversed a pool of unsteady air. But NASA and private industry may soon have a better way: they are designing a sort of infrared radar that would let planes scan the sky for agitated particles in the air characteristic of CAT. NASA plans to test the device but does not know when it will be operational. In the meantime, the Federal Aviation Administration is improving the pilot reporting system by equipping planes with software that measures even mild turbulence and flashes data to the ground, where computers collate the information and beam it back up to all planes in the area.

Of course, the most advanced turbulence-warning system on earth will not do a bit of good unless passengers heed those warnings by using the low-tech but highly effective anti-turbulence device known as the seat belt. Since 1980 only two serious turbulence-related injuries were suffered by properly strapped-in passengers. And although United says the FASTEN SEAT BELT sign was on during Flight 826, many passengers were, as passengers often do, simply ignoring it. □

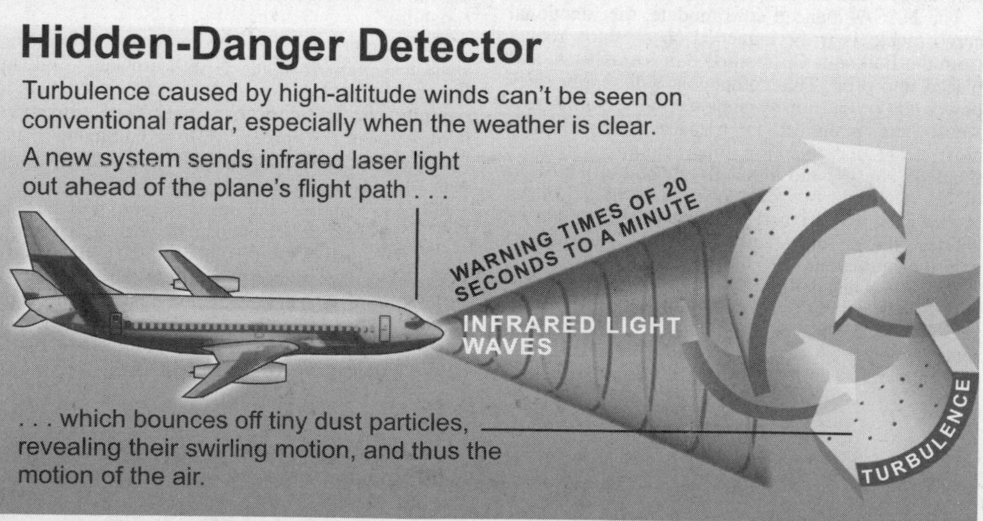

Hidden-Danger Detector
Turbulence caused by high-altitude winds can't be seen on conventional radar, especially when the weather is clear.
A new system sends infrared laser light out ahead of the plane's flight path . . .
WARNING TIMES OF 20 SECONDS TO A MINUTE
INFRARED LIGHT WAVES
TURBULENCE
. . . which bounces off tiny dust particles, revealing their swirling motion, and thus the motion of the air.

Source: Coherent Technologies

TIME Graphic by Steve Hart

Hunting the Predators

The government threatens to fine big airlines for trying to run low-priced competitors out of town

By ADAM ZAGORIN TIME

With only a pair of brand-new Boeing 737s sporting brightly colored orange-and-green tail fins, Pro Air Inc. is one of America's newest passenger airlines. Launched in Detroit's City Airport in July 1997 by former Boeing lawyer Kevin Stamper, Pro Air offers fares as much as 85% less than giant Northwest Airlines' on comparable routes. Passengers flocked to Pro Air, but Northwest, which dominates traffic in Detroit, was not about to let Pro Air grab share. Northwest quickly cut prices and added seats to Pro Air destinations, including Baltimore, Md.; Newark, N.J.; and Indianapolis, Ind. Under this assault, Pro Air had to abandon one of its Indianapolis routes, as well as a $69 one-way trip to Milwaukee, Wis. Before you could say "Put your tray tables in their upright and locked positions," Northwest jacked up some Milwaukee seats to more than $200, according to Pro Air.

Airlines like Northwest have routinely blown new competitors out of the sky with such tactics, on the theory that letting a low-cost start-up get started up is a bad strategy. Just look at what Southwest Airlines has done. But the tactic—matching low prices and adding more seats, even if it means absorbing losses—has virtually shut out new competition and kept fares high. "The most grievous government failure has been [not to] prosecute what appear to have been flagrant cases of predatory competition by major airlines against new competitors," says Alfred Kahn, the former Civil Aeronautics Board chairman who got deregulation off the ground.

The feds have now begun to stir. According to Secretary of Transportation Rodney Slater, a potential solution to the problem of predatory behavior by big airlines is imposing fines on them. "There is growing concern that the major carriers are willing to lose money—lots of it—in the short run to drive off competition," says Slater. Meanwhile, the Justice Department has begun an investigation into possible anticompetitive practices.

The megacarriers are making life miserable for discount airlines. Five, including Pan Am, Sun Jet, and Air South, have recently failed. The stragglers, which include Frontier Airlines and Reno Air, have lost a combined $200 million. The big airlines, by contrast, logged record earnings in 1997 of more than $5 billion, a rise of 28%, their fourth consecutive annual increase. No wonder. In 1997 business-class fares increased 16%, and average air fares have risen 9%. Meanwhile, the price of jet fuel, the airlines' biggest cost item, keeps dropping.

The big carriers say the start-ups flop because they are undercapitalized and poorly run, offering limited routes and flights, with no frequent-flyer clubs and other features. It is a circular argument, of course. The low fares of the upstarts are based on a cost structure that doesn't have such extras as frequent-flyer programs. And the big airlines force them to burn through their start up capital by stepping up the price wars.

American, United, Delta, and Northwest contend that Slater's warnings amount to interference in a tough market. "The small airlines want sympathy, so they accuse us of competing vigorously in the marketplace, which is and should be perfectly legal," argues Jon Austin, a spokesman for Northwest. And a smart strategy, perhaps. But now the big carriers have managed to attract the attention of both the Transportation and Justice departments. As Microsoft can attest, a smart business strategy isn't necessarily smart politics. □

Famous Firsts in Aviation

1782 **First balloon flight.** Jacques and Joseph Montgolfier of Annonay, France, sent up a small smoke-filled balloon about mid-November.

1783 **First hydrogen-filled balloon flight.** Jacques A. C. Charles, Paris physicist, supervised construction by A. J. and M. N. Robert of a 13-ft.-in-diameter balloon that was filled with hydrogen. It got up to about 3,000 ft. and traveled about 16 mi. in a 45-min flight (Aug. 27).

First human balloon flights. A Frenchman, Jean Pilâtre de Rozier made the first captive-balloon ascension (Oct. 15). With the Marquis d'Arlandes, Pilâtre de Rozier made the first free flight, reaching a peak altitude of about 500 ft., and traveling about 5½ mi. in 20 min (Nov. 21).

1784 **First powered balloon.** Gen. Jean Baptiste Marie Meusnier developed the first propeller-driven and elliptically shaped balloon—the crew cranking three propellers on a common shaft to give the craft a speed of about 3 mph.

First balloon flight by a woman. Mme. Thible, a French opera singer (June 4).

1793 **First balloon flight in America.** Jean Pierre Blanchard, a French pilot, made it from Philadelphia to near Woodbury, Gloucester County, N.J., in a little over 45 min (Jan. 9).

1794 **First military use of the balloon.** Jean Marie Coutelle, using a balloon built for the French Army, made two 4-hour observation ascents. The military purpose of the ascents seems to have been to damage the enemy's morale.

1797 **First parachute jump.** André-Jacques Garnerin dropped from about 6,500 ft. over Monceau Park in Paris in a 23-ft. diameter parachute made of white canvas with a basket attached (Oct. 22).

1843 **First air transport company.** In London, William S. Henson and John Stringfellow filed articles of incorporation for the Aerial Transit Company (March 24). It failed.

1852 **First dirigible.** Henri Giffard, a French engineer, flew in a controllable (more or less) steam-engine powered balloon, 144 ft. long and 39 ft. in diameter, inflated with 88,000 cubic ft. of coal gas. It reached 6.7 mph on a flight from Paris to Trappe (Sept. 24).

1860 **First aerial photographers.** Samuel Archer King and William Black made two photos of Boston, which are still in existence.

1872 **First gas-engine-powered dirigible.** Paul Haenlein, a German engineer, flew in a semi-rigid-frame dirigible, powered by a 4-cylinder internal-combustion engine running on coal gas drawn from the supporting bag.

1873 **First transatlantic attempt.** *The New York Daily Graphic* sponsored the attempt with a 400,000 cu. ft. balloon carrying a lifeboat. A rip in the bag during inflation brought collapse of the balloon and the project.

1897 **First successful metal dirigible.** An all-metal dirigible, designed by David Schwarz, a Hungarian, took off from Berlin's Tempelhof Field and, powered by a 16-hp Daimler engine, got several miles before leaking gas caused it to crash (Nov. 13).

1900 **First Zeppelin flight.** Germany's Count Ferdinand von Zeppelin flew the first of his long series of rigid-frame airships. It attained a speed of 18 mph and got 3½ mi. before its steering gear failed (July 2).

1903 **First successful heavier-than-air machine flight.** Aviation was really born on the sand dunes at Kitty Hawk, N.C., when Orville Wright crawled to his prone position between the wings of the biplane he and his brother Wilbur had built, opened the throttle of their home-made 12-hp engine, and took to the air. He covered 120 ft. in 12 sec. Later that day, in one of four flights, Wilbur stayed up 59 sec and covered 852 ft. (Dec. 17).

1904 **First airplane maneuvers.** Orville Wright made the first turn with an airplane (Sept. 15); five days later his brother Wilbur made the first complete circle.

1905 **First airplane flight over half an hour.** Orville Wright kept his craft up 33 min, 17 sec (Oct. 4).

1906 **First European airplane flight.** Alberto Santos-Dumont, a Brazilian, flew a heavier-than-air machine at Bagatelle Field, Paris (Sept. 13).

1908 **First airplane fatality.** Lt. Thomas E. Selfridge, U.S. Army Signal Corps, was in a group of officers evaluating the Wright plane at Fort Myer, Va. He was up about 75 ft. with Orville Wright when the propeller hit a bracing wire and was broken, throwing the plane out of control, killing Selfridge and seriously injuring Wright (Sept. 17).

1909 **First cross-Channel flight.** Louis Blériot flew in a 25-hp Blériot VI monoplane from Les Baraques near Calais, France, and landed near Dover Castle, England, in a 26.61-mi. (38-km), 37-min flight across the English Channel (July 25).

First International Aviation Competition Meeting. American Glenn Curtis narrowly beat France's Louis Blériot in the main event and won the Gordon Bennett Cup. Meet held at Rheims, France (Aug. 22–28).

1910 **First licensed woman pilot.** Baroness Raymonde de la Roche of France, who learned to fly in 1909, received ticket No. 36 on March 8.

First flight from shipboard. Lt. Eugene Ely, USN, took a Curtiss plane off from the deck of the cruiser *Birmingham* at Hampton Roads, Va., and flew to Norfolk (Nov. 14). The following January he reversed the process, flying from Camp Selfridge to the deck of the armored cruiser *Pennsylvania* in San Francisco Bay (Jan. 18).

First aircraft to take off from water. Henri Fabrer in a Gnome-powered floatplane, at Martigues, France (March 28).

1911 **First U.S. woman pilot.** Harriet Quimby, a magazine writer, got ticket No. 37, making her the second licensed female pilot in the world.

1912 **First woman's cross-Channel flight.** Harriet Quimby flew from Dover, England, across the English Channel and landed at Hardelot, France (25 mi. south of Calais), in a Blériot monoplane loaned to her by Louis Blériot (April 16). She was later killed in a flying accident over Dorchester Bay during a Harvard-Boston aviation meet on July 1, 1912.

First parachute jump from a powered airplane. Albert Berry jumped in a test over Jefferson Barracks military post, St. Louis (March 1). Some sources credit Grant Morton as making first jump in 1911.

1913 **First multi-engined aircraft.** Built and flown by Igor Ivan Sikorsky while still in his native Russia.

1914 **First aerial combat.** In August, Allied and German pilots and observers started shooting at each other with pistols and rifles—with negligible results.

1915 **First air raids on England.** German Zeppelins started dropping bombs on four English communities (Jan. 19).

1918 **First U.S. air squadron.** The U.S. Army Air Corps made its first independent raids over enemy lines, in DH-4 planes (British-designed) powered with 400-hp American-designed Liberty engines (April 8).

First regular airmail service. Operated for the Post Office Department by the Army, the first regular service was inaugurated with one round trip a day (except Sunday) between Washington, D.C., and New York City (May 15).

1919 **First transatlantic flight.** The NC-4, one of four Curtiss flying boats commanded by Lt. Comdr. Albert C. Read, reached Lisbon, Portugal (May 27), after hops from Trepassy Bay, Newfoundland, to Horta, Azores (May 16–17), to Ponta Delgada (May 20). The Liberty-powered craft was piloted by Walter Hinton.

First nonstop transatlantic flight. Capt. John Alcock and Lt. Arthur Whitten Brown, British World War I flyers, made the 1,900 mi. trip from St. John's, Newfoundland, to Clifden, Ireland, in 16 hours, 12 min in a Vickers-Vimy bomber with two 350-hp Rolls-Royce engines (June 15–16).

First lighter-than-air transatlantic flight. The British dirigible R-34, commanded by Maj. George H. Scott, left Firth of Forth, Scotland (July 2), and touched down at Mineola, L.I., 108 hours later. The eastbound trip was made in 75 hours (completed July 13).

First scheduled London-Paris passenger service (using airplanes). Aircraft Travel and Transport inaugurated London-Paris service (Aug. 25).

Aviation Web Sites

U.S. Air Force: www.af.mil
Strategic Air Command Museum: www.omahafreenet.org/sacmuzm
National Air & Space Museum: www.nasm.si.edu
International Women's Air & Space Museum: www.infinet.com/~iwasm
American Airpower Heritage Museum: www.avdigest.com/aahm/aahm.html
Aviation History Online Museum: www.aviation-history.com
National Aviation Museum of Canada: www.aviation.nmstc.ca
Confederate Air Force: www.avdigest.com/caf/caf.html
National Aeronautic Association: www.naa.ycg.org
Airports Council International: www.airports.org
Civil Air Patrol: www.cap.af.mil
Federal Aviation Administration: www.faa.gov
National Transportation Safety Board: www.ntsb.gov

Later the company started the first trans-channel mail service on the same route (Nov. 10).

First free-fall parachute jump. Leslie Irvin jumped over McCook Field, Dayton, Ohio, to prove that one won't lose consciousness during a delayed free-fall using a manually operated parachute (April 28).

1921 First U.S. black female pilot. Bessie Coleman received license June 15. Was killed April 30, 1926, in flying accident.

First naval vessel sunk by aircraft. Two battleships being scrapped by treaty were sunk by bombs dropped from Army planes in demonstration put on by Brig. Gen. William S. Mitchell (July 21).

First helium balloon. The C-7, non-rigid Navy dirigible was first to use non-inflammable helium as lifting gas, making a flight from Hampton Roads, Va., to Washington, D.C. (Dec. 1).

1922 First member of Caterpillar Club. Lt. (later Maj. Gen.) Harold Harris bailed out of a crippled plane he was testing at McCook Field, Dayton, Ohio (Oct. 20), and became the first man to join the Caterpillar Club—those whose lives have been saved by parachute.

1923 First nonstop transcontinental flight. Lts. John A. Macready and Oakley Kelly flew a single-engine Fokker T-2 nonstop from New York to San Diego, a distance of just over 2,500 mi. in 26 hours, 50 min (May 2–3).

First autogyro flight. Juan de la Cierva, a brilliant Spanish mathematician, made the first successful flight in a rotary wing aircraft in Madrid (June 9).

1924 First round-the-world flight. Four Douglas Cruiser biplanes of the U.S. Army Air Corps took off from Seattle under command of Maj. Frederick Martin (April 6). 175 days later, two of the planes (Lt. Lowell Smith's and Lt. Erik Nelson's) landed in Seattle after a circuitous route—one source saying 26,345 mi., another saying 27,553 mi.

1926 First polar flight. Then–Lt. Cmdr. Richard E. Byrd, acting as navigator, and Floyd Bennett as pilot, flew a trimotor Fokker from Kings Bay, Spitsbergen, over the North Pole and back in 15 ½ hours (May 8–9).

1927 First solo, nonstop transatlantic flight. Charles Augustus Lindbergh lifted his Wright-powered Ryan monoplane, *Spirit of St. Louis,* from Roosevelt Field, L.I., to stay aloft 33 hours 39 min and travel 3,600 mi. to Le Bourget Field outside Paris (May 20–21). Although 91 persons in 13 separate flights crossed the Atlantic before him, he flew directly between two great world cities and did it alone.

First transatlantic passenger. Charles A. Levine was piloted by Clarence D. Chamberlin from Roosevelt Field, L.I., to Eisleben, Germany, in a Wright-powered Bellanca (June 4–5).

1928 First east-west transatlantic crossing. Baron Guenther von Huenefeld, piloted by German Capt. Hermann Koehl and Irish Capt. James Fitzmaurice, left Dublin for New York City (April 12) in a single-engine all-metal Junkers-monoplane. Some 37 hours later, they crashed on Greely Island, Labrador. Rescued.

First U.S.–Australia flight. Sir Charles Kingsford-Smith and Capt. Charles T. P. Ulm, Australians, and two American navigators, Harry W. Lyon and James Warner, crossed the Pacific from Oakland to Brisbane. They went via Hawaii and the Fiji Islands in a trimotor Fokker (May 31–June 8).

First transarctic flight. Sir Hubert Wilkins, an Australian explorer, and Carl Ben Eielson, who served as pilot, flew from Point Barrow, Alaska, to Spitsbergen (mid-April).

1929 First of the endurance records. With Air Corps Maj. Carl Spaatz in command and Capt. Ira Eaker as chief pilot, an Army Fokker, aided by refueling in the air, remained aloft 150 hours 40 min at Los Angeles (Jan. 1–7).

First round-the-world airship flight. The LZ-127, known as the *Graf Zeppelin,* flew 21,300 miles in 20 days and 4 hours. Also set distance record (August).

First blind flight. James H. Doolittle proved the feasibility of instrument-guided flying when he took off and landed entirely on instruments (Sept. 24).

First rocket-engine flight. Fritz von Opel, a German auto maker, stayed aloft in his small rocket-powered craft for 75 sec, covering nearly 2 mi. (Sept. 30).

First South Pole flight. Comdr. Richard E. Byrd, with Bernt Balchen as pilot, Harold I. June, radio operator, and Capt. A. C. McKinley, photographer, flew a trimotor Fokker from the Bay of Whales, Little America, over the South Pole and back (Nov. 28–29).

1930 First Paris–New York nonstop flight. Dieudonné Coste and Maurice Bellonte, French pilots, flew a Hispano-powered Breguet biplane from Le Bourget Field to Valley Stream, L.I., in 37 hours, 18 min (Sept. 2–3).

1931 First flight into the stratosphere. Auguste Piccard, a Swiss physicist, and Charles Knipfer ascended in a balloon from Augsburg, Germany, and reached a height of 51,793 ft. in a 17-hour flight that terminated on a glacier near Innsbruck, Austria (May 27).

First nonstop transpacific flight. Hugh Herndon and Clyde Pangborn took off from Sabishiro Beach, Japan, dropped their landing gear, and flew 4,860 mi. to near Wenatchee, Wash., in 41 hours 13 min (Oct. 4–5).

World's 25 Busiest Airports in 1997

ACI 1997 Worldwide Airport Traffic Statistics

	Airport	Total passengers	1996–1997 % change	Airport	Total cargo	1996–1997 % change
1.	Chicago, O'Hare (ORD)	70,385,073	1.8	Memphis (MEM)	2,233,489	15.5
2.	Atlanta, Hartsfield (ATL)	68,205,769	7.7	Los Angeles (LAX)	1,872,862	8.9
3.	Dallas/Ft. Worth (DFW)	60,488,713	4.2	Hong Kong (HKG)	1,813,266	14.0
4.	Los Angeles (LAX)	60,142,588	3.7	Miami (MIA)	1,765,784	3.3
5.	London, Heathrow (LHR)	58,142,836	3.8	Tokyo, Narita (NRT)	1,738,795	6.9
6.	Tokyo, Haneda (HND)	49,302,268	5.7	New York (JFK)	1,667,581	1.9
7.	San Francisco (SFO)	40,493,959	3.2	Seoul (SEL)	1,567,638	15.1
8.	Frankfurt/Main (FRA)	40,262,691	3.9	Frankfurt/Main (FRA)	1,514,267	1.1
9.	Seoul (SEL)	36,757,716	5.9	Chicago, O'Hare (ORD)	1,407,307	11.7
10.	Paris, Charles de Gaulle (CDG)	35,293,378	11.3	Singapore (SIN)	1,358,044	12.1
11.	Denver, Stapleton (DEN)	34,969,021	8.3	Louisville (SDF)	1,345,693	–1.7
12.	Miami (MIA)	34,533,268	3.1	London, Heathrow (LHR)	1,260,068	10.5
13.	Amsterdam (AMS)	31,569,977	13.6	Anchorage (ANC)	1,259,827	17.4
14.	Detroit (DTW)	31,541,650	3.0	Amsterdam, Schiphol (AMS)	1,207,282	7.3
15.	New York (JFK)	31,355,268	0.6	Paris, Charles de Gaulle (CDG)	1,072,207	9.5
16.	Newark (EWR)	30,915,857	6.2	Newark (EWR)	1,043,494	8.9
17.	Phoenix (PHX)	30,659,143	0.8	Taipei (TPE)	913,520	14.7
18.	Las Vegas (LAS)	30,305,822	–0.5	Atlanta (ATL)	864,944	8.1
19.	Minneapolis/St. Paul (MSP)	30,208,256	5.0	Dayton (DAY)	813,180	6.0
20.	Hong Kong (HKG)	29,006,565	–4.0	Dallas/Ft. Worth (DFW)	810,687	4.7
21.	Houston (IAH)	28,705,213	8.4	San Francisco (SFO)	780,029	9.6
22.	St. Louis (STL)	27,661,144	1.4	Bangkok (BKK)	771,064	9.7
23.	Orlando (MCO)	27,305,249	6.9	Osaka (KIX)	744,937	25.7
24.	London, Gatwick (LGW)	26,961,453	10.8	Tokyo, Haneda (HND)	696,498	3.8
25.	Toronto (YYZ)	26,094,527	7.6	Oakland (OAK)	678,083	10.2

Top 50 ACI airports, January–December 1997. Total Passengers: enplaned and deplaned, passengers in transit counted once. Cargo: load and unloaded freight and mail (in metric tons). *Source:* Airport Council International, Geneva, Switzerland.

1932 First woman's transatlantic solo. Amelia Earhart, flying a Pratt & Whitney Wasp-powered Lockheed Vega, flew alone from Harbor Grace, Newfoundland, to Ireland in approximately 15 hours (May 20–21).

First westbound transatlantic solo. James A. Mollison, a British pilot, took a de Havilland Puss Moth from Portmarnock, Ireland, to Pennfield, New Brunswick (Aug. 18).

First woman airline pilot. Ruth Rowland Nichols, first woman to hold three international records at the same time—speed, distance, altitude—was employed by N.Y.–New England Airways.

1933 First round-the-world solo. Wiley Post took a Lockheed Vega, *Winnie Mae,* 15,596 mi. around the world in 7 days, 18 hours, 49½ min (July 15–22).

1937 First successful helicopter flight. Hanna Reitsch, a German pilot, flew Dr. Heinrich Focke's FW-61 in free, fully controlled flight at Bremen (July 4). Ms. Reitsch was also the first woman civil and military aviation test pilot.

1939 First turbojet flight. Just before their invasion of Poland, the Germans flew a Heinkel He-178 plane powered by a Heinkel S3B turbojet (Aug. 27).

1940 First wartime use of military gliders. German commandos made a successful glider assault on Belgium's Fort Eben-Emael during WWII (May 10).

1941–1945 Most combat missions flown by a pilot in any war. Captain Hans-Ulrich Rudel of Germany flew 2,530 combat missions during WWII while flying a JU-87 Stuka dive bomber. He survived the war.

1942–1945 Top-scoring fighter pilot of any war. German Luftwaffe ace Maj. Erich Hartmann scored 352 victories all while flying a Messerschmitt BF 109 during WWII. He was involved in 800 dogfights, and flew 1,425 missions. Maj. Hartmann survived the war.

1942 First and only enemy bombing of U.S. mainland. During World War II, a floatplane launched from a Japanese submarine off Cape Blanco, Oregon, dropped incendiary bombs on the Oregon forest in two attempts to start forest fires and terrorize American civilians, but the bombs did little damage (Sept. 9 and 29).

First American jet plane flight. Robert Stanley, chief pilot for Bell Aircraft Corp., flew the Bell XP-59 *Airacomet* at Muroc Army Base, Calif. (Oct. 1).

First woman fighter pilot to shoot down an enemy aircraft. Soviet Lieutenant Lilya Litvyak, flying a Yak-1 fighter of the women's 586th Fighter Aviation Regiment, shot down two German planes over Stalingrad on Sept. 13, 1942.

1944 First production stage rocket-engine fighter plane. The German Messerschmitt Me 163B *Komet* (test flown 1941) became operational in June 1944. Some 350 of these delta-wing fighters were built before WWII in Europe ended.

1947 First piloted supersonic flight in an airplane. Capt. Charles E. Yeager, U.S. Air Force, flew the X-1 rocket-powered research plane built by Bell Aircraft Corp., faster than the speed of sound at Muroc Air Force Base, California (Oct. 14).

1949 First round-the-world nonstop flight. Capt. James Gallagher and USAF crew of 13 flew a Boeing B-50A Superfortress around the world nonstop from Ft. Worth, returning to same point:

23,452 mi. in 94 hours, 1 min, with four aerial refuelings enroute (Feb. 27–March 2).

1950 First nonstop transatlantic jet flight. Col. David C. Schilling (USAF) flew 3,300 mi. from England to Limestone, Maine, in 10 hours, 1 min (Sept. 22).

1951 First solo across North Pole. Charles F. Blair, Jr., flew a converted P-51 (May 29).

1952 First jetliner service. The De Havilland Comet flight was inaugurated by BOAC between London and Johannesburg, South Africa (May 2). Flight, including stops, took 23 hours, 38 min.

First transatlantic helicopter flight. Capt. Vincent H. McGovern and 1st Lt. Harold W. Moore piloted two Sikorsky H-19s from Westover, Mass., to Prestwick, Scotland (3,410 mi.). Trip was made in five steps, with a flying time of 42 hours, 25 min (July 15–31).

First transatlantic round trip in same day. A British Canberra twin-jet bomber flew from Aldergrove, Northern Ireland, to Gander, Newfoundland, and back in 7 hours, 59 min flying time (Aug. 26).

1955 First transcontinental round trip in same day. Lt. John M. Conroy piloted an F-86 Sabrejet across U.S. (Los Angeles–New York) and back—5,085 mi.—in 11 hours, 33 min, 27 sec (May 21).

1957 First round-the-world, nonstop jet plane flight. Maj. Gen. Archie J. Old, Jr., USAF, led a flight of three Boeing B-52 bombers, powered with eight 10,000-lb.-thrust Pratt & Whitney Aircraft J57 engines around the world in 45 hours, 19 min; distance 24,325 mi.; average speed 525 mph (completed Jan. 18).

1958 First transatlantic jet passenger service. BOAC, New York to London (Oct. 4). Pan American started daily service, New York to Paris (Oct. 26).

First domestic jet passenger service. National Airlines inaugurated service between New York and Miami (Dec. 10).

1968 Prototype of world's first supersonic airliner. The Soviet-designed Tupolev Tu-144 made its first flight, Dec. 31. It first achieved supersonic speed on June 5, 1969.

1973 First female pilot of a major U.S. scheduled airline. Emily H. Warner became employed by Frontier Airlines on January 29 as second officer on a Boeing 737.

1976 First regularly scheduled commercial supersonic transport (SST) flights begin. Air France and British Airways inaugurated service (January 21). Air France flew the Paris–Rio de Janeiro route; B.A., the London–Bahrain. Both airlines began SST service to Washington, D.C. (May 24).

1977 First successful man-powered aircraft. Paul MacCready, an aeronautical engineer from Pasadena, Calif., was awarded the Kremer Prize for creating the world's first successful man-powered aircraft. The *Gossamer Condor* was flown by Bryan Allen over the required 3-mile course on Aug. 23.

1978 First successful transatlantic balloon flight. Three Albuquerque, N.M., men, Ben Abruzzo, Larry Newman, and Maxie Anderson, completed the crossing (Aug. 16.; landed, Aug. 17) in their helium-filled balloon, *Double Eagle II.*

1979 First man-powered aircraft to fly across the English Channel. The Kremer Prize for the Channel crossing was won by Bryan Allen who flew the *Gossamer Albatross* from Folkestone, England to Cap Gris-Nez, France, in 2 hours, 55 min (June 12).

1980 First successful balloon flight over the North Pole. Sidney Conn and his wife Eleanor, in hot-air balloon *Joy of Sound* (April 11).

First nonstop transcontinental balloon flight, and also record for longest overland voyage in a balloon. Maxie Anderson and his son, Kris, completed four-day flight from Fort Baker, Calif., to successful landing outside Matane, Quebec, on May 12 in their helium-filled balloon, *Kitty Hawk.*

First long-distance solar-powered flight. Janice Brown, a 98-lb former teacher, flew a tiny experimental solar-powered aircraft, *Solar Challenger,* six miles in 22 min near Marana, Ariz. (Dec. 3). The craft was powered by a 2.75-hp engine.

First solar-powered aircraft to fly across the English Channel. Stephen R. Ptacek flew the 210-lb *Solar Challenger* at an average speed of 30 mph from Cormeilles-en-Vexin near Paris to the Royal Manston Air Force Base on England's southeastern coast in 5 hours, 30 min (July 7).

1984 First solo transatlantic balloon flight. Joe W. Kittinger landed Sept. 18 near Savona, Italy, in his helium-filled balloon *Rosie O'Grady's Balloon of Peace* after a flight of 3,535 miles from Caribou, Me.

1986 First nonstop flight around the world without refueling. From Edwards AFB, Calif., Dick Rutan and Jeana Yeager flew in *Voyager* around the world (24,986.727 mi.), returning to Edwards in 216 hours, 3 min, 44 sec (Dec. 14–23).

1987 First transatlantic hot-air balloon flight. Richard Branson and Per Lindstrand flew 2,789.6 miles from Sugarloaf Mt., Maine, to Ireland in the hot-air balloon *Virgin Atlantic Flyer* (July 2–4).

1991 First transpacific hot-air balloon flight. Richard Branson and Per Lindstrand flew about 6,700 miles from Miyakonyo, Japan, to 150 miles west of Yellowknife, Northwest Territories, Canada (Jan. 15–17).

1993 First woman to co-pilot a commercial supersonic plane. Barbara Harmer, British Airways, flew as first officer on the Concorde from London to New York City (March 25).

1995 First solo transpacific balloon flight. Steve Fossett made a flight of more than 5,430 miles from Seoul, South Korea, to Leader,

Active Pilot Certificates Held

Year	Total	Airline transport	Commercial	Private
1970	720,028	31,442	176,585	299,491
1980	814,667	63,652	182,097	343,276
1985	722,376	79,192	155,929	320,086
1990	702,659	107,732	149,666	299,111
1994	654,088	117,434	138,728	284,236
1995	639,184	123,877	133,980	261,399
1996	622,261	127,486	129,187	254,002
1997	616,342	130,858	125,300	247,604

NOTE: Includes other pilot categories—student 96,101, helicopter 6,801, glider 9,394, and recreational 284. Also nonpilot, i.e., mechanic, parachute rigger, etc. (Nonpilot total, 540,892). Data as of Dec. 31, 1997. *Source:* Department of Transportation, Federal Aviation Administration.

Saskatchewan, Canada, in a helium-filled balloon. Also set record for distance (Feb. 18–21, 1995).

1998 **World record duration balloon flight.** Bertrand Piccard, Wim Verstraeten, and Andy Elson made a flight of 9 days, 17 hrs., 55 min from Château d'Oex, Switzerland to Okpo, Myanmar in the *Breitling Orbiter 2,* (Jan. 28–Feb. 7, 1997). Record pending verification.

World Class Helicopter Records

Selected records. *Source:* National Aeronautic Association.

Great Circle Distance Without Landing

International: 2,213.04 mi.; 3,561.55 km.

Robert G. Ferry (U.S.) in Hughes YOH-6A helicopter powered by Allison T-63-A-5 engine; from Culver City, Calif., to Ormond Beach, Fla., April 6–7, 1966.

Distance, Closed Circuit

International: 1,739.96 mi.; 2,800.20 km.

Jack Schweibold (U.S.) in Hughes YOH-6A helicopter powered by Allison T-62-A-5 engine; Edwards Air Force Base, Calif., March 26, 1966.

Altitude Without Payload

International: 40,820 ft.; 12,442 m.

Jean Boulet (France) in Alouette SA 315-001 *Lama* powered by Artouste IIIB 735 KW engine; Istres, France, June 21, 1972.

Altitude in Horizontal Flight

International: 36,122 ft.; 11,010 m.

CWO James K. Church, (U.S.) in Sikorsky CH-54B helicopter powered by two P&W JFTD-12 engines; Stratford, Conn., Nov. 4, 1971.

Speed Around the World, Eastbound

40.99 mph; 65.97 kph.

Joe Ronald Bower (U.S.) pilot, in Bell JetRanger III, powered by one Allison 250-C20J (317 shp), covered 23,800 miles in 24 days, 4 hours, 36 min. June 28–July 22, 1994.

Speed Around the World, Westbound

57.01 mph; 91.75 kph.

Joe Ronald Bower (U.S.) pilot, John W. Williams (U.S.), co-pilot in Bell 430 powered by 2 Allison 250–C40, (811 shp), Aug. 17–Sept. 3, 1996.

Absolute World Records, Balloons

Selected records. *Source:* National Aeronautic Association.

Altitude (USA)

113,739.9 ft.; 34,668 m.

Cmdr. M.D. Ross (USNR) and Lt. Cmdr. V.A. Prather, *Lee Lewis Memorial,* Gulf of Mexico, May 4, 1961.

Distance (USA)

15,200 mi; 24,462 km.

J. Stephen Fossett, *Solo Spirit.* Mendoza, Argentina to crash landing in Coral Sea, Aug. 7–16, 1998. Record pending verification.

Duration (USA)

146 h., 44 min.

J. Stephen Fossett, *Cameron R-210.* St. Louis, Mo. to Sultanpur, India, Jan. 14–20, 1997.

Absolute World Records

(Maximum Performance in Any Class)

Source: National Aeronautic Association

Speed Around the World, Nonstop, Nonrefueled

Speed (mph)	Date	Plane	Pilots	Place
115.65	Dec. 14–23, 1986	*Voyager*	Dick Rutan & Jeana Yeager (U.S.)	Edwards AFB, Calif.—Edwards AFB, Calif.

Distance, Great Circle Without Landing, also Distance, Closed Circuit Without Landing

Distance (mi.)	Date	Plane	Pilots	Place
24,986.727	Dec. 14–23, 1986	*Voyager*	Dick Rutan & Jeana Yeager (U.S.)	Edwards AFB, Calif.—Edwards AFB, Calif.

Speed Over a Straight Course

Speed (mph)	Date	Plane type	Pilot	Place
2,193.16	July 28, 1976	Lockheed SR-71A	Capt. Eldon W. Joersz (USAF)	Beale AFB, Calif.

Speed Over A Closed Circuit

Speed (mph)	Date	Plane type	Pilot	Place
2,092.294	July 27, 1976	Lockheed SR-71A	Maj. Adolphus H. Bledsoe, Jr. (USAF)	Beale AFB, Calif.

Altitude

Height (ft)	Date	Plane type	Pilot	Place
123,523.58	Aug. 31, 1977	MIG-25, E-266M	Alexander Fedotov (U.S.S.R.)	U.S.S.R.

Altitude in Horizontal Flight

Height (ft)	Date	Pilot	Place
85,068.997	July 28, 1976	Capt. Robert C. Helt (USAF)	Beale AFB, Calif.

Altitude, Aircraft Launched From A Carrier Airplane

Height (ft)	Date	Plane type	Pilot	Place
314,750.00	July 17, 1962	N. American X-15-1	Maj. Robert White (USAF)	Edwards AFB, Calif.

The National Aviation Hall of Fame

Dedicated to honoring and preserving the history of outstanding air and space pioneers, the Aviation Hall of Fame was established in Dayton, Ohio, on October 5, 1962, with five Daytonians as its founding fathers: James W. Jacobs, Gregory C. Karas, John A. Lombard, Larry E. O'Neil, and Gerald E. Weller. The first annual enshrinement ceremonies were held in December that same year. The United States Congress passed Public Law 88-372 in July 1964 granting the NAHF a national charter.

For additional information, contact the National Aviation Hall of Fame, Dayton Convention Center, Dayton, Ohio, 45402, (937) 226–0800.

(With year of enshrinement)

Allen, William McPherson (1971)
Andrews, Frank M. (1986)
Armstrong, Harry George (1998)
Armstrong, Neil Alden (1979)
Arnold, Henry Harley (1967)
Atwood, J. Leland (1984)
Balchen, Bernt (1973)
Baldwin, Thomas Scott (1964)
Beachey, Lincoln (1966)
Beech, Olive Ann (1981)
Beech, Walter Herschel (1977)
Bell, Alexander Graham (1965)
Bell, Lawrence Dale (1977)
Bellanca, Giuseppe Mario (1993)
Bendix, Vincent Hugo (1991)
Boeing, William Edward (1966)
Bong, Richard L. (1986)
Borman, Frank (1982)
Boyd, Albert (1084)
Bradley, Mark E. (1992)
Brown, George Scratchley (1985)
Brukner, Clayton J. (1997)
Byrd, Richard Evelyn (1968)
Cessna, Clyde Vernon (1978)
Chamberlin, Clarence Duncan (1976)
Chanute, Octave (1963)
Chennault, Claire Lee (1972)
Cochran, Jacqueline (1972)
Collins, Michael (1985)
Combs, Harry B. (1996)
Conrad, Charles, Jr. (1980)
Crawford, Frederick C. (1993)
Crossfield, A. Scott (1983)
Cunningham, Alfred Austell (1965)
Curtiss, Glenn Hammond (1964)
Dargue, Herbert A. (1997)
Davis, Jr. Benjamin O. (1994)
deSeversky, Alexander P. (1970)
Doolittle, James Harold (1967)
Douglas, Donald Wills (1969)
Draper, Charles Stark (1981)
Eaker, Ira Clarence (1970)
Earhart, Amelia (1968)
Eielson, Carl Benjamin (1985)
Ellyson, Theodore Gordon (1964)
Ely, Eugene Burton (1965)
Everest, Frank K. (1989)
Fairchild, Sherman Mills (1979)
Fleet, Rueben Hollis (1975)
Fokker, Anthony Herman Gerard (1980)
Ford, Henry (1984)
Foss, Joseph Jacob (1984)
Foulois, Benjamin Delahauf (1963)
Frye, William John (1992)
Gabreski, Francis Stanley (1978)
Gentile, Dominic S. (1995)
Gilruth, Robert R. (1994)
Glenn, John Herschel, Jr. (1976)
Goddard, George William (1976)
Goddard, Robert Hutchings (1966)
Godfrey, Arthur (1987)
Goldwater, Barry Morris (1982)
Grissom, Virgil I. (1987)
Gross, Robert Ellsworth (1970)
Grumman, Leroy Randle (1972)
Guggenheim, Harry Frank (1971)
Haughton, Daniel J. (1987)
Hegenberger, Albert Francis (1976)
Heinemann, Edward Henry (1981)
Hoover, Robert A. (1988)
Ingalls, David Sinton (1983)
James, Daniel, Jr. (1993)
Jeppesen, Elrey B. (1000)
Johnson, Clarence Leonard (1974)
Johnston, Alvin M. (1993)
Jones, Thomas V. (1992)
Kenney, George Churchill (1971)
Kettering, Charles Franklin (1979)
Kindelberger, James Howard (1972)
Kittinger, Jr., Joe W. (1997)
Knabenshue, A. Roy (1965)
Knight, William J. (1988)
Lahm, Frank Purdy (1963)
Langley, Samuel Pierpont (1963)
Lear, William Powerll, Sr. (1978)
LeMay, Curtis Emerson (1972)
LeVier, Anthony William (1978)
Lindbergh, Anne Morrow (1979)
Lindbergh, Charles Augustus (1967)
Link, Edwin Albert (1976)
Lockheed, Allan H. (1986)
Loening, Grover (1969)
Lovell, James Arthur, Jr. (1998)
Lufbery, Raoul Gervais (1998)
Luke, Frank, Jr. (1975)
Macready, John Arthur (1968)
Macready, Paul B. (1991)
Martin, Glenn Luther (1966)
McCampbell, David (1996)
McDonnell, James Smith (1977)
Meyer, John C. (1988)
Mitchell, William (1966)
Mitscher, Marc A. (1988)
Montgomery, John Joseph (1964)
Moorer, Thomas H. (1987)
Moss, Sanford Alexander (1976)
Neumann, Gerhard (1986)
Nichols, Ruth Rowland (1992)
Norden, Carl L. (1994)
Northrop, John Knudsen (1974)
Pangborn, Clyde Edward (1995)
Patterson, William Allan (1976)
Piper, William Thomas, Sr. (1980)
Pitcairn, Harold Frederick (1995)
Post, Wiley Hardeman (1969)
Read, Albert Cushing (1965)
Reeve, Robert Campbell (1965)
Rentschler, Frederick Brant (1982)
Richardson, Holden Chester (1978)
Rickenbacker, Edward Vernon (1965)
Rodgers, Calbraith Perry (1964)
Rogers, Will (1977)
Rushworth, Robert A. (1990)
Rutan, Elbert L. (1995)
Ryan, T. Claude (1974)
Schirra, Walter M., Jr. (1986)
Schriever, Bernard Adolf (1980)
Selfridge, Thomas Etholen (1965)
Shepard, Alan Bartlett, Jr. (1977)
Sikorsky, Igor Ivan (1968)
Six, Robert Forman (1980)
Slayton, Donald K. "Deke" (1996)
Smith, C.R. (1974)
Spaatz, Carl Andrew (1967)
Sperry, Elmert Ambrose, Sr. (1973)
Sperry, Lawrence Burst, Sr. (1981)
Stafford, Thomas P. (1997)
Stanley, Robert M. (1990)
Stapp, John Paul (1985)
Stearman, Lloyd C. (1989)
Taylor, Charles Edward (1965)
Thomas, Lowell (1992)
Tibbets, Paul W., Jr. (1996)
Towers, John Henry (1966)
Trippe, Juan Terry (1970)
Turner, Roscoe (1975)
Twining, Nathan Farragut (1976)
Vandenberg, Hoyt S. (1991)
von Braun, Wernher (1982)
von Karman, Theodore (1983)
von Ohain, Hans P. (1990)
Vought, Chance M. (1989)
Wade, Leigh (1974)
Walden, Henry W. (1964)
Wells, Edward Curtis (1991)
Williams, Sam Barlow (1998)
Wilson, Thornton Arnold (1983)
Woolman, Collett Everman (1994)
Wright, Orville (1962)
Wright, Wilbur (1962)
Yeager, Charles Elwood (1973)
Young, John W. (1988)

The Seven Wonders of the World

Since ancient times, people have put together many "seven wonders" lists; examples include the Seven Wonders of the Natural World, the Seven Wonders of the Modern World, and the Seven Natural Wonders of the U.S. The content of these lists tends to vary, and none is definitive. The original list of seven wonders is the Seven Wonders of the Ancient World, which is made up of a selection of ancient architectural and sculptural accomplishments. The seven wonders that are most widely agreed upon as being in the original list are outlined below. Asterisk indicates photo can be found in the Headline History section.

The Pyramids of Egypt.* A group of three pyramids, *Khufu, Khafra,* and *Menkaura* at Giza, outside modern Cairo, is often called the first wonder of the world. The largest pyramid, built by Khufu (Cheops), a king of the fourth dynasty, had an original estimated height of 482 ft. (now approximately 450 ft.). The base has sides 755 ft. long. It contains 2,300,000 blocks; the average weight of each is 2.5 tons. Estimated date of construction is 2800 B.C.E. Of all the Ancient Wonders, the pyramids alone survive.

Hanging Gardens of Babylon. Often listed as the second wonder, these gardens were supposedly built by Nebuchadnezzar about 600 B.C.E. to please his queen, Amuhia. They are also associated with the mythical Assyrian queen, Semiramis. Archeologists surmise that the gardens were laid out atop a vaulted building, with provisions for raising water. The terraces were said to rise from 75 to 300 ft.

The Walls of Babylon, also built by Nebuchadnezzar, are sometimes referred to as the second (or the seventh) wonder instead of the Hanging Gardens.

Statue of Zeus (Jupiter) at Olympia. The work of Phidias (5th century B.C.E.), this colossal figure in gold and ivory was reputedly 40 ft. high. All trace of it is lost, except for reproductions on coins.

Temple of Artemis (Diana) at Ephesus. A beautiful structure, begun about 350 B.C.E., in honor of a non-Hellenic goddess who later became identified with the Greek goddess of the same name. The temple, with Ionic columns 60 ft. high, was destroyed by invading Goths in C.E. 262.

Mausoleum at Halicarnassus. This famous monument was erected by Queen Artemisia in memory of her husband, King Mausolus of Caria in Asia Minor, who died in 353 B.C.E. Some remains of the structure are in the British Museum. This shrine is the source of the modern word "mausoleum."

Colossus at Rhodes. This bronze statue of Helios (Apollo), about 105 ft. high, was the work of the sculptor Chares, who reputedly labored for 12 years before completing it in 280 B.C.E. It was destroyed during an earthquake in 224 B.C.E.

Pharos of Alexandria. The seventh wonder was the Pharos (lighthouse) of Alexandria, built by Sostratus of Cnidus during the 3rd century B.C.E. on the island of Pharos off the coast of Egypt. It was destroyed by an earthquake in the 13th century.

Famous Structures

Ancient

The *Great Sphinx of Egypt,* one of the wonders of ancient Egyptian architecture, adjoins the pyramids of Giza and has a length of 240 ft. Built in the 4th dynasty, it is approximately 4,500 years old. A 10-year, $2.5 million restoration project was completed in 1998. Other Egyptian buildings of note include the *Temples of Karnak, Edfu,* and the *Tombs at Beni Hassan.*

The *Parthenon of Greece,** built on the Acropolis in Athens, was the chief temple to the goddess Athena. It was believed to have been completed by 438 B.C.E. The present temple remained intact until the 5th century C.E. Today, though the Parthenon is in ruins, its majestic proportions are still discernible.

Other great structures of ancient Greece were the *Temples at Paestum* (about 540 and 420 B.C.E.); the *Temple of Poseidon* (about 460 B.C.E.); the *Temple of Apollo* at Corinth (about 540 B.C.E.); the *Temple of Apollo* at Bassae (about 450–420 B.C.E.); the famous *Erechtheum* atop the Acropolis (about 421–405 B.C.E.); the *Temple of Athena Niké* at Athens (about 426 B.C.E.); the *Olympieum* at Athens (174 B.C.E.–C.E. 131); the *Athenian Treasury* at Delphi (about 515 B.C.E.); the *Propylaea* of the Acropolis at Athens (437–432 B.C.E.); the *Theater of Dionysus* at Athens (about 350–325 B.C.E.); the *House of Cleopatra* at Delos (138 B.C.E.); and the *Theater* at Epidaurus (about 325 B.C.E.).

The *Colosseum (Flavian Amphitheater) of Rome,* the largest and most famous of the Roman amphitheaters, was opened for use C.E. 80. Elliptical in shape, it consisted of three stories and an upper gallery, rebuilt in stone in its present form in the third century C.E. Its seats rise in tiers, which in turn are buttressed by concrete vaults and stone piers. It could seat between 40,000 and 50,000 spectators. It was principally used for gladiatorial combat.

The *Pantheon* at Rome, begun by Agrippa in 27 B.C.E. as a temple, was rebuilt in its present circular form by Hadrian (C.E. 118–128). Literally the Pantheon was intended as a temple of "all the gods." It is remarkable for its perfect preservation today, and it has served continuously for 20 centuries as a place of worship.

Famous Roman arches include the *Arch of Constantine* (about C.E. 315) and the *Arch of Titus* (about C.E. 80).

Later European

St. Mark's Cathedral in Venice (1063–1067), one of the great examples of Byzantine architecture, was begun in the 9th century. Partly destroyed by fire in 976, it was later rebuilt as a Byzantine edifice.

Other famous examples of Byzantine architecture are *St. Sophia* in Istanbul (532–537); *San Vitale* in Ravenna (542); *St. Paul's Outside the Walls,* Rome (5th century); *Assumption Cathedral* in the Kremlin, Moscow (begun in 1475); and *St. Lorenzo Outside the Walls,* Rome, begun in 588.

The *Cathedral Group* at Pisa (1067–1173), one of the most celebrated groups of structures built in Romanesque-style, consists of the cathedral, the cathedral's baptistery, and the *Leaning Tower.** This trio forms a group by itself in the northwest corner of the city. The cathedral and baptistery are built in varicolored marble. The campanile *(Leaning Tower)* is 179 ft. high and leans more than 16 ft. out of the perpendicular. There is little reason to believe that the architects intended to have the tower lean.

Other examples of Romanesque architecture include the *Vézelay Abbey* in France (1130); the *Church of Notre-Dame-du-Port* at Clermont-Ferrand in France (1100); the *Church of San Zeno* (begun in 1138) at Verona; and *Durham Cathedral* in England.

The *Alhambra* (1248–1354), located in Granada, Spain, is universally esteemed as one of the greatest masterpieces of Muslim architecture. Designed as a palace and fortress for the Moorish monarchs of Granada, it is surrounded by a heavily fortified wall more than a mile in perimeter. The location of the Alhambra in the Sierra Nevada provides a magnificent setting for this jewel of Moorish Spain.

The *Tower of London* is a group of buildings and towers covering 13 acres along the north bank of the Thames. The central *White Tower,* begun in 1078 during the reign of William the Conqueror, was originally a fortress and royal residence, but was later used as a prison. The *Bloody Tower* is associated with Anne Boleyn and other notables.

Westminster Abbey, in London, was begun in 1045 and completed in 1065. It was rebuilt and enlarged in 1245–1250.

Notre-Dame de Paris (begun in 1163), one of the great examples of Gothic architecture, is a twin-towered church with a steeple over the crossing and immense flying buttresses supporting the masonry at the rear of the church.

Other famous Gothic structures are *Chartres Cathedral** (France; 12th century); *Sainte Chapelle* (Paris, France; 1246–1248); *Laon Cathedral* (France; 1160–1205); *Reims Cathedral* (France; about 1210–1250; rebuilt after its almost complete destruction in World War I); *Rouen Cathedral* (France; 13th–16th centuries); *Amiens Cathedral* (France; 1218–1269); *Beauvais Cathedral* (France; begun 1247); *Salisbury Cathedral* (England; 1220–1260); *York Minster* or the *Cathedral of St. Peter* (England; begun in the 7th century); *Milan Cathedral* (Italy; begun 1386); and *Cologne Cathedral* (Germany; 13th–19th centuries; badly damaged in World War II).

*The Duomo** (cathedral) in Florence was founded in 1298, completed by Brunelleschi, and consecrated in 1436. The oval-shaped dome dominates the entire structure.

The *Vatican* is a group of buildings in Rome comprising the official residence of the pope. The *Basilica of St. Peter,* the largest church in the Christian world, was begun in 1450. The *Sistine Chapel,* begun in 1473, is noted for the art masterpieces of Michelangelo, Botticelli, and others. The *Basilica of the Savior* (known as *St. John Lateran*) is the first-ranking Catholic Church in the world, for it is the cathedral of the pope.

Other examples of Renaissance architecture are the *Palazzo Riccardi,* the *Palazzo Pitti,* and the *Palazzo Strozzi* in Florence; the *Farnese Palace* in Rome; *Palazzo Grimani* (completed about 1550) in Venice; the *Escorial* (1563–93) near Madrid; the *Town Hall* of Seville (1527–32); the *Louvre,* Paris; the *Château* at Blois, France; *St. Paul's Cathedral,* London (1675–1710; badly damaged in World War II); the *École Militaire,* Paris (1752); the *Pazzi Chapel,* Florence, designed by Brunelleschi (1429); and the *Palace of Fontainebleau* and the *Château de Chambord* in France.

The *Palace of Versailles* in France, containing the famous Hall of Mirrors, was built during the reign of Louis XIV and served as the royal palace until 1793.

Outstanding European buildings of the 18th and 19th centuries are the *Superga* at Turin (Italy); the *Hôtel-Dieu* in Lyons; the *Belvedere Palace* at Vienna; the *Royal Palace* of Stockholm; the *Bank of England,* the *British Museum,* the *University of London,* and the *Houses of Parliament,* all in London; and the *Panthéon,* the *Church of the Madeleine,* the *Bourse,* the *Palais de Justice,* and the *Opera House,* all in Paris.

The *Eiffel Tower,* in Paris, was built for the Exposition of 1889 by Alexandre Eiffel. It is 984-ft. high (1,056 ft., including the television tower).

Asiatic and African

The *Taj Mahal** (1632–1650), at Agra, India, built by Shah Jahan as a tomb for his wife, is considered by some as the most perfect example of the Mogul style and by others as the most beautiful building in the world. Four slim white minarets flank the building, which is topped by a white dome; the entire structure is made of marble. Other examples of Indian architecture are the temples at Benares and Tanjore.

Among famed Muslim edifices are the *Dome of the Rock* or *Mosque of Omar,* Jerusalem (C.E. 691); the *Citadel* (1166) and the *Tombs of the Mamelukes* (15th century), in Cairo; the *Tomb of Humayun* in Delhi; the *Blue Mosque* (1468) at Tabriz; and the *Tamerlane Mausoleum* at Samarkand.

Angkor Wat, outside the city of Angkor Thom, Cambodia, is one of the most beautiful examples of Cambodian or Khmer architecture. The sanctuary was built during the 12th century.

The Great Wall of China (228 B.C.E.?), designed specifically as a defense against nomadic tribes, has large watch towers that could be called buildings. It was erected by Emperor Ch'in Shih Huang Ti and is 1,400 miles long. Built mainly of earth and stone, it varies in height between 18 and 30 ft.

Typical of Chinese architecture are the pagodas or temple towers. Among some of the better-known pagodas are the *Great Pagoda of the Wild Geese* at Sian (founded in 652); *Nan t'a* (11th century) at

Fang Shan; and the *Pagoda of Sung Yueh Ssu* (C.E. 523) at Sung Shan, Honan.

Other well-known Chinese buildings are the *Drum Tower* (1273), the *Three Great Halls* in the Purple Forbidden City (1627), *Buddha's Perfume Tower* (19th century), the *Porcelain Pagoda,* and the *Summer Palace,* all at Beijing.

United States

Rockefeller Center, in New York City, extends from 5th Ave. to the Avenue of the Americas between 48th and 52nd Sts. (and halfway to 7th Ave. between 47th and 51st Sts.). It occupies more than 22 acres and has 19 buildings.

The Cathedral of St. John the Divine, at 112th St. and Amsterdam Ave. in New York City, was begun in 1892 and is now in the final stages of completion. When completed, it will be the largest cathedral in the world: 601-ft. long, 146-ft. wide at the nave, 320-ft. wide at the transept. The east end is designed in Romanesque-Byzantine style, and the nave and west end are Gothic.

St. Patrick's Cathedral, at Fifth Ave. and 50th St. in New York City, has a seating capacity of 2,500. The nave was opened in 1877, and the cathedral was dedicated in 1879.

The World Trade Center, in New York City, was dedicated in 1973. Its twin towers are 110 stories high (1,350 ft.), and the complex contains over 9-million sq-ft. of office space. A restaurant is on the 107th floor of the North Tower.

San Francisco's *Golden Gate Bridge,* completed in 1937, is one of the most recognizable structures in the U.S. Designed by Joseph B. Strauss, this elegant suspension bridge has a main span of 4,200 feet.

* Photos of these structures can be found in the Headline History section.

Notable Modern Bridges

Name	Location	Length of main span		Year
		feet	meters	completed
Suspension	**United States**			
Verrazano-Narrows	Lower New York Bay	4,260	1,298	1964
Golden Gate	San Francisco Bay	4,200	1,280	1937
Mackinac Straits	Michigan	3,800	1,158	1957
George Washington	Hudson River at New York City	3,500	1,067	1931
Tacoma Narrows II	Puget Sound at Tacoma, Wash.	2,800	853	1950
San Francisco–Oakland Bay[1]	San Francisco Bay	2,310	704	1936
Bronx-Whitestone	East River, New York City	2,300	701	1939
Delaware Memorial[1]	Delaware River near Wilmington, Del.	2,150	655	1951, 1968
Seaway Skyway	St. Lawrence River at Ogdensburg, N.Y.	2,150	655	1960
Walt Whitman	Delaware River at Philadelphia	2,000	610	1957
Ambassador International	Detroit River at Detroit	1,850	564	1929
Throgs Neck	East River, New York City	1,800	549	1961
Benjamin Franklin	Delaware River at Philadelphia	1,750	533	1926
	International			
Akashi Kaikyo	Hyogo, Japan	6,529	1,990	1998
Storebælt	Denmark	5,328	1,624	1998
Humber	Hull, England	4,626	1,410	1981
Jiangyin Yangtze	China	4,543	1,385	UC99
Tsing Ma Bridge	Hong Kong	4,518	1,377	1997
High Coast Bridge	Västernorrland, Sweden	3,969	1,210	1997
Minami Bisan-Seto	Japan	3,668	1,118	1988
Second Bosporus	Istanbul, Turkey	3,576	1,090	1988
First Bosporus	Istanbul, Turkey	3,524	1,074	1973
Third Kurushima	Japan	3,379	1,030	UC99
Second Kurushima	Japan	3,346	1,020	UC99
Ponte 25 de Abril	Tagus River at Lisbon, Portugal	3,323	1,013	1966
Forth Road	Queensferry, Scotland	3,300	1,006	1964
Kita Bisan-Seto	Japan	3,248	990	1988
Severn	Severn River at Beachley, England	3,240	988	1966
Shimotsui Straits	Japan	3,084	940	1988
Xiling Yangtze	Three Gorges Dam, China	2,952	900	1996
Ohnaruto	Japan	2,874	876	1988
Pierre Laporte	Quebec, Canada	2,190	668	1970
Cantilever	**United States**			
Commodore John Barry	Chester, Pa.	1,644	501	1974
Greater New Orleans[1]	Mississippi River, La.	1,576	480	1958
Transbay Bridge	San Francisco Bay	1,400	427	1936
	International			
Quebec Railway	St. Lawrence River at Quebec, Canada	1,800	549	1917
Forth Railway[1]	Queensferry, Scotland	1,710	521	1890
Minato Ohashi	Osaka, Japan	1,673	510	1974
Howrah	Hooghly River at Calcutta, India	1,500	457	1943

Name	Location	Length of main span: feet	meters	Year completed
Steel Arch	**United States**			
New River Gorge	Fayetteville, W. Va.	1,700	518	1977
Bayonne	Kill Van Kull at Bayonne, N.J.	1,675	510	1931
	International			
Sydney Harbor	Sydney, Australia	1,670	509	1932
Zdákov	Vltava River, Czech Republic	1,244	380	1967
Port Mann	Fraser River at Vancouver, British Columbia	1,200	366	1964
Cable-Stayed	**United States**			
Dame Point	Jacksonville, Florida	1,300	396	1988
Houston Ship Channel	Baytown, Texas	1,250	381	1995
Hale Boggs Memorial	Luling, Louisiana	1,222	373	1983
Sunshine Skyway	Tampa, Florida	1,200	366	1987
	International			
Tatara	Ehime, Japan	2,920	890	UC99
Ponte de Normandie	Le Havre, France	2,808	856	1995
Qingzhou Minjiang	Fuzhou, China	1,985	605	1996
Yang Pu	Shanghai, China	1,975	602	1993
Xupu	Shanghai, China	1,936	590	1997
Meiko Chuo	Aichi, Japan	1,936	590	1997
Skarnsundet Bridge	near Trondheim, Norway	1,739	530	1991
Tsurumi Tsubasa	Kanagawa, Japan	1,673	510	1995
Oresund	Denmark/Sweden	1,614	492	UC2000
Ikuchi	Honshu-Shikoku, Japan	1,608	490	1991
Higashi Kobe	Hyogo, Japan	1,591	485	1991
Ting Kau	Hong Kong	1,558	475	1997
Seohae	Korea	1,542	470	UC2000
Alex Fraser	Vancouver, B.C., Canada	1,525	465	1986
Yokohama-ko-odan	Kanagawa, Japan	1,509	460	1989
Second Hooghly	Calcutta, India	1,500	457	1992
Second Severn Crossing	Severn River, England	1,496	456	1996
Dartford	Thames River, Dartford, England	1,476	450	1992
Dao Kanong	Chao Phraya River, Bangkok, Thailand	1,476	450	1987
Chongqing 2nd Bridge	Sichuan Province, China	1,457	444	1996
Continuous Truss	**United States**			
Astoria	Columbia River at Astoria, Oregon	1,232	376	1966
Croton Reservoir	Croton, N.Y.	1,052	321	1970
Ravenswood	Ohio River, Ravenswood, W. Va.	902	275	1981
	International			
Oshima	Oshima Island, Japan	1,066	325	1976
Tenmon	Kumamoto, Japan	984	300	1966
Kuronoseto	Nagashima-Kyushu, Japan	984	300	1974
Graf Spee	Germany	839	256	1936
Concrete Arch	**United States**			
Natchez Trace Pkwy.	Franklin, Tenn.	582	177	1994
Westinghouse	Pittsburgh, Pa.	460	140	1931
Jack's Run	Pittsburgh, Pa.	400	120	1930
Cappelen	Minneapolis, Minn.	400	120	1923
	International			
Krk (I)	Krk, Croatia	1,280	390	1979
Gladesville	Parramatta River at Sydney, Australia	1,000	305	1964
Amizade	Paraná River at Foz do Iguassu, Brazil	951	290	1964
Arrábida	Porto, Portugal	886	270	1963
Sandö	Angerman River at Kramfors, Sweden	866	264	1943
Northumberland Strait	(Connects Canada to Prince Edward Island)	820	250	1997
Sibenik	Sibenik, Yugoslavia	808	246	1966
Krk (II)	Krk, Croatia	800	244	1979
Fiumarella	Catanzaro, Italy	758	231	1961
Zaporozhe	Old Dnepr River, Ukraine	748	228	1952
Segmental Construction	**United States**			
Jesse H. Jones Memorial	Houston Ship Channel, Texas	750	228	1982

1. Twin span. NOTE: UC = under construction. *Source:* Federal Highway Administration.

World's Tallest Buildings

Building, City	Year	Stories	Height m	Height ft.
Suyong Bay Tower 88, Pusan	UC02	88	462	1,516
Shanghai World Financial Center, Shanghai	UC01	95	460	1,509
Petronas Tower 1, Kuala Lumpur	UC98	88	452	1,483
Petronas Tower 2, Kuala Lumpur	UC98	88	452	1,483
Sears Tower, Chicago	1974	110	442	1,450
Sudirman Office & Ritz Carlton Hotel, Jakarta	UC00	81	427	1,400
Jin Mao Building, Shanghai	UC98	88	421	1,380
World Trade Center One, New York	1972	110	417	1,368
World Trade Center Two, New York	1973	110	415	1,362
Plaza Rakyat, Kuala Lumpur	UC98	77	382	1,254
Empire State Building, New York	1931	102	381	1,250
Central Plaza, Hong Kong	1992	78	374	1,227
Bank of China Tower, Hong Kong	1989	70	369	1,209
T & C Tower, Kaoshiung	1997	85	348	1,140
Amoco Building, Chicago	1973	80	346	1,136
John Hancock Center, Chicago	1969	100	344	1,127
Shun Hing Square, Shenzen	1996	69	325	1,066
Sky Central Plaza, Guangzhou	1997	80	322	1,056
Chicago Beach Tower Hotel, Dubai	UC98	60	321	1,053
Baiyoke Tower II, Bangkok	1997	90	320	1,050
Chrysler Building, New York	1930	77	319	1,046
BDNI Center —Tower A, Jakarta	UC99	62	317	1,040
NationsBank Plaza, Atlanta	1993	55	312	1,023
First Interstate World Center, Los Angeles	1990	75	310	1,018
AT&T Corporate Center, Chicago	1989	60	307	1,007
Texas Commerce Tower, Houston	1982	75	305	1,000
Two Prudential Plaza, Chicago	1990	64	303	995
Ryugyong Hotel, Pyongyang	1995	105	300	984
Commerzbank Tower, Frankfurt	1997	56	299	981
First Interstate Bank Plaza, Houston	1983	71	296	972
Landmark Tower, Yokohama	1993	70	296	971
311 South Wacker Drive, Chicago	1990	65	293	961
The Centre, Hong Kong	UC98	69	292	958
American International Building, New York	1932	67	290	952
First Canadian Place, Toronto	1975	72	290	951
Society Tower, Cleveland	1991	57	290	950
One Liberty Place, Philadelphia	1987	61	287	945
Columbia Seafirst Center, Seattle	1984	76	287	943
40 Wall Street, New York	1930	72	283	927
NationsBank Plaza, Dallas	1985	72	281	921
Nanjing Xi Lu, Shanghai	UC98	62	281	923
Overseas Union Bank Centre, Singapore	1986	66	280	919
United Overseas Bank Plaza, Singapore	1992	66	280	919
Republic Plaza, Singapore	1995	66	280	919
Citicorp Center, New York	1977	59	279	915
Scotia Plaza, Toronto	1989	68	275	902
Transco Tower, Houston	1983	64	275	901
Renaissance Tower, Dallas	1975	56	270	886
900 North Michigan Ave., Chicago	1989	66	265	871
NationsBank Corporate Center, Charlotte	1992	60	265	871
SunTrust Plaza, Atlanta	1992	60	265	871
Water Tower Place, Chicago	1976	74	262	859
First Interstate Tower, Los Angeles	1974	62	262	858
Canada Trust Tower, Toronto	1990	51	261	856
Tianjin World Trade Center, Tianjin	UC99	64	260	853
Transamerica Pyramid, San Francisco	1972	48	260	853
G.E. Building, New York	1933	70	259	850
One First National Plaza, Chicago	1969	60	259	850
Two Liberty Place, Philadelphia	1990	58	258	848
Messeturm, Frankfurt	1990	63	257	843
USX Tower, Pittsburgh	1970	64	256	841
Rinku Gate Tower, Osaka	1996	56	256	840
World Trade Center, Osaka	1995	55	252	827
IBM Tower, Atlanta	1987	50	250	820
BNI City Tower, Jakarta	1995	46	250	820
Al Falsaliah Center, Riyadh	UC00	n.a.	250	820
Korea Life Insurance Company, Seoul	1985	60	249	817
CitySpire, New York	1989	75	248	814
Rialto Tower, Melbourne	1985	63	248	814
One Chase Manhattan Plaza, New York	1961	60	248	813
MetLife, New York	1963	59	246	808
Shin Kong Life Tower, Taipei	1993	51	244	801
Malayan Bank, Kuala Lumpur	1988	50	244	799
Tokyo City Hall, Tokyo	1991	48	243	797
Woolworth Building, New York	1913	57	241	792
Mellon Bank Center, Philadelphia	1991	54	241	792
John Hancock Tower, Boston	1976	60	240	788
BDNI Center— Tower B, Jakarta	UC99	45	240	788
Bank One Center, Dallas	1987	60	240	787
JR Central Towers, Nagoya	UC99	53	240	787
Commerce Court West, Toronto	1973	57	239	784
Graha Kuningan, Jakarta	UC98	52	239	784
Moscow State University, Moscow	1953	26	239	784
Empire Tower, Kuala Lumpur	1994	62	238	781
NationsBank Center, Houston	1984	56	238	780

NOTE: Height does not include TV towers and antennas. *n.a.* = figures not available. *Source:* Council on Tall Buildings and Urban Habitat, Lehigh University.

World's Highest Dams

Name	River, country, or state	Structural height: feet	Structural height: meters	Gross reservoir capacity: thousands of acre feet	Gross reservoir capacity: millions of cubic meters	Year completed
Rogun	Vakhsh, Tajikistan	1099	335	9,404	11,600	1985
Ching-p'ing	Ya-lung, China	1030	314	n.a.	n.a.	UC
Nurek	Vakhsh, Tajikistan	984	300	8,512	10,500	1980
Hsiao-wang	Mekong, China	971	296	n.a.	n.a.	UC
Grande Dixence	Dixence, Switzerland	935	285	324	400	1962
Lung-t'an	Hung-shui, China	935	285	n.a.	n.a.	UC
Inguri	Inguri, Georgia	892	272	801	1,100	1984
Boruca	Térraba, Costa Rica	876	267	n.a.	n.a.	UC
Chicoasén	Grijalva, Mexico	869	265	1,346	1,660	1981
Vaiont	Vaiont, Italy	869	265	137	169	1961
Tehri	Bhagirathi, India	856	261	2,869	3,540	UC
Kinshau	Tons, India	830	253	1,946	2,400	1985
Guavio	Orinoco, Colombia	820	250	811	1,000	1989
Mica	Columbia, Canada	794	242	20,000	24,670	1972
Sayano-Shushensk	Yenisei, Russia	794	242	25,353	31,300	1980
Mihoesti	Aries, Romania	794	242	5	6	1983
Chivor	Batá, Colombia	778	237	661	815	1975
Mauvoisin	Drance de Bagnes, Switzerland	777	237	146	180	1957
Oroville	Feather, California	770	235	3,538	4,299	1968
Chirkey	Sulak, Ukraine	764	233	2,252	2,780	1977
Bhakra	Sutlej, India	741	226	8,002	9,870	1963
El Cajón	Humuya, Honduras	741	226	4,580	5,650	1984
Hoover	Colorado, Arizona/Nevada	726	221	28,500	35,154	1936
Contra	Verzasca, Switzerland	722	220	70	86	1965
Dabaklamm	Dorferbach, Austria	722	220	191	235	UC
Mratinje	Piva, Herzegovina	722	220	713	880	1973
Dworshak	N. Fk. Clearwater, Idaho	717	219	3,453	4,259	1974
Glen Canyon	Colorado, Arizona	710	216	27,000	33,304	1964
Toktogul	Naryn, Kyrgyzstan	705	215	15,800	19,500	1978
Daniel Johnson	Manicouagan, Canada	703	214	115,000	141,852	1968
San Roque	Agno, Philippines	689	210	803	990	UC
Luzzone	Brenno di Luzzone, Switzerland	682	208	71	87	1963
Keban	Firat, Turkey	679	207	25,110	31,000	1974
Dez	Dez, Abi, Iran	666	203	2,707	3,340	1963
Almendra	Tormes, Spain	662	202	2,148	2,649	1970
Kölnbrein	Malta, Austria	656	200	166	205	1977
Karun	Karun, Iran	656	200	2,351	2,900	1976
Altinkaya	Kizil Irmak, Turkey	640	195	4,672	5,763	1986
New Bullards Bar	No. Yuba, California	637	194	960	1,184	1968
Lakhwar	Yamuna, India	630	192	470	580	1985
New Melones	Stanislaus, California	625	191	2,400	2,960	1979
Itaipu	Paraná, Brazil/Paraguay	623	190	23,510	29,000	1982
Kurobe 4	Kurobe, Japan	610	186	162	199	1964
Swift	Lewis, Washington	610	186	756	932	1958
Mossyrock	Cowlitz, Washington	607	185	1,300	1,603	1968
Oymopinar	Manavgat, Turkey	607	185	251	310	1983
Atatürk	Firat, Turkey	604	184	39,482	48,700	1990
Shasta	Sacramento, California	602	183	4,550	5,612	1945
Bennett WAC	Peace, Canada	600	183	57,006	70,309	1967
Karakaya	Firat, Turkey	591	180	7,767	9,580	1986
Tignes	Isère, France	591	180	186	230	1952
Amir Kabir (Karad)	Karadj, Iran	591	180	166	205	1962
Tachien	Tachia, Taiwan	591	180	188	232	1974
Dartmouth	Mitta-Mitta, Australia	591	180	3,243	4,000	1978
Özköy	Gediz, Turkey	591	180	762	940	1983
Emosson	Barberine, Switzerland	590	180	184	225	1974
Zillergrundl	Ziller, Austria	590	180	73	90	1986
Los Leones	Los Leones, Chile	587	179	86	106	1986
New Don Pedro	Tuolumne, California	585	178	2,030	2,504	1971
Alpa-Gera	Cormor, Italy	584	178	53	65	1965

NOTE: UC = under construction. *n.a.* = figures not available. *Source:* Department of the Interior, Bureau of Reclamation and *International Water Power and Dam Construction.*

World's Largest Dams

Dam	Location	Volume (thousands) Cubic meters	Cubic yards	Year completed
Syncrude Tailings	Canada	540,000	706,320	UC
Chapetón	Argentina	296,200	311,539	UC
Pati	Argentina	238,180	274,026	UC
New Cornelia Tailings	United States	209,500	274,026	1973
Tarbela	Pakistan	121,720	159,210	1976
Kambaratinsk	Kyrgyzstan	112,200	146,758	UC
Fort Peck	Montana	96,049	125,628	1940
Lower Usuma	Nigeria	93,000	121,644	1990
Cipasang	Indonesia	90,000	117,720	UC
Atatürk	Turkey	84,500	110,522	1990
Yacyretá-Apipe	Paraguay/Argentina	81,000	105,944	UC
Guri (Raul Leoni)	Venezuela	78,000	102,014	1986
Rogun	Tajikistan	75,500	98,750	1985
Oahe	South Dakota	70,339	92,000	1963
Mangla	Pakistan	65,651	85,872	1967
Gardiner	Canada	65,440	85,592	1968
Afsluitdijk	Netherlands	63,400	82,927	1932
Oroville	California	59,639	78,008	1968
San Luis	California	59,405	77,700	1967
Nurek	Tajikistan	58,000	75,861	1980
Garrison	North Dakota	50,843	66,500	1956
Cochiti	New Mexico	48,052	62,850	1975
Tabka (Thawra)	Syria	46,000	60,168	1976
Bennett W.A.C.	Canada	43,733	57,201	1967
Tucuruíi	Brazil	43,000	56,242	1984
Boruca	Costa Rica	43,000	56,242	UC
High Aswan (Sadd-el-Aali)	Egypt	43,000	56,242	1970
San Roque	Philippines	43,000	56,242	UC
Kiev	Ukraine	42,841	56,034	1964
Dantiwada Left Embankment	India	41,040	53,680	1965
Saratov	Russia	40,400	52,843	1967
Mission Tailings 2	Arizona	40,088	52,435	1973
Fort Randall	South Dakota	38,227	50,000	1953
Kanev	Ukraine	37,860	49,520	1976
Mosul	Iraq	36,000	47,086	1982
Kakhovka	Ukraine	35,640	46,617	1955
Itumbiara	Brazil	35,600	46,563	1980
Lauwerszee	Netherlands	35,575	46,532	1969
Beas	India	35,418	46,325	1974
Oosterschelde	Netherlands	35,000	45,778	1986

NOTE: UC = under construction. *Source:* Department of the Interior, Bureau of Reclamation and *International Water Power and Dam Construction.*

World's Largest Hydroelectric Plants

Name of Dam	Location	Rated capacity (MW) Present	Ultimate	Year of initial operation
Itaipu	Brazil/Paraguay	12,600	12,600	1984
Guri (Raul Leoni)	Venezuela	2,800	10,060	1968
Tucuruíi	Brazil	—	7,500	1985
Grand Coulee	Washington	6,494	6,494	1942
Sayano-Shushensk	Former U.S.S.R.	—	6,400	1980
Krasnoyarsk	Russia	6,096	6,096	1968
Corpus-Posadas	Argentina/Paraguay	—	6,000	UC
LaGrande 2	Canada	5,328	5,328	1982
Churchill Falls	Canada	5,225	5,225	1971
Bratsk	Siberia.	4,100	4,600	1964
Ust'-Ilimsk	Russia	3,675	4,500	1974
Cabora Bassa	Mozambique	2,075	4,150	1974
Yacyretá-Apipe	Argentina/Paraguay	—	4,050	UC
Rogun	Tajikistan	—	3,600	1985
Paulo Afonso	Brazil	3,409	3,409	1954
Salto Santiago	Brazil	1,332	3,333	1980

Name of Dam	Location	Rated capacity (MW) Present	Ultimate	Year of initial operation
Pati (Chapetón)	Argentina	—	3,300	UC
Iha Solteira	Brazil	3,200	3,200	1973
Inga I	Zaire	360	2,820	1974
Gezhouba	China	965	2,715	1981
John Day	Oregon/Washington	2,160	2,700	1969
Nurek	Tajikistan	900	2,700	1976
Revelstoke	Canada	900	2,700	1984
Sáo Simao	Brazil	2,680	2,680	1979
LaGrande 4	Canada	2,637	2,637	1984
Mica	Canada	1,736	2,610	1976
Volgograd—22nd Congress	Russia	2,560	2,560	1958
Fos do Areia	Brazil	2,511	2,511	1983
Itaparica	Brazil	—	2,500	1985
Bennett W.A.C.	Canada	2,116	2,416	1969
Chicoasén	Mexico	—	2,400	1980
Atatürk	Turkey	—	2,400	1990
Bakun	Balui, Bakun Rapids, Malaysia	—	2,400	UC2002
LaGrande 3	Canada	2,310	2,310	1982
Volga—V.I. Lenin	Russia	2,300	2,300	1955
Iron Gates I	Romania/Yugoslavia	2,300	2,300	1970
Iron Gates II	Romania/Yugoslavia	270	2,160	1983
Bath County	Virginia	—	2,100	1985
High Aswan (Saad-el-Aali)	Egypt	2,100	2,100	1967
Tarbela	Pakistan	1,400	2,100	1977
Piedra del Aquila	Argentina		2,100	1993
Itumbiara	Brazil	2,080	2,080	1980
Chief Joseph	Washington	2,069	2,069	1956
McNary	Oregon	980	2,030	1954
Green River	North Carolina	—	2,000	1980
Tehri	India	—	2,000	UC
Cornwall	New York	—	2,000	1978
Ludington	Michigan	1,979	1,979	1973
Robert Moses—Niagara	New York	1,950	1,950	1961

Note: MW = mogawatts, UC = under construction. *Source:* Department of the Interior, Bureau of Reclamation and *International Water Power and Dam Construction.*

Famous Ship Canals

Name	Location	Length (miles)[1]	Width (feet)	Depth (feet)	Locks	Year opened
Albert	Belgium	80.0	53.0	16.5	6	1939
Amsterdam-Rhine	Netherlands	45.0	164.0	41.0	3	1952
Beaumont-Port Arthur	United States	40.0	200.0	34.0	—	1916
Chesapeake and Delaware	United States	19.0	250.0	27.0	—	1927
Houston	United States	50.0	(2)	40.0	—	1914
Kiel (Nord-Ostsee Kanal)	Germany	61.3	144.0	36.0	4	1895
Panama	Panama	50.7	110.0	41.0	12	1914
St. Lawrence Seaway	U.S. and Canada	2,400.0[3]	(4)	—	—	1959
Montreal to Prescott	U.S. and Canada	11.5	80.0	30.0	7	1959
Welland	Canada	27.5	80.0	27.0	8	1931
Sault Ste. Marie	Canada	1.2	60.0	16.8	1	1895
Sault Ste. Marie	United States	1.6	80.0	25.0	4	1915
Suez	Egypt	100.6[5]	197.0	36.0	—	1869

1. Statute miles. 2. 300–400 feet. 3. From Montreal to Duluth. 4. 442–550 feet; there are 11.5 miles of locks, 80-feet wide and 30-feet deep. 5. From Port Said lighthouse to entrance channel in Suez roads. *Source:* American Society of Civil Engineers.

Notable Tunnels

Name	Location	Length mi.	Length km	Year completed
Railroad, excluding subways				
Seikan	Tsugaru Strait, Japan	33.5	53.6	1988
Channel[1]	English Channel, England–France	31.1	49.8	1994
Simplon (I and II)	Alps, Switzerland–Italy	12.3	19.8	1906 & 1922
Apennine	Bologna–Florence, Italy	11.5	18.5	1934
St. Gotthard	Swiss Alps	9.3	14.9	1880
Lötschberg	Swiss Alps	9.1	14.6	1911
Mont Cénis	French Alps	8.5[2]	13.7	1871
New Cascade	Cascade Mountains, Washington	7.8	12.6	1929
Vosges	Vosges, France	7.0	11.3	1940
Flathead	Rocky Mountains, Montana	7.0	11.3	1970
Arlberg	Austrian Alps	6.3	10.1	1884
Moffat	Rocky Mountains, Colorado	6.2	9.9	1928
Shimizu	Shimizu, Japan	6.1	9.8	1931
Rimutaka	Wairarapa, New Zealand	5.5	8.9	1955
Vehicular				
St. Gotthard	Alps, Switzerland	10.2	16.4	1980
Pinglin Highway	near Taipei, Taiwan	8.0	12.9	UC99
Trans-Tokyo Bay I and II	Tokyo, Japan	5.8	9.3	1997
Store Baelt	Great Belt, Denmark	5.0	8.0	1995
Mt. Blanc	Alps, France–Italy	7.5	12.1	1965
Mt. Ena	Japan Alps, Japan	5.3	8.5	1976[3]
Great St. Bernard	Alps, Switzerland–Italy	3.4	5.5	1964
Mount Royal	Montreal, Canada	3.2	5.1	1918
Lincoln	Hudson River, New York–New Jersey	1.6	2.6	1937
Queensway Road	Mersey River, Liverpool, England	2.2	3.5	1934
Brooklyn-Battery	East River, New York City	1.7	2.7	1950
Holland	Hudson River, New York–New Jersey	1.6	2.6	1927
Fort McHenry	Baltimore, Maryland	1.7	2.7	1985
Hampton Roads	Norfolk, Virginia	1.4	2.3	1957
Queens-Midtown	East River, New York City	1.3	2.1	1940
Liberty Tubes	Pittsburgh, Pennsylvania	1.2	1.9	1923
Baltimore Harbor	Baltimore, Maryland	1.2	1.9	1957
Allegheny Tunnels	Pennsylvania Turnpike	1.2	1.9	1940[4]

1. Twin-rail. One tunnel for passenger trains, the other for shuttle trains carrying vehicles plus a central service tunnel. 2. Lengthened to its present 8.5 miles in 1881. 3. Parallel tunnel begun in 1976. 4. Parallel tunnel built in 1965, twin tunnel in 1966. *Source:* American Society of Civil Engineers and International Bridge, Tunnel & Turnpike Association, Wittiker's.

World's Largest Subway Systems

(by 1997 usage)

City	Date system completed	Number of riders in 1997 (in millions)	Length (km)
Moscow	1935	3,160	200+
Tokyo	1927	2,740	169.3
Mexico City	n.a.	1,420	n.a.
Seoul	n.a.	1,390	n.a.
New York City	1904	1,130	320.0
Paris	1900	1,120	200.9
Osaka	1933	1,000	99.1
Hong Kong	n.a.	779	28.2
London	1863	770	391.0
São Paulo	n.a.	701	n.a.

Note: *n.a.* indicates that no figures were available.

Explorations

(All years are C.E. unless B.C.E. is specified.)

Country or place	Event	Explorer	Date
AFRICA			
Sierra Leone	Explored	Hanno, Carthaginian seaman	c. 520 B.C.E.
Zaire River (Congo)	Mouth visited[1]	Diogo Cão, Portuguese explorer	c. 1484
Cape of Good Hope	Rounded	Bartolomeu Diaz, Portuguese explorer	1488
Gambia River	Explored	Mungo Park, Scottish explorer	1795
Sahara	Crossed	Dixon Denham and Hugh Clapperton, English explorers	1822–1823
Zambezi River	Explored[1]	David Livingstone, Scottish explorer	1851
Sudan	Explored	Heinrich Barth, German explorer	1852–1855
Victoria Falls	Explored[1]	David Livingstone, Scottish explorer	1855
Lake Tanganyika	Explored[1]	Richard Burton and John Speke, British explorers	1858
Zaire River (Congo)	Traced	Sir Henry M. Stanley, British explorer	1877
ASIA			
Punjab (India)	Invaded	Alexander the Great, King of Macedonia	327 B.C.E.
China	Explored	Marco Polo, Italian traveler	c. 1272
Tibet	Visited	Odoric of Pordenone, Italian monk	c. 1325
Southern China	Explored	Niccolò dei Conti, Venetian traveler	c. 1440
India	Explored (Cape route)	Vasco da Gama, Portuguese navigator	1498
Japan	Visited	St. Francis Xavier of Spain, missionary	1549
Arabia	Explored	Carsten Niebuhr, German explorer	1762
China	Explored	Ferdinand Richthofen, German scientist	1868
Mongolia	Explored	Nikolai M. Przhevalsky, Russian explorer	1870–1873
Central Asia	Explored	Svon Hedin, Swedish scientist	1890–1908
EUROPE			
Shetland Islands	Visited	Pytheas of Massilia (Marseille), Greek navigator and geographer	c. 325 B.C.E.
North Cape	Rounded	Ottar, Norwegian explorer	c. 870
Iceland	Colonized	Norwegian noblemen	c. 890–900
NORTH AMERICA			
Greenland	Colonized	Eric the Red, Norwegian	c. 985
Labrador; Nova Scotia (?)	Explored[1]	Leif Ericson, Norse explorer	1000
West Indies	Explored[1]	Christopher Columbus, Italian	1492
North America	Coast explored[1]	Giovanni Caboto (John Cabot), for British	1497
Pacific Ocean	Sighted[1]	Vasco Núñez de Balboa, Spanish explorer	1513
Florida	Explored	Ponce de León, Spanish explorer	1513
Mexico	Conquered	Hernando Cortés, Spanish adventurer	1519–1521
St. Lawrence River	Explored[1]	Jacques Cartier, French navigator	1534
Southwest United States	Explored	Francisco Coronado, Spanish explorer	1540–1542
Colorado River	Explored[1]	Hernando de Alarcón, Spanish explorer	1540
Mississippi River	Explored[1]	Hernando de Soto, Spanish explorer	1541
Frobisher Bay	Explored[1]	Martin Frobisher, English seaman	1576
Maine Coast	Explored	Samuel de Champlain, French explorer	1604
Jamestown, Va.	Settled	John Smith, English colonist	1607
Hudson River	Explored	Henry Hudson, English navigator	1609
Hudson Bay (Canada)	Explored[1]	Henry Hudson	1610
Baffin Bay	Explored[1]	William Baffin, English navigator	1616
Lake Michigan	Navigated	Jean Nicolet, French explorer	1634
Arkansas River	Explored[1]	Jacques Marquette and Louis Jolliet, French explorers	1673
Mississippi River	Explored	Sieur de La Salle, French explorer	1682
Bering Strait	Explored[1]	Vitus Bering, Danish explorer	1728
Alaska	Explored[1]	Vitus Bering	1741
Mackenzie River (Canada)	Explored[1]	Sir Alexander Mackenzie, Scottish-Canadian explorer	1789
Northwest United States	Explored	Meriwether Lewis and William Clark, American explorers	1804–1806
Northeast Passage (Arctic Ocean)	Navigated	Nils Nordenskjöld, Swedish explorer	1879
Greenland	Explored	Robert Peary, American explorer	1892
Northwest Passage	Navigated	Roald Amundsen, Norwegian explorer	1906

Country or place	Event	Explorer	Date
SOUTH AMERICA			
Continent	Explored	Christopher Columbus, Italian	1498
Brazil	Explored[1]	Pedro Alvarez Cabral, Portuguese	1500
Peru	Conquered	Francisco Pizarro, Spanish explorer	1532–1533
Amazon River	Explored	Francisco Orellana, Spanish explorer	1541
Cape Horn	Explored[1]	Willem C. Schouten, Dutch navigator	1615
OCEANIA			
Papua New Guinea	Explored	Jorge de Menezes, Portuguese explorer	1526
Australia	Explored	Abel Janszoon Tasman, Dutch navigator	1642
Tasmania	Explored[1]	Abel Janszoon Tasman	1642
Australia	Explored	John McDouall Stuart, English explorer	1828
Australia	Explored	Robert Burke and William Willis, Australian explorers	1861
New Zealand	Sighted (and named)	Abel Janszoon Tasman, Dutch navigator	1642
New Zealand	Explored	James Cook, English navigator	1769
ARCTIC, ANTARCTIC, AND MISCELLANEOUS			
Africa, Middle East, South and Southeast Asia, and Europe	Explored	Ibn Batuta, greatest Arab traveler	1325–1349
Ocean exploration	Expedition	Ferdinand Magellan's ships circled globe for Spain	1519–1522
Galápagos Islands	Explored	Diego de Rivadeneira, Spanish captain	1535
Spitsbergen	Explored	Willem Barents, Dutch navigator	1596
Antarctic Circle	Crossed	James Cook, English navigator	1773
Antarctica	Explored[1]	Nathaniel Palmer, American whaler (archipelago) and Fabian Gottlieb von Bellingshausen, Russian admiral (mainland)	1820–1821
Antarctica	Explored	Charles Wilkes, American explorer	1840
North Pole	Reached[2]	Robert E. Peary, American explorer	1909
South Pole	Reached	Roald Amundsen, Norwegian explorer	1911

1. First European to reach the area. 2. Admiral Peary's claim to have reached the pole has been disputed from the beginning—as was the claim made by his former colleague, Dr. Frederick Cook, who has been generally dismissed as a charlatan. The credit ultimately went to Peary, a claim officially backed by the U.S. Congress. But recent scholarship, including evidence culled from the journals and diaries of both Cook and Peary, has cast doubt on both explorers' veracity. If it is the case that neither reached the pole, then the credit goes to Joseph Fletcher, who landed a U.S. Air Force C-47 plane there in 1952.

The Continents and the Theory of Continental Drift

A continent is defined as a large unbroken land mass completely surrounded by water, although in some cases continents are (or were in part) connected by land bridges. The seven continents are North America, South America, Europe, Asia, Africa, Australia, and Antarctica. The island groups in the Pacific are often called "Oceania," but this name does *not* imply that scientists consider them the remains of a continent.

When describing a continent, it is important to remember that there is a fundamental difference between a deep ocean, like the Atlantic, and shallow seas, like the Baltic and most of the North Sea, which are merely flooded portions of a continent. Another and entirely different point to remember is that political considerations have often overridden geographical facts when it came to naming continents.

Geographically, Europe, including the British Isles, is a large western peninsula of the continent of Asia; and many geographers, when referring to Europe and Asia, speak of the Eurasian continent. But traditionally, Europe is counted as a separate continent, with the Ural and the Caucasus mountains forming the line of demarcation between Europe and Asia. To the south of Europe, Asia has an odd-shaped peninsula jutting westward, which has a large number of political subdivisions. The northern section is taken up by Turkey; to the south of Turkey there are Syria, Iraq, Israel, Jordan, Saudi Arabia, and a number of smaller Arab countries. All these are part of Asia. Traditionally, the island of Cyprus in the Mediterranean is also considered to be part of Asia.

The Indonesian archipelago is divided between the Asian and Australian continents at Wallace's Line—an imaginary boundary demarcating the faunal differences between Asia and Australia. In the case of the Americas, the problem arises as to whether they should be considered one or two continents. There are good arguments on both sides, but since there is now a land bridge between North and South America (in the past it was often flooded) and since no part of the sea east of the land bridge is deep ocean, it is more logical to consider the Americas as one continent.

The first comprehensive theory of continental drift was suggested by the German meteorologist Alfred Wegener in 1912. The hypothesis asserts that the continents consist of lighter rocks that rest on heavier crustal material—similar to the manner in which icebergs float on water. Wegener contended that the relative positions of the continents are not rigidly fixed but are slowly moving—at a rate of about one yard per century. Through most of geologic time the world was made up of a single continent that eventually separated into the seven continents we have today.

Plate-Tectonics Theory

Source: U.S. Dept. of the Interior, Geological Survey.

According to the generally accepted plate-tectonics theory, scientists believe that Earth's surface is broken into a number of shifting slabs or plates, which average about 50 miles in thickness. These plates move relative to one another above a hotter, deeper, more mobile zone at average rates as great as a few inches per year. Most of the world's active volcanoes are located along or near the boundaries between shifting plates and are called plate-boundary volcanoes. However, some active volcanoes are not associated with plate boundaries, and many of these so-called intra-plate volcanoes form roughly linear chains in the interior of some oceanic plates. The Hawaiian Islands provide perhaps the best example of an intra-plate volcanic chain, developed by the northwest-moving Pacific plate passing over an inferred "hot spot" that initiates the magma-generation and volcano-formation process. The peripheral areas of the Pacific Ocean Basin, containing the boundaries of several plates, are dotted by many active volcanoes that form the so-called Ring of Fire. The Ring provides excellent examples of plate-boundary volcanoes, including Mt. St. Helens.

World Land Areas and Elevations

Area	Approximate land area sq km	Approximate land area sq mi.	Percent of total land area	Elevation, feet: Highest	Elevation, feet: Lowest
WORLD	148,429,000	57,308,738	100.0%	Mt. Everest, Asia, 29,028 ft. (8,848 m)	Antarctica, ice covered—8,327 ft. below sea level (–2,538 m)
ASIA (includes the Middle East)	44,579,000	17,212,041	30.0	Mt. Everest, Tibet-Nepal, 29,028 ft. (8,848 m)	Dead Sea, Israel-Jordan, 1,312 ft. below sea level (–408 m)
AFRICA	30,065,000	11,608,156	20.3	Mt. Kilimanjaro, Tanzania, 19,340 ft. (5,895 m)	Lake Assal, Djibouti, 512 ft. below sea level (–156 m)
NORTH AMERICA	24,256,000	9,365,290	16.3	Mt. McKinley, Alaska, 20,320 ft. (6,194 m)	Death Valley, Calif., 282 ft. below sea level (–86 m)
SOUTH AMERICA (includes Central America and the Caribbean)	17,819,000	6,879,952	8.9	Mt. Aconcagua, Argentina, 22,834 ft. (6,960 m)	Valdes Peninsula, Argentina 131 ft. below sea level (–40 m)
ANTARCTICA	13,209,000	5,100,021	8.9	Vinson Massif, Ellsworth Mts., 16,066 ft. (4,897 m)	Ice covered 8,327 ft. below sea level (–2,538 m)
EUROPE (includes the recently independent states of the former Soviet Union)	9,938,000	3,837,082	6.7	Elbrus, Russia/Georgia, 18,510 ft. (5,642 m)	Caspian Sea, Russia/Kazakhstan 92 ft. below sea level (–28 m)
AUSTRALIA (includes Oceania)	7,687,000	2,967,966	5.2	Kosciusko, Australia 7,316 ft. (7,310 m)	Lake Eyre, Australia, 52 ft. below sea level (–16 m)

Source: National Geographic Society.

Volcanoes of the World

About 550 volcanoes have erupted on Earth's surface since recorded history; far more have erupted unobserved on the ocean floor. Almost two-thirds of volcanoes are located in the Northern Hemisphere. About 60 volcanoes are active each year. Most volcanoes exist at the boundaries of Earth's crustal plates, such as the famous Ring of Fire that surrounds the Pacific Ocean plate. Of the world's active volcanoes, about 60% are along the perimeter of the Pacific, about 17% on mid-oceanic islands, about 14% in an arc along the south of the Indonesian islands, and about 9% in the Mediterranean area, Africa, and Asia Minor. Fifty volcanoes have erupted in the United States since recorded history, and the United States ranks third, behind Indonesia and Japan, in the number of historically active volcanoes.

Current Volcanic Activity

Volcano	Date of last eruption or activity	Volcano	Date of last eruption or activity
Adatara, Honshu, Japan	Sept. 7, 1997	Momotombo, Nicaragua	April 4, 1996
Akutan, Alaska	March 10, 1996	Monowai Seamount, Kermadec Islands	Dec. 5, 1997
Amukta, Alaska	Sept. 17, 1996	Montserrat, West Indies	July 3, 1998
Arenal, Costa Rica	May 5, 1998	Mount Hili Aludo	May 13, 1997
Axial Seamount	Jan. 25–28, 1998	Mount Karangetang, Indonesia	April 19, 1997
Barren Island, Indian Ocean	Dec. 20, 1994	Mount Peuet Sague, Indonesia	April 27, 1998
Bezymianny, Kamchatka, Russia	Dec. 5, 1997	Mount St. Helens	July 1, 1998
Cerro Negro, Nicaragua	Nov. 30, 1995	Northern Gorda Ridge	Feb. 28, 1996
Chiginagak, Alaska	Nov. 7, 1997	Okmok, Alaska	May. 2, 1997
Eastern Gemini Seamount, Vanuatu	Feb. 23, 1996	Pacaya, Guatemala	May 21, 1998
Etna, Sicily, Italy	Aug. 18, 1998	Papandayan, Java, Indonesia	July 1, 1998
Fernandina, Galapagos	Jan. 25, 1995	Pavlof, Alaska	June 3, 1997
Fogo, Cape Verde	April 2, 1995	Piparo, Trinidad	Feb. 22, 1997
Grimsvotn Volcano, Iceland	Sept. 30, 1996	Piton de la Fournaise, Reunion, Indian Ocean	March 9, 1998
Hakkoda, Japan	July 12, 1997	Popocatepetl, Mexico	Aug. 16, 1998
Hosho, Kyushu, Japan	Oct. 12, 1995	Rabaul, Papua, New Guinea	May 28, 1997
Iwate-san, Honshu, Japan	July 10, 1998	Rincon de la Vieja, Costa Rica	Feb. 16, 1998
Karymsky, Kamchatka, Russia	April 21, 1998	Ruapehu, New Zealand	Oct. 1997
Kilauea, Hawaii	1983–continuing	Ruby Seamount, Mariana Islands	Oct. 25, 1995
Kiluchevskoi, Russia	Jan. 20, 1997	Sakura-Jima, Japan	Jan. 24, 1998
Komaga-take, Hokkaido, Japan	March 5, 1996	San Cristobal, Nicaragua	May 20, 1997
Korovin, Alaska	June 30, 1998	Semeru, Java, Indonesia	1967–continuing
Krakatau, Indonesia	April 3, 1996	Sheveluch, Kamchatka, Russia	July 31, 1997
Loihi Seamount, Hawaii	July 26, 1996	Shishaldin, Alaska	June 3, 1997
Long Valley caldera, California	April 2, 1996	Stromboli, Italy	Aug. 23, 1998
Maderas, Nicaragua	Sept. 27, 1996	White Island, New Zealand	Aug. 21, 1998
Manam, Papua New Guinea	May 28, 1997	Yellowstone, Wyoming	Jan. 9, 1998
McDonald Island, Australia	Dec. 1996	Zacatecas, Mexico	June 1997
Merapi, Indonesia	July 20, 1998		
Metis Shoal, Tonga	June 6, 1995		

Note: Activity through August 1998. *Source:* Volcano World, University of North Dakota (http://volcano.und.nodak.edu).

The Nature of Volcanoes

Source: United States Geological Survey.

Volcanoes are built by the accumulation of their own eruptive products—lava, bombs (crusted over ash flows), and tephra (airborne ash and dust). A volcano is most commonly a conical hill or mountain built around a vent that connects with reservoirs of molten rock below the surface of Earth. The term volcano also refers to the opening or vent through which the molten rock and associated gases are expelled.

Driven by buoyancy and gas pressure, the molten rock, which is lighter than the surrounding solid rock, forces its way upward and may ultimately break though zones of weaknesses in Earth's crust. If so, an eruption begins, and the molten rock may pour from the vent as nonexplosive lava flows, or it may shoot violently into the air as dense clouds of lava fragments. Larger fragments fall back around the vent, and accumulations of fall-back fragments may move downslope as ash flows under the force of gravity. Some of the finer ejected materials may be carried by the wind and fall to the ground many miles away. The finest ash particles may be injected miles into the atmosphere and carried many times around the world by stratospheric winds before settling out.

Molten rock below the surface of Earth that rises in volcanic vents is known as magma, but after it erupts from a volcano it is called lava. Originating many tens of miles beneath the ground, the ascending magma commonly contains some crystals, fragments of surrounding (unmelted) rocks, and dissolved gases, but it is primarily a liquid composed of oxygen, silicon, aluminum, iron, magnesium, calcium, sodium, potassium, titanium, and manganese. Magmas also contain many other chemical elements in trace quantities. Upon cooling, the liquid magma may precipitate crystals of various minerals until solidification is complete to form an igneous or magmatic rock.

Lava is red hot when it pours or blasts out of a vent but soon changes to dark red, gray, black, or some other color as it cools and solidifies. Very hot, gas-rich lava containing abundant iron and magnesium is fluid and flows like hot tar, whereas cooler, gas-poor lava high in silicon, sodium, and potassium flows sluggishly, like thick honey, or in other cases, like pasty, blocky masses.

All magmas contain dissolved gases, and as they rise to the surface to erupt, the confining pressures are reduced and the dissolved gases are liberated either quietly or explosively. If the lava is a thin fluid (not viscous), the gases may escape easily. But if the lava is thick and pasty (highly viscous), the gases will not move freely but will build up tremendous pressure, and ultimately escape with explosive violence. Gases in lava may be compared with the gas in a bottle of a carbonated soft drink. If you put your thumb over the top of the bottle and shake it vigorously, the gas separates from the drink and forms bubbles. When you remove your thumb abruptly, there is a miniature explosion of gas and liquid. The gases in lava behave in somewhat the same way. Their sudden expansion causes the terrible explosions that throw out great masses of solid rock as well as lava, dust, and ashes.

The violent separation of gas from lava may produce rock froth called pumice. Some of this froth is so light—because of the many gas bubbles—that it floats on water. In many eruptions, the froth is shattered explosively into small fragments that are hurled high into the air in the form of volcanic cinders (red or black), volcanic ash (commonly tan or gray), and volcanic dust. □

The Deadliest Volcanic Eruptions

Deaths	Volcano	Year	Major cause of deaths
92,000	Tambora, Indonesia	1815	Starvation
36,417	Krakatau, Indonesia	1883	Tsunami
29,025	Mt. Pelee, Martinique	1902	Ash flows
25,000	Ruiz, Colombia	1985	Mudflows
14,300	Unzen, Japan	1792	Volcano collapse, tsunami
9,350	Laki, Iceland	1783	Starvation
5,110	Kelut, Indonesia	1919	Mudflows
4,011	Galunggung, Indonesia	1882	Mudflows
3,500	Vesuvius, Italy	1631	Mudflows, lava flows
3,360	Vesuvius, Italy	79	Ash flows and falls
2,957	Papandayan, Indonesia	1772	Ash flows
2,942	Lamington, Papua New Guinea	1951	Ash flows
2,000	El Chichon, Mexico	1982	Ash flows
1,680	Soufriere, St. Vincent	1902	Ash flows
1,475	Oshima, Japan	1741	Tsunami
1,377	Asama, Japan	1783	Ash flows, mudflows
1,335	Taal, Philippines	1911	Ash flows
1,200	Mayon, Philippines	1814	Mudflows
1,184	Agung, Indonesia	1963	Ash Flows
1,000	Cotopaxi, Ecuador	1877	Mudflows
800	Pinatubo, Philippines	1991	Roof collapses and disease
700	Komagatake, Japan	1640	Tsunami
700	Ruiz, Colombia	1845	Mudflows
500	Hibok-Hibok, Philippines	1951	Ash flows

Source: Volcano World, University of North Dakota (http://volcano.und.nodak.edu).

Indonesian Volcanoes

Indonesia has 130 active volcanoes, more than any other country.

Mt. Merapi, Java (9,554 ft.; 2,912 m), is the most active, and has had at least 12 eruptions causing fatalities. The last eruption was in July 1998.

Mt. Bromo, Java (7,639 ft.; 2,329 m), has erupted 53 times since 1804, most recently in 1984.

Mt. Semeru, Java (12,060 ft.; 3,339 m), the highest mountain on the island, was active in 1997.

The most famous of Indonesian volcanoes is Krakatau, a small volcanic island in the Sunda Strait between Sumatra and Java. Its eruption in 1883 was one of the world's most violent. Giant 40-meter tidal waves hurled ashore blocks of coral weighing as much as 600 tons. More than 36,000 people were killed. Three months after the eruption a volcanic dust veil surrounded Earth, acting as a solar filter that lowered the global temperature as much as 1.2°C in the year following the eruption. The most recent volcanic activity took place on the island of Anak Krakatau ("Child of Krakatau"—a remnant of the main island) in May 1997.

Principal Types of Volcanoes

Source: U.S. Dept. of Interior, Geological Survey.

Geologists generally group volcanoes into four main kinds—cinder cones, composite volcanoes, shield volcanoes, and lava domes.

Cinder Cones

Cinder cones are the simplest type of volcano. They are built from particles and blobs of congealed lava ejected from a single vent. As the gas-charged lava is blown violently into the air, it breaks into small fragments that solidify and fall as cinders around the vent to form a circular or oval cone. Most cinder cones have a bowl-shaped crater at the summit and rarely rise more than a thousand feet or so above their surroundings. Cinder cones are numerous in western North America as well as throughout other volcanic terrains of the world.

Composite Volcanoes

Composite volcanoes—sometimes called *stratovolcanoes*—are typically deep-sided, symmetrical cones of large dimension built of alternating layers of lava flows, volcanic ash, cinders, blocks, and bombs and may rise as much as 8,000 feet above their bases. Some of the most beautiful mountains in the world are composite volcanoes, including Mt. Fuji in Japan, Mt. Cotopaxi in Ecuador, Mt. Shasta in California, Mt. Hood in Oregon, and Mt. St. Helens and Mt. Rainier in Washington.

Most composite volcanoes have a crater at the summit that contains a central vent or a clustered group of vents. Lavas either flow through breaks in the crater wall or issue from fissures on the flanks of the cone. Lava, solidified within the fissures, forms *dikes* that act as ribs which greatly strengthen the cone.

The essential feature of a composite volcano is a conduit system through which magma from a reservoir deep in Earth's crust rises to the surface. The volcano is built up by the accumulation of material erupted through the conduit and increases in size as lava, cinders, and ash are added to its slopes.

Shield Volcanoes

Shield volcanoes are built almost entirely of fluid lava flows. Flow after flow pours out in all directions from a central summit vent, or group of vents, building a broad, gently sloping cone of flat, domical shape, with a profile much like that of a warrior's shield. They are built up slowly by the accretion of thousands of flows of highly fluid basaltic (from *basalt,* a hard, dense dark volcanic rock) lava that spread widely over great distances, and then cool as thin, gently dipping sheets. Lavas also commonly erupt from vents along fractures (rift zones) that develop on the flanks of the cone. Some of the largest volcanoes in the world are shield volcanoes. In northern California and Oregon, many shield volcanoes have diameters of 3 or 4 miles and heights of 1,500 to 2,000 feet. The Hawaiian Islands are composed of linear chains of these volcanoes, including Kilauea and Mauna Loa on the island of Hawaii.

In some shield volcano eruptions, basaltic lava pours out quietly from long fissures instead of central vents and floods the surrounding countryside with lava flow upon lava flow, forming broad plateaus. Lava plateaus of this type can be seen in Iceland, southeastern Washington, eastern Oregon, and southern Idaho.

Lava Domes

Volcanic or lava domes are formed by relatively small, bulbous masses of lava too viscous to flow any great distance; consequently, on extrusion, the lava piles over and around its vent. A dome grows largely by expansion from within. As it grows its outer surface cools and hardens, then shatters, spilling loose fragments down its sides. Some domes form craggy knobs or spines over the volcanic vent, whereas others form short, steep-sided lava flows known as *coulees.* Volcanic domes commonly occur within the craters or on the flanks of large composite volcanoes. The nearly circular Novarupta Dome that formed during the 1912 eruption of Katmai Volcano, Alaska, measures 800 feet across and 200 feet high. The internal structure of this dome—defined by layering of lava fanning upward and outward from the center—indicates that it grew largely by expansion from within. Mt. Pelée in Martinique, West Indies, and Lassen Peak and Mono domes in California, are examples of lava domes.

Submarine Volcanoes

Submarine volcanoes and volcanic vents are common features on certain zones of the ocean floor. Some are active at the present time and, in shallow water, disclose their presence by blasting steam and rock-debris high above the surface of the sea. Many others lie at such great depths that the tremendous weight of the water above them results in high, confining pressure and prevents the formation and release of steam and gases. Even very large, deep-water eruptions may not disturb the ocean floor.

The famous black sand beaches of Hawaii were created virtually instantaneously by the violent interaction between hot lava and sea water.

Earth's Greatest Volcanic Field

The largest known concentration of active volcanoes on Earth was discovered by scientists aboard the research vessel *Melville* (Nov. 1992–Jan. 1993). The vast volcanic cluster is situated under the South Pacific Ocean, 600 miles northwest of Easter Island.

A total of 1,133 seamounts and volcanic cones were found in the area which is about the size of New York state. Some of them rise to a height of almost 7,000 feet and their peaks are 2,500 to 5,000 feet below the ocean's surface. □

Earthquakes

The Severity of an Earthquake

Source: National Earthquake Information Center, U.S. Geological Survey.

The severity of an earthquake can be expressed in terms of both intensity and magnitude. The two terms are quite different, however, and they are often confused. Intensity is based on the observed effects of ground shaking on people, buildings, and natural features. It varies from place to place within the disturbed region depending on the location of the observer with respect to the earthquake epicenter. Magnitude is related to the amount of seismic energy released at the hypocenter of the earthquake. It is based on the amplitude of the earthquake waves recorded on instruments, which have a common calibration. The magnitude of an earthquake is thus represented by a single, instrumentally determined value.

Earthquakes are the result of forces deep within Earth's interior that continuously affect its surface. The energy from these forces is stored in a variety of ways within the rocks. When this energy is released suddenly—by shearing movements along faults in the crust of Earth, for example—an earthquake results. The area of the fault where the sudden rupture takes place is called the focus or hypocenter of the earthquake. The point on Earth's surface directly above the focus is called the epicenter of the earthquake.

The Richter Magnitude Scale

Seismic waves are the vibrations from earthquakes that travel through Earth; they are recorded on instruments called seismographs. Seismographs record a zig-zag trace that shows the varying amplitude of ground oscillations beneath the instrument. Sensitive seismographs, which greatly magnify these ground motions, can detect strong earthquakes from sources anywhere in the world. The time, location, and magnitude of an earthquake can be determined from the data recorded by seismograph stations.

The Richter magnitude scale was developed in 1935 by Charles F. Richter of the California Institute of Technology as a mathematical device to compare the size of earthquakes. The magnitude of an earthquake is determined from the logarithm of the amplitude of waves recorded by seismographs. Adjustments are included in the magnitude formula to compensate for the variation in the distance between the various seismographs and the epicenter of the earthquakes. On the Richter Scale, magnitude is expressed in whole numbers and decimal fractions. For example, a magnitude of 5.3 might be computed for a moderate earthquake, and a strong earthquake might be rated as magnitude 6.3. Because of the logarithmic basis of the scale, each whole number increase in magnitude represents a tenfold increase in measured amplitude; as an estimate of energy, each whole number step in the magnitude scale corresponds to the release of about 31 times more energy than the amount associated with the preceding whole number value.

Great earthquakes, such as the 1964 Good Friday earthquake in Alaska, have magnitudes of 8.0 or higher. On the average, one earthquake of such size occurs somewhere in the world each year. Although the Richter Scale has no upper limit, the largest known shocks have had magnitudes in the 8.8 to 8.9 range.

The Richter Scale is not used to express damage. An earthquake in a densely populated area that results in many deaths and considerable damage may have the same magnitude as a shock in a remote area that does nothing more than frighten the wildlife. Large-magnitude earthquakes that occur beneath the oceans may not even be felt by humans.

More Accurate Magnitude Scales

The Richter scale has been largely abandoned by seismologists because it isn't very accurate for the biggest earthquakes, those in the range of 8 or 9. Because it is based on readings taken close to quakes, 100 miles or so, it is less precise in other parts of the world where the nearest seismograph may be many hundreds of miles away.

New ways have been developed to rate the magnitude of the quake in numbers similar to the familiar Richter scale. The U.S. Geological Survey's National Earthquake Information Center in Golden, Colorado, uses surface-wave magnitude, which measures the seismic waves crackling around Earth's surface. Other seismologists use a measure known as the moment magnitude, which is based on the size of the fault on which an earthquake occurs and the amount Earth slips. So nowadays, when most seismologists announce a magnitude number, they no longer say "on the Richter scale."

The Modified Mercalli Intensity Scale

The effect of an earthquake on Earth's surface is called the intensity. The intensity scale consists of a series of certain key responses such as people awakening, movement of furniture, damage to chimneys, and finally—total destruction. Although numerous intensity scales have been developed over the last several hundred years to evaluate the effects of earthquakes, the one currently used in the United States is the Modified Mercalli (MM) Intensity Scale. It was developed in 1931 by the American seismologists Harry Wood and Frank Neumann. This scale, composed of 12 increasing levels of intensity that range from imperceptible shaking to catastrophic destruction, is designated by Roman numerals. It does not have a mathematical basis; instead it is an arbitrary ranking based on observed effects.

The Modified Mercalli Intensity value assigned to a specific site after an earthquake has a more meaningful measure of severity to the nonscientist than the magnitude because intensity refers to the effects actually experienced at that place. After the occurrence of widely felt earthquakes, the Geological Survey mails questionnaires to postmasters in the disturbed area requesting the information so that intensity values can be assigned. The results of this postal canvass and information furnished by other sources are used to assign an intensity value, and to compile isoseismal maps that show the extent of various levels of intensity within the felt area. The maximum observed intensity generally occurs near the epicenter. □

Frequency of Earthquakes Worldwide[1]

Descriptor	Magnitude	Annual Average	Descriptor	Magnitude	Annual Average
Great	8 or higher	1	Light	4–4.9	c.6,200
Major	7–7.9	18	Minor	3–3.9	c.49,000
Strong	6–6.9	120	Very minor	2–3	c.1,000[2]
Moderate	5–5.9	800	Very minor	1–2	c.8,000[2]

1. Since 1900. 2. Per day. *Source:* National Earthquake Information Center, U.S. Geological Survey.

Number of Earthquakes Worldwide, 1987–1997

Magnitude	1987	1988	1990	1991	1992	1993	1994	1995	1996	1997
8.0–9.9	0	0	0	0	0	1	2	3	1	0
7.0–7.9	11	8	12	11	23	15	13	22	21	18
6.0–6.9	112	93	115	105	104	141	161	185	160	124
5.0–5.9	1,437	1,485	1,635	1,469	1,541	1,449	1,542	1,327	1,223	1,099
4.0–4.9	4,146	4,018	4,493	4,372	5,196	5,034	4,544	8,140	8,794	8,522
3.0–3.9	1,806	1,932	2,457	2,952	4,643	4,263	5,000	5,002	4,869	4,537
2.0–2.9	1,037	1,479	2,364	2,927	3,068	5,390	5,369	3,838	2,388	2,448
1.0–1.9	102	118	474	801	887	1,177	779	645	295	392
0.1–0.9	0	3	0	1	2	9	17	19	1	4
No magnitude	2,639	3,575	5,062	3,878	4,084	3,997	1,944	1,826	2,186	3680
Total	11,290	12,711	16,612	16,516	19,548	21,476	19,371	21,007	19,938	20,824

Source: National Earthquake Information Center, U.S. Geological Survey.

Major Earthquakes Around the World, 1998

(through Aug. 1998)

Date	Location	Magnitude[1]
Jan. 4, 1998	Loyalty Islands region (S. Pacific Sea)	7.4
Jan. 30, 1998	Near coast, northern Chile	7.0
March 25, 1998	Balleny Islands region	8.3[2]
March 29, 1998	Fiji Islands region	7.2
April 1, 1998	Off coast, southern Chile	7.0
May 3, 1998	Southeast of Taiwan	7.5
July 16, 1998	Santa Cruz Islands (S. Pacific Sea)	7.1
July 17, 1998	Papua New Guinea	7.1[3]
Aug 4, 1998	Near coast of Ecuador	7.1[3]
Aug. 20, 1998	Bonnin Islands, Japan	7.0

NOTE: A major earthquake is defined here as having a magnitude of 7.0 or more. 1. Unless otherwise indicated, magnitudes listed are moment magnitudes, the newest, more uniformly applicable magnitude scale. 2. Energy magnitude. 3. Surface wave magnitude. *Source:* National Earthquake Information Center, U.S. Geological Survey.

The Ten Largest Earthquakes in the World: 1900–1994

Country or place	Date	Magnitude
Chile	May 22, 1960	9.5
Alaska	March 28, 1964	9.2
Russia	Nov. 4, 1952	9.0
Ecuador	Jan. 31, 1906	8.8
Alaska	March 9, 1957	8.8
Kuril Islands	Nov. 6, 1958	8.7
Alaska	Feb. 4, 1965	8.7
India	Aug. 15, 1950	8.6
Argentina	Nov. 11, 1922	8.5
Indonesia	Feb. 1, 1938	8.5

Source: National Earthquake Information Center, U.S. Geological Survey.

The Fifteen Largest Earthquakes in the United States

Rank	Magnitude	Date	Location
1.	9.2	March 28, 1964	Prince William Sound, Alaska
2.	8.8	March 9, 1957	Andreanof Islands, Alaska
3.	8.7	Feb. 4, 1965	Rat Islands, Alaska
4.	8.3	Nov. 10, 1938	East of Shumagin Islands, Alaska
5.	8.3	July 10, 1958	Lituya Bay, Alaska
6.	8.2	Sept. 10, 1899	Yakutat Bay, Alaska
7.	8.2	Sept. 4, 1899	Near Cape Yakataga, Alaska
8.	8.0	May 7, 1986	Andreanof Islands, Alaska
9.	7.9	Feb. 7, 1812	New Madrid, Missouri
10.	7.9	Jan. 9, 1857	Fort Tejon, California
11.	7.9	April 3, 1868	Ka'u District, Island of Hawaii
12.	7.9	Oct. 9, 1900	Kodiak Island, Alaska
13.	7.9	Nov. 30, 1987	Gulf of Alaska
14.	7.8	March 26, 1872	Owens Valley, California
15.	7.8	Feb. 24, 1892	Imperial Valley, California

Source: National Earthquake Information Center, U.S. Geological Survey.

The Fifteen Largest Earthquakes in the Contiguous United States

Rank	Magnitude	Date	Location
1.	7.9	Feb. 7, 1812	New Madrid, Missouri
2.	7.9	Jan. 9, 1857	Fort Tejon, California
3.	7.8	March 26, 1872	Owens Valley, California
4.	7.8	Feb. 24, 1892	Imperial Valley, California
5.	7.7	Dec. 16, 1811	New Madrid, Missouri area
6.	7.7	April 18, 1906	San Francisco, California
7.	7.7	Oct. 3, 1915	Pleasant Valley, Nevada
8.	7.6	Jan. 23, 1812	New Madrid, Missouri
9.	7.6	June 28, 1992	Landers, California
10.	7.5	July 21, 1952	Kern County, California
11.	7.3	Nov. 4, 1927	West of Lompoc, California
12.	7.3	Dec. 16, 1954	Dixie Valley, Nevada
13.	7.3	Aug. 18, 1959	Hebgen Lake, Montana
14.	7.3	Oct. 28, 1983	Borah Peak, Idaho
15.	7.3	Jan. 31, 1922	West of Eureka, California

Source: National Earthquake Information Center, U.S. Geological Survey. NOTE: Widely differing magnitudes have been computed for some of these earthquakes; the values differ according to the methods and data used.

Highest Mountain Peaks of the World

(*See* p. 501 for U.S. peaks.)

Mountain peak	Range	Location	Height feet	Height meters
Everest	Himalayas	Nepal/Tibet	29,028	8,848
K2 (Godwin Austen)	Karakoram	Pakistan/China	28,250	8,611
Kanchenjunga	Himalayas	India/Nepal	28,169	8,586
Lhotse I	Himalayas	Nepal/Tibet	27,940	8,516
Makalu I	Himalayas	Nepal/Tibet	27,766	8,463
Cho Oyu	Himalayas	Nepal/Tibet	26,906	8,201
Dhaulagiri	Himalayas	Nepal	26,795	8,167
Manaslu I	Himalayas	Nepal	26,781	8,163
Nanga Parbat	Himalayas	Pakistan	26,660	8,125
Annapurna	Himalayas	Nepal	26,545	8,091
Gasherbrum I	Karakoram	Pakistan/China	26,470	8,068
Broad Peak	Karakoram	Pakistan/China	26,400	8,047
Gosainthan (Shishma Pangma)	Himalayas	Tibet	26,397	8,046
Gasherbrum II	Karakoram	Pakistan/China	26,360	8,035
Annapurna II	Himalayas	Nepal	26,041	7,937
Gyachung Kang	Himalayas	Nepal	25,910	7,897
Disteghil Sar	Karakoram	Pakistan	25,858	7,882
Himalchuli	Himalayas	Nepal	25,801	7,864
Nuptse	Himalayas	Nepal	25,726	7,841
Nanda Devi	Himalayas	India	25,663	7,824
Masherbrum	Karakoram	Kashmir [1]	25,660	7,821
Rakaposhi	Karakoram	Pakistan	25,551	7,788
Kanjut Sar	Karakoram	Pakistan	25,461	7,761
Kamet	Himalayas	India/Tibet	25,446	7,756
Namcha Barwa	Himalayas	Tibet	25,445	7,756
Gurla Mandhata	Himalayas	Tibet	25,355	7,728
Ulugh Muztagh	Kunlun	Tibet	25,340	7,723
Kungur	Muztagh Ata	China	25,325	7,719
Tirich Mir	Hindu Kush	Pakistan	25,230	7,690
Saser Kangri	Karakoram	India	25,172	7,672
Makalu II	Himalayas	Nepal	25,120	7,657
Minya Konka (Gongga Shan)	Daxue Shan	China	24,900	7,590
Kula Kangri	Himalayas	Bhutan	24,783	7,554
Chang-tzu	Himalayas	Tibet	24,780	7,553
Muztagh Ata	Muztagh Ata	China	24,757	7,546
Skyang Kangri	Himalayas	Kashmir	24,750	7,544
Communism Peak	Pamirs	Tajikistan	24,590	7,495
Jongsong Peak	Himalayas	Nepal	24,472	7,459
Pobeda Peak	Tien Shan	Kyrgyzstan	24,406	7,439
Sia Kangri	Himalayas	Kashmir	24,350	7,422
Haramosh Peak	Karakoram	Pakistan	24,270	7,397
Istoro Nal	Hindu Kush	Pakistan	24,240	7,388
Tent Peak	Himalayas	Nepal	24,165	7,365
Chomo Lhari	Himalayas	Tibet/Bhutan	24,040	7,327
Chamlang	Himalayas	Nepal	24,012	7,319
Kabru	Himalayas	Nepal	24,002	7,316
Alung Gangri	Himalayas	Tibet	24,000	7,315
Baltoro Kangri	Himalayas	Kashmir	23,990	7,312
Muztagh Ata (K-5)	Kunlun	China	23,890	7,282
Mana	Himalayas	India	23,860	7,273
Baruntse	Himalayas	Nepal	23,688	7,220
Nepal Peak	Himalayas	Nepal	23,500	7,163
Amne Machin	Kunlun	China	23,490	7,160
Gauri Sankar	Himalayas	Nepal/Tibet	23,440	7,145
Badrinath	Himalayas	India	23,420	7,138
Nunkun	Himalayas	Kashmir	23,410	7,135
Lenin Peak	Pamirs	Tajikistan/Kyrgyzstan	23,405	7,134
Pyramid	Himalayas	Nepal	23,400	7,132
Api	Himalayas	Nepal	23,399	7,132
Pauhunri	Himalayas	India/China	23,385	7,128
Trisul	Himalayas	India	23,360	7,120
Korzhenevski Peak	Pamirs	Tajikistan	23,310	7,105
Kangto	Himalayas	Tibet	23,260	7,090
Nyainqentanglha	Nyainqentanglha Shan	China	23,255	7,088

Mountain peak	Range	Location	Height feet	Height meters
Trisuli	Himalayas	India	23,210	7,074
Dunagiri	Himalayas	India	23,184	7,066
Revolution Peak	Pamirs	Tajikistan	22,880	6,974
Aconcagua	Andes	Argentina	22,834	6,960
Ojos del Salado	Andes	Argentina/Chile	22,664	6,908
Bonete	Andes	Argentina/Chile	22,546	6,872
Tupungato	Andes	Argentina/Chile	22,310	6,800
Moscow Peak	Pamirs	Tajikistan	22,260	6,785
Pissis	Andes	Argentina	22,241	6,779
Mercedario	Andes	Argentina/Chile	22,211	6,770
Huascarán	Andes	Peru	22,205	6,768
Llullaillaco	Andes	Argentina/Chile	22,057	6,723
El Libertador	Andes	Argentina	22,047	6,720
Cachi	Andes	Argentina	22,047	6,720
Kailas	Himalayas	Tibet	22,027	6,714
Incahuasi	Andes	Argentina/Chile	21,720	6,620
Yerupaja	Andes	Peru	21,709	6,617
Kurumda	Pamirs	Tajikistan	21,686	6,610
Galan	Andes	Argentina	21,654	6,600
El Muerto	Andes	Argentina/Chile	21,463	6,542
Sajama	Andes	Bolivia	21,391	6,520
Nacimiento	Andes	Argentina	21,302	6,493
Illampu	Andes	Bolivia	21,276	6,485
Illimani	Andes	Bolivia	21,201	6,462
Coropuna	Andes	Peru	21,083	6,426
Laudo	Andes	Argentina	20,997	6,400
Ancohuma	Andes	Bolivia	20,958	6,388
Cuzco (Ausangate)	Andes	Peru	20,945	6,384

1. Kashmir is divided between India and Pakistan, with both countries disputing the boundaries. *Source:* National Geographic Society.

World's Greatest Man-Made Lakes[1]

Name of dam	Location	Millions of cubic meters	Thousands of acre-feet	Year completed
Owen Falls	Uganda	204,800	166,000	1954
Kariba	Zimbabwe	181,592	147,218	1959
Bratsk	Siberia	169,270	137,220	1964
High Aswan (Sadd-el-Aali)	Egypt	168,000	136,200	1970
Akosombo	Ghana	148,000	120,000	1965
Daniel Johnson	Canada	141,852	115,000	1968
Guri (Raul Leoni)	Venezuela	136,000	110,256	1986
Krasnoyarsk	Siberia	73,300	59,425	1967
Bennett W.A.C.	Canada	70,309	57,006	1967
Zeya	Russia	68,400	55,452	1978
Cabora Bassa	Mozambique	63,000	51,075	1974
LaGrande 2	Canada	61,720	50,037	1982
LaGrande 3	Canada	60,020	48,659	1982
Ust'-Ilimsk	Russia	59,300	48,075	1980
Volga-V.I. Lenin	Russia	58,000	47,020	1955
Caniapiscau	Canada	53,790	43,608	1981
Pati (Chapetón)	Argentina	53,700	43,535	UC
Upper Wainganga	India	50,700	41,103	1987
Sáo Felix	Brazil	50,600	41,022	1986
Bukhtarma	Former U.S.S.R.	49,740	40,325	1960
Atatürk (Karababa)	Turkey	48,700	39,482	1990
Cerros Colorados	Argentina	48,000	38,914	1973
Irkutsk	Russia	46,000	37,290	1956
Tucuruí	Brazil	36,375	29,489	1984
Vilyuy	Russia	35,900	29,104	1967
Sanmenxia	China	35,400	28,700	1960
Hoover	Nevada/Arizona	35,154	28,500	1936
Sobridinho	Brazil	34,200	27,726	1981
Glen Canyon	Arizona	33,304	27,000	1964
Jenpeg	Canada	31,790	25,772	1975

1. Formed by construction of dams. NOTE: UC = under construction. *Source:* Department of the Interior, Bureau of Reclamation and *International Water Power and Dam Construction.*

Oceans and Seas

Name	Area sq mi.	Area sq km	Average depth feet	Average depth meters	Greatest known depth feet	Greatest known depth meters	Place of greatest known depth
Pacific Ocean	64,000,000	165,760,000	13,215	4,028	36,198	11,033	Mariana Trench
Atlantic Ocean	31,815,000	82,400,000	12,880	3,926	30,246	9,219	Puerto Rico Trench
Indian Ocean	25,300,000	65,526,700	13,002	3,963	24,460	7,455	Sunda Trench
Arctic Ocean	5,440,200	14,090,000	3,953	1,205	18,456	5,625	77°45′N; 175°W
Mediterranean Sea[1]	1,145,100	2,965,800	4,688	1,429	15,197	4,632	Off Cape Matapan, Greece
Caribbean Sea	1,049,500	2,718,200	8,685	2,647	22,788	6,946	Off Cayman Islands
South China Sea	895,400	2,319,000	5,419	1,652	16,456	5,016	West of Luzon
Bering Sea	884,900	2,291,900	5,075	1,547	15,659	4,773	Off Buldir Island
Gulf of Mexico	615,000	1,592,800	4,874	1,486	12,425	3,787	Sigsbee Deep
Okhotsk Sea	613,800	1,589,700	2,749	838	12,001	3,658	146°10′E; 46°50′N
East China Sea	482,300	1,249,200	617	188	9,126	2,782	25°16′N; 125°E
Hudson Bay	475,800	1,232,300	420	128	600	183	Near entrance
Japan Sea	389,100	1,007,800	4,429	1,350	12,276	3,742	Central Basin
Andaman Sea	308,100	797,700	2,854	870	12,392	3,777	Off Car Nicobar Island
North Sea	222,100	575,200	308	94	2,165	660	Skagerrak
Red Sea	169,100	438,000	1,611	491	7,254	2,211	Off Port Sudan
Baltic Sea	163,000	422,200	180	55	1,380	421	Off Gotland

1. Includes Black Sea and Sea of Azov. NOTE: For Caspian Sea, *see* Large Lakes of the World.

Large Lakes of the World

(Area more than 1,600 sq miles)

Name and location	Area sq mi.	Area km	Length mi.	Length km	Maximum depth feet	Maximum depth meters
Caspian Sea, Azerbaijan-Russia-Kazakhstan-Turkmenistan-Iran[1]	152,239	394,299	745	1,199	3,104	946
Superior, U.S.-Canada	31,820	82,414	383	616	1,333	406
Victoria, Tanzania-Uganda	26,828	69,485	200	322	270	82
Aral, Kazakhstan-Uzbekistan	25,659	66,457	266	428	223	68
Huron, U.S.-Canada	23,010	59,596	247	397	750	229
Michigan, U.S.	22,400	58,016	321	517	923	281
Tanganyika, Tanzania-Congo	12,700	32,893	420	676	4,708	1,435
Baikal, Russia	12,162	31,500	395	636	5,712	1,741
Great Bear,Canada	12,000	31,080	232	373	270	82
Nyasa, Malawi-Mozambique-Tanzania	11,600	30,044	360	579	2,316	706
Great Slave, Canada	11,170	28,930	298	480	2,015	614
Chad,[2] Chad-Niger-Nigeria	9,946	25,760	—	—	23	7
Erie, U.S.-Canada	9,930	25,719	241	388	210	64
Winnipeg, Canada	9,094	23,553	264	425	204	62
Ontario, U.S.-Canada	7,520	19,477	193	311	778	237
Balkhash, Kazakhstan	7,115	18,428	376	605	87	27
Ladoga, Russia	7,000	18,130	124	200	738	225
Onega, Russia	3,819	9,891	154	248	361	110
Titicaca, Bolivia-Peru	3,141	8,135	110	177	1,214	370
Nicaragua, Nicaragua	3,089	8,001	110	177	230	70
Athabaska, Canada	3,058	7,920	208	335	407	124
Rudolf, Kenya	2,473	6,405	154	248	—	—
Reindeer, Canada	2,444	6,330	152	245	—	—
Eyre, South Australia	2,400[3]	6,216	130	209	varies	varies
Issyk-Kul, Kyrgyzstan	2,394	6,200	113	182	2,297	700
Urmia,[2] Iran	2,317	6,001	81	130	49	15
Torrens, South Australia	2,200	5,698	130	209	—	—
Vänern, Sweden	2,141	5,545	87	140	322	98
Winnipegosis, Canada	2,086	5,403	152	245	59	18
Mobutu Sese Seko, Uganda	2,046	5,299	100	161	180	55
Nettilling, Baffin Island, Canada	1,950	5,051	70	113	—	—
Nipigon, Canada	1,870	4,843	72	116	—	—
Manitoba, Canada	1,817	4,706	140	225	22	7
Great Salt, U.S.	1,800	4,662	75	121	15–25	5–8
Kioga, Uganda	1,700	4,403	50	80	about 30	9
Koko-Nor, China	1,630	4,222	66	106	—	—

1. The Caspian Sea is called "sea" because the Romans, finding it salty, named it *Mare Caspium.* Many geographers, however, consider it a lake because it is land-locked. 2. Figures represent high-water data. 3. Varies with the rainfall of the wet season. It has been reported to dry up almost completely on occasion

Principal Rivers of the World

(*See* pp. 499–501 for other U.S. rivers.)

River	Source	Outflow	Approx. length miles	Approx. length km
Nile	Tributaries of Lake Victoria, Africa	Mediterranean Sea	4,180	6,690
Amazon	Glacier-fed lakes, Peru	Atlantic Ocean	3,912	6,296
Mississippi-Missouri-Red Rock	Source of Red Rock, Montana	Gulf of Mexico	3,710	5,970
Yangtze Kiang	Tibetan plateau, China	China Sea	3,602	5,797
Ob	Altai Mts., Russia	Gulf of Ob	3,459	5,567
Huang Ho (Yellow)	Eastern part of Kunlan Mts., west China	Gulf of Chihli	2,900	4,667
Yenisei	Tannu-Ola Mts., western Tuva, Russia	Arctic Ocean	2,800	4,506
Paraná	Confluence of Paranaiba and Grande rivers	Río de la Plata	2,795	4,498
Irtish	Altai Mts., Russia	Ob River	2,758	4,438
Zaire (Congo)	Confluence of Lualab and Luapula rivers, Congo	Atlantic Ocean	2,716	4,371
Heilong (Amur)	Confluence of Shilka (Russia) and Argun (Manchuria) rivers	Tatar Strait	2,704	4,352
Lena	Baikal Mts., Russia	Arctic Ocean	2,652	4,268
Mackenzie	Head of Finlay River, British Columbia, Canada	Beaufort Sea (Arctic Ocean)	2,635	4,241
Niger	Guinea	Gulf of Guinea	2,600	4,184
Mekong	Tibetan highlands	South China Sea	2,500	4,023
Mississippi	Lake Itasca, Minnesota	Gulf of Mexico	2,348	3,779
Missouri	Confluence of Jefferson, Gallatin, and Madison rivers, Montana	Mississippi River	2,315	3,726
Volga	Valdai plateau, Russia	Caspian Sea	2,291	3,687
Madeira	Confluence of Beni and Maumoré rivers, Bolivia-Brazil boundary	Amazon River	2,012	3,238
Purus	Peruvian Andes	Amazon River	1,993	3,207
São Francisco	Southwest Minas Gerais, Brazil	Atlantic Ocean	1,987	3,198
Yukon	Junction of Lewes and Pelly rivers, Yukon Territory, Canada	Bering Sea	1,979	3,185
St. Lawrence	Lake Ontario	Gulf of St. Lawrence	1,900	3,058
Rio Grande	San Juan Mts., Colorado	Gulf of Mexico	1,885	3,034
Brahmaputra	Himalayas	Ganges River	1,800	2,897
Indus	Himalayas	Arabian Sea	1,800	2,897
Danube	Black Forest, Germany	Black Sea	1,766	2,842
Euphrates	Confluence of Murat Nehri and Kara Su rivers, Turkey	Shatt-al-Arab	1,739	2,799
Darling	Central part of Eastern Highlands, Australia	Murray River	1,702	2,739
Zambezi	11°21′S, 24°22′E, Zambia	Mozambique Channel	1,700	2,736
Tocantins	Goiás, Brazil	Pará River	1,677	2,699
Murray	Australian Alps, New South Wales	Indian Ocean	1,609	2,589
Nelson	Head of Bow River, western Alberta, Canada	Hudson Bay	1,600	2,575
Paraguay	Mato Grosso, Brazil	Paraná River	1,584	2,549
Ural	Southern Ural Mts., Russia	Caspian Sea	1,574	2,533
Ganges	Himalayas	Bay of Bengal	1,557	2,506
Amu Darya (Oxus)	Nicholas Range, Pamir Mts., Turkmenistan	Aral Sea	1,500	2,414
Japurá	Andes, Colombia	Amazon River	1,500	2,414
Salween	Tibet, south of Kunlun Mts.	Gulf of Martaban	1,500	2,414
Arkansas	Central Colorado	Mississippi River	1,459	2,348
Colorado	Grand County, Colorado	Gulf of California	1,450	2,333
Dnieper	Valdai Hills, Russia	Black Sea	1,419	2,284
Ohio-Allegheny	Potter County, Pennsylvania	Mississippi River	1,306	2,102

River	Source	Outflow	Approx. length miles	km
Irrawaddy	Confluence of Nmai and Mali rivers, northeast Burma	Bay of Bengal	1,300	2,092
Orange	Lesotho	Atlantic Ocean	1,300	2,092
Orinoco	Serra Parima Mts., Venezuela	Atlantic Ocean	1,281	2,062
Pilcomayo	Andes Mts., Bolivia	Paraguay River	1,242	1,999
Xi Jiang (Si Kiang)	Eastern Yunnan Province, China	China Sea	1,236	1,989
Columbia	Columbia Lake, British Columbia, Canada	Pacific Ocean	1,232	1,983
Don	Tula, Russia	Sea of Azov	1,223	1,968
Sungari	China-North Korea boundary	Amur River	1,215	1,955
Saskatchewan	Canadian Rocky Mts.	Lake Winnipeg	1,205	1,939
Peace	Stikine Mts., British Columbia, Canada	Great Slave River	1,195	1,923
Tigris	Taurus Mts., Turkey	Shatt-al-Arab	1,180	1,899

Large Islands of the World

Island	Location and political affiliation	Area sq mi.	sq km
Greenland	North Atlantic (Danish)	839,999	2,175,597
New Guinea	Southwest Pacific (Irian Jaya, Indonesian, west part; Papua New Guinea, east part)	316,615	820,033
Borneo	West mid-Pacific (Indonesian, south part, Brunei and Malaysian, north part)	286,914	743,107
Madagascar	Indian Ocean (Malagasy Republic)	226,657	587,042
Baffin	North Atlantic (Canadian)	183,810	476,068
Sumatra	Northeast Indian Ocean (Indonesian)	182,859	473,605
Honshu	Sea of Japan-Pacific (Japanese)	88,925	230,316
Great Britain	Off coast of NW Europe (England, Scotland, and Wales)	88,758	229,883
Ellesmere	Arctic Ocean (Canadian)	82,119	212,688
Victoria	Arctic Ocean (Canadian)	81,930	212,199
Sulawesi (Celebes)	West mid-Pacific (Indonesian)	72,986	189,034
South Island	South Pacific (New Zealand)	58,093	150,461
Java	Indian Ocean (Indonesian)	48,990	126,884
North Island	South Pacific (New Zealand)	44,281	114,688
Cuba	Caribbean Sea (republic)	44,218	114,525
Newfoundland	North Atlantic (Canadian)	42,734	110,681
Luzon	West mid-Pacific (Philippines)	40,420	104,688
Iceland	North Atlantic (republic)	39,768	102,999
Mindanao	West mid-Pacific (Philippines)	36,537	94,631
Ireland	West of Great Britain (republic, south part; United Kingdom, north part)	32,597	84,426
Hokkaido	Sea of Japan—Pacific (Japanese)	30,372	78,663
Hispaniola	Caribbean Sea (Dominican Republic, east part; Haiti, west part)	29,355	76,029
Tasmania	South of Australia (Australian)	26,215	67,897
Sri Lanka (Ceylon)	Indian Ocean (republic)	25,332	65,610
Sakhalin (Karafuto)	North of Japan (Russian)	24,560	63,610
Banks	Arctic Ocean (Canadian)	23,230	60,166
Devon	Arctic Ocean (Canadian)	20,861	54,030
Tierra del Fuego	Southern tip of South America (Argentinian, east part; Chilean, west part)	18,605	48,187
Kyushu	Sea of Japan—Pacific (Japanese)	16,223	42,018
Melville	Arctic Ocean (Canadian)	16,141	41,805
Axel Heiberg	Arctic Ocean (Canadian)	15,779	40,868
Southampton	Hudson Bay (Canadian)	15,700	40,663

Highest Waterfalls of the World

Waterfall	Location	River	Height feet	Height m
Angel	Venezuela	Tributary of Caroni	3,281	1,000
Tugela	Natal, South Africa	Tugela	3,000	914
Cuquenán	Venezuela	Cuquenán	2,000	610
Sutherland	South Island, New Zealand	Arthur	1,904	580
Takkakaw	British Columbia	Tributary of Yoho	1,650	503
Ribbon (Yosemite)	California	Creek flowing into Yosemite	1,612	491
Upper Yosemite	California	Yosemite Creek, tributary of Merced	1,430	436
Gavarnie	Southwest France	Gave de Pau	1,384	422
Vettisfoss	Norway	Mörkedola	1,200	366
Widows' Tears (Yosemite)	California	Tributary of Merced	1,170	357
Staubbach	Switzerland	Staubbach (Lauterbrunnen Valley)	984	300
Middle Cascade (Yosemite)	California	Yosemite Creek, tributary of Merced	909	277
King Edward VIII	Guyana	Courantyne	850	259
Gersoppa	India	Sharavati	829	253
Kaieteur	Guyana	Potaro	822	251
Skykje	Norway	In Skykjedal (valley Inner Hardinger Fjord)	820	250
Kalambo	Tanzania-Zambia	—	720	219
Fairy (Mt. Rainier Park)	Washington	Stevens Creek	700	213
Trummelbach	Switzerland	Trummelbach (Lauterbrunnen Valley)	700	213
Aniene (Teverone)	Italy	Tiber	680	207
Cascata delle Marmore	Italy	Velino, tributary of Nera	650	198
Maradalsfos	Norway	Stream flowing into Ejkisdalsvand (lake)	643	196
Feather	California	Fall River	640	195
Maletsunyane	Lesotho	Maletsunyane	630	192
Bridalveil (Yosemite)	California	Yosemite Creek	620	189
Multnomah	Oregon	Multnomah Creek, tributary of Columbia	620	189
Vøringsfos	Norway	Bjoreia	597	182
Nevada (Yosemite)	California	Merced	594	181
Skjeggedal	Norway	Tysso	525	160
Marlna	Guyana	Tributary tributary of Potaro	500	152
Tequendama	Colombia	Funza, tributary of Magdalena	425	130
King George's	Cape of Good Hope, South Africa	Orange	400	122
Illilouette (Yosemite)	California	Illilouette Creek, tributary of Merced	370	113
Victoria	Zimbabwe-Zambia boundary	Zambezi	355	108
Handöl	Sweden	Handöl Creek	345	105
Lower Yosemite	California	Yosemite	320	98
Comet (Mt. Rainier Park)	Washington	Van Trump Creek	320	98
Vernal (Yosemite)	California	Merced	317	97
Virginia	Northwest Territories, Canada	South Nahanni, tributary of Mackenzie	315	96
Lower Yellowstone	Wyoming	Yellowstone	310	94

NOTE: Niagara Falls (New York-Ontario), though of great volume, has parallel drops of only 158 and 167 feet.

Principal Deserts of the World

Desert	Location	Approximate size	Approx. elevation, ft.
Atacama	North Chile	400 mi. long	7,000–13,500
Black Rock	Northwest Nevada	About 1,000 sq mi.	2,000–8,500
Colorado	Southeast California from San Gorgonio Pass to Gulf of California	200 mi. long and a maximum width of 50 mi.	Few feet above to 250 below sea level
Dasht-e-Kavir	Southeast of Caspian Sea, Iran	—	2,000
Dasht-e-Lut	Northeast of Kerman, Iran	—	1,000
Gobi (Shamo)	Covers most of Mongolia	500,000 sq mi.	3,000–5,000
Great Arabian	Most of Arabia	1,500 mi. long	—
Great Basin	Southwestern United States	190,000 sq mi.	
Dahna	Northeast of Nejd	400 mi. by 30 mi.	—
Rub' al-Khali	South portion of Nejd	Over 200,000 sq. mi.	—
Syrian (Al-Hamad)	North of lat. 30°N	—	1,850
Great Australian	Western portion of Australia	About one half the continent	600–1,000
Great Salt Lake	West of Great Salt Lake to Nevada—Utah boundary	About 110 mi. by 50 mi.	4,500
Kalahari	South Africa—South-West Africa	About 120,000 sq mi.	Over 3,000
Kara Kum	Southwest Turkmenistan	115,000 sq mi.	—

Desert	Location	Approximate size	Approx. elevation, ft.
Kavir	Central Iran	100,000 sq mi.	
Kyzyl Kum	Uzbekistan and Kazakhstan	Over 100,000 sq. mi.	160–2,000
Libyan	Libya, Egypt, Sudan	Over 500,000 sq mi.	—
Lut	Eastern Iran	20,000 sq mi.	
Mojave	North of Colorado Desert and south of Death Valley, southeast California	15,000 sq mi.	2,000
Namib	Southwestern Africa	52,000 sq mi.	
Nubian	From Red Sea to great west bend of the Nile, Sudan	—	2,500
Painted Desert	Northeast Arizona	Over 7,000 sq mi.	High plateau, 5,000
Sahara	North Africa to about lat. 15°N and from Red Sea to Atlantic Ocean	3,200 mi. greatest length along lat. 20°N; area over 3,500,000 sq mi.	440 below sea level to 11,000 above; avg. elevation, 1,400–1,600
Sonoran	Southwestern Arizona, southeastern California, and northwestern Mexico	120,000 sq mi.	—
Takla Makan	Southcentral Sinkiang, China	Over 100,000 sq mi.	—
Thar (Indian)	Pakistan-India	Nearly 100,000 sq mi.	Over 1,000

Some Major Types of Deserts

Source: U.S. Geological Survey.

Trade wind deserts: Trade winds, which are steady tropical winds, heat up as they move toward the equator. These dry winds dissipate cloud cover, allowing more sunlight to heat the land. Most of the major deserts, including the world's largest, the Sahara, lie in areas crossed by the trade winds.

Midaltitude deserts: Occurring between 30° and 50° N and S, midaltitude deserts are interior drainage basins far from oceans and have a wide range of annual temperatures.

Rain shadow deserts: Tall mountain ranges prevent moisture-rich clouds from reaching areas on the protected side of the range. As air rises over the mountain, water is precipitated and the air loses its moisture content. A desert is formed in the "shadow" of the range.

Coastal deserts: Generally found on the western edges of continents near the tropics of Cancer and Capricorn, these deserts are affected by cold ocean currents that parallel the coast. A coastal desert, the Atacama of South America, is Earth's driest desert: its measurable rainfall averages 1 millimeter every 5–20 years.

Interesting Caves and Caverns of the World

Aggtelek. In village of same name, northern Hungary. Large stalactitic cavern about five miles long.

Altamira Cave. Near Santander, Spain. Contains animal paintings (Old Stone Age art) on roof and walls.

Antiparos. On island of same name in the Grecian Archipelago. Some stalactites are 20 ft. long. Brilliant colors and fantastic shapes.

Blue Grotto. On island of Capri, Italy. Cavern hollowed out in limestone by constant wave action. Now half filled with water because of sinking coast. Name derived from unusual blue light permeating the cave. Source of light is a submerged opening, light passing through the water.

Carlsbad Caverns. Southeast New Mexico. Largest underground labyrinth yet discovered. Three levels: 754-, 900-, and 1,320 ft. below the surface.

Fingal's Cave. On island of Staffa off coast of western Scotland. Penetrates about 200 ft. inland. Contains basaltic columns almost 40 ft. high.

Jenolan Caves. In Blue Mountain plateau, New South Wales, Australia. Beautiful stalactitic formations.

Kent's Cavern. Near Torquay, England. Source of much information on Paleolithic humans.

Luray Cavern. Near Luray, Va. Has large stalactitic and stalagmitic columns of many colors.

Mammoth Cave. Limestone cavern in central Kentucky. Cave area is about 10 miles in diameter but has over 300 miles of irregular subterranean passageways at various levels. Temperature remains fairly constant at 54°F.

Peak Cavern or Devil's Hole. Derbyshire, England. About 2,250 ft. into a mountain. Lowest part is about 600 ft. below the surface.

Postojna (Postumia) Grotto. Near Postumia in Julian Alps, about 25 miles northeast of Trieste. Stalactitic cavern, largest in Europe. Piuca (Pivka) River flows through part of it. Caves have numerous beautiful stalactites.

Singing Cave. Iceland. A lava cave; name derived from echoes of people singing in it.

Wind Cave. In Black Hills of South Dakota. Limestone caverns with stalactites and stalagmites almost entirely missing. Variety of crystal formations called "boxwork."

Wyandotte Cave. In Crawford County, southern Indiana. A limestone cavern with five levels of passages; one of the largest in North America. "Monumental Mountain," approximately 135 ft. high, is believed to be one of the world's largest underground "mountains."

Latitude and Longitude of World Cities

(and time corresponding to 12:00 noon, eastern standard time)

City	Latitude °	Latitude ′	Longitude °	Longitude ′	Time
Aberdeen, Scotland	57	9 N	2	9 W	5:00 p.m.
Adelaide, Australia	34	55 S	138	36 E	2:30 a.m.[1]
Algiers, Algeria	36	50 N	3	0 E	6:00 p.m.
Amsterdam, Netherlands	52	22 N	4	53 E	6:00 p.m.
Ankara, Turkey	39	55 N	32	55 E	7:00 p.m.
Asunción, Paraguay	25	15 S	57	40 W	1:00 p.m.
Athens, Greece	37	58 N	23	43 E	7:00 p.m.
Auckland, New Zealand	36	52 S	174	45 E	5:00 a.m.[1]
Bangkok, Thailand	13	45 N	100	30 E	midnight
Barcelona, Spain	41	23 N	2	9 E	6:00 p.m.
Beijing, China	39	55 N	116	25 E	1:00 a.m.[1]
Belém, Brazil	1	28 S	48	29 W	2:00 p.m.
Belfast, Northern Ireland	54	37 N	5	56 W	5:00 p.m.
Belgrade, Yugoslavia	44	52 N	20	32 E	6:00 p.m.
Berlin, Germany	52	30 N	13	25 E	6:00 p.m.
Birmingham, England	52	25 N	1	55 W	5:00 p.m.
Bogotá, Colombia	4	32 N	74	15 W	12:00 noon
Bombay, India	19	0 N	72	48 E	10:30 p.m.
Bordeaux, France	44	50 N	0	31 W	6:00 p.m.
Bremen, Germany	53	5 N	8	49 E	6:00 p.m.
Brisbane, Australia	27	29 S	153	8 E	3:00 a.m.[1]
Bristol, England	51	28 N	2	35 W	5:00 p.m.
Brussels, Belgium	50	52 N	4	22 E	6:00 p.m.
Bucharest, Romania	44	25 N	26	7 E	7:00 p.m.
Budapest, Hungary	47	30 N	19	5 E	6:00 p.m.
Buenos Aires, Argentina	34	35 S	58	22 W	2:00 p.m.
Cairo, Egypt	30	2 N	31	21 E	7:00 p.m.
Calcutta, India	22	34 N	88	24 E	10:30 p.m.
Canton, China	23	7 N	113	15 E	1:00 a.m.[1]
Cape Town, South Africa	33	55 S	18	22 E	7:00 p.m.
Caracas, Venezuela	10	28 N	67	2 W	1:00 p.m.
Cayenne, French Guiana	4	49 N	52	18 W	1:00 p.m.
Chihuahua, Mexico	28	37 N	106	5 W	11:00 a.m.
Chongqing, China	29	46 N	106	34 E	1:00 a.m.[1]
Copenhagen, Denmark	55	40 N	12	34 E	6:00 p.m.
Córdoba, Argentina	31	28 S	64	10 W	2:00 p.m.
Dakar, Senegal	14	40 N	17	28 W	5:00 p.m.
Darwin, Australia	12	28 S	130	51 E	2:30 a.m.[1]
Djibouti, Djibouti	11	30 N	43	3 E	8:00 p.m.
Dublin, Ireland	53	20 N	6	15 W	5:00 p.m.
Durban, South Africa	29	53 S	30	53 E	7:00 p.m.
Edinburgh, Scotland	55	55 N	3	10 W	5:00 p.m.
Frankfurt, Germany	50	7 N	8	41 E	6:00 p.m.
Georgetown, Guyana	6	45 N	58	15 W	1:15 p.m.
Glasgow, Scotland	55	50 N	4	15 W	5:00 p.m.
Guatemala City, Guatemala	14	37 N	90	31 W	11:00 a.m.
Guayaquil, Ecuador	2	10 S	79	56 W	12:00 noon
Hamburg, Germany	53	33 N	10	2 E	6:00 p.m.
Hammerfest, Norway	70	38 N	23	38 E	6:00 p.m.
Havana, Cuba	23	8 N	82	23 W	12:00 noon
Helsinki, Finland	60	10 N	25	0 E	7:00 p.m.
Hobart, Tasmania	42	52 S	147	19 E	3:00 a.m.[1]
Iquique, Chile	20	10 S	70	7 W	1:00 p.m.
Irkutsk, Russia	52	30 N	104	20 E	1:00 a.m.
Jakarta, Indonesia	6	16 S	106	48 E	0:30 a.m.[1]
Johannesburg, South Africa	26	12 S	28	4 E	7:00 p.m.
Kingston, Jamaica	17	59 N	76	49 W	12:00 noon
Kinshasa, Congo	4	18 S	15	17 E	6:00 p.m.
La Paz, Bolivia	16	27 S	68	22 W	1:00 p.m.
Leeds, England	53	45 N	1	30 W	5:00 p.m.
Lima, Peru	12	0 S	77	2 W	12:00 noon
Lisbon, Portugal	38	44 N	9	9 W	5:00 p.m.
Liverpool, England	53	25 N	3	0 W	5:00 p.m.
London, England	51	32 N	0	5 W	5:00 p.m.
Lyons, France	45	45 N	4	50 E	6:00 p.m.
Madrid, Spain	40	26 N	3	42 W	6:00 p.m.
Manchester, England	53	30 N	2	15 W	5:00 p.m.
Manila, Philippines	14	35 N	120	57 E	1:00 a.m.[1]
Marseilles, France	43	20 N	5	20 E	6:00 p.m.
Mazatlán, Mexico	23	12 N	106	25 W	10:00 a.m.
Mecca, Saudi Arabia	21	29 N	39	45 E	8:00 p.m.
Melbourne, Australia	37	47 S	144	58 E	3:00 a.m.[1]
Mexico City, Mexico	19	26 N	99	7 W	11:00 a.m.
Milan, Italy	45	27 N	9	10 E	6:00 p.m.
Montevideo, Uruguay	34	53 S	56	10 W	2:00 p.m.
Moscow, Russia	55	45 N	37	36 E	8:00 p.m.
Munich, Germany	48	8 N	11	35 E	6:00 p.m.
Nagasaki, Japan	32	48 N	129	57 E	2:00 a.m.[1]
Nagoya, Japan	35	7 N	136	56 E	2:00 a.m.[1]
Nairobi, Kenya	1	25 S	36	55 E	8:00 p.m.
Nanjing (Nanking), China	32	3 N	118	53 E	1:00 a.m.[1]
Naples, Italy	40	50 N	14	15 E	6:00 p.m.
Newcastle-on-Tyne, England	54	58 N	1	37 W	5:00 p.m.
Odessa, Ukraine	46	27 N	30	48 E	8:00 p.m.
Osaka, Japan	34	32 N	135	30 E	2:00 a.m.[1]
Oslo, Norway	59	57 N	10	42 E	6:00 p.m.
Panama City, Panama	8	58 N	79	32 W	12:00 noon
Paramaribo, Suriname	5	45 N	55	15 W	1:30 p.m.
Paris, France	48	48 N	2	20 E	6:00 p.m.
Perth, Australia	31	57 S	115	52 E	1:00 a.m.[1]
Plymouth, England	50	25 N	4	5 W	5:00 p.m.
Port Moresby, Papua New Guinea	9	25 S	147	8 E	3:00 a.m.[1]
Prague, Czech Republic	50	5 N	14	26 E	6:00 p.m.
Rangoon, Burma	16	50 N	96	0 E	11:30 p.m.
Reykjavik, Iceland	64	4 N	21	58 W	4:00 p.m.
Rio de Janeiro, Brazil	22	57 S	43	12 W	2:00 p.m.
Rome, Italy	41	54 N	12	27 E	6:00 p.m.
Salvador, Brazil	12	56 S	38	27 W	2:00 p.m.
Santiago, Chile	33	28 S	70	45 W	1:00 p.m.
St. Petersburg, Russia	59	56 N	30	18 E	8:00 p.m.
Sao Paulo, Brazil	23	31 S	46	31 W	2:00 p.m.
Shanghai, China	31	10 N	121	28 E	1:00 a.m.[1]
Singapore, Singapore	1	14 N	103	55 E	0:30 a.m.[1]
Sofia, Bulgaria	42	40 N	23	20 E	7:00 p.m.
Stockholm, Sweden	59	17 N	18	3 E	6:00 p.m.
Sydney, Australia	34	0 S	151	0 E	3:00 a.m.[1]
Tananarive, Madagascar	18	50 S	47	33 E	8:00 p.m.
Teheran, Iran	35	45 N	51	45 E	8:30 p.m.
Tokyo, Japan	35	40 N	139	45 E	2:00 a.m.[1]
Tripoli, Libya	32	57 N	13	12 E	7:00 p.m.
Venice, Italy	45	26 N	12	20 E	6:00 p.m.
Veracruz, Mexico	19	10 N	96	10 W	11:00 a.m.
Vienna, Austria	48	14 N	16	20 E	6:00 p.m.
Vladivostok, Russia	43	10 N	132	0 E	3:00 a.m.[1]
Warsaw, Poland	52	14 N	21	0 E	6:00 p.m.
Wellington, New Zealand	41	17 S	174	47 E	5:00 a.m.[1]
Zürich, Switzerland	47	21 N	8	31 E	6:00 p.m.

1. On the following day.

Miscellaneous Data for the United States

Highest point: Mt. McKinley, Alaska	20,320 ft. (6,198 m)
Lowest point: Death Valley, Calif.	282 ft. (86 m) below sea level
Approximate mean elevation	2,500 ft. (763 m)
Points farthest apart (50 states): Log Point, Elliot Key, Fla., and Kure Island, Hawaii	5,859 mi. (9,429 km)
Geographic center (50 states): in Butte County, S.D. (west of Castle Rock)	44°58′N lat.103°46′W long.
Geographic center (48 conterminous states): In Smith County, Kan. (near Lebanon)	39°50′N lat. 98°35′W long.
Boundaries:	
Between Alaska and Canada	1,538 mi. (2,475 km)
Between the 48 conterminous states and Canada (incl. Great Lakes)	3,987 mi. (6,416 km)
Between the United States and Mexico	1,933 mi. (3,111 km)

Source: U.S. Geological Survey.

Extreme Points of the United States (50 States)

Extreme point	Latitude	Longitude	Distance[1] mi.	Distance[1] km
Northernmost point: Point Barrow, Alaska	71°23′ N	156°29′ W	2,507	4,034
Easternmost point: West Quoddy Head, Me.	44°49′ N	66°57′ W	1,788	2,997
Southernmost point: Ka Lae (South Cape), Hawaii	18°55′ N	155°41′ W	3,463	5,573
Westernmost point: Cape Wrangell, Alaska (Attu Island)	52°55′ N	172°27′ E	3,625	5,833

1. From geographic center of United States (incl. Alaska and Hawaii), west of Castle Rock, S.D., 44°58′ lat., 103°46′ W long. If measured from the prime meridian in Greenwich, England, Cape Wrangell, Attu Island, Alaska, would be the easternmost point.

The Continental Divide

The Continental Divide is a ridge of high ground that runs irregularly north and south through the Rocky Mountains and separates eastward-flowing from westward-flowing streams. The waters that flow eastward empty into the Atlantic Ocean, chiefly by way of the Gulf of Mexico; those that flow westward empty into the Pacific.

Rivers of the United States
(350 or more miles long)

Alabama-Coosa (600 mi.; 966 km): From junction of Oostanula and Etowah R. in Georgia to Mobile R.

Altamaha-Ocmulgee (392 mi.; 631 km): From junction of Yellow R. and South R., Newton Co. in Georgia to Atlantic Ocean.

Apalachicola-Chattahoochee (524 mi.; 843 km): From Towns Co. in Georgia to Gulf of Mexico in Florida.

Arkansas (1,459 mi.; 2,348 km): From Lake Co. in Colorado to Mississippi R. in Arkansas.

Brazos (923 mi.; 1,490 km): From junction of Salt Fork and Double Mountain Fork in Texas to Gulf of Mexico.

Canadian (906 mi.; 1,458 km): From Las Animas Co. in Colorado to Arkansas R. in Oklahoma.

Cimarron (600 mi.; 966 km): From Colfax Co. in New Mexico to Arkansas R. in Oklahoma.

Colorado (1,450 mi.; 2,333 km): From Rocky Mountain National Park in Colorado to Gulf of California in Mexico.

Colorado (862 mi.; 1,387 km): From Dawson Co. in Texas to Matagorda Bay.

Columbia (1,243 mi.; 2,000 km): From Columbia Lake in British Columbia to Pacific Ocean (entering between Oregon and Washington).

Colville (350 mi.; 563 km): From Brooks Range in Alaska to Beaufort Sea.

Connecticut (407 mi.; 655 km): From Third Connecticut Lake in New Hampshire to Long Island Sound in Connecticut.

Cumberland (720 mi.; 1,159 km): From junction of Poor and Clover Forks in Harlan Co. in Kentucky to Ohio R.

Delaware (390 mi.; 628 km): From Schoharie Co. in New York to Liston Point, Delaware Bay.

Gila (649 mi.; 1,044 km): From Catron Co. in New Mexico to Colorado R. in Arizona.

Green (360 mi.; 579 km): From Lincoln Co. in Kentucky to Ohio R. in Kentucky.

Green (730 mi.; 1,175 km): From Sublette Co. in Wyoming to Colorado R. in Utah.

Illinois (420 mi.; 676 km): From St. Joseph Co. in Indiana to Mississippi R. at Grafton in Illinois.

James (sometimes called *Dakota*) (710 mi.; 1,143 km): From Wells Co. in North Dakota to Missouri R. in South Dakota.

Kanawha-New (352 mi.; 566 km): From junction of North and South Forks of New R. in North Carolina, through Virginia and West Virginia (New River becoming Kanawha River), to Ohio River.

Kansas (743 mi.; 1,196 km): From source of Arikaree R. in Elbert Co., Colorado, to Missouri R. at Kansas City, Kansas.

Koyukuk (470 mi.; 756 km): From Brooks Range in Alaska to Yukon R.

Kuskokwim (724 mi.; 1,165 km): From Alaska Range in Alaska to Kuskokwim Bay.

Coastline of the United States

State	General coastline[1]	Tidal shoreline[2]
	Lengths, statute miles	
Atlantic Coast:		
Maine	228	3,478
New Hampshire	13	131
Massachusetts	192	1,519
Rhode Island	40	384
Connecticut	—	618
New York	127	1,850
New Jersey	130	1,792
Pennsylvania	—	89
Delaware	28	381
Maryland	31	3,190
Virginia	112	3,315
North Carolina	301	3,375
South Carolina	187	2,876
Georgia	100	2,344
Florida (Atlantic)	580	3,331
Total Atlantic coast	2,069	28,673
Gulf Coast:		
Florida (Gulf)	770	5,095
Alabama	53	607
Mississippi	44	359
Louisiana	397	7,721
Texas	367	3,359
Total Gulf coast	1,631	17,141
Pacific Coast:		
California	840	3,427
Oregon	296	1,410
Washington	157	3,026
Hawaii	750	1,052
Alaska (Pacific)	5,580	31,383
Total Pacific coast	7,623	40,298
Arctic Coast:		
Alaska (Arctic)	1,060	2,521
Total Arctic coast	1,060	2,521
States Total	**12,383**	**88,633**

1. Figures are lengths of general outline of seacoast. Measurements made with unit measure of 30 minutes of latitude on charts as near scale of 1:1,200,000 as possible. Coastline of bays and sounds is included to point where they narrow to width of unit measure, and distance across at such point is included. 2. Figures obtained in 1939-1940 with recording instrument on largest-scale maps and charts then available. Shoreline of outer coast, offshore islands, sounds, bays, rivers, and creeks is included to head of tidewater, or to point where tidal waters narrow to width of 100 feet. *Source:* Department of Commerce, National Oceanic and Atmospheric Administration, National Ocean Service.

Licking (350 mi.; 563 km): From Magoffin Co. in Kentucky to Ohio R. at Cincinnati in Ohio.

Little Missouri (560 mi.; 901 km): From Crook Co. in Wyoming to Missouri R. in North Dakota.

Milk (625 mi.; 1,006 km): From junction of forks in Alberta Province to Missouri R.

Mississippi (2,348 mi.; 3,779 km): From Lake Itasca in Minnesota to mouth of Southwest Pass in Louisiana.

Mississippi-Missouri-Red Rock (3,710 mi.; 5,970 km): From source of Red Rock R. in Montana to mouth of Southwest Pass in Louisiana.

Missouri (2,315 mi.; 3,726 km): From junction of Jefferson R., Gallatin R., and Madison R. in Montana to Mississippi R. near St. Louis.

Missouri-Red Rock (2,540 mi.; 4,090 km): From source of Red Rock R. in Montana to Mississippi R. near St. Louis.

Mobile-Alabama-Coosa (645 mi.; 1,040 km): From junction of Etowah R. and Oostanula R. in Georgia to Mobile Bay.

Neosho (460 mi.; 740 km): From Morris Co. in Kansas to Arkansas R. in Oklahoma.

Niobrara (431 mi.; 694 km): From Niobrara Co. in Wyoming to Missouri R. in Nebraska.

Noatak (350 mi.; 563 km): From Brooks Range in Alaska to Kotzebue Sound.

North Canadian (800 mi.; 1,290 km): From Union Co. in New Mexico to Canadian R. in Oklahoma.

North Platte (618 mi.; 995 km): From Jackson Co. in Colorado to junction with So. Platte R. in Nebraska to form Platte R.

Ohio (981 mi.; 1,579 km): From junction of Allegheny R. and Monongahela R. at Pittsburgh to Mississippi R. between Illinois and Kentucky.

Ohio-Allegheny (1,306 mi.; 2,102 km): From Potter Co. in Pennsylvania to Mississippi R. at Cairo in Illinois.

Osage (500 mi.; 805 km): From east-central Kansas to Missouri R. near Jefferson City in Missouri.

Ouachita (605 mi.; 974 km): From Polk Co. in Arkansas to Red R. in Louisiana.

Pearl (411 mi.; 661 km): From Neshoba County in Mississippi to Gulf of Mexico (Mississippi-Louisiana).

Pecos (926 mi.; 1,490 km): From Mora Co. in New Mexico to Rio Grande in Texas.

Pee Dee-Yadkin (435 mi.; 700 km): From Watauga Co. in North Carolina to Winyah Bay in South Carolina.

Pend Oreille-Clark Fork (531 mi.; 855 km): Near Butte in Montana to Columbia R. on Washington-Canada border.

Platte (990 mi.; 1593 km): From source of Grizzly Creek in Jackson Co., Colorado, to Missouri R. south of Omaha, Nebraska.

Porcupine (569 mi.; 916 km): From Yukon Territory, Canada, to Yukon R. in Alaska.

Potomac (383 mi.; 616 km): From Garrett Co. in Maryland to Chesapeake Bay at Point Lookout in Maryland.

Powder (375 mi.; 603 km): From junction of forks in Johnson Co. in Wyoming to Yellowstone R. in Montana.

Red (1,290 mi.; 2,080 km): From source of Tierra Blanca Creek in Curry County, New Mexico to Mississippi R. in Louisiana.

Red (also called *Red River of the North*) (545 mi.; 877 km): From junction of Otter Tail R. and Bois de Sioux R. in Minnesota to Lake Winnipeg in Manitoba, Canada.

Republican (445 mi.; 716 km): From junction of North Fork and Arikaree R. in Nebraska to junction with Smoky Hill R. in Kansas to form the Kansas R.

Rio Grande (1,900 mi.; 3,060 km): From San Juan Co. in Colorado to Gulf of Mexico.

Roanoke (380 mi.; 612 km): From junction of forks in Montgomery Co. in Virginia to Albemarle Sound in North Carolina.

Sabine (380 mi.; 612 km): From junction of forks in Hunt Co. in Texas to Sabine Lake between Texas and Louisiana.

Sacramento (377 mi.; 607 km): From Siskiyou Co. in California to Suisun Bay.

Saint Francis (425 mi.; 684 km): From Iron Co. in Missouri to Mississippi R. in Arkansas.

Salmon (420 mi.; 676 km): From Custer Co. in Idaho to Snake R.

San Joaquin (350 mi.; 563 km): From junction of forks in Madera Co. in California to Suisun Bay.

San Juan (360 mi.; 579 km): From Archuleta Co. in Colorado to Colorado R. in Utah.

Santee-Wateree-Catawba (538 mi.; 866 km): From McDowell Co. in North Carolina to Atlantic Ocean in South Carolina.

Smoky Hill (540 mi.; 869 km): From Cheyenne Co. in Colorado to junction with Republican R. in Kansas to form Kansas R.

Snake (1,038 mi.; 1,670 km): From Ocean Plateau in Wyoming to Columbia R. in Washington.

South Platte (424 mi.; 682 km): From Park Co. in Colorado to junction with North Platte R. in Nebraska to form Platte R.

Stikine (379 mi.; 610 km): From British Columbia in Canada to Stikine Strait near Wrangell, Alaska.

Susquehanna (444 mi.; 715 km): From Otsego Lake in New York to Chesapeake Bay in Maryland.

Tanana (659 mi.; 1,060 km): From Wrangell Mts. in Yukon Territory, Canada, to Yukon R. in Alaska.

Tennessee (652 mi.; 1,049 km): From junction of Holston R. and French Broad R. in Tennessee to Ohio R. in Kentucky.

Tennessee-French Broad (886 mi.; 1,417 km): From Transylvania Co. in North Carolina to Ohio R. at Paducah in Kentucky.

Tombigbee (525 mi.; 845 km): From junction of forks in Itawamba Co. in Mississippi to Mobile R. in Alabama.

Trinity (360 mi.; 579 km): From junction of forks in Dallas Co. in Texas to Galveston Bay.

Wabash (512 mi.; 824 km): From Darke Co. in Ohio to Ohio R. between Illinois and Indiana.

Washita (500 mi.; 805 km): From Hemphill Co. in Texas to Red R. in Oklahoma.

White (722 mi.; 1,160 km): From Madison Co. in Arkansas to Mississippi R.

Wisconsin (430 mi.; 692 km): From Vilas Co. in Wisconsin to Mississippi R.

Yellowstone (692 mi.; 1,110 km): From Park Co. in Wyoming to Missouri R. in North Dakota.

Yukon (1,979 mi.; 3,185 km): From source of McNeil R. in Yukon Territory, Canada, to Bering Sea in Alaska.

Mountain Peaks in the United States Higher than 14,000 Feet

Name	State	Height (ft.)	Name	State	Height (ft.)	Name	State	Height (ft.)
Mt. McKinley	Alaska	20,320	Castle Peak	Colo.	14,265	Mt. Eolus	Colo.	14,083
Mt. St. Elias	Alaska	18,008	Quandary Peak	Colo.	14,265	Windom Peak	Colo.	14,082
Mt. Foraker	Alaska	17,400	Mt. Evans	Colo.	14,264	Mt. Columbia	Colo.	14,073
Mt. Bona	Alaska	16,500	Longs Peak	Colo.	14,255	Mt. Augusta	Alaska	14,070
Mt. Blackburn	Alaska	16,390	Mt. Wilson	Colo.	14,246	Missouri Mtn.	Colo.	14,067
Mt. Sanford	Alaska	16,237	White Mtn.	Calif.	14,246	Humboldt Peak	Colo.	14,064
Mt. Vancouver	Alaska	15,979	North Palisade	Calif.	14,242	Mt. Bierstadt	Colo.	14,060
South Buttress	Alaska	15,885	Mt. Cameron	Colo.	14,238	Sunlight Peak	Colo.	14,059
Mt. Churchill	Alaska	15,638	Mt. Shavano	Colo.	14,229	Split Mtn.	Calif.	14,058
Mt. Fairweather	Alaska	15,300	Crestone Needle	Colo.	14,197	Handies Peak	Colo.	14,048
Mt. Hubbard	Alaska	14,950	Mt. Belford	Colo.	14,197	Culebra Peak	Colo.	14,047
Mt. Bear	Alaska	14,831	Mt. Princeton	Colo.	14,197	Mt. Lindsey	Colo.	14,042
East Buttress	Alaska	14,730	Mt. Yale	Colo.	14,196	Ellingwood Point	Colo.	14,042
Mt. Hunter	Alaska	14,573	Mt. Bross	Colo.	14,172	Middle Palisade	Calif.	14,040
Browne Tower	Alaska	14,530	Kit Carson Mtn.	Colo.	14,165	Little Bear Peak	Colo.	14,037
Mt. Alverstone	Alaska	14,500	Mt. Wrangell	Alaska	14,163	Mt. Sherman	Colo.	14,036
Mt. Whitney	Calif.	14,494[1]	Mt. Sill	Calif.	14,163	Redcloud Peak	Colo.	14,034
University Peak	Alaska	14,470	Mt. Shasta	Calif.	14,162	Mt. Langley	Calif.	14,027
Mt. Elbert	Colo.	14,433	El Diente Peak	Colo.	14,159	Conundrum Peak	Colo.	14,022
Mt. Massive	Colo.	14,421	Point Success	Wash.	14,158	Mt. Tyndall	Calif.	14,019
Mt. Harvard	Colo.	14,420	Maroon Peak	Colo.	14,156	Pyramid Peak	Colo.	14,018
Mt. Rainier	Wash.	14,410	Tabeguache Mtn.	Colo.	14,155	Wilson Peak	Colo.	14,017
Mt. Williamson	Calif.	14,370	Mt. Oxford	Colo.	14,153	Wetterhorn Peak	Colo.	14,015
La Plata Peak	Colo.	14,361	Mt. Sill	Calif.	14,153	North Maroon Peak	Colo.	14,014
Blanca Peak	Colo.	14,345	Mt. Sneffels	Colo.	14,150	San Luis Peak	Colo.	14,014
Uncompahgre Peak	Colo.	14,309	Mt. Democrat	Colo.	14,148	Middle Palisade	Calif.	14,012
Crestone Peak	Colo.	14,294	Capitol Peak	Colo.	14,130	Mt. Muir	Calif.	14,012
Mt. Lincoln	Colo.	14,286	Liberty Cap	Wash.	14,112	Mt. of the Holy Cross	Colo.	14,005
Grays Peak	Colo.	14,270	Pikes Peak	Colo.	14,110	Huron Peak	Colo.	14,003
Mt. Antero	Colo.	14,269	Snowmass Mtn.	Colo.	14,092	Thunderbolt Peak	Calif.	14,003
Torreys Peak	Colo.	14,267	Mt. Russell	Calif.	14,088	Sunshine Peak	Colo.	14,001

1. National Geodetic Survey. *Source:* Department of the Interior, U.S. Geological Survey.

Highest, Lowest, and Mean Elevations in the United States

State	Elevation ft.[1]	Highest point	Elevation ft.	Lowest point	Elevation ft.
Alabama	500	Cheaha Mountain	2,405	Gulf of Mexico	Sea level
Alaska	1,900	Mt. McKinley	20,320	Pacific Ocean	Sea level
Arizona	4,100	Humphreys Peak	12,633	Colorado River	70
Arkansas	650	Magazine Mountain	2,753	Ouachita River	55
California	2,900	Mt. Whitney	14,494	Death Valley	–282[2]
Colorado	6,800	Mt. Elbert	14,433	Arkansas River	3,350
Connecticut	500	Mt. Frissell, on south slope	2,380	Long Island Sound	Sea level
Delaware	60	Ebright Road, Del.–Pa. state line	448	Atlantic Ocean	Sea level
D.C.	150	Tenleytown, at Reno Reservoir	410	Potomac River	1
Florida	100	Sec. 30, T6N, R20W, Walton County [4]	345	Atlantic Ocean	Sea level
Georgia	600	Brasstown Bald	4,784	Atlantic Ocean	Sea level
Hawaii	3,030	Puu Wekiu, Mauna Kea	13,796	Pacific Ocean	Sea level
Idaho	5,000	Borah Peak	12,662	Snake River	710
Illinois	600	Charles Mound	1,235	Mississippi River	279
Indiana	700	Franklin Township, Wayne County	1,257	Ohio River	320
Iowa	1,100	Sec. 29, T100N, R41W, Osceola County	1,670	Mississippi River	480
Kansas	2,000	Mt. Sunflower	4,039	Verdigris River	679
Kentucky	750	Black Mountain	4,139	Mississippi River	257
Louisiana	100	Driskill Mountain	535	New Orleans	–8[2]
Maine	600	Mt. Katahdin	5,267	Atlantic Ocean	Sea level
Maryland	350	Backbone Mountain	3,360	Atlantic Ocean	Sea level
Massachusetts	500	Mt. Greylock	3,487	Atlantic Ocean	Sea level
Michigan	900	Mt. Arvon	1,979	Lake Erie	572
Minnesota	1,200	Eagle Mountain	2,301	Lake Superior	600
Mississippi	300	Woodall Mountain	806	Gulf of Mexico	Sea level
Missouri	800	Taum Sauk Mountain	1,772	St. Francis River	230
Montana	3,400	Granite Peak	12,799	Kootenai River	1,800
Nebraska	2,600	Johnson Township, Kimball County	5,424	Missouri River	840
Nevada	5,500	Boundary Peak	13,140	Colorado River	479
New Hampshire	1,000	Mt. Washington	6,288	Atlantic Ocean	Sea level
New Jersey	250	High Point	1,803	Atlantic Ocean	Sea level
New Mexico	5,700	Wheeler Peak	13,161	Red Bluff Reservoir	2,842
New York	1,000	Mt. Marcy	5,344	Atlantic Ocean	Sea level
North Carolina	700	Mt. Mitchell	6,684	Atlantic Ocean	Sea level
North Dakota	1,900	White Butte	3,506	Red River	750
Ohio	850	Campbell Hill	1,549	Ohio River	455
Oklahoma	1,300	Black Mesa	4,973	Little River	289
Oregon	3,300	Mt. Hood	11,239	Pacific Ocean	Sea level
Pennsylvania	1,100	Mt. Davis	3,213	Delaware River	Sea level
Rhode Island	200	Jerimoth Hill	812	Atlantic Ocean	Sea level
South Carolina	350	Sassafras Mountain	3,560	Atlantic Ocean	Sea level
South Dakota	2,200	Harney Peak	7,242	Big Stone Lake	966
Tennessee	900	Clingmans Dome	6,643	Mississippi River	178
Texas	1,700	Guadalupe Peak	8,749	Gulf of Mexico	Sea level
Utah	6,100	Kings Peak	13,528	Beaverdam Wash	2,000
Vermont	1,000	Mt. Mansfield	4,393	Lake Champlain	95
Virginia	950	Mt. Rogers	5,729	Atlantic Ocean	Sea level
Washington	1,700	Mt. Rainier	14,410	Pacific Ocean	Sea level
West Virginia	1,500	Spruce Knob	4,861	Potomac River	240
Wisconsin	1,050	Timms Hill	1,951	Lake Michigan	579
Wyoming	6,700	Gannett Peak	13,804	Belle Fourche River	3,099
United States	2,500	Mt. McKinley (Alaska)	20,320	Death Valley (California)	-282[2]

1. Approximate mean elevation. 2. Below sea level. *Source:* U.S. Geological Survey.

Latitude and Longitude of U.S. and Canadian Cities

(and time corresponding to 12:00 noon, eastern standard time)

City	Lat. °	Lat. ′	Long. °	Long. ′	Time
Albany, N.Y.	42	40	73	45	12:00 noon
Albuquerque, N.M.	35	05	106	39	10:00 a.m.
Amarillo, Tex.	35	11	101	50	11:00 a.m.
Anchorage, Alaska	61	13	149	54	8:00 a.m.
Atlanta, Ga.	33	45	84	23	12:00 noon
Austin, Tex.	30	16	97	44	11:00 a.m.
Baker, Ore.	44	47	117	50	9:00 a.m.
Baltimore, Md.	39	18	76	38	12:00 noon
Bangor, Maine	44	48	68	47	12:00 noon
Birmingham, Ala.	33	30	86	50	11:00 a.m.
Bismarck, N.D.	46	48	100	47	11:00 a.m.
Boise, Idaho	43	36	116	13	10:00 a.m.
Boston, Mass.	42	21	71	5	12:00 noon
Buffalo, N.Y.	42	55	78	50	12:00 noon
Calgary, Alberta	51	1	114	1	10:00 a.m.
Carlsbad, N.M.	32	26	104	15	10:00 a.m.
Charleston, S.C.	32	47	79	56	12:00 noon
Charleston, W. Va.	38	21	81	38	12:00 noon
Charlotte, N.C.	35	14	80	50	12:00 noon
Cheyenne, Wyo.	41	9	104	52	10:00 a.m.
Chicago, Ill.	41	50	87	37	11:00 a.m.
Cincinnati, Ohio	39	8	84	30	12:00 noon
Cleveland, Ohio	41	28	81	37	12:00 noon
Columbia, S.C.	34	0	81	2	12:00 noon
Columbus, Ohio	40	0	83	1	12:00 noon
Dallas, Tex.	32	46	96	46	11:00 a.m.
Denver, Colo.	39	45	105	0	10:00 a.m.
Des Moines, Iowa	41	35	93	37	11:00 a.m.
Detroit, Mich.	42	20	83	3	12:00 noon
Dubuque, Iowa	42	31	90	40	11:00 a.m.
Duluth, Minn.	46	49	92	5	11:00 a.m.
Eastport, Maine	44	54	67	0	12:00 noon
El Centro, Calif.	32	38	115	33	9:00 a.m.
El Paso, Tex.	31	46	106	29	10:00 a.m.
Eugene, Ore.	44	3	123	5	9:00 a.m.
Fargo, N.D.	46	52	96	48	11:00 a.m.
Flagstaff, Ariz.	35	13	111	41	10:00 a.m.
Fort Worth, Tex.	32	43	97	19	11:00 a.m.
Fresno, Calif.	36	44	119	48	9:00 a.m.
Grand Junction, Colo.	39	5	108	33	10:00 a.m.
Grand Rapids, Mich.	42	58	85	40	12:00 noon
Havre, Mont.	48	33	109	43	10:00 a.m.
Helena, Mont.	46	35	112	2	10:00 a.m.
Honolulu, Hawaii	21	18	157	50	7:00 a.m.
Hot Springs, Ark.	34	31	93	3	11:00 a.m.
Houston, Tex.	29	45	95	21	11:00 a.m.
Idaho Falls, Idaho	43	30	112	1	10:00 a.m.
Indianapolis, Ind.	39	46	86	10	12:00 noon
Jackson, Miss.	32	20	90	12	11:00 a.m.
Jacksonville, Fla.	30	22	81	40	12:00 noon
Juneau, Alaska	58	18	134	24	8:00 a.m.
Kansas City, Mo.	39	6	94	35	11:00 a.m.
Key West, Fla.	24	33	81	48	12:00 noon
Kingston, Ont., Can.	44	15	76	30	12:00 noon
Klamath Falls, Ore.	42	10	121	44	9:00 a.m.
Knoxville, Tenn.	35	57	83	56	12:00 noon
Las Vegas, Nev.	36	10	115	12	9:00 a.m.
Lewiston, Idaho	46	24	117	2	9:00 a.m.
Lincoln, Neb.	40	50	96	40	11:00 a.m.
London, Ont.	43	2	81	34	12:00 noon
Long Beach, Calif.	33	46	118	11	9:00 a.m.
Los Angeles, Calif.	34	3	118	15	9:00 a.m.
Louisville, Ky.	38	15	85	46	12:00 noon
Manchester, N.H.	43	0	71	30	12:00 noon
Memphis, Tenn.	35	9	90	3	11:00 a.m.
Miami, Fla.	25	46	80	12	12:00 noon
Milwaukee, Wis.	43	2	87	55	11:00 a.m.
Minneapolis, Minn.	44	59	93	14	11:00 a.m.
Mobile, Ala.	30	42	88	3	11:00 a.m.
Montgomery, Ala.	32	21	86	18	11:00 a.m.
Montpelier, Vt.	44	15	72	32	12:00 noon
Montreal, Que., Can.	45	30	73	35	12:00 noon
Moose Jaw, Sask., Can.	50	37	105	31	10:00 a.m.
Nashville, Tenn.	36	10	86	47	11:00 a.m.
Nelson, B.C., Can.	49	30	117	17	9:00 a.m.
Newark, N.J.	40	44	74	10	12:00 noon
New Haven, Conn.	41	19	72	55	12:00 noon
New Orleans, La.	29	57	90	4	11:00 a.m.
New York, N.Y.	40	47	73	58	12:00 noon
Nome, Alaska	64	25	165	30	8:00 a.m.
Oakland, Calif.	37	48	122	16	9:00 a.m.
Oklahoma City, Okla.	35	26	97	28	11:00 a.m.
Omaha, Neb.	41	15	95	56	11:00 a.m.
Ottawa, Ont., Can.	45	24	75	43	12:00 noon
Philadelphia, Pa.	39	57	75	10	12:00 noon
Phoenix, Ariz.	33	29	112	4	10:00 a.m.
Pierre, S.D.	44	22	100	21	11:00 a.m.
Pittsburgh, Pa.	40	27	79	57	12:00 noon
Port Arthur, Ont., Can.	48	30	89	17	12:00 noon
Portland, Maine	43	40	70	15	12:00 noon
Portland, Ore.	45	31	122	41	9:00 a.m.
Providence, R.I.	41	50	71	24	12:00 noon
Quebec, Que., Can.	46	49	71	11	12:00 noon
Raleigh, N.C.	35	46	78	39	12:00 noon
Reno, Nev.	39	30	119	49	9:00 a.m.
Richfield, Utah	38	46	112	5	10:00 a.m.
Richmond, Va.	37	33	77	29	12:00 noon
Roanoke, Va.	37	17	79	57	12:00 noon
Sacramento, Calif.	38	35	121	30	9:00 a.m.
St. John, N.B., Can.	45	18	66	10	1:00 p.m.
St. Louis, Mo.	38	35	90	12	11:00 a.m.
Salt Lake City, Utah	40	46	111	54	10:00 a.m.
San Antonio, Tex.	29	23	98	33	11:00 a.m.
San Diego, Calif.	32	42	117	10	9:00 a.m.
San Francisco, Calif.	37	47	122	26	9:00 a.m.
San Jose, Calif.	37	20	121	53	9:00 a.m.
San Juan, P.R.	18	30	66	10	1:00 p.m.
Santa Fe, N.M.	35	41	105	57	10:00 a.m.
Savannah, Ga.	32	5	81	5	12:00 noon
Seattle, Wash.	47	37	122	20	9:00 a.m.
Shreveport, La.	32	28	93	42	11:00 a.m.
Sioux Falls, S.D.	43	33	96	44	11:00 a.m.
Sitka, Alaska	57	10	135	15	9:00 a.m.
Spokane, Wash.	47	40	117	26	9:00 a.m.
Springfield, Ill.	39	48	89	38	11:00 a.m.
Springfield, Mass.	42	6	72	34	12:00 noon
Springfield, Mo.	37	13	93	17	11:00 a.m.
Syracuse, N.Y.	43	2	76	8	12:00 noon
Tampa, Fla.	27	57	82	27	12:00 noon
Toledo, Ohio	41	39	83	33	12:00 noon
Toronto, Ont., Can.	43	40	79	24	12:00 noon
Tulsa, Okla.	36	09	95	59	11:00 a.m.
Victoria, B.C., Can.	48	25	123	21	9:00 a.m.
Virginia Beach, Va.	36	51	75	58	12:00 noon
Washington, D.C.	38	53	77	02	12:00 noon
Wichita, Kan.	37	43	97	17	11:00 a.m.
Wilmington, N.C.	34	14	77	57	12:00 noon
Winnipeg, Man., Can.	49	54	97	7	11:00 a.m.

Mason and Dixon's Line

Mason and Dixon's Line (often called the Mason-Dixon Line) is the boundary between Pennsylvania and Maryland, running at a north latitude of 39°43′19.11″. The greater part of it was surveyed from 1763–1767 by Charles Mason and Jeremiah Dixon, English astronomers who had been appointed to settle a dispute between the colonies. As the line was partly the boundary between the free and the slave states, it has come to signify the division between the North and the South.

Geysers in the United States

Geysers are natural hot springs that intermittently eject a column of water and steam into the air. They exist in many parts of the volcanic regions of the world such as Japan and South America but their greatest development is in Iceland, New Zealand, and Yellowstone National Park.

There are 120 named geysers in Yellowstone National Park, Wyoming, and perhaps half that number unnamed. Most of the geysers and the 4,000 or more hot springs are located in the western portion of the park. The most important are the following:

Norris Geyser Basin has 24 or more active geysers; the number varies. There are scores of steam vents and hot springs. *Steamboat* is the largest active geyser in the world, sending water more than 300 ft. into the air for 3 to 20 minutes. It emits water every few minutes, but its major eruptions are infrequent and erratic. *Valentine* erupts 50–75 ft. at intervals varying from 18 hr. to 3 days or more. *Minuté* erupts 15–20 ft. high, several hours apart. Others include: *Fearless, Veteran, Vixen, Corporal, Whirligig, Little Whirligig,* and *Pinwheel.*

Lower Geyser Basin has at least 18 active geysers. *Fountain* throws water 50–75 ft. in all directions at unpredictable intervals. *Clepsydra* erupts violently from 4 vents up to 30 ft. *Great Fountain* plays every 8 to 15 hr. in spurts from 30 to 90 ft. high.

Midway Geyser Basin has vast steaming terraces of red, orange, pink and other colors; there are pools and springs, including the beautiful *Grand Prismatic Spring. Excelsior* crater discharges boiling water into Firehole River at the rate of 6 cu ft. per second.

Giant erupts up to 200 ft. at intervals of 2½ days to 3 mo; eruptions last about 1½ hr. *Daisy* sends water up to 75 ft. but is irregular and frequently inactive.

Old Faithful, the most famous geyser in the park, sends up a column varying from 116 to 175 ft. at intervals of about 65 min, varying from 33 to 90 min. Eruptions last about 4 min, during which time about 12,000 gal. are discharged.

Giantess seldom erupts, but during its active period sends up streams 150–200 ft.

Lion plays up to 60 ft. every 2–4 days when active; *Little Cub* up to 10 ft. every 1–2 hr. *Big Cub* and *Lioness* seldom erupt.

There are no geysers in the Mammoth Hot Springs area. The formation is travertine. Sides of a hill are steps and terraces over which flow the steaming waters of hot springs laden with minerals. Each step is tinted by algae to many shades of orange, pink, yellow, brown, green, and blue. Terraces are white where no water flows.

One Lake or Two?

It is a widely accepted fact that Lake Superior, with an area of 31,820 square miles is the world's largest freshwater lake. However, this fact is based on a historical inaccuracy in the naming of Lake Huron and Lake Michigan. What should have been considered one body of water, Lake Michigan-Huron with an area of 45,410 square miles, was mistakenly given two names, one for each lobe. The explorers in colonial times incorrectly believed each lobe to be a separate lake because of their great size.

Why should the two lakes be considered one? The Huron Lobe and the Michigan Lobe are at the same elevation and are connected by the 120-foot deep Mackinac Strait, also at the same elevation. Lakes are separated from each other by streams and rivers. The Strait of Mackinac is not a river. It is 3.6 to 5 miles wide, wider than most lakes are long. In essence, it is just a narrowing, not a separation of the two lobes of Lake Michigan-Huron.

The flow between the two lakes can reverse. Because of the large connecting channel, the two can equalize rapidly whenever a water level imbalance occurs. Gauge records for the lakes clearly show them to have identical water level regimes and mean long-term behavior; that is, they are hydrologically considered to be one lake.

Historical names are not easily changed. The separate names for the lake are a part of history and are also legally institutionalized since Lake Michigan is treated as American and Lake Huron is bisected by the international boundary between the United States and Canada.

Of all the world's freshwater lakes, North America's Great Lakes are unique. Their five basins combine to form a single watershed with one common outlet to the ocean. The total volume of the lakes is about 5,475 cubic miles, more than 6,000 trillion gallons.

The Great Lakes are Superior, with an area of 31,820 square miles (82,414 km) shared by the United States and Canada; Huron, with an area of 23,010 square miles (59,596 sq km) shared by the United States and Canada; Michigan, with an area of 22,400 square miles (58,016 sq km) entirely in the United States; Erie, with an area of 9,930 square miles (25,719 km) shared by the United States and Canada; and Ontario, with an area of 7,520 square miles (19,477 km) shared by the United States and Canada.

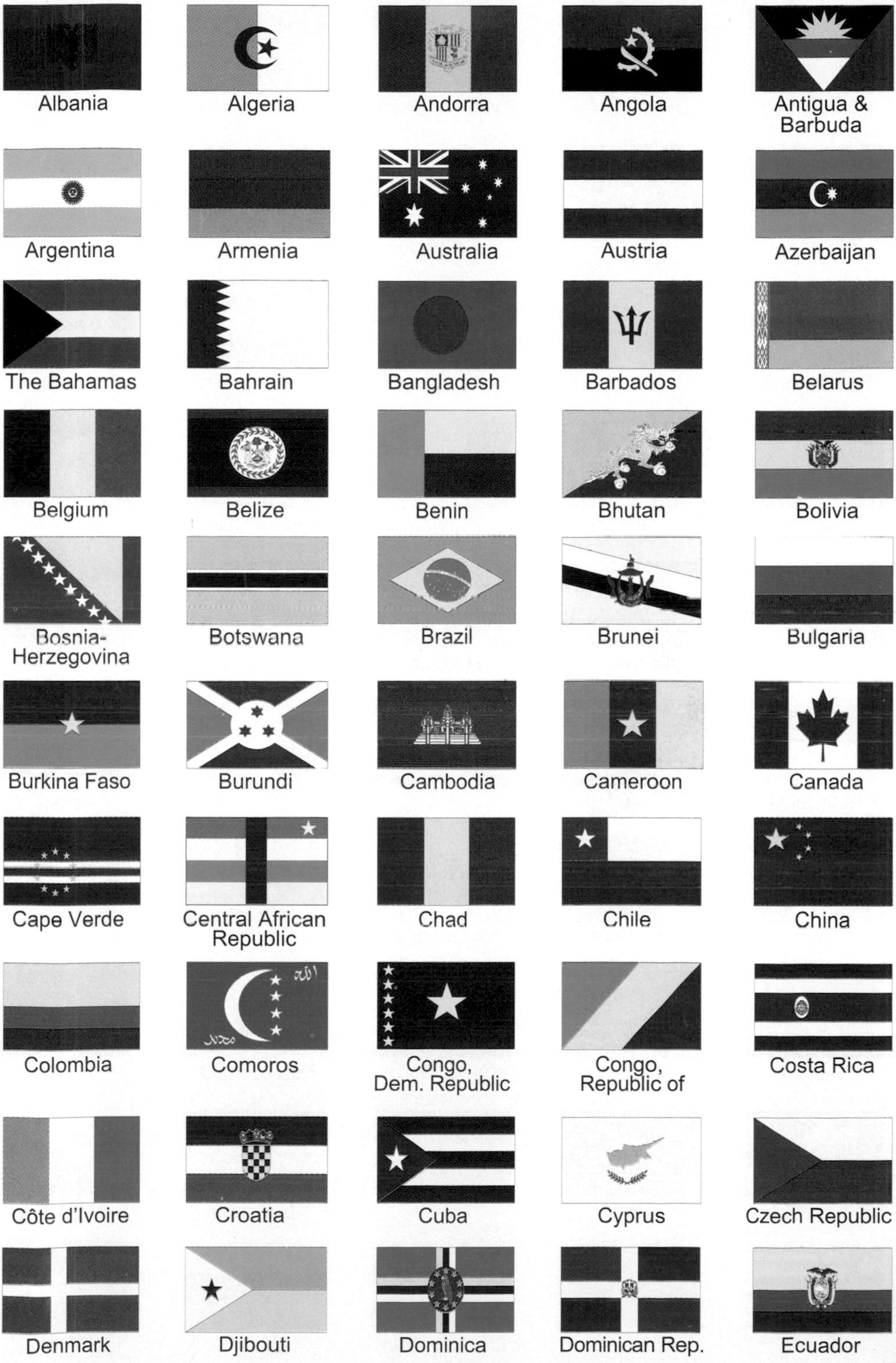

Albania

Algeria

Andorra

Angola

Antigua & Barbuda

Argentina

Armenia

Australia

Austria

Azerbaijan

The Bahamas

Bahrain

Bangladesh

Barbados

Belarus

Belgium

Belize

Benin

Bhutan

Bolivia

Bosnia-Herzegovina

Botswana

Brazil

Brunei

Bulgaria

Burkina Faso

Burundi

Cambodia

Cameroon

Canada

Cape Verde

Central African Republic

Chad

Chile

China

Colombia

Comoros

Congo, Dem. Republic

Congo, Republic of

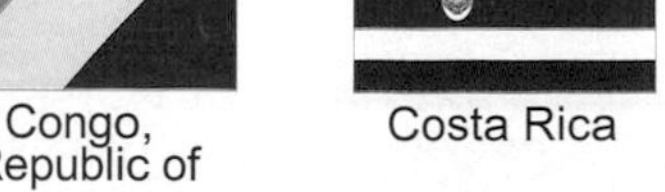

Costa Rica

Côte d'Ivoire

Croatia

Cuba

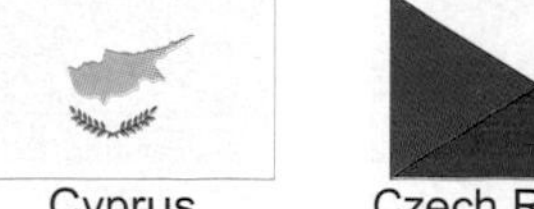

Cyprus

Czech Republic

Denmark

Djibouti

Dominica

Dominican Rep.

Ecuador

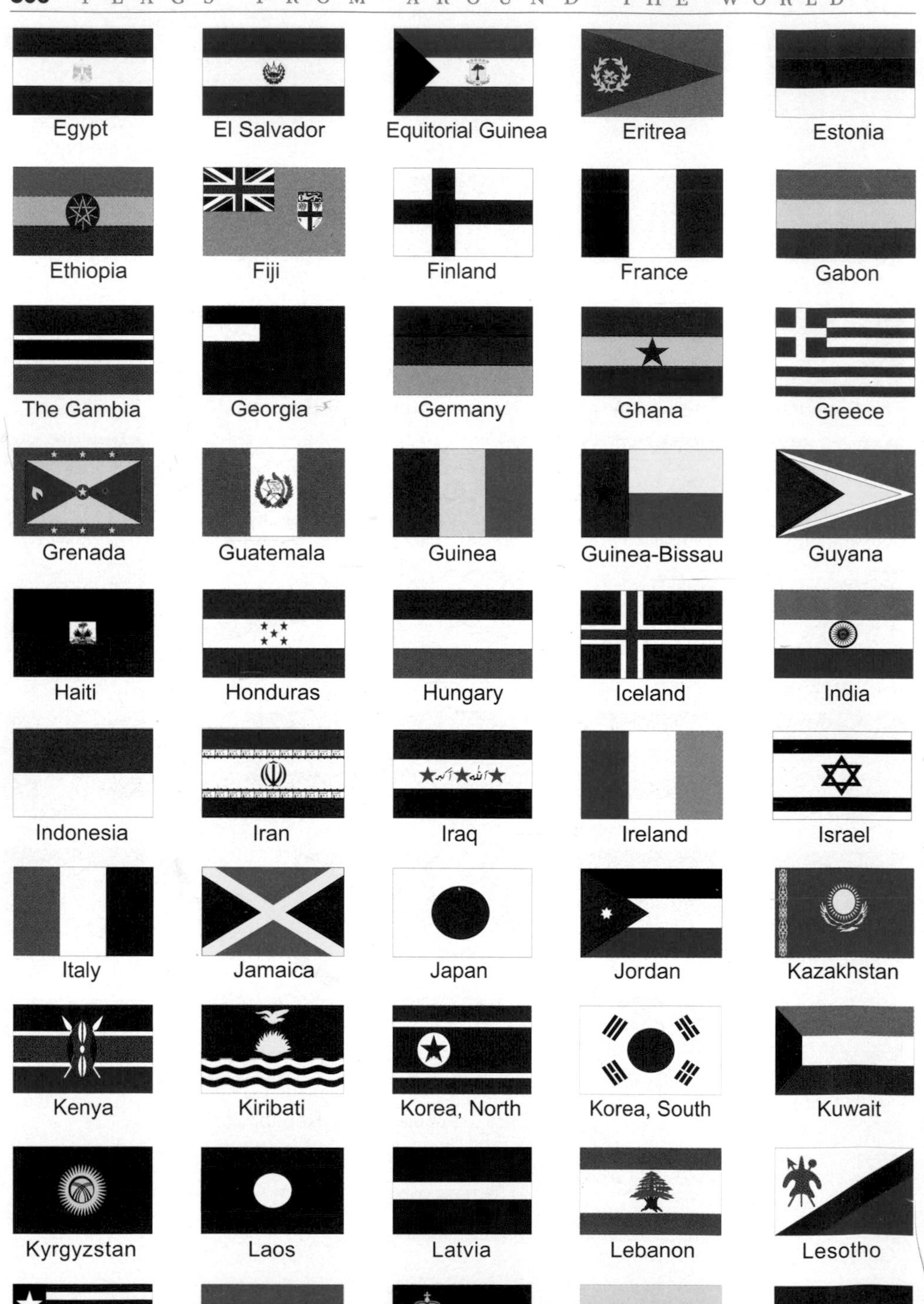

Egypt
El Salvador
Equitorial Guinea
Eritrea
Estonia
Ethiopia
Fiji
Finland
France
Gabon
The Gambia
Georgia
Germany
Ghana
Greece
Grenada
Guatemala
Guinea
Guinea-Bissau
Guyana
Haiti
Honduras
Hungary
Iceland
India
Indonesia
Iran
Iraq
Ireland
Israel
Italy
Jamaica
Japan
Jordan
Kazakhstan
Kenya
Kiribati
Korea, North
Korea, South
Kuwait
Kyrgyzstan
Laos
Latvia
Lebanon
Lesotho
Liberia
Libya
Liechtenstein
Lithuania
Luxembourg

Macedonia

Madagascar

Malawi

Malaysia

Maldives

Mali

Malta

Marshall Is.

Mauritania

Mauritius

Mexico

Micronesia

Moldova

Monaco

Mongolia

Morocco

Mozambique

Myanmar

Namibia

Nauru

Nepal

The Netherlands

New Zealand

Nicaragua

Niger

Nigeria

Norway

Oman

Pakistan

Palau

Panama

Papua New Guinea

Paraguay

Peru

The Philippines

Poland

Portugal

Qatar

Romania

Russia

Rwanda

St. Kitts & Nevis

St. Lucia

St. Vincent & The Grenadines

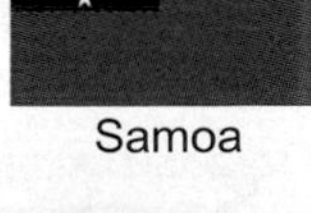
Samoa

San Marino

São Tomé & Príncipe

Saudi Arabia

Senegal

Seychelles

Sierra Leone

Singapore

Slovakia

Slovenia

Solomon Is.

Somalia

South Africa

Spain

Sri Lanka

The Sudan

Suriname

Swaziland

Sweden

Switzerland

Syria

Taiwan

Tajikistan

Tanzania

Thailand

Togo

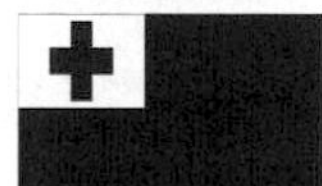
Tonga

Trinidad & Tobago

Tunisia

Turkey

Turkmenistan

Tuvalu

Uganda

Ukraine

United Arab Emirates

United Kingdom

United States

Uruguay

Uzbekistan

Vanuatu

Vatican City

Venezuela

Vietnam

Yemen

Yugoslavia

Zambia

Zimbabwe

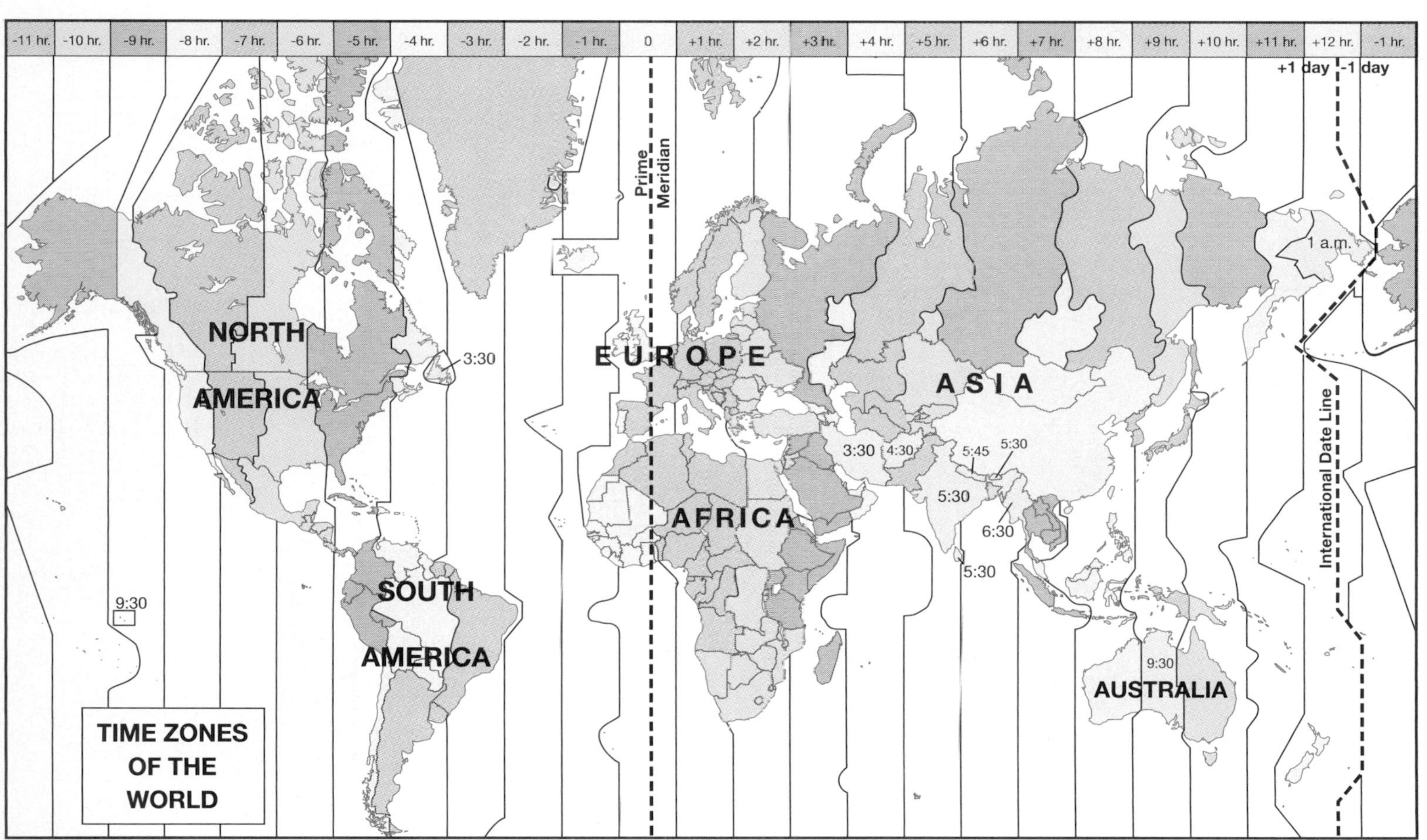
TIME ZONES OF THE WORLD
-11 hr.
-10 hr.
-9 hr.
-8 hr.
-7 hr.
-6 hr.
-5 hr.
-4 hr.
-3 hr.
-2 hr.
-1 hr.
0
+1 hr.
+2 hr.
+3 hr.
+4 hr.
+5 hr.
+6 hr.
+7 hr.
+8 hr.
+9 hr.
+10 hr.
+11 hr.
+12 hr.
-1 hr.
+1 day
-1 day
Prime Meridian
International Date Line
NORTH AMERICA
SOUTH AMERICA
EUROPE
AFRICA
ASIA
AUSTRALIA
3:30
9:30
1 a.m.
3:30
4:30
5:45
5:30
5:30
6:30
5:30
9:30

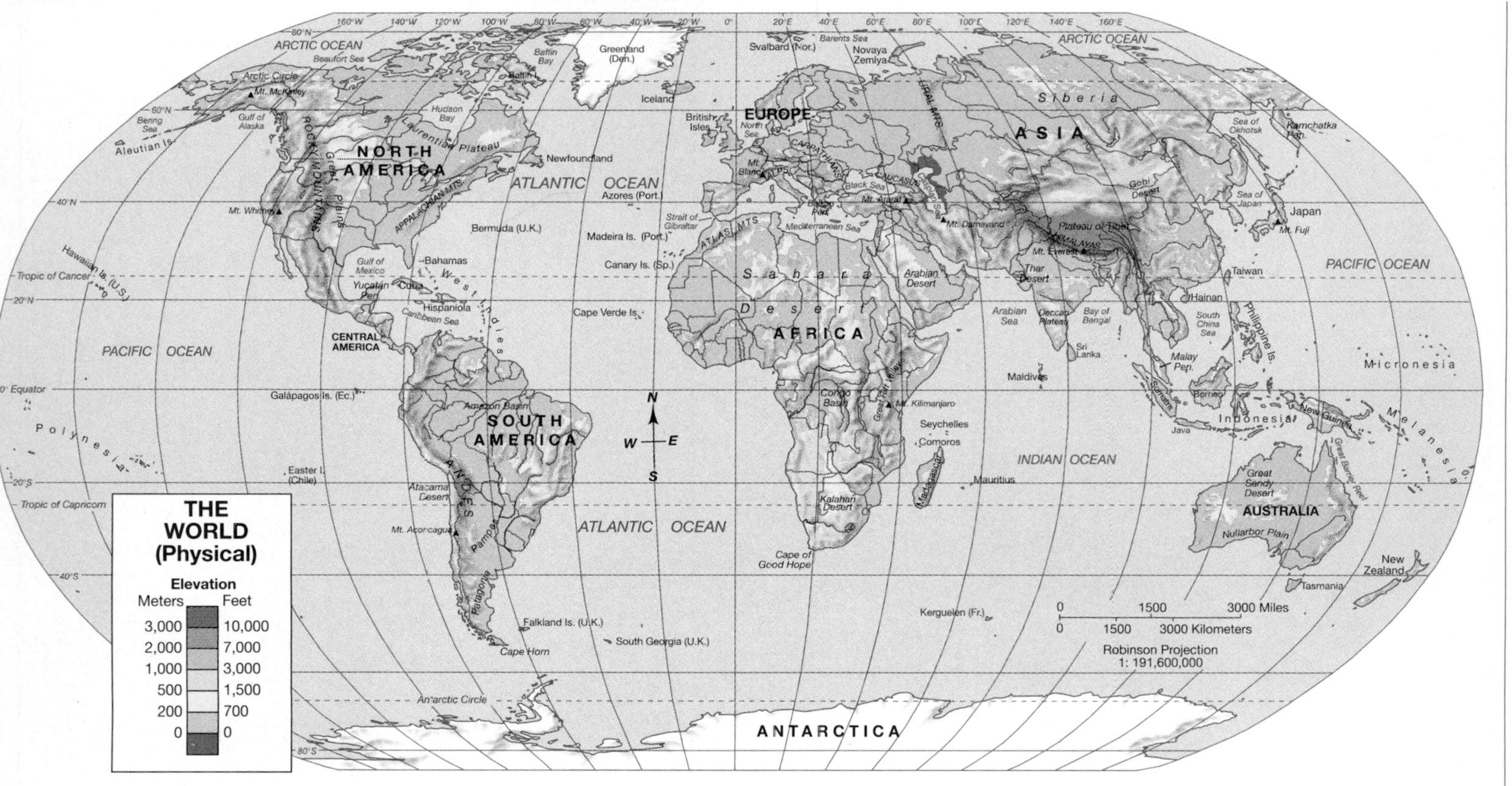
THE WORLD (Physical)
Elevation
Meters Feet
3,000 10,000
2,000 7,000
1,000 3,000
500 1,500
200 700
0 0
0 1500 3000 Miles
0 1500 3000 Kilometers
Robinson Projection
1: 191,600,000
ARCTIC OCEAN
Beaufort Sea
Arctic Circle
Mt. McKinley
Gulf of Alaska
Bering Sea
Aleutian Is.
Hudson Bay
Baffin Bay
Greenland (Den.)
Iceland
NORTH AMERICA
Laurentian Plateau
ROCKY MOUNTAINS
Great Plains
APPALACHIAN MTS.
Mt. Whitney
Newfoundland
ATLANTIC OCEAN
Azores (Port.)
Bermuda (U.K.)
Madeira Is. (Port.)
Canary Is. (Sp.)
Strait of Gibraltar
Gulf of Mexico
Bahamas
Yucatán Pen.
Cuba
West Indies
Hispaniola
Caribbean Sea
Cape Verde Is.
Hawaiian Is. (U.S.)
Tropic of Cancer
CENTRAL AMERICA
PACIFIC OCEAN
Equator
Galápagos Is. (Ec.)
Polynesia
Easter I. (Chile)
Tropic of Capricorn
SOUTH AMERICA
Amazon Basin
ANDES
Atacama Desert
Mt. Aconcagua
Pampas
Patagonia
Falkland Is. (U.K.)
Cape Horn
South Georgia (U.K.)
Antarctic Circle
ANTARCTICA
Svalbard (Nor.)
Barents Sea
Novaya Zemlya
EUROPE
British Isles
North Sea
Mt. Blanc
ALPS
CARPATHIANS
Black Sea
CAUCASUS
Caspian Sea
URAL MTS.
Mt. Ararat
Mediterranean Sea
ATLAS MTS.
Sahara Desert
AFRICA
Arabian Desert
Congo Basin
Great Rift Valley
Mt. Kilimanjaro
Seychelles
Comoros
Madagascar
Kalahari Desert
Cape of Good Hope
Mauritius
Kerguelen (Fr.)
INDIAN OCEAN
Siberia
ASIA
Sea of Okhotsk
Kamchatka Pen.
Gobi Desert
Sea of Japan
Japan
Mt. Fuji
Plateau of Tibet
HIMALAYAS
Mt. Everest
Mt. Damavand
Thar Desert
Arabian Sea
Deccan Plateau
Bay of Bengal
Sri Lanka
Maldives
Taiwan
Hainan
South China Sea
Philippine Is.
Malay Pen.
Sumatra
Borneo
Java
Indonesia
New Guinea
Micronesia
Melanesia
Great Barrier Reef
Great Sandy Desert
AUSTRALIA
Nullarbor Plain
Tasmania
New Zealand
N
S
E
W

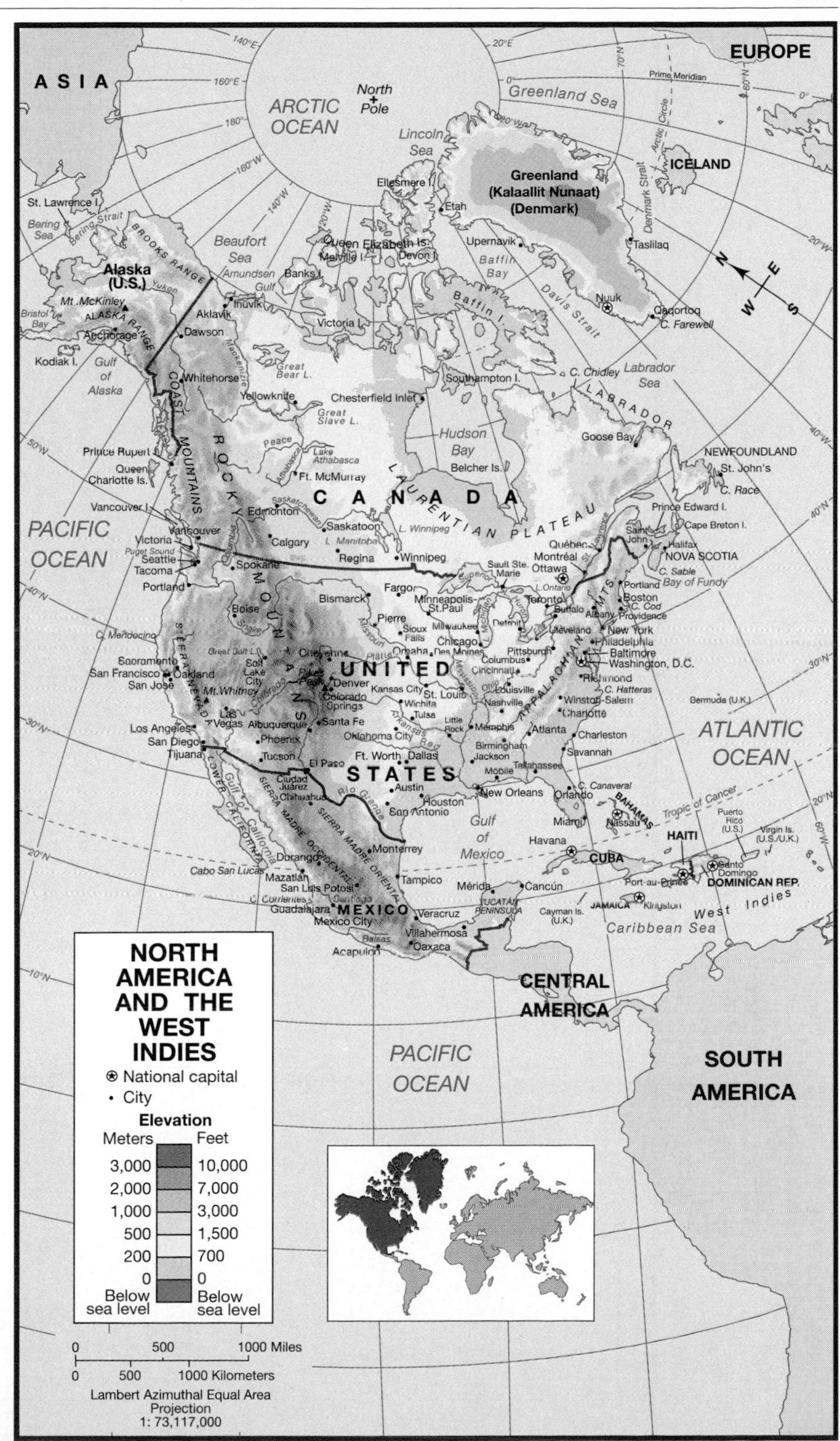
NORTH AMERICA AND THE WEST INDIES
National capital
City
Elevation
Meters
Feet
3,000
10,000
2,000
7,000
1,000
3,000
500
1,500
200
700
0
0
Below sea level
Below sea level
0
500
1000 Miles
0
500
1000 Kilometers
Lambert Azimuthal Equal Area Projection
1: 73,117,000
ASIA
EUROPE
ARCTIC OCEAN
North Pole
Greenland Sea
Lincoln Sea
Prime Meridian
Arctic Circle
ICELAND
Greenland (Kalaallit Nunaat) (Denmark)
Ellesmere I.
Etah
Denmark Strait
Taslilaq
St. Lawrence I.
Bering Sea
Bering Strait
Beaufort Sea
Queen Elizabeth Is.
Melville I.
Devon I.
Upernavik
Baffin Bay
BROOKS RANGE
Alaska (U.S.)
Yukon
Amundsen Gulf
Banks I.
Baffin I.
Davis Strait
Nuuk
Qaqortoq
C. Farewell
Mt. McKinley
Bristol Bay
ALASKA RANGE
Anchorage
Inuvik
Aklavik
Dawson
Victoria I.
Kodiak I.
Gulf of Alaska
Great Bear L.
Mackenzie
Whitehorse
Southampton I.
C. Chidley
Labrador Sea
LABRADOR
Yellowknife
Chesterfield Inlet
Great Slave L.
COAST MOUNTAINS
ROCKY MOUNTAINS
Hudson Bay
Goose Bay
Prince Rupert
Queen Charlotte Is.
Peace
Lake Athabasca
Athabasca
Ft. McMurray
Belcher Is.
NEWFOUNDLAND
St. John's
C. Race
CANADA
LAURENTIAN PLATEAU
Vancouver I.
Edmonton
Saskatchewan
Prince Edward I.
Cape Breton I.
PACIFIC OCEAN
Vancouver
Victoria
Puget Sound
Seattle
Tacoma
Portland
Calgary
Saskatoon
L. Winnipeg
L. Manitoba
Regina
Winnipeg
Québec
Montréal
Ottawa
Saint John
Halifax
NOVA SCOTIA
C. Sable
Bay of Fundy
Spokane
Sault Ste. Marie
L. Superior
L. Ontario
Portland
Boston
C. Cod
Providence
Fargo
Bismarck
Minneapolis-St.Paul
Toronto
Buffalo
Albany
New York
Philadelphia
Baltimore
Washington, D.C.
Boise
Snake
Pierre
Sioux Falls
Milwaukee
Detroit
Cleveland
Chicago
Pittsburgh
Columbus
Cincinnati
Richmond
C. Mendocino
SIERRA NEVADA
Great Salt L.
Salt Lake City
Cheyenne
Omaha
Des Moines
Platte
Missouri
Mississippi
Ohio
Sacramento
San Francisco
Oakland
San Jose
Pikes Peak
Denver
UNITED STATES
Kansas City
St. Louis
Louisville
C. Hatteras
APPALACHIAN MTS.
Mt. Whitney
Colorado
Colorado Springs
Wichita
Nashville
Winston-Salem
Charlotte
Bermuda (U.K.)
Las Vegas
Albuquerque
Santa Fe
Tulsa
Arkansas
Little Rock
Memphis
Atlanta
Charleston
ATLANTIC OCEAN
Los Angeles
San Diego
Tijuana
Phoenix
Oklahoma City
Red
Birmingham
Jackson
Savannah
Tucson
Ft. Worth
Dallas
El Paso
Mobile
Tallahassee
LOWER CALIFORNIA
Ciudad Juárez
Chihuahua
SIERRA MADRE OCCIDENTAL
SIERRA MADRE ORIENTAL
Austin
Rio Grande
Houston
San Antonio
New Orleans
C. Canaveral
Orlando
BAHAMAS
Tropic of Cancer
Puerto Rico (U.S.)
Gulf of California
Miami
Nassau
HAITI
Virgin Is. (U.S./U.K.)
Gulf of Mexico
Monterrey
Havana
CUBA
Santo Domingo
DOMINICAN REP.
Durango
Cabo San Lucas
Tampico
Mazatlán
San Luis Potosí
Mérida
Cancún
Port-au-Prince
C. Corrientes
Santiago
Guadalajara
MEXICO
Mexico City
YUCATÁN PENINSULA
Cayman Is. (U.K.)
JAMAICA
Kingston
West Indies
Veracruz
Caribbean Sea
Balsas
Villahermosa
Oaxaca
Acapulco
CENTRAL AMERICA
PACIFIC OCEAN
SOUTH AMERICA
N
E
S
W

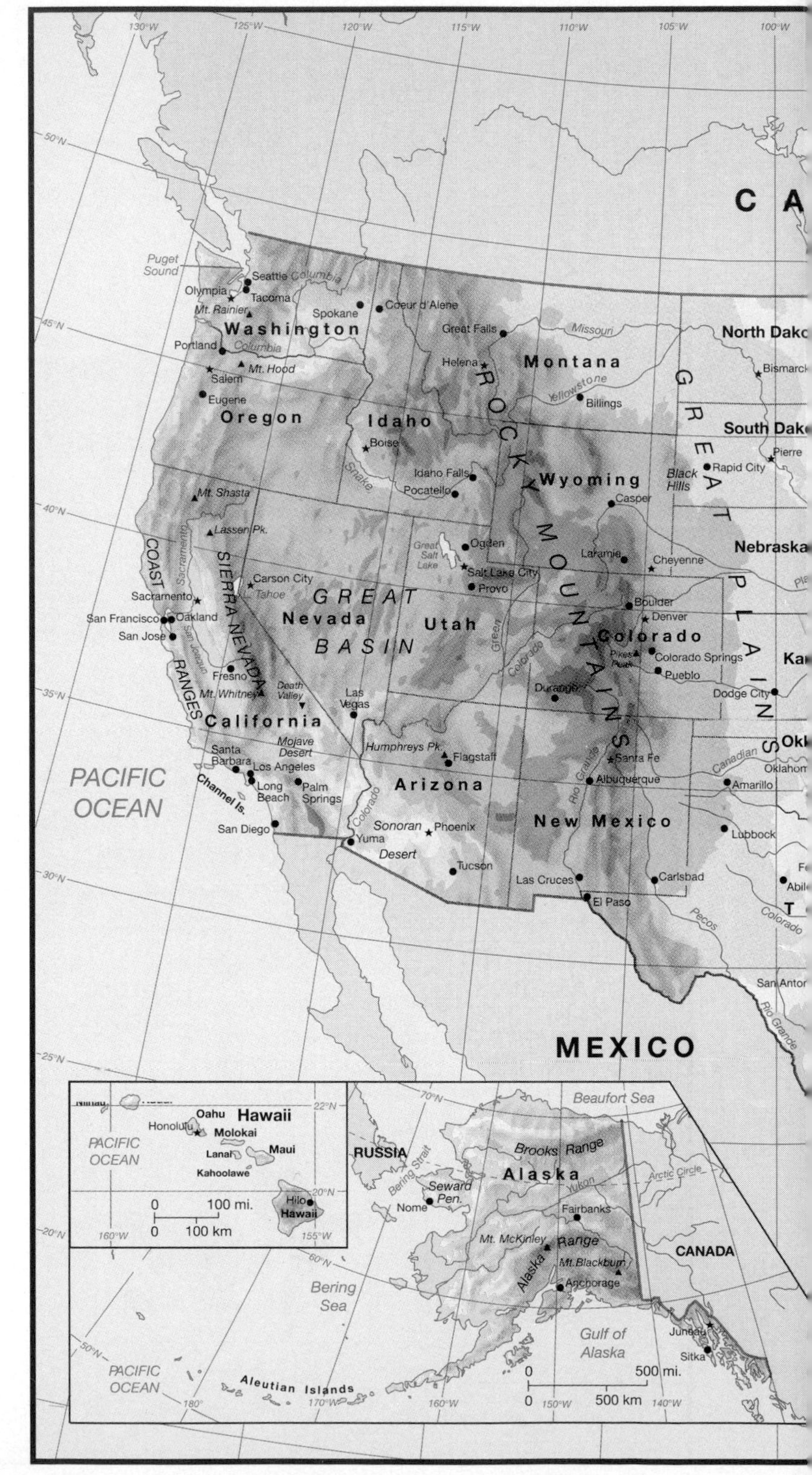
PACIFIC OCEAN
MEXICO
Puget Sound
Seattle
Olympia
Tacoma
Mt. Rainier
Spokane
Coeur d'Alene
Washington
Portland
Columbia
Mt. Hood
Salem
Eugene
Oregon
Idaho
Boise
Snake
Great Falls
Helena
Montana
Missouri
Yellowstone
Billings
ROCKY MOUNTAINS
GREAT PLAINS
North Dako
Bismarck
South Dak
Pierre
Rapid City
Black Hills
Idaho Falls
Pocatello
Wyoming
Casper
Mt. Shasta
Lassen Pk.
COAST RANGES
SIERRA NEVADA
Sacramento
Great Salt Lake
Ogden
Salt Lake City
Provo
Laramie
Cheyenne
Nebraska
Carson City
Tahoe
GREAT BASIN
Nevada
Utah
Green
Boulder
Denver
Colorado
Pikes Peak
Colorado Springs
Pueblo
San Francisco
Oakland
San Jose
San Joaquin
Fresno
Mt. Whitney
Death Valley
Las Vegas
Durango
Dodge City
California
Mojave Desert
Santa Barbara
Los Angeles
Long Beach
Palm Springs
Channel Is.
Humphreys Pk.
Flagstaff
Santa Fe
Rio Grande
Albuquerque
Canadian
Amarillo
Arizona
San Diego
Yuma
Sonoran Desert
Phoenix
New Mexico
Lubbock
Tucson
Las Cruces
El Paso
Carlsbad
Pecos
San Anton
C A
50°N
45°N
40°N
35°N
30°N
25°N
20°N
130°W
125°W
120°W
115°W
110°W
105°W
100°W
Hawaii
Oahu
Honolulu
Molokai
Lanai
Maui
Kahoolawe
Hilo
Hawaii
0 100 mi.
0 100 km
Beaufort Sea
RUSSIA
Bering Strait
Brooks Range
Alaska
Arctic Circle
Yukon
Seward Pen.
Nome
Fairbanks
Mt. McKinley
Alaska Range
Mt. Blackburn
Anchorage
CANADA
Bering Sea
Gulf of Alaska
Juneau
Sitka
Aleutian Islands
0 500 mi.
0 500 km

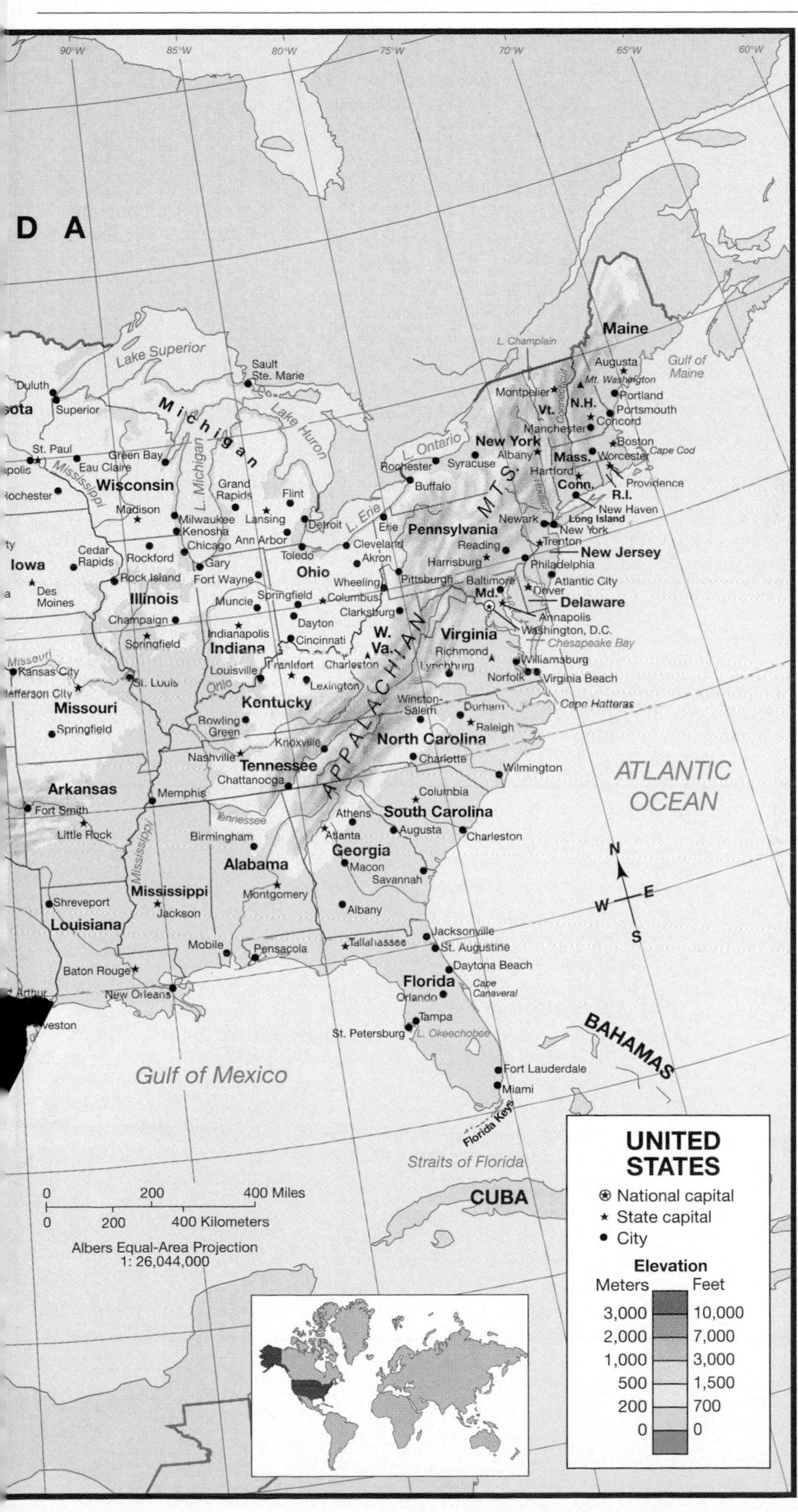
90°W
85°W
80°W
75°W
70°W
65°W
60°W
D A
Lake Superior
Sault Ste. Marie
Duluth
Superior
St. Paul
Eau Claire
Green Bay
Michigan
Lake Huron
L. Michigan
Mississippi
Wisconsin
Rochester
Madison
Milwaukee
Kenosha
Chicago
Grand Rapids
Lansing
Flint
Detroit
Ann Arbor
Toledo
L. Erie
Erie
Cleveland
Akron
Cedar Rapids
Iowa
Des Moines
Rockford
Gary
Rock Island
Fort Wayne
Ohio
Illinois
Muncie
Springfield
Columbus
Wheeling
Champaign
Dayton
Clarksburg
Indianapolis
Cincinnati
Springfield
Indiana
Missouri
Kansas City
Jefferson City
Missouri
Springfield
St. Louis
Louisville
Frankfort
Lexington
Ohio
Kentucky
Charleston
W. Va.
Bowling Green
Knoxville
Nashville
Tennessee
Chattanooga
Arkansas
Fort Smith
Little Rock
Memphis
Tennessee
Birmingham
Alabama
Mississippi
Mississippi
Jackson
Shreveport
Louisiana
Montgomery
Mobile
Pensacola
Baton Rouge
New Orleans
Gulf of Mexico
L. Champlain
Maine
Augusta
Gulf of Maine
Mt. Washington
Montpelier
Portland
Connecticut
Vt.
N.H.
Portsmouth
Concord
Manchester
L. Ontario
New York
Albany
Boston
Cape Cod
Rochester
Syracuse
Mass.
Worcester
Hartford
Buffalo
Hudson
Conn.
Providence
R.I.
New Haven
Newark
Long Island
New York
Pennsylvania
Trenton
Reading
New Jersey
Harrisburg
Philadelphia
Pittsburgh
Baltimore
Atlantic City
Md.
Dover
Delaware
Annapolis
Washington, D.C.
Chesapeake Bay
Virginia
Richmond
Lynchburg
Williamsburg
Norfolk
Virginia Beach
Cape Hatteras
APPALACHIAN MTS.
Winston-Salem
Durham
Raleigh
North Carolina
Charlotte
Wilmington
Columbia
South Carolina
Athens
Atlanta
Augusta
Charleston
Georgia
Macon
Savannah
Albany
Jacksonville
Tallahassee
St. Augustine
Daytona Beach
Florida
Cape Canaveral
Orlando
Tampa
St. Petersburg
L. Okeechobee
Fort Lauderdale
Miami
Florida Keys
Straits of Florida
CUBA
BAHAMAS
ATLANTIC OCEAN
N
E
W
S
0 200 400 Miles
0 200 400 Kilometers
Albers Equal-Area Projection
1: 26,044,000
UNITED STATES
National capital
State capital
City
Elevation
Meters
Feet
3,000
10,000
2,000
7,000
1,000
3,000
500
1,500
200
700
0
0

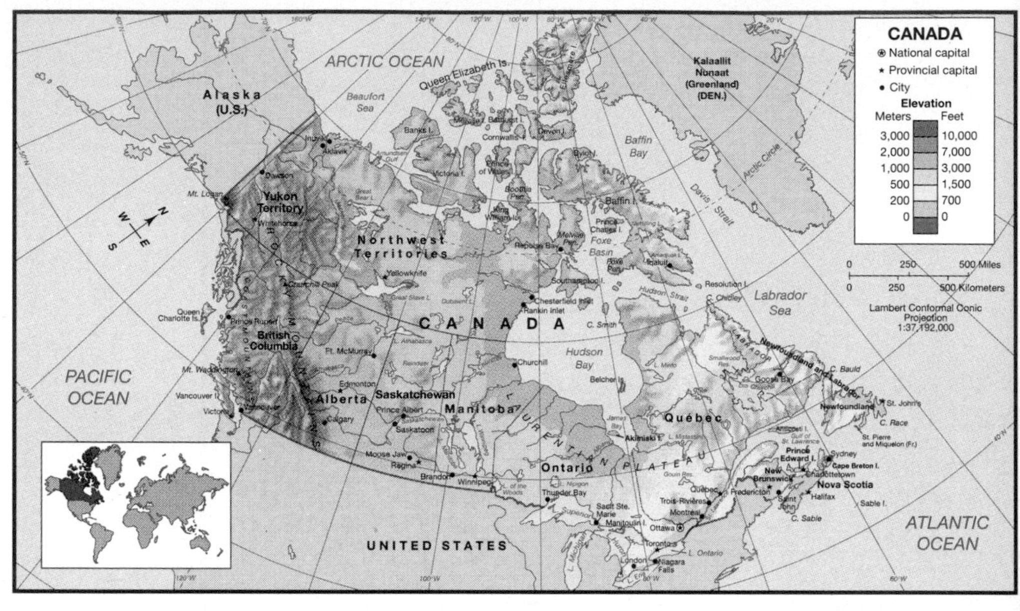
CANADA
National capital
Provincial capital
City
Elevation
Meters Feet
3,000 10,000
2,000 7,000
1,000 3,000
500 1,500
200 700
0 0
Lambert Conformal Conic Projection 1:37,192,000
ARCTIC OCEAN
PACIFIC OCEAN
ATLANTIC OCEAN
Alaska (U.S.)
Kalaallit Nunaat (Greenland) (DEN.)
Yukon Territory
Northwest Territories
British Columbia
Alberta
Saskatchewan
Manitoba
Ontario
Québec
Newfoundland and Labrador
New Brunswick
Nova Scotia
Prince Edward I.
CANADA
UNITED STATES
Hudson Bay
Baffin Bay
Labrador Sea
Beaufort Sea
Queen Elizabeth Is.

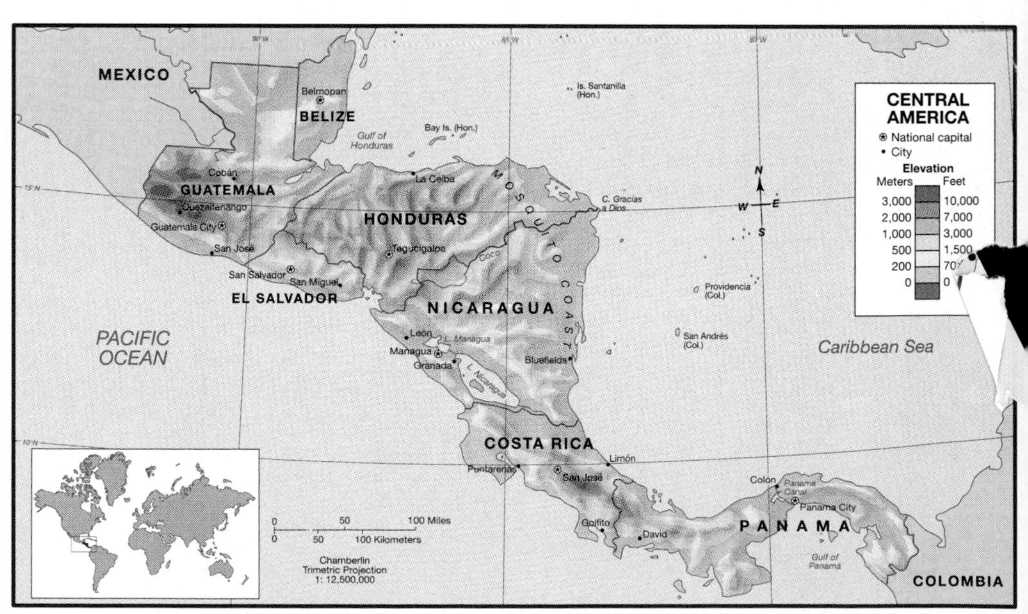
CENTRAL AMERICA
National capital
City
Elevation
Meters Feet
3,000 10,000
2,000 7,000
1,000 3,000
500 1,500
200 700
0 0
Chamberlin Trimetric Projection 1: 12,500,000
MEXICO
BELIZE
GUATEMALA
HONDURAS
EL SALVADOR
NICARAGUA
COSTA RICA
PANAMA
COLOMBIA
PACIFIC OCEAN
Caribbean Sea
Gulf of Honduras
Belmopan
Guatemala City
Tegucigalpa
San Salvador
Managua
San José
Panama City

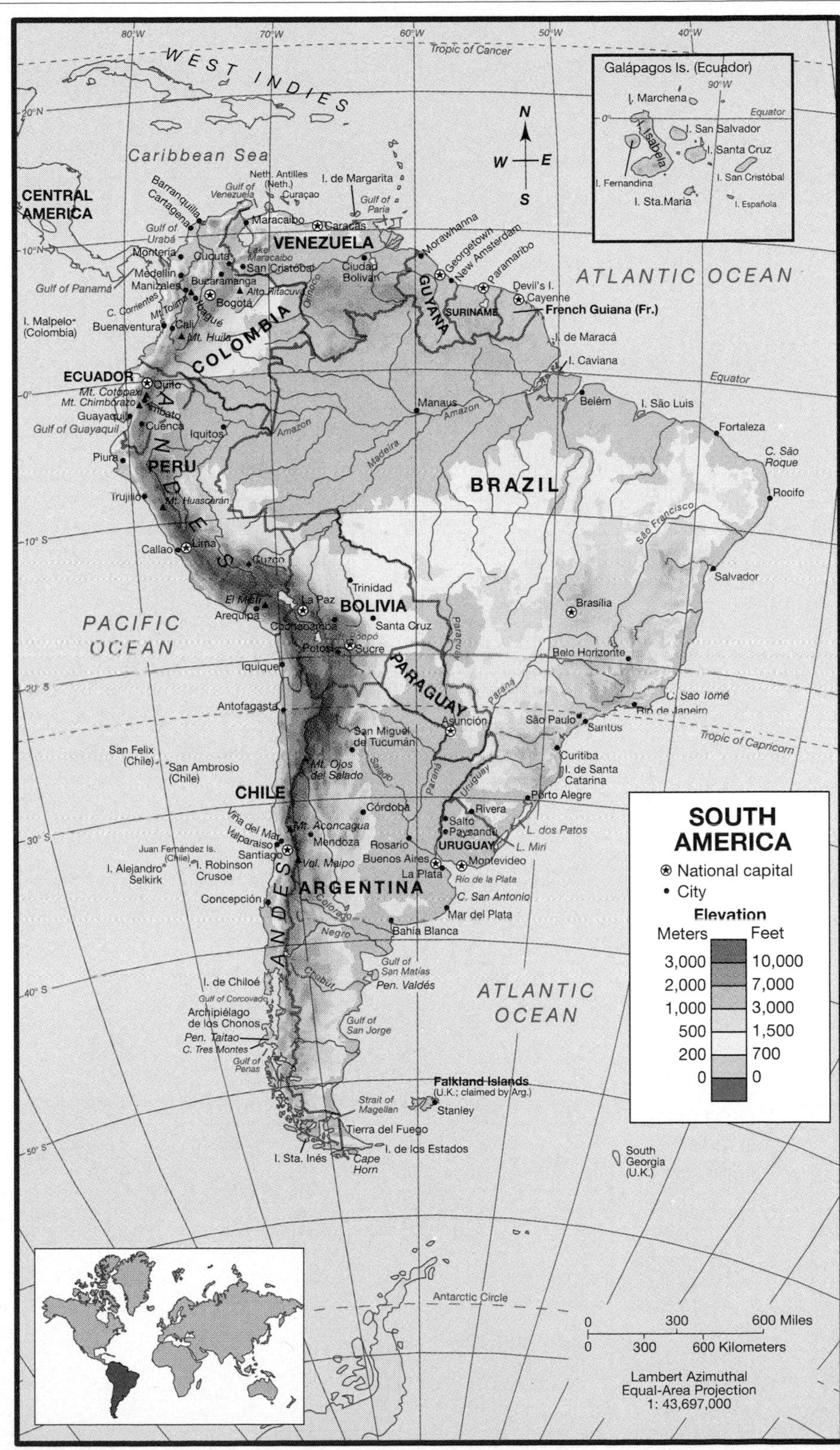
SOUTH AMERICA
National capital
City
Elevation
Meters
Feet
3,000
10,000
2,000
7,000
1,000
3,000
500
1,500
200
700
0
0
Galápagos Is. (Ecuador)
90°W
I. Marchena
Equator
I. San Salvador
I. Isabela
I. Santa Cruz
I. Fernandina
I. San Cristóbal
I. Sta.Maria
I. Española
80°W
70°W
60°W
50°W
40°W
Tropic of Cancer
WEST INDIES
20°N
10°N
0°
10° S
20° S
30° S
40° S
50° S
N
W
E
S
Caribbean Sea
CENTRAL AMERICA
Neth. Antilles (Neth.)
Gulf of Venezuela
Curaçao
I. de Margarita
Gulf of Paria
Barranquilla
Cartagena
Gulf of Urabá
Maracaibo
Caracas
VENEZUELA
Lake Maracaibo
Montería
Cúcuta
San Cristóbal
Ciudad Bolívar
Orinoco
Morawhanna
Georgetown
New Amsterdam
Paramaribo
GUYANA
SURINAME
Devil's I.
Cayenne
French Guiana (Fr.)
ATLANTIC OCEAN
Medellín
Manizales
Bucaramanga
Alto Ritacuva
Bogotá
Gulf of Panamá
C. Corrientes
Mt. Tolima
Ibagué
I. Malpelo (Colombia)
Buenaventura
Cali
Mt. Huila
COLOMBIA
I. de Maracá
I. Caviana
ECUADOR
Quito
Mt. Cotopaxi
Mt. Chimborazo
Ambato
Guayaquil
Gulf of Guayaquil
Cuenca
Iquitos
Amazon
Manaus
Equator
Belém
I. São Luis
Fortaleza
Madeira
Piura
PERU
C. São Roque
BRAZIL
Recife
Trujillo
Mt. Huascarán
São Francisco
ANDES
Callao
Lima
Cuzco
Trinidad
Salvador
El Misti
Arequipa
La Paz
BOLIVIA
Brasília
PACIFIC OCEAN
Cochabamba
Santa Cruz
L. de Poopó
Potosí
Sucre
Paraguay
Iquique
Belo Horizonte
PARAGUAY
Paraná
C. São Tomé
Rio de Janeiro
Antofagasta
Asunción
São Paulo
Santos
San Miguel de Tucumán
Tropic of Capricorn
San Felix (Chile)
San Ambrosio (Chile)
Mt. Ojos del Salado
Salado
Curitiba
I. de Santa Catarina
Uruguay
CHILE
Porto Alegre
Córdoba
Rivera
Viña del Mar
Mt. Aconcagua
Salto
Paysandú
L. dos Patos
Valparaíso
Mendoza
Rosario
L. Mirí
Juan Fernández Is. (Chile)
Santiago
URUGUAY
I. Alejandro Selkirk
I. Robinson Crusoe
Vol. Maipo
Buenos Aires
Montevideo
La Plata
Río de la Plata
ARGENTINA
Concepción
C. San Antonio
Mar del Plata
Colorado
Negro
Bahía Blanca
Gulf of San Matías
Chubut
Pen. Valdés
I. de Chiloé
Gulf of Corcovado
ATLANTIC OCEAN
Archipiélago de los Chonos
Gulf of San Jorge
Pen. Taitao
C. Tres Montes
Gulf of Penas
Falkland Islands (U.K.; claimed by Arg.)
Strait of Magellan
Stanley
Tierra del Fuego
I. de los Estados
I. Sta. Inés
Cape Horn
South Georgia (U.K.)
Antarctic Circle
0
300
600 Miles
0
300
600 Kilometers
Lambert Azimuthal Equal-Area Projection
1: 43,697,000

WESTERN EUROPE
National capital
City
Elevation
Meters
Feet
3,000
10,000
2,000
7,000
1,000
3,000
500
1,500
200
700
0
0
0
200
400 Miles
0
200
400 Kilometers
Azimuthal Equal-Area Projection
1: 31,019,000
ARCTIC OCEAN
Barents Sea
Norwegian Sea
ATLANTIC OCEAN
North Sea
Baltic Sea
Bay of Biscay
Mediterranean Sea
Tyrrhenian Sea
Ionian Sea
Adriatic Sea
Ligurian Sea
EASTERN EUROPE
AFRICA
ICELAND
Reykjavík
Akureyri
Seydhisfjördhur
Denmark Strait
Arctic Circle
Jan Mayen (Norway)
Faroe Is. (Den.)
Rockall (U.K.)
Shetland Is. (U.K.)
Orkney Is.
Hebrides
UNITED KINGDOM
SCOTLAND
Inverness
Glasgow
Edinburgh
Newcastle-upon-Tyne
N. IRELAND
Belfast
IRELAND
Galway
Dublin
Limerick
Cork
C. Clear
Manchester
Leeds
Liverpool
Sheffield
Bradford
ENGLAND
WALES
Cardiff
Birmingham
Bristol
London
Southampton
Portsmouth
Land's End
English Channel
Channel Is. (U.K.)
NORWAY
Trondheim
Kristiansund
Ålesund
Bergen
Oslo
Drammen
Stavanger
Arendal
Kristiansand
Lillehammer
SWEDEN
LAPLAND
Kiruna
Sundsvall
Gävle
Stockholm
Göteborg
Visby
Gotland (Sw.)
Öland
Malmö
FINLAND
Oulu
Vaasa
Kuopio
Tampere
Turku
Helsinki
Espoo
Kotka
Ahvenanmaa (Finland)
Gulf of Bothnia
G. of Finland
Hammerfest
North Cape
Vardø
DENMARK
JUTLAND
Ålborg
Århus
Odense
Copenhagen
Bornholm (Den.)
Skagerrak
Kattegat
Frisian Is.
NETHERLANDS
Amsterdam
The Hague
Rotterdam
Utrecht
BELGIUM
Antwerp
Brussels
Liège
LUX.
GERMANY
Kiel
Lübeck
Hamburg
Bremen
Hannover
Berlin
Magdeburg
Dortmund
Essen
Düsseldorf
Cologne
Bonn
Leipzig
Dresden
Frankfurt
Mannheim
Nuremberg
Stuttgart
Munich
FRANCE
Calais
Lille
Cherbourg
Le Havre
Rouen
Reims
Brest
Paris
Versailles
Orléans
Nantes
Strasbourg
Vichy
Lyon
Bordeaux
Biarritz
Toulouse
Nîmes
Marseille
Nice
Grenoble
MASSIF CENTRAL
G. of Lions
SWITZ.
Basel
Zürich
Bern
Geneva
Mt. Blanc
LIECHTENSTEIN
AUSTRIA
Vienna
Linz
Salzburg
Innsbruck
Graz
ALPS
JURA MTS.
ITALY
Milan
Turin
Genoa
Venice
Trieste
Bologna
Ravenna
SAN MARINO
Florence
Pisa
Siena
Perugia
VATICAN CITY
Rome
Naples
Bari
Brindisi
Mt. Vesuvius
Reggio di Calabria
Messina
Palermo
Catania
Sicily
Mt. Etna
C. Passero
APENNINES
G. of Taranto
G. of Squillace
Corsica (Fr.)
Ajaccio
Str. of Bonifacio
Sardinia (It.)
Cagliari
MONACO
MALTA
Valletta
SPAIN
PORTUGAL
Porto
Braga
Coimbra
Lisbon
Setúbal
Évora
Salamanca
Madrid
Toledo
Bilbao
Saragossa
Barcelona
Valencia
Seville
Córdoba
Granada
Cádiz
Málaga
Almería
Gibraltar (U.K.)
Cueta (Sp.)
C. Ortegal
CANTABRIAN MTS.
PYRENEES
ANDORRA
SIERRA DE GUADARRAMA
SIERRA MORENA
C. St. Vincent
Gulf of Cádiz
Strait of Gibraltar
C. Gata
C. Palos
C. Nao
C. Creus
Balearic Is.
Majorca
Minorca
Palma
Ibiza

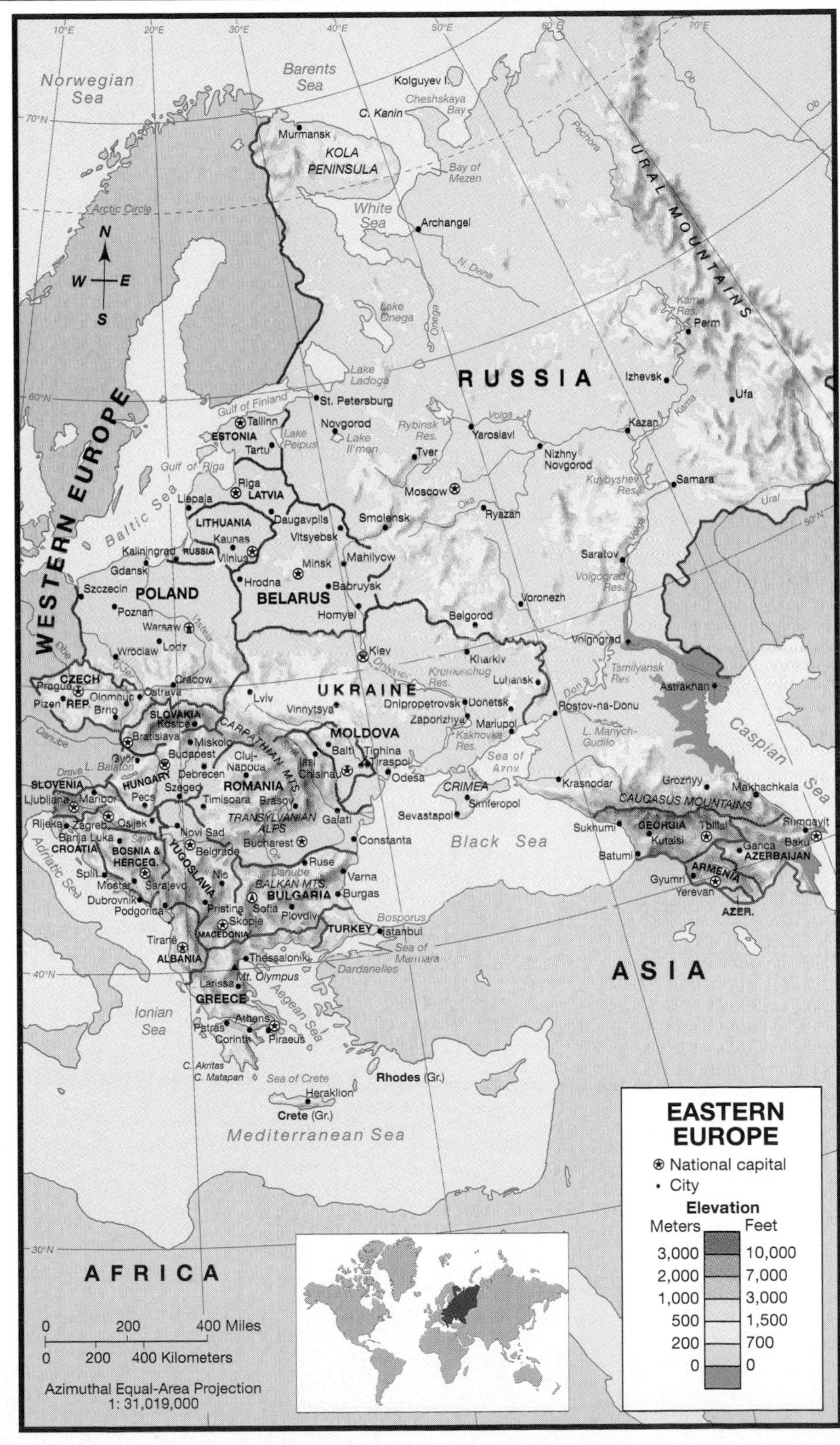
EASTERN EUROPE
National capital
City
Elevation
Meters
Feet
3,000
10,000
2,000
7,000
1,000
3,000
500
1,500
200
700
0
0
0
200
400 Miles
0
200
400 Kilometers
Azimuthal Equal-Area Projection
1: 31,019,000
RUSSIA
UKRAINE
POLAND
BELARUS
WESTERN EUROPE
AFRICA
ASIA
Norwegian Sea
Barents Sea
White Sea
Black Sea
Caspian Sea
Mediterranean Sea
Ionian Sea
Aegean Sea
Adriatic Sea
Baltic Sea
Sea of Azov
Sea of Marmara
Sea of Crete
KOLA PENINSULA
URAL MOUNTAINS
CAUCASUS MOUNTAINS
CARPATHIAN MTS.
TRANSYLVANIAN ALPS
BALKAN MTS.
CRIMEA
Arctic Circle
Moscow
St. Petersburg
Kiev
Minsk
Warsaw
Riga
Tallinn
Vilnius
Bucharest
Budapest
Sofia
Belgrade
Athens
Prague
Bratislava
Chisinau
Tbilisi
Yerevan
Baku
Skopje
Tirane
Sarajevo
Zagreb
Ljubljana
ESTONIA
LATVIA
LITHUANIA
MOLDOVA
ROMANIA
HUNGARY
SLOVAKIA
CZECH REP.
SLOVENIA
CROATIA
BOSNIA & HERCEG.
YUGOSLAVIA
MACEDONIA
ALBANIA
GREECE
BULGARIA
TURKEY
GEORGIA
ARMENIA
AZERBAIJAN
AZER.
Rhodes (Gr.)
Crete (Gr.)

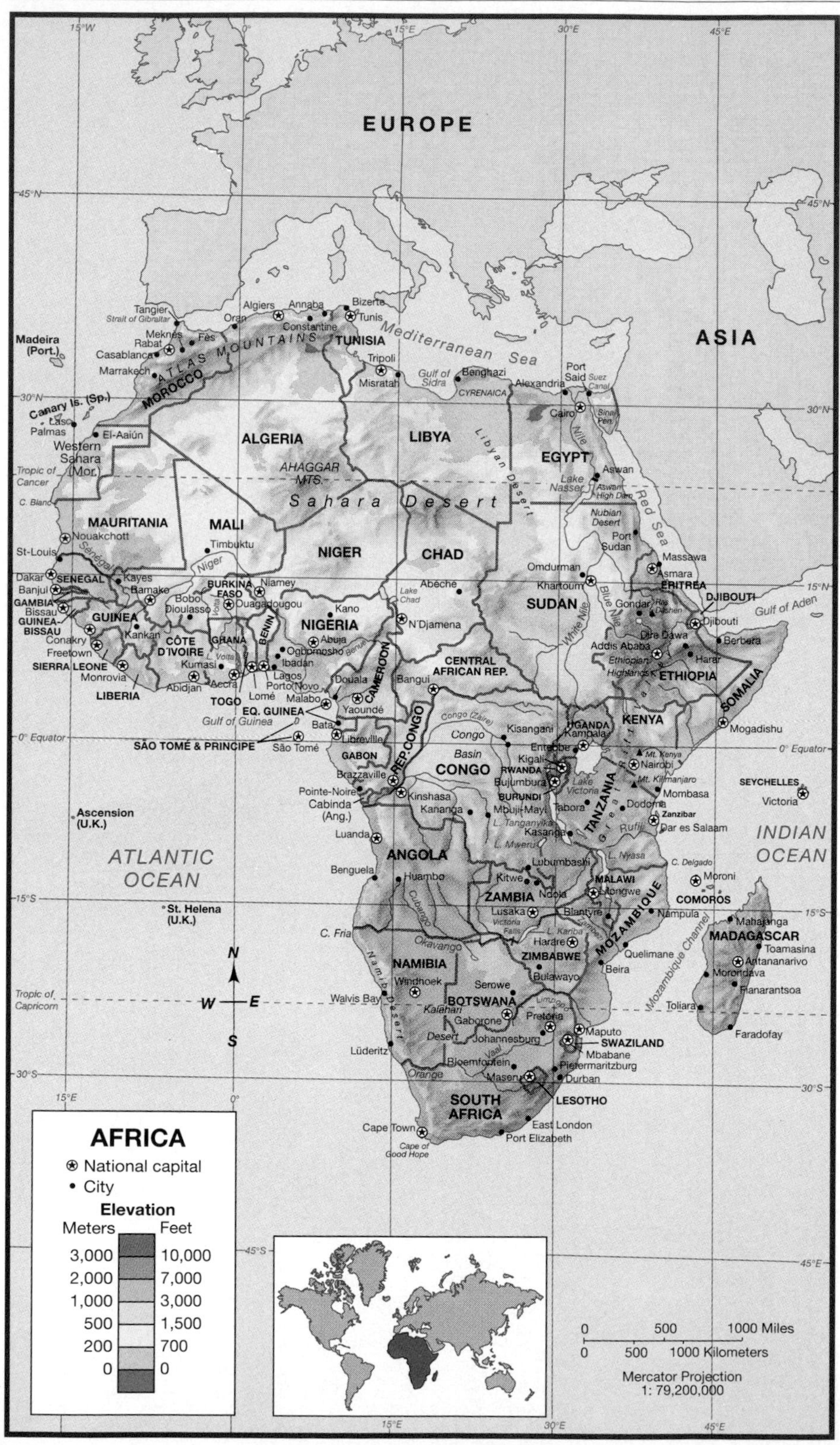
EUROPE
ASIA
AFRICA
National capital
City
Elevation
Meters
Feet
3,000
10,000
2,000
7,000
1,000
3,000
500
1,500
200
700
0
0
ATLANTIC OCEAN
INDIAN OCEAN
Mediterranean Sea
Red Sea
Gulf of Aden
Gulf of Guinea
Mozambique Channel
ATLAS MOUNTAINS
AHAGGAR MTS.
Sahara Desert
Libyan Desert
Nubian Desert
Kalahari Desert
Namib Desert
Congo Basin
Ethiopian Highlands
MOROCCO
ALGERIA
TUNISIA
LIBYA
EGYPT
Western Sahara (Mor.)
MAURITANIA
MALI
NIGER
CHAD
SUDAN
ERITREA
DJIBOUTI
ETHIOPIA
SOMALIA
SENEGAL
GAMBIA
GUINEA-BISSAU
GUINEA
SIERRA LEONE
LIBERIA
CÔTE D'IVOIRE
BURKINA FASO
GHANA
TOGO
BENIN
NIGERIA
CAMEROON
CENTRAL AFRICAN REP.
EQ. GUINEA
SÃO TOMÉ & PRINCIPE
GABON
REP. CONGO
CONGO
UGANDA
KENYA
RWANDA
BURUNDI
TANZANIA
ANGOLA
ZAMBIA
MALAWI
MOZAMBIQUE
ZIMBABWE
NAMIBIA
BOTSWANA
SOUTH AFRICA
SWAZILAND
LESOTHO
MADAGASCAR
COMOROS
SEYCHELLES
Madeira (Port.)
Canary Is. (Sp.)
Ascension (U.K.)
St. Helena (U.K.)
Cabinda (Ang.)
Tangier
Strait of Gibraltar
Rabat
Meknès
Fès
Casablanca
Marrakech
Oran
Algiers
Annaba
Constantine
Bizerte
Tunis
Tripoli
Misratah
Gulf of Sidra
Benghazi
CYRENAICA
Alexandria
Port Said
Suez Canal
Cairo
Sinai Pen.
Nile
Aswan
Lake Nasser
Aswan High Dam
Port Sudan
Massawa
Asmara
Las Palmas
El-Aaiún
Tropic of Cancer
C. Blanc
Nouakchott
Timbuktu
St-Louis
Senegal
Dakar
Banjul
Bissau
Kayes
Bamako
Niger
Bobo Dioulasso
Niamey
Ouagadougou
Conakry
Freetown
Kankan
Monrovia
Kumasi
Abidjan
Accra
Lomé
Volta
L. Volta
Ogbomosho
Ibadan
Lagos
Porto Novo
Abuja
Kano
Benue
Lake Chad
N'Djamena
Abeche
Omdurman
Khartoum
Blue Nile
White Nile
Gondar
Ras Dashen
Djibouti
Dire Dawa
Berbera
Addis Ababa
Harar
Douala
Malabo
Yaoundé
Bata
Libreville
São Tomé
Bangui
Congo (Zaire)
Kisangani
Entebbe
Kampala
Kigali
Bujumbura
Lake Victoria
Nairobi
Mt. Kenya
Mt. Kilimanjaro
Mombasa
Mogadishu
Victoria
Brazzaville
Pointe-Noire
Kinshasa
Kananga
Mbuji-Mayi
Tabora
Dodoma
Zanzibar
Dar es Salaam
L. Tanganyika
Kasanga
L. Mweru
Rufiji
Luanda
Lubumbashi
L. Nyasa
C. Delgado
Moroni
Benguela
Huambo
Kitwe
Ndola
Lilongwe
Cubango
Lusaka
Blantyre
Nampula
Victoria Falls
L. Kariba
Zambezi
C. Fria
Okavango
Harare
Quelimane
Beira
Mahajanga
Toamasina
Antananarivo
Morondava
Fianarantsoa
Toliara
Faradofay
Windhoek
Serowe
Bulawayo
Limpopo
Walvis Bay
Tropic of Capricorn
Gaborone
Pretoria
Maputo
Johannesburg
Mbabane
Vaal
Lüderitz
Bloemfontein
Pietermaritzburg
Orange
Maseru
Durban
East London
Port Elizabeth
Cape Town
Cape of Good Hope
N
S
W
E
45°N
30°N
15°N
0° Equator
15°S
30°S
45°S
15°W
0°
15°E
30°E
45°E
0
500
1000 Miles
0
500
1000 Kilometers
Mercator Projection
1: 79,200,000

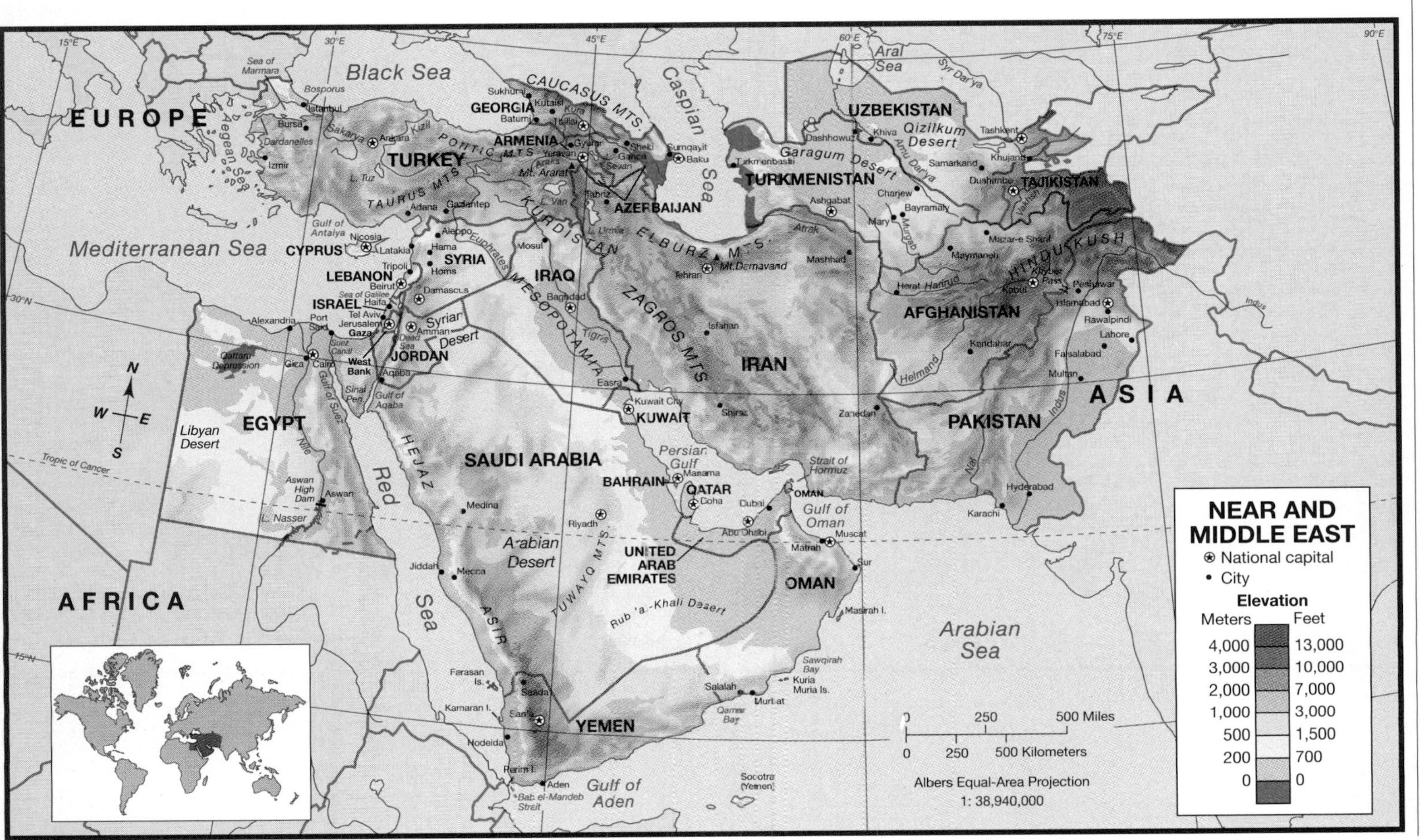
NEAR AND MIDDLE EAST
National capital
City
Elevation
Meters Feet
4,000 13,000
3,000 10,000
2,000 7,000
1,000 3,000
500 1,500
200 700
0 0
0 250 500 Miles
0 250 500 Kilometers
Albers Equal-Area Projection
1: 38,940,000
EUROPE
ASIA
AFRICA
Black Sea
Caspian Sea
Mediterranean Sea
Aegean Sea
Sea of Marmara
Aral Sea
Red Sea
Persian Gulf
Gulf of Oman
Arabian Sea
Gulf of Aden
Gulf of Aqaba
Gulf of Suez
Gulf of Antalya
TURKEY
GEORGIA
ARMENIA
AZERBAIJAN
TURKMENISTAN
UZBEKISTAN
TAJIKISTAN
AFGHANISTAN
PAKISTAN
IRAN
IRAQ
SYRIA
LEBANON
ISRAEL
JORDAN
CYPRUS
EGYPT
SAUDI ARABIA
KUWAIT
BAHRAIN
QATAR
UNITED ARAB EMIRATES
OMAN
YEMEN
West Bank
Gaza
CAUCASUS MTS.
PONTIC MTS.
TAURUS MTS.
ELBURZ MTS.
ZAGROS MTS.
HINDU KUSH
KURDISTAN
MESOPOTAMIA
HEJAZ
ASIR
TUWAYQ MTS.
Syrian Desert
Arabian Desert
Rub 'al-Khali Desert
Libyan Desert
Qizilkum Desert
Garagum Desert
Qattara Depression
Sinai Pen.
Tropic of Cancer
Istanbul
Ankara
Izmir
Bursa
Adana
Gaziantep
Nicosia
Beirut
Tripoli
Damascus
Homs
Hama
Aleppo
Latakia
Haifa
Tel Aviv
Jerusalem
Amman
Aqaba
Cairo
Giza
Alexandria
Port Said
Suez Canal
Aswan
Aswan High Dam
L. Nasser
Nile
Baghdad
Mosul
Basra
Kuwait City
Manama
Doha
Abu Dhabi
Dubai
Muscat
Matrah
Sur
Salalah
Riyadh
Medina
Mecca
Jiddah
Sanaa
Saada
Hodeida
Aden
Tehran
Tabriz
Esfahan
Shiraz
Mashhad
Zahedan
Mt. Damavand
Mt. Ararat
Tbilisi
Yerevan
Baku
Sumqayit
Ganca
Kutaisi
Batumi
Sukhumi
Gyumri
Ashgabat
Turkmenbashi
Dashhowuz
Khiva
Charjew
Mary
Bayramaly
Samarkand
Tashkent
Khujand
Dushanbe
Kabul
Herat
Kandahar
Mazar-e Sharif
Maymanah
Khyber Pass
Islamabad
Rawalpindi
Peshawar
Lahore
Faisalabad
Multan
Hyderabad
Karachi
Indus
Tigris
Euphrates
Amu Darya
Syr Darya
Murgab
Helmand
Atrak
Strait of Hormuz
Bab el-Mandeb Strait
Socotra (Yemen)
Kuria Muria Is.
Masirah I.
Farasan Is.
Kamaran I.
Perim I.
Bosporus
Dardanelles
N
S
E
W
15°E
30°E
45°E
60°E
75°E
90°E
30°N
15°N

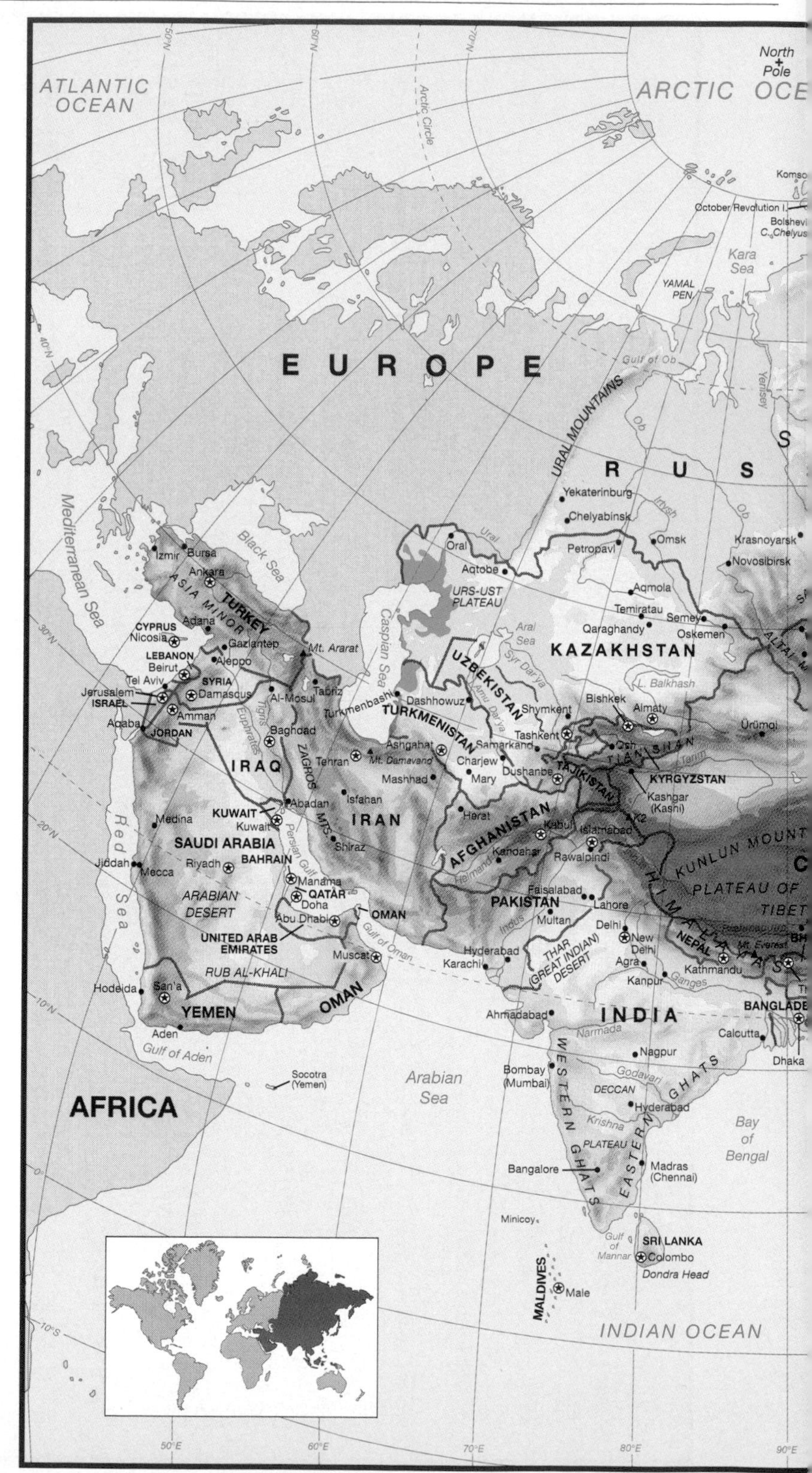

ATLANTIC OCEAN
ARCTIC OCE
North Pole
Arctic Circle
50°N
60°N
70°N
40°N
30°N
20°N
10°N
0°
10°S
50°E
60°E
70°E
80°E
90°E
Komso
October Revolution I.
Bolshevi
C. Chelyus
Kara Sea
YAMAL PEN.
Gulf of Ob
Yenisey
Ob
E U R O P E
URAL MOUNTAINS
R U S S
Yekaterinburg
Chelyabinsk
Irtysh
Ural
Oral
Petropavl
Omsk
Krasnoyarsk
Novosibirsk
Aqtobe
URS-UST PLATEAU
Aqmola
Temirtau
Qaraghandy
Semey
Oskemen
ALTAI
Aral Sea
Syr Dar'ya
KAZAKHSTAN
L. Balkhash
Mediterranean Sea
Black Sea
Caspian Sea
Izmir
Bursa
Ankara
ASIA MINOR
TURKEY
Adana
CYPRUS
Nicosia
Gaziantep
Mt. Ararat
LEBANON
Beirut
Aleppo
Tel Aviv
SYRIA
Damascus
Jerusalem
ISRAEL
Amman
Aqaba
JORDAN
Al-Mosul
Tabriz
Tigris
Euphrates
Baghdad
IRAQ
ZAGROS MTS.
UZBEKISTAN
Dashhowuz
Amu Dar'ya
Turkmenbashi
TURKMENISTAN
Ashgabat
Mt. Damavand
Tehran
Mashhad
Samarkand
Tashkent
Shymkent
Bishkek
Almaty
Ürümqi
Charjew
Mary
Dushanbe
TAJIKISTAN
Osh
TIAN SHAN
Tarim
KYRGYZSTAN
Kashgar (Kashi)
Isfahan
IRAN
Abadan
KUWAIT
Kuwait
Herat
AFGHANISTAN
Kabul
Islamabad
K2
KUNLUN MOUNT
Medina
Red Sea
Persian Gulf
Shiraz
SAUDI ARABIA
BAHRAIN
Riyadh
Kandahar
Rawalpindi
Helmand
Jiddah
Mecca
Manama
QATAR
Doha
ARABIAN DESERT
PLATEAU OF TIBET
Faisalabad
PAKISTAN
Lahore
Indus
Multan
Abu Dhabi
OMAN
Delhi
New Delhi
HIMALAYAS
Mt. Everest
NEPAL
Kathmandu
UNITED ARAB EMIRATES
Gulf of Oman
Muscat
Hyderabad
Karachi
THAR (GREAT INDIAN) DESERT
Agra
Kanpur
Ganges
RUB AL-KHALI
Hodeida
San'a
YEMEN
OMAN
Ahmadabad
INDIA
BANGLADE
Narmada
Calcutta
Dhaka
Aden
Gulf of Aden
Nagpur
Socotra (Yemen)
Arabian Sea
Bombay (Mumbai)
WESTERN GHATS
Godavari
DECCAN
EASTERN GHATS
Hyderabad
AFRICA
Krishna
PLATEAU
Bay of Bengal
Bangalore
Madras (Chennai)
Minicoy
Gulf of Mannar
SRI LANKA
Colombo
Dondra Head
MALDIVES
Male
INDIAN OCEAN

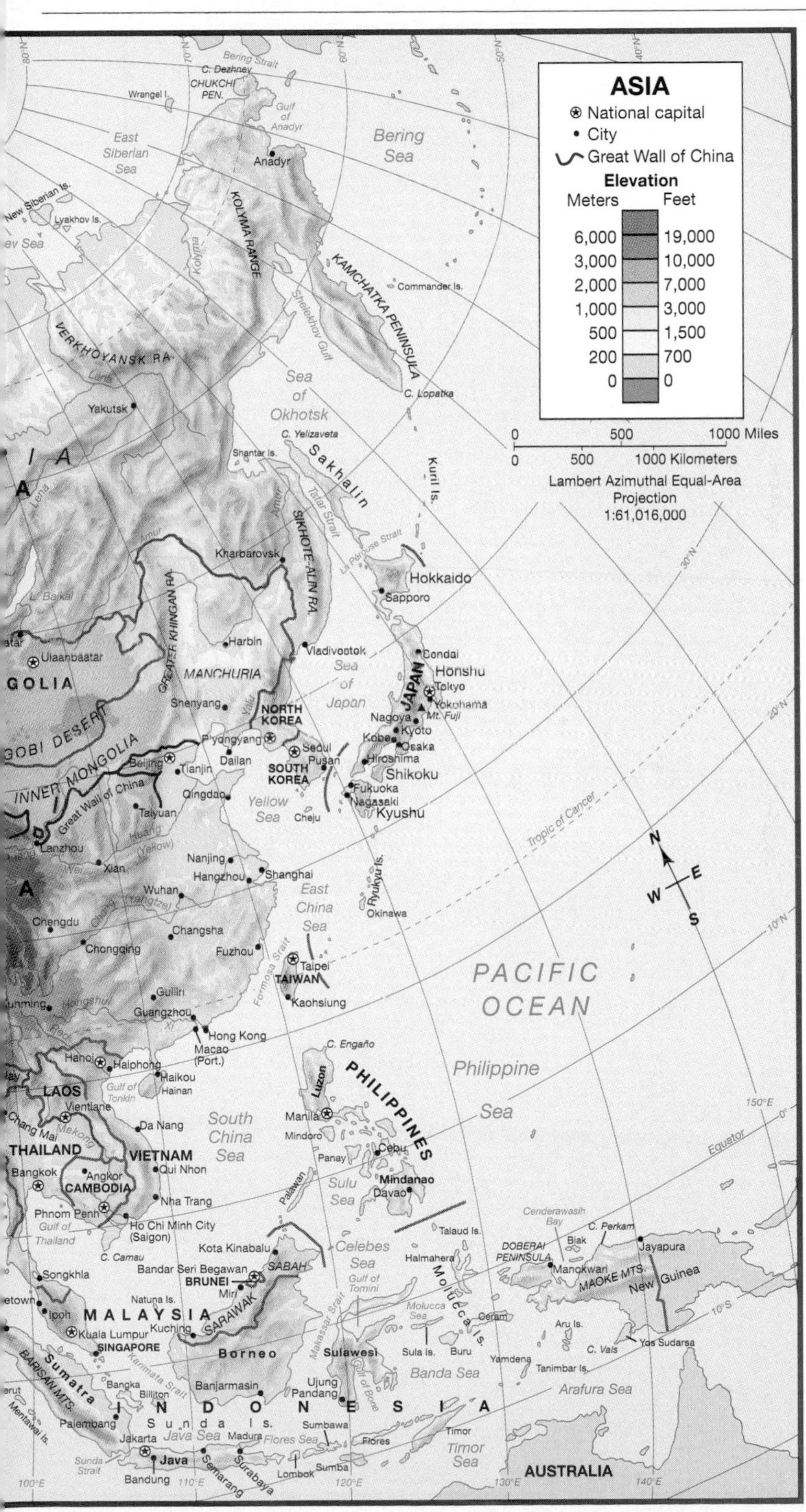
ASIA
National capital
City
Great Wall of China
Elevation
Meters
Feet
6,000
19,000
3,000
10,000
2,000
7,000
1,000
3,000
500
1,500
200
700
0
0
0
500
1000 Miles
0
500
1000 Kilometers
Lambert Azimuthal Equal-Area Projection
1:61,016,000
Bering Sea
East Siberian Sea
Sea of Okhotsk
Sea of Japan
Yellow Sea
East China Sea
South China Sea
Philippine Sea
PACIFIC OCEAN
Sulu Sea
Celebes Sea
Banda Sea
Arafura Sea
Java Sea
Flores Sea
Timor Sea
Molucca Sea
Gulf of Tonkin
Gulf of Thailand
Gulf of Anadyr
Gulf of Tomini
Gulf of Bone
Shelekhov Gulf
Bering Strait
Tatar Strait
La Pérouse Strait
Formosa Strait
Makassar Strait
Karimata Strait
Sunda Strait
C. Dezhnev
CHUKCHI PEN.
Wrangel I.
New Siberian Is.
Lyakhov Is.
Anadyr
KOLYMA RANGE
Kolyma
KAMCHATKA PENINSULA
Commander Is.
C. Lopatka
VERKHOYANSK RA.
Lena
Yakutsk
C. Yelizaveta
Shantar Is.
Sakhalin
Kuril Is.
Amur
Kharbarovsk
SIKHOTE-ALIN RA.
GREATER KHINGAN RA.
L. Baikal
Hokkaido
Sapporo
Harbin
Vladivostok
Ulaanbaatar
MANCHURIA
Sendai
Honshu
JAPAN
Tokyo
Yokohama
Mt. Fuji
Nagoya
Kyoto
Kobe
Osaka
Hiroshima
Shikoku
Fukuoka
Nagasaki
Kyushu
Shenyang
Yalu
NORTH KOREA
P'yongyang
Dalian
Seoul
Pusan
SOUTH KOREA
Cheju
GOBI DESERT
INNER MONGOLIA
Beijing
Tianjin
Great Wall of China
Qingdao
Taiyuan
Huang (Yellow)
Lanzhou
Wei
Xian
Nanjing
Hangzhou
Shanghai
Ryukyu Is.
Okinawa
Wuhan
Chang (Yangtze)
Chengdu
Changsha
Chongqing
Fuzhou
Taipei
TAIWAN
Kaohsiung
Guilin
Kunming
Hongshui
Guangzhou
Xi
Red
Hong Kong
Macao (Port.)
Hanoi
Haiphong
Haikou
Hainan
LAOS
Vientiane
Chiang Mai
Mekong
THAILAND
Da Nang
VIETNAM
Qui Nhon
Bangkok
Angkor
CAMBODIA
Nha Trang
Phnom Penh
Ho Chi Minh City (Saigon)
C. Camau
Songkhla
C. Engaño
Luzon
PHILIPPINES
Manila
Mindoro
Panay
Cebu
Mindanao
Davao
Palawan
Talaud Is.
Kota Kinabalu
SABAH
Bandar Seri Begawan
BRUNEI
Miri
SARAWAK
Natuna Is.
MALAYSIA
Ipoh
Kuala Lumpur
Kuching
SINGAPORE
Borneo
Sumatra
BARISAN MTS.
Mentawai Is.
Bangka
Billiton
Banjarmasin
Palembang
INDONESIA
Sunda Is.
Jakarta
Java
Bandung
Semarang
Madura
Surabaya
Lombok
Sumba
Sumbawa
Flores
Timor
Sulawesi
Ujung Pandang
Halmahera
Moluccas Is.
Sula Is.
Buru
Ceram
Cenderawasih Bay
C. Perkam
DOBERAI PENINSULA
Biak
Manokwari
Jayapura
MAOKE MTS.
New Guinea
Aru Is.
Yamdena
Tanimbar Is.
C. Vals
Yos Sudarso
AUSTRALIA
Tropic of Cancer
Equator
N
E
S
W
80°N
70°N
60°N
50°N
40°N
30°N
20°N
10°N
0°
10°S
100°E
110°E
120°E
130°E
140°E
150°E

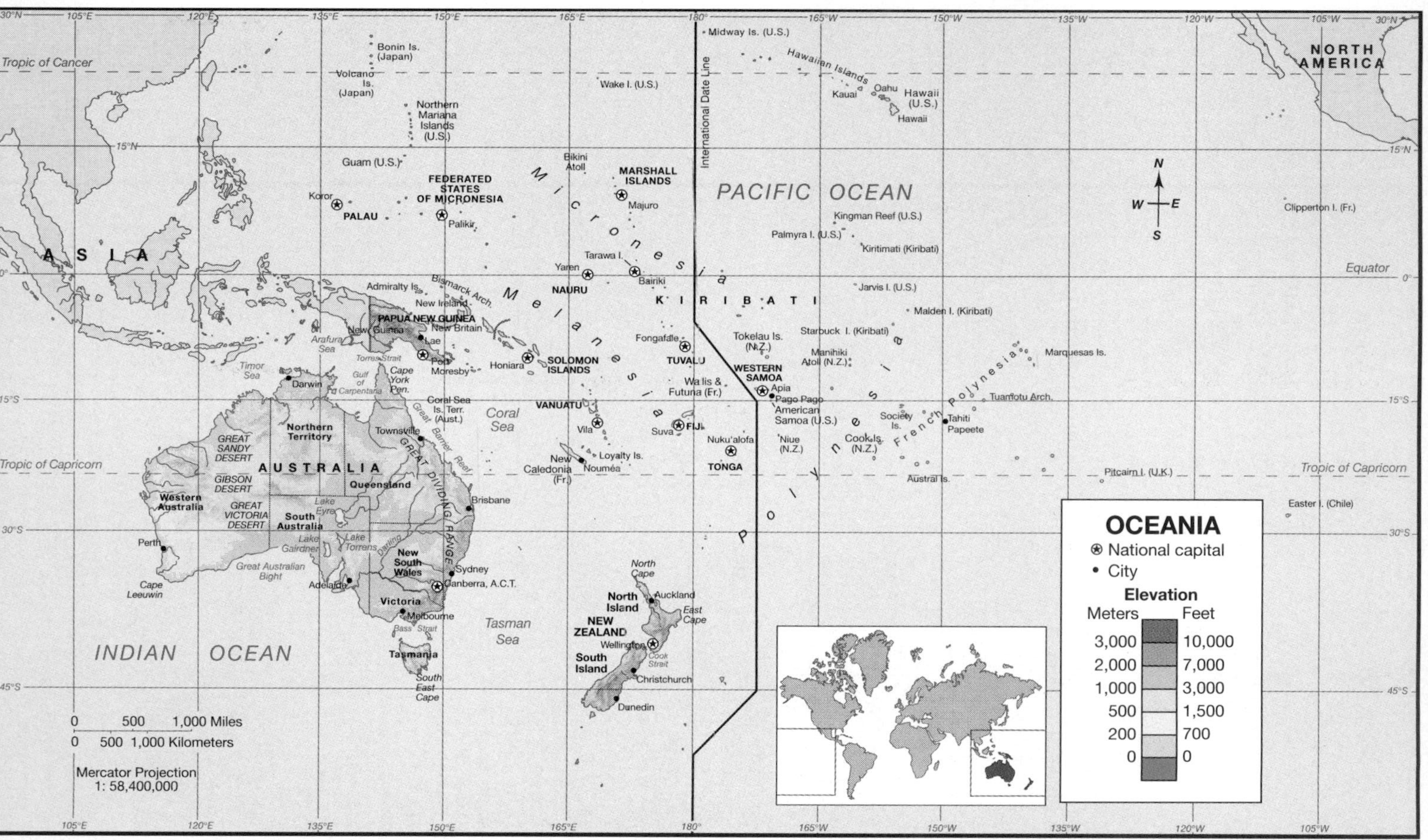

OCEANIA
National capital
City
Elevation
Meters Feet
3,000 10,000
2,000 7,000
1,000 3,000
500 1,500
200 700
0 0
0 500 1,000 Miles
0 500 1,000 Kilometers
Mercator Projection
1: 58,400,000
PACIFIC OCEAN
INDIAN OCEAN
NORTH AMERICA
ASIA
AUSTRALIA
Micronesia
Melanesia
Polynesia
French Polynesia
KIRIBATI
Equator
Tropic of Cancer
Tropic of Capricorn
International Date Line
Western Australia
Northern Territory
South Australia
Queensland
New South Wales
Victoria
Tasmania
GREAT SANDY DESERT
GIBSON DESERT
GREAT VICTORIA DESERT
GREAT DIVIDING RANGE
Great Barrier Reef
Great Australian Bight
Perth
Darwin
Adelaide
Melbourne
Sydney
Canberra, A.C.T.
Brisbane
Townsville
Cape York Pen.
Gulf of Carpentaria
Arafura Sea
Timor Sea
Coral Sea
Tasman Sea
Torres Strait
Bass Strait
Darling
Lake Eyre
Lake Torrens
Lake Gairdner
Cape Leeuwin
South East Cape
PAPUA NEW GUINEA
New Guinea
New Britain
New Ireland
Bismarck Arch.
Admiralty Is.
Port Moresby
Lae
SOLOMON ISLANDS
Honiara
VANUATU
Vila
New Caledonia (Fr.)
Nouméa
Loyalty Is.
Coral Sea Is. Terr. (Aust.)
FIJI
Suva
TONGA
Nuku'alofa
TUVALU
Fongafale
Wallis & Futuna (Fr.)
WESTERN SAMOA
Apia
Pago Pago
American Samoa (U.S.)
Niue (N.Z.)
Tokelau Is. (N.Z.)
Cook Is. (N.Z.)
NAURU
Yaren
Tarawa I.
Bairiki
MARSHALL ISLANDS
Majuro
Bikini Atoll
FEDERATED STATES OF MICRONESIA
Palikir
PALAU
Koror
Guam (U.S.)
Northern Mariana Islands (U.S.)
Bonin Is. (Japan)
Volcano Is. (Japan)
Wake I. (U.S.)
Midway Is. (U.S.)
Hawaiian Islands
Kauai
Oahu
Hawaii (U.S.)
Hawaii
Palmyra I. (U.S.)
Kingman Reef (U.S.)
Kiritimati (Kiribati)
Jarvis I. (U.S.)
Malden I. (Kiribati)
Starbuck I. (Kiribati)
Manihiki Atoll (N.Z.)
Society Is.
Tahiti
Papeete
Tuamotu Arch.
Marquesas Is.
Austral Is.
Pitcairn I. (U.K.)
Easter I. (Chile)
Clipperton I. (Fr.)
NEW ZEALAND
North Island
South Island
North Cape
East Cape
Auckland
Wellington
Cook Strait
Christchurch
Dunedin
N
W
E
S

REUTERS/MIKE BLAKE/ARCHIVE

HOMERIC FEAT: After a season-long duel, two baseball sluggers—Mark McGwire of the St. Louis Cardinals and Sammy Sosa of the Chicago Cubs—broke Roger Maris's record for the most home runs hit in a season. Here, McGwire ties Maris with his 61st homer.

BELOW: REUTERS/NBC-TV/ARCHIVE. ABOVE: RTV/ARCHIVE

WHITE HOUSE SCANDAL: In a terse four-minute address on Aug. 17, left, President Bill Clinton acknowledged that he had conducted an "inappropriate" sexual affair with a White House intern in her 20s, Monica Lewinsky. Clinton had publicly denied the affair in January. Bottom left, Clinton is seen embracing Lewinsky in a videotape as they celebrate Democratic wins in the November 1996 election at the White House.

IN THE SPOTLIGHT: On this page, three key figures in the White House sex scandal. Top right, Monica Lewinsky. Bottom left, Linda Tripp, a Pentagon employee who secretly taped Lewinsky discussing her relations with the President. Bottom right, independent counsel Kenneth Starr, the former U.S. Solicitor General who led the inquiry.

STARR: ARNOLD SACHS/CNP/ARCHIVE. TRIPP: REUTERS/MARK WILSON/ARCHIVE. LEWINSKY: REUTERS/HO/ARCHIVE

TERROR'S TOLL: In a pair of carefully calculated terrorist attacks, bombs exploded at the U.S. embassies in Kenya and Tanzania at exactly the same time on Aug. 7, leaving 257 dead and more than 5,000 injured. Thirteen days later, the U.S. struck back against the Saudi billionaire it charged with planning the bombings, Osama bin Laden, right. U.S. cruise missiles were fired against two targets: a training camp for terrorists in Afghanistan and a chemical factory in Sudan the U.S. claimed was producing components of nerve gas. Above, searching for survivors near the U.S. embassy in Nairobi.

TOP: REUTERS/CORINNE DUFKA/ARCHIVE. BOTTOM: REUTERS/ARCHIVE

RIGHT: REUTERS/HO/ARCHIVE. ABOVE: REUTERS/PAUL CARTE/*REGISTER GUARD*/ARCHIVE

SCHOOL MASSACRES: In a series of five shootings that began in 1997, students opened fire at their schools, killing 15 and wounding 44. At top, Kip Kinkel, who shot his parents, then killed two at his school in Springfield, Ore. Above, a service for his victims.

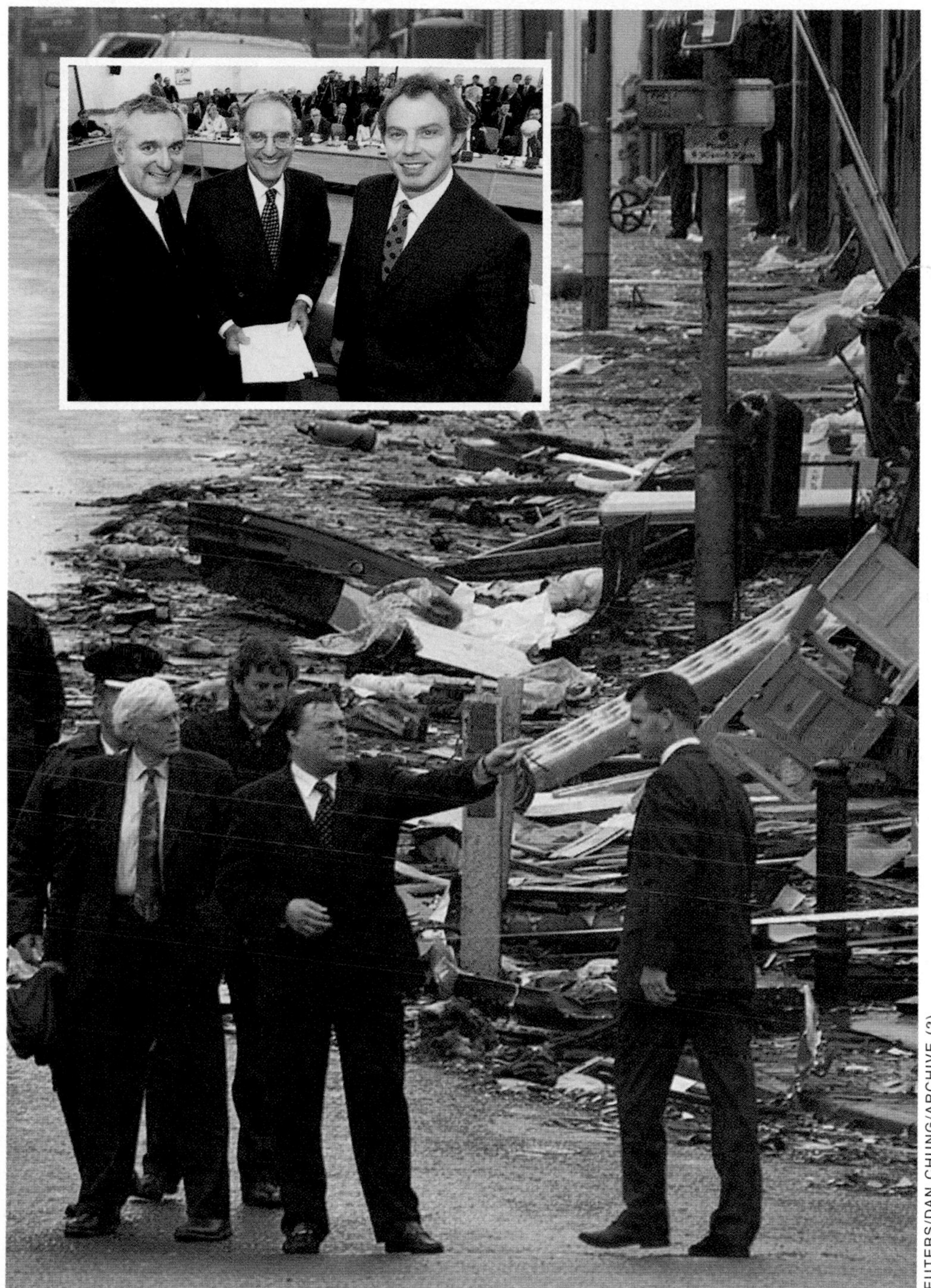

REUTERS/DAN CHUNG/ARCHIVE (2)

WAGING PEACE: An agreement reached on Good Friday promised to put an end to decades of violence between Protestants and Roman Catholics in Northern Ireland. U.S. diplomat George Mitchell, inset center, helped broker the peace with British Prime Minister Tony Blair, right, and Irish PM Bertie Ahern. In August, a bomb exploded in the small town of Omagh, killing 28. An Irish Republican Army group claimed responsibility.

JOURNEY TO MOSCOW: Refusing to cancel a long-planned summit meeting, President Clinton visited Russia in early September, even as President Boris Yeltsin was trying to form a new government and the devalued ruble threatened to paralyze the economy.

JOURNEY TO BEIJING: In June President Clinton embarked on a nine-day visit to China. Above, he is welcomed by President Jiang Xemin, who had visited America in 1997. Clinton championed human rights in a speech that was broadcast live on Chinese TV.

NUCLEAR RACE IN ASIA: India's Hindu nationalist Prime Minister, A.B. Vajpayee, shocked the world by testing a nuclear weapon in May, ushering in a nuclear arms race in southern Asia. Within days India's neighbor and longtime enemy, heavily Muslim Pakistan, exploded a device of its own. Above, Indians burn President Clinton in effigy after the U.S. leader declared his opposition to the test.

REVOLT IN INDONESIA: In May, after a series of unprecedented public protests against his regime, right, Indonesian dictator Suharto was forced from office after 32 years in power. Avoiding the possibility of more serious violence, Suharto resigned and appointed longtime political ally B.J. Habibie to lead the nation.

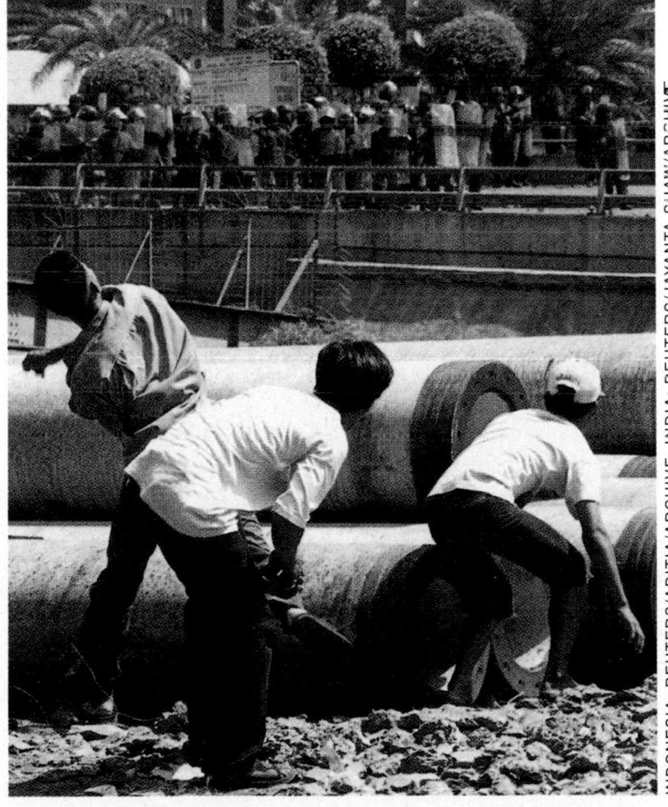

INDONESIA: REUTERS/ADITIA/ARCHIVE. INDIA: REUTERS/JAYANTA SHAW/ARCHIVE

REUTERS/PAUL HANNA/ARCHIVE

JOURNEY TO HAVANA: In a moment that would have seemed incredible only a few years ago, President Fidel Castro welcomed Pope John Paul II to heavily Roman Catholic Cuba in January. The papal visit came as Castro—head of one of the world's last communist nations—found himself isolated and suffering from ongoing U.S. economic sanctions. The Pope spoke against the sanctions—but also in favor of religious freedom.

MARKET WOES: World stock markets were hit by a downturn that began in Asia, then spread to the U.S., where the long-running bull market finally faltered. Traders in Japan, left, and the U.S., above, suffered.

U.S. v. MICROSOFT? Microsoft mogul Bill Gates, left, and fellow computer-company CEOs testify at a Senate hearing on marketing practices in the software and Internet industries, even as the Justice Department pursued an antitrust suit against Microsoft.

GATES: RON SACHS/CNP/ARCHIVE. JAPAN: REUTERS/ERIKO SUGITA/ARCHIVE. U.S.:REUTERS/PETER MORGAN/ARCHIVE

REUTERS/HO/ARCHIVE. INSET: REUTERS/GARY HERSHORN/ARCHIVE

UNSINKABLE: Director James Cameron, inset, scored an artistic and financial triumph with *Titanic,* starring Leonardo DiCaprio and Kate Winslet. The blockbuster, which cost $200 million to make, earned $700 million at the box office and snagged 11 Oscars.

REUTERS/RAY STUBBLEBINE/ ARCHIVE

TOPS: Michael Jordan of the Chicago Bulls hefts the National Basketball Association championship trophy. For the sixth time in his outstanding career, Jordan led the Bulls to the N.B.A. title, besting the Utah Jazz in six games. Jordan was named the series MVP.

REUTERS/BLAKE SELL/ARCHIVE

TARA TRIUMPHS: At the Winter Olympics in Nagano, Japan, American Tara Lipinski, 15, broke Sonja Henie's 70-year-old record in becoming the youngest figure skater to win a gold medal. Lipinski bested favored teammate Michelle Kwan, 17, to take the gold.

FRANK SINATRA: The legendary singer died of a heart attack at 82 in May after a long illness. Considered the champion of classic American pop singing, Sinatra enjoyed one of the longest careers in show business, from his days as a Big Band singer in the 1930s through his teen-idol period in the '40s, to success in Hollywood and Las Vegas in the decades that followed. His legacy is secure, thanks to his 1,414 studio recordings.

The Personality Genes

Does DNA shape behavior? A pioneering biologist offers some answers

By J. MADELEINE NASH TIME

What is it that makes us who we are? What, for that matter, accounts for the quirks and foibles, talents and traits that make up anyone's personality? Dean Hamer, a molecular biologist at the National Institutes of Health, is not content merely to ask such questions; he is trying to answer them as well. A pioneer in the field, Hamer is exploring the role genes play in governing the very core of our individuality. "You have about as much choice in some aspects of your personality as you do in the shape of your nose or the size of your feet," contend Dean Hamer and his coauthor Peter Copeland in their provocative book, *Living with Our Genes.*

Until recently, research into behavioral genetics was dominated by psychiatrists and psychologists, who based their most compelling conclusions about the importance of genes on studies of identical twins. For example, psychologist Michael Bailey of Northwestern University famously demonstrated that if one identical twin is gay, there is about a 50% likelihood that the other will be too. Seven years ago, Hamer picked up where the twin studies left off, homing in on specific strips of DNA that appear to influence everything from mood to sexual orientation.

Early Studies

The results of Hamer's first foray into behavioral genetics, published by the journal *Science* in 1993, ignited a furor that has yet to die down. According to Hamer and his colleagues, male homosexuality appeared to be linked to a stretch of DNA at the very tip of the X chromosome, the chromosome men inherit from their mothers. Three years later, in 1996, Hamer and his collaborators at NIH seconded an Israeli group's finding that linked a gene on chromosome 11 to the personality trait psychologists call novelty seeking. That same year Hamer's lab helped pinpoint another gene, this time on chromosome 17, that appears to play a role in regulating anxiety.

Unlike the genes that are responsible for physical traits, Hamer emphasizes, these genes do not cause people to become homosexuals, thrill-seeking rock climbers, or anxiety-ridden worrywarts. The biology of personality is much more complicated than that. Rather, what genes appear to do, says Hamer, is subtly bias the psyche so that different individuals react to similar experiences in surprisingly different ways.

Intriguing as these findings are, other experts caution that none has been unequivocally replicated by other research teams. Why? One possibility is that, despite all of Hamer's work, the links between these genes and these particular personality traits do not, in fact, exist. There is, however, another, more tantalizing possibility. Consider the genes that give tomatoes their flavor, suggests Hamer's colleague Dr. Dennis Murphy of the National Institute of Mental Health. Even a simple trait like acidity is controlled not by a single gene but by as many as 30 that operate in concert. In the same way, he speculates, many genes are involved in setting up temperamental traits and psychological vulnerabilities; each gene contributes just a little bit to the overall effect.

Influential, Not Deterministic

Hunting down the genes that influence personality remains a dauntingly difficult business. Although DNA is constructed out of a mere four chemicals—adenine, guanine, cytosine, thymine—it can take as many as a million combinations to spell out a single human gene. Most of these genes vary from individual to individual by only one chemical letter in a thousand, and it is precisely these minute differences that Hamer and his colleagues are trying to identify. Of particular interest are variations that may affect the operation of such brain chemicals as dopamine and serotonin, which are well-known modulators of mood. The so-called novelty-seeking gene, for example, is thought to affect how efficiently nerve cells absorb dopamine. The so-called anxiety gene is postulated to affect serotonin's action.

How can this be? After all, as Hamer and Copeland observe in their book, ". . . genes are not switches that say 'shy' or 'outgoing' or 'happy' or 'sad.' Genes are simply chemicals that direct the combination of more chemicals." What genes do is order up the production of proteins in organs like the kidney, the skin, and also the brain. Thus, Hamer speculates, one version of the novelty-seeking gene may make a protein that is less efficient at absorbing dopamine. Since dopamine is the chemical that creates sensations of pleasure in response to intense experiences, people who inherit this gene might seek to stimulate its production by seeking out thrills.

Still, as critics emphasize and Hamer himself acknowledges, genes alone do not control the chemistry of the brain. Ultimately, it is the environment that determines how these genes will express themselves. What people are born with, Hamer says, are temperamental traits. What they can acquire through experience is the ability to control these traits by exercising that intangible part of personality called character. □

Following Our Noses

Animals—and perhaps humans—communicate volumes through smell

By JEFFREY KLUGER TIME

If you're an animal, there are few things as valuable as a good nose. In a world without speech, it's often scent alone that tells you if a stranger is in the mood to mate or in distress, is preparing to attack or about to retreat in fear. The chemicals that carry these odorless messages are called pheromones, and while most animals produce them, the highest animals—humans—were thought to be above such crude olfactory signals.

All that may have changed. In an article in the March 1998 issue of *Nature,* psychologist Martha McClintock of the University of Chicago reported what may be the best evidence yet of human pheromones. In an elegantly straightforward experiment, she was able to speed up and slow down the monthly cycles of a group of women by exposing them to a whiff of sweat from other women. The ovulatory command, she believes, was carried by pheromones. If McClintock is right, the implications could be sweeping, offering not just new insights into human communication but practical medical applications as well. "Once you establish that pheromones exist," McClintock says, "the question becomes how far-ranging they can be."

The Olfactory Powers of Animals

For most scientists, pheromones are nothing new. In the 1930s entomologists first noticed that female moths are able to excite males even when the males can neither see nor hear them. The males, they discovered, "smell" the females with their antennae. When the fragrance was isolated, it was able to stimulate millions of moths with concentrations of less than one 300-millionth of an ounce.

When substances this potent hit the sensory systems of a relatively unsophisticated animal, they pack a big behavioral wallop. Pheromones emitted by queen bees prevent other females from maturing sexually, ensuring that the queen's genes remain dominant. Among fish, scent markers released by females cause male sperm counts to quintuple overnight. When injured by a predator, some amphibians emit a compound that warns others of their species to keep out of harm's way.

It is in mammals that the pheromonal chatter climaxes. Countless species—from wolves to musk oxen—claim territory by urinating around their borders, an olfactory keep off the grass sign if there ever was one. Male voles use urine as a potent aphrodisiac, excreting a chemical that causes females to ovulate within 48 hours. "Identify anything that's of biological significance to animals," says Rachel Herz of the Monell Chemical Senses Center in Philadelphia, "and it's usually mediated by scent."

Human Experiments

Uncovering similar tendencies in humans wasn't easy; McClintock began looking nearly 30 years ago. As an undergraduate at Wellesley College, she noticed that the women in her dormitory often developed remarkably similar menstrual patterns. In other animals, this kind of synchrony has survival advantages. "When you see others successfully rearing young," McClintock says, "it means it's a good time for you too."

The phenomenon intrigued McClintock, and she and coresearcher Kathleen Stern recruited a group of 29 women and asked nine of them to wear pads under their arms for several hours, either before ovulation or just after. When the pads were wiped under the noses of the other women, the results were remarkable. Pre-ovulation pads shortened menstrual cycles by as many as 14 days in 68% of the women. When exposed to ovulation-phase pads, a different 68% experienced cycles that were as many as 12 days longer. Clearly, something was bringing the group into synch.

Among other scientists, the reaction to the study has been mostly positive—but questions remain. Even if human pheromones exist, it's not clear how the body processes them. Mammals and reptiles detect pheromones with a tiny nasal cavity called a vomeronasal organ, or VNO. Anatomists don't think humans have a VNO and aren't sure we would need one to perceive pheromones.

McClintock, meanwhile, is pushing ahead. Pheromone treatments designed to regulate ovulation, she says, could serve as fertility enhancers for couples who want to conceive and as contraceptives for those who don't. Other researchers think mood-altering pheromones could alleviate depression and stress. Still others think the chemicals might even control prostate activity in men, reducing the risk of cancer. New insights into how the body works, it seems, aren't right under our noses, but inside them. □

Scientific Classification

Classification, or taxonomy, is a system of categorizing living things. There are seven divisions in the system: (1) Kingdom; (2) Phylum or Division; (3) Class; (4) Order; (5) Family; (6) Genus; (7) Species.

Kingdom is the broadest division. There is no consensus about the number of kingdoms, though most scientists support a four-kingdom (Animalia, Plantae, Protista, and Monera) or five-kingdom (Animalia, Plantae, Protista, Monera, and Fungi) system. The lowest, most basic division is species, which consists of organisms that resemble each other and are capable of interbreeding to produce fertile offspring. Species are identified by two names (binomial nomenclature). The first is the genus, the second is the species. □

Chemical Elements

Element	Symbol	Atomic no.	Atomic wt.	Specific gravity	Melting point °C	Boiling point °C	No. of isotopes[1]	Discoverer	Year
Actinium	Ac	89	227[2]	10.07[2]	1050	3200±300	11	Debierne	1899
Aluminum	Al	13	26.9815	2.6989	660.37	2467	8	Wöhler	1827
Americum	Am	95	243[6]	13.67	994±4	2607	13[3]	Seaborg et al.	1944
Antimony	Sb	51	121.75	6.61	630.74	1750	29	Early historic times	—
Argon	Ar	18	39.948	1.7837[4]	–189.2	–185.7	8	Rayleigh and Ramsay	1894
Arsenic (gray)	As	33	74.9216	5.73	817 (28 atm.)	613[5]	14	Albertus Magnus	1250?
Astatine	At	85	210	—	302	337	21	Corson et al.	1940
Barium	Ba	56	137.34	3.5	725	1640	25	Davy	1808
Berkelium	Bk	97	247[6]	14.00[7]	—	—	8[3]	Seaborg et al.	1949
Berylium	Be	4	9.01218	1.848	1278±5	2970 (5 mm.)	6	Vauquelin	1798
Bismuth	Bi	83	208.9806	9.747	271.3	1560±5	19	Geoffroy	1753
Bohrium	Bh	107	262	—	—	—	—	Armbruster and Münzenberg	1981
Boron	B	5	10.81	2.37[8]	2300	2550[5]	6	Gay-Lussac and Thénard; Davy	1808
Bromine	Br	35	79.904	3.12[4]	–7.2	58.78	19	Balard	1826
Cadmium	Cd	48	112.40	8.65	320.9	765	22	Stromeyer	1817
Calcium	Ca	20	40.08	1.55	839±2	1484	14	Davy	1808
Californium	Cf	98	251[6]	—	—	—	12[3]	Seaborg et al.	1950
Carbon	C	6	12.011	1.8-3.5[9]	–3550	4827	7	Prehistoric	—
Cerium	Ce	58	140.12	6.771	798±3	3257	19	Berzelius and Hisinger; Klaproth	1803
Cesium	Cs	55	132.9055	1.873	28.40	678.4	22	Bunsen and Kirchoff	1860
Chlorine	Cl	17	35.453	1.56[4]	–100.98	–34.6	11	Scheele	1774
Chromium	Cr	24	51.996	7.18-7.20	1857±20	2672	9	Vauquelin	1797
Cobalt	Co	27	58.9332	8.9	1495	2870	14	Brandt	c.1735
Copper	Cu	29	63.546	8.96	1083.4±0.2	2567	11	Prehistoric	—
Curium	Cm	96	247[6]	13.51[2]	1340±40	—	13[3]	Seaborg et al.	1944
Dubnium	Db	105	262	—	—	—	—	Ghiorso et al.	1970
Dysprosium	Dy	66	162.50	8.540	1409	2335	21	Boisbaudran	1886
Einsteinium	Es	99	254[6]	—	—	—	12[3]	Ghiorso et al.	1952
Erbium	Er	68	167.26	9.045	1522	2510	16	Mosander	1843
Europium	Eu	63	151.96	5.283	822±5	1597	21	Demarcay	1896
Fermium	Fm	100	257[6]	—	—	—	10[3]	Ghiorso et al.	1953
Fluorine	F	9	18.9984	1.108[4]	–219.62	–188.14	6	Moissan	1886
Francium	Fr	87	223[6]	—	27[2]	677[2]	21	Perey	1938
Gadolinium	Gd	64	157.25	7.898	1311±1	3233	17	Marignac	1880
Gallium	Ga	31	69.72	5.904	29.78	2403	14	Boisbaudran	1875
Germanium	Ge	32	72.59	5.323	937.4	2830	17	Winkler	1886
Gold	Au	79	196.9665	19.32	1064.43	2807	21	Prehistoric	—
Hafnium	Hf	72	178.49	13.31	2227±20	4602	17	Coster and von Hevesy	1923
Hassium	Hs	108	265	—	—	—	—	Armbruster and Münzenberg	1983
Helium	He	2	4.00260	0.1785[4]	–272.2 (26 atm.)	–268.934	5	Janssen	1868
Holmium	Ho	67	164.9303	8.781	1470	2720	29	Delafontaine and Soret	1878
Hydrogen	H	1	1.0080	0.070[4]	–259.14	–252.87	3	Cavendish	1766
Indium	In	49	114.82	7.31	156.61	2080	34	Reich and Richter	1863
Iodine	I	53	126.9045	4.93	113.5	184.35	24	Cortois	1811
Iridium	Ir	77	192.22	22.42	2410	4130	25	Tennant	1803
Iron	Fe	26	55.847	7.894	1535	2750	10	Prehistoric	—
Krypton	Kr	36	83.80	3.733[4]	–156.6	–152.30±0.10	23	Ramsay and Travers	1898
Lanthanum	La	57	138.9055	6.166	920±5	3454	19	Mosander	1839
Lawrencium	Lr	103	257[6]	—	—	—	20[3]	Ghiorso et al.	1961
Lead	Pb	82	207.2	11.35	327.502	1740	29	Prehistoric	—
Lithium	Li	3	6.941	0.534	180.54	1347	5	Arfvedson	1817
Lutetium	Lu	71	174.97	9.835	1656±5	3315	22	Urbain	1907
Magnesium	Mg	12	24.305	1.738	648.8±0.5	1090	8	Black	1755
Manganese	Mn	25	54.9380	7.21-7.44[10]	1244±3	1962	11	Gahn, Scheele, and Bergman	1774
Meitnerium	Mt	109	266	—	—	—	—	GSI, Darmstadt, West Germany	1982
Mendelevium	Md	101	256[6]	—	—	—	3[3]	Ghiorso et al.	1955
Mercury	Hg	80	200.59	13.546	–38.87	356.58	26	Prehistoric	—
Molybdenum	Mo	42	95.94	10.22	2617	4612	20	Scheele	1778
Neodymium	Nd	60	144.24	6.80 & 7.004[10]	1010	3127	16	von Welsbach	1885
Neon	Ne	10	20.179	0.89990 (g/10°C/1 atm)	–248.67	–246.048	8	Ramsay and Travers	1898
Neptunium	Np	93	237.0482	20.25	6400±1	3902	15[3]	McMillan and Abelson	1940
Nickel	Ni	28	58.71	8.902	1453	2732	11	Cronstedt	1751
Niobium (Columbium)	Nb	41	92.9064	8.57	2468±10	4742	24	Hatchett	1801
Nitrogen	N	7	14.0067	0.808[4]	–209.86	–195.8	8	Rutherford	1772
Nobelium	No	102	254[6]	—	—	—	7[3]	Ghiorso et al.	1957
Osmium	Os	76	190.2	22.57	3045±30	5027±100	19	Tennant	1803

Element	Symbol	Atomic no.	Atomic wt.	Specific gravity	Melting point °C	Boiling point °C	No. of isotopes[1]	Discoverer	Year
Oxygen	O	8	15.9994	1.14[4]	–218.4	–182.962	8	Priestley	1774
Palladium	Pd	46	106.4	12.02	1552	3140	21	Wollaston	1803
Phosphorous	P	15	30.9738	1.82 (white)	44.1	280	7	Brand	1669
Platinum	Pt	78	195.09	21.45	1772	3827±100	32	Ulloa	1735
Plutonium	Pu	94	244[6]	19.84	641	3232	16[3]	Seaborg et al.	1940
Polonium	Po	84	210[6]	9.32	254	962	34	Curie	1898
Potassium	K	19	39.102	0.862	63.65	774	10	Davy	1807
Praseodymium	Pr	59	140.9077	6.772	931±4	3212	15	von Weisbach	1885
Promethium	Pm	61	145[6]	—	≈1080	2460	14	Marinsky et al.	1945
Protactinium	Pa	91	231.0359	15.37[2]	<1600	—	14	Hahn and Meitner	1917
Radium	Ra	88	226.0254	5.0?	700	1140	15	P. and M. Curie	1898
Radon	Rn	86	222[6]	4.4[4]	–71	–61.8	20	Dorn	1900
Rhenium	Re	75	186.2	21.02	3180	5627[7]	21	Noddack, Berg, and Tacke	1925
Rhodium	Rh	45	102.9055	12.41	1966±3	3727±100	20	Wollaston	1803
Rubidium	Rb	37	85.4678	1.532	38.89	688	20	Bunsen and Kirchoff	1861
Rutherfordium	Rf	104	261	—	—	—	—	Ghiorso et al.	1969
Ruthenium	Ru	44	101.07	12.44	2310	3900	16	Klaus	1844
Samarium	Sm	62	150.4	7.536	1072±5	1778	17	Boisbaudran	1879
Scandium	Sc	21	44.9559	2.989	1539	2832	15	Nilson	1879
Seaborgium	Sg	106	263	—	—	—	—	Ghiorso et al.	1974
Selenium	Se	34	78.96	4.79 (gray)	217	684.9±1	20	Berzelius	1817
Silicon	Si	14	28.086	2.33	1410	2355	8	Berzelius	1824
Silver	Ag	47	107.868	10.5	961.93	2212	27	Prehistoric	—
Sodium	Na	11	22.9898	0.971	97.81±0.03	882.9	7	Davy	1807
Strontium	Sr	38	87.62	2.54	769	1384	18	Davy	1808
Sulfur	S	16	32.06	2.07[11]	112.8	444.674	10	Prehistoric	—
Tantalum	Ta	73	180.9479	16.654	2996	5425±100	19	Ekeberg	1801
Technetium	Tc	43	98.062	11.50[2]	2172	4877	23	Perrier and Segré	1937
Tellurium	Te	52	127.60	6.24	449.5±0.3	989.8±3.8	29	von Reichenstein	1782
Terbium	Tb	65	158.9254	8.234	1360±4	3041	24	Mosander	1843
Thallium	Tl	81	204.37	11.85	303.5	1457±10	28	Crookes	1861
Thorium	Th	90	232.0381	11.72	1750	4790	12	Berzelius	1828
Thulium	Tm	69	168.9342	9.314	1545±15	1727	18	Cleve	1879
Tin	Sn	50	118.69	7.31 (white)	231.9681	2270	28	Prehistoric	—
Titanium	Ti	22	47.90	4.55	1660±10	3287	9	Gregor	1791
Tungsten (Wolfram)	W	74	183.85	19.3	3410±20	5660	22	J. and F. d'Elhuyar	1783
Uranium	U	92	238.029	19.05	1132.3±0.8	3818	15	Peligot	1841
Vanadium	V	23	50.9414	6.11	1890±10	3380	9	del Rio	1801
Xenon	Xe	54	131.30	3.52[4]	–111.9	–107.1±3	31	Ramsay and Travers	1898
Ytterbium	Yb	70	173.04	6.972	824±5	1193	16	Marignac	1878
Yttrium	Y	39	88.9059	4.457	1523±8	3337	21	Gadolin	1794
Zinc	Zn	30	65.38	7.133	419.58	907	15	Prehistoric	—
Zirconium	Zr	40	91.22	6.506[2]	1852±2	4377	20	Klaproth	1789

1. Isotopes are different forms of the same element having the same atomic number but different atomic weights. 2. Calculated figure. 3. Artificially produced. 4. Liquid. 5. Sublimation point. 6. Mass number of the isotope of longest known life. 7. Estimated. 8. Amorphous. 9. Depending on whether amorphous, graphite, or diamond. 10. Depending on allotropic form. 11. Rhombic. ≈ means "approximately." < means "less than."

The Elements

Elements are the building blocks of nature. Water, for example, is a compound consisting of the elements hydrogen and oxygen. Each element is a pure substance that cannot be split up into any simpler pure substance.

The smallest particle of an element that can exist is an atom. An atom consists of subatomic particles. The most important of these are protons, which have positive electrical charges; electrons, which have negative electrical charges; and neutrons, which are electrically neutral.

The atomic number of an element is the number of protons in one atom of the element. Each element has a different atomic number. For example, the atomic numbers of hydrogen and oxygen are 1 and 8, respectively.

Elements with atomic numbers 1 (hydrogen) to 92 (uranium) occur naturally on Earth. Those with atomic numbers 93 (neptunium) onwards are artificial. They have to be synthesized from elements with lower atomic numbers. Element 100 is named fermium. Elements with atomic numbers 101 onwards are known as the transfermium elements. They are also known as heavy elements because their atoms have very large masses compared with atoms of hydrogen, the lightest of all elements.

The heaviest element synthesized to date is element 112. One atom of this element was synthesized by scientists at the Heavy-Ion Research Center (Gesellschaft für Schwerionenforschung [GSI]) in Darmstadt, Germany, in February 1996. It was made by bombarding the element lead (atomic number 82) with a high-energy beam of atoms of the element zinc (atomic number 30). The atom existed for a fraction of a second before splitting up. Elements 110 and 111 were discovered by the same group of scientists in 1994.

Names for the six new heavy elements were approved on August 31, 1997, by the International Union of Pure and Applied Chemistry (IUPAC) in Geneva. Elements 110, 111, and 112 have not yet been named.

A Weighty Discovery in Particle Physics

In June 1998, an international team of Japanese and U.S. physicists unveiled strong evidence that elusive subatomic particles known as neutrinos have mass (or weight). These findings run counter to the standard model of particle physics—the basic theory about the structure of matter—which holds that these electrically neutral, weakly interacting particles have no mass. The discovery means that existing theoretical models of matter must now be revised to include neutrinos with mass.

Neutrinos occur in three states: electron, muon, and tau, with the names signifying what is produced when a neutrino collides with another particle. Observers do not see the neutrinos themselves, but can detect the creation of electrons and muons from faint flashes of light following a particle collision.

The physicists used the giant Super-Kamiokande—the world's biggest neutrino detector buried deep underground in Mozumi, Japan. In the experiment, conducted in a 50,000-ton tank of purified water, neutrinos created when cosmic rays bombard Earth's upper atmosphere were counted relative to the number expected to penetrate the cavern. The experimenters found that the number of electron-neutrinos detected was relatively constant with theorized totals, while the number of muon-neutrinos was significantly lower. This indicated that they were disappearing into another state, or "flavor," such as an undetected tau-neutrino, or possibly another type.

Theorists expected that two-thirds of the neutrinos detected would be of muon "flavor," and one-third would be electron-neutrinos, but the experiment resulted in too few muon-neutrinos.

The scientists concluded that the only explanation that made sense, given the data, is that muon-neutrinos were oscillating, or changing from one type of neutrino to another, which could occur only if they have mass.

The new findings may help astrophysicists trying to find the missing matter in the universe. Some estimates conclude that perhaps 90 percent of the universe's mass is "missing," much of it assumed to be invisible dark matter that emits no light and is therefore not visible with current observing equipment. The missing mass may eventually be found to exist in the form of neutrinos. □

Table of Geological Periods

It is now generally assumed that planets are formed by the accretion of gas and dust in a cosmic cloud, but there is no way of estimating the length of this process. Our Earth acquired its present size, more or less, between 4,000 million and 5,000 million years ago. Life on Earth originated about 2,000 million years ago, but there are no good fossil remains from periods earlier than the Cambrian, which began about 550 million years ago. The largely unknown past before the Cambrian Period is referred to as the Pre-Cambrian and is subdivided into the Lower (or older) and Upper (or younger) Pre-Cambrian—also called the Archaeozoic and Proterozoic Eras.

The known geological history of Earth since the beginning of the Cambrian Period is subdivided into three eras, each of which includes a number of periods. They, in turn, are subdivided into subperiods. In a subperiod, a certain section may be especially well known because of rich fossil finds. Such a section is called a formation, and it is usually identified by a place name.

Paleozoic Era

This era began 550 million years ago and lasted for 355 million years. The name was compounded from Greek *palaios* (old) and *zoön* (animal).

Period	Duration[1]	Subperiods	Events
Cambrian (from *Cambria,* Latin name for Wales)	70	Lower Cambrian Middle Cambrian Upper Cambrian	Invertebrate sea life of many types, proliferating during this and the following period
Ordovician (from Latin *Ordovices,* people of early Britain)	85	Lower Ordovician Upper Ordovician	First known fishes
Silurian (from Latin *Silures,* people of early Wales)	40	Lower Silurian Upper Silurian	Gigantic sea scorpions
Devonian (from Devonshire in England)	50	Lower Devonian Upper Devonian	Proliferation of fishes and other forms of sea life, land still largely lifeless
Carboniferous (from Latin *carbo* = coal + *fero* = to bear)	85	Lower or Mississippian Upper or Pennsylvanian	Period of maximum coal formation in swampy forests; early insects and first known amphibians
Permian (from district of Perm in Russia)	25	Lower Permian Upper Permian	Early reptiles and mammals; earliest form of turtles

1. In millions of years.

Mesozoic Era

This era began 195 million years ago and lasted for 135 million years. The name was compounded from Greek *mesos* (middle) and *zoön* (animal). Popular name: Age of Reptiles.

Period	Duration[1]	Subperiods	Events
Triassic (from *trias* = triad)	35	Lower or Buntsandstein (from German *bunt* = colorful + *sandstein* = sandstone). Middle or Muschelkalk (from German *muschel* = shell + *kalk* = limestone). Upper or Keuper (old miner's term)	Early saurians
Jurassic (from Jura Mountains)	35	Lower or Black Jurassic, or Lias (from French *liais* = hard stone) Middle or Brown Jurassic, or Dogger (old provincial English for ironstone) Upper or White Jurassic, or Malm (Middle English for sand)	Many seagoing reptiles; early large dinosaurs; somewhat later, flying reptiles (pterosaurs), earliest known birds
Cretaceous (from Latin *creta* = chalk)	65	Lower Cretaceous Upper Cretaceous	Maximum development of dinosaurs; birds proliferating; opossumlike mammals

1. In millions of years.

Cenozoic Era

This era began 60 million years ago and includes the geological present. The name was compounded from Greek *kainos* (new) and *zoön* (animal). Popular name: Age of Mammals.

Period	Duration[1]	Subperiods	Events
Tertiary (originally thought to be the third of only three periods)	c. 60	Paleocene (from Greek *palaios* = old + *kainos* = new). Eocene (from Greek *eos* = dawn + *kainos* = new). Oligocene (from Greek *oligos* = few + *kainos* = new). Miocene (from Greek *meios* = less + *kainos* = new). Pliocene (from Greek *pleios* = more + *kainos* = new)	First mammals other than marsupials. Formation of amber, rich insect fauna, early bats, steady increase of large mammals. Mammals closely resembling present types; protohumans
Pleistocene (from Greek *pleistos* = most + *kainos* = new) (popular name: Ice Age)	1	Four major glaciations, named Günz, Mindel, Riss, and Würm, originally the name of rivers. Last glaciation ended 10,000 to 15,000 years ago	Various forms of early humans
Holocene (from Greek *holos* = entire + *kainos* = new)		The present	The last 3,000 years are called "history"

1. In millions of years.

Classification of the Dinosaurs

Dinosaurs ("terrible lizards") belong to a large group of reptiles called Archosauria ("ruling reptiles"). They are classified into two distinct orders, which are distinguished by their pelvic differences.

Saurischia ("lizard hipped"). All members of this order had modern lizardlike pelvises and clawed feet. Saurischians roamed Earth from the Middle Triassic to the end of the Cretaceous period. They included carnivores and plant eaters. Members of the order included Allosaurus ("different lizard"), Apatosaurus ("deceptive lizard"), which was formerly called Brontosaurus, and Tyrannosaurus ("tyrant lizard"). The group is divided into two suborders: **Theropoda** ("beast footed") and **Sauropodomorpha** ("lizard-footed forms"). The Velociraptor ("swift robber") was a theropod.

Ornithiscia ("bird hipped"). All Ornithischian dinosaurs had pelvises similar to those of modern birds, had hoofed toes. All were herbivores. These dinosaurs lived throughout the world from the Middle Triassic to the end of the Cretaceous period. Members of the order included Iguanodon ("iguana tooth"), Stegosaurus ("plated lizard"), and Triceratops ("three-horned face"). The order is divided into four suborders: **Ornithopoda** ("bird footed"), **Stegosauria** ("plated lizards"), **Ankylosauria** ("armored lizards"), and **Certopsia** ("horned faces").

Four-Million-Year-Old Prehumans Walked Erect

In May 1998, a research team led by Dr. Meave G. Leakey, curator of paleontology at the National Museums of Kenya, announced that it had dated the age of the prehuman fossil specimens the team found in Africa at between 4.1 million and 4.2 million years old, making a case for the earliest known humanlike species to walk upright.

The fossils were discovered in 1995 at Kanapoi, southwest of Lake Turkana in northern Kenya, and Allia Bay, east of the lake. They were determined to be the remains of a new species of australopithecine (southern ape), a prehuman ancestor that stood and walked erect. The oldest *Australopithecus* skeleton found so far is "Lucy," discovered in 1974. The new hominid species was named *Australopithecus anamensis*, after the native word *anam,* which means "lake." (Some *anamensis* fossils were originally discovered in that area in 1955.)

When the Kenyan fossils were discovered, scientists were unable to accurately determine their age because the earliest geological layer associated with the fossils was mostly powdery volcanic ash. The best dating technique, known as the 40 Argon/39 Argon method, requires crystals. Since then, researchers have managed to sift through the ashes to get enough good crystals to make a definite determination of their age. The anthropologists also unearthed 38 new fossils at the site that painted a more complete picture of the species.

The *Australopithecus anamensis* species is an important branch of the human family. It had a small brain, humanlike limbs, and primitive jaws shaped more like a chimpanzee's than like a modern human's. *Anamensis* also had a characteristically primitive feature known as sexual dimorphism—large differences between the sexes in overall body size and teeth. The males were much larger than the females and had bigger canine teeth. Among the new fossils was a wrist bone with the primitive features of a chimpanzee wrist. But the leg bone found is more like a modern human's, with a structure that allowed for walking upright on two legs instead of on all fours as a chimp would. These features show that the human body didn't evolve all at once, but in bits and pieces like a mosaic, depending on which piece natural selection was acted on at the time. □

Major Discoveries about Human Ancestors

Living and extinct human beings and their near human ancestors are called "hominids" and belong to the *Hominidae* family of primates. They are not to be confused with "hominoids," which belong to the *Hominoidea* family of primates and include apes and humans. Scientists theorize that the human and ape lines branched off from a common ancestor 8 million to 6 million years ago.

Years ago	Species	Discovered	Remarks
c. 4.4 million	*Ardipithecus ramidus*	1994 in Ethiopia	Oldest known human ancestor. Had chimpanzee-like skull.
c. 4.2 million	*Australopithecus anamensis*	1995, two sites at Lake Turkana in Kenya: Kanapoi and Allia Bay	Possible ancestor of *A. afarensis* (Lucy). Walked upright.
c. 3.2 million	*Australopithecus afarensis*	1974 at Hadar in the Afar triangle of eastern Ethiopia	Nicknamed "Lucy." Her skeleton was 3.5 feet (100 cm.) tall. Had apelike skull. Walked fully upright. Lived in family groups throughout eastern Africa.
c. 2.5 million	*Australopithecus africanus*	1924 at Taung, northern Cape Province, South Africa	Descendant of "Lucy." Lived in social groups.
c. 2 million	*Australopithecus robustus*	1938 in Kromdraai, South Africa	Was related to *A. africanus*
c. 2 million	*Homo habilis* ("skillful man")	1960 in Olduvai Gorge, Tanzania	First brain expansion; is believed to have used stone tools.
c. 1.8 million	*Homo erectus* ("upright man")	1891 at Trinil, Java	Brain size twice that of australopithecine species. Controversy exists whether "Java Man," as he was called, is a direct ancestor of *Homo sapiens* or instead developed on a separate evolutionary tract. He is, however, the first hominid to use fire and the hand axe, and to live in caves.
c. 100,000(?)	*Homo sapiens* ("knowing or wise man")	1868, Cro-Magnon, France	Anatomically modern humans

The Nation's Highest Science and Technology Honors

The National Medal of Science

The National Medal of Science, established by Congress in 1959, is administered by the National Science Foundation. The medal honors the contributions made by outstanding individuals who have significantly advanced knowledge in the following fields: physics, biology, chemistry, mathematics, engineering, and sociology and other behavioral sciences.

The 1998 National Medal of Science and Medal of Technology recipients will not be announced until late in 1998, past our publishing deadline. The list of 1997 winners is the latest available at press time.

1997 Medal of Science Recipients

William K. Estes, Emeritus Professor of Psychology at Harvard University in Cambridge, Mass., for fundamental theories of cognition and learning that transformed the field of experimental psychology and led to the development of quantitative cognitive science. His pioneering methods of quantitative modeling and insistence on rigor and precision established the standard for modern psychological science.

Darieane C. Hoffman, Director of the Glenn T. Seaborg Institute for Transactinium Science at Lawrence Berkeley National Laboratory in Berkeley, Calif., for her discovery of plutonium in nature and for her numerous contributions to our understanding of radioactive decay, notably of heavy nuclei. She is an internationally recognized leader in nuclear chemistry, particularly in the fields of nuclear fission, properties of actinide elements, and reactions of heavy ions.

Harold S. Johnston, Emeritus Professor of Chemistry at the University of California in Berkeley, Calif., for understanding the chemistry of nitrogen compounds and their role and reactions in Earth's stratosphere and in urban areas. His chemical and environmental research, along with his commitment to science in the service of society, has resulted in pivotal contributions to the understanding and conservation of Earth's atmosphere.

Marshall N. Rosenbluth, Professor of Physics at the University of California in San Diego, Calif., for his fundamental contributions to plasma physics, his leadership in the quest to develop controlled thermonuclear fusion, and his wide-ranging technical contributions to national security. His theoretical studies of the behavior of plasmas and their instabilities provided a significant foundation for the design and development of prototype devices for fusion power.

Martin Schwarzschild, Emeritus Higgins Professor of Astronomy (recently deceased) at Princeton University in Princeton, N.J., for his seminal contributions to the theory of the evolution of stars and his creative insights into the dynamics of galaxies. His research forms the basis of much of contemporary astrophysics, and the many students he trained are among today's leaders in the field.

James D. Watson, President of Cold Spring Harbor Laboratory in Cold Spring Harbor, N.Y., for five decades of scientific and intellectual leadership in molecular biology, starting with his co-discovery of the doublehelix structure of DNA. He was a forceful advocate for the Human Genome Project and shaped that effort as the founding Director of the National Center for Human Genome Research.

Robert A. Weinberg, Member of the Whitehead Institute for Biomedical Research and Professor of Biology at the Massachusetts Institute of Technology in Cambridge, Mass., for crucial discoveries that clarified the genetic basis of human cancers. His work has influenced virtually all major aspects of our current understanding of the origins of cancer, from mutations affecting certain cellular genes, to the development of diagnostic tests for such mutations, to the description of the combination of events that produce cancer.

George W. Wetherill, Member of the Department of Terrestrial Magnetism of the Carnegie Institute of Washington in Washington, D.C., for his fundamental contributions to measuring astronomical time scales and to understanding how Earth-like planets may be created in evolving solar systems. His pioneering achievements include developing precise radiometric techniques for dating the age of meteorites, and creating conceptual models and computer algorithms for the accretion of a few solid, terrestrial planets by collision with smaller neighbors.

Shing-Tung Yau, Professor of Mathematics at Harvard University in Cambridge, Mass., for profound contributions to mathematics that have had great impact on fields as diverse as topology, algebraic geometry, general relativity, and string theory. His work insightfully combines two different mathematical approaches and has resulted in the solution of several long-standing and important problems in mathematics.

The National Medal of Technology

The National Medal of Technology, established by Congress in 1980, is administered by the U.S. Department of Commerce. The medal is awarded for technological innovation and the advancement of U.S. global competitiveness. The medal also recognizes groundbreaking contributions that commercialize a technology, create jobs, improve productivity, or stimulate the nation's growth and development in other ways.

1997 Medal of Technology Recipients

Norman R. Augustine, Chairman and CEO of Lockheed Martin Corp. in Bethesda, Md., for visionary leadership in maintaining the United States' preeminence in the aerospace industry, and for championing technical and managerial solutions to the challenges in civil and defense systems. **Category:** Technology Management.

Ray M. Dolby, Founder and Chairman, Dolby Laboratories, Inc., in San Francisco, Calif., for

inventing technologies that have dramatically improved sound recording and reproduction, fostering their adoption worldwide, and maintaining a vision that has kept the world listening for more than 30 years. **Category:** General Product and Process Innovation; Technology Transfer.

Robert S. Ledley, Director of Medical Computing and Biophysics and Professor of Radiology, Physiology, and Biophysics at Georgetown University Medical Center in Washington, D.C., for pioneering contributions to biomedical computing and engineering, including the invention of the whole-body CT scanner, and for his role in developing automated chromosome analysis for prenatal diagnosis of birth defects. **Category:** General Product and Process Innovation.

Team Award (Jointly): Vinton Cerf, Senior Vice President of Data Architecture at MCI in Reston, Va., and **Robert E. Kahn,** President of the Corporation for National Research Initiatives in Reston, Va., for creating and sustaining development of Internet protocols and continuing to provide leadership in the emerging industry of internetworking. **Category:** Technology Transfer.

1998 Westinghouse Science Talent Search Winners

The Westinghouse Science Talent Search, now in its 57th year, is the nation's oldest and most prestigious science competition for high school students. The contest is sponsored by the Westinghouse Electric Corporation's Westinghouse Foundation and Science Service. Winners were announced at the National Academy of Sciences, March 8, 1998, in Washington, D.C. Awards are given to 40 finalists. The remaining 30 finalists receive awards of $1,000 each.

Top Ten Winners

First Place: $40,000 scholarship, Christopher Colin Mihelich, 17, Carmel, Ind., Park Tudor School, for study of properties of polynomials having applications to geometry and combinatorics.

Second Place: $30,000 scholarship, Ravi Vikram Shah, 17, Tempe, Ariz., Corona del Sol High School, for investigation of changes in repair genes in DNA from tumors resistant to various concentrations of cancer drugs.

Third Place: $20,000 scholarship, Parker Rouse Conrad, 17, New York City, Collegiate School, for study of two types of receptors crucial to understanding the function of nerve cells.

Fourth Place: $15,000 scholarship, Sohini Ramachandran, 15, Fair Oaks, Calif., Rio Americano High School, for project linking plant genetics and human migration by mathematically analyzing short sequences of DNA from American and Old World plant populations.

Fifth Place: $15,000 scholarship, Travis Jeremy Schedler, 17, Carbondale, Ill., Illinois Mathematics and Science Academy in Aurora, for project involving quantum group theory (Yang-Baxter equation), a subject at the interface of mathematics and physics.

Sixth Place: $15,000 scholarship, William J. "BJ" Greenleaf, 18, Rochester, Minn., Mayo High School, for an investigation of more effective ultrasound gene-transfer methods.

Seventh Place: $10,000 scholarship, Ann Kromsky, 17, Corona, Calif., Corona High School, for investigation of how children learn a language.

Eighth Place: $10,000 scholarship, Jonathan Adam Kelner, 17, Old Westbury, N.Y., The Wheaton School, for work on probability formulas that explain behavior of quarks.

Ninth Place: $10,000 scholarship, Patrick William Goodwill, 17, Plano, Texas, Academy of Mathematics and Science in Denton, for project in physical chemistry creating a sensor for detecting contaminants in semiconductor processing.

Tenth Place: $10,000 scholarship, Jessie Keith Anttila-Hughs, 17, New York City, Stuyvesant High School, for project designed to understand how the nervous system works in myasthenia gravis, a neuromuscular disease.

75-Million-Year-Old Dinosaur Voice Heard Again

A team of computer scientists and paleontologists from Sandia National Laboratories and the New Mexico Museum of Natural History and Science Museum has recreated the sound that a Parasaurolophus dinosaur made when it lived during the late Cretaceous period. The team accomplished this feat by using a rare 4.5 foot long fossil of the dinosaur's skull, computed tomography (CT) scans, and powerful supercomputers.

The Parasaurolophus had a bony tubular crest that extended back from the top of its head. Many scientists believed the crest, containing a labyrinth of air cavities and shaped like a trombone, might have been used to produce distinctive sounds. Once a 3-D model of the crest was created, the computer was able to simulate blowing air through it to amplify the tones it was capable of making. As expected, the dinosaur apparently emitted a resonating low-frequency rumbling sound that could change in pitch.

Each Parasaurolophus probably had a voice that was distinctive enough not only to distinguish it from other dinosaurs, but from other Parasaurolophuses. The sound may have been somewhat birdlike, and they may have made songs of some sort to call to one another. □

Roundup of Recent Discoveries

Prehistoric Eggs

The earliest fossil animal embryos, dating from the Precambrian era, were found by American, Taiwanese, and Chinese scientists in phosphate deposits in China's Guizhou province. Some of these remarkably preserved, 570-million-year-old fossils are no larger than a grain of sand and show detailed multiple-cell division. This discovery indicates that multicellular animal life evolved earlier than researchers had previously thought.

Warp-Speed Computers

Simulating nuclear-weapon explosions requires the ability to calculate what happens to billions of data points in a fraction of a second. The Department of Energy (DOE) has contracted IBM Corporation to build a 10-trillion-operation-per-second computer system so that it can calculate the effects of weapons in our nation's stockpile without detonating real nuclear bombs.

This advanced supercomputer is slated for installation at the DOE's Lawrence Livermore National Laboratory in the year 2000. It will be the world's fastest computer, capable of 10 TeraOps (10 trillion operations per second). It would take a person with a handheld calculator 10 million years to do the same number of calculations that the 10-TeraOps computer will be able to do in one second. Even faster computers are on the way. The DOE plans to build a 30- and a 100-TeraOps computer system in the future.

Slimy Cave Critters

Researchers exploring a mile-deep area of a Mexican cavern called Cueva De Villa Luiz (Cave of the Lighted House), in the state of Tabasco, discovered strange viscous colonies of single-cell organisms hanging from the cave's limestone walls and ceiling. The unidentified bacteria were dubbed "snot-tites" because they hang in slimy white masses resembling stalactites. These bizarre microorganisms—found nowhere else—get most of their energy by oxidizing sulfur from the noxious hydrogen-sulfide fumes in the cave. They excrete drops of acid as strong as battery acid.

Dinosaur-Bird Link?

Two new fossil animals with distinct imprints of feathers and many dinosaur features were found in China's Liaoning province. Dating back more than 120 million years, the feathered specimens add considerable weight to the theory that birds evolved directly from dinosaurs.

One of the new species, *Protarchaeopteryx robusta,* has symmetrical feathers similar to those of modern flightless birds, suggesting that it could not fly. The other new species, called *Caudipteryx zoui,* is covered with primitive feathers that also lacked the aerodynamic quality necessary for flight.

In addition, a 65- to 70-million-year-old bird fossil was discovered by a team of international scientists on the African island nation of Madagascar. The fossil, named *Rahona ostromi,* offers evidence of a close relationship between dinosaurs and birds. The creature had a two-foot wingspan and what seem to be well-developed feathers, indicating that it was a capable flyer. Unlike most birds, however, it also had a long bony tail, and a large, sickle-like killing claw at the end of a thick second toe on the hind foot. This unique toe-and-claw is identical to that of theropod dinosaurs called "maniraptorans," which many scientists believe gave rise to birds.

Meanwhile, skeptics of the theory that birds descended from dinosaurs cite studies of modern bird and reptile embryos that suggest that birds and dinosaurs took different evolutionary paths. They found that bird wings developed from "fingers" corresponding to the digits of the human hand—the index, middle, and ring fingers—while reptile forelimbs have three digits corresponding to the human thumb, index, and middle fingers. Critics claim that these developmental differences cannot be reconciled.

Misbehaving Universe

Scientists have long thought that the effect of gravity between the galaxies would eventually slow the acceleration rate of the expanding universe that was created by the force of the Big Bang. This assumption is now being questioned. Astronomers studying supernovas (exploding stars) have discovered evidence that the universe may in fact be gaining momentum.

Although they cannot explain why galaxies seem to be moving away from each other at a faster rate, some astronomers theorize that a mysterious antigravity force in the cosmos may be causing the universe to gain speed.

Celestial "Old Faithful"

NASA researchers observing a disk of matter surrounding a black hole in the constellation Aquilla have discovered that the disk periodically hurls jets of hot gas in opposite directions from the black hole at nearly the speed of light (650 million miles per hour). At half-hour intervals the black hole replenishes the disk by pulling fresh material from the surface of a nearby "companion" star and then undergoing another disruption, behaving much like a heavenly version of Old Faithful geyser in Yellowstone Park. Each eruption is estimated to eject 100 trillion tons of matter, using an amount of energy equivalent to six trillion times the annual energy consumption of the entire United States.

Ancient Innards

A 113-million-year-old baby dinosaur fossil was found in the Pietraroia limestone formation in Italy's Benevento province with much of its soft tissue intact, including muscles, intestines, and liver. The extraordinary discovery of this prehistoric creature's

fossilized organs is expected to provide scientists with important information about dinosaur anatomy.

The nine-inch dinosaur specimen was named Scipionyx and belongs to the group called theropods, which includes *Tyrannosaurus rex* and velociraptors. Although the unique fossil was discovered by an amateur paleontologist a decade ago, it was not recognized as dinosaur remains until recently. It is the first dinosaur fossil ever found in Italy.

Earth Drags Space and Time

Einstein's theory of relativity predicts that large rotating objects should drag space and time around themselves as they turn. The first direct evidence of this phenomena was announced in March 1998 by an international team of NASA and other scientists, who discovered that Earth does indeed drag time and space around itself as it rotates. The researchers detected this effect, called "frame-dragging," by precisely measuring shifts in the orbits of two Earth-orbiting satellites (LAGEOS I and II). The team found that the plane of the orbits of the two satellites shifted about six feet (two meters) per year in the direction of Earth's rotation.

Frame-dragging is not unlike the effect of a bowling ball spinning in molasses. As the ball spins, it pulls the molasses around itself. Anything stuck in the molasses will also move around the ball. Similarly, as Earth rotates, it pulls nearby space and time around itself. This pull shifts the orbits of satellites near Earth.

Solar-System Snapshot

NASA astronomers have discovered evidence of a solar system like our own forming around a youthful star known as HR 4796, some 220 light-years from Earth in the constellation Centaurus. (A light-year is about 5.88 trillion miles.) An infrared image taken by NASA shows a swirling disc of dust around the star. In the middle of the disc is an empty region that may have been swept clean when its dusty material was pulled into newly formed planetary bodies. Scientists think that this may be what our solar system looked like at the end of its main planetary formation phase.

The diameter of the planetary-forming disc orbiting the star is about 200 astronomical units (A.U.). The diameter of the cleared inner region is about 100 A.U., slightly larger than our own solar system. The hole in the doughnut-shaped disc is typical of what would be left by a moving celestial body, offering indirect evidence that a planet has been formed.

The discovery was made on March 16, 1998, from the new giant 10-meter (33-foot) Keck II telescope atop Mauna Kea, Hawaii, and confirmed by astronomers at Chile's Cerro Tololo Observatory.

Galactic Water Cloud

In April 1998 a team of U.S. astronomers reported finding a massive concentration of water vapor within the Orion molecular cloud, a giant interstellar gas cloud located near the Orion nebula. This gas cloud, which is a trillion miles across, generates enough water molecules in a single day to fill the Earth's oceans 60 times over.

Researchers believe the cloud provides an important clue to the origin of water in the solar system. Eventually, the water vapor in the cloud will freeze, turning into small ice particles. Similar ice particles are thought to have been present within the gas cloud from which our solar system formed.

The measurements were made by the Infrared Space Observatory (ISO) satellite, launched in November 1995 by the European Space agency and with the participation of NASA.

A Saharan Stonehenge

Scientists have confirmed that an assembly of huge stone slabs in Egypt's Sahara Desert is the oldest known astronomical alignment of megaliths in the world. Known as Nabta, the site is 6,500 to 6,000 years old, predating Stonehenge and similar prehistoric sites by about 1,000 years.

The site consists of a 12-foot-in-diameter stone circle, a series of flat, tomblike stone structures, and five lines of standing and toppled megaliths. Some of the slabs are nine feet high. Two sets of slabs are aligned in a north-south direction, while another pair provides a line of sight toward the summer-solstice horizon. An east-west alignment of megaliths is present, as are geometrical lines involving about a dozen additional stone monuments, the significance of which is not understood.

Dolly's Bonnie Baby

Dolly, the first mammal successfully cloned from an adult cell, gave birth to a healthy female lamb named Bonnie on April 14, 1998, at Roslin Institute in Edinburgh. The birth of Dolly's lamb confirmed the ability of clones to produce healthy offspring naturally. Dolly was mated with David, a 4-year-old Welsh Mountain ram.

Neanderthals Had Gift for Gab

Duke University scientists studying hypoglossal canal size in fossil skulls of Neanderthals and other ancestral humans have found evidence that some of these ancient species were probably capable of human speech as long as 400,000 years ago.

The hypoglossal canal is a bony channel that transmits messages from the cranial nerves that control voluntary movements of the tongue muscles. The canal is nearly twice as large in modern humans than in apes and chimpanzees who are incapable of speech. The hypoglossal canal size of Neanderthal and archaic Homo sapiens is similar to those of modern humans. Assuming that the size of the hypoglossal canal and its nerves indicate of the tongue's motor-control and vocal capabilities, it can be inferred that these species could coordinate their tongues to form humanlike speech.

Blockbuster Big Bang

In May 1998 astronomers announced that they had measured the most violent explosion ever found in the cosmos—a stupendous gamma-ray burst that released a hundred times more energy than they had theorized previously, making it the most powerful explosion since the Big Bang. The unprecedented gamma-ray burst, designated GRB 971214, was observed by researchers using satellites from NASA's Compton Gamma Ray Observatory (which measured brightness) and the Italian/Dutch BeppoSax (which pinpointed location). Although the

burst was discovered in mid-December 1997, its distance from Earth had just been calculated.

The burst originated in a faint galaxy about 12 billion light-years from Earth. Although the explosion lasted a mere 50 seconds, the energy released was almost equal to the amount of energy radiated by our entire galaxy over a couple of centuries. The cosmic fireball released several hundred times more energy than an exploding star or supernova, and its flash was as bright as the entire universe.

Gamma-ray bursts are mysterious flashes of high-energy radiation that appear from random directions in space and typically last a few seconds. First detected by U.S. Air Force Vela satellites in the 1960s, their origin remains unknown.

Mammals and Dinosaurs Coexisted

Overwhelming evidence from the largest evolutionary study of gene sequences ever performed suggests that the major group of mammals and birds emerged well before the mass extinction of the dinosaurs 65 million years ago.

According to the research done by a scientific team at Penn State, mammals were definitely living on Earth during the Cretaceous period, from 70 million to 100 million years ago. Scientists don't know what these mammals looked like or if they were very abundant, but the genes of their descendants seem to confirm their existence.

The research team sifted through many thousands of vertebrate gene sequences from hundreds of species to find those that develop mutations at a constant rate over time. They then used these sequences to trace the history of each species back to its time of origin. For many species, research yielded origin dates similar to those based on fossil dating; for others, however, genetic clues pointed to a much earlier time.

The study suggests that the evolution of mammals occurred gradually, as a result of the isolation of breeding groups when the continents broke apart, rather than suddenly, by the rapid filling of ecological niches left vacant when the dinosaurs became extinct.

Down Memory's Divided Lane

Psychologists studying patients with brain damage have concluded that the left side of the brain is used for language tasks and the right side for spatial and pictorial information. Scientists who make images of the brain at work, however, have concluded that the left side is used for memorization and the right side for retrieval.

A new study by researchers at Washington University School of Medicine at St. Louis found that when a person is told to remember a word, a region on the left side of the brain is activated. When a person is told to remember an image, a region on the right side is activated. Both regions are activated when a person is asked to recall an image they can name.

First Extrasolar World Image

In 1998 astronomers using the Hubble Space Telescope took the first direct photograph of what may be a planet outside our solar system. Previous extrasolar planets have been discovered only by indirect means such as gravitational wobbles in their parent stars. The young planet, called TMR 1C, is located within a star-forming region in the constellation Taurus. It appears to lie at the end of a 130-billion-mile-long filament structure, suggesting that it had been flung from the vicinity of a newly forming pair of binary stars.

At a distance of 450 light-years, the same distance as the newly formed stars, this possible planet would be 10,000 times less luminous than the sun. It is estimated that if the planet is a few hundred thousand years old, the same age as the newly formed star system that may have ejected it, then it is two to three times the mass of Jupiter, the largest planet in our solar system.

Cosmic Dust Doomed Dinosaurs?

A controversial study by researchers at the University of Florida and Carnegie Institution theorizes that space dust in Earth's atmosphere and changes in the planet's orbit may have started the gradual extinction of dinosaurs and other life thousands of years before a massive asteroid collision dealt the final blow.

Currently, Earth is accumulating about 30,000 metric tons of cosmic dust from interplanetary space each year. The scientists found that most of this dust comes from just three families of asteroids (Eos, Themis, and Koronis) in the solar system's asteroid belt. As Earth orbits the sun, it passes through this cloud of dust particles, capturing some of the dust in its atmosphere. The study showed that the amount of dust captured depends on the shape (ellipticity) and tilt (inclination) of Earth's orbit. These vary periodically due to the gravitational pull of other planets. The dust buildup rises and falls in about 100,000 periods that correspond to ice-age cycles.

Space dust could remain at high levels in the atmosphere for periods of thousands of years, and any associated cooling would also persist for this length of time. If the amount of dust in Earth's atmosphere altered the climate, the change would cause gradual extinction. □

Inventions & Discoveries

See also Famous Firsts in Aviation, Nobel Prizes.

Adrenaline: (isolation of) John Jacob Abel, U.S., 1897.
Aerosol can: Erik Rotheim, Norway, 1926.
Air brake: George Westinghouse, U.S., 1868.
Air conditioning: Willis Carrier, U.S., 1911.
Airship: (non-rigid) Henri Giffard, France, 1852; (rigid) Ferdinand von Zeppelin, Germany, 1900.
Aluminum manufacture: (by electrolytic action) Charles M. Hall, U.S., 1866.
Anatomy, human: (*De fabrica corporis humani,* an illustrated systematic study of the human body) Andreas Vesalius, 1543; (comparative: parts of an organism are correlated to the functioning whole) Georges Cuvier, 1799–1805.

Anesthetic: (first use of anesthetic—ether—on humans) Crawford W. Long, U.S., 1842.

Antibiotics: (first demonstration of antibiotic effect) Louis Pasteur, Jules-François Joubert, France, 1887; (discovery of penicillin, first modern antibiotic) Alexander Fleming, England, 1928; (penicillin's infection-fighting properties) Howard Florey, Ernst Chain, England, 1940.

Antiseptic: (surgery) Joseph Lister, England, 1867.

Antitoxin, diphtheria: Emil von Behring, Germany, 1890.

Appliances, electric: (fan) Schuyler Wheeler, U.S., 1882; (flatiron) Henry W. Seely, U.S., 1882; (stove) Hadaway, U.S., 1896; (washing machine) Alva Fisher, U.S., 1906.

Aqualung: Jacques-Yves Cousteau, Emile Gagnan, France, 1943.

Aspirin: Dr. Felix Hoffman, Germany, 1899.

Astronomical calculator: The Antikythera device, first century B.C.E., Greece. Found off island of Antikythera in 1900.

Atom: (nuclear model of) Ernest Rutherford, England, 1911.

Atomic theory: (ancient) Leucippus, Democritus, Greece, c.500 B.C.E.; Lucretius, Rome c.100 B.C.E.; (modern) John Dalton, England, 1808.

Automobile: (first with internal combustion engine, 250 rpm) Karl Benz, Germany, 1885; (first with practical high-speed internal combustion engine, 900 rpm) Gottlieb Daimler, Germany, 1885; (first true automobile, not carriage with motor) René Panhard, Emile Lavassor, France, 1891; (carburetor, spray) Charles E. Duryea, U.S., 1892.

Autopilot: (for aircraft) Elmer A. Sperry, U.S., c.1910, first successful test, 1912, in a Curtiss flying boat.

Avogadro's law: (equal volumes of all gases at the same temperature and pressure contain equal number of molecules) Amedeo Avogadro, 1811.

Bacteria: Anton van Leeuwenhoek, The Netherlands, 1683.

Balloon, hot-air: Joseph and Jacques Montgolfier, France, 1783.

Barbed wire: (most popular) Joseph E. Glidden, U.S., 1873.

Bar codes: (computer-scanned binary signal code): (retail trade use) Monarch Marking, U.S. 1970; (industrial use) Plessey Telecommunications, England, 1970.

Barometer: Evangelista Torricelli, Italy, 1643.

Bicycle: Karl D. von Sauerbronn, Germany, 1816; (first modern model) James Starley, England, 1884.

Science Web Sites

National Science Foundation: www.nsf.gov
National Academy of Science: www2.nas.edu/nas/
American Association for the Advancement of Science: www.aaas.org/
Federation of American Scientists: www.fas.org
The Franklin Institute of Science Museum: sln.fi.edu/tfi/welcome.html
Bio Online: www.bio.com
Science News Online: www.sciencenews.org
Popular Science: www.popsci.com
Periodic Table of Elements: mwanal.lanl.gov/cst/imagemap/periodic/periodic.html
Dinosauria Online: www.dinosauria.com/
Discovery Channel Online: www.discovery.com
Fermilab: www.fnal.gov/
Argonne National Laboratory: www.anl.gov/
American Geophysical Union: earth.agu.org/kosmos/homepage.html
Artificial Life Online: alife.santafe.edu/
Newton (for K–12 teachers and students): www.newton.dep.anl.gov
Field Museum (Chicago): www.bvis.uic.edu/museum/home.html
Santa Barbara Museum of Natural History: www.sbnature.org
Inventors Hall of Fame: www.invent.org/
The Smithsonian Web: www.si.edu/newstart.htm

Big Bang theory: (the universe originated with a huge explosion) Edwin Hubble, U.S., 1929; (confirmed) Arno Penzias, Robert Wilson, U.S., 1965.

Blood, circulation of: William Harvey, England, 1628.

Boyle's law: (relation between pressure and volume in gases) Robert Boyle, Ireland, 1662.

Braille: Louis Braille, France, 1829.

Bridges: (suspension, iron chains) James Finley, Pa., 1800; (wire suspension) Marc Seguin, Lyons, 1825; (truss) Ithiel Town, U.S., 1820.

Bullet: (conical) Claude Minié, France, 1849.

Calculating machine: (logarithms: made multiplying easier and thus calculators practical) John Napier, Scotland, 1614; (slide rule) William Oughtred, England, 1632; (digital calculator) Blaise Pascal, 1642; (multiplication machine) Gottfried Leibniz, Germany, 1671; (important 19th-century contributors to modern machine) Frank S. Baldwin, Jay R. Monroe, Dorr E. Felt, W. T. Ohdner, William Burroughs, all U.S.; ("analytical engine" design, included concepts of programming, taping) Charles Babbage, England, 1835.

Calculus: Isaac Newton, England, 1669; (differential calculus) Gottfried Leibniz, Germany, 1684.

Camera: (hand-held) George Eastman, U.S., 1888; (Polaroid Land) Edwin Land, U.S., 1948.

"Canals" of Mars: Giovanni Schiaparelli, Italy, 1877.

Carpet sweeper: Melville R. Bissell, U.S., 1876.

Car radio: William Lear, Elmer Wavering, U.S., 1929, manufactured by Galvin Manufacturing Co., "Motorola."

Cells: (word used to describe microscopic examination of cork) Robert Hooke, 1665; (theory: cells are common structural and functional unit of all living organisms) Theodor Schwann, Matthias Schleiden, 1838–1839.

Cement, Portland: Joseph Aspdin, England, 1724.

Chewing gum: (spruce-based) John Curtis, U.S., 1848; (chicle-based) Thomas Adams, U.S., 1870.

Cholera bacterium: Robert Koch, Germany, 1883.

Circuit, integrated: (theoretical) G.W.A. Dummer, England, 1952; (phase-shift oscillator) Jack S. Kilby, Texas Instruments, U.S., 1959.

Classification of plants: (first modern, based on comparative study of forms) Andrea Cesalpino, 1583; (classification of plants and animals by genera and species) Carolus Linnaeus, Sweden, 1737–1753.

Clock, pendulum: Christian Huygens, The Netherlands, 1656.

Coca-Cola: John Pemberton, U.S., 1886.

Combustion: (nature of) Antoine Lavoisier, France, 1777.

Compact disk: RCA, U.S., 1972.

Computer: (differential analyzer, mechanically operated) Vannevar Bush, U.S., 1928; (Mark I, first information-processing digital computer) Howard Aiken, U.S., 1944; (ENIAC, Electronic Numerical Integrator and Calculator, first all-electronic) J. Presper Eckert, John W. Mauchly, U.S., 1946; (stored-program concept) John von Neumann, U.S., 1947.

Concrete: (reinforced) Joseph Monier, France, 1877.

Condensed milk: Gail Borden, U.S., 1853.

Conditioned reflex: Ivan Pavlov, Russia, c.1910.

Conservation of electric charge: (the total electric charge of the universe or any closed system is constant) Benjamin Franklin, U.S., 1751–1754.

Contagion theory: (infectious diseases caused by living agent transmitted from person to person) Girolamo Fracastoro, Italy, 1546.

Continental drift theory: Antonio Snider-Pellegrini, 1858.

Contraceptive, oral: Gregory Pincus, Min Chuch Chang, John Rock, Carl Djerassi, U.S., 1951.

Converter, Bessemer: William Kelly, U.S., 1851.

Cosmetics: Egypt, c.4000 B.C.E.

Cotton gin: Eli Whitney, U.S., 1793.

Crossbow: China, c.300 B.C.E.

Cyclotron: Ernest O. Lawrence, U.S., 1931.

Deuterium: (heavy hydrogen) Harold Urey, U.S., 1931.

Disease: (chemicals in treatment of) crusaded by Philippus Paracelsus, 1527–1541; (germ theory) Louis Pasteur, France, 1862–1877.

DNA: (deoxyribonucleic acid) Friedrich Meischer, Germany, 1869; (determination of double-helical structure) Rosalind Elsie Franklin, F. H. Crick, England, James D. Watson, U.S., 1953.

Dyes: (aniline, start of synthetic dye industry) William H. Perkin, 1856.

Dynamite: Alfred Nobel, Sweden, 1867.

Electric cooking utensil: (first) patented by St. George Lane-Fox, England, 1874.

Electric generator (dynamo): (laboratory model) Michael Faraday, England, 1832; Joseph Henry, U.S., c.1832; (hand-driven model) Hippolyte Pixii, France, 1833; (alternating-current generator) Nikola Tesla, U.S., 1892.

Thomas Alva Edison (1847–1931) *Library of Congress*

Electric lamp: (arc lamp) Sir Humphrey Davy, England, 1801; (fluorescent lamp) A.E. Becquerel, France, 1867; (incandescent lamp) Sir Joseph Swann, England, Thomas A. Edison, U.S., contemporaneously, 1870s; (carbon arc street lamp) Charles F. Brush, U.S., 1879; (first widely marketed incandescent lamp) Thomas A. Edison, U.S., 1879; (mercury vapor lamp) Peter Cooper Hewitt, U.S., 1903; (neon lamp) Georges Claude, France, 1911; (tungsten filament) Irving Langmuir, U.S., 1915.

Electrocardiography: Demonstrated by Augustus Waller, 1887; (first practical device for recording activity of heart) Willem Einthoven, 1903, Dutch physiologist.

Electromagnet: William Sturgeon, England, 1823.

Electron: Sir Joseph J. Thompson, England, 1897.

Elevator, passenger: (safety device permitting use by passengers) Elisha G. Otis, U.S., 1852; (elevator utilizing safety device) 1857.

$E = mc^2$: (equivalence of mass and energy) Albert Einstein, Switzerland, 1907.

Engine, internal combustion: No single inventor. Fundamental theory established by Sadi Carnot, France, 1824; (two-stroke) Etienne Lenoir, France, 1860; (ideal operating cycle for four-stroke) Alphonse Beau de Roche, France, 1862; (operating four-stroke) Nikolaus Otto, Germany, 1876; (diesel) Rudolf Diesel, Germany, 1892; (rotary) Felix Wankel, Germany, 1956.

Evolution: (organic) Jean-Baptiste Lamarck, 1809; (by natural selection) Charles Darwin, England, 1859.

Exclusion principle: (no two electrons in an atom can occupy the same energy level) Wolfgang Pauli, 1925.

Expanding universe theory: (galaxies are receding from each other at speeds proportionate to their distance) George Lemaître, 1927.

Falling bodies, law of: Galileo Galilei, Italy, 1590.

Fermentation: (microorganisms as cause of) Louis Pasteur, France, c.1860.

Fiber optics: Narinder Kapany, England, 1955.

Fibers, man-made: (nitrocellulose fibers treated to change flammable nitrocellulose to harmless cellulose, precursor of rayon) Sir Joseph Swann, England, 1883; (rayon) Count Hilaire de Chardonnet, France, 1889; (Celanese) Henry and Camille Dreyfuss, U.S., England, 1921; (research on polyesters and polyamides, basis for modern man-made fibers) U.S., England, Germany, 1930s; (nylon) Wallace H. Carothers, U.S., 1935.

Frozen food: Clarence Birdseye, U.S. 1924.

Gene transfer: (human) Steven Rosenberg, R. Michael Blaese, W. French Anderson, U.S., 1989.

Geometry, elements of: Euclid, Alexandria, Egypt, c.300 B.C.E.; (analytic) René Descartes, France; and Pierre de Fermat, Switzerland, 1637.

Gravitation, law of: Sir Isaac Newton, England, c.1665 (published 1687).

Gunpowder: China, c.700.

Gyrocompass: Elmer A. Sperry, U.S., 1905.

Gyroscope: Léon Foucault, France, 1852.

Halley's Comet: Edmund Halley, 1705.

Heart, artificial: Dr. Robert Jarvik, U.S., 1982.

Helicopter: (double rotor) Heinrich Focke, Germany, 1936; (single rotor) Igor Sikorsky, U.S., 1939.

Helium first observed on sun: Sir Joseph Lockyer, England, 1868.

Heredity, laws of: Gregor Mendel, Austria, 1865.

Holograph: Dennis Gabor, England, 1947.

Home videotape systems (VCR): (Betamax) Sony, Japan, 1975; (VHS) Matsushita, Japan, 1975.

Ice age theory: Louis Agassiz, 1840.

Induction, electric: Joseph Henry, U.S., 1828.

Insulin: Sir Frederick G. Banting, J. J. R. MacLeod, Canada, 1922.

Intelligence testing: Alfred Binet, Theodore Simon, France, 1905.

Interferon: Alick Isaacs, Jean Lindemann, England, Switzerland, 1957.

Isotopes: (concept of) Frederick Soddy, England, 1912; (stable isotopes) J. J. Thompson, England, 1913; (existence demonstrated by mass spectrography) Francis W. Ashton, 1919.

Jet propulsion: (engine) Sir Frank Whittle, England, Hans von Ohain, Germany, 1930; (aircraft) *Heinkel He 170*, 1939.

Kinetic theory of gases: (molecules of a gas are in a state of rapid motion) Daniel Bernoulli, 1738.

Laser: (theoretical work on) Charles H. Townes, Arthur L. Schawlow, U.S., N. Basov, A. Prokhorov, U.S.S.R., 1958; (first working model) T. H. Maiman, U.S., 1960.

Lawn mower: Edwin Budding, John Ferrabee, England, 1830–1831.

LCD (liquid crystal display): Hoffmann-La Roche, Switzerland, 1970.

Lens, bifocal: Benjamin Franklin, U.S., c.1760.

Leyden jar: (prototype electrical condenser) Canon E. G. von Kleist of Kamin, Pomerania, 1745; independently evolved by Cunaeus and P. van Musschenbroek, University of Leyden, Holland, 1746, from where name originated.

Light, nature of: (wave theory) Christian Huygens, The Netherlands, 1678; (electromagnetic theory) James Clerk Maxwell, England, 1873.

Light, speed of: (theory that light has finite velocity) Olaus Roemer, Denmark, 1675.

Lightning rod: Benjamin Franklin, U.S., 1752.

Locomotive: (steam powered) Richard Trevithick, England, 1804; (first practical, due to multiple-fire-tube boiler) George Stephenson, England, 1829; (largest steam-powered) Union Pacific's "Big Boy," U.S., 1941.

Lock, cylinder: Linus Yale, U.S., 1851.

Loom: (horizontal, two-beamed) Egypt, c.4400 B.C.E.;(Jacquard drawloom, pattern controlled by punch cards) Jacques de Vaucanson, France, 1745, Joseph-Marie Jacquard, 1801; (flying shuttle) John Kay, England, 1733; (power-driven loom) Edmund Cartwright, England, 1785.

Machine gun: James Puckle, England, 1718; Richard J. Gatling, U.S., 1861.

Magnet, Earth is: William Gilbert, 1600.

Match: (phosphorus) François Derosne, France, 1816; (friction) Charles Sauria, France, 1831; (safety) J. E. Lundstrom, Sweden, 1855.
Measles vaccine: John F. Enders, Thomas Peebles, U.S., 1953.
Metric system: revolutionary government of France, 1790–1801.
Microphone: Charles Wheatstone, England, 1827.
Microscope: (compound) Zacharias Janssen, The Netherlands, 1590; (electron) Vladimir Zworykin et al., U.S., Canada, Germany, 1932–1939.
Microwave oven: Percy Spencer, U.S., 1947.
Motion, laws of: Isaac Newton, England, 1687.
Motion pictures: Thomas A. Edison, U.S., 1893.
Motion pictures, sound: Product of various inventions. First picture with synchronized musical score: *Don Juan,* 1926; with spoken dialogue: *The Jazz Singer,* 1927; both Warner Bros.
Motor, electric: Michael Faraday, England, 1822; (alternating-current) Nikola Tesla, U.S., 1892.
Motorcycle: (motor tricycle) Edward Butler, England, 1884; (gasoline-engine motorcycle) Gottlieb Daimler, Germany, 1885.
National Science Foundation: established by U.S. Congress, 1950 based on report by Vannevar Bush, 1945.
Neptune: (discovery of) Johann Galle, 1846.
Neptunium: (first transuranic element, synthesis of) Edward M. McMillan, Philip H. Abelson, U.S., 1940.
Neutron: James Chadwick, England, 1932.
Neutron-induced radiation: Enrico Fermi et al., Italy, 1934.
Nitroglycerin: Ascanio Sobrero, Italy, 1846.
Nuclear fission: Otto Hahn, Fritz Strassmann, Germany, 1938.
Nuclear reactor: Enrico Fermi, et al., 1942.
Ohm's law: (relationship between strength of electric current, electromotive force, and circuit resistance) Georg S. Ohm, Germany, 1827.
Oil well: Edwin L. Drake, U.S., 1859.
Oxygen: (isolation of) Joseph Priestley, 1774; Carl Scheele, 1773.
Ozone: Christian Schönbein, Germany, 1839.
Pacemaker: (internal) Clarence W. Lillehie, Earl Bakk, U.S., 1957.
Paper China, c.100 C.E.
Parachute: Louis S. Lenormand, France, 1783.
Pen: (fountain) Lewis E. Waterman, U.S., 1884; (ball-point, for marking on rough surfaces) John H. Loud, U.S., 1888; (ball-point, for handwriting) Lazlo Biro, Argentina, 1944.
Periodic law: (that properties of elements are functions of their atomic weights) Dmitri Mendeleev, Russia, 1869.
Periodic table: (arrangement of chemical elements based on periodic law) Dmitri Mendeleev, Russia, 1869.
Phonograph: Thomas A. Edison, U.S., 1877.
Photography: (first paper negative, first photograph, on metal) Joseph Nicéphore Niepce, France, 1816–1827; (discovery of fixative powers of hyposulfite of soda) Sir John Herschel, England, 1819; (first direct positive image on silver plate, the daguerreotype) Louis Daguerre, based on work with Niepce, France, 1839; (first paper negative from which a number of positive prints could be made) William Talbot, England, 1841. Work of these four men, taken together, forms basis for all modern photography. (First color images) Alexandre Becquerel, Claude Niepce de Saint-Victor, France, 1848–1860; (commercial color film with three emulsion layers, Kodachrome) U.S., 1935.
Photovoltaic effect: (light falling on certain materials can produce electricity) Edmund Becquerel, France, 1839.
Piano: (Hammerklavier) Bartolommeo Cristofori, Italy, 1709; (pianoforte with sustaining and damper pedals) John Broadwood, England, 1873.
Planetary motion, laws of: Johannes Kepler, Germany, 1609, 1619.
Plant respiration and photosynthesis: Jan Ingenhousz, 1779.
Plastics: (first material, nitrocellulose softened by vegetable oil, camphor, precursor to Celluloid) Alexander Parkes, England, 1855; (Celluloid, involving recognition of vital effect of camphor) John W. Hyatt, U.S., 1869; (Bakelite, first completely synthetic plastic) Leo H. Baekeland, U.S., 1910; (theoretical background of macromolecules and process of polymerization on which modern plastics industry rests) Hermann Staudinger, Germany, 1922.
Plate tectonics: Alfred Wegener, Germany, 1912–1915.
Plow, forked: Mesopotamia, before 3000 B.C.E.
Plutonium, synthesis of: Glenn T. Seaborg, Edwin M. McMillan, Arthur C. Wahl, Joseph W. Kennedy, U.S., 1941.
Polio, vaccine against: (vaccine made from dead virus strains) Jonas E. Salk, U.S., 1954; (vaccine made from live virus strains) Albert Sabin, U.S., 1960.
Positron: Carl D. Anderson, U.S., 1932.
Pressure cooker: (early version) Denis Papin, France, 1679.
Printing: (block) Japan, c.700; (movable type) Korea, c.1400; Johann Gutenberg, Germany, c.1450 (lithography, offset) Aloys Senefelder, Germany, 1796; (rotary press) Richard Hoe, U.S., 1844; (linotype) Ottmar Mergenthaler, U.S., 1884.

Johann Gutenberg (c. 1400–1468)

Probability theory: René Descartes, France; and Pierre de Fermat, Switzerland, 1654.
Proton: Ernest Rutherford, England, 1919.
Psychoanalysis: Sigmund Freud, Austria, c.1904.
Pulsars: Jocelyn Bell Bunnell, England, 1968.
Quantum theory: (general) Max Planck, Germany, 1900; (sub-atomic) Niels Bohr, Denmark, 1913; (quantum mechanics) Werner Heisenberg, Erwin Schrödinger, Germany, 1925.
Quarks: Jerome Friedman, Henry Kendall, Richard Taylor, U.S., 1967.
Quasars: Marten Schmidt, U.S., 1963.
Rabies immunization: Louis Pasteur, France, 1885.
Radar: (limited to one-mile range) Christian Hulsmeyer, Germany, 1904; (pulse modulation, used for measuring height of ionosphere) Gregory Breit, Merle Tuve, U.S., 1925; (first practical radar—radio detection and ranging) Sir Robert Watson-Watt, England, 1934–1935.
Radio: (electromagnetism, theory of) James Clerk Maxwell, England, 1873; (spark coil, generator of electromagnetic waves) Heinrich Hertz, Germany, 1886; (first practical system of wireless telegraphy) Guglielmo Marconi, Italy, 1895; (vacuum electron tube, basis for radio telephony) Sir John Fleming, England, 1904; (triode amplifying tube) Lee de Forest, U.S., 1906; (regenerative circuit, allowing long-distance sound reception) Edwin H. Armstrong, U.S., 1912; (frequency modulation—FM) Edwin H. Armstrong, U.S., 1933.
Radioactivity: (X-rays) Wilhelm K. Roentgen, Germany, 1895; (radioactivity of uranium) Henri Becquerel, France, 1896; (radioactive elements, radium and polonium in uranium ore) Marie Sklodowska-Curie, Pierre Curie, France, 1898; (classification of alpha and beta particle radiation) Pierre Curie, France, 1900; (gamma radiation) Paul-Ulrich Villard, France, 1900; (carbon dating) Willard F. Libby et al., U.S., 1955.

Radio signals, extraterrestrial: first known radio noise signals were received by U.S. engineer, Karl Jansky, originating from the Galactic Center, 1931.

Radio waves: (cosmic sources, led to radio astronomy) Karl Jansky, U.S., 1932.

Razor: (safety, successfully marketed) King Gillette, U.S., 1901; (electric) Jacob Schick, U.S., 1928, 1931.

Reaper: Cyrus McCormick, U.S., 1834.

Refrigerator: Alexander Twining, U.S., James Harrison, Australia, 1850; (first with a compressor device) the Domelse, Chicago, U.S., 1913.

Refrigerator ship: (first) the *Frigorifique,* cooling unit designed by Charles Teller, France, 1877.

Relativity: (special and general theories of) Albert Einstein, Switzerland, Germany, U.S., 1905–1953.

Revolver: Samuel Colt, U.S., 1835.

Richter scale: Charles F. Richter, U.S., 1935.

Rifle: (muzzle-loaded) Italy, Germany, c.1475; (breech-loaded) England, France, Germany, U.S., c.1866; (bolt-action) Paul von Mauser, Germany, 1889; (automatic) John Browning, U.S., 1918.

Rocket: (liquid-fueled) Robert Goddard, U.S., 1926.

Roller bearing: (wooden for cartwheel) Germany or France, c.100 B.C.E.

Rotation of earth: Jean Bernard Foucault, France, 1851.

Royal Observatory, Greenwich: established by Charles II of England, John Flamsteed first Astronomer Royal.

Rubber: (vulcanization process) Charles Goodyear, U.S., 1839.

Saccharin: Constantine Fuhlberg, Ira Remsen, U.S., 1879.

Safety pin: Walter Hunt, U.S., 1849.

Saturn, ring around: Christian Huygens, The Netherlands, 1659.

"Scotch" tape: Richard Drew, U.S., 1929.

Screw propeller: Sir Francis P. Smith, England, 1836; John Ericsson, England, worked independently of and simultaneously with Smith, 1837.

Seismograph: (first accurate) John Milne, England, 1880.

Sewing machine: Elias Howe, U.S., 1846; (continuous stitch) Isaac Singer, U.S., 1851.

Solar energy: First realistic application of solar energy using parabolic solar reflector to drive caloric engine on steam boiler, John Ericsson, U.S., 1860s.

Solar system, universe: (sun-centered universe) Nicolaus Copernicus, Warsaw, 1543; (establishment of planetary orbits as elliptical) Johannes Kepler, Germany, 1609; (infinity of universe) Giordano Bruno, Italian monk, 1584.

Spectrum: (heterogeneity of light) Sir Isaac Newton, England, 1665–1666.

Spectrum analysis: Gustav Kirchhoff, Robert Bunsen, Germany, 1859.

Spermatozoa: Anton van Leeuwenhoek, The Netherlands, 1683.

Spinning: (spinning wheel) India, introduced to Europe in Middle Ages; (Saxony wheel, continuous spinning of wool or cotton yarn) England, c.1500–1600; (spinning jenny) James Hargreaves, England, 1764; (spinning frame) Sir Richard Arkwright, England, 1769; (spinning mule, completed mechanization of spinning, permitting production of yarn to keep up with demands of modern looms) Samuel Crompton, England, 1779.

Star catalog: (first modern) Tycho Brahe, Denmark, 1572.

Steam engine: (first commercial version based on principles of French physicist Denis Papin) Thomas Savery, England, 1639; (atmospheric steam engine) Thomas Newcomen, England, 1705; (steam engine for pumping water from collieries) Savery, Newcomen, 1725; (modern condensing, double acting) James Watt, England, 1782.

Steamship: Claude de Jouffroy d'Abbans, France, 1783; James Rumsey, U.S., 1787; John Fitch, U.S., 1790. All preceded Robert Fulton, U.S., 1807, credited with launching first commercially successful steamship.

Stethoscope: René Laënnec, France, 1819.

Sulfa drugs: (parent compound, para-aminobenzenesulfanomide) Paul Gelmo, Austria, 1908; (antibacterial activity) Gerhard Domagk, Germany, 1935.

Superconductivity: (theory) Bardeen, Cooper, Scheiffer, U.S., 1957.

Symbolic logic: George Boule, 1854; (modern) Bertrand Russell, Alfred North Whitehead, England, 1910–1913.

Tank, military: Sir Ernest Swinton, England, 1914.

Tape recorder: (magnetic steel tape) Valdemar Poulsen, Denmark, 1899.

Teflon: DuPont, U.S., 1943.

Samuel F. B. Morse (1791–1872)
Library of Congress

Telegraph: Samuel F. B. Morse, U.S., 1837.

Telephone: Alexander Graham Bell, U.S., 1876.

Telescope: Hans Lippershey, The Netherlands, 1608; (astronomical) Galileo Galilei, Italy, 1609; (reflecting) Isaac Newton, England, 1668.

Television: (Iconoscope–T.V. camera table), Vladimir Zworkin, U.S., 1923, and also kinescope (cathode ray tube), 1928; (mechanical disk-scanning method) successfully demonstrated by J.K. Baird, England, C.F. Jenkins, U.S., 1926; (first all-electric television image), 1927, Philo T. Farnsworth, U.S; (color, mechanical disk) Baird, 1928; (color, compatible with black and white) George Valensi, France, 1938; (color, sequential rotating filter) Peter Goldmark, U.S., first introduced, 1951; (color, compatible with black and white) commercially introduced in U.S., National Television Systems Committee, 1953.

Thermodynamics: (first law: energy cannot be created or destroyed, only converted from one form to another) Julius von Mayer, Germany, 1842; James Joule, England, 1843; (second law: heat cannot of itself pass from a colder to a warmer body) Rudolph Clausius, Germany, 1850; (third law: the entropy of ordered solids reaches zero at the absolute zero of temperature) Walter Nernst, Germany, 1918.

Thermometer: (open-column) Galileo Galilei, c.1593; (clinical) Santorio Santorio, Padua, c.1615; (mercury, also Fahrenheit scale) Gabriel D. Fahrenheit, Germany, 1714; (centigrade scale) Anders Celsius, Sweden, 1742; (absolute-temperature, or Kelvin, scale) William Thompson, Lord Kelvin, England, 1848.

Tire, pneumatic: Robert W. Thompson, England, 1845; (bicycle tire) John B. Dunlop, Northern Ireland, 1888.

Toilet, flush: Product of Minoan civilization, Crete, c.2000 B.C.E. Alleged invention by "Thomas Crapper" is untrue.

Tractor: Benjamin Holt, U.S., 1900.

Transformer, electric: William Stanley, U.S., 1885.

Transistor: John Bardeen, William Shockley, Walter Brattain, U.S., 1948.

Tuberculosis bacterium: Robert Koch, Germany, 1882.

Typewriter: Christopher Sholes, Carlos Glidden, U.S., 1867.

Uncertainty principle: (that position and velocity of an object cannot both be measured exactly, at the same time) Werner Heisenberg, Germany, 1927.

Uranus: (first planet discovered in recorded history) William Herschel, England, 1781.

Vaccination: Edward Jenner, England, 1796.

Vacuum cleaner: (manually operated) Ives W. McGaffey, 1869; (electric) Hubert C. Booth, England, 1901; (upright) J. Murray Spangler, U.S., 1907.

Van Allen (radiation) Belt: (around the earth) James Van Allen, U.S., 1958.

Video disk: Philips Co., The Netherlands, 1972.

Vitamins: (hypothesis of disease deficiency) Sir F. G. Hopkins, Casimir Funk, England, 1912; (vitamin A) Elmer V. McCollum, M. Davis, U.S., 1912–1914; (vitamin B) McCollum, U.S., 1915–1916; (thiamin, B_1) Casimir Funk, England, 1912; (riboflavin, B_2) D. T. Smith, E. G. Hendrick, U.S., 1926; (niacin) Conrad Elvehjem, U.S., 1937; (B_6) Paul Gyorgy, U.S., 1934; (vitamin C) C. A. Hoist, T. Froelich, Norway, 1912; (vitamin D) McCollum, U.S., 1922; (folic acid) Lucy Wills, England, 1933.

Voltaic pile: (forerunner of modern battery, first source of continuous electric current) Alessandro Volta, 1800.

Wallpaper: Europe, 16th and 17th century.

Wassermann test: (for syphilis) August von Wassermann, Germany, 1906.

Wheel: (cart, solid wood) Mesopotamia, c.3800–3600 B.C.E.

Windmill: Persia, c.600.

Xerography: Chester Carlson, U.S., 1938.

Zero: India, c.600; (absolute zero temperature, cessation of all molecular energy) William Thompson, Lord Kelvin, England, 1848.

Zipper: W. L. Judson, U.S., 1891.

The National Inventors Hall of Fame

The Inventors Hall of Fame, located in Akron, Ohio, was established in 1973 by the National Council of Patent Law Associations, now the National Council of Intellectual Property Law Associations, and the Patent and Trademark Office of the U.S. Department of Commerce.

The 1998 Class of Inductees

Begun, S. Joseph, 1905–1995 (Danzig, Germany, now Gdansk, Poland) MAGNETIC RECORDING. Early recording machines of the 1920s were cumbersome at best. Sound was recorded magnetically on rapidly spinning reels of steel wire, and editing could only be done with wire cutters and welding equipment. In 1934, Begun built the first tape recorder for broadcasting, which was later used in the 1936 Olympics. After WWII, he continued to work on magnetic recording media based on coating paper and plastic tape with ferrmagnetic powder suspensions. Begun developed the first consumer tape recorder in the U.S. under the trade name Sound Mirror. He also negotiated the first sourcing agreement for magnetic tape with 3M—which later became a billion-dollar product line.

Engelbart, Douglas, 1925– (near Portland, Oregon) X-Y POSITION INDICATOR FOR A DISPLAY SYSTEM: THE MOUSE. Douglas Engelbart envisioned a computer that would work in the modern office and made it a practical reality. In 1963, he began research at the Augmentation Research Center at Stanford Research Institute (SRI), and developed a pioneering hypermedia groupware system called NLS (for oN-Line System). NLS introduced two-dimensional computerized text editing using the mouse to position a pointer into the text. He first demonstrated NLS in 1968. This was the world debut of the mouse, hypermedia, and on-screen video teleconferencing. His project became the second host on ARPANET—the predecessor of the Internet.

Fergason, James L., 1934– (Wakenda, Missouri) LIQUID CRYSTAL DISPLAY (LCD). Liquid crystal displays were originally based on a concept that used a large amount of powder, provided a limited life, and poor visual contrast. Fergason overcame these obstacles in 1969 with his discovery of the twisted nematic field effect, which forms the basis of modern LCDs. In 1970, he founded the International Crystal Company (ILIXCO), which pioneered the way for digital watch displays by selling field effect LCDs to the Gruen Watch Company. He also founded the American Liquid Crystal Company, and then, in 1981, Optical Shields Ltd., of which he is now president. His company produced LCD products to protect the eyes against inner sources of radiation like laser weapons and welding arcs.

Mullis, Kary Banks, 1944– (North Carolina) PCR, THE POLYMERASE CHAIN REACTION. Mullis invented PCR, the process for amplifying nucleic acids, in 1993 while at Cetus Corporation. PCR has revolutionized the fields of microbiology, medical diagnostics, and forensics. PCR allows scientists to identify a fragment of DNA genetic code and then reproduce it infinitely. It is used to discover faulty genes in hereditary diseases and diagnose viral and bacterial infections, including HIV. Police can get decisive information from a single drop of blood or a hair. Other uses include determining genetic ties and evolutionary connections between animal species including extinct animals whose remains are fossilized. It was used to identify the remains of Russia's last czar, Nicolas II.

Nobel, Alfred, 1833–1896 (Stockholm, Sweden) IMPROVED EXPLOSIVE COMPOUND: DYNAMITE. Accidents in the manufacturing and handling of nitroglycerin made Nobel aware of its danger in the fluid state. After much experimenting, he invented dynamite in 1866—nitroglycerine absorbed by a very porous dynamite clay. Easily handled, solid, and malleable, nitroglycerine was transformed into a useful explosive making mining, railroad building, and other construction safer, more efficient, and cheaper. Upon his death, he willed the bulk of his fortune to a foundation that would award prizes annually for advancements in physics, chemistry, physiology or medicine, literature, and peace.

Timken, Henry, 1831–1909 (Bremen, Germany) TAPERED ROLLER BEARINGS. The bearings that existed in the late 19th century worked well at reducing friction but ran into problems when wheels had to bear heavy loads from the sides, as when vehicles turn. Henry Timken tackled the problem and created a tapered roller bearing in 1898. A year later, he established the Timkin Roller Bearing Axle Company which grew rapidly as the product was in great demand by cars, trucks, and tractors. By 1923, 90% of the country's production came from Timkin. His slogan "Wherever wheels and shafts turn," describes the widespread use for bearings—trains, conveyors, elevators, aircraft engines, even space shuttle landing wheels.

Of Networks and Nations

A glimpse inside the Information Marketplace of the future

By MICHAEL DERTOUZOS TIME

We are constantly told that information technology will take us to a gleaming, gigabyte-infested other world called Cyberspace. Baloney! The Industrial Revolution didn't take us to Motorspace; it brought motors into our lives. The Information Revolution will do the same, introducing new tools that we will use to serve our ancient human needs. This new movement is not about multimedia, virtual reality, or even the mighty World Wide Web. It is about an emerging Information Marketplace in which computers and their users everywhere will buy, sell, and freely exchange information and "information work."

When people talk about information, they think of the traditional content of books, newspapers, television, and radio, which represent about 5% of the U.S. economy. No one talks about information work—the activity people and machines perform when they transform information—which accounts for 60% of the U.S. economy. Information work will take many guises in the Information Marketplace. Imagine a doctor in Sri Lanka examining a homeless person in a San Francisco clinic who is connected by means of a few electrodes to a diagnostic kiosk, with a nurse standing by. The doctor provides human information work—his medical diagnostic skills—for $2.00 a "visit." The Information Marketplace will bring this and many other new tools into our lives through the electronic bulldozers and electronic proximity.

New Tools for Old Problems

In the industrial era, mechanical bulldozers allowed workers to throw away their shovels and offload their muscle-work on machines. Today we squint our eyes and scorch our brains in front of inscrutable email headers and pages of impenetrable text. We are still shoveling with our eyes and brains but dismiss the drudgery because our silicon-studded shovels make us feel modern. It's time we shed the shovels and exploited electronic bulldozers.

New tools like e-forms will make this easier than it sounds. To fill in a travel e-form, for example, all I have to type or say out loud is: "Computer, take us to Athens this weekend." My machine knows that "us" means two, and that we prefer business class. It calls the airline computer, and after a few exchanges, the machines complete the booking. It takes me three seconds to give my command and it takes the machines ten minutes to finish the job—a 20,000% productivity gain. Electronic bulldozer tools like this will get much of our information work done. We will increase our productivity further by making our machines truly easier to use. One good way is to speak to them. Speech-understanding systems are finally becoming technologically mature and affordable.

The changes arising from the second major new force—electronic proximity—will be just as large. As the Information Marketplace develops, we'll be closer to a thousand times more people than we were with the automobile. Within a decade, half a billion people and machines will be squeezed into one gigantic electronic city block. The closeness will lead to powerful benefits through groupwork and telework, but also to infopredators and new kinds of crime. I don't expect the ratio of good to bad will change; the angels and devils are within us, not in our machines.

New Global Networks

Electronic proximity will strengthen tribalism. Ethnic groups scattered across the globe will have a way to unite, perhaps even extending the meaning of a "nation" from a land mass to an ethnic network. At the same time, electronic proximity will strengthen diversity, because when people from different ethnic groups meet within a "tribe" of classical-music buffs, for example, they'll get to know one another within that subgroup. This won't lead to a universal global culture, but a thin veneer of shared norms. It will also give rise to new projects that have worthy human purposes, like a Virtual Compassion Corps that could match the providers of human help to those worldwide who need it. Electronic proximity will ultimately lead to increased democratization, not so much because information will traverse national borders, but because even totalitarian nations will want to participate in the major new economic force of the 21st century. To do so, they will have to play by the rules of engagement made by the predominantly democratic nations that will establish the Information Marketplace.

The Information Marketplace will create problems, too. Unless we intervene, it will increase the gap between rich and poor nations, because the rich will be able to afford the electronic bulldozers while the poor will not. Electronic proximity will inundate us with infojunk, creating a need for human intermediaries who can help us find what we want. And electronic proximity will be perceived by some as a license to attack cultures that took thousands of years to build. National leaders will no doubt use politics and technology to protect their cultures against such info-assaults. They will also need to negotiate how to handle "cross-border" information violations, as they did earlier with international crime and trade. Because of the widespread changes it will foster, the Information Revolution will earn its place in history as the third socio-economic movement, following the Agrarian and Industrial Revolutions. Maybe then, having understood the plow, the motor, and the computer, we'll dare go beyond artifacts and embark upon the fourth revolution—striving to understand ourselves. □

Internet Timeline

1969 ARPA (Advanced Research Projects Agency) goes online in December, connecting four major U.S. universities. Designed for research, education, and government organizations, it provides a communications network linking the country in the event that a military attack destroys conventional communications systems.

1972 Electronic mail is introduced. Queen Elizabeth sends her first email in 1976.

1973 Transmission Control Protocol/Internet Protocol (TCP/IP) is designed and in 1983 it becomes the standard for communicating between computers over the Internet. One of these protocols, FTP (file transfer protocol), allows users to log onto a remote computer, list the files on that computer, and download files from that computer.

1989 The first effort to index the Internet is created by Peter Deutsch at McGill University in Montreal, who devises Archie, an archive of FTP sites. Another indexing system, WAIS (Wide Area Information Server), is developed by Brewster Kahle of Thinking Machines Corp. Tim Berners-Lee of CERN (European Laboratory for Particle Physics) develops a new technique for distributing information on the Internet, which eventually is called the World Wide Web. The Web is based on hypertext, which permits the user to connect from one document to another at different sites on the Internet via hyperlinks (specially programmed words, phrases, buttons, or graphics). Unlike other Internet protocols, such as FTP and email, the Web is accessible through a graphical user interface.

1991 Gopher, the first user-friendly interface, is created at the University of Minnesota and named after the school mascot. Gopher becomes the most popular interface for several years.

1993 Mosaic is developed by Marc Andreeson at the National Center for Supercomputing Applications (NCSA). It becomes the dominant navigating system for the World Wide Web, which at this time accounts for merely 1% of all Internet traffic.

1994 U.S. White House launches Web page. Initial commerce sites are established and mass marketing campaigns are launched via email, introducing the term "spamming" to the Internet vocabulary.

1996 Approximately 45 million people are using the Internet, with roughly 30 million of those in North America (United States and Canada), 9 million in Europe, and 6 million in Asia/Pacific (Australia, Japan, etc.). 43.2 million (44%) of U.S. households own a personal computer, and 14 million of them are online.

1998 More than 20% of all U.S. households have access to the Internet, up from 13% at the end of 1996.

Sources for this timeline include International Data Corporation, the W3C Consortium, and the Internet Society.

Internet Resource Guide

If you're like most 'Net neophytes, you're a bit overwhelmed by the possibility of accessing a worldwide network of information, and probably also frustrated that it's not better organized and easier to find what you're looking for. Here are a few tips to finding your way around the Internet, as well as some addresses that should serve as a starting place for you to explore this brave new world.

Generally, you can determine the "genre" of a site based on a 3-character extension in the address. If it ends in ".gov" it is a government site (e.g., www.whitehouse.gov); ".edu" is an educational institution (e.g., www.harvard.edu); ".com" is a company (e.g., www.infoplease.com); and ".org" is an organization (e.g., www.un.org)—likely nonprofit, or it would appear as a ".com." The default is for addresses in the U.S., so international addresses usually also include a two-character country code (e.g., "uk" for United Kingdom, "de" for Germany, "fr" for France, "nl" for the Netherlands, etc.). Chances are, if you're looking for information on a company or a college, you could access a "home page" of data over the Internet by typing "www.[name of company].com" or "www.[name of institution].edu."

Not all addresses are that simple, though. If you can't find what you need, go to a search engine, many of which are available at home.netscape.com/escapes/search/. Search engines maintain an index of words that appear on Internet sites within their stated scope (some are worldwide, others are industry- or topic-specific). The engine will return a list of sites containing your search terms. You may go to those sites by simply clicking on the address (all underlined terms on the Internet are "links" that provide direct access to other information simply by clicking on the term).

To get you started, here are a few topically arranged addresses. Many of these sites also offer links to other sites with more information. Though the Internet may at first appear to be a labyrinth full of dead ends and wrong turns, the journey itself is almost always interesting.

Leisure

Books

Amazon.com www.amazon.com

This Seattle-based bookseller offers over a million titles. Visitors can browse the shelves, search for a specific book by title, author, and subject, write a review, and purchase books for delivery within a week or so. Editors keep visitors apprised of new books within their interest categories via email messages.

New York Times Books www.nytimes.com/books

Updated daily with book-related news and reviews, it includes the complete *Sunday Book Review* archive (searchable by author and title), the first chapters from a selection of bestsellers and recently reviewed books, expanded bestseller lists, forums, and RealAudio clips of world-class authors reading from their own works.

Entertainment

broadcast.com www.broadcast.com

This is what multimedia is all about. With a set of speakers and the free RealPlayer plugin (available through the site), you can watch TV shows, see movie trailers, tune in to radio stations from across the country, follow live sports events, or listen to various albums, audio books, or recorded concerts of your choice.

The Dilbert Zone www.unitedmedia.com/comics/dilbert

The best features of this site are its two-week archive of "Dilbert" comic strips and its Daily Mental Workout brainteaser. Naturally, there is a separate (easier) workout for managers, so don't be intimidated by this site, ostensibly favored only by the technically adept.

Interesting Places for Kids www.starport.com/places/forKids

This site is a collection of links of interest to children. Many contain art or writing by children, others gear their content toward children. This site is sure to ease parents' fears about their children surfing the 'Net.

Mr. Showbiz www.mrshowbiz.com

Whether your 'Biz is music, television, or movies, this site has some insider info for you. With features, chat rooms, biographies, news items, and polls on current events, this is the place to keep up with all the folks who keep you up.

Sony www.sony.com

Sony's sprawling empire, from music to television to movies to home video, is all represented here. Find out about the latest movie release or plans for a new television show, or play in the online arcade.

Movies

Disney www.disney.com

Want to find out what went on behind the scenes of the latest Disney film? Plan a vacation to Disneyland? Or chat with the stars of an upcoming movie? This is the place to do it, with content to suit adults and kids.

Internet Movie Database www.imdb.com

An exceptionally valuable resource for any movie buff, this site offers biographical and professional information on just about anyone you can think of who ever had anything to do with the movies or television, along with awards, plot summaries, goofs, and reviews.

Museums

Boston's Museum of Fine Arts www.mfa.org

This site's latest incarnation is surprisingly more focused on providing background and contextual information about art rather than images of the art itself. Check out the "past exhibitions" section for more images (along with supporting text).

The Louvre mistral.culture.fr/louvre/louvrea.htm

Though the site contains some of the world's most famous art, the images take a long time to download and there are remarkably few of them to look at once the page has loaded. Still, it's cool to tell your friends you went to see the Mona Lisa at the Louvre today.

The National Museum of American Art www.nmaa.si.edu:80

A Web-friendly site that creatively melds technology and art to provide innovative and interactive tours of several exhibitions. The site is updated regularly, and with content from America's art gallery, it is worth visiting often.

Music

Billboard Online www.billboard.com

A great site for music enthusiasts, Billboard Online posts all its recent charts plus interesting features, album and concert reviews, a music news column that's updated twice daily, and lists of recent and upcoming releases. There's also a cool concert search function so you can track your favorite bands as they tour.

Shopping

American Greetings www.americangreetings.com

With a calendar of card-worthy holidays and the ability to order all your cards for the year in a single visit, there's really no longer any excuse for forgetting your mother-in-law's birthday.

AutoWeb www.autoweb.com

Now you can find out everything you need to know about the car you want to trade in and its potential replacements *before* heading into the dealership. You can also post autos for sale and browse other postings from around the U.S.

Egghead www.egghead.com

It only makes sense that one should be able to order software online. At egghead.com, not only can shoppers search for the software of their dreams; they can download certain titles and start using them right away. Now that's instant gratification.

HomeScout www.homescout.com

With listings of over 300,000 homes for sale nationwide, this should be the first stop for anyone seeking summary information on homes in their old (or new) neighborhood. Links to local real estate brokers provide detailed listings. Other features include a mortgage calculator, home-buying FAQs, and discounts on home-related purchases.

Imall www.imall.com

Dozens of vendors offer products, from audio to automotive, and tools to toys. Those looking to save more than their energy will like the Daily Deals, which can be emailed directly to visitors if they so choose. Transactions are made through a secure commerce server.

Sports

CBS SportsLine www.cbs.sportsline.com

An inclusive sports resource with more than 300,000 pages of content including up-to-the-minute scores and sports news, schedules, live broadcasts, biographies, and stats. The site is quick and searchable. Extra benefits are available to paying subscribers.

ESPN SportsZone ESPN.SportsZone.com

Here you will find a real-time scoreboard, the latest sports news, insightful reviews, a vast archive of sports history and statistics, and an online ticketing service. "Insiders" will enjoy extra benefits once they've paid the membership fee. ESPN cable viewers will enjoy the presence of familiar sportscasters on the site.

Media

Online Magazines

Salon Magazine www.salonmagazine.com

This site's frequently updated columns, travel section, and reviews of music, books, games, and comics have become a "daily fix" for many visitors. *Salon* is risqué, funny, on-the-mark, and no doubt the most original magazine online.

Slate www.slate.com

For a magazine designed for the Web community, this site does very little to take advantage of its medium. Its content, however, makes up for its lack of Web pyrotechnics. The brainchild of Michael Kinsley, this subscription-only site features incisive commentary and reviews as well as a stellar cast of contributors.

Suck www.suck.com

Launched by staff at Wired Ventures, this satirical magazine is targeted exclusively to online readers. The 15,000 daily visitors to the site attest to the popularity of its content ("things that suck") and its format (a single column of double-spaced text that you would never find in print).

Magazines

Discover www.discover.com

This site contains the complete text of *Discover* magazine's current issue, as well as a searchable archive, listings for television counterpart the Discovery Channel, a directory of other science-related Web sites, and a marketplace for Discovery-related items (videos, books, etc.).

Entertainment Weekly www.pathfinder.com/ew

This glitzy online counterpart to the weekly magazine edition is enhanced with archives of previous movie reviews, interviews, photos, and a slick interface.

Fortune www.pathfinder.com/fortune

Features all you'd expect to find in the magazine, accessible through an attractive interface, plus a stock quote service, searchable archives, and Web-only offers for free gifts and trial copies.

Money Magazine www.pathfinder.com/money

The content echoes its print counterpart, plus it includes a stock quote service (including personal portfolio tracking), links to other Web sites, and tips on goal-oriented saving and investing (for home, college, retirement, etc.).

People Magazine www.people.com

Features all the catty, behind-the-scenes scoop of the print magazine, but goes much further to include daily feeds (Rosie Report, horoscopes, what happened in the lives of celebrities on this date) and weekly features found only on the online site.

TIME Magazine www.pathfinder.com/time

Accessible via a clear, crisp interface that features good use of color and photos, the content is everything in the print counterpart plus online-only features such as daily newsfeeds, searching, and a multimedia section.

U.S. News and World Report www.usnews.com

In addition to all the news on current events you'd expect to find, this site includes an extensive education section and a "News You Can Use" section with information on health, gardening, taxes, travel, and personal finance.

News

Networks

CNN Interactive www.cnn.com

Whether you need up-to-the-minute information about breaking news, or a resource to help you pinpoint the date of a recent event, this is the site to find it. Most stories include photos, audio, or QuickTime video clips, and links to other sites, with content ranging from world events, travel, and finance, to sports, weather, and trivia.

MSNBC www.msnbc.com

A cooperative venture between Microsoft Corp. and NBC has produced this news-and-information-driven site, with instant access to top stories, current events, and online discussions. Search capability is simple to use and provides just what users would expect.

Yahoo! News www.yahoo.com/headlines

Though Yahoo! was first known as a search engine, it is also a great resource for timely and authoritative news information, covering domestic, international, business, high tech, entertainment, and sports categories. You'll find newswire press releases, plus a seven-day searchable archive, stock quotes, and weather information.

Newspapers

New York Times www.nytimes.com

Everything you find inside the inky pages of the paper edition can be found here, plus a few extra features especially for the Web edition.

San Jose Mercury News www.sjmercury.com

With all the usual newspaper sections, plus "Good Morning Silicon Valley," "Mortgage Watch," and customizable comics, it's easy to see why this site is so popular. Offering a savvy combination of content and technology, the Mercury News is a prime example of what a well-conceived and executed Web site can offer.

Wall Street Journal Interactive Edition www.wsj.com

The online *Journal* offers all the news and analysis of its print counterpart, plus a whole lot more: continually updated news from the regional U.S., European, and Asian editions; a clipping service; company profiles; and links to audio files. The first two weeks are free, and the subscription price is lower for subscribers to the print *Journal*.

Health & Medicine Resources

New England Journal of Medicine www.nejm.org

Turn here for expert opinions backed by authoritative research. Full-text articles published in the weekly journal are provided here, with a searching capability. The professional focus and lack of images may make the site seem intimidating, but the content is valuable.

The National Library of Medicine www.nlm.nih.gov

A wealth of information for health professionals and patients alike, this site offers published data sheets, symposia proceedings, and results of studies. The focus is on the data, though, not on how pretty it is or how well the site is displayed, so it helps if you know what you're looking for.

Health Risk Assessment www.youfirst.com

This site provides a free, in-depth assessment of your current health and habits versus others in your age group. You may choose to set up your own personal health "ticker"—a confidential profile that is automatically updated with research or publications in your indicated areas of interest.

HealthWWWeb www.healthwwweb.com

Focusing on natural health and alternative therapies, the site has introductory articles on such topics as acupuncture and herbal medicines, and more focused articles on vegetarian diets and nutritional food substitutes.

Reference

Careers and Education

The Monster Board www.monster.com

An excellent resource if you are looking for a new job or even a new career. In addition to 30,000 job postings (searchable by location, category, keyword, and company), you can create an online resume, locate job fairs, read company profiles, and learn about different professions.

Peterson's www.petersons.com

The Peterson's site is at least as useful as the company's popular print guides. Here you can search for colleges and grad schools that match your criteria, find profiles for specific schools, fill out the Universal Application, and get information on standardized tests, financial aid, careers, and employers.

Company Information

Hoover's Online www.hoovers.com

Allows users to search for information on 2,700+ public and private companies, but you can only see the profiles if you subscribe to the service (though there are sample profiles provided free at the site).

General Information

Britannica Online www.eb.com

The entire contents of the *Encyclopedia Britannica* are available on this site. An authoritative and invaluable source, eb.com is available only to subscribers.

Virtual Reference Desk www.refdesk.com

A collection of links to free reference resources of all types on the Web, ranging in content from biographies to weights and measures. Also includes links to networks (such as A&E Biography) and other topic-specific sites. Good starting place for research, but you will ultimately bookmark your chosen resources and bypass this page.

Government Information

Central Intelligence Agency www.odci.gov/cia

The real resource here is the *World Factbook,* which provides valuable information on all the countries of the world, as well as worldwide aggregate statistics. You can find the population of Afghanistan, the literacy rate of Zimbabwe, and everything in between.

U.S. Census Bureau www.census.gov

Excellent and authoritative information about the U.S. is available from this site. Includes statistics on population as well as education, economy, law enforcement, births, deaths, income, poverty, law enforcement, and agriculture. All information is available free of charge.

History

The History Net www.thehistorynet.com

Students of all ages should bookmark this site. Sponsored by the Cowles History Group, it includes information on world and U.S. history, a daily quiz, personality profiles, and selected magazines. It has valuable information, though finding it with the site search is somewhat stupefying.

Travel

Agencies

Business Travel Resource www.thetrip.com

Full-service site for business (or leisure) travel. Users can define a profile that automatically applies your preferences regarding airlines, meals, hotels, and car rentals to any reservations you make. Offers electronic ticketing (where available from suppliers) and flight status information.

Guides

Fodor's www.fodors.com

An excellent resource for planning a trip or just thinking about being somewhere else, this site offers trip-planning resources, including restaurant and hotel indices, currency converter, travel advisories, and language preparation with useful phrases (including pronunciations) in four languages.

Weather

IntelliCast www.intellicast.com

For those interested in current or future weather conditions at home or abroad, this site provides instant access to local forecasts around the world. Travelers can plan ahead with the regional forecasts arranged by month.

Women

Women In Technology International www.witi.com

WITI strives to enhance the status of women in science and technology. At the same time, women in all professional fields can acquire the knowledge needed to keep up in today's ever-changing world of technology.

Women's Wire www.womenswire.com

This hip magazine has sections devoted to the topics women care about: news, health, stock market, career advice, managing your money, fashion, celebrities, and horoscopes. The editors comb the online news sources daily to find stories their readers will find interesting, and their choices are right on target.

Computer Glossary

ASCII American Standard Code for Information Interchange, an encoding system for converting keyboard characters and instructions into the binary number code that the computer understands.

bit (short for "binary digit"). The smallest piece of computer information, either the number 0 or 1. Through "machine language," the computer interprets a series of 0s and 1s to form numbers, letters, punctuation marks, and symbols.

boot To start up a computer.

browser Software used to navigate the Internet. Netscape Navigator and Microsoft Internet Explorer are today's most popular browsers for accessing the World Wide Web.

bug A malfunction due to an error in the program or a defect in the equipment.

byte Most computers use combinations of eight bits, called bytes, to represent one character of data or instructions. For example, the word "cat" has three characters, and it would be represented by three bytes.

CD-ROM Compact Disc Read-Only Memory. Similar to a CD music disc, but designed for computers, a single disc can hold an entire library of books, such as encyclopedias or other reference works, and multimedia programs for quick, convenient viewing.

chip A tiny wafer of silicon containing miniature electric circuits that can store millions of bits of information.

client A single user of a network application run off a server. A client/server architecture allows many people to use the same data simultaneously; the program's main component (the data) resides on a centralized server, with smaller components (user interface) on each client.

cyberspace Slang for the Internet.

database A collection of similar information stored in a file, for example, a database of addresses. This information may be created and stored in a database management system (DBMS).

debug Computer slang for finding and correcting equipment defects or malfunctions in the program.

desktop publishing Use of a personal computer in combination with text, graphics, and page layout programs to produce publication-quality documents.

directory A list of files stored in the computer.

disk Two distinct types: the so-called "hard disk" that is inside the computer and stores vast amounts of data (new computers currently come standard with 1–2 gigabyte hard drives); and the "floppy" disk, which is portable, 3.5″ square, and can store about 1.4 megabytes of data (the name is a vestige of early 5.25″ disks, which were flexible).

disk drive The equipment that a floppy disk is inserted into so that information may be stored on or retrieved from the disk.

documentation The instruction manual for a piece of hardware or software.

domain The name of a network or computer linked to the Internet. It is found in an email address after an @ sign. The email address of this almanac, for example, is ipa@infoplease.com, "infoplease.com" being its domain. A domain ends with an abbreviation indicating its type (e.g., ".com" stands for company, ".gov" for government, ".org" for organization, and ".edu" for educational institution).

DOS Disk Operating System. An operating system designed for early IBM-compatible PCs.

email Electronic mail; messages, including memos or letters, sent electronically between networked computers that may be across the office or around the world.

file A set of data that is stored in the computer.

fonts Sets of typefaces (or characters) that come in different styles and sizes.

FTP File Transfer Protocol. The format and rules for transferring files from a host to a remote computer.

gigabyte (GB) One thousand megabytes.

glitch The cause of an unexpected malfunction.

gopher An Internet search tool that allows users to access textual information through a series of menus.

GUI Graphical User Interface. A system that simplifies selecting computer commands by enabling the user to point to symbols or illustrations (called "icons") on the computer screen with a mouse.

groupware Software that allows networked individuals to form groups and collaborate on documents, programs, or databases.

hacker A person with technical expertise who enjoys tinkering with computer systems to produce additional features. Also one who intentionally accesses all or part of a computer or a computer system without authorization to do so (a crime in some states).

hard copy A paper printout of what you have prepared on the computer.

hardware The physical and mechanical components of a computer system. They include electronic circuitry, chips, screens, disk drives, keyboards, modems, and printers.

home page The main page of a Web site used to greet visitors, provide information about the site, or to direct the viewer to other pages on the site.

HTML Hypertext Markup Language. A standard of text markup conventions used for documents on the World Wide Web. Browsers interpret the codes to give the text formatting (such as bold, blue, or italic).

HTTP Hypertext Transfer Protocol. A common system used to request and send HTML documents on the World Wide Web. It is the first portion of all URL addresses on the World Wide Web (e.g., http://www.whitehouse.gov).

hypermedia Integrates audio, graphics, and/or video through links embedded in the main application.

hypertext A system for organizing text through links, as opposed to a menu-driven hierarchy such as Gopher. Most Web pages include hypertext links to other pages at that site, or to other sites on the World Wide Web.

icons Symbols or illustrations appearing on the computer screen that indicate program files or other computer functions.

input Data that goes into a computer device.

interface The interconnections that allow a device, a program, or a person to interact. Hardware interfaces are the cables that connect the device to its power source and to other devices. Software interfaces allow the program to communicate with other programs (such as the operating system), and user interfaces allow the user to communicate with the program (e.g., via mouse, menu commands, icons, voice commands, etc.).

Internet An international conglomeration of interconnected computer networks. Developed in the 1970s to allow government and university researchers to share information, the Internet is not controlled by any single source. Its original focus was research and communications, but it continues to expand, offering a wide array of resources for business and home users.

Java An object-oriented programming language; allows users to create small programs or applications ("applets") to enhance Web sites. Java was designed specifically for programs (particularly multimedia) to be used over the Internet.

kilobyte (K or KB) Equal to 1,024 bytes.

laptop and notebook Small, lightweight, portable battery-powered computers that can fit onto your lap. They have a thin, flat, liquid crystal display screen.

megabyte (MB) Equal to 1,048,576 bytes, usually rounded off to one million bytes.

memory A computer device or series of devices that store information. Computer memory is measured in terms of the amount of information it can store, commonly in megabytes or gigabytes.

menu A list of options that users can choose from.

merge To combine two or more files into a single file.

Mhz An abbreviation for Megahertz. One million Hertz. One million cycles per second. Unit of measure for band and bandwidth, or for processor speed of a computer CPU, in millions of computer clock cycles per second. For example, the Pentium is currently available in 133 Mhz, 166 Mhz, and 200 Mhz models.

microprocessor A complete central processing unit (CPU) contained on a single silicon chip.

modem A device that connects two computers together over a telephone line by converting the computer's data into an audio signal.

monitor A video display terminal.

mouse A small hand-held device, similar to a "trackball," used to control the position of the cursor on the video display; movements of the mouse on a desktop correspond to movements of the cursor on the screen.

multimedia Software programs that combine text and graphics with sound, video, and animation. A **multimedia PC** contains the hardware to support these capabilities.

MS-DOS An early operating system developed by Microsoft Corporation.

network Computers that are connected to other computers.

OS/2 An operating system with a graphical user interface, developed by IBM for IBM PCs and compatible computers.

output Data that come out of a computer device.

PC Personal computer.

Pentium chip Intel's fifth generation of sophisticated high-speed microprocessors. Pentium means "the fifth element."

personal computer (PC) A single-user computer containing a central processing unit (CPU) and one or more memory circuits.

Power PC A competitor to the Pentium chip. It is a new generation of powerful sophisticated microprocessors produced from an Apple-IBM-Motorola alliance.

printer A mechanical device for printing your computer's output on paper. The three major types of printers are **dot matrix,** in which individual letters are made up of a series of tiny ink dots formed by punching a ribbon with the ends of tiny wires; **ink jet,** which sprays tiny droplets of ink particles onto paper; and **laser,** which uses a beam of light to reproduce the image of each page, before dry toner is applied to the image and transferred to paper.

program A precise series of instructions written in a computer language that tells the computer what to do and how to do it. Programs are also called "software" or "applications."

programming language A series of instructions written by a programmer according to a given set of rules or conventions ("syntax"). High-level programming languages are independent of the device on which the application (or program) will eventually run; low-level languages are specific to each program or platform. Programming language instructions are converted into programs in language specific to a particular machine or operating system ("machine language") so that the computer can interpret and carry out the instructions. Some common programming languages are BASIC, C, C++, dBASE, FORTRAN, and Perl.

push technology Internet tool that delivers specific information directly to a user's desktop, eliminating the need to surf for it. PointCast, which delivers news in user-defined categories, is a popular example of this technology.

RAM Random Access Memory. One of two basic types of memory. Portions of programs are stored in RAM when the program is launched so that the program will run faster. Though a PC has a fixed amount of RAM, only portions of it will be accessed by the computer at any given time.

ROM Read-Only Memory. One of two basic types of memory. ROM contains only permanent information put there by the manufacturer; information in ROM cannot be altered, nor can the memory be dynamically allocated by the computer or its operator.

scanner An electronic device that uses light-sensing equipment to scan paper images such as text, photos, and illustrations and translate the images into signals that the computer can then store, modify, or distribute.

search engine Software that makes it possible to look for and retrieve material on the Internet, particularly the Web. Some popular search engines are Alta Vista, Yahoo!, Web Crawler, and Lycos.

server A computer that shares its resources and information with other computers, called clients, on a network.

software Computer programs; also called "applications."

spreadsheet Software that allows one to calculate numbers in a format that is similar to pages in a conventional ledger.

surfing Exploring the Internet.

trackball Input device that controls the position of the cursor on the screen; the unit is mounted near the keyboard, and movement is controlled by moving a ball.

URL Uniform Resource Locator. The protocol for identifying a document on the Web; the Web address (e.g., www.census.gov).

USENET A large unmoderated and unedited bulletin board on the Internet that offers thousands of forums, called newsgroups. These range from newsgroups exchanging information on scientific advances to celebrity fan clubs.

user friendly A program or device whose use is intuitive to people with a nontechnical background.

virtual reality (VR) A technology that allows you to experience and interact with images in a simulated three-dimensional environment. For example, you could design a room in a house on your computer and actually feel that you are walking around in it even though it was never built. (The holodeck in the science-fiction TV series *Star Trek: Voyager* would be the ultimate virtual reality.) Current technology requires the user to wear a special helmet, viewing goggles, gloves, and other equipment that is wired to the computer.

virus An unauthorized piece of computer code attached to a computer program or portions of a computer system that secretly spreads from one computer to another by shared disks and over telephone lines.

Windows A graphical environment developed by Microsoft Corp. that enables users to select commands by pointing to illustrations or symbols with a mouse.

World Wide Web ("WWW" or "the Web") A network of servers on the Internet that use hypertext-linked databases and files. It was developed in 1989 by Tim Berners-Lee, a British computer scientist, and is now the primary platform of the Internet. The feature that distinguishes the Web from other Internet applications is its ability to display graphics in addition to text.

word processor A computer system or program for setting, editing, revising, correcting, storing, and printing text.

Countries With the Most Computers

(in millions)

Country[1]	Computers in use	1985	1988	1989	1991	1992	1993	1994	1995	2000[2]
United States	Total computers	21.50	40.80	47.60	62.00	68.20	76.50	85.80	96.20	160.50
	Total PCs	19.10	37.90	44.50	58.60	64.60	72.60	81.50	91.50	154.00
Japan	Total computers	2.10	5.10	6.40	9.20	10.80	12.60	14.90	18.30	46.80
	Total PCs	1.80	4.70	5.90	8.70	10.20	12.00	14.20	17.40	45.00
Germany	Total computers	1.90	4.20	5.20	7.30	8.70	10.40	12.30	14.20	29.80
	Total PCs	1.60	3.90	4.90	6.90	8.30	9.90	11.70	13.50	28.60
United Kingdom	Total computers	2.10	4.30	5.20	7.20	8.40	9.60	10.90	12.60	26.00
	Total PCs	1.80	3.90	4.80	6.80	7.90	9.10	10.40	12.00	25.00
France	Total computers	1.30	3.10	4.00	5.70	6.50	7.50	8.60	10.00	21.80
	Total PCs	1.10	2.90	3.70	5.40	6.20	7.10	8.20	9.50	21.00
Canada	Total computers	0.90	2.00	2.50	3.70	4.30	5.20	6.20	7.20	15.30
	Total PCs	0.80	1.90	2.40	3.50	4.10	5.00	5.90	6.90	14.70
Italy	Total computers	0.90	2.10	2.60	3.70	4.30	5.00	5.90	6.70	17.50
	Total PCs	0.80	1.90	2.40	3.50	4.10	4.80	5.60	6.40	16.80
Australia	Total computers	0.34	0.95	1.24	2.10	2.70	3.40	4.00	4.80	10.20
	Total PCs	0.28	0.87	1.15	1.96	2.60	3.20	3.80	4.60	9.80
South Korea	Total computers	0.13	0.28	0.43	1.00	1.40	1.90	2.60	3.50	10.60
	Total PCs	0.10	0.26	0.40	0.90	1.30	1.80	2.50	3.40	10.20
Spain	Total computers	0.20	0.50	0.79	1.44	1.80	2.30	2.90	3.50	8.10
	Total PCs	0.17	0.46	0.73	1.35	1.70	2.20	2.70	3.30	7.80
Netherlands	Total computers	0.32	0.76	1.02	1.65	2.00	2.40	2.80	3.30	7.10
	Total PCs	0.27	0.70	0.95	1.55	1.90	2.30	2.70	3.20	6.80
China	Total computers	0.12	0.28	0.40	0.67	0.92	1.34	2.00	2.90	13.30
	Total PCs	0.09	0.25	0.36	0.63	0.87	1.26	1.90	2.80	12.70
Russia	Total computers	0.10	0.23	0.34	0.65	0.93	1.37	1.90	2.70	9.20
	Total PCs	0.08	0.20	0.31	0.61	0.88	1.29	1.80	2.60	8.80
Mexico	Total computers	0.15	0.37	0.49	0.87	1.21	1.61	2.05	2.60	6.30
	Total PCs	0.12	0.34	0.46	0.82	1.14	1.52	1.94	2.40	6.00
Brazil	Total computers	0.10	0.24	0.31	0.62	0.91	1.27	1.76	2.40	7.80
	Total PCs	0.08	0.22	0.29	0.59	0.86	1.20	1.67	2.30	7.50
Worldwide Total	Total computers	38.10	79.40	97.00	136.90	159.20	186.90	218.80	257.20	556.90
	Total PCs	33.20	73.40	90.60	129.40	150.80	177.40	208.00	245.00	535.60

1. List represents the fifteen countries with the most computers. 2. Projected. *Source:* Karen Petska-Juliussen and Egil Juilussen, *8th Annual Computer Industry Almanac,* Copyright © 1996 by Computer Industry Almanac Inc., 800-377-6810 (U.S. only).

Computers Per Capita

Rank	Computers/1000 People	1985	1988	1989	1991	1992	1993	1994	1995	2000[1]
1.	United States	90.1	166.0	191.7	245.4	266.9	296.6	329.2	364.7	580.0
2.	Australia	21.5	58.4	75.3	120.5	155.0	191.9	222.7	264.3	525.7
3.	Norway	28.4	61.2	77.7	120.7	148.2	180.5	218.5	259.5	515.4
4.	Canada	36.4	77.4	96.2	136.6	157.5	189.0	219.2	254.8	511.9
5.	Denmark	25.9	58.6	76.7	127.3	153.8	184.6	217.2	252.5	510.2
6.	Finland	25.4	56.2	76.0	119.3	146.2	178.8	211.0	245.5	505.0
7.	Sweden	24.5	58.5	77.0	114.2	139.6	169.9	204.0	244.1	508.9
8.	New Zealand	25.7	57.2	73.5	115.6	136.4	159.8	191.2	224.8	499.2
9.	United Kingdom	36.4	74.8	90.7	125.7	144.8	164.8	187.4	216.5	441.1
10.	Netherlands	22.4	51.9	69.2	109.7	131.1	156.9	184.3	214.8	450.3
11.	Switzerland	24.2	53.0	70.2	109.0	126.6	149.5	174.3	201.6	443.7
12.	Singapore	17.8	46.5	59.7	84.7	104.8	126.9	153.8	188.8	412.0
13.	Belgium	20.1	47.0	63.2	100.2	117.3	138.3	161.2	188.6	405.2
14.	Ireland	23.8	54.1	68.3	102.0	117.4	136.1	159.1	186.4	404.1
15.	Germany	24.0	54.2	67.6	91.5	108.6	129.2	151.3	174.6	361.8
	Europe	14.3	31.7	40.8	60.2	71.0	83.5	97.3	113.4	248.9
	Worldwide	7.8	15.4	18.5	25.2	29.1	33.6	38.8	44.9	90.3

1. Projected. *Source:* Karen Petska-Juliussen and Egil Juliussen, *8th Annual Computer Industry Almanac,* Copyright © 1996 by Computer Industry Almanac Inc., 800-377-6810 (U.S. only).

Top 15 Countries in Internet Usage

1997 rank	Country	Internet users (in thousands)	% share of total
1.	United States	54,675	54.70
2.	Japan	7,965	7.97
3.	United Kingdom	5,828	5.83
4.	Canada	4,325	4.33
5.	Germany	4,064	4.07
6.	Australia	3,347	3.35
7.	Netherlands	1,386	1.39
8.	Sweden	1,311	1.31
9.	Finland	1,250	1.25
10.	France	1,175	1.17
11.	Norway	1,007	1.01
12.	Spain	920	0.92
13.	Brazil	861	0.86
14.	Italy	841	0.84
15.	Switzerland	767	0.77
	Total Top 15 countries	**89,720**	**89.76**
	Total Europe	**21,961**	**21.97**
	Total Worldwide	**99,960**	**100.00**

Source: Karen Petska-Juliussen and Egil Juliussen, *8th Annual Computer Industry Almanac,* Copyright © 1996 by Computer Industry Almanac Inc., 800-377-6810 (U.S. only).

Top 15 Countries in Internet Usage Per Capita

1997 rank	Country	Internet users (per 1,000 people)
1.	Finland	244.5
2.	Norway	231.1
3.	Iceland	227.3
4.	United States	203.4
5.	Australia	178.0
6.	New Zealand	155.9
7.	Canada	148.9
8.	Sweden	147.3
9.	Singapore	141.2
10.	Denmark	125.6
11.	Switzerland	107.1
12.	United Kingdom	99.5
13.	Netherlands	88.9
14.	Hong Kong	64.9
15.	Japan	63.1
	Average Top 15 Countries	**148.5**
	Average Europe	**44.1**
	Average Worldwide	**16.9**

Source: Karen Petska-Juliussen and Egil Juliussen, *8th Annual Computer Industry Almanac,* Copyright © 1996 by Computer Industry Almanac Inc., 800-377-6810 (U.S. only).

Conversion Factors

To change	To	Multiply by	To change	To	Multiply by
acres	square feet	43,560	liters	quarts (liquid)	1.0567
acres	square miles	.001562	meters	feet	3.2808
atmospheres	cms. of mercury	76	meters	miles	.0006214
Btu	kilowatt-hour	.0002928	meters	yards	1.0936
Btu/hour	watts	.2931	metric tons	tons (long)	.9842
bushels	cubic inches	2150.4	metric tons	tons (short)	1.1023
centimeters	inches	.3937	miles	kilometers	1.6093
centimeters	feet	.03281	miles	feet	5280
circumference	radians	6.283	miles (nautical)	miles (statute)	1.1516
cubic feet	cubic meters	.0283	miles (statute)	miles (nautical)	.8684
cubic meters	cubic feet	35.3145	miles/hour	feet/minute	88
cubic meters	cubic yards	1.3079	millimeters	inches	.0394
cubic yards	cubic meters	.7646	ounces avdp.	grams	28.3495
fathoms	feet	6.0	ounces	pounds	.0625
feet	meters	.3048	ounces (troy)	ounces (avdp)	1.09714
feet	miles (nautical)	.0001645	pecks	liters	8.8096
feet	miles (statute)	.0001894	pints (dry)	liters	.5506
feet/second	miles/hour	.6818	pints (liquid)	liters	.4732
furlongs	feet	660.0	pounds ap or t	kilograms	.3782
furlongs	miles	.125	pounds avdp	kilograms	.4536
gallons (U.S.)	liters	3.7853	pounds	ounces	16
grains	grams	.0648	quarts (dry)	liters	1.1012
grams	ounces avdp	.0353	quarts (liquid)	liters	.9463
grams	pounds	.002205	radians	degrees	57.30
hectares	acres	2.4710	rods	meters	5.029
hectoliters	bushels (U.S.)	2.8378	rods	feet	16.5
horsepower	watts	745.7	square feet	square meters	.0929
hours	days	.04167	square kilometers	square miles	.3861
inches	millimeters	25.4000	square meters	square feet	10.7639
inches	centimeters	2.5400	square miles	square kilometers	2.5900
kilograms	pounds avdp or t	2.2046	square yards	square meters	.8361
kilometers	miles	.6214	tons (long)	metric tons	1.016
kilowatts	horsepower	1.341	tons (short)	metric tons	.9072
knots	nautical miles/hour	1.0	tons (long)	pounds	2240
knots	statute miles/hour	1.151	tons (short)	pounds	2000
liters	gallons (U.S.)	.2642	watts	Btu/hour	3.4129
liters	pints (dry)	1.8162	watts	horsepower	.001341
liters	pints (liquid)	2.1134	yards	meters	.9144
liters	quarts (dry)	.9081	yards	miles	.0005682

Fahrenheit and Celsius (Centigrade) Scales

°Celsius	°Fahrenheit	°Celsius	°Fahrenheit
–273.15	–459.67	30	86
–250	–418	35	95
–200	–328	40	104
–150	–238	45	113
–100	–148	50	122
–50	–58	55	131
–40	–40	60	140
–30	–22	65	149
–20	–4	70	158
–10	14	75	167
0	32	80	176
5	41	85	185
10	50	90	194
15	59	95	203
20	68	100	212
25	77		

Zero on the Fahrenheit scale represents the temperature produced by the mixing of equal weights of snow and common salt.

	°Fahrenheit	°Celsius
Boiling point of water	212°	100°
Freezing point of water	32°	0°
Absolute zero	–459.6°	–273.1°

Absolute zero is theoretically the lowest possible temperature, the point at which all molecular motion would cease.

To convert Fahrenheit to Celsius (Centigrade), subtract 32 and multiply by 5⁄9.

To convert Celsius (Centigrade) to Fahrenheit, multiply by 9⁄5 and add 32.

Roman Numerals

Roman numerals are expressed by letters of the alphabet and are rarely used today except for formality or variety.

There are three basic principles for reading Roman numerals:

1. A letter repeated once or twice repeats its value that many times (XXX = 30, CC = 200, etc.).
2. One or more letters placed after another letter of greater value increases the greater value by the amount of the smaller. (VI = 6, LXX = 70, MCC = 1200, etc.).
3. A letter placed before another letter of greater value decreases the greater value by the amount of the smaller. (IV = 4, XC = 90, CM = 900, etc.).

Letter	Value	Letter	Value	Letter	Value	Letter	Value	Letter	Value
I	1	VII	7	XL	40	C	100	$\overline{C}$	100,000
II	2	VIII	8	L	50	D	500	$\overline{D}$	500,000
III	3	IX	9	LX	60	M	1,000	$\overline{M}$	1,000,000
IV	4	X	10	LXX	70	$\overline{V}$	5,000		
V	5	XX	20	LXXX	80	$\overline{X}$	10,000		
VI	6	XXX	30	XC	90	$\overline{L}$	50,000		

Mean and Median

The arithmetic mean, also called the average, of a series of quantities is obtained by finding the sum of the quantities and dividing it by the number of quantities. In the series 1, 3, 5, 18, 19, 20, 25, the mean or average is 13—in other words, 91 divided by 7.

The median of a series is that point which so divides it that half the quantities are on one side, half on the other. In the above series, the median is 18.

The median often better expresses the common-run, since it is not, as is the mean, affected by an excessively high or low figure. In the series 1, 3, 4, 7, 55, the median of 4 is a truer expression of the common-run than is the mean of 14.

Prime Numbers between 1 and 1,000

	2	3	5	7	11	13	17	19	23
29	31	37	41	43	47	53	59	61	67
71	73	79	83	89	97	101	103	107	109
113	127	131	137	139	149	151	157	163	167
173	179	181	191	193	197	199	211	223	227
229	233	239	241	251	257	263	269	271	277
281	283	293	307	311	313	317	331	337	347
349	353	359	367	373	379	383	389	397	401
409	419	421	431	433	439	443	449	457	461
463	467	479	487	491	499	503	509	521	523
541	547	557	563	569	571	577	587	593	599
601	607	613	617	619	631	641	643	647	653
659	661	673	677	683	691	701	709	719	727
733	739	743	751	757	761	769	773	787	797
809	811	821	823	827	829	839	853	857	859
863	877	881	883	887	907	911	919	929	937
941	947	953	967	971	977	983	991	997	(1009)

Definitions of Gold Terminology

The term "fineness" defines a gold content in parts per thousand. For example, a gold nugget containing 885 parts of pure gold, 100 parts of silver, and 15 parts of copper would be considered 885-fine.

The word "karat" indicates the proportion of solid gold in an alloy based on a total of 24 parts. Thus, 14-karat (14K) gold indicates a composition of 14 parts of gold and 10 parts of other metals.

The term "gold-filled" is used to describe articles of jewelry made of base metal that are covered on one or more surfaces with a layer of gold alloy. No article having a gold alloy portion of less than one twentieth by weight may be marked "gold-filled." Articles may be marked "rolled gold plate" provided the proportional fraction and fineness designations are also shown.

Electroplated jewelry items carrying at least 7 millionths of an inch of gold on significant surfaces may be labeled "electroplate." Plate thicknesses less than this may be marked "gold-flashed" or "gold-washed."

Portraits and Designs of U.S. Paper Currency

Currency[1]	Portrait	Design on back
$1	Washington	ONE between obverse and reverse of Great Seal of U.S.
$2[2]	Jefferson	Monticello
$2[3]	Jefferson	"The Signing of the Declaration of Independence"
$5	Lincoln	Lincoln Memorial
$10	Hamilton	U.S. Treasury Building
$20	Jackson	White House
$50[4]	Grant	U.S. Capitol
$100[5]	Franklin	Independence Hall
$500	McKinley	Ornate FIVE HUNDRED
$1,000	Cleveland	Ornate ONE THOUSAND
$5,000	Madison	Ornate FIVE THOUSAND
$10,000	Chase	Ornate TEN THOUSAND
$100,000[6]	Wilson	Ornate ONE HUNDRED THOUSAND

1. Denominations of $500 and higher were discontinued in 1969. 2. Discontinued in 1966. 3. New issue, April 1976. 4. New issue, Fall 1997. 5. New issue, March 1996. 6. For use only in transactions between Federal Reserve System and Treasury Department.

Customary U.S. Weights and Measures

Linear Measure

12 inches (in.) = 1 foot (ft.)
3 feet = 1 yard (yd)
$5\frac{1}{2}$ yards = 1 rod (rd), pole, or perch ($16\frac{1}{2}$ ft.)
40 rods = 1 furlong (fur) = 220 yds = 660 ft.
8 furlongs = 1 statute mile (mi.) = 1,760 yds = 5,280 ft.
3 land miles = 1 league
5,280 feet = 1 statute or land mile
6,076.11549 feet = 1 international nautical mile

Area Measure

144 square inches = 1 sq ft.
9 square feet = 1 sq yd = 1,296 sq in.
$30\frac{1}{4}$ square yards = 1 sq rd = $272\frac{1}{4}$ sq ft.
160 square rods = 1 acre = 4,840 sq yds = 43,560 sq ft.
640 acres = 1 sq mi.
1 mile square = 1 section (of land)
6 miles square = 1 township = 36 sections = 36 sq mi.

Cubic Measure

1,728 cubic inches = 1 cu ft.
27 cubic feet = 1 cu yd

Liquid Measure

When necessary to distinguish the liquid pint or quart from the dry pint or quart, the word "liquid" or the abbreviation "liq" should be used in combination with the name or abbreviation of the liquid unit.

4 gills (gi) = 1 pint (pt) (= 28.875 cu in.)
2 pints = 1 quart (qt) (= 57.75 cu in.)
4 quarts = 1 gallon (gal) (= 231 cu in.) = 8 pts = 32 gills

Apothecaries' Fluid Measure

60 minims (min.) = 1 fluid dram (fl dr) (= 0.2256 cu in.)
8 fluid drams = 1 fluid ounce (fl oz) (= 1.8047 cu in.)
16 fluid ounces = 1 pt (= 28.875 cu in.) = 128 fl drs
2 pints = 1 qt (= 57.75 cu in.) = 32 fl oz = 256 fl drs
4 quarts = 1 gal (= 231 cu in.) = 128 fl oz = 1,024 fl drs

Dry Measure

When necessary to distinguish the dry pint or quart from the liquid pint or quart; the word "dry" should be used in combination with the name or abbreviation of the dry unit.

2 pints = 1 qt (=67.2006 cu in.)
8 quarts = 1 peck (pk) (=537.605 cu in.) = 16 pts
4 pecks = 1 bushel (bu) (= 2,150.42 cu in.) = 32 qts

Avoirdupois Weight

When necessary to distinguish the avoirdupois dram from the apothecaries' dram, or to distinguish the avoirdupois dram or ounce from the fluid dram or ounce, or to distinguish the avoirdupois ounce or pound from the troy or apothecaries' ounce or pound, the word "avoirdupois" or the abbreviation "avdp" should be used in combination with the name or abbreviation of the avoirdupois unit. (The "grain" is the same in avoirdupois, troy, and apothecaries' weights.)

$27\frac{11}{32}$ grains = 1 dram (dr)
16 drams = 1 oz = $437\frac{1}{2}$ grains
16 ounces = 1 lb = 256 drams = 7,000 grains
100 pounds = 1 hundredweight (cwt)[1]
20 hundredweights = 1 ton (tn) = 2,000 lbs[1]

In "gross" or "long" measure, the following values are recognized:

112 pounds = 1 gross or long cwt[1]
20 gross or long hundredweights = 1 gross or long ton = 2,240 lbs[1]

1. When the terms "hundredweight" and "ton" are used unmodified, they are commonly understood to mean the 100-pound hundredweight and the 2,000-pound ton, respectively; these units may be designated "net" or "short" when necessary to distinguish them from the corresponding units in gross or long measure.

Units of Circular Measure

Second (′) = —
Minute (′) = 60 seconds
Degree (°) = 60 minutes
Right angle = 90 degrees
Straight angle = 180 degrees
Circle = 360 degrees

Troy Weight

24 grains = 1 pennyweight (dwt)
20 pennyweights = 1 ounce troy (oz t) = 480 grains
12 ounces troy = 1 pound troy (lb t) = 240 pennyweights = 5,760 grains

Apothecaries' Weight

20 grains = 1 scruple (s ap)
3 scruples = 1 dram apothecaries' (dr ap) = 60 grains
8 drams apothecaries' = 1 ounce apothecaries' (oz ap) = 24 scruples = 480 grains
12 ounces apothecaries' = 1 pound apothecaries' (lb ap) = 96 drams apothecaries' = 288 scruples = 5,760 grains

Gunter's or Surveyor's Chain Measure

7.92 inches = 1 link (li)
100 links = 1 chain (ch) = 4 rods = 66 ft.
80 chains = 1 statute mile = 320 rods = 5,280 ft.

The International System (Metric)

Source: Department of Commerce, National Bureau of Standards.

The International System of Units is a modernized version of the metric system, established by international agreement, that provides a logical and interconnected framework for all measurements in science, industry, and commerce. The system is built on a foundation of seven basic units, and all other units are derived from them. (Use of metric weights and measures was legalized in the United States in 1866, and our customary units of weights and measures are defined in terms of the meter and kilogram.)

Length. Meter. Up until 1983, the meter was defined as 1,650,763.73 wavelengths in vacuum of the orange-red line of the spectrum of krypton-86. Since then, it is equal to the distance traveled by light in a vacuum in 1/299,792,45 of a second.

Time. Second. The second is defined as the duration of 9,192,631,770 cycles of the radiation associated with a specified transition of the cesium-133 atom.

Mass. Kilogram. The standard for the kilogram is a cylinder of platinum-iridium alloy kept by the International Bureau of Weights and Measures at Paris. A duplicate at the National Bureau of Standards serves as the mass standard for the United States. The kilogram is the only base unit still defined by a physical object.

Temperature. Kelvin. The Kelvin is defined as the fraction 1/273.16 of the thermodynamic temperature of the triple point of water; that is, the point at which water forms an interface of solid, liquid, and vapor. This is defined as 0.01°C on the Centigrade or Celsius scale and 32.02°F on the Fahrenheit scale. The temperature 0°K is called "absolute zero."

Electric Current. Electric current. The ampere is defined as that current that, if maintained in each of two long parallel wires separated by one meter in free space, would produce a force between the two wires (due to their magnetic fields) of 2×10^{-7} newton for each meter of length. (A newton is the unit of force that when applied to one kilogram mass would experience an acceleration of one meter per second per second.)

Luminous Intensity. Candela. The candela is defined as the luminous intensity of 1/600,000 of a square meter of a cavity at the temperature of freezing platinum (2,042°K).

Amount of Substance. Mole. The mole is the amount of substance of a system that contains as many elementary entities as there are atoms in 0.012 kilogram of carbon-12.

Tables of Metric Weights and Measures

Linear Measure

10 millimeters (mm) = 1 centimeter (cm)
10 centimeters = 1 decimeter (dm) = 100 millimeters
10 decimeters = 1 meter (m) = 1,000 millimeters
10 meters = 1 dekameter (dam)
10 dekameters = 1 hectometer (hm) = 100 meters
10 hectometers = 1 kilometer (km) = 1,000 meters

Area Measure

100 square millimeters (mm^2) = 1 sq centimeter (cm^2)
10,000 square centimeters = 1 sq meter (m^2) = 1,000,000 sq millimeters
100 square meters = 1 are (a)
100 ares = 1 hectare (ha) – 10,000 sq meters
100 hectares = 1 sq kilometer (km^2) = 1,000,000 sq meters

Volume Measure

10 milliliters (ml) = 1 centiliter (cl)
10 centiliters = 1 deciliter (dl) = 100 milliliters
10 deciliters = 1 liter (l) = 1,000 milliliters
10 liters = 1 dekaliter (dal)
10 dekaliters = 1 hectoliter (hl) = 100 liters
10 hectoliters = 1 kiloliter (kl) = 1,000 liters

Cubic Measure

1,000 cubic millimeters (mm^3) = 1 cu centimeter (cm^3)
1,000 cubic centimeters = 1 cu decimeter (dm^3) = 1,000,000 cu millimeters
1,000 cubic decimeters = 1 cu meter (m^3) = 1 stere = 1,000,000 cu centimeters = 1,000,000,000 cu millimeters

Weight

10 milligrams (mg) = 1 centigram (cg)
10 centigrams = 1 decigram (dg) = 100 milligrams
10 decigrams = 1 gram (g) = 1,000 milligrams
10 grams = 1 dekagram (dag)
10 dekagrams = 1 hectogram (hg) = 100 grams
10 hectograms = 1 kilogram (kg) = 1,000 grams
1,000 kilograms = 1 metric ton (t)

Kelvin Scale

Absolute zero, –273.15° on the Celsius (Centigrade) scale, is 0° Kelvin. Thus, Kelvin is equivalent to Celsius plus 273.15. The freezing point of water, 0°C and 32°F, is 273.15°K. The conversion formula is K° = C° + 273.15.

Metric and U.S. Equivalents

1 angstrom[1] (light wave measurement)	0.1 millimicron 0.000 1 micron 0.000 000 1 millimeter 0.000 000 004 inch
1 cable's length	120 fathoms 720 feet 219.456 meters
1 centimeter	0.3937 inch
1 decimeter	3.937 inches
1 dekameter	32.808 feet
1 fathom	6 feet 1.8288 meters
1 foot	0.3048 meter
1 furlong	10 chains (surveyor's) 660 feet 220 yards 1/8 statute mile 201.168 meters
1 inch	2.54 centimeters
1 kilometer	0.621 mile
1 league (land)	3 statute miles 4.828 kilometers
1 meter	39.37 inches 1.094 yards
1 micron	0.001 millimeter 0.000 039 37 inch
1 mil	0.001 inch 0.025 4 millimeter
1 mile (statute or land)	5,280 feet 1.609 kilometers
1 mile (nautical international)	1.852 kilometers 1.151 statute miles 0.999 U.S. nautical miles
1 millimeter	0.03937 inch
1 millimicron (m+GRKm)	0.001 micron 0.000 000 039 37 inch
1 nanometer	0.001 micrometer or 0.000 000 039 37 inch
1 point (typography)	0.013 837 inch 1/72 inch (approximately) 0.351 millimeter
1 rod, pole, or perch	16½ feet 5.0292 meters
1 yard	0.9144 meter

Areas or Surfaces

1 acre	43,560 square feet 4,840 square yards 0.405 hectare
1 are	119.599 square yards 0.025 acre
1 hectare	2.471 acres
1 square centimeter	0.155 square inch
1 square decimeter	15.5 square inches
1 square foot	929.030 square centimeters
1 square inch	6.4516 square centimeters
1 square kilometer	0.386 square mile 247.105 acres
1 square meter	1.196 square yards 10.764 square feet
1 square mile	258.999 hectares
1 square millimeter	0.002 square inch
1 square rod, square pole or square perch	25.293 square meters
1 square yard	0.836 square meters

Capacities or Volumes

1 barrel, liquid	31 to 42 gallons[2]
1 bushel (U.S.) struck measure	2,150.42 cubic inches 35.238 liters
1 bushel, heaped (U.S.)	2,747.715 cubic inches 1.278 bushels, struck measure[3]
1 cord (firewood)	128 cubic feet
1 cubic centimeter	0.061 cubic inch
1 cubic decimeter	61.024 cubic inches
1 cubic foot	7.481 gallons 28.316 cubic decimeters
1 cubic inch	0.554 fluid ounce 4.433 fluid drams 16.387 cubic centimeters
1 cubic meter	1.308 cubic yards
1 cubic yard	0.765 cubic meter

1 cup, measuring	8 fluid ounces ½ liquid pint
1 dram, fluid or liquid (U.S.)	⅛ fluid ounces 0.226 cubic inch 3.697 milliliters 1.041 British fluid drachms
1 dekaliter	2.642 gallons 1.135 pecks
1 gallon (U.S.)	231 cubic inches 3.785 liters 0.833 British gallon 128 U.S. fluid ounces
1 gallon (British Imperial)	277.42 cubic inches 1.201 U.S. gallons 4.546 liters 160 British fluid ounces
1 hectoliter	26.418 gallons 2.838 bushels
1 liter	1.057 liquid quarts 0.908 dry quart 61.024 cubic inches
1 milliliter	0.271 fluid dram 16.231 minims 0.061 cubic inch
1 ounce, fluid or liquid (U.S.)	1.805 cubic inch 29.574 milliliters 1.041 British fluid ounces
1 peck	8.810 liters
1 pint, dry	33.600 cubic inches 0.551 liter
1 pint, liquid	28.875 cubic inches 0.473 liter
1 quart, dry (U.S.)	67.201 cubic inches 1.101 liters 0.969 British quart
1 quart, liquid (U.S.)	57.75 cubic inches 0.946 liter 0.833 British quart
1 quart (British)	69.354 cubic inches 1.032 U.S. dry quarts 1.201 U.S. liquid quarts
1 tablespoon, measuring	3 teaspoons 4 fluid drams ½ fluid ounce
1 teaspoon, measuring	⅓ tablespoon 1⅓ fluid drams
1 carat	200 milligrams 3.086 grains
1 dram, apothecaries'	60 grains 3.888 grams
1 dram, avoirdupois	27 11/32 (=27.344) grains 1.772 grams
1 grain	64.798 91 milligrams
1 gram	15.432 grains 0.035 ounce, avoirdupois
1 kilogram	2.205 pounds
1 microgram (μg—the Greek letter mu in combination with the letter g)	0.000 001 gram
1 milligram	0.015 grain
1 ounce, avoirdupois	437.5 grains 0.911 troy or apothecaries', ounce 28.350 grams
1 ounce, troy or apothecaries'	480 grains 1.097 avoirdupois ounces 31.103 grams
1 pennyweight	1.555 grams
1 point	0.01 carat 2 milligrams
1 pound, avoirdupois	7,000 grains 1.215 troy or apothecaries' pounds 453.592 37 grams
1 pound, troy or apothecaries'	5,760 grains 0.823 avoirdupois pound 373.242 grams
1 ton, gross or long[4]	2,240 pounds 1.12 net tons 1.016 metric tons
1 ton, metric	2,204.623 pounds 0.984 gross ton 1.102 net tons
1 ton, net or short	2,000 pounds 0.893 gross ton 0.907 metric ton

1. The angstrom is basically defined as 10^{-10} meter. 2. There is a variety of "barrels" established by law or usage. For example, federal taxes on fermented liquors are based on a barrel of 31 gallons; many state laws fix the "barrel for liquids" at 31½ gallons; one state fixes a 36-gallon barrel for cistern measurement; federal law recognizes a 40-gallon barrel for "proof spirits"; by custom, 42 gallons compose a barrel of crude oil or petroleum products for statistical purposes, and this equivalent is recognized "for liquids" by four states. 3. Frequently recognized as 1¼ bushels, struck measure. 4. The gross or long ton is used commercially in the United States to only a limited extent, usually in restricted industrial fields. These units are the same as the British "ton."

Conversion of Miles to Kilometers and Kilometers to Miles

Miles	Kilometers	Miles	Kilometers	Miles	Kilometers	Kilometers	Miles	Kilometers	Miles	Kilometers	Miles
1	1.6	8	12.8	60	96.5	1	0.6	8	4.9	60	37.2
2	3.2	9	14.4	70	112.6	2	1.2	9	5.5	70	43.4
3	4.8	10	16.0	80	128.7	3	1.8	10	6.2	80	49.7
4	6.4	20	32.1	90	144.8	4	2.4	20	12.4	90	55.9
5	8.0	30	48.2	100	160.9	5	3.1	30	18.6	100	62.1
6	9.6	40	64.3	1,000	1609.0	6	3.7	40	24.8	1,000	621.0
7	11.2	50	80.4			7	4.3	50	31.0		

Bolts and Screws: Conversion from Fractions of an Inch to Millimeters

Inch	mm	Inch	mm	Inch	mm	Inch	mm
1/64	0.40	17/64	6.75	33/64	13.10	49/64	19.45
1/32	0.79	9/32	7.14	17/32	13.50	25/32	19.84
3/64	1.19	19/64	7.54	35/64	13.90	51/64	20.24
1/16	1.59	5/16	7.94	9/16	14.29	13/16	20.64
5/64	1.98	21/64	8.33	37/64	14.69	53/64	21.03
3/32	2.38	11/32	8.73	19/32	15.08	27/32	21.43
7/64	2.78	23/64	9.13	39/64	15.48	55/64	21.83
1/8	3.18	3/8	9.53	5/8	15.88	7/8	22.23
9/64	3.57	25/64	9.92	41/64	16.27	57/64	22.62
5/32	3.97	13/32	10.32	21/32	16.67	29/32	23.02
11/64	4.37	27/64	10.72	43/64	17.06	59/64	23.42
3/16	4.76	7/16	11.11	11/16	17.46	15/16	23.81
13/64	5.16	29/64	11.51	45/64	17.86	61/64	24.21
7/32	5.56	15/32	11.91	23/32	18.26	31/32	24.61
15/64	5.95	31/64	12.30	47/64	18.65	63/64	25.00
1/4	6.35	1/2	12.70	3/4	19.05	1	25.40

Cooking Measurement Equivalents

16 tablespoons = 1 cup
12 tablespoons = 3/4 cup
10 tablespoons + 2 teaspoons = 2/3 cup
8 tablespoons = 1/2 cup
6 tablespoons = 3/8 cup
5 tablespoons + 1 teaspoon = 1/3 cup
4 tablespoons = 1/4 cup

2 tablespoons = 1/8 cup
2 tablespoons + 2 teaspoons = 1/6 cup
1 tablespoon = 1/16 cup
2 cups = 1 pint
2 pints = 1 quart
3 teaspoons = 1 tablespoon
48 teaspoons = 1 cup

U.S.–Metric Cooking Conversions

U.S. to Metric

Capacity		Weight	
1/5 teaspoon	1 milliliter	1 oz	28 grams
1 teaspoon	5 ml	1 pound	454 grams
1 tablespoon	15 ml		
1 fluid oz	30 ml		
1/5 cup	50 ml		
1 cup	240 ml		
2 cups (1 pint)	470 ml		
4 cups (1 quart)	.95 liter		
4 quarts (1 gal.)	3.8 liters		

Metric to U.S.

Capacity		Weight	
1 milliliter	1/5 teaspoon	1 gram	.035 ounce
5 ml	1 teaspoon	100 grams	3.5 ounces
15 ml	1 tablespoon	500 grams	1.10 pounds
100 ml	3.4 fluid oz	1 kilogram	2.205 pounds
240 ml	1 cup		35 oz
1 liter	34 fluid oz		
	4.2 cups		
	2.1 pints		
	1.06 quarts		
	0.26 gallon		

Prefixes and Multiples

Prefix	Suffix	Equivalent	Multiple/submultiple	Prefix	Suffix	Equivalent	Multiple/submultiple
atto	a	quintillionth part	10^{-18}	deci	d	tenth part	10^{-1}
femto	f	quadrillionth part	10^{-15}	deka	da	tenfold	10
pico	p	trillionth part	10^{-12}	hecto	h	hundredfold	10^{2}
nano	n	billionth part	10^{-9}	kilo	k	thousandfold	10^{3}
micro	μ	millionth part	10^{-6}	mega	M	millionfold	10^{6}
milli	m	thousandth part	10^{-3}	giga	G	billionfold	10^{9}
centi	c	hundredth part	10^{-2}	tera	T	trillionfold	10^{12}

Common Formulas

Circumference

Circle: $C = \pi d$, in which π is 3.1416 and d the diameter.

Area

Triangle: $A = \frac{ab}{2}$, in which a is the base and b the height.

Square: $A = a^2$, in which a is one of the sides.

Rectangle: $A = ab$, in which a is the base and b the height.

Trapezoid: $A = \frac{h(a+b)}{2}$, in which h is the height, a the longer parallel side, and b the shorter.

Regular pentagon: $A = 1.720a^2$, in which a is one of the sides.

Regular hexagon: $A = 2.598a^2$, in which a is one of the sides.

Regular octagon: $A = 4.828a^2$, in which a is one of the sides.

Circle: $A = \pi r^2$, in which π is 3.1416 and r the radius.

Volume

Cube: $V = a^3$, in which a is one of the edges.

Rectangular prism: $V = abc$, in which a is the length, b is the width, and c the depth.

Pyramid: $V = \frac{Ah}{3}$, in which A is the area of the base and h the height.

Cylinder: $V = \pi r^2 h$, in which π is 3.1416, r the radius of the base, and h the height.

Cone: $V = \frac{\pi r^2 h}{3}$, in which π is 3.1416, r the radius of the base, and h the height.

Sphere: $V = \frac{4 \pi r^3}{3}$, in which π is 3.1416 and r the radius.

Temperature Scales

Degrees Fahrenheit to Degrees Celsius:

$$T_C = \frac{5}{9} (T_F - 32)$$

Degrees Celsius to Degrees Fahrenheit:

$$T_F = \frac{9}{5} T_C + 32$$

Degrees Celsius to Kelvin:

$$T_K = T_C + 273.15$$

Miscellaneous

Distance in feet traveled by falling body:
$d = 16t^2$, in which t is the time in seconds.

Speed of sound in feet per second through any given temperature of air:

$V = \frac{1087 \sqrt{273 + t}}{16.52}$, in which t is the temperature Celsius.

Cost in cents of operation of electrical device:

$C = \frac{Wtc}{1000}$, in which W is the number of watts, t the time in hours, and c the cost in cents per kilowatt-hour.

Conversion of matter into energy (Einstein's Theorem): $E = mc^2$, in which E is the energy in ergs, m the mass of the matter in grams, and c the speed of light in centimeters per second:

$$(c^2 = 9 \times 10^{20})$$

Decimal Equivalents of Common Fractions

1/2	.5000	1/10	.1000	2/7	.2857	3/11	.2727	5/9	.5556	7/11	.6364
1/3	.3333	1/11	.0909	2/9	.2222	4/5	.8000	5/11	.4545	7/12	.5833
1/4	.2500	1/12	.0833	2/11	.1818	4/7	.5714	5/12	.4167	8/9	.8889
1/5	.2000	1/16	.0625	3/4	.7500	4/9	.4444	6/7	.8571	8/11	.7273
1/6	.1667	1/32	.0313	3/5	.6000	4/11	.3636	6/11	.5455	9/10	.9000
1/7	.1429	1/64	.0156	3/7	.4286	5/6	.8333	7/8	.8750	9/11	.8182
1/8	.1250	2/3	.6667	3/8	.3750	5/7	.7143	7/9	.7778	10/11	.9091
1/9	.1111	2/5	.4000	3/10	.3000	5/8	.6250	7/10	.7000	11/12	.9167

Miscellaneous Units of Measure

acre An area of 43,560 square feet. Originally, the area a yoke of oxen could plow in one day.

agate Originally a measurement of type size (5½ points). Now equal to 1/14 inch. Used in printing for measuring column length.

ampere Unit of electric current. A potential difference of one volt across a resistance of one ohm produces a current of one ampere.

astronomical unit (A.U.) 93,000,000 miles, the average distance of the earth from the sun. Used for astronomy.

bale A large bundle of goods. In the U.S., the approximate weight of a bale of cotton is 500 pounds. The weight varies in other countries.

board foot (fbm) 144 cubic inches (12 in. × 12 in. × 1 in.). Used for lumber.

bolt 40 yards. Used for measuring cloth.

Btu British thermal unit. Amount of heat needed to increase the temperature of one pound of water by one degree Fahrenheit (252 calories).

carat (c) 200 milligrams or 3.086 grains troy. Originally the weight of a seed of the carob tree in the Mediterranean region. Used for weighing precious stones.

chain (ch) A chain 66 feet or one-tenth of a furlong in length, divided into 100 parts called links. One mile is equal to 80 chains. Used in surveying and sometimes called Gunter's or Surveyor's chain.

cubit 18 inches or 45.72 cm. Derived from distance between elbow and tip of middle finger.

decibel Unit of relative loudness. One decibel is the smallest amount of change detectable by the human ear.

ell, English 1¼ yards or 1/32 bolt. Used for measuring cloth.

freight, ton (also called measurement ton) 40 cubic feet of merchandise. Used for cargo freight.

great gross 12 gross or 1728.

gross 12 dozen or 144.

hand 4 inches or 10.16 cm. Derived from the width of the hand. Used for measuring the height of horses at withers.

hertz Modern unit for measurement of electromagnetic wave frequencies (equivalent to "cycles per second").

hogshead (hhd) 2 liquid barrels or 14,653 cubic inches.

horsepower The power needed to lift 33,000 pounds a distance of one foot in one minute (about 1½ times the power an average horse can exert). Used for measuring power of steam engines, etc.

karat (kt) A measure of the purity of gold, indicating how many parts out of 24 are pure. For example: 18-karat gold is ¾ pure. Sometimes spelled *carat.*

knot Not a distance, but the rate of speed of one nautical mile per hour. Used for measuring speed of ships.

league Rather indefinite and varying measure, but usually estimated at 3 miles in English-speaking countries.

light-year 5,880,000,000,000 miles, the distance light travels in a vacuum in a year at the rate of 186,281.7 miles (299,792 kilometers) per second. (If an astronomical unit were represented by one inch, a light-year would be represented by about one mile.) Used for measurements in interstellar space.

magnum Two-quart bottle. Used for measuring wine, etc.

ohm Unit of electrical resistance. A circuit in which a potential difference of one volt produces a current of one ampere has a resistance of one ohm.

parsec Approximately 3.26 light-years of 19.2 million miles. Term is combination of first syllables of *par*allax and *sec*ond, and distance is that of imaginary star when lines drawn from it to both Earth and the Sun form a maximum angle or parallax of one second (1/3600 degree). Used for measuring interstellar distances.

pi (π) 3.14159265+. The ratio of the circumference of a circle to its diameter. For practical purposes, the value is used to four decimal places: 3.1416.

pica 1/6 inch or 12 points. Used in printing for measuring column width, etc.

pipe 2 hogsheads. Used for measuring wine and other liquids.

point .013837 (approximately 1/72) inch or 1/12 pica. Used in printing for measuring type size.

quintal 100,000 grams or 220.46 pounds avoirdupois.

quire Used for measuring paper. Sometimes 24 sheets but more often 25. There are 20 quires to a ream.

ream Used for measuring paper. Sometimes 480 sheets, but more often 500 sheets.

roentgen International Unit of radiation exposure produced by X-rays.

score 20 units.

sound, speed of Usually placed at 1,088 ft. per second at 32°F at sea level. It varies at other temperatures and in different media.

span 9 inches or 22.86 cm. Derived from the distance between the end of the thumb and the end of the little finger when both are outstretched.

square 100 square feet. Used in building.

stone Legally 14 pounds avoirdupois in the U.K.

therm 100,000 Btus.

township U.S. land measurement of almost 36 square miles. The south border is 6 miles long. The east and west borders, also 6 miles long, follow the meridians, making the north border slightly less than 6 miles long. Used in surveying.

tun 252 gallons, but often larger. Used for measuring wine and other liquids.

watt Unit of power. The power used by a current of one ampere across a potential difference of one volt equals one watt.

Clean As a Breeze

With smarter energy options becoming more accessible, fossil fuels may soon go the way of the dinosaurs

By CHRISTOPHER FLAVIN TIME

Over the past several years, a new crop has sprouted across the broad, fertile plains of northern Germany. Sprinkled among the barns and silos are thousands of 100-ft.-tall towers topped by sleek, fiberglass blades that whirl slowly in the breeze. Functioning as clean, trim powerhouses, these modern windmills turn even gentle currents of air into strong currents of electricity, energizing the region's businesses and homes without hurting the environment.

Half a world away, on the Indonesian island of Java, hundreds of rural families have mounted small, silvery panels on poles near their homes. Made of silicon semiconductor chips similar to the microprocessors found in computers, the solar cells convert the energy of sunshine into electricity. These almost magical devices make it possible for people living a day's walk from the nearest power lines to turn on light bulbs, radios, and TV sets for the first time.

In Europe, Southeast Asia, and all sorts of places in between, something remarkable is happening. New, carbon-free energy technologies that do not rely on fossil fuels are moving from experimental curiosity to commercial reality, economically turning sunlight, wind, and other renewable resources into useful forms of energy. Although the new devices provide less than 1% of the world's energy, they are advancing rapidly. These are the technologies that could provide the blueprint for an engineering solution to the problems of global warming and climate change.

It's been nearly a century since the world has had a comparable opportunity. Much of the energy system now in place was created in an explosion of invention that began around 1890 and was largely finished by 1910. Cities all over the world were transformed as automobiles and electric lights replaced horse-drawn carriages and gas lamps. Old technologies that had prevailed for centuries became obsolete in a matter of years, and the 20th century emerged as the age of fossil fuels.

We may be at a similar turning point today. Thanks to a potent combination of government incentives and private investment, technologies that use synthetic materials, advanced electronics, and biotechnology are sweeping through the energy industry. They could foster a new generation of mass-produced machines that efficiently and cleanly provide the energy that enables people to take a hot shower, sip a cold beer, or surf the Internet. The transition to a 21st-century energy system is gathering speed on at least four fronts:

• **Here Comes the Sun** The world market for solar cells has gone from $340 million in 1988 to roughly $1 billion in 1991—a growth spurt brought on by a 95% decline in the cost of these devices since the 1970s. Although the electricity they put out is still far more expensive than that produced by conventional generators, solar cells are the least expensive source of power for rural homes not connected to a region's electric grid. Further advances may make solar power an economically attractive option for many urban buildings within the next decade.

That prospect is stirring excitement around the globe. In Japan, housing companies have introduced a type of dwelling with silicon roof tiles that generate enough electricity to meet most of a family's needs. Spurred by government incentives, construction of some 70,000 of these houses is expected in the next several years. In Switzerland and Germany, dozens of office buildings have been built with solar cells integrated into the glass of south-facing walls, allowing the windows to produce power while transmitting filtered sunlight.

• **Blowing in the Wind** The global wind-power industry, a $2 billion-a-year business, has seen its market nearly quadruple since 1992. Two decades of research have yielded a thoroughly modern wind turbine with tough fiber-glass blades and electronic controls. The cost of the electricity produced is comparable to that of fossil-fuel power and still falling.

Thousands of wind turbines have been installed in a dozen European countries. In 1997 Denmark got 6% of its electricity from wind power. Developers have started to install windmills in the shallow North Sea, whose winds could one day meet much of Europe's power needs. The boom is also being felt in Asia, where wind-power companies, in joint ventures with Europeans, are installing turbines in India and China.

• **No Smoke in Your Eyes** Several companies in Europe and the U.S. are marketing a new generation of micro-power plants small enough to fit in your basement. Not only do they generate electricity, but their excess heat warms the house. These new-age power plants are based on tiny engines and produce electricity less expensively than multibillion-dollar coal and nuclear plants.

An even more advanced technology, the fuel cell, is being pioneered by a small Canadian company called Ballard Power Systems. The fuel cell combines hydrogen and oxygen to generate electricity cleanly and quietly; the only waste it produces is water. Small, mass-produced, and without moving parts, the devices are a spin-off of the U.S. space program, which uses them to meet the electricity needs of the shuttle fleet. Fuel cells could one day sit in millions of basements producing power and hot water without fossil fuels.

• **Take the T-Bird Away** After 80 years of dominance by the internal-combustion engine, a new kind of automobile is on the way. Several major auto manufacturers are designing hybrid electric cars that have twice the fuel economy and half the carbon-dioxide emissions of today's vehicles. The sticker price is admittedly a few thousand dollars higher but is largely offset by lower fuel bills. Toyota brought the first such car to the market in Japan in December 1997, and other carmakers will quickly follow suit.

Like the computer industry, with which it shares many technologies, the clean-energy business is being led by dozens of entrepreneurial start-up companies, many of them financed with venture capital. But as business has boomed in the past few years, major corporations have jumped in. The lure is obvious: the use of wind and solar power is growing more than 25% a year, while the markets for coal and oil are expanding only 1% to 2%.

How quickly the world's energy systems are transformed will depend in part on whether fossil-fuel prices remain low and the entrenched opposition of many oil and electric-power companies can be overcome. In the 1980s, California provided tax incentives and access to the power grid for new energy sources, which enabled the state to dominate renewable-energy markets worldwide. Similar incentives and access have been offered by European countries in the 1990s. Sometimes such measures are needed to overcome the momentum of a century's investment in fossil fuels.

Although many economists argue that it will be difficult and expensive to find an alternative to oil and coal—and that we should delay the transition for as long as possible—their position is based on a technological pessimism that seems out of place today. The first automobiles and computers were difficult to use and expensive, but the pioneers persevered and made improvements, and ultimately triumphed in the marketplace.

Just as automobiles followed horses and computers displaced typewriters, so can the advance of technology make today's smokestacks and gas-powered cars look primitive, inefficient, and uneconomical. Unlike fossil fuels, renewable energy never runs out, and geologists will not have to travel to the Alaskan North Slope or the shores of the Caspian Sea to find new sources. The sunlight falling on the surface of the earth each day contains 6,000 times as much energy as is used by all countries combined. Studies show that covering the existing flat-roof space of many cities with solar cells could meet half to three-quarters of their electricity needs. In the U.S., North Dakota, South Dakota, and Texas together are swept by sufficient wind to meet the electricity needs of the entire country.

The coming generation of new energy technologies offers a ray of hope. In order to wean ourselves from the fossil fuels that are choking the planet, we need reliable alternatives. If anything can be done to accelerate the new technologies, we may all breathe a little easier. □

Renewable Energy Consumption in U.S. by Source, 1990–1997

(quadrillion Btu)

Year	Biofuels[1]	Geothermal energy[2]	Conventional hydroelectric power[3, 4]	Solar energy[5]	Wind energy[6]	Total
1990	2.632	r0.355	r3.123	r0.063	0.023	r6.197
1991	2.642	r0.365	r3.205	r0.066	0.027	r6.304
1992	2.788	r0.379	r2.863	0.068	0.030	r6.128
1993	2.784	r0.393	r3.147	r0.071	0.031	r6.426
1994	2.838	r0.395	r2.969	r0.072	0.036	r6.309
1995	r2.846	r0.339	r3.472	r0.073	0.033	r6.763
1996	r2.938	r0.352	r3.914	0.075	r0.035	r7.315
1997e	2.723	0.366	3.942	0.075	0.039	7.145

1. Wood, wood waste, wood liquors, peat, railroad ties, wood sludge, spent sulfite liquors, agricultural waste, straw, tires, fish oils, tall oil, sludge waste, waste alcohol, municipal solid waste, landfill gases, other waste, and ethanol blended into motor gasoline. 2. Includes electricity imports from Mexico that are derived from geothermal energy. Includes grid-connected electricity, and geothermal heat pump and direct use energy. Excludes shaft power and remote electrical power. 3. Hydroelectricity generated by pumped storage is not included in renewable energy. 4. Includes electricity net imports from Canada that are derived from hydroelectric power. 5. Includes solar thermal and photovoltaic energy. 6. Includes only grid-connected electricity. Excludes direct heat applications. r = revised. e = estimated. *Source:* Energy Information Administration (EIA), Office of Coal, Nuclear, Electric and Alternative Fuels estimates, and Oregon Institute of Technology.

Energy Overview

Source: Annual Energy Review, 1997.

Production

Historically, three fossil fuels have accounted for the bulk of domestic energy production, which by 1997 totaled 72.3 quadrillion Btu. Coal accounted for the largest share of domestic energy production in 1949–1951 and, after a long hiatus, again in 1982 and in 1984 through 1997. In the interim, first crude oil and then natural gas dominated domestic production. In 1997, coal production totaled 23.2 quadrillion Btu. Dry natural gas production totaled 19.5 quadrillion Btu and crude oil production totaled 13.6 quadrillion Btu. Natural gas plant liquids accounted for another 2.5 quadrillion Btu.

Net generation of electricity by electric utilities increased throughout the 1949–1996 period, registering only two year-to-year declines (during the 1982 recession and again in 1992). However, the rate of growth of electricity net generation slowed during the 48-year period. From 1949 through 1979, the annual growth rate averaged 7.1%, whereas from 1980 through 1996, the annual growth rate averaged 1.9%. After the mid-1970s, coal and nuclear fuels provided increasing shares of fuel input for electricity generation, displacing substantial quantities of petroleum and, to a lesser extent, natural gas.

Hydroelectric generation (conventional and pumped storage) accounted for over 1.4 quadrillion Btu of electricity in 1949, and from the 1970s through 1995 usually provided about 3 quadrillion Btu per year. In 1988, the second year of drought, hydroelectric generation totaled only 2.3 quadrillion Btu, but it reached a record high in 1997 of 3.7 quadrillion Btu.

Other renewable energy sources also contributed to the domestic energy supply. Biofuels, a category that includes wood and waste, contributed 2.7 quadrillion Btu to the 1997 total. Geothermal, solar, and wind energy combined contributed 0.5 quadrillion Btu. Renewable energy production (including conventional hydroelectric power and excluding hydroelectric pumped storage) totaled 6.9 quadrillion Btu, 9.6% of U.S. total energy production.

Consumption

Energy consumption more than doubled during the 1949–1973 period, increasing from 30.5 quadrillion Btu in 1949 to 74.3 quadrillion Btu in 1973, and the U.S. economy grew at about the same rate. The domestic energy market was dominated by rapid growth in petroleum and natural gas consumption, which more than tripled during the period. After the 1973 oil shock, energy consumption fluctuated, influenced by dramatic changes in oil prices, changes in the rate of growth of the domestic economy, and such factors as concerns about the effect of energy use on the environment. The post-1973 low point of energy consumption, 70.5 quadrillion Btu, occurred in 1983 following a period of very high oil prices. The highest level of energy consumption, 94.2 quadrillion Btu, occurred in 1997, following several years when oil prices were low.

The composition of demand after 1973 reflected an increasing emphasis on electricity generated by coal, nuclear, and renewable energy sources and on non-electric utility use of renewable sources. In 1973, petroleum and natural gas accounted for 77% of total energy consumption; by 1995, their share had declined to 63%.

Changing Patterns of Trade

From 1958 forward, the United States consumed more energy than it produced, and the difference was met by energy imports. Net imports of energy (primarily petroleum) grew rapidly through 1973, as demand for cheap foreign oil eroded quotas on petroleum imports. The oil embargo of 1973–1974, coupled with the increase in the price of crude oil, interrupted growth in petroleum net imports; nevertheless, they climbed to a peak of 18 quadrillion Btu in 1977. That year, U.S. dependence on foreign sources of petroleum reached an all-time high of 47%. A second round of price increases in 1979 through 1981 suppressed demand for foreign oil. In 1985, petroleum net imports totaled 9.0 quadrillion Btu, and U.S. dependence fell to 27% of consumption. Subsequently, petroleum net imports increased every year through 1989, when U.S. dependence on foreign sources of petroleum reached 42% of consumption. In 1996, petroleum net imports rose to 18 quadrillion Btu and U.S. dependence on them equaled 46%—the second highest level in 19 years.

Natural gas trade was limited to border countries until the advent of shipping natural gas in liquefied form in the late 1960s. In 1997, natural gas net imports reached the record level of 2.9 quadrillion Btu.

Throughout the 1949–1997 period, the United States was a net exporter of coal. In 1997, coal net exports totaled 2.0 quadrillion Btu. □

World Greenhouse Gas Emissions

Source: Annual Energy Review, 1997.

As concerns about global warming continue to mount, attention is turning again to the so-called "greenhouse effect" and the gas emissions thought to cause it. Anthropogenic, or human-caused, emissions are suspected to be the chief cause of the greenhouse effect.

Carbon Dioxide. Carbon dioxide is the largest component of human-caused emissions, accounting for 5.5 billion metric tons of gas in 1996, up from 4.7 billion metric tons in 1985. Emissions caused by the burning of fossil fuels totaled 1.5 billion metric tons in 1996. (There is one metric ton of carbon in every 3.667 metric tons of carbon dioxide gas.) Consumption of petroleum products to fuel automobiles, burning of coal to produce electricity, and use of natural gas, were the biggest sources of carbon dioxide emissions in 1996.

Energy Web Sites

U.S. Department of Energy: www.doe.gov
Energy Efficiency and Renewable Energy Network (EREN): www.eren.doe.gov
Federal Energy Regulatory Commission: www.ferc.fed.us
Energy Information Administration (EIA): www.eia.doe.gov
Nuclear Regulatory Commission (NRC): www.nrc.gov
National Renewable Energy Laboratory (NREL): www.nrel.gov
Alliance to Save Energy: www.ase.org
Natural Resources Defense Council: www.nrdc.org
American Council for an Energy-Efficient Economy: www.aceee.org
The Center for Renewable Energy and Sustainable Technology (Solstice): www.solstice.crest.org

Methane. Energy-related activities also accounted for the largest share of methane emissions (11.6 million metric tons) in 1996. Landfills were responsible for another 10.3 million metric tons, and agricultural sources (such as digestive processes in ruminant animals like cattle, sheep, and goats, and the anaerobic decomposition of organic materials in animal waste and rice paddies) emitted 8.8 million metric tons in 1996.

Nitrous Oxide. Emissions of nitrous oxide, which, molecule for molecule, has a warming potential greater than either carbon dioxide or methane, dropped to 0.4 million metric tons of gas per year after having stayed at 0.5 million from 1991 through 1995.

Electric Power Generation. In 1996, electric utilities and nonutility power producers (NPPs) combined emitted 2.7 billion short tons of carbon dioxide, 13.7 million short tons of sulfur dioxide, and 9.1 million short tons of nitrogen oxides. Emissions of carbon dioxide and nitrogen oxides were 13.5% and 3.1% higher, respectively, than in 1989, the earliest year for which data for both utilities and NPPs are available. Sulfur dioxide emissions fell 17.7% over the period, due primarily to greater use of lower-sulfur coal and of scrubbers at electric utility coal-fired generating units.

NPPs raised their total net electric output by 27% between 1992 and 1995 at a cost of a 9% increase in carbon dioxide emissions. Electric utilities' total net output increased 7% during the period, while their emissions of carbon dioxide rose 4%. The ratio difference is due in part to fuel use patterns: NPPs rely on natural gas for 52% of their output and natural gas has the lowest carbon content of the fossil fuels. Electric utilities produce 54% of their output using coal, which has the highest carbon content.

Nuclear Power Generation Status

Source: Annual Energy Review, 1997.

Nuclear electric power production in 1996 totaled 629 billion kilowatt-hours, down from 675 billion kilowatt-hours in 1996. At the end of 1997, there were 107 licensed operable nuclear generating units in the United States, most of them located east of the Mississippi River. No new plants had been ordered or announced in 1997.

The Three Mile Island accident in 1979 greatly increased concerns about the safety of nuclear power plants. In response to these concerns, new regulations governing the operation and construction of nuclear facilities were implemented. The new guidelines made nuclear plants even more expensive to build and run, which has also contributed to the decline in the number of planned nuclear units. □

Largest Nuclear Power Plants in the United States

Plant	Operating utility	Capacity (net MWe)	Year operative
Palo Verde 3, Ariz.	Arizona Public Service	1253	1987
South Texas 1, Tex.	Houston Lighting & Power	1251	1988
South Texas 2 , Tex.	Houston Lighting & Power	1251	1989
Palo Verde 1, Ariz.	Arizona Public Service	1249	1985
Palo Verde 2, Ariz.	Arizona Public Service	1249	1986
Comanche Peak 1, Tex.	Texas Utilities	1215	1990
Comanche Peak 2, Tex.	Texas Utilities	1215	1993
Grand Gulf 1, Miss.	System Energy Resources	1179	1984
Perry 1, Ohio	Cleveland Electric Illuminating	1169	1986
Vogtle 1, Ga.	Georgia Power	1164	1987
Vogtle 2 , Ga.	Georgia Power	1164	1989
Wolf Creek, Kans.	Wolf Creek Nuclear Operating	1163	1985
Sequoyah 1, Tenn.	Tennessee Valley Authority	1162	1980
Seabrook 1, N.H.	Public Service of N.H.	1162	1990
Catawba 1, S.C.	Duke Power Co.	1129	1985
Catawba 2, S.C.	Duke Power Co.	1129	1986
McGuire 1, N.C.	Duke Power Co.	1129	1981
McGuire 2, N.C.	Duke Power Co.	1129	1983
Callaway, Mo.	Union Electric	1125	1984
Watts Bar 1, Tenn.	Tennessee Valley Authority	1122	1996
Byron 1, Ill.	Commonwealth Edison	1120	1985
Byron 2, Ill.	Commonwealth Edison	1120	1987
Millstone 3, Conn.	Northeast Nuclear Energy	1120	1986
Limerick 2 , Pa.	Philadelphia Electric	1115	1989
Washington 2, Wash.	General Electric Company	1107	1984
Sequoyah 2, Tenn.	Tennessee Valley Authority	1106	1981
Salem 1, N.J.	Public Service Electric & Gas	1106	1976
Salem 2, N.J.	Public Service Electric & Gas	1106	1981
Fermi 2, Mich.	Detroit Edison	1098	1985
Susquehanna 2, Pa.	Pennsylvania Power & Light	1094	1984

Source: Department of Energy, Energy Information Administration.

Motor Vehicle Fuel Consumption and Travel

	1960	1965	1970	1975	1980	1985	1990	1995	1996
Number registered (thousands)[1]									
Passenger car	61,671	75,258	89,244	106,706	121,601	127,885	133,700	128,387	129,728
Total	73,858	90,358	111,242	137,913	161,490	177,133	193,057	205,427	210,236
Vehicle-miles traveled (millions)									
Passenger car	587,000	723,000	917,000	1,034,000	1,112,000	1,247,000	1,408,000	1,438,000	1,468,000
Total	719,000	888,000	1,110,000	1,328,000	1,527,000	1,775,000	2,144,000	2,423,000	2,482,000
Fuel consumed (million gallons)									
Passenger car	41,171	49,723	67,819	74,140	69,982	71,518	69,568	68,072	68,897
Total	57,880	71,104	92,329	108,984	114,960	121,301	130,755	143,834	146,676
Average miles traveled per vehicle (thousands)									
Passenger car	9.5	9.6	10.3	9.7	9.1	9.7	10.5	11.2	11.3
Total	9.7	9.8	10.0	9.6	9.5	10.0	11.1	11.8	11.8
Average miles traveled per gallon									
Passenger car	14.3	14.5	13.5	13.9	15.9	17.4	20.2	21.1	21.3
Total	12.4	12.5	12.0	12.2	13.3	14.6	16.4	16.8	16.9
Average fuel consumed per vehicle (gallons)									
Passenger car	668	661	760	695	576	559	520	530	531
Total	784	787	830	790	712	685	677	700	698

1. Includes personal passenger vehicles, buses, and motor trucks. *Source:* U.S. Department of Transportation.

Major Air Pollutants

Pollutant	Sources	Effects
Ozone. A colorless gas that is the major constituent of photochemical smog at Earth's surface. In the upper atmosphere (stratosphere), however, ozone is beneficial, protecting us from the sun's harmful rays.	Ozone is formed in the lower atmosphere as a result of chemical reactions between oxygen, volatile organic compounds, and nitrogen oxides in the presence of sunlight, especially during hot weather. Sources of such harmful pollutants include vehicles, factories, landfills, industrial solvents, and numerous small sources such as gas stations, and farm and lawn equipment.	Ozone causes significant health and environmental problems at Earth's surface. It can irritate the respiratory tract, produce impaired lung function and cause throat irritation, chest pain, cough, and lung inflammation. It can also reduce the yield of agricultural crops and injure forests and other vegetation. Ozone is the most injurious pollutant to plant life.
Carbon Monoxide. Odorless and colorless gas emitted in the exhaust of motor vehicles and other kinds of engines where there is incomplete fossil fuel combustion.	Automobiles, buses, trucks, small engines, and some industrial processes. High concentrations can be found in confined spaces like parking garages, poorly ventilated tunnels, or along roadsides during periods of heavy traffic.	Reduces the ability of blood to deliver oxygen to vital tissues, affecting primarily the cardiovascular and nervous systems. Lower concentrations have been shown to adversely affect individuals with heart disease; higher concentrations can cause dizziness, headaches, and fatigue.
Nitrogen Dioxide. Light brown gas at lower concentrations; in higher concentrations becomes an important component of unpleasant-looking brown, urban haze.	Result of burning fuels in utilities, industrial boilers, cars, and trucks.	One of the major pollutants that causes smog and acid rain. Can harm humans and vegetation when concentrations are sufficiently high.
Particulate Matter. Solid matter or liquid droplets from smoke, dust, fly ash and condensing vapors that can be suspended in the air for long periods of time.	Industrial processes, smelters, automobiles, burning industrial fuels, woodsmoke, dust from paved and unpaved roads, construction, and agricultural ground breaking.	These microscopic particles can affect breathing and respiratory health, causing increased respiratory disease and lung damage, and possibly premature death.
Sulfur Dioxide. Colorless gas, odorless at low concentrations but pungent at very high concentrations.	Emitted largely from industrial, institutional, utility and apartment-house furnaces and boilers, as well as petroleum refineries, smelters, paper mills, and chemical plants.	One of the major pollutants that cause smog. Can also, at high concentrations, affect human health, especially among asthmatics, and acidify lakes and streams.
Lead. Lead and lead compounds can adversely affect human health through either ingestion of lead-contaminated soil, dust, paint, or direct inhalation.	Transportation sources using lead in their fuels, coal combustion, smelters, car battery plants, and combustion of garbage containing lead products.	Elevated lead levels can adversely affect mental development, kidney function, and blood chemistry. Young children are particularly at risk.

Pollutant	Sources	Effects
Toxic Air Pollutants. Includes pollutants such as arsenic, asbestos, and benzenes.	Chemical plants, industrial processes, motor vehicle emissions and fuels, and building materials.	Known or suspected to cause cancer, respiratory effects, birth defects, and reproductive and other serious health effects.
Stratospheric Ozone Depleters. Chemicals such as chlorofluorocarbons (CFCs), halons, carbon tetrachloride, and methyl chloroform. These chemicals rise to the upper atmosphere where they destroy the protective ozone layer.	Industrial household refrigeration, cooling and cleaning processes, car and home air conditioners, some fire extinguishers, and plastic foam products.	Increased exposure to UV radiation could potentially cause an increase in skin cancer, cataracts, suppression of the human immune response system, and environmental damage.
Greenhouse gases. Gases that build up in the atmosphere that may induce global climate change or the "greenhouse effect." They include carbon dioxide, methane, and nitrous oxide.	The main man-made source of carbon dioxide emissions is fossil fuel combustion for energy-use and transportation. Methane comes from landfills, cud-chewing livestock, coal mines, and rice paddies. Nitrous oxide results from industrial processes, such as nylon fabrication.	The extent of the effects of climate change on human health and the environment is still uncertain, but could include increased global temperature, increased severity and frequency of storms and other "weather extremes," melting of the polar ice cap, and sea-level rise.

Source: Environmental Protection Agency, EPA 450–K-92–002, October 1992.

International Energy

Source: Department of Energy, Energy Information Administration

World Leaders

Worldwide energy production of 375 quadrillion Btu in 1996 was 55 quadrillion Btu greater than in 1987. The relative contributions of the four leading energy producers changed markedly over the ten-year period.

In 1987, the former U.S.S.R. was the leading producer of energy and its production of 67 quadrillion Btu accounted for 20.9% of the world total. The United States, the second leading producer, accounted for 65 quadrillion Btu, a 20.3% share.

As of December 31, 1991, the U.S.S.R. ceased to exist as a political entity. Three of the U.S.S.R.'s constituent republics (Russia, Ukraine, and Kazakhstan) together produced 46 quadrillion Btu of energy in 1994. That year the United States produced 71 quadrillion Btu. In 1996, the United States produced more energy than any other country, at 73 quadrillion Btu. Russia, on it own, dropped to number two, producing 40 quadrillion Btu of energy.

Energy production in China, the third-largest producer of energy from 1987 through 1996, increased throughout the 10-year period. In 1987, China produced 26 quadrillion Btu of energy, much of which was coal. By 1996, Chinese production had reached 37 quadrillion Btu.

At 13 quadrillion Btu, Canada was the fourth-largest producer of energy in 1987. During the remainder of the 10-year period, Saudi Arabia nearly doubled its energy production, increasing from 11 quadrillion Btu in 1987 to 20 quadrillion Btu in 1996. Saudi Arabia has been the fourth-largest producer of energy since 1990.

Crude Oil Production in 1996

World production of crude oil totaled 64.0 million barrels per day in 1996, up 2.5% from the 1995 level. The most noticeable production increases occurred in Norway (up 12%), Venezuela (up 11%), and Nigeria (up 10%). Production declined 1.4% in the United States to 6.5 million barrels per day, and 2.0% in Russia to 5.9 million barrels per day. In Saudi Arabia, the largest producer of crude oil in 1996, production was essentially unchanged at 8.2 million barrels per day. Crude oil production by all members of the Organization of Petroleum Exporting Countries (OPEC) combined rose to 26.8 million barrels per day and accounted for 42% of the world total in 1996.

Natural Gas Production in 1996

World production of dry natural gas totaled 82 trillion cubic feet and, on a Btu basis, equaled 22% of world energy production in 1996. In 1995 (the most recent figures available), Russia was the major producer of natural gas and accounted for 21 trillion cubic feet, a 27% share of the world total. The United States was the second —largest producer in 1995 and accounted for 19 trillion cubic feet, a 24% share.

Coal Production in 1996

World production of coal totaled 5.2 billion short tons and, on a Btu basis, equaled 25% of world energy production in 1996. China, the leading producer, accounted for 1.5 billion short tons in 1996. Coal production in the United States, the second leading producer, totaled 1.1 billion short tons. India accounted for 311 million short tons and Russia for 302 million short tons.

Electricity Generation

As of January 1, 1996, world electricity installed capacity at all sites (including nonutility power producers) totaled 3.0 billion kilowatts. Most of the capacity (66%) was fossil fuel-fired. Hydroelectric generating capacity accounted for 22% and nuclear electric generating capacity accounted for 12%. Renewable sources, such as biofuels and geothermal, solar, and wind energy, accounted for less than 1% of the world total.

World net electricity generation totaled 12.8 trillion kilowatthours in 1995. Fossil fuel-fired net generation totaled 7.8 trillion kilowatthours. The United

States, with 2.3 trillion kilowatthours, was by far the largest producer of fossil fuel–fired net generation. China's net generation totaled 756 billion kilowatthours and Germany's totaled 570 billion kilowatthours. World hydroelectric power net generation in 1995 totaled 2.5 trillion kilowatthours, up 5% from the 1994 level. The top five countries in hydroelectric power net generation (Canada, the United States, Brazil, Russia, and China) together accounted for half of the world's total. In 1995, nuclear-based electricity gross generation totaled 2.2 trillion kilowatthours. The U.S. share of the world total was 31%. France accounted for 16% and Japan for 13% of the world total.

Petroleum Prices and Demand

Following Iraq's invasion of Kuwait in August 1990, the average price of crude oil rose to $22.22 per barrel, the highest in five years, and year-to-year growth in world petroleum consumption of only 1% was the lowest in those years. In 1991, following the resolution of the war in the Persian Gulf, the average price of crude oil fell to $19.06 per barrel. World consumption of petroleum rose 0.9% to 67 million barrels per day. In 1992 through 1994, the average price of crude oil fell further, reaching $15.59 per barrel. In real terms, the 1994 price was the lowest in 21 years. In 1995, the price rose 11% to $17.23 per barrel, while world consumption increased to 70 million barrels per day.

From 1960 through 1996, the United States consumed more petroleum by far than any other country. In 1996, U.S. consumption accounted for 26% of the 72 million barrels per day consumed worldwide. Japan consumed 5.9 million barrels per day. China and Russia accounted for 3.5 million barrels per day and 2.7 million barrels per day, respectively.

Dry Natural Gas Consumption in 1996

Although natural gas can be transported across borders in pipelines and some natural gas is shipped as liquefied natural gas, in general, natural gas tends to be consumed closer to its site of production than does petroleum. Not surprisingly, the two top producers of dry natural gas in 1996 were also the top consumers. U.S. consumption of dry natural gas totaled 21.9 trillion cubic feet, equal to 112% of its production. Russia consumed 14.5 trillion cubic feet, an amount equal to 68% of its production of dry natural gas. Germany, the third-largest consumer of natural gas, consumed 3.7 trillion cubic feet and the United Kingdom consumed 3.2 trillion cubic feet.

Coal Consumption in 1996

World coal consumption in 1996 totaled 5.2 billion short tons, up for the sixth year in a row. China, the United States, and India, the leading producers of coal, were also the leading consumers. China consumed 1.5 billion short tons, the United States consumed 983 million short tons, India consumed 321 million short tons, and Germany consumed 290 million short tons of coal in 1996. □

Threatened and Endangered Species

(as of June 30, 1998)

Source: U.S. Fish and Wildlife Service, Dept. of the Interior.

Group	Endangered[1]		Threatened[2]		Total listings[3]	Species with recovery plans[4]
	U.S.	Foreign	U.S.	Foreign		
Mammals	59	251	8	16	334	43
Birds	75	178	15	6	274	77
Reptiles	14	66	20	14	114	30
Amphibians	9	8	7	1	25	11
Fishes	68	11	42	0	121	79
Snails	15	1	7	0	23	19
Clams	61	2	8	0	71	45
Crustaceans	16	0	3	0	19	7
Insects	28	4	9	0	41	21
Arachnids	5	0	0	0	5	4
Flowering plants	525	1	114	0	640	408
Conifers	2	0	0	2	4	1
Ferns & others	26	0	2	0	28	26
Total	**903**	**522**	**235**	**39**	**1,699**	**771**

1. *Endangered species* are those in danger of extinction. 2. *Threatened species* are those likely to become an endangered species within the foreseeable future. 3. Separate populations of a species listed both as endangered and threatened are tallied only once, for the endangered population. Those species are the argali, leopard, gray wolf, piping plover, roseate tern, chimpanzee, green sea turtle, olive ridley sea turtle, stellar sea lion, and saltwater crocodile. 4. There are 488 approved recovery plans sponsored by the endangered species program of the U.S. Fish and Wildlife Service. They are dedicated to restoring species to a secure status in the wild. Some recovery plans cover more than one species, and a few species have separate plans covering different parts of their ranges. Recovery plans are drawn up only for species in the United States.

U.S. Zoos and Aquariums

Source: The facilities listed are members of, and accredited by, the American Zoo and Aquarium Association (AZA) to ensure that they are maintaining professional standards. The AZA also accredits facilities outside of the United States. Their Web site is www.aza.org.

Abilene Zoological Gardens, Tex.
African Safari Wildlife Park, Port Clinton, Tex.
Akron Zoological Park, Ohio
Alameda Park Zoo, Alamogordo, N.M.
Albuquerque Biological Park, N.M.
Alexandria Zoological Park, La.
Aquarium for Wildlife Conservation, The, Brooklyn, N.Y.
Aquarium of the Americas, New Orleans, La.
Arizona-Sonora Desert Museum, Tucson
Audubon Park and Zoological Garden, New Orleans
John Ball Zoological Garden, Grand Rapids, Mich.
Baltimore Zoo, The, Md.
Beardsley Zoological Gardens, Bridgeport, Conn.
Belle Isle Aquarium, Royal Oak, Minn.
Belle Isle Zoo, Detroit
Bergen County Zoological Park, Paramus, N.J.
Bermuda Aquarium, Museum, and Zoo, Flatts, Fla.
Binder Park Zoo, Battle Creek, Mich.
Birch Aquarium, La Jolla, Calif.
Birmingham Zoo, Ala.
Blank Park Zoo, Des Moines, Iowa
Bramble Park Zoo, Watertown, S.D.
Brandywine Zoo, Wilmington, Del.
Brevard Zoo, Melbourne, Fla.
Bronx Zoo/Wildlife Conservation Park, N.Y.
Brookfield Zoo, Ill.
Brookgreen Gardens, Murrells Inlet, S.C.
Buffalo Zoological Gardens, N.Y.
Burnet Park Zoo, Syracuse, N.Y.
Busch Gardens, Tampa, Fla.
Caldwell Zoo, Tyler, Tex.
Cameron Park Zoo, Waco, Tex.
Cape May County Park Zoo, Cape May Court House, N.J.
Central Florida Zoological Park, Lake Monroe, Fla.
Central Park Wildlife Center, New York, N.Y.
Chaffee Zoological Gardens of Fresno, Calif.
Chahinkapa Zoo, Wahpeton, N.D.
Chehaw Wild Animal Park, Albany, Ga.
Cheyenne Mountain Zoological Park, Colorado Springs
Cincinnati Zoo and Botanical Garden, Ohio
Cleveland Metroparks Zoo, Ohio
Columbus Zoological Gardens, Ohio
Dakota Zoo, Bismarck, N.D.
Dallas Aquarium at Fair Park, Tex.
Dallas World Aquarium, Tex.
Dallas Zoo, Tex.
Denver Zoological Gardens, Colo.
Detroit Zoological Park, Mich.
Dickerson Park Zoo, Springfield, Mo.
Discovery Island Zoological Park, Lake Buena Vista, Fla.
El Paso Zoo, Tex.
Emporia Zoo, Kan.
Erie Zoo, Pa.
Florida Aquarium, Tampa, Fla.
Folsom Children's Zoo & Botanical Garden, Lincoln, Neb.
Fort Wayne Children's Zoo, Ind.
Fort Worth Zoological Park, Tex.
Fossil Rim Wildlife Center, Glen Rose, Tex.
Franklin Park Zoo, Boston, Mass.
Glen Oak Zoo, Peoria, Ill.
Great Plains Zoo & Museum, Sioux Falls, S.D.
Greater Baton Rouge Zoo, La.
Greenville Zoo, S.C.
Happy Hollow Park and Zoo, San Jose, Calif.
Honolulu Zoo, Hawaii
Houston Zoological Gardens, Tex.
Hutchinson Zoo, Hutchinson, Kans.
Indianapolis Zoo, Ind.
International Crane Foundation, Baraboo, Wis.
Jackson Zoological Park, Miss.
Jacksonville Zoological Park, Fla.
Kansas City Zoological Gardens, Mo.
Knoxville Zoological Gardens, Tenn.
Lake Superior Zoological Gardens, Duluth, Minn.
Lincoln Park Zoological Gardens, Chicago
Little Rock Zoological Garden, Ark.
Living Desert, The, Palm Desert, Calif.
Living Seas, The, Lake Buena Vista, Fla.
Los Angeles Zoo, Calif.
Louisville Zoological Garden, Ky.
Lowry Park Zoological Garden, Tampa, Fla.
Marine World Africa USA, Vallejo, Calif.
Memphis Zoological Garden and Aquarium, Tenn.
Mesker Park Zoo, Evansville, Ind.
Metro Washington Park Zoo, Portland, Ore.
Miami Metrozoo, Fla.
Micke Grove Zoo, Lodi, Calif.
Miller Park Zoo, Bloomington, Ill.
Mill Mountain Zoo, Roanoke, Va.
Milwaukee County Zoological Gardens, Wis.
Minnesota Zoological Garden, Apple Valley, Minn.
Monterey Bay Aquarium, Calif.
Montgomery Zoo, Ala.
Mystic Marinelife Aquarium, Mystic, Conn.
National Aquarium in Baltimore, Md.
National Aviary in Pittsburgh, Pa.
National Zoo Conservation & Research Center, Front Royal, Va.
National Zoological Park, Washington, D.C.
New England Aquarium, Boston
New Jersey State Aquarium at Camden
North Carolina Aquarium at Fort Fisher, Kure Beach
North Carolina Aquarium at Pine Knoll Shores, Atlantic Beach
North Carolina Aquarium on Roanoke Island, Manteo
North Carolina Zoological Park, Asheboro
North Eastern Wisconsin Zoo, Green Bay, Wis.
Northwest Trek Wildlife Park, Eatonville, Wash.
NZP Conservation Research Center, Front Royal, Va.
Oakland Zoo, The, Calif.
Oglebay's Good Zoo, Wheeling, W.Va.
Oklahoma City Zoological Park, Okla.
Omaha's Henry Doorly Zoo, Neb.
Charles Paddock Zoo, Atascadero, Calif.
Palm Beach Zoo at Dreher Park, West Palm Beach, Fla.
Parrot Jungle and Gardens, Miami, Fla.
Clyde Peeling's Reptiland Ltd., Allenwood, Pa.
Philadelphia Zoological Garden, Pa.
Phoenix Zoo, The, Ariz.
Pittsburgh Zoo, Pa.
Point Defiance Zoo and Aquarium, Tacoma, Wash.
Gladys Porter Zoo, Brownsville, Tex.
Potawatomi Zoo, South Bend, Ind.
Potter Park Zoological Gardens, Lansing, Mich.
Prospect Park Wildlife Center, Brooklyn, N.Y.
Pueblo Zoo, Colo.
Queens Wildlife Center, Flushing, N.Y.
Racine Zoological Gardens, Wis.
Rainforest at Moody Gardens, Inc., Galveston, Tex.
Reid Park Zoo, Tucson, Ariz.
Lee Richardson Zoo, Garden City, Kan.
Riverbanks Zoological Park and Botanical Garden, Columbia, S.C.
Riverside Zoo, Scottsbluff, Neb.
Henson Robinson Zoo, Springfield, Ill.

Roosevelt Zoo, Minot, N.D.
Ross Park Zoo, Binghamton, N.Y.
Sacramento Zoo, Calif.
St. Augustine Alligator Farm, Fla.
St. Catherine's Wildlife Conservation Center, Midway, Ga.
St. Louis Zoological Park, Mo.
St. Paul's Como Zoo, Minn.
Salisbury Zoological Park, Md.
San Antonio Zoological Gardens and Aquarium, Tex.
San Diego Wild Animal Park, Calif.
San Diego Zoo, Calif.
San Francisco Zoological Gardens, Calif.
Santa Ana Zoo, Calif.
Santa Barbara Zoological Gardens, Calif.
Sea Life Park Hawaii, Waimanalo
Sea World of California, San Diego
Sea World of Florida, Orlando
Sea World of Ohio, Aurora
Sea World of Texas, San Antonio
Seattle Aquarium, The, Wash.
Sedgwick County Zoo, Wichita, Kan.
Seneca Park Zoo, Rochester, N.Y.
Sequoia Park Zoo, Eureka, Calif.
John G. Shedd Aquarium, Chicago
Silver Springs, Silver Springs, Fla.
Staten Island Zoo, N.Y.
Steinhart Aquarium, San Francisco, Calif.
Sunset Zoological Park, Manhattan, Kan.
Tautphaus Park Zoo, Idaho Falls, Idaho
Tennessee Aquarium, Chattanooga, Tenn.
Texas State Aquarium, Corpus Christi
Texas Zoo, The, Victoria, Tex.
Toledo Zoological Gardens, Ohio
Topeka Zoological Park, Kan.
Tracy Aviary, Salt Lake City, Utah
Trevor Zoo, Millbrook, N.Y.
Ellen Trout Zoo, Lufkin, Tex.
Tulsa Zoo and Living Museum, Okla.
Utah's Hogle Zoo, Salt Lake City
Utica Zoo, N.Y.
Henry Vilas Zoo, Madison, Wis.
Virginia Zoological Park, Norfolk, Va.
Waikiki Aquarium, Hawaii
Wildlife Safari, Winston, Ore.
Wildlife World Zoo, Litchfield Park, Ariz.
The Wilds, Cumberland, Ohio
Roger Williams Park Zoo, Providence, R.I.
Woodland Park Zoological Gardens, Seattle
The ZOO, Gulf Breeze, Fla.
Zoo Atlanta, Ga.
ZOOAMERICA North American Wildlife Park, Hershey, Pa.

Animal Names: Male, Female, and Young

Animal	Male	Female	Young	Animal	Male	Female	Young	Animal	Male	Female	Young
Ass	Jack	Jenny	Foal	Duck	Drake	Duck	Duckling	Sheep	Ram	Ewe	Lamb
Bear	Boar	Sow	Cub	Elephant	Bull	Cow	Calf	Swan	Cob	Pen	Cygnet
Cat	Tom	Queen	Kitten	Fox	Dog	Vixen	Cub	Swine	Boar	Sow	Piglet
Cattle	Bull	Cow	Calf	Goose	Gander	Goose	Gosling	Tiger	Tiger	Tigress	Cub
Chicken	Rooster	Hen	Chick	Horse	Stallion	Mare	Foal	Whale	Bull	Cow	Calf
Deer	Buck	Doe	Fawn	Lion	Lion	Lioness	Cub	Wolf	Dog	Bitch	Pup
Dog	Dog	Bitch	Pup	Rabbit	Buck	Doe	Bunny				

Source: James G. Doherty, General Curator, The Wildlife Conservation Society.

Gestation, Incubation, and Longevity of Certain Animals

Animal	Gestation or incubation, in days & (average)	Longevity, in years & (record exceptions)	Animal	Gestation or incubation, in days & (average)	Longevity, in years & (record exceptions)
Ass	365	18-20 (63)	Horse	329-345 (336)	20-25 (50+)
Bear	180-240[1]	15-30 (47)	Human	253-303	([2])
Cat	52-69 (63)	10-12 (26+)	Kangaroo	32-39[1]	4-6 (23)
Chicken	22	7-8 (14)	Lion	105-113 (108)	10 (29)
Cow	c. 280	9-12 (39)	Monkey	139-270[1]	12-15[1] (29)
Deer	197-300[1]	10-15 (26)	Mouse	19-31[1]	1-3 (4)
Dog	53-71 (63)	10-12 (24)	Parakeet (Budgerigar)	17-20 (18)	8 (12+)
Duck	21-35[1](28)	10 (15)	Pig	101-130 (115)	10 (22)
Elephant	510-730[1] (624)	30-40 (71)	Pigeon	11-19	10-12 (39)
Fox	51-63[1]	8-10 (14)	Rabbit	30-35 (31)	6-8 (15)
Goat	136-160 (151)	12 (17)	Rat	21	3 (5)
Groundhog	31-32	4-9	Sheep	144-152[1] (151)	12 (16)
Guinea pig	58-75 (68)	3 (6)	Squirrel	44	8-9 (15)
Hamster, golden	15-17	2 (8)	Whale	365-547[1]	—
Hippopotamus	220-255 (240)	30 (49+)	Wolf	60-63	10-12 (16)

1. Depending on kind. 2. For life expectancy charts, *see* Expectation of Life in the United States. *Source:* James G. Doherty, General Curator, The Wildlife Conservation Society.

Animal Group Terminology

Source: James G. Doherty, General Curator, The Wildlife Conservation Society.

ants: colony
bears: sleuth, sloth
bees: grist, hive, swarm
birds: flight, volery
cattle: drove
cats: clutter, clowder
chicks: brood, clutch
clams: bed
cranes: sedge, seige
crows: murder
doves: dule
ducks: brace, team
elephants: herd
elks: gang
finches: charm
fish: school, shoal, draught
foxes: leash, skulk
geese: flock, gaggle, skein
gnats: cloud, horde
goats: trip
gorillas: band
hares: down, husk
hawks: cast
hens: brood
hogs: drift
horses: pair, team
hounds: cry, mute, pack
kangaroos: troop
kittens: kindle, litter
larks: exaltation
lions: pride
locusts: plague
magpies: tidings
mules: span
nightingales: watch
oxen: yoke
oysters: bed
parrots: company
partridges: covey
peacocks: muster, ostentation
pheasants: nest, bouquet
pigs: litter
ponies: string
quail: bevy, covey
rabbits: nest
seals: pod
sheep: drove, flock
sparrows: host
storks: mustering
swans: bevy, wedge
swine: sounder
toads: knot
turkeys: rafter
turtles: bale
vipers: nest
whales: gam, pod
wolves: pack, route
woodcocks: fall

Speed of Animals

Most of the following measurements are for maximum speeds over approximate quarter-mile distances. Exceptions—which are included to give a wide range of animals—are the lion and elephant, whose speeds were clocked in the act of charging; the whippet, which was timed over a 200-yard course; the cheetah over a 100-yard distance; humans for a 15-yard segment of a 100-yard run; and the black mamba, six-lined race runner, spider, giant tortoise, three-toed sloth, and garden snail, which were measured over various small distances.

Animal	Speed (mph)	Animal	Speed (mph)	Animal	Speed (mph)
Cheetah	70.00	Mongolian wild ass	40.00	Human	27.89
Pronghorn antelope	61.00	Greyhound	39.35	Elephant	25.00
Wildebeest	50.00	Whippet	35.50	Black mamba snake	20.00
Lion	50.00	Rabbit (domestic)	35.00	Six-lined race runner	18.00
Thomson's gazelle	50.00	Mule deer	35.00	Squirrel	12.00
Quarter horse	47.50	Jackal	35.00	Pig (domestic)	11.00
Elk	45.00	Reindeer	32.00	Chicken	9.00
Cape hunting dog	45.00	Giraffe	32.00	Spider (Tegeneария atrica)	1.17
Coyote	43.00	White-tailed deer	30.00	Giant Tortoise	0.17
Gray fox	42.00	Wart hog	30.00	Three-toed sloth	0.15
Hyena	40.00	Grizzly bear	30.00	Garden snail	0.03
Zebra	40.00	Cat (domestic)	30.00		

Source: Natural History Magazine, March 1974, copyright 1974. The American Museum of Natural History; and James G. Doherty, General Curator, The Wildlife Conservation Society.

Top Twenty Most Visited National Park Sites, 1997

Rank	Name and location	Number of visitors
1.	Blue Ridge Parkway, National Va.	18,373,279
2.	Golden Gate National Recreation Area, Calif.	13,803,382
3.	Great Smoky Mountains National Park, Tenn.	9,965,075
4.	Lake Mead National Recreation Area, Nev.	8,528,420
5.	Gateway National Recreation Area, N.Y.	6,807,945
6.	Natchez Trace Parkway, Miss.	5,992,978
7.	George Washington Memorial Parkway, Va.	5,844,294
8.	Grand Canyon National Park, Ariz.	4,791,668
9.	Delaware Water Gap National Recreation Area, Pa. & N.J.	4,752,100
10.	Statue of Liberty National Monument, N.Y.	4,738,388
11.	Gulf Islands National Seashore, Fla.–Miss.	4,697,014
12.	Cape Cod National Seashore, Mass.	4,508,454
13.	Castle Clinton National Monument, N.Y.	4,109,013
14.	Olympic National Park, Wash.	3,846,709
15.	Yosemite National Park, Calif.	3,669,970
16.	San Francisco Maritime National Historic Park, Calif.	3,530,687
17.	Cuyahoga Valley National Recreation Area, Ohio	3,527,837
18.	Jefferson National Expansion Memorial, Mo.	3,420,076
19.	Colonial National Historic Park, Va.	3,218,180
20.	Independence National Historic Park, Pa.	3,155,195
21.	Rocky Mountain National Park, Colo.	2,965,354
22.	Chattahoochee River National Recreation Area, Ga.	2,957,698
23.	Yellowstone National Park, Wyo.–Mont.–Idaho	2,889,512
24.	Acadia National Park, Maine	2,760,306
25.	Boston National Historic Park, Mass.	2,707,789

Source: Department of the Interior, National Park Service. www.nps.gov

The National Park System

Source: Department of the Interior, National Park Service.

The National Park System of the United States is administered by the National Park Service, a bureau of the Department of the Interior. Started with the establishment of Yellowstone National Park on March 1, 1872, the system includes not only the most extraordinary and spectacular scenic exhibits in the United States, but also a large number of sites distinguished either for their historic or prehistoric importance or scientific interest, or for their superior recreational assets. The National Park System is made up of 376 areas covering more than 83 million acres in every state except Delaware. It also includes areas in the District of Columbia, American Samoa, Guam, Puerto Rico, and the Virgin Islands. A comprehensive list of the areas follows. See also the excellent Web site of the Park Service: www.nps.gov.

Note: n.a. means "not available."

NATIONAL PARKS

Name, location, and year authorized	Acreage	Outstanding characteristics
Acadia (Maine), 1919	46,998.43	Rugged seashore on Mt. Desert Island and adjacent mainland
Arches (Utah), 1971	73,378.98	Unusual stone arches, windows, pedestals caused by erosion
Badlands (S.D.), 1978	242,755.94	Arid land of fossils, prairie, bison, deer, bighorn, antelope
Big Bend (Tex.), 1935	801,163.21	Mountains and desert bordering the Rio Grande
Biscayne (Fla.), 1980	172,924.07	Aquatic, coral reef park south of Miami; was a national monument, 1968–1980
Bryce Canyon (Utah), 1924	35,835.08	Area of grotesque eroded rocks brilliantly colored
Canyonlands (Utah), 1964	337,570.43	Colorful wilderness with impressive red-rock canyons, spires, arches
Capitol Reef (Utah), 1971	241,904.26	Highly colored sedimentary rock formations in high, narrow gorges
Carlsbad Caverns (N.M.), 1930	46,766.45	The world's largest known caves
Channel Islands (Calif.), 1980	249,353.77	Area is rich in marine mammals, sea birds, endangered species, and archeology
Crater Lake (Ore.), 1902	183,224.05	Deep blue lake in heart of inactive volcano
Death Valley (Calif.-Nev.), 1994	3,367,627.68	Largest desert, surrounded by high mountains, containing the lowest point in the Western hemisphere
Denali (Alaska), 1917	4,741,800.00	Mt. McKinley National Park was renamed and enlarged by Act of Dec. 2, 1980. Contains Mt. McKinley, N. America's highest mountain (20,320 ft.)
Dry Tortugas (Fla.), 1992	64,700.00	Formerly Ft. Jefferson National Monument. Located 70 miles off Key West. Features an underwater nature trail
Everglades (Fla.), 1934	1,507,850.00	Subtropical area with abundant bird and animal life
Gates of the Arctic (Alaska), 1980	7,523,898.00	Diverse north central wilderness contains part of Brooks Range
Glacier (Mont.), 1910	1,013,572.42	Rocky Mountain scenery with many glaciers and lakes
Glacier Bay (Alaska), 1980	3,224,794.00	Park was a national monument 1925–1980; popular for wildlife, whale-watching, glacier-calving, and scenery
Grand Canyon (Ariz.), 1919	1,217,158.32	Mile-deep gorge, 4 to 18 miles wide, 217 miles long
Grand Teton (Wyo.), 1929	309,994.72	Picturesque range of high mountain peaks
Great Basin (Nev.), 1986	77,180.00	Exceptional scenic, biologic, and geologic attractions
Great Smoky Mts. (N.C.-Tenn), 1926	521,621.00	Highest mountain range east of Black Hills; luxuriant plant life
Guadalupe Mountains (Tex.), 1966	86,415.97	Contains highest point in Texas: Guadalupe Peak (8,751 ft.)
Haleakala (Hawaii), 1960	28,091.14	World-famous 10,023-ft. Haleakala volcano (dormant)
Hawaii Volcanoes (Hawaii), 1916	209,695.38	Spectacular volcanic area; luxuriant vegetation at lower levels
Hot Springs (Ark.), 1921	5,549.46	47 mineral hot springs said to have therapeutic value
Isle Royale (Mich.), 1931	571,790.11	Largest wilderness island in Lake Superior; moose, wolves, lakes
Joshua Tree (Calif.), 1936	792,749.87	Desert region featuring Joshua trees and a great variety of plants and animals.
Katmai (Alaska), 1980	3,674,540.87	Expansion may assure brown bear's preservation. Park was national monument 1918–1980; is known for fishing, 1912 eruption, bears
Kenai Fjords (Alaska), 1980	670,642.79	Mountain goats, marine mammals, birdlife are features at this seacoast park near Seward
Kings Canyon (Calif.), 1940	461,901.20	Huge canyons; high mountains; giant sequoias
Kobuk Valley (Alaska), 1980	1,750,736.86	Native culture and anthropology center around the broad Kobuk River in northwest Alaska
Lake Clark (Alaska), 1980	2,636,839.00	Park provides scenic and wilderness recreation across Cook Inlet from Anchorage
Lassen Volcanic (Calif.), 1916	106,372.36	Exhibits of impressive volcanic phenomena
Mammoth Cave (Ky.), 1926	52,830.19	Vast limestone labyrinth with underground river
Mesa Verde (Colo.), 1906	52,121.93	Best-preserved prehistoric cliff dwellings in United States
Mount Rainier (Wash.), 1899	235,612.50	Single-peak glacial system; dense forests, flowered meadows

Name, location, and year authorized	Acreage	Outstanding characteristics
National Park of American Samoa, 1988	9,000.00	Samoa National Park, American Samoa: two rain forest preserves and a coral reef on the island of Ofu are home to unique tropical animals. The park also includes several thousand acres on the islands of Tutuila and Ta'u
North Cascades (Wash.), 1968	504,780.94	Roadless Alpine landscape; jagged peaks; mountain lakes; glaciers
Olympic (Wash.), 1938	922,651.01	Finest Pacific Northwest rain forest; scenic mountain park
Petrified Forest (Ariz.), 1962	93,532.57	Extensive natural exhibit of petrified wood
Redwood (Calif.), 1968	110,232.40	Coastal redwood forests; contains world's tallest known tree (369.2 ft.)
Rocky Mountain (Colo.), 1915	265,727.15	Section of the Rocky Mountains; 107 named peaks over 10,000 ft.
Saguaro (Ariz.), 1994	91,452.95	Giant saguaro cacti, unique to the Sonoran Desert, sometimes reach a height of 50 ft. in this cactus forest
Sequoia (Calif.), 1890	402,482.38	Giant sequoias; magnificent High Sierra scenery, including Mt. Whitney
Shenandoah (Va.), 1926	197,388.98	Tree-covered mountains; scenic Skyline Drive
Theodore Roosevelt (N.D.), 1978	70,446.89	Scenic valley of Little Missouri River; T.R. Ranch; wildlife
Virgin Islands (U.S. V.I.), 1956	14,688.87	Beaches; lush hills; prehistoric Carib Indian relics
Voyageurs (Minn.), 1971	218,035.33	Wildlife, canoeing, fishing, and hiking
Wind Cave (S.D.), 1903	28,295.03	Limestone caverns in Black Hills; buffalo herd
Wrangell-St. Elias (Alaska), 1980	8,323,617.68	Largest Park System area has abundant wildlife, second highest peak in U.S. (Mt. St. Elias); adjoins Canadian park
Yellowstone (Wyo.-Mont.-Idaho), 1872	2,219,790.71	World's greatest geyser area; abundant falls, wildlife, and canyons
Yosemite (Calif.), 1890	761,236.20	Mountains; inspiring gorges and waterfalls; giant sequoias
Zion (Utah), 1919	146,597.61	Multicolored gorge in heart of southern Utah desert

National Historical Parks

Name and location	*Total acreage*
Appomattox Court House (Va.)	1,774.81
Boston (Mass.)	41.03
Chaco Culture (N.M.)	33,974.29
Chesapeake and Ohio Canal (Md.-W.Va.-D.C.)	19,236.60
Colonial (Va.)	9,352.60
Cumberland Gap (Ky.-Tenn.-Va.)	20,454.02
Dayton Aviation Heritage (Ohio)	85.65
George Rogers Clark (Ind.)	26.17
Harpers Ferry (W.Va.-Md.)	2,287.48
Hopewell Culture (Ohio)	1,134.44
Independence (Pa.)	44.88
Jean Lafitte (La.)	20,020.00
Kalaupapa (Hawaii)	10,778.88
Kaloko-Honokohau (Hawaii)	1,160.91
Keewenaw (Mich.)	1,870.00
Klondike Goldrush (Alaska-Wash.)	13,191.35
Lowell (Mass.)	136.86
Lyndon B. Johnson (Tex.)	1,570.15
Marsh-Billings (Vt.)	643.07
Minuteman (Mass.)	935.55
Morristown (N.J.)	1,683.61
Natchez (Miss.)	108.26
Nez Perce (Idaho)	2,122.75
Pecos (N.M.)	6,670.65
Pu'uhonua a Honaunau (Hawaii)	181.80
Salt River Bay (U.S. V.I.)	945.00
San Antonio Missions (Tex.)	819.19
San Francisco Maritime (Calif.)	31.18
San Juan Island (Wash.)	1,751.99
Saratoga (N.Y.)	3,392.42
Sitka (Alaska)	106.83
Tumacacori (Ariz.)	46.52
Valley Forge (Pa.)	3,466.47
War in the Pacific (Guam)	1,960.07
Women's Rights (N.Y.)	6.80
Zuni-Cibola (N.M.)	800.00

National Monuments

Name and location	*Total acreage*
Agate Fossil Beds (Neb.)	3,055.22
Alibates Flint Quarries (Tex.)	1,370.97
Aniakchak (Alaska)	137,176.00
Aztec Ruins (N.M.)	319.73
Bandelier (N.M.)	32,737.20
Black Canyon (Colo.)	20,766.14
Booker T. Washington (Va.)	223.92
Buck Island Reef (U.S. V.I.)	880.00
Cabrillo (Calif.)	137.06
Canyon de Chelly (Ariz.)	83,840.00
Cape Krusenstern (Alaska)	659,807.00
Capulin Volcano (N.M.)	792.84
Casa Grande (Ariz.)	472.50
Castillo de San Marcos (Fla.)	20.51
Castle Clinton (N.Y.)	1.00
Cedar Breaks (Utah)	6,154.60
Chiricahua (Ariz.)	11,984.73
Colorado (Colo.)	20,453.93
Congaree Swamp (S.C.)	22,200.00
Craters of the Moon (Idaho)	53,440.05
Devils Postpile (Calif.)	798.46
Devils Tower (Wyo.)	1,346.91
Dinosaur (Utah-Colo.)	210,844.02
Effigy Mounds (Iowa)	1,481.39
El Malpais (N.M.)	114,275.95
El Morro (N.M.)	1,278.72
Florissant Fossil Beds (Colo.)	5,998.09
Fort Frederica (Ga.)	241.42
Fort Matanzas (Fla.)	227.76
Fort McHenry (Md.)	43.26
Fort Pulaski (Ga.)	5,623.10
Fort Stanwix (N.Y.)	15.52
Fort Sumter (S.C.)	194.60
Fort Union (N.M.)	720.60
Fossil Butte (Wyo.)	8,198.00
George Washington Birthplace (Va.)	553.23
George Washington Carver (Mo.)	210.00
Gila Cliff Dwellings (N.M.)	533.13

Name and location	Total acreage
Grand Portage (Minn.)	709.97
Great Sand Dunes (Colo.)	38,662.18
Hagerman Fossil Beds (Idaho)	4,345.59
Hohokam Pima (Ariz.)	1,690.00
Homestead (Neb.)	195.11
Hovenweep (Utah-Colo.)	784.93
Jewel Cave (S.D.)	1,273.51
John Day Fossil Beds (Ore.)	14,014.58
Lava Beds (Calif.)	46,559.87
Little Big Horn Battlefield (Mont.)	765.34
Montezuma Castle (Ariz.)	857.69
Muir Woods (Calif.)	553.55
Natural Bridges (Utah)	7,636.49
Navajo (Ariz.)	360.00
Ocmulgee (Ga.)	701.54
Oregon Caves (Ore.)	487.98
Organ Pipe Cactus (Ariz.)	330,688.86
Petroglyph (N.M.)	7,240.33
Pinnacles (Calif.)	16,265.44
Pipe Spring (Ariz.)	40.00
Pipestone (Minn.)	281.78
Poverty Point (La.)	910.85
Rainbow Bridge (Utah)	160.00
Russell Cave (Ala.)	310.45
Salinas (N.M.)	1,071.42
Scotts Bluff (Neb.)	3,003.03
Statue of Liberty (N.Y.-N.J.)	58.38
Sunset Crater (Ariz.)	3,040.00
Timpanogos Cave (Utah)	250.00
Tonto (Ariz.)	1,120.00
Tuzigoot (Ariz.)	800.62
Walnut Canyon (Ariz.)	3,541.46
White Sands (N.M.)	143,732.92
Wupatki (Ariz.)	35,442.13
Yucca House (Colo.)	33.87

National Preserves

Name and location	Total acreage
Aniakchak (Alaska)	465,603.00
Bering Land Bridge (Alaska)	2,698,000.00
Big Cypress (Fla.)	716,000.00
Big Thicket (Tex.)	96,679.68
Denali (Alaska)	1,334,200.00
Gates of the Arctic (Alaska)	948,629.00
Glacier Bay (Alaska)	58,406.00
Katmai (Alaska)	418,699.30
Lake Clark (Alaska)	1,407,293.00
Little River Canyon (Ala.)	13,669.00
Mojave (Calif.)	1,450,000.00
Noatak (Alaska)	6,570,000.00
Tall Grass Prairie (Kans.)	180.00
Timucuan Ecological and Historic Preserve (Fla.)	46,000.00
Wrangell-St. Elias (Alaska)	4,852,773.31
Yukon-Charley (Alaska)	2,526,509.46

National Reserves

Name and location	Total acreage
City of Rocks (Idaho)	14,407.19
Ebey's Landing (Wash.)	19,000.00

National Military Parks

Name and location	Total acreage
Chickamauga and Chattanooga (Ga.-Tenn.)	8,119.11
Fredericksburg and Spotsylvania (Va.)	7,787.26
Gettysburg Nat. Mil. Park (Pa.)	5,906.30
Guilford Courthouse (N.C.)	220.25
Horseshoe Bend (Ala.)	2,040.00
Kings Mountain (S.C.)	3,945.29
Pea Ridge (Ark.)	4,300.35
Shiloh Nat. Park (Tenn.)	3,972.87
Vicksburg Nat. Mil. Park (Miss.)	1,736.47

National Battlefields

Name and location	Total acreage
Antietam (Md.)	3,255.89
Big Hole (Mont.)	655.61
Cowpens (S.C.)	841.56
Fort Donelson (Tenn.)	551.69
Fort Necessity (Pa.)	902.80
Monocacy (Md.)	1,647.01
Moores Creek (N.C.)	86.52
Petersburg (Va.)	2,744.10
Stones River (Tenn.)	708.32
Tupelo (Miss.)	1.00
Wilson's Creek (Mo.)	1,749.91

National Battlefield Parks

Name and location	Total acreage
Kennesaw Mountain (Ga.)	2,884.14
Manassas (Va.)	5,071.62
Richmond (Va.)	820.59

National Battlefield Site

Name and location	Total acreage
Brices Cross Roads (Miss.)	1.00

National Historic Sites

Name and location	Total acreage
Abraham Lincoln Birthplace (Ky.)	116.50
Adams (Mass.)	13.54
Allegheny Portage Railroad (Pa.)	1,249.20
Andersonville (Ga.)	494.61
Andrew Johnson (Tenn.)	16.68
Bent's Old Fort (Colo.)	799.80
Boston African-American (Mass.)	n.a.
Brown v. Board of Education (Kans.)	1.85
Carl Sandburg Home (N.C.)	263.52
Charles Pinckney (S.C.)	28.45
Christiansted (U.S. V.I.)	27.15
Clara Barton (Md.)	8.59
Edgar Allan Poe (Pa.)	0.52
Edison (N.J.)	21.25
Eisenhower (Pa.)	690.46
Eleanor Roosevelt (N.Y.)	180.50
Eugene O'Neill (Calif.)	13.19
Ford's Theatre (Lincoln Museum) (D.C.)	0.29
Fort Bowie (Ariz.)	1,000.00
Fort Davis (Tex.)	460.00
Fort Laramie (Wyo.)	832.85
Fort Larned (Kan.)	718.39
Fort Point (Calif.)	29.00
Fort Raleigh (N.C.)	152.93
Fort Scott (Kan.)	16.69
Fort Smith (Ark.-Okla.)	75.00
Fort Union Trading Post (N.D.-Mont.)	443.80
Fort Vancouver (Wash.)	208.89
Frederick Douglass Home (D.C.)	8.53
Frederick Law Olmsted (Mass.)	1.75
Friendship Hill (Pa.)	674.56
Golden Spike (Utah)	2,735.28
Grant-Kohrs Ranch (Mont.)	1,498.38
Hampton (Md.)	62.04
Harry S. Truman (Mo.)	6.67
Herbert Hoover (Iowa)	186.80
Home of F. D. Roosevelt (N.Y.)	290.34
Hopewell Furnace (Pa.)	848.06
Hubbell Trading Post (Ariz.)	160.09
James A. Garfield (Ohio)	7.82
Jimmy Carter (Ga.)	70.54

Name and location	Total acreage
John F. Kennedy (Mass.)	0.09
John Muir (Calif.)	344.73
Knife River Indian Villages (N.D.)	1,758.35
Lincoln Home (Ill.)	12.24
Longfellow (Mass.)	1.98
Maggie L. Walker (Va.)	1.29
Manzanar National Historic Site (Calif.)	800.00
Martin Luther King, Jr. (Ga.)	36.95
Martin Van Buren (N.Y.)	39.58
Mary McLeod Bethune Council House (D.C.)	0.07
Ninety Six (S.C.)	989.14
Palo Alto Battlefield (Tex.)	3,357.42
Pennsylvania Avenue (D.C.)	n.a.
Puukohola Heiau (Hawaii)	86.24
Sagamore Hill (N.Y.)	83.02
Saint-Gaudens (N.H.)	148.23
Saint Paul's Church (N.Y.)	6.13
Salem Maritime (Mass.)	9.02
San Juan (P.R.)	75.13
Saugus Iron Works (Mass.)	8.51
Springfield Armory (Mass.)	54.93
Steamtown (Pa.)	62.48
Theodore Roosevelt Birthplace (N.Y.)	0.11
Theodore Roosevelt Inaugural (N.Y.)	1.03
Thomas Stone (Md.)	328.25
Tuskegee Institute (Ala.)	57.92
Ulysses S. Grant (Mo.)	9.60
Vanderbilt Mansion (N.Y.)	211.65
Washita Battlefield (Okla.)	330.28
Weir Farm (Conn.)	60.76
Whitman Mission (Wash.)	98.15
William Howard Taft (Ohio)	3.07

National Memorials

Name and location	Total acreage
Arkansas Post (Ark.)	389.18
Arlington House, the Robert E. Lee Memorial (Va.)	27.91
Chamizal (Tex.)	54.90
Coronado (Ariz.)	4,750.22
De Soto (Fla.)	26.84
Federal Hall (N.Y.)	0.45
Fort Caroline (Fla.)	138.39
Fort Clatsop (Ore.)	125.20
Franklin Delano Roosevelt Memorial (D.C.)	7.50
General Grant (N.Y.)	0.76
Hamilton Grange (N.Y.)	0.11
Jefferson National Expansion Memorial (Mo.)	90.96
Johnstown Flood (Pa.)	164.12
Korean War Veterans (D.C.)	2.20
Lincoln Boyhood (Ind.)	199.65
Lincoln Memorial (D.C.)	107.43
Lyndon Baines Johnson Memorial Grove on the Potomac (D.C.)	17.00
Mount Rushmore (S.D.)	1,278.45
Perry's Victory and International Peace Memorial (Ohio)	25.38
Roger Williams (R.I.)	4.56
Thaddeus Kosciuszko (Pa.)	0.02
Theodore Roosevelt Island (D.C.)	88.50
Thomas Jefferson Memorial (D.C.)	18.36
USS Arizona Memorial (Hawaii)	10.50
Vietnam Veterans Memorial (D.C.)	2.00
Washington Monument (D.C.)	106.01
Wright Brothers (N.C.)	428.44

Name and location	Total acreage

National Seashores

Name and location	Total acreage
Assateague Island (Md.-Va.)	39,721.85
Canaveral (Fla.)	57,661.69
Cape Cod (Mass.)	43,569.09
Cape Hatteras (N.C.)	30,319.43
Cape Lookout (N.C.)	28,243.36
Cumberland Island (Ga.)	36,415.39
Fire Island (N.Y.)	19,578.55
Gulf Islands (Fla.-Miss.)	135,607.15
Padre Island (Tex.)	130,434.27
Point Reyes (Calif.)	71,057.03

National Parkways

Name and location	Total acreage
Blue Ridge (Va.-N.C.)	87,992.21
George Washington Memorial (Va.-Md.)	7,247.63
John D. Rockefeller, Jr., Memorial (Wyo.)	23,777.22
Natchez Trace (Miss.-Tenn.-Ala.)	51,747.59

National Lakeshores

Name and location	Total acreage
Apostle Islands (Wis.)	69,371.89
Indiana Dunes (Ind.)	15,139.02
Pictured Rocks (Mich.)	73,235.53
Sleeping Bear Dunes (Mich.)	71,189.40

National Wild and Scenic Rivers

Name and location	Total acreage
Alagnak Wild River (Alaska)	30,800.00
Bluestone National Scenic River (W. Va.)	4,309.51
Delaware (N.Y.-N.J.-Pa.)	1,973.33
Great Egg Harbor River (N.J.)	n.a.
Missouri National Recreational River (Neb.-S.D.)	n.a.
Obed Wild & Scenic River (Tenn.)	5,121.78
Rio Grande Wild & Scenic (Tex.)	9,600.00
St. Croix (Minn.-Wis.)	67,456.27
Upper Delaware (N.Y.-N.J.-Pa.)	75,000.00

National Rivers

Name and location	Total acreage
Big South Fork National River & Recreation Area (Ky.-Tenn.)	125,000.00
Buffalo (Ark.)	94,309.49
Mississippi National River & Recreation Area (Minn.)	53,775.00
New River Gorge (W.Va.)	70,911.69
Niobrara/Missouri National Scenic Riverways (Neb.-S.D.)	n.a.
Ozark (Mo.)	80,790.04

National Recreation Areas

Name and location	Total acreage
Amistad (Tex.)	58,500.00
Bighorn Canyon (Wyo.-Mont.)	120,296.22
Boston Harbor Islands (Mass.)	1,482.25
Chattahoochee River (Ga.)	9,238.81
Chickasaw (Okla.)	9,888.83
Coulee Dam (Wash.)	100,390.31
Curecanti (Colo.)	41,972.42
Cuyahoga Valley (Ohio)	32,524.76
Delaware Water Gap (Pa.-N.J.)	67,191.66
Gateway (N.Y.-N.J.)	26,601.27
Gauley River (W. Va.)	11,145.07
Glen Canyon (Ariz.-Utah)	1,236,880.00
Golden Gate (Calif.)	74,441.36
Lake Chelan (Wash.)	61,886.98
Lake Mead (Ariz.-Nev.)	1,495,665.52
Lake Meredith (Tex.)	44,977.63
Ross Lake (Wash.)	117,574.59
Santa Monica Mountains (Calif.)	150,050.00
Whiskeytown-Shasta-Trinity (Calif.)	42,503.46

Name and location	Total acreage
National Scenic Trail	
Appalachian (Maine-N.H.-Vt.-Mass.-Conn.-N.Y.-N.J.- Pa.-Md.-W.Va.-Va.-N.C.-Tenn., Ga.)	172,109.93
Natchez Trace (Ga.-Ala.-Tenn.)	10,995.00
Potomac Heritage (D.C.-Md.-Va.-Pa.)	n.a.
International Historic Site	
Saint Croix Island (Maine)	35.39
Affiliated Areas	
(National Historic Sites unless otherwise noted.)	
American Memorial Park (N. Mariana Is.)	133.00
Benjamin Franklin (Pa.)[1]	n.a.
Blackstone River Valley National Heritage Corridor (Mass.-R.I.)	n.a.
Chicago Portage (Ill.)	91.20
Chimney Rock (Neb.)	83.36
David Berger (Ohio)[1]	n.a.
Delaware and Lehigh Navigation Canal National Heritage Corridor (Pa.)	n.a.
Father Marquette (Mich.)[1]	52.00
Gloria Dei Church (Pa.)	3.71
Green Springs Historic District (Va.)	5,490.59
Historic Camden (S.C.)	n.a.
Ice Age Scenic Trail (Wis.)	n.a.
Ice Age (Wis.)[2]	32,500.00
Iditarod National Historic Trail (Alaska)	n.a.
Illinois and Michigan Canal National Heritage Corridor	n.a.
International Peace Garden (N.D.)	2,330.30
Jamestown (Va.)	20.63
Lewis & Clark Natl. Historic Trail (Ill.-Mo.-Kan.-Neb.-Iowa-Idaho-S.D.-N.D.-Mont.- Ore.-Wash.)	n.a.
Mary McLeod Bethune Council House (D.C.)	n.a.
McLoughlin House (Ore.)	0.63
Mormon Pioneer Natl. Historic Trail (Ill.-Iowa-Neb.-Wyo.-Utah)	n.a.
North Country Nat'l Scenic Trail (N.Y.-Pa.-Ohio-Mich.-Wis.-Minn.-N.D.)	n.a.
Oregon Natl. Historic Trail (Mo.-Kan.-Neb.-Wyo.-Idaho-Ore.-Wash.)	n.a.
Overmountain Victory Trail (Mo. to Ore.)	n.a.
Pinelands Natl. Reserve (N.J.)	n.a.
Red Hill Patrick Henry (Va.)[1]	n.a.
Roosevelt-Campobello International Park (Canada)	2,721.50
Santa Fe National Historic Trail (Mo. to N.M.)	n.a.
Sewell-Belmont House National Historic Site (D.C.)	0.35
Touro Synagogue (R.I.)	0.23
Trail of Tears National Historic Trail (N.C. to Okla.)	n.a.

1. National Memorial. 2. National Scientific Reserve.

Name and location	Total acreage
National Cemeteries[1]	
Andersonville (Ga.)	494.61
Andrew Johnson (Tenn.)	16.68
Antietam (Md.)	11.36
Battleground (D.C.)	1.03
Fort Donelson (Tenn.)	15.30
Fredericksburg (Va.)	12.00
Gettysburg (Pa.)	20.58
Little Big Horn (Mont.)	765.34
Poplar Grove (Va.)	8.72
Shiloh (Tenn.)	10.05
Stones River (Tenn.)	719.81
Vicksburg (Miss.)	116.28
Yorktown (Va.)	2.91

1. The National Cemeteries are not independent areas of the National Park System; each is part of a military park, battlefield, etc., except Battleground. Their acreage is kept separately. Arlington National Cemetery is under the Department of the Army.

Name and location	Total acreage
Other Parks	
Catoctin Mountain (Md.)	5,770.22
Constitution Gardens (D.C.)	52.00
Fort Washington Park (Md.)	341.00
Greenbelt (Md.)	1,175.99
National Capital Parks (D.C.)	6,546.92
National Mall (D.C.)	146.35
Piscataway (Md.)	4,440.52
Prince William Forest (Va.)	18,571.55
Rock Creek Park (D.C.)	1,754.37
White House (D.C.)	18.07
Wolf Trap Farm Park for the Performing Arts (Va.)	130.28

National Historic Landmarks Designated in 1997

Secretary of the Interior Bruce Babbitt announced the designation of 16 new National Historic Landmarks on December 9, 1997. Among the new landmarks, which are located in 11 different states and one U.S. territory, are President Franklin D. Roosevelt's private retreat in Hyde Park, N.Y.; an Alabama church that had significance in the civil rights movement in the 1960s; three stops on the Underground Railroad; a California immigration station; and a shipwreck from the Spanish-American War.

Brown Chapel, A.M.E. Church (Selma, Ala.)
Cincinnati Observatory (Cincinnati, Ohio)
Farm Creek Section (nr. East Peoria, Ill.)
Johnson House (Philadelphia, Pa.)
Kake Cannery (Kake, Alaska)
Monument Avenue Historic District (Richmond, Va.)
N.C. Wyeth House and Studio (Chadds Fords, Pa.)
New York State Inebriate Asylum (Binghamton, N.Y.)
Old State House (Little Rock, Ark.)
Riversdale Mansion (Riverdale, Md.)
Rokeby (Ferrisburgh, Vt.)
S.S. *Antonio López* (nr. Dorado, Puerto Rico)
Top Cottage (Hyde Park, N.Y.)
Union Square (New York, N.Y.)
U.S. Immigration Station, Angel Island (Tiburon, Calif.)
Wilson Bruce Evans House (Oberlin, Ohio)

Make Way for La Niña, El Niño's Alter Ego

The wild weather continues with the arrival of El Niño's sister

By J. MADELEINE NASH TIME

The latest coming of El Niño, the mysterious, periodic warming of Pacific Ocean waters that leads to nasty extremes in the weather, is among the worst on record, and the impact has varied wildly from one region to another. While floods have soaked the Americas and deadly storms have pelted China, droughts have parched Australia and fueled fires in Southeast Asia and Brazil.

But as bad as this El Niño has been, the future may hold no relief. The period following an El Niño often brings a cooling of those same Pacific seas—a climatic pattern known as La Niña, which generally produces sharp reversals of weather patterns around the globe. Some scientists now say that we may witness an unusually strong La Niña, which has added a new urgency to a long-running scientific mission: the quest to understand El Niño and La Niña.

Improving Predictions

This cycle of disturbances may already be the most studied weather phenomenon of all time. For months, and in some cases years, meteorologists have been poring over weather maps, running supercomputer simulations, studying coral reefs and tree rings—all in an effort to probe the dynamics of water temperatures in the Pacific.

Some researchers want to learn what causes El Niño/La Niña and what keeps the cycle churning. Others want to measure the effect on human life. At the same time, El Niño gives scientists a rare chance to study a phenomenon that transcends the short-term weather forecasts that are the bread and butter of meteorologists. In many ways, El Niño may be a test case for the kind of large-scale weather effects some scientists predict will accompany the climate changes caused by global warming.

Like global warming, El Niño—or rather, the climate cycle that produces El Niño—does not generate weather per se: rather, it alters the context in which weather takes place. The distinction here is a critical one. "Climate," as social scientist Michael Glantz of the National Center for Atmospheric Research, likes to say, "is what you expect. Weather is what you get." Sometimes there can be a wide gulf between the two. In Australia, for example, El Niño caused extremely dry conditions that had farmers fearing disaster. But as it turns out, some rain did fall—just in time to rescue the wheat harvest. Does that mean the drought predictions were wrong? Not at all, says Nicholas Graham, a climate modeler at the University of California at San Diego's Scripps Institution of Oceanography. Think of what El Niño does as the equivalent of rigging a roulette wheel so that it comes up black 40% of the time and red 60% of the time, Graham suggests. "Just because it comes up black once," he says, "you don't conclude the roulette wheel isn't rigged."

In trying to improve their power of prediction, researchers are building on a scientific investigation that began in the 1920s, when the British meteorologist Sir Gilbert Walker linked swings in atmospheric pressure over the Pacific to a calamitous failure of the Indian monsoon 50 years earlier. In the 1960s, UCLA meteorologist Jacob Bjerknes suggested that El Niño was governed by the same swings in atmospheric pressure. The way El Niño works, scientists are now convinced, is that high pressure in the eastern Pacific sends trade winds blowing to the West. Because these winds push water before them like an invisible plow, the sea's surface actually measures about a half-meter higher around Indonesia and Australia than it does off the coast of Peru. When

WHAT NORMALLY HAPPENS

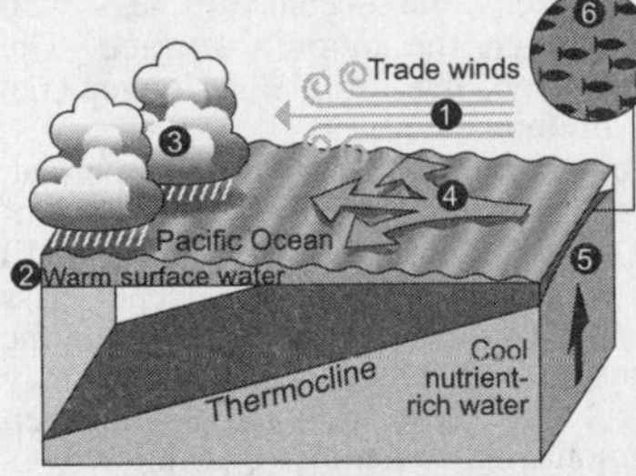

1 Tropical trade winds blow from east to west across the equatorial Pacific Ocean.

2 The winds drag the surface water along with them, causing the ocean in Asia to be about 2 ft. (60 cm) higher than the ocean along the coast of South America.

3 The winds pick up moisture as they blow across the ocean, then release it as monsoon rains over Indonesia.

4 The surface water moves westward and is diverted poleward near the equator by the effect of the earth's rotation.

5 The divergent flow causes an upwelling of deep water, which is cooler, especially in the eastern Pacific, where the transition layer between warmer, shallower water and cooler, bottom water (known as the thermocline) is close to the surface.

6 As the cool water comes up into the sunlight, plankton feed on the nutrients. These creatures support vast amounts of marine life in the waters off Peru and Chile.

THE EL NIÑO PHENOMENON

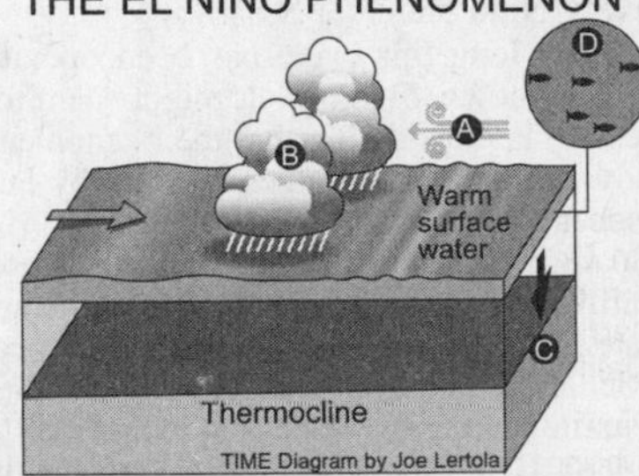

A The trade winds weaken, and the warm water stays in the eastern Pacific.

B The monsoon rains fall over the middle of the Pacific instead of over Southeast Asia.

C The thermocline flattens.

D Marine-life population drops as the nutrients that support it are withdrawn.

the pressure drops and trade winds slacken, the water sloshes back downhill, to the East.

This eastward flow is central to the physics that drive El Niño, says Scripps' Nicholas Graham. The sloshing sends waves across the ocean like ripples in a pond. These waves, in turn, push down on the so-called thermocline, a layer of cooler water that normally mingles with the warmer water at the surface. As the thermocline sinks to greater depths, the mixing stops, temperatures at the sea's surface rise, and an El Niño begins.

These ripples can be thousands of kilometers long, but since they travel 30 m or more beneath the surface they are hard to detect directly. So scientists use satellites to pick up the subtle undulations in sea level produced as the ripples pass by. That's how NASA oceanographer Anthony Busalacchi could see early in 1997 that swarms of undersea waves had started to head out across the Pacific toward the coast of Peru; he followed them as they slammed into the continental shelf, then split, heading sharply south toward Chile and north toward Alaska. The warm water created by the south-moving ripples created a heat wave that sent residents of Santiago flocking to nearby beaches in the middle of their winter, while the north-moving waves triggered a sharp rise in ocean temperatures off the U.S. West Coast, delighting sportfishermen by attracting tropical species like marlin to usually frigid waters.

As El Niño Ebbs, La Niña Flows

These subsurface waves explain more than the origin and propagation of El Niños. They also explain how El Niños end. When the waves first hit the South American coast, some reflect back, like sound bouncing off a wall. When the reflected waves reach Asia, they rebound again. But this double bounce inverts their effect: instead of depressing the thermocline, these twice-reflected waves now lift it up. Cool water dilutes the warmer liquid at the surface, causing a temperature drop in the eastern Pacific—and that decrease is known as La Niña. Thus, observes Ants Leetmaa, director of the National Climate Prediction Center, "each El Niño contains the seeds of its own destruction." For every Niño there's a Niña.

How long this cycle has been operating, no one really knows. Finding out might seem to be a hopeless task, considering that the phenomenon was discovered only about a century ago by Peruvian fishermen. (It was they who called it El Niño, the Spanish name for the Christ child whose December birthday occurs at the peak of the disturbance.) But late in 1997, Columbia University oceanographer Richard Fairbanks was floating in the equatorial Pacific gathering data that could tell researchers about El Niños going back thousands of years. Working aboard the research vessel *Moana Wave*, Fairbanks spent weeks at El Niño's very epicenter, a patch of ocean near Christmas Island in the Republic of Kiribati, 2,100 km from Hawaii. Using a powerful oil drill, he and his colleagues repeatedly bored into ancient reef beds buried beneath the sea floor, pulling up chunks of coral as white as sun-bleached bone.

Measuring El Niño

Corals, it turns out, are like miniature thermometers and rain gauges. When water temperatures rise, these small creatures incorporate less strontium into their skeletons than they do under cooler conditions. Their oxygen content, meanwhile, records salinity swings, which in turn can be used to estimate rainfall. And warm temperatures and heavy rainfall—here, at least—are the telltale markers of El Niño.

Corals are not the only recorders of climate history. Trees too can faithfully preserve evidence of long-past climate patterns. David Stahle of the University of Arkansas Tree Ring Lab recently presented data derived from teaks in Java and firs in Mexico and the American Southwest that date back to 1706. The thicker the trees' growth rings, the more rain fell that year. According to Stahle, "it looks as if a substantial shift occurred after 1880." After that date, the rainfall patterns typical of El Niño start to recur on average every 4.9 years instead of every 7.5 years, while patterns typical of La Niña show up at 4.2-year intervals versus once a decade.

Out of all this information, a crude picture begins to emerge. It appears the El Niño cycle is more variable than scientists previously imagined, subject to protean swings of mood that can last from decades to thousands of years. To account for this eccentric behavior, many scientists invoke the science of chaos, which says slight differences now—a barely perceptible increase in wind speed, for example—can lead to a dramatic change down the road. The El Niño cycle may resemble a chaotic pendulum whose swings never retrace the same path. Yet there is a rhythm to the swings, like a jazzman's improvisations, endlessly circling a central theme.

While all these climate cycles seem to involve both atmosphere and oceans, more and more scientists are abandoning their long-held belief that air currents run the show. The atmosphere is fickle, they observe. Storms form, then quickly dissipate, so whatever information they contain about the conditions that created them is quickly lost. By contrast, ocean gyres—surface currents that follow a sweeping circular route—take anywhere from 10 to 20 years to complete a single journey, making them perfect vehicles for transmitting messages into the future. With the exception of the tropical Pacific, unfortunately, the oceans are less well monitored than even the moon's surface. The changes they undergo, moreover, take longer than any scientist's lifetime.

That's why corals and tree rings are so important. They are like a tape recording of the various instruments in the climate orchestra, ranging from El Niño's high-frequency violin to the deeper bass tones struck by longer-term cycles. By studying the hidden rhythms in these signals, scientists may finally be able to see how the parts fit together, sometimes harmonizing, sometimes clashing.

Over the next few years, researchers hope to shed light not only on El Niño's past but on its future as well. For if the atmosphere warms because of the buildup of greenhouse gases, the El Niño cycle could very well change. We will never have a complete picture of the planet's complex, unpredictable climate patterns, but as this scientific quest moves forward, we could get useful glimpses of what lies ahead. □

Climate of 100 Selected U.S. Cities

	Average monthly temperature (°F)[1]				Precipitation		Snowfall	
					Average annual			
City	Jan.	April	July	Oct.	(in.)[1]	(days)[2]	Average annual (in.)[2]	Years[2]
Albany, N.Y.	21.1	46.6	71.4	50.5	35.74	134	65.5	38
Albuquerque, N.M.	34.8	55.1	78.8	57.4	8.12	59	10.6	45
Anchorage, Alaska	13.0	35.4	58.1	34.6	15.20	115	69.2	41[3]
Asheville, N.C.	36.8	55.7	73.2	56.0	47.71	124	17.5	20
Atlanta, Ga.	41.9	61.8	78.6	62.2	48.61	115	1.9	50
Atlantic City, N.J.	31.8	51.0	74.4	55.5	41.93	112	16.4	40[3]
Austin, Texas	49.1	68.7	84.7	69.8	31.50	83	0.9	43
Baltimore, Md.	32.7	54.0	76.8	56.9	41.84	113	21.8	34
Baton Rouge, La.	50.8	68.4	82.1	68.2	55.77	108	0.1	34[3]
Billings, Mont.	20.9	44.6	72.3	49.3	15.09	96	57.2	50
Birmingham, Ala.	42.9	62.8	80.1	62.6	54.52	117	1.3	41
Bismark, N.D.	6.7	42.5	70.4	46.1	15.36	96	40.3	45
Boise, Idaho	29.9	48.6	74.6	51.9	11.71	92	21.4	45
Boston, Mass.	29.6	48.7	73.5	54.8	43.81	127	41.8	49[3]
Bridgeport, Conn.	29.5	48.6	74.0	56.0	41.56	117	26.0	36
Buffalo, N.Y.	23.5	45.4	70.7	51.5	37.52	169	92.2	41
Burlington, Vt.	16.6	42.7	69.6	47.9	33.69	153	78.2	41
Caribou, Maine	10.7	37.3	65.1	43.1	36.59	160	113.3	45
Casper, Wyo.	22.2	42.1	70.9	47.1	11.43	95	80.5	34
Charleston, S.C.	47.9	64.3	80.5	65.8	51.59	113	0.6	42
Charleston, W.Va.	32.9	55.3	74.5	55.9	42.43	151	31.5	37
Charlotte, N.C.	40.5	60.3	78.5	60.7	43.16	111	6.1	45
Cheyenne, Wyo.	26.1	41.8	68.9	47.5	13.31	98	54.1	49
Chicago, Ill.	21.4	48.8	73.0	53.5	33.34	127	40.3	26
Cleveland, Ohio	25.5	48.1	71.6	53.2	35.40	156	53.6	43
Columbia, S.C.	44.7	63.8	81.0	63.4	49.12	109	1.9	37
Columbus, Ohio	27.1	51.4	73.8	53.9	36.97	137	28.3	37[3]
Concord, N.H.	19.9	44.1	69.5	48.3	36.53	125	64.5	43
Dallas-Ft. Worth, Texas	44.0	65.9	86.3	67.9	29.46	78	3.1	31
Denver, Colo.	29.5	47.4	73.4	51.9	15.31	88	59.8	50
Des Moines, Iowa	18.6	50.5	76.3	54.2	30.83	107	34.7	45
Detroit, Mich.	23.4	47.3	71.9	51.9	30.97	133	40.4	26
Dodge City, Kan.	29.5	54.3	80.0	57.7	20.66	78	19.5	42
Duluth, Minn.	6.3	38.3	65.4	44.2	29.68	135	77.4	41[3]
El Paso, Texas	44.2	63.6	82.5	63.6	7.82	47	5.2	45
Fairbanks, Alaska	–12.7	30.2	61.5	25.1	10.37	106	67.5	33
Fargo, N.D.	4.3	42.1	70.6	46.3	19.59	100	35.9	42
Grand Junction, Colo.	25.5	51.7	78.9	54.9	8.00	72	26.1	38
Grand Rapids, Mich.	22.0	46.3	71.4	50.9	34.35	143	72.4	21
Hartford, Conn.	25.2	48.8	73.4	52.4	44.39	127	50.0	30
Helena, Mont.	18.1	42.3	67.9	45.1	11.37	96	47.9	44
Honolulu, Hawaii	72.6	75.7	80.1	79.5	23.47	100	0.0	38[3]
Houston, Texas	51.4	68.7	83.1	69.7	44.76	105	0.4	50
Indianapolis, Ind.	26.0	52.4	75.1	54.8	39.12	125	23.1	53[3]
Jackson, Miss.	45.7	65.1	81.9	65.0	52.82	109	1.2	21
Jacksonville, Fla.	53.2	67.7	81.3	69.5	52.76	116	T	43
Juneau, Alaska	21.8	39.1	55.7	41.8	53.15	220	102.8	41
Kansas City, Mo.	28.4	56.9	80.9	59.6	29.27	98	20.0	43
Knoxville, Tenn.	38.2	59.6	77.6	59.5	47.29	127	12.3	42
Las Vegas, Nev.	44.5	63.5	90.2	67.5	4.19	26	1.4	36
Lexington, Ky.	31.5	55.1	75.9	56.8	45.68	131	16.3	40
Little Rock, Ark.	39.9	62.4	82.1	63.1	49.20	104	5.4	42
Long Beach, Calif.	55.2	60.9	72.8	67.5	11.54	32	T	41[3]
Los Angeles, Calif.	56.0	59.5	69.0	66.3	12.08	36	T	49
Louisville, Ky.	32.5	56.6	77.6	57.7	43.56	125	17.5	37
Madison, Wisc.	15.6	45.8	70.6	49.5	30.84	118	40.8	36
Memphis, Tenn.	39.6	62.6	82.1	62.9	51.57	107	5.5	34
Miami, Fla.	67.1	75.3	82.5	77.9	57.55	129	0.0	42
Milwaukee, Wisc.	18.7	44.6	70.5	50.9	30.94	125	47.0	44
Minneapolis-St. Paul, Minn.	11.2	46.0	73.1	49.6	26.36	115	48.9	46
Mobile, Ala.	50.8	68.0	82.2	68.5	64.64	123	0.3	43
Montgomery, Ala.	46.7	65.2	81.7	65.3	49.16	108	0.3	40
Mt. Washington, N.H.	5.1	22.4	48.7	30.5	89.92	209	246.8	52
Nashville, Tenn.	37.1	59.7	79.4	60.2	48.49	119	11.1	43
Newark, N.J.	31.2	52.1	76.8	57.2	42.34	122	28.2	43
New Orleans, La.	52.4	68.7	82.1	69.2	59.74	114	0.2	38[3]
New York, N.Y.	31.8	51.9	76.4	57.5	42.82	119	26.1	40[3]

City	Average monthly temperature (°F)[1]				Precipitation		Snowfall	
	Jan.	April	July	Oct.	Average annual (in.)[1]	(days)[2]	Average annual (in.)[2]	Years[2]
Norfolk, Va.	39.9	58.2	78.4	61.3	45.22	115	7.9	36
Oklahoma City, Okla.	35.9	60.2	82.1	62.3	30.89	82	9.0	45
Olympia, Wash.	37.2	47.3	63.0	50.1	50.96	164	18.0	43
Omaha, Neb.	20.2	52.2	77.7	54.5	30.34	98	31.1	49[3]
Philadelphia, Pa.	31.2	52.9	76.5	56.5	41.42	117	21.9	42[3]
Phoenix, Ariz.	52.3	68.1	92.3	73.4	7.11	36	T	47[3]
Pittsburgh, Pa.	26.7	50.1	72.0	52.5	36.30	154	44.6	32
Portland, Maine	21.5	42.8	68.1	48.5	43.52	128	72.4	44
Portland, Ore.	38.9	50.4	67.7	54.3	37.39	154	6.8	44
Providence, R.I.	28.2	47.9	72.5	53.2	45.32	124	37.1	31
Raleigh, N.C.	39.6	59.4	77.7	59.7	41.76	112	7.7	40
Reno, Nev.	32.2	46.4	69.5	50.3	7.49	51	25.3	42
Richmond, Va.	36.6	57.9	77.8	58.6	44.07	113	14.6	47
Roswell, N.M.	41.4	61.9	81.4	61.7	9.70	52	11.4	37[3]
Sacramento, Calif.	45.3	58.2	75.6	63.9	17.10	58	0.1	36[3]
Salt Lake City, Utah	28.6	49.2	77.5	53.0	15.31	90	59.1	56
San Antonio, Texas	50.4	69.6	84.6	70.2	29.13	81	0.4	42
San Diego, Calif.	56.8	61.2	70.3	67.5	9.32	43	T	44
San Francisco, Calif.	48.5	54.8	62.2	60.6	19.71	63	T	57
Savannah, Ga.	49.1	66.0	81.2	66.9	49.70	111	0.3	34
Seattle-Tacoma, Wash.	39.1	48.7	64.8	52.4	38.60	158	12.8	40
Sioux Falls, S.D.	12.4	46.4	74.0	49.4	24.12	96	39.9	39
Spokane, Wash.	25.7	45.8	69.7	47.5	16.71	114	51.5	37
Springfield, Ill.	24.6	53.3	76.5	56.0	33.78	114	24.5	37
St. Louis, Mo.	28.8	56.1	78.9	57.9	33.91	111	19.8	48[3]
Tampa, Fla.	59.8	71.5	82.1	74.4	46.73	107	T	38
Toledo, Ohio	23.1	47.8	71.8	51.7	31.78	137	38.3	29
Tucson, Ariz.	51.1	64.9	86.2	70.4	11.14	52	1.2	44
Tulsa, Okla.	35.2	61.0	83.2	62.6	38.77	89	9.0	46
Vero Beach, Fla.	61.9	71.7	81.1	75.2	51.41	n.a.	n.a.	0
Washington, D.C.	35.2	56.7	78.9	59.3	39.00	112	17.0	41[3]
Wichita, Kan.	29.6	56.3	81.4	59.1	28.61	85	16.4	31
Wilmington, Del.	31.2	52.4	76.0	56.3	41.38	117	20.9	37

1. Based on 30-year period 1951–80. Data latest available. 2. Data through 1984 based on number of years as indicated in Years column. 3. For snowfall data where number of years differs from that for precipitation data. T = trace. n.a. = not available. *Source:* National Oceanic and Atmospheric Administration.

Wind Chill Factors

Wind speed (mph)	Thermometer reading (°F)																
	35	30	25	20	15	10	5	0	–5	–10	–15	–20	–25	–30	–35	–40	–45
5	33	27	21	19	12	7	0	–5	–10	–15	–21	–26	–31	–36	–42	–47	–52
10	22	16	10	3	–3	–9	–15	–22	–27	–34	–40	–46	–52	–58	–64	–71	–77
15	16	9	2	–5	–11	–18	–25	–31	–38	–45	–51	–58	–65	–72	–78	–85	–92
20	12	4	–3	–10	–17	–24	–31	–39	–46	–53	–60	–67	–74	–81	–88	–95	–103
25	8	1	–7	–15	–22	–29	–36	–44	–51	–59	–66	–74	–81	–88	–96	–103	–110
30	6	–2	–10	–18	–25	–33	–41	–49	–56	–64	–71	–79	–86	–93	–101	–109	–116
35	4	–4	–12	–20	–27	–35	–43	–2	–58	–67	–74	–82	–89	–97	–105	–113	–120
40	3	–5	–13	–21	–29	–37	–45	–53	–60	–69	–76	–84	–92	–100	–107	–115	–123
45	2	–6	–14	–22	–30	–38	–46	–54	–62	–70	–78	–85	–93	–102	–109	–117	–125

NOTE: This chart gives equivalent temperatures for combinations of wind speed and temperature. For example, the combination of a temperature of 10° Fahrenheit and a wind blowing at 10 mph has a cooling power equal to –9° F. Wind speeds of higher than 45 mph have little additional cooling effect.

Recorded Weather Extremes

Highest average annual mean temperature (world): Dallol, Ethiopia (Oct. 1960–Dec. 1966), 94° F (35° C). **(U.S.):** Key West, Fla. (30-year normal), 78.2° F (25.7° C).

Lowest average annual mean temperature (world): Plateau Station, Antarctica, –70° F (–7° C). **(U.S.):** Barrow, Alaska (30-year normal), 9.3° F (–13° C).

Greatest average yearly rainfall (world): Cherrapunji, India (74-year avg), 450 in. (1,143 cm). **(U.S.):** Mt. Waialeale, Kauai, Hawaii (32-year avg), 460 in. (1,168 cm).

Minimum average yearly rainfall (world): Arica, Chile (59-year avg), 0.03 in. (0.08 cm) (no rainfall for 14 consecutive years). **(U.S.):** Death Valley, Calif. (42-year avg), 1.63 in. (4.14 cm). Bagdad, Calif., holds the U.S. record for the longest period with no measurable rain, 767 days, from Oct. 3, 1912 to Nov. 8, 1914.

Hottest summer average in Western Hemisphere (U.S.): Death Valley, Calif., 98° F (36.7° C).

Longest hot spell (world): Marble Bar, W. Australia, 100° F (38° C) (or above) for 162 consecutive days, Oct. 30, 1923 to Apr. 7, 1924.

Largest hailstone (U.S.): Coffeyville, Kans., 17.5 in. (44.5 cm), Sept. 3, 1979.

World and U.S. Extremes of Climate

Highest Recorded Temperatures

	Place	Date	Degrees Fahrenheit	Degrees Centigrade
World (Africa)	El Azizia, Libya	Sept. 13, 1922	136	58
North America (U.S.)	Death Valley, Calif.	July 10, 1913	134	57
Asia	Tirat Tsvi, Israel	June 21, 1942	129	54
Australia	Cloncurry, Queensland	Jan. 16, 1889	128	53
Europe	Seville, Spain	Aug. 4, 1881	122	50
South America	Rivadavia, Argentina	Dec. 11, 1905	120	49
Canada	Midale and Yellow Grass, Saskatchewan, Canada	July 5, 1937	113	45
Persian Gulf (sea-surface)		Aug. 5, 1924	96	36
Antarctica	Vanda Station	Jan. 5, 1974	59	15
South Pole		Dec. 27, 1978	7.5	–14

Lowest Recorded Temperatures

	Place	Date	Degrees Fahrenheit	Degrees Centigrade
World (Antarctica)	Vostok	July 21, 1983	–129	–89
Asia	Verkhoyansk/Oimekon	Feb. 6, 1933	–90	–68
Greenland	Northice	Jan. 9, 1954	–87	–66
North America (excl. Greenland)	Snag, Yukon, Canada	Feb. 3, 1947	–81	–63
United States	Prospect Creek, Alaska	Jan. 23, 1971	–80	–62
U.S. (excl. Alaska)	Rogers Pass, Mont.	Jan. 20, 1954	–70	–56.5
Europe	Ust 'Shchugor, Russia	n.a.	–67	–55
South America	Sarmiento, Argentina	June 1, 1907	–27	–33
Africa	Ifrane, Morocco	Feb. 11, 1935	–11	–24
Australia	Charlotte Pass, N.S.W.	June 29, 1994	–9	–22

Greatest Rainfalls

	Place	Date	Inches	Centimeters
1 minute (World)	Unionville, Md.	July 4, 1956	1.23	3.1
20 minutes (World)	Curtea-de-Arges, Romania	July 7, 1889	8.1	20.5
42 minutes (World)	Holt, Mo.	June 22, 1947	12	30.5
12 hours (World)	Grand Ilet, La Réunion	Jan. 26, 1980	46	114
24 hours (World)	Foc-Foc, La Réunion	Jan. 7–8, 1966	72	182.5
24 hours (N. Hemisphere)	Paishih, Taiwan	Sept. 10–11, 1963	49	125
24 hours (Australia)	Bellenden Ker, Queensland	Jan. 4, 1979	44	114
24 hours (U.S.)	Alvin, Tex.	July 25–26, 1979	43	109
24 hours (Canada)	Ucluelet Brynnor Mines, British Columbia	Oct. 6, 1967	19	49
5 days (World)	Commerson, La Réunion	Jan. 23–28, 1980	156	395
1 month (World)	Cherrapunji, India	July 1861	366	930
12 months (World)	Cherrapunji, India	Aug. 1860–Aug. 1861	1,042	2,647
12 months (U.S.)	Kukui, Maui, Hawaii	Dec. 1981–Dec. 1982	739	1878

Greatest Snowfalls

	Place	Date	Inches	Centimeters
1 month (U.S.)	Tamarack, Calif.	Jan. 1911	390	991
24 hours (N. America)	Silver Lake, Colo.	April 14–15, 1921	76	195.6
24 hours (Alaska)	Thompson Pass	Dec. 29, 1955	62	157.5
19 hours (France)	Bessans	April 5–6, 1969	68	173
1 storm (N. America)	Mt. Shasta Ski Bowl, Calif.	Feb. 13–19, 1959	189	480
1 storm (Alaska)	Thompson Pass	Dec. 26–31, 1955	175	445.5
1 season (N. America)	Paradise Ranger Sta., Wash.	1971–1972	1,122	2,850
1 season (Alaska)	Thompson Pass	1952–1953	974.5	2,475
1 season (Canada)	Revelstoke Mt. Copeland, British Columbia	1971–1972	964	2,446.5

Source: U.S. Army Corps of Engineers, Engineer Topographic Laboratories.

Apparent Temperature for Values of Room Temperature and Relative Humidity

Relative Humidity (%)

Room temperature (°F)	0	10	20	30	40	50	60	70	80	90	100
75	68	69	71	72	74	75	76	76	77	78	79
74	66	68	69	71	72	73	74	75	76	77	78
73	65	67	68	70	71	72	73	74	75	76	77
72	64	65	67	68	70	71	72	73	74	75	76
71	63	64	66	67	68	70	71	72	73	74	75
70	63	64	65	66	67	68	69	70	71	72	73
69	62	63	64	65	66	67	68	69	70	71	72
68	61	62	63	64	65	66	67	68	69	70	71
67	60	61	62	63	64	65	66	67	68	68	69
66	59	60	61	62	63	64	65	66	67	67	68
65	59	60	61	61	62	63	64	65	65	66	67
64	58	59	60	60	61	62	63	64	64	65	66
63	57	58	59	59	60	61	62	62	63	64	64
62	56	57	58	58	59	60	61	61	62	63	63
61	56	57	57	58	59	59	60	60	61	61	62
60	55	56	56	57	58	58	59	59	60	60	61

Source: National Oceanic and Atmospheric Administration, Environmental Data and Information Service and National Climatic Center.

Tropical Storms and Hurricanes, 1886–1997

	Jan.-April	May	June	July	Aug.	Sept.	Oct.	Nov.	Dec.	Total
Number of tropical storms (incl. hurricanes)	4	14	60	78	234	319	197	46	6	958
Number of tropical storms that reached hurricane intensity	1	3	24	40	160	202	100	24	3	557

Source: National Hurricane Center.

Record Highest Temperatures by State

State	Temp. °F	Temp. °C	Date	Station	Elevation in feet
Alabama	112	44	Sept. 5, 1925	Centerville	345
Alaska	100	38	June 27, 1915	Fort Yukon	est. 420
Arizona	128	53	June 29, 1994	Lake Havasu	785
Arkansas	120	49	Aug. 10, 1936	Ozark	396
California	134	57	July 10, 1913	Greenland Ranch	-178
Colorado	118	48	July 11, 1888	Bennett	5,484
Connecticut	106	41	July 15, 1995	Danbury	457
Delaware	110	43	July 21, 1930	Millsboro	20
D.C.	106	41	July 20, 1930	Washington	410
Florida	109	43	June 29, 1931	Monticello	207
Georgia	113	45	May 27, 1978	Greenville	860
Hawaii	100	38	Apr. 27, 1931	Pahala	850
Idaho	118	48	July 28, 1934	Orofino	1,027
Illinois	117	47	July 14, 1954	E. St. Louis	410
Indiana	116	47	July 14, 1936	Collegeville	672
Iowa	118	48	July 20, 1934	Keokuk	614
Kansas	121	49	July 24, 1936*	Alton (near)	1,651
Kentucky	114	46	July 28, 1930	Greensburg	581
Louisiana	114	46	Aug. 10, 1936	Plain Dealing	268
Maine	105	41	July 10, 1911*	North Bridgton	450
Maryland	109	43	July 10, 1936*	Cumberland & Frederick	623; 325
Massachusetts	107	42	Aug. 2, 1975	New Bedford & Chester	120; 640
Michigan	112	44	July 13, 1936	Mio	963
Minnesota	114	46	July 6, 1936*	Moorhead	904
Mississippi	115	46	July 29, 1930	Holly Springs	600
Missouri	118	48	July 14, 1954*	Warsaw & Union	687; 560
Montana	117	47	July 5, 1937	Medicine Lake	1,950
Nebraska	118	48	July 24, 1936*	Minden	2,169
Nevada	125	52	June 29, 1994	Laughlin	680
New Hampshire	106	41	July 4, 1911	Nashua	125
New Jersey	110	43	July 10, 1936	Runyon	18
New Mexico	122	50	June 27, 1994	Lakewood	3,418
New York	108	42	July 22, 1926	Troy	35
North Carolina	110	43	Aug. 21, 1983	Fayetteville	81
North Dakota	121	49	July 6, 1936	Steele	1,857
Ohio	113	45	July 21, 1934*	Gallipolis (near)	673
Oklahoma	120	49	June 29, 1994*	Tipton	1,251
Oregon	119	48	Aug. 10, 1898	Pendleton	1,074
Pennsylvania	111	44	July 10, 1936*	Phoenixville	100
Rhode Island	104	40	Aug. 2, 1975	Providence	51
South Carolina	111	44	June 28, 1954*	Camden	170
South Dakota	120	49	July 5, 1936	Gannvalley	1,750
Tennessee	113	45	Aug. 9, 1930*	Perryville	377
Texas	120	49	Aug. 12, 1936	Seymour	1,291
Utah	117	47	July 5, 1895	Saint George	2,880
Vermont	105	41	July 4, 1911	Vernon	310
Virginia	110	43	July 15, 1954	Balcony Falls	725
Washington	118	48	Aug. 5, 1961*	Ice Harbor Dam	475
West Virginia	112	44	July 10, 1936*	Martinsburg	435
Wisconsin	114	46	July 13, 1936	Wisconsin Dells	900
Wyoming	114	46	July 12, 1900	Basin	3,500

* Also on earlier dates at the same or other places. *Source:* National Climatic Data Center, Asheville, N.C., and Storm Phillips, STORMFAX, INC.

Record Lowest Temperatures by State

State	Temp. °F	Temp. °C	Date	Station	Elevation in feet
Alabama	–27	–33	Jan. 30, 1966	New Market	760
Alaska	–80	–62	Jan. 23, 1971	Prospect Creek	1,100
Arizona	–40	–40	Jan. 7, 1971	Hawley Lake	8,180
Arkansas	–29	–34	Feb. 13, 1905	Pond	1,250
California	–45	–43	Jan. 20, 1937	Boca	5,532
Colorado	–61	–52	Feb. 1, 1985	Maybell	5,920
Connecticut	–32	–36	Feb. 16, 1943	Falls Village	585
Delaware	–17	–27	Jan. 17, 1893	Millsboro	20
D.C.	–15	–26	Feb. 11, 1899	Washington	410
Florida	–2	–19	Feb. 13, 1899	Tallahassee	193
Georgia	–17	–27	Jan. 27, 1940	CCC Camp F-16	est. 1,000
Hawaii	7	–14	Jan. 23, 1997	Mauna Kea	13,770
Idaho	–60	–51	Jan. 18, 1943	Island Park Dam	6,285
Illinois	–35	–37	Feb. 3, 1996	Elizabeth	880
Indiana	–36	–38	Jan. 19, 1994	New Whiteland	785
Iowa	–47	–44	Feb. 3, 1996	Elkader	745
Kansas	–40	–40	Feb. 13, 1905	Lebanon	1,812
Kentucky	–37	–38	Jan. 19, 1994	Shelbyville	730
Louisiana	–16	–27	Feb. 13, 1899	Minden	194
Maine	–48	–44	Jan. 19, 1925	Van Buren	510
Maryland	–40	–40	Jan. 13, 1912	Oakland	2,461
Massachusetts	–35	–37	Jan. 12, 1981	Chester	640
Michigan	–51	–46	Feb. 9, 1934	Vanderbilt	785
Minnesota	–60	–51	Feb. 2, 1996	Tower	1,400
Mississippi	–19	–28	Jan. 30, 1966	Corinth	420
Missouri	–40	–40	Feb. 13, 1905	Warsaw	700
Montana	–70	–57	Jan. 20, 1954	Rogers Pass	5,470
Nebraska	–47	–44	Feb. 12, 1899	Camp Clarke	3,700
Nevada	–50	–46	Jan. 8, 1937	San Jacinto	5,200
New Hampshire	–46	–43	Jan. 28, 1925	Pittsburg	1,575
New Jersey	–34	–37	Jan. 5, 1904	River Vale	70
New Mexico	–50	–46	Feb. 1, 1951	Gavilan	7,350
New York	–52	–47	Feb. 18, 1979*	Old Forge	1,720
North Carolina	–34	–37	Jan. 21, 1985	Mt. Mitchell	6,525
North Dakota	–60	–51	Feb. 15, 1936	Parshall	1,929
Ohio	–39	–39	Feb. 10, 1899	Milligan	800
Oklahoma	–27	–33	Jan. 18, 1930	Watts	958
Oregon	–54	–48	Feb. 10, 1933*	Seneca	4,700
Pennsylvania	–42	–41	Jan. 5, 1904	Smethport	est. 1,500
Rhode Island	–25	–32	Feb. 5, 1996	Greene	425
South Carolina	–20	–28	Jan. 18, 1977	Caesars Head	3,100
South Dakota	–58	–50	Feb. 17, 1936	McIntosh	2,277
Tennessee	–32	–36	Dec. 30, 1917	Mountain City	2,471
Texas	–23	–31	Feb. 8, 1933*	Seminole	3,275
Utah	–69	–56	Feb. 1, 1985	Peters Sink	8,095
Vermont	–50	–46	Dec. 30, 1933	Bloomfield	915
Virginia	–30	–34	Jan. 22, 1985	Mountain Lake	3,870
Washington	–48	–44	Dec. 30, 1968	Mazama & Winthrop	2,120; 1,765
West Virginia	–37	–38	Dec. 30, 1917	Lewisburg	2,200
Wisconsin	–54	–48	Jan. 24, 1922	Danbury	908
Wyoming	–63	–53	Feb. 9, 1933	Moran	6,770

* Also on earlier dates at the same or other places. *Source:* National Climatic Data Center, Asheville, N.C., and Storm Phillips, STORMFAX, INC.

Record Monthly High and Low Temperatures in the United States

Source: National Climatic Data Center, Asheville, N.C., and Storm Phillips, STORMFAX, Inc.

January

The highest temperature ever recorded for the month of January occurred on January 17, 1936, and again in 1954, in Laredo, Tex. (elevation 421 ft.), where the temperature reached 98° F.

The lowest temperature ever recorded for the month of January occurred on January 20, 1954, in Rogers Pass, Mont. (elevation 5,470 ft.), where the temperature fell to –70° F.

February

The highest temperature ever recorded for the month of February occurred on February 3, 1963, in Montezuma, Ariz. (elevation 735 ft.), where the temperature reached 105° F.

The lowest temperature ever recorded for the month of February occurred on February 1, 1985, at the Peters Sink station in Utah (elevation 8,095 ft.), where the temperature fell to –69° F.

March

The highest temperature ever recorded for the month of March occurred on March 31, 1954, in Rio Grande City, Tex. (elevation 168 ft.), where the temperature reached 108° F.

The lowest temperature ever recorded for the month of March occurred on March 17, 1906, in Snake River, Wyo. (elevation 6,862 ft.), where the temperature dropped to –50° F.

April

The highest temperature ever recorded for the month of April occurred on April 25, 1898, at Volcano Springs, Calif. (elevation –220 ft.), where the temperature reached 118° F.

The lowest temperature ever recorded for the month of April occurred on April 5, 1945, in Eagle Nest, N.M. (elevation 8,250 ft.), where the temperature dropped to –36° F.

May

The highest temperature ever recorded for the month of May occurred on May 27, 1896, in Salton, Calif. (elevation –263 ft.), where the temperature reached 124° F.

The lowest temperature ever recorded for the month of May occurred on May 7, 1964, in White Mountain 2, Calif. (elevation 12,470 ft.), where the temperature dropped to –15° F.

June

The highest temperature ever recorded for the month of June occurred on June 23, 1902, at Volcano Springs, Calif. (elevation –220 ft.), where the temperature reached 129° F.

The lowest temperature ever recorded for the month of June occurred on June 13, 1907, in Tamarack, Calif. (elevation 8,000 ft.), where the temperature dropped to 2° F.

July

The highest temperature ever recorded for the month of July occurred on July 10, 1913, at Greenland Ranch, Calif. (elevation –178 ft.), where the temperature reached 134° F.

The lowest temperature ever recorded for the month of July occurred on July 21, 1911, at Painter, Wyo. (elevation 6,800 ft.), where the temperature fell to 10° F.

August

The highest temperature ever recorded for the month of August occurred on August 12, 1933, at Greenland Ranch, Calif. (elevation –178 ft.), where the temperature reached 127° F.

The lowest temperature ever recorded for the month of August occurred on August 25, 1910, in Bowen, Mont. (elevation 6,080 ft.), where the temperature fell to 5° F.

September

The highest temperature ever recorded for the month of September occurred on September 2, 1950, in Mecca, Calif. (elevation –175 ft.), where the temperature reached 126° F.

The lowest temperature ever recorded for the month of September occurred on September 24, 1926, at Riverside Ranger Station, Mont. (elevation 6,700 ft.), where the temperature fell to –9° F.

October

The highest temperature ever recorded for the month of October occurred on October 5, 1917, in Sentinel, Ariz. (elevation 685 ft.), where the temperature reached 116° F.

The lowest temperature ever recorded for the month of October occurred on October 29, 1917, in Soda Butte, Wyo. (elevation 6,600 ft.), where the temperature fell to –33° F.

November

The highest temperature ever recorded for the month of November occurred on November 12, 1906, in Craftonville, Calif. (elevation 1,759 ft.), where the temperature reached 105° F.

The lowest temperature ever recorded for the month of November occurred on November 16, 1959, at Lincoln, Mont. (elevation 5,130 ft.), where the temperature fell to –53° F.

December

The highest temperature ever recorded for the month of December occurred on December 8, 1938, in La Mesa, Calif. (elevation 539 ft.), where the temperature reached 100° F.

The lowest temperature ever recorded for the month of December occurred on December 19, 1924, at Riverside Ranger Station, Mont. (elevation 6,700 ft.), where the temperature fell to –59° F.

Temperature Extremes in the United States

Source: National Oceanic and Atmospheric Administration, Environmental Data and Information Service, and National Climatic Center

The Highest Temperature Extremes

Greenland Ranch, California, with 134° F on July 10, 1913, holds the record for the highest temperature ever officially observed in the United States. This station was located in barren Death Valley, 178 feet below sea level. Death Valley is about 140 miles long, four to six miles wide, and oriented north to south in southwestern California. Much of the valley is below sea level and is flanked by towering mountain ranges with Mt. Whitney, the highest landmark in the 48 conterminous states, rising to 14,495 feet above sea level, less than 100 miles to the west. Death Valley has the hottest summers in the Western Hemisphere, and is the only known place in the United States where nighttime temperatures sometimes remain above 100° F.

The highest annual normal (1941–1970 mean) temperature in the United States, 78.2° F, and the highest summer (June–August) normal temperature, 92.8° F, are for Death Valley, California. The highest winter (December–February) normal temperature is 72.8° F for Honolulu, Hawaii.

Amazing temperature rises of 40° to 50° F in a few minutes occasionally may be brought about by chinook winds.[1]

Some Outstanding Temperature Rises

In 12 hours: 83° F, Granville, N.D., Feb. 21, 1918, from –33° F to 50° F from early morning to late afternoon.

In 15 minutes: 42° F, Fort Assiniboine, Mont., Jan. 19, 1892, from –5° F to 37° F.

In seven minutes: 34° F, Kipp, Mont., Dec. 1, 1896. The observer also reported that a total rise of 80° F occurred in a few hours and that 30 inches of snow disappeared in half a day.

In two minutes: 49° F, Spearfish, S.D., Jan. 22, 1943, from –4° F at 7:30 A.M. to 45° F at 7:32 A.M.

The Lowest Temperature Extremes

The lowest temperature on record in the United States, –79.8° F, was observed at Prospect Creek Camp in the Endicott Mountains of northern Alaska (latitude 66°48′N, longitude 150°40′W) on Jan. 23, 1971. The lowest ever recorded in the conterminous 48 states, –69.7° F, occurred at Rogers Pass, in Lewis and Clark County, Mont., on Jan. 20, 1954. Rogers Pass is in mountainous and heavily forested terrain about one half of a mile east of and 140 feet below the summit of the Continental Divide.

The lowest annual normal (1941–1970 mean) temperature in the United States is 9.3° F for Barrow, Alaska, which lies on the Arctic coast. Barrow also has the coolest summers (June–August) with a normal temperature of 36.4° F. The lowest winter (December–February) normal temperature, is –15.7° F for Barter Island on the Arctic coast of northeast Alaska.

In the 48 conterminous states, Mt. Washington, N.H. (elevation 6,262 feet), has the lowest annual normal temperature, 26.9° F, and the lowest normal summer temperature, 46.8° F. A few stations in the northeastern United States and in the upper Rocky Mountains have normal annual temperatures in the 30s; summer normal temperatures at these stations are in the low 50s. Winter normal temperatures are lowest in northeastern North Dakota, 5.6° F for Langdon Experiment Farm, and in northwestern Minnesota, 5.3° F for Hallock.

Some Outstanding Temperature Falls

In 24 hours: 100° F, Browing, Mont., Jan. 23–24, 1916, from 44° F to –56° F.

In 12 hours: 84° F, Fairfield, Mont., Dec. 24, 1924, from 63° F at noon to –21° F at midnight.

In 2 hours: 62° F, Rapid City, S.D., Jan. 12, 1911, from 49° F at 6:00 A.M. to –13° F at 8:00 A.M.

In 27 minutes: 58° F, Spearfish, S.D., Jan. 22, 1943, from 54° F at 9:00 A.M. to –4° F at 9:27 A.M.

In 15 minutes: 47° F, Rapid City, S.D., Jan. 10, 1911, from 55° F at 7:00 A.M. to 8° F. at 7:15 A.M.

1. A warm, dry wind that descends from the eastern slopes of the Rocky Mountains, causing a rapid rise in temperature.

Tornado Facts and Myths

Tornadoes, violently rotating columns of air extending from a thunderstorm to the ground, are among nature's most virulent storms. In an average year, 800 tornadoes are reported across the United States, resulting in 80 deaths and more than 1,500 injuries. The worst tornadoes are capable of tremendous destruction with wind speeds of 250 miles per hour or more.

Tornadoes can occur anywhere in the U.S. at any time of the year. In the southern states, the peak tornado season is March through May, while peak months in the northern states are during the summer.

Myth: Areas near rivers, lakes, and mountains are safe from tornadoes.

Fact: No place is safe. In the late 1980s, a tornado swept through Yellowstone National Park leaving a path of destruction up and down a 10,000-foot mountain.

Myth: The low pressure in a tornado causes buildings to "explode" as the tornado passes overhead.

Fact: Violent winds exceeding 200 miles per hour and debris slamming into buildings cause most structural damage.

Myth: Windows should be opened before a tornado approaches to equalize pressure and minimize damage.

Fact: Opening windows allows damaging winds to enter the structure and wastes precious time. Leave the windows alone; instead, immediately go to a safe place.

The following lists are not all-inclusive due to space limitations. Only disasters involving great loss of life and/or property, historical interest, or unusual circumstances are listed. Data as of early Sept. 1998. For later disasters *see* Current Events: What Happened in 1998.

WORST UNITED STATES DISASTERS

AIRCRAFT

1979 **May 25, Chicago:** American Airlines DC-10 lost left engine upon take-off and crashed seconds later, killing all 272 persons aboard and three on the ground in worst U.S. air disaster.

DAM

1928 **March 12, Santa Paula, Calif.:** collapse of St. Francis Dam left 450 dead.

DROUGHT

1930s **Many states:** longest drought of 20th century. Peak periods were 1930, 1934, 1936, 1939, and 1940. During 1934, dry regions stretched solidly from N.Y. and Pa. across the Great Plains to the Calif. coast. A great "dust bowl" covered 50 million acres in south central plains during winter of 1935-1936.

EARTHQUAKE

1906 **April 18, San Francisco:** earthquake accompanied by fire razed more than 4 sq mi.; more than 500 dead or missing.

EPIDEMIC

1918 **Nationwide:** Spanish influenza killed over 500,000 Americans.

EXPLOSION

1947 **April 16–18, Texas City, Tex.** most of the city destroyed by a fire and subsequent explosion on the French freighter *Grandcamp* carrying a cargo of ammonium nitrate. At least 516 were killed and over 3,000 injured.

FIRE

1871 **Oct. 8, Peshtigo, Wis.:** over 1,200 lives lost and 2 billion trees burned in forest fire.

FLOOD

1889 **May 31, Johnstown, Pa.:** more than 2,200 died in flood.

HURRICANE

1900 **Aug. 27–Sept. 15, Galveston, Tex.:** The "Galveston Hurricane" killed over 6,000 from devastation due to both winds and tidal wave.

MARINE

1865 **April 27, Mississippi River, Tenn.:** boiler explosion on Mississippi River steamboat, *Sultana,* near Memphis; 1,547 killed.

MINE

1907 **Dec. 6, Monongha, W. Va.:** coal mine explosion killed 361.

OIL SPILL

1989 **Mar. 24, Prince William Sound, Alaska:** tanker, *Exxon Valdez,* hit an undersea reef and released 10 million plus gallons of oil into the waters.

RAILROAD

1918 **July 9, Nashville, Tenn.:** 101 killed in a two-train collision near Nashville.

SUBMARINE

1963 **April 10, North Atlantic:** atomic-powered submarine, *Thresher,* sank; 129 dead.

TERRORIST ATTACK

1995 **April 19, Oklahoma City:** car bomb exploded outside Federal office building, collapsing wall and floors. 168 persons were killed, including 19 children and one person who died in rescue effort. Over 220 buildings sustained damage. Timothy McVeigh and Terry Nichols later convicted in the antigovernment plot to avenge the Branch Davidian standoff in Waco, Tex. exactly two years earlier. (*See* Miscellaneous Disasters.)

TORNADO

1925 **March 18, Mo., Ill., and Ind.:** great tri-state tornado; 695 deaths. Eight additional tornadoes in Ky., Tenn., and Ala. raised day's toll to 792 dead.

WINTER STORM

1888 **March 11–14, East Coast:** The Blizzard of 1888. 400 people died; as much as five feet of snow. Damage was estimated at $20 million.

EARTHQUAKES AND VOLCANIC ERUPTIONS

C.E. 79 **Aug. 24, Italy:** eruption of Mt. Vesuvius buried cities of Pompeii and Herculaneum, killing thousands.

1556 **Jan. 24, Shaanxi (Shensi) Province, China:** most deadly earthquake in history; 830,000 killed.

1755 **Nov. 1, Portugal:** one of the most severe of recorded earthquakes leveled Lisbon and was felt as far away as southern France and North Africa; 10,000–20,000 killed in Lisbon.

1811 **Dec. 16, Mississippi Valley nr. New Madrid, Mo.:** earthquake reversed the course of the Mississippi River. Fatalities unknown due to sparse population in area. Aftershocks and tremors continued into 1812. It has been estimated that three of the series of earthquakes had surface-wave magnitudes of 8.6, 8.4, and 8.8 on the Richter Scale. It is the largest series of earthquakes known to have occurred in North America.

1883 **Aug. 26–28, Netherlands Indies:** eruption of Krakatau; violent explosions destroyed two-thirds of island. Sea waves occurred as far away as Cape Horn, and possibly England. Estimated 36,000 dead.

1886 **Aug. 31, Charleston, S.C.:** 60 persons killed and damage to city extensive. The magnitude was 7.7 on the Richter Scale.

1902 **May 8, Martinique, West Indies:** Mt. Pelée erupted and wiped out city of St. Pierre; 40,000 dead.

1906 **April 18, San Francisco:** earthquake accompanied by fire razed more than 4 sq mi.; more than 500 dead or missing.

1908 **Dec. 28, Messina, Sicily:** about 85,000 killed and city totally destroyed.

1915 **Jan. 13, Avezzano, Italy:** earthquake left 29,980 dead.

1920 **Dec. 16, Gansu (Kansu) Province, China:** earthquake killed 200,000.

1923 **Sept. 1, Japan:** earthquake destroyed third of Tokyo and most of Yokohama; more than 140,000 killed.

1933 **March 10, Long Beach, Calif.:** 117 left dead by earthquake.

1935 **May 31, India:** earthquake at Quetta killed an estimated 50,000.

1939 **Jan. 24, Chile:** earthquake razed 50,000 sq mi.; about 30,000 killed.

Dec. 27, Northern Turkey: severe quakes destroyed city of Erzingan; about 100,000 casualties.

1950 **Aug. 15, India:** earthquake affected 30,000 sq mi. in Assam; 20,000–30,000 believed killed.

1964 **March 27, Alaska:** strongest earthquake ever to strike North America hit 80 miles east of Anchorage; followed by seismic wave 50 feet high that traveled 8,445 miles at 450 miles per hour; 117 killed.

1970 **May 31, Peru:** earthquake left 50,000 dead, 17,000 missing.

1972 **Dec. 22, Managua, Nicaragua:** earthquake devastated city, leaving up to 6,000 dead.

1976 **Feb. 4, Guatemala:** quake left over 23,000 dead.

July 28, Tangshan, China: earthquake devastated 20-sq-mi. area of city, leaving estimated 242,000 dead.

Aug. 17, Mindanao, Philippines: earthquake and tidal wave left up to 8,000 dead or missing.

1978 **Sept. 16, Tabas, Iran:** earthquake destroyed city in eastern Iran, leaving 25,000 dead.

1985 **Sept. 19–20, Mexico:** earthquake registering 8.1 on Richter scale struck central and southwestern regions, devastating part of Mexico City and three coastal states. An estimated 25,000 killed.

Nov. 14–16, Colombia: eruption of Nevada del Ruiz, 85 miles northwest of Bogotá. Mud slides buried most of the town of Armero and devastated Chinchiná. About 25,000 killed.

1988 **Dec. 7, Armenia:** earthquake measuring 6.9 on the Richter scale killed nearly 25,000, injured 15,000, and left at least 400,000 homeless.

1989 **Oct. 17, San Francisco Bay Area:** earthquake measuring 7.1 on Richter Scale killed 67 and injured over 3,000. Over 100,000 buildings damaged or destroyed; damage cost city billions of dollars.

1990 **June 21, Northwestern Iran:** earthquake measuring 7.7 on Richter Scale destroyed cities and villages in Caspian Sea area. At least 50,000 dead, over 60,000 injured, and 400,000 homeless.

1994 **Jan. 17, San Fernando Valley, Calif.:** earthquake measuring 6.6 on Richter Scale killed 61 and injured over 8,000. Damage estimated at $13–20 billion.

1995 **Jan.17, Osaka, Kyoto, Kobe, Japan:** 5,100 killed and 26,800 injured, estimated damage $100 billion. Epicenter 12 miles under Awaji Island in the Inland Sea. Magnitude: 7.2.

1997 **May 12, Northeastern Iran:** severe earthquake measuring 7.1 on Richter Scale left more than 1,500 people dead and at least 4,460 injured.

1997 **June–Sept., Southern Montserrat:** ongoing eruption of Soufriere Hills volcano since July 1995; killed 20 persons in major eruption on June 25, 1997, rendered southern two-thirds of Montserrat uninhabitable, and forced some 8,000 of the island's 12,000 residents to abandon the island.

1998 **May 30, Northern Afghanistan:** magnitude 7.1 earthquake and aftershocks killed an estimated 5,000 and injured at least 1,500. A Feb. 4th quake in same area killed about 2,300.

MAJOR U.S. EPIDEMICS

1793 **Philadelphia:** more than 4,000 residents died from yellow fever.

1832 **July–Aug., New York City:** over 3,000 people killed in a cholera epidemic.

Oct., New Orleans: cholera took the lives of 4,340 people.

1848 **New York City:** more than 5,000 deaths caused by cholera.

1853 **New Orleans:** yellow fever killed 7,790.

1867 **New Orleans:** 3,093 perished from yellow fever.

1878 **Southern States:** over 13,000 people died from yellow fever in lower Mississippi Valley.

1916 **Nationwide:** over 7,000 deaths occurred and 27,363 cases were reported of polio (infantile paralysis) in America's worst polio epidemic.

1918 **March–Nov., Nationwide:** outbreak of Spanish influenza killed over 500,000 people in the worst single U.S. epidemic.

1949 **Nationwide:** 2,720 deaths occurred from polio and 42,173 cases were reported.

1952 **Nationwide:** polio killed 3,300; 57,628 cases reported; worst epidemic since 1916.

1981 **1981 to Dec. 1997:** total U.S. AIDS cases reported to Centers for Disease Control: 641,086; total AIDS deaths reported: 390,692.

FLOODS, AVALANCHES, AND TIDAL WAVES

1228 **Holland:** 100,000 people reputedly drowned by sea flood in Friesland.

1642 **China:** rebels destroyed Kaifeng seawall; 300,000 drowned.

1896 **June 15, Sanriku, Japan:** earthquake and tidal wave killed 27,000.

1889 **May 31, Johnstown, Pa.:** more than 2,200 died in flood.

1953 **Northwest Europe:** storm followed by floods devastated North Sea coastal areas. Netherlands was hardest hit with 1,794 dead.

1959 **Dec. 2, Frejus, France:** flood caused by collapse of Malpasset Dam left 412 dead.

1960 **Agadir, Morocco:** 10,000–12,000 dead as earthquake set off tidal wave and fire, destroying most of city.

1962 **Jan. 10, Peru:** avalanche down Huascaran, extinct Andean volcano, killed more than 3,000.

1963 **Oct. 9, Italy:** landslide into the Vaiont Dam; flood killed about 2,000.

1966 **Oct. 21, Aberfan, Wales:** avalanche of coal, waste, mud, and rocks killed 144 people, including 116 children in school.

1969 **Jan. 18–26, Southern Calif.:** floods and mudslides from heavy rains caused widespread property damage; at least 100 dead. Another downpour (Feb. 23–26) caused further floods and mudslides; at least 18 dead.

1970 **Nov. 13, East Pakistan:** 200,000 killed by cyclone-driven tidal wave from Bay of Bengal. Over 100,000 missing.

1972 **Feb. 26, Man, W. Va.:** more than 118 died when slag-pile dam collapsed under pressure of torrential rains and flooded 17-mile valley.

June 9–10, Rapid City, S.D.: flash flood caused 237 deaths and $160 million in damage.

June 20, Eastern Seaboard: tropical storm Agnes, in ten-day rampage, caused widespread flash floods. Death toll 129; 115,000 left homeless; damage estimated at $3.5 billion.

1976 **Aug. 1, Loveland, Colo.:** flash flood along Route 34 in Big Thompson Canyon left 139 dead.

1988 **Aug.–Sept., Bangladesh:** heaviest monsoon in 70 years inundated three-fourths of country, killing more than 1,300 and leaving 30 million homeless. Damage estimated at over $1 billion.

1993 **June–Aug., Ill., Iowa, Kan., Ky., Minn., Mo., Neb., N.D., S.D., Wis.:** two months of heavy rain caused Mississippi River and tributaries to flood in ten states, causing almost 50 deaths and about $12 billion in damage to property and agriculture in Midwest. Almost 70,000 left homeless.

1997 **Dec. 1996–Jan. 1997, U.S. West Coast:** torrential rains and snowmelt produced severe floods in parts of Calif., Ore., Wash., Idaho, Nev., and Mont., causing 36 deaths and about $2–3 billion in damage.

1998 **July 17, Papua New Guinea:** spurred by undersea earthquake, three tsunamis wiped out entire villages in the northwestern province of Sepik. One tidal wave reported by survivor to be 30 ft. high. At least 2,000 found or presumed dead. Many who were injured by the tsunamis were later killed by deadly gangrene infections.

TROPICAL STORMS

Cyclones, typhoons, and hurricanes are the same kind of tropical storms but are called by different names in different areas of the world.

CYCLONES

1864 **Oct. 5, India:** most of Calcutta denuded by cyclone; 70,000 killed.

1942 **Oct. 16, India:** cyclone devastated Bengal; about 40,000 lives lost.

1960 **Oct. 10, East Pakistan:** cyclone and tidal wave killed about 6,000.

1963 **May 28–29, East Pakistan:** cyclone killed about 22,000 along coast.

1965 **May 11–12 and June 1–2, East Pakistan:** cyclones killed about 47,000.

Dec. 15, Karachi, Pakistan: cyclone killed about 10,000.

1970 **Nov. 12–13, East Pakistan:** cyclone and tidal waves killed 200,000 and another 100,000 were reported missing.

1971 **Sept. 29, Orissa State, India:** cyclone and tidal wave off the Bay of Bengal killed as many as 10,000.

1974 **Dec. 25, Darwin, Australia:** cyclone destroyed nearly the entire city, causing mass evacuation; 50 reported dead.

1977 **Nov. 19, Andhra Pradesh, India:** cyclone and tidal wave claimed lives of 20,000.

1991 **April 30, Southeastern Bangladesh:** cyclone killed over 131,000 and left as many as 9 million homeless. Thousands of survivors died from hunger and water-borne disease.

U.S. HURRICANES

(U.S. deaths only, except where noted)

1775 **Sept. 2–Sept. 9, N.C. to Nova Scotia:** called the "Hurricane of Independence," it is believed that 4,170 in the U.S. and Canada died in the storm.

1856 **Aug. 11, Last Island, La.:** 400 died.

1893 **Aug. 28, Savannah, Ga., Charleston, S.C., Sea Islands, S.C.:** at least 1,000 died.

1900 **Aug. 27–Sept. 15, Galveston, Tex. and Texas Gulf Coast:** more than 6,000 died in hurricane and tidal wave. The "Galveston Hurricane" is considered the deadliest in U.S. history.

1909 **Sept. 10–21, La. and Miss.:** 350 deaths.

1915 **Aug. 5–23, East Tex. and La.:** 275 killed.

1919 **Sept. 2–15, Fla., La., and Tex.:** 287 deaths, and 488 deaths at sea.

1926 **Sept. 11–22, Fla. and Ala.:** 243 deaths.

1928 **Sept. 6–20, Southern Fla.:** 1,836 died and 1,870 injured.

1935 **Aug. 29–Sept. 10, Southern Fla.:** 408 killed.

1938 **Sept. 10–22, Long Island and Southern New England:** 600 deaths; 1,764 injured.

1944 **Sept. 9–16, N.C. to New England:** 46 deaths, and 344 deaths at sea.

1947 **Sept. 4–21, Fla. and Mid-Gulf Coast:** 51 killed.

1954 **Aug. 25–31, N.C. to New England:** "Carol" killed 60 and injured 1,000 in Long Island-New England area.

Oct. 5–18, S.C. to N.Y.: "Hazel" killed 95 in U.S.; about 400–1,000 in Haiti; 78 in Canada.

1955 **Aug. 7–21, N.C. to New England:** "Diane" took 184 lives.

1957 **June 25–28. Tex. to Ala.:** "Audrey" wiped out Cameron, La., causing 390 deaths.

1960 **Aug. 29–Sept. 13, Fla. to New England:** "Donna" killed 50 in the U.S. 115 deaths in Antilles—mostly from flash floods in Puerto Rico.

1961 **Sept. 3–15, Tex. coast:** "Carla" devastated Texas gulf cities, taking 46 lives.

1965 **Aug. 27–Sept. 12, Southern Fla. and La.:** "Betsy" killed 75 people.

1969 Aug. 14–22, Miss., La., Ala., Va., and W. Va.: 256 killed and 68 persons missing as a result of "Camille."

1972 June 14–23, Fla. to N.Y.: "Agnes" caused 117 deaths (50 in Pa.).

1979 Aug. 25–Sept. 7, Caribbean Islands to New England: "David" caused five U.S. deaths; 1,200 in the Dominican Republic.

1980 Aug. 3–10, Caribbean Islands to Tex. Gulf: "Allen" killed 28 in U.S.; over 200 in Caribbean.

1989 Sept. 10–22, Caribbean Sea, S.C., and N.C.: "Hugo" claimed 49 U.S. lives (71 killed overall); $4.2 billion paid in insurance claims.

1992 Aug. 22–26, South Fla., La., and Bahamas: Gulf Coast hurricane "Andrew," with damage estimated at $15–$20 billion, is most costly hurricane in U.S. history.

OTHER HURRICANES

1926 Oct. 20, Cuba: worst hurricane in 80 years, 650 reported dead.

1930 Sept. 3 Santo Domingo: hurricane killed about 2,000 and injured 6,000.

1934 Sept. 21, Japan: hurricane killed more than 4,000 on Honshu.

1955 Sept. 19, Mexico: "Hilda" took 200 lives.

Sept. 22–28, Caribbean: "Janet" killed 200 in Honduras and 300 in Mexico.

1961 Oct. 31, British Honduras: "Hattie" devastated capital Belize, killed at least 400.

1963 Oct. 2–7, Caribbean: "Flora" killed up to 7,000 in Haiti and Cuba.

1966 Sept. 24–30, Caribbean area: "Inez" killed 293.

1974 Sept. 20, Honduras: "Fifi" struck northern section of country, leaving 8,000 dead, 100,000 homeless.

1988 Sept. 12–17, Caribbean Sea and Gulf of Mexico: "Gilbert," worst Atlantic storm ever recorded, took at least 260 lives and caused some 39 tornadoes in Tex.

1997 Oct. 8–10, southern Mexico: "Pauline" devastated resort city of Acapulco and villages along the coast in states of Oaxaca and Guerrero, leaving 217 dead and 20,000 homeless.

TORNADOES

1884 Feb. 19: tornadoes in Miss., Ala., N.C., S.C., Tenn., Ky., and Ind. caused estimated 800 deaths.

1925 March 18: tornadoes in Mo., Ill., Ind., Ky., Tenn., and Ala. killed 792.

1932 March 21: outbreak of tornadoes in Ala., Miss., Ga., and Tenn. killed 268.

1936 April 5–6: series of tornadoes in Ark., Ala., Tenn., Ga., and S.C. killed 498.

1952 March 21–22: tornadoes in Ark., Tenn., Mo., Miss., Ala., and Ky. caused 343 deaths.

1953 May 11: a single tornado struck Waco, Tex., killing 114.

June 8: tornado killed 116 in Flint, Mich.

1965 April 11: tornadoes in Iowa, Ill., Ind., Ohio, Mich., and Wis. caused 256 deaths.

1974 April 3–4: a series of tornadoes in East, South, and Midwest killed approximately 315.

TYPHOONS

1906 Sept. 18, Hong Kong: typhoon with tsunami killed an estimated 10,000 persons.

1949 Dec. 5, off Korea: typhoon struck fishing fleet; several thousand men reported dead.

1959 Aug. 20, Fukien province, China: "Iris" killed 2,334.

Sept. 27, Honshu, Japan: "Vera" killed an estimated 4,464.

1960 June 9, Fukien province, China: "Mary" caused at least 1,600 deaths.

1984 Sept. 2–3, Philippines: "Ike" hit seven major islands, leaving 1,300 dead.

1991 Nov. 5, Central Philippines: flash floods triggered by tropical storm "Thelma" killed about 3,000 people. Leyte city of Ormoc was worst hit.

NUCLEAR POWER PLANT ACCIDENTS

1952 Dec. 12, Chalk River, nr. Ottawa, Canada: a partial meltdown of the reactor's uranium fuel core resulted after the accidental removal of four control rods. Although millions of gallons of radioactive water accumulated inside the reactor, there were no injuries.

1957 Oct. 7, Windscale Pile No. 1, north of Liverpool, England: fire in a graphite-cooled reactor spewed radiation over the countryside, contaminating a 200-sq-mi area.

South Ural Mountains: explosion of radioactive wastes at Soviet nuclear weapons factory 12 miles from city of Kyshtym forced the evacuation of over 10,000 people from a contaminated area. No casualties were reported by Soviet officials.

1976 nr. Greifswald, East Germany: radioactive core of reactor in the Lubmin nuclear power plant nearly melted down due to the failure of safety systems during a fire.

1979 March 28, Three Mile Island, nr. Harrisburg, Pa.: one of two reactors lost its coolant, which caused the radioactive fuel to overheat and caused a partial meltdown. Some radioactive material was released.

1986 April 26, Chernobyl, nr. Kiev, former U.S.S.R.: explosion and fire in the graphite core of one of four reactors released radioactive material that spread over part of the Soviet Union, Eastern Europe, Scandinavia, and later Western Europe. 31 claimed dead. Total casualties are unknown and estimates run into the thousands. Worst such accident to date.

FIRES AND EXPLOSIONS

1666 Sept. 2, England: "Great Fire of London" destroyed St. Paul's Church, etc. Damage £10 million.

1835 Dec. 16, New York City: 530 buildings destroyed by fire.

1871 Oct. 8, Chicago: the "Chicago Fire" burned 17,450 buildings, killed 250 persons; $196 million damage.

Oct. 8, Peshtigo, Wis.: over 1,200 lives lost and 2 billion trees burned in forest fire.

1872 Nov. 9, Boston: fire destroyed 800 buildings; $75 million damage.

1876 Dec. 5, New York City: fire in Brooklyn Theater killed more than 300.

1881 **Dec. 8, Vienna:** at least 620 died in fire at Ring Theatre.

1894 **Sept. 1, Minn.:** forest fire over 480-square-mile area destroyed six towns and killed 480 people.

1900 **May 1, Scofield, Utah:** explosion of blasting powder in coal mine killed 200.
June 30, Hoboken, N.J.: piers of North German Lloyd Steamship line burned; 326 dead.

1903 **Dec. 30, Chicago:** Iroquois Theatre fire killed 602.

1906 **March 10, France:** explosion in coal mine in Courrières killed 1,060.

1907 **Dec. 6, Monongha, W. Va.:** coal mine explosion killed 361.
Dec. 19, Jacobs Creek, Pa.: explosion in coal mine left 239 dead.

1909 **Nov. 13, Cherry, Ill.:** explosion in coal mine killed 259.

1911 **March 25, New York City:** fire in Triangle Shirtwaist Factory fatal to 145.

1913 **Oct. 22, Dawson, N.M.:** coal mine explosion left 263 dead.

1917 **April 10, Eddystone, Pa.:** explosion in munitions plant killed 133.
Dec. 6, Canada: 1,600 people died when French ammunition ship *Mont Blanc* collided with Belgium steamer in Halifax Harbor.

1930 **April 21, Columbus, Ohio:** fire in Ohio State Penitentiary killed 320 convicts.

1937 **March 18, New London, Tex.:** explosion destroyed schoolhouse; 294 killed.

1942 **April 26, Manchuria:** explosion in Honkeiko Colliery killed 1,549.
Nov. 28, Boston: Coconut Grove nightclub fire killed 491.

1944 **July 6, Hartford, Conn.:** fire and ensuing stampede in main tent of Ringling Brothers Circus killed 168, injured 487.
July 17, Port Chicago, Calif.: 322 killed when ammunition ships exploded.
Oct. 20, Cleveland: liquid-gas tanks exploded, killing 130.

1946 **Dec. 7, Atlanta:** fire in Winecoff Hotel killed 119.

1947 **April 16–18, Texas City, Tex.:** most of the city destroyed by a fire and subsequent explosion on the French freighter *Grandcamp* carrying a cargo of ammonium nitrate. At least 516 were killed and over 3,000 injured.

1948 **Dec. 3, Shanghai:** Chinese passenger ship *Kiangya,* carrying refugees fleeing Communist troops during civil war, struck an old mine, exploded, and sank off Shanghai. Over 3,000 people were believed killed.

1949 **Sept. 2, China:** fire on Chongqing (Chungking) waterfront killed 1,700.

1954 **May 26, off Quonset Point, R.I.:** explosion and fire aboard aircraft carrier *Bennington* killed 103 crewmen.

1956 **Aug. 7, Colombia:** about 1,100 reported killed when seven army ammunition trucks exploded at Cali.
Aug. 8, Belgium: 262 died in coal mine fire at Marcinelle.

1960 **Jan. 21, Coalbrook, South Africa:** coal mine explosion killed 437.
Nov. 13, Syria: 152 children killed in moviehouse fire.

1961 **Dec. 17, Niteroi, Brazil:** circus fire fatal to 323.

1962 **Feb. 7, Saarland, West Germany:** coal mine gas explosion killed 298.

1963 **Nov. 9, Japan:** explosion in coal mine at Omuta killed 447.

1965 **May 28, India:** coal mine fire in state of Bihar killed 375.
June 1, near Fukuoka, Japan: coal mine explosion killed 236.

1967 **May 22, Brussels:** fire in L'Innovation, major department store, left 322 dead.
July 29, off North Vietnam: fire on U.S. carrier *Forrestal* killed 134.

1969 **Jan. 14, Pearl Harbor, Hawaii:** nuclear aircraft carrier *Enterprise* ripped by explosions; 27 dead, 82 injured.

1970 **Nov. 1, Saint-Laurent-du-Pont, France:** fire in dance hall killed 146 young people.

1972 **May 13, Osaka, Japan:** 118 people died in fire in nightclub on top floor of Sennichi department store.
June 6, Wankie, Rhodesia: explosion in coal mine killed 427.

1973 **Nov. 29, Kumamoto, Japan:** fire in Taiyo department store killed 101.

1974 **Feb. 1, Sao Paulo, Brazil:** fire in upper stories of bank building killed 189 persons, many of whom leaped to their deaths.

1975 **Dec. 27, Dhanbad, India:** explosion in coal mine followed by flooding from nearby reservoir left 372 dead.

1977 **May 28, Southgate, Ky.:** fire in Beverly Hills Supper Club; 167 dead.

1978 **July 11, Tarragona, Spain:** 140 killed at coastal campsite when tank truck carrying liquid gas overturned and exploded.
Aug. 20, Abadan, Iran: nearly 400 killed when arsonists set fire to crowded theater.

1982 **Dec. 18–21, Caracas, Venezuela:** power-plant fire left 128 dead.

1986 **Dec. 31, San Juan, P.R.:** arson fire in Dupont Plaza Hotel set by three employees killed 96.

1989 **June 3, Ural Mountains:** liquefied petroleum gas leaking from a pipeline running alongside the Trans-Siberian railway near Uta, 72 miles east of Moscow, exploded and destroyed two passing passenger trains. About 500 travelers were killed and 723 injured of an estimated 1,200 passengers on both trains.
Oct. 23, Pasadena, Tex.: a huge explosion followed by a series of others and a raging fire at a plastics manufacturing plant owned by Phillips Petroleum Co. killed 22 and injured more than 80 persons. A large leak of ethylene was presumed to be the cause.

1990 **March 25, New York City:** arson fire in illegal Happy Land Social Club, Bronx, killed 87.

1991 **Oct. 20–23, Oakland-Berkeley, Calif.:** brush fire in drought-stricken area destroyed over 3,000 homes and apartments. At least 24 persons died, damage estimated at $1.5 billion.

1993 **May 10, near Bangkok, Thailand:** Fire in doll factory killed at least 187 persons and injured 500 others. World's deadliest factory fire.

SHIPWRECKS

1833 **May 11, *Lady of the Lake:*** bound from England to Quebec, struck iceberg; 215 perished.

1853 **Sept. 29, *Annie Jane:*** emigrant vessel off coast of Scotland; 348 died.

1865 **April 27, *Sultana:*** boiler explosion on Mississippi River steamboat, near Memphis, 1,547 killed.

1898 **Nov. 26, *City of Portland:*** 157 died nr. Cape Cod.

1904 **June 15, *General Slocum:*** excursion steamer burned in East River, N.Y.; 1,021 perished.

1912 **March 5, *Principe de Asturias:*** Spanish steamer struck rock off Sebastien Point; 500 drowned.

April 15, *Titanic:* sank after colliding with iceberg; 1,513 died.

1914 **May 29, *Empress of Ireland:*** sank after collision in St. Lawrence River; 1,024 perished.

1915 **July 24, *Eastland:*** Great Lakes excursion steamer overturned in Chicago River; 812 died.

1928 **Nov. 12, *Vestris:*** British steamer sank in gale off Va.; 110 died.

1934 **Sept. 8, *Morro Castle:*** 134 killed in fire off Asbury Park, N.J.

1939 **May 23, *Squalus:*** submarine with 59 men sank off Hampton Beach, N.H.; 33 saved.

June 1, Submarine *Thetis:* sank in Liverpool Bay, England; 99 perished.

1942 **Oct. 2, *Queen Mary:*** rammed and sank a British cruiser; 338 aboard the cruiser died.

1945 **April 9:** U.S. ship, loaded with aerial bombs, exploded at Bari, Italy; at least 360 killed.

1948 **Nov.:** unidentified Chinese troopship evacuating Nationalist troops from Manchuria sank nr. Yingkow, killing an estimated 6,000 persons.

1949 **Sept. 17, *Noronic:*** Canadian Great Lakes cruise ship burned at Toronto dock; about 130 died.

1952 **April 26, *Hobson:*** minesweeper collided with aircraft carrier *Wasp* and sank during night maneuvers in mid-Atlantic; 176 persons lost.

1953 **Jan. 9, *Chang Tyong-Ho:*** South Korean ferry foundered off Pusan; 249 reported dead.

Jan. 31, *Princess Victoria:* British ferry sank in Irish Sea; 133 lost.

1956 **July 25, *Andrea Doria:*** Italian liner collided with Swedish liner *Stockholm* off Nantucket Island, Mass., sank next day; 52, mostly passengers on Italian ship, dead or unaccounted for; over 1,600 rescued.

1962 **April 8, *Dara:*** British liner exploded and sank in Persian Gulf; 236 dead. Caused by time bomb.

1963 **April 10, *Thresher:*** atomic-powered submarine sank in North Atlantic; 129 dead.

May 4: United Arab Republic ferry capsized and sank in upper Nile; over 200 died.

1968 **Late May, *Scorpion:*** nuclear submarine sank in Atlantic 400 miles S.W. of Azores; 99 dead. (Located Oct. 31.)

1970 **Dec. 15:** ferry in Korean Strait capsized; 261 lost.

1976 **Oct. 20, *George Prince:*** Mississippi River ferry rammed by Norwegian tanker *Frosta* nr. Luling, La.; 77 dead.

1983 **May 25, *10th of Ramadan:*** Nile steamer, caught fire and sank in Lake Nasser, near Aswan, Egypt; 272 dead and 75 missing.

1987 **March 9:** British ferry capsized after leaving Belgian port of Zeebrugge with 500 aboard; 134 drowned. Water rushing through open bow is believed to be probable cause.

Dec. 20.: over 1,500 killed when passenger ferry *Dona Paz* collided with oil tanker *Victor* off Mindoro Is., 110 miles south of Manila.

1990 **April 7, *Scandinavian Star:*** suspected arson fire aboard Danish-owned North Sea ferry killed at least 110 passengers in Skagerrak Strait off Norway.

April 7: double-decker ferry sank in Gyaing River in Myanmar (Burma) during a storm and 215 persons were believed drowned.

1991 **Dec. 14:** ferry carrying 569 passengers sank in Red Sea off coast of Safaga, Egypt, after hitting a coral reef. Over 460 people believed drowned.

1993 **Feb. 17, *Neptune:*** triple-deck ferry capsized off southern peninsula of Haiti during a squall. Over 1,000 passengers believed drowned. About 300 survived the sinking.

1994 **Sept. 28, *Estonia:*** passenger ferry capsized off coast of Southwest Finland and sank in a stormy Baltic Sea. Only about 140 of the estimated 1,040 passengers aboard survived.

MYSTERIOUS DISAPPEARANCES

1872 ***Mary Celeste:*** the brigantine set sail from New York harbor for Genoa, Italy, on Nov. 5. A British brigantine, the *DeGratia,* discovered the ship derelict on Dec. 5 and boarded her. Everyone aboard the *Mary Celeste* had vanished—her captain, his family, and its 14-man crew. The ship was in perfect order with ample supplies and there was no sign of violence or trouble. The fate of the crew remains unknown.

1928 **Dec. 22, *Köbenhavn:*** the five-masted Danish steel barque, a sail-training ship with a crew of 75 including 45 boy cadets, sailed from the River Plate for Melbourne, Australia, on Dec. 14. The last radio contact with the ship was made on Dec. 22 and all was well. The *Köbenhavn* and its crew disappeared without a trace and no one knows what happened to it.

AIRCRAFT ACCIDENTS

(150 deaths or more, with exceptions)

1921 **Aug. 24, England:** British dirigible *AR-2* broke in two on trial trip near Hull; 62 died.

1925 **Sept. 3, Caldwell, Ohio:** U.S. dirigible *Shenandoah* broke apart; 14 dead.

1930 **Oct. 5, Beauvais, France:** British dirigible *R 101* crashed, killing 47.

1933 **April 4, N.J.:** U.S. dirigible *Akron* crashed; 73 died.

1937 **May 6, Lakehurst, N.J.:** German zeppelin *Hindenburg* destroyed by fire at tower mooring; 36 killed.

1945 **July 28, New York City:** U.S. Army bomber crashed into Empire State Building; 13 dead.

1960 **Dec. 16, New York City:** United and Trans World planes collided in fog, crashed in two boroughs, killing 134 in air and on ground.

1961 **Feb. 15, nr. Brussels:** 72 on board and farmer on ground killed in crash of Sabena plane; U.S. figure skating team wiped out.

1966 **Dec. 24, Binh Thai, South Vietnam:** crash of military-chartered plane into village killed 129.

1971 **July 30, Morioka, Japan:** Japanese Boeing 727 and F-86 fighter collided in mid-air; 162 died.

1972 **Aug. 14, East Berlin, East Germany:** Soviet-built East German Ilyushin plane crashed, killing 156.

Dec. 3, Santa Cruz de Tenerife, Canary Islands: Spanish charter jet carrying West German tourists crashed on take-off; all 155 aboard killed.

1973 **Jan. 22, Kano, Nigeria:** 171 Nigerian Muslims returning from Mecca and five crewmen died in crash.

1973 **Feb. 21, Sinai:** civilian Libyan Arab Airlines Boeing 727 shot down by Israeli fighters after it had strayed off course; 108 died, five survived. Officials claimed that the pilot had ignored fighters' warnings to land.

1974 **March 3, Paris:** Turkish DC-10 jumbo jet crashed in forest shortly after take-off; all 346 passengers and crew killed.

Dec. 4, Colombo, Sri Lanka: Dutch DC-8 carrying Muslims to Mecca crashed on landing approach, killing all 191 persons aboard.

1975 **April 4, near Saigon, Vietnam:** Air Force Galaxy C-5A crashed after take-off, killing 172, mostly Vietnamese children.

Aug. 3, Agadir, Morocco: Chartered Boeing 707, returning Moroccan workers home after vacation in France, plunged into mountainside; all 188 aboard killed.

1976 **Sept. 10, Zagreb, Yugoslavia:** midair collision between British Airways Trident and Yugoslav charter DC-9 fatal to all 176 persons aboard.

1977 **March 27, Santa Cruz de Tenerife, Canary Islands:** Pan American and KLM Boeing 747s collided on runway. All 249 on KLM plane and 333 of 394 aboard Pan Am jet killed. Total of 582 is highest for any type of aviation disaster.

1978 **Jan. 1, Bombay:** Air India 747 with 213 aboard exploded and plunged into sea minutes after takeoff.

Sept. 25, San Diego, Calif.: Pacific Southwest plane collided in midair with Cessna. All 135 on airliner, 2 in Cessna, and 7 on ground killed for total of 144.

Nov. 15, Colombo, Sri Lanka: chartered Icelandic Airlines DC-8, carrying 249 Muslim pilgrims from Mecca, crashed in thunderstorm during landing approach; 183 killed.

1979 **May 25, Chicago:** American Airlines DC-10 lost left engine upon take-off and crashed seconds later, killing all 272 persons aboard and three on the ground in worst U.S. air disaster.

Nov. 26, Jidda, Saudi Arabia: Pakistan International Airlines 707 carrying pilgrims returning from Mecca crashed on takeoff; all 156 aboard killed.

Nov. 28, Mt. Erebus, Antarctica: Air New Zealand DC-10 crashed on sightseeing flight; 257 killed.

1980 **Aug. 19, Riyadh, Saudi Arabia:** all 301 aboard Saudi Arabian jet killed when burning plane made safe landing but passengers were unable to escape.

1981 **Dec. 1, Ajaccio, Corsica:** Yugoslav DC-9 Super 80 carrying tourists crashed into mountain on landing approach, killing all 178 aboard.

1983 **Aug. 30, nr. island of Sakhalin off Siberia:** South Korean civilian jetliner Boeing 747, flight KAL-007, shot down by Soviet fighter after it strayed off course into Soviet airspace. All 269 aboard killed. Secret Soviet documents released in Oct. 1992 reveal that the plane was flying a straight course for two hours with its navigational lights on and did not take evasive action. Crew was unaware of its location and never saw the Soviet fighter that downed them. The Soviet fighter did not give a warning by firing tracer bullets as originally claimed. Recorded conversations indicated that the crew members did not know what hit them.

Nov. 26, Madrid: a Columbian Avianca Boeing 747 crashed near Mejorada del Campó Airport killing 183 persons aboard. Eleven people survived the accident.

1985 **June 23, off coast of Ireland:** Air-India Boeing 747 exploded over Atlantic; all 329 aboard were killed.

Aug. 12, Japan: Japan Air Lines Boeing 747 crashed into a mountain, killing 520 of the 524 aboard.

Dec. 12, Gander, Newfoundland: a chartered Arrow Air DC-8, bringing American soldiers home for Christmas, crashed on takeoff. All 256 aboard died.

1987 **May 9, Poland:** Polish airliner, Ilyushin 62M, on charter flight to N.Y., crashed after takeoff from Warsaw, killing 183.

Aug. 16, Detroit: Northwest Airlines McDonnell Douglas MD-30 plunged to heavily traveled boulevard, killing 156. Girl, 4, only survivor.

Nov. 26, south of Mauritius: South African Airways Boeing 747 went down in rough seas; 160 died.

Nov. 29, Burma: Korean Air Boeing 747 jetliner exploded from bomb planted by North Korean agents and crashed into sea, killing all 115 aboard.

1988 **July 3, Persian Gulf:** U.S. Navy cruiser *Vincennes* shot down Iran Air A300 Airbus, killing 290 persons, after mistaking it for an attacking jet fighter.

Aug. 28, Ramstein Air Force Base, West Germany: three jets from Italian Air Force acrobatic team collided in mid-air during air show and crashed, killing 70 persons, including the pilots and spectators on the ground. It is worst air-show disaster in history.

Dec. 21, Lockerbie, Scotland: a N.Y.-bound Pan-Am Boeing 747 exploded in flight from a terrorist bomb and crashed into Scottish village, killing all 259 aboard and 11 on the ground. Passengers included 35 Syracuse University students and many U.S. military personnel.

1989 **June 7, Paramaribo, Suriname:** a Surinam Airways DC-8 carrying 174 passengers and nine crew members crashed into the jungle while making a third attempt to land in a thick fog, killing 168 aboard.

1991 **July 11, Jedda, Saudi Arabia:** Canadian-chartered DC-8 carrying pilgrims returning to Nigeria crashed after takeoff, killing 261 persons.

1994 **April 14, Northern Iraq:** two American F-15C fighter aircraft mistook two U.S. Army black-hawk helicopters for Russian-made Iraqi MI-24 helicopters and shot them down over no-fly zone, killing all 26 on board.

April 26, Nagoya, Japan: a China Airlines A-300 Airbus from Taiwan crash-landed and exploded on the tarmac. Only seven of the 271 passengers aboard survived.

June 6, Xian, China: a Russian-built Tupolev-154 airliner of China Northwest Airlines crashed 10 minutes after takeoff, killing all 160 aboard.

1995 **Dec. 20, near Cali, Colombia:** 160 people killed when American Airlines Boeing 757 crashed in Andean Mountains.

1996 **Jan. 8, Kinshasa, Zaire:** a Russian-built Antonov-32 cargo plane crashed after takeoff from Kinshasa into the center of the city, killing over 350 people and injuring at least 470.

Feb. 5, off coast of Puerto Plata, Dominican Republic: a Boeing 737 crashed into Atlantic Ocean after takeoff, killing 189.

July 18, off coast of Long Island, N.Y.: a TWA Boeing 747-100 bound for Paris from New York exploded over waters of eastern L.I. and crashed into Atlantic Ocean, killing all 230 aboard.

Nov. 12, near New Delhi, India: shortly after takeoff, Saudi Arabian Airlines Boeing 747 collided in midair with Kazak Airlines Ilysuhin 76 plane approaching the New Delhi airport. All 349 passengers and crew were killed; the world's worst midair collision

1997 **Aug. 6, Guam:** South Korean Air Boeing 747-300 from Seoul crashed into jungle near Agana International Airport killing 227 persons; 27 survived.

Sept. 26, nr. northern Indonesia: Indonesian Garuda Airlines A-300 Airbus jetliner crashed while approaching Medan Airport, Sumatra, killing all 234 persons aboard.

1998 **Feb. 3, Mt. Cermis, Italy:** low-flying U.S. Marine surveillance jet on training flight accidentally cut ski-lift cable-car line, causing all 20 people aboard to fall some 260 feet to their deaths.

Feb. 16, Taipei, Taiwan: China Airlines Airbus 300 jumbo jet crashed while trying to land in fog at Chiang Ki-Shek International Airport, killing all 197 passengers and crew and at least seven persons on the ground.

Sept. 2, Nova Scotia, Canada: Swissair flight from New York to Geneva crashed off Canadian coast, killing all 229 aboard. 136 Americans were on the McDonnell Douglas MD-11.

SPACE ACCIDENTS

1967 **Jan. 27, *Apollo 1*:** a fire aboard the space capsule on the ground at Cape Kennedy, Fla. killed astronauts Virgil I. Grissom, Edward H. White, and Roger Chaffee.

April 23–24, *Soyuz 1*: Vladimir M. Komarov was killed when his craft crashed after its parachute lines, released at 23,000 feet for reentry, became snarled.

1971 **June 6–30, *Soyuz 11*:** three cosmonauts, Georgi T. Dolrovolsky, Vladislav N. Volkov, and Viktor I. Patsayev, found dead in the craft after its automatic landing. Apparent cause of death was loss of pressurization in the space craft during reentry into the earth's atmosphere.

1980 **March 18, U.S.S.R.** a Vostok rocket exploded on its launch pad while being refueled, killing 50 at the Plesetsk Space Center.

1986 **Jan 28, *Challenger* Space Shuttle:** exploded 73 seconds after lift off, killing all seven crew members. They were: Christa McAuliffe, Francis R. Scobee, Michael J. Smith, Judith A. Resnick, Ronald E. McNair, Ellison S. Onizuka, and Gregory B. Jarvis. A booster leak ignited the fuel, causing the explosion.

RAILROAD ACCIDENTS

NOTE: Very few passengers were killed in a single U.S. train wreck up until 1853. These early trains ran slowly and made short trips, night travel was rare, and there were not many of them in operation.

1831 **June 17:** the boiler exploded on America's first passenger locomotive, *The Best Friend of Charleston,* killing the fireman. He was the first person in America to be killed in a railroad accident.

1833 **Nov. 8, nr. Heightstown, N.J.:** world's first train wreck and first passenger fatalities recorded. A 24-passenger Camden & Amboy train derailed due to a broken axle, killing two passengers and injuring all others. Former President John Quincy Adams and Cornelius Vanderbilt, who later made a fortune in railroads, were aboard the train.

1853 **May 6, Norwalk, Conn:** a New Haven Railroad train ran through an open drawbridge and plunged into the Norwalk River. Forty-six passengers were crushed to death or drowned. This was the first major drawbridge accident.

1856 **July 17, Camp Hill, Pa.:** two Northern Penn trains crashed head-on. Sixty-six church school children bound for a picnic died in the flaming wreckage.

1876 **Dec. 29, Ashtabula, Ohio:** a Lake Shore train fell into the Ashtabula River when the bridge it was crossing collapsed during a snowstorm. Ninety-two were killed.

1887 **Aug. 10, nr. Chatsworth, Ill.:** a burning railroad trestle collapsed while a Toledo, Peoria & Western train was crossing, killing 81 and injuring 372.

1904 **Aug. 7, Eden, Colo.:** train derailed on bridge during flash flood; 96 killed.

1910 **March 1, Wellington, Wash.:** two trains swept into canyon by avalanche; 96 dead.

1915 **May 22, Gretna, Scotland:** two passenger trains and troop train collided; 227 killed.

1917 **Dec. 12, Modane, France:** nearly 550 killed in derailment of troop train near mouth of Mt. Cenis tunnel.

1918 **July 9, Nashville, Tenn.:** 101 killed in a two-train collision near Nashville.

Nov. 1, New York City: derailment of subway train in Malbone St. tunnel in Brooklyn left 92 dead.

1926 **March 14, Virilla River Canyon, Costa Rica:** an over-crowded train carrying pilgrims derailed while crossing the Colima Bridge, killing over 300 people and injuring hundreds more.

1939 Dec. 22, nr. Magdeburg, Germany: more than 125 killed in collision; 99 killed in another wreck near Friedrichshafen.

1943 Dec. 16, nr. Rennert, N.C.: 72 killed in derailment and collision of two Atlantic Coast Line trains.

1944 March 2, nr. Salerno, Italy: 521 suffocated when Italian train stalled in tunnel.

1949 Oct. 22, nr. Nowy Dwor, Poland: more than 200 reported killed in derailment of Danzig-Warsaw express.

1950 Nov. 22, Richmond Hill, N.Y.: 79 died when one Long Island Rail Road commuter train crashed into rear of another.

1951 Feb. 6, Woodbridge, N.J.: 85 died when Pennsylvania Railroad commuter train plunged through temporary overpass.

1952 Oct. 8, Harrow-Wealdstone, England: two express trains crashed into commuter train; 112 dead.

1957 Sept. 1, nr. Kendal, Jamaica: about 175 killed when train plunged into ravine.

Sept. 29, nr. Montgomery, West Pakistan: express train crashed into standing oil train; nearly 300 killed.

Dec. 4, St. John's, England: 92 killed, 187 injured as one commuter train crashed into another in fog.

1960 Nov. 14, Pardubice, Czechoslovakia: two trains collided; 110 dead, 106 injured.

1962 May 3, nr. Tokyo: 163 killed and 400 injured when train crashed into wreckage of collision between inbound freight train and outbound commuter train.

1963 Nov. 9, nr. Yokohama, Japan: two passenger trains crashed into derailed freight, killing 162.

1964 July 26, Custoias, Portugal: passenger train derailed; 94 dead.

1970 Feb. 4, nr. Buenos Aires: 236 killed when express train crashed into standing commuter train.

1972 July 21, Seville, Spain: head-on crash of two passenger trains killed 76.

Oct. 6, nr. Saltillo, Mexico: train carrying religious pilgrims derailed and caught fire, killing 204 and injuring over 1,000.

Oct. 30, Chicago: two Illinois Central commuter trains collided during morning rush hour; 45 dead and over 200 injured.

1974 Aug. 30, Zagreb, former Yugoslavia: train entering station derailed, killing 153 and injuring over 60.

1981 June 6, nr. Mansi, India: driver of train carrying over 500 passengers, braked to avoid hitting cow, causing train to plunge off a bridge into Baghmati River; 268 passengers were reported killed, but at least 300 more were missing.

1982 July 11, Tepic, Mexico: Nogales-Guadalajara train plunged down mountain gorge killing 120.

1989 Jan. 15, Maizdi Khan, Bangladesh: a train carrying Muslim pilgrims crashed head-on with a mail train killing at least 110 persons and injuring as many as 1,000. Many people were riding on the roof of the trains and between the cars.

1989 Aug. 10, nr. Los Mochis, Mexico: a second-class passenger train traveling from Mazatlán to Mexicali, plunged off a bridge at Puente del Rio Bamoa into the river and killed an estimated 85 people and injured 107.

1990 Jan. 4, Sangi village, Sindh province, Pakistan: an overcrowded sixteen-car passenger train was switched to the wrong track and rammed into a standing freight train. At least 210 persons were killed and 700 were believed injured in what is said to be Pakistan's worst train disaster.

1993 Sept. 22, nr. Mobile, Ala.: Amtrak's *Sunset Limited,* en route to Miami, jumped rails on weakened bridge that had been damaged by a barge, and plunged in Big Bayou Canot, killing 47 persons.

1995 Aug. 20, Firozabad, Northern India: a speeding passenger train rammed another train that was stalled after hitting a cow. About 300 persons were killed and over 400 injured.

1997 March 3, Punjab province, Pakistan: passenger train crashed due to failed brakes, killing 119 and injuring at least 80 persons.

1998 June 3, nr. Eschede, Germany: Inter City Express passenger train traveling at 125 m.p.h. crashed into support pier of an overpass, killing 98. Is nation's worst postwar train accident. Crash may have been caused by a defective wheel.

OIL SPILLS

1978 March 16, off Portsall, France: wrecked supertanker *Amoco Cadiz* spilled 68 million gallons, causing widespread environmental damage over 100 miles of Brittany coast—world's largest tanker disaster.

1979 June 8, Gulf of Mexico: exploratory oil well, Ixtoc 1, blew out, spilling an estimated 140 million gallons of crude oil into the open sea. Although it is the largest known oil spill, it had a low environmental impact.

1989 Mar. 24, Prince William Sound, Alaska: tanker, *Exxon Valdez,* hit an undersea reef and spilled 10 million plus gallons of oil into the waters, causing the worst oil spill in U.S. history.

Dec. 19, off Las Palmas, the Canary Islands: explosion in Iranian supertanker, the *Kharg-5,* tore through its hull and caused 19 million gallons of crude oil to spill out into the Atlantic Ocean about 400 miles north of Las Palmas, forming a 100-square-mile oil slick.

1991 Jan. 25, Southern Kuwait: during the Persian Gulf War, Iraq deliberately released an estimated 460 million gallons of crude oil into the Persian Gulf from tankers at Mina al-Ahmadi and Sea Island Terminal 10 miles off Kuwait. Spill had little military significance. On Jan. 27, U.S. warplanes bombed pipe systems to stop the flow of oil.

1994 Aug. 12, nr. Ursinsk, Russia: huge oil spill from ruptured pipeline.

Sept. 8, Russia: a dam built to contain oil burst and spilled oil into Kolva River tributary. U.S. Energy Department estimated spill at 2 million barrels. Russian state-owned oil company claimed spill was only 102,000 barrels.

1996 Feb. 15, off Welsh coast: supertanker, *Sea Empress* ran aground at port of Milford Haven, Wales, spewed out 70,000 tons of crude oil, and created a 25-mile slick.

SPORTS DISASTERS

1955 **June 11, Le Mans, France:** racing car in Grand Prix hurtled into grandstand, killing 82 spectators.

1964 **May 24, Lima, Peru:** more than 300 soccer fans killed and over 500 injured during riot and panic following unpopular ruling by referee in Peru vs. Argentina soccer game. It is worst soccer disaster on record.

1971 **Jan. 2, Glasgow, Scotland:** 66 killed in crush at Glasgow Rangers home stadium when fans trying to leave encountered fans trying to return to stadium after hearing that a late goal had been scored.

1982 **Oct. 20, Moscow:** according to *Sovietsky Sport,* as many as 340 died at Lenin Stadium when exiting soccer fans collided with returning fans after final goal was scored. All the fans had been crowded into one section of stadium by police.

1985 **May 11, Bradford, England:** 56 burned to death and over 200 injured when fire engulfed main grandstand at Bradford's soccer stadium.

May 29, Brussels, Belgium: drunken group of British soccer fans supporting Liverpool club stormed stand filled with Italian supporters of Juventus team before European Champion's Cup final. While British fans attacked rival spectators at the Heysel Stadium, concrete retaining wall collapsed and 39 persons were crushed or trampled to death, 32 of them Italians. More than 400 persons were injured.

1988 **March 12, Katmandu, Nepal:** some 80 soccer fans seeking cover during a violent hail storm at the national stadium were trampled to death in a stampede because the stadium doors were locked.

1989 **April 15, Sheffield, England:** 94 killed and 170 injured at Hillsborough stadium when throngs of Liverpool soccer fans, many without tickets, collapsed a stadium barrier in a mad rush to see the game between Liverpool and Nottingham Forest. It is Britain's worst soccer disaster.

1996 **Oct. 16, Guatemala City:** at least 84 killed and 147 injured by stampeding soccer fans before a 1998 World Cup qualifying match between Guatemala and Peru held at Mateo Flores National Stadium.

TERRORIST ATTACKS IN U.S.

1920 **Sept. 16, New York City:** TNT bomb planted in unattended horse-drawn wagon exploded on Wall Street opposite House of Morgan, killing 35 persons and injuring hundreds more. Bolshevist or anarchist terrorists believed responsible but crime never solved.

1975 **Jan. 24, New York City:** bomb set off in historical Fraunces Tavern killed four and injured more than 50 persons. Puerto Rican nationalist group (FALN) claimed responsibility and police tied 13 other bombings to it.

1993 **Feb. 26, New York City:** bomb exploded in basement garage of World Trade Center; killed six and injured at least 1,040 others. Six Middle Eastern men were later convicted in this act of vengeance for the Palestinian people. They claimed to be retaliating against U.S. support for the Israeli government.

1995 **April 19, Oklahoma City:** car bomb exploded outside Federal office building, collapsing wall and floors. 168 persons were killed, including 19 children and one person who died in rescue effort. Over 220 buildings sustained damage. Timothy McVeigh and Terry Nichols later convicted in the antigovernment plot to avenge the Branch Davidian standoff in Waco, Tex. exactly two years earlier. (*See* Miscellaneous Disasters.)

MISCELLANEOUS DISASTERS

1888 **March 11–14, East Coast:** The Blizzard of 1888. 400 people died; as much as five feet of snow. Damage was estimated at $20 million.

1928 **March 12, Santa Paula, Calif.:** collapse of St. Francis Dam left 450 dead.

1930s **Many states:** longest drought of the 20th century. Peak periods were 1930, 1934, 1936, 1939, and 1940. During 1934, dry regions stretched solidly from N.Y. and Pa. across the Great Plains to the Calif. coast. A great "dust bowl" covered some 50 million acres in the south central plains during the winter of 1935–1936.

1958 **Jan.–Oct., Austria, France, Germany, Italy, and Switzerland:** 283 people were killed in mountain climbing accidents in Alps Mountains.

1980 **Jan. 20, Sincelejo, Colombia:** bleachers at a bullring collapsed, leaving 222 dead.

March 30, Stavanger, Norway: floating hotel in North Sea collapsed, killing 123 oil workers.

1981 **July 18, Kansas City, Mo.:** suspended walkway in Hyatt Regency Hotel collapsed; 113 dead, 186 injured.

1984 **Dec. 3, Bhopal, India:** toxic gas, methyl isocyanate, seeped from Union Carbide insecticide plant, killed more than 2,000, injured about 150,000.

1987 **Sept. 18. Goiânia, Brazil:** 244 people contaminated with cesium-137 that was removed from a steel cylinder taken from a cancer-therapy machine in an abandoned clinic and sold as scrap. Four people died in worst radiation disaster in Western Hemisphere.

1988 **July 6, North Sea off Scotland:** 166 workers killed in explosion and fire on Occidental Petroleum's *Piper Alpha* rig in North Sea; 64 survivors. It is the world's worst offshore oil disaster.

1990 **July 2, Mecca, Saudi Arabia:** a stampede in a 1,800 foot-long pedestrian tunnel leading from Mecca to a tent city for pilgrims killed 1,426 pilgrims who were trampled to death.

1991 **Nov. 29, near Coalinga, Calif.:** a massive traffic accident occurred during a severe dust storm involving 104 vehicles in a pileup on Interstate 5; 17 persons killed.

1993 **April 19, Waco, Tex.:** 51-day stalemate between federal agents and members of Christian Branch Davidian cult ended in a fiery tragedy after federal agents botched their assault on the sect's compound. Earlier, on Feb. 28, four agents were shot to death in failed attack on heavily armed

compound. About 80 Branch Davidians, including at least 17 children, died when the compound burned to the ground in a suspicious blaze. Jurors in the criminal trial of surviving cult members were unable to determine who fired the first shot on Feb. 28. Surviving Davidians dispute the government's version of how the cult members died.

1995 **June 29, Seoul, Korea:** five-story wing of Sampoong Department Store collapsed, killing at least 206 people, injuring 910 others.

July 12–17, U.S. Midwest and Northeast: over 800 persons, including 560 in Chicago, died in record heat wave.

1996 **May 10–11, Mt. Everest, Nepal:** eight climbers died near summit during storm on mountain. Is worst single loss of lives to occur in a season on Mt. Everest. Another four died over the remaining course of the month.

1997 **April 15, Mecca, Saudia Arabia:** fire and stampede in pilgrim's encampment killed 217 and injured at least 1,300.

1998 **Aug. 7, Nairobi, Kenya, and Dar es Salaam, Tanzania:** U.S. embassies bombed by terrorists, killing 243 in Nairobi and 10 in Tanzania; more than 1,000 injured.

WARTIME DISASTERS

1915 **May 6, off the coast of Ireland:** despite German warnings in newspapers, the Cunard Liner *Lusitania* sailed from N.Y. for Liverpool, England, on May 1st and was sunk by a German submarine. 1,198 passengers and crew, 128 of them Americans, died. Unknown to the passengers, the ship was carrying a cargo of small arms. Disaster contributed to entry of the U.S. into World War I.

1916 **Feb. 26, Mediterranean:** 3,100 people died when the French cruiser *Provence* was sunk by a German submarine.

1940 **Sept. 13, Atlantic Ocean:** luxury liner S.S. *City of Benares* sailed from Liverpool with over 90 British children who were being evacuated to Canada to escape harm during World War II. About 600 miles out to sea, the ship was torpedoed by a German submarine during the night and only 13 of the children survived the disaster.[1]

1941 **Dec. 7, Pearl Harbor, Hawaii:** 1,177 crewmen killed when U.S. Battleship *Arizona* was sunk during a surprise attack on the American naval base by Japanese warplanes. The devastating air strike, which damaged or destroyed every battleship in the U.S. Pacific fleet, is the worst naval catastrophe in U.S. history.

1943 **Nov. 26, Mediterranean Sea:** 1,105 U.S. soldiers died when the British troopship HMT *Rohna*, was sunk by a German air-to-surface guided missile. It is the worst U.S. troopship disaster.

Dec., Bari Harbor, Italy: U.S. ship, damaged during German bombing attack, leaked mustard gas into harbor, killing 83 U.S. servicemen and nearly 1,000 civilians.

1944 **Sept. 12, South China Sea:** U.S. submarines torpedoed and sank two Japanese troop ships, the *Kachidoki Maru* and the *Rakuyo Maru*. Unknown to the submarines, the Japanese, in disregard for the rules of treatment of prisoners of war, had forced 2,000 British, Australian, and American POWs into the holds of the ships which were designed to hold only 300 troops. Later, when the subs discovered the tragedy, they sought to rescue as many survivors as possible. Japanese vessels picked up most of *Kachidoki Maru*'s prisoners but abandoned those from the *Rakuyo Maru,* taking only the Japanese survivors. Of the 1,300 POWs aboard the *Rakuyo Maru,* 159 were rescued, but only seven lived.

Oct. 24, South China Sea: the *Arisan Maru* carrying 1,800 American prisoners was torpedoed by a U.S. submarine and sunk. The Japanese destroyer escort rescued Japanese military and civilian personnel and left the POWs to their fate. It is estimated that only ten prisoners survived the disaster.

Dec. 17–18, Philippine Sea: a typhoon struck U.S. Third Fleet's Task Force 38, sank three destroyers, damaged seven other ships, destroyed 186 aircraft, and killed 800 officers and men.

1945 **Jan. 30, Baltic Sea:** 7,700 persons died in world's largest marine disaster when the Nazi passenger ship *Wilhelm Gustoff* carrying Germans fleeing Poland was torpedoed by a Soviet submarine.

May 3: several days before World War II ended in Europe, the German passenger ship, *Cap Arcona,* carrying about 6,000, of which an estimated 5,000 were concentration camp prisoners, was sunk by British aircraft. An estimated 5,000 persons were killed.

May 4, Gearhart Mountain, south-central Ore.: six people on a picnic, including a mother and her unborn child, were the only persons ever killed by a balloon-carried bomb launched from Japan. During the war, Japan launched some 6,000 FUGO ("windship weapon") balloons to drift across the Pacific to the U.S. and Canada, each carrying bombs and incendiaries for starting forest fires and creating death and havoc among the American people. Although over 200 of the deadly balloons floated to the U.S. before the war ended, the government kept it a secret from the American people.

July 29, nr. Leyte Gulf, Philippines: heavy cruiser *Indianapolis* torpedoed and sunk by a Japanese submarine. Of the crew of 1,199 men, only 316 survived. Due to Navy blundering, the warship was not reported missing when it did not arrive at Leyte on July 31 as scheduled and therefore no search was ever made for crew. The survivors were discovered by a Navy patrol plane 82 hours after the ship had gone down.

1991 **Feb., Kuwait:** during Persian Gulf War, Iraqi troops systematically dynamited and set fire to 650 of Kuwait's 950 oil wells, causing world's worst man-made environmental disaster. Total of 749 wells damaged. Last of oil fires extinguished on Nov. 6, 1991.

1. During the war (1939–1945), some 10,000 children were evacuated to stay with foster parents in the United States and Canada. The sinking of the *City of Benares* ended the British government's evacuation program.

U.S. Societies and Associations

Source: Questionnaires to organizations. Names are listed alphabetically according to key word in title; figure in parentheses is year of founding; other figure is membership.

The following is a partial list selected for general readership interest. A comprehensive listing of approximately 23,000 national and international organizations can be found in the *Encyclopedia of Associations,* 31st ed., 1996, published by Gale Research Company, 835 Penobscot Building, 645 Griswold St., Detroit, Mich. 48226-4049, available in most public libraries.

AARP (American Association of Retired Persons) (1958): 601 E. St. N.W., Washington, D.C. 20049. 33,000,000. Phone: (202) 434-2277. www.aarp.org.

Abortion Federation, National (1977): 1755 Mass. Ave., Suite 600, Washington, D.C. 20036. Phone: (202) 667-5881 or (800) 772-9100. www.prochoice.org.

Accountants, American Institute of Certified Public (1887): 1211 Avenue of the Americas, New York, N.Y. 10036-8775. 330,000. Phone: (212) 596-6200. www.aicpa.org.

ACSM: American Congress on Surveying and Mapping (1941): 5410 Grosvenor Lane, Suite 100, Bethesda, Md. 20814. 8,000. Phone: (301) 493-0200. www.landsurveyor.com/acsm.

Actors' Equity Association (1913): 165 W. 46th St., New York, N.Y. 10036. Phone: (212) 869-8530.

Actuaries, Society of (1949): 475 N. Martingale Rd., Suite 800, Schaumburg, Ill. 60173-2226. 16,900. Phone: (847) 706-3500. www.soa.org.

Aeronautic Association, National (1905): 1815 N. Fort Myer Dr., Suite 700, Arlington, Va. 22209. 300,000. Phone: (703) 527-0226. www.naa.ycg.org.

Aerospace Medical Association (1929): 320 S. Henry St., Alexandria, Va. 22314-3579. 4,000. Phone: (703) 739-2240. www.asma.org.

African-American Institute, The (1953): 380 Lexington Ave., New York, N.Y. 10168-4298. Phone: (212) 949-5666.

AFS Intercultural Programs—USA (American Field Service) (1947): 198 Madison Avenue, 8th floor, New York, N.Y. 10016. 100,000. Phone: (212) 299-9000 or (800) AFS-INFO. www.afs.org.

Agricultural History Society (1919): 1301 New York Ave. N.W., Washington, D.C. 20005-4788. 1,400. Phone: (202) 219-0786. www.public.iastate.edu/nhistory_info/aghistory.htm.

Agronomy, American Society of (1907): 677 S. Segoe Rd., Madison, Wis. 53711-1086. 11,400. Phone: (608) 273-8080; fax: (608) 273-2021. www.agronomy.org.

Aircraft Association, Experimental (1953): P.O. Box 3086, Oshkosh, Wis. 54903-3086. 170,000. Phone: (920) 426-4800. www.eaa.org.

Aircraft Owners and Pilots Association (1939): 421 Aviation Way, Frederick, Md. 21701-4798. 340,000. Phone: (301) 695-2000; fax: (301) 695-2375. www.aopa.org.

Air Force Association (1946): 1501 Lee Highway, Arlington, Va. 22209-1198. 170,000. Phone: (703) 247-5800. www.afa.org.

Air Line Pilots Association (1931): 1625 Massachusetts Ave. N.W., Washington, D.C. 20036 and 535 Herndon Pkwy., Herndon, Va. 20170. 49,000. Phone: (703) 689-2270. www.alpa.org.

Al-Anon Family Group Headquarters, Inc. For families and friends of alcoholics. (1951): 1600 Corporate Landing Pkwy., Virginia Beach, Va. 23456-5617. 33,000 groups worldwide. Phone: (757) 563-1600. www.al-anon.org.

Alcoholics Anonymous (1935): General Service Office, A.A. World Services, Inc., 475 Riverside Dr., 11th Floor, New York, N.Y. 10115. 2,000,000. Phone: (212) 870-3400. www.aa.org.

Alcohol Problems, American Council on (1895): 3426 Bridgeland Dr., Bridgeton, Mo. 63044. Phone: (314) 739-5944.

Alexander Graham Bell Association for the Deaf (1890): 3417 Volta Place N.W., Washington, D.C. 20007. 6,200. Phone: (202) 337-5220 V, TTY. www.agbell.org.

Alzheimer's Association (1980): 919 N. Michigan Ave., Suite 1000, Chicago, Ill. 60611-1676. More than 200 Chapters in all 50 states, over 2,000 Family Support Groups. Phone: (312) 335-8700; (800) 272-3900. www.alz.org.

American Academy of Allergy, Asthma and Immunology (1943): 611 E. Wells St., Milwaukee, Wis. 53202. 5,000. Phone: (414) 272-6071. www.aaaai.org.

American Alliance for Health, Physical Education, Recreation and Dance (1885): 1900 Association Dr., Reston, Va. 20191. 25,000. Phone: (703) 476-3400. www.aahperd.org.

American Automobile Association (1902): 1000 AAA Dr., Heathrow, Fla. 32746-5063. Phone: (407) 444-7000. www.aaa.com.

American Civil Liberties Union (1920): 125 Broad St., 18th Floor, New York, N.Y. 10004. 275,000. www.aclu.org.

American Contract Bridge League (1927): 2990 Airways Blvd., Memphis, Tenn. 38116-3847. Phone: (901) 332-5586; fax: (901) 398-7754. www.acbl.org.

American Federation of Labor and Congress of Industrial Organizations (AFL-CIO) (1955): 815 16th St. N.W., Washington, D.C. 20006. 14,500,000. Phone: (202) 637-5000. www.aflcio.org.

American Federation of Musicians of the United States and Canada (1896): 1501 Broadway, Suite 600, Paramount Bldg., New York, N.Y. 10036. Phone: (212) 869-1330. www.afm.org.

American Forests (1875): P.O. Box 2000, Washington, D.C. 20013. 115,000. Phone: (202) 667-3300. www.amfor.org.

American Foundrymen's Society, Inc. (1896): 505 State St., Des Plaines, Ill. 60016-8399. 13,000. Phone: (847) 824-0181. www.afsinc.org.

American Friends Service Committee (1917): 1501 Cherry St., Philadelphia, Pa. 19102-1479. Phone: (215) 241-7000. www.afsc.org.

American Geographical Society, The (1871): 120 Wall St., Ste. 100, New York, N.Y. 10005. 1,500. Phone: (212) 422-5456; fax: (212) 422-5480. email: amgeosoc@earthlink.net.

American Geriatrics Society (1942): 770 Lexington Ave., Suite 300, New York, N.Y. 10021. 6,000. Phone: (212) 308-1414; fax: (212) 832-8646. www.americangeriatrics.org.

American Heart Association (1924): 7272 Greenville Ave., Dallas, Tex. 75231-4596. 4,200,000 volunteers. Phone: (800) AHA-USA1. www.amhrt.org.

American Historical Association (1884): 400 A St. S.E., Washington, D.C. 20003. 15,000. Phone: (202) 544-2422. email: aha@theaha.org. chnm.gmu.edu/aha.

American Indian Affairs, Association on (1923): Tekakwitha Complex, Agency Road #7, Box 268, Sisseton, S.D. 57262. 40,000. Phone: (605) 698-3998 or 3787.

American Jewish Committee (1906): 165 East 56th Street, New York, N.Y. 10022. 70,000. Phone: (212) 751-4000; fax: (212) 319-0975. www.ajc.org.

American Kennel Club (1884): 51 Madison Ave., New York, N.Y. 10010. 505 member clubs. Phone: (212) 696-8200; (919) 233-9767 (customer service). www.akc.org.

American Legion, The (1919): P.O. Box 1055, Indianapolis, Ind. 46206. 2,900,000. Phone: (317) 630-1200. www.legion.org.

American Legion Auxiliary (1919): 777 N. Meridian St., Indianapolis, Ind. 46204. 1,000,000. Phone: (317) 635-6291. www.legion-aux.org.

American Mensa, Ltd. (1960): 201 Main St., Suite 1101, Fort Worth, Texas 76102. 50,000. Phone: (817) 332-2600. www.us.mensa.org.

American Montessori Society (1960): 281 Park Avenue South, 6th floor, New York, N.Y. 10010. Phone: (212) 358-1250; fax: (212) 358-1256. www.amshq.org.

American Museum of Natural History (1869): Central Park West at 79th St., New York, N.Y. 10024-5192. 500,000. Phone: (212) 769-5100. www.amnh.org.

American Planning Association (1909): Administrative Offices: 122 S. Michigan Ave., Chicago, Ill. 60603. 30,000. Phone: (312) 431-9100. Headquarters: 1776 Massachusetts Ave. N.W., Washington, D.C. 20036. Phone: (202) 872-0611. www.planning.org.

Americans for Democratic Action, Inc. (1947): 1625 K St. N.W., Suite 210, Washington, D.C. 20006. 70,000. Phone: (202) 785-5980. www.apaction.org.

American Society for Nutritional Sciences (1928): 9650 Rockville Pike, Bethesda, Md. 20814-3990. 3,600. Phone: (301) 530-7050. www.faseb.org/asns.

American Society for Public Administration (ASPA) (1939): 1120 G St. N.W., Suite 700, Washington, D.C. 20005. 12,000. Phone: (202) 393-7878. www.aspanet.org.

American Universities, Association of (1900): 1200 New York Avenue NW, Suite 550, Washington, D.C. 20005. Phone: (202) 408-7500. www.tulane.edu:80/naau.

American Water Resources Association (1964): 950 Herndon Parkway, Ste. 300, Herndon, Va. 20170–5531. 4,000. Phone: (703) 904-1225. fax: (703) 904-1228. email: awrahq@aol.com. www.awra.org.

Amnesty International/USA (1961): 322 Eighth Ave., New York, N.Y. 10001-4808. 300,000. Phone: (212) 807-8400. www.amnesty-usa.org.

AMVETS (American Veterans of World War II, Korea, and Vietnam) (1944): 4647 Forbes Blvd., Lanham, Md. 20706-4380. 250,000. Phone: (301) 459-9600. www.amvets.org.

Animals, The American Society for the Prevention of Cruelty to (ASPCA) (1866): 424 E. 92nd St., New York, N.Y. 10128. 400,000+. Phone: (212) 876-7700. www.aspca.org.

Animals, The Fund For, Inc. (1967): 200 W. 57th St., New York, N.Y. 10019. 175,000. Phone: (212) 246-2096. www.envirolink.org/arrs/fund.

Anthropological Association, American (1902): 4350 N. Fairfax Dr., Suite 640, Arlington, Va. 22203-1620. 11,500. Phone: (703) 528-1902. www.ameranthassn.org.

Anti-Defamation League of B'nai B'rith (1913): 823 United Nations Plaza, New York, N.Y. 10017-3560. Phone: (212) 885-7700. www.adl.org.

Anti-Vivisection Society, The American (1883): 801 Old York Rd., #204, Jenkintown, Pa. 19046-1685. 15,000. Phone: (215) 887-0816; fax: (215) 887-2088. email: aavsonline@aol.com. www.aavs.org.

Appraisers, American Society of (1936): 555 Herndon Parkway, Suite 125, Herndon, VA 20170. 6,500. Phone: (800) ASA-VALU or (703) 478-2228. www.appraisers.org.

Arboriculture, International Society of (1924): P.O. Box GG, Savoy, Ill. 61874-9902. 8,000. Phone: (217) 355-9411; fax (217) 355-9516. www.ag.uiuc.edu/~isa.

Archaeological Institute of America (1879): 656 Beacon St., Boston, Mass. 02215-2010. 11,000. Phone: (617) 353-9361. email: aia@bu.edu. www.archaeological.org.

Architects, The American Institute of (1857): 1735 New York Ave. N.W., Washington, D.C. 20006-5292. 59,000. Phone: (202) 626-7300. www.aia.org.

Architectural Historians, Society of (1940): 1365 N. Astor St., Chicago, Ill. 60610-2144. 4,000. Phone: (312) 573-1365; fax: (312) 573-1141. www.sah.org.

Army, Association of the United States (1950): 2425 Wilson Blvd., Arlington, Va. 22210-3385. 100,000+. Phone: (703) 841-4300. www.ausa.org.

Arthritis Foundation (1948): 1330 West Peachtree St., Atlanta, Ga. 30309. 150 local offices. Phone: (404) 872-7100; (800) 283-7800. www.arthritis.org.

Arts, National Endowment for the (1965): 1100 Pennsylvania Ave. N.W., Washington, D.C. 20506. Phone: (202) 682-5400. arts.endow.gov.

ASM International ® (1913): Materials Park, Ohio 44073-0002. 44,000. Phone: (800) 336-5152; fax: (440) 338-4634. www.asm-intl.org.

Association for Investment Management and Research (1990): 5 Boar's Head Lane, P.O. Box 3668, Charlottesville, Va. 22903. 30,000. Phone: (804) 980-3668. www.aimr.com.

Astronomical Society, American (1899): 2000 Florida Ave. Suite 400, Washington, D.C. 20009. 6,300. Phone: (202) 328-2010. www.aas.org.

Atheists, American (1963): P.O. Box 140195, Austin, Texas 78714. 40,000 Families. Phone: (512) 458-1244. www.athiests.org.

Audubon Society, National (1905): 700 Broadway, New York, N.Y. 10003-9562. 550,000. Phone: (212) 979-3000. www.audubon.org.

Authors League of America (1912): 330 W. 42nd St., 29th Floor, New York, N.Y. 10036-6902. 14,000. Phone: (212) 564-8350.

Autism Society of America (1965): 7910 Woodmont Ave., Suite 650, Bethesda, Md. 20814. 18,000+. Phone: (301) 657-0881; (800) 3AUTISM. www.autism-society.org.

Automobile Club, National (1924): Bayside Plaza, 188 The Embarcadero, #300, San Francisco, Calif. 94105. 200,000. Phone: (415) 777-4000.

Bar Association, American (1878): 750 N. Lake Shore Dr., Chicago, Ill. 60611-4497. 371,000. Phone: (312) 988-5000. www.abanet.org.

Barber Shop Quartet Singing in America, Society for the Preservation and Encouragement of (SPEBSQSA, Inc.) (1938): 6315 Third Ave., Kenosha, Wis., 53143-5199. 38,000. Phone: (800) 876-SING. www.spebsqa.org.

Better Business Bureaus, Council of (1970): 4200 Wilson Blvd., Suite 800, Arlington, Va. 22203-1838. Phone: (703) 276-0100; fax: (703) 525-8277. www.bbb.org.

Bible Society, American (1816): 1865 Broadway, New York, N.Y. 10023-9980. Phone: (800) 32-BIBLE. www.americanbible.org.

Biblical Literature, Society of (1880): 1201 Clairmont Rd., Suite 300, Decatur, Ga. 30030. 8,000 members, 1,200 subscribers. Phone: (404) 636-4744; fax: (404) 248-0815; or (404) 727-2345 for membership services. www.sb/-site.org.

Big Brothers Big Sisters of America (1977): 230 N. 13th St., Philadelphia, Pa. 19107. Phone: (215) 567-7000. www.bbbsa.org.

Biochemistry and Molecular Biology, American Society for (1906): 9650 Rockville Pike, Bethesda,

Md. 20814. 9,600. Phone: (301) 530-7145. www.faseb.org/asbmb.

Biological Sciences, American Institute of (1947): 1444 Eye St. N.W., Washington, D.C. 20005. 5,000. Phone: (202) 628-1500. www.aibs.org.

Blind, American Council of the (1961): 1155 15th St. N.W., Suite 720, Washington, D.C. 20005. 40,000. Phone: (202) 467-5081. www.acb.org.

Blind, National Federation of the (1940): 1800 Johnson St., Baltimore, Md. 21230. 50,000. Phone: (410) 659-9314. www.nfb.org.

B'nai B'rith International (1843): 1640 Rhode Island Ave. N.W., Washington, D.C. 20036-3278. 500,000. Phone: (202) 857-6600. www.bnaibrith.org.

Booksellers Association, American (1900): 828 So. Broadway, Tarrytown, N.Y. 10591. 4,500. Phone: (914) 591-2665, (800) 637-0037. www.bookweb.org.

Boys & Girls Clubs of America (1906): 1230 West Peachtree St. N.W., Atlanta, Ga., 30309-3447. 2,600,000 youth served. Phone: (404) 815-5700; fax: (404) 815-5757. www.bgca.org.

Boy Scouts of America (1910): 1325 W. Walnut Hill Lane, P.O. Box 152079, Irving, Tex. 75015-2079. 5,378,546. Phone: (972) 580-2000. www.bsa.scouting.org.

Broadcasters, National Association of (1922): 1771 N St. N.W., Washington, D.C. 20036-2891. Phone: (202) 429-5300. www.nab.org.

Brookings Institution, The (1916): 1775 Massachusetts Ave. N.W., Washington, D.C. 20036-2188. Phone: (202) 797-6000. www.brookings.org.

Business Education Association, National (1946): 1914 Association Dr., Reston, Va. 20191-1596. 16,000. Phone: (703) 860-8300; fax: (703) 620-4483. email: nbea@nbea.org; www.nbea.org.

Business Women's Association, American (1949): 9100 Ward Parkway, P.O. Box 8728, Kansas City, Mo. 64114-0728. 80,000. Phone: (816) 361-6621; fax: (816) 361-4991. email: abwa@abwahq.org. www.abwahq.org.

Camp Fire Boys and Girls (1910): 4601 Madison Ave., Kansas City, Mo. 64112-1278. 670,000. Phone: (816) 756-1950. www.campfire.org.

Camping Association, The American (1910): 5000 State Rd. 67 N., Martinsville, Ind. 46151-7902. 5,500, 2,000+ camps. Phone: (765) 342-8456. www.aca-camps.org.

Cancer Society, American (1913): 1599 Clifton Rd. N.E., Atlanta, Ga. 30329. Over 2 million volunteers. Phone: (800) ACS-2345 or check local listings. www.cancer.org.

CARE, Inc. (1945): 151 Ellis St. NE, Atlanta, Ga. 30303-2439. Programs in 62 developing countries. Phone: (800) 521-CARE. www.care.org.

Carnegie Endowment for International Peace (1910): 1779 Massachusetts Ave., N.W., Washington, D.C. 20036–2103. Phone: (202) 483-7600; fax: (202) 483-1840. www.ceip.org.

Catholic Charities USA (1910): 1731 King St., Alexandria, Va. 22314. 1,400 agencies and institutions. Phone: (703) 549-1390. www.catholiccharitiesusa.org.

Catholic Daughters of the Americas (1903): 10 W. 71st St., New York, N.Y. 10023. 125,000. Phone: (212) 877-3041.

Catholic War Veterans of the U.S.A. Inc. (1935): 441 N. Lee St., Alexandria, Va. 22314. 25,000. Phone: (703) 549-3622.

Cerebral Palsy Associations, Inc., United (1949): 1660 L St. N.W., Suite 700, Washington, D.C. 20036. 153 affiliates. Phone: (202) 973-7197/TT, (800) 872-5827. www.ucpa.org.

Chamber of Commerce of the U.S. (1912): 1615 H St. N.W., Washington, D.C. 20062-2000. 220,000. Phone: (800) 649-9719. www.uschamber.org.

Chemical Engineers, American Institute of (1908): 345 E. 47th St., New York, N.Y. 10017-2395. 55,000. Phone: (212) 705-7338. www.aiche.org.

Chemical Society, American (1876): 1155 16th St. N.W., Washington, D.C. 20036. 151,024. Phone: (202) 872-4600. www.acs.org.

Chess Federation, United States (1939): 3054 NYS Rte. 9W, New Windsor, N.Y. 12553. 50,000+. Phone: (914) 562-8350; (800) 388-KING. www.uschess.org.

Child Labor Committee, National (1904): 1501 Broadway, Rm. 1111, New York, N.Y. 10036. Phone: (212) 840-1801.

Children's Book Council (1945): 568 Broadway, Suite 404, New York, N.Y. 10012. 80 imprints. Phone: (212) 966-1990; fax: (212) 966-2073. email: staff@cbcbooks.org. www.cbcbooks.org.

Child Welfare League of America (1920): 440 First St. N.W., Suite 310, Washington, D.C. 20001-2085. Phone: (202) 638-2952. www.cwla.org.

Chiropractic Association, American (1963): 1701 Clarendon Blvd., Arlington, Va. 22209. 22,000. Phone: (703) 276-8800, (800) 986-4636; fax: (703) 243-2593. www.amerchiro.org.

Cities, National League of (1924): 1301 Pennsylvania Ave. N.W., Washington, D.C. 20004. 18,000 cities and towns. Phone: (202) 626-3000. www.ncl.org.

Civil Air Patrol, National Headquarters (1941): 105 S. Hansell St., Bldg. 714, Maxwell AFB, Ala. 36112-6332. 54,493. Phone: (334) 953-4287. www.capaf.mil.

Civil Engineers, American Society of (1852): 1801 Alexander Bell Dr., Reston, Va. 20191-4400. 120,000. Phone: (800) 548–ASCE (2723). www.asce.org.

Clinical Pathologists, American Society of (1922): 2100 W. Harrison St., Chicago, Ill. 60612-3798. 77,200. Phone: (312) 738-1336; fax: (312) 738-9798. www.ascp.org.

The College Fund/UNCF (1944): 8260 Willow Oaks Corporate Dr., P.O. Box 10444, Fairfax, Va. 22031-4511. Phone: (703) 205-3400; fax: (703) 205-3576. www.uncf.org.

Colleges and Employers, National Association of (formerly College Placement Council) (1956): 62 E. Highland Ave., Bethlehem, Pa. 18017. 3,200. Phone: (800) 544-5272. www.jobweb.org.

Common Cause (1970): 1250 Connecticut Ave. N.W., Washington, D.C. 20036. 250,000. Phone: (202) 833-1200; fax: (202) 659-3716. www.commoncause.org.

Community Cultural Center Association, American (1978): 149 Cannongate III, Nashua, N.H. 03063. Phone: (603) 886-2748.

Composer/USA, National Association of (1932): P.O. Box 49256, Barrington Station, Los Angeles, Calif. 90049. 600. Phone: (310) 541-8213. www.thebook.com/nacusa.

Congress of Racial Equality (CORE) (1942): 30 Cooper Square, New York, N.Y. 10003. Nationwide network of chapters. Phone: (212) 598-4000; fax: (212) 598-4000. www.core-online.org.

Conscientious Objectors, Central Committee for (1948): 1515 Cherry St., Philadelphia, Pa. 19102. Phone: (215) 563-8787.
655 Sutter St., Suite 514, San Francisco, Calif. 94102. Phone: (415) 474-3002. www.libertynet.org/ccco.

Conservation Engineers, Association of (1961): Attn: Jim Price, Secretary, c/o Arkansas Game & Fish Commission, #2 Natural Resources Drive, Little Rock, Ark. 72205.

Consumer Federation of America (1968): 1424 16th St. N.W., Suite 604, Washington, D.C. 20036. 240 member organizations. Phone: (202) 387-6121.

Consumers League, National (1899): 1701 K St. N.W., Suite 1200, Washington, D.C. 20006. Phone: (202) 835-3323. www.natlconsumersleague.org.

Consumers Union (1936): 101 Truman Ave., Yonkers, N.Y. 10703-1057. 4.6 million subscribers to *Consumer Reports Magazine.* Phone: (914) 378-2000.

Counselors, American College of (1984): 8038 Camellia Lane, Indianapolis, Ind. 46219. Phone: (317) 898-3211.

Country Music Association (1958): One Music Circle South, Nashville, Tenn. 37203. 7,000+. Phone: (615) 244-2840. www.countrymusic.org.

Credit Management, National Association of (1896): 8815 Centre Park Dr., Suite 200, Columbia, Md. 21045. Phone: (410) 740-5560. www.nacm.org.

Credit Union National Association (1934): P.O. Box 431, Madison, Wis. 53701. 51 state leagues representing 12,400 credit unions. Phone: (800) 356-9655. www.cuna.org.

Crime and Delinquency, National Council on (1907): 685 Market St., #620, San Francisco, Calif. 94105. Criminal justice research, nationwide membership. Phone: (415) 896-6223. www.nccd.com.

CSA/USA, Celiac Sprue Association/United States of America, Inc., P.O. Box 31700, Omaha, Neb. 68131-0700. 6 regions in U.S., 74 chapters, 36 active resource units. Phone: (402) 558-0600; fax: (402) 558-1347.

Dairy Council, National (1915): 10255 W. Higgins Rd., Suite 900 Rosemont, Ill. 60018-5616. Phone: (847) 803-2000; fax: (847) 803-2077. www.ndc.org.

Daughters of the American Revolution, National Society (1890): 1776 D St. N.W., Washington, D.C. 20006. 180,000. Phone: (202) 628-1776. www.dar.org.

Deaf, National Association of the (1880): 814 Thayer Ave., Silver Spring, Md. 20910. Phone: (301) 587-1788 V; (301) 587-1789 TTY. www.nad.org.

Defenders of Wildlife (1947): 1101 14th St. N.W., #1400, Washington, D.C. 20005. 200,000 members and supporters. Phone: (202) 682-9400. www.defenders.org.

Dental Association, American (1859): 211 E. Chicago Ave., Chicago, Ill. 60611. 141,000. Phone: (312) 440-2500. www.ada.org.

Diabetes Association, American (1940): 1660 Duke St., Alexandria, Va. 22314. Phone: (703) 549-1500. www.diabetes.org/depault.htm.

Dignity (1969): 1500 Massachusetts Ave. N.W., Suite 11, Washington, D.C. 20005. 5,000. Phone: (202) 861-0017 and (800) 877-8797. www.dignityusa.org.

Disabled American Veterans (1920): 807 Maine Ave. S.W., Washington, D.C. 20024. 1,400,000. Phone: (202) 554-3501. www.dav.org.

Dowsers, Inc., The American Society of (1961): P.O. Box 24, Danville, Vt. 05828-0024. 5,000. Phone: (800) 711-9530; fax: (802) 748-8565. email: ASD@dowsers.org. www.newhampshire.com/dowsers.org.

Ducks Unlimited, Inc. (1937): One Waterfowl Way, Memphis, Tenn. 38120. 600,000. Phone: (901) 758-3825. www.ducks.org.

Earthwatch (1972): 680 Mt. Auburn St., Box 403N, Watertown, Mass. 02272. 75,000. Phone: (800) 776-0188; fax: (617) 926-8532. www.earthwatch.org.

Eastern Star, Order of, General Grand Chapter (1876): 1618 New Hampshire Ave. N.W., Washington, D.C. 20009. 1,207,301. Phone: (202) 667-4737.

Easter Seal Society, The National (1919): 230 W. Monroe, Suite 1800, Chicago, Ill. 60606-4802. 109 state and local affiliate societies operating 500 service sites. Phone: (312) 726-6200; (312) 726-4258 TDD. www.seals.com.

Economic Association, American (1885): 2014 Broadway, Suite 305, Nashville, Tenn. 37203-2418. 22,000. 5,500 inst. subscribers. Phone: (615) 322-2595. www.vanderbilt.edu/AEA.

Edison Electric Institute (1933): 701 Pennsylvania Ave. N.W., Washington, D.C. 20004-2696. www.eei.org.

Education, American Council on (ACE), (1918): One Dupont Circle N.W., Washington, D.C. 20036-1193. 1,600+ colleges and universities and 200+ higher education associations. Phone: (202) 939-9300. www.acenet.edu.

Educational Exchange, Council on International (1947): 205 E. 42nd St., New York, N.Y. 10017. 265. Phone: (212) 822-2600. www.ciee.org.

Educational Research Association, American (1916): 1230 17th St. N.W., Washington, D.C. 20036. 22,000. Phone: (202) 223-9485. aera.net.

Education Association, National (1857): 1201 16th St. N.W., Washington, D.C. 20036-3290. 2.2 million. Phone: (202) 833-4000. www.nea.org.

Electrochemical Society, The (1902): 10 S. Main St., Pennington, N.J. 08534-2896. 7,000. Phone: (609) 737-1902; fax: (609) 737-2743. email: ecs@electrochem.org. www.electrochem.org.

Elks of the U.S.A., Benevolent and Protective Order of the (1868): 2750 N. Lakeview Ave., Chicago, Ill. 60614. 1,300,000. Phone: (773) 477-2750. www.elks.org/default.cfm.

Energy Engineers, Association of (1977): 4025 Pleasantdale Rd., Suite 420, Atlanta, Ga. 30340. 8,500. Phone: (770) 447-5083 ext. 210; fax: (770) 446-3969. email: info@aeecenter.org. www.aeecenter.org.

English-Speaking Union of the United States (1920): 16 E. 69th St., New York, N.Y. 10021. 18,000. Phone: (212) 879-6800. www.english-speakingunion.org.

Entomological Society of America (1889): 9301 Annapolis Rd., Lanham, Md. 20706-3115. 7,400+. Phone: (301) 731-4535; fax: (301) 731-4538. email: esa@entsoc.org. www.entsoc.org.

Esperanto League for North America, The (1952): P.O. Box 1129, El Cerrito, Calif. 94530. Over 1,000. Phone: (800) 377-3726. www.esperanto-usa.org.

Exceptional Children, The Council for (1922): 1920 Association Dr., Reston, Va. 20191-1589. 54,000. Voice phone: (800) CEC-SPED; TTY: (703) 264-9446; fax: (703) 264-9494. email: cec@cec.sped.org. www.cec.sped.org.

Exploration Geophysicists, Society of (1930): P.O. Box 702740, Tulsa, Okla. 74170-2740. 15,000+. Phone: (918) 497-5500. www.seg.org.

Family and Consumer Sciences, American Association of (1909): 1555 King St., Alexandria, Va. 22314. 14,500. Phone: (703) 706-4600. www.aafcs.org.

Family Campers & RVers (1949): 4804 Transit Rd., Bldg. 2, Depew, N.Y. 14043-4906. 15,000 families. Phone: (716) 668-6242; fax: (716) 668-6242. www.pgh.net/~dscott/fcrv.html.

Family Physicians, American Academy of (1947): 8880 Ward Pkwy., Kansas City, Mo. 64114-2797. 84,000. Phone: (816) 333-9700. www.aafp.org.

Family Relations, National Council on (1938): 3989 Central Ave. N.E., #550, Minneapolis, Minn. 55421-3921. 3,800. Phone: (612) 781-9331. www.ncfr.com.

Farm Bureau Federation, American (1919): 225 Touhy Ave., Park Ridge, Ill. 60068. 4.7 million member families. Phone: (847) 685-8600. www.fb.com.

Federal Bar Association (1920): 1815 H St. N.W., Suite 408, Washington, D.C. 20006-3697. 15,000. Phone: (202) 638-0252; fax: (202) 775-0295. www.fedbar.org.

Federal Employees, National Federation of (1917): 1016 16th St. N.W., Washington, D.C. 20036. Rep. 150,000. Phone: (202) 862-4400.

Fellowship of Reconciliation (1915): Box 271, Nyack, N.Y. 10960. 20,000. Phone: (914) 358-4601. www.nonviolence.org.

Female Executives, National Association for (1972): 30 Irving Place, New York, N.Y. 10003. 200,000. Phone: (212) 477-2200. www.nafe.com.

FFA Organization, National (1928): 5632 Mt. Vernon Memorial Hwy., P.O. Box 15160, Alexandria, Va. 22309-0160. 449,814. Phone: (703) 360-3600. www.agriculture.com/contents/FFA.

Fire Protection Association, National (1896): One Batterymarch Park, P.O. Box 9101, Quincy, Mass. 02269-9101. 68,000. Phone: (617) 770-3000. www.nfpa.org.

Flag Foundation, National (1968): Flag Plaza, Pittsburgh, Pa. 15219-3630. 3,000+. Phone: (412) 261-1776. www.usflag.org/usflag/nff.html.

Fleet Reserve Association (1924): 125 N. West St., Alexandria, Va. 22314-2754. 162,000. Phone: (703) 683-1400; (800) 372-1924. email: news-fra@fra.org. www.fra.org.

Foreign Policy Association (1918): 470 Park Ave. So., New York, N.Y. 10016. Phone: (212) 481-8100. www.fpa.org.

Foreign Relations, Council on (1921): 58 E. 68th St., New York, N.Y. 10021. 3,300. Phone: (212) 734-0400. www.foreignrelations.org.

Foreign Study, American Institute for (1965): 102 Greenwich Ave., Greenwich, Conn. 06830. Phone: (203) 869-9090; (800) 727-AIFS. www.aifs.org.

Forensic Sciences, American Academy of (1948): 410 N. 21st St., Suite 203/80904, P.O. Box 669, Colorado Springs, Colo. 80901-0669. 4,315. Phone: (719) 636-1100; fax: (719) 636-1993. www.aafs.org.

Foresters, Society of American (1900): 5400 Grosvenor Lane, Bethesda, Md. 20814-2198. 19,000. Phone: (301) 897-8720. www.safnet.org.

4-H Program (early 1900s): Room 3441-S, U.S. Department of Agriculture, Washington, D.C. 20250. 5.6 million. Phone: (202) 720-2908. www.4h-usa.org.

Freedom of Information Center (1958): 127 Neff Annex, Univ. of Missouri, Columbia, Mo. 65211. Phone: (573) 882-4856. www.missouri.edu/~foiwww.

French Institute/Alliance Française (1898): 22 E. 60th St., New York, N.Y. 10022-1077. 9,000. Phone: (212) 355-6100. www.fiaf.org.

Friends of Animals Inc. (1957): 777 Post Rd., Suite 205, Darien, Conn. 06820. 120,000. Phone: (203) 656-1522. www.envirolink.org/orgs/foa.

Friends of the Earth (1969): 1025 Vermont Ave. N.W., Suite 300, Washington, D.C. 20005. 35,000. Phone: (202) 783-7400. www.foe.org.

Future Homemakers of America, Inc. (1945): 1910 Association Dr., Reston, Va. 20191. 230,000. Phone: (703) 476-4900. www.fhahero.org.

Gamblers Anonymous: Box 17173, Los Angeles, Calif. 90017. Phone: (213) 386-8789. www.gamblersanonymous.org.

Gay and Lesbian Task Force, National (1973): 2320 17th St. N.W., Washington, D.C. 20009-2702. 35,000 members. Phone: (202) 332-6483. www.ngltf.org.

Genealogical Society, National (1903): 4527 17th St. N., Arlington, Va. 22207-2399. 17,000+. Phone: (703) 525-0050; fax: (703) 525-0052. www.genealogy.org/~ngs.

Geographers, Association of American (1904): 1710 16th St. N.W., Washington, D.C. 20009-3198. 7,000. Phone: (202) 234-1450; fax: (202) 234-2744. email: gaia@aag.org. www.aag.org.

Geographic Education, National Council for (1915): 16A Leonard Hall, Indiana University of Pennsylvania, Indiana, Pa. 15705. 3,700. Phone: (724) 357-6290. www.ncge.org.

Geographic Society, National (1888): 1145 17th St. N.W., Washington, D.C. 20036. 9,200,000. Phone: (202) 857-7000. www.nationalgeographic.com.

Geological Institute, American (1948): 4220 King St., Alexandria, Va. 22302-1502. 31 geoscience societies representing 100,000 geoscientists. Phone: (703) 379-2480. www.agiweb.org/.

Geological Society of America, Inc. (1888): 3300 Penrose Pl., P.O. Box 9140, Boulder, Colo. 80301. 15,000. Phone: (303) 447-2020. www.geosociety.org.

German American National Congress, The (Deutsch-Amerikanischer National Kongress—D.A.N.K.) (1958): 4740 N. Western Ave., Executive Office, Chicago, Ill. 60625-2097. Phone: (773) 275-1100. www.dank.org.

Gideons International, The (1889): 2900 Lebanon Rd., Nashville, Tenn. 37214-0800. 125,000. Phone: (615) 883-8533. www.gideons.org.

Gifted, The Association for the (1958): The Council for Exceptional Children, 1920 Association Dr., Reston, Va. 20191-1589. 2,200. Phone: (703) 620-3660.

Girl Scouts of the U.S.A. (1912): 420 Fifth Ave., New York, N.Y. 10018. 2,500,000. Phone: (212) 852-8000. www.gsusa.org.

Girls Incorporated (1945): 30 E. 33rd St., New York, N.Y. 10016. 350,000. Phone: (212) 689-3700. www.girlsinc.org.

Graphoanalysis Society, International (1929): 111 N. Canal St., Chicago, Ill. 60606. 10,000. Phone: (312) 930-9446. www.igas.com.

Gray Panthers (1970): P.O. Box 21477, Washington, D.C. 20009-9477. Over 50 chapters (networks). Phone: (202) 466-3132.

Greenpeace (1971): 1436 U St. N.W., Washington, D.C. 20009. 600,000. Phone: (202) 462-1177. www.greenpeaceusa.org.

Guide Dog Foundation for the Blind, Inc.® (1946): 371 E. Jericho Turnpike, Smithtown, N.Y. 11787-2976. 100,000. Phone: (516) 265-2121; (800) 548-4337; fax: (516) 361-5192. www.guidedog.org.

Hadassah, The Women's Zionist Organization of America (1912): 50 W. 58th St., New York, N.Y. 10019. 385,000. Phone: (212) 355-7900. www.hadassah.org.

Handgun Control, Inc. (1974): 1225 Eye St. N.W., Washington, D.C. 20005. 380,000. Phone: (202) 898-0792.www.handguncontrol.org.

Heating, Refrigerating and Air-Conditioning Engineers, Inc., American Society of (1894): 1791 Tullie Circle N.E., Atlanta, Ga. 30329. 50,000. Phone: (404) 636-8400. www.ashrae.org.

Helicopter Association International (1948): 1635 Prince St., Alexandria, Va. 22314. Phone: (703) 683-4646; fax: (703) 683-4745. www.rotor.com.

Historians, The Organization of American (1907): Indiana Univ., 112 N. Bryan St., Bloomington, Ind. 47408. 12,000. Phone: (812) 855-7311. www.indiana.edu/~oah.

Historic Preservation, National Trust for (1949): 1785 Massachusetts Ave. N.W., Washington, D.C. 20036. 275,000. Phone: (202) 588-6000. www.nationaltrust.org.

Horse Council, Inc., American (1969): 1700 K St. N.W., #300, Washington, D.C. 20006. More than 190 organizations and 2,400 individuals. Phone: (202) 296-4031.

Horse Shows Association, Inc., American (1917): 220 E. 42nd St., New York, N.Y. 10017-5876. 65,000. Phone: (212) 972-2473. www.ahsa.org.

Horticultural Association, National Junior (1935): 1424 N. 8th, Durant, Okla. 74701. 12,500. Phone: (405) 924-0771.

Horticultural Society, American (1922): 7931 East Boulevard Dr., Alexandria, Va. 22308. 22,000. Phone: (703) 768-5700 or (800) 777-7931; fax: (703) 768-8700. www.ahs.org.

Hostelling International—American Youth Hostels (1934): 733 15th St. N.W., Suite 840, Washington, D.C. 20005. 124,000. Phone: (202) 783-6161 for membership and reservations. www.hiayh.org.

Humane Association, American (1877): 63 Inverness Drive East, Englewood, Colo. 80112-5117. Phone: (303) 792-9900. www.amerhumane.org.

Humane Association, The American—Children's Division (1877): 63 Inverness Drive East, Englewood, Colo. 80112. Phone: (303) 792-9900; fax: (303) 792-5333. email: children@amerhumane.org. www.amerhumane.org.

Humane Society of the United States (1954): 2100 L St. N.W., Washington, D.C. 20037. 5,000,000. Phone: (202) 452-1100. www.hsus.org.

Humanities, National Endowment for the (1965): 1100 Pennsylvania Ave. N.W., Washington, D.C. 20506. Phone: (202) 606-8400. www.neh.fed.us.

Hydrogen Energy, International Association for (1975): P.O. Box 248266, Coral Gables, Fla. 33124. 2,500. Phone: (305) 284-4666.

Industrial Engineers, Institute of (1948): 25 Technology Park/Atlanta, Norcross, Ga. 30092. 24,000. Phone: (770) 449-0461.

International Credit Association (ICA) (1912): P.O. Box 419–57, St. Louis, Mo. 63141-1757. 7,500 members, 100 local associations. Phone: (314) 991-3030; fax: (314) 991-3029. email: icahdqtrs@stlnet.com. www.ica-credit.org.

Izaak Walton League of America (1922): 707 Conservation Lane, Gaithersburg, Md. 20878-2983. 50,000. Phone: (301) 548-0150. www.iwla.org

Jewish Community Centers Association (JCC) of North America (1917): 15 E. 26th St., New York, N.Y. 10010-1579. 275+ affiliated Jewish Community Centers, YM-YWHAs, and camps serving 1 million+ members. Phone: (212) 532-4949; fax: (212) 481-4174. email: info@jcca.org. www.jcca.org.

Jewish Congress, American (1918): 15 E. 84th St., New York, N.Y. 10028. 50,000. Phone: (212) 879-4500. www.ajcongress.org.

Jewish Historical Society, American (1892): 2 Thornton Rd., Waltham, Mass. 02154. 3,500. Phone: (781) 891-8110; fax: (617) 899-9208. email: ajhs@ajhs.org. www.ajhs.org.

Jewish War Veterans of the U.S.A. (1896): 1811 R St. N.W., Washington, D.C. 20009-1659. Phone: (202) 265-6280. www.penfed.org/jwv/home.htm.

Jewish Women, National Council of (1893): 53 W. 23rd St., New York, N.Y. 10010. 90,000. Phone: (212) 645-4048; fax: (212) 645-7466. www.ncjw.org.

John Birch Society (1958): P.O. Box 8040, Appleton, Wis. 54913. Under 100,000. Phone: (920) 749-3780; fax: (920) 749-5062. www.jbs.org.

Journalists, Society of Professional, (1909): 16 S. Jackson, Greencastle, Ind. 46135. 13,500. Phone: (765) 653-3333. www.spj.org.

Judaism, American Council for (1943): P.O. Box 9009, Alexandria, Va. 22304. 10,000. Phone: (703) 836-2546.

Junior Achievement Inc. (1919): One Education Way, Colorado Springs, Colo. 80906-4477. 2.3 million. Phone: (719) 540-8000. www.ja.org.

Junior Chamber of Commerce, The United States, Jaycees (1920): P.O. Box 7, Tulsa, Okla. 74102-0007. 113,000. Phone: (918) 584-2481; fax: (918) 584-4422. www.usjaycees.org.

Junior Leagues International, Inc., Association of (1921): 660 First Ave., New York, N.Y. 10016-3241. 293 Leagues, 200,000 members. Phone: (212) 683-1515.

Junior Statesmen of America (1934): 60 E. Third Ave., Suite 320, San Mateo, Calif. 94401. 15,000. Phone: (650) 347-1600 or (800) 334-5353. www.jsa.org.

Kiwanis International (1915): 3636 Woodview Trace, Indianapolis, Ind. 46268-3196. 316,000. Phone: (317) 875-8755. email: kiwanismail@kiwanis.org. www.kiwanis.org.

Knights of Columbus (1882): One Columbus Plaza, New Haven, Conn. 06510-3326. 1,600,000. Phone: (203) 772-2130. www.kofc-supreme-council.org.

Knights Templar, Grand Encampment of (1816): 5097 N. Elston Ave., Suite 101, Chicago, Ill. 60630-2460. 220,000. Phone: (773) 777-3300.

La Leche League International (1956): 1400 N. Meacham Rd., P.O. Box 4079, Schaumburg, Ill. 60168-4079. 50,000. Phone: (847) 519-7730. www.lalecheleague.org.

Law, American Society of International (1906): 2223 Massachusetts Ave. N.W., Washington, D.C. 20008. 4,300. Phone: (202) 939-6000.

League of Women Voters of the U.S. (1920): 1730 M St. N.W., Washington, D.C. 20036. Phone: (202) 429-1965; fax: (202) 429-0854. www.lwv.org.

Legal Aid and Defender Association, National (1911): 1625 K St. N.W., Suite 800, Washington, D.C. 20006. 2,400. Phone: (202) 452-0620.

Legal Secretaries, National Association of (1950): 314 East 3rd St., Suite 210, Tulsa, Okla. 74120. 6,000. Phone: (918) 582-5188. www.nals.org.

Leukemia Society of America (1949): 600 Third Ave., 4th Floor, New York, N.Y. 10016. Phone: (212) 573-8484. www.leukemia.org.

Library Association, American (1876): 50 E. Huron St., Chicago, Ill. 60611. 57,000. Phone: (312) 944-6780; (800) 545-2433. www.ala.org.

Lions Clubs International (1917): 300 22nd St., Oak Brook, Ill. 60521-8842. 1,419,408. Phone: (630) 571-5466. www.lionet.com.

Lung Association, American (1904): 1740 Broadway, New York, N.Y. 10019-4374. 99 constituent and affiliate associations. Phone: (800) LUNG-USA; (800) 586-4872. www.lungusa.org.

Magazine Editors, American Society of (1963): 919 Third Ave., 22nd Floor, New York, N.Y. 10022. 800. Phone: (212) 872-3700.

Management Accountants, Institute of (1919): 10 Paragon Dr., Montvale, N.J. 07645-1759. 80,000. Phone: (201) 573-9000. www.rutgers.edu/accounting/raw/ima.

Management Association, American (1923): 1601 Broadway, New York, N.Y. 10019-7420. 70,000. Phone: (212) 586-8100. www.tregistry.com/ama.htm.

Management Consultants, Institute of (1968): 521 Fifth Ave., 35th Floor, New York, N.Y. 10175-3598. 2,600 individuals. Phone: (212) 697-8262.

Manufacturers, National Association of (1895): 1331 Pennsylvania Ave. N.W., Washington, D.C. 20004-1790. Approx. 14,000. Phone: (202) 637-3000. www.nam.org.

March of Dimes Birth Defects Foundation (1938): 1275 Mamaroneck Ave., White Plains, N.Y. 10605. 104 chapters. Phone: (914) 428-7100, (888) 663-4637; tty: (914) 997-4764; fax: (914) 997-4763. email: resourcecenter@modimes.org. www.modimes.org.

Marine Conservation, Center for (1972): 1725 De Sales St. N.W., Suite 600, Washington, D.C. 20036. 120,000. Phone: (202) 429-5609. www.cmc-ocean.org.

Marine Corps Association (1913): P.O. Box 1775, 715 Broadway, Quantico, Va. 22134. 100,723. Phone: (703) 640-6161; (800) 336-0291. www.mca-marines.org.

Marine Technology Society (1963): 1828 L St. N.W., Suite 906, Washington, D.C. 20036-5104. 2,000+. Phone: (202) 775-5966; fax: (202) 429-9417. www.cms.udel.edu/mts.

Masons, Royal Arch, General Grand Chapter International (1797): P.O. Box 489, Danville, Ky. 40423-0489. 230,000. Phone: (606) 236-0757.

Mathematical Association of America (1915): 1529 18th St. N.W., Washington, D.C. 20036. 30,000. Phone: (202) 387-5200. www.maa.org.

Mathematical Society, American (1888): P.O. Box 6248, Providence, R.I. 02940-6248. 30,000. Phone: (401) 455-4000. email: ams@ams.org. www.ams.org.

Mayflower Descendants, General Society of (1897): 4 Winslow St., P.O. Box 3297, Plymouth, Mass. 02361. 25,000. Phone: (508) 746-3188.

Mechanical Engineers, American Society of (1880): 345 E. 47th St., New York, N.Y. 10017. 125,000. Phone: (800) THE-ASME. www.asme.org.

Medical Association, American (1847): 515 N. State St., Chicago, Ill. 60610-4377. Phone: (312) 464-5000. www.ama-assn.org.

Mental Health Association, National (1909): 1021 Prince St., Alexandria, Va., 22314-2971. 330+ affiliates. Phone: (703) 684-7722; 800-969-NMHA; TDD 800-433-5959; fax: (703) 684-5968. email: nmhainfo@aol.com. www.nmha.org

Meteorological Society, American (1919): 45 Beacon St., Boston, Mass. 02108-3693. 11,000. Phone: (617) 227-2425. www.ametsoc.org/ams.

Military Chaplains Association of the U.S.A. (1925): P.O. Box 42660, Washington, D.C. 20015-0660. 1,500. Phone: (202) 574-2423. www.wrldnet.net/~cma.

Mining, Metallurgical, and Petroleum Engineers, The American Institute of (1871): 345 E. 47th St., New York, N.Y. 10017. 4 Member Societies: Society for Mining, Metallurgy and Exploration, The Minerals, Metals & Materials Society, Iron & Steel Society, Society of Petroleum Engineers. Phone: (212) 705-7695; fax: (212) 371–9622. email: AIMENY@aol.com. www.idis.com/aime.

Model Aeronautics, Academy of (1936): 5151 East Memorial Dr., Muncie, Ind. 47302. 150,000. Phone: (765) 287-1256. www.modelaircraft.org.

Modern Language Association of America (1883): 10 Astor Place, New York, N.Y. 10003. 32,000. Phone: (212) 475-9500. www.mla.org.

Moose International, Inc. (1888): Mooseheart, Ill. 60539. 1,600,000. Phone: (630) 859-2000. www.mooseintl.org.

Mothers Against Drunk Driving (MADD) (1980): P.O. Box 541688, Dallas, Tex. 75354-1688. 3 million members and supporters. Victim hotline: (800) GET-MADD. www.madd.org.

Motion Picture Arts & Sciences, Academy of (1927): 8949 Wilshire Blvd., Beverly Hills, Calif. 90211-1972. Phone: (310) 247-3000. www.ampas.org.

Multiple Sclerosis Society, National (1946): 733 Third Ave., New York, N.Y. 10017-3288. 350,000. Phone: (212) 986-3240; (800) FIGHT MS (344-4867). www.nmss.org.

Muscular Dystrophy Association (1950): 3300 East Sunrise Dr., Tucson, Ariz. 85718. 2,300,000 volunteers. Phone: (520) 529-2000. www.mdausa.org.

Museums, American Association of (1906): 1575 Eye St., NW, Suite 400, Washington, D.C. 20005. 15,000. Phone: (202) 289-1818; fax: (202) 289-6578, tty: (202) 289-8439. www.aam-us.org.

Muzzle Loading Rifle Association, National (1933): P.O. Box 67, Friendship, Ind. 47021. 25,000. Phone: (812) 667-5131. www.nmlra.org.

NAFSA: Association of International Educators (1948): 1875 Connecticut Ave. N.W., Suite 1000, Washington, D.C. 20009-5728. 7,500. Phone: (202) 462-4811. www.nafsa.org.

National Abortion and Reproductive Rights Action League (NARAL) (1969): 1156 15th St. N.W., Washington, D.C. 20005. 500,000. Phone: (202) 973-3000. www.naral.org.

National Association for the Advancement of Colored People (1909): 4805 Mt. Hope Dr., Baltimore, Md. 21215-3297. 500,000+. Phone: (410) 358-8900. www.naacp.org.

National Conference for Community and Justice, The (founded as The Natl. Conf. of Christians & Jews) (1927): 71 Fifth Ave., New York, N.Y. 10003. Phone: (212) 206-0006. www.nccj.org.

National Cooperative Business Association (formerly Cooperative League of the U.S.A.) (1916): 1401 New York Ave. N.W., Suite 1100, Washington, D.C. 20005. Phone: (202) 638-6222. www.cooperative.org.

National Council of the Churches of Christ in the USA (1950): 475 Riverside Drive, Rm. 850, New York, N.Y. 10115. 34 Protestant and Orthodox communions. Phone: (212) 870-2227. www.ncccusa.org.

National Grange of the Order of Patrons of Husbandry, (1867): 1616 H St. N.W., Washington, D.C. 20006-4999. 300,000. Phone: (202) 628-3507; fax: (202) 347-1091. www.grange.org.

National Press Club (1908): National Press Bldg., 529 14th St. N.W., 13th floor, Washington, D.C. 20045. 4,500. Phone: (202) 662-7500. ncp.press.org.

National PTA (National Congress of Parents and Teachers) (1897): 330 N. Wabash Ave., Suite 2100, Chicago, Ill. 60611-3690. 6.5 million. Phone: (312) 670-6782. email: info@pta.org. www.pta.org.

National Rifle Association of America (1871): 11250 Waples Mill Rd., Fairfax, Va. 22030. 3,300,000. Phone: (703) 267-1000. www.nra.org.

National Urban League, Inc. (1910): 120 Wall St., New York, N.Y. 10005. 115 affiliates in 34 states and D.C. Phone: (212) 558-5300. www.nul.org.

National Wildlife Federation (1936): 8925 Leesburg Pike, Vienna, VA 22184. 4,000,000+. Phone: (703) 790-4000. www.nwf.org.

Nature Conservancy, The (1951): 1815 N. Lynn St., Arlington, Va. 22209. 830,000. Phone: (703) 841-5300. www.tnc.org.

Naval Architects and Marine Engineers, The Society of (1893): 601 Pavonia Ave., Jersey City, N.J. 07306. 11,000. Phone: (201) 798-4800; fax: (201) 798-4975. www.sname.org.

Naval Engineers, American Society of (1888): 1452 Duke St., Alexandria, Va. 22314. 6,800. Phone: (703) 836-6727; fax: (703) 836-7491. www.jhuapl.edu/ASNE.

Naval Institute, United States (1873): 118 Maryland Ave., Annapolis, Md. 21402-5035. 90,000. Phone: (410) 268-6110. www.usni.org.

Navigation, The Institute of (1945): 1800 Diagonal Rd., Suite 480, Alexandria, Va. 22314. 3,800. Phone: (703) 683-7101; fax: (703) 683-7105. email: membership@ion.org. www.ion.org.

Navy League of the United States (1902): 2300 Wilson Blvd., Arlington, Va. 22201-3308. 71,500. Phone: (703) 528-1775. www.navyleague.org.

NDIA (National Defense Industrial Association) (1919): 2111 Wilson Blvd., Arlington, Va. 22201-3061. 28,000 individual, 900 corporate. Phone: (703) 522-1820. www.ndia.org.

Neurofibromatosis Foundation, Inc., The National (1978): 95 Pine St., 16th Floor, New York, NY 10005. 38,000. Phone: (800) 323-7938; in NY State (212) 344-NNFF; fax: (212) 747-0004. email: nnff@aol.com. www.nf.org.

Newspaper Association of America (1887): 1921 Gallows Rd., Suite 600, Vienna, Va. 22180. Phone (703) 902-1600. www.naa.org.

Nondestructive Testing, Inc., The American Society for (1941): 1711 Arlingate Lane, P.O. Box 28518, Columbus, Ohio 43228-0518. 10,240. Phone: (800) 222-ASNT. www.asnt.org.

NOT SAFE (National Organization Taunting Safety and Fairness Everywhere) (1980): P.O. Box 5743, Montecito, Calif. 93150. 975. Phone: (805) 969-6217.

Nuclear Society, American (1954): 555 N. Kensington Ave., La Grange Park, Ill. 60526. 14,700. Phone: (708) 352-6611. www.ans.org.

Numismatic Association, American (1891): 818 N. Cascade Ave., Colorado Springs, Colo. 80903-3279. 30,000. Phone: (719) 632-2646. email: ana@money.org. www.money.org.

Nurses Association, American (1896): 600 Maryland Ave. S.W., Suite 100, Washington, D.C. 20024-2571.

170,000. Phone: (800) 274-4ANA. www.nursingworld.org.

Odd Fellows, Sovereign Grand Lodge, Independent Order of (1819): 422 North Trade St., Winston-Salem, N.C. 27101-2830. 460,000. Phone: (910) 725-5955. www.ioof.org.

Olympic Committee, United States (1921): One Olympic Plaza, Colorado Springs, Colo. 80909-5760. Phone: (719) 632-5551. www.olympic-usa.org.

Optimist International (1919): 4494 Lindell Blvd., St. Louis, Mo. 63108. 155,000. Phone: (314) 371-6000. www.optimist.org.

Optometric Association, American (1898): 243 N. Lindbergh Blvd., St. Louis, Mo. 63141. 32,000. Phone: (314) 991-4100. www.aoanet.org.

Ornithologists' Union, American (1883): c/o National Museum of Natural History, NHB E607, MRC-116, Smithsonian Institution, Washington, D.C. 20560. 5,000. Phone: (202) 357-2051. www.pica.wru.umt.edu/aou/aou.html.

Overeaters Anonymous, Inc. (1960): P.O. Box 44020, Rio Rancho, N. Mex. 87174-4020. 150,000. Phone: (505) 891-2664. www.overeatersanonymous.org.

Parents, Families and Friends of Lesbians and Gays (1981): 1101 14th St. N.W., Suite 1030, Washington, D.C. 20005. 67,000+ members. 400 chapters in 12 countries. Phone: (202) 638-4200. www.pflag.org.

Parents Without Partners (1957): 401 N. Michigan Ave., Chigaco, Ill. 60611-4267. Phone: (312) 644-6610. www.parentswithoutpartners.org.

Peace Action (a merger of SANE and the Nuclear Weapons Freeze Campaign) (1957): 1819 H St. N.W., Suite 420, Washington D.C. 20006-3603. 50,000. Phone: (202) 862-9740. www.webcom.com/peaceact.

People For the American Way (1980): 2000 M St. N.W., Suite 400, Washington, D.C. 20036. 300,000. Phone: (202) 467-4999. www.pfaw.org.

Petroleum Geologists, American Association of (1917): P.O. Box 979, Tulsa, Okla. 74101-0979. 31,500. Phone: (918) 584-2555. www.geobyte.com.

Pharmaceutical Association, American (1852): 2215 Constitution Ave. N.W., Washington, D.C. 20037. 50,000. Phone: (202) 628-4410. www.aphanet.org.

Philatelic Society, American (1886): P.O. Box 8000, State College, Pa. 16803. 57,000. Phone: (814) 237-3803. www.west.net/~stamps1/aps.html.

Photogrammetry and Remote Sensing, American Society for (1934): 5410 Grosvenor Lane, Suite 210, Bethesda, Md. 20814-2160. Phone: (301) 493-0290; fax: (301) 493-0208. email: asprs@asprs.org. www.asprs.org/asprs.

Photographic Society of America (1934): 3000 United Founders Blvd., Suite 103, Oklahoma City, Okla. 73112. Phone: (405) 843-1437. www.psa-photo.org.

Physical Society, The American (1899): One Physics Ellipse, College Park, Md. 20740-3844. 41,000. Phone: (301) 209-3269. www.aps.org.

Physical Therapy Association, American (APTA) (1921): 1111 N. Fairfax St., Alexandria, Va. 22314. 70,000. Phone: (703) 684-2782. www.apta.org.

Physics, American Institute of (1931): One Physics Ellipse, College Park, Md. 20740-3843. 125,000. Phone: (301) 209-3100. www.aip.org.

Pilot International (1921): Pilot International Headquarters, 244 College St., P.O. Box 4844, Macon, Ga. 31208-4844. 17,000. Phone: (912) 743-7403.

Planetary Society, The (1979): 65 N. Catalina Ave., Pasadena, Calif. 91106. 100,000. Phone: (818) 793-5100. www.planetary.org.

Planned Parenthood® Federation of America, Inc., (1916): 810 Seventh Ave., New York, N.Y. 10019. 150 affiliates. Phone: (212) 541-7800; fax: (212) 245-1845. www.plannedparenthood.org.

Plastics Engineers, Society of (1942): 14 Fairfield Dr., Brookfield, Conn. 06804-0403. 37,000. Phone: (203) 775-0471. www.4spe.org.

Police, American Federation of (1966): Records Center, 3801 Biscayne Blvd., Miami, Fla. 33137. 100,000. Phone: (305) 573-0070.

Police, International Association of Chiefs of (1893): 515 N. Washington St., Alexandria Va. 22314-2357. 14,000. Phone: (703) 836-6767. www.theiacp.org.

Political and Social Science, American Academy of (1889): 3937 Chestnut St., Philadelphia, Pa. 19104. Phone: (215) 386-4594.

Political Science, Academy of (1880): 475 Riverside Dr., Suite 1274, New York, N.Y. 10115-1274. 8,500. Phone: (212) 870-2500.

Prevent Blindness America (1908): 500 E. Remington Rd., Schaumburg, Ill. 60173-5611. 25 affiliates and divisions. Phone: (847) 843-2020; (800) 331-2020. www.preventblindness.org.

Professional Engineers, National Society of (1934): 1420 King St., Alexandria, Va. 22314. 69,000. Phone: (703) 684-2800; fax: (703) 836-4875. www.nspe.org.

Professional Photographers of America, Inc. (1880): 57 Forsyth St. N.W., Suite 1600, Atlanta, Ga. 30303. 14,000. Phone: (404) 522-8600. www.apa-world.org.

Psychiatric Association, American (1844): 1400 K St. N.W., Washington, D.C. 20005. 40,537. Phone: (202) 682-6000. www.psych.org.

Psychoanalytic Association, The American (1911): 309 E. 49th St., New York, N.Y. 10017. 3,116 psychoanalysts. Phone: (212) 752-0450; fax: (212) 593-0571. email: apsaorg@compuserve.com.

Psychological Association, American (1892): 750 First St. N.E., Washington, D.C. 20002-4242. 151,000. Phone: (202) 336-5500; TDD: (202) 336-5662. www.apa.org.

Public Health Association, American (1872): 1015 15th St. N.W., Suite 300, Washington, D.C. 20005-2600. 50,000+. Phone: (202) 789-5600. www.apha.org.

Puppeteers of America (1937): 5 Cricklewood Path, Pasadena, Calif. 91107-1002. Phone: (818) 797-5748. www.puppeteers.com

Quality, The American Society for (1946): 611 E. Wisconsin Ave., P.O. Box 3005, Milwaukee, Wis. 53201-3005. 135,000+. Phone: (414) 272-8575. www.asq.org.

Railroads, Association of American (1934): 50 F St. N.W., Washington, D.C. 20001-1564. Phone: (202) 639-2100. www.aar.org.

Recording Arts & Sciences, Inc., National Academy of (1958): 3402 Pico Blvd., Santa Monica, Calif. 90405. 10,000. Phone: (310) 392-3777. www.grammy.com.

Red Cross, American (1881): 17th and D Sts. N.W., Washington, D.C. 20006. Approx. 1,650 chapters. Phone: (202) 737-8300. www.redcross.org.

Rehabilitation Association, National (1925): 633 S. Washington St., Alexandria, Va. 22314-4193. 12,000. Phone: (703) 836-0850. www.nationalrehab.org.

Reserve Officers Association of the United States (1922): 1 Constitution Ave. N.E., Washington, D.C. 20002. 93,000. Phone: (202) 479-2200. www.roa.org.

Retired Federal Employees, National Association: 606 N. Washington St., Alexandria, Va. 22314-1943. 500,000. Phone: (703) 838-7760. www.narfe.org.

Reye's Syndrome Foundation, National (1974): P.O. Box 829, Bryan, Ohio 43506. Phone: (800) 233-7393; fax: (419) 636-3366. email: reyessyn@mail.bright.net. www.bright.net/~reyessyn.

RID-USA (Remove Intoxicated Drivers) (1978): Box 520, Schenectady, N.Y. 12301. Over 150/41 state chapters. Phone: (518) 372-0034/(518) 393-HELP; fax: (518) 370-4917.

Right to Life, Committee, Inc., National (1973): 419 7th St. N.W., Suite 500, Washington, D.C. 20004. Phone: (202) 626-8800. www.nrlcorg.

Rotary International (1905): One Rotary Center, 1560 Sherman Ave., Evanston, Ill. 60201. 1,195,500 in 155 countries and 35 geographical regions. Phone: (847) 866-3000. www.rotary.org.

SAE (Society of Automotive Engineers) (1905): 400 Commonweatlh Dr., Warrendale, Pa. 15096-0001. 71,000. Phone: (412) 776-4841. www.sae.org.

Safety Council, National (1913): 1121 Spring Lake Dr., Itasca, Il. 60143-3201. Phone: (630) 285-1121. www.nsc.org.

Salvation Army, The (1865): National Headquarters, 615 Slaters Lane, P.O. Box 269, Alexandria, Va. 22313. 453,150. Phone: (703) 684-5500. www.salvationarmy.org.

Save-the-Redwoods League (1918): 114 Sansome St., Suite 605, San Francisco, Calif. 94104. 45,000. Phone: (415) 362-2352. www.savetheredwoods.org.

Science, American Association for the Advancement of (1848): 1200 New York Ave. N.W., Washington, D.C. 20005. 143,000. Phone: (202) 326-6400. www.aaas.org.

Science and Health, American Council on (1978): 1995 Broadway, 2nd Floor, New York, N.Y. 10023-5860. Phone: (212) 362-7044; fax: (212) 362-4919. email: acsh@acsh.org. www.acsh.org.

Science Fiction Society, World (1939): c/o Southern California Institute for Fan Interests, P.O. Box 8442, Van Nuys, Calif. 91409. 6,000. Phone: (818) 366-3827. www.wsfs.org.

Scientists, Federation of American (FAS) (1945): 307 Massachusetts Ave. N.E., Washington, D.C. 20002. 4,000. Phone: (202) 546-3300. www.fas.org.

SCRABBLE® Association, National (1972): P.O. Box 700, Front Street Garden, Greenport, N.Y. 11944. 15,000. Phone: (516) 477-0033.

Screen Actors Guild (1933): 5757 Wilshire Blvd., 90036. 90,000. Phone: (213) 954-1600. www.sag.com.

Sculpture Society, National (1893): 1177 Ave. of the Americas, New York, N.Y. 10036. 4,500. Phone: (212) 764-5645. www.sculptor.org/NSS

Seeing Eye Inc., The (1929): P.O. Box 375, Morristown, N.J. 07963-0375. Phone: (973) 539-4425. www.seeingeye.org.

Senior Citizens, National Alliance of (1974): 1744 Riggs Place, N.W., 3rd Floor, Washington, D.C. 20009. 117,000. Phone: (202) 986-0117.

Shriners of North America and Shriners Hospitals for Children, The (1872 and 1922): Box 31356, Tampa, Fla. 33631-3356. 600,000. Phone: (813) 281-0300. www.shrinershq.org.

Sierra Club (1892): 85 2nd Street, San Francisco, Calif. 94105-3441. 550,000. Phone: (415) 977-5500. www.sierraclub.org.

SIETAR INTERNATIONAL (The International Society for Intercultural Education, Training and Research) (1974): 808 17th St. N.W., Suite 200, Washington, D.C. 20006-3910. 2,000+. Phone: (202) 466-7883; fax: (202) 223-9569. email: SIETAR@compuserve.com. aspin.asu.edu/~sietar

Simon Wiesenthal Center (1978): 9786 W. Pico Blvd., Los Angeles, Calif. 90035-4792. 375,000 member families. Phone: (310) 553-9036. www.wiesenthal.com.

Small Business United, National (1937): 1156 15th St. N.W., Washington, D.C. 20005-1711. 65,000+. Phone: (202) 293-8830; fax: (202) 872-8543. email: nsbu@nsbu.org. www.nsbu.org.

Social Work Education, Council on (1952): 1600 Duke St., Alexandria, Va. 22314-3421. Phone: (703) 683-8080; fax: (703) 683-8099. www.cswe.org.

Social Workers, National Association of (1955): 750 First St. N.E., Suite 700, Washington, D.C. 20002-4241. Phone: (202) 408-8600. www.naswdc.org.

Society for Integrative and Comparitive Biology (formerly the American Society of Zoologists) (1890): 401 N. Michigan Ave., Chicago, Ill. 60611. 2,200. Phone: (312) 527-6697; (800) 955-1236; fax: (312) 245-1085. email: sicb@sba.com. www.sicb.org.

Soil and Water Conservation Society (1945): 7515 N.E. Ankeny Rd., Ankeny, Iowa 50021-9764. 10,000. Phone: (515) 289-2331; fax: (515) 289-1227. email: swcs@swcs.org. www.swcs.org.

Songwriters Guild of America, The (1931): 1500 Harbor Blvd., Weehawken, N.J. 07087-6732. Phone: (201) 867-7603. www.songwriters.org/new/home.htm.

Sons of Italy in America, Order (1905): 219 E St. N.E., Washington, D.C. 20002. 475,000. Phone: (202) 547-2900. www.osia.org.

Sons of the American Revolution, National Society of the (1889): 1000 S. 4th St., Louisville, Ky. 40203. 27,000. Phone: (502) 589-1776. www.sar.org.

Soroptimist International of the Americas (1921): Two Penn Center Plaza, Suite 1000, Philadelphia, Pa. 19102-1883. 50,000. Phone: (215) 557-9300. www.siahq.com.

Southern Early Childhood Association (formerly SACUS) (1948): P.O. Box 55930, Little Rock, Ark. 72215-5930. 19,300. Phone: (501) 663-0353; (800) 304-7322; fax: (501) 663-2114. email: seca@aristotle.net. www.seca50.org.

Space Education Association, U.S. (1973): Global Operations Center, 231 School Lane, P.O. Box 249, Rheems, Pa. 17570-0249. Voice/Fax: (717) 367-5196.

Space Society, National (1974): 600 Pennsylvania Ave., S.E., Suite 201, Washington, D.C. 20003-4316. Phone: (202) 543-1900; fax: (202) 546-4189. www.nss.org/.

Special Olympics International, Inc. (1968): 1325 G St. N.W., Suite 500, Washington, D.C., 20005-3104. 1,000,000. Phone: (202) 628-3630. www.specialolympics.org.

Speech-Language-Hearing Association, American (1925): 10801 Rockville Pike, Rockville, Md. 20852. 87,000. Phone: (301) 897-5700. www.asha.org.

Sports Car Club of America Inc. (1944): 9033 E. Easter Place, Englewood, Colo. 80112-2105. 54,000. Phone: (303) 694-7222. www.scca.com.

Statistical Association, American (1839): 1429 Duke St., Alexandria, Va. 22314. 19,000. www.amstat.org.

Student Association, United States (1947): 1413 K Street, NW, 10th Floor, Washington, D.C. 20005. 350 schools (3.5 million students) Phone: (202) 347-8772. www.essential.org/ussa.

Surgeons, American College of (1913): 55 E. Erie St., Chicago, Ill. 60611-2797. 58,000+. Phone: (312) 664-4050. www.facs.org.

Symphony Orchestra League, American (1942): 1156 15th St. N.W., Suite 800, Washington, D.C. 20005-1704. 5,500. Phone: (202) 776-0212.

TASH: The Association for Persons with Severe Handicaps (1976): 29 W. Susquehanna Ave., Suite 210, Baltimore, Md. 21204. 8,500. Phone: (410) 828-TASH. www.tash.org.

Teachers, American Federation of (1916): 555 New Jersey Ave. N.W., Washington, D.C., 20001. 900,000+. Phone: (202) 879-4400. www.aft.org.

Testing & Materials, American Society for (1898): 100 Barr Harbor Dr., W. Conshohocken, Pa. 19428-2959. 34,000. Phone: (610) 832-9500. www.astm.org.

The Arc, a national organization on mental retardation (1950): 500 E. Border St., Suite 300, Arlington, Texas 76010. 140,000 members, 1,200 state and local chapters. Phone: (817) 261-6003. www.thearc.org.

Theatre Guild, Inc. (1919): 226 W. 47th St., New York, N.Y. 10036. 72,000. Phone: (212) 873-0676.

Theosophical Society in America, The (1875): P.O. Box 270, Wheaton, Ill. 60189-0270. 4,400. Phone: (630) 668-1571. www.theosophical.org.

Tin Can Sailors, Inc. (1976): P.O. Box 100, Somerset, Mass. 02726-0100. 16,000+. Phone: (508) 677-0515. www.destroyers.org.

Toastmasters International (1924): P.O. Box 9052, Mission Viejo, Calif. 92690-7052, and 23182 Arroyo Vista, Rancho Santa Margarita, Calif. 92688. 180,000. Phone: (714) 858-8255, club information voice mail: (800) 9WE-SPEAK; fax: (714) 858-1207. email: tminfo@toastmasters.org. www.toastmasters.org.

TOUGHLOVE International (1977): P.O. Box 1069, Doylestown, Pa. 18901. 300 registered groups. Phone: (215) 348-7090; (800) 333-1069.

TransAfrica Forum (1981): 1744 R. St. N.W., Washington, D.C. 20009. Phone: (202) 797-2301; fax: (202) 797-2382. email: transforum@igc.org. www.igc.apc.org/transafrica.

Travel Agents, American Society of (ASTA) (1931): 1101 King St., Alexandria, Va. 22314. 28,500. Phone: (703) 739-2782. www.astanet.com.

Travelers Aid International (1851); 1612 K St. N.W., Suite 506, Washington, D.C. 20006. Phone: (202) 546-9112; fax: (202) 546-1127.

Tuberous Sclerosis Association, Inc., National (1975): 8181 Professional Place, Suite 110, Landover, Md. 20785. 5,000. Phone: (301) 459-9888; (800) 225-6872; fax: (301) 459-0394. email: ntsa@aol.com. www.ntsa.org.

UFOs, National Investigations Committee on (1967): 14617 Victory Blvd., Suite 4, Van Nuys, Calif. 91411. Phone: (818) 989-5942; fax: (818) 989-2165.

UNICEF, U.S. Committee for (1947): 333 E. 38th St., New York, N.Y. 10016. 20,000 volunteers. Phone: (212) 686-5522. www.unicefusa.org.

Union of Concerned Scientists (1969): 2 Brattle Square, Cambridge, Mass. 02238-9105. 70,000. Phone: (617) 547-5552. www.ucsusa.org.

United Daughters of the Confederacy® (1894): 328 N. Boulevard, Richmond, Va. 23220-4057. 24,000. Phone: (804) 355-1636. www.hsv.tis.net/~maxs/UDC.

United Jewish Appeal (1939): 99 Park Ave., New York, N.Y. 10016. Phone: (212) 818-9100. www.uja.org.

United Way of America (1918): 701 N. Fairfax St., Alexandria, Va. 22314-2045. 1,800 local United Ways. Phone: (703) 836-7100; fax: (703) 683-7840. www.unitedway.org.

University Foundation, International (1973): 1301 S. Noland Rd., Independence, Mo. 64055. 67,000. Phone: (816) 461-3633. www.tiu.com.

University Women, American Association of (1881): 1111 16th St. N.W., Washington, D.C. 20036. 135,000. Phone: (202) 785-7700. www.aaww.org.

USO (United Service Organizations) (1941): World Headquarters, Washington Navy Yard, 901 M St., S.E., Bldg. 198, Washington, D.C. 20374-5096. Phone: (202) 610-5700. www.uso.org.

Variety Clubs International (1927): 1560 Broadway, Suite 1209, New York, N.Y. 10036. 15,000. Phone: (212) 704-9872.

Veterans Committee, American (AVC) (1944): Bethesda, Md. 20817. 15,000. Phone & fax: (301) 320-6490.

Veterans of Foreign Wars of the U.S. (1899): 406 W. 34th St., Kansas City, Mo. 64111. VFW and Auxiliary, 2,850,000. Phone: (816) 756-3390. www.vfw.org.

Veterinary Medical Association, American (1863): 1931 N. Meacham Rd., Suite 100, Schaumburg, Ill. 60173-4360. 57,700. Phone: (847) 925-8070. www.avma.org.

Volunteers of America (1896): 110 South Union Street, 2nd Floor, Alexandria, Va. 22314-3324. Provides human services in more than 400 communities. Phone: (703) 548-2288; 1-800-899-0089. www.voa.org.

War Resisters League (1923): 339 Lafayette St., New York, N.Y. 10012. 12,000. Phone: (212) 228-0450; fax: (212) 228-6193. email: wrl@igc.apc.org. www.nonviolence.org/wrl.

Washington Legal Foundation (1977): 2009 Massachusetts Ave., N.W., Washington, D.C. 20036. 100,000. Phone: (202) 588-0302. www.wlf.org.

Water Quality Association (1974): 4151 Naperville Rd., Lisle, Ill. 60532. 2,500. Phone: (630) 505-0160; fax: (630) 505-9637. www.wqa.org.

Welding Society, American (1919): 550 N.W. LeJeune Rd., Miami, Fla. 33126. 48,000. Phone: (305) 443-9353; (800) 443-9353. www.amweld.org.

Wildlife Fund, World (1961): 1250 24th St. N.W., Washington, D.C. 20037-1175. 1.2 million. Phone: (202) 293-4800. www.wwf.org.

Woman's Christian Temperance Union, National (1874): 1730 Chicago Ave., Evanston, Ill. 60201. Under 20,000. Phone: (847) 864-1396. www.wctu.org.

Women, National Organization for (NOW) (1966): 1000 16th St. N.W., Suite 700, Washington, D.C. 20036-5705. 270,000. Phone: (202) 331-0066. www.now.org.

Women Police, The International Association of (1915): RR1, Box 149, Deer Isle, Me. 04627. 3,000. Phone: (207) 348-6976; fax: (207) 348-6171. www.iawp.org.

Women's American ORT (1927): 315 Park Ave. South, New York, N.Y. 10010. Chapters throughout the U.S. Phone: (212) 505-7700.

Women's Educational and Industrial Union (1877): 356 Boylston St., Boston, Mass. 02116. 1,500. Phone: (617) 536-5651; fax: (617) 247-8826.

Women's International League for Peace and Freedom (1915): 1213 Race St., Philadelphia, Pa. 19107-1691. 10,000. Phone: (215) 563-7110. www.wilpf.org.

World Future Society (1966): 7910 Woodmont Ave., Suite 450, Bethesda, Md. 20814. 30,000. Phone: (301) 656-8274; fax: (301) 951-0394. www.wfs.org.

World Health, American Association for (1953): 1825 K St. N.W., Washington, D.C. 20036. Phone: (202) 466-5883, fax: (202) 466-5896. email: AAWHstaff@aol.com. www.aawhworldhealth.org.

World Peace, International Association of Educators for (1969): P.O. Box 3282, Mastin Lake Station, Huntsville, Ala. 35810-0282. 25,000. Phone: (205) 534-5501. www.homeplanet.org/iaewp.

World Peace Foundation (1910): One Eliot Square, Cambridge, Mass. 02138. Phone: (617) 491-5085; fax: (617) 491-8588. www.wpf.org.

Worldwatch Institute (1974): 1776 Massachusetts Ave. N.W., Washington, D.C. 20036. Global environmental research organization. Phone: (202) 452-1999; fax: (202) 296-296-7365. email: worldwatch@worldwatch.org. www.worldwatch.org.

Writers Union, National (1983): 113 University Place, 6th Floor, New York, N.Y. 10003. 4,500. Phone: (212) 254-0279. www.nwu.org.

YMCA of the USA (1844): 101 N. Wacker Dr., Chicago, Ill. 60606. 13,500,000. Phone: (312) 977-0031. www.ymca.net.

Young Women's Christian Association of the U.S.A. (1858 in U.S.A., 1855 in England): Empire State Building, 350 Fifth Ave., 3rd floor, New York, N.Y. 10118. 1,000,000. Phone: (212) 273-7800. www.ywca.org.

Zionist Organization of America (1897): ZOA House, 4 E. 34th St., New York, N.Y. 10016. 110,000. Phone: (212) 481-1500; fax: (212) 481-1515. www.zoa.org.

First Aid to Crossword Puzzlers

We cannot begin to list all the odd words you might encounter in your daily and Sunday crossword puzzles, for such words run into the many thousands. But we have tried to include those that turn up most frequently, as well as many others that should be of help to you when you are unable to go any further.

We do not guarantee that the definitions in your puzzle will be exactly the same as ours, although we have checked every word with a standard dictionary and have followed its definition.

In nearly every case, we have used as the key word the principal noun of the definition, rather than any adjective, adjective phrase, or noun used as an adjective. And, to simplify your searching, we have grouped the words according to the number of spaces you have to fill.

Words of Two Letters

Ambary, DA
And (French, Latin), ET
Article (Arabic), AL
(French), LA, LE, UN
(Spanish), EL, LA, UN
At the (French), AU
(Spanish), AL
Behold, LO
Bird: Hawaiian, OO
Birthplace: Abraham's, UR
Bone, OS
Buddha, FO
Butterfly: Peacock, IO
Champagne, AY
Chaos, NU
Chief: Burmese, BO
Coin: Roman, AS
Siamese, AT
Concerning, RE
Dialect: Chinese, WU
Double (Egy. relig.), KA
Drama: Japanese, NO
Egg (comb. form), OO
Esker, OS
Eye (Scotch), EE
Factor: Amplification, MU
Fifty (Greek), NU
Fish: Carplike, ID
Force, OD
Forty (Greek), MU
From (French, Latin, Spanish), DE
(Latin prefix), AB
From the (French), DU
God: Babylonian, EA, ZU
Egyptian sun, RA
Hindu unknown, KA
Semitic, EL
Goddess: Babylonian, AI
Greek earth, GE
Gold (heraldry), OR
Gulf: Arctic, OB
Heart (Egy. relig.), AB
Indian: South American, GE
King: Of Bashan, OG
Language: Artificial, RO
Assamese, AO
Lava: Hawaiian, AA
Letter: Greek, MU, NU, PI, XI
Hebrew, HE, PE
Lily: Palm, TI
Measure: Annamese, LY
Chinese, HO, HU, KO, LI, MU, PU, TO, TU
Japanese, GO, JO, MO, RI, SE, TO
Metric land, AR
Netherlands, EL
Portuguese, PE
Siamese, WA
Swedish, AM
Type, EM, EN
Monk: Buddhist, BO
Month: Jewish, AB
Mouth, OS
Mulberry: Indian, AL
Native: Burmese, WA
Note: Of Scale, DO, FA, MI, LA, RE, TI
Of (French, Latin, Spanish), DE
Of the (French), DU
One (Scotch), AE
Pagoda: Chinese, TA
Plant: East Indian fiber, DA
Ridge: Sandy, AS, OS
River: Russian, OB
Sloth: Three-toed, AI
Soul (Egy. relig.), BA
Sound: Hindu mystic, OM
Suffix: Comparative, ER
To the: French, AU
Spanish, AL
Tree: Buddhist sacred, BO
Tribe: Assamese, AO
Type: Jumbled, PI
Weight: Annamese, TA
Chinese, LI
Danish, ES
Japanese, MO
Roman, AS
Whirlwind: Faeroe Is., OE
Yes (German), JA
(Italian, Spanish), SI
(Russian), DA

Words of Three Letters

Adherent: IST
Again, BIS
Age, ERA
Antelope: African, GNU, KOB
Apricot: Japanese, UME
Article (German), DAS, DEM, DEN, DER, DES, DIE, EIN
(French), LES, UNE
(Spanish), LAS, LOS, UNA
Banana: Polynesian, FEI
Barge, HOY
Bass: African, IYO
Beak, NEB, NIB
Beard: Grain, AWN
Beetle: June, DOR
Being, ENS
Berry: Hawthorn, HAW
Beverage: Hawaiian, AVA
Bird: Australian, EMU
Crowlike, JAY
Extinct, MOA
Fabulous, ROC
Frigate, IWA
Parson, POE, TUE, TUI
Sea, AUK
Blackbird, ANI, ANO
Born, NEE
Bronze: Roman, AES
Bugle: Yellow, IVA
By way of, VIA
Canton: Swiss, URI
Cap: Turkish, FEZ
Catnip, NEP
Character: In "Faerie Queene," UNA
Coin (Money of account):
Afghan, PUL
Albanian, LEK
British Guiana, BIT
Bulgarian, LEV, LEW
French, ECU, SOU
Indian, PIE
Japanese, SEN, YEN
Korean, WON
Lithuanian, LIT
Macao, Timor, AVO
Palestinian, MIL
Persian, PUL
Peruvian, SOL
Rumanian, BAN, LEU, LEY
Scandinavian, ORE
Siamese, ATT
Collection: Facts, ANA
Commune: Belgian, ANS, ATH
Netherlands, EDE, EPE
Community: Russian, MIR
Constellation: Southern, ARA
Contraction: Poetic, EEN, EER, OER
Covering: Apex of roof, EPI
Crab: Fiddler, UCA
Crag: Rocky, TOR
Cry: Crow, rook, raven, CAW
Cup: Wine, AMA
Cymbal, Oriental, TAL, ZEL
Disease: Silkworm, UJI
Division: Danish territorial, AMT
Geologic, EON
Doctrine, ISM
Dowry, DOT
Dry (French), SEC
Dynasty: Chinese, CHI, HAN, SUI, WEI, YIN
Eagle: Sea, ERN
Earth (comb. form), GEO
Egg: Louse, NIT
Eggs: Fish, ROE
Emmet, ANT
Enzyme, ASE
Equal (comb. form), ISO
Extension: building, ELL
Far (comb. form), TEL
Farewell, AVE
Fiber: Palm, TAL
Finial, EPI
Fish: Carplike, IDE
Pikelike, GAR
Flatfish, DAB
Fleur-de-lis, LIS, LYS
Food: Hawaiian, POI
Formerly, NEE
Friend (French), AMI
Game: Card, LOO
Garment: Camel-hair, ABA
Gateway, DAR
Gazelle: Tibetan, GOA
Genus: Ducks, AIX
Grasses, POA
Grasses (maize), ZEA
Herbs or shrubs, IVA
Lizards, UTA
Rodents (incl. house mice), MUS
Ruminants (incl. cattle), BOS
Swine, SUS
Gibbon: Malay, LAR
God: Assyrian, SIN
Babylonian, ABU, ANU, BEL, HEA, SIN, UTU
Irish sea, LER
Phrygian, MEN
Polynesian, ORO
Goddess: Babylonian, AYA
Etruscan, UNI
Hindu, SRI, UMA, VAC
Teutonic, RAN
Governor: Algerian, DEY
Turkish, BEY
Grampus, ORC
Grape, UVA
Grass: Meadow, POA
Gypsy, ROM
Hail, AVE
Hare: Female, DOE
Hawthorn, HAW
Hay: Spread for drying, TED
Herb: Japanese, UDO
Perennial, PIA
Used for blue dye, WAD
Herd: Whales, GAM, POD
Hero: Spanish, CID
High (music), ALT
Honey (pharm.), MEL
Humorist: American, ADE
I (Latin), EGO
I love (Latin), AMO
Indian: Algonquian, FOX, SAC, WEA
Chimakuan, HOH
Keresan, SIA
Mayan, MAM
Shoshonean, UTE
Siouan, KAW, OTO
South American, ITE, ONA, URO, URU, YAO
Tierra del Fuego, ONA
Wakashan, AHT
Ingot, PIG
Inlet: Narrow, RIA
Island: Cyclades, IOS
Dodecanese, COS, KOS
(French), ILE
River, AIT
Jackdaw, DAW

John (Gaelic), IAN
Keelbill, ANI, ANO
Kiln, OST
King: British legendary LUD
Kobold, NIS
Lace: To make, TAT
Lamprey, EEL
Language: Artificial, IDO
Bantu, ILA
Siamese, LAO, TAI
Leaf: Palm, OLA, OLE
Leaving, ORT
Left: Cause to turn, HAW
Letter: Greek, CHI, ETA, PHI, PSI, RHO, TAU
Hebrew, MEM, NUN, SIN, TAV, VAU
Lettuce, COS
Life (comb. form), BIO
Lily: Palm, TOI
Lizard, EFT
Louse: Young, NIT
Love (Anglo-Irish), GRA
Lute: Oriental, TAR
Macaw: Bralizian, ARA
Marble, TAW
Match: Shooting (French), TIR
Meadow, LEA
Measure: Abyssinian, TAT
Algerian, PIK
Annamese, GON, MAU, NGU, VUO, SAO, TAO, TAT
Arabian, DEN, SAA
Belgian, VAT
Bulgarian, OKA, OKE
Chinese, FEN, TOU, YIN
Cloth, ELL
Cyprus, OKA, OKE, PIK
Czech, LAN, SAH
Danish, FOD, MIL, POT
Dominican Republic, ONA
Dutch, old, AAM
East Indian, KIT
Egyptian, APT, HEN, PIK, ROB
Electric, MHO, OHM
Energy, ERG
English, PIN
Estonian, TUN
French, POT
German, AAM
Greek, PIK
Hebrew, CAB, HIN, KOR, LOG
Hungarian, AKO
Icelandic, FET
Indian, GAZ, GUZ, JOW, KOS
Japanese, BOO, CHO, KEN, RIN, SHO, SUN, TAN
Malabar, ADY
Metric land, ARE
Netherlands, KAN, KOP, MUD, VAT, ZAK
Norwegian, FOT, POT
Persian, GAZ, GUZ, MOU, ZAR, ZER
Polish, CAL
Rangoon, DHA, LAN
Roman, PES, URN
Russian, FUT, LOF
Scotch, COP
Siamese, KEN, NIU, RAI, SAT, SEN, SOK, WAH, YOT
Somaliland, TOP
Spanish, PIE
Straits Settlements, PAU, TUN
Swedish, ALN, FOT, MIL, REF, TUM
Swiss, POT
Tunisian, SAA
Turkish, OKA, OKE, PIK
Wire, MIL
Württemberg, IMI
Yarn, LEA
Yugoslavian, OKA, RIF
Milk, LAC
Milkfish, AWA
Moccasin, PAC
Money: Yap stone, FEI
Money of Account (also Coin):
Anglo-Saxon, ORA, ORE
French, SOU
Indian, LAC
Japanese, RIN
Oman, GAJ
Virgin Islands, BIT
Monkey: Capuchin, SAI
Morsel, ORT
Mother: Peer Gynt's, ASE
Mountain: Asia Minor, IDA
Mulberry: Indian, AAL, ACH, AWL
Muttonbird: New Zealand, OII
Nahoor, SNA
Native: Mindanao, ATA
Neckpiece, BOA
Newt, EFT
No (Scotch), NAE
Note: Guido's highest, ELA
Of scale, SOL
Nursemaid: Oriental, AMA, IYA
Ocher: Yellow, SIL
One (Scotch), YIN
Ornament: Pagoda, TEE
Oven: Polynesian, UMU
Ox: Tibetan, YAK
Pagoda: Chinese, TAA
Parrot: Hawk, HIA
New Zealand, KEA
Part: Footlike, PES
Particle: Electrified, ION
Pasha, DEY
Pass: Mountain, COL
Paste: Rice, AME
Pea: Indian split, DAL
Peasant: Philippine, TAO
Penpoint, NEB, NIB
Piece out, EKE
Pigeon, NUN
Pine: Textile screw, ARA
Pistol (slang), GAT
Pit: Baking, IMU
Plant: Pepper, AVA
Play: By Capek, RUR
Poem: Old French, DIT
Porgy: Japanese, TAI
Priest: Biblical high, ELI
Prince Ethiopian, RAS
Pseudonym: Dickens', BOZ
Queen: Fairy, MAB
Quince: Bengal, BEL
Record: Ship's, LOG
Refuse: Flax (Scotch), PAB, POB
Resin, LAC
Resort, SPA
Revolver (slang), GAT
Right: Cause to turn, GEE
River: Scotch or English, DEE
(Spanish), RIO
Swiss, AAR
Room: Harem, ODA
Rootstock: Fern, ROI
Rose (Persian), GUL
Ruff: Female, REE
Rule: Indian, RAJ
Sailor, GOB, TAR
Saint: Female (abbr.), STE
Islamic, PIR
Salt, SAL
Sash: Japanese, OBI
Scrap, ORT
Seed: Poppy, MAW
Small, PIP
Self, EGO
Serpent: Vedic sky, AHI
Sesame, TIL
Sheep: Female, EWE
Indian, SHA
Male, RAM
Sheepfold (Scotch), REE
Shelter, LEE
Shield, ECU
Shooting match (French), TIR
Shrew: European, ERD
Shrub: Evergreen, YEW
Silkworm, ERI
Snake, ASP, BOA
Soak, RET
Son-in-law: Mohammed's, ALI
Sorrel: Wood, OCA
Spade: Long, narrow, LOY
Spirit: Malignant, KER
Spot: Playing-card, PIP
Spread for drying, TED
Spring: Mineral, SPA
Sprite: Water, NIX
Statesman: Japanese, ITO
Stern: Toward, AFT
Stomach: Bird's, MAW
Street (French), RUE
Summer (French), ETE
Sun, SOL
Swamp, BOG, FEN
Swan: Male, COB
Tea: Chinese, CHA
Temple: Shinto, SHA
Thing (law), RES
Title: Etruscan, LAR
Monk's, FRA
Portuguese, DOM
Spanish, DON
Turkish, AGA, BEY
Tool: Cutting, ADZ, AXE
Mining, GAD
Piercing, AWL
Tree: Candlenut, AMA
Central American, EBO
East Indian, SAJ, SAL
Evergreen, YEW
Hawaiian, KOA, KOU
Indian, BEL, DAR
Linden, LIN
New Zealand, AKE
Philippine, DAO, TUA, TUI
Rubber, ULE
South American, APA
Tribe: New Zealand, ATI
Turmeric, REA
Twice, BIS
Twin: Siamese, ENG
Uncle (dialect), EAM, EME
Veil: Chalice, AER, AIR
Vessel: Wine, AMA
Vestment: Ecclesiastical, ALB
Vetch: Bitter, ERS
Victorfish, AKU
Vine: New Zealand, AKA
Philippine, IYO
Wallaba, APA
Wapiti, ELK
Water (French), EAU
Waterfall, LIN
Watering place: Prussian, EMS
Weave: Designating plain, UNI
Weight: Annamese, CAN
Bulgarian, OKA, OKE
Burmese, MOO, VIS
Chinese, FEN, HAO, KIN, SSU, TAN, YIN
Cyprus, OKA, OKE
Danish, LOD, ORT, VOG
East Indian, TJI
Egyptian, KAT, OKA, OKE
English, for wool, TOD
German, LOT
Greek, MNA, OKA, OKE
Indian, SER
Japanese, FUN, KIN, RIN, SHI
Korean, KON
Malacca, KIP
Mongolian, LAN
Netherlands, ONS
Norwegian, LOD
Polish, LUT
Rangoon, PAI
Roman, BES
Russian, LOT
Siamese, BAT, HAP, PAI
Swedish, ASS, ORT
Turkish, OKA, OKE
Yugoslavian, OKA, OKE
Whales: Herd, GAM, POD
Wildebeest, GNU
Wing, ALA
Witticism, MOT
Wolframite, CAL
Worm: African, LOA
Wreath: Hawaiian, LEI
Yale, ELI
Yam: Hawaiian, HOI
Yes (French), OUI
Young: Bring forth, EAN
Z (letter), ZED

Words of Four Letters

Aborigine: Borneo, DYAK
Agave, ALOE
Animal: Footless, APOD
Ant: White, ANAI, ANAY
Antelope: African, ASSE, BISA, GUIB, KOBA, KUDU, ORYX, POKU, PUKU, TOPI, TORA
Apoplexy: Plant, ESCA
Apple, POME
Apricot, ANSU
Ardor, ELAN
Armadillo, APAR, PEBA, PEVA, TATU
Ascetic: Islamic, SUFI
Association: Chinese, TONG
Astronomer: Persian, OMAR
Avatar: Of Vishnu, RAMA
Axillary, ALAR
Band: Horizontal (heraldry), FESS
Barracuda, SPET
Bark: Mulberry, TAPA
Base: Column, DADO
Bearing (heraldry), ORLE
Beer: Russian, KVAS
Beige, ECRU
Being, ESSE
Beverage: Japanese rice, SAKE
Bird: Asian, MINA, MYNA
Egyptian sacred, IBIS
Extinct, DODO, MAMO
Flightless, KIWI
Gull-like, TERN
Hawaiian, IIWI, MAMO
Parson, KOKO
Unfledged, EYAS
Birds: As class, AVES
Black, EBON
(French), NOIR
Blackbird: European, MERL
Boat: Flat-bottomed, DORY
Bone: Forearm, ULNA
Bones, OSSA
Box, Japanese, INRO

Bravo (rare), EUGE
Buffalo: Indian wild, ARNA
Bull (Spanish), TORO
Burden, ONUS
Cabbage: Sliced, SLAW
Caliph: Islamic, OMAR
Canoe: Malay, PRAU, PROA
Cap: Military, KEPI
Cape, NESS
Capital: Ancient Irish, TARA
Case: Article, ETUI
Cat: Wild, BALU, EYRA
Chalcedony, SARD
Chamber: Indian ceremonial, KIVA
Channel: Brain, ITER
Cheese: Dutch, EDAM
Chest: Sepulchral stone, CIST
Chieftain: Arab, EMIR
Church: Part of, APSE, NAVE
  (Scotch), KIRK
Claim (law), LIEN
Cluster: Flower, CYME
Coin: Chinese, TAEL, YUAN
  German, MARK
  Indian, ANNA
  Iranian, RIAL
  Italian, LIRA
  Moroccan, OKIA
  Siamese, BAHT
  South American, PESO
  Spanish, DURO, PESO
  Turkish, PARA
Commune: Belgian, AATH
Composition: Musical, OPUS
Compound: Chemical, DIOL
Constellation: Southern, PAVO
Council: Russian, DUMA
Counsel, REDE
Covering: Seed, ARIL
Cross: Egyptian, ANKH
Cry: Bacchanalian, EVOE
Cup (Scotch), TASS
Cupbearer, SAKI
Dagger, DIRK
  Malay, KRIS
Dam: River, WEIR
Dash, ELAN
Date: Roman, IDES
Dawn: Pertaining to, EOAN
Dean: English, INGE
Decay: In fruit, BLET
Deer: Sambar, MAHA
Disease: Skin, ACNE
Disk: Solar, ATEN
Dog: Hunting, ALAN
Drink: Hindu intoxicating, SOMA
Duck, SMEE, SMEW, TEAL
Dynasty: Chinese, CHEN, CHIN, CHOU,
  CHOW, HSIA, MING, SUNG, TANG,
  TSIN
  Mongol, YUAN
Eagle: Biblical, GIER
  Sea, ERNE
Egyptian: Christian, COPT
Ear: Pertaining to, OTIC
Entrance: Mine, ADIT
Esau, EDOM
Escutcheon: Voided, ORLE
Eskers, OSAR
Evergreen: New Zealand, TAWA
Fairy: Persian, PERI
Family: Italian, ESTE
Far (comb. form), TELE
Farewell, VALE
Father (French), PERE
Fennel: Philippine, ANIS
Fever: Malarial, AGUE
Fiber: East Indian, JUTE
Firn, NEVE
Fish: Carplike, DACE
  Hawaiian, ULUA
  Herringlike, SHAD
  Mackerellike, CERO
  Marine, HAKE
  Sea, LING, MERO, OPAH
  Spiny-finned, GOBY

Food: Tropical, TARO
Foot: Metric, IAMB
Formerly, ERST
Founder: Of Carthage, DIDO
France: Southern, MIDI
Furze, ULEX
Gaelic, ERSE
Gaiter, SPAT
Game: Card, FARO, SKAT
Garlic: European wild, MOLY
Garment: Hindu, SARI
  Roman, TOGA
Gazelle, CORA
Gem, JADE, ONYX, OPAL, RUBY
Genus: Amphibians (incl. frogs), RANA
  Amphibians (incl. tree toads), HYLA
  Antelopes, ORYX
  Auks, ALCA, URIA
  Bees, APIS
  Birds (American ostriches), RHEA
  Birds (cranes), CRUS
  Birds (magpies), PICA
  Birds (peacocks), PAVO
  Cetaceans, INIA
  Ducks (incl. mallards), ANAS
  Fishes (burbots), LOTA
  Fishes (incl. bowfins), AMIA
  Geese (snow geese), CHEN
  Gulls, XEMA
  Herbs, ARUM, GEUM
  Insects (water scorpions), NEPA
  Lilies, ALOE
  Mammals (mankind), HOMO
  Orchids, DISA
  Owls, ASIO, BUBO, OTUS
  Palms, NIPA
  Sea birds, SULA
  Sheep, OVIS
  Shrubs, Eurasian, ULEX
  Shrubs (hollies), ILEX
  Shrubs (incl. Virginia Willow), ITEA
  Shrubs, tropical, EVEA
  Snakes (sand snakes), ERYX
  Swans, OLOR
  Trees, chocolate, COLA
  Trees (ebony family), MABA
  Trees (incl. maples), ACER
  Trees (olives), OLEA
  Trees, tropical, EVEA
  Turtles, EMYS
Goat: Wild, IBEX, KRAS, TAHR, TAIR,
  THAR
God: Assyrian, ASUR
  Babylonian, ADAD, ADDU, ENKI,
  ENZU, IRRA, NABU, NEBO, UTUG
  Celtic, LLEU, LLEW
  Hindu, AGNI, CIVA, DEVA, DEWA,
  KAMA, RAMA, SIVA, VAYU
  Phrygian, ATYS
  Semitic, BAAL
  Teutonic, HLER
Goddess: Babylonian, ERUA, GULA
  Hawaiian, PELE
  Hindu, DEVI, KALI, SHRI, VACH
Gooseberry: Hawaiian, POHA
Gourd, PEPO
Grafted (heraldry), ENTE
Grandfather (obsolete), AIEL
Grandparents: Pertaining to, AVAL
Grass: Hawaiian, HILO
Gray (French), GRIS
Green (heraldry), VERT
Groom: Indian, SYCE
Half (prefix), DEMI, HEMI, SEMI
Hamlet, DORP
Hammer-head: Part of, PEEN
Handle, ANSA
Harp: Japanese, KOTO
Hartebeest, ASSE, TORA
Hautboy, OBOE
Hawk: Taken from nest (falconry), EYAS
Hearing (law), OYER
Heater: For liquids, ETNA
Herb: Aromatic, ANET, DILL
  Fabulous, MOLY
  Perennial, GEUM, SEGO

  Pot, WORT
  Used for blue dye, WADE, WOAD
Hill: Flat-topped, MESA
  Sand, DENE, DUNE
Hoarfrost, RIME
Hog: Immature female, GILT
Holly, ILEX
House: Cow, BYRE
  (Spanish), CASA
Ice: Floating, FLOE
Image, ICON, IKON
Incarnation: Of Vishnu, RAMA
Indian: Algonquian, CREE, SAUK
  Central American, MAYA
  Iroquoian, ERIE
  Mexican, CORA
  Peruvian, CANA, INCA, MORO
  Shoshonean, HOPI
  Siouan, OTOE
  Southwestern, HOPI, PIMA, YUMA,
  ZUNI
Insect: Immature, PUPA
Instrument: Stringed, LUTE, LYRE
Ireland, EIRE, ERIN
Jacket: English, ETON
Jail (British), GAOL
Jar, OLLA
Judge: Islamic, CADI
Juniper: European, CADE
Kiln, OAST, OVEN
King: British legendary, LUDD, NUDD
Kiss, BUSS
Knife: Philippine, BOLO
Koran: Section of, SURA
Laborer: Spanish American, PEON
Lake: Mountain, TARN
  (Scotch), LOCH
Lamp: Miner's, DAVY
Landing place: Indian, GHAT
Language: Buddhist, PALI
  Japanese, AINU
Latvian, LETT
Layer: Of iris, UVEA
Leaf: Palm, OLAY, OLLA
Legislature: Ukrainian, RADA
Lemur, LORI
Leopard, PARD
Let it stand, STET
Letter: Greek, BETA, IOTA, ZETA
  Hebrew, AYIN, BETH, CAPH, KOPH,
  RESH, SHIN, TETH, YODH
  Papal, BULL
Lily, ALOE
Literature: Hindu sacred, VEDA
Lizard, GILA
  Monitor, URAN
Loquat, BIWA
Magistrate: Genoese or Venetian, DOGE
Man (Latin), HOMO
Mark: Omission, DELE
armoset: South American, MICO
Meadow: Fertile, VEGA
Measure: Electric, VOLT, WATT
  Force, DYNE
  Hebrew, OMER
  Printing, PICA
  Spanish or Portuguese, VARA
  Swiss land, IMMI
Medley, OLIO
Merganser, SMEW
Milk (French), LAIT
Molding, GULA
  Curved, OGEE
Mongoose: Crab-eating, URVA
Monk: Tibetan, LAMA
Monkey: African, MONA, WAAG
  Ceylonese, MAHA
  Cochin-China, DOUC
  South American, SAKI, TITI
Monkshood, ATIS
Month: Jewish, ADAR, ELUL, IYAR
Mother (French), MERE
Mountain: Thessaly, OSSA
Mouse: Meadow, VOLE
Mythology: Norse, EDDA
Nail (French), CLOU

Native: Philippine, MORO
Nest: Of pheasants, NIDE
Network, RETE
No (German), NEIN
Noble: Islamic, AMIR
Notice: Death, OBIT
Novel: By Zola, NANA
Nursemaid: Oriental AMAH, AYAH, EYAH
Nut: Philippine, PILI
Oak: Holm, ILEX
Oil (comb. form), OLEO
Ostrich: American, RHEA
Oven, KILN, OAST
Owl: Barn, LULU
Ox: Celebes wild, ANOE
  Extinct wild, URUS
Palm, ATAP, NIPA, SAGO
Parliament, DIET
Parrot: New Zealand, KAKA
Pass: Indian mountain, GHAT
Passage: Closing (music), CODA
Peach: Clingstone, PAVY
Peasant: Indian, RYOT
  Old English, CARL
Pepper: Australasian, KAVA
Perfume, ATAR
Persia, IRAN
Person: Extraordinary, ONER
Pickerel or pike, ESOX
Pitcher, EWER
Plant: Aromatic, NARD
  Century, ALOE
  Indigo, ANIL
  Pepper, KAVA
Platform: Raised, DAIS
Plum: Wild, SLOE
Pods: Vegetable, OKRA, OKRO
Poem: Epic, EPOS
Poet: Persian, OMAR
  Roman, OVID
Poison, BANE
  Arrow, INEE
Porkfish, SISI
Portico: Greek, STOA
Premium, AGIO
Priest: Islamic, IMAM
Prima donna, DIVA
Prong: Fork, TINE
Pseudonym: Lamb's, ELIA
Queen: Carthaginian, DIDO
  Hindu, RANI
Rabbit, CONY
Race: Of Japan, AINU
Rail: Ducklike, COOT
  North American, SORA
Redshank, CLEE
Refuse: After pressing, MARC
Regiment: Turkish, ALAI
Reliquary, ARCA
Resort: Italian, LIDO
Ridges: Sandy, ASAR, OSAR
River: German, ELBE, ODER
  Italian, ADDA
  Siberian, LENA
Road: Roman, ITER

Rockfish: California, RENA
Rodent: Mouselike, VOLE
  South American, PACA
Rootstock, TARO
Salamander, NEWT
Salmon: Silver, COHO
  Young, PARR
Same (Greek), HOMO
  (Latin), IDEM
Sauce: Fish, ALEC
School: English, ETON
Seaweed, AGAR, ALGA, KELP
Secular, LAIC
Sediment, SILT
Seed: Dill, ANET
  Of vetch, TARE
Serf, ILOT
Sesame, TEEL
Settlement: Eskimo, ETAH
Shark: Atlantic, GATA
  European, TOPE
Sheep: Wild, UDAD
Sheltered, ALEE
Shield, EGIS
Ship: Jason's, ARGO
  Left side of, PORT
  Two-masted, BRIG
Shrine: Buddhist, TOPE
Shrub: New Zealand, TUTU
Sign: Magic, RUNE
Silkworm, ERIA
Skin: Beaver, PLEW
Skink: Egyptian, ADDA
Slave, ESNE
Sloth: Two-toed, UNAU
Smooth, LENE
Snow: Glacial, NEVE
Soapstone, TALC
Society: African secret, EGBO, PORO
Son: Of Seth, ENOS
Song (German), LIED
  Unaccompanied, GLEE
Sound: Lung, RALE
Sour, ACID
Sow: Young, GILT
Spike: Brad-shaped, BROB
Spirit: Buddhist evil, MARA
Stake: Poker, ANTE
Star: Temporary, NOVA
Starch: East Indian, SAGO
Stone: Precious, OPAL
Strap: Bridle, REIN
Strewn (heraldry), SEME
Sweetsop, ATES, ATTA
Sword: Fencing, EPEE, FOIL
Tambourine: African, TAAR
Tapir: Brazilian, ANTA
Tax, CESS
Tea: South American, MATE
Therefore (Latin), ERGO
Thing: Extraordinary, ONER
Three (dice, cards, etc.), TREY
Thrush: Hawaiian, OMAO
Tide, NEAP

Tipster: Racing, TOUT
Tissue, TELA
Title: Etruscan, LARS
  Hindu, BABU
  Indian, RAJA
  Islamic, EMIR, IMAM
  Persian, BABA
  Spanish, DONA
  Turkish, AGHA, BABA
Toad: Largest-known, AGUA
  Tree, HYLA
Tool: Cutting, ADZE
Track: Deer, SLOT
Tract: Sandy, DENE
Tree: Apple, SORB
  Central American, EBOE
  East Indian, TEAK
  Eucalyptus, YATE
  Guiana and Trinidad, MORA
  Javanese, UPAS
  Linden, LIME, LINN, TEIL, TILL
  Sandarac, ARAR
  Sassafras, AGUE
  Tamarisk salt, ATLE
Tribe: Moro, SULU
Trout, CHAR
Vessel: Arab, DHOW
Vestment: Ecclesiastical, COPE
Vetch, TARE
Vine: East Indian, SOMA
Violinist: Famous, AUER
Vortex, EDDY
Wampum, PEAG
Wapiti, STAG
Waste: Allowance for, TRET
Watchman: Indian, MINA
Water (Spanish), AGUA
Waterfall, LINN
Wavy (heraldry), ONDE, UNDE
Wax, CERE
  Chinese, PELA
Weed: Biblical, TARE
Weight: Ancient, MINA
  Danish (pl.), ESER
  East Asian, TAEL
  Greek, MINA
  Siamese, BAHT
Well done (rare), EUGE
Whale, CETE
  Killer, ORCA
  White, HUSE, HUSO
Whirlpool, EDDY
Wife: Of Geraint, ENID
Willow: Virginia, ITEA
Wine, PORT
Winged, ALAR
  (Heraldry), AILE
Wings, ALAE
Withered, SERE
Without (French), SANS
Wool: To comb, CARD
Work, OPUS
Wrong: Civil, TORT
Young: Bring forth, YEAN

Words of Five Letters

Abode of dead: Babylonian, ARALU
Aborigine: Borneo DAYAK
Aftersong, EPODE
Aloe, AGAVE
Animal: Footless, APODE
Ant, EMMET
Antelope: African, ADDAX, BEISA, CAAMA, ELAND, GUIBA, ORIBI, TIANG
  Goat, GORAL, SEROW
  Indian, SASIN
  Siberian, SAIGA
Arch: Pointed, OGIVE
Armadillo, APARA, POYOU, TATOU
Arrowroot, ARARU
Artery: Trunk, AORTA
Association: Russian, ARTEL
  Secret, CABAL
Author: English, READE

Automaton, GOLEM, ROBOT
Award: Motion-picture, OSCAR
Basket: Fishing, CREEL
Beer: Russian, KVASS
Bible: Islamic, KORAN, QUR'AN
Bird: Asian, MINAH, MYNAH
  Indian, SHAMA
  Larklike, PIPIT
  Loonlike, GREBE
  Oscine, VIREO
  South American, AGAMI
  Swimming, GREBE
Black: (French), NOIRE
  (Heraldry), SABLE
Blackbird: European, MERLE, OUSEL, OUZEL
Block: Glacial, SERAC
Blue (heraldry), AZURE
Boat: Eskimo, BIDAR, UMIAK

Bobwhite, COLIN, QUAIL
Bone (comb. form), OSTEO
  Leg, TIBIA
  Thigh, FEMUR
Broom: Twig, BESOM
Brother (French), FRERE
  Moses, AARON
Canoe: Eskimo, BIDAR, KAYAK
Cape: Papal, FANON, ORALE
Caravansary, SERAI
Card: Old playing, TAROT
Caterpillar: New Zealand, AWETO
Catkin, AMENT
Cavity: Stone, GEODE
Cephalopod, SQUID
Cetacean, WHALE
Chariot, ESSED
Cheek: Pertaining to, MALAR
Chieftain: Arab, EMEER

Child (Scotch), BAIRN
Cigar, CLARO
Coating: Seed, TESTA
Cockatoo: Palm, ARARA
Coin: Costa Rican, COLON
Danish, KRONE
Ecuadorian, SUCRE
English, GROAT, PENCE
French, FRANC
German, KRONE, TALER
Hungarian, PENGO
Icelandic, KRONA
Indian, RUPEE
Iraqi, DINAR
Norwegian, KRONE
Polish, ZLOTY
Russian, COPEC, KOPEK, RUBLE
Swedish, KRONA
Turkish, ASPER
Yugoslav, DINAR
Collar: Papal, FANON, ORALE
Roman, RABAT
Commune: Italian, TREIA
Composition: Choral, MOTET
Compound: Chemical, ESTER
Conceal (law), ELOIN
Council: Ecclesiastical, SYNOD
Court: Anglo-Saxon, GEMOT
Inner, PATIO
Crest: Mountain, ARETE
Crown: Papal, TIARA
Cuttlefish, SEPIA
Date: Roman, NONES
Decree: Islamic, IRADE
Russian, UKASE
Deposit: Loam, LOESS
Desert: Gobi, SHAMO
Devilfish, MANTA
Disease: Cereals, ERGOT
Disk, PATEN
Dog: Wild, DHOLE, DINGO
Dormouse, LEROT
Drum, TABOR
Duck: Sea, EIDER
Dynasty: Chinese, CHING, LIANG, SHANG
Earthquake, SEISM
Eel, ELVER, MORAY
Ermine: European, STOAT
Ether: Crystalline, APIOL
Fabric: Velvetlike, PANNE
Fabulist, AESOP
Family: Italian, CENCI
Fiber: West Indian, SISAL
Fig: Smyrna, ELEME, ELEMI
Figure: Of speech, TROPE
Finch: European, SERIN
Fish: American small, KILLY
Flower: Garden, ASTER
Friend (Spanish), AMIGO
Fruit: Tropical, MANGO
Fungus: Rye, ERGOT
Furze, GORSE
Gateway, TORAN, TORII
Gem, AGATE, BERYL, PEARL, TOPAZ
Genus: Barnacles, LEPAS
Bears, URSUS
Birds (loons), GAVIA
Birds (nuthatches), SITTA
Cats, FELIS
Dogs, CANIS
Fishes (chiros), ELOPS
Fishes (perch), PERCA
Geese, ANSER
Grasses, STIPA
Grasses (incl. oats), AVENA
Gulls, LARUS
Hares, rabbits, LEPUS
Hawks, BUTEO
Herbs, old world, INULA
Herbs, trailing or climbing, APIOS
Herbs, tropical, TACCA, URENA
Horses, EQUUS
Insects (olive flies), DACUS
Lice, plant, APHIS
Lichens, USNEA
Lizards, AGAMA
Moles, TALPA
Mollusks, OLIVA
Monkeys, CEBUS
Palms, ARECA
Pigeons, GOURA
Plants (amaryllis family), AGAVE
Ruminants (goats), CAPRA
Shrubs, Asiatic, SABIA
Shrubs (heath), ERICA
Shrubs (incl. raspberry), RUBUS
Shrubs, tropical, IXORA, TREMA, URENA
Ticks, ARGAS
Trees (of elm family), TREMA, ULMUS
Trees, tropical, IXORA, TREMA
Goat: Bezoar, PASAN
God: Assyrian, ASHIR, ASHUR, ASSUR
Babylonian, DAGAN, SIRIS
Gaelic, DAGDA
Hindu, BHAGA, INDRA, SHIVA
Japanese, EBISU
Philistine, DAGON
Phrygian, ATTIS
Teutonic, AEGIR, GYMIR
Welsh, DYLAN
Goddess: Babylonian, ISTAR, NANAI
Hindu, DURGA, GAURI, SHREE
Group: Of six, HEXAD
Grove: Sacred to Diana, NEMUS
Growing out, ENATE
Guitar: Hindu, SITAR
Gull: PEWEE, PEWIT
Hartebeest, CAAMA
Headdress: Jewish or Persian, TIARA
Liturgical, MITER, MITRE
Heath, ERICA
Herb: Grasslike marsh, SEDGE
Heron, EGRET
Hog: Young, SHOAT, SHOTE
Image, EIKON
Indian: Cariban, ARARA
Iroquoian, HURON
Mexican, AZTEC, OPATA, OTOMI
Muskhogean, CREEK
Siouan, OSAGE, TETON
Spanish American, ARARA, CARIB
Inflorescence: Racemose, AMENT
Insect: Immature, LARVA
Intrigue, CABAL
Iris: Yellow, SEDGE
Juniper, GORSE, RETEM
Kidneys: Pertaining to, RENAL
King: British legendary, LLUDD
Kite: European, GLEDE
Kobold, NISSE
Land: Cultivated, ARADA, ARADO
Landholder (Scotch), LAIRD, THANE
Language: Dravidian, TAMIL
Lariat, LASSO, REATA
Laughing, RIANT
Lawgiver: Athenian, DRACO, SOLON
Leaf: Calyx, SEPAL
Fern, FROND
Lemur, LORIS
Letter: English, AITCH
Greek, ALPHA, DELTA, GAMMA, KAPPA, OMEGA, SIGMA, THETA
Hebrew, ALEPH, CHETH, GIMEL, SADHE, ZAYIN
Lichen, USNEA
Lighthouse, PHARE
Lizard: Old World, AGAMA
Loincloth, DHOTI
Louse: Plant, APHID
Macaw: Brazilian, ARARA
Mahogany: Philippine, ALMON
Mammal: Badgerlike, RATEL
Civetlike, GENET
Giraffelike, OKAPI
Raccoonlike, COATI
Man (French), HOMME
Marble, AGATE
Mark: Insertion, CARET
Market place: Greek, AGORA
Marsupial: Australian, KOALA
Measure: Electric, FARAD, HENRY
Energy, JOULE
Metric, LITER, STERE
Printing, AGATE
Russian, VERST
Mixture: Smelting, MATTE
Mohicans: Last of, UNCAS
Molding: Convex, OVOLO, TORUS
Mole, TALPA
Monkey: African, PATAS
Capuchin, SAJOU
Howling, ARABA
Monkshood, ATEES
Month: Jewish, NISAN, SIVAN, TEBET
Museum (French), MUSEE
Musketeer, ATHOS
Native: Aleutian, ALEUT
New Zealand, MAORI
Neckpiece: Ecclesiastical, AMICE
Nerve (comb. form), NEURO
Nest: Eagle's or hawk's, AERIE
Insect's, NIDUS
Net: Fishing, SEINE
Newsstand, KIOSK
Nitrogen, AZOTE
Noble: Islamic, AMEER
Nodule: Stone, GEODE
Nostrils, NARES
Notched irregularly, EROSE
Nymph: Islamic, HOURI
Official: Roman, EDILE
Oleoresin, ELEMI
Opening: Mouthlike, STOMA
Oration: Funeral, ELOGE
Ostiole, STOMA
Page: Left-hand, VERSO
Right-hand, RECTO
Palm, ARECA, BETEL
Park: Colorado, ESTES
Perfume, ATTAR
Philosopher: Greek, PLATO
Pillar: Stone, STELA, STELE
Pinnacle: Glacial, SERAC
Plain, LLANO
Plant: Century, AGAVE
Climbing, LIANA
Dwarf, CUMIN
East Asian perennial, RAMIE
Medicinal, SENNA
Mustard family, CRESS
Plate: Communion, PATEN
Poem: Lyric, EPODE
Point: Lowest, NADIR
Poplar, ABELE, ALAMO, ASPEN
Porridge: Spanish American, ATOLE
Post: Stair, NEWEL
Priest: Islamic, IMAUM
Protozoan, AMEBA
Queen: (French), REINE
Hindu, RANEE
Rabbit, CONEY
Rail, CRAKE
Red (heraldry), GULES
Religion: Moslem, Muslim, ISLAM
Resin, ELEMI
Revoke (law), ADEEM
Rich man, MIDAS, NABOB
Ridge: Sandy, ESKAR, ESKER
River: French, LOIRE, SEINE
Rockfish: California, REINA
Rootstock: Fragrant, ORRIS
Ruff: Female, REEVE
Sack: Pack, KYACK
Salt: Ethereal, ESTER
Saltpeter, NITER, NITRE
Salutation: Eastern, SALAM
Sandpiper: Old World, TEREK
Scented, OLENT
School: Fish, SHOAL
French public, LYCEE
Scriptures: Islamic, KORAN
Seaweeds, ALGAE
Seed: Aromatic, ANISE
Seraglio, HAREM, SERAI
Serf, HELOT
Sheep: Wild, AUDAD

Sheeplike, OVINE
Shield, AEGIS
Shoe: Wooden, SABOT
Shoots: Pickled bamboo, ACHAR
Shot: Billiard, CAROM, MASSE
Shrine: Buddhist, STUPA
Shrub: Burning bush, WAHOO
  Ornamental evergreen, TOYON
  Used in tanning, SUMAC
Silk: Watered, MOIRE
Sister (French), SOEUR
  (Latin), SOROR
Six: Group of, HEXAD
Skeleton: Marine, CORAL
Slave, HELOT
Snake, ABOMA, ADDER, COBRA, RACER
Soldier: French, POILU
  Indian, SEPOY
Sour, ACERB
Spirit: Air, ARIEL
Staff: Shepherd's, CROOK
Starwort, ASTER
Steel (German), STAHL
Stockade: Russian, ETAPE
Stop (nautical), AVAST
Storehouse, ETAPE
Subway: Parisian, METRO
Tapestry, ARRAS
Tea: Paraguayan, YERBA
Temple: Hawaiian, HEIAU
Terminal: Positive, ANODE
Theater: Greek, ODEON, ODEUM
Then (French), ALORS
Thread: Surgical, SETON
Thrush: Wilson's, VEERY
Title: Hindu, BABOO
  Indian, RAJAH, SAHEB, SAHIB
  Islamic, EMEER, IMAUM
Tree: Buddhist sacred, PIPAL
  East Indian cotton, SIMAL
  Hickory, PECAN
  Light-wooded, BALSA
  Malayan, TERAP
  Mediterranean, CAROB
  Mexican, ABETO
  Mexican pine, OCOTE
  New Zealand, MAIRE
  Philippine, ALMON
  Rain, SAMAN
  South American, UMBRA
  Tamarack, LARCH
  Tamarisk salt, ATLEE
  West Indian, ACANA
Trout, CHARR
Troy, ILION, ILIUM
Twin: Siamese, CHANG
Vestment: Ecclesiastical, STOLE
Violin: Famous, AMATI, STRAD
Volcano: Mud, SALSE
Wampum, PEAGE
War cry: Greek, ALALA
Wavy (heraldry), UNDEE
Weight: Jewish, GERAH
Wen, TALPA
Wheat, SPELT
Wheel: Persian water, NORIA
Whitefish, CISCO
Willow, OSIER
Window: Bay, ORIEL
Wine, MEDOC, RHINE, TINTA, TOKAY
Winged, ALATE
Woman (French), FEMME
Year: Excess of solar over lunar, EPACT
Zoroastrian, PARSI

Words of Six or More Letters

Agave, MAGUEY
Alkaloid: Crystalline, ESERIN, ESERINE
Alligator, CAYMAN
Amphibole, EDENITE, URALITE
Ant: White, TERMITE
Antelope: African, DIKDIK, DUIKER, GEMSBOK, IMPALA, KOODOO
  European, CHAMOIS
  Indian, NILGAI, NILGAU, NILGHAI, NILGHAU
Ape: Asian or East Indian, GIBBON
Appendage: Leaf, STIPEL, STIPULE
Armadillo, PELUDO, TATOUAY
Arrowroot, ARARAO
Ascetic: Jewish, ESSENE
Ass: Asian wild, ONAGER
Avatar: Of Vishnu, KRISHNA
Babylonian, ELAMITE
Badge: Shoulder, EPAULET
Baldness, ALOPECIA
Barracuda, SENNET
Bark: Aromatic, SINTOC
Bearlike, URSINE
Beetle, ELATER
Bible: Zoroastrian, AVESTA
Bird: Sea, PETREL
  South American, SERIEMA
  Wading, AVOCET, AVOSET
Bone: Leg, FIBULA
Branched, RAMATE
Brother (Latin), FRATER
Bunting: European, ORTOLAN
Call: Trumpet, SENNET
Canoe: Eskimo, BAIDAR, OOMIAK
Caravansary, IMARET
Cat: Asian or African, CHEETAH
  Leopardlike, OCELOT
Cenobite: Jewish, ESSENE
Centerpiece: Table, EPERGNE
Cetacean, DOLPHIN, PORPOISE
Chariot, ESSEDA, ESSEDE
Chief: Seminole, OSCEOLA
Claim: Release as (law), REMISE
Clock: Water, CLEPSYDRA
Cloud, CUMULUS, NIMBUS
Coach: French hackney, FIACRE
Coin: Czech, KORUNA
  Ethiopian, TALARI
  Finnish, MARKKA
  German, THALER
  Greek, DRACHMA
  Haitian, GOURDE
  Honduran, LEMPIRA
  Hungarian, FORINT
  Indo-Chinese, PIASTER
  Netherlands, GUILDER
  Panamanian, BALBOA
  Paraguayan, GUARANI
  Portuguese, ESCUDO
  Russian, COPECK, KOPECK, ROUBLE
  Spanish, PESETA
  Venezuelan, BOLIVAR
Communion: Last holy, VIATICUM
Conceal (law), ELOIGN
Confection, PRALINE
Construction: Sentence, SYNTAX
Convexity: Shaft of column, ENTASIS
Court: Anglo-Saxon, GEMOTE
Cow: Sea, DUGONG, MANATEE
Cylindrical, TERETE
Dagger, STILETTO
  Malay, CREESE, KREESE
Date: Roman, CALENDS, KALENDS
Deer, CARIBOU, WAPITI
Disease: Plant, ERINOSE
Doorkeeper, OSTIARY
Dragonflies: Order of, ODANATA
Drink: Of gods, NECTAR
Drum: TABOUR
  Moorish, ATABAL, ATTABAL
Duck: Fish-eating, MERGANSER
  Sea, SCOTER
Dynasty: Chinese, MANCHU
Eel, CONGER
Edit, REDACT
Envelope: Flower, PERIANTH
Eskimo, AMERIND
Ether: Crystalline, APIOLE
Excuse (law), ESSOIN
Eyespots, OCELLI
Fabric, ESTAMENE, ESTAMIN, ETAMINE
Falcon: European, KESTREL
Figure: Used as column, CARYATID, TELAMON
Fine: For punishment, AMERCE
Fish: Asian fresh-water, GOURAMI
  Pikelike, BARRACUDA
Five: Group of, PENTAD
Fly: African, TSETSE
Foot: Metric, ANAPEST, IAMBUS
Foxlike, VULPINE
Frying pan, SPIDER
Fur, KARAKUL
Galley: Greek or Roman, BIREME, TRIREME
Game: Card, ECARTE
Garment: Greek, CHLAMYS
Gateway, GOPURA, TORANA
Genus: Birds (ravens, crows), CORVUS
  Eels, CONGER
  Fishes, ANABAS
  Foxes, VULPES
  Herbs, ANEMONE
  Insects, CICADA
  Lemurs, GALAGO
  Mints (incl. catnip), NEPETA
  Mollusks, ANOMIA, ASTARTE, TEREDO
  Mollusks (incl. oysters), OSTREA
  Monkeys (spider monkeys), ATELES
  Thrushes (incl. robins), TURDUS
  Trees (of elm family), CELTIS
  Trees (inc. dogwood), CORNUS
  Trees, tropical American, SAPOTA
  Wrens, NANNUS
Gibbon, SIAMANG, WOUWOU
Gland: Salivary, RACEMOSE
Goat: Bezoar, PASANG
Goatlike, CAPRINE
God: Assyrian, ASHSHUR, ASSHUR
  Babylonian, BABBAR, MARDUK, MERODACH, NANNAR, NERGAL, SHAMASH
  Hindu, BRAHMA, KRISHNA, VISHNU
  Tahitian, TAAROA
Goddess: Babylonian, ISHTAR
  Hindu, CHANDI, HAIMAVATI, LAKSHMI, PARVATI, SARASVATI, SARASWATI
Government, POLITY
Governor: Persian, SATRAP
Grandson (Scotch), NEPOTE
Group: Of five, PENTAD
  Of nine, ENNEAD
  Of seven, HEPTAD
Hare: in first year, LEVERET
Harpsichord, SPINET
Herb: Alpine, EDELWEISS
  Chinese, GINSENG
  South African, FREESIA
Hermit, EREMITE
Hero: Legendary, PALADIN
Heron, BITTERN
Horselike, EQUINE
Hound: Short-legged, BEAGLE
House (French), MAISON
Idiot, CRETIN
Implement: Stone, NEOLITH
Incarnation: Hindu, AVATAR
Indian, APACHE, COMANCHE, PAIUTE, SENECA
Inn: Turkish, IMARET
Insects: Order of, DIPTERA
Instrument: Japanese banjolike, SAMISEN
  Musical, CLAVIER, SPINET
Interstice, AREOLA
Ironwood, COLIMA
Juniper: Old Testament, RAETAM
Kettledrum, ATABAL
King: Fairy, OBERON
Kneecap, PATELLA
Knife, MACHETE
Langur: Sumatran, SIMPAI
Legislature: Spanish, CORTES

Lemur: African, GALAGO
Madagascar, AYEAYE
Letter: Greek, EPSILON, LAMBDA, OMICRON, UPSILON
Hebrew, DALETH, LAMEDH, SAMEKH
Lighthouse, PHAROS
Lizard, IGUANA
Llama, ALPACA
Lockjaw, TETANUS
Locust, CICADA, CICALA
Macaw: Brazilian, MARACAN
Maid: Of Astolat, ELAINE
Mammal: Madagascar, TENDRAC, TENREC
Man (Spanish), HOMBRE
Marmoset: South American, TAMARIN
Marsupial, BANDICOOT, WOMBAT
Massacre, POGROM
Mayor: Spanish, ALCALDE
Measure: Electric, AMPERE, COULOMB, KILOWATT
Medicine: Quack, NOSTRUM
Member: Religious order, CENOBITE
Molasses, TREACLE
Monkey: African, GRIVET, NISNAS
Asian, LANGUR
Philippine, MACHIN
South American, PINCHE, SAIMIRI, SAMIRI, SAPAJOU
Monster, CHIMERA, GORGON
(Comb. form), TERATO
Cretan, MINOTAUR
Month: Jewish, HESHVAN, KISLEV, SHEBAT, TAMMUZ, TISHRI, VEADAR
Mountain: Asia Minor, ARARAT
Mulct, AMERCE
Musketeer, ARAMIS, PORTHOS
Nearsighted, MYOPIC
Net, TRAMMEL
New York City, GOTHAM
Nine: Group of, ENNEAD
Nobleman: Spanish, GRANDEE
Official: Roman, AEDILE
Onyx: Mexican, TECALI
Order: Dragonflies, ODANATA
Insects, DIPTERA
Organ: Plant, PISTIL
Ornament: Shoulder, EPAULET
Overcoat: Military, CAPOTE
Ox: Wild, BANTENG
Oxidation: Bronze or copper, PATINA
Paralysis: Incomplete, PARESIS
Pear: Alligator, AVOCADO
Persimmon: Mexican, CHAPOTE
Pipe: Peace, CALUMET
Plaid (Scotch), TARTAN
Plain, PAMPAS, STEPPE, TUNDRA
Plant: Buttercup family, ANEMONE
Century, MAGUEY
On rocks, LICHEN
Plowing: Fit for, ARABLE
Poem: Heroic, EPOPEE
Six-lined, SESTET
Point: Highest, ZENITH
Potion: Love, PHILTER, PHILTRE
Protozoan, AMOEBA
Punish, AMERCE
Purple (heraldry), PURPURE
Queen: Fairy, TITANIA
Race: Skiing, SLALOM
Rat, BANDICOOT, LEMMING
Retort, RIPOST, RIPOSTE
Ring: Harness, TERRET
Little, ANNULET
Rodent: Jumping, JERBOA
Spanish American, AGOUTI, AGOUTY
Sailor: East Indian, LASCAR
Salmon: Young, GRILSE
Salutation: Eastern, SALAAM
Sandpiper, PLOVER
Sandy, ARENOSE
Sapodilla, SAPOTA, SAPOTE
Saw: Surgical, TREPAN
Seven: Group of, HEPTAD
Sexes: Common to both, EPICENE
Shawl: Mexican, SERAPE
Sheathing: Flower, SPATHE
Sheep: Wild, AOUDAD, ARGALI
Shipworm, TEREDO
Shoes: Mercury's winged, TALARIA
Shortening: Syllable, SYSTOLE
Shrub, SPIRAEA
Sickle-shaped, FALCATE
Silver (heraldry), ARGENT
Snake, ANACONDA
Speech: Loss of, APHASIA
Spiral, HELICAL
Staff: Bishop's, CROSIER, CROZIER
Stalk: Plant, PETIOLE
State: Swiss, CANTON
Studio, ATELIER
Swan: Young, CYGNET
Swimming, NATANT
Sword-shaped, ENSATE
Terminal: Negative, CATHODE
Third (music), TIERCE
Thrust: Fencing, RIPOST, RIPOSTE
Tile: Pertaining to, TEGULAR
Tomb: Empty, CENOTAPH
Tooth (comb. form), ODONTO
Tower: Islamic, MINARET
Tree: African timber, BAOBAB
Black gum, TUPELO
East Indian, MARGOSA
Locust, ACACIA
Malayan, SINTOC
Marmalade, SAPOTE
Urn: Tea, SAMOVAR
Vehicle, LANDAU, TROIKA
Verbose, PROLIX
Viceroy: Egyptian, KHEDIVE
Vulture: American, CONDOR
Warehouse (French), ENTREPOT
Whale: White, BELUGA
Whirlpool, VORTEX
Will: Addition to, CODICIL
Having left, TESTATE
Wind, CHINOOK, MONSOON, SIMOOM, SIMOON, SI ROCCO
Window: In roof, DORMER
Wine, BARBERA, BURGUNDY, CABERNET, CHABLIS, CHIANTI, CLARET, MUSCATEL, RIESLING, SAUTERNE, SHERRY, ZINFANDEL
Wolfish, LUPINE
Woman: Boisterous, TERMAGANT
Woolly, LANATE
Workshop, ATELIER
Zoroastrian, PARSEE

Old Testament Names

We do not pretend that this list is all-inclusive. We list only those names that occur most often in crossword puzzles.

Aaron: First high priest of Jews; son of Amram; brother of Miriam and Moses; father of Abihu, Eleazer, Ithamar, and Nadab.
Abel: Son of Adam; slain by Cain.
Abigail: Wife of Nabal; later, wife of David.
Abihu: Son of Aaron.
Abimelech: King of Gerar.
Abner: Commander of army of Saul and Ishbosheth; slain by Joab.
Abraham (or Abram): Patriarch; forefather of the Jews; son of Terah; husband of Sarah; father of Isaac and Ishmael.
Absalom: Son of David and Maacah; revolted against David; slain by Joab.
Achish: King of Gath; gave refuge to David.
Achsa (or Achsah): Daughter of Caleb; wife of Othniel.
Adah: Wife of Lamech.
Adam: First man; husband of Eve; father of Cain, Abel, and Seth.
Adonijah: Son of David and Haggith.
Agag: King of Amalek; spared by Saul; slain by Samuel.
Ahasuerus: King of Persia; husband of Vashti and, later, Esther; sometimes identified with Xerxes the Great.
Ahijah: Prophet; foretold accession of Jeroboam.
Ahinoam: Wife of David.
Amasa: Commander of army of David; slain by Joab.
Amnon: Son of David and Ahinoam; ravished Tamar; slain by Absalom.
Amram: Husband of Jochebed; father of Aaron, Miriam and Moses.
Asenath: Wife of Joseph.
Asher: Son of Jacob and Zilpah.
Balaam: Prophet; rebuked by his donkey for cursing God.
Barak: Jewish captain; associated with Deborah.
Baruch: Secretary to Jeremiah.
Bathsheba: Wife of Uriah; later, wife of David.
Belshazzar: Crown prince of Babylon.
Benaiah: Warrior of David; proclaimed Solomon King.
Ben-Hadad: Name of several kings of Damascus.
Benjamin: Son of Jacob and Rachel.
Bezaleel: Chief architect of tabernacle.
Bilbah: Servant of Rachel; mistress of Jacob.
Bildad: Comforter of Job.
Boaz: Husband of Ruth; father of Obed.
Cain: Son of Adam and Eve; slayer of Abel; father of Enoch.
Cainan: Son of Enos.
Caleb: Spy sent out by Moses to visit Canaan; father of Achsa.
Canaan: Son of Ham.
Chilion: Son of Elimelech; husband of Orpah.
Cush: Son of Ham; father of Nimrod.
Dan: Son of Jacob and Bilhah.
Daniel: Prophet; saved from lions by God.
Deborah: Hebrew prophetess; helped Israelites conquer Canaanites.
Delilah: Mistress and betrayer of Samson.
Elam: Son of Shem.
Eleazar: Son of Aaron; succeeded him as high priest.
Eli: High priest and judge; teacher of Samuel; father of Hophni and Phinehas.
Eliakim: Chief minister of Hezekiah.
Eliezer: Servant of Abraham.
Elihu: Comforter of Job.
Elijah (or Elias): Prophet; went to heaven in chariot of fire.
Elimelech: Husband of Naomi; father of Chilion and Mahlon.
Eliphaz: Comforter of Job.

Elisha (or Eliseus): Prophet; successor of Elijah.
Elkanah: Husband of Hannah; father of Samuel.
Enoch: Son of Cain.
Enoch: Father of Methuselah.
Enos: Son of Seth; father of Cainan.
Ephraim: Son of Joseph.
Esau: Son of Isaac and Rebecca; sold his birthright to his brother Jacob.
Esther: Jewish wife of Ahasuerus; saved Jews from Haman's plotting.
Eve: First woman; created from rib of Adam.
Ezra (or Esdras): Hebrew scribe and priest.
Gad: Son of Jacob and Zilpah.
Gehazi: Servant of Elisha.
Gideon: Israelite hero; defeated Midianites.
Goliath: Philistine giant; slain by David.
Hagar: Handmaid of Sarah; concubine of Abraham; mother of Ishmael.
Haggith: Mother of Adonijah.
Ham: Son of Noah; father of Cush, Mizraim, Phut, and Canaan.
Haman: Chief minister of Ahasuerus; hanged on gallows prepared for Mordecai.
Hannah: Wife of Elkanah; mother of Samuel.
Hanun: King of Ammonites.
Haran: Brother of Abraham; father of Lot.
Hazael: King of Damascus.
Hephzi-Bah: Wife of Hezekiah; mother of Mannaseh.
Hiram: King of Tyre.
Holofernes: General of Nebuchadnezzar; slain by Judith.
Hophni: Son of Eli.
Isaac: Hebrew patriarch; son of Abraham and Sarah; half brother of Ishmael; husband of Rebecca; father of Esau and Jacob.
Ishmael: Son of Abraham and Hagar; half brother of Isaac.
Issachar: Son of Jacob and Leah.
Ithamar: Son of Aaron.
Jabal: Son of Lamech and Adah.
Jabin: King of Hazor.
Jacob: Hebrew patriarch; founder of Israel; son of Isaac and Rebecca; husband of Leah and Rachel; father of Asher, Benjamin, Dan, Gad, Issachar, Joseph, Judah, Levi, Naphtali, Reuben, Simeon, and Zebulun.
Jael: Slayer of Sisera.
Japheth: Son of Noah.
Jehoiada: High priest; husband of Jehoshabeath; revolted against Athaliah and made Joash King of Judah.
Jehoshabeath (or Jehosheba): Daughter of Jehoram of Judah; wife of Jehoiada.
Jephthah: Judge in Israel; sacrificed his only daughter because of vow.
Jesse: Son of Obed; father of David.
Jethro: Midianite priest; father of Zipporah.
Jezebel: Phoenician princess; wife of Ahab; mother of Ahaziah, Athaliah, and Jehoram.
Joab: Commander in chief under David; slayer of Abner, Absalom, and Amasa.
Job: Patriarch; underwent many afflictions; comforted by Bildad, Elihu, Eliphaz and Zophar.
Jochebed: Wife of Amram.
Jonah: Prophet; cast into sea and swallowed by great fish.
Jonathan: Son of Saul; friend of David.
Joseph: Son of Jacob and Rachel; sold into slavery by his brothers; husband of Asenath; father of Ephraim and Manassah.
Joshua: Successor of Moses; son of Nun.
Jubal: Son of Lamech and Adah.
Judah: Son of Jacob and Leah.
Judith: Slayer of Holofernes.
Kish: Father of Saul.
Laban: Father of Leah and Rachel.
Lamech: Son of Methuselah; father of Noah.
Lamech: Husband of Adah and Zillah; father of Jabal, Jubal, and Tubal-Cain.
Leah: Daughter of Laban; wife of Jacob.
Levi: Son of Jacob and Leah.
Lot: Son of Haran; escaped destruction of Sodom.
Maacah: Mother of Absalom and Tamar.
Mahlon: Son of Elimelech; first husband of Ruth.
Manasseh: Son of Joseph.
Melchizedek: King of Salem.
Methuselah: Patriarch; son of Enoch; father of Lamech.
Michal: Daughter of Saul; wife of David.
Miriam: Prophetess; daughter of Amram; sister of Aaron and Moses.
Mizraim: Son of Ham.
Mordecai: Uncle of Esther; with her aid, saved Jews from Haman's plotting.
Moses: Prophet and lawgiver; son of Amram; brother of Aaron and Miriam; husband of Zipporah.
Naaman: Syrian captain; cured of leprosy by Elisha.
Nabal: Husband of Abigail.
Naboth: Owner of vineyard; stoned to death because he would not sell it to Ahab.
Nadab: Son of Aaron.
Nahor: Father of Terah.
Naomi: Wife of Elimelech; mother-in-law of Ruth.
Naphtali: Son of Jacob and Bilhah.
Nathan: Prophet; reproved David for causing Uriah's death.
Nebuchadnezzar (or Nebuchadrezzar): King of Babylon; destroyer of Jerusalem.
Nehemiah: Jewish leader; empowered by Artaxerxes to rebuild Jerusalem.
Nimrod: Mighty hunter; son of Cush.
Noah: Patriarch; son of Lamech; escaped Deluge by building Ark; father of Ham, Japheth and Shem.
Nun (or Non): Father of Joshua.
Obed: Son of Boaz; father of Jesse.
Og: King of Bashan.
Orpah: Wife of Chilion.
Othniel: Kenezite; judge of Israel; husband of Achsa.
Phinehas: Son of Eleazer.
Phinehas: Son of Eli.
Phut (or Put): Son of Ham.
Potiphar: Egyptian official; bought Joseph.
Rachel: Wife of Jacob.
Rebecca (or Rebekah): Wife of Isaac.
Reuben: Son of Jacob and Leah.
Ruth: Wife of Mahlon, later of Boaz; daughter-in-law of Naomi.
Samson: Judge of Israel; famed for strength; betrayed by Delilah.
Samuel: Hebrew judge and prophet; son of Elkanah.
Sarah (or Sara, Sarai): Wife of Abraham.
Sennacherib: King of Assyria.
Seth: Son of Adam; father of Enos.
Shem: Son of Noah; father of Elam.
Simeon: Son of Jacob and Leah.
Sisera: Canaanite captain; slain by Jael.
Tamar: Daughter of David and Maachah; ravished by Amnon.
Terah: Son of Nahor; father of Abraham.
Tubal-Cain: Son of Lamech and Zillah.
Uriah: Husband of Bathsheba; sent to death in battle by David.
Vashti: Wife of Ahasuerus; set aside by him.
Zadok: High priest during David's reign.
Zebulun (or Zabulon): Son of Jacob and Leah.
Zillah: Wife of Lamech.
Zilpah: Servant of Leah; mistress of Jacob.
Zipporah: Daughter of Jethro; wife of Moses.
Zophar: Comforter of Job.

Kings of Judah and Israel

Kings Before Division of Kingdom

Saul: First King of Israel; son of Kish; father of Ish-Bosheth, Jonathan and Michal.
Ish-Bosheth (or Eshbaal): King of Israel; son of Saul.
David: King of Judah; later of Israel; son of Jesse; husband of Abigail, Ahinoam, Bathsheba, Michal, etc.; father of Absalom, Adonijah, Amnon, Solomon, Tamar, etc.
Solomon: King of Israel and Judah; son of David; father of Rehoboam.
Rehoboam: Son of Solomon; during his reign the kingdom was divided into Judah and Israel.

Kings of Judah (Southern Kingdom)

Rehoboam: First King.
Abijah (or Abijam or Abia): Son of Rehoboam.
Asa: Probably son of Abijah.
Jehoshaphat: Son of Asa.
Jehoram (or Joram): Son of Jehoshaphat; husband of Athaliah.
Ahaziah: Son of Jehoram and Athaliah.
Athaliah: Daughter of King Ahab of Israel and Jezebel; wife of Jehoram.
Joash (or Jehoash): Son of Ahaziah.

Amaziah: Son of Joash.
Uzziah (or Azariah): Son of Amaziah.
Jotham: Regent, later King; son of Uzziah.
Ahaz: Son of Jotham.
Hezekiah: Son of Ahaz; husband of Hephzi-Bah.
Manasseh: Son of Hezekiah and Hephzi-Bah.
Amon: Son of Manasseh.
Josiah (or Josias): Son of Amon.
Jehoahaz (or Joahaz): Son of Josiah.
Jehoiachin: Son of Jehoiakim.
Jehoiakim: Son of Josiah.
Zedekiah: Son of Josiah; kingdom overthrown by Babylonians under Nebuchadnezzar.

Kings of Israel (Northern Kingdom)

Jeroboam I: Led secession of Israel.
Nadab: Son of Jeroboam I.
Baasha: Overthrew Nadab.
Elah: Son of Baasha.
Zimri: Overthrew Elah.
Omri: Overthrew Zimri.
Ahab: Son of Omri; husband of Jezebel.
Ahaziah: Son of Ahab.
Jehoram (or Joram): Son of Ahab.
Jehu: Overthrew Jehoram.
Jehoahaz (or Joahaz): Son of Jehu.
Jehoash (or Joash): Son of Jehoahaz.
Jeroboam II: Son of Jehoash.
Zechariah: Son of Jeroboam II.
Shallum: Overthrew Zechariah.
Menahem: Overthrew Shallum.
Pekahiah: Son of Menahem.
Pekah: Overthrew Pekahiah.
Hoshea: Overthrew Pekah; kingdom overthrown by Assyrians under Sargon II.

Prophets

Major. Isaiah, Jeremiah, Ezekiel, Daniel.
Minor. Hosea, Obadiah, Nahum, Haggai, Joel, Jonah, Habakkuk, Zechariah, Amos, Micah, Zephaniah, Malachi.

Greek and Roman Mythology

Most of the Greek deities were adopted by the Romans, although in many cases there was a change of name. In the list below, information is given under the Greek name; the name in parentheses is the Roman equivalent. However, all Latin names are listed with cross-references to the Greek ones. In addition, there are several deities that are exclusively Roman.

Acheron: One of several **Rivers of Underworld:** Acheron (woe), Cocytus (wailing), Lethe (forgetfulness), Phlegethon (fire), Styx (across which souls of dead were ferried by Charon).
Achilles: Greek warrior; slew Hector at Troy; slain by Paris, who wounded him in his vulnerable heel.
Actaeon: Hunter; surprised Artemis bathing; changed by her to stag; and killed by his dogs.
Admetus: King of Thessaly; his wife, Alcestis, offered to die in his place.
Adonis: Beautiful youth loved by Aphrodite.
Aeacus: One of three judges of dead in Hades; son of Zeus.
Aeëtes: King of Colchis; father of Medea; keeper of Golden Fleece.
Aegeus: Father of Theseus; believing Theseus killed in Crete, he drowned himself; Aegean Sea named for him.
Aegisthus: Son of Thyestes; slew Atreus; with Clytemnestra, his paramour, slew Agamemnon; slain by Orestes.
Aegyptus: Brother of Danaus; his sons, except Lynceus, slain by Danaides.
Aeneas: Trojan; son of Anchises and Aphrodite; after fall of Troy, led his followers eventually to Italy; loved and deserted Dido.
Aeolus: One of several **Winds:** Aeolus (keeper of winds), Boreas (Aquilo) (north wind), Eurus (east wind), Notus (Auster) (south wind), Zephyrus (Favonius) (west wind).
Aeson: King of Iolcus; father of Jason; overthrown by his brother Pelias; restored to youth by Medea.
Aether: Personification of sky.
Aethra: Mother of Theseus.
Agamemnon: King of Mycenae; son of Atreus; brother of Menelaus; leader of Greeks against Troy; slain on his return home by Clytemnestra and Aegisthus.
Aglaia: One of several **Graces:** Beautiful goddesses: Aglaia (Brilliance), Euphrosyne (Joy), and Thalia (Bloom); daughters of Zeus.
Ajax: Greek warrior; killed himself at Troy because Achilles's armor was awarded to Odysseus.
Alcestis: Wife of Admetus; offered to die in his place but saved from death by Hercules.
Alcmene: Wife of Amphitryon; mother by Zeus of Hercules.
Alcyone: One of several **Pleiades:** Alcyone, Celaeno, Electra, Maia, Merope, Sterope or Asterope, Taygeta; seven daughters of Atlas; transformed into heavenly constellation, of which six stars are visible (Merope is said to have hidden in shame for loving a mortal).
Alecto: One of several **Furies:** Avenging spirits; Alecto, Megaera, and Tisiphone; known also as Erinyes or Eumenides.
Alectryon: Youth changed by Ares into cock.
Althaea: Wife of Oeneus; mother of Meleager.
Amazons: Female warriors in Asia Minor; supported Troy against Greeks.
Amphion: Musician; husband of Niobe; charmed stones to build fortifications for Thebes.
Amphitrite: Sea goddess; wife of Poseidon.
Amphitryon: Husband of Alcmene.
Anchises: Father of Aeneas.
Ancile: Sacred shield that fell from heavens; palladium of Rome.
Andraemon: Husband of Dryope.
Andromache: Wife of Hector.
Andromeda: Daughter of Cepheus; chained to cliff for monster to devour; rescued by Perseus.
Anteia: Wife of Proetus; tried to induce Bellerophon to elope with her.
Anteros: God who avenged unrequited love.
Antigone: Daughter of Oedipus; accompanied him to Colonus; performed burial rite for Polynices and hanged herself.
Antinoüs: Leader of suitors of Penelope; slain by Odysseus.
Aphrodite (Venus): Goddess of love and beauty; daughter of Zeus; mother of Eros.
Apollo: God of beauty, poetry, music; later identified with Helios as Phoebus Apollo; son of Zeus and Leto.
Aquilo: One of several **Winds:** Aeolus (keeper of winds), Boreas (Aquilo) (north wind), Eurus (east wind), Notus (Auster) (south wind), Zephyrus (Favonius) (west wind).
Arachne: Maiden who challenged Athena to weaving contest; changed to spider.
Ares (Mars): God of war; son of Zeus and Hera.
Argo: Ship in which Jason and followers sailed to Colchis for Golden Fleece.
Argus: Monster with hundred eyes; slain by Hermes; his eyes placed by Hera into peacock's tail.
Ariadne: Daughter of Minos; aided Theseus in slaying Minotaur; deserted by him on island of Naxos and married to Dionysus.
Arion: Musician; thrown overboard by pirates but saved by dolphin.
Artemis (Diana): Goddess of moon; huntress; twin sister of Apollo.
Asclepius (Aesculapius): Mortal son of Apollo; slain by Zeus for raising dead; later deified as god of medicine. Also known as Asklepios.
Astarte: Phoenician goddess of love; variously identified with Aphrodite, Selene, and Artemis.
Astraea: Goddess of Justice; daughter of Zeus and Themis.
Atalanta: Princess who challenged her suitors to a foot race; Hippomenes won race and married her.
Athena (Minerva): Goddess of wisdom; known poetically as Pallas Athene; sprang fully armed from head of Zeus.
Atlas: Titan; held world on his shoulders as punishment for warring against Zeus; son of Iapetus.
Atreus: King of Mycenae; father of Menelaus and Agamemnon; brother of Thyestes, three of whose sons he slew and served to him at banquet; slain by Aegisthus.
Atropos: One of several **Fates:** Goddesses of destiny; Clotho (Spinner of thread of life), Lachesis (Determiner of length), and Atropos (Cutter of thread); also called Moirae. Identified by Romans with their goddesses of fate, Nona, Decuma, and Morta; called Parcae.
Auster: One of several **Winds:** Aeolus (keeper of winds), Boreas (Aquilo) (north wind), Eurus (east wind), Notus (Auster) (south wind), Zephyrus (Favonius) (west wind).

Avernus: Infernal regions; name derived from small vaporous lake near Vesuvius which was fabled to kill birds and vegetation.
Bellerophon: Corinthian hero; killed Chimera with aid of Pegasus; tried to reach Olympus on Pegasus and was thrown to his death.
Bellona: Roman goddess of war.
Boreas: One of several **Winds:** Aeolus (keeper of winds), Boreas (Aquilo) (north wind), Eurus (east wind), Notus (Auster) (south wind), Zephyrus (Favonius) (west wind).
Briareus: Monster of hundred hands; son of Uranus and Gaea.
Briseis: Captive maiden given to Achilles; taken by Agamemnon in exchange for loss of Chryseis, which caused Achilles to cease fighting, until death of Patroclus.
Cadmus: Brother of Europa; planter of dragon seeds from which first Thebans sprang.
Calliope: One of several **Muses,** Goddesses presiding over arts and sciences: Calliope (epic poetry), Clio (history), Erato (lyric and love poetry), Euterpe (music), Melpomene (tragedy), Polymnia or Polyhymnia (sacred poetry), Terpsichore (choral dance and song), Thalia (comedy and bucolic poetry), Urania (astronomy); daughters of Zeus and Mnemosyne.
Calypso: Sea nymph; kept Odysseus on her island Ogygia for seven years.
Cassandra: Daughter of Priam; prophetess who was never believed; slain with Agamemnon.
Castor: One of **Dioscuri,** Twins Castor and Pollux; sons of Leda by Zeus.
Celaeno: One of several **Pleiades:** Alcyone, Celaeno, Electra, Maia, Merope, Sterope or Asterope, Taygeta; seven daughters of Atlas; transformed into heavenly constellation, of which six stars are visible (Merope is said to have hidden in shame for loving a mortal).
Centaurs: Beings half man and half horse; lived in mountains of Thessaly.
Cephalus: Hunter; accidentally killed his wife Procris with his spear.
Cepheus: King of Ethiopia; father of Andromeda.
Cerberus: Three-headed dog guarding entrance to Hades.
Chaos: Formless void; personified as first of gods.
Charon: Boatman on Styx who carried souls of dead to Hades; son of Erebus.
Charybdis: Female monster; personification of whirlpool.
Chimera: Female monster with head of lion, body of goat, tail of serpent; killed by Bellerophon.
Chiron: Most famous of centaurs.
Chronos: Personification of time.
Chryseis: Captive maiden given to Agamemnon; his refusal to accept ransom from her father Chryses caused Apollo to send plague on Greeks besieging Troy.
Circe: Sorceress; daughter of Helios; changed Odysseus's men into swine.
Clio: One of several **Muses:** Goddesses presiding over arts and sciences: Calliope (epic poetry), Clio (history), Erato (lyric and love poetry), Euterpe (music), Melpomene (tragedy), Polymnia or Polyhymnia (sacred poetry), Terpsichore (choral dance and song), Thalia (comedy and bucolic poetry), Urania (astronomy); daughters of Zeus and Mnemosyne.
Clotho: One of several **Fates:** Goddesses of destiny; Clotho (Spinner of thread of life), Lachesis (Determiner of length), and Atropos (Cutter of thread); also called Moirae. Identified by Romans with their goddesses of fate; Nona, Decuma, and Morta; called Parcae.
Clytemnestra: Wife of Agamemnon, whom she slew with aid of her paramour, Aegisthus; slain by her son Orestes.
Cocytus: One of several **Rivers of Underworld:** Acheron (woe), Cocytus (wailing), Lethe (forgetfulness), Phlegethon (fire), Styx (across which souls of dead were ferried by Charon).
Creon: Father of Jocasta; forbade burial of Polynices; ordered burial alive of Antigone.
Creüsa: Princess of Corinth, for whom Jason deserted Medea; slain by Medea, who sent her poisoned robe; also known as Glaüke.
Creusa: Wife of Aeneas; died fleeing Troy.
Cronus (Saturn): Titan; god of harvests; son of Uranus and Gaea; dethroned by his son Zeus.
Cybele: Anatolian nature goddess; adopted by Greeks and identified with Rhea.
Cyclopes: Race of one-eyed giants (singular: Cyclops).
Daedalus: Athenian artificer; father of Icarus; builder of Labyrinth in Crete; devised wings attached with wax for him and Icarus to escape Crete.
Danae: Princess of Argos; mother of Perseus by Zeus, who appeared to her in form of golden shower.
Danaïdes: Daughters of Danaüs; at his command, all except Hypermnestra slew their husbands, the sons of Aegyptus.
Danaüs: Brother of Aegyptus; father of Danaïdes; slain by Lynceus.
Daphne: Nymph; pursued by Apollo; changed to laurel tree.
Decuma: One of several **Fates:** Goddesses of destiny; Clotho (Spinner of thread of life), Lachesis (Determiner of length), and Atropos (Cutter of thread); also called Moirae. Identified by Romans with their goddesses of fate; Nona, Decuma, and Morta; called Parcae.
Deino: One of several **Graeae:** Sentinels for Gorgons; Deino, Enyo, and Pephredo; had one eye among them, which passed from one to another.
Demeter (Ceres): Goddess of agriculture; mother of Persephone.
Dido: Founder and queen of Carthage; stabbed herself when deserted by Aeneas.
Diomedes: Greek hero; with Odysseus, entered Troy and carried off Palladium, sacred statue of Athena.
Diomedes: Owner of man-eating horses, which Hercules, as ninth labor, carried off.
Dione: Titan goddess; mother by Zeus of Aphrodite.
Dionysus (Bacchus): God of wine; son of Zeus and Semele.
Dioscuri: Twins Castor and Pollux; sons of Leda by Zeus.
Dryads: Wood nymphs.
Dryope: Maiden changed to Hamadryad.
Echo: Nymph who fell hopelessly in love with Narcissus; faded away except for her voice.
Electra: Daughter of Agamemnon and Clytemnestra; sister of Orestes; urged Orestes to slay Clytemnestra and Aegisthus.
Electra: One of several **Pleiades:** Alcyone, Celaeno, Electra, Maia, Merope, Sterope or Asterope, Taygeta; seven daughters of Atlas; transformed into heavenly constellation, of which six stars are visible (Merope is said to have hidden in shame for loving a mortal).
Elysium: Abode of blessed dead.
Endymion: Mortal loved by Selene.
Enyo: One of several **Graeae:** Sentinels for Gorgons; Deino, Enyo, and Pephredo; had one eye among them, which passed from one to another.
Eos (Aurora): Goddess of dawn.
Epimetheus: Brother of Prometheus; husband of Pandora.
Erato: One of several **Muses:** Goddesses presiding over arts and sciences: Calliope (epic poetry), Clio (history), Erato (lyric and love poetry), Euterpe (music), Melpomene (tragedy), Polymnia or Polyhymnia (sacred poetry), Terpsichore (choral dance and song), Thalia (comedy and bucolic poetry), Urania (astronomy); daughters of Zeus and Mnemosyne.
Erebus: Spirit of darkness; son of Chaos.
Erinyes: One of several **Furies:** Avenging spirits; Alecto, Megaera, and Tisiphone; known also as Erinyes or Eumenides.
Eris: Goddess of discord.
Eros (Amor or Cupid): God of love; son of Aphrodite.
Eteocles: Son of Oedipus, whom he succeeded to rule alternately with Polynices; refused to give up throne at end of year; he and Polynices slew each other.
Eumenides: One of several **Furies:** Avenging spirits; Alecto, Megaera, and Tisiphone; known also as Erinyes or Eumenides.
Euphrosyne: One of several **Graces:** Beautiful goddesses: Aglaia (Brilliance), Euphrosyne (Joy), and Thalia (Bloom); daughters of Zeus.
Europa: Mortal loved by Zeus, who, in form of white bull, carried her off to Crete.
Eurus: One of several **Winds:** Aeolus (keeper of winds), Boreas (Aquilo) (north wind), Eurus (east wind), Notus (Auster) (south wind), Zephyrus (Favonius) (west wind).
Euryale: One of several **Gorgons:** Female monsters; Euryale, Medusa, and Stheno; had snakes for hair; their glances turned mortals to stone.
Eurydice: Nymph; wife of Orpheus.
Eurystheus: King of Argos; imposed twelve labors on Hercules.
Euterpe: One of several **Muses:** Goddesses presiding over arts and sciences: Calliope (epic poetry), Clio (history), Erato (lyric and love poetry), Euterpe (music), Melpomene (tragedy), Polymnia or Polyhymnia (sacred poetry), Terpsichore (choral dance and song), Thalia (comedy and bucolic poetry), Urania (astronomy); daughters of Zeus and Mnemosyne.
Fates: Goddesses of destiny; Clotho (Spinner of thread of life), Lachesis (Determiner of length), and Atropos (Cutter of thread); also called Moirae. Identified by Romans with their goddesses of fate; Nona, Decuma, and Morta; called Parcae.
Fauns: Roman deities of woods and groves.
Favonius: One of several **Winds:** Aeolus (keeper of winds), Boreas (Aquilo) (north wind), Eurus (east wind), Notus (Auster) (south wind), Zephyrus (Favonius) (west wind).

Flora: Roman goddess of flowers.
Fortuna: Roman goddess of fortune.
Furies: Avenging spirits; Alecto, Megaera, and Tisiphone; known also as Erinyes or Eumenides.
Gaea: Goddess of earth; daughter of Chaos; mother of Titans; known also as Ge, Gea, Gaia, etc.
Galatea: Statue of maiden carved from ivory by Pygmalion; given life by Aphrodite.
Galatea: Sea nymph; loved by Polyphemus.
Ganymede: Beautiful boy; successor to Hebe as cupbearer of gods.
Glaucus: Mortal who became sea divinity by eating magic grass.
Golden Fleece: Fleece from ram that flew Phrixos to Colchis; Aeëtes placed it under guard of dragon; carried off by Jason.
Gorgons: Female monsters; Euryale, Medusa, and Stheno; had snakes for hair; their glances turned mortals to stone.
Graces: Beautiful goddesses: Aglaia (Brilliance), Euphrosyne (Joy), and Thalia (Bloom); daughters of Zeus.
Graeae: Sentinels for Gorgons; Deino, Enyo, and Pephredo; had one eye among them, which passed from one to another.
Hades (Dis): Name sometimes given Pluto; also, abode of dead, ruled by Pluto.
Haemon: Son of Creon; promised husband of Antigone; killed himself in her tomb.
Hamadryads: Tree nymphs.
Harpies: Monsters with heads of women and bodies of birds.
Hebe (Juventas): Goddess of youth; cupbearer of gods before Ganymede; daughter of Zeus and Hera.
Hecate: Goddess of sorcery and witchcraft.
Hector: Son of Priam; slayer of Patroclus; slain by Achilles.
Hecuba: Wife of Priam.
Helen: Fairest woman in world; daughter of Zeus and Leda; wife of Menelaus; carried to Troy by Paris, causing Trojan War.
Heliades: Daughters of Helios; mourned for Phaëthon and were changed to poplar trees.
Helios (Sol): God of sun; later identified with Apollo.
Helle: Sister of Phrixos; fell from ram of Golden Fleece; water where she fell named Hellespont.
Hephaestus (Vulcan): God of fire; celestial blacksmith; son of Zeus and Hera; husband of Aphrodite.
Hera (Juno): Queen of heaven; wife of Zeus.
Hercules: Hero and strong man; son of Zeus and Alcmene; performed twelve labors or deeds to be free from bondage under Eurystheus; after death, his mortal share was destroyed, and he became immortal. Also known as Herakles or Heracles. Labors: (1) killing Nemean lion; (2) killing Lernaean Hydra; (3) capturing Erymanthian boar; (4) capturing Cerynean hind; (5) killing man-eating Stymphalian birds; (6) procuring girdle of Hippolyte; (7) cleaning Augean stables; (8) capturing Cretan bull; (9) capturing man-eating horses of Diomedes; (10) capturing cattle of Geryon; (11) procuring golden apples of Hesperides; (12) bringing Cerberus up from Hades.
Hermes (Mercury): God of physicians and thieves; messenger of gods; son of Zeus and Maia.
Hero: Priestess of Aphrodite; Leander swam Hellespont nightly to see her; drowned herself at his death.
Hesperus: Evening star.
Hestia (Vesta): Goddess of hearth; sister of Zeus.
Hippolyte: Queen of Amazons; wife of Theseus.
Hippolytus: Son of Theseus and Hippolyte; falsely accused by Phaedra of trying to kidnap her; slain by Poseidon at request of Theseus.
Hippomenes: Husband of Atalanta, whom he beat in race by dropping golden apples, which she stopped to pick up.
Hyacinthus: Beautiful youth accidentally killed by Apollo, who caused flower to spring up from his blood.
Hydra: Nine-headed monster in marsh of Lerna; slain by Hercules.
Hygeia: Personification of health.
Hyman: God of marriage.
Hyperion: Titan; early sun god; father of Helios.
Hypermnestra: Daughter of Danaüs; refused to kill her husband Lynceus.
Hypnos (Somnus): God of sleep.
Iapetus: Titan; father of Atlas, Epimetheus, and Prometheus.
Icarus: Son of Daedalus; flew too near sun with wax-attached wings and fell into sea and was drowned.
Io: Mortal maiden loved by Zeus; changed by Hera into heifer.
Iobates: King of Lycia; sent Bellerophon to slay Chimera.
Iphigenia: Daughter of Agamemnon; offered as sacrifice to Artemis at Aulis; carried by Artemis to Tauris where she became priestess; escaped from there with Orestes.
Iris: Goddess of rainbow; messenger of Zeus and Hera.
Ismene: Daughter of Oedipus; sister of Antigone.
Iulus: Son of Aeneas.
Ixion: King of Lapithae; for making love to Hera he was bound to endlessly revolving wheel in Tartarus.
Janus: Roman god of gates and doors; represented with two opposite faces.
Jason: Son of Aeson; to gain throne of Ioclus from Pelias, went to Colchis and brought back Golden Fleece; married Medea; deserted her for Creüsa.
Jocasta: Wife of Laius; mother of Oedipus; unwittingly became wife of Oedipus; hanged herself when relationship was discovered.
Lachesis: One of several **Fates:** Goddesses of destiny; Clotho (Spinner of thread of life), Lachesis (Determiner of length), and Atropos (Cutter of thread); also called Moirae. Identified by Romans with their goddesses of fate; Nona, Decuma, and Morta; called Parcae.
Laius: Father of Oedipus, by whom he was slain.
Laocoön: Priest of Apollo at Troy; warned against bringing wooden horse into Troy; destroyed with his two sons by serpents sent by Athena.
Lares: Roman ancestral spirits protecting descendants and homes.
Lavinia: Wife of Aeneas after defeat of Turnus.
Leander: Swam Hellespont nightly to see Hero; drowned in storm.
Leda: Mortal loved by Zeus in form of Swan; mother of Helen, Clytemnestra, Dioscuri.
Lethe: One of several **Rivers of Underworld:** Acheron (woe), Cocytus (wailing), Lethe (forgetfulness), Phlegethon (fire), Styx (across which souls of dead were ferried by Charon).
Leto (Latona): Mother by Zeus of Artemis and Apollo.
Lucina: Roman goddess of childbirth; identified with Juno.
Lynceus: Son of Aegyptus; husband of Hypermnestra; slew Danaüs.
Maia: Daughter of Atlas; mother of Hermes.
Maia: One of several **Pleiades:** Alcyone, Celaeno, Electra, Maia, Merope, Sterope or Asterope, Taygeta; seven daughters of Atlas; transformed into heavenly constellation, of which six stars are visible (Merope is said to have hidden in shame for loving a mortal).
Manes: Souls of dead Romans, particularly of ancestors.
Marsyas: Shepherd; challenged Apollo to music contest and lost; flayed alive by Apollo.
Medea: Sorceress; daughter of Aeëtes; helped Jason obtain Golden Fleece; when deserted by him for Creüsa, killed her children and Creüsa.
Medusa: Gorgon; slain by Perseus, who cut off her head.
Megaera: One of several **Furies:** Avenging spirits; Alecto, Megaera, and Tisiphone; known also as Erinyes or Eumenides.
Meleager: Son of Althaea; his life would last as long as brand burning at his birth; Althaea quenched and saved it but destroyed it when Meleager slew his uncles.
Melpomene: One of several **Muses:** Goddesses presiding over arts and sciences: Calliope (epic poetry), Clio (history), Erato (lyric and love poetry), Euterpe (music), Melpomene (tragedy), Polymnia or Polyhymnia (sacred poetry), Terpsichore (choral dance and song), Thalia (comedy and bucolic poetry), Urania (astronomy); daughters of Zeus and Mnemosyne.
Memnon: Ethiopian king; made immortal by Zeus; son of Tithonus and Eos.
Menelaus: King of Sparta; son of Atreus; brother of Agamemnon; husband of Helen.
Merope: One of several **Pleiades:** Alcyone, Celaeno, Electra, Maia, Merope, Sterope or Asterope, Taygeta; seven daughters of Atlas; transformed into heavenly constellation, of which six stars are visible; said to have hidden in shame for loving a mortal.
Mezentius: Cruel Etruscan king; ally of Turnus against Aeneas; slain by Aeneas.
Midas: King of Phrygia; given gift of turning to gold all he touched.
Minos: King of Crete; after death, one of three judges of dead in Hades; son of Zeus and Europa.
Minotaur: Monster, half man and half beast, kept in Labyrinth in Crete; slain by Theseus.
Mnemosyne: Goddess of memory; mother by Zeus of Muses.
Moirae: One of several **Fates:** Goddesses of destiny; Clotho (Spinner of thread of life), Lachesis (Determiner of length), and Atropos (Cutter of thread); also called Moirae. Identified by Romans with their goddesses of fate; Nona, Decuma, and Morta; called Parcae.
Momus: God of ridicule.
Morpheus: God of dreams.

Morta: One of several **Fates:** Goddesses of destiny; Clotho (Spinner of thread of life), Lachesis (Determiner of length), and Atropos (Cutter of thread); also called Moirae. Identified by Romans with their goddesses of fate; Nona, Decuma, and Morta; called Parcae.

Muses: Goddesses presiding over arts and sciences: Calliope (epic poetry), Clio (history), Erato (lyric and love poetry), Euterpe (music), Melpomene (tragedy), Polymnia or Polyhymnia (sacred poetry), Terpsichore (choral dance and song), Thalia (comedy and bucolic poetry), Urania (astronomy); daughters of Zeus and Mnemosyne.

Naiads: Nymphs of waters, streams, and fountains.

Napaeae: Wood nymphs.

Narcissus: Beautiful youth loved by Echo; in punishment for not returning her love, he was made to fall in love with his image reflected in pool; pined away and became flower.

Nemesis: Goddess of retribution.

Neoptolemus: Son of Achilles; slew Priam; also known as Pyrrhus.

Nereids: Sea nymphs; attendants on Poseidon.

Nestor: King of Pylos; noted for wise counsel in expedition against Troy.

Nike: Goddess of victory.

Niobe: Daughter of Tantalus; wife of Amphion; her children slain by Apollo and Artemis; changed to stone but continued to weep her loss.

Nona: One of several **Fates:** Goddesses of destiny; Clotho (Spinner of thread of life), Lachesis (Determiner of length), and Atropos (Cutter of thread); also called Moirae. Identified by Romans with their goddesses of fate; Nona, Decuma, and Morta; called Parcae.

Notus: One of several **Winds:** Aeolus (keeper of winds), Boreas (Aquilo) (north wind), Eurus (east wind), Notus (Auster) (south wind), Zephyrus (Favonius) (west wind).

Nymphs: Beautiful maidens; inferior deities of nature.

Nyx (Nox): Goddess of night.

Oceanids: Ocean nymphs; daughters of Oceanus.

Oceanus: Eldest of Titans; god of waters.

Odysseus (Ulysses): King of Ithaca; husband of Penelope; wandered ten years after fall of Troy before arriving home.

Oedipus: King of Thebes; son of Laius and Jocasta; unwittingly murdered Laius and married Jocasta; tore his eyes out when relationship was discovered.

Oenone: Nymph of Mount Ida; wife of Paris, who abandoned her; refused to cure him when he was poisoned by arrow of Philoctetes at Troy.

Oreads: Mountain nymphs.

Orestes: Son of Agamemnon and Clytemnestra; brother of Electra; slew Clytemnestra and Aegisthus; pursued by Furies until his purification by Apollo.

Orion: Hunter; slain by Artemis and made heavenly constellation.

Orpheus: Famed musician; son of Apollo and Muse Calliope; husband of Eurydice.

Pales: Roman goddess of shepherds and herdsmen.

Palinurus: Aeneas' pilot; fell overboard in his sleep and was drowned.

Pan (Faunus): God of woods and fields; part goat; son of Hermes.

Pandora: Opener of box containing human ills; mortal wife of Epimetheus.

Parcae: One of several **Fates:** Goddesses of destiny; Clotho (Spinner of thread of life), Lachesis (Determiner of length), and Atropos (Cutter of thread); also called Moirae. Identified by Romans with their goddesses of fate; Nona, Decuma, and Morta; called Parcae.

Paris: Son of Priam; gave apple of discord to Aphrodite, for which she enabled him to carry off Helen; slew Achilles at Troy; slain by Philoctetes.

Patroclus: Great friend of Achilles; wore Achilles' armor and was slain by Hector.

Pegasus: Winged horse that sprang from Medusa's body at her death; ridden by Bellerophon when he slew Chimera.

Pelias: King of Ioclus; seized throne from his brother Aeson; sent Jason for Golden Fleece; slain unwittingly by his daughters at instigation of Medea.

Pelops: Son of Tantalus; his father cooked and served him to gods; restored to life; Peloponnesus named for him.

Penates: Roman household gods.

Penelope: Wife of Odysseus; waited faithfully for him for ten years while putting off numerous suitors.

Pephredo: One of several **Graeae:** Sentinels for Gorgons; Deino, Enyo, and Pephredo; had one eye among them, which passed from one to another.

Periphetes: Giant; son of Hephaestus; slain by Theseus.

Persephone (Proserpine): Queen of infernal regions; daughter of Zeus and Demeter; wife of Pluto.

Perseus: Son of Zeus and Danaë; slew Medusa; rescued Andromeda from monster and married her.

Phaedra: Daughter of Minos; wife of Theseus; caused the death of her stepson, Hippolytus.

Phaethon: Son of Helios; drove his father's sun chariot and was struck down by Zeus before he set world on fire.

Philoctetes: Greek warrior who possessed Hercules' bow and arrows; slew Paris at Troy with poisoned arrow.

Phineus: Betrothed of Andromeda; tried to slay Perseus but turned to stone by Medusa's head.

Phlegethon: One of several **Rivers of Underworld:** Acheron (woe), Cocytus (wailing), Lethe (forgetfulness), Phlegethon (fire), Styx (across which souls of dead were ferried by Charon).

Phosphor: Morning star.

Phrixos: Brother of Helle; carried by ram of Golden Fleece to Colchis.

Pirithous: Son of Ixion; friend of Theseus; tried to carry off Persephone from Hades; bound to enchanted rock by Pluto.

Pleiades: Alcyone, Celaeno, Electra, Maia, Merope, Sterope or Asterope, Taygeta; seven daughters of Atlas; transformed into heavenly constellation, of which six stars are visible (Merope is said to have hidden in shame for loving a mortal).

Pluto (Dis): God of Hades; brother of Zeus.

Plutus: God of wealth.

Pollux: One of **Dioscuri:** Twins Castor and Pollux; sons of Leda by Zeus.

Polymnia: One of several **Muses:** Goddesses presiding over arts and sciences: Calliope (epic poetry), Clio (history), Erato (lyric and love poetry), Euterpe (music), Melpomene (tragedy), Polymnia or Polyhymnia (sacred poetry), Terpsichore (choral dance and song), Thalia (comedy and bucolic poetry), Urania (astronomy); daughters of Zeus and Mnemosyne.

Polynices: Son of Oedipus; he and his brother Eteocles killed each other; burial rite, forbidden by Creon, performed by his sister Antigone.

Polyphemus: Cyclops; devoured six of Odysseus's men; blinded by Odysseus.

Polyxena: Daughter of Priam; betrothed to Achilles, whom Paris slew at their betrothal; sacrificed to shade of Achilles.

Pomona: Roman goddess of fruits.

Pontus: Sea god; son of Gaea.

Poseidon (Neptune): God of sea; brother of Zeus.

Priam: King of Troy; husband of Hecuba; ransomed Hector's body from Achilles; slain by Neoptolemus.

Priapus: God of regeneration.

Procris: Wife of Cephalus, who accidentally slew her.

Procrustes: Giant; stretched or cut off legs of victims to make them fit iron bed; slain by Theseus.

Proetus: Husband of Anteia; sent Bellerophon to Iobates to be put to death.

Prometheus: Titan; stole fire from heaven for man. Zeus punished him by chaining him to rock in Caucasus where vultures devoured his liver daily.

Proteus: Sea god; assumed various shapes when called on to prophesy.

Psyche: Beloved of Eros; punished by jealous Aphrodite; made immortal and united with Eros.

Pygmalion: King of Cyprus; carved ivory statue of maiden which Aphrodite gave life as Galatea.

Pyramus: Babylonian youth; made love to Thisbe through hole in wall; thinking Thisbe slain by lion, killed himself.

Python: Serpent born from slime left by Deluge; slain by Apollo.

Quirinus: Roman war god.

Remus: Brother of Romulus; slain by him.

Rhadamanthus: One of three judges of dead in Hades; son of Zeus and Europa.

Rhea (Ops): Daughter of Uranus and Gaea; wife of Cronus; mother of Zeus; identified with Cybele.

Rivers of Underworld: Acheron (woe), Cocytus (wailing), Lethe (forgetfulness), Phlegethon (fire), Styx (across which souls of dead were ferried by Charon).

Romulus: Founder of Rome; he and Remus suckled in infancy by she-wolf; slew Remus; deified by Romans.

Sarpedon: King of Lycia; son of Zeus and Europa; slain by Patroclus at Troy.

Satyrs: Hoofed demigods of woods and fields; companions of Dionysus.

Sciron: Robber; forced strangers to wash his feet, then hurled them into sea where tortoise devoured them; slain by Theseus.

Scylla: Female monster inhabiting rock opposite Charybdis; menaced passing sailors.

Selene: Goddess of moon.

Semele: Daughter of Cadmus; mother by Zeus of Dionysus; demanded Zeus appear before her in all his splendor and was destroyed by his lightnings.
Sibyis: Various prophetesses; most famous, Cumaean sibyl, accompanied Aeneas into Hades.
Sileni: Minor woodland deities similar to satyrs (singular: silenus). Sometimes Silenus refers to eldest of satyrs, son of Hermes or of Pan.
Silvanus: Roman god of woods and fields.
Sinis: Giant; bent pines, by which he hurled victims against side of mountain; slain by Theseus.
Sirens: Minor deities who lured sailors to destruction with their singing.
Sisyphus: King of Corinth; condemned in Tartarus to roll huge stone to top of hill; it always rolled back down again.
Sphinx: Monster of Thebes; killed those who could not answer her riddle; slain by Oedipus. Name also refers to other monsters having body of lion, wings, and head and bust of woman.
Sterope: One of several **Pleiades:** Alcyone, Celaeno, Electra, Maia, Merope, Sterope or Asterope, Taygeta; seven daughters of Atlas; transformed into heavenly constellation, of which six stars are visible (Merope is said to have hidden in shame for loving a mortal).
Stheno: One of several **Gorgons:** Female monsters; Euryale, Medusa, and Stheno; had snakes for hair; their glances turned mortals to stone.
Styx: One of several **Rivers of Underworld:** Acheron (woe), Cocytus (wailing), Lethe (forgetfulness), Phlegethon (fire), Styx (across which souls of dead were ferried by Charon).
Symplegades: Clashing rocks at entrance to Black Sea; Argo passed through, causing them to become forever fixed.
Syrinx: Nymph pursued by Pan; changed to reeds, from which he made his pipes.
Tantalus: Cruel king; father of Pelops and Niobe; condemned in Tartarus to stand chin-deep in lake surrounded by fruit branches; as he tried to eat or drink, water or fruit always receded.
Tartarus: Underworld below Hades; often refers to Hades.
Taygeta: One of several **Pleiades:** Alcyone, Celaeno, Electra, Maia, Merope, Sterope or Asterope, Taygeta; seven daughters of Atlas; transformed into heavenly constellation, of which six stars are visible (Merope is said to have hidden in shame for loving a mortal).
Telemachus: Son of Odysseus; made unsuccessful journey to find his father.
Tellus: Roman goddess of earth.
Terminus: Roman god of boundaries and landmarks.
Terpsichore: One of several **Muses:** Goddesses presiding over arts and sciences: Calliope (epic poetry), Clio (history), Erato (lyric and love poetry), Euterpe (music), Melpomene (tragedy), Polymnia or Polyhymnia (sacred poetry), Terpsichore (choral dance and song), Thalia (comedy and bucolic poetry), Urania (astronomy); daughters of Zeus and Mnemosyne.
Terra: Roman earth goddess.
Thalia: One of several **Graces:** Beautiful goddesses: Aglaia (Brilliance), Euphrosyne (Joy), and Thalia (Bloom); daughters of Zeus. Also one of several **Muses:** Goddesses presiding over arts and sciences: Calliope (epic poetry), Clio (history), Erato (lyric and love poetry), Euterpe (music), Melpomene (tragedy), Polymnia or Polyhymnia (sacred poetry), Terpsichore (choral dance and song), Thalia (comedy and bucolic poetry), Urania (astronomy); daughters of Zeus and Mnemosyne.
Thanatos (Mors): God of death.
Themis: Titan goddess of laws of physical phenomena; daughter of Uranus; mother of Prometheus.
Theseus: Son of Aegeus; slew Minotaur; married and deserted Ariadne; later married Phaedra.
Thisbe: Beloved of Pyramus; killed herself at his death.
Thyestes: Brother of Atreus; Atreus killed three of his sons and served them to him at banquet.
Tiresias: Blind soothsayer of Thebes.
Tisiphone: One of several **Furies:** Avenging spirits; Alecto, Megaera, and Tisiphone; known also as Erinyes or Eumenides.
Titans: Early gods from which Olympian gods were derived; children of Uranus and Gaea.
Tithonus: Mortal loved by Eos; changed into grasshopper.
Triton: Demigod of sea; son of Poseidon.
Turnus: King of Rutuli in Italy; betrothed to Lavinia; slain by Aeneas.
Urania: One of several **Muses:** Goddesses presiding over arts and sciences: Calliope (epic poetry), Clio (history), Erato (lyric and love poetry), Euterpe (music), Melpomene (tragedy), Polymnia or Polyhymnia (sacred poetry), Terpsichore (choral dance and song), Thalia (comedy and bucolic poetry), Urania (astronomy); daughters of Zeus and Mnemosyne.
Uranus: Personification of Heaven; husband of Gaea; father of Titans; dethroned by his son Cronus.
Vertumnus: Roman god of fruits and vegetables; husband of Pomona.
Winds: Aeolus (keeper of winds), Boreas (Aquilo) (north wind), Eurus (east wind), Notus (Auster) (south wind), Zephyrus (Favonius) (west wind).
Zephyrus: One of several **Winds:** Aeolus (keeper of winds), Boreas (Aquilo) (north wind), Eurus (east wind), Notus (Auster) (south wind), Zephyrus (Favonius) (west wind).
Zeus (Jupiter): Chief of Olympian gods; son of Cronus and Rhea; husband of Hera.

Norse Mythology

Aesir: Chief gods of Asgard.
Andvari: Dwarf; robbed of gold and magic ring by Loki.
Angerbotha (Angrbotha): Giantess; mother by Loki of Fenrir, Hel, and Midgard serpent.
Asgard (Asgarth): Abode of gods.
Ask (Aske, Askr): First man; created by Odin, Hoenir, and Lothur.
Asynjur: Goddesses of Asgard.
Atli: Second husband of Gudrun; invited Gunnar and Hogni to his court, where they were slain; slain by Gudrun.
Audhumia (Audhumbla): Cow that nourished Ymir; created Buri by licking ice cliff.
Balder (Baldr, Baldur): God of light, spring, peace, joy; son of Odin; slain by Hoth at instigation of Loki.
Bifrost: Rainbow bridge connecting Midgard and Asgard.
Bragi (Brage): God of poetry; husband of Ithunn.
Branstock: Great oak in hall of Volsungs; into it, Odin thrust Gram, which only Sigmund could draw forth.
Brynhild: Valkyrie; wakened from magic sleep by Sigurd; married Gunnar; instigated death of Sigurd; killed herself and was burned on pyre beside Sigurd.
Bur (Bor): Son of Buri; father of Odin, Hoenir, and Lothur.
Buri (Bori): Progenitor of gods; father of Bur; created by Audhumla.
Embla: First woman; created by Odin, Hoenir, and Lothur.
Fafnir: Son of Rodmar, whom he slew for gold in Otter's skin; in form of dragon, guarded gold; slain by Sigurd.
Fenrir: Wolf; offspring of Loki; swallows Odin at Ragnarok and is slain by Vitharr.
Forseti: Son of Balder.
Frey (Freyr): God of fertility and crops; son of Njorth; originally one of Vanir.
Freya (Freyja): Goddess of love and beauty; sister of Frey; originally one of Vanir.
Frigg (Frigga): Goddess of sky; wife of Odin.
Garm: Watchdog of Hel; slays, and is slain by, Tyr at Ragnarok.
Gimle: Home of blessed after Ragnarok.
Giuki: King of Nibelungs; father of Gunnar, Hogni, Guttorm, and Gudrun.
Glathsehim (Gladsheim): Hall of gods in Asgard.
Gram (meaning "Angry"): Sigmund's sword; rewelded by Regin; used by Sigurd to slay Fafnir.
Greyfell: Sigmund's horse; descended from Sleipnir.
Grimhild: Mother of Gudrun; administered magic potion to Sigurd which made him forget Brynhild.
Gudrun: Daughter of Giuki; wife of Sigurd; later wife of Atli and Jonakr.
Gunnar: Son of Giuki; in his semblance Sigurd won Brynhild for him; slain at hall of Atli.
Guttorm: Son of Giuki; slew Sigurd at Brynhild's request.
Heimdall (Heimdallr): Guardian of Asgard.
Hel: Goddess of dead and queen of underworld; daughter of Loki.
Hiordis: Wife of Sigmund; mother of Sigurd.
Hoenir: One of creators of Ask and Embla; son of Bur.
Hogni: Son of Giuki; slain at hall of Atli.
Hoth (Hoder, Hodur): Blind god of night and darkness; slayer of Balder at instigation of Loki.
Ithunn (Ithun, Iduna): Keeper of golden apples of youth; wife of Bragi.
Jonakr: Third husband of Gudrun.

Jormunrek: Slayer of Swanhild; slain by sons of Gudrun.
Jotunnheim (Jotunheim): Abode of giants.
Lif and Lifthrasir: First man and woman after Ragnarok.
Loki: God of evil and mischief; instigator of Balder's death.
Lothur (Lodur): One of creators of Ask and Embla.
Midgard (Midgarth): Abode of mankind; the earth.
Midgard Serpent: Sea monster; offspring of Loki; slays, and is slain by, Thor at Ragnarok.
Mimir: Giant; guardian of well in Jotunnheim at root of Yggdrasill; knower of past and future.
Mjollnir: Magic hammer of Thor.
Nagifar: Ship to be used by giants in attacking Asgard at Ragnarok; built from nails of dead men.
Nanna: Wife of Balder.
Nibelungs: Dwellers in northern kingdom ruled by Giuki.
Niflheim (Nifelheim): Outer region of cold and darkness; abode of Hel.
Njorth: Father of Frey and Freya; originally one of Vanir.
Norns: Demigoddesses of fate: Urth (Urdur) (past), Verthandi (Verdandi) (present), Skuld (future).
Odin (Othin): Head of Aesir; creator of world with Vili and Ve; equivalent to Woden (Wodan, Wotan) in Teutonic mythology.
Otter: Son of Rodmar; slain by Loki; his skin filled with gold hoard of Andvari to appease Rodmar.
Ragnarok: Final destruction of present world in battle between gods and giants; some minor gods will survive, and Lif and Lifthrasir will repeople world.
Regin: Blacksmith; son of Rodmar; foster-father of Sigurd.
Rerir: King of Huns; son of Sigi.
Rodmar: Father of Regin, Otter, and Fafnir; demanded Otter's skin be filled with gold; slain by Fafnir, who stole gold.
Sif: Wife of Thor.
Siggeir: King of Goths; husband of Signy; he and his sons slew Volsung and his sons, except Sigmund; slain by Sigmund and Sinflotli.
Sigi: King of Huns; son of Odin.
Sigmund: Son of Volsung; brother of Signy, who bore him Sinflotli; husband of Hiordis, who bore him Sigurd.
Signy: Daughter of Volsung; sister of Sigmund; wife of Siggeir; mother by Sigmund of Sinflotli.
Sigurd: Son of Sigmund and Hiordis; wakened Brynhild from magic sleep; married Gudrun; slain by Guttorm at instigation of Brynhild.
Sigyn: Wife of Loki.
Sinflotli: Son of Sigmund and Signy.
Skuld: One of several **Norns:** Demigoddesses of fate: Urth (Urdur) (Past), Verthandi (Verdandi) (Present), Skuld (Future).
Sleipnir (Sleipner): Eight-legged horse of Odin.
Surt (Surtr): Fire demon; slays Frey at Ragnarok.
Svartalfaheim: Abode of dwarfs.
Swanhild: Daughter of Sigurd and Gudrun; slain by Jormunrek.
Thor: God of thunder; oldest son of Odin; equivalent to Germanic deity Donar.
Tyr: God of war; son of Odin; equivalent to Tiu in Teutonic mythology.
Ull (Ullr): Son of Sif; stepson of Thor.
Urth: One of several **Norns:** Demigoddesses of fate: Urth (Urdur) (past), Verthandi (Verdandi) (present), Skuld (future).
Valhalla (Valhall): Great hall in Asgard where Odin received souls of heroes killed in battle.
Vali: Odin's son: Ragnarok survivor.
Valkyries: Virgins, messengers of Odin, who selected heroes to die in battle and took them to Valhalla; generally considered as nine in number.
Vanir: Early race of gods; three survivors, Njorth, Frey, and Freya, are associated with Aesir.
Ve: Brother of Odin; one of creators of world.
Verthandi: One of several **Norns:** Demigoddesses of fate: Urth (Urdur) (past), Verthandi (Verdandi) (present), Skuld (future).
Vili: Brother of Odin; one of creators of world.
Vingolf: Abode of goddesses in Asgard.
Vitharr (Vithar): Son of Odin; survivor of Ragnarok.
Volsung: Descendant of Odin, and father of Signy, Sigmund; his descendants were called Volsungs.
Yggdrasill: Giant ash tree springing from body of Ymir and supporting universe; its roots extended to Asgard, Jotunnheim, and Niffheim.
Ymir (Ymer): Primeval frost giant killed by Odin, Vili, and Ve; world created from his body; also, from his body sprang Yggdrasill.

Egyptian Mythology

Aaru: Abode of the blessed dead.
Amen (Amon, Ammdn): One of chief Theban deities; united with sun god under form of Amen-Ra.
Amenti: Region of dead where souls were judged by Osiris.
Anubis: Guide of souls to Amenti; son of Osiris; jackal-headed.
Apis: Sacred bull, an embodiment of Ptah; identified with Osiris as Osiris-Apis or Serapis.
Geb (Keb, Seb): Earth god; father of Osiris; represented with goose on head.
Hathor (Athor): Goddess of love and mirth; cow-headed.
Horus: God of day; son of Osiris and Isis; hawk-headed.
Isis: Goddess of motherhood and fertility; sister and wife of Osiris.
Khepera: God of morning sun.
Khnemu (Khnum, Chnuphis, Chnemu, Chnum): Ram-headed god.
Khonsu (Khensu, Khuns): Son of Amen and Mut.
Mentu (Ment): Solar deity, sometimes considered god of war; falcon-headed.
Min (Khem, Chem): Principle of physical life.
Mut (Maut): Wife of Amen.
Nephthys: Goddess of the dead; sister and wife of Set.
Nu: Chaos from which world was created, personified as a god.
Nut: Goddess of heavens; consort of Geb.
Osiris: God of underworld and judge of dead; son of Geb and Nut.
Ptah (Phtha): Chief deity of Memphis.
Ra: God of the Sun, the supreme god; son of Nut; Pharaohs claimed descent from him; represented as lion, cat, or falcon.
Serapis: God uniting attributes of Osiris and Apis.
Set (Seth): God of darkness or evil; brother and enemy of Osiris.
Shu: Solar deity; son of Ra and Hathor.
Tem (Atmu, Atum, Tum): Solar deity.
Thoth (Dhouti): God of wisdom and magic; scribe of gods; ibis-headed

American Crossword Puzzle Tournament

April 3–5, 1998, Stamford, Connecticut

The oldest and largest crossword puzzle tournament in the United States is directed by Will Shortz, the crossword puzzle editor of *The New York Times.* Competitors face eight puzzles and are scored on accuracy and speed.

1978 Nancy Schuster, Rego Park, N.Y.
1979 Miriam Raphael, Port Chester, N.Y.
1980 Daniel Pratt, Fort Meade, Md.
1981 Philip Cohen, Aliquippa, Pa.
1982 Stanley Newman, Brooklyn, N.Y.
1983 David Rosen, Buffalo, N.Y.
1984 John McNeill, Austin, Tex.
1985 David Rosen, Buffalo, N.Y.
1986 David Rosen, Buffalo, N.Y.
1987 David Rosen, New York, N.Y.
1988 Douglas Hoylman, Chevy Chase, Md.
1989 Jon Delfin, New York, N.Y.
1990 Jon Delfin, New York, N.Y.
1991 Jon Delfin, New York, N.Y.
1992 Douglas Hoylman, Chevy Chase, Md.
1993 Trip Payne, Atlanta, Ga.
1994 Douglas Hoylman, Chevy Chase, Md.
1995 Jon Delfin, New York, N.Y.
1996 Douglas Hoylman, Chevy Chase, Md.
1997 Douglas Hoylman, Chevy Chase, Md.
1998 Trip Payne, Atlanta, Ga.

A Concise Guide to Style

This section discusses and illustrates the basic conventions of American capitalization, punctuation, and italicization.

Capitalization

Capitalize the following:

1. The first word of a sentence: Some spiders are poisonous; others are not. Are you my new neighbor?
2. The first word of a direct quotation, except when the quotation is split: Joyce asked, "Do you think that the lecture was interesting?" "No," I responded, "it was very boring." Tom Paine said, "The sublime and the ridiculous are often so nearly related that it is difficult to class them separately."
3. The first word of each line in a poem in traditional verse: Half a league, half a league,/Half a league onward,/All in the valley of Death/Rode the six hundred.—Alfred, Lord Tennyson
4. The names of people, of organizations and their members, of councils and congresses, and of historical periods and events: Marie Curie, Benevolent and Protective Order of Elks, an Elk, Protestant Episcopal Church, an Episcopalian, the Democratic Party, a Democrat, the Nuclear Regulatory Commission, the U.S. Senate, the Middle Ages, World War I, the Battle of Britain.
5. The names of places and geographic divisions, districts, regions, and locales: Richmond, Vermont, Argentina, Seventh Avenue, London Bridge, Arctic Circle, Eastern Hemisphere, Continental Divide, Middle East, Far North, Gulf States, East Coast, the North, the South Shore.

   Do not capitalize words indicating compass points unless a specific region is referred to: Turn north onto Interstate 91.
6. The names of rivers, lakes, mountains, and oceans: Ohio River, Lake Como, Rocky Mountains, Atlantic Ocean.
7. The names of ships, aircraft, satellites, and space vehicles: U.S.S. *Arizona, Spirit of St. Louis,* the spy satellite Ferret-D, *Voyager II*, the space shuttle *Challenger*.
8. The names of nationalities, races, tribes, and languages: Spanish, Maori, Bantu, Russian.
9. Words derived from proper names, except in their extended senses: the Byzantine Empire. *But:* byzantine office politics.
10. Words indicating family relationships when used with a person's name as a title: Aunt Toni and Uncle Jack. *But:* my aunt and uncle, Toni and Jack Walker.
11. A title (i.e., civil, judicial, military, royal and noble, religious, and honorary) when preceding a name: Justice Marshall, General Jackson, Mayor Daley, Queen Victoria, Lord Mountbatten, Pope John Paul II, Professor Jacobson, Senator Byrd.
12. All references to the President and Vice President of the United States: The President has entered the hall. The Vice President presides over the Senate.
13. All key words in titles of literary, dramatic, artistic, and musical works: the novel *The Old Man and the Sea,* the short story "Notes from Underground," an article entitled "On Passive Verbs," James Dickey's poem "In the Tree House at Night," the play *Cat on a Hot Tin Roof,* Van Gogh's *Wheat Field and Cypress Trees,* Beethoven's *Emperor Concerto.*
14. *The* in the title of a newspaper if it is a part of the title: *The Wall Street Journal. But:* the New York *Daily News.*
15. The first word in the salutation and in the complimentary close of a letter: My dear Carol, Yours sincerely.
16. Epithets and substitutes for the names of people and places: Old Hickory, Old Blood and Guts, The Oval Office, the Windy City.
17. Words used in personifications: When is not Death at watch/Within those secret waters?/ What wants he but to catch/Earth's heedless sons and daughters?—Edmund Blunden
18. The pronoun *I:* I told them that I had heard the news.
19. Names for the Deity and sacred works: God, the Almighty, Jesus, Allah, the Supreme Being, the Bible, the Qu'ran, the Talmud.
20. Days of the week, months of the year, holidays, and holy days: Tuesday, May, Independence Day, Passover, Ramadan, Christmas.
21. The names of specific courts: The Supreme Court of the United States, the Massachusetts Appeals Court, the United States Court of Appeals for the First Circuit.
22. The names of treaties, accords, pacts, laws, and specific amendments: Panama Canal Treaty, Treaty of Paris, Geneva Accords, Warsaw Pact countries, Sherman Antitrust Law, Labor Management Relations Act, took the Fifth Amendment.
23. Registered trademarks and service marks: Day-Glo®, Comsat®.
24. The names of geologic eras, periods, epochs, and strata and the names of prehistoric divisions: Paleozoic Era, Precambrian, Pleistocene, Age of Reptiles, Bronze Age, Stone Age.
25. The names of constellations, planets, and stars: Milky Way, Southern Crown, Saturn, Jupiter, Uranus, Polaris.
26. Genus but not species names in binomial nomenclature: *Rana pipiens.*

27. New Latin names of classes, families, and all groups higher than genera in botanical and zoological nomenclature: Nematoda.
    But do not capitalize derivatives from such names: nematodes.
28. Many abbreviations and acronyms: Dec., Tues., Lt. Gen., M.F.A., UNESCO, MIRV.

Italicization

Use italics to:

1. Indicate titles of books, plays, and epic poems: *War and Peace, The Importance of Being Earnest, Paradise Lost.*
2. Indicate titles of magazines and newspapers: *New York* magazine, *The Wall Street Journal,* the New York *Daily News.*
3. Set off the titles of motion pictures and radio and television programs: *Star Wars, All Things Considered, Masterpiece Theater.*
4. Indicate titles of major musical compositions: Handel's *Messiah,* Adam's *Giselle.*
5. Set off the names of paintings and sculpture: *Mona Lisa, Pietà.*
6. Indicate words, letters, or numbers that are referred to: The word *hiss* is onomatopoeic. *Can't* means *won't* in your lexicon. You form your *n*'s like *u*'s. A *6* looks like an inverted *9.*
7. Indicate foreign words and phrases not yet assimilated into English: *C'est la vie* was the response to my complaint.
8. Indicate the names of plaintiff and defendant in legal citations: *Roe* v. *Doe.*
9. Emphasize a word or phrase: When you appear on the national news, you are *somebody.* Use this device sparingly.
10. Distinguish New Latin names of genera, species, subspecies, and varieties in botanical and zoological nomenclature: *Homo sapiens.*
11. Set off the names of ships and aircraft: U.S.S. *Arizona, Spirit of St. Louis.*

Punctuation

Apostrophe

1. Indicates the possessive case of singular and plural nouns, indefinite pronouns, and surnames combined with designations such as *Jr., Sr.,* and *II:* my sister's husband, my three sisters' husbands, anyone's guess, They answer each other's phones, John Smith, Jr.'s car.
2. Indicates joint possession when used with the last of two or more nouns in a series: Doe and Roe's report.
3. Indicates individual possession or authorship when used with each of two or more nouns in a series: Smith's, Roe's, and Doe's reports.
4. Indicates the plurals of words, letters, and figures used as such: 60's and 70's; *x*'s, *y*'s, and *z*'s.
5. Indicates omission of letters in contractions: aren't, that's, o'clock.
6. Indicates omission of figures in dates: the class of '63.

Brackets

1. Enclose words or passages in quoted matter to indicate insertion of material written by someone other than the author: A tough but nervous, tenacious but restless race [the Yankees]; materially ambitious, yet prone to introspection. . . . —Samuel Eliot Morison
2. Enclose material inserted within matter already in parentheses: (Vancouver [B.C.] January 1, 19—).

Colon

1. Introduces words, phrases, or clauses that explain, amplify, or summarize what has gone before: Suddenly I realized where we were: Rome.
   "There are two cardinal sins from which all the others spring: impatience and laziness." —Franz Kafka
2. Introduces a long quotation: In his original draft of the *Declaration of Independence,* Jefferson wrote: "We hold these truths to be sacred and undeniable; that all men are created equal and independent, that from that equal creation they derive rights inherent and inalienable. . . ."
3. Introduces a list: We need the following items: pens, paper, pencils, blotters, and erasers.
4. Separates chapter and verse numbers in Biblical references: James 1:4.
5. Separates city from publisher in footnotes and bibliographies: Chicago: Riverside Press, 1983.
6. Separates hour and minute(s) in time designations: 9:30 a.m., a 9:30 meeting.
7. Follows the salutation in a business letter: Sir or Madam:

Comma

1. Separates the clauses of a compound sentence connected by a coordinating conjunction: A difference exists between the musical works of Handel and Haydn, and it is a difference worth noting.
   The comma may be omitted in short compound sentences: I heard what you said and I am furious. I got out of the car and I walked and walked.
2. Separates *and* or *or* from the final item in a series of three or more (optional): Red, yellow, and blue may be mixed to produce all colors.
3. Separates two or more adjectives modifying the same noun if *and* could be used between them without altering the meaning: a solid, heavy gait. *But:* a polished mahogany dresser.
4. Sets off nonrestrictive clauses or phrases (i.e., those that if eliminated would not affect the meaning of the sentences): The burglar, who had entered through the patio, went straight to the silver chest.
   The comma should not be used when a clause is restrictive (i.e., essential to the meaning of the sentence): The burglar who had entered through the patio went straight to the silver chest; the other burglar searched for the wall safe.
5. Sets off words or phrases in apposition to a noun or noun phrase: Plato, the famous Greek philosopher, was a student of Socrates.
   The comma should not be used if such words or phrases precede the noun: The Greek philosopher Plato was a student of Socrates.
6. Sets off transitional words and short expressions that require a pause in reading or speaking: Unfortunately, my friend was not well traveled.

Did you, after all, find what you were looking for? I live with my family, of course.

7. Sets off words used to introduce a sentence: No, I haven't been to Paris. Well, what do you think we should do now?
8. Sets off a subordinate clause or a long phrase that precedes a principal clause: By the time we found the restaurant, we were starved. Of all the illustrations in the book, the most striking are those of the tapestries.
9. Sets off short quotations and sayings: The candidate said, "Actions speak louder than words." "Talking of axes," said the Duchess, "chop off her head."—Lewis Carroll
10. Indicates omission of a word or words: To err is human; to forgive, divine.
11. Sets off the year from the month in full dates: Nicholas II of Russia was shot on July 16, 1918.

    But note that when only the month and the year are used, no comma appears: Nicholas II of Russia was shot in July 1918.
12. Sets off city and state in geographic names: Atlanta, Georgia, is the transportation center of the South. 34 Beach Drive, Bedford, VA 24523.
13. Separates series of four or more figures into thousands, millions, etc.: 67,000; 200,000.
14. Sets off words used in direct address: "I tell you, folks, all politics is applesauce."—Will Rogers. Thank you for your expert assistance, Dolores.
15. Separates a tag question from the rest of a sentence: You forgot your keys again, didn't you?
16. Sets off sentence elements that could be misunderstood if the comma were not used: Some time after, the actual date for the project was set.
17. Follows the salutation in a personal letter and the complimentary close in a business or personal letter: Dear Jessica, Sincerely yours, Fred.
18. Sets off titles and degrees from surnames and from the rest of a sentence: Walter T. Prescott, Jr.; Gregory A. Rossi, S.J.; Susan P. Green, M.D., presented the case.

Dash

1. Indicates a sudden break or abrupt change in continuity: "If—if you'll just let me explain—" the student stammered. And the problem—if there really is one—can then be solved.
2. Sets apart an explanatory, a defining, or an emphatic phrase: Foods rich in protein—meat, fish, and eggs—should be eaten on a daily basis.

    More important than winning the election, is governing the nation. That is the test of a political party—the acid, final test.—Adlai E. Stevenson
3. Sets apart parenthetical matter: Wolsey, for all his faults—and he had many—was a great statesman, a man of natural dignity with a generous temperament. . . .—Jasper Ridley
4. Marks an unfinished sentence: "But if my bus is late—" he began.
5. Sets off a summarizing phrase or clause: The vital measure of a newspaper is not its size but its spirit—that is its responsibility to report the news fully, accurately, and fairly.—Arthur H. Sulzberger
6. Sets off the name of an author or source, as at the end of a quotation: A poet can survive everything but a misprint.—Oscar Wilde

Ellipses

1. Indicate, by three spaced points, omission of words or sentences within quoted matter: Equipped by education to rule in the nineteenth century, . . . he lived and reigned in Russia in the twentieth century.—Robert K. Massie
2. Indicate, by four spaced points, omission of words at the end of a sentence: The timidity of bureaucrats when it comes to dealing with . . . abuses is easy to explain. . . . —*New York*
3. Indicate, when extended the length of a line, omission of one or more lines of poetry:

    Roll on, thou deep and dark blue ocean—roll!
    . . . .
    Man marks the earth with ruin—his control
    Stops with the shore.—Lord Byron
4. Are sometimes used as a device, as for example, in advertising copy:

    To help you Move and Grow
    with the Rigors of
    Business in the 1980's . . .
    and Beyond.—*Journal of Business Strategy*

Exclamation Point

1. Terminates an emphatic or exclamatory sentence: Go home at once! You've got to be kidding!
2. Terminates an emphatic interjection: Encore!

Hyphen

1. Indicates that part of a word of more than one syllable has been carried over from one line to the next:

    During the revolution, the nation was beset with problems—looting, fighting, and famine.
2. Joins the elements of some compounds: great-grandparent, attorney-at-law, ne'er-do-well.
3. Joins the elements of compound modifiers preceding nouns: high-school students, a fire-and-brimstone lecture, a two-hour meeting.
4. Indicates that two or more compounds share a single base: four- and six-volume sets, eight- and nine-year olds.
5. Separates the prefix and root in some combinations; check a dictionary when in doubt about the spelling: anti-Nazi, re-elect, co-author, re-form/reform, re-cover/recover, re-creation/recreation.
6. Substitutes for the word *to* between typewritten inclusive words or figures: pp. 145–155, the Boston–New York air shuttle.
7. Punctuates written-out compound numbers from 21 through 99: forty-six years of age, a person who is forty-six, two hundred fifty-nine dollars.

Parentheses

1. Enclose material that is not essential to a sentence and that if not included would not alter its meaning: After a few minutes (some say less) the blaze was extinguished.

2. Often enclose letters or figures to indicate subdivisions of a series: A movement in sonata form consists of the following elements: (1) the exposition, (2) the development, and (3) the recapitulation.
3. Enclose figures following and confirming written-out numbers, especially in legal and business documents: The fee for my services will be two thousand dollars ($2,000.00).
4. Enclose an abbreviation for a term following the written-out term, when used for the first time in a text: The patient is suffering from acquired immune deficiency syndrome (AIDS).

Period

1. Terminates a complete declarative or mild imperative sentence: There could be no turning back as war's dark shadow settled irrevocably across the continent of Europe.—W. Bruce Lincoln. Return all the books when you can. Would you kindly affix your signature here.
2. Terminates sentence fragments: Gray clouds—and what looks like a veil of rain falling behind the East German headland. A pair of ducks. A tired or dying swan, head buried in its back feathers, sits on the sand a few feet from the water's edge.—Anthony Bailey
3. Follows some abbreviations: Dec., Rev., St., Blvd., pp., Co.

Question Mark

1. Punctuates a direct question: Have you seen the new play yet? Who goes there? *But:* I wonder who said "Nothing is easy in war." I asked if they planned to leave.
2. Indicates uncertainty: Ferdinand Magellan (1480?–1521), Plato (427?–347 B.C.E.).

Quotation Marks

1. Double quotation marks enclose direct quotations: "What was Paris like in the Twenties?" our daughter asked. "Ladies and Gentlemen," the Chief Usher said, "the President of the United States." Robert Louis Stevenson said that "it is better to be a fool than to be dead." When advised not to become a lawyer because the profession was already overcrowded, Daniel Webster replied, "There is always room at the top."
2. Double quotation marks enclose words or phrases to clarify their meaning or use or to indicate that they are being used in a special way: This was the border of what we often call "the West" or "the Free World." "The Windy City" is a name for Chicago.
3. Double quotation marks set off the translation of a foreign word or phrase: *die Grenze,* "the border."
4. Double quotation marks set off the titles of series of books, of articles or chapters in publications, of essays, of short stories and poems, of individual radio and television programs, and of songs and short musical pieces: "The Horizon Concise History" series; an article entitled "On Reflexive Verbs in English"; Chapter Nine, "The Prince and the Peasant"; Pushkin's "The Queen of Spades"; Tennyson's "Ode on the Death of the Duke of Wellington"; "The Bob Hope Special"; Schubert's "Death and the Maiden."
5. Single quotation marks enclose quotations within quotations: The blurb for the piece proclaimed, "Two years ago at Geneva, South Vietnam was virtually sold down the river to the Communists. Today the spunky little . . . country is back on its own feet, thanks to 'a mandarin in a sharkskin suit who's upsetting the Red timetable.'"—Frances FitzGerald

Put commas and periods inside quotation marks; put semicolons and colons outside. Other punctuation, such as exclamation points and question marks, should be put inside the closing quotation marks only if part of the matter quoted.

Semicolon

1. Separates the clauses of a compound sentence having no coordinating conjunction: Do not let us speak of darker days; let us rather speak of sterner days.—Winston Churchill
2. Separates the clauses of a compound sentence in which the clauses contain internal punctuation, even when the clauses are joined by conjunctions: Skis in hand, we trudged to the lodge, stowed our lunches, and donned our boots; and the rest of our party waited for us at the lifts.
3. Separates elements of a series in which items already contain commas: Among those at the diplomatic reception were the Secretary of State; the daughter of the Ambassador to the Court of St. James's, formerly of London; and two United Nations delegates.
4. Separates clauses of a compound sentence joined by a conjunctive adverb, such as *however, nonetheless,* or *hence:* We insisted upon a hearing; however, the Grievance Committee refused.
5. May be used instead of a comma to signal longer pauses for dramatic effect: But I want you to know that when I cross the river my last conscious thought will be of the Corps; and the Corps; and the Corps.—General Douglas MacArthur

Virgule

1. Separates successive divisions in an extended date: fiscal year 1998/99.
2. Represents *per:* 35 km/hr, 1,800 ft./sec.
3. Means *or* between the words *and* and *or:* Take water skis and/or fishing equipment when you visit the beach this summer.
4. Separates two or more lines of poetry that are quoted and run in on successive lines of a text: The student actress had a memory lapse when she came to the lines "Double, double, toil and trouble/Fire burn and cauldron bubble/Eye of newt and toe of frog/Wool of bat and tongue of dog" and had to leave the stage in embarrassment.

Forms of Address

Source: Webster's II New Riverside University Dictionary. © 1984 by Houghton Mifflin Company.

Academics

Dean, college or university. *Address:* Dean ________. *Salutation:* Dear Dean________

President. *Address:* President ________ ________. *Salutation:* Dear President ________.

Professor, college or university. *Address:* Professor ________ ________. *Salutation:* Dear Professor ________.

Clerical and Religious Orders

Abbot. *Address:* The Right Reverend ________ ________, O.S.B. Abbot of ________. *Salutation:* Right Reverend Abbot or Dear Father Abbot.

Archbishop, Eastern Orthodox. *Address:* The Most Reverend Joseph, Archbishop of ________. *Salutation:* Your Eminence.

Archbishop, Roman Catholic. *Address:* The Most Reverend ________ ________, Archbishop of ________. *Salutation:* Your Excellency.

Archdeacon, Episcopal. *Address:* The Venerable ________ ________, Archdeacon of ________. *Salutation:* Venerable Sir or Dear Archdeacon ________.

Bishop, Episcopal. *Address:* The Right Reverend ________ ________, Bishop of ________. *Salutation:* Right Reverend Sir or Dear Bishop ________.

Bishop, other Protestant. *Address:* The Reverend ________ ________. *Salutation:* Dear Bishop ________.

Bishop, Roman Catholic. *Address:* The Most Reverend ________ ________, Bishop of ________. *Salutation:* Your Excellency or Dear Bishop ________.

Brotherhood, Roman Catholic. *Address:* Brother ________ ________, C.F.C. *Salutation:* Dear Brother or Dear Brother Joseph.

Brotherhood, superior of. *Address:* Brother Joseph C.F.C. Superior. *Salutation:* Dear Brother Joseph.

Cardinal. *Address:* His Eminence Joseph Cardinal Stone. *Salutation:* Your Eminence.

Clergyman/woman, Protestant. *Address:* The Reverend ________ ________ or The Reverend ________ ________, D.D. *Salutation:* Dear Mr./Ms. ________ or Dear Dr. ________.

Dean of a cathedral, Episcopal. *Address:* The Very Reverend ________ ________, Dean of ________. *Salutation:* Dear Dean ________.

Monsignor. *Address:* The Right Reverend Monsignor ________ ________. *Salutation:* Dear Monsignor.

Patriarch, Greek Orthodox. *Address:* His All Holiness Patriarch Joseph. *Salutation:* Your All Holiness.

Patriarch, Russian Orthodox. *Address:* His Holiness the Patriarch of ________. *Salutation:* Your Holiness.

Pope. *Address:* His Holiness The Pope. *Salutation:* Your Holiness or Most Holy Father.

Priest, Roman Catholic. *Address:* The Reverend ________ ________, S.J. *Salutation:* Dear Reverend Father or Dear Father.

Rabbi, man or woman. *Address:* Rabbi ________ ________ or ________ ________, D.D. *Salutation:* Dear Rabbi ________ or Dear Dr. ________.

Sisterhood, Roman Catholic. *Address:* Sister ________ ________, C.S.J. *Salutation:* Dear Sister or Dear Sister ________.

Sisterhood, superior of. *Address:* The Reverend Mother Superior, S.C. *Salutation:* Reverend Mother.

Diplomats

Ambassador, U.S. *Address:* The Honorable ________ ________ The Ambassador of the United States. *Salutation:* Sir/Madam or Dear Mr./Madam Ambassador.

Ambassador to the U.S. *Address:* His/Her Excellency ________ ________, The Ambassador of ________. *Salutation:* Excellency or Dear Mr./Madam Ambassador.

Chargé d'Affaires, U.S. *Address:* The Honorable ________ ________, United States Chargé d'Affaires. *Salutation:* Dear Mr./Ms. ________.

Consul, U.S. *Address:* ________ ________, Esq., United States Consul. *Salutation:* Dear Mr./Ms. ________.

Minister, U.S. or to U.S. *Address:* The Honorable ________ ________, The Minister of ________. *Salutation:* Sir/Madam or Dear Mr./Madame Minister.

Secretary General, United Nations. *Address:* His/Her Excellency ________ ________, Secretary General of the United Nations. *Salutation:* Dear Mr./Madam/Madame Secretary General.

United Nations Representative (Foreign). *Address:* His/Her Excellency ________ ________, Representative of ________ to the United Nations. *Salutation:* Excellency or My dear Mr./Madame ________.

United Nations Representative (U.S.) *Address:* The Honorable ________ ________, United States Representative to the United Nations. *Salutation:* Sir/Madam or Dear Mr./Ms. ________.

Government Officials

Assemblyman. *Address:* The Honorable ________ ________. *Salutation:* Dear Mr./Ms. ________.

Associate Justice, U.S. Supreme Court. *Address:* Mr./Madam Justice ________ ________. *Salutation:* Dear Mr./Madam Justice or Sir/Madam.

Attorney General, U.S. *Address:* The Honorable ________ ________, Attorney General of the United States. *Salutation:* Dear Mr./Madam or Attorney General.

Cabinet member. *Address:* The Honorable ________ ________, Secretary of ________. *Salutation:* Sir/Madam or Dear Mr./Madam Secretary.

Chief Justice, U.S. Supreme Court. *Address:* The Chief Justice of the United States. *Salutation:* Dear Mr./Madame Chief Justice.

Commissioner (federal, state, local). *Address:* The Honorable ________ ________. *Salutation:* Dear Mr./Ms. ________.

Governor. *Address:* The Honorable ________ ________, Governor of ________. *Salutation:* Dear Governor ________.

Judge, federal. *Address:* The Honorable ________ ________, Judge of the United States District Court for the ________, District of ________. *Salutation:* Sir/Madam or Dear Judge ________.

Judge, state or local. *Address:* The Honorable ________ ________, Judge of the Court of ________. *Salutation:* Dear Judge ________.

Lieutenant Governor. *Address:* The Honorable ________ ________, Lieutenant Governor of ________. *Salutation:* Dear Mr./Ms. ________.

Mayor. *Address:* The Honorable ________ ________, Mayor of ________. *Salutation:* Dear Mayor ________.

President, U.S. *Address:* The President. *Salutation:* Dear Mr./Madam President.

President, U.S., former. *Address:* The Honorable ________ ________. *Salutation:* Dear Mr./Madam ________.

Representative, state. *Address:* The Honorable ________ ________. *Salutation:* Dear Mr./Ms. ________.

Representative, U.S. *Address:* The Honorable ________ ________, United States House of Representatives. *Salutation:* Dear Mr./Ms. ________.

Senator, state. *Address:* The Honorable ________ ________. The State Senate, State Capitol. *Salutation:* Dear Senator ________.

Senator, U.S. *Address:* The Honorable ________ ________, United States Senate. *Salutation:* Dear Senator ________.

Speaker, U.S. House of Representatives. *Address:* The Honorable ________ ________, Speaker of the House of Representatives. *Salutation:* Dear Mr./Madam Speaker.

Vice President, U.S. *Address:* The Vice President of the United States. *Salutation:* Sir/Madam or Dear Mr./Madam Vice President.

Military and Naval Officers

Rank. *Address:* Full rank, USN (or USCG, USAF, USA, USMC). *Salutation:* Dear (full rank) ________.

Professions

Attorney. *Address:* Mr./Ms. ________ ________, Attorney at law or ________ ________, Esq. *Salutation:* Dear Mr./Ms. ________.

Dentist. *Address:* ________ ________, D.D.S. *Salutation:* Dear Dr. ________.

Physician. *Address:* ________ ________, M.D. *Salutation:* Dear Dr. ________.

Veterinarian. *Address:* ________ ________, D.V.M. *Salutation:* Dear Dr. ________.

Foreign Words and Phrases

The English meanings given below are not necessarily literal translations. Foreign words and phrases should be set in italics (or underlined if written in long-hand) if their meanings are likely to be unknown to the reader. Whether the expression is familiar or unfamiliar, however, is a matter of judgment. Below, all foreign words have been italicized for the sake of emphasis.

ad absurdum [Lat.]: to the point of absurdity. "He tediously repeated his argument *ad absurdum.*"

ad hominem [Lat.]: attacking an opponent's character rather than answering his argument. "As usual, any attempt on my part to discuss the matter rationally was met with an *ad hominem* attack on my perceived personality flaws."

ad infinitum [Lat.]: to infinity. "The lecture seemed to drone on *ad infinitum.*"

ad nauseam [Lat.]: to a sickening degree. "The politician uttered one platitude after another *ad nauseam.*"

aficionado [Span.]: an ardent devotee. "I was surprised at what a baseball *aficionado* she had become."

annus mirabilis [Lat.]: wonderful year. "Last year was the *annus mirabilis* for my company."

au courant [Fr.]: up-to-date. "The shoes, the hair, the clothes—every last detail of her dress, in fact—was utterly *au courant.*"

beau geste [Fr.]: a fine or noble gesture, often futile. "My fellow writers supported me by writing letters of protest to the publisher, but their *beau geste* could not prevent the inevitable."

beau monde [Fr.]: high society. "Such elegant decor would impress even the *beau monde.*"

bête noire [Fr.]: something or someone particularly disliked. "Talk of the good old college days way back when had become his *bête noire,* and he began to avoid his school friends."

bona fide [Lat.]: in good faith; genuine. "For all her reticence and modesty, it was clear that she was a *bona fide* expert in her field."

bon mot [Fr.]: a witty remark or comment. "One *bon mot* after another flew out of his mouth, charming the audience."

bon vivant [Fr.]: a person who lives luxuriously and enjoys good food and drink. "It's true he's quite the *bon vivant,* but when he gets down to business he conducts himself like a Spartan."

carpe diem [Lat.]: seize the day. "So what if you have an 8:00 a.m. meeting tomorrow and a full day of appointments? *Carpe diem!*"

carte blanche [Fr.]: unrestricted power to act on one's own. "I may have *carte blanche* around the office, but at home I'm a slave to my family's demands."

caveat emptor [Lat.]: let the buyer beware. "Before you leap at that real estate deal, *caveat emptor!*"

comme ci comme ça [Fr.]: so-so. "The plans for the party strike me as *comme ci comme ça.*"

comme il faut [Fr.]: as it should be; fitting. "His end was truly *comme il faut.*"

coup de grâce [Fr.]: finishing blow. "After an already wildly successful day, the *coup de grâce* came when she won best all-around athlete."

cri de coeur [Fr.]: heartfelt appeal. "About to leave the podium, he made a final *cri de coeur* to his people to end the bloodshed."

de gustibus non est disputandum [Lat.]: there is no arguing in matters of taste. "Shaking his head at the tinsel-town ostentation of the casino, he mumbled, '*de gustibus non est disputandum.*'"

de rigueur [Fr.]: strictly required, as by etiquette, usage, or fashion. "Loudly proclaiming one's support for radical causes had become *de rigueur* among her crowd."

deus ex machina [Lat.]: a contrived device to resolve a situation. "Stretching plausibility, the movie concluded with a *deus ex machina* ending in which everyone was rescued at the last minute."

dolce vita [Ital.]: sweet life; the good life perceived as one of physical pleasure and self-indulgence. "My vacation this year is going to be two uninterrupted weeks of *dolce vita.*"

***Doppelgänger** [Ger.]: a ghostly double or counterpart of a living person. "I could not shake the sense that some shadowy *Doppelgänger** echoed my every move."

ecce homo [Lat.]: behold the man. "The painting depicted the common Renaissance theme, *ecce homo*—Christ wearing the crown of thorns."

éminence grise [Fr.]: gray eminence; power behind the throne. "All but the most unperceptive realized that the general was the *éminence grise* behind the puppet ruler."

enfant terrible [Fr.]: an incorrigible child; an outrageously outspoken or bold person. "Again he played the role of *enfant terrible,* jolting us with his blunt assessment; yet I was secretly thrilled that the truth had come out in such a flagrant manner."

entre nous [Fr.]: between ourselves; confidentially. "*Entre nous,* their marriage is on the rocks."

ex cathedra [Lat.]: with authority; used especially of those pronouncements of the pope that are considered infallible. "I resigned myself to obeying; my father's opinions were *ex cathedra* in our household."

ex post facto [Lat.]: retroactively. "I certainly hope that the change in policy will be honored *ex post facto.*"

fait accompli [Fr.]: an accomplished fact, presumably irreversible. "There's no use protesting—it's a *fait accompli.*"

faux pas [Fr.]: a social blunder. "Suddently, she realized she had unwittingly committed yet another *faux pas.*"

***Feinschmecker** [Ger.]: gourmet. "No, I don't think McDonald's will do; he's much too much of a *Feinschmecker.*"

flagrante delicto [Lat.]: in the act. "The detective realized that without hard evidence he had no case; he would have to catch the culprit *flagrante delicto.*"

glasnost [Rus.]: open and frank discussion: initiated by Mikhail Gorbachev in 1985 in the Soviet Union. "Once the old chairman retired, the spirit of *glasnost* pervaded the department."

hoi polloi [Gk.]: the common people. "Marie Antoinette recommended cake to the *hoi polloi.*"

in loco parentis [Lat.]: in the place of a parent. "Put those cigarettes away young man; while you're with me consider my word *in loco parentis.*"

in medias res [Lat.]: in the middle of things. "The story began *in medias res;* it was clear from the first lines that some kind of horrendous calamity had already befallen the characters."

in situ [Lat.]: situated in the original or natural position. "I prefer seeing statues *in situ* rather than in the confines of a museum."

in vino veritas [Lat.]: in wine there is truth. "By the end of drunken banquet, several of the guests had made a good deal of their private lives public, prompting the host to murmur to his wife, '*in vino veritas.*'"

ipso facto [Lat.]: by the fact itself. "An extremist, *ipso facto,* cannot become part of a coalition."

je ne sais quoi [Fr.]: I know not what; an elusive quality. "She couldn't explain it, but there was something *je ne sais quoi* about him that she found devastatingly attractive."

***Kinder, Kirche, Küche** [Ger.]: children, church, kitchen. "She realized that her entire life had been devoted to *Kinder, Kirche, Küche.*"

mano a mano [Span.]: a direct confrontation or conflict. "'Stay out of it,' he admonished his friends, 'I want to handle this guy *mano a mano.*'"

mea culpa [Lat.]: I am to blame. "His *mea culpa* was so offhand that I hardly think he meant it."

memento mori [Lat.]: a reminder that you must die. "The skull rested on the mantlepiece as a *memento mori.*"

modus operandi [Lat.]: a method of operating. "Her *modus operandi* is to sugar-coat the truth so thoroughly that the news almost seems welcome."

mot juste [Fr.]: the exact, appropriate word. "'Rats!' screamed the defiant three-year-old, immensely proud of his *mot juste.*"

ne plus ultra [Fr.]: the most intense degree of a quality or state. "Pulling it from the box, he realized he was face to face with the *ne plus ultra* of computers."

nom de guerre [Fr.]: pseudonym. "He went by his *nom de guerre* when frequenting trendy nightclubs."

nom de plume [Fr.]: pen name. "Deciding it was time to sit down and write a novel, the would-be writer spent the first several hours deciding upon a suitably dashing *nom de plume.*"

nota bene [Ital.]: note well; take notice. "She appended her suggestions to the manuscript, underlining the words *nota bene* for added emphasis."

persona non grata [Lat.]: unacceptable or unwelcome person. "Once I was cut out of the will, I became *persona non grata* among my relatives."

pro bono [Lat.]: done or donated without charge; free. "The lawyer's *pro bono* work gave him a sense of value that his work on behalf of the corporation could not."

quid pro quo [Lat.]: something for something; an equal exchange. "She vowed that when she had the means, she would return his favors *quid pro quo.*"

sans souci [Fr.]: carefree. "Their mood was definitely *sans souci.*"

savoir faire [Fr.]: the ability to say and do the correct thing. "She presided over the gathering with impressive *savoir faire.*"

sic transit gloria mundi [Lat.]: thus passes away the glory of the world. "Watching the aging former football quarterback lumber down the street, potbellied and dissipated, his friend shook his head in disbelief and muttered, '*sic transit gloria mundi.*'"

sine qua non [Lat.]: indispensable. "Lemon is the *sine qua non* of this recipe."

terra incognita [Lat.]: unknown territory. "When the conversation suddenly switched from contemporary fiction to medieval Albanian playwrights, he felt himself entering *terra incognita.*"

tout le monde [Fr.]: everybody; everyone of importance. "Don't miss the event; it's bound to be attended by *tout le monde.*"

veni, vidi, vici [Lat.]: I came, I saw, I conquered. "After the takeover the business mogul gloated, '*veni, vidi, vici.*'"

verboten [Ger.]: forbidden, as by law; prohibited. "That topic, I am afraid, is *verboten* in this household."

vox populi [Lat.]: the voice of the people. "My sentiments echo those of the *vox populi.*"

***Wanderjahr** [Ger.]: a year or period of travel, especially following one's schooling. "The trio took off on their *Wanderjahr* soon after they graduated, planning to circle the globe by bicycle."

***Weltanschauung** [Ger.]: a comprehensive conception or image of the universe and of humanity's relation to it. "His *Weltanschauung* gradually metamorphized from a grim and pessimistic one to a sunny, but no less complex, view."

***Zeitgeist** [Ger.]: the spirit of the time; general trend of thought or feeling characteristic of a particular period of time. "She blamed it on the *Zeitgeist,* which encouraged hedonistic excess."

*German nouns are capitalized. A familiar German expression that is not italicized, however, should be lowercased, following the English conventions of not capitalizing common nouns. "His proclivities leaned more to the occult than to the philosophical: a poltergeist he could understand; the *Zeitgeist* he could not."

Easily Confused Words

allusion / illusion Allusion is a noun that means an indirect reference: "The speech made allusions to the final report." Illusion is a noun that means a misconception: "The policy is designed to give an illusion of reform."

alternately / alternatively Alternately is an adverb that means in turn; one after the other: "We alternately spun the wheel in the game." Alternatively is an adverb that means on the other hand; one or the other: "You can choose a large bookcase or, alternatively, you can buy two small ones."

beside / besides Beside is a preposition that means next to: "Stand here beside me. "Besides is an adverb that means also: "Besides, I need to tell you about the new products my company offers."

bimonthly / semimonthly Bimonthly is an adjective that means every two months: "I brought the cake for the bimonthly office party." Bimonthly is also a noun that means a publication issued every two months: "The bimonthly magazine will soon become a monthly publication." Semimonthly is an adjective that means happening twice a month: "We have semimonthly meetings on the 1st and the 15th."

cite / site Cite is a verb that means to quote as an authority or example: "I cited several eminent scholars in my study of water resources." It also means to recognize formally: "The public official was cited for service to the city." It can also mean to summon before a court of law: "Last year the company was cited for pollution violations." Site is a noun meaning location: "They chose a new site for the factory just outside town."

complement / compliment Complement is a noun or verb that means something that completes or makes up a whole: "The red sweater is a perfect complement to the outfit." Compliment is a noun or verb that means an expression of praise or admiration: "I received many compliments about my new outfit."

concurrent / consecutive Concurrent is an adjective that means simultaneous or happening at the same time as something else: "The concurrent strikes of several unions crippled the economy." Consecutive means successive or following one after the other: "The union called three consecutive strikes in one year."

connote / denote Connote is a verb that means to imply or suggest: "The word 'espionage' connotes mystery and intrigue." Denote is a verb that means to indicate or refer to specifically: "The symbol for 'pi' denotes the number 3.14159."

discreet / discrete Discreet is an adjective that means prudent, circumspect, or modest: "Their discreet comments about the negotiations led the reporters to expect an early settlement." Discrete is an adjective that means separate or individually distinct: "Each company in the conglomerate operates as a discrete entity."

disinterested / uninterested Disinterested is an adjective that means unbiased or impartial: "We appealed to the disinterested mediator to facilitate the negotiations." Uninterested is an adjective that means not interested or indifferent: "They seemed uninterested in our offer."

emigrant / immigrant / migrant Emigrant is a noun that means one who leaves one's native country to settle in another: "The emigrants spent four weeks aboard ship before landing in Los Angeles." Immigrant is a noun that means one who enters and settles in a new country: "Most of the immigrants easily found jobs." Migrant is a noun that means one who travels from one region to another, especially in search of work: "The migrants worked in the strawberry fields on the west coast, then traveled east to harvest wheat."

foreword / forward Foreword is a noun that means an introductory note or preface: "In my foreword I explained my reasons for writing the book." Forward is an adjective or adverb that means toward the front: "I sat in the forward section of the bus. Please step forward when your name is called." Forward is also a verb that means to send on: "Forward the letter to the customer's new address."

farther / further Farther is an adjective and adverb that means to or at a more distant point: "We drove 50 miles today; tomorrow, we will travel 100 miles farther." Further is an adjective and adverb that means to or at a greater extent or degree: "We won't be able to suggest a solution until we are further along in our evaluation of the problem." It can also mean in addition or moreover: "They stated further that they would not change the policy."

few / less Few is an adjective that means small in number. It is used with countable objects: "This department has few employees." Less is an adjective that means small in amount or degree. It is used with objects of indivisible mass: "Which jar holds less water?"

figuratively / literally Figuratively is an adverb that means metaphorically or symbolically: "Happening upon the shadowy figure, they figuratively jumped out of their shoes." Literally is an adverb that means word for word or according to the exact meaning of the words: "I translated the Latin passage literally."

hanged / hung Hanged is the past tense and past participle of hang when the meaning is to execute by suspending by the neck: "They hanged the prisoner for treason." "The convicted killer was hanged at dawn." Hung is the past tense and participle of hang when the meaning is to suspend from above with no support from below: "I hung the painting on the wall." "The painting was hung at a crooked angle."

it's / its It's is a contraction for it is, whereas its is the possessive form of it: "It's a shame that we cannot talk about its size."

laid / lain / lay Laid is the past tense and the past participle of the verb lay and not the past tense of lie. Lay is the past tense of the verb lie and lain is the past participle: "He laid his books down and lay down on the couch, where he has lain for an hour."

principal / principle Principal is a noun that means a person who holds a high position or plays an important role: "The school principal has 20 years of teaching experience. The principals in the negotiations will meet tomorrow at 10 o'clock." It also means a sum of money on which interest accrues: "The depositors were guaranteed they would not lose their principal." Principal is also an adjective that means chief or leading: "The necessity of moving to another city was the principal reason I turned down the job offer." Principle is a noun that means a rule or standard: "They refused to compromise their principles."

stationary / stationery Stationary is an adjective that means fixed or unmoving: "They maneuvered around the stationary barrier in the road." Stationery is a noun that means writing materials: "We printed the letters on company stationery."

American Sign Language and the Manual Alphabet

Sign language for the deaf was first systematized in France during the eighteenth century by Abbot Charles-Michel l'Epée. French Sign Language (FSL) was brought to the United States in 1816 by Thomas Gallaudet, founder of the American School for the Deaf in Hartford, Connecticut. He developed American Sign Language (ASL), a language of gestures and hand symbols that express words and concepts. It is the fourth most used language in the United States today.

Along with sign language and lip reading, many deaf people communicate with the manual alphabet, which uses finger positions that correspond to the letters of the alphabet to spell out words.

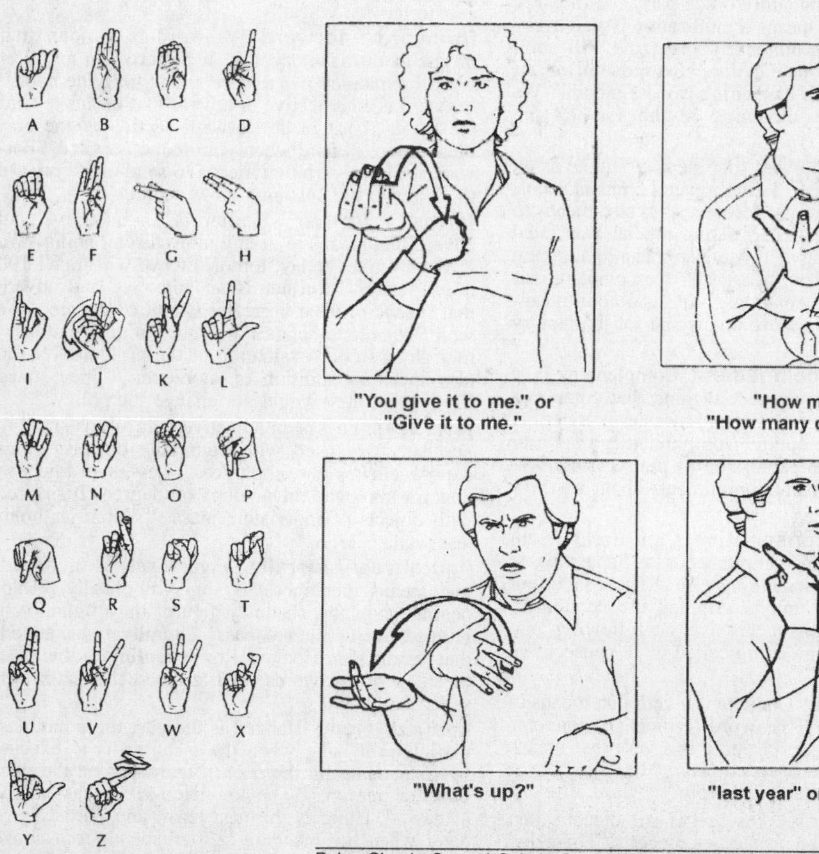

American Manual Alphabet

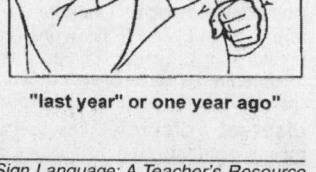

"You give it to me." or "Give it to me."

"How many?" or "How many do you want?"

"What's up?"

"last year" or one year ago"

Baker-Shenk, C., and Cokely, D., *American Sign Language: A Teacher's Resource Text on Grammar and Culture* (1980). Washington, D.C.: Gallaudet University Press.

PEOPLE

Many public figures not listed here may be found elsewhere in the almanac.

U.S. Presidents
U.S. Vice Presidents
Families of U.S. Presidents
U.S. Governors
U.S. Congress
U.S. Supreme Court Members
U.S. Government Officials
British Prime Ministers
Kings of England
Kings of France
Kings of Judah and Israel
Kings of Prussia
Kings of Russia
Sports Personalities

Names in parentheses indicate a person's original name or nickname. Locations in parentheses are the present-day name of the birthplace. Dates of birth appear as month/day/year. **Boldface** years in parentheses are dates of **(birth–death).**

Information has been gathered from many sources, including the individuals themselves. However, the almanac cannot guarantee the accuracy of every item.

A

Aalto, Alvar (architect); Kuortane, Finland **(1898–1976)**
Abbado, Claudio (orchestra conductor); Milan, Italy, 1933
Abbott, Bud (William Abbott) (comedian); Asbury Park, N.J. **(1898–1974)**
Abbott, George (stage producer); Forestville, N.Y. **(1887–1995)**
Abelard, Peter (theologian); nr. Nantes, France **(1079–1142)**
Abernathy, Ralph (civil rights leader); Linden, Ala. **(1926–1990)**
Abraham, F(ahrid) Murray (actor); Pittsburgh, 10/24/39
Achebe, Chinua (writer); Ogidi, Nigeria, 11/16/30
Acheson, Dean (statesman); Middletown, Conn. **(1893–1971)**
Acuff, Roy Claxton (musician); nr. Maynardsville, Tenn. **(1903–1992)**
Adams, Abigail (First Lady, writer); Weymouth, Mass. **(1744–1818)**
Adams, Charles Francis (diplomat); Boston **(1807–1886)**
Adams, Don (actor); New York City, 4/19/26
Adams, Edie (Edie Enke) (actress); Kingston, Pa., 4/16/29
Adams, Franklin Pierce (columnist, author); Chicago **(1881–1960)**
Adams, Gerry (political leader); West Belfast, Northern Ireland, 10/6/48
Adams, Henry Brooks (historian); Boston **(1838–1918)**
Adams, Joey (comedian); New York City, 1/6/11
Adams, John (2nd U.S. president); Braintree (Quincy), Mass. **(1735–1826)**
Adams, John Quincy (6th U.S. president); Braintree (Quincy), Mass. **(1767–1848)**
Adams, Maude (Maude Kiskadden) (actress); Salt Lake City **(1872–1953)**
Adams, Samuel (American Revolutionary patriot); Boston **(1722–1803)**
Adams, Scott (cartoonist); Catskill, N.Y., 6/8/57
Adamson, Joy (naturalist); Troppau, Silesia **(1910–1980)**
Addams, Charles (cartoonist); Westfield, N.J. **(1912–1988)**
Addams, Jane (social worker); Cedarville, Ill. **(1860–1935)**
Adderley, Julian "Cannonball" (jazz saxophonist); Tampa, Fla. **(1928–1975)**
Ade, George (humorist); Kentland, Ind. **(1866–1944)**
Adenauer, Konrad (statesman); Cologne, Germany **(1876–1967)**
Adler, Alfred (psychoanalyst); Vienna **(1870–1937)**
Adler, Larry (musician); Baltimore, 2/10/14
Adler, Richard (songwriter); New York City, 8/3/21
Aeschylus (dramatist); Eleusis (Greece) **(525–456 B.C.E.)**
Aesop (fabulist); Samos?, Greece, fl. c. 500 B.C.E.
Agnew, Spiro (political figure); Baltimore **(1905–1996)**
Aiello, Danny (actor); New York City, 6/20/33
Aiken, Conrad (poet); Savannah, Ga. **(1889–1973)**
Ailey, Alvin (choreographer); Rogers, Tex. **(1931–1989)**
Akhmatova, Anna (poet); Odessa, Ukraine **(1889–1966)**
Akihito, Tsugunomiya (Emperor of Japan); Tokyo, 12/23/33
Albanese, Licia (operatic soprano); Bari, Italy, 7/22/13
Albee, Edward (playwright); Washington, D.C., 3/12/28
Albers, Josef (painter); Bottrop, Germany **(1888–1976)**
Albert, Eddie (Edward Albert Heimberger) (actor); Rock Island, Ill., 4/22/08
Albert, Edward (actor); Los Angeles, 2/20/51
Albertson, Jack (actor); Malden, Mass. **(1907–1981)**
Albright, Lola (actress); Akron, Ohio, 7/20/25
Albright, Madeleine (diplomat, U.S. Secretary of State); Prague, Czechoslovakia, 5/15/37
Alcott, Louisa May (novelist); Germantown, Pa. **(1832–1888)**
Alda, Alan (actor); New York City, 1/28/36
Alda, Robert (Alphonso d'Abruzzo) (actor); New York City **(1914–1986)**
Alden, John (American Pilgrim); England **(c. 1599–1687)**
Alexander, Jane (Quigley) (actress); Boston, 10/28/39
Alexander, Jason (Jay Scott Greenspan) (actor); Newark, N.J., 9/23/59
Alexander the Great (monarch, conqueror); Pella, Macedonia (Greece) **(356–323 B.C.E.)**
Alger, Horatio (author); Revere, Mass. **(1834–1899)**
Algren, Nelson (novelist); Detroit **(1909–1981)**
Allen, Debbie (dancer-choreographer, actress); Houston, 1/16/50
Allen, Ethan (American Revolutionary soldier); Litchfield, Conn. **(1738–1789)**
Allen, Fred (John Florence Sullivan) (comedian); Cambridge, Mass. **(1894–1956)**
Allen, Gracie (Grace Ethel Cecile Rosalie Allen) (comedienne); San Francisco **(1906–1964)**
Allen, Mel (Melvin Israel) (sportscaster); Birmingham, Ala. **(1913–1996)**
Allen, Peter (actor, songwriter); Tenterfield, Australia **(1944–1992)**
Allen, Steve (TV entertainer); New York City, 12/26/21
Allen, Woody (Allen Stewart Konigsberg) (actor, writer, director); Brooklyn, N.Y., 12/1/35
Allende, Isabel (novelist); Lima, Peru, 8/2/42
Alley, Kirstie (actress); Wichita, Kans., 1/12/55
Allison, Fran (actress); LaPorte City, Iowa **(1908?–1989)**
Allman, Gregg (singer); Nashville, Tenn., 12/8/47
Allyson, June (Ella Geisman) (actress); New York City, 10/7/17
Alonso, Alicia (ballet dancer); Havana, 12/21/21?
Alpert, Herb (band leader); Los Angeles, 3/31/35?
Alsop, Joseph W., Jr. (journalist); Avon, Conn. **(1910–1989)**
Alsop, Stewart (journalist); Avon, Conn. **(1914–1974)**
Altman, Robert (director); Kansas City, Mo., 2/20/25
Amanpour, Christiane (broadcast journalist); London, 1958
Amati, Nicola (violin maker); Cremona, Italy **(1596–1684)**
Ambler, Eric (suspense writer); London, 6/28/09
Ameche, Don (Dominic Amici) (actor); Kenosha, Wis. **(1908–1993)**
Amis, Kingsley (novelist); London **(1922–1995)**
Amory, Cleveland (writer, conservationist); Nahant, Mass., 9/2/17
Amos (Freeman F. Gosden) (radio comedian); Richmond, Va. **(1899–1982)**
Amos, John (actor); Newark, N.J., 12/27/41
Amsterdam, Morey (actor); Chicago **(1914–1996)**
Andersen, Hans Christian (author of fairy tales); Odense, Denmark **(1805–1875)**
Anderson, Gillian (actress); Chicago, 8/9/68
Anderson, Harry (actor); Newport, R.I., 10/14/52
Anderson, Ib (ballet dancer); Copenhagen, 12/14/54
Anderson, Jack (journalist); Long Beach, Calif., 10/19/22
Anderson, Dame Judith (actress); Adelaide, Australia **(1898–1992)**
Anderson, Lindsay (Gordon) (director); Bangalore, India **(1923–1994)**
Anderson, Loni (actress); St. Paul, Minn., 8/5/45
Anderson, Lynn (singer); Grand Forks, N.D., 9/26/47
Anderson, Marian (contralto); Philadelphia **(1897–1993)**
Anderson, Maxwell (dramatist); Atlantic, Pa. **(1888–1959)**
Anderson, Richard Dean (actor); Minneapolis, Minn., 1/23/50
Anderson, Robert (playwright); New York City, 4/28/17
Anderson, Sherwood (novelist); Camden, Ohio **(1876–1941)**
Andress, Ursula (actress); Bern, Switzerland, 3/19/38

Andrews, Julie (Julia Wells) (actress, singer); Walton-on-Thames, England, 10/1/35
Andrews, La Verne (singer); Minneapolis **(1916–1967)**
Andrews, Maxene (singer); Minneapolis **(1918–1995)**
Andrews, Patti (singer); Minneapolis, 2/16/20
Andy (Charles J. Correll) (radio comedian); Peoria, Ill. **(1890–1972)**
Angeles, Victoria de los (Victoria Gamez Cima) (operatic soprano); Barcelona, 11/1/24
Angelico, Fra (Guido di Pietro; Giovanni de Fiesole) (painter); nr. Florence **(c. 1400–1455)**
Angelou, Maya Marguerite Johnson (poet, novelist); St. Louis, 4/4/28
Aniston, Jennifer (Jennifer Anistonapoulos) (actress); Sherman Oaks, Calif., 2/11/69
Anka, Paul (singer, composer); Ottawa, 7/30/41
Annan, Kofi (diplomat, U.N. Secretary General); Kumasi, Ghana, 4/8/38
Ann-Margret (Ann-Margaret Olsson) (actress); Valsjobyn, Sweden, 4/28/41
Anouilh, Jean (playwright); Bordeaux, France **(1910–1987)**
Anthony, Susan Brownell (woman suffragist); Adams, Mass. **(1820–1906)**
Antonioni, Michelangelo (director); Ferrara, Italy, 9/29/12
Antony, Mark (Marcus Antonius) (statesman); Rome **(c. 83–30 B.C.E.)**
Anuszkiewicz, Richard (painter); Erie, Pa., 5/23/30
Aquinas, St. Thomas (philosopher); nr. Aquino (Italy) **(1225–1274)**
Arafat, Yasir (Mohammed Abdel-Raouf Arafat al Qudwa al Husseini) (Chairman of the Palestine Liberation Organization); Cairo, Egypt, 8/24/29
Arbuckle, Roscoe "Fatty" (actor, director); Smith Center, Kans. **(1887–1933)**
Archimedes (physicist, mathematician); Syracuse, Sicily **(287–212 B.C.E.)**
Archipenko, Alexandre (sculptor); Kiev, Ukraine **(1887–1964)**
Arden, Elizabeth (Florence Nightingale Graham) (cosmetics executive); Woodbridge, Canada **(1891–1966)**
Arden, Eve (Eunice Quedens) (actress); Mill Valley, Calif. **(1912–1990)**
Arendt, Hannah (historian); Hannover, Germany **(1906–1975)**
Aristophanes (dramatist); Athens **(c. 448–c. 385 B.C.E.)**
Aristotle (philosopher); Stagirus, Macedonia **(384–322 B.C.E.)**
Arkin, Adam (actor); New York City, 8/19/57
Arkin, Alan (actor, director); New York City, 3/26/34
Arledge, Roone (TV executive); Forest Hills, N.Y., 7/8/31
Arlen, Harold (Hyman Arluck) (composer); Buffalo, N.Y. **(1905–1986)**
Armani, Georgio (fashion designer); Piacenza, Italy, 7/11/34
Armstrong, Louis ("Satchmo") (musician); New Orleans **(1900–1971)**
Arnaz, Desi (Desiderio Arnaz) (actor, producer); Santiago, Cuba **(1917–1986)**
Arness, James (James Aurness) (actor); Minneapolis, 5/26/23
Arno, Peter (cartoonist); New York City **(1904–1968)**
Arnold, Benedict (American Revolutionary War general, charged with treason); Norwich, Conn. **(1741–1801)**
Arnold, Eddy (singer); Henderson, Tenn., 5/15/18
Arnold, Matthew (poet, critic); Laleham, England **(1822–1888)**
Arp, Jean (sculptor, painter); Strasbourg (France) **(1887–1966)**
Arpino, Gerald (choreographer); Staten Island, N.Y., 1/14/28
Arquette, Cliff (actor); Toledo, Ohio **(1905–1974)**
Arquette, Rosanna (actress); New York City, 8/10/59
Arrau, Claudio (pianist); Chillán, Chile **(1903–1991)**
Arroyo, Martina (soprano); New York City, 2/2/40
Arthur, Bea (Bernice Frankel) (actress); New York City, 5/13/23
Arthur, Chester Alan (21st U.S. president); Fairfield, Vt. **(1830–1886)**
Arthur, Jean (Gladys Greene) (actress); New York City **(1900–1991)**
Ashcroft, Dame Peggy (actress); Croydon, England **(1907–1991)**
Ashkenazy, Vladimir (concert pianist); Gorki, U.S.S.R., 7/6/37
Ashley, Elizabeth (actress); Ocala, Fla., 8/30/39
Ashton, Sir Frederick William Mallandaine (choreographer); Guayaquil, Ecuador **(1904–1988)**
Asimov, Isaac (author); Petrovichi, Russia **(1920–1992)**
Asner, Edward (actor); Kansas City, Mo., 11/15/29
Assante, Armand (actor); New York City, 10/4/49
Astaire, Fred (Frederick Austerlitz) (dancer, actor); Omaha, Neb. **(1899–1987)**
Astin, John (actor, director); Baltimore, 3/30/30
Astor, Brooke (socialite, philanthropist); Portsmouth, N.H., 3/16/05
Astor, John Jacob (financier); Waldorf (Germany) **(1763–1848)**
Astor, Mary (Lucile Langhanke) (actress); Quincy, Ill. **(1906–1987)**
Ataturk, Kemal (Mustafa Kemal) (Turkish soldier, statesman); Salonika (Greece) **(1881–1938)**
Atkins, Chet (guitarist); nr. Luttrell, Tenn., 6/20/24
Attenborough, Richard (actor, director); Cambridge, England, 8/29/23
Attila (King of Huns) **(406?–453)**
Attucks, Crispus (American Revolutionary Patriot); Boston **(c. 1723–1770)**
Atwill, Lionel (actor); Croydon, England **(1885–1946)**
Auberjonois, Rene (actor); New York City, 6/1/40
Auchincloss, Louis (author); Lawrence, N.Y., 9/27/17
Auden, W(ystan) H(ugh) (poet); York, England **(1907–1973)**
Audubon, John James (naturalist, painter); Haiti **(1785–1851)**
Auer, Leopold (violinist, teacher); Veszprém, Hungary **(1845–1930)**
Augustine, Saint (Aurelius Augustinus) (theologian); Tagaste, Numidia (Algeria) **(354–430)**
Augustus (Gaius Octavius) (Roman emperor); Rome **(63 B.C.E.–C.E. 14)**
Aumont, Jean-Pierre (actor); Paris, 1/5/13
Aung, San Suu Kyi (human rights activist); Rangoon, Burma, 6/19/45
Austen, Jane (novelist); Steventon, England **(1775–1817)**
Autry, Gene (singer, actor); Tioga, Tex., 9/29/07
Avalon, Frankie (singer); Philadelphia, 9/18/39
Avedon, Richard (photographer); New York City, 5/15/23
Avery, Milton (painter); Altmar, N.Y. **(1893–1965)**
Ax, Emanuel (pianist); Lvov, Ukraine, 6/8/49
Axelrod, George (playwright); New York City, 6/9/22
Ayckbourn, Alan (playwright); London, 4/12/39
Aykroyd, Dan (actor); Ottawa, Ont., Canada, 7/1/52
Ayres, Lew (actor); Minneapolis **(1908–1996)**
Aznavour, Charles (singer, composer); Paris, 5/22/24

B

Bacall, Lauren (Betty Joan Perske) (actress); New York City, 9/16/24
Bach, Carl Phillipp Emanuel (composer); Weimar, Germany **(1714–1788)**
Bach, Johann Sebastian (composer); Eisenach, Germany **(1685–1750)**
Bacharach, Burt (songwriter); Kansas City, Mo., 5/12/29
Backus, Jim (actor); Cleveland **(1913–1989)**
Bacon, Francis (philosopher, essayist); London **(1561–1626)**
Bacon, Francis (painter); Dublin **(1910–1992)**
Bacon, Kevin (actor); Philadelphia, 7/8/58
Bacon, Roger (philosopher, scientist); Ilchester, England **(c. 1214–1294?)**
Baez, Joan (folk singer); Staten Island, N.Y., 1/9/41
Bailey, F. Lee (lawyer); Waltham, Mass., 6/10/33
Bailey, Pearl (singer); Newport News, Va. **(1918–1990)**
Bain, Conrad (actor); Lethbridge, Alberta, Canada, 2/4/23
Baio, Scott (actor); Brooklyn, N.Y., 9/22/61
Baird, Bil (William B. Baird) (puppeteer); Grand Island, Neb. **(1904–1987)**
Baker, Anita (singer); Toledo, Ohio, 1958
Baker, Carroll (actress); Johnstown, Pa., 5/28/31
Baker, Josephine (singer, dancer); St. Louis **(1906–1975)**
Baker, Russell (columnist); Loudoun County, Va., 8/14/25
Balanchine, George (choreographer); St. Petersburg, Russia **(1904–1983)**
Balboa, Vasco Nuñez de (explorer); Jerez de los Caballeros (Spain) **(1475–1517)**
Baldwin, Alec (actor); Massapequa, N.Y., 4/3/58
Baldwin, James (novelist); New York City **(1924–1987)**
Balenciaga, Cristóbal (fashion designer); Guetaria, Spain **(1895–1972)**
Ball, Lucille (Lucille Désirée Ball) (actress, producer); Celoron (nr. Jamestown), N.Y. **(1911–1989)**
Ballard, Kaye (Catherine Gloria Balotta) (actress); Cleveland, 11/20/26
Balmain, Pierre (fashion designer); St.-Jean-de-Maurienne, France **(1914–1982)**
Balsam, Martin (actor); Bronx, New York **(1919–1996)**
Balzac, Honoré de (novelist); Tours, France **(1799–1850)**
Bancroft, Anne (Annemarie Italiano) (actress); New York City, 9/17/31
Banderas, Antonio (José Antonio Dominguez Banderas) (actor, model); Málaga, Spain, 8/10/60
Bankhead, Tallulah (actress); Huntsville, Ala. **(1903–1968)**
Banneker, Benjamin (mathematician, astronomer); Endicott, Md. **(1731–1806)**

Banting, Fredrick Grant (physiologist); Alliston, Ont., Canada **(1891–1941)**
Baraka, Imamu Amiri (LeRoi Jones) (playwright); Newark, N.J., 10/7/34
Baranski, Christine (actress); Buffalo, N.Y., 5/2/52
Barber, Red (Walter Lanier) (sportscaster); Columbus, Miss. **(1908–1992)**
Barber, Samuel (composer); West Chester, Pa. **(1910–1981)**
Barbie, Klaus (Nazi, "The Butcher of Lyon"); Bad Godesberg, Germany **(1913–1991)**
Bardot, Brigitte (Camille Javal) (actress); Paris, 9/28/34
Barenboim, Daniel (concert pianist, conductor); Buenos Aires, 11/15/42
Barker, Bob (host); Darrington, Wash., 12/12/23
Barnard, Christiaan N. (heart surgeon); Beauford West, South Africa, 10/8/22
Barnum, Phineas Taylor (showman); Bethel, Conn. **(1810–1891)**
Barrie, Sir James Matthew (author); Kirriemuir, Scotland **(1860–1937)**
Barry, Gene (Eugene Klass) (actor); New York City, 6/14/21
Barry, John (naval officer); County Wexford, Ireland **(1745–1803)**
Barrymore, Diana (actress); New York City **(1921–1960)**
Barrymore, Drew (actress); Los Angeles, 2/22/75
Barrymore, Ethel (Ethel Blythe) (actress); Philadelphia **(1879–1959)**
Barrymore, Georgiana Drew (actress); Philadelphia **(1856–1893)**
Barrymore, John (John Blythe) (actor); Philadelphia **(1882–1942)**
Barrymore, Lionel (Lionel Blythe) (actor); Philadelphia **(1878–1954)**
Barrymore, Maurice (Herbert Blythe) (actor, playwright); Agra, India **(1847–1905)**
Barth, John (novelist); Cambridge, Md., 5/27/30
Barthelme, Donald (novelist); Philadelphia **(1931 –1989)**
Barthelmess, Richard (actor); New York City **(1897–1963)**
Bartholomew, Freddie (actor); London **(1924–1992)**
Bartók, Béla (composer); Nagyszentmiklo, Hungary (Romania) **(1881–1945)**
Barton, Clara (founder of American Red Cross); Oxford, Mass. **(1821–1912)**
Baruch, Bernard Mannes (statesman); Camden, S.C. **(1870–1965)**
Baryshnikov, Mikhail Nikolayevich (ballet dancer, artistic director); Riga, Latvia, 1/27/48
Basehart, Richard (actor); Zanesville, Ohio **(1914–1984)**
Basie, Count (William Basie) (band leader); Red Bank, N.J. **(1904–1984)**
Basinger, Kim (actress); Athens, Ga., 12/8/53
Bassett, Angela (actress); New York City, 8/16/58
Bassey, Shirley (singer); Cardiff, Wales, 1/8/37
Batchelor, Clarence Daniel (political cartoonist); Osage City, Kans. **(1888–1977)**
Bateman, Jason (actor); Rye, N.Y., 1/14/69
Bateman, Justine (actress); Rye, N.Y., 2/19/66
Bates, Alan (actor); Allestree, England, 2/17/34
Bates, Kathy (Kathleen Doyle Bates) (actress); Memphis, Tenn., 6/28/48
Battle, Kathleen (soprano); Portsmouth, Ohio, 8/13/48
Baudelaire, Charles Pierre (poet); Paris **(1821–1867)**
Baxter, Anne (actress); Michigan City, Ind. **(1923–1985)**
Baxter, Meredith (actress); Los Angeles, 6/21/47
Bean, Orson (Dallas Frederick Burrows) (actor); Burlington, Vt., 7/22/28
Beardsley, Aubrey Vincent (illustrator); Brighton, England **(1872–1898)**
Beaton, Cecil (photographer, designer); London **(1904–1980)**
Beatty, Clyde (animal trainer); Chillicothe, Ohio **(1903–1965)**
Beatty, Warren (Henry Warren Beaty) (actor, producer); Richmond, Va., 3/30/37
Beaumont, Francis (dramatist); Grace-Dieu, England **(1584–1616)**
Becket, Thomas à (Archbishop of Canterbury); London **(1118?–1170)**
Beckett, Samuel (playwright); Dublin **(1906–1989)**
Beckmann, Max (painter); Leipzig, Germany **(1884–1950)**
Bede, Saint ("The Venerable Bede") (scholar); Monkwearmouth, England **(673–735)**
Beecham, Sir Thomas (conductor); St. Helens, England **(1879–1961)**
Beecher, Henry Ward (clergyman); Litchfield, Conn. **(1813–1887)**
Beerbohm, Sir Max (author); London **(1872–1956)**
Beery, Noah (actor); Kansas City, Mo. **(1884–1946)**
Beery, Noah, Jr. (actor); New York City **(1913–1994)**
Beery, Wallace (actor); Kansas City, Mo. **(1886–1949)**
Beethoven, Ludwig van (composer); Bonn (Germany) **(1770–1827)**
Begin, Menachem (Israeli Prime Minister); Brest-Litovsk, Belarus **(1913–1992)**
Begley, Ed (actor); Hartford, Conn. **(1901–1970)**
Beiderbecke, Bix (jazz musician); Davenport, Iowa **(1903–1931)**
Belafonte, Harry (singer, actor); New York City, 3/1/27
Belafonte-Harper, Shari (actress); New York City, 9/22/54
Belasco, David (dramatist, producer); San Francisco **(1854–1931)**
Bel Geddes, Barbara (actress); New York City, 10/31/22
Bell, Alexander Graham (inventor); Edinburgh, Scotland **(1847–1922)**
Bell, Quentin (author, artist); England **(1910–1996)**
Bellamy, Edward (author); Chicopee Falls, Mass. **(1850–1898)**
Bellamy, Ralph (actor); Chicago **(1904–1991)**
Bellini, Giovanni (painter); Venice **(c. 1430–1516)**
Bellow, Saul (novelist); Lachine, Que., Canada, 6/10/15
Bellows, George Wesley (painter, lithographer); Columbus, Ohio **(1882–1925)**
Belmondo, Jean-Paul (actor); Neuilly-sur-Seine, France, 4/9/33
Belushi, Jim (actor); Chicago, 6/15/54
Belushi, John (comedian, actor); Chicago **(1949–1982)**
Benchley, Peter Bradford (novelist); New York City, 5/8/40
Benchley, Robert Charles (humorist); Worcester, Mass. **(1889–1945)**
Bendix, William (actor); New York City **(1906–1964)**
Benedict, Ruth Fulton (anthropologist); New York City **(1887–1948)**
Benes, Eduard (statesman); Kozlany, former Czechoslovakia **(1884–1948)**
Benét, Stephen Vincent (poet, story writer); Bethlehem, Pa. **(1898–1943)**
Benét, William Rose (poet, novelist); Ft. Hamilton, Brooklyn, N.Y. **(1886–1950)**
Ben-Gurion, David (David Green) (statesman); Plónsk (Poland) **(1886–1973)**
Bening, Annette (actress); Topeka, Kans., 5/29/58
Benjamin, Richard (actor, director); New York City, 5/22/38
Bennett, Enoch Arnold (novelist, dramatist); Hanley, England **(1867–1931)**
Bennett, James Gordon (editor); Keith, Scotland **(1795–1872)**
Bennett, Joan (actress); Palisades, N.J. **(1910–1990)**
Bennett, Robert Russell (composer); Kansas City, Mo. **(1894–1981)**
Bennett, Tony (Anthony Benedetto) (singer); Astoria, Queens, N.Y., 8/3/26
Benny, Jack (Benjamin Kubelsky) (comedian); Chicago **(1894–1974)**
Benson, Robby (actor); Dallas, 1/21/56
Bentham, Jeremy Heinrich (economist); London **(1748–1832)**
Benton, Thomas Hart (painter); Neosho, Mo. **(1889–1975)**
Berenger, Tom (actor); Chicago, 5/31/50
Berg, Alban (composer); Vienna **(1885–1935)**
Berg, Gertrude (writer, actress); New York City **(1899–1966)**
Bergen, Candice (actress); Beverly Hills, Calif., 5/9/46
Bergen, Edgar (ventriloquist); Chicago **(1903–1978)**
Bergen, Polly (Nellie Paulina Burgin) (actress, singer); Knoxville, Tenn., 7/14/30
Bergerac, Cyrano de (poet); Paris **(1619–1655)**
Bergman, Ingmar (film director); Uppsala, Sweden, 7/14/18
Bergman, Ingrid (actress); Stockholm **(1918–1982)**
Bergson, Henri (philosopher); Paris **(1859–1941)**
Berkeley, Busby (William Berkeley Enos) (choreographer, director); Los Angeles **(1895–1976)**
Berle, Milton (Milton Berlinger) (comedian); New York City, 7/12/08
Berlin, Irving (Israel Baline) (songwriter); Temum, Russia **(1888–1989)**
Berlioz, Louis Hector (composer); La Côte-Saint-André, France **(1803–1869)**
Berman, Lazar (concert pianist); Leningrad (St. Petersburg, Russia), 2/26/30
Berman, Shelley (Sheldon Berman) (comedian); Chicago, 2/3/26
Bernardi, Herschel (actor); New York City **(1922–1986)**
Bernardin, Joseph Cardinal (prelate); Columbia, S.C. **(1928–1996)**
Bernhardt, Sarah (Rosine Bernard) (actress); Paris **(1844–1923)**
Bernini, Gian Lorenzo (sculptor, painter); Naples (Italy) **(1598–1680)**
Bernoulli, Jacques (scientist); Basel, Switzerland **(1654–1705)**
Bernsen, Corbin (actor); North Hollywood, Calif., 7/7/54
Bernstein, Leonard (conductor); Lawrence, Mass. **(1918–1990)**
Berry, Chuck (Charles Edward Berry) (singer, guitarist); San Jose, Calif., 1/15/26
Berry, Ken (actor); Moline, Ill., 11/3/30
Berry, Richard (songwriter); Extension, S.C. **(1935–1997)**
Berryman, John (poet); McAlester, Okla. **(1914–1972)**
Bertinelli, Valerie (actress); Wilmington, Del., 4/23/60
Bethune, Mary McCleod (educator); Mayesville, S.C. **(1875–1955)**
Betjeman, Sir John (Poet Laureate); London **(1906–1984)**

Bettelheim, Bruno (psychoanalyst); Vienna **(1903–1990)**
Bickford, Charles (actor); Cambridge, Mass. **(1889–1967)**
Bierce, Ambrose Gwinnett (journalist); Meigs County, Ohio **(1842–1914?)**
Bikel, Theodore (actor, folk singer); Vienna, 5/2/24
Bing, Sir Rudolf (opera manager); Vienna, 1/9/02
Bingham, George Caleb (painter); Augusta Co., Va. **(1811–1879)**
Binoche, Juliette (actress); Paris, 3/9/64
Bishop, Joey (Joseph Gottlieb) (comedian); New York City, 2/3/19
Bismarck-Schönhausen, Prince Otto Eduard Leopold von (statesman); Schönhausen, Germany **(1815–1898)**
Bisset, Jacqueline (actress); Weybridge, England, 9/13/44
Bixby, Bill (actor); San Francisco **(1934–1993)**
Bizet, Georges (Alexandre César Léopold Bizet) (composer); Paris **(1838–1875)**
Bjoerling, Jussi (tenor); Stora Tuna, Sweden **(1911–1960)**
Black, Karen (actress); Park Ridge, Ill., 7/1/42
Black, Shirley Temple (former actress); Santa Monica, Calif., 4/23/28
Blackmer, Sidney (actor); Salisbury, N.C. **(1898–1973)**
Blackstone, Sir William (jurist); London **(1723–1780)**
Blackwell, Elizabeth (physician, educator); England **(1821–1910)**
Blades, Ruben (actor, musician, composer); Panama City, Panama, 7/16/48
Blake, Amanda (Beverly Louise Neill) (actress); Buffalo, N.Y. **(1929–1989)**
Blake, Eubie (James Hubert) (pianist); Baltimore **(1883–1983)**
Blake, Robert (Michael Gubitosi) (actor); Nutley, N.J., 9/18/33
Blake, William (poet, artist); London **(1757–1827)**
Blanc, Mel (Melvin Jerome) (actor, voice specialist); San Francisco **(1908–1989)**
Blass, Bill (fashion designer); Fort Wayne, Ind., 6/22/22
Bleeth, Yasmine (model, actress); New York City, 6/14/68
Bloch, Ernest (composer); Geneva **(1880–1959)**
Blondell, Joan (actress); New York City **(1909–1979)**
Bloom, Claire (actress); London, 2/15/31
Bloomgarden, Kermit (producer); Brooklyn, N.Y. **(1904–1976)**
Blume, Judy (Judy Sussman) (young adult novelist); Elizabeth, N.J., 2/12/38
Bly, Nellie (pseud. for Elizabeth Seaman) (journalist); Cochrane Mills, Pa. **(1867–1922)**
Bly, Robert (poet, critic); Madison, Minn., 12/23/26
Boccaccio, Giovanni (author); Paris **(1313–1375)**
Boccherini, Luigi (Rodolfo) (composer); Lucca, Italy **(1743–1805)**
Boccioni, Umberto (painter, sculptor); Reggio di Calabria, Italy **(1882–1916)**
Bochco, Steven (TV producer, writer); New York City, 12/16/43
Bock, Jerry (composer); New Haven, Conn., 11/23/28
Bogarde, Dirk (Derek Van den Bogaerde) (film actor, director); London, 3/28/21
Bogart, Humphrey DeForest (actor); New York City **(1899–1957)**
Bogdanovich, Peter (producer, director); Kingston, N.Y., 7/30/39
Bohlen, Charles E. (diplomat); Clayton, N.Y. **(1904–1974)**
Bohr, Niels (atomic physicist); Copenhagen **(1885–1962)**
Bok, Sissela (Sissela Ann Myrdal) (scholar); Stockholm, 12/2/34
Bolger, Ray (dancer, actor); Dorchester, Mass **(1904–1987)**
Bolivar, Simón (South American liberator); Caracas, Venezuela **(1783–1830)**
Bologna, Giovanni da (sculptor); Douai (France) **(1529–1608)**
Bombeck, Erma (author, columnist); Dayton, Ohio **(1927–1996)**
Bonaparte, Napoleon (Emperor of the French); Ajaccio, Corsica (France) **(1769–1821)**
Bond, Julian (Georgia legislator); Nashville, Tenn., 1/14/40
Bonet, Lisa (actress); San Francisco, 11/16/67
Bonham Carter, Helena (actress); London, 5/23/66
Bon Jovi, Jon (musician, songwriter); Sayreville, N.J., 3/2/62
Bonnard, Pierre (painter); Fontenayaux-Roses, France **(1867–1947)**
Bono, Sonny (Salvatore Bono) (singer, politician); Detroit **(1935–1997)**
Boone, Daniel (frontiersman); nr. Reading, Pa. **(1734–1820)**
Boone, Pat (Charles Boone) (singer); Jacksonville, Fla., 6/1/34
Boone, Richard (actor); Los Angeles **(1917–1981)**
Boorstin, Daniel (historian); Atlanta, 10/1/14
Booth, Edwin Thomas (actor); Bel Air, Md. **(1833–1893)**
Booth, Evangeline Cory (religious leader); London **(1865–1950)**
Booth, John Wilkes (actor; assassin of Lincoln); Harford County, Md. **(1838–1865)**
Booth, Shirley (Thelma Booth Ford) (actress); New York City **(1907–1992)**
Borden, Lizzy (Elizabeth Andrew Borden) (accused murderer); Fall River, Mass. **(1860–1927)**
Borge, Victor (pianist, comedian); Copenhagen, 1/3/09
Borgia, Cesare (nobleman, soldier); Rome **(1476–1507)**
Borgia, Lucrezia (Duchess of Ferrara); Rome **(1480–1519)**
Borgnine, Ernest (actor); Hamden, Conn., 1/24/17
Borromini, Francesco (architect); Bissone (Italy) **(1599–1667)**
Bosch, Hieronymus (Hieronymus van Aeken) (painter); Hertogenbosch (Netherlands) **(c. 1450–1516)**
Bosley, Tom (actor); Chicago, 10/1/27
Bostwick, Barry (actor); San Mateo, Calif., 2/24/45
Boswell, James (diarist, biographer); Edinburgh, Scotland **(1740–1795)**
Botticelli, Sandro (Alessandro di Mariano dei Filipepi) (painter); Florence (Italy) **(1444–1510)**
Bottoms, Timothy (actor); Santa Barbara, Calif., 8/30/50
Boulez, Pierre (conductor); Montbrison, France, 3/26/25
Bourke-White, Margaret (photographer); New York City **(1906–1971)**
Boutros-Ghali, Boutros (ex-Secretary General of the U.N.); Cairo, Egypt, 11/14/22
Bow, Clara (actress); Brooklyn, N.Y. **(1905–1965)**
Bowen, Catherine Drinker (biographer); Haverford, Pa. **(1897–1973)**
Bowie, David (David Robert Jones) (actor, musician); London, 1/8/47
Bowie, James (soldier); Burke County, Ga. **(1799–1836)**
Bowles, Chester (diplomat); Springfield, Mass. **(1901–1986)**
Boxleitner, Bruce (actor); Elgin, Ill., 5/12/50
Boyce, William (composer); London? **(1710–1779)**
Boyd, Bill ("Hopalong Cassidy") (actor); Cambridge, Ohio **(1895–1972)**
Boyd, Stephen (Stephen Millar) (actor); Belfast, Northern Ireland **(1928–1977)**
Boyer, Charles (actor); Figeac, France **(1897–1978)**
Boy George (George Alan O'Dowd) (singer); London, 1961
Boyle, Peter (actor); Philadelphia, 10/18/33
Boyle, Robert (scientist); Lismore Castle, Munster, Ireland **(1627–1691)**
Bracken, Eddie (actor); Astoria, Queens, N.Y., 2/7/20
Bradbury, Ray Douglas (science-fiction writer); Waukegan, Ill., 8/22/20
Bradlee, Benjamin C. (editor); Boston, 8/26/21
Bradley, Ed (broadcast journalist); Philadelphia, 6/22/41
Bradley, Omar N. (5-star general); Clark, Mo. **(1893–1981)**
Bradley, Thomas (mayor of Los Angeles); Calvert, Tex., 12/29/17
Brady, Mathew (early photographer); Warren Co., N.Y. **(c. 1823–1896)**
Brahe, Tycho (astronomer); Knudstrup, Denmark **(1546–1601)**
Brahms, Johannes (composer); Hamburg **(1833–1897)**
Braille, Louis (teacher of blind); Coupvray, France **(1809–1862)**
Brailowsky, Alexander (pianist); Kiev, Ukraine **(1896–1976)**
Bramante, Donato D'Agnolo (architect); Monte Asdrualdo (now Fermignano, Italy) **(1444–1514)**
Branagh, Kenneth (actor, director, writer, producer); Belfast, Northern Ireland, 12/10/60
Brancusi, Constantin (sculptor); Pestisansi, Romania **(1876–1957)**
Brandauer, Klaus Maria (Klaus Maria Steng) (actor); Bad Aussee, Steiermark, Austria , 6/22/44
Brando, Marlon (actor); Omaha, Neb., 4/3/24
Brandt, Willy (Herbert Frahm) (ex-Chancellor); Lübeck, Germany **(1913–1992)**
Braque, Georges (painter); Argenteuil, France **(1882–1963)**
Brazelton, T(homas) Berry II (pediatrician, writer); Waco, Tex., 5/10/18
Brecht, Bertolt (dramatist, poet); Augsburg, Bavaria **(1898–1956)**
Brel, Jacques (singer, composer); Brussels **(1929–1978)**
Brennan, Walter (actor); Lynn, Mass. **(1894–1974)**
Brennan, William J., Jr. (jurist); Newark, N.J. **(1906–1997)**
Breslin, Jimmy (journalist); Jamaica, Queens, N.Y., 10/17/30
Breton, André (writer); Tinchebray, France **(1896–1966)**
Breuer, Marcel (architect, designer); Pécs, Hungary **(1902–1981)**
Brewster, Kingman, Jr. (ex-president of Yale); Longmeadow, Mass. **(1919–1988)**
Brezhnev, Leonid I. (Communist Party Secretary); Dneprodzerzhinsk, Ukraine **(1906–1982)**
Brice, Fanny (Fannie Borach) (comedienne); New York City **(1892–1951)**
Bridges, Beau (actor); Los Angeles, 12/9/41
Bridges, Jeff (actor); Los Angeles, 12/4/49
Bridges, Lloyd (actor); San Leandro, Calif. **(1913–1998)**
Brinkley, David (TV newscaster); Wilmington, N.C., 7/10/20
Britten, Benjamin (composer); Lowestoft, England **(1913–1976)**
Brodsky, Joseph Alexandrovitch (poet); St. Petersburg, Russia **(1940–1996)**
Brody, Jane (journalist); Brooklyn, N.Y., 5/19/41

Brokaw, Tom (TV newscaster); Webster, S.D., 2/6/40
Brolin, James (actor); Los Angeles, 7/18/40
Bromfield, Louis (novelist); Mansfield, Ohio **(1896–1956)**
Bronson, Charles (Charles Buchinsky) (actor); Ehrenfield, Pa., 11/3/21
Brontë, Charlotte (novelist); Thornton, England **(1816–1855)**
Brontë, Emily Jane (novelist); Thornton, England **(1818–1848)**
Bronzino, Agnolo (painter); Monticelli (Italy) **(1503–1572)**
Brook, Peter (director); London, 3/21/25
Brooke, Rupert (poet); Rugby, England **(1887–1915)**
Brooks, Albert (Albert Einstein) (actor, writer, director); Beverly Hills, Calif., 7/22/47
Brooks, Avery (actor) 4/18/49
Brooks, Geraldine (Geraldine Stroock) (actress); New York City **(1925–1977)**
Brooks, Gwendolyn (poet); Topeka, Kans., 6/7/17
Brooks, Mel (Melvin Kaminsky) (writer, film director); Brooklyn, N.Y., 6/28/26
Brosnan, Pierce (actor); County Meath, Ireland, 5/16/52
Brothers, Joyce (Bauer) (psychologist, author, radio-TV personality); New York City, 9/20/28
Broun, Matthew Heywood Campbell (journalist); Brooklyn, N.Y. **(1888–1939)**
Brown, Charles Brockden (novelist); Philadelphia **(1771–1810)**
Brown, Helen Gurley (editor, author); Green Forest, Ark., 2/18/22
Brown, James (singer); Augusta, Ga., 5/3/34
Brown, Joe E. (comedian); Holgate, Ohio **(1892–1973)**
Brown, John (abolitionist); Torrington, Conn. **(1800–1859)**
Brown, Les (band leader); Reinerton, Pa., 3/14/12
Brown, Margaret Wise (children's author); Brooklyn, N.Y. **(1910–1962)**
Brown, Trisha (choreographer); Aberdeen, Wash., 11/25/36
Browne, Jackson (singer, guitarist); Heidelberg, Germany, 10/9/48
Browning, Elizabeth Barrett (poet); Durham, England **(1806–1861)**
Browning, Robert (poet); London **(1812–1889)**
Brubeck, Dave (musician); Concord, Calif., 12/6/20
Bruce, Lenny (comedian); Long Island, N.Y. **(1926–1966)**
Bruce, Nigel (actor); Ensenada, Mexico **(1895–1953)**
Brueghel, Pieter (painter); nr. Breda, Flanders (Netherlands) **(c. 1520–1569)**
Bruhn, Erik (Belton Evers) (ballet dancer); Copenhagen **(1928–1986)**
Brunelleschi, Filippo (architect); Florence (Italy) **(1377–1446)**
Bruno, Giordano (philosopher); Nola, Italy **(1548–1600)**
Brutus, Marcus Junius (Roman politician) **(85–42 B.C.E.)**
Bryan, William Jennings (orator, politician); Salem, Ill. **(1860–1925)**
Bryant, Anita (singer); Barnsdall, Okla., 3/25/40
Bryant, William Cullen (poet, editor); Cummington, Mass. **(1794–1878)**
Brynner, Yul (Taidje Khan) (actor); Sakhalin Island, Russia **(1920–1985)**
Brzezinski, Zbigniew (ex-presidential adviser); Warsaw, 3/28/28
Buber, Martin (philosopher, theologian); Vienna **(1878–1965)**
Buchanan, Edgar (actor); Humansville, Mo. **(1903–1979)**
Buchanan, Pat (politician); Washington, D.C., 11/2/38
Buchholz, Horst (actor); Berlin, 12/4/33
Büchner, Georg (dramatist); Goddelau, Germany **(1813–1837)**
Buchwald, Art (Arthur Buchwald) (columnist); Mount Vernon, N.Y., 10/20/25
Buck, Pearl S(ydenstricker) (author); Hillsboro, W. Va. **(1892–1973)**
Buckley, Christopher (writer); New York City, 1952
Buckley, William F., Jr. (journalist); New York City, 11/24/25
Buffalo Bill (William Frederick Cody) (scout); Scott County, Iowa **(1846–1917)**
Buffett, Jimmy (singer, writer); Mobile, Ala., 12/25/46
Buffett, Warren (investment expert); Omaha, Neb., 8/30/30
Bujold, Genevieve (actress); Montreal, 7/1/42
Bujones, Fernando (ballet dancer); Miami, Fla., 3/9/55
Bulgakov, Mikhail (novelist); Kiev, Ukraine **(1891–1940)**
Bullins, Ed (playwright); Philadelphia, 7/2/35
Bumbry, Grace (mezzo-soprano); St. Louis, 1/4/37
Bunche, Ralph J. (statesman); Detroit **(1904–1971)**
Bundy, McGeorge (educator); Boston **(1919–1996)**
Bundy, William Putnam (editor); Washington, D.C., 9/24/17
Buñuel, Luis (film director); Calanda, Spain **(1900–1983)**
Bunyan, John (preacher, author); Elstow, England **(1628–1688)**
Burbank, Luther (horticulturist); Lancaster, Mass. **(1849–1926)**
Burke, Adm. Arleigh A. (ex-Chief of Naval Operations); Boulder, Colo. **(1901–1996)**
Burke, Billie (comedienne); Washington, D.C. **(1885–1970)**
Burke, Delta (actress); Orlando, Fla., 7/30/56
Burke, Edmund (statesman); Dublin **(1729–1797)**
Burne-Jones, Edward Coley (painter); Birmingham, England **(1833–1898)**
Burnett, Carol (comedienne); San Antonio, 4/26/33
Burney, Fanny (Frances) (writer); King's Lynn, England **(1752–1840)**
Burns, George (Nathan Birnbaum) (comedian); New York City **(1896–1996)**
Burns, Ken (documentary filmmaker); Brooklyn, N.Y., 7/29/53
Burns, Robert (poet); Alloway, Scotland **(1759–1796)**
Burr, Aaron (political leader); Newark, N.J. **(1756–1836)**
Burr, Raymond (William Stacey Burr) (actor); New Westminster, British Columbia, Canada **(1917–1993)**
Burroughs, Edgar Rice (novelist); Chicago **(1875–1950)**
Burroughs, William S. (author); St. Louis **(1914–1997)**
Burrows, Abe (playwright, director); New York City **(1910–1985)**
Burstyn, Ellen (Edna Rae Gillooly) (actress); Detroit, 12/7/32
Burton, LeVar (actor, director); Landsthul, Germany, 2/16/57
Burton, Richard (Richard Jenkins) (actor); Pontrhydfen, Wales **(1925–1984)**
Burton, Tim (filmmaker); Burbank, Calif., 8/25/58
Bush, George Herbert Walker (41st U.S. president); Milton, Mass., 6/12/24
Butkus, Dick (actor); Chicago, 12/9/42
Butler, Samuel (author); Langar, England **(1835–1902)**
Butterworth, Charles (actor); South Bend, Ind. **(1896–1946)**
Buttons, Red (Aaron Chwatt) (actor); New York City, 2/5/19
Buzzi, Ruth (comedienne); Wequetequock, Conn., 7/24/36
Byrd, Richard Evelyn (polar explorer); Winchester, Va. **(1888–1957)**
Byrne, Gabriel (actor); Dublin, 5/12/50
Byron, George Gordon (6th Baron Byron) (poet); London **(1788–1824)**

C

Caan, James (actor); Queens, New York, 3/26/39
Caballé, Montserrat (soprano); Barcelona, Spain, 4/12/33
Cabot, John (Giovanni Caboto) (navigator); Genoa **(1450–1498)**
Cabot, Sebastian (navigator); Venice **(c. 1476–1557)**
Cadmus, Paul (painter, etcher); New York City, 12/17/04
Caesar, Irving (lyricist); New York City **(1895–1996)**
Caesar, Gaius Julius (statesman); Rome **(100–44 B.C.E.)**
Caesar, Sid (comedian); Yonkers, N.Y., 9/8/22
Cage, Nicolas (Nicolas Coppola) (actor); Long Beach, Calif., 1/7/64
Cagney, James (actor); New York City **(1899–1986)**
Cahn, Sammy (songwriter); New York City **(1913–1993)**
Caine, Michael (Maurice J. Micklewhite) (actor); London, 3/14/33
Calder, Alexander (sculptor); Lawnton, Pa. **(1898–1976)**
Calderón del al Barca, Pedro (dramatist); Madrid **(1600–1681)**
Caldwell, Erskine (novelist); White Oak, Ga. **(1903–1987)**
Caldwell, Sarah (opera director, conductor); Maryville, Mo., 3/6/24
Caldwell, Taylor (novelist); Manchester, England **(1900–1985)**
Caldwell, Zoe (actress); Hawthorn, Australia, 9/14/33
Calhern, Louis (Carl Henry Vogt) (actor); Brooklyn, N.Y. **(1895–1956)**
Calhoun, John Caldwell (statesman); nr. Calhoun Mills, S.C. **(1782–1850)**
Caligula Gaius Caesar (Roman emperor); Antium, Latium **(12–41)**
Calisher, Hortense (novelist); New York City, 12/20/11
Callas, Maria (Maria Calogeropoulos) (dramatic soprano); New York City **(1923–1977)**
Calloway, Cab (Cabell Calloway) (band leader); Rochester, N.Y. **(1907–1994)**
Calvin, John (Jean Chauvin) (religious reformer); Noyon, Picardy **(1509–1564)**
Calvin, Melvin (chemist, Nobel laureate); St. Paul, Minn. **(1911–1997)**
Cambridge, Godfrey (comedian); New York City **(1933–1976)**
Cameron, James (director); Kapuskasing, Ont., Canada, 8/16/54
Cameron, Rod (Rod Cox) (actor); Calgary, Alberta, Canada **(1912–1983)**
Campbell, Glen (singer); nr. Delight, Ark., 4/22/38
Campbell, Neve (actress); Guelph, Ont., Canada, 10/3/73
Camus, Albert (author); Mondovi, Algeria **(1913–1960)**
Canaletto (Giovanni Antonio Canale) (painter); Venice **(1697–1768)**
Candy, John (actor, comedian); Toronto **(1950–1994)**
Caniff, Milton (cartoonist); Hillsboro, Ohio **(1907–1988)**
Cannon, Dyan Samille Diane Friesen (actress); Tacoma, Wash., 1/4/37
Cantinflas (Mario Moreno-Reyes) (comedian); Mexico City **(1911–1993)**
Cantor, Eddie (Edward Iskowitz) (actor); New York City **(1892–1964)**
Capone, Al(fonse) (gangster); Naples, Italy **(1899–1947)**

Capote, Truman (novelist); New Orleans **(1924–1984)**
Capp, Al (Alfred Gerald Caplin) (cartoonist); New Haven, Conn. **(1909–1979)**
Capra, Frank (film producer, director); Palermo, Italy **(1897–1991)**
Caputo, Phil (Philip Joseph Caputo) (author, journalist); Chicago, 6/10/41
Caravaggio, Michelangelo Merisi da (painter); Caravaggio (Italy) **(1573–1610)**
Cardin, Pierre (fashion designer); nr. Venice, 7/7/22
Cardinale, Claudia (actress); Tunis, Tunisia, 4/15/39
Carey, Drew (actor, producer); Cleveland, 5/23/58
Carey, Harry (actor); New York City **(1878–1947)**
Carey, Macdonald (actor); Sioux City, Iowa **(1913–1994)**
Carlin, George (comedian); Bronx, N.Y., 5/12/37
Carlisle, Kitty (singer, actress); New Orleans, 9/3/15
Carlyle, Thomas (essayist, historian); Ecclefechan, Scotland **(1795–1881)**
Carmichael, Hoagy (Hoagland Howard) (songwriter); Bloomington, Ind. **(1899–1981)**
Carne, Judy (Joyce Botterill) (singer); Northampton, England, 4/27/39
Carnegie, Andrew (industrialist); Dunfermline, Scotland **(1835–1919)**
Carney, Art (actor); Mt. Vernon, N.Y., 11/4/18
Caron, Leslie (actress); Paris, 7/1/31
Carr, Vikki (Florencia Bisenta de Casillas Martinez Cordona) (singer); El Paso, Tex., 7/19/42
Carracci, Annibale (painter); Bologna (Italy) **(1560–1609)**
Carracci, Lodovico (painter); Bologna (Italy) **(1555–1619)**
Carradine, David (actor); Hollywood, Calif., 12/8/36
Carradine, John (actor); New York City **(1906–1988)**
Carradine, Keith (actor); San Mateo, Calif., 8/8/49
Carreras, José (tenor); Barcelona, Spain, 12/5/46
Carroll, Diahann (Carol Diahann Johnson) (singer, actress); Bronx, N.Y., 7/17/35
Carroll, Leo G. (actor); Weedon, England **(1892–1972)**
Carroll, Lewis (Charles Lutwidge Dodgson) (author, mathematician); Daresbury, England **(1832–1898)**
Carson, Jack (actor); Carmen, Man., Canada **(1910–1963)**
Carson, Johnny (TV entertainer); Corning, Iowa, 10/23/25
Carson, Kit (Christopher Carson) (scout); Madison County, Ky. **(1809–1868)**
Carson, Rachel (biologist, author); Springdale, Pa. **(1907–1964)**
Carter, Dixie (actress); McLemoresville, Tenn., 5/25/39
Carter, Jack (comedian); New York City, 6/24/23
Carter, James Earl, Jr. (39th U.S. president); Plains, Ga., 10/1/24
Carter, Lynda (actress); Phoenix, Ariz., 7/24/51
Cartier, Jacques (explorer); Saint-Malo, Brittany (France) **(1491–1557)**
Cartier-Bresson, Henri (photographer); Chanteloup, France, 8/22/08
Cartland, Barbara (author); England, 7/9/01
Caruso, Enrico (Errico Caruso) (tenor); Naples, Italy **(1873–1921)**
Carver, George Washington (botanist); Diamond Grove, Mo. **(1864–1943)**
Cary, Arthur Joyce Lunel (novelist); Londonderry, Ireland **(1888–1957)**
Casals, Pablo (cellist); Vendrell, Spain **(1876–1973)**
Casanova de Seingalt, Giovanni Jacopo (adventurer); Venice **(1725–1798)**
Cash, Johnny (singer); nr. Kingsland, Ark., 2/26/32
Cass, Peggy (comedienne); Boston, 5/21/24
Cassatt, Mary (painter); Allegheny, Pa. **(1844–1926)**
Cassavetes, John (director); New York City **(1929–1989)**
Cassidy, David (singer); New York City, 4/12/50
Cassidy, Jack (actor); Richmond Hill, Queens, N.Y. **(1927–1976)**
Cassidy, Shaun (actor); Los Angeles, 9/27/58
Cassini, Oleg (Oleg Lolewski-Cassini) (fashion designer); Paris, 4/11/13
Castagno, Andrea del (painter); San Martino a Corella (Italy) **(c. 1421–1457)**
Castle, Irene (Irene Foote) (actress, dancer); New Rochelle, N.Y. **(1893–1969)**
Castle, Vernon Blythe (dancer, aviator); Norwich, England **(1887–1918)**
Castro Ruz, Fidel (Premier); Mayari, Oriente, Cuba, 8/13/26
Cather, Willa Sibert (novelist); Winchester, Va. **(1876–1947)**
Cato, Marcus Porcius (called Cato the Elder) (statesman); Tusculum (Italy) **(234–149 B.C.E.)**
Catt, Carrie Chapman Lane (woman suffragist); Ripon, Wis. **(1859–1947)**
Catton, Bruce (historian); Petoskey, Mich. **(1899–1978)**
Catullus, Gaius Valerius (poet); Verona **(c. 84–c. 54 B.C.E.)**
Cavallaro, Carmen (band leader); New York City **(1913–1989)**
Cavett, Dick (Richard Cavett) (TV entertainer); Gibbon, Neb., 11/19/36
Ceausecu, Nicolae (head of state); Scorniscesti, Romania **(1918–1989)**
Céline, Louis Ferdinand (pseud. of Louis Fuch Destouches) (novelist); Paris **(1894–1961)**
Cellini, Benvenuto (goldsmith, sculptor); Florence (Italy) **(1500–1571)**
Cervantes Saavedra, Miguel de (novelist); Alcalá de Henares, Spain **(1547–1616)**
Cézanne, Paul (painter); Aix-en-Provence, France **(1839–1906)**
Chagall, Marc (painter); Vitebsk, Russia **(1887–1985)**
Chaliapin, Feodor Ivanovitch (operatic basso); Kazan, Russia **(1873–1938)**
Chamberlain, Arthur Neville (statesman); Edgbaston, England **(1869–1940)**
Chamberlain, Richard (actor, producer); Los Angeles, 3/31/35
Champion, Gower (choreographer); Geneva, Ill. **(1921–1980)**
Champion, Marge (actress, dancer); Los Angeles, 9/2/23
Champlain, Samuel de (explorer); nr. Rochefort, France **(1567–1635)**
Chan, Jackie (Chan Kwong Sang) (actor); Hong Kong, 4/7/54
Chancellor, John (TV commentator); Chicago **(1927–1996)**
Chandler, Jeff (actor); Brooklyn, N.Y. **(1918–1961)**
Chandler, Raymond (writer); Chicago **(1883–1959)**
Chanel, "Coco" (Gabriel Bonheur) (fashion designer); Issoire, France **(1883–1971)**
Chaney, Lon (actor); Colorado Springs, Colo. **(1883–1930)**
Channing, Carol (actress); Seattle, 1/31/23
Channing, Stockard (Susan Stockard) (actress); New York City, 2/13/44
Chaplin, Geraldine (actress); Santa Monica, Calif., 7/31/44
Chaplin, Sir Charles (actor); London **(1889–1977)**
Charisse, Cyd (Tula Finklea) (dancer, actress); Amarillo, Tex., 3/8/21
Charlemagne (Holy Roman Emperor); birthplace unknown **(742–814)**
Charles, Ray (Ray Charles Robinson) (pianist, singer, songwriter); Albany Ga., 9/23/30
Charo (Maria Rosario Pilar Martinez) (actress); Murcia, Spain, 1/15/51
Chase, Chevy (Cornelius Crane Chase) (comedian); New York City, 10/8/43
Chase, Lucia (founder Ballet Theatre [now American Ballet Theatre]); Waterbury, Conn. **(1907–1986)**
Chateaubriand, François René de (writer, statesman); St. Malo, France **(1768–1848)**
Chaucer, Geoffrey (poet); London **(c. 1340–1400)**
Chávez, Carlos (composer); nr. Mexico City **(1899–1978)**
Chavez, Cesar (labor leader); nr. Yuma, Ariz. **(1927–1993)**
Chayefsky, Paddy (Sidney Chayefsky) (playwright); New York City **(1923–1981)**
Checker, Chubby (Ernest Evans) (performer); Philadelphia, 10/3/41
Cheever, John (novelist); Quincy, Mass. **(1912–1982)**
Chekhov, Anton Pavlovich (dramatist, short-story writer); Taganrog, Russia **(1860–1904)**
Cher (Cherilyn Sarkisian La Piere) (actress, singer); El Centro, Calif., 5/20/46
Cherubini, Luigi (composer); Florence **(1760–1842)**
Chesterton, Gilbert Keith (author); Kensington, England **(1874–1936)**
Chesnutt, Charles Waddell (author); Cleveland **(1858–1932)**
Chevalier, Maurice (entertainer); Paris **(1888–1972)**
Chiang Kai-shek (Chief of State); Feng-hwa, China **(1887–1975)**
Child, Julia (food expert); Pasadena, Calif., 8/15/12
Chippendale, Thomas (cabinet-maker); Otley, England **(1718–1779)**
Chirico, Giorgio de (painter); Vólos, Greece **(1888–1978)**
Chisholm, Shirley Anita St. Hill (U.S. Representative); Brooklyn, N.Y., 11/30/24
Chlumsky, Anna (actress); Chicago, 12/3/80
Chomsky, (Avram) Noam (linguist, educator, activist); Philadelphia, 12/7/28
Chopin, Frédéric François (composer); nr. Warsaw **(1810–1849)**
Chopin, Kate O'Flaherty (author); St. Louis **(1851–1904)**
Christie, Agatha (mystery writer); Torquay, England **(1890–1976)**
Christie, Julie (actress); Chukua, India, 4/14/41
Chung, Connie (broadcast journalist); Washington, D.C., 8/20/46
Churchill, Sir Winston Leonard Spencer (statesman); Blenheim Palace, Oxfordshire, England **(1874–1965)**
Cicero, Marcus Tullius (orator, statesman); Arpinum (Italy) **(106–43 B.C.E.)**

Cid, El (Rodrigo [or Ruy] Dìez de Bivar) (Spanish national hero); nr. Burgos, Spain **(c. 1043–1099)**
Cilento, Diane (actress); Queensland, Australia, 10/5/33
Cimabue, Giovanni (painter); Florence (Italy) **(c. 1240–c. 1302)**
Cimino, Michael (director, writer, producer); New York City, 1943
Claire, Ina (Ina Fagan) (actress); Washington, D.C. **(1895–1985)**
Clancy, Tom (novelist); Baltimore, 4/12/47
Clapton, Eric (singer, guitarist); Ripley, England, 3/30/45
Clark, Dick (TV personality); Mt. Vernon, N.Y., 11/30/29
Clark, Mary Higgins (writer); New York City, 12/24/31
Clark, Petula (singer); Epsom, England, 11/15/34
Clark, Roy (country music artist); Meherrin, Va., 4/15/33
Clark, William (explorer); Caroline County, Va. **(1770–1838)**
Clarke, Arthur C. (science fiction writer); Minehead, England, 12/16/17
Claude Lorrain (Claude Gellée) (painter); Champagne, France **(1600–1682)**
Clausewitz, Karl von (military strategist); Burg (Germany) **(1780–1831)**
Clay, Henry (statesman); Hanover County, Va. **(1777–1852)**
Clay, Lucius D. (banker, ex-general); Marietta, Ga. **(1897–1978)**
Clayburgh, Jill (actress); New York City, 4/30/44
Cleary, Beverly (Beverly Atlee Bunn) (children's author); McMinnville, Ore., 1916
Cleaver, Eldridge (Leroy) (author, activist); Wabbaseka, Ark. **(1935–1998)**
Cleese, John (writer, actor); Weston-super-Mare, England, 10/27/39
Clemenceau, Georges (statesman); Mouilleron-en-Pareds, Vondée, France **(1841–1929)**
Cleopatra (Queen of Egypt); Alexandria, Egypt **(69–30 B.C.E.)**
Cleveland, Stephen Grover (22nd & 24th U.S. president); Caldwell, N.J. **(1837–1908)**
Cliburn, Van (Harvey Lavan Cliburn, Jr.) (concert pianist); Shreveport, La., 7/12/34
Clift, Montgomery (actor); Omaha, Neb. **(1920–1966)**
Cline, Patsy (singer); Winchester, Va. **(1933–1963)**
Clinton, William Jefferson (42nd U.S. president); Hope, Ark., 8/19/46
Clooney, George (actor); Lexington, Ky., 5/6/61
Clooney, Rosemary (singer); Maysville, Ky., 5/23/28
Close, Glenn (actress); Greenwich, Conn., 3/19/47
Clurman, Harold (stage producer); New York City **(1901–1980)**
Cobb, Irvin Shrewsbury (humorist); Paducah, Ky. **(1876–1944)**
Cobb, Lee J. (Leo Jacob Cobb) (actor); New York City **(1911–1976)**
Coburn, Charles Douville (actor); Savannah, Ga. **(1877–1961)**
Coburn, James (actor); Laurel, Neb., 8/31/28
Coca, Imogene (comedienne); Philadelphia, 11/18/08
Cocker, Joe (John Robert Cocker) (singer); Sheffield, England, 5/20/44
Coco, James (actor); New York City **(1929–1987)**
Cocteau, Jean (author); Maison-Lafitte, France **(1891–1963)**
Cohan, George Michael (actor, dramatist); Providence, R.I. **(1878–1942)**
Colbert, Claudette (Lily Chauchoin) (actress); Paris **(1903–1996)**
Cole, Nat "King" (singer); Montgomery, Ala. **(1919–1965)**
Cole, Natalie (singer); Los Angeles, 2/6/50
Cole, Paula (alternative musician); Rockport, Mass., 4/15/68
Cole, Thomas (painter); Lancashire, England **(1801–1848)**
Coleman, Dabney (actor); Austin, Tex., 1/3/32
Coleridge, Samuel Taylor (poet); Ottery St. Mary, England **(1772–1834)**
Colette (Sidonie-Gabrielle Colette) (novelist); St.-Sauveur, France **(1873–1954)**
Collingwood, Charles (TV commentator); Three Rivers, Mich. **(1917–1985)**
Collins, Joan (actress); London, 5/23/33
Collins, Judy (singer); Seattle, 5/1/39
Colman, Ronald (actor); Richmond, England **(1891–1958)**
Colonna, Jerry (comedian); Boston **(1905–1986)**
Coltrane, John (jazz musician); Hamlet, N.C. **(1926–1967)**
Columbo, Russ (singer, bandleader); San Francisco **(1908–1934)**
Columbus, Christopher (Cristoforo Colombo) (explorer); Genoa (Italy) **(1451–1506)**
Comden, Betty (writer); New York City, 5/3/19
Comenius, Johann Amos (educational reformer); Nivnice, Moravia (Czech Republic) **(1592–1670)**
Commager, Henry Steele (historian); Pittsburgh **(1902–1998)**
Como, Perry (Pierino Como) (singer); Canonsburg, Pa., 5/18/12
Compton, Karl Taylor (physicist); Wooster, Ohio **(1887–1954)**
Comte, Auguste (philosopher); Montpellier, France **(1798–1857)**
Conant, James B. (educator, statesman); Dorchester, Mass. **(1893–1978)**
Condon, Eddie (jazz musician); Goodland, Ind. **(1905–1973)**
Confucius (K'ung Fu-tzu) (philosopher); Shantung province, China **(c. 551–479 B.C.E.)**
Congreve, William (dramatist); nr. Leeds, England **(1670–1729)**
Connelly, Marc (playwright); McKeesport, Pa. **(1890–1980)**
Connery, Sean (actor); Edinburgh, Scotland, 8/25/30
Conniff, Ray (band leader); Attleboro, Mass., 11/6/16
Connors, Chuck (actor); Brooklyn, N.Y. **(1921–1992)**
Connors, Mike (Krekor Ohanian) (actor); Fresno, Calif., 8/15/25
Conrad, Joseph (Teodor Jozef Konrad Korzeniowski) (novelist); Berdichev, Ukraine **(1857–1924)**
Conrad, Robert (Conrad Robert Falk) (actor); Chicago, 3/1/35
Conrad, William (actor); Louisville, Ky. **(1920–1994)**
Conried, Hans (Frank Foster) (actor); Baltimore **(1915–1982)**
Conroy, Pat (author); Atlanta, 10/26/45
Constable, John (painter); East Bergholt, Suffolk, England **(1776–1837)**
Constantine II (ex-king of Greece); Athens, 6/2/40
Constantine, Michael (actor); Reading, Pa., 5/22/27
Conte, Richard (actor); New York City **(1916–1975)**
Conti, Tom (actor); Paisley, Scotland, 11/22/41
Convy, Bert (actor, host); St. Louis **(1933–1991)**
Conway, Tim (comedian); Chagrin Falls, Ohio, 12/15/33
Coogan, Jackie (actor); Los Angeles **(1914–1984)**
Cook, Peter (actor, writer); Torquay, England **(1937–1995)**
Cooke, Alistair (Alfred Alistair) (TV narrator, journalist); Manchester, England, 11/20/08
Cooke, Jack Kent (business executive); Hamilton, Ont., Canada **(1912–1997)**
Cooley, Denton A(rthur) (heart surgeon); Houston, 8/22/20
Coolidge, John Calvin (30th U.S. president); Plymouth, Vt. **(1872–1933)**
Coolidge, Rita (singer); Nashville, Tenn., 5/1/45
Cooper, Alice (Vincent Furnier) (rock musician); Detroit, 2/4/48
Cooper, Gary (Frank James Cooper) (actor); Helena, Mont. **(1901–1961)**
Cooper, Dame Gladys (actress); Lewisham, England **(1898–1971)**
Cooper, Jackie (actor, director); Los Angeles, 9/15/22
Cooper, James Fenimore (novelist); Burlington, N.J. **(1789–1851)**
Cooper, Peter (industrialist, philanthropist); New York City **(1791–1883)**
Copernicus, Nicolaus (Mikolaj Kopernik) (astronomer); Thorn, Poland **(1473–1543)**
Copland, Aaron (composer); Brooklyn, N.Y. **(1900–1990)**
Copley, John Singleton (painter); Boston **(1738–1815)**
Copperfield, David (David Kotkin) (illusionist); Metuchen, N.J., 9/16/56
Coppola, Francis Ford (film director); Detroit, 4/7/39
Corelli, Arcangelo (composer); Fusignano, Italy **(1653–1713)**
Corelli, Franco (operatic tenor); Ancona, Italy, 4/8/23
Corneille, Pierre (dramatist); Rouen, France **(1606–1684)**
Cornell, Katharine (actress); Berlin **(1893–1974)**
Corot, Jean Baptiste Camille (painter); Paris **(1796–1875)**
Correggio, Antonio Allegri da (painter); Correggio (Italy) **(1494–1534)**
Corsaro, Frank (opera director); New York harbor, 12/22/24
Cortés (or Cortez), Hernando (explorer); Medellin, Spain **(1485–1547)**
Cosby, Bill (actor); Philadelphia, 7/12/37
Cosell, Howard (Howard Cohen) (sportscaster); Winston-Salem, N.C. **(1918–1995)**
Costello, Elvis (Declan Patrick McManus) (singer, musician, songwriter); London, 1954
Costello, Lou (comedian); Paterson, N.J. **(1908–1959)**
Costner, Kevin (actor); Los Angeles, 1/18/55
Cotten, Joseph (actor); Petersburg, Va. **(1905–1994)**
Couperin, François (composer); Paris **(1668–1733)**
Courbet, Gustave (painter); Ornans, France **(1819–1877)**
Couric, Katie (TV host); Arlington, Va., 1/7/57
Courtenay, Tom (actor); Hull, England, 2/25/37
Cousins, Norman (publisher); Union Hill, N.J. **(1915–1990)**
Cousteau, Jacques-Yves (marine explorer); St. André-de-Cubzac, France **(1910–1997)**
Covey, Stephen R. (author); Salt Lake City, 10/24/32
Coward, Sir Noel (playwright, actor); Teddington, England **(1899–1973)**
Cowles, Gardner, Jr. (newspaper publisher); Algona, Iowa **(1903–1985)**
Cowper, William (poet); Great Berkhamstead, England **(1731–1800)**
Cox, Archibald (Watergate prosecutor); Plainfield, N.J., 5/17/12
Cox, Courteney (actress); Birmingham, Ala., 6/15/64
Cozzens, James Gould (novelist); Chicago **(1903–1978)**

Crabbe, Buster (Clarence Crabbe) (actor); Oakland, Calif. **(1908–1983)**
Cranach, Lucas, the elder (painter); Kronach (Germany) **(1472–1553)**
Crane, Hart (poet); Garrettsville, Ohio **(1899–1932)**
Crane, Stephen (novelist, poet); Newark, N.J. **(1871–1900)**
Cranmer, Thomas (churchman); Aslacton, England **(1489–1556)**
Crawford, Broderick (actor); Philadelphia **(1911–1986)**
Crawford, Cheryl (stage producer); Akron, Ohio **(1902–1986)**
Crawford, Joan (Lucille LeSueur) (actress, business executive); San Antonio **(1908–1977)**
Crazy Horse (Lakota Indian leader); nr. Bear Butte, S.D. **(1840?–1877)**
Crenna, Richard (actor); Los Angeles, 11/30/27
Crespin, Régine (operatic soprano); Marseilles, France, 2/23/29
Crichton, (John) Michael (novelist); Chicago, 10/23/42
Crick, Francis Harry Compton (scientist, Nobel laureate); Northampton, England, 6/8/16
Crisp, Donald (actor); London **(1880–1974)**
Croce, Benedetto (philosopher); Peseasseroli, Aquila, Italy **(1866–1952)**
Croce, Jim (singer); Philadelphia **(1942–1973)**
Crockett, Davy (David) (frontiersman); Greene County, Tenn. **(1786–1836)**
Cromwell, Oliver (statesman); Huntingdon, England **(1599–1658)**
Cronin, A. J. (Archibald J. Cronin) (novelist); Cardross, Scotland **(1896–1981)**
Cronkite, Walter (TV newscaster); St. Joseph, Mo., 11/4/16
Cronyn, Hume (actor); London, Ont., Canada, 7/18/11
Crosby, Bing (Harry Lillis) (singer, actor); Tacoma, Wash. **(1904–1977)**
Crosby, Bob (musician); Spokane, Wash. **(1913–1993)**
Crosby, Cathy Lee (actress); Los Angeles, 12/2/48
Crosby, Norm (comedian); Boston, 9/15/27
Cross, Ben (Bernard) (actor); Paddington, England, 12/16/47
Cross, Milton (opera commentator); New York City **(1897–1975)**
Crouse, Russel (playwright); Findlay, Ohio **(1893–1966)**
Cruise, Tom (Thomas Mapother IV) (actor, producer); Syracuse, N.Y., 7/3/62
Crystal, Billy (comedian, actor); Long Beach, N.Y., 3/14/47
Cugat, Xavier (band leader); Barcelona, Spain **(1900–1990)**
Cukor, George (film director); New York City **(1899–1983)**
Cullen, Bill (William Lawrence Cullen) (radio and TV entertainer); Pittsburgh **(1920–1990)**
Cullen, Countee (poet); New York City **(1903–1946)**
Culp, Robert (actor); Berkeley, Calif., 8/16/30
cummings, e. e. (Edward Estlin Cummings) (poet); Cambridge, Mass. **(1894–1962)**
Cummings, Robert (actor); Joplin, Mo. **(1908–1990)**
Cunningham, Merce (choreographer); Centralia, Wash., 4/16/19
Curie, Marie (Marja Sklodowska) (physical chemist, Nobel laureate); Warsaw **(1867–1934)**
Curie, Pierre (physicist); Paris **(1859–1906)**
Curtin, Jane (actress); Cambridge, Mass., 9/6/47
Curtin, Phyllis (soprano); Clarksburg, W. Va., 12/3/27
Curtis, Jamie Lee (actress); Los Angeles, 11/22/58
Curtis, Tony (Bernard Schwartz) (actor); Bronx, N.Y., 6/3/25
Curzon, Clifford (concert pianist); London **(1907–1982)**
Cusack, John (actor); Chicago, 6/28/66
Custer, George Armstrong (army officer); New Rumley, Ohio **(1839–1876)**

D

Dafoe, Willem (William Dafoe, Jr.) (actor); Appleton, Wis., 7/22/55
da Gama, Vasco (explorer); Sines, Portugal **(1460–1524)**
Daguerre, Louis (photographic pioneer); nr. Paris **(1787–1851)**
Dahl, Arlene (actress); Minneapolis, 8/11/28
Dale, Jim (actor, singer, songwriter); Rothwell, England, 8/15/35
Daley, Richard J. (Mayor of Chicago); Chicago **(1902–1976)**
Dali, Salvador (painter); Figueras, Spain **(1904–1989)**
Dalton, John (chemist); nr. Cockermouth, England **(1766–1844)**
Dalton, Timothy (actor); Colwyn Bay, Wales, U.K ., 3/21/46
Daly, Tyne (actress); Madison, Wis., 2/21/46
d'Amboise, Jacques (ballet dancer); Dedham, Mass., 7/28/34
Damone, Vic (Vito Farinola) (singer); Brooklyn, N.Y., 6/12/28
Damrosch, Walter Johannes (orchestra conductor); Breslau (Poland) **(1862–1950)**
Dana, Charles Anderson (editor); Hinsdale, N.H. **(1819–1897)**
Dandridge, Dorothy (actress); Cleveland **(1923–1965)**
Danes, Claire (actress); New York City, 4/12/79
Dangerfield, Rodney (Jacob Cohen) (actor, comedian); Babylon, N.Y., 11/22/22
Daniels, Bebe (Virginia Daniels) (actress); Dallas **(1901–1971)**
Daniels, William (actor); Brooklyn, N.Y., 3/31/27
Danilova, Alexandra (ballet dancer); Peterhof, Russia **(1904–1997)**
Dannay, Frederic (novelist, pseudonym Ellery Queen); Brooklyn, N.Y. **(1905–1982)**
Danner, Blythe (actress); Philadelphia, 2/3/43
D'Annunzio, Gabriele (soldier, author); Francaville at Mare, Pescara, Italy **(1863–1938)**
Danson, Ted (actor); San Diego, Calif., 12/29/47
Dante (or Durante) Alighieri (poet); Florence (Italy) **(1265–1321)**
Danton, Georges Jacques (French Revolutionary leader); Arcis-sur-Aube, France **(1759–1794)**
Danza, Tony (actor); Brooklyn, N.Y., 4/21/51
Darnell, Linda (actress); Dallas **(1921–1965)**
Darren, James (actor); Philadelphia, 6/8/36
Darrow, Clarence Seward (lawyer); Kinsman, Ohio **(1857–1938)**
Darwell, Jane (actress); Palmyra, Mo. **(1879–1967)**
Darwin, Charles Robert (naturalist); Shrewsbury, England **(1809–1882)**
daSilva, Howard (actor); Cleveland **(1909–1986)**
Dassin, Jules (film director); Middletown, Conn., 12/18/11
Daumier, Honoré (caricaturist); Marseilles, France **(1808–1879)**
David, Jacques-Louis (painter); Paris **(1748–1825)**
David (King of Israel and Judah) died c. 973 B.C.E.
Davidson, John (singer, actor); Pittsburgh, 12/13/41
Davies, Marion (Marion Douras) (actress); New York City **(1897–1961)**
Davies, (William) Robertson (writer); Thamesville, Ont., Canada **(1913–1996)**
Davis, Angela (social activist); Birmingham, Ala., 1/26/44
Davis, Ann B. (actress); Schenectady, N.Y., 5/5/26
Davis, Lt. Gen. Benjamin O., Jr. (Air Force general); Washington, D.C., 12/18/12
Davis, Brig. Gen. Benjamin O., Sr. (U.S. Army general); Washington, D.C. **(1877–1970)**
Davis, Bette (actress); Lowell, Mass. **(1908–1989)**
Davis, Geena (Virginia Davis) (actress); Wareham, Mass., 1/21/57
Davis, Jefferson (President of the Confederacy); Christian (now Todd) County, Ky. **(1808–1889)**
Davis, Judy (actress); Perth, Australia, 1955
Davis, Mac (singer); Lubbock, Tex., 1/21/42
Davis, Miles (jazz trumpeter); Alton, Ill. **(1926–1991)**
Davis, Ossie (actor, writer); Cogdell, Ga., 12/18/17
Davis, Sammy, Jr. (actor, singer); New York City **(1925–1990)**
Davis, Skeeter (Mary Francis Penick) (singer); Dry Ridge, Ky., 12/30/31
Davis, Stuart (painter); Philadelphia **(1894–1964)**
Dawson, Richard (actor, host); Gosport, Hampshire, England, 11/20/32
Day, Doris (Doris von Kappelhoff) (singer, actress); Cincinnati, 4/3/24
Dayan, Moshe (ex-Defense Minister of Israel); Dagania, Palestine **(1915–1981)**
Day-Lewis, Daniel (actor); London, 4/29/58
Dean, James (actor); Marion, Ind. **(1931–1955)**
Dean, Jimmy (singer); Seth Ward, nr. Plainview, Tex., 8/10/28
De Bakey, Michael E. (heart surgeon); Lake Charles, La., 9/7/08
de Beauvoir, Simone (novelist, philosopher); Paris **(1908–1986)**
Debs, Eugene Victor (Socialist leader); Terre Haute, Ind. **(1855–1926)**
Debussy, Claude Achille (composer); St. Germain-en-Laye, France **(1862–1918)**
DeCamp, Rosemary (actress); Prescott, Ariz., 11/14/10
De Carlo, Yvonne (Peggy Yvonne Middleton) (actress); Vancouver, B.C., Canada, 9/1/24
de Chirico, Giorgio (painter); Volos, Greece **(1888–1978)**
Dee, Ruby (Ruby Ann Wallace) (actress); Cleveland, 10/27/24
Dee, Sandra (Alexandra Zuck) (actress); Bayonne, N.J., 4/23/42
Degas, Hilaire Germain Edgar (painter); Paris **(1834–1917)**
de Gaulle, Charles André Joseph Marie (soldier, statesman); Lille, France **(1890–1970)**
de Havilland, Olivia (actress); Tokyo, 7/1/16
de Kooning, Willem (artist); Rotterdam **(1904–1997)**
Delacroix, Eugène (painter); Charenton-St. Maurice, France **(1798–1863)**
Delany, Dana (actress); New York City, 3/15/56
de la Renta, Oscar (fashion designer); Santo Domingo, Dominican Republic, 7/22/32
Delaunay, Robert (painter); Paris **(1885–1941)**
De Laurentiis, Dino (film producer); Torre Annunziata, Bay of Naples, Italy, 8/8/18
della Robbia, Andrea (sculptor); Florence **(1435–1525)**
della Robbia, Luca (sculptor); Florence **(1400–1482)**

Delon, Alain (actor); Sceaux, France, 11/8/35
DeLuise, Dom (actor, comedian); Brooklyn, N.Y., 8/1/33
Demarest, William (actor); St. Paul, Minn. **(1892–1983)**
de Mille, Agnes (choreographer); New York City **(1905–1993)**
De Mille, Cecil Blount (film director); Ashfield, Mass. **(1881–1959)**
Demosthenes (orator); Athens **(384?–322 B.C.E.)**
Deneuve, Catherine (actress); Paris, 10/22/43
Deng Xiaoping (Chinese leader); Sichuan province, China **(1904–1997)**
De Niro, Robert (actor, director); New York City, 8/17/43
Dennehy, Brian (actor); Bridgeport, Conn., 7/9/39
Denning, Richard (actor); Poughkeepsie, N.Y., 3/27/14
Dennis, Sandy (actress); Hastings, Neb. **(1937–1992)**
Denny, Reginald (actor); Richmond, England **(1891–1967)**
Denver, John (Henry John Deutschendorf, Jr.) (singer, actor); Roswell, N.M. **(1943–1997)**
De Palma, Brian (film director); Newark, N.J., 9/11/40
Depp, Johnny (actor); Owensboro, Ky., 6/9/63
Derain, André (painter); Chatou, Seine-et-Oise, France **(1880–1954)**
Derek, John (actor, director); Los Angeles **(1926–1998)**
Dern, Bruce (actor); Winnetka, Ill., 6/4/36
Dern, Laura (actress); Los Angeles, 2/10/67
Dershowitz, Alan (lawyer); Brooklyn, N.Y., 9/1/38
Derrida, Jacques (philosopher); El-Biar, Algeria, 7/15/30
Descartes, René (philosopher, mathematician); La Haye, France **(1596–1650)**
De Seversky, Alexander P. (aviator); Tiflis (Tlilisi, Georgia) **(1894–1974)**
De Sica, Vittorio (film director); Sora, Italy **(1901–1974)**
Desmond, Johnny (composer); Detroit **(1921–1985)**
Desmond, William (actor); Dublin **(1878–1949)**
De Soto, Hernando (explorer); Barcarrota, Spain **(c. 1500–1542)**
De Valera, Eamon (ex-President of Ireland); New York City **(1882–1975)**
Devane, William (actor); Albany, N.Y., 9/5/39
Devine, Andy (actor); Flagstaff, Ariz. **(1905–1977)**
DeVito, Danny (Daniel Michael DeVito) (actor, director); Neptune, N.J., 11/17/44
De Vries, Peter (novelist); Chicago **(1910–1993)**
de Waart, Edo (conductor); Amsterdam, the Netherlands, 6/1/41
Dewey, George (admiral); Montpelier, Vt. **(1837–1917)**
Dewey, John (philosopher, educator); Burlington, Vt. **(1859–1952)**
Dewey, Thomas E. (political figure); Owosso, Mich. **(1902–1971)**
Dewhurst, Colleen (actress); Montreal **(1926–1991)**
De Wolfe, Billy (actor); Wollaston, Mass. **(1907–1974)**
Dey, Susan (actress); Pekin, Ill., 12/10/52
Diaghilev, Sergei (ballet impressario); Novgorod, Russia **(1872–1929)**
Diamond, Neil (singer); Brooklyn, N.Y., 1/24/41
Diana (Diana Frances Spencer) (Princess of Wales); Sandringham, England **(1961–1997)**
Diaz, Cameron (actress, model); San Diego, Calif., 8/30/72
DiCaprio, Leonardo (actor); Los Angeles, 11/11/74
Dichter, Misha (pianist); Shanghai, 9/27/45
Dickens, Charles John Huffam (novelist); Portsea, England **(1812–1870)**
Dickey, James (writer); Atlanta **(1923–1997)**
Dickinson, Angie (Angeline Brown) (actress); Kulm, N.D., 9/30/31
Dickinson, Emily Elizabeth (poet); Amherst, Mass. **(1830–1886)**
Diddley, Bo (Elias McDaniel) (guitarist); McComb, Miss., 12/30/28
Diderot, Denis (encyclopedist); Langres, France **(1713–1784)**
Dietrich, Marlene (Maria Magdalena von Losch) (actress); Berlin **(1901–1992)**
Diller, Phyllis (Phyllis Driver) (comedienne); Lima, Ohio, 7/17/17
Dine, Jim (painter); Cincinnati, 6/16/35
Dinesen, Isak (Karen Blixen) (author); Rungsted, Denmark **(1885–1962)**
Dinkins, David (ex-Mayor of New York City); Trenton, N.J., 7/10/27
Diogenes (philosopher); Sinope (Turkey) **(c. 412–323 B.C.E.)**
Dion (Dion DiMucci) (singer); Bronx, N.Y., 7/18/39
Dion, Celine (musician); Charlemagne, Que., Canada, 3/30/68
Dior, Christian (fashion designer); Granville, France **(1905–1957)**
Disney, Walt(er) Elias (film animator, producer); Chicago **(1901–1966)**
Disraeli, Benjamin (Earl of Beaconsfield) (statesman); London **(1804–1881)**
Dix, Dorothea (civil rights reformer); Hampden, Maine **(1802–1887)**
Dixon, Jeane (Jeane Pinckert) (seer); Medford, Wis. **(1918–1997)**
Dobbs, Mattiwilda (soprano); Atlanta, 7/11/25
Doctorow, E(dgar) L(aurence) (novelist); New York City, 1/6/31
Dole, Elizabeth (public official); Salisbury, N.C., 7/29/36
Dole, Robert (political figure); Russell, Kans., 7/22/23
Dolin, Anton (dancer); Slinfold, England **(1904–1983)**
Domingo, Placido (tenor); Madrid, 1/21/41
Domino, Fats (Antoine) (musician); New Orleans, 2/26/28
Donahue, Phil (TV host); Cleveland, 12/21/35
Donahue, Troy (Merle Johnson) (actor); New York City, 1/27/36
Donaldson, Sam (broadcast journalist); El Paso, Tex., 3/11/34
Donat, Robert (actor); Withington, England **(1905–1958)**
Donatello (Donato Niccolò di Betto Bardi) (sculptor); Florence **(c. 1386–1466)**
Donlevy, Brian (actor); Portadown, Ireland **(1899–1972)**
Donne, John (poet); London **(1573–1631)**
Donovan (Donovan Leitch) (singer, songwriter); Glasgow, Scotland, 2/10/46
Doolittle, James H. (ex-Air Force general); Alameda, Calif. **(1896–1993)**
Doohan, James (actor); Vancouver, B.C., 3/20/20
Dorati, Antal (orchestra conductor); Budapest **(1906–1988)**
Dorn, Michael (actor); Luling, Tex., 12/9/52
Dorris, Michael (anthropologist, writer); Louisville, Ky. **(1945–1997)**
Dorsey, Jimmy (band leader); Shenandoah, Pa. **(1904–1957)**
Dorsey, Thomas Andrew (father of gospel music); Villa Rice, Ga. **(1899–1993)**
Dorsey, Tommy (band leader); Mahanoy Plane, Pa. **(1905–1956)**
Dos Passos, John (author); Chicago **(1896–1970)**
Dostoevski, Fyodor Mikhailovich (novelist); Moscow **(1821–1881)**
Dotrice, Roy (actor); Guernsey, Channel Islands, England, 5/26/23
Douglas, Aaron (painter); Topeka, Kans. **(1900–1979)**
Douglas, Helen Gahagan (ex-Representative); Boonton, N.J. **(1900–1980)**
Douglas, Kirk (Issur Danielovitch) (actor); Amsterdam, N.Y., 12/9/16
Douglas, Melvyn (Melvyn Hesselberg) (actor); Macon, Ga. **(1901–1981)**
Douglas, Michael (actor, producer); New Brunswick, N.J., 9/25/44
Douglas, Mike (Michael D. Dowd, Jr.) (TV host); Chicago, 8/11/25
Douglas, Stephen Arnold (politician); Brandon, Vt. **(1813–1861)**
Douglass, Frederick (abolitionist, author, orator); Tuckahoe, Md. **(1817–1895)**
Dow, Charles (financier); Sterling, Conn. **(1851–1902)**
Down, Lesley-Ann (actress); London, 3/17/54
Downey, Robert, Jr. (actor, director); New York City, 4/4/65
Downs, Hugh (broadcast journalist); Akron, Ohio, 2/14/21
Doyle, Sir Arthur Conan (novelist, spiritualist); Edinburgh, Scotland **(1859–1930)**
Doyle, David (actor); Lincoln, Neb. **(1929–1997)**
Drake, Sir Francis (navigator); Tavistock, England **(1545–1596)**
Dreiser, Theodore (writer); Terre Haute, Ind. **(1871–1945)**
Dreyfus, Alfred (French army officer); Mulhouse, (France) **(1859–1935)**
Dreyfuss, Richard (actor); Brooklyn, N.Y., 10/29/47
Drury, Allen (novelist); Houston **(1918–1998)**
Dryden, John (poet); Northamptonshire, England **(1631–1700)**
Dryer, Fred (ex-NFL player, actor); Hawthorne, Calif., 7/6/46
Dubček, Alexander (ex-President of Czechoslovakia); Uhroved, former Czechoslovakia **(1921–1992)**
Dubinsky, David (David Dobnievski) (labor leader); Brest-Litovsk (Belarus) **(1892–1982)**
Du Bois, W(illiam) E(dward) B(urghardt) (scholar, activist); Great Barrington, Mass. **(1868–1963)**
Duchamp, Marcel (painter); Blainville, France **(1887–1968)**
Duchin, Eddy (pianist, bandleader); Cambridge, Mass. **(1909–1951)**
Duchin, Peter (pianist, band leader); New York City, 7/28/37
Duchovny, David (actor); New York City, 8/7/60
Dufay, Guillaume (composer); Cambrai, France **(c. 1400–1474)**
Duff, Howard (actor); Bremerton, Wash. **(1917–1990)**
Duffy, Julia (actress); Minneapolis, Minn., 6/27/50
Dufy, Raoul (painter); Le Havre, France **(1877–1953)**
Dukakis, Olympia (actress); Lowell, Mass., 6/20/31
Duke, James B. (industrialist); nr. Durham, N.C. **(1856–1925)**
Duke, Patty (Anna Marie Duke) (actress); New York City, 12/14/46
Dullea, Keir (actor); Cleveland, 5/30/36
Dulles, Allen Welsh (ex-Director of CIA); Watertown, N.Y. **(1893–1969)**
Dulles, John Foster (political figure); Washington, D.C. **(1888–1959)**
Dumas, Alexandre (called Dumas fils) (novelist); Paris **(1824–1895)**
Dumas, Alexandre (called Dumas père) (novelist); Villers-Cotterets, France **(1802–1870)**
du Maurier, Daphne (novelist); London **(1907–1989)**
du Maurier, George Louis Palmella Busson (novelist); Paris **(1834–1896)**
Dumont, Margaret (actress); Brooklyn, N.Y. **(1889–1965)**
Dunaway, Faye (actress); Bascom, Fla., 1/14/41

Dunbar, Paul Laurence (poet, novelist); Dayton, Ohio **(1872–1906)**
Duncan, Isadora (dancer); San Francisco **(1878–1927)**
Duncan, Sandy (actress); Henderson, Tex., 2/20/46
Dunham, Katherine (dancer, choreographer); Chicago, 6/22/09
Dunne, Irene (actress); Louisville, Ky. **(1898–1990)**
Duns Scotus, John (theologian); Duns, Scotland **(1265–1303)**
Du Pont, Pierre S. (economist); Paris **(1739–1817)**
Durante, Jimmy (comedian); New York City **(1893–1980)**
Duras, Marguerite (Donnadieu) (novelist, dramatist); Gia Dinh (Vietnam) **(1914–1996)**
Durbin, Deanna (Edna Mae) (actress); Winnipeg, Canada, 12/4/22
Dürer, Albrecht (painter, engraver); Nürnberg(Germany) **(1471–1528)**
Durning, Charles (actor); Highland Falls, N.Y., 2/28/23
Durrell, Lawrence George (novelist); Julundur, India **(1912–1990)**
Duse, Eleonora (actress); Chioggia, Italy **(1859–1924)**
Dussault, Nancy (actress); Pensacola, Fla., 6/30/36
Duvall, Robert (actor, director, producer); San Diego, Calif., 1/5/31
Duvall, Shelley (actress); Houston, 7/7/49
Dvořák, Antonin (composer); Nelahozeves (Czechoslovakia) **(1841–1904)**
Dylan, Bob (Robert Zimmerman) (folk singer, composer); Duluth, Minn., 5/24/41
Dysart, Richard (actor); Brighton, Mass., 3/30/29

E

Eakins, Thomas (painter, sculptor); Philadelphia **(1844–1916)**
Earhart, Amelia (aviator); Atchison, Kans. **(1898–1937)**
Earp, Wyatt Berry Stapp (sheriff, gunfighter); Monmouth, Ill. **(1848–1929)**
Eastman, George (camera inventor); Waterville, N.Y. **(1854–1932)**
Eastwood, Clint (actor, director, producer); San Francisco, 5/31/30
Ebert, Roger (film critic); Urbana, Ill., 6/18/42
Ebsen, Buddy (Christian Ebsen, Jr.) (actor); Belleville, Ill., 4/2/08
Eckstine, Billy (singer); Pittsburgh **(1914–1993)**
Eddy, Mary Baker (founder of Christian Science Church); Bow, N.H. **(1821–1910)**
Eddy, Nelson (baritone, actor); Providence, R.I. **(1901–1967)**
Edel, Leon (author); Pittsburgh **(1907–1997)**
Edelman, Marian Wright (social activist); Bennettsville, S.C., 6/6/39
Eden, Sir Anthony (Earl of Avon) (ex-Prime Minister); Durham, England **(1897–1977)**
Eden, Barbara (actress); Tucson, Ariz., 8/23/34
Edison, Thomas Alva (inventor); Milan, Ohio **(1847–1931)**
Edwards, Anthony (actor); Santa Barbara, Calif., 7/19/62
Edwards, Blake (film writer, producer); Tulsa, Okla., 7/26/22
Edwards, Jonathan (theologian); East Windsor, Conn. **(1703–1758)**
Edwards, Ralph (TV and radio producer); Merino, Colo., 6/13/13
Edwards, Vincent (Vincent Edward Zoino) (actor); Brooklyn, N.Y. **(1928–1996)**
Eglevsky, André (ballet dancer); Moscow **(1917–1977)**
Ehrlich, Paul (bacteriologist); Strzelin (Poland) **(1854–1915)**
Eichmann, (Karl) Adolf (Nazi, mass murderer); Solingen, Germany **(1906–1962)**
Eikenberry, Jill (actress); New Haven, Conn., 1/21/47
Einstein, Albert (physicist); Ulm, Germany **(1879–1955)**
Eisenhower, Dwight David (34th U.S. president); Denison, Tex. **(1890–1969)**
Eisenhower, Milton S. (educator); Abilene, Kans. **(1899–1985)**
Eisenstaedt, Alfred (photographer, photojournalist); Dirschau (Prussia, now Tczew, Poland) **(1898–1995)**
Ekland, Britt (Britt-Marie) (actress); Stockholm, 10/6/42
Elgar, Sir Edward (composer); Worcester, England **(1857–1934)**
Elgart, Larry (band leader); New London, Conn., 3/20/22
El Greco (Domenicos Theotocopoulos) (painter); Candia, Crete (Greece) **(c. 1541–1614)**
Elion, Gertrude B. (chemist, Nobel laureate); New York City, 1/23/18
Eliot, George (Mary Ann Evans) (novelist); Chilvers Coton, England **(1819–1880)**
Eliot, Thomas Stearns (poet); St. Louis **(1888–1965)**
Elizabeth I (Queen of England); Greenwich, England **(1533–1603)**
Elizabeth II (Queen of England); London, 4/21/26
Elizondo, Hector (actor); New York City, 12/22/36
Ellington, Duke (Edward Kennedy) (jazz musician); Washington, D.C. **(1899–1974)**
Elliot, "Mama" Cass (Ellen Naomi Cohen) (singer); Baltimore **(1941–1974)**
Elliott, Sam (actor); Sacramento, Calif., 8/9/44
Ellison, Lawrence J. (computer industry executive); New York City, 1944
Ellison, Ralph (novelist); Oklahoma City, Okla. **(1914–1994)**
Ellsberg, Daniel (activist); Chicago, 4/7/31
Elman, Mischa (violinist); Stalnoye, Ukraine **(1891–1967)**
Emerson, Ralph Waldo (philosopher, poet); Boston **(1803–1882)**
Enesco, Georges (composer); Dorohoi, Romania **(1881–1955)**
Engels, Friedrich (Socialist writer); Barmen (Germany) **(1820–1895)**
Englund, Robert (actor); Glendale, Calif., 6/6/49
Entremont, Philippe (concert pianist); Rheims, France, 6/7/34
Ephron, Nora (writer, director); New York City, 5/19/41
Epicurus (philosopher); Samos (Greece) **(341–270 B.C.E.)**
Epstein, Sir Jacob (sculptor); New York City **(1880–1959)**
Erasmus, Desiderius (Gerhard Gerhards) (scholar); Rotterdam **(1469–1536)**
Erdrich, (Karen) Louise (writer); Little Falls, Minn., 7/6/54
Erickson, Leif (actor); Alameda, Calif. **(1911–1986)**
Ericson, Leif (navigator) c. 10th century C.E.
Erikson, Erik H. (psychoanalyst); Frankfurt, Germany **(1902–1994)**
Ernst, Max (painter); Bruhl, Germany **(1891–1976)**
Erté (Romain de Tirtoff) (artist, designer); St. Petersburg, Russia **(1892–1990)**
Euclid (mathematician); Megara (Greece), fl. 300 B.C.E.
Euler, Leonhard (mathematician); Basel, Switzerland **(1707–1783)**
Euripides (dramatist); Salamis (Greece) **(c. 484–407 B.C.E.)**
Evans, Dale (born Lucille Wood Smith but raised as Frances Octavia Smith) (actress, singer); Uvalde, Tex., 10/30/12
Evans, Dame Edith (actress); London **(1888–1976)**
Evans, Linda (actress); Hartford, Conn., 11/18/42
Evans, Maurice (actor); Dorchester, England **(1901–1989)**
Everett, Chad (Raymond Lee Cramton) (actor); South Bend, Ind., 6/11/36
Evers, Charles (civil rights leader); Decatur, Miss., 9/14/22
Evers, Medgar (civil rights leader); Decatur, Miss. **(1925–1963)**
Evers-Williams, Myrlie (civil rights leader); Vicksburg, Miss., 3/17/33

F

Fabares, Shelley (actress); Santa Monica, Calif., 1/19/44
Fabian (Fabian Anthony Forte) (singer); Philadelphia, 2/6/43
Fabray, Nanette (Nanette Fabarés) (actress); San Diego, Calif., 10/27/22
Fahrenheit, Gabriel (German physicist); Danzig (Poland) **(1686–1736)**
Fairbanks, Douglas (Douglas Ulman) (actor); Denver **(1883–1939)**
Fairbanks, Douglas, Jr. (actor); New York City, 12/9/09
Fairchild, Morgan (Patsy Ann McClenny) (actress); Dallas, 2/3/50
Faith, Percy (conductor); Toronto **(1908–1976)**
Falk, Peter (actor); New York City, 9/16/27
Falla, Manuel de (composer); Cadiz, Spain **(1876–1946)**
Faludi, Susan (journalist, writer); New York City, 4/18/59
Falwell, Jerry (fundamentalist preacher); Lynchburg, Va., 8/11/33
Faraday, Michael (physicist); Newington, England **(1791–1867)**
Farentino, James (actor); Brooklyn, N.Y., 2/24/38
Farmer, James (civil rights leader); Marshall, Tex., 1/12/20
Farr, Jamie (actor); Toledo, Ohio, 7/1/34
Farrar, Geraldine (soprano, actress); Melrose, Mass. **(1882–1967)**
Farrell, Eileen (operatic soprano); Willimantic, Conn., 2/13/20
Farrell, James T. (novelist); Chicago **(1904–1979)**
Farrell, Mike (actor); St. Paul, Minn., 2/6/39
Farrell, Suzanne (Roberta Sue Ficker) (ballet dancer); Cincinnati, 8/16/45
Farrow, Mia (actress); Los Angeles, 2/9/46
Fasanella, Ralph (painter); New York City **(1914–1997)**
Fassbinder, Rainer Werner (film, stage director); Bad Wörishofen, (Germany) **(1946–1982)**
Fast, Howard (novelist); New York City, 11/11/14
Faubus, Orval E(ugene) (governor of Arkansas); Combs, Ark. **(1910–1994)**
Faulkner, William (novelist); New Albany, Miss. **(1897–1962)**
Fauré, Gabriel Urbain (composer); Pamiers, France **(1845–1924)**
Fawcett, Farrah (Mary Farrah Leni Fawcett) (actress); Corpus Christi, Tex., 2/2/47
Faye, Alice (Ann Leppert) (actress); New York City **(1912–1998)**
Feiffer, Jules (cartoonist); New York City, 1/26/29
Feininger, Lyonel (painter); New York City **(1871–1956)**
Feldman, Marty (actor, screenwriter, director); London **(1938–1982)**
Feldon, Barbara (actress); Pittsburgh, 3/12/41
Feliciano, José (singer); Larez, Puerto Rico, 9/10/45
Felker, Clay S. (editor, publisher); St. Louis, 10/2/25
Fell, Norman (actor); Philadelphia, 3/24/23
Fellini, Federico (film director); Rimini, Italy **(1920–1993)**
Fender, Freddie (Baldemar Huerta) (singer); San Benito, Tex., 6/4/37

Ferber, Edna (novelist); Kalamazoo, Mich. **(1885–1968)**
Ferguson, Maynard (jazz trumpeter); Verdun, Que., Canada, 5/4/28
Ferlinghetti, Lawrence (poet, writer, translator); Yonkers, N.Y., 3/24/19
Fermi, Enrico (atomic physicist); Rome **(1901–1954)**
Fernandel (Fernand Joseph Desire Contandin) (actor); Marseilles, France **(1903–1971)**
Ferraro, Geraldine Anne (political figure); New York City, 8/26/35
Ferrer, José (actor, director); Santurce, Puerto Rico **(1912–1992)**
Ferrer, Mel (actor); Elberon, N.J., 8/25/17
Fetchit, Stepin (Lincoln Theodore Perry) (comedian); Key West, Fla. **(1902–1985)**
Fiedler, Arthur (conductor); Boston **(1894–1979)**
Field, Eugene (poet); St. Louis **(1850–1895)**
Field, Marshall (merchant); nr. Conway, Mass. **(1834–1906)**
Field, Sally (actress); Pasadena, Calif., 11/6/46
Fielding, Henry (novelist); nr. Glastonbury, England **(1707–1754)**
Fields, W. C. (William Claude Dukenfield) (comedian); Philadelphia **(1880–1946)**
Fiennes, Ralph (actor); Suffolk, England, 12/22/62
Fierstein, Harvey (Forbes) (playwright, actor); Brooklyn, 6/6/54
Filene, Edward A. (merchant) **(1860–1937)**
Fillmore, Millard (13th U.S. president); Locke, Cayuga County, N.Y. **(1800–1874)**
Finch, Peter (actor); Kensington, England **(1916–1977)**
Finney, Albert (actor); Salford, England, 5/9/36
Firkusny, Rudolf (pianist); Napajedia, former Czechoslovakia **(1912–1994)**
Fischer-Dieskau, Dietrich (baritone); Berlin, 5/28/25
Fishburne, Laurence (actor); Augusta, Ga., 7/30/61
Fisher, Carrie (actress); Los Angeles, 10/21/56
Fisher, Eddie (Edwin) (singer); Philadelphia, 8/10/28
Fitzgerald, Barry (William Joseph Shields) (actor); Dublin **(1888–1961)**
Fitzgerald, Ella (singer); Newport News, Va. **(1918–1996)**
Fitzgerald, F. Scott (Francis Scott Key Fitzgerald) (novelist); St. Paul, Minn. **(1896–1940)**
Fitzgerald, Geraldine (actress); Dublin, 11/24/14
Fitzgerald, Pegeen (radio broadcaster); Norcatur, Kans. **(1910–1989)**
Flack, Roberta (singer); Black Mountain, N.C., 2/10/40
Flagstad, Kirsten (Wagnerian soprano); Hamar, Norway **(1895–1962)**
Flatt, Lester Raymond (bluegrass musician); Overton County, Tenn. **(1914–1979)**
Flaubert, Gustave (novelist); Rouen, France **(1821–1880)**
Fleming, Sir Alexander (bacteriologist); Lochfield, Scotland **(1881–1955)**
Fleming, Rhonda (Marilyn Louis) (actress); Los Angeles, 8/10/23
Fletcher, John (dramatist); Rye, Sussex, England **(1579–1625)**
Flynn, Errol (actor); Hobart, Tasmania **(1909–1959)**
Fodor, Eugene (violinist); Turkey Creek, Colo., 3/5/50
Fokine, Michel (dancer, choreographer); St. Petersburg, Russia **(1880–1942)**
Fonda, Henry (actor); Grand Island, Neb. **(1905–1982)**
Fonda, Jane (actress); New York City, 12/21/37
Fonda, Peter (actor); New York City, 2/23/39
Fontaine, Frank (singer, comedian); Cambridge, Mass. **(1920–1979)**
Fontaine, Joan (Joan de Havilland) (actress); Tokyo, 10/22/17
Fontanne, Lynn (actress); London **(1887–1983)**
Fonteyn, Dame Margot (Margaret Hookham) (ballet dancer); Reigate, England **(1919–1991)**
Foote, Shelby (historian); Greenville, Miss., 11/17/16
Forbes, Malcolm S(tevenson) (publisher, sportsman); Brooklyn, N.Y. **(1919–1990)**
Ford, Gerald Rudolph (38th U.S. president); Omaha, Neb., 7/14/13
Ford, Glenn (Gwyllyn Ford) (actor); Ste.-Christine, Que., Canada, 5/1/16
Ford, Harrison (actor); Chicago, 7/13/42
Ford, Henry (industrialist); Greenfield, Mich. **(1863–1947)**
Ford, John (film director); Cape Elizabeth, Maine **(1895–1973)**
Ford, Tennessee Ernie (Ernie Jennings Ford) (singer); Bristol, Tenn. **(1919–1991)**
Forrester, Maureen (contralto); Montreal, 7/25/30
Forsythe, John (actor); Penn's Grove, N.J., 1/29/18
Fosdick, Harry Emerson (clergyman); Buffalo, N.Y. **(1878–1968)**
Fosse, Bob (Robert Louis Fosse) (choreographer, director); Chicago **(1927–1987)**
Foster, Jodie (Alicia Christian Foster) (actress, director, producer); Los Angeles, 11/19/62
Foster, Stephen Collins (composer); nr. Pittsburgh **(1826–1864)**
Fountain, Pete (jazz musician); New Orleans, 7/3/30
Fox, Matthew (actor); Crowheart, Wy., 7/14/66
Fox, Michael J. (actor, producer); Edmonton, Alta., Canada, 6/9/61
Foxx, Redd (John Elroy Sanford) (actor, comedian); St. Louis **(1922–1991)**
Foy, Eddie, Jr. (dancer, actor); New Rochelle, N.Y. **(1905–1983)**
Fra Angelico (Giovanni da Fiesole) (painter); Vicchio in the Mugello, Tuscany (Italy) **(c. 1387–1455)**
Fracci, Carla (ballet dancer); Milan, Italy, 8/20/36
Fragonard, Jean Honoré (painter); Grasse, France **(1732–1806)**
Frakes, Jonathan (actor); Bethlehem, Pa., 8/19/52
Frampton, Peter (rock musician); Beckenham, England, 4/20/50
France, Anatole (Jacques Anatole François Thibault) (author); Paris **(1844–1924)**
Francescatti, Zino (violinist); Marseilles, France **(1902–1991)**
Franciosa, Anthony (Anthony Papaleo) (actor); New York City, 10/25/28
Francis, Anne (actress); Ossining, N.Y., 7/16/30
Francis, Arlene (Arlene Francis Kazanjian) (actress); Boston, 10/20/08
Francis, Connie (Concetta Franconero) (singer); Newark, N.J., 12/12/38
Francis, Genie (actress); Englewood, N.J., 5/26/62
Francis of Assisi, Saint (Giovanni Francesco Barnardone) (founder of Franciscans); Assisi, Italy **(1182–1226)**
Franck, César Auguste (composer); Liège (Belgium) **(1822–1890)**
Franco Bahamonde, Francisco (Chief of State); El Ferrol, Spain **(1892–1975)**
Frankenthaler, Helen (artist); New York City, 12/12/28
Frankl, Victor E. (psychiatrist); Vienna **(1905–1997)**
Franklin, Aretha (singer); Memphis, Tenn., 3/25/42
Franklin, Benjamin (statesman, scientist); Boston **(1706–1790)**
Franklin, Bonnie (actress); Santa Monica, Calif., 1/6/44
Franklin, John Hope (historian); Rentiesville, Okla., 1/2/15
Frann, Mary (actress); St. Louis, 2/27/43
Franz, Dennis (Dennis Schlachta) (actor); Chicago, 10/28/44
Frazer, Sir James George (anthropologist); Glasgow, Scotland **(1854–1941)**
Freeman, Morgan (actor); Memphis, Tenn., 6/1/37
Freud, Sigmund (psychoanalyst); Moravia, Czech Repubic **(1856–1939)**
Frey, Glenn (musician); Detroit, 11/6/48
Frick, Henry Clay (industrialist); Westmoreland Co., Pa. **(1849–1919)**
Friedan, Betty (Betty Naomi Goldstein) (feminist); Peoria, Ill., 2/4/21
Fromm, Erich (psychoanalyst); Frankfurt-am-Main, Germany **(1900–1980)**
Frost, David (TV entertainer); Tenterden, England, 4/7/39
Frost, Robert Lee (poet); San Francisco **(1874–1963)**
Fry, Christopher (playwright); Bristol, England, 12/18/07
Fugard, Athol (playwright); Middleburg, South Africa, 6/11/32
Fulbright, J. William (politician); Sumner, Mo. **(1905–1995)**
Fuller, Charles (playwright); Philadelphia, 3/5/39
Fuller, R(ichard) Buckminster (Jr.) (architect, educator); Milton, Mass. **(1895–1983)**
Fulton, Robert (inventor); Lancaster County, Pa. **(1765–1815)**
Funicello, Annette (actress); Utica, N.Y., 10/22/42
Funt, Allen (TV producer); Brooklyn, N.Y., 9/16/14

Gabin, Jean (actor); Paris **(1904–1976)**
Gable, (William) Clark (actor); Cadiz, Ohio **(1901–1960)**
Gabo, Naum (sculptor); Briansk, Russia **(1890–1977)**
Gabor, Eva (actress); Budapest **(1920–1995)**
Gabor, Zsa Zsa (Sari) (actress); Budapest, 2/6/17
Gabrieli, Giovanni (composer); Venice **(c. 1557–1612)**
Gaddis, William (novelist); New York City, 12/29/22
Gainsborough, Thomas (painter); Sudbury, Suffolk, England **(1727–1788)**
Galbraith, John Kenneth (economist); Iona Station, Ont., Canada, 10/15/08
Galilei, Galileo (astronomer, physicist); Pisa, Italy **(1564–1642)**
Gallico, Paul (novelist); New York City **(1897–1976)**
Gallup, George H. (poll taker); Jefferson, Iowa **(1901–1984)**
Galsworthy, John (novelist, dramatist); Coombe, England **(1867–1933)**
Galway, James (flutist); Belfast, Northern Ireland, 12/8/39
Gambling, John A. (radio broadcaster); New York City, 1930
Gandhi, Indira (Indira Nehru) (Prime Minister); Allahabad, India **(1917–1984)**
Gandhi, Mohandas Karamchand (called Mahatma Gandhi) (Hindu leader); Porbandar, India **(1869–1948)**
Gannett, Frank E. (editor, publisher) **(1876–1957)**

Garagiola, Joe (Joseph Henry Garagiola) (sportscaster); St. Louis, 2/12/26
Garbo, Greta (Greta Gustafsson) (actress); Stockholm **(1905–1990)**
Garcia, Andy (Andres Arturo Garcia-Menendez) (actor); Havana, Cuba, 4/12/56
Garcia, Jerry (rock musician); San Francisco **(1942–1995)**
Garcia Lorca, Frederico (poet, dramatist); Fuente Vaqueros, Spain **(1898–1936)**
Garden, Mary (soprano); Aberdeen, Scotland **(1874–1967)**
Gardenia, Vincent (actor); Naples, Italy **(1922–1992)**
Gardner, Ava (actress); Smithfield, N.C. **(1922–1990)**
Gardner, Erle Stanley (novelist); Malden, Mass. **(1889–1970)**
Garfield, James Abram (20th U.S. president); Cuyahoga County, Ohio **(1831–1881)**
Garfunkel, Art (Arthur) (singer); Newark, N.J., 11/5/41
Garibaldi, Giuseppe (Italian nationalist leader); Nice, France **(1807–1882)**
Garland, Judy (Frances Gumm) (actress, singer); Grand Rapids, Minn. **(1922–1969)**
Garner, Erroll (jazz pianist); Pittsburgh **(1921–1977)**
Garner, James (James Bumgarner) (actor); Norman, Okla., 4/7/28
Garner, Peggy Ann (actress); Canton, Ohio **(1932–1984)**
Garr, Teri (actress); Lakewood, Ohio, 12/11/49
Garrison, William Lloyd (abolitionist); Newburyport, Mass. **(1805–1879)**
Garroway, Dave (TV host); Schenectady, N.Y. **(1913–1982)**
Garson, Greer (actress); County Down, Northern Ireland **(1903–1996)**
Garth, Jennie (actress); Urbana, Ill., 4/3/72
Garvey, Marcus Moziah (black nationalist leader); Jamaica **(1887–1940)**
Gassman, Vittorio (film actor, director); Genoa, Italy, 9/1/22
Gates, Bill (William Henry Gates III) (software pioneer); Seattle, 10/28/55
Gates, Henry Louis, Jr. (scholar); Keyser, W. Va., 9/16/50
Gaudí, Antonio (architect); Reus, Spain **(1852–1926)**
Gauguin, Eugène Henri Paul (painter); Paris **(1848–1903)**
Gautama Buddha (Prince Siddhartha) (philosopher); Kapilavastu (India) **(c. 563–c. 483 B.C.E.)**
Gavin, John (actor, diplomat); Los Angeles, 4/8/35
Gavras, Konstantinos (Costa-Gavras) (film director); Loutra-Iraias, Greece, 2/13/33
Gaye, Marvin (singer); Washington, D.C. **(1939–1984)**
Gayle, Crystal (Brenda Gayle Webb) (singer); Paintsville, Ky., 1/9/51
Gaynor, Janet (actress); Philadelphia **(1906–1984)**
Gaynor, Mitzi (Francesca Mitzi Marlene de Czanyi von Gerber) (actress); Chicago, 9/4/31
Gazzara, Ben (Biagio Anthony Gazzara) (actor); New York City, 8/28/30
Gedda, Nicolai (tenor); Stockholm, 7/11/25
Genet, Jean (playwright); Paris **(1910–1986)**
Genghis Khan (Temujin) (conqueror); nr. Lake Baikal, Russia **(1162–1227)**
Gentry, Bobbie (Roberta Streeter) (singer); Chickasaw Co., Miss., 7/27/44
George, David Lloyd (statesman); Manchester, England **(1863–1945)**
George, Henry (economist, reformer); Philadelphia **(1839–1897)**
Gere, Richard (actor); Philadelphia, 8/29/49
Gericault, Jean Louis (painter); Rouen, France **(1791–1824)**
Geronimo (Goyathlay) (Apache chieftain); Arizona **(1829–1909)**
Gershwin, George (composer); Brooklyn, N.Y. **(1898–1937)**
Gershwin, Ira (lyricist); New York City **(1896–1983)**
Getty, J. Paul (oil executive); Minneapolis **(1892–1976)**
Getz, Stan (saxophonist); Philadelphia **(1927–1991)**
Ghiberti, Lorenzo (goldsmith, sculptor); Florence **(1378–1455)**
Ghostley, Alice (actress); Eve, Mo., 8/14/26
Giacometti, Alberto (sculptor); Switzerland **(1901–1966)**
Giannini, Giancarlo (actor); La Spezia, Italy, 8/1/42
Gibbon, Edward (historian); Putney, England **(1737–1794)**
Gibson, Charles Dana (illustrator); Roxbury, Mass. **(1867–1944)**
Gibson, Henry (actor, comedian); Germantown, Pa., 9/21/35
Gibson, Mel (actor, director, producer); Peekskill, N.Y., 1/3/56
Gide, André (author); Paris **(1869–1951)**
Gielgud, Sir John (actor); London, 4/14/04
Gifford, Kathie Lee (Kathie Lee Epstein) (talk show host); Paris, 8/16/53
Gilbert, Melissa (actress); Los Angeles, 5/8/64
Gilbert, Walter (chemist, Nobel laureate); Boston, 3/21/32
Gilbert, Sir William Schwenck (librettist); London **(1836–1911)**
Gilels, Emil (concert pianist); Odessa, Ukraine **(1916–1985)**
Gillespie, Dizzy (John Birks Gillespie) (jazz trumpeter); Cheraw, S.C. **(1917–1993)**
Gilligan, Carol (Friedman) (psychologist); New York City, 11/28/36
Gilpin, Peri (actress); Waco, Tex., 5/27/61
Gimbel, Bernard F. (merchant); Vincennes, Ind. **(1885–1966)**
Gingrich, Newt (politician); Harrisburg, Pa., 6/17/43
Ginsberg, Allen (poet); Newark, N.J. **(1926–1997)**
Giordano, Luca (painter); Naples, Italy **(1632–1705)**
Giorgione (painter); Castelfranco (Italy) **(c. 1477–1510)**
Giotto di Bondone (painter); Vespignamo (Italy) **(c. 1266–1337)**
Giovanni, Nikki (poet); Knoxville, Tenn., 6/7/43
Giroud, Françoise (French government official); Geneva, 9/21/16
Gish, Dorothy (actress); Massillon, Ohio **(1898–1968)**
Gish, Lillian (Lillian de Guiche) (actress); Springfield, Ohio **(1893–1993)**
Givenchy, Hubert (fashion designer); Beauvais, France, 2/21/27
Gladstone, William Ewart (statesman); Liverpool, England **(1809–1898)**
Glaser, Paul Michael (actor, director); Cambridge, Mass., 3/25/43
Glass, Philip (composer); Baltimore, 1/31/37
Gleason, Jackie (comedian); Brooklyn, N.Y. **(1916–1987)**
Gless, Sharon (actress); Los Angeles, 5/31/43
Glover, Danny (actor); San Francisco, 7/22/47
Gluck, Christoph Willibald (composer); Erasbach (Germany) **(1714–1787)**
Gobel, George (comedian); Chicago **(1920–1991)**
Godard, Jean Luc (film director); Paris, 12/3/30
Goddard, Paulette (Marion Levy) (actress); Great Neck, N.Y. **(1911–1990)**
Goddard, Robert Hutchings (father of modern rocketry); Worcester, Mass. **(1882–1945)**
Godfrey, Arthur (entertainer); New York City **(1903–1983)**
Goebbels, Joseph Paul (Nazi leader); Rheydt, Germany **(1897–1945)**
Goering, Hermann (Nazi leader); Rosenheim, Germany **(1893–1946)**
Goethals, George Washington (engineer); Brooklyn, N.Y. **(1858–1928)**
Goethe, Johann Wolfgang von (poet, playwright, novelist); Frankfurt-am-Main, Germany **(1749–1832)**
Gogol, Nikolai Vasilievich (novelist); nr. Mirgorod, Ukraine **(1809–1852)**
Goldberg, Rube (cartoonist); San Francisco **(1883–1970)**
Goldberg, Whoopi (Caryn Johnson) (actress); New York City, 11/13/49
Goldblum, Jeff (actor); Pittsburgh, 10/22/52
Golden, Harry (Harry Goldhurst) (author); New York City **(1902–1981)**
Goldman, Emma (anarchist); Kovno, Lithuania **(1869–1940)**
Goldsmith, Oliver (dramatist, poet); County Longford, Ireland **(1728–1774)**
Goldwyn, Samuel (Schmuel Gelbfisz) (film producer); Warsaw **(1879–1974)**
Gompers, Samuel (labor leader); London **(1850–1924)**
Goodall, Jane (Baroness van Lawick-Goodall) (ethologist); London, 4/3/34
Goodman, Benny (clarinetist); Chicago **(1909–1986)**
Goodman, John (actor); St. Louis, 6/20/52
Goodwin, Doris (Helen) Kearns (historian); Rockville Center, N.Y., 1/4/43
Goodyear, Charles (inventor); New Haven, Conn. **(1800–1860)**
Gorbachev, Mikhail Sergeyevich (Soviet leader); Privolnoye, (Russia), 3/2/31
Gordimer, Nadine (novelist, short-story writer); Springs, South Africa, 12/20/23
Gordon, Dexter (jazz musician); Los Angeles **(1923–1990)**
Gordon, Ruth (actress); Wollaston, Mass. **(1896–1985)**
Gordy, Berry, Jr. (record company executive); Detroit, 11/28/29
Gorey, Edward (St. John) (illustrator, author); Chicago, 2/22/25
Gorki, Maxim (Alexei Maximovich Peshkov) (author); Nizhni Novgorod, Russia **(1868–1936)**
Gorky, Arshile (painter); Armenia **(1904–1948)**
Gormé, Eydie (singer); Bronx, N.Y., 8/16/32
Gorshin, Frank (actor); Pittsburgh, 4/5/34
Gossett, Louis, Jr. (actor); Brooklyn, N.Y., 5/27/36
Gottschalk, Louis Moreau (pianist, composer); New Orleans **(1829–1869)**
Gould, Chester (cartoonist); Pawnee, Okla. **(1900–1985)**
Gould, Elliott (Elliott Goldstein) (actor); Brooklyn, N.Y., 8/29/38
Gould, Glenn (concert pianist); Toronto **(1932–1982)**
Gould, Morton (composer); Richmond Hill, Queens, N.Y. **(1913–1996)**

Gould, Stephen Jay (paleontologist, science writer); New York City, 9/10/41
Goulet, Robert (singer); Lawrence, Mass., 11/26/33
Gounod, Charles François (composer); Paris **(1818–1893)**
Goya y Lucientes, Francisco José de (painter); Fuendetodos, Spain **(1746–1828)**
Grable, Betty (actress); St. Louis **(1916–1973)**
Grace, Princess of Monaco (Grace Kelly) (ex-actress); Philadelphia **(1929–1982)**
Graham, Bill (Wolfgang Grajonca) (rock impresario); Berlin **(1930–1991)**
Graham, Billy (William F. Graham) (evangelist); Charlotte, N.C., 11/7/18
Graham, Katharine Meyer (newspaper publisher); New York City, 6/16/17
Graham, Martha (choreographer); Pittsburgh **(1894–1991)**
Grainger, Percy Aldridge (pianist, composer); Melbourne, Australia **(1882–1961)**
Gramm, Donald (Grambach) (bass-baritone); Milwaukee **(1927–1983)**
Grammer, Kelsey (actor); St. Thomas, V.I., 2/21/55
Granger, Stewart (James Stewart) (actor); London **(1913–1993)**
Grant, Cary (Alexander Archibald Leach) (actor); Bristol, England **(1904–1986)**
Grant, Lee (Lyova Haskell Rosenthal) (actress); New York City, 10/31/30
Grant, Ulysses Simpson (18th U.S. president); Point Pleasant, Ohio **(1822–1885)**
Grass, Günter (novelist); Danzig, (Poland), 10/16/27
Graves, Nancy (Stevenson) (artist); Pittsfield, Mass. **(1940–1996)**
Graves, Peter (Peter Aurness) (actor); Minneapolis, 3/18/26
Graves, Robert (writer); London **(1895–1985)**
Gray, Linda (actress); Santa Monica, Calif., 9/12/40
Gray, Thomas (poet); London **(1716–1771)**
Greco, José (dancer); Montorio nei Frentani, Italy, 12/23/18
Greeley, Horace (journalist, politician); Amherst, N.H. **(1811–1872)**
Green, Adolph (actor, lyricist); New York City, 12/2/15
Green, Al (singer); Forrest City, Ark., 4/13/46
Greene, Graham (novelist); Berkhamsted, England **(1904–1991)**
Greene, Lorne (actor); Ottawa **(1915–1987)**
Greene, Shecky (comedian, actor); Chicago, 4/8/25
Greenstreet, Sydney (actor); Sandwich, England **(1879–1954)**
Greer, Germaine (feminist); Melbourne, Australia, 1/29/39
Gregory, Cynthia (ballet dancer); Los Angeles, 7/8/46
Gregory, Dick (comedian); St. Louis, 10/12/32
Gregory, Lady (Isabella) Augusta (playwright); Roxborough, Ireland **(1852–1932)**
Greuze, Jean-Baptiste (painter); Tournus, France **(1725–1805)**
Grey, Joel (Joel Katz) (actor); Cleveland, 4/11/32
Grey, Zane (author); Zanesville, Ohio **(1875–1939)**
Grieg, Edvard Hagerup (composer); Bergen, Norway **(1843–1907)**
Griffin, Merv (TV host, producer); San Mateo, Calif., 7/6/25
Griffith, Andy (actor); Mount Airy, N.C., 6/1/26
Griffith, David Lewelyn Wark (film producer); La Grange, Ky. **(1875–1948)**
Griffith, Melanie (actress); New York City, 8/9/57
Grigorovich, Yuri (choreographer); Leningrad (St. Petersburg, Russia), 1/1/27
Grimes, Tammy (actress); Lynn, Mass., 1/30/34
Grimm, Jacob (author of fairy tales); Hanau (Germany) **(1785–1863)**
Grimm, Wilhelm (author of fairy tales); Hanau (Germany) **(1786–1859)**
Gris, Juan (José Victoriano González) (painter); Madrid **(1887–1927)**
Grisham, John (attorney, author); Jonesboro, Ark., 2/8/55
Grodin, Charles (actor); Pittsburgh, 4/21/35
Groening, Matt (animator, producer); Portland, Ore., 2/14/54
Gromyko, Andrei A. (diplomat); Starye Gromyki, Russia **(1909–1989)**
Gropius, Walter (architect); Berlin **(1883–1969)**
Gropper, William (painter, illustrator); New York City **(1897–1977)**
Gross, Michael (actor); Chicago, 6/21/47
Grosz, George (painter); Germany **(1893–1959)**
Grove, Andrew (Andras Grof) (computer industry executive); Budapest, Hungary, 9/2/36
Grünewald, Matthias (Mathis Gothart Neithart) (painter); Würzburg, Germany **(c. 1470–1528)**
Guggenheim, Meyer (capitalist); Langnau, Switzerland **(1828–1905)**
Guillaume, Robert (actor); St. Louis, 11/30/27
Guinness, Sir Alec (actor); London, 4/2/14
Guitry, Sacha (Alexandre Guitry) (actor, film director); St. Petersburg, Russia **(1885–1957)**
Gumbel, Bryant Charles (TV newscaster); New Orleans, 9/29/48
Gunther, John (author); Chicago **(1901–1970)**
Gutenberg, Johann (printer); Mainz (Germany) **(c. 1397–1468)**
Guthrie, Arlo (singer); New York City, 7/10/47
Guthrie, Woody (folk singer, composer); Okemah, Okla. **(1912–1967)**
Gwenn, Edmund (actor); London **(1875–1959)**
Gwynne, Fred (actor); New York City **(1926–1993)**

H

Hackett, Bobby (trumpeter); Providence, R.I. **(1915–1976)**
Hackett, Buddy (Leonard Hacker) (comedian, actor); Brooklyn, N.Y., 8/31/24
Hackman, Gene (actor); San Bernardino, Calif., 1/30/31
Hagen, Uta (actress); Göttingen, Germany, 6/12/19
Haggard, Merle (songwriter); Bakersfield, Calif., 4/6/37
Hagman, Larry (Larry Hageman) (actor); Weatherford, Tex., 9/21/31
Haig, Alexander Meigs, Jr. (ex-Secretary of State, ex-general); Bala-Cynwyd, Pa., 12/2/24
Haile Selassie (Ras Tafari Makonnen) (ex-Emperor); Ethiopia **(1892–1975)**
Hailey, Arthur (novelist); Luton, England, 4/5/20
Halberstam, David (journalist); New York City, 4/10/34
Hale, Alan (actor, director); Washington, D.C. **(1892–1950)**
Hale, Barbara (actress); DeKalb, Ill., 4/18/21
Hale, Edward Everett (clergyman, author); Boston **(1822–1909)**
Hale, Nathan (American Revolutionary officer); Coventry, Conn. **(1755–1776)**
Halevi, Judah (Jewish poet); Toledo, Spain **(1085–1140)**
Haley, Alex (writer); Ithaca, N.Y. **(1921–1992)**
Haley, Jack (actor); Boston **(1899–1979)**
Hall, Arsenio (comedian, talk show host); Cleveland, 2/12/58
Hall, Donald (Andrew, Jr.) (poet); New Haven, Conn., 9/20/28
Hall, Huntz (actor); New York City, 8/15/19
Hall, Monty (TV personality); Winnipeg, Canada, 8/25/23
Halley, Edmund (astronomer); London **(1656–1742)**
Hals, Frans (painter); Antwerp (Netherlands) **(c. 1580–1666)**
Halsey, William Frederick, Jr. (naval officer); Elizabeth, N.J. **(1882–1959)**
Hamel, Veronica (actress); Philadelphia, 11/20/43
Hamilton, Alexander (statesman); Nevis, British West Indies **(1755–1804)**
Hamilton, Alice (physician, reformer); New York City **(1869–1970)**
Hamilton, Edith (scholar); Dresden, Germany **(1867–1963)**
Hamilton, George (actor); Memphis, Tenn., 8/12/39
Hamlin, Harry (actor); Pasadena, Calif., 10/30/51
Hamlisch, Marvin (composer, pianist); New York City, 6/2/44
Hammarskjöld, Dag (U.N. Secretary-General); Jönköping, Sweden **(1905–1961)**
Hammerstein, Oscar, II (librettist, stage producer); New York City **(1895–1960)**
Hampton, Lionel (vibraharpist, band leader); Birmingham, Ala., 4/12/13
Hamsun, Knut (Knut Pedersen) (novelist); Lom, Norway **(1859–1952)**
Hancock, Herbie (jazz musician); Chicago, 4/12/40
Hancock, John (statesman); Braintree, Mass. **(1737–1793)**
Hand, Learned (jurist); Albany, N.Y. **(1872–1961)**
Handel, George Frederick (Georg Friedrich Händel) (composer); Halle (Germany) **(1685–1759)**
Handy, William Christopher (blues composer); Florence, Ala. **(1873–1958)**
Hanks, Tom (actor, director, writer); Concord, Calif., 7/9/56
Hannah, Daryl (actress); Chicago, 12/19/60
Hannibal (Carthaginian general); North Africa **(247–182 B.C.E.)**
Hansberry, Lorraine (playwright); Chicago **(1930–1965)**
Hanson, Howard (conductor); Wahoo, Neb. **(1896–1981)**
Harburg, E. Y. "Yip" (songwriter); New York City **(1896–1981)**
Harding, Warren Gamaliel (29th U.S. president); Morrow County, Ohio **(1865–1923)**
Hardwicke, Sir Cedric (actor); Stourbridge, England **(1893–1964)**
Hardy, Oliver (comedian); Atlanta **(1892–1957)**
Hardy, Thomas (novelist); Dorsetshire, England **(1840–1928)**
Harkness, Edward S. (business executive); Cleveland **(1874–1940)**
Harlow, Jean (Harlean Carpentier) (actress); Kansas City, Mo. **(1911–1937)**
Harmon, Mark (actor); Burbank, Calif., 9/2/51
Harnick, Sheldon (lyricist); Chicago, 4/30/24
Harper, Valerie (actress); Suffern, N.Y., 8/22/40
Harrell, Lynn (cellist); New York City, 1/30/44

Harrelson, Woody (actor); Midland, Tex., 7/23/61
Harriman, Pamela (ambassador); Farnborough, England **(1920–1997)**
Harriman, W. (William) Averell (ex-Governor of New York); New York City **(1891–1986)**
Harrington, Pat, Jr. (actor, comedian); New York City, 8/13/29
Harris, Barbara (Sandra Markowitz) (actress); Evanston, Ill., 7/25/35
Harris, Ed (actor); Englewood, N.J., 11/28/50
Harris, Emmylou (singer); Birmingham, Ala., 4/2/47
Harris, Julie (actress); Grosse Pointe Park, Mich., 12/2/25
Harris, Phil (actor, band leader); Linton, Ind. **(1906–1995)**
Harris, Richard (actor); Limerick, Ireland, 10/1/33
Harris, Rosemary (actress); Ashby, England, 9/19/30
Harris, Roy (composer); Lincoln County, Okla. **(1898–1979)**
Harrison, Benjamin (23rd U.S. president); North Bend, Ohio **(1833–1901)**
Harrison, George (singer, songwriter); Liverpool, England, 2/25/43
Harrison, Gregory (actor); Avalon, Catalina Island, Calif., 5/31/50
Harrison, Sir Rex (Reginald Carey) (actor); Huyton, England **(1908–1990)**
Harrison, William Henry (9th U.S. president); Charles City County, Va. **(1773–1841)**
Hart, Lorenz (lyricist); New York City **(1895–1943)**
Hart, Mary (Mary Johanna Harum) (host); Sioux Falls, S.D., 11/8/50
Hart, Melissa Joan (actress); Sayville, N.Y., 4/18/76
Hart, Moss (playwright); New York City **(1904–1961)**
Hart, William S. (actor); Newburgh, N.Y. **(1862–1946)**
Harte, Bret (Francis Brett Harte) (author); Albany, N.Y. **(1836–1902)**
Hartford, Huntington (George Huntington Hartford II) (A.&P. heir); New York City, 4/18/11
Hartford, John (singer, banjoist); New York City, 12/30/37
Hartley, Mariette (actress); New York City, 6/21/40
Hartman, David Downs (TV newscaster); Pawtucket, R.I., 5/19/35
Hartman, Phil (actor, comedian); Brantford, Ont., Canada **(1948–1998)**
Hartman Black, Lisa (actress); Houston, 6/1/56
Harvey, Laurence (Larushka Skikne) (actor); Joniskis, Lithuania **(1928–1973)**
Harvey, William (physician); Folkestone, England **(1578–1657)**
Hasselhoff, David (actor, producer); Baltimore, 7/17/52
Hatcher, Teri (actress); Sunnyvale, Calif., 12/8/64
Havel, Vaclav (political leader, dramatist, poet); Prague, 10/5/36
Havoc, June (Ellen Evangeline Hovick) (actress); Seattle, 11/8/16
Hawke, Ethan (actor); Austin, Tex., 11/6/70
Hawking, Stephen (physicist, astronomer); Oxford, England, 1/8/42
Hawkins, Coleman (jazz musician); St. Joseph, Mo. **(1904–1969)**
Hawkins, Jack (actor); London **(1910–1973)**
Hawn, Goldie (actress, producer); Washington, D.C., 11/21/45
Haworth, Jill (actress); Sussex, England, 8/15/45
Hawthorne, Nathaniel (novelist); Salem, Mass. **(1804–1864)**
Hay, John Milton (statesman); Salem, Ind. **(1838–1905)**
Hayakawa, Sessue (actor); Honshu, Japan **(1890–1973)**
Hayden, Melissa (ballet dancer); Toronto, 4/25/23
Hayden, Sterling (Sterling Relyea Walter) (actor, writer); Montclair, N.J. **(1916–1986)**
Haydn, Franz Joseph (composer); Rohrau (Austria) **(1732–1809)**
Hayes, Helen (Helen Hayes Brown) (actress); Washington, D.C. **(1900–1993)**
Hayes, Isaac (composer); Covington, Tenn., 8/20/42
Hayes, Peter Lind (comedian, singer); San Francisco **(1915–1998)**
Hayes, Rutherford Birchard (19th U.S. president); Delaware, Ohio **(1822–1893)**
Hayward, Leland (producer); Nebraska City, Neb. **(1902–1971)**
Hayward, Susan (Edythe Marrener) (actress); Brooklyn, N.Y. **(1918–1975)**
Hayworth, Rita (Margarita Cansino) (actress); New York City **(1918–1987)**
Head, Edith (costume designer); Los Angeles **(1907–1981)**
Heaney, Seamus (poet); Londonderry, Northern Ireland, 4/13/39
Hearst, William Randolph (publisher); San Francisco **(1863–1951)**
Hearst, William Randolph, Jr. (publisher); New York City **(1908–1993)**
Heatherton, Joey (actress); Rockville Centre, N.Y., 9/14/44
Hecht, Ben (author); New York City **(1894–1964)**
Heckart, Eileen (actress); Columbus, Ohio, 3/29/19
Heflin, Van (Emmet Evan Heflin) (actor); Walters, Okla. **(1910–1971)**
Hefner, Hugh (publisher); Chicago, 4/9/26
Hegel, Georg Wilhelm Friedrich (philosopher); Stuttgart (Germany) **(1770–1831)**
Heidegger, Martin (existentialist philosopher); Messkirch, Germany **(1889–1976)**
Heifetz, Jascha (concert violinist); Vilna, Russia **(1901–1987)**
Heine, Heinrich (Harry) (poet); Düsseldorf, Germany **(1797–1856)**
Heinemann, Gustav (ex-President of Germany); Schweim, Germany **(1899–1976)**
Heisenberg, Werner Karl (physicist); Würzburg, Germany **(1901–1976)**
Held, Anna (comedienne); Paris **(1873?–1918)**
Heller, Joseph (novelist); Brooklyn, N.Y., 5/1/23
Hellman, Lillian (playwright); New Orleans **(1905–1984)**
Helmond, Katherine (actress); Galveston, Tex., 7/5/34
Helms, Jesse (politician); Monroe, N.C., 10/18/21
Helmsley, Leona (business executive); New York City, c. 1920
Hemingway, Ernest Miller (novelist); Oak Park, Ill. **(1899–1961)**
Hemingway, Margaux (actress); Portland, Ore. **(1955–1996)**
Hemmings, David (actor); Guilford, England, 11/2/41
Henderson, Florence (actress); Dale, Ind., 2/14/34
Henderson, Skitch (Lyle Russell Cedric) (conductor, pianist); Birmingham, England?, 1/27/18
Hendrix, Jimi (James Marshall Hendrix) (guitarist); Seattle **(1942–1970)**
Henley, Beth (playwright-actress); Jackson, Miss., 5/8/52
Henley, Don (musician); Linden, Tex., 7/22/47
Henner, Marilu (actress); Chicago, 4/6/52
Henning, Doug (magician, actor); Winnipeg, Canada, 5/3/47
Henreid, Paul (actor); Trieste **(1908–1992)**
Henri, Robert (painter); Cincinnati **(1865–1926)**
Henry VIII (King of England); Greenwich, England **(1491–1547)**
Henry, O. (William Sydney Porter) (story writer); Greensboro, N.C. **(1862–1910)**
Henry, Patrick (statesman); Hanover County, Va. **(1736–1799)**
Henson, Jim (puppeteer); Greenville, Miss. **(1936–1990)**
Hepburn, Audrey (actress); Brussels **(1929–1993)**
Hepburn, Katharine (actress); Hartford, Conn., 5/12/07
Hepplewhite, George (furniture designer); England **(?–1786)**
Hepworth, Barbara (sculptor); Wakefield, England **(1903–1975)**
Herbert, George (poet); Montgomery Castle, Wales **(1593–1633)**
Herbert, Victor (composer); Dublin **(1859–1924)**
Herblock (Herbert L. Block) (political cartoonist); Chicago, 10/13/09
Herman, Pee-wee (Paul Rubenfeld) (comedian); Peekskill, N.Y., 8/27/52
Herman, Woody (Woodrow Charles Herman) (band leader); Milwaukee **(1913–1987)**
Herod (called Herod the Great) (King of Judea) **(73–4 B.C.E.)**
Herodotus (historian); Halicarnassus, Asia Minor (Turkey) **(c. 484–425 B.C.E.)**
Herrick, Robert (poet); London **(1591–1674)**
Herschbach, Dudley Robert (chemist, Nobel laureate); San Jose, Calif., 6/18/32
Herschel, William (Frederich Wilhelm Herschel) (astronomer); Hannover, Germany **(1738–1822)**
Hershey, Barbara (Barbara Herzstein) (actress); Hollywood, Calif., 2/5/48
Herzog, Chaim (Israeli statesman); Belfast, Northern Ireland **(1918–1997)**
Hesburgh, Theodore M. (educator); Syracuse, N.Y., 5/2/17
Hesseman, Howard (actor); Salem, Ore., 2/27/40
Heston, Charlton (actor); Evanston, Ill., 10/4/24
Heyerdahl, Thor (ethnologist, explorer); Larvik, Norway, 10/6/14
Hill, Anita (lawyer, professor); Lone Tree, Okla., 7/30/56
Hill, Benny (comedian); Southampton, England **(1925–1992)**
Hillary, Sir Edmund (mountain climber); New Zealand, 7/20/19
Hillerman, John (actor); Denison, Tex., 12/20/32
Hilton, Conrad (hotelier); San Antonio, N.M. **(1887–1979)**
Hindemith, Paul (composer); Hanau, Germany **(1895–1963)**
Hindenburg, Paul von (Paul Ludwig Hans Anton von Hindenburg und Beneckendorff) (German field marshal, president); Poznan (Poland) **(1847–1934)**
Hines, Earl "Fatha" (jazz pianist); Duquesne, Pa. **(1905–1983)**
Hines, Gregory (dancer, actor); New York City, 2/14/46
Hines, Jerome (Jerome Heinz) (basso); Los Angeles, 11/8/21
Hippocrates (physician); Cos, Greece **(c. 460–c. 377 B.C.E.)**
Hirohito (Emperor); Tokyo **(1901–1989)**
Hiroshige, Ando (painter); Edo (Tokyo) **(1797–1858)**
Hirsch, Judd (actor); New York City, 3/15/35
Hirschfeld, Al (Albert) (cartoonist); St. Louis, 6/21/03
Hirschhorn, Joseph Herman (financier, speculator, art collector); Mitau, Latvia **(1899–1981)**
Hirt, Al (trumpeter); New Orleans, 11/7/22
Hiss, Alger (public official); Baltimore **(1904–1996)**
Hitchcock, Alfred J. (film director); London **(1899–1980)**
Hitler, Adolf (German dictator); Braunau, Austria **(1889–1945)**
Hobbes, Thomas (philosopher); Westport, England **(1588–1679)**

Hobson, Laura Z. (Laura K. Zametkin) (novelist); New York City **(1900–1986)**
Ho Chi Minh (Nguyen That Tranh) (Vietnamese nationalist leader); Kim Lien (Vietnam) **(1890–1969)**
Hockney, David (artist); Bradford, England, 7/9/37
Hodgkin, Dorothy Mary Crowfoot (chemist, Nobel laureate); Cairo, Egypt **(1910–1994)**
Hoffa, James R(iddle) (labor leader); Brazil, Ind. **(1913–1975?; presumed murdered.)**
Hoffman, Dustin (actor, director); Los Angeles, 8/8/37
Hofmann, Hans (painter); Germany **(1880–1966)**
Hoffmann, Roald (chemist, Nobel laureate); Zloczow, Poland, 7/18/37
Hofstadter, Richard (historian); Buffalo, N.Y. **(1916–1970)**
Hogan, Paul (actor); Lightning Ridge, N.S.W., Australia, 10/8/39
Hogarth, William (painter, engraver); London **(1697–1764)**
Hokusai, Katsushika (artist); Yedo, Japan **(1760–1849)**
Holbein, Hans (the Elder) (painter); Augsburg (Germany) **(c. 1465–1524)**
Holbein, Hans (the Younger) (painter); Augsburg (Germany) **(c. 1497–1543)**
Holbrook, Hal (actor); Cleveland, 2/17/25
Holden, William (William Franklin Beedle, Jr.) (actor); O'Fallon, Ill. **(1918–1981)**
Holder, Geoffrey (dancer); Port-of-Spain, Trinidad, 8/1/30
Holiday, Billie (Eleanora Fagan) (jazz-blues singer); Baltimore **(1915–1959)**
Holliman, Earl (actor); Delhi, La., 9/11/28
Holly, Buddy (singer); Lubbock, Tex. **(1936–1959)**
Holm, Celeste (actress); New York City, 4/29/19
Holmes, Oliver Wendell (jurist); Boston **(1841–1935)**
Home, Lord (Alexander Frederick Douglas-Home) (diplomat); London, 7/2/03
Homer, Winslow (painter); Boston **(1836–1910)**
Homer (Greek poet) fl. 850 B.C.E.
Honegger, Arthur (composer); Le Havre, France **(1892–1955)**
Hook, Sidney (philosopher); New York City **(1902–1989)**
Hooker, John Lee (blues guitarist, singer, songwriter); Clarksdale, Miss., 8/22/20
Hoover, Herbert Clark (31st U.S. president); West Branch, Iowa **(1874–1964)**
Hoover, J. Edgar (FBI director); Washington, D.C. **(1895–1972)**
Hope, Bob (Leslie Townes Hope) (comedian); London, 5/29/03
Hopkins, Sir Anthony (actor); Port Talbot, Wales, 12/31/37
Hopkins, Gerald Manley (poet); Stratford, England **(1844–1899)**
Hopkins, Johns (financier); Anne Arundel County, Md. **(1795–1873)**
Hopper, Dennis (actor); Dodge City, Kans., 5/17/36
Hopper, Edward (painter); Nyack, N.Y. **(1882–1967)**
Horace (Quintus Horatius Flaccus) (poet); Venosa (Italy) **(65–8 B.C.E.)**
Horne, Lena (singer); Brooklyn, N.Y., 6/30/17
Horne, Marilyn (mezzo-soprano); Bradford, Pa., 1/16/34
Horowitz, Vladimir (pianist); Kiev, Ukraine **(1903–1989)**
Horsley, Lee (actor); Muleshoe, Tex., 5/15/55
Horton, Edward Everett (comedian); Brooklyn, N.Y. **(1887–1970)**
Hoskins, Bob (actor); Bury St. Edmunds, England, 10/26/42
Houdini, Harry (Ehrich Weiss) (magician); Appleton, Wis. **(1874–1926)**
Houseman, John (Jacques Haussmann) (producer, director, actor); Bucharest **(1902–1988)**
Housman, A(lfred) E(dward) (poet); Fockburg, England **(1859–1936)**
Houston, Charles Hamilton (civil rights lawyer); Washington, D.C. **(1895–1950)**
Houston, Samuel (political leader); Rockbridge County, Va. **(1793–1863)**
Houston, Whitney (singer); Newark, N.J., 8/9/63
Howard, Ken (actor); El Centro, Calif., 3/28/44
Howard, Leslie (Leslie Stainer) (actor); London **(1893–1943)**
Howard, Ron (actor, producer, director); Duncan, Okla., 3/1/54
Howard, Trevor (actor); Kent, England **(1916–1988)**
Howe, Elias (inventor); Spencer, Mass. **(1819–1867)**
Howe, Irving (literary critic); New York City **(1920–1993)**
Howe, Julia Ward (poet, reformer); New York City **(1819–1910)**
Hudson, Henry (English navigator) **(fl. 1607–1611)**
Hudson, Rock (born Roy Scherer, Jr.; took Roy Fitzgerald as legal name) (actor); Winnetka, Ill. **(1925–1985)**
Huggins, Nathan Irvin (historian); Chicago **(1927–1989)**
Hughes, Charles Evans (jurist); Glens Falls, N.Y. **(1862–1948)**
Hughes, Howard (industrialist, film producer); Houston **(1905–1976)**
Hughes, Langston (poet); Joplin, Mo. **(1902–1967)**
Hugo, Victor Marie (author); Besançon, France **(1802–1885)**
Hulce, Tom (actor); Detroit, 12/6/53
Hume, David (philosopher); Edinburgh, Scotland **(1711–1776)**
Humperdinck, Engelbert (composer); Siegburg (Germany) **(1854–1921)**
Humperdinck, Engelbert (Arnold Dorsey) (singer); Madras, India, 5/2/36
Hunt, Helen (actress); Los Angeles, 6/15/63
Hunter, Holly (actress); Atlanta, 3/20/58
Hunter, Kim (Janet Cole) (actress); Detroit, 11/12/22
Hunter, Tab (Arthur Andrew Gelien) (actor); New York City, 7/11/31
Hunter-Gault, Charlayne (activist, broadcast journalist); Due West, S.C., 2/27/42
Huntley, Chet (TV newscaster); Cardwell, Mont. **(1911–1974)**
Hurok, Sol (Solomon Hurok) (impresario); Pogar, Russia **(1884–1974)**
Hurst, Fannie (novelist); Hamilton, Ohio **(1889–1968)**
Hurston, Zora Neale (author); Eatonville, Fla. **(1901–1960)**
Hurt, John (actor); Shirebrook, England, 1/22/40
Hurt, William (actor); Washington, D.C., 3/20/50
Hus, Jan (Bohemian religious reformer); Husinetz, nr. Budweis (Czech Republic) **(c. 1369–1415)**
Husing, Ted (sportscaster); New York City **(1901–1962)**
Hussein I (King); Jordan, 11/14/35
Hussein, Saddam (al-Tikriti) (Iraqi President); Tikrit, Iraq, 4/28/37
Huston, Anjelica (actress); Los Angeles, 7/8/51
Huston, John (actor, director, writer); Nevada, Mo. **(1906–1987)**
Huston, Walter (Walter Houghston) (actor); Toronto **(1884–1950)**
Hutchins, Robert M. (educator); Brooklyn, N.Y. **(1899–1977)**
Hutton, Betty (Betty Thornburg) (actress); Battle Creek, Mich., 2/26/21
Hutton, Lauren (actress, model); Charleston, S.C., 11/17/43
Hutton, Timothy (actor); Los Angeles, 8/16/60
Huxley, Aldous (author); Godalming, England **(1894–1963)**
Huxley, Sir Julian S. (biologist, author); London **(1887–1975)**
Huxley, Thomas Henry (biologist); Ealing, England **(1825–1895)**

I

Iacocca, Lee (Lido Anthony) (business executive); Allentown, Pa., 10/15/24
Ian, Janis (singer); New York City, 5/7/51
Ibsen, Henrik (dramatist); Skien, Norway **(1828–1906)**
Inge, William (playwright); Independence, Kans. **(1913–1973)**
Ingres, Jean Auguste Dominique (painter); Montauban, France **(1780–1867)**
Inness, George (painter); nr. Newburgh, N.Y. **(1825–1894)**
Ionesco, Eugene (playwright); Slatina, Romania **(1912–1994)**
Ireland, Jill (actress); London **(1936–1990)**
Ireland, Patricia (feminist, social activist); Oak Park, Ill., 10/19/45
Irons, Jeremy (actor); Cowes, Isle of Wight, England, 9/19/48
Irving, Amy (actress); Palo Alto, Calif., 9/10/53
Irving, John (Winslow) (writer); Exeter, N.H., 3/2/42
Irving, Washington (author); New York City **(1783–1859)**
Isherwood, Christopher (novelist, playwright); nr. Dilsey and High Lane, England **(1904–1986)**
Iturbi, José (concert pianist); Valencia, Spain **(1895–1980)**
Ives, Burl (Icle Ivanhoe) (singer); Hunt, Ill. **(1909–1995)**
Ives, Charles E(dward) (composer); Danbury, Conn. **(1874–1954)**
Ivins, Molly (journalist); Monterey, Calif., 8/30/44
Ivory, James (director, producer); Berkeley, Calif., 6/7/28

J

Jackson, Andrew (7th U.S. president); Waxhaw, S.C. **(1767–1845)**
Jackson, Anne (actress); Millvale, Pa., 9/3/26
Jackson, Glenda (actress); Cheshire, England, 5/9/36
Jackson, Janet (singer); Gary, Ind., 5/16/66
Jackson, Rev. Jesse (civil rights leader); Greenville, S.C., 10/8/41
Jackson, Kate (actress); Birmingham, Ala., 10/29/49
Jackson, Mahalia (gospel singer); New Orleans **(1911–1972)**
Jackson, Maynard (mayor of Atlanta); Dallas, 3/23/38
Jackson, Michael (singer); Gary, Ind., 8/29/58
Jackson, Samuel L. (actor); Washington, D.C., 12/21/48
Jackson, Thomas Jonathan ("Stonewall") (general); Clarksburg, Va. (now W. Va.) **(1824–1863)**
Jacobi, Derek (actor); Leytonstone, England, 10/22/38
Jacobs, Jane (urbanologist); Scranton, Pa., 5/1/16
Jaffe, Susan (ballet dancer); Washington, D.C., 1963?
Jagger, Mick (Michael Phillip Jagger) (singer); Dartford, England, 7/26/43
James, Harry (trumpeter); Albany, Ga. **(1916–1983)**
James, Henry (novelist); New York City **(1843–1916)**
James, Jesse Woodson (outlaw); Clay County, Mo. **(1847–1882)**

James, William (psychologist); New York City **(1842–1910)**
Jameson, (Margaret) Storm (novelist); Whitby, England **(1897–1986)**
Janis, Byron (pianist); McKeesport, Pa., 3/24/28
Janis, Conrad (actor, musician); New York City, 2/11/28
Janssen, David (David Meyer) (actor); Naponee, Neb. **(1930–1980)**
Jaworkski, Leon (Watergate special prosecutor); Waco, Tex. **(1905–1982)**
Jay, John (statesman, jurist); New York City **(1745–1829)**
Jeanmaire, Renée (dancer); Paris, 4/29/24
Jefferson, Thomas (3rd U.S. president); Shadwell, Va. **(1743–1826)**
Jemison, Mae C. (astronaut, physician); Decatur, Ala., 10/17/56
Jenner, Edward (physician); Berkeley, England **(1749–1823)**
Jennings, Peter (news anchor); Toronto, 7/29/38
Jennings, Waylon (singer); Littlefield, Tex., 6/15/37
Jessel, George (entertainer); New York City **(1898–1981)**
Jessup, Philip C. (diplomat); New York City **(1897–1986)**
Jillian, Ann (actress); Cambridge, Mass., 1/29/51
Joan of Arc (Jeanne d'Arc) (saint, patriot); Domremy-la-Pucelle, France **(1412–1431)**
Jobs, Steven Paul (computer industry pioneer); San Francisco, 1955
Joel, Billy (singer); New York City, 5/9/49
Joffrey, Robert (Abdullah Jaffa Bey Khan) (choreographer); Seattle **(1930–1988)**
John, Elton (Reginald Kenneth Dwight) (singer, pianist); Pinner, England, 3/25/47
Johns, Jasper (painter, sculptor); Augusta, Ga., 5/15/30
Johnson, Andrew (17th U.S. president); Raleigh, N.C. **(1808–1875)**
Johnson, Don (actor); Flatt Creek, Mo., 12/15/49
Johnson, James Weldon (author, educator); Jacksonville, Fla. **(1871–1938)**
Johnson, Lyndon Baines (36th U.S. president); Stonewall, Tex. **(1908–1973)**
Johnson, Philip Cortelyou (architect); Cleveland, 7/8/06
Johnson, Samuel (lexicographer, author); Lichfield, England **(1709–1784)**
Johnson, Van (actor); Newport, R.I., 8/20/16
Johnson, Virginia (human sexuality expert); Springfield, Mo., 2/11/25
Joliot-Curie, Frédéric (chemist, Nobel laureate); Paris **(1900–1958)**
Joliot-Curie, Irène (Irène Curie) (chemist, Nobel laureate); France **(1897–1956)**
Jolliet, Louis (Louis Joliet) (explorer); Beaupré, Canada **(1645–1700)**
Jolson, Al (Asa Yoelson) (actor, singer); St. Petersburg, Russia **(1886–1950)**
Jones, Dean (actor); Morgan County, Ala., 1/25/35
Jones, George (singer); Saratoga, Tex., 9/12/31
Jones, Inigo (architect); London **(1573–1652)**
Jones, James (novelist); Robinson, Ill. **(1921–1977)**
Jones, James Earl (actor); Arkabutla, Miss., 1/17/31
Jones, Jennifer (Phylis Isley) (actress); Tulsa, Okla., 3/2/19
Jones, John Paul (John Paul) (naval officer); Scotland **(1747–1792)**
Jones, Quincy (composer); Chicago, 3/14/33
Jones, Shirley (singer, actress); Smithtown, Pa., 3/31/34
Jones, Spike (host, orchestra leader); Long Beach, Calif. **(1911–1965)**
Jones, Tom (Thomas Jones Woodward) (singer); Pontypridd, Wales, 6/7/40
Jones, Tommy Lee (actor); San Saba, Tex., 9/15/46
Jong, Erica (writer); New York City, 3/26/42
Jonson, Ben (Benjamin Jonson) (poet, dramatist); Westminster, England **(1572–1637)**
Joplin, Janis (singer); Port Arthur, Tex. **(1943–1970)**
Joplin, Scott (ragtime pianist, composer); Texarkansas, Tex. **(1868–1917)**
Jordan, Barbara (U.S. Representative); Houston **(1936–1996)**
Joseph (Chief Joseph) (Nez Perce Indian leader); eastern Ore. **(1841–1904)**
Josquin des Prés (usually known as Josquin) (composer); Conde-sur-L'Escaut?, Hainaut (Belgium) **(c. 1445–1521)**
Jourdan, Louis (Louis Gendre) (actor); Marseilles, France, 6/19/19
Joyce, James (novelist); Dublin **(1882–1941)**
Juárez, Benito Pablo (statesman); Guelatao, Mexico **(1806–1872)**
Judd, Ashley (actress); Los Angeles, 4/19/68
Julia, Raul (Raúl Rafael Carlos Julia y Arcelay) (actor); San Juan, P.R. **(1940–1994)**
Jung, Carl Gustav (psychoanalyst); Basel, Switzerland **(1875–1961)**
Jurado, Katy (Maria Christina Jurado Garcia) (actress); Guadalajara, Mexico, 1/16/24

K

Kabalevsky, Dmitri (composer); St. Petersburg, Russia **(1904–1987)**
Kafka, Franz (author); Prague **(1883–1924)**
Kádár, János (Communist Party leader); Hungary **(1912–1989)**
Kahn, Gus (songwriter); Coblenz, Germany **(1886–1941)**
Kahn, Louis I. (architect); Oesel Island, Estonia **(1901–1974)**
Kahn, Madeline (actress); Boston, 9/29/42
Kandinsky, Wassily (painter); Moscow **(1866–1944)**
Kanin, Garson (playwright); Rochester, N.Y., 11/24/12
Kant, Immanuel (philosopher); Königsberg (Kaliningrad, Russia) **(1724–1804)**
Kantor, MacKinlay (novelist); Webster City, Iowa **(1904–1977)**
Kaplan, Justin (writer, editor); New York City, 9/5/25
Karan, Donna (fashion designer); Forest Hills, N.Y., 10/2/48
Karloff, Boris (William Henry Pratt) (actor); London **(1887–1969)**
Kasem, Casey (disc jockey); Detroit, 4/27/32
Kaufman, George S. (playwright); Pittsburgh **(1889–1961)**
Kavner, Julie (actress); Los Angeles, 9/7/51
Kaye, Danny (David Daniel Kominski) (comedian); Brooklyn, N.Y. **(1913–1987)**
Kaye, Sammy (band leader); Cleveland **(1910–1987)**
Kazan, Elia (director); Constantinople, Turkey, 9/7/09
Kazan, Lainie (Levine) (singer); New York City, 5/15/40
Kazantzakis, Nikos (writer); Herakleion, Crete **(1883–1957)**
Keach, Stacy (actor); Savannah, Ga., 6/2/41
Keaton, Buster (Joseph Frank Keaton) (comedian); Piqua, Kans. **(1896–1966)**
Keaton, Diane (actress); Los Angeles, 1/5/46
Keaton, Michael (Michael Douglas) (actor); Robinson Township, Pa., 9/9/51
Keats, John (poet); London **(1795–1821)**
Keel, Howard (Harold Clifford Leek) (singer, actor); Gillespie, Ill., 4/13/19
Keeler, Ruby (Ethel Hilde Keeler) (actress, dancer); Halifax, Nova Scotia, Canada **(1910–1993)**
Kefauver, Estes (legislator); Madisonville, Tenn **(1903–1963)**
Keitel, Harvey (actor); Brooklyn, N.Y., 5/13/39
Keith, Brian (Robert Brian Keith, Jr.) (actor); Bayonne, N.J. **(1921–1997)**
Keller, Helen Adams (author, educator); Tuscumbia, Ala. **(1880–1968)**
Kelley, DeForest (actor); Atlanta, 1/20/20
Kelly, Emmett (clown); Sedan, Kans. **(1898–1979)**
Kelly, Gene (dancer, actor); Pittsburgh **(1912–1996)**
Kelly, Walt (cartoonist); Philadelphia **(1913–1973)**
Kempis, Thomas à (mystic); Kempis, Prussia (Germany) **(1380–1471)**
Kendall, Henry W. (physicist, Nobel laureate); Boston, 12/9/26
Kennan, George F. (diplomat); Milwaukee, 2/16/04
Kennedy, Arthur (actor); Worcester, Mass. **(1914–1990)**
Kennedy, George (actor); New York City, 2/18/25
Kennedy, John Fitzgerald (35th U.S. president); Brookline, Mass. **(1917–1963)**
Kennedy, John F., Jr. (publisher); Washington, D.C., 11/25/60
Kennedy, Joseph P. (financier); Boston **(1888–1969)**
Kennedy, Robert Francis (legislator); Brookline, Mass. **(1925–1968)**
Kennedy, Rose Fitzgerald (President's mother); Boston **(1890–1995)**
Kent, Allegra (ballet dancer); Santa Monica, Calif., 8/11/38
Kent, Rockwell (painter); Tarrytown Heights, N.Y. **(1882–1971)**
Kenton, Stan (Stanley Newcomb) (jazz musician); Wichita, Kans. **(1912–1979)**
Kepler, Johannes (astronomer); Weil (Germany) **(1571–1630)**
Kercheval, Ken (actor); Wolcottville, Ind., 7/15/35
Kerensky, Alexander Fedorovich (statesman); Simbirsk, Russia **(1881–1970)**
Kern, Jerome David (composer); New York City **(1885–1945)**
Kerns, Joanna (actress); San Francisco, 2/12/53
Kerr, Deborah (actress); Helensburgh, Scotland, 9/30/21
Kettering, Charles F. (engineer, inventor); nr. Loudonville, Ohio **(1876–1958)**
Key, Francis Scott (lawyer, author of national anthem); Frederick (Carroll) County, Md. **(1779–1843)**
Keyes, Frances Parkinson (novelist); Charlottesville, Va. **(1885–1970)**
Keynes (John Maynard Keynes) (economist); Cambridge, England **(1883–1946)**
Khachaturian, Aram (composer); Tiflis, Russia (Tbilisi, Georgia) **(1903–1978)**

Khomeini, Ayatollah Ruhollah (Islamic religious leader); Iran **(1900–1989)**
Khrushchev, Nikita S. (Soviet leader); Kalinovka, nr. Kursk, Ukraine **(1894–1971)**
Kidd, Michael (choreographer); Brooklyn, N.Y., 8/12/19
Kidd, William (called Captain Kidd) (pirate); Greenock, Scotland **(c. 1645–1701)**
Kidder, Margot (actress); Yellowknife, N.W.T., Canada, 10/17/48
Kidman, Nicole (actress); Honolulu, 6/20/67
Kiepura, Jan (tenor); Sosnowiec, Poland **(1902–1966)**
Kieran, John (writer); New York City **(1892–1981)**
Kierkegaard, Sören Aalys (philosopher); Copenhagen **(1813–1855)**
Kiesinger, Kurt Georg (diplomat); Ebingen, Germany **(1904–1988)**
Kiley, Richard (actor, singer); Chicago, 3/31/22
Kilmer, Alfred Joyce (poet); New Brunswick, N.J. **(1886–1918)**
King, Alan (Irwin Alan Kniberg) (entertainer); Brooklyn, N.Y., 12/26/27
King, B.B. (Riley King) (guitarist); Itta Bena, Miss., 9/16/25
King, Carole (singer, songwriter); Brooklyn, N.Y., 2/9/41
King, Coretta Scott (civil rights leader); Marion, Ala., 4/27/27
King, Larry (TV host); New York City, 11/19/33
King, Martin Luther, Jr. (civil rights leader); Atlanta **(1929–1968)**
King, Stephen (writer); Portland, Maine, 9/21/47
Kingsley, Ben (Krishna Bhanji) (actor); Snainton, England, 12/31/43
Kingsley, Sidney (Sidney Kirschner) (playwright); New York City **(1906–1995)**
Kingsolver, Barbara (writer); Annapolis, Md., 4/8/55
Kingston, Maxine Hong (novelist); Stockton, Calif., 10/27/40
Kinsey, Alfred Charles (human sexuality expert); Hoboken, N.J. **(1894–1956)**
Kinski, Nastassja (Nastassja Nakszynski) (actress); West Berlin, 1/24/61
Kipling, Rudyard (author); Bombay (Mumbai) **(1865–1936)**
Kipnis, Alexander (basso); Ukraine **(1891–1978)**
Kirby, George (comedian); Chicago **(1923–1995)**
Kirchner, Ernst Ludwig (painter); Aschaffenburg, Germany **(1880–1938)**
Kirk, Grayson (educator); Jeffersonville, Ohio **(1903–1997)**
Kirkland, Gelsey (ballet dancer); Bethlehem, Pa., 12/29/52
Kirkpatrick, Jeane Jordan (educator-public affairs); Duncan, Okla., 11/19/26
Kirkpatrick, Ralph (harpsichordist); Leominster, Mass. **(1911–1984)**
Kirstein, Lincoln (dance, theater executive); Rochester, N.Y. **(1907–1996)**
Kirsten, Dorothy (soprano); Montclair, N.J. **(1910–1992)**
Kissinger, Henry (Heinz Alfred Kissinger) (ex-U.S. Secretary of State); Furth, Germany, 5/27/23
Kitt, Eartha (singer); North, S.C., 1/26/28
Klee, Paul (painter); Münchenbuchsee, nr. Bern, Switzerland **(1879–1940)**
Klein, Calvin (fashion designer); Bronx, N.Y., 11/19/42
Klein, Robert (comedian); New York City, 2/8/42
Kleist, Henrich von (poet); Frankfurt an der Oder (Germany) **(1777–1811)**
Klemperer, Otto (conductor); Breslau (Poland) **(1885–1973)**
Klemperer, Werner (actor); Cologne, Germany, 3/22/20
Klimt, Gustav (painter); Vienna **(1862–1918)**
Kline, Kevin (actor); St. Louis, 10/24/47
Klugman, Jack (actor); Philadelphia, 4/27/22
Knight, Gladys (singer); Atlanta, 5/28/44
Knight, Ted (Tadeus Wladyslaw Konopka) (actor); Terryville, Conn. **(1923–1986)**
Knight, John S. (publisher); Bluefield, W. Va. **(1894–1981)**
Knopf, Alfred A. (publisher); New York City **(1892–1984)**
Knotts, Don (actor); Morgantown, W. Va., 7/21/24
Knox, John (religious reformer); Haddington, East Lothian, Scotland **(1505–1572)**
Koch, Robert (physician); Klausthal (Germany) **(1843–1910)**
Koenig, Walter (actor); Chicago, 9/14/36
Koestler, Arthur (novelist); Budapest **(1905–1983)**
Kokoschka, Oskar (painter); Póchlarn Austria **(1886–1980)**
Kollwitz, Käthe (graphic artist, sculptor); Königsberg, (Russia) **(1867–1945)**
Koop, C. Everett (ex-Surgeon General); Brooklyn, N.Y., 10/14/16
Kooper, Al (singer, pianist); Brooklyn, N.Y., 2/5/44
Kopell, Bernie (actor); New York City, 6/21/33
Koppel, Ted (broadcast journalist); Lancashire, England, 2/8/40
Korman, Harvey (actor); Chicago, 2/15/27
Kosciusko, Thaddeus (Tadeusz Andrzej Bonawentura Kosciuszko) (military officer; Grand Duchy of Lithuania) **(1746–1817)**
Kossuth, Lajos (patriot); Monok, Hungary **(1802–1894)**
Kostelanetz, André (orchestra conductor); St. Petersburg, Russia **(1901–1980)**
Kosygin, Aleksei N. (Premier); St. Petersburg, Russia **(1904–1980)**
Koussevitzky, Serge (Sergei) Alexandrovitch (orchestra conductor); Vishni Volochek, Tver, Russia **(1874–1951)**
Kramer, Stanley E. (film producer, director); New York City, 9/29/13
Kràus, Lili (pianist); Budapest **(1905–1986)**
Kreisler, Fritz (violinist, composer); Vienna **(1875–1962)**
Kresge, S. S. (merchant); Bald Mount, Pa. **(1867–1966)**
Krips, Josef (orchestra conductor); Vienna **(1902–1974)**
Kristofferson, Kris (singer); Brownsville, Tex., 6/22/36
Krupa, Gene (drummer); Chicago **(1909–1973)**
Krupp, Alfred (munitions magnate); Essen, Germany **(1812–1887)**
Kubelik, Rafael (conductor); Bychory, former Czechoslovakia **(1914–1996)**
Kublai Khan (Mongol conqueror) **(1216–1294)**
Kubrick, Stanley (producer, director); New York City, 7/26/28
Kudrow, Lisa (actress); Encino, Calif., 7/30/63
Kuralt, Charles (TV journalist); Wilmington, N.C. **(1934–1997)**
Kurosawa, Akira (film director); Tokyo **(1910–1998)**
Kurtz, Efrem (conductor); St. Petersburg, Russia **(1900–1995)**
Kurtz, Swoosie (actress); Omaha, Neb., 9/6/44

L

LaBelle, Patti (singer, actress); Philadelphia, 5/24/44
Ladd, Cheryl (Cheryl Stoppelmoor) (actress); Huron, S.D., 7/12/51
Ladd, Diane (actress); Meridian, Miss., 11/29/32
Lafayette, Marquis de (Marie Joseph Paul Yves Roch Gilbert du Motier) (military officer); Auvergne, France **(1757–1834)**
Lafitte, Jean (pirate); Bayonne? France **(1780–1826)**
La Follette, Robert Marin (politician); Primrose, Wis. **(1855–1925)**
La Fontaine, Jean de (poet); Château-Thierry, France **(1621–1695)**
La Guardia, Fiorello Henry (Mayor of New York); New York City **(1882–1947)**
Lahti, Christine (actress, director); Birmingham, Mich., 4/4/50
Laine, Frankie (Frank Paul LoVecchio) (singer); Chicago, 3/30/13
Laird, Melvin (ex-Secretary of Defense); Omaha, Neb., 9/1/22
Lamarck, Chevalier de (Jean Baptiste Pierre Antoine de Monet) (naturalist); Bazantin, France **(1744–1829)**
Lamas, Lorenzo (actor); Los Angeles, 1/20/58
Lamb, Charles (Elia) (essayist); London **(1775–1834)**
L'Amour, Louis (author); Jamestown, N.D. **(1908–1988)**
Lancaster, Burt (actor); New York City **(1913–1994)**
Landau, Martin (actor); Brooklyn, N.Y., 6/20/31
Landers, Ann (Esther Pauline Friedman) (columnist); Sioux City, Iowa, 7/4/18
Landon, Michael (Eugene Maurice Orowitz) (actor, director, producer); Forest Hills, Queens, N.Y. **(1936–1991)**
Lane, Abbe (Abigail Francine Lassman) (singer); New York City, 1933
Lane, Burton (songwriter); New York City **(1912–1997)**
Lang, Fritz (film director); Vienna **(1890–1976)**
Lang, Paul Henry (music critic); Budapest **(1901–1991)**
Lange, Hope (actress); Redding Ridge, Conn., 11/28/33
Lange, Jessica (actress); Cloquet, Minn., 4/20/49
Langella, Frank (actor); Bayonne, N.J., 1/1/40
Langford, Frances (singer); Lakeland, Fla., 4/4/13
Langmuir, Irving (chemist); Brooklyn, N.Y. **(1881–1957)**
Langtry, Lillie (Emily Le Breton) (actress); Island of Jersey **(1852–1929)**
Lansbury, Angela (actress, producer); London, 10/16/25
Lansing, Robert (Robert Howell Brown) (actor); San Diego, Calif. **(1928–1994)**
Lanza, Mario (Alfred Arnold Cocozza) (singer, actor); Philadelphia **(1921–1959)**
Lao-tse (Li Erh) (philosopher); Honan Province, China **(c. 604–531 B.C.E.)**
Lardner, Ring (Ringgold Wilmar Lardner) (story writer); Niles, Mich. **(1885–1933)**
La Rouchefoucauld, Francois duc de (author); Paris **(1613–1680)**
Larroquette, John (actor); New Orleans, 11/25/47
Larson, Gary (cartoonist); Tacoma, Wash., 8/14/50
La Salle, Eriq (actor); Hartford, Conn., 7/23/62
La Salle, Sieur de (Robert Cavelier) (explorer); Rouen, France **(1643–1687)**
Lasch, Christopher (historian, social critic); Omaha, Neb. **(1932–1994)**
La Tour, Georges de (painter); Vic-sur-Seille, France **(1593–1652)**
Lauder, Sir Harry (Harry MacLennan) (singer); Portobello, Scotland **(1870–1950)**
Lauer, Matt (TV host); New York City, 12/20/57
Laughton, Charles (actor); Scarborough, England **(1899–1962)**

Lauper, Cyndi (singer); New York City, 6/20/53
Laurel, Stan (Arthur Jefferson) (comedian); Ulverston, England **(1890–1965)**
Laurents, Arthur (playwright); New York City, 7/14/18
Laurie, Piper (Rosetta Jacobs) (actress); Detroit, 1/22/32
Lavin, Linda (actress); Portland, Maine, 10/15/37
Lavoisier, Antoine-Laurent (chemist); Paris **(1743–1794)**
Lawford, Peter (actor); London **(1923–1984)**
Lawless, Lucy (Lucy Ryan) (actress); Auckland, New Zealand, 3/29/68
Lawrence, David Herbert (novelist); Nottingham, England **(1885–1930)**
Lawrence, Jacob (painter); Atantic City, N.J., 9/7/17
Lawrence, Marjorie (singer); Deans Marsh, Australia **(1908–1979)**
Lawrence, Martin (actor); Frankfurt, Germany, 4/16/65
Lawrence, Sharon (actress); Charlotte, N.C., 6/29/62
Lawrence, Steve (Sidney Leibowitz) (singer); Brooklyn, N.Y., 7/8/35
Lawrence of Arabia (Thomas Edward Lawrence, later changed to Shaw) (author, soldier); Tremadoc, Wales **(1888–1935)**
Lawrence, Vicki (actress); Inglewood, Calif., 3/26/49
Leach, Penelope (Balchin) (child psychologist, writer); London, 11/19/37
Leach, Robin (host, producer); London, 8/29/41
Leachman, Cloris (actress); Des Moines, Iowa, 4/30/26
Leadbelly, (Huddie Ledbetter) (blues singer, guitarist); Mooringsport, La. **(1885–1949)**
Leakey, Louis Seymour Bazett (anthropologist); Kabete, Kenya **(1903–1972)**
Leakey, Mary (anthropologist); London **(1913–1996)**
Leakey, Richard (paleoanthropologist, wildlife conservationist); Kenya, 12/19/44
Lean, David (film director); Croydon, England **(1908–1991)**
Lear, Edward (nonsense poet); London **(1812–1888)**
Lear, Evelyn (Shulman) (soprano); Brooklyn, N.Y., 1/8/26
Lear, Norman (TV producer); New Haven, Conn., 7/27/22
Learned, Michael (actress); Washington, D.C., 4/9/39
Leary, Timothy (psychologist, LSD advocate); Springfield, Mass. **(1920–1996)**
Le Blanc, Matt (actor); Newton, Mass., 7/25/67
le Carré, John (David John Moore Cornwell) (novelist); Poole, England, 10/19/31
Le Corbusier (Charles Edouard Jeanneret) (architect); La Chaux-de-Fonds, Switzerland **(1887–1965)**
Lee, Christopher (actor); London, 5/27/22
Lee, Manfred B. (pseudonym Ellery Queen) (novelist); Brooklyn, N.Y. **(1905–1971)**
Lee, Michele (actress, singer); Los Angeles, 6/24/42
Lee, Peggy (Norma Engstrom) (singer); Jamestown, N.D., 5/26/20
Lee, Robert Edward (Confederate general); Stratford Estate, Va. **(1807–1870)**
Lee, Spike (Shelton Jackson Lee) (actor, director, writer, producer); Atlanta, 3/20/57
Leeuwenhoek, Anton van (zoologist); Delft (Netherlands) **(1632–1723)**
Lehár Franz (composer); Komárom (Hungary) **(1870–1948)**
Lehman, Herbert H. (Governor, Senator); New York City **(1878–1963)**
Lehmann, Lotte (soprano); Perleberg (Germany) **(1888–1976)**
Lehrer, Jim (TV newscaster); Wichita, Kans., 5/19/34
Leibniz, Gottfried W. von (scientist); Leipzig (Germany) **(1646–1716)**
Leibovitz, Annie (photographer); Westbury, Conn., 10/2/49
Leigh, Janet (Jeanette Helen Morrison) (actress); Merced, Calif., 7/6/27
Leigh, Jennifer Jason (Jennifer Morrow) (actress); Los Angeles, 2/5/62
Leigh, Vivien (Vivian Mary Hartley) (actress); Darjeeling, India **(1913–1967)**
Leinsdorf, Erich (conductor); Vienna **(1912–1993)**
Lemmon, Jack (actor); Boston, 2/8/25
Lenin, Vladimir (Vladimir Ilich Ulyanov) (Soviet leader); Simbirsk, Russia **(1870–1924)**
Lennon, John (singer, songwriter); Liverpool, England **(1940–1980)**
Leno, Jay (comedian, TV host); New Rochelle, N.Y., 4/28/50
Leonard, Sheldon (Sheldon Leonard Bershad) (actor, producer); New York City **(1907–1997)**
Leonardo da Vinci, (painter, scientist); Vinci, Tuscany (Italy) **(1452–1519)**
Lerner, Alan Jay (lyricist); New York City **(1918–1986)**
Lerner, Max (columnist); Minsk, Russia **(1902–1992)**
Lessing, Doris (novelist); Kermanshah, Iran, 10/22/19
Letterman, David (TV host, producer); Indianapolis, 4/12/47
Levant, Oscar (pianist); Pittsburgh **(1906–1972)**
Levenson, Sam (humorist); New York City **(1911–1980)**
Levi, Carlo (novelist); Turin, Italy **(1902–1975)**
Levine, James (music director, Metropolitan Opera); Cincinnati, 6/23/43
Levine, Joseph E. (film producer); Boston **(1905–1987)**
Lewis, C(live) S(taples) (author); Belfast, Northern Ireland **(1898–1963)**
Lewis, Gilbert Newton (chemist, Nobel laureate); Weymouth, Mass. **(1875–1946)**
Lewis, Jerry (Joseph Levitch) (comedian, film director); Newark, N.J., 3/16/26
Lewis, Jerry Lee (singer); Ferriday, La., 9/29/35
Lewis, John Llewellyn (labor leader); Lucas, Iowa **(1880–1969)**
Lewis, Meriwether (explorer); Albemarle Co., Va. **(1774–1809)**
Lewis, (Percy) Wyndham (artist, writer); Bay of Fundy, Maine (at sea) **(1884–1957)**
Lewis, Shari (Shari Hurwitz) (puppeteer); New York City **(1934–1998)**
Lewis, Sinclair (novelist); Sauk Centre, Minn. **(1885–1951)**
Ley, Willy (science writer); Berlin **(1906–1969)**
Liberace (Wladziu Liberace) (pianist); West Allis, Wis. **(1919–1987)**
Lichtenstein, Roy (painter); New York City **(1923–1997)**
Lie, Trygve Halvdan (first U.N. Secretary-General); Oslo **(1896–1968)**
Light, Judith (actress); Trenton, N.J., 2/9/49
Lightfoot, Gordon (singer, songwriter); Orillia, Ont., Canada, 11/17/38
Limbaugh, Rush (political commentator); Cape Girardeau, Mo., 1/12/51
Lin, Maya (architect, sculptor); Athens, Ohio, 10/5/59
Lin Yutang (author); Changchow, China **(1895–1976)**
Lincoln, Abraham (16th U.S. president); Hardin (Larue) County, Ky. **(1809–1865)**
Lind, Jenny (Johanna Maria Lind) (soprano); Stockholm **(1820–1887)**
Lindbergh, Anne Morrow (author); Englewood, N.J., 6/22/06
Lindbergh, Charles A. (aviator); Detroit **(1902–1974)**
Linden, Hal (Harold Lipshitz) (actor); New York City, 3/20/31
Lindsay, Howard (playwright); Waterford, N.Y. **(1889–1968)**
Lindstrom, Pia (TV newscaster); Stockholm, 11/?/38
Linkletter, Art (radio-TV personality); Moose Jaw, Sask., Canada, 7/17/12
Linnaeus, Carolus (Carl von Linné) (botanist); Råshult, Sweden **(1707–1778)**
Liotta, Ray (actor); Union, N.J., 12/18/55
Lipchitz, Jacques (sculptor); Druskieniki, Latvia **(1891–1973)**
Lippi, Fra Filippo (painter); Florence **(1406–1469)**
Lippmann, Walter (columnist, author, political analyst); New York City **(1889–1974)**
Lister, (Joseph Lister) (surgeon); Upton, England **(1827–1912)**
Liszt, Franz (composer, pianist); Raiding (Hungary) **(1811–1886)**
Lithgow, John (actor); Rochester, N.Y., 6/6/45
Little, Rich (impressionist); Ottawa, 11/26/38
Livingstone, David (missionary, explorer); Lanarkshire, Scotland **(1813–1873)**
L. L. Cool J (James Todd Smith) (rap artist); New York City, 1/14/68
Llewellyn, Richard (novelist); St. David's, Wales **(1906–1983)**
Lloyd George, David (Earl of Dwyfor) (statesman); Manchester, England **(1863–1945)**
Lloyd Webber, Andrew (composer); London, 3/22/48
Locke, Alain L. (philosopher); Philadelphia **(1886–1954)**
Locke, John (philosopher); Somersetshire, England **(1632–1704)**
Lockhart, June (actress); New York City, 6/25/25
Lodge, Henry Cabot (legislator); Boston **(1850–1924)**
Lodge, Henry Cabot, Jr. (diplomat); Nahant, Mass. **(1902–1985)**
Loesser, Frank (composer); New York City **(1910–1969)**
Loewe, Frederick (composer); Vienna **(1901–1988)**
Logan, Joshua (director, producer); Texarkana, Tex. **(1908–1988)**
Lollobrigida, Gina (Luigina Lollobrigida) (actress); Subiaco, Italy, 7/4/27
Lombard, Carole (Jane Alice Peters) (actress); Ft. Wayne, Ind. **(1908–1942)**
Lombardo, Guy (band leader); London, Ont., Canada **(1902–1977)**
London, George (baritone); Montreal **(1920–1985)**
London, Jack (John Griffith London) (novelist); San Francisco **(1876–1916)**
Long, Huey Pierce (politician); Winnfield, La. **(1893–1935)**
Long, Shelley (actress); Fort Wayne, Ind., 8/23/49
Longfellow, Henry Wadsworth (poet); Portland, Maine **(1807–1882)**
Longworth, Alice Roosevelt (social figure); New York City **(1884–1980)**
Loos, Anita (novelist); Sissons, Calif. **(1888–1981)**
Lopez, Trini (singer); Dallas, 5/15/37

Lopez, Vincent (band leader); Brooklyn, N.Y. **(1895–1975)**
Lord, Jack (John Joseph Ryan) (actor); New York City **(1920–1998)**
Loren, Sophia (Sofia Scicolone) (actress); Rome, 9/20/34
Lorenz, Konrad (ethologist); Vienna **(1903–1989)**
Lorre, Peter (Laszlo Löewenstein) (actor); Rosenberg, former Czechoslovakia **(1904–1964)**
Loudon, Dorothy (actress, singer); Boston, 9/17/33
Louis-Dreyfus, Julia (actress); New York City, 1/13/61
Louis XIV (King of France); St.-Germain-en-Laye, France **(1638–1715)**
Louise, Tina (actress); New York City, 2/11/37
Love, Susan (surgeon, oncologist, activist); Long Branch, N.J., 2/9/48
Lovecraft, Howard Phillips (author); Providence, R.I. **(1890–1937)**
Lovett, Lyle (country singer, songwriter); Klein, Tex., 11/1/56
Lowell, Amy (poet); Brookline, Mass. **(1874–1925)**
Lowell, James Russell (poet); Cambridge, Mass. **(1819–1891)**
Lowell, Robert (poet); Boston **(1917–1977)**
Loy, Myrna (Myrna Williams) (actress); nr. Helena, Mont. **(1905–1993)**
Loyola, St. Ignatius of (Iñigo de Oñez y Loyola) (founder of Jesuits); Gúipuzcoa Province, Spain **(1491–1556)**
Lubitsch, Ernst (film director); Berlin **(1892–1947)**
Lucas, George (film director); Modesto, Calif., 5/14/44
Lucci, Susan (actress); Scarsdale, N.Y., 12/23/46
Luce, Clare Boothe (playwright, former Ambassador); New York City **(1903–1987)**
Luce, Henry Robinson (editor, publisher); Tengchow, China **(1898–1967)**
Ludlum, Robert (author); New York City, 5/25/27
Lugosi, Béla (Béla Blasko) (actor); Lugos, Hungary **(1888–1956)**
Lukas, J. Anthony (author); New York City **(1933–1997)**
Lukas, Paul (actor); Budapest **(1895–1971)**
Lully, Jean Baptiste (French composer); Florence **(1639–1687)**
Lumet, Sidney (director); Philadelphia, 6/25/24
Lunden, Joan (TV host); Fair Oaks, Calif., 9/19/50
Lunt, Alfred (actor); Milwaukee **(1892–1977)**
Lupino, Ida (actress, director); London **(1918–1995)**
LuPone, Patti (actress, singer); Northport, N.Y., 4/21/49
Luther, Martin (religious reformer); Eisleben (East Germany) **(1483–1546)**
Lynn, Loretta (singer); Butcher's Hollow, Ky., 4/14/35

M

Ma, Yo-Yo (cellist); Paris, 10/7/55
Maazel, Lorin (conductor); Neuilly, France, 3/5/30
MacArthur, Charles (playwright); Scranton, Pa. **(1895–1956)**
MacArthur, Douglas (five-star general); Little Rock Barracks, Ark. **(1880–1964)**
MacArthur, James (actor); Los Angeles, 12/8/37
Macaulay, Thomas Babington (author); Rothley Temple, England **(1800–1859)**
MacDermot, Galt (composer); Montreal, 12/19/28
MacDonald, James Ramsay (statesman); Lossiemouth, Scotland **(1866–1937)**
MacDonald, Jeanette (actress, soprano); Philadelphia **(1907–1965)**
Macdonald, Ross (Kenneth Millar) (mystery writer); Los Gatos, Calif. **(1915–1983)**
MacDowell, Edward Alexander (composer); New York City **(1861–1908)**
MacDowell, Andie (Rosalie Anderson MacDowell) (actress); Gaffney, S.C., 4/21/58
MacFadden, Bernarr (physical culturist); nr. Mill Spring, Mo. **(1868–1955)**
Machaut, Guillaume de (composer); Marchault, France **(1300–1377)**
Machiavelli, Niccolò (political philosopher); Florence (Italy) **(1469–1527)**
Mackie, Bob (designer); Monterey Park, Calif., 3/24/40
MacLaine, Shirley (Shirley MacLean Beaty) (actress); Richmond, Va., 4/24/34
MacLeish, Archibald (poet); Glencoe, Ill. **(1892–1982)**
Macmillan, Harold (ex-Prime Minister); London **(1894–1986)**
MacMurray, Fred (actor); Kankakee, Ill. **(1908–1991)**
MacNeil, Cornell (baritone); Minneapolis, 9/24/22
MacNeil, Robert (TV newscaster); Montreal, 1/19/31
MacNicol, Peter (actor); Dallas, 4/10/54
MacRae, Gordon (singer); East Orange, N.J. **(1921–1986)**
MacRae, Sheila (comedienne); London, 9/24/24
Madison, Guy (Robert Moseley) (actor); Bakersfield, Calif. **(1922–1996)**
Madison, James (4th U.S. president); Port Conway, Va. **(1751–1836)**
Madonna (Madonna Louise Ciccone) (singer, actress); Bay City, Mich., 8/16/58
Maeterlinck, Count Maurice (author); Ghent, Belgium **(1862–1949)**
Magellan, Ferdinand (Fernando de Magalhaes) (navigator); Sabrosa, Portugal **(c. 1480–1521)**
Magliozzi, Ray ("Car Talk" host); Cambridge, Mass., 3/30/49
Magliozzi, Tom ("Car Talk" host); Cambridge, Mass., 6/28/37
Magritte, René (painter); Belgium **(1898–1967)**
Magsaysay, Ramón (statesman); Iba, Luzon, Philippines **(1907–1957)**
Mahan, Alfred Thayer (naval historian); West Point, N.Y. **(1840–1914)**
Mahler, Gustav (composer, conductor); Kalischt (Czechoslovakia) **(1860–1911)**
Mahoney, John (actor); Manchester, England, 6/20/40
Mailer, Norman (novelist); Long Branch, N.J., 1/31/23
Maillol, Aristide (sculptor); Banyuls-sur-Mer, Rousillion, France **(1861–1944)**
Maimonides, Moses (Jewish philosopher); Cordoba, Spain **(1135–1204)**
Mainbocher (Main Rousseau Bocher) (fashion designer); Chicago **(1891–1976)**
Majors, Lee (Harvey Lee Yeary) (actor); Wyandotte, Mich., 4/23/40
Makarova, Natalia (ballet dancer); Leningrad (St. Petersburg, Russia), 11/21/40
Makeba, Miriam (singer); Johannesburg, South Africa, 3/4/32
Malamud, Bernard (novelist); Brooklyn, N.Y. **(1914–1986)**
Malcolm X (Malcolm Little; el Hajj Ma lik el-Shabazz) (Black nationalist, religious leader); Omaha, Neb. **(1925–1965)**
Malden, Karl (Karl Mladen Sekulovich) (actor); Chicago, 3/22/13
Malkovich, John (actor); Christopher, Ill., 12/9/53
Mallarmé, Stephane (poet, essayist); Paris **(1842–1898)**
Malle, Louis (director); Thumeries, France **(1932–1995)**
Malone, Dorothy (actress); Chicago, 1/30/25
Malraux, André (author); Paris **(1901–1976)**
Malthus, Thomas Robert (economist); nr. Dorking, England **(1766–1834)**
Maltin, Leonard (film critic and historian); New York City, 12/18/50
Mamet, David (playwright); Chicago, 11/30/47
Manchester, Melissa (singer); Bronx, N.Y., 2/15/51
Manchester, William (writer); Attleboro, Mass., 4/1/22
Mancini, Henry (composer, conductor); Cleveland **(1924–1994)**
Mandela, Nelson (Rolihlahla) (South African political activist); Umtata, Transkei, 6/11/18
Mandela, Winnie (Nomzamo) (South African political activist); Pondoland district of the Transkei, 1936?
Mandrell, Barbara (singer); Houston, 12/25/48
Manet, Edouard (painter); Paris **(1832–1883)**
Mangione, Chuck (hornist, pianist, composer); Rochester, N.Y., 11/29/40
Manilow, Barry (singer); Brooklyn, N.Y., 6/17/46
Mankiewicz, Frank F. (columnist); New York City, 5/16/24
Mankiewicz, Joseph L. (film writer, director); Wilkes-Barre, Pa. **(1909–1993)**
Mann, Horace (educator); Franklin, Mass. **(1796–1859)**
Mann, Thomas (novelist); Lübeck, Germany **(1875–1955)**
Mannes, Marya (writer); New York City **(1904–1990)**
Mansfield, Jayne (Jayne Palmer) (actress); Bryn Mawr, Pa. **(1932–1967)**
Mansfield, Katherine (story writer); Wellington, New Zealand **(1888–1923)**
Mantegna, Andrea (painter); Isola di Carturo, Italy **(1431–1506)**
Mantegna, Joe (actor); Chicago, 11/13/47
Mantovani, Annunzio (conductor); Venice **(1905–1980)**
Mao Zedong (Tse-tung) (Chinese leader); Shao Shan, China **(1893–1976)**
Mapplethorpe, Robert (photographer); Floral Park, Queens, N.Y. **(1946–1989)**
Marat, Jean Paul (French revolutionist); Boudry, Neuchâtel, Switzerland **(1743–1793)**
Marceau, Marcel (mime); Strasbourg, France, 3/22/23
March, Fredric (Frederick Bickel) (actor); Racine, Wis. **(1897–1975)**
Marchand, Nancy (actress); Buffalo, N.Y., 6/19/28
Marconi, Guglielmo (inventor); Bologna, Italy **(1874–1937)**
Marcus Aurelius (Marcus Annius Verus) (Roman emperor); Rome **(121–180)**
Marcus, Rudolph Arthur (chemist, Nobel laureate); Montreal, 7/21/23
Marcuse, Herbert (philosopher); Berlin **(1898–1979)**
Margaret Rose (Princess); Glamis Castle, Angus, Scotland, 8/21/30

Margrethe II (Queen); Copenhagen, 4/16/40
Margulies, Julianna (actress); Spring Valley, N.Y., 6/8/65
Marie Antoinette (Josephe Jeanne Marie Antoinette) (Queen of France); Vienna **(1755–1793)**
Marisol (Escobar) (Venezuelan-American sculptor); Paris, 1930
Markham, Edwin (poet); Oregon City, Ore. **(1852–1940)**
Markova, Dame Alicia (Lilian Alice Marks) (ballet dancer); London, 12/1/10
Marley, Bob (singer, songwriter); Kingston, Jamaica **(1945–1981)**
Marlowe, Christopher (dramatist); Canterbury, England **(1564–1593)**
Marquand, J(ohn) P(hillips) (novelist); Wilmington, Del. **(1893–1960)**
Marquette, Jacques (missionary, explorer); Laon, France **(1637–1675)**
Marriner, Neville (conductor); Lincoln, England, 4/15/24
Marsalis, Wynton (musician); New Orleans, 10/18/61
Marshall, E.G. (actor); Owatonna, Minn. **(1910–1998)**
Marshall, George Catlett (general); Uniontown, Pa. **(1880–1959)**
Marshall, Herbert (actor); London **(1890–1968)**
Marshall, John (jurist); nr. Germantown, Va. **(1755–1835)**
Marshall, Penny (Penny Marscharelli) (actress, director, producer); Bronx, N.Y., 10/15/42
Marshall, Thurgood (U.S. Supreme Court justice); Baltimore **(1908–1993)**
Martin, Dean (Dino Crocetti) (singer, actor); Steubenville, Ohio **(1917–1995)**
Martin, Mary (singer, actress); Weatherford, Tex. **(1913–1990)**
Martin, Steve (actor, writer, producer); Waco, Tex., 8/14/45
Martin, Tony (Alvin Morris) (singer); San Francisco, 12/25/13
Martinelli, Giovanni (tenor); Montagnana, Italy **(1885–1969)**
Martins, Peter (dancer, choreographer); Copenhagen, 10/27/45
Marvell, Andrew (poet); Winestead, England **(1621–1678)**
Marvin, Lee (actor); New York City **(1924–1987)**
Marx, Chico (Leonard) (comedian); New York City **(1891–1961)**
Marx, Groucho (Julius) (comedian); New York City **(1890–1977)**
Marx, Harpo (Arthur) (comedian); New York City **(1893–1964)**
Marx, Karl (Socialist writer); Treves (Germany) **(1818–1883)**
Marx, Zeppo (Herbert) (comedian); New York City **(1901–1979)**
Mary Stuart Mary, Queen of Scots (Queen of Scotland); Linlithgow, Scotland **(1542–1587)**
Masaccio, (Tommaso di Giovanni di Simone Cassai) (painter); San Giovanni Valdarno, Tuscany **(1401–c. 1428)**
Masaryk, Jan Garrigue (statesman); Prague (Czech Republic) **(1886–1948)**
Masaryk, Thomas Garrigue (statesman); Hodonin (Czech Republic) **(1850–1937)**
Masefield, John (poet), Ledbury, England **(1878–1967)**
Masekela, Hugh (trumpeter); Wilbank, South Africa, 4/4/39
Mason, Jackie (Jacob Moshe Maza) (comedian); Sheboygan, Wis., 6/9/31
Mason, James (actor); Huddersfield, England **(1909–1984)**
Mason, Marsha (actress); St. Louis, 4/3/42
Massenet, Jules Emile Frédéric (composer); Montaud, France **(1842–1912)**
Massine, Léonide (choreographer); Moscow **(1895–1979)**
Masters, Edgar Lee (poet); Garnett, Kans. **(1869–1950)**
Masters, William (human sexuality expert); Cleveland, 12/27/15
Mastroianni, Marcello (actor); Fontana Liri, Italy **(1924–1996)**
Mather, Cotton (clergyman); Boston **(1663–1728)**
Mathis, Johnny (singer); San Francisco, 9/30/35
Matisse, Henri (painter); Le Cateau, France **(1869–1954)**
Matthau, Walter (Walter Matuschanskayasky) (actor); New York City, 10/1/20
Mature, Victor (actor); Louisville, Ky., 1/29/15
Maugham, W(illiam) Somerset (author); Paris **(1874–1965)**
Mauldin, Bill (political cartoonist); Mountain Park, N.M., 10/29/21
Maupassant, Henri René Albert Guy de (story writer); Normandy, France **(1850–1893)**
Maurois, André (Emile Herzog) (author); Elbauf, France **(1885–1967)**
Maximilian (Ferdinand Maximilian Joseph) (Emperor of Mexico); Vienna **(1832–1867)**
Maxwell, James Clerk (physicist); Edinburgh, Scotland **(1831–1879)**
Maxwell, (Ian) Robert (publisher); Selo Slatina, Czechoslavakia **(1923–1991)**
May, Elaine (Elaine Berlin) (entertainer, writer); Philadelphia, 4/21/32
May, Rollo (psychologist); Ada, Ohio **(1909–1994)**
Mayall, John (singer, songwriter); Manchester, England, 11/29/33
Mayer, Louis B. (movie executive); Minsk, Russia **(1885–1957)**
Mayo, Charles H. (surgeon); Rochester, Minn. **(1865–1939)**
Mayo, Charles W. (surgeon); Rochester, Minn. **(1898–1968)**
Mayo, Virginia (Jones) (actress); St. Louis, 11/30/20
Mayo, William J. (surgeon); Le Sueur, Minn. **(1861–1939)**
Mayron, Melanie (actress); Philadelphia, 10/20/52
Mazzini, Giuseppe (patriot); Genoa **(1805–1872)**
McBride, Patricia (ballet dancer); Teaneck, N.J., 8/23/42
McCallum, David (actor); Glasgow, Scotland, 9/19/33
McCambridge, Mercedes (actress); Joliet, Ill., 3/17/18
McCarthy, Eugene J. (ex-Senator); Watkins, Minn., 3/29/16
McCarthy, Joseph Raymond (Senator); Grand Chute, Wis. **(1908–1957)**
McCarthy, Kevin (actor); Seattle, 2/15/14
McCarthy, Mary (novelist); Seattle **(1912–1989)**
McCartney, Paul (singer, songwriter); Liverpool, England, 6/18/42
McClanahan, Rue (actress); Healdton, Okla., 2/21/35
McClellan, George Brinton (general); Philadelphia **(1826–1885)**
McClintock, Barbara (geneticist); Hartford, Conn. **(1902–1992)**
McCloy, John J. (lawyer, banker); Philadelphia **(1895–1989)**
McCormack, John (tenor); Athlone, Ireland **(1884–1945)**
McCormack, John W. (ex-Speaker of House); Boston **(1891–1980)**
McCormick, Cyrus Hall (inventor); Rockbridge County, Va. **(1809–1884)**
McCracken, James (dramatic tenor); Gary, Ind. **(1926–1988)**
McCrea, Joel (actor); Los Angeles **(1905–1990)**
McCullers, Carson (novelist); Columbus, Ga. **(1917–1967)**
McDermott, Dylan (actor); Waterbury, Conn., 10/26/62
McDormand, Frances (actress); Illinois, 6/23/57
McDowall, Roddy (actor); London, 9/17/28
McDowell, Malcolm (actor); Leeds, England, 6/15/43
McFadden, Gates (actress); Cuyahoga Falls, Ohio, 8/28/49
McFarland, Spanky (George Emmett) (actor); Fort Worth, Tex. **(1928–1993)**
McGavin, Darren (actor); San Joaquin, Calif., 5/7/22
McGinley, Phyllis (poet, writer); Ontario, Ore. **(1905–1978)**
McGoohan, Patrick (actor); Astoria, Queens, N.Y., 3/19/28
McGovern, Maureen (singer); Youngstown, Ohio, 7/27/49
McGregor, Ewan (actor); Crieff, Scotland, 3/31/71
McGuire, Dorothy (actress); Omaha, Neb., 6/14/19
McKellen, Ian (actor); Burnley, England, 5/25/39
McKinley, William (25th U.S. president); Niles, Ohio **(1843–1901)**
McKuen, Rod (singer, composer); Oakland, Calif., 4/29/33
McLaughlin, John (guitarist); Yorkshire, England, 1/4/42
McLean, Don (singer, songwriter); New Rochelle, N.Y., 10/2/45
McLuhan, Marshall (Herbert Marshall) (communications writer); Edmonton, Alta., Canada **(1911–1980)**
McMahon, Ed (TV personality); Detroit, 3/6/23
McMurtry, Larry (novelist); Wichita Falls, Tex., 6/3/36
McQueen, Butterfly (Thelma) (actress); Tampa, Fla. **(1911–1995)**
McQueen, Steve (Terence Stephen McQueen) (actor); Indianapolis **(1930–1980)**
McRaney, Gerald (actor); Collins, Miss., 8/19/47
Mead, Margaret (anthropologist); Philadelphia **(1901–1978)**
Meadows, Audrey (actress); Wu Chang, China **(1924–1996)**
Meadows, Jayne (actress); Wu Chang, China, 9/27/26
Meaney, Colm (actor); Dublin, 5/30/53
Meany, George (labor leader); New York City **(1894–1980)**
Meara, Anne (actress); New York City, 9/20/29
Medici, Lorenzo de' (called Lorenzo the Magnificent) (Florentine ruler); Florence (Italy) **(1449–1492)**
Mehta, Zubin (conductor); Bombay (Mumbai), 4/29/36
Meir, Golda (Golda Myerson, nee Mabovitz) (ex-Premier of Israel); Kiev, Ukraine **(1898–1978)**
Melba, Dame Nellie (Helen Porter Mitchell) (soprano); nr. Melbourne, Australia **(1861–1931)**
Melchior, Lauritz (Lebrecht Hommel) (heroic tenor); Copenhagen **(1890–1973)**
Mellon, Andrew William (financier); Pittsburgh **(1855–1937)**
Melville, Herman (novelist); New York City **(1819–1891)**
Mencken, Henry Louis (writer); Baltimore **(1880–1956)**
Mendel, Gregor Johann (geneticist); Heinzendorf, Austrian Silesia **(1822–1884)**
Mendeleyev, Dmitri Ivanovich (chemist); Tobolsk, Russia **(1834–1907)**
Mendelssohn-Bartholdy, Jakob Ludwig Felix (composer); Hamburg **(1809–1847)**
Mendès-France, Pierre (ex-Premier); Paris **(1905–1982)**
Mengele, Josef (Nazi, "Angel of Death"); Günzberg, Germany **(1911–1979)**
Mennin, Peter (Peter Mennini) (composer); Erie, Pa. **(1923–1983)**
Menninger, William C. (psychiatrist); Topeka, Kans. **(1899–1966)**
Menotti, Gian Carlo (composer); Cadegliano, Italy, 7/7/11
Menuhin, Yehudi (violinist, conductor); New York City, 4/22/16

Menzies, Robert Gordon (ex-Prime Minister); Jeparit, Australia **(1894–1978)**
Mercer, Johnny (songwriter); Savannah, Ga. **(1909–1976)**
Mercer, Mabel (singer); Burton-on-Trent, England **(1900–1984)**
Merchant, Ismail (Ismail Noormohamed Abdul Rehman) (film producer); Bombay (Mumbai), 12/25/36
Meredith, Burgess (actor); Cleveland **(1908–1997)**
Merman, Ethel (Ethel Zimmerman) (singer, actress); Astoria, Queens, N.Y. **(1909–1984)**
Merrick, David (David Margulois) (stage producer); St. Louis, 11/27/12
Merrill, Robert (baritone); Brooklyn, N.Y., 6/4/19
Merton, Thomas (clergyman, writer); France **(1915–1968)**
Mesmer, Franz Anton (physician); Itzmang, nr. Constance (Germany) **(1733–1815)**
Mesta, Perle (social figure); Sturgis, Mich. **(1889–1975)**
Metacom, (King Philip) (Wampanoag Indian sachem); (southeastern Mass.) **(1640–1676)**
Metternich, Prince Klemens Wenzel Nepomuk Lothar von (statesman); Coblenz (Germany) **(1773–1859)**
Mfume, Kweisi (Frizzell Gray) (politician, NAACP leader); Baltimore, 10/24/48
Michaels, Lorne (producer); Toronto, 11/17/44
Michelangelo Buonarroti (painter, sculptor, architect); Caprese (Italy) **(1475–1564)**
Michener, James A. (novelist); New York City **(1907–1997)**
Mickiewicz, Adam (Polish poet); Zozie, Belorussia (Belarus) **(1798–1855)**
Midler, Bette (singer, actress, producer); Honolulu, 12/1/45
Mielziner, Jo (stage designer); Paris **(1901–1976)**
Mies van der Rohe, Ludwig (architect, designer); Aachen, Germany **(1886–1969)**
Mikoyan, Anastas I. (diplomat); Sanain, Armenia **(1895–1978)**
Milhaud, Darius (composer); Aix-en-Provence, France **(1892–1974)**
Mill, John Stuart (philosopher); London **(1806–1873)**
Milland, Ray (Reginald Truscott-Jones) (actor); Neath, Wales **(1907–1986)**
Millay, Edna St. Vincent (poet); Rockland, Maine **(1892–1950)**
Miller, Ann (Lucille Ann Collier) (dancer, actress); Cherino, Tex., 4/12/23
Miller, Arthur (playwright); New York City, 10/17/15
Miller, Glenn (band leader); Clarinda, Iowa **(1904–1944)**
Miller, Henry (novelist); New York City **(1891–1980)**
Miller, Jason (John Miller) (playwright, actor); New York City, 4/22/39
Miller, Mitch (Mitchell) (musician); Rochester, N.Y., 7/4/11
Miller, Roger (singer); Fort Worth **(1936–1992)**
Millet, Jean François (painter); Gruchy, France **(1814–1875)**
Millett, Kate (feminist); St. Paul, Minn., 9/14/34
Millikan, Robert A. (physicist); Morrison, Ill. **(1869–1953)**
Mills, Donna (actress); Chicago, 12/11/41
Mills, Hayley (actress); London, 4/18/46
Mills, Juliet (actress); London, 11/21/41
Milne, A(lan) A(lexander) (author); London **(1882–1956)**
Milner, Martin (actor); Detroit, 12/28/31
Milnes, Sherrill (baritone); Downers Grove, Ill., 1/10/35
Milstein, Nathan (concert violinist); Odessa (Ukraine) **(1904–1992)**
Milton, John (poet); London **(1608–1674)**
Mimieux, Yvette (actress); Hollywood, Calif., 1/8/41
Mingus, Charles (jazz composer); Nogales, Ariz. **(1922–1979)**
Minnelli, Liza (singer, actress); Hollywood, Calif., 3/12/46
Minnelli, Vincente (film director); Chicago **(1913–1986)**
Minuit, Peter (Governor of New Amsterdam); Wesel (Germany) **(1580–1638)**
Miranda, Carmen (Maria do Carmo da Cunha) (singer, dancer); Lisbon **(1909–1955)**
Miró, Joan (painter); Barcelona **(1893–1983)**
Mirren, Helen (Ilynea Lydia Mironoff) (actress); London, 7/26/45
Mitchell, John N. (former Attorney General); Detroit **(1913–1988)**
Mitchell, Joni (Roberta Joan Anderson) (singer, songwriter); Ft. Macleod, Canada, 11/7/43
Mitchell, Margaret (novelist); Atlanta **(1900–1949)**
Mitchell, Maria (astronomer); Nantucket, Mass. **(1818–1889)**
Mitchum, Robert (actor); Bridgeport, Conn. **(1917–1997)**
Mitropoulos, Dimitri (orchestra conductor); Athens **(1896–1960)**
Mitterand, François (Maurice) (ex-prime minister of France); Jarnac, France **(1916–1996)**
Mix, Tom (actor); Mix Run, Pa. **(1880–1940)**
Mobutu Sese Seko (Zairean dictator); Lisala, Congo **(1930–1997)**
Modigliani, Amedeo (painter); Leghorn, Italy **(1884–1920)**
Moffo, Anna (soprano); Wayne, Pa., 6/27/34
Mohammed (prophet); Mecca (Saudi Arabia) **(570–632)**
Molière (Jean Baptiste Poquelin) (dramatist); Paris **(1622–1673)**
Molina, Mario (chemist, Nobel laureate); Mexico City, 3/19/43
Moll, Richard (actor); Pasadena, Calif., 1/13/43?
Molnar, Ferenc (dramatist); Budapest **(1878–1952)**
Molotov, Vyacheslav M. (V. M. Skryabin) (diplomat); Kukarka, Russia **(1890–1986)**
Mondrian, Piet (painter); Amersfoort, Netherlands **(1872–1944)**
Monet, Claude (painter); Paris **(1840–1926)**
Monk, Meredith (choreographer, composer, performing artist); Lima, Peru, 11/20/42
Monk, Thelonious (pianist); Rocky Mount, N.C. **(1918–1982)**
Monroe, James (5th U.S. president); Westmoreland County, Va. **(1758–1831)**
Monroe, Marilyn (Norma Jean Mortenson or Baker) (actress); Los Angeles **(1926–1962)**
Monroe, Vaughn (Wilton) (band leader); Akron, Ohio **(1912–1973)**
Monsarrat, Nicholas (novelist); Liverpool, England **(1910–1979)**
Montaigne, Michel Eyquem de (essayist); nr. Bordeaux, France **(1533–1592)**
Montalban, Ricardo (actor); Mexico City, 11/25/20
Montand, Yves (Ivo Livi) (actor, singer); Florence, Italy **(1921–1991)**
Montesquieu, Charles-Louis de Secondat, baron de La Brède and de, (philosopher); nr. Bordeaux, France **(1689–1755)**
Montessori, Maria (physician, educator); Chiaravalle, Italy **(1870–1952)**
Monteux, Pierre (conductor); Paris **(1875–1964)**
Monteverdi, Claudio (composer); Cremona Italy **(1567–1643)**
Montezuma II (Aztec emperor); Mexico **(1466–1520)**
Montgomery, Elizabeth (actress); Hollywood, Calif. **(1938–1995)**
Montgomery, Robert (Henry, Jr.) (actor); Beacon, N.Y. **(1904–1981)**
Montgomery of Alamein, 1st Viscount of Hindhead (Sir Bernard Law Montgomery) (military leader); London **(1887–1976)**
Montoya, Carlos (guitarist); Madrid **(1903–1993)**
Moore, Clayton (Jack Moore) (actor); Chicago, 9/14/14
Moore, Clement Clarke (author); New York City **(1779–1863)**
Moore, Demi (actress); Roswell, N.M., 11/11/62
Moore, Dudley (actor, writer, musician); Dagenham, England, 4/19/35
Moore, Garry (Thomas Garrison Morfit) (TV personality); Baltimore **(1915–1993)**
Moore, Grace (soprano); Jellico, Tenn. **(1901–1947)**
Moore, Henry (sculptor); Castleford, England **(1898–1986)**
Moore, Marianne (poet); Kirkwood, Mo. **(1887–1972)**
Moore, Mary Tyler (actress); Brooklyn, N.Y., 12/29/36
Moore, Melba (Beatrice) (singer, actress); New York City, 10/27/45
Moore, Roger (actor); London, 10/14/27
Moore, Thomas (poet); Dublin **(1779–1852)**
Moorehead, Agnes (actress); Clinton, Mass. **(1906–1974)**
Moranis, Rick (actor); Toronto, 4/18/53
More, Henry (philosopher); Grantham, England **(1614–1687)**
More, Sir Thomas (statesman, author); London **(1478–1535)**
Moreno, Rita (Rosita Dolores Alverio) (actress); Humacao, P.R., 12/11/31
Morgan, Harry (Harry Bratsburg) (actor); Detroit, 4/10/15
Morgan, John Pierpont (financier); Hartford, Conn. **(1837–1913)**
Moriarty, Michael (actor); Detroit, 4/5/41
Morini, Erica (concert violinist); Vienna **(1904–1995)**
Morison, Samuel Eliot (historian); Boston **(1887–1976)**
Morley, Christopher Darlington (novelist); Haverford, Pa. **(1890–1957)**
Morris, Mark (choreographer); Seattle, 8/29/56
Morris, William (poet, craftsman); Walthamstow, England **(1834–1896)**
Morrison, Jim (James Douglas Morrison) (singer, songwriter); Melbourne, Fla. **(1943–1971)**
Morrison, Toni (Chloe Anthony Wofford) (novelist); Lorain, Ohio, 2/18/31
Morrison, Van (singer); Belfast, Northern Ireland, 8/31/45
Morse, Marston (mathematician); Waterville, Maine **(1892–1977)**
Morse, Robert (actor); Newton, Mass., 5/18/31
Morse, Samuel Finley Breese (painter, inventor); Charlestown, Mass. **(1791–1872)**
Morton, Jelly Roll (Ferdinand Joseph La Menthe) (jazz composer); New Orleans **(1890–1941)**
Moseley-Braun, Carol (U.S. Senator); Chicago, 8/16/47
Moses, Grandma (Mrs. Anna Mary Robertson Moses) (painter); Greenwich, N.Y. **(1860–1961)**
Moses, Robert (urban planner); New Haven, Conn. **(1888–1981)**
Mostel, Zero (Samuel Joel Mostel) (actor); Brooklyn, N.Y. **(1915–1977)**
Mother Teresa (Agnes Gonxha Bojaxhiu) (nun); Skopje, Macedonia **(1910–1997)**
Motherwell, Robert (artist, "action" painter); Aberdeen, Wash. **(1915–1991)**

Mott, Lucretia (Coffin) (feminist, reformer); Nantucket, Mass. **(1793–1880)**
Moussorgsky, Modest Petrovich (composer); Karev, Russia **(1839–1881)**
Moyers, Bill D. (Billy Don) (journalist); Hugo, Okla., 6/5/34
Moynihan, Daniel Patrick (New York Senator); Tulsa, Okla., 3/16/27
Mozart, Wolfgang Amadeus (Johannes Chrysostomus Wolfgangus Theophilus Mozart) (composer); Salzburg (Austria) **(1756–1791)**
Mudd, Roger (TV newscaster); Washington, D.C., 2/9/28
Muggeridge, Malcolm (Thomas) (writer); Croydon, England **(1903–1990)**
Muhammad, (founder of Islam); Mecca (Saudi Arabia) **(c. 570–632)**
Muhammad, Elijah (Elijah Poole) (religious leader); Sandersville, Ga. **(1897–1975)**
Mulgrew, Kate (actress); Dubuque, Iowa, 4/29/55
Mulhare, Edward (actor); Ireland **(1923–1997)**
Mulliken, Robert Sanderson (chemist, Nobel laureate); Newburyport, Mass. **(1896–1986)**
Mumford, Lewis (cultural historian, city planner); Flushing, Queens, N.Y. **(1895–1990)**
Munch, Edvard (painter); Löten, Norway **(1863–1944)**
Munchhausen, Karl Friedrick Hieronymus, baron von (anecdotist); Hannover, Germany **(1720–1797)**
Muni, Paul (Muni Weisenfreund) (actor); Lemburg, (Ukraine) **(1895–1967)**
Muñoz Marin, Luis (ex-governor of Puerto Rico); San Juan, P.R. **(1898–1980)**
Munsel, Patrice (soprano); Spokane, Wash., 5/14/25
Murdoch, Iris (novelist); Dublin, 7/15/19
Murdoch, Rupert (publisher); Melbourne, Australia, 3/11/31
Murillo, Bartolomé Esteban (painter); Seville, Spain **(1617–1682)**
Murphy, Audie (actor, war hero); Kingston, Tex. **(1924–1971)**
Murphy, Eddie (actor, comedian); Brooklyn, N.Y., 4/3/61
Murphy, George (actor, dancer, ex-Senator); New Haven, Conn. **(1902–1992)**
Murray, Arthur (dance teacher); New York City **(1895–1991)**
Murray, Bill (actor, comedian); Wilmette, Ill., 9/21/50
Murray, Kathryn (dance teacher); Jersey City, N.J., 1906
Murrow, Edward R. (commentator, government official); Greensboro, N.C. **(1908–1965)**
Musil, Robert (novelist); Klagenfurt, Austria **(1880–1942)**
Muskie, Edmund (political figure); Rumford, Maine **(1914–1996)**
Mussolini, Benito (Italian dictator); Dovia, Forli, Italy **(1883–1945)**
Muti, Riccardo (orchestra conductor); Naples, Italy, 7/28/41
Mutter, Anne-Sophie (violinist); Rheinfelden, Germany, 6/29/63
Myers, Mike (actor, writer, comedian); Scarborough, Ont., Canada, 5/25/63
Myerson, Bess (consumer advocate); Bronx, N.Y., 7/16/24
Myhrvold, Nathan (software industry executive); Santa Monica?, Calif., 1959
Myrdal, Gunnar (sociologist, economist); Gustaf Parish, Sweden **(1898–1987)**

N

Nabokov, Vladimir (novelist); St. Petersburg, Russia **(1899–1977)**
Nabors, Jim (actor, singer); Sylacauga, Ala., 6/12/32
Nader, Ralph (consumer advocate); Winsted, Conn., 2/27/34
Nash, Graham (singer); Blackpool, England, 1942
Nash, Ogden (poet); Rye, N.Y. **(1902–1971)**
Nasser, Gamal Abdel (statesman); Beni Mor, Egypt **(1918–1970)**
Nast, Thomas (cartoonist); Landau (Germany) **(1840–1902)**
Nation, Carry Amelia (temperance leader); Garrard County, Ky. **(1846–1911)**
Natta, Giulio (chemist, Nobel laureate); Imperia, Italy **(1903–1979)**
Natwick, Mildred (actress); Baltimore **(1905–1994)**
Nazimova, Alla (actress); Yalta, Crimea, Russia **(1879–1945)**
Neagle, Anna (Marjorie Robertson) (actress); London **(1908–1986)**
Neal, Patricia (actress); Packard, Ky., 1/20/26
Neeson, Liam (William John) (actor); Ballymena, Northern Ireland, 6/7/52
Neff, Hildegard (actress); Ulm, Germany, 12/28/25
Negri, Pola (Apolina Mathias-Chalupec) (actress); Bromberg (Poland) **(1899–1987)**
Nehru, Jawaharlal (first Prime Minister of India); Allahabad, India **(1889–1964)**
Neill, Sam (Nigel Neill) (actor); Omagh, Northern Ireland, 9/14/47
Nelligan, Kate (actress); London, Ont., Canada, 3/16/51
Nelson, Barry (Robert Haakon Nielsen) (actor); San Francisco, 4/16/20
Nelson, David (actor); New York City, 10/24/36
Nelson, Harriet Hilliard (Peggy Lou Snyder) (actress); Des Moines, Iowa **(1909–1994)**
Nelson, Ozzie (Oswald) (actor); Jersey City, N.J. **(1907–1975)**
Nelson, Ricky (Eric) (singer, actor); Teaneck, N.J. **(1940–1985)**
Nelson, Viscount Horatio (naval officer); Burnham Thorpe, England **(1758–1805)**
Nelson, Willie (singer); Waco, Tex., 4/30/33
Nenni, Pietro (Socialist leader); Faenza, Italy **(1891–1980)**
Nero (Nero Claudius Caesar Drusus Germanicus) (Roman emperor); Antium, (Italy) **(37–68)**
Nero, Peter (pianist); New York City, 5/22/34
Netanyahu, Benjamin (Binyamin) (Israeli Prime Minister); Tel Aviv, Israel, 10/21/49
Neuwirth, Bebe (Beatrice Neuwirth) (actress); Newark, N.J., 12/31/58
Nevelson, Louise (sculptor); Kiev, Russia **(1899–1988)**
Newhart, Bob (actor); Chicago, 9/5/29
Newhouse, Samuel I. (publisher); New York City **(1895–1979)**
Newley, Anthony (actor, songwriter); London, 9/24/31
Newman, Edwin (news commentator); New York City, 1/25/19
Newman, John Henry (prelate); London **(1801–1890)**
Newman, Paul (actor, director); Cleveland, 1/26/25
Newman, Randy (singer); Los Angeles, 11/28/43
Newton, Huey (black activist); New Orleans **(1942–1989)**
Newton, Sir Isaac (mathematician, scientist); nr. Grantham, England **(1642–1727)**
Newton, Wayne (singer); Norfolk, Va., 4/3/42
Newton-John, Olivia (singer); Cambridge, England, 9/26/48
Nichols, Nichelle (actress); Robbins, Ill., 12/28/33
Nichols, Mike (Michael Peschkowsky) (stage and film director); Berlin, 11/6/31
Nicholson, Jack (actor, director, writer); Neptune, N.J., 4/22/37
Nielsen, Leslie (actor); Regina, Sask., Canada, 2/11/26
Nietzsche, Friedrich Wilhelm (philosopher); nr. Lützen, Saxony (Germany) **(1844–1900)**
Nightingale, Florence (nurse); Florence, Italy **(1820–1910)**
Nijinsky, Vaslav (ballet dancer); Warsaw **(1890–1950)**
Nilsson, Birgit (soprano); West Karup, Sweden, 5/17/23
Nilsson, Harry (singer, songwriter); Brooklyn, N.Y. **(1941–1994)**
Nimitz, Chester W. (naval officer); Fredericksburg, Tex. **(1885–1966)**
Nimoy, Leonard (actor, director, writer, producer); Boston, 3/26/31
Nin, Anais (author, diarist); Neuilly, France **(1903–1977)**
Niven, David (actor); Kirriemuir, Scotland **(1910–1983)**
Nixon, Richard Milhous (37th U.S. president); Yorba Linda, Calif. **(1913–1994)**
Nizer, Louis (lawyer, author); London **(1902–1994)**
Nobel, Alfred Bernhard (industrialist); Stockholm **(1833–1896)**
Noguchi, Isamu (sculptor); Los Angeles **(1904–1988)**
Nolan, Lloyd (actor); San Francisco **(1902–1985)**
Nolte, Nick (actor); Omaha, Neb., 2/8/40
Norell, Norman (Norman Levinson) (fashion designer); Noblesville, Ind. **(1900–1972)**
Norman, Jessye (soprano); Augusta, Ga., 9/15/45
Norman, Marsha (Marsha Williams) (playwright); Louisville, Ky., 9/21/47
Normand, Mabel (actress); Boston **(1894–1930)**
Norstad, Gen. Lauris (ex-commander of NATO forces); Minneapolis **(1907–1988)**
North, John Ringling (circus director); Baraboo, Wis. **(1903–1985)**
North, Oliver (ex-military officer); San Antonio, 10/7/43
North, Sheree (actress); Los Angeles, 1/17/33
Norton, Eleanor Holmes (New York City government official, lawyer); Washington, D.C., 6/13/37
Nostradamus (Michel de Notredame) (astrologer); St. Rémy, France **(1503–1566)**
Novaes, Guiomar (pianist); São João de Boa Vista, Brazil **(1895–1979)**
Novak, Kim (Marilyn Novak) (actress); Chicago, 2/13/33
Novarro, Ramon (Ramon Samaniegoes) (actor); Durango, Mexico **(1899–1968)**
Novello, Ivor (actor, playwright, composer); Cardiff, Wales **(1893–1951)**
Nugent, Elliott (actor, director); Dover, Ohio **(1899–1980)**
Nureyev, Rudolf (ballet dancer); Siberia **(1938–1993)**
Nyro, Laura (singer, songwriter); Bronx, N.Y. **(1947–1997)**

O

Oakie, Jack (actor); Sedalia, Mo. **(1903–1978)**
Oakley, Annie (Phoebe Anne Oakley Mozee) (markswoman); Darke County, Ohio **(1860–1926)**
Oates, Joyce Carol (novelist); Lockport, N.Y., 6/16/38
Oberon, Merle (Estelle Merle O'Brien Thompson) (actress); Calcutta, India **(1911–1979)**

Oberth, Hermann (rocketry and space flight pioneer); Nagyszeben, Austria-Hungary (Sibiu, Romania) **(1894–1989)**
O'Brian, Hugh (Hugh J. Krampe) (actor); Rochester, N.Y., 4/19/25
O'Brien, Conan (TV personality); Brookline, Mass., 4/18/63
O'Brien, Edmond (actor); New York City **(1915–1985)**
O'Brien, Margaret (Angela Maxine O'Brien) (actress); San Diego, Calif., 1/15/37
O'Brien, Pat (William Joseph O'Brien, Jr.) (actor); Milwaukee **(1899–1983)**
O'Casey, Sean (playwright); Dublin **(1881–1964)**
Ochs, Adolph Simon (publisher); Cincinnati **(1858–1935)**
O'Connor, Carroll (actor); New York City, 8/2/24
Odets, Clifford (playwright); Philadelphia **(1906–1963)**
Odetta (Odetta Holmes) (folk singer, actress); Birmingham, Ala., 12/31/30
O'Donnell, Rosie (actress, talk show host); Commack, N.Y., 3/21/62
Offenbach, Jacques (composer); Cologne, Germany **(1819–1880)**
O'Hara, John (novelist); Pottsville, Pa. **(1905–1970)**
O'Hara, Maureen (Maureen FitzSimons) (actress); Dublin, 8/17/20
Ohlsson, Garrick (pianist); Bronxville, N.Y., 4/3/48
Ohrbach, Jerry (actor, singer); Bronx, N.Y., 10/20/35
Oistrakh, David (concert violinist); Odessa, Russia **(1908–1974)**
O'Keeffe, Georgia (painter); Sun Prairie, Wis. **(1887–1986)**
Oland, Warner (actor); Umea, Sweden **(1880–1938)**
Oldenburg, Claes (painter); Stockholm, 1/28/29
Oldman, Gary (actor, director); London, 3/21/58
Oliphant, Patrick B. (editorial cartoonist); Adelaide, Australia, 7/24/35
Oliver, Edna May (actress); Malden, Mass. **(1883–1942)**
Olivier, Sir Laurence (actor); Dorking, England **(1907–1989)**
Olmos, Edward James (actor); East Los Angeles, 2/24/47
Olmsted, Frederick Law (landscape architect); Hartford, Conn. **(1822–1903)**
Olsen, Ole (John Sigvard Olsen) (comedian); Peru, Ind. **(1892–1963)**
Omar Khayyam (poet, astronomer); Nishapur (Iran) (died c. 1123)
Onassis, Aristotle (shipping executive); Smyrna, Turkey **(1906–1975)**
Onassis, Christina (shipping executive); New York City **(1950–1988)**
Onassis, Jacqueline Kennedy (Jacqueline Bouvier) (First Lady); Southampton, N.Y. **(1929–1994)**
O'Neal, Ryan (Patrick) (actor); Los Angeles, 4/20/41
O'Neal, Tatum (actress); Los Angeles, 11/5/63
O'Neill, Eugene Gladstone (playwright); New York City **(1888–1953)**
O'Neill, Jennifer (actress); Rio de Janeiro, 2/20/49
Oppenheimer, J. Robert (nuclear physicist); New York City **(1904–1967)**
Orbach, Jerry (actor); New York City, 10/20/35
Orff, Carl (composer); Munich, Germany **(1895–1982)**
Orlando, Tony (Michael Anthony Orlando Cassavitis) (singer); New York City, 4/3/44
Ormandy, Eugene (conductor); Budapest **(1899–1985)**
Ormond, Julia (actress); Epsom, Surrey, England, 1/4/65
Orozco, José Clemente (painter); Zapotlán, Jalisco, Mexico **(1883–1949)**
Orwell, George (Eric Arthur Blair) (British author); Motihari, India **(1903–1950)**
Osborn, Paul (playwright); Evansville, Ind. **(1901–1988)**
Osborne, John (playwright); London **(1929–1994)**
Osler, Sir William (physician); Bondhead, Ont., Canada **(1849–1919)**
Osmond, Donny (singer, actor); Ogden, Utah, 12/9/57
Osmond, Marie (Olive Marie) (singer, actress); Ogden, Utah, 10/13/59
O'Sullivan, Maureen (actress); County Roscommon, Ireland **(1911–1997)**
Oswald, Lee Harvey (presumed assassin); New Orleans **(1939–1963)**
Otis, Elisha (inventor); Halifax, Vt. **(1811–1861)**
O'Toole, Peter (actor); Connemara, Ireland, 8/2/32
Ovid (Publius Ovidius Naso) (poet); Sulmona (Italy) **(43 B.C.E.–C.E. 17)**
Owens, Buck (Alvis Edgar Owens) (singer); Sherman, Tex., 8/12/29
Ozawa, Seiji (orchestra conductor); Fentian (Shenyan), Manchuria, 7/1/35

Paar, Jack (TV personality); Canton, Ohio, 5/1/18
Pacino, Al (Alfred) (actor); New York City, 4/25/40
Packard, Vance (author); Granville Summit, Pa. **(1914–1996)**
Paderewski, Ignace Jan (pianist, statesman); Kurylowka, Russian Podolia **(1860–1941)**
Paganini, Nicolò (violinist); Genoa (Italy) **(1782–1840)**
Page, Geraldine (actress); Kirksville, Mo. **(1924–1987)**
Page, Patti (Clara Ann Fowler) (singer, entertainer); Claremore, Okla., 11/8/27
Pagels, Elaine Hiesey (religious scholar); Palo Alto, Calif., 2/13/43
Paglia, Camille (writer, social critic); Endicott, N.Y., 4/2/47
Paine, Thomas (political philosopher); Thetford, England **(1737–1809)**
Palance, Jack (Walter Palanuik) (actor); Lattimer, Pa., 2/18/19
Palestrina, Giovanni Pierluigi da (composer); Palestrina, Italy **(1526–1594)**
Paley, William S. (broadcasting executive); Chicago **(1901–1990)**
Palladio, Andrea (architect); Padua or Vicenza (Italy) **(1508–1580)**
Palmerston, Henry John Templeton (3rd Viscount) (statesman); Broadlands, England **(1784–1865)**
Paltrow, Gwyneth (actress); Los Angeles, 9/28/73
Papanicolaou, George N. (physician); Coumi, Greece **(1883–1962)**
Papas, Irene (Lelekou) (actress); Chiliomodian, Greece, 3/9/26
Papp, Joseph (Joseph Papirofsky) (stage producer, director); Brooklyn, N.Y. **(1921–1991)**
Paracelsus, Philippus (Aureolus Theophrastus Bombastus von Hohenheim) (physican); Einsiedeln, Switzerland **(1493–1541)**
Park, Chung Hee (President of South Korea); Sangmo-ri, Korea **(1917–1979)**
Parker, Charlie "Bird" (jazz musician); Kansas City, Kans. **(1920–1955)**
Parker, Dorothy (Dorothy Rothschild) (author); West End, N.J. **(1893–1967)**
Parker, Fess (actor); Fort Worth, Tex., 8/16/25
Parker, Suzy (model, actress); San Antonio, 10/28/33
Parkinson, C(yril) Northcote (historian); Durham, England **(1909–1993)**
Parkman, Francis (historian); Boston **(1823–1893)**
Parks, Bert (Bert Jacobson) (entertainer); Atlanta **(1914–1992)**
Parks, Gordon (film director); Ft. Scott, Kans., 11/30/12
Parks, Rosa (civil rights activist); Tuskegee, Ala., 2/4/13
Parnell, Charles Stewart (statesman); Avondale, Ireland **(1846–1891)**
Parnis, Mollie (Mollie Parnis Livingston) (fashion designer); New York City **(1905?–1992)**
Parsons, Estelle (actress); Marblehead, Mass., 11/20/27
Parton, Dolly (singer); Locust Ridge, Tenn., 1/19/46
Pascal, Blaise (philosopher); Clermont, France **(1623–1662)**
Pasternak, Boris Leonidovich (author); Moscow **(1890–1960)**
Pasternak, Joseph (film producer); Silagy-Somlyo, Romania **(1901–1991)**
Pasteur, Louis (chemist); Dôle, France **(1822–1895)**
Pastor, Tony (Antonio) (actor, theater manager); New York City **(1837–1908)**
Pater, Walter (Horatio) (writer); London **(1839–1894)**
Patinkin, Mandy (Mandel) (actor, singer); Chicago, 11/30/52
Paton, Alan (author); Pietermaritzburg, South Africa **(1903–1988)**
Patti, Adelina (soprano); Madrid **(1843–1919)**
Patton, George Smith, Jr. (general); San Gabriel, Calif. **(1885–1945)**
Paul, Alice (feminist, woman suffragist); Moorestown, N.J. **(1885–1977)**
Paul, Les (Lester William Polfus) (guitarist); Waukesha, Wis., 6/9/15
Paul VI (Giovanni Battista Montini) (Pope); Concesio, nr. Brescia, Italy **(1897–1978)**
Pauley, Jane (Margaret Jane Pauley) (TV newscaster); Indianapolis, 10/31/50
Pauling, Linus Carl (chemist, Nobel laureate); Portland, Ore. **(1901–1994)**
Pavarotti, Luciano (tenor); Modena, Italy, 10/12/35
Pavlov, Ivan Petrovich (physiologist); Ryazan district, Russia **(1849–1936)**
Pavlova, Anna (ballet dancer); St. Petersburg, Russia **(1885–1931)**
Peale, Norman Vincent (clergyman); Bowersville, Ohio **(1898–1993)**
Pearl, Minnie (Sarah Ophelia Colley Cannon) (comedienne, singer); Centerville, Tenn., 10/25/12
Pears, Peter (tenor); Farnham, England **(1910–1986)**
Pearson, Drew (Andrew Russel Pearson) (columnist); Evanston, Ill. **(1897–1969)**
Pearson, Lester B. (statesman); Toronto **(1897–1972)**
Peary, Robert Edwin (explorer); Cresson, Pa. **(1856–1920)**
Peck, Gregory (Eldred Gregory Peck) (actor); La Jolla, Calif., 4/5/16
Peckinpah, Sam (film director); Fresno, Calif. **(1925–1984)**
Peerce, Jan (tenor); New York City **(1904–1984)**
Pegler, (James) Westbrook (columnist); Minneapolis **(1894–1969)**

Pei, I(eoh) M(ing) (architect); Canton, China, 4/26/17
Penn, Arthur (director); Philadelphia, 9/27/22
Penn, Sean (actor, filmmaker); Los Angeles, 8/17/60
Penn, William (American colonist); London **(1644–1718)**
Penney, James C. (merchant); Hamilton, Mo. **(1875–1971)**
Peppard, George (actor); Detroit **(1928–1994)**
Pepys, Samuel (diarist); Bampton, England **(1633–1703)**
Perelman, S(idney) J(oseph) (writer); Brooklyn, N.Y. **(1904–1979)**
Pergolesi, Giovanni Battista (composer); Jesi, Italy **(1710–1736)**
Pericles (statesman); Athens died 429 B.C.E.
Perkins, Anthony (actor); New York City **(1932–1992)**
Perkins, Frances (social reformer); Boston **(1882–1965)**
Perlman, Itzhak (violinist); Tel Aviv, Israel, 8/31/45
Perlman, Rhea (actress); Brooklyn, N.Y., 3/31/48
Perón, Isabel (María Estela Martínez Cartas) (former chief of state); La Rioja, Argentina, 2/4/31
Perón, Juan D. (statesman); nr. Lobos, Argentina **(1895–1974)**
Perón, Maria Eva Duarte de (political leader); Los Toldos, Argentina **(1919–1952)**
Perot, H. Ross (business executive); Texarkana, Tex., 6/27/30
Perrine, Valerie (actress, dancer); Galveston, Tex., 9/3/43
Perry, Matthew (actor); Williamstown, Mass., 8/19/69
Pershing, John Joseph (general); Linn County, Mo. **(1860–1948)**
Pestalozzi, Johann (educator); Zurich, Switzerland **(1746–1827)**
Peters, Bernadette (Bernadette Lazzara) (actress); New York City, 2/28/48
Peters, Brock (actor, singer); New York City, 7/2/27
Peters, Jean (actress); Canton, Ohio, 10/15/26
Peters, Roberta (Roberta Peterman) (soprano); New York City, 5/4/30
Petit, Roland (choreographer, dancer); Villemombe, France, 1924
Petrarch (Francesco Petrarca) (poet); Arezzo (Italy) **(1304–1374)**
Pfeiffer, Michelle (actress); Santa Ana, Calif., 4/29/58
Philbin, Regis (talk show host); New York City, 8/25/33
Philip (Philip Mountbatten) (Duke of Edinburgh); Corfu, Greece, 6/10/21
Piaf, Edith (Edith Gassion) (singer); Paris **(1916–1963)**
Piatigorsky, Gregor (cellist); Ekaterinoslav, Russia **(1903–1976)**
Piazza, Marguerite (soprano); New Orleans, 5/6/26
Picasso, Pablo (painter, sculptor); Málaga, Spain **(1881–1973)**
Pickett, Wilson (singer); Prattville, Ala., 3/18/41
Pickford, Mary (Gladys Mary Smith) (actress); Toronto **(1893–1979)**
Picon, Molly (actress); New York City **(1898–1992)**
Pidgeon, Walter (actor); East St. John, N.B., Canada **(1898–1984)**
Hyde Pierce, David (actor); Saratoga Springs, N.Y., 4/3/59
Pierce, Franklin (14th U.S. president); Hillsboro, N.H. **(1804–1869)**
Pileggi, Mitch (actor); Portland, Ore., 4/5/52
Pinkett-Smith, Jada (actress); Baltimore, 9/18/71
Pinter, Harold (playwright); London, 10/10/30
Pinza, Ezio (basso); Rome **(1892–1957)**
Pirandello, Luigi (dramatist, novelist); nr. Girgenti, Italy **(1867–1936)**
Piranesi, Giambattista (artist); Mestre, Italy **(1720–1778)**
Pissaro, Camille Jacob (painter); St. Thomas (U.S. Virgin Islands) **(1830–1903)**
Piston, Walter (composer); Rockland, Maine **(1894–1976)**
Pitman, Sir [Isaac] James (educator, publisher); Bath, England **(1901–1985)**
Pitt, Brad (actor); Shawnee, Okla., 12/18/64
Pitt, William ("Younger Pitt") (statesman); nr. Bromley, England **(1759–1806)**
Pitts, ZaSu (actress); Parsons, Kans. **(1898–1963)**
Pius XII (Eugenio Pacelli) (Pope); Rome **(1876–1958)**
Pizarro, Francisco (explorer); Trujillo, Spain **(c. 1476–1541)**
Planck, Max (physicist); Kiel, Germany **(1858–1947)**
Plath, Sylvia (poet); Boston **(1932–1963)**
Plato (Aristocles) (philosopher); Athens **(c. 427–347 B.C.E.)**
Pleasence, Donald (actor); Worksop, England **(1919–1995)**
Pleshette, Suzanne (actress); New York City, 1/31/37
Plimpton, George (author); New York City, 3/18/27
Plisetskaya, Maya (ballet dancer); Moscow, 11/20/25
Plowright, Joan (actress); Brigg, England, 10/28/29
Plummer, Christopher (actor); Toronto, 12/13/29
Plutarch (biographer); Chaeronea (Greece) **(c. 46–c. 120)**
Pocahontas (Matoaka) (American Indian princess); (Virginia) **(c. 1595–1617)**
Podhoretz, Norman (author); Brooklyn, N.Y., 1/16/30
Poe, Edgar Allan (poet, story writer); Boston **(1809–1849)**
Poitier, Sidney (actor, director); Miami, Fla., 2/20/27
Polanski, Roman (director); Paris, 8/18/33
Polk, James Knox (11th U.S. president); Mecklenburg County, N.C. **(1795–1849)**
Pollard, Michael J. (actor); Passaic, N.J., 5/30/39
Pollock, Jackson (painter); Cody, Wyo. **(1912–1956)**
Polo, Marco (traveler); Venice **(c. 1254–1324)**
Pol Pot, (Cambodian dictator); Kompong Thom, Cambodia **(1925–1998)**
Pompadour, Mme. de (Jeanne Antoinette Poisson) (courtesan); Versailles **(1721–1764)**
Pompey (Gnaeus Pompeius Magnus) (general); Rome **(106–48 B.C.E.)**
Ponce de León, Juan (explorer); Servas, Spain **(c. 1460–1521)**
Pons, Lily (coloratura soprano); Cannes, France **(1904–1976)**
Ponselle, Rosa (soprano); Meriden, Conn. **(1897–1981)**
Ponti, Carlo (director); Milan, Italy, 12/11/13
Pontormo, Jacopo da (painter); Pontormo, Italy **(1492–1557)**
Pope, Alexander (poet); London **(1688–1744)**
Porter, Cole (songwriter); Peru, Ind. **(1891–1964)**
Porter, Katherine Anne (novelist); Indian Creek, Tex. **(1891–1980)**
Post, Wiley (aviator); Grand Plain, Tex. **(1900–1935)**
Poston, Tom (actor); Columbus, Ohio, 10/17/27
Potëmkin, Grigori Aleksandrovich, Prince (statesman); Khizovo (Khizov, Belarus) **(1739–1791)**
Potok, Chaim (author); New York City, 2/17/29
Potter, (Helen) Beatrix (author, illustrator); South Kensington, Middlesex, England **(1866–1943)**
Poulenc, Francis (composer); Paris **(1899–1963)**
Pound, Ezra (poet); Hailey, Idaho **(1885–1972)**
Poussin, Nicolas (painter); Villers, France **(1594–1665)**
Powell, Adam Clayton, Jr. (Congressman); New Haven, Conn. **(1908–1972)**
Powell, Colin L. (retired general); New York City, 4/5/37
Powell, Dick (actor); Mt. View, Ark. **(1904–1963)**
Powell, Eleanor (actress, tap dancer); Springfield, Mass. **(1912–1982)**
Powell, Jane (Suzanne Burce) (actress, singer); Portland, Ore., 4/1/29
Powell, William (actor); Pittsburgh **(1892–1984)**
Power, Tyrone (actor); Cincinnati, Ohio **(1914–1958)**
Powers, Stefanie (Stefania Zofia Federkiewcz) (actress); Hollywood, Calif., 11/12/42
Praxiteles (sculptor); Athens **(c. 370–c. 330 B.C.E.)**
Preminger, Otto (director, producer); Vienna **(1906–1986)**
Prentiss, Paula (Paula Ragusa) (actress); San Antonio, 3/4/39
Presley, Elvis (singer, actor); Tupelo, Miss. **(1935–1977)**
Presley, Priscilla (actress); Brooklyn, N.Y., 5/24/45
Preston, Robert (Robert Preston Meservey) (actor); Newton Highlands, Mass. **(1918–1987)**
Previn, André (conductor); Berlin, 4/6/29
Previn, Dory (singer); Rahway, N.J., 10/22/29?
Price, Leontyne (Mary) (soprano); Laurel, Miss., 2/10/27
Price, Ray (country music artist); Perryville, Tex., 1/12/26
Price, Vincent (actor); St. Louis **(1911–1993)**
Pride, Charley (singer); Sledge, Miss., 3/18/38?
Priestley, Jason (actor, producer); Vancouver, B.C., Canada, 8/28/69
Priestley, J. B. (John B.) (author); Bradford, England **(1894–1984)**
Priestley, Joseph (chemist); nr. Leeds, England **(1733–1804)**
Primrose, William (violist); Glasgow, Scotland **(1904–1982)**
Prince (Prince Roger Nelson) (singer); Minneapolis, 6/7/58
Prince, Harold (stage producer); New York City, 1/30/28
Principal, Victoria (actress); Fukuoka, Japan, 1/3/45
Prinze, Freddie (actor); New York City **(1954–1977)**
Pritchett, V(ictor) S(awdon) (literary critic); Ipswich, England **(1900–1997)**
Procter, William (scientist); Cincinnati **(1872–1951)**
Prokofiev, Sergei Sergeevich (composer); St. Petersburg, Russia **(1891–1953)**
Proulx, E. Annie (novelist); Norwich, Conn., 8/22/35
Proust, Marcel (novelist); Paris **(1871–1922)**
Provine, Dorothy (actress); Deadwood, S. Dak., 1/20/37
Prowse, Juliet (actress); Bombay (Mumbai) **(1936–1996)**
Pryor, Richard (comedian); Peoria, Ill., 12/1/40
Ptolemy (Claudius Ptolemaeus) (astronomer, geographer); Ptolemais Hermii, (Egypt), fl. 2nd cent.
Pucci, Emilio (Marchese di Barsento) (fashion designer); Naples, Italy **(1914–1992)**
Puccini, Giacomo (composer); Lucca, Italy **(1858–1924)**
Puente, Tito (band leader); New York City, 4/20/23
Pulaski, Casimir (military officer); Podolia, Poland **(1748–1779)**
Pulitzer, Joseph (publisher); Makó (Hungary) **(1847–1911)**
Pullman, Bill (actor); Delphi, N.Y., 12/17/53
Pullman, George (inventor); Brockton, N.Y. **(1831–1897)**
Purcell, Henry (composer); London **(1658–1695)**
Pusey, Nathan M. (educator); Council Bluffs, Iowa, 4/4/07

Pushkin, Alexander Sergeevich (poet, dramatist); Moscow **(1799–1837)**
Puzo, Mario (novelist); New York City, 10/15/21
Pyle, Ernest Taylor (journalist); Dana, Ind. **(1900–1945)**
Pythagoras (mathematician, philosopher); Samos (Greece) **(c. 582–c. 507C.E.)**

Q

Qaddafi, Muammar al- (Libyan leader); Libya, 1942
Quaid, Dennis (actor); Houston, 4/9/54
Quaid, Randy, (actor); Houston, 10/1/50
Quayle, Anthony (actor); Ainsdale, England **(1913–1989)**
Queen, Ellery: pen name of Frederic Dannay and Manfred B. Lee
Queler, Eve (conductor); New York City, 1/1/36
Quennell, Sir Peter Courtney (biographer); Bromley, England **(1905–1993)**
Quindlen, Anna (writer); Philadelphia, 7/8/53
Quinn, Aidan (actor); Chicago, 3/8/59
Quinn, Anthony (Antonio Quiñones) (actor); Chihuahua, Mexico, 4/21/16

R

Rabe, David (playwright); Dubuque, Iowa, 3/10/40
Rabelais, François (satirist); nr. Chinon, France **(c. 1490–1553)**
Rabi, I(sidor) I(saac) (physicist); Rymanow (Poland) **(1898–1988)**
Rabin, Yitzhak (former Israeli Prime Minister); Jerusalem **(1922–1995)**
Rachmaninoff, Sergei Wassilievitch (pianist, composer); Oneg Estate, Novgorod, Russia **(1873–1943)**
Racine, Jean Baptiste (dramatist); La Ferté-Milon, France **(1639–1699)**
Radner, Gilda (comedienne); Detroit **(1946–1989)**
Raft, George (actor); New York City **(1895–1980)**
Rainier III (Prince); Monaco, 5/31/23
Rains, Claude (actor); London **(1889–1967)**
Raitt, Bonnie (singer); Burbank, Calif., 11/8/49
Raitt, John (actor, singer); Santa Ana, Calif., 1/19/17
Raleigh, Sir Walter (courtier, navigator); London **(1552?–1618)**
Rambeau, Marjorie (actress); San Francisco **(1889–1970)**
Rameau, Jean-Philippe (composer); Dijon, France **(1683–1764)**
Rampal, Jean-Pierre (Louis) (flutist); Marseilles, France, 7/1/22
Rand, Ayn (novelist, philosopher); St. Petersburg, Russia **(1905–1982)**
Randall, Tony (Leonard Rosenberg) (actor); Tulsa, Okla., 2/26/20
Randolph, A(sa) Philip (labor leader); Crescent City, Fla. **(1889–1979)**
Rankin, Jeannette (pacifist); Missoula, Mont. **(1880–1973)**
Raphael (Raffaello Santi) (painter, architect); Urbino (Italy) **(1483–1520)**
Rasputin, Grigori Efimovich (monk); Tobolsk Province, Russia **(1872–1916)**
Rathbone, Basil (Philip St. John Basil Rathbone) (actor); Johannesburg, South Africa **(1892–1967)**
Rather, Dan (TV newscaster); Wharton, Tex., 10/31/31
Rattigan, Terence (playwright); London **(1911–1977)**
Rauschenberg, Robert (painter); Port Arthur, Tex., 10/22/25
Ravel, Maurice Joseph (composer); Ciboure, France **(1875–1937)**
Ray, Aldo (DaRe) (actor); Pen Argyl, Pa. **(1926–1991)**
Ray, Gene Anthony (actor, dancer); Harlem, N.Y., 5/24/63
Ray, Man (painter); Philadelphia **(1890–1976)**
Ray, Satyajat (film director); Calcutta **(1921–1992)**
Raye, Martha (Margie Yvonne Reed) (comedienne, actress); Butte, Mont. **(1916–1994)**
Reagan, Ronald Wilson (40th U.S. president); Tampico, Ill., 2/6/11
Reasoner, Harry (TV commentator); Dakota City, Iowa **(1923–1991)**
Redding, Otis (singer); Dawson, Ga. **(1941–1967)**
Reddy, Helen (singer); Melbourne, Australia, 10/25/41
Redford, Robert (Charles Robert Redford, Jr.) (actor); Santa Monica, Calif., 8/18/37
Redgrave, Lynn (actress); London, 3/8/43
Redgrave, Sir Michael (actor); Bristol, England **(1908–1985)**
Redgrave, Vanessa (actress); London, 1/30/37
Redon, Odilon (artist); Bordeaux, France **(1840–1916)**
Reed, Donna (Donna Belle Mullenger) (actress); Denison, Iowa **(1921–1986)**
Reed, Rex (critic); Ft. Worth, 10/2/40
Reed, Walter (army surgeon); Belroi, Va. **(1851–1902)**
Reese, Della (Deloreese Patricia Early) (singer, actress); Detroit, 7/6/32
Reeve, Christopher (actor, activist); New York City, 9/25/52
Reeves, Jim (singer); Panola County, Tex. **(1923–1964)**
Reich, Robert (Clinton Cabinet Member); Scranton, Pa., 6/24/46
Reich, Steve (composer); New York City, 10/3/36
Reid, Wallace (actor); St. Louis **(1891–1923)**
Reiner, Carl (actor); New York City, 3/20/22
Reiner, Fritz (conductor); Budapest **(1888–1963)**
Reiner, Robert (actor, director, writer, producer); Bronx, N.Y., 3/6/45
Reinhardt, Max (Max Goldmann) (theater producer); nr. Vienna **(1873–1943)**
Reiser, Paul (actor, producer); New York City, 3/30/57
Remarque, Erich Maria (novelist); Osnabrük, Germany **(1898–1970)**
Rembrandt (Rembrandt Harmensz van Rijn) (painter); Leyden, (Netherlands) **(1605–1669)**
Remick, Lee (Ann) (actress); Boston **(1935–1991)**
Rennert, Günther (opera director, producer); Essen, Germany, 4/1/11
Rennie, Michael (actor); Bradford, England **(1909–1971)**
Reno, Janet (U.S. Attorney General); Miami, Fla., 7/21/38
Renoir, Jean (film director, writer); Paris **(1894–1979)**
Renoir, Pierre Auguste (painter); Limoges, France **(1841–1919)**
Resnais, Alain (film director); Vannes, France, 6/3/22
Resnik, Regina (mezzo-soprano); New York City, 8/30/22
Respighi, Ottorino (composer); Bologna, Italy **(1879–1936)**
Reston, James (journalist); Clydebank, Scotland **(1909–1995)**
Reuther, Walter (labor leader); Wheeling, W. Va. **(1907–1970)**
Revere, Paul (silversmith, hero of famous ride); Boston **(1735–1818)**
Revson, Charles (business executive); Boston **(1906–1975)**
Reynolds, Burt (actor, director, producer); Lansing, Mich., 2/11/36
Renolds, Debbie (Marie Frances Reynolds) (actress); El Paso, Tex., 4/1/32
Reynolds, Sir Joshua (painter); nr. Plymouth, England **(1723–1792)**
Reynolds, Marjorie (Marjorie Goodspeed) (actress); Buhl, Idaho **(1921–1997)**
Rhodes, Cecil John (South African statesman); Bishop Stortford, England **(1853–1902)**
Rice, Anne (novelist); New Orleans, 10/14/41
Rice, Elmer (Elmer Leopold Reizenstein) (playwright); New York City **(1892–1967)**
Rice, Grantland (sports writer); Murfreesboro, Tenn. **(1880–1954)**
Rich, Buddy (Bernard) (drummer); Brooklyn, N.Y. **(1917–1987)**
Rich, Charlie (singer); Colt, Ark. **(1932–1995)**
Richard I the Lion-hearted (King of England); Oxford, England **(1157–1199)**
Richards, Ann (Dorothy Ann Willis) (ex-governor of Texas); Lakeview, Tex., 9/1/33
Richards, Keith (rock singer); Dartford, England, 12/18/43
Richards, Michael (actor); California, 8/24/49
Richardson, Elliot L. (ex-Cabinet member); Boston, 7/20/20
Richardson, Sir Ralph (actor); Cheltenham, England **(1902–1983)**
Richardson, Tony (director); Shipley, England **(1928–1991)**
Richelieu, Duc de (Armand Jean du Plessis) (cardinal); Paris **(1585–1642)**
Richie, Lionel (singer, songwriter); Tuskegee, Ala., 6/20/49
Richter, Charles Francis (seismologist); Hamilton, Ohio **(1900–1985)**
Richter, Sviatoslav (pianist); Zhitomir, Ukraine, 3/20/14
Rickenbacker, Edward V. (aviator); Columbus, Ohio **(1890–1973)**
Rickles, Don (comedian); New York City, 5/8/26
Rickover, Vice Admiral Hyman G. (atomic energy expert); Russia **(1900–1986)**
Riddle, Nelson (composer); Hackensack, N.J. **(1921–1985)**
Ride, Sally K(risten) (astronaut, astrophysicist); Encino, Calif., 5/26/51
Ridgway, General Matthew B. (ex-Army Chief of Staff); Ft. Monroe, Va. **(1895–1993)**
Riemenschneider, Tilman (sculptor); Osterode, Germany **(c. 1460–1531)**
Rigg, Diana (actress); Doncaster, England, 7/20/38
Riley, James Whitcomb (poet); Greenfield, Ind. **(1849–1916)**
Rilke, Rainer Maria (poet); Prague **(1875–1926)**
Rimbaud, (Jean Nicolas) Arthur (poet); Charleville, France **(1854–1891)**
Rimes, LeAnn (singer); Jackson, Miss., 8/28/82
Rimsky-Korsakov, Nikolai Andreevich (composer); Tikhvin, Russia **(1844–1908)**
Rinehart, Mary (née Roberts) (novelist); Pittsburgh **(1876–1958)**
Ritchard, Cyril (actor, director); Sydney, Australia **(1898–1977)**
Ritter, John (Jonathan) (actor); Burbank, Calif., 9/17/48
Ritter, Tex (Woodward Maurice Ritter) (singer); Panola County, Tex. **(1905–1973)**
Ritter, Thelma (actress); Brooklyn, N.Y. **(1905–1969)**

Rivera, Chita (Dolores Conchita Figuero del Rivero) (dancer, actress, singer); Washington, D.C., 1/23/33
Rivera, Diego (painter); Guanajuato, Mexico **(1886–1957)**
Rivera, Geraldo (Miguel Rivera) (TV host); New York City, 7/4/43
Rivers, Joan (comedienne); Brooklyn, N.Y., 6/8/33
Rivers, Larry (Yitzroch Loiza Grossberg) (painter); New York City, 8/17/23
Roach, Hal (film producer); Elmira, N.Y. **(1892–1992)**
Robards, Jason, Jr. (actor); Chicago, 7/22/22
Robards, Jason, Sr. (actor); Hillsdale, Mich. **(1892–1963)**
Robinson, Robert (chemist, Nobel laureate); Chesterfield, Derbyshire, England **(1885–1975)**
Robbins, Harold (Harold Rubin) (novelist); New York City **(1916–1997)**
Robbins, Jerome (Jerome Rabinowitz) (choreographer); New York City **(1918–1998)**
Robbins, Marty (singer); Glendale, Ariz. **(1925–1982)**
Robbins, Tim (Timothy Francis) (actor, director); West Covina, Calif., 10/16/58
Roberts, Cokie (Mary Martha Corinne Morrison Claiborne Boggs) (broadcast journalist); New Orleans, 12/27/43
Roberts, Eric (actor); Biloxi, Miss., 4/18/56
Roberts, Julia (actress); Smyrna, Ga., 10/28/67
Roberts, Oral (Granville) (evangelist, publisher); nr. Ada, Okla., 1/24/18
Robertson, Cliff (Clifford Parker Robertson III) (actor); La Jolla, Calif., 9/9/25
Robertson, Dale (Dayle) (actor); Oklahoma City, 7/14/23
Robeson, Paul (singer, actor); Princeton, N.J. **(1898–1976)**
Robespierre, Maximilien François Marie Isidore de (French Revolutionist); Arras, France **(1758–1794)**
Robinson, Bill "Bojangles" (Luther) (dancer); Richmond, Va. **(1878–1949)**
Robinson, Edward G. (Emanuel Goldenberg) (actor); Bucharest **(1893–1973)**
Robinson, Edwin Arlington (poet); Head Tide, Maine **(1869–1935)**
Robinson, Smokey (singer, songwriter); Detroit, 2/19/40
Rochester (Eddie Anderson) (actor); Oakland, Calif. **(1905–1977)**
Rockefeller, David (banker); New York City, 6/12/15
Rockefeller, John Davison (business executive); Richford, N.Y. **(1839–1937)**
Rockefeller, John Davison, Jr. (industrialist); Cleveland **(1874–1960)**
Rockefeller, John D., 3rd (philanthropist); New York City **(1906–1978)**
Rockefeller, Laurance S. (conservationist); New York City, 5/26/10
Rockwell, Norman (painter, illustrator); New York City **(1894–1978)**
Roddenberry, Gene (creator of *Star Trek*); El Paso, Tex. **(1921–1991)**
Rodgers, Jimmie (singer); Meridian, Miss. **(1897–1933)**
Rodgers, Richard (composer); New York City **(1902–1979)**
Rodin, François Auguste René (sculptor); Paris **(1840–1917)**
Rodzinski, Artur (conductor); Spalato, Dalmatia **(1894–1958)**
Roeg, Nicolas (film director); London, 8/15/28
Roentgen, Wilhelm Konrad (physicist); Lennep, Prussia **(1845–1923)**
Roethke, Theodore (poet); Saginaw, Mich. **(1908–1963)**
Rogers, Buddy (Charles) (actor); Olathe, Kans., 8/13/04
Rogers, Carl (psychologist); Oak Park, Ill. **(1902–1987)**
Rogers, Fred (TV producer, host); Latrobe, Pa., 3/20/28
Rogers, Ginger (Virginia McMath) (dancer, actress); Independence, Mo. **(1911–1995)**
Rogers, Kenny (singer); Houston, 8/21/38
Rogers, Roy (Leonard Frank Sly) (actor); Cincinnati **(1911–1998)**
Rogers, Wayne (actor); Birmingham, Ala., 4/7/33
Rogers, Will (William Penn Adair Rogers) (humorist); Oologah, Okla. **(1879–1935)**
Rogers, William P. (ex-Secretary of State); Norfolk, N.Y., 6/23/13
Roland, Gilbert (actor); Juarez, Mexico **(1905–1994)**
Rolland, Romain (author); Clamecy, France **(1866–1944)**
Rollins, Sonny (saxophonist); New York City, 9/7/30
Romberg, Sigmund (composer); Szeged (Hungary) **(1887–1951)**
Rome, Harold (composer); Hartford, Conn. **(1908–1993)**
Romero, Cesar (actor); New York City **(1907–1994)**
Romney, George W. (automobile executive, governor); Chihuahua, Mexico **(1907–1995)**
Romulo, Carlos P. (diplomat, educator); Manila **(1899–1985)**
Ronsard, Pierre de (poet); La Possonnière nr. Couture, France **(1524–1585)**
Ronstadt, Linda (singer); Tucson, Ariz., 7/30/46
Rooney, Andy (TV personality); Albany, N.Y., 1/14/19
Rooney, Mickey (Joe Yule, Jr.) (actor); Brooklyn, N.Y., 9/23/20
Roosevelt, Anna Eleanor (reformer, humanitarian); New York City **(1884–1962)**
Roosevelt, Franklin Delano (32nd U.S. president); Hyde Park, N.Y. **(1882–1945)**
Roosevelt, Theodore (26th U.S. president); New York City **(1858–1919)**
Rorem, Ned (composer); Richmond, Ind., 10/23/23
Rose, Billy (showman); New York City **(1899–1966)**
Rose, Leonard (concert cellist); Washington, D.C. **(1918–1984)**
Roseanne, (Roseanne Barr) (actress); Salt Lake City, 11/3/52
Rosenberg, Ethel (spy); New York City **(1915–1953)**
Rosenberg, Julius (spy); New York City **(1918–1953)**
Ross, Betsy (Betsey Griscom) (flagmaker); Philadelphia **(1752–1836)**
Ross, Diana (singer); Detroit, 3/26/44
Ross, Katharine (actress); Hollywood, Calif., 1/29/42
Rossellini, Isabella (model, actress); Rome, Italy, 6/18/52
Rossellini, Roberto (film director); Rome **(1906–1977)**
Rossetti, Christina Georgina (poet); London **(1830–1894)**
Rossetti, Dante Gabriel (painter, poet); London **(1828–1882)**
Rossini, Gioacchino Antonio (composer); Pesaro, Italy **(1792–1868)**
Rosten, Leo (writer); Lodz, Poland **(1908–1997)**
Rostand, Edmond (dramatist); Marseilles, France **(1868–1918)**
Rostow, Walt Whitman (economist); New York City, 10/7/16
Rostropovich, Mstislav (cellist, conductor); Baku, (Azerbaijan), 3/27/27
Roth, Henry (writer); Tysmenica (Ukraine) **(1906–1995)**
Roth, Philip (novelist); Newark, N.J., 3/19/33
Rothko, Mark (Marcus Rothkovich) (painter); Russia **(1903–1970)**
Rouault, Georges (painter); Paris **(1871–1958)**
Roundtree, Richard (actor); New Rochelle, N.Y., 9/7/42
Rousseau, Henri (painter); Laval, France **(1844–1910)**
Rousseau, Jean Jacques (philosopher); Geneva **(1712–1778)**
Rovere, Richard H. (journalist); Jersey City, N.J., 5/5/15
Rowan, Carl Thomas (journalist); Ravenscroft, Tenn., 8/11/25
Rowan, Dan (comedian); Beggs, Okla. **(1922–1987)**
Rowlands, Gena (actress); Cambria, Wis., 6/19/30
Royko, Mike (columnist); Chicago **(1932–1997)**
Rubens, Sir Peter Paul (painter); Siegen (Germany) **(1577–1640)**
Rubinstein, Arthur (concert pianist); Lódz (Poland) **(1887–1982)**
Rubinstein, Helena (cosmetics executive); Krakow (Poland) **(1882?–1965)**
Rubinstein, John (actor, composer); Los Angeles, 12/8/46
Rudel, Julius (conductor); Vienna, 3/6/21
Ruffo, Titta (baritone); Italy **(1878–1953)**
Runyon, (Alfred) Damon (journalist); Manhattan, Kans. **(1884–1945)**
Rushdie, (Ahmed) Salman (novelist); Bombay (Mumbai), 6/19/47
Rusk, Dean (ex-Sec. of State); Cherokee County, Ga. **(1909–1994)**
Ruskin, John (art critic); London **(1819–1900)**
Russell, Lord Bertrand (Arthur William) (mathematician, philosopher); Trelleck, Wales **(1872–1970)**
Russell, Jane (actress); Bemidji, Minn., 6/21/21
Russell, Ken (film director); Southhampton, England, 4/3/27
Russell, Kurt (actor); Springfield, Mass., 3/17/51
Russell, Leon (pianist, singer); Lawton, Okla., 4/2/41
Russell, Lillian (Helen Louise Leonard) (soprano); Clinton, Iowa **(1861–1922)**
Russell, Mark (satirist); Buffalo, N.Y., 8/23/32
Russell, Nipsy (comedian); Atlanta, 10/13/24
Russell, Rosalind (actress); Waterbury, Conn. **(1912–1976)**
Russell, Theresa (Theresa Paup) (actress); San Diego, Calif., 3/20/57
Rustin, Bayard (civil rights leader); West Chester, Pa. **(1910–1987)**
Rutherford, Dame Margaret (actress); London **(1892–1972)**
Ryan, Jeri (actress); Munich, Germany, 2/22/68
Ryan, Meg (Margaret Mary Emily Anne Hyra) (actress); Fairfield, Conn., 11/19/61
Ryan, Robert (actor); Chicago **(1909–1973)**
Rydell, Bobby (Robert Ridarelli) (singer); Philadelphia, 4/26/42
Ryder, Winona (Winona Horowitz) (actress); Winona, Minn., 10/29/71
Rysanek, Leonie (dramatic soprano); Vienna **(1928–1998)**

Saarinen, Eero (architect); Finland **(1910–1961)**
Sabin, Albert B. (polio researcher); Bialystok (Poland) **(1906–1993)**
Sabu (Dastagir) (actor); Karapur, India **(1924–1963)**
Sacagawea, (Shoshone Indian guide); Lemhi River valley, (Idaho) **(c. 1786–1812)**
Sachs, Jeffrey D. (economist, educator); Michigan, 1954

Sadat, Anwar el- (President); Egypt **(1918–1981)**
Sade, Marquis de (Donatien Alphonse François, Comte de Sade) (libertine, writer); Paris **(1740–1814)**
Safer, Morley (TV newscaster); Toronto, 11/8/31
Sagan, Carl (Edward) (astronomer, science writer); New York City **(1934–1996)**
Sagan, Françoise (novelist); Cajarc, France, 6/21/35
Sahl, Mort (Morton Lyon Sahl) (comedian); Montreal, 5/11/27
Saint, Eva Marie (actress); Newark, N.J., 7/4/24
St. Denis, Ruth (dancer, choreographer); Newark, N.J. **(1878–1968)**
St. James, Susan (Susan Miller) (actress); Los Angeles, 8/14/46
St. John, Jill (actress); Los Angeles, 8/19/40
St. Johns, Adela Rogers (journalist, author); Los Angeles **(1894–1988)**
Sainte-Marie, Buffy (Beverly) (folk singer); Craven, Sask., Canada, 2/20/41
Saint-Gaudens, Augustus (sculptor); Dublin **(1848–1907)**
Saint-Laurent, Yves (Henri Donat Mathieu) (fashion designer); Oran, Algeria, 8/1/36
Saint-Saens, Charles Camille (composer); Paris **(1835–1921)**
Sakharov, Andrei Dmitriyevich (nuclear physicist, peace activist); Russia **(1921–1989)**
Sales, Soupy (Milton Hines) (television entertainer); Franklinton, N.C., 1/6/26
Salinger, J(erome) D(avid) (novelist); New York City, 1/1/19
Salisbury, Harrison E. (journalist); Minneapolis **(1908–1993)**
Salk, Jonas (polio researcher); New York City **(1914–1995)**
Salk, Lee (psychologist); New York City **(1926–1992)**
Salomon, Haym (American Revolution financier); Leszno, Poland **(1740–1785)**
Sand, George (Amandine Lucille Aurore Dudevant, née Dupin) (novelist); Paris **(1804–1876)**
Sandburg, Carl (poet, biographer); Galesburg, Ill. **(1878–1967)**
Sanders, George (actor); St. Petersburg, Russia **(1906–1972)**
Sands, Tommy (singer); Chicago, 8/27/37
Sanger, Margaret (birth control advocate); Corning, N.Y. **(1883–1966)**
San Giacomo, Laura (actress); Hoboken, N.J., 11/14/62
Santayana, George (philosopher); Madrid **(1863–1952)**
Sappho (poet); Lesbos (Greece) **(610 B.C.E.–580 B.C.E.)**
Sarandon, Susan (Susan Tomalin) (actress); New York City, 10/4/46
Sargent, John Singer (painter); Florence, Italy **(1856–1925)**
Sarnoff, David (radio executive); Minsk, (Belarus) **(1891–1971)**
Saroyan, William (novelist); Fresno, Calif. **(1908–1981)**
Sarrazin, Michael (actor); Que., Canada, 5/22/40
Sarto, Andrea del (Andrea Domenico d'Agnolo di Francesco) (painter); Florence (Italy) **(1486–1531)**
Sartre, Jean-Paul (existentialist writer); Paris **(1905–1980)**
Sassoon, Vidal (hair stylist); London, 1/17/28
Satie, Erik (Alfred Leslie) (composer); Paris **(1866–1925)**
Saul (King of Israel) fl. 11th cent. B.C.E.
Savalas, Telly (Aristoteles) (actor); Garden City, N.Y. **(1924–1994)**
Savonarola, Girolamo (religious reformer); Ferrara, Italy **(1452–1498)**
Sawyer, Diane (broadcast journalist); Glasgow, Ky., 12/22/45
Sayão, Bidú (soprano); Rio de Janeiro, 5/11/02
Scaasi, Arnold (Arnold Isaacs) (fashion designer); Montreal,
Scarlatti, Alessandro (composer); Palermo, Italy **(1659–1725)**
Scarlatti, Domenico (composer); Naples, Italy **(1685–1757)**
Scavullo, Francesco (photographer); Staten Island, N.Y., 1/16/29
Schama, Simon (historian); London, 2/13/45
Schapiro, Meyer (Meir) (art historian); Siauliai, Lithuania **(1904–1906)**
Schary, Dore (producer, writer); Newark, N.J. **(1905–1980)**
Schell, Maximilian (actor); Vienna, 12/8/30
Schiaparelli, Elsa (fashion designer); Rome **(1890–1973)**
Schiff, Dorothy (newspaper publisher); New York City **(1903–1989)**
Schiller, Johann Christoph Friedrich von (dramatist, poet); Marbach (Germany) **(1759–1805)**
Schipa, Tito (tenor); Lecce, Italy **(1890–1965)**
Schippers, Thomas (conductor); Kalamazoo, Mich. **(1930–1977)**
Schlegel, Friedrich von (philosopher); Hannover, Germany **(1772–1829)**
Schlesinger, Arthur M., Jr. (historian); Columbus, Ohio, 10/15/17
Schnabel, Artur (pianist, composer); Lipnik, Austria **(1882–1951)**
Schneider, Romy (Rose-Marie Albach-Retty) (actress); Vienna **(1938–1982)**
Schoenberg, Arnold (composer); Vienna **(1874–1951)**
Schomberg, Arthur (bibliophile, antiquarian); San Juan, P.R. **(1874–1938)**
Schopenhauer, Arthur (philosopher); Danzig (Poland) **(1788–1860)**
Schubert, Franz Peter (composer); Vienna **(1797–1828)**
Schulberg, Budd (novelist); New York City, 3/27/14
Schulz, Charles M. (cartoonist); Minneapolis, 11/26/22
Schuman, Robert (statesman); Luxembourg **(1886–1963)**
Schuman, William (composer); New York City **(1910–1992)**
Schumann, Robert Alexander (composer); Zwickau (Germany) **(1810–1856)**
Schumann-Heink, Ernestine (contralto); nr. Prague **(1861–1936)**
Schwartz, Arthur (songwriter); Brooklyn, N.Y. **(1900–1984)**
Schwarzenegger, Arnold (bodybuilder, actor); Graz, Austria, 7/30/47
Schwarzkopf, Elisabeth (soprano); Jarotschin, Poznán, (Poland), 12/9/15
Schwarzkopf, H. Norman (retired general); Trenton, N.J., 8/22/34
Schweitzer, Albert (humanitarian); Kaysersburg, Upper Alsace **(1875–1965)**
Schwimmer, David (actor); New York City, 11/12/66
Scofield, Paul (actor); Hurstpierpoint, England, 1/21/22
Scorsese, Martin (actor, writer, director, producer); Flushing, N.Y., 11/17/42
Scott, George C. (actor); Wise, Va., 10/18/27
Scott, Hazel (singer, pianist); Port of Spain, Trinidad **(1920–1981)**
Scott, Lizabeth (Emma Matzo) (actress); Scranton, Pa., 9/29/23
Scott, Randolph (Randolph Crane) (actor); Orange County, Va. **(1898–1987)**
Scott, Robert Falcon (explorer); Devonport, England **(1868–1912)**
Scott, Sir Walter (novelist); Edinburgh, Scotland **(1771–1832)**
Scott, Zachary (actor); Austin, Tex. **(1914–1965)**
Scotto, Renata (operatic soprano); Savona, Italy, 2/24/36
Scruggs, Earl Eugene (bluegrass musician); Cleveland County, N.C., 1/6/24
Seaborg, Glenn Theodore (chemist, Nobel laureate); Ishpeming, Mich., 4/19/12
Seattle, (Chief Seattle) (Suquamish Indian leader); Blake Island (Wash.) **(c. 1786–1866)**
Sebastian, John (composer); New York City, 3/17/44
Seberg, Jean (actress); Marshalltown, Iowa **(1938–1979)**
Sedaka, Neil (singer); Brooklyn, N.Y., 3/13/39
Sedgwick, Kyra (actress); New York City, 8/19/65
Seeger, Pete (folk singer); New York City, 5/3/19
Segal, Erich (novelist); Brooklyn, N.Y., 6/16/37
Segal, George (actor); New York City, 2/13/36
Segovia, Andrés (guitarist); Linares, Spain **(1893–1987)**
Seinfeld, Jerry (comedian); Brooklyn, N.Y., 4/29/54
Selleck, Tom (actor); Detroit, 1/29/45
Sellars, Peter (theater director); Pittsburgh, 1958?
Sellers, Peter (actor); Southsea, England **(1925–1980)**
Selznick, David O. (producer); Pittsburgh **(1902–1965)**
Sendak, Maurice (Bernard) (children's book author, illustrator); Brooklyn, N.Y., 6/10/28
Sennett, Mack (Michael Sinnott) (film producer); Richmond, Que., Canada **(1880–1960)**
Sequoyah, (Cherokee linguist); Taskigi, Tenn. **(c. 1770–1843)**
Serkin, Peter (pianist); New York City, 7/24/47
Serkin, Rudolf (pianist); Eger (Czech Republic) **(1903–1991)**
Serling, Rod (writer, TV host); Syracuse, N.Y. **(1924–1975)**
Sessions, Roger (composer); Brooklyn, N.Y. **(1896–1985)**
Seurat, Georges (painter); Paris **(1859–1891)**
Seuss, Dr. (Theodor Seuss Geisel) (author, illustrator); Springfield, Mass. **(1904–1991)**
Sevareid, Eric (TV commentator); Velva, N.D. **(1912–1991)**
Severinsen, Doc (Carl) (band leader); Arlington, Ore., 7/7/27
Sexton, Anne (poet); Newton, Mass. **(1928–1974)**
Seymour, Jane (Joyce Penelope Wilhelmina Frankenburg) (actress); Wimbledon, England, 2/15/51
Shabazz, Betty (Betty Sanders) (civil rights activist); Detroit **(1936–1997)**
Shaffer, Peter (playwright); Liverpool, England, 5/15/26
Shaham, Gil (violinist); Urbana, Ill., 1971
Shahn, Ben(jamin) (painter); Kaunas, Lithuania **(1898–1969)**
Shakespeare, William (dramatist); Stratford on Avon, England **(1564–1616)**
Shandling, Garry (comedian, actor, producer); Chicago, 11/29/49
Shange, Ntozake (Paulette Williams) (poet, playwright); Trenton, N.J., 10/18/48
Shankar, Ravi (sitar player); Benares, India, 4/7/20
Sharif, Omar (Michael Shalhoub) (actor); Alexandria, Egypt, 4/10/32
Shatner, William (actor); Montreal, 3/22/31
Shaw, Artie (Arthur Arshawsky) (band leader); New York City, 5/23/10
Shaw, George Bernard (dramatist); Dublin **(1856–1950)**
Shaw, Irwin (novelist); Brooklyn, N.Y. **(1913–1984)**

Shaw, Robert (actor); Lancashire, England **(1927–1978)**
Shaw, Robert (chorale conductor); Red Bluff, Calif., 4/30/16
Shawn, Ted (Edwin Myers Shawn) (dancer, choreographer); Kansas City, Mo. **(1891–1972)**
Shearer, Moira (ballet dancer); Dunfermline, Scotland, 1/17/26
Shearer, Norma (actress); Montreal **(1900–1983)**
Shearing, George (pianist); London, 8/13/20
Sheen, Fulton J. (Peter Sheen) (Roman Catholic bishop); El Paso, Ill. **(1895–1979)**
Sheen, Martin (Ramon Estevez) (actor); Dayton, Ohio, 8/3/40
Shelley, Mary Wollstonecraft Godwin (writer); London **(1797–1851)**
Shelley, Percy Bysshe (poet); nr. Horsham, England **(1792–1822)**
Shepard, Sam (Samuel Shepard Rogers) (playwright); Ft. Sheridan, Ill., 11/5/43
Shepherd, Cybill (actress); Memphis, Tenn., 2/18/50
Sheraton, Thomas (furniture designer); Stockton-on-Tees, England **(1751–1806)**
Sheridan, Ann (Clara Lou Sheridan) (actress); Denton, Tex. **(1915–1967)**
Sheridan, Philip (army officer); Albany, N.Y. **(1831–1888)**
Sheridan, Richard Brinsley (dramatist); Dublin **(1751–1816)**
Sherman, William Tecumseh (army officer); Lancaster, Ohio **(1820–1891)**
Sherwood, Robert Emmet (playwright); New Rochelle, N.Y. **(1896–1955)**
Shevardnadze, Eduard Amvrosiyevich (State Council Chairman, Georgia); Mamati, (Georgia), 1/25/28
Shields, Brooke (actress); New York City, 5/31/65
Shire, Talia (Coppola) (actress); Lake Success, N.Y., 4/25/46
Shirer, William L. (journalist, historian); Chicago **(1904–1993)**
Sholokhov, Mikhail (novelist); Veshenskaya, Russia **(1905–1984)**
Shore, Dinah (Frances Rose Shore) (singer); Winchester,Tenn. **(1917–1994)**
Short, Bobby (Robert Waltrip Short) (singer, pianist); Danville, Ill., 9/15/24
Short, Martin (actor); Hamilton, Ont., Canada, 3/26/50
Shostakovich, Dmitri (composer); St. Petersburg, Russia **(1906–1975)**
Shriner, Herb (humorist, host); Toledo, Ohio **(1918–1970)**
Shriver, Maria (TV co-host); Chicago, 11/6/55
Shriver, Sargent (Robert Sargent Shriver, Jr.) (business executive); Westminster, Md., 11/9/15
Shulman, Max (novelist); St. Paul, Minn. **(1919–1988)**
Sibelius, Jean (Johann Julius Christian Sibelius) (composer); Tavastehus (Finland) **(1865–1957)**
Sidney, Sir Philip (poet); Penshurst, England **(1554–1586)**
Sidney, Sylvia (Sophia Kosow) (actress); New York City, 8/8/10
Siegfried and Roy (illusionists) **Siegfried Fischbacher**; Rosenheim, Bavaria, Germany, 1939 **Roy Uwe Ludwig Horn**; Nordenham, nr. Bremen, Germany, 1944
Siepi, Cesare (basso); Milan, Italy, 2/10/23
Signoret, Simone (Simone Kaminker) (actress); Wiesbaden, Germany **(1921–1985)**
Sihanouk, Norodom (King of Cambodia); Cambodia, 10/31/22
Sikorsky, Igor I. (inventor); Kiev, Ukraine **(1889–1972)**
Sills, Beverly (Belle Silverman) (soprano, opera director); Brooklyn, N.Y., 5/25/29
Sills, Milton (actor); Chicago **(1882–1930)**
Silone, Ignazio (Secondo Tranquilli) (novelist); Pescina del Marsi, Italy **(1900–1978)**
Silver, Ron (Ron Zimelman) (actor); New York City, 7/2/46
Silverheels, Jay (Harold J. Smith) (actor); Brantfort, Ont., Canada **(1919–1980)**
Silverman, Fred (broadcasting executive); New York City, 9/13/37
Silvers, Phil (Philip Silversmith) (comedian); Brooklyn, N.Y. **(1912–1985)**
Sim, Alastair (actor); Edinburgh, Scotland **(1900–1976)**
Simenon, Georges (Georges Sim) (mystery writer); Liège, Belgium **(1903–1989)**
Simmons, Jean (actress); Crouch Hill, London, 1/31/29
Simon, Carly (singer, songwriter); New York City, 6/25/45
Simon, Neil (playwright); Bronx, N.Y., 7/4/27
Simon, Norton (business executive); Portland, Ore. **(1907–1993)**
Simon, Paul (singer, songwriter); Newark, N.J., 11/5/42
Simon, Simone (actress); Marseilles, France, 4/23/14
Simone, Nina (Eunice Kathleen Waymoa) (singer, pianist); Tryon, N.C., 2/21/33
Sinatra, Frank (Francis Albert Sinatra) (singer, actor); Hoboken, N.J. **(1915–1998)**
Sinclair, Upton Beall (novelist); Baltimore **(1878–1968)**
Singer, Isaac Bashevis (novelist); Radzymin (Poland) **(1904–1991)**
Singleton, John (writer, director); Los Angeles, 1/6/68
Sinise, Gary (actor, director); Chicago, 3/17/55
Siqueiros, David (painter); Chihuahua, Mexico **(1896–1974)**
Sirtis, Marina (actress); London, 3/29/64
Siskel, Gene (film critic); Chicago, 1/26/46
Sisley, Alfred (painter); Paris **(1839–1899)**
Sitting Bull (Prairie Sioux Indian Chief); on Grand River, S.D. **(c. 1835–1890)**
Skelton, Red (Richard) (comedian); Vincennes, Ind. **(1913–1997)**
Skerritt, Tom (actor); Detroit, 8/25/43
Skinner, B(urrhus) F(rederic) (psychologist); Susquehanna, Pa. **(1904–1990)**
Skinner, Otis (actor); Cambridge, Mass. **(1858–1942)**
Slatkin, Leonard (conductor); Los Angeles, 9/1/44
Sloan, Alfred P., Jr. (industrialist); New Haven, Conn. **(1875–1965)**
Sloan, John (painter); Lock Haven, Pa. **(1871–1951)**
Smalley, Richard E. (chemist, Nobel laureate); Akron, Ohio, 6/6/43
Smetana, Bedrich (composer); Litomysl (Czech Republic) **(1824–1884)**
Smith, Adam (economist); Kirkaldy, Scotland **(1723–1790)**
Smith, Alexis (actress); Penticon, Canada **(1921–1993)**
Smith, Alfred Emanuel (politician); New York City **(1873–1944)**
Smith, Bessie (blues singer); Chattanooga, Tenn. **(1894–1937)**
Smith, Sir C. Aubrey (actor); London **(1863–1948)**
Smith, David (sculptor); Decatur, Ind. **(1906–1965)**
Smith, Harry (TV co-anchor); Hammond, Ind., 8/21/51
Smith, Howard K. (TV commentator); Ferriday, La., 5/12/14
Smith, Jaclyn (actress); Houston, 10/26/47
Smith, John (American colonist); Willoughby, Lincolnshire, England **(1580–1631)**
Smith, Joseph (religious leader); Sharon, Vt. **(1805–1844)**
Smith, Kate (Kathryn) (singer); Greenville, Va. **(1909–1986)**
Smith, Dame Maggie (actress); Ilford, England, 12/28/34
Smith, Patti Lee (singer, songwriter); Chicago, 12/30/46
Smith, Red (Walter) (sports columnist); Green Bay, Wis. **(1905–1982)**
Smith, Will (actor, rap singer); Philadelphia, 9/25/68
Smits, Jimmy (actor); New York City, 7/9/55
Smollet, Tobias (novelist); Dalquhurn, Scotland **(1721–1771)**
Smothers, Dick (Richard) (comedian); New York City, 11/20/39
Smothers, Tom (Thomas) (comedian); New York City, 2/2/37
Snow, Lord (Charles Percy) (author); Leicester, England **(1905–1980)**
Snowdon, Earl of (Anthony Armstrong-Jones) (photographer); London, 3/7/30
Snyder, Tom (TV personality); Milwaukee, 5/12/36
Socrates (philosopher); Athens **(469–399 B.C.E.)**
Solomon (King of Israel); Jerusalem, fl. 950 B.C.E.
Solon (lawgiver); Salamis (Greece) **(c. 630–559 B.C.E.)**
Solti, Sir Georg (conductor); Budapest **(1912–1997)**
Solzhenitsyn, Aleksandr (novelist); Kislovodsk, Russia, 12/11/18
Somers, Suzanne (Suzanne Mahoney) (actress); San Bruno, Calif., 10/16/46
Somes, Michael (ballet dancer); Horsley, England **(1917–1994)**
Sommer, Elke (Elke Schletz) (actress); Berlin, 11/5/42
Sondheim, Stephen (composer); New York City, 3/22/30
Sontag, Susan (author, film director); New York City, 1/28/33
Sophocles (dramatist); nr. Athens **(c. 496–406 B.C.E.)**
Sorbo, Kevin (actor); Mound, Minn., 9/24/58
Sorvino, Mira (actress); Tenafly, N.J., 9/28/67
Sorvino, Paul (actor); Brooklyn, N.Y., 4/13/39
Sothern, Ann (Harriette Lake) (actress); Valley City, N.D., 1/22/09
Soul, David (David Solberg) (actor); Chicago, 8/28/43
Sousa, John Philip (composer); Washington, D.C. **(1854–1932)**
Soyer, Raphael (painter); Borisoglebsk, Russia **(1899–1987)**
Spaak, Paul-Henri (statesman); Brussels **(1899–1972)**
Spacek, Sissy (Mary Elizabeth Spacek) (actress); Quitman, Tex., 12/25/49
Spacey, Kevin (actor); South Orange, N.J., 7/28/59
Spark, Muriel (novelist); Edinburgh, Scotland, 2/1/18
Spector, Phil (rock producer); Bronx, N.Y., 12/25/40
Spelling, Aaron (producer); Dallas, 4/22/28
Spencer, Herbert (philosopher); Derby, England **(1820–1903)**
Spender, Stephen (poet); nr. London **(1909–1995)**
Spengler, Oswald (philosopher); Blankenburg (Germany) **(1880–1936)**
Spenser, Edmund (poet); London **(1552?–1599)**
Spewack, Bella (playwright); Hungary **(1899–1990)**
Spiegel, Sam (producer); Jaroslaw (Poland) **(1901–1985)**
Spielberg, Steven (director, producer, writer, actor); Cincinnati, 12/18/47
Spillane, Mickey (Frank Spillane) (mystery writer); Brooklyn, N.Y., 3/9/18
Spiner, Brent (actor); Houston, 2/2/49

Spinoza, Baruch (philosopher); Amsterdam (Netherlands) **(1632–1677)**
Spitalny, Phil (orchestra leader) **(1890–1970)**
Spivak, Lawrence (TV producer); Brooklyn, N.Y. **(1900–1994)**
Spock, Benjamin (pediatrician); New Haven, Conn. **(1903–1998)**
Springsteen, Bruce (singer, songwriter); Freehold, N.J., 9/23/49
Sproul, Robert G. (educator); San Francisco **(1891–1975)**
Squanto, (Wampanoag Indian emissary); Patuxet (Plymouth Bay, Mass.) **(c. 1590–1622)**
Stack, Robert (Robert Modini) (actor); Los Angeles, 1/13/19
Stafford, Jo (singer); Coalinga, Calif., 11/12/18
Stahl, Lesley (broadcast journalist); Lynn, Mass., 12/16/41
Stalin, Joseph Vissarionovich (Iosif V. Dzhugashvili) (Soviet leader); nr. Tiflis (Tbilisi, Georgia) **(1879–1953)**
Stallone, Sylvester (actor, writer, director); New York City, 7/6/46
Stamp, Terence (actor); London, 1938
Stander, Lionel (actor); New York City **(1908–1994)**
Stanislavski (Konstantin Sergeevich Alekseev) (stage producer); Moscow **(1863–1938)**
Stanley, Sir Henry Morton (John Rowlands) (explorer); Denbigh, Wales **(1841–1904)**
Stanley, Kim (Patricia Reid) (actress); Tularosa, N.M., 2/11/25
Stans, Maurice H. (ex-Secretary of Commerce); Shakope, Minn. **(1908–1998)**
Stanton, Elizabeth Cady (woman suffragist); Johnstown, N.Y. **(1815–1902)**
Stanton, Frank (broadcasting executive); Muskegon, Mich., 3/20/08
Stanwyck, Barbara (Ruby Stevens) (actress); Brooklyn, N.Y. **(1907–1990)**
Stapleton, Jean (Jeanne Murray) (actress); New York City, 1/19/23
Stapleton, Maureen (actress); Troy, N.Y., 6/21/25
Starker, Janós (cellist); Budapest, 7/5/26
Starr, Kay (Starks) (singer); Dougherty, Okla., 7/21/22
Starr, Ringo (Richard Starkey) (singer, songwriter); Liverpool, England, 7/7/40
Stassen, Harold E. (ex-government official); West St. Paul, Minn., 4/13/07
Staudinger, Hermann (chemist, Nobel laureate); Worms, Germany **(1881–1965)**
Steber, Eleanor (soprano); Wheeling, W. Va. **(1916–1990)**
Steegmuller, Francis (biographer); New Haven, Conn. **(1906–1994)**
Steel, Danielle (Danielle Fernande Schuelein-Steel) (novelist); New York City, 8/14/47
Steele, Tommy (singer); London, 12/17/36
Stegner, Wallace (Earle) (novelist, critic); Lake Mills, Iowa **(1909–1993)**
Steichen, Edward Jean (photographer, artist); Luxembourg **(1879–1973)**
Steiger, Rod (Rodney Steiger) (actor); Westhampton, N.Y., 4/14/25
Stein, Gertrude (author); Allegheny, Pa. **(1874–1946)**
Steinbeck, John Ernst (novelist); Salinas, Calif. **(1902–1968)**
Steinberg, David (comedian); Winnipeg, Man., Canada, 8/19/42
Steinberg, William (conductor); Cologne, Germany **(1899–1978)**
Steinem, Gloria (feminist, publisher); Toledo, Ohio, 3/25/34
Steinmetz, Charles (electrical engineer); Breslau (Poland) **(1865–1923)**
Stendhal (Marie Henri Beyle) (novelist); Grenoble, France **(1783–1842)**
Stern, Isaac (concert violinist); Kreminlecz, Russia, 7/21/20
Sterne, Laurence (novelist); Clonmel, Ireland **(1713–1768)**
Stevens, Cat (Steven Georgiou) (singer, songwriter); London, 7/21/47
Stevens, Connie (Concetta Ingolia) (singer); Brooklyn, N.Y., 8/8/38
Stevens, George (film director); Oakland, Calif. **(1905–1975)**
Stevens, Risë (mezzo-soprano); New York City, 6/11/13
Stevens, Wallace (poet); Reading, Pa. **(1879–1955)**
Stevenson, Adlai Ewing (statesman); Los Angeles **(1900–1965)**
Stevenson, McLean (actor); Bloomington, Ill. **(1929–1996)**
Stevenson, Parker (actor); Philadelphia, 6/4/52
Stevenson, Robert Louis Balfour (novelist, poet); Edinburgh, Scotland **(1850–1894)**
Stewart, James (actor); Indiana, Pa. **(1908–1997)**
Stewart, Martha (entrepreneurial homemaker); Nutley, N.J., 8/3/41
Stewart, Patrick (actor); Mirfield, England, 7/13/49
Stewart, Rod (Roderick David) (singer); London, 1/10/45
Stieglitz, Alfred (photographer); Hoboken, N.J. **(1864–1946)**
Stiers, David Ogden (actor); Peoria, Ill., 10/31/42
Stiller, Jerry (actor); Brooklyn, N.Y., 6/8/29
Stills, Stephen (singer, songwriter); Dallas, 1/3/45
Sting (Gordon Matthew Sumner) (singer, composer); Wallsend, England, 10/2/51
Stipe, Michael (singer); Decatur, Ga., 1/4/60
Stockwell, Dean (actor); North Hollywood, Calif., 3/5/36
Stoker, Bram (novelist); Dublin **(1847–1912)**
Stokes, Carl (TV newscaster); Cleveland, 6/21/27
Stokowski, Leopold (conductor); London **(1882–1977)**
Stone, Edward Durell (architect); Fayetteville, Ark. **(1902–1978)**
Stone, I(sidor) F(einstein) (journalist); Philadelphia **(1907–1989)**
Stone, Irving (Irving Tennenbaum) (novelist); San Francisco **(1903–1989)**
Stone, Lucy (woman suffragist); nr. West Brookfield, Mass. **(1818–1893)**
Stone, Oliver (director, writer, producer); New York City, 9/15/46
Stone, Robert (novelist); Brooklyn, N.Y., 8/21/37
Stone, Sharon (actress); Meadville, Pa., 3/10/58
Stone, Sly (Sylvester Stone) (rock musician) 1944
Stooges, The Three (comedy team) **Moe Howard** (Moses Horwitz); Brooklyn, N.Y. **(1897–1975) Shemp Howard** (Samuel Horwitz); Brooklyn, N.Y. **(1900–1955) Larry Fine** (Laurence Feinburg); Philadelphia **(1911–1974) Curly Howard** (Jerome Horwitz); Brooklyn, N.Y. **(1906–1952)**
Stoppard, Tom (Thomas Straussler) (playwright); Zlin, (Slovakia), 7/3/37
Stout, Rex (mystery writer); Noblesville, Ind. **(1886–1975)**
Stowe, Harriet Elizabeth Beecher (novelist); Litchfield, Conn. **(1811–1896)**
Stowe, Madeleine (actress); Eagle Rock, Calif., 8/18/58
Strachey, (Giles) Lytton (biographer); London **(1880–1932)**
Stradivari, Antonio (violinmaker); Cremona (Italy) **(1644–1737)**
Straight, Beatrice (actress); Old Westbury, N.Y., 8/2/18
Strasberg, Lee (stage director); Budanov, Austria **(1901–1982)**
Strasberg, Susan (actress); New York City, 5/22/38
Stratas, Teresa (soprano); Toronto, 5/26/38
Straus, Oskar (composer); Vienna **(1870–1954)**
Strauss, Johann (composer); Vienna **(1825–1899)**
Strauss, Lewis L. (naval officer, scientist); Charleston, W. Va. **(1896–1974)**
Strauss, Peter (actor); New York City, 2/20/47
Strauss, Richard (composer); Munich, Germany **(1864–1949)**
Stravinsky, Igor (composer); Orlenbaum, Russia **(1882–1971)**
Streep, Meryl (Mary Louise) (actress); Summit, N.J., 6/22/49
Streisand, Barbra (singer, actress, director, producer, writer); Brooklyn, N.Y., 4/24/42
Strindberg, (Johan) August (dramatist); Stockholm **(1849–1912)**
Stritch, Elaine (actress); Detroit, 2/2/25
Struthers, Sally Ann (actress); Portland, Ore., 7/28/48
Stuart, Gilbert Charles (painter); Rhode Island **(1755–1828)**
Stuart, James Ewell Brown (known as Jeb) (Confederate army officer); Patrick County, Va. **(1833–1864)**
Sturges, Preston (Edmond P. Biden) (director, screenwriter, playwright); Chicago **(1898–1959)**
Stuyvesant, Peter (Governor of New Amsterdam); West Friesland (Netherlands) **(1592–1672)**
Styne, Jule (Julius Kerwin Stein) (songwriter); London **(1905–1994)**
Styron, William (William Clark Styron, Jr.) (novelist); Newport News, Va., 6/11/25
Suharto, (President of Indonesia); Sedaju-Godean, Java, 2/20/21
Sukarno, (Indonesian leader); Surabaja, Java **(1901–1970)**
Sullavan, Margaret Brooke (actress); Norfolk, Va. **(1911–1960)**
Sullivan, Sir Arthur Seymour (composer); London **(1842–1900)**
Sullivan, Barry (Patrick Barry) (actor); New York City **(1912–1994)**
Sullivan, Ed (columnist, TV personality); New York City **(1901–1974)**
Sullivan, Frank (Francis John) (humorist); Saratoga Springs, N.Y. **(1892–1976)**
Sullivan, Louis Henry (architect); Boston **(1856–1924)**
Sulzberger, Arthur Ochs (newspaper publisher); New York City, 2/5/26
Sumac, Yma (singer); Ichocan, Peru, 9/10/27
Summer, Donna (La Donna Andrea Gaines) (singer); Boston, 12/31/48
Sun Ra (Herman "Sunny" Blount) (jazz composer); Birmingham, Ala. **(1914?–1993)**
Sun Tzu (writer, military strategist); China **(fl. c. 500–320 B.C.E.)**
Sun Yat-sen (statesman); nr. Macao **(1866–1925)**
Susann, Jacqueline (novelist); Philadelphia **(1918–1974)**
Susskind, David (TV producer); New York City **(1920–1987)**
Sutherland, Donald (actor); St. John, N.B., Canada, 7/17/34
Sutherland, Joan (soprano); Sydney, Australia, 11/7/26
Suzuki, Pat (actress); Cressey, Calif., 1931
Swados, Elizabeth (composer, playwright); Buffalo, N.Y., 2/5/51
Swanson, Gloria (Gloria May Josephine Svensson) (actress); Chicago **(1899–1983)**
Swarthout, Gladys (soprano); Deepwater, Mo. **(1904–1969)**
Swayze, John Cameron (news commentator); Wichita, Kans. **(1906–1995)**

Swayze, Patrick (actor, dancer); Houston, 8/18/54
Swenenborg, Emanuel (scientist, philosopher, mystic); Stockholm **(1688–1772)**
Swift, Jonathan (satirist); Dublin **(1667–1745)**
Swinburne, Algernon Charles (poet); London **(1837–1909)**
Swit, Loretta (actress); Passaic, N.J., 11/4/37
Swope, Herbert Bayard (journalist); St. Louis **(1882–1958)**
Sydow, von, Max (Carl Adolf von Sydow) (actor); Lund, Sweden, 4/10/29
Symons, Arthur (poet, critic); Milford Haven, Wales **(1865–1945)**
Synge, John Millington (dramatist); nr. Dublin **(1871–1909)**
Szilard, Leo (physicist); Budapest **(1898–1964)**

T

Taft, Robert Alphonso (legislator); Cincinnati **(1889–1953)**
Taft, William Howard (27th U.S. president); Cincinnati **(1857–1930)**
Tagore, Sir Rabindranath (poet); Calcutta **(1861–1941)**
Tallchief, Maria (ballet dancer); Fairfax, Okla., 1/24/25
Talleyrand-Pèrigord, Charles Maurice de (statesman); Paris **(1754–1838)**
Talmadge, Norma (actress); Niagara Falls, N.Y. **(1897–1957)**
Talvela, Martti (basso); Hiitola, Finalnd **(1935–1989)**
Tamerlane (Timur) (Mongol conqueror); nr. Samarkand (Turkestan) **(c. 1336–1405)**
Tamiroff, Akim (actor); Baku (Azerbaijan) **(1899–1972)**
Tan, Amy (novelist); Oakland, Calif., 2/19/52
Tandy, Jessica (actress); London **(1909–1994)**
Tarbell, Ida Minerva (author, biographer); Erie Co., Pa. **(1857–1944)**
Tarkington, (Newton) Booth (novelist); Indianapolis **(1869–1946)**
Tartikoff, Brandon (television executive); Freeport, N.Y. **(1949–1997)**
Tate, Allen (John Orley) (poet, critic); Winchester, Ky. **(1899–1979)**
Tate, Sharon (actress); Dallas **(1943–1969)**
Tati, Jacques (Jacques Tatischeff) (actor); Pecq, France **(1908–1982)**
Taylor, Deems (composer); New York City **(1885–1966)**
Taylor, Elizabeth (actress); London, 2/27/32
Taylor, Harold (educator); Toronto, 9/28/14
Taylor, James (singer, songwriter); Boston, 3/12/48
Taylor, Laurette (Laurette Cooney) (actress); New York City **(1884–1946)**
Taylor, Gen. Maxwell D. (former Army Chief of Staff); Keytesville, Mo. **(1901–1987)**
Taylor, Paul (choreographer); Wilkinsburg, Pa., 7/29/30
Taylor, Rod (actor), Sydney, Australia, 1/11/30
Taylor, Zachary (12th U.S. president); Montebello, Orange County, Va. **(1784–1850)**
Tchaikovsky, Peter (Pëtr) Ilich (composer); Votkinsk, Russia **(1840–1893)**
Teasdale, Sara (poet); St. Louis **(1884–1933)**
Tebaldi, Renata (lyric soprano); Pesaro, Italy, 1/2/22
Tecumseh (Shawnee Indian chief); nr. Springfield, Ohio **(1768–1813)**
Te Kanawa, Kiri (soprano); Gisborne, New Zealand, 3/6/44
Telemann, Georg Philipp (composer); Magdeburg (Germany) **(1681–1767)**
Teller, Edward (atomic physicist); Budapest, 1/15/08
Templeton, Alec Andrew (pianist, composer); Cardiff, Wales **(1910–1963)**
Tennille, Toni (singer); Montgomery, Ala., 5/8/43
Tennyson, Alfred (1st Baron Tennyson) (poet); Somersby, England **(1809–1892)**
Tenskwatawa (Shawnee prophet); Old Piqua, Ohio **(c. 1770–c. 1835)**
Terhune, Albert Payson (novelist, journalist); Newark, N.J. **(1872–1942)**
Terkel, Studs (writer, interviewer); New York City, 5/16/12
Terry, Ellen Alicia (actress); Coventry, England **(1848–1928)**
Terry-Thomas (Thomas Terry Hoar Stevens) (actor); London **(1911–1990)**
Tesla, Nikola (electrical engineer, inventor); Smiljan (Croatia) **(1856–1943)**
Thackeray, William Makepeace (novelist); Calcutta **(1811–1863)**
Thalberg, Irving G. (producer); Brooklyn, N.Y. **(1899–1936)**
Thant, U (U.N. statesman); Pantanaw (Burma) **(1909–1974)**
Tharp, Twyla (dancer, choreographer); Portland, Ind., 7/1/42
Thatcher, Margaret (former Prime Minister); Grantham, England, 10/13/25
Thebom, Blanche (mezzo-soprano); Monessen, Pa., 9/19/19
Theodorakis, Mikis (composer); Chios, Greece, 7/29/25
Thicke, Alan (actor, composer); Kirland Lake, Ont., Canada, 3/1/47
Thieu, Nguyen Van (ex-President of South Vietnam); Trithuy (Vietnam), 4/5/23
Thomas, Danny (Amos Jacobs) (entertainer, TV producer); Deerfield, Mich. **(1912–1991)**
Thomas, Dylan Marials (poet); Carmarthenshire, Wales **(1914–1953)**
Thomas, JonathanTaylor (actor); Bethlehem, Pa., 9/8/81
Thomas, Lowell (explorer, commentator); Woodington, Ohio **(1892–1981)**
Thomas, Marlo (actress); Detroit, 11/21/43
Thomas, Michael Tilson (conductor); Hollywood, Calif., 12/21/44
Thomas, Norman Mattoon (Socialist leader); Marion, Ohio **(1884–1968)**
Thomas, Philip Michael (actor); Columbus, Ohio, 5/26/49
Thomas, Richard (actor); New York City, 6/13/51
Thompson, Dorothy (writer); Lancaster, N.Y. **(1894–1961)**
Thompson, Emma (actress); London, 4/15/59
Thompson, Hunter (Stockton) (writer); Louisville, Ky., 7/18/39
Thompson, Sada (actress); Des Moines, Iowa, 9/27/29
Thomson, Virgil (Garnett) (composer); Kansas City, Mo. **(1896–1989)**
Thoreau, Henry David (naturalist, author); Concord, Mass. **(1817–1862)**
Thorndike, Dame Sybil (actress); Gainsborough, England **(1882–1976)**
Thorne-Smith, Courtney (actress); San Francisco, 11/8/67
Thurber, James Grover (author, cartoonist); Columbus, Ohio **(1894–1961)**
Thurman, Robert A. F. (scholar, Indo-Tibetan Buddhist studies); New York City, 8/6/40
Thurmond, (James) Strom (U.S. Senator); Edgefield, S.C., 12/5/02
Tibbett, Lawrence (baritone); Bakersfield, Calif. **(1896–1960)**
Tiberius Caesar Augustus (Roman emperor); Capri **(42 B.C.E.–C.E. 37)**
Tiegs, Cheryl (model, actress); Minnesota, 9/25/47
Tierney, Gene (actress); Brooklyn, N.Y. **(1920–1991)**
Tillich, Paul (philosopher, theologian); Starzeddel, Germany **(1886–1965)**
Tillstrom, Burr (puppeteer); Chicago **(1917–1985)**
Tintoretto, Il (Jacopo Robusti) (painter); Venice **(1518–1594)**
Tiny Tim (Herbert Khaury) (entertainer); New York City **(1930–1996)**
Tiomkin, Dmitri (composer); St. Petersburg, Russia **(1894–1979)**
Titian (Tiziano Vecelli) (painter); Pieve di Cadore (Italy) **(1477–1576)**
Tito (Josip Broz or Brozovich) (President of Yugoslavia); Croatia (former Yugoslavia) **(1892–1980)**
Tocqueville, Alexis de (writer); Verneuil, France **(1805–1859)**
Todd, Michael (producer); Minneapolis **(1907–1958)**
Todd, Richard (actor); Dublin, 6/11/19
Todd, Thelma (actress); Lawrence, Mass. **(1905–1935)**
Tolkien, J(ohn) R(onald) R(euel) (fantasy writer); Bloemfontein, South Africa **(1892–1973)**
Tolstoy, Count Leo (Lev) Nikolaevich (novelist); Tula Province, Russia **(1828–1910)**
Tomlin, Lily (actress, comedienne); Detroit, 9/1/36
Tone, Franchot (actor); Niagara Falls, N.Y. **(1905–1968)**
Tormé, Mel (Melvin) (singer); Chicago, 9/13/25
Torn, Rip (Elmore Torn, Jr.) (actor, director); Temple, Tex., 2/6/31
Torquamada, Tomásde (Spanish Inquisitor); Valladolid, Spain **(1420–1498)**
Toscanini, Arturo (orchestra conductor); Parma, Italy **(1867–1957)**
Totenberg, Nina (broadcast journalist); New York City, 1/14/44
Toulouse-Lautrec (Henri Marie Raymond de Toulouse-Lautrec Monfa) (painter); Albi, France **(1864–1901)**
Toynbee, Arnold J. (historian); London **(1889–1975)**
Tracy, Spencer (actor); Milwaukee **(1900–1967)**
Traubel, Helen (Wagnerian soprano); St. Louis **(1903–1972)**
Travanti, Daniel J. (actor); Kenosha, Wis., 3/7/40
Travolta, John (actor); Englewood, N.J., 2/18/54
Treacher, Arthur (actor); Brighton, England **(1894–1975)**
Tree, Sir Herbert Beerbohm (actor, manager); London **(1853–1917)**
Trevor, Claire (Wemlinger) (actress); New York City, 3/9/09
Trigère, Pauline (fashion designer); Paris, 11/4/12
Trilling, Diana (writer); New York City **(1905–1996)**
Trilling, Lionel (author, educator); New York City **(1905–1975)**
Trollope, Anthony (novelist); London **(1815–1882)**
Trotsky, Leon (Lev Davidovich Bronstein) (statesman); Elisavetgrad, Russia **(1879–1940)**
Troyanos, Tatiana (mezzo-soprano); New York City **(1938–1993)**
Trudeau, Garry (cartoonist); New York City, 1948
Trudeau, Pierre Elliott (former Prime Minister); Montreal, 10/18/19
Truffaut, François (film director); Paris **(1932–1984)**

Trujillo y Molina, Rafael Leonidas (dictator); San Cristóbal, Dominican Republic **(1891–1961)**
Truman, Harry S. (33rd U.S. president); near Lamar, Mo. **(1884–1972)**
Truman, Margaret (author); Independence, Mo., 2/17/24
Trump, Donald (business executive); New York City, 6/14/46
Truth, Sojourner (Isabella) (preacher, abolitionist); Ulster Co., N.Y. **(c. 1797–1883)**
Tryon, Thomas (actor, novelist); Hartford, Conn. **(1926–1991)**
Tsiolkovsky, Konstantin E. (father of cosmonautics); Izhevskoye, Russia **(1857–1935)**
Tsongas, Paul E. (politician); Lowell, Mass. **(1941–1997)**
Tubman, Harriet (Araminta) (abolitionist); Dorchester Co., Md. **(c. 1820–1913)**
Tuchman, Barbara (Wertheim) (historian, author); New York City **(1912–1989)**
Tucker, Forrest (actor); Plainfield, Ind. **(1919–1986)**
Tucker, Richard (tenor); New York City **(1914–1975)**
Tucker, Sophie (Sophia Kalish) (singer); Russia **(1884–1966)**
Tudor, Antony (choreographer); London **(1909–1987)**
Tune, Tommy (dancer, choreographer); Wichita Falls, Tex., 2/28/39
Turgenev, Ivan Sergeevich (novelist); Orel, Russia **(1818–1883)**
Turner, Frederick J. (historian); Portage, Wis. **(1861–1932)**
Turner, Ike (singer); Clarksdale, Miss., 11/5/31
Turner, Janine (actress); Lincoln, Neb., 12/6/62
Turner, Joseph M.W. (painter); London **(1775–1851)**
Turner, Kathleen (actress); Springfield, Mo., 6/19/54
Turner, Lana (Julia Jean Mildred Frances Turner) (actress); Wallace, Idaho **(1920–1995)**
Turner, Nat (civil rights leader); Southampton County, Va. **(1800–1831)**
Turner, Ted (business executive); Cincinnati, 11/19/38
Turner, Tina (Annie Mae Bullock) (singer); Nut Bush, Tenn., 11/26/39
Turpin, Ben (comedian); New Orleans **(1874–1940)**
Twain, Mark (Samuel Langhorne Clemens) (author); Florida, Mo. **(1835–1910)**
Tweed, William Marcy (politician); New York City **(1823–1878)**
Twiggy (Leslie Hornby) (model); London, 9/19/49
Twining, Gen. Nathan F. (former Air Force Chief of Staff); Monroe, Wis. **(1897–1982)**
Twitty, Conway (Harold Lloyd Jenkins) (singer, guitarist); Friars Point, Miss. **(1933–1993)**
Tyler, John (10th U.S. president); Charles City County, Va. **(1790–1862)**
Tyson, Cicely (actress); New York City, 12/19/33

U

Uccello, Paolo (painter); Florence **(1397–1475)**
Udall, Stewart L. (ex-Secretary of the Interior); St. Johns, Ariz., 1/31/20
Uggams, Leslie (singer, actress); New York City, 5/25/43
Ulanova, Galina (ballet dancer); St. Petersburg, Russia **(1910–1998)**
Ullman, Tracey (actress, singer); Slough, England, 12/30/59
Ullmann, Liv (actress); Tokyo, 12/16/39
Untermeyer, Louis (anthologist, poet); New York City **(1885–1977)**
Updike, John (novelist); Shillington, Pa., 3/18/32
Urey, Harold C. (chemist, Nobel laureate); Walkerton, Ind. **(1893–1981)**
Uris, Leon (novelist); Baltimore, 8/3/24
Ustinov, Peter (actor, producer); London, 4/16/21
Utrillo, Maurice (painter); Paris **(1883–1955)**

V

Vaccaro, Brenda (actress); Brooklyn, N.Y., 11/18/39
Vadim, Roger (Roger Vadim Plemiannikov) (film director); Paris, 1/26/28
Valentine, Karen (actress); Santa Rosa, Calif., 5/25/47
Valentino, Rudolph (Rodolpho d'Antonguolla) (actor); Castellaneta, Italy **(1895–1926)**
Valentino (Valentino Garavani) (fashion designer); nr. Milan, Italy, 5/11/32
Valéry, Paul (Ambroise Toussaint Jules) (poet, critic); Sète, France **(1871–1945)**
Vallee, Rudy (Hubert Prior Rudy Vallée) (band leader, singer); Island Pond, Vt. **(1901–1986)**
Valli, Frankie (Frank Castellaccio) (singer); Newark, N.J., 5/3/37
Van Allen, James Alfred (space physicist); Mt. Pleasant, Iowa, 9/7/14
Van Buren, Abigail (Pauline Esther Friedman) (columnist); Sioux City, Iowa, 7/4/18
Van Buren, Martin (8th U.S. president); Kinderhook, N.Y. **(1782–1862)**
Vance, Vivian (Vivian Jones) (actress); Cherryvale, Kans. **(1912–1979)**
Vanderbilt, Alfred G. (sportsman); London, 9/22/12
Vanderbilt, Cornelius (financier); Port Richmond, N.Y. **(1794–1877)**
Vanderbilt, Gloria (fashion designer); New York City, 2/20/24
Van Doren, Carl (writer, educator); Hope, Ill. **(1885–1950)**
Van Doren, Mamie (actress); Rowena, S.D., 2/6/33
Van Dyke, Dick (actor); West Plains, Mo., 12/13/25
Vandyke (or Van Dyck), Sir Anthony (painter); Antwerp (Belgium) **(1599–1641)**
Van Eyck, Jan (painter); Maeseyck (Belgium) **(c. 1390–1441)**
Van Fleet, Jo (actress); Oakland, Calif. **(1915–1996)**
van Gogh, Vincent (painter); Groot Zundert, Brabant (Belgium) **(1853–1890)**
van Hamel, Martine (ballet dancer); Brussels, 11/16/45
Van Heusen, Jimmy (Edward Chester Babcock) (songwriter); Syracuse, N.Y. **(1913–1990)**
Van Patten, Dick (actor); Richmond Hill, N.Y., 12/9/28
Van Peebles, Melvin (playwright); Chicago, 9/21/32
Vasari, Giorgio (art historian); Arezzo, Italy **(1511–1574)**
Vaughan, Sarah (singer); Newark, N.J. **(1924–1990)**
Vaughan Williams, Ralph (composer); Down Ampney, England **(1872–1958)**
Vaughn, Robert (actor); New York City, 11/22/32
Veblen, Thorstein (economist, social critic); Cato Township, Wis. **(1857–1929)**
Veidt, Conrad (actor); Potsdam, Germany **(1893–1943)**
Velázquez, Diego Rodriguez de Silva y (painter); Seville, Spain **(1599–1660)**
Venturi, Robert (Charles) (architect); Philadelphia, 6/25/25
Verdi, Giuseppe (composer); Roncole (Italy) **(1813–1901)**
Verdon, Gwen (actress); Culver City, Calif., 1/13/25
Vereen, Ben (actor, singer); Miami, Fla., 10/10/46
Verlaine, Paul (poet); Metz, France **(1844–1896)**
Vermeer, Jan (or Jan van der Meer van Delft) (painter); Delft (Netherlands) **(1632–1675)**
Verne, Jules (author); Nantes, France **(1828–1905)**
Veronese, Paolo (Paolo Cagliari) (painter); Verona **(1528–1588)**
Verrazano, Giovanni da (navigator); Florence (Italy) **(c. 1485–1528)**
Verrett, Shirley (mezzo-soprano); New Orleans, 5/31/33
Versace, Gianni (fashion designer); Reggio, Italy **(1946–1997)**
Vesalius, Andreas (anatomist); Brussels **(1515–1564)**
Vespucci, Amerigo (navigator); Florence (Italy) **(1454–1512)**
Vickers, Jon (tenor); Prince Albert, Sask., Canada, 10/29/26
Vico, Giovanni Battista (philosopher); Naples, Italy **(1668–1744)**
Victoria (Queen of England); London **(1819–1901)**
Vidal, Gore (novelist); West Point, N.Y., 10/3/25
Vidor, King (film director, producer); Galveston, Tex. **(1895–1982)**
Vigoda, Abe (actor); New York City, 2/24/21
Villa, Pancho (Doroteo Arango) (revolutionary); Hacienda de Rio Grande, San Juan del Rio, Mexico **(1877–1923)**
Villella, Edward (ballet dancer); Bayside, Queens, N.Y., 10/1/36
Villon, François (François de Montcorbier) (poet); Paris **(1431–1463)**
Vinton, Bobby (singer); Canonsburg, Pa., 4/16/35
Virgil (or Vergil) (Publius Vergilius Maro) (poet); nr. Mantua (Italy) **(70–19 B.C.E.)**
Vishnevskaya, Galina (soprano); St. Petersburg (Russia), 10/25/26
Vivaldi, Antonio (composer); Venice **(1678–1741)**
Vlaminck, Maurice de (painter); Paris **(1876–1958)**
Voight, Jon (actor); Yonkers, N.Y., 12/29/38
Volta, Alessandro (scientist); Como, Italy **(1745–1827)**
Voltaire (François Marie Arouet) (author); Paris **(1694–1778)**
von Aroldingen, Karin (Karin Awny Hannelore Reinbold von Aroedingen and Eltzinger) (ballet dancer); Greiz (Germany), 7/9/41
von Braun, Wernher (rocket scientist); Wirsitz, Germany **(1912–1977)**
von Furstenberg, Betsy (Elizabeth Caroline Maria Agatha Felicitas Therese von Furstenberg-Hedringen) (actress); Nelheim-Heusen, Germany, 8/16/35
von Fürstenberg, Diane (Diane Simone Michelle Halfin) (fashion designer); Brussels, 12/31/46
von Hindenburg, Paul (statesman); Posen (Poland) **(1847–1934)**
von Karajan, Herbert (conductor); Salzburg (Austria) **(1908–1989)**
Vonnegut, Kurt, Jr. (novelist); Indianapolis, 11/11/22
Von Stade, Frederica (mezzo-soprano); Somerville, N.J., 6/1/45
Von Stroheim, Erich Oswald Hans Carl Maria von Nordenwall (actor, director); Vienna **(1885–1957)**
Von Zell, Harry (announcer); Indianapolis **(1906–1981)**
Vreeland, Diana (Diana Da Iziel) (fashion journalist, museum consultant); Paris **(1903?–1989)**

W

Wagner, Lindsay (actress); Los Angeles, 6/22/49
Wagner, Robert (actor); Detroit, 2/10/30
Wagner, Robert F. (ex-Mayor of New York City); New York City **(1910–1991)**
Wagner, Wilhelm Richard (composer); Leipzig (Germany) **(1813–1883)**
Waits, Tom (blues singer); Pomona, Calif., 12/7/49
Waldheim, Kurt (ex-U.N. Secretary-General); St. Andrae-Wörden, Austria, 12/21/18
Walesa, Lech (Polish labor leader and ex-president); Popowo, Poland, 9/29/43
Walker, Alice (novelist, poet); Eatonon, Ga., 2/9/44
Walker, Nancy (Ann Myrtle Swoyer) (actress, comedienne); Philadelphia **(1922–1992)**
Walker, Robert (actor); Salt Lake City **(1918–1951)**
Walker, T-Bone (blues singer); Linden, Tex. **(1910–1975)**
Wallace, DeWitt (publisher); St. Paul, Minn. **(1889–1981)**
Wallace, George C. (ex-governor); Clio, Ala. **(1919–1998)**
Wallace, Irving (novelist); Chicago **(1916–1990)**
Wallace, Mike (Myron Wallace) (TV interviewer, commentator); Brookline, Mass., 5/9/18
Wallach, Eli (actor); Brooklyn, N.Y., 12/7/15
Wallenberg, Raoul (diplomat, humanitarian); Stockholm **(1912–1947)**
Wallenstein, Alfred (conductor); Chicago **(1898–1983)**
Waller, Thomas "Fats" (pianist); New York City **(1904–1943)**
Wallis, Hal (film producer); Chicago **(1899–1986)**
Walpole, Horace (statesman, novelist); London **(1717–1797)**
Waltari, Mika (novelist); Helsinki **(1903–1979)**
Walter, Bruno (Bruno Walter Schlesinger) (orchestra conductor); Berlin **(1876–1962)**
Walters, Barbara (TV commentator); Boston, 9/25/31
Walton, Izaak (author); Stafford, England **(1593–1683)**
Wambaugh, Joseph (author, screenwriter); East Pittsburgh, 1/22/37
Wanamaker, John (merchant); Philadelphia **(1838–1922)**
Wanamaker, Sam (actor, director); Chicago **(1919–1993)**
Ward, Barbara (economist); York, England **(1914–1981)**
Warhol, Andy (Warhola) (artist); McKeesport, Pa. **(1928–1987)**
Waring, Fred (band leader); Tyrone, Pa. **(1900–1984)**
Warner, H. B. (Henry Bryan Warner Lickford) (actor); London **(1876–1958)**
Warren, Lesley Ann (actress); New York City, 8/16/46
Warren, Robert Penn (novelist); Guthrie, Ky. **(1905–1989)**
Warrick, Ruth (actress); St. Joseph, Mo., 6/29/15
Warwick, Dionne (singer); East Orange, N.J., 12/12/41
Washington, Booker Taliaferro (educator); Franklin County, Va. **(1856–1915)**
Washington, Denzel (actor); Mt. Vernon, N.Y., 12/28/54
Washington, George (1st U.S. president); Westmoreland County, Va. **(1732–1799)**
Washington, Harold (ex-mayor of Chicago); Chicago **(1922–1987)**
Waters, Ethel (actress, singer); Chester, Pa. **(1896–1977)**
Waters, Muddy (McKinley Morganfield) (singer, guitarist); Rolling Fork, Miss. **(1915–1983)**
Waterston, Sam (actor); Cambridge, Mass., 11/15/40
Watson, James Dewey (scientist, Nobel laureate); Chicago, 4/6/28
Watson, Thomas John (industrialist); Campbell, N.Y. **(1874–1956)**
Watt, James (inventor); Greenock, Scotland **(1736–1819)**
Watteau, Jean-Antoine (painter); Valanciennes, France **(1684–1721)**
Wattleton, Faye (family planning advocate); St. Louis, 7/8/43
Watts, André (concert pianist); Nuremberg, Germany, 6/20/46
Waugh, Alec (Alexander Raban Waugh) (novelist); London **(1898–1981)**
Waugh, Evelyn (novelist); London **(1903–1966)**
Wayne, Anthony (military officer); Waynesboro (family farm), nr. Paoli, Pa. **(1745–1796)**
Wayne, David (David McMeekan) (actor); Traverse City, Mich. **(1914–1995)**
Wayne, John (Marion Michael Morrison) (actor); Winterset, Iowa **(1907–1979)**
Weaver, Dennis (actor); Joplin, Mo., 6/4/25
Weaver, Fritz (actor); Pittsburgh, 1/19/26
Weaver, Sigourney (actress); New York City, 10/8/49
Webb, Clifton (Webb Parmelee Hollenbeck) (actor); Indianapolis **(1893–1966)**
Webb, Jack (actor, producer); Santa Monica, Calif. **(1920–1982)**
Weber, Karl Maria Friedrich Ernst von (composer); nr. Lübeck (Germany) **(1786–1826)**
Webster, Daniel (statesman); Salisbury, N.H. **(1782–1852)**
Webster, Margaret (producer, director, actress); New York City **(1905–1973)**
Webster, Noah (lexicographer); West Hartford, Conn. **(1758–1843)**
Weill, Kurt (composer); Dessau, (Germany) **(1900–1950)**
Weir, Peter (director); Sydney, Australia, 8/21/44
Weizmann, Chaim (statesman); Grodno Province, Russia **(1874–1952)**
Welch, Raquel (Raquel Tejada) (actress); Chicago, 9/5/40
Weld, Tuesday (Susan Ker Weld) (actress); New York City, 8/27/43
Welk, Lawrence (band leader); Strasburg, N.D. **(1903–1992)**
Welles, Orson (actor, director, producer); Kenosha, Wis. **(1915–1985)**
Wellington, Duke of (Arthur Wellesley) (statesman); Ireland **(1769–1852)**
Wells, H(erbert) G(eorge) (author); Bromley, England **(1866–1946)**
Wells, Ida Bell (Barnett) (journalist); Holly Springs, Miss. **(1862–1931)**
Welty, Eudora (novelist); Jackson, Miss., 4/13/09
Wenner, Jann (publisher); New York City, 1/7/46
Werfel, Franz (novelist); Prague **(1890–1945)**
Werner, Oskar (Josef Schliessmayer) (actor, director); Vienna **(1922–1984)**
Wertheimer, Linda (radio journalist); Carlsbad, N.M., 3/19/43
Wertmueller, Lina (Arcanguela Felice Assunta W. von Elgg) (director); Rome, 8/14/28
Wesley, John (religious leader); Epworth Rectory, Lincolnshire, England **(1703–1791)**
West, Benjamin (painter); Springfield, Pa. **(1738–1820)**
West, Dame Rebecca (Cicily Fairfield) (novelist); County Kerry, Ireland **(1892–1983)**
West, Jessamyn (novelist); nr. North Vernon, Ind. **(1902–1984)**
West, Mae (actress); Brooklyn, N.Y. **(1893–1980)**
West, Nathanael (Nathan Weinstein) (novelist); New York City **(1902–1940)**
Westheimer, Ruth (Karola Ruth Siegel) (human sexuality expert); Frankfurt, Germany, 1928
Westinghouse, George (inventor); Central Bridge, N.Y. **(1846–1914)**
Westmoreland, William Childs (ex-Army Chief of Staff); Saxon, S.C., 3/26/14
Weyden, Roger van der (painter); Tournai (Belgium) **(c. 1400–1464)**
Wharton, Edith Newbold (née Jones) (novelist); New York City **(1862–1937)**
Wheatley, Phillis (poet); Senegal **(c. 1753–1784)**
Wheeler, Bert (Albert Jerome Wheeler) (comedian); Paterson, N.J. **(1895–1968)**
Whistler, James Abbott McNeill (painter, etcher); Lowell, Mass. **(1834–1903)**
Whitaker, Forest (actor); Longview, Tex., 7/15/61
White, Betty (actress); Oak Park, Ill., 1/17/22
White, Edmund (writer); Cincinnati, Ohio, 1/13/40
White, E(lwyn) B(rooks) (author); Mt. Vernon, N.Y. **(1899–1985)**
White, Pearl (actress); Green Ridge, Mo. **(1889–1938)**
White, Stanford (architect); New York City **(1853–1906)**
White, Theodore H. (historian); Boston **(1915–1986)**
White, Vanna (TV personality); Conway, S.C., 2/18/57
White, William Allen (journalist); Emporia, Kans. **(1868–1944)**
Whitehead, Alfred North (mathematician, philosopher); Isle of Thanet, England **(1861–1947)**
Whiteman, Paul (band leader); Denver **(1891–1967)**
Whiting, Margaret (singer, actress); Detroit, 7/22/24
Whitman, Walt (Walter) (poet); West Hills, N.Y. **(1819–1892)**
Whitmore, James (actor); White Plains, N.Y., 10/1/21
Whitney, Cornelius Vanderbilt (sportsman); New York City **(1899–1992)**
Whitney, Eli (inventor); Westboro, Mass. **(1765–1825)**
Whitney, John Hay (publisher); Ellsworth, Maine **(1904–1982)**
Whittier, John Greenleaf (poet); Haverhill, Mass. **(1807–1892)**
Wideman, John Edgar (writer); Washington, D.C., 6/14/41
Widmark, Richard (actor); Sunrise, Minn., 12/26/14
Wiesel, Elie (Eliezer) (author); Signet, Romania, 9/30/28
Wiesenthal, Simon (Nazi hunter); Buchach (Ukraine), 12/31/08
Wilde, Cornel (film actor, producer); New York City **(1915–1989)**
Wilde, Oscar Fingal O'Flahertie Wills (author); Dublin **(1854–1900)**
Wilder, Billy (Samuel Wilder) (film producer, director); Vienna, 6/22/06
Wilder, Gene (Jerome Silberman) (actor, writer, director, producer); Milwaukee, 6/11/35
Wilder, Thornton (author); Madison, Wis. **(1897–1975)**
Wilding, Michael (actor); Westcliff, England **(1912–1979)**
Wilkins, Roy (civil rights leader); St. Louis **(1901–1981)**
William, Prince (heir to British throne); London, 6/21/82
Williams, Andy (singer); Wall Lake, Iowa, 12/3/30
Williams, Anson (actor, director); Los Angeles, 9/25/49

Williams, Billy Dee (actor); New York City, 4/6/37
Williams, Cindy (actress); Van Nuys, Calif., 8/22/47
Williams, Edward Bennett (lawyer); Hartford, Conn. **(1920–1988)**
Williams, Emlyn (actor, playwright); Mostyn, Wales **(1905–1987)**
Williams, Esther (actress); Los Angeles, 8/8/23
Williams, Gluyas (cartoonist); San Francisco **(1888–1982)**
Williams, Hank, Sr. (Hiram King Williams) (singer); Georgiana, Ala. **(1923–1953)**
Williams, Joe (singer); Cordele, Ga., 12/12/18
Williams, John T. (composer, conductor); Queens, N.Y., 2/8/32
Williams, Paul (singer, composer, actor); Omaha, Neb., 9/19/40
Williams, Robin (actor, producer); Chicago, 7/21/52
Williams, Roger (clergyman); London **(1603?–1683)**
Williams, Tennessee (Thomas L. Williams) (playwright); Columbus, Miss. **(1911–1983)**
Williams, William Carlos (physician, poet); Rutherford, N.J. **(1883–1963)**
Williamson, Nicol (actor); Hamilton, Scotland, 9/14/38
Willkie, Wendell Lewis (lawyer); Elwood, Ind. **(1892–1944)**
Willis, Bruce (actor); Germany, 3/19/55
Willson, Meredith (composer); Mason City, Iowa **(1902–1984)**
Wilson, August (poet, writer, playwright); Pittsburgh, 1945
Wilson, Don (radio and TV announcer); Lincoln, Neb. **(1900–1982)**
Wilson, Dooley (actor, musician); Tyler, Tex. **(1894–1953)**
Wilson, Edmund (literary critic, author); Red Bank, N.J. **(1895–1972)**
Wilson, Flip (Clerow) (comedian); Jersey City, N.J., 12/8/33
Wilson, Harold (ex-Prime Minister); Huddersfield, England **(1916–1995)**
Wilson, Nancy (singer); Chillicothe, Ohio, 2/20/37
Wilson, Sloan (novelist); Norwalk, Conn., 5/8/20
Wilson, Thomas Woodrow (28th U.S. president); Staunton, Va. **(1856–1924)**
Winchell, Walter (columnist); New York City **(1897–1972)**
Windsor, Duchess of (Bessie Wallis Warfield) Blue Ridge Summit, Pa. **(1896–1986)**
Windsor, Duke of (formerly King Edward VIII of England); Richmond Park, England **(1894–1972)**
Winfrey, Oprah (TV host, actress, producer); Kosciusko, Miss., 1/29/54
Winger, Debra (Mary Debra) (actress); Cleveland, 5/17/55
Winkler, Henry (actor, director, producer); New York City, 10/30/45
Winningham, Mare (actress); Phoenix, Ariz., 5/16/59
Winter, Johnny (guitarist); Leland, Miss., 2/23/44
Winters, Jonathan (comedian); Dayton, Ohio, 11/11/25
Winters, Shelley (Shirley Schrift) (actress); East St. Louis, Ill., 8/18/22
Winthrop, John (first Governor, Massachusetts Bay Colony); Suffolk, England **(1588–1649)**
Wise, Stephen Samuel (rabbi); Budapest **(1874–1949)**
Withers, Jane (actress); Atlanta, 4/12/26
Wittig, Georg F. K. (chemist, Nobel laureate); Berlin, Germany **(1897–1987)**
Wittgenstein, Ludwig (Josef Johann) (philosopher); Vienna **(1889–1951)**
Wodehouse, P(elham) G(renville) (novelist); Guildford, England **(1881–1975)**
Wolf, Scott (actor); Boston, 6/4/68
Wolfe, Thomas Clayton (novelist); Asheville, N.C. **(1900–1938)**
Wolfe, Tom (journalist); Richmond, Va., 3/2/31
Wolff, Tobias (author); Birmingham, Ala., 6/19/45
Wolsey, Thomas (prelate, statesman); Ipswich, England **(c. 1475–1530)**
Wonder, Stevie (Steveland Judkins, later Steveland Morris) (singer, songwriter); Saginaw, Mich., 5/13/50
Wong, Anna May (Lu Tsong Wong) (actress); Los Angeles **(1907–1961)**
Wood, Grant (painter); Anamosa, Iowa **(1892–1942)**
Wood, Natalie (Natasha Viparaeff) (actress); San Francisco **(1938–1981)**
Woods, James (actor); Vernal, Utah, 4/18/47
Woodhouse, Barbara (Blackburn) (dog trainer, author, TV personality); Rathfarnham, Ireland **(1910–1988)**
Woodruff, Judy (broadcast journalist); Tulsa, Okla., 11/20/46
Woodson, Carter G. (historian); New Canton, Va. **(1875–1950)**
Woodward, Edward (actor); Croydon, England, 6/1/30
Woodward, Joanne (actress); Thomasville, Ga., 2/27/30
Woodward, Robert Burns (chemist, Nobel laureate); Boston **(1917–1979)**
Woolf, Adeline Virginia (née Stephens) (novelist); London **(1882–1941)**
Woollcott, Alexander (author, critic); Phalanx, N.J. **(1887–1943)**
Woolley, Monty (Edgar Montillion Woolley) (actor); New York City **(1888–1963)**
Woolworth, Frank (merchant); Rodman, N.Y. **(1852–1919)**
Wopat, Tom (actor); Lodi, Wis., 9/9/50
Wordsworth, William (poet); Cockermouth, England **(1770–1850)**
Wouk, Herman (novelist); New York City, 5/27/15
Wovoka, (Jack Wilson) (Paiute Indian religious leader); (western Nev.) **(c. 1858–1932)**
Wray, Fay (actress); Alberta, Canada, 9/14/07
Wren, Sir Christopher (architect); East Knoyle, England **(1632–1723)**
Wright, Frank Lloyd (architect); Richland Center, Wis. **(1869–1959)**
Wright, Martha (singer); Seattle, 3/23/26
Wright, Orville (inventor); Dayton, Ohio **(1871–1948)**
Wright, Richard (novelist); nr. Natchez, Miss. **(1908–1960)**
Wright, Wilbur (inventor); Millville, Ind. **(1867–1912)**
Wyatt, Jane (actress); Campgaw, N.J., 8/12/12
Wycliffe, John (church reformer); Hipswell, England **(1320–1384)**
Wyeth, Andrew (painter); Chadds Ford, Pa., 7/12/17
Wyle, Noah (actor); Hollywood, Calif., 6/4/71
Wyler, William (director); Mulhouse (France) **(1902–1981)**
Wyman, Jane (Sarah Jane Fulks) (actress); St. Joseph, Mo., 1/4/14
Wynette, Tammy (Virginia Wynette Pugh) (singer); Tupelo, Miss. **(1942–1998)**
Wynn, Ed (Isaiah Edwin Leopold) (comedian); Philadelphia **(1886–1966)**
Wynn, Keenan (actor); New York City **(1916–1986)**

Xavier, St. Francis (Jesuit missionary); Pamplona, Navarre (Spain) **(1506–1552)**
Xenophon (soldier, historian, essayist); Athens **(c. 435–c. 355 B.C.E.)**
Xerxes, the Great (king); Persian Empire **(c. 519–465 B.C.E.)**

Yeats, William Butler (poet); nr. Dublin **(1865–1939)**
Yevtushenko, Yevgeny (poet); Zima (Russia), 7/18/33
York, Michael (actor); Fulmer, England, 3/27/42
York, Susannah (Fletcher) (actress); London, 1/9/42
Yorty, Samuel W. (ex-Mayor of Los Angeles); Lincoln, Neb., 10/1/09
Yothers, Tina (actress); Whittier, Calif., 5/5/73
Young, Alan (actor); North Shield, England, 11/19/19
Young, Andrew (civil rights leader); New Orleans, 3/12/32
Young, Brigham (religious leader); Whitingham, Vt. **(1801–1877)**
Young, Gig (Byron Barr) (actor); St. Cloud, Minn. **(1917–1978)**
Young, Loretta (Gretchen Young) (actress); Salt Lake City, 1/6/13
Young, Neil (singer, songwriter); Toronto, 11/12/45
Young, Robert (actor); Chicago **(1907–1998)**
Youngman, Henny (comedian); Whitechapel, London **(1906–1998)**

Z

Zanuck, Darryl F. (producer); Wahoo, Neb. **(1902–1979)**
Zappa, Frank (Francis Vincent Zappa, Jr.) (singer, songwriter); Baltimore **(1940–1993)**
Zeffirelli, Franco (director); Florence, Italy, 2/12/23
Zemeckis, Robert (filmmaker); Chicago, 1952
Zenger, John Peter (printer, journalist); (Germany) **(1697–1746)**
Zhou Enlai (Premier); Hualyin, China **(1898–1976)**
Ziegfeld, Florenz (theatrical producer); Chicago **(1869–1932)**
Ziegler, Karl (chemist, Nobel laureate); Helsa, Germany **(1898–1973)**
Zimbalist, Efrem (concert violinist); Rostov-on-Don, Russia **(1889–1985)**
Zimbalist, Efrem, Jr. (actor); New York City, 11/30/23
Zimbalist, Stephanie (actress); New York City, 10/8/56
Zinnemann, Fred (director); Vienna **(1907–1997)**
Zola, Emile (novelist); Paris **(1840–1902)**
Zoroaster (religious leader); Persian Empire **(c. 628–c. 551 B.C.E.)**
Zukerman, Pinchas (violinist); Tel Aviv, Israel, 7/16/48
Zukor, Adolph (movie executive); Risce, Hungary **(1873–1976)**
Zurbarán, Francisco de (painter); Fuentes de Cantos, Spain **(1598–1664)**
Zweig, Stefan (author); Vienna **(1881–1942)**
Zwingli, Huldrych (humanist); Wildaus, Switzerland **(1484–1531)**

Nobel Prizes

For years not listed, no award was made. *(See* October 1998 Current Events for 1998 winners.)

PEACE

1901 Henri Dunant (Switzerland); Frederick Passy (France)
1902 Elie Ducommun and Albert Gobat (Switzerland)
1903 Sir William R. Cremer (U.K.)
1904 Institut de Droit International (Belgium)
1905 Bertha von Suttner (Austria)
1906 Theodore Roosevelt (U.S.)
1907 Ernesto T. Moneta (Italy) and Louis Renault (France)
1908 Klas P. Arnoldson (Sweden) and Frederik Bajer (Denmark)
1909 Auguste M. F. Beernaert (Belgium) and Baron Paul H. B. B. d'Estournelles de Constant de Rebecque (France)
1910 Bureau International Permanent de la Paix (Switzerland)
1911 Tobias M. C. Asser (Holland) and Alfred H. Fried (Austria)
1912 Elihu Root (U.S.)
1913 Henri La Fontaine (Belgium)
1917 International Red Cross
1919 Woodrow Wilson (U.S.)
1920 Léon Bourgeois (France)
1921 Karl H. Branting (Sweden) and Christian L. Lange (Norway)
1922 Fridtjof Nansen (Norway)
1925 Sir Austen Chamberlain (U.K.) and Charles G. Dawes (U.S.)
1926 Aristide Briand (France) and Gustav Stresemann (Germany)
1927 Ferdinand Buisson (France) and Ludwig Quidde (Germany)
1929 Frank B. Kellogg (U.S.)
1930 Lars O. J. Söderblom (Sweden)
1931 Jane Addams and Nicholas M. Butler (U.S.)
1933 Sir Norman Angell (U.K.)
1934 Arthur Henderson (U.K.)
1935 Karl von Ossietzky (Germany)
1936 Carlos de S. Lamas (Argentina)
1937 Lord Cecil of Chelwood (U.K.)
1938 Office International Nansen pour les Réfugiés (Switzerland)
1944 International Red Cross
1945 Cordell Hull (U.S.)
1946 Emily G. Balch and John R. Mott (U.S.)
1947 American Friends Service Committee (U.S.) and British Society of Friends' Service Council (U.K.)
1949 Lord John Boyd Orr (Scotland)
1950 Ralph J. Bunche (U.S.)
1951 Léon Jouhaux (France)
1952 Albert Schweitzer (French Equatorial Africa)
1953 George C. Marshall (U.S.)
1954 Office of U.N. High Commissioner for Refugees
1957 Lester B. Pearson (Canada)
1958 Rev. Dominique Georges Henri Pire (Belgium)
1959 Philip John Noel-Baker (U.K.)
1960 Albert John Luthuli (South Africa)
1961 Dag Hammarskjöld (Sweden)
1962 Linus Pauling (U.S.)
1963 Intl. Comm. of Red Cross; League of Red Cross Societies (both Geneva)
1964 Rev. Dr. Martin Luther King, Jr. (U.S.)
1965 UNICEF (United Nations Children's Fund)
1968 René Cassin (France)
1969 International Labour Organization
1970 Norman E. Borlaug (U.S.)
1971 Willy Brandt (West Germany)
1973 Henry A. Kissinger (U.S.); Le Duc Tho (North Vietnam)[1]
1974 Eisaku Sato (Japan); Sean MacBride (Ireland)
1975 Andrei D. Sakharov (U.S.S.R.)
1976 Mairead Corrigan and Betty Williams (both Northern Ireland)
1977 Amnesty International
1978 Menachem Begin (Israel) and Anwar el-Sadat (Egypt)
1979 Mother Teresa of Calcutta (India)
1980 Adolfo Pérez Esquivel (Argentina)
1981 Office of the United Nations High Commissioner for Refugees
1982 Alva Myrdal (Sweden) and Alfonso García Robles (Mexico)
1983 Lech Walesa (Poland)
1984 Bishop Desmond Tutu (South Africa)
1985 International Physicians for the Prevention of Nuclear War
1986 Elie Wiesel (U.S.)
1987 Oscar Arias Sánchez (Costa Rica)
1988 U.N. Peacekeeping Forces
1989 Dalai Lama (Tibet)
1990 Mikhail S. Gorbachev (U.S.S.R.)
1991 Daw Aung San Suu Kyi (Burma)
1992 Rigoberta Menchú (Guatemala)
1993 F. W. de Klerk and Nelson Mandela (both South Africa)
1994 Yasir Arafat (Palestine) and Yitzhak Rabin (Israel)
1995 Joseph Rotblat and Pugwash Conference on Science and World Affairs (U.K.)
1996 Carlos Filipe Ximenes Belo and José Ramos-Horta (East Timor)
1997 International Campaign to Ban Landmines and Jody Williams (U.S.)

1. Le Duc Tho refused prize, charging that peace had not yet really been established in South Vietnam.

LITERATURE

1901 René F. A. Sully Prudhomme (France)
1902 Theodor Mommsen (Germany)
1903 Björnstjerne Björnson (Norway)
1904 Frédéric Mistral (France) and José Echegaray (Spain)
1905 Henryk Sienkiewicz (Poland)
1906 Giosuè Carducci (Italy)

1907 Rudyard Kipling (U.K.)
1908 Rudolf Eucken (Germany)
1909 Selma Lagerlöf (Sweden)
1910 Paul von Heyse (Germany)
1911 Maurice Maeterlinck (Belgium)
1912 Gerhart Hauptmann (Germany)
1913 Rabindranath Tagore (India)
1915 Romain Rolland (France)
1916 Verner von Heidenstam (Sweden)
1917 Karl Gjellerup (Denmark) and Henrik Pontoppidan (Denmark)
1919 Carl Spitteler (Switzerland)
1920 Knut Hamsun (Norway)
1921 Anatole France (France)
1922 Jacinto Benavente (Spain)
1923 William B. Yeats (Ireland)
1924 Wladyslaw Reymont (Poland)
1925 George Bernard Shaw (Ireland)
1926 Grazia Deledda (Italy)
1927 Henri Bergson (France)
1928 Sigrid Undset (Norway)
1929 Thomas Mann (Germany)
1930 Sinclair Lewis (U.S.)
1931 Erik A. Karlfeldt (Sweden)
1932 John Galsworthy (U.K.)
1933 Ivan G. Bunin (Russia)
1934 Luigi Pirandello (Italy)
1936 Eugene O'Neill (U.S.)
1937 Roger Martin du Gard (France)
1938 Pearl S. Buck (U.S.)
1939 Frans Eemil Sillanpää (Finland)
1944 Johannes V. Jensen (Denmark)
1945 Gabriela Mistral (Chile)
1946 Hermann Hesse (Switzerland)
1947 André Gide (France)
1948 Thomas Stearns Eliot (U.K.)
1949 William Faulkner (U.S.)
1950 Bertrand Russell (U.K.)
1951 Pär Lagerkvist (Sweden)
1952 François Mauriac (France)
1953 Sir Winston Churchill (U.K.)
1954 Ernest Hemingway (U.S.)
1955 Halldór Kiljan Laxness (Iceland)
1956 Juan Ramón Jiménez (Spain)
1957 Albert Camus (France)
1958 Boris Pasternak (U.S.S.R.) (declined)
1959 Salvatore Quasimodo (Italy)
1960 St. John Perse (Alexis St.-Léger Léger) (France)
1961 Ivo Andric (Yugoslavia)
1962 John Steinbeck (U.S.)
1963 Giorgios Seferis (Seferiades) (Greece)
1964 Jean-Paul Sartre (France) (declined)
1965 Mikhail Sholokhov (U.S.S.R.)
1966 Shmuel Yosef Agnon (Israel) and Nelly Sachs (Sweden)
1967 Miguel Angel Asturias (Guatemala)
1968 Yasunari Kawabata (Japan)
1969 Samuel Beckett (Ireland)
1970 Aleksandr Solzhenitsyn (U.S.S.R.)
1971 Pablo Neruda (Chile)
1972 Heinrich Böll (Germany)
1973 Patrick White (Australia)
1974 Eyvind Johnson and Harry Martinson (both Sweden)
1975 Eugenio Montale (Italy)
1976 Saul Bellow (U.S.)
1977 Vicente Aleixandre (Spain)
1978 Isaac Bashevis Singer (U.S.)
1979 Odysseus Elytis (Greece)
1980 Czeslaw Milosz (U.S.)
1981 Elias Canetti (Bulgaria)
1982 Gabriel García Márquez (Colombia)
1983 William Golding (U.K.)
1984 Jaroslav Seifert (Czechoslovakia)
1985 Claude Simon (France)
1986 Wole Soyinka (Nigeria)
1987 Joseph Brodsky (U.S.)
1988 Naguib Mahfouz (Egypt)
1989 Camilo José Cela (Spain)
1990 Octavio Paz (Mexico)
1991 Nadine Gordimer (South Africa)
1992 Derek Walcott (Trinidad)
1993 Toni Morrison (U.S.)
1994 Kenzaburo Oe (Japan)
1995 Seamus Heaney (Ireland)
1996 Wislawa Szymborska (Poland)
1997 Dario Fo (Italy)

PHYSICS

1901 Wilhelm K. Roentgen (Germany), for discovery of Roentgen rays
1902 Hendrik A. Lorentz and Pieter Zeeman (Netherlands), for work on influence of magnetism upon radiation
1903 A. Henri Becquerel (France), for work on spontaneous radioactivity; and Pierre and Marie Curie (France), for study of radiation
1904 John Strutt (Lord Rayleigh) (U.K.), for discovery of argon in investigating gas density
1905 Philipp Lenard (Germany), for work with cathode rays
1906 Sir Joseph Thomson (U.K.), for investigations on passage of electricity through gases
1907 Albert A. Michelson (U.S.), for spectroscopic and metrologic investigations
1908 Gabriel Lippmann (France), for method of reproducing colors by photography
1909 Guglielmo Marconi (Italy) and Ferdinand Braun (Germany), for development of wireless
1910 Johannes D. van der Waals (Netherlands), for work with the equation of state for gases and liquids
1911 Wilhelm Wien (Germany), for his laws governing the radiation of heat
1912 Gustaf Dalén (Sweden), for discovery of automatic regulators used in lighting lighthouses and light buoys
1913 Heike Kamerlingh-Onnes (Netherlands), for work leading to production of liquid helium
1914 Max von Laue (Germany), for discovery of diffraction of Roentgen rays passing through crystals
1915 Sir William Bragg and William L. Bragg (U.K.), for analysis of crystal structure by X-rays
1917 Charles G. Barkla (U.K.), for discovery of Roentgen radiation of the elements
1918 Max Planck (Germany), discoveries in connection with quantum theory
1919 Johannes Stark (Germany), discovery of Doppler effect in Canal rays and decomposition of spectrum lines by electric fields
1920 Charles E. Guillaume (Switzerland), for discoveries of anomalies in nickel-steel alloys
1921 Albert Einstein (Germany), for discovery of the law of the photoelectric effect

1922 Niels Bohr (Denmark), for investigation of structure of atoms and radiations emanating from them

1923 Robert A. Millikan (U.S.), for work on elementary charge of electricity and photoelectric phenomena

1924 Karl M. G. Siegbahn (Sweden), for investigations in X-ray spectroscopy

1925 James Franck and Gustav Hertz (Germany), for discovery of laws governing impact of electrons upon atoms

1926 Jean B. Perrin (France), for work on discontinuous structure of matter and discovery of the equilibrium of sedimentation

1927 Arthur H. Compton (U.S.), for discovery of Compton phenomenon; and Charles T. R. Wilson (U.K.), for method of perceiving paths taken by electrically charged particles

1928 In 1929, the 1928 prize was awarded to Sir Owen Richardson (U.K.), for work on the phenomenon of thermionics and discovery of the Richardson Law

1929 Prince Louis Victor de Broglie (France), for discovery of the wave character of electrons

1930 Sir Chandrasekhara Raman (India), for work on diffusion of light and discovery of the Raman effect

1932 In 1933, the prize for 1932 was awarded to Werner Heisenberg (Germany), for creation of the quantum mechanics

1933 Erwin Schrödinger (Austria) and Paul A. M. Dirac (U.K.), for discovery of new fertile forms of the atomic theory

1935 James Chadwick (U.K.), for discovery of the neutron

1936 Victor F. Hess (Austria), for discovery of cosmic radiation; and Carl D. Anderson (U.S.), for discovery of the positron

1937 Clinton J. Davisson (U.S.) and George P. Thomson (U.K.), for discovery of diffraction of electrons by crystals

1938 Enrico Fermi (Italy), for identification of new radioactivity elements and discovery of nuclear reactions effected by slow neutrons

1939 Ernest Orlando Lawrence (U.S.), for development of the cyclotron

1943 Otto Stern (U.S.), for detection of magnetic momentum of protons

1944 Isidor Isaac Rabi (U.S.), for work on magnetic movements of atomic particles

1945 Wolfgang Pauli (Austria), for work on atomic fissions

1946 Percy Williams Bridgman (U.S.), for studies and inventions in high-pressure physics

1947 Sir Edward Appleton (U.K.), for discovery of layer that reflects radio short waves in the ionosphere

1948 Patrick M. S. Blackett (U.K.), for improvement on Wilson chamber and discoveries in cosmic radiation

1949 Hideki Yukawa (Japan), for mathematical prediction, in 1935, of the meson

1950 Cecil Frank Powell (U.K.), for method of photographic study of atom nucleus, and for discoveries about mesons

1951 Sir John Douglas Cockcroft (U.K.) and Ernest T. S. Walton (Ireland), for work in 1932 on transmutation of atomic nuclei

1952 Edward Mills Purcell and Felix Bloch (U.S.), for work in measurement of magnetic fields in atomic nuclei

1953 Fritz Zernike (Netherlands), for development of "phase contrast" microscope

1954 Max Born (U.K.), for work in quantum mechanics; and Walther Bothe (Germany), for work in cosmic radiation

1955 Polykarp Kusch and Willis E. Lamb, Jr. (U.S.), for atomic measurements

1956 William Shockley, Walter H. Brattain, and John Bardeen (all U.S.), for developing electronic transistor

1957 Tsung Dao Lee and Chen Ning Yang (China), for disproving principle of conservation of parity

1958 Pavel A. Cherenkov, Ilya M. Frank, and Igor E. Tamm (all U.S.S.R.), for work resulting in development of cosmic-ray counter

1959 Emilio Segre and Owen Chamberlain (both U.S.), for demonstrating the existence of the anti-proton

1960 Donald A. Glaser (U.S.), for invention of "bubble chamber" to study subatomic particles

1961 Robert Hofstadter (U.S.), for determination of shape and size of atomic nucleus; Rudolf Mössbauer (Germany), for method of producing and measuring recoil-free gamma rays

1962 Lev D. Landau (U.S.S.R.), for his theories about condensed matter

1963 Eugene Paul Wigner, Maria Goeppert Mayer (both U.S.), and J. Hans D. Jensen (Germany), for research on structure of atom and its nucleus

1964 Charles Hard Townes (U.S.), Nikolai G. Basov, and Aleksandr M. Prochorov (both U.S.S.R.), for developing maser and laser principle of producing high-intensity radiation

1965 Richard P. Feynman, Julian S. Schwinger (both U.S.), and Shinichiro Tomonaga (Japan), for research in quantum electrodynamics

1966 Alfred Kastler (France), for work on energy levels inside atom

1967 Hans A. Bethe (U.S.), for work on energy production of stars

1968 Luis Walter Alvarez (U.S.), for study of subatomic particles

1969 Murray Gell-Mann (U.S.), for study of subatomic particles

1970 Hannes Alfvén (Sweden), for theories in plasma physics; and Louis Néel (France), for discoveries in antiferromagnetism and ferromagnetism

1971 Dennis Gabor (U.K.), for invention of holographic method of three-dimensional imagery

1972 John Bardeen, Leon N. Cooper, and John Robert Schrieffer (all U.S.), for theory of superconductivity, where electrical resistance in certain metals vanishes above absolute zero temperature

1973 Ivar Giaever (U.S.), Leo Esaki (Japan), and Brian D. Josephson (U.K.), for theories that have advanced and expanded the field of miniature electronics

1974 Antony Hewish (U.K.), for discovery of pulsars; Martin Ryle (U.K.), for using

radiotelescopes to probe outer space with high degree of precision

1975 James Rainwater (U.S.), Ben Mottelson, and Aage N. Bohr (both Denmark), for showing that the atomic nucleus is asymmetrical

1976 Burton Richter and Samuel C. C. Ting (both U.S.), for discovery of subatomic particles known as J and psi

1977 Philip W. Anderson, John H. Van Vleck (both U.S.), and Nevill F. Mott (U.K.), for work underlying computer memories and electronic devices

1978 Arno A. Penzias and Robert W. Wilson (both U.S.), for work in cosmic microwave radiation; Piotr L. Kapitsa (U.S.S.R.), for basic inventions and discoveries in low-temperature physics

1979 Steven Weinberg, Sheldon L. Glashow (both U.S.), and Abdus Salam (Pakistan), for developing theory that electromagnetism and the "weak" force, which causes radioactive decay in some atomic nuclei, are facets of the same phenomenon

1980 James W. Cronin and Val L. Fitch (both U.S.), for work concerning the asymmetry of subatomic particles

1981 Nicolaas Bloembergen, Arthur L. Schawlow (both U.S.), and Kai M. Siegbahn (Sweden), for developing technologies with lasers and other devices to probe the secrets of complex forms of matter

1982 Kenneth G. Wilson (U.S.), for analysis of changes in matter under pressure and temperature

1983 Subrahmanyam Chandrasekhar and William A. Fowler (both U.S.), for complementary research on processes involved in the evolution of stars

1984 Carlo Rubbia (Italy) and Simon van der Meer (Netherlands), for their role in discovering three subatomic particles, a step toward developing a single theory to account for all natural forces

1985 Klaus von Klitzing (Germany), for developing an exact way of measuring electrical conductivity

1986 Ernst Ruska, Gerd Binnig (both Germany), and Heinrich Rohrer (Switzerland), for work on microscopes

1987 K. Alex Müller (Switzerland) and J. Georg Bednorz (Germany), for their discovery of high-temperature superconductors

1988 Leon M. Lederman, Melvin Schwartz, and Jack Steinberger (all U.S.), for research that improved the understanding of elementary particles and forces

1989 Norman F. Ramsey (U.S.), for work leading to development of the atomic clock, and Hans G. Dehmelt (U.S.) and Wolfgang Paul (Germany), for developing methods to isolate atoms and subatomic particles

1990 Richard E. Taylor (Canada), Jerome I. Friedman, and Dr. Henry W. Kendall (both U.S.), for their "breakthrough in our understanding of matter" that confirmed the reality of quarks

1991 Pierre-Gilles de Gennes (France), for his discoveries about the ordering of molecules in substances ranging from "super" glue to an exotic form of liquid helium

1992 George Charpak (France), for his inventions of particle detectors

1993 Joseph H. Taylor and Russell A. Hulse (both U.S.), for their discovery of a binary pulsar

1994 Clifford G. Shull (U.S.) and Bertram N. Brockhouse (Canada), for adapting beams of neutrons as probes to explore the atomic structure of matter

1995 Martin L. Perl and Frederick Reines (both U.S.), for their discoveries of "two of nature's most remarkable subatomic particles"—the tau and the neutrino

1996 David M. Lee, Robert C. Richardson, and Douglas D. Osheroff (all U.S.), for their discovery of superfluity in helium-3

1997 Steven Chu, William D. Phillips (both U.S.), and Claude Cohen-Tannoudji (France), for developing a method to cool and trap atoms using light from lasers

CHEMISTRY

1901 Jacobus H. van't Hoff (Netherlands), for laws of chemical dynamics and osmotic pressure in solutions

1902 Emil Fischer (Germany), for experiments in sugar and purin groups of substances

1903 Svante A. Arrhenius (Sweden), for his electrolytic theory of dissociation

1904 Sir William Ramsay (U.K.), for discovery and determination of place of inert gaseous elements in air

1905 Adolf von Baeyer (Germany), for work on organic dyes and hydroaromatic combinations

1906 Henri Moissan (France), for isolation of fluorine, and introduction of electric furnace

1907 Eduard Buchner (Germany), discovery of cell-less fermentation and investigations in biological chemistry

1908 Sir Ernest Rutherford (U.K.), for investigations into disintegration of elements

1909 Wilhelm Ostwald (Germany), for work on catalysis and investigations into chemical equilibrium and reaction rates

1910 Otto Wallach (Germany), for work in the field of alicyclic compounds

1911 Marie Curie (France), for discovery of elements radium and polonium

1912 Victor Grignard (France), for reagent discovered by him; and Paul Sabatier (France), for methods of hydrogenating organic compounds

1913 Alfred Werner (Switzerland), for linking up atoms within the molecule

1914 Theodore W. Richards (U.S.), for determining atomic weight of many chemical elements

1915 Richard Willstätter (Germany), for research into coloring matter of plants, especially chlorophyll

1918 Fritz Haber (Germany), for synthetic production of ammonia

1920 Walther Nernst (Germany), for work in thermochemistry

1921 Frederick Soddy (U.K.), for investigations into origin and nature of isotopes

1922 Francis W. Aston (U.K.), for discovery of isotopes in nonradioactive elements and for discovery of the whole number rule

1923 Fritz Pregl (Austria), for method of microanalysis of organic substances discovered by him
1925 In 1926, the 1925 prize was awarded to Richard Zsigmondy (Germany), for work on the heterogeneous nature of colloid solutions
1926 Theodor Svedberg (Sweden), for work on disperse systems
1927 In 1928, the 1927 prize was awarded to Heinrich Wieland (Germany), for investigations of bile acids and kindred substances
1928 Adolf Windaus (Germany), for investigations on constitution of the sterols and their connection with vitamins
1929 Sir Arthur Harden (U.K.) and Hans K. A. S. von Euler-Chelpin (Sweden), for research of fermentation of sugars
1930 Hans Fischer (Germany), for work on coloring matter of blood and leaves and for his synthesis of hemin
1931 Karl Bosch and Friedrich Bergius (both Germany), for invention and development of chemical high-pressure methods
1932 Irving Langmuir (U.S.), for work in realm of surface chemistry
1934 Harold C. Urey (U.S.), for discovery of heavy hydrogen
1935 Frédéric and Irène Joliot-Curie (both France), for synthesis of new radioactive elements
1936 Peter J. W. Debye (Netherlands), for investigations on dipole moments and diffraction of X-rays and electrons in gases
1937 Walter N. Haworth (U.K.), for research on carbohydrates and vitamin C; and Paul Karrer (Switzerland), for work on carotenoids, flavins, and vitamins A and B
1938 Richard Kuhn (Germany), for carotenoid study and vitamin research (declined)
1939 Adolf Butenandt (Germany), for work on sexual hormones (declined the prize); and Leopold Ruzicka (Switzerland), for work with polymethylenes
1943 Georg Hevesy De Heves (Hungary), for work on use of isotopes as indicators
1944 Otto Hahn (Germany), for work on atomic fission
1945 Artturi Illmari Virtanen (Finland), for research in the field of conservation of fodder
1946 James B. Sumner (U.S.), for crystallizing enzymes; John H. Northrop and Wendell M. Stanley (both U.S.), for preparing enzymes and virus proteins in pure form
1947 Sir Robert Robinson (U.K.), for research in plant substances
1948 Arne Tiselius (Sweden), for biochemical discoveries and isolation of mouse paralysis virus
1949 William Francis Giauque (U.S.), for research in thermodynamics, especially effects of low temperature
1950 Otto Diels and Kurt Alder (both Germany), for discovery of diene synthesis enabling scientists to study structure of organic matter
1951 Glenn T. Seaborg and Edwin H. McMillan (both U.S.), for discovery of plutonium
1952 Archer John Porter Martin and Richard Laurence Millington Synge (both U.K.), for development of partition chromatography
1953 Hermann Staudinger (Germany), for research in giant molecules
1954 Linus C. Pauling (U.S.), for study of forces holding together protein and other molecules
1955 Vincent du Vigneaud (U.S.), for work on pituitary hormones
1956 Sir Cyril Hinshelwood (U.K.) and Nikolai N. Semenov (U.S.S.R.), for parallel research on chemical reaction kinetics
1957 Sir Alexander Todd (U.K.), for research with chemical compounds that are factors in heredity
1958 Frederick Sanger (U.K.), for determining molecular structure of insulin
1959 Jaroslav Heyrovsky (Czechoslovakia), for development of polarography, an electrochemical method of analysis
1960 Willard F. Libby (U.S.), for "atomic time clock" to measure age of objects by measuring their radioactivity
1961 Melvin Calvin (U.S.), for establishing chemical steps during photosynthesis
1962 Max F. Perutz and John C. Kendrew (U.K.), for mapping protein molecules with X-rays
1963 Carl Ziegler (Germany) and Giulio Natta (Italy), for work in uniting simple hydrocarbons into large molecule substances
1964 Dorothy Mary Crowfoot Hodgkin (U.K.), for determining structure of compounds needed in combatting pernicious anemia
1965 Robert B. Woodward (U.S.), for work in synthesizing complicated organic compounds
1966 Robert Sanderson Mulliken (U.S.), for research on bond holding atoms together in molecule
1967 Manfred Eigen (Germany), Ronald G. W. Norrish, and George Porter (both U.K.), for work in high-speed chemical reactions
1968 Lars Onsager (U.S.), for development of system of equations in thermodynamics
1969 Derek H. R. Barton (U.K.) and Odd Hassel (Norway), for study of organic molecules
1970 Luis F. Leloir (Argentina), for discovery of sugar nucleotides and their role in biosynthesis of carbohydrates
1971 Gerhard Herzberg (Canada), for contributions to knowledge of electronic structure and geometry of molecules, particularly free radicals
1972 Christian Boehmer Anfinsen, Stanford Moore, and William Howard Stein (all U.S.), for pioneering studies in enzymes
1973 Ernst Otto Fischer (W. Germany) and Geoffrey Wilkinson (U.K.), for work that could solve problem of automobile exhaust pollution
1974 Paul J. Flory (U.S.), for developing analytic methods to study properties and molecular structure of long-chain molecules
1975 John W. Cornforth (Australia) and Vladimir Prelog (Switzerland), for research on structure of biological molecules such as antibiotics and cholesterol
1976 William N. Lipscomb, Jr. (U.S.), for work on the structure and bonding mechanisms of boranes
1977 Ilya Prigogine (Belgium), for contributions to nonequilibrium thermodynamics, particularly the theory of dissipative structures
1978 Peter Mitchell (U.K.), for contributions to the understanding of biological energy transfer

1979 Herbert C. Brown (U.S.) and Georg Wittig (West Germany), for developing a group of substances that facilitate very difficult chemical reactions

1980 Paul Berg, Walter Gilbert (both U.S.), and Frederick Sanger (U.K.), for developing methods to map the structure and function of DNA, the substance that controls the activity of the cell

1981 Roald Hoffmann (U.S.) and Kenichi Fukui (Japan), for applying quantum-mechanics theories to predict the course of chemical reactions

1982 Aaron Klug (U.K.), for research in the detailed structures of viruses and components of life

1983 Henry Taube (U.S.), for research on how electrons transfer between molecules in chemical reactions

1984 R. Bruce Merrifield (U.S.), for research that revolutionized the study of proteins

1985 Herbert A. Hauptman and Jerome Karle (both U.S.), for their outstanding achievements in the development of direct methods for the determination of crystal structures

1986 Dudley R. Herschback, Yuan T. Lee (both U.S.), and John C. Polanyi (Canada), for their work on "reaction dynamics"

1987 Donald J. Cram, Charles J. Pederson (both U.S.), and Jean-Marie Lehn (France), for wide-ranging research that has included the creation of artificial molecules that can mimic vital chemical reactions of the processes of life

1988 Johann Deisenhofer, Robert Huber, and Hartmut Michel (all West Germany), for unraveling the structure of proteins that play a crucial role in photosynthesis

1989 Thomas R. Cech and Sidney Altman (both U.S.), for their discovery, independently, that RNA could actively aid chemical reactions in the cells

1990 Elias James Corey (U.S.), for developing new ways to synthesize complex molecules ordinarily found in nature

1991 Richard R. Ernst (Switzerland), for refinements he developed in nuclear magnetic-resonance spectroscopy

1992 Rudolph A. Marcus (U.S.), for his mathematical analysis of how the overall energy in a system of interacting molecules changes and induces an electron to jump from one molecule to another

1993 Kary B. Mullis (U.S.) and Michael Smith (Canada), for their contributions to the science of genetics

1994 George A. Olah (U.S.), University of Southern California in Los Angeles, for research that opened new ways to break apart and rebuild compounds of carbon and hydrogen

1995 F. Sherwood Rowland, Mario Molina (both U.S.), and Paul Crutzen (Netherlands), for their pioneering work in explaining the chemical processes that deplete the earth's ozone shield

1996 Richard E. Smalley, Robert F. Curl, Jr. (both U.S.), and Harold W. Kroto (U.K.), for discovery of a new class of carbon molecule

1997 Paul D. Boyer (U.S.), Jens C. Skou (Denmark), and John E. Walker (U.K.), for discoveries about a molecule that allows the human body to store and transfer energy between cells

PHYSIOLOGY OR MEDICINE

1901 Emil A. von Behring (Germany), for work on serum therapy against diphtheria

1902 Sir Ronald Ross (U.K.), for work on malaria

1903 Niels R. Finsen (Denmark), for his treatment of lupus vulgaris with concentrated light rays

1904 Ivan P. Pavlov (U.S.S.R.), for work on the physiology of digestion

1905 Robert Koch (Germany), for work on tuberculosis

1906 Camillo Golgi (Italy) and Santiago Ramón y Cajal (Spain), for work on structure of the nervous system

1907 Charles L. A. Laveran (France), for work with protozoa in the generation of disease

1908 Paul Ehrlich (Germany) and Elie Metchnikoff (U.S.S.R.), for work on immunity

1909 Theodor Kocher (Switzerland), for work on the thyroid gland

1910 Albrecht Kossel (Germany), for achievements in the chemistry of the cell

1911 Allvar Gullstrand (Sweden), for work on the dioptrics of the eye

1912 Alexis Carrel (France), for work on vascular ligature and grafting of blood vessels and organs

1913 Charles Richet (France), for work on anaphylaxy

1914 Robert Bárány (Austria), for work on physiology and pathology of the vestibular system

1919 Jules Bordet (Belgium), for discoveries in connection with immunity

1920 August Krogh (Denmark), for discovery of regulation of capillaries' motor mechanism

1922 In 1923, the 1922 prize was shared by Archibald V. Hill (U.K.), for discovery relating to heat-production in muscles; and Otto Meyerhof (Germany), for correlation between consumption of oxygen and production of lactic acid in muscles

1923 Sir Frederick Banting (Canada) and John J. R. Macleod (Scotland), for discovery of insulin

1924 Willem Einthoven (Netherlands), for discovery of the mechanism of the electrocardiogram

1926 Johannes Fibiger (Denmark), for discovery of the Spiroptera carcinoma

1927 Julius Wagner-Jauregg (Austria), for use of malaria inoculation in treatment of dementia paralytica

1928 Charles Nicolle (France), for work on typhus exanthematicus

1929 Christiaan Eijkman (Netherlands), for discovery of the antineuritic vitamins; and Sir Frederick Hopkins (U.K.), for discovery of growth-promoting vitamins

1930 Karl Landsteiner (U.S.), for discovery of human blood groups

1931 Otto H. Warburg (Germany), for discovery of the character and mode of action of the respiratory ferment

1932 Sir Charles Sherrington (U.K.) and Edgar D. Adrian (U.S.), for discoveries of the function of the neuron

1933 Thomas H. Morgan (U.S.), for discoveries on hereditary function of the chromosomes
1934 George H. Whipple, George R. Minot, and William P. Murphy (U.S.), for discovery of liver therapy against anemias
1935 Hans Spemann (Germany), for discovery of the organizer effect in embryonic development
1936 Sir Henry Dale (U.K.) and Otto Loewi (Germany), for discoveries on chemical transmission of nerve impulses
1937 Albert Szent-Györgyi von Nagyrapolt (Hungary), for discoveries on biological combustion
1938 Corneille Heymans (Belgium), for determining importance of sinus and aorta mechanisms in the regulation of respiration
1939 Gerhard Domagk (Germany), for antibacterial effect of prontocilate
1943 Henrik Dam (Denmark) and Edward A. Doisy (U.S.), for analysis of vitamin K
1944 Joseph Erlanger and Herbert Spencer Gasser (both U.S.), for work on functions of the nerve threads
1945 Sir Alexander Fleming, Ernst Boris Chain, and Sir Howard Florey (all U.K.), for discovery of penicillin
1946 Herman J. Muller (U.S.), for hereditary effects of X-rays on genes
1947 Carl F. and Gerty T. Cori (U.S.), for work on animal starch metabolism; Bernardo A. Houssay (Argentina), for study of pituitary
1948 Paul Mueller (Switzerland), for discovery of insect-killing properties of DDT
1949 Walter Rudolf Hess (Switzerland), for research on brain control of body; and Antonio Caetano de Abreu Freire Egas Moniz (Portugal), for development of brain operation
1950 Philip S. Hench, Edward C. Kendall (both U.S.), and Tadeus Reichstein (Switzerland), for discoveries about hormones of adrenal cortex
1951 Max Theiler (South Africa), for development of anti-yellow-fever vaccine
1952 Selman A. Waksman (U.S.), for co-discovery of streptomycin
1953 Fritz A. Lipmann (Germany-U.S.) and Hans Adolph Krebs (Germany-U.K.), for studies of living cells
1954 John F. Enders, Thomas H. Weller, and Frederick C. Robbins (all U.S.), for work with cultivation of polio virus
1955 Hugo Theorell (Sweden), for work on oxidation enzymes
1956 Dickinson W. Richards, Jr., André F. Cournand (both U.S.), and Werner Forssmann (Germany), for new techniques in treating heart disease
1957 Daniel Bovet (Italy), for development of drugs to relieve allergies and relax muscles during surgery
1958 Joshua Lederberg (U.S.), for work with genetic mechanisms; George W. Beadie and Edward L. Tatum (both U.S.), for discovering how genes transmit hereditary characteristics
1959 Severo Ochoa and Arthur Kornberg (both U.S.), for discoveries related to compounds within chromosomes that play a vital role in heredity
1960 Sir Macfarlane Burnet (Australia) and Peter Brian Medawar (U.K.), for discovery of acquired immunological tolerance
1961 Georg von Bekesy (U.S.), for discoveries about physical mechanisms of stimulation within cochlea
1962 James D. Watson (U.S.), Maurice H. F. Wilkins, and Francis H. C. Crick (both U.K.), for determining structure of deoxyribonucleic acid (DNA)
1963 Alan Lloyd Hodgkin, Andrew Fielding Huxley (both U.K.), and Sir John Carew Eccles (Australia), for research on nerve cells
1964 Konrad E. Bloch (U.S.) and Feodor Lynen (Germany), for research on mechanism and regulation of cholesterol and fatty-acid metabolism
1965 François Jacob, André Lwolff, and Jacques Monod (all France), for study of regulatory activities in body cells
1966 Charles Brenton Huggins (U.S.), for studies in hormone treatment of cancer of prostate; Francis Peyton Rous (U.S.), for discovery of tumor-producing viruses
1967 Haldan K. Hartline, George Wald, and Ragnar Granit (all U.S.), for work on human eye
1968 Robert W. Holley, Har Gobind Khorana, and Marshall W. Nirenberg (all U.S.), for studies of genetic code
1969 Max Delbruck, Alfred D. Hershey, and Salvador E. Luria (all U.S.), for study of mechanism of virus infection in living cells
1970 Julius Axelrod (U.S.), Ulf S. von Euler (Sweden), and Sir Bernard Katz (U.K.), for studies of how nerve impulses are transmitted within the body
1971 Earl W. Sutherland, Jr. (U.S.), for research on how hormones work
1972 Gerald M. Edelman (U.S.), and Rodney R. Porter (U.K.), for research on the chemical structure and nature of antibodies
1973 Karl von Frisch, Konrad Lorenz (both Austria), and Nikolaas Tinbergen (Netherlands), for their studies of individual and social behavior patterns
1974 George E. Palade, Christian de Duve (both U.S.), and Albert Claude (Belgium), for contributions to understanding inner workings of living cells
1975 David Baltimore, Howard M. Temin, and Renato Dulbecco (all U.S.), for work in interaction between tumor viruses and genetic material of the cell
1976 Baruch S. Blumberg and D. Carleton Gajdusek (both U.S.), for discoveries concerning new mechanisms for the origin and dissemination of infectious diseases
1977 Rosalyn S. Yalow, Roger C. L. Guillemin, and Andrew V. Schally (all U.S.), for research in role of hormones in chemistry of the body
1978 Daniel Nathans, Hamilton Smith (both U.S.), and Werner Arber (Switzerland), for discovery of restriction enzymes and their application to problems of molecular genetics
1979 Allan McLeod Cormack (U.S.) and Godfrey Newbold Hounsfield (U.K.), for developing computed axial tomography (CAT scan) X-ray technique

1980 Baruj Benacerraf, George D. Snell (both U.S.), and Jean Dausset (France), for discoveries that explain how the structure of cells relates to organ transplants and diseases

1981 Roger W. Sperry, David H. Hubel (both U.S.), and Torsten N. Wiesel (Sweden), for studies vital to understanding the organization and functioning of the brain

1982 Sune Bergstrom, Bengt Samuelsson (both Sweden), and John R. Vane (U.K.), for research in prostaglandins, hormonelike substances involved in a wide range of illnesses

1983 Barbara McClintock (U.S.), for her discovery of mobile genes in the chromosomes of a plant that change the future generations of plants they produce

1984 Cesar Milstein (U.K./Argentina), Georges J. F. Kohler (West Germany), and Niels K. Jerne (U.K./Denmark), for their work in immunology

1985 Michael S. Brown and Joseph L. Goldstein (both U.S.), for their work, which has drastically widened our understanding of the cholesterol metabolism and increased our possibilities to prevent and treat atherosclerosis and heart attacks

1986 Rita Levi-Montalcini (dual U.S./Italy) and Stanley Cohen (U.S.), for their contributions to the understanding of substances that influence cell growth

1987 Susumu Tonegawa (Japan), for his discoveries of how the body can suddenly marshal its immunological defenses against millions of different disease agents that it has never encountered before

1988 Gertrude B. Elion, George H. Hitchings (both U.S.), and Sir James Black (U.K.), for their discoveries of important principles for drug treatment

1989 J. Michael Bishop and Harold E. Varmus (both U.S.), for their unifying theory of cancer development

1990 Joseph E. Murray and E. Donnall Thomas (both U.S.), for their pioneering work in transplants

1991 Erwin Neher and Bert Sakmann (both Germany), for their research, particularly for the development of a technique called patch clamp

1992 Edmond H. Fischer and Edwin G. Krebs (both U.S.), for their discovery of a regulatory mechanism affecting almost all cells

1993 Phillip A. Sharp (U.S.) and Richard J. Roberts (U.K.), for their independent discovery in 1977 of "split genes"

1994 Alfred G. Gilman and Martin Rodbell (both U.S.), for discovery of G-proteins that help cells respond to outside signals

1995 Edward B. Lewis, Eric F. Wieschaus (both U.S.), and Christiane Nüsslein-Volhard (Germany), for studies of the fruit fly that will help explain congenital malformations in humans

1996 Peter C. Doherty (Australia) and Rolf M. Zinkernagel (Switzerland), for discoveries about how the immune system recognizes virus-infected cells

1997 Stanley B. Prusiner (U.S.), for discovery of a new type of germ, called prions, that causes degenerative brain disorders

ECONOMIC SCIENCE

1969 Ragnar Frisch (Norway) and Jan Tinbergen (Netherlands), for work in econometrics (application of mathematics and statistical methods to economic theories and problems)

1970 Paul A. Samuelson (U.S.), for efforts to raise the level of scientific analysis in economic theory

1971 Simon Kuznets (U.S.), for developing concept of using a country's gross national product to determine its economic growth

1972 Kenneth J. Arrow (U.S.) and Sir John R. Hicks (U.K.), for theories that help to assess business risk and government economic and welfare policies

1973 Wassily Leontief (U.S.), for devising the input-output technique to determine how different sectors of an economy interact

1974 Gunnar Myrdal (Sweden) and Friedrich A. von Hayek (U.K.), for pioneering analysis of the interdependence of economic, social, and institutional phenomena

1975 Leonid V. Kantorovich (U.S.S.R.) and Tjalling C. Koopmans (U.S.), for work on the theory of optimum allocation of resources

1976 Milton Friedman (U.S.), for work in consumption analysis and monetary history and theory, and for demonstration of complexity of stabilization policy

1977 Bertil Ohlin (Sweden) and James E. Meade (U.K.), for contributions to theory of international trade and international capital movements

1978 Herbert A. Simon (U.S.), for research into the decision-making process within economic organizations

1979 Sir Arthur Lewis (U.K.) and Theodore Schultz (U.S.), for work on economic problems of developing nations

1980 Lawrence R. Klein (U.S.), for developing models for forecasting economic trends and shaping policies to deal with them

1981 James Tobin (U.S.), for analyses of financial markets and their influence on spending and saving by families and businesses

1982 George J. Stigler (U.S.), for work on government regulation in the economy and the functioning of industry

1983 Gerard Debreu (U.S.), in recognition of his work on the basic economic problem of how prices operate to balance what producers supply with what buyers want

1984 Sir Richard Stone (U.K.), for his work to develop the systems widely used to measure the performance of national economics

1985 Franco Modigliani (U.S.), for his pioneering work in analyzing the behavior of household savers and the functioning of financial markets

1986 James M. Buchanan (U.S.), for his development of new methods for analyzing economic and political decision-making

1987 Robert M. Solow (U.S.), for seminal contributions to the theory of economic growth

1988 Maurice Allais (France), for his pioneering development of theories to better understand market behavior and the efficient use of resources

1989 Trygve Haavelmo (Norway), for his pioneering work in methods for testing economic theories

1990 Harry M. Markowitz, William F. Sharpe, and Merton H. Miller (all U.S.), whose work provided new tools for weighing the risks and rewards of different investments and for valuing corporate stocks and bonds

1991 Ronald Coase (U.S.), for his pioneering work in how property rights and the cost of doing business affect the economy

1992 Gary S. Becker (U.S.), for "having extended the domain of economic theory to aspects of human behavior which had previously been dealt with—if at all—by other social science disciplines"

1993 Robert W. Fogel and Douglass C. North (both U.S.), for their work in economic history

1994 John F. Nash, John C. Harsanyi (both U.S.), and Reinhard Selten (Germany), for their pioneering work in game theory

1995 Robert E. Lucas, Jr. (U.S.), for having had the greatest influence on macroeconomic research since 1970

1996 James A. Mirrlees (U.K.) and William Vickrey (U.S.), for "their fundamental contributions to the economic theory of incentives"

1997 Robert C. Merton and Myron S. Scholes (both U.S.), for developing a formula that determines the value of stock options and other derivatives

Motion Picture Academy Awards (Oscars)

1928

Picture: *Wings,* Paramount
Director: Frank Borzage, *Seventh Heaven;* Lewis Milestone, *Two Arabian Nights*
Actress: Janet Gaynor, *Seventh Heaven, Street Angel, Sunrise*
Actor: Emil Jannings, *The Way of All Flesh, The Last Command*

1929

Picture: *The Broadway Melody,* MGM
Director: Frank Lloyd, *The Divine Lady*
Actress: Mary Pickford, *Coquette*
Actor: Warner Baxter, *In Old Arizona*

1930

Picture: *All Quiet on the Western Front,* Universal
Director: Lewis Milestone, *All Quiet on the Western Front*
Actress: Norma Shearer, *The Divorcee*
Actor: George Arliss, *Disraeli*

1931

Picture: *Cimarron,* RKO Radio
Director: Norman Taurog, *Skippy*
Actress: Marie Dressler, *Min and Bill*
Actor: Lionel Barrymore, *A Free Soul*

1932

Picture: *Grand Hotel,* MGM
Director: Frank Borzage, *Bad Girl*
Actress: Helen Hayes, *The Sin of Madelon Claudet*
Actor: Fredric March, *Dr. Jekyll and Mr, Hyde,* and Wallace Beery, *The Champ*

1933

Picture: *Cavalcade,* Fox
Director: Frank Lloyd, *Cavalcade*
Actress: Katharine Hepburn, *Morning Glory*
Actor: Charles Laughton, *The Private Life of Henry VIII*

1934

Picture: *It Happened One Night,* Columbia
Director: Frank Capra, *It Happened One Night*
Actress: Claudette Colbert, *It Happened One Night*
Actor: Clark Gable, *It Happened One Night*

1935

Picture: *Mutiny on the Bounty,* MGM
Director: John Ford, *The Informer*
Actress: Bette Davis, *Dangerous*
Actor: Victor McLaglen, *The Informer*

1936

Picture: *The Great Ziegfeld,* MGM
Director: Frank Capra, *Mr. Deeds Goes to Town*
Actress: Luise Rainer, *The Great Ziegfeld*
Actor: Paul Muni, *The Story of Louis Pasteur*
Supporting Actress: Gale Sondergaard, *Anthony Adverse*
Supporting Actor: Walter Brennan, *Come and Get It*

1937

Picture: *The Life of Emile Zola,* Warner Bros.
Director: Leo McCarey, *The Awful Truth*
Actress: Luise Rainer, *The Good Earth*
Actor: Spencer Tracy, *Captains Courageous*
Supporting Actress: Alice Brady, *In Old Chicago*
Supporting Actor: Joseph Schildkraut, *The Life of Emile Zola*

1938

Picture: *You Can't Take It with You,* Columbia
Director: Frank Capra, *You Can't Take It with You*
Actress: Bette Davis, *Jezebel*
Actor: Spencer Tracy, *Boys Town*
Supporting Actress: Fay Balnter, *Jezebel*
Supporting Actor: Walter Brennan, *Kentucky*

1939

Picture: *Gone with the Wind,* Selznick MGM
Director: Victor Fleming, *Gone with the Wind*
Actress: Vivien Leigh, *Gone with the Wind*
Actor: Robert Donat, *Goodbye, Mr. Chips*
Supporting Actress: Hattie McDaniel, *Gone with the Wind*
Supporting Actor: Thomas Mitchell, *Stagecoach*

1940

Picture: *Rebecca*, Selznick–United Artists
Director: John Ford, *The Grapes of Wrath*
Actress: Ginger Rogers, *Kitty Foyle*
Actor: James Stewart, *The Philadelphia Story*
Supporting Actress: Jane Darwell, *The Grapes of Wrath*
Supporting Actor: Walter Brennan, *The Westerner*

1941

Picture: *How Green Was My Valley,* 20th Century–Fox
Director: John Ford, *How Green Was My Valley*
Actress: Joan Fontaine, *Suspicion*
Actor: Gary Cooper, *Sergeant York*
Supporting Actress: Mary Astor, *The Great Lie*
Supporting Actor: Donald Crisp, *How Green Was My Valley*

1942

Picture: *Mrs. Miniver,* MGM
Director: William Wyler, *Mrs. Miniver*
Actress: Greer Garson, *Mrs. Miniver*
Actor: James Cagney, *Yankee Doodle Dandy*
Supporting Actress: Teresa Wright, *Mrs. Miniver*
Supporting Actor: Van Heflin, *Johnny Eager*

1943

Picture: *Casablanca,* Warner Bros.
Director: Michael Curtiz, *Casablanca*

Actress: Jennifer Jones, *The Song of Bernadette*
Actor: Paul Lukas, *Watch on the Rhine*
Supporting Actress: Katina Paxinou, *For Whom the Bell Tolls*
Supporting Actor: Charles Coburn, *The More the Merrier*

1944

Picture: *Going My Way,* Paramount
Director: Leo McCarey, *Going My Way*
Actress: Ingrid Bergman, *Gaslight*
Actor: Bing Crosby, *Going My Way*
Supporting Actress: Ethel Barrymore, *None But the Lonely Heart*
Supporting Actor: Barry Fitzgerald, *Going My Way*

1945

Picture: *The Lost Weekend,* Paramount
Director: Billy Wilder, *The Lost Weekend*
Actress: Joan Crawford, *Mildred Pierce*
Actor: Ray Milland, *The Lost Weekend*
Supporting Actress: Anne Revere, *National Velvet*
Supporting Actor: James Dunn, *A Tree Grows in Brooklyn*

1946

Picture: *The Best Years of Our Lives,* Goldwyn–RKO Radio
Director: William Wyler, *The Best Years of Our Lives*
Actress: Olivia de Havilland, *To Each His Own*
Actor: Fredric March, *The Best Years of Our Lives*
Supporting Actress: Anne Baxter, *The Razor's Edge*
Supporting Actor: Harold Russell, *The Best Years of Our Lives*

1947

Picture: *Gentleman's Agreement,* 20th Century–Fox
Director: Elia Kazan, *Gentleman's Agreement*
Actress: Loretta Young, *The Farmer's Daughter*
Actor: Ronald Colman, *A Double Life*
Supporting Actress: Celeste Holm, *Gentleman's Agreement*
Supporting Actor: Edmund Gwenn, *Miracle on 34th Street*

1948

Picture: *Hamlet,* Rank–Two Cities–UI
Director: John Huston, *Treasure of Sierra Madre*
Actress: Jane Wyman, *Johnny Belinda*
Actor: Laurence Olivier, *Hamlet*
Supporting Actress: Claire Trevor, *Key Largo*
Supporting Actor: Walter Huston, *Treasure of Sierra Madre*

1949

Picture: *All the King's Men,* Rossen–Columbia
Director: Joseph L. Mankiewicz, *A Letter to Three Wives*
Actress: Olivia de Havilland, *The Heiress*
Actor: Broderick Crawford, *All the King's Men*
Supporting Actress: Mercedes McCambridge, *All the King's Men*
Supporting Actor: Dean Jagger, *Twelve O'Clock High*

1950

Picture: *All About Eve,* 20th Century–Fox
Director: Joseph L. Mankiewicz, *All About Eve*
Actress: Judy Holliday, *Born Yesterday*
Actor: José Ferrer, *Cyrano de Bergerac*
Supporting Actress: Josephine Hull, *Harvey*
Supporting Actor: George Sanders, *All About Eve*

1951

Picture: *An American in Paris,* MGM
Director: George Stevens, *A Place in the Sun*
Actress: Vivien Leigh, *A Streetcar Named Desire*
Actor: Humphrey Bogart, *The African Queen*
Supporting Actress: Kim Hunter, *A Streetcar Named Desire*
Supporting Actor: Karl Malden, *A Streetcar Named Desire*

1952

Picture: *The Greatest Show on Earth,* DeMille–Paramount
Director: John Ford, *The Quiet Man*
Actress: Shirley Booth, *Come Back, Little Sheba*
Actor: Gary Cooper, *High Noon*
Supporting Actress: Gloria Grahame, *The Bad and the Beautiful*
Supporting Actor: Anthony Quinn, *Viva Zapata!*

1953

Picture: *From Here to Eternity,* Columbia
Director: Fred Zinnemann, *From Here to Eternity*
Actress: Audrey Hepburn, *Roman Holiday*
Actor: William Holden, *Stalag 17*
Supporting Actress: Donna Reed, *From Here to Eternity*
Supporting Actor: Frank Sinatra, *From Here to Eternity*

1954

Picture: *On the Waterfront,* Horizon–American Corp., Columbia
Director: Elia Kazan, *On the Waterfront*
Actress: Grace Kelly, *The Country Girl*
Actor: Marlon Brando, *On the Waterfront*
Supporting Actress: Eva Marie Saint, *On the Waterfront*
Supporting Actor: Edmond O'Brien, *The Barefoot Contessa*

1955

Picture: *Marty,* Hecht and Lancaster, United Artists
Director: Delbert Mann, *Marty*
Actress: Anna Magnani, *The Rose Tattoo*
Actor: Ernest Borgnine, *Marty*
Supporting Actress: Jo Van Fleet, *East of Eden*
Supporting Actor: Jack Lemmon, *Mister Roberts*

1956

Picture: *Around the World in 80 Days,* Michael Todd Co., Inc.–United Artists
Director: George Stevens, *Giant*
Actress: Ingrid Bergman, *Anastasia*
Actor: Yul Brynner, *The King and I*
Supporting Actress: Dorothy Malone, *Written on the Wind*
Supporting Actor: Anthony Quinn, *Lust for Life*

1957

Picture: *The Bridge on the River Kwai,* Horizon Films, Columbia
Director: David Lean, *The Bridge on the River Kwai*
Actress: Joanne Woodward, *The Three Faces of Eve*
Actor: Alec Guinness, *The Bridge on the River Kwai*
Supporting Actress: Miyoshi Umeki, *Sayonara*
Supporting Actor: Red Buttons, *Sayonara*

1958

Picture: *Gigi,* Arthur Freed Productions, Inc., MGM
Director: Vincente Minnelli, *Gigi*
Actress: Susan Hayward, *I Want to Live!*
Actor: David Niven, *Separate Tables*
Supporting Actress: Wendy Hiller, *Separate Tables*
Supporting Actor: Burl Ives, *The Big Country*

1959

Picture: *Ben-Hur,* MGM
Director: William Wyler, *Ben-Hur*
Actress: Simone Signoret, *Room at the Top*
Actor: Charlton Heston, *Ben-Hur*
Supporting Actress: Shelley Winters, *The Diary of Anne Frank*
Supporting Actor: Hugh Griffith, *Ben-Hur*

1960

Picture: *The Apartment,* Mirisch Co., Inc., United Artists
Director: Billy Wilder, *The Apartment*
Actress: Elizabeth Taylor, *Butterfield 8*
Actor: Burt Lancaster, *Elmer Gantry*
Supporting Actress: Shirley Jones, *Elmer Gantry*
Supporting Actor: Peter Ustinov, *Spartacus*

1961

Picture: *West Side Story,* Mirisch Pictures, Inc., and B and P Enterprises, Inc., United Artists
Director: Robert Wise and Jerome Robbins, *West Side Story*
Actress: Sophia Loren, *Two Women*
Actor: Maximillian Schell, *Judgment at Nuremberg*

Supporting Actress: Rita Moreno, *West Side Story*
Supporting Actor: George Chakiris, *West Side Story*

1962

Picture: *Lawrence of Arabia,* Horizon Pictures, Ltd.–Columbia
Director: David Lean, *Lawrence of Arabia*
Actress: Anne Bancroft, *The Miracle Worker*
Actor: Gregory Peck, *To Kill a Mockingbird*
Supporting Actress: Patty Duke, *The Miracle Worker*
Supporting Actor: Ed Begley, *Sweet Bird of Youth*

1963

Picture: *Tom Jones,* A Woodfall Production, United Artists–Lopert Pictures
Director: Tony Richardson, *Tom Jones*
Actress: Patricia Neal, *Hud*
Actor: Sidney Poitier, *Lilies of the Field*
Supporting Actress: Margaret Rutherford, *The V.I.P.s*
Supporting Actor: Melvyn Douglas, *Hud*

1964

Picture: *My Fair Lady,* Warner Bros.
Director: George Cukor, *My Fair Lady*
Actress: Julie Andrews, *Mary Poppins*
Actor: Rex Harrison, *My Fair Lady*
Supporting Actress: Lila Kedrova, *Zorba the Greek*
Supporting Actor: Peter Ustinov, *Topkapi*

1965

Picture: *The Sound of Music,* Argyle Enterprises Production, 20th Century–Fox
Director: Robert Wise, *The Sound of Music*
Actress: Julie Christie, *Darling*
Actor: Lee Marvin, *Cat Ballou*
Supporting Actress: Shelley Winters, *A Patch of Blue*
Supporting Actor: Martin Balsam, *A Thousand Clowns*

1966

Picture: *A Man for All Seasons,* Highland Films, Ltd., Production, Columbia
Director: Fred Zinnemann, *A Man for All Seasons*
Actress: Elizabeth Taylor, *Who's Afraid of Virginia Woolf?*
Actor: Paul Scofield, *A Man for All Seasons*
Supporting Actress: Sandy Dennis, *Who's Afraid of Virginia Woolf?*
Supporting Actor: Walter Matthau, *The Fortune Cookie*

1967

Picture: *In the Heat of the Night,* Mirisch Corp. Productions, United Artists
Director: Mike Nichols, *The Graduate*
Actress: Katharine Hepburn, *Guess Who's Coming to Dinner*
Actor: Rod Steiger, *In the Heat of the Night*
Supporting Actress: Estelle Parsons, *Bonnie and Clyde*
Supporting Actor: George Kennedy, *Cool Hand Luke*

1968

Picture: *Oliver!,* Columbia Pictures
Director: Sir Carol Reed, *Oliver!*
Actress: Katharine Hepburn, *The Lion in Winter* and Barbra Streisand, *Funny Girl*
Actor: Cliff Robertson, *Charly*
Supporting Actress: Ruth Gordon, *Rosemary's Baby*
Supporting Actor: Jack Albertson, *The Subject Was Roses*

1969

Picture: *Midnight Cowboy,* Jerome Hellman–John Schlesinger Production, United Artists
Director: John Schlesinger, *Midnight Cowboy*
Actress: Maggie Smith, *The Prime of Miss Jean Brodie*
Actor: John Wayne, *True Grit*
Supporting Actress: Goldie Hawn, *Cactus Flower*
Supporting Actor: Gig Young, *They Shoot Horses, Don't They?*

1970

Picture: *Patton,* Frank McCarthy–Franklin J. Schaffner Production, 20th Century–Fox
Director: Franklin J. Schaffner, *Patton*
Actress: Glenda Jackson, *Women in Love*
Actor: George C. Scott, *Patton*
Supporting Actress: Helen Hayes, *Airport*
Supporting Actor: John Mills, *Ryan's Daughter*

1971

Picture: *The French Connection,* D'Antoni Productions, 20th Century–Fox
Director: William Friedkin, *The French Connection*
Actress: Jane Fonda, *Klute*
Actor: Gene Hackman, *The French Connection*
Supporting Actress: Cloris Leachman, *The Last Picture Show*
Supporting Actor: Ben Johnson, *The Last Picture Show*

1972

Picture: *The Godfather,* Albert S. Ruddy Production, Paramount
Director: Bob Fosse, *Cabaret*
Actress: Liza Minnelli, *Cabaret*
Actor: Marlon Brando, *The Godfather*
Supporting Actress: Eileen Heckart, *Butterflies Are Free*
Supporting Actor: Joel Gray, *Cabaret*

1973

Picture: *The Sting,* Universal–Bill/Phillips–George Roy Hill Production, Universal
Director: George Roy Hill, *The Sting*
Actress: Glenda Jackson, *A Touch of Class*
Actor: Jack Lemmon, *Save the Tiger*
Supporting Actress: Tatum O'Neal, *Paper Moon*
Supporting Actor: John Houseman, *The Paper Chase*

1974

Picture: *The Godfather, Part II,* Coppola Co. Production, Paramount
Director: Francis Ford Coppola, *The Godfather, Part II*
Actress: Ellen Burstyn, *Alice Doesn't Live Here Anymore*
Actor: Art Carney, *Harry and Tonto*
Supporting Actress: Ingrid Bergman, *Murder on the Orient Express*
Supporting Actor: Robert De Niro, *The Godfather, Part II*

1975

Picture: *One Flew Over the Cuckoo's Nest,* Fantasy Films Production, United Artists
Director: Milos Forman, *One Flew Over the Cuckoo's Nest*
Actress: Louise Fletcher, *One Flew Over the Cuckoo's Nest*
Actor: Jack Nicholson, *One Flew Over the Cuckoo's Nest*
Supporting Actress: Lee Grant, *Shampoo*
Supporting Actor: George Burns, *The Sunshine Boys*

1976

Picture: *Rocky,* Robert Chartoff–Irwin Winkler Production, United Artists
Director: John G. Avildsen, *Rocky*
Actress: Faye Dunaway, *Network*
Actor: Peter Finch, *Network*
Supporting Actress: Beatrice Straight, *Network*
Supporting Actor: Jason Robards, *All the President's Men*

1977

Picture: *Annie Hall,* Jack Rollins–Charles H. Joffe Production, United Artists
Director: Woody Allen, *Annie Hall*
Actress: Diane Keaton, *Annie Hall*
Actor: Richard Dreyfuss, *The Goodbye Girl*
Supporting Actress: Vanessa Redgrave, *Julia*
Supporting Actor: Jason Robards, *Julia*

1978

Picture: *The Deer Hunter,* Michael Cimino Film Production, Universal
Director: Michael Cimino, *The Deer Hunter*
Actress: Jane Fonda, *Coming Home*
Actor: Jon Voight, *Coming Home*
Supporting Actress: Maggie Smith, *California Suite*
Supporting Actor: Christopher Walken, *The Deer Hunter*

1979

Picture: *Kramer vs. Kramer,* Stanley Jaffe Production, Columbia Pictures
Director: Robert Benton, *Kramer vs. Kramer*
Actress: Sally Field, *Norma Rae*
Actor: Dustin Hoffman, *Kramer vs. Kramer*
Supporting Actress: Meryl Streep, *Kramer vs. Kramer*
Supporting Actor: Melvyn Douglas, *Being There*

1980

Picture: *Ordinary People,* Wildwood Enterprises Production, Paramount
Director: Robert Redford, *Ordinary People*
Actress: Sissy Spacek, *Coal Miner's Daughter*
Actor: Robert De Niro, *Raging Bull*
Supporting Actress: Mary Steenburgen, *Melvin and Howard*
Supporting Actor: Timothy Hutton, *Ordinary People*

1981

Picture: *Chariots of Fire,* Enigma Productions, Ladd Company/Warner Bros.
Director: Warren Beatty, *Reds*
Actress: Katharine Hepburn, *On Golden Pond*
Actor: Henry Fonda, *On Golden Pond*
Supporting Actress: Maureen Stapleton, *Reds*
Supporting Actor: John Gielgud, *Arthur*

1982

Picture: *Gandhi,* Indo-British Films Production/Columbia
Director: Richard Attenborough, *Gandhi*
Actress: Meryl Streep, *Sophie's Choice*
Actor: Ben Kingsley, *Gandhi*
Supporting Actress: Jessica Lange, *Tootsie*
Supporting Actor: Louis Gossett, Jr., *An Officer and a Gentleman*

1983

Picture: *Terms of Endearment,* Paramount
Director: James L. Brooks, *Terms of Endearment*
Actress: Shirley MacLaine, *Terms of Endearment*
Actor: Robert Duvall, *Tender Mercies*
Supporting Actress: Linda Hunt, *The Year of Living Dangerously*
Supporting Actor: Jack Nicholson, *Terms of Endearment*

1984

Picture: *Amadeus,* Orion Pictures
Director: Milos Forman, *Amadeus*
Actress: Sally Field, *Places in the Heart*
Actor: F. Murray Abraham, *Amadeus*
Supporting Actress: Dame Peggy Ashcroft, *A Passage to India*
Supporting Actor: Haing S. Ngor, *The Killing Fields*

1985

Picture: *Out of Africa,* Universal
Director: Sydney Pollack, *Out of Africa*
Actress: Geraldine Page, *The Trip to Bountiful*
Actor: William Hurt, *Kiss of the Spider Woman*
Supporting Actress: Anjelica Huston, *Prizzi's Honor*
Supporting Actor: Don Ameche, *Cocoon*

1986

Picture: *Platoon,* Orion Pictures
Director: Oliver Stone, *Platoon*
Actress: Marlee Matlin, *Children of a Lesser God*
Actor: Paul Newman, *The Color of Money*
Supporting Actress: Dianne Wiest, *Hannah and Her Sisters*
Supporting Actor: Michael Caine, *Hannah and Her Sisters*

1987

Picture: *The Last Emperor,* Columbia Pictures
Director: Bernardo Bertolucci, *The Last Emperor*
Actress: Cher, *Moonstruck*
Actor: Michael Douglas, *Wall Street*
Supporting Actress: Olympia Dukakis, *Moonstruck*
Supporting Actor: Sean Connery, *The Untouchables*

1988

Picture: *Rain Man,* United Artists
Director: Barry Levinson, *Rain Man*
Actress: Jodie Foster, *The Accused*
Actor: Dustin Hoffman, *Rain Man*
Supporting Actress: Geena Davis, *The Accidental Tourist*
Supporting Actor: Kevin Kline, *A Fish Called Wanda*

1989

Picture: *Driving Miss Daisy,* Warner Brothers
Director: Oliver Stone, *Born on the Fourth of July*
Actress: Jessica Tandy, *Driving Miss Daisy*
Actor: Daniel Day-Lewis, *My Left Foot*
Supporting Actress: Brenda Fricker, *My Left Foot*
Supporting Actor: Denzel Washington, *Glory*

1990

Picture: *Dances With Wolves,* Orion
Director: Kevin Costner, *Dances With Wolves*
Actress: Kathy Bates, *Misery*
Actor: Jeremy Irons, *Reversal of Fortune*
Supporting Actress: Whoopi Goldberg, *Ghost*
Supporting Actor: Joe Pesci, *Goodfellas*

1991

Picture: *The Silence of the Lambs,* Orion
Director: Jonathan Demme, *The Silence of the Lambs*
Actress: Jodie Foster, *The Silence of the Lambs*
Actor: Anthony Hopkins, *The Silence of the Lambs*
Supporting Actress: Mercedes Ruehl, *The Fisher King*
Supporting Actor: Jack Palance, *City Slickers*

1992

Picture: *Unforgiven,* Warner Brothers
Director: Clint Eastwood, *Unforgiven*
Actress: Emma Thompson, *Howards End*
Actor: Al Pacino, *Scent of a Woman*
Supporting Actress: Marisa Tomei, *My Cousin Vinny*
Supporting Actor: Gene Hackman, *Unforgiven*

1993

Picture: *Schindler's List,* Universal
Director: Steven Spielberg, *Schindler's List*
Actress: Holly Hunter, *The Piano*
Actor: Tom Hanks, *Philadelphia*
Supporting Actress: Anna Paquin, *The Piano*
Supporting Actor: Tommy Lee Jones, *The Fugitive*

1994

Picture: *Forrest Gump,* Paramount
Director: Robert Zemeckis, *Forrest Gump*
Actress: Jessica Lange, *Blue Sky*
Actor: Tom Hanks, *Forrest Gump*
Supporting Actress: Dianne Wiest, *Bullets Over Broadway*
Supporting Actor: Martin Landau, *Ed Wood*

1995

Picture: *Braveheart,* Paramount
Director: Mel Gibson, *Braveheart*
Actress: Susan Sarandon, *Dead Man Walking*
Actor: Nicolas Cage, *Leaving Las Vegas*
Supporting Actress: Mira Sorvino, *Mighty Aphrodite*
Supporting Actor: Kevin Spacey, *The Usual Suspects*

1996

Picture: *The English Patient,* Miramax
Director: Anthony Minghella, *The English Patient*
Actress: Frances McDormand, *Fargo*
Actor: Geoffrey Rush, *Shine*
Supporting Actress: Juliette Binoche, *The English Patient*
Supporting Actor: Cuba Gooding, Jr., *Jerry Maguire*

1997

Picture: *Titanic,* 20th Century Fox and Paramount
Director: James Cameron, *Titanic*
Actress: Helen Hunt, *As Good As It Gets*
Actor: Jack Nicholson, *As Good As It Gets*
Supporting Actress: Kim Basinger, *L.A. Confidential*
Supporting Actor: Robin Williams, *Good Will Hunting*

Other Academy Awards for 1997

Art direction: Peter Lamont, *Titanic*
Cinematography: Russell Carpenter, *Titanic*
Costume design: Deborah L. Scott, *Titanic*
Documentary (feature): Rabbi Marvin Hier and Richard Trank, *The Long Way Home;* **(short subject):** Donna Dewey and Carol Pasternak, *A Story of Healing*
Editing: Conrad Buff, James Cameron, and Richard A. Harris, *Titanic*
Foreign-language film: *Character,* The Netherlands
Makeup: Rick Baker and David LeRoy Anderson, *Men in Black*
Music (original musical or comedy score): Anne Dudley, *The Full Monty;* **(original dramatic score):** James Horner, *Titanic;* **(original song):** James Horner (music) and Will Jennings (lyrics), "My Heart Will Go On," *Titanic*

Screenplay, adapted: Brian Helgeland and Curtis Hanson, *L.A. Confidential*

Screenplay, original: Ben Affleck and Matt Damon, *Good Will Hunting*

Short subject (live action): Chris Tashima and Chris Donahue, *Visas and Virtue;* **(animated):** Jan Pinkava, *Geri's Game*

Sound: Gary Rydstrom, Tom Johnson, Gary Summers, and Mark Ulano, *Titanic*

Sound effects editing: Tom Bellfort and Christopher Boyes, *Titanic*

Visual effects: Robert Legato, Mark Lasoff, Thomas L. Fisher, and Michael Kanfer, *Titanic*

Pulitzer Prize Awards

(For years not listed, no award was made.)

PULITZER PRIZES IN JOURNALISM

Meritorious Public Service

1918 *New York Times;* also special award to Minna Lewinson and Henry Beetle Hough
1919 *Milwaukee Journal*
1921 *Boston Post*
1922 *New York World*
1923 *Memphis Commercial Appeal*
1924 *New York World*
1926 *Columbus* (Ga.) *Enquirer Sun*
1927 *Canton* (Ohio) *Daily News*
1928 *Indianapolis Times*
1929 *New York Evening World*
1931 *Atlanta Constitution*
1932 *Indianapolis News*
1933 *New York World–Telegram*
1934 *Medford* (Ore.) *Mail Tribune*
1935 *Sacramento Bee*
1936 *Cedar Rapids* (Iowa) *Gazette*
1937 *St. Louis Post–Dispatch*
1938 *Bismarck* (N.D.) *Tribune*
1939 *Miami Daily News*
1940 *Waterbury* (Conn.) *Republican* and *American*
1941 *St. Louis Post–Dispatch*
1942 *Los Angeles Times*
1943 *Omaha World–Herald*
1944 *New York Times*
1945 *Detroit Free Press*
1946 *Scranton* (Pa.) *Times*
1947 *Baltimore Sun*
1948 *St. Louis Post–Dispatch*
1949 (Lincoln) *Nebraska State Journal*
1950 *Chicago Daily News;* and *St. Louis Post–Dispatch*
1951 *Miami Herald;* and *Brooklyn Eagle*
1952 *St. Louis Post–Dispatch*
1953 *Whiteville* (N.C.) *News Reporter;* and *Tabor City* (N.C.) *Tribune*
1954 *Newsday* (Garden City, N.Y.)
1955 *Columbus* (Ga.) *Ledger* and *Sunday Ledger–Enquirer*
1956 *Watsonville* (Calif.) *Register–Pajaronian*
1957 *Chicago Daily News*
1958 (Little Rock) *Arkansas Gazette*
1959 *Utica* (N.Y.) *Observer Dispatch* and *Utica Daily Press*
1960 *Los Angeles Times*
1961 *Amarillo* (Tex.) *Globe–Times*
1962 *Panama City* (Fla.) *News–Herald*
1963 *Chicago Daily News*
1964 *St. Petersburg* (Fla.) *Times*
1965 *Hutchinson* (Kan.) *News*
1966 *Boston Globe*
1967 *Louisville Courier–Journal* and *Milwaukee Journal*
1968 *Riverside* (Calif.) *Press–Enterprise*
1969 *Los Angeles Times*
1970 *Newsday* (Garden City, N.Y.)
1971 *Winston–Salem* (N.C.) *Journal and Sentinel*
1972 *New York Times*
1973 *Washington Post*
1974 *Newsday* (Garden City, N.Y.)
1975 *Boston Globe*
1976 *Anchorage* (Alaska) *Daily News*
1977 *Lufkin* (Tex.) *News*
1978 *Philadelphia Inquirer*
1979 *Point Reyes* (Calif.) *Light*
1980 Gannett News Service
1981 *Charlotte* (N.C.) *Observer*
1982 *Detroit News*
1983 *Jackson* (Miss.) *Clarion–Ledger*
1984 *Los Angeles Times*
1985 *The Fort Worth Star–Telegram*
1986 *Denver Post*
1987 *Pittsburgh Press,* reporting by Andrew Schneider and Matthew Brelis
1988 *Charlotte* (N.C.) *Observer*
1989 *Anchorage Daily News*
1990 *Philadelphia Inquirer* and *Washington* (N.C.) *Daily News*
1991 *Des Moines Register,* reporting by Jane Schorer
1992 *Sacramento Bee* for "The Sierra in Peril" series by Tom Knudson
1993 *Miami Herald*
1994 *The Akron* (Ohio) *Beacon Journal*
1995 *The Virgin Islands Daily News*
1996 *The News and Observer* (Raleigh, N.C.)
1997 *The Times–Picayune* (New Orleans, La.)
1998 *Grand Forks* (N.D.) *Herald*

Editorial

1917 *New York Tribune*
1918 *Louisville Courier–Journal*
1920 Harvey E. Newbranch *(Omaha Evening World–Herald)*
1922 Frank M. O'Brien *(New York Herald)*

1923 William Allen White (*Emporia* [Kan.] *Gazette*)
1924 *Boston Herald*; special prize: Frank I. Cobb (*New York World*)
1925 *Charleston* (S.C.) *News and Courier*
1926 Edward M. Kingsbury (*New York Times*)
1927 F. Lauriston Bullard (*Boston Herald*)
1928 Grover Cleveland Hall (*Montgomery* [Ala.] *Advertiser*)
1929 Louis Isaac Jaffe (*Norfolk Virginian–Pilot*)
1931 Charles S. Ryckman (*Fremont* [Neb.] *Tribune*)
1933 *Kansas City* (Mo.) *Star*
1934 E. P. Chase (*Atlantic* [Iowa] *News Telegraph*)
1936 Felix Morley (*Washington Post*); George B. Parker (Scripps–Howard Newspapers)
1937 John W. Owens (*Baltimore Sun*)
1938 W. W. Waymack (*Des Moines Register and Tribune*)
1939 Ronald G. Callvert (*Portland Oregonian*)
1940 Bart Howard (*St. Louis Post–Dispatch*)
1941 Reuben Maury (*New York Daily News*)
1942 Geoffrey Parsons (*New York Herald Tribune*)
1943 Forrest W. Seymour (*Des Moines Register and Tribune*)
1944 Henry J. Haskell (*Kansas City* [Mo.] *Star*)
1945 George W. Potter (*Providence* [R.I.] *Journal–Bulletin*)
1946 Hodding Carter ([Greenville, Miss.] *Delta Democrat–Times*)
1947 William H. Grimes (*Wall Street Journal*)
1948 Virginius Dabney (*Richmond Times–Dispatch*)
1949 John H. Crider (*Boston Herald*); Herbert Elliston (*Washington Post*)
1950 Carl M. Saunders (*Jackson* [Mich.] *Citizen Patriot*)
1951 William H. Fitzpatrick (*New Orleans States*)
1952 Louis LaCoss (*St. Louis Globe–Democrat*)
1953 Vermont C. Royster (*Wall Street Journal*)
1954 Don Murray (*Boston Herald*)
1955 Royce Howes (*Detroit Free Press*)
1956 Lauren K. Soth (*Des Moines Register and Tribune*)
1957 Buford Boone (*Tuscaloosa* [Ala.] *News*)
1958 Harry S. Ashmore (*Arkansas Gazette*)
1959 Ralph McGill (*Atlanta Constitution*)
1960 Lenoir Chambers (*Virginian–Pilot*)
1961 William J. Dorvillier (*San Juan* [P.R.] *Star*)
1962 Thomas M. Storke (*Santa Barbara* [Calif.] *News–Press*)
1963 Ira B. Harkey, Jr. (*Pascagoula* [Miss.] *Chronicle*)
1964 Hazel Brannon Smith (*Lexington* [Miss.] *Advertiser*)
1965 John R. Harrison (*Gainesville* [Fla.] *Daily Sun*)
1966 Robert Lasch (*St. Louis Post–Dispatch*)
1967 Eugene Patterson (*Atlanta Constitution*)
1968 John S. Knight (Knight Newspapers)
1969 Paul Greenberg (*Pine Bluff* [Ark.] *Commercial*)
1970 Phillip L. Geyelin (*Washington Post*)
1971 Horance G. Davis, Jr. (*Gainesville* [Fla.] *Sun*)
1972 John Strohmeyer (*Bethlehem* [Pa.] *Globe Times*)
1973 Roger Bourne Linscott (*Berkshire Eagle* [Pittsfield, Mass.])
1974 F. Gilman Spencer (*Trenton* [N.J.] *Trentonian*)
1975 John Daniell Maurice (*Charleston* [W. Va.] *Daily Mail*)
1976 Philip P. Kerby (*Los Angeles Times*)
1977 Warren L. Lerude, Foster Church, and Norman F. Cardoza (*Reno* [Nev.] *Gazette* and *Nevada State Journal*)
1978 Meg Greenfield (*Washington Post*)
1979 Edwin M. Yoder, Jr. (*Washington Star*)
1980 Robert L. Bartley (*Wall Street Journal*)
1982 Jack Rosenthal (*New York Times*)
1983 *Miami Herald*
1984 Albert Scardino (*Georgia Gazette*)
1985 Richard Aregood (*Philadelphia Daily News*)
1986 Jack Fuller (*Chicago Tribune*)
1987 Jonathan Freedman (*San Diego Tribune*)
1988 Jane E. Healy (*Orlando Sentinel*)
1989 Lois Wille (*Chicago Tribune*)
1990 Thomas J. Hylton (*Pottstown* [Pa.] *Mercury*)
1991 Ron Casey, Harold Jackson, and Joey Kennedy (*Birmingham* [Ala.] *News*)
1992 Maria Henson (*Lexington* [Ky.] *Herald–Leader*)
1994 R. Bruce Dold (*Chicago Tribune*)
1995 Jeffrey Good (*St. Petersburg* [Fla.] *Times*)
1996 Robert B. Semple, Jr. (*New York Times*)
1997 Michael Gartner (*Daily Tribune* [Ames, Iowa])
1998 Bernard L. Stein (*The Riverdale Press* [Bronx, N.Y.])

Correspondence

1929 Paul Scott Mowrer (*Chicago Daily News*)
1930 Leland Stowe (*New York Herald Tribune*)
1931 H. R. Knickerbocker (*Philadelphia Public Ledger* and *New York Evening Post*)
1932 Walter Duranty (*New York Times*); Charles G. Ross (*St. Louis Post–Dispatch*)
1933 Edgar Ansel Mowrer (*Chicago Daily News*)
1934 Frederick T. Birchall (*New York Times*)
1935 Arthur Krock (*New York Times*)
1936 Wilfred C. Barber (*Chicago Tribune*)
1937 Anne O'Hare McCormick (*New York Times*)
1938 Arthur Krock (*New York Times*)
1939 Louis P. Lochner (Associated Press)
1940 Otto D. Tolischus (*New York Times*)
1941 Group award[1]
1942 Carlos P. Romulo (*Philippines Herald*)
1943 Hanson W. Baldwin (*New York Times*)
1944 Ernie Pyle (Scripps–Howard Newspaper Alliance)
1945 Harold V. (Hal) Boyle (Associated Press)
1946 Arnaldo Cortesi (*New York Times*)
1947 Brooks Atkinson (*New York Times*)

1. For the public services and the individual achievements of American news reporters in the war zones.

Editorial Cartooning

1922 Rollin Kirby (*New York World*)
1924 Jay Norwood Darling (*New York Tribune*)
1925 Rollin Kirby (*New York World*)
1926 D. R. Fitzpatrick (*St. Louis Post–Dispatch*)
1927 Nelson Harding (*Brooklyn Eagle*)
1928 Nelson Harding (*Brooklyn Eagle*)
1929 Rollin Kirby (*New York World*)
1930 Charles R. Macauley (*Brooklyn Eagle*)
1931 Edmund Duffy (*Baltimore Sun*)
1932 John T. McCutcheon (*Chicago Tribune*)
1933 H. M. Talburt (*Washington Daily News*)
1934 Edmund Duffy (*Baltimore Sun*)
1935 Ross A. Lewis (*Milwaukee Journal*)
1937 C. D. Batchelor (*New York Daily News*)
1938 Vaughn Shoemaker (*Chicago Daily News*)
1939 Charles G. Werner (*Daily Oklahoman* [Oklahoma City])
1940 Edmund Duffy (*Baltimore Sun*)
1941 Jacob Burck (*Chicago Times*)

1942 Herbert L. Block (NEA Service)
1943 Jay Norwood Darling *(New York Herald Tribune)*
1944 Clifford K. Berryman *(Washington Evening Star)*
1945 Bill Mauldin (United Features Syndicate)
1946 Bruce Alexander Russell *(Los Angeles Times)*
1947 Vaughn Shoemaker *(Chicago Daily News)*
1948 Reuben L. Goldberg *(New York Sun)*
1949 Lute Pease *(Newark Evening News)*
1950 James T. Berryman *(Washington Evening Star)*
1951 Reg (Reginald W.) Manning (*Arizona Republic* [Phoenix])
1952 Fred L. Packer *(New York Mirror)*
1953 Edward D. Kuekes *(Cleveland Plain Dealer)*
1954 Herbert L. Block *(Washington Post* and *Times–Herald)*
1955 Daniel R. Fitzpatrick *(St. Louis Post–Dispatch)*
1956 Robert York *(Louisville Times)*
1957 Tom Little *(Nashville Tennessean)*
1958 Bruce M. Shanks *(Buffalo Evening News)*
1959 Bill Mauldin *(St. Louis Post–Dispatch)*
1961 Carey Orr *(Chicago Tribune)*
1962 Edmund S. Valtman *(Hartford Times)*
1963 Frank Miller *(Des Moines Register)*
1964 Paul Conrad (formerly of *Denver Post,* later on *Los Angeles Times*)
1966 Don Wright *(Miami News)*
1967 Patrick B. Oliphant *(Denver Post)*
1968 Eugene Gray Payne *(Charlotte* [N.C.] *Observer)*
1969 John Fischetti *(Chicago Daily News)*
1970 Thomas F. Darcy (*Newsday* [Garden City, N.Y.])
1971 Paul Conrad *(Los Angeles Times)*
1972 Jeffrey K. MacNelly *(Richmond* [Va.] *News Leader)*
1974 Paul Szep *(Boston Globe)*
1975 Garry Trudeau (Universal Press Syndicate)
1976 Tony Auth *(Philadelphia Inquirer)*
1977 Paul Szep *(Boston Globe)*
1978 Jeffrey K. MacNelly *(Richmond* [Va.] *News Leader)*
1979 Herbert L. Block *(Washington Post)*
1980 Don Wright *(Miami News)*
1981 Mike Peters *(Dayton* [Ohio] *Daily News)*
1982 Ben Sargent *(Austin* [Tex.] *American–Statesman)*
1983 Richard Locher *(Chicago Tribune)*
1984 Paul Conrad *(Los Angeles Times)*
1985 Jeff MacNelly *(Chicago Tribune)*
1986 Jules Feiffer *(Village Voice)*
1987 Berke Breathed (*Washington Post* Writers Group)
1988 Doug Marlette *(Atlanta Constitution* and *Charlotte* [N.C.] *Observer)*
1989 Jack Higgins *(Chicago Sun–Times)*
1990 Tom Toles *(Buffalo News)*
1991 Jim Borgman *(Cincinnati Inquirer)*
1992 Signe Wilkinson *(Philadelphia Daily News)*
1993 Stephen R. Benson *(Arizona Republic)*
1994 Michael P. Ramirez *(The Commercial Appeal,* Memphis)
1995 Mike Luckovich *(The Atlanta Constitution)*
1996 Jim Morin *(The Miami Herald)*
1997 Walt Handelsman *(The Times–Picayune)*
1998 Stephen P. Breen *(The Asbury Park* [N.J.] *Press)*

News Photography

1942 Milton Brooks *(Detroit News)*
1943 Frank Noel (Associated Press)
1944 Frank Filan (Associated Press); Earle L. Bunker *(Omaha World–Herald)*
1945 Joe Rosenthal (Associated Press)
1947 Arnold Hardy
1948 Frank Cushing *(Boston Traveler)*
1949 Nat Fein *(New York Herald Tribune)*
1950 Bill Crouch *(Oakland Tribune)*
1951 Max Desfor (Associated Press)
1952 John Robinson and Don Ultang *(Des Moines Register & Tribune)*
1953 William M. Gallagher *(Flint* [Mich.] *Journal)*
1954 Mrs. Walter M. Schau
1955 John L. Gaunt, Jr. *(Los Angeles Times)*
1956 *New York Daily News*
1957 Harry A. Trask *(Boston Traveler)*
1958 William C. Beall *(Washington Daily News)*
1959 William Seaman *(Minneapolis Star)*
1960 Andrew Lopez (United Press International)
1961 Yasushi Nagao (Mainichi Newspapers, Tokyo)
1962 Paul Vathis (Harrisburg [Pa.] bureau of Associated Press)
1963 Hector Rondon (*La Republica,* Caracas, Venezuela)
1964 Robert H. Jackson *(Dallas Times Herald)*
1965 Horst Faas (Associated Press)
1966 Kyoichi Sawada (United Press International)
1967 Jack R. Thornell (Associated Press)
1968 News: Rocco Morabito *(Jacksonville* [Fla.] *Journal);* features: Toshio Sakai (United Press International)
1969 Spot news: Edward T. Adams (Associated Press); features: Moneta Sleet, Jr.
1970 Spot news: Steve Starr (Associated Press); features: Dallas Kinney *(Palm Beach Post)*
1971 Spot news: John Paul Filo (*Valley Daily News* and *Daily Dispatch* [Tarentum and New Kensington, Pa.]); features: Jack Dykinga *(Chicago Sun–Times)*
1972 Spot news: Horst Faas and Michel Laurent (Associated Press); features: Dave Kennerly (United Press International)
1973 Spot news: Huynh Cong Ut *(Associated Press);* features: Brian Lanker *(Topeka Capital–Journal)*
1974 Spot news: Anthony K. Roberts (Associated Press); features: Slava Veder (Associated Press)
1975 Spot news: Gerald H. Gay *(Seattle Times);* features: Matthew Lewis *(Washington Post)*
1976 Spot news: Stanley J. Forman *(Boston Herald–American);* features: photographic staff of *Louisville Courier–Journal* and *Times*
1977 Spot news: Neal Ulevich (Associated Press) and Stanley J. Forman *(Boston Herald–American);* features: Robin Hood *(Chattanooga News–Free Press)*
1978 Spot news: John Blair, freelance, Evansville, Ind.; features: J. Ross Baughman (Associated Press)
1979 Spot news: Thomas J. Kelly, 3rd *(Pottstown* [Pa.] *Mercury);* features: photographic staff of *Boston Herald–American*
1980 Features: Erwin H. Hagler *(Dallas Times Herald)*
1981 Spot news: Larry C. Price *(Fort Worth Star–Telegram);* features: Taro M. Yamasaki *(Detroit Free Press)*

1982 Spot news: Ron Edmonds (Associated Press); features: John H. White *(Chicago Sun–Times)*
1983 Spot news: Bill Foley (Associated Press); features: James B. Dickman *(Dallas Times Herald)*
1984 Spot news: Stan Grossfeld *(Boston Globe)*; features: Anthony Suau *(Denver Post)*
1985 Spot news: photographic staff of *Register*, Santa Ana, Calif.; features: Stan Grossfeld *(Boston Globe)*
1986 Spot news: Michel duCille and Carol Guzy *(Miami Herald)*; features: Tom Gralish *(Philadelphia Inquirer)*
1987 Spot news: Kim Komenich *(San Francisco Examiner)*; features: David Peterson *(Des Moines Register)*
1988 Spot news: Scott Shaw *(Odessa* [Texas] *American)*; features: Michel duCille *(Miami Herald)*
1989 Spot news: Ron Olshwanger *(St. Louis Post–Dispatch)*; features: Manny Crisostomo *(Detroit Free Press)*
1990 Spot news: *Oakland Tribune*; features: David C. Turnley *(Detroit Free Press)*
1991 Spot news: Greg Marinovich (Associated Press); features: William Snyder *(Dallas Morning News)*
1992 Spot news: Associated Press staff; features: John Kaplan *(Herald* [Monterey, Calif.] and *Pittsburgh Post–Gazette)*
1993 Spot news: William Snyder and Ken Geiger *(Dallas Morning News)*; features: Associated Press
1994 Spot news: Paul Watson *(Toronto Star)*; features: Kevin Carter, freelancer for *New York Times*
1995 Spot news: Carol Guzy *(Washington Post)*; features: Associated Press Staff
1996 Spot news: Charles Porter IV, freelance photographer for Associated Press; features: Stephanie Walsh, freelance photographer for Newhouse News Service
1997 Spot news: Annie Wells (*The Press Democrat* [Santa Rosa, Calif.]); features: Alexander Zemlianichenko (Associated Press)
1998 Spot news: Martha Rial *(The Pittsburgh Post–Gazette)*; features: Clarence Williams *(The Los Angeles Times)*

National Telegraphic Reporting

1942 Louis Stark *(New York Times)*
1944 Dewey L. Fleming *(Baltimore Sun)*
1945 James Reston *(New York Times)*
1946 Edward A. Harris *(St. Louis Post–Dispatch)*
1947 Edward T. Folliard *(Washington Post)*

National Reporting

1948 Bert Andrews *(New York Herald Tribune)*; Nat S. Finney *(Minneapolis Tribune)*
1949 C. P. Trussell *(New York Times)*
1950 Edwin O. Guthman *(Seattle Times)*
1952 Anthony Leviero *(New York Times)*
1953 Don Whitehead (Associated Press)
1954 Richard Wilson (Cowles Newspapers)
1955 Anthony Lewis *(Washington Daily News)*
1956 Charles L. Bartlett *(Chattanooga Times)*
1957 James Reston *(New York Times)*
1958 Relman Morin (Associated Press) and Clark Mollenhoff *(Des Moines Register & Tribune)*
1959 Howard Van Smith *(Miami News)*
1960 Vance Trimble (Scripps–Howard Newspaper Alliance)
1961 Edward R. Cony *(Wall Street Journal)*
1962 Nathan G. Caldwell and Gene S. Graham *(Nashville Tennessean)*
1963 Anthony Lewis *(New York Times)*
1964 Merriman Smith (United Press International)
1965 Louis M. Kohlmeier *(Wall Street Journal)*
1966 Haynes Johnson *(Washington Evening Star)*
1967 Stanley Penn and Monroe Karmin *(Wall Street Journal)*
1968 Howard James *(Christian Science Monitor)*; Nathan K. (Nick) Kotz *(Des Moines Register* and *Minneapolis Tribune)*
1969 Robert Cahn *(Christian Science Monitor)*
1970 William J. Eaton *(Chicago Daily News)*
1971 Lucinda Franks and Thomas Powers (United Press International)
1972 Jack Anderson *(United Feature Syndicate)*
1973 Robert Boyd and Clark Hoyt *(Knight Newspapers)*
1974 Jack White *(Providence* [R.I.] *Journal–Bulletin)*; James R. Polk *(Washington Star–News)*
1975 Donald L. Barlett and James B. Steele *(Philadelphia Inquirer)*
1976 James Risser *(Des Moines Register)*
1977 Walter Mears (Associated Press)
1978 Gaylord D. Shaw *(Los Angeles Times)*
1979 James Risser *(Des Moines Register)*
1980 Bette Swenson Orsini and Charles Stafford *(St. Petersburg Times)*
1981 John M. Crewdson *(New York Times)*
1982 Rick Atkinson *(Kansas City* [Mo.] *Times)*
1983 *Boston Globe*
1984 John N. Wilford *(New York Times)*
1985 Thomas J. Knudson *(Des Moines Register)*
1986 Craig Flournoy and George Rodrigue *(Dallas Morning News)* and Arthur Howe *(Philadelphia Inquirer)*
1987 *Miami Herald*, staff; *New York Times*, staff
1988 Tim Weiner *(Philadelphia Inquirer)*
1989 Donald L. Barlett and James B. Steele *(Philadelphia Inquirer)*
1990 Ross Anderson, Bill Dietrich, Mary Ann Gwinn, and Eric Nalder *(Seattle Times)*
1991 Marjie Lundstrom and Rochelle Sharpe (Gannett News Service)
1992 Jeff Taylor and Mike McGraw *(Kansas City Star)*
1993 David Marannis *(Washington Post)*
1994 Eileen Welsome *(Albuquerque* [N.M.] *Tribune)*
1995 Tony Horwitz *(Wall Street Journal)*
1996 Alix M. Freedman *(Wall Street Journal)*
1997 Staff of the *Wall Street Journal*
1998 Russell Carollo and Jeff Nesmith *(Dayton* [Ohio] *Daily News)*

International Telegraphic Reporting

1942 Laurence Edmund Allen (Associated Press)
1943 Ira Wolfert (North American Newspaper Alliance, Inc.)
1944 Daniel De Luce (Associated Press)
1945 Mark S. Watson *(Baltimore Sun)*
1946 Homer W. Bigart *(New York Herald Tribune)*
1947 Eddy Gilmore (Associated Press)

International Reporting

1948 Paul W. Ward *(Baltimore Sun)*
1949 Price Day *(Baltimore Sun)*
1950 Edmund Stevens *(Christian Science Monitor)*

1951 Keyes Beech and Fred Sparks *(Chicago Daily News);* Homer Bigart and Marguerite Higgins *(New York Herald Tribune);* Relman Morin and Don Whitehead (Associated Press)
1952 John M. Hightower (Associated Press)
1953 Austin C. Wehrwein *(Milwaukee Journal)*
1954 Jim G. Lucas (Scripps–Howard Newspapers)
1955 Harrison E. Salisbury *(New York Times)*
1956 William Randolph Hearst, Jr., and Frank Conniff (Hearst Newspapers); Kingsbury Smith (INS)
1957 Russell Jones (United Press)
1958 *New York Times*
1959 Joseph Martin and Philip Santora *(New York Daily News)*
1960 A. M. Rosenthal *(New York Times)*
1961 Lynn Heinzerling (Associated Press)
1962 Walter Lippmann (New York Herald Tribune Syndicate)
1963 Hal Hendrix *(Miami News)*
1964 Malcolm W. Browne (Associated Press); David Halberstam *(New York Times)*
1965 J. A. Livingston *(Philadelphia Bulletin)*
1966 Peter Arnett (Associated Press)
1967 R. John Hughes *(Christian Science Monitor)*
1968 Alfred Friendly *(Washington Post)*
1969 William Tuohy *(Los Angeles Times)*
1970 Seymour M. Hersh (Dispatch News Service)
1971 Jimmie Lee Hoagland *(Washington Post)*
1972 Peter R. Kann *(Wall Street Journal)*
1973 Max Frankel *(New York Times)*
1974 Hedrick Smith *(New York Times)*
1975 William Mullen and Ovie Carter *(Chicago Tribune)*
1976 Sydney H. Schanberg *(New York Times)*
1978 Henry Kamm *(New York Times)*
1979 Richard Ben Cramer *(Philadelphia Inquirer)*
1980 Joel Brinkley and Jay Mather *(Louisville Courier–Journal)*
1981 Shirley Christian *(Miami Herald)*
1982 John Darnton *(New York Times)*
1983 Thomas L. Friedman *(New York Times)*
1984 Karen E. House *(Wall Street Journal)*
1985 Josh Friedman, Dennis Bell, and Ozier Muhammad *(Newsday)*
1986 Lewis M. Simons, Pete Carey, and Katherine Ellison *(San Jose Mercury News)*
1987 Michael Parks *(Los Angeles Times)*
1988 Thomas L. Friedman *(New York Times)*
1989 Bill Keller *(New York Times);* Glenn Frankel *(Washington Post)*
1990 Nicholas D. Kristof and Sheryl WuDunn *(New York Times)*
1991 Caryle Murphy *(Washington Post);* Serge Schmemann *(New York Times)*
1992 Patrick J. Sloyan *(Newsday)*
1993 John F. Burns *(New York Times);* Roy Gutman *(Newsday)*
1994 *Dallas Morning News* team
1995 Mark Fritz (Associated Press)
1996 David Rohde *(Christian Science Monitor)*
1997 John F. Burns *(New York Times)*
1998 *New York Times* staff

Reporting

1917 Herbert B. Swope *(New York World)*
1918 Harold A. Littledale *(New York Evening Post)*
1920 John J. Leary, Jr. *(New York World)*
1921 Louis Seibold *(New York World)*
1922 Kirke L. Simpson (Associated Press)
1923 Alva Johnston *(New York Times)*
1924 Magner White *(San Diego Sun)*
1925 James W. Mulroy and Alvin H. Goldstein *(Chicago Daily News)*
1926 William Burke Miller *(Louisville Courier–Journal)*
1927 John T. Rogers *(St. Louis Post–Dispatch)*
1929 Paul Y. Anderson *(St. Louis Post–Dispatch)*
1930 Russell D. Owen *(New York Times);* special award: W. O. Dapping *(Auburn* [N.Y.] *Citizen)*
1931 A. B. MacDonald *(Kansas City* [Mo.] *Star)*
1932 W. C. Richards, D. D. Martin, J. S. Pooler, F. D. Webb, and J. N. W. Sloan *(Detroit Free Press)*
1933 Francis A. Jamieson (Associated Press)
1934 Royce Brier *(San Francisco Chronicle)*
1935 William H. Taylor *(New York Herald Tribune)*
1936 Lauren D. Lyman *(New York Times)*
1937 John J. O'Neill *(New York Herald Tribune);* William Leonard Laurence *(New York Times);* Howard W. Blakeslee (Associated Press); Gobind Behari Lal (Universal Service); David Dietz (Scripps–Howard Newspapers)
1938 Raymond Sprigle *(Pittsburg Post–Gazette)*
1939 Thomas L. Stokes *(New York World–Telegram)*
1940 S. Burton Heath *(New York World–Telegram)*
1941 Westbrook Pegler *(New York World–Telegram)*
1942 Stanton Delaplane *(San Francisco Chronicle)*
1943 George Weller *(Chicago Daily News)*
1944 Paul Schoenstein and associates *(New York Journal–American)*
1945 Jack S. McDowell *(San Francisco Call–Bulletin)*
1946 William Leonard Laurence *(New York Times)*
1947 Frederick Woltman *(New York World–Telegram)*
1948 George E. Goodwin *(Atlanta Journal)*
1949 Malcolm Johnson *(New York Sun)*
1950 Meyer Berger *(New York Times)*
1951 Edward S. Montgomery *(San Francisco Examiner)*
1952 George de Carvalho *(San Francisco Chronicle)*
1953 Editorial staff *(Providence Journal and Evening Bulletin);*[1] Edward J. Mowery *(New York World–Telegram and Sun)*[2]
1954 *Vicksburg* (Miss.) *Sunday Post–Herald;*[1] Alvin Scott McCoy *(Kansas City* [Mo.] *Star)*[2]
1955 Mrs. Caro Brown *(Alice* [Tex.] *Daily Echo);*[1] Roland Kenneth Towery *(Cuero* [Tex.] *Record)*[2]
1956 Lee Hills *(Detroit Free Press);*[1] Arthur Daley *(New York Times)*[2]
1957 *Salt Lake Tribune;*[1] Wallace Turner and William Lambert *(Portland Oregonian)*[2]
1958 *Fargo* [N.D.] *Forum;*[1] George Beveridge *(Washington* [D.C.] *Evening Star)*[2]
1959 Mary Lou Werner *(Washington* [D.C.] *Evening Star);*[1] John Harold Brislin *(Scranton* [Pa.] *Tribune & Scrantonian)*[2]
1960 Jack Nelson *(Atlanta Constitution);*[1] Miriam Ottenberg *(Washington Evening Star)*[2]
1961 Sanche de Gramont *(New York Herald Tribune);*[1] Edgar May *(Buffalo Evening News)*[2]
1962 Robert D. Mullins (*Deseret News,* Salt Lake City);[1] George Bliss *(Chicago Tribune)*[2]
1963 Sylvan Fox, Anthony Shannon, and William Longgood *(New York World–*

Telegram and Sun);[1] Oscar Griffin, Jr. (former editor of *Pecos* [Tex.] *Independent and Enterprise*, now on staff of *Houston Chronicle)*[2]

1. Reporting under pressure of edition deadlines.
2. Reporting not under pressure of edition deadlines.

General Local Reporting

1964 Norman C. Miller *(Wall Street Journal)*
1965 Melvin H. Ruder (*Hungry Horse News*, Columbia Falls, Mont.)
1966 *Los Angeles Times* staff
1967 Robert V. Cox *(Chambersburg* [Pa.] *Public Opinion)*
1968 *Detroit Free Press* staff
1969 John Fetterman *(Louisville Times* and *Courier–Journal)*
1970 Thomas Fitzpatrick *(Chicago Sun–Times)*
1971 *Akron* (Ohio) *Beacon* staff
1972 Richard Cooper and John Machacek *(Rochester* [N.Y.] *Times–Union)*
1973 *Chicago Tribune*
1974 Arthur M. Petacque and Hugh F. Hough *(Chicago Sun–Times)*
1975 *Xenia* (Ohio) *Daily Gazette*
1976 Gene Miller *(Miami Herald)*
1977 Margo Huston *(Milwaukee Journal)*
1978 Richard Whitt *(Louisville Courier–Journal)*
1979 Staff of *San Diego* (Calif.) *Evening Tribune*
1980 Staff of *Philadelphia Inquirer*
1981 *Longview* (Wash.) *Daily News*
1982 *Kansas City* (Mo.) *Star* and *Kansas City* (Mo.) *Times*
1983 *Fort Wayne* (Ind.) *News–Sentinel*
1984 *Newsday*

General News Reporting

1985 Thomas Turcol *(Virginian–Pilot and Ledger–Star)*
1986 Edna Buchanan *(Miami Herald)*
1987 *Akron Beacon Journal* staff
1988 *Alabama Journal* (Montgomery) staff; *Lawrence* (Mass.) *Eagle–Tribune* staff
1989 *Louisville Courier–Journal* staff
1990 *San Jose* (Calif.) *Mercury News*

Spot News Reporting

1991 *Miami Herald* staff
1992 *New York Newsday* staff
1993 *Los Angeles Times* staff
1994 *New York Times* staff
1995 *Los Angeles Times* staff
1996 Robert D. McFadden *(New York Times)*
1997 *Newsday* staff (Long Island, N.Y.)
1998 Discontinued

Breaking News Reporting

1998 *Los Angeles Times* staff

Special Local Reporting

1964 James V. Magee, Albert V. Gaudiosi, and Frederick A. Meyer *(Philadelphia Bulletin)*
1965 Gene Goltz *(Houston Post)*
1966 John A. Frasca *(Tampa Tribune)*
1967 Gene Miller *(Miami Herald)*
1968 J. Anthony Lukas *(New York Times)*
1969 Albert L. Delugach and Denny Walsh *(St. Louis Globe–Democrat)*
1970 Harold Eugene Martin *(Montgomery Advertiser)*
1971 William Hugh Jones *(Chicago Tribune)*
1972 Timothy Leland, Gerard N. O'Neill, Stephen A. Kurkjian, and Ann DeSantis *(Boston Globe)*
1973 Sun Newspapers of Omaha, Neb.
1974 William Sherman *(New York Daily News)*
1975 *Indianapolis Star*
1976 *Chicago Tribune*
1977 Acel Moore and Wendell Rawls, Jr. *(Philadelphia Inquirer)*
1978 Anthony R. Dolan *(Stamford* [Conn.] *Advocate)*
1979 Gilbert M. Gaul and Elliot G. Jaspin *(Pottsville* [Pa.] *Republican)*
1980 Nils J. Bruzelius, Alexander B. Hawes, Jr., Stephen A. Kurkjian, Robert M. Porterfield, and Joan Vennochi *(Boston Globe)*
1981 Clark Hallas and Robert B. Lowe (*Arizona Daily Star*, Tucson)
1982 Paul Henderson *(Seattle Times)*
1983 Loretta Tofani *(Washington Post)*
1984 Kenneth Cooper, Joan FitzGerald, Jonathan Kaufman, Norman Lockman, Gary McMillan, Kirk Scharfenberg, and David Wessel *(Boston Globe)*

Investigative Reporting

1985 Lucy Morgan, Jack Reed *(St. Petersburg* [Fla.] *Times)*, and William K. Marimow *(Philadelphia Inquirer)*
1986 Jeffrey A. Marx and Michael M. York *(Lexington* [Ky.] *Herald Leader)*
1987 Daniel R. Biddle, H. G. Bissinger, and Fredric N. Tulsky *(Philadelphia Inquirer)*
1988 Dean Baquet, William C. Gaines, and Ann Marie Lipinski *(Chicago Tribune)*
1989 Bill Dedman *(Atlanta Journal and Constitution)*
1990 Lou Kilzer and Chris Ison *(Minneapolis–St. Paul Star Tribune)*
1991 Joseph T. Hallinan and Susan M. Headden *(Indianapolis Star)*
1992 Lorraine Adams and Dan Malone *(Dallas Morning News)*
1993 Jeff Brazil and Steve Berry *(Orlando* [Fla.] *Sentinel)*
1994 *Providence* (R.I.) *Journal–Bulletin* staff
1995 Stephanie Saul and Brian Donovan *(Newsday)*
1996 *Orange County Register* staff (Santa Ana, Calif.)
1997 Eric Nalder, Deborah Nelson, and Alex Tizon *(Seattle Times)*
1998 Gary Cohn and Will Englund (*The Sun* [Baltimore, Md.])

Feature Writing

1979 Jon D. Franklin *(Baltimore Evening Sun)*
1980 Madeleine Blais *(Miami Herald)*
1981 Teresa Carpenter (*Village Voice*, New York)
1982 Saul Pett (Associated Press)
1983 Nan Robertson *(New York Times)*
1984 Peter M. Rinearson *(Seattle Times)*
1985 Alice Steinbach *(Baltimore Sun)*
1986 John Camp *(St. Paul Pioneer Press and Dispatch)*
1987 Steve Twomey *(Philadelphia Inquirer)*
1988 Jacqui Banaszynski *(St. Paul Pioneer Press Dispatch)*
1989 David Zucchino *(Philadelphia Inquirer)*
1990 Dave Curtin *(Colorado Springs Gazette Telegraph)*

1991 Sheryl James *(St. Petersburg* [Fla.] *Times)*
1992 Howell Raines *(New York Times)*
1993 George Lardner, Jr. *(Washington Post)*
1994 Isabel Wilkerson *(New York Times)*
1995 Ron Suskind *(Wall Street Journal)*
1996 Rick Bragg *(New York Times)*
1997 Lisa Pollak *(Baltimore Sun)*
1998 Thomas French *(St. Petersburg* [Fla.] *Times)*

Commentary

1970 Marquis W. Childs *(St. Louis Post–Dispatch)*
1971 William A. Caldwell (*Record* [Hackensack, N.J.])
1972 Mike Royko *(Chicago Daily News)*
1973 David S. Broder *(Washington Post)*
1974 Edwin A. Roberts, Jr. *(National Observer)*
1975 Mary McGrory *(Washington Star)*
1976 Walter W. (Red) Smith *(New York Times)*
1977 George F. Will (*Washington Post* Writers Group)
1978 William Safire *(New York Times)*
1979 Russell Baker *(New York Times)*
1980 Ellen H. Goodman *(Boston Globe)*
1981 Dave Anderson *(New York Times)*
1982 Art Buchwald (*Los Angeles Times* Syndicate)
1983 Claude Sitton *(Raleigh* [N.C.] *News & Observer)*
1984 Vermont Royster *(Wall Street Journal)*
1985 Murray Kempton *(Newsday)*
1986 Jimmy Breslin *(New York Daily News)*
1987 Charles Krauthammer (*Washington Post* Writers Group)
1988 Dave Barry *(Miami Herald)*
1989 Clarence Page *(Chicago Tribune)*
1990 Jim Murray *(Los Angeles Times)*
1991 Jim Hoagland *(Washington Post)*
1992 Anna Quindlen *(New York Times)*
1993 Liz Balmaseda *(Miami Herald)*
1994 William Raspberry *(Washington Post)*
1995 Jim Dwyer *(New York Newsday)*
1996 E. R. Shipp *(New York Daily News)*
1997 Eileen McNamara *(Boston Globe)*
1998 Mike McAlary *(New York Daily News)*

Criticism

1970 Ada Louise Huxtable *(New York Times)*
1971 Harold C. Schonberg *(New York Times)*
1972 Frank Peters, Jr. *(St. Louis Post–Dispatch)*
1973 Ronald Powers *(Chicago Sun–Times)*
1974 Emily Genauer (Newsday Syndicate)
1975 Roger Ebert *(Chicago Sun–Times)*
1976 Alan M. Kriegsman *(Washington Post)*
1977 William McPherson *(Washington Post)*
1978 Walter Kerr *(New York Times)*
1979 Paul Gapp *(Chicago Tribune)*
1980 William A. Henry, 3rd *(Boston Globe)*
1981 Jonathan Yardley *(Washington Star)*
1982 Martin Bernheimer *(Los Angeles Times)*
1983 Manuela Hoelterhoff *(Wall Street Journal)*
1984 Paul Goldberger *(New York Times)*
1985 Howard Rosenberg *(Los Angeles Times)*
1986 Donal Henahan *(New York Times)*
1987 Richard Eder *(Los Angeles Times)*
1988 Tom Shales *(Washington Post)*
1989 Michael Skube (*News and Observer* [Raleigh, N.C.])
1990 Allan Temko *(San Francisco Chronicle)*
1991 David Shaw *(Los Angeles Times)*
1993 Michael Dirda *(Washington Post)*
1994 Lloyd Schwartz *(Boston Phoenix)*
1995 Margo Jefferson *(New York Times)*
1996 Robert Campbell *(Boston Globe)*
1997 Tim Page *(Washington Post)*
1998 Michiko Kakutani *(New York Times)*

Explanatory Journalism

1985 Jon Franklin *(Baltimore Evening Sun)*
1986 *New York Times*
1987 Jeff Lyon and Peter Gorner *(Chicago Tribune)*
1988 Daniel Hertzberg and James B. Stewart *(Wall Street Journal)*
1989 David Hanners, William Snyder, and Karen Blessen *(Dallas Morning News)*
1990 David A. Vise and Coll *(Washington Post)*
1991 Susan C. Faludi *(Wall Street Journal)*
1992 Robert S. Capers and Eric Lipton *(Hartford Courant)*
1993 Mike Toner *(Atlanta Journal–Constitution)*
1994 Ronald Kotulak *(Chicago Tribune)*
1995 Leon Dash and Lucian Perkins *(Washington Post)*
1996 Laurie Garrett (*Newsday* [Long Island, N.Y.])
1997 Michael Vitez, Ron Cortes, and April Saul *(Philadelphia Inquirer)*
1998 Paul Salopek *(Chicago Tribune)*

Specialized Reporting

1985 Randall Savage and Jackie Crosby *(Macon* [Ga.] *Telegraph and News)*
1986 Andrew Schneider and Mary Pat Flaherty *(Pittsburgh Press)*
1987 Alex S. Jones *(New York Times)*
1988 Walt Bogdanich *(Wall Street Journal)*
1989 Edward Humes *(Orange County Register)*
1990 Tamar Stieber (*Albuquerque* (N.M.) *Journal)*

Beat Reporting

1991 Natalie Angier *(New York Times)*
1992 Deborah Blum *(Sacramento Bee)*
1993 Paul Ingrassia and Joseph B. White *(Wall Street Journal)*
1994 Eric Freedman and Jim Mitzelfeld *(Detroit News)*
1995 David M. Shribman *(Boston Globe)*
1996 Bob Keeler (*Newsday* [Long Island, N.Y.])
1997 Byron Acohido *(Seattle Times)*
1998 Linda Greenhouse *(New York Times)*

PULITZER PRIZES IN LETTERS

Fiction[1]

1918 *His Family,* Ernest Poole
1919 *The Magnificent Ambersons,* Booth Tarkington
1921 *The Age of Innocence,* Edith Wharton
1922 *Alice Adams,* Booth Tarkington
1923 *One of Ours,* Willa Cather
1924 *The Able McLaughlins,* Margaret Wilson
1925 *So Big,* Edna Ferber
1926 *Arrowsmith,* Sinclair Lewis
1927 *Early Autumn,* Louis Bromfield
1928 *The Bridge of San Luis Rey,* Thornton Wilder
1929 *Scarlet Sister Mary,* Julia Peterkin
1930 *Laughing Boy,* Oliver La Farge
1931 *Years of Grace,* Margaret Ayer Barnes
1932 *The Good Earth,* Pearl S. Buck
1933 *The Store,* T. S. Stribling
1934 *Lamb in His Bosom,* Caroline Miller
1935 *Now in November,* Josephine Winslow Johnson
1936 *Honey in the Horn,* Harold L. Davis
1937 *Gone With the Wind,* Margaret Mitchell
1938 *The Late George Apley,* John Phillips Marquand

1939 *The Yearling,* Marjorie Kinnan Rawlings
1940 *The Grapes of Wrath,* John Steinbeck
1942 *In This Our Life,* Ellen Glasgow
1943 *Dragon's Teeth,* Upton Sinclair
1944 *Journey in the Dark,* Martin Flavin
1945 *A Bell for Adano,* John Hersey
1947 *All the King's Men,* Robert Penn Warren
1948 *Tales of the South Pacific,* James A. Michener
1949 *Guard of Honor,* James Gould Cozzens
1950 *The Way West,* A. B. Guthrie, Jr.
1951 *The Town,* Conrad Richter
1952 *The Caine Mutiny,* Herman Wouk
1953 *The Old Man and the Sea,* Ernest Hemingway
1955 *A Fable,* William Faulkner
1956 *Andersonville,* MacKinlay Kantor
1958 *A Death in the Family,* James Agee
1959 *The Travels of Jaimie McPheeters,* Robert Lewis Taylor
1960 *Advise and Consent,* Allen Drury
1961 *To Kill a Mockingbird,* Harper Lee
1962 *The Edge of Sadness,* Edwin O'Connor
1963 *The Reivers,* William Faulkner
1965 *The Keepers of the House,* Shirley Ann Grau
1966 *Collected Stories of Katherine Anne Porter,* Katherine Anne Porter
1967 *The Fixer,* Bernard Malamud
1968 *The Confessions of Nat Turner,* William Styron
1969 *House Made of Dawn,* N. Scott Momaday
1970 *Collected Stories,* Jean Stafford
1972 *Angle of Repose,* Wallace Stegner
1973 *The Optimist's Daughter,* Eudora Welty
1975 *The Killer Angels,* Michael Shaara
1976 *Humboldt's Gift,* Saul Bellow
1978 *Elbow Room,* James Alan McPherson
1979 *The Stories of John Cheever,* John Cheever
1980 *The Executioner's Song,* Norman Mailer
1981 *A Confederacy of Dunces,* John Kennedy Toole
1982 *Rabbit Is Rich,* John Updike
1983 *The Color Purple,* Alice Walker
1984 *Ironweed,* William Kennedy
1985 *Foreign Affairs,* Alison Lurie
1986 *Lonesome Dove,* Larry McMurtry
1987 *A Summons to Memphis,* Peter Taylor
1988 *Beloved,* Toni Morrison
1989 *Breathing Lessons,* Anne Tyler
1990 *The Mambo Kings Play Songs of Love,* Oscar Hijeulos
1991 *Rabbit at Rest,* John Updike
1992 *A Thousand Acres,* Jane Smiley
1993 *A Good Scent From a Strange Mountain,* Robert Olen Butler
1994 *The Shipping News,* E. Annie Proulx
1995 *The Stone Diaries,* Carol Shields
1996 *Independence Day,* Richard Ford
1997 *Martin Dressler: The Tale of an American Dreamer,* Steven Millhauser
1998 *American Pastoral,* Philip Roth

1. Before 1948, award was for novels only.

History of United States

1917 *With Americans of Past and Present Days,* J. J. Jusserand, Ambassador of France to United States
1918 *A History of the Civil War, 1861–1865,* James Ford Rhodes
1920 *The War With Mexico,* Justin H. Smith
1921 *The Victory at Sea,* William Sowden Sims, in collaboration with Burton J. Hendrick
1922 *The Founding of New England,* James Truslow Adams
1923 *The Supreme Court in United States History,* Charles Warren
1924 *The American Revolution—A Constitutional Interpretation,* Charles Howard McIlwain
1925 *A History of the American Frontier,* Frederic L. Paxson
1926 *The History of the United States,* Edward Channing
1927 *Pinckney's Treaty,* Samuel Flagg Bemis
1928 *Main Currents in American Thought,* Vernon Louis Parrington
1929 *The Organization and Administration of the Union Army, 1861–1865,* Fred Albert Shannon
1930 *The War of Independence,* Claude H. Van Tyne
1931 *The Coming of the War: 1914,* Bernadotte E. Schmitt
1932 *My Experiences in the World War,* John J. Pershing
1933 *The Significance of Sections in American History,* Frederick J. Turner
1934 *The People's Choice,* Herbert Agar
1935 *The Colonial Period of American History,* Charles McLean Andrews
1936 *The Constitutional History of the United States,* Andrew C. McLaughlin
1937 *The Flowering of New England,* Van Wyck Brooks
1938 *The Road to Reunion, 1865–1900,* Paul Herman Buck
1939 *A History of American Magazines,* Frank Luther Mott
1940 *Abraham Lincoln: The War Years,* Carl Sandburg
1941 *The Atlantic Migration, 1607–1860,* Marcus Lee Hansen
1942 *Reveille in Washington,* Margaret Leech
1943 *Paul Revere and the World He Lived In,* Esther Forbes
1944 *The Growth of American Thought,* Merle Curti
1945 *Unfinished Business,* Stephen Bonsal
1946 *The Age of Jackson,* Arthur M. Schlesinger, Jr.
1947 *Scientists Against Time,* James Phinney Baxter, 3rd
1948 *Across the Wide Missouri,* Bernard DeVoto
1949 *The Disruption of American Democracy,* Roy Franklin Nichols
1950 *Art and Life in America,* Oliver W. Larkin
1951 *The Old Northwest, Pioneer Period 1815–1840,* R. Carlyle Buley
1952 *The Uprooted,* Oscar Handlin
1953 *The Era of Good Feelings,* George Dangerfield
1954 *A Stillness at Appomattox,* Bruce Catton
1955 *Great River: The Rio Grande in North American History,* Paul Horgan
1956 *The Age of Reform,* Richard Hofstadter
1957 *Russia Leaves the War: Soviet–American Relations, 1917–1920,* George F. Kennan
1958 *Banks and Politics in America: From the Revolution to the Civil War,* Bray Hammond
1959 *The Republican Era: 1869–1901,* Leonard D. White, assisted by Jean Schneider
1960 *In the Days of McKinley,* Margaret Leech
1961 *Between War and Peace: The Potsdam Conference,* Herbert Feis
1962 *The Triumphant Empire: Thunder-Clouds Gather in the West,* Lawrence H. Gipson

1963 *Washington, Village and Capital, 1800–1878,* Constance McLaughlin Green
1964 *Puritan Village: The Formation of a New England Town,* Sumner Chilton Powell
1965 *The Greenback Era,* Irwin Unger
1966 *Life of the Mind in America,* Perry Miller
1967 *Exploration and Empire: The Explorer and Scientist in the Winning of the American West,* William H. Goetzmann
1968 *The Ideological Origins of the American Revolution,* Bernard Bailyn
1969 *Origins of the Fifth Amendment,* Leonard W. Levy
1970 *Present at the Creation: My Years in the State Department,* Dean Acheson
1971 *Roosevelt: The Soldier of Freedom,* James McGregor Burns
1972 *Neither Black Nor White: Slavery and Race Relations in Brazil and the United States,* Carl N. Degler
1973 *People of Paradox: An Inquiry Concerning the Origin of American Civilization,* Michael Kammen
1974 *The Americans: The Democratic Experience, Vol. 3,* Daniel J. Boorstin
1975 *Jefferson and His Time,* Dumas Malone
1976 *Lamy of Santa Fe,* Paul Horgan
1977 *The Impending Crisis: 1841–1861,* David M. Potter
1978 *The Invisible Hand: The Managerial Revolution in American Business,* Alfred D. Chandler, Jr.
1979 *The Dred Scott Case: Its Significance in Law and Politics,* Don E. Fehrenbacher
1980 *Been in the Storm So Long,* Leon F. Litwack
1981 *American Education: The National Experience; 1783–1876,* Lawrence A. Cremin
1982 *Mary Chesnut's Civil War,* C. Vann Woodward, editor
1983 *The Transformation of Virginia, 1740–1790,* Rhys L. Isaac
1985 *The Prophets of Regulation,* Thomas K. McCraw
1986 *The Heavens and the Earth: A Political History of the Space Age,* Walter A. McDougall
1987 *Voyagers to the West: A Passage in the Peopling of America on the Eve of the Revolution,* Bernard Bailyn
1988 *The Launching of Modern American Science 1846–1876,* Robert V. Bruce
1989 *Parting the Waters,* Taylor Branch; *Battle Cry of Freedom,* James M. McPherson
1990 *In Our Image: America's Empire in the Philippines,* Stanley Karnow
1991 *A Midwife's Tale: The Life of Martha Ballard, Based on Her Diary 1785–1812,* Laurel Thatcher Ulrich
1992 *The Fate of Liberty: Abraham Lincoln and Civil Liberties,* Mark E. Neely, Jr.
1993 *The Radicalism of the American Revolution,* Gordon S. Wood
1995 *No Ordinary Time: Franklin and Eleanor Roosevelt: The Home Front in World War II,* Doris Kearns Goodwin
1996 *William Cooper's Town: Power and Persuasion on the Frontier of the Early American Republic,* Alan Taylor
1997 *Original Meanings: Politics and Ideas in the Making of the Constitution,* Jack N. Rakove
1998 *Summer for the Gods: The Scopes Trial and America's Continuing Debate Over Science and Religion,* Edward J. Larson

Biography or Autobiography

1917 *Julia Ward Howe,* Laura E. Richards and Maude Howe Elliott, assisted by Florence Howe Hall
1918 *Benjamin Franklin, Self-Revealed,* William Cabell Bruce
1919 *The Education of Henry Adams,* Henry Adams
1920 *The Life of John Marshall,* Albert J. Beveridge
1921 *The Americanization of Edward Bok,* Edward Bok
1922 *A Daughter of the Middle Border,* Hamlin Garland
1923 *The Life and Letters of Walter H. Page,* Burton J. Hendrick
1924 *From Immigrant to Inventor,* Michael Idvorsky Pupin
1925 *Barrett Wendell and His Letters,* M. A. DeWolfe Howe
1926 *The Life of Sir William Osler,* Harvey Cushing
1927 *Whitman,* Emory Holloway
1928 *The American Orchestra and Theodore Thomas,* Charles Edward Russell
1929 *The Training of an American: The Earlier Life and Letters of Walter H. Page,* Burton J. Hendrick
1930 *The Raven,* Marquis James
1931 *Charles W. Eliot,* Henry James
1932 *Theodore Roosevelt,* Henry F. Pringle
1933 *Grover Cleveland,* Allan Nevins
1934 *John Hay,* Tyler Dennett
1935 *R. E. Lee,* Douglas S. Freeman
1936 *The Thought and Character of William James,* Ralph Barton Perry
1937 *Hamilton Fish,* Allan Nevins
1938 *Pedlar's Progress,* Odell Shepard; *Andrew Jackson,* Marquis James
1939 *Benjamin Franklin,* Carl Van Doren
1940 *Woodrow Wilson: Life and Letters,* Vols. VII and VIII, Ray Stannard Baker
1941 *Jonathan Edwards,* Ola E. Winslow
1942 *Crusader in Crinoline,* Forrest Wilson
1943 *Admiral of the Ocean Sea,* Samuel Eliot Morison
1944 *The American Leonardo: The Life of Samuel F. B. Morse,* Carleton Mabee
1945 *George Bancroft: Brahmin Rebel,* Russel Blaine Nye
1946 *Son of the Wilderness,* Linnie Marsh Wolfe
1947 *The Autobiography of William Allen White*
1948 *Forgotten First Citizen: John Bigelow,* Margaret Clapp
1949 *Roosevelt and Hopkins,* Robert E. Sherwood
1950 *John Quincy Adams and the Foundations of American Foreign Policy,* Samuel Flagg Bemis
1951 *John C. Calhoun: American Portrait,* Margaret Louise Coit
1952 *Charles Evans Hughes,* Merlo J. Pusey
1953 *Edmund Pendleton, 1721–1803,* David J. Mays
1954 *The Spirit of St. Louis,* Charles A. Lindbergh
1955 *The Taft Story,* William S. White
1956 *Benjamin Henry Latrobe,* Talbot F. Hamlin
1957 *Profiles in Courage,* John F. Kennedy

1958 *George Washington,* Douglas Southall Freeman (Vols. 1–6) and John Alexander Carroll and Mary Wells Ashworth (Vol. 7)
1959 *Woodrow Wilson, American Prophet,* Arthur Walworth
1960 *John Paul Jones,* Samuel Eliot Morison
1961 *Charles Sumner and the Coming of the Civil War,* David Donald
1963 *Henry James: Vol. II, The Conquest of London, 1870–1881; Vol. III, The Middle Years, 1881–1895,* Leon Edel
1964 *John Keats,* Walter Jackson Bate
1965 *Henry Adams* (3 Vols.), Ernest Samuels
1966 *A Thousand Days,* Arthur M. Schlesinger, Jr.
1967 *Mr. Clemens and Mark Twain,* Justin Kaplan
1968 *Memoirs, 1925–1950,* George F. Kennan
1969 *The Man From New York,* B. L. Reid
1970 *Huey Long,* T. Harry Williams
1971 *Robert Frost: The Years of Triumph, 1915–1938,* Lawrence Thompson
1972 *Eleanor and Franklin: The Story of Their Relationship Based on Eleanor Roosevelt's Private Papers,* Joseph P. Lash
1973 *Luce and His Empire,* W. A. Swanberg
1974 *O'Neill, Son and Artist,* Louis Sheaffer
1975 *The Power Broker: Robert Moses and the Fall of New York,* Robert A. Caro
1976 *Edith Wharton: A Biography,* Richard W. B. Lewis
1977 *A Prince of Our Disorder,* John E. Mack
1978 *Samuel Johnson,* Walter Jackson Bate
1979 *Days of Sorrow and Pain: Leo Baeck and the Berlin Jews,* Leonard Baker
1980 *The Rise of Theodore Roosevelt,* Edmund Morris
1981 *Peter the Great,* Robert K. Massie
1982 *Grant: A Biography,* William S. McFeely
1983 *Growing Up,* Russell Baker
1984 *Booker T. Washington,* Louis R. Harlan
1985 *The Life and Times of Cotton Mather,* Kenneth Silverman
1986 *Louise Bogan: A Portrait,* Elizabeth Frank
1987 *Bearing the Cross: Martin Luther King, Jr., and the Southern Christian Leadership Conference,* David J. Garrow
1988 *Look Homeward: A Life of Thomas Wolfe,* David Herbert Donald
1989 *Oscar Wilde,* Richard Ellmann
1990 *Machiavelli in Hell,* Sebastian de Grazia
1991 *Jackson Pollock: An American Saga,* Steven Naifeh and Gregory White Smith
1992 *Fortunate Son: The Healing of a Vietnam Vet,* Lewis B. Puller, Jr.
1993 *Truman,* David McCullough
1994 *W. E. B. DuBois: Biography of a Race, 1868–1919,* David Levering Lewis
1995 *Harriet Beecher Stowe: A Life,* Joan D. Hedrick
1996 *God: A Biography,* Jack Miles
1997 *Angela's Ashes: A Memoir,* Frank McCourt
1998 *Personal History,* Katharine Graham

Poetry[1]

1918 *Love Songs,* Sara Teasdale
1919 *Old Road to Paradise,* Margaret Widdemer; *Corn Huskers,* Carl Sandburg
1922 *Collected Poems,* Edwin Arlington Robinson
1923 *The Ballad of the Harp-Weaver; A Few Figs from Thistles;* eight sonnets in *American Poetry, 1922, A Miscellany,* Edna St. Vincent Millay
1924 *New Hampshire: A Poem With Notes and Grace Notes,* Robert Frost
1925 *The Man Who Died Twice,* Edwin Arlington Robinson
1926 *What's O'Clock,* Amy Lowell
1927 *Fiddler's Farewell,* Leonora Speyer
1928 *Tristram,* Edwin Arlington Robinson
1929 *John Brown's Body,* Stephen Vincent Benét
1930 *Selected Poems,* Conrad Aiken
1931 *Collected Poems,* Robert Frost
1932 *The Flowering Stone,* George Dillon
1933 *Conquistador,* Archibald MacLeish
1934 *Collected Verse,* Robert Hillyer
1935 *Bright Ambush,* Audrey Wurdemann
1936 *Strange Holiness,* Robert P. T. Coffin
1937 *A Further Range,* Robert Frost
1938 *Cold Morning Sky,* Marya Zaturenska
1939 *Selected Poems,* John Gould Fletcher
1940 *Collected Poems,* Mark Van Doren
1941 *Sunderland Capture,* Leonard Bacon
1942 *The Dust Which Is God,* William Rose Benét
1943 *A Witness Tree,* Robert Frost
1944 *Western Star,* Stephen Vincent Benét
1945 *V-Letter and Other Poems,* Karl Shapiro
1947 *Lord Weary's Castle,* Robert Lowell
1948 *The Age of Anxiety,* W. H. Auden
1949 *Terror and Decorum,* Peter Viereck
1950 *Annie Allen,* Gwendolyn Brooks
1951 *Complete Poems,* Carl Sandburg
1952 *Collected Poems,* Marianne Moore
1953 *Collected Poems, 1917–1952,* Archibald MacLeish
1954 *The Waking,* Theodore Roethke
1955 *Collected Poems,* Wallace Stevens
1956 *Poems—North & South,* Elizabeth Bishop
1957 *Things of This World,* Richard Wilbur
1958 *Promises: Poems, 1954–1956,* Robert Penn Warren
1959 *Selected Poems, 1928–1958,* Stanley Kunitz
1960 *Heart's Needle,* William Snodgrass
1961 *Times Three: Selected Verse From Three Decades,* Phyllis McGinley
1962 *Poems,* Alan Dugan
1963 *Pictures From Breughel,* William Carlos Williams
1964 *At the End of the Open Road,* Louis Simpson
1965 *77 Dream Songs,* John Berryman
1966 *Selected Poems,* Richard Eberhart
1967 *Live or Die,* Anne Sexton
1968 *The Hard Hours,* Anthony Hecht
1969 *Of Being Numerous,* George Oppen
1970 *Untitled Subjects,* Richard Howard
1971 *The Carrier of Ladders,* William S. Merwin
1972 *Collected Poems,* James Wright
1973 *Up Country,* Maxine Winokur Kumin
1974 *The Dolphin,* Robert Lowell
1975 *Turtle Island,* Gary Snyder
1976 *Self-Portrait in a Convex Mirror,* John Ashbery
1977 *Divine Comedies,* James Merrill
1978 *Collected Poems,* Howard Nemerov
1979 *Now and Then: Poems, 1976–1978,* Robert Penn Warren
1980 *Selected Poems,* Donald Rodney Justice
1981 *The Morning of the Poem,* James Schuyler
1982 *The Collected Poems,* Sylvia Plath
1983 *Selected Poems,* Galway Kinnell
1984 *American Primitive,* Mary Oliver
1985 *Yin,* Carolyn Kizer
1986 *The Flying Change,* Henry Taylor

1987 *Thomas and Beulah,* Rita Dove
1988 *Partial Accounts: New and Selected Poems,* William Meredith
1989 *New and Collected Poems,* Richard Wilbur
1990 *The World Doesn't End,* Charles Simic
1991 *Near Changes,* Mona Van Duyn
1992 *Selected Poems,* James Tate
1993 *The Wild Iris,* Louise Gluck
1994 *Neon Vernacular,* Yusef Komunyakaa
1995 *Simple Truth,* Philip Levine
1996 *The Dream of the Unified Field,* Jorie Graham
1997 *Alive Together: New and Selected Poems,* Lisel Mueller
1998 *Black Zodiac,* Charles Wright

1. The poetry prize was established in 1922. The 1918 and 1919 awards were made from gifts provided by the Poetry Society.

General Nonfiction

1962 *The Making of the President, 1960,* Theodore H. White
1963 *The Guns of August,* Barbara W. Tuchman
1964 *Anti-Intellectualism in American Life,* Richard Hofstadter
1965 *O Strange New World,* Howard Mumford Jones
1966 *Wandering Through Winter,* Edwin Way Teale
1967 *The Problem of Slavery in Western Culture,* David Brion Davis
1968 *Rousseau and Revolution,* Will and Ariel Durant
1969 *So Human an Animal,* Rene Jules Dubos; *The Armies of the Night,* Norman Mailer
1970 *Gandhi's Truth,* Erik H. Erikson
1971 *The Rising Sun,* John Toland
1972 *Stilwell and the American Experience in China, 1911–1945,* Barbara W. Tuchman
1973 *Fire in the Lake: The Vietnamese and the Americans in Vietnam,* Frances FitzGerald; *Children of Crisis* (Vols. 1 and 2), Robert M. Coles
1974 *The Denial of Death,* Ernest Becker
1975 *Pilgrim at Tinker Creek,* Annie Dillard
1976 *Why Survive? Being Old in America,* Robert N. Butler
1977 *Beautiful Swimmers: Watermen, Crabs and the Chesapeake Bay,* William W. Warner
1978 *The Dragons of Eden,* Carl Sagan
1979 *On Human Nature,* Edward O. Wilson
1980 *Gödel, Escher, Bach: An Eternal Golden Braid,* Douglas R. Hofstadter
1981 *Fin-de–Siecle Vienna: Politics and Culture,* Carl E. Schorske
1982 *The Soul of a New Machine,* Tracy Kidder
1983 *Is There No Place on Earth for Me?,* Susan Sheehan
1984 *Social Transformation of American Medicine,* Paul Starr
1985 *The Good War: An Oral History of World War II,* Studs Terkel
1986 *Move Your Shadow: South Africa, Black and White,* Joseph Lelyveld; *Common Ground: A Turbulent Decade in the Lives of Three American Families,* J. Anthony Lukas
1987 *Arab and Jew: Wounded Spirits in a Promised Land,* David K. Shipler
1988 *The Making of the Atomic Bomb,* Richard Rhodes
1989 *A Bright Shining Lie,* Neil Sheehan
1990 *And Their Children After Them,* Dale Maharidge and Michael Williamson
1991 *The Ants,* Bert Holldobler and Edward O. Wilson
1992 *The Prize: The Epic Quest for Oil, Money and Power,* Daniel Yergin
1993 *Lincoln at Gettysburg: The Words That Remade America,* Garry Wills
1994 *Lenin's Tomb: The Last Days of the Soviet Empire,* David Remick
1995 *The Beak of the Finch: A Story of Evolution in Our Time,* Jonathan Weiner
1996 *The Haunted Land: Facing Europe's Ghosts After Communism,* Tina Rosenberg
1997 *Ashes to Ashes: America's Hundred-Year Cigarette War, the Public Health, and the Unabashed Triumph of Philip Morris,* Richard Kluger
1998 *Guns, Germs, and Steel: The Fates of Human Societies,* Jared Diamond

PULITZER PRIZES IN MUSIC

1943 *Secular Cantata No. 2, A Free Song,* William Schuman
1944 *Symphony No. 4* (Op. 34), Howard Hanson
1945 *Appalachian Spring,* Aaron Copland
1946 *The Canticle of the Sun,* Leo Sowerby
1947 *Symphony No. 3,* Charles Ives
1948 *Symphony No. 3,* Walter Piston
1949 *Louisiana Story* music, Virgil Thomson
1950 *The Consul,* Gian Carlo Menotti
1951 Music for opera *Giants in the Earth,* Douglas Stuart Moore
1952 *Symphony Concertante,* Gail Kubik
1954 *Concerto for Two Pianos and Orchestra,* Quincy Porter
1955 *The Saint of Bleecker Street,* Gian Carlo Menotti
1956 *Symphony No. 3,* Ernst Toch
1957 *Meditations on Ecclesiastes,* Norman Dello Joio
1958 *Vanessa,* Samuel Barber
1959 *Concerto for Piano and Orchestra,* John La Montaine
1960 *Second String Quartet,* Elliott Carter
1961 *Symphony No. 7,* Walter Piston
1962 *The Crucible,* Robert Ward
1963 *Piano Concerto No. 1,* Samuel Barber
1966 *Variations for Orchestra,* Leslie Bassett
1967 *Quartet No. 3,* Leon Kirchner
1968 *Echoes of Time and the River,* George Crumb
1969 *String Quartet No. 3,* Karel Husa
1970 *Time's Encomium,* Charles Wuorinen
1971 *Synchronisms No. 6 for Piano and Electronic Sound,* Mario Davidowsky
1972 *Windows,* Jacob Druckman
1973 *String Quartet No. 3,* Elliott Carter
1974 *Notturno,* Donald Martino
1975 *From the Diary of Virginia Woolf,* Dominick Argento
1976 *Air Music,* Ned Rorem
1977 *Visions of Terror and Wonder,* Richard Wernick
1978 *Déjà Vu for Percussion Quartet and Orchestra,* Michael Colgrass
1979 *Aftertones of Infinity,* Joseph Schwantner
1980 *In Memory of a Summer Day,* David Del Tredici
1982 *Concerto for Orchestra,* Roger Sessions
1983 *Three Movements for Orchestra,* Ellen T. Zwilich

1984 *Canti del Sole,* Bernard Rands
1985 *Symphony RiverRun,* Stephen Albert
1986 *Wind Quintet IV,* George Perle
1987 *The Flight Into Egypt,* John Harbison
1988 *12 New Etudes for Piano,* William Bolcom
1989 *Whispers Out of Time,* Roger Reynolds
1990 *Duplicates: A Concerto for Two Pianos and Orchestra,* Mel Powell
1991 *Symphony,* Shulamit Ran
1992 *The Face of the Night, The Heart of the Dark,* Wayne Peterson
1993 *Trombone Concerto,* Christopher Rouse
1994 *Of Reminiscences and Reflections,* Gunther Schuller
1995 *Stringmusic,* Morton Gould
1996 *Lilacs,* George Walker
1997 *Blood on the Field,* Wynton Marsalis
1998 *String Quartet No. 2, Musica Instrumentalis,* Aaron Jay Kernis

PULITZER PRIZES IN DRAMA

1918 *Why Marry?* Jesse Lynch Williams
1920 *Beyond the Horizon,* Eugene O'Neill
1921 *Miss Lulu Bett,* Zona Gale
1922 *Anna Christie,* Eugene O'Neill
1923 *Icebound,* Owen Davis
1924 *Hell-Bent Fer Heaven,* Hatcher Hughes
1925 *They Knew What They Wanted,* Sidney Howard
1926 *Craig's Wife,* George Kelly
1927 *In Abraham's Bosom,* Paul Green
1928 *Strange Interlude,* Eugene O'Neill
1929 *Street Scene,* Elmer L. Rice
1930 *The Green Pastures,* Marc Connelly
1931 *Alison's House,* Susan Glaspell
1932 *Of Thee I Sing,* George S. Kaufman, Morrie Ryskind, and Ira Gershwin
1933 *Both Your Houses,* Maxwell Anderson
1934 *Men in White,* Sidney Kingsley
1935 *The Old Maid,* Zöe Akins
1936 *Idiot's Delight,* Robert E. Sherwood
1937 *You Can't Take It With You,* Moss Hart and George S. Kaufman
1938 *Our Town,* Thornton Wilder
1939 *Abe Lincoln in Illinois,* Robert E. Sherwood
1940 *The Time of Your Life,* William Saroyan
1941 *There Shall Be No Night,* Robert E. Sherwood
1943 *The Skin of Our Teeth,* Thornton Wilder
1945 *Harvey,* Mary Chase
1946 *State of the Union,* Russel Crouse and Howard Lindsay
1948 *A Streetcar Named Desire,* Tennessee Williams
1949 *Death of a Salesman,* Arthur Miller
1950 *South Pacific,* Richard Rodgers, Oscar Hammerstein II, and Joshua Logan
1952 *The Shrike,* Joseph Kramm
1953 *Picnic,* William Inge
1954 *The Teahouse of the August Moon,* John Patrick
1955 *Cat on a Hot Tin Roof,* Tennessee Williams
1956 *The Diary of Anne Frank,* Frances Goodrich and Albert Hackett
1957 *Long Day's Journey Into Night,* Eugene O'Neill
1958 *Look Homeward, Angel,* Ketti Frings
1959 *J. B.* Archibald MacLeish
1960 *Fiorello!* George Abbott, Jerome Weidman, Jerry Bock, and Sheldon Harnick
1961 *All the Way Home,* Tad Mosel
1962 *How to Succeed in Business Without Really Trying,* Frank Loesser and Abe Burrows
1965 *The Subject Was Roses,* Frank D. Gilroy
1967 *A Delicate Balance,* Edward Albee
1969 *The Great White Hope,* Howard Sackler
1970 *No Place to Be Somebody,* Charles Gordone
1971 *The Effect of Gamma Rays on Man-in-the-Moon Marigolds,* Paul Zindel
1973 *That Championship Season,* Jason Miller
1975 *Seascape,* Edward Albee
1976 *A Chorus Line,* Conceived by Michael Bennett
1977 *The Shadow Box,* Michael Cristofer
1978 *The Gin Game,* Donald L. Coburn
1979 *Buried Child,* Sam Shepard
1980 *Talley's Folly,* Lanford Wilson
1981 *Crimes of the Heart,* Beth Henley
1982 *A Soldier's Play,* Charles Fuller
1983 *'Night, Mother,* Marsha Norman
1984 *Glengarry Glen Ross,* David Mamet
1985 *Sunday in the Park with George,* Stephen Sondheim and James Lapine
1987 *Fences,* August Wilson
1988 *Driving Miss Daisy,* Alfred Uhry
1989 *The Heidi Chronicles,* Wendy Wasserstein
1990 *The Piano Lesson,* August Wilson
1991 *Lost in Yonkers,* Neil Simon
1992 *The Kentucky Cycle,* Robert Schenkkan
1993 *Angels in America: Millennium Approaches,* Tony Kushner
1994 *Three Tall Women,* Edward Albee
1995 *The Young Man from Atlanta,* Horton Foote
1996 *Rent,* Jonathan Larson
1990 *How I Learned to Drive,* Paula Vogel

SPECIAL CITATIONS

1938 *Edmonton* [Alberta] *Journal,* special bronze plaque for editorial leadership in defense of freedom of the press in province of Alberta
1941 *New York Times,* for the public educational value of its foreign news report
1944 Byron Price, director of the Office of Censorship, for the creation and administration of the newspaper and radio codes; Mrs. William Allen White, for her husband's interest and services during the past seven years as a member of the Advisory Board of the Graduate School of Journalism, Columbia University; Richard Rodgers and Oscar Hammerstein II, for their musical *Oklahoma!*
1945 The cartographers of the American press, for their war maps
1947 (Pulitzer centennial year.) Columbia University and the Graduate School of Journalism, for their efforts to maintain and advance the high standards governing the Pulitzer Prize awards; the *St. Louis Post–Dispatch,* for its unswerving adherence to the public and professional ideals of its founder and its leadership in American journalism
1948 Dr. Frank D. Fackenthal, for his interest and service
1951 Cyrus L. Sulzberger *(New York Times),* for his exclusive interview with Archbishop Stepinac in a Yugoslav prison
1952 *Kansas City Star,* for coverage of 1951 floods; Max Kase *(New York Journal–American),* for exposures of bribery in basketball
1953 *New York Times,* for its 17-year publication of "Review of the Week," and Lester Markel, its founder

1957 Kenneth Roberts, for his historical novels
1958 Walter Lippmann *(New York Herald Tribune)*, for his "wisdom, perception and high sense of responsibility" in his commentary on national and international affairs
1960 Garrett Mattingly, for *The Armada*
1961 *American Heritage Picture History of the Civil War,* as a distinguished example of American book publishing
1964 Gannett Newspapers, Rochester, N.Y.
1973 James Thomas Flexner, for his biography *George Washington*
1974 Roger Sessions, for his "life's work in music"
1976 John Hohenberg, for "services for 22 years as Administrator of the Pulitzer Prizes"; Scott Joplin, for his contributions to American music
1977 Alex Haley, for his novel, *Roots*
1978 E. B. White of *New Yorker* magazine and Richard L. Strout of *The Christian Science Monitor*
1982 Milton Babbitt, "for his life's work as a distinguished and seminal American composer"
1984 Theodor Seuss Geisel (Dr. Seuss), for "books full of playful rhymes, nonsense words and strange illustrations"
1985 William Schuman, for "more than half a century of contribution to American music as a composer and educational leader"
1987 Joseph Pulitzer Jr., "for extraordinary services to American journalism and letters during his 31 years as chairman of the Pulitzer Prize Board and for his accomplishments as an editor and publisher"
1992 *Maus,* Art Spiegelman
1996 Herb Caen *(San Francisco Chronicle)*, "for his extraordinary and continuing contribution as a voice and conscience of his city"
1998 George Gershwin

1997 National Society of Film Critics Awards

The National Society of Film Critics includes 48 leading critics from major U.S. publications and media outlets.

Best Picture: *L.A. Confidential*
Best Actor: Robert Duvall, *The Apostle*
Best Actress: Julie Christie, *Afterglow*
Best Supporting Actor: Burt Reynolds, *Boogie Nights*
Best Supporting Actress: Julianne Moore, *Boogie Nights*
Best Director: Curtis Hanson, *L.A. Confidential*
Best Screenplay: Curtis Hanson and Brian Helgeland, *L.A. Confidential*
Best Cinematography: Roger Deakins, *Kundun*
Best Foreign Film: *La Promesse* (Belgium)
Best Documentary: *Fast, Cheap & Out of Control*
Special Award: *Nightjohn,* Charles Burnett

1997 Broadcast Film Critics Association Awards

The Broadcast Film Critics Association, formed in 1995, includes 84 television, radio, and online movie critics.

Best Picture: *L.A. Confidential*
Best Actor: Jack Nicholson, *As Good As It Gets*
Best Actress: Helena Bonham Carter, *The Wings of the Dove*
Best Supporting Actor: Anthony Hopkins, *Amistad*
Best Supporting Actress: Joan Cusack, *In & Out*
Best Director: James Cameron, *Titanic*
Best Adapted Screenplay: Curtis Hanson and Brian Helgeland, *L.A. Confidential*
Best Original Screenplay: Ben Affleck and Matt Damon, *Good Will Hunting*
Best Made-for-TV Picture: *Don King: Only in America* (HBO)
Best Child Performance: Jurnee Smollett, *Eve's Bayou*
Lifetime Achievement: Robert Wise

1997 Golden Globe Awards

The Golden Globe Awards, honoring excellence in film and television, are presented by the Hollywood Foreign Press Association.

MOTION PICTURE

Best Drama: *Titanic*
Best Actor in a Drama: Peter Fonda, *Ulee's Gold*
Best Actress in a Drama: Judi Dench, *Mrs. Brown*
Best Musical or Comedy: *As Good As It Gets*
Best Actor in a Musical or Comedy: Jack Nicholson, *As Good As It Gets*
Best Actress in a Musical or Comedy: Helen Hunt, *As Good As It Gets*
Best Supporting Actor: Burt Reynolds, *Boogie Nights*
Best Supporting Actress: Kim Basinger, *L.A. Confidential*
Best Director: James Cameron, *Titanic*
Best Screenplay: Matt Damon and Ben Affleck, *Good Will Hunting*
Best Original Score: James Horner, *Titanic*
Best Original Song: "My Heart Will Go On," *Titanic*
Best Foreign Film: *Ma Vie en Rose* (Belgium)
Cecil B. DeMille Award for Lifetime Achievement: Shirley MacLaine

TELEVISION

Best Series, Drama: *The X–Files* (Fox)
Best Actor in a Drama: Anthony Edwards, *ER*
Best Actress in a Drama: Christine Lahti, *Chicago Hope*
Best Series, Musical or Comedy: *Ally McBeal* (Fox)
Best Actor in a Musical or Comedy Series: Michael J. Fox, *Spin City*
Best Actress in a Musical or Comedy Series: Calista Flockhart, *Ally McBeal*
Best Miniseries or Movie Made for Television: *George Wallace* (TNT)

Best Actor in a Miniseries or Movie Made for Television: Ving Rhames, *Don King: Only in America*

Best Actress in a Miniseries or Movie Made for Television: Alfre Woodard, *Miss Evers' Boys*

Best Supporting Actor in a Series, Miniseries, or Movie Made for Television: George C. Scott, *12 Angry Men*

Best Supporting Actress in a Series, Miniseries, or Movie Made for Television: Angelina Jolie, *George Wallace*

1998 New York Drama Critics Circle Awards

Best Play: *Art*
Best American Play: *Pride's Crossing*
Best Musical: *The Lion King*
Special Citation: *Cabaret*

1998 Obie Awards

The Obie Awards are presented by *The Village Voice* to honor superior off-Broadway theater.

Best Play: Richard Foreman, *Pearls for Pigs, Benita Canova*

Direction: Ivo van Hove, *More Stately Mansions;* David Esbjornson, *Therese Raquin;* Jo Bonney, sustained excellence of direction

Performance: Lea DeLaria, *On the Town;* Mary Testa, *On the Town* and *From Above;* Tim Hopper, *More Stately Mansions;* David Patrick Kelly, sustained excellence of performance; Joseph Wiseman, *I Can't Remember Anything;* Heather Gillespie, *Mamba's Daughters;* Kate Valk, sustained excellence of performance; Marie Mullen, *The Beauty Queen of Leenane;* Matthew Maguire, *I Don't Know Who He Was and I Don't Know What He Said;* Yvette Freeman, *Dinah Was;* Adriane Lenox, *Dinah Was;* Elizabeth Marvel, *Therese Raquin* and *Misalliance;* J. Smith Cameron, *As Bees in Honey Drown;* Brian Murray, sustained excellence of performance; Joan MacIntosh, *More Stately Mansions*

Design: Darron L. West, soundscape for *Bob;* Mimi Jordan Sherin, lighting design for *Bob*

Special Citations: Target Margin Theater, *Mamba's Daughters;* David Herskovits, Thomas Cabaniss, Lenore Doxsee, Erika Belsey, David Zinn, Tim Schellenbaum, John Cameron Mitchell, *Hedwig and the Angry Inch;* Stephen Trask, *Hedwig and the Angry Inch;* Mark Bennett, sustained excellence of sound design; Alan Johnson, sustained excellence of musical direction and pianism; Karen Finley, *The American Chestnut;* Philim McDermott, Lee Simpson, Julian Crouch, Guy Dartnell, Ben Park, and Steve Tiplady, creators of *70 Hill Lane;* Buzz Cohen, distinguished stage management

Sustained Achievement: Jennifer Tipton

Ross Wetzsteon Award: Doug Aibel and the Vineyard Theater for sustained support of artists and creativity in the theater

1998 Tony (Antoinette Perry) Awards

The Tony Awards are theater awards recognizing talent in plays and musicals.

Play: *Art*
Musical: *The Lion King*
Revival—Play: *A View From the Bridge*
Revival—Musical: *Cabaret*
Actor—Play: Anthony LaPaglia, *A View From the Bridge*
Actress—Play: Marie Mullen, *The Beauty Queen of Leenane*
Actor—Musical: Alan Cumming, *Cabaret*
Actress—Musical: Natasha Richardson, *Cabaret*
Featured Actor—Play: Tom Murphy, *The Beauty Queen of Leenane*
Featured Actress—Play: Anna Manahan, *The Beauty Queen of Leenane*
Featured Actor—Musical: Ron Rifkin, *Cabaret*
Featured Actress—Musical: Audra McDonald, *Ragtime*
Director—Play: Garry Hynes, *The Beauty Queen of Leenane*
Director—Musical: Julie Taymor, *The Lion King*
Book—Musical: *Ragtime*
Score—Musical: *Ragtime*
Orchestration: William David Brohn, *Ragtime*
Scenic Designer: Richard Hudson, *The Lion King*
Costume Designer: Julie Taymor, *The Lion King*
Choreographer: Garth Fagan, *The Lion King*
Lighting Designer: Donald Holder, *The Lion King*
Regional Theater: Denver Center Theatre Company
Special Awards: Edward E. Colton, theatrical attorney; Ben Edwards, set design

1998 National Magazine Awards

General Excellence: *Double Take* (circulation less than 100,000); *Preservation* (circulation 100,000 to 400,000); *Outside* (circulation 400,000 to 1,000,000); *Rolling Stone* (circulation more than 1,000,000)
Personal Service: *Men's Journal*
Special Interests: *Entertainment Weekly*
Reporting: *Rolling Stone*
Essays and Criticism: *The New Yorker*
Feature Writing: *Harper's Magazine*
Public Interest: *The Atlantic Monthly*
Design: *Entertainment Weekly*
Fiction: *The New Yorker*
Single-Topic Issue: *The Sciences*
Photography: *W*
General Excellence in New Media: *The Sporting News Online*

Major Grammy Awards for Recording in 1997

Record: "Sunny Came Home," Shawn Colvin
Album: *Time Out of Mind,* Bob Dylan
Song: "Sunny Came Home," Shawn Colvin and John Leventhal, songwriters
New Artist: Paula Cole
Female Pop Vocal: "Building a Mystery," Sarah McLachlan
Male Pop Vocal: "Candle in the Wind 1997," Elton John
Pop Duo or Group with Vocals: "Virtual Insanity," Jamiroquai
Pop Collaboration with Vocals: "Don't Look Back," John Lee Hooker with Van Morrison
Pop Instrumental: "Last Dance," Sarah McLachlan
Dance Recording: "Carry On," Donna Summer and Giorgio Moroder
Pop Album: *Hourglass,* James Taylor
Traditional Pop Album: *Tony Bennett on Holiday*, Tony Bennett
Female Rock Vocal: "Criminal," Fiona Apple
Male Rock Vocal: "Cold Irons Bound," Bob Dylan
Rock Duo or Group with Vocals: "One Headlight," the Wallflowers
Hard Rock: "The End Is the Beginning Is the End," the Smashing Pumpkins
Metal: "Ænima," Tool
Rock Instrumental: "Block Rockin' Beats," the Chemical Brothers
Rock Song: "One Headlight," Jakob Dylan, songwriter
Rock Album: *Blue Moon Swamp*, John Fogerty
Alternative Album: *OK Computer*, Radiohead
Female R&B Vocal: "On & On," Erykah Badu
Male R&B Vocal: "I Believe I Can Fly," R. Kelly
R&B Duo or Group with Vocals: "No Diggity," Blackstreet

R&B Song: "I Believe I Can Fly," R. Kelly, songwriter
R&B Album: *Baduizm*, Erykah Badu
Rap Solo: "Men in Black," Will Smith
Rap Duo or Group: "I'll Be Missing You," Puff Daddy and Faith Evans featuring 112
Rap Album: *No Way Out*, Puff Daddy and the Family
Female Country Vocal: "How Do I Live," Trisha Yearwood
Male Country Vocal: "Pretty Little Adriana," Vince Gill
Country Duo or Group with Vocals: "Looking in the Eyes of Love," Alison Krauss and Union Station
Country Collaboration with Vocals: "In Another's Eyes," Trisha Yearwood and Garth Brooks
Country Instrumental: "Little Liza Jane," Alison Krauss and Union Station
Country Song: "Butterfly Kisses," Bob Carlisle and Randy Thomas, songwriters
Country Album: *Unchained*, Johnny Cash
Bluegrass Album: *So Long So Wrong*, Alison Krauss and Union Station
New Age Album: *Oracle*, Michael Hedges
Contemporary Jazz: *Into the Sun*, Randy Brecker
Jazz Vocal: *Dear Ella*, Dee Dee Bridgewater
Jazz Instrumental, Solo: "Stardust," Doc Cheatham and Nicholas Payton
Jazz Instrumental, Individual or Group: *Beyond the Missouri Sky*, Charlie Haden and Pat Metheny
Large Jazz Ensemble: *Joe Henderson Big Band*, Joe Henderson Big Band
Latin Jazz: *Habana*, Roy Hargrove's Crisol
Rock Gospel Album: *Welcome to the Freak Show: dc Talk Live in Concert*, dc Talk
Pop/Contemporary Gospel Album: *Much Afraid*, Jars of Clay
Southern Gospel, Country Gospel or Bluegrass Gospel Album: *Amazing Grace 2: A Country Salute to Gospel*, various artists
Traditional Soul Gospel Album: *I Couldn't Hear Nobody Pray*, the Fairfield Four
Contemporary Soul Gospel Album: *Brothers*, Take 6
Gospel Album by a Choir or Chorus: *God's Property From Kirk Franklin's Nu Nation*, God's Property; Kirk Franklin, Choir Director
Latin Pop: *Romances*, Luis Miguel
Latin Rock/Alternative: *Fabulosos Calavera*, Los Fabulosos Cadillacs
Tropical Latin: *Buena Vista Social Club*, Ry Cooder
Mexican-American/Tejano: *En Tus Manos*, La Mafia
Traditional Blues: *Don't Look Back*, John Lee Hooker
Contemporary Blues: *Senor Blues*, Taj Mahal
Traditional Folk: *L'Amour ou la Folie*, BeauSoleil
Contemporary Folk: *Time Out of Mind*, Bob Dylan
Reggae Album: *Fallen is Babylon*, Ziggy Marley and the Melody Makers
World Music Album: *Nascimento*, Milton Nascimento
Polka Album: *Living on Polka Time*, Jimmy Sturr
Musical Album for Children: *All Aboard!*, John Denver
Spoken Word Album for Children: *Winnie-The-Pooh*, Charles Kuralt
Spoken Word or Non-Musical Album: *Charles Kuralt's Spring*, Charles Kuralt
Spoken Comedy Album: *Roll With the New*, Chris Rock
Musical Show Album: *Chicago: the Musical*
Instrumental Composition: "Aung San Suu Kyi," Wayne Shorter, composer
Instrumental Composition for a Motion Picture or for Television: *The English Patient*, Gabriel Yared, composer
Song Written Specifically for a Motion Picture or for Television: "I Believe I Can Fly" (from *Space Jam*), R. Kelly, songwriter
Instrumental Arrangement: "Straight, No Chaser," Bill Holman, arranger
Instrumental Arrangement with Accompanying Vocals: "Cotton Tail," Slide Hampton, arranger
Historical Album: *Anthology of American Folk Music (1997 Edition Expanded)*
Producer: Babyface
Classical Producer: Steven Epstein
Classical Album: *Premieres: Cello Concertos (Works of Danielpour, Kirchner, Rouse)*, Philadelphia Orchestra
Orchestral: *Berlioz: Symphonie Fantastique; Tristia*, Pierre Boulez conducting the Cleveland Orchestra and Chorus
Opera: *Wagner: Die Meistersinger von Nurnberg*, Sir Georg Solti conducting the Chicago Symphony Orchestra and Chorus
Choral: *Adams: Harmonium/Rachmaninoff: The Bells*, Robert Shaw, conductor
Instrumental Soloist with Orchestra: *Premieres: Cello Concertos (Works of Danielpour, Kirchner, Rouse)*, Yo-Yo Ma, violoncello; David Zinman, conductor
Instrumental Soloist without Orchestra: *Bach: Suites for Solo Cello Nos. 1–6*, Janos Starker, cello
Chamber Music: *Beethoven: The String Quartets*, Emerson String Quartet
Small Ensemble Performance (with or without Conductor): "Hindemith: Kammermusik No. 1 With Finale 1921, Op. 24 No. 1," Claudio Abbado conducting members of the Berliner Philharmonic
Classical Vocal: *An Italian Songbook (Works of Bellini, Donizetti, Rossini)*, Cecilia Bartoli
Classical Contemporary Composition: "Adams: El Dorado," John Adams, composer
Music Video, Short Form: "Got 'Till It's Gone," Janet Jackson; Mark Romanek and Aris McGarry, video directors
Music Video, Long Form: *Alanis Morissette: Jagged Little Pill, Live*, Alanis Morissette and Steve Purcell, video directors

1997 George Foster Peabody Awards for Broadcasting

State Farm: Good Neighbor or Bad Faith?: *KGO Radio, San Francisco*
Flood of the Century: *KFGO, Fargo, N.D.*
Will the Circle Be Unbroken?: *Southern Regional Council, Atlanta*
Dietrich Bonhoeffer: The Cost of Freedom: *Focus on the Family, Colorado Springs, Colo.*
Jazz from Lincoln Center: *Murray Street Enterprise, New York, for National Public Radio*
Military Medicine: *WRAL–TV, Raleigh, N.C.*
The Trial of Pol Pot: *ABC News/Nightline*
Richard Rodrigues Essays on American Life: *The NewsHour with Jim Lehrer, PBS*
The Castro: *KQED–TV, San Francisco*
Liberty! The American Revolution: *KTCA, Twin Cities Public Television, St. Paul, Minn., in association with Middlemarch Films*
Hello Mr. President: *Barraclough Carey Productions for Channel 4, London, and The History Channel, New York*
A Healthy Baby Girl: *P.O.V./The American Documentary; a co-presentation with the Independent Television Service*
Look for Me Here: 299 Days in the Life of Nora Lenihan: *New England Cable News, Newton, Mass.*
In the Land of the Deaf: *Les Films d'Ici, La Sept-Cinema, Centre European Cinematographique RhoneAlpes, presented on Bravo/The Independent Film Channel*
Blue Note: A History of Modern Jazz: *Euroarts Entertainment, OHG & SDR arte, in association with Bravo and Denmark Radio*
Divided Highways: The Interstates and the Transformation of American Life: *Florentine Films/Hott Productions and WETA–TV, Washington, D.C.*
The American Experience: The Presidents Series: *WGBH–TV, Boston*
The American Experience: Troublesome Creek—A Midwestern: *WGBH–TV, Boston*
The Nazis: A Warning from History: *BBC, London*

Body Doubles: The Twin Experience: *Home Box Office and Carlton Television, in association with the Canadian Broadcasting Corporation*
City Arts: *Thirteen/WNET, New York*
Ellen: The Puppy Episode: *ABC, The Black/Marlens Company in association with Touchstone Television*
Homicide: Life on the Street: *NBC, Fatima Productions, New York*
Nothing Sacred: *ABC, Sarabande Productions in association with 20th Century Fox TV*
Mobil Masterpiece Theatre: The Tenant of Wildfell Hall: *WGBH–TV, Boston, and BBC, London*
Don King: Only in America: *HBO Pictures and the Thomas Carter Company*
George Wallace: *TNT, a Mark Carliner Production*
The Eddie Files: *FASE Productions, Los Angeles, for PBS*
Wishbone: *Big Feats! Entertainment, an entertainment unit of Lyrick Studios, for PBS*
Nickelodeon: The Big Help: *Nickelodeon, New York*
CBS News: Sunday Morning: *CBS, New York*
Carol Marin: In recognition of nearly two decades of distinguished investigative reporting that demonstrates a personal commitment to ethics and integrity in local broadcast journalism.
CBS News: 60 Minutes: *CBS, New York*
R.E. "Ted" Turner: A titanic figure in modern electronic communication whose pioneering efforts in station ownership, cable and satellite, entertainment and sports programming, and broadcast journalism have revolutionized media in America and worldwide.

Alfred I. du Pont–Columbia University Broadcast News Awards

Administered by Columbia University, the awards recognize excellence in television and radio broadcasting. This year's awards were given for work broadcast between July 1, 1996, and June 30, 1997.

GOLD BATON

Frontline, for remarkable quality and sustained commitment to controversial and sensitive stories as exemplified by four programs: "Murder, Money and Mexico," "The Choice '96," "Secret Daughter," and "Innocence Lost: The Plea" (WGBH–TV, Boston)

SILVER BATONS

Television Awards: *PrimeTime Live:* "Debt Reckoning" (ABC News); "Why Can't We Live Together?" (NBC News and Scripps Howard News Prods.); "Enter the Jury Room" (CBS News)
Major-Market Television: WABC–TV (New York) for "Room 104: The Overcrowding Crisis," about a first-grade classroom in Brooklyn
Small-Market Television: Wisconsin Public Television for "Welcome to Poverty Hollow," which followed three families in an innovative anti-poverty effort in northern Wisconsin that responded to the state's new welfare reform system; KTCA–TV (St. Paul, Minn.) for *NewsNight Minnesota:* "Unisys," a series of reports about the impact of downsizing on long-term employees of the Unisys Corporation

Independent Television Productions: The Center for New American Media for "Vote for Me: Politics in America" (PBS); Blowback Productions for "CIA: America's Secret Warriors" (Discovery Channel); Jon Else, Sandra Itkoff, and Marc Reisner for "An American Nile" (PBS); KCET (Los Angeles) and the BBC for "The Great War and the Shaping of the 20th Century" (PBS)

Radio Awards: KUSC (Los Angeles) for *Marketplace,* which proves that reporting on economic issues can be approached with energy and flair (Public Radio International)

Major Emmy Awards for TV in 1997

Drama Series: *Law & Order* (NBC)
- **Actress:** Gillian Anderson, *The X–Files*
- **Actor:** Dennis Franz, *NYPD Blue*
- **Supporting actress:** Kim Delaney, *NYPD Blue*
- **Supporting actor:** Hector Elizondo, *Chicago Hope*

Comedy Series: *Frasier* (NBC)
- **Actress:** Helen Hunt, *Mad About You*
- **Actor:** John Lithgow, *3rd Rock From the Sun*
- **Supporting actress:** Kristen Johnston, *3rd Rock From the Sun*
- **Supporting actor:** Michael Richards, *Seinfeld*

Variety, Music, or Comedy Series: *Tracey Takes On . . .* (HBO)
Variety, Music, or Comedy Special: *Chris Rock: Bring the Pain* (HBO)
Miniseries or Special: *Prime Suspect 5: Errors of Judgment* (PBS)
- **Actress:** Alfre Woodard, *Miss Evers' Boys*
- **Actor:** Armand Assante, *Gotti*
- **Supporting actress:** Diana Rigg, *Rebecca*
- **Supporting actor:** Beau Bridges, *The Second Civil War*

Made for TV Movie: *Miss Evers' Boys* (HBO)
Individual Performance, Variety, or Music Program: Bette Midler, *Bette Midler: Diva Las Vegas*

1998 TV Daytime Emmy Awards

Outstanding Drama Series: *All My Children* (ABC)
Lead Actor in a Drama Series: Eric Braeden, *The Young and the Restless* (CBS)
Lead Actress in a Drama Series: Cynthia Watros, *Guiding Light* (CBS)
Supporting Actor in a Drama Series: Steve Burton, *General Hospital* (ABC)
Supporting Actress in a Drama Series: Julia Barr, *All My Children* (ABC)
Younger Actor in a Drama Series: Jonathan Jackson, *General Hospital* (ABC)
Younger Actress in a Drama Series: Sarah Brown, *General Hospital* (ABC)
Outstanding Children's Series: *Reading Rainbow* (PBS)
Outstanding Children's Special: *In His Father's Shoes* (SHO)
Outstanding Children's Animated Program: *Arthur* (PBS)
Outstanding Children's Animated Program (special class): *The New Batman/Superman Adventures* (WB)
Performer in a Children's Series: Bill Nye, *Disney Presents Bill Nye the Science Guy* (syndicated)
Performer in a Children's Special: Robert Richard, *In His Father's Shoes* (SHO)
Performer in an Animated Program: Louie Anderson, *Life With Louie* (FOX)
Outstanding Preschool Children's Series: *Sesame Street* (PBS)
Special Class Program: *1997 Macy's Thanksgiving Day Parade* (NBC)
Outstanding Game Show: *Jeopardy!* (syndicated)
Outstanding Game-Show Host: Pat Sajak, *Wheel of Fortune* (syndicated)
Outstanding Talk Show: *The Rosie O'Donnell Show* (syndicated)

Outstanding Talk-Show Host: Oprah Winfrey, *The Oprah Winfrey Show* (syndicated) and Rosie O'Donnell, *The Rosie O'Donnell Show* (syndicated)

Outstanding Service Show: *The Pet Department* (FX)

Outstanding Service-Show Host: Steve Thomas, *This Old House* (PBS)

Drama Series Writing Team: *All My Children* (ABC)

1997 National Book Awards

The National Book Awards are presented by the Association of American Publishers. (Called the American Book Awards 1980–1986; reverted to original name in 1987.)

Fiction: *Cold Mountain,* Charles Frazier (Atlantic Monthly Press)

Nonfiction: *American Sphinx: The Character of Thomas Jefferson,* Joseph J. Ellis (Knopf)

Poetry: *Effort at Speech: New and Selected Poems,* William Meredith (Triquarterly Books/Northwestern University Press)

Young People's Literature: *Dancing on the Edge,* Han Nolan (Harcourt Brace)

1997 National Book Critics Circle Awards

Fiction: *The Blue Flower,* Penelope Fitzgerald (Mariner/ Houghton Mifflin)

General Nonfiction: *The Spirit Catches You and You Fall Down,* Anne Fadiman (Farrar, Straus & Giroux)

Biography or Autobiography: *Ernie Pyle's War: America's Eyewitness to World War II,* James Tobin (Free Press)

Poetry: *Black Zodiac,* Charles Wright (Farrar, Straus & Giroux)

Criticism: *Making Waves,* Mario Vargas Llosa (Farrar, Straus & Giroux)

Newbery Medal

1998 Newbery Medal and Honor Books

The Newbery Medal is awarded annually by the American Library Association for the most distinguished contribution to American literature for children.

Newbery Medal for Best Book: *Out of the Dust,* Karen Hesse (Scholastic Press)

Newbery Honor Books: *Lily's Crossing,* Patricia Reilly Giff (Delacorte Press); *Ella Enchanted,* Gail Carson Levine (HarperCollins); *Wringer,* Jerry Spinelli (Joanna Cotler Books/HarperCollins)

1922–1997

1922 *The Story of Mankind,* Hendrick Willem Van Loon
1923 *The Voyages of Dr. Doolittle,* Hugh A. Lofting
1924 *The Dark Frigate,* Charles Boardman Hawes
1925 *Tales from Silver Lands,* Charles Joseph Finger
1926 *Shen of the Sea,* Arthur Bowie Chrisman
1927 *Smoky, the Cow Horse,* Will James
1928 *Gay-Neck, the Story of a Pigeon,* Dhan Gopal Mukerji
1929 *The Trumpeter of Krakow,* Eric P. Kelly
1930 *Hitty, Her First Hundred Years,* Rachel Field
1931 *The Cat Who Went to Heaven,* Elizabeth Jane Coatsworth
1932 *Waterless Mountain,* Laura Adams Armer
1933 *Young Fu of the Upper Yangtze,* Elizabeth Foreman Lewis
1934 *Invincible Louisa,* Cornelia Meigs
1935 *Dobry,* Monica Shannon
1936 *Caddie Woodlawn,* Carol Ryrie Brink
1937 *Roller Skates,* Ruth Sawyer
1938 *The White Stag,* Kate Seredy
1939 *Thimble Summer,* Elizabeth Enright
1940 *Daniel Boone,* James Henry Daugherty
1941 *Call it Courage,* Armstrong Sperry
1942 *The Matchlock Gun,* Walter Dumax Edmonds
1943 *Adam of the Road,* Elizabeth Janet Gray
1944 *Johnny Tremain,* Esther Forbes
1945 *Rabbit Hill,* Robert Lawson
1946 *Strawberry Girl,* Lois Lenski
1947 *Miss Hickory,* Carolyn Sherwin Bailey
1948 *The Twenty-One Balloons,* William Pène du Bois
1949 *King of the Wind,* Marguerite Henry
1950 *The Door in the Wall,* Marguerite de Angeli
1951 *Amos Fortune, Free Man,* Elizabeth Yates
1952 *Ginger Pye,* Eleanor Estes
1953 *Secret of the Andes,* Ann Nolan Clark
1954 *. . . And Now Miguel,* Joseph Krumgold
1955 *The Wheel on the School,* Meindert DeJong
1956 *Carry On, Mr. Bowditch,* Jean Lee Latham
1957 *Miracles on Maple Hill,* Virginia Eggertsen Sorensen
1958 *Rifles for Watie,* Harold Keith
1959 *The Witch of Blackbird Pond,* Elizabeth George Speare
1960 *Onion John,* Joseph Krumgold
1961 *Island of the Blue Dolphins,* Scott O'Dell
1962 *The Bronze Bow,* Elizabeth George Speare
1963 *A Wrinkle in Time,* Madeleine L'Engle
1964 *It's Like This, Cat,* Emily Cheney Neville
1965 *Shadow of a Bull,* Maia Wojciechowska
1966 *I, Juan de Pareja,* Elizabeth Borton de Treviño
1967 *Up a Road Slowly,* Irene Hunt
1968 *From the Mixed-Up Files of Mrs. Basil E. Frankweiler,* E. L. Konigsburg
1969 *The High King,* Lloyd Alexander
1970 *Sounder,* William H. Armstrong
1971 *Summer of the Swans,* Betsy Cromer Byars
1972 *Mrs. Frisby and the Rats of NIMH,* Robert C. O'Brien
1973 *Julie of the Wolves,* Jean Craighead George
1974 *The Slave Dancer,* Paula Fox
1975 *M. C. Higgins, the Great,* Virginia Hamilton
1976 *The Grey King,* Susan Cooper
1977 *Roll of Thunder, Hear My Cry,* Mildred D. Taylor
1978 *Bridge to Terabithia,* Katherine Paterson
1979 *The Westing Game,* Ellen Raskin
1980 *A Gathering of Days: A New England Girl's Journal, 1830–32,* Joan W. Blos
1981 *Jacob Have I Loved,* Katherine Paterson

1982 *A Visit to William Blake's Inn: Poems for Innocent and Experienced Travelers,* Nancy Willard
1983 *Dicey's Song,* Cynthia Voigt
1984 *Dear Mr. Henshaw,* Beverly Cleary
1985 *The Hero and the Crown,* Robin McKinley
1986 *Sarah, Plain and Tall,* Patricia MacLachlan
1987 *The Whipping Boy,* Sid Fleischman
1988 *Lincoln: A Photobiography,* Russell Freedman
1989 *Joyful Noise: Poems for Two Voices,* Paul Fleischman
1990 *Number the Stars,* Lois Lowry
1991 *Maniac Magee: a Novel,* Jerry Spinelli
1992 *Shiloh,* Phyllis Reynolds Naylor
1993 *Missing May,* Cynthia Rylant
1994 *The Giver,* Lois Lowry
1995 *Walk Two Moons,* Sharon Creech
1996 *The Midwife's Apprentice,* Karen Cushman
1997 *The View from Saturday,* E. L. Konigsburg

Caldecott Medal

1998 Caldecott Medal and Honor Books

The Caldecott Medal is awarded annually by the American Library Association for the most distinguished American picture book for children.

Caldecott Medal for Best Picture Book: *Rapunzel,* illustrated and retold by Paul O. Zelinsky (Dutton)

Caldecott Honor Books: *Harlem,* illustrated by Christopher Myers, written by Walter Dean Myers (Scholastic Press); *The Gardener,* illustrated by David Small, written by Sarah Stewart (Farrar, Straus & Giroux); *There Was an Old Lady Who Swallowed a Fly,* illustrated and retold by Simms Taback (Viking)

1938–1997

1938 *Animals of the Bible, a Picture Book,* text selected by Helen Dean Fish, illustrated by Dorothy P. Lathrop
1939 *Mei Li,* written and illustrated by Thomas Handforth
1940 *Abraham Lincoln,* written and illustrated by Ingrid and Edgar Parin D'Aulaire
1941 *They Were Strong and Good,* written and illustrated by Robert Larson
1942 *Make Way for Ducklings,* written and illustrated by Robert McCloskey
1943 *The Little House,* written and illustrated by Virginia Lee Burton
1944 *Many Moons,* written by James Thurber, illustrated by Louis Slobodkin
1945 *Prayer for a Child,* written by Elizabeth Orton Jones
1946 *The Rooster Crows,* written and illustrated by Maud and Miska Petersham
1947 *The Little Island,* written by Golden MacDonald, illustrated by Leonard Weisgard
1948 *White Snow, Bright Snow,* written by Alvin Tresselt, illustrated by Roger Duvoisin
1949 *The Big Snow,* written and illustrated by Berta and Elmer Hader
1950 *Song of the Swallows,* written and illustrated by Leo Politi
1951 *The Egg Tree,* written and illustrated by Katherine Milhous
1952 *Finders Keepers,* written by William Lipkind, illustrated by Nicolas Mordivinoff
1953 *The Biggest Bear,* written and illustrated by Lynd Ward
1954 *Madeline's Rescue,* written and illustrated by Ludwig Bemelmans
1955 *Cinderella, or, The Little Glass Slipper,* translated and illustrated by Marcia Brown
1956 *Frog Went A-Courtin',* retold by John Langstaff, illustrated by Feodor Rojankovsky
1957 *A Tree is Nice,* written by Janice May Udry, illustrated by Marc Simont
1958 *Time of Wonder,* written and illustrated by Robert McCloskey
1959 *Chanticleer and the Fox,* adapted and illustrated by Barbara Cooney
1960 *Nine Days to Christmas,* written by Marie Hall Ets and Aurora Labastida, illustrated by Marie Hall Ets
1961 *Baboushka and the Three Kings,* written by Ruth Robbins, illustrated by Nicolas Sidjakov
1962 *Once a Mouse,* retold and illustrated by Marcia Brown
1963 *The Snowy Day,* written and illustrated by Ezra Jack Keats
1964 *Where the Wild Things Are,* written and illustrated by Maurice Sendak
1965 *May I Bring a Friend?,* written by Beatrice Schenk de Regniers, illustrated by Beni Montresor
1966 *Always Room for One More,* written by Sorche Nic Leodhas, illustrated by Nonny Hogrogian
1967 *Sam, Bangs and Moonshine,* written and illustrated by Evaline Ness
1968 *Drummer Hoff,* written by Barbara Emberley, illustrated by Ed Emberley
1969 *The Fool of the World and the Flying Ship,* retold by Arthur Ransome, illustrated by Uri Shulevitz
1970 *Sylvester and the Magic Pebble,* written and illustrated by William Steig
1971 *A Story, A Story: An African Tale,* retold and illustrated by Gail E. Haley
1972 *One Fine Day,* written and illustrated by Nonny Hogrogian
1973 *The Funny Little Woman,* retold by Arlene Mosel, illustrated by Blair Lent
1974 *Duffy and the Devil,* retold by Harve Zemach, illustrated by Margot Zemach
1975 *Arrow to the Sun: A Pueblo Indian Tale,* adapted and illustrated by Gerald H. McDermott
1976 *Why Mosquitos Buzz in People's Ears (An African Tale),* retold by Verna Aardema, illustrated by Leo and Diane Dillon
1977 *Ashanti to Zulu: African Traditions,* written by Margaret Musgrove, illustrated by Leo and Diane Dillon
1978 *Noah's Ark,* written by Jacob Revius, illustrated by Peter Spier
1979 *The Girl Who Loved Wild Horses,* written and illustrated by Paul Goble
1980 *Ox-Cart Man,* written by Donald Hall, illustrated by Barbara Cooney

1981 *Fables,* written and illustrated by Arnold Lobel
1982 *Jumanji,* written and illustrated by Chris Van Allsburg
1983 *Shadow,* translated and illustrated by Marcia Brown
1984 *The Glorious Flight: Across the Channel with Louise Blériot,* written and illustrated by Alice and Martin Provensen
1985 *St. George and the Dragon,* retold by Margaret Hodges, illustrated by Trina Schart Hyman
1986 *The Polar Express,* written and illustrated by Chris Van Allsburg
1987 *Hey, Al,* written by Arthur Yorinks, illustrated by Richard Egielski
1988 *Owl Moon,* written by Jane Yolen, illustrated by John Schoenherr
1989 *Song and Dance Man,* written by Karen Ackerman, illustrated by Stephen Gammell
1990 *Lon Po Po: A Red-Riding Hood Story from China,* translated and illustrated by Ed Young
1991 *Black & White,* written and illustrated by David Macaulay
1992 *Tuesday,* written and illustrated by David Wiesner
1993 *Mirette on the High Wire,* written and illustrated by Emily Arnold McCully
1994 *Grandfather's Journey,* written and illustrated by Allen Say
1995 *Smoky Night,* written by Eve Bunting, illustrated by David Diaz
1996 *Officer Buckle and Gloria,* written and illustrated by Peggy Rathmann
1997 *Golem,* written and illustrated by David Wisniewski

Other American Library Association Awards for Children's Books, 1998

Coretta Scott King Awards, honoring black authors and illustrators: (author): *Forged by Fire,* Sharon Draper (Atheneum); **(illustrator):** *In Daddy's Arms I Am Tall,* Javaka Steptoe (Lee & Low)

Coretta Scott King Honor Books: (author): *I Thought My Soul Would Rise and Fly: The Diary of Patsy, a Freed Girl,* Joyce Hansen (Scholastic Press); *Bayard Rustin: Behind the Scenes of the Civil Rights Movement,* James Haskins (Hyperion Press); **(illustrator):** *Ashley Bryan's ABC of African-American Poetry,* Ashley Bryan (Atheneum); *The Hunterman and the Crocodile: A West African Folktale,* Baba Wague Diakite (Scholastic Press); *Harlem,* Christopher Myers (Scholastic Press)

1998 Pura Belpre Awards, honoring Latino writers and illustrators: (author): *Parrot in the Oven,* Victor Martinez (Joanna Cotler Books); **(illustrator):** *Snapshots from The Wedding,* illustrated by Stephanie Garcia, written by Gary Soto (Putnam)

Pura Belpre Honor Awards: (author): *Spirits of the High Mesa,* Floyd Martinez (Arte Publico); *Laughing Tomatoes and Other Spring Poems* (Children's Book Press); **(illustrator):** *The Golden Flower,* Enrique Sanchez (Simon & Schuster); *My Family,* Carmen Lomas Garza (Children's Book Press); *Gathering the Sun,* Simon Silva (Lee & Shepard)

Mildred Batchelder Award, for best book originally published in a foreign language: *The Robber and Me,* by Josef Holub, originally published in German (Henry Holt & Co,)

Margaret A. Edwards Award, for outstanding literature for young adults: Madeleine L'Engle, a lifetime achievement award

Laura Ingalls Wilder Award, for lasting contributions to children's literature: Russell Freedman

Bollingen Prize in Poetry

This $25,000 award is given biennially. It is administered by Yale University and the Bollingen Foundation.

1949 Ezra Pound
1950 Wallace Stevens
1951 John Crowe Ransom
1952 Marianne Moore
1953 Archibald MacLeish and William Carlos Williams
1954 W. H. Auden
1955 Léonie Adams and Louise Bogan
1956 Conrad Aiken
1957 Allen Tate
1958 e. e. cummings
1959 Theodore Roethke
1960 Delmore Schwartz
1961 Yvor Winters
1962 John Hall Wheelock and Richard Eberhart
1963 Robert Frost
1965 Horace Gregory
1967 Robert Penn Warren
1969 John Berryman and Karl Shapiro
1971 Richard Wilbur and Mona Van Duyn
1973 James Merrill
1975 Archie Randolph Ammons
1977 David Ignatow
1979 W. S. Merwin
1981 Howard Nemerov and May Swenson
1983 Anthony Hecht and John Hollander
1985 John Ashbery and Fred Chappell
1987 Stanley Kunitz
1989 Edgar Bowers
1991 Laura Riding Jackson and Donald Justice
1993 Mark Strand
1995 Kenneth Koch
1997 Gary Snyder

1998 Kingsley Tufts Poetry Prize

This $50,000 award is given to a poet for a book published in the previous year. Established in 1992, it is administered by the Claremont (California) Graduate School.

1993 Susan Mitchell, *Rapture*
1994 Yusef Komunyakaa, *Neon Vernacular*
1995 Thomas Lux, *Split Horizon*
1996 Deborah Digges, *Rough Music*
1997 Campbell McGrath, *Spring Comes to Chicago*
1998 John Koethe, *Falling Water*

1998 MacArthur Foundation Awards

The MacArthur Foundation awards monetary prizes each year in order to provide financial assistance for selected innovators.

Janine Antoni, 34, artist; New York
Ida Applebroog, 68, painter and social critic; New York
Ellen Barry, 44, attorney; Oakland, Calif.
Tim Berners-Lee, 43, computer scientist; Lexington, Mass.
Linda Bierds, 53, poet; Bainbridge Island, Wash.
Bernadette Brooten, 47, professor of religion; Cambridge, Mass.
John Carlstrom, 41, astrophysicist; Chicago
Mike Davis, 52, historian; Pasadena, Calif.
Nancy Folbre, 45, economist; Montague, Mass.
Avner Greif, 42, economist; Stanford, Calif.
Kun-Liang Guan, 35, biochemist; Ann Arbor, Mich.
Gary Hill, 47, video artist; Seattle
Edward Hirsch, 48, poet and essayist; Houston
Ayesha Jalal, 42, historian; New York
Charles Johnson, 50, writer and cartoonist; Seattle
Leah Krubitzer, 37, neuroscientist; Davis, Calif.
Stewart Kwoh, 49, lawyer and human rights leader; Los Angeles
Charles Lewis, 44, founder of Center for Public Integrity; Alexandria, Va.
William McDonald, 46, cattle rancher; Douglas, Ariz.
Peter Miller, 33, history scholar; Berlin, Germany
Don Mitchell, 36, cultural geographer; Syracuse, N.Y.
Rebecca Nelson, 37, plant pathologist; Lima, Peru
Elinor Ochs, 53, linguistic anthropologist; Pacific Palisades, Calif.
Ishmael Reed, 60, writer and publisher; Oakland, Calif.
Benjamin Santer, 43, atmospheric scientist; Livermore, Calif.
Karl Sims, 36, computer scientist; Cambridge, Mass.
Dorothy Q. Thomas, 38, human rights and women's rights worker; New York
Leonard Zeskind, 48, human rights activist; Kansas City, Mo.
Mary Zimmerman, 37, director and playwright; Evanston, Ill.

Presidential Medal of Freedom

The nation's highest civilian award, the Presidential Medal of Freedom recognizes exceptional meritorious service. The medal was established by President Truman in 1945 to recognize notable service in the war. In 1963, President Kennedy reintroduced it as an honor for distinguished civilian service in peace time. Shown below are only those medals awarded during President Clinton's administration.

1993* Arthur Ashe, Jr. (athlete, tennis)
1993 William J. Brennan, Jr. (jurist)
1993 Marjory Stoneman Douglas (conservationist)
1993 J. William Fulbright (public servant)
1993* Thurgood Marshall (jurist)
1993 General Colin L. Powell [1](soldier)
1993* Joseph L. Raugh, Jr. (civil rights and labor activist)
1993 Martha Raye (entertainer)
1993 John Minor Wisdom (public servant)
1994 Herbert Block (cartoonist)
1994* Cesar Chavez (labor leader)
1994 Arthur Flemming (government servant)
1994 James Grant (executive director, UNICEF)
1994 Dorothy Height (civil rights leader)
1994 Barbara Jordan (public servant)
1994 Lane Kirkland (labor leader)
1994 Robert H. Michel (public servant)
1994 R. Sargent Shriver (government servant)
1995 Peggy Charren (children's television advocate)
1995 William Thaddeus Coleman, Jr. (public servant and civil rights advocate)
1995 Joan Ganz Cooney (children's television advocate)
1995 John Hope Franklin (historian)
1995 A. Leon Higginbotham, Jr. (jurist and civil rights advocate)
1995 Frank M. Johnson, Jr. (jurist)
1995 C. Everett Koop (public health worker)
1995 Gaylord A. Nelson (public servant and conservationist)
1995 Walter P. Reuther (labor leader)
1995 James W. Rouse (urban planner)
1995* William C. Velasquez (voting rights advocate)
1995 Lew R. Wasserman (media executive)
1996 James Scott Brady (gun control advocate)
1996 Cardinal Joseph Bernadin (Catholic leader)
1996 Millard D. Fuller (founder, Habitat for Humanity)
1996 David Alan Hamburg (physician and children's advocate)
1996 John H. Johnson (founder, *Ebony* and *Jet*)
1996 Eugene M. Lang (founder, "I Have a Dream" Foundation)
1996 Jan Nowak-Jezioranski (WWII Polish resistence fighter)
1996 Antonia Pantoja (Puerto Rican educational and economic advocate)
1996 Rosa Parks (civil rights leader)
1996 Ginetta Sagan (advocate for political prisoners)
1996 Morris Udall (public servant)
1997 Robert Dole (public servant)
1997 William J. Perry (soldier)
1998 Arnold Aronson (civil rights advocate)
1998 Brooke Astor (philanthropist)
1998 Robert Coles (psychiatrist and author)
1998 Justin Dart, Jr. (founder of Americans with Disabilities Act)
1998 James Farmer (civil rights leader)
1998 Frances Hesselbein (former leader of the Girl Scouts of America)
1998 Fred Korematsu (activist redressing Japanese-American internment in WWII)
1998 Sol M. Linowitz (jurist)
1998 Wilma Mankiller (former Cherokee Nation leader)
1998 Margaret Murie (environmentalist)
1998 Mario G. Obledo (activist for Mexican-American civil rights)
1998 Elliot L. Richardson (public servant)
1998 David Rockefeller (philanthropist)
1998* Albert Shanker (educator)
1998 Adm. Elmo R. Zumwalt, Jr. (soldier)

1. With Distinction. NOTE: An asterisk following a year denotes a posthumous award.

Enrico Fermi Award

The $100,000 award is given in recognition of scientific and technical achievement in atomic energy, Awarded by the president, it is the U.S. government's oldest science and technology award,

1954 Enrico Fermi
1956 John von Neumann
1957 Ernest O. Lawrence
1958 Eugene P. Wigner
1959 Glenn T. Seaborg
1961 Hans A. Bethe
1962 Edward Teller
1963 J. Robert Oppenheimer
1964 Hyman G. Rickover
1966 Otto Hahn, Lise Meitner, and Fritz Strassman
1968 John A. Wheeler
1969 Walter H. Zinn
1970 Norris E. Bradbury
1971 Shields Warren and Stafford L. Warren
1972 Manson Benedict
1976 William L. Russell
1978 Harold M. Agnew and Wolfgang K. H. Panofsky
1980 Alvin M. Weinberg and Rudolf E. Peirls
1981 W. Bennett Lewis
1982 Herbert Anderson and Seth Neddermeyer
1983 Alexander Hollaender and John Lawrence
1984 Robert R. Wilson and Georges Vendryès
1985 Norman C. Rasmussen and Marshall N. Rosenblath
1986 Ernest D. Courant and M. Stanley Livingston
1987 Luis W. Alvarez and Gerald F. Tape
1988 Richard B. Setlow and Victor F. Weisskopf
1989 Award not given
1990 George A. Cowan and Robley D. Evans
1991 Award not given
1992 Leon M. Lederman, Harold Brown, and John S. Foster, Jr.
1993 Freeman J. Dyson and Liane B. Russell
1994 Award not given
1995 Ugo Fano and Martin Kamen
1996 Richard Garwin, Mortimer Elkind, and H. Rodney Withers

Fields Medal Winners

The Fields Medal has been awarded since 1936 by the International Congress of Mathematicians in Toronto to recognize outstanding mathematics achievement.

1936 Lars Valerian Ahlfors (Harvard University) and Jesse Douglas (Massachusetts Institute of Technology)
(Fields Medals were not awarded during World War II)
1950 Laurent Schwarts (University of Nancy) and Alte Selberg (Institute for Advanced Study, Princeton)
1954 Kunihiko Kodaira (Princeton University) and Jean-Pierre Serre (University of Paris)
1958 Klaus Friedrich Roth (University of London) and René Thom (University of Strasbourgh)
1962 Lars V. Hörmander (University of Stockholm) and John Willard Milnor (Princeton University)
1966 Michael Francis Atiyah (Oxford University), Paul Joseph Cohen (Stanford University), Alexander Grothendieck (University of Paris), and Stephen Smale (University of California, Berkeley)
1970 Alan Baker (Cambridge University), Heisuke Hironaka (Harvard University), Serge P. Novikov (Moscow University), and John Griggs Thompson (Cambridge University)
1974 Enrico Bombieri (University of Pisa) and David Bryant Mumford (Harvard University)
1978 Pierre René Deligne (Institut des Hautes Études Scientifiques), Charles Louis Fefferman (Princeton University), Gregori Alexandrovitch Margulis (Moscow University), and Daniel G. Quillen (Massachusetts Institute of Technology)
1982 Alain Connes (Institut des Hautes Études Scientifiques), William P. Thurston (Princeton University), and Shing-Tung Yau (Institute for Advanced Study, Princeton)
1986 Simon Donaldson (Oxford University), Gerd Faltings (Princeton University), and Michael Freedman (University of California, San Diego)
1990 Vladimir Drinfeld (Phys. Inst. Kharkov), Vaughan Jones (University of California, Berkeley), Shigefumi Mori (University of Kyoto), and Edward Witten (Institute for Advanced Study, Princeton)
1994 Pierre-Louis Lions (Université de Paris–Dauphine), Jean-Christophe Yoccoz (Université de Paris–Sud), Jean Bourgain (Institute for Advanced Study, Princeton), and Efim Zelmanov (University of Wisconsin)

Recipients of Kennedy Center Honors

The Kennedy Center Honors recognize the lifetime achievements of selected American performing artists.

1978 Marian Anderson (contralto), Fred Astaire (dancer-actor), Richard Rodgers (Broadway composer), Arthur Rubinstein (pianist), George Balanchine (choreographer)

1979 Ella Fitzgerald (jazz singer), Henry Fonda (actor), Martha Graham (choreographer), Tennessee Williams (playwright), Aaron Copland (composer)

1980 James Cagney (actor), Leonard Bernstein (composer-conductor), Agnes de Mille (choreographer), Lynn Fontanne (actress), Leontyne Price (soprano)

1981 Count Basie (jazz composer-pianist), Cary Grant (actor), Helen Hayes (actress), Jerome Robbins (choreographer), Rudolf Serkin (pianist)

1982 George Abbott (Broadway producer), Lillian Gish (actress), Benny Goodman (jazz clarinetist), Gene Kelly (dancer-actor), Eugene Ormandy (conductor)

1983 Katherine Dunham (dancer-choreographer), Elia Kazan (director-author), James Stewart (actor), Virgil Thomson (music critic-composer), Frank Sinatra (singer)
1984 Lena Horne (singer), Danny Kaye (comedian-actor), Gian Carlo Menotti (composer), Arthur Miller (playwright), Isaac Stern (violinist)
1985 Merce Cunningham (dancer-choreographer), Irene Dunne (actress), Bob Hope (comedian), Alan Jay Lerner (lyricist-playwright), Frederick Loewe (composer), Beverly Sills (soprano)
1986 Lucille Ball (comedienne), Ray Charles (musician), Yehudi Menuhin (violinist), Antony Tudor (choreographer), Hume Cronyn and Jessica Tandy (husband-and-wife acting team)
1987 Perry Como (singer), Bette Davis (actress), Sammy Davis, Jr., (entertainer), Nathan Milstein (violinist), Alwin Nikolais (choreographer)
1988 Alvin Ailey (choreographer), George Burns (comedian-actor), Myrna Loy (actress), Alexander Schneider (violinist), Roger L. Stevens (theatrical producer and the Kennedy Center's founding chairman)
1989 Harry Belafonte (singer-actor), Claudette Colbert (actress), Alexandra Danilova (ballerina), Mary Martin (actress), William Schuman (composer)
1990 Dizzy Gillespie (jazz trumpeter), Katharine Hepburn (actress), Risë Stevens (mezzo-soprano), Jule Styne (composer), Billy Wilder (director)
1991 Roy Acuff (country songwriter and singer), Betty Comden and Adolph Green (co-authors of books and lyrics of musicals), the brothers Fayard and Harold Nicholas (dancers), Gregory Peck (actor), Robert Shaw (choral director)
1992 Lionel Hampton (jazz musician), Paul Newman (actor), Joanne Woodward (actress), Ginger Rogers (dancer-actress), Mstislav Rostropovich (cellist-conductor), Paul Taylor (choreographer)
1993 Johnny Carson (talk-show host), Arthur Mitchell (dancer and choreographer), Georg Solti (conductor), Stephen Sondheim (composer and lyricist), Marion Williams (gospel singer)
1994 Kirk Douglas (actor), Aretha Franklin (singer), Morton Gould (composer), Harold Prince (producer and director), Pete Seeger (folk singer)
1995 Jacques D'Ambroise (choreographer), Marilyn Horne (mezzo soprano), B. B. King (blues singer), Sidney Poitier (actor), Neil Simon (playwright)
1996 Edward Albee (playwright), Benny Carter (jazz musician), Johnny Cash (musician), Jack Lemmon (actor), Maria Tallchief (ballerina)
1997 Lauren Bacall (actress), Bob Dylan (songwriter and singer), Charlton Heston (actor), Jessye Norman (soprano), Edward Villella (ballet dancer and director)
1998 Bill Cosby (actor and comedian), John Kander and Fred Ebb (Broadway composer and lyricist team), Willie Nelson (singer and songwriter), André Previn (composer and conductor), Shirley Temple Black (actress)

The Spingarn Medal

The Spingarn Medal is awarded annually by the National Association for the Advancement of Colored People (NAACP) for outstanding achievement by a black American.

1915 Ernest E. Judd
1916 Charles Young
1917 Harry T. Burleigh
1918 William Stanley Braithwaite
1919 Archibald H. Grimke
1920 W. E. B. Du Bois
1921 Charles S. Gilpin
1922 Mary B. Talbert
1923 George Washington Carver
1924 Roland Hayes
1925 James Weldon Johnson
1926 Carter G. Woodson
1927 Anthony Overton
1928 Charles W. Chesnutt
1929 Mordecai Wyatt Johnson
1930 Henry A. Hunt
1931 Richard Berry Harrison
1932 Robert Russa Moton
1933 Max Yergan
1934 William T. B. Williams
1935 Mary McLeod Bethune
1936 John Hope
1937 Walter White
1938 No award
1939 Marian Anderson
1940 Louis T. Wright
1941 Richard Wright
1942 A. Philip Randolph
1943 William H. Hastie
1944 Charles Drew
1945 Paul Robeson
1946 Thurgood Marshall
1947 Percy Julian
1948 Channing H. Tobias
1949 Ralph J. Bunche
1950 Charles Hamilton Houston
1951 Mabel Keaton Staupers
1952 Harry T. Moore
1953 Paul R. Williams
1954 Theodore K. Lawless
1955 Carl Murphy
1956 Jackie Robinson
1957 Martin Luther King. Jr.
1958 Daisy Bates and the Little Rock Nine
1959 Edward Kennedy (Duke) Ellington
1960 Langston Hughes
1961 Kenneth B. Clark
1962 Robert C. Weaver
1963 Medgar Evers
1964 Roy Wilkins
1965 Leontyne Price
1966 John H. Johnson
1967 Edward W. Brooke III
1968 Sammy Davis, Jr.
1969 Clarence M. Mitchell, Jr.
1970 Jacob Lawrence
1971 Leon Howard Sullivan
1972 Gordon Parks
1973 Wilson C. Riles
1974 Damon Keith
1975 Hank Aaron
1976 Alvin Ailey
1977 Alex Haley
1978 Andrew Young
1979 Rosa L. Parks
1980 Rayford W. Logan
1981 Coleman Young
1982 Benjamin E. Mays
1983 Lena Horne
1984 Tom Bradley
1985 Bill Cosby
1986 Benjamin L. Hooks
1987 Percy Ellis Sutton
1988 Frederick Douglass Patterson
1989 Jesse Jackson
1990 L. Douglas Wilder
1991 Colin T. Powell
1992 Barbara Jordan
1993 Dorothy Irene Height
1994 Maya Angelou
1995 John Hope Franklin
1996 A. Leon Higginbotham, Jr.
1997 Carl Rowan
1998 Myrlie Evers-Williams

U.S. Symphony Orchestras and Their Music Directors

(With expenses over $1,050,000)

Akron Symphony Orchestra: Alan Balter
Alabama Symphony Ochestra: Douglas Gerhart[1]
American Composers Orchestra: Dennis Russell Davies
American Symphony Orchestra: Leon Botstein
Arkansas Symphony Orchestra: David Itkin
Aspen Chamber Symphony: David Zinman
Atlanta Symphony: Yoel Levi
Austin Symphony: Peter Bay
Baltimore Symphony: David Zinman
Baton Rouge Symphony: James Paul
Boca Pops: Crafton Beck[2]
Boston Symphony: Seiji Ozawa
Boston Symphony Chamber Players: Malcolm Lowe
Boulder Philharmonic Orchestra: Theodor Kuchar
Brooklyn Philharmonic: Robert Spano
Buffalo Philharmonic Orchestra: Jo Ann Falletta
Cedar Rapids Symphony: Christian Tiemeyer
Charleston Symphony: David Stahl
Charlotte Symphony: Peter McCoppin
Chattanooga Symphony & Opera Association: Robert Bernhardt
Chicago Sinfonietta: Paul Freeman
Chicago Symphony: Daniel Barenboim
Cincinnati Symphony: Jesus Lopez-Cobos
Cleveland Orchestra: Christoph von Dohnanyi
Colorado Springs Symphony: Yaacov Bergman
Colorado Symphony (Denver): Marin Alsop
Columbus Symphony: Alessandro Siciliani
Dallas Symphony: Andrew Litton
Dayton Philharmonic: Neal Gittleman
Delaware Symphony: Stephen Gunzenhauser
Des Moines Symphony: Joseph Giunta
Detroit Symphony: Neeme Jarvi
Elgin Symphony Orchestra: Robert L. Hanson[2]
El Paso Symphony Orchestra: Gurer Aykal
Erie Philharmonic: Peter Bay
Evansville Philharmonic Orchestra: Alfred Savia
Florida Orchestra: Jahja Ling
Florida Philharmonic Orchestra: James Judd
Florida Symphonic Pops: Dr. Crafton Beck [2]
Florida West Coast Symphony Orchestra: Paul C. Wolfe[2]
Fort Wayne Philharmonic: Edvard Tchivzhel
Fort Worth Symphony: John Giordano
Fresno Philharmonic Orchestra: Raymond Harvey
Grand Rapids Symphony: Catherine Comet
Grant Park Symphony (Chicago): Hugh Wolff[3]
Greensboro Symphony Orchestra: Stuart Malina
Greenville Symphony Orchestra: David Politt
Handel & Haydn Society: Christopher Hogwood[4]
Harrisburg Symphony Orchestra: Richard Westerfield
Hartford Symphony: Michael Lankester
Honolulu Symphony Society: Samuel Wong
Houston Symphony: Christopher Eschenbach
Hudson Valley Philharmonic (Poughkeepsie): Randall Craig Fleischer
Indianapolis Symphony: Raymond Leppard
Jacksonville Symphony: Roger Nierenberg
Kalamazoo Symphony Orchestra: Yoshimi Takeda
Kansas City Symphony: William McGlaughlin
Kennedy Center Opera House Orchestra: Heinze Frickle
Knoxville Symphony: Kirk Trevor
Little Orchestra Society of New York: Dino Anagnost
Long Beach Symphony: JoAnn Falletta
Long Island Philharmonic: David Lockington
Los Angeles Chamber Orchestra: Jeffrey Kahane
Los Angeles Philharmonic: Esa-Pekka Salonen
Louisianna Philharmonic Orchestra: Klauspeter Seibel
Louisville Orchestra: Max Bragado-Darman
Madison Symphony Orchestra: John De Main
Memphis Symphony: Alan Balter
Milwaukee Symphony Orchestra: Andreas Delfs
Minnesota Orchestra: Eiji Oue
Mississippi Symphony: Colman Pearce
Monterey County Symphony: Clark Suttle
Music Academy of the West Summer Festival Orchestra: Carleen Landes[4]
Music of the Baroque: Thomas S. Wikman
Naples Philharmonic: Christopher Seaman
Nashville Symphony: Kenneth D. Schermerhorn
National Sininietta: Burton A. Zipser[4]
National Symphony (D.C.): Leonard Slatkin
New Haven Symphony: Michael Palmer
New Jersey Symphony: Zdenek Macal[4]
New Mexico Symphony: David Lockington
New West Symphony: Boris Brott[2]
New World Symphony (Fla.): Michael Tilson Thomas[4]
New York Chamber Symphony of the 92nd St. Y: Gerard Schwarz
New York Philharmonic: Kurt Masur
New York Pops: Skitch Henderson
North Carolina Symphony: Gerhardt Zimmermann
Northeastern Pennsylvania Philharmonic: Hugh Keelan
Ohio Chamber Orchestra: David Lockington[1]
Oklahoma City Philharmonic: Joel A. Levine
Omaha Symphony: Victor Yampolsky
Omaha Symphony Chamber Orchestra: Gary L. Good[1]
Oregon Symphony: James DePreist
Pacific Symphony (Calif.): Carl St. Clair
Palm Beach Pops: Bob Lappin
Philadelphia Orchestra: Wolfgang Sawallisch
Philharmonia Baroque Orchestra: Nicholas McGegan
Phoenix Symphony: Hermann Michael
Pittsburgh Symphony Orchestra: Mariss Jansons
Portland Symphony: Hermann Michael
Puerto Rico Symphony: Eugene Kohn[5]
Quad City Symphony Orchestra Association: Kim Allen Giunta
Rhode Island Philharmonic: Larry Rachleff
Richmond Symphony: George Manahan
River City Brass Band: Denis Colwell
Rochester Philharmonic: Robert Bernhardt[3]
St. Louis Symphony: Hans Vonk
St. Paul Chamber Orchestra: Hugh Wolff
San Antonio Symphony: Christopher Wilkins
San Francisco Symphony: Michael Tilson Thomas
San Jose Symphony: Leonid Grin
Santa Barbara Symphony Orchestra: Gisele Ben-Dor
Santa Rosa Symphony: Jeffrey Kahane
Savannah Symphony: Philp B. Greenberg
Seattle Symphony: Gerard Schwarz
Shreveport Symphony: Dennis Simons
Spokane Symphony: Fabio Mechetti
Springfield Symphony (Mass.): Mark Russell Smith
Stamford Symphony Orchestra: Leonard Slatkin
Symphony of United Nations: Joseph Eger

Syracuse Symphony: Fabio Mechetti
Toledo Symphony: Andrew Massey
Tucson Symphony: George Hanson
Tulsa Philharmonic: Bernard Rubenstein
Utah Symphony: Joseph Silverstein
Virginia Symphony: JoAnn Falletta
Westchester Philharmonic: Paul Lustig Dunkel[2]
West Virginia Symphony: Thomas B. Conlin[4]
Wichita Symphony: Zuohuang Chen
Winston-Salem Piedmont Triad Symphony: Peter J. Perret
Youngstown Symphony Orchestra: Isaiah Jackson

1. Executive Director. 2. Conductor. 3. Principal Conductor. 4. Artistic Director. 5. Music Conductor. *Source:* American Symphony Orchestra League.

U.S. Opera Companies

(Budgets $2,000,000 and over)

American Musical Theatre of San Jose (Calif.), Dianna Shuster, Art. Dir.
Arizona Opera Company (Tucson, Phoenix), Glynn Ross, Gen. Dir.
Aspen Opera Theater Center (Colo.), Robert Harth, Pres. and CEO
Atlanta Opera, The (Ga.), William Fred Scott, Art. Dir.
Austin Lyric Opera (Tex.), Joseph McClain, Gen. Dir.
Baltimore Opera Company (Md.), Michael Harrison, Gen. Dir.
Boston Lyric Opera Company (Mass.), Janice Mancini Del Sesto, Gen. Dir.
Central City Opera House Association (Colo.), Daniel R. Rule, Gen. Mgr.
Cincinnati Opera Association (Ohio), James de Blasis, Art. Dir.
Civic Light Opera (Pittsburgh), Charles Gray, Exec. Dir.
Cleveland Opera (Ohio), David Bamberger, Gen. Dir.
Dallas Opera, The (Tex.), Plato S. Karayanis, Gen. Dir.
Florentine Opera Company (Milwaukee), Dennis W. Hanthorn, Gen. Dir.
Florida Grand Opera (Miami), Robert M. Heuer, Gen. Mgr. and CEO
Glimmerglass Opera (Cooperstown, N.Y.), Paul Kellogg, Art. Dir.
Goodspeed Opera House (East Haddam, Conn.), Michael Price, Exec. Dir.
Hawaii Opera Theatre (Honolulu), J. Mario Ramos, Gen. Dir. and Art. Dir.
Houston Grand Opera Association (Tex.), R. David Gockley, Gen. Dir.
Kentucky Opera (Louisville), Thomson Smillie, Gen. Dir.
Long Beach Civic Light Opera (Calif.), J. Phillip Keene III, Exec. Dir.
Los Angeles Music Center Opera (Calif.), Peter Hemmings, Gen. Dir.
Lyric Opera of Chicago (Ill.), Ardis Krainik, Gen. Dir.
Lyric Opera of Kansas City (Mo.), Russell Patterson, Gen. Art. Dir.
Metro Lyric Opera (Allenhurst, N.J.), Era M. Tognoli, Gen. Dir. and Art. Dir.
Metropolitan Opera Association, (N.Y.), James Levine, Art. Dir.
Michigan Opera Theatre (Detroit), David DiChiera, Gen. Dir.
Minnesota Opera, The (Minneapolis), Kevin Smith, Pres. and Gen. Dir.
New York City Opera (N.Y.), Paul Kellogg, Gen. Dir.
New York City Opera National Company (N.Y.), Clifford Kellas, Tour Coord.
Ohio Light Opera (Wooster), James Stuart, Art. Dir.
Opera Colorado (Denver), Nathaniel Merrill, Pres. and Gen. Dir.
Opera Company of Philadelphia (Pa.), Robert B. Driver, Gen. Dir.
Opera Pacific (Irvine, Calif.), David DiChiera, Art. Dir.
Opera Theatre of St. Louis (Mo.), Charles MacKay, Gen. Dir.
Orlando Opera Company Inc. (Fla.), Robert Swedberg, Gen. Dir.
Palm Beach Opera Inc. (Fla.), Herbert P. Benn, Gen. Dir.
Pittsburgh Opera, Inc. (Pa.), Tito Capobianco, Art. Dir.
Portland Opera Association (Ore.), Robert Bailey, Gen. Dir.
San Diego Civic Light Opera Association (Calif.), Leon Drew, Gen. Mgr.
San Diego Opera (Calif.), Ian D. Campbell, Gen. Dir.
San Francisco Opera (Calif.), Lotfi Mansouri, Gen. Dir.
San Francisco Opera Center (Calif.), Richard Harrell, Dir.
Santa Barbara Civic Light Opera (Calif.), Paul Iannacone, Exec. Prod.
Santa Fe Opera (N.M.), John Crosby, Gen. Dir.
Sarasota Opera Association (Fla.), Deane Carroll Allyn, Exec. Dir.
Seattle Opera Association (Wash.), Speight Jenkins, Gen. Dir.
Virginia Opera (Norfolk), Peter Mark, Gen. Dir.
Utah Opera Company (Salt Lake City), Anne Ewers, Gen. Dir.
Washington Opera, The (D.C.), Placido Domingo, Art. Dir. Designate

Source: Musical America International Directory of the Performing Arts, 1996 edition.

U.S. Dance Companies

(Budgets $2,500,000 and over)

Alvin Ailey American Dance Theatre (1958): Judith Jamison, Art. Dir.
American Ballet Theatre (1940): Kevin McKenzie, Art. Dir.
Atlanta Ballet Company (1929): John McFall, Art. Dir. and CEO
Ballet Florida (1986): Marie Hale, Art. Dir.
BalletMet Columbus (1978): David Nixon, Art. Dir.
Ballet West (1968[1]): John Hart, Art. Dir.
Boston Ballet (1964): Anna-Marie Holmes, Art. Dir.
Cincinnati Ballet (1955): Victoria Morgan, Art. Dir.
Cleveland San Jose Ballet (1976): Richard Bennett, Exec. Dir.
Colorado Ballet (1961): Martin Fredmann, Art. Dir.
Merce Cunningham Dance Company (1952): Merce Cunningham, Art. Dir.
Dance Theater of Harlem (1968): Arthur Mitchell, Art. Dir.
Feld Ballet New York (1974): Eliot Feld, Dir.
Martha Graham Dance Company (1927): Ron Protas, Art. Dir.
Houston Ballet (1968): Ben Stevenson, Art. Dir.
Joffrey Ballet of Chicago (1954): Gerald Arpino, Art. Dir.
Los Angeles Ballet (1995[2]): Andrew Deneau, Gen. Dir.
Miami City Ballet (1986): Edward Villella, Art. Dir.
Milwaukee Ballet (1970): Basil Thompson, Art. Dir.
New York City Ballet (1948): Peter Martins, Ballet-Master-in-Chief

Ocheami-Afrikan Dance Company (1978): Kofe Anang, Art. Dir.
Pacific Northwest Ballet (1972): Kent Stowell and Francia Russell, Art. Dirs.
Pittsburgh Ballet Theater (1970): Patricia Wilde, Art. Dir.
San Francisco Ballet (1933): Helgi Tomasson, Art. Dir.
Paul Taylor Dance Company (1954): Paul Taylor, Dir.
Streb/Ringside (1985): Elizabeth Streb, Art. Dir.

NOTE: Year founded appears in parentheses after name. 1. Prior company founded 1963, name changed to Ballet West in 1968. 2. Originally founded 1954, survived several reincarnations, the most recent of which was begun in 1995. *Source: Musical America International Directory of the Performing Arts,* 1996 edition.

Bestselling Books, 1997

Source: Publishers Weekly

Hardcover Fiction

1. *The Partner,* John Grisham
2. *Cold Mountain,* Charles Frazier
3. *The Ghost,* Danielle Steel
4. *The Ranch,* Danielle Steel
5. *Special Delivery,* Danielle Steel
6. *Unnatural Exposure,* Patricia Cornwell
7. *The Best Laid Plans,* Sidney Sheldon
8. *Pretend You Don't See Her,* Mary Higgins Clark
9. *Cat & Mouse,* James Patterson
10. *Hornet's Nest,* Patricia Cornwell

Hardcover Nonfiction

1. *Angela's Ashes,* Frank McCourt
2. *Simple Abundance,* Sarah Ban Breathnach
3. *Midnight in the Garden of Good and Evil,* John Berendt
4. *The Royals,* Kitty Kelley
5. *Joy of Cooking,* Irma S. Rombauer, Marion Rombauer Becker, and Ethan Becker
6. *Diana: Her True Story,* Andrew Morton
7. *Into Thin Air,* Jon Krakauer
8. *Conversations with God, Book I,* Neale Donald Walsch
9. *Men Are from Mars, Women Are from Venus,* John Gray
10. *Eight Weeks to Optimum Health,* Andrew Weil

Trade Paperbacks

1. *Don't Sweat the Small Stuff and It's All Small Stuff,* Richard Carlson
2. *Chicken Soup for the Woman's Soul,* Jack Canfield, Mark Victor Hansen, et al
3. *She's Come Undone,* Wally Lamb
4. *Chicken Soup for the Mother's Soul,* Jack Canfield, Mark Victor Hansen, et al.
5. *Wizard and Glass,* Stephen King
6. *Stones from the River,* Ursula Hegi
7. *Prescription for Nutritional Healing,* James F. & Phyllis A. Balch
8. *Windows 95 for Dummies, 2nd ed.,* Andy Rathbone
9. *Chicken Soup for the Christian Soul,* Jack Canfield, Mark Victor Hansen, et al.
10. *Songs in Ordinary Time,* Mary McGarry Morris

Mass Market Paperbacks

1. *The Runaway Jury,* John Grisham
2. *Five Days in Paris,* Danielle Steel
3. *Malice,* Danielle Steel
4. *Silent Honor,* Danielle Steel
5. *Executive Orders,* Tom Clancy
6. *Moonlight Becomes You,* Mary Higgins Clark
7. *Desperation,* Stephen King
8. *My Gal Sunday,* Mary Higgins Clark
9. *Airframe,* Michael Crichton
10. *Cause of Death,* Patricia Cornwell

All-Time Children's Bestselling Books

From the date of publication (in parentheses) through the end of 1995.

Source: Publishers Weekly

Hardcovers

1. *The Poky Little Puppy,* Janette Sebring Lowrey (1942)
2. *The Tale of Peter Rabbit,* Beatrix Potter (1902)
3. *Tootle,* Gertrude Crampton (1945)
4. *Saggy Baggy Elephant,* Kathryn and Byron Jackson (1955)
5. *Scuffy the Tugboat,* Gertrude Crampton (1955)
6. *Pat the Bunny,* Dorothy Kunhardt (1940)
7. *Green Eggs and Ham,* Dr. Seuss (1960)
8. *The Cat in the Hat,* Dr. Seuss (1957)
9. *The Littlest Angel,* Charles Tazewell (1946)
10. *One Fish, Two Fish, Red Fish, Blue Fish,* Dr. Seuss (1960)

Paperbacks

1. *Charlotte's Web,* E.B. White, illus. by Garth Williams (1974)
2. *The Outsiders,* S.E. Hinton (1968)
3. *Tales of a Fourth Grade Nothing,* Judy Blume (1976)
4. *Shane,* Jack Schaeffer (1983)
5. *Are You There, God? It's Me, Margaret,* Judy Blume (1972)
6. *Where the Red Fern Grows,* Wilson Rawls (1974)
7. *A Wrinkle in Time,* Madeleine L'Engle (1973)
8. *Island of the Blue Dolphins,* Scott O'Dell (1971)
9. *Little House on the Prairie,* Laura Ingalls Wilder, illus. by Garth Williams (1971)
10. *Little House in the Big Woods,* Laura Ingalls Wilder, illus. by Garth Williams (1971)

Major City Public Libraries

City (branches)	Volumes	Circulation	Budget (millions)
Akron-Summit County, Ohio (17)	1,087,517	3,571,966	$16.7
Albuquerque, N.M. (15)	1,534,121	2,913,328	8.1
Annapolis, Md. (15)	1,310,359	5,002,677	11.9
*Atlanta-Fulton County (31)	1,960,000	2,704,000	19.5
Austin, Tex. (19)	1,450,046	2,433,992	11.6
Baltimore (29)	2,600,000	1,518,524	22.8
Baton Rouge, La. (9)	1,100,603	2,465,857	14.2
*Birmingham, Ala. (19)	1,039,000	1,701,817	10.5
*Boston (25)	6,581,736	3,500,000	30.1
Buffalo-Erie County, N.Y. (53)	3,600,000[1]	8,827,234	25.0
*Charleston-Kanawna County, W.Va. (8)	612,435	1,040,000	4.8
Charlotte, N.C. (22)	1,430,257	5,646,750	17.4
Chicago (81)	6,465,991[2]	7,839,041	69.2
Cincinnati (41)	4,585,127	12,564,004	42.6
Cleveland (27)	3,479,931[3]	5,525,663	41.0
Columbus Metropolitan, Ohio (21)	2,384,752	11,862,449	34.1
Dallas (22)	2,722,736	4,077,655	17.6
*Dayton-Montgomery County, Ohio (20)	1,633,332	6,206,420	16.0
Denver (21)	4,223,938	7,477,619	23.7
Des Moines, Iowa (5)	611,105	1,370,947	4.5
Detroit (24)	2,746,571	1,594,963	26.5
*El Paso (10)	1,277,003[4]	1,731,820	6.6[5]
Erie, Pa. (6)	425,593	1,634,880	3.5
Evansville-Vanderburgh, Ind. (7)	803,380	1,432,278	6.2
Fairfax County, Va. (19)	2,100,000	9,400,000	19.7
Fort Wayne-Allen County, Ind. (14)	3,231,808[3]	4,208,205	15.0
Fort Worth (10)	2,029,363	4,388,337	7.9
*Grand Rapids, Mich. (5)	976,640	1,084,540	6.2
Greenville City-County, S.C. (11)	957,846	1,891,781	8.5
Hawaii State Public Library System (49)[6]	3,517,989[2]	7,374,583	20.8
Houston (34)	4,385,879	5,906,886	27.1
Independence, Mo. (29)	2,475,762	6,431,129	20.3
Indianapolis-Marion County (21)	1,714,960	8,275,441	26.5
Jackson-Hinds County, Miss. (15)	583,324	820,523	2.9
Jacksonville, Fla. (18)	2,687,980	3,693,283	14.3
Kansas City, Mo. (9)	2,009,420	2,275,774	12.8
Knoxville, Tenn. (16)	719,956	1,966,233	5.6
Lincoln, Neb. (7)	606,024	2,028,000	4.9
Long Beach, Calif. (11)	1,093,155	2,459,131	10.9
Los Angeles County (88)	6,945,639[7]	15,300,000	57.9
Louisville, Ky. (16)	1,033,008[2]	3,104,300	11.7
Madison, Wis. (8)	756,680	2,555,233	7.4
Memphis, Tenn. (21)	1,720,046	3,737,834	14.2
Miami-Dade County, Fla. (31)	3,983,968	10,667,327	34.8
Milwaukee (12)	2,447,499	3,024,239	19.2
Minneapolis (14)	2,114,887	2,651,753	16.9
Nashville-Davidson County, Tenn. (18)	700,171[7]	2,072,921	10.3
*Newark, N.J. (11)	1,400,000	1,400,000	9.4
New Orleans (15)	953,867	1,116,525	6.3
New York City:			
New York Public Library			
Branches (82)	11,466,261	11,194,409	104.0
Research	41,452,558	—	94.0
Brooklyn Public Library (60)	6,495,084	10,078,269	55.0
Queens Borough Public Library (62)	8,640,540	15,280,937	58.6
Norfolk, Va. (11)	970,112	383,844	3.8
Oklahoma City-County (12)	871,657	4,168,000	11.8
Omaha, Neb. (9)	728,235	2,289,858	8.9[8]
Philadelphia (52)	7,983,088	6,530,277	38.8
Phoenix, Ariz. (12)	1,764,965	5,686,766	17.5
Pittsburgh (20)	2,004,299	3,029,038	18.0
Portland-Multnomah County, Ore. (14)	1,435,637	7,757,882	24.1
Providence, R.I. (9)	1,004,746	708,405	5.0
*Richmond, Va. (10)	814,723	814,752	3.7
*Rochester, N.Y. (10)	2,000,000	1,582,730	10.6
Sacramento, Calif. (23)	1,343,224	3,587,042	16.5
*St. Louis (15)	4,895,532	2,196,246	16.5
*St. Paul (12)	1,050,555[9]	2,400,918	7.8
*St. Petersburg, Fla. (6)	448,938	1,107,342	3.2
Salt Lake County, Utah (16)	1,552,750	6,017,265	15.2
San Antonio (18)	1,681,040	3,450,299	15.9
San Diego, Calif. (33)	2,465,162	6,370,488	22.6[10]
San Francisco, Calif. (26)	2,124,162[7]	4,345,072	36.3
San Jose, Calif. (18)	1,434,351[11]	5,000,199	31.3
Seattle (22)	2,414,767[11]	4,580,780	24.5
Springfield, Mass. (8)	758,092	852,494	5.0
Tampa, Fla. (17)	2,163,613	3,436,618	15.3
Tucson, Ariz. (19)	1,146,000	4,900,000	13.6
Tulsa City-County, Okla. (21)	1,040,574	3,719,407	10.2
*Washington, D.C. (27)	2,163,321[2]	1,803,599	19.7
Wichita, Kan. (12)	970,882	1,821,287	4.7
*Winston-Salem-Forsyth County, N.C. (9)	400,000	2,100,000	6.0
Worcester, Mass. (2)	628,820	630,206	3.1
Youngstown-Mahoning County, Ohio (22)	670,880	1,857,432	9.0

1. Includes books and audio material. 2. Book collection only. 3. Includes government documents, bound periodicals, bound series. 4. Includes books, periodicals, records, films, government documents (collection weeded). 5. Budget includes both general and bonded funds. 6. Statewide system. 7. Includes books and audiovisual materials; excludes microforms. 8. Includes benefits, indirect costs, and county funding. 9. Includes books, audiovisual materials, government documents, and musical scores. 10. Includes local funds, grants, and capital improvements. 11. Includes all library materials. *Did not reply to questionnaire with updated information.

Poets Laureate of the United States

Robert Penn Warren	1986–1987
Richard Wilbur	1987–1988
Howard Nemerov	1988–1990
Mark Strand	1990–1991
Joseph Brodsky	1991–1992
Mona Van Duyn	1992–1993
Rita Dove	1993–1995
Robert Hass	1995–1997
Robert Pinsky	1997–

NOTE: The post was established in 1985. Appointment is for a one-year term, but is renewable.

Poets Laureate of England

Edmund Spenser	1591–1599	Laurence Eusden	1718–1730	Alfred Austin	1896–1913
Samuel Daniel	1599–1619	Colley Cibber	1730–1757	Robert Bridges	1913–1930
Ben Jonson	1619–1637	William Whitehead	1757–1785	John Masefield	1930–1967
William Davenant	1638–1668	Thomas Warton	1785–1790	Cecil Day-Lewis	1967–1972
John Dryden[1]	1670–1689	Henry James Pye	1790–1813	Sir John Betjeman	1972–1984
Thomas Shadwell	1689–1692	Robert Southey	1813–1843	Ted Hughes	1984–
Nahum Tate	1692–1715	William Wordsworth	1843–1850		
Nicholas Rowe	1715–1718	Alfred Lord Tennyson	1850–1892		

1. First to bear the title officially.

Longest Broadway Runs

Show	Dates[1]	Performances
1. Cats	10/82–present	6,533
2. A Chorus Line	10/75–4/90	6,137
3. Oh, Calcutta!	9/76–8/89	5,962
4. Les Misérables	3/87–present	4,615
5. The Phantom of the Opera	1/88–present	4,318
6. 42nd Street	8/80–1/89	3,485
7. Grease	2/72–4/80	3,388
8. Fiddler on the Roof	9/64–7/72	3,242
9. Life With Father	11/39–7/47	3,224
10. Tobacco Road	12/33–5/41	3,182
11. Miss Saigon	4/91–present	2,980
12. Hello Dolly	1/64–12/70	2,844
13. My Fair Lady	3/56–9/62	2,717
14. Annie	4/77–1/83	2,377
15. Man of La Mancha	11/65–6/71	2,329
16. Abie's Irish Rose	5/22–10/27	2,327
17. Oklahoma!	3/43–5/48	2,212
18. Pippin	10/72–6/77	1,944
19. South Pacific	4/49–1/54	1,925
20. The Magic Show	5/74–12/78	1,920
21. Gemini	6/77–9/81	1,819
22. Deathtrap	2/78–6/82	1,793
23. Harvey	11/44–1/49	1,775
24. Dancin'	3/78–6/82	1,774
25. La Cage Aux Folles	6/83–11/87	1,761

1. As of 5/31/98 *Source:* League of American Theatres and Producers.

Top 10 Classical Albums, 1997

1. *David Helfgott Plays Rachmaninov,* David Helfgott (RCA Victor/BMG Classics)
2. *Appalachia Waltz,* Ma/Meyer/O'Connor (Sony Classical)
3. *The Vienna I Love,* Andre Rieu (Philips/PolyGram Classics)
4. *In Gabriel's Garden,* Wynton Marsalis (Sony Classical)
5. *The Classical Album,* Vanessa-Mae (Angel/Angel Records)
6. *Chant D'Amour,* Cecilia Bartoli (London/PolyGram Classics)
7. *From Holland With Love,* Andre Rieu (Philips/PolyGram Classics)
8. *Grace,* Kathleen Battle (Sony Classical)
9. *In Concert,* Carreras, Domingo, Pavarotti (Mehta) (London/PolyGram Classics)
10. *Paul McCartney's Standing Stone,* London Symphony Orchestra (Foster) (MPL/EMI Classics/Angel Records)

Source: © 1998 BPI Communications Inc. Used with permission from *Billboard*/SoundScan/BDS.

Top 10 Country Singles, 1997

1. "It's Your Love," Tim McGraw (with Faith Hill) (Curb)
2. "One Night At A Time," George Strait (MCA Nashville)
3. "Carrying Your Love With Me," George Strait (MCA Nashville)
4. "On The Verge," Collin Raye (Epic)
5. "How Your Love Makes Me Feel," Diamond Rio (Arista Nashville)
6. "Rumor Has It," Clay Walker (Giant/Reprise)
7. "(This Ain't) No Thinkin' Thing," Trace Adkins (Capitol Nashville)
8. "Better Man, Better Off," Tracy Lawrence (Atlantic)
9. "She's Got It All," Kenny Chesney (BNA)
10. "I Left Something Turned On At Home," Trace Adkins (Capitol Nashville)

Source: © 1998 BPI Communications Inc. Used with permission from *Billboard*/SoundScan/BDS.

Top 10 Country Albums, 1997

1. *Blue,* LeAnn Rimes (Curb)
2. *Did I Shave My Legs For This?* Deana Carter (Capitol Nashville)
3. *Unchained Melody/The Early Years,* LeAnn Rimes (Curb)
4. *Carrying Your Love With Me,* George Strait (MCA Nashville)
5. *Everywhere,* Tim McGraw (Curb)
6. *You Light Up My Life—Inspirational Songs,* LeAnn Rimes (Curb)
7. *Everything I Love,* Alan Jackson (Arista Nashville)
8. *(Songbook) A Collection of Hits,* Trisha Yearwood (MCA Nashville)
9. *What If It's You,* Reba McEntire (MCA Nashville)
10. *The Greatest Hits,* Clint Black (RCA)

Source: © 1998 BPI Communications Inc. Used with permission from *Billboard*/SoundScan/BDS.

Top 10 Pop Singles, 1997

1. "Candle In The Wind 1997/Something About the Way You Look Tonight," Elton John (Rocket/A&M)
2. "You Were Meant For Me/Foolish Games," Jewel (Atlantic)
3. "I'll Be Missing You," Puffy Daddy & Faith Evans (Featuring 112) (Bad Boy/Arista)
4. "Un-Break My Heart," Toni Braxton (LaFace/Arista)
5. "Can't Nobody Hold Me Down," Puff Daddy (Featuring Mase) (Bad Boy/Arista)
6. "I Believe I Can Fly," (from *Space Jam*) R. Kelly (Warner Sunset/Atlantic/Jive)
7. "Don't Let Go (Love)," (from *Set it Off*) En Vogue (EastWest/EEG)
8. "Return Of The Mack," Mark Morrison (Atlantic)
9. "How Do I Live," LeAnn Rimes (Curb)
10. "Wannabe," Spice Girls (Virgin)

Source: © 1998 BPI Communications Inc. Used with permission from *Billboard*/SoundScan/BDS.

Top 10 Pop Albums, 1997

1. *Spice,* Spice Girls (Virgin)
2. *Tragic Kingdom,* No Doubt (Trauma/Interscope)
3. *Falling Into You,* Celine Dion (550 Music/Epic)
4. *Space Jam,* Soundtrack (Warner Sunset/Atlantic/AG)
5. *Pieces Of You,* Jewel (Atlantic/AG)
6. *Blue,* LeAnn Rimes (Curb)
7. *Bringing Down The Horse,* The Wallflowers (Interscope)
8. *Life After Death,* The Notorious B.I.G. (Bad Boy/Arista)
9. *Secrets,* Toni Braxton (LaFace/Arista)
10. *No Way Out,* Puff Daddy & The Family (Bad Boy/Arista)

Source: © 1998 BPI Communications Inc. Used with permission from *Billboard*/SoundScan/BDS.

Top 10 R&B Singles, 1997

1. "In My Bed," Dru Hill (Island)
2. "I'll Be Missing You," Puff Daddy & Faith Evans (Featuring Mase) (Bad Boy/Arista)
3. "G.H.E.T.T.O.U.T.," Changing Faces (Big Beat/Atlantic)
4. "Can't Nobody Hold Me Down," Puff Daddy (Featuring Mase) (Bad Boy/Arista)
5. "You Make Me Wanna...," Usher (LaFace/Arista)
6. "I Belong To You (Every Time I See Your Face)," Rome (Grand Jury/RCA)
7. "I Believe I Can Fly," from *Space Jam*) R. Kelly (Warner Sunset/Atlantic/Jive)
8. "Cupid," 112 (Bad Boy/Arista)
9. "On & On," Erykah Badu (Kedar/Universal)
10. "Get It Together," 702 (Biv 10/Motown)

Source: © 1998 BPI Communications Inc. Used with permission from *Billboard*/SoundScan/BDS.

Top R & B Albums, 1997

1. *Life After Death,* The Notorious B.I.G. (Bad Boy/Arista)
2. *Baduizm,* Erykah Badu (Kedar/Universal)
3. *The Don Killuminati: The 7 Day Theory,* Makaveli (Death Row/Interscope)
4. *Share My World,* Mary J. Blige (MCA)
5. *No Way Out,* Puff Daddy & The Family (Bad Boy/Arista)
6. *Ill Na Na,* Foxy Brown (Violator/Def Jam/Mercury)
7. *God's Property,* God's Property From Kirk Franklin's Nu Nation (B-Rite/Interscope)
8. *Another Level,* BLACKstreet (Interscope)
9. *Wu-Tang Forever,* Wu-Tang Clan (Loud/RCA)
10. *One In A Million,* Aaliyah (Blackground/Atlantic/AG)

Source: © 1998 BPI Communications Inc. Used with permission from *Bilboard*/SoundScan/BDS.

Best of 1997

Top Single: "Candle in the Wind/Something About the Way You Look Tonight," Elton John
Top Album: *Spice,* Spice Girls
Top Female Singles Artist: Toni Braxton
Top Male Singles Artist: Elton John
Top Singles Group: Spice Girls
New Pop Artist: Spice Girls
Top Country Artist: Leann Rimes
Top R&B Artist: Dru Hill
Top Adult Contemporary Artist: Toni Braxton
Top Jazz Artist: Tony Bennett
Top Classical Artist: David Helfgott

Source: © 1998 BPI Communications Inc. Used with permission from *Billboard*/SoundScan/BDS.

Top 15 Concert Grosses of 1997

Amusement Business annually ranks domestic and international concert grosses and touring acts. (gross ticket sales; total attendance; venue)

1. **Michael Jackson (7/12, 7/15, 7/17),** $9,236,685; 212,601; Wembley Stadium, London
2. **Three Tenors in Concert: Jose Carreras, Placido Domingo, Luciano Pavarotti (1/4),** $8,089,051; 50,688; SkyDome, Toronto
3. **The Rolling Stones, Foo Fighters (10/16, 10/17),** $6,823,242; 118,610; Giants Stadium, East Rutherford, N.J.
4. **U2, Audio Web, The Longpigs (8/22, 8/23),** $6,753,356; 144,308; Wembley Stadium, London
5. **U2, Fun Lovin' Criminals, The Longpigs (5/31, 6/1, 6/3),** $6,499,131; 129,644; Giants Stadium, East Rutherford, N.J.
6. **The Rolling Stones, Blues Traveler (9/23, 9/25),** $6,260,600; 107,186; Soldier Field, Chicago, Ill.
7. **U2, Fun Lovin' Criminals (6/27–6/29),** $5,956,587; 116,972; Soldier Field, Chicago, Ill.
8. **Michael Jackson (7/4, 7/6),** $5,879,068; 142,170; Olympia Stadium, Munich, Germany
9. **Three Tenors in Concert: Jose Carreras, Placido Domingo, Luciano Pavarotti (12/31/96),** $5,544,099; 41,872; B.C. Place Stadium, Vancouver
10. **The Rolling Stones, Wallflowers (11/9–11/10),** $4,338,429; 90,519; Dodger Stadium, Los Angeles, Calif.
11. **U2 (9/20),** $5,294,117; 150,000; Festival Site, Reggio Emilia, Italy
12. **The Rolling Stones, Sheryl Crow (10/20),** $4,839,760; 84,696; Foxboro (Mass.) Stadium
13. **U2, Fun Lovin' Criminals (7/1–7/2),** $4,789,124; 93,946; Foxboro (Mass.) Stadium
14. **Phish: The Great Went (8/16, 8/17),** $4,337,184; 123,172; Former Loring Air Force Base, Limestone, Maine
15. **Michael Jackson (8/24, 8/26),** $4,166,735; 97,106; Olympic Stadium, Helsinki, Finland

Source: © 1998 BPI Communications Inc. Used with permission from *Amusement Business.*

The Rock and Roll Hall of Fame

1986
Chuck Berry
James Brown
Ray Charles
Sam Cooke
Fats Domino
The Everly Brothers
Buddy Holly
Jerry Lee Lewis
Elvis Presley
Little Richard
Nonperformers
Alan Freed
Sam Phillips
Early Influences
Robert Johnson
Jimmie Rodgers
Jimmy Yancey
Lifetime Achievement
John Hammond

1987
The Coasters
Eddie Cochran
Bo Diddley
Aretha Franklin
Marvin Gaye
Bill Haley
B.B. King
Clyde McPhatter
Ricky Nelson
Roy Orbison
Carl Perkins
Smokey Robinson
Joe Turner
Muddy Waters
Jackie Wilson
Nonperformers
Leonard Chess
Ahmet Ertegun
Jerry Leiber and Mike Stoller
Jerry Wexler
Early Influences
Louis Jordan
T-Bone Walker
Hank Williams

1988
The Beach Boys
The Beatles
The Drifters
Bob Dylan
The Supremes
Nonperformer
Berry Gordy, Jr.
Early Influences
Woody Guthrie
Leadbelly
Les Paul

1989
Dion
Otis Redding
The Rolling Stones
The Temptations
Stevie Wonder
Nonperformer
Phil Spector
Early Influences
The Ink Spots
Bessie Smith
The Soul Stirrers

1990
Hank Ballard
Bobby Darin
The Four Seasons
The Four Tops
The Kinks
The Platters
Simon and Garfunkel
The Who
Nonperformers
Gerry Goffin and Carole King
Brian Holland, Eddie Holland, and Lamont Dozier
Early Influences
Louis Armstrong
Charlie Christian
Ma Rainey

1991
LaVern Baker
The Byrds
John Lee Hooker
The Impressions
Wilson Pickett
Jimmy Reed
Ike and Tina Turner
Nonperformers
Dave Bartholomew
Ralph Bass
Early Influence
Howlin' Wolf
Lifetime Achievement
Nesuhi Ertegun

1992
Bobby "Blue" Bland
Booker T. and the MG's
Johnny Cash
Jimi Hendrix Experience
Isley Brothers
Sam and Dave
The Yardbirds
Nonperformers
Leo Fender
Bill Graham
Doc Pomus
Early Influences
Elmore James
Professor Longhair

1993
Ruth Brown
Cream
Creedence Clearwater Revival
The Doors
Etta James
Frankie Lymon and the Teenagers
Van Morrison
Sly and the Family Stone
Nonperformers
Dick Clark
Milt Gabler
Early Influence
Dinah Washington

1994
The Animals
The Band
Duane Eddy
The Grateful Dead
Elton John
John Lennon
Bob Marley
Rod Stewart
Nonperformer
Johnny Otis
Early Influence
Willie Dixon

1995
The Allman Brothers Band
Al Green
Janis Joplin
Led Zeppelin
Martha and the Vandellas
Neil Young
Frank Zappa
Nonperformer
Paul Ackerman
Early Influence
The Orioles

1996
David Bowie
Jefferson Airplane
Little Willie John
Gladys Knight and the Pips
Pink Floyd
The Shirelles
The Velvet Underground
Nonperformer
Tom Donahue
Early Influence
Pete Seeger

1997
The Bee Gees
Buffalo Springfield
Crosby, Stills and Nash
The Jackson Five
Joni Mitchell
Parliament-Funkadelic
The (Young) Rascals
Nonperformer
Syd Nathan
Early Influences
Mahalia Jackson
Bill Monroe

1998
The Eagles
Fleetwood Mac
Mamas and Papa
Lloyd Price
Santana
Gene Vincent
Nonperformer
Allen Toussaint
Early Influence
"Jelly Roll" Morton

Top 10 Video Sales, 1997

1. *Riverdance—The Show,* (Columia TriStar Home Video)
2. *Lord of the Dance,* (PolyGram Video)
3. *Independence Day,* (FoxVideo)
4. *Jerry Maguire,*(Columia TriStar Home Video)
5. *101 Dalmations,* (Buena Vista Home Video)
6. *Space Jam,* (Warner Home Video)
7. *Toy Story,* (Buena Vista Home Video)
8. *Bambi,* (Buena Vista Home Video)
9. *Star Wars Trilogy—Special Edition,* (FoxVideo)
10. *The Hunchback of Notre Dame,* (Buena Vista Home Video)

Source: © 1998 BPI Communications Inc. Used with permission from *Billboard*/SoundScan/BDS.

Top 10 Video Rentals, 1997

1. *Fargo,* (PolyGram Video)
2. *Scream,* (Buena Vista Home Video)
3. *Donnie Brasco,* (Columbia TriStar Home Video)
4. *Sling Blade,* (Buena Vista Home Video)
5. *Absolute Power,* (Warner Home Video)
6. *The First Wives Club,* (Paramount Home Video)
7. *Sleepers,* (Warner Home Video)
8. *Phenomenon,* (Buena Vista Home Video)
9. *Ransom,* (Buena Vista Home Video)
10. *Jerry Maguire,* (Columbia TriStar Home Video)

Source: © 1998 BPI Communications Inc. Used with permission from *Billboard*/SoundScan/BDS.

The Recording Industry Association of America's Top-Selling Certified Albums of All Time

The RIAA certifies recordings that sell 500,000 or more copies as gold, those selling 1,000,000 or more as platinum, and those selling 2,000,000 or more as multi-platinum.

25 Million

Thriller, Michael Jackson (Epic)

24 Million

Eagles—Their Greatest Hits 1971–1975, Eagles (Elektra)

22 Million

The Wall, Pink Floyd (Columbia)

18 Million

Greatest Hits Volume I & II, Billy Joel (Columbia)

17 Million

Led Zeppelin IV, Led Zeppelin (Swan Song)
Rumours, Fleetwood Mac (Warner Bros.)

16 Million

Back in Black, AC/DC (Atco)
The Beatles, The Beatles (Capitol)
The Bodyguard, (Soundtrack) Whitney Houston (Arista)
Boston, Boston (Epic)

15 Million

Born in the U.S.A., Bruce Springsteen (Columbia)
Cracked Rear View, Hootie & the Blowfish (Atlantic)
Jagged Little Pill, Alanis Morissette (Maverick)

14 Million

Appetite for Destruction, Guns 'N Roses (Geffen)
The Beatles 1967–1970 , The Beatles (Capitol)
Hotel California, Eagles (Elektra)

13 Million

Bat Out of Hell, Meat Loaf (Epic)
The Beatles 1962–1966, The Beatles (Capitol)
The Dark Side of the Moon, Pink Floyd (Capitol)
Greatest Hits, Elton John (Rocket)
No Fences, Garth Brooks (Liberty)
Purple Rain, (Soundtrack) Prince and the Revolution (Warner Bros.)

12 Million

II, Boyz II Men (Motown)
Bruce Springsteen & the E Street Band Live 1975–'85, (Box set), Bruce Springsteen (Columbia)
Kenny Rogers' Greatest Hits, Kenny Rogers (Capitol Nashville)
Slippery When Wet, Bon Jovi (Mercury)
Whitney Houston, Whitney Houston (Arista)

11 Million

Abbey Road, The Beatles (Capitol)
Breathless, Kenny G (Arista)
Candle in the Wind 1997/Something, You Look Tonight (Single), Elton John (Rocket)
Dirty Dancing, Soundtrack (RCA)
Hysteria, Def Leppard (Mercury)
James Taylor's Greatest Hits, James Taylor (Warner Bros.)
Ropin' the Wind, Garth Brooks (Liberty)
Sgt. Pepper's Lonely Hearts Club Band, The Beatles (Capitol)
Saturday Night Fever, (Soundtrack) Bee Gees (RSO)

10 Million

Best of the Doobies, Doobie Brothers (Warner Bros.)
Can't Slow Down, Lionel Richie (Motown)
Crazy, Sexy, Cool TLC (LaFace)
Eliminator, ZZ Top (Warner Bros.)
Faith, George Michael (Columbia)
Falling Into You, Celine Dion (550 Music)
The Joshua Tree, U2 (Island)
The Lion King, Soundtrack (Walt Disney)
Metallica, Metallica (Elektra)
Music Box, Mariah Carey (Columbia)
Please Hammer Don't Hurt 'Em, Hammer (Capitol)
Tapestry, Carole King (Ode)
Ten, Pearl Jam (Epic)
Unplugged, Eric Clapton (Reprise)
Van Halen, Van Halen (Warner Bros.)
The Woman in Me, Shania Twain (Mercury Nashville)

9 Million

1984, Van Halen (Warner Bros.)
Aerosmith's Greatest Hits, Aerosmith (Columbia)
Brothers in Arms, Dire Straits (Warner Bros.)
CooleyHighHarmony, Boyz II Men (Motown)
Daydream, Mariah Carey (Columbia)
Dookie, Green Day (Reprise)
Eagles Greatest Hits Volume II, Eagles (Elektra)
Escape, Journey (Columbia)
Greatest Hits, Journey (Columbia)
Hi Infidelity, R.E.O. Speedwagon (Epic)
The Hits, Garth Brooks (Capitol Nashville)
Legend, Bob Marley & the Wailers (Island)
Like a Virgin, Madonna (Sire)
Nevermind, Nirvana (DGC)
Pyromania, Def Leppard (Mercury)
The Sign, Ace of Base (Arista)
Some Gave All, Billy Ray Cyrus (Mercury)
The Stranger, Billy Joel (Columbia)
Whitney, Whitney Houston (Arista)

8 Million

Bad, Michael Jackson (Epic)
The Beatles Anthology, Volume I, The Beatles (Capitol)
Footloose, Soundtrack (Columbia)
Grease, (Soundtrack) Olivia Newton-John and John Travolta (RSO)
Hangin' Tough, New Kids on the Block (Columbia)
Mariah Carey, Mariah Carey (Columbia)
Mellon Collie and the Infinite Sadness, Smashing Pumkins (Virgin)
Time, Love & Tenderness, Michael Bolton (Columbia)
Toni Braxton, Toni Braxton (LaFace)
Whitesnake, Whitesnake (Geffen)

7 Million

52nd Street, Billy Joel (Columbia)
Achtung Baby, U2 (Island)
All Eyez on Me, 2PAC (Death Row/Interscope)
An Innocent Man, Billy Joel (Columbia)
August & Everything After, Counting Crows (Geffen)
Deja Vu, Crosby, Stills, Nash & Young (Atlantic)
Don't Be Cruel, Bobby Brown (MCA)
Don't Look Back, Boston (Epic)
Forever Your Girl, Paula Abdul (Virgin)
Garth Brooks, Garth Brooks (Capitol Nashville)
Get a Grip, Aerosmith (Geffen)
Glass Houses, Billy Joel (Columbia)
Greatest Hits, Patsy Cline (MCA)
Miracles, Kenny G (Arista)
New Jersey, Bon Jovi (Mercury)
No Jacket Required, Phil Collins (Atlantic)
No Need to Argue, The Cranberries (Island)
Off the Wall, Michael Jackson (Epic)
Pump, Aerosmith (Geffen)
Sports, Huey Lewis & the News (Chrysalis)
Throwing Copper, Live (Radioactive)
Time Pieces/Best of Eric Clapton, Eric Clapton (Polydor)
Top Gun, Soundtrack (Columbia)
To the Extreme, Vanilla Ice (SBK)
Tragic Kingdom, No Doubt (Trauma/Interscope)
True Blue, Madonna (Sire)
Tuesday Night Music Club, Sheryl Crow (A&M)
Waiting to Exhale, Soundtrack (Arista)

Dollar Value of Recordings[1]

(in millions, net after returns)

	1986	1990	1994	1995	1996
CD	930.1	3,451.6	8,464.5	9,377.4	9,934.7
CD single	n.a.	6.0	56.1	110.9	184.1
Cassette	2,499.5	3,472.4	2,976.4	2,303.6	1,905.3
Cassette single	n.a.	257.9	274.9	236.3	189.3
LP/EP	983.0	86.5	17.8	25.1	36.8
Vinyl single	228.1	94.4	47.2	46.7	47.5
Music video	n.a.	172.3	231.1	220.3	236.1

1. List price value. *Source:* Recording Industry Association of America, Inc.

Top Specials 1997–98[1]

Rank	Program name (network) [first telecast]	Rating (% of TV households)
1.	Academy Awards (ABC) [3/23/98]	34.9%
2.	Seinfeld Clipshow Special (NBC) [5/14/98]	33.6
3.	Seinfeld (NBC) [4/23/98]	20.3
4.	Third Rock from Sun Special (NBC) [1/25/98]	19.7
5.	Grammy Awards (CBS) [2/25/98]	17.0

1. Sept. 22, 1997–May 20, 1998. *Source:* Nielsen Media Research. © 1998, Nielsen Media Research.

Top 15 Regularly Scheduled Network Programs, 1997–98[1]

Rank	Program name (network)	Total percent of TV households
1.	Seinfeld (NBC)	22.0%
2.	E.R. (NBC)	20.7
3.	Veronica's Closet (NBC)	16.8
4.	Friends (NBC)	16.4
4.	NFL Monday Night Foodball (ABC)	15.0
6.	Touched By An Angel (CBS)	14.4
7.	60 Minutes (CBS)	13.9
8.	Union Square (NBC)	13.6
9.	CBS Sunday Movie (CBS)	13.3%
10.	Frasier (NBC)	12.0
10.	Home Improvement (ABC)	12.0
10.	Just Shoot Me (NBC)	12.0
13.	Dateline NBC Tues. (NBC)	11.5
13.	NFL Monday Showcase (ABC)	11.5
15.	Dateline NBC Mon. (NBC)	11.4

1. Sept. 22, 1997–May 20, 1998. *Source:* Nielsen Media Research. © 1998, Nielsen Media Research.

Top 15 Syndicated TV Programs 1997–98 Season

Rank	Program [2]	Rating (% U.S.)[1]
1.	Wheel of Fortune–Syn	11.8%
2.	Jeopardy	9.8
2.	Home Improvement–Syn (AT)	8.1
4.	Seinfeld–Syn	7.4
5.	Oprah Winfrey Show	7.3
6.	X-Files–Syn	7.0
7.	Buena Vista I	6.5
8.	ESPN NFL Football	6.5
9.	Jerry Springer (AT)	6.4%
10.	Entertainment Tonight	6.1
10.	X-Files–Syn (AT)	6.1
12.	Simpsons M–F (AT)	5.8
13.	Wheel of Fortune–Wknd	5.5
13.	Xena	5.5
15.	Frasier–Syn	5.2

1. Sept. 22, 1997–May 20, 1998. 2. Programs airing 3 or less weeks have been excluded from this ranking. Note: (AT) = Additional Telecasts; station programming provides additional viewing opportunities. *Source:* Nielsen Media Research. © 1998, Nielsen Media Research.

Top Sports Shows 1997–98[1]

Rank	Program name (network)	Description	Rating (% of TV households)
1.	Super Bowl XXXII (NBC)	Green Bay vs. Denver	44.5%
2.	Super Bowl XXXII Postgame (NBC)	Green Bay vs. Denver	33.4
3.	Super Bowl XXXII Kickoff (NBC)	Green Bay vs. Denver	32.5
4.	Fox NFC Championship (Fox)	Green Bay at San Francisco	26.2
5.	AFC Championship Game (NBC)	Denver at Pittsburgh	25.0
6.	NBC World Series Game 7 (NBC)	Cleveland at Florida	24.5
7.	XVIII Winter Olympics (CBS)	Fri., 2/20/98	23.2
8.	NFL Playoff Game-Sun. (NBC)	Denver at Kansas City	22.9
9.	XVIII Winter Olympics (CBS)	Weds., 2/18/98	20.7
10.	XVIII Winter Olympics (CBS)	Sun., 2/08/98	20.2
10.	Fox NFC Playoff-Sun. (Fox)	Tampa Bay at Green Bay	20.2

1. Sept. 22, 1997–May 20, 1998. *Source:* Nielsen Media Research. © 1998, Nielsen Media Research.

Top-Rated TV Movies 1997–98[1]

Rank	Program name (network)	Rating (% of TV households)	Rank	Program name (network)	Rating (% of TV households)
1.	What the Deaf Man Heard (CBS)	23.0%	9.	The Echo of Thunder (CBS)	16.4%
2.	Merlin, Part I (NBC)	21.7	10.	The Long Way Home (CBS)	15.7
3.	Merlin, Part II (NBC)	20.6	11.	The Wedding: Part 2 (ABC)	15.6
4.	Before Women Had Wings (ABC)	18.8	12.	1,000 Men and a Baby (CBS)	15.4
5.	Cinderella (ABC)	18.7	13.	Miracle in the Woods (CBS)	14.8
6.	Borrowed Hearts (CBS)	18.4	13.	Bella Mafia, Pt. 1 of 2 (CBS)	14.8
7.	The Wedding: Part I (ABC)	16.8	15.	The Love Letter (CBS)	14.4
8.	Ellen Foster (CBS)	16.5			

1. Sept. 22, 1997–May 24, 1998. *Source:* Nielsen Media Research. © 1998, Nielsen Media Research.

Hours of TV Usage Per Week by Household Income

	Under $30,000	$30,000+	$40,000+	$50,000+	$60,000+
Nov. 1993	53 hr. 35 min.	50 hr. 34 min.	50 hr. 24 min. (includes $50,000+)		47 hr. 13 min.
Nov. 1994	53 hr. 46 min.	52 hr. 05 min.	50 hr. 04 min. (includes $50,000+)		46 hr. 42 min.
Nov. 1995	52 hr. 25 min.	51 hr. 44 min.	48 hr. 53 min.		46 hr. 02 min.
Nov. 1996	55 hr. 26 min.	49 hr. 43 min.	49 hr. 03 min.	48 hr. 23 min.	47 hr. 32 min.
Nov. 1997	56 hr. 17 min.	51 hr. 04 min.	50 hr. 34 min.	49 hr. 44 min.	48 hr. 43 min.

Source: Nielsen Media Research. © 1998, Nielsen Media Research.

Television Set Ownership
(January 1998)

Households with	Number	Percent
Color TV sets	97,020,000	99%
B&W only	980,000	1
Two or more sets	72,520,000	74
One set	25,480,000	26
Cable	72,520,000	74
Total TV households	**98,000,000**	**98**

Source: Nielsen Media Research. © 1998, Nielsen Media Research.

Persons Viewing Primetime[1]
(in millions)

	Total persons
Monday	96.69
Tuesday	94.18
Wednesday	91.10
Thursday	96.92
Friday	80.74
Saturday	77.14
Sunday	88.58

1. Average minute audiences May 1998. NOTE: Prime time is 8:00–11:00 p.m. (EST) except Sun. 7:00–11:00 p.m. *Source:* Nielsen Media Research. © 1998, Nielsen Media Research.

Source of Household Viewing—Primetime
Pay Cable, Basic Cable, and Non-Cable Households
(Monday–Sunday, 8:00–11:00 p.m.)

	Nov. 1997			Nov. 1996			Nov. 1995			Nov. 1994		
	Pay cable	Basic cable	Non-cable	Pay cable	Basic cable	Non-cable	Pay cable	Basic cable	Non-cable	Pay cable	Basic cable	Non-cable
% TV usage	66.7	60.8	55.7	67.6	60.2	54.9	67.2	60.9	54.4	67.0	61.2	58.1
Pay cable	7.1	—	—	8.2	—	—	9.2	—	—	9.3	—	—
Cable-originated programming	28.5	26.9	—	27.0	24.2	—	25.9	23.6	—	22.1	20.5	—
Other-on-air stations	6.8	5.7	10.1	7.0	6.2	9.2	6.9	5.4	9.3	7.2	7.8	12.7
Network affiliated stations	36.4	34.4	39.3	37.6	35.3	42.2	38.1	37.5	44.3	41.6	40.7	50.6
Network share	55	57	71	56	59	77	57	62	81	62	67	87

Source: Nielsen Media Research, NTI Cable Status Report. © 1998, Nielsen Media Research.

Average Hours of Household TV Usage
(in hours and minutes per day)

	Yearly average	February	July		Yearly average	February	July
1985–1986	7 hr. 10 min.	7 hr. 48 min.	6 hr. 37 min.	1991–1992	7 hr. 04 min.	7 hr. 32 min.	6 hr. 39 min.
1986–1987	7 hr. 05 min.	7 hr. 35 min.	6 hr. 32 min.	1992–1993	7 hr. 09 min.	7 hr. 41 min.	6 hr. 47 min.
1987–1988	6 hr. 59 min.	7 hr. 38 min.	6 hr. 31 min.	1993–1994	7 hr. 15 min.	7 hr. 51 min.	6 hr. 53 min.
1988–1989	7 hr. 02 min.	7 hr. 32 min.	6 hr. 27 min.	1994–1995	7 hr. 02 min.	7 hr. 39 min.	6 hr. 46 min.
1989–1990	6 hr. 55 min.	7 hr. 16 min.	6 hr. 24 min.	1995–1996	7 hr. 17 min.	7 hr. 38 min.	6 hr. 58 min.
1990–1991	6 hr. 56 min.	7 hr. 30 min.	6 hr. 26 min.	1996–1997	7 hr. 11 min.	7 hr. 28 min.	6 hr. 49 min.

Source: Nielsen Media Research. © 1998, Nielsen Media Research.

Weekly TV Viewing by Age

(in hours and minutes)

	Time per week				Time per week		
	Nov. 1997	Nov. 1996	Nov. 1995		Nov. 1997	Nov. 1996	Nov. 1995
Women 18–24 years old	25 hr. 22 min.	24 hr. 32 min.	24 hr. 52 min.	Men 55 and over	36 hr. 17 min.	37 hr. 08 min.	37 hr. 58 min.
Women 25–54	31 hr. 45 min.	30 hr. 44 min.	31 hr. 45 min.	Female teens	19 hr. 60 min.	18 hr. 19 min.	19 hr. 59 min.
Women 55 and over	41 hr. 50 min.	41 hr. 50 min.	42 hr. 20 min.	Male teens	19 hr. 60 min.	19 hr. 59 min.	20 hr. 38 min.
Men 18–24	20 hr. 30 min.	20 hr. 20 min.	21 hr. 20 min.	Children 6–11	19 hr. 49 min.	19 hr. 59 min.	21 hr. 40 min.
Men 25–54	28 hr. 44 min.	28 hr. 04 min.	28 hr. 23 min.	Children 2–5	26 hr. 02 min.	23 hr. 21 min.	24 hr. 52 min.

Source: Nielsen Media Research. © 1998, Nielsen Media Research.

Audience Composition by Selected Program Type[1]

(Average Minute Audience)

	General drama	Situation comedy	Informational[2] 6:00–7:00 p.m.	Feature films	All regular network programs 7:00–11:00 p.m.
Women (18 and over)	6,592,000	5,414,000	5,787,000	6,810,000	6,436,000
Men (18 and over)	4,398,000	3,557,000	4,376,000	4,672,000	4,708,000
Teens (12–17)	724,000	951,000	230,000	946,000	831,000
Children (2–11)	793,000	1,141,000	435,000	1,403,000	1,045,000
Total persons (2+)	12,508,000	11,063,000	10,827,000	13,831,000	13,019,000

1. All figures are estimated for November 1997. 2. Multiweekly viewing. *Source:* Nielsen Media Research. © 1998, Nielsen Media Research.

Movie Revenues

All-Time Box Office Grosses[1]

1.	*Titanic* (1997)	$581,889,889
2.	*Star Wars* (1977)	460,987,469
3.	*E.T.* (1982)	399,804,539
4.	*Jurassic Park* (1993)	356,839,725
5.	*Forrest Gump* (1994)	329,690,974
6.	*The Lion King* (1994)	312,855,561
7.	*Return of the Jedi* (1983)	309,161,884
8.	*Independence Day* (1996)	306,169,255
9.	*The Empire Strikes Back* (1980)	290,268,568
10.	*Home Alone* (1990)	285,016,000
11.	*Jaws* (1975)	260,000,000
12.	*Batman* (1989)	251,188,924
13.	*Men in Black* (1997)	250,147,615
14.	*Raiders of the Lost Ark* (1981)	245,034,358
15.	*Twister* (1996)	241,708,908
16.	*Beverly Hills Cop* (1984)	234,760,478
17.	*The Lost World: Jurassic Park* (1997)	229,074,524
18.	*Ghostbusters* (1984)	220,858,490
19.	*Mrs. Doubtfire* (1993)	219,194,773
20.	*Ghost* (1990)	217,631,306
21.	*Aladdin* (1992)	217,350,219
22.	*Back to the Future* (1985)	210,609,762
23.	*Terminator 2* (1991)	204,466,562
24.	*Indiana Jones and the Last Crusade* (1989)	197,171,806
25.	*Gone With the Wind* (1939)	193,597,756

Top 25 Movies of 1997[2]

1.	*Men in Black* (Sony/Columbia)	$250,147,615
2.	*Titanic* (Paramount)	242,748,914
3.	*The Lost World: Jurassic Park* (Universal)	229,074,525
4.	*Liar Liar* (Universal)	181,395,380
5.	*Air Force One* (Sony/Columbia)	171,880,017
6.	*Star Wars: Special Edition* (Fox)	138,247,327
7.	*My Best Friend's Wedding* (Sony/TriStar)	126,805,112
8.	*Face/Off* (Paramount)	112,273,211
9.	*Tomorrow Never Dies* (MGM/UA)	111,815,560
10.	*Batman & Robin* (Warner Bros.)	107,285,004
11.	*George of the Jungle* (Buena Vista)	105,263,257
12.	*Con Air* (Buena Vista/Touchstone)	100,927,613
13.	*Contact* (Warner Bros.)	100,769,177
14.	*Hercules* (Buena Vista/Disney)	99,105,066
15.	*Scream 2* (Miramax)	93,597,728
16.	*Flubber* (Buena Vista)	87,190,216
17.	*Conspiracy Theory* (Warner Bros.)	75,912,202
18.	*I Know What You Did Last Summer* (Sony/Columbia)	70,287,258
19.	*The Empire Strikes Back: Special Edition* (Fox)	67,594,302
20.	*Dante's Peak* (Universal)	67,090,725
21.	*As Good as It Gets* (Sony/TriStar)	66,831,247
22.	*Anaconda* (Sony/Columbia)	65,885,767
23.	*The Fifth Element* (Sony/Columbia)	63,820,180
24.	*In & Out* (Paramount)	63,774,581
25.	*The Saint* (Paramount)	61,355,436

1. As of June 6, 1998. 2. As of Jan. 19, 1998. Including reissues. *Source:* Exhibitor Relations Co. Inc.

Miss America Winners

1921 Margaret Gorman, Washington, D.C.
1922–23 Mary Campbell, Columbus, Ohio
1924 Ruth Malcolmson, Philadelphia, Pa.
1925 Fay Lamphier, Oakland, Calif.
1926 Norma Smallwood, Tulsa, Okla.
1927 Lois Delaner, Joliet, Ill.
1933 Marion Bergeron, West Haven, Conn.
1935 Henrietta Leaver, Pittsburgh, Pa.
1936 Rose Coyle, Philadelphia, Pa.
1937 Bette Cooper, Bertrand Island, N.J.
1938 Marilyn Meseke, Marion, Ohio
1939 Patricia Donnelly, Detroit, Mich.
1940 Frances Marie Burke, Philadelphia, Pa.
1941 Rosemary LaPlanche, Los Angeles, Calif.
1942 JoCaroll Dennison, Tyler, Texas
1943 Jean Bartel, Los Angeles, Calif.
1944 Venus Ramey, Washington, D.C.
1945 Bess Myerson, New York, N.Y.
1946 Marilyn Buferd, Los Angeles, Calif.
1947 Barbara Walker, Memphis, Tenn.
1948 BeBe Shopp, Hopkins, Minn.
1949 Jacque Mercer, Litchfield, Ariz.
1951 Yolande Betbeze, Mobile, Ala.
1952 Coleen Kay Hutchins, Salt Lake City, Utah
1953 Neva Jane Langley, Macon, Ga.
1954 Evelyn Margaret Ay, Ephrata, Pa.
1955 Lee Meriwether, San Francisco, Calif.
1956 Sharon Ritchie, Denver, Colo.
1957 Marian McKnight, Manning, S.C.
1958 Marilyn Van Derbur, Denver, Colo.
1959 Mary Ann Mobley, Brandon, Miss.
1960 Lynda Lee Mead, Natchez, Miss.
1961 Nancy Fleming, Montague, Mich.
1962 Maria Fletcher, Asheville, N.C.
1963 Jacquelyn Mayer, Sandusky, Ohio
1964 Donna Axum, El Dorado, Ark.
1965 Vonda Kay Van Dyke, Phoenix, Ariz.
1966 Deborah Irene Bryant, Overland Park, Kan.
1967 Jane Anne Jayroe, Laverne, Okla.
1968 Debra Dene Barnes, Moran, Kan.
1969 Judith Anne Ford, Belvidere, Ill.
1970 Pamela Anne Eldred, Birmingham, Mich.
1971 Phyllis Ann George, Denton, Texas
1972 Laurie Lea Schaefer, Columbus, Ohio
1973 Terry Anne Meeuwsen, DePere, Wis.
1974 Rebecca Ann King, Denver, Colo.
1975 Shirley Cothran, Fort Worth, Texas
1976 Tawney Elaine Godin, Yonkers, N.Y.
1977 Dorothy Kathleen Benham, Edina, Minn.
1978 Susan Perkins, Columbus, Ohio
1979 Kylene Baker, Galax, Va.
1980 Cheryl Prewitt, Ackerman, Miss.
1981 Susan Powell, Elk City, Okla.
1982 Elizabeth Ward, Russellville, Ark.
1983 Debra Maffett, Anaheim, Calif.
1984 Vanessa Williams, Milwood, N.Y.[1]
1984 Suzette Charles, Mays Landing, N.J.
1985 Sharlene Wells, Salt Lake City, Utah
1986 Susan Akin, Meridian, Miss.
1987 Kellye Cash, Memphis, Tenn.
1988 Kaye Lani Rae Rafko, Monroe, Mich.
1989 Gretchen Elizabeth Carlson, Anoka, Minn.
1990 Debbye Turner, Mexico, Mo.
1991 Marjorie Judith Vincent, Oak Park, Ill.
1992 Carolyn Suzanne Sapp, Honolulu, Hawaii
1993 Leanza Cornett, Jacksonville, Fla.
1994 Kimberly Clarice Aiken, Columbia, S.C.
1995 Heather Whitestone, Birmingham, Ala.
1996 Shawntel Smith, Muldrow, Okla.
1997 Tara Dawn Holland, Overland Park, Kan.
1998 Katherine Shindle, Evanston, Ill.

1. Resigned July 23, 1984.

Top 100 Daily Newspapers in the United States

By circulation, as of September 30, 1997

Newspapers	Circulation
Wall Street Journal (New York, N.Y.)	1,774,880
USA Today (Arlington, Va.)	1,629,665
Times (New York, N.Y.)	1,074,741
Times (Los Angeles,)	1,050,176
Post (Washington, D.C.)	775,894
Daily News (New York, N.Y.)	721,256
Tribune (Chicago)	653,554
Newsday (Long Island, N.Y.)	568,914
Chronicle (Houston)	549,101
Sun-Times (Chicago)	484,379
Chronicle (San Francisco)	484,218
Morning News (Dallas)	481,032
Globe (Boston)	476,966
Arizona Republic (Phoenix)	437,118
Post (New York, N.Y.)	436,226
Inquirer (Philadelphia)	428,233
Star-Ledger (Newark, N.J.)	406,010
Star-Tribune (Minneapolis)	387,412
Free Press (Detroit)	384,624
Plain Dealer (Cleveland)	383,586
Union-Tribune (San Diego)	375,598
Herald (Miami)	356,803
Register (Orange County, Calif.)	356,520
Oregonian (Portland)	342,454
Times (St. Petersburg, Fla.)	342,189
Post (Denver)	337,372
Post-Dispatch (St. Louis)	313,594
Sun (Baltimore)	312,826
Rocky Mountain News (Denver)	302,953
Constitution (Atlanta)	296,669
Mercury News (San Jose, Calif.)	290,811
Journal Sentinel (Milwaukee)	288,173
Bee (Sacramento, Calif.)	281,471
Herald (Boston)	277,106
Star (Kansas City, Mo.)	276,349
News (Buffalo, N.Y.)	262,085
Times-Picayune (New Orleans)	260,552
Sentinel (Orlando, Fla.)	258,037
Sun-Sentinel (Fort Lauderdale, Fla.)	257,118
News (Detroit)	246,638
Dispatch (Columbus, Ohio)	246,095
Post-Gazette (Pittsburgh, Pa.)	243,024
Tribune (Tampa, Fla.)	240,990
Observer (Charlotte, N.C.)	239,016
Investor's Business Daily (Los Angeles)	234,596
Star-Telegram (Fort Worth, Tex.)	229,701
Courier-Journal (Louisville, Ky.)	228,185
Times (Seattle)	227,162
World-Herald (Omaha, Neb.)	225,761
Star (Indianapolis)	224,372

Newspapers	Circulation
Express-News (San Antonio, Tex.)	216,232
Courant (Hartford, Conn.)	210,800
Times-Dispatch (Richmond, Va.)	209,690
Daily Oklahoman (Oklahoma City)	204,376
Daily News (Los Angeles)	201,669
Virginian-Pilot (Norfolk, Va.)	200,696
Pioneer Press (St. Paul, Minn.)	200,275
Post-Intelligencer (Seattle)	197,921
Enquirer (Cincinnati)	194,328
American-Statesman (Austin, Tex.)	178,643
Democrat and Chronicle (Rochester, N.Y.)	176,762
Times-Union (Jacksonville, Fla.)	176,346
Daily News (Philadelphia)	175,290
Commercial Appeal (Memphis)	174,938
Palm Beach Post (West Palm Beach, Fla.)	174,171
Democrat-Gazette (Little Rock, Ark.)	170,766
Journal (Providence, R.I.)	170,292
Register (Des Moines, Iowa)	164,912
Press-Enterprise (Riverside, Calif.)	162,551
World (Tulsa, Okla.)	162,186
Daily News (Dayton, Ohio)	159,072
Review-Journal (Las Vegas)	158,441
Asbury Park Press (Neptune, N.J.)	156,821
News & Observer (Raleigh, N.C.)	153,408
Bee (Fresno, Calif.)	152,718
News (Birmingham, Ala.)	150,346
Tennessean (Nashville)	146,914
Record (Bergen County, N.J.)	146,089
Blade (Toledo, Ohio)	145,800
Beacon Journal (Akron, Ohio)	145,055
Press (Grand Rapids, Mich.)	138,907
Daily Herald (Arlington Heights, Ill.)	132,090
Tribune (Salt Lake City)	129,836
Morning Call (Allentown, Pa.)	128,581
News Tribune (Tacoma, Wash.)	128,498
News Journal (Wilmingon, Del.)	123,869
State (Columbia, S.C.)	121,699
Examiner (San Francisco)	120,856
Spokesman-Review (Spokane, Wash.)	116,391
News-Sentinel (Knoxville, Tenn.)	115,264
Journal (Albuquerque)	113,694
Herald-Leader (Lexington, Ky.)	112,139
Journal (Atlanta)	108,876
Telegram & Gazette (Worcester, Mass.)	108,769
Post & Courier (Charleston, S.C.)	108,637
Herald-Tribune (Sarasota, Fla.)	108,271
La Opinion (Los Angeles)	106,790
Clarion-Ledger (Jackson, Miss.)	104,375
Press-Telegram (Long Beach, Calif.)	104,078
Advertiser (Honolulu)	102,236

Source: Newspaper Association of America.

Top 100 Daily Newspapers in the World According to 1997 Circulation

Newspaper	Circulation
Yomiuri Shimbun (Japan)	14,562,436
Asahi Shimbun (Japan)	12,722,651
Sichuan Ribao (China)	8,000,000
Mainichi Shimbun (Japan)	5,833,095
Bild (Germany)	5,674,400
O Diario (Portugal)	5,666,915
Nihon Keizai Shimbun (Japan)	4,640,109
Chunichi Shimbun (Japan)	4,323,142
Sun (England)	3,863,822
Renmin Ribao (China)	3,000,000
Sankei Shimbun (Japan)	2,893,451
Gongren Ribao (China)	2,500,000
Daily Mirror (England)	2,375,579
Chosun Ilbo (South Korea)	2,225,000
Daily Mail (England)	2,220,225
Dong-A Ilbo (South Korea)	2,150,000
Hokkaido Shimbun (Japan)	1,982,919
Eleftherotypia (Greece)	1,858,316
Wall Street Journal (United States)	1,774,880
Xin Min Wan Bao (China)	1,750,000
Yangcheng Wnbao (China)	1,730,000
Kerala Kaumudi (India)	1,720,000
Wen Hui Bao Daily (China)	1,700,000
USA Today (United States)	1,629,665
Joong-Ang Daily News (South Korea)	1,500,000
Economic Daily (China)	1,500,000
Rodong Sinmun (North Korea)	1,500,000
NRZ (Germany)	1,496,300
Kyung-Hyang Daily News (South Korea)	1,478,537
Sports Nippon (Japan)	1,473,135
Shizuoka Shimbun (Japan)	1,426,713
Sankei Sports (Japan)	1,367,734
West Deutche Allgemeine (Germany)	1,313,400
United Daily News (Taiwan)	1,300,000
China Times (Taiwan)	1,270,000
O Estado de Sao Paulo (Brazil)	1,230,160
Hochi Shimbun (Japan)	1,223,847
Daily Express (England)	1,216,188
Jang Daily (Pakistan)	1,200,000
Jang Lahore (Pakistan)	1,200,000
Akhbar El Yom/Al Akhbar (Egypt)	1,159,339
Hankook Ilbo (South Korea)	1,156,000
Tokyo Shimbun (Japan)	1,119,352
Daily Telegraph (England)	1,086,461
Neue Kronenzeitung (Austria)	1,079,726
New York Times (United States)	1,074,741
Los Angeles Times (United States)	1,050,176
Nishi Nippon Shimbun (Japan)	1,035,472
Nikkan Sports (Japan)	1,020,191
Jiefang Ribao (China)	1,000,000
Nanfang Ribao (China)	1,000,000
Nongmin Ribao (China)	1,000,000
Zhongguo Qingnian (China)	1,000,000
Al Akhbar (Egypt)	980,000
Guangming Ribao (China)	950,000
Corriere della Sera (Italy)	932,067
Al Ahram (Egypt)	900,000
Al Goumhouriya (Egypt)	900,000
Seoul Shinmun (South Korea)	900,000
Xin Hua Ribao (China)	900,000
Times of India (India)	876,858
Kyoto Shimbun (Japan)	838,593
Chugoku Shimbun (Japan)	829,627
Jang (Pakistan)	820,000
Beijing Wnbao (China)	800,000
Hubei Ribao (China)	800,000
Jiefangjun Ribao (China)	800,000
Trybuna Slaska (Poland)	800,000
La Gazzetta dello Sport (Italy)	798,243
La Repubblica (Italy)	796,262
Ouest-France (France)	790,133
Kobe Shimbun (Japan)	785,052
Washington Post (United States)	775,894
Holos Ukrainy (Ukraine)	768,000

Newspaper	Circulation	Newspaper	Circulation
The Times (England)	766,341	*Daily Record* (Scotland)	696,332
De Telegraf (Netherlands)	751,400	*Diario Insular* (Portugal)	684,143
Gazeta Wyborcza (Poland)	750,000	*Granma Internacional* (Cuba)	675,000
Zero Hora (Brazil)	727,188	*China Daily News* (Taiwan)	670,000
Diario dos Campos (Brazil)	725,000	*Chicago Tribune* (United States)	653,554
Sabah (Turkey)	722,950	*Guangxi Ribao* (China)	650,000
New York Daily News (United States)	721,256	*Kahoku Shimpo* (Japan)	644,158
Jornal da Tarde (Brazil)	709,793	*The Daily Star* (England)	639,388
Beijing Ribao (China)	700,000	*Malayala Manorama* (India)	630,068
Chongqing Ribao (China)	700,000	*La Nacion* (Argentina)	630,000
Clarin (Argentina)	700,000	*Hurriyet* (Turkey)	615,579
Thai Rath (Thailand)	700,000	*Herald Sun* (Australia)	600,000
Zhejiang Ribao (China)	700,000	*Hurriyet* (Pakistan)	600,000

Source: Newspaper Association of America.

Top 100 Consumer Magazines 1997

Rank	Magazine	Circulation	Rank	Magazine	Circulation
1.	*Modern Maturity*	20,454,478	51.	*Outdoor Life*	1,367,321
2.	*NRTA/AARP Bulletin*	20,432,489	52.	*Boys' Life*	1,360,791
3.	*Reader's Digest*	15,086,390	53.	*Golf Magazine*	1,317,945
4.	*TV Guide*	13,171,025	54.	*Entertainment Weekly*	1,300,611
5.	*National Geographic Magazine*	9,013,113	55.	*Consumers Digest*	1,289,365
6.	*Better Homes & Gardens*	7,614,737	56.	*Rolling Stone*	1,256,915
7.	*Family Circle*	5,054,263	57.	*Soap Opera Digest*	1,241,259
8.	*Good Housekeeping*	4,643,428	58.	*Discover*	1,203,879
9.	*Ladies' Home Journal*	4,513,629	59.	*New Woman*	1,190,598
10.	*McCall's*	4,255,784	60.	*PC Magazine*	1,153,952
11.	*Woman's Day*	4,163,248	61.	*PC World*	1,143,710
12.	*Time*	4,150,223	62.	*Self*	1,141,405
13.	*People Weekly*	3,507,936	63.	*Mademoiselle*	1,136,570
14.	*Car & Travel Magazine*	3,349,118	64.	*US*	1,133,236
15.	*Sports Illustrated*	3,280,233	65.	*The Family Handyman*	1,123,464
16.	*Newsweek*	3,276,457	66.	*Endless Vacation*	1,121,173
17.	*Prevention*	3,251,555	67.	*Car and Driver*	1,117,783
18.	*Playboy*	3,172,451	68.	*Parenting Magazine*	1,115,467
19.	*Redbook*	2,830,133	69.	*Bon Appetit*	1,104,018
20.	*Home & Away*	2,764,696	70.	*Kiplinger's Personal Finance*	1,100,211
21.	*The American Legion Magazine*	2,753,678	71.	*Vogue*	1,100,084
22.	*National Enquirer*	2,716,626	72.	*Scholastic Parent & Child*	1,100,021
23.	*Avenues*	2,557,269	73.	*Vanity Fair*	1,095,607
24.	*Cosmopolitan*	2,525,317	74.	*Scouting*	1,084,344
25.	*Southern Living*	2,493,772	75.	*The American Hunter*	1,059,010
26.	*Seventeen*	2,472,194	76.	*Motor Trend*	1,047,692
27.	*Martha Stewart Living*	2,315,638	77.	*AAA Going Places*	1,044,628
28.	*U.S. News & World Report*	2,220,236	78.	*Globe*	1,041,747
29.	*Star*	2,219,164	79.	*Weight Watchers Magazine*	1,034,082
30.	*NEA Today*	2,182,775	80.	*Country Home*	1,032,905
31.	*YM*	2,145,817	81.	*Health*	1,029,498
32.	*Smithsonian*	2,070,968	82.	*Sesame Street Magazine*	1,009,041
33.	*Glamour*	2,066,500	83.	*Home*	1,008,304
34.	*Money*	1,941,841	84.	*PC/Computing*	1,006,285
35.	*Ebony*	1,835,496	85.	*American Homestyle & Gardening*	1,004,721
36.	*V.F.W. Magazine*	1,812,631	86.	*Essence*	1,000,238
37.	*Field & Stream*	1,753,630	87.	*Travel & Leisure*	997,435
38.	*Parents*	1,739,527	88.	*Jet*	973,482
39.	*Teen*	1,661,048	89.	*FamilyFun*	969,487
40.	*Country Living*	1,615,567	90.	*In Style*	965,213
41.	*Life*	1,576,889	91.	*Shape*	931,950
42.	*Popular Science*	1,560,130	92.	*Victoria*	924,184
43.	*Golf Digest*	1,539,759	93.	*Elle*	916,817
44.	*Men's Health*	1,506,145	94.	*Business Week*	915,149
45.	*Woman's World*	1,486,668	95.	*True Story Plus*	911,219
46.	*American Rifleman*	1,480,074	96.	*Today's Homeowner*	909,637
47.	*Sunset*	1,448,229	97.	*American Health — For Women*	907,529
48.	*First for Women*	1,433,114	98.	*Country America*	904,017
49.	*Popular Mechanics*	1,425,043	99.	*Penthouse*	883,581
50.	*Cooking Light*	1,409,417	100.	*House Beautiful*	875,055

Average paid circulation for the six months ending Dec. 31, 1997. *Source:* Publishers Information Bureau.

States and Territories

Data for state populations are the latest available from the U.S. Census Bureau. NOTE: Persons of Hispanic origin can be of any race. "American Indian" includes American Indians, Eskimos, and Aleuts. "Asian" includes Asians and Pacific Islanders. Largest cities include incorporated places only, as defined by the U.S. Census Bureau. They do not include adjacent or suburban areas. For secession and readmission dates of the former Confederate states, *see* the Confederate States of America.

For lists of governors, senators, and representatives, *see* the Governors of the Fifty States, the Senate, and the House of Representatives.

Alabama

Capital: Montgomery
Governor: Fob James, Jr., R (to Jan. 1999)
Lieut. Governor: Don Siegelman, D (to Jan. 1999)
Senators: Jeff Sessions, R (to Jan. 2003); Richard C. Shelby, R (to Jan. 1999)
Secy. of State: Jim Bennett, R (to Jan. 1999)
Treasurer: Lucy Baxley, D (to Jan. 1999)
Atty. General: William Pryor, R (to Jan. 1999)
Auditor: Pat Duncan, D (to Jan. 1999)
Organized as territory: March 3, 1817
Entered Union (rank): Dec. 14, 1819 (22)
Present constitution adopted: 1901
Motto: *Audemus jura nostra defendere* (We dare defend our rights)
State symbols: flower, Camellia (1959); **bird,** Yellowhammer (1927); **song,** "Alabama" (1931); **tree,** Southern pine (longleaf) (1949); **salt water fish,** Tarpon (1955); **fresh water fish,** Largemouth bass (1975); **horse,** Racking horse (1975); **mineral,** Hematite (1967); **rock,** Marble (1969); **game bird,** Wild turkey (1980); **dance,** Square dance (1981); **nut,** Pecan (1982); **fossil,** species *Basilosaurus Cetoides* (1984); **butterfly,** Eastern Tiger Swallowtail (1989); **insect,** Monarch butterfly (1989); **reptile,** Alabama red-bellied turtle (1990); **gemstone,** Star Blue Quartz (1990); **shell,** Scaphella junonia johnstoneae (1990)
Nickname: Yellowhammer State
Origin of name: May come from Choctaw meaning "thicket-clearers" or "vegetation-gatherers"
10 largest cities (1996 est.): Birmingham, 258,543; Mobile, 202,581; Montgomery, 196,363; Huntsville, 170,424; Tuscaloosa, 82,379; Dothan, 55,944; Hoover, 55,464; Decatur, 53,797; Gadsden, 41,155; Florence, 38,999
Land area (rank): 50,750 sq mi. (131,443 sq km) (28)
Geographic center: In Chilton Co., 12 mi. SW of Clanton
Number of counties: 67
Largest county (area): Baldwin (1,590 sq mi.)
Largest county (1995 pop. est.): Jefferson, 657,827
State forests: 21 (48,000 ac.)
State parks: 22 (45,614 ac.)
1997 resident population est.: 4,319,154
1990 census population (rank): 4,040,587 (22). **Male:** 1,936,162; **Female:** 2,104,425. **White:** 2,975,797 (73.6%); **Black:** 1,020,705 (25.3%); **American Indian:** 16,506 (0.4%); **Asian:** 21,797 (0.5%); **Other race:** 5,782 (0.1%); **Hispanic:** 24,629 (0.6%). **1990 percent population under 18:** 26.2; **65 and over:** 12.9; **median age:** 33.0.

Spanish explorers are believed to have arrived at Mobile Bay in 1519, and the territory was visited in 1540 by the explorer Hernando de Soto. The first permanent European settlement in Alabama was founded by the French at Fort Louis de la Mobile in 1702. The British gained control of the area in 1763 by the Treaty of Paris, but had to cede almost all the Alabama region to the U.S. after the American Revolution. The Confederacy was founded at Montgomery in February 1861 and, for a time, the city was the Confederate capital.

During the last part of the 19th century, the economy of the state slowly improved. At Tuskegee Institute, founded in 1881 by Booker T. Washington, Dr. George Washington Carver carried out his famous agricultural research.

In the 1950s and '60s, Alabama was the site of such landmark civil-rights actions as the bus boycott in Montgomery (1955–56) and the "Freedom March" from Selma to Montgomery (1965).

Today paper, chemicals, rubber and plastics, apparel and textiles, and primary metals constitute the leading industries of Alabama. Continuing as a major manufacturer of coal, iron, and steel, Birmingham is also noted for its world-renowned medical center, especially for heart surgery. The state ranks high in the production of poultry, soybeans, milk, vegetables, livestock, wheat, cattle, cotton, peanuts, fruits, hogs, and corn.

Points of interest include the Helen Keller birthplace "Ivy Green" at Tuscumbia, the Space and Rocket Center at Huntsville, the White House of the Confederacy, the restored state Capitol, the Civil Rights Memorial, the Shakespeare Festival Theater Complex in Montgomery, the Civil Rights Institute in Birmingham, the Russell Cave near Bridgeport, the Bellingrath Gardens at Theodore, the USS *Alabama* at Mobile, Mound State Monument near Tuscaloosa, and the Gulf Coast area.

Famous natives and residents: Hank Aaron, baseball player; Ralph Abernathy, civil rights activist; Tallulah Bankhead, actress; Hugo L. Black, jurist; George Washington Carver, educator, agricultural chemist; Nat "King" Cole, entertainer; Marva Collins, educator; Kenneth Gibson, first black mayor of major eastern city (Newark); Lionel Hampton, jazz musician; W. C. Handy, composer; Kate Jackson, actress; Helen Keller, author and educator; Coretta Scott King, civil rights leader; Harper Lee, writer; Joe Louis, boxer; Willie Mays, baseball player; Jim Nabors, actor; Jesse Owens, athlete; Rosa Parks, civil rights activist; Wayne Rogers, actor; Tascaluza, Choctaw chief; George Wallace, former governor; William Weatherford (Red Eagle), Creek leader; Heather Whitestone, Miss America (1995).

Alaska

Capital: Juneau
Governor: Tony Knowles, D (to Dec. 1998)
Lieut. Governor: Fran Ulmer, D (to Dec. 1998)
Senators: Frank H. Murkowski, R (to Jan. 1999); Ted Stevens, R (to Jan. 2003)
Commissioner of Administration: Mark Boyer
Atty. General: Bruce M. Bothelho, D
Organized as territory: 1912
Entered Union (rank): Jan. 3, 1959 (49)
Constitution ratified: April 24, 1956
Motto: North to the Future
State symbols: flower, Forget-me-not (1949); **tree,** Sitka spruce (1962); **bird,** Willow ptarmigan (1955); **fish,** King salmon (1962); **song,** "Alaska's Flag" (1955); **gem,** Jade (1968); **marine mammal,** Bowhead Whale (1983); **fossil,** Woolly Mammoth (1986); **mineral,** Gold (1968); **sport,** Dog Mushing (1972)
Nickname: The state is commonly called "The Last Frontier" or "Land of the Midnight Sun"
Origin of name: Corruption of Aleut word meaning "great land" or "that which the sea breaks against"
10 largest cities (1996 est.): Anchorage, 250,505; Fairbanks, 32,960; Juneau, 29,756; Sitka, 8,510; Ketchikan, 8,274; Kenai, 7,706; Kodiak, 7,677; Bethel, 5,952; Wasilla, 5,350; Homer, 4608
Land area (rank): 570,374 sq mi. (1,477,267 sq km) (1)
Geographic center: 60 mi. NW of Mt. McKinley
Number of boroughs: 16
Largest borough (1995 pop. est.): Anchorage, 251,335
State parks: more than 100 (3.5 million acres)
1997 resident population est.: 609,311
1990 resident census population (rank): 550,043 (49). **Male:** 289,867; **Female:** 260,176. **White:** 415,492 (75.5%); **Black:** 22,451 (4.1%); **American Indian:** 85,698 (15.6%); **Asian:** 19,728 (3.6%); **Other race:** 6,675 (1.2%); **Hispanic:** 17,803 (3.2%). **1990 percent population under 18:** 31.3; **65 and over:** 4.1; **median age:** 29.4

Vitus Bering, a Dane working for the Russians, and Alexei Chirikov discovered the Alaskan mainland and the Aleutian Islands in 1741. The tremendous land mass of Alaska—equal to one-fifth of the continental U.S.—was unexplored in 1867 when Secretary of State William Seward arranged for its purchase from the Russians for $7,200,000. The transfer of the territory took place on Oct. 18, 1867. Despite a price of about two cents an acre, the purchase was widely ridiculed as "Seward's Folly." The first official census (1880) reported a total of 33,426 Alaskans, all but 430 being of aboriginal stock. The Gold Rush of 1898 resulted in a mass influx of more than 30,000 people. Since then, Alaska has contributed billions of dollars' worth of products to the U.S. economy.

In 1968, a large oil and gas reservoir near Prudhoe Bay on the Arctic Coast was found. The Prudhoe Bay reservoir, with an estimated recoverable 10 billion barrels of oil and 27 trillion cubic feet of gas, is twice as large as any other oil field in North America. The Trans-Alaska pipeline was completed in 1977 at a cost of $7.7 billion. On June 20, oil started flowing through the 800-mile-long pipeline from Prudhoe Bay to the port of Valdez.

Other industries important to Alaska's economy are fisheries, wood and wood products, furs, and tourism.

Denali National Park and Mendenhall Glacier in North Tongass National Forest are of interest, as is the large totem pole collection at Sitka National Historical Park. The Katmai National Park includes the "Valley of Ten Thousand Smokes," an area of active volcanoes.

Famous natives and residents: Clarence L. Andrews, author; Aleksandr Baranov, first governor of Russian America; Margaret Elizabeth Bell, author; Benny Benson, designed state flag at age 13; Vitus Bering, explorer; Charles E. Bunnell, educator; Susan Butcher, sled-dog racer; William A. Egan, first state governor; Carl Ben Eielson, pioneer pilot; Henry E. Gruennig, political leader; B. Frank Heintzleman, territorial governor; Walter J. Hickel, former governor; Sheldon Jackson, educator and missionary; Joe Juneau, prospector; Austin Lathrop, industrialist; Sydney Lawrence, painter; Ray Mala, actor; Virgil F. Partch, cartoonist; Joe Redington, Sr., sled-dog musher and promoter; Peter Trinble Rowe, first Episcopal bishop; Ivan Popov-Veniaminov (St. Innocent), Russian Orthodox missionary; Ferdinand Wrangel, educator; Samuel Hall Young, founder of first American church.

Arizona

Capital: Phoenix
Governor: Jane Dee Hull, R (to Jan. 1999)
Senators: Jon Kyl, R (to Jan. 2001); John McCain (to Jan. 1999)
Secy. of State: Betsey Bayless, R (to Jan. 1999)
Atty. General: Grant Woods, R (to Jan. 1999[1])
Treasurer: Tony West, R (to Jan. 1999)
Organized as territory: Feb. 24, 1863
Entered Union (rank): Feb. 14, 1912 (48)
Present constitution adopted: 1911
Motto: *Ditat Deus* (God enriches)
State symbols: flower: Flower of saguaro cactus (1931); **bird:** Cactus wren (1931); **colors:** Blue and old gold (1915); **song:** "Arizona March Song" (1919); **tree:** Palo Verde (1954); **neckwear:** Bola tie (1971); **fossil:** Petrified wood (1988); **gemstone:** Turquoise (1974); **animals: mammal,** Ringtail (1986); **reptile,** Arizona Ridgenose rattlesnake (1986); **fish,** Arizona trout (1986); **amphibian,** Arizona tree frog (1986)
Nickname: Grand Canyon State
Origin of name: From the Indian "Arizonac," meaning "little spring" or "young spring"
10 largest cities (1996 est.): Phoenix, 1,159,014; Tucson, 449,002; Mesa, 344,764; Glendale, 182,219; Scottsdale, 179,012; Tempe, 162,701; Chandler, 142,918; Peoria, 76,045; Gilbert, 64,326; Yuma, 60,519
Land area (rank): 114,000 sq mi. (296,400 sq km) (6)
Geographic center: In Yavapai Co., 55 mi. ESE of Prescott
Number of counties: 15
Largest county (1996 est.): Maricopa, 2,634,625
State parks: 24
1997 resident population est.: 4,554,966
1990 resident census population (rank): 3,665,228 (24). **Male:** 1,810,691; **Female:** 1,854,537. **White:** 2,963,186 (80.8%); **Black:** 110,524 (3.0%); **American Indian:** 203,527 (5.6%); **Asian:** 55,206 (1.5%); **Other race:** 332,785 (9.1%); **Hispanic:** 688,338 (18.8%). **1990 percent population under 18:** 26.8; **65 and over:** 13.1; **median age:** 32.2

1. Ran unopposed.

Marcos de Niza, a Spanish Franciscan friar, was the first European to explore Arizona. He entered the area in 1539 in search of the mythical Seven Cities of Gold. Although he was followed a year later by another gold seeker, Francisco Vásquez de Coronado, most of the early settlement was for missionary purposes. In 1775 the Spanish established Fort Tucson. In 1848, after the Mexican War, most of the Arizona territory became part of the U.S., and the southern portion of the territory was added by the Gadsden Purchase in 1853.

In 1973 one of the world's most massive dams, the New Cornelia Tailings, was completed near Ajo.

Arizona history is rich in legends of America's Old West. It was here that the great Indian chiefs Geronimo and Cochise led their people against the frontiersmen. Tombstone, Ariz., was the site of the West's most famous shoot-out—the gunfight at the O.K. Corral. Today, Arizona has one of the largest U.S. Indian populations; more than 14 tribes are represented on 20 reservations.

Manufacturing has become Arizona's most important industry. Principal products include electrical, communications, and aeronautical items. The state produces over half the country's copper. Agriculture is also important to the state's economy.

State attractions include the Grand Canyon, the Petrified Forest, and the Painted Desert. Hoover Dam, Lake Mead, Fort Apache, and the reconstructed London Bridge at Lake Havasu City are of particular interest.

Famous natives and residents: Apache Kid, Indian outlaw; Erma Bombeck, humorist and writer; Lynda Carter, actress; Cesar Chavez, labor leader; Cochise, Apache chief; Alice Cooper, singer and songwriter; Wyatt Earp, marshall; Max Ernst, painter; Geronimo (Goyathlay), Apache chief; Barry Goldwater, politician; Zane Grey, novelist; Carl Trumbull Hayden, politician; George W. P. Hunt, first state governor; Bill Keane, cartoonist; Eusebio Kino, missionary; Percival Lowell, astronomer; Frank Luke, Jr., WWI fighter ace; Charles Mingus, jazz musician and composer; Carlos Montezuma, doctor and Indian spokesman; Sandra Day O'Connor, jurist; William O'Neill, frontier sheriff; Alexander M. Patch, general; William H. Pickering, astronomer; Linda Ronstadt, singer; Paolo Soleri, architect; Clyde W. Tombaugh, astronomer; Tanya Tucker, singer; Stewart Udall, former Secretary of the Interior; Pauline Weaver, frontier person; Frank Lloyd Wright, architect.

Arkansas

Capital: Little Rock
Governor: Mike Huckabee, R (to Jan. 1999)
Lieut. Governor: Winthrop Rockefeller, R (to 1999)
Senators: Dale Bumpers, D (to Jan. 1999); Tim Hutchinson, R (to Jan. 2003)
Secy. of State: Sharon Priest, D (to Jan. 1999)
Atty. General: Winston Bryant, D (to Jan. 1999)
Auditor of State: Gus Wingfield, D (to Jan. 2003)
Treasurer of State: Jimmie Lou Fisher, D (to Jan. 1999)
Land Commissioner: Charles Daniels, D (to Jan. 1999)
Organized as territory: March 2, 1819
Entered Union (rank): June 15, 1836 (25)
Present constitution adopted: 1874
Motto: *Regnat populus* (The people rule)
State symbols: flower, Apple Blossom (1901); **tree,** Pine (1939); **bird,** Mockingbird (1929); **insect,** Honeybee (1973); **song,** "Arkansas" (1963)
Nickname: The Natural State
Origin of name: From the Quapaw Indians
10 largest cities (1996 est.): Little Rock, 175,752; Fort Smith, 75,776; North Little Rock, 60,468; Pine Bluff, 54,165; Jonesboro, 52,656; Fayetteville, 52,360; Springdale, 38,572; Hot Springs, 36,255; Conway, 35,827; Rogers, 35,355
Land area (rank): 52,075 sq mi. (134,875 sq km) (27)
Geographic center: In Pulaski Co., 12 mi. NW of Little Rock
Number of counties: 75
Largest county (1995 pop. est.): Pulaski, 352,240
State parks: 44
1997 resident population est.: 2,522,819
1990 resident population (rank): 2,350,725 (33). **Male:** 1,133,076; **Female:** 1,217,649. **White:** 1,944,744 (82.7%); **Black:** 373,912 (15.9%); **American Indian:** 12,773 (0.5%); **Asian:** 12,530 (0.5%); **Other race:** 6,766 (0.3%); **Hispanic:** 19,876 (0.8%). **1990 percent population under 18:** 26.4; **65 and over:** 14.9; **median age:** 33.8.

Hernando de Soto, in 1541, was among the early European explorers to visit the territory. It was a Frenchman, Henri de Tonti, who in 1686 founded the first permanent white settlement—the Arkansas Post. In 1803 the area was acquired by the U.S. as part of the Louisiana Purchase.

Food products are the state's largest employing sector, with lumber and wood products a close second. Arkansas is also a leader in the production of cotton, rice, and soybeans. It also has the country's only active diamond mine; located near Murfreesboro, it is operated as a tourist attraction.

Hot Springs National Park, and Buffalo National River in the Ozarks are major state attractions.

Blanchard Springs Caverns, the Arkansas Territorial Restoration at Little Rock, and the Arkansas Folk Center in Mountain View are of interest.

Famous natives and residents: G. M. "Broncho Billy" Anderson, actor; Maya Angelou, author and poet; Katharine Susan Anthony, author; Helen Gurley Brown, editor; Glen Campbell, singer; Hattie Caraway, first elected woman senator; Johnny Cash, singer; Eldridge Cleaver, black activist; William Jefferson Clinton, 42nd President; Dizzy Dean, baseball player; Orval Faubus, former governor; John Gould Fletcher, writer; James W. Fulbright, former senator; John H. Johnson, publisher; Alan Ladd, actor; Douglas MacArthur, 5-star general; John Paul McConnell, U.S. Air Force officer; Ben Murphy, actor; Frank Pace, Jr., public official; Ben Piazza, actor; Albert Pike, pioneer teacher and lawyer; Dick Powell, actor; Opie P. Read, writer; Jenny D. Rice-Meyrowitz, painter; Brehon Burke Somervell, World Wars I and II U.S. Army officer; Mary Steenburgen, actress; Edward Durrell Stone, architect; William C. Warfield, concert singer and actor.

California

Capital: Sacramento
Governor: Pete Wilson, R (to Jan. 1999)
Lieut. Governor: Gray Davis, D (to Jan. 1999)
Senators: Barbara Boxer, D (to Jan. 1999); Dianne Feinstein, D (to Jan. 2001)
Secy. of State: Bill Jones, R (to Jan. 1999)
Controller: Cathleen Connell, D (to Jan. 1999)
Atty. General: Dan Lungren, R (to Jan. 1999)
Treasurer: Matt Fong, R (to Jan. 1999)
Supt. of Public Instruction: David Meaney
Entered Union (rank): Sept. 9, 1850 (31)
Present constitution adopted: 1879
Motto: *Eureka* (I have found it)
State symbols: flower, Golden poppy (1903); **tree,** California redwoods (*Sequoia sempervirens & Sequoia gigantea)* (1937 % 1953); **bird,** California valley quail (1931); **animal,** California grizzly bear (1953); **fish,** California golden trout (1947); **colors,** Blue and gold (1951); **song,** "I Love You, California" (1951)
Nickname: Golden State
Origin of name: From a book, *Las Sergas de Esplandián,* by Garcia Ordóñez de Montalvo, c. 1500
10 largest cities (1996 est.): Los Angeles, 3,553,638; San Diego, 1,171,121; San Jose, 838,744; San Francisco, 735,315; Long Beach, 421,904; Fresno, 396,011; Sacramento, 376,243; Oakland, 367,230; Santa Ana, 302,419; Anaheim, 288,945
Land area (rank): 155,973 sq mi. (403,970 sq km) (3)
Geographic center: In Madera Co., 35 mi. NE of Madera

Number of counties: 58
Largest county (1995 pop. est.): Los Angeles, 9,138,789
State forests: 8 (70,283 ac.)
State parks and beaches: 180 (723,000 ac.)
1997 resident population est.: 32,268,301
1990 resident population (rank): 29,760,021 (1). **Male:** 14,897,627; **Female:** 14,862,394. **White:** 20,524,327 (69.9%); **Black:** 2,208,801 (7.4%); **American Indian:** 242,164 (0.8%); **Asian:** 2,845,659 (9.6%); **Other race:** 3,939,070 (13.2%); **Hispanic:** 7,687,938 (25.8%). **1990 percent population under 18:** 26.0; **65 and over:** 10.5; **median age:** 31.5.

Although California was sighted by Spanish navigator Juan Rodríguez Cabrillo in 1542, its first Spanish mission (at San Diego) was not established until 1769. California became a U.S. territory in 1847 when Mexico surrendered it to John C. Frémont. On Jan. 24, 1848, James W. Marshall discovered gold at Sutter's Mill, starting the California Gold Rush and bringing settlers to the state in large numbers.

In 1964, the U.S. Census Bureau estimated that California had become the most populous state, surpassing New York. California also leads the country in personal income and consumer expenditures.

Leading industries include manufacturing (transportation equipment, machinery, and electronic equipment), agriculture, biotechnology, and tourism. Principal natural resources include timber, petroleum, cement, and natural gas.

More immigrants settle in California than any other state—more than one-third of the nation's total in 1994. Asians and Pacific Islanders led the influx.

Death Valley, in the southeast, is 282 feet below sea level, the lowest point in the nation. Mt. Whitney (14,491 ft.) is the highest point in the contiguous 48 states. Lassen Peak is one of two active U.S. volcanoes outside of Alaska and Hawaii; its last eruptions were recorded in 1917. The General Sherman Tree in Sequoia National Park is estimated to be 3,500 years old and a stand of bristlecone pine trees in the White Mountains may be over 4,000 years old.

Other points of interest include Yosemite National Park, Disneyland, Hollywood, the Golden Gate Bridge, San Simeon State Park, and Point Reyes National Seashore.

Famous natives and residents: Gertrude Atherton, author; David Belasco, playwright and producer; Shirley Temple Black, actress, ambassador; Dave Brubeck, musician; Luther Burbank, horticulturalist; Julia Child, chef; Joe DiMaggio, baseball player; James H. Doolittle, air force general; Isadora Duncan, dancer; John Frémont, explorer; Robert Frost, poet; Henry George, economist; Richard "Pancho" Gonzales, tennis player; George E. Hale, astronomer; Bret Harte, writer; William Randolph Hearst, publisher; Sidney Howard, playwright; Collis Potter Huntington, financier; Helen Hunt Jackson, writer; Robinson Jeffers, poet; Anthony M. Kennedy, jurist; Jack London, author; James W. Marshall, first discovered gold; Aimee Semple McPherson, evangelist; Marilyn Monroe, actress; John Muir, naturalist; Richard M. Nixon, President; Isamu Noguchi, sculptor; Frank Norris, novelist; Kathleen Norris, novelist; George S. Patton, Jr., general; Robert Redford, actor; Sally K. Ride, astronaut; William Saroyan, author; Junípero Serra, missionary; Upton Sinclair, novelist; Leland Stanford, railroad magnate; Lincoln Steffens, journalist, author; John Steinbeck, author; Adlai Stevenson, statesman; Johann Sutter, pioneer; Michael Tilson Thomas, conductor; Earl Warren, jurist.

Colorado

Capital: Denver
Governor: Roy Romer, D (to Jan. 1999)
Lieut. Governor: Gail Schoettler, D (to Jan. 1999)
Senators: Wayne A. Allard (to Jan. 2003); Ben Nighthorse Campbell (to Jan. 1999)
Secy. of State: Vikki Buckley, R (to Jan 1999)
Treasurer: Bill Owens, R (to Jan. 1999)
Controller: Cliff Hall, R (appointed)
Atty. General: Gale Norton, R (to Jan. 1999)
Organized as territory: Feb. 28, 1861
Entered Union (rank): Aug. 1, 1876 (38)
Present constitution adopted: 1876
Motto: *Nil sine Numine* (Nothing without Providence)
State symbols: flower, Rocky Mountain columbine (1899); **tree,** Colorado blue spruce (1939); **bird,** Lark bunting (1931); **animal,** Rocky Mountain bighorn sheep (1961); **gemstone,** Aquamarine (1971); **colors,** Blue and white (1911); **song,** "Where the Columbines Grow" (1915); **fossil,** Stegosaurus (1991)
Nickname: Centennial State
Origin of name: From the Spanish, "ruddy" or "red"
10 largest cities (1996 est.): Denver, 497,840; Colorado Springs, 345,127; Aurora, 252,341; Lakewood, 134,999; Fort Collins, 104,196; Pueblo, 99,406; Arvada, 96,340; Westminster, 93,115; Boulder, 90,928; Greeley, 68,593
Land area (rank): 103,730 sq mi. (268,660 sq km) (8)
Geographic center: In Park Co., 30 mi. NW of Pikes Peak
Number of counties: 63
Largest county (1995 pop. est.): Denver, 494,462
State forests: 1 (71,000 ac.)
State parks: 44
1997 resident population est.: 3,892,644
1990 resident census population (rank): 3,294,394 (26). **Male:** 1,631,295; **Female:** 1,663,099. **White:** 2,095,474 (88.2%); **Black:** 133,146 (4.0%); **American Indian:** 27,776 (0.8%); **Asian:** 59,862 (1.8%); **Other race:** 168,136 (5.1%); **Hispanic:** 424,302 (12.9%). **1990 percent population under 18:** 26.1; **65 and over:** 10.0; **median age:** 32.5

First visited by Spanish explorers in the 1500s, the territory was claimed for Spain by Juan de Ulibarri in 1706. The U.S. obtained eastern Colorado as part of the Louisiana Purchase in 1803, the central portion in 1845 with the admission of Texas as a state, and the western part in 1848 as a result of the Mexican War.

Colorado has the highest mean elevation of any state, with more than 1,000 Rocky Mountain peaks over 10,000 feet high and 54 towering above 14,000 feet. Pikes Peak, the most famous of these mountains, was discovered by U.S. Army Lieut. Zebulon M. Pike in 1806.

Once primarily a mining and agricultural state, Colorado's economy is now driven by the service-producing industries, which provide jobs for approximately 82.4 percent of the state's non-farm work force. Tourism expenditures in the state total approximately 6 billion dollars annually. Tourist expenditures on the ski industry account for 1.8 billion dollars annually, approximately a third of the total tourist expenditures. The main tourist attractions in the state include Rocky Mountain National Park, Curecanti National Recreation Area, Mesa Verde National Park, the Great Sand Dunes and Dinosaur National Monuments, Colorado National Monument, and the Black Canyon of the Gunnison National Monument.

The two primary facets of Colorado's manufacturing industry are food and kindred products, and printing and publishing.

The mining industry, which includes oil and gas, coal, and metal mining, was important to Colorado's economy, but it now employs only 1.2 percent of the state's workforce. Denver is home to companies that control half of the nation's gold production. The farm industry, which is primarily concentrated in livestock, is also an important element of the state's economy. The primary crops in Colorado are corn, hay, and wheat.

Famous natives and residents: William E. Barrett, writer; William Bent, fur trader and pioneer; Charles F. Brannan, lawyer and public official; M. Scott Carpenter, astronaut; Lon Chaney, actor; Mary Coyle Chase, playwright; Jack Dempsey, boxer; Ralph Edwards, entertainer; John Evans, physician, educator; Douglas Fairbanks, actor; John Thomas Fante, writer; Eugene Fodor, violinist; Gene Fowler, writer; Erick Hawkins, choreographer; Homer Lea, soldier, writer; Ted Mack, TV host; Jaye P. Morgan, singer; Peg Murray, actress; Ouray, Ute Indian chief; Anne Parrish, writer; Barbara Rush, actress; Horace A. Tabor, silver king and lieut. governor; Lowell Thomas, commentator and author; Dalton Trumbo, screenwriter, novelist; Byron R. White, jurist; Paul Whiteman, conductor; Don Wilson, announcer.

Connecticut

Capital: Hartford
Governor: John G. Rowland, R (to Jan. 1999)
Lieut. Governor: M. Jodi Rell, R (to Jan. 1999)
Senators: Christopher J. Dodd, D (to Jan. 1999); Joseph I. Lieberman, D (to Jan. 2001)
Secy. of State: Miles S. Rapoport, D (to Jan. 1999)
Comptroller: Nancy Wyman, D (to Jan. 1999)
Treasurer: Christopher B. Burnham, R (to Jan. 1999)
Atty. General: Richard Blumenthal, D (to Jan. 1999)
Entered Union (rank): Jan. 9, 1788 (5)
Present constitution adopted: Dec. 30, 1965
Motto: *Qui transtulit sustinet* (He who transplanted still sustains)
State symbols: flower, Mountain Laurel (1907); **tree,** White Oak (1947); **animal,** Sperm Whale (1975); **bird,** American Robin (1943); **hero,** Nathan Hale (1985); **heroine,** Prudence Crandall (1995); **insect,** Praying Mantis (1977); **mineral,** Garnet (1977); **song,** "Yankee Doodle" (1978); **ship,** USS *Nautilus* (SSN571) (1983); **shellfish,** Eastern Oyster (1989); **fossil,** *Eubrontes Giganteus* (1991)
Official designation: *Constitution State* (1959)
Nickname: Nutmeg State
Origin of name: From an Indian word (Quinnehtukqut) meaning "beside the long tidal river"
10 largest cities (1996 est.): Bridgeport, 137,990; Hartford, 133,086; New Haven, 124,665; Stamford, 110,056; Waterbury, 106,412; Norwalk, 77,977; New Britain, 71,512; Danbury, 65,506; Bristol, 59,619; Meriden, 57,189
Land area (rank): 4,845 sq mi. (12,550 sq km) (48)
Geographic center: In Hartford Co., at East Berlin
Number of counties: 8
Largest county (1995 pop. est.): Hartford 835,589
State forests: 30 (144,768 ac.)
State parks: 90 (31,729 ac.)
1997 resident population est.: 3,269,858
1990 resident population (rank): 3,287,116 (27). **Male:** 1,592,873; **Female:** 1,694,243. **White:** 2,859,353 (87.0%); **Black:** 274,269 (8.3%); **American Indian:** 6,654 (0.2%); **Asian:** 50,698 (1.5%); **Other race:** 96,142 (2.9%); **Hispanic:** 213,116 (6.5%). **1990 percent population under 18:** 22.8; **65 and over:** 13.6; **median age:** 34.4.

The Dutch navigator, Adriaen Block, was the first European of record to explore the area, sailing up the Connecticut River in 1614. In 1633, Dutch colonists built a fort and trading post near present-day Hartford, but soon lost control to English Puritans migrating south from the Massachusetts Bay Colony.

English settlements, established in the 1630s at Windsor, Wethersfield, and Hartford, united in 1639 to form the Connecticut Colony and adopted the *Fundamental Orders.*

The colony's royal charter of 1662 was exceptionally liberal. When Gov. Edmund Andros tried to seize it in 1687, it was hidden in the Hartford Oak, commemorated in Charter Oak Place.

Connecticut played a prominent role in the Revolutionary War, serving as the Continental Army's major supplier. Sometimes called the "Arsenal of the Nation," the state became one of the most industrialized in the nation.

Today, Connecticut factories produce weapons, sewing machines, jet engines, helicopters, motors, hardware and tools, cutlery, clocks, locks, ball bearings, silverware, and submarines. Hartford has the oldest U.S. newspaper still being published—the *Hartford Courant,* established 1764—and is the insurance capital of the nation.

Poultry, fruit, and dairy products account for the largest portion of farm income, and Connecticut's shade-grown tobacco is acknowledged to be the state's most valuable crop per acre.

Connecticut is a popular resort area with its 250-mile Long Island Sound shoreline and many inland lakes. Among the major points of interest are Yale University's Gallery of Fine Arts and Peabody Museum. Other famous museums include the P. T. Barnum, Winchester Gun, and American Clock and Watch. The town of Mystic features a recreated 19th-century New England seaport and the Mystic Marinelife Aquarium.

Famous natives and residents: Dean Acheson, statesman; Ethan Allan, American Revolutionary soldier; Benedict Arnold, American Revolutionary general; P. T. Barnum, showman; Henry Ward Beecher, clergyman; John Brown, abolitionist; Oliver Ellsworth, jurist; Eileen Farrell, soprano; Charles Goodyear, inventor; Nathan Hale, American Revolutionary officer; Dorothy Hamill, ice skater; Katharine Hepburn, actress; Charles Ives, composer; Edwin H. Land, inventor; John Pierpont Morgan, financier; Frederick Law Olmsted, landscape designer; Rosa Ponselle, soprano; Adam Clayton Powell, Jr., congressman; Benjamin Spock, pediatrician; Harriet Beecher Stowe, author; Mark Twain, author; Morris R. Waite, jurist; Noah Webster, lexicographer.

Delaware

Capital: Dover
Governor: Thomas R. Carper, D (to Jan. 2001)
Lieut. Governor: Ruth Ann Minner, D (to Jan. 2001)
Senators: Joseph R. Biden, Jr., D (to Jan. 2003); William V. Roth, Jr., R (to Jan. 2001)
Secy. of State: Edward J. Freel, D (Pleasure of Governor)
State Treasurer: Janet C. Rzewnicki, R (to Jan. 2001)
Atty. General: M. Jane Brady, R (to Jan. 2001)
Entered Union (rank): Dec. 7, 1787 (1)
Present constitution adopted: 1897
Motto: Liberty and independence
State symbols: colors, Colonial blue and buff; **flower,** Peach blossom (1895); **tree,** American holly (1939); **bird,** Blue Hen chicken (1939); **insect,** Ladybug (1974); **fish,** Weakfish, *Cynoscion regalis* (1981); **song,** "Our Delaware"

Nicknames: Diamond State; First State; Small Wonder
Origin of name: From Delaware River and Bay; named in turn for Sir Thomas West, Baron De La Warr
10 largest cities (1996 est.): Wilmington, 69,490; Dover, 30,414; Newark, 27,870; Milford, 6,557; Seaford, 6,400; Elsmere, 5,787; Smyrna, 5,502; New Castle 4,912; Middletown, 4,291; Georgetown, 4,029
Land area (rank): 1,982 sq mi. (5,153 sq km) (49)
Geographic center: In Kent Co., 11 mi. S of Dover
Number of counties: 3
Largest county (1997 pop. est.): New Castle, 474,838
State forests: 3 (9,353 ac.)
State parks: 13
1998 resident population est.: 739,337
1990 resident census population (rank): 666,168 (46). **Male:** 322,968; **Female:** 343,200. **White:** 535,094 (80.3%); **Black:** 112,460 (16.9%); **American Indian:** 2,019 (0.3%); **Asian:** 9,057 (1.4%); **Other race:** 7,538 (1.1%); **Hispanic:** 15,820 (2.4%). **1990 percent population under 18:** 24.5; **65 and over:** 12.1; **median age:** 32.9.

Henry Hudson, sailing under the Dutch flag, is credited with Delaware's discovery in 1609. The following year, Capt. Samuel Argall of Virginia named Delaware for his colony's governor, Thomas West, Baron De La Warr. An attempted Dutch settlement failed in 1631. Swedish colonization began at Fort Christina (now Wilmington) in 1638, but New Sweden fell to Dutch forces led by New Netherlands' Gov. Peter Stuyvesant in 1655.

England took over the area in 1664 and it was transferred to William Penn as the southern Three Counties in 1682. Semiautonomous after 1704, Delaware fought as a separate state in the American Revolution and became the first state to ratify the constitution in 1787.

During the Civil War, although a slave state, Delaware did not secede from the Union.

In 1802, Ëleuthère Irénée du Pont established a gunpowder mill near Wilmington that laid the foundation for Delaware's huge chemical industry. Delaware's manufactured products now also include vulcanized fiber, textiles, paper, medical supplies, metal products, machinery, machine tools, and automobiles.

Delaware also grows a great variety of fruits and vegetables and is a U.S. pioneer in the food-canning industry. Corn, soybeans, potatoes, and hay are important crops. Delaware's broiler-chicken farms supply the big Eastern markets, and fishing and dairy products are other important industries.

Points of interest include the Fort Christina Monument, Hagley Museum, Holy Trinity Church (erected in 1698, the oldest Protestant church in the United States still in use), and Winterthur Museum, in and near Wilmington; central New Castle, an almost unchanged late 18th-century capital; and the Delaware Museum of Natural History.

Popular recreation areas include Cape Henlopen, Delaware Seashore, Trapp Pond State Park, and Rehoboth Beach.

Famous natives and residents: Richard Allen, founder of the African Methodist Episcopal Church; Valerie Bertinelli, actress; Robert Montgomery Bird, playwright and novelist; Henry S. Canby, editor and author; Annie Jump Cannon, astronomer; Elizabeth Margaret Chandler, author; Felix Darley, artist; John Dickinson, statesman; E. I. du Pont, industrialist; Oliver Evans, inventor; Thomas Garrett, abolitionist; Henry Heimlich, surgeon, inventor; Wilham Julius "Judy" Johnson, basketball player; J. P. Marquand, novelist; Howard Pyle, artist and author; George Read, jurist, signer of Declaration of Independence; Jay Saunders Redding, educator and author; Caesar Rodney, patriot, signer of Declaration of Independence; Frank Stephens, sculptor; Estelle Taylor, actress; George Alfred Townsend, journalist and author.

District of Columbia

See Washington, D.C., listing in U.S. Cities.

Florida

Capital: Tallahassee
Governor: Lawton Chiles, D (to Jan. 1999)
Lieut. Governor: Buddy McKay, D (to Jan. 1999)
Senators: Bob Graham, D (to Jan. 1999); Connie Mack III, R (to Jan. 2001)
Secy. of State: Sandra B. Mortham, R (to Jan. 1999)
Comptroller: Bob Milligan, R (to Jan. 1999)
Commissioner of Agriculture: Bob Crawford, D (to Jan. 1999)
Atty. General: Bob Butterworth, D (to Jan. 1999)
Organized as territory: March 30, 1822
Entered Union (rank): March 3, 1845 (27)
Present constitution adopted: 1969
Motto: In God we trust (1868)
State symbols: flower, Orange blossom (1909); **bird,** Mockingbird (1927); **song,** "Suwannee River" (1935)
Nickname: Sunshine State (1970)
Origin of name: From the Spanish, meaning "feast of flowers" (Easter)
10 largest cities (1996 est.): Jacksonville (CC[1]), 679,792; Miami, 365,127; Tampa, 285,206; St. Petersburg, 235,988; Hialeah, 204,684; Orlando, 173,902; Fort Lauderdale, 151,805; Tallahassee, 136,812; Hollywood, 127,894; Coral Springs, 105,275
Land area (rank): 53,997 sq mi. (139,852 sq km) (26)
Geographic center: In Hernando Co., 12 mi. NNW of Brooksville
Number of counties: 67
Largest county (1996 pop. est.): Dade, 2,013,821
State forests: 35 (550,000 ac.)
State parks: 147 (456,972 ac.)
1997 resident population est.: 14,653,945
1990 resident census population (rank): 12,937,926 (4). **Male:** 6,261,719; **Female:** 6,676,207. **White:** 10,749,285 (83.1%); **Black:** 1,759,534 (13.6%); **American Indian:** 36,335 (0.3%); **Asian:** 154,302 (1.2%); **Other race:** 238,470 (1.8%); **Hispanic:** 1,574,143 (12.2%). **1990 percent population under 18:** 22.2; **65 and over:** 18.3; **median age:** 36.4.

1. Consolidated City (Coextensive with Duval County).

In 1513, Ponce De Leon, seeking the mythical "Fountain of Youth," discovered and named Florida, claiming it for Spain. Later, Florida would be held at different times by Spain and England until Spain finally sold it to the United States in 1819. (Incidentally, France established a colony named Fort Caroline in 1564 in the state that was to become Florida.)

Florida's early-19th-century history as a U.S. territory was marked by wars with the Seminole Indians that did not end until 1842, although a treaty was actually never signed.

One of the nation's fastest-growing states, Florida's population has gone from 2.8 million in 1950 to more than 12.9 million in 1990.

Florida's economy rests on a solid base of tourism (in 1992 the state entertained more than 40.5 million visitors from all over the world), manufacturing, agriculture, and international trade.

In recent years, oranges, grapefruit, and tomatoes led Florida's agricultural-product list, followed by vegetables, potatoes, melons, strawberries, sugar cane, dairy products, cattle and calves, and forest products.

Major tourist attractions are Miami Beach, Palm Beach, St. Augustine (founded in 1565, thus the oldest permanent city in the U.S.), Daytona Beach, and Fort Lauderdale on the East Coast. West Coast resorts include Sarasota, Tampa, Key West, and St. Petersburg. The Orlando area, where Disney World is located on a 27,000-acre site, is Florida's most popular tourist destination.

Also drawing many visitors are the NASA Kennedy Space Center's Spaceport USA, located in the town of Kennedy Space Center, Everglades National Park, and the Epcot Center.

Famous natives and residents: Julian "Cannonball" Adderley, jazz saxophonist; Pat Boone, singer; Fernando Bujones, ballet dancer; Steve Carlton, baseball player; Fay Dunaway, actress; Stepin Fetchit (Lincoln Theodore Perry), comedian; Lue Gim Gong, horticulturist; Dwight Gooden, baseball player; Zora Neale Hurston, writer; Daniel James, four-star general; James Weldon Johnson, author and educator; Frances Langford, singer; Little Richard, singer; Butterfly McQueen, actress; Jim Morrison, singer; Osceola, Seminole Indian leader; Sidney Poitier, actor; A. Philip Randolph, labor leader; Marjorie Kinnan Rawlings, author; Burt Reynolds, actor; Charles and John Ringling, circus entrepreneurs; Joseph W. Stilwell, army general; Norman E. Thargard, astronaut; Clarence Thomas, jurist; Ben Vereen, actor.

Georgia

Capital: Atlanta
Governor: Zell Miller, D (to Jan. 1999)
Lieut. Governor: Pierre Howard, D (to Jan. 1999)
Senators: Max Cleland, D (to Jan. 2003); Paul Coverdell, R (to Jan. 1999)
Secy. of State: Lewis A. Massey, D (to Jan. 1999)
Insurance Commissioner: John Oxendine, D (to Jan. 1999)
Atty. General: Thurbert Baker, D (to Jan. 1999)
Entered Union (rank): Jan. 2, 1788 (4)
Present constitution adopted: 1977
Motto: Wisdom, justice, and moderation
State symbols: flower, Cherokee rose (1916); **tree,** Live oak (1937); **bird,** Brown thrasher (1935); **song,** "Georgia on My Mind" (1922)
Nicknames: Peach State, Empire State of the South
Origin of name: In honor of George II of England
10 largest cities (1996 est.): Atlanta, 401,907; Columbus[1], 182,828; Savannah, 136,262; Macon, 113,352; Athens-Clarke County, 89,405; Albany, 78,591; Roswell, 55,462; Marietta, 50,937; Warner Robins, 45,559; Valdosta, 41,816
Land area (rank): 57,919 sq mi. (150,010 sq km) (21)
Geographic center: In Twiggs Co., 18 mi. SE of Macon
Number of counties: 159
Largest county (1995 pop. est.): Fulton, 700,689
State forests: 25,258,000 ac. (67% of total state area)
State parks: 53 (42,600 ac.)
1997 resident population est.: 7,486,242
1990 resident census population (rank): 6,478,216 (11). **Male:** 3,144,503; **Female:** 3,333,713. **White:** 4,600,148 (71.0%); **Black:** 1,746,565 (27.0%); **American Indian:** 13,348 (0.2%); **Asian:** 75,781 (1.2%); **Other race:** 42,374 (0.7%); **Hispanic:** 108,922 (1.7%). **1990 percent population under 18:** 26.7; **65 and over:** 10.1; **median age:** 31.6.

1. Consolidated City (Coextensive with Muscogee County).

Hernando de Soto, the Spanish explorer, first traveled parts of Georgia in 1540. British claims later conflicted with those of Spain. After obtaining a royal charter, Gen. James Oglethorpe established the first permanent settlement in Georgia in 1733 as a refuge for English debtors. In 1742, Oglethorpe defeated Spanish invaders in the Battle of Bloody Marsh.

A Confederate stronghold, Georgia was the scene of extensive military action during the Civil War. Union General William T. Sherman burned Atlanta and destroyed a 60-mile-wide path to the coast, where he captured Savannah in 1864.

The largest state east of the Mississippi, Georgia is typical of the changing South with an ever-increasing industrial development. Atlanta, largest city in the state, is the communications and transportation center for the Southeast and the area's chief distributor of goods.

Georgia leads the nation in the production of paper and board, tufted textile products, and processed chicken. Other major manufactured products are transportation equipment, food products, apparel, and chemicals.

Important agricultural products are corn, cotton, tobacco, soybeans, eggs, and peaches. Georgia produces twice as many peanuts as the next leading state. From its vast stands of pine come more than half the world's resins and turpentine and 74.4 percent of the U.S. supply. Georgia is also a leader in the production of marble, kaolin, barite, and bauxite.

Principal tourist attractions in Georgia include the Okefenokee National Wildlife Refuge, Andersonville Prison Park and National Cemetery, Chickamauga and Chattanooga National Military Park, the Little White House at Warm Springs where Pres. Franklin D. Roosevelt died in 1945, Sea Island, the enormous Confederate Memorial at Stone Mountain, Kennesaw Mountain National Battlefield Park, and Cumberland Island National Seashore.

Famous natives and residents: Conrad Aiken, poet; James Bowie, soldier; James Brown, singer; Jim Brown, actor and athlete; Erskine Caldwell, writer; James E. Carter, former president; Ray Charles, singer; Lucius D. Clay, banker and former general; Ty Cobb, baseball player; Ossie Davis, actor and writer; James Dickey, poet; Mattiwilda Dobbs, soprano; Melvyn Douglas, actor; Rebecca Latimer Felton, first appointed woman U.S. senator; Roosevelt Grier, entertainer and former athlete; Oliver Hardy, comedian; Joel Chandler Harris, journalist and author; Larry Holmes, boxer; Miriam Hopkins, actress; Harry James, trumpeter; Jasper Johns, painter and sculptor; Bobby Jones, golfer; Stacy Keach, actor; DeForest Kelley, actor; Martin Luther King, Jr., civil rights leader; Gladys Knight, singer; Joseph R. Lamar, jurist; Juliette Gordon Low, U.S. Girl Scouts founder; Carson McCullers, novelist; Johnny Mercer, songwriter; Margaret Mitchell, novelist; Elijah Muhammad, religious leader; Jessye Norman, soprano; Otis Redding, singer; Burt Reynolds, actor; Jackie Robinson, baseball player; Dean Rusk, former secretary of state; Nipsey Russell, comedian; Alice Walker, author; Joanne Woodward, actress.

Hawaii

Capital: Honolulu (on Oahu)
Governor: Benjamin Cayetano, D (to Dec. 1998)
Lieut. Governor: Mazie Hirono, D
Senators: Daniel K. Akaka, D (to Jan. 2001); Daniel K. Inouye, D (to Jan. 1999)
Comptroller: Raymond Sato
Atty. General: Margery Bronster
Organized as territory: 1900
Entered Union (rank): Aug. 21, 1959 (50)
Motto: *Ua Mau Ke Ea O Ka Aina I Ka Pono* (The life of the land is perpetuated in righteousness)
State symbols: flower, Hibiscus (yellow) (1988); **song,** "Hawaii Ponoi" (1967); **bird,** Nene (hawaiian goose) (1957); **tree,** Kukui (Candlenut) (1959)
Nickname: Aloha State (1959)
Origin of name: Uncertain. The islands may have been named by Hawaii Loa, their traditional discoverer. Or

they may have been named after Hawaii or Hawaiki, the traditional home of the Polynesians.

10 largest cities[1] (1996 est.): Honolulu, 377,059; Hilo, 37,808; Kailua, 36,818; Kaneohe, 35,448; Waipahu, 31,435; Pearl City, 30,993; Waimalu, 29,967; Mililani Town, 29,359; Schofield Barracks, 19,597; Wahiawa, 17,386

Land area (rank): 6,423.4 sq mi. (16,636.5 sq km) (47)

Geographic center: Between islands of Hawaii and Maui

Number of counties: Four plus one non-functioning county (Kalawao)

Largest county (1997 pop. est.): Honolulu, 869,857

State parks and historic sites: 19

1997 resident population est.: 1,186,602

1990 resident census population (rank): 1,108,229 (41). **Male:** 563,891; **Female:** 544,338. **White:** 369,616 (33.4%); **Black:** 27,195 (2.5%); **American Indian:** 5,099 (0.5%); **Asian:** 685,236 (61.8%); **Other race:** 21,083 (1.9%); **Hispanic:** 81,390 (7.3%). **1990 percent population under 18:** 25.3; **65 and over:** 11.3; **median age:** 32.6

1. Census Designated Place. There are no political boundaries to Honolulu or any other place, but statistical boundaries are assigned under state law.

First settled by Polynesians sailing from other Pacific islands between C.E. 300 and 600, Hawaii was visited in 1778 by British Captain James Cook, who called the group the Sandwich Islands.

Hawaii was a native kingdom throughout most of the 19th century, when the expansion of the vital sugar industry (pineapple came after 1898) meant increasing U.S. business and political involvement. In 1893, Queen Liliuokalani was deposed and a year later the Republic of Hawaii was established with Sanford B. Dole as president. Then, following its annexation in 1898, Hawaii became a U.S. territory in 1900.

The Japanese attack on the naval base at Pearl Harbor on Dec. 7, 1941, was directly responsible for U.S. entry into World War II.

Hawaii, 2,397 miles west-southwest of San Francisco, is a 1,523-mile chain of islets and eight main islands—Hawaii, Kahoolawe, Maui, Lanai, Molokai, Oahu, Kauai, and Niihau. The Northwestern Hawaiian Islands, other than Midway, are administratively part of Hawaii.

The temperature is mild and Hawaii's soil is fertile for tropical fruits and vegetables. Cane sugar, pineapple, and flowers and nursery products are the chief products. Hawaii also grows coffee, bananas, and nuts. The tourist business is Hawaii's largest source of outside income.

Hawaii's highest peak is Mauna Kea (13,796 ft.). Mauna Loa (13,679 ft.) is the largest volcanic mountain in the world in cubic content.

Among the major points of interest are Hawaii Volcanoes National Park (Hawaii), Haleakala National Park (Maui), Puuhonua o Honaunau National Historical Park (Hawaii), Polynesian Cultural Center (Oahu), the USS *Arizona* Memorial at Pearl Harbor, The National Memorial Cemetery of the Pacific (Oauhu), and Iolani Palace (the only royal palace in the U.S.), Bishop Museum, and Waikiki Beach (all in Honolulu).

Famous natives and residents: Salevaa Atisanoe (Konishiki), sumo wrestler; George Ariyoshi, first Japanese-American elected governor; Hiram Bingham, missionary; Charles R. Bishop, banker and philanthropist; Tia Carrere, singer, actress; Samuel N. Castle, missionary, founder of Castle & Cooke Ltd. with Amos S. Cooke, missionary and educator; Father Damien, leper-colony worker; Sanford B. Dole, territorial governor; Jean Erdman, dancer, choreographer; Hiram L. Fong, first Chinese-American senator; Don Ho, entertainer; Daniel K. Inouye, senator; Gerrit P. Judd, advisor to the Hawaiian king; Kaahumanu, Hawaiian queen; Duke Paoa Kahanamoku, Olympic swimming champion; Kamehameha I, first Hawaiian king; Kamehameha V, last of the dynasty; George Parsons Lathrop, journalist and poet; Liliuokalani, queen, last Hawaiian monarch; Bette Midler, singer; Ellison Onizuka, astronaut; Kawaipuna Prejean, Hawaiian activist, proponent of Hawaiian sovereignty; Chad Rowan, Yokozuna, sumo wrestler; Harold Sakata, actor; Carolyn Suzanne Sapp, Miss America (1991); James Shigeta, actor; Claus Spreckels, developer of Hawaiian sugar industry; Don Stroud, actor.

Idaho

Capital: Boise

Governor: Philip E. Batt, R (to Jan. 1999)

Lieut. Governor: C. L. "Butch" Otter, R (to Jan. 1999)

Senators: Larry E. Craig, R (to Jan. 2003); Dirk Kempthorne, R (to Jan. 1999)

Secy. of State: Pete T. Cenarrusa, R (to Jan. 1999)

State Auditor: J. D. Williams, D (to Jan. 1999)

Atty. General: Alan G. Lance, R (to Jan. 1999)

Treasurer: Lydia Justice Edwards, R (to Jan. 1999)

Organized as territory: March 3, 1863

Entered Union (rank): July 3, 1890 (43)

Present constitution adopted: 1890

Motto: *Esto perpetua* (It is forever)

State symbols: flower, Syringa (1931); **tree,** White pine (1935); **bird,** Mountain bluebird (1931); **horse,** Appaloosa (1975), **gem,** Star garnet (1967); **song,** "Here We Have Idaho"; **folk dance,** Square Dance; **fish,** Cutthroat trout (1990); **fossil,** Hagerman horse fossil (1988)

Nicknames: Gem State; Spud State; Panhandle State

Origin of name: Unknown. Though popularly believed to be an Indian word, it is an invented name whose meaning is unknown.

10 largest cities (1996 est.): Boise, 152,737; Pocatello, 51,344; Idaho Falls, 48,079; Nampa, 37,558; Twin Falls, 31,989; Coeur d'Alene, 31,076; Lewiston, 30,271; Caldwell, 21,089; Meridian, 20,627; Moscow, 20,101

Land area (rank): 82,751 sq mi. (214,325 sq km) (11)

Geographic center: In Custer Co., at Custer, SW of Challis

Number of counties: 44, plus small part of Yellowstone National Park

Largest county (1997 pop. est.): Ada, 267,168

State forests: 881,000 ac.

State parks: 23 (46,664 ac.)

1997 resident population est.: 1,210,232

1990 resident census population (rank): 1,006,749 (42). **Male:** 500,956; **Female:** 505,793. **White:** 950,451 (94.4%); **Black:** 3,370 (0.3%); **American Indian:** 13,780 (1.4%); **Asian:** 9,365 (0.9%); **Other race:** 29,783 (3.0%); **Hispanic:** 52,927 (5.3%). **1990 percent population under 18:** 30.6; **65 and over:** 12.0; **median age:** 31.5.

After its acquisition by the U.S. as part of the Louisiana Purchase in 1803, the region was explored by Meriwether Lewis and William Clark in 1805–06. Northwest boundary disputes with Great Britain were settled by the Oregon Treaty in 1846 and the first permanent U.S. settlement in Idaho was established by the Mormons at Franklin in 1860.

After gold was discovered on Orofino Creek in 1860, prospectors swarmed into the territory, but left little more than a number of ghost towns.

In the 1870s, growing white occupation of Indian lands led to a series of battles between U.S. forces and the Nez Percé, Bannock, and Sheepeater tribes.

Mining, lumbering, and irrigation farming have been important for years. Idaho produces more than one fifth of all the silver mined in the U.S. It also ranks high among the states in antimony, lead, cobalt, garnet, phosphate rock, vanadium, zinc, mercury, and gold.

Idaho's most impressive growth began when World War II military needs made processing agricultural products a big industry, particularly the dehydrating and freezing of potatoes. The state produces about one fourth of the nation's potato crop, as well as wheat, apples, corn, barley, sugar beets, and hops.

With the growth of winter sports, tourism now outranks mining in dollar revenue. Idaho's many streams and lakes provide fishing, camping, and boating sites. The nation's largest elk herds draw hunters from all over the world and the famed Sun Valley resort attracts thousands of visitors to its swimming and skiing facilities.

Other points of interest are the Craters of the Moon National Monument; Nez Percé National Historic Park, which includes many sites visited by Lewis and Clark; and the State Historical Museum in Boise.

Famous natives and residents: Joe Albertson, grocery chain founder; Cecil Andrus, former governor; T. H. Bell, educator; Ezra Taft Benson, Eisenhower's Secretary of Agriculture, pres. LDS church, marketing specialist; William E. Borah, former senator; Gutzon Borglum, Mt. Rushmore sculptor; Carol R. Brink, author; Frank F. Church, former senator; Fred Dubois, senator; Vardis Fisher, novelist; Lawrence H. Gipson, historian; Ernest Hemingway, author; Mariel Hemingway, actress; Chief Joseph, Nez Percé chief; Harmon Killebrew, baseball player; Jerry Kramer, football player, author; Ezra Pound, poet; Sacagawea, Shoshonean guide; J. R. Simplot, industrialist; Robert E. Smylie, political leader; Henry Spalding, missionary; Frank Steunenberg, former governor; Picabo Street, skier; David Tompson, founded first trading post; Lana Turner, actress.

Illinois

Capital: Springfield
Governor: Jim Edgar, R (to Jan. 1999)
Lieut. Governor: Bob Kustra, R (to Jan. 1999)
Senators: Richard J. Durbin, D (to Jan. 2003); Carol Moseley-Braun, D (to Jan. 1999)
Atty. General: Jim Ryan, R (to Jan. 1999)
Secy. of State: George H. Ryan, R (to Jan. 1999)
Comptroller: Loleta Didrickson, R (to Jan. 1999)
Treasurer: Judith Barr Topinka, R (to Jan. 1999)
Organized as territory: Feb. 3, 1809
Entered Union (rank): Dec. 3, 1818 (21)
Present constitution adopted: 1970
Motto: State sovereignty, national union
State symbols: flower, Violet (1908); **tree,** White oak (1973); **bird,** Cardinal (1929); **animal,** White-tailed deer (1982); **fish,** Bluegill (1987); **insect,** Monarch butterfly (1975); **song,** "Illinois" (1925); **mineral,** Fluorite (1965)
Nickname: Prairie State
Origin of name: Unknown. It is an invented name whose meaning, if any, is unknown
10 largest cities (1996 est.): Chicago, 2,721,547; Rockford, 143,531; Aurora, 116,405; Springfield, 112,921; Peoria, 112,306; Naperville, 107,001; Joliet, 86,749; Elgin, 86,034; Decatur, 81,369; Arlington Heights Village, 76,740
Land area (rank): 55,593 sq mi. (143,987 sq km) (24)
Geographic center: In Logan County 28 mi. NE of Springfield
Number of counties: 102
Largest county (1995 pop. est.): Cook, 5,136,877
Public use areas: 187 (275,000 ac.), incl. state parks, memorials, forests and conservation areas
1997 resident population est.: 11,895,849
1990 resident census population (rank): 11,430,602 (6). **Male:** 5,552,233; **Female:** 5,878,369. **White:** 8,952,978 (78.3%); **Black:** 1,694,273 (14.8%); **American Indian:** 21,836 (0.2%); **Asian:** 285,311 (2.5%); **Other race:** 476,204 (4.2%); **Hispanic:** 904,446 (7.9%). **1990 percent population under 18:** 25.8; **65 and over:** 12.6; **median age:** 32.8.

French explorers Jacques Marquette and Louis Joliet, in 1673, were the first Europeans of record to visit the region. In 1699 French settlers established the first permanent settlement at Cahokia, near present-day East St. Louis.

Great Britain obtained the region at the end of the French and Indian War in 1763. The area figured prominently in frontier struggles during the Revolutionary War and in Indian wars during the early 19th century.

Significant episodes in the state's early history include the growing migration of Eastern settlers following the opening of the Erie Canal in 1825; the Black Hawk War, which virtually ended the Indian troubles in the area; and the rise of Abraham Lincoln from farm laborer to President.

Today, Illinois stands high in manufacturing, coal mining, agriculture, and oil production. The sprawling Chicago district (including a slice of Indiana) is a great iron and steel producer, meat packer, grain exchange, and railroad center. Chicago is also famous as a Great Lakes port.

Illinois ranks third in the nation in export of agricultural products, first in corn and soybeans, and third in hog production. An important dairy state, Illinois is also a leader in corn, oats, wheat, barley, rye, truck vegetables, and the nursery products.

The state manufactures a great variety of industrial and consumer products: railroad cars, clothing, furniture, tractors, liquor, watches, and farm implements are just some of the items made in its factories and plants.

Central Illinois is noted for shrines and memorials associated with the life of Abraham Lincoln. In Springfield are the Lincoln Home, the Lincoln Tomb, and the restored Old State Capitol. Other points of interest are the home of Mormon leader Joseph Smith in Nauvoo and, in Chicago: the Art Institute, Field Museum, Museum of Science and Industry, Shedd Aquarium, Adler Planetarium, Merchandise Mart, and Chicago Portage National Historic Site.

Famous natives and residents: Franklin Pierce Adams, author; Jane Addams, social worker; Mary Astor, actress; Jack Benny, comedian; Black Hawk, Sauk Indian chief; Harry A. Blackmun, jurist; Ray Bradbury, author; William Jennings Bryan, orator and politician; Edgar Rice Burroughs, novelist; Gower Champion, choreographer; John Chancellor, TV commentator; Raymond Chandler, writer; Jimmy Connors, tennis champion; James Gould Cozzens, novelist; Richard J. Daley, former mayor of Chicago; Miles Davis, musician; Peter DeVries, novelist; Walt Disney, film animator and producer; John Dos Passos, author; James T. Farrell, novelist; Betty Friedan, feminist; Benny Goodman, musician; John Gunther, author; Ernest Hemingway, author; Charlton Heston, actor; Wild Bill Hickok, scout; William Holden, actor; Rock Hudson, actor; Burl Ives, singer; James Jones, novelist; John Jones, civil rights leader; Quincy Jones, composer; Keokuk (Watchful Fox), chief of the Sac and Fox Indians; Walter Kerr, drama critic; Archibald MacLeish, poet; David Mamet, playwright; Robert A. Millikan, physicist; Sherrill

Milnes, baritone; Bill Murray, actor; Bob Newhart, actor and comedian; William S. Paley, broadcasting executive; Drew Pearson, columnist; Richard Pryor, comedian and actor; Ronald Reagan, former President and actor; Carl Sandburg, poet; Sam Shepard, playwright; William L. Shirer, author and historian; John Paul Stevens, jurist; McLean Stevenson, actor; Preston Sturges, director; Gloria Swanson, actress; Carl Van Doren, writer and educator; Melvin Van Peebles, playwright; Irving Wallace, novelist; Alfred Wallenstein, conductor; Raquel Welch, actress; Florenz Ziegfield, theatrical producer.

Indiana

Capital: Indianapolis
Governor: Frank O'Bannon, D (to Jan. 2001)
Lieut. Governor: Joseph E. Kernan, D (to Jan. 2001)
Senators: Dan Coats, R (to Jan. 1999); Richard G. Lugar, R (to Jan. 2001)
Secy. of State: Sue Anne Gilroy, R (to Feb. 1999)
Treasurer: Joyce Brinkman, R (to Feb. 1999)
Atty. General: Jeffrey A. Modisett, D (to Jan. 2001)
Auditor: Morris Wooden, R (to Dec. 1998)
Organized as territory: May 7, 1800
Entered Union (rank): Dec. 11, 1816 (19)
Present constitution adopted: 1851
Motto: The Crossroads of America
State symbols: flower, Peony (1957); **tree,** Tulip tree (1931); **bird,** Cardinal (1933); **song,** "On the Banks of the Wabash, Far Away" (1913); **river,** Wabash
Official language: English
Nickname: Hoosier State
Origin of name: Meaning "land of Indians"
10 largest cities (1996 est.): Indianapolis, 746,737; Fort Wayne, 184,783; Evansville, 123,456; Gary, 110,975; South Bend, 102,100; Hammond, 80,081; Muncie, 69,058; Bloomington, 66,479; Anderson, 59,131; Terre Haute, 54,585
Land area (rank): 35,870 sq mi. (92,904 sq km) (38)
Geographic center: In Boone Co., 14 mi. NNW of Indianapolis
Number of Counties: 92
Largest county (1997 pop. est.): Marion, 813,670
State parks: 23 (56,409 ac.)
State historic sites: 17 (2,007 ac.)
1997 resident population est.: 5,864,108
1990 census population (rank): 5,544,159 (14). **Male:** 2,688,281; **Female:** 2,855,878. **White:** 5,020,700 (90.6%); **Black:** 432,092 (7.8%); **American Indian:** 12,720 (0.2%); **Asian:** 37,617 (0.7%); **Other race:** 41,030 (0.7%); **Hispanic:** 98,788 (1.8%). **1990 percent population under 18:** 26.3; **65 and over:** 12.6; **median age:** 32.8.

First explored for France by sieur de la Salle in 1679–1680, the region figured importantly in the Franco-British struggle for North America that culminated with British victory in 1763.

George Rogers Clark led American forces against the British in the area during the Revolutionary War and, prior to becoming a state, Indiana was the scene of frequent Indian uprisings until the victory of Gen. William Henry Harrison at Tippecanoe in 1811.

Indiana's 41-mile Lake Michigan waterfront—one of the world's great industrial centers—turns out iron, steel, and oil products. Products include automobile parts and accessories, mobile homes and recreational vehicles, truck and bus bodies, aircraft engines, farm machinery, and fabricated structural steel. Wood office furniture and pharmaceuticals are also manufactured.

The state is a leader in agriculture with corn the principal crop. Hogs, soybeans, wheat, oats, rye, tomatoes, onions, and poultry also contribute heavily to Indiana's agricultural output. Much of the building limestone used in the U.S. is quarried in Indiana, which is also a large producer of coal.

Wyandotte Cave, one of the largest in the U.S., is located in Crawford County in southern Indiana, and West Baden and French Lick are well known for their mineral springs. Other attractions include Indiana Dunes National Lakeshore, Indianapolis Motor Speedway, Lincoln Boyhood National Memorial, and the George Rogers Clark National Historical Park.

Famous natives and residents: George Ade, humorist; Leon Ames, actor; Anne Baxter, actress; Albert J. Beveridge, political leader; Larry Bird, basketball player; Bill Blass, fashion designer; Frank Borman, astronaut; Hoagy Carmichael, songwriter; James Dean, actor; Eugene V. Debs, Socialist leader; Lloyd C. Douglas, author; Theodore Dreiser, writer; Bernard F. Gimbel, merchant; Virgil Grissom, astronaut; Phil Harris, actor and band leader; John Milton Hay, statesman; James R. Hoffa, labor leader; Michael Jackson, singer; Buck Jones, actor; Alfred C. Kinsey, zoologist; David Letterman, TV host and comedian; Eli Lilly, pharmaceuticals manufacturer; Carole Lombard, actress; Shelley Long, actress; Marjorie Main, actress; James McCracken, tenor; Joaquin Miller, poet; Paul Osborn, playwright; Cole Porter, songwriter; Gene Stratton Porter, naturalist and author; Ernest Taylor Pyle, journalist; J. Danforth Quayle, former vice president; James Whitcomb Riley, poet; Knute Rockne, football coach; Ned Rorem, composer; Red Skelton, comedian; Rex Stout, mystery writer; Booth Tarkington, author; Twyla Tharp, dancer and choreographer; Forrest Tucker, actor; Harold C. Urey, physicist; Kurt Vonnegut, Jr., author; Dan Wakefield, author; Robert Wise, director; Jessamyn West, novelist; Wendell Willkie, lawyer; Wilbur Wright, inventor.

Iowa

Capital: Des Moines
Governor: Terry E. Branstad, R (to Jan. 1999)
Lieut. Governor: Joy Corning, R (to Jan. 1999)
Senators: Chuck Grassley, R (to Jan. 1999); Tom Harkin, D (to Jan. 2003)
Secy. of State: Paul Pate, R (to Jan. 1999)
Treasurer: Michael L. Fitzgerald, D (to Jan. 1999)
Atty. General: Tom Miller, D (to Jan. 1999)
Organized as territory: June 12, 1838
Entered Union (rank): Dec. 28, 1846 (29)
Present constitution adopted: 1857
Motto: Our liberties we prize and our rights we will maintain
State symbols: flower, Wild rose (1897); **bird,** Eastern goldfinch (1933); **colors,** Red, white, and blue (in state flag); **song,** "Song of Iowa"
Nickname: Hawkeye State
Origin of name: Probably from an Indian word meaning "this is the place," or "the Beautiful Land"
10 largest cities (1996 est.): Des Moines, 193,422; Cedar Rapids, 113,482; Davenport, 97,010; Sioux City, 83,791; Waterloo, 65,022; Iowa City, 60,923; Dubuque, 57,312; Council Bluffs, 55,569; Ames, 47,698; West Des Moines, 40,380
Land area (rank): 55,875 sq mi. (144,716 sq km) (23)
Geographic center: In Story Co., 5 mi. NE of Ames
Number of counties: 99
Largest county (1997 pop. est.): Polk, 354,850
State forests: 5 (28,000 ac.)
State parks: 84 (49,237)
1997 resident population est.: 2,852,423
1990 resident census population (rank): 2,776,755 (30). **Male:** 1,344,802; **Female:** 1,431,953. **White:** 2,683,090 (96.6%); **Black:** 48,090 (1.7%); **American Indian:** 7,349 (0.3%); **Asian:** 25,476 (0.9%); **Other race:** 12,750 (0.5%); **Hispanic:** 32,647 (1.2%). **1990 percent population under 18:** 25.9; **65 and over:** 15.3; **median age:** 34.0

The first Europeans to visit the area were the French explorers Father Jacques Marquette and Louis Joliet in 1673. The U.S. obtained control of the area in 1803 as part of the Louisiana Purchase.

During the first half of the 19th century, there was heavy fighting between white settlers and Indians. Lands were taken from the Indians after the Black Hawk War in 1832 and again in 1836 and 1837.

When Iowa became a state in 1846, its capital was Iowa City; the more centrally located Des Moines became the new capital in 1857. At that time, the state's present boundaries were also drawn.

Although Iowa produces a tenth of the nation's food supply, the value of Iowa's manufactured products is twice that of its agriculture. Major industries are food and associated products, non-electrical machinery, electrical equipment, printing and publishing, and fabricated products.

Iowa stands in a class by itself as an agricultural state. Its farms sell over $10 billion worth of crops and livestock annually. Iowa leads the nation in all corn, soybean, livestock, and hog marketings, with about 25% of the pork supply and 6% of the grain-fed cattle. Iowa's forests produce hardwood lumber, particularly walnut, and its mineral products include cement, limestone, sand, gravel, gypsum, and coal.

Tourist attractions include the Herbert Hoover birthplace and library near West Branch; the Amana Colonies; Fort Dodge Historical Museum, Fort, and Stockade; the Iowa State Fair at Des Moines in August; and the Effigy Mounds National Monument, a prehistoric Indian burial site at Marquette.

Famous natives and residents: Bix Beiderbecke, jazz musician; Norman Borlang, plant pathologist, geneticist, and Nobel Peace Prize winner; William "Buffalo Bill" F. Cody, scout; Johnny Carson, TV entertainer; Gardner Cowles, Jr., publisher; Simon Estes, bass-baritone; William Frawley, actor; George H. Gallup, poll taker; Susan Glaspell, writer; Herbert Hoover, former president; MacKinlay Kantor, novelist; Charles A. Kettering, inventor; Ann Landers, columnist; Cloris Leachman, actress; John L. Lewis, labor leader; Glenn L. Martin, aviator and manufacturer; Elsa Maxwell, writer; Frederick L. Maytag, inventor and manufacturer; Glenn Miller, bandleader; Harriet Nelson, actress; Nathan M. Pusey, educator; David Rabe, playwright; Harry Reasoner, TV commentator; Donna Reed, actress; Lillian Russell, soprano; Robert Schiller, evangelist; Wallace Stegner, novelist and critic; Billy Sunday, evangelist; James A. Van Allen, space physicist; Abigail Van Buren, columnist; Henry A. Wallace, statesman and vice president; John Wayne, actor; Andy Williams, singer; Meredith Willson, composer; Grant Wood, painter.

Kansas

Capital: Topeka
Governor: Bill Graves, R (to Jan. 1999)
Lieut. Governor: Gary Sherrer, R (to Jan. 1999)
Senators: Sam Brownback, R (to Jan. 2003); Pat Roberts, R (to Jan. 2003)
Secy. of State: Ron Thornburgh, R (to Jan. 1999)
Treasurer: Sally Thompson, D (to Jan. 1999)
Atty. General: Carla Stovall, R (to Jan. 1999)
Commission of Insurance: Kathleen Sebelius, D (to Jan. 1999)
Organized as territory: May 30, 1854
Entered Union (rank): Jan. 29, 1861 (34)
Present constitution adopted: 1859
Motto: *Ad astra per aspera* (To the stars through difficulties)
State symbols: flower, Sunflower (1903); **tree,** Cottonwood (1937); **bird,** Western meadowlark (1937); **animal,** Buffalo (1955); **song,** "Home on the Range" (1947)
Nicknames: Sunflower State; Jayhawk State
Origin of name: From a Sioux word meaning "people of the south wind"
10 largest cities (1996 est.): Wichita, 329,395; Kansas City, 142,654; Overland Park, 131,053; Topeka, 119,658; Olathe, 78,666; Lawrence, 71,887; Salina, 44,176; Shawnee, 43,006; Manhattan, 42,117; Leavenworth, 39,431
Land area (rank): 81,823 sq mi. (211,922 sq km) (13)
Geographic center: In Barton Co., 15 mi. NE of Great Bend
Number of counties: 105
Largest county (1995 pop. est.): Sedgwick, 419,333
State parks: 22 (14,394 ac.)
1997 resident population est.: 2,594,840
1990 resident census population (rank): 2,477,574 (32). **Male:** 1,214,645; **Female:** 1,262,929. **White:** 2,231,986 (90.1%); **Black:** 143,076 (5.8%); **American Indian:** 21,965 (0.9%); **Asian:** 31,750 (1.3%); **Other race:** 48,797 (2.0%); **Hispanic:** 93,670 (3.8%). **1990 percent population under 18:** 26.7; **65 and over:** 13.8; **median age:** 32.9.

Spanish explorer Francisco de Coronado, in 1541, is considered the first European to have traveled this region. Sieur de la Salle's extensive land claims for France (1682) included present-day Kansas. Ceded to Spain by France in 1763, the territory reverted back to France in 1800 and was sold to the U.S. as part of the Louisiana Purchase in 1803.

Lewis and Clark, Zebulon Pike, and Stephen H. Long explored the region between 1803 and 1819. The first permanent settlements in Kansas were outposts—Fort Leavenworth (1827), Fort Scott (1842), and Fort Riley (1853)—established to protect travelers along the Santa Fe and Oregon Trails.

Just before the Civil War, the conflict between the pro- and anti-slavery forces earned the region the grim title of Bleeding Kansas.

Today, wheat fields, oil-well derricks, herds of cattle, and grain-storage elevators are chief features of the Kansas landscape. A leading wheat-growing state, Kansas also raises corn, sorghums, oats, barley, soybeans, and potatoes. Kansas stands high in petroleum production and mines zinc, coal, salt, and lead. It is also the nation's leading producer of helium.

Wichita is one of the nation's leading aircraft-manufacturing centers, ranking first in production of private aircraft. Kansas City is an important transportation, milling, and meat-packing center.

Points of interest include the Kansas Museum of History at Topeka, the Eisenhower boyhood home and the new Eisenhower Memorial Museum and Presidential Library at Abilene, John Brown's cabin at Osawatomie, recreated Front Street in Dodge City, Fort Larned (once the most important military post on the Santa Fe Trail), and Fort Leavenworth and Fort Riley.

Famous natives and residents: Roscoe "Fatty" Arbuckle, actor; Clarence D. Batchelor, political cartoonist; Gwendolyn Brooks, poet; Walter P. Chrysler, auto manufacturer; Clark M. Clifford, former secretary of defense; John Steuart Curry, painter; Amelia Earhart, aviator; Milton S. Eisenhower, educator; Gary Hart, politician; William Inge, playwright; Walter Johnson, baseball pitcher; Osa L. Johnson, documentary film producer; Buster Keaton, comedian; Emmett Kelly, clown; Stan Kenton, jazz musician; James Lehrer, broadcast journalist; Edgar Lee Masters, poet; Mary McCarthy, actress; Hattie McDaniel, actress; William C. Menninger, psychiatrist; Gordon Parks, film director; Zasu Pitts, actress; Samuel Ramey, opera singer; Charles Robinson, statesman and first governor; Charles (Buddy) Rogers, actor; Damon Runyon, journalist; Eugene W. Smith, photojournalist; Milburn Stone, actor; John Cameron

Swayze, news commentator; William Allen White, journalist; Charles E. Whittaker, jurist; Jess Willard, boxer.

Kentucky

Capital: Frankfort
Governor: Paul E. Patton, D (to Dec. 1999)
Lieut. Governor: Stephen L. Henry, D (to Dec. 1999)
Senators: Wendell H. Ford, D (to Jan. 1999); Mitch McConnell, R (to Jan. 2003)
Secy. of State: John Y. Brown III, D (to Dec. 1999)
Treasurer: Ed Hatchett, D (to Dec. 1999)
Auditor: John Kennedy Hamilton, D (to Dec. 1999)
Atty. General: A.B. Chandler III, D (to Dec. 1999)
Entered Union (rank): June 1, 1792 (15)
Present constitution adopted: 1891
Motto: United we stand, divided we fall
State symbols: tree, Tulip poplar (1994); **flower,** Goldenrod; **bird,** Kentucky cardinal; **song,** "My Old Kentucky Home"
Nickname: Bluegrass State
Origin of name: From an Iroquoian word "Ken-tah-ten" meaning "land of tomorrow"
10 largest cities (1996 est.): Louisville, 260,689; Lexington-Fayette, 239,942; Owensboro, 54,350; Bowling Green, 44,208; Covington, 40,971; Hopkinsville, 28,317; Frankfort, 26,535; Paducah, 26,601; Henderson, 26,456; Richmond, 26,227
Land area (rank): 39,732 sq mi. (102,907 sq km) (36)
Geographic center: In Marion Co., 3 mi. NNW of Lebanon
Number of counties: 120
Largest county (1995 pop. est.): Jefferson, 672,918
State forests: 9 (44,173 ac.)
State parks: 43 (40,574 ac.)
1997 resident population est.: 3,908,124
1990 resident census population (rank): 3,685,296 (23). **Male:** 1,785,235; **Female:** 1,900,061. **White:** 3,391,832 (92.0%); **Black:** 262,907 (7.1%); **American Indian:** 5,769 (0.2%); **Asian:** 17,812 (0.5%); **Other race:** 6,976 (0.2%); **Hispanic:** 21,984 (0.6%). **1990 percent population below age 18:** 25.9; **65 and over:** 12.7; **median age:** 33.0.

Kentucky was the first region west of the Allegheny Mountains to be settled by American pioneers. James Harrod established the first permanent settlement at Harrodsburg in 1774; the following year Daniel Boone, who had explored the area in 1767, blazed the Wilderness Trail and founded Boonesboro.

Politically, the Kentucky region was originally part of Virginia, but early statehood was gained in 1792. During the Civil War, as a slaveholding state with a considerable abolitionist population, Kentucky was caught in the middle of the conflict, supplying both Union and Confederate forces with thousands of troops.

In recent years, manufacturing has shown important gains, particularly in automotive assembly and parts manufacturing. Kentucky also prides itself on producing some of the nation's best tobacco, horses, and whiskey. Corn, soybeans, wheat, fruit, hogs, cattle, and dairy products are among the agricultural items produced.

Among the manufactured items produced in the state are motor vehicles, furniture, aluminum ware, brooms, apparel, lumber products, machinery, textiles, and iron and steel products. Kentucky also produces significant amounts of petroleum, natural gas, fluorspar, clay, and stone. However, coal accounts for 90% of the total mineral income.

Louisville, the largest city, famed for the Kentucky Derby at Churchill Downs, is also the location of a large state university, whiskey distilleries, and cigarette factories. The Bluegrass country around Lexington is the home of some of the world's finest race horses. Other attractions are Mammoth Cave, the George S. Patton, Jr., Military Museum at Fort Knox, and Old Fort Harrod State Park.

Famous natives and residents: John Adair, pioneer and political leader; Muhammad Ali, boxer; Alben W. Barkley, former vice president; Louis D. Brandeis, jurist; John Mason Brown, critic; Kit Carson, scout; Champ Clark, politician; Rosemary Clooney, singer; Irvin S. Cobb, humorist; Jefferson Davis, president of the Confederacy; Irene Dunne, actress; Crystal Gayle, singer; David W. Griffith, film producer; John M. Harlan, jurist; Elizabeth Hardwick, writer; Casey Jones, celebrated locomotive engineer; Abraham Lincoln, former president; Loretta Lynn, singer; Carry Amelia Nation, temperance leader; Patricia Neal, actress; George Reeves, actor; Wiley B. Rutledge, jurist; Diane Sawyer, broadcast journalist; Phil Simms, football player; Adlai Stevenson, former vice president; Allen Tate, poet and critic; Hunter Thompson, writer; Frederick M. Vinson, jurist; Robert Penn Warren, novelist.

Louisiana

Capital: Baton Rouge
Governor: Murphy J. "Mike" Foster, R (to Jan. 2000)
Lieut. Governor: Kathleen Blanco, D (to Jan. 2000)
Senators: John B. Breaux, D (to Jan. 1999); Mary Landrieu, D (to Jan. 2003)
Secy. of State: W. Fox McKeithen, R (to Jan. 2000)
Treasurer: Ken Duncan, D (to Jan. 2000)
Atty. General: Richard P. Ieyoub, D (to Jan. 2000)
Organized as territory: March 26, 1804
Entered Union (rank): April 30, 1812 (18)
Present constitution adopted: 1974
Motto: Union, justice, and confidence
State symbols: flower, Magnolia (1900); **tree,** Bald cypress (1963); **bird,** Pelican (1958); **songs,** "Give Me Louisiana" and "You Are My Sunshine"
Nicknames: Pelican State; Sportsman's Paradise; Creole State; Sugar State
Origin of name: In honor of Louis XIV of France
10 largest cities (1996 est.): New Orleans, 476,625; Baton Rouge, 215,882; Shreveport, 191,558; Lafayette, 104,899; Kenner, 72,345; Lake Charles, 71,445; Bossier City, 55,686; Monroe, 54,588; Alexandria, 46,051; New Iberia, 32,513
Land area (rank): 43,566 sq mi. (112,836 sq km) (33)
Geographic center: In Avoyelles Parish, 3 mi. SE of Marksville
Number of parishes (counties): 64
Largest parish (1995 pop. est.): Orleans, 481,913
State forests: 1 (8,000 ac.)
State parks: 30 (13,932 ac.)
1997 resident population est.: 4,351,769
1990 resident census population (rank): 4,219,973 (21). **Male:** 2,031,386; **Female:** 2,188,587. **White:** 2,839,138 (67.3%); **Black:** 1,299,281 (30.8%); **American Indian:** 18,541 (0.4%); **Asian:** 41,099 (1.0%); **Other race:** 21,914 (0.5%); **Hispanic:** 93,044 (2.2%). **1990 percent population under 18:** 29.1; **65 and over:** 11.1; **median age:** 31.0.

Louisiana has a rich, colorful historical background. Early Spanish explorers were Alvárez Piñeda, 1519; Álvar Núñez Cabeza de Vaca, 1528; and Hernando De Soto in 1541. Sieur de la Salle reached the mouth of the Mississippi and claimed all the land drained by it and its tributaries for Louis XIV of France in 1682.

Louisiana became a French crown colony in 1731, was ceded to Spain in 1763, returned to

France in 1800, and sold by Napoleon to the U.S. as part of the Louisiana Purchase (with large territories to the north and northwest) in 1803.

In 1815, Gen. Andrew Jackson's troops defeated a larger British army in the Battle of New Orleans, neither side aware that the treaty ending the War of 1812 had been signed.

Louisiana is a leader in natural gas, salt, petroleum, and sulfur production. Much of the oil and sulfur comes from offshore deposits. The state also produces large crops of sweet potatoes, rice, sugar cane, pecans, soybeans, corn, and cotton.

Leading manufactures include chemicals, processed food, petroleum and coal products, paper, lumber and wood products, transportation equipment, and apparel.

Louisiana marshes supply most of the nation's muskrat fur as well as that of opossum, raccoon, mink, and otter, and large numbers of game birds.

Major points of interest include New Orleans with its French Quarter and Superdome, plantation homes near Natchitoches and New Iberia, Cajun country in the Mississippi Delta region, Chalmette National Historical Park, and the state capital at Baton Rouge.

Famous natives and residents: Louis Armstrong, musician; Geoffrey Beene, fashion designer; Truman Capote, writer; Kitty Carlisle, singer and actress; Van Cliburn, concert pianist; Michael De Bakey, heart surgeon; Fats Domino, musician; Louis Moreau Gottschalk, pianist and composer; Bryant Gumbel, TV newscaster; Lillian Hellman, playwright; Al Hirt, trumpeter; Mahalia Jackson, gospel singer; Jean Laffite, privateer; Dorothy Lamour, actress; John A. Lejeune, Marine Corps general; Elmore Leonard, author; Jerry Lee Lewis, singer; Huey P. Long, politician; Wynton Marsalis, musician; Jelly Roll Morton, jazz musician and composer; Huey Newton, black activist; Marguerite Piazza, soprano; Paul Prudhomme, chef; Howard K. Smith, TV commentator; Ben Turpin, comedian; Ray Walston, actor; Edward Douglas White, jurist.

Maine

Capital: Augusta
Governor: Angus S. King, Jr., I (to Jan. 1999)
Senators: Susan Collins, R (to Jan. 2003); Olympia J. Snowe (to Jan. 2001)
Secy. of State: Dan A. Gwadosky, D (to Jan. 1999)
Controller: Carol Whitney, R (to Jan. 1999)
Atty. General: Andrew Ketterer, D (to Jan. 1999)
Entered Union (rank): March 15, 1820 (23)
Present constitution adopted: 1820
Motto: *Dirigo* (I lead)
State symbols: flower, White pine cone and tassel (1895); **tree,** White pine tree (1945); **bird,** Chickadee (1927); **fish,** Landlocked salmon (1969); **mineral,** Tourmaline (1971); **song,** "State of Maine Song" (1937); **animal,** Moose (1979); **cat,** Maine Coon Cat (1985); **fossil,** Pertica quadrifaria (1985); **insect,** Honeybee (1975)
Nickname: Pine Tree State
Origin of name: First used to distinguish the mainland from the offshore islands. It has been considered a compliment to Henrietta Maria, queen of Charles I of England. She was said to have owned the province of Mayne in France.
10 largest cities (1996 est.): Portland, 63,123; Lewiston, 36,830; Bangor, 31,649; Auburn, 22,997; South Portland, 22,985; Biddeford, 20,788; Augusta, 20,441; Westbrook, 16,459; Waterville, 16,450; Saco, 15,681
Largest town (1990 census): Brunswick, 20,906
Land area (rank): 30,865 sq mi. (79,939 sq km) (39)
Geographic center: In Piscataquis Co., 18 mi. N of Dover-Foxcroft
Number of counties: 16
Largest county (1995 pop. est.): Cumberland, 248,526
State forests: 1 (21,000 ac.)
State parks: 26 (247,627 ac.)
State historic sites: 18 (403 ac.)
1997 resident population est.: 1,242,051
1990 resident census population (rank): 1,227,928 (38). **Male:** 597,850; **Female:** 630,078. **White:** 1,208,360 (98.4%); **Black:** 5,138 (0.4%); **American Indian:** 5,998 (0.5%); **Asian:** 6,683 (0.5%); **Other race:** 1,749 (0.1%); **Hispanic:** 6,829 (0.6%).

John Cabot and his son, Sebastian, are believed to have visited the Maine coast in 1498. However, the first permanent English settlements were not established until more than a century later, in 1623.

The first naval action of the Revolutionary War occurred in 1775 when colonials captured the British sloop *Margaretta* off Machias on the Maine coast. In that same year, the British burned Falmouth (now Portland).

Long governed by Massachusetts, Maine became the 23rd state as part of the Missouri Compromise in 1820.

Maine produces 98% of the nation's low-bush blueberries. Farm income is also derived from apples, potatoes, dairy products, and vegetables, with poultry and eggs the largest items.

The state is one of the world's largest pulp-paper producers. It ranks second in boot-and-shoe manufacturing. With almost 89% of its area forested, Maine turns out wood products from boats to toothpicks.

Maine leads the world in the production of the familiar flat tins of sardines, producing more than 75 million of them annually. Lobstermen normally catch 51% of the nation's total of lobsters. The 1995 catch was 36.5 million pounds, the second-largest lobster catch in history.

A scenic seacoast, beaches, lakes, mountains, and resorts make Maine a popular vacationland. There are more than 2,500 lakes and 5,000 streams, plus 26 state parks to attract hunters, fishermen, skiers, and campers.

Major points of interest are Bar Harbor, Allagash National Wilderness Waterway, the Wadsworth-Longfellow House in Portland, Roosevelt Campobello International Park, and the St. Croix Island National Monument.

Famous natives and residents: F. Lee Bailey, defense attorney; Charles F. Browne (Artemus Ward), humorist; Cyrus Curtis, publisher; Dorothea Dix, civil rights reformer; John Ford, film director; Melville Fuller, jurist; Marsden Hartley, painter; Henry Wadsworth Longfellow, poet; Sarah Orne Jewett, author; Stephen King, writer; Linda Lavin, actress; Edna St. Vincent Millay, poet; Marston Morse, mathematician; Frank Munsey, publisher; Walter Piston, composer; George Putnam, publisher; Kenneth Roberts, historical novelist; Edwin Arlington Robinson, poet; Margaret Chase Smith, politician; Samantha Smith, peacemaker and actress; John Hay Whitney, publisher.

Maryland

Capital: Annapolis
Governor: Parris N. Glendening, D (to Jan. 1999)
Lieut. Gov.: Kathleen Kennedy Townsend, D (to Jan. 1999)
Senators: Barbara A. Mikulski, D (to Jan. 1999); Paul S. Sarbanes, D (to Jan. 2001)
Secy. of State: John T. Willis, D (to Jan. 1999)
Comptroller of the Treasury: Louis L. Goldstein, D (to Jan. 1999)

Treasurer: Lucille Maurer, D (to Jan. 1999)
Atty. General: J. Joseph Curran, Jr., D (to Jan. 1999)
Entered Union (rank): April 28, 1788 (7)
Present constitution adopted: 1867
Motto: *Fatti maschii, parole femine* (Manly deeds, womanly words)
State symbols: bird, Baltimore oriole (1947); **boat,** Skipjack (1985); **crustacean,** Maryland Blue Crab (1989); **dog,** Chesapeake Bay retriever (1964); **flower,** Black-eyed susan (1918); **tree,** White oak (1941); **fish,** Rockfish (1965); **folk dance,** Square dance (1994); **fossil shell,** *Ecphora gardnerae gardnerae* (Wilson) (1994); **insect,** Baltimore checkerspot butterfly (1973); **song,** "Maryland! My Maryland!" (1939); **sport,** Jousting (1962)
Nicknames: Free State; Old Line State
Origin of name: In honor of Henrietta Maria (queen of Charles I of England)
10 largest cities (1996 est.): Baltimore, 675,401; Frederick, 46,227; Rockville, 46,019; Gaithersburg, 45,361; Bowie, 40,181; Hagerstown, 34,633; Annapolis, 33,234; College Park, 24,987; Cumberland, 22,341; Greenbelt, 21,840
Land area (rank): 9,775 sq mi. (25,316 sq km) (42)
Geographic center: In Prince Georges Co., 4½ mi. NW of Davidsonville
Number of counties: 23, and 1 independent city
Largest county (1995 pop. est.): Montgomery, 809,569
State forests: 13 (132,944 ac.)
State parks: 47 (87,670 ac.)
1997 resident population est.: 5,094,289
1990 resident census population (rank): 4,781,468 (19). **Male:** 2,318,671; **Female:** 2,462,797. **White:** 3,393,964 (71.0%); **Black:** 1,189,899 (24.9%); **American Indian:** 12,972 (0.3%); **Asian:** 139,719 (2.9%); **Other race:** 44,914 (0.9%); **Hispanic:** 125,102 (2.6%). **1990 percent population under 18:** 24.3; **65 and over:** 10.8; **median age:** 33.0

Maryland was inhabited by Indians as early as circa 10,000 B.C.E. Permanent Indian villages were established by circa C.E. 1000.

In 1608, Capt. John Smith explored Chesapeake Bay. Charles I granted a royal charter for Maryland to Cecil Calvert, Lord Baltimore, in 1632, and English settlers, many of whom were Roman Catholic, landed on St. Clement's (now Blakistone) Island in 1634. Religious freedom, granted all Christians in the Toleration Act passed by the Maryland assembly in 1649, was ended by a Puritan revolt, 1654–58.

From 1763 to 1767, Charles Mason and Jeremiah Dixon surveyed Maryland's northern boundary line with Pennsylvania. In 1791, Maryland ceded land to form the District of Columbia.

In 1814, when the British unsuccessfully tried to capture Baltimore, the bombardment of Fort McHenry inspired Francis Scott Key to write the words to "The Star-Spangled Banner."

The Baltimore clipper-ship trade developed during the 19th century. During the Civil War, Maryland remained a Union state even while the battles of South Mountain (1862), Antietam (1862), and Monocacy (1864) were fought on her soil.

In 1904, the Great Fire of Baltimore occurred. In 1937, the City of Greenbelt, a New Deal model community, was chartered.

Maryland's Eastern Shore and Western Shore embrace the Chesapeake Bay, and the many estuaries and rivers create one of the longest waterfronts of any state. The Bay produces more seafood—oysters, crabs, clams, fin fish—than any comparable body of water. Important agricultural products, in order of cash value, are greenhouse and nursery products, chickens, dairy products, soybeans, corn, eggs, vegetables, melons, and wheat. Maryland is a leader in vegetable canning. Stone, coal, sand, gravel, cement, and clay are the chief mineral products.

Manufacturing industries produce food and kindred products, instruments, chemicals, printing and publishing, transportation equipment, and primary metals. Baltimore, home of the Johns Hopkins University and Hospital, ranks as the nation's second port in foreign tonnage. Annapolis, site of the U.S. Naval Academy, has one of the earliest state houses (1772–79) still in regular use by a state government.

Among the popular attractions in Maryland are the Fort McHenry National Monument; Harpers Ferry and Chesapeake and Ohio Canal National Historic Parks; Antietam National Battlefield; National Aquarium, USS *Constellation,* and Maryland Science Center at Baltimore's Inner Harbor; Historic St. Mary's City; Jefferson Patterson Historical Park and Museum at St. Leonard; U.S. Naval Academy in Annapolis; Goddard Space Flight Center at Greenbelt; Assateague Island National Park Seashore; Ocean City beach resort; and Catoctin Mountain, Fort Frederick, and Piscataway parks.

Famous natives and residents: Benjamin Banneker, almanacker and mathematician-astronomer; John Barth, writer; Eubie Blake, musician; John Wilkes Booth, actor and Lincoln assassin; Francis X. Bushman, actor; James M. Cain, writer; Samuel Chase, jurist; Frederick Douglass, abolitionist; John Hurst Fletcher, Methodist bishop and educator; Christopher Gist, frontiersman; Philip Glass, composer; Matthew Henson, reached North Pole with Peary; Billie Holiday, jazz-blues singer; Johns Hopkins, financier; Reverdy Johnson, lawyer and statesman; Thomas Johnson, political leader; Francis Scott Key, laywer and author of the words to the national anthem; Thurgood Marshall, jurist; H. L. Mencken, writer; Hezekiah Niles, journalist; Charles Wilson Peale, painter; Frank Perdue, farmer, businessman; James R. Randall, journalist and writer of the state song; Babe Ruth, baseball player; Upton Sinclair, novelist; Roger B. Taney, jurist; George Alfred Townsend (Gath), journalist; Harriet Tubman, abolitionist; Leon Uris, novelist; Frank Zappa, singer.

Massachusetts

Capital: Boston
Governor: Argeo Paul Cellucci, R (to Jan. 1999)
Senators: Edward M. Kennedy, D (to Jan. 2001); John F. Kerry, D (to Jan. 2003)
Secy. of the Commonwealth: William F. Galvin, D (to Jan. 1999)
Treasurer & Receiver-General: Joseph D. Malone, R (to Jan. 1999)
Auditor of the Commonwealth: A. Joseph DeNucci, D (to Jan. 1999)
Atty. General: L. Scott Harshbarger, D (to Jan. 1999)
Present constitution drafted: 1780 (oldest U.S. state constitution in effect today)
Entered Union (rank): Feb. 6, 1788 (6)
Motto: *Ense petit placidam sub libertate quietem* (By the sword we seek peace, but peace only under liberty)
State symbols: flower, Mayflower (1918); **tree,** American elm (1941); **bird,** Chickadee (1941); **song,** "All Hail to Massachusetts" (1966); **beverage,** Cranberry juice (1970); **insect,** Ladybug (1974); **muffin,** Corn muffin; **dessert,** Boston cream pie
Nicknames: Bay State; Old Colony State
Origin of name: From two Indian words meaning "Great Mountain Place"
10 largest cities (1996 est.): Boston, 558,394; Worcester, 166,350; Springfield, 149,948; Lowell,

100,973; New Bedford, 96,903; Cambridge, 93,707; Brockton, 92,324; Fall River, 90,865; Quincy, 85,532; Lynn, 80,563

Land area (rank): 7,838 sq mi. (20,300 sq km) (45)

Geographic center: In Worcester Co., in S part of city of Worcester

Number of counties: 14

Largest county (1995 pop. est.): Middlesex, 1,408,450

State forests and parks: 129 (242,000 ac.)[1]

1997 resident population est.: 6,117,520

1990 resident census population (rank): 6,016,425 (13). **Male:** 2,888,745; **Female:** 3,127,680. **White:** 5,405,374 (89.8%); **Black:** 300,130 (5.0%); **American Indian:** 12,241 (0.2%); **Asian:** 143,392 (2.4%); **Other race:** 155,288 (2.6%); **Hispanic:** 287,549 (4.8%). **1990 percent population under 18:** 22.5; **65 and over:** 13.6; **median age:** 33.6.

1. The Metropolitan District Commission, an agency of the Commonwealth serving municipalities in the Boston area, has about 14,000 acres of parkways and reservations under its jurisdiction.

Massachusetts has played a significant role in American history since the Pilgrims, seeking religious freedom, founded Plymouth Colony in 1620. As one of the most important of the 13 colonies, Massachusetts became a leader in resisting British oppression. In 1773, the Boston Tea Party protested unjust taxation. The Minute Men started the American Revolution by battling British troops at Lexington and Concord on April 19, 1775.

During the 19th century, Massachusetts was famous for the vigorous intellectual activity of its renowned writers and educators and for its expanding commercial fishing, shipping, and manufacturing interests.

Massachusetts pioneered the manufacture of textiles and shoes. Today, these industries have been replaced in importance by activity in the electronics and communications equipment fields.

The state's cranberry crop is the nation's largest. Also important are dairy and poultry products, nursery and greenhouse produce, vegetables, and fruit.

Tourism has become an important factor in the economy of the state because of its numerous recreational areas and historical landmarks. Cape Cod has summer theaters, water sports, and an artists' colony at Provincetown. Tanglewood, in the Berkshires, features the summer concerts of the Boston Symphony.

Among the many other points of interest are Old Sturbridge Village in Sturbridge in central Massachusetts, Minute Man National Historical Park between Lexington and Concord, and, in Boston: Old North Church, Old State House, Faneuil Hall, the USS *Constitution,* and the John F. Kennedy Library and Museum.

Famous natives and residents: John Adams, former president; John Quincy Adams, former president; Samuel Adams, patriot; Horatio Alger, novelist; Susan B. Anthony, woman suffragist; Clara Barton, American Red Cross founder; Leonard Bernstein, conductor; George Bush, former president; William Cullen Bryan, poet and editor; Luther Burbank, horticulturalist; John Cheever, novelist; John Singleton Copley, painter; e.e. cummings, poet; Jacques d'Amboise, ballet dancer; Bette Davis, actress; Cecil B. DeMille, film director; Emily Dickinson, poet; Ralph Waldo Emerson, philosopher and poet; Geraldine Farrar, soprano, actress; Benjamin Franklin, statesman and scientist; Buckminster Fuller, architect and educator; Robert Goddard, father of modern rocketry; John Hancock, statesman; Nathaniel Hawthorne, novelist; Oliver Wendell Holmes, jurist; Winslow Homer, painter; Elias Howe, inventor; John F. Kennedy, former president; Amy Lowell, poet; James Russell Lowell, poet; Robert Lowell, poet; Horace Mann, educator; Cotton Mather, clergyman; Samuel F. B. Morse, painter and inventor; Edgar Allan Poe, writer; Paul Revere, silversmith and Revolutionary War figure; Dr. Seuss (Theodore Geisel), author and illustrator; David Souter, jurist; Lucy Stone, woman suffragist; Louis Henry Sullivan, architect; Henry David Thoreau, author; Barbara Walters, TV commentator; James McNeill Whistler, painter; Eli Whitney, inventor; John Greenleaf Whittier, poet.

Michigan

Capital: Lansing

Governor: John M. Engler, R (to Jan. 1999)

Lieut. Governor: Connie Binsfeld, R (to Jan. 1999)

Senators: Spencer Abraham, R (to Jan. 2001); Carl Levin, D (to Jan. 2003)

Secy. of State: Candace S. Miller, R (to Jan. 1999)

Atty. General: Frank J. Kelley, D (to Jan. 1999)

Organized as territory: Jan. 11, 1805

Entered Union (rank): Jan. 26, 1837 (26)

Present constitution adopted: April 1, 1963, (effective Jan. 1, 1964)

Motto: *Si quaeris peninsulam amoenam circumspice* (If you seek a pleasant peninsula, look around you)

State symbols: flower, Apple blossom (1897); **bird,** Robin (1931); **mammal,** White-tailed Deer (1997) **fishes,** Trout (1965), Brook trout (1988); **gem,** Isle Royal Greenstone (Chlorastrolite) (1972); **stone,** Petoskey Stone (1965); **tree,** White pine (1955); **soil,** Kalkaska Soil series (1990); **reptile,** Painted turtle (1996); **flag,** "Blue charged with the arms of the state" (1911)

Nickname: Wolverine State

Origin of name: From Indian word "Michigana" meaning "great or large lake"

10 largest cities (1996 est.): Detroit, 1,000,272; Grand Rapids, 188,242; Warren, 138,078; Flint, 134,881; Lansing, 125,736; Sterling Heights, 118,698; Ann Arbor, 108,758; Livonia, 105,099; Dearborn, 91,418; Westland, 90,798

Land area (rank): 58,110 sq mi.(22)

Geographic center: In Wexford Co., 5 mi. NNW of Cadillac

Number of counties: 83

Largest county (1995 pop. est.): Wayne, 2,055,500

State parks and recreation areas: 96 (265,000 ac.)

1997 resident population est.: 9,773,892

1990 resident census population (rank): 9,295,297 (8). **Male:** 4,512,781; **Female:** 4,787,516. **White:** 7,756,086 (83.4%); **Black:** 1,291,706 (13.9%); **American Indian:** 55,638 (0.6%); **Asian:** 104,983 (1.1%); **Other race:** 86,884 (0.9%); **Hispanic:** 201,596 (2.2%). **1990 percent population under 18:** 26.5; **65 and over:** 11.9; **median age:** 32.6.

Indian tribes were living in the Michigan region when the first European, Étienne Brulé of France, arrived in 1618. Other French explorers, including Jacques Marquette, Louis Joliet, and sieur de la Salle, followed, and the first permanent settlement was established in 1668 at Sault Ste. Marie. France was ousted from the territory by Great Britain in 1763, following the French and Indian War.

After the Revolutionary War, the U.S. acquired most of the region, which remained the scene of constant conflict between the British and U.S. forces and their respective Indian allies through the War of 1812.

Bordering on four of the five Great Lakes, Michigan is divided into Upper and Lower peninsulas by the Straits of Mackinac, which link lakes Michigan and Huron. The two parts of the state are connected by the

Mackinac Bridge, one of the world's longest suspension bridges. To the north, connecting lakes Superior and Huron, are the busy Sault Ste. Marie Canals.

While Michigan ranks first among the states in production of motor vehicles and parts, it is also a leader in many other manufacturing and processing lines, including prepared cereals, machine tools, airplane parts, refrigerators, hardware, steel springs, and furniture.

The state produces important amounts of iron, copper, iodine, gypsum, bromine, salt, lime, gravel, and cement. Michigan's farms grow apples, cherries, beans, pears, grapes, potatoes, and sugar beets. Michigan's forests contribute significantly to the state's economy. Forest-based industries (wood product industry, tourism, and recreation) support nearly 180,000 jobs and contribute over $18 billion to the state economy. With 10,083 inland lakes and 3,288 miles of Great Lakes shoreline, Michigan is a prime area for both commercial and sport fishing.

Points of interest are the automobile plants in Dearborn, Detroit, Flint, Lansing, and Pontiac; Mackinac Island; Pictured Rocks and Sleeping Bear Dunes National Lakeshores; Greenfield Village in Dearborn; and the many summer resorts along both the inland and Great Lakes.

Famous natives and residents: Nelson Algren, novelist; Ralph J. Bunche, statesman, Ellen Burstyn, actress; Bruce Catton, historian; Roger Chaffee, astronaut; Francis Ford Coppola, film director; Thomas E. Dewey, politician; Edna Ferber, novelist; Henry Ford, industrialist; Ali Haji-Sheikh, football player; Julie Harris, actress; Earvin "Magic" Johnson, basketball player; Ring Lardner, writer; Charles A. Lindbergh, aviator; Madonna, singer; Dick Martin, comedian; Terry McMillan, author; John N. Mitchell, former attorney general; Ted Nugent, singer; Gilda Radner, comedienne; Della Reese, singer; Jason Robards, Sr., actor; Diana Ross, singer; Steven Seagal, actor; Bob Seger, singer; Tom Selleck, actor; Thomas Schippers, conductor; Potter Stewart, jurist; Lily Tomlin, actress; Danny Thomas, entertainer; Margaret Whiting, singer; Robin Williams, comedian and actor; Stevie Wonder, singer.

Minnesota

Capital: St. Paul
Governor: Arne Carlson, R (to Jan. 1999)
Lieut. Governor: Joanne Benson, R (to Jan. 1999)
Senators: Rod Grams, R (to Jan. 2001); Paul D. Wellstone, D (to Jan. 2003)
Secy. of State: Joan Anderson Growe, D (to Jan. 1999)
State Auditor: Judi Dutcher, R (to Jan. 1999)
Atty. General: Hubert H. Humphrey III, D (to Jan. 1999)
State Treasurer: Michael McGrath, D (to Jan. 1999)
Organized as territory: March 3, 1849
Entered Union (rank): May 11, 1858 (32)
Present constitution adopted: 1858
Motto: L'Étoile du Nord (The North Star)
State symbols: flower, Showy lady slipper (1902); **tree,** Red (or Norway) pine (1953); **bird,** Common loon (also called Great Northern Diver) (1961); **song,** "Hail Minnesota" (1945); **fish,** Walleye (1965); **mushroom,** Morel (1984)
Nicknames: North Star State; Gopher State; Land of 10,000 Lakes
Origin of name: From a Dakota Indian word meaning "sky-tinted water"
10 largest cities (1996 est.): Minneapolis, 358,785; St. Paul, 259,606; Bloomington, 86,664; Duluth, 83,699; Rochester, 75,638; Coon Rapids, 62,790; Brooklyn Park, 61,335; Plymouth, 60,103; Eagan, 57,294; Burnsville, 57,087
Land area (rank): 79,617 sq mi. (206,207 sq km) (14)
Geographic center: In Crow Wing Co., 10 mi. SW of Brainerd
Number of counties: 87
Largest county (1995 pop. est.): Hennepin, 1,053,467
State forests: 56 (3,200,000+ ac.)
State parks: 66 (226,000 ac.)
1997 resident population est.: 4,685,549
1990 resident census population (rank): 4,375,099 (20). **Male:** 2,145,183; **Female:** 2,229,916. **White:** 4,130,395 (94.4%); **Black:** 94,944 (2.2%); **American Indian:** 49,909 (1.1%); **Asian:** 77,886 (1.8%); **Other race:** 21,965 (0.5%); **Hispanic:** 53,884 (1.2%). **1990 percent population under 18:** 26.7; **65 and over:** 12.5; **median age:** 32.5.

Following the visits of several French explorers, fur traders, and missionaries, including Jacques Marquette, Louis Joliet, and sieur de la Salle, the region was claimed for Louis XIV by Daniel Greysolon, sieur Duluth, in 1679.

The U.S. acquired eastern Minnesota from Great Britain after the Revolutionary War and 20 years later bought the western part from France in the Louisiana Purchase of 1803. Much of the region was explored by U.S. Army Lt. Zebulon M. Pike before the northern strip of Minnesota bordering Canada was ceded by Britain in 1818.

The state is rich in natural resources. A few square miles of land in the north in the Mesabi, Cuyuna, and Vermillion ranges produce more than 75% of the nation's iron ore. The state's farms rank high in yields of corn, wheat, rye, alfalfa, and sugar beets. Other leading farm products include butter, eggs, milk, potatoes, green peas, barley, soybeans, oats, and livestock.

Minnesota's factory production includes nonelectrical machinery, fabricated metals, flour-mill products, plastics, electronic computers, scientific instruments, and processed foods. It is also one of the nation's leaders in the printing and paper-products industries.

Minneapolis is the trade center of the Midwest; and the headquarters of the world's largest supercomputer and grain distributor. St. Paul is the nation's biggest publisher of calendars and law books. These "twin cities" are the nation's third-largest trucking center. Duluth has the nation's largest inland harbor and now handles a significant amount of foreign trade. Rochester is the home of the Mayo Clinic, an internationally famous medical center.

Today, tourism is a major revenue producer in Minnesota, with arts, fishing, hunting, water sports, and winter sports bringing in millions of visitors each year.

Among the most popular attractions are the St. Paul Winter Carnival; the Tyrone Guthrie Theatre, the Institute of Arts, Walker Art Center, and Minnehaha Park, in Minneapolis; Boundary Waters Canoe Area; Voyageurs National Park; North Shore Drive; the Minnesota Zoological Gardens; and the state's more than 10,000 lakes.

Famous natives and residents: LaVerne, Maxene, and Patti Andrews, singers; Warren E. Burger, jurist; William E. Colby, former director of the CIA; William Demarest, actor; William O. Douglas, jurist; Bob Dylan, singer and composer; F. Scott Fitzgerald, novelist; Judy Garland, singer and actress; J. Paul Getty, oil executive; Cass Gilbert, architect; Duane Hanson, sculptor; Hubert H. Humphrey, senator and vice president; Jessica Lange, actress; Sinclair Lewis, novelist; Cornell MacNeil, baritone;

Roger Maris, baseball player; E. G. Marshall, actor; Charles H. Mayo, surgeon; William J. Mayo, surgeon; Eugene J. McCarthy, former senator; Kate Millett, feminist; Gen. Lauris Norstad, former commander of NATO forces; Westbrook Pegler, columnist; John Sargent Pillsbury, businessman; Marion Ross, actress; Jane Russell, actress; Harrison E. Salisbury, journalist; Charles M. Schulz, cartoonist; Max Shulman, novelist; Maurice H. Stans, former secretary of commerce; Harold E. Stassen, former government official; Michael Todd, producer; Frederick Weyerhaeuser, businessman; Gig Young, actor.

Mississippi

Capital: Jackson
Governor: Kirk Fordice, R (to Jan. 2000)
Lieut. Governor: Ronnie Musgrove, D (to Jan. 2000)
Senators: Thad Cochran, R (to Jan. 2003); Trent Lott, R (to Jan. 2001)
Secy. of State: Eric Clark, D (to Jan. 2000)
Treasurer: Marshall Bennett, D (to Jan. 2000)
Auditor: Phil Bryant, R (to Jan. 2000)
Atty. General: Mike Moore, D (to Jan. 2000)
Agriculture and Commerce Commissioner: Lester Spell, D (to Jan. 2000)
Insurance Commissioner: George Dale, D (to Jan. 2000)
Organized as territory: April 7, 1798
Entered Union (rank): Dec. 10, 1817 (20)
Present constitution adopted: 1890
Motto: *Virtute et armis* (By valor and arms)
State symbols: flower, Flower or bloom of the magnolia or evergreen magnolia (1952); **wildflower,** Coreopsis (1991); **tree,** Magnolia (1938); **bird,** Mockingbird (1944); **song,** "Go, Mississippi" (1962); **stone,** Petrified wood (1976); **fish,** Largemouth or black bass (1974); **insect,** Honeybee (1980); **shell,** Oyster shell (1974); **water mammal,** Bottlenosed dolphin or porpoise (1974); **fossil,** Prehistoric whale (1981); **land mammal,** White-tailed deer (1974), Red fox (1997); **waterfowl,** Wood duck (1974); **beverage,** Milk (1984); **butterfly,** Spicebush Swallowtail (1991); **dance,** Square dance (1995)
Nickname: Magnolia State
Origin of name: From an Indian word meaning "Father of Waters"
10 largest cities (1996 est.): Jackson, 192,923; Gulfport, 64,829; Biloxi, 48,414; Hattiesburg, 47,803; Greenville, 42,933; Meridian, 40,835; Tupelo, 35,194; Vicksburg, 27,056; Pascagoula, 27,026; Columbus, 22,724
Land area (rank): 46,914 sq mi. (121,506 sq km) (31)
Geographic center: In Leake Co., 9 mi. WNW of Carthage
Number of counties: 82
Largest county (1995 pop. est.): Hinds, 251,031
State forests: 1 (1,760 ac.)
State parks: 27 (16,763 ac.)
1997 resident population est.: 2,730,501
1990 resident census population (rank): 2,573,216 (31). **Male:** 1,230,617; **Female:** 1,342,599. **White:** 1,633,461 (63.5%); **Black:** 915,057 (35.6%); **American Indian:** 8,525 (0.3%); **Asian:** 13,016 (0.5%); **Other race:** 3,157 (0.1%); **Hispanic:** 15,931 (0.6%). **1990 percent population under 18:** 29.0; **65 and over:** 12.5; **median age:** 31.2.

First explored for Spain by Hernando De Soto, who discovered the Mississippi River in 1540, the region was later claimed by France. In 1699, a French group under Sieur d'Iberville established the first permanent settlement near present-day Ocean Springs.

Great Britain took over the area in 1763 after the French and Indian War, ceding it to the U.S. in 1783 after the Revolution. Spain did not relinquish its claims until 1798, and in 1810 the U.S. annexed West Florida from Spain, including what is now southern Mississippi.

For a little more than one hundred years, from shortly after the state's founding through the Great Depression, cotton was the undisputed king of Mississippi's largely agrarian economy. Over the last half-century, however, Mississippi has progressively deepened its commitment to diversification by balancing agricultural output with increased industrial activity.

Today, agriculture continues as a major segment of the state's economy. While the most acreage is devoted to soybeans, cotton is the largest cash crop—Mississippi remains third in the nation in cotton production. The state's farmlands yield important harvests of corn, peanuts, pecans, rice, sugar cane, sweet potatoes, soybeans, and food grains as well as poultry, eggs, meat animals, dairy products, feed crops, and horticultural crops. Mississippi remains the world's leading producer of pond-raised catfish. Mississippi boasts 100,000 of the 140,000 total acres nationwide of catfish ponds.

The state abounds in historical landmarks and is the home of the Vicksburg National Military Park. Other National Park Service areas are Brices Cross Roads National Battlefield Site, Tupelo National Battlefield, and part of Natchez Trace National Parkway. Pre-Civil War mansions are the special pride of Natchez, Oxford, Columbus, Vicksburg, and Jackson.

Famous natives and residents: Red Barber, sportscaster; Jimmy Buffett, singer and songwriter; Craig Claiborne, columnist and restaurant critic; Bo Diddley, guitarist; Charles Evers, civil rights leader; Medgar Evers, civil rights leader; William Faulkner, novelist; Shelby Foote, historian; Richard Ford, novelist; John Grisham, novelist; Barry Hannah, novelist; Beth Henley, playwright and actress; Jim Henson, puppeteer; James Earl Jones, actor; B. B. King, guitarist; Mary Ann Mobley, actress; Willie Morris, writer; Elvis Presley, singer and actor; Leontyne Price, soprano; William Raspberry, columnist; Jerry Rice, football player; Jimmie Rodgers, singer; Sela Ward, actress; Muddy Waters, singer and guitarist; Eudora Welty, novelist; Tennessee Williams, playwright; Oprah Winfrey, talk-show host and actress; Richard Wright, novelist; Tammy Wynette, country music star; Zig Ziglar, speaker and author.

Missouri

Capital: Jefferson City
Governor: Mel Carnahan, D (to Jan. 2001)
Lieut. Governor: Roger Wilson, D (to Jan. 2001)
Senators: John Ashcroft, R (to Jan. 2001); Christopher S. Bond, R (to Jan. 1999)
Secy. of State: Rebecca ("Bekki") McDowell Cook, D (to Jan. 2001)
Auditor: Margaret Kelly, R (to Jan. 1999)
Treasurer: Bob Holden, D (to Jan. 2001)
Atty. General: Jeremiah "Jay" W. Nixon, D (to Jan. 2001)
Organized as territory: June 4, 1812
Entered Union (rank): Aug. 10, 1821 (24)
Present constitution adopted: 1945
Motto: *Salus populi suprema lex esto* (The welfare of the people shall be the supreme law)
State symbols: flower, Hawthorn (1923); **bird,** Bluebird (1927); **fish,** paddlefish (1997), channel catfish (1997); **song,** "Missouri Waltz" (1949); **fossil,** Crinoid (1989); **musical instrument,** Fiddle (1987); **rock,** Mozarkite (1967); **mineral,** Galena (1967); **insect,** Honeybee (1985); **tree,** Flowering dogwood (1955); **tree nut,** Eastern black walnut (1990); **animal,** Mule (1995); **dance,** Square dance (1995); **Missouri Day,** third Wednesday in October (1915)
Nickname: Show-me State

Origin of name: Named after the Missouri Indian tribe. "Missouri" means "town of the large canoes."
10 largest cities (1996 est.): Kansas City, 441,259; St. Louis, 351,565; Springfield, 143,407; Independence, 110,303; Columbia, 76,756; St. Joseph, 71,711; Lee's Summit, 61,861; St. Charles, 56,525; Florissant, 50,491; St. Peter's, 48,493
Land area (rank): 68,898 sq mi. (178,446 sq km) (18)
Geographic center: In Miller Co., 20 mi. SW of Jefferson City
Number of counties: 114, plus 1 independent city
Largest county (1996 pop. est.): St. Louis, 1,003,807
Conservation areas[1]: leased, 287 (194,381 ac.); owned, 785 (761,863 ac.)
Conservation accesses: leased, 72; owned, 251
State parks and historic sites: 79 (134,496 ac.)
1997 resident population est.: 5,402,058
1990 resident census population (rank): 5,117,073 (15). **Male:** 2,464,315; **Female:** 2,652,758. **White:** 4,486,228 (87.7%); **Black:** 548,208 (10.7%); **American Indian:** 19,835 (0.4%); **Asian:** 41,277 (0.8%); **Other race:** 21,525 (0.4%); **Hispanic:** 61,702 (1.2%). **1990 percent population under 18:** 25.7; **65 and over:** 14.0; **median age:** 33.5.

1. Includes wildlife areas, natural history areas, state forests, and tower sites.

Hernando De Soto visited the Missouri area in 1541. France's claim to the entire region was based on sieur de la Salle's travels in 1682. French fur traders established Ste. Genevieve in 1735 and St. Louis was first settled in 1764.

The U.S. gained Missouri from France as part of the Louisiana Purchase in 1803, and the territory was admitted as a state following the Missouri Compromise of 1820. Throughout the pre–Civil War period and during the war, Missourians were sharply divided in their opinions about slavery and in their allegiances, supplying both Union and Confederate forces with troops. However, the state itself remained in the Union.

Historically, Missouri played a leading role as a gateway to the West, St. Joseph being the eastern starting point of the Pony Express, while the much-traveled Santa Fe and Oregon trails began in Independence. Now a popular vacationland, Missouri has 11 major lakes and numerous fishing streams, springs, and caves. Bagnell Dam, across the Osage River in the Ozarks, completed in 1931, created one of the largest man-made lakes in the world, covering 65,000 acres.

Missouri's economy relies on a diversified industrial base. Service industries provide more income and jobs than any other segment, and include a growing tourism and travel sector. Wholesale and retail trade, manufacturing, and agriculture also play significant roles in the state's economy. Missouri is a leading producer of transportation equipment (including automobile manufacturing and auto parts), beer and beverages, and defense and aerospace technology. Food processing is the state's fastest-growing industry, well suited to the state's blend of agricultural, natural, energy, and transportation resources. Missouri mines produce 90% of the nation's principal (non-recycled) lead supply.

Missouri's largest corporate employers include McDonnell-Douglas/Boeing, Wal-Mart, Washington University, Schnuck Markets, Barnes Hospital, Chrysler Corporation, Ford Motor Company, May Department Stores, Trans World Airlines, and Southwestern Bell. The state's top agricultural products include grain, sorghum, hay, corn, soybeans, wheat, oats, barley, tobacco, and rice. A well-established grape and wine program brings together aspects of agriculture, manufacturing, and tourism to support a vibrant vintner industry.

Tourism draws hundreds of thousands of visitors to a number of Missouri points of interest: the country-music shows of Branson; Bass Pro Shops national headquarters (Springfield); the Gateway Arch at the Jefferson National Expansion (St. Loius); Mark Twain's boyhood home and cave (Hannibal); the Harry S Truman home and library (Independence); the scenic beauty of the Ozark National Scenic Riverways; and the Pony Express and Jesse James museums (St. Joseph). The state's different lakes regions also attract fishermen and sun-seekers from throughout the Midwest.

Famous natives and residents: Robert Altman, film director; Burt Bacharach, songwriter; Josephine Baker, singer and dancer; Wallace Beery, actor; Robert Russell Bennett, composer; Yogi Berra, baseball player; Thomas Hart Benton, painter; Bill Bradley, basketball player and former N.J. senator; Omar N. Bradley, five-star general; Grace Bumbry, soprano; William Burroughs, writer; Sarah Caldwell, opera director and conductor; Martha Jane Canary (Calamity Jane), frontierswoman; George Washington Carver, scientist; Walter Cronkite, TV newscaster; Robert Cummings, actor; Jane Darwell, actress; Walt Disney, artist; T. S. Eliot, poet; Redd Foxx, actor and comedian; Betty Grable, actress; Dick Gregory, comic and activist; Jean Harlow, actress; George Hearn, actor; Edwin Hubble, astronomer; Langston Hughes, poet; John Huston, film director; Jesse James, outlaw; Scott Joplin, composer; Marianne Moore, poet; Geraldine Page, actress; James C. Penney, merchant; John Joseph Pershing, general; Vincent Price, actor; Joseph Pulitzer, journalist; Ginger Rogers, dancer and actress; Sacajawea, Indian guide for Lewis and Clark; Casey Stengel, baseball player; Gladys Swarthout, soprano; Sara Teasdale, poet; Virgil Thomson, composer; Harry S Truman, former president; Mark Twain, author; Dick Van Dyke, actor; Ruth Warrick, actress; Dennis Weaver, actor; Mary Wickes, actress; Laura Ingalls Wilder, author; Roy Wilkins, civil rights leader.

Montana

Capital: Helena
Governor: Marc Racicot, R (to Jan. 2001)
Lieut. Governor: Judy Martz, R (to Jan. 2001)
Senators: Max Baucus, D (to Jan. 2003); Conrad R. Burns, R (to Jan. 2001)
Secy. of State: Mike Cooney, D (to Jan. 2001)
Auditor: Mark O'Keefe, D (to Jan. 2001)
Atty. General: Joe Mazurek, D (to Jan. 2001)
Organized as territory: May 26, 1864
Entered Union (rank): Nov. 8, 1889 (41)
Present constitution adopted: 1972
Motto: *Oro y plata* (Gold and silver)
State symbols: flower, Bitterroot (1895); **tree,** Ponderosa pine (1949); **stones,** Sapphire and agate (1969); **bird,** Western meadowlark (1981); **song,** "Montana" (1945)
Nickname: Treasure State
Origin of name: Chosen from Latin dictionary by J. M. Ashley. It is a Latinized Spanish word meaning "mountainous."
10 largest cities (1996 est.): Billings, 91,195; Great Falls, 57,758; Missoula, 51,204; Butte-Silver Bow[1], 34,051; Bozeman, 28,522; Helena, 27,982; Kalispell, 15,678; Havre, 10,232; Anaconda–Deer Lodge County, 10,093; Miles City, 8,882
Land area (rank): 145,556 sq mi. (376,991 sq km) (4)
Geographic center: In Fergus Co., 12 mi. W of Lewistown
Number of counties: 56, plus small part of Yellowstone National Park

Largest county (1995 pop. est.): Yellowstone, 124,655
State forests: 7 (214,000 ac.)
State parks and recreation areas: 110 (18,273 ac.)
1997 resident population est.: 878,810
1990 resident census population (rank): 799,065 (44). **Male:** 395,769; **Female:** 403,296. **White:** 741,111 (92.7%); **Black:** 2,381 (0.3%); **American Indian:** 47,679 (6.0%); **Asian:** 4,259 (0.5%); **Other race:** 3,635 (0.5%); **Hispanic:** 12,174 (1.5%). **1990 percent population under 18:** 27.8; **65 and over:** 13.3; **median age:** 33.8.

1. Consolidated City.

First explored for France by François and Louis-Joseph Verendrye in the early 1740s, much of the region was acquired by the U.S. from France as part of the Louisiana Purchase in 1803. Before western Montana was obtained from Great Britain in the Oregon Treaty of 1846, American trading posts and forts had been established in the territory.

The major Indian Wars (1867–1877) included the famous 1876 Battle of the Little Big Horn, better known as "Custer's Last Stand," in which Cheyennes and Sioux defeated George A. Custer and more than 200 of his men in southeastern Montana.

Much of Montana's early history was concerned with mining with copper, lead, zinc, silver, coal, and oil as principal products. Butte is the center of the area that once supplied half of the U.S. copper.

Fields of grain cover much of Montana's plains. It ranks high among the states in wheat and barley, with rye, oats, flaxseed, sugar beets, and potatoes as other important crops. Sheep and cattle raising make significant contributions to the economy.

Tourist attractions include hunting, fishing, skiing, and dude ranching. Glacier National Park, on the Continental Divide, is a scenic and vacation wonderland with 60 glaciers, 200 lakes, and many streams with good trout fishing.

Other major points of interest include the Custer Battlefield National Monument, Virginia City, Yellowstone National Park, Museum of the Plains Indians at Browning, and the Fort Union Trading Post and Grant-Kohr's Ranch National Historic Sites.

Famous natives and residents: Dorothy Baker, author; Dirk Benedict, actor; W. A. (Tony) Boyle, labor union official; Gary Cooper, actor; John Cowan, prospector and founder of Last Chance Gulch (now Helena); Alfred Bertram Guthrie, Pulitzer Prize–winning author; Chet Huntley, TV newscaster; Will James, writer and artist; Dorothy Johnson, author; Evel Knievel, daredevil motorcyclist; Myrna Loy, actress; David Lynch, filmmaker; Mike Mansfield, former senator; George Montgomery, actor; Jeannette Rankin, first woman elected to Congress; Martha Raye, actress; Charles M. Russell, Old West painter; Michael Smuin, choreographer; Lester C. Thurow, economist and educator.

Nebraska

Capital: Lincoln
Governor: Ben Nelson, D (to Jan. 1999)
Lieut. Governor: Kim Robak, D (to Jan. 1999)
Senators: Chuck Hagel, R (to Jan. 2003); Robert J. Kerrey, D (to Jan. 2001)
Secy. of State: Scott Moore, R (to Jan. 1999)
Atty. General: Don Stenberg, R (to Jan. 1999)
Auditor: John Breslow, R (to Jan. 1999)
Treasurer: David Heineman, R (to Jan. 1999)
Organized as territory: May 30, 1854
Entered Union (rank): March 1, 1867 (37)
Present constitution adopted: Oct. 12, 1875 (extensively amended 1919–20)
Motto: Equality before the law
State symbols: flower, Goldenrod (1895); **tree,** Cottonwood (1972); **bird,** Western meadowlark (1929); **insect,** Honeybee (1975); **gemstone,** Blue agate (1967); **rock,** Prairie agate (1967); **fossil,** Mammoth (1967); **song,** "Beautiful Nebraska" (1967); **soil,** Typic Arguistolls, Holdrege Series (1979); **mammal,** Whitetail deer (1981); **grass,** Little Bluestem (1969)
Nicknames: Cornhusker State (1945); Beef State
Origin of name: From an Oto Indian word meaning "flat water"
10 largest cities (1996 est.): Omaha, 364,253; Lincoln, 209,192; Bellevue, 42,807; Grand Island, 41,177; Kearney, 27,314; Fremont, 24,223; Norfolk, 23,423; North Platte, 23,369; Hastings, 22,008; Columbus, 20,848
Land area (rank): 76,644 sq mi. (198,508 sq km) (15)
Geographic center: In Custer Co., 10 mi. NW of Broken Bow
Number of counties: 93
Largest county (1995 pop. est.): Douglas, 434,147
State parks: 86 areas, historical and recreational; 8 major areas
1997 resident population est.: 1,656,870
1990 resident census population (rank): 1,578,417 (36). **Male:** 769,439; **Female:** 808,946. **White:** 1,480,558 (93.8%); **Black:** 57,404 (3.6%); **American Indian:** 12,410 (0.8%); **Asian:** 12,422 (0.8%); **Other race:** 15,591 (1.0%); **Hispanic:** 36,969 (2.3%). **1990 percent population under 18:** 27.2; **65 and over:** 14.1; **median age:** 33.0.

French fur traders first visited Nebraska in the late 1600s. Part of the Louisiana Purchase in 1803, Nebraska was explored by Lewis and Clark in 1804–1806.

Robert Stuart pioneered the Oregon Trail across Nebraska in 1812–1813 and the first permanent white settlement was established at Bellevue in 1823. Western Nebraska was acquired by treaty following the Mexican War in 1848. The Union Pacific began its transcontinental railroad at Omaha in 1865. In 1937, Nebraska became the only state in the Union to have a unicameral (one-house) legislature. Members are elected to it without party designation.

Nebraska is a leading grain-producer with bumper crops of grain sorghum, corn, and wheat. More varieties of grass, valuable for forage, grow in this state than in any other in the nation. The state's sizable cattle and hog industries make Dakota City and Lexington among the nation's largest meat-packing centers.

Manufacturing has become diversified in Nebraska, strengthening the state's economic base. Firms making electronic components, auto accessories, pharmaceuticals, and mobile homes have joined such older industries as clothing, farm machinery, chemicals, and transportation equipment. Oil was discovered in 1939 and natural gas in 1949.

Among the principal attractions are Agate Fossil Beds, Homestead, and Scotts Bluff National Monuments; Chimney Rock National Historic Site; a recreated pioneer village at Minden; SAC Museum near Ashland; the Stuhr Museum of the Prairie Pioneer with 57 original 19th-century buildings near Grand Island; the Sheldon Memorial Art Gallery and the Lied Center for the Performing Arts located on the University of Nebraska campus in Lincoln; the State Capitol in Lincoln; the Joslyn Art Museum in Omaha; the Henry Doorly Zoo in Omaha; and the University of Nebraska State Museum in Lincoln.

Famous natives and residents: Grace Abbott, social worker; Bess Streeter Aldrich, author; Grover Cleveland Alexander, Hall of Fame pitcher; Fred Astaire, dancer and actor; Max Baer, boxer; Bil Baird, puppeteer; George Beadle, geneticist; Marlon Brando, actor; William Jennings Bryan, three-time U.S. presidential candidate; Warren Buffett, investor; Johnny Carson, TV host; Willa Cather, author; Dick Cavett, TV entertainer; Richard B. Cheney, former secretary of Defense; Montgomery Clift, actor; James Coburn, actor; William "Buffalo Bill" Cody, showman of the Old West; Sandy Dennis, actress; Mignon Eberhart, author; Harold "Doc" Edgerton, inventor; Ruth Etting, singer and actress; Fr. Edward J. Flanagan, founder of Boys Town; Henry Fonda, actor; Gerald Ford, former president; Bob Gibson, baseball player; Hoot Gibson, actor; Howard Hanson, conductor; Leland Hayward, producer; Robert Henri, painter; David Janssen, actor; Susette La Flesche, Omaha Indian artist; Francis La Flesche, ethnologist; Melvin Laird, politician and former secretary of defense; Frank W. Leahy, football coach; Harold Lloyd, actor; Malcolm X, civil rights advocate; Irish McCalla, actress; Dorothy McGuire, actress; Julius Sterling Morton, politician and journalist; John G. Neihardt, epic poet; Nick Nolte, actor; George W. Norris, U.S. Senator; John J. Pershing, Army leader and founder of Pershing Rifles; Nathan Pound, dean of Harvard Law School and botanist; Red Cloud, Indian rights advocate; Mari Sandoz, author; Standing Bear, Indian rights advocate; Inga Swenson, actress; Robert Taylor, actor; Paul Williams, singer, composer, and actor; Julie Wilson, singer and actress; Darryl F. Zanuck, film producer.

Nevada

Capital: Carson City
Governor: Robert J. Miller, D (to Jan. 1999)
Lieut. Governor: Lonnie L. Hammargren, R (to Jan. 1999)
Senators: Richard H. Bryan, D (to Jan. 2001); Harry Reid, D (to Jan. 1999)
Secy. of State: Dean Heller, R (to Jan. 1999)
Treasurer: Bob Seale, R (to Jan. 1999)
Controller: Darrel R. Daines, R (to Jan. 1999)
Atty. General: Frankie Sue Del Papa, D (to Jan. 1999)
Organized as territory: March 2, 1861
Entered Union (rank): Oct. 31, 1864 (36)
Present constitution adopted: 1864
Motto: All for Our Country
State symbols: flower, Sagebrush (1959); **trees,** Single-leaf pinon (1953) and Bristlecone pine (1987); **bird,** Mountain bluebird (1967); **animal,** Desert bighorn sheep (1973); **colors,** Silver and blue (1983); **song,** "Home Means Nevada" (1933); **rock,** Sandstone (1987); **precious gemstone,** Virgin Valley Black Fire Opal (1987); **semiprecious gemstone,** Nevada Turquoise (1987); **grass,** Indian Ricegrass (1977); **metal,** Silver (1977); **fossil,** Ichthyosaur (1977); **fish,** Lahontan Cutthroat Trout (1981); **reptile,** Desert tortoise (1989); **state artifact,** Tule duck decoy (1995)
Nicknames: Sagebrush State; Silver State; Battle Born State
Origin of name: Spanish: "snowcapped"
10 largest cities (1996 est.): Las Vegas, 376,906; Reno, 155,499; Henderson, 122,339; North Las Vegas, 78,659; Sparks, 59,496; Carson City, 47,237; Elko, 19,371; Boulder City, 14,249; Winnemucca, 7,668; Fallon, 7,654
Land area (rank): 109,806 sq mi. (284,397 sq km) (7)
Geographic center: In Lander Co., 26 mi. SE of Austin
Number of counties: 16, plus 1 independent city
Largest county (1995 pop. est.): Clark, 992,593
State parks: 20 (150,000 ac., including leased lands)
1997 resident population est.: 1,676,809
1990 resident census population (rank): 1,201,833 (39). **Male:** 611,880; **Female:** 589,953. **White:** 1,012,695 (84.3%); **Black:** 78,771 (6.6%); **American Indian:** 19,637 (1.6%); **Asian:** 38,127 (3.2%); **Other race:** 52,603 (4.4%); **Hispanic:** 124,419 (10.4%). **1990 percent population under 18:** 24.7; **65 and over:** 10.6; **median age:** 33.3.

Trappers and traders, including Jedediah Smith, and Peter Skene Ogden, entered the Nevada area in the 1820s. In 1843–1845, John C. Fremont and Kit Carson explored the Great Basin and Sierra Nevada.

In 1848 following the Mexican War, the U.S. obtained the region and the first permanent settlement was a Mormon trading post near present-day Genoa.

The driest state in the nation, with an average annual rainfall of only about 7 inches, much of Nevada is uninhabited, sagebrush-covered desert. The wettest part of state receives about 40 inches of precipitation per year, while the driest spot has less than four inches per year.

Nevada was made famous by the discovery of the fabulous Comstock Lode in 1859 and its mines have produced large quantities of gold, silver, copper, lead, zinc, mercury, barite, and tungsten. Oil was discovered in 1954. Gold now far exceeds all other minerals in value of production.

In 1931, the state created two industries, divorce and gambling. For many years, Reno and Las Vegas were the "divorce capitals of the nation." More liberal divorce laws in many states have ended this distinction, but Nevada is the gambling and entertainment capital of the U.S. State gambling taxes account for 40.1% of general fund tax revenues. Although Nevada leads the nation in per capita gambling revenue, it ranks only fourth in total gambling revenue.

Near Las Vegas, on the Colorado River, stands Hoover Dam, which impounds the waters of Lake Mead, one of the world's largest artificial lakes.

The state's agricultural crop consists mainly of hay, alfalfa seed, barley, wheat, and potatoes.

Nevada manufactures gaming equipment; lawn and garden irrigation devices; titanium products; seismic and machinery monitoring devices; and specialty printing.

Major resort areas flourish in Lake Tahoe, Reno, and Las Vegas. Recreation areas include those at Pyramid Lake, Lake Tahoe, and Lake Mead and Lake Mohave, both in Lake Mead National Recreation Area. Among the other attractions are Hoover Dam, Virginia City, and Great Basin National Park (includes Lehman Caves).

Famous natives and residents: Eva Adams, former director of U.S. Mint; Andre Agassi, tennis player; Raymond T. Baker, former director of U.S. Mint; Helen Delich Bentley, government official and newspaperwoman; Robert Caples, painter; Walter Van Tilburg Clark, writer; Henry Comstock, prospector of "Comstock Lode" fame; Abby Dalton, actress; Michele Greene, actress; Sarah Winnemucca Hopkins, author and Paiute interpreter and peacemaker; Jack Kramer, tennis player; Paul Laxalt, politician; William Lear, aviation inventor; Robert C. Lynch, surgeon; John W. Mackay, benefactor, one of Big Four of Comstock Lode; Emma Nevada, opera singer; Thelma "Pat" Nixon, former First Lady; James W. Nye, territory governor and former senator; Lute Pease, cartoonist and Pulitzer Prize winner; Edna Purviance, actress; Patty Sheehan, golfer; Jack Wilson, Paiute Indian prophet; George Wingfield, mining millionaire.

New Hampshire

Capital: Concord
Governor: Jeanne Shaheen, D (to Jan. 1999)
Senators: Judd Gregg, R (to Jan. 1999); Bob Smith, R (to Jan. 2003)
Treasurer: Georgie A. Thomas, R (to Dec. 1998)
Secy. of State: William M. Gardner, D (to Dec. 1998)
Atty. General: Philip T. McLaughlin (to March 2001)
Entered Union (rank): June 21, 1788 (9)
Present constitution adopted: 1784
Motto: Live free or die
State symbols: flower, Purple lilac (1919); **tree,** White birch (1947); **animal,** White-tailed deer (1983); **insect,** Ladybug (1977); **saltwater fish,** Striped bass (1994); **freshwater fish,** Brook trout (1995); **amphibian,** Spotted newt (1985); **butterfly,** Karner Blue (1992); **bird,** Purple finch (1957); **songs,** "Old New Hampshire" (1949) and "New Hampshire, My New Hampshire" (1963)
Nickname: Granite State
Origin of name: From the English county of Hampshire
10 largest cities (1996 est.): Manchester, 100,967; Nashua, 81,094; Concord, 37,021; Rochester, 27,704; Dover, 25,766; Portsmouth, 25,034; Keene, 22,325; Laconia, 16,264; Claremont, 13,970; Lebanon, 12,571
Land area (rank): 8,969 sq mi. (23,231 sq km) (44)
Geographic center: In Belknap Co., 3 mi. E of Ashland
Number of counties: 10
Largest county (1995 pop. est.): Hillsborough, 349,572
State forests and parks: 210 (156,398 ac.)
1997 resident population est.: 1,172,709
1990 resident census population (rank): 1,109,252 (41). **Male:** 543,544; **Female:** 565,708. **White:** 1,087,433 (98.0%); **Black:** 7,198 (0.6%); **American Indian:** 2,134 (0.2%); **Asian:** 9,343 (0.8%); **Other race:** 3,144 (0.3%); **Hispanic:** 11,333 (1.0%). **1990 percent population under 18:** 25.1; **65 and over:** 11.3; **median age:** 32.8.

Under an English land grant, Capt. John Smith sent settlers to establish a fishing colony at the mouth of the Piscataqua River, near present-day Rye and Dover, in 1623. Capt. John Mason, who participated in the founding of Portsmouth in 1630, gave New Hampshire its name.

After a 38-year period of union with Massachusetts, New Hampshire was made a separate royal colony in 1679. As leaders in the revolutionary cause, New Hampshire delegates received the honor of being the first to vote for the Declaration of Independence on July 4, 1776. New Hampshire is the only state that ever played host at the formal conclusion of a foreign war when, in 1905, Portsmouth was the scene of the treaty ending the Russo-Japanese War.

Abundant water power early turned New Hampshire into an industrial state, and manufacturing is the principal source of income in the state. The most important industrial products are electrical and other machinery, textiles, pulp and paper products, and stone and clay products.

Dairy and poultry farming and growing fruit, truck vegetables, corn, potatoes, and hay are the major agricultural pursuits.

Tourism, because of New Hampshire's scenic and recreational resources, now brings over $3.5 billion into the state annually.

Vacation attractions include Lake Winnipesaukee, largest of 1,300 lakes and ponds; the 724,000-acre White Mountain National Forest; Daniel Webster's birthplace near Franklin; Strawbery Banke, restored building of the original settlement at Portsmouth; and the famous "Old Man of the Mountain" granite head profile, the state's official emblem, at Franconia.

Famous natives and residents: Sherman Adams, former governor and presidential advisor; Salmon P. Chase, jurist; Charles Anderson Dana, editor; Mary Baker Eddy, founder of the Christian Science Church; Dustin Farnum, actor; Thomas Green Fessenden, journalist and satirical poet; Daniel Chester French, sculptor; Horace Greeley, journalist and politician; Sarah J. Hale, editor; John Irving, writer; Benjamin F. Keith, theater entrepreneur; Jackson Hall Kelly, promoter of Oregon settlement; John Langdon, political leader; Sharon Christa McAuliffe, teacher and astronaut; Franklin Pierce, former president; Augustus Saint-Gaudens, sculptor; Alan Shepard, astronaut; Harlan F. Stone, jurist; Daniel Webster, statesman; Henry Wilson, politician and former vice president; Noah Worcester, clergyman and pacifist.

New Jersey

Capital: Trenton
Governor: Christine Todd Whitman, R (to Jan. 2002)
Senators: Robert Torricelli, D (to Jan. 2003); Frank R. Lautenberg, D (to Jan. 2001)
Secy. of State: Lonna R. Hooks, R (to Jan. 2002)
Treasurer: James A. DiEleuterio, Jr., R (to Jan. 2002)
Atty. General: Peter Verniero, R (to Jan. 2002)
Chief Justice: Deborah T. Poritz, R
Entered Union (rank): Dec. 18, 1787 (3)
Present constitution adopted: 1947
Motto: Liberty and prosperity
State symbols: flower, Purple violet (1913); **bird,** Eastern goldfinch (1935); **insect,** Honeybee (1974); **tree,** Red oak (1950); **animal,** Horse (1977); **colors,** Buff and blue (1965); **folk dance,** Square dance; **dinosaur,** Hadrosaurus Foulkii, **fish,** Brook trout; **shell,** Knobbed whelk
Nickname: Garden State
Origin of name: From the Channel Isle of Jersey
10 largest cities (1996 est.)[1]: Newark, 268,510; Jersey City, 229,039; Paterson, 150,270; Elizabeth, 110,149; Trenton, 85,437; Camden, 84,844; Clifton, 71,305; East Orange, 70,534; Bayonne, 60,499; Union City, 57,126
Land area (rank): 7,419 sq mi. (19,215 sq km) (46)
Geographic center: In Mercer Co., 5 mi. SE of Trenton
Number of counties: 21
Largest county (1995 pop. est.): Bergen, 845,189
State forests: 11
State parks: 35 (67,111 ac.)
1997 resident population est.: 8,052,849
1990 resident census population (rank): 7,730,188 (9). **Male:** 3,735,685; **Female:** 3,994,503. **White:** 6,130,465 (79.3%); **Black:** 1,036,825 (13.4%); **American Indian:** 14,970 (0.2%); **Asian:** 272,521 (3.5%); **Other race:** 275,407 (3.6%); **Hispanic:** 739,861 (9.6%). **1990 percent population under 18:** 23.3; **65 and over:** 13.4; **median age:** 34.5.

New Jersey's early colonial history was involved with that of New York (New Netherlands), of which it was a part. One year after the Dutch surrender to England in 1664, New Jersey was organized as an English colony under Gov. Philip Carteret.

In 1676 the colony was divided between Carteret and a company of English Quakers who had obtained the rights belonging to John, Lord Berkeley. New Jersey became a united, crown colony in 1702, administered by the royal governor of New York. Finally, in 1738, New Jersey was separated from New York under its own royal governor, Lewis Morris.

Because of its key location between New York City and Philadelphia, New Jersey saw much fighting during the American Revolution.

Today, New Jersey, an area of wide industrial diversification, is known as the Crossroads of the East. Products from over 15,000 factories can be delivered overnight to almost 60 million people, representing 12 states and the District of Columbia. The greatest single industry is chemicals; New Jersey is one of the foremost research centers in the world. Many large oil refineries are located in northern New Jersey. Other important manufactures are pharmaceuticals, instruments, machinery, electrical goods, and apparel.

Of the total land area, 36% is forested (1992). Farmland is declining. In 1995 there were about 9,000 farms, with over 850,000 acres under harvest. The state ranks high in the production of almost all garden vegetables. Tomatoes, asparagus, corn, and blueberries are important crops, and poultry and dairy farming make significant contributions to the state's economy.

Tourism is the second-largest industry in New Jersey. The state has numerous resort areas on 127 miles of Atlantic coastline. In 1977, New Jersey voters approved legislation allowing legalized casino gambling in Atlantic City. Points of interest include the Delaware Water Gap, the Edison National Historic Site in West Orange, Princeton University, Liberty State Park, Jersey City, and the N.J. State Aquarium in Camden (opened 1992).

Famous natives and residents: Bud Abbott, comedian; Charles Addams, cartoonist; Edwin Aldrin, astronaut; Count Basie, band leader; Joan Bennett, actress; Jon Bon Jovi, musician; William J. Brennan, jurist; Aaron Burr, political leader; James Fenimore Cooper, novelist; Lou Costello, comedian; Stephen Crane, writer; Helen Gahagan Douglas, former representative; Allen Ginsberg, poet; William Frederick Halsey, Jr., admiral; Alfred Joyce Kilmer, poet; Ernie Kovacs, comedian; Jerry Lewis, comedian and film director; Anne Morrow Lindbergh, author; Norman Mailer, novelist; Patricia McBride, ballerina; Richard Nixon, former president; Dorothy Parker, author; Joe Piscopo, comedian and actor; Paul Robeson, singer and actor; Philip Roth, novelist; Ruth St. Denis, dancer and choreographer; Antonin Scalia, jurist; H. Norman Schwarzkopf, general; Frank Sinatra, singer and actor; Bruce Springsteen, musician; Alfred Stieglitz, photographer; Albert Payson Terhune, journalist and novelist; Sarah Vaughan, singer; William Carlos Williams, physician and poet; Edmund Wilson, literary critic and author.

New Mexico

Capital: Santa Fe
Governor: Gary Johnson, R (to Jan. 1999)
Lieut. Governor: Walter Bradley, R (to Jan. 1999)
Senators: Jeff Bingaman, D (to Jan. 2001); Pete V. Domenici, R (to Jan. 2003)
Secy. of State: Stephanie Gonzales, D (to Jan. 1999)
Atty. General: Tom Udall, D (to Jan. 1999)
State Auditor: Robert E. Vigil, D (to Jan. 1999)
State Treasurer: Michael A. Montoya, D (to Jan. 1999)
Commissioner of Public Lands: Ray Powell, D (to Jan. 1999)
Organized as territory: Sept. 9, 1850
Entered Union (rank): Jan. 6, 1912 (47)
Present constitution adopted: 1911
Motto: *Crescit eundo* (It grows as it goes)
State symbols: flower, Yucca (1927); **tree,** Pinon (1949); **animal,** Black bear (1963); **bird,** Roadrunner (1949); **fish,** Cutthroat trout (1955); **vegetables,** Chili and frijol (1965); **gem,** Turquoise (1967); **colors,** Red and yellow of old Spain (1925); **song,** "O Fair New Mexico" (1917); **Spanish-language song,** "Asi Es Nuevo Méjico" (1971); **poem,** A Nuevo México (1991); **grass,** Blue gramma; **fossil,** Coelophysis; **cookie,** Bizcochito (1989); **insect,** Tarantula hawk wasp (1989)
Nicknames: Land of Enchantment; Sunshine State
Origin of name: From the country of Mexico
10 largest cities (1996 est.): Albuquerque, 419,681; Las Cruces, 74,779; Santa Fe, 66,522; Roswell, 47,559; Rio Rancho, 46,565; Farmington, 37,936; Clovis, 34,663; Alamogordo, 27,596; Hobbs, 27,986; Carlsbad, 26,535
Land area (rank): 121,365 sq mi. (314,334 sq km) (5)
Geographic center: In Torrance Co., 12 mi. SSW of Willard
Number of counties: 33
Largest county (1995 pop. est.): Bernalillo, 522,328
State-owned forested land: 933,000 ac.
State parks: 29 (105,012 ac.)
1997 resident population est.: 1,729,751
1990 resident census population (rank): 1,515,069 (37). **Male:** 745,253; **Female:** 769,816. **White:** 1,146,028 (75.6%); **Black:** 30,210 (2.0%); **American Indian:** 134,355 (8.9%); **Asian:** 14,124 (0.9%); **Other race:** 190,352 (12.6%); **Hispanic:** 579,224 (38.2%). **1990 percent population under 18:** 29.5; **65 and over:** 10.8; **median age:** 31.3.

Francisco Vásquez de Coronado, a Spanish explorer searching for gold, traveled the region that became New Mexico in 1540–42. In 1598 the first Spanish settlement was established on the Rio Grande River by Juan de Onate; in 1610 Santa Fe was founded and made the capital of New Mexico.

The U.S. acquired most of New Mexico in 1848, as a result of the Mexican War, and the remainder in the 1853 Gadsden Purchase. Union troops captured the territory from the Confederates during the Civil War. With the surrender of Geronimo in 1886, the Apache Wars and most of the Indian conflicts in the area were ended.

Since 1945, New Mexico has been a leader in energy research and development with extensive experiments conducted at Los Alamos Scientific Laboratory and Sandia Laboratories in the nuclear, solar, and geothermal areas.

Minerals are the state's richest natural resource and New Mexico is one of the U.S. leaders in output of uranium and potassium salts. Petroleum, natural gas, copper, gold, silver, zinc, lead, and molybdenum also contribute heavily to the state's income.

The principal manufacturing industries include food products, chemicals, transportation equipment, lumber, electrical machinery, and stone-clay-glass products. More than two-thirds of New Mexico's farm income comes from livestock products, especially sheep. Cotton, pecans, and sorghum are the most important field crops. Corn, peanuts, beans, onions, chilies, and lettuce are also grown.

Tourist attractions in New Mexico include the Carlsbad Caverns National Park, Inscription Rock at El Morro National Monument, the ruins at Fort Union, Billy the Kid mementos at Lincoln, the White Sands and Gila Cliff Dwellings National Monuments, and the Chaco Culture National Historical Park.

Famous natives and residents: Kathy Baker, actress; Judy Blume, author; Ernest L. Blumenshein, artist; William "Billy the Kid" Bonney, outlaw; Richard Bradford, author; Ralph Bunche, Nobel Peace Prize winner; Bruce Cabot, actor; Glen Campbell, singer; Kit Carson, army scout and trapper; Dennis Chavez, former senator; John Chisum, cattle king; Mangus Coloradas, Apache leader; Edward Condon,

physicist; Bill Daily, actor; John Denver, singer; Bo Diddley, blues guitarist; Patrick Garrett, lawman; Greer Garson, actress; Sid Gutierrez, astronaut; William Hanna, animator; Neil Patrick Harris, actor; Carl Hatch, former senator; Tony Hillerman, author; Conrad Hilton, hotel executive; Dennis Hopper, actor; Peter Hurd, artist; Preston Jones, playwright and actor; Ralph Kiner, baseball player and sportscaster; Nancy Lopez, golfer; Maria Martínez, San Ildefonso Pueblo potter; Demi Moore, actress; Jim Morrison, singer and songwriter; Bill Mauldin, political cartoonist; Popé, San Juan Pueblo medicine man and leader; Georgia O'Keeffe, painter; Harrison Schmitt, astronaut and U.S. representative; Kim Stanley, actress; Slim Summerville, actor; Clyde Tombaugh, astronomer; Al Unser, Bobby Unser, auto racers; Victorio, Apache chief; Linda Wertheimer, NPR correspondent; Kathy Whitworth, golfer.

New York

Capital: Albany
Governor: George Pataki, R (to Jan. 1999)
Lieut. Governor: Elizabeth McCaughey, R (to Jan. 1999)
Senators: Alfonse M. D'Amato, R (to Jan. 2003); Daniel Patrick Moynihan, D (to Jan. 2001)
Secy. of State: Alexander Treadwell, R (to Jan. 1999)
Comptroller: Carl McCall, D (to Jan. 1999)
Atty. General: Dennis Vacco, R (to Jan. 1999)
Entered Union (rank): July 26, 1788 (11)
Present constitution adopted: 1777 (last revised 1938)
Motto: *Excelsior* (Ever upward)
State symbols: animal, Beaver (1975); **fish,** Brook trout (1975); **gem,** Garnet (1969); **flower,** Rose (1955); **tree,** Sugar maple (1956); **bird,** Bluebird (1970); **insect,** Ladybug (1989); **song,** "I Love New York" (1980)
Nickname: Empire State
Origin of name: In honor of the Duke of York
10 largest cities (1996 est.): New York, 7,380,906; Buffalo, 310,548; Rochester, 221,594; Yonkers, 190,316, Syracuse, 155,865; Albany, 103,564; New Rochelle, 67,369; Mount Vernon, 67,112; Schenectady, 62,893; Utica, 61,368
Land area (rank): 47,224 sq mi. (122,310 sq km) (30)
Geographic center: In Madison Co., 12 mi. S of Oneida and 26 mi. SW of Utica
Number of counties: 62
Largest county (1997 pop. est.): Kings, 2,240,385
State forest preserves: Adirondacks, 2,500,000 ac.; Catskills, 250,000 ac.
State parks: 150 (250,000 ac.)
1997 resident population est.: 18,137,226
1990 resident census population (rank): 17,990,455 (2). **Male:** 8,625,673; **Female:** 9,364,782. **White:** 13,385,255 (74.4%); **Black:** 2,859,055 (15.9%); **American Indian:** 62,651 (0.3%); **Asian:** 693,760 (3.9%); **Other race:** 989,734 (5.5%); **Hispanic:** 2,214,026 (12.3%). **1990 percent population under 18:** 23.7; **65 and over:** 13.1; **median age:** 33.9.

Giovanni da Verrazano, an Italian-born navigator sailing for France, discovered New York Bay in 1524. Henry Hudson, an Englishman employed by the Dutch, reached the bay and sailed up the river now bearing his name in 1609, the same year that northern New York was explored and claimed for France by Samuel de Champlain.

In 1624 the first permanent Dutch settlement was established at Fort Orange (now Albany); one year later Peter Minuit is said to have purchased Manhattan Island from the Indians for trinkets worth about $24 and founded the Dutch colony of New Amsterdam (now New York City), which was surrendered to the English in 1664.

For a short time, New York City was the U.S. capital and George Washington was inaugurated there as first president on April 30, 1789.

New York's extremely rapid commercial growth may be partly attributed to Governor De Witt Clinton, who pushed through the construction of the Erie Canal (Buffalo to Albany), which was opened in 1825. Today, the 559-mile Governor Thomas E. Dewey Thruway connects New York City with Buffalo and with Connecticut, Massachusetts, and Pennsylvania express highways. Two toll-free superhighways, the Adirondack Northway (linking Albany with the Canadian border) and the North-South Expressway (crossing central New York from the Pennsylvania border to the Thousand Islands) have been opened.

New York, with the great metropolis of New York City, is the spectacular nerve center of the nation. It is a leader in manufacturing, foreign trade, commercial and financial transactions, book and magazine publishing, and theatrical production.

New York City is not only a national but an international leader. A leading seaport, its John F. Kennedy International Airport is one of the busiest airports in the world. It is the largest manufacturing center in the country and its apparel industry is the city's largest manufacturing employer, with printing and publishing second.

Nearly all the rest of the state's manufacturing is done on Long Island, along the Hudson River north to Albany, and through the Mohawk Valley, Central New York, and Southern Tier regions to Buffalo. The St. Lawrence seaway and power projects have opened the North Country to industrial expansion and have given the state a second seacoast.

The state ranks fourth in the nation in manufacturing, with 982,000 employees in 1995. The principal industries are apparel, printing and publishing, leather products, instruments, and electronic equipment. The convention and tourist business is one of the state's most important sources of income.

New York farms raise cattle and calves, produce corn and poultry, and raise vegetables and fruits. The state is a leading wine producer.

Among the major points of interest are Castle Clinton, Fort Stanwix, and Statue of Liberty National Monuments; Niagara Falls; U.S. Military Academy at West Point; National Historic Sites that include homes of Franklin D. Roosevelt at Hyde Park and Theodore Roosevelt in Oyster Bay and New York City; National Memorials, including Grant's Tomb and Federal Hall in New York City; Fort Ticonderoga; the Baseball Hall of Fame in Cooperstown; and the United Nations, skyscrapers, museums, theaters, and parks in New York City.

Famous natives and residents: Kareem Abdul-Jabbar, basketball player; Lucille Ball, actress; Humphrey Bogart, actor; James Cagney, actor; Maria Callas, soprano; Benjamin N. Cardozo, jurist; Paddy Chayefsky, playwright; Peter Cooper, industrialist and philanthropist; Aaron Copland, composer; Sammy Davis, Jr., actor and singer; Agnes de Mille, choreographer; Eamon De Valera, former president of Ireland; George Eastman, inventor; Millard Fillmore, former president; Lou Gehrig, baseball player; George Gershwin, composer; Learned Hand, jurist; Edward Hopper, painter; Julia Ward Howe, poet and reformer; Charles Evans Hughes, jurist; Washington Irving, author; Henry James, novelist; John Jay, jurist; Michael Jordan, basketball player; Jerome Kern, composer; Rockwell Kent, painter; Vince Lombardi, football coach; Chico, Groucho, Harpo, and Zeppo Marx, comedians; Herman Melville, author; Ethel Merman, singer and actress; Ogden Nash, poet; Eugene O'Neill, playwright; Red Jacket, Seneca chief; John D. Rockefeller, industrialist; Norman Rockwell, painter and illustrator; Mickey Rooney, actor; Anna Eleanor Roosevelt, reformer

and humanitarian; Franklin D. Roosevelt, former president; Theodore Roosevelt, former president; Jonas Salk, polio researcher; Margaret Sanger, birth control leader; Barbara Stanwyck, actress; Risë Stevens, mezzo-soprano; Richard Tucker, tenor; Martin Van Buren, former president; Mae West, actress; Walt Whitman, poet; Edith Wharton, novelist.

North Carolina

Capital: Raleigh
Governor: James B. Hunt, Jr., D (to Jan. 2001)
Lieut. Governor: Dennis A. Wicker, D (to Jan. 2001)
Senators: Lauch Faircloth, R (to Jan. 1999); Jesse Helms, R (to Jan. 2003)
Secy. of State: Elaine F. Marshall, D (to Jan. 2001)
Treasurer: Harlan E. Boyles, D (to Jan. 2001)
Auditor: Ralph Campbell, D (to Jan. 2001)
Atty. General: Michael Easley, D (to Jan. 2001)
Entered Union (rank): Nov. 21, 1789 (12)
Present constitution adopted: 1971
Motto: *Esse quam videri* (To be rather than to seem)
State symbols: flower, Dogwood (1941); **tree,** Pine (1963); **bird,** Cardinal (1943); **mammal,** Gray squirrel (1969); **insect,** Honeybee (1973); **reptile,** Eastern box turtle (1979); **gemstone,** Emerald (1973); **shell,** Scotch bonnet (1965); **historic boat,** Shad Boat (1987); **beverage,** Milk (1987); **rock,** Granite (1979); **dog,** Plott Hound (1989); **song,** "The Old North State" (1927); **colors,** Red and blue (1945)
Nickname: Tar Heel State
Origin of name: In honor of Charles I of England
10 largest cities (1996 est.): Charlotte, 441,297; Raleigh, 243,835; Greensboro, 195,426; Winston-Salem, 153,541; Durham, 149,799; Fayetteville, 79,631; Cary, 75,676; High Point, 74,417; Jacksonville, 69,889; Asheville, 64,067
Land area (rank): 48,718 sq mi. (126,180 sq km) (29)
Geographic center: In Chatham Co., 10 mi. NW of Sanford
Number of counties: 100
Largest county (1996 pop. est.): Mecklenburg, 592,257
State forests: 1
State parks: 30 (125,000 ac.)
1997 resident population est.: 7,428,194
1990 resident census population (rank): 6,628,637 (10). **Male:** 3,214,290; **Female:** 3,414,347. **White:** 5,008,491 (75.6%); **Black:** 1,456,323 (22.0%); **American Indian:** 80,155 (1.2%); **Asian:** 52,166 (0.8%); **Other race:** 31,502 (0.5%); **Hispanic:** 76,726 (1.2%). **1990 percent population under 18:** 24.2; **65 and over:** 12.1; **median age:** 33.1.

English colonists, sent by Sir Walter Raleigh, unsuccessfully attempted to settle Roanoke Island in 1585 and 1587. Virginia Dare, born there in 1587, was the first child of English parentage born in America.

In 1653 the first permanent settlements were established by English colonists from Virginia near the Roanoke and Chowan rivers. The region was established as an English proprietary colony in 1663–65 and its early history was the scene of Culpepper's Rebellion (1677), the Quaker-led Cary Rebellion of 1708, the Tuscarora Indian War in 1711–13, and many pirate raids.

During the American Revolution, there was relatively little fighting within the state, but many North Carolinians saw action elsewhere. Despite considerable pro-Union, anti-slavery sentiment, North Carolina joined the Confederacy.

North Carolina is the nation's largest furniture, tobacco, brick, and textile producer. It holds second place in the Southeast in population and first place in the value of its industrial and agricultural production. This production is highly diversified, with metalworking, chemicals, and paper constituting enormous industries. Tobacco, corn, cotton, hay, peanuts, and vegetable crops are of major importance. It is the country's leading producer of mica and lithium.

Tourism is also important, with travelers and vacationers spending more than $1 billion annually in North Carolina. Sports include year-round golfing, skiing at mountain resorts, both fresh- and salt-water fishing, and hunting.

Among the major attractions are the Great Smoky Mountains, the Blue Ridge National Parkway, the Cape Hatteras and Cape Lookout National Seashores, the Wright Brothers National Memorial at Kitty Hawk, Guilford Courthouse and Moores Creek National Military Parks, Carl Sandburg's home near Hendersonville, and the Old Salem Restoration in Winston-Salem.

Famous natives and residents: David Brinkley, TV newscaster; Howard Cosell, sportscaster; Virginia Dare, first person born in America to English parents; James B. Duke, industrialist; Roberta Flack, singer; Ava Gardner, actress; Richard Gatling, inventor; Billy Graham, evangelist; Kathryn Grayson, singer and actress; Jesse Helms, politician; O. Henry, writer; Barbara Howar, broadcaster and writer; Andrew Johnson, former president; Charles Kuralt, TV journalist; Sugar Ray Leonard, boxer; Dolley Madison, former first lady; Ronni Milsap, country music singer; Thelonious Monk, pianist; Alfred Moore, jurist; Edward R. Murrow, commentator and government official; Walter Hines Page, journalist and ambassador; Floyd Patterson, boxer; Richard Petty, auto racer; James K. Polk, former president; Soupy Sales, comedian; Earl Scruggs, bluegrass musician; Randy Travis, musician; John Scott Trotter, orchestra leader; Thomas Wolfe, novelist.

North Dakota

Capital: Bismarck
Governor: Edward T. Schafer, R (to 2000)
Lieut. Governor: Rosemarie Myrdal, R (to Dec. 15, 2000)
Senators: Kent Conrad, D (to Jan. 2001); Byron L. Dorgan, D (to Jan. 1999)
Secy. of State: Alvin A. Jaeger, R (to Dec. 31, 2000)
Auditor: Robert R. Peterson, R (to Dec. 31, 2000)
Treasurer: Kathi Gilmore, D (to Dec. 31, 2000)
Atty. General: Heidi Heitkamp, D (to Dec. 31, 2000)
Organized as territory: March 2, 1861
Entered Union (rank): Nov. 2, 1889 (39)
Present constitution adopted: 1889
Motto: Liberty and union, now and forever: one and inseparable
State symbols: tree, American elm (1947); **bird,** Western meadowlark (1947); **song,** "North Dakota Hymn" (1947); **fish,** Northern Pike (1969); **grass,** Western wheatgrass (1977); **fossil,** Teredo petrified wood (1967); **beverage,** Milk (1983); **state march,** Spirit of the Land (1975); **flower,** Wild prairie rose (1907); **equine,** Nokota horse (1993); **dance,** Square dance (1995)
Nickname: Sioux State; Flickertail State; Peace Garden State
Origin of name: From the Sioux tribe, meaning "allies"
10 largest cities (1996 est.): Fargo, 83,778; Bismarck, 53,514; Grand Forks, 50,675; Minot, 35,926; Dickinson, 16,094; Mandan, 15,648; Jamestown, 14,983; West Fargo, 13,566; Williston, 12,718; Wahpeton, 9,039
Land area (rank): 68,994 sq mi. (178,695 sq km) (17)
Geographic center: In Sheridan Co., 5 mi. SW of McClusky
Number of counties: 53
Largest county (1995 pop. est.): Cass, 111,440
State parks: 14 (14,922.6 ac.)
1997 resident population est.: 640,883

1990 resident census population (rank): 638,800 (47). **Male:** 318,201; **Female:** 320,599. **White:** 604,142 (94.6%); **Black:** 3,524 (0.6%); **American Indian:** 25,917 (4.1%); **Asian:** 3,462 (0.5%); **Other race:** 1,755 (0.3%); **Hispanic:** 4,665 (0.7%). **1990 percent population under 18:** 27.5; **65 and over:** 14.3; **median age:** 32.4.

North Dakota was explored in 1738–40 by French Canadians led by sieur de la Verendrye. In 1803, the U.S. acquired most of North Dakota from France in the Louisiana Purchase. Lewis and Clark explored the region in 1804–06 and the first settlements were made at Pembina in 1812 by Scottish and Irish families while this area was still in dispute between the U.S. and Great Britain.

In 1818, the U.S. obtained the northeastern part of North Dakota by treaty with Great Britain and took possession of Pembina in 1823.

North Dakota is the most rural of all the states, with farms covering more than 90% of the land. North Dakota ranks first in the nation's production of spring and durum wheat, and the state's coal and oil reserves are plentiful.

Other agricultural products include barley, rye, sunflowers, dry edible beans, honey, oats, flaxseed, sugar beets, hay, beef cattle, sheep, and hogs.

Recently, manufacturing industries have grown, especially food processing and farm equipment. The state also produces natural gas, lignite, salt, clay, sand, and gravel.

The Garrison Dam on the Missouri River provides extensive irrigation and produces 400,000 kilowatts of electricity for the Missouri Basin areas.

Known for its waterfowl, grouse, and deer hunting and bass, trout, and northern pike fishing, North Dakota has 20 state parks and recreation areas. Points of interest include the International Peace Garden near Dunseith, Fort Union Trading Post National Historic Site, the State Capitol at Bismarck, the Badlands, Theodore Roosevelt National Park, and Fort Lincoln, now a state park, from which Gen. George Custer set out on his last campaign in 1876.

Famous natives and residents: Lynn Anderson, singer; Maxwell Anderson, playwright; Dr. Robert H. Bahmer, U.S. archivist; Elizabeth Bodine, humanitarian; Dr. Anne Carlsen, educator; Ronald N. Davies, jurist; Angie Dickinson, actress; Ivan Dmitre, artist; Phyllis Frelich, actress; Bertin C. Gamble, founder of Gamble-Skogmo; William H. Gass, writer and philosopher; Rev. Richard C. Halverson, U.S. Senate chaplain; Phil D. Jackson, basketball player and coach; Dr. Leon O. Jacobson, researcher and educator; Harold K. Johnson, former army general; David C. Jones, U.S. Army general; Louis L'Amour, author; Peggy Lee, singer; William Lemke, former representative; Roger Maris, baseball player; Marquis de Mores, cattleman who established Medora; Gerald P. Nye, former senator; Casper Oimoen, skier; Arthur Peterson, radio and TV actor; Cliff (Fido) Purpur, hockey player and coach; James Rosenquist, painter; Harold Schafer, founder of Gold Seal Co.; Eric Sevareid, TV commentator; Ann Sothern, actress; Dorothy Stickney, actress; Edward K. Thompson, *Life* magazine editor; Era Bell Thompson, *Ebony* magazine editor; Tommy Tucker, band leader; Lawrence Welk, band leader; Larry Woiwode, writer.

Ohio

Capital: Columbus
Governor: George V. Voinovich, R (to Jan. 1999)
Lieut. Governor: Nancy Putnam-Hollister, R (to Jan. 1999)
Senators: Mike DeWine, R (to Jan. 2001); John H. Glenn, Jr., D (to Jan. 1999)
Secy. of State: Bob Taft, R (to Jan. 1999)
Auditor: Jim Petro, R (to Jan. 1999)
Treasurer: J. Kenneth Blackwell, R (to Jan. 1999)
Atty. General: Betty D. Montgomery, R (to Jan. 1999)
Entered Union (rank): March 1, 1803 (17)
Present constitution adopted: 1851
Motto: With God, all things are possible
State symbols: flower, Scarlet carnation (1904); **tree,** Buckeye (1953); **bird,** Cardinal (1933); **insect,** Ladybug (1975); **gemstone,** Flint (1965); **song,** "Beautiful Ohio" (1969); **drink,** Tomato juice (1965)
Nickname: Buckeye State
Origin of name: From an Iroquoian word meaning "great river"
10 largest cities (1996 est.): Columbus, 657,053; Cleveland, 498,246; Cincinnati, 345,818; Toledo, 317,606; Akron, 216,882; Dayton, 172,947; Youngstown, 87,405; Parma, 85,006; Canton, 81,079; Lorain, 69,800
Land area (rank): 40,953 sq mi. (106,067 sq km) (35)
Geographic center: In Delaware Co., 25 mi. NNE of Columbus
Number of counties: 88
Largest county (1996 pop. est.): Cuyahoga, 1,401,552
State forests: 19 (172,744 ac.)
State parks: 71 (198,027 ac.)
1997 resident population est.: 11,186,331
1990 resident census population (rank): 10,847,115 (7). **Male:** 5,226,340; **Female:** 5,620,775. **White:** 9,521,756 (87.8%); **Black:** 1,154,826 (10.6%); **American Indian:** 20,358 (0.2%); **Asian:** 91,179 (0.8%); **Other race:** 58,996 (0.5%); **Hispanic:** 139,696 (1.3%). **1990 percent population under 18:** 25.8; **65 and over:** 13.0; **median age:** 33.3.

First explored for France by sieur de la Salle in 1669, the Ohio region became British property after the French and Indian War. Ohio was acquired by the U.S. after the Revolutionary War in 1783. In 1788, the first permanent settlement was established at Marietta, capital of the Northwest Territory.

The 1790s saw severe fighting with the Indians in Ohio; a major battle was won by Maj. Gen. Anthony Wayne at Fallen Timbers in 1794. In the War of 1812, Commodore Oliver H. Perry defeated the British in the Battle of Lake Erie on Sept. 10, 1813.

Ohio is one of the nation's industrial leaders, ranking third in the value of manufactured products. Important manufacturing centers are located in or near Ohio's major cities. Akron is known for rubber; Canton for roller bearings; Cincinnati for jet engines and machine tools; Cleveland for auto assembly and parts, refining, and steel; Dayton for office machines, refrigeration, and heating and auto equipment; Youngstown and Steubenville for steel; and Toledo for glass and auto parts.

The state's thousands of factories almost overshadow its importance in agriculture and mining. Its fertile soil produces soybeans, corn, oats, grapes, and clover. More than half of Ohio's farm receipts come from dairy farming and sheep and hog raising. Ohio is the top state in lime production and among the leaders in coal, clay, salt, sand, and gravel. Petroleum, gypsum, cement, and natural gas are also important.

Tourism is a valuable revenue producer, bringing in $9.9 billion in 1996, and ranking 7th among the 50 states. Attractions include the Rock and Roll Hall of Fame, Indian burial grounds at Mound City Group National Monument, Perry's Victory International Peace Memorial, the Pro Football Hall of Fame at Canton, and the homes of presidents Grant, Taft, Hayes, Harding, and Garfield.

Famous natives and residents: Neil Armstrong, astronaut; Kathleen Battle, soprano; George Bellows, painter and lithographer; Ambrose Bierce, journalist; Erma Bombeck, columnist; Bill Boyd (Hopalong Cassidy), actor; Milton Caniff, cartoonist; Hart Crane, poet; George Armstrong Custer, army officer; Dorothy Dandridge, actress; Doris Day, singer and actress; Clarence Darrow, lawyer; Ruby Dee, actress; Rita Dove, former U.S. poet laureate; Hugh Downs, TV broadcaster; Thomas A. Edison, inventor; Clark Gable, actor; James A. Garfield, former president; Lillian Gish, actress; John Glenn, astronaut and senator; Ulysses S. Grant, former president; Warren G. Harding, former president; Rutherford Hayes, former president; Benjamin Harrison, former president; William Dean Howells, novelist and critic; Zane Grey, author; Robert Henri, painter; Kenisaw Mountain Landis, first baseball commissioner; Dean Martin, singer and actor; William McKinley, former president; Paul Newman, actor; Jack Nicklaus, golfer; Annie Oakley, markswoman; Norman Vincent Peale, clergyman; Tyrone Power, actor; Judith Resnik, astronaut; Eddie Rickenbacker, aviator; Arthur M. Schlesinger, Jr., historian; William Tecumseh Sherman, army general; Gloria Steinem, feminist; William H. Taft, former president; Tecumseh, Shawnee Indian chief; Lowell Thomas, explorer and commentator; James Thurber, author and cartoonist; Orville Wright, inventor; Cy Young, baseball player.

Oklahoma

Capital: Oklahoma City
Governor: Frank Keating, R (to Jan. 1999)
Lieut. Governor: Mary Fallin, R (to Jan. 1999)
Senators: James M. Inhofe, R (to Jan. 2003); Don Nickles, R (to Jan. 1999)
Secy. of State: Tom Cole, R (to Jan. 1999)
Treasurer: Robert Butkin, D (to Jan. 1999)
Atty. General: Drew Edmondson, D (to Jan. 1999)
Organized as territory: May 2, 1890
Entered Union (rank): Nov. 16, 1907 (46)
Present constitution adopted: 1907
Motto: *Labor omnia vincit* (Labor conquers all things)
State symbols: flower, Mistletoe (1893); **tree,** Redbud (1937); **bird,** Scissor-tailed flycatcher (1951); **animal,** Bison (1972); **reptile,** Mountain boomer lizard (1969); **stone,** Rose Rock (barite rose) (1968); **colors,** Green and white (1915); **song,** "Oklahoma" (1953); **beverage,** Milk; **butterfly,** Black swallowtail; **fish,** White or Sand bass; **folk dance,** Square dance; **furbearer,** Raccoon; **game animal,** White-tailed deer; **grass,** Indiangrass; **insect,** Honeybee; **musical instrument,** Fiddle; **poem,** "Howdy Folks," David Randolph Milsten; **waltz,** "Oklahoma Wind"; **wildflower,** Indian blanket
Nickname: Sooner State
Origin of name: From two Choctaw Indian words meaning "red people"
10 largest cities (1996 est.): Oklahoma City, 469,852; Tulsa, 378,491; Norman, 90,228; Lawton, 82,582; Broken Arrow, 69,175; Edmond, 63,475; Midwest City, 54,252; Enid, 45,724; Moore, 44,472; Stillwater, 38,487
Land area (rank): 68,679 sq mi. (177,877 sq km) (19)
Geographic center: In Oklahoma Co., 8 mi. N of Oklahoma City
Number of counties: 77
Largest county (1995 pop. est.): Oklahoma, 625,337
State parks: 36 (57,487 ac.)
1997 resident population est.: 3,317,091
1990 resident census population (rank): 3,145,585 (28). **Male:** 1,530,819; **Female:** 1,614,766. **White:** 2,583,512 (82.1%); **Black:** 233,801 (7.4%); **American Indian:** 252,420 (8.0%); **Asian:** 33,563 (1.1%); **Other race:** 42,289 (1.3%); **Hispanic:** 86,160 (2.7%). **1990 percent population under 18:** 26.6; **65 and over:** 13.5; **median age:** 33.2.

Francisco Vásquez de Coronado first explored the region for Spain in 1541. The U.S. acquired most of Oklahoma in 1803 in the Louisiana Purchase from France; the Western Panhandle region became U.S. territory with the annexation of Texas in 1845.

Set aside as Indian Territory in 1834, the region was divided into Indian Territory and Oklahoma Territory on May 2, 1890. The two were combined to make a new state, Oklahoma, on Nov. 16, 1907.

On April 22, 1889, the first day homesteading was permitted, 50,000 people swarmed into the area. Those who tried to beat the noon starting gun were called "Sooners," hence the state's nickname.

Oil made Oklahoma a rich state, but natural-gas production has now surpassed it. Oil refining, meat packing, food processing, and machinery manufacturing (especially construction and oil equipment) are important industries.

Other minerals produced in Oklahoma include helium, gypsum, zinc, cement, coal, copper, and silver.

Oklahoma's rich plains produce bumper yields of wheat, as well as large crops of sorghum, hay, cotton, and peanuts. More than half of Oklahoma's annual farm receipts are contributed by livestock products, including cattle, dairy products, and broilers.

Tourist attractions include the National Cowboy Hall of Fame in Oklahoma City, the Will Rogers Memorial in Claremore, the Cherokee Cultural Center with a restored Cherokee village, the restored Fort Gibson Stockade near Muskogee, the Lake Texoma recreation area, Pari-Mutual horse racing at Remington Park in Oklahoma City, and Blue Ribbon Downs in Sallisaw.

Famous natives and residents: Johnny Bench, baseball player; John Berryman, poet; Garth Brooks, singer; Iron Eyes Cody, Cherokee actor; L. Gordon Cooper, astronaut; Ralph Ellison, writer; James Garner, actor; Owen K. Garriott, astronaut; Vince Gill, singer; Chester Gould, cartoonist; Woody Guthrie, singer and composer; Roy Harris, composer; Paul Harvey, broadcaster; Van Heflin, actor; Ron Howard, actor and director; Ben Johnson, actor; Jennifer Jones, actress; Jeane Kirkpatrick, educator and public-affairs spokesperson; Shannon Lucid, astronaut; Wilma P. Mankiller, principal chief of the Cherokee Nation of Oklahoma; Mickey Mantle, baseball player; Reba McEntire, singer; Shannon Miller, Olympic gymnast; Bill Moyers, journalist; Daniel Patrick Moynihan, N.Y. senator; Patti Page, singer; Mary Kay Place, actress and writer; Tony Randall, actor; Oral Roberts, evangelist; Dale Robertson, actor; Will Rogers, humorist; Dan Rowan, comedian; Thomas P. Stafford, astronaut; Maria Tallchief, ballerina; Jim Thorpe, athlete; Alfre Woodard, actress.

Oregon

Capital: Salem
Governor: John A. Kitzhaber, D (to Jan. 1999)
Senators: Gordon Smith, R (to Jan. 2003); Ron Wyden, D (to Jan. 1999)
Secy. of State: Phil Keisling, D (to Jan. 1999)
Treasurer: James A. Hill, D (to Jan. 1999)
Atty. General: Theodore R. Kulongoski, D (to Jan. 1999)
Organized as territory: Aug. 14, 1848
Entered Union (rank): Feb. 14, 1859 (33)
Present constitution adopted: 1859
Motto: *Alis volat Propriis* (She flies with her own wings) (1987)
State symbols: flower, Oregon grape (1899); **tree,** Douglas fir (1939); **animal,** Beaver (1969); **bird,** Western meadowlark (1927); **fish,** Chinook salmon (1961); **rock,** Thunderegg (1965); **colors,** Navy blue and gold (1959); **song,** "Oregon, My Oregon" (1927);

insect, Swallowtail butterfly (1979); **dance,** Square dance (1997); **nut,** Hazelnut (1989); **gemstone** Sunstone (1987)
Nickname: Beaver State
Origin of name: Unknown. However, it is generally accepted that the name, first used by Jonathan Carver in 1778, was taken from the writings of Maj. Robert Rogers, an English army officer.
10 largest cities (1996 est.): Portland, 480,824; Eugene, 123,718; Salem, 122,566; Gresham, 81,583; Beaverton, 63,224; Medford, 56,067; Hillsboro, 52,479; Springfield, 49,430; Corvallis, 47,518; Albany, 37,919
Land area (rank): 96,003 sq mi. (248,647 sq km) (10)
Geographic center: In Crook Co., 25 mi. SSE of Prineville
Number of counties: 36
Largest county (1996 pop. est.): Multnomah, 636,000
State forests: 820,000 ac.
State parks: 240 (93,330 ac.)
1997 resident population est.: 3,243,487
1990 resident census population (rank): 2,842,321 (29). **Male:** 1,397,073; **Female:** 1,445,248. **White:** 2,636,787 (92.8%); **Black:** 46,178 (1.6%); **American Indian:** 38,496 (1.4%); **Asian:** 69,269 (2.4%); **Other race:** 51,591 (1.8%); **Hispanic:** 112,707 (4.0%). **1990 percent population under 18:** 25.5; **65 and over:** 13.8; **median age:** 34.5.

Spanish and English sailors are believed to have sighted the Oregon coast in the 1500s and 1600s. Capt. James Cook, seeking the Northwest Passage, charted some of the coastline in 1778. In 1792, Capt. Robert Gray, in the *Columbia,* discovered the river named after his ship and claimed the area for the U.S.

In 1805 the Lewis and Clark expedition explored the area. John Jacob Astor's fur depot, Astoria, was founded in 1811. Disputes for control of Oregon between American settlers and the Hudson Bay Company were finally resolved in the 1846 Oregon Treaty in which Great Britain gave up claims to the region.

Oregon has a $3.3 billion lumber and wood products industry, and an $859 million paper and allied manufacturing industry. Its salmon-fishing industry is one of the world's largest.

In agriculture, the state leads in growing peppermint, cover seed crops, blackberries, boysenberries, loganberries, black raspberries, and hazelnuts. It is second in raising hops, raspberries, sweet cherries, prunes, snap beans, and onions. Oregon has the only nickel smelter in the United States.

With the low-cost electric power provided by Bonneville Dam, McNary Dam, and other dams in the Pacific Northwest, Oregon has developed steadily as a manufacturing state. Leading manufactures are lumber and plywood, metalwork, machinery, aluminum, chemicals, paper, food packing, and electronic equipment.

Crater Lake National Park, Mount Hood, and Bonneville Dam on the Columbia are major tourist attractions. Oregon Dunes National Recreation Area has been established near Florence. Other points of interest include the Oregon Caves National Monument, Cape Perpetua in Siuslaw National Forest, Columbia River Gorge between The Dalles and Troutdale, Hells Canyon, Newberry Volcanic National Monument, and John Day Fossil Beds National Monument.

Famous natives and residents: James Beard, food expert; Raymond Carver, writer and poet; Homer C. Davenport, political cartoonist; David Douglas, botanist; Abigail Scott Duniway, women's suffrage advocate; John E. Frohnmeyer, former chairman of the National Endowment for the Arts; Robert Gray, sea captain and discoverer of Columbia River; Matt Groening, cartoonist; Mark Hatfield, senator; Donald P. Hodel, former secretary of the Interior; Chief Joseph, Nez Percé chief; Dave Kingman, baseball player; Ursula LeGuin, writer; Edwin Markham, poet; Phyllis McGinley, author; Linus Pauling, chemist; Jane Powell, actress and singer; John Reed, poet and author; Harvey W. Scott, editor; Doc Severinsen, band leader; Norton Simon, business executive; Paul M. Simon, Illinois senator; William E. Stafford, poet; Sally Struthers, actress.

Pennsylvania

Capital: Harrisburg
Governor: Tom Ridge, R (to Jan. 1999)
Lieut. Governor: Mark Schweiker, R (to Jan. 1999)
Senators: Rick Santorum, R (to Jan. 2001); Arlen Specter, R (to Jan. 1999)
Secy. of the Commonwealth: Yvette Kane, R (at the pleasure of the governor)
Auditor General: Robert P. Casey, Jr., D (to Jan. 2001)
Atty. General: D. Michael Fisher, R (to Jan. 2001)
Entered Union (rank): Dec. 12, 1787 (2)
Present constitution adopted: 1968
Motto: Virtue, liberty, and independence
State symbols: flower, Mountain laurel (1933); **tree,** Hemlock (1931); **bird,** Ruffed grouse (1931); **dog,** Great Dane (1965); **colors,** Blue and gold (1907); **song,** "Pennsylvania" (1990)
Nickname: Keystone State
Origin of name: In honor of Adm. Sir William Penn, father of William Penn. It means "Penn's Woodland."
10 largest cities (1996 est.): Philadelphia, 1,478,002; Pittsburgh, 350,363; Erie, 105,270; Allentown, 102,211; Scranton, 77,189; Reading, 75,723; Bethlehem, 70,245; Lancaster, 53,597; Harrisburg, 50,886; Altoona, 50,101
Land area (rank): 44,820 sq mi. (116,083 sq km) (32)
Geographic center: In Centre Co., 2½ mi. SW of Bellefonte
Number of counties: 67
Largest county (1995 pop. est.): Philadelphia, 1,498,971
State forests: 1,991,526 ac.
State parks: 114 (277,164.18 ac.)
19957 resident population est.: 12,019,661
1990 resident census population (rank): 11,881,643 (5). **Male:** 5,694,265; **Female:** 6,187,378. **White:** 10,520,201 (88.5%); **Black:** 1,089,795 (9.2%); **American Indian:** 14,733 (0.1%); **Asian:** 137,438 (1.2%); **Other race:** 119,476 (1.0%); **Hispanic:** 232,262 (2.0%). **1990 percent population under 18:** 23.5; **65 and over:** 15.4; **median age:** 35.

Rich in historic lore, Pennsylvania territory was disputed in the early 1600s among the Dutch, the Swedes, and the English. England acquired the region in 1664 with the capture of New York and in 1681 Pennsylvania was granted to William Penn, a Quaker, by King Charles II.

Philadelphia was the seat of the federal government almost continuously from 1776 to 1800; there the Declaration of Independence was signed in 1776 and the U.S. Constitution drawn up in 1787. Valley Forge, of Revolutionary War fame, and Gettysburg, site of the pivotal battle of the Civil War, are both in Pennsylvania. The Liberty Bell is located in a glass pavilion across from Independence Hall in Philadelphia.

With the decline of the coal, steel, and railroad industries, Pennsylvania's industry has diversified, though the state still leads the country in the production of specialty steel. Pennsylvania is a leader in

the production of chemicals, food, and electrical machinery and produces 10% of the nations's cement. Also important are brick and tiles, glass, limestone, and slate. Data processing is also increasingly important.

Pennsylvania's 9 million agricultural acres (6 million acres for crops and pasture, 3 million acres in farm woodlands) produce a wide variety of crops, and its 55,535 farms are the backbone of the state's economy. Leading products are milk, poultry, and eggs, a variety of fruits, sweet corn, potatoes, mushrooms, cheese, beans, hay, maple syrup, and even Christmas trees.

Pennsylvania has the largest rural population in the nation. The state's farmers sell more than $3.3 billion in crops and livestock annually, and agribusiness and food-related industries account for another $35 billion in economic activity annually.

Tourists now spend approximately $6 billion in Pennsylvania annually. Among the chief attractions are the Gettysburg National Military Park, Valley Forge National Historical Park, Independence National Historical Park in Philadelphia, the Pennsylvania Dutch region, the Eisenhower farm near Gettysburg, and the Delaware Water Gap National Recreation Area.

Famous natives and residents: Louisa May Alcott, novelist; Marian Anderson, contralto; Maxwell Anderson, dramatist; Samuel Barber, composer; John Barrymore, actor; Donald Barthelme, author; Stephen Vincent Benet, poet and story writer; Daniel Boone, frontiersman; Ed Bradley, TV anchorman; James Buchanan, former president; Alexander Calder, sculptor; Rachel Carson, biologist and author; Mary Cassatt, painter; Henry Steele Commager, historian; Bill Cosby, actor; Stuart Davis, painter; Jimmy and Tommy Dorsey, band leaders; W. C. Fields, comedian; Stephen Foster, composer; Robert Fulton, inventor; Grace, Princess of Monaco; Martha Graham, choreographer; Alexander Haig, former secretary of state; Marilyn Horne, mezzo-soprano; Lee Iacocca, auto executive; Reggie Jackson, baseball player; Gene Kelly, dancer and actor; Gelsey Kirkland, ballerina; S. S. Kresge, merchant; Mario Lanza, actor and singer; George C. Marshall, five-star general; George McClellan, former general; Margaret Mead, anthropologist; Andrew Mellon, financier; Tom Mix, actor; Arnold Palmer, golfer; Robert E. Peary, explorer; Man Ray, painter; Mary Roberts Rinehart, novelist; Betsy Ross, flagmaker; B. F. Skinner, psychologist; John Sloan, painter; Gertrude Stein, author; James Stewart, actor; John Updike, novelist; Honus Wagner, baseball player; Fred Waring, band leader; Ethel Waters, singer and actress; Anthony Wayne, military officer; August Wilson, poet, writer, and playwright; Wallis Warfield, Duchess of Windsor; Andrew Wyeth, painter.

Rhode Island

Capital: Providence
Governor: Lincoln Almond, R (to Jan. 1999)
Lieut. Governor: Bernard Jackvony, R (to Jan. 1999)
Senators: John H. Chafee, R (to Jan. 2001); Jack Reed, D (to Jan. 2003)
Secy. of State: Jim Langevin, D (to Jan. 1999)
Atty. General: Jeffery B. Pine, D (to Jan. 1999)
General Treasurer: Nancy J. Mayer, D (to Jan. 1999)
Entered Union (rank): May 29, 1790 (13)
Present constitution adopted: 1843
Motto: Hope
State symbols: flower, Violet (unofficial) (1968); **tree,** Red maple (official) (1964); **bird,** Rhode Island Red (official) (1954); **shell,** Quahog (official); **mineral,** Bowenite (1966); **stone,** Cumberlandite (1966); **colors,** Blue, white, and gold (in state flag); **song,** "Rhode Island" (1946)
Nickname: The Ocean State
Origin of name: From the Greek Island of Rhodes
Largest cities (1996 est.): Providence, 152,558; Warwick, 84,514; Cranston, 74,324; Pawtucket, 69,068; East Providence, 48,389; Woonsocket, 41,817; Newport, 24,295; Central Falls, 16,620
Land area (rank): 1,045 sq mi. (2,706 sq km) (50)
Geographic center: In Kent Co., 1 mi. SSW of Compton
Number of counties: 5
Largest county (1995 pop. est.): Providence, 580,015
State forests: 11 (20,900 ac.)
State parks: 17 (14,000 ac.)
1997 resident population est.: 987,429
1990 resident census population (rank): 1,003,464 (43). **Male:** 481,496; **Female:** 521,968. **White:** 917,375 (91.4%); **Black:** 38,861 (3.9%); **American Indian:** 4,071 (0.4%); **Asian:** 18,325 (1.8%); **Other race:** 24,832 (2.5%); **Hispanic:** 45,752 (4.6%). **1990 percent population under 18:** 22.5; **65 and over:** 15.0; **median age:** 34.

From its beginnings, Rhode Island has been distinguished by its support for freedom of conscience and action, started by Roger Williams, who was exiled by the Massachusetts Bay Colony Puritans in 1636, and was the founder of the present state capital, Providence. Williams was followed by other religious exiles who founded Pocasset, now Portsmouth, in 1638 and Newport in 1639.

Rhode Island's rebellious, authority-defying nature was further demonstrated by the burnings of the British revenue cutters *Liberty* and *Gaspee* prior to the Revolution, by its early declaration of independence from Great Britain in May 1776, its refusal to participate actively in the War of 1812, and by Dorr's Rebellion of 1842, which protested property requirements for voting.

Rhode Island, smallest of the fifty states, is densely populated and highly industrialized. It is a primary center for jewelry manufacturing in the U.S. Electronics, metal, plastic products, and boat and ship construction are other important industries. Non-manufacturing employment includes research in health, medicine, and the ocean environment. Providence is a wholesale distribution center for New England.

Two of New England's fishing ports are at Galilee and Newport. Rural areas of the state support small-scale farming, including grapes for local wineries, turf grass, and nursery stock. Tourism is one of Rhode Island's largest industries, generating over a billion dollars a year in revenue.

Newport became famous as the summer capital of society in the mid–19th century. Touro Synagogue (1763) is the oldest in the U.S. Other points of interest include the Roger Williams National Memorial in Providence, Samuel Slater's Mill in Pawtucket, the General Nathanael Greene Homestead in Coventry, and Block Island.

Famous natives and residents: Harry Anderson, actor; George M. Cohan, actor and dramatist; Eddie Dowling, actor and stage producer; Nelson Eddy, baritone and actor; Ann Smith Franklin, printer and almanac publisher; Charles Gorham, silversmith; Spalding Gray, writer, performance artist; Bobby Hackett, trumpeter; David Hartman, TV newscaster; Ruth Hussey, actress; Anne Hutchinson, religious leader; Thomas H. Ince, film producer; Wilbur John, Quaker leader; Van Johnson, actor; Clarence King, first director of the U.S. Geological Survey; Galway Kinnell, poet; Oliver LaFarge, writer; Irving R. Levine, news correspondent; H. P. Lovecraft, author; Ida Lewis, lighthouse keeper; John McLaughlin, political commentator, broadcaster; Dana C. Munro, educator and historian; Matthew C. Perry, naval officer; Oliver Hazard Perry, naval officer; King Philip (Metacomet), Indian leader;

Gilbert Stuart, painter; Sarah Helen (Power) Whitman, poet; Jemima Wilkinson, religious leader; Roger Williams, clergyman and founder of Rhode Island; Leonard Woodcock, labor union official.

South Carolina

Capital: Columbia
Governor: David M. Beasley, R (to Jan. 1999)
Lieut. Governor: Robert L. Peeler, R (to Jan. 1999)
Senators: Ernest F. Hollings, D (to Jan. 1999); Strom Thurmond, R (to Jan. 2003)
Secy. of State: Jim Miles, R (to Jan. 1999)
Comptroller General: Earle E. Morris, Jr., D (to Jan. 1999)
Atty. General: Charles M. Condon, R (to Jan. 1999)
Entered Union (rank): May 23, 1788 (8).
Present constitution adopted: 1895
Mottoes: *Animis opibusque parati* (Prepared in mind and resources) and *Dum spiro spero* (While I breathe, I hope)
State symbols: flower, Carolina yellow jessamine (1924); **tree,** Palmetto tree (1939); **bird,** Carolina wren (1948); **song,** "Carolina" (1911)
Nickname: Palmetto State
Origin of name: In honor of Charles I of England
10 largest cities (1996 est.): Columbia, 112,773; Charleston, 71,052; North Charleston, 59,923; Greenville, 57,064; Rock Hill, 44,061; Spartanburg, 42,136; Sumter, 38,565; Mount Pleasant, 34,262; Florence, 30,168; Hilton Head Island, 29,088
Land area (rank): 30,111 sq mi. (77,988 sq km) (40)
Geographic center: In Richland Co., 13 mi. SE of Columbia
Number of counties: 46
Largest county (1995 pop. est.): Greenville, 339,908
State forests: 4 (124,052 ac.)
State parks: 50 (61,726 ac.)
1997 resident population est.: 3,760,181
1990 resident census population (rank): 3,486,703 (25). **Male:** 1,688,510; **Female:** 1,798,193. **White:** 2,406,974 (69.0%); **Black:** 1,039,884 (29.8%); **American Indian:** 8,246 (0.2%); **Asian:** 22,382 (0.6%); **Other race:** 9,217 (0.3%); **Hispanic:** 30,551 (0.9%) **1990 percent population under 18:** 26.4; **65 and over:** 11.4; **median age:** 32.0

Following exploration of the coast in 1521 by Francisco de Gordillo, the Spanish tried unsuccessfully to establish a colony near present-day Georgetown in 1526 and the French also failed to colonize Parris Island near Fort Royal in 1562.

The first English settlement was made in 1670 at Albemarle Point on the Ashley River, but poor conditions drove the settlers to the site of Charleston (originally called Charles Town). South Carolina, officially separated from North Carolina in 1729, was the scene of extensive military action during the Revolution and again during the Civil War. The Civil War began in 1861 as South Carolina troops fired on federal Fort Sumter in Charleston Harbor and the state was the first to secede from the Union.

Once primarily agricultural, South Carolina has built so many large textile and other mills that today its factories produce eight times the output of its farms in cash value. Charleston makes asbestos, wood, pulp, and steel products; chemicals, machinery, and apparel are also important.

Farms have become fewer but larger in recent years. South Carolina grows more peaches than any other state except California; it ranks fifth in overall tobacco production. Other farm products include cotton, peanuts, sweet potatoes, soybeans, corn, and oats. Poultry and dairy products are also important revenue producers.

Points of interest include Fort Sumter National Monument, Fort Moultrie, Fort Johnson, and aircraft carrier USS *Yorktown* in Charleston Harbor; the Middleton, Magnolia, and Cypress Gardens in Charleston; Cowpens National Battlefield; and the Hilton Head resorts.

Famous natives and residents: Bernard Baruch, statesman; Mary McLeod Bethune, educator; James F. Byrnes, senator, jurist and secretary of state; John C. Calhoun, statesman; Mark Clark, general; Joe Frazier, prize fighter; Althea Gibson, tennis champion; Dizzy Gillespie, jazz trumpeter; DuBose Heyward, poet, playwright, and novelist; Andrew Jackson, former president; Jesse Jackson, civil rights leader; Eartha Kitt, singer; Francis Marion ("Swamp Fox"), Revolutionary general; Ronald McNair, astronaut; John Rutledge, jurist; Strom Thurmond, politician; Charles Townes, physicist; William Westmoreland, former army chief of staff; Vanna White, TV personality.

South Dakota

Capital: Pierre
Governor: William J. Janklow, R (to Jan. 1999)
Lieut. Governor: Carole Hillard, R (to Jan. 1999)
Senators: Thomas A. Daschle, D (to Jan. 1999); Tim Johnson, D (to Jan. 2003)
Atty. General: Mark Barnett, R (to Jan. 1999)
Secy. of State: Joyce Hazeltine, R (to Jan. 1999)
Auditor: Vern Larson, R (to Jan. 1999)
Treasurer: Richard Butler, D (to Jan. 1999)
Organized as territory: March 2, 1861
Entered Union (rank): Nov. 2, 1889 (40)
Present constitution adopted: 1889
Motto: Under God the people rule
State symbols: flower, American pasqueflower (1903); **grass,** Western wheat grass (1970); **soil,** Houdek (1990); **tree,** Black Hills spruce (1947); **bird,** Ring-necked pheasant (1943); **insect,** Honeybee (1978); **animal,** Coyote (1949); **mineral stone,** Rose quartz (1966); **gemstone,** Fairburn agate (1966); **colors,** Blue and gold (in state flag); **song,** "Hail! South Dakota" (1943); **fish,** Walleye (1982); **musical instrument,** Fiddle (1989)
Nicknames: Mount Rushmore State; Coyote State
Origin of name: From the Sioux tribe, meaning "allies"
10 largest cities (1996 est.): Sioux Falls, 113,223; Rapid City, 57,642; Aberdeen, 25,088; Watertown, 19,619; Brookings, 17,413; Mitchell, 14,191; Yankton, 13,969; Pierre, 13,422; Huron, 12,428; Vermillion, 10,521
Land area (rank): 75,898 sq mi. (196,575 sq km) (16)
Geographic center: In Hughes Co., 8 mi. NE of Pierre
Number of counties: 67 (64 county governments)
Largest county (1995 pop. est.): Minnehaha, 135,641
State forests: None[1]
State parks: 13 plus 39 recreational areas (87,269 ac.)[2]
1997 resident population est.: 737,973
1990 resident census population (rank): 696,004 (45). **Male:** 342,498; **Female:** 353,506. **White:** 637,515 (91.6%); **Black:** 3,258 (0.5%); **American Indian:** 50,575 (7.3%); **Asian:** 3,123 (0.4%); **Other race:** 1,533 (0.2%); **Hispanic:** 5,252 (0.8%). **1990 percent population under 18:** 28.5; **65 and over:** 14.7; **median age:** 32.5.

1. No designated state forests; about 13,000 ac. of state land is forestland. 2. Acreage includes 39 recreation areas and 80 roadside parks, in addition to 12 state parks.

Exploration of this area began in 1743 when Louis-Joseph and François Verendrye came from France in search of a route to the Pacific.

The U.S. acquired the region as part of the Louisiana Purchase in 1803 and it was explored by Lewis and Clark in 1804–06. Fort Pierre, the first permanent settlement, was established in 1817. In 1831, the first Missouri River steamboat reached the fort.

Settlement of South Dakota did not begin in earnest until the arrival of the railroad in 1873 and the discovery of gold in the Black Hills the following year.

South Dakota's economy in recent years has benefitted from an expanding and diversifying industrial base. Agriculture is a cultural and economic mainstay, but it no longer leads the state in employment or share of gross state product. Durable-goods manufacturing and private services have evolved as the drivers of the economy. Tourism is also a booming industry in the state, generating approximately $1 billion worth of economic activity each year.

South Dakota leads the nation in the production of hay and oats, and ranks second among the states in the production of rye, flaxseed, and sunflower seed.

South Dakota is the nation's second leading producer of gold and the Homestake Mine is the richest in the U.S. Other minerals produced include berylium, bentonite, granite, silver, and uranium.

The Black Hills are the highest mountains east of the Rockies. Mt. Rushmore, in this group, is famous for the likenesses of Washington, Jefferson, Lincoln, and Theodore Roosevelt, which were carved in granite by Gutzon Borglum. A memorial to Crazy Horse is also being carved in granite near Custer.

Other tourist attractions include the Badlands; the World's Only Corn Palace, in Mitchell; and the city of Deadwood, where Wild Bill Hickok was killed in 1876 and where gambling was recently legalized to truly recapture the city's Old West flavor.

Famous natives and residents: Sparky Anderson, baseball manager; Gertrude Bonnin (Zitkala-Sa), Sioux writer and pan-Indian activist; Tom Brokaw, TV newscaster; Robert Casey, writer; Myron Floren, accordionist; Joseph J. Foss, WW II Marine fighter ace; Mary Hart, TV host; Crazy Horse, Oglala chief; Oscar Howe, Sioux artist; Hubert H. Humphrey, former vice president; Cheryl Ladd, actress; Ernest Orlando Lawrence, physicist; Russell Means, American Indian activist; George McGovern, politician; Arthur C. Mellette, first governor; Dorothy Provine, actress; Rain-in-the-Face, Hunkpapa Sioux chief; Red Cloud, chief of the Oglala Sioux; Ben Reifel, Brulé Sioux congressman; Ole Edvart Rölvaag, writer; Sitting Bull, chief of Hunkpappa Sioux; Norm Van Brocklin, football player; Mamie Van Doren, actress.

Tennessee

Capital: Nashville
Governor: Don Sundquist, R (to Jan. 1999)
Lieut. Governor: John S. Wilder, D (to Jan. 1999)
Senators: William H. Frist, R (to Jan. 2001); Fred Thompson, R (to Jan. 2003)
Secy. of State: Riley C. Darnell, D (to Jan. 1999)
Atty. General: J. Knox Walkup, D (to Aug. 2005)
Treasurer: Steve Adams, D (to Jan. 1999)
Entered Union (rank): June 1, 1796 (16)
Present constitution adopted: 1870; amended 1953, 1960, 1966, 1972, 1978
Motto: Agriculture and Commerce (1987)
Slogan: Tennessee—America at its best! (1965)
State symbols: flower, Iris (1933); **tree,** Tulip poplar (1947); **bird,** Mockingbird (1933); **horse,** Tennessee walking horse; **animal,** Raccoon (1971); **wild flower,** Passion flower (1973); **songs,** "Tennessee Waltz" (1965); "My Homeland, Tennessee" (1925); "When It's Iris Time in Tennessee" (1935), "My Tennessee" (1955); "Rocky Top" (1982); "Tennessee" (1992)
Nickname: Volunteer State
Origin of name: Of Cherokee origin; the exact meaning is unknown
10 largest cities (1996 est.): Memphis, 696,725; Nashville-Davidson (CC[1]), 511,263; Knoxville, 167,535; Chattanooga, 150,425; Clarksville, 94,879; Johnson City, 55,542; Murfreesboro, 53,966; Jackson, 50,406; Kingsport, 41,335; Hendersonville, 37,261
Land area (rank): 41,220 sq mi. (106,759 sq km) (34)
Geographic center: In Rutherford Co., 5 mi. NE of Murfreesboro
Number of counties: 95
Largest county (1995 pop. est.): Shelby, 865,058
State forests: 13 (155,000 ac.)
State parks: 50 (133,000 ac.)
1997 resident population est.: 5,368,198
1990 resident census population (rank): 4,877,185 (17). **Male:** 2,348,928; **Female:** 2,528,257. **White:** 4,048,068 (83.0%); **Black:** 778,035 (16.0%); **American Indian:** 10,039 (0.2%); **Asian:** 31,839 (0.7%); **Other race:** 9,204 (0.2%); **Hispanic:** 32,741 (0.7%). **1990 percent population under 18:** 24.9; **65 and over:** 12.7; **median age:** 33.6.

1. Consolidated City.

First visited by the Spanish explorer Hernando de Soto in 1540, the Tennessee area would later be claimed by both France and England as a result of the 1670s and 1680s explorations of Jacques Marquette and Louis Joliet, sieur de la Salle, and the Englishmen James Needham and Gabriel Arthur.

Great Britain obtained the region following the French and Indian War in 1763. It was rapidly occupied by settlers moving in from Virginia and the Carolinas.

During 1784–87, the settlers formed the "state" of Franklin, which was disbanded when the region was allowed to send representatives to the North Carolina legislature. In 1790 Congress organized the territory south of the Ohio River, and Tennessee joined the Union in 1796.

Although Tennessee joined the Confederacy during the Civil War, there was much pro-Union sentiment in the state, which was the scene of extensive military action.

The state is now predominantly industrial; the majority of its population lives in urban areas. Among the most important products are chemicals, textiles, apparel, electrical machinery, furniture, and leather goods. Other lines include food processing, lumber, primary metals, and metal products. The state is known as the U.S. hardwood-flooring center and ranks first in the production of marble, zinc, pyrite, and ball clay.

Tennessee is one of the leading tobacco-producing states in the nation. Its farming income is derived from livestock and dairy products, as well as corn, cotton, and soybeans.

With six other states, Tennessee shares the extensive federal reservoir developments on the Tennessee and Cumberland River systems. The Tennessee Valley Authority operates a number of dams and reservoirs in the state.

Among the major points of interest are the Andrew Johnson National Historic Site at Greenville, the American Museum of Atomic Energy at Oak Ridge, Great Smoky Mountains National Park,

the Hermitage (home of Andrew Jackson near Nashville), Rock City Gardens near Chattanooga, and three National Military Parks.

Famous natives and residents: James Agee, writer; Eddy Arnold, singer; Chet Atkins, guitarist; Julian Bond, Georgia legislator; Davy Crockett, frontiersman; David G. Farragut, first American admiral; Lester Flatt, bluegrass musician; Tennessee Ernie Ford, singer; Abe Fortas, jurist; Aretha Franklin, singer; Nikki Giovanni, poet; Al Gore, Jr., vice president; Red Grooms, artist; Isaac Hayes, composer; Benjamin L. Hooks, civil rights activist; Cordell Hull, former secretary of state; Andrew Jackson, former president; Andrew Johnson, former president; Estes Kefauver, legislator; Anita Kerr, singer; Grace Moore, soprano; Dolly Parton, singer; Minnie Pearl, singer and comedienne; James K. Polk, president; Grantland Rice, sportswriter; Carl Rowan, journalist; Wilma Rudolph, sprinter; Sequoia, Cherokee scholar and educator; Cybil Shepherd, actress; Dinah Shore, actress and singer; Tina Turner, singer; Alvin York, World War I hero.

Texas

Capital: Austin
Governor: George W. Bush, R (to Jan. 1999)
Lieut. Governor: Bob Bullock, D (to Jan. 1999)
Senators: Phil Gramm, R (to Jan. 2003); Kay Bailey Hutchison, R (to Jan. 2001)
Secy. of State: Alberto Gonzales (apptd. by gov.)
Comptroller: John Sharp, D (to Jan. 1999)
Atty. General: Dan Morales, D (to Jan. 1999)
Entered Union (rank): Dec. 29, 1845 (28)
Present constitution adopted: 1876
Motto: Friendship
State symbols: flower, Bluebonnet (1901); **tree,** Pecan (1919); **bird,** Mockingbird (1927); **song,** "Texas, Our Texas" (1929); **fish,** Guadalupe bass (1989); **seashell,** Lightning whelk (1987); **dish,** Chili (1977); **folk dance,** Square dance (1991); **fruit,** Texas Red grapefruit (1993); **gem,** Texas blue topaz (1969); **gemstone cut,** Lone Star Cut (1977); **grass,** Sideoats grass (1971); **reptile,** Horned lizard (1993); **stone,** Petrified palmwood (1969); **plant,** Prickly pear cactus; **insect,** Monarch butterfly; **pepper,** Jalapeño pepper; **mammal,** Longhorn; **small mammal,** Armadillo; **flying mammal,** Mexican free-tailed bat
Nickname: Lone Star State
Origin of name: From an Indian word meaning "friends"
10 largest cities (1996 est.): Houston, 1,744,058; Dallas, 1,067,816; San Antonio, 1,053,292; El Paso, 599,865; Austin, 541,278; Fort Worth, 479,716; Arlington, 294,816; Corpus Christi, 280,260; Lubbock, 193,565; Plano, 192,280
Land area (rank): 261,914 sq mi. (678,358 sq km) (2)
Geographic center: In McCulloch Co., 15 mi. NE of Brady
Number of counties: 254
Largest county (1995 pop. est.): Harris, 3,076,867
State forests: 5 (7,609 ac.)
State parks: 218 (206 developed)
1997 resident population est.: 19,439,337
1990 resident census population (rank): 16,986,510 (3). **Male:** 8,365,963; **Female:** 8,620,547. **White:** 12,774,762 (75.2%); **Black:** 2,021,632 (11.9%); **American Indian:** 65,877 (0.4%); **Asian:** 319,459 (1.9%); **Other race:** 1,804,780 (10.6%); **Hispanic:** 4,339,905 (25.5%). **1990 percent population under 18:** 28.5; **65 and over:** 10.1; **median age:** 30.8.

Spanish explorers, including Álvar Núñez Cabeza de Vaca and Francisco Vásquez de Coronado, were the first to visit the region in the 16th and 17th centuries, settling at Ysleta near El Paso in 1682. In 1685, sieur de la Salle established a short-lived French colony at Matagorda Bay.

Americans, led by Stephen F. Austin, began to settle along the Brazos River in 1821 when Texas was controlled by Mexico, recently independent from Spain. In 1836, following a brief war between the American settlers in Texas and the Mexican government, the Independent Republic of Texas was proclaimed with Sam Houston as president. This war was famous for the battles of the Alamo and San Jacinto. After Texas became the 28th U.S. state in 1845, border disputes led to the Mexican War of 1846–48.

Today, Texas, second only to Alaska in land area, leads all other states in such categories as oil, cattle, sheep, and cotton. Possessing enormous natural resources, Texas is a major agricultural state and an industrial giant.

Sulfur, salt, helium, asphalt, graphite, bromine, natural gas, cement, and clays are among the state's valuable resources. Chemicals, oil refining, food processing, machinery, and transportation equipment are among the major Texas manufacturing industries.

Texas ranches and farms produce beef cattle, poultry, rice, pecans, peanuts, sorghum, and an extensive variety of fruits and vegetables.

Millions of tourists spend well over $20.6 billion annually visiting more than 70 state parks, recreation areas, and points of interest such as the Gulf Coast resort area, the Lyndon B. Johnson Space Center in Houston, the Alamo in San Antonio, the state capital in Austin, and the Big Bend and Guadalupe Mountains National Parks.

Famous natives and residents: Alvin Ailey, choreographer; Mary Kay Ash, cosmetics entrepreneur; Steven Fuller Austin, founding father of Texas; Gene Autry, singer and actor; Carol Burnett, comedienne; Cyd Charisse, actress and dancer; Denton A. Cooley, heart surgeon; Joan Crawford, actress; Dwight David Eisenhower, former president and general; A. J. Foyt, auto racer; Ben Hogan, golfer; Howard Hughes, industrialist and film producer; Jack Johnson, boxer; Lyndon B. Johnson, former president; George Jones, singer; Tommy Lee Jones, actor; Scott Joplin, composer; Trini Lopez, singer; Mary Martin, singer and actress; Spanky McFarland, actor; Audie Murphy, actor and war hero; Chester Nimitz, admiral; Sandra Day O'Connor, jurist; Buck Owens, singer; Katherine Anne Porter, novelist; Wiley Post, aviator; Dan Rather, TV newscaster; Robert Rauschenberg, painter; Tex Ritter, singer; Rip Torn, actor and director; Tommy Tune, dancer and choreographer; Dooley Wilson, actor and musician; Babe Didrikson Zaharias, athlete and golfer.

Utah

Capital: Salt Lake City
Governor: Mike O. Leavitt, R (to Jan. 2001)
Lieut. Governor: Olene Walker, R (to Jan. 2001)
Senators: Robert F. Bennett, R (to Jan. 1999); Orrin G. Hatch, R (to Jan. 2001)
Atty. General: Jan Graham, D (to Jan. 2001)
Organized as territory: Sept. 9, 1850
Entered Union (rank): Jan. 4, 1896 (45)
Present constitution adopted: 1896
Motto: Industry
State symbols: flower, Sego lily (1911); **tree,** Blue spruce (1933); **bird,** California gull (1955); **emblem,** Beehive (1959); **song,** "Utah, We Love Thee" (1953); **gem,** Topaz; **animal,** Rocky Mountain Elk (1971); **insect,** Honeybee (1983); **grass,** Indian rice grass (1990); **fossil,** Allosaurus (1988); **cooking pot,** Dutch oven (1997); **fish,** Bonneville cutthroat trout (1997); **fruit,** Cherry (1997); **mineral,** Copper; **rock,** Coal (1991)
Nickname: Beehive State
Origin of name: From the Ute tribe, meaning "people of the mountains"

10 largest cities (1996 est.): Salt Lake City, 172,575; Provo, 99,606; West Valley City, 99,136; Sandy, 94,593; Orem, 79,736; Ogden, 65,720; West Jordan, 57,600; Layton, 50,906; St. George, 42,763; Bountiful, 39,595
Land area (rank): 82,168 sq mi. (212,816 sq km) (12)
Geographic center: In Sanpete Co., 3 mi. N. of Manti
Number of counties: 29
Largest county (1996 pop. est.): Salt Lake, 827,818
National parks: 5
National monuments: 6
State parks/forests: 45 (64,097 ac.)
1997 resident population est.: 2,059,148
1990 resident census population (rank): 1,722,850 (35). **Male:** 855,759; **Female:** 867,091. **White:** 1,615,845 (93.8%); **Black:** 11,576 (0.7%); **American Indian:** 24,283 (1.4%); **Asian:** 33,371 (1.9%); **Other race:** 37,775 (2.2%); **Hispanic:** 84,597 (4.9%). **1990 percent population under 18:** 36.4; **65 and over:** 8.7; **median age:** 26.2.

The region was first explored for Spain by Franciscan friars Escalante and Dominguez in 1776. In 1824 the famous American frontiersman Jim Bridger discovered the Great Salt Lake.

Fleeing the religious persecution encountered in eastern and middle-western states, the Mormons reached the Great Salt Lake in 1847 and began to build Salt Lake City. The U.S. acquired the Utah region in the treaty ending the Mexican War in 1848 and the first transcontinental railroad was completed with the driving of a golden spike at Promontory Summit in 1869.

Mormon difficulties with the federal government about polygamy did not end until the Mormon Church renounced the practice in 1890, six years before Utah became a state.

Rich in natural resources, Utah has long been a leading producer of copper, gold, silver, lead, zinc, and molybdenum. Oil has also become a major product. Utah shares rich oil shale deposits with Colorado and Wyoming. Utah also has large deposits of low sulphur coal.

Ranked eighth among the states in number of sheep in 1989, Utah also produces large crops of alfalfa, winter wheat, and beans.

Utah's traditional industries of agriculture and mining are complemented by increased tourism business and growing aerospace, biomedical, and computer-related businesses. Utah is home to computer software giant Novell.

Utah is a great vacationland with 11,000 miles of fishing streams and 147,000 acres of lakes and reservoirs. Among the many tourist attractions are Arches, Bryce Canyon, Canyonlands, Capitol Reef, and Zion National Parks; Dinosaur, Natural Bridges, and Rainbow Bridge National Monuments; the Mormon Tabernacle in Salt Lake City; and Monument Valley. Salt Lake City will be the site of the 2002 Winter Olympics.

Famous natives and residents: Maude Adams, actress; Roseanne, actress; Frank Borzage, film director and producer; John M. Browning, inventor; Butch Cassidy, outlaw; Laraine Day, actress; Bernard De Voto, writer; Avard Fairbanks, sculptor; Philo Farnsworth, television pioneer; Jake Garn, senator; John Gilbert, actor; J. Willard Marriott, restaurant and hotel chain founder; Peter Skene Ogden, fur trader and trapper; Merlin Olsen, football player; Donny Osmond, Marie Osmond, singers; Ivy Baker Priest, former U.S. treasurer; Lee Greene Richards, painter; Leroy Robertson, composer; Brent Scowcroft, business executive and consultant; Reed Smoot, first Morman elected to U.S. Senate; Mack Swain, actor; Everett Thorpe, painter; Robert Walker, actor; James Woods, actor; Brigham Young, territory governor and religious leader; Loretta Young, actress.

Vermont

Capital: Montpelier
Governor: Howard B. Dean, D (to Jan. 1999)
Lieut. Governor: Douglas A. Racine, D (to Jan. 1999)
Senators: James M. Jeffords, R (to Jan. 2001); Patrick J. Leahy, D (to Jan. 1999)
Secy. of State: James F. Milne, R (to Jan. 1999)
Treasurer: James H. Douglas, R (to Jan. 1999)
Auditor of Accounts: Edward S. Flanagan, D (to Jan. 1999)
Atty. General: William Sorrell, D (to Jan. 1999)
Entered Union (rank): March 4, 1791 (14)
Present constitution adopted: 1793
Motto: Vermont, Freedom and Unity
State symbols: flower, Red clover (1894); **tree,** Sugar maple (1949); **bird,** Hermit thrush (1941); **animal,** Morgan horse (1961); **insect,** Honeybee (1978); **song,** "Hail, Vermont!" (1938)
Nickname: Green Mountain State
Origin of name: From the French "vert mont," meaning "green mountain"
10 largest cities (1994): Burlington, 38,306; Rutland, 17,489; Bennington, 16,247; South Burlington, 13,170; Barre, 9,466; Essex Junction, 8,702; Montpelier, 8,042; St. Albans, 7,650; Winooski, 6,219; Newport, 4,354
Land area (rank): 9,249 sq mi. (23,956 sq km) (43)
Geographic center: In Washington Co., 3 mi. E of Roxbury
Number of counties: 14
Largest county (1995 pop. est.): Chittenden, 139,041
State forests: 34 (113,953 ac.)
State parks: 45 (31,325 ac.)
1997 resident population est.: 588,978
1990 resident census population (rank): 562,758 (48). **Male:** 275,492; **Female:** 287,266. **White:** 555,088 (98.6%); **Black:** 1,951 (0.3%); **American Indian:** 1,696 (0.3%); **Asian:** 3,215 (0.6%); **Other race:** 808 (0.1%); **Hispanic:** 3,661 (0.7%). **1990 percent population under 18:** 25.4; **65 and over:** 11.8; **median age:** 33.0.

The Vermont region was explored and claimed for France by Samuel de Champlain in 1609 and the first French settlement was established at Fort Ste. Anne in 1666. The first English settlers moved into the area in 1724 and built Fort Drummer on the site of present-day Brattleboro. England gained control of the area in 1763 after the French and Indian War.

First organized to drive settlers from New York out of Vermont, the Green Mountain Boys, led by Ethan Allen, won fame by capturing Fort Ticonderoga from the British on May 10, 1775, in the early days of the Revolutionary War.

In 1777 Vermont adopted its first constitution abolishing slavery and providing for universal male suffrage without property qualifications. In 1791 Vermont became the fourteenth state to join the Union.

Vermont leads the nation in the production of monument granite, marble, and maple syrup. It is also a leader in the production of talc.

Vermont's rugged, rocky terrain discourages extensive agricultural farming, but is well suited to raising fruit trees, and to dairy farming. Vermont has the highest proportion of dairy cows to humans in the nation.

Principal industrial products include electrical equipment, fabricated metal products, printing and publishing, and paper and allied products.

Tourism is a major industry in Vermont. Vermont's many famous ski areas include Stowe, Killington, Mt. Snow, Bromley, Jay Peak, and Sugarbush. Hunting and fishing also attract many visitors to Vermont each year. Among the many points of interest are the Green Mountain National Forest, Bennington Battle Monument, the Calvin Coolidge Homestead at Plymouth, and the Marble Exhibit in Proctor.

Famous natives and residents: Chester A. Arthur, former president; Orson Bean, actor; Calvin Coolidge, former president; George Dewey, admiral; John Dewey, philosopher and educator; Stephen A. Douglas, politician; James Fisk, financial speculator; Wilbur Fisk, clergyman and educator; Richard Morris Hunt, architect; William Morris Hunt, painter; Elisha Otis, inventor; Moses Pendleton, choreographer; Joseph Smith, religious leader; Ernest Thompson, actor and writer; Rudy Vallee, singer and band leader; Henry Wells, pioneer entrepreneur (Wells Fargo & Co.); Brigham Young, religious leader.

Virginia

Capital: Richmond
Governor: James S. Gilmore, III, R (to Jan. 2002)
Lieut. Governor: John H. Hager, R (to Jan. 2002)
Senators: Charles S. Robb, D (to Jan. 2001); John W. Warner, R (to Jan. 2003)
Secy. of the Commonwealth: Anne P. Petera (apptd. by governor)
Comptroller: William E. Landsidle (apptd. by governor)
Atty. General: Mark L. Earley
Entered Union (rank): June 25, 1788 (10)
Present constitution adopted: 1970
Motto: *Sic semper tyrannis* (Thus always to tyrants)
State symbols: flower, American dogwood (1918); **bird,** Cardinal (1950); **dog,** American foxhound (1966); **shell,** Oyster shell (1974)
Nicknames: The Old Dominion; Mother of Presidents
Origin of name: In honor of Elizabeth "Virgin Queen" of England
10 largest cities (1996 est.): Virginia Beach, 430,385; Norfolk, 233,430; Richmond, 198,267; Chesapeake, 192,342; Newport News, 176,122; Arlington CDP, 175,334; Hampton, 138,757; Alexandria, 117,586; Portsmouth, 101,308; Roanoke, 95,548
Land area (rank): 39,598 sq mi. (102,558 sq km) (37)
Geographic center: In Buckingham Co., 5 mi. SW of Buckingham
Number of counties: 95, plus 40 independent cities
Largest county (1995 pop. est.): Fairfax, 887,205
State forests: 11 (50,636 ac.)
State parks and recreational parks: 28 (63,000 ac.)[1]
1997 resident population est.: 6,733,996
1990 resident census population (rank): 6,187,358 (12). **Male:** 3,033,974; **Female:** 3,153,384. **White:** 4,791,739 (77.4%); **Black:** 1,162,994 (18.8%); **American Indian:** 15,282 (0.2%); **Asian:** 159,053 (2.6%); **Other race:** 58,290 (0.9%); **Hispanic:** 160,288 (2.6%). **1990 percent population under 18:** 24.3; **65 and over:** 10.7; **median age:** 32.6.

1. Does not include portion of Breaks Interstate Park (Va.-Ky., 1,200 ac.) that lies in Virginia.

The history of America is closely tied to that of Virginia, particularly in the Colonial period. Jamestown, founded in 1607, was the first permanent English settlement in North America and slavery was introduced there in 1619. The surrenders ending both the American Revolution (Yorktown) and the Civil War (Appomattox) occurred in Virginia. The state is called the "Mother of Presidents" because eight chief executives of the United States were born there.

Today, Virginia has a large number of diversified manufacturing industries, including transportation equipment, textiles, food processing, and printing. Other important lines are electronic and other electric equipment, chemicals, apparel, lumber and wood products, furniture, and industrial machinery and equipment.

Agriculture remains an important sector in the Virginia economy and the state ranks among the top 10 in the U.S. in tomatoes, tobacco, peanuts, summer potatoes, turkeys, apples, broilers, and sweet potatoes. Other crops include corn, vegetables, and barley. Famous for Smithfield hams, Virginia also has a large dairy industry.

Coal mining accounts for roughly 75% of Virginia's mineral output, and lime, kyanite, and stone are also mined.

Points of interest include Mt. Vernon and other places associated with George Washington; Monticello, home of Thomas Jefferson; Stratford, home of the Lees; Richmond, capital of the Confederacy and of Virginia; and Williamsburg, the restored Colonial capital.

The Chesapeake Bay Bridge-Tunnel spans the mouth of Chesapeake Bay, connecting Cape Charles with Norfolk. Consisting of a series of low trestles, two bridges and two mile-long tunnels, the complex is 18 miles (29 km) long. It was opened in 1964.

Other attractions are the Shenandoah National Park, Fredericksburg and Spotsylvania National Military Park, the Booker T. Washington birthplace near Roanoke, Arlington House (the Robert E. Lee Memorial), the Skyline Drive, and the Blue Ridge National Parkway.

Famous natives and residents: Richard Arlen, actor; Arthur Ashe, tennis player; Pearl Bailey, singer; Russell Baker, columnist; Warren Beatty, actor; George Bingham, painter; Richard E. Byrd, polar explorer; Willa Cather, novelist; Roy Clark, country music artist; William Clark, explorer; Henry Clay, statesman; Joseph Cotten, actor; Ella Fitzgerald, singer; William H. Harrison, former president; Patrick Henry, statesman; Sam Houston, political leader; Thomas Jefferson, former president; Robert E. Lee, Confederate general; Meriwether Lewis, explorer; Shirley MacLaine, actress; James Madison, former president; John Marshall, jurist; Cyrus McCormick, inventor; James Monroe, former president; Opochancanough, Powhatan leader; John Payne, actor; Walter Reed, army surgeon; Matthew Ridgway, former Army Chief of Staff; Bill "Bojangles" Robinson, dancer; George C. Scott, actor; Sam Snead, golfer; James "Jeb" Stuart, Confederate army officer; Zachary Taylor, former president; Nat Turner, civil rights leader; John Tyler, former president; Booker T. Washington, educator; George Washington, first president; Woodrow Wilson, former president; Tom Wolfe, journalist.

Washington

Capital: Olympia
Governor: Gary Locke, D (to 2001)
Lieut. Governor: Brad Owen, D (to 2001)
Senators: Slade Gorton, R (to Jan. 2001); Patty Murray, D (to Jan. 1999)
Secy. of State: Ralph Munro, R (to 2001)
State Treasurer: Michael J. Murphy (to 2001)
Atty. General: Christine Gregoire, D (to 2001)
Organized as territory: March 2, 1853
Entered Union (rank): Nov. 11, 1889 (42)
Present constitution adopted: 1889
Motto: *Al-Ki* (Indian word meaning "by and by")
State symbols: flower, Coast Rhododendron (1949); **tree,** Western hemlock (1947); **bird,** Willow goldfinch (1951); **fish,** Steelhead trout (1969); **gem,** Petrified wood (1975); **colors,** Green and gold (1925); **song,** "Washington, My Home" (1959); **folk song,** "Roll On Columbia, Roll On" (1987); **dance,** Square dance (1979)

Nicknames: Evergreen State; Chinook State
Origin of name: In honor of George Washington
10 largest cities (1996 est.): Seattle, 524,704; Spokane, 186,562; Tacoma, 179,114; Bellevue, 92,267; Everett, 81,028; Federal Way, 68,088; Yakima, 65,110; Bellingham, 61,043; Vancouver, 59,982; Kennewick, 51,184
Land area (rank): 66,582 sq mi. (172,447 sq km) (20)
Geographic center: In Chelan Co., 10 mi. WSW of Wenatchee
Number of counties: 39
Largest county (1995 pop. est.): King, 1,595,243
State forest lands: 1,922,880 ac.
State parks: 215 (231,861 ac.)[1]
1997 resident population est.: 5,610,362
1990 resident census population (rank): 4,866,692 (18). **Male:** 2,413,747; **Female:** 2,452,945. **White:** 4,308,937 (88.5%); **Black:** 149,801 (3.1%); **American Indian:** 81,483 (1.7%); **Other race:** 115,513 (2.4%); **Hispanic:** 214,570 (4.4%). **1990 percent population under 18:** 25.9; **65 and over:** 11.8; **median age:** 33.1.

1. Parks and undeveloped areas administered by State Parks and Recreation Commission. Dept. of Wildlife administers wildlife and recreation areas totaling 428,989.5 acres.

As part of the vast Oregon Country, Washington territory was visited by Spanish, American, and British explorers—Bruno Heceta for Spain in 1775, the American Capt. Robert Gray in 1792, and Capt. George Vancouver for Britain in 1792–1794. Lewis and Clark explored the Columbia River region and coastal areas for the U.S. in 1805–1806.

Rival American and British settlers and conflicting territorial claims threatened war in the early 1840s. However, in 1846 the Oregon Treaty set the boundary at the 49th parallel and war was averted.

Washington is a leading lumber producer. Its rugged surface is rich in stands of Douglas fir, hemlock, ponderosa and white pine, spruce, larch, and cedar. The state holds first place in apples, lentils, dry edible peas, hops, pears, red raspberries, spearmint oil, and sweet cherries, and ranks high in apricots, asparagus, grapes, peppermint oil, and potatoes. Livestock and livestock products make important contributions to total farm revenue and the commercial fishing catch of salmon, halibut, and bottomfish makes a significant contribution to the state's economy.

Manufacturing industries in Washington include aircraft and missiles, shipbuilding and other transportation equipment, lumber, food processing, metals and metal products, chemicals, and machinery.

The Columbia River contains one-third of the potential water power in the U.S., harnessed by such dams as the Grand Coulee, one of the greatest power producers in the world. Washington has over 1,000 dams built for a variety of purposes including irrigation, power, flood control, and water storage. Its abundance of electrical power makes Washington one of the nation's major producers of refined aluminum.

Among the major points of interest: Mt. Rainier, Olympic, and North Cascades. In 1980, Mount St. Helens, a peak in the Cascade Range in Southwestern Washington, erupted on May 18th. Also of interest are National Parks; Whitman Mission and Fort Vancouver National Historic Sites; and the Pacific Science Center and the Space Needle, in Seattle.

Famous natives and residents: Bob Barker, TV host; Dyan Cannon, actress; Carol Channing, actress; Judy Collins, singer; Bing Crosby, singer and actor; Bob Crosby, musician; Merce Cunningham, choreographer; Howard Duff, actor; Frances Farmer, actress; Bill Gates, software executive; Jimi Hendrix, guitarist; Frank Herbert, writer; Robert Joffrey, choreographer; Gypsy Rose Lee, entertainer; Hank Ketcham, cartoonist; Mary McCarthy, novelist; Guthrie McClintic, theatrical producer and director; John McIntire, actor; Robert Motherwell, artist; Patrice Munsel, soprano; Ella Raines, actress; Jimmy Rogers, singer; Francis Scobee, astronaut; Seattle, Dwamish, Suquamish chief; Jeff Smith, TV cook; Smohalla, Indian prophet and chief; Adam West, actor; Martha Wright, singer; Audrey Wurdemann, poet.

West Virginia

Capital: Charleston
Governor: Cecil H. Underwood, R (to Jan. 2001)
Senators: Robert C. Byrd, D (to Jan. 2001); John D. Rockefeller IV, D (to Jan. 2003)
Secy. of State: Ken Heckler, D (to Jan. 1997)
State Auditor: Glen Gainer (to Jan. 1997)
Atty. General: Darrell McGraw, D (to Jan. 1997)
Entered Union (rank): June 20, 1863 (35)
Present constitution adopted: 1872
Motto: *Montani semper liberi* (Mountaineers are always free)
State symbols: flower, Rhododendron (1903); **tree,** Sugar maple (1949); **bird,** Cardinal (1949); **animal,** Black bear (1973); **colors,** Blue and gold (official) (1863); **songs,** "West Virginia, My Home Sweet Home," "The West Virginia Hills," and "This Is My West Virginia" (adopted by Legislature in 1947, 1961, and 1963 as official state songs)
Nickname: Mountain State
Origin of name: In honor of Elizabeth "Virgin Queen" of England
10 largest cities (1996 est.): Charleston, 56,098; Huntington, 53,941; Wheeling, 33,311; Parkersburg, 32,766; Morgantown, 26,919; Weirton, 21,731; Fairmont, 19,731; Beckley, 18,353; Clarksburg, 17,410; Martinsburg, 14,541
Land area (rank): 24,087 sq mi. (62,384 sq km) (41)
Geographic center: In Braxton Co., 4 mi. E of Sutton
Number of counties: 55
Largest county (1995 pop. est.): Kanawha, 206,195
State forests: 9 (79,502 ac.)
State parks: 35 (74,508 ac.)
1997 resident population est.: 1,815,787
1990 resident census population (rank): 1,793,477 (34). **Male:** 861,536; **Female:** 931,941. **White:** 1,725,523 (96.2%); **Black:** 56,295 (3.1%); **American Indian:** 2,458 (0.1%); **Asian:** 7,459 (0.4%); **Other race:** 1,742 (0.1%); **Hispanic:** 8,489 (0.5%). **1990 percent population under 18:** 24.7; **65 and over:** 15.0; **median age:** 35.4.

West Virginia's early history from 1609 until 1863 is largely shared with Virginia, of which it was a part until Virginia seceded from the Union in 1861. Then the delegates of 40 western counties formed their own government, which was granted statehood in 1863.

First permanent settlement dates from 1731 when Morgan Morgan founded Mill Creek. In 1742 coal was discovered on the Coal River, an event that would be of great significance in determining West Virginia's future.

The state usually ranks third in total coal production with about 15% of the U.S. total. It also is a leader in steel, glass, aluminum, and chemical manufactures; natural gas; oil; quarry products; and hardwood lumber.

Major cash farm products are poultry and eggs, dairy products, apples, and feed crops. Nearly 75% of West Virginia is covered with forests.

Tourism is increasingly popular in mountainous West Virginia and visitors spent $2.475 billion in

1990. More than a million acres have been set aside in 35 state parks and recreation areas and in 9 state forests and national forests.

Major points of interest include Harpers Ferry and New River Gorge National River, The Greenbrier and Berkeley Springs resorts, the scenic railroad at Cass, and the historic homes in the Eastern Panhandle.

Famous natives and residents: George Brett, baseball player; Pearl S. Buck, author; Phyllis Curtin, soprano; Martin R. Delany, first Black Army major; Billy Dixon, frontiersman and scout; Joanne Dru, actress; Thomas "Stonewall" Jackson, Confederate general; John S. Knight, publisher; Don Knotts, actor; Peter Marshall, TV host; Kathy Mattea, country music superstar; Whitney D. Morrow, banker and diplomat; Mary Lou Retton, gymnast; Walter Reuther, labor leader; Eleanor Steber, soprano; Lewis L. Strauss, naval officer and scientist; Cyrus Vance, government official; William Lyne Wilson, legislator and university president; Chuck Yeager, test pilot and Air Force general.

Wisconsin

Capital: Madison
Governor: Tommy G. Thompson, R (to Jan. 1999)
Lieut. Governor: Scott McCallum, R (to Jan. 1999)
Senators: Russell D. Feingold, D (to Jan. 1999); Herb Kohl, D (to Jan. 2001)
Secy. of State: Douglas J. La Follette, D (to Jan. 1999)
State Treasurer: Jack C. Voight, R (to Jan. 1999)
Atty. General: James E. Doyle, D (to Jan. 1999)
Superintendent of Public Instruction: John Benson, Nonpartisan (to July 2001)
Organized as territory: July 4, 1836
Entered Union (rank): May 29, 1848 (30)
Present constitution adopted: 1848
Motto: Forward
State symbols: flower, Wood violet (1949); **tree,** Sugar maple (1949); **grain,** corn (1990); **bird,** Robin (1949); **animal,** Badger; **wild life animal,** White-tailed deer (1957); **domestic animal,** Dairy cow (1971); **insect,** Honeybee (1977); **fish,** Musky (Muskellunge) (1955); **song,** "On Wisconsin"; **mineral,** Galena (1971); **rock,** Red Granite (1971); **symbol of peace:** Mourning Dove (1971); **soil,** Antigo Silt Loam (1983); **fossil,** Trilobite (1985); **dog,** American Water Spaniel (1986); **beverage,** Milk (1988); **dance,** Polka (1994)
Nickname: Badger State
Origin of name: French corruption of an Indian word whose meaning is disputed
10 largest cities (1996 est.): Milwaukee, 590,503; Madison, 197,630; Green Bay, 102,076; Kenosha, 86,888; Racine, 82,572; Appleton, 65,862; West Allis, 60,550; Waukesha, 60,197; Janesville, 58,960; Eau Claire, 58,872
Land area (rank): 54,314 sq mi. (140,673 sq km) (25)
Geographic center: In Wood Co., 9 mi. SE of Marshfield
Number of counties: 72
Largest county (1995 pop. est.): Milwaukee, 931,242
State forests: 9 (476,004 ac.)
State parks & scenic trails: 45 parks, 14 trails (66,185 ac.)
1997 resident population est.: 5,169,677
1990 resident census population (rank): 4,891,769 (16). **Male:** 2,392,935; **Female:** 2,498,834. **White:** 4,512,523 (92.2%); **Black:** 244,539 (5.0%); **American Indian:** 39,387 (0.8%); **Asian:** 53,583 (1.1%); **Other race:** 41,737 (0.9%); **Hispanic:** 93,194 (1.9%). **1980 percent population under 18:** 26.4; **65 and over:** 13.3; **median age:** 32.9.

The Wisconsin region was first explored for France by Jean Nicolet, who landed at Green Bay in 1634. In 1660 a French trading post and Roman Catholic mission were established near present-day Ashland.

Great Britain obtained the region in settlement of the French and Indian War in 1763; the U.S. acquired it in 1783 after the Revolutionary War. However, Great Britain retained actual control until after the War of 1812. The region was successively governed as part of the territories of Indiana, Illinois, and Michigan between 1800 and 1836, when it became a separate territory.

Wisconsin is a leading state in milk and cheese production. In 1996 the state ranked first in the number of milk cows (1,410,000) and produced 29% of the nation's total output of cheese. Other important farm products are peas, beans, beets, corn, potatoes, oats, hay, and cranberries.

The chief industrial products of the state are automobiles, machinery, furniture, paper, beer, and processed foods. Wisconsin ranks second among the 47 paper-producing states.

Wisconsin is a pioneer in social legislation, providing pensions for the blind (1907), aid to dependent children (1913), and old-age assistance (1925). In labor legislation, the state was the first to enact an unemployment compensation law (1932) and the first in which a workman's compensation law actually took effect. Wisconsin had the first state-wide primary-election law and the first successful income-tax law. In April 1984, Wisconsin became the first state to adopt the Uniform Marital Property Act. The act took effect on January 1, 1986.

The state has over 14,000 lakes, of which Winnebago is the largest. Water sports, ice-boating, and fishing are popular, as are skiing and hunting. Public parks and forests take up one-seventh of the land, with 45 state parks, 9 state forests, 14 state trails, 3 recreational areas, and 2 national forests.

Among the many points of interest are the Apostle Islands National Lakeshore; Ice Age National Scientific Reserve; the Circus World Museum at Baraboo; the Wolf, St. Croix, and Lower St. Croix national scenic riverways; and the Wisconsin Dells.

Famous natives and residents: Don Ameche, actor; Ray Chapman Andrews, naturalist and explorer; Walter Annenberg, media tycoon and philanthropist; Carrie Catt, woman suffragist; John R. Commons, economist; Tyne Daly, actress; August Derleth, author; Jeanne Dixon, seer; Zona Gale, novelist; Eric Heiden, skater; Woody Herman, band leader; Hildegarde, singer; Harry Houdini, magician; Hans V. Kaltenborne, journalist; Pee Wee King, singer; George F. Kennan, diplomat; Robert La Follette, politician; William D. Leahy, Fleet Admiral; Liberace, pianist; Charles Litel, actor; Allen Ludden, TV host; Alfred Lunt, actor; Frederic March, actor; Jackie Mason, comedian; John Ringling North, circus director; Pat O'Brien, actor; Georgia O'Keeffe, painter; Charlotte Rae, actress; William H. Rehnquist, jurist; Gena Rowlands, actress; Tom Snyder, newscaster; Spencer Tracy, actor; Thorstein Veblen, economist; Orson Welles, actor and producer; Thornton Wilder, author; Charles Winninger, actor; Frank Lloyd Wright, architect.

Wyoming

Capital: Cheyenne
Governor: Jim Geringer, R (to Jan. 1999)
Senators: Mike Enzi, R (to Jan. 2003); Craig Thomas, R (to Jan. 2001)
Secy. of State: Diana Ohman, R (to Jan. 1999)
Auditor: Dave Ferrari, R (to Jan. 1999)
Supt. of Public Instruction: Judy Catchpole, R (to Jan. 1999)
Treasurer: Stanford S. Smith, R (to Jan. 1999)
Atty. General: Bill Hill, R (apptd. by Governor)

Organized as territory: May 19, 1869
Entered Union (rank): July 10, 1890 (44)
Present constitution adopted: 1890
Motto: Equal rights (1955)
State symbols: flower, Indian paintbrush (1917); **tree,** Cottonwood (1947); **bird,** Meadowlark (1927); **gemstone,** Jade (1967); **insignia,** Bucking horse (unofficial); **song,** "Wyoming" (1955)
Nickname: Equality State
Origin of name: From the Delaware Indian word, meaning "mountains and valleys alternating"; the same as the Wyoming Valley in Pennsylvania
10 largest cities (1996 est.): Cheyenne, 53,729; Casper, 48,800; Laramie, 26,583; Rock Springs, 19,742; Gillette, 19,202; Sheridan, 14,730; Green River, 13,289; Evanston, 11,514; Riverton, 10,050; Rawlins, 8,947
Land area (rank): 97,105 sq mi. (251,501 sq km) (9)
Geographic center: In Fremont Co., 58 mi. ENE of Lander
Number of counties: 23, plus Yellowstone National Park
Largest county (1996 pop. est.): Laramie, 79,175
State parks and historic sites: 23 (58,498 ac.)
1997 resident population est.: 479,743
1990 resident census population (rank): 453,588 (50). **Male:** 227,007; **Female:** 226,581. **White:** 427,061 (94.2%); **Black:** 3,606 (0.8%); **American Indian:** 9,479 (2.1%); **Asian:** 2.806 (0.6%); **Other race:** 10,636 (2.3%); **Hispanic:** 25,751 (5.7%). **1990 percent population under 18:** 29.9; **65 and over:** 10.4; **median age:** 32.0.

The U.S. acquired the land comprising Wyoming from France as part of the Louisiana Purchase in 1803. John Colter, a fur-trapper, is the first white man known to have entered present Wyoming. In 1807 he explored the Yellowstone area and brought back news of its geysers and hot springs.

Robert Stuart pioneered the Oregon Trail across Wyoming in 1812–13 and, in 1834, Fort Laramie, the first permanent trading post in Wyoming, was built. Western Wyoming was obtained by the U.S. in the 1846 Oregon Treaty with Great Britain and as a result of the treaty ending the Mexican War in 1848.

When the Wyoming Territory was organized in 1869 Wyoming women became the first in the nation to obtain the right to vote. In 1925 Mrs. Nellie Tayloe Ross was elected first woman governor in the United States.

Wyoming's towering mountains and vast plains provide spectacular scenery, grazing lands for sheep and cattle, and rich mineral deposits.

Mining, particularly oil and natural gas, is the most important industry. Wyoming has the world's largest sodium carbonate (natrona) deposits and has the nation's second largest uranium deposits.

Wyoming ranks second among the states in wool production. In January 1995, it ranked third in sheep and lambs, exceeded only by Texas and California; it also had 1,410,000 cattle. Principal crops include wheat, oats, sugar beets, corn, potatoes, barley, and alfalfa.

Second in mean elevation to Colorado, Wyoming has many attractions for the tourist trade, notably Yellowstone National Park. Cheyenne is famous for its annual "Frontier Days" celebration. Flaming Gorge, the Fort Laramie National Historic Site, and Devils Tower and Fossil Butte National Monuments are other National points of interest.

Famous natives and residents: James Bridger, trapper, guide and storyteller; Dick Cheney, former Secretary of Defense; Buffalo Bill Cody, scout; John Colter, trader and first white man to enter Wyoming; June E. Downey, educator; Thomas Fitzpatrick, mountain man and guide; Curt Gowdy, sportscaster; Tom Horn, detective; Isabel Jewell, actress; Velma Linford, writer; Esther Morris, first woman judge; Ted Olson, writer; John "Portugee" Phillips, frontiersman; Jackson Pollock, painter; Nellie Tayloe Ross, first woman elected governor of a state; Alan K. Simpson, senator; Jedediah S. Smith, mountain man and first American to reach California from the East; Alan Swallow, publisher and author; Willis Van Devanter, Supreme Court justice; Francis E. Warren, first state governor; Chief Washakie, chief of the Shoshone; James G. Watt, former secretary of the Interior.

U.S. Territories and Outlying Areas

Puerto Rico

COMMONWEALTH OF PUERTO RICO

Governor: Pedro Rosselló, New Progressive Party (1993; reelected 1997)
Capital and largest city (1990 pop.): San Juan, 437,745
Other large cities (1990 pop.): Bayamón, 220,262; Ponce, 190,900; Carolina, 177,806
Land area: 3,459 sq mi. (8,959 sq km)
1998 est. population: 3,857,000; average annual rate of natural increase: 0.9%; birth rate: 17/1,000; infant mortality rate: 12/1,000; density per sq mi.: 1,115
Nickname: Island of Enchantment
Languages: Spanish and English (both official). **Ethnicity/Race:** Almost entirely Hispanic. **Religions:** Roman Catholic 85%, Protestant denominations and other 15%. **Literacy rate:** 90% **Currency:** U.S. dollars
Economic Summary: Gross Product (FY 1997): $32.1 billion; per capita: $8,403; real growth rate: 3.2%; inflation: 5.1% (1996 est.); unemployment: 14% (FY95/96 est.); Labor force (1996): 1,267,000; 25% services, 23% government, 20% commerce, 15% manufacturing, 6% communications and transportation, 5% construction, 3% agriculture, 3% other. Exports: $22.9 billion (f.o.b. 1996). Imports: $19.1 billion (c.i.f. 1996). Industries: pharmaceuticals, electronics, apparel, food products (livestock products, chickens, sugarcane, coffee, pineapples, plantains, bananas); tourism. The U.S. is the major trade partner.

The Commonwealth of Puerto Rico is located in the Caribbean Sea, about 1,000 miles east southeast of Miami, Fla. A possession of the United States, it consists of the island of Puerto Rico—smallest of the Greater Antilles, measuring about 100 miles from east to west and 35 miles north to south—plus the adjacent islets of Vieques, Culebra, and Mona. Puerto Rico has a mountainous tropical ecosystem with very little flat land and few mineral resources.

Puerto Rico's executive power resides in the governor, who is elected directly for a term of four years. A bicameral legislature consists of a 27-member Senate and a 51-member House of Representatives, all elected for four-year terms. From 1940 to 1968, Puerto Rican politics was dominated by a party advocating voluntary association with the U.S. Since then, the New Progressive Party, a party favoring U.S. statehood, has won five of eight

gubernatorial elections—including the last two. Puerto Rican voters have twice had the opportunity to express themselves directly on political status alternatives. In 1967, the outcome was commonwealth 60%; statehood 39%; independence 1%. In 1993, commonwealth dropped to 48.6%; statehood rose to 46.3%; independence polled 4.4%; and 0.6% of the ballots were blank or spoiled.

Under the commonwealth formula, residents of Puerto Rico lack voting representation in Congress and the right to participate in presidential elections. Also, funding caps limit their access to several key federal programs. As U.S. citizens, Puerto Ricans are subject to military service and most Federal laws. Residents of the Commonwealth pay no Federal income tax on locally-generated earnings, but Puerto Rico government income tax rates are set at a level that closely parallels Federal-plus-state levies on the mainland.

When Christopher Columbus arrived there in 1493, the island was inhabited by the peaceful Arawak Indians, who were being challenged by the warlike Carib Indians. Puerto Rico remained economically undeveloped until 1830, when the island gradually developed a plantation economy founded on three export crops: sugarcane, coffee, and tobacco.

After Puerto Ricans began to press for political independence, the island was granted broad powers of self-government by Spain in 1897. But during the Spanish-American War of 1898 American troops invaded the island and Spain ceded it to the U.S. Since then, Puerto Rico has remained an unincorporated U.S. territory. Its people were granted American citizenship under the Jones Act in 1917; were permitted to elect their own governor, beginning in 1948; and now fully administer their internal affairs under a constitution approved by the U.S. Congress in 1952. In spite of broad popular support for the autonomy of the commonwealth government and a rapidly modernizing industrial society, there were expressions of dissatisfaction. Puerto Rican extremists dramatized their desire for independence with an attempt to assassinate President Truman on Nov. 1, 1950, and on March 1, 1954, they wounded five congressmen in an attack in the U.S. Capitol.

A self-help program of economic development and social welfare (called "Operation Bootstrap") was forged in the 1940s by Puerto Rican leader and subsequent four-time Governor Luis Muñoz Marín. In a little more than four decades, much of the island's crushing poverty was eliminated. This was done partly through emphasis on the development of manufacturing and service industries, the latter related to an enormous growth in tourism. Also during this period, many Puerto Ricans migrated to large cities on the mainland U.S.

Puerto Rico is a major hub of Caribbean commerce, finance, tourism, and communications. San Juan is one of the world's busiest cruise ship ports, and Puerto Rico's standard of living continues to be among the highest in the hemisphere. Its future political status, however, remains unclear. On March 4, 1998, the U.S. House of Representatives passed a bill that called for binding elections in Puerto Rico to decide the island's permanent political status.

Guam

TERRITORY OF GUAM

Governor: Carl T. C. Gutierrez (1995)
Capital: Agaña; population (1990) 1,139
Land area: 212 sq mi. (549 sq km)
1998 est. population: 148,060; average annual rate of natural increase: 2.1%; birth rate: 25/1,000; infant mortality rate: 8/1,000; density per sq mi.: 698
1996 est. net migration: 3 migrants per 1,000 population
Languages: English and Chamorro, most residents are bilingual; Japanese also widely spoken. **Ethnicity/Race:** Chamorro, 47%; Filipino, 25%; Caucasian, 10%; Chinese, Japanese, Korean, and other, 18%. **Religions:** Roman Catholic 98% and other 2%. **Literacy rate:** 99% **Currency:** U.S. dollars
Economic Summary: Gross national product (1996 est.): $3 billion; per capita: $19,000; real growth rate: n.a.; inflation: 11% (1993); unemployment: 7.3% (Dec. 1994). Labor force (1994): 66,460; 30.6% government, 69.4% private. Industries: U.S. military, tourism, transshipment services, concrete products, printing and publishing, food processing, textiles. Exports: $34 million (f.o.b., 1984); Imports: $493 million (c.i.f., 1984).

Guam is the largest and southernmost island in the Marianas Archipelago. The island is sharply divided into a northern coralline limestone plateau and a southern chain of volcanic hills.

Today Guam is an unincorporated, organized territory of the United States. It is "unincorporated" because not all of the provisions of the U.S. constitution apply to the territory. It is an "organized" territory because the Congress provided the territory with an Organic Act in 1950 which organized the government much as a constitution would. The people of Guam have been U.S. citizens since 1950. They have been represented in the U.S. Congress since 1973 by a non-voting delegate, but do not participate in presidential elections. The executive branch includes a popularly-elected governor, who serves a four-year term. The legislative branch is a 21-member unicameral legislature whose members are elected every two years.

Guam was probably visited by the Portuguese navigator Ferdinand Magellan (sailing for Spain) in 1521. Guam was formally claimed by Spain in 1565, and its people were forced into submission and conversion to Roman Catholicism, beginning in 1668. After the Spanish-American War of 1898, Spain ceded Guam to the United States. From 1899 to 1949, the U.S. Navy administered Guam, except for 1941–1944 when Japanese forces seized and occupied the island. Guam was liberated by American military forces in the summer of 1944. Guam's economy is based on two main sources of revenue: tourism and U.S. military spending (U.S. Naval and Air Force bases occupy one-third of the land on Guam). Federal expenditures (FY94): $1,048 million; $457 million for wages and salaries and $295 million for purchases in the local economy. Due to the relocation of some U.S. defense missions to Guam from the Philippines, defense spending is expected to remain high—at the half-billion dollars a year level. Guam's sophisticated business service envionment is attracting regional distribution centers of foreign and domestic companies. Today, more than 300 U.S. foreign sales corporations have set up

offices in Guam. The tourism industry has grown rapidly over the past 20 years.

U.S. Virgin Islands

VIRGIN ISLANDS OF THE UNITED STATES

Governor: Roy L. Schneider (1995)
Capital: Charlotte Amalie (on St. Thomas), population (1990): 12,331
Land area: 140 sq mi (363 sq km): St. Croix, 84 sq. mi. (218 sq km), St. Thomas, 32 sq mi (83 sq km), St. John, 20 sq mi. (52 sq km)
Population (est. 1998): 118,211; average annual rate of natural increase: 1.1%; birth rate: 16/1,000; infant mortality rate: 10/1,000; density per sq mi.: 844
Languages: English (official), but Spanish and French are also spoken. **Ethnicity/Race:** West Indian, 74% (45% born in the Virgin Islands and 29% born elsewhere in the West Indies), U.S. mainland, 13%; Puerto Rican, 5%; other, 8%; black, 80%, white, 15%, other, 5%; 14% of Hispanic origin. **Religions:** Baptist 42%, Roman Catholic 34%, Episcopalian 17%, other 7%. **Literacy rate:** 90% **Currency:** U.S. dollars
Economic Summary: Gross Domestic Product (1989): $1.34 billion; per capita: $11,052; real growth rate: n.a.; inflation: n.a.; unemployment: 6.2% (March 1994). Labor force (1992): 48,620. Industries: tourism, petroleum refining, watch assembly, rum distilling, construction, pharmaceuticals, textiles, electronics. Exports: $1.8 billion (f.o.b., 1992); Imports: $2.2 billion (c.i.f., 1992). **Aid:** Western (non-U.S.) countries, official development assistance and other official flows, and bilateral commitments (1970–1989): $42 million.

The Virgin Islands, consisting of nine main islands and some 75 islets, were explored by Columbus in 1493. They were inhabited by the Carib people. Since 1666, England has held six of the main islands; the other three (St. Croix, St. Thomas, and St. John), as well as about 50 of the islets, were eventually acquired by Denmark, which named them the Danish West Indies. In 1917, these islands were purchased by the U.S. from Denmark for $25 million.

Congress granted U.S. citizenship to Virgin Islanders in 1927; and, in 1931, administration was transferred from the Navy to the Department of the Interior. Universal suffrage was given in 1936 to all persons who could read and write the English language. The governor was elected by popular vote for the first time in 1970; previously he had been appointed by the president of the U.S. A unicameral 15-person legislature serves the Virgin Islands, and Congressional legislation gave the islands a non-voting representative in Congress.

The government is organized under the Organic Act of the Virgin Islands, passed by the U.S. Congress in 1936, amended in 1954 and subsequently. The governor, elected to a four-year term, appoints heads of the executive branches and administrative assistants for St. Croix and St. John with approval of the unicameral legislature, or Senate, whose 15 members are elected to four-year terms. Residents of the islands substantially enjoy the same rights as those enjoyed by mainlanders with one important exception: citizens of the U.S. Virgin Islands who are residents may not vote in presidential elections. Independence appears not to be the goal for the islands, and statehood continues to be only a remote possibility.

Tourism is the primary economic activity, accounting for more than 70% of the GDP and 70% of employment. Tourist expenditures are estimated to be over $791.5 million annually. The Virgin Islands economy has a diversified blend of heavy and light manufacturing industries, including a major oil refinery, alumina production, a rum distillery, watch assembly plants, pharmaceutical, garment-making, and sensitive-instrument assembly operations. All goods made in the Virgin Islands qualify for duty-free entry into the United States.

American Samoa

TERRITORY OF AMERICAN SAMOA

Governor: Tauese Pita Sunia (1997)
Capital: Pago Pago, population 1990: 3,519
Land area: 77 sq mi (199 sq km)
Population (July 1998 est.): 62,093; average rate of natural increase: 2.3%; birth rate 27/1,000; infant mortality rate: 10/1,000; density per sq mi.: 806
Languages: Samoan (closely related to Hawaiian and other Polynesian languages) and English; most people are bilingual. **Ethnicity/Race:** Samoan (Polynesian), 89%; Tongan, 4%; Caucasian, 2%; other, 6%. **Religions:** Christian Congregationalist 50%, Roman Catholic 20%, Protestant denominations and other 30%. **Literacy rate:** 99% **Currency:** U.S. dollars
Economic Summary: Gross Domestic Product (1991): $128 million; per capita: $2,600; real growth rate: n.a.; inflation: 7%; unemployment: 12% (1991). Labor force: 14,400 (1990). Exports: $306 million (f.o.b., 1989); Imports: $360.3 million (c.i.f., 1989). **Aid (1991):** $21 million in operational funds and $1,227,000 in construction for capital–improvement projects from the U.S. Department of Interior.

American Samoa, a group of five volcanic islands and two coral atolls located some 2,600 miles south of Hawaii in the South Pacific, is an unincorporated, unorganized territory of the U.S., administered by the Department of the Interior. It includes the eastern Samoan islands of Tutuila, Aunu'u, and Rose; three islands (Ta'u, Olosega, and Ofu) of the Manu'a group; and Swains Island. Around 1000 B.C.E. Proto-polynesians established themselves in the islands, and their descendants are one of the few remaining societies of Polynesians. The Dutch navigator Jacob Roggeveen sighted the Manu'a Islands in 1722. American Samoa has been a territory of the United States since April 17, 1900, when the High Chiefs of Tutuila signed the first of two Deeds of Cession for the islands to the U.S. (Congress ratified the Deeds in 1929). Swains Island, which is privately owned, came under U.S. administration in 1925.

Until World War II the United States operated a coaling station and naval base in Pago Pago. During the war, the islands were an important U.S. Marines staging area. In 1960 American Samoa ratified its territorial constitution and has since developed a modern, self-governing political system. American Samoans elect a governor, lieutenant governor, and legislature. The legislature (Fono) consists of two houses: the Senate, selected by village chiefs (matai) for four-year terms, and the House of Representatives, elected by the general population for two-year terms. The Secretary of the Interior appoints the Chief Justice and the Associate Justice of the High Court of American Samoa. In 1981, American Samoa sent its first non-voting representative to the U.S. Congress. The people of American Samoa are U.S. nationals, not U.S. citizens, but many have become naturalized American citizens. Economic activity is strongly linked to the U.S., with which American Samoa does 80–90% of its foreign trade.

Tuna–fishing and tuna–processing plants are the backbone of the private sector, with canned tuna the primary export ($300 million annually). Transfers from the U.S. government add substantially to American Samoa's economic well-being.

Northern Mariana Islands

THE COMMONWEALTH OF THE NORTHERN MARIANA ISLANDS, OR CNMI

Governor: Pedro P. Tenorio (1998)
Capital: Chalan Kanoa (on Saipan)
Total area: 184.17 sq mi. (477 sq km)
Population (1998 est.): 66,561; average annual rate of natural increase: 2.1%; birth rate: 23/1,000; infant mortality: 7/1,000; density per sq mi.: 361. Most reside on Saipan, which is also the seat of government; Rota, Agrihan, and Tinian are also inhabited. About half the population are U.S. citizens; the remainder are temporary alien workers.
Languages: English (official), Chamorro, Carolinian. **Ethnicity/Race:** Chamorro, Carolinians, other Micronesians, Caucasian, Japanese, Chinese, Korean. **Religions:** Primarily Roman Catholic **Literacy rate:** 97% **Currency:** U.S. dollars
Economic Summary: The government of the CNMI benefits substantially from U.S. financial assistance. Gross national product (1994 est.): $524 million. Labor force: 7,476 indigenous; 22,560 foreign workers (1995). Exports (mostly garments to the U.S.): $514 million; Imports: $587 million. The U.S. and Japan are the major trade partners.

The Northern Mariana Islands, east of the Philippines and south of Japan, include the islands of Rota, Saipan, Tinian, Pagan, Guguan, Agrihan, and Aguijan. Although sighted by Ferdinand Magellan in 1521 as he sailed for Spain, the islands were not settled by Europeans until 1668, when missionaries converted the indigenous Chamorro people to Catholicism. They were ruled successively by Spain, Germany, and Japan before they became a U.N. Trusteeship (administered by the U.S.) after World War II. The Commonwealth of the Northern Mariana Islands (CNMI) became part of the United States pursuant to P.L. 94-241 on November 3, 1986. Spanish cultural traditions are still strong. Tourism is the leading employer, affecting about 50% of the work force. Seventy-five percent of the tourists are Japanese. The chief agricultural products are copra and coconuts, fruits, cattle, and vegetables.

Midway Islands

Total area: 2 sq mi. (5 sq km)
Population (1995 est.): no indigenous inhabitants; 453 U.S. military personnel.

Midway Island, lying about 1,150 miles west-northwest of Hawaii, was first explored by Captain N. C. Brooks on July 5, 1859, in the name of the United States. The atoll was formally declared a U.S. possession in 1867, and in 1903 Theodore Roosevelt made it a naval reservation. The island was renamed "Midway" by the U.S. Navy in recognition of its geographic location on the route between California and Japan. Air traffic across the Pacific increased the island's importance in the mid-1930s; the San Francisco–Manila mail route included a regular stop on Midway. Its military importance was soon recognized, and the Navy began building an air and submarine base there in 1940. The Battle of Midway, which took place from June 3–6, 1942, and featured aircraft based on carriers, was considered a turning point in World War II. After the war, the strategic importance of the island declined; the Midway stop for commercial air traffic was eliminated in 1950, and the air base closed in 1992.

The Midway Islands consist of a circular atoll, 6 miles in diameter, that encloses two islands. Eastern Island, on its southeast side, is triangular in shape, and about 1.2 miles long. Sand Island, on its south side, is about 2.25 miles long in a northeast-southwest direction. A National Wildlife Refuge was set up on Midway under an agreement with the Fish and Wildlife Service of the U.S. Dept. of the Interior, to protect the island's diverse and abundant wildlife. The Midway Islands are within a Naval Defensive Sea Area. The Navy Department maintains an installation and has jurisdiction over the atoll.

Wake Island

Total area: 2.5 sq mi. (6.5 sq km)
Comparative size: about 11 times the size of the Mall in Washington, D.C.
Population (1995 est.): no indigenous inhabitants; 302 U.S. military personnel and civilian contractors.
Economy: The economic activity is limited to providing services to U.S. military personnel and contractors on the island. All food and manufactured goods must be imported.

Wake Island, about halfway between Midway and Guam, is an atoll consisting of the three islets of Wilkes, Peale, and Wake. They were discovered by the British in 1796 and annexed by the U.S. in 1899. In 1938, Pan American Airways established a seaplane base, and Wake Island was used as a commercial base for several years. On Dec. 8, 1941, it was attacked by the Japanese, who finally took possession on Dec. 23. It was surrendered by the Japanese on Sept. 4, 1945. The president, acting pursuant to the Hawaii Omnibus Act, assigned responsibility for Wake to the secretary of the Interior in 1962. The Department of Transportation exercised civil administration of Wake through an agreement with the Department of the interior until June 1972, at which time the Department of the Air Force assumed responsibility. The government of Wake Island has been administered by the U.S. Army and Strategic Defense Command since Oct. 1, 1994.

Johnston Atoll

Land area: 1.08 sq. mi. (2.8 sq km); density per sq mi.: 1,111
Population (July 1997 est.): no indigenous inhabitants; 1,200 U.S. military and civilian personnel

Johnston is a coral atoll about 700 miles southwest of Hawaii. It consists of four small islands—Johnston Island, Sand Island, Hikina Island, and Akau Island—which lie on a reef about 9 miles long in a northeast-southwest direction. The atoll was discovered by Capt. Charles James Johnston of HMS *Cornwallis* in 1807. In 1858 it was claimed by Hawaii, and later became a U.S. possession. Johnston Atoll is a Naval Defensive Sea Area and Airspace Reservation and is closed to the public. The airspace entry control has been suspended but is subject to immediate reinstatement without notice. The atoll is managed cooperatively by the Defense Nuclear Agency and the Fish and Wildlife Service of the U.S. Department of the Interior as part of the National Wildlife Refuge system. In the early 1990s,

the U.S. government opened a facility for destroying chemical weapons on Johnston Atoll.

Baker, Howland, and Jarvis Islands

These Pacific islands, claimed by the United States under the Guano Act of 1856, were placed under the control of the Department of the Interior by President Franklin D. Roosevelt on May 13, 1936. The three islands have a tropical climate with scant rainfall, constant wind, and a burning sun. The guano deposits on the islands were exhausted in the 19th century. Baker Island is a saucer-shaped atoll with an area of approximately one square mile. It is about 1,650 miles from Hawaii. Howland Island, 36 miles to the northwest, is approximately one and a half miles long and half a mile wide. It is a low-lying, nearly level, sandy, coral island surrounded by a narrow fringing reef. Howland Island is related to the tragic disappearance of Amelia Earhart and Fred J. Noonan during their round-the-world flight in 1937. They left New Guinea on July 2, 1937, for Howland, but were never seen again. Jarvis Island is several hundred miles to the east and approximately one and three-quarter miles long by one mile wide. It is a sandy coral island surrounded by a narrow fringing reef.

Baker, Howland, and Jarvis have been uninhabited since 1942. In 1974, the islands became part of the National Wildlife Refuge System, administered by the Fish and Wildlife Service of the U.S. Department of the Interior.

Kingman Reef

Kingman Reef, located about 1,000 miles south of Hawaii, was discovered by Capt. E. Fanning in 1798, but named for Capt. W. E. Kingman, who rediscovered it in 1853. The reef, drying only on its northeast, east, and southeast edges, is of an atoll character. The reef is triangular in shape, with its apex northward; it is about 9.5 miles long, east to west, and 5 miles wide, north to south, within the 100-fathom curve. The island is uninhabited. A United States possession since 1922, Kingman Reef is a Naval Defensive Sea Area and Airspace Reservation, and is closed to the public. The Airspace Entry Control has been suspended, but is subject to immediate reinstatement without notice. No vessel, except those authorized by the secretary of the navy, shall be navigated in the area within the 3-mile limit.

Navassa Island

Navassa Island is located in the Caribbean Sea, 99.4 miles (160 km) south of the U.S. Naval Base at Guantanamo, Cuba, between Cuba, Haiti, and Jamaica. The island has a total area of 2 sq mi. (5.2 sq km). It is an unincorporated territory of the United States, administered by the Office of Insular Affairs within the U.S. Department of the Interior. Visitors require permission from the Office of Insular Affairs to land on the island. The U.S. is responsible for its defense. In the 19th century, the island's guano deposits were mined. The workers on this desolate island were badly treated, and once mutinied, killing their supervisors. The island's terrain consists of a raised coral and limestone plateau, ringed by vertical cliffs. Navassa is uninhabited except by transient Haitian fisherman. The island is also claimed by Haiti.

Palmyra Atoll

Palmyra Atoll is an incorporated territory of the U.S., privately owned, but administered by the Office of Insular Affairs, U.S. Department of the Interior. The atoll has a total area of 4.6 sq mi. (11.9 sq km). The U.S. is responsible for its defense. It is located in the North Pacific Ocean, 994 miles (1,600) kilometers south-southwest of Honolulu, almost halfway between Hawaii and American Samoa. It was used as a military base by the U.S. during World War II, but was not attacked. The atoll consists of about 50 islets covered with dense vegetation, coconut trees, and balsa-like trees almost 100 feet (30 meters) high. Palmyra Atoll is uninhabited.

Tabulated Data on State Governments

State	Governor: Term, years	Governor: Annual salary	Legislature[1]: Membership U[3]	Membership L[4]	Term, years U[3]	Term, years L[4]	Salaries of members[5]		Highest Court[2]: Members	Term, years	Annual salary
Alabama	4[6]	$ 87,643	35	105	4	4	$ 10	per diem	9	6	$115,695[7]
Alaska	4	81,648	20	40	4	2	24,012[8]	per annum	5	3[9]	99,996[7]
Arizona	4	75,000	30	60	2	2	15,000	per annum	5	6	114,257[7]
Arkansas	4	60,000	35	100	4	2	12,500	per annum	7	8	95,216[7]
California	4	114,000	40	80	4	2	72,500	per annum	7	12	127,276[7]
Colorado	4	70,000	35	65	4	2	17,500	per annum	7	10	91,000[7]
Connecticut	4	78,000	36	151	2	2	16,760	per annum	7	8	113,042[7]
Delaware	4[10]	107,000	21	41	4	2	28,300	per annum	5	12	121,200[7]
Florida	4[6]	110,962	40	120	4[6]	2[11]	26,388	per annum	7	6	137,314
Georgia[6]	4	111,480	56	180	2	2	11,348	per annum	7	6	124,310
Hawaii	4	94,780	25	51	4	2	32,000	per annum	5	10	93,780[7]
Idaho	4	92,500	35	70	2	2	12,360[8]	per annum	5	6	90,791[7]
Illinois	4	114,439	59	118	4-2	2	50,802	per annum	7	10	122,892
Indiana	4[6]	77,200	50	100	4	2	11,600	per annum	5	2[9]	81,000
Iowa	4	98,300	50	100	4	2	20,120	per annum	9	8	106,700[7]
Kansas	4	80,355	40	125	4	2	138	per diem[12]	7	6	82,005[7]

State	Governor: Term, years	Governor: Annual salary	Legislature[1]: Membership U[3]	Legislature[1]: Membership L[4]	Legislature[1]: Term, years U[3]	Legislature[1]: Term, years L[4]	Legislature[1]: Salaries of members[5]		Highest Court[2]: Members	Highest Court[2]: Term, years	Highest Court[2]: Annual salary
Kentucky	4	95,525	38	100	4	2	105.58	per diem[13]	7	8	103,741[7]
Louisiana	4	95,000	39	105	4	4	16,800	per annum	7	10	85,000
Maine	4	70,000	35	151	2	2	18,000	per biennium	7	7	80,392
Maryland	4[6]	120,000	47	141	4	4	29,700	per annum	7	10	107,300[7]
Massachusetts	4	100,000	40	160	2	2	46,410	per annum	7	([15])	95,880[7]
Michigan	4	127,300	38	110	4	2	53,192	per annum	7	8	124,770
Minnesota	4	114,000	67	134	4[15]	2	27,979	per annum	7	6	83,494
Mississippi	4	83,160	52	122	4	4	10,000	per session	9	8	90,800[7]
Missouri	4[10]	107,269	34	163	4[16]	2	27,580	per annum	7	12	108,783[7]
Montana	4	59,310	50	100	4	2	55	per diem	7	8	68,874
Nebraska	4[6]	65,000	49[17]	—	4[17]	—	12,000	per annum	7	6	101,649
Nevada	4	90,000	21	42	4	2	7,800	per biennium	5	6	107,600
New Hampshire	2	86,235	24	([18])	2	2	200	per biennium	5	([14])	95,628[7]
New Jersey	4[6]	130,000[19]	40	80	4[16]	2	35,000	per annum	7	7[20]	128,800[7]
New Mexico	4[6]	90,000	42	70	4	2	104	per diem	5	8	79,567[7]
New York	4	130,000	61	150	2	2	57,500	per annum	7	14	125,000[7]
North Carolina	4[6]	91,938	50	120	2	2	13,026	per annum	7	8	89,532[7]
North Dakota	4	75,372	49	98	4	4	111	per diem[21]	5	10	82,164[7]
Ohio	4	115,752	33	99	4	2	42,427	per annum	7	6	101,150[7]
Oklahoma	4	101,140	48	101	4	2	38,400	per annum	([22])	6	97,807[7]
Oregon	4[6]	80,000	30	60	4	2	1,092	per month	7	6	83,700
Pennsylvania	4[6]	125,000	50	203	4	2	47,000	per annum	7	10	119,750[7]
Rhode Island	4	69,900	50	100	2	2	10,000	per annum	5	([23])	104,403
South Carolina	4	106,078	46	124	4	2	10,400	per annum	5	10	106,061[7]
South Dakota	4[6]	84,739	35	70	2	2	6,000	per biennium	5	3[24]	82,701[7]
Tennessee	4	85,000	33	99	4	2	16,500	per annum	5	8	101,820
Texas	4	99,122	31	150	4	2	7,200	per annum	9	6	94,686[7]
Utah	4	90,700	29	75	4	2	100	per diem	5	3[8]	98,500[7]
Vermont	2	96,661	30	150	2	2	510[25]	per week	5	6	83,072[7]
Virginia	4[13]	110,000	40	100	4	2	17,640[26]	per annum	7	12	112,044[7]
Washington	4[27]	121,000	49	98	4[11]	2	28,300	per annum	9	6	112,078
West Virginia	4[6]	72,000	34	100	4	2	15,000	per annum	5	12	72,000
Wisconsin	4	102,882	33	99	4	2	39,211	per annum	7	10	100,690[7]
Wyoming	4	95,000	30	60	4	2	125	per diem	5	8	85,000

1. Known as *General Assembly* in Ark., Colo., Conn., Del., Ga., Ill., Iowa, Ind., Ky., Md., Mo., N.C., Ohio, Pa., R.I., S.C., Tenn., Vt., Va.; *Legislative Assembly* in N.D., Ore.; *General Court* in Mass., N.H.; *Legislature* in other states. Meets biennially in Calif., Ky., Maine, Mont., Nev., N.J., N.D., Ore., Pa., Texas. Wyoming Legislature has regular general session on odd-numbered years and a budget session on even-numbered years. Arkansas General Assembly meets every other year for 60 days in odd numbered years. Ohio General Assembly meets when deemed necessary. Legislative bodies meet annually in other states. 2. Known as *Court of Appeals* in Md., N.Y.; *Supreme Court of Virginia* in Va.; *Supreme Judicial Court* in Maine, Mass.; *Supreme Court* in other states. 3. Upper house: *Senate* in all states except Neb., which has a single-house legislative body, "the Legislature." 4. Lower house: *Assembly* in Calif., Nev., N.Y., Wis.; *House of Delegates* in Md., Va., W.Va.; *General Assembly* in N.J.; *House of Representatives* in other states. 5. Base salary. Does not include additional payments for expenses, mileage, special sessions, etc., or additional per diem payments. 6. May not serve third consecutive term. 7. Chief justice receives a higher salary. 8. Leaders receive a higher salary. 9. Initial term; thereafter elected popularly for 10-year term. 10. May serve only two terms, consecutive or otherwise. 11. Have term limitations. 12. When in session, plus $600/mo. when not in session. 13. During 1998 session, plus $1,003 per month when not in session. Beginning calendar year 1999: $151 per diem and $1,435 per month when not in session. 14. Until 70 years old. 15. Every 10 years (the year after census) term is only for 2 years. 16. Legislators may serve only 8 years in each house, 16 combined. 17. Unicameral legislature. 18. Constitutional number: 375-400. 19. Legislated salary; salary received is $85,000. 20. Second term receive tenure, mandatory retirement at 70. 21. When in session, plus $250 per month when not in session. 22. Nine members in supreme court, highest in civil cases; five in Court of Criminal Appeals. 23. Term of good behavior. 24. Subsequent terms, eight years. 25. To limit of $13,000 per biennium; $100 per diem for Special Session. 26. Upper house receives higher salary. 27. No person is eligible who would have served during 8 of the previous 14 years. NOTE: Salaries are rounded to nearest dollar. *Source:* questionnaires to the states.

Land and Water Area of States, 1990

(in square miles)

State	Rank (total area)	Land[1] area	Water[2] area	Total area
Alabama	30	50,750.23	1,672.71	52,422.94
Alaska	1	570,373.55	86,050.59	656,424.14
Arizona	6	113,642.26	364.00	114,006.26
Arkansas	29	52,075.29	1,107.07	53,182.36
California	3	155,973.09	7,734.06	163,707.15
Colorado	8	103,729.54	370.78	104,100.32
Connecticut	48	4,845.39	698.26	5,543.65
Delaware	49	1,954.62	534.76	2,489.38
Dist. of Columbia	—	61.41	6.95	68.36
Florida	22	53,997.08	11,761.00	65,758.08
Georgia	24	57,918.73	1,522.49	59,441.22
Hawaii	43	6,423.34	4,508.24	10,931.58
Idaho	14	82,750.93	822.84	83,573.77
Illinois	25	55,593.29	2,324.55	57,917.84
Indiana	38	35,870.18	549.91	36,420.09
Iowa	26	55,874.90	400.64	56,275.54
Kansas	15	81,823.02	458.98	82,282.00
Kentucky	37	39,732.31	678.93	40,411.24
Louisiana	31	43,566.03	8,277.44	51,843.47
Maine	39	30,864.55	4,522.78	35,387.33
Maryland	42	9,774.65	2,632.80	12,407.45
Massachusetts	44	7,837.98	2,716.81	10,554.79
Michigan	11	56,809.18	40,001.04	96,810.22
Minnesota	12	79,616.66	7,326.05	86,942.71
Mississippi	32	46,913.64	1,519.95	48,433.59
Missouri	21	68,898.01	810.80	69,708.81
Montana	4	145,556.34	1,489.82	147,046.16
Nebraska	16	76,877.73	480.67	77,358.40
Nevada	7	109,805.89	761.02	110,566.91
New Hampshire	46	8,969.36	381.57	9,350.93
New Jersey	47	7,418.84	1,303.11	8,721.95
New Mexico	5	121,364.54	233.69	123,598.23
New York	27	47,223.85	7,250.71	54,474.56
North Carolina	28	48,718.08	5,103.27	53,821.35
North Dakota	19	68,994.24	1,709.59	70,703.83
Ohio	34	40,952.59	3,874.94	44,827.53
Oklahoma	20	68,678.57	1,224.33	69,902.90
Oregon	9	96,002.58	2,383.17	98,385.75
Pennsylvania	33	44,819.61	1,238.63	46,058.24
Rhode Island	50	1,044.98	500.12	1,545.10
South Carolina	40	30,111.12	1,895.99	32,007.11
South Dakota	17	75,897.74	1,223.72	77,121.46
Tennessee	36	41,219.52	926.49	42,146.01
Texas	2	261,914.26	6,686.70	268,600.96
Utah	13	82,168.15	2,735.97	84,904.12
Vermont	45	9,249.33	365.67	9,615.00
Virginia	35	39,597.79	3,171.09	42,768.88
Washington	18	66,581.95	4,720.70	71,302.65
West Virginia	41	24,086.55	144.89	24,231.44
Wisconsin	23	54,313.71	11,189.50	65,503.21
Wyoming	10	97,104.55	713.56	97,818.11
U.S. Total		**3,536,341.73**	**251,083.35**	**3,787,425.08**

1. Dry land and land temporarily or partially covered by water, such as marshland, swamps, etc.; streams and canals under one-eighth statute mile wide; and lakes, reservoirs, and ponds under 40 acres. 2. Permanent inland water surface, such as lakes, reservoirs, and ponds having an area of 40 acres or more; streams, sloughs, estuaries, and canals one-eighth statute mile or more in width; deeply indented embayments and sounds, and other coastal waters behind or sheltered by headlands or islands separated by less than 1 nautical mile of water, and islands under 40 acres in area. Excludes areas of oceans, bays, sounds, etc. lying within U.S. jurisdiction but not defined as inland water. *Source:* Department of Commerce, Bureau of the Census.

State Capitals and Largest Cities

State	Capital	Largest city
Alabama	Montgomery	Birmingham
Alaska	Juneau	Anchorage
Arizona	Phoenix	Phoenix
Arkansas	Little Rock	Little Rock
California	Sacramento	Los Angeles
Colorado	Denver	Denver
Connecticut	Hartford	Bridgeport
Delaware	Dover	Wilmington
Florida	Tallahassee	Jacksonville
Georgia	Atlanta	Atlanta
Hawaii	Honolulu	Honolulu
Idaho	Boise	Boise
Illinois	Springfield	Chicago
Indiana	Indianapolis	Indianapolis
Iowa	Des Moines	Des Moines
Kansas	Topeka	Wichita
Kentucky	Frankfort	Louisville
Louisiana	Baton Rouge	New Orleans
Maine	Augusta	Portland
Maryland	Annapolis	Baltimore
Massachusetts	Boston	Boston
Michigan	Lansing	Detroit
Minnesota	St. Paul	Minneapolis
Mississippi	Jackson	Jackson
Missouri	Jefferson City	Kansas City
Montana	Helena	Billings
Nebraska	Lincoln	Omaha
Nevada	Carson City	Las Vegas
New Hampshire	Concord	Manchester
New Jersey	Trenton	Newark
New Mexico	Santa Fe	Albuquerque
New York	Albany	New York City
North Carolina	Raleigh	Charlotte
North Dakota	Bismarck	Fargo
Ohio	Columbus	Columbus
Oklahoma	Oklahoma City	Oklahoma City
Oregon	Salem	Portland
Pennsylvania	Harrisburg	Philadelphia
Rhode Island	Providence	Providence
South Carolina	Columbia	Columbia
South Dakota	Pierre	Sioux Falls
Tennessee	Nashville	Memphis
Texas	Austin	Houston
Utah	Salt Lake City	Salt Lake City
Vermont	Montpelier	Burlington
Virginia	Richmond	Virginia Beach
Washington	Olympia	Seattle
West Virginia	Charleston	Charleston
Wisconsin	Madison	Milwaukee
Wyoming	Cheyenne	Cheyenne

Source: U.S. Bureau of the Census, 1990 figures.

50 Largest Cities of the United States

(According to 1996 Census Bureau data)

Data supplied by Bureau of the Census and by the cities in response to questionnaires. Ranking of 50 largest cities based on July 1, 1996, census estimates. Per capita personal income data is given for the Metropolitan Statistical Area (MSA), the Primary Metropolitan Statistical Area (PMSA), the New England County Metropolitan Area (NECMA), or the Consolidated Metropolitan Statistical Area (CMSA), as noted, and is for 1992, unless otherwise noted. Average daily temperature data is from *County and City Data Book*. Population breakdown figures only available for original 1990 census data. For the revised 1990 census total population figures, see "Top 50 Cities in the U.S. by Estimated 1996 Population and Rank." NOTE: Persons of Hispanic origin may be of any race.

Albuquerque, N.M.

Mayor: Jim Baca (to Dec. 2001)
1996 est. population (rank): 419,681 (37)
1990 census population (rank): 384,736 (38); **% change,** 9.1; **Male,** 186,584; **Female,** 198,152; **White,** 301,010 (78.3%); **Black,** 11,484 (3.0%); **American Indian, Eskimo, or Aleut,** 11,708 (3.0%); **Asian or Pacific Islander,** 6,660 (1.7%); **Other race,** 53,874; **Hispanic origin,** 132,706 (34.5%). **1990 population under 18:** 25.0%; **65 and over:** 11.1%; **median age:** 32.5.
Land area: 163 sq mi. (422 sq km); **Alt.:** 4,958 ft.
Avg. daily temp.: Jan., 34.8° F; July, 78.8° F
Churches: 211; **City-owned parks:** 189; **Radio stations:** 43 (AM, 17; FM, 26); **Television stations:** 11
Civilian Labor Force: 224,003; **Unemployed:** 10,305, **Percent:** 4.6; **Per capita personal income (MSA) 1992:** $17,758
Chamber of Commerce: Greater Albuquerque Chamber of Commerce, 401 2nd St., N.W., Albuquerque, N.M. 87125. Albuquerque Hispanic Chamber of Commerce, 202 Central Ave., S.E., Albuquerque, N.M. 87102

Albuquerque is the largest city in New Mexico and the seat of Bernalillo County. It is situated in west central New Mexico on the upper Rio Grande River. Early Spanish settlers arrived there in the mid-1600s. The old town was founded in 1706 by Don Francisco Cuervo y Valdés, the governor of New Mexico, and named after the Duke of Albuquerque, the viceroy of New Spain. During the Civil War, Confederate forces briefly occupied the city in 1862. The new town section was founded in 1880. In 1883, Albuquerque became the county seat and was incorporated as a city in 1891.

The city is noted as a center for health and medical services in the region, and government agencies, nuclear research, banking, and tourism are important to the economy. There is a growing high-tech center in Albuquerque and Intel Corp.'s largest manufacturing facility is located there.

Famous natives: Erna Fergusson, author; Annabeth Gish, actress; Fred Haney, baseball player, executive; Ernie Pyle, World War II war correspondent; Slim Summerville, actor; Al and Bobby Unser, auto racers.

Atlanta, Ga.[1]

Mayor: Bill Campbell (to Jan. 2002)
1996 est. population (rank): 401,907 (38)[2]
1990 census population (rank): 394,017 (36); **% change,** 2.0; **Male,** 187,877; **Female,** 206,140; **White,** 122,327 (31.1%); **Black,** 264,262 (67.1%); **American Indian, Eskimo, or Aleut,** 563 (0.1%); **Asian or Pacific Islander,** 3,498 (0.9%); **Other race,** 3,367; **Hispanic origin,** 7,525 (1.9%). **1990 population under 18:** 24.1%; **65 and over:** 11.3%; **median age:** 31.5.
City land area: 136 sq mi. (352.2 sq km); **Alt.:** Highest, 1,050 ft.; lowest, 940 ft.
Avg. daily temp.: Jan., 41.9° F; July, 78.6° F
Churches: 1,500; **City-owned parks:** 277 (3,178 ac.); **Radio stations:** AM, 7; FM, 20; **Television stations:** 8 commercial; 2 PBS
Civilian Labor Force (1996): 1,976,970; **Unemployed:** 75,260, **Percent:** 3.8; **Per capita personal income (MSA) 1996:** $25,563
Chamber of Commerce: Metro Atlanta Chamber of Commerce, 235 International Blvd., Atlanta, Ga. 30303

1. Information is gathered on the 20-county MSA. 2. 1996 est. population: 3,505,970 (metro area).

Atlanta, the largest city and capital of Georgia, is the seat of Fulton County. It is situated in the northwest part of the state at the base of the Blue Ridge Mountains near the Chattahoochee River. The first European settler was Hardy Ivy, who built a cabin there in 1833.

The town was founded as Terminus in 1837 as the end of the Georgia railroad line (Western and Atlantic Railroad) and became incorporated as Marthasville in 1843 in honor of ex-governor Lumpkin's daughter Martha. It was renamed Atlanta in 1845 and incorporated as a city in 1847. The name was suggested by the railroad's chief engineer, J. Edgar Thomson, and was derived from its location at the end of the Georgia and Atlantic railroad line. The city later became the capital of Georgia in 1868.

During the Civil War, the city was burned and almost completely destroyed while occupied by General W. T. Sherman's troops in November 1864. It was quickly rebuilt after the war and it grew rapidly due to the expansion of the railroads in the southwest. Atlanta's diverse economy is led by the service, communications, retail trade, manufacturing, and finance and insurance industries. The convention business is also important, and the 1996 Summer Olympic Games were held there.

Famous natives: Hank Aaron, baseball player; Arrested Development, recording artists; Jimmy Carter, former president; Ray Charles, singer; James Dickey, poet; Mattivilda Dobbs, soprano; Walt Frazier, basketball player; Oliver Hardy, comedian; Evander Holyfield, boxer; Allan Jackson, singer; Bobby Jones, golfer; DeForest Kelley, actor; Martin Luther King, Jr., civil rights leader and Nobel Peace Prize winner; Gladys Knight, singer; Kriss Kross, recording artists; Margaret Mitchell, novelist; Bert Parks, entertainer; Eric Roberts, actor; Julia Roberts, actress; Ferroll Sams, author; Doug Stone, singer; Pamela Stone, comedienne; Gwen Torrence, Olympic athlete; Lee Tracy, actor; Travis Tritt, singer; Ted Turner, TBS and CNN founder; Jane Withers, actress; Joanne Woodward, actress; Andrew Young, civil rights activist.

Austin, Tex.

Mayor: Kirk Watson (to May 2000)
1996 est. population (rank): 541,278 (22)[1]
1990 census population (rank): 465,622 (27); **% change,** 16.2; **Male,** 232,473; **Female,** 233,149; **White,** 328,542 (70.6%); **Black,** 57,868 (12.4%); **American Indian, Eskimo, or Aleut:,** 1,756 (0.4%); **Asian or Pacific Islander,** 14,141 (3.0%); **Other race,** 63,315; **Hispanic origin,** 106,868 (23.0%). **1990 population under 18:** 23.1%; **65 and over:** 7.4%; **median age:** 28.9
Land area: 116 sq mi. (300 sq km); **Alt.:** From 425 ft. to over 1000 ft.
Avg. daily temp.: Jan., 49.1° F; July, 84.7° F
Churches: 353 churches, representing 45 denominations; **City-owned parks and playgrounds:** 169 (11,800 ac.); **Radio stations:** AM, 6; FM, 12; **Television stations:** 3 commercial; 1 PBS; 1 independent
Civilian Labor Force (1995): 616,300; **Unemployed:** 20,338, **Percent:** 3.3; **Per capita personal income:** $18,770, Austin–San Marcos (MSA)
Chamber of Commerce: Greater Austin Chamber of Commerce, P.O. Box 1967, Austin, Tex. 78767

1. 1997 est. population 561,045.

Austin, the capital and seat of Travis County, is the fifth-largest city in Texas. It is situated in the south central part of the state on the Colorado River. The site was called Waterloo in 1838 and in 1839 was incorporated as a city and chosen to become the capital of the independent Republic of Texas. Waterloo was renamed Austin in honor of Stephen F. Austin, the founder of the Texas Republic. It became the permanent capital of the state of Texas in 1870.

Austin's growth was spurred by several developments after the Civil War—the railroads reached the city in the 1870s; it was crossed by the important Chisholm cattle trail; and it became the seat of the state university in 1883.

Austin has a growing commercial and diversified manufacturing sector. Civilian government employment is 28% of the labor force and is important to the economy. As home to the University of Texas, Austin is a major center for research and development, and is nationally recognized as a high-technology center. The city has a new convention center downtown.

Famous natives: Don Baylor, baseball player and manager; Earl Campbell, football player; Liz Carpenter, author; Dabney Coleman, actor; Ben Crenshaw, golfer; Michael Dell, founder Dell Computer Corp.; Tobe Hooper, film director; Lady Bird Johnson, former First Lady; Tom Kite, golfer; James Michener, author; Willie Nelson, musician; Amado Pena, artist; Darrell Royal, football coach; Zachary Scott, actor; Jerry Jeff Walker, musician; Dalhart Windberg, artist.

Baltimore, Md.

Mayor: Kurt L. Schmoke (to Dec. 1999)
1996 est. population (rank): 675,401 (15)
1990 census population (rank): 736,014 (13); **% change,** –8.2; **Male,** 343,513; **Female:** 392,501; **White:** 287,753 (39.1%); **Black:** 435,768 (59.2%); **American Indian, Eskimo, or Aleut:** 2,555 (0.3%); **Asian or Pacific Islander:** 7,942 (1.1%); **Other race:** 1,996; **Hispanic origin:** 7,602 (1.0%). **1990 population under 18:** 24.4%; **65 and over:** 13.7%; **Median age:** 32.6.
Land area: 80.3 sq mi. (208 sq km); **Alt.:** Highest, 490 ft.; lowest, sea level
Avg. daily temp.: Jan., 35.5° F; July, 79.9° F
Churches: Roman Catholic, 72; Jewish, 50; Protestant and others, 344; **City-owned parks:** 347 park areas and tracts (6,314 ac.); **Radio stations:** AM, 10; FM, 11; **Television stations:** 7 (including Home Shopping Network)
Civilian Labor Force: 333,043; **Unemployed:** 35,531, **Percent:** 10.7; **Per capita personal income (PMSA) 1992:** $22,412
Chamber of Commerce: Greater Baltimore Committee, 111 S. Calvert St., Ste. 1500, Baltimore, Md. 21202

Baltimore is the largest city in Maryland and is situated in the northern part of the state on the Patapsco River estuary, an arm of Chesapeake Bay. The city is independent and is in no county.

The site was settled in the early 17th century and founded as a town in 1729. The town was named after Lord Baltimore, the founder of Maryland, and was incorporated as a city in 1797. It has an excellent harbor and has been a principal port since the 18th century. Baltimore was a pioneer ship-building center and the Baltimore clipper, one of the best sailing ships of its day, was used extensively in world trade. It ranks today as the nation's second port in foreign tonnage.

Baltimore's economy is focused on manufacturing, in steel, heavy and light industries; ship construction; and scientific research and development.

Famous natives: Larry Adler, musician; John Astin, actor; Eubie Blake, pianist; Francis X. Bushman, actor; Charlie Chase, actor; Hans Conried, actor; Mildred Dunnock, actress; "Mama" Cass Elliot, singer; Barry Farber, broadcaster; Paul Ford, actor; Philip Glass, composer; Billie Holiday, singer; Barry Levinson, director; H. L. Mencken, writer; Babe Ruth, baseball player; Upton Sinclair, novelist; Leon Uris, novelist; Frank Zappa, musician.

Boston, Mass.

Mayor: Thomas Menino (to Dec. 2001)
1996 est. population (rank): 558,394 (20)
1990 census population (rank): 574,283 (20); **% change,** –2.8; **Male,** 275,972; **Female,** 298,311; **White,** 360,875 (62.8%); **Black,** 146,945 (25.6%); **American Indian, Eskimo, or Aleut,** 1,884 (0.3%); **Asian or Pacific Islander,** 30,388 (5.3%); **Other race,** 34,191; **Hispanic origin,** 61,955 (10.8%). **1990 population under 18:** 19.1%; **65 and over:** 11.5%; **median age:** 30.3.
Land area: 47.2 sq mi. (122 sq km); **Alt.:** Highest, 330 ft.; lowest, sea level
Avg. daily temp.: Jan., 29.6° F; July, 73.5° F
Churches: Protestant, 187; Roman Catholic, 72; Jewish, 28; others, 100; **City-owned parks, playgrounds, etc.:** 2,276.36 ac.; **Radio stations:** AM, 9; FM, 12; **Television stations:** 10
Civilian Labor Force (1995): 284,448; **Unemployed:** 14,036, **Percent:** 4.9; **Per capita personal income (NECMA) 1992:** $24,109[1]
Chamber of Commerce: Boston Chamber of Commerce, 600 Atlantic Ave., Boston, Mass. 02210

1. Boston-Lawrence-Salem-Lowell-Brockton NECMA.

Boston is the capital and seat of Suffolk County, and the largest city in Massachusetts. It is located in the eastern part of the state at the head of Boston Bay. It was incorporated as a city in 1822. No city in the U.S. is richer in historical associations than Boston, and no city has retained more of its original buildings as memorials to America's past.

Puritans from England settled at Boston in 1630, only ten years after the Pilgrims had landed at Plymouth in 1620. They named their new town Boston,

after the former home of many of the Pilgrims in Lincolnshire, England. Fourteen years later, the pioneer Bostonians set aside the first public park in the U.S.—the Boston Common. The following year, 1635, they opened the first free public school in America. Today, the Boston metropolitan area is home to 68 colleges and universities.

Boston is a major industrial, financial, and educational hub and has one of the finest ports in the world. The port of Boston ships more than $8.5 billion worth of goods each year.

Although the city's banking and financial services, insurance, and real-estate sectors declined in the early '90s, other industries continue to grow, especially in the health care field. Boston has 25 medical research institutions, more than any other U.S. city, and its health care industry is growing at a rate of about 3% a year. The city's unique cultural and historic heritage makes it a center of tourism and its hotel industry ranks first in the nation in occupancy. Boston's other businesses are in high technology, biotechnology, software, and electronics.

Famous natives: Samuel Adams, patriot; John Singleton Copley, painter; Ralph Waldo Emerson, philosopher and poet; Arthur Fiedler, conductor; Benjamin Franklin, statesman and scientist; Edward Everett Hale, clergyman and author; Oliver Wendell Holmes, jurist; Winslow Homer, painter; Joseph P. Kennedy, financier; Jack Lemmon, actor; Robert Lowell, poet; Edgar Allan Poe, writer; Paul Revere, patriot and silversmith; John L. Sullivan, boxer; Barbara Walters, TV journalist.

Charlotte, N.C.

Mayor: Pat McCrory (to Nov. 1999)
1996 est. population: 441,297 (32)[1]
1990 census population (rank): 395,934 (35); **% change,** 11.5; **Male,** 188,088; **Female,** 207,846; **White,** 259,760 (65.6%); **Black,** 125,827 (31.8%); **American Indian, Eskimo, or Aleut:** 1,425 (0.4%); **Asian or Pacific Islander:** 7,211 (1.8%); **Other race,** 1,711; **Hispanic origin,** 5,571 (1.4%). **1990 population under 18:** 24.2%; **65 and over:** 9.8%; **median age:** 32.1.
Land area: 234 sq mi. (606.2 sq km); **Alt.:** 765 ft.
Avg. daily temp.: Jan., 40.5° F; July, 78.5° F
Churches: Protestant, over 400; Roman Catholic, 8; Jewish, 3; Greek Orthodox, 1; **City-owned parks and parkways:** 130; **Radio stations:** AM, 10; FM, 17; **Television stations:** 4 commercial; 2 PBS
Civilian Labor Force (1997): 341,010; **Unemployed:** 9,200, **Percent:** 3.0; **Per capita personal income (MSA) 1997:** $15,586[2]
Chamber of Commerce: Charlotte Chamber, P.O. Box 32785, Charlotte, N.C., 28232

1.1997 est. population: 470,553. 2. Charlotte–Gastonia Rock Hill, N.C.–S.C.

Charlotte, North Carolina's largest city and the seat of Mecklenburg County, is located in the southern part of the state near the South Carolina border. It was named for King George III of England's wife, Charlotte Sophia of Mecklenburg-Strelitz.

Settled about 1750, Charlotte was incorporated as a city in 1768 and made the county seat in 1774. Charlotte was a leading Confederate city during the Civil War and was the last meeting place of the full Confederate cabinet.

From 1800 to 1848, Charlotte was the center of U.S. gold production. A branch of the U.S. mint operated from there from 1837 to 1913.

The city has a highly diversified economy and is a foremost center for distribution, retailing, technology, and manufacturing. It is the second-largest banking center in the U.S. It is the seat of the University of North Carolina at Charlotte.

Famous natives: Romare Bearden, artist; Richard G. Darman, government official; Billy Graham, evangelist; Charles Gwathmey, architect; Hamilton Jordan, government official; Donald Schollander, swimmer; Randolph Scott, actor.

Chicago, Ill.

Mayor: Richard M. Daley (to April 1999)
1996 est. population (rank): 2,721,547 (3)
1990 census population (rank): 2,783,726 (3); **% change,** –2.2; **Male,** 1,334,705; **Female,** 1,449,021; **White,** 1,263,524 (45.4%); **Black,** 1,087,711 (39.1%); **American Indian, Eskimo, or Aleut,** 7,064 (0.3%); **Asian or Pacific Islander,** 104,118 (3.7%); **Other race,** 321,309; **Hispanic origin,** 545,852 (19.6%). **1990 population under 18:** 26.0%; **65 and over:** 11.9%; **median age:** 31.3.
Land area: 228.469 sq mi. (592 sq km); **Alt.:** Highest, 672 ft.; lowest, 578.5 ft.
Avg. daily temp. (1997): Jan., 19.9° F; July, 73.2° F
Churches: Protestant, 850; Roman Catholic, 252; Jewish, 51; **City-owned parks:** 547; **Radio stations (1997):** AM, 26; FM, 43; **Television stations:** 14
Civilian Labor Force (PMSA 1996): 4,120,400; **Unemployed:** 194,400, **Percent:** 4.7; **Per capita personal income (PMSA) 1994:** $25,865
Chamber of Commerce: Chicagoland Chamber of Commerce, 200 N. LaSalle, Chicago, Ill. 60601

Chicago is the largest city in Illinois and the seat of Cook County. Built directly on the lake front, it stretches for 22 miles along the southwestern shore of Lake Michigan.

The first white men known to have visited Chicago were Louis Joliet and Jacques Marquette in 1673. The first permanent white settler in the area was John Kinzie, sometimes called the Father of Chicago, who took over a trading post in 1796 that had been established 1791 by Jean-Baptiste Point du Sable, a French-speaking black fur trapper. Fort Dearborn, a blockhouse and stockade, was built in 1804, but was evacuated in 1812, with more than half of its garrison massacred at what is now the foot of 18th Street. Not until 1830 was the town laid out. The name Chicago is thought to come from the Algonquian Indian word Chicagou meaning "strong" or "powerful." Some early Frenchmen believed that the name was derived from the Algonquian word for "onion place" because wild onions grew there.

Chicago was incorporated as a village in 1833 and as a city in 1837. Thirty-four years later it was destroyed in the great Chicago fire of 1871.

Chicago is a major Great Lakes port and the commercial, financial, industrial, and cultural center of the Midwest. The manufacturing industries dominate the wholesale and retail trade, and trade in agricultural commodities is important to the economy. The Chicago Board of Trade is the largest agricultural futures market in the world.

Famous natives: Jack Benny, comedian; Edgar Rice Burroughs, author; Raymond Chandler, author; Hillary Rodham Clinton, lawyer and First Lady; Michael Crichton, author; Walt Disney, filmmaker; John Dos Passos, author; Bobby Fischer, chess player; Bob Fosse, choreographer and director; Benny Goodman, clarinetist; Dorothy Hamill, figure skater; Quincy Jones, composer; Gene Krupa, drummer; Dorothy Malone, actress; David Mamet, playwright; Bob Newhart, comedian; Kim Novak, actress;

Donald O'Connor, actor; William L. Shirer, journalist and historian; Preston Sturges, film director; Gloria Swanson, actress; Melvin Van Peebles, playwright; Alfred Wallenstein, conductor; Robin Williams, comedian and actor; Robert Young, actor.

Cincinnati, Ohio

Mayor: Roxanne Qualls (to Nov. 1999)
City Manager: John F. Shirey
1996 est. population (rank): 345,818 (49)
1990 census population (rank): 364,040 (45); **% change,** –5.0; **Male,** 169,305; **Female,** 194,735; **White,** 220,285 (60.5%); **Black,** 138,1312 (37.9%); **American Indian, Eskimo, or Aleut,** 660 (0.2%); **Asian or Pacific Islander,** 4,030 (1.1%); **Other race,** 933; **Hispanic origin,** 2,386 (0.7%). **1990 population under 18:** 25.1%; **65 and over:** 13.9%; **median age:** 30.9.
Land area: 78.1 sq mi. (202 sq km); **Alt.:** Highest, 960 ft.; lowest, 441 ft.
Avg. daily temp.: Jan., 30.3° F; July, 76.1° F
Churches: 850; **City-owned parks:** 96 (4,345 ac.); **Radio stations:** AM, 10; FM, 15 (Greater Cincinnati); **Television stations:** 8
Civilian Labor Force: 188,161; **Unemployed:** 14,318, **Percent:** 7.6; **Per capita personal income (PMSA) 1992:** $20,517[1]
Chamber of Commerce: Cincinnati Chamber of Commerce, 441 Vine St. Suite 300, Cincinnati, Ohio 45202

1. Ohio–Ky.–Ind.

Cincinnati is the third largest city in Ohio and the seat of Hamilton County. It is located on the Ohio River.

Cincinnati began as part of the Miami Purchase of 1788. The first settlement, Columbia, was begun by Benjamin Stites that same year. The town of Losantiville was founded in 1788 on a plateau above the Ohio River by Mathias Denman, Robert Patterson, and Israel Ludlow. Its strategic location in the Western Territory led to the building of Ft. Washington, the most ambitious military establishment in the territory. The community of Losantiville that grew up around the fort was renamed Cincinnati in 1790 by Gen. Arthur St. Clair, commander of Ft. Washington and first governor of the Northwest Territory, after the Revolutionary officers' Society of the Cincinnati, founded by George Washington. It was incorporated as a village in 1802 and chartered as a city in 1819.

The city began to flourish as a commercial hub with the arrival of the first steamboat in 1811, the completion of the Miami and Erie Canal in 1827, and the coming of the first railroad in 1843.

Cincinnati is a port of entry and more than 46 million tons pass through each year. The city has a diverse economy and is a major center for manufacturing, wholesaling, and retailing, as well as insurance and finance companies and health services. Prominent manufacturing groups include: transportation equipment, which includes aircraft engines and auto parts; food and kindred products; metal working; general industrial machinery; chemicals; fabricated metal products; printing and publishing.

Famous natives: Eddie Arcaro, jockey; Theda Bara, actress; Doris Day, actress; Jim Dine, painter; Suzanne Farrell, ballerina; Robert Henri, painter; James Levine, music director; Adolph Ochs, publisher; Tyrone Power, actor; William Procter, scientist; Roy Rogers, actor; Pete Rose, baseball player; Steven Spielberg, filmmaker; Roger Staubach, football player; Robert A. Taft, legislator; William Howard Taft, former president.

Cleveland, Ohio

Mayor: Michael R. White (to Dec. 2001)
1996 est. population (rank): 498,246 (25)
1990 census population (rank): 505,616 (24); **% change,** –1.5; **Male,** 237,211; **Female,** 268,405; **White,** 250,234 (49.5%); **Black,** 235,405 (46.6%); **American Indian, Eskimo, or Aleut,** 1,562 (0.3%); **Asian or Pacific Islander,** 5,115 (1.0%); **Other race,** 13,300; **Hispanic origin,** 23,197 (4.6%). **1990 population under 18:** 26.9%; **65 and over:** 14.0%; **median age:** 31.9.
Land area: 79 sq mi. (205 sq km); **Alt.:** Highest, 1048 ft.; lowest, 573 ft.
Avg. daily temp.: Jan., 25.5° F; July, 71.6° F
Churches [1]: Protestant, 980; Roman Catholic, 187; Jewish, 31; Eastern Orthodox, 22; **City-owned parks:** 41 (1,930 ac.); **Radio stations:** AM, 15; FM, 17; **Television stations:** 7
Civilian Labor Force: 209,700; **Unemployed:** 19,900, **Percent:** 9.7; **Per capita personal income (PMSA) 1992:** $21,533[1]
Chamber of Commerce: Greater Cleveland Growth Association, 200 Tower City Center, Cleveland, Ohio 44113

1. Cleveland–Lorain–Elyria.

Cleveland is the second-largest city in Ohio and the seat of Cuyahoga County. It is located in the northeastern part of the state on Lake Erie. In the colonial era, the Cleveland area was known as the Connecticut Western Reserve, part of a land grant made to Connecticut by King Charles II in 1662. The city was founded in 1796 by Gen. Moses Cleaveland, who was the head surveyor of the Connecticut Land Company. This company had bought three million acres in what is now northern Ohio. A permanent settlement was founded in 1799, named after the general, and the spelling was shortened to Cleveland. The city was incorporated in 1836.

Cleveland's industrial growth was stimulated by the opening of the Ohio and Erie canals in 1832 and, later, the advent of the Civil War with the corresponding demand for machinery, railroad equipment, ships, and other items.

The port of Cleveland is the largest overseas general cargo port on Lake Erie. Greater Cleveland has long been famous as a diversified durable goods manufacturing area. Following the national trend, Cleveland has been shifting to a more services-based economy. Greater Cleveland is a world corporate center for leading national and multinational companies in industries ranging from transportation, insurance, retailing, and utilities, to commercial banking and finance.

Famous natives: Jim Backus, actor; Drew Carey, actor and comedian; Dorothy Dandridge, actress; Ruby Dee, actress; Phil Donahue, talk-show host; Joel Grey, actor; Arsenio Hall, talk-show host; Margaret Hamilton, actress; Philip Johnson, architect; Henry Mancini, composer; Burgess Meredith, actor; Paul Newman, actor; Carl Stokes, jurist.

Colorado Springs, Colo.

Mayor: Mary Lou Makepeace (to 2001)
1996 est. population (rank): 345,127 (50)
1990 census population (rank): 281,140 (54); **% change,** 22.8; **Male,** 137,611; **Female,** 143,529; **White,** 241,513 (85.9%); **Black,** 19,746 (7.0%); **American Indian, Eskimo, or Aleut,** 2,335 (0.8%); **Asian or Pacific Islander,** 6,845 (2.4%); **Other race,** 10,701; **Hispanic origin,** 25,662 (9.1%).

1990 population under 18: 26.7%; **65 and over:** 9.2%; **median age:** 31.1.
Land area: 183.2 sq mi. (474.49 sq km); **Alt.:** 6,035 ft.
Avg. daily temp.: Jan., 28.8° F; July, 71.2° F
Churches: Protestant, 400+; Roman Catholic, 20; Jewish, 3; others, **City parks and playgrounds:** 156 (10,762 ac.); **Radio stations:** AM, 7; FM, 17; **Television stations:** 7
Civilian Labor Force: 138,239; **Unemployed:** 10,084, **Percent:** 6.68; **Per capita personal income (1989):** $14,243
Chamber of Commerce: Colorado Springs Chamber of Commerce, 2 N. Cascade Ave., Suite 110, Colorado Springs, Colo. 80903

Colorado Springs is the second-largest city in Colorado, after Denver. It is the seat of El Paso County, making up about three-quarters of the county's population. It is located on the edge of the Rocky Mountains, with Pikes Peak (alt. 14,110 feet) towering beside it to the west. To the east begin the Great Plains.

The city was founded in 1871. General William Jackson Palmer, a Pennsylvania-born Civil War veteran, came across the scenic spot in his railroad travels and was inspired to begin a new resort community there. The subsequent development of Colorado Springs was influenced in part by an influx of English tourists later in the 1870s and by the discovery of gold in nearby Cripple Creek in the 1890s. The discovery brought a great deal of wealth to Colorado Springs. Millionaire businessmen and philanthropists, such as Spencer Penrose, Charles Tutt, and Winfield Scott Stratton, helped to establish the city's infrastructure and shape its popularity as a tourist destination.

During World War II, Colorado Springs sold a large amount of land just south of the city to the military. The U.S. Army established Fort Carson as a training facility. The military presence in Colorado Springs would continue to grow, with the establishment of the United States Air Force Academy there in the 1950s, and later, the construction of Peterson Air Force Base, Falcon Air Force Base, and Cheyenne Mountain Air Force Base. The bases are all home to space command centers (with Cheyenne Mountain housing the headquarters for the North American Aerospace Defense Command [NORAD]) and have collectively earned Colorado Springs its national reputation as the leading center for military space operations.

The city's economy is still based heavily on tourism. In more recent years, Colorado Springs has gained a strong foothold in the electronics, high-technology, and manufacturing industries. The city is also a large center for amateur sports, as it is home to the headquaraters of the U.S. Olympic Committee and Olympic Training Center facility.

Famous natives: Bert Andrews, journalist; Kelly Bishop, actress; Spring Byington, actress; Lon Chaney, actor; Marjorie Daw, actress; Marceline Day, actress; Rich "Goose" Gossage, baseball player; Helen Hunt Jackson, writer and poet; Chase Masterson, actress; Sherry Stringfield, actress.

Columbus, Ohio

Mayor: Gregory S. Lashutka (to Nov. 1999)
1996 est. population (rank): 657,053 (16)
1990 census population (rank): 632,910 (16); **% change,** 3.8; **Male,** 305,574; **Female,** 327,336; **White,** 471,025 (74.4%); **Black,** 142,748 (22.6%); **American Indian, Eskimo, or Aleut,** 1,469 (0.2%); **Asian or Pacific Islander,** 14,993 (2.4%); **Other race,** 2,675; **Hispanic origin,** 6,741 (1.1%). **1990 population under 18:** 23.7%; **65 and over:** 9.2%; **median age:** 29.4.
Land area: 209 sq mi. (541.5 sq km); **Alt.:** Highest, 902 ft.; lowest, 702 ft.
Avg. daily temp.: Jan., 27.1° F; July, 73.8° F
Churches: Protestant, 436; Roman Catholic, 62; Jewish, 5; Other, 8; **City-owned parks:** 203 (12,891 ac.); **Radio stations:** AM, 10; FM, 16; **Television stations:** 9 commercial, 3 PBS
Civilian Labor Force (1995): 554,733; **Unemployed:** 18,233, **Percent:** 3.3; **Per capita personal income:** $13,151
Chamber of Commerce: Columbus Area Chamber of Commerce, P.O. Box 1527, Columbus, Ohio 43216

Columbus, the largest city in Ohio, is the state capital and the seat of Franklin County. It is located in central Ohio on the Scioto River.

The first structures near downtown Columbus were earthen mounds constructed by Indian tribes known as Mound Builders. The Indians lived alone in Central Ohio until the 1700s, when the first explorers entered the Midwest. The first permanent settlement was founded by a surveyor from Kentucky, Lucas Sullivant, in 1797 and was named Franklinton. The site was laid out as the state capital in 1812 and named to honor Christopher Columbus. It became the capital in 1816. Columbus was chartered as a city in 1834 and annexed Franklinton in 1870. The city's growth was stimulated by the development of transportation facilities—a feeder to the Ohio Canal completed in 1832, the National Road in 1833, and the arrival of the railroad in 1850.

Columbus is a port of entry and a major industrial, commercial, manufacturing, and cultural center. It is the seat of Ohio State University. The city has enjoyed steady growth over the years due to its economic diversity—no single activity dominates the economy.

Famous natives: Warner Baxter, actor; George Bellows, painter; Michael Feinstein, singer and pianist; Eileen Heckart, actress; Jack Nicklaus, golfer; Tom Poston, actor; Eddie Rickenbacker, aviator; Arthur M. Schlesinger, historian; James Thurber, writer; Nancy Wilson, singer.

Dallas, Tex.

Mayor: Ron Kirk (to 1999)
City Manager: John Ware (apptd. Nov. 1993)
1996 est. population (rank): 1,053,292 (9)
1990 census population (rank): 1,006,877 (8); **% change,** 4.6; **Male,** 495,141; **Female,** 511,736; **White,** 556,760 (55.3%); **Black,** 296,994 (29.5%); **American Indian, Eskimo, or Aleut,** 4,792 (0.5%); **Asian or Pacific Islander,** 21,952 (2.2%); **Other race,** 126,379; **Hispanic origin,** 210,240 (20.9%). **1990 population under 18:** 25.0%; **65 and over:** 9.7%; **median age:** 30.6.
Land area: 378 sq mi. (979 sq km); **Alt.:** Highest, 750 ft.; lowest, 375 ft.
Avg. daily temp.: Jan., 45.0° F; July, 86.3° F
Churches: 1,974 (in Dallas Co.); **City-owned parks:** 296 (47,025 ac.); **Radio stations:** AM, 19; FM, 30; **Television stations:** 10 commercial, 1 PBS
Civilian Labor Force: 570,661; **Unemployed:** 50,526, **Percent:** 8.9; **Per capita personal income (PMSA) 1992:** $22,424
Chamber of Commerce: Dallas Chamber of Commerce, 1201 Elm, Dallas, Tex. 75270

Dallas is the second-largest city in Texas and is the seat of Dallas County. It is situated 185 miles northeast of Austin on the Trinity River near the junction of its three forks. It was first settled by Tennessee lawyer John Neely Bryan as a trading post on the Trinity River in 1841. Many historians believe that John Neely Bryan named the city after George Mifflin Dallas, vice president under James K. Polk, but there is no official agreement on this. It was incorporated as a town in 1856 and a city in 1871. The city developed as a cotton market in the 1870s and became the chief cotton-producing region of Texas.

The economy is highly diversified and the city is the leading commercial, marketing, and industrial center of the southwest. The insurance business is important, and the service sector has experienced rapid growth. Dallas is also a popular tourist and convention city.

Famous natives: Tex Avery, animator and director; Robby Benson, actor; Ernie Banks, baseball player; Bebe Daniels, actress; Linda Darnell, actress; Lee Elder, golfer; Morgan Fairchild, actress; Trini Lopez, singer; Aaron Spelling, producer; Stephen Stills, singer; Sharon Tate, actress; Lee Trevino, golfer.

Denver, Colo.

Mayor: Wellington Webb (to July 1999)
1996 est. population (rank): 497,840 (26)
1990 census population (rank): 467,610 (26); **% change,** 6.5; **Male,** 227,517; **Female,** 240,093; **White,** 337,198 (72.1%); **Black,** 60,046 (12.8%); **American Indian, Eskimo, or Aleut,** 5,381 (1.2%); **Asian or Pacific Islander,** 11,005 (2.4%); **Other race,** 53,980; **Hispanic origin,** 107,382 (23.0%); **1990 population under 18:** 22.0%; **65 and over:** 13.9%; **median age:** 33.9.
Land area: 154.63 sq mi. (400.5 sq km); **Alt.:** Highest, 5,494 ft.; lowest, 5,140 ft.
Avg. daily temp.: Jan., 29.5° F; July, 73.3° F
Churches:[1] Protestant, 859; Roman Catholic, 60; Jewish, 13; **City-owned parks:** 205 (4,166 ac.); **City-owned mountain parks:** 40 (13,600 ac.); **Radio stations:** AM, 23; FM, 20[1]; **Television stations:** 17[1]
Civilian Labor Force: 245,495[2], **Unemployed:** 17,527[2]; **Percent:** 7.1[2]; **Per capita personal income (PMSA) 1992:** $22,930
Chamber of Commerce: Greater Denver Chamber of Commerce, 1445 Market Street, Denver, Colo. 80202

1. Metropolitan area. 2. Denver City/County.

Denver is the largest city in Colorado. It is the state capital and the seat of Denver County. It lies at the foot of the Rocky Mountains and is situated at the junction of the South Platte River and Cherry Creek. The city was born in 1858, when gold was discovered in the sands of Cherry Creek, and it began as a tough village of cabins, shacks, and tents. It was incorporated as a city in 1861 and became the territorial capital in 1867. The city is named for James W. Denver, governor of the Kansas Territory, which included part of Colorado. The city prospered from the famous gold and silver mines of the 1870s and the 1880s.

Denver International Airport, the first major new airport to be opened in the U.S. in 21 years, opened to passenger traffic on Feb. 28, 1995, at a cost of $4.9 billion. At 53 square miles, it is the largest airport in North America.

Denver is an important cultural, industrial, transportation, tourist, and marketing center. It is also a regional center for many federal government agencies and a leader in the development of western energy resources.

Denver's fastest-growing industries include contract construction, real estate, retail trade, and government.

Famous natives: Tim Allen, comedian and actor; Ward Bond, actor; Douglas Fairbanks, Sr., actor; John Hart, newsman; Pat Hingle, actor; Ted Mack, TV host; Barbara Rush, actress; Alan K. Simpson, senator; Paul Whiteman, bandleader; Don Wilson, announcer.

Detroit, Mich.

Mayor: Dennis W. Archer (to 2002)
1996 est. population (rank): 1,000,272 (10)
1990 census population (rank): 1,027,974 (7); **% change,** –2.7; **Male,** 476,814; **Female,** 551,160; **White,** 222,316 (21.6%); **Black,** 777,916 (75.7%); **American Indian, Eskimo, or Aleut,** 3,655 (0.4%); **Asian or Pacific Islander,** 8,461 (0.8%); **Other race,** 15,626; **Hispanic origin,** 28,473 (2.8%). **1990 population under 18:** 29.4%; **65 and over:** 12.2%; **median age:** 30.8.
Land area: 143 sq mi. (370 sq km); **Alt.:** Highest, 685 ft.; lowest, 574 ft.
Avg. daily temp.: Jan., 23.4° F; July, 71.9° F
Churches:[1] Protestant, 1,165; Roman Catholic, 89; Jewish, 2; **City-owned parks:** 56 parks (3,843 ac.); 393 sites (5,838 ac.); **Radio stations:** AM, 27; FM, 30 (includes 3 in Windsor, Ont.); **Television stations:** 8[2] (includes 1 in Windsor, Ont.)
Civilian Labor Force (1997): 394,050; **Unemployed:** 31,100; **Percent:** 7.9; **Per capita personal income:** $21,000
Chamber of Commerce: Detroit Regional Chamber of Commerce, One Woodward Avenue, P.O. Box 33840, Detroit MI 48232-0840

1. Six-county metropolitan area. 2. Within four counties of Metro Detroit.

Detroit, the largest city in Michigan, is situated in the southeastern part of the state on the Detroit River. It is the seat of Wayne County. Detroit was incorporated as a city in 1815 and reincorporated in 1824.

Detroit is the oldest city of any size west of the seaboard colonies, having been founded by Antoine de la Mothe Cadillac on July 24, 1701, more than a century before Chicago was founded. The French were the first settlers and they gave the city its name from their word meaning "strait," referring to the 27-mile-long Detroit River, which connects Lake Erie and Lake St. Clair. The river forms part of the international boundary, and marks the only point where Canada lies directly south of U.S. territory.

Because of its strategic location, Detroit was fought over by the French, the British, and the Indians. It was the headquarters for the British forces in the Northwest Territory during the American Revolutionary War.

The first steam vessel, the *Walk-in-the-Water*, made its appearance on the Great Lakes in 1818, and Detroit was the western terminus for most of its voyages from Buffalo. Its link to all the important cities on the Great Lakes made it a major exporting port.

Detroit is one of the largest manufacturing cities in the U.S. and is the center of the automobile manufacturing industry, which has experienced a decline to foreign competition in the past decade. The health and medical care sector is important to

the economy, and employment in the finance, insurance, and real-estate industries has inched up in the Detroit metropolitan area since 1991.

Famous natives: Ralph Bunche, statesman; Francis Ford Coppola, director; Charles Lindbergh, aviator; Madonna, singer; John Mitchell, former U.S. Attorney General; George Peppard, actor; Gilda Radner, comedian; Della Reese, singer; Sugar Ray Robinson, boxer; Diana Ross, singer; Tom Selleck, actor; Margaret Whiting, singer.

El Paso, Tex.

Mayor: Carlos Ramirez (to May 1999)
1996 est. population (rank): 599,865 (17)[1]
1990 census population (rank): 515,342 (22); **% change,** 16.4; **Male,** 247,163; **Female,** 268,179; **White,** 396,122 (76.9%); **Black,** 17,708 (3.4%); **American Indian, Eskimo, or Aleut,** 2,239 (0.4%); **Asian or Pacific Islander,** 5,956 (1.2%); **Other race,** 93,317; **Hispanic origin,** 355,669 (69.0%). **1990 population under 18:** 31.9%; **65 and over:** 8.7%; **median age:** 28.7
Land area: 247.4 sq mi. (641 sq km); **Alt.:** 4,000 ft.
Avg. daily temp.: Jan., 44.2° F; July, 82.5° F
Churches: Protestant, 320; Roman Catholic, 39; Jewish, 3; others, 20; **City-owned parks:** 116[2] (1,180 ac.); **Radio Stations:** AM, 18; FM, 17; **Television stations:** 6
Civilian Labor Force (1995): 285,100; **Unemployed:** 31,100, **Percent:** 10.9; **Per capita personal income:** $12,790
Chamber of Commerce: El Paso Chamber of Commerce and El Paso Hispanic Chamber of Commerce, 10 Civic Center Plaza, El Paso, Tex. 79944

1. 1997 est. population: 596,804. 2. Includes 109 developed and 7 undeveloped parks.

El Paso, the fourth-largest city in Texas and the seat of El Paso County, is located in the far western part of the state on the north bank of the Rio Grande River, opposite the Mexican city of Ciudad Juárez on the south bank.

In 1581, Spanish explorers came through the Pass of the North to test the missionary and mining possibilities of New Mexico. The area had been inhabited for centuries by various Indian groups. On April 30, 1598, Juan de Onate took formal possession of the area for King Philip II of Spain and subsequently crossed the Rio Grande River near a site west of the present downtown El Paso that he called "El Paso del Rio del Norte," meaning the crossing of the river—the first use of the name "El Paso." In 1659, the mission of Nuestra Senora de Guadalupe was founded on a site that is present-day downtown Ciudad Juárez; the mission is still in use today. In 1682, Spanish colonists from Mexico founded the settlement of Ysleta within the site of the present-day city. However, it wasn't until 1827 that the first permanent settlement at El Paso was established by Juan María Ponce de León. The city's real growth started with the arrival of the Southern Pacific Railroad in 1881. El Paso was incorporated as a city in 1873.

In 1888, Mexico changed the name of Paso del Norte to Ciudad Juárez in honor of Benito Juárez. Later, in 1967, the United States agreed to cede a long-disputed part of El Paso to Mexico due to changes in the course of the Rio Grande, which forms the international boundary between the two countries. El Paso and its sister city of Ciudad Juárez across the U.S./Mexico border are inexorably joined by culture and economy. El Paso and Juárez make up the largest international metroplex in the world.

El Paso is an important port of entry to the U.S. from Mexico. The apparel industry plays a major role in the El Paso area. The high technology, medical device manufacturing, plastics, refining, automotive, food processing, and defense-related industries are important to the economy. El Paso's service sector has experienced the healthiest growth since 1983. El Paso is also a major tourist resort.

Famous natives: Manuel Acosta, artist; Don Bluth, animation director; Vicki Carr, singer; Sam Donaldson, newsman; Judith Ivey, actress; Guy Kibbee, actor; Sandra Day O'Connor, Supreme Court justice; Debbie Reynolds, actress; Irene Ryan, actress.

Fort Worth, Tex.

Mayor: Kenneth Barr (to May 1999)
City Manager: Bob Terrell
1996 est. population (rank): 479,716 (28)[1]
1990 census population (rank): 447,619 (28); **% change,** 7.2; **Male,** 220,268; **Female:** 227,351; **White,** 285,549 (63.8%); **Black,** 98,532 (22.0%); **American Indian, Eskimo, or Aleut,** 1,914 (0.4%); **Asian or Pacific Islander,** 8,910 (2.0%); **Other race,** 52,714; **Hispanic origin,** 87,345 (19.5%). **1990 population under 18:** 26.6%; **65 and over:** 11.2%; **median age:** 30.3.
Land area: 300.6 sq mi. (778.8 sq km); **Alt.:** Highest, 780 ft.; lowest, 520 ft.
Avg. daily temp.: Jan., 44.2° F; July, 82.5° F
Churches: 941, representing 72 denominations; **City-owned parks:** 195 (6,321 ac. plus 3,500 ac. in Nature Center); **Radio stations:** AM, 5; FM, 20; **Television stations:** 15 (9 local)
Civilian Labor Force (1996): 244,188; **Unemployed:** 13,758, **Percent:** 5.63; **Per capita personal income (MSA) 1992:** $20,250[2]
Chamber of Commerce: Fort Worth Chamber of Commerce, 777 Taylor Street, Suite 900, Fort Worth, Tex. 76102

1. 1997 est. population: 484,500. 2. Fort Worth–Arlington.

Fort Worth, seat of Tarrant County, is situated in the north central part of Texas on the Trinity River.

The city was founded by Major Ripley Arnold in 1849 as a military outpost on the Trinity River to protect settlers moving westward from frequent Indian attacks. It was named after Gen. William J. Worth, the commander of the Texas army. Fort Worth was incorporated in 1873. Its growth was stimulated in the 1870s by the proximity to the Chisholm cattle trail. It prospered as a meat-packing and shipping center when the Texas and Pacific Railway arrived in 1876, and later experienced a new boom when oil was discovered nearby in 1917. The establishment of military installations in the area during both world wars also spurred the economy.

Fort Worth has traditionally been a diverse center of manufacturing and is not dependent on the oil or financial sectors. The city's industries range from clothing and food products to jet fighters, helicopters, computers, pharmaceuticals, and plastics. Fort Worth is a national leader in aviation products, electronic equipment, and refrigeration equipment. It is home to a multitude of major corporate headquarters, offices, and distribution centers.

Famous natives: Robert Bass, financier; Kate Capshaw, actress; Sandra Heynie, golfer; Patricia Highsmith, writer; Spanky McFarland, actor; R. Bruce Merrifield, Nobelist in chemistry; Roger Miller, singer; Fess Parker, actor; Rex Reed, critic; Johnny Rutherford, auto racer; Liz Smith, columnist.

Fresno, Calif.

Mayor: Jim Patterson (to May 2000)
City Manager: Jeffrey M. Reid
1996 est. population (rank): 396,011 (39)
1990 census population (rank): 354,202 (47); **% change,** 11.8; **Male,** 172,241; **Female,** 181,961; **White,** 209,604 (59.2%); **Black,** 29,409 (8.3%); **American Indian, Eskimo, or Aleut,** 3,729 (1.1%); **Asian or Pacific Islander,** 44,358 (12.5%); **Other race,** 67,102; **Hispanic origin,** 105,787 (29.9%). **1990 population under 18:** 31.7%; **65 and over:** 10.1%; **median age:** 28.4.
Land area: 99.38 sq mi. (257.39 sq km); **Alt.:** 328 ft.
Avg. daily temp.: Jan., 45.5° F; July, 81.0° F
Churches: 450 (approximate); **City-owned parks:** 38 (690 ac.); **Radio stations:** AM 11[1]; FM 13[1]; Bilingual 1; **Television stations:** 8[1]
Civilian Labor Force: 174,496; **Unemployed:** 22,708, **Percent:** 13.0; **Per capita personal income (MSA) 1992:** $16,376
Chamber of Commerce: Fresno County and City Chamber of Commerce, P.O. Box 1469, 2331 Fresno St., Fresno, Calif. 93716

1. Metropolitan area.

Fresno is located in central California, 184 miles southeast of San Francisco and 222 miles northwest of Los Angeles. It is the seat of Fresno County. Fresno was incorporated as a city in 1885.

Fresno began as a station for the Central Pacific Railroad in 1872 and was made the seat of Fresno County in 1874. The city's name is Spanish for the ash trees that the early explorers found in the area.

Fresno is the world capital of the agribusiness, with 250 different crops produced by 7,500 farmers on 1.9 million irrigated acres, worth $3 billion a year. Fresno county's top five agricultural products are grapes, cotton, tomatoes, cattle and calves, and turkeys. The city is also a trade, financial, media, and commercial center. Its diverse industries include agricultural chemicals, farm equipment, canned fruit and vegetables, clothing, computer software, electric wire, pumps, glass, and plastic products.

Famous natives: Mike Connors, actor; Maynard Dixon, painter; Bruce Furniss, swimmer; Jon Hall, actor; Daryle Lamonica, football player; Sam Peckinpah, director; William Saroyan, novelist; Tom Seaver, baseball player.

Honolulu, Hawaii

Mayor: Jeremy Harris (to Jan. 2001)
1996 est. population (rank): 423,475 (35)
1990 census population (rank): 365,272 (44)[1]; **% change,** 15.9; **Male,** 186,371; **Female,** 190,688; **White,** 104,038 (27.6%); **Black,** 7,371 (1.95%); **American Indian, Eskimo, or Aleut,** 1,197 (0.3%); **Asian or Pacific Islander,** 259,629 (68.9%); **Other race,** 4,824 (1.3%); **Hispanic origin,** 18,017 (4.8%). **1990 population under 18:** 19.8%; **65 and over:** 15.5%; **median age:** n.a.
Land area: 600 sq mi. (1554 sq km); **Alt.:** Highest, 4,003 ft.; lowest, sea level
Avg. daily temp.: Jan., 72.6° F; July, 81° F
Churches: Roman Catholic, 39; Buddhist, 51; Jewish, 2; Protestant and others, 402; **City-owned parks:** 6,146 ac.; **Radio stations:** AM, 17; FM, 15; **Television stations:** 10
Civilian Labor Force (1997 avg.): 425,950[2]; **Unemployed:** 22,500[2], **Percent:** 5.3[2]; **Per capita personal income (1994):** $27,040
Chamber of Commerce: Chamber of Commerce of Hawaii, 1132 Bishop St., Suite 200, Honolulu, Hawaii 96813

1. Census Designated Place; the census bureau does not include the entire city and county in its census of Honolulu. If it did, the 1990 census and rank would be 836,231 (12). 2. City and county.

Honolulu is the capital (on Oahu) and largest city in Hawaii. It is also the seat of Honolulu County. The city and county of Honolulu include the entire island of Oahu, the major island of the state of Hawaii, and most of the Northwestern Hawaiian Islands, from Nihoa to Kure Atoll, except Midway. It is situated in the central Pacific Ocean 2,397 miles west-southwest of San Francisco. Honolulu's name means "sheltered harbor" and derives from the native words hono, meaning "a bay," and lulu, meaning "sheltered."

Honolulu's early history was one of turbulence and conflict. One of the last areas on the globe to be explored and exploited by Europeans (it was first visited by British Captain James Cook in 1778), Hawaii was subject to strong pressures from many forces, including American missionaries, who arrived in 1820, and opportunistic whalers. These whalers were among those who built Honolulu originally, bringing trade, commerce, and prosperity that led to expansion into the sugar and pineapple industries.

As early as 1814, Russia tried to move in and Russian soldiers built a bastion at the harbor's edge. The British flag was raised in 1843 and French forces occupied Honolulu in 1849. Each time control was given back to the independent kingdom without bloodshed. In 1898, a group of Americans completed a project attempted at intervals during the previous 65 years—annexation to the United States. Honolulu was incorporated as a city in 1907.

Honolulu was bombed by Japan in a surprise attack on the unprepared U.S. naval base at Pearl Harbor on Dec. 7, 1941. This action forced the United States to enter World War II. "Remember Pearl Harbor," became a famous American wartime slogan.

Hawaiian statehood in 1959 and the viability of commercial air travel to the island brought boom times to Honolulu. Tourism is the city's principal industry, followed by federal defense expenditures and agricultural exports (chiefly pineapples).

Famous natives: Hiram Bingham, explorer; Jean Erdman, dancer and choreographer; Hiram Fong, senator; Daniel Inouye, senator; Duke Kahanamoku, surfer and Olympian swimmer; Bette Midler, actress and singer; Kelly Preston, actress; Louise Morgan Sill, author; Don Stroud, actor; Merlin D. Tuttle, biologist and wildlife photographer.

Houston, Tex.

Mayor: Lee P. Brown (to Dec. 1999)
1996 est. population (rank): 1,744,058 (4)
1990 census population (rank): 1,630,553 (4); **% change,** 7.0; **Male,** 809,048; **Female,** 821,505; **White,** 859,069 (52.7%); **Black,** 457,990 (28.1%); **American Indian, Eskimo, or Aleut,** 4,126 (0.3%); **Asian or Pacific Islander,** 67,113 (4.1%); **Other race,** 242,255; **Hispanic origin,** 450,483 (27.6%). **1990 population under 18:** 26.7%; **65 and over:** 8.3%; **median age:** 30.4.
Land area: 594.03 sq mi. (1,521 sq km); **Alt.:** Highest, 120 ft.; lowest, sea level

Avg. daily temp.: Jan., 51.4° F; July, 83.1° F
Churches: 1,750[1]; **City-owned parks:** 307 (32,598 ac.); **Radio stations:** AM, 22; FM, 32[1]; **Television stations:** 13 commercial, 1 PBS
Civilian Labor Force: 979,931; **Unemployed:** 65,315, **Percent:** 6.7; **Per capita personal income (PMSA) 1992:** $21,737
Chamber of Commerce: Greater Houston Partnership, 1200 Smith, Suite 700, Houston, Tex. 77002

1. Harris County.

Houston, the largest city in Texas and seat of Harris County, is located in the southeastern part of the state near the Gulf of Mexico.

Sam Houston was the commander-in-chief of the Texas troops who fought a successful war of rebellion against the domination by Mexico, which had been in possession of Texas. On April 21, 1836, Houston's men won a decisive victory in which the Mexican dictator, Gen. Santa Anna, was taken prisoner and forced to sign the treaty that launched the Republic of Texas. In September, a constitution was ratified, and Houston was elected president. The Texas Republic was recognized by the U.S. and by the major European powers. The present city of Houston was incorporated in 1837 and named after Sam Houston; it was the Republic's first capital.

The port of Houston is a leader in the U.S. in foreign tonnage handled. The city is a major business, financial, science, and technology center. Houston is outstanding in oil and natural-gas production and is the energy capital of the world. It is the home of one of the largest medical facilities in the world—the Texas Medical Center—and the focus of the aerospace industry. The Lyndon B. Johnson Space Center is the nation's headquarters for manned spaceflight.

Famous natives: Debbie Allen, choreographer; Lance Alworth, football player; Denton Cooley, heart surgeon; Jim Demaret, golfer; Allen Drury, novelist; Shelly Duvall, actress; A. J. Foyt, auto racer; Howard Hughes, industrialist; Barbara C. Jordan, educator, lawyer and politician; Barbara Mandrell, singer; Annette O'Toole, actress; Dennis and Randy Quaid, actors; Kenny Rogers, singer; Patrick Swayze, actor and dancer.

Indianapolis, Ind.

Mayor: Stephen Goldsmith (to Dec. 31, 1999)
1996 est. population (rank): 746,737 (12)
1990 census population (rank)[2]: 741,952 (12); **% change,** 0.6; **Male,** 352,309; **Female,** 389,643; **White,** 564,447 (77.2%); **Black,** 166,031 (22.4%); **American Indian, Eskimo, or Aleut,** 1,580 (0.2%); **Asian or Pacific Islander,** 6,943 (0.9%); **Other race,** 2,951; **Hispanic origin,** 7,790 (1.0%). **1990 population under 18:** 25.6%; **65 and over:** 11.5%; **median age:** 31.8.
Land area: 352 sq mi. (912 sq km); **Alt.:** Highest, 840 ft.; lowest, 700 ft.
Avg. daily temp.: Jan., 26.0 F; July, 75.1° F
Churches: 1,200[1]; **City-owned parks:** 130 (9,375 ac.); **Radio stations:** AM, 8[3]; FM, 17[3]; **Television stations:** 7[1]
Civilian Labor Force: 441,780[1] **Unemployed:** 20,820[1], **Percent:** 4.7[1]; **Per capita personal income (MSA) 1992:** $20,992
Chamber of Commerce: Indianapolis Chamber of Commerce, 320 N. Meridian St., Indianapolis, Ind. 46204

1. Marion County. 2. Consolidated city. 3. Metropolitan area.

Indianapolis, the largest city in Indiana and seat of Marion County, is located in the central part of the state on the West Fork of the White River. Its name derives from combining "Indiana" with "polis," the Greek word for city.

Indianapolis was settled in 1820, and in 1825 its site was chosen as the state capital. It was incorporated as a city in 1832 and reincorporated in 1838. The city's growth began when the railroad reached it in 1847. Toward the end of the 19th century, the discovery of nearby natural gas and the start of the automobile industry hastened its industrial expansion. On Jan. 1, 1970, Indianapolis merged with surrounding Marion County.

Indianapolis is an important center of a rich agricultural region and a major grain and livestock market. It is also a focal point of commerce, transportation, and manufacturing for the region. Some leading industries are electronics, pharmaceuticals, and food processing. The financial sector, and service and insurance industries are growing rapidly.

Indianapolis is the site of the world-famous 500-mile automobile race and the Indiana State Fair.

Famous natives: Monte Blue, actor; David Letterman, TV host; Steve McQueen, actor; Jane Pauley, TV newscaster; Booth Tarkington, author; Kurt Vonnegut, Jr., author; Harry Von Zell, announcer; Clifton Webb, actor.

Jacksonville, Fla.

Mayor: John Delaney (to June 30, 1999)
1996 est. population (rank): 679,792 (14)
1990 census population (rank)[1]: 672,971 (15); **% change,** 1.0; **Male,** 328,737; **Female,** 344,234; **White,** 489,604 (77.1%); **Black,** 163,902 (24.4%); **American Indian, Eskimo, or Aleut,** 1,904 (0.3%); **Asian or Pacific Islander,** 12,940 (1.9%); **Other race,** 4,621; **Hispanic origin,** 17,333 (2.6%). **1990 population under 18:** 25.9%; **65 and over:** 10.7%; **median age:** 31.5.
Land area: 759.6 sq mi. (1,967 sq km); **Alt.:** Highest, 71 ft.; lowest, sea level
Avg. daily temp.: Jan., 53.2° F; July, 81.3° F
Churches: Protestant, 794; Roman Catholic, 21; Jewish, 5; others, 22; **City-owned parks and playgrounds:** 138 (1,522 ac.); **Radio stations:** AM, 14; FM, 16; **Television stations:** 6 commercial, 1 PBS, 1 religious
Civilian Labor Force: 328,211; **Unemployed:** 24,051, **Percent:** 7.3; **Per capita personal income (MSA) 1992:** $19,146
Chamber of Commerce: Jacksonville Area Chamber of Commerce, Jacksonville, Fla. 32202

1. Consolidated city.

Jacksonville, Florida's largest city, is located in Duval County in the northeast corner of Florida, on the banks of the St. Johns River and adjacent to the Atlantic Ocean. It is the largest metropolitan area in northeast Florida and southeast Georgia.

Starting in the 16th century, French, Spanish, and English explorers and colonists were attracted to the region by the St. Johns River. The site was settled by Lewis Hogans in 1816. Jacksonville was laid out in 1822 and was named after Gen. Andrew Jackson, the first military governor of Florida. It was incorporated as a city in 1832.

During the Civil War, much of the city was destroyed by Union forces who occupied Jacksonville four times. The city was rebuilt and, following the development of its harbor and the railroads, fast became the transportation hub and leading industrial city in Florida by the 1880s. In 1968, Jacksonville annexed Duval county.

Jacksonville is the transportation hub and distribution focal point in the state. The strength of the

city's economy lies in its broad diversification. The area's economy is balanced among distribution, financial services, biomedical, consumer goods, information services, manufacturing, and other industries. Jacksonville has the largest deepwater port in the South Atlantic and is the leading port in the U.S. for automobile imports.

Famous natives: Mae Axton, songwriter; Pat Boone, singer; Judy Canova, comedian; Harold Carmichael, football player; Merion C. Cooper, producer and director; Billy Daniels, vocalist; Storm Davis, athlete; Bob Hayes, athlete; Wanda Hendrix, actress; James Weldon Johnson, author and educator; John Rosamond Johnson, musician and composer; Mark McCumber, pro golfer; Ray Mercer, boxer; Charles "Hoss" Singleton, songwriter; Bill Terry, member of Baseball Hall of Fame; Donnie Van Zant, rock musician; Ronnie Van Zant, rock musician; Leeroy Yarbrough, auto racer.

Kansas City, Mo.

Mayor: Emanuel Cleaver II (to April 1999)
City Manager: Robert L. Collins (apptd. July 1997)
1996 est. population (rank): 441,259 (33)
1990 census population (rank): 435,146 (31); **% change:** 1.4; **Male,** 206,965; **Female,** 228,181; **White,** 290,572 (66.8%); **Black,** 128,768 (29.6%); **American Indian, Eskimo, or Aleut,** 2,144 (0.5%); **Asian or Pacific Islander,** 5,239 (1.2%); **Other race,** 8,423; **Hispanic origin,** 17,017 (3.9%). **1990 population under 18:** 24.8%; **65 and over:** 12.9%; **median age:** 32.8.
Land area: 317 sq mi. (821 sq km); **Alt.:** Highest, 1,014 ft.; lowest, 722 ft.
Avg. daily temp.: Jan., 28.4° F; July, 80.9 F
Churches: 1,100 churches of all denominations[1]; **City-owned parks and playgrounds:** 189 (10,647 ac.); **Radio stations:** AM, 14; FM, 19[1]; **Television stations:** 7[1]
Civilian Labor Force: 239,600; **Unemployed:** 15,400, **Percent:** 6.4; **Per capita personal income (MSA) 1992:** $24,576[2]
Chamber of Commerce: Chamber of Commerce of Greater Kansas City, 911 Main St., Kansas City, Mo. 64105

1. Metropolitan area. 2. Kansas City, Mo.–Kan.

Kansas City is the largest city in Missouri. It is located in the western part of the state, at the junction of the Missouri and Kansas rivers. Kansas City is located in Jackson, Clay, Platte, and Cass counties.

In 1821, the year Missouri entered the Union, French trader François Chouteau came from St. Louis to establish a trading post on the site of the present city to take advantage of the growing fur trade with the Kansa, Osage, Wyandotte, and other tribes. In 1833, a settlement was laid out by John Calvin McCoy and developed, called the town of Westport Landing. The community became the Town of Kansas and was incorporated as a city in 1850 and renamed Kansas City in 1889. The city's name reflects its Native American heritage—its site was within the territory of the Kansa or Kaw Indians.

The city grew rapidly in the mid-1880s as the starting point for gold prospectors and settlers heading westward. The coming of the Missouri-Pacific Railroad in 1865 and the spanning of the Missouri River by the Hannibal Bridge in 1869 also contributed to the city's growth, and it prospered as a center for the nation's cattle business.

The Kansas City metropolitan area, once known primarily for agriculture and manufacturing, has expanded its economic base to include strong growth in areas of telecommunications, banking and finance, and the service industry. A transportation hub since the 1800s, the area enjoys a national and regional prominence as a distribution and manufacturing center. Kansas City ranks nationally as first in greeting-card publishing, frozen food storage and distribution, and first in hard winter-wheat marketing, second in wheat flour production, and third in auto and truck assembly. The area is one of ten federal regional centers and employs over 25,000 in local, state, and federal government. The city is also a regional center for health care, employing over 55,000 in this industry.

Famous natives: Robert Altman, director; Edward Asner, actor; Burt Bacharach, composer; Noah and Wallace Beery, actors; Robert Russell Bennett, composer; Jeanne Eagels, actress; Jean Harlow, actress; Ted Shawn, dancer and choreographer; Casey Stengel, baseball player; Virgil Thompson, composer; Tom Watson, golfer.

Las Vegas, Nev.

Mayor: Jan Jones (to May 1999)
1996 est. population (rank): 376,906 (41)
1990 census population (rank): 258,295 (63); **% change:** 45.9; **Male,** 130,981; **Female,** 127,314; **White,** 202,549 (78.4%); **Black,** 29,529 (11.4%); **American Indian, Eskimo, or Aleut,** 2,282 (0.9%); **Asian or Pacific Islander,** 9,325 (3.6%); **Other race,** 14,610; **Hispanic origin,** 32,369 (12.5%); **1990 population under 18:** 25.0%; **65 and over:** 10.3%; **median age:** 32.5.
Land area: 83.3 sq mi. (1,215.7 sq km); **Alt.:** 2,174 ft.
Avg. daily temp.: Jan., 45.5° F; July, 91° F
Churches: over 500 churches and synagogues; **Radio stations:** AM 8; FM 18; **Television stations:** 7
Civilian Labor Force: (1990 census): 131,001; **Unemployed:** 19,043, **Percent:** 4.9; **Per capita personal income (MSA) 1992:** $19,994
Chamber of Commerce: 3720 Howard Hughes Parkway, Las Vegas, NV 89109

Las Vegas, seat of Clark County in southeastern Nevada, is the largest city in the state and one of the fastest-growing cities in the United States. Between April 1990 and July 1994, the Las Vegas metropolitan area population increased by 26%, growing from 852,646 to 1,076,267.

The area was discovered by Spanish explorers in 1829. The site of Las Vegas ("The Meadows" in Spanish) was originally a watering place for travelers on their way to southern California. It was first settled by Mormons in 1855, who were attracted by its artesian springs. They abandoned their settlement two years later in 1857 and the U.S. Army established Fort Baker there in 1864. In 1867, Las Vegas was detached from the Arizona Territory and joined with Nevada.

The town was established in 1905 and started to grow with the arrival of the San Pedro, Los Angeles, and Salt Lake Railroad in 1905. However, its growth did not really begin until shortly after 1931, when the Nevada legislature legalized gambling in an effort to lift the state from the Great Depression. The construction of nearby Hoover Dam economically aided the area as well.

The Las Vegas that we know today basically began after World War II when the idea of large hotels along the brand new "Strip" was developed. Las Vegas is the Marriage Capital of America. There are 50 wedding chapels in the city. Tourism and the convention industry are the city's major sources of

income. In addition, manufacturing, government, warehousing, and trucking are major sources of employment. Many high-technology companies are also located there. Three of the reasons for that are the city's proximity to sophisticated military technology centers like Nellis Air Force Base, the top-secret Nuclear Testing Grounds, and the College of Engineering at the University of Nevada, Las Vegas.

Las Vegas has a favorable business climate: taxes are relatively low, and there are neither city nor state income taxes. This is because gambling and sales taxes, paid by tourists, have allowed the city and state governments to avoid personal and corporate income taxes.

Popular nearby tourist attractions are Hoover Dam and Lake Mead (the largest man-made lake in the U.S.), Lake Mojave, the Mt. Charleston Recreation Area, Red Rock Canyon, and the Death Valley National Monument.

Famous natives: Andre Agassi, tennis player; Clara Bow, actress; Howard Hughes, industrialist and film producer; Jack Kramer, tennis player; Phyllis McGuire, singer; Benjamin Siegel, hotel-casino promoter; Orson Welles, actor and producer; Joe Williams, jazz singer.

Long Beach, Calif.

Mayor: Beverly O'Neill (to April 2002)
City Manager: James C. Hankla
1996 est. population (rank): 421,904 (36)
1990 census population (rank): 429,433 (32); **% change,** –1.8; **Male,** 216,685; **Female,** 212,748; 1996 est. population breakdown: **White,** 168,074 (39.1%); **Black,** 63,376 (14.8%); **American Indian, Eskimo, or Aleut,** 2,322 (0.5%); **Asian or Pacific Islander,** 66,767 (15.6%); **Hispanic origin,** 125,269 (29.3%). **1990 population under 18:** 25.5%; **65 and over:** 10.8%; **median age:** 30.0.
Land area: 49.8 sq mi. (129 sq km); **Alt.:** Highest, 170 ft.; lowest, sea level
Avg. daily temp.: Jan., 55.2° F; July, 72.8° F
Churches: 236; **City-owned parks:** 64 (2,000 ac.); **Radio stations:** AM, 2; FM, 2; **Television stations:** 8 (metro area)
Civilian Labor Force: 212,700; **Unemployed:** 11,800, **Percent:** 5.6; **Per capita personal income (MSA) 1992:** $21,434[1]
Chamber of Commerce: Long Beach Area Chamber of Commerce, One World Trade Center, Suite 350, Long Beach, Calif. 90831-0350

1. Los Angeles–Long Beach MSA.

Long Beach is the fifth-largest city in California and is situated on San Pedro Bay, south of Los Angeles, in Los Angeles County.

The town was laid out and settled in 1881 by developer W. E. Willmore, who sold lots in the site as a seaside resort community called Willmore City. It was renamed Long Beach for its 8½-mi. beach in 1884. The city was incorporated in 1888 and reincorporated in 1897.

Long Beach is a major industrial port. The services and manufacturing industries together account for over 50% of the local economy. Retail trade and government are the next largest sectors, accounting for an additional 30% of employment. Tourism is also important to the economy. Minor industries include transportation, communication and utilities, wholesale trade, finance, insurance, and real estate. Long Beach's economy has been adversely affected by cutbacks in the defense and aircraft production industries.

Famous natives: Jack Anderson, journalist; Jennife Bartlett, artist; Barbara Britton, actress; Nicholas Cage, actor; Spike Jones, orchestra leader; Sally Kellerman, actress; Billie Jean King, tennis player; Martha Rae Watson, track star; Heather Watts, dancer.

Los Angeles, Calif.

Mayor: Richard Riordan (to June 2001)
1996 est. population (rank): 3,553,638 (2)
1990 census population (rank): 3,485,398 (2); **% change,** 2.0; **Male,** 1,750,055; **Female,** 1,735,343; **White,** 1,841,182 (52.8%); **Black,** 487,674 (14.0%); **American Indian, Eskimo, or Aleut,** 16,379 (0.5%); **Asian or Pacific Islander,** 341,807 (9.8%); **Other race,** 798,356; **Hispanic origin,** 1,391,411 (39.9%). **1990 population under 18:** 24.8%; **65 and over:** 10.0%; **median age:** 30.7.
Land area: 467.4 sq mi. (1,210.57 sq km); **Alt.:** Highest, 5,081 ft.; lowest, sea level
Avg. daily temp.: Jan., 57.2° F; July, 74.1° F
Churches: 2,000 of all denominations; **City-owned parks:** 355 (15,357 ac.); **Radio stations:** AM, 35; FM, 53; **Television stations:** 19
Civilian Labor Force: 1,827,505; **Unemployed:** 198,626, **Percent:** 10.9; **Per capita personal income (PMSA) 1992:** $21,434[1]
Chamber of Commerce: Los Angeles Chamber of Commerce, 404 S. Bixel St., Los Angeles, Calif. 90017

1. Los Angeles–Long Beach.

Los Angeles is the largest city in California and the second-largest urban area in the nation. It is located in the southern part of the state on the Pacific Ocean. It is the seat of Los Angeles County. Geographically, it extends more than 40 miles from the mountains to the sea.

The Spanish explorer Gaspar de Portolá visited the site in 1769. On Sept. 4, 1781, the Mexican provincial governor, Filipe de Neve, founded "El Pueblo de Nuestra Señora la Reina de Los Angeles"—meaning "The Village of Our Lady, the Queen of the Angels." The pueblo became the capital of the Mexican province, Alta California, and it was the last place to surrender to the U.S. at the time of the American occupation in 1847. By the Treaty of Guadalupe Hidalgo in 1848, Mexico ceded California to the United States and Los Angeles was incorporated as a city in 1850.

The city's phenomenal growth was brought about primarily by its equable climate, which attracted people and industry from all parts of the nation; the development of its citrus-fruit industry; the discovery of oil in the area during the early 1890s; the development of its man-made harbor—its port is one of the busiest in the U.S.; and the growth of the motion picture industry in the early 20th century. Today, Hollywood is a suburb of Los Angeles.

Los Angeles is a major hub of shipping, manufacturing, industry, and finance, and is world-renowned in the entertainment and communications fields. It is a favorite vacation destination and attracts millions of tourists to the area each year from all over the world.

Los Angeles County is the nation's largest manufacturing center, surpassing Chicago, New York, and Detroit. The ports of Los Angeles and Long Beach are second only to New York as the largest customs district in the United States.

Major employers in the Los Angeles Five-County area are in the business and management sector. Growth in the key wholesale industries—apparel and textiles, furniture, jewelry, and toys—and the boom

ı industrial trade have been forecast for the region ın the 1990s. Other important sectors are health services and international trade and investment. The aerospace and technology industries have declined due to defense cutbacks but are still expected to be a viable part of the region's economy.

Famous natives: Busby Berkeley, choreographer and director; Marge Champion, dancer and choreographer; Jackie Coogan, actor; Jackie Cooper, actor; Linda Fratianne, figure skater; Jodie Foster, actress and director; John Gavin, actor and diplomat; Pancho Gonzalez, tennis player; Cynthia Gregory, ballerina; Jerome Hines, basso; Dustin Hoffman, actor; Theodore Harold Maiman, laser inventor; Marilyn Monroe, actress; Isamu Noguchi, sculptor; Leonard Slotkin, conductor; Duke Snider, baseball player; Adlai E. Stevenson, statesman; Madeleine Stowe, actress; Darryl Strawberry, baseball player.

Memphis, Tenn.

Mayor: W. W. Herenton (to Dec. 1999)
1996 est. population (rank): 596,725 (18)
1990 census population (rank): 610,337 (18); **% change,** –2.2; **Male,** 285,010; **Female,** 325,327; **White,** 268,600 (43.4%); **Black,** 334,737 (54.8%); **American Indian, Eskimo, or Aleut,** 960 (0.2%); **Asian or Pacific Islander,** 4,805 (0.8%); **Other race,** 1,235; **Hispanic origin,** 4,455 (0.7%). **1990 population under 18:** 26.9%; **65 and over:** 12.2%; **median age:** 31.5.
Land area: 277 sq mi. (702 sq km); **Alt.:** Highest, 417 ft.
Avg. daily temp.: Jan., 39.6° F; July, 82.1° F
Churches: 2000+; **Parks and playgrounds:** 230 (13,291 ac.); **Radio stations:** AM, 14; FM, 15; **Television stations:** 6
Civilian Labor Force: 292,819; **Unemployed:** 25,640, **Percent:** 8.8; **Per capita personal income (MSA) 1992:** $19,517
Chamber of Commerce: Memphis Area Chamber of Commerce, P.O. Box 224, Memphis, Tenn. 38103

Memphis, the largest city in Tennessee and the seat of Shelby County, is located in the southwestern corner of the state, on the Mississippi River.

The first settlers of Memphis were the Chickasaw Indians, who had a village named Chisca there on the bluffs overlooking the Mississippi River. Hernando de Soto, in 1541, is said to have had his first glimpse of the Mississippi from the site of Memphis; in the next century, Louis Joliet and Jacques Marquette stopped there to trade with the Indians. The French explorer Sieur de La Salle tried to claim the region for France in 1682 and built Fort Prudhomme there. The area was ceded to the United States by the Chickasaw Indians in 1818. Memphis was officially established in 1819 by three enterprising businessmen from Nashville, James Winchester, John Overton, and future president Andrew Jackson. Jackson named it after the ancient Egyptian city because of its Nilelike site on the Mississippi River. Memphis was incorporated as a city in 1826 and became an important Mississippi River port.

During the Civil War, Memphis was a Confederate military center. In 1862, Federal forces won a gunboat battle on the river at Memphis and General Sherman was enabled to take the city.

Memphis's population was devastated by several yellow-fever epidemics during the 1870s. The city did not recover its prosperity until the end of the 19th century.

Memphis is one of the country's largest inland ports and is known as "America's Distribution Center," serving the northeast, southeast, and southwest regions of the country. Memphis is a leader in agribusiness, cultivating soybeans, rice, grain sorghum, winter wheat, and corn, and raising livestock. The city is the world's largest trading center for spot cotton, handling over 40% of the nation's spot cotton crops annually. It is the largest hardwood lumber trading and processing center in the world and is estimated to be the nation's third-largest total food processor.

Health care and related activities such as medical education and biomedical research are Memphis's largest industries, bringing over $2.5 billion a year to the local economy. Also important are high-technology communications.

Famous natives: Kathy Bates, actress; Dixie Carter, actress; Rosalind Cash, singer; Aretha Franklin, singer; Morgan Freeman, actor; Al Green, singer; George Hamilton, actor; Anfernee "Penny" Hardaway, basketball player; Isaac Hayes, singer; Hal Holbrook, actor; Benjamin Hooks, organization official; Hal Needham, director; Charlie Rich, singer; Cybill Shepherd, actress; Robert Siodmak, director; Fred Smith, business executive; Rufus Thomas, singer; Kemmons Wilson, business executive.

Miami, Fla.

Mayor: Joe Carollo (to Nov. 2001)
City manager: Edward Marquez (apptd. Nov. 1996)
1996 est. population (rank): 365,127 (44)
1990 census population (rank): 358,548 (46); **% change,** 1.8; **Male,** 173,223; **Female,** 185,325; **White,** 235,358 (65.6%); **Black,** 98,207 (27.4%); **American Indian, Eskimo, or Aleut,** 545 (0.2%); **Asian or Pacific Islander,** 2,272 (0.6%); **Other race,** 22,166; **Hispanic origin,** 223,964 (62.5%). **1990 population under 18:** 23.0%; **65 and over,** 16.6%; **median age,** 36.0.
Land area: 34.3 sq mi. (89 sq km); **Water area:** 19.5 sq mi.; **Alt.:** Average, 12 ft.
Avg. daily temp.: Jan., 67.1° F; July, 82.4° F
Churches (Dade County): Protestant, 850; Roman Catholic, 61; Jewish, 64; **City-owned parks (Miami):** 109; **Radio stations (Dade County):** 29; **Television stations (Dade County):** 9 TV, 1 Cable
Civilian Labor Force: 181,684; **Unemployed:** 21,348, **Percent:** 11.8; **Per capita personal income (PMSA) 1992:** $17,124
Chamber of Commerce: Greater Miami Chamber of Commerce, 1601 Biscayne Blvd., Miami, Fla. 33132

Miami, the second-largest city in Florida and seat of Dade County, is located in the southeastern part of the state, on Biscayne Bay.

The area was once the home of the Tequesta Indians until they were nearly wiped out by European diseases and warfare brought on by two centuries of Spanish control of Florida. Miami was founded in 1870 near the site of Ft. Dallas, built in 1835 during the Seminole Indian wars. The city's name is probably derived from "Mayaimi," an Indian word for "big water."

Miami is the only U.S. city to have been conceived by a woman. Julia Tuttle, a Clevelander, arrived there in 1891 and bought several hundred acres on the bank of the Miami River. She convinced New York financier Henry M. Flagler of the area's vast potential and persuaded him to extend his Florida East Coast Railroad to Miami in 1896, the year the city was incorporated. Flagler dredged Miami Harbor, built the renowned Royal Palm Hotel, which opened Jan. 1, 1897, and promoted the area as a winter playground. Tourists flocked there and, by 1910, the city was a thriving recreational

area. Miami survived the collapse of a land speculation boom in the 1920s, and severe hurricanes in 1926 and 1935, and continued to grow in the aftermath of these disasters.

Miami experienced one of its most monumental population boosts during the 1960s when about 260,000 Cuban refugees arrived on its shore seeking freedom. They made a great impact on Miami, now a bilingual metropolis, and spurred economic growth.

Miami is an international banking and finance center and the city has the greatest concentration of international and Edge Act banks[1] in North America; these constitute a major employment base. Greater Miami[2] has a highly diversified economy with over 170 multinational Miami-based companies, a bevy of Fortune 500 companies, and a rapidly growing manufacturing and distribution center. Miami ranks number one in Florida for total manufacturing income, employment, and number of manufacturing establishments. Greater Miami is the nation's leader in biomedical technology and the health care sector is a major industry. It is also part of an area known as the Computer Coast of Florida, and its growing technologies include computers, electrical engineering, and plastics manufacturing.

Miami is one of the world's leading year-round resort centers with tourism contributing over 60% of the area's economy. The city is a major transportation hub and the port of Miami is the world's largest cruise port and a major seaport for cargo. The famous island resort of Miami Beach, incorporated in 1915, is part of Greater Miami and is connected to Miami by four causeways.

1. Edge Act banks may make only foreign loans and accept foreign deposits. 2. Greater Miami is made up of 27 municipalities of which the city of Miami is the largest.

Famous natives: Fernando Bujones, dancer; Steve Carlton, baseball player; Debbie Harry, singer; Dick Howser, baseball player and manager; Sidney Poitier, actor; Janet Reno, attorney general of the U.S.; Ben Vereen, actor; Ellen Zwilich, composer.

Milwaukee, Wis.

Mayor: John O. Norquist (to April 2000)
1996 est. population (rank): 590,503 (19)
1990 census population (rank): 628,088 (17); **% change,** –6.0; **Male,** 296,837; **Female,** 331,251; **White,** 398,033 (63.4%); **Black,** 191,255 (30.5%); **American Indian, Eskimo, or Aleut,** 5,858 (0.9%); **Asian or Pacific Islander,** 11,817 (1.9%); **Other race,** 21,125; **Hispanic origin,** 39,409 (6.3%). **1990 population under 18:** 27.4%; **65 and over:** 12.4%; **median age:** 30.3.
Land area: 95.8 sq mi. (248 sq km); **Alt.:** 580.60 ft.
Avg. daily temp.: Jan., 18.7° F; July, 70.5° F
Churches: 411; **County-owned parks:** 14,785 ac.; **Radio stations:** AM, 9; FM, 18; **Television stations:** 11
Civilian Labor Force (1995): 296,700; **Unemployed:** 14,900, **Percent:** 5.0; **Per capita personal income (PMSA) 1993:** $22,786
Chamber of Commerce: Metropolitan Milwaukee Association of Commerce, 828 N. Broadway, Milwaukee, Wis. 53202; Milwaukee Minority Chamber of Commerce, 2821 N. 4th St., Milwaukee, Wis. 53212; Hispanic Chamber of Commerce, 1125 W. National Ave., Milwaukee, Wis. 53204

Milwaukee, the largest city in Wisconsin and seat of Milwaukee County, is located in the southeastern part of the state on Lake Michigan.

French missionaries visited the site of Milwaukee in the seventeenth century, but it was not until 1795 that Jacques Vieau established a fur-trading post there. The first permanent white settler, Vieau's son-in-law, Solomon Juneau, an agent of the American Fur Company, made his home there in 1818. The settlement merged with several neighboring villages in 1838 to form Milwaukee, and the city was incorporated in 1846. Its name is derived from the Algonquian Indian word Milo-aki, meaning "beautiful land." A large wave of German immigrants arrived after 1848 and contributed greatly to the city's political, economic, and cultural development.

Milwaukee is one of the great industrial centers in the country and one of the largest Great Lakes ports. Currently, port commerce runs over 3.3 million tons per year.

Its economy was forged by heavy industries but is now diversified. Manufacturing remains strong and Milwaukee manufacturers are national leaders in lithographic commercial printing and the production of medical diagnostic instruments, small gasoline engines, malt beverages, iron and steel forgings, mining and construction machinery, robotics, speed changers and drives, and electronic controls. Milwaukee's high-tech manufacturing community is the ninth-largest among the nation's 31 major metropolitan areas. Once known as a "beer town," less than 1% of Milwaukee's workforce is involved in beer production. However, beer still plays an important role and almost 11% of the nation's malt beverage is produced there.

Tourism is important to the economy. About 5 million people visit Milwaukee every year.

Famous natives: Donald Gramm, bass-baritone; Woody Herman, band leader; Al Jarreau, singer; George F. Kennan, diplomat; Alfred Lunt, actor; Douglas MacArthur, army general; Pat O'Brien, actor; Tom Snyder, TV personality; Speech, member of the rap group "Arrested Development;" Spencer Tracy, actor; Gene Wilder, actor; Jerry and David Zucker, film producers.

Minneapolis, Minn.

Mayor: Sharon Sayles Belton (to Jan. 2002)
1996 est. population (rank): 358,785 (46)
1990 census population (rank): 368,383 (42); **% change,** –2.6; **Male,** 178,671; **Female,** 189,712; **White,** 288,967 (78.4%); **Black,** 47,948 (13.0%); **American Indian, Eskimo, or Aleut,** 12,335 (3.3%); **Asian or Pacific Islander,** 15,723 (4.3%); **Other race,** 3,410; **Hispanic origin,** 7,900 (2.1%). **1990 population under 18:** 20.6%; **65 and over:** 13.0%; **median age:** 31.7
Land area: 58.7 sq mi. (143 sq km); **Alt.:** Highest, 945 ft.; lowest, 695 ft.
Avg. daily temp.: Jan., 11.2° F; July, 73.1° F
Churches: 419; **City-owned parks:** 153; **Radio stations:** AM, 17; FM, 15 (metro area); **Television stations:** 6 (metro area)
Civilian Labor Force: 204,477; **Unemployed:** 9,905, **Percent:** 4.8; **Per capita personal income (MSA) 1992:** $23,284[1]
Chamber of Commerce: Greater Minneapolis Chamber of Commerce, Young Quinlan Building, 81 S. Ninth Street, Suite 200, Minneapolis, Minn. 55402-3223

1. Minneapolis–St. Paul Minn.–Wis.

Minneapolis, the largest city in Minnesota and the seat of Hennepin County, is located in the southeast central part of the state on the Mississippi River. It is adjacent to its "twin city" of St. Paul. The

Minneapolis–St. Paul Standard Metropolitan Statistical Area is the 15th-largest in the United States.

In 1680, Father Louis Hennepin visited the future site of Minneapolis and gave the Falls of St. Anthony their name. Lieutenant Zebulon Pike made a treaty with the Sioux Indians in 1805–06 by which they ceded to the whites land, including the Falls of St. Anthony and the site of Minneapolis. Fort Snelling was built in 1819–20 and, in 1823, the government built a lumber and flour mill. Flour milling became the major industry of early Minneapolis and made the city the milling capital of the world. The town of St. Anthony was established on the east bank of the Mississippi in 1848 and the town of Minneapolis grew up on the opposite bank of the river. The name Minneapolis is a combination of the Dakota Sioux word "minna," for water, and the Greek word "polis," for city. Minneapolis was incorporated as a city in 1867, and in 1872 the city of St. Anthony (chartered in 1860) was annexed to it. After the spread of the railroads in the 1870s, Minneapolis became the gateway to the Northern Great Plains.

Minneapolis is a center of industry and commerce serving a large agricultural region. During the 20th century, manufacturing, food processing, milling, computers, health services, and graphic arts developed as Minneapolis's major industries. Sixteen Fortune 500 industrial and 17 Fortune service companies are headquartered there. The city is the home of the world's largest cash grain market and is the headquarters of the Ninth Federal Reserve Bank.

Famous natives: La Verne, Maxene, and Patti Andrews, singers; James Arness, actor; Lew Ayres, actor; Patty Berg, golfer; Virginia Bruce, actress; J. Paul Getty, oil executive; Peter Graves, actor; George Roy Hill, director; Cornell MacNeil, baritone; Ralph Meeker, actor; Westbrook Pegler, columnist; Prince, singer; Harrison Salisbury, journalist; Charles Schulz, cartoonist; Ann Tyler, writer; Bud Wilkinson, football coach; David Winfield, baseball player.

Nashville-Davidson, Tenn.

Mayor: Philip N. Bredesen (to Aug. 1999)
1996 est. population (rank): 511,263 (24)[1]
1990 census population (rank)[2]**:** 510,784 (23); **% change,** 0.1; **Male,** 242,492; **Female,** 268,292; **White,** 381,740 (78.2%); **Black,** 119,273 (23.4%); **American Indian, Eskimo, or Aleut,** 1,162 (0.2%); **Asian or Pacific Islander,** 7,081 (1.4%); **Other race,** 1,528; **Hispanic origin,** 4,775 (0.9%). **1990 population under 18:** 22.8%; **65 and over:** 11.6%; **median age:** 32.6.
Land area: 533 sq mi. (1,380 sq km); **Altitude:** Highest, 1,100 ft.; lowest, approx. 400 ft.
Avg. daily temp.: Jan., 36.7° F; July, 76.6° F
Churches: Protestant, 781; Roman Catholic, 18; Jewish, 3; **City-owned parks:** 76 (6,650 ac.); **Radio stations:** AM, 15; FM, 19; **Television stations:** 11
Civilian Labor Force (1997): 313,636; **Unemployed:** 9,225, **Percent:** 2.9; **Per capita personal income (1995):** $23,655
Chamber of Commerce: Nashville Area Chamber of Commerce, 161 Fourth Ave. North, Nashville, Tenn. 37219

1. 1997 est. population: 536,650. 2. Consolidated city.

The consolidated city of Nashville-Davidson is the capital and second-largest city in Tennessee and is located in the north central part of the state on the Cumberland River. It is the seat of Davidson County.

During the winter of 1779–80, James Robertson and John Donelson founded a settlement at Big Salt Lick by the Cumberland River at the present site of the city. They built forts on both sides of the river, naming one of them Fort Nashborough in honor of Francis Nash, a Revolutionary War general. In 1784, the town was named Nashville and was incorporated as a city in 1806.

Nashville became the capital of Tennessee in 1843 and was the seat of Davidson County until 1963, when it merged with the county to become Nashville-Davidson.

Nashville's best-known industries are recording, publishing, and the distribution of music, especially country music. The city is a port of entry and an important industrial and commercial center serving the Upper South. Its diverse economy includes automobiles, apparel, publishing, insurance, and banking. Health care services is the largest industry. Nashville is the home of several religious organizations and is a major tourist attraction and convention center.

Famous natives: Gregg Allman, singer; Rita Coolidge, singer; Al Gore, vice president; Red Grooms, artist; Barbara Howar, hostess and writer; Minnie Pearl, comedienne; Annie Potts, actress; Paula Robeson, flutist; Dinah Shore, actress and singer.

New Orleans, La.

Mayor: Marc H. Morial (to Feb. 2002)
1996 est. population (rank): 476,625 (29)
1990 census population (rank): 496,938 (25); **% change,** –4.1; **Male,** 230,883; **Female,** 266,055; **White,** 173,554 (34.9%); **Black,** 307,728 (61.9%); **American Indian, Eskimo, or Aleut,** 759 (0.2%); **Asian or Pacific Islander,** 9,678 (1.9%); **Other race,** 5,219; **Hispanic origin,** 17,238 (3.5%). **1990 population under 18:** 27.5%; **65 and over,** 13.0%; **median age,** 31.6.
Land area: 199.4 sq mi. (516 sq km); **Alt.:** Highest, 15 ft.; lowest, –4 ft.
Avg. daily temp.: Jan., 52.4° F; July, 77° F
Churches: 712; **City-owned parks:** 165 (299 ac.); **Radio stations:** AM, 12; FM, 14; **Television stations:** 7
Civilian Labor Force: 205,610[1]; **Unemployed:** 15,055[1], **Percent:** 7.3[1]; **Per capita personal income (MSA) 1992:** $18,087
Chamber of Commerce: The Chamber/New Orleans and the River Region, 301 Camp Street, New Orleans, La. 70130

1. New Orleans City/Orleans Parish.

New Orleans, the largest city in Louisiana and seat of Orleans Parish, is located in the southeastern part of the state, between the Mississippi River and Lake Ponchartrain.

One of the few cities of the nation that has been under three flags, New Orleans has belonged to Spain, France, and the U.S. The French founded it in 1718 and named it in honor of the Duke of Orleans. In 1762, France ceded the city and the territory to Spain. In 1800, the territory was returned to France, but government authorities did not take over until 1803, only 20 days before the region became part of the U.S. in the Louisiana Purchase.

New Orleans is famous for its French Quarter, which attracts tourists and gourmets. The Mardi Gras—a week of carnival held in New Orleans before the beginning of Lent—is the most spectacular festival in the U.S., and is a popular tourist attraction. Tourism has grown rapidly in recent years and New Orleans hosts more than seven million visitors annually.

New Orleans is one of the world's greatest international ports, one of the largest in the nation, and a major focus of the city's economy. New Orleans is home to the corporate offices of oil companies with major offshore operations in the Gulf of Mexico, as well as the distribution and service centers of offshore equipment suppliers and fabricators.

The manufacturing industry is a significant part of the economy, with petroleum, petrochemical, shipbuilding, and aerospace industries all playing a role. The New Orleans region also functions as a mining, processing, and transportation center for other minerals, principally sulfur. Service industries are playing a larger role, with health care and telecommunications leading the way. The information services sector is one of the fastest-growing, and the New Orleans region is widely regarded as a leading center of medicine and health care in the South.

Famous natives: Louis Armstrong, musician; Truman Capote, author; Fats Domino, musician; Louis Gottschalk, pianist and composer; Bryant Gumbel, TV personality; Lillian Hellman, playwright and author; Al Hirt, musician; Mahalia Jackson, singer; Dorothy Lamour, actress; Wynton Marsalis, musician; Huey Newton, activist; Marguerite Piazza, soprano; Rusty Staub, baseball player; Ben Turpin, comedian; Shirley Verrett, mezzo-soprano; Carl Weathers, actor; Del Williams, football player.

New York, N.Y.

Mayor: Rudolph W. Guiliani (to Dec. 2001)
Borough Presidents: Bronx, Fernando Ferrer; Brooklyn, Howard Golden; Manhattan, C. Virginia Fields; Queens, Claire Shulman; Staten Island, Guy V. Molinari
1996 est. population (rank): 7,380,906 (1)
1990 census population (rank): 7,322,564 (1)[1]; **% change,** 0.8; **Male,** 3,437,687; **Female,** 3,884,877; **White,** 3,827,088 (52.2%); **Black,** 2,102,512 (28.7%); **American Indian, Eskimo, or Aleut,** 27,531 (0.4%); **Asian or Pacific Islander,** 512,719 (7.0%); **Other race,** 852,714; **Hispanic origin,** 1,783,511 (24.4%).[1] **1990 population under 18:** 23.0%; **65 and over:** 13.0%; **median age:** 33.7.
Land area: 321.8 sq mi. (826.68 sq km) (Queens, 112.1; Brooklyn, 81.8; Staten Island, 60.2; Bronx, 44.0; Manhattan, 23.7); **Alt.:** Highest, 410 ft.; lowest, sea level
Avg. daily temp.: Jan., 31.8° F; July, 76.7° F
Churches: Protestant, 1,766; Jewish, 1,256; Roman Catholic, 437; Orthodox, 66; **City-owned parks:** 1,701 (27,118 ac.); **Radio stations:** AM, 13; FM, 18; **Television stations:** 6 commercial, 1 public
Civilian Labor Force: 3,311,000; **Unemployed:** 359,000, **Percent:** 10.8; **Per capita personal income (PMSA) 1992:** $27,039
Chamber of Commerce: New York Chamber of Commerce and Industry, One Battery Park Plaza, New York, N.Y. 10004

1. Race breakdown figures according to N.Y.C. Dept. of City Planning: White, non-Hispanic, 3,163,125; Black, non-Hispanic, 1,847,049; American Indian, non-Hispanic, 17,871; Asian, non-Hispanic, 489,157; Hispanic, 1,783,511.

New York City is the largest city in the United States. It is located in the southern part of New York State, at the mouth of the Hudson River (also known as North River as it passes Manhattan Island).

In 1609, Henry Hudson, who worked for the Dutch East India Company, sailed up the river that now bears his name and went as far as Albany. Five years later, a permanent settlement was established at what is now New York, but it was originally called New Amsterdam by the Dutch governors. One of them, Peter Minuit, was said to have bought Manhattan Island from the Indians for $24 worth of beads, buttons, and trinkets. In 1664, Great Britain's Duke of York sent a fleet that quietly seized the settlement from the Dutch, without bloodshed, and rechristened the colony in honor of the duke.

Control of New York passed to the young U.S. at the end of the Revolutionary War, and George Washington was inaugurated president in New York's old City Hall. Congress met in New York from 1785 to 1790.

In 1898, when Greater New York was chartered, the city expanded to include the following five boroughs, which are also counties in New York State: Manhattan (New York County); Brooklyn (Kings County); Bronx (Bronx County); Queens (Queens County); and Staten Island (Richmond County). There is a growing effort among Staten Island residents to separate from Greater New York and become an independent city of Staten Island.

The Big Apple is the most populous city in the United States, a major world capital, and a world leader in finance, the arts, and communications. The city is also the center of advertising, fashion, publishing, and radio broadcasting in the United States. New York has many museums, art galleries, and educational institutions. The port of New York is one of the finest in the world. The city is the home of the United Nations and is headquarters for some of the world's largest corporations.

Famous natives: Kareem Abdul-Jabbar, basketball player; Woody Allen, actor and director; Robert Anderson, playwright; Martina Arroyo, soprano; Jean Arthur, actress; Lauren Bacall, actress; James Baldwin, novelist; Harry Belafonte, singer and actor; Humphrey Bogart, actor; James Cagney, actor; Maria Callas, soprano; Paddy Chayefsky, playwright; Aaron Copland, composer; Sammy Davis, Jr., singer and actor; Agnes de Mille, choreographer; Robert De Niro, actor; Eamon De Valera, former president of Ireland; Gertrude Elion, Nobel Prize winner in medicine; Lou Gehrig, baseball player; George Gershwin, composer; Ira Gershwin, lyricist; Jackie Gleason, actor; Hank Greenberg, baseball player; Rita Hayworth, actress; Lena Horne, singer; Julia Ward Howe, poet and reformer; Washington Irving, author; Henry James, novelist; John Jay, statesman and jurist; Michael Jordan, basketball player; Jerome Kern, composer; Sandy Koufax, baseball player; Michael Landon, actor; Roy Lichtenstein, painter; Vince Lombardi, football player and coach; Chico, Groucho, Harpo, and Zeppo Marx, comedians; Herman Melville, novelist; Yehudi Menuhin, violinist; Ethel Merman, singer and actress; James Michener, novelist; Arthur Miller, playwright; Eugene O'Neill, playwright; J. Robert Oppenheimer, nuclear physicist; Al Pacino, actor; Jan Peerce, tenor; Roberta Peters, soprano; Elmer Rice, playwright; Jerome Robbins, choreographer; Norman Rockwell, painter and illustrator; Eleanor Roosevelt, reformer and humanitarian; Theodore Roosevelt, former president; Jonas Salk, polio researcher; Beverly Sills, soprano; Neil Simon, playwright; Risë Stevens, mezzo-soprano; Barbra Streisand, singer and actress; Ed Sullivan, TV personality; Fats Waller, pianist; Mae West, actress; Edith Wharton, novelist; Rosalyn Yalow, Nobel Prize winner in medicine.

akland, Calif.

ayor: Elihu Mason Harris (to Jan. 1999)
ity Manager (interim): Kofi Bonner
996 est. population (rank): 367,230 (43)[1]
1990 census popultion (rank): 372,242 (39); **% change,** –1.3; **Male,** 178,824; **Female,** 193,418; **White,** 120,849 (32.5%); **Black,** 163,335 (43.9%); **American Indian, Eskimo, or Aleut,** 2,371 (0.6%); **Asian or Pacific Islander,** 54,931 (14.8%); **Other race,** 30,756; **Hispanic origin,** 51,711 (13.9%). **1990 population under 18,** 24.9%; **65 and over,** 12.0%; **median age:** 32.7.
Land area: 53.9 sq mi. (140 sq km); **Alt.:** Highest, 1,700 ft.; lowest, sea level
Avg. daily temp.: Jan., 49.0° F; July, 63.7° F
Churches: 374, representing over 78 denominations in the City; over 500 churches in Alameda County; **City-owned parks:** 2,196 ac.; **Radio stations:** AM, 1; **Television stations:** 1 commercial
Civilian Labor Force: 180,624; **Unemployed:** 18,148, **Percent:** 10.0; **Per capita personal income (PMSA) 1992:** $24,359
Chamber of Commerce: Oakland Chamber of Commerce, 475 Fourteenth St., Oakland, Calif. 94612-1903

1. 1997 est. population: 386,100

Oakland is located in the west central part of California on the east side of San Francisco Bay. It is the seat of Alameda County.

Don Luis Peralta first settled the site of Oakland in 1820 when he established the Rancho San Antonio. The gold rush of 1849 attracted more people to the area and the city's population continued to grow after a ferry service to San Francisco was started in 1851. Oakland was incorporated as a town in 1852 and as a city in 1854. It was named after the numerous oak trees found in the area. Oakland became the western terminus of the Central Pacific Railroad in 1869 and the seat of Alameda County in 1873.

During the latter part of the 19th century and also in 1910, additional territory was annexed to Oakland and the city assumed its present size. In 1906, thousands of people fled to Oakland in the aftermath of the San Francisco earthquake and settled there permanently, furthering the city's growth. Oakland's economic development continued to rise with the opening of the San Francisco–Oakland Bay Bridge in 1936.

Oakland is a major center of culture and commerce. It is an important container shipping port and the terminus of three transcontinental railroads. Oakland's industries include shipbuilding, food processing, chemicals, pharmaceuticals, electrical and high technology manufacturing. Oakland is also a leading importer of foreign cars. The city is the headquarters of many national and international corporations.

Famous natives: Buster Crabbe, actor; Frederick Cottrell, inventor; Dennis Eckersley, athlete; Hammer, singer, dancer, and songwriter; Rod McKuen, singer and composer; Russ Meyer, producer and director; Eddie (Anderson) Rochester, actor; George Stevens, director; Amy Tan, writer; Jo Van Fleet, actress.

Oklahoma City, Okla.

Mayor: Kirk Humphreys (to April 2002)
City Manager: Glen E. Deck
1996 est. population (rank): 469,852 (30)
1990 census population (rank): 444,719 (29); **% change,** 5.7; **Male,** 214,466; **Female,** 230,253; **White,** 332,539 (74.8%); **Black,** 71,064 (16.0%); **American Indian, Eskimo, or Aleut,** 18,794 (4.2%); **Asian or Pacific Islander,** 10,491 (2.4%); **Other race,** 11,831; **Hispanic origin,** 22,033 (5.0%). **1990 population under 18:** 26.0%; **65 and over:** 11.9%; **median age:** 32.4.
Land area: 608.2 sq mi. (1,575 sq km); **Alt.:** Highest, 1,320 ft.; lowest, 1,140 ft.
Avg. daily temp.: Jan., 35.9° F; July, 82.1° F
Churches: Roman Catholic, 25; Jewish, 2; Protestant and others, 741; **City-owned parks:** 138 (3,944 ac.); **Television stations:** 8; **Radio stations:** AM, 10; FM, 14
Civilian Labor Force: 524,530; **Unemployed:** 15,500, **Percent:** 3.2; **Per capita personal income (MSA) 1994:** $16,006
Chamber of Commerce: Greater Oklahoma City Chamber of Commerce, 123 Park Ave., Oklahoma City, Okla. 73102

Oklahoma City, the state capital and seat of Oklahoma County, is the largest city in Oklahoma. It is located in the central part of the state on the North Canadian River.

Oklahoma City sprang into being almost overnight. On April 22, 1889, the government threw open the territory for settlement, and there was a classic rush across the line to stake claims. Within a short time, a sprawling tent city sprang up near the Santa Fe railroad tracks and Oklahoma City was a bustling town of 10,000. The city was incorporated in 1890 and replaced Guthrie as the state capital in 1910. Oil was discovered in the city in 1928 and petroleum production became a mainstay of the city's economy.

Oklahoma City is the wholesale and distributing center for the state, and the city's stockyards are the largest stocker and feeder cattle market in the world. Following the decline of the energy sector, Oklahoma City is fostering a private entrepreneurial environment and a more diversified economy. Within the service sector, health services are projected to grow, followed by retail trade and business services. Aerospace, distribution, and telecommunications have been targeted for business attraction. Nearby Tinker Air Force Base, one of the world's largest air depots, is a major city employer.

Famous natives: Johnny Bench, baseball; Lon Chaney, Jr., actor; Ralph Ellison, writer; Kay Francis, actress; Dale Robertson, actor; Ted Shackleford, actor; Pamela Tiffin, actress; Vince Gill, country singer.

Omaha, Neb.

Mayor: Hal Daub (to 2001)
1996 est. population (rank): 364,253 (45)
1990 census population (rank): 335,795 (48); **% change,** 8.5; **Male,** 160,392; **Female,** 175,403; **White,** 281,603 (83.9%); **Black,** 43,989 (13.1%); **American Indian, Eskimo, or Aleut,** 2,274 (0.7%); **Asian or Pacific Islander,** 3,412 (1.0%); **Other race,** 4,517; **Hispanic origin,** 10,288 (3.1%). **1990 population under 18:** 25.4%; **65 and over:** 12.9%; **median age:** 32.2.
Land area: 112 sq mi. (290 sq km); **Alt.:** Highest, 1,270 ft.
Avg. daily temp.: Jan., 20.2° F; July, 77.7° F
Churches: Protestant, 246; Roman Catholic, 44; Jewish, 4; **City-owned parks:** 164 (over 7,400 ac.); **Radio stations:** AM, 7; FM, 13; **Television stations:** 4

Civilian Labor Force: 177,387; **Unemployed:** 8,298, **Percent:** 4.7; **Per capita personal income (MSA) 1992:** $20,242[1]
Chamber of Commerce: Omaha Chamber of Commerce, 1301 Harney St., Omaha, Neb. 68102

1. Omaha, Neb.–Iowa.

Omaha, the largest city in Nebraska and the seat of Douglas County, is located in the eastern part of the state on the west bank of the Missouri River, opposite Council Bluffs, Iowa.

The area was visited by the Lewis and Clark expedition in 1804, and the U.S. Army built Ft. Atkinson nearby in 1819. Pierre Cabanne established a fur-trading post at the site in 1825. The first Mormon migrants wintered there in 1846–1847 on their way to Utah. The city grew rapidly as the most northerly supply point for overland wagons to the Far West.

The city was officially founded in 1854 after the Nebraska Territory was opened for settlement. It was named for the Omaha Indians living nearby, whose tribal name means "those who go upstream or against the current." Omaha was incorporated as a city in 1857 and was the capital of the Nebraska Territory from 1855 to 1867. The city continued to thrive as a point of entry and a major transportation center when the Union Pacific trans-continental railroad arrived in 1869.

Omaha is a major market for food processing, telecommunications, and insurance. Other important industries include electrical equipment and finance as well as printing and publishing.

Famous natives: Fred Astaire, dancer and actor; Max Baer, boxer; Ronald Boone, former NBA professional; Robert Boozer, former NBA professional; Marlon Brando, actor; Montgomery Clift, actor; Gerald Ford, former president; Bob Gibson, baseball player; Swoosie Kurtz, actress; Melvin Laird, former secretary of defense; Dorothy McGuire, actress; Nick Nolte, actor; Gale Sayers, football player; Malcolm X, political activist; Paul Williams, singer and composer.

Philadelphia, Pa.

Mayor: Edward G. Rendell (to Jan. 2000)
1995 est. population (rank): 1,478,002 (5)
1990 census population (rank): 1,585,577 (5); **% change,** –6.8; **Male,** 737,763; **Female,** 847,814; **White,** 848,586 (53.5%); **Black,** 631,936 (39.9%); **American Indian, Eskimo, or Aleut,** 3,454 (0.2%); **Asian or Pacific Islander,** 43,522 (2.7%); **Other race,** 58,079; **Hispanic origin,** 89,193 (5.6%). **1990 population under 18:** 23.9%; **65 and over:** 15.2%; **median age:** 33.2.
Land area: 136 sq mi. (352 sq km); **Alt.:** Highest, 440 ft.; lowest, sea level
Avg. daily temp.: Jan., 31.2° F; July, 76.5° F
Churches: Roman Catholic, 133; Jewish, 55; Protestant and others, 830; **City-owned parks:** 630 (10,252 ac.); **Radio stations:** AM, 40[1]; FM, 43[1]; **Television stations:** 14[1]
Civilian Labor Force (1997 est.): 652,126[1]; **Unemployed:** 41,085[1], **Percent:** 8.8[2]; **Per capita personal income (PMSA) 1994:** $25,220[1]
Chamber of Commerce: Philadelphia Chamber of Commerce, 1234 Market Street, Suite 1800, Philadelphia, Pa. 19107

1. Philadelphia City/County.

Philadelphia, the largest city in Pennsylvania and seat of Philadelphia County (coterminous), is located in the southeastern part of the state at the junction of the Schuylkill and Delaware Rivers.

Philadelphia, the City of Brotherly Love, was settled in 1681 by Capt. William Markham, who, with a small band of colonists, was sent out by his cousin, William Penn. Penn arrived the following year.

In the period before the American Revolution, the city outstripped all others in the colonies in education, arts, science, industry, and commerce. In 1774–1776, the First and Second Continental Congresses met in Philadelphia; and, from 1781–1783, the city was the capital of the U.S. under the Articles of Confederation. In 1790, it became the nation's capital under the Constitution and remained so until the seat of the federal government moved to Washington in 1800.

Within a half-century of the founding of the nation at Independence Hall, Philadelphia had emerged as the "world's greatest workshop." The steam locomotives and hat factories of the 19th century have been replaced by diverse manufacturing specialties such as chemicals (including pharmaceuticals), medical devices, transportation equipment, and printing and publishing. In the services sector, Philadelphia is a major net "exporter" in subsectors such as health services, insurance carriers, legal services, and architecture and engineering services.

The city abounds in landmarks of early American history, including Independence Hall and the Liberty Bell.

Famous natives: Marian Anderson, contralto; Frankie Avalon, singer and actor; John, Lionel, and Ethel Barrymore, actors; Edmund Bacon, city planner; Kevin Bacon, actor; Boyz II Men, R&B group; Mary Cassatt, artist; Wilt Chamberlain, basketball player; Chubby Checker, singer; Bill Cosby, actor; Stuart Davis, painter; Thomas Eakins, painter and sculptor; Fabian, singer; W. C. Fields, comedian; Benjamin Franklin, inventor and statesman; Frank Furness, architect; Stan Getz, saxophonist; Grace (Kelly), Princess of Monaco; Walt Kelly, cartoonist; Jack Klugman, actor; Patti LaBelle, singer; Mario Lanza, singer and actor; George McClellan, general; Margaret Mead, anthropologist; Edgar Allen Poe, author; Anna Quindlen, writer and Pulitzer Prize winner; Man Ray, painter; Betsy Ross, flagmaker; Bobby Rydell, singer; Will Smith, actor; Jacqueline Susann, novelist; Robert Venturi, architect.

Phoenix, Ariz.

Mayor: Skip Rimsza (to Oct. 1999)
City Manager: Frank Fairbanks (apptd. May 1990)
1996 est. population (rank): 1,159,014 (7)[1]
1990 census population (rank): 983,403 (9); **% change,** 17.9; **Male,** 487,589; **Female,** 495,814; **White,** 803,332 (81.6%); **Black,** 51,053 (5.2%); **American Indian, Eskimo, or Aleut,** 18,225 (1.9%); **Asian or Pacific Islander,** 16,303 (1.7%); **Other race,** 94,490; **Hispanic origin,** 197,103 (20.0%). **1990 population under 18:** 27.2%; **65 and over,** 9.7%; **median age,** 31.1.
Land area: 469.7 sq mi. (1,216.8 sq km); **Alt.:** Highest, 2,740 ft..; lowest, 1,017 ft.
Avg. daily temp.: Jan., 53.6° F; July, 93.5° F
City-owned parks: 200 (30,412 ac.); **Radio stations:** AM, 20; FM, 20; **Television stations:** 9 commercial; 1 PBS
Civilian Labor Force: 1,482,000; **Unemployed:** 51,200, **Percent:** 3.3; **Per capita personal income (MSA) 1992:** $19,018
Chamber of Commerce: Phoenix Chamber of Commerce, 201 N. Central, Phoenix, Ariz. 85073

1. 1997 est. population: 1,187,944.

Phoenix, the capital of Arizona and seat of Maricopa County, is the largest city in the state. It is located in the center of Arizona, on the Salt River.

The prehistoric Hohokam Indians first settled the area about 300 B.C.E. and dug a system of extensive irrigation canals for farming. The Indian culture mysteriously broke up in the 1400s. The site was permanently resettled again by Jack Swilling and "Lord Darrell" Duppa about 1867. Because the city was founded on the ruins of the ancient civilization, it was named Phoenix after the legendary Phoenix bird that could regenerate itself. The irrigation canals were restored for farming, and ranching and prospecting began in the surrounding area. The city quickly grew as an important trading center.

Phoenix was incorporated as a city in 1881 and was made the territorial capital in 1889. It became the state capital when Arizona was admitted to the Union in 1912.

Phoenix is a center of agriculture and commerce. Major industries include government, agricultural products, aerospace technology, electronics, air-conditioning, leather goods, and Indian arts and crafts. The city of Phoenix is renowned as a leader in local government management and received the 1993 Bertelsmann Foundation award for the best-managed city in the world.

Famous natives: Lynda Carter, actress; Joan Ganz Cooney, TV executive; Alice Cooper, musician; Arthur A. Fletcher, government official; Barry Goldwater, politician; Stevie Nicks, musician; Charles S. Robb, politician; Mare Winningham, actress.

Pittsburgh, Pa.

Mayor: Tom Murphy (to Jan. 2002)
1996 est. population (rank): 350,363 (48)
1990 census population (rank): 369,879 (40); **% change,** –5.3; **Male,** 171,722; **Female,** 198,157; **White,** 266,791 (72.1%); **Black,** 95,362 (25.8%); **American Indian, Eskimo, or Aleut,** 671 (0.2%); **Asian or Pacific Islander,** 5,937 (1.6%); **Other race,** 1,118; **Hispanic origin,** 3,468 (0.9%). **1990 population under 18:** 19.8%; **65 and over,** 17.9%; **median age:** 34.6.
Land area: 55.5 sq mi. (144 sq km); **Alt.:** Highest, 1,240 ft.; lowest, 715 ft.
Avg. daily temp.: Jan., 26.7° F; July, 72.0° F
Churches: Protestant, 348; Roman Catholic, 86; Jewish, 28; Orthodox, 26; **City-owned parks and playgrounds:** 270 (2,572 ac.); **Radio stations:** AM, 12; FM, 20; **Television stations:** 11
Civilian Labor Force: 164,600; **Unemployed:** 7,400, **Percent:** 4.5; **Per capita personal income (MSA) 1996 :** $24,957
Chamber of Commerce: The Chamber of Commerce of Greater Pittsburgh, 3 Gateway Center, Pittsburgh, Pa. 15222

Pittsburgh, the second-largest city in Pennsylvania and seat of Allegheny County, is located in the southwestern part of the state at the junction where the Allegheny and Monongahela rivers join to form the Ohio River.

Some of the first inhabitants of the area were the Shawnee, Seneca, Delaware, and Iroquois Indians who had left the area by 1754. That year a detachment of troops from Virginia put a fort on the site of present Pittsburgh (Ft. Prince George), considering it a strategic spot. Following the original Virginia settlers, the French seized the spot and named it Ft. Duquesne; in 1758, the British took it away from the French. The British built a new fort and named it after the British prime minister, William Pitt. A town developed around the fort and was incorporated as the City of Pittsburgh in 1816.

By the late 1800s, Pittsburgh had become a world leader in iron and steelmaking, and it remained so for nearly a century. In the early 1980s, the country's domestic steel industry collapsed, causing major upheavals in Pittsburgh's manufacturing sector.

The Pittsburgh region underwent a successful diversified economic transition, shifting from heavy industries to light manufacturing, advanced technologies such as industrial automation, advanced materials, software engineering, and biomedical technology, medicine, education, finance, and corporate services. Pittsburgh is a national leader in health care services and is the world's leading center for organ transplantation. The city is a hub of international business and was ranked eighth by Fortune 500 as a major corporate headquarters center.

Pittsburgh is also a major U.S. transportation center and is one of the nation's largest inland ports in terms of tonnage.

Famous natives: Rachel Carson, ecologist; Henry Steele Commager, historian; Bill Cullen, radio and TV entertainer; John Davidson, singer and actor; Billy Eckstine, singer; Erroll Garner, jazz pianist; Scott Glenn, actor; Martha Graham, dancer and choreographer; George S. Kaufman, playwright; Michael Keaton, actor; Gene Kelly, actor and dancer; Oscar Levant, pianist; Andrew Mellon, financier; Adolphe Menjou, actor; William Powell, actor; Mary Roberts Rinehart, novelist; Peter Sellars, theater director; David O. Selznick, producer; Joseph Wambaugh, novelist; Andy Warhol, artist; August Wilson, playwright.

Portland, Ore.

Mayor: Vera Katz (to Jan. 2001)
1996 est. population (rank).: 480,824 (27)
1990 census population (rank): 437,319 (30); **% change,** 9.9; **Male,** 211,914; **Female,** 225,405; **White,** 370,135 (84.4%); **Black,** 33,530 (7.7%); **American Indian, Eskimo, or Aleut,** 5,399 (1.2%); **Asian or Pacific Islander,** 23,185 (5.3%); **Other race,** 5,070; **Hispanic origin,** 13,874 (3.2%). **1990 population under 18:** 21.9%; **65 and over,** 14.6%; **median age:** 34.5.
Land area: 137.8 sq mi. (357 sq km); **Alt.:** Highest, 1073 ft.; lowest, sea level
Avg. daily temp.: Jan., 38.9° F; July, 67.7° F
Churches: Protestant, 450; Roman Catholic, 48; Jewish, 9; Buddhist, 6; other, 190; **City-owned parks:** 200 (over 9,400 ac.); **Radio stations:** AM: 14, FM: 14; **Television stations:** 5 commercial, 1 public
Civilian Labor Force: 248,724; **Unemployed:** 18,372, **Percent:** 7.4; **Per capita personal income (PMSA) 1992:** $20,681
Chamber of Commerce: Portland Chamber of Commerce, 221 NW 2nd Ave., Portland, Ore. 97209

Portland, the largest city in Oregon and seat of Multnomah County, is located in the northwestern part of the state on the Willamette River.

Lewis and Clark camped at the site of Portland in 1805 on their expedition across the continent. Portland was founded in 1845 and was almost called Boston after the city in Massachusetts. Its two founders, Amos Lovejoy from Massachusetts and Francis Pettygrove from Maine, flipped a coin to decide the name of the new town. Pettygrove won the toss and named the place Portland after his hometown in Maine. Portland was incorporated as a city in 1851.

Portland's growth was stimulated during the 1850s as a supply base for the California gold rush, the

development of its salmon and lumber industries, and by the arrival of the railroad in 1883. The city continued to grow during 1879 to 1900 as a supply point for the Alaska gold rush and as the site of the Lewis and Clark Centennial Exposition in 1905.

The port of Portland leads the west in grain exports and is among the top five auto-import centers in the United States. The port ranks third in overall volume behind Los Angeles and Long Beach.

Portland has a diverse economy with a broad base of manufacturing, distribution, wholesale and retail trade, regional government, and business services. Major manufacturing industries include machinery, electronics, metals, transportation equipment, and lumber and wood products. High technology is a thriving part of Portland's economy, with over 500 high-tech companies located in the metropolitan area. Tourism is also important to Portland's economy.

Famous natives: James Beard, food expert; Pietro Belluschi, architect; Richard Fosbury, high jumper; Matt Groening, cartoonist; Margaux Hemingway, actress; Phil Knight, founder of Nike; Terrance Knox, actor; Jeff Lorber, jazz musician; Linus Pauling, chemist; Jane Powell, singer and actress; Ahmad Rashad, football player and sportscaster; Susan Ruttan, actress; Pat Schroeder, congressperson; Doc Severinson, band leader; Norton Simon, business executive; Sally Ann Struthers, actress; Gus Van Sant, film director; Lindsay Wagner, actress; Mitch Williams, baseball pitcher.

Sacramento, Calif.

Mayor: Joe Serna, Jr. (to March 2000)
1996 est. population (rank): 376,243 (41)
1990 census population (rank): 369,365 (42); **% change,** 1.9; **Male,** 178,737; **Female,** 190,628; **White,** 221,963 (60.1%); **Black,** 56,521 (15.3%); **American Indian, Eskimo, or Aleut,** 4,561 (1.2%); **Asian or Pacific Islander,** 55,426 (15.0%); **Other race,** 30,894; **Hispanic origin,** 60,007 (16.2%). **1990 population under 18:** 26.2%; **65 and over,** 12.1%; **median age:** 31.8.
Land area: 123 sq mi. (318.7 sq km)
Avg. daily temp.: Jan., 53.5° F; July, 88.4° F
City park & recreational facilities: 134+ (1,427+ ac.); **Television stations:** 7
Civilian Labor Force: 188,670; **Unemployed:** 13,070, **Percent:** 6.9; **Per capita personal income (PMSA) 1992:** $23,038
Chamber of Commerce: Sacramento Chamber of Commerce, 917 7th St., Sacramento, Calif. 95814; West Sacramento Chamber of Commerce, 834-C Jefferson Blvd., Sacramento, Calif. 95691

Sacramento is the capital and seventh-largest city in California and is the seat of Sacramento County. It is located in the north central part of the state at the confluence of the Sacramento and American rivers.

In 1839, German-born Swiss citizen John Augustus Sutter obtained a grant from the Mexican governor to establish a colony for fellow Swiss emigrants on a large tract of land in the vicinity that he named New Helvetia (New Switzerland), and established Fort Sutter there as a trading post.

After gold was discovered on Sutter's property in 1848, the settlement rapidly expanded as the prominent supply point for gold prospectors coming from the East. Sacramento was laid out in 1848 and named after California's principal river, which ran beside it. The river's name in Spanish honors the Holy Sacrament. It became incorporated as a city in 1849 and was made the state capital in 1854. Sacramento was the terminus of the first railroad in 1856 and the western terminus of the Pony Express in 1860.

The city has always been a hub of river transportation and is a major deep-water port connected to the Pacific Ocean. Sacramento's economy is highly diversified and, along with state government and military installations, its industries include aerospace, high technology, furniture, chemicals, pharmaceuticals, meat packing, and food processing of crops from the Central Valley.

The defense sector of the economy declined and Mather Air Force Base and the Army Depot were closed in 1995.

Famous natives: Joan Didion, author; Mark Goodson, TV producer; Tom Hanks, actor; Henry Hathaway, director; Anthony M. Kennedy, Supreme Court justice; Molly Ringwald, actress.

St. Louis, Mo.

Mayor: Clarence Harmon (to April 2001)
1996 est. population (rank): 351,565 (47)
1990 census population (rank): 396,685 (34); **% change,** –11.4; **Male,** 180,680; **Female,** 216,005; **White,** 202,085 (50.9%); **Black,** 188,408 (47.5%); **American Indian, Eskimo, or Aleut,** 950 (0.2%); **Asian or Pacific Islander,** 3,733 (0.9%); **Other race,** 1,509; **Hispanic origin,** 5,124 (1.3%). **1990 population under 18:** 25.2%; **65 and over:** 16.6%; **median age:** 32.8.
Land area: 61.4 sq mi. (159 sq km); **Alt.:** Highest, 616 ft.; lowest, 413 ft.
Avg. daily temp.: Jan., 28.8° F; July, 78.9° F
Churches: 900[1]; **City-owned parks:** 89 (2,639 ac.); **Radio stations:** AM, 21; FM 27[1]; **Television stations:** 6 commercial; 1 PBS
Civilian Labor Force: 179,278; **Unemployed:** 14,379, **Percent:** 8.0; **Per capita personal income (MSA) 1992:** $22,700[2]
Chamber of Commerce: St. Louis Regional Commerce and Growth Association, 100 S. Fourth St., Ste. 500, St. Louis, Mo. 63102

1. Metropolitan area. 2. St. Louis, Mo.–Ill.

St. Louis, the second-largest city in Missouri, is located in the east central part of the state on the Mississippi River. The city is independent and is not part of any county.

St. Louis was founded by the French in 1764 when Auguste Chouteau established a fur-trading post and Pierre Laclède Liguest, a New Orleans merchant, founded a town in February 1764 at the present site. They named it after King Louis XV of France and his patron saint, Louis IX. From 1770 to 1803, St. Louis was a Spanish possession and retroceded to France in 1803 in accordance with the Treaty of San Ildefonso (1800), only to be acquired by the U.S. as part of the Louisiana purchase that year.

The town was incorporated in 1809. From 1812 to 1821, St. Louis was the capital of the Missouri Territory and was incorporated as a city in 1822.

John Jacob Astor opened the Western branch of the American Fur Company in 1819 and the city prospered during the early part of the 19th century as a center for the transportation of the fur trade. St. Louis's commercial growth continued as a major transportation hub with the development of steamboat traffic and the later expansion of the railroads in the 1850s. The world-famous Louisiana Purchase Exposition was held here in 1904.

Manufacturing is important to the city's economy, and its highly developed industries include automobiles, aircraft and space technology, metal fabrication, beer, steelmaking, chemicals, food processing, and storage and distribution.

The giant stainless steel Gateway Arch, 630 feet high, standing on the banks of the Mississippi symbolizes St. Louis as the Gateway to the West.

Famous natives: Josephine Baker, singer; Yogi Berra, baseball player; Grace Bumbry, mezzo-soprano; Morris Carnovsky, actor; T. S. Eliot, poet; Eugene Field, poet; Redd Foxx, comedian; Joe Garagiola, baseball player; John Goodman, actor; Betty Grable, actress; Dick Gregory, comedian; Al Hirschfeld, cartoonist; Kevin Kline, actor; David Merrick, producer; Vincent Price, actor; Judy Rankin, golfer; Leon Spinks, boxer; Herbert Bayard Swope, journalist; Sara Teasdale, poet; Helen Traubel, soprano; Roy Wilkins, civil rights leader.

San Antonio, Tex.

Mayor: Howard Peak (to June 1999)
City Manager: Alexander E. Briseno (apptd. April 27, 1990)
1996 est. population (rank): 1,067,816 (8)[1]
1990 census population (rank): 935,933 (10); **% change,** 14.1; **Male,** 450,695; **Female,** 485,238; **White,** 676,082 (72.3%); **Black,** 65,884 (7.0%); **American Indian, Eskimo, or Aleut,** 3,303 (0.4%); **Asian or Pacific Islander,** 10,703 (1.1%); **Other race,** 179,961; **Hispanic origin,** 520,282 (55.6%). **1990 population under 18:** 29.0%; **65 and over:** 10.5%; **median age:** 29.8.
Land area: 399.7 sq mi. (1035.5 sq km); **Alt.:** 700 ft.
Avg. daily temp.: Jan., 51.2° F; July, 86.1° F
City-owned parks: 6,717 ac.; **Radio stations:** AM, 20; FM, 22; **Television stations:** 9
Civilian Labor Force: 695,110; **Unemployed:** 32,177, **Percent:** 4.6; **Per capita personal income (MSA) 1992:** $17,282
Chamber of Commerce: Greater San Antonio Chamber of Commerce, P.O. Box 1628, 602 E. Commerce, San Antonio, Tex. 78296

1. 1997 est. population: 1,115,600.

San Antonio, the third-largest city in Texas and the seat of Bexar County, is located in the south central part of the state, on the San Antonio River.

The site of San Antonio was first visited in 1691 by a Franciscan friar on the feast day of St. Anthony and was named San Antonio de Padua in his honor. San Antonio was permanently settled on May 1, 1718, when the Spanish governor of Coahuila and Texas, Martin de Alarcón, founded the presidio (a fort) of San Antonio de Bejar (Bexar) and the mission of San Antonio de Valero (later called the Alamo[1]) on the site of a Coahuiltecan Indian village. San Antonio remained almost continuously under Spanish rule until 1812, when Mexico won its independence from Spain.

During the outbreak of the Texas revolution (1835) against the tyranny of Mexican dictator General Santa Anna, San Antonio was captured by a small band of rebels who occupied the fortified mission of the Alamo in December 1835. The historic battle of the Alamo was fought there (Feb. 24 to March 6, 1836) and its 183 besieged defenders were massacred by Santa Anna's troops. Their heroism aroused the anger and fighting spirit of Texans to shout their famous battle cry "Remember the Alamo!" and defeat the Mexicans six weeks later (April 21, 1836) at the battle of San Jacinto. Texas became an independent republic in 1836 and San Antonio was incorporated as a city on Jan. 5, 1837.

After the Civil War, San Antonio prospered as a major shipping point for cattle with the arrival of the railroad in 1877. The city has been an important military center since World War II and is the home to five of the largest military installations in the nation, including Fort Sam Houston, constructed in 1876. San Antonio is a leading livestock center and one of the largest produce exchange markets. The city's industries are highly diversified and tourism is important to the economy.

1. Spanish for the cottonwood tree.

Famous natives: Carol Burnett, comedienne; Cody Carlson, football player; Henry G. Cisneros, secretary of HUD; Joan Crawford, actress; Cito Gaston, baseball manager; Ann Harding, actress; Jesse James Leija, boxer; Emilio Navaira, Tejano music singer; Oliver North, military officer and government official; Suzy Parker, model and actress; Paula Prentiss, actress; Kyle Rote, football player; David R. Scott, astronaut; John Silber, university president; Patsy Torres, Tejano music singer; Edward H. White, astronaut.

San Diego, Calif.

Mayor: Susan Golding (to 2000)
City Manager: Michael Uberuaga (apptd. Nov. 1997)
1996 est. population (rank): 1,171,121 (6)
1990 census population (rank): 1,110,549 (6); **% change,** 5.5; **Male,** 566,464; **Female,** 544,085; **White,** 745,406 (67.1%); **Black,** 104,261 (9.4%); **American Indian, Eskimo, or Aleut,** 6,800 (0.6%); **Asian or Pacific Islander,** 130,945 (11.8%); **Other race,** 123,137; **Hispanic origin,** 229,519 (20.7%). **1990 population under 18:** 23.1%; **65 and over:** 10.2%; **median age:** 30.5.
Land area: 330.7 sq miles (857 sq km); **Alt.:** Highest, 1,591 ft.; lowest, sea level
Avg. daily temp.: Jan., 56.8° F; July, 70.3° F
Churches: Roman Catholic, 39; Jewish, 9; Protestant, 334; Eastern Orthodox, 8; other, 18; **City park and recreation facilities:** 164 (17,207 ac.); **Radio stations:** AM, 8; FM, 18; **Television stations:** 9
Civilian Labor Force: 548,687; **Unemployed:** 41,301, **Percent:** 7.5; **Per capita personal income (MSA) 1992:** $20,384
Chamber of Commerce: San Diego Chamber of Commerce, 402 West Broadway, Suite 1000, San Diego, Calif. 92101

San Diego is the second-largest city in California. It is located in the southwestern part of the state, on San Diego Bay.

Portuguese navigator Juan Rodríguez Cabrillo claimed the bay in 1542 for Spain. The site was named San Miguel by Cabrillo. On Nov. 12, 1602, Don Sebastian de Viscaíno came ashore with his party on the day of St. Didacus (San Diego in Spanish) and celebrated a mass in the saint's honor. By coincidence, Viscaíno's flagship was named *San Diego*. He renamed the place San Diego after the 15th-century saint.

In 1769, Franciscan Father Junípero Serra established the first California mission there—San Diego del Alcala. In 1822, Mexico won control of the town after it declared its independence from Spain. In 1846, during the Mexican War, San Diego was seized by the United States and incorporated into a city in 1850 after California joined the Union that same year.

Today, San Diego's excellent natural harbor is a busy commercial port and a hub of U.S. naval

operations. However, the naval training center at San Diego is slated to be closed due to defense cutbacks. Other leading industries are electronics, aerospace and missiles, medical and scientific research, oceanography, and agriculture. Its magnificent climate and proximity to Mexico have made tourism a significant part of the city's economy.

Famous natives: Billy Casper, golfer; Florence Chadwick, swimmer; Dennis Conner, yacht racer; Ted Danson, actor; Robert Duvall, actor; Nanette Fabray, actress; Robert Lansing, actor; Margaret O'Brien, actress; Carol Vaness, soprano; Ted Williams, baseball player; Mickey Wright, golfer.

San Francisco, Calif.

Mayor: Willie L. Brown, Jr. (to Jan. 2000)
1996 est. population (rank): 735,315 (13)
1990 census population (rank): 723,959 (14); **% change,** 1.6; **Male,** 362,497; **Female,** 361,462; **White,** 387,783 (53.6%); **Black,** 79,039 (10.9%); **American Indian, Eskimo, or Aleut,** 3,456 (0.5%); **Asian or Pacific Islander,** 210,876 (29.1%); **Other race,** 42,805; **Hispanic origin,** 100,717 (13.9%). **1990 population under 18:** 16.1%; **65 and over:** 14.6%; **median age:** 35.8.
Land area: 46.1 sq mi. (120 sq km); **Alt.:** Highest, 925 ft.; lowest, sea level
Avg. daily temp.: Jan., 48.5° F; July, 62.2° F
Churches: 540 of all denominations; **City-owned parks and squares:** 225; **Radio stations:** 29; **Television stations:** 10
Civilian Labor Force (1995): 398,000[1]; **Unemployed (S.F. residents):** 26,000[1], **Percent:** 6.4[1]; **Per capita personal income (PMSA) 1992:** $31,262
Chamber of Commerce: Greater San Francisco Chamber of Commerce, 465 California St., San Francisco, Calif. 94104

1. San Francisco City/County.

San Francisco, the fourth-largest city in California, is coextensive with San Francisco County. It is located in the northern part of the state between the Pacific Ocean and San Francisco Bay. A narrow arm of land embraces San Francisco Bay, the largest land-locked harbor in the world, and shelters it from the Pacific Ocean. On this arm of land is San Francisco, a city on hills, almost surrounded by water.

A Franciscan father who was sailing with Sebastián Rodríguez Cermeño named the bay San Francisco on Nov. 7, 1595. In 1776, the Spaniards established a presidio, or military post, and a Franciscan mission on the end of the beautiful peninsula. In the following year, a little town called Yerba Buena, Spanish for "Good Herb," because mint grew in abundance, was founded around the mission.

In 1846, during the Mexican War, Yerba Buena was taken over by the United States. It was renamed San Francisco in 1847 and became incorporated as a city in 1850.

When gold was discovered in California in 1848, the city's population jumped to 10,000, and it experienced turbulent years until order was established by Vigilance Committees, first in 1851, and again in 1856. Then followed a period of more orderly growth and the foundations of the great commerce and industry of today were laid.

In 1906, San Francisco experienced the nation's worst earthquake, which, together with the fire that followed, practically destroyed the city. The city was quickly rebuilt and grew rapidly as a leading transportation, industrial, and cultural center. In the 19th century, the American explorer and sol[dier] John C. Frémont, known as The Pathfinder, nam[ed] the entrance to the bay the Golden Gate, and th[e] famous bright orange Golden Gate Bridge was dedi[-]cated in May 1937.

Not just where the city meets the bay, but a vital part of the economic and cultural fabric of northern California, the port of San Francisco covers 7½ miles of waterfront as diverse and changing as the city itself. The port is home to a broad range of commercial, maritime, and public activities including ship repair, passenger cruising, ferry and excursion boats, commercial and sport fishing, and public parks. Its major shipping terminals serve shipping lines from around the world. The port also manages over 23 million sq ft. of commercial real estate including office, retail, industrial, parking, and warehouse facilities. Fisherman's Wharf, Alcatraz, Hyde St. Pier, and Pier 39 all make the port of San Francisco one of the world's leading visitor destinations.

San Francisco inspires entrepreneurs to start their own businesses, and small businesses have a very important place in the economy. More than 80% of the city's 33,800 businesses have fewer than 15 employees. The high-technology industries of electronics and biotechnology are well represented throughout the Bay Area. With nearly 30% of the worldwide biotechnology labor force, and 360 biotech firms, the Bay Area has been appropriately called "Bionic Bay." Tourism is one of San Francisco's largest industries and the largest employer of city residents. Nearly 13.4 million persons visit San Francisco each year and annual visitor spending is $231 million, providing 66,400 jobs.

The military has played an important role in the San Francisco and the Bay Area's economy, but its impact will decline due to defense cutbacks. San Francisco is also the banking and financial center of the West and is home to a Federal Reserve Bank and a United States Mint. More than 60 foreign banks maintain offices there.

Famous natives: Gracie Allen, comedienne; Luis Walter Alvarez, Nobel Prize winner in physics; David Belasco, dramatist and producer; Mel Blanc, actor and voice specialist; Rosemary Casals, tennis player; Isadora Duncan, dancer; Clint Eastwood, actor; Robert Frost, poet; Rube Goldberg, cartoonist; William Randolph Hearst, publisher; Bruce Lee, actor; Mervyn LeRoy, director; Jack London, novelist; Johnny Mathis, singer; Lloyd Nolan, actor; O. J. Simpson, football player; Robert G. Sproul, educator; Irving Stone, novelist; Natalie Wood, actress.

San Jose, Calif.

Mayor: Susan Hammer (to Dec. 31, 1998)
City Manager: Regina V.K. Williams (apptd. Nov. 1994)
1996 population (est): 838,744 (11)[1]
1990 census population (rank): 782,248 (11); **% change,** 7.2; **Male,** 397,709; **Female,** 384,539; **White,** 491,280 (62.8%); **Black,** 36,790 (4.7%); **American Indian, Eskimo, or Aleut,** 5,416 (0.7%); **Asian or Pacific Islander,** 152,815 (19.5%); **Other race,** 95,947; **Hispanic origin,** 208,388 (26.6%). **1990 population under 18:** 26.7%; **65 and over:** 7.2%; **median age:** 30.4.
Land area: 180.8 sq mi. (468.27 sq km); **Alt.:** Highest, 4,372 ft.; lowest, sea level
Avg. daily temp.: Jan., 49.5° F; July, 68.8° F
Churches: 403; **City-owned parks and playgrounds:** 152 (3,136 ac.); **Radio stations:** 14; **Television stations:** 4

Civilian Labor Force: 420,686; **Unemployed:** 33,484, **Percent:** 8.0; **Per capita personal income (PMSA) 1992:** $25,924[1]
Chamber of Commerce: San Jose Chamber of Commerce, One Paseo de San Antonio, San Jose, Calif. 95113

1. 1997 est. population: 873,300

San Jose, the third-largest city in California and seat of Santa Clara County, is located in the northern part of the state in the Santa Clara Valley near San Francisco Bay, 50 miles south of downtown San Francisco.

San Jose was founded on Nov. 29, 1777, by Spanish colonizers who named the settlement Pueblo de San José de Guadalupe in honor of Saint Joseph and after the Guadalupe River on which the pueblo (town) was situated. The town was the first city to be established in California.

After California became a U.S. territory in 1847, San Jose became the first state capital from December 1849 to 1852 and was incorporated as a city in 1850. The city developed commercially as a supply base for gold prospectors and, when the railroad connected it with San Francisco in 1864, it became the distribution point for agricultural products from the Santa Clara Valley.

Today, the city continues to be the distribution and food-processing center for the surrounding rich agricultural region, which produces seasonal fruits and grapes. More than 50 wineries grace the valley.

Computers are big business here and San Jose is the capital of Silicon Valley (Santa Clara), the nation's center of high technology, where more than 3,000 high-tech companies are located. Silicon Valley is also one of the world's leading centers for medical treatment and research. Heart transplants, gene splicing, and transportable baby incubators were developed there.

San Jose has healthy retail, transportation, and tourism industries as well, and is the primary center for real estate and industrial development in the area.

Famous natives: "Fatty" Arbuckle, actor; Chuck Berry, singer and guitarist; Cesar Chavez, labor leader; Peggy Fleming, figure skater; Farley Granger, actor; Edmund Lowe, actor; Jim Plunkett, football player.

Seattle, Wash.

Mayor: Paul Schell (to Dec. 31, 2001)
1996 est. population (rank): 524,704 (23)
1990 census population (rank): 516,259 (21); **% change,** 1.6; **Male,** 252,042; **Female,** 264,217; **White,** 388,858 (75.3%); **Black,** 51,948 (10.1%); **American Indian, Eskimo, or Aleut,** 7,326 (1.4%); **Asian or Pacific Islander,** 60,819 (11.8%); **Other race,** 7,308 (1.4%); **Hispanic origin,** 18,349 (3.6%). **1990 population under 18:** 16.5%; **65 and over:** 15.2%; **median age:** 34.9.
Land area: 144.6 sq mi. (375 sq km); **Alt.:** Highest, 521 ft.; lowest, sea level
Avg. daily temp.: Jan., 41.1° F; July, 64.5° F
Churches: Roman Catholic, 35; Jewish, 13; Protestant, 490; others, 19; **City-owned parks, playgrounds, etc.:** 397 (6,000+ ac.); **Radio stations:** AM, 18; FM, 24; **Television stations:** 7
Civilian Labor Force (1996): (3 counties) 1,201,137; **Unemployed:** 39,637, **Percent:** 3.3; **Per capita personal income:** $32,459
Chamber of Commerce: Greater Seattle Chamber of Commerce, 1301 5th Ave., Suite 2400, Seattle, Wash. 98101-2603

Seattle is the largest city in Washington and the seat of King County. A city of steep hills, Seattle lies in western Washington between two bodies of water—Puget Sound on the west and Lake Washington on the east. Its fine landlocked harbor has made Seattle one of the major ports in the United States.

Seattle was first settled by five pioneer families from Illinois at Alki Point at the south end of Elliott Bay in 1851. They moved in 1852 to the eastern shore of the bay and laid out a town in 1853. It was named Seattle after a friendly Suquamish Indian Chief (Seattle is only an approximation of his name).

Seattle successfully withstood an Indian attack in 1856 and was incorporated as a city in 1869. A disastrous fire almost destroyed the entire business district in 1889. When the Great Northern Railway arrived in 1893, the city became a major rail terminus and it grew rapidly. It was a boom town during the Alaska gold rush of 1897 and continued to prosper as a major Pacific port of entry with the opening of the Panama Canal in 1914.

Seattle is the region's commercial and transportation hub and the center of manufacturing, trade, and finance. Its important diversified industries include aircraft, lumber and forest products, fishing, high technology, food processing, boat building, machinery, fabricated metals, chemicals, pharmaceuticals, and apparel.

Famous natives: Chester Carlson, Xerox inventor; Carol Channing, actress; Judy Collins, singer; Fred Couples, golfer; Gail Devers, athlete; Frances Farmer, actress; William Gates, Microsoft founder; June Havoc, actress; Jimi Hendrix, guitarist; Robert Joffrey, choreographer; Gypsy Rose Lee, entertainer; Mary Livingstone, comedienne; Kevin McCarthy, actor; Mary McCarthy, novelist; Jeff Smith, food expert; Martha Wright, singer.

Tucson, Ariz.

Mayor: George Miller (to Dec. 1999)
1996 est. population (rank): 449,002 (31)[1]
1990 census population (rank): 405,390 (33); **% change,** 10.8; **Male,** 197,319; **Female,** 208,071; **White,** 305,055 (74.6%); **Black,** 17,366 (4.3%); **American Indian, Eskimo, or Aleut,** 6,464 (1.6%); **Asian or Pacific Islander,** 8,901 (2.2%); **Other race,** 67,604; **Hispanic origin,** 118,595 (29.3%). **1990 population under 18:** 24.5%; **65 and over:** 12.6%; **median age:** 30.6.
Land area: 162 sq mi. (419 sq km); **Alt.:** 2,400 ft.
Avg. daily temp.: Jan., 51.1° F; July, 86.2° F
Churches: Protestant, 340; Roman Catholic, 42; other, 150; **City-owned parks and parkways:** (25,349 ac.); **Radio stations:** AM, 15; FM, 17; **Television stations:** 3 commercial; 1 educational; 3 other
Civilian Labor Force (1997): 364,700; **Unemployed:** 10,300, **Percent:** 2.8; **Per capita personal income (1997):** $22,307
Chamber of Commerce: Tucson Metropolitan Chamber of Commerce, P.O. Box 991, Tucson, Ariz. 85702

1. 1997 est. population: 452,298.

Tucson is the second-largest city in Arizona and the seat of Pima County. It is located in the southeastern part of the state on the Santa Cruz River.

The site was originally settled by the prehistoric Hohokam Indians (300 B.C.E.–C.E.1400s). The first Europeans to visit the area were Spanish missionaries in the 17th century. In 1700, the Jesuit missionary explorer Father Eusebio Fancisco Kino founded the mission of San Xavier del Bac close by the Papago Indian village of Stjukshon (later called

Tucson). Stjukshon is an Indian word meaning "village of the dark spring at the foot of the mountain." The Papago Indians are descendants of the ancient Hohokam peoples.

In 1776, Spanish colonists from Mexico constructed a presidio (fort) at Tucson as protection against the hostile Apache Indians and also established the mission of San Jose de Tucson nearby. Tucson remained a military outpost under Spanish rule and later Mexican control until the area was sold to the United States as part of the Gadsden Purchase in 1853. Tucson was the capital of the Arizona Territory from 1867 to 1877. It was incorporated as a city in 1877. The town grew rapidly when the Southern Pacific Railroad arrived in 1880 and silver and copper deposits were discovered nearby.

Tucson is a popular vacation and health resort due to its sunny, mild, and dry climate and unique desert location. Tourism is important to the city's economy. Major industries include aerospace and missile production, high technology, optics, biotechnology, environmental technology, software, and electronics. Tucson is also the commercial center for the surrounding area's agriculture and mining industries.

Famous natives: Rose E. Bird, jurist; Dennis De Concini, senator; Barbara Eden, actress; Linda Ronstadt, singer.

Tulsa, Okla.

Mayor: M. Susan Savage (to May 2002)
1996 est. population (rank): 378,491 (40)
1990 census population (rank): 367,302 (43); **% change,** 3.0; **Male,** 175,538; **Female,** 191,764; **White,** 291,444 (79.3%); **Black,** 49,825 (13.6%); **American Indian, Eskimo, or Aleut,** 17,091 (4.7%); **Asian or Pacific Islander,** 5,133 (1.4%); **Other race,** 3,809; **Hispanic origin,** 9,564 (2.6%). **1990 population under 18:** 24.4%; **65 and over:** 12.7%; **median age:** 33.1.
Land area: 191.5 sq mi. (497.1 sq km); **Alt.:** 674 ft.
Avg. daily temp.: Jan., 35.2° F; July, 83.2° F
Churches: Protestant, 593; Roman Catholic, 32; Jewish, 2; others, 4; **City parks and playgrounds:** 121 (6,050 ac.); **Radio stations:** AM, 9; FM, 21; **Television stations:** 7 commercial; 1 PBS; 1 cable
Civilian Labor Force (1997): 398,700; **Unemployed:** 12,200, **Percent:** 3.1; **Per capita personal income (1995):** $20,479
Chamber of Commerce: Metropolitan Tulsa Chamber of Commerce, 616 S. Boston, Tulsa, Okla. 74119

Tulsa, the second-largest city in Oklahoma and seat of Tulsa County, is located in the northeastern part of the state on the Arkansas River.

Tulsa was settled in the 1830s by Creek Indians from Alabama who were forcibly sent to the area (then part of Indian Territory) under the Indian Removal Act of 1830. Creek medicine men planted ashes from their old home at the new site and the Creeks named their new village "Tulsy," meaning old town, in memory of their former home in Tallassee, Alabama. In time, the village became the town of Tulsa.

The coming of the first railroad in 1882 attracted white settlers to Tulsa and the town developed into a cattle-shipping center. When enormous oil deposits were discovered at nearby Red Fork in 1901 and at Glenn Pool in 1905, the city experienced rapid growth as a center of a booming petroleum industry. Tulsa was incorporated as a city in 1898 and chartered in 1908.

Tulsa is the center of the state's petroleum industry and has a diversified economy. Important industries include aerospace, chemicals, computer parts, automobile glass, fabricated metals, and industrial machinery. The city became a major inland port when the Tulsa Port of Catoosa opened in 1971. It is the national headquarters of the U.S. Junior Chamber of Commerce (Jaycees).

Famous natives: Garth Brooks, singer; Blake Edwards, director; Paul Harvey, commentator; Jennifer Jones, actress; Henry R. Kravis, investment banker; Daniel Patrick Moynihan, senator; Tony Randall, actor; Alfre Woodard, actress; Judy Woodruff, journalist.

Virginia Beach, Va.

Mayor: Meyera E. Obendorf (to June 2000)
1996 est. population (rank): 430,385 (34)
1990 census population (rank): 393,069 (37); **% change,** 9.5; **Male,** 199,571; **Female,** 193,498; **White,** 316,408 (80.5%); **Black,** 54,671 (13.9%); **American Indian, Eskimo, or Aleut,** 1,384 (0.4%); **Asian or Pacific Islander,** 17,025 (4.3%); **Other race,** 3,581; **Hispanic origin,** 12,137 (3.1%); **1990 population under 18:** 28.0%; **65 and over:** 5.9%; **median age:** 28.9.
Land area: 258.7 sq mi. (670 sq km); **Alt.:** 12 ft.
Avg. daily temp.: Jan., 39.9° F; July, 78.4° F
Churches: Protestant, 159; Catholic, 8; Jewish, 4; **City-owned parks:** 182 (1,748 ac.); **Radio stations:** AM 18, FM 26; **Television stations:** 4 commercial, 1 PBS, 1 cable
Civilian Labor Force: 194,579; **Unemployed:** 11,541, **Percent:** 5.9; **Per capita personal income (MSA) 1992:** $18,077[1]
Chamber of Commerce: Hampton Roads Chamber of Commerce, 4512 Virginia Beach Blvd., Virginia Beach, Va., 23456

1. Norfolk–Virginia Beach–Newport News.

Virginia Beach, the largest city in Virginia, is located in the southeasternmost portion of the state on the Atlantic coastline. It is independent and is not part of any county.

The first English settlers to set foot in America landed at Cape Henry at the tip of Virginia Beach on April 29, 1607. They were led by John Smith on his way to establishing Jamestown. The first permanent settlement within the city limits was made at Lynnhaven Bay in 1621. Cape Henry became an important port for British merchant ships calling on America, and it was here that the French Fleet led by Admiral Comte de Grasse blockaded the British Fleet during the American Revolution.

Virginia Beach gained its reputation as a famous vacation resort in the 19th century, following the building of a railroad connecting its oceanfront with Norfolk and the construction of its first hotel in 1883. Virginia Beach was incorporated as a town in 1906 and as a city in 1952. In 1963, Princess Anne County and Virginia Beach merged and gave the present city an area of 310 square miles of oceanfront.

Tourism is the mainstay of the economy and 2.5 million people visit Virginia Beach overnight each year. Virginia Beach's economy is supported by four nearby military bases and diverse industries, including agriculture (165 farms), computer software, engineering, and technical services.

Famous natives and residents: V. C. Andrews, novelist; Raymond Brian Buckland, occult writer; Edgar Cayce, psychic; Ann Woodruff Compton, news correspondent; D. J. Dozier, football and baseball player; George

Eastman, inventor; Scott McKenzie, singer; Juice Newton, singer; Kenneth S. Reightler, Jr., astronaut; Pat Robertson, evangelist; Grace Sherwood, accused witch; Henry Walke, naval officer in Mexican and Civil wars; Pernell "Sweet Pea" Whitaker, boxer; Skip Wilkins, wheelchair athlete.

Washington, D.C.

Created municipal corporation: Feb. 21, 1871
Mayor: Marion Barry (to Jan. 1999)
Motto: *Justitia omnibus* (Justice to all)
Flower: American beauty rose; **Tree:** Scarlet oak
1996 est. population: 543,213 (21)
1990 census population (rank): 606,900 (19); **% change,** –10.5; **Male,** 282,970; **Female,** 323,930; **White,** 179,667 (29.6%); **Black,** 399,604 (65.8%); **American Indian, Eskimo, or Aleut,** 1,466 (0.2%); **Asian or Pacific Islander,** 11,214 (1.8%); **Other race,** 14,949; **Hispanic origin,** 32,710 (5.4%)
Land area: 68.25 sq mi. (177 sq km); **Alt.:** Highest, 420 ft.; lowest, sea level
Avg. daily temp.: Jan., 35.2° F; July, 78.9° F
Churches: Protestant, 610; Roman Catholic, 132; Jewish, 9; **City parks:** 753 (7,725 ac.); **Radio stations:** AM, 9; FM, 38; **Television stations:** 19
Civilian Labor Force: 276,000; **Unemployed:** 23,000, **Percent:** 8.4; **Per capita personal income (PMSA) 1992:** $26,817[1]
Board of Trade: Greater Washington Board of Trade, 1129 20th Street, N.W., Washington, D.C. 20036
Chamber of Commerce: D.C. Chamber of Commerce, 1319 F St., NW, Washington, D.C. 20004

1. Washington, D.C.–Md.–Va.–W.Va.

The District of Columbia—identical with the City of Washington—is the capital of the United States and the first carefully planned capital in the world. It is located between Virginia and Maryland on the Potomac River. The district is named after Columbus.

D.C. history began in 1790 when Congress directed selection of a new capital site, 100 square miles, along the Potomac. When the site was determined, it included 30.75 square miles on the Virginia side of the river. In 1846, however, Congress returned that area to Virginia, leaving the 68.25 square miles ceded by Maryland in 1788. The seat of government was transferred from Philadelphia to Washington on Dec. 1, 1800, and President John Adams became the first resident in the White House.

The city was planned and partly laid out by Major Pierre Charles L'Enfant, a French engineer. This work was perfected and completed by Major Andrew Ellicott and Benjamin Banneker, a freeborn black man, who was an astronomer and mathematician. In 1814, during the War of 1812, a British force fired the capital including the White House.

Until Nov. 3, 1967, the District of Columbia was administered by three commissioners appointed by the president. On that day, a government consisting of a mayor-commissioner and a 9-member council, all appointed by the president with the approval of the Senate, took office. On May 7, 1974, the citizens of the District of Columbia approved a Home Rule Charter, giving them an elected mayor and 13-member council—their first elected municipal government in more than a century. The district also has one non-voting member in the House of Representatives and an elected Board of Education.

On Aug. 22, 1978, Congress passed a proposed constitutional amendment to give Washington, D.C., voting representation in the Congress. The amendment had to be ratified by at least 28 state legislatures within seven years to become effective. As of 1985 it died.

A petition asking for the district's admission to the Union as the 51st state was filed in Congress on September 9, 1983. The district is continuing this drive for statehood.

The federal government and tourism are the mainstays of the city's economy, and many unions, business, professional, and nonprofit organizations are headquartered there.

Famous natives: Edward Albee, playwright; Billie Burke, comedienne; Ina Claire, actress; John Foster Dulles, statesman; Duke Ellington, musician; Jane Greer, actress; Goldie Hawn, actress; Helen Hayes, actress; J. Edgar Hoover, former director of the F.B.I.; William Hurt, actor; Noor al-Hussein, queen of Jordan; Michael Learned, actress; Roger Mudd, newscaster; Eleanor Holmes Norton, government official; Chita Rivera, dancer and actress; Leonard Rose, cellist; John Philip Sousa, composer; Frances Sternhagen, actress.

Top 50 Cities in the U.S. by Estimated 1996 Population and Rank

	Revised 4/1/90 population census	7/1/96 population estimate	Numerical population change 1990–1996	Percent population change 1990–1996	Size rank 1990	Size rank 1996
New York, N.Y.	7,322,564	7,380,906	58,342	0.8	1	1
Los Angeles, Calif.	3,485,557	3,553,638	68,081	2.0	2	2
Chicago, Ill.	2,783,726	2,721,547	-62,179	–2.2	3	3
Houston, Tex.	1,637,859	1,744,058	106,199	6.5	4	4
Philadelphia, Pa.	1,585,577	1,478,002	–107,575	–6.8	5	5
San Diego, Calif.	1,110,623	1,171,121	60,498	5.4	6	6
Phoenix, Ariz.	984,310	1,159,014	174,704	17.7	9	7
San Antonio, Tex.	959,295	1,067,816	108,521	11.3	10	8
Dallas, Tex.	1,007,618	1,053,292	45,674	4.5	8	9
Detroit, Mich.	1,027,974	1,000,272	–27,702	–2.7	7	10
San Jose, Calif.	782,224	838,744	56,520	7.2	11	11
Indianapolis (remainder),[1] Ind.	731,278	746,737	15,459	2.1	13	12
San Francisco, Calif.	723,959	735,315	11,356	1.6	14	13
Jacksonville (remainder),[1] Fla.	635,230	679,792	44,562	7.0	15	14
Baltimore, Md.	736,014	675,401	–60,613	–8.2	12	15
Columbus, Ohio	632,945	657,053	24,108	3.8	16	16

	Revised 4/1/90 population census	7/1/96 population estimate	Numerical population change 1990–1996	Percent population change 1990–1996	Size rank 1990	Size rank 1996
El Paso, Tex.	515,342	599,865	84,523	16.4	22	17
Memphis, Tenn.	618,652	596,725	–21,927	–3.5	18	18
Milwaukee, Wis.	628,088	590,503	–37,585	–6.0	17	19
Boston, Mass.	574,283	558,394	–15,889	–2.8	20	20
Washington, D.C.	606,900	543,213	–63,687	–10.5	19	21
Austin, Tex.	472,020	541,278	69,258	14.7	26	22
Seattle, Wash.	516,259	524,704	8,445	1.6	21	23
Nashville-Davidson (remainder),[1] Tenn.	488,366	511,263	22,897	4.7	25	24
Cleveland, Ohio	505,616	498,246	–7,370	–1.5	23	25
Denver, Colo.	467,610	497,840	30,230	6.5	27	26
Portland, Ore.	463,634	480,824	17,190	3.7	28	27
Fort Worth, Tex.	447,619	479,716	32,097	7.2	29	28
New Orleans, La.	496,938	476,625	–20,313	–4.1	24	29
Oklahoma City, Okla.	444,724	469,852	25,128	5.7	30	30
Tucson, Ariz.	411,480	449,002	37,522	9.1	34	31
Charlotte, N.C.	419,539	441,297	21,758	5.2	33	32
Kansas City, Mo.	434,829	441,259	6,430	1.5	31	33
Virginia Beach, Va.	393,089	430,385	37,296	9.5	37	34
Honolulu CDP,[2] Hawaii	377,059	423,475	46,416	12.3	39	35
Long Beach, Calif.	429,321	421,904	–7,417	–1.7	32	36
Albuquerque, N.M.	384,915	419,681	34,766	9.0	38	37
Atlanta, Ga.	393,929	401,907	7,978	2.0	36	38
Fresno, Calif.	354,091	396,011	41,920	11.8	47	39
Tulsa, Okla.	367,302	378,491	11,189	3.0	44	40
Las Vegas, Nev.	258,204	376,906	118,702	46.0	63	41
Sacramento, Calif.	369,365	376,243	6,878	1.9	42	42
Oakland, Calif.	372,242	367,230	–5,012	–1.3	40	43
Miami, Fla.	358,648	365,127	6,479	1.8	46	44
Omaha, Neb	342,862	364,253	21,391	6.2	48	45
Minneapolis, Minn.	368,383	358,785	–9,598	–2.6	43	46
St. Louis, Mo.	396,685	351,565	–45,120	–11.4	35	47
Pittsburgh, Pa.	369,879	350,363	–19,516	–5.3	41	48
Cincinnati, Ohio	364,114	345,818	–18,296	–5.0	45	49
Colorado Springs, Colo.	281,140	345,127	63,987	23.1	54	50

1. The term "remainder" following a city name indicates that it is part of a consolidated city-county government and that the populations of other incorporated places in the county have been excluded from the population totals shown here. 2. Honolulu CDP (census designated place) is not incorporated as a city but is recognized for census purposes as a large urban place. Honolulu CDP is coextensive with Honolulu Judicial District within the city and county of Honolulu. NOTE: 1990 population figures in this table reflect most recent revisions by the Census Bureau. They are not the same as those used in the individual city profiles. *Source:* U.S. Bureau of the Census.

Tabulated Data on City Governments

	Mayor			Council or Commission			
City	Term, years	Salary[1]	City manager's salary[1,2]	Name	Members	Term, years	Salary[1,3]
Albuquerque, N.M.	4	$ 73,500	—	Council	9	4	$ 7,028
Atlanta, Ga.	4	100,000	—	Council	18	4	22,000
Austin, Tex.	3	35,000	$125,000	Council	7	3	30,000
Baltimore, Md.	4	95,000	—	Council	19	4	37,000
Boston, Mass.	4	110,000	—	Council	13	2	54,500
Charlotte, N.C.	2	20,000	129,728	Council	11	2	12,000
Chicago, Ill.	4	170,000	—	Council	50	4	75,000
Cincinnati, Ohio	2	50,121	148,800	Council	9	2	46,621
Cleveland, Ohio	4	101,286	—	Council	21	4	47,751
Colorado Springs, Colo.	4	6,200	120,000	Council	9	4	6,200
Columbus, Ohio	4	98,000	—	Council	7	4	25,000
Dallas, Tex.	2	50[4]	179,001	Council	15	2	50[4]
Denver, Colo.	4	97,812	—	Council	13	4	43,000
Detroit, Mich.	4	143,000	—	Council	9	4	66,000
El Paso, Tex.	2	25,000	—	Council	8[5]	2	15,000
Fort Worth, Tex.	2	75[4]	140,195	Council	9[5]	2	75[4]

City	Mayor		City manager's salary[1,2]	Council or Commission			
	Term, years	Salary[1]		Name	Members	Term, years	Salary[1,3]
Fresno, Calif.	4	99,000	120,000	Council	8[5]	4	28,800
Honolulu, Hawaii	4	100,000	95,000[6]	Council	9	4	38,500
Houston, Tex.	6	133,005	—	Council	14	2	36,614
Indianapolis, Ind.	4	83,211	—	Council	29	4	14,705
Jacksonville, Fla.	2	110,000	105,000[7]	Council	19	4	24,000
Kansas City, Mo.	4	61,800	127,500	Council	13[5]	4	28,800
Las Vegas, Nev.	4	75,800	112,499	Council	4	4	33,480
Long Beach, Calif.	4	88,228	173,500	Council	9	4	22,057
Los Angeles, Calif.	4[8]	139,607	193,224[6]	Council	15	4	107,390
Memphis, Tenn.	4	110,000	98,000[6]	Council	13	4	20,100
Miami, Fla.	4	97,000	96,000	Commission	5	4	5,000
Milwaukee, Wis.	4	115,851	—	Council	17	4	54,159
Minneapolis, Minn.	4	73,486	95,888	Council	13	4	54,578
Nashville, Tenn.	4	75,000	8,900[9]	Council	40	4	6,900
New Orleans, La.	4	90,000	57,900	Council	7	4	42,500
New York, N.Y.	4	165,000	138,000[9]	Council	51	4	70,500
Oakland, Calif.	4	97,740	147,090[10]	Council	9[5]	4	47,880[8,11]
Oklahoma City, Okla.	4	2,000	100,000	Council	8	4	20[12]
Omaha, Neb.	4	86,252	—	Council	7	4	25,150
Philadelphia, Pa.	4	110,000	95,000[7]	Council	17	4	65,000
Phoenix, Ariz.	4	37,500	146,000	Council	9[5]	4	35,000
Pittsburgh, Pa.	4	81,222	—	Council	9	4	46,312
Portland, Ore.	4	83,416	—	Council	4	4	70,261
Sacramento, Calif,	4	1,652[13]	124,963	Council	9	4	1,251[13]
St. Louis, Mo.	4	71,266	—	Board of Alderman	29	4	18,500
San Antonio, Tex.	2	3,000[14]	115,000	Council	11[5]	2	20[4]
San Diego, Calif.	4	71,992	162,792	Council	8	4	54,021
San Francisco, Calif.	4	142,610	131,612	Bd. of Supvrs.	11	4	23,928
San Jose, Calif.	4	87,550	158,000	Council	10	4	58,240
Seattle, Wash.	4	115,654	—	Council	9	4	73,377
Tucson, Ariz.	4	36,000	127,000	Council	7[5]	4	18,000
Tulsa, Okla.	4	70,000	—	Council	9	2	12,000
Virginia Beach, Va.	4	20,000	125,000	Council	11	4	18,000
Washington, D.C.	4	90,705	115,700	Council	13	4	71,885

1. Annual salary unless otherwise indicated; does not include additional payments for expenses, special sessions, etc. 2. City manager's term is indefinite and at will of council (or mayor). 3. In some cities, leaders receive a higher salary. 4. Per council meeting, with an annual cap. 5. Including mayor. 6. Appointed by mayor, approved by council. 7. Appointed by mayor; not subject to council confirmation. 8. At mayor's request; limited to 2 terms. 9. No city manager; salary is for deputy or vice mayor. 10. Denotes average based on range. 11. Council also serves as the Redevelopment Agency for which there is additional compensation. 12. Per council meeting; not to exceed 5 meetings a month. 13. Per month. 14. Plus council pay. *Source:* Questionnaires to the cities.

U.S. Cities with Population Over 50,000

ZIP codes provided below indicate the primary ZIP code for each city; please consult a ZIP code directory to find the appropriate ZIP code for a particular address. NOTE: Census Designated Place (CDP)—a statistical area comprising a densely settled concentration of population that is not incorporated but which resembles an incorporated place in that local people can identify it with a name.

City	ZIP code	1996 pop. est.	1996 rank
Alabama			
Birmingham	35203	258,543	63
Decatur	35601	53,797	508
Dothan	36302	55,944	479
Hoover City	35216	55,464	487
Huntsville	35813	170,424	111
Mobile	36601	202,581	79
Montgomery	36119	196,363	82
Tuscaloosa	35401	82,379	280
Alaska			
Anchorage	99501	250,505	66
Arizona			
Chandler	85225	142,918	134
Flagstaff	86004	55,094	489
Gilbert	85234	64,326	393
Glendale	85301	182,219	100
Mesa	85201	344,764	51
Peoria	85345	76,045	314
Phoenix	85026	1,159,014	7
Scottsdale	85251	179,012	102
Tempe	85282	162,701	116
Tucson	85726	449,002	31
Yuma	85364	60,519	422
Arkansas			
Fort Smith	72917	75,776	316
Jonesboro	72401	52,656	520
Little Rock	72231	175,752	106
North Little Rock	72114	60,468	424
Pine Bluff	71601	54,165	502
California			
Alameda	94501	76,042	315
Alhambra	91715	83,644	276
Anaheim	92803	288,945	57
Antioch	94509	76,293	312
Apple Valley	92307	54,865	490
Arcadia	91006	50,483	559
Bakersfield	93380	205,508	77
Baldwin Park	91706	71,414	342

City	ZIP code	1996 pop. est.	1996 rank
Bellflower	90706	63,220	400
Berkeley	94704	103,243	206
Buena Park	90622	71,999	336
Burbank	91505	96,579	230
Camarillo	93010	57,090	467
Carlsbad	92008	69,069	358
Carson	90745	86,516	263
Cerritos	90703	53,645	511
Chino	91710	64,723	391
Chula Vista	92010	151,963	122
Clovis	93612	63,246	398
Compton	90221	91,700	242
Concord	94520	114,850	172
Corona	91720	100,208	217
Costa Mesa	92628	100,938	214
Daly City	94015	97,649	224
Davis	95616	52,321	527
Diamond Bar	91765	54,138	503
Downey	90241	93,073	238
El Cajon	92020	92,057	241
El Monte	91731	110,026	188
Encinitas	92024	57,873	452
Escondido	92025	116,184	170
Fairfield	94533	85,610	266
Fontana	92335	104,124	203
Fountain Valley	92708	55,790	482
Fremont	94537	187,800	94
Fresno	93706	396,011	39
Fullerton	92634	120,188	163
Garden Grove	92642	149,208	129
Gardena	90247	53,104	517
Glendale	92109	184,321	97
Glendora	91740	51,500	532
Hawthorne	90250	72,942	334
Hayward	94544	121,631	162
Hemet	92543	51,350	534
Hesperia	92345	60,605	420
Huntington Beach	92647	190,751	90
Huntington Park	90255	57,251	463
Inglewood	90311	111,040	183
Irvine	92713	127,873	152
Laguna Niguel	92607	51,701	530
La Habra	90631	53,704	510
La Mesa	90241	54,844	491
Laguna Niguel	92654	51,701	460
Lake Forest	92630	73,117	333
Lakewood	90714	75,462	321
Lancaster	93534	115,675	171
Livermore	94550	64,647	392
Lodi	95240	54,585	496
Long Beach	90809	421,904	36
Los Angeles	90052	3,553,638	2
Lynwood	90262	62,916	402
Merced	95340	58,099	450
Milpitas	95035	58,626	441
Mission Viejo	92690	84,689	271
Modesto	95350	178,559	103
Montebello	90640	60,281	425
Monterey Park	91754	61,912	410
Moreno Valley	92388	140,932	136
Mountain View	94041	70,619	347
Napa	94558	65,030	392
National City	92050	51,071	542
Newport Beach	92658	69,658	355
Norwalk	90650	100,209	216
Oakland	94615	367,230	43
Oceanside	92054	145,941	130
Ontario	91761	144,854	136
Orange	92613	119,890	164
Oxnard	93030	151,009	124
Palmdale	93550	106,540	196
Palo Alto	94303	58,304	445
Paramount	90723	50,793	551
Pasadena	91109	134,116	146
Pico Rivera	90660	59,968	430
Pittsburg	94565	50,813	549
Pleasanton	94566	57,275	462
Pomona	91768	134,706	145
Rancho Cucamonga	91739	116,613	168
Redding	96049	76,616	311
Redlands	92373	66,693	384
Redondo Beach	92077	62,367	407
Redwood City	94063	71,140	344
Rialto	92376	82,320	281
Richmond	94802	91,018	245
Riverside	92517	255,069	64
Rosemead	91770	52,700	519
Roseville	95678	62,649	406
Sacramento	95813	376,243	42
Salinas	93907	111,757	181
San Bernardino	92403	183,474	98
San Buenaventura (Ventura)	93001	97,205	225
San Diego	92199	1,171,121	6
San Francisco	94188	735,315	13
San Jose	95101	838,744	11
San Leandro	94577	69,976	352
San Mateo	94402	90,161	251
San Rafael	94901	50,439	560
Santa Ana	92799	302,419	55
Santa Barbara	93102	86,154	264
Santa Clara	95050	98,726	223
Santa Clarita	91380	125,153	155
Santa Cruz	95060	51,155	540
Santa Maria	93454	67,012	375
Santa Monica	90406	88,471	253
Santa Rosa	95402	121,879	161
Santee	92071	55,934	480
Simi Valley	93065	106,974	195
South Gate	90280	88,125	254
South San Francisco	94080	57,357	459
Stockton	95213	232,660	71
Sunnyvale	94086	125,156	154
Thousand Oaks	91359	113,368	174
Torrance	90510	136,183	142
Tustin	92681	62,222	408
Union City	94587	58,294	446
Upland	91786	67,095	373
Vacaville	95687	81,355	285
Vallejo	94590	109,593	189
Victorville	92392	67,089	374
Visalia	93277	87,787	257
Vista	92083	78,494	303
Walnut Creek	94596	62,786	405
West Covina	91790	101,526	210
Westminster	92684	82,425	279
Whittier	90605	78,740	298
Yorba Linda	92686	58,124	449
Colorado			
Arvada	80001	96,340	231
Aurora	80010	252,341	65
Boulder	80302	90,928	246
Colorado Springs	80910	345,127	50
Denver	80201	497,840	26
Fort Collins	80521	104,196	202
Greeley	80631	68,593	362
Lakewood	80215	134,999	143
Longmont	80501	58,318	444
Pueblo	81003	99,406	221
Thornton	80229	67,217	371
Westminster	80030	93,115	237
Connecticut			
Bridgeport	06602	137,990	139
Bristol	06010	59,619	432
Danbury	06810	65,506	383
Hartford	06101	133,086	147
Meriden	06450	57,189	465
New Britain	06050	71,512	340
New Haven	06511	124,665	156
Norwalk	06856	77,977	305
Stamford	06910	110,056	187
Waterbury	06701	106,412	197
West Haven	06616	52,153	528
Delaware			
Wilmington	19850	69,490	356
District of Columbia			
Washington	20066	543,213	21
Florida			
Boca Raton	33431	68,507	366

City	ZIP code	1996 pop. est.	1996 rank
Boynton Beach	33436	50,742	553
Cape Coral	33990	88,053	256
Clearwater	34618	100,132	219
Coral Springs	33075	105,275	215
Davie	33329	58,501	442
Daytona Beach	32114	65,203	434
Delray Beach	33444	50,720	554
Fort Lauderdale	33310	151,805	123
Fort Myers	33907	50,489	543
Gainesville	32602	87,295	259
Hialeah	33010	204,684	78
Hollywood	33022	127,894	151
Jacksonville (remainder)	32203	679,792	14
Lakeland	33805	73,157	363
Largo	34640	65,793	384
Lauderhill	33152	50,522	557
Margate	33063	50,575	556
Melbourne	32901	67,631	381
Miami	33152	365,127	44
Miami Beach	33119	94,540	235
Miramar	33023	50,956	543
North Miami	33261	50,757	552
Ocala	32678	53,225	504
Orlando	32862	173,902	108
Palm Bay	32901	74,982	324
Pembroke Pines	33084	100,662	219
Pensacola	32501	59,162	442
Plantation	33318	78,674	306
Pompano Beach	33060	74,583	332
Port St. Lucie	34985	75,532	322
Sarasota	34230	50,891	547
St. Petersburg	33730	235,988	69
Sunrise	33322	77,592	320
Tallahassee	32301	136,812	140
Tamarac	33309	51,081	541
Tampa	33630	285,206	58
West Palm Beach	33406	79,305	299
Georgia			
Albany	31706	78,591	302
Athens–Clarke County (remainder)	30601	89,405	252
Atlanta	30304	401,907	38
Columbus (remainder)	31908	182,828	99
Macon	31201	113,352	175
Marietta	30060	50,937	544
Roswell	30075	55,462	488
Savannah	31402	136,262	141
Hawaii			
Honolulu CDP	96820	423,475	35
Idaho			
Boise City	83708	152,737	120
Pocatello	83201	51,344	535
Illinois			
Arlington Heights	60005	76,740	310
Aurora	60505	116,405	169
Bloomington	61701	57,365	458
Bolingbrook	60440	51,312	536
Champaign	61820	64,002	396
Chicago	60607	2,721,547	3
Cicero	60650	70,915	346
Decatur	62523	81,369	284
Des Plaines	60018	54,836	492
Downers Grove	60515	50,089	566
Elgin	60120	86,034	265
Evanston	60201	71,593	339
Joliet	60436	86,749	261
Mount Prospect	60056	54,040	504
Naperville	60540	107,001	194
Oak Lawn	60455	57,696	455
Oak Park	60301	51,585	531
Peoria	61601	112,306	179
Rockford	61125	143,531	132
Schaumburg	60194	74,294	329
Skokie	60077	58,635	440
Springfield	62703	112,921	177
Waukegan	60085	74,166	330
Wheaton	60187	54,173	501
Indiana			
Anderson	46011	59,131	435
Bloomington	47408	66,479	379
Evansville	47708	123,456	158
Fort Wayne	46802	184,783	96
Gary	46401	110,975	184
Hammond	46320	80,081	292
Indianapolis (remainder)	46206	746,737	12
Muncie	47302	69,058	360
South Bend	46624	102,100	208
Terre Haute	47808	54,585	496
Iowa			
Cedar Rapids	52401	113,482	173
Council Bluffs	51501	55,569	485
Davenport	52802	97,010	227
Des Moines	50318	193,422	85
Dubuque	52001	57,312	460
Iowa City	52240	60,923	419
Sioux City	51101	83,791	273
Waterloo	50703	65,022	387
Kansas			
Kansas City	66106	142,654	135
Lawrence	66044	71,887	338
Olathe	66061	78,666	300
Overland Park	66204	131,053	150
Topeka	66603	119,658	165
Wichita	67276	320,395	52
Kentucky			
Lexington-Fayette	40511	239,942	68
Louisville	40231	260,689	61
Owensboro	42301	54,350	498
Louisiana			
Baton Rouge	70821	215,882	75
Bossier City	71111	55,686	484
Kenner	70062	72,345	335
Lafayette	70501	104,899	201
Lake Charles	70601	71,445	341
Monroe	71203	54,588	494
New Orleans	70113	476,625	29
Shreveport	71102	191,558	89
Maine			
Portland	04101	63,123	401
Maryland			
Baltimore	21233	675,401	15
Massachusetts			
Boston	02205	558,394	20
Brockton	02402	92,324	239
Cambridge	02139	93,707	236
Chicopee	01020	54,532	497
Fall River	02720	90,865	248
Haverhill	01830	53,952	506
Lawrence	01842	68,807	361
Lowell	01853	100,973	212
Lynn	01901	80,563	290
Malden	02148	52,749	518
Medford	02155	56,190	475
New Bedford	02740	96,903	228
Newton	02164	80,238	291
Quincy	02369	85,532	267
Somerville	02143	74,356	327
Springfield	01101	149,948	127
Taunton	02780	51,937	529
Waltham	02154	57,214	464
Worcester	01613	166,350	114
Michigan			
Ann Arbor	48103	108,758	191
Battle Creek	49016	53,430	515
Dearborn	48120	91,418	243
Dearborn Heights	48127	61,504	414
Detroit	48283	1,000,272	10
Farmington Hills	48333	79,918	293
Flint	48502	134,881	144
Grand Rapids	49501	188,242	93
Kalamazoo	49001	77,460	307
Lansing	48924	125,736	153
Livonia	48150	105,099	200
Pontiac	48343	70,471	337
Rochester Hills	48309	67,408	349
Roseville	48066	51,275	537
Royal Oak	48068	64,942	388
Saginaw	48605	65,014	377
Southfield	48037	76,184	313

City	ZIP code	1996 pop. est.	1996 rank
St. Clair Shores	48080	64,065	389
Sterling Heights	48311	118,698	166
Taylor	48180	71,939	313
Troy	48099	79,120	293
Warren	48090	138,078	138
Westland	48185	90,798	249
Wyoming	49509	66,571	368
Minnesota			
Bloomington	55431	86,664	262
Brooklyn Park	55429	61,335	416
Burnsville	55337	57,087	468
Coon Rapids	55433	62,790	404
Duluth	55806	83,699	275
Eagan	55121	57,294	461
Minneapolis	55401	358,785	46
Minnetonka	55345	50,219	563
Plymouth	55441	60,103	427
Rochester	55901	75,638	319
St. Cloud	56301	50,801	550
St. Paul	55101	259,606	62
Mississippi			
Gulfport	39500	64,829	390
Jackson	39205	192,923	86
Missouri			
Columbia	65201	76,756	309
Florissant	63033	50,491	558
Independence	64050	110,303	185
Kansas City	64108	441,259	33
Lee's Summit	64063	61,861	411
Springfield	65801	143,407	133
St. Charles	63301	56,525	474
St. Joseph	64501	70,208	351
St. Louis	63155	351,565	47
Montana			
Billings	59101	91,195	244
Great Falls	59401	57,758	453
Missoula	59801	51,201	538
Nebraska			
Lincoln	68501	200,192	76
Omaha	68108	364,253	45
Nevada			
Henderson	89015	122,339	160
Las Vegas	89199	376,906	41
North Las Vegas	89030	78,659	301
Reno	89510	155,499	118
Sparks	89431	59,496	433
New Hampshire			
Manchester	03103	100,967	213
Nashua	03060	81,094	287
New Jersey			
Bayonne	07002	60,499	423
Camden	08101	84,844	270
Clifton	07015	71,305	343
East Orange	07019	70,534	348
Elizabeth	07207	110,149	186
Jersey City	07303	229,039	72
Newark	07101	268,510	60
Passaic	07055	57,039	470
Paterson	07510	150,270	126
Trenton	08650	85,437	268
Union City	07087	57,126	466
Vineland	08360	55,906	481
New Mexico			
Albuquerque	87101	419,681	37
Las Cruces	88001	74,779	323
Santa Fe	87501	66,522	378
New York			
Albany	12288	103,564	204
Buffalo	14240	310,548	54
Mount Vernon	10551	67,112	372
New Rochelle	10802	67,369	369
New York	10199	7,380,906	1
Niagara Falls	14302	58,357	443
Rochester	14692	221,594	73
Schenectady	12305	62,893	403
Syracuse	13220	155,865	117
Troy	12180	52,518	522
Utica	13504	61,368	415
Yonkers	10702	190,316	91

City	ZIP code	1996 pop. est.	1996 rank
North Carolina			
Asheville	28810	64,067	394
Cary	27511	75,676	318
Charlotte	28228	441,297	32
Durham	27701	149,799	128
Fayetteville	28302	79,631	295
Gastonia	28052	56,575	473
Greensboro	27420	195,426	83
Greenville	27833	54,602	493
High Point	27260	74,417	326
Jacksonville	28540	69,889	353
Raleigh	27611	243,835	67
Rocky Mount	27801	52,635	521
Wilmington	28402	62,192	409
Winston-Salem	27102	153,541	119
North Dakota			
Bismarck	58501	53,514	513
Fargo	58102	83,778	274
Grand Forks	58201	50,675	555
Ohio			
Akron	44309	216,882	74
Canton	44711	81,079	288
Cincinnati	45234	345,818	49
Cleveland	44101	498,246	25
Cleveland Heights	44118	54,293	499
Columbus	43216	657,053	16
Dayton	45401	172,947	109
Elyria	44035	56,729	472
Euclid	44117	52,472	525
Hamilton	45011	61,833	412
Kettering	45429	58,204	448
Lakewood	44107	55,731	483
Lorain	44052	69,800	354
Mansfield	44901	50,906	546
Mentor	44060	50,251	562
Parma	44129	85,006	269
Springfield	45501	67,460	367
Toledo	43601	317,606	53
Warren	44481	50,343	545
Youngstown	44501	87,405	258
Oklahoma			
Broken Arrow	74012	69,175	357
Edmond	73034	63,475	397
Lawton	73501	82,582	277
Midwest City	73125	54,252	500
Norman	73069	90,228	250
Oklahoma City	73125	469,852	30
Tulsa	74103	378,491	40
Oregon			
Beaverton	97005	63,224	399
Eugene	97401	123,718	157
Gresham	97030	81,583	283
Hillsboro	97123	52,479	524
Medford	97501	56,067	477
Portland	97208	480,824	27
Salem	97301	122,566	159
Pennsylvania			
Allentown	18101	102,211	207
Altoona	16601	50,101	565
Bethlehem	18016	70,245	350
Erie	16515	105,270	199
Harrisburg	17107	50,886	548
Lancaster	17604	53,597	512
Philadelphia	19104	1,478,002	5
Pittsburgh	15290	350,363	48
Reading	19612	75,723	317
Scranton	18505	77,189	308
Rhode Island			
Cranston	02920	74,324	328
Pawtucket	02860	69,068	359
Providence	02904	152,558	121
Warwick	02886	84,514	272
South Carolina			
Charleston	29423	71,052	345
Columbia	29292	112,773	178
Greenville	29602	57,064	469
North Charleston	29406	59,923	431
South Dakota			
Rapid City	57701	57,642	456

City	ZIP code	1996 pop. est.	1996 rank
Sioux Falls	57101	113,223	176
Tennessee			
Chattanooga	37421	150,425	125
Clarksville	37040	94,879	233
Jackson	38301	50,406	561
Johnson City	37601	55,542	486
Knoxville	37950	167,535	113
Memphis	38101	596,725	18
Murfreesboro	37130	53,966	505
Nashville-Davidson (remainder)	37229	511,263	24
Texas			
Abilene	79604	108,476	192
Amarillo	79120	169,588	112
Arlington	76010	294,816	56
Austin	78710	541,278	22
Baytown	77520	68,156	364
Beaumont	77707	111,224	182
Brownsville	78520	132,091	148
Bryan	77801	58,247	447
Carrollton	75006	96,757	229
College Station	77840	58,757	439
Corpus Christi	78469	280,260	56
Dallas	75260	1,053,292	9
Denton	76201	73,483	331
El Paso	79910	599,865	17
Fort Worth	76161	479,716	28
Galveston	77550	60,048	428
Garland	75040	190,055	92
Grand Prairie	75051	109,231	190
Harlingen	78550	56,893	471
Houston	77201	1,744,058	4
Irving	75015	176,993	104
Killeen	76541	78,022	304
Laredo	78041	164,899	115
Lewisville	75067	61,517	413
Longview	75602	74,572	325
Lubbock	79402	193,565	84
McAllen	78501	103,352	205
Mesquite	75149	111,947	180
Midland	79711	97,162	226
Missouri City	77459	55,958	478
North Richland Hills	76182	53,214	516
Odessa	79761	90,883	247
Pasadena	77501	131,620	149
Plano	75075	192,280	88
Port Arthur	77640	57,701	454
Richardson	75080	81,133	286
Round Rock	78664	52,479	524
San Angelo	76902	88,098	255
San Antonio	78284	1,067,816	8
Temple	76501	51,394	533
Tyler	75712	82,185	287
Victoria	77901	61,059	416
Waco	76702	108,412	193
Wichita Falls	76307	100,138	218
Utah			
Layton	84040	50,906	546
Ogden	84401	65,720	382
Orem	84057	79,736	294
Provo	84601	99,606	220
Salt Lake City	84199	172,575	110
Sandy	84070	94,593	294
West Jordan	84084	57,600	457
West Valley City	84199	99,136	222
Virginia			
Alexandria	22313	117,586	167
Arlington CDP	22210	175,334	107
Chesapeake	23320	192,342	87
Danville	24541	53,472	514
Hampton	23670	138,757	137
Lynchburg	24506	67,250	370
Newport News	23607	176,122	105
Norfolk	23501	233,430	70
Portsmouth	23707	101,308	211
Richmond	23232	198,267	80
Roanoke	24022	95,548	232
Suffolk	23434	58,901	437
Virginia Beach	23450	430,385	34
Washington			
Bellevue	98009	92,267	240
Bellingham	98225	61,043	418
Everett	98201	81,028	289
Federal Way	98063	68,088	365
Kennewick	99336	51,184	539
Seattle	98109	524,704	23
Spokane	99210	186,562	95
Tacoma	98413	179,114	101
Vancouver	98661	59,982	429
Yakima	98903	65,110	385
West Virginia			
Charleston	25301	56,098	476
Huntington	25704	53,941	507
Wisconsin			
Appleton	54911	65,862	380
Eau Claire	54703	58,872	438
Green Bay	54303	102,076	209
Janesville	53545	58,960	436
Kenosha	53140	86,888	260
La Crosse	54601	50,212	564
Madison	53714	197,630	81
Milwaukee	53203	590,503	19
Oshkosh	54901	57,957	451
Racine	53403	82,572	278
Waukesha	53186	60,197	426
West Allis	53214	60,550	421
Wyoming			
Cheyenne	82001	53,729	509

Firsts in U.S. Cities

Famous first	City	Date
Ambulance	Cincinnati, Ohio	prior to 1865
Aquarium	Chicago, Ill.	1893
Automobile service station	Pittsburgh, Pa.	Dec. 1, 1913
Baseball stadium	Pittsburgh, Pa.	June 30, 1909
Cathedral	Baltimore, Md.	1851
Computer	Philadelphia, Pa.	1946
Daily newspaper	Philadelphia, Pa.	Sept. 21, 1784
Department store	Salt Lake City, Utah	1868
Electric company	New York, N.Y.	Oct. 15, 1878
Elevator	New York, N.Y.	1850
Hospital	Philadelphia, Pa.	Feb. 11, 1752
Motion picture theater	Los Angeles, Calif.	April 2, 1902
Opera house	San Francisco, Calif.	Oct. 15, 1932
Parking meter	Oklahoma City, Okla.	July 16, 1935
Public museum	Charleston, S.C.	Jan. 12, 1773
Railroad station	Baltimore, Md.	1830
Revolving restaurant	Seattle, Wash.	May 22, 1961
Skyscraper	Chicago, Ill.	1885
Subway	Boston, Mass.	Sept. 1, 1897
Traffic light	Cleveland, Ohio	Aug. 5, 1914
Zoological garden	Philadelphia, Pa.	July 1, 1874

See also Firsts in America.

Profile of the United States

This profile was created by the editors of the almanac from many data sources. Most figures are approximate. For additional details about the U.S., please refer to the appropriate sections of the almanac.

Geography

Number of states: 50
Land area (1990): 3,536,341. Share of world land area (1990): 6.2%
Northernmost point: Point Barrow, Alaska
Easternmost point: West Quoddy Head, Maine
Southernmost point: Ka Lae (South Cape), Hawaii
Westernmost point: Cape Wrangell, Alaska[1]
Geographic center: in Butte County, S.D. (44′ 58′ N. lat., 103′ 46′ W. long.)

1. The extreme points are measured from the geographic center of the United States (incl. Alaska and Hawaii), west of Castle Rock, S.D., 44° 58′ N. lat., 103° 46′ W. long. If measured from the prime meridian in Greenwich, England, Cape Wrangell, Alaska, would be the easternmost point.

Population

Total[1] (1998): 269,816,000
Center of population (1990): 9.7 miles northwest of Steelville in Crawford County, Missouri.
Males (1998): 132,152,000
Females (1998): 137,664,000
White (1998): 222,790,000 (82.6% of pop.)
Black (1998): 34,333,000 (12.7% of pop.)
Asian and Pacific Islander (1998): 10,339,000 (3.8% of pop.)
American Indian, Eskimo, and Aleut (1998): 2,354,000 (0.9% of pop.)
Hispanic origin (can be of any race) (1998): 30,307,000 (11.2% of pop.)
Median age (1998): 35.2
Baby boomers (1992): 77,000,000
Rural population (1990): 66,964,000
Metropolitan population (1990): 192,725,741
Families (1997): 70,241,000
Average family size (1997): 3.19
Home ownership (1995): 64.7% of pop.
Married (March 1997): 116,751,000
Never married (March 1997): 57,388,000
Divorced (March 1997) 19,347,000
Unmarried couples (1995): 3,661,000
Single parents (1995): female, 12,514,000; male, 3,513,000
Widowed (March 1997): 13,749,000

1. Excludes the United States Armed Forces overseas.

Vital Statistics

Births (1997): 3,882,000 (14.5 per 1,000)
Deaths (1997): 2,294,000 (8.6 per 1,000)
Marriages (1997): 2,384,000 (8.9 per 1,000)
Divorces (1997): 1,163,000 (4.3 per 1,000)
Infant mortality rate (1997): 7.0 per 1,000
Legal abortions (1995): 1,210,883
Life expectancy (1996): Total U.S., both sexes, 76.1; total men, 73.0; total women, 79.0; white men, 73.8; white women, 79.6; black men, 66.1; black women, 74.2.

Civilian Labor Force

All (1997): 136,285,000 (4.95% are unemployed)
Males (1996): 72,087,000 (5.4% are unemployed)
Females (1996): 61,857,000 (5.4% are unemployed)
Work at home (telecommuters, est. 1997): 23.3 million
Farms (1997): 2,060,000; total acres (1997): 968,000,000. Farm population (1994): 5,024,000; percent of civilian population, 1.8%.

Income and Credit

Gross Domestic Product (1997): $7,636.0 billion
Federal budget (est. 1998): total receipts, $1,667.8 billion; total outlays, $1,657.9 billion; total deficit, $10 billion
Personal income per capita (1997): $25,660
Median family income (1996): $51,518
Individual shareholders (1992): 51,300,000
Number below poverty level (1996): white, 24,650,000; black, 9,694,000; Hispanic, 8,697,000

Education

Elementary school pupils, grades 1–8 (1996): 31,500,000
Secondary school pupils, grades 9–12 (1996): 15,300,000
Dropout rate, grades 10–12 (1996): 4.7%
College enrollment (1996): 15,200,000
Number of college students age 25 and older (1996): 6,200,000 (40.9%)
Money spent on public elementary and secondary education (1994–95): $260,142,000
Public school teachers (1996): 2,611,000; elementary, 1,535,000; secondary, 1,077,000; private elementary and secondary school teachers (1994): 378,000
Average salary for public school teachers (1997): $39,580

Conveniences

Radio stations (July 1997): AM, 4,987; FM, 4,932
Television stations (July 1997): 1,092; cable, est. 9,000
Registered automobiles (est. 1996): 129,728,341
Newspaper circulation (1995): 58,193,391
Cable TV subscribers (1998): 72,520,000
Total TV households (1998): 97,000,000
TV Homes with VCRs (est. 1997): 74%
Households with computers (1997): 31.9% of pop.

Crime

Total arrests (est. 1996): 9,974,944; Under 18 years, 2,103,658; Males, 7,918,554; Females, 2,056,390
Child neglect and abuse cases (1995): 1,000,502
Prisoners under sentence of death (1995): 3,054
Law enforcement officers killed (1995): 130
Total murder victims (1996): 15,848
Violent crime (1996): 2,700,000
Household property crimes (1996): 27,400,000

Population

Colonial Population Estimates (in round numbers)

Year	Population	Year	Population
1610	350	1700	250,900
1620	2,300	1710	331,700
1630	4,600	1720	466,200
1640	26,600	1730	629,400
1650	50,400	1740	905,600
1660	75,100	1750	1,170,800
1670	111,900	1760	1,593,600
1680	151,500	1770	2,148,100
1690	210,400	1780	2,780,400

Covers years before the establishment of the U.S. Census in 1790. *See* following page for National Census figures, 1790 to 1990.

Total Population

Area	1990	1980	1970
50 states of U.S.	248,709,873	226,545,805	203,302,031
48 conterminous	247,051,601	225,179,263	202,229,535
Alaska	550,043	401,851	302,583
Hawaii	1,108,229	964,691	769,913
American Samoa	46,773	32,297	27,159
Canal Zone	(1)	(1)	44,198
Corn Islands	—	—	(2)
Guam	133,152	105,979	84,996
Johnston Atoll	n.a.	327	1,007
Midway	(3)	453	2,220
Puerto Rico	3,522,037	3,196,520	2,712,033
Swan Islands	n.a.	n.a.	22
Trust Ter. of Pac. Is.	15,122[5]	132,929[4]	90,940
Virgin Is. of U.S.	101,809	96,569	62,468
Wake Island	(3)	302	1,647
Population abroad	922,819	995,546	1,737,836
Armed forces	910,611	515,408	1,057,776
Total	**253,451,585**	**231,106,727**	**208,066,557**

1. Reverted to Panama. 2. Returned to Nicaragua April 25, 1971. 3. No indigenous population. 4. Includes Northern Mariana Islands. 5. Palau only Trust Territory remaining. NOTE: n.a. = not available. *Source:* U.S. Bureau of the Census; Web: www.census.gov.

National Censuses[1]

Year	Resident population[2]	Land area, sq mi.	Pop. per sq mi.
1790	3,929,214	864,746	4.5
1800	5,308,483	864,746	6.1
1810	7,239,881	1,681,828	4.3
1820	9,638,453	1,749,462	5.5
1830	12,866,020	1,749,462	7.4
1840	17,069,453	1,749,462	9.8
1850	23,191,876	2,940,042	7.9
1860	31,443,321	2,969,640	10.6
1870	39,818,449	2,969,640	13.4
1880	50,155,783	2,969,640	16.9
1890	62,947,714	2,969,640	21.2
1900	75,994,575	2,969,834	25.6
1910	91,972,266	2,969,565	31.0
1920	105,710,620	2,969,451	35.6
1930	122,775,046	2,977,128	41.2
1940	131,669,275	2,977,128	44.2
1950	150,697,361	2,974,726	50.7
1960	179,323,175	3,540,911	50.6
1970	203,302,031	3,540,023	57.4
1980	226,545,805	3,539,289	64.0
1990	248,709,873	3,536,278	70.3

1. Beginning with 1960, figures include Alaska and Hawaii. 2. Excludes armed forces overseas. *Source:* U.S. Bureau of the Census; Web: www.census.gov.

Resident Population of the United States: Estimates, by Sex, Race, and Hispanic Origin, with Median Age, 1998

(in thousands)

	Total population	% of population	Median age	Male population	Female population
All races	269,816	100.0%	35.2	132,152	137,664
White	222,790	82.6	36.3	109,681	113,109
Black	34,333	12.7	29.9	16,310	18,023
American Indian, Eskimo, and Aleut	2,354	0.9	27.4	1,169	1,185
Asian and Pacific Islander	10,339	3.8	31.2	4,992	5,347
Hispanic origin (of any race)	30,307	11.2	26.5	15,573	14,734

NOTE: Percentages add up to more than 100% because Hispanics may be of any race and are therefore counted under more than one category. *Source:* U.S. Bureau of the Census; Web: www.census.gov.

Population Distribution by Age, Race, Nativity, and Sex

	Age						Race and Nativity				
							White[1]				
Year	Total	Under 5	5–19	20–44	45–64	65 and over	Total	Native born	Foreign born	Black	Other races[1]
Percent Distribution											
1860[2]	100.0%	15.4%	35.8%	35.7%	10.4%	2.7%	85.6%	72.6 %	13.0 %	14.1%	0.3%
1870[2]	100.0	14.3	35.4	35.4	11.9	3.0	87.1	72.9	14.2	12.7	0.2
1880[2]	100.0	13.8	34.3	35.9	12.6	3.4	86.5	73.4	13.1	13.1	0.3
1890[3]	100.0	12.2	33.9	36.9	13.1	3.9	87.5	73.0	14.5	11.9	0.3
1900	100.0	12.1	32.3	37.7	13.7	4.1	87.9	74.5	13.4	11.6	0.5
1910	100.0	11.6	30.4	39.0	14.6	4.3	88.9	74.4	14.5	10.7	0.4
1920	100.0	10.9	29.8	38.4	16.1	4.7	89.7	76.7	13.0	9.9	0.4
1930	100.0	9.3	29.5	38.3	17.4	5.4	89.8	78.4	11.4	9.7	0.5
1940	100.0	8.0	26.4	38.9	19.8	6.8	89.8	81.1	8.7	9.8	0.4
1950	100.0	10.7	23.2	37.6	20.3	8.1	89.5	82.8	6.7	10.0	0.5
1960	100.0	11.3	27.1	32.2	20.1	9.2	88.6	83.4	5.2	10.5	0.9
1970[2]	100.0	8.4	29.5	31.7	20.6	9.8	87.6	83.4	4.3	11.1	1.4
1980	100.0	7.2	24.8	37.1	19.6	11.3	83.1	n.a.	n.a.	11.7	5.2
1990	100.0	7.6	21.3	40.1	18.6	12.5	83.9	n.a.	n.a.	12.3	3.8
Males per 100 Females											
1860[2]	104.7	102.4	101.2	107.9	111.5	98.3	105.3	103.7	115.1	99.6	260.8
1870[2]	102.2	102.9	101.2	99.2	114.5	100.5	102.8	100.6	115.3	96.2	400.7
1880[2]	103.6	103.0	101.3	104.0	110.2	101.4	104.0	102.1	115.9	97.8	362.2
1890[3]	105.0	103.6	101.4	107.3	108.3	104.2	105.4	102.9	118.7	99.5	165.2
1900	104.4	102.1	100.9	105.8	110.7	102.0	104.9	102.8	117.4	98.6	185.2
1910	106.0	102.5	101.3	108.1	114.4	101.1	106.6	102.7	129.2	98.9	185.6
1920	104.0	102.5	100.8	102.8	115.2	101.3	104.4	101.7	121.7	99.2	156.6
1930	102.5	103.0	101.4	100.5	109.1	100.5	102.9	101.1	115.8	97.0	150.6
1940	100.7	103.2	102.0	98.1	105.2	95.5	101.2	100.1	111.1	95.0	140.5
1950	98.6	103.9	102.5	96.2	100.1	89.6	99.0	98.8	102.0	93.7	129.7
1960	97.1	103.4	102.7	95.6	95.7	82.8	97.4	97.6	94.2	93.3	109.7
1970[2]	94.8	104.0	103.3	95.1	91.6	72.1	95.3	95.9	83.8	90.8	100.2
1980	94.5	104.7	104.0	98.1	90.7	67.6	94.8	n.a.	n.a.	89.6	100.3
1990	95.1	104.8	105.0	99.8	92.5	67.2	95.9	n.a.	n.a.	89.8	96.5

1. The 1980 and 1990 census data for white and other races categories are not directly comparable to those shown for the preceding years because of changes in the way some persons reported their race, as well as changes in procedures relating to racial classification. 2. Excludes persons for whom age is not available. 3. Excludes persons enumerated in the Indian Territory and on Indian reservations. NOTES: Data exclude armed forces overseas. Beginning in 1960, includes Alaska and Hawaii. n.a. = not available. *Source:* U.S. Bureau of the Census; Web: www.census.gov.

Ratio of Males to Females, by Age Group, 1950–1996

(number of males per 100 females, total resident population)

Age	1950 (Apr. 1)	1960 (Apr. 1)	1970 (Apr. 1)	1980 (Apr. 1)	1990[1] (Apr. 1)	1996 (July 1)
All ages	**98.6**	**97.1**	**94.8**	**94.5**	**95.1**	**95.8**
Under 14 years	103.7	103.4	103.9	104.6	104.9	104.9
14 to 24 years	98.2	98.7	98.7	101.9	104.6	105.7
25 to 44 years	96.4	95.7	95.5	97.4	98.9	99.4
45 to 64 years	100.1	95.7	91.6	90.7	92.5	93.8
65 years and over	89.6	82.8	72.1	67.6	67.2	69.5

Source: U.S. Bureau of the Census, *U.S. Census of Population: 1950,* vol. II, part 1; *1960,* vol. I, part 1; *1970,* vol. 1, part B; *Current Population Reports,* P25-1095 and P25-1130; Population Paper Listings PPL-57.

Resident Population of the United States: Estimates, by Age and Sex, 1998

	Both sexes	Male	Female
Population, all ages	269,816,000	132,152,000	137,664,000
Median age	35.2	34.0	36.4
Five-year age groups			
Under 5 years	19,033,000	9,739,000	9,294,000
5 to 9 years	19,905,000	10,192,000	9,712,000
10 to 14 years	19,162,000	9,819,000	9,343,000
15 to 19 years	19,425,000	10,009,000	9,416,000
20 to 24 years	17,664,000	9,061,000	8,602,000
25 to 29 years	18,647,000	9,359,000	9,288,000
30 to 34 years	20,201,000	10,071,000	10,131,000
35 to 39 years	22,600,000	11,278,000	11,322,000
40 to 44 years	21,848,000	10,844,000	11,004,000
45 to 49 years	18,792,000	9,235,000	9,557,000
50 to 54 years	15,752,000	7,671,000	8,081,000
55 to 59 years	12,307,000	5,915,000	6,392,000
60 to 64 years	10,234,000	4,835,000	5,400,000
65 to 69 years	9,590,000	4,391,000	5,199,000
70 to 74 years	8,779,000	3,843,000	4,936,000
75 to 79 years	7,183,000	2,979,000	4,203,000
80 to 84 years	4,703,000	1,752,000	2,951,000
85 to 89 years	2,525,000	798,000	1,727,000
90 to 94 years	1,091,000	283,000	808,000
95 to 99 years	315,000	68,000	247,000
100 years and over	61,000	11,000	50,000
Special age categories			
18 years and over	200,030,000	96,375,000	103,656,000
65 years and over	34,247,000	14,125,000	20,122,000

Source: U.S. Bureau of the Census; Web: www.census.gov.

Population Trends by Region

	July 1990	July 1993	July 1994	July 1995	July 1996	July 1997
United States	**249,439,545**	**257,752,702**	**260,292,437**	**262,760,639**	**265,179,411**	**267,636,061**
Northeast[1]	**50,873,469**	**51,241,529**	**51,349,083**	**51,428,139**	**51,502,371**	**51,588,281**
New England	13,219,210	13,211,485	13,241,007	13,280,586	13,326,211	13,378,545
Middle Atlantic	37,654,259	38,030,044	38,108,076	38,147,553	38,176,160	38,209,736
Midwest[2]	**59,763,595**	**61,085,537**	**61,452,399**	**61,837,876**	**62,181,664**	**62,460,453**
East North Central	42,075,499	42,996,425	43,228,928	43,483,513	43,713,327	43,889,857
West North Central	17,688,096	18,089,112	18,223,471	18,354,363	18,468,337	18,570,596
South[3]	**85,731,322**	**89,357,816**	**90,606,513**	**91,824,747**	**93,009,528**	**94,187,161**
South Atlantic	43,756,608	45,681,858	46,337,861	46,962,293	47,588,515	48,230,168
East South Central	15,208,424	15,702,898	15,877,321	16,044,096	16,187,380	16,325,977
West South Central	26,766,290	27,973,060	28,391,331	28,818,358	29,233,633	29,631,016
West[4]	**53,071,159**	**56,067,820**	**56,884,442**	**57,669,877**	**58,485,848**	**59,400,166**
Mountain	13,716,651	14,841,564	15,314,473	15,752,130	16,124,450	16,482,103
Pacific	39,354,508	41,226,256	41,569,969	41,917,747	42,361,398	42,918,063

1. The Northeast region includes the New England division: Connecticut, Maine, Massachusetts, New Hampshire, Rhode Island, and Vermont; and the Middle Atlantic division: New Jersey, New York, and Pennsylvania. 2. The Midwest region includes the East North Central division: Illinois, Indiana, Michigan, Ohio, and Wisconsin; and the West North Central division: Iowa, Kansas, Minnesota, Missouri, Nebraska, North Dakota, and South Dakota. 3. The South region includes the South Atlantic division: Delaware, District of Columbia, Florida, Georgia, Maryland, North Carolina, South Carolina, Virginia, and West Virginia; the East South Central division: Alabama, Kentucky, Mississippi, and Tennessee; and the West South Central division: Arkansas, Louisiana, Oklahoma, and Texas. 4. The West region includes the Mountain division: Arizona, Colorado, Idaho, Montana, Nevada, New Mexico, Utah, and Wyoming; and the Pacific division: Alaska, California, Hawaii, Oregon, and Washington. NOTE: Estimates of the Population of States: Annual Time Series, July 1, 1990, to July 1, 1997 (includes revised April 1, 1990, census population counts). These data were released to the public December 31, 1997. The estimated population is the computed number of persons living in an area (resident population) as of July 1. *Source:* Population Estimates Program, Population Division, U.S. Bureau of the Census; Web: www.census.gov/population.

Population by State

State	1990	Percent change, 1980–1990	Pop. per sq mi., 1990	Pop. rank, 1990	1980	1950	1900	1790
Alabama	4,040,587	3.8%	79.6	22	3,893,888	3,061,743	1,828,697	—
Alaska	550,403	36.9	1.0	49	401,851	128,643	63,592	—
Arizona	3,665,228	34.8	32.3	24	2,718,215	749,587	122,931	—
Arkansas	2,350,725	2.8	45.1	33	2,286,435	1,909,511	1,311,564	—
California	29,760,021	25.7	190.4	1	23,667,902	10,586,223	1,485,053	—
Colorado	3,294,394	14.0	31.8	26	2,889,964	1,325,089	539,700	—
Connecticut	3,287,116	5.8	674.7	27	3,107,576	2,007,280	908,420	237,946
Delaware	666,168	12.1	344.8	46	594,338	318,085	184,735	59,096
D.C.	606,900	–4.9	—	—	638,333	802,178	278,718	—
Florida	12,937,926	32.7	238.9	4	9,746,324	2,771,305	528,542	—
Georgia	6,478,216	18.6	109.9	11	5,463,105	3,444,578	2,216,331	82,548
Hawaii	1,108,229	14.9	172.5	41	964,691	499,794	154,001	—
Idaho	1,006,749	6.7	12.2	42	943,935	588,637	161,772	—
Illinois	11,430,602	0.0	205.4	6	11,426,518	8,712,176	4,821,550	—
Indiana	5,544,159	1.0	154.2	14	5,490,224	3,934,224	2,516,462	—
Iowa	2,776,755	–4.7	49.6	30	2,913,808	2,621,073	2,231,853	—
Kansas	2,477,574	4.8	30.3	32	2,363,679	1,905,299	1,470,495	—
Kentucky	3,685,296	0.7	92.9	23	3,660,777	2,944,806	2,147,174	73,677
Louisiana	4,219,973	0.3	94.8	21	4,205,900	2,683,516	1,381,625	—
Maine	1,227,928	9.2	39.6	38	1,124,660	913,774	694,466	96,540
Maryland	4,781,468	13.4	486.0	19	4,216,975	2,343,001	1,188,044	319,728
Massachusetts	6,016,425	4.9	768.9	13	5,737,037	4,690,514	2,805,346	378,787
Michigan	9,295,297	0.4	163.2	8	9,262,078	6,371,766	2,420,982	—
Minnesota	4,375,099	7.3	55.0	20	4,075,970	2,982,483	1,751,394	—
Mississippi	2,573,216	2.1	54.5	31	2,520,638	2,178,914	1,551,270	—
Missouri	5,117,073	4.1	74.2	15	4,916,686	3,954,653	3,106,665	—
Montana	799,065	1.6	5.5	44	786,690	591,024	243,329	—
Nebraska	1,578,385	0.5	20.6	36	1,569,825	1,325,510	1,066,300	—
Nevada	1,201,833	50.1	10.9	39	800,493	160,083	42,335	—
New Hampshire	1,109,252	20.5	123.3	40	920,610	533,242	411,588	141,885
New Jersey	7,730,188	5.0	1,035.1	9	7,364,823	4,835,329	1,883,669	184,139
New Mexico	1,515,069	16.3	12.5	37	1,302,894	681,187	195,310	—
New York	17,990,455	2.5	379.7	2	17,558,072	14,830,192	7,268,894	340,120
North Carolina	6,628,637	12.7	135.7	10	5,881,766	4,061,929	1,893,810	393,751
North Dakota	638,800	–2.1	9.0	47	652,717	619,636	319,146	—
Ohio	10,847,115	0.5	264.5	7	10,797,630	7,946,627	4,157,545	—
Oklahoma	3,145,585	4.0	45.8	28	3,025,290	2,233,351	790,391[1]	—
Oregon	2,842,321	7.9	29.5	29	2,633,105	1,521,341	413,536	—
Pennsylvania	11,881,643	0.1	264.7	5	11,863,895	10,498,012	6,302,115	434,373
Rhode Island	1,003,464	5.9	951.1	43	947,154	791,896	428,556	68,825
South Carolina	3,486,703	11.7	115.4	25	3,121,820	2,117,027	1,340,316	249,073
South Dakota	696,004	0.8	9.1	45	690,768	652,740	401,570	—
Tennessee	4,877,185	6.2	118.5	17	4,591,120	3,291,718	2,020,616	35,691
Texas	16,986,510	19.4	64.8	3	14,229,191	7,711,194	3,048,710	—
Utah	1,722,850	17.9	20.9	35	1,461,037	688,862	276,749	—
Vermont	562,758	10.0	60.7	48	511,456	377,747	343,641	85,425
Virginia	6,187,358	15.7	155.8	12	5,346,818	3,318,680	1,854,184	747,610[2]
Washington	4,866,692	17.8	73.1	18	4,132,156	2,378,963	518,103	—
West Virginia	1,793,477	–8.0	73.8	34	1,949,644	2,005,552	958,800	—
Wisconsin	4,891,769	4.0	89.9	16	4,705,767	3,434,575	2,069,042	—
Wyoming	453,588	–3.4	4.7	50	469,557	290,529	92,531	—
Total U.S.	**248,709,873**	**9.8**	**—**	**—**	**226,545,805**	**151,325,798**	**76,212,168**	**3,929,214**

1. Includes population of Indian Territory, 1900: 392,960. 2. Until 1863, Virginia included what is now West Virginia. *Source:* U.S. Bureau of the Census; Web: www.census.gov.

Estimated 1994 Population of Metro Areas Over One Million

Metropolitan statistical area (MSA) or Consolidated metropolitan statistical area (CMSA)	July 1994
New York–Northern New Jersey–Long Island, N.Y.–N.J.–Conn.–Pa. (CMSA)	19,796,000
Los Angeles–Riverside–Orange County, Calif. (CMSA)	15,302,000
Chicago–Gary–Kenosha, Ill.–Ind.–Wis. (CMSA)	8,527,000
Washington–Baltimore, D.C.–Md.–Va.–W.Va. (CMSA)	7,051,000
San Francisco–Oakland–San Jose, Calif. (CMSA)	6,513,000
Philadelphia–Wilmington–Atlantic City, Pa.–N.J.–Del.–Md. (CMSA)	5,959,000
Boston–Worcester–Lawrence, Mass.–N.H.–Maine–Conn. (CMSA)	5,497,000
Detroit–Ann Arbor–Flint, Mich. (CMSA)	5,256,000
Dallas–Fort Worth, Tex. (CMSA)	4,362,000
Houston–Galveston–Brazoria, Tex. (CMSA)	4,099,000
Miami–Fort Lauderdale, Fla. (CMSA)	3,408,000
Atlanta, Ga. (MSA)	3,331,000
Seattle–Tacoma–Bremerton, Wash. (CMSA)	3,226,000
Cleveland–Akron, Ohio (CMSA)	2,899,000
Minneapolis–St. Paul, Minn.–Wis. (MSA)	2,688,000
San Diego, Calif. (MSA)	2,632,000
St. Louis, Mo.–Ill. (MSA)	2,536,000
Phoenix–Mesa, Ariz. (MSA)	2,473,000
Pittsburgh, Pa. (MSA)	2,402,000
Denver–Boulder–Greeley, Colo. (CMSA)	2,190,000
Tampa–St. Petersburg–Clearwater, Fla. (MSA)	2,157,000
Portland–Salem, Ore.–Wash. (CMSA)	1,982,000
Cincinnati–Hamilton, Ohio–Ky.–Ind. (CMSA)	1,894,000
Kansas City, Mo.–Kans. (MSA)	1,647,000
Milwaukee–Racine, Wis. (CMSA)	1,637,000
Sacramento–Yolo, Calif. (CMSA)	1,588,000
Norfolk–Virginia Beach–Newport News, Va.–N.C. (MSA)	1,529,000
Indianapolis, Ind. (MSA)	1,462,000
San Antonio, Tex. (MSA)	1,437,000
Columbus, Ohio (MSA)	1,423,000
Orlando, Fla. (MSA)	1,361,000
New Orleans, La. (MSA)	1,309,000
Charlotte–Gastonia–Rock Hill, N.C.–S.C. (MSA)	1,260,000
Buffalo–Niagara Falls, N.Y. (MSA)	1,189,000
Salt Lake City–Ogden, Utah (MSA)	1,178,000
Hartford, Conn. (MSA)	1,151,000
Providence–Fall River–Warwick, R.I.–Mass. (MSA)	1,129,000
Greensboro–Winston-Salem–High Point, N.C. (MSA)	1,107,000
Rochester, N.Y. (MSA)	1,091,000
Las Vegas, Nev.–Ariz.	1,076,000
Nashville, Tenn. (MSA)	1,070,000
Memphis, Tenn.–Ark.–Miss. (MSA)	1,056,000
Oklahoma City, Okla. (MSA)	1,007,000

NOTE: These estimates are consistent with the population as enumerated in the 1990 census, and have not been adjusted for census coverage errors. *Source:* U.S. Bureau of the Census; Web: www.census.gov.

Getting to Work in the City

Commuting characteristics for the 15 largest cities by population, 1990

		Means of transportation (%)				
City of residence	Total workers 16 years and over	Drove alone	Carpool	Public transit	Other Means[1]	Average travel time to work (min.)
New York, N.Y.	3,183,088	24.0%	8.5%	53.4%	14.0%	36.5
Los Angeles, Calif.	1,629,096	65.2	15.4	10.5	8.9	26.5
Chicago, Ill.	1,181,677	46.3	14.8	29.7	9.2	31.5
Houston, Tex.	772,957	71.7	15.5	6.5	6.3	24.7
Philadelphia, Pa.	640,577	44.7	13.2	28.7	13.5	27.4
San Diego, Calif.	560,913	70.7	12.8	4.2	12.2	20.4
Dallas, Tex.	500,566	72.5	15.2	6.7	5.7	24.0
Phoenix, Ariz.	473,966	73.7	15.1	3.3	7.9	23.0
San Jose, Calif.	400,932	76.9	14.6	3.5	5.1	25.5
San Antonio, Tex.	395,551	73.4	15.5	4.9	6.2	21.7
San Francisco, Calif.	382,309	38.5	11.5	33.5	16.5	26.9
Indianapolis, Ind.	362,777	78.0	13.4	3.3	5.2	20.8
Detroit, Mich.	325,054	67.8	16.1	10.7	5.3	24.7
Jacksonville, Fla.	312,958	75.5	14.2	2.7	7.6	21.6
Baltimore, Md.	307,679	50.9	16.8	22.0	10.2	26.0

1. Includes commuting by motorcycle, bicycle, walking, and all other means. Also includes those who worked at home. NOTE: Percentages may not add up to 100%, due to rounding. *Source:* U.S. Bureau of the Census; Web: www.census.gov.

Persons 65 Years Old and Over—Characteristics, by Sex, 1980–1996

Characteristic	Total 1980	Total 1990	Total 1996	Male 1980	Male 1990	Male 1996	Female 1980	Female 1990	Female 1996
Total[1] (million)	**24.2**	**29.6**	**32.0**	**9.9**	**12.3**	**13.4**	**14.2**	**17.2**	**18.7**
White (million)	21.9	26.5	28.6	9.0	11.0	12.0	12.9	15.4	16.6
Black (million)	2.0	2.5	2.6	0.8	1.0	1.0	1.2	1.5	1.6
Percent below poverty level[2]	15.2%	11.4%	10.5%	11.1%	7.8%	6.2%	17.9%	13.9%	13.6%
Percent distribution									
Marital status:									
Single	5.5%	4.6%	4.0%	4.9%	4.2%	4.0%	5.9%	4.9%	4.1%
Married	55.4	56.1	56.3	78.0	76.5	75.6	39.5	41.4	42.6
Spouse present	53.6	54.1	54.1	76.1	74.2	73.2	37.9	39.7	40.4
Spouse absent	1.8	2.0	2.2	1.9	2.3	2.4	1.7	1.7	2.0
Widowed	35.7	34.2	33.3	13.5	14.2	14.7	51.2	48.6	46.8
Family status:									
In families[3]	67.6	66.7	66.6	83.0	81.9	79.9	56.8	55.8	57.0
Nonfamily householders	31.2	31.9	32.2	15.7	16.6	18.5	42.0	42.8	42.0
Secondary individuals	1.2	1.4	1.2	1.3	1.5	1.6	1.1	1.4	0.9
Living arrangements:									
Living in household	99.8	99.7	100.0	99.9	99.9	100.0	99.7	99.5	100.0
Living alone	30.3	31.0	31.1	14.9	15.7	17.4	41.0	42.0	40.9
Spouse present	53.6	54.1	54.1	76.1	74.3	73.2	37.9	39.7	40.4
Living with someone else	15.9	14.6	14.8	8.9	9.9	9.4	20.8	17.8	18.7
Not in household	0.2	0.3	—	0.1	0.1	—	0.3	0.5	—
Years of school completed:									
8 years or less	43.1	28.5	19.4	45.3	30.0	20.3	41.6	27.5	18.8
1 to 3 years of high school	16.2	16.1	15.7[5]	15.5	15.7	14.3[5]	16.7	16.4	16.7[5]
4 years of high school	24.0	32.9	33.9[6]	21.4	29.0	29.4[6]	25.8	35.6	37.2[6]
1 to 3 years of college	8.2	10.9	17.0[7]	7.5	10.8	17.1[7]	8.6	11.0	16.9[7]
4 years or more of college	8.6	11.6	13.9[8]	10.3	14.5	18.9[8]	7.4	9.5	10.4[8]
Labor force participation:[9]									
Employed	12.2	11.5	11.6	18.4	15.9	16.3	7.8	8.4	8.2
Unemployed	0.4	0.4	0.4	0.6	0.5	0.6	0.3	0.3	0.3
Not in labor force	87.5	88.1	87.9	81.0	83.6	83.1	91.9	91.3	91.4

NOTE: (—) Represents zero. 1. Includes other races, not shown separately. 2. Poverty status based on income in preceding year. 3. Excludes those living in unrelated subfamilies. 4. In group quarters other than institutions. 5. Represents those who completed 9th to 12th grade, but have no high school diploma. 6. High school graduate. 7. Some college or associate degree. 8. Bachelor's or advanced degree. 9. Annual averages of monthly figures (from U.S. Bureau of Labor Statistics, *Employment and Earnings,* January issues. Data beginning 1994 not directly comparable with earlier years). *Source:* Except as noted, U.S. Bureau of the Census, *Current Population Reports.*

Immigration

Immigrants to U.S. by Country of Origin

Figures are totals, not annual averages, and were tabulated as follows: 1820–1867, alien passengers arrived; 1868–1891 and 1895–1897, immigrant aliens arrived; 1892–1894 and 1898 to present, immigrant aliens admitted. From 1989 totals include legalized immigrants. (Data before 1906 relate to country whence alien came; 1906–1980, to country of last permanent residence; 1981 to present data based on country of birth.)

Countries	1996	1820–1996	1981–90	1971–80	1961–70	1951–60	1941–50	1820–1940
Europe:								
Albania[1]	4,007	12,230	479	329	98	59	85	2,040
Austria[2]	554	2,664,728	4,636	9,478	20,621	67,106	24,860	2,534,617
Belgium	651	212,894	5,706	5,329	9,192	18,575	12,189	158,205
Bulgaria[3]	2,066	78,029	2,342	1,188	619	104	375	65,856
Former Czechoslovakia[1]	1,389	156,848	11,500	6,023	3,273	918	8,347	120,013
Denmark	608	374,287	5,380	4,439	9,201	10,984	5,393	335,025
Estonia[1]	280	2,254	137	91	163	185	212	506
Finland[1]	602	40,315	3,265	2,868	4,192	4,925	2,503	19,593
France	3,079	795,259	23,124	25,069	45,237	51,121	38,809	594,998
Germany[2]	6,748	7,105,301	70,111	74,414	190,796	477,765	226,578	6,021,951
Greece	1,452	704,679	29,130	92,369	85,969	47,608	8,973	430,608

Countries	1996	1820–1996	1981–90	1971–80	1961–70	1951–60	1941–50	1820–1940
Hungary[2]	1,183	167,871	9,764	6,550	5,401	36,637	3,469	1,609,158
Ireland	1,731	4,780,891	32,823	11,490	32,966	48,362	14,789	4,580,557
Italy	2,501	5,353,213	32,894	129,368	214,111	185,491	57,661	4,719,223
Latvia[1]	736	6,603	359	207	510	352	361	1,192
Lithuania[1]	1,080	7,967	482	248	562	242	683	2,201
Luxembourg[1]	32	3,284	234	307	556	684	820	565
Netherlands	1,423	382,109	11,958	10,492	30,606	52,277	14,860	253,759
Norway[4]	354	756,448	3,901	3,941	15,484	22,935	10,100	697,095
Poland[5]	8,481	743,376	97,390	37,234	53,539	9,985	7,571	414,755
Portugal	3,766	518,753	40,020	101,710	76,065	19,588	7,423	256,044
Romania[6]	5,198	246,657	39,963	12,393	2,531	1,039	1,076	156,945
Spain	1,591	289,611	15,698	39,141	44,659	7,894	2,898	170,123
Sweden[4]	1,098	1,398,578	10,211	6,531	17,116	21,697	10,665	1,325,208
Switzerland	677	362,792	7,076	8,235	18,453	17,675	10,547	295,680
United Kingdom	13,657	5,197,150	142,123	137,374	213,822	202,824	139,306	4,266,561
Former U.S.S.R.[7]	2,588	3,749,777	84,081	38,961	2,465	671	571	3,343,361
Former Yugoslavia[3]	2,011	158,540	19,182	30,540	20,381	8,225	1,576	56,787
Other Europe	3,605	65,875	2,661	4,049	4,904	9,799	3,447	36,060
Total Europe	147,581	36,410,452	705,630	800,368	1,123,492	1,325,727	621,147	32,468,776
Asia:								
China[8]	25,106	1,232,740	388,686	124,326	34,764	9,657	16,709	382,173
India	44,859	703,339	261,841	164,134	27,189	1,973	1,761	9,873
Israel	3,126	152,473	36,353	37,713	29,602	25,476	476	—
Japan[9]	6,011	498,333	43,248	49,775	39,988	46,250	1,555	277,591
Turkey	3,657	425,601	20,843	13,399	10,142	3,519	798	361,236
Other Asia	207,413	5,010,282	2,042,025	1,198,831	285,957	66,374	15,729	44,053
Total Asia[10]	268,248	8,000,844	2,066,455	1,588,178	427,642	153,249	37,028	1,074,926
America:								
Canada and Newfoundland[11]	15,825	4,348,541	119,204	169,939	413,310	377,952	171,718	3,005,728
Central America	44,289	1,153,217	458,753	134,640	101,330	44,751	21,665	49,154
Mexico[12]	163,572	5,246,392	1,653,250	640,294	453,937	299,811	60,589	778,255
South America	61,769	1,588,408	455,977	295,741	257,954	91,628	21,831	121,302
West Indies	116,801	3,372,716	892,392	741,126	470,213	123,091	49,725	446,971
Other America[12]	51	117,574	1,352	995	19,630	59,711	29,276	56
Total America	340,540	15,945,081	3,580,928	1,982,735	1,716,374	996,944	354,804	4,401,466
Africa	52,889	561,569	192,212	80,779	28,954	14,092	7,367	26,060
Australia and New Zealand	2,750	160,870	20,169	23,788	19,562	11,506	13,805	54,437
Pacific Islands[13]	—	63,034	21,041	17,454	5,560	1,470	746	11,089
Countries not specified[14]	5	272,254	196	12	93	12,491	142	253,689
Total all countries	**605,793**	**61,207,884**	**7,338,062**	**4,493,314**	**3,321,677**	**2,515,479**	**1,035,039**	**38,290,443**

1. Countries established since beginning of World War I are included with countries to which they belonged. 2. Data for Austria-Hungary not reported until 1861. Austria and Hungary recorded separately after 1905, Austria included with Germany 1938–45. 3. Bulgaria, Serbia, Montenegro first reported in 1899. Bulgaria reported separately since 1920. In 1920, separate enumeration for Kingdom of Serbs, Croats, Slovenes; since 1922, recorded as Yugoslavia. 4. Norway included with Sweden 1820–68. 5. Included with Austria-Hungary, Germany, and Russia 1899–1919. 6. No record of immigration until 1880. 7. From 1931–63, the U.S.S.R. was broken down into European U.S.S.R. and Asian U.S.S.R. Since 1964, total U.S.S.R. has been reported in Europe. 8. Beginning in 1957, China includes Taiwan. 9. No record of immigration until 1861. 10. From 1934, Asia included Philippines; before 1934, recorded in separate tables as insular travel. 11. Includes all British North American possessions, 1820–98. 12. No record of immigration, 1886–93. 13. Included with "Countries not specified" prior to 1925. 14. Includes 32,897 persons returning in 1906 to their homes in U.S. NOTE: Data are latest available. *Source:* Department of Justice, Immigration and Naturalization Service.

The Foreign-Born Population in the United States, 1990 and 1980

25 most common places of birth

1990 rank	Place of Birth	Number	Percent	1980 rank	Place of birth	Number	Percent
	United States	**19,767,316**	**100.0%**		**United States**	**14,079,906**	**100.0%**
1	Mexico	4,298,014	21.7	1	Mexico	2,199,221	15.6
2	Philippines	912,674	4.6	2	Germany	849,384	6.0
3	Canada	744,830	3.8	3	Canada	842,859	6.0
4	Cuba	736,971	3.7	4	Italy	831,922	5.9
5	Germany	711,929	3.6	5	United Kingdom	669,149	4.8
6	United Kingdom	640,145	3.2	6	Cuba	607,814	4.3
7	Italy	580,592	2.9	7	Philippines	501,440	3.6
8	Korea	568,397	2.9	8	Poland	418,128	3.0
9	Vietnam	543,262	2.7	9	Soviet Union	406,022	2.9
10	China	529,837	2.7	10	Korea	289,885	2.1
11	El Salvador	465,433	2.4	11	China	286,120	2.0
12	India	450,406	2.3	12	Vietnam	231,120	1.6
13	Poland	388,328	2.0	13	Japan	221,794	1.6
14	Dominican Republic	347,858	1.8	14	Portugal	211,614	1.5
15	Jamaica	334,140	1.7	15	Greece	210,998	1.5
16	Soviet Union	333,725	1.7	16	India	206,087	1.5
17	Japan	290,128	1.5	17	Ireland	197,817	1.4
18	Colombia	286,124	1.4	18	Jamaica	196,811	1.4
19	Taiwan	244,102	1.2	19	Dominican Republic	169,147	1.2
20	Guatemala	225,739	1.1	20	Yugoslavia	152,967	1.1
21	Haiti	225,393	1.1	21	Austria	145,607	1.0
22	Iran	210,941	1.1	22	Hungary	144,368	1.0
23	Portugal	210,122	1.1	23	Colombia	143,508	1.0
24	Greece	177,398	0.9	24	Iran	121,505	0.9
25	Laos	171,577	0.9	25	France	120,215	0.9

Source: U.S. Bureau of the Census, 1993; Web: www.census.gov.

Facts About the Foreign-Born Population in the U.S., 1997

Source: U.S. Bureau of the Census, *Current Population Reports,* P20–507, March 1998.

- In 1997, the foreign-born population of the United States numbered 25.8 million persons or 9.7% of the total population.
- Five states had a larger percentage foreign born than the United States: California (24.8%), New York (19.6%), Florida (16.4%), New Jersey (15.4%), and Texas (11.3%). There was no statistical difference between Florida and New Jersey.
- Persons born in Central America, South America, or the Caribbean accounted for 51% of the total foreign-born population (13.1 million). About 27% of the foreign born were from Asia, and 17% came from Europe.
- Seven million persons, or 27% of the foreign born in the United States in 1997, were born in Mexico.
- In March 1997, about 35% of the foreign born were naturalized citizens, and about 65% were not citizens.
- About one-quarter of both the native-born and foreign born populations aged 25 years and over had completed four or more years of college (not statistically different). On the other hand, 34.7% of the foreign born over the age of 25 had not completed high school, compared with 15.6% of the comparable native-born population.
- In March 1997, 8.4% of the noncitizen, foreign-born persons in the labor force were unemployed, compared with 4.3% of naturalized, foreign-born citizens and 5.4% of the native born.
- The poverty rate for naturalized citizens was 10.4% in 1996, lower than the rate for foreign-born noncitizens (26.8%), and the native born (12.9%).
- In March 1997, there was a statistical difference between the percentages of the native born (3.3%) and the foreign born (4.9%) receiving public assistance.

Immigrants Admitted as Permanent Residents Under Refugee Acts, by Country of Birth, 1971–1994

Covers immigrants who were allowed to enter the United States under 1953 Refugee Relief Act and later acts; Hungarian parolees under July 1958 act; refugee-escapee parolees under July 1960 act; conditional entries by refugees under Oct. 1965 act; Cuban parolees under Nov. 1966 act; beginning 1978, Indochina refugees under Oct. 1977 act; beginning 1980, refugee-parolees under the Oct. 1978 act, and asylees under the March 1980 act; and beginning 1981, refugees under the March 1980 act.

Country of birth	1971–80, total	1981–90, total	1991–93, total	1994
Total	**539,447**	**1,013,620**	**383,459**	**121,434**
Europe[1]	71,858	155,512	158,862	54,978
Albania	395	353	1,812	733
Bulgaria	1,238	1,197	1,176	138
Czechoslovakia	3,646	8,204	1,097	41
Greece	478	1,408	194	65
Hungary	4,358	4,942	1,126	37
Poland	5,882	33,889	6,448	334
Romania	6,812	29,798	12,901	1,199
Soviet Union, former[2]	31,309	72,306	130,955	50,756
Azerbaijan	n.a.	n.a.	n.a.	2,668
Belarus	n.a.	n.a.	n.a.	5,156
Moldova	n.a.	n.a.	n.a.	2,154
Russia	n.a.	n.a.	n.a.	10,359
Ukraine	n.a.	n.a.	n.a.	19,366
Uzbekistan	n.a.	n.a.	n.a.	3,211
Spain	5,317	736	183	55
Yugoslavia	11,297	324	201	506
Asia[1]	210,683	712,092	154,967	45,768
Afghanistan	542	22,946	6,415	1,665
Cambodia	7,739	114,064	5,053	557
China[3]	13,760	7,928	2,673	774
Hong Kong	3,468	1,916	358	82
Iran	364	46,773	15,483	2,186
Iraq	6,851	7,540	2,414	4,400
Laos	21,690	142,964	23,700	4,482
Philippines	216	3,403	592	103
Syria	1,336	2,145	463	34
Thailand	1,241	30,259	11,375	3,076
Turkey	1,193	1,896	204	156
Vietnam	150,266	324,453	83,947	27,318
North America[1]	252,633	121,840	53,205	14,204
Cuba	251,514	113,367	29,475	11,998
El Salvador	45	1,383	2,803	275
Nicaragua	36	5,590	18,793	6
South America	1,244	1,976	1,223	383
Africa[1]	2,991	22,149	15,155	6,078
Egypt	1,473	426	105	37
Ethiopia	1,307	18,542	10,532	2,530
Other	38	51	47	23

n.a. = not available. 1. Includes other countries, not shown separately. 2. Includes other republics and unknown republics, not shown separately. 3. Includes Taiwan. *Source:* U.S. Immigration and Naturalization Service, *Statistical Yearbook,* annual, and releases.

Marital Status and Household Characteristics

Marriages and Divorces, 1900–1997

Year	Marriage Number	Marriage Rate[2]	Divorce[1] Number	Divorce[1] Rate[2]
1900	709,000	9.3	55,751	0.7
1910	948,166	10.3	83,045	0.9
1920	1,274,476	12.0	170,505	1.6
1930	1,126,856	9.2	195,961	1.6
1940	1,595,879	12.1	264,000	2.0
1950	1,667,231	11.1	385,144	2.6
1960	1,523,000	8.5	393,000	2.2
1965	1,800,000	9.3	479,000	2.5
1970	2,158,802	10.6	708,000	3.5
1975	2,152,662	10.1	1,036,000	4.9
1980	2,406,708	10.6	1,182,000	5.2
1982	2,495,000	10.8	1,180,000	5.1
1983	2,444,000	10.5	1,179,000	5.0
1984	2,487,000	10.5	1,155,000	4.9
1985	2,425,000	10.2	1,187,000	5.0
1986	2,400,000	10.0	1,159,000	4.8
1987	2,421,000	9.9	1,157,000	4.8
1988	2,389,000	9.7	1,183,000	4.8
1989	2,404,000	9.7	1,163,000	4.7
1990	2,448,000	9.8	1,175,000	4.7
1991	2,371,000	9.4	1,187,000	4.7
1992	2,362,000	9.2	1,215,000	4.8
1993	2,334,000	9.0	1,187,000	4.6
1994	2,362,000	9.1	1,191,000	4.6
1995	2,336,000	8.9	1,169,000	4.4
1996	2,344,000	8.8	1,150,000	4.3
1997	2,384,000	8.9	1,163,000	4.3

1. Includes annulments. 2. Per 1,000 population. Divorce rates for 1941–1946 are based on population including armed forces overseas. Marriage rates are based on population excluding armed forces overseas. NOTE: Marriage and divorce figures for most years include some estimated data. Alaska is included beginning 1959, Hawaii beginning 1960. *Source:* Department of Health and Human Services, National Center for Health Statistics; Web: www.dhhs.gov.

Households, Families, and Married Couples

	Households		Families		Married couples
Date	Number	Average population per household	Number	Average population per family	Number
June 1890	12,690,000	4.93	—	—	—
April 1930	29,905,000	4.11	—	—	25,174,000
April 1940	34,949,000	3.67	32,166,000	3.76	28,517,000
March 1950	43,554,000	3.37	39,303,000	3.54	36,091,000
April 1955	47,874,000	3.33	41,951,000	3.59	37,556,000
March 1960[1]	52,799,000	3.33	45,111,000	3.67	40,200,000
March 1965	57,436,000	3.29	47,956,000	3.70	42,478,000
March 1970	63,401,000	3.14	51,586,000	3.58	45,373,000
March 1975	71,120,000	2.94	55,712,000	3.42	47,547,000
March 1980	80,776,000	2.76	59,550,000	3.29	49,714,000
March 1985	86,789,000	2.69	62,706,000	3.23	51,114,000
March 1990	93,347,000	2.63	66,090,000	3.17	53,256,000
March 1995	98,990,000	2.65	69,305,000	3.19	54,944,000
March 1996	99,627,000	2.65	69,594,000	3.20	53,567,000
Dec. 1997	101,018,000	2.64	70,241,000	3.19	53,604,000

1. First year in which figures for Alaska and Hawaii are included. *Source:* U.S. Bureau of the Census; Web: www.census.gov.

Singles in the United States

The ratio of unmarried men per 100 unmarried women in U.S. Metro Areas, 1990

Highest Ratio Men to Women

Rank	Metro Area	Ratio
1	Jacksonville, N.C. MSA	223.64
2	Killeen–Temple, Tex. MSA	122.75
3	Fayetteville, N.C. MSA	117.66
4	Brazoria, Tex. PMSA	116.71
5	Lawton, Okla. MSA	115.63
6	State College, Pa. MSA	112.98
7	Clarksville–Hopkinsville, Tenn. -Ky. MSA	112.71
8	Anchorage, Alaska MSA	112.45
9	Salinas–Seaside–Monterey, Calif. MSA	112.01
10	Bryan–College Station, Tex. MSA	111.40
11	Bremerton, Wash. MSA	108.30
12	San Diego, Calif. MSA	105.33
13	Honolulu, Hawaii MSA	105.22
14	Las Vegas, Nev. MSA	104.65
15	Yuma, Ariz. MSA	104.64
16	Grand Forks, N.D. MSA	104.19
17	San Jose, Calif. PMSA	103.63
18	Reno, Nev. MSA	103.52
19	Lafayette–West Lafayette, Ind. MSA	102.01
20	Fort Walton Beach, Fla. MSA	101.70
21	Vallejo–Fairfield–Napa, Calif. PMSA	101.68
22	Lake County, Ill. PMSA	101.56
23	Champaign–Urbana–Rantoul, Ill. MSA	101.33
24	Jackson, Miss. MSA	101.24
25	Colorado Springs, Colo. MSA	99.42

Lowest Ratio Men to Women

Rank	Metro Area	Ratio
1	Sarasota, Fla. MSA	65.57
2	Bradenton, Fla. MSA	68.41
3	Altoona, Pa. MSA	69.42
4	Springfield, Ill. MSA	69.63
5	Jacksonville, Tenn. MSA	69.72
6	Gadsden, Ala. MSA	69.86
7	Wheeling, W.Va.–Ohio MSA	70.48
8	Charleston, W.Va. MSA	70.65
9	St. Joseph, Mo. MSA	70.93
10	Lynchburg, Va. MSA	71.04
11	Roanoke, Va. MSA	71.09
12	Asheville, N.C. MSA	71.14
13	Shreveport, La. MSA	71.54
14	Birmingham, Ala. MSA	71.63
15	Danville, Va. MSA	71.72
16	Pittsburgh, Pa. PMSA	72.04
17	Monroe, La. MSA	72.06
18	Owensboro, Ky. MSA	72.14
19	Pittsburgh–Beaver Valley, Pa. (CMSA)	72.16
20	Florence, Ala. MSA	72.20
21	Sherman–Denison, Tex. MSA	72.27
22	Florence, S.C. MSA	72.32
23	Huntington–Ashland, W.Va.–Ky.–Ohio MSA	72.67
24	Cumberland, Md.–W.Va. MSA	72.73
25	Steubenville–Weirton, Ohio–W.Va. MSA	72.87

NOTE: Unmarried includes never-married, widowed, and divorced persons, 15 years or older. Metro Areas as defined June 30, 1990. The presence of a military base, college or university, etc. in a metropolitan area may have a significant impact on the size of the ratio. MSA—Metropolitan Statistical Area. CMSA—Consolidated Metropolitan Statistical Area. PMSA—Primary Metropolitan Statistical Area. *Source:* U.S. Bureau of the Census; Web: www.census.gov.

Characteristics of Unmarried-Couple Households, 1995

(in thousands)

Characteristics	Number	Percent
Unmarried-couple households	3,668	100.0%
Age of householders:		
Under 25 years	742	20.2
25–44 years	2,188	59.7
45–64 years	558	15.2
65 years and over	180	4.9

Characteristics	Number	Percent
Presence of children:		
No children under 15 years	2,349	64.0%
Some children under 15 years	1,319	36.0
Sex of householders:		
Male	2,076	56.6
Female	1,593	43.4

Source: U.S. Bureau of the Census; Web: www.census.gov.

Persons Living Alone, by Sex and Age

(in thousands)

Sex and Age[1]	1995 Number	1995 Percent	1994 Number	1994 Percent	1990 Number	1990 Percent	1980 Number	1980 Percent	1970 Number	1970 Percent
Both sexes										
15 to 24 years	1,196	5.0%	1,126	4.8%	1,210	5.3%	1,726	9.4%	556	5.1%
25 to 44 years	7,316	29.6	7,235	30.6	7,110	30.9	4,729	25.8	1,604	14.8
45 to 64 years	6,377	26.0	5,967	25.3	5,502	23.9	4,514	24.7	3,622	33.4
65 years and over	9,844	39.8	9,285	39.3	9,176	39.9	7,328	40.1	5,071	46.7
Total, 15 years and over	**24,732**	**100.0**	**23,613**	**100.0**	**22,999**	**100.0**	**18,296**	**100.0**	**10,851**	**100.0**
Male										
15 to 24 years	623	3.0	570	6.0	674	7.4	947	13.6	274	2.5
25 to 44 years	4,476	44.1	4,359	46.2	4,231	46.8	2,920	41.9	933	8.6
45 to 64 years	2,787	11.0	2,473	26.2	2,203	24.3	1,613	23.2	1,152	10.6
65 years and over	2,254	22.2	2,037	21.6	1,942	21.5	1,486	21.3	1,174	10.8
Total, 15 years and over	**10,140**	**100.0**	**9,439**	**100.0**	**9,049**	**100.0**	**6,966**	**100.0**	**3,532**	**100.0**
Female										
15 to 24 years	572	2.0	557	3.9	536	3.8	779	6.9	282	2.6
25 to 44 years	2,839	19.5	2,872	20.3	2,881	20.7	1,809	16.0	671	6.2
45 to 64 years	3,589	15.0	3,493	24.6	3,300	23.7	2,901	25.6	2,470	22.8
65 years and over	7,591	52.0	7,248	51.1	7,233	51.8	5,842	51.6	3,897	35.9
Total, 15 years and over	**14,592**	**100.0**	**14,171**	**100.0**	**13,950**	**100.0**	**11,330**	**100.0**	**7,319**	**100.0**

1. Prior to 1980, data are for persons 14 years and older. NOTE: Details may not add up to 100% because of rounding. *Source:* U.S. Bureau of the Census; Web: www.census.gov.

Families Maintained by Women, No Husband Present

(in thousands)

	1995 Number	1995 Percent	1990 Number	1990 Percent	1980 Number	1980 Percent	1970 Number	1970 Percent	1960 Number	1960 Percent
Age of women:										
Under 35 years	4,089	33.5%	3,699	34.0%	3,015	34.6%	1,364	24.4%	796	17.7%
35 to 44 years	3,502	28.7	2,929	26.9	1,916	22.0	1,074	19.2	940	20.9
45 to 64 years	3,094	25.3	2,790	25.6	2,514	28.9	2,021	36.1	1,731	38.5
65 years and over	1,536	12.6	1,471	13.5	1,260	14.5	1,131	20.2	1,027	22.9
Median age	40.4	—	40.7	—	41.7	—	48.5	—	50.1	—
Presence of children:										
No own children under 18 years	4,606	37.7	4,290	39.4	3,260	37.4	2,665	47.7	2,397	53.3
With own children under 18 years	7,615	62.3	6,599	60.6	5,445	62.6	2,926	52.3	2,097	46.7
Total own children under 18 years	13,419	—	11,378	—	10,204	—	6,694	—	4,674	—
Average per family	1.10	—	1.04	—	1.17	—	1.20	—	1.04	—
Average per family with children	1.76	—	1.72	—	1.87	—	2.29	—	2.24	—
Race:										
White	8,031	65.7	7,306	67.1	6,052	69.5	4,165	74.5	3,547	78.9
Black[1]	3,716	30.4	3,275	30.1	2,495	28.7	1,382	24.7	947	21.1
Other	473	3.9	309	2.8	158	1.8	44	0.8	n.a.	n.a.
Marital status:										
Married, husband absent	2,160	17.7	1,947	17.9	1,769	20.3	1,326	23.7	1,099	24.5
Widowed	2,283	18.7	2,536	23.3	2,570	29.5	2,396	42.9	2,325	51.7
Divorced	4,537	37.1	3,949	36.3	3,008	34.6	1,259	22.5	694	15.4
Never married	3,240	26.5	2,457	22.6	1,359	15.6	610	10.9	376	8.4
Total	**12,220**	**100.0**	**10,890**	**100.0**	**8,705**	**100.0**	**5,591**	**100.0**	**4,494**	**100.0**

1. Includes other races in 1960. NOTE: n.a. = not available. (—) as shown in this table, means "not applicable." *Source:* U.S. Bureau of the Census; Web: www.census.gov.

Median Age at First Marriage

Year	Males	Females	Year	Males	Females	Year	Males	Females
1890	26.1	22.0	1940	24.3	21.5	1990	26.1	23.9
1900	25.9	21.9	1950	22.8	20.3	1993	26.5	24.5
1910	25.1	21.6	1960	22.8	20.3	1994	26.7	24.5
1920	24.6	21.2	1970	23.2	20.8	1995	26.9	24.5
1930	24.3	21.3	1980	24.7	22.0	1996	27.1	24.8

Source: U.S. Bureau of the Census; Web: www.census.gov.

Selected Family Characteristics

Characteristics[1]	1995 Number (thousands)	1995 Median income
ALL RACES		
All households	99,627	$34,076
Age of householder		
Under 65 years	78,141	39,148
15 to 24 years	5,282	20,979
25 to 34 years	19,225	34,701
35 to 44 years	23,226	43,465
45 to 54 years	18,008	48,058
55 to 64 years	12,401	38,077
65 years and over	21,486	19,096
65 to 74 years	11,908	23,031
75 years and over	9,578	15,342
Region		
Northeast	19,695	36,111
Midwest	23,707	35,839
South	35,143	30,942
West	21,082	35,979
Type of household		
Family household	69,594	41,224
Married-couple family	53,567	47,129
Male householder, no wife present	3,513	33,534
Female householder, no husband present	12,514	21,348
Number of earners		
No earner	21,281	13,102
1 earner	33,538	27,567
2 earners or more	44,809	52,813
2 earners	35,320	50,000
3 earners	6,982	63,191
4 earners or more	2,507	74,243
Size of household		
1 person	24,900	17,063
2 persons	32,526	35,700
3 persons	16,724	42,244
4 persons	15,118	49,531
5 persons	6,631	45,710
6 persons	2,357	44,263
7 persons or more	1,372	39,013
WHITE		
All households	84,511	35,766
Age of householder		
Under 65 years	65,186	41,481
15 to 24 years	4,254	22,203
25 to 34 years	15,730	36,912
35 to 44 years	19,373	45,924
45 to 54 years	15,214	50,607
55 to 64 years	10,614	40,150
65 years and over	19,326	19,590
65 to 74 years	10,583	23,816
75 years and over	8,743	15,807
Region		
Northeast	16,959	$37,772
Midwest	21,095	37,220
South	28,297	32,917
West	18,160	36,390
Type of household		
Family household	58,869	43,265
Married-couple family	47,873	47,608
Male householder, no wife present	2,712	35,129
Female householder, no husband present	8,284	24,431
Number of earners		
No earner	17,964	14,267
1 earner	27,639	29,175
2 earners or more	38,907	53,990
2 earners	30,701	50,910
3 earners	6,058	64,311
4 earners or more	2,149	75,092
Size of household		
1 person	21,194	17,512
2 persons	28,615	36,939
3 persons	13,873	44,997
4 persons	12,659	51,611
5 persons	5,350	49,073
6 persons	1,856	47,249
7 persons or more	965	41,109
BLACK		
All households	11,577	22,393
Age of householder		
Under 65 years	9,799	24,545
15 to 24 years	774	12,825
25 to 34 years	2,633	21,871
35 to 44 years	2,889	28,097
45 to 54 years	2,118	30,210
55 to 64 years	1,385	21,842
65 years and over	1,777	13,246
65 to 74 years	1,064	15,925
75 years and over	713	9,886
Region		
Northeast	2,165	21,947
Midwest	2,153	22,027
South	6,163	22,567
West	1,096	23,416
Type of household		
Family household	8,055	26,838
Married-couple family	3,713	41,362
Male householder, no wife present	573	27,071
Female householder, no husband present	3,769	15,589

Characteristics[1]	1995 Number (thousands)	1995 Median income
Number of earners		
No earner	2,764	$ 7,651
1 earner	4,678	20,268
2 earners or more	4,135	42,341
2 earners	3,310	40,357
3 earners	624	48,737
4 earners or more	201	67,415
Size of household		
1 person	3,055	13,229
2 persons	3,034	24,133
3 persons	2,197	25,578
4 persons	1,715	32,086
5 persons	919	27,630
6 persons	366	28,028
7 persons or more	291	28,908
HISPANIC ORIGIN[2]		
All households	7,939	22,860
Age of householder		
Under 65 years	7,041	24,399
15 to 24 years	749	16,854
25 to 34 years	2,195	23,187
35 to 44 years	2,109	26,492
45 to 54 years	1,181	29,441
55 to 64 years	808	22,859
65 years and over	898	13,513
65 to 74 years	609	14,561
75 years and over	289	12,277
Region		
Northeast	1,368	$19,936
Midwest	535	27,777
South	2,725	21,907
West	3,311	24,368
Type of household		
Family household	6,287	25,491
Married-couple family	4,247	30,195
Male householder, no wife present	436	25,053
Female householder, no husband present	1,604	14,755
Number of earners		
No earner	1,363	7,486
1 earner	2,923	18,062
2 earners or more	3,654	36,963
2 earners	2,712	34,170
3 earners	651	43,709
4 earners or more	290	56,612
Size of household		
1 person	1,260	11,074
2 persons	1,788	22,127
3 persons	1,528	22,977
4 persons	1,508	27,903
5 persons	964	26,701
6 persons	523	29,114
7 persons or more	368	30,180

1. Household data as of March 1995. 2. Persons of Hispanic origin may be of any race. NOTE: Data are the latest available. *Source:* U.S. Bureau of the Census, *Current Population Reports;* Web: www.census.gov.

Births

Live Births by Age and Race of Mother

Year[1]/race	Total	Age of Mother: Under 15	15–19	20–24	25–29	30–34	35–39	40–44	45–49
1940	2,558,647	3,865	332,667	799,537	693,268	431,468	222,015	68,269	7,558
1945	2,858,449	4,028	298,868	832,746	785,299	554,906	296,852	78,853	6,897
1950	3,631,512	5,413	432,911	1,155,167	1,041,360	610,816	302,780	77,743	5,322
1955	4,014,112	6,181	493,770	1,290,939	1,133,155	732,540	352,320	89,777	5,430
1960	4,257,850	6,780	586,966	1,426,912	1,092,816	687,722	359,908	91,564	5,182
1965	3,760,358	7,768	590,894	1,337,350	925,732	529,376	282,908	81,716	4,614
1970	3,731,386	11,752	644,708	1,418,874	994,904	427,806	180,244	49,952	3,146
1975	3,144,198	12,642	582,238	1,093,676	936,786	375,500	115,409	26,319	1,628
1980	3,612,258	10,169	552,161	1,226,200	1,108,291	550,354	140,793	23,090	1,200
1985	3,760,561	10,220	467,485	1,141,320	1,201,350	696,354	214,336	28,334	1,162
1990	4,158,212	11,657	521,826	1,093,730	1,277,108	886,063	317,583	48,607	1,638
1995	3,899,589	12,242	499,873	965,547	1,063,539	904,666	383,745	67,250	2,727
1996	3,914,953	11,242	494,272	951,247	1,078,411	904,329	400,810	71,663	2,980
White	3,113,014	5,570	346,509	731,148	884,787	753,589	331,044	57,973	2,395
Black	596,039	5,227	131,059	180,093	133,437	94,256	43,614	8,067	285
American Indian[2]	38,456	208	7,851	12,334	9,026	5,867	2,630	524	17
Asian or Pacific Islander	167,444	237	8,853	27,672	51,161	50,617	23,521	5,099	284
Hispanic origin[3]	697,829	3,084	118,612	213,685	184,368	118,677	49,280	9,711	412

1. Data for 1940–55 are adjusted for under-registration. Beginning 1960, only registered births are shown. Data for 1960–70 based on a 50% sample of births. For 1972–84, based on 100% of births in selected states and on 50% sample in all other states. Beginning 1989, births are tabulated by race of mother; previously based on race of child. 2. Includes births to Aleuts and Eskimos. 3. Persons of Hispanic origin may be any race. NOTE: Data refer only to births occurring within the U.S. *Source:* Department of Health and Human Services, National Center for Health Statistics; Web: www.dhhs.gov.

Live Births by Sex and Sex Ratio

	Total[1, 2]			White			Black		
Year	Male	Female	Males per 1,000 females	Male	Female	Males per 1,000 females	Male	Female	Males per 1,000 females
1985	1,927,983	1,832,578	1,052	1,536,646	1,454,727	1,056	308,575	299,618	1,030
1986	1,924,868	1,831,679	1,051	1,523,914	1,446,525	1,053	315,788	305,433	1,034
1987	1,951,153	1,858,241	1,050	1,535,517	1,456,971	1,054	325,259	316,308	1,028
1988	2,002,424	1,907,086	1,050	1,562,675	1,483,487	1,053	341,441	330,535	1,033
1989	2,069,490	1,971,468	1,050	1,606,757	1,525,234	1,053	360,131	349,264	1,031
1990	2,129,495	2,028,717	1,050	1,654,928	1,570,415	1,054	367,455	357,121	1,029
1991	2,101,518	2,009,389	1,046	1,659,077	1,582,196	1,049	346,455	336,147	1,031
1992	2,082,097	1,982,917	1,050	1,641,811	1,559,867	1,053	342,726	330,907	1,036
1993	2,048,861	1,951,379	1,050	1,616,332	1,533,501	1,054	333,984	324,891	1,028
1994	2,022,589	1,930,178	1,048	1,599,803	1,521,401	1,051	322,554	313,837	1,028
1995	1,996,355	1,930,234	1,049	1,588,427	1,510,458	1,052	308,115	297,024	1,031
1996	1,990,480	1,901,014	1,047	—	—	1,050	—	—	1,028

NOTE: (—) Data not available. 1. Excludes births to nonresidents of U.S. 2. Includes races other than white and black. *Source:* Department of Health and Human Services, National Center for Health Statistics; Web: www.dhhs.gov.

Births, Birth Rates, and Teenage Birth Rates by State, 1996

State	Number of births	Birth rate	Teenage birth rate
United States[1]	3,891,494	14.7	54.4
Alabama	60,488	14.2	69.2
Alaska	10,037	16.5	46.4
Arizona	75,322	17.0	73.9
Arkansas	36,371	14.5	75.4
California	539,433	16.9	62.6
Colorado	55,807	14.6	49.5
Connecticut	44,469	13.6	37.4
Delaware	10,155	14.0	56.9
D.C.	8,390	15.4	102.1
Florida	189,392	13.2	58.9
Georgia	114,043	15.5	68.2
Hawaii	18,401	15.5	48.1
Idaho	18,625	15.7	47.2
Illinois	183,180	15.5	57.1
Indiana	83,513	14.3	56.1
Iowa	37,139	13.0	37.8
Kansas	36,651	14.2	49.6
Kentucky	52,706	13.6	61.5
Louisiana	65,204	15.0	66.7
Maine	13,774	11.1	31.4
Maryland	71,533	14.1	46.1
Massachusetts	80,276	13.2	32.2
Michigan	133,387	13.9	46.5
Minnesota	63,700	13.7	32.1
Mississippi	40,987	15.1	75.5
Missouri	73,832	13.8	53.7
Montana	10,856	12.3	38.6
Nebraska	23,286	14.1	38.7
Nevada	26,125	16.3	69.6
New Hampshire	14,520	12.5	28.6
New Jersey	114,306	14.3	35.4
New Mexico	27,228	15.9	70.9
New York	263,963	14.5	41.8
North Carolina	104,470	14.3	63.5
North Dakota	8,347	13.0	32.3
Ohio	151,692	13.6	50.4
Oklahoma	46,193	14.0	63.4
Oregon	43,658	13.6	50.8
Pennsylvania	148,338	12.3	39.3
Rhode Island	12,652	12.8	42.5
South Carolina	51,117	13.8	62.9
South Dakota	10,473	14.3	39.5
Tennessee	73,754	13.9	66.1
Texas	330,406	17.3	73.5
Utah	42,087	21.0	42.8
Vermont	6,767	11.5	30.1
Virginia	92,354	13.8	45.5
Washington	77,945	14.1	45.0
West Virginia	20,750	11.4	50.3
Wisconsin	67,106	13.0	36.8
Wyoming	6,286	13.1	44.0
Puerto Rico	63,141	16.7	74.8
Virgin Islands	1,905	16.8	54.9
Guam	4,259	29.4	116.8

1. Excludes data for Puerto Rico, Virgin Islands, and Guam. NOTE: Data by place of residence. Rates are per 1,000 population. *Source:* Department of Health and Human Services, National Center for Health Statistics; Web: www.dhhs.gov.

Selected Characteristics of Births, by Race of Mother, 1996

Characteristic	All races	White	Black	American Indian[1]	Asian or Pacific Islander
Percentage of mothers who:					
Had prenatal care beginning in the first trimester	81.9	84.0	71.4	67.7	81.2
Had late or no prenatal care	4.0	3.3	7.3	8.6	3.9
Were tobacco users[2]	13.6	14.7	10.2	21.3	3.3
Were alcohol users[3]	1.4	1.3	2.0	4.0	0.4
Gained less than 16 lbs[4]	11.1	10.0	16.8	15.1	9.2
Had Caesarean births	20.7	20.6	21.7	18.1	18.6
Median weight gain[4]	30.4	30.6	29.1	30.1	30.0
Percentage of infants who:					
Were born prior to 37 full weeks	11.0	9.8	17.4	11.9	10.0
Weighed less than 1,500 grams (3 lb 4 oz.)	1.4	1.1	3.0	1.2	1.0
Weighed less than 2,500 grams (5 lb 8 oz.)	7.4	6.3	13.0	6.5	7.1
Weighed 4,000 grams (8 lb 4 oz.) or more	10.2	11.4	5.4	12.3	6.0
Had five-minute Apgar scores of less than 7[5]	1.4	1.2	2.5	1.4	1.0

1. Includes births to Aleuts and Eskimos. 2. Excludes data for Calif., Ind., N.Y. (but includes N.Y.C.), and S.D., which did not report tobacco use on birth certificate. 3. Excludes data for Calif. and S.D., which did not report alcohol use on birth certificate. 4. Excludes data for Calif., which did not report weight gain on birth certificate. 5. Excludes data for Calif. and Tex., which did not report Apgar scores on birth certificate. Apgar scores are derived from evaluations of five major signs at one minute and five minutes after birth. Each sign is given a score of 0–2 for a total of ten possible points; scores of 7–10 are considered normal, 4–7 may require resuscitative measures, and 0–3 require immediate resuscitation. The signs and scores (0-1-2) are as follows: Activity or muscle tone (absent—arms and legs flexed—active movement); Pulse (absent—below 100 bpm—above 100 bpm); Grimace or reflex irritability (no response—grimace—sneeze, cough, pulls away); Appearance or skin color (blue-gray, pale all over—normal, except for extremities—normal over entire body); Respiration (absent—slow, irregular—good, crying). NOTE: Data for Hispanic origin not available. *Source:* U.S. Department of Health and Human Services; Web: www.dhhs.gov.

Contraceptive Use by Women, 15 to 44 Years Old, 1995

Contraceptive status and method	All women	Age: 15–24 years	Age: 25–34 years	Age: 35–44 years	Marital status: Never married	Marital status: Currently married	Marital status: Formerly married
All women (in thousands)	**60,201**	**18,002**	**20,758**	**21,440**	**22,679**	**29,673**	**7,849**
Percent distribution							
Sterile[1]	29.7	2.6	25.0	57.0	6.9	43.2	45.1
Surgically sterile	27.9	1.8	23.6	54.0	5.7	41.1	42.5
Nonsurgically sterile[2]	1.7	0.7	1.3	2.8	1.1	2.0	2.2
Pill	17.3	23.1	23.7	6.3	20.4	15.6	14.6
IUD	0.5	0.1	0.6	0.8	0.3	0.7	0.4
Diaphragm	1.2	0.2	1.2	2.0	0.5	1.8	0.9
Condom	13.1	13.9	15.0	10.7	13.9	13.3	10.1
Periodic abstinence	1.5	0.5	1.8	2.0	0.6	2.3	0.7
Withdrawal	2.0	1.6	2.3	1.9	1.5	2.3	1.8
Other methods[3]	3.9	5.6	4.2	2.1	4.6	3.3	3.9

1. Total sterile includes male sterile for unknown reasons. 2. Persons sterile from illness, accident, or congenital conditions. 3. Includes implants, injectables, morning-after-pill, suppository, Today(TM) sponge, and less frequently used methods. *Source:* U.S. National Center for Health Statistics. From *Statistical Abstract of the United States 1997.*

Abortion Statistics, 1972–1995

	1972	1980	1985	1990	1995
Reported no. legal abortions	586,760	1,297,606	1,328,570	1,429,577	1,210,883
Abortion ratio[1]	180	359	354	345	311
Abortion rate[2]	13	25	24	24	20
	Percentage distribution				
Age group (yrs)					
≤19	32.6%	29.2%	26.3%	22.4%	20.1%
20–24	32.5	35.5	34.7	33.2	32.5
≥25	34.9	35.3	39.0	44.4	47.4
Marital status					
Married	29.7	23.1	19.3	21.7	20.3
Unmarried	70.3	76.9	80.7	78.3	79.7

1. Number of legal induced abortions per 1,000 live births. 2. Number of legal induced abortions per 1,000 women aged 15–44 years. *Source:* U.S. Department of Health and Human Services, *Morbidity and Mortality Weekly Report,* vol. 46, no. 48.

Mortality

U.S. Annual Death Rates

Year	Rate	Year	Rate	Year	Rate
1900	17.2	1948	9.9	1973	9.3
1905	15.9	1949	9.7	1974	9.1
1910	14.7	1950	9.6	1975	8.8
1915	13.2	1951	9.7	1976	8.8
1920	13.0	1952	9.6	1977	8.6
1925	11.7	1953	9.6	1978	8.7
1930	11.3	1954	9.2	1979	8.5
1931	11.1	1955	9.3	1980	8.7
1932	10.9	1956	9.4	1982	8.5
1933	10.7	1957	9.6	1983	8.6
1934	11.1	1958	9.5	1984	8.6
1935	10.9	1959	9.4	1985	8.7
1936	11.6	1960	9.5	1986	8.7
1937	11.3	1962	9.5	1987	8.7
1938	10.6	1963	9.6	1988	8.8
1939	10.6	1964	9.4	1989	8.7
1940	10.8	1965	9.4	1990	8.6
1941	10.5	1966	9.5	1991	8.5
1942	10.3	1967	9.4	1992	8.5
1943	10.9	1968	9.7	1993	8.8
1944	10.6	1969	9.5	1994	8.8
1945	10.6	1970[1]	9.5	1995	8.8
1946	10.0	1971	9.3	1996	8.8
1947	10.1	1972	9.4	1997	8.6

1. First year for which deaths of nonresidents are excluded. 2. Provisional. NOTE: Includes only deaths occurring within the registration states. Beginning with 1933, area includes entire U.S.; with 1959 includes Alaska, and with 1960 includes Hawaii. Excludes fetal deaths. Rates per 1,000 population residing in area, as of April 1 for 1940, 1950, 1960, 1970, and 1980, and estimated as of July 1 for all other years. *Sources:* Department of Health and Human Services, National Center for Health Statistics; Web: www.dhhs.gov.

15 Leading Causes of Death in the U.S., 1996

Rank[1]	Causes of death	Number	Death rate	Age-adjusted death rate 1996	1995	Percent change
	All causes	2,322,421	875.4	494.1	503.9	–1.9%
1	Diseases of heart	733,834	276.6	134.6	138.3	–2.7
2	Malignant neoplasms, including neoplasms of lymphatic and hematopoietic tissues	544,278	205.2	129.1	129.9	–0.6
3	Cerebrovascular diseases	160,431	60.5	26.5	26.7	–0.7
4	Chronic obstructive pulmonary diseases and allied conditions	106,146	40.0	21.0	20.8	1.0
5	Accidents and adverse effects	93,874	35.4	30.1	30.5	–1.3
	Motor vehicle accidents	43,449	16.4	16.2	16.3	–0.6
	All other accidents and adverse effects	50,425	19.0	13.9	14.2	–2.1
6	Pneumonia and influenza	82,579	31.1	12.6	12.9	–2.3
7	Diabetes mellitus	61,559	23.2	13.6	13.3	2.3
8	Human immunodeficiency virus infection	32,655	12.3	11.6	15.6	–25.6
9	Suicide	30,862	11.6	10.8	11.2	–3.6
10	Chronic liver disease and cirrhosis	25,135	9.5	7.5	7.6	–1.3
11	Nephritis, nephrotic syndrome, and nephrosis	24,392	9.2	4.3	4.3	—
12	Septicemia	21,395	8.1	4.1	4.1	—
13	Alzheimer's disease	21,166	8.0	2.7	2.7	—
14	Homicide and legal intervention	20,738	7.8	8.4	9.4	–10.6
15	Atherosclerosis	16,803	6.3	2.2	2.3	–4.3
	All other causes	346,574	130.6	n.a.	n.a.	n.a.

1. Rank based on number of deaths. n.a. = data not available. *Source:* U.S. National Center for Health Statistics, *Monthly Vital Statistics Report,* vol. 46, no. 1.

Expectation of Life by Sex, 1850–1995

Calendar period	Age 0	10	20	30	40	50	60	70	80
White males									
1850[1]	38.3	48.0	40.1	34.0	27.9	21.6	15.6	10.2	5.9
1890[1]	42.50	48.45	40.66	34.05	27.37	20.72	14.73	9.35	5.40
1900–1902[2]	48.23	50.59	42.19	34.88	27.74	20.76	14.35	9.03	5.10
1909–1911[2]	50.23	51.32	42.71	34.87	27.43	20.39	13.98	8.83	5.09
1919–1921[3]	56.34	54.15	45.60	37.65	29.86	22.22	15.25	9.51	5.47
1929–1931	59.12	54.96	46.02	37.54	29.22	21.51	14.72	9.20	5.26
1939–1941	62.81	57.03	47.76	38.80	30.03	21.96	15.05	9.42	5.38
1949–1951	66.31	58.98	49.52	40.29	31.17	22.83	15.76	10.07	5.88
1959–1961[5]	67.55	59.78	50.25	40.98	31.73	23.22	16.01	10.29	5.89
1969–1971[6]	67.94	59.69	50.22	41.07	31.87	23.34	16.07	10.38	6.18
1979–1981	70.82	61.98	52.45	43.31	34.04	25.26	17.56	11.35	6.76
1990	72.7	63.5	54.0	44.7	35.6	26.7	18.7	12.1	7.1
1993	73.1	63.8	54.2	44.9	35.9	27.0	18.9	12.3	7.1
1995	73.4	64.1	54.5	45.2	36.1	27.3	19.3	12.5	7.2
White females									
1850[1]	40.5	47.2	40.2	35.4	29.8	23.5	17.0	11.3	6.4
1890[1]	44.46	49.62	42.03	35.36	28.76	22.09	15.70	10.15	5.75
1900–1902[2]	51.08	52.15	43.77	36.42	29.17	21.89	15.23	9.59	5.50
1909–1911[2]	53.62	53.57	44.88	36.96	29.26	21.74	14.92	9.38	5.35
1919–1921[3]	58.53	55.17	46.46	38.72	30.94	23.12	15.93	9.94	5.70
1929–1931	62.67	57.65	48.52	39.99	31.52	23.41	16.05	9.98	5.63
1939–1941	67.29	60.85	51.38	42.21	33.25	24.72	17.00	10.50	5.88
1949–1951	72.03	64.26	54.56	45.00	35.64	26.76	18.64	11.68	6.59
1959–1961[5]	74.19	66.05	56.29	46.63	37.13	28.08	19.69	12.38	6.67
1969–1971[6]	75.49	66.97	57.24	47.60	38.12	29.11	20.79	13.37	7.59
1979–1981	78.22	69.21	59.44	49.76	40.16	30.96	22.45	14.89	8.65
1990	79.4	70.1	60.3	50.6	41.0	31.6	23.0	15.4	9.0
1993	79.5	70.1	60.3	50.6	41.0	31.7	23.0	15.3	8.9
1995	79.6	70.2	60.4	50.6	41.0	31.7	23.0	15.4	8.9
All other males[4]									
1900–1902[2]	32.54	41.90	35.11	29.25	23.12	17.34	12.62	8.33	5.12
1909–1911[2]	34.05	40.65	33.46	27.33	21.57	16.21	11.67	8.00	5.53
1919–1921[3]	47.14	45.99	38.36	32.51	26.53	20.47	14.74	9.58	5.83
1929–1931	47.55	44.27	35.95	29.45	23.36	17.92	13.15	8.78	5.42
1939–1941	52.33	48.54	39.74	32.25	25.23	19.18	14.38	10.06	6.46
1949–1951	58.91	52.96	43.73	35.31	27.29	20.25	14.91	10.74	7.07
1959–1961[5]	61.48	55.19	45.78	37.05	28.72	21.28	15.29	10.81	6.87
1969–1971[6]	60.98	53.67	44.37	36.20	28.29	21.24	15.35	10.68	7.57
1979–1981	65.63	57.40	47.87	39.13	30.64	22.92	16.54	11.36	7.22
1990	67.0	58.5	49.0	40.3	31.9	23.9	17.0	11.4	7.0
1993	67.3	58.6	49.2	40.6	32.2	24.3	17.3	11.5	6.9
1995	67.9	59.1	49.6	40.8	32.4	24.6	17.6	11.7	7.0
All other females[4]									
1900–1902[2]	35.04	43.02	36.89	30.70	24.37	18.67	13.60	9.62	6.48
1909–1911[2]	37.67	42.84	36.14	29.61	23.34	17.65	12.78	9.22	6.05
1919–1921[3]	46.92	44.54	37.15	31.48	25.60	19.76	14.69	10.25	6.58
1929–1931	49.51	45.33	37.22	30.67	24.30	18.60	14.22	10.38	6.90
1939–1941	55.51	50.83	42.14	34.52	27.31	21.04	16.14	11.81	8.00
1949–1951	62.70	56.17	46.77	38.02	29.82	22.67	16.95	12.29	8.15
1959–1961[5]	66.47	59.72	50.07	40.83	32.16	24.31	17.83	12.46	7.66
1969–1971[6]	69.05	61.49	51.85	42.61	33.87	25.97	19.02	13.30	9.01
1979–1981	74.00	65.64	55.88	46.39	37.16	28.59	20.49	14.44	9.17
1990	75.2	66.6	56.8	47.3	38.1	29.2	21.3	14.5	8.8
1993	75.5	66.7	56.9	47.4	38.2	29.5	21.4	14.5	8.7
1995	75.7	66.8	57.0	47.5	38.3	29.6	21.5	14.5	8.7

1. Massachusetts only; white and nonwhite combined, the latter being about 1% of the total. 2. Original Death Registration States. 3. Death Registration States of 1920. 4. Data for periods 1900–1902 to 1929–1931 relate to blacks only. 5. Alaska and Hawaii included beginning in 1959. 6. Deaths of nonresidents of the United States excluded starting in 1970. *Sources:* Department of Health and Human Services, National Center for Health Statistics; Web: www.dhhs.gov.

Life Expectancy at Birth by Race and Sex, 1940–1996

	All races			White			Black		
Year	Both sexes	Male	Female	Both sexes	Male	Female	Both sexes	Male	Female
1996	76.1	73.0	79.0	76.8	73.8	79.6	70.3	66.1	74.2
1995	75.8	72.5	78.9	76.5	73.4	79.6	69.6	65.2	73.9
1994	75.7	72.4	79.0	76.5	73.3	79.6	69.5	64.9	73.9
1993	75.5	72.2	78.8	76.3	73.1	79.5	69.2	64.6	73.7
1992	75.8	72.3	79.1	76.5	73.2	79.8	69.6	65.0	73.9
1991	75.5	72.0	78.9	76.3	72.9	79.6	69.3	64.6	73.8
1990	75.4	71.8	78.8	76.1	72.7	79.4	69.1	64.5	73.6
1989	75.1	71.7	78.5	75.9	72.5	79.2	68.8	64.3	73.3
1988	74.9	71.4	78.3	75.6	72.2	78.9	68.9	64.4	73.2
1987	74.9	71.4	78.3	75.6	72.1	78.9	69.1	64.7	73.4
1986	74.7	71.2	78.2	75.4	71.9	78.8	69.1	64.8	73.4
1985	74.7	71.1	78.2	75.3	71.8	78.7	69.3	65.0	73.4
1984	74.7	71.1	78.2	75.3	71.8	78.7	69.5	65.3	73.6
1983	74.6	71.0	78.1	75.2	71.6	78.7	69.4	65.2	73.5
1982	74.5	70.8	78.1	75.1	71.5	78.7	69.4	65.1	73.6
1981	74.1	70.4	77.8	74.8	71.1	78.4	68.9	64.5	73.2
1980	73.7	70.0	77.4	74.4	70.7	78.1	68.1	63.8	72.5
1979	73.9	70.0	77.8	74.6	70.8	78.4	68.5	64.0	72.9
1978	73.5	69.6	77.3	74.1	70.4	78.0	68.1	63.7	72.4
1977	73.3	69.5	77.2	74.0	70.2	77.9	67.7	63.4	72.0
1976	72.9	69.1	76.8	73.6	69.9	77.5	67.2	62.9	71.6
1975	72.6	68.8	76.6	73.4	69.5	77.3	66.8	62.4	71.3
1974	72.0	68.2	75.9	72.8	69.0	76.7	66.0	61.7	70.3
1973	71.4	67.6	75.3	72.2	68.5	76.1	65.0	60.9	69.3
1972[1]	71.2	67.4	75.1	72.0	68.3	75.9	64.7	60.4	69.1
1971	71.1	67.4	75.0	72.0	68.3	75.8	64.6	60.5	68.9
1970	70.8	67.1	74.7	71.7	68.0	75.6	64.1	60.0	68.3
1960	69.7	66.6	73.1	70.6	67.4	74.1	—	—	—
1950	68.2	65.6	71.1	69.1	66.5	72.2	—	—	—
1940	62.9	60.8	65.2	64.2	62.1	66.6	—	—	—

(—) Data not available. 1. Deaths based on a 50-percent sample. *Source:* U.S. National Center for Health Statistics, *Monthly Vital Statistics Report*; Web: www.dhhs.gov.

Accidental Deaths by Principal Types

Year	Motor vehicle	Falls	Drowning[1]	Fire, burns[2]	Suffocation by ingested object	Firearms	Poison (solid, liquid)	Poison by gas
1987	48,700	11,300	5,300	4,800	3,200	1,400	4,400	1,000
1988	49,000	12,000	5,000	5,000	3,600	1,400	5,300	1,000
1989	46,900	12,400	4,600	4,400	3,900	1,600	5,600	900
1990	46,300	12,400	5,200	4,300	3,200	1,400	5,700	800
1991	43,500	12,200	4,600	4,200	2,900	1,400	5,600	800
1992	40,300	12,400	4,300	4,000	2,700	1,400	5,200	700
1993	42,000	13,500	4,800	4,000	2,900	1,600	6,500	700
1994	43,000	13,300	4,000	4,200	3,000	1,500	8,000	700
1995	43,900	12,600	4,500	4,100	2,800	1,400	10,000	600
1996	43,300	14,100	3,900	3,200	3,000	1,400	9,800	600

1. Includes drowning in water transport accidents. 2. Includes burns by fire and deaths resulting from conflagration regardless of nature of injury. NOTE: Figures are latest available. *Source:* National Safety Council.

Improper Driving as Factor in Accidents

	Fatal accidents		Injury accidents		All accidents	
Kind of improper driving	1995	1994	1995	1994	1995	1994
Improper driving	**68.1%**	**63.7**	**73.5%**	**65.7**	**75.5%**	**67.2**
Speed too fast or unsafe	19.8	19.5	13.9	11.2	14.0	11.9
Right of way	15.2	15.1	25.5	24.1	22.9	21.3
Failed to yield	*10.2*	*9.1*	*18.1*	*15.0*	*17.0*	*14.5*
Passed stop sign	*2.2*	*2.6*	*2.4*	*3.1*	*1.9*	*2.5*
Disregarded signal	*3.0*	*3.4*	*5.0*	*6.0*	*4.0*	*4.3*
Drove left of center	9.1	9.4	2.4	2.5	2.2	2.3
Improper overtaking	1.5	1.6	1.3	1.2	1.5	1.4

Kind of improper driving	Fatal accidents 1995	Fatal accidents 1994	Injury accidents 1995	Injury accidents 1994	All accidents 1995	All accidents 1994
Made improper turn	2.3%	2.6%	2.8%	2.9%	4.2%	4.1%
Followed too closely	0.5	0.5	7.0	5.9	7.2	5.6
Other improper driving	19.7	15.0	20.7	17.9	23.6	20.6
No improper driving stated	**31.9**	**36.3**	**26.5**	**34.3**	**24.5**	**32.8**
Total	**100.0%**	**100.0%**	**100.0%**	**100.0%**	**100.0%**	**100.0%**

NOTE: Figures are latest available. *Source:* Motor-vehicle reports from 11 (1993) and 17 (1994) state traffic authorities to National Safety Council.

Deaths by Firearms, 1979–1995

Year	All races: Number of deaths	All races: Death rate[1]	White: Number of deaths	White: Death rate[1]	Black: Number of deaths	Black: Death rate[1]
1979	33,019	14.7	24,234	12.5	8,304	31.6
1980	33,780	14.9	24,849	12.8	8,505	31.9
1981	34,050	14.8	25,237	12.8	8,324	30.7
1982	32,957	14.2	25,071	12.7	7,415	27.0
1983	31,099	13.3	24,038	12.1	6,589	23.6
1984	31,331	13.3	24,419	12.2	6,449	22.9
1985	31,566	13.3	24,507	12.1	6,565	23.0
1986	33,373	13.9	25,339	12.5	7,494	25.9
1987	32,895	13.6	24,789	12.1	7,586	25.9
1988	33,989	13.9	24,892	12.1	8,475	28.5
1989	34,776	14.1	25,023	12.1	9,077	30.1
1990	37,155	14.9	26,299	12.6	10,175	33.4
1991	38,317	15.2	26,455	12.5	11,025	35.4
1992	37,776	14.8	26,120	12.3	10,906	34.5
1993	39,595	15.4	26,948	12.5	11,763	36.6
1994	38,505	14.8	26,403	12.2	11,223	34.4
1995	35,957	13.7	25,438	11.7	9,643	29.1

1. On an annual basis, per 100,000 population in specified group. *Source:* Centers for Disease Control and Prevention, *Monthly Vital Statistics Report,* vol. 45, no. 11(s)2.

Number of Deaths and Death Rates from Selected Types of Cancer, 1996

(rates per 100,000 population)

Cause of death	1996 Number	1996 Rate	1995 Number	1995 Rate
Cancer (malignant neoplasms)[1]	544,278	205.2	538,455	204.9
Esophagus	11,328	4.3	10,969	4.2
Stomach	13,448	5.1	13,645	5.2
Colon, rectum, rectosigmoid junction, and anus	57,058	21.5	57,333	21.8
Pancreas	27,596	10.4	26,766	10.2
Trachea, bronchus, and lung	153,331	57.8	151,200	57.5
Skin	7,348	2.8	6,907	2.6
Cervix	4,537	1.7	4,503	1.7
Uterus	6,277	2.4	6,237	2.4
Ovary	13,271	5.0	13,342	5.1
Prostate	34,405	13.0	34,475	13.1
Bladder	11,553	4.4	11,084	4.2
Kidney and other and unspecified urinary organs	11,598	4.4	11,555	4.4
Brain and other and unspecified parts of nervous system	12,334	4.6	12,063	4.6
Hodgkin's disease	1,420	0.5	1,431	0.5
Malignant lymphoma other than Hodgkin's disease	23,055	8.7	22,522	8.6

1. Includes figures from all types of cancer, including those not shown. *Source:* U.S. National Center for Health Statistics, *Monthly Vital Statistics Report,* vol. 46, no. 1; Web: www.dhhs.gov.

Cumulative AIDS Deaths in the United States through 1997[1]

Race/ethnicity and age at death[2]	Males, cumulative total	Females, cumulative total	Cumulative total
White, not Hispanic			
Under 15	532	398	930
15–24	2,437	438	2,875
25–34	51,591	4,162	55,753
35–44	73,682	4,191	77,873
45–54	32,790	1,603	34,393
55 or older	13,801	1,537	15,338
All ages	175,018	12,354	187,372
Black, not Hispanic			
Under 15	1,314	1,289	2,603
15–24	2,247	1,213	3,460
25–34	30,321	10,014	40,335
35–44	43,038	11,942	54,980
45–54	17,677	3,809	21,486
55 or older	7,490	1,717	9,207
All ages	102,198	30,023	132,221
Hispanic			
Under 15	584	530	1,114
15–24	1,254	437	1,691
25–34	18,577	3,986	22,563
35–44	22,995	4,085	27,080
45–54	8,992	1,383	10,375
55 or older	3,650	665	4,315
All ages	56,119	11,098	67,217
Asian/Pacific Islander			
Under 15	18	15	33
15–24	32	5	37
25–34	651	68	719
35–44	1,010	88	1,098
45–54	480	53	533
55 or older	214	39	253
All ages	2,406	270	2,676
American Indian/ Alaska Native			
Under 15	11	8	19
15–24	25	3	28
25–34	318	52	370
35–44	322	45	367
45–54	97	16	113
55 or older	34	7	41
All ages	811	131	942
All racial/ethnic groups			
Under 15	2,461	2,242	4,703
15–24	6,000	2,098	8,089
25–34	101,520	18,286	119,806
35–44	141,155	20,359	161,514
45–54	60,076	6,867	66,943
55 or older	25,211	3,967	29,178
All ages	336,795	53,897	390,692

1. Data for deaths occurring in 1997 are incomplete and not tabulated separately, but are included in the cumulative totals. Tabulations for 1995 and 1996 may increase as additional deaths are reported to CDC. 2. Data tabulated under "all ages" include 495 persons whose age at death is unknown. Data tabulated under "all racial/ethnic groups" include 271 persons whose race/ethnicity is unknown. *Source:* Centers for Disease Control, *HIV/AIDS Surveillance Report,* vol. 8, no. 2.

Miscellaneous

New Cases of Cancer and Survival Rates

	Estimated new cases,[1] 1997 (thousands)			Five-year relative survival rate (percent)							
				White				Black			
Site	Total	Male	Female	1974–78	1979–83	1984–88	1989–92	1974–78	1979–83	1984–88	1989–92
All Sites[2]	**1,382**	**786**	**597**	**52.6%**	**53.8%**	**57.9%**	**62.7%**	**40.4%**	**40.6%**	**42.5%**	**46.7%**
Lung	178	98	80	13.7	14.4	14.3	15.1	11.2	12.5	11.6	10.7
Breast[3]	182	1	180	76.1	77.7	83.5	86.9	63.6	65.1	67.9	71.2
Colon and rectum	131	66	65	52.5	56.3	62.0	63.8	45.7	48.7	51.5	53.2
Prostate	335	335	n.a.	71.0	76.2	83.6	94.6	62.8	63.4	68.7	79.6
Bladder	55	40	15	74.8	78.6	81.5	83.0	50.5	58.7	60.1	63.5
Corpus uteri	35	n.a.	35	88.7	84.3	85.9	87.6	60.8	54.3	57.7	56.2
Non-Hodgkin's lymphoma[4]	54	30	23	47.8	52.0	54.1	52.3	48.2	51.1	47.1	42.0
Oral cavity and pharynx	31	21	10	55.2	55.4	56.4	55.5	36.6	32.9	35.0	32.9
Leukemia[4]	28	16	12	36.3	38.5	42.5	43.1	31.6	31.5	34.5	29.1
Melanoma of skin	40	23	17	81.0	83.1	87.1	87.6	57.9	64.2	66.0	69.5
Pancreas	28	13	14	1.9	2.7	2.7	4.1	1.8	4.3	4.8	3.5
Kidney	29	17	12	54.9	56.1	61.6	64.3	53.4	58.4	57.4	59.3
Stomach	22	14	8	15.6	16.8	18.6	19.3	16.3	17.5	19.7	21.6
Ovary	27	n.a.	27	37.6	39.8	41.7	51.0	41.6	39.2	40.8	45.0
Cervix uteri[5]	15	n.a.	15	69.9	68.8	71.5	71.2	63.6	61.4	56.5	60.6

n.a. = not applicable 1. Estimates provided by American Cancer Society are based on rates from the National Cancer Institute's SEER program. 2. Includes other sites not shown separately. 3. Survival rates for female only. 4. All types combined. 5. Invasive cancer only. *Note:* The five-year relative survival rate, which is derived by adjusting the observed survival rate for expected mortality, represents the likelihood that a person will not die from causes directly related to their cancer within five years. *Source:* U.S. National Institutes of Health, National Cancer Institute, *Cancer Statistics Review*, annual.

AIDS Cases Reported, by Patient Characteristic

Characteristic	1981–1996 total	1990	1992	1994	1996
Total	**562,549**	**41,595**	**45,789**	**77,268**	**66,886**
Age:					
Under 5 years old	5,743	585	610	750	485
5 to 12 years old	1,521	139	139	220	175
13 to 19 years old	2,633	173	148	399	381
20 to 29 years old	99,137	8,077	7,888	12,636	9,778
30 to 39 years old	255,260	18,815	20,615	35,006	29,990
40 to 49 years old	140,718	9,651	11,540	20,359	18,891
50 to 59 years old	41,761	2,926	3,405	5,848	5,321
Over 60 years old	15,776	1,229	1,444	2,049	1,865
Sex:					
Male	477,518	36,726	39,457	63,447	53,293
Female	85,031	4,869	6,332	13,821	13,593
Race/Ethnic Group:					
Non-Hispanic White	268,746	22,302	22,446	32,808	26,324
Non-Hispanic Black	203,025	13,205	16,052	30,972	28,764
Hispanic	84,443	5,672	6,766	12,577	10,865
Other/unknown	6,335	416	525	911	933
Transmission category:					
Males, 13 years and over	473,770	36,335	39,082	62,972	52,958
Men who have sex with men	284,410	23,843	24,482	35,296	26,937
Injecting drug use	99,698	6,956	8,040	15,145	11,491
Men who have sex with men and injecting drug use	35,825	2,793	3,144	4,328	2,874
Hemophilia/coagulation disorder	4,220	332	324	478	297
Heterosexual contact[1]	9,279	260	611	1,854	2,168
Heterosexual contact with injecting drug user	6,121	460	627	919	792
Transfusion[2]	4,435	452	347	384	275
Undetermined[3]	29,782	1,239	1,507	4,568	8,124
Females, 13 years and over	81,515	4,536	5,958	13,325	13,268
Injecting drug use	37,027	2,325	2,966	5,853	4,534
Hemophilia/coagulation disorder	170	15	10	27	16
Heterosexual contact[1]	16,539	503	963	3,381	3,401
Heterosexual contact with injecting drug user	13,916	1,037	1,320	2,014	1,744
Transfusion[2]	3,234	336	258	316	263
Undetermined[3]	10,629	320	441	1,734	3,310

1. Includes persons who have had heterosexual contact with a person with human immunodeficiency virus (HIV) infection or at risk of HIV infection. 2. Receipt of blood transfusion, blood components, or tissue. 3. Includes persons for whom risk information is incomplete (because of death, refusal to be interviewed, or loss to follow-up), persons still under investigation, men reported only to have had heterosexual contact with prostitutes, and interviewed persons for whom no specific risk is identified. *Source:* U.S. Centers for Disease Control and Prevention, HIV/AIDS Surveillance Reports. From *Statistical Abstract of the United States 1997.*

Percent Persons Not Covered by Health Insurance, by State, 1996

State	Percent	State	Percent	State	Percent
Alabama	12.9%	Kentucky	15.4%	North Dakota	9.8%
Alaska	13.5	Louisiana	20.9	Ohio	11.5
Arizona	24.1	Maine	12.1	Oklahoma	17.0
Arkansas	21.7	Maryland	11.4	Oregon	15.3
California	20.1	Massachusetts	12.4	Pennsylvania	9.5
Colorado	16.6	Michigan	8.9	Rhode Island	9.9
Connecticut	11.0	Minnesota	10.2	South Carolina	17.1
Delaware	13.4	Mississippi	18.5	South Dakota	9.5
D.C.	14.8	Missouri	13.2	Tennessee	15.2
Florida	18.9	Montana	13.6	Texas	24.3
Georgia	17.8	Nebraska	11.4	Utah	12.0
Hawaii	8.6	Nevada	15.6	Vermont	11.1
Idaho	16.5	New Hampshire	9.5	Virginia	12.5
Illinois	11.3	New Jersey	16.7	Washington	13.5
Indiana	10.6	New Mexico	22.3	West Virginia	14.9
Iowa	11.6	New York	17.0	Wisconsin	8.4
Kansas	11.4	North Carolina	16.0	Wyoming	13.5

Note: These estimates should not be used to rank the states. Results from different samplings could easily show different estimates and rankings because of small sampling sizes. For example, the high noncoverage for Texas is not statistically different from that of New Mexico. *Source:* U.S. Bureau of the Census, *March 1997 Current Population Survey.*

Mental Health: Lifetime Prevalence of Psychiatric Disorders, 1990–92

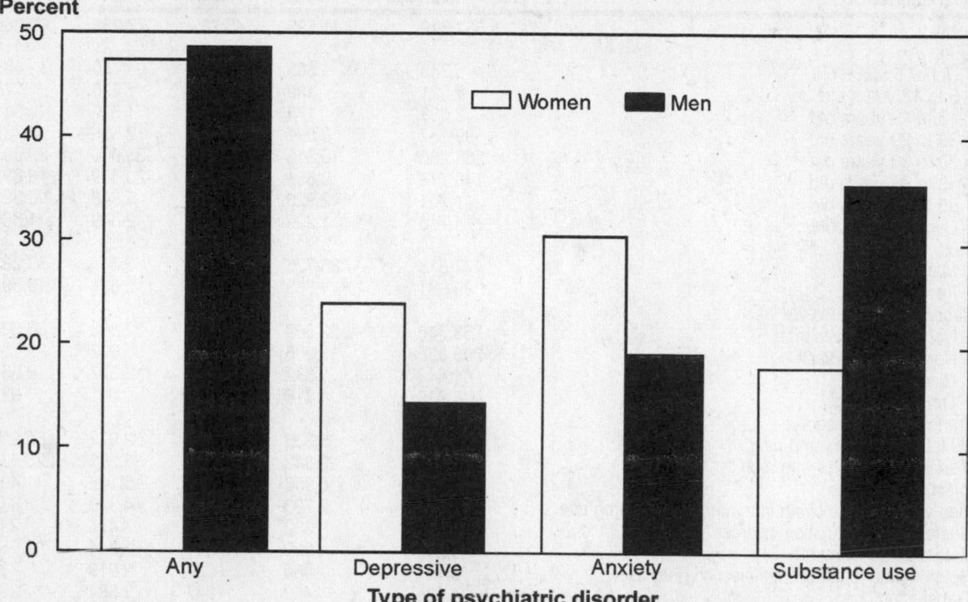

NOTES: Persons 15–54 years are represented. The presence of a psychiatric disorder did not have to be formally diagnosed for persons to be included as having had a disorder. The category "Any Disorder" includes disorders not included in the specific types shown. *Source:* University of Michigan, Institute for Social Research/Survey Research Center, National Comorbidity Survey.

Self-Perception of Being Overweight

Age	Percent of overweight people who think they are overweight					
	Total[1]		Non-Hispanic white		Non-Hispanic black	
	Male	Female	Male	Female	Male	Female
Total	**83.4%**	**91.8%**	**86.2%**	**94.2%**	**71.9%**	**87.4%**
20 to 39 years old	84.5	94.5	88.8	97.4	73.4	90.9
40 to 59 years old	89.0	95.4	92.1	98.0	74.0	93.4
60 years old and over	73.0	83.6	74.6	86.5	63.7	71.7

Age	Percent of population not overweight who think they are overweight					
	Total[1]		Non-Hispanic white		Non-Hispanic black	
	Male	Female	Male	Female	Male	Female
Total	**25.3%**	**47.9%**	**28.1%**	**50.2%**	**13.1%**	**37.5%**
20 to 39 years old	24.8	49.5	28.1	51.4	10.1	41.1
40 to 59 years old	27.6	56.5	30.7	59.6	19.6	46.5
60 years old and over	23.2	35.3	24.7	38.6	12.6	13.5

1. Includes other races and persons of Hispanic origin not shown separately. *Source:* Federation of American Societies for Experimental Biology, Life Sciences Research Office, *Third Report on Nutrition Monitoring in the United States, 1995.* From *Statistical Abstract of the United States 1997.*

Persons Below Poverty Level

Race and Hispanic Origin, Age, and Region, 1996

	Number	Percent		Number	Percent
Total[1]	36,529	13.7%	45 to 54 years	2,516	7.6%
White	24,650	11.2	55 to 59 years	1,086	9.4
Black	9,694	28.4	60 to 64 years	1,134	11.5
Asian and Pacific Islander	1,454	14.5	65 years and over	3,428	10.8
Hispanic origin[2]	8,697	29.4	Northeast	6,558	12.7
Under 18 years	14,463	20.5	Midwest	6,654	10.7
18 to 24 years	4,466	17.9	South	14,098	15.1
25 to 34 years	5,093	12.7	West	9,219	15.4
35 to 44 years	4,343	9.9			

1. Includes races not shown separately. 2. Persons of Hispanic origin may be of any race. *Source:* "Income, Poverty, and Valuation of Noncash Benefits," *Current Population Reports,* U.S. Bureau of the Census; Web: www.census.gov.

Weighted Average Poverty Thresholds for Families of Specified Size, 1960–1996

Calendar year	Individual	2 persons	Families of 3 persons or more: 3 persons	4 persons	5 persons	6 persons	7 persons
1960	$1,490	$ 1,924	$ 2,359	$ 3,022	$ 3,560	$ 4,002	$ 4,921
1965	1,582	2,048	2,514	3,223	3,797	4,264	5,248
1970	1,954	2,525	3,099	3,968	4,680	5,260	6,468
1975	2,724	3,506	4,293	5,500	6,499	7,316	9,022
1980	4,190	5,363	6,565	8,414	9,966	11,269	12,761
1985	5,469	6,998	8,573	10,989	13,007	14,696	16,656
1990	6,652	8,509	10,419	13,359	15,792	17,839	20,241
1995	7,763	9,933	12,158	15,569	18,408	20,804	23,552
1997	8,178	10,468	12,803	16,404	19,387	21,880	24,825

Source: U.S. Bureau of the Census; Web: www.census.gov.

State Unemployment Compensation

Average Weekly Benefit, 1997

State	Avg. wkly. benefit	State	Avg. wkly. benefit	State	Avg. wkly. benefit
United States	**$192.76**	Kentucky	$175.91	Ohio	$207.99
Alabama	144.67	Louisiana	132.61	Oklahoma	176.78
Alaska	175.76	Maine	151.75	Oregon	198.14
Arizona	146.52	Maryland	195.93	Pennsylvania	227.50
Arkansas	198.24	Massachusetts	262.85	Puerto Rico	94.25
California	151.85	Michigan	221.75	Rhode Island	223.63
Colorado	212.73	Minnesota	242.00	South Carolina	168.62
Connecticut	211.37	Mississippi	142.24	South Dakota	155.68
Delaware	193.70	Missouri	154.21	Tennessee	163.31
D.C.	233.48	Montana	166.09	Texas	195.87
Florida	191.94	Nebraska	162.81	Utah	193.08
Georgia	162.47	Nevada	203.88	Vermont	173.52
Hawaii	268.83	New Hampshire	165.26	Virgin Islands	165.96
Idaho	187.20	New Jersey	258.50	Virginia	179.20
Illinois	217.41	New Mexico	158.00	Washington	239.62
Indiana	185.90	New York	203.78	West Virginia	180.20
Iowa	205.03	North Carolina	198.27	Wisconsin	188.47
Kansas	204.41	North Dakota	176.11	Wyoming	181.80

Average weekly benefit for weeks of total unemployment. *Source:* Department of Labor, Employment and Training Admin.

Top 20 Charities in the U.S., 1997

1997 Rank	Charity	Private support	1996 rank
1.	Salvation Army (Alexandria, Va.)	$1,012,403,000	1
2.	American Red Cross (Washington)	479,928,282	2
3.	American Cancer Society (Atlanta)	426,695,000	4
4.	Emory University (Atlanta)	415,406,381	54
5.	Catholic Charities USA (Alexandria, Va.)	386,545,894	3
6.	Second Harvest (Chicago)	351,376,162	5
7.	YMCA of the USA (Chicago)	340,337,000	11
8.	Habitat for Humanity International (Americus, Ga.)	334,737,000	17
9.	Boys & Girls Clubs of America (Atlanta)	321,757,180	8
10.	Stanford University (Palo Alto, Calif.)	312,887,120	12
11.	Harvard University (Cambridge, Mass.)	309,360,000	7
12.	Fidelity Investments Charitable Gift Fund (Boston)	298,186,219	22
13.	American Heart Association (Dallas)	273,989,000	10
14.	YWCA of the USA (New York)	265,352,445	9
15.	Boy Scouts of America (Irving, Tex.)	233,230,000	14
16.	Gifts in Kind International (Alexandria, Va.)	223,871,836	24
17.	Shriners Hospitals for Children (Tampa, Fla.)	220,123,000	18
18.	Cornell University (Ithaca, N.Y.)	219,746,000	20
19.	Campus Crusade for Christ International (Orlando, Fla.)	212,794,000	23
20.	Nature Conservancy (Arlington, Va.)	203,886,056	15

Source: The Chronicle of Philanthropy, Oct. 30, 1997. Reprinted with permission.

Percent of Adult Population Doing Volunteer Work, 1995

Age, sex, race, and Hispanic origin	Percent of population volunteering	Average hours volunteered per week
Total	48.8%	4.2
18–24 years	38.4	2.8
25–34 years	50.8	4.3
35–44 years	55.0	4.3
45–54 years	55.3	4.5
55–64 years	47.9	4.8
65–74 years	44.7	4.1
75 years and over	33.7	4.4
Male	45.1	4.2
Female	52.2	4.2
White	51.9	4.2
Black	35.3	4.5
Hispanic[1]	40.4	4.3

Educational attainment and household income	Percent of population volunteering	Average hours volunteered per week
Elementary school	18.7%	(B)
Some high school	26.1	3.3
High-school graduate	43.1	4.0
Technical, trade, or business school	51.2	4.4
Some college	56.3	3.9
College graduate	70.7	4.8
Under $10,000	34.7	3.6
10,000–19,999	34.3	3.2
20,000–29,999	41.2	3.7
30,000–39,999	46.0	3.7
40,000–49,999	52.7	5.8
50,000–59,999	64.1	5.9
60,000–74,999	56.4	4.4
75,000–99,999	64.8	4.0
100,000 or more	69.4	4.4

Type of activity	Percent of population involved in activity
Arts, culture, humanities	6.2%
Education	17.5
Environment	7.1
Health	13.2
Human services	12.7
Informal	20.3
International, foreign	1.6

Type of activity	Percent of population involved in activity
Political organizations	3.8%
Private, community foundations	2.7
Public and societal benefit	6.7
Recreation—adults	7.3
Religion	25.8
Work-related organizations	7.9
Youth development	15.4

(B) = Base figure too small to meet statistical standards for reliability. 1. Hispanic persons may be of any race. NOTE: Covers persons 18 years and over. Volunteers are persons who worked in some way to help others for no monetary pay during the previous year. Based on a sample survey conducted during the spring of the following years and subject to sampling variability. *Source: Statistical Abstract of the United States 1997.*

Participation in Various Leisure Activities, 1992

	Adult population (mil.)	Attendance at: Movies	Sports events	Amuse-ment park	Participation in: Exercise program	Playing sports	Outdoor activities[1]	Home improvement/ repair	Gardening
Total	**185.8**	**59%**	**37%**	**50%**	**60%**	**39%**	**34%**	**48%**	**55%**
Sex: Male	89.0	60	44	51	61	50	39	53	46
Female	96.8	59	30	50	59	29	29	42	62
Race: White	158.8	60	38	51	61	40	37	50	57
Black	21.1	54	32	45	51	32	10	32	39
Other	5.9	62	20	46	51	38	28	31	42
Age: 18 to 24 years	24.1	82	51	68	67	59	43	33	31
25 to 34 years	42.4	70	47	68	67	52	41	47	51
35 to 44 years	39.8	68	43	58	62	44	42	58	57
45 to 54 years	27.7	58	35	44	62	34	36	57	64
55 to 64 years	21.2	40	23	30	56	21	21	53	63
65 to 74 years	18.3	34	20	29	50	18	21	42	63
75 to 96 years	12.3	19	7	14	34	7	5	20	55
Education: Grade school	14.3	16	9	24	24	10	11	24	44
Some high school	18.6	35	19	35	39	18	21	34	50
High-school graduate	69.4	54	33	51	55	34	31	47	53
Some college	39.2	21	45	59	71	49	42	53	55
College graduate	26.2	77	51	58	75	55	42	52	61
Graduate school	18.1	81	51	54	79	57	51	65	65

1. Camping, hiking, canoeing. *Source:* U.S. National Endowment for the Arts, *Arts Participation in America: 1982 to 1992.*

Household Pet Ownership, 1986

Item	Dog	Cat	Pet bird	Horse
Households owning companion pets[1] (millions)	31.20	27.00	4.60	1.50
Percent of all households	31.60%	27.30%	4.60%	1.50%
Average number owned	1.70	2.20	2.70	2.70
Total companion pet population[1] (millions)	52.90	59.10	12.60	4.00
Households obtaining veterinary care[2]	88.70%	72.90%	15.80%	66.30%
Average visits per household per year	2.60	1.90	0.20	2.30
Average annual costs per household	$ 186.80	$ 112.24	$10.95	$226.26
Total expenditures	$5,828.00	$3,030.00	$50.00	$339.00
Percent distribution of households owning pets				
Annual household income: Under $12,500	12.70%	13.90%	17.30%	9.50%
$12,500 to $24,999	19.10	19.70	20.90	20.30
$25,000 to $39,999	21.60	21.50	22.00	21.80
$40,000 to $59,999	21.50	21.20	17.50	23.10
$60,000 and over	25.20	23.70	22.30	25.40
Family size:[1] One person	13.20%	16.80%	12.70%	12.10%
Two persons	31.00	32.60	27.90	29.10
Three persons	21.40	20.60	20.40	22.00
Four or more persons	34.50	29.90	38.90	36.70

NOTE: Based on a sample survey of 80,000 households in 1996. 1. As of December. 2. During 1996. *Source:* American Veterinary Medical Association, Schaumburg, Ill., *U.S. Pet Ownership and Demographics Sourcebook, 1997.* Reprinted with permission.

The Big Bank Theory

Big, bigger, biggest: with a wave of mergers, big banks chart an aggressive course that may rewrite the way you save and invest

By JOSHUA COOPER RAMO TIME

The first half of 1998 was peppered with the kind of earthmoving financial deals that would have seemed impossible a decade ago. On the same day that the $60 billion BankAmerica-NationsBank deal was announced, Banc One announced plans to merge its $116 billion bank with the $115 billion First Chicago NBD Corp. All this came just a week after insurance and brokerage giant Travelers Group announced plans to tie the knot with Citicorp, the second-largest bank in the U.S.—a $76 billion marriage of two industry titans.

In just two decades we've gone from a world of simple mortgages and passbook savings to a universe of Roth IRAS, 401(k) plans, personal-risk-management scenarios, and collateralized-mortgage obligations. Years ago, mutual funds were thought to save investors the hassle of choosing among thousands of stocks. Yet today, small investors have to choose among some 7,000 mutual funds—there are almost as many of them as there are stocks.

Bits vs. Banks

At the center of this new world is a conflict between consolidation and disintermediation (a word that sounds like a tropical disease but means the removal of intermediaries, such as banks, from financial transactions). The disintermediation camp—led by software firms like Microsoft and Intuit—believes that the future will belong to companies that master the technology of this new era and give investors complete control over their finances with sophisticated products balancing risk/reward and cost/value. The opposite camp—led by the banking industry—argues that the future belongs to huge financial institutions that will package investments and provide investors with everything from insurance to car loans to airplane tickets.

Sure enough, one of the selling points of these megadeals is the idea that smart software will reshape the relationship between banks and customers. In a nonstop tango of bits and bills, the computers at the new Citigroup or at BankAmerica will zip through accounts looking for better ways to make money for both you and the bank. And the banks will use that efficiency to lever into the most profitable parts of the financial world: investment banking, stock underwriting, and insurance.

The fundamental idea driving this revolution is that technology and finance have become one and the same. And nowhere is that truer than in the world of cold, hard cash, which is transforming currency from paper in your wallet to instantly transferable, easily traceable "cybercash." (*See* next article.)

The Role of Derivatives

The prophet of the new age of bigger banks and digital dollars is financial expert Charles Sanford Jr., of Bankers Trust. In a speech to a gathering of economics sachems in 1993, he explained that all investments can be characterized by two variables: risk and reward, which tend to be proportional. If you want more reward, generally it means taking a bigger risk. Home mortgages are fairly riskless for lenders, but the return is tiny—perhaps 6%. Lending money to the government of Malaysia is fairly lucrative, but the double-digit interest rate brings with it risks of a devaluation, a government coup, or a default.

If all investments—from insurance policies to vacation loans—could be broken into tiny packages of risk that could be put into a computer, they could be auctioned on a global network. Investors seeking varying levels of risk and return at different times would buy these chunks of risk. Because these risk bundles were derived from the underlying investments, they were called derivatives.

The idea proved to be hugely popular. By allowing institutions to manage their financial risk more carefully, derivatives offered the possibility of locking in greater rewards at lower risks. Suddenly what seemed to be the first immutable law of finance—you can't get a bigger reward without a bigger risk—was up for grabs. Alas, derivatives aren't inherently good: just ask the citizens of Orange County who lost millions of dollars in public money when a derivatives deal blew up in 1994.

Nonetheless, derivatives have changed the rules of the game forever. Average investors who are now pouring money into mutual funds and stocks will soon have access to hundreds of other investment options—everything from distressed Japanese real estate to Russian oil futures—marketed and packaged by giant banks like BankAmerica or by fund companies like Fidelity Investments and the Vanguard Group. "This is like the automobile's coming," says Sanford. "We'd always had transportation—people walked, eventually they rode donkeys—but the automobile was a break from everything that came before it. Risk management will do that to finance. It's a total break."

In Sanford's vision, every financial asset, from the mortgage you hold on your house to the items you've charged on your credit card, will become part of a giant, interconnected financial universe. And each piece of your superportfolio, called a "wealth account," will be understood as an instrument designed to match your financial needs with the available options.

Wealth accounts will precisely balance your demand for investment and consumption. Your

checking deposits, for instance, might be programmed to scour an electronic Web looking for interest-bearing investments overnight while you sleep. You'll be able to draw instantly on assets in one area to create liabilities in another, say pay for your sports car by instantly drawing on the wealth inherent in your vacation house. Finance could become a banker-free zone.

Of course, all this has risks of its own. Taking complex finance out of the hands of Wall Street rocket scientists and putting it into the hands of consumers or even inexperienced bankers is hardly a riskless activity. In fact, the China Syndrome aspect of all this interconnected finance is among its most worrisome features. What if the whole interconnected computer network crashes? (Hell, what if just your part does?) What if a hacker breaks in at the wrong place? What if the bank's investments fail? Industry insiders—the folks who have designed the systems—argue that the infrastructure they have built is secure enough to survive any tampering and that the markets themselves will factor in the risks of rogue or inexperienced traders. □

Welcome to the Age of Digital Dollars

Financial experts agree: greenbacks are out—cybercash is in

By JOSHUA COOPER RAMO TIME

Paper money is amazing stuff: easily transferable, widely accepted, portable (especially U.S. dollars), storable, exchangeable, and pretty durable. But if you lose paper cash it's gone; sit on it and it may lose its value overnight.

Enter electronic cash. Instead of storing value on paper, wrap it in a string of digits that's more portable and (more important) smarter than its paper counterpart. Smart money? Well, yes. Because digital cash is endlessly mutable, you can control it much more precisely than paper money. The $2,000 check you send to your daughter at college for expenses could be spent on books . . . or beer. Digital cash takes that relatively simple transaction—passing an allowance—and makes it into a much more intelligent process. And one that hardly requires something as old-fashioned as a bank.

For starters, you can send the money over the Internet encoded in an E-mail instead of sending a check. This saves you the trouble of balancing the checkbook at the end of the month, and it offers greater flexibility: you can transfer the money from any source—mutual fund, money market, checking account—your daughter can store the money any way she wants—on her laptop, on a debit card, even (in the not too distant future) on a chip implanted under her skin. And, perhaps best of all, digital cash offers greater control. You can program the money to be spent only in specific ways, some for books, some for food and movies.

Smart, digital cash may also address some of the other problems of paper money. If you lose your digital cash, you will be able to replace it instantly by invalidating the lost digits and replacing them with a fresh set. And unlike paper money—which stops earning interest as it shoots out of the ATM slot—smart money can keep earning interest until the moment you spend it.

This "cash-interest phenomenon" may sound trivial, but it's a link to a whole other revolution in finance: the dissolution of the government monopoly on money. After all, if some small bank in Luxembourg or Belize is willing to pay you more interest on your digital cash, who are you to argue? As long as the bank's digits are widely accepted, there is no need to stick with government-issued numbers. Government money will still exist, but so will dozens of digital currencies, each tailored to a specific need and convertible and exchangeable. The best money, in short, will be the smartest money. Says Howard Greenspan, president of the Toronto-based Heraclitus Corp., a management consulting firm: "In the electronic city, the final step in the evolution of money is being taken. Money is being demonetized. Money is being eliminated."

"Money Tracks"

One of the great hopes for traceable, bit-based cash is that it will do away with whole categories of cash-based crime. DigiCash founder David Chaum argues that the traceability of electronic cash will mean the end of some types of crime. "What kidnapper would take a ransom payment by check?"

But Chaum assumes that these electronic transactions will be traceable—something that's sort of a jump ball in the theory of electronic finance these days. One school of theorists, led by Chaum, argues that electronic cash needs to be "one-way anonymous" so that people transferring money can always see where it goes, while people receiving money won't know where it comes from. This one-way mirror transfer makes it easier to keep track of where money is spent and why. But who really wants to leave "money tracks"?

Electronic cash can also be two-way anonymous—totally untraceable and a dream for international criminals. The cybermoney revolution might make some forms of tax evasion very easy, and even calls into question the role of the Federal Reserve as arbiter of the nation's money supply. "The more such innovations succeed, the less the public has to rely on central banks as direct sources of exchange media," University of Georgia economics professor George Selgin has written.

When will the smart money revolution hit Main Street? Not for a few more years, at the least. Digital cash, for all its charms, is still climbing a tough road to acceptance. "Between 40% and 50% of transactions today use cash and checks," says Steve Cone, an executive at Fidelity Investments. That figure won't change too soon. While it's enticing (or annoying, if you're a cyber-Luddite) to imagine the day of the digital dollar—don't start burning your money just yet. □

Major Business Events

January 1998

SBC Buys SNET for $4.4 Billion (Jan. 5): In a consolidation of regional telephone services, SBC will expand its wireless offerings to include wireless, long-distance, and Internet services in Connecticut, and will expand its wireless services within Massachusetts and to Rhode Island. SBC already provides these services to Boston, upstate New York, and the Washington–Baltimore area.

Justice Files Charges Against Tobacco Firm (Jan. 7): DNA Plant Technology agrees to plead guilty to conspiracy to violate the tobacco-seed export law for its role in a scheme to manipulate the nicotine levels in cigarettes. These are the first criminal charges to be brought as a result of the investigation of the tobacco industry.

AT&T Goes Local (Jan. 8): In a bid to enter the local telephone market, AT&T will purchase Teleport Communications Group in a stock swap valued at $11.3 billion. **Restructuring Eliminates 15,000 Jobs (Jan. 22):** As part of its bid to enter the local market, AT&T announces plans to cut 15,000–18,000 jobs. **Record Profits Announced (Jan. 26):** Surprisingly strong fourth-quarter profits have no effect on plans to eliminate jobs.

Texas Wins Tobacco Trial (Jan. 17): The $15.3 billion settlement is the largest to date in the series of lawsuits against the tobacco industry that seek to recover state funds spent treating smokers.

Microsoft Agrees to DOJ Terms (Jan. 22): In what was termed a "partial settlement," Microsoft agrees to provide hardware manufacturers with a version of its operating system that allows its Internet browser to be disabled without adversely affecting other functionality. The charge that Microsoft has violated the 1995 consent decree by forcing Windows licensees to use other Microsoft products has yet to be resolved.

Compaq to Buy Digital for $9.6 Billion (Jan. 26): The largest computer industry deal ever would create a firm with $38 billion in annual sales, still less than half that of industry leader IBM.

"Smoking is a Factor in Lung Cancer and Heart Disease" (Jan. 29): Testifying before Congress, executives from five tobacco companies admit for the first time that smoking causes health problems and that nicotine could be considered addictive. In 1994 congressional testimony, other representatives from these same firms had denied that nicotine was addictive.

Prozac Pushes Profits (Jan. 29): Eli Lilly reports 23 percent increase in fourth-quarter profits, largely due to increased sales of Prozac.

February 1998

White House Submits Balanced Budget (Feb. 2): Clinton's budget calls for $1.73 trillion in spending with increases in programs to improve technology, education, and health care, funded in part by a settlement from tobacco firms and through increased taxes on corporations. The projected surplus of $9.5 billion sparks debate over who should benefit: Republicans want to use it to fund a tax cut, liberal Democrats want to increase social programs, and the president wants to save Social Security.

Outplacement Firms Busy in January (Feb. 5): Layoffs soared 66 percent in January over the same month in 1997, and up 24 percent over the previous month. Telecommunications led the way, with more than 18,000 jobs lost, mostly at AT&T.

Dow Resumes its Record Ways (Feb. 10 et seq.): The first eight months of 1997 saw the Dow gain 1,300 points, but turmoil in Asia put a damper on investor enthusiasm in the closing months of the year. It began trading near record levels again in February, breaking records on three consecutive closes to end the day at 8369.60 on February 12. **Blue Chips Set Sixth Straight Record, Over 8400 (Feb. 18):** Technology and pharmaceuticals lead the way to a close of 8451.06. **Dow Over 8500 (Feb. 27):** The Dow closes out the month 8.1 percent higher, at 8545.72.

Columbia/HCA Fraud Comes to Light (Feb. 10): Federal documents reveal details of Medicare fraud in the latest in a series of allegations that the health-care giant sought to defraud the government.

"Big Four" Back to "Big Five" (Feb. 13): KPMG Peat Marwick and Ernst & Young decide they don't want to become the world's largest accounting firm, after all, calling off merger discussions begun in October 1997.

FDA Approves Once-Daily Asthma Drug from Merck (Feb. 23): Chronic asthma sufferers can put the inhaler on the shelf and take a pill once a day instead. Singulair is remarkable for its once-daily dosage and its approval for use in preventing asthma attacks in both adults and children as young as six.

Apple Kills Newton (Feb. 27): The handheld computer unit of Apple will close, its 200 employees transferred to other projects.

March 1998

Microsoft Fesses Up (March 3): Microsoft chairman Bill Gates admitted in testimony before Congress that the company restricts its partner companies from promoting rival browser software from Netscape.

Nasdaq and AMEX to Merge (March 12): The technology-laden Nasdaq with its "virtual exchange" announces plans to merge with the original street-corner American Stock Exchange to better compete with the NYSE.

Reynolds Knew Government Cigarette Findings Were Inaccurate (March 16): Company documents show that the firm knew that smokers inhale twice as much tar and nicotine as government testing indicated.

DOJ Expands Microsoft Inquiry (March 17): Justice will also investigate Microsoft's practices and policies relating to developing Java software programs. Java is a standard developed by rival Sun Microsystems Inc. **(March. 20):** Meanwhile, HP plans to release its own variant of Java, splintering the alliance against Microsoft.

Random House Bought by Bertelsmann (March 24): Consolidation in the publishing industry continues, leaving fewer, larger companies to provide markets for authors and content for movies.

Grove to Step Down (March 27): Intel's legendary CEO will step aside in May to make way for Craig Barrett. Grove, who was *Time* magazine's 1997 Man of the Year, will retain his position as chairman.

April 1998

Reynolds and Philip Morris Announce Cigarette Price Hike (April 4): Facing reduced profits as a result of the pending legislation to regulate the tobacco industry, the market leaders announce a five-cent per pack increase.

Justice May Expand Microsoft Probe (April 6): Investigators contend there is evidence the software giant seeks to illegally monopolize software for running personal computers. **States to File Separate Suit (April 9):** Several states are planning to file a separate antitrust suit against Microsoft.

Travelers and Citicorp to Merge in $83 Billion Deal (April 6): In the largest financial services deal ever, the two firms would become Citigroup, pending regulatory approval.

Dow Closes Above 9000 (April 6): The Dow closed at 9033.23 on news of mergers in the financial community. It took nine months for the Dow to advance 1,000 points, compared to just five months between the 7000 and 8000 milestones. **Dow Reaches 9100 (April 14):** Strong economic news leads the DJIA to close at 9110.20.

Consolidation of the Banking Industry Continues (April 13): BankAmerica and NationsBank will merge in a deal worth about $60 billion, resulting in the single largest bank in the U.S., with $570 billion in assets. Separately, Banc One and First Chicago will merge in a $30 billion stock swap that will create the second-largest bank credit-card firm. **(April 17):** Canadian Imperial and Toronto Dominion announce plans to merge into Canada's second-largest bank in a $15 billion stock swap. **(April 23):** Bank of New York makes bid for Mellon Bank, which Mellon rebuffs.

Tobacco Round 2 (April 29): After taking on a class-action suit from state attorneys general, the tobacco industry faces another attack from those seeking to recover costs incurred to treat smoking-related illnesses. This time it's the insurance industry, led by Blue Cross and Blue Shield, in suits filed in New York, Chicago, and Seattle.

Disney Buys Internet Publisher (April 30): Apparently Disney liked the trial size well enough to buy the whole company, having purchased an initial stake in Starwave Corp., a web site developer, in 1997. The purchase increases Disney's Internet presence, which is already evident in ESPN's SportsZone, one of the most popular sites on the Internet. Financial terms for the remaining stake were not disclosed. Starwave Corp. was founded by Microsoft co-founder Paul Allen.

May 1998

Microsoft Legal Woes Threaten Release (May 4): In an effort to intimidate investigators into cancelling proposed examinations of Microsoft's Windows 98 operating system, Microsoft warns of dire consequences for the entire computer industry if its release of the product is delayed by investigations. **Justice Files Suit (May 20):** The DOJ joined with 20 state attorneys general to file suit against Microsoft alleging antitrust violations in its operating system products. It is expected to be one of the biggest antitrust suits in U.S. history, rivaling those of Standard Oil, IBM, and AT&T.

Daimler and Chrysler Merge to Become World's Fifth-Largest Automaker (May 6): The new firm, Daimler-Chrysler Corp., will have corporate headquarters in Stuttgart, Germany, and Auburn Hills, Michigan.

Compaq Acquisition Leads to 15,000 Digital Job Cuts (May 6): Digital will see its work force shrink by 27 percent to 39,000, or about one third of its size during the 1980s. The cuts come as the personal computer giant assimilates the company that first offered minicomputers as alternatives to mainframes, only to lose market share to increasingly powerful personal computers.

Tobacco Industry Settles Rather Than Risk Jury Verdict in Minnesota (May 8): In a virtual echo of the settlements with Florida and Mississippi, the tobacco industry agrees to pay $6 billion to reimburse the state for Medicaid payments to treat smoking-related illnesses. The deal calls for restrictions on tobacco advertising, including a ban on paid placement of tobacco paraphernalia in movies and on television. **RJR and Philip Morris Earnings Hit (May 15):** The firms will take a total of $1.1 billion in charges to their earnings to cover costs of the Minnesota settlement.

New "Love Bug" Has a Bug (May 15): Volkswagen recalled all new Beetles sold in the U.S. and Canada because of faulty wiring that may cause the popular cars to catch fire. The company denies that it has received any reports of injuries resulting from the problem.

Pete's Wicked Rich (May 22): The trend-setting lager purveyor, Pete's Brewing Company, is sold to a Texas beer distributor for $68 million. Pete's Wicked Ale will now be distributed alongside imported beers Moosehead and Corona in the market for niche-market brews.

June 1998

VW Wins Bidding War Against BMW (June 5): British luxury car maker Rolls-Royce agrees to $703 million offered by Volkswagen. BMW cancels its agreement to supply engines for Rolls-Royce. **Audi Buys Lamborghini (June 12):** A week after acquiring the automotive jewel in the British crown, German automaker VW's luxury unit, Audi, buys Italian sports car maker Lamborghini, whose cars offer 500-horsepower engines under their sporty little hoods.

More Banks Merge (June 8): Norwest and Wells Fargo announce plans to merge in a $34 billion deal that will create the nation's seventh-largest bank once other mergers are completed. With 90,000 employees in 21 states, the bank will offer services from Ohio to California.

Japanese Economy in First Recession in 24 Years (June 12): Japan's gross domestic product contracted for the second consecutive quarter, which defines a recession. The GDP dropped 0.4 percent in October–December 1997, and another 1.3 percent in January–March 1998. The economic powerhouse of East Asia had not seen a drop in GDP for two consecutive quarters since the 1974–75 fiscal year.

Ronald McLayoff (June 18): The fast-food chain announces plans to eliminate 525 jobs from its corporate work force, the first such reduction in the company's history.

GM Strike Idles North American Plants (June 19 et seq.): A strike by workers at a Michigan parts supplier expands to affect the entire North American operations of General Motors as talks between management and the UAW drag on. Without parts, production facilities are idled and inventories at retailers are dwindling. GM takes a public stand against the UAW, cuts off medical benefits to striking workers, and calls on managers worldwide to cut cash expenditures where possible. The UAW threatens strikes in other plants.

Round 1: Microsoft, by Decision (June 24): Microsoft wins its first-round fight with the DOJ when a federal panel of judges rules it can integrate its Windows and Internet software.

AT&T Goes Cable (June 25): With a resounding $37.3 billion deal to buy cable giant Tele-Communications Inc., Ma Bell has made it clear that her future lies in convergence. Since cable companies have access to the local phone market, rivals see the acquisition as an end-run at the antitrust act that got AT&T out of the local business in the first place.

Compaq Cuts Manufacturing Jobs (June 30): The first 5,000 casualties of the DEC-Compaq merger have received their pink slips.

July 1998

GM is Uncompetitive (July 7): Analysts estimate the firm would need to cut at least 50,000 hourly jobs just to remain competitive with rival automakers. The strike has cost GM more than $1 billion. **GM Earnings Plummet 81% (July 14):** In the wake of the ongoing strike by some 9,000 workers at two parts plants, the company-wide shutdown now jeopardizes production of 1999 model year vehicles. GM files suit in federal court against the UAW, claiming the strike violates the current contract. **(July 27):** Seven weeks after it was called, the strike at GM is over, though it may take as much as 10 days to return to full production at the affected plants.

Deal? What Deal? (July 10): UPS backs away from its promise to Teamsters that ended the August 1997 strike, opting not to create 2,000 new full-time jobs by the end of July 1998.

Tropicana Becomes a Foot Soldier in the Cola Wars (July 21): Pepsico buys Tropicana in a $3.3 billion deal in a bid to enter the juice market and compete against rival Minute Maid, owned by Coca-Cola.

Communications Consolidation Continues (July 27): British Telecom and AT&T enter into a joint venture to provide voice, video, and data to customers on both sides of the Atlantic. Meanwhile, BellAtlantic and GTE agree to a $55 billion stock swap to marry GTE's Internet and long-distance business to BellAtlantic's local services. Both deals face regulatory scrutiny, and analysts decry the deals as bad for competition.

August 1998

Is it a "Correction" Yet? (Aug. 5): Stock prices tumble, sending the Dow down nearly 300 points in its third-largest point loss ever. The 3.4% drop in the index comes up short of the 10% loss that defines a "correction," but many individual stocks have seen their prices drop more than 10% from the highs experienced only weeks before. **Yes! (Aug. 31):** Concerns about the Russian economy send the U.S. stock markets wobbling, then tumbling. After four straight days of losses, culminating in a 513 point drop on August 31, the Dow closes at 7,539, wiping out all of this year's gains.

Manufacturing Jobs Disappear in Expanding Economy (Aug. 11): Despite all the news about the shallow labor pool and low unemployment, the U.S. economy shed some 176,000 manufacturing jobs in July.

Transatlantic Mergers Continue (Aug. 11): In the largest industrial merger ever, British Petroleum announces plans to buy Amoco in a $48 billion stock swap.

Russian Ruble Devalued (Aug. 17): After a turbulent week that rocked Russia's stock markets and cut short President Yeltsin's vacation, Yeltsin allows the Russian currency to lose one third of its value and announces a three-month hiatus in repayment of ruble-denominated foreign debt. **Yeltsin Dissolves Government (Aug. 23):** For the second time in a year, President Yeltsin dismisses his government. This time, he replaces his prime minister with Chernomyrdin, the man he had ousted in the previous dissolution.

Dow Milestones

Date	Milestone	Close	Date	Milestone	Close
Feb. 13, 1997	7000	7022.44	July 30, 1997	8200	8254.89
May 5, 1997	7100	7214.49	Feb. 11, 1998	8300	8314.55
May 5, 1997	7200	7214.49	Feb. 18, 1998	8400	8451.06
May 15, 1997	7300	7333.55	Feb. 7, 1998	8500	8545.72
June 6, 1997	7400	7435.78	Mar. 10, 1998	8600	8643.12
June 10, 1997	7500	7539.27	Mar. 16, 1998	8700	8718.85
June 12, 1997	7600	7711.47	Mar. 19, 1998	8800	8803.05
June 12, 1997	7700	7711.47	Mar. 20, 1998	8900	8906.43
July 3, 1997	7800	7895.81	April 6, 1998	9000	9033.23
July 9, 1997	7900	7962.31	April 14, 1998	9100	9110.20
July 16, 1997	8000	8038.88	May 13, 1998	9200	9211.84
July 24, 1997	8100	8116.93	July 16, 1998	9300	9328.19

Top Stocks by Market Value

Rank 1997	Rank 1996	Company name	Shares outstanding (millions)	Market value (millions)
1.	1.	General Electric Co.	3,714	272,504
2.	2.	Coca-Cola Co.	3,441	229,268
3.	3.	Exxon Corp.	2,984	182,561
4.	4.	Merck & Co., Inc.	1,484	157,668
5.	6.	Philip Morris Co. Inc.	2,806	127,145
6.	10.	Procter & Gamble Co.	1,487	118,667
7.	5.	Intel Corp.	1,635	114,859
8.	8.	Intl. Business Machines Corp.	1,035	108,226
9.	12.	Bristol-Myers Squibb Co.	1,129	106,832
10.	13.	Pfizer Inc.	1,379	102,846
11.	9.	Johnson & Johnson	1,535	101,106
12.	11.	AT&T Corp.	1,625	99,561
13.	17.	Wal-Mart Stores, Inc.	2,300	90,707
14.	14.	American International Group, Inc.	759	82,552
15.	7.	Microsoft Corp.	1,212	78,326
16.	29.	Eli Lilly and Co.	1,123	78,196
17.	55.	BellAtlantic Corp.	788	71,710
18.	15.	E.I. du Pont de Nemours and Co.	1,155	69,389
19.	45.	SBC Communications Inc.	929	68,078
20.	25.	Gillette Co.	676	67,861
21.	21.	Walt Disney Co.	683	67,689
22.	19.	Hewlett-Packard Co.	1,042	65,096
23.	16.	Mobil Corp.	894	64,520
24.	27.	Federal National Mortgage Assoc.	1,129	64,429
25.	18.	Citicorp	506	64,015
26.	43.	Schering-Plough Corp.	1,015	63,041
27.	22.	Berkshire Hathaway Inc.	1,377	62,920
28.	20.	PepsiCo, Inc.	1,725	62,860
29.	31.	BellSouth Corp.	1,010	56,884
30.	30.	Cisco Systems Inc.	1,015	56,586
31.	36.	BankAmerica Corp.	775	56,553
32.	23.	Chevron Corp.	712	54,862
33.	28.	American Home Products Corp.	711	54,387
34.	24.	GTE Corp.	983	51,382
35.	33.	Abbott Laboratories	777	50,949
36.	49.	Lucent Technologies Inc.	637	50,853
37.	47.	Schlumberger Ltd.	618	49,728
38.	44.	Ford Motor Co.	1,020	49,670
39.	38.	Boeing Co.	1,000	48,935
40.	34.	Chase Manhattan Corp.	441	48,236
41.	51.	NationsBank Corp.	781	47,468
42.	41.	Ameritech Corp.	588	47,359
43.	40.	Royal Dutch Petroleum Co.	868	47,017
44.	26.	General Motors Corp.	757	45,871
45.	56.	Compaq Computer Corp.	763	43,081
46.	57.	Home Depot, Inc.	730	43,001
47.	32.	Amoco Corp.	492	41,856
48.	58.	American Express Co.	467	41,638
49.	59.	Allstate Corp.	450	40,894
50.	60.	Warner-Lambert Co.	321	39,762

Based on closing prices on December 31, 1997. *Source:* New York Stock Exchange *1997 Fact Book* and SEC filings.

Most Active Stocks on NYSE, 1997

Rank 1997	Rank 1996	Company name	Share volume (in thousands)
1	7	Compaq Computer Corp.	1,231,586
2	13	Philip Morris Co. Inc.	1,107,800
3	2	AT&T Corp.	1,052,683
4	1	Micron Technology Inc.	1,003,273
5	3	PepsiCo, Inc.	879,811
6	4	Intl. Business Machines Corp.	875,731
7	19	General Electric Co.	840,513
8	17	Coca-Cola Co.	753,484
9	5	Wal-Mart Stores, Inc.	736,662
10	–	Columbia/HCA Healthcare Corp.	700,831
11	26	Telecomm Brasil Telebras	679,371
12	16	Merck & Co., Inc.	655,795
13	28	Seagate Technology Inc.	645,831
14	14	Hewlett-Packard Co.	643,351
15	–	Boeing Co.	638,715
16	9	Motorola Inc.	627,382
17	34	Exxon Corp.	592,177
18	22	Chrysler Corp.	581,771
19	8	Ford Motor Co.	574,653
20	18	Chase Manhattan Corp.	565,005
21	10	Bay Networks Inc.	562,513
22	29	CBS Corp.	550,720
23	32	Johnson and Johnson	540,415
24	11	Federal National Mortgage Assn.	538,457
25	20	General Motors Corp.	537,686
26	–	First Data Corp.	533,873
27	12	Telefonos de Mexico	530,243
28	23	Texas Instruments	526,501
29	46	Pfizer Inc.	520,192
30	31	Waste Management, Inc.	489,494
31	24	Citicorp	481,059
32	6	Kmart Corp.	476,423
33	–	Advanced Micro Devices	473,586
34	–	NationsBank Corp.	470,558
35	27	McDonald's Corp.	469,380
36	–	DuPont de Nemours (E.I.) and Co.	459,866
37	–	IOMEGA Corp.	445,106
38	–	Travelers Group Inc.	437,864
39	–	CUC International Inc.	435,002
40	–	Bristol-Myers Squibb	434,324
41	21	LSI Logic Corp.	429,650
42	37	Lucent Technologies Inc.	428,986
43	–	NIKE Inc.	411,189
44	42	GTE Corp.	404,908
45	30	Pharmacia Upjohn Inc.	399,475
46	–	Western Digital Corp.	395,100
47	–	Banc One Corp.	394,909
48	44	Sears Roebuck	391,017
49	45	BankAmerica Corp.	383,553
50	–	Electronic Data Sys. Corp.	380,530

As of December 31, 1997. *Source:* New York Stock Exchange *1997 Fact Book.*

Largest U.S. Businesses

Rank 1997	Rank 1996	Company name	Revenues ($ millions)
1	1	General Motors Corp.	178,174
2	1	Ford Motor Co.	153,627
3	3	Exxon Corp.	122,379
4	4	Wal-Mart Stores, Inc.	119,299
5	5	General Electric Co.	90,840
6	6	Intl. Business Machines Corp.	78,508
7	9	Chrysler Corp.	61,147
8	8	Mobil Corp.	59,978
9	10	Philip Morris Cos. Inc.	56,114
10	7	AT&T Corp.	53,261
11	36	Boeing Co.	45,800
12	11	Texaco	45,187
13	12	State Farm Insurance Cos.	43,957
14	16	Hewlett-Packard Co.	42,895
15	14	E.I. du Pont de Nemours and Co.	41,304
16	17	Sears Roebuck	41,296
17	40	Travelers Group Inc.	37,609
18	13	Prudential Ins. Co. of America	37,073
19	15	Chevron Corp.	36,376
20	18	Procter & Gamble Co.	35,764
21	20	Citicorp	34,697
22	19	Amoco Corp.	32,836
23	22	Kmart Corp.	32,183
24	30	Merrill Lynch and Co.	31,731
25	33	J.C. Penney	30,546
26	23	American International Group	30,520
27	25	Chase Manhattan Corp.	30,381
28	99	Bell Atlantic Corp.	30,194
29	24	Motorola Inc.	29,794
30	88/86	TIAA-CREF	29,348
31	21	PepsiCo, Inc.	29,292
32	26	Lockheed Martin	28,069
33	29	Federal National Mortgage Assoc.	27,777
34	27	Dayton Hudson	27,757
35	—	Morgan Stanley Dean Witter Discover	27,132
36	28	Kroger	26,567
37	—	Lucent Technologies Inc.	26,360
38	43	Intel Corp.	25,070
39	32	Allstate Corp.	24,949
40	85	SBC Communications Inc.	24,856
41	34	United Technologies	24,713
42	60	Compaq Computer Corp.	24,584
43	35	Metropolitan Life Insurance	24,374
44	50	Home Depot	24,156
45	31	ConAgra	24,002
46	48	Merck & Co. Inc.	23,637
47	38	BankAmerica Corp.	23,585
48	41	GTE Corp.	23,260
49	39	Johnson & Johnson	22,629
50	65	Safeway	22,484
51	55	Walt Disney Co.	22,473
52	37	United Parcel Service	22,458
53	49	Costco	21,874
54	62	NationsBank Corp.	21,734
55	42	USX	21,057
56	53	BellSouth Corp.	20,561
57	94	Enron	20,273
58	44	International Paper	20,096
59	54	Cigna	20,038
60	45	Dow Chemical	20,018
61	57	Sara Lee	19,734

Rank 1997	Rank 1996	Company name	Revenues ($ millions)
62	59	MCI Communications	19,653
63	46	Loews	19,648
64	52	Atlantic Richfield	19,272
65	56	American Stores	19,139
66	68	Caterpillar	18,925
67	63	New York Life Insurance	18,899
68	58	Coca-Cola Co.	18,868
69	47	Columbia/HCA Healthcare	18,819
70	61	AMR	18,570
71	67	Aetna	18,540
72	51	Xerox Corp.	18,166
73	64	American Express Co.	17,760
74	73	J.P. Morgan & Co.	17,701
75	71	UAL	17,378
76	66	RJR Nabisco Holdings	17,057
77	80	Lehman Brothers Holdings	16,883
78	76	Bristol-Myers Squibb Co.	16,701
79	—	Ingram Micro	16,582
80	70	Supervalu	16,552
81	—	Duke Energy	16,309
82	77	Ameritech Corp.	15,998
83	75	Federated Department Stores	15,668
84	74	Phillips Petroleum	15,424
85	—	PG&E Corp.	15,400
86	69	Fleming	15,373
87	—	US West	15,352
88	—	Electronic Data Systems	15,236
89	81	Minnesota Mining & Mfg.	15,070
90	82	Sprint	14,874
91	72	Eastman Kodak Co.	14,713
92	89	Albertson's	14,690
93	84	AlliedSignal	14,472
94	92	SYSCO	14,455
95	—	Federal Home Loan Mortgage	14,399
96	—	First Union Corp.	14,329
97	—	Fluor	14,299
98	83	American Home Products Corp.	14,196
99	93	Archer Daniels Midland	13,853
100	—	Raytheon	13,674

Note: Dash indicates the company was not in the top 100 in 1996. *Source:* 1998 Fortune 500, © 1998 Time, Inc. All rights reserved. For more detailed information, visit *Fortune* on the web, www.fortune.com/fortune500.

Corporate Profits[1]

(in billions of dollars)

Item	1998[2]	1997	1996	1995	1990	1985	1980	1975	1970
Domestic industries	$651.0	$636.7	$578.2	$511.7	$236.4	$190.8	$161.9	$107.6	$62.4
Financial	125.8	119.5	103.5	97.6	18.7	21.0	26.9	11.8	12.1
Nonfinancial	525.2	517.2	474.7	414.1	217.7	169.7	134.9	95.8	50.2
Manufacturing	221.5	224.7	205.5	181.3	88.8	73.0	72.9	52.6	26.6
Wholesale and retail trade	113.2	106.9	87.2	68.8	41.5	49.7	23.6	21.3	9.5
Other	96.5	95.0	90.3	77.6	87.5	47.0	38.4	21.9	14.1
Rest of world	103.0	98.6	95.9	86.7	56.9	31.8	29.9	13.0	6.5
Total	**754.0**	**735.3**	**674.1**	**598.4**	**293.3**	**222.6**	**191.7**	**120.6**	**68.9**

1. Corporate profits before tax with inventory valuation adjustment. 2. First quarter (seasonally adjusted at annual rates). *Source:* U.S. Bureau of Economic Analysis, *Survey of Current Business,* June 1996, web: www.bea.doc.gov.

Life Insurance in Force

(in millions of dollars)

As of Dec. 31	Ordinary	Group	Industrial	Credit	Total
1915	$ 16,650	$ 100	$ 4,279	—	$ 21,029
1930	78,576	9,801	17,963	$ 73	106,413
1945	101,550	22,172	27,675	365	151,762
1950	149,116	47,793	33,415	3,844	234,168
1955	216,812	101,345	39,682	14,493	372,332
1960	341,881	175,903	39,563	29,101	586,448
1965	499,638	308,078	39,818	53,020	900,554
1970	734,730	551,357	38,644	77,392	1,402,123
1975	1,083,421	904,695	39,423	112,032	2,139,571
1980	1,760,474	1,579,355	35,994	165,215	3,541,038
1985	3,247,289	2,561,595	28,250	215,973	6,053,107
1990	5,366,982	3,753,506	24,071	248,038	9,392,597
1994	6,407,399	4,441,730	18,947	189,398	11,057,474
1995	6,815,630	4,603,297	18,134	201,083	11,638,144
1996	7,294,079	5,066,621	18,064	210,746	12,589,510

Source: American Council of Life Insurance.

Leading Advertising Agencies in Revenues
(in thousands of dollars)

Rank	Agency	1997 revenues	Percent change	1997 billings	Percent change
1	McCann-Erickson	$1,796,820	13.4%	$13,770,100	19.7%
2	DDB Needham	1,591,207	11.9	11,680,049	11.7
3	BBDO Worldwide	1,466,679	9.4	11,632,947	7.1
4	J. Walter Thompson	1,177,000*	5.0	8,000,000	5.0
5	Ogilvy & Mather	1,052,895	6.7	8,839,187	6.7
6	Young & Rubicam	1,015,415	11.7	9,667,711	9.2
7	Ammirati Puris Lintas Worldwide	973,471	6.8	7,275,798	9.5
8	Grey Advertising	954,966	9.8	6,369,500	9.6
9	MVBMS/EURO RSCG Worldwide	952,005	8.2	7,128,996	8.4
10	Leo Burnett Co.	878,008	1.4	5,977,061	2.7
11	Foote, Cone & Belding	650,000*	–10.5	6,101,505	–10.4
12	D'Arcy Masius Benton & Bowles	606,768	14.0	5,806,630	13.3
13	TBWA	550,260	17.1	3,961,792	16.7
14	The Lowe Group	502,801	5.6	3,652,554	9.5
15	Bozell	380,000*	20.9	3,077,000	22.1
16	Saatchi & Saatchi	230,000	10.0	2,295,700	0.5
17	Bates Worldwide	116,000*	1.8	1,974,075	1.7
18	Campbell-Ewald	95,600*	15.0	982,000*	14.9
19	Arnold Communications	90,754	24.1	752,685	36.5
20	Campbell Mithun Esty	86,700*	10.0	863,700	10.0

*Estimated. *Source: Adweek,* Top 20 U.S.-Based Agency Networks, March 30, 1998, edition. © 1998 Adweek. Used with permission of *Adweek.*

New Business Concerns and Business Failures

Incorporations and failures	1995[1]	1994	1993	1992	1991	1990	1989	1985	1980
New incorporations (1,000)	768	741	707	667	629	647	677	664	534
Failures, number (1,000)	71.2	71.6	86.1	97.1	88.1	60.7	50.4	57.1	11.7
Rate per 10,000 concerns	90	86	96	110	107	74	65	115	42

1. Preliminary. NOTE: Data are most recent available. *Sources:* U.S. Bureau of Economic Analysis and Dun & Bradstreet Corporation. From *Statistical Abstract of the United States 1997,* web: www.census.gov/stat_abstract.

World's Largest Banks[1]
(in millions of U.S. dollars)

Rank	Bank	Assets
1	Bank of Tokyo-Mitsubishi Ltd., Japan	$691,920.3
2	Deutsche Bank AG, Frankfurt, Ger.	580,069.0
3	Sumitomo Bank Ltd., Osaka, Japan	483,730.4
4	Credit Suisse Group, Zurich, Switz.	473,829.8
5	HSBC Holdings, Plc., London, U.K.	471,037.8
6	Dai-Ichi Kangyo Bank Ltd., Tokyo, Japan	433,102.9
7	Sanwa Bank Ltd., Osaka, Japan	427,979.6
8	Credit Agricole Mutuel, Paris, France	419,763.2
9	Fuji Bank Ltd., Tokyo, Japan	414,173.0
10	ABN-AMRO Bank, N.V., Amsterdam, Neth.	412,771.9
11	Societe Generale, Paris, France	410,842.2
12	Sakura Bank Ltd., Tokyo, Japan	399,491.5
13	Union Bank of Switzerland, Zurich, Switz.	395,086.5
14	Norin Chunkin Bank, Tokyo, Japan	392,553.5
15	BarclaysBank Plc., London, U.K.	385,950.3
16	Dresdner Bank, Frankfurt, Ger.	371,371.0
17	Industrial Bank of Japan Ltd., Tokyo, Japan	369,954.0
18	Chase Manhattan Corp., New York, U.S.	365,521.0
19	Banque Nationale de Paris, France	339,648.2
20	Westdeutsche Landesbank Girozentrale, Duesseldorf, Ger.	335,816.2
21	Citicorp, New York, U.S.	310,897.0
22	ING Bank, Amsterdam, Neth.	307,559.6
23	NatWest Group, London, U.K.	304,941.8
24	Swiss Bank Corp., Basel, Switz.	300,259.1
25	Commerzbank, Frankfurt, Ger.	286,946.6
26	Mitsubishi Trust & Banking Corp., Tokyo, Japan	$269,524.4
27	NationsBank Corp., Charlotte, N.C., U.S.	264,562.0
28	Tokai Bank Ltd., Nagoya, Japan	262,423.7
29	JP Morgan & Co., Inc., New York, U.S.	262,159.0
30	BankAmerica Corp., San Francisco, U.S.	260,159.0
31	Lloyds TSB Group Inc., London, U.K.	260,042.8
32	Sumitomo Trust & Banking Co. Ltd., Osaka, Japan	254,189.7
33	Credit Lyonnais, Paris, France	250,149.9
34	Bayerische Vereinsbank AG, Munich, Ger.	249,830.6
35	Abbey National, Plc., London, U.K.	248,040.3
36	Compagnie Financiere de Paribas, Paris, France	245,061.1
37	Mitsui Trust & Banking Co., Ltd., Tokyo, Japan	241,916.0
38	Bayerische Landesbank Girozentrale, Munich, Ger.	241,714.0
39	Asahi Bank Ltd., Tokyo, Japan	219,939.4
40	Halifax Plc., Leeds, U.K.	215,625.4
41	Rabobank Group, Utrecht, Neth.	208,739.6
42	Deutsche Genossenschaftsbank, Frankfurt, Ger.	207,768.9
43	Bayerische Hypotheken-und Wechsel-Bank AG, Munich, Ger.	203,567.0
44	Dexia Belgium, Brussels, Belgium	202,958.5
45	Bankgesellschaft Berlin AG, Berlin, Ger.	197,364.8
46	Long Term Credit Bank of Japan Ltd., Tokyo, Japan	188,497.4

Rank	Bank	Assets
47	Royal Bank of Canada, Toronto, Can.	$ 171,218.5
48	Grupo Santander, Spain	170,927.0
49	Canadian Imperial Bank of Commerce, Toronto, Can.	166,472.4
50	Yasuda Trust & Banking Co., Ltd., Tokyo, Japan	$ 165,784.2

1. Based on total assets held on December 31, 1997. *Source: American Banker,* August 6, 1998. Reprinted with permission. Copyright © American Banker/Bond Buyer.

Domestic Freight Traffic by Major Carriers

(in billions of ton-miles)[1]

Year	Railroads		Trucks		Oil pipeline		Inland waterways[2]		Air		Total
	Amt.	%	Amt.	%	Amt.	%	Amt.	%	Amt.	%	
1940	379	61.3%	62	10.0%	59	9.6%	118	19.1%	0.01	—	618
1945	691	67.3	67	6.5	127	12.3	143	13.9	0.09	—	1,028
1950	597	56.2	173	16.3	129	12.1	163	15.4	0.32	—	1,062
1955	632	49.5	223	17.5	203	16.0	217	17.0	0.48	—	1,274
1960	579	44.1	285	21.7	229	17.4	220	16.8	0.78	—	1,314
1965	709	43.3	359	21.9	306	18.7	262	16.0	1.91	0.1%	1,638
1970	771	39.8	412	21.3	431	22.3	319	16.4	3.27	0.2	1,936
1975	759	36.7	454	22.0	507	24.6	342	16.5	3.73	0.2	2,066
1980	932	37.5	555	22.3	588	23.6	407	16.4	4.84	0.2	2,487
1985	895	36.4	610	24.8	564	22.9	382	15.5	6.71	0.3	2,458
1986	889	35.6	632	25.3	578	23.1	393	15.7	7.34	0.3	2,499
1987	972	36.8	663	25.1	587	22.2	411	15.6	8.67	0.3	2,642
1988	1,028	37.0	700	25.2	601	21.6	438	15.8	9.33	0.3	2,776
1989	1,070	37.8	716	25.3	584	20.6	449	15.9	10.21	0.4	2,829
1990	1,091	37.7	735	25.4	584	20.2	475	16.4	10.42	0.4	2,895
1991	1,100	37.9	758	26.1	579	19.9	459	15.8	9.96	0.3	2,906
1992	1,138	37.6	815	27.0	589	19.5	470	15.5	10.99	0.4	3,023
1993	1,183	38.1	861	27.7	593	19.1	456	14.7	11.54	0.4	3,105
1994	1,275	39.1	908	27.8	591	18.1	475	14.6	12.03	0.4	3,261
1995	1,375	40.4	921	27.1	599	17.6	497	14.6	12.72	0.4	3,405
1996	1,426	40.2	972	27.4	631	17.8	471	13.3	13.36	0.4	3,546

1. Mail and express included, except railroads for 1970. 2. Rivers, canals, and domestic traffic on Great Lakes. NOTE: Data are the most recent available. *Source: Transportation in America* by Rosalyn Wilson.

Tonnage Handled by Principal U.S. Ports

Top 50 Ports Ranked in Total Tons

1996 rank	1995 rank	Port	1996 tonnage
1	1	Port of South Louisiana	189,814,564
2	2	Houston, Tex.	148,182,876
3	3	New York, N.Y. & N.J.	131,601,244
4	6	New Orleans, La.	83,726,470
5	4	Baton Rouge, La.	81,009,253
6	8	Corpus Christi, Tex.	80,460,088
7	5	Valdez, Alaska	77,116,459
8	7	Port of Plaquemines, La.	66,910,237
9	9	Long Beach, Calif.	58,395,243
10	12	Texas City, Tex.	56,393,758
11	14	Pittsburgh, Pa.	50,874,367
12	11	Mobile, Ala.	50,863,944
13	10	Tampa, Fla.	49,292,651
14	15	Norfolk Harbor, Va.	49,260,972
15	16	Lake Charles, La.	49,096,325
16	17	Los Angeles, Calif.	45,689,232
17	19	Baltimore, Md.	43,552,356
18	20	Philadelphia, Pa.	41,882,200
19	18	Duluth-Superior, Minn./Wis.	41,398,293
20	13	Port Arthur, Tex.	37,157,786
21	30	Beaumont, Tex.	35,705,109
22	23	St. Louis, Mo./Ill.	30,161,905
23	21	Portland, Ore.	29,733,913
24	25	Pascagoula, Miss.	29,342,671
25	27	Chicago, Ill.	27,886,169
26	24	Huntington, W. Va.	27,478,215
27	28	Paulsboro, N.J.	25,038,524
28	29	Newport News, Va.	24,787,261
29	33	Freeport, Tex.	24,570,954
30	26	Seattle, Wash.	23,546,789
31	32	Richmond, Calif.	21,802,748
32	31	Tacoma, Wash.	21,490,783
33	37	Boston, Mass.	20,103,978
34	35	Port Everglades, Fla.	18,896,571
35	34	Detroit, Mich.	18,603,745
36	36	Savannah, Ga.	17,598,389
37	38	Memphis, Tenn.	17,299,836
38	39	Indiana Harbor, Ind.	16,892,858
39	40	Jacksonville, Fla.	16,736,773
40	42	Cleveland, Ohio	16,720,837
41	43	Lorain, Ohio	15,977,949
42	50	Portland, Maine	15,242,802
43	41	San Juan, P.R.	15,112,223
44	46	Anacortes, Wash.	13,843,669
45	44	Toledo, Ohio	13,031,631
46	47	Cincinnati, Ohio	12,803,247
47	22	Marcus Hook, Pa.	12,365,946
48	49	Honolulu, Hawaii	12,010,003
49	53	Galveston, Tex.	11,640,754
50	45	Oakland, Calif.	11,229,862

Source: U.S. Department of the Army, Corps of Engineers.

Motor Vehicle Data

	1996	1995	1990	1980	1970	1960
U.S. passenger cars and taxis registered (thousands)	129,728	128,387	133,700	121,601	89,244	61,671
Total mileage of U.S. passenger cars (millions)	1,467,703	1,438,294	1,417,823	1,121,810	919,679	587,012
Total fuel consumption of U.S. passenger cars (millions of gallons)	68,897	68,317	71,989	71,883	67,820	41,169
World registration of cars, trucks, and buses (thousands)	671,358	646,759	582,982	411,113	246,368	126,955
U.S. registration of cars, trucks, and buses (thousands)	206,365	200,446	188,655	155,796	108,418	73,858
U.S. share of world registration of cars, trucks, and buses	30.7%	31.0%	32.4%	37.9%	44.0%	58.2%

Source: American Automobile Manufacturers Association.

State Motor Vehicle Registrations, 1996

(in thousands)

State	Autos	Buses[1]	Trucks	Motorcycles	Total
Alabama	1,761	9	1,554	37	3,324
Alaska	228	2	301	13	531
Arizona	1,766	4	1,212	72	2,983
Arkansas	862	6	765	17	1,633
California	15,399	44	9,771	526	25,214
Colorado	1,901	6	1,527	94	3,433
Connecticut [2]	1,941	9	658	48	2,609
Delaware	398	2	193	10	593
District of Columbia	200	3	35	1	237
Florida	7,286	41	3,562	203	10,889
Georgia	3,841	16	2,426	73	6,283
Hawaii	505	4	276	25	786
Idaho	485	4	573	34	1,061
Illinois	6,293	16	2,507	171	8,817
Indiana	3,167	25	2,024	96	5,216
Iowa	1,654	10	1,206	132	2,869
Kansas	1,158	4	948	49	2,110
Kentucky	1,606	12	1,078	37	2,696
Louisiana	1,903	21	1,394	37	3,318
Maine	578	3	378	27	959
Maryland	2,570	11	1,053	38	3,635
Massachusetts	3,544	11	1,147	91	4,702
Michigan	5,091	25	2,895	150	8,010
Minnesota	2,273	15	1,573	116	3,861
Mississippi	1,268	10	904	30	2,182
Missouri	2,576	12	1,762	54	4,350
Montana	437	3	533	21	973
Nebraska	807	6	665	18	1,479
Nevada	619	2	475	22	1,096
New Hampshire[2]	737	2	374	52	1,112
New Jersey[2]	4,398	20	1,404	92	5,822
New Mexico	772	3	769	31	1,545
New York[2]	7,985	45	2,606	136	10,636
North Carolina	3,508	35	2,216	68	5,759
North Dakota	338	2	339	16	679
Ohio	6,609	34	3,128	220	9,770
Oklahoma	1,686	15	1,381	59	3,082
Oregon	1,528	13	1,310	61	2,851
Pennsylvania[2]	5,936	35	2,670	179	8,640
Rhode Island[2]	511	2	183	17	696
South Carolina	1,764	15	1,012	39	2,791
South Dakota	370	3	378	25	751
Tennessee	2,997	17	1,817	79	4,831
Texas	7,579	76	5,832	149	13,487
Utah	811	1	632	23	1,445
Vermont	301	2	200	18	503
Virginia	3,638	17	1,921	57	5,576
Washington	2,637	8	1,958	104	4,603
West Virginia	802	3	601	16	1,406
Wisconsin	2,473	13	1,486	170	3,972
Wyoming	232	3	328	15	562
Total	**129,728**	**697**	**75,940**	**3,871**	**206,365**

NOTE: Includes federal, state, county, and municipal vehicles, but not military vehicles. 1. Numbers reflect Federal Highway Administration estimates of buses in operation rather than the registration counts of the states. 2. The following farm trucks, registered at a nominal fee and restricted to use in the vicinity of the owner's farm, are not included in the table: Connecticut, 9,666; New Hampshire, 4,427; New Jersey, 6,588; New York, 31,395; Pennsylvania, 22,790; and Rhode Island, 1,041. *Source:* Federal Highway Administration, September 1997.

Domestic and Export Factory Sales of Motor Vehicles

(in thousands)

	From plants in the United States								
	Passenger cars			Motor trucks and buses			Total motor vehicles		
Year	Total	Domestic	Exports	Total	Domestic	Exports	Total	Domestic	Exports
1970	6,547	6,187	360	1,692	1,566	126	8,239	7,753	486
1975	6,713	6,073	640	2,272	2,003	269	8,985	8,076	909
1980	6,400	5,840	560	1,667	1,464	203	8,067	7,304	763
1985	8,002	7,337	665	3,464	3,234	231	11,467	10,571	896
1990	6,050	5,502	548	3,725	3,455	270	9,775	8,957	818
1991	5,407	4,874	533	3,388	3,050	338	8,795	7,924	871
1992	5,685	5,165	520	4,062	3,702	360	9,747	8,847	880
1993	5,962	5,473	489	4,895	4,471	424	10,857	9,944	913
1994	6,549	5,964	585	5,640	5,139	501	12,189	11,103	1,088
1995	6,310	5,788	522	5,713	5,211	502	12,023	10,999	1,024
1996	6,141	5,617	524	5,776	5,249	527	11,917	10,866	1,051
1997	6,070	5,534	536	6,153	5,489	664	12,223	11,023	1,200

Source: American Automobile Manufacturers Association.

Passenger Car Production by Make

Companies and models	1997	1995	1990	1985	1980	1975	1970
American Motors Corp.	—	—	—	109,919	164,725	323,704	276,127
Chrysler Corp.							
Plymouth	155,563	129,571	212,354	369,487	293,342	443,550	699,031
Dodge	241,058	331,253	361,769	482,388	263,169	354,482	405,699
Chrysler	44,096	121,022	136,339	414,193	82,463	102,940	158,614
Imperial	—	—	16,280	—	—	1,930	10,111
Total	**440,717**	**576,846**	**726,742**	**1,266,068**	**638,974**	**902,902**	**1,273,455**
Ford Motor Corp.							
Ford	913,440	1,012,818	933,466	1,098,627	929,627	1,301,414	1,647,918
Mercury	229,866	225,308	221,436	374,446	324,528	405,104	310,463
Lincoln	146,482	157,584	222,449	163,077	52,793	101,520	58,771
Total	**1,209,788**	**1,395,710**	**1,377,351**	**1,636,150**	**1,306,948**	**1,808,038**	**2,017,152**
General Motors Corp/							
Chevrolet	650,820	665,955	1,025,379	1,691,254	1,737,336	1,687,091	1,504,614
Pontiac	600,506	574,455	649,255	702,617	556,429	523,469	422,212
Oldsmobile	277,086	391,216	418,742	1,168,982	783,225	654,342	439,632
Buick	287,655	393,879	405,123	1,001,461	783,575	535,820	459,931
Cadillac	169,912	186,113	252,540	322,765	203,991	278,404	152,859
Saturn	271,612	301,540	4,245	—	—	—	—
Toyota/Cavalier	12,033	1,978	—	—	—	—	—
Total	**2,269,624**	**2,515,136**	**2,755,284**	**4,887,079**	**4,064,556**	**3,679,126**	**2,979,248**
Volkswagen of America	—	—	—	96,458	197,106	—	—
Honda	648,268	552,995	435,437	238,159	145,337	—	—
Nissan	279,510	333,234	95,844	43,810	—	—	—
Toyota	554,110	516,878	321,523	—	—	—	—
Mitsubishi[1]	184,675	218,161	148,379	—	—	—	—
Auto Alliance[2]	100,116	148,932	184,428	—	—	—	—
Subaru Legacy	102,180	80,669	32,461	—	—	—	—
BMW	58,293	11,872	—	—	—	—	—
Industry total [3]	**5,927,281**	**6,350,433**	**6,077,449**	**8,184,821**	**6,375,506**	**6,716,951**	**6,550,128**

1. Produces Misubishi and Chrysler/Dodge/Eagle vehicles. 2. Formerly listed as Mazda; includes Mazda MX-6 and 626 and Ford Probe. 3. Industry total may not be the sum of models and companies listed due to timing of company reports. *Source:* American Automobile Manufacturers Association.

Livestock on Farms

(in thousands)

Type	1998	1996	1994	1990	1985	1980	1975	1970	1965
Cattle[1]	99,501	103,487	100,988	95,816	109,582	111,242	132,028	112,369	109,000
Dairy cows[1]	9,191	9,416	9,528	10,015	10,311	10,758	11,220	13,303	16,981
Sheep[1]	7,616	8,461	9,714	11,358	10,716	12,699	14,515	20,423	25,127
Swine[2]	60,915	58,264	57,904	53,788	64,462	67,318	54,693	57,046	56,106
Chickens[3]	403,495	384,622	379,640	357,241	347,443	400,585	384,101	422,096	401,813
Turkeys[4]	n.a.	302,708	286,605	282,445	185,427	165,243	124,165	116,139	105,914

Except as noted, these figures represent the number of animals on a given day, rather than the number produced over the year. 1. As of January 1. 2. As of December 1 of the previous year. 3. As of December 1 of previous year; excludes commercial broilers. 4. Inventory data on turkeys is not available; represents the number produced. *Source:* U.S. Department of Agriculture, National Agricultural Statistics Service, web: www.usda.gov/nass.

Farm Income
(in millions of dollars)

Year	Cash receipts from marketings		Government payments	Total cash income[1]
	Crops	Livestock, livestock products		
1930	$ 3,868	$ 5,187	—	$ 9,055
1935	2,977	4,143	$ 573	7,693
1940	3,469	4,913	723	9,105
1945	9,655	12,008	742	22,405
1950	12,356	16,105	283	28,764
1955	13,523	15,967	229	29,842
1960	15,023	18,989	703	34,958
1965	17,479	21,886	2,463	42,215
1970	20,977	29,532	3,717	54,768
1975	45,813	43,089	807	90,707
1980	71,746	67,991	1,285	143,295
1985	74,293	69,822	$ 7,705	$ 157,854
1990	80,131	89,843	9,298	186,824
1991	82,060	86,735	8,214	184,858
1992	84,853	86,350	9,169	188,160
1993	87,500	90,200	13,402	200,100
1994	93,100	88,200	7,900	198,300
1995	100,700	87,000	7,300	205,000
1996	109,400	92,900	7,300	220,600
1997[2]	108,900	92,600	7,900	220,800
1998[2]	106,700	91,300	7,400	216,400

1. Includes items not listed. 2. Forecast. *Source:* U.S. Department of Agriculture, Economic Research Service, web: www.usda.gov.

Agricultural Output by States, 1997 Crops

State	Corn (1,000 bu)	Wheat (1,000 bu)	Cotton[2] (1,000 ba[3])	Potatoes (1,000 cwt)	Tobacco (1,000 lb)	Cattle (1,000 head)	Swine (1,000 head)
Alabama	23,055	4,200	550	1,148	—	209	107
Arizona	8,500	8,775	865	1,705	—	471	10
Arkansas	21,875	39,360	1,730	—	—	31	188
California	44,200	43,680	2,620	16,188	—	1,030	1,937
Colorado	150,380	94,700	—	28,037	—	2,595	43
Connecticut[1]	—	—	—	—	3,572	—	—
Delaware	15,840	5,329	—	966	—	38[4]	230[4]
Florida	6,400	585	135	8,181	19,635	—	126
Georgia	55,000	15,840	1,900	—	89,320	—	310
Hawaii	—	—	—	—	—	19	41
Idaho	6,200	114,060	—	135,430	—	742	102
Illinois	1,425,450	70,150	—	1,495	—	1,034	8,456
Indiana	719,550	38,280	—	1,323	18,690	47	4,914
Iowa	1,656,000	1,134	—	273	—	1,049	24,450
Kansas	386,100	506,000	17	—	—	7,369	—
Kentucky	120,510	28,620	—	—	427,715	54	2,195
Louisiana	57,330	4,255	985	—	—	30	39
Maine[1]	—	—	—	19,170	—	—	—
Maryland	37,350	14,620	—	952	12,000	—[4]	—[4]
Massachusetts[1]	—	—	—	675	1,876	—	—
Michigan	263,250	33,480	—	14,250	—	491	—
Minnesota	857,850	78,890	—	20,440	—	1,121	6,992
Mississippi	50,290	7,525	1,810	—	—	—	—
Missouri	332,920	57,200	580	1,479	7,490	110	3,529
Montana	1,890	185,630	—	3,328	—	18	20
Nebraska	1,151,700	70,300	—	9,204	—	7,408	5,776
Nevada	—	1,575	—	2,967	—	1	2
New England	—	—	—	—	—	35	26
New Hampshire[1]	—	—	—	—	—	—	—
New Jersey	10,044	2,040	—	594	—	25	—
New Mexico	14,875	9,975	105	4,022	—	24	2
New York	75,400	7,560	—	8,408	—	94	49
North Carolina	77,430	34,840	930	3,420	714,120	188	9,274
North Dakota	59,895	267,695	—	21,525	—	—	46
Ohio	462,300	68,670	—	1,175	18,620	160	1,096
Oklahoma	26,600	178,200	200	—	—	46	3,216
Oregon	4,290	63,430	—	27,161	—	18	175
Pennsylvania	97,515	9,100	—	3,190	15,360	973	2,339
Rhode Island[1]	—	—	—	208	—	—	—
South Carolina	32,495	15,000	400	—	126,360	—	—
South Dakota	333,200	99,213	—	1,050	—	261	5,045
Tennessee	66,300	16,650	656	—	104,488	62	—
Texas	248,400	118,900	5,355	3,447	—	6,615	333
Utah	3,105	9,174	—	915	—	—	17
Vermont[1]	—	—	—	—	—	—	—
Virginia	30,225	17,000	139	1,463	111,112	26	4,121
Washington	18,050	168,080	—	88,060	—	933	—

State	Corn (1,000 bu)	Wheat (1,000 bu)	Cotton[2] (1,000 ba[3])	Potatoes (1,000 cwt)	Tobacco (1,000 lb)	Cattle (1,000 head)	Swine (1,000 head)
West Virginia	3,515	486	—	—	3,060	17	10
Wisconsin	402,600	8,075	—	27,923	5,453	1,643	351
Wyoming	7,695	8,276	—	140	—	6	5
Total U.S.	**9,365,574**	**2,526,552**	**18,977**	**459,912**	**1,678,821**	**36,317**	**91,960**

1. Individual state estimates not always available. 2. Production ginned and to be ginned. 3. 480-lb net weight bales. 4. The cattle and pig totals for Maryland are included with those for Delaware. *Source:* U.S. Department of Agriculture, National Agricultural Statistics Service, web: www.usda.gov/nass.

Farm Indexes

(1990–92 = 100)

Year	Prices paid by farmers[1]	Prices rec'd by farmers[2]	Ratio	Year	Prices paid by farmers[1]	Prices rec'd by farmers[2]	Ratio
1975	47	73	155	1993	103	101	98
1980	75	98	137	1994	106	100	94
1985	86	91	106	1995	110	102	92
1990	99	104	105	1996	115	110	96
1991	100	100	99	1997	116	104	90
1992	101	98	98				

1. Commodities, interest, and taxes and wage rates. 2. All crops and livestock. *Source:* U.S. Department of Agriculture, National Agricultural Statistics Service, web: www.usda.gov/nass.

Estimated Annual Retail and Wholesale Sales by Kind of Business

(in millions of dollars)

Kind of business	1997	1995
Retail sales, total	2,566,209	2,329,310
Building materials stores	116,106	98,191
Automotive dealers	625,682	556,708
Furniture, home furnishings, and equipment stores	146,679	130,348
General merchandise stores	331,496	297,962
Food stores	429,805	407,302
Gasoline service stations	158,693	149,555
Apparel and accessory stores	117,826	110,936
Eating and drinking places	236,159	222,081
Drug and proprietary stores	98,182	84,705
Liquor stores	23,964	21,700
Merchant wholesale sales, total	2,500,109	2,265,732
Durable goods, total	1,311,313	1,179,197
Motor vehicles and automotive parts and supplies	216,561	202,556
Furniture and home furnishings	40,929	40,861
Lumber and other construction materials	90,161	77,139
Professional and commercial equipment and supplies	237,036	194,647
Metals and minerals except petroleum	107,887	100,514
Electrical goods	201,156	169,776
Hardware, plumbing, and heating equipment	75,970	67,622
Machinery, equipment, and supplies	206,441	182,748
Miscellaneous durable goods	135,172	143,334
Nondurable goods, total	1,188,796	1,086,535
Paper and paper products	84,813	81,976
Drugs, drug proprietaries, and druggists' sundries	113,641	95,039
Apparel, piece goods, and notions	82,805	70,583
Groceries and related products	327,538	304,695
Farm-product raw materials	125,302	113,691
Chemical and allied products	55,673	47,774
Petroleum and petroleum products	166,475	150,560
Beer, wine, and distilled alcoholic beverages	54,955	54,060
Miscellaneous nondurable goods	177,594	168,157

Source: U.S. Bureau of the Census, web: www.census.gov.

Imports and Exports of Leading Commodities

by Principal SITC Groupings (in millions of dollars)

Item	Cumulative 1997 Exports	Cumulative 1997 Imports
Selected commodities [1]		
ADP equipment; office machines	43,632	75,001
Airplanes and airplate parts	38,756	9,583
Alcoholic bev., distilled	385	2,186
Aluminum	3,761	5,558
Animal feeds	4,623	649
Artwork/antiques	1,114	3,587
Basketware, etc.	2,492	3,360
Cereal flour	1,244	1,328
Chemicals	69,461	50,326
Cigarettes and tobacco	5,962	1,203
Clothing	8,388	48,407
Coal	3,565	654
Coffee	7	3,575
Copper	1,442	3,254
Cork, wood, lumber	5,136	8,185
Corn	5,417	103
Cotton, raw, and linters	2,709	20
Crude fertilizers	1,627	1,340
Crude oil	780	54,091
Fish and preparations	2,630	7,687
Footwear	802	14,018
Furniture and bedding	3,942	11,143
Gem diamonds	108	7,599
Glass	2,115	1,750
Glassware	814	1,555
Gold, nonmonetary	5,673	3,028
Hides and skins	1,503	129
Iron and steel mill production	5,634	14,292
Jewelry	730	4,587

Item	Cumulative 1997 Exports	Imports
Lighting, plumbing	1,537	2,945
Liquified propane/butane	297	1,159
Live animals	684	1,654
Machinery	158,318	159,639
Meat and preparations	6,894	2,656
Metal manufactures, n.e.s.	10,297	12,229
Metal ores; scrap	4,672	4,156
Mineral fuels, other	3,357	1,863
Natural gas	320	5,223
Nickel	346	1,144
Oils/fats, vegetable	1,397	1,375
Optical goods	1,703	2,494
Paper and paperboard, printed matter, and pulp	18,764	17,213
Petroleum preparations	3,885	13,871
Photographic equipment	3,867	5,747
Plastic articles, n.e.s.	5,098	5,682
Platinum	440	1,959
Pottery	101	1,685
Records/magnetic media	6,814	4,144
Rice	932	217
Rubber articles, n.e.s.	1,246	1,553
Rubber tires and tubes	2,395	3,417
Scientific instruments	23,997	13,947
Ships, boats	1,366	876
Silver and bullion	641	472
Soybeans	7,479	86
Spacecraft	828	187
Sugar	3	958
Televisions, VCRs, etc.	24,024	36,685
Textile yarn, fabric	8,978	11,949
Toys/games/sporting goods	3,830	17,372
Travel goods	331	3,842
Vegetables and fruits	7,483	7,744
Vehicles	55,268	112,767
Watches/clocks/parts	309	2,837
Wheat	4,178	359
Wood manufactures	1,960	4,670
Total, selected categories:		
Manufactured goods [1]	549,061	728,574
Agricultural commodities [1]	55,654	35,148
Mineral fuels [1]	12,328	77,840
Total [2]	**688,896**	**870,723**

Notes: SITC = Standard International Trade Classification; n.e.s. = not elsewhere specified. 1. Domestic exports 2. Total exports (domestic and foreign). Details may not equal totals due to rounding. Data not seasonally adjusted. *Source:* U.S. Bureau of the Census, Foreign Trade Division, web: www.census.gov.

Economic Outlook Through 2006

The Bureau of Labor Statistics released its biennial update of the employment outlook for the coming decade in the November 1997 issue of *Monthly Labor Review*. Highlights of the report follow.

Slower Growth in the Labor Force

The gradual slowdown in the rate of labor-force expansion continues to be one of the fundamental forces shaping the employment outlook. The slowdown is itself a reflection of very long-term swings in fertility. At the same time, immigration has become an increasingly important source of population and labor-force growth, moderating to some degree the slowing of population and labor-force growth.

The labor force will increase by about 15 million persons (or 11 percent) over the next 10 years, reaching 149 million by 2006. By comparison, the labor force expanded by some 16 million persons (or 14 percent) over the past 10 years. Significant shifts are expected in its demographic structure. The result will be a continuation of the aging of the labor force seen in the previous decade. By 2006, the median age of the labor force will approach 41 years, a level not seen in the United States since the 1960s.

Changing Complexion of the Labor Force

Women will continue to increase their share of the labor force, although at a slower rate than in the past. Labor force participation for women overall is projected to rise by about 2 percentage points, half the increase of the preceding decade. By 2006, women's share of the labor force will increase by just 1.2 percentage points, to 47.4 percent, compared with increases of 1.7 points between 1986 and 1996, and 4 points between 1976 and 1986.

Significant compositional shifts are also expected along racial/ethnic lines. Although white non-Hispanics are expected to continue to account for by far the largest share of the labor force in 2006 (73 percent, compared with 75 percent in 1996 and 80 percent in 1986), their rate of growth is considerably below that of the black, Asian, and Hispanic groups. Continued rapid growth of the Hispanic population makes it likely that this group will become the second-largest ethnic grouping, replacing blacks, by 2006 or shortly thereafter.

Output

As the natural increase of the population slows, immigration has become a major factor in determining the prospects for labor-force growth. The results are a labor force that is not only larger, but one that is younger and has a different ethnic mix and higher overall participation rate.

The moderating growth in the labor force will also affect potential output and total employment. Overall, real gross domestic product is projected to increase 2.1 percent per year over the projection period, compared with 2.3 percent over the preceding 10-year period. The slowdown reflects lower employment growth, partially offset by a modest improvement in productivity.

One of the most striking features of the macroeconomic outlook is the growing internationalization of the U.S. economy. By 2006, exports and imports are each expected to approach 20 percent of gross domestic product. Investment spending also shows strong growth, nearly 50 percent faster than the overall economy. Both of these trends are fueled in large part by strong demand for computers and a broad array of other high technology products.

Unemployment

The projected growth of gross domestic product, slower labor-force growth, and a favorable inflation outlook combine to allow the unemployment rate to

remain at relatively low levels. The trade and federal budget deficits also respond favorably to projected economic conditions, with the trade deficit reduced substantially in real terms and the federal budget deficit virtually eliminated.

Mirroring the slowdown in labor-force growth, total employment is expected to expand more slowly in the 1996–2006 period than it did in the preceding 10 years. The economy is expected to add 18.6 million new jobs by 2006, compared with a gain of 21 million between 1986 and 1996. As was the case in the previous BLS projection, all of this growth occurs in the service-producing sector, including net gains of 3.6 million in business services, 3.2 million in health services, and 2.3 million in retail trade. Although manufacturing shows a slight decline overall, some industries, particularly those benefiting from strong exports and capital spending, show moderation or even reversal of previously projected employment declines.

Industry

While the overall picture of industrial structure has not changed dramatically, a number of sectors do show significant changes from previous projections. The computer and data-processing services sector, for example, is now expected to add 1.3 million jobs, twice the number previously projected.

The growth and shifting industrial structure of the U.S. economy has major implications for the pattern of occupational demand over the next 10 years. At the major group level, professionals; managers; technicians; and service, marketing, and sales workers are all expected to increase their share of total employment. Meanwhile, occupational groups such as administrative support; precision production, craft and repair; and fabricators, laborers and operators will experience a declining share.

The shifting industrial structure has a major impact on the relative growth of occupations. The three fastest growing occupations, for example, are computer specialties, reflecting, in large part, the expected rapid expansion of the computer and data-processing services industry. Similarly, as a result of rapid employment growth in health services, half of the 30 fastest growing occupations are health-care related.

Education and Training

The projections also show that differing growth prospects among occupations have important implications for education. While the economy will continue to generate large numbers of jobs at all educational levels, the results also show that employment in occupations requiring an associate degree or higher will grow considerably faster than those with lesser educational requirements.

The new BLS projections describe an economy that is gradually slowing in response to demographic factors, but is nevertheless expected to produce 18 million new jobs by 2006—as well as a much larger number of job openings to meet replacement needs. The effects of the long-term trend toward sevice-producing activities is evident, as computer and health-related occupations dominate the list of the fastest growing jobs. On the other hand, the decline in manufacturing jobs seems to have come to at least a temporary halt, as the growing internationalization and computerization of the economy provides significant demand for technology-related manufactured products. Finally, while the economy will generate job opportunities at all educational and skill levels, the increasing role of technology means that the fastest-growing jobs are most likely to be those requiring relatively more extensive education and training. □

Industry Output and Employment Projections to 2006

Over the 1996–2006 period, total employment in the United States is projected to increase by 18.6 million to 151 million. The projected annual average rate of growth is 1.3 percent, slower than the 1.7 percent annual average rate of growth from 1986 to 1996. Most of the increase (95 percent) comes from nonfarm wage and salary jobs, as agricultural employment is expected to decline by 24,000. Private household wage and salary jobs also are projected to decline, by 153,000. The remaining portion of growth in total jobs is accounted for by an increase of 1.2 million in nonagricultural self-employed and unpaid family workers.

The macroeconomic factors whose combined influence most affects the growth of total employment are increases in the labor force, in productivity, and in the nation's gross domestic product, or GDP. In the latest round of Bureau of Labor Statistics (BLS) projections, the labor force grows at an annual average rate of 1.1 percent during the 1996–2006 projection period. This is a slowing in the rate of growth compared to the 1.3-percent annual average rate of increase posted over the 1986–96 period. The growth rate of the nonfarm labor productivity index is projected to average 1.1 percent per year from 1996 through 2006, an increase from the 0.7 percent rate of change during the previous 10 years. The rate of growth for GDP during the projection period is 2.1 percent, a slight decline from the 2.3 percent average annual increase during the 1986–96 period. The overall picture, then, is one of an economy in which the rate of growth of both the labor force and GDP is slowing, but output, as measured by GDP, continues to outpace labor force growth because of productivity gains.

Services

The service-producing sector, excluding private households, has a projected increase of 17.6 million nonfarm wage and salary jobs, from 94.3 million in 1996 to 111.9 million by 2006. Within the service-producing sector, employment growth is highly concentrated. During the 1986–96 period, 11.2 million, or 56 percent, of the 20.1 million increase in service-producing sector employment was concentrated in the services division. The projected 11.3 million gain in wage and salary jobs in the services division over the 1996–2006 period accounts for almost two thirds of the projected 17.6 million increase in employment in the service-producing sector. The addition of job growth for retail trade (2.3 million) and for state and local government (1.8 million) to that for the services division accounts for 87 percent of the projected job gains in the service-producing sector.

Goods

The goods-producing sector, excluding agricultural products, has a slight projected increase of 20,000 wage and salary jobs, with employment remaining essentially stable at 24.4 million over the 1996–2006 period. However, strong productivity gains allow real gross duplicated output to grow at a projected 2.3 percent annual rate. At the major industry level on the goods-producing side, only construction is projected to post an employment gain. From the 1996 level of 5.4 million, construction is expected to add 500,000 jobs to reach a projected 2006 jobs level of 5.9 million. Employment in mining is projected to decline by 131,000, from a level of 574,000 in 1996 to 443,000 in 2006. Over the 1986–96 period, mining lost 204,000 jobs. Manufacturing is expected to decline by 350,000 jobs, from 18.5 million in 1996 to 18.2 million in 2006. The decline for manufacturing is about 30 percent less than the reduction of 493,000 jobs recorded over the previous 10-year period, 1986–96.

Rate of Employment Growth or Decline, by Industry, 1996–2006

Industry description	Change (in thousands of jobs) 1996–2006	Average annual rate of change 1996–2006
Fastest growing		
Computer and data-processing services	1,301.2	7.6%
Health services	796.4	5.3
Management and public relations	526.8	4.8
Miscellaneous transportation services	123.1	4.8
Residential care	397.7	4.8
Personnel supply services	1,393.3	4.3
Water and sanitation	118.2	4.2
Individual and miscellaneous social services	419.6	4.1
Offices of health practitioners	1,294.5	3.9
Amusement and recreation services	456.7	3.5
Automobile parking, repair, and services	345.9	3.3
Nursing and personal care facilities	644.8	3.2
Producers, orchestras, and entertainers	52.9	3.0
Miscellaneous equipment rental and leasing	82.4	3.0
Security and commodity brokers	189.0	3.0
Passenger transportation arrangement	64.3	2.7
Child day-care services	164.2	2.6
Miscellaneous business services	576.5	2.5
Museums, botanical, and zoological gardens	24.1	2.5
Nondepository; holding and investment offices	202.6	2.5%
Most rapidly declining		
Coal mining	–44.4	–6.0
Watches, clocks, and parts	–2.6	–4.0
Footwear, except rubber and plastic	–15.7	–4.0
Search and navigation equipment	–51.2	–3.8
Crude petroleum, natural gas, and gas liquids	–46.7	–3.7
Luggage, handbags, and leather products	–15.0	–3.6
Tobacco products	–11.1	–3.1
Metal cans and shipping containers	–10.4	–3.1
Apparel	–167.8	–3.0
Tires and inner tubes	–20.2	–2.9
Photographic equipment and supplies	–19.8	–2.6
Electrical industrial apparatus	–33.6	–2.4
Petroleum refining	–20.7	–2.3
Household appliances	–24.6	–2.2
Blast furnaces and basic steel products	–43.6	–2.0
State and local government enterprises	–108.0	–2.0
Electric distribution equipment	–14.2	–1.9
Private households	–152.8	–1.8
Beverages	–29.2	–1.8
Metal mining	–8.8	–1.8

Source: U.S. Department of Labor, Bureau of Labor Statistics, *Monthly Labor Review* web: stats.bls.gov/.

Poverty and Income in the United States

Source: U.S. Bureau of the Census, *Poverty in the United States: 1996* and *Money Income in the United States: 1996*, both issued September 1997.

The number of persons below the official government poverty level was 36.5 million in 1996, representing 13.7 percent of the nation's population. Neither the number of poor nor the poverty rate showed a significant difference from the 1995 figure of 36.4 million and a poverty rate of 13.8 percent.

Age

In 1996, the poverty rate for all persons under 18 years old was 20.5 percent. The poverty rate for those aged 18 to 64 was 11.4 percent, about the same as that for ages 65 and over (10.8 percent).

The elderly are under-represented in the poverty population. These persons 65 and over are approximately 12 percent of the total population but make up only 9 percent of the poor. However, a higher proportion of elderly (7.6 percent) than nonelderly (4.4 percent) were concentrated just over their respective poverty thresholds (between 100 percent and 125 percent of their thresholds); 19 percent of the nation's 12.8 million "near poor" persons were elderly.

Persons under age 18 continue to represent a very large segment of the poor (40 percent) even though they are only a little more than one fourth of the total population.

Persons Below the Poverty Level, 1975–1996

(in thousands)

Year	All persons	White	Black	Hispanic origin[1]	Year	All persons	White	Black	Hispanic origin[1]
1975	25,877	17,770	7,545	2,991	1986	32,370	22,183	8,983	5,117
1976	24,975	16,713	7,595	2,783	1987	32,221	21,195	9,520	5,422
1977	24,720	16,416	7,726	2,700	1988	31,745	20,715	9,356	5,357
1978	24,497	16,259	7,625	2,607	1989	31,528	20,785	9,302	5,430
1979	26,072	17,214	8,050	2,921	1990	33,585	22,326	9,837	6,006
1980	29,272	19,699	8,579	3,491	1991	35,708	23,747	10,242	6,339
1981	31,822	21,553	9,173	3,713	1992	38,014	25,259	10,827	7,592
1982	34,398	23,517	9,697	4,301	1993	39,265	26,226	10,877	8,126
1983	35,303	23,984	9,882	4,633	1994	38,059	25,379	10,196	8,416
1984	33,700	22,955	9,490	4,806	1995	36,425	24,423	9,872	8,574
1985	33,064	22,860	8,926	5,236	1996	36,529	24,650	9,694	8,697

1. Persons of Hispanic origin may be of any race. *Source:* U.S. Bureau of the Census, web: www.census.gov.

Children under age six have been particularly vulnerable to poverty. In 1996, the overall poverty rate for related children under six years of age was 22.7 percent. Of related children under six years old living in families with a female householder, no spouse present, 58.8 percent were poor, compared to 11.5 percent of such young children in married-couple families.

Race and Hispanic Origin

In 1996, the poverty rate was 11.2 percent for whites, 8.6 percent for non-Hispanic whites, and 28.4 percent for blacks. For persons of Hispanic origin (who may be of any race) the poverty rate was 29.4 percent. For Asians and Pacific Islanders, the largest component of persons of other races, the poverty rate was 14.5 percent in 1996.

Even though the poverty rate for whites was lower than that for the other racial and ethnic groups, the majority of poor persons in 1996 were white (67.5 percent), and 45.1 percent were non-Hispanic white.

None of the racial or ethnic groups showed a significant change between 1995 and 1996 in the number of poor or the poverty rate.

Families

There was no significant change in either the number of poor families or in their poverty rate between 1995 and 1996. The poverty rate for families was 11.0 percent in 1996 compared with 10.8 percent in 1995. Married couples had a 1996 poverty rate of 5.6 percent, the same as for 1995.

There was no significant change for black or Hispanic-origin families overall. For families with a female householder, no spouse present, the poverty rate was 32.6 percent, largely unchanged from 32.4 percent in 1995. Female-householder families were over-represented among the poor. While 54 percent of all poor families had a female householder with no spouse present, only 18 percent of all families in the United States had a female householder. Neither of these figures was statistically different from their respective 1995 estimates.

Income

For the second consecutive year, the real median income of households in the United States increased in 1996. Median household income in 1996 was $35,492, an increase of 1.2 percent over 1995.

Race and Hispanic Origin

Among the race and Hispanic-origin groups, Asian and Pacific Islander households had the highest median household income in 1996 ($43,276), and black and Hispanic-origin households had the lowest ($23,482 and $24,906, respectively). Households maintained by white persons had a median income of $37,161.

Households of Hispanic origin saw a 5.8 percent increase in real median household income in 1996 over 1995. There were no significant changes in real household income for white, black, or Asian and Pacific Islander households in the same period.

Year-Round, Full-Time Workers

The real median earnings of year-round, full-time women workers 15 years old and over increased by 2.4 percent to $23,710 in 1996, while those of men declined by 0.9 percent to $32,144. Earnings of men have been declining steadily since 1993, and have declined by 3.3 percent since 1990. Though this is generally not good news, the decline in men's earnings has narrowed the wage gap between men and women to an all-time low. In 1996 women earned about 74 cents for every dollar men earned.

Per Capita Income

Overall, per capita income increased significantly in real terms between 1995 and 1996 for all but one of the race/ethnic-origin groups. The per

Poverty Thresholds

The poverty thresholds in 1996 were as follows: one person under 65: $8,163; age 65 and over, $7,525; two persons: householder under 65, $10,564; householder 65 and over, $9,491; three persons, $12,516; four persons, $16,036; five persons, $18,952; six persons, $21,389; seven persons, $24,268; eight persons, $27,091; nine or more persons, $31,971.

capita income of whites, blacks, and Hispanics increased by 1.8 percent, 5.2 percent, and 4.9 percent, respectively, though the percent change for Asians and Pacific Islanders was not significant. Per capita incomes were $19,181 for whites, $11,899 for blacks, $17,921 for Asians and Pacific Islanders and $10,048 for Hispanic-origin populations. The 1996 per capita income was $18,136 for the total population.

Percent of Persons in Poverty, by State: 1991–1996

State	1996 Percent	1995 Percent	1993 Percent	1991 Percent
Alabama	17.1%	20.1%	17.4%	19.0%
Alaska	7.7	7.1	9.1	12.0
Arizona	18.3	16.1	15.4	15.5
Arkansas	16.1	14.9	20.0	17.4
California	16.8	16.7	18.2	16.3
Colorado	9.7	8.8	9.9	10.6
Connecticut	10.7	9.7	8.5	9.0
Delaware	9.5	10.3	10.2	7.7
D.C.	23.2	22.2	26.4	18.6
Florida	15.2	16.2	17.8	15.7
Georgia	13.5	12.1	13.5	17.1
Hawaii	11.2	10.3	8.0	7.8
Idaho	13.2	14.5	13.1	14.1
Illinois	12.3	12.4	13.6	13.8
Indiana	8.6	9.6	12.2	15.8
Iowa	10.9	12.2	10.3	9.8
Kansas	11.0	10.8	13.1	12.4
Kentucky	15.9	14.7	20.4	18.8
Louisiana	20.1	19.7	26.4	19.2
Maine	11.2	11.7	15.4	14.2
Maryland	10.2	10.1	9.7	9.3
Massachusetts	10.6	11.0	10.7	11.3
Michigan	11.7	12.2	15.4	14.2
Minnesota	9.5	9.2	11.6	13.1
Mississippi	22.1	23.5	24.7	23.8
Missouri	9.5	9.4	16.1	14.9
Montana	16.2%	15.3%	14.9%	15.5%
Nebraska	9.9	9.6	10.3	9.8
Nevada	9.6	11.1	9.8	11.6
New Hampshire	5.9	5.3	9.9	7.4
New Jersey	8.5	7.8	10.9	10.0
New Mexico	25.4	25.3	17.4	23.0
New York	16.6	16.5	16.4	15.7
North Carolina	12.4	12.6	14.4	14.6
North Dakota	11.5	12.0	11.2	14.7
Ohio	12.1	11.5	13.0	13.5
Oklahoma	16.9	17.1	19.9	17.2
Oregon	11.5	11.2	11.8	13.6
Pennsylvania	11.9	12.2	13.2	11.2
Rhode Island	10.8	10.6	11.2	10.7
South Carolina	16.5	19.9	18.7	16.5
South Dakota	13.2	14.5	14.2	14.3
Tennessee	15.7	15.5	19.6	15.5
Texas	17.0	17.4	17.4	18.0
Utah	8.1	8.4	10.7	13.0
Vermont	11.5	10.3	10.0	12.7
Virginia	11.3	10.2	9.7	10.0
Washington	12.2	12.5	12.1	9.7
West Virginia	17.6	16.7	22.2	17.9
Wisconsin	8.7	8.5	12.6	10.0
Wyoming	12.1	12.2	13.3	9.9

Source: Poverty in the United States, 1996, Current Population Reports, U.S. Bureau of the Census, web: www.census.gov.

How to Raise and Spend $1.7 Trillion

Government estimates for receipts and outlays for fiscal year 1999.

WHERE IT WOULD COME FROM...

Other 5%
Excise Taxes 4%
Corporate Income Taxes 11%
Individual Income Taxes 46%
Payroll Taxes 34%

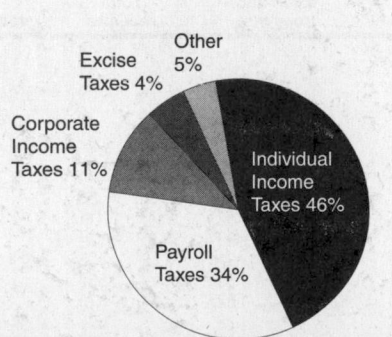

...AND HOW IT WOULD BE SPENT

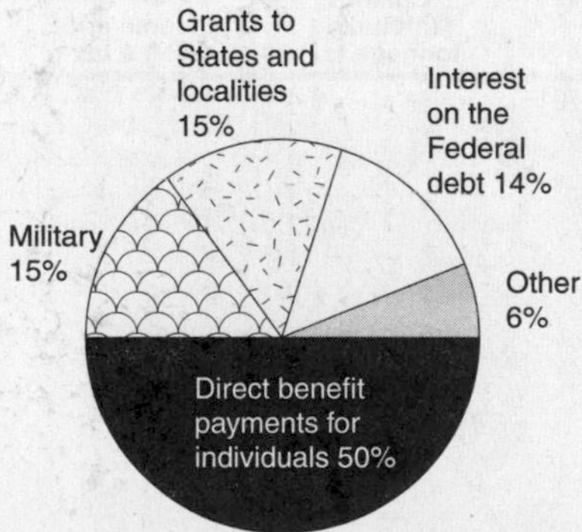

Source: Office of Management and Budget

The Federal Budget—Receipts and Outlays

(in billions of dollars)

	Actual			Estimate	
	1995	1996	1997	1998	1999
Receipts by Source					
Individual income taxes	$ 590.2	$ 656.4	$ 737.5	$ 767.8	$ 791.5
Corporation income taxes	157.0	171.8	182.3	190.8	198.0
Social insurance and retirement receipts	484.5	509.4	539.4	571.4	595.9
Excise taxes	57.5	54.0	56.9	55.5	72.0
Estate and gift taxes	15.6	17.2	19.8	20.4	20.5
Customs duties	20.9	18.7	17.9	18.4	18.2
Miscellaneous receipts	28.6	25.5	25.5	33.5	46.7
Total receipts	1,355.2	1,453.1	1,579.3	1,657.9	1,742.7
Outlays by Function					
National defense	272.1	265.7	270.5	264.1	265.5
Human resources	923.8	958.3	1,002.3	1,049.0	1,100.5
Education, training, employment, and social services	54.3	52.0	53.0	55.1	59.5
Health	115.4	119.4	123.8	131.8	141.5
Medicare	159.9	174.2	190.0	198.1	207.3
Income security	220.5	226.0	230.9	239.3	252.8
Social security	335.8	349.7	365.3	381.5	396.2
Veterans benefits and services	37.9	37.0	39.3	43.1	43.3
Physical resources	59.2	64.2	60.0	81.1	78.9
Energy	4.9	2.8	1.5	0.4	(1.0)
Natural resources and environment	22.1	21.6	21.4	23.8	23.2
Commerce and housing credit	(17.8)	(10.5)	(14.6)	3.5	3.5
Transportation	39.4	39.6	40.8	41.5	42.3
Community and regional development	10.6	10.7	11.0	11.8	10.9
Net interest	232.2	241.1	244.0	242.7	241.8
Other functions	73.0	68.8	74.4	77.3	89.0
International affairs	16.4	13.5	15.2	14.5	14.5
General science, space and technology	16.7	16.7	17.2	17.1	17.6
Agriculture	9.8	9.2	9.0	10.6	11.0
Administration of justice	16.2	17.5	20.2	22.3	25.5
General government	13.8	11.9	12.8	12.9	17.2
Allowances	—	—	—	—	3.3
Undistributed offsetting receipts	(44.5)	(37.6)	(50.0)	(46.4)	(42.5)
Total Outlays	1,515.7	1,560.5	1,601.2	1,667.8	1,733.2
Total Deficit or Surplus	–160.5	–107.3	–21.9	9.9	9.5

NOTE: The fiscal year is from October 1 to September 30. *Source:* Budget of the United States Government, Fiscal Year 1999, web: www.access.gpo.gov/su_docs/budget99/maindown.html.

Receipts and Outlays of the Federal Government

(in millions of dollars)

From 1789 to 1842, the federal fiscal year ended December 31; from 1844 to 1976, on June 30; and beginning 1977, on September 30.

	Receipts					
		Internal revenue				
	Customs (including tonnage tax)[1]	Income and profits tax	Other	Miscellaneous taxes and receipts	Total receipts	Net receipts[2]
1789–1791	$ 4	—	—	—	$ 4	$ 4
1800	9	—	$ –1	$ 1	11	11
1810	9	—	—	1	9	9
1820	15	—	—	3	18	18
1830	22	—	—	3	25	25
1840	14	—	—	6	20	20
1850	40	—	—	4	44	44
1860	53	—	—	3	56	56
1870	195	—	185	32	411	411
1880	187	—	124	23	334	334
1890	230	—	143	31	403	403
1900	233	—	295	39	567	567
1910	334	—	290	52	675	675
1915	210	$ 80	335	72	698	683
1929	602	2,331	607	493	4,033	3,862
1939	319	2,189	2,972	188	5,668	4,979
1944	431	34,655	7,030	3,325	45,441	43,563

	Receipts					
		Internal revenue				
	Customs (including tonnage tax)[1]	Income and profits tax	Other	Miscellaneous taxes and receipts	Total receipts	Net receipts[2]
1945	$ 355	$ 35,173	$ 8,729	$ 3,494	$ 47,750	$ 44,362
1950	423	28,263	11,186	1,439	41,311	36,422
1956	705	56,639	20,564	389	78,297	74,547
1960	1,123	67,151	28,266	1,190	97,730	92,492
1965	1,478	79,792	39,996	1,598	122,863	116,833
1970	2,494	138,689	65,276	3,424	209,883	193,743
1975	3,782	202,146	108,371	6,711	321,010	280,997
1980	7,482	359,927	192,436	12,797	572,641	520,050
1985	12,079	474,074	311,092	18,576	815,821	733,996
1988	16,198	495,376	377,469	19,909	(4)	908,953
1989	16,334	549,273	402,200	22,800	(4)	990,691
1990	16,707	560,391	426,893	27,470	(4)	1,031,462
1991	15,949	565,913	449,577	22,846	(4)	1,054,265
1992	17,359	576,234	470,401	26,459	(4)	1,090,453
1993	18,802	627,200	488,934	18,290	(4)	1,153,226
1994	20,099	683,123	531,924	22,041	(4)	1,257,187
1995	19,300	747,247	556,721	27,309	(4)	1,350,578
1996	18,670	828,241	534,948	25,534	(4)	1,407,393
1997	17,928	919,759	539,371	25,465	(4)	1,579,292
1998	18,363	958,610	571,374	33,535	(4)	1,657,858

	Outlays					
Year	Department of Defense (Army, 1789–1950)	Department of the Navy	Interest on public debt	All other	Net outlays[3]	Surplus (+) or deficit (–)
1789–1791	$ 1	—	$ 2	$ 1	$ 4	—
1800	3	$ 3	3	1	11	—
1810	2	2	3	1	8	$ +1
1820	3	4	5	6	18	—
1830	5	3	2	5	15	+10
1840	7	6	—	11	24	–4
1850	9	8	4	18	40	+4
1860	16	12	3	32	63	–7
1870	58	22	129	101	310	+101
1880	38	14	96	120	268	+66
1890	45	22	36	215	318	+85
1900	135	56	40	290	521	+46
1910	190	123	21	359	694	–19
1915	202	142	23	379	746	–63
1929	426	365	678	1,658	3,127	+734
1939	695	673	941	6,533	8,841	–3,862
1944	49,438	26,538	2,609	16,401	94,986	–51,423
1945	50,490	30,047	3,617	14,149	98,303	–53,941
1950	5,789	4,130	5,750	23,875	39,544	–3,122
1956	35,693	—	6,787	27,981	70,460	+4,087
1960	43,969	—	9,180	39,075	92,223	+269
1965	47,179	—	11,346	59,904	118,430	–1,596
1970	78,360	—	19,304	98,924	196,588	–2,845
1975	87,471	—	32,665	205,969	326,105	–45,108
1980	136,138	—	74,860	368,013	579,011	–58,961
1985	244,054	—	178,945	513,810	936,809	–202,813
1988	290,349	—	151,711	621,995	1,064,055	–155,102
1989	303,600	—	169,100	649,943	1,142,643	–123,785
1990	299,355	—	183,790	768,725	1,251,850	–220,388
1991	273,292	—	194,541	855,924	1,323,757	–269,492
1992	298,350	—	199,439	883,005	1,380,794	–290,340
1993	291,186	—	198,811	918,635	1,408,532	–255,306
1994	281,451	—	202,957	976,149	1,460,557	–203,370
1995	271,895	—	232,175	1,010,364	1,514,434	–163,856
1996	265,748	—	241,090	1,053,674	1,560,512	–153,119
1997	270,473	—	244,013	1,357,222	1,601,235	–21,943
1998	264,112	—	242,694	1,425,121	1,667,815	–9,957

1. Beginning 1933, tonnage tax is included in "Other receipts." 2. Net receipts equal total receipts less (a) appropriations to federal old-age and survivors' insurance trust fund beginning fiscal year 1939 and (b) refunds of receipts beginning fiscal year 1933. 3. Includes Air Force 1950–65 (in millions): 1950, $3,521; 1956, $16,750; 1960, $19,065; 1965, $18,471. 4. Net receipts are now the total receipts. Public Law 99-177 moved two social security trust funds off-budget. *Source:* Budget of the United States Government, Fiscal Year 1999, web: www.access.gpo.gov/su_docs/budget99/maindown.html.

Social Welfare Expenditures Under Public Programs

(in millions of dollars)

Year and source of funds	Social insurance	Public aid	Health and medical programs[1]	Veterans' programs	Education	Housing	Other social welfare	All health and medical care[2]	Total social welfare	Total social welfare as: Percent of gross domestic product	Total social welfare as: Percent of total govt. outlays
Federal											
1982	$ 250,551	$ 52,485	$ 14,598	$ 24,463	$ 11,917	$ 7,176	$ 6,500	$ 90,776	$ 367,691	11.8%	52.5%
1984	288,743	58,480	16,622	25,970	13,010	10,226	7,349	103,927	420,399	11.4	50.2
1986	326,588	65,615	19,926	27,072	15,022	10,164	7,977	125,730	472,364	11.2	47.6
1988	358,412	74,137	22,681	28,845	16,952	14,006	8,112	149,102	523,144	11.0	49.1
1990	422,257	92,858	27,204	30,428	18,374	16,612	8,905	190,616	616,639	11.2	51.4
1992	495,710	138,704	31,872	34,212	20,188	17,950	10,677	249,528	749,312	12.6	57.1
1993	534,310	151,851	35,209	36,034	20,455	18,006	10,838	275,390	804,702	12.4	60.0
1994	557,389	162,675	34,770	37,262	24,084	24,724	11,718	n.a.	852,622	12.5	51.4
State and Local											
1982	52,481	28,367	19,195	245	121,957	778	5,154	40,738	228,178	7.4	62.6
1984	52,378	32,206	20,383	301	139,046	1,306	5946	44,540	251,569	7.0	58.9
1986	63,816	37,464	24,408	373	163,495	1,872	6,728	53,884	298,158	7.3	58.2
1988	73,783	46,237	29,859	409	202,416	2,550	7,368	70,511	362,622	7.5	60.1
1990	91,565	53,953	36,263	488	240,011	2,856	9,012	85,775	434,148	7.9	68.0
1992	121,266	69,241	39,163	555	272,011	2,668	10,855	104,559	515,758	8.7	70.6
1993	123,018	69,214	41,294	572	311,455	1,748	11,832	106,372	559,183	8.6	81.2
1994	126,458	75,351	44,526	633	320,112	2,045	12,899	n.a.	582,023	8.5	74.0
Total											
1982	303,033	80,852	33,793	24,708	133,874	7,954	11,654	131,514	595,869	19.2	55.7
1984	341,120	90,685	37,006	26,275	152,056	11,532	13,295	148,467	671,969	18.3	52.8
1986	390,404	103,079	44,334	27,445	178,518	12,036	14,705	179,614	770,522	18.5	47.9
1988	432,195	120,375	52,540	29,254	219,368	16,556	15,480	219,613	885,766	18.5	52.8
1990	513,823	146,811	63,467	30,916	258,385	19,468	17,918	276,391	1,050,788	19.2	56.7
1992	616,975	207,945	71,035	34,767	292,198	20,617	21,532	354,058	1,265,070	21.3	61.6
1993	657,328	221,065	74,503	36,606	331,910	19,803	22,670	381,762	1,363,884	21.1	66.7
1994	683,847	238,025	79,296	37,895	344,196	26,769	24,617	407,910	1,434,645	21.0	58.2
Percent of total, by type											
1986	50.7	13.4	5.8	3.6	23.2	1.6	1.9	23.3	100.0	(3)	(3)
1988	48.8	13.6	5.9	3.3	24.8	1.9	1.7	24.8	100.0	(3)	(3)
1990	49.0	14.0	6.0	3.0	25.0	2.0	1.0	26.0	100.0	(3)	(3)
1992	48.8	16.4	5.6	2.7	23.1	1.6	1.7	28.0	100.0	(3)	(3)
1993	46.7	16.2	5.5	2.7	24.3	1.5	1.7	28.0	100.0	(3)	(3)
1994	47.7	16.6	5.5	2.6	24.0	1.9	1.7	28.4	100.0	(3)	(3)
Federal spending as a percent of total											
1986	83.6	63.7	44.9	98.6	8.4	84.4	54.2	70.0	61.3	(3)	(3)
1988	82.9	61.6	43.2	98.6	7.7	84.6	52.4	67.9	59.1	(3)	(3)
1990	82.0	63.0	43.0	98.0	7.0	85.0	50.0	69.0	59.0	(3)	(3)
1992	80.3	66.7	44.9	98.4	6.9	87.1	49.6	70.5	59.2	(3)	(3)
1993	81.3	68.7	44.6	98.4	6.2	90.9	47.8	72.4	59.0	(3)	(3)
1994	81.5	68.3	43.8	98.3	7.0	92.4	47.6	72.0	59.4	(3)	(3)

1. Excludes program parts of social insurance, public aid, veterans, and other social welfare. 2. Combines health and medical programs with medical services provided in connection with social insurance, public aid, veterans, and other social welfare programs. 3. Not applicable. NOTE: Figures are most recent available. *Source:* Social Security Administration, web: www.ssa.gov.

Distribution of Federal Funds by State and Territory, Fiscal Year 1997

(in millions of dollars)

State/Territory	Total	Grants to state and local governments	Salaries and wages	Direct payments to individuals	Procurement	Other programs
Alabama	$ 24,563	$ 3,483	$ 2,902	$14,177	$ 3,231	$ 771
Alaska	4,701	1,303	1,284	1,056	856	201
Arizona	22,108	3,355	2,574	12,872	2,636	671
Arkansas	12,668	2,283	1,067	8,339	455	524
California	160,874	27,014	17,587	84,090	26,247	5,936
Colorado	19,702	2,444	3,386	9,332	3,494	1,046
Connecticut	17,864	2,905	1,353	10,045	2,918	643
Delaware	3,452	629	383	2,186	157	97
District of Columbia	23,112	2,740	11,598	2,845	4,184	1,746

State/Territory	Total	Grants to state and local governments	Salaries and wages	Direct payments to individuals	Procurement	Other programs
Florida	$ 82,060	$ 8,504	$ 7,666	$ 56,224	$ 8,083	$ 1,583
Georgia	35,778	5,469	5,707	18,839	4,774	989
Hawaii	8,266	1,184	2,330	3,430	1,077	244
Idaho	5,683	936	627	2,981	888	251
Illinois	52,818	9,296	5,404	32,892	3,190	2,035
Indiana	25,115	3,539	1,781	15,741	2,329	1,724
Iowa	13,557	1,977	943	8,003	806	1,829
Kansas	12,507	1,620	1,589	7,287	989	1,023
Kentucky	21,261	3,702	2,273	11,773	2,755	758
Louisiana	23,156	4,457	2,066	13,171	2,777	686
Maine	7,184	1,378	755	3,840	1,018	193
Maryland	39,137	3,950	7,556	15,749	8,477	3,405
Massachusetts	37,378	6,365	2,824	19,716	6,121	2,352
Michigan	40,652	7,237	2,741	27,371	2,010	1,292
Minnesota	20,088	3,952	1,638	11,243	1,684	1,572
Mississippi	15,026	2,626	1,542	8,590	1,727	541
Missouri	31,697	4,231	3,033	16,365	6,324	1,744
Montana	5,132	991	595	2,525	260	762
Nebraska	7,809	1,227	974	4,384	521	703
Nevada	7,085	983	824	4,512	550	216
New Hampshire	5,041	842	480	3,022	487	211
New Jersey	39,537	6,602	3,476	24,525	4,097	837
New Mexico	12,441	2,152	1,595	4,679	3,534	480
New York	95,622	24,384	7,039	55,163	5,778	3,258
North Carolina	34,731	6,284	4,887	20,298	1,960	1,301
North Dakota	4,331	1,074	575	1,828	229	624
Ohio	50,707	8,327	4,298	32,186	4,605	1,293
Oklahoma	17,317	2,510	2,629	10,206	1,188	785
Oregon	14,633	2,853	1,422	9,107	580	671
Pennsylvania	65,314	10,268	5,267	42,286	5,126	2,368
Rhode Island	5,879	1,144	709	3,443	356	228
South Carolina	18,815	2,987	2,077	10,887	2,404	460
South Dakota	4,149	982	511	2,034	253	370
Tennessee	28,558	4,555	2,624	16,209	4,386	784
Texas	88,332	13,184	10,897	47,835	13,293	3,124
Utah	8,436	1,355	1,388	4,125	1,206	363
Vermont	2,728	601	267	1,581	150	129
Virginia	52,908	3,518	11,312	20,026	16,254	1,798
Washington	30,321	4,496	4,574	15,295	4,601	1,355
West Virginia	10,409	2,100	863	6,649	502	295
Wisconsin	20,805	3,617	1,363	13,481	1,307	1,037
Wyoming	2,643	762	375	1,250	149	108
American Samoa	170	121	2	25	4	18
Guam	835	125	359	192	121	39
Northern Marianas	76	35	2	25	4	10
Puerto Rico	10,970	3,719	730	5,800	318	404
Virgin Islands	625	371	41	149	8	56
Undistributed	22,054	1,032	1,381	—	19,641	
United States	**1,428,818**	**229,778**	**166,145**	**781,880**	**193,074**	**57,942**

Source: Consolidated Federal Funds Report, Fiscal Year 1997.

Unemployment Rate in the Civilian Labor Force

Year	Rate	Year	Rate	Year	Rate	Year	Rate	Year	Rate	Year	Rate
1920	5.2%	1946	3.9%	1966	3.8%	1986	7.0%	1996	5.4%	Sept.	4.9%
1928	4.2	1948	3.8	1968	3.6	1987	6.2	1997	4.9	Oct.	4.8
1930	8.7	1950	5.3	1970	4.9	1988	5.4	Jan.	5.4	Nov.	4.6
1932	23.6	1952	3.0	1972	5.6	1989	5.3	Feb.	5.3	Dec.	4.7
1934	21.7	1954	5.5	1974	5.6	1990	5.5	March	5.2	1998	
1936	16.9	1956	4.1	1976	7.7	1991	6.7	April	5.0	Jan.	4.7
1938	19.0	1958	6.8	1978	6.0	1992	7.4	May	4.8	Feb.	4.6
1940	14.6	1960	5.5	1980	7.1	1993	6.8	June	5.0	March	4.7
1942	4.7	1962	5.5	1982	9.7	1994	6.1	July	4.9	April	4.3
1944	1.2	1964	5.2	1984	7.5	1995	5.6	Aug.	4.9		

NOTE: Estimates prior to 1940 are based on sources other than direct enumeration. *Source:* U.S. Department of Labor, Bureau of Labor Statistics, web: stats.bls.gov.

Employed and Unemployed Workers

By Full- and Part-Time Status, Sex, and Age

(in thousands)

	1997[2]	1996[2]	1995[2]	1994[2]	1993[1]	1990[1]	1985	1980	1970
Men, 20 yr. and over									
Employed	66,524	64,897	64,085	63,294	62,335	61,678	56,562	53,101	45,581
Full time	61,057	59,543	58,707	57,707	57,010	57,055	52,425	49,699	43,138
Part time	5,467	5,354	5,377	5,587	5,345	4,623	4,137	3,403	2,444
Unemployed	2,826	3,147	3,239	3,627	4,287	3,239	3,715	3,353	1,638
Full time	2,623	2,899	2,988	3,359	4,011	3,000	3,479	3,167	1,502
Part time	203	248	251	269	276	239	236	186	137
Women, 20 yr. and over									
Employed	57,647	53,310	54,396	53,606	52,099	50,535	44,154	38,492	26,952
Full time	43,698	41,953	40,943	40,183	40,209	39,138	33,604	29,391	20,654
Part time	13,949	13,357	13,453	13,423	11,890	11,397	10,550	9,102	6,297
Unemployed	2,187	2,783	2,819	3,049	3,288	2,596	3,129	2,615	1,349
Full time	1,785	2,258	2,265	2,506	2,670	2,079	2,536	2,135	1,077
Part time	402	525	554	543	619	517	593	480	271
Total 16 yr. and over									
Employed	130,785	126,707	124,900	123,060	120,259	118,793	107,150	99,303	78,678
Full time	106,618	103,537	101,679	99,772	99,114	98,666	88,535	82,564	66,752
Part time	24,167	23,170	23,220	23,288	21,145	20,128	18,615	16,742	11,924
Unemployed	5,957	7,236	7,404	7,996	8,940	7,047	8,312	7,637	4,093
Full time	4,846	5,803	5,909	6,513	7,305	5,677	6,793	6,269	3,206
Part time	1,111	1,433	1,495	1,483	1,635	1,369	1,519	1,369	889
Total 16–19 yr.									
Employed	6,614	6,499	6,419	6,161	5,805	6,581	6,434	7,710	6,144
Full time	1,863	2,041	2,029	1,883	1,895	2,473	2,507	3,474	2,960
Part time	4,751	4,458	4,390	4,278	3,910	4,107	3,927	4,237	3,183
Unemployed	944	1,307	1,346	1,320	1,365	1,212	1,468	1,669	1,106
Full time	438	646	657	648	625	598	777	966	626
Part time	506	661	689	672	740	614	690	701	480

1. Revised; data beginning in 1990 are not directly comparable with earlier years due to the introduction of 1990 census-based population controls, adjusted for the estimated under-count. 2. Data beginning in 1994 are not directly comparable with earlier years due to the introduction of a major redesign of the Current Population Survey. *Source:* Current Population Survey, web: www.bls.census.gov/cps/pubsmain.htm.

Persons in the Labor Force

	Labor force[1]		Percent in labor force in[2]			Labor force[1]		Percent in labor force in[2]	
Year	Number (thousands)	Percent of working-age population	Farm occupation	Nonfarm occupation	Year	Number (thousands)	Percent of working-age population	Farm occupation	Nonfarm occupation
1840	5,420	46.6%	68.6%	31.4%	1920	42,434	51.3%	27.0%	73.0%
1850	7,697	46.8	63.7	36.3	1930	48,830	49.5	21.4	78.6
1860	10,533	47.0	58.9	41.1	1940	52,789	52.2	17.4	82.6
1870	12,925	45.8	53.0	47.0	1950	60,054	53.5	11.6	88.4
1880	17,392	47.3	49.4	50.6	1960	69,877	55.3	6.0	94.0
1890	23,318	49.2	42.6	57.4	1970	82,049	58.2	3.1	96.9
1900	29,073	50.2	37.5	62.5	1980	106,085	62.0	2.2	97.8
1910	37,371	52.2	31.0	69.0	1990	125,182	65.3	1.6	98.4

1. For 1830 to 1930, the data relate to the population and gainful workers at ages 10 and over. For 1940 to 1960, the data relate to the population and labor force at ages 14 and over; for 1970 and 1980, the data relate to the population and labor force at age 16 and over. For 1940 to 1980, the data include the Armed Forces. 2. The farm and nonfarm percentages relate only to the experienced civilian labor force. *Source:* U.S. Bureau of the Census, web: www.census.gov.

Unemployment Rate, 1995–1997

	Men			Women				Men			Women		
Race, and age	1995	1996	1997	1995	1996	1997	Race, and age	1995	1996	1997	1995	1996	1997
Total, 16 and over	5.6	5.4	4.9	5.6	5.4	5.0	Total, 25 and over	4.3	4.1	3.6	4.4	4.3	3.9
White	4.9	4.7	4.2	4.8	4.7	4.2	White	3.8	3.6	3.2	3.9	3.8	3.3
Black	10.6	11.1	10.2	10.2	10.0	9.9	Black	7.5	8.0	6.9	7.3	7.4	7.6

Annual averages. *Source:* Bureau of Labor Statistics, U.S. Department of Labor, web: stats.bls.gov.

Employment Status of Women

(in thousands)

Labor force status	1997[2]	1996[2]	1995[2]	1994[2]	1993[1]	1992[1]	1991[1]	1990[1]	1989
In the labor force	63,036	61,857	60,944	60,239	58,795	58,141	57,178	56,829	56,030
16 to 19 years of age	3,837	3,763	3,729	3,585	3,408	3,345	3,470	3,698	3,818
20 years and over	59,199	58,094	57,215	56,655	55,388	54,796	53,708	53,131	52,212
Employed	59,873	58,501	57,523	56,610	54,910	54,052	53,496	53,689	53,027
16 to 19 years of age	3,260	3,190	3,127	3,005	2,811	2,724	2,862	3,154	3,282
20 years and over	56,613	55,311	54,396	53,606	52,099	51,328	50,634	50,535	49,745
Unemployed	3,162	3,356	3,421	3,629	3,885	4,090	3,683	3,140	3,003
16 to 19 years of age	577	573	602	580	597	621	608	544	536
20 years and over	2,585	2,783	2,819	3,049	3,288	3,469	3,074	2,596	2,467
Not in the labor force	42,382	42,528	42,462	42,221	42,711	42,394	42,468	41,957	41,601
Women as percent of labor force	46.2%	46.2%	46.1%	46.0%	45.5%	45.4%	45.3%	45.2%	45.2%
Total civilian noninstitutional population of women	105,418	104,385	103,406	102,460	101,506	100,535	99,646	98,787	97,630

1. Revised; data beginning in 1990 are not directly comparable with earlier years due to the introduction of 1990 census-based population controls, adjusted for estimated under-count. 2. Data beginning in 1994 are not directly comparable with earlier years due to the introduction of a major redesign of the Current Population Survey. *Source:* Current Population Survey, web: www.bls.census.gov/cps/cpsmain.htm.

Employment Status by Race and Major Occupational Groups

	1997		1996		1995	
Race and occupational group	Number (in thousands)	Percent distribution	Number (in thousands)	Percent distribution	Number (in thousands)	Percent distribution
White						
Managerial and professional specialty	33,089	30.1%	32,127	29.8%	31,323	29.4%
Executive, administrative, and managerial	16,420	14.9	15,848	14.7	15,398	14.5
Professional specialty	16,669	15.2	16,279	15.1	15,924	15.0
Technical, sales, and administrative support	32,624	29.7	32,127	29.8	32,184	30.2
Technicians and related support	3,571	3.3	3,342	3.1	3,361	3.2
Sales occupations	13,730	12.5	13,476	12.5	13,366	12.6
Administrative support, including clerical	15,323	13.9	15,309	14.2	15,457	14.5
Service occupations	13,604	12.4	13,476	12.5	13,208	12.4
Precision production, craft, and repair	12,472	11.4	11,967	11.1	11,949	11.2
Operators, fabricators, and laborers	14,813	13.5	14,662	13.6	14,496	13.6
Farming, forestry, fishing	3,254	3.0	3,342	3.1	3,330	3.1
Total	**109,856**	**100.0**	**107,808**	**100.0**	**106,490**	**100.0**
Black						
Managerial and professional specialty	2,764	19.8%	2,708	20.0%	2,651	20.0%
Executive, administrative, and managerial	1,267	9.1	1,219	9.0	1,233	9.3
Professional specialty	1,497	10.7	1,490	11.0	1,418	10.7
Technical, sales, and administrative support	4,032	28.9	3,873	28.6	3,808	28.7
Technicians and related support	410	2.9	366	2.7	378	2.8
Sales occupations	1,271	9.1	1,219	9.0	1,183	8.9
Administrative support, including clerical	2,352	16.8	2,289	16.9	2,248	16.9
Service occupations	3,092	22.1	2,966	21.9	2,880	21.7
Precision production, craft, and repair	1,144	8.2	1,070	7.9	1,073	8.1
Operators, fabricators, and laborers	2,781	19.9	2,790	20.6	2,712	20.4
Farming, forestry, and fishing	156	1.1	135	1.0	154	1.2
Total	**13,969**	**100.0**	**13,542**	**100.0**	**13,279**	**100.0**

Note: Workers are 16 years or older. *Source:* U.S. Department of Labor, Bureau of Labor Statistics, web: stats.bls.gov.

Occupations of Employed Women

Occupations	1997	1996	1995	1994	1992	1990	1988	1986
Managerial and professional	30.8%	30.3%	29.4%	28.7%	27.4%	26.2%	25.2%	23.7%
Technical, sales, administrative support	41.0	41.4	41.9	42.4	43.8	44.4	44.6	45.6
Service occupations	17.4	17.5	17.7	17.8	17.9	17.7	17.9	18.3
Precision production, craft and repair	2.1	2.1	2.1	2.2	2.1	2.2	2.3	2.4
Operators, fabricators, laborers	7.6	7.6	7.6	7.7	7.9	8.5	8.9	8.9
Farming, forestry, fishing	1.1	1.2	1.3	1.2	1.0	1.0	1.1	1.1

NOTE: Percentage of female labor force (16 years of age and over) employed in each occupation, annual averages. Details may not add up to totals because of rounding. *Source:* U.S. Department of Labor, Bureau of Labor Statistics, web: stats.bls.gov.

Mothers Participating in Labor Force

Year	Percentage of mothers with children: Under 18 years	6 to 17 years	Under 6 years[1]
1955	27.0%	38.4%	18.2%
1965	35.0	45.7	25.3
1975	47.3	54.8	38.8
1980	56.6	64.3	46.8
1985	62.1	69.9	53.5
1986	62.8	70.4	54.4
1987	64.7	72.0	56.7
1988	65.1	73.3	56.1
1989	65.7	74.2	56.7
1990	66.7	74.7	58.2
1991	66.6	74.4	58.4
1992	67.2	75.9	58.0
1993	67.0	75.4	57.9
1994	68.4	76.0	60.3
1995	69.7	76.4	62.3
1996	70.2	77.2	62.3
1997	72.1	78.1	65.0

1. May also have older children. NOTE: 1955 data are for April; 1965 and 1975–94 data are for March. *Source:* U.S. Department of Labor, Bureau of Labor Statistics, web: stats.bls.gov.

Women in the Civilian Labor Force

Year	Number[1] (thousands)	% Female population aged 16 and over[1]	% of Labor force population aged 16 and over[1]
1900	5,319	18.8%	18.3%
1910	7,445	21.5	19.9
1920	8,637	21.4	20.4
1930	10,752	22.0	22.0
1940	12,845	25.4	24.3
1950	18,389	33.9	29.6
1960	23,240	37.7	33.4
1970	31,543	43.3	38.1
1980	45,487	51.5	42.5
1990[2]	56,829	57.5	45.2
1993	58,795	57.9	45.5
1994[3]	60,239	58.8	46.0
1996	61,857	59.3	46.2
1997	63,036	59.8	46.2

1. For 1900–1930, data relate to population and labor force aged 10 and over; for 1940, to population and labor force aged 14 and over; beginning 1950, to civilian population and labor force aged 16 and over. 2. Data beginning in 1990 are not strictly comparable with data for prior years because population controls were adjusted. 3. Data beginning 1994 are not strictly comparable with data for prior years because of a major redesign of the Current Population Survey (household survey) questionnaire and collection methodology. *Source:* U.S. Department of Labor, Women's Bureau.

Job-Related Work at Home
(numbers in thousands)

Characteristic	Total	Rate[1]	Worked at home percent distribution by class of worker[2]: Wage and salary: Paid	Wage and salary: Unpaid	Self-employed[3]: Total	Self-employed[3]: Home-based business
Total, 16 years and over	21,478	17.8%	17.0%	51.5%	30.1%	19.2%
Men	11,202	17.3	15.0	50.1	33.8	19.3
Women	10,275	18.3	19.1	53.1	26.2	19.2
Occupation						
Managerial and professional specialty	13,120	36.7	14.0	61.7	23.5	13.1
Executive, administrative, and managerial	5,940	34.0	14.6	54.8	29.8	17.1
Professional specialty	7,180	39.2	13.5	67.5	18.2	9.7
Technical, sales, and administrative support	5,457	15.0	25.0	40.7	32.0	18.6
Technicians and related support	417	10.6	26.9	60.3	11.3	8.6
Sales occupations	3,356	22.4	19.1	39.1	40.4	21.5
Administrative support, including clerical	1,684	9.7	36.3	39.0	20.5	15.4
Service occupations	1,250	7.2	20.4	23.0	54.0	49.3
Precision production, craft, and repair	1,145	8.2	10.1	26.5	62.0	49.2
Operators, fabricators, and laborers	506	2.9	14.4	31.2	51.1	42.5
Industry						
Mining	73	12.3	(4)	(4)	(4)	(4)
Construction	1,330	16.2	10.3	20.0	66.8	54.6
Manufacturing	2,318	11.5	22.3	62.7	14.2	8.3
Transportation and public utilities	963	10.9	21.2	56.2	21.0	13.7
Wholesale trade	1,202	24.4	28.5	42.8	27.7	15.4
Retail trade	1,964	9.2	14.7	36.9	47.3	27.1
Finance, insurance, and real estate	2,008	25.7	16.4	48.6	33.1	14.5
Services	10,954	25.1	14.8	55.6	28.3	18.8
Public administration	666	12.3	29.5	69.2	—	—
Race and Hispanic origin						
White	19,646	19.2	17.0	50.7	30.9	19.7
Black	1,117	8.5	16.6	64.8	16.2	12.1
Hispanic origin	830	7.2	17.5	53.9	27.8	18.8

1. Refers to the number of persons working at home as a percent of the total at work. 2. Excludes unpaid family workers, not shown separately. 3. Includes both the incorporated and unincorporated self-employed. 4. Data not shown where the base is less than 75,000. NOTE: Data refer to employed persons in nonagricultural industries who reported work at home during the survey reference week as part of their primary job. Dash represents zero. *Source:* U.S. Department of Labor, Bureau of Labor Statistics, web: stats.bls.gov.

Unemployment by Marital Status, Sex, and Race[1]

Marital status and race	Number (in thousands)		Unemployment rate		Number (in thousands)		Unemployment rate	
	Jan. 1997	Jan. 1998	Jan. 1997	Jan. 1998	Jan. 1997	Jan. 1998	Jan. 1997	Jan. 1998
White	3,438	2,945	5.6%	4.7%	2,475	2,281	4.8%	4.4%
Married, spouse present	1,285	1,147	3.3	3.0	995	906	3.4	3.1
Widowed, divorced, or separated	520	404	7.3	5.5	508	579	5.1	5.7
Single (never married)	1,633	1,393	10.2	8.5	973	796	8.2	6.4
Black	851	749	11.9	10.3	816	741	10.2	9.0
Married, spouse present	180	183	5.5	5.4	136	117	5.4	4.5
Widowed, divorced, or separated	111	87	9.9	7.4	167	153	7.5	6.8
Single (never married)	560	478	20.5	17.5	513	472	15.7	14.0
Total	4,477	3,882	6.2	5.3	3,457	3,186	5.6	5.0
Married, spouse present	1,532	1,408	3.5	3.2	1,203	1,097	3.6	3.3
Widowed, divorced, or separated	666	508	7.8	5.7	709	768	5.6	5.9
Single (never married)	2,279	1,967	11.5	9.8	1,544	1,322	9.8	8.0

1. Persons 16 years and over. *Source: Employment & Earnings,* February 1998, U.S. Department of Labor, Bureau of Labor Statistics, web: stats.bls.gov.

Employment Status by Industry

(in millions of persons)

Category	1997	1996	1995	1990	1985	1980	1970	1950	1945	1932	1929
Employment Status[1]											
Civilian noninstitutional population	203.1	200.6	198.6	189.2	178.2	167.7	137.1	105.0	94.1	—	—
Civilian labor force	136.3	133.9	132.3	125.8	115.5	106.9	82.8	62.2	53.9	—	—
Civilian labor force participation rate	67.1	66.8	66.6	66.5	64.8	63.8	60.4	59.2	57.2	—	—
Employed	129.6	126.7	124.9	118.8	107.2	99.3	78.7	58.9	52.8	38.9	47.6
Employment-population ratio	63.8	63.2	62.9	62.8	60.1	59.2	57.4	56.1	56.1	—	—
Agriculture	3.4	3.4	3.4	3.2	3.2	3.4	3.5	7.2	8.6	10.2	10.5
Nonagricultural industries	126.2	123.3	121.5	115.6	104.0	95.9	75.2	51.8	44.2	28.8	37.2
Unemployed	6.7	7.2	7.4	7.1	8.3	7.6	4.1	3.3	1.0	12.1	1.6
Unemployment rate	4.9	5.4	5.6	5.6	7.2	7.1	4.9	5.3	1.9	23.6	3.2
Not in labor force	66.8	66.6	66.3	63.3	62.7	60.8	54.3	42.8	40.2	—	—
Industry											
Total nonfarm employment	122.3	119.5	117.2	109.4	97.4	90.4	70.9	45.2	40.4	23.6	31.3
Goods-producing industries	24.7	24.3	24.2	24.9	24.8	25.7	23.6	18.5	17.5	8.6	13.3
Mining	0.6	0.6	0.6	0.7	0.9	1.0	0.6	0.9	0.8	0.7	1.1
Construction	5.6	5.4	5.2	5.1	4.7	4.3	3.6	2.4	1.1	1.0	1.5
Manufacturing: durable goods	10.9	10.7	10.7	10.7	11.5	12.2	11.2	8.1	9.1	—	—
Nondurable goods	7.6	7.8	7.8	7.8	7.8	8.1	8.2	7.2	6.4	—	—
Services-producing industries	97.5	95.3	93.0	84.5	72.5	64.7	47.3	26.7	22.9	15.0	18.0
Transportation and public utilities	6.4	6.3	6.2	5.8	5.2	5.1	4.5	4.0	3.9	2.8	3.9
Trade, wholesale	6.7	6.6	6.4	6.2	5.7	5.3	4.0	2.6	2.0	—	—
Retail	22.1	21.6	21.2	19.6	17.3	15.0	11.0	6.7	5.4	—	—
Finance, insurance, and real estate	7.1	7.0	6.8	6.7	5.9	5.2	3.6	1.9	1.5	—	—
Services	35.6	34.4	33.1	27.9	21.9	17.9	11.5	5.4	4.2	—	—
Federal government	2.7	2.8	2.8	2.8	2.9	2.9	2.7	1.9	2.8	—	—
State and local government	17.0	16.7	16.5	15.2	13.5	13.4	9.8	4.1	3.1	2.7	2.5

1. For 1929–45, figures on employment status relate to persons 14 years and over; beginning in 1950, 16 years and over. Data for 1990–93 have been revised. Data beginning in 1990 are not directly comparable with earlier years due to the introduction of 1990 census-based population controls, adjusted for the estimated under-count. Data beginning in 1994 are not directly comparable with earlier years because of the introduction of a major redesign of the Current Population Survey. *Source:* U.S. Department of Labor, *Monthly Labor Review.*

Labor Unions in the U.S.

Selected Characteristics of Union Workers

	Percent of employed population that are members of unions[1]		Percent of employed population that are represented by unions[2]	
	1997	1996	1997	1996
Sex and age				
Total, 16 years and over	14.1%	14.5%	15.6%	16.2%
16 to 24 years	5.2	5.5	6.1	6.3
25 years and over	15.8	16.3	17.5	18.1
Men, 16 years and over	16.3	16.9	17.7	18.4
16 to 24 years	6.3	6.7	7.1	7.5
25 years and over	18.2	18.8	19.8	20.5
Women, 16 years and over	11.6	12.0	13.4	13.8
16 to 24 years	4.0	4.2	5.0	5.0
25 years and over	13.1	13.5	15.0	15.5
Race, Hispanic origin, and sex[3]				
White	13.6	14.0	15.1	15.7
Men	16.0	16.4	17.4	17.9
Women	10.9	11.3	12.6	13.1
Black	17.9	18.9	20.1	21.2
Men	20.2	21.6	22.2	23.7
Women	16.0	16.5	18.3	19.0
Hispanic origin	11.8	12.9	13.5	14.6
Men	12.6	13.7	14.3	15.0
Women	10.6	11.8	12.2	13.9
Full- or part-time status[4]				
Full-time workers	15.6	16.2	17.3	18.1
Part-time workers	7.0	7.1	8.0	8.2

1. Data refer to members of a labor union or an employee association similar to a union. 2. Data refer to members of a labor union or an employee association similar to a union as well as workers who report no union affiliation but whose jobs are covered by a union or an employee association contract. 3. 16 years and over. 4. The distinction between full- and part-time workers is based on hours usually worked. *Source:* U.S. Census Bureau, Bureau of Labor Statistics, web: www.bls.census.gov/cps.

Weekly Earnings of Union-Affiliated Workers

Race, Origin, Gender	1997 Total	1997 Members of unions[1]	1997 Represented by unions[2]	1997 Non-union	1996 Total	1996 Members of unions[1]	1996 Represented by unions[2]	1996 Non-union
Total	$503	$640	$632	$478	$490	$615	$610	$462
Men	579	683	679	539	557	653	651	520
Women	431	577	568	411	418	549	543	398
White	519	663	654	494	506	635	630	480
Men	595	699	695	569	580	675	673	544
Women	444	595	587	421	428	572	564	408
Black	400	533	523	371	387	507	502	356
Men	432	577	573	396	412	526	522	380
Women	375	504	496	349	362	485	480	336
Hispanic origin	351	506	501	331	339	484	482	319
Men	371	538	526	348	356	511	511	330
Women	318	440	430	309	316	436	433	305

NOTE: Median weekly earnings of those 16 years and older. 1. Data refer to members of a labor union or an employee association similar to a union. 2. Data refer to members of a labor union or an employee association similar to a union as well as workers who report no union affiliation but whose jobs are covered by a union or an employee association contract. *Source:* U.S. Census Bureau, Bureau of Labor Statistics, web: www.bls.census.gov/cps.

National Labor Organizations with Membership Over 100,000

Members[1]	Union
775,000	United International Union of Automobile, Aerospace and Agricultural Implement Workers of America[2]
110,000	Bakery, Confectionery, and Tobacco Workers International Union
123,041	International Association of Bridge, Structural, Ornamental and Reinforcing Iron Workers
510,000	*United Brotherhood of Carpenters and Joiners of America
600,000	Communications Workers of America
2,300,000	National Education Association, (Ind.)
750,000	International Brotherhood of Electrical Workers
125,000	International Union of Electronic, Electrical, Salaried, Machine and Furniture Workers

Members[1]	Union
215,000	International Association of Fire Fighters
1,400,000	United Food and Commercial Workers International Union
600,000	American Federation of Government Employees
150,000	Graphic Communications International Union
300,000	*Hotel Employees and Restaurant Employees International Union
750,000	Laborers' International Union of North America
315,000	National Association of Letter Carriers
600,000	International Association of Machinists and Aerospace Workers[2]
200,000	Mine Workers of America, United
250,000	Union of Needletrades, Industrial and Textile Employees[3]
182,000	American Nurses Association (Ind.)
130,000	Office and Professional Employees International Union
400,000	International Union of Operating Engineers
130,000	International Brotherhood of Painters and Allied Trades
250,000	United Paperworkers International Union
291,000	United Association of Journeymen and Apprentices of the Plumbing and Pipe Fitting Industry of the United States and Canada
366,000	American Postal Workers Union
100,000	Retail, Wholesale, and Department Store Union
1,100,000	Service Employees International Union
134,000	Sheet Metal Workers' International Association
1,300,000	American Federation of State, County and Municipal Employees
700,000	United Steelworkers of America[2]
940,000	American Federation of Teachers
1,400,000	International Brotherhood of Teamsters
160,000	Amalgamated Transit Union
135,000	Transportation • Communications International Union
125,000	United Transportation Union

Note: List is arranged alphabetically by keyword. 1. Data are for 1998, except *, which did not respond to *Information Please* mailings. Unless otherwise noted, unions are AFL-CIO affiliated. 2. These three unions announced on July 27, 1995, they will merge over a five-year period. 3. Merger of the International Ladies Garment Workers' Union and the Amalgamated Clothing and Textile Workers Union.

Work Stoppages Involving 1,000 Workers or More

Year	Work stoppages	Workers involved (thousands)	Days idle (thousands)	Year	Work stoppages	Workers involved (thousands)	Days idle (thousands)
1950	424	1,698	30,390	1988	40	118	4,381
1960	222	896	13,260	1989	51	452	16,996
1970	381	2,468	52,761	1990	44	185	5,926
1975	235	965	17,563	1991	40	392	4,584
1980	187	795	20,844	1992	35	364	3,989
1983	81	909	17,461	1993	35	184	3,981
1984	68	391	8,499	1994	45	322	5,020
1985	61	584	7,079	1995	28	176	5,736
1986	72	900	11,861	1996	37	273	4,887
1987	46	174	4,456	1997	29	339	4,497

NOTE: Refers to stoppages that began in the year. Days idle is total for all stoppages in effect. Workers are counted more than once if they were involved in more than one stoppage during the year. *Source:* U.S. Department of Labor, Bureau of Labor Statistics, *Monthly Labor Review,* March 1998, web: stats.bls.gov.

Earnings Distribution of Full-Time Workers, by Sex, 1996

	Number (in thousands)			Distribution (% of total)			Women as a % of each earnings level
	Total	Men	Women	Total	Men	Women	
$7,499 or less	10,323	4,876	5,447	9.2%	7.5%	11.6%	52.8%
$7,500 to $12,499	10,978	5,168	5,810	9.8	7.9	12.4	52.9
$12,500 to $19,999	17,966	8,424	9,541	16.0	12.9	20.3	53.1
$20,000 to $29,999	24,098	12,735	11,363	21.4	19.5	24.2	47.2
$30,000 to $39,999	17,120	10,545	6,575	15.2	16.1	14.0	38.4
$40,000 to $49,999	10,401	7,068	3,336	9.3	10.8	7.1	32.1
$50,000 to $59,999	6,048	4,454	1,597	5.4	6.8	3.4	26.4
$60,000 to $74,999	4,879	3,835	1,044	4.3	5.9	2.2	21.4
$75,000 to $99,999	2,225	791	203	2.0	1.2	0.4	9.1
$100,000 and Over	2,733	2,338	395	2.4	3.6	0.8	14.5
Total	112,387	65,409	46,978				

Source: U.S. Bureau of the Census, web: www.census.gov.

Manufacturing Industries—Weekly Earnings and Hours

Industry	1997 Earnings	1997 Hours worked	1980 Earnings	1980 Hours worked	1970 Earnings	1970 Hours worked
All manufacturing	$553.14	42.0	$288.62	39.7	$133.73	39.8
Durable goods	588.07	42.8	310.78	40.1	143.07	40.3
Lumber and wood products	441.16	41.0	252.18	38.5	117.51	39.7
Furniture and fixtures	424.11	40.2	209.17	38.1	108.58	39.2
Primary metal industries	683.38	44.9	391.78	40.1	159.17	40.5
Iron and steel foundries	638.02	46.1	328.00	40.0	151.03	40.6
Nonferrous foundries	524.94	43.6	291.27	39.9	138.16	39.7
Fabricated metal products	547.84	42.7	300.98	40.4	143.67	40.7
Hardware, cutlery, hand tools	754.29	42.7	275.89	39.3	132.33	40.1
Structural metal products	510.25	41.1	291.85	40.2	142.61	40.4
Industrial machinery and equipment	613.02	43.6	328.00	41.0	154.95	41.1
Electric and electronic equipment	533.40	42.0	276.21	39.8	130.54	39.8
Transportation equipment	783.20	44.5	379.61	40.6	163.22	40.3
Motor vehicles and equipment	814.05	45.0	394.00	40.0	170.07	40.3
Nondurable goods	504.71	40.9	255.45	39.0	120.43	39.1
Food and kindred products	474.54	41.3	271.95	39.7	127.98	40.5
Tobacco manufactures	746.88	38.9	294.89	38.1	110.00	37.8
Textile mill products	414.83	41.4	203.31	40.1	97.76	39.9
Apparel and other textile products	308.55	37.4	161.42	35.4	84.37	35.3
Paper and allied products	658.12	43.7	330.85	42.2	144.14	41.9
Printing and publishing	502.81	38.5	279.36	37.1	147.78	37.7
Chemicals and allied products	716.26	43.2	344.45	41.5	153.50	41.6
Petroleum and allied products	870.62	43.1	422.18	41.8	182.76	42.7
Leather and leather products	343.68	38.4	169.09	36.7	92.63	37.2

Source: U.S. Department of Labor, Bureau of Labor Statistics, *Employment & Earnings,* March 1998.

Nonmanufacturing Industries—Weekly Earnings and Hours

Industry	1997 Earnings	1997 Hours worked	1990 Earnings	1990 Hours worked	1970 Earnings	1970 Hours worked
General building contracting	$579.11	38.2	$487.08	37.7	$184.40	36.3
Local and transportation	433.95	38.2	376.65	38.2	142.30	42.1
Telephone communications	732.34	41.8	578.74	40.9	131.60	39.4
Radio and TV broadcasting	598.69	35.3	438.61	34.7	147.45	38.2
Electric, gas, and sanitary services	807.06	42.1	636.76	41.7	172.64	41.5
Wholesale trade	515.71	38.4	411.48	38.1	137.60	40.0
Retail trade	241.03	28.9	195.26	28.8	82.47	33.8
Services						
Hotels, tourist courts, motels	263.58	30.9	214.68	30.8	68.16	34.6
Laundries and dry cleaning plants	274.85	34.1	232.22	34.0	77.47	35.7
Business services	395.97	33.5	n.a.	n.a.	n.a.	n.a.
Advertising	615.98	36.6	n.a.	n.a.	n.a.	n.a.
Computer and data-processing services	762.94	38.3	n.a.	n.a.	n.a.	n.a.
Auto repair, services, parking	381.58	36.1	n.a.	n.a.	n.a.	n.a.
Health services	437.58	33.0	n.a.	n.a.	n.a.	n.a.
Mining						
Metal mining	790.76	44.4	602.07	42.7	165.68	42.7
Bituminous coal and lignite mining	880.88	45.5	740.52	44.0	186.41	40.8
Nonmetallic minerals	671.66	47.2	524.12	45.3	155.11	44.7

Source: U.S. Department of Labor, Bureau of Labor Statistics, *Employment & Earnings,* March 1998.

Full-Time Workers by Occupation and Sex, 1997

Occupation	Total: Number of workers (in thousands)	Total: Median weekly earnings	Men: Number of workers (in thousands)	Men: Median weekly earnings	Women: Number of workers (in thousands)	Women: Women's earnings as a percent of men's
Total, 16 years and over	93,578	$503	53,220	$579	40,358	74.4%
Managerial and professional specialty	28,252	738	14,359	875	13,893	72.2
Executive, administrative, and managerial	13,965	725	7,466	868	6,500	69.7
Professional specialty	14,287	750	6,894	883	7,393	75.0
Mathematical and computer scientists	1,328	908	916	947	411	88.9
Health assessment and treating occupations	2,043	716	309	862	1,734	81.3
Teachers, except college and university	3,810	655	980	733	2,830	86.4
Technical, sales, and administrative support	26,791	456	10,239	588	16,552	68.5
Technicians and related support	3,494	582	1,803	667	1,691	74.7
Sales occupations	9,405	482	5,174	603	4,231	58.4
Administrative support, including clerical	13,892	419	3,262	514	10,630	78.4
Service occupations	10,172	313	5,071	372	5,101	75.8
Private household	348	215	24	—	324	$213[1]
Protective services	1,961	550	1,654	575	308	78.4
Service occupations, except private household and protective services	7,863	296	3,393	317	4,469	88.3
Food preparation and service occupations	2,956	276	1,514	295	1,442	87.5
Precision production, craft, and repair	11,495	548	10,511	569	984	67.1
Mechanics and repairers	4,020	578	3,860	581	160	84.2
Construction trades	3,878	536	3,813	538	65	82.7
Operators, fabricators, and laborers	15,338	401	11,709	436	3,630	71.8
Machine operators, assemblers, and inspectors	7,235	390	4,610	449	2,625	69.7
Transportation and material-moving occupations	4,325	498	4,033	505	292	73.9
Handlers, equipment cleaners, helpers, and laborers	3,779	329	3,065	343	713	87.2
Farming, forestry, and fishing	1,530	295	1,331	302	198	85.1

Dash indicates base is less than 50,000, so no data are provided. 1. Since the men's earnings are effectively zero, it is not possible to calculate a percentage. The number is the median weekly earnings for women. *Source:* U.S. Department of Labor, Bureau of Labor Statistics, *Employment & Earnings,* January 1998, web: stats.bls.gov.

Earnings by Sex and Race, 1948–1996

Year	Median Earnings, All races: Men	Median Earnings, All races: Women	Earnings as a Percentage of Men's (All races): All races: Women	White: Men	White: Women	Black[1]: Men	Black[1]: Women	Hispanic origin[2]: Men	Hispanic origin[2]: Women
1996	$ 23,834	$ 12,815	53.8%	104.7%	54.4%	69.2%	49.4%	64.8%	39.8%
1995	22,562	12,130	53.8	105.9	54.6	70.9	48.6	65.8	39.6
1994	21,720	11,466	52.8	104.4	53.5	69.0	48.5	66.8	39.7
1993	21,102	11,046	52.3	104.2	53.4	69.2	45.1	64.9	38.4
1992[3]	20,455	10,714	52.4	104.6	53.6	63.9	43.4	65.5	40.6
1991	20,469	10,476	51.2	104.5	52.4	63.3	43.1	67.5	39.1
1990	20,293	10,070	49.6	104.3	50.8	63.4	41.0	66.4	37.1
1989	19,893	9,624	48.4	104.9	49.3	63.4	39.6	67.4	38.4
1988	18,908	8,884	47.0	105.6	48.1	63.7	38.9	68.9	37.0
1987	17,786	8,295	46.6	106.3	47.8	63.1	39.1	68.8	37.3
1986	17,114	7,610	44.5	105.5	45.3	63.2	38.4	67.4	37.0
1985	16,311	7,217	44.2	104.9	45.1	66.0	38.5	70.1	36.9
1984	15,600	6,868	44.0	105.6	44.5	60.6	39.5	71.2	37.4
1983	14,631	6,319	43.2	105.3	43.9	61.3	37.9	77.1	36.9
1978	10,935	4,068	37.2	104.7	37.6	62.7	33.9	76.6	34.6
1973	8,056	2,796	34.7	104.9	35.0	63.5	31.6	77.0	32.9
1968	5,980	2,019	33.8	104.8	34.8	62.2	27.6	—	—
1963	4,511	1,372	30.4	106.5	31.9	55.4	21.3	—	—
1958	3,743	1,176	31.4	106.2	34.2	52.9	20.0	—	—
1953	3,221	1,166	36.2	105.2	40.1	58.1	23.5	—	—
1948	2,396	1,009	42.1	104.8	47.3	56.9	20.5	—	—

Year-round, full-time workers, aged 15 years and over. Income in 1996 CPI-U-X1 adjusted dollars. Dash indicates data are not available. 1. Prior to 1967, data are for black and other races. 2. Persons of Hispanic origin may be of any race. *Source:* Current Population Reports, Series P60, U.S. Bureau of the Census, web: www.census.gov.

Median Four-Person Family Income

(in current dollars)

Year	Income	Percent change	Year	Income	Percent change	Year	Income	Percent change
1996	$ 51,518	3.7%	1988	$ 39,051	6.1%	1980	$ 24,332	8.6%
1995	49,687	5.7	1987	36,812	6.0	1979	22,395	9.6
1994	47,012	4.1	1986	34,716	5.9	1978	20,428	9.1
1993	45,161	2.1	1985	32,777	5.4	1977	18,723	8.1
1992	44,251	2.8	1984	31,097	6.6	1976	17,315	9.3
1991	43,056	3.9	1983	29,184	5.7	1975	15,848	7.5
1990	41,151	1.7	1982	27,619	5.1			
1989	40,763	4.4	1981	26,274	8.0			

Source: Income Statistics Branch/HHES Division, U.S. Bureau of the Census, web: www.census.gov.

Per Capita Personal Income

Year	Amount	Year	Amount	Year	Amount	Year	Amount	Year	Amount	Year	Amount
1935	$ 474	1965	$ 2,773	1981	$ 10,949	1986	$ 14,597	1991	$ 19,638	1996[1]	$ 24,457
1945	1,223	1970	3,893	1982	11,480	1987	15,638	1992	20,582	1997[2]	25,660
1950	1,501	1975	5,851	1983	12,098	1988	16,615	1993	21,223		
1955	1,881	1979	8,638	1984	13,114	1989	17,696	1994	22,045		
1960	2,219	1980	9,910	1985	13,896	1990	18,635	1995	23,196		

1. Revised. 2. Preliminary. *Source:* U.S. Department of Commerce, *Survey of Current Business,* web: www.doc.gov.

Per Capita Income and Personal Consumption Expenditures

(in current dollars)

				Personal Consumption Expenditures			
Year	Gross national product	Personal income	Disposable personal income	Durable goods	Nondurable goods	Services	Total
1950	$ 1,900	$ 1,504	$ 1,368	$ 203	$ 648	$ 416	$ 1,267
1955	2,456	1,901	1,687	235	755	570	1,560
1960	2,851	2,265	1,986	240	847	741	1,829
1965	3,268	2,840	2,505	327	987	954	2,268
1970	4,951	4,056	3,489	418	1,318	1,385	3,121
1975	7,401	6,081	5,291	627	1,927	2,135	4,689
1980	11,985	9,916	8,421	963	2,992	3,653	7,607
1985	16,776	13,895	11,861	1,555	3,807	5,622	10,985
1990	21,737	18,477	15,695	1,910	4,748	7,888	14,547
1991	22,500	19,100	16,700	1,800	5,000	8,700	15,400
1992	23,340	19,802	17,346	1,881	5,053	9,101	16,035
1993	24,576	20,810	18,153	2,083	5,185	9,683	16,951
1994	25,774	21,846	19,003	2,266	5,342	10,126	17,734
1995	27,545	23,233	20,214	2,305	5,648	10,767	18,719
1996	28,759	24,457	21,117	2,389	5,779	11,441	19,608
1997	30,088	25,660	21,969	2,461	5,943	12,074	20,478

Source: U.S. Department of Commerce, *Survey of Current Business,* May 1998, web: www.doc.gov.

Total Household Income by Race

	White			Black			Hispanic[1]		
Income range	1996	1980	1967	1996	1980	1967	1996	1980	1972
Number of households[2]	85,059	71,872	54,188	12,109	8,847	5,728	8,225	3,906	2,655
Percent distribution									
Under $5,000	2.6%	2.7%	5.4%	8.2%	7.9%	11.6%	5.1%	5.0%	3.9%
$5,000 to $9,999	7.4	8.6	8.6	14.9	18.0	16.4	12.1	11.7	8.7
$10,000 to $14,999	8.2	7.7	7.2	11.6	12.9	13.6	11.9	10.7	12.4
$15,000 to $24,999	15.1	16.0	15.7	17.7	19.8	22.6	21.0	21.2	21.8
$25,000 to $34,999	13.7	14.5	19.2	13.9	13.2	15.9	15.0	16.2	19.8
$35,000 to $49,999	16.7	19.7	21.6	14.0	14.4	11.7	15.0	16.9	19.0
$50,000 to $74,999	18.8	18.9	15.2	12.4	10.0	5.8	12.3	12.8	10.7
$75,000 to $99,999	8.5	7.3	4.2	4.7	2.8	1.5	4.2	3.6	2.4
$100,000 and over	8.9	4.8	2.8	2.7	1.0	0.9	3.5	1.9	1.5
Median income	$37,161	$35,620	$32,197	$23,482	$20,521	$18,694	$24,906	$26,025	$27,129

NOTE: Income in 1996 CPI-U-X1 adjusted dollars. Households as of March 1 of the following year. 1. Persons of Hispanic origin may be of any race. 2. As of March of the following year. *Source:* U.S. Bureau of the Census, web: www.census.gov/hhes/www/income96.html.

Per Capita Personal Income by State

State	1980	1990	1996[1]	1997[2]	State	1980	1990	1996[1]	1997[2]
Alabama	$ 7,465	$ 14,899	$20,056	$20,842	Montana	8,342	14,743	19,278	20,046
Alaska	13,007	20,887	24,597	25,305	Nebraska	8,895	17,379	22,975	23,803
Arizona	8,854	16,262	21,335	22,364	Nevada	10,848	20,248	26,059	26,791
Arkansas	7,113	13,779	18,967	19,585	New Hampshire	9,150	20,231	26,772	28,047
California	11,021	20,656	25,368	26,570	New Jersey	10,966	24,182	31,265	32,654
Colorado	10,143	18,818	25,740	27,051	New Mexico	7,940	14,213	18,814	19,587
Connecticut	11,532	25,426	34,174	36,263	New York	10,179	22,322	29,221	30,752
Delaware	10,059	19,719	27,782	29,022	North Carolina	7,780	16,284	22,244	23,345
Dist. of Columbia	12,251	24,643	34,172	35,852	North Dakota	8,642	15,320	20,479	20,271
Florida	9,246	18,785	24,198	25,255	Ohio	9,399	17,547	23,493	24,661
Georgia	8,021	17,121	23,028	24,061	Oklahoma	9,018	15,117	19,574	20,556
Hawaii	10,129	20,905	25,421	26,034	Oregon	9,309	17,201	23,111	24,393
Idaho	8,105	15,304	19,865	20,478	Pennsylvania	9,353	18,884	24,851	26,058
Illinois	10,454	20,159	26,855	28,202	Rhode Island	9,227	19,035	24,613	25,760
Indiana	8,914	16,815	22,633	23,604	South Carolina	7,392	15,101	19,898	20,755
Iowa	9,226	16,683	22,330	23,102	South Dakota	7,800	15,628	20,749	21,447
Kansas	9,880	17,639	23,133	24,379	Tennessee	7,711	15,903	22,032	23,018
Kentucky	7,679	14,751	19,773	20,657	Texas	9,439	16,747	22,324	23,656
Louisiana	8,412	14,279	19,709	20,680	Utah	7,671	14,063	19,384	20,432
Maine	7,760	17,041	21,087	22,078	Vermont	7,957	17,444	22,545	23,401
Maryland	10,394	22,088	27,676	28,969	Virginia	9,413	19,543	25,255	26,438
Massachusetts	10,103	22,248	29,808	31,524	Washington	10,256	19,268	25,277	26,718
Michigan	9,801	18,239	24,588	25,560	West Virginia	7,764	13,964	18,225	18,957
Minnesota	9,673	18,784	25,699	26,797	Wisconsin	9,364	17,399	23,390	24,475
Mississippi	6,573	12,578	17,561	18,272	Wyoming	11,018	16,905	21,587	22,648
Missouri	8,812	17,407	22,984	24,001	**United States**	**9,494**	**18,667**	**24,436**	**25,598**

1. Revised. 2. Preliminary. *Source:* U.S. Department of Commerce, Bureau of Economic Analysis, *Survey of Current Business,* web: www.bea.doc.gov.

Median Income of Households with Selected Characteristics, 1996

	White		Black		Hispanic Origin[1]		All Races	
Characteristic	As a % of all white households	Median income	As a % of all black households	Median income	As a % of all Hispanic households	Median income	As a % of all households	Median income
Overall		$ 37,161		$ 23,482		$ 24,906		$ 35,492
Region								
Northeast	20%	40,120	19%	22,177	17%	20,859	20%	37,406
Midwest	25	38,057	19	23,314	7	30,177	24	36,579
South	33	35,214	54	23,277	34	24,814	35	32,422
West	22	37,281	9	30,176	41	25,619	21	37,125
Type of household								
Family households	69	45,382	70	27,496	81	27,152	70	43,082
Married-couple families	56	50,302	32	42,069	55	32,379	53	49,858
Single-father household	3	36,938	5	30,995	6	28,322	4	35,658
Single-mother household	10	24,375	33	16,256	20	14,535	13	21,564
Nonfamily households	31	21,536	30	15,454	19	15,705	30	20,973
Male living alone	10	25,098	11	16,447	7	14,506	10	24,050
Female living alone	15	14,890	15	11,529	8	9,746	15	14,626
Size of household								
One person	25	18,426	26	13,772	15	11,894	25	17,897
Two persons	34	39,039	26	24,844	22	22,258	32	37,283
Three persons	17	47,529	19	26,321	20	27,078	17	44,814
Four persons	15	53,704	16	32,943	20	30,048	15	51,405
Five persons	6	51,102	8	31,806	12	30,356	7	47,841
Six persons	2	44,782	3	30,931	7	27,510	2	42,438
Seven persons or more	1	45,241	2	27,317	5	34,864	1	40,337
Number of earners								
No earners	21	14,579	23	7,612	16	7,912	21	13,320
One	33	29,592	40	20,658	36	18,883	34	27,895
Two	36	53,362	29	42,539	35	34,835	35	52,416
Three	7	63,919	6	51,894	10	47,044	7	62,428
Four or more	3	78,898	2	71,429	4	58,055	3	78,504

1. Persons of Hispanic origin may be of any race. *Source:* U.S. Bureau of the Census, *Money Income in the United States: 1996,* web: www.census.gov.

Gross Domestic Product or Expenditure[1]

(in billions of dollars)

Item	1997	1996	1995	1994	1990	1987	1980	1970
Gross domestic product	$8,083.4	$7,636.0	$7,245.8	$6,931.4	$5,513.8	$4,539.9	$2,708.0	$1,010.7
GDP in chained (1992) dollars	7,191.4	6,928.4	6,739.0	6,604.2	6,138.7	5,648.4	4,611.9	3,388.2
Personal consumption expenditures	5,488.6	5,207.6	4,924.3	4,698.7	3,742.6	3,052.2	1,748.1	646.5
Durable goods	659.4	634.5	606.4	580.9	465.9	403.0	212.5	85.3
Nondurable goods	1,592.7	1,534.7	1,486.1	1,429.7	1,217.7	1,011.1	682.9	270.4
Services	3,236.5	3,038.4	2,831.8	2,688.1	2,059.0	1,637.4	852.7	290.8
Gross private domestic investment	1,237.6	1,116.5	1,065.3	1,014.4	802.6	749.3	467.6	150.3
Residential	327.5	309.2	289.8	287.7	215.7	225.2	123.3	41.4
Nonresidential	845.4	781.4	738.5	667.2	587.0	497.8	353.8	106.7
Change in business inventories	64.6	25.9	37.0	59.5	0	26.3	–9.5	2.3
Net export of goods and services	–96.7	–94.8	–102.3	–96.4	–74.4	–143.1	–14.7	1.2
Government purchases	1,453.9	1,406.7	1,358.5	1,314.7	1,042.9	881.5	507.1	212.7
Federal	524.8	520.0	516.7	516.3	424.9	384.9	209.1	100.1
State and local	929.1	886.7	841.7	798.4	618.0	496.6	298.0	112.6

1. Current dollars except as noted. *Source:* U.S. Bureau of Economic Analysis, *Survey of Current Business,* February 1997, web: www.bea.doc.gov.

National Income by Type

(in billions of dollars)

Type of income	1997	1995	1990	1985	1980	1975	1970	1965	1960
National income	$ 6,649.7	$ 5,828.9	$ 4,611.9	$ 3,351.5	$ 2,216.1	$ 1,295.5	$ 836.6	$ 587.8	$ 426.2
Compensation of employees	4,703.6	4,222.7	3,352.8	2,425.7	1,653.9	951.3	618.1	399.8	296.7
Wages and salaries	3,878.6	3,433.2	2,757.5	1,995.7	1,377.6	814.7	551.5	363.7	272.8
Supplements to wages and salaries	825.0	789.5	595.2	430.0	276.3	136.6	66.6	36.1	23.8
Proprietors' income[1,2]	544.5	486.1	361.0	257.4	167.9	116.5	78.0	63.5	50.5
Farm	40.7	27.9	36.3	24.5	13.8	24.2	14.8	13.0	11.5
Business and professional	503.8	458.2	324.6	232.5	154.1	92.3	63.2	50.4	39.1
Rental income[1]	147.9	111.7	61.4	49.1	35.3	26.6	24.7	22.5	19.1
Corporate profits[1,2]	805.0	604.8	369.5	282.2	167.1	121.1	75.7	80.9	48.8
Net interest	448.7	403.6	467.3	337.2	191.9	80.0	40.0	21.1	11.2

1. Includes capital consumption adjustment. 2. Includes inventory valuation adjustment. *Source:* U.S. Department of Commerce, Bureau of Economic Analysis, *Survey of Current Business,* May 1998, web: www.bea.doc.gov.

Producer Price Indexes by Major Commodity Groups

(1982 = 100)

Commodity	1997	1995	1990	1985	1980	1975	1970
All commodities	**126.7**	**124.7**	**116.3**	**103.2**	**89.8**	**58.4**	**38.1**
Farm products	110.1	107.4	112.2	95.1	102.9	77.0	45.8
Processed foods and feeds	132.9	127.0	121.9	103.5	95.9	72.6	44.6
Textile products and apparel	122.5	120.8	114.9	102.9	89.7	67.4	52.4
Hides, skins, and leather products	153.5	153.7	141.7	108.9	94.7	56.5	42.0
Fuels and related products and power	82.8	78.0	82.2	91.4	82.8	35.4	15.3
Chemicals and allied products	143.5	142.5	123.6	103.7	89.0	62.0	35.0
Rubber and plastic products	123.1	124.3	113.6	101.9	90.1	62.2	44.9
Lumber and wood products	181.9	178.1	129.7	106.6	101.5	62.1	39.9
Pulp, paper, and allied products	171.2	172.2	141.3	113.3	86.3	59.0	37.5
Metals and metal products	130.6	134.5	123.0	104.4	95.0	61.5	38.7
Machinery and equipment	125.4	126.6	120.7	107.2	86.0	57.9	40.0
Furniture and household durables	130.7	128.2	119.1	107.1	90.7	67.5	51.9
Nonmetallic mineral products	133.7	129.0	114.7	108.6	88.4	54.4	35.3
Transportation equipment	141.5	139.7	121.5	107.9	82.9	56.7	41.9

Source: U.S. Department of Labor, Bureau of Labor Statistics, Division of Industrial Prices and Price Indexes, web: stats.bls.gov

Per Capita Consumption of Principal Foods[1]

Food	1996	1994	1992	1990	Food	1996	1994	1992	1990
Red meat[2]	112.8	114.8	114.1	112.3	Fruits[4]	283.2	277.9	261.0	266.8
Poultry[2]	64.4	63.3	60.8	56.3	Peanuts	5.7	5.8	6.2	6.0
Fish and shellfish[2]	14.7	15.1	14.7	15.0	Vegetables	412.5	404.7	394.8	386.4
Eggs	30.5	30.6	30.3	30.2	Sugar	66.2	65.0	64.6	64.4
Fluid milk and cream[3]	223.6	226.3	230.5	233.4	Corn sweeteners[5]	84.5	81.0	76.2	71.1
Ice cream	15.9	16.1	16.3	15.8	Flour and cereal products	198.5	194.1	186.2	182.0
Cheese	27.7	26.8	26.0	24.8	Soft drinks (gal)	52.0	51.3	48.5	46.3
Butter	4.3	4.8	4.4	4.4	Coffee bean equivalent	9.0	8.2	10.0	10.3
Margarine	11.1	11.4	10.6	9.7	Cocoa (chocolate liquor equivalent)	n.a.	3.9	4.6	4.3
Total fats and oils[3]	65.8	68.6	67.4	62.8					

1. Data are on a retail-weight basis unless otherwise indicated. Final consumer products from a combination of primary food groups, such as bakery products, are measured and reported in the form of their primary ingredients, such as flour, shortening, and eggs. 2. Boneless, trimmed equivalent. 3. Fat-content basis. 4. Excludes wine grapes. 5. Dry basis. NOTE: Data are most recent available. *Source:* U.S. Department of Agriculture, Economic Research Service, web: www.usda.gov.

Consumer Credit

(installment credit outstanding; in billions of dollars, not seasonally adjusted)

Holder	1998[4]	1997	1996	1995	1990	1985	1980	1975
Commercial banks	$ 499.5	$ 511.6	$ 529.4	$ 507.8	$ 347.1	$ 245.1	$ 147.0	$ 82.9
Finance companies	153.2	154.9	154.5	152.6	133.3	111.7	62.3	32.7
Credit unions	149.8	146.7	144.1	131.9	93.1	72.7	44.0	25.7
Retailers[1]	65.1	67.7	79.7	85.1	43.5	43.0	28.7	18.2
Other[2]	47.0	46.3	44.7	40.1	57.0	53.8	20.1	9.2
Pools[3]	326.8	272.1	271.9	214.4	77.9	—	—	—
Total	**1,241.4**	**1,199.3**	**1,224.4**	**1,131.9**	**751.9**	**526.3**	**302.1**	**168.7**

1. Starting in 1994, source includes retailers and gasoline companies in nonfinancial business category. 2. Includes mutual savings banks, savings and loan associations, and gasoline companies (until 1994). 3. Beginning 1989, outstanding balances of pools upon which securities have been issued; these balances are no longer on the balance sheets for the loan originators. 4. Preliminary data as of May 1998. *Source:* Federal Reserve Board, web http://www.bog.frb.fed.us.

Consumer Price Index for All Urban Consumers

(1982–84 = 100)

Group	March 1998	March 1997	March 1996	March 1995
All items	158.8	160.0	155.7	151.4
Food	158.9	156.6	151.6	147.4
Alcoholic beverages	163.8	162.1	157.4	153.1
Apparel and upkeep	132.8	134.5	134.8	134.4
Men's and boys' apparel	132.7	129.2	129.1	127.2
Women's and girls' apparel	126.0	130.1	129.9	131.5
Footwear	127.7	127.0	128.1	125.9
Housing, total	155.6	155.9	151.7	147.4
Rent	169.9	165.1	160.6	156.7
Gas and electricity	118.8	123.4	118.2	117.1
Fuel oil, coal, bottled gas	94.5	105.5	99.3	89.0
House operation[1]	124.5	125.4	124.6	122.6
House furnishings	109.0	111.1	111.7	111.2
Transportation	139.9	144.9	141.2	138.0
Medical care	239.3	233.4	226.6	218.4
Personal care	155.6	151.8	149.4	146.0
Tobacco products	254.0	238.2	230.8	222.5
Entertainment	161.8	162.1	158.4	152.6
Personal and educational expenses	263.6	255.8	244.1	232.0

1. Combines house furnishings and operation. *Source:* U.S. Department of Labor, Bureau of Labor Statistics, *Monthly Labor Review,* May 1998, web: stats.bls.gov.

The Public Debt

Year	Gross debt: Amount (in millions)	Gross debt: Per capita
1800 (Jan. 1)	$ 83	$ 15.87
1860 (June 30)	65	2.06
1865	2,678	75.01
1900	1,263	16.60
1920	24,299	228.23
1925	20,516	177.12
1930	16,185	131.51
1935	28,701	225.55
1940	42,968	325.23
1945	258,682	1,848.60
1950	256,087[1]	1,688.30
1955	272,807[1]	1,650.63
1960	284,093[1]	1,572.31
1965	313,819[1]	1,612.70
1970	370,094[1]	1,807.09
1975	533,189	2,496.90
1980	907,701	3,969.55
1985	1,823,103	7,598.51
1990	3,233,313	12,823.28
1994	4,643,711	17,805.64
1995	4,973,983	18,928.53
1996	5,217,305	19,681.26
1997	5,355,085	20,006.08
1998	5,529,921	20,474.79

Note: Figures as of July for each year. 1. Adjusted to exclude issues to the International Monetary Fund and other international lending institutions to conform to the budget presentation. *Source:* U.S. Department of the Treasury, Financial Management Service, web: www.publicdebt.treas.gov/opd/opdpenny.htm.

Foreign Investment by U.S. Businesses

	1997	1996	1995		1997	1996	1995
Western Europe	$585.5	$468.8	$362.0	Japan	$ 120.4	$126.4	$128.5
United Kingdom	277.8	185.4	137.6	Latin America and Other Western Hemisphere	103.3	76.8	32.0
France	56.7	42.8	31.3	Mexico	26.1	22.1	18.8
Germany	47.9	40.5	31.7	Other countries	113.1	137.8	129.7
Netherlands	77.4	64.8	52.9	Australia	33.9	26.1	21.8
Spain	25.9	22.8	17.7	Hong Kong	27.7	37.3	24.3
Sweden	36.6	34.2	23.6	**Total holdings**	**1,001.30**	**876.8**	**699.1**
Switzerland	47.6	33.9	30.4				
Canada	79.0	67.0	46.9				

Source: U.S. Department of Commerce, Bureau of Economic Analysis, web: www.bea.doc.gov.

Balance of International Payments

(in billions of dollars)

Item	1997[1]	1995	1990	1985	1980	1975	1970	1965	1960
Exports of goods, services, and income	$1,167.6	$ 969.2	$ 652.9	$ 366.0	$ 343.2	$ 157.9	$ 68.4	$ 42.7	$ 30.5
Goods, adjusted, excluding military	678.3	575.9	389.5	214.4	224.0	107.1	42.5	26.5	19.7
Services	253.2	210.6	133.1	54.0	44.7	23.2	11.4	7.2	4.6
Transfers under U.S. military agency sales contracts	15.2	13.4	9.8	9.0	8.2	3.9	1.5	0.8	0.3
Receipts of income on U.S. assets abroad	236.0	182.7	130.0	90.0	75.9	25.4	11.8	7.4	4.6
Imports of goods and services	–1,295.5	–1,082.3	–722.7	–461.2	–333.9	–132.6	–60.0	–32.8	–23.7
Goods, adjusted, excluding military	–877.3	–749.4	–497.6	–339.0	–249.3	–98.0	–39.9	–21.5	–14.8
Services	–167.9	–142.2	–106.9	–58.0	–41.4	–22.0	–14.7	–9.2	–7.7
Direct defense expenditures	–11.3	–9.8	–17.1	–12.0	–10.7	–4.8	–4.9	–3.0	–3.1
Payments of income on foreign assets in U.S.	–250.3	–190.7	–118.1	–65.0	–43.2	–12.6	–5.5	–2.1	–1.2
Unilateral transfers, excluding military grants, net	–38.5	–35.1	–22.3	–15.0	–7.0	–4.6	–3.3	–2.9	–2.3
U.S. assets abroad, net	–426.9	–307.9	–57.7	–27.7	–86.1	–39.7	–9.3	–5.7	–4.1
U.S. government assets abroad, net	0.2	–0.3	2.9	–2.8	–5.2	–3.5	–1.6	–1.6	–1.1
U.S. private assets abroad, net	–426.1	–297.8	–58.5	–26.0	–71.5	–35.4	–10.2	–5.3	–5.1
Foreign assets in U.S., net	690.5	424.5	86.3	127.1	50.3	15.6	6.4	0.7	2.3
Statistical discrepancy	–97.1	31.5	63.5	23.0	29.6	5.5	–0.2	–0.5	–1.0
Balance on goods, services, and income	–127.9	–113.1	–69.7	–106.8	9.5	25.2	8.5	10.0	6.9
Balance on current account	–166.4	–148.2	–92.1	–118.0	3.7	18.4	2.4	5.4	2.8

1. Preliminary. NOTE: — denotes debits. Only selected items within each category are shown. *Source:* U.S. Department of Commerce, Bureau of Economic Analysis, *Survey of Current Business,* April 1998, web: www.bea.doc.gov.

U.S. Direct Investment in Other Countries, 1997

(in millions of dollars)

	All industries	Petroleum	Manufacturing	Wholesale trade	Banking	Finance, insurance, real estate	Services	Other industries
All countries	**$860,723**	**$85,726**	**$288,290**	**$69,080**	**$34,359**	**$280,920**	**$40,874**	**$61,475**
Canada	99,859	12,738	45,892	7,307	1,047	19,050	4,667	9,159
Europe	420,934	29,793	142,528	34,620	17,312	153,625	24,824	18,232
Belgium	17,403	237	8,788	2,102	252	4,066	1,364	594
France	34,615	1,045	15,887	2,857	781	8,996	4,118	930
Germany	43,931	2,648	20,462	2,538	1,065	13,816	1,713	1,689
Ireland	14,476	(*)	8,462	352	(*)	5,113	321	22
Italy	17,749	(*)	12,223	2,122	379	842	1,089	(*)
Netherlands	64,648	2,623	14,682	4,936	(*)	35,732	4,617	(*)
Spain	11,642	194	6,432	1,472	2,031	639	432	442
Switzerland	35,203	1,144	3,723	8,151	3,341	16,786	1,880	177
United Kingdom	138,765	14,228	38,267	7,389	6,886	54,023	7,569	10,402

	All industries	Petro-leum	Manu-facturing	Wholesale trade	Banking	Finance, insurance, real estate	Services	Other industries
Latin America and Other Western Hemisphere	$172,481	$ 9,462	$47,496	$ 8,358	$ 4,939	$81,403	$5,424	$15,399
South America	67,112	6,824	31,005	2,297	3,851	9,395	2,779	10,962
Brazil	35,727	1,769	22,584	656	1,489	4,711	1,602	2,915
Central America	48,881	1,264	15,919	2,475	622	23,758	971	3,873
Mexico	25,395	109	15,119	862	510	4,079	924	3,792
Panama	20,958	724	102	509	89	19,585	33	-83
Other Western Hemisphere	56,489	1,374	572	3,587	466	48,250	1,674	565
Bermuda	33,092	150	(*)	1,607	0	29,822	1,407	(*)
United Kingdom Islands, Caribbean	12,143	236	(*)	102	634	11,040	24	(*)
Africa	10,253	5,872	1,899	198	299	834	115	1,038
Middle East	8,959	3,438	1,744	271	741	1,878	408	479
Asia and Pacific	142,704	20,442	48,731	18,327	10,020	24,131	5,437	15,616
Australia	26,125	1,206	7,506	2,569	2,181	4,779	1,805	6,080
China	5,013	899	2,696	363	107	636	63	250
Hong Kong	19,065	624	2,755	5,237	1,859	3,049	1,155	4,387
Japan	35,569	4,686	14,293	5,628	565	8,839	1,177	380
Singapore	17,514	3,329	7,851	1,874	694	3,154	528	85

* Suppressed to avoid disclosure of data of individual companies. *Source:* U.S. Department of Commerce, Bureau of Economic Analysis, web: www.bea.doc.gov.

U.S. Contributions to International Organizations

Organization	1997	1996
United Nations and affiliated agencies:		
Food and Agriculture Organization	$ 68	$ 75
International Atomic Energy Agency	64	63
International Civil Aviation Organization	12	13
International Labor Organization	54	65
International Maritime Organization	1	1
International Telecommunications Union	7	8
United Nations	331	311
Universal Postal Union	1	2
World Health Organization	87	97
World Intellectual Property Organization	1	1
World Meteorological Organization	10	12
Subtotal	636	648
Inter-American organizations:		
Inter-American Institute for Cooperation on Agriculture	15	16
Organization of American States	51	52
Pan American Health Organization	46	48
Subtotal	112	116
Regional organizations:		
Asia Pacific Economic Cooperation	1	1
North Atlantic Assembly	1	1
North Atlantic Treaty Organization	44	37
Organization for Economic Cooperation and Development	55	65
South Pacific Commission	1	1
Subtotal	102	105
Other international organizations:		
World Trade Organization/ General Agreement on Tariffs and Trade	12	13
Customs Cooperation Council	3	4
International Agency for Research on Cancer	1	2
Intl. Center for Study of Preservation & Restoration of Cultural Properties	1	1
International Bureau of Weights and Measures	1	1
International Seabed Authority	$ 0	$ 0
International Tribunal of the Law of the Sea	0	0
International Grains Council	0	0
Interparliamentary Union	1	1
Organization for Prohibition of Chemical Weapons	12	0
Other international organizations	2	1
Subtotal	33	23
Arrearage Payment	0	0
U.N. Tax Credit	0	0
U.N. Buydown	19	0
Total	**902**	**892**
International peacekeeping activities:		
U.N. Disengagement Observer Force	7	8
U.N. Interim Force in Lebanon	25	16
U.N. Angola Verification Mission	59	52
U.N. Iraq–Kuwait Observer Mission	4	3
U.N. Mission for the Referendum in the Western Sahara	0	0
War Crimes Tribunal–Rwanda	0	0
U.N. Operations in the Former Yugoslavia	155	122
War Crimes Tribunal–Yugoslavia	0	0
U.N. Peacekeeping Operation in Guatemala	1	0
U.N. Observer Mission in Georgia	3	1
U.N. Mission in Haiti	17	40
U.N. Observer Mission in Liberia	6	6
U.N. Assistance Mission for Rwanda	0	14
U.N. Force in Cyprus	7	3
U.N. Mission in Tajikistan	1	2
Payment of Prior Year Balances	50	92
Total	**335**	**359**

NOTE: All years are fiscal years. All amounts in millions. *Source:* Budget of the United States Government Fiscal Year 1999.

The articles and opinions in this section are for general information only and are not intended to provide specific advice or recommendations for any individual.

Married to the Market

What crash? Only 11 years after the plunge of '87, average Joes and Janes have more money, and faith, in the market than ever before

By **DANIEL KADLEC** TIME

Worried about retirement? Don't be. Little Biff and Betsy are just a few years from college? No sweat. Vacation house? Go ahead. Heck, chuck all your financial concerns, including those about social time bombs like a deficit-ridden federal budget and the financial squeeze on Social Security.

You just need to keep the faith with your fellow believers: the stock-obsessed masses in mutual funds and investment clubs, trading online and standing in line a dozen deep at the corner Fidelity or Schwab office. Only 11 years after the most devastating one-day plunge in history, Americans are married to the market in confounding degrees. They have the trust of a newlywed that stocks will be a lifetime mate. The average person has more invested in the market than in the house that shelters him. Stocks account for more than 40% of the average household's financial assets, more than in any period in history. The percentage of adult Americans who own stock has risen from 10.4% in 1965 to 43% today.

Doesn't anyone remember October 19, 1987, that lose-your-lunch Monday when the Dow Jones industrial average plunged 23% and sent shrieks issuing from the canyons of Wall Street? Even when the market—prompted by the Asian financial crisis that began in Thailand—plunged from its July 1998 peak of 9,337 points to below 8,000 in August, small investors stayed the course.

Perhaps they recalled that the '87 carnage was quickly repaired and never did ripple in a way that would curb consumer spending and dampen the economy, as many feared might happen at the time. Just two years after the crash, the Dow was setting records again and the investing public had learned, rightly or wrongly, to buy when the market drops. The bigger the decline, the greater the opportunity. So goes the dogma of the day, and it is ironic that the greatest one-day plunge ever—the 1929 crash was a mere 12%—was the springboard for today's equity culture, which professes one elixir for every financial ailment: buy-and-hold.

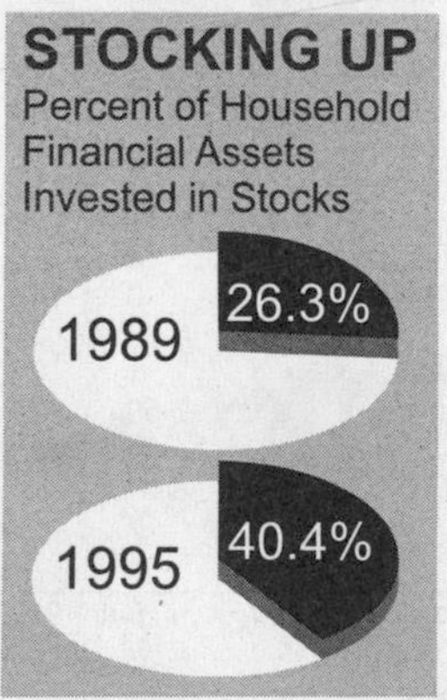

Risky Behavior or Common Sense?

Clearly, the market is a proven wealth builder that can and should benefit all participants in a free-market economy. However, investing in stocks isn't the sure thing that today's equity culture assumes. Even in up markets, some stocks go down and stay down. Ask anyone who owned shares of U.S. Surgical in 1991. Johnson & Johnson invaded the little company's niche in surgical supplies, and the stock, once worth $120 a share, is now below $30. U.S. Surgical is hardly an isolated case. Biotechnology stocks fell 80% in a 1992 bloodbath, and many have not fully recovered. Scores of stocks are down in an up market.

Sure, buy-and-hold is all but foolproof for those with diverse portfolios, an endless time horizon, and supreme confidence that they'll never need to raise money in a pinch. But how about the other 99% of humanity? For them, the market holds risk, and some sense of that risk is precisely what's missing today and, oddly, what may make the market riskier than ever.

Contrary to cult thinking, outsized returns year in and year out are not a birthright wholly detached from the possibility of getting wiped out. Only curmudgeons like Federal Reserve Chairman Alan Greenspan and gray-haired money managers who lived through the tough 1970s markets speak of such things. Everyone else goes on merrily leveraging his or her financial future to an institution that has demonstrated through history a penchant for stomping on anyone who dares to take it for granted.

Success Stories

Practically everyone has a bull-market story, and collectively these tales illustrate the depth of the market's penetration into our social consciousness. Barton Biggs, the veteran investment strategist at Morgan Stanley Dean Witter, recalls a party at his summer house. The septic system backed up, and the plumber who came to save the party did so in more ways than one. The plumber recognized Biggs from his TV appearances and immediately commenced quizzing him on the market. "I told him I would be cautious at this point," Biggs says. The plumber begged to differ. To the amusement of all within earshot, "he told me I was as full of it as my septic system." The plumber went on to say he was plumbing part time now because he made more money trading stocks.

Ray DeVoe, who writes the DeVoe Report, an investment newsletter, conducted a series of interviews in the summer of 1997 at small-town grocery

stores. He found that late in the month an increasing number of shoppers were buying as little as $20 worth of groceries with a credit card. Many were cash short because they were having $100 or $200 a month automatically debited from their checking account and plunked into a stock fund.

Plenty of hard numbers confirm this love affair with stocks. There are more financial newsletters, books, and personal-finance magazines than ever. A total of $2.2 trillion resides in stock mutual funds, 12 times the $186 billion that was there in 1987. Net inflows are about $20 billion a month. New funds are forming at the rate of three a day. In the U.S. there are more mutual funds that own stocks than there are stocks listed on the New York Stock Exchange.

In Stocks We Trust

Society as a whole, not just individuals through mutual funds and 401(k) plans, has placed a gargantuan bet on the stock market. Even governments see the market as a means to an end. The state of Louisiana recently passed a law allowing its pension-fund managers to put as much as 65% of their assets into the stock market, up from the previous cap of 55%.

And of course there is the controversial debate over whether the Social Security system should begin owning stocks rather than government bonds exclusively. Proponents such as Democratic Senator John Kerry of Massachusetts and Republican Congressman John Porter of Illinois say the higher returns are the best way to fix the Social Security–funding problem. (Without changes, the system will be broke by 2029.) "It would give every American worker control over his or her retirement destiny," Porter maintains.

The immense faith in stocks led Washington to cut the capital-gains tax rate in August 1997. The cut had been in the works for years. It didn't become feasible, though, until enough voters owned enough stock (which they implicitly believed would deliver capital gains) to conclude that such a cut would be good not just for the rich but for everybody.

Is it all misguided devotion? Hardly. Since 1926 the Standard & Poor's 500 has risen 10.9% a year on average, beating bonds, money-market funds, gold, collectibles, tulips, and most other things. That long-term statistic is the holy scripture for today's investors, the thing that gives them faith when they fleetingly wonder how much higher their stocks can go.

Keeping the Faith

There is no reason to suspect that the long-term growth rate will change much—and you should be terrified by that thought. If the 10.9% figure is reliable, as everyone assumes, then a period of grossly subpar returns must be coming. The S&P 500, including dividends, has returned an average 33% annually since 1994. To revert to the long-term trend line over, say, the next four years, the S&P 500 would have to register no gain. Indeed, a handful of Wall Street pros sees something on that order starting. Charles Clough, chief investment strategist at Merrill Lynch, expects total return from stocks to be 4% to 6% a year in the next five years. Biggs says the market might return nil to 2% a year in the next five years and 5% a year in the next 10.

But that's not at all what Wade Brown, a 31-year-old financial manager in Lindon, Utah, has in mind. "Every time I've lost on a stock it's because of impatience," he says. "As I look back, the stock has always gone back up." He's banking on a run to get his portfolio to $1 million in four years. "Age 35 is what I've been thinking," he says matter-of-factly. "That's the only milestone that has crossed my mind." Age 35? A million dollars? Where does such confidence spring from? Lots of places, and most of them quite valid. Baby Boomers are saving for retirement, not spending their hearts out. The fall of communism is opening the door to global trade. Technology is making everyone more efficient, which keeps inflation and interest rates low even as corporate profits mushroom.

A Never-Ending Bull Market?

That, in a nutshell, is the new era you have heard so much about, and it's real, at least for now. Such perfect economic conditions have persisted through most of the '90s and led to a uniquely placid period in the market. As a society in love with stocks, we've never quite been here, so no one can be sure what to expect. When pushed, market veterans liken today's fervor to 1929 or 1968, both bull-market peaks. Because of key differences between now and those periods, however, few predict imminent disaster. But it's worth noting that after the '29 crash the S&P 500, excluding dividends, didn't fully recover for 25 years. And the '68 peak was part of a sideways market that lasted 18 years. Some believe a long dry spell like the one after the '68 bust, which included a 46% decline in the market in 1973–1974, will be our model. Others say the model will be the even more disturbing decline of stocks in Japan since 1989. There, the market has fallen 63%, and assets in mutual funds have plunged 93%.

Such a turnabout would offer a stiff test for this equity culture. "If you're 30 or 40, it's nothing to worry about," says Biggs. The market always comes back. But if you're 55 or 60 and letting bills pile up while you buy stocks, the risks are acute because you have less time. Minuscule returns over a long period could mean that you won't have as much money in retirement as you thought, or that you'll have to work longer, and if you need money during the worst of the drought, you'll have to sell at the bottom. A serious market dive of 40% could sap consumer confidence and bring on a recession, always tough on those who have been taking on debt.

But the biggest risk is the one that has trampled investors so often in the past. With a big market drop, the equity culture—the faith—just dies out as investors see other assets start to zoom higher, as gold and real estate did in the '70s. They shift to those asset classes and end up missing huge initial gains when stocks eventually, inevitably, bounce back. That kind of behavior destroys any argument for the public's easily attaining the long-term average annual returns that stocks offer.

For the equity culture to be true Nirvana, it must be permanent. Buy-and-hold means buy and hold a diverse portfolio through thick and thin. But where money is concerned, the age-old forces of greed and fear will always rule. Most investors won't stick with their stocks through years of drought any more than baseball fans will keep filling the stadium for a last-place team. And that's the risk. □

Two New Tax-Saving IRAs

Individual Retirement Accounts (IRAs) became more attractive on January 1, 1998, with the creation of the "Roth IRA" (named for Senate Finance Committee Chairman William Roth of Delaware) and the new "Education IRA."[1]

Specifically: A Roth IRA doesn't qualify you for a tax deduction, but all qualified earnings and withdrawals will be tax-free after five years when you begin withdrawing and are at least 59½ years old. Another advantage of the new retirement account is that it has much higher income limits for eligibility than the traditional, deductible IRAs. Singles with an annual adjusted gross income (AGI) of less than $110,000 and married couples filing jointly with an AGI of less than $160,000 are eligible for the new IRA. By contrast, the AGI limits of the traditional IRA are under $30,000 for singles and below $50,000 for couples filing jointly in 1998.

The combined maximum that can be contributed into either type of IRA remains the same at $2,000 per year, but with the Roth account, you can continue to make annual contributions after age 70½.

In the case of a married couple filing jointly, up to $2,000 can be contributed to each spouse's IRA (even if one spouse has little or no compensation). This means that the total contributions that can be made to both types of IRAs can be as much as $4,000 annually.

Withdrawals up to $10,000 from any IRA can be made before age 59½ without paying a 10% penalty only if the money is used to buy a first home or pay for college tuition. However, withdrawals will be subject to income taxes.

Mandatory distributions are not required from a Roth IRA at age 70½ as they are with traditional IRAs. With a Roth account, you can decide your own timetable for withdrawals or choose not to withdraw any funds after the five-year holding period. In fact, you never have to take any distributions.

Younger workers may especially benefit from these provisions because they have many working years ahead to make contributions and accumulate a large nest egg of tax-free cash for when they retire.

Single or married taxpayers can convert a traditional IRA to a Roth account if their income for the year is $100,000 or less, but they have to pay tax on the value of the converted IRA.

Whether you should choose a Roth IRA over a traditional one depends on your specific situation, such as how many years remain before retirement, your present and future tax-brackets, and your goals after retirement. You should discuss which IRA suits you best with a lawyer, financial, or investment adviser before making a definite decision.

Depending on their income levels, many families (including many middle-class households) can qualify for the new "Education IRA," a nondeductible savings account set up to pay for their child's college expenses. The account, which is similar to an IRA, enables qualifying parents to contribute up to $500 per year for each child under 18 years old and allows the earnings to grow tax-free. However, you do not qualify if you are contributing to a qualified state tuition program.

Unlike the other IRAs, there is no requirement that the contributor have any earned income or be under age 70½. Married couples filing joint returns with adjusted income of $150,000 or less and singles with an adjusted income of $95,000 or less, are permitted to make the full $500 contribution. The allowable contribution diminishes with higher income levels.

Summary of IRA Choices

Traditional, deductible IRA

Eligibility: Persons who do not participate in an employer's retirement plan; those who do but are married and file jointly, and have an annual AGI under $50,000 in 1998; and single persons whose AGI is less than $30,000 in 1998.

Tax Rules: Contributions and earnings are not taxed until withdrawal. Must begin to take distributions at age 70½. Distributions taken before age 59½ are subject to a 10% penalty except in cases where withdrawals up to $10,000 are used for purchasing first home, or for education.

Roth IRA

Eligibility: Married persons filing jointly whose AGI is less than $150,000 in 1998 and single persons whose AGI is under $95,000 in 1998.

Tax Rules: Contributions are not tax deductible. Earnings and withdrawals are not taxed as long as the account is held for five years and account holder is at least 59½ years old when distributions are taken. No minimum withdrawals required at age 70½. Distributions taken before age 59½ are subject to a 10% penalty except in cases where withdrawals up to $10,000 are for purchasing first home, or for education.

1. The new retirement accounts discussed here are only meant to provide readers with general information and are not intended to cover the subject in its entirety. These IRA changes do not apply to 401(k) and Keogh retirement plans.

New Savings Bonds Are Inflation-Indexed

Source: U.S. Treasury Department, Bureau of Public Debt.

A new type of savings bond that is indexed to inflation became available Sept. 1, 1998. Known as the "I-Bond" (Series I Inflation-Indexed Savings Bond), it guarantees that inflation won't eat away the value of Americans' hard-earned savings. The I-Bonds also protect you from potential deflation. Even if deflation is greater than the fixed interest rate, the I-Bond's value will remain the same.

I-Bond Advantages

There are several advantages to purchasing I-Bonds. You can defer federal taxes on their earnings for up to 30 years (the final maturity date or other taxable disposition, whichever occurs first) and they are also exempt from both state and local income taxes. You don't have to do anything to get these benefits, they are built right into I-Bonds.

Other advantages are that they usually increase in value every month, and interest is compounded semiannually. The bonds are liquid and can be turned into cash at any time after they have been held for six months. Investors redeeming bonds before five years are assessed a penalty amounting to three months' worth of earnings. Individuals are limited to purchases of up to $30,000 worth of I-Bonds each calendar year. I-bonds are safe and backed by the U.S. government.

Bonds Honor Prominent Americans

The new bonds, which are sold in denominations of $50 to $5,000, honor eight distinguished Americans for their significant contributions to the nation's past, present, and future. The eight Americans featured on the bonds include:

- $50 I-Bond: Helen Keller, noted author and advocate for individuals with disabilities. Ms. Keller is also responsible for Braille becoming the standard for printed communications for the blind.
- $75 I-Bond: Dr. Hector Garcia, a leading advocate for Mexican-American veterans' rights, an activist in the Latino civil rights movement, and the founder of the American GI forum.
- $100 I-Bond: Dr. Martin Luther King, Jr., one of the nation's most prominent civil rights leaders. Dr. King was also a minister and Nobel Peace Prize recipient.
- $200 I-Bond: Chief Joseph, Nez Perce Chief, one of the greatest Native American leaders.
- $500 I-Bond: General George Marshall, U.S. Army Chief of Staff during World War II, Secretary of State and Defense, author of the Marshall Plan, and Nobel Peace Prize recipient.
- $1,000 I-Bond: Albert Einstein, physicist and creator of the theory of relativity. Einstein was also a Noble Prize recipient for physics.
- $5,000 I-Bond: Marian Anderson, world-renowned vocalist and the first African-American to sing at the Metropolitan Opera.
- $10,000 I-Bond: Spark Matsunaga, former U.S. Senator and Congressman, and a World War II hero.

Six of the eight I-Bonds ($50, $75, $100, $1000, and $5000) went on sale in September 1998. The rest are available as of May 1999.

How Earnings Rates Are Set

The I-Bond earnings rate is a combination of two separate rates: a fixed rate of return and a semiannual inflation rate. Each May and November, the Treasury announces a fixed rate of return that applies to all I-Bonds issued during the six-month period beginning with the effective date of the announcement, May 1 or November 1. The fixed rate for any given I-Bond will never change.

Also, every May and November, the Treasury determines a semiannual inflation rate based on changes in the Consumer Price Index for all Urban consumers (CPI-U). The semiannual inflation rate announced in May is a measure of inflation from the previous October through March; the rate announced in November is a measure of inflation from the previous April through September. The semiannual inflation rate is then combined with the fixed rate of an I-Bond to determine the bond's earning rate for the next six months. □

Buying a Home

Source: U.S. Department of Housing and Urban Development.

Shopping for a Loan

Your choice of a lender and type of loan will influence not only your settlement costs, but also the monthly cost of your mortgage loan. There are many types of lenders and types of loans to choose from. Many banks, savings associations, mortgage companies, and credit unions provide home mortgage loans. You can often find a listing of some mortgage lenders in the yellow pages and a listing of rates in your local newspaper.

Mortgage Brokers

Some companies, known as "mortgage brokers" offer to find you a mortgage lender willing to make you a loan. A mortgage broker may operate as an independent business and may not be operating as your "agent" or representative. Your mortgage broker may be paid by the lender, by you as the borrower, or by both. You may wish to ask about the fees that the mortgage broker will receive for its services.

Government Programs

You may be eligible for a loan insured through the Federal Housing Administration (FHA) or guaranteed by the Department of Veterans Affairs or similar programs operated by cities or states. These programs usually require a smaller downpayment. Ask lenders about these programs. You can get more information about these programs from the agencies that run them.

CLOs

Computer loan origination systems, or CLOs, are computer terminals sometimes available in real estate offices or other locations to help you sort through the various types of loans offered by different lenders. The CLO operator may charge a fee for the services the CLO offers. This fee may be paid by you or by the lender that you select.

Types of Loans

Loans can have a fixed interest rate or a variable interest rate. Fixed rate loans have the same principal and interest payments during the loan term. Variable rate loans can have any one of a number of "indexes" and "margins" which determine how and when the rate and payment amount change. If you apply for a variable rate loan, also known as an adjustable rate mortgage (ARM), you should receive a disclosure and booklet (as required by the Truth in Lending Act) that will further describe the ARM. Most loans can be repaid over a term of 30 years or less. Most loans have equal monthly payments. The amounts can change from time to time on an ARM depending on changes in the interest rate. Some

loans have short terms and a large final payment called a "balloon." You should shop for the type of home mortgage loan terms that best suit your needs.

Interest Rate, "Points," & Other Fees

Often the price of a home mortgage loan is stated in terms of an interest rate, points, and other fees. A "point" is a fee that equals one percent of the loan amount. Points are usually paid to the lender, mortgage broker, or both, at the settlement or upon the completion of the escrow. Often, you can pay fewer points in exchange for a higher interest rate or more points for a lower rate. Ask your lender or mortgage broker about points and other fees. A document called the Truth in Lending Disclosure Statement will show you the "Annual Percentage Rate" (APR) and other payment information about the loan for which you have applied. The APR takes into account not only the interest rate, but also the points, mortgage broker fees, and certain other fees that you have to pay. Ask for the APR before you apply, to help you find the loan that is best for you. Also ask if your loan will have a charge or a fee for making payments before they are due ("prepayment penalty"). You may be able to negotiate the terms of the prepayment penalty.

Lender-Required Settlement Costs

Your lender may require you to obtain certain settlement services, such as a new survey, mortgage insurance, or title insurance. It may also order and charge you for other settlement-related services, such as the appraisal or credit report. A lender may also charge other fees, such as fees for loan processing, document preparation, underwriting, flood certification, or an application fee. You may wish t ask for an estimate of fees and settlement costs before choosing a lender. Some lenders offer "no cost" or "no point" loans but normally cover these fees by charging a higher interest rate.

Financial Web Sites

FinanceNet www.financenet.gov
The Syndicate
www.moneypages.com/syndicate/index.html
Invest-o-Rama www.investorama.com/
American Association of Individual Investors
www.aaii.org
Mutual Funds Homepage www.fundsinteractive.com
Foreign Exchange Rates
www.cnnfn.com/markets/currencies.html
U.S. Securities and Exchange Commission
www.sec.gov
Federal Deposit Insurance Corporation
www.fdic.gov
FannieMae www.fanniemae.com
United States Treasury www.ustreas.gov
U.S. Savings Bonds
www.publicdebt.treas.gov/sav/sav.html
Debt Counselors of America www.dca.org
Pension and Welfare Benefits Administration
www.dol.gov/dol/pwba
MetLife Online (Annuities, etc.) www.lifeadvice.com
American Express (financial information)
www.americanexpress.com
American Consumer Credit Counseling
www.consumercredit.com/financial
New York Stock Exchange www.nyse.com
American Stock Exchange www.amex.com
NASDAQ www.nasdaq.com
Chicago Mercantile Exhange www.cme.com
Institute of Certified Financial Planners
www.icfp.org

Comparing Loan Costs

Comparing APRs may be an effective way to shop for a loan. However, you must compare similar loan products for the same loan amount. For example, compare two 30-year fixed rate loans for $100,000. Loan A, with an APR of 8.35%, is less costly than Loan B, with an APR of 8.56%, over the loan term. Before you decide on a loan, you should also consider the up-front cash you will be required to pay for each of the two loans.

Another effective shopping technique is to compare identical loans with different up-front points and other fees. As an example, assume that you are offered two 30-year fixed rate loans for $100,000, both at 8% and with equal monthly payments, but the up-front costs are different. Loan A is set at 2 points ($2,000) and has lender-required costs of $1,800, totalling $3,800 in costs. Loan B is set at 2¼ points ($2,250) and has lender-required costs of $1,200, totalling $3,450 in costs. A comparison of the up-front costs shows Loan B requires $350 less than Loan A. However, your individual situation (how long you plan to stay in your house) and your tax situation (points can usually be deducted for the tax year that you purchase a house) may affect your choice of loans.

Lock-Ins

"Locking in" your rate or points at the time of application or during the processing of your loan will keep the rate and/or points from changing until settlement or closing of the escrow process. Ask your lender if there is a fee to lock-in the rate and whether the fee reduces the amount you have to pay for points. Find out how long the lock-in is effective, what happens if it expires, and whether the lock-in fee is refundable if your application is rejected.

Tax and Insurance Payments

Your monthly mortgage payment will be used to repay the money you borrowed plus interest. Part of your monthly payment may be deposited into an "escrow account" (also known as a "reserve" or "impound" account) so your lender or servicer can pay your real estate taxes, property insurance, mortgage insurance and/or flood insurance. Ask your lender or mortgage broker if you will be required to set up an escrow or impound account for taxes and insurance payments.

Transfer of Your Loan

While you may start the loan process with a lender or mortgage broker, you could find that after settlement another company may be collecting the payments on your loan. Collecting loan payments is often known as "servicing" the loan. Your lender or broker should disclose whether it expects to service your loan or to transfer the servicing to someone else.

Mortgage Insurance

Private mortgage insurance and government mortgage insurance protect the lender against default and enable the lender to make a loan which the lender considers a higher risk. Lenders often require mortgage insurance for loans where the downpayment is less than 20% of the sales price. You may be billed monthly, annually, by an initial lump sum, or through some combination of these practices for your mortgage insurance premium. Ask your lender if mortgage insurance is required and how much it will cost. Mortgage insurance should not be confused with mortgage life, credit life, or disability insurance, which are designed to pay off a mortgage in the event of a borrower's death or disability. You may also be offered "lender paid" mortgage insurance (LPMI). Under LPMI plans, the lender purchases the mortgage insurance and pays the premiums to the insurer. The lender will increase your interest rate to pay for the premiums—but LPMI may reduce your settlement costs. You cannot cancel LPMI or government mortgage insurance during the life of your loan. However, it may be possible to cancel private mortgage insurance at some point, such as when your loan balance is reduced to a certain amount. Before you commit to paying for mortgage insurance, find out the specific requirements for cancellation.

Flood Hazard Areas

Most lenders will not lend you money to buy a home in a flood hazard area unless you pay for flood insurance. Some government loan programs will not allow you to purchase a home that is located in a flood hazard area. Your lender may charge you a fee to check for flood hazards. You should be notified if flood insurance is required. If a change in flood insurance maps brings your home within a flood hazard area after your loan is made, your lender or servicer may require you to buy flood insurance at that time. □

Mortgage Qualifications for Buying a Home

Source: Fannie Mae.

Your History

Your job history is important and it will be a major factor in whether you qualify for a loan. If you have been working continuously for two years or more, you are considered to have steady employment. However, you do not have to have held the same job for two years in order to be approved for a loan. Job moves that result in equal or more pay and continue to use proven skills are a plus for you. If there are good reasons why you haven't worked continuously for the last two years, you can explain them to the mortgage lender.

How you paid your bills in the past also gives a lender some indication of how you can be expected to pay them in the future. You will be asked to list all your debts, the amount of your monthly payments, and the number of months or years left to pay on the debts. Your lender will order a credit report to verify the information that you give.

Payment Options

When you buy a home, you need money for a down payment and closing costs. The amount of the down payment may vary, but generally you must make a down payment that equals at least 5% of the purchase price. Closing costs can be expensive, depending upon where you live.

The mortgage lender will want proof that you have saved the funds that you will use for a down payment and part or all of the closing costs. If the funds are in a savings account, the lender will ask the financial institution to verify the amount and the length of time that the funds have been in your account. The lender wants to make sure that you are not borrowing all the money you will use for the down payment and closing costs.

The amount of your monthly payment depends upon the amount you borrow, the interest rate, and the repayment period or "term." The shorter the term, the higher your monthly payment. For that reason, most home buyers repay their mortgage over the longest term possible, usually 30 years.

Housing Expense Guidelines

When you first approach a lender about financing your mortgage, it will use the following two commonly accepted guidelines to help determine your ability to make mortgage payments:

1. Your monthly housing costs (including mortgage payments, property taxes, homeowner and mortgage insurance, and homeowner's fees) should total no more than 28% of your monthly gross (before taxes) income. In addition to your regular pay, your income can include funds you receive from overtime work, a part-time job, or a second job; retirement, VA, and Social Security benefits; disability, welfare, and unemployment benefits; alimony; and child support.

2. Your monthly housing costs plus other long-term debts such as payments on car loans, student loans, or other installment debt (debts with more than ten months left to repay) should total no more than 36% of your monthly gross income. Depending upon your household income, you may be eligible for special assistance programs. These programs may make it easier for you to get a larger mortgage loan than you normally would be able to, using the above qualifying rules.

How Large a Mortgage Do You Qualify For?

This chart can help you find out how large a mortgage you might qualify for based on your annual income and the interest rate currently being quoted for 30-year fixed-rate mortgages. Rather than using the normal 28% ratio, this chart uses a 25% ratio and assumes that the amount you need to set aside to pay for taxes and insurance would amount to approximately the 3% difference. This simplified approach should give you a fairly accurate answer.

Interest rates	Annual income $15,000	$20,000	$25,000	$30,000	$35,000	$40,000
6.5%	$49,400	$65,900	$82,400	$98,800	$115,300	$131,800
7.0	47,000	62,600	78,300	93,900	109,600	125,300
7.5	44,600	59,600	74,500	89,400	104,300	119,200
8.0	45,000	56,700	70,900	85,100	99,300	113,500
8.5	40,600	54,100	67,700	81,200	94,800	108,300
9.0	38,800	51,700	64,700	77,700	90,600	103,500
9.5	37,200	49,500	61,900	74,300	86,700	99,100
10.0	35,600	47,400	59,300	71,200	83,000	94,900
10.5	34,200	45,500	56,900	68,300	79,700	91,100
	$45,000	**$50,000**	**$55,000**	**$60,000**	**$65,000**	**$70,000**
6.5%	$148,300	$164,800	$181,300	$197,700	$214,200	$230,000
7.0	140,900	156,600	172,300	187,900	203,600	219,200
7.5	134,100	149,000	163,900	178,800	193,700	208,600
8.0	127,700	141,900	156,100	170,300	184,500	198,700
8.5	121,900	135,400	149,000	162,500	176,100	189,600
9.0	116,500	129,400	142,400	155,300	168,200	181,200
9.5	111,400	123,800	136,200	148,600	161,000	173,400
10.0	106,800	118,600	130,500	142,400	154,300	166,100
10.5	102,400	113,800	125,200	136,600	148,000	159,400

Source: Fannie Mae.

Calculate Your Mortgage Payment

Use this chart to calculate how much your monthly mortgage payment might be, based on a 30-year term. Let's suppose that you want to purchase a house that costs $50,000. If you make a $5,000 down payment, you would need a $45,000 mortgage. As you can see on the chart, the monthly payment on a $45,000 mortgage at 8% interest is $330. The $330 monthly payment only covers the principal, or a portion of the amount you borrowed, and interest on the mortgage loan. There are other expenses that will be added to your monthly payment. These include taxes and homeowner's insurance. If your down payment is less than 20%, you may need to pay private mortgage insurance. These costs vary depending upon where you live and the cost of your home, but they can add a hundred dollars or more to your monthly payment. In addition, if you are thinking about buying a unit in a condo or cooperative building, or a house in a planned unit development, you may also need to pay monthly homeowner's fees to cover maintenance expenses or special assessments related to the common areas.

Loan amount	Interest rates 6.5%	7%	7.5%	8%	8.5%	9%	9.5%	10%	10.5%
$20,000	$126	$133	$140	$147	$154	$161	$168	$176	$183
25,000	158	166	175	183	192	201	210	219	229
30,000	190	200	210	220	231	241	252	263	274
35,000	221	233	245	257	269	282	294	307	320
40,000	253	266	280	294	308	322	336	351	366
45,000	284	299	315	330	346	362	378	395	412
50,000	316	333	350	367	384	402	420	439	457
55,000	348	366	385	404	423	443	462	483	503
60,000	380	399	420	440	461	483	505	527	549
65,000	411	432	454	477	500	523	547	570	595
70,000	442	466	489	514	538	563	589	614	640
75,000	474	499	524	550	577	603	631	658	686
80,000	506	532	559	587	615	644	673	702	732
85,000	537	566	594	624	654	684	715	746	778
90,000	569	599	629	660	692	724	757	790	823
95,000	600	632	664	697	730	764	799	834	869
100,000	632	665	699	734	769	805	841	878	915

Source: Fannie Mae.

1998 Study of Housing Costs

According to the E &Y Kenneth Leventhal Eighth Annual Housing Costs Study, Oklahoma City remained the city where housing took the smallest bite from employee paychecks in 1998. New York City took the biggest bite. E &Y Kenneth Leventhal is the real estate group of Ernst & Young LLP. Housing costs are based on the average cost of amenitized for-sale and rental housing for mid-level executives. American companies use the study as an evaluation tool in making relocation and expansion decisions.

Oklahoma City, the most affordable market, required only 21.3% of median family income to rent a luxury apartment and 13.6% of income to afford a four-bedroom, single-family home. In contrast, the average buyer pays 41.8% of median family income to rent a similar apartment and 45.3% of income to buy a four-bedroom residence in the New York City metro area.

The ten most affordable housing markets in order of rank are: Oklahoma City, Richmond, Kansas City, Knoxville, Raleigh-Durham, Indianapolis, Tulsa, Houston, Charlotte, and Dallas-Fort Worth.

The ten least affordable housing markets in order of rank are: New York City, San Francisco, Los Angeles, Boston, Oakland-East Bay, Pittsburgh, El Paso, Miami, San Jose, and Honolulu.

The study made several other observations:

High Cost Markets "Settle for Less": The study does not imply that most professional households in New York spend more than two-fifths of their income on housing. Rather, it indicates that many households in high-cost housing regions must "settle" for less housing—either by buying smaller homes or by staying in rental housing.

Regional Variations Persist: Homeowners in coastal California and those in northeastern markets still pay roughly twice as much of their income to acquire housing as those in many urban areas in the Central and Southeast United States.

Southeast Offers Most Affordable Housing: The region extending from Texas north to Missouri has five of the ten most affordable large housing markets in the country.

Affordable "Pockets" Within the Costly Coasts: Not all of California and the Northeast are inordinately costly. In both Sacramento and Riverside–San Bernardino, housing requires less than 24% of the median local family income. Orange County required 25%.

Better value may also soon surface in Hawaii, where home ownership hasn't been very accessible in recent years. The value of a Honolulu mid-management home has dropped by $100,000 in two years.

In the Northeast, Newark–North New Jersey continues to offer low housing prices, requiring 29% of median local family income compared to the 43% cost across the Hudson in New York City.

Boston's housing affordability continues to worsen, primarily due to rising rents during the past year. □

How to Measure the Shrinking Value of the Dollar

Source: Martin Lefkowitz, Economist, U.S. Chamber of Commerce.

How to use this table. This table provides a method for translating dollar values from the past 52 years into 1998 dollars. For example: What weekly salary would you need to earn in 1998 to equal the purchasing power of a weekly salary of $100 in 1970? Take the 1970 multiplier, 4.22, times $100 and you would need to earn $422 a week in 1998 to achieve the same salary.

Year	Value of dollar in 1998 dollars	Year	Value of dollar in 1998 dollars	Year	Value of dollar in 1998 dollars
1946	$8.39	1964	$5.28	1982	$1.70
1947	7.03	1965	5.20	1983	1.64
1948	6.79	1966	5.05	1984	1.58
1949	6.88	1967	4.90	1985	1.52
1950	6.79	1968	4.70	1986	1.49
1951	6.30	1969	4.46	1987	1.44
1952	6.18	1970	4.22	1988	1.38
1953	6.13	1971	4.04	1989	1.32
1954	6.09	1972	3.92	1990	1.25
1955	6.11	1973	3.69	1991	1.20
1956	6.02	1974	3.32	1992	1.17
1957	5.83	1975	3.04	1993	1.13
1958	5.66	1976	2.88	1994	1.10
1959	5.63	1977	2.70	1995	1.07
1960	5.53	1978	2.51	1996	1.04
1961	5.47	1979	2.25	1997	1.02
1962	5.42	1980	1.99	1998	1.00
1963	5.35	1981	1.80		

Credit Cards Lose Their Charm

Consumers are saddled with growing fees, shrinking grace periods, and extra penalties

By STACY PERMAN TIME

For consumers, the world of plastic is not looking so fantastic anymore. The industry has been consolidating in an attempt to get back on the gravy train it once rode. With fewer big competitors, the remaining card issuers are getting less generous. AT&T's initial no-fee offer, for example, inspired a wink of inducements from other issuers, each upping the ante with low initial rates and rebates. And consumers snapped them up, stuffing an average of seven cards in their wallets.

But for many in the industry, profits have melted under the costs of these incentives. They fell 24% in 1996—dropping 300% from the mid-1980s—and remained flat last year, pounded by a wave of delinquencies as consumers maxed out their debt. "The credit-card free-for-all has come back to haunt the industry," says Robert McKinley, president of RAM Research. To stanch the southern flow of profits, card issuers are seeking to edge up their income by retrenching on offers and charging penalties, new fees, and higher rates.

The trend gained momentum when GE Capital (the finance arm of General Electric) announced it would slap a $25 annual penalty on holders of its GE Rewards MasterCard who did not accrue interest-bearing debt. Since then, issuers have come up with a slew of punitive measures—er, fees—that squeeze responsible cardholders as well as slackers. Just a few years ago, no company charged a late fee of more than $18; today almost half do. Even grace periods are shrinking from the average 25 to 30 days to 20 days, which means some customers could get hit with a finance charge even before receiving a bill.

Some 55 million to 60 million households owe more than $7,000 on their plastic, according to the Consumer Federation of America. That means they already pay at least $1,000 a year in fees and interest. The average interest rate is 18.84%, up from 17.7% the year before. Mellon Bank of Pittsburgh, Pa., assesses its cardholders $15 for not charging during a six-month period. If you cancel your card account with Advanta Bank of Wilmington, Del., it may impose a $25 fee as a parting gift. Warns McKinley: "There are going to be more costs associated with cards in the future." And that future is now. □

Credit Card Use: 1989 to 1995

General purpose credit cards include Mastercard, Visa, Optima, and Discover cards. All dollar figures are given in constant 1995 dollars based on consumer price index data as published by U.S. Bureau of Labor Statistics.

Age of family head and family income[1]	Percent having a general purpose credit card	Percent having a balance after last month's bills	Median balance[2]	Percent of cardholding families who— Almost always pay off the balance	Sometimes pay off the balance	Hardly ever pay off the balance
1989, total	55.8%	52.0%	$1,200	53.1%	21.5%	25.4%
1992, total	62.2	52.8	1,100	52.8	19.6	27.6
1995, total	**66.4**	**56.3**	**1,500**	**51.9**	**20.4**	**27.7**
Under 35 years old	59.0	69.2	1,500	40.2	23.5	36.3
35 to 44 years old	68.5	68.1	1,900	40.7	26.9	32.4
45 to 54 years old	75.4	64.8	1,800	47.1	22.5	30.4
55 to 64 years old	71.9	48.0	1,800	59.3	18.4	22.3
65 to 74 years old	68.3	30.8	800	72.0	12.9	15.1
75 years old and over	54.6	18.2	700	85.8	2.5	11.7
Less than $10,000	26.3	55.8	1,000	56.4	12.4	31.2
$10,000 to $24,999	53.3	57.0	1,500	50.9	17.2	31.9
$25,000 to $49,999	75.0	59.2	1,500	47.6	20.9	31.5
$50,000 to $99,999	93.1	59.4	2,000	49.7	25.3	25.1
$100,000 and more	97.1	35.4	2,100	73.7	17.2	9.1

1. Families include one-person units. 2. Among families having a balance. *Source:* Board of Governors of the Federal Reserve System, *Statistical Abstract of the U.S., 1997*, www.census.gov/stat_abstract/.

Measuring the New CPI

It's official: inflation is even lower than you thought

By **DANIEL KADLEC** TIME

Inflation has been all but wiped off the worry screen of most Americans. But not of politicians and government statistics moles, who adjusted the Consumer Price Index downward in 1998 for the fourth consecutive year. Stifle that yawn. The CPI, the nation's principal gauge of inflation, is not just a measure of the price of a quart of milk or a gallon of gas. It is easily the most important weapon in the government's considerable measurements arsenal. It forms the basis for annual benefits adjustments to some 80 million voters, from union workers and Social Security recipients to government retirees. Funding for food stamps and school lunches is pegged to the CPI, as are income tax exemptions and deductions and the break points between tax brackets.

"Virtually everything we do in the economy depends on the CPI," says Michael Boskin, Stanford University economics professor and former chair of the Council of Economic Advisers. In 1996 Boskin headed a Senate commission that concluded that the CPI overstates annual inflation by about a percentage point. That means the low CPI of 1.7% in 1997 might really have been less than 1%—a huge difference. Boskin's startling assertion accelerated the drive to find a new CPI formula while politicians began drooling over the prospect of reallocating billions of dollars freed by reduced CPI-pegged spending. The CPI formula has been tinkered with in 1995, '96, and '97, refiguring food, housing, and medical costs. Those changes shaved .3 of a percentage point off the annual rate. In 1997 the Bureau of Labor Statistics (BLS) began tracking an experimental CPI, for the first time trying to account for rational behavior: substituting chicken for beef, for instance, when beef prices rise. That formula will be eventually incorporated in the official CPI and will trim an additional .2 of a percentage point off the annual rate.

The 1998 change in the CPI was a real haircut. For the first time in 11 years, the BLS compiled a new "market basket" of goods to track, adding things like cellular phones and auto leases and making personal computers more prominent. The BLS, which monitors some 80,000 items, added one major category, education and communication, catapulting the CPI into the information age. All the latest revisions will shave about .1 of a percentage point off the annual rate, bringing the four-year cumulative effect on the CPI to .6 of a percentage point. The White House predicts that turning a few more knobs will bring that figure to .7. Put that into real dollars, and the government saves $4 billion a year.

Officials say accuracy, not parsimony, is the goal. "Consumption patterns change," notes BLS commissioner Katharine Abraham. "New products enter the market. Old ones are modified or disappear. The market basket of today is totally different from that of a generation ago." There is a gold lining of sorts. The overstated inflation rate has kept interest rates unduly high because lenders account for inflation in setting rates. Allen Sinai of Primark Decision Economics believes that even with the changes, the CPI may be a full point too high. "Effectively, there is no inflation," he says. Now the government is making it official. □

Consumer Tips

Source: U.S. Office of Consumer Affairs.

Consumer Information Catalog

The *Consumer Information Catalog* lists approximately 200 free or low-cost federal booklets with helpful information for consumers. Topics include careers and education, cars, childcare, the environment, federal benefits, financial planning, food and nutrition, health, housing, small businesses, and more. This free catalog is published quarterly by the Consumer Information Center of the U.S. General Services Administration. Single copies of the catalog only may be ordered by sending your name and address to *Catalog,* Consumer Information Center, Pueblo, CO 81009, or on the Internet at www.pueblo.gsa.gov, or by calling 719-948-4000.

Nonprofit groups that can distribute 25 copies or more each quarter may automatically receive copies by writing for a bulk mail card.

Consumer Web Sites

Consumer Information Center: www.pueblo.gsa.gov
Consumer World: www.consumerworld.org
National Fraud Information Center: www.fraud.org
Federal Trade Commission: www.ftc.gov
Consumer Product Safety Commission: www.cpsc.gov
U.S. Dept. of Transportation: www.dot.gov/safety.htm
Project OPEN (National Consumer League): www.isa.net/project-open
American Council on Consumer Interests: riker.ps.missouri.edu/dh/acci
Consumer Alert: www.consumeralert.org/index.htm
Copyright Information: lcweb.loc.gov/copyright/
Better Business Bureau: www.bbb.org
U.S. Dept. of Justice: www.usdoj.gov
Federal Consumer Information: www.consumer.gov
Consumer Union Advocacy: www.consunion.org

Copyrights

Source: Copyright Office, Washington, D.C.

Copyright is a form of protection provided by the laws of the United States to the creators of "original works of authorship," including literary, dramatic, musical, artistic, and certain other intellectual works. This protection is available to both published and unpublished works. The Copyright Act generally gives the owner of copyright the exclusive right to do and to authorize others to do the following:

- To reproduce the copyrighted work;
- To prepare derivative works based upon the copyrighted work;
- To distribute copies or phonorecords of the copyrighted work to the public by sale or other transfer of ownership, or by rental, lease, or lending;
- To perform the copyrighted work publicly; and
- To display the copyrighted work publicly.

It is illegal for anyone to violate these rights. However, they are limited by the doctrine of "fair use," or by a "compulsory license" under which certain limited uses of copyrighted works are permitted in exchange for payment. For further information about the limitations of any of these rights, consult the Copyright Act or write to the Copyright Office.

Copyright protection exists from the time the work is created in fixed form; that is, it is an incident of the process of authorship. The copyright in the work of authorship immediately becomes the property of the author who created it. Only the author, or those deriving their rights through the author, can rightfully claim copyright.

In the case of works made for hire, the employer and not the employee is presumptively considered the author. The copyright statute defines a "work made for hire" as:

- A work prepared by an employee within the scope of his or her employment; or
- A work specially ordered or commissioned for use as a contribution to a collective work, as a part of a motion picture or other audiovisual work, as a translation, as a supplementary work, as a compilation, as an instructional text, as a test, as answer material for a test, or as an atlas, if the parties expressly agree in a written instrument signed by them that the work shall be considered a work made for hire. . . .

The authors of a joint work are co-owners of the copyright in the work, unless there is an agreement to the contrary.

Copyright in each separate contribution to a periodical or other collective work is distinct from copyright in the collective work as a whole and vests initially with the author of the contribution.

Two General Principles:

- Mere ownership of a book, manuscript, painting, or any other copy or phonorecord does not give the possessor the copyright. The law provides that transfer of ownership of any material object that embodies a protected work does not of itself convey any rights in the copyright.
- Minors may claim copyright, but state laws may regulate the business dealings involving copyrights owned by minors. For information on relevant state laws, consult an attorney.

Copyright is secured automatically when the work is created, and a work is "created" when it is fixed in a copy or phonorecord for the first time. "Copies" are material objects from which a work can be read or visually perceived, such as books, manuscripts, sheet music, film, videotape, or microfilm. "Phonorecords" are material objects embodying fixations of sounds (excluding, by statutory definition, motion picture soundtracks), such as cassette tapes, CDs, or LPs. Thus, for example, a song (the "work") can be fixed in sheet music ("copies") or in phonograph disks ("phonorecords"), or both.

If a work is prepared over a period of time, the part of the work that is fixed on a particular date constitutes the created work as of that date.

Copyright protection is available for all unpublished works, regardless of the nationality or domicile of the author. Published works are eligible for copyright protection in the United States if any one of the several conditions regarding the nationality of the authors or place of publication is met. Check with the Copyright Office for details.

What Works Are Protected

Copyright protects "original works of authorship" including the following categories:

- literary works;
- musical works, including any accompanying words;
- dramatic works, including any accompanying music;
- pantomimes and choreographic works;
- pictorial, graphic, and sculptural works;
- motion pictures and other audiovisual works;
- sound recordings; and
- architectural works.

These categories should be viewed quite broadly. For example, computer programs and most "compilations" are registrable as "literary works." Maps and architectural plans are registrable as "pictorial, graphic, and sculptural works."

Several categories of material are generally not eligible for statutory copyright protection. These include among others:

- Works that have not been fixed in a tangible form of expression. For example, choreographic works that have not been notated or recorded, or improvisational speeches or performances that have not been written or recorded.
- Titles, names, short phrases, and slogans; familiar symbols or designs; mere variations of typographic ornamentation, lettering, or coloring; mere listings of ingredients or contents.
- Ideas, procedures, methods, systems, processes, concepts, principles, discoveries, or devices, as distinguished from a description, explanation, or illustration.
- Works consisting entirely of information that is common property and containing no original authorship. For example, standard calendars, height and weight charts, tape measures and rulers, and lists or tables taken from public documents or other common sources.

Notice of Copyright

When a work is published, it may bear a notice of copyright to identify the year of publication and the

name of the copyright owner and to inform the public that the work is protected by copyright. Use of the notice is recommended because it informs the public that the work is protected by copyright, identifies the copyright owners, and shows the year of first publication.

Furthermore, in the event that a work is infringed, if a proper notice of copyright appears on the published copy or copies to which a defendant in a copyright infringement suit had access, then no weight shall be given to such a defendant's interposition of a defense based on innocent infringement in mitigation of actual or statutory damages, except as provide in section 504(c) (2) of the copyright code. Innocent infringement occurs when the infringer did not realize that the work was protected.

The use of the copyright notice is the responsibility of the copyright owner and does not require advance permission from, or registration with, the Copyright Office.

Form of Notice for Visually Perceptible Copies

The notice for visually perceptible copies should contain all of the following three elements:

1. The symbol © (the letter C in a circle), or the word "Copyright," or the abbreviation "Copr.";
2. The year of publication of the work; and
3. The name of the owner of copyright in the work, or an abbreviation by which the name can be recognized, or a generally known alternative designation of the owner.

Example: © 1999 John Doe

Form of Notice for Sound Recordings

The copyright notice for phonorecords of sound recordings should contain the following three elements:

1. The symbol ℗ (the letter P in a circle);
2. The year of first publication of the sound recording; and
3. The name of the owner of copyright in the sound recording, or an abbreviation by which the name can be recognized, or a generally known alternative designation of the owner. If the producer of the sound recording is named on the phonorecord labels or containers, and if no other name appears in conjunction with the notice, the producer's name shall be considered a part of the notice.

Example: ℗ 1999 A.B.C., Inc.

NOTE: Since questions may arise from the use of variant forms of the notice, any form of the notice other than those given here should not be used without first seeking legal advice.

Position of Notice

The notice should be positioned so as to "give reasonable notice of the claim of copyright." The Copyright Office has issued regulations concerning the form and position of the copyright notice. For more information, contact them directly.

Publications Incorporating United States Government Works

Works by the U.S. Government are not eligible for copyright protection, though portions of these works may be eligible. Example:

© 1998 Jane Brown. Copyright claimed in Chapters 7–10, exclusive of U.S. Government maps.

Unpublished Works

To avoid an inadvertent publication without notice, the author or other owner of copyright may wish to place a copyright notice on any copies or phonorecords that leave his or her control. An appropriate notice for an unpublished work is "Unpublished work © 1999 Jane Doe."

Copyright Protection Endurance

Works Originally Created On or After Jan. 1, 1978

A work that is created on or after January 1, 1978, is automatically protected from the moment of its creation, and is ordinarily given a term of the author's life, plus 50 years. In the case of a joint work prepared by two or more authors who did not work for hire, the term lasts for 50 years after the last surviving author's death. For works made for hire, and for anonymous and pseudonymous works (unless the author's identity is revealed in Copyright Office records), the duration of copyright will be 75 years from publication or 100 years from creation, whichever is shorter.

Works Originally Created Before Jan. 1, 1978

Works that were created but not published or registered for copyright before January 1, 1978, have been automatically brought under the statute and are now given federal copyright protection. The duration of copyright in these works will generally be computed in the same way as for works created on or after January 1, 1978. The law provides that in no case will the term of copyright for works in this category expire before December 31, 2002, and for works published on or before December 31, 2002, the term of copyright will not expire before December 31, 2027. Works that were created and published or registered before January 1, 1978, generally enjoy a copyright term of 75 years from the date of publication or registration. Check with the Copyright Office for details.

International Copyright Protection

There is no "international copyright" that will automatically protect an author's work throughout the entire world. Protection against unauthorized use in a particular country depends basically on the national laws of that country. However, most countries do offer protection to foreign works under certain conditions, and these conditions have been greatly simplified by international copyright treaties and conventions.

In general, copyright registration is a legal formality intended to make a public record of the basic facts of a particular copyright but is not a condition of copyright protection. However, the copyright law provides several inducements or advantages to encourage copyright owners to make registration:

- It establishes a public record of the copyright claim.
- Before an infringement suit may be filed in court, registration is necessary for works of U.S. origin and for foreign works not originating in a Berne Union country.
- If made before or within five years of publication, registration will establish *prima facie* evidence in court of the validity of the copyright and of the facts stated in the certificate.

• If registration is made within three months after publication of the work or prior to an infringement of the work, statutory damages and attorney's fees will be available to the copyright owner in court actions. Otherwise, only an award of actual damages and profits is available to the copyright owner.

• Registration allows the copyright owner to record the registration with the U.S. Customs Service for protection against the importation of infringing copies.

For a list of countries that maintain copyright relations with the United States, request Circular 38a from the Copyright Office.

Copyright Registration

Copyright registration makes a public record of the basic facts of a particular copyright. Even though registration is not a requirement for protection, the copyright law provides several incentives to encourage copyright owners to register. They include the following:

• Registration establishes a public record of the copyright claim;

• Before an infringement suit may be filed in court, registration is necessary for works of U.S. origin and for foreign works not originating in a Berne Convention country. (For more information on when a work is of U.S. origin, request Circular 93);

• If made before or within five years of publication, registration will establish prima facie evidence in court of the validity of the copyright and of the facts stated in the certificate; and

• If registration is made within three months after publication of the work or prior to an infringement of the work, statutory damages, and attorney's fees will be available to the copyright owner in court actions. Otherwise, only an award of actual damages and profits is available to the copyright owner.

• Copyright registration allows the owner of the copyright to record the registration with the U.S. Customs Service for protection against the importation of infringing copies. For additional information, request Publication No. 563 from IPR Branch, Franklin Court, Suite 4000, U.S. Customs Service, 1301 Constitution Ave., N.W., Washington, D.C. 20229.

Registration may be made at any time within the life of the copyright. When a work has been registered in unpublished form, it is not necessary to make another registration when the work becomes published (although the copyright owner may register the published edition, if desired).

To register a work, send the following three elements in the same envelope or package to the Registrar of Copyrights, Copyright Office, Library of Congress, Washington, D.C. 20559-6000:

1. A properly completed application form;
2. A nonrefundable filing fee of $20 for each application;
3. A nonreturnable deposit of the work that is being registered. Generally the deposit is two copies if the work is published and one copy if the work is unpublished. The application form details the specific deposit requirements.

A copyright registration is effective on the date the Copyright Office receives all of the required elements in acceptable form, regardless of how long it takes to process the application and mail the certificate of registration. The time the Copyright Office requires to process an application varies, depending on the amount of material the office is receiving. If you apply for copyright registration, you will not receive an acknowledgment that your application has been received (the office receives more than 600,000 applications annually), but you can expect:

• A letter or telephone call from a Copyright Office staff member if further information is needed, or

• A certificate of registration indicating that the work has been registered, or if the application cannot be accepted, a letter explaining why it has been rejected.

Requests to have certificates sent by Federal Express or another mail service cannot be honored. If you want to know the date that the Copyright Office receives your material, send it by registered or certified mail and request a return receipt.

For More Information

Information on registration and application forms may be obtained free of charge by writing or calling the Copyright Office. Circular 1 contains general copyright information, including a list of application forms for copyright registration. Address inquiries to the Copyright Office, Publications Section, LM-455, Library of Congress, Washington, D.C. 20559-6000. To speak with an information specialist, call 202-707-3000 (TTY: 202-707-6737) between 8:30 a.m.–5:00 p.m., Eastern Time, Monday to Friday, except federal holidays. Recorded information is available 24 hours a day. To receive information via fax, call 202-707-2600. Registration forms are not available via fax.

Copyright information, including the most frequently requested circulars, is available via the Internet. Internet site addresses are www.lcweb.loc.gov/copyright/ and gopher.marvel.loc.gov.port70.

Copyright Office records of registrations and other related documents from 1978 forward are also available over the Internet via the above addresses or telnet directly to LOCIS (Library of Congress Information System) at locis.loc.gov.

Trademarks

Source: Department of Commerce, Patent and Trademark Office.

A trademark may be defined as a word, letter, device, or symbol, as well as any combination of these, which is used in connection with merchandise and which points distinctly to the origin of the goods.

Certificates of registration of trademarks are issued under the seal of the Patent and Trademark Office and may be registered by the owner if he or she is engaged in interstate or foreign commerce. Federal jurisdiction over trademarks arises under the commerce clause of the Constitution. Effective November 16, 1989, applications to register may also be based on a "bona fide intention to use the

mark in commerce." Trademarks may be registered by foreign owners who comply with our law, as well as by citizens of foreign countries with which the U.S. has treaties relating to trademarks. American citizens may register trademarks in foreign countries by complying with the laws of those countries. The right to registration and protection of trademarks in many foreign countries is guaranteed by treaties.

General jurisdiction in trademark cases involving Federal Registrations is given to Federal courts. Adverse decisions of examiners on applications for registration are appealable to the Trademark Trial and Appeal Board, whose affirmances, and decisions in *inter partes* proceedings, are subject to court review. Before adopting a trademark, a person should make a search of prior marks to avoid infringing unwittingly upon them.

The duration of a trademark registration is 10 years, but it may be renewed indefinitely for 10-year periods, provided the trademark is still in use at the time of expiration.

The application fee is $245 per class.

Patents

Source: Department of Commerce, Patent and Trademark Office.

A patent, in the most general sense, is a document issued by a government, conferring some special right or privilege. The term is now restricted mainly to patents for inventions; occasionally, land patents.

The grant of a patent for an invention gives the inventor the privilege, for a limited period of time, of excluding others from making, using, or selling a certain article.

In the U.S., the law provides that a patent may be granted, for a term of 20[1] years from the date of application, to any person who has invented or discovered any new and useful art, machine, manufacture, or composition of matter, as well as any new and useful improvements thereof. A patent may also be granted to a person who has invented or discovered and asexually reproduced a new and distinct variety of plant (other than a tuber-propagated one) or has invented a new, original and ornamental design for an article of manufacture for a term of 20 years and 14 years, respectively.

A patent is granted only upon a regularly filed application, complete in all respects; upon payment of the fees; and upon determination that the disclosure is complete and that the invention is new, useful, and, in view of the prior art, unobvious to one skilled in the art. The disclosure must be of such nature as to enable others to reproduce the invention.

A complete application, which must be addressed to the Commissioner of Patents and Trademarks, Washington, D.C. 20231, consists of a specification with one or more claims; oath or declaration; drawing (whenever the nature of the case admits of it); and a basic filing fee of $395.[2] The filing fee is not returned to the applicant if the patent is refused. If the patent is allowed, another fee of $660[2] is required before the patent is issued. The fee for design patent application is $165; the issue fee is $225.[2] The fee for a plant patent application is $270; the issue fee is $335. Maintenance fees are required on utility patents at stipulated intervals.

Applications are ordinarily considered in the order in which they are received. Patents are not granted for printed matter, for methods of doing business, or for devices for which claims contrary to natural laws are made. Applications for a perpetual-motion machine have been made from time to time, but until a working model is presented that actually fulfills the claim, no patent will be issued.

1. As a result of the GATT Uruguay Round implementing legislation, the term of utility and plant patents is 20 years measured from the date of filing an application in the U.S. effective June 8, 1995. 2. Fees quoted are for small entity applicants as of Oct. 1, 1997. Fees are double for corporations.

Beware of Illegal Patent Services

It is illegal under patent law (35 USC 33) for anyone to hold himself out as qualified to prepare and prosecute patent applications unless he is registered with the Patent Office. Also, Patent Office regulations forbid registered practitioners advertising for patent business. Some inventors, unaware of this, enter into binding contracts with persons and firms which advertise their assistance in making patent searches, preparing drawings, specifications, and patent applications, only to discover much later that their applications require the services of fully qualified agents or attorneys.

National Consumer Organizations

Alliance Against Fraud In Telemarketing (AAFT), c/o National Consumers League, 1701 K St., N.W., Ste. 1200, Washington, D.C. 20006, 202-835-3323, 202-835-0747 (fax).

The Alliance, coordinated by the National Consumers League, is an international coalition of public interest groups, trade associations, labor unions, businesses, law enforcement agencies, consumer reporters and consumer protection agencies. AAFT members promote cooperative educational efforts to alert potential victims to the threat of telemarketing fraud and steps consumers can take to protect themselves.

American Association of Retired Persons (AARP), Consumer Affairs Section, 601 E St., N.W., Washington, D.C. 20049, 800-424-3410, 202-434-6466 (fax).

AARP's Consumer Affairs Section advocates on behalf of mid-life and older consumers, develops and distributes consumer information, and educates the private sector about the specific needs of older consumers. It offers programs and materials on housing, insurance, funeral practices, eligibility for public benefits, financial security, transportation and consumer protection issues, with special focus on the needs and problems of older consumers.

American Council on Consumer Interests (ACCI), 240 Stanley Hall, University of Missouri, Columbia, Mo. 65211–0001, 573-882-3817, 573-884-6571 (fax), acci@showme.missouri.edu.
Contact: Anita B. Metzen, Executive Director.

Serving the professional needs of consumer educators, researchers and policymakers, ACCI publications and educational programs foster the production, synthesis and dissemination of information in the consumer interest.

American Council on Science and Health (ACSH), 1995 Broadway, 2nd Fl., New York, N.Y. 10023-5860, 212-362-7044, 212-362-4919 (fax).

A nonprofit public education group, ACSH's goal is to provide up-to-date, sound information on the relationship among health and chemicals, foods, lifestyles, and the environment. Booklets and special reports on a variety of topics are available, as is a quarterly magazine, *Priorities.*

Bankcard Holders of America (BHA), 524 Branch Dr., Salem, Va. 24153, 540-389-5445, 540-389-3020 (fax).

A nonprofit organization, BHA assists consumers in saving money on credit, getting out of debt and resolving credit problems. It offers lists of low-rate and secured credit cards, more than 20 guidebooks and educational brochures on credit topics, and a newsletter.

Better Business Bureau *See* Council of Better Business Bureaus, Inc. (CBBB)

Call for Action, 3400 Idaho Ave., N.W., Washington, D.C. 20016-3046, Network Hotline 202-362-3813, 202-537- 0585 (fax).

An international nonprofit hotline, Call for Action is affiliated with radio and television stations and helps consumers and small businesses through mediation of marketplace disputes. A list of the affiliated radio and television stations is available by contacting the hotline.

Center for Auto Safety (CAS), 2001 S St., N.W., Ste. 410, Washington, D.C. 20009, 202-328-7700.

CAS advocates on behalf of consumers in auto safety and quality, fuel efficiency, emissions and related issues. For advice on specific problems, consumers should write to CAS, including a brief statement of the problem or question, year, make and model of the vehicle, and a stamped self-addressed envelope.

Center for Science in the Public Interest (CSPI), 1875 Connecticut Ave., N.W., Ste. 300, Washington, D.C. 20009, 202-332-9110, 202-265-4954 (fax).

A nonprofit, membership organization, CSPI conducts research, education and advocacy on nutrition, health, food safety and related issues, and publishes the monthly *Nutrition Action Healthletter,* as well as other consumer materials.

Citizen Action, 1730 Rhode Island Ave., N.W., Ste. 403, Washington, D.C. 20036, 202-775-1580, 202-296-4054 (fax).

Citizen Action works on behalf of its 3 million members and 32 state organizations on health care reform, environment and energy issues.

Community Nutrition Institute (CNI), 910 17th St., N.W., Ste. 413, Washington, D.C. 20006, 202-776-0595, 202-776-0599 (fax).

An advocate for programs and services to enable consumers to enjoy a diet that is adequate, safe and healthy, CNI also works to increase citizen participation in the state and federal policy and administrative processes to achieve these goals. CNI publishes *Nutrition Week,* a newsletter covering nutrition and food safety issues.

Congress of Consumer Organizations (COCO), P.O. Box 158, Newton Centre, Mass. 02159, 617-552-8184, 617-552-2380 (fax), www.essential.org.

COCO publishes a monthly newsletter, the *COCO INTERCOM,* on a broad range of consumer issues.

Congress Watch, 215 Pennsylvania Ave., S.E., Washington, D.C. 20003, 202-546-4996, 202-547-7392 (fax).

An arm of Public Citizen, Congress Watch works for consumer-related legislation, regulation and policies in such areas as trade, health and safety, and campaign financing, and has publications available on the issues with which it deals.

Consumer Action (CA), 116 New Montgomery, St. 233, San Francisco, Calif. 94105, 415-777-9635 (consumer hotline, 10 a.m.–2 p.m., PST), 415-777-9456 (voice/ttd), 415-777-5267 (fax).

An education and advocacy organization specializing in credit, finance and telecommunications issues, Consumer Action offers a multilingual consumer complaint hotline, free information on its surveys of banks and long-distance telephone companies, and consumer education materials in as many as eight languages.

Consumer Alert, 1001 Connecticut Ave., N.W., Ste. 1128, Washington, D.C. 20036, 202-467-5809, 202-467-5814 (fax). www.consumeralert.org.

Consumer Alert is a nonprofit, membership organization whose mission is to inform the public about the consumer benefits of competitive enterprise, advancing competition as the best regulator of business. A bimonthly newsletter and other materials are available.

Consumer Federation of America (CFA), 1424 16th St., Ste. 604, Washington, D.C. 20036, 202-387-6121, 202-265-7989 (fax).

Made up of more than 240 organizations representing 50 million consumers, CFA is a consumer advocacy and education organization. Issues on which it currently represents consumer interests before Congress and federal regulatory agencies include telephone service, insurance and financial services, product safety, indoor air pollution, health care, product liability and utility rates. It develops and distributes studies of various consumer issues, as well as consumer guides in book and pamphlet form. In addition, CFA publishes several newsletters. The National Insurance Consumer Organization (NICO) has merged with CFA and is now known as CFA Insurance Group.

Consumers for World Trade (CWT), 2000 L St., N.W., Ste. 200, Washington, D.C. 20036, 202-785-4835, 202-416-1734 (fax).

A nonprofit organization, CWT supports trade expansion and liberalization to promote economic growth and increase consumer choice and price competition in the marketplace. Various publications are available.

Consumers Union of U.S., Inc. (CU), 101 Truman Ave., Yonkers, N.Y. 10703-1057, 914-378-2000, 914-378-2900 (fax). Available online via CompuServe.

A nonprofit, independent organization, CU researches and tests consumer goods and services and disseminates the results in its monthly magazine, *Consumer Reports,* as well as other publications and media.

Council of Better Business Bureaus, Inc. (CBBB), 4200 Wilson Blvd., Suite 800, Arlington, Va. 22203–1838, 703-276-0100, 703-525-8277 (fax), www.bbb.org

Sponsored by national companies and the nation's Better Business Bureaus, the Council of Better Business Bureaus provides coordination and leadership to the 163 Better Business Bureaus (BBBs) in the United States, offers a national advertising review program, dispute resolution services, an advisory service that reports on national charities, consumer information services, and voluntary industry guidelines for advertising and selling products and services.

Families USA Foundation, 1334 G St., N.W., Washington, D.C. 20005, 202-628-3030, 202-347-2417 (fax), info@familiesusa.org.

A national, nonprofit membership organization committed to access to affordable health and long-term care, Families USA works to educate and mobilize consumers on health

care issues. In addition to its two grassroots advocacy networks, a.s.a.p., a network of health and long-term care reform activists, and HealthLink USA, a nationwide health reform computer network for public interest groups, Families USA develops and distributes reports and other materials on health and long-term care issues.

Health Research Group (HRG), 1600 20th St., N.W., Washington, D.C. 20009, 202-885-1000.

A division of Public Citizen, HRG works for protection against unsafe foods, drugs, medical devices, and workplaces, and advocates for greater consumer control over personal health decisions. A monthly *Health Letter* and other publications are available.

National Association of Consumer Agency Administrators (NACAA), 1010 Vermont Ave., N.W., Ste. 514, Washington, D.C. 20005, 202-347-7395, 202-347-2563 (fax).

An association of the administrators of local, state and federal government consumer protection agencies, NACAA provides training programs, public policy studies, and conferences, professional publications and other member services.

National Association of State Utility Consumer Advocates (NASUCA), 1133 15th St., N.W., Ste. 50, Washington, D.C. 20005, 202-727-3908, 202-727-3911 (fax), nacaa@essential.org.

A national organization of 41 utility ratepayer advocate offices in 38 states and the District of Columbia, NASUCA members represent millions of consumers served by investor-owned gas, telephone, electric, and water companies before Congress, state regulatory commissions, the courts, the Federal Energy Regulatory Commission and the Federal Communications Commission.

National Coalition for Consumer Education (NCCE), 295 Main St., Ste. 200, Madison, N.J. 07940, 201-377-8987, 201-377-4828 (fax).

The coalition brings together people and resources from government, business, education, consumer organizations, and the media to educate consumers about such important issues as financial management, health and safety, and the environment. The coalition develops and provides educational materials and resources to consumer educators, but does not handle requests from individuals.

National Consumers League (NCL), 1701 K St., N.W., Ste. 1201, Washington, D.C. 20006, 202-835-3323, 202-835-0747 (fax).

Founded in 1899, NCL is America's pioneer consumer advocacy organization. The league is a nonprofit, membership organization working for consumer health and safety protection and fairness in the marketplace and workplace. Current principal issue areas include consumer fraud, food and drug safety, fair labor standards, child labor, health care, the environment, financial services, and telecommunications. The league develops and distributes consumer education materials and newsletters.

National Foundation For Consumer Credit, Inc. (NFCC), 8611 2nd Ave., Ste. 100, Silver Spring, Md. 20910, 301-589-5600 or 800-388-2227, 301-495-5623 (fax).

A membership organization for nonprofit community organizations that are often called Consumer Credit Counseling Service agencies and are in more than 1,100 locations in the United States and Canada. The agencies educate and counsel individuals and families on credit issues. Consumers are taught to budget and use credit wisely and may be helped to resolve their credit problems. The 800 number provides the location of the nearest agency.

National Fraud Information Center (NFIC), P.O. Box 65868, Washington, D.C. 20035, 800-876-7060 (TDD available), 202-835-0767 (fax), www.fraud.org.

A project of the National Consumers League, the center's toll-free hotline assists consumers with information to help them avoid becoming victims of fraud, referral to appropriate law enforcement agencies and professional associations, and assistance in filing complaints. The center also provides professionals involved in consumer fraud prevention and enforcement with telecommunications systems and data links to improve fraud regulation, prevention, and law enforcement.

National Institute for Consumer Education (NICE), 559 Gary M. Owen Bldg., 300 W. Michigan Ave., Ypsilanti, Mich. 48197 734-487-2292, 734-487-7153 (fax).

A consumer education resource and professional development center for K–12 classroom teachers, business, government, labor and community educators, NICE conducts training programs, develops teaching guides and resource lists, and manages a national clearinghouse of consumer education materials, including videos, software programs, textbooks, and curriculum guides.

National Insurance Consumer Organization (NICO) *See* Consumer Federation of America (CFA)

National Senior Citizens Law Center, 1101 14th St. N.W., Suite 400, Washington, D.C. 20005, 202-289-6976, 202-289-7224 (fax), nsclc@nsclc.org (email), www.nsclc.org.

The National Senior Citizens Law Center (NSCLC) was established in 1972 to help older Americans live their lives in dignity and freedom from poverty, through legal work in support of elderly poor clients, client groups, and Elder Law attorneys. NSCLC attorneys are knowledgeable in a broad range of legal issues and practice areas that affect the security and welfare of older persons of limited income.

Public Citizen, Inc., 1600 20th St., N.W., Washington, D.C. 20009, 202-885-1000.

A national, nonprofit membership organization representing consumer interests through lobbying, litigation, research, and publications, Public Citizen represents consumer interests in Congress, the courts, government agencies and the media. Primary current areas of interest include product liability, health care delivery, safe medical devices and medications, open and ethical government, and safe and sustainable energy use.

Public Voice for Food and Health Policy, 1101 14th St., N.W., Washington, D.C. 20005, 202-371-1840, 202-371-1910 (fax), pvoice@ix.netcom.com.

A national research, education, and advocacy organization, Public Voice works for food, agriculture policies, and practices that improve the safety, health, and affordability of the food supply and protect the environment. Public Voice develops and distributes consumer information materials on pesticide reduction, nutrition labeling, and seafood safety.

Society of Consumer Affairs Professionals in Business (SOCAP), 801 N. Fairfax St., Ste. 404, Alexandria, Va. 22314, 703-519-3700, 703-549-4886 (fax).

An international professional organization, SOCAP provides training, conferences, and publications to encourage and maintain the integrity of business in transactions with consumers; to encourage and promote effective communication and understanding among business, government and consumers; and to define and advance the consumer affairs profession.

U.S. Public Interest Research Group (U.S. PIRG), 218 D St., S.E., Washington, D.C. 20003, 202-546-9707, pirg@pirg.org (email), www.pirg.org.

This is the national lobbying office for state PIRGs, consumer/environmental advocacy groups active in 33 states, that lobby and publish reports on issues, including credit bureau errors; bank fees and services; toy, ATV, and product safety; toxic chemicals in art supplies and other consumer products; and recycling, over-packaging and green consumerism. U.S. PIRG does not handle individual consumer complaints directly, but measures complaint levels to gauge the need for remedial legislation.

Why Do Schoolkids Kill?

The spate of recent schoolboy massacres may be an aberration. But the question remains: Why are students murdering students?

By RICHARD LACAYO TIME

It is a grisly report card. October 1997: in Pearl, Miss., a 16-year-old kills his mother and two classmates and wounds seven others. December 1997: in West Paducah, Ky., a 14-year-old kills three students and wounds five. Two weeks later, in Stamps, Ark., a 14-year-old kills two students. March 1998: in Jonesboro, Ark., a 13-year-old and an 11-year-old kill four classmates and a teacher, and wound ten. April 1998: in Edinboro, Pa., a 14-year-old kills a teacher and wounds three students at a school dance. May 1998: in Springfield, Ore., a 15-year-old kills a student and his parents, and wounds 23 others. June 1998: in Richmond, Va., a 14-year-old wounds a teacher and a school aide. With the exception of the parents who were killed, all the shootings took place on school premises.

In the past five years there have been more than a dozen multiple killings committed by children at American schools. Everyone knows that late-20th-century America is not for the faint of heart. But how did it become a place where kids gun down other kids? Among the experts, the search for a new vocabulary is well under way. Psychologists share the assumptions of most parents on the question of how the psychological terrain that might make a kid capable of killing is prepared. These days Mom and Dad are not always home much. The extended family of the past is gone. A feckless popular culture has moved into the vacuum.

"Television and the movies have never, in my experience, turned a responsible youngster into a criminal," says Stanton Samenow, author of *Before It's Too Late: Why Some Kids Get into Trouble and What Parents Can Do About It.* "But a youngster who is already inclined toward antisocial behavior hears of a particular crime, and it feeds an already fertile mind." Most children resist the worst temptations, he says. The trick is to recognize the ones who do not.

Absentee Parents

In a great many households, work, divorce, or both have removed parents for much of the day. When the grownups are out, or even when one is there but not mindful, children are left to the mercies of a peer culture shaped by the media, the ultimate in crazed nannies. Armed with video-game joysticks and TV remotes—a funny word, with its false promise that it keeps you at a distance from whatever excitements it bounces you through—kids are whiplashed from one bit of blood sport to another, from South Park and Jerry Springer to Mortal Kombat on Nintendo. Ordinary kids may be a bit desensitized to violence. More susceptible kids are pushed toward a dangerous mental precipice.

All that remains is for their world to be bristling with real firearms, which it often is—a third of all households have at least one gun. But child development experts say that for kids who never develop an internal brake on their own aggression, the pop culture of weaponry makes a difference. "The violence in the media and the easy availability of guns are what's driving the slaughter of innocents," says Barry Krisberg, president of the National Council on Crime and Delinquency in San Francisco.

As for media violence, the debate there is fast approaching the same point that discussions about the health impact of tobacco reached some time ago—it's over. Few researchers bother any longer to dispute that bloodshed on TV and in the movies has an effect on the kids who witness it. Added to the mix now are video games, at least the ones built around the model of hunt and kill. Captivated by effects that are ever more graphic, game boys learn to associate gusts of "blood" with the primal gratifications of scoring.

Reading the Warning Signs

"Many boys have impulse-control problems," says Gil Noam, a professor of education and medicine at Harvard. "They don't think, What are going to be the consequences for the rest of my life?" Bringing them through the treacherous pathways of mass culture takes a watchful adult. Things that merely amuse a grownup can injure a child, whose brain undergoes a powerful development surge before age 14.

There is a special problem for boys, who were the shooters in all of the dozen multiple killings at American schools in the past five years. When boys are ready to detonate, the signs are harder to read. Girls are more likely to decline into such inward-directed aggressions as depression or eating disorders. They are also more likely to put their feelings into words, an early warning that boys don't always offer. "The signals of boys tend to be discipline problems," says Michael Gurian, author of *The Wonder of Boys.*

Given all that, the real wonder may be that schoolboy massacres are still an aberration. But like crime generally, juvenile violence involving guns has actually been in decline since 1994. In 1998 the National Center for Education Statistics, in a survey requested by President Clinton, found the incidence of serious crime in schools to be flat. In the past year, only 10% reported a rape, robbery, or fight involving a weapon. But again, like crime generally, violent juvenile crime has stabilized at a rate that would have seemed very high 30 years ago, making the recent declines more like nicks in a high plateau. □

How to Punish Kids Who Kill?

By **CHARLOTTE FALTERMAYER** TIME

Twenty-seven of the states do not have age restrictions in prosecuting juveniles as adults. In those states where age is a barrier to punishment, many are asking: If the law cannot effectively go after the kids, can it not punish the parents? According to the National Conference of State Legislatures in Denver, 42 states have enacted laws making parents responsible in one form or another for their children's crimes. Of those states, 17 make parents criminally liable.

In 1989 Florida passed the first child access prevention law (or CAP law), which holds adults—often parents and legal guardians—accountable if they allow guns to fall into underage hands. Fourteen other states have enacted similar legislation, and CAP laws are pending in a number of others.

Shannan Wilber, attorney at the Youth Law Center in San Francisco, says that unlike parent-responsibility laws, CAP laws draw a direct causal relationship between adults and the crimes committed by juveniles. "Where there is a closer connection," she says, "such as a parent's possession of firearms and failure to keep them away from their kids, it's easier to connect that to a subsequent criminal act by the child. It's more concrete."

Critics of CAP laws say they are open to too much prosecutorial discretion and interfere with the way parents maintain control over their households. Joe Sudbay, director of state legislation at Handgun Control Inc. in Washington, says that's nonsense: "The whole point of these laws is not to punish. The point is to prevent." Do they? According to a study published in the *Journal of the American Medical Association* last October, unintentional deaths dropped 23% among children younger than 15 years old in the years covered by CAP laws. □

How Old Is Old Enough?

Under some provisions, the minimum age at which a child can be tried as an adult

15	Louisiana
14	Alabama, Arkansas, California, Connecticut, Hawaii, Idaho, Iowa, Kansas, Kentucky, Minnesota, Missouri, New Jersey, New Mexico, North Dakota, Texas, Utah, Virginia, Wisconsin
13	Illinois, North Carolina
12	Colorado
10	Vermont
7	New York

No age minimum
Alaska
Arizona
Delaware
Florida
Georgia
Indiana
Maine
Maryland
Massachusetts
Michigan
Mississippi
Montana
Nebraska
Nevada
New Hampshire
Ohio
Oklahoma
Oregon
Pennsylvania
Rhode Island
South Carolina
South Dakota
Tennessee
Washington
Washington, D.C.
West Virginia
Wyoming

Sources: National Center for Juvenile Justice; National Conference of State Legislatures. © TIME, April 6, 1998.

GRADING THE STATES ON JUVENILE GUN CONTROL

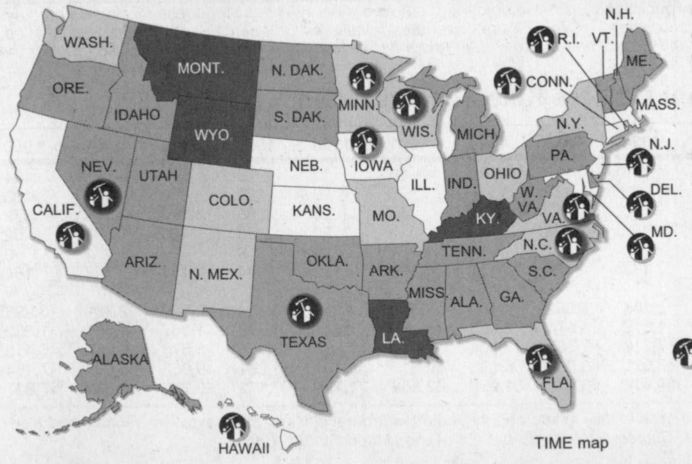

TIME map

Handgun Inc., which lobbies for gun control in Washington, has graded the states for what they have done to protect children from gun violence and accidents. The ratings are based on the presence of laws the advocacy group deems essential to protecting young people from violence, including prohibitions on juvenile handgun sales and possession as well as child access prevention laws, which require adults to keep firearms, including hunting rifles, away from children.

States with child access prevention Laws

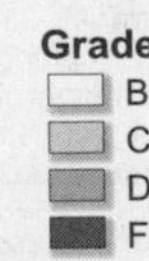

Total Arrests Under Age 21: 1996

	Number of arrests	Percent		Number of arrests	Percent
Total, under 21	3,568,260	32.2%	17	511,553	4.6%
Total, under 18	2,103,658	19.0	18	526,435	4.7
Total, under 15	679,449	6.1	19	499,616	4.5
15	418,656	3.8	20	438,551	4.0
16	494,000	4.5	21	398,610	3.6

NOTE: Based on reports furnished to the FBI by 9,666 agencies covering a 1996 estimated population of 189,927,000. *Source:* Department of Justice, Federal Bureau of Investigation, *Uniform Crime Reports for the United States, 1996.*

Murder Victims, by Weapons Used

		Weapons used or cause of death						
		Guns						
Year	Murder victims, total	Total	Percent	Cutting or stabbing	Blunt object[1]	Strangulation, hands, fists, feet, or pushing	Arson[2]	All other[3]
1965	8,773	5,015	57.2%	2,021	505	894	226	112
1970	13,649	9,039	66.2	2,424	604	1,031	353	198
1975	18,642	12,061	64.7	3,245	1,001	1,646	193	496
1980	21,860	13,650	62.0	4,212	1,094	1,666	291	947
1985	17,545	10,296	58.7	3,694	972	1,491	243	849
1990	20,045	12,847	64.1	3,503	1,075	1,424	287	909
1991	21,676	14,373	66.3	3,430	1,099	1,529	195	847
1992	22,716	15,489	68.2	3,296	1,040	1,445	203	1,043
1993	23,180	16,136	69.6	2,967	1,022	1,482	217	1,168
1994	22,084	15,463	70.0	2,802	912	1,452	196	1,079
1995	20,232	13,790	68.2	2,557	918	1,438	166	968
1996	15,848	10,744	67.8	2,142	733	1,182	151	726

1. Refers to club, hammer, etc. 2. Before 1973, includes drowning. 3. Includes poison, explosives, unknown, drowning, asphyxiation, narcotics, other means, and weapons not stated. *Source:* Department of Justice, Federal Bureau of Investigation, *Uniform Crime Reports for the United States, 1996.*

Federal Prosecutions of Public Corruption: 1980 to 1995

(Prosecution of persons who have corrupted public office in violation of Federal Criminal Statutes.)

Prosecution status	1995	1994	1993	1992	1991	1990	1989	1988	1985	1980
Total:[1] Indicted	1,051	1,165	1,371	1,189	1,452	1,176	1,348	1,274	1,157	727
Convicted	878	969	1,362	1,081	1,194	1,084	1,149	1,067	997	602
Awaiting trial	323	332	403	380	346	300	375	288	256	213
Federal officials: Indicted	527	571	627	624	803	615	695	629	563	123
Convicted	438	488	595	532	665	583	610	529	470	131
Awaiting trial	120	124	133	139	149	103	126	86	90	16
State officials: Indicted	61	99	113	84	115	96	71	66	79	72
Convicted	61	97	133	92	77	79	54	69	66	51
Awaiting trial	23	17	39	24	42	28	18	14	20	28
Local officials: Indicted	236	248	309	232	242	257	269	276	248	247
Convicted	191	202	272	211	180	225	201	229	221	168
Awaiting trial	89	96	132	91	88	98	122	79	49	82

1. Includes individuals who are neither public officials nor employees, but who were involved with public officials or employees in violating the law, now shown separately. NOTE: Figures are latest available. *Source:* U.S. Department of Justice, *Report to Congress on the Activities and Operations of the Public Integrity Section*, annual, from *Statistical Abstract of the United States 1997.*

Law Enforcement Officers Killed or Assaulted:[1] 1980 to 1995

	1995	1994	1993	1992	1991	1990	1989	1988	1987	1980
Northeast	16	18	12	16	16	13	23	17	24	31
Midwest	19	29	27	15	26	20	22	18	31	23
South	61	50	57	68	55	68	68	77	51	72
West	32	30	22	23	17	23	23	39	40	32
Puerto Rico	2	6	11	7	8	8	8	—	1	6
Total killed	**130**	**133**	**129**	**129**	**122**	**132**	**144**	**151**	**147**	**164**
Assaults										
Firearm	2,277	3,168	4,002	4,455	3,532	3,662	3,154	2,759	2,789	3,295
Knife or cutting instrument	1,325	1,513	1,574	2,095	1,493	1,641	1,379	1,367	1,561	1,653
Other dangerous weapon	6,299	7,210	7,551	8,604	7,014	7,390	5,778	5,573	5,685	5,415
Hands, fists, feet, etc.	46,634	53,021	53,848	66,098	50,813	59,101	51,861	49,053	53,807	47,484
Total assaulted	**56,535**	**64,912**	**66,975**	**81,252**	**62,852**	**71,794**	**62,172**	**58,752**	**63,842**	**57,847**

1. Covers officers killed feloniously and accidentally in line of duty; includes federal officers. 1988 excludes Florida and Kentucky. NOTE: Data are latest available. *Source: Statistical Abstract of the United States, 1997.*

Summary of Hate Crime Statistics, 1996

	Number of incidents	Number of offenses	Number of victims	Number of known offenders
Bias motivation				
Race:	5,396	6,767	6,994	6,122
Anti-white	1,106	1,384	1,445	1,783
Anti-black	3,674	4,469	4,600	3,701
Anti-American Indian/Alaskan Native	51	69	71	56
Anti-Asian/Pacific Islander	355	527	544	374
Anti-multi-racial group	210	318	334	208
Ethnicity/national origin:	940	1,163	1,207	1,095
Anti-Hispanic	564	710	728	734
Anti-other ethnicity/national origin	376	453	479	361
Religion:	1,401	1,500	1,535	523
Anti-Jewish	1,109	1,182	1,209	371
Anti-Catholic	35	37	38	17
Anti-Protestant	75	80	81	44
Anti-Islamic	27	33	33	16
Anti-other religious group	129	139	145	64
Anti-multi-religious group	24	27	27	11
Anti-atheism/agnosticism/etc.	2	2	2	0
Sexual orientation:	1,016	1,256	1,281	1,180
Anti-male homosexual	757	927	940	925
Anti-female homosexual	150	185	192	150
Anti-homosexual	84	94	99	93
Anti-heterosexual	15	38	38	4
Anti-bisexual	10	12	12	8
Multiple bias	6	20	22	15
Total	8,759	10,706	11,039	8,935

Source: U.S. Department of Justice, *Uniform Crime Reports.*

Crime Index by State, 1996

State	Crime index total	Rate per 100,000 inhab-itants	Violent crime	Property crime	Murder and non-neg-ligent man-slaughter
Ala.	205,962	4,820.1	24,159	181,803	444
Alaska	33,084	5,450.4	4,417	28,667	45
Ariz.	312,927	7,067.0	27,963	284,964	377
Ark.	117,951	4,699.2	13,161	104,790	219
Calif.	1,660,131	5,207.8	274,996	1,385,135	2,916
Colo.	195,681	5,118.5	15,463	180,218	180
Conn.	138,414	4,227.7	13,490	124,924	158
Del.	35,488	4,894.9	4,845	30,643	31
D.C.[1]	64,599	11,896.7	13,411	51,188	397
Fla.[4]	1,079,623	7,497.4	151,350	928,273	1,077
Ga.	463,952	6,309.7	46,966	416,986	630
Hawaii	77,961	6,584.5	3,322	74,639	40
Idaho	47,709	4,012.5	3,177	44,532	43
Ill.[2]	629,762	5,315.8	104,985	524,777	1,179
Ind.	262,742	4,498.2	31,366	231,376	420
Iowa	104,067	3,648.9	7,771	96,296	53
Kans.[2]	120,414	4,681.7	10,642	109,772	170
Ky.	122,979	3,166.3	12,448	110,531	228
La.	297,556	6,838.8	40,426	257,130	762
Maine	42,189	3,394.1	1,553	40,636	25
Md.	307,461	6,061.9	47,230	260,231	588
Mass.	233,758	3,837.1	39,122	194,636	157
Mich.	490,971	5,117.5	60,951	430,020	722
Minn.	207,891	4,463.1	15,782	192,109	167
Miss.	122,842	4,522.9	13,261	109,581	301
Mo.	272,450	5,084.0	31,669	240,781	433
Mont.[2]	39,499	4,493.6	1,415	38,084	34
Nebr.	73,292	4,436.6	7,182	66,110	48
Nev.	96,052	5,992.0	13,005	83,047	220
N.H.	32,809	2,823.5	1,373	31,436	20
N.J.	346,116	4,332.9	42,459	303,657	338
N.M.	113,097	6,602.3	14,399	98,698	197
N.Y.	751,456	4,132.3	132,206	619,250	1,353
N.C.	404,684	5,526.2	43,068	361,616	619
N.D.	17,189	2,669.1	541	16,648	14
Ohio	497,831	4,455.7	47,896	449,935	538
Okla.	186,602	5,652.9	19,710	166,892	223
Ore.	192,132	5,996.6	14,837	177,295	129
Pa.	409,004	3,392.5	52,140	356,864	686
P.R.[3]	99,788	n.a.	20,147	79,641	868
R.I.	39,536	3,993.5	3,437	36,099	25
S.C.	229,861	6,214.1	36,875	192,986	332
S.D.	21,740	2,969.9	1,297	20,443	9
Tenn.	289,904	5,449.3	41,175	248,729	503
Tex.	1,092,002	5,708.9	123,270	968,732	1,477
Utah	119,717	5,985.9	6,638	113,079	63
Vt.	17,687	3,002.9	714	16,973	11
Va.	264,882	3,968.3	22,782	242,100	500
Wash.	326,968	5,909.4	23,857	303,111	255
W.Va.	45,346	2,483.4	3,836	41,510	69
Wis.	197,182	3,821.4	13,039	184,143	204
Wyo.	20,462	4,254.1	1,201	19,261	16

NOTE: The Crime Index is composed of the violent and property crime categories. In 1996, 25% of the index offenses reported to law enforcement agencies were violent crimes and 74% were property crimes. Violent crimes are murder, forcible rape, robbery, and aggravated assault. Property crimes are burglary, larceny-theft, and auto-theft. Data are not included for the property crime of arson. 1. Includes offenses reported by the zoological police. 2. Complete data were not available for the states of Illinois, Kansas, Kentucky, and Montana; therefore it was necessary that their crime counts be estimated. 3. n.a. = not available. The 1996 Bureau of Census population for Puerto Rico was not available; therefore no rates per 100,000 inhabitants are provided. 4. Florida state total for 1996 was supplied by the Florida Department of Law Enforcement. *Source: F.B.I. Uniform Crime Reports for the United States, 1996.*

Crime Rates for Selected Large Cities: 1995

(Offenses known to the police per 100,000 population.)

City ranked by population size, 1995[1]	Violent crime				Property crime		
	Murder	Forcible rape	Robbery	Aggravated assault	Burglary	Larceny-theft	Motor vehicle theft
New York, N.Y.	16.1	32.4	809.9	714.8	1,009.5	2,500.7	992.9
Los Angeles, Calif.	24.5	45.9	840.5	1,123.6	1,192.2	3,120.1	1,333.2
Chicago, Ill.	30.0	(n.a.)	1,094.1	1,425.7	1,463.3	4,417.9	1,316.3
Houston, Tex.	18.2	48.3	531.7	685.3	1,431.7	3,573.5	1,299.4
Philadelphia, Pa.	28.2	50.5	889.8	467.7	1,056.6	3,028.5	1,556.3
San Diego, Calif.	7.9	29.9	280.2	638.8	890.6	2,634.8	1,066.0
Phoenix, Ariz.	19.7	37.9	340.1	669.8	1,929.9	5,749.4	2,133.3
Dallas, Tex.	26.5	81.8	566.1	858.1	1,603.0	4,708.6	1,620.0
Detroit, Mich.	47.6	110.7	1,010.3	1,238.9	2,242.7	4,353.3	2,935.2
San Antonio, Tex.	14.2	65.8	234.5	203.3	1,396.2	5,237.5	842.3
Honolulu, Hawaii	4.3	24.7	155.7	142.7	1,150.4	5,304.8	845.2
San Jose, Calif.	4.6	47.0	146.9	609.5	665.6	2,399.6	513.5
Las Vegas, Nev.	14.9	72.0	467.8	645.5	1,540.0	3,837.1	1,007.1
San Francisco, Calif.	13.4	41.2	876.1	545.9	965.2	4,625.5	1,122.9
Baltimore, Md.	45.6	95.9	1,594.1	1,282.5	2,326.4	6,405.3	1,568.6
Jacksonville, Fla.	12.7	92.0	430.0	878.3	1,839.2	4,904.1	844.6
Columbus, Ohio	12.1	99.6	521.2	404.2	2,058.1	4,995.1	1,102.2
Milwaukee, Wisc.	22.2	59.4	586.4	414.3	1,344.0	4,214.0	1,822.6
Memphis, Tenn.	29.0	125.8	926.3	688.2	2,568.7	3,958.2	2,217.8
Washington, D.C.	65.2	52.7	1,239.0	1,304.7	1,838.3	5,826.9	1,839.7
El Paso, Tex.	6.3	41.0	182.3	608.8	648.6	4,919.2	657.7
Boston, Mass.	17.4	68.8	653.2	998.2	1,211.3	4,721.5	1,822.4
Seattle, Wash.	7.7	49.1	417.9	451.3	1,452.1	6,792.9	1,311.4
Charlotte, N.C.	16.4	67.3	542.0	1,070.3	1,830.2	5,379.6	670.8
Nashville-Davidson, Tenn.	20.1	93.0	510.8	1,166.5	1,572.7	5,798.0	1,549.6
Austin, Tex.	8.8	58.8	255.1	450.6	1,436.2	5,238.6	683.8
Denver, Colo.	16.0	63.3	279.3	502.7	1,464.9	3,511.2	1,036.1
Cleveland, Ohio	26.1	139.2	853.2	627.8	1,553.9	2,780.2	1,829.6
New Orleans, La.	74.5	100.0	1098.0	960.0	2,101.1	4,609.0	2,018.4
Fort Worth, Tex.	23.5	72.1	426.9	638.5	1,593.2	4,807.1	1,056.0
Portland, Oreg.	9.4	92.9	501.1	1,322.7	1,703.6	6,451.7	1,987.0
Oklahoma City, Okla.	48.7	101.5	343.8	798.7	2,234.9	6,877.0	1,097.1
Long Beach, Calif.	18.3	39.2	636.2	601.8	1,279.0	3,213.3	1,243.0
Tucson, Ariz.	14.4	64.9	264.9	861.8	1,332.3	8,274.8	1,344.3
Kansas City, Mo.	24.0	105.5	751.0	1,304.2	2,187.9	5,903.1	1,524.4
Virginia Beach, Va.	3.7	22.7	109.9	85.8	668.6	3,496.7	264.5
Albuquerque, N.M.	12.6	70.5	386.7	658.3	1,992.3	5,589.8	1,190.1
Atlanta, Ga.	45.5	109.1	1,300.9	2,191.0	2,892.1	8,463.5	2,065.6
St. Louis, Mo.	54.9	73.5	1,382.8	1,841.3	2,878.6	7,696.6	2,155.2
Sacramento, Calif.	15.2	42.0	566.5	515.1	2,129.3	4,932.4	2,123.7
Fresno, Calif.	18.3	54.6	557.5	826.3	1,966.0	5,290.2	3,196.4
Tulsa, Okla.	8.0	67.0	251.1	829.1	1,610.0	3,444.5	1,167.2
Miami, Fla.	29.0	52.3	1,498.7	1,833.3	2,607.2	7,271.1	2,332.1
Minneapolis, Minn.	26.8	161.6	992.4	797.3	2,243.2	6,069.2	1,254.9
Pittsburgh, Pa.	16.3	68.5	585.4	308.9	1,014.1	3,182.0	954.7
Cincinnati, Ohio	13.9	113.4	599.0	563.4	1,491.6	4,172.9	531.8
Toledo, Ohio	10.8	85.8	436.5	353.7	1,944.0	4,574.8	989.0
Buffalo, N.Y.	19.8	83.5	907.8	1,016.0	2,270.2	3,560.9	1,347.0
Wichita, Kans.	13.2	65.1	287.2	335.5	1,721.0	4,950.3	849.3
Mesa, Ariz.	5.2	39.4	156.2	611.7	1,467.4	5,233.6	1,381.2
Colorado Springs, Colo.	5.5	63.8	128.2	285.1	1,062.1	4,792.6	427.8
Tampa, Fla.	16.2	95.6	905.9	1995.6	2,284.4	6,821.1	2,063.6
Santa Ana, Calif.	24.6	22.6	422.2	390.4	746.5	2,530.4	1,060.3
Arlington, Tex.	3.1	52.7	178.2	647.2	1,102.9	4,209.7	786.1
Anaheim, Calif.	8.8	26.8	356.5	480.7	1,107.7	3,090.8	1,064.7
Corpus Christi, Tex.	11.0	77.0	179.6	717.4	1,348.9	7,580.4	518.2
Louisville, Ky.	18.3	49.5	583.9	543.9	1,639.9	3,227.7	1,085.7
St. Paul, Minn.	9.5	88.1	351.6	509.6	1,614.9	4,241.0	842.6
Newark, N.J.	39.2	83.0	2,105.8	1,757.3	2,831.7	4,904.1	3,790.8
Birmingham, Ala.	44.7	91.6	797.1	1,522.6	2,363.6	6,024.1	1,359.3
Aurora, Colo.	7.0	53.7	213.7	487.6	948.0	4,348.2	519.5
Norfolk, Va.	21.7	72.6	530.2	356.8	1,285.2	5,227.2	954.7

1. Crime data are not available for Indianapolis, Ind., and Albuquerque, N.M., in 1995. 2. The rate for forcible rape is not shown because the forcible rape figures were not in accordance with national Uniform Crime Reporting guidelines. *Source: Statistical Abstract of the United States, 1997.*

Arrests by Race, 1996

Offense charged	White	Black	American Indian or Alaskan Native	Asian or Pacific Islander
	Percent distribution[1]			
Total	**66.9%**	**30.7%**	**1.3%**	**1.2%**
Murder[2]	42.8	54.9	.8	1.5
Forcible rape	56.1	41.6	1.1	1.2
Robbery	39.8	58.2	.5	1.5
Aggravated assault	59.6	38.1	1.0	1.3
Burglary	67.9	29.8	1.1	1.3
Larceny—theft	64.8	32.2	1.3	1.8
Motor vehicle theft	56.6	40.2	1.2	2.0
Arson	74.1	24.0	1.0	1.0
Other assaults	62.4	35.1	1.3	1.2
Forgery and counterfeiting	64.1	33.6	.6	1.8
Fraud	63.0	35.8	.5	.8
Embezzlement	63.1	34.9	.5	1.5
Stolen property—buying, receiving, possessing	57.6	40.3	.8	1.3
Vandalism	73.1	24.2	1.4	1.2
Weapons—carrying, possessing, etc.	58.0	40.1	.7	1.2
Prostitution and commercialized vice	59.0	38.3	.7	2.0
Sex offenses, except forcible rape and prostitution	73.9%	23.7%	1.1%	1.3%
Drug abuse violation	60.4	38.4	.5	.6
Gambling	45.4	50.6	.4	3.6
Offenses against family and children	65.6	31.6	1.1	1.7
Driving under the influence	86.7	10.4	1.7	1.3
Liquor laws	80.9	16.0	2.5	.7
Drunkenness	81.1	16.2	2.4	.4
Disorderly conduct	62.4	35.7	1.3	.7
Vagrancy	54.3	43.4	1.9	.4
All other offenses except traffic	63.6	34.0	1.2	1.2
Suspicion	67.6	30.8	1.2	.5
Curfew and loitering law violations	72.9	24.5	1.2	1.4
Runaways	78.2	16.7	1.2	4.0

1. Because of rounding, the percentages may not add up to total. 2. Includes non-negligent manslaughter. *Source: Uniform Crime Reports, 1996.*

Total Arrest Trends by Sex, 1987 and 1996

Offense	Male 1987	Male 1996	Male Percent change	Female 1987	Female 1996	Female Percent change
Total	**7,061,872**	**7,918,554**	**+12.1%**	**1,512,860**	**2,056,390**	**+35.9%**
Murder[1]	12,247	12,062	–1.5	1,719	1,384	–19.5
Forcible rape	24,551	21,505	–12.4	299	247	–17.4
Robbery	93,885	101,998	+8.6	8,431	11,091	+31.6
Aggravated assault	209,782	284,004	+35.4	31,716	61,640	+94.3
Burglary	264,041	209,076	–20.8	24,442	27,190	+11.2
Larceny—theft	663,264	655,775	–1.1	297,624	337,434	+13.4
Motor vehicle theft	106,604	104,562	–1.9	11,454	16,427	+43.4
Arson	10,144	10,431	+2.8	1,603	1,860	+16.0
Other assaults	454,944	695,386	+52.9	81,583	177,644	+117.7
Forgery and counterfeiting	39,931	51,372	+28.7	21,056	28,105	+33.5
Fraud	127,472	168,385	+32.1	98,537	116,746	+18.5
Embezzlement	5,355	5,633	+5.2	3,329	4,619	+38.8
Stolen property—buying, receiving, possessing	86,771	84,867	–2.2	11,419	14,435	+26.4
Vandalism	160,482	182,709	+13.9	19,222	29,336	+52.6
Weapons—carrying, possessing, etc.	123,403	135,565	+9.9	10,177	11,637	+14.3
Prostitution and commercialized vice	29,335	30,657	+4.5	56,253	46,097	–18.1
Sex offenses, except forcible rape and prostitution	62,263	59,062	–5.1	5,026	5,324	+5.9
Drug abuse violations	554,554	857,057	+54.5	99,872	173,831	+74.1
Gambling	16,811	13,834	–17.7	2,747	2,206	–19.7
Offenses against family and children	30,037	61,308	+104.1	6,493	19,263	+196.7
Driving under the influence	983,915	756,935	–23.1	127,476	130,246	+2.2
Liquor laws	320,504	352,456	+10.0	69,066	83,737	+21.2
Drunkenness	547,595	422,605	–22.8	54,833	57,656	+5.1
Disorderly conduct	389,340	437,824	+12.5	90,856	116,257	+28.0
Vagrancy	27,324	16,168	–40.8	3,439	4,135	+20.2
All other offenses, except traffic	1,624,731	2,039,086	+25.5	297,922	465,210	+56.2
Curfew and loitering law violations	47,039	93,756	+99.3	15,277	38,991	+155.2
Runaways	45,548	54,476	+19.6	60,989	73,642	+20.7

1. Includes non-negligent manslaughter. *Source:* Department of Justice, Federal Bureau of Investigation, *Uniform Crime Reports for the United States, 1996.*

Characteristics of the Prison Population, 1998

Characteristic	Number	Percent
Gender		
Male	97,679	93.0%
Female	7,411	7.0
Inmates by race		
White	59,314	56.4
Black	42,391	40.3
Asian	1,777	1.7
Native American	1,608	1.5
Ethnicity		
Hispanic	29,694	28.3
Non-Hispanic	75,396	71.7
Citizenship		
United States	76,526	72.8
Mexico	10,234	9.7
Colombia	4,307	4.1
Cuba	2,785	2.7
Other/Unknown	11,229	10.7
Average inmate age	37	
Sentence imposed		
Under 1 year	1,710	1.8
1–3 years	11,940	12.8%
3–5 years	12,560	13.5
5–10 years	28,091	30.1
10–15 years	18,801	20.1
15–20 years	8,223	8.8
20+ years	9,404	10.1
Life	2,601	2.8
Type of offense		
Drug offenses	55,624	59.1
Robbery	8,725	9.3
Firearms, explosives, arson	8,423	8.9
Extortion, fraud, bribery	5,257	5.6
Property offenses	5,414	5.8
Violent offenses	2,371	2.5
Immigration	3,904	4.1
Continuing criminal enterprise	671	0.7
White collar	660	0.7
Courts or corrections	604	0.6
National security	67	0.1
Miscellaneous	2,393	2.6

Source: Federal Bureau of Prisons.

Number of Persons Executed, by Jurisdiction, 1930–1996

State	Number executed since 1930	1977[1]
U.S. total	4,217	358
Texas	404	107
Georgia	388	22
New York	329	—
California	296	4
North Carolina	271	8
Florida	208	38
South Carolina	173	11
Ohio	172	—
Mississippi	158	4
Louisiana	156	23
Pennsylvania	154	2
Alabama	148	13
Arkansas	130	12
Virginia	129	37
Kentucky	103	—
Illinois	98	8
Tennessee	93	—
Missouri	85	23
New Jersey	74	—
Maryland	69	1
Oklahoma	68	8
Washington	49	2
Colorado	47	—
Indiana	45	4
Arizona	44	6
District of Columbia	40	—
West Virginia	40	—
Nevada	35	6
Federal system	33	—
Massachusetts	27	—
Connecticut	21	—
Delaware	20	8
Oregon	20	1
Utah	18	5
Iowa	18	—
Kansas	15	—
Wyoming	8	1
New Mexico	8	—
Montana	7	1
Nebraska	6	2
Idaho	4	1
Vermont	4	—
New Hampshire	1	—
South Dakota	1	—

1. In 1972 the Supreme Court ruled that capital punishment, as it was then administered, was "cruel and unusual" and therefore unconstitutional. On July 1, 1976, however, the Court overturned the ruling by a 7–2 decision, and capital punishment was reinstated. *Source: Capital Punishment, 1996.*

Women On Death Row
(as of 2/9/98)

State	Total	White	Black
Total	42	29	13
California	8	6	2
Texas	6	4	2
Pennsylvania	4	1	3
Florida	3	3	0
Alabama	3	2	1
Oklahoma	3	2	1
North Carolina	3	3	0
Illinois	2	0	2
Missouri	2	2	0
Tennessee	2	2	0
Mississippi	1	1	0
Arizona	1	1	0
Idaho	1	1	0
Nevada	1	0	1
Louisiana	1	0	1
New Jersey	1	1	0

Source: Capital Punishment 1996 and the Death Penalty Information Center.

Characteristics of Prisoners Under Sentence of Death[1]

Characteristic	1980	1990	1995
White	418	1,368	1,730
Black and other	270	978	1,324
Under 20 years	11	8	20
20 to 24 years	173	168	264
25 to 34 years	334	1,110	1,068
35 to 54 years	186	1,006	1,583
55 years and over	10	64	119
Years of schooling completed:			
7 years or less	68	178	191
8 years	74	186	195
9 to 11 years	204	775	979
12 years	162	729	995
More than 12 years	43	209	272
Unknown	163	279	422
Marital status:			
Never married	268	998	1,412
Married	229	632	718
Divorced[2]	217	726	924
Time elapsed since sentencing:			
Less than 12 months	185	231	287
12 to 47 months	389	753	784
48 to 71 months	102	438	423
72 months and over	38	934	1,560
Legal status at arrest:			
Not under sentence	384	1,345	1,764
Parole or probation[3]	115	578	866
Prison or escaped	45	128	110
Unknown	170	305	314
Total	**688**	**2,346**	**3,054**

1. For 1980 and 1990 revisions to the total number of prisoners were not carried to the characteristics except for race. 2. Includes widows, widowers, and unknown. 3. Includes persons on mandatory conditional release, work release, leave, AWOL, or bail. NOTE: As of Dec. 31. Excludes prisoners under sentence of death confined in local correctional systems pending appeal or who had not been committed to prison. *Source:* U.S. Bureau of Justice Statistics, *Capital Punishment*, annual, from *Statistical Abstract of the United States, 1997*.

Methods of Execution

State	Minimum age	Method
Alabama	16	Electrocution
Alaska	—	No death penalty
Arizona[1]	none	Lethal injection or gas
Arkansas[2]	14	Lethal injection or electrocution
California[3]	18	Lethal gas or injection
Colorado	18	Lethal injection
Connecticut	18	Lethal injection
Delaware[4]	16	Lethal injection or hanging
D.C.	—	No death penalty
Florida	16	Electrocution
Georgia	17	Electrocution
Hawaii	—	No death penalty
Idaho	none	Lethal injection or firing squad
Illinois	18	Lethal injection
Indiana	16	Lethal injection
Iowa	—	No death penalty
Kansas	18	Lethal injection
Kentucky	16	Electrocution
Louisiana	none	Lethal injection
Maine	—	No death penalty
Maryland[5]	18	Lethal injection or gas
Massachusetts	—	No death penalty
Michigan	—	No death penalty
Minnesota	—	No death penalty
Mississippi[6]	16	Lethal injection or gas
Missouri	16	Lethal injection or gas
Montana	none	Hanging or lethal injection
Nebraska	18	Electrocution
Nevada	16	Lethal injection
New Hampshire[7]	17	Lethal injection or hanging
New Jersey	18	Lethal injection
New Mexico	18	Lethal injection
New York	18	Lethal injection
North Carolina	17	Lethal gas or injection
North Dakota	—	No death penalty
Ohio	18	Electrocution or lethal injection
Oklahoma[8]	16	Lethal injection, electrocution, or firing squad
Oregon	18	Lethal injection
Pennsylvania	none	Lethal injection
Rhode Island	—	No death penalty
South Carolina	none	Electrocution or lethal injection
South Dakota	none	Lethal injection
Tennessee	18	Electrocution
Texas	17	Lethal injection
Utah	none	Firing squad or lethal injection
Vermont	—	No death penalty
Virginia	14	Electrocution or lethal injection
Washington	18	Hanging or lethal injection
West Virginia	—	No death penalty
Wisconsin	—	No death penalty
Wyoming[9]	16	Lethal injection or gas
U.S. (Fed. Govt.)[10]	18	Lethal injection
American Samoa	—	No death penalty
Guam	—	No death penalty
Puerto Rico	—	No death penalty
Virgin Islands	—	No death penalty

1. Arizona authorizes lethal injection for persons sentenced after 11/15/92; those sentenced before that date may select lethal injection or lethal gas. 2. Arkansas authorizes lethal injection for persons committing a capital offense after 7/4/83; those who committed the offense before that date may select lethal injection or electrocution. 3. Use of lethal gas is currently prohibited in California pending a legal challenge in Federal court. 4. Delaware authorizes lethal injection for those whose capital offense occurred after 6/13/86; those who committed the offense before that date may select lethal injection or hanging. 5. Maryland authorizes lethal injection for all inmates, as of 3/25/94. One inmate, convicted prior to that date, has selected lethal gas for method of execution. 6. Mississippi authorizes lethal injection for those convicted after 7/1/84 and lethal gas for those convicted earlier. 7. New Hampshire authorizes hanging only if lethal injection cannot be given. 8. Oklahoma authorizes electrocution if lethal injection is ever held to be unconstitutional and firing squad if both lethal injection and electrocution are held unconstitutional. 9. Wyoming authorizes lethal gas if lethal injection is ever held to be unconstitutional. 10. The method of execution of Federal prisoners is lethal injection, pursuant to 28 CFR, Part 26. For offenses under the Violent Crime Control and Law Enforcement Act of 1994, the method is that of the state in which the conviction took place, pursuant to 18 USC 3596. *Source: Capital Punishment,* 1996.

Motor Vehicle Laws, 1998

State	Age for license: Motor-cycle	Age for license: Moped	Age for driver's license[1]: Regular	Age for driver's license[1]: Learner's	Age for driver's license[1]: Restrictive	Driver's license duration	Fee	Annual safety inspection required
Alabama	16	14	16	15[5]	14[11]	4 yrs.	$20.00	no[15]
Alaska	16	14	16	14	14[6,]	5	15.00	no[15]
Arizona	16	16[6]	18	15 yrs.,7 mo.[5, 6]	16[6]	Until 60	10–25.00[12]	no[17]
Arkansas	16	10[10]	16	14-16[5]	14[6,9]	4	14.00	yes
California	18[19]	16[19]	18	15[4, 7, 8]	16[4]	4	12.00	no[17]
Colorado	16	16	21	15½[6, 9]	15¼[6, 8, 9]	5	15.00	no[18]
Connecticut	16	16	16[4]	16[4]		4	28.50–43.50[12]	no
Delaware	18[19]	16	18	15 10 mo.[4]	16[4, 6]	5	12.50	yes
D. C.	16	16	18	([5, 7])	16[6]	4	20.00	yes[21]
Florida	16	15	16	15[5]	15[6]	4 or 6	20.00	no[17]
Georgia	16	15	16	15	16[6]	4	15.00	no[17]
Hawaii	15	15	18	15[5, 7]	15[6]	4 or 6[2]	6/12.00	yes
Idaho	16[19]	16[19]	17	15[4, 5, 7]	15[3, 4]	4	20.50	no[17]
Illinois	18	16[19]	18	([5])	16[4, 6]	4 or 5	10.00	no[17]
Indiana	16	15	18	16[7, 8]	16 1 mo.[4, 6]	4[13]	6.00	no[17]
Iowa	18[19]	14	18	14	16[4, 6]	4[2]	8/16.00	no[15]
Kansas	14	14	16	([5])	14	4-6	12–21.00[12]	no[15]
Kentucky	16	16	18	([5])	16[6]	4	8.00	no
Louisiana	15	15	15[27]	14[6]	17[3]	4	18.00	yes
Maine	16[4]	15[4]	17	15[4, 7]	15[4]	6	30.00	no[17]
Maryland	18[19]	16	18[26]	15¾[5, 9]	16[4, 6]	5	30.00	no[17, 20]
Massachusetts	17	16	17	16	16½[3 4, 6]	5	33.75	yes[18]
Michigan	18[19]	15	18	14¾[4, 6, 7]	16[4, 6]	2-4	12.00	no
Minnesota	18[22]	15	18	([5])	16[4]	4	18.50/37.50	no[15,17]
Mississippi	15	15	16	([5])		4[27]	20.00	yes
Missouri	15.5[4]	16	16	15½[23]	15½[23]	3	7.50	yes[17]
Montana	15[4]	15[4]	18		15[4, 6]	4 or 8[10]	16.00/32.00	no
Nebraska	16	16	16	15[7]	14	4	15.00	no
Nevada	16	16	16[6]	15½[5, 6, 9]	14[3, 6]	4	15.50–20.50[12]	no[17]
New Hampshire	18[19]	16[4]	18[19]		16[4]	4	32.00	yes[21]
New Jersey	17	15	17		16	4	16/18.00	yes
New Mexico	16	13	16	15[4]	14[9]	4	13.00	no
New York	17	16	17[4]	16	16[6]	5	28.00	yes[18]
North Carolina	18	16	18	15[4, 6, 9]	16	5	18.75	yes[17]
North Dakota	16	14	16	([5])	14[4, 6]	4	10.00	no[15]
Ohio	18	14	18	15½[4,6]	14[11]	4	10.75	no[15,17]
Oklahoma	14	14	16	([8])	15½[4]	4	19.00	yes[17]
Oregon	16[19]	16	16	15[6, 9]	14	4	26.25	no[15,17,24]
Pennsylvania	16	16	16	16[6, 7]	16[6]	4	29.00	yes[17]
Rhode Island	16	16	18[19]	([5])	16[4]	5	30.00	yes[18]
South Carolina	16	14	16	15[9]	15	5	12.50	no
South Dakota	16	14	16	14[7]	14[3]	4 or 5	8.00	no
Tennessee	16	14	16	15[7]	14	5	19.50	no[17]
Texas	18[19]	15	18[19]	15	15[4, 7]	4-6	16–24.00	yes[17]
Utah	16	16	16[4, 6]	16	15¾[8, 9]	5	15/20.00	yes[17]
Vermont	18	16	18	15[5, 9]	16[7]	2 or 4	12/20.00	yes
Virginia	18[19]	16	18	15[5, 6, 7]	16[4, 6]	5	12.00	yes[17]
Washington	18[19]	16	18[19]	15[8]	16[4]	4	14.00	no[17]
West Virginia	18[19]	16	18	15[9]	16	5	13.00	yes
Wisconsin	18[19]	16	18[19]	15½[5]	16[4, 6]	8	18.00	no[17]
Wyoming	18	15[22]	16[6]	15[6, 7]	15[6, 7]	4	20.00	no

1. Full driving privileges at age given in "Regular" column. A license restricted or qualified in some manner may be obtained at age given in "Restricted" column. 2. 4 years if under 18 or over 70. 3. Hours of operation restricted. 4. Must have completed approved driver education course. 5. Learner's permit required. 6. Guardian's or parental consent required. 7. Driver with learner's permit must be accompanied by locally licensed operator 18 years or older. 8. Must be enrolled in driver education course. 9. Driver with learner's permit must be accompanied by locally licensed operator 21 years or older. 10. Up to 50 cc. 11. Restricted to mopeds. 12. License fee is prorated by age. 13. 3 years if over 75. 14. Individual inspection upon reasonable grounds. 15. State troopers are authorized to inspect at their discretion. 16. For more information, contact the Montana Title and Registration Bureau, Motor Vehicle Division. 17. Annual emissions test in some counties. 18. Annual or bi-annual emissions test for entire state. 19. 18; 16 if approved driver training course completed. 20. All used vehicles upon resale or transfer. 21. Required on out-of-state or salvaged vehicles. Emissions tested in some counties. 22. May obtain instruction permit with motorcycle endorsement. 23. Driver with learner's permit must be accompanied by licensed parent of guardian. 24. Biennial emission inspection in the Portland metro area and Rogue Valley. 25. All first-time new licensees must complete state-approved pre-licensing course. 26. All new drivers must complete 3-hour alcohol-awareness program. 27. 1 year if under 18. NOTES: A driver's license is required in every state. All states have an *implied consent* Chemical Test Law for alcohol. *Source:* Reprinted with permission of the American Automobile Association, Heathrow, Fla.

Standards: The States Go Their Own Ways

By **JAMES COLLINS** TIME

In 1983 a national report entitled "A Nation at Risk" asserted that American schoolchildren need to start getting more out of their educations if the U.S. is to remain socially and economically healthy. Since then, Congress has been debating the merits of implementing national educational standards. President Clinton's efforts to generate support for such a system have not fared too well. The voluntary tests he proposed in his January 1998 State of the Union address met with strong criticism from conservatives, who argued that they would bring too much federal control over education, and the proposal became immobilized in a congressional committee. In a sense, though, the fate of Clinton's initiative may be largely irrelevant because the question of standards is being vigorously addressed by the states themselves.

Inspired in part by an education summit that took place in May 1996, 44 states are revising their standards, and five more are writing them for the first time (Iowa is the lone holdout). The term *standards* in this case refers to something quite specific: official, written guidelines that define what a state expects its public school students to know and be able to do. Some states have set standards for every grade; others measure students' progress over periods of several years.

The argument for academic standards is simple: as in any other endeavor, the people engaged in education need clear goals and a way to determine whether those goals have been met. "When you put rigorous standards in place," says Sandra Feldman, president of the American Federation of Teachers, "it helps parents, teachers, and students to know what the expectations are, and it helps measure whether students are meeting those expectations. This is a method of knowing whether children are learning what they need to be learning at a certain age."

In order for standards to improve schools, say proponents, three conditions must be met: the standards themselves must be explicit; students must be tested on whether they have met them; and finally, schools and students alike must be held accountable when they fall short of expectations. Among the states, however, the quality of standards varies widely: some are so vague that they can hardly be considered standards at all, while others are highly specific. The accompanying map shows which states so far, in the view of the American Federation of Teachers, have written strong standards and which have not. Most states assess their students' achievements with tests, but using the results to actually improve quality is often difficult. Only a few states impose sanctions on underperforming schools and students. One place accountability has been established is Virginia, where Governor George Allen announced that any school with a pass rate of less than 70% will lose its accreditation.

Clinton may get the national standards he wants without even trying. Patty Sullivan, director of education legislation at the National Governors' Association, reports, "Every state that begins working on standards calls and says, 'Which are the states with the best standards? Can you send a copy to us?'" The end result, Sullivan predicts, will be that you'll find they aren't that different from state to state. When all 49 of these states are finished developing their standards, the country may end up eating its cake and having it too: de facto national standards created by the individual states. □

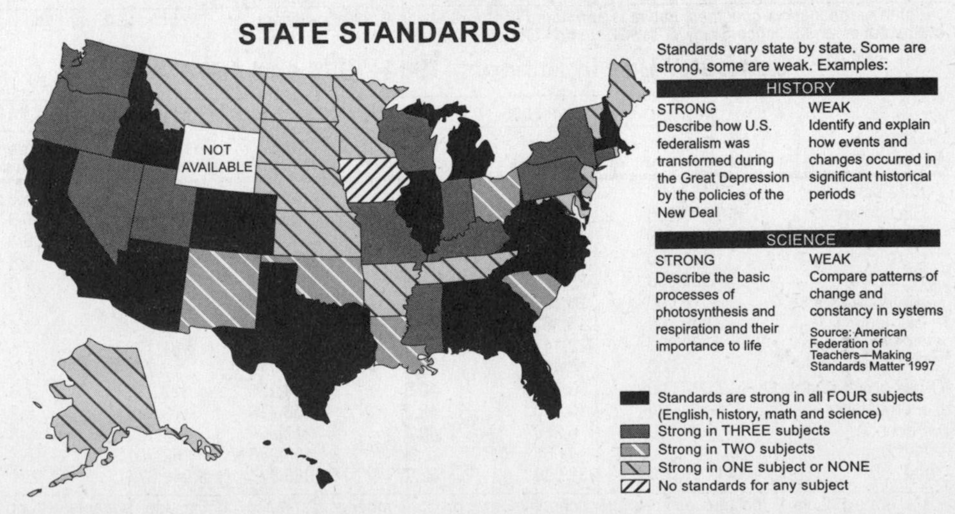

STATE STANDARDS
NOT AVAILABLE
Standards vary state by state. Some are strong, some are weak. Examples:
HISTORY
STRONG
Describe how U.S. federalism was transformed during the Great Depression by the policies of the New Deal
WEAK
Identify and explain how events and changes occurred in significant historical periods
SCIENCE
STRONG
Describe the basic processes of photosynthesis and respiration and their importance to life
WEAK
Compare patterns of change and constancy in systems
Source: American Federation of Teachers—Making Standards Matter 1997
Standards are strong in all FOUR subjects (English, history, math and science)
Strong in THREE subjects
Strong in TWO subjects
Strong in ONE subject or NONE
No standards for any subject

Mathematics and Science Achievement Around the World

Rank	Country	Average achievement	Rank	Country	Average achievement
	Eighth grade* achievement in mathematics			**Eighth grade* achievement in science**	
1	Singapore	643	1	Singapore	607
2	Korea	607	2	Czech Republic	574
3	Japan	605	3	Japan	571
4	Hong Kong	588	4	Korea	565
5	Belgium (Flanders)	565	4	Bulgaria	565
6	Czech Republic	564	5	Netherlands	560
7	Slovak Republic	547	5	Slovenia	560
8	Switzerland	545	6	Austria	558
9	Netherlands	541	7	Hungary	554
9	Slovenia	541	8	England	552
10	Bulgaria	540	9	Belgium (Flanders)	550
11	Austria	539	10	Australia	545
12	France	538	11	Slovak Republic	544
13	Hungary	537	12	Russian Federation	538
14	Russian Federation	535	12	Ireland	538
15	Australia	530	13	Sweden	535
16	Ireland	527	14	United States	534
16	Canada	527	15	Germany	531
17	Belgium (Wallonia)	526	15	Canada	531
18	Thailand	522	16	Norway	527
18	Israel	522	17	New Zealand	525
19	Sweden	519	17	Thailand	525
20	Germany	509	18	Israel	524
21	New Zealand	508	19	Hong Kong	522
22	England	506	19	Switzerland	522
23	Norway	503	20	Scotland	517
24	Denmark	502	20	Spain	517
25	United States	500	21	France	498
26	Scotland	498	22	Greece	497
27	Latvia (LSS)	493	23	Iceland	494
28	Spain	487	24	Romania	486
28	Iceland	487	25	Latvia (LSS)	485
29	Greece	484	26	Portugal	480
30	Romania	482	27	Denmark	478
31	Lithuania	477	28	Lithuania	476
32	Cyprus	474	29	Belgium (Wallonia)	471
33	Portugal	454	30	Iran, Islamic Rep.	470
34	Iran, Islamic Rep.	428	31	Cyprus	463
35	Kuwait	392	32	Kuwait	430
36	Colombia	385	33	Colombia	411
37	South Africa	354	34	South Africa	326

* Eighth grade in most countries. Latvia is annotated LSS for Latvian Speaking Schools only. *Source:* IEA Third International Mathematics and Science Study (TIMSS), Boston College, 1994–95.

Computer Use in Schools, 1984–1985 and 1997–1998

Level	1984–1985 Total enrollment	1984–1985 Number of computers[1]	1984–1985 Students per computer[2]	1997–1998 Total enrollment	1997–1998 Number of computers[1]	1997–1998 Students per computer[2]
Public schools	39,186,000	569,825	63.5	46,769,320	7,415,007	6.3
Elementary	19,373,000	215,393	79.3	23,499,195	3,401,082	6.9
Middle/junior high	6,662,000	100,331	61.2	8,549,137	1,348,058	6.3
Senior high	11,191,000	228,726	51.5	12,287,093	2,180,520	5.6
K–12/other	1,959,000	25,375	45.8	2,433,895	485,345	5.0
Catholic schools	2,813,000	28,427	73.5	2,652,781	311,822	8.5
Elementary	2,065,000	15,863	85.1	1,969,779	222,942	8.8
Secondary	700,000	12,147	57.8	631,263	81,178	7.8
K–12/other	48,000	417	n.a.	51,739	7,701	6.7
Other private schools	2,093,000	33,731	40.5	2,444,226	323,045	7.6
Elementary	1,049,000	13,400	42.7	1,058,216	129,249	8.2
Secondary	79,000	6,266	40.1	217,964	41,335	5.3
K–12/other	965,000	14,065	n.a.	1,168,046	152,461	7.7
Total	**44,091,000**	**631,983**	**62.7**	**51,866,327**	**8,049,875**	**6.4**

n.a. = not available 1. Includes estimates for schools not reporting number of computers. 2. Excludes schools with no computers. *Source:* Market Data Retrieval, Shelton, Conn., unpublished data (copyright).

Public Schools with Access or Planned Access to the Internet, 1994–1996

School characteristic	Percent of schools with Internet access			Percent of instructional rooms with Internet access			Percent of schools without Internet access in 1996 that plan for access by the year 2000
	1994	1995	1996	1994	1995	1996	
Total[1]	35%	50%	65%	3%	8%	14%	87%
Instructional level:							
Elementary	30	46	61	3	8	13	85
Secondary	49	65	77	4	8	16	93
Size of enrollment:							
Less than 300	30	39	57	3	9	15	83
300 to 999	35	52	66	3	8	13	88
1,000 or more	58	69	80	3	4	16	87
Percent minority enrollment:							
Less than 6 percent	n.a.	52	65	n.a.	9	18	86
6 to 20 percent	n.a.	58	72	n.a.	10	18	88
21 to 49 percent	n.a.	54	65	n.a.	9	12	95
50 percent or more	n.a.	40	56	n.a.	3	5	78
Percent of students eligible for free or reduced-price school lunch:							
Less than 11 percent	n.a.	62	78	n.a.	9	18	88
11 to 30 percent	n.a.	59	72	n.a.	10	16	92
31 to 70 percent	n.a.	47	58	n.a.	7	14	84
71 percent or more	n.a.	31	53	n.a.	3	7	85

n.a. = not available. 1. Includes combined schools. NOTE: Excludes special education, vocational education, and alternative based on sample and subject to sampling error. *Source:* U.S. National Center for Education Statistics, "Advanced Telecommunications in U.S. Public Elementary and Secondary Schools, Fall 1996."

Funding for Public Elementary and Secondary Education, 1986–1987 to 1994–1995

(In thousands except percent)

School year	Total	Federal	State	Local[1]	% Federal	% State	% Local[1]
1986–87	$158,523,693	$10,146,013	$ 78,830,437	$ 69,547,243	6.4%	49.7%	43.9%
1987–88	169,561,974	10,716,687	84,004,415	74,840,873	6.3	49.5	44.1
1988–89	191,210,310	11,872,419	91,158,363	88,179,529	6.2	47.4	46.1
1989–90	207,752,932	12,700,784	98,238,633	96,813,516	6.1	47.3	46.6
1990–91	223,340,537	13,776,066	105,324,533	104,239,939	6.2	47.2	46.7
1991–92	234,588,732	15,493,330	108,783,449	110,311,953	6.6	46.4	47.0
1992–93	248,496,276	17,267,351	113,396,992	117,831,933	6.9	45.6	47.4
1993–94[2]	247,626,000	17,261,000	113,403,000	116,961,000	7.0	45.8	47.2
1994–95	260,142,000	18,336,000	117,462,000	124,344,000	7.0	45.2	47.8

1. Includes a relatively small amount from nongovernmental sources (gifts, tuition, and transportation fees from patrons). 2. Revised from previously published figures. *Source:* U.S. Department of Education, Digest of Education Statistics 1996.

High School and College Graduates

School year	High school			College[1]		
	Men	Women	Total	Men	Women	Total
1900	38,075	56,808	94,883	22,173	5,237	27,410
1910	63,676	92,753	156,429	28,762	8,437	37,199
1920	123,684	187,582	311,266	31,980	16,642	48,622
1929–30	300,376	366,528	666,904	73,615	48,869	122,484
1939–40	578,718	642,757	1,221,475	109,546	76,954	186,500
1949–50	570,700	629,000	1,199,700	328,841	103,217	432,058
1959–60	898,000	966,000	1,858,000[2]	254,063	138,377	392,440
1969–70	1,433,000	1,463,000	2,889,000[2]	451,097[2]	341,219[2]	792,316[2]
1974–75	1,541,000	1,599,000	3,133,000[2]	504,841[2]	418,092[2]	922,933[2]
1978–79	1,531,800	1,602,400	3,101,000[2]	477,344[2]	444,046[2]	921,390[2]
1979–80	1,500,000	1,558,000	3,043,000[2]	473,611[2]	455,806[2]	929,417[2]

School year	High school Men	High school Women	High school Total	College[1] Men	College[1] Women	College[1] Total
1980–81	1,483,000	1,537,000	3,020,000	469,883[2]	465,257[2]	935,140[2]
1981–82	1,474,000	1,527,000	2,995,000[2]	473,364[2]	479,634[2]	952,998[2]
1982–83	1,437,000	1,451,000	2,888,000	479,140	490,370	969,510
1983–84	n.a.	n.a.	2,767,000	482,319	491,990	974,309
1984–85	n.a.	n.a.	2,677,000	482,528	496,949	979,477
1985–86	n.a.	n.a.	2,643,000	485,923	501,900	987,823
1986–87	n.a.	n.a.	2,694,000	480,854	510,485	991,339
1987–88	n.a.	n.a.	2,773,000	480,782[2]	510,482[2]	991,264[2]
1988–89	n.a.	n.a.	2,727,000	483,346	535,409	1,018,755
1989–90	n.a.	n.a.	2,586,000[2]	491,696	559,648	1,051,344
1990–91	n.a.	n.a.	2,503,000	504,045	590,493	1,094,538
1991–92	n.a.	n.a.	2,482,000	520,811	615,742	1,136,553
1992–93	n.a.	n.a.	2,490,000	532,881	632,297	1,165,178
1993–94	n.a.	n.a.	2,479,000	532,422	636,853	1,169,275
1994–95	n.a.	n.a.	2,531,000[2,3]	526,131[2]	634,003[2]	1,160,134[2]
1995–96	n.a.	n.a.	2,557,000[2,3]	531,000[2]	655,000[2]	1,186,000[2]
1996–97	n.a.	n.a.	2,623,000	528,000[2]	655,000	1,183,000[2]

1. Bachelors's degrees. Includes first-professional degrees for years 1900–1960. 2. Revised from previously published data. 3. Public high school graduates based on state estimates. 4. Projected. n.a. = not available. NOTE: Includes graduates from public and private schools. Beginning in 1959–60, figures include Alaska and Hawaii. Because of rounding, details may not add to totals. Most recent data available. *Source:* Department of Education, National Center for Education Statistics.

Differences in Educational Attainment by Race, Hispanic Origin, and Age: 1997

Source: U.S. Bureau of the Census, Current Population Survey, March 1997.

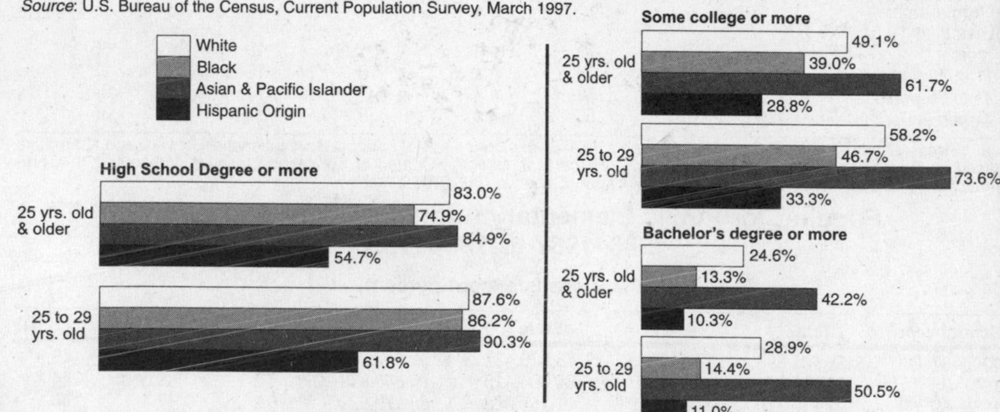

School Enrollment by Grade, Type of Institution, and Race

(in thousands)

Grade level and type of institution	White Oct. 1996[3]	White Oct. 1990[3]	White Oct. 1980[4]	Black Oct. 1996[3]	Black Oct. 1990[3]	Black Oct. 1980[4]	All races[1] Oct. 1996[3]	All races[1] Oct. 1990[3]	All races[1] Oct. 1980[4]
Nursery school: Public	1,314	896	432	459	283	180	1,868	1,212	633
Private	1,969	1,961	1,205	243	148	115	2,344	2,188	1,354
Kindergarten: Public	2,596	2,609	2,172	545	574	440	3,353	3,322	2,690
Private	567	472	423	89	62	50	680	567	486
Grades 1–8: Public	21,763	20,997	19,743	4,839	4,431	4,058	28,116	26,615	24,398
Private	2,905	2,359	2,768	317	199	202	3,351	2,676	3,051
Grades 9–12: Public	10,809	9,429	12,056[2]	2,281	1,937	2,200[2]	13,865	11,911	14,556[2]
Private	1,048	810	—	97	65	—	1,184	906	—
College: Public	9,566	9,049	8,875[2]	1,519	1,120	1,007[2]	12,014	10,754	10,180[2]
Private	2,622	2,439	—	381	274	—	3,212	2,869	—
Total: Public	46,048	42,954	—	9,643	8,344	—	59,216	53,823	—
Private	9,111	8,041	—	1,127	748	—	10,771	9,204	—
Grand Total	**55,159**	**50,995**	**47,673**	**10,770**	**9,092**	**8,251**	**69,987**	**63,027**	**57,348**

1. Includes persons of Hispanic origin. 2. Total public and private. Breakdown not available. 3. Estimates controlled to 1990 census base. 4. Estimates controlled to 1970 census base. *Source:* Department of Commerce, Bureau of the Census.

Major U.S. College and University Libraries, 1997

Top 50 based on number of volumes in library

Academic institution	Volumes	Microforms	Academic institution	Volumes	Microforms
Harvard	13,617,133	8,146,817	Iowa	3,822,656	5,934,537
Yale	9,932,080	6,475,762	U. of Pittsburgh	3,819,100	3,768,023
U. of Illinois, Urbana	9,024,298	4,749,496	Rutgers	3,633,792	5,285,009
U. of California, Berkeley	8,628,028	5,798,420	New York U.	3,629,897	4,138,289
U. of Texas	7,495,275	5,351,849	U. of Kansas	3,532,810	3,094,881
U. of California, Los Angeles	7,010,234	5,871,355	U. of Georgia	3,458,298	5,643,843
U. of Michigan	6,973,162	5,643,000	U. of Southern California	3,417,928	5,658,731
Columbia	6,905,609	5,217,558	U. of Florida	3,317,781	6,208,462
Stanford	6,865,158	4,972,783	Arizona State	3,278,332	6,612,808
U. of Chicago	6,116,978	2,356,427	Washington U.-St. Louis	3,234,005	2,894,196
Cornell	6,113,346	7,164,967	Johns Hopkins	3,224,741	3,765,177
Indiana	5,916,992	3,981,111	SUNY-Buffalo	3,047,830	4,939,762
U. of Wisconsin	5,824,639	4,395,889	Wayne State	3,002,261	3,453,750
U. of Washington	5,715,202	6,526,689	South Carolina	2,998,228	4,525,128
Princeton	5,516,141	4,479,269	U. of Rochester	2,962,157	4,132,302
U. of Minnesota	5,490,668	5,391,112	Louisiana State	2,950,442	5,022,323
Ohio State	5,087,336	4,364,755	U. of California, Davis	2,949,213	3,765,683
North Carolina	4,819,186	4,189,938	Brown	2,932,818	1,620,278
Duke	4,645,050	3,381,313	U. of Hawaii	2,925,821	5,729,691
U. of Pennsylvania	4,546,667	3,155,776	U. of Connecticut	2,828,359	4,228,154
U. of Arizona	4,442,961	5,425,646	U. of Massachusetts	2,826,284	2,259,861
U. of Virginia	4,433,628	4,841,744	U. of Missouri	2,816,452	6,450,139
Michigan State	4,118,032	5,175,541	U. of Colorado	2,715,702	5,685,353
Pennsylvania State	3,934,344	3,434,019	Syracuse	2,712,132	3,688,001
Northwestern	3,893,005	3,385,241	U. of Kentucky	2,679,084	5,727,331

1. Includes reels of microfilm and number of microcards, microprint sheets, and microfiches. *Source:* Association of Research Libraries.

College and University Endowments, 1996–1997

Top 75, in millions of dollars

Institution	Endowment[1]	Voluntary support	Expenditures[2]	Institution	Endowment[1]	Voluntary support	Expenditures[2]
Harvard Univ.	11,161.8	427.6	1,531.8	Rockefeller Univ.	803.1	37.5	110.9
Yale Univ.	5,794.1	203.2	962.3	Georgia Inst. of Tech.	775.4	76.9	462.7
Princeton Univ.	5,099.7	133.9	296.6	Ohio State Univ.	767.7	129.0	1,024.4
Stanford Univ.	4,667.0	312.3	1,072.0	Grinnell Col.	754.6	12.0	45.5
Columbia Univ.	3,038.9	201.8	1,234.6	Swarthmore Col.	748.2	14.9	64.9
Massachusetts Inst. of Tech.	3,023.6	137.4	834.0	Univ. of N.C.–Chapel Hill	719.9	108.0	783.7
Washington Univ.	2,844.7	92.8	n.a.	Wellesley Col.	691.1	36.5	101.0
Texas A&M Univ.	2,629.0	106.6	833.4	Smith Col.	683.4	34.7	104.5
Univ. of Pennsylvania	2,535.3	174.5	882.2	Washington and Lee Univ.	680.2	19.5	54.9
Northwestern Univ.	2,447.7	124.6	785.7	Boston Col.	676.9	26.6	219.3
William Marsh Rice Univ.	2,300.0	51.6	197.4	Texas Christian Univ.	675.5	21.2	104.4
Cornell Univ.	2,155.9	220.6	996.2	Univ. of Richmond	672.0	18.6	88.0
Univ. of Michigan	2,045.2	157.9	1,473.9	Williams Col.	663.6	23.9	74.9
Univ. of Chicago	2,031.0	129.2	639.7	Univ. of Delaware	662.8	25.4	318.6
Univ. of Notre Dame	1,515.2	95.2	301.7	Baylor Col. of Medicine	659.0	27.8	501.7
Mayo Foundation	1,430.9	86.7	294.5	Southern Methodist Univ.	645.5	32.1	178.2
Univ. of Calif.–Berkeley	1,361.3	181.1	954.0	Univ. of Wisconsin–Madison	636.4	212.6	1,081.7
Vanderbilt Univ.	1,311.9	78.1	561.9	Univ. of Kansas	620.4	47.0	446.2
Dartmouth Col.	1,277.8	100.1	291.6	Univ. of Pittsburgh	614.7	55.0	745.2
Duke Univ.	1,190.5	220.0	658.1	Wake Forest Univ.	614.7	37.8	425.7
Case Western Reserve Univ.	1,158.0	75.3	376.5	Indiana Univ.	608.9	116.4	1,126.6
Johns Hopkins Univ.	1,156.6	164.6	1,542.1	Carnegie-Mellon Univ.	592.0	90.0	354.0
Univ. of Minnesota	1,126.8	136.0	1,339.0	Pomona Col.	587.9	26.7	56.3
California Inst. of Tech.	1,027.0	67.1	408.4	Univ. of Calif.–San Francisco	564.2	105.4	769.5
Univ. of Texas–Austin	1,020.7	106.8	834.1	Univ. of Cincinnati	558.0	39.2	481.7
Brown Univ.	965.2	67.4	236.9	Univ. of Nebraska	556.1	88.2	716.8
Univ. of Virginia	961.6	109.3	583.3	Univ. of Tulsa	547.6	20.2	73.3
Univ. of Rochester	942.5	37.0	349.9	Middlebury Col.	542.8	18.7	88.3
Univ. of Calif.–Los Angeles	890.8	197.8	1,324.8	Univ. of Illinois	537.9	127.5	1,768.6
New York Univ.	878.4	109.8	1,143.2	George Washington Univ.	534.2	26.3	426.6
Purdue Univ.	870.4	65.0	730.0				

Institution	Endowment[1]	Voluntary support	Expenditures[2]
Berea Col.	521.8	19.7	35.4
Pennsylvania State Univ.	517.9	94.9	1,155.2
St. Louis Univ.	513.3	24.0	192.3
Lehigh Univ.	511.2	29.2	170.3
Boston Univ.	494.2	50.3	642.0
Univ. of Washington	488.7	150.0	1,077.7
Univ. of Iowa	486.1	80.8	644.5
Univ. of Tennessee	482.0	63.1	783.6
Trinity Univ.	476.6	24.1	54.1
Amherst Col.	474.1	31.7	70.9
Vassar Col.	473.0	18.9	73.9
Baylor Univ.	468.3	59.2	153.8
Macalester Col.	448.3	9.2	52.9
Wesleyan Univ.	439.7	12.8	89.8

1. Endowment is market value at fiscal year-end 1997. 2. Data for expenditures is not necessarily comparable across institutions, as the schools do not all use the same standards in reporting expenditures. NOTES: List includes only institutions that participated in the 1996–1997 Voluntary Support of Education Survey. State systems that submitted combined endowments above the current cut-off are not included. *Source:* Survey of Voluntary Support of Education 1997. Council for Aid to Education, N.Y.

Average Earnings by Educational Attainment, Sex, and Race, 1996

Educational attainment	Total, both sexes	Total, male	Total, female	White, both sexes	Black, both sexes	Hispanic, both sexes
Overall	$28,106	$34,705	$20,570	$28,844	$21,978	$19,439
Advanced degree	61,317	74,406	42,625	61,779	48,731	49,873
Bachelor's degree	38,112	46,702	28,701	38,936	31,955	32,955
Some college or Associate degree	25,181	31,426	18,933	25,511	23,628	22,209
High school graduate	22,154	27,642	16,161	22,782	18,722	18,528
Not a high school graduate	15,011	17,826	10,421	15,358	13,110	13,287

Source: Census Bureau, Current Population Survey, March 1997 Update.

Mean Earnings of Workers 18 Years and Over by Educational Attainment, 1975 to 1995

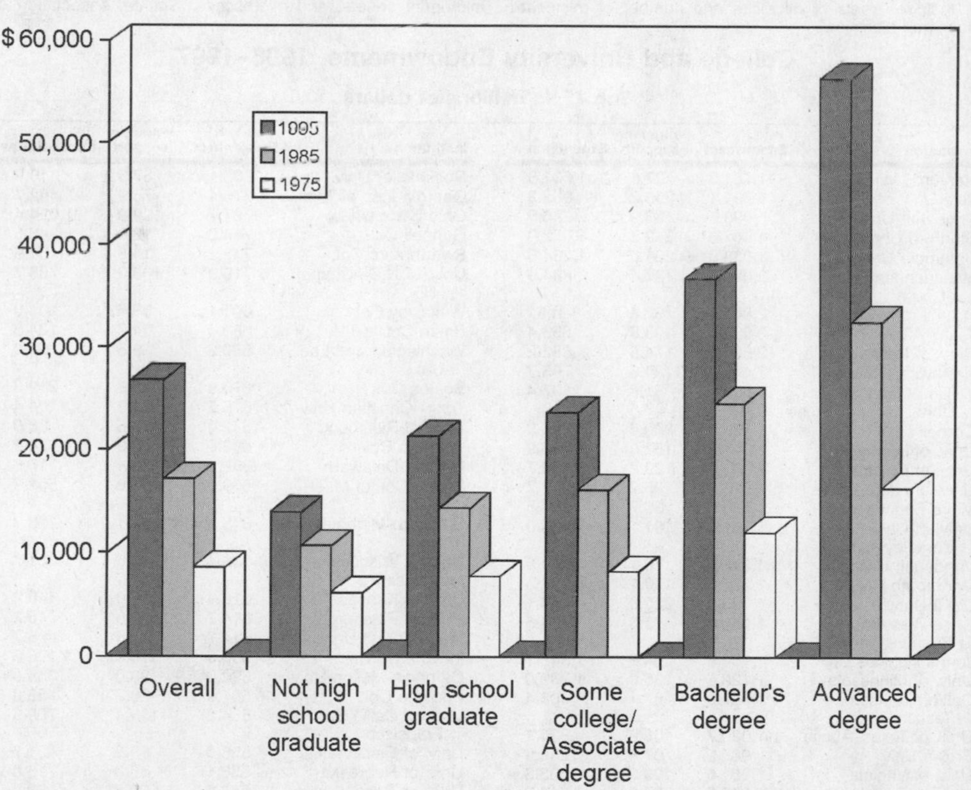

Source: Census Bureau, Current Population Survey

Family Reading

	Percentage of 3- to 5-year-olds[1] who were read to daily by a family member		
	1993	1995	1996
Overall	53%	58%	57%
Gender			
Male	51	57	56
Female	54	59	57
Race and Hispanic origin[2]			
White, non-Hispanic	59	65	64
Black, non-Hispanic	39	43	44
Hispanic	37	38	39
Poverty status			
Above poverty threshold	56	62	61
At or below poverty threshold	44	48	46
Family type			
Two parents	55	61	61
One or no parent	46	49	46
Mother's education[3]			
Less than high school	37	40	37
High school/GED	48	48	49
Vocational/technical or some college	57	64	62
College graduate	71	76	77
Mother's employment status[3]			
35 hours or more per week	52	55	54
Less than 35 hours per week	56	63	59
Not in labor force	55	60	59

1. Estimates based on children who have yet to enter kindergarten. 2. Persons of Hispanic origin may be of any race. 3. Children without mothers in the home are not included. *Source:* U.S. Department of Education, National Center for Education Statistics.

Accredited U.S. Senior Colleges and Universities

Source: The information below comes to us from *The Princeton Review's Complete Book of Accredited Colleges, 1999 Edition.*

Schools are listed alphabetically within each state and are accredited four-year institutions offering at least a Bachelor's degree. Tuition, room, and board listed are average annual figures (including fees) subject to fluctuation, usually covering two semesters, two out of three trimesters, or three out of four quarters, depending on the school calendar. Note that some schools include room and board expenses within the tuition figures rather than reporting them separately. For further information, write to the registrar of the school concerned.

(P) = private; (Pub) = public.

Institution name; city, state ZIP (control)	Students	Percent Accepted	Percent Women	Tuition In-state	Tuition Out-of-state	Room and board
ALABAMA						
Alabama A&M University; Huntsville, Ala. 35801 (Pub)	3,745	64%	52%	$ 1,932	$ 3,864	$2,678
Alabama State University; Montgomery, Ala. 36101 (Pub)	4,456	68		1,800	3,600	3,330
Athens State College; Athens, Ala. 35611 (Pub)	1,271		62	1,656	3,312	4,800
Auburn University; Auburn Univ., Ala. 36849 (Pub)	18,229	86	48	2,820	2,820	4,930
Auburn University–Montgomery; Montgomery, Ala. 36124-4023 (Pub)	5,645		61	2,289	6,867	2,160
Birmingham–Southern College; Birmingham, Ala. 35254 (P)	1,443	96	58	13,750	13,750	5,370
Faulkner University; Montgomery, Ala. 36109 (P)	1,892	75	60	10,260	10,260	
Huntingdon College; Montgomery, Ala. 36106 (P)	673	75	59	10,100	10,100	5,000
Jacksonville State University; Jacksonville, Ala. 36265-5781 (Pub)	6,477	93	55	2,040	4,080	2,870
Judson College (Ala.); Marion, Ala. 36756 (P)	233		100	6,900	6,900	4,300
Miles College; Birmingham, Ala. 35208 (P)	1,215			6,750	6,750	
Oakwood College; Huntsville, Ala. 35896 (P)	1,666	82		10,638	10,638	
Samford University; Birmingham, Ala. 35229 (P)	2,919	91	62	9,904	9,904	4,406
Spring Hill College; Mobile, Ala. 36608 (P)	1,149	90	61	13,670	13,670	5,250
Stillman College; Tuscaloosa, Ala. 35403 (P)	913	77		8,300	8,300	
Talladega College; Talladega, Ala. 35160 (P)	642	38	65	5,666	5,666	2,964
Troy State University; Troy, Ala. 36082 (Pub)	5,382	73	56	2,055	4,110	3,480
Troy State University at Dothan; Dothan, Ala. 36304 (Pub)	2,100	14		2,100	4,200	
Troy State University at Montgomery; Montgomery, Ala. 36103 (Pub)	2,800		59	1,980	3,160	
Tuskegee University; Tuskegee, Ala. 36088 (P)	2,618	65	60	8,662	8,662	4,104
University of Alabama–Birmingham; Birmingham, Ala. 35294 (Pub)	10,358	90	56	2,520	5,040	3,090
University of Alabama–Huntsville; Huntsville, Ala. 35899 (Pub)	5,173	85	50	2,832	5,938	3,700
University of Alabama–Tuscaloosa; Tuscaloosa, Ala. 35487 (Pub)	14,447	81	52	1,342	3,608	3,800
University of Mobile; Mobile, Ala. 36663 (P)	1,856	87	62	7,350	7,350	4,080
University of Montevallo; Montevallo, Ala. 35115 (Pub)	3,125	75	68	2,970	5,940	3,242
University of North Alabama; Florence, Ala. 35632-0001 (Pub)	4,962	76	57	2,064	4,128	3,260
University of South Alabama; Mobile, Ala. 36688-0002 (Pub)	10,159	93	55	2,640	5,280	2,883
University of West Alabama; Livingston, Ala. 35470 (Pub)	1,838	76	53	2,280	4,560	2,460

Institution name; city, state ZIP (control)	Students	Percent Accepted	Percent Women	Tuition In-state	Tuition Out-of-state	Room and board
ALASKA						
Alaska Pacific University; Anchorage, Alaska 99508 (P)	361	84%	61%	$12,220	$12,220	
Sheldon Jackson College; Sitka, Alaska 99835 (P)	202	100		6,850	6,850	$4,500
University of Alaska–Anchorage; Anchorage, Alaska 99508 (Pub)	16,746	81	56	2,168	6,428	7,650
University of Alaska–Fairbanks; Fairbanks, Alaska 99775 (Pub)	7,393	79	59	2,168	6,428	7,650
University of Alaska–Southeast; Juneau, Alaska 99801 (Pub)	2,782	88	55	2,168	6,428	7,650
ARIZONA						
Arizona State University; Tempe, Ariz. 85287-0112 (Pub)	33,497	78	51	1,988	8,640	4,500
Embry-Riddle Aeronautical University (Ariz.); Prescott, Ariz. 86301-3720 (P)	1,512	87	17	9,600	9,600	4,950
Grand Canyon University; Phoenix, Ariz. 85017 (P)	1,789	83	64	8,670	8,670	3,860
Northern Arizona University; Flagstaff, Ariz. 86011 (Pub)	14,058	81	57	2,160	8,076	3,546
Prescott College; Prescott, Ariz. 86301 (P)	718	74	63	11,500	11,500	4,706
University of Arizona; Tucson, Ariz. 85721-0041 (Pub)	25,617	82	52	1,940	8,308	4,930
Western International University; Phoenix, Ariz. 85021 (P)	820	18		3,960	3,960	
ARKANSAS						
Arkansas Baptist College; Little Rock, Ark. 72202 (P)	411	54		4,258	4,258	
Arkansas State University; State University, Ark. 72467 (Pub)	8,983	79	56	2,000	5,090	2,840
Arkansas Tech University; Russellville, Ark. 72801 (Pub)	4,541	90	53	2,178	4,356	2,925
Harding University; Searcy, Ark. 72149 (P)	3,573	60	56	7,590	7,590	3,988
Henderson State University; Arkadelphia, Ark. 71999-0001 (Pub)	3,354	93	58	1,980	3,960	4,152
Hendrix College; Conway, Ark. 72032 (P)	1,034	89	55	10,690	10,690	4,160
John Brown University; Siloam Spring, Ark. 72761 (P)	1,295	68	54	9,482	9,482	4,478
Lyon College; Batesville, Ark. 72503 (P)	511	53	54	9,750	9,750	4,418
Ouachita Baptist University; Arkadelphia, Ark. 71923 (P)	1,619	81	50	7,970	7,970	3,040
Philander Smith College; Little Rock, Ark. 72202 (P)	851	31	67	3,288	3,288	2,746
Southern Arkansas University–Magnolia; Magnolia, Ark. 71753-5000 (Pub)	2,142	91	62	1,848	2,856	2,530
University of Arkansas–Fayetteville; Fayetteville, Ark. 72701 (Pub)	11,844	74	46	2,604	7,084	4,030
University of Arkansas–Little Rock; Little Rock, Ark. 72204-1099 (Pub)	8,559	74	59	1,131	2,916	2,435
University of Arkansas–Monticello; Monticello, Ark. 71656 (Pub)	2,200	68	56	1,680	3,888	2,930
University of Arkansas–Pine Bluff; Pine Bluff, Ark. 71601 (Pub)	3,425	88	59	1,944	5,136	3,470
University of Central Arkansas; Conway, Ark. 72035 (Pub)	7,914	75	61	2,392	4,364	2,920
University of the Ozarks; Clarksville, Ark. 72830 (P)	573	96	55	7,750	7,750	3,750
Williams Baptist College; Walnut Ridge, Ark. 72476 (P)	564	79	55	7,122	7,122	
CALIFORNIA						
Art Center College of Design; Pasadena, Calif. 91103 (P)	1,334	61		17,180	17,180	
Azusa Pacific University; Azusa, Calif. 91702 (P)	2,279	88	60	13,020	13,020	4,482
Biola University; La Mirada, Calif. 90639 (P)	2,153	88	60	15,214	15,214	4,990
Brooks Institute of Photography; Santa Barbara, Calif. 93108 (P)	302	89	32	15,000	15,000	
California Baptist College; Riverside, Calif. 92504 (P)	1,675	70	58	8,190	8,190	4,594
California College of Arts and Crafts; San Francisco, Calif. 94107 (P)	991	62	59	15,850	15,850	4,894
California Institute of Technology; Pasadena, Calif. 91125 (P)	904	23		18,950	18,950	5,881
California Institute of the Arts; Valencia, Calif. 91355 (P)	724	40	40	18,190	18,190	5,450
California Lutheran University; Thousand Oaks, Calif. 91360 (P)	1,659	81	54	15,415	15,415	5,985
California Maritime Academy of California State University; Vallejo, Calif. 94590-0644 (Pub)	389	70	12	1,506	7,380	5,801
California Polytechnic State University-San Luis Obispo; San Luis Obis, Calif. 93407 (Pub)	15,761	38	43	1,506	7,380	5,801
California State Polytechnic University-Pomona; Pomona, Calif. 91768 (Pub)	15,073	70	43	1,506	7,380	5,801
California State University–Bakersfield; Bakersfield, Calif. 93311 (Pub)	4,309	68	62	1,506	7,380	5,801
California State University–Chico; Chico, Calif. 95929-0722 (Pub)	12,506	83	53	1,506	7,380	5,801
California State University–Dominguez Hills; Carson, Calif. 90747 (Pub)	8,323	74		1,506	7,380	5,801
California State University–Fresno; Fresno, Calif. 93740 (Pub)	14,100	71	55	1,506	7,380	5,801
California State University–Fullerton; Fullerton, Calif. 92634-6808 (Pub)	20,743	77	57	1,506	7,380	5,801
California State University–Hayward; Hayward, Calif. 94542 (Pub)	9,905	62	63	1,506	7,380	5,801
California State University–Long Beach; Long Beach, Calif. 90840 (Pub)	21,094	83	55	1,506	7,380	5,801
California State University–Los Angeles; Los Angeles, Calif. 90032 (Pub)	13,995	53	59	1,506	7,380	5,801
California State University–Northridge; Northridge, Calif. 91330 (Pub)	21,720	82	55	1,506	7,380	5,801

Institution name; city, state ZIP (control)	Students	Percent Accepted	Percent Women	Tuition In-state	Tuition Out-of-state	Room and board
California State University–Sacramento; Sacramento, Calif. 95819 (Pub)	18,713	65%	54%	$ 1,506	$ 7,380	$5,801
California State University–San Bernardino; San Bernardino, Calif. 92407 (Pub)	11,007	70	59	1,506	7,380	5,801
California State University–San Marcos; San Marcos, Calif. 92096-0001 (Pub)	1,284		66	1,506	7,380	5,801
California State University–Stanislaus; Turlock, Calif. 95382 (Pub)	4,886	69	63	1,506	7,380	5,801
Chapman University; Orange, Calif. 92866 (P)	2,404	89	56	25,104	25,104	
Christian Heritage College; El Cajon, Calif. 92019-1157 (P)	617	75	60	10,240	10,240	4,500
Claremont McKenna College; Claremont, Calif. 91711 (P)	979	32	44	19,800	19,800	7,070
Cogswell Polytechnical College; Sunnyvale, Calif. 94089-1299 (P)	400	58		5,900	5,900	3,200
College of Notre Dame (Calif.); Belmont, Calif. 94002 (P)	813	77	65	22,075	22,075	
Concordia University (Calif.); Irvine, Calif. 92612-3299 (P)	970	80	65	13,600	13,600	5,480
Dominican College of San Rafael; San Rafael, Calif. 94901-2298 (P)	1,026	81	79	15,840	15,840	7,246
Fresno Pacific University; Fresno, Calif. 93702 (P)	816	75	65	12,480	12,480	4,950
Golden Gate University; San Francisco, Calif. 94105 (P)	1,519	44	57	8,500	8,500	
Harvey Mudd College; Claremont, Calif. 91711-5990 (P)	665	43	24	20,754	20,754	7,691
Holy Names College; Oakland, Calif. 94619-1699 (P)	537	70	81	14,300	14,300	6,400
Humboldt State University; Arcata, Calif. 95521-8299 (Pub)	6,670	77	52	1,958	5,904	5,391
John F. Kennedy University; Orinda, Calif. 94563 (P)	318		75	7,380	7,380	
LaSierra University; Riverside, Calif. 92515 (P)	1,385	76	52	14,220	14,220	4,137
Loma Linda University; Loma Linda, Calif. 92350 (P)	1,255		69	15,540	15,540	
Loyola Marymount University; Los Angeles, Calif. 90045-8350 (P)	4,282	66	57	16,296	16,296	6,854
Menlo College; Atherton, Calif. 94027 (P)	522	93	39	15,980	15,980	6,800
Mills College; Oakland, Calif. 94613 (P)	771		100	21,740	21,740	
Monterey Institute of International Studies; Monterey, Calif. 93901 (P)	36	21	60	18,200	18,200	5,802
Mount Saint Mary's College (Calif.); Los Angeles, Calif. 90049 (P)	1,644	81	94	15,452	15,452	6,300
National University; La Jolla, Calif. 92037 (P)	4,451		54	20,400	20,400	
New College of California; San Francisco, Calif. 94102 (P)	1,402	90	57	8,200	8,200	
Northrop University; Los Angeles, Calif. 90045 (P)				12,270	12,270	
Occidental College; Los Angeles, Calif. 90041 (P)	1,739	73	52	27,804	27,804	
Otis College of Art & Design; Los Angeles, Calif. 90045 (P)	707	70	59	15,900	15,900	4,490
Pacific Christian College; Fullerton, Calif. 92631 (P)	822	90		11,784	11,784	
Pacific Oaks College; Pasadena, Calif. 91103 (P)	221		89	10,800	10,800	
Pacific Union College; Angwin, Calif. 94508 (P)	1,455	67	53	14,055	14,055	4,305
Patten College; Oakland, Calif. 94601-2699 (P)	636	62		8,972	8,972	
Pepperdine University; Malibu, Calif. 90263 (P)	3,175	56	57	28,960	28,960	
Pitzer College; Claremont, Calif. 91711 (P)	871	62	59	28,574	28,574	
Point Loma Nazarene College; San Diego, Calif. 92106 (P)	2,027	88	61	12,210	12,210	5,220
Pomona College; Claremont, Calif. 91711 (P)	1,421	31		21,420	21,420	8,270
Saint John's Seminary; Camarillo, Calif. 93012 (P)		23		8,920	8,920	
Saint Mary's College (Calif.); Moraga, Calif. 94575 (P)	2,200	84	81	16,674	16,674	6,990
Samuel Merritt College; Oakland, Calif. 94609-5108 (P)	286	63	88	14,560	14,560	3,330
San Diego State University; San Diego, Calif. 92182 (Pub)	24,899	80	55	1,854	5,904	6,730
San Francisco Art Institute; San Francisco, Calif. 94133 (P)	538	70	54	25,431	25,431	
San Francisco Conservatory of Music; San Francisco, Calif. 94122 (P)	161	64	53	17,400	17,400	
San Francisco State University; San Francisco, Calif. 94132 (Pub)	19,102	72	57	1,904	7,808	6,240
San Jose State University; San Jose, Calif. 95112-0001 (Pub)	21,753	77	52	2,017	7,380	5,306
Santa Clara University; Santa Clara, Calif. 95053 (P)	4,282	66	54	16,455	16,455	7,026
Scripps College; Claremont, Calif. 91711 (P)	734	45	99	26,330	26,330	
Simpson College and Graduate School; Redding, Calif. 96003 (P)	955	72	65	8,200	8,200	4,100
Sonoma State University; Rohnert Park, Calif. 94928 (Pub)	5,984	80	63	2,130	2,130	5,769
Southern California College; Costa Mesa, Calif. 92626 (P)	1,190	86	58	11,320	11,320	4,860
Southern California College of Optometry; Fullerton, Calif. 92631 (P)				16,200	16,200	
Stanford University; Stanford, Calif. 94305-3005 (P)	7,127	15	51	22,110	22,110	7,769
The Master's College; Santa Clarita, Calif. 91321 (P)	917	82	52	12,440	12,440	4,700
Thomas Aquinas College; Santa Paula, Calif. 93060 (P)	219	84		14,900	14,900	4,300
United States International University; San Diego, Calif. 92131 (P)	401	59	54	12,015	12,015	5,040
University of California-Berkeley; Berkeley, Calif. 94720-5800 (Pub)	21,751	31	47	4,212	13,596	5,946
University of California-Davis; Davis, Calif. 95616 (Pub)	19,184	70	54	4,174	13,596	5,946
University of California-Irvine; Irvine, Calif. 92717 (Pub)	14,240	71	53	4,064	13,596	5,946

Institution name; city, state ZIP (control)	Students	Percent		Tuition		Room and board
		Accepted	Women	In-state	Out-of-state	
University of California-Los Angeles; Los Angeles, Calif. 90095 (Pub)	23,925	36%	53%	$ 4,050	$13,596	$5,946
University of California-Riverside; Riverside, Calif. 92521 (Pub)	8,381	84	53	4,212	13,596	5,946
University of California-San Diego; La Jolla, Calif. 92093-0337 (Pub)	15,140	50	50	4,212	13,596	5,946
University of California-Santa Barbara; Santa Barbara, Calif. 93106 (Pub)	16,281	78	53	3,988	13,562	6,899
University of California-Santa Cruz; Santa Cruz, Calif. 95064 (Pub)	8,629	83	60	4,212	13,596	5,946
University of Judaism; Los Angeles, Calif. 90077 (P)	105	83	62	13,910	13,910	7,290
University of La Verne; La Verne, Calif. 91750 (P)	2,953	74	57	15,500	15,500	4,820
University of Redlands; Redlands, Calif. 92373-0999 (P)	1,415	80	55	18,940	18,940	7,224
University of San Diego; San Diego, Calif. 92110-2492 (P)	4,356	81	57	21,360	21,360	
University of San Francisco; San Francisco, Calif. 94117-1080 (P)	4,695	76	63	15,850	15,850	7,260
University of Southern California; Los Angeles, Calif. 90089 (P)	15,430	46	49	20,078	20,078	6,748
University of the Pacific; Stockton, Calif. 95211 (P)	2,800	84	56	19,365	19,365	5,770
University of West Los Angeles; Culver City, Calif. 90230 (Pub)	181					
Western State Univ. College of Law-Orange County; Fullerton, Calif. 92631 (P)	227			12,780	12,780	
Westmont College; Santa Barbara, Calif. 93108 (P)	1,320	86	60	21,940	21,940	
Whittier College; Whittier, Calif. 90608-0634 (P)	1,301	70	55	23,847	23,847	
Woodbury University; Burbank, Calif. 91510 (P)	877	78	53	15,800	15,800	6,268
COLORADO						
Adams State College; Alamosa, Colo. 81102 (Pub)	2,039	86	60	1,494	5,428	4,424
Colorado Christian University; Lakewood, Colo. 80226 (P)	1,625	85	58	9,720	9,720	5,160
Colorado College; Colorado Springs, Colo. 80903 (P)	2,016	53	54	25,080	25,080	
Colorado School of Mines; Golden, Colo. 80401 (Pub)	2,405	80	24	4,540	14,468	4,920
Colorado State University; Fort Collins, Colo. 80523 (Pub)	18,477	78	51	2,258	9,480	4,878
Colorado Technical University; Colorado Springs, Colo. 80907 (P)	1,232	49	21	6,075	6,075	
Fort Lewis College; Durango, Colo. 81301 (Pub)	4,440	90	48	1,618	7,684	4,236
Johnson and Wales University-Vail; Vail, Colo. 81657 (P)	46	82	26	18,858	18,858	
Loretto Heights College; Denver, Colo. 80236 (P)	1,100			23,000	23,000	
Mesa State College; Grand Junction, Colo. 81502-2647 (Pub)	4,882	92	56	1,540	5,826	4,800
Metropolitan State College of Denver; Denver, Colo. 80217 (Pub)	17,624	83	56	1,445	5,914	3,906
Regis University; Denver, Colo. 80221-1099 (P)	1,178	82	54	15,600	15,600	6,200
United States Air Force Academy; USAF Academy, Colo. 80840 (Pub)	4,096	15	16	0	0	0
University of Colorado–Boulder; Boulder, Colo. 80309 (Pub)	20,006	80	47	2,877	14,927	4,545
University of Colorado–Colorado Springs; Colorado Springs, Colo. 80933-7150 (Pub)	4,700	76	59	2,154	8,716	4,790
University of Colorado–Denver; Denver, Colo. 80217 (Pub)	7,510	76	54	1,944	10,416	
University of Denver; Denver, Colo. 80208 (P)	3,491	82	58	16,740	16,740	5,538
University of Northern Colorado; Greeley, Colo. 80639 (Pub)	9,653	80	59	1,942	8,710	4,420
University of Southern Colorado; Pueblo, Colo. 81001 (Pub)	4,744	76	56	1,766	8,250	4,656
Western State College of Colorado; Gunnison, Colo. 81231 (Pub)	2,517	86	41	1,440	6,418	4,649
CONNECTICUT						
Albertus Magnus College; New Haven, Conn. 06511 (P)	1,404	67	66	13,264	13,264	6,136
Central Connecticut State University; New Britain, Conn. 06050 (Pub)	9,032	69	51	2,062	6,674	5,472
Charter Oak State College; Newington, Conn. 06111-2646 (Pub)	1,232		50			
Connecticut College; New London, Conn. 06320 (P)	1,808	40	58	29,475	29,475	
Eastern Connecticut State University; Willimantic, Conn. 06226 (Pub)	4,335	81	57	2,062	6,674	5,048
Fairfield University; Fairfield, Conn. 06430-5195 (P)	4,269	68	52	18,800	18,800	7,234
Quinnipiac College; Hamden, Conn. 06518-1940 (P)	4,197	62	66	15,740	15,740	7,590
Sacred Heart University; Fairfield, Conn. 06432 (P)	2,300	85	55	13,972	13,972	6,870
Saint Joseph College (Conn.); West Hartford, Conn. 06117 (P)	1,200	87	99	19,100	19,100	
Southern Connecticut State University; New Haven, Conn. 06515 (Pub)	7,567	75	57	2,062	6,674	5,794
Teikyo Post University; Waterbury, Conn. 06723-2540 (P)	1,550	83	66	17,600	17,600	
Trinity College (Conn.); Hartford, Conn. 06106 (P)	2,044	43	47	21,710	21,710	6,320
United States Coast Guard Academy; New London, Conn. 06320 (Pub)	827	11		3,000	3,000	
University of Bridgeport; Bridgeport, Conn. 06601 (P)	1,098	83	53	13,000	13,000	6,810
University of Connecticut; Storrs, Conn. 06269 (Pub)	11,437	70	51	4,158	12,676	5,544
University of Hartford; West Hartford, Conn. 06117-1599 (P)	5,387	78	52	17,190	17,190	7,200
University of New Haven; West Haven, Conn. 06516 (P)	2,885	84	37	13,500	13,500	6,160
Wesleyan University; Middletown, Conn. 06459-0265 (P)	2,796	33	52	27,940	27,940	

Institution name; city, state ZIP (control)	Students	Percent Accepted	Percent Women	Tuition In-state	Tuition Out-of-state	Room and board
Western Connecticut State University; Danbury, Conn. 06810-9972 (Pub)	4,428	74%	54%	$ 2,062	$ 6,674	$5,170
Yale University; New Haven, Conn. 06520 (P)	5,435	18	49	23,780	23,780	7,050
DELAWARE						
Delaware State University; Dover, Del. 19901 (Pub)	3,057	44	57	7,672	11,332	4,522
Goldey-Beacom College; Wilmington, Del. 19808 (P)	894	77	48	9,915	9,915	
University of Delaware; Newark, Del. 19716 (Pub)	17,916	65	58	4,120	11,750	4,770
Wesley College; Dover, Del. 19901 (P)		85		15,553	15,553	
Wilmington College (Del.); New Castle, Del. 19720 (P)	583		62	4,752	4,752	
DISTRICT OF COLUMBIA						
American University; Washington, D.C. 20016 (P)	5,427	79	59	19,200	19,200	7,655
Corcoran School of Art; Washington, D.C. 20006 (P)	514	54	59	13,440	13,440	4,000
Gallaudet University; Washington, D.C. 20002 (P)	1,251	62	56	10,800	10,800	
George Washington University; Washington, D.C. 20052 (P)	7,830	49	52	21,320	21,320	7,880
Georgetown University; Washington, D.C. 20057 (P)	6,177	21	53	22,248	22,248	8,416
Howard University; Washington, D.C. 20059 (P)	6,120	60	62	8,750	8,750	5,250
Mount Vernon College; Washington, D.C. 20007 (P)	341		99	22,770	22,770	
Southeastern University; Washington, D.C. 20024 (P)	175	64	58	6,660	6,660	
The Catholic University of America; Washington, D.C. 20064 (P)	2,316	69	55	17,325	17,325	7,360
Trinity College (D.C.); Washington, D.C. 20017-1094 (P)	1,069	76	100	19,930	19,930	
University of the District of Columbia; Washington, D.C. 20008 (Pub)	10,004		56	1,008	4,032	
FLORIDA						
Barry University; Miami Shores, Fla. 33161-6695 (P)	4,685	49	66	13,290	13,290	5,850
Bethune-Cookman College; Daytona Beach, Fla. 32114-3099 (P)	2,523	72	57	8,047	8,047	4,984
Clearwater Christian College; Clearwater, Fla. 34619 (P)	554	85		7,600	7,600	3,500
Eckerd College; St. Petersburg, Fla. 33711 (P)	1,443	76	57	17,500	17,500	4,810
Edward Waters College; Jacksonville, Fla. 32209 (P)				4,800		4,300
Embry–Riddle Aeronautical University (Fla.); Daytona Beach, Fla. 32114-3900 (P)	4,336	85	14	9,600	9,600	4,600
Flagler College; St. Augustine, Fla. 32085-1027 (P)	1,655	47	63	5,950	5,950	3,680
Florida A&M University; Tallahassee, Fla. 32307 (Pub)	9,878	60	58	1,891	7,898	3,458
Florida A&M University/Florida State University (FAMU/FSU); Tallahassee, Fla. 32307-3200 (Pub)	9,765	81	56	1,585	6,318	3,360
Florida Atlantic University; Boca Raton, Fla. 33431 (Pub)	15,288	74	59	2,022	7,940	4,680
Florida Institute of Technology; Melbourne, Fla. 32901-6975 (P)	1,843	85	31	15,510	15,510	4,870
Florida International University; Miami, Fla. 33199 (Pub)	24,136	75	56	1,790	6,695	4,380
Florida Memorial College; Miami, Fla. 33054 (P)	1,488		63	5,420	5,420	2,428
Florida Southern College; Lakeland, Fla. 33801-5698 (P)	1,775	76	59	11,114	11,114	5,600
Florida State University; Tallahassee, Fla. 32306 (Pub)	23,685	72	55	1,882	7,127	4,472
Jacksonville University; Jacksonville, Fla. 32211 (P)	1,857	64	54	13,360	13,360	4,900
Johnson and Wales University-North Miami; North Miami, Fla. 33181 (P)	1,054	79	40	15,378	15,378	3,930
Lynn University; Boca Raton, Fla. 33431-5598 (P)	1,638	77	55	16,700	16,700	6,250
New College of the University of South Florida; Sarasota, Fla. 34243-2197 (Pub)	604	62		2,475	10,513	4,242
Nova Southeastern University; Fort Lauderda, Fla. 33314-7721 (P)	4,040	78	70	10,350	10,350	5,797
Palm Beach Atlantic College; West Palm Beach, Fla. 33416 (P)	1,543	80	59	10,500	10,500	4,700
Ringling School of Art & Design; Sarasota, Fla. 34234 (P)	853	58	35	13,845	13,845	7,000
Rollins College; Winter Park, Fla. 32789-4499 (P)	1,480	70	59	24,430	24,430	
Saint John Vianney College Seminary; Miami, Fla. 33165 (P)		100		10,400	10,400	
Saint Leo College; Saint Leo, Fla. 33574 (P)	902	68	60	15,040	15,040	
Saint Thomas University; Miami, Fla. 33054 (P)	2,326	68	53	14,800	14,800	
Southeastern College of Assemblies of God; Lakeland, Fla. 33801-6099 (P)	1,069	77	49	4,350	4,350	3,274
Stetson University; DeLand, Fla. 32720 (P)	1,908	88	57	15,850	15,850	5,730
University of Central Florida; Orlando, Fla. 32816 (Pub)	23,729	65	54	1,829	7,074	3,610
University of Florida; Gainesville, Fla. 32611 (Pub)	31,535	59	50	1,926	7,843	
University of Miami; Coral Gables, Fla. 33124-4616 (P)	8,395	57	54	20,034	20,034	7,606
University of North Florida; Jacksonville, Fla. 32224 (Pub)	8,662	70	58	2,106	8,320	3,796
University of South Florida; Tampa, Fla. 33620-9951 (Pub)	25,775	66	57	2,085	8,002	4,830
University of Tampa; Tampa, Fla. 33606-1490 (P)	2,334	93	60	13,890	13,890	4,780
University of West Florida; Pensacola, Fla. 32514 (Pub)	6,389	89	59	1,985	7,902	2,144
Warner Southern College; Lake Wales, Fla. 33853-8725 (P)	646	53	57	7,938	7,938	4,043
Webber College; Babson Park, Fla. 33827 (P)	413		46	7,390	7,390	3,384
GEORGIA						
Agnes Scott College; Decatur, Ga. 30030 (P)	752	82	100	14,825	14,825	6,230
Albany State University; Albany, Ga. 31705 (Pub)	2,817	70	64	1,680	4,461	3,105
Armstrong Atlantic State University; Savannah, Ga. 31419 (Pub)	5,140	82	69	1,962	6,423	4,116

Institution name; city, state ZIP (control)	Students	Percent Accepted	Percent Women	Tuition In-state	Tuition Out-of-state	Room and board
Augusta State University; Augusta, Ga. 30904-2200 (Pub)	4,726	77%	64%	$ 1,680	$ 6,141	
Berry College; Mount Berry, Ga. 30149-5031 (P)	1,875	69	62	14,058	14,058	
Brenau University; Gainesville, Ga. 30501 (P)	1,567	74	85	11,280	11,280	$6,610
Brewton-Parker College; Mount Vernon, Ga. 30445 (P)	1,682	70	54	5,560	5,560	2,250
Clark Atlanta University; Atlanta, Ga. 30314 (P)	4,391	70	70	9,650	9,650	5,800
Columbus State University; Columbus, Ga. 31907 (Pub)	4,584	73	62	1,941	6,402	4,130
Covenant College; Lookout Mount, Ga. 30750 (P)	884	83	54	13,400	13,400	4,250
Emory University; Atlanta, Ga. 30322 (P)	5,996	44	55	21,870	21,870	7,100
Fort Valley State College; Fort Valley, Ga. 31030 (Pub)	2,124			1,833	4,677	3,075
Georgia College & State University; Milledgeville, Ga. 31061 (Pub)	4,296	97	63	1,921	5,800	3,909
Georgia Institute of Technology; Atlanta, Ga. 30332-0320 (Pub)	9,524	61	28	2,310	9,240	5,700
Georgia Southern University; Statesboro, Ga. 30460 (Pub)	14,000	70	45	2,055	5,934	3,735
Georgia Southwestern College; Americus, Ga. 31709 (Pub)	2,071	75	63	2,067	5,946	3,130
Georgia State University; Atlanta, Ga. 30303 (Pub)	16,828	60	61	2,250	9,000	3,789
Kennesaw State College; Marietta, Ga. 30061 (Pub)	10,994	86	59	1,730	6,950	
LaGrange College; LaGrange, Ga. 30240 (P)	922	79	59	13,911	13,911	
Mercer University; Macon, Ga. 31207 (P)	4,019	87	64	15,462	15,462	5,070
Mercer University Atlanta; Atlanta, Ga. 30341 (P)	235			7,650	7,650	
Morehouse College; Atlanta, Ga. 30314 (P)	3,000	68	0	13,676	13,676	
Morris Brown College; Atlanta, Ga. 30314 (P)	1,891	66	58	11,994	11,994	
North Georgia College; Dahlonega, Ga. 30597 (Pub)	2,792	66		1,584	5,427	3,157
Oglethorpe University; Atlanta, Ga. 30319 (P)	1,220	94	60	16,660	16,660	5,140
Paine College; Augusta, Ga. 30910 (P)	812			9,240	9,240	
Piedmont College; Demorest, Ga. 30535-0010 (P)	1,010	66	61	8,200	8,200	3,930
Savannah College of Art & Design; Savannah, Ga. 31402-3146 (P)	2,947	75	41	18,800	18,800	6,375
Savannah State University; Savannah, Ga. 31402 (Pub)	2,822		56	2,130	6,009	3,495
Shorter College; Rome, Ga. 30165-4298 (P)	836	83	65	8,150	8,150	4,050
Southern Polytechnic State University; Marietta, Ga. 30060 (Pub)	3,340	80	17	1,851	5,730	3,525
Spelman College; Atlanta, Ga. 30314 (P)	1,899	54	100	14,280	14,280	
State University of West Georgia; Carrollton, Ga. 30118 (Pub)	6,172	86	61	1,730	5,220	3,532
The Atlanta College of Art; Atlanta, Ga. 30309 (P)	395	86		14,700	14,700	
Toccoa Falls College; Toccoa Falls, Ga. 30598 (P)	987	69	54	7,728	7,728	3,782
University of Georgia; Athens, Ga. 30602 (Pub)	22,000	56	54	2,930	9,621	9,860
Valdosta State University; Valdosta, Ga. 31698 (Pub)	8,524	73	59	2,140	6,600	3,525
Wesleyan College; Macon, Ga. 31210 (P)	477	70	100	15,000	15,000	5,300
West Georgia College, Carrollton, Ga. 30118 (Pub)	6,189	65	60	1,989	5,868	3,471
HAWAII						
Brigham Young University (Hawaii); Laie Oahu, Hawaii 96762 (P)	2,294	47	62	2,665	2,665	4,900
Chaminade University of Honolulu; Honolulu, Hawaii 96816 (P)	1,920	84	54	15,730	15,730	
Hawaii Pacific University; Honolulu, Hawaii 96813 (P)	7,286	71	51	7,920	7,920	7,800
University of Hawaii-Hilo; Hilo, Hawaii 96720-4091 (Pub)	2,723	64	61	1,344	6,960	3,400
University of Hawaii-Manoa; Honolulu, Hawaii 96822 (Pub)	12,029	69	54	2,928	9,408	5,078
University of Hawaii-West Oahu; Pearl City, Hawaii 96782 (Pub)	648			1,752	6,888	
IDAHO						
Albertson College; Caldwell, Idaho 83605 (P)	671	87	53	15,600	15,600	4,050
Boise State University; Boise, Idaho 83725 (Pub)	13,287	87	57	1,964	7,310	3,370
Idaho State University; Pocatello, Idaho 83209 (Pub)	9,876	85	56	726	5,674	3,580
Lewis-Clark State College; Lewiston, Idaho 83501 (Pub)	2,981	85	59	1,868	6,830	3,130
Northwest Nazarene College; Nampa, Idaho 83686 (P)	1,116	46	57	12,141	12,141	3,519
University of Idaho; Moscow, Idaho 83844-4140 (Pub)	11,027	92	43	2,136	6,000	3,830
ILLINOIS						
Augustana College (Ill.); Rock Island, Ill. 61201-2296 (P)	2,277	81	59	16,017	16,017	4,842
Aurora University; Aurora, Ill. 60506 (P)	1,270	80	60	11,700	11,700	4,491
Barat College; Lake Forest, Ill. 60045 (P)	730	95	77	12,950	12,950	5,100
Benedictine University; Lisle, Ill. 60532 (P)	2,838	92	52	6,300	6,300	4,791
Blackburn College; Carlinville, Ill. 62626 (P)	448	74	46	7,795	7,795	3,240
Bradley University; Peoria, Ill. 61625 (P)	4,916	89	53	13,240	13,240	5,150
Chicago State University; Chicago, Ill. 60628 (Pub)	7,237	43	70	2,158	7,253	5,825
Columbia College (Ill); Chicago, Ill. 60605-1996 (P)	5,355		48	9,544	9,544	4,750
Concordia University (Ill); River Forest, Ill. 60305-1499 (P)	1,170	95	68	11,904	11,904	4,852
DePaul University; Chicago, Ill. 60604 (P)	9,691	78	57	18,250	18,250	
Dominican University; River Forest, Ill. 60305 (P)	913	85	72	13,600	13,600	4,880
Eastern Illinois University; Charleston, Ill. 61920-3099 (Pub)	10,225	75	57	2,152	6,564	3,919
East-West University; Chicago, Ill. 60605 (P)	342			6,450	6,450	
Elmhurst College; Elmhurst, Ill. 60181 (P)	2,842	72	65	12,770	12,770	5,104
Eureka College; Eureka, Ill. 61530 (P)	502	80	49	14,540	14,540	4,400
Greenville College; Greenville, Ill. 62246-0159 (P)	955	75	56	12,576	12,576	4,750
Illinois College; Jacksonville, Ill. 62650 (P)	909	84	57	9,500	9,500	4,200

Institution name; city, state ZIP (control)	Students	Percent Accepted	Percent Women	Tuition In-state	Tuition Out-of-state	Room and board
Illinois Institute of Technology; Chicago, Ill. 60616 (P)	2,262	68%	18%	$17,000	$17,000	$5,090
Illinois State University; Normal, Ill. 61790-2200 (Pub)	17,366	79	57	3,038	9,113	3,975
Illinois Wesleyan University; Bloomington, Ill. 61702-2900 (P)	2,021	60	53	18,375	18,375	4,825
Judson College (Ill.); Elgin, Ill. 60123 (P)	331	77		15,160	15,160	
Kendall College; Evanston, Ill. 60201 (P)	497			13,929	13,929	
Knox College; Galesburg, Ill. 61401 (P)	1,195	79	55	18,855	18,855	5,076
Lake Forest College; Lake Forest, Ill. 60045 (P)	1,171	78	55	19,800	19,800	5,000
Lewis University; Romeoville, Ill. 60441 (P)	3,078	85	56	14,416	14,416	
Loyola University of Chicago; Chicago, Ill. 60611 (P)	7,669	79	63	20,610	20,610	
MacMurray College; Jacksonville, Ill. 62650 (P)	669	76	57	14,940	14,940	
Malinckrodt College; Wilmette, Ill. 60091 (P)				4,500	4,500	
McKendree College; Lebanon, Ill. 62254 (P)	1,848	91	61	10,500	10,500	4,170
Mennonite College of Nursing; Bloomington, Ill. 61701 (P)	175			11,390	11,390	
Millikin University; Decatur, Ill. 62522 (P)	1,997	86	57	13,988	13,988	5,070
Monmouth College (Ill.); Monmouth, Ill. 61462 (P)	1,043	79	60	15,120	15,120	4,410
National College of Chiropractic; Lombard, Ill. 60148 (P)	850			12,349	12,349	
National-Louis University; Evanston, Ill. 60201 (P)	3,076	76	72	14,928	14,928	
North Central College; Naperville, Ill. 60566 (P)	2,267	82	58	13,725	13,725	4,950
North Park University; Chicago, Ill. 60625 (P)	1,582	87	62	15,420	15,420	5,030
Northeastern Illinois University; Chicago, Ill. 60625 (Pub)	7,524	69	61	2,789	7,157	
Northern Illinois University; DeKalb, Ill. 60115 (Pub)	15,855	72	54	4,347	9,106	4,310
Northwestern University; Evanston, Ill. 60204-3060 (P)	7,670	29	52	20,244	20,244	6,630
Olivet Nazarene University; Bourbonnais, Ill. 60901 (P)	1,700	82	55	11,178	11,178	4,696
Parks College of Saint Louis University; Cahokia, Ill. 62206 (P)	803		10	19,010	19,010	
Principia College; Elsah, Ill. 62028 (P)	552	79	53	14,481	14,481	5,586
Quincy University; Quincy, Ill. 62301 (P)	1,051	76	52	13,040	13,040	4,390
Rockford College; Rockford, Ill. 61108 (P)	1,043	41	69	20,400	20,400	
Roosevelt University; Chicago, Ill. 60605 (P)	4,180	75	61	15,496	15,496	
Saint Xavier University; Chicago, Ill. 60655 (P)	2,283	83	72	12,450	12,450	5,184
School of the Art Institute of Chicago; Chicago, Ill. 60603 (P)	1,430	76	57	21,300	21,300	
Southern Illinois University-Carbondale; Carbondale, Ill. 62901-6806 (Pub)	17,817	67	43	2,850	8,550	3,745
Southern Illinois University-Edwardsville; Edwardsville, Ill. 62026 (Pub)	8,610	86	58	2,081	6,242	4,066
Trinity Christian College; Palos Heights, Ill. 60463 (P)	618	94	65	12,260	12,260	4,870
Trinity International University; Deerfield, Ill. 60015 (P)	1,177	72	55	12,840	12,840	4,800
University of Chicago; Chicago, Ill. 60637 (P)	3,690	62	47	22,902	22,902	7,606
University of Illinois at Urbana-Champaign; Urbana, Ill. 61801 (Pub)	36,019	68	35	3,150	8,580	5,078
University of Illinois-Chicago; Chicago, Ill. 60607-7128 (Pub)	16,283	62	54	2,956	8,868	5,526
Vandercook College of Music; Chicago, Ill. 60616 (P)	62		40	10,000	10,000	5,100
West Suburban College of Nursing; Oak Park, Ill. 60302 (P)	141			15,823	15,823	
Western Illinois University; Macomb, Ill. 61455-1390 (Pub)	9,703	70	51	2,119	6,358	3,838
Wheaton College (Ill.); Wheaton, Ill. 60187-5593 (P)	2,321	55	51	17,650	17,650	
INDIANA						
Anderson University; Anderson, Ind. 46012-3495 (P)	1,929	77	60	13,110	13,110	4,330
Ball State University; Muncie, Ind. 47306 (Pub)	16,983	89	53	3,316	8,872	4,120
Bethel College (Ind.); Mischawaka, Ind. 46545 (P)	1,443	85	67	11,500	11,500	3,700
Butler University; Indianapolis, Ind. 46208 (P)	3,165	85	60	16,280	16,280	5,570
Calumet College of Saint Joseph; Whiting, Ind. 46394 (P)	1,125		69	5,460	5,460	
DePauw University; Greencastle, Ind. 46135 (P)	2,334	88	55	17,650	17,650	5,840
Earlham College; Richmond, Ind. 47374 (P)	1,025	83	58	18,056	18,056	4,544
Franklin College; Franklin, Ind. 46131-2598 (P)	917	86	53	12,210	12,210	4,080
Goshen College; Goshen, Ind. 46526-4794 (P)	1,014	42	60	11,950	11,950	4,150
Grace College and Seminary; Winona Lake, Ind. 46590 (P)	765	88	53	14,102	14,102	
Hanover College; Hanover, Ind. 47243 (P)	1,092	86	53	10,175	10,175	4,440
Huntington College; Huntington, Ind. 46750 (P)	767	87	57	15,500	15,500	
Indiana Institute of Technology; Fort Wayne, Ind. 46803 (P)	1,380	65	35	11,500	11,500	4,430
Indiana State University; Terre Haute, Ind. 47809 (Pub)	9,180	88	52	3,196	7,916	4,143
Indiana University East; Richmond, Ind. 47374 (Pub)	2,351	100		2,611	6,773	
Indiana University Northwest; Gary, Ind. 46408 (Pub)	4,620	53		2,823	7,326	
Indiana University-Purdue Univ. Fort Wayne; Fort Wayne, Ind. 46805 (Pub)	9,815	98	56	3,213	7,361	
Indiana Wesleyan University; Marion, Ind. 46953 (P)	1,947	72	62	14,302	14,302	
Manchester College; N. Manchester, Ind. 46962 (P)	1,056	83	49	13,180	13,180	4,770
Marian College; Indianapolis, Ind. 46222 (P)	1,352	56	66	15,652	15,652	
Oakland City University; Oakland City, Ind. 47660 (P)	1,016	96	46	10,946	10,946	
Purdue University-Calumet; Hammond, Ind. 46323 (Pub)	8,345		51	2,262	5,688	5,345
Purdue University-West Lafayette; West Lafayett, Ind. 47907 (Pub)	29,122	89	43	3,352	11,184	4,800
Rose-Hulman Institute of Technology; Terre Haute, Ind. 47803 (P)	1,480	68		23,300	23,300	
Saint Joseph's College (Ind.); Rensselaer, Ind. 47978 (P)	926	82	55	13,470	13,470	4,900

Institution name; city, state ZIP (control)	Students	Percent Accepted	Percent Women	Tuition In-state	Tuition Out-of-state	Room and board
Saint Mary-of-the-Woods College; Saint Mary-of-the-Woods, Ind. 47876 (P)		86%		$16,510	$16,510	
Saint Mary's College (Ind.); Notre Dame, Ind. 46556 (P)	1,347	82	99%	14,738	14,738	$5,197
Taylor University; Upland, Ind. 46989-1001 (P)	1,884	69	53	13,270	13,270	4,410
Tri-State University; Angola, Ind. 46703 (P)	1,116	81	29	11,900	11,900	4,950
University of Evansville; Evansville, Ind. 47722 (P)	3,085	91	56	14,400	14,400	4,560
University of Indianapolis; Indianapolis, Ind. 46227 (P)	2,846	88	68	13,470	13,470	4,690
University of Notre Dame; Notre Dame, Ind. 46556 (P)	7,838	40	45	19,800	19,800	5,060
University of Saint Francis; Fort Wayne, Ind. 46808 (P)	794	82	65	10,310	10,310	4,270
University of Southern Indiana; Evansville, Ind. 47712 (Pub)	7,870	99	60	2,700	6,617	2,100
Valparaiso University; Valparaiso, Ind. 46383 (P)	2,887	88	56	14,560	14,560	3,930
Wabash College; Crawfordsville, Ind. 47933-0352 (P)	793	69	0	15,400	15,400	4,780
IOWA						
Briar Cliff College; Sioux City, Iowa 51104 (P)	1,011	83	68	15,192	15,192	
Buena Vista University; Storm Lake, Iowa 50588 (P)	2,473	90	62	18,583	18,583	
Central College; Pella, Iowa 50219 (P)	1,236	86	57	13,232	13,232	4,592
Clarke College; Dubuque, Iowa 52001-3198 (P)	1,079	85	68	12,688	12,688	4,886
Coe College; Cedar Rapids, Iowa 52402 (P)	1,253	84	54	16,800	16,800	4,760
Cornell College; Mount Vernon, Iowa 52314-1098 (P)	1,079	81	58	17,770	17,770	4,850
Divine Word College; Epworth, Iowa 52045 (P)				8,700	8,700	
Dordt College; Sioux Center, Iowa 51250 (P)	1,301	93	50	14,480	14,480	3,030
Drake University; Des Moines, Iowa 50311 (P)	3,417	93	61	16,000	16,000	4,870
Grand View College; Des Moines, Iowa 50316-1599 (P)	1,433	85	65	11,340	11,340	3,775
Grinnell College; Grinnell, Iowa 50112 (P)	1,363	69	56	17,998	17,998	5,414
Iowa State University; Ames, Iowa 50011 (Pub)	20,717	91	43	2,666	8,944	3,958
Iowa Wesleyan College; Mount Pleasan, Iowa 52641 (P)	804	82	66	11,640	11,640	3,900
Loras College; Dubuque, Iowa 52004 (P)	1,736	81	52	15,800	15,800	
Luther College; Decorah, Iowa 52101-1042 (P)	2,400	92	60	20,730	20,730	
Maharishi International University; Fairfield, Iowa 52557 (P)		99	43	18,560	18,560	
Marycrest International University; Davenport, Iowa 52804 (P)	905	63	60	14,974	14,974	
Morningside College; Sioux City, Iowa 51106 (P)	1,178	94	57	15,130	15,130	
Mount Mercy College; Cedar Rapids, Iowa 52402 (P)	1,131	87	70	12,440	12,440	3,800
Mount Saint Clare College; Clinton, Iowa 52733-2967 (P)	523	86	60	11,500	11,500	4,020
Northwestern College (Iowa); Orange City, Iowa 51041 (P)	1,177	93	59	15,125	15,125	
Saint Ambrose University; Davenport, Iowa 52803-2898 (P)	1,970	85	58	17,660	17,660	4,810
Simpson College (Iowa); Indianola, Iowa 50125 (P)	1,958	87	55	13,095	13,095	4,290
University of Dubuque; Dubuque, Iowa 52001 (P)	672	85	45	16,490	16,490	
University of Iowa; Iowa City, Iowa 52242 (Pub)	18,913	84	54	2,666	9,788	4,152
University of Northern Iowa; Cedar Falls, Iowa 50614 (Pub)	11,767	84	57	2,666	7,220	3,636
Upper Iowa University; Fayette, Iowa 52142 (P)	640	74	20	10,240	10,240	3,958
Wartburg College; Waverly, Iowa 50677 (P)	1,528	85	57	14,140	14,140	4,100
William Penn College; Oskaloosa, Iowa 52577 (P)	737	79	46	11,320	11,320	3,840
KANSAS						
Baker University; Baldwin City, Kans. 66006 (P)	1,424	79	51	11,300	11,300	4,650
Benedictine College; Atchison, Kans. 66002 (P)	873	91	46	11,500	11,500	4,450
Bethany College (Kans.); Lindsborg, Kans. 67456-1897 (P)	667	60	47	10,540	10,540	3,610
Bethel College (Kans.); North Newton, Kans. 67117 (P)	610	92	57	10,290	10,290	4,200
Emporia State University; Emporia, Kans. 66801 (Pub)	4,495	100	61	1,406	5,516	3,480
Fort Hays State University; Hays, Kans. 67601 (Pub)	4,346	98	53	2,061	6,530	3,600
Friends University; Wichita, Kans. 67213 (P)	1,968	61	56	12,645	12,645	
Kansas State University; Manhattan, Kans. 66506 (Pub)	16,936	66	47	1,965	8,270	3,640
Kansas Wesleyan University; Salina, Kans. 67401 (P)	675	72		12,620	12,620	
McPherson College; McPherson, Kans. 67460 (P)	426		47	14,090	14,090	
Mid America Nazarene University; Olathe, Kans. 66062 (P)	1,266	100	55	11,368	11,368	
Newman University; Wichita, Kans. 67213 (P)	1,517	80	67	12,270	12,270	
Ottawa University; Ottawa, Kans. 66067-3399 (P)	521	62	43	9,560	9,560	3,620
Pittsburg State University; Pittsburg, Kans. 66762 (Pub)	4,973	93	48	2,016	6,280	3,316
Saint Mary College (Kans.); Leavenworth, Kans. 66048 (P)	839	96	72	14,700	14,700	
Southwestern College; Winfield, Kans. 67156 (P)	810	94	52	9,860	9,860	4,004
Sterling College; Sterling, Kans. 67579 (P)	457	70	47	10,076	10,076	3,884
Tabor College; Hillsboro, Kans. 67063 (P)	516	67	49	15,480	15,480	
University of Kansas; Lawrence, Kans. 66045 (Pub)	16,659	62	51	1,965	8,269	3,850
University of Kansas, Medical Center; Kansas City, Kans. 66160-7116 (Pub)				1,965	8,270	
Washburn University; Topeka, Kans. 66621 (Pub)	5,370	96	61	6,050	6,590	3,950
Wichita State University; Wichita, Kans. 67260 (Pub)	10,536	76	57	1,665	7,195	3,800
KENTUCKY						
Alice Lloyd College; Pippa Passes, Ky. 41844 (P)	501	51	50	6,360	6,360	2,680
Asbury College; Wilmore, Ky. 40390 (P)	1,258	89	58	11,880	11,880	3,390
Bellarmine College; Louisville, Ky. 40205 (P)	2,275	94	64	11,600	11,600	3,820
Berea College; Berea, Ky. 40404 (P)	1,464	35	58	3,168	3,168	
Brescia College; Owensboro, Ky. 42301 (P)	621	84	64	8,790	8,790	3,764
Campbellsville University; Campbellsville, Ky. 42718-2799 (P)	1,496	66	56	11,600	11,600	

Institution name; city, state ZIP (control)	Students	Percent Accepted	Percent Women	Tuition In-state	Tuition Out-of-state	Room and board
Centre College; Danville, Ky. 40422 (P)	1,001	85%	49%	$19,400	$19,400	$4,800
Cumberland College; Williamsburg, Ky. 40769 (P)	1,596	64	55	8,798	8,798	3,976
Eastern Kentucky University; Richmond, Ky. 40475 (Pub)	13,424	95	57	2,060	5,660	
Georgetown College; Georgetown, Ky. 40324 (P)	1,309	89	57	10,600	10,600	4,050
Kentucky Christian College; Grayson, Ky. 41143 (P)	529	86		9,212	9,212	
Kentucky State University; Frankfort, Ky. 40601 (Pub)	2,203	63	59	1,920	5,760	3,276
Kentucky Wesleyan College; Owensboro, Ky. 42301 (P)	777	85	58	9,220	9,220	4,500
Lindsey Wilson College; Columbia, Ky. 42728 (P)	1,006		51	8,640	8,640	4,230
Morehead State University; Morehead, Ky. 40351 (Pub)	6,823	89	57	2,270	6,110	2,400
Murray State University; Murray, Ky. 42071-0009 (Pub)	7,120	66	55	2,300	6,140	3,540
Northern Kentucky University; Highland Heig, Ky. 41099 (Pub)	10,602	100	59	2,120	5,720	3,439
Pikeville College; Pikeville, Ky. 41501 (P)	814	100		9,550	9,550	
Spalding University; Louisville, Ky. 40203 (P)	1,128	85	81	10,300	10,300	2,790
Thomas More College; Crestview Hil, Ky. 41017 (P)	1,324	81	56	11,578	11,578	4,500
Transylvania University; Lexington, Ky. 40508-1797 (P)	918	93	54	13,400	13,400	4,990
University of Kentucky; Lexington, Ky. 40506 (Pub)	17,008	78	51	2,400	7,200	3,388
University of Louisville; Louisville, Ky. 40292-0001 (Pub)	14,548	89	53	2,400	7,200	4,982
Western Kentucky University; Bowling Green, Ky. 42101 (Pub)	12,338	97	58	1,920	5,760	
LOUISIANA						
Centenary College of Louisiana; Shreveport, La. 71134-1188 (P)	743	85	55	16,150	16,150	
Dillard University; New Orleans, La. 70122 (P)	1,584	90	78	8,500	8,500	4,464
Grambling State University; Grambling, La. 71245 (Pub)	6,828	76	58	2,208	7,358	2,636
Louisiana College; Pineville, La. 71359 (P)	1,003	81	59	6,210	6,210	3,112
Louisiana State University and A&M College; Baton Rouge, La. 70803 (Pub)	22,714	79	52	2,301	5,901	3,772
Louisiana State University-Baton Rouge; Baton Rouge, La. 70803 (Pub)	22,714	79	52	2,711	6,311	3,772
Louisiana State University-Shreveport; Shreveport, La. 71115 (Pub)	3,354	99	70	1,950	5,290	1,827
Louisiana Tech University; Ruston, La. 71272 (Pub)	7,997	98	48	2,367	5,367	
Loyola University New Orleans; New Orleans, La. 70118 (P)	3,380	91	61	13,466	13,466	6,040
McNeese State University; Lake Charles, La. 70609 (Pub)	7,045	99	58	2,012	5,542	2,310
Nicholls State University; Thibodaux, La. 70310 (Pub)	6,355	92	59	2,336	5,376	2,820
Northeast Louisiana University; Monroe, La. 71209 (Pub)	9,800	92	60	1,644	4,044	3,380
Northwestern State University of Louisiana; Natchitoches, La. 71497 (Pub)	8,303	100	64	2,030	6,320	2,416
Our Lady of Holy Cross College; New Orleans, La. 70131 (P)	1,134	99	77	5,280	5,280	
Saint Joseph Seminary College; St. Benedict, La. 70457 (P)	62			10,200	10,200	
Southeastern Louisiana University; Hammond, La. 70402 (Pub)	13,571	91	60	2,200	5,464	2,400
Southern University and Agricultural and Mechanical College; Shreveport, La. 71107 (Pub)	1,345		69	1,104	2,394	
Southern University of New Orleans; New Orleans, La. 70126 (P)	4,500			1,662		
Southern University-Baton Rouge; Baton Rouge, La. 70813 (Pub)	7,976		57	2,028	4,808	3,228
Tulane University; New Orleans, La. 70118-5680 (P)	5,174	76	66	23,204	23,204	6,710
University of New Orleans; New Orleans, La. 70148 (Pub)	11,891	88	57	2,362	7,888	3,150
University of Southwestern Louisiana; Lafayette, La. 70504-1008 (Pub)	15,611	99	57	1,650	6,882	
Xavier University of Louisiana; New Orleans, La. 70125 (P)	2,994	91	71	8,100	8,100	4,700
MAINE						
Bates College; Lewiston, Maine 04240 (P)	1,611	36	51	28,650	28,650	
Bowdoin College; Brunswick, Maine 04011 (P)	1,605	34	50	22,460	22,460	6,115
Colby College; Waterville, Maine 04901-8840 (P)	1,753	34	52	30,420	30,420	
College of the Atlantic; Bar Harbor, Maine 04609 (P)	286	60	67	18,048	18,048	5,265
Husson College; Bangor, Maine 04401 (P)	952	82	63	8,700	8,700	4,740
Maine College of Art; Portland, Maine 04101 (P)	283	88	53	19,920	19,920	
Maine Maritime Academy; Castine, Maine 04420 (Pub)	635	78		4,374	8,029	5,022
Nasson College; Springvale, Maine 04083 (P)		66	56	6,300	6,300	
Saint Joseph's College (Maine); Windham, Maine 04062-1198 (P)	744		64	11,340	11,340	5,530
Thomas College; Waterville, Maine 04901 (P)	731	96	62	10,850	10,850	5,025
Unity College; Unity, Maine 04988-0532 (P)	523	89		15,380	15,380	
University of Maine-Augusta; Augusta, Maine 04330-9410 (Pub)	7,846			2,400	6,210	
University of Maine-Farmington; Farmington, Maine 04938 (Pub)	2,337	74	67	3,300	8,070	4,412
University of Maine-Fort Kent; Fort Kent, Maine 04743 (Pub)	767	87	61	3,030	7,410	3,910
University of Maine-Machias; Machias, Maine 04654 (Pub)	884	81	63	3,030	7,410	4,185
University of Maine-Orono; Orono, Maine 04469-5713 (Pub)	6,962	75	48	3,870	10,950	5,152
University of Maine-Presque Isle; Presque Isle, Maine 04769 (Pub)	1,413	80	60	3,570	10,110	3,970
University of New England; Biddeford, Maine 04005 (P)	1,386	73	74	14,320	14,320	5,595

Institution name; city, state ZIP (control)	Students	Percent Accepted	Percent Women	Tuition In-state	Tuition Out-of-state	Room and board
University of Southern Maine; Gorham, Maine 04038-1088 (Pub)	8,217	72%	48%	$ 3,540	$ 9,810	$4,875
Westbrook College; Portland, Maine 04103 (P)	458	66		14,320	14,320	5,820
MARYLAND						
Baltimore Hebrew University; Baltimore, Md. 21215 (P)	204		68	4,800	4,800	
Bowie State University; Bowie, Md. 20715 (Pub)	2,960	34	61	2,814	5,542	4,427
Capitol College; Laurel, Md. 20708 (P)	634	93	18	10,512	10,512	3,146
College of Notre Dame of Maryland; Baltimore, Md. 21210 (P)	2,353	83	92	13,846	13,846	6,130
Columbia Union College; Takoma Park, Md. 20912 (P)	1,172	79	60	14,940	14,940	
Coppin State College; Baltimore, Md. 21216 (Pub)	2,931	55	64	2,867	6,872	4,884
Frostburg State University; Frostburg, Md. 21532 (Pub)	4,305	76	51	3,092	7,352	5,034
Goucher College; Baltimore, Md. 21204-2794 (P)	1,085	78	73	19,450	19,450	7,015
Hood College; Frederick, Md. 21701 (P)	1,022	77	88	16,700	16,700	3,700
Johns Hopkins University; Baltimore, Md. 21218 (P)	4,702	40	38	26,705	26,705	
Loyola College (Md.); Baltimore, Md. 21210 (P)	3,284	70	55	18,200	18,200	7,240
Maryland Institute, College of Art; Baltimore, Md. 21217 (P)	991	63	54	17,250	17,250	5,740
Morgan State University; Baltimore, Md. 21239 (Pub)	5,356	47		1,853	4,405	5,296
Mount Saint Mary's College (Md.); Emmitsburg, Md. 21727 (P)	1,398	82	53	15,900	15,900	6,450
Peabody Conservatory of Music-John Hopkins University; Baltimore, Md. 21202 (P)	600			24,640	24,640	
Saint John's College (Md.); Annapolis, Md. 21404 (P)	455	65		21,990	21,990	6,100
Saint Mary's College of Maryland; St. Mary's City, Md. 20686 (Pub)	1,682	61	59	5,800	10,050	5,645
Salisbury State University; Salisbury, Md. 21801 (Pub)	5,391	59	58	2,856	7,066	5,390
Sojourner Douglass College; Baltimore, Md. 21205 (P)	262			3,190	3,190	
Towson University; Towson, Md. 21252-0001 (Pub)	13,366	64	59	3,080	8,158	5,044
United States Naval Academy; Annapolis, Md. 21402 (Pub)	3,994	17	16	0	0	0
University of Baltimore; Baltimore, Md. 21201 (Pub)	1,925		53	4,460	10,589	
University of Maryland-Baltimore County; Baltimore, Md. 21228 (Pub)	8,808	61	50	3,890	8,298	5,456
University of Maryland-College Park; College Park, Md. 20742 (Pub)	24,454	65	48	3,894	10,416	5,667
University of Maryland-Eastern Shore; Princess Anne, Md. 21853 (Pub)	2,862	75	58	2,577	7,219	4,530
Villa Julie College; Stevenson, Md. 21153 (P)	1,000		82	9,400	9,400	3,500
Washington College; Chestertown, Md. 21620 (P)	1,050	84	57	18,750	18,750	5,740
Western Maryland College; Westminster, Md. 21157 (P)	1,510	83	56	22,200	22,200	5,350
MASSACHUSETTS						
American International College; Springfield, Mass. 01109 (P)	1,426	77	52	11,800	11,800	5,692
Amherst College; Amherst, Mass. 01002 (P)	1,642	20		23,730	23,730	6,280
Anna Maria College; Paxton, Mass. 01612-1198 (P)	868	88	60	11,600	11,600	5,256
Assumption College; Worcester, Mass. 01615 (P)	2,221	81	63	14,700	14,700	6,100
Atlantic Union College; South Lancaster, Mass. 01561 (P)	1,193	94	52	12,125	12,125	3,900
Babson College; Babson Park, Mass. 02157-0310 (P)	1,692	49		20,360	20,360	8,110
Bentley College; Waltham, Mass. 02154-4705 (P)	4,134	66	45	17,000	17,000	7,800
Berklee College of Music; Boston, Mass. 02215 (P)	2,933	75	22	22,880	22,880	
Boston College; Chestnut Hill, Mass. 02167 (P)	8,921	39		20,760	20,760	7,770
Boston Conservatory; Boston, Mass. 02215 (P)	333	45	73	15,300	15,300	7,150
Boston University; Boston, Mass. 02215 (P)	15,394	53	57	22,830	22,830	7,870
Bradford College; Haverhill, Mass. 01835-7393 (P)	586	80	63	16,500	16,500	6,850
Brandeis University; Waltham, Mass. 02254-9110 (P)	3,036	54	56	23,360	23,360	6,970
Bridgewater State College; Bridgewater, Mass. 02325 (Pub)	7,364	69	60	1,270	5,950	4,343
Clark University; Worcester, Mass. 01610-1477 (P)	1,903	77	70	21,300	21,300	4,150
College of the Holy Cross; Worcester, Mass. 01610-2395 (P)	2,730	50	53	21,600	21,600	7,100
Curry College; Milton, Mass. 02186 (P)	1,442	81	51	15,860	15,860	6,050
Eastern Nazarene College; Quincy, Mass. 02170 (P)	1,508	78		13,860	13,860	
Elms College; Chicopee, Mass. 01013 (P)	883	93	95	12,950	12,950	5,000
Emerson College; Boston, Mass. 02116-1511 (P)	2,983	60	58	18,112	18,112	8,480
Emmanuel College; Boston, Mass. 02115 (P)	1,353	86	85	20,225	20,225	
Endicott College; Beverly, Mass. 01915 (P)	1,230	83	72	12,970	12,970	6,885
Fitchburg State College; Fitchburg, Mass. 01420 (Pub)	2,800	59	58	1,270	6,450	4,410
Framingham State College; Framingham, Mass. 01701 (Pub)	4,261	70	63	1,210	6,450	4,000
Gordon College; Wenham, Mass. 01984 (P)	1,348	79	65	15,100	15,100	5,295
Hampshire College; Amherst, Mass. 01002 (P)	1,152	66		24,280	24,280	6,435
Harvard and Radcliffe Colleges; Cambridge, Mass. 02138 (P)	6,630	11	46	21,342	21,342	7,514
Hellenic College; Brookline, Mass. 02146 (P)	64	63		7,600	7,600	5,900
Lesley College; Cambridge, Mass. 02138 (P)	1,478	75	87	14,300	14,300	6,700
Massachusetts College of Art; Boston, Mass. 02115 (Pub)	2,178	49	61	1,260	7,400	6,400
Massachusetts College of Liberal Arts; North Adams, Mass. 01247 (Pub)	1,552	63	59	3,377	8,617	4,900
Massachusetts College of Pharmacy & Allied Health; Boston, Mass. 02215 (P)	1,200		61	14,900	14,900	7,800

Institution name; city, state ZIP (control)	Students	Percent Accepted	Percent Women	Tuition In-state	Tuition Out-of-state	Room and board
Massachusetts Institute of Technology; Cambridge, Mass. 02139 (P)	4,828	25%	39%	$27,150	$27,150	
Massachusetts Maritime Academy; Buzzards Bay, Mass. 02532 (Pub)	791			1,390	6,634	$3,960
Merrimack College; North Andover, Mass. 01845 (P)	2,000	60	50	15,110	15,110	7,230
Mount Holyoke College; South Hadley, Mass. 01075 (P)	1,849	65	100	23,200	23,200	6,820
Mount Ida College; Newton, Mass. 02159 (P)	2,009	80	60	19,720	19,720	
New England College of Optometry; Boston, Mass. 02215 (P)				22,449	22,449	
New England Conservatory of Music; Boston, Mass. 02115 (P)	387	45	50	18,750	18,750	8,600
Nichols College; Dudley, Mass. 01571 (P)	1,266	84	49	16,944	16,944	
Northeastern University; Boston, Mass. 02115 (P)	19,691	70	50	14,030	14,030	5,510
Pine Manor College; Chestnut Hill, Mass. 02167 (P)	307	88	100	11,000	11,000	6,900
Regis College; Weston, Mass. 02193-1571 (P)	1,111	87	99	16,000	16,000	7,200
Salem State College; Salem, Mass. 01970 (Pub)	8,607		57	1,150	6,450	4,005
School of the Museum of Fine Arts; Boston, Mass. 02115 (P)	522		61	15,490	15,490	
Simmons College; Boston, Mass. 02115 (P)	1,251	69	100	17,984	17,984	7,228
Simon's Rock of Bard College; Great Barrington, Mass. 01230 (P)	334	39	56	24,440	24,440	
Smith College; Northampton, Mass. 01063 (P)	2,630	52	100	21,360	21,360	7,560
Springfield College; Springfield, Mass. 01109 (P)	2,046	55	51	18,630	18,630	
Stonehill College; Easton, Mass. 02357-5610 (P)	2,715	57	59	15,130	15,130	7,350
Suffolk University; Boston, Mass. 02108 (P)	3,070	72	56	19,996	19,996	
Tufts University; Medford, Mass. 02155 (P)	4,749	32	52	23,106	23,106	7,108
University of Massachusetts-Amherst; Amherst, Mass. 01003 (Pub)	19,065	73	49	5,234	12,474	4,500
University of Massachusetts-Boston; Boston, Mass. 02125-3393 (Pub)	9,612	54	55	2,004	8,842	
University of Massachusetts-Dartmouth; N. Dartmouth, Mass. 02747-2300 (Pub)	5,655	68	54	1,574	7,250	4,828
University of Massachusetts-Lowell; Lowell, Mass. 01854 (Pub)	9,542	81	38	4,422	10,069	
Wellesley College; Wellesley, Mass. 02481 (P)	2,300	40	100	22,530	22,530	6,990
Wentworth Institute of Technology; Boston, Mass. 02115 (P)	3,094	78	14	12,000	12,000	6,400
Western New England College; Springfield, Mass. 01119 (P)	3,103	76	37	11,130	11,130	6,544
Westfield State College; Westfield, Mass. 01086 (Pub)	4,194	65	51	1,270	5,440	4,440
Wheaton College (MA); Norton, Mass. 02766 (P)	1,443	73	67	21,640	21,640	6,620
Wheelock College; Boston, Mass. 02215 (P)	730	78	95	16,096	16,096	6,300
Williams College; Williamstown, Mass. 01267 (P)	2,028	26	49	23,860	23,860	6,480
Worcester Polytechnic Institute; Worcester, Mass. 01609 (P)	2,744	78	22	18,710	18,710	6,240
Worcester State College; Worcester, Mass. 01602 (Pub)	4,733	59	63	1,270	5,950	4,140
MICHIGAN						
Adrian College; Adrian, Mich. 49221 (P)	1,049	81	49	13,150	13,150	4,320
Albion College; Albion, Mich. 49224 (P)	1,500	91	53	16,640	16,640	4,890
Alma College; Alma, Mich. 48801-1599 (P)	1,407	90	57	14,424	14,424	5,250
Andrews University; Berrien Springs, Mich. 49104 (P)	1,847	34	57	11,685	11,685	3,630
Aquinas College; Grand Rapids, Mich. 49506-1799 (P)	1,881	92	65	13,168	13,168	4,432
Calvin College; Grand Rapids, Mich. 49546 (P)	4,029	98	57	12,225	12,225	4,340
Center for Creative Studies; Detroit, Mich. 48202 (P)	921	76	40	14,280	14,280	5,500
Central Michigan University; Mount Pleasant, Mich. 48859 (Pub)	16,409	77	58	3,066	7,961	4,320
Cleary College; Ypsilanti, Mich. 48197 (P)	644	60	68	7,521	7,521	
Davenport College of Business; Grand Rapids, Mich. 49503 (P)				10,035	10,035	
Detroit College of Business; Dearborn, Mich. 48126 (P)	6,354	100	79	6,516	6,516	
Eastern Michigan University; Ypsilanti, Mich. 48197 (Pub)	17,701	74	59	2,984	9,874	2,300
Ferris State University; Big Rapids, Mich. 49307 (Pub)	9,075	96	43	3,808	7,850	4,792
Grand Rapids Baptist College; Grand Rapids, Mich. 49505 (P)		89		11,132	11,132	
Grand Valley State University; Allendale, Mich. 49401 (Pub)	11,734	85	60	3,362	7,342	5,000
Hillsdale College; Hillsdale, Mich. 49242 (P)	1,238	83	51	12,840	12,840	5,710
Hope College; Holland, Mich. 49422-9000 (P)	2,911	95	59	15,380	15,380	4,884
Kalamazoo College; Kalamazoo, Mich. 49006 (P)	1,241	88		18,630	18,630	5,619
Kendall College of Art and Design; Grand Rapids, Mich. 49503 (P)	527	62	54	10,500	10,500	
Kettering University; Flint, Mich. 48504 (P)	2,482	76		14,112	14,112	3,848
Lake Superior State University; Sault Sainte, Mich. 49783-1699 (Pub)	3,224	94	50	3,642	7,158	4,646
Lawrence Technological University; Southfield, Mich. 48075 (P)	3,073	80	24	11,436	11,436	
Madonna University; Livonia, Mich. 48150-1173 (P)	3,307	86	77	6,310	6,310	4,508
Marygrove College; Detroit, Mich. 48221 (P)	1,087	52	85	13,166	13,166	
Michigan State University; East Lansing, Mich. 48824 (Pub)	33,308	81	53	4,223	11,288	4,052
Michigan Technological University; Houghton, Mich. 49913 (Pub)	5,674	96	26	3,822	9,576	4,420
Northern Michigan University; Marquette, Mich. 49855 (Pub)	7,144	91	51	2,880	5,160	4,340
Northwood University; Midland, Mich. 48640 (P)	2,694	93	45	10,980	10,980	5,010
Oakland University; Rochester, Mich. 48309 (Pub)	11,178	84	65	3,448	10,718	4,555

		Percent		Tuition		Room
Institution name; city, state ZIP (control)	Students	Accepted	Women	In-state	Out-of-state	and board
Olivet College; Olivet, Mich. 49076 (P)	824	83%	56%	$12,762	$12,762	$4,094
Rochester College; Rochester Hills, Mich. 48307 (P)	418		51	6,524	6,524	3,700
Sacred Heart Major Seminary; Detroit, Mich. 48206 (P)	179			9,045	9,045	
Saginaw Valley State University; University Center, Mich. 48710 (Pub)	6,451	92	60	3,184	6,681	4,375
Saint Mary's College (Mich.); Orchard Lake, Mich. 48328 (P)	310	70	43	5,352	5,352	5,600
Siena Heights College; Adrian, Mich. 49221 (P)	993	94	55	14,190	14,190	
Spring Arbor College; Spring Arbor, Mich. 49283 (P)	1,916	99	57	14,350	14,350	
University of Detroit Mercy; Detroit, Mich. 48219-0900 (P)	4,275	77	66	13,350	13,350	5,380
University of Michigan-Ann Arbor; Ann Arbor, Mich. 48109-1316 (Pub)	23,939	69	50	6,070	18,910	5,486
University of Michigan-Dearborn; Dearborn, Mich. 48128 (Pub)	6,744	77	55	2,928	10,650	
University of Michigan-Flint; Flint, Mich. 48502 (Pub)	5,984	83	62	3,309	9,823	
Wayne State University; Detroit, Mich. 48202 (Pub)	19,248	81	57	3,150	7,020	3,271
Western Michigan University; Kalamazoo, Mich. 49008 (Pub)	20,217	83	54	3,061	7,770	4,398
William Tyndale College; Farmington Hills, Mich. 48331-3147 (P)	615	86	53	6,300	6,300	3,300
MINNESOTA						
Augsburg College; Minneapolis, Minn. 55454 (P)	2,641	83	61	14,470	14,470	5,134
Bemidji State University; Bemidji, Minn. 56601 (Pub)	4,342		54	2,594	5,798	3,085
Bethel College (Minn.); Saint Paul, Minn. 55112 (P)	2,391	81	63	13,840	13,840	4,950
Carleton College; Northfield, Minn. 55057 (P)	1,880	51	52	21,750	21,750	4,440
College of Saint Benedict; Saint Joseph, Minn. 56374 (P)	1,980	92	100	15,424	15,424	4,861
Concordia College–Moorhead; Moorhead, Minn. 56562 (P)	2,931	92	63	12,040	12,040	3,525
Concordia College–Saint Paul; St. Paul, Minn. 55104-5494 (P)	1,027		58	12,658	12,658	4,726
Crown College; St. Bonifacius, Minn. 55375 (P)	656	98	61	12,260	12,260	
Gustavus Adolphus College; St. Peter, Minn. 56082 (P)	2,418	83	56	20,710	20,710	
Hamline University; Saint Paul, Minn. 55104 (P)	1,655	84	57	18,718	18,718	
Macalester College; St. Paul, Minn. 55105 (P)	1,774	55	56	19,673	19,673	5,593
Mankato State University; Mankato, Minn. 56002 (Pub)	10,350	85	53	2,582	5,769	2,965
Martin Luther College; New Ulm, Minn. 56073-3965 (P)	811	89	48	4,130	4,130	2,285
Minneapolis College of Art & Design; Minneapolis, Minn. 55404 (P)	541	83	44	16,750	16,750	3,600
Moorhead State University; Moorhead, Minn. 56563 (Pub)	0,140		64	2,355	5,307	3,256
North Central Bible College; Minneapolis, Minn. 55404 (P)	1,041	91		9,910	9,910	
Northwestern College (Minn.); St. Paul, Minn. 55113-1598 (P)	1,664	70	60	13,920	13,920	4,173
Saint Cloud State University; Saint Cloud, Minn. 56301 (Pub)	12,570	76	53	2,897	5,847	3,105
Saint John's University (Minn.); Collegeville, Minn. 56321 (P)	1,696	87	0	15,424	15,424	4,740
Saint Mary's University of Minnesota; Winona, Minn. 55987-1399 (P)	1,718	88	52	12,750	12,750	4,270
Saint Olaf College; Northfield, Minn. 55057-1098 (P)	2,975	78	59	17,140	17,140	4,180
Southwest State University; Marshall, Minn. 56258 (Pub)	2,900	73	56	2,648	5,965	3,000
The College of Saint Catherine; Saint Paul, Minn. 55105 (P)	2,342	89	99	14,144	14,144	4,402
The College of Saint Scholastica; Duluth, Minn. 55811 (P)	1,383	91	73	14,970	14,970	4,134
University of Minnesota-Crookston; Crookston, Minn. 56716 (Pub)	2,074			3,368	9,350	
University of Minnesota-Duluth; Duluth, Minn. 55812 (Pub)	7,785	78	49	3,708	10,588	3,912
University of Minnesota-Minneapolis; Minneapolis, Minn. 55455-0213 (Pub)	32,342	80	52	3,976	11,378	4,311
University of Minnesota-Morris; Morris, Minn. 56267 (Pub)	1,970	84	57	4,090	10,787	5,448
University of St. Thomas; St. Paul, Minn. 55105-1096 (P)	5,127	89	53	15,296	15,296	4,972
Winona State University; Winona, Minn. 55987-5838 (Pub)	6,500	66	56	2,500	5,600	3,150
MISSISSIPPI						
Alcorn State University; Lorman, Miss. 39096 (Pub)	2,555	36	61	2,685	5,546	2,427
Belhaven College; Jackson, Miss. 39202 (P)	1,217	90	63	9,490	9,490	3,660
Delta State University; Cleveland, Miss. 38733 (Pub)	3,443		61	2,354	4,948	2,400
Jackson State University; Jackson, Miss. 39217 (Pub)	5,250	55	56	2,688	5,546	3,800
Millsaps College; Jackson, Miss. 39210 (P)	1,209	81	56	13,660	13,660	5,526
Mississippi College; Clinton, Miss. 39058 (P)	2,333	83	57	11,200	11,200	
Mississippi State University; Mississippi State, Miss. 39762 (Pub)	12,622	78	44	1,996	4,816	4,100
Mississippi University for Women; Columbus, Miss. 39701 (Pub)	3,085	75	83	2,284	4,786	2,557
Mississippi Valley State University; Itta Bena, Miss. 38941 (Pub)	2,169	25	58	2,278	4,780	2,490
Rust College; Holly Springs, Miss. 38635 (P)	875	32	60	5,025	5,025	2,275
Tougaloo College; Tougaloo, Miss. 39174 (P)	982	50	69	6,250	6,250	3,000
University of Mississippi; University, Miss. 38677 (Pub)	8,616	77	53	2,036	5,551	3,090
University of Southern Mississippi; Hattiesburg, Miss. 39406 (Pub)	10,647	72	57	2,590	5,410	2,560
William Carey College; Hattiesburg, Miss. 39401 (P)	1,762	52	68	6,500	6,500	2,700

Institution name; city, state ZIP (control)	Students	Percent Accepted	Percent Women	Tuition In-state	Tuition Out-of-state	Room and board
MISSOURI						
Avila College; Kansas City, Mo. 64145 (P)	899	91%		$10,800	$10,800	$4,400
Central Methodist College; Fayette, Mo. 65248 (P)	1,258	88	60%	10,350	10,350	4,110
Central Missouri State University; Warrensburg, Mo. 64093 (Pub)	8,685	93	54	2,640	4,080	
College of the Ozarks; Point Lookout, Mo. 65726 (P)	1,563	14	55	2,200	2,200	
Columbia College (Mo.); Columbia, Mo. 65216 (P)	7,384	81	57	9,522	9,522	4,270
Culver-Stockton College; Canton, Mo. 63435 (P)	994	82	62	9,650	9,650	4,450
Drury College; Springfield, Mo. 65802 (P)	1,351	93	53	13,356	13,356	
Evangel College; Springfield, Mo. 65802 (P)	1,616	88	56	8,390	8,390	3,440
Fontbonne College; Saint Louis, Mo. 63105 (P)	1,387	88	67	10,650	10,650	4,700
Hannibal-LaGrange College; Hannibal, Mo. 63401 (P)	1,086		65	10,070	10,070	
Harris-Stowe State College; Saint Louis, Mo. 63103 (Pub)	1,723		65	1,992	3,924	
Kansas City Art Institute; Kansas City, Mo. 64111 (P)	607	70	44	20,310	20,310	
Lincoln University (Mo.); Jefferson City, Mo. 65102 (Pub)	3,306	90	53	2,016	4,032	2,976
Lindenwood College; Saint Charles, Mo. 63301 (P)	2,891	55	55	14,700	14,700	
Maryville University of Saint Louis; Saint Louis, Mo. 63141-7299 (P)	2,548	80	72	11,600	11,600	5,200
Missouri Baptist College; Saint Louis, Mo. 63141 (P)	2,373	75	56	11,480	11,480	
Missouri Southern State College; Joplin, Mo. 64801-1595 (Pub)	5,485	99	56	2,205	4,410	3,370
Missouri Valley College; Marshall, Mo. 65340 (P)	1,192	82		14,700	14,700	
Missouri Western State College; Saint Joseph, Mo. 64507 (Pub)	5,124	100	62	2,406	4,422	3,302
Northwest Missouri State University; Maryville, Mo. 64468 (Pub)	5,304	84	55	2,722	4,732	3,890
Park College; Parkville, Mo. 64152 (P)	1,053	89	65	4,590	4,590	4,600
Rockhurst College; Kansas City, Mo. 64110-2561 (P)	2,049	89	56	11,900	11,900	4,920
Saint Louis College of Pharmacy; Saint Louis, Mo. 63110 (P)	793	87	62	12,000	12,000	5,050
Saint Louis University; Saint Louis, Mo. 63103 (P)	9,786	71	56	16,100	16,100	5,702
Southeast Missouri State University; Cape Girardea, Mo. 63701 (Pub)	7,799	90	58	2,889	5,379	4,080
Southwest Baptist University; Bolivar, Mo. 65613 (P)	2,498	66		10,331	10,331	
Southwest Missouri State University; Springfield, Mo. 65804 (Pub)	18,811	90	54	2,670	5,340	3,472
Stephens College; Columbia, Mo. 65215 (P)	933	88	95	14,830	14,830	5,790
Truman State University; Kirksville, Mo. 63501 (Pub)	6,050	81	57	3,408	6,024	
University of Missouri-Columbia; Columbia, Mo. 65211 (Pub)	17,346	80	53	3,630	10,851	
University of Missouri-Kansas City; Kansas City, Mo. 64110 (Pub)	5,632	62	53	3,330	6,624	5,600
University of Missouri-Rolla; Rolla, Mo. 65409 (Pub)	4,112	97	25	3,855	11,523	4,490
University of Missouri-Saint Louis; St. Louis, Mo. 63121 (Pub)	12,844	81	77	3,744	11,187	4,000
Washington University; St. Louis, Mo. 63130-4899 (P)	6,082	40	50	22,200	22,200	6,922
Webster University; Saint Louis, Mo. 63119 (P)	3,169	64	65	11,400	11,400	5,100
Westminster College (Mo.); Fulton, Mo. 65251-1299 (P)	654	84	41	12,300	12,300	4,450
William Jewell College; Liberty, Mo. 64068 (P)	1,184	89	58	11,584	11,584	3,560
William Woods University; Fulton, Mo. 65251 (P)	847	82	83	12,600	12,600	5,000
MONTANA						
Carroll College (Mont.); Helena, Mont. 59625 (P)	1,206	96	61	11,490	11,490	4,540
Montana State University-Billings; Billings, Mont. 59101 (Pub)	3,857	100	63	2,517	6,976	4,050
Montana State University-Bozeman; Bozeman, Mont. 59717 (Pub)	10,401	84	44	1,954	6,969	4,025
Montana State University-Northern; Havre, Mont. 59501 (Pub)	1,509	100	52	2,349	6,661	3,700
Montana Tech of the University of Montana; Butte, Mont. 59701 (Pub)	1,823	83	41	2,365	6,769	3,712
Rocky Mountain College; Billings, Mont. 59102-1796 (P)	777	90	56	11,068	11,068	3,978
University of Great Falls; Great Falls, Mont. 59405 (P)	1,001	100	68	7,350	7,350	3,520
University of Montana; Missoula, Mont. 59812 (Pub)	10,608	83	53	2,776	7,714	4,236
Western Montana College; Dillon, Mont. 59725 (Pub)	1,122	85	56	1,826	4,280	3,800
NEBRASKA						
Chadron State College; Chadron, Neb. 69337 (Pub)	2,553	100	56	1,732	3,465	3,120
Clarkson College; Omaha, Neb. 68131 (P)	380	39	89	6,528	6,528	2,040
College of Saint Mary; Omaha, Neb. 68124 (P)	1,001	81	97	11,434	11,434	4,290
Concordia College (Neb.); Seward, Neb. 68434 (P)	1,087	84	56	11,310	11,310	3,786
Creighton University; Omaha, Neb. 68178 (P)	3,979	92	59	12,858	12,858	5,190
Dana College; Blair, Neb. 68008 (P)	594	90	54	11,130	11,130	3,880
Doane College; Crete, Neb. 68333 (P)	1,456	90	57	11,530	11,530	3,550
Hastings College; Hastings, Neb. 68902 (P)	1,075	74	53	13,884	13,884	
Midland Lutheran College; Fremont, Neb. 68025 (P)	1,062	89	55	12,810	12,810	3,450
Nebraska Methodist College of Nursing and Allied Health; Omaha, Neb. 68114 (P)	395	97	89	7,860	7,860	1,250
Nebraska Wesleyan University; Lincoln, Neb. 68504 (P)	1,709	98	59	13,804	13,804	
Peru State College; Peru, Neb. 68421 (Pub)	1,618	88	52	1,650	3,465	2,950
Union College; Lincoln, Neb. 68506 (P)	2,042	90		12,670	12,670	
University of Nebraska-Kearney; Kearney, Neb. 68849 (Pub)	7,141	96	53	1,823	3,413	3,280

Institution name; city, state ZIP (control)	Students	Percent Accepted	Percent Women	Tuition In-state	Tuition Out-of-state	Room and board
University of Nebraska-Lincoln; Lincoln, Neb. 68588 (Pub)	18,246	81%	47%	$ 1,884	$ 5,118	$3,700
University of Nebraska-Omaha; Omaha, Neb. 68182 (Pub)	12,078	96	53	2,626	5,646	
Wayne State College; Wayne, Neb. 68787 (Pub)	3,201	99	56	3,348	7,471	
NEVADA						
Deep Springs College; Dyer, Nev. 89010 (P)	26	15	0	0	0	0
Sierra Nevada College; Incline Villa, Nev. 89450 (P)	540	97	40	10,800	10,800	5,600
University of Nevada-Las Vegas; Las Vegas, Nev. 89154 (Pub)	14,931	72	53	1,995	7,840	5,380
University of Nevada-Reno; Reno, Nev. 89557 (Pub)	9,150	86	51	1,656	7,426	5,200
NEW HAMPSHIRE						
Colby-Sawyer College; New London, N.H. 03257 (P)	775	80	65	17,120	17,120	6,530
Daniel Webster College; Nashua, N.H. 03063 (P)	536	81	30	19,060	19,060	
Dartmouth College; Hanover, N.H. 03755 (P)	4,275	22	44	23,790	23,790	6,801
Franklin Pierce College; Rindge, N.H. 03461-0060 (P)	1,420	75	48	16,440	16,440	5,400
Keene State College; Keene, N.H. 03435 (Pub)	4,187	77	56	3,240	8,740	4,660
New England College; Henniker, N.H. 03242 (P)	978	85	42	16,842	16,842	6,062
New Hampshire College; Manchester, N.H. 03106-1045 (P)	5,622	81	38	12,990	12,990	5,980
Notre Dame College (N.H.); Manchester, N.H. 03104 (P)	781	90	78	13,300	13,300	6,400
Plymouth State College; Plymouth, N.H. 03264 (Pub)	4,015	86	50	3,620	8,920	4,706
Rivier College; Nashua, N.H. 03060 (P)	1,757	88	83	12,990	12,990	5,525
Saint Anselm College; Manchester, N.H. 03102 (P)	2,007	79	56	20,260	20,260	
University of New Hampshire; Durham, N.H. 03824 (Pub)	10,400	76	68	6,555	15,275	4,636
University of New Hampshire at Manchester; Manchester, N.H. 03102 (Pub)	10,649			3,920	10,860	
NEW JERSEY						
Bloomfield College; Bloomfield, N.J. 07003 (P)	1,997	66	69	9,500	9,500	4,850
Caldwell College; Caldwell, N.J. 07006 (P)	1,716	67	69	11,600	11,600	5,600
Centenary College; Hackettstown, N.J. 07840 (P)	899	83	76	12,900	12,900	5,800
College of Saint Elizabeth; Morristown, N.J. 07960-6989 (P)	1,403	82	89	12,500	12,500	6,200
Drew University; Madison, N.J. 07940 (P)	1,542	74	58	21,702	21,702	6,392
Fairleigh Dickinson University, Florham-Madison Campus; Madison, N.J. 07940 (P)	2,234	75	56	13,280	13,280	5,864
Fairleigh Dickinson University, Teaneck Campus; Teaneck, N.J. 07555 (P)	2,077	64	55	18,464	18,464	
Felician College; Lodi, N.J. 07644 (P)	978	73	85	8,550	8,550	
Georgian Court College; Lakewood, N.J. 08701 (P)	1,488	91	91	14,832	14,832	
Jersey City State College; Jersey City, N.J. 07305 (Pub)	6,359	62	60	2,880	4,898	5,000
Kean University; Union, N.J. 07083 (Pub)	9,879	70	63	3,212	4,829	5,316
Monmouth University (N.J.); W. Long Branch, N.J. 07764-1898 (P)	5,300	85	57	14,520	14,520	6,448
Montclair State University; Upper Montclair, N.J. 07043 (Pub)	9,203	46	60	3,446	4,906	5,658
New Jersey Institute of Technology; Newark, N.J. 07102 (Pub)	4,995	67	19	4,638	8,982	6,382
Princeton University; Princeton, N.J. 08544 (P)	4,601	13	46	23,820	23,820	6,711
Ramapo College of New Jersey; Mahwah, N.J. 07430 (Pub)	4,681	49	55	3,159	5,529	6,002
Richard Stockton College of New Jersey; Pomona, N.J. 08240 (Pub)	6,040	48	57	2,816	4,544	4,760
Rider University; Lawrenceville, N.J. 08648-3099 (P)	3,878	84	60	15,120	15,120	6,270
Rowan University; Glassboro, N.J. 08028 (Pub)	8,055	51	57	4,240	7,370	5,326
Rutgers University-Camden College of Arts & Sciences; Camden, N.J. 08101 (Pub)	2,188	60	59	4,262	8,676	5,314
Rutgers University-Camden Region; Camden, N.J. 08102 (Pub)	3,293	60	56	4,262	8,676	5,314
Rutgers University-College of Engineering; Piscataway, N.J. 08854-8097 (Pub)	2,206	71	22	4,732	9,626	5,314
Rutgers University-College of Nursing; Newark, N.J. 07102-1896 (Pub)	393	29	89	4,262	8,676	5,314
Rutgers University-College of Pharmacy; Piscataway, N.J. 08854-8097 (Pub)	879	37	62	4,732	9,626	5,314
Rutgers University-Cook College; Piscataway, N.J. 08854-8097 (Pub)	3,284	64	51	4,732	9,626	5,314
Rutgers University-Douglass College; Piscataway, N.J. 08854-8097 (Pub)	3,014	70	100	4,262	8,676	5,314
Rutgers University-Livingston College; Piscataway, N.J. 00854-8097 (Pub)	3,160	60	39	4,262	8,676	5,314
Rutgers University-Mason Gross School of the Arts; Piscataway, N.J. 08854-8097 (Pub)	546	23	56	4,262	8,676	5,314
Rutgers University-New Brunswick Region; Piscataway, N.J. 08854-8097 (Pub)	26,615	57	54	4,732	9,626	5,314
Rutgers University-Newark College of Arts & Sciences; Newark, N.J. 07102-1896 (Pub)	3,621	57	54	4,262	8,676	5,314
Rutgers University-Newark Region; Newark, N.J. 07102-1896 (Pub)	5,804	54	56	4,262	8,676	5,314
Rutgers University-Rutgers College; Piscataway, N.J. 08854-8097 (Pub)	10,680	48	51	4,262	8,676	5,314
Saint Peter's College; Jersey City, N.J. 07306 (P)	3,211	79	57	14,100	14,100	5,060
Seton Hall University; South Orange, N.J. 07079-2680 (P)	5,500	80	52	18,410	18,410	

Institution name; city, state ZIP (control)	Students	Percent Accepted	Percent Women	Tuition In-state	Tuition Out-of-state	Room and board
Stevens Institute of Technology; Hoboken, N.J. 07030 (P)	1,451	67%	22%	$19,900	$19,900	$6,960
The College of New Jersey; Ewing, N.J. 08628-0718 (Pub)	5,386	45		3,791	6,620	5,996
Thomas Edison State College; Trenton, N.J. 08608 (Pub)	8,575	100	41	495	880	
Westminster Choir College of Rider University; Princeton, N.J. 08540 (P)	280	58		20,744	20,744	
William Paterson University; Wayne, N.J. 07470 (Pub)	7,654	47	59	3,380	5,360	5,100
NEW MEXICO						
College of Santa Fe; Santa Fe, N.M. 87505-7634 (P)	1,240	84	63	13,000	13,000	4,724
College of the Southwest; Hobbs, N.M. 88240 (P)	579	83	74	7,514	7,514	
Eastern New Mexico University; Portales, N.M. 88130 (Pub)	3,296	99	56	1,752	6,510	3,104
New Mexico Highlands University; Las Vegas, N.M. 87701 (Pub)	2,054	94	52	1,782	7,122	2,171
New Mexico Institute of Mining & Technology; Socorro, N.M. 87801 (Pub)	1,135	76	37	1,450	5,988	3,530
New Mexico State University; Las Cruces, N.M. 88003-8001 (Pub)	11,872	80	52	2,165	8,174	2,980
Saint John's College (N.M.); Santa Fe, N.M. 87501 (P)	383	83	44	20,500	20,500	6,200
University of New Mexico; Albuquerque, N.M. 87131 (Pub)	15,056	74	56	2,346	7,848	4,954
Western New Mexico University; Silver City, N.M. 88061 (Pub)	1,758	100		1,516	4,652	2,260
NEW YORK						
Adelphi University; Garden City, N.Y. 11530 (P)	4,787		66	20,850	20,850	
Albany College of Pharmacy; Albany, N.Y. 12208 (P)	652	77	58	11,250	11,250	3,400
Alfred University; Alfred, N.Y. 14802 (P)	2,201	84	49	25,406	25,406	
Arnold & Marie Schwartz College of Pharmacy & Health Science; Brooklyn, N.Y. 11201 (P)	660			7,900	7,900	
Audrey Cohen College; New York, N.Y. 10013 (P)	1,017	79	79	8,800	8,800	
Bard College; Annandale-on-Hudson, N.Y. 12504 (P)	1,141	51	59	28,512	28,512	
Barnard College; New York, N.Y. 10027 (P)	2,313	46	100	21,600	21,600	8,898
Binghamton University (State University of New York); Binghamton, N.Y. 13902-6001 (Pub)	9,460	42	53	3,400	8,300	5,114
Boricua College; New York, N.Y. 10032 (P)	1,072		78	6,100	6,100	
Canisius College; Buffalo, N.Y. 14208 (P)	2,779	84	47	14,170	14,170	6,070
City University of New York–Baruch College; New York, N.Y. 10010 (Pub)	12,730	57	57	3,200	6,800	
City University of New York–Brooklyn College; Brooklyn, N.Y. 11210 (Pub)	11,478	83	58	3,200	6,800	
City University of New York–City College; New York, N.Y. 1003-9198 (Pub)	9,020	60	51	3,200	6,800	
City University of New York–College of Staten Island; Staten Island, N.Y. 10314 (Pub)	10,640		58	3,200	6,800	
City University of New York–Hunter College; New York, N.Y. 10021 (Pub)	14,601	54	71	3,200	6,800	1,840
City University of New York–John Jay College of Criminal Justice; New York, N.Y. 10019 (Pub)	9,772		56	2,450	5,050	
City University of New York–Lehman College; Bronx, N.Y. 10468 (Pub)	7,698	51	72	3,200	6,800	
City University of New York–Medgar Evers College; Brooklyn, N.Y. 11225 (Pub)	5,401	100		3,200	6,800	
City University of New York–Queens College; Flushing, N.Y. 11367 (Pub)	12,440	67	61	3,200	6,800	
City University of New York–York College; Jamaica, N.Y. 11451 (Pub)	6,869	100	68	3,200	6,800	
Clarkson University; Potsdam, N.Y. 13699 (P)	2,424	82	25	18,250	18,250	6,510
Colgate University; Hamilton, N.Y. 13346 (P)	2,893	42	51	23,715	23,715	6,235
College of Aeronautics; East Elmhurst, N.Y. 11369 (P)	1,102	91	5	7,350	7,350	3,924
College of Insurance; New York, N.Y. 10007 (P)	575	97	52	20,830	20,830	
College of Mount Saint Vincent; Riverdale, N.Y. 10471-1093 (P)	1,262	68	82	13,000	13,000	6,240
College of New Rochelle; New Rochelle, N.Y. 10805-2339 (P)	5,344	64	85	11,300	11,300	5,850
Columbia University; New York, N.Y. 10027 (P)	3,570	50	49	28,044	28,044	
Concordia College (N.Y.); Bronxville, N.Y. 10708 (P)	599	82	60	12,590	12,590	5,750
Cooper Union; New York, N.Y. 10003 (P)	853	16	36	8,300	8,300	9,600
Cornell University; Ithaca, N.Y. 14853 (P)	13,294	34		30,427	30,427	
Daemen College; Amherst, N.Y. 14226 (P)	1,830	69	71	11,000	11,000	5,800
Dominican College of Blauvelt; Orangeburg, N.Y. 10962 (P)	1,675	75	75	10,350	10,350	6,250
Dowling College; Long Island, N.Y. 11769-1999 (P)	3,375	93	58	11,940	11,940	5,705
D'Youville College; Buffalo, N.Y. 14201 (P)	1,221	53	74	9,840	9,840	4,760
Eastman School of Music; Rochester, N.Y. 14604-2599 (P)	487	30	53	19,540	19,540	7,289
Elmira College; Elmira, N.Y. 14901 (P)	1,576	75	69	19,876	19,876	6,680
Eugene Lang College; New York, N.Y. 10011 (P)	408	73	68	18,600	18,600	9,005
Fashion Institute of Technology; New York, N.Y. 10001 (P)		50		7,405	7,405	
Fordham University; New York, N.Y. 10023 (P)	6,121	69	57	18,295	18,295	7,810
Hamilton College; Clinton, N.Y. 13323 (P)	1,716	42	48	23,600	23,600	5,850
Hartwick College; Oneonta, N.Y. 13820 (P)	1,494	90	53	26,050	26,050	
Hobart and William Smith Colleges; Geneva, N.Y. 14456 (P)	1,843	76	53	22,983	22,983	6,565

Institution name; city, state ZIP (control)	Students	Percent Accepted	Percent Women	Tuition In-state	Tuition Out-of-state	Room and board
Hofstra University; Hempstead, N.Y. 11549 (P)	8,568	83%	54%	$12,790	$12,790	$6,730
Houghton College; Houghton, N.Y. 14744 (P)	1,411	85	62	12,344	12,344	4,238
Iona College; New Rochelle, N.Y. 10801 (P)	3,612	76	56	13,100	13,100	7,720
Ithaca College; Ithaca, N.Y. 14850-7020 (P)	5,629	70	55	17,662	17,662	7,652
Juilliard School; New York, N.Y. 10023 (P)	465	11		14,400	14,400	8,100
Keuka College; Keuka Park, N.Y. 14478 (P)	938	84	71	15,530	15,530	
Laboratory Institute of Merchandising; New York, N.Y. 10022 (P)	217	83	97	11,800	11,800	
Le Moyne College; Syracuse, N.Y. 13214-1399 (P)	2,290	80	61	13,830	13,830	6,230
Long Island University-Brooklyn; Brooklyn, N.Y. 11201 (P)	4,193	59	66	17,480	17,480	
Long Island University-C.W. Post; Brookville, N.Y. 11548 (P)	4,613	79	59	13,920	13,920	5,880
Long Island University-Southampton; Southampton, N.Y. 11968 (P)	1,273	85	58	19,580	19,580	
Manhattan College; Riverdale, N.Y. 10471 (P)	2,536	81	45	7,200	7,200	7,250
Manhattan School of Music; New York, N.Y. 10027 (P)	409	35	50	17,830	17,830	5,000
Manhattanville College; Purchase, N.Y. 10577 (P)	1,145	70	69	23,800	23,800	
Mannes College of Music; New York, N.Y. 10024 (P)	106	18	50	20,580	20,580	
Marist College; Poughkeepsie, N.Y. 12601-1387 (P)	4,062	61	58	13,434	13,434	7,662
Marymount College; Tarrytown, N.Y. 10591-3796 (P)	898	84	95	13,770	13,770	7,400
Marymount Manhattan College; New York, N.Y. 10021 (P)	2,140	88	81	12,500	12,500	6,000
Medaille College; Buffalo, N.Y. 14214 (P)	914	67	74	14,675	14,675	
Mercy College; Dobbs Ferry, N.Y. 10522 (P)	5,868	90	58	7,800	7,800	7,500
Molloy College; Rockville Centre, N.Y. 11571-5002 (P)	1,981		81	9,600	9,600	
Mount Saint Mary College; Newburgh, N.Y. 12550 (P)	1,640	87	68	9,870	9,870	5,250
Nazareth College of Rochester; Rochester, N.Y. 14618-3790 (P)	1,796	73	76	13,120	13,120	6,130
New York Institute of Technology; Old Westbury, N.Y. 11568 (P)	6,737	78	30	10,630	10,630	6,480
New York University; New York, N.Y. 10011 (P)	17,553	40	59	22,586	22,586	8,170
Niagara University; Niagara University, N.Y. 14109 (P)	2,452	86	61	12,390	12,390	6,078
Nyack College; Nyack, N.Y. 10960 (P)	1,011	73	55	14,080	14,080	
Pace University-New York; New York, N.Y. 10038 (P)	9,042	76	61	13,470	13,470	6,100
Pace University-White Plains; White Plains, N.Y. 10603 (P)		99		18,050	18,050	
Parsons School of Design; New York, N.Y. 10011 (P)	1,788	50	72	19,270	19,270	8,857
Polytechnic University-Brooklyn; Brooklyn, N.Y. 11201 (P)	1,588	81	14	22,130	22,130	
Pratt Institute; Brooklyn, N.Y. 11205 (P)	2,272	55	46	17,642	17,642	7,530
Rensselaer Polytechnic Institute; Troy, N.Y. 12180 (P)	4,348	83	26	21,030	21,030	7,456
Roberts Wesleyan College; Rochester, N.Y. 14624-1997 (P)	1,134	89		15,468	15,468	
Rochester Institute of Technology; Rochester, N.Y. 14623-5604 (P)	10,326	78	34	16,083	16,083	6,501
Russell Sage College; Troy, N.Y. 12180 (P)	1,021	96	100	14,350	14,350	6,050
Saint Bonaventure University; Saint Bonaventure, N.Y. 14778 (P)	2,032	94	52	13,280	13,280	5,400
Saint John Fisher College; Rochester, N.Y. 14618 (P)	2,000	78	55	17,630	17,630	
Saint John's University (N.Y.); Jamaica, N.Y. 11439 (P)	13,889	86	56	11,800	11,800	
Saint Joseph's College (Brooklyn); Brooklyn, N.Y. 11205 (P)	1,381	66	73	8,350	8,350	
Saint Joseph's College (N.Y.); Patchogue, N.Y. 11772 (P)	2,756	76	78	8,595	8,595	
Saint Lawrence University; Canton, N.Y. 13617 (P)	1,921	71	49	21,175	21,175	6,340
Saint Thomas Aquinas College; Sparkill, N.Y. 10976 (P)	2,038	77	58	11,100	11,100	6,910
Sarah Lawrence College; Bronxville, N.Y. 10708-5999 (P)	1,111	46	76	23,640	23,640	7,612
School of Visual Arts; New York, N.Y. 10010 (P)	4,903	61	48	13,650	13,650	
Siena College; Loudonville, N.Y. 12211 (P)	2,700	77	60	13,075	13,075	5,835
Skidmore College; Saratoga Springs, N.Y. 12866 (P)	2,543	48	61	22,853	22,853	6,640
State University of New York at Albany; Albany, N.Y. 12222 (Pub)	11,047	61	48	3,400	8,300	5,420
State University of New York at Buffalo; Buffalo, N.Y. 14260 (Pub)	15,552	72	46	3,400	8,300	5,420
State University of New York at Stony Brook; Stony Brook, N.Y. 11794-1901 (Pub)	12,392	57	48	3,400	8,300	5,594
State University of New York College at Brockport; Brockport, N.Y. 14420 (Pub)	6,574	58	54	3,400	8,300	5,420
State University of New York College at Buffalo; Buffalo, N.Y. 14222 (Pub)	9,421	60	57	3,400	8,300	5,420
State University of New York College at Cortland; Cortland, N.Y. 13045 (Pub)	5,146	64	55	3,400	8,300	5,420
State University of New York College at Fredonia; Fredonia, N.Y. 14063 (Pub)	4,331	62	57	3,400	8,300	5,420
State University of New York College at Geneseo; Geneseo, N.Y. 14454 (Pub)	5,245	56	66	3,400	8,300	4,700
State University of New York College at New Paltz; New Paltz, N.Y. 12561 (Pub)	6,074	43	63	3,400	8,300	5,420
State University of New York College at Old Westbury; Old Westbury, N.Y. 11568 (Pub)	3,790	88	57	3,400	8,300	5,420
State University of New York College at Oneonta; Oneonta, N.Y. 13820 (Pub)	5,036	69	60	3,400	8,300	5,420

Institution name; city, state ZIP (control)	Students	Percent Accepted	Percent Women	Tuition In-state	Tuition Out-of-state	Room and board
State University of New York College at Oswego; Oswego, N.Y. 13126 (Pub)	6,818	67%	53%	$ 3,400	$ 8,300	$5,420
State University of New York College at Plattsburgh; Plattsburgh, N.Y. 12901-2681 (Pub)	5,319	67	57	3,400	8,300	5,420
State University of New York College at Potsdam; Potsdam, N.Y. 13676 (Pub)	3,548	82	57	3,400	8,300	5,420
State University of New York College at Purchase; Purchase, N.Y. 10577 (Pub)	3,217	54	57	3,400	8,300	5,420
State University of New York College of Environmental Science and Forestry; Syracuse, N.Y. 13210 (Pub)	1,185			3,400	8,300	7,060
State University of New York Empire State College; Saratoga Springs, N.Y. 12866 (Pub)	7,213		52	3,400	8,300	5,420
State University of New York Maritime College; Bronx, N.Y. 10465 (Pub)	646			3,400	8,300	5,420
Syracuse University; Syracuse, N.Y. 13244 (P)	10,400	60	53	18,440	18,440	7,751
The College of Saint Rose; Albany, N.Y. 12203 (P)	2,637	80	70	11,968	11,968	5,966
The Jewish Theological Seminary of America; New York, N.Y. 10027 (P)	435			13,840	13,840	
Touro College; New York, N.Y. 10001 (P)	6,812	64	68	11,400	11,400	
Union College (N.Y.); Schenectady, N.Y. 12308 (P)	2,042	52	48	22,929	22,929	6,417
United States Merchant Marine Academy; Kings Point, N.Y. 11024 (Pub)	980	58		0	0	0
United States Military Academy; West Point, N.Y. 10996 (Pub)	4,087	14		0	0	0
University of Rochester; Rochester, N.Y. 14627-001 (P)	4,663	54	50	20,540	20,540	7,160
Utica College of Syracuse University; Utica, N.Y. 13502 (P)	1,762	85		15,654	15,654	5,932
Vassar College; Poughkeepsie, N.Y. 12604 (P)	2,352	42	62	22,670	22,670	6,620
Wadhams Hall Seminary College; Ogdensburg, N.Y. 13669 (P)	51	82		8,690	8,690	
Wagner College; Staten Island, N.Y. 10301 (P)	1,648	71	59	16,800	16,800	6,200
Webb Institute; Glen Cove, N.Y. 11542 (P)	86	48		6,050	6,050	
Wells College; Aurora, N.Y. 13026 (P)	312	84	99	17,100	17,100	5,900
Yeshiva University; New York, N.Y. 10033 (P)	1,990		43	14,920	14,920	4,750
NORTH CAROLINA						
Appalachian State University; Boone, N.C. 28608 (Pub)	10,878	61	52	900	8,028	3,190
Barber Scotia College; Concord, N.C. 28025 (P)	500	60	46	6,000	6,000	3,300
Barton College; Wilson, N.C. 27893 (P)	1,303	88	68	9,462	9,462	4,278
Belmont Abbey College; Belmont, N.C. 28012 (P)	834	31	55	11,094	11,094	5,978
Bennett College; Greensboro, N.C. 27401 (P)	664	70	100	6,400	6,400	3,525
Campbell University; Buies Creek, N.C. 27506 (P)	2,231	62	55	9,993	9,993	3,630
Catawba College; Salisbury, N.C. 28144 (P)	1,283	86	50	11,352	11,352	4,500
Chowan College; Murfreesboro, N.C. 27855 (P)	755	76	41	11,470	11,470	4,600
Davidson College; Davidson, N.C. 28036 (P)	1,623	36	49	20,658	20,658	6,126
Duke University; Durham, N.C. 27708 (P)	6,367	30	49	23,200	23,200	6,978
East Carolina University; Greenville, N.C. 27858 (Pub)	14,780	77	58	916	8,028	3,680
Elizabeth City State College; Elizabeth City, N.C. 27909 (Pub)	1,937	72	63	628	6,360	4,952
Elon College; Elon College, N.C. 27244 (P)	3,533	63	58	15,712	15,712	4,170
Fayetteville State University; Fayetteville, N.C. 28301-4298 (Pub)	3,249	87	64	900	8,028	3,400
Gardner-Webb University; Boiling Springs, N.C. 28017 (P)	2,402	87	65	10,190	10,190	4,630
Greensboro College; Greensboro, N.C. 27401-1875 (P)	1,051	81	54	10,182	10,182	4,700
Guilford College; Greensboro, N.C. 27410 (P)	1,402	81	56	14,796	14,796	5,400
High Point University; High Point, N.C. 27262 (P)	2,411	84	60	1,040	1,040	5,300
Johnson C. Smith University; Charlotte, N.C. 28216 (P)	1,283	61	59	8,126	8,126	3,846
Lees-McRae College; Banner Elk, N.C. 28604 (P)	462		43	13,700	13,700	
Lenoir-Rhyne College; Hickory, N.C. 28603 (P)	1,474	86	63	15,740	15,740	
Livingstone College/Hood Theological Seminary; Salisbury, N.C. 28144 (P)				9,540	9,540	
Mars Hill College; Mars Hill, N.C. 28754 (P)	1,300	87	51	12,700	12,700	
Meredith College; Raleigh, N.C. 27607 (P)	2,367	86	99	8,840	8,840	3,900
Methodist College; Fayetteville, N.C. 28311 (P)	1,720	89	45	11,250	11,250	4,400
Montreat College; Montreat, N.C. 28757 (P)	678		50	10,042	10,042	3,940
Mount Olive College; Mount Olive, N.C. 28365 (P)	970			11,390	11,390	
North Carolina A&T State University; Greensboro, N.C. 27411 (Pub)	6,598	65	50	1,662	8,790	3,850
North Carolina Central University; Durham, N.C. 27707 (Pub)	4,125	70	64	874	8,028	3,384
North Carolina School of the Arts; Winston-Salem, N.C. 27117-2189 (Pub)	656	45		1,401	9,858	3,970
North Carolina State University; Raleigh, N.C. 27695 (Pub)	21,900	75	41	2,270	11,256	4,350
North Carolina Wesleyan College; Rocky Mount, N.C. 27804 (P)	1,700	82	50	11,100	11,100	
Pfeiffer College; Misenheimer, N.C. 28109 (P)	847	81	51	10,230	10,230	1,860
Queens College; Charlotte, N.C. 28274 (P)	1,273	73	80	9,410	9,410	5,830
Saint Andrews Presbyterian College; Laurinburg, N.C. 28352 (P)	662	84	54	16,490	16,490	
Saint Augustine's College; Raleigh, N.C. 27610 (P)	1,639	50	59	4,656	4,656	4,088

Institution name; city, state ZIP (control)	Students	Percent Accepted	Percent Women	Tuition In-state	Tuition Out-of-state	Room and board
Salem College; Winston-Salem, N.C. 27108 (P)	887	87%	98%	$12,690	$12,690	$7,610
Shaw University; Raleigh, N.C. 27601 (P)	2,327	76	63	6,030	6,030	4,174
University of North Carolina-Asheville; Asheville, N.C. 28804 (Pub)	3,137	60	57	752	7,046	3,826
University of North Carolina-Chapel Hill; Chapel Hill, N.C. 27599 (Pub)	15,362	37	60	2,161	10,693	
University of North Carolina-Charlotte; Charlotte, N.C. 28223-0001 (Pub)	13,822	76	54	900	8,028	3,446
University of North Carolina-Greensboro; Greensboro, N.C. 27412 (Pub)	9,741	76	66	1,036	9,490	4,044
University of North Carolina-Pembroke; Pembroke, N.C. 28372-1510 (Pub)	3,034	88	55	1,566	8,664	3,202
University of North Carolina-Wilmington; Wilmington, N.C. 28403 (Pub)	8,621	60	60	900	8,028	4,260
Wake Forest University; Winston-Salem, N.C. 27109 (P)	3,877	42	50	23,600	23,600	
Warren Wilson College; Asheville, N.C. 28815 (P)	652	86	60	12,850	12,850	4,350
Western Carolina University; Cullowhee, N.C. 28723 (Pub)	5,674	85	51	874	8,028	3,090
Wingate University; Wingate, N.C. 28174 (P)	1,119	85	47	11,600	11,600	4,300
Winston-Salem State University; Winston-Salem, N.C. 27110 (Pub)	2,865	80	67	1,446	7,486	
NORTH DAKOTA						
Dickinson State University; Dickinson, N.D. 58601-4896 (Pub)	1,736	100	58	1,756	4,690	2,568
Jamestown College; Jamestown, N.D. 58405 (P)	1,072	96	60	11,500	11,500	
Mayville State University; Mayville, N.D. 58257 (Pub)	756	99	50	1,680	4,886	2,835
Minot State University; Minot, N.D. 58707 (Pub)	3,120	99	62	2,139	5,262	2,984
North Dakota State University; Fargo, N.D. 58105 (Pub)	8,500	81	42	2,236	5,970	3,135
University of Mary; Bismarck, N.D. 58504 (P)	1,934	95	63	7,900	7,900	3,150
University of North Dakota; Grand Forks, N.D. 58202 (Pub)	8,528	68	49	2,677	6,411	3,117
Valley City State University; Valley City, N.D. 58072 (Pub)	1,054	94	56	1,756	4,690	2,910
OHIO						
Antioch College; Yellow Springs, Ohio 45387 (P)	611	79	65	21,628	21,628	4,176
Art Academy of Cincinnati; Cincinnati, Ohio 45202 (P)	187	82	49	9,990	9,990	
Ashland University; Ashland, Ohio 44805 (P)	2,938	89	56	13,725	13,725	5,070
Baldwin-Wallace College; Berea, Ohio 44017 (P)	4,700	83	52	13,490	13,490	5,060
Bluffton College; Bluffton, Ohio 45817 (P)	1,028	87	55	12,375	12,375	5,121
Bowling Green State University; Bowling Green, Ohio 43403 (Pub)	14,535	83	57	4,190	8,930	4,150
Capital University; Columbus, Ohio 43209-2394 (P)	2,715	82	64	15,260	15,260	4,400
Case Western Reserve University; Cleveland, Ohio 44106 (P)	3,609	79	41	18,400	18,400	5,240
Cedarville College; Cedarville, Ohio 45314 (P)	2,559	82	54	9,936	9,936	4,716
Central State University; Wilberforce, Ohio 45384 (Pub)	1,954	66	49	1,106	2,431	1,565
Cleveland Institute of Art; Cleveland, Ohio 44106 (P)		81		17,026	17,026	
Cleveland Institute of Music; Cleveland, Ohio 44106 (P)	220	31	50	17,120	17,120	5,380
Cleveland State University; Cleveland, Ohio 44115 (Pub)	11,660	98	52	1,728	3,456	4,848
College of Mount Saint Joseph; Cincinnati, Ohio 45233 (P)	2,242	86	67	11,900	11,900	5,050
College of Wooster; Wooster, Ohio 44691-2636 (P)	1,714	86	52	18,380	18,380	5,070
Columbus College of Art and Design; Columbus, Ohio 43215 (P)	1,494	63	43	12,600	12,600	5,900
Defiance College; Defiance, Ohio 43512 (P)	738	80	55	13,800	13,800	3,780
Denison University; Granville, Ohio 43023 (P)	2,025	78	52	20,080	20,080	5,590
Franciscan University of Steubenville; Steubenville, Ohio 43952-1763 (P)	1,605	92	60	16,100	16,100	4,730
Franklin University; Columbus, Ohio 43215 (P)	4,005	100	33	5,152	5,152	
Heidelberg College; Tiffin, Ohio 44883 (P)	1,232	86	53	16,100	16,100	5,148
Hiram College; Hiram, Ohio 44234 (P)	818	88	81	16,720	16,720	5,594
John Carroll University; Cleveland, Ohio 44118 (P)	3,512	90	52	14,620	14,620	5,804
Kent State University; Kent, Ohio 44242-0001 (Pub)	21,000	88	44	4,228	7,768	4,152
Kenyon College; Gambier, Ohio 43022 (P)	1,551	70	54	22,990	22,990	4,110
Lake Erie College; Painesville, Ohio 44077 (P)	512	80	31	17,355	17,355	
Lourdes College; Sylvania, Ohio 43560 (P)	1,364	78	83	6,576	6,576	
Malone College; Canton, Ohio 44709 (P)	1,894	88	59	14,500	14,500	
Marietta College; Marietta, Ohio 45750 (P)	1,219	76	51	16,590	16,590	4,774
Miami University; Oxford, Ohio 45056 (Pub)	14,732	77	55	4,482	10,582	
Mount Union College; Alliance, Ohio 44601 (P)	1,407		49	16,890	16,890	
Mount Vernon Nazarene College; Mount Vernon, Ohio 43050 (P)	1,835	94	29	9,830	9,830	3,843
Muskingum College; New Concord, Ohio 43762 (P)	1,201	82	49	14,130	14,130	
Notre Dame College of Ohio; South Euclid, Ohio 44121 (P)	597	73	98	12,774	12,774	5,248
Oberlin College; Oberlin, Ohio 44074 (P)	2,946	54	58	23,174	23,174	6,238
Ohio Dominican College; Columbus, Ohio 43219 (P)	1,883	92	66	12,940	12,940	
Ohio Northern University; Ada, Ohio 45810 (P)	2,505	94	51	19,815	19,815	4,875
Ohio State University-Columbus; Columbus, Ohio 43210 (Pub)	35,647	79	48	3,906	11,088	5,800
Ohio State University-Lima; Lima, Ohio 45804 (Pub)	1,281	56	59	3,960	11,088	5,800

Institution name; city, state ZIP (control)	Students	Percent		Tuition		Room and board
		Accepted	Women	In-state	Out-of-state	
Ohio State University-Mansfield; Mansfield, Ohio 44906 (Pub)	1,225			$ 3,906	$11,088	$5,800
Ohio State University-Marion; Marion, Ohio 43302 (Pub)	1,060			3,906	11,088	5,800
Ohio State University-Newark; Newark, Ohio 43055 (Pub)	1,522	54%	61%	3,906	11,088	5,800
Ohio University-Athens; Athens, Ohio 45701 (Pub)	16,271	75	55	4,275	8,973	5,076
Ohio University-Chillicothe; Chillicothe, Ohio 45601 (Pub)	1,565			3,102	7,581	5,800
Ohio University-Eastern; West Saint Clairsville, Ohio 43950-9724 (Pub)	1,000			2,613	6,276	
Ohio University-Lancaster; Lancaster, Ohio 43130 (Pub)	1,500					
Ohio University-Southern; Ironton, Ohio 45638-2214 (Pub)				2,865	2,988	
Ohio Wesleyan University; Delaware, Ohio 43015 (P)	1,893	82	52	20,040	20,040	6,370
Otterbein College; Westerville, Ohio 43081 (P)	2,475	85	64	19,749	19,749	
Pontifical College Josephinum; Columbus, Ohio 43235 (P)	42	100		8,740	8,740	
Shawnee State University; Portsmouth, Ohio 45662 (Pub)	3,223	66	63	2,976	5,151	4,096
The Union Institute; Cincinnati, Ohio 45206 (P)	802	73	58	5,952	5,952	
Tiffin University; Tiffin, Ohio 44883 (P)	1,150		50	13,610	13,610	
University of Akron; Akron, Ohio 44325-2001 (P)	4,035	100	52	7,548	7,548	
University of Cincinnati; Cincinnati, Ohio 45221-0091 (Pub)	20,976	85	47	4,509	11,186	5,958
University of Dayton; Dayton, Ohio 45469 (P)	6,662	93	51	14,170	14,170	4,670
University of Findlay; Findlay, Ohio 45840 (P)	3,155	78	47	14,320	14,320	5,510
University of Rio Grande; Rio Grande, Ohio 45674 (P)	1,971	93	58	7,170	7,170	
University of Toledo; Toledo, Ohio 43606 (Pub)	16,911	95	53	3,952	9,544	4,194
Urbana University; Urbana, Ohio 43078-2091 (P)	530	79		13,686	13,686	
Ursuline College; Pepper Pike, Ohio 44124 (P)	1,065	84		8,856	8,856	4,330
Walsh University; North Canton, Ohio 44720 (P)	1,261	53	54	10,900	10,900	5,110
Wilberforce University; Wilberforce, Ohio 45384 (P)	775	25	65	7,760	7,760	4,260
Wilmington College (Ohio); Wilmington, Ohio 45177 (P)	1,033	80	50	16,080	16,080	
Wittenberg University; Springfield, Ohio 45501 (P)	2,088	79	58	18,958	18,958	5,006
Wright State University; Dayton, Ohio 45435 (Pub)	11,843	90	53	3,930	7,860	4,545
Xavier University (Ohio); Cincinnati, Ohio 45207 (P)	3,915	85	60	14,400	14,400	6,150
Youngstown State University; Youngstown, Ohio 44555 (Pub)	11,146	75	55	2,826	6,609	
OKLAHOMA						
Bartlesville Wesleyan College; Bartlesville, Okla. 74006 (P)	571	60		8,200	8,200	3,800
Cameron University; Lawton, Okla. 73505 (Pub)	5,009	94	51	1,479	3,363	2,600
East Central University; Ada, Okla. 74820 (Pub)	3,786		58	1,106	3,323	2,200
Langston University; Langston, Okla. 73050 (Pub)	3,864	62	57	1,857	2,532	2,944
Mid-America Bible College; Oklahoma City, Okla. 73170 (P)	512			6,796	6,796	
Northeastern State University; Tahlequah, Okla. 74464 (Pub)	7,075	91	50	1,686	3,891	2,520
Northwestern Oklahoma State University; Alva, Okla. 73717 (Pub)	1,501	90	54	1,830	4,340	2,316
Oklahoma Baptist University; Shawnee, Okla. 74801 (P)	2,412	95	59	7,660	7,660	3,300
Oklahoma Christian University of Science and Arts; Oklahoma City, Okla. 73136 (P)	1,593	90	47	8,200	8,200	3,840
Oklahoma City University; Oklahoma City, Okla. 73106 (P)	2,174	83	56	8,380	8,380	3,990
Oklahoma Panhandle State University; Goodwell, Okla. 73939 (Pub)	1,589	100		1,290	3,765	2,330
Oklahoma State University; Stillwater, Okla. 74078 (Pub)	14,732	88	47	2,200	5,950	4,420
Oral Roberts University; Tulsa, Okla. 74171 (P)	2,788	61	57	10,160	10,160	4,728
Phillips University; Enid, Okla. 73701 (P)	525	85	49	6,685	6,685	3,900
Southeastern Oklahoma State University; Durant, Okla. 74701-0609 (Pub)	3,476	99	54	1,395	3,900	2,619
Southern Nazarene University; Bethany, Okla. 73008 (P)	1,536	100	55	11,134	11,134	
Southwestern College of Christian Ministries; Bethany, Okla. 73008 (P)				5,409	5,409	
Southwestern Oklahoma State University; Weatherford, Okla. 73096 (Pub)	4,004	99	56	1,380	3,735	2,216
University of Central Oklahoma; Edmond, Okla. 73034 (Pub)	11,288	96	57	1,372	3,713	2,481
University of Oklahoma; Norman, Okla. 73019 (Pub)	16,219	88	47	1,745	5,785	3,800
University of Science & Arts of Oklahoma; Chickasha, Okla. 73018 (Pub)	1,393	91	65	1,725	4,208	2,025
University of Tulsa; Tulsa, Okla. 74104 (P)	2,909	83	52	12,850	12,850	4,550
OREGON						
Blue Mountain College; Pendleton, Ore. 97801 (P)	417	75		6,200	6,200	
Eastern Oregon State College; La Grande, Ore. 97850 (Pub)	2,168	61	53	2,316	2,316	4,165
George Fox University; Newberg, Ore. 97132 (P)	1,667	87	60	15,950	15,950	5,120
Lewis & Clark College; Portland, Ore. 97219-7899 (P)	1,858	66	58	19,176	19,176	6,046
Linfield College; McMinnville, Ore. 97128-6894 (P)	2,709	88	64	16,830	16,830	5,180
Marylhurst University; Marylhurst, Ore. 97036-0261 (P)	931		74	7,812	7,812	5,700
Mount Angel Seminary; St. Benedict, Ore. 97373 (P)				7,050	7,050	
Northwest Christian College; Eugene, Ore. 97401 (P)	384	97		14,300	14,300	
Oregon Health Sciences University; Portland, Ore. 97201-3098 (Pub)	146					
Oregon Institute of Technology; Klamath Falls, Ore. 97601 (Pub)	1,626	76	67	3,309	10,083	3,910

Institution name; city, state ZIP (control)	Students	Percent Accepted	Percent Women	Tuition In-state	Tuition Out-of-state	Room and board
Oregon State University; Corvallis, Ore. 97331 (Pub)	11,430		43%	$ 3,432	$10,420	$4,851
Pacific Northwest College of Art; Portland, Ore. 97209 (P)	280	29%	56	14,742	14,742	
Pacific University; Forest Grove, Ore. 97116 (P)	1,700	85	60	16,694	16,694	4,579
Portland State University; Portland, Ore. 97207 (Pub)	11,397	81	54	3,060	9,108	5,850
Reed College; Portland, Ore. 97202 (P)	1,316	70	54	30,470	30,470	
Southern Oregon University; Ashland, Ore. 97520 (Pub)	4,097	77	53	3,045	9,063	4,182
University of Oregon; Eugene, Ore. 97403-1217 (Pub)	13,762	90	52	3,750	12,500	5,200
University of Portland; Portland, Ore. 97203 (P)	2,078	92	53	16,200	16,200	4,990
Warner Pacific College; Portland, Ore. 97215 (P)	594	87	62	11,190	11,190	4,100
Western Baptist College; Salem, Ore. 97301 (P)	701	91	61	12,750	12,750	4,820
Western Oregon University; Monmouth, Ore. 97361 (Pub)	3,862	56	59	3,096	9,108	4,410
Willamette University; Salem, Ore. 97301 (P)	1,862	82	55	26,770	26,770	
PENNSYLVANIA						
Academy of the New Church; Bryn Athyn, Pa. 19009 (P)	132			8,169	8,169	
Albright College; Reading, Pa. 19612 (P)	1,100	86	65	18,240	18,240	5,612
Allegheny College; Meadville, Pa. 16335 (P)	1,890	81	53	20,020	20,020	
Allentown College of Saint Francis de Sales; Center Valley, Pa. 18034 (P)	1,751	76		11,600	11,600	5,470
Alvernia College; Reading, Pa. 19607 (P)	1,214	77	67	11,280	11,280	5,200
Baptist Bible College of Pennsylvania; Clarks Summit, Pa. 18411 (P)	533	46		7,530	7,530	4,534
Beaver College; Glenside, Pa. 19038 (P)	1,637	75	73	16,520	16,520	6,900
Bloomsburg University of Pennsylvania; Bloomsburg, Pa. 17815 (Pub)	6,920	58	62	3,468	8,824	3,368
Bryn Mawr College; Bryn Mawr, Pa. 19010-2899 (P)	1,226	58	100	21,020	21,020	7,590
Bucknell University; Lewisburg, Pa. 17837 (P)	3,376	54	48	21,870	21,870	5,355
Cabrini College; Radnor, Pa. 19087 (P)	1,685	87	70	13,900	13,900	6,900
California University of Pennsylvania; California, Pa. 15419 (Pub)	4,779	75	53	3,468	8,566	3,992
Carlow College; Pittsburgh, Pa. 15213-3165 (P)	2,056	81	93	10,730	10,730	4,692
Carnegie Mellon University; Pittsburgh, Pa. 15213 (P)	4,875	43	34	20,275	20,275	6,225
Cedar Crest College; Allentown, Pa. 18104-6196 (P)	1,673	75	96	20,735	20,735	
Chatham College; Pittsburgh, Pa. 15232 (P)	551	92	98	15,184	15,184	5,526
Chestnut Hill College; Philadelphia, Pa. 19118-2693 (P)	764	83	100	14,648	14,648	6,510
Cheyney University of Pennsylvania; Cheyney, Pa. 19319 (Pub)	1,059	71	50	2,954	8,824	4,528
Clarion University of Pennsylvania; Clarion, Pa. 16214 (Pub)	5,900	91	57	7,749	7,804	3,480
College Misericordia; Dallas, Pa. 18612 (P)	1,545	64	74	19,270	19,270	
Combs College of Music; Philadelphia, Pa. 19119 (P)				9,400	9,400	
Delaware Valley College; Doylestown, Pa. 18901 (P)	2,095	75	50	14,706	14,706	5,826
Dickinson College; Carlisle, Pa. 17013 (P)	1,842	79	57	22,250	22,250	6,030
Drexel University; Philadelphia, Pa. 19104-2875 (P)	7,702	68	35	14,726	14,726	7,488
Duquesne University; Pittsburgh, Pa. 15228 (P)	5,572	65	57	13,041	13,041	5,978
East Stroudsburg University of Pennsylvania; East Stroudsburg, Pa. 18301-2999 (Pub)	4,821	71	57	3,468	8,824	3,720
Eastern College; St. Davids, Pa. 19087-3696 (P)	1,744	51	65	13,200	13,200	5,654
Edinboro University of Pennsylvania; Edinboro, Pa. 16444 (Pub)	6,455	78	57	3,468	8,824	3,674
Elizabethtown College; Elizabethtown, Pa. 17022-2298 (P)	1,703	76	68	17,050	17,050	5,200
Franklin & Marshall College; Lancaster, Pa. 17604-3003 (P)	1,843	54	49	23,164	23,164	5,400
Gannon University; Erie, Pa. 16541 (P)	2,684	83	57	12,460	12,460	5,600
Geneva College; Beaver Falls, Pa. 15010 (P)	1,763	84	53	15,300	15,300	
Gettysburg College; Gettysburg, Pa. 17325 (P)	2,243	72	53	27,468	27,468	5,038
Gratz College; Philadelphia, Pa. 19141 (P)	350			4,200	4,200	
Grove City College; Grove City, Pa. 16127-2104 (P)	2,268	42	50	6,740	6,740	3,912
Gwynedd-Mercy College; Gwynedd Valley, Pa. 19437 (P)	1,502	55	80	12,775	12,775	5,900
Haverford College; Haverford, Pa. 19041 (P)	1,147	34		22,644	22,644	7,370
Holy Family College; Philadelphia, Pa. 19114 (P)	2,057	78	75	10,800	10,800	
Immaculata College; Immaculata, Pa. 19345 (P)	2,540	91	57	12,500	12,500	6,200
Indiana University of Pennsylvania; Indiana, Pa. 15705 (Pub)	12,158	63	55	3,368	8,566	3,332
Juniata College; Huntingdon, Pa. 16652-2119 (P)	1,204	85	56	17,500	17,500	4,965
King's College (Penn.); Wilkes-Barre, Pa. 18711 (P)	2,077	83	51	13,390	13,390	6,020
Kutztown University of Pennsylvania; Kutztown, Pa. 19530 (Pub)	6,932	73	58	4,101	9,297	3,910
Lafayette College; Easton, Pa. 18042 (P)	2,185	58	46	21,964	21,964	6,841
LaRoche College; Pittsburgh, Pa. 15237 (P)	1,219	91		14,910	14,910	
LaSalle University; Philadelphia, Pa. 19141 (P)	4,031	84	60	23,205	23,205	7,195
Lebanon Valley College; Annville, Pa. 17003 (P)	1,645	76	61	21,910	21,910	
Lehigh University; Bethlehem, Pa. 18015 (P)	4,483	55	39	21,350	21,350	6,220
Lincoln University (Penn.); Lincoln University, Pa. 19352 (P)	1,211		58	8,181	8,181	4,440
Lock Haven University of Pennsylvania; Lock Haven, Pa. 17745 (Pub)	3,465	81	54	3,468	8,824	3,880
Lycoming College; Williamsport, Pa. 17701-5192 (P)	1,455	80	57	16,500	16,500	4,700

Institution name; city, state ZIP (control)	Students	Percent Accepted	Percent Women	Tuition In-state	Tuition Out-of-state	Room and board
Mansfield University of Pennsylvania; Mansfield, Pa. 16933 (Pub)	2,698	86%	57%	$ 3,468	$ 8,824	$3,468
Marywood University; Scranton, Pa. 18509 (P)	1,710	82	74	14,208	14,208	6,200
Medical College of Pennsylvania/Hahnemann University; Philadelphia, Pa. 19102 (P)				15,000	15,000	
Mercyhurst College; Erie, Pa. 16546 (P)	2,635	77	52	12,000	12,000	4,884
Messiah College; Grantham, Pa. 17027-0800 (P)	2,616	87	61	12,900	12,900	5,500
Millersville University of Pennsylvania; Millersville, Pa. 17551-0302 (Pub)	6,662	58	58	3,468	8,824	4,510
Moore College of Art & Design; Philadelphia, Pa. 19103 (P)	370	62	100	19,434	19,434	
Moravian College; Bethlehem, Pa. 18018 (P)	1,712	82	58	17,570	17,570	5,720
Mount Aloysius College; Cresson, Pa. 16630 (P)	1,399	54	76	9,460	9,460	4,580
Muhlenberg College; Allentown, Pa. 18104-5596 (P)	1,910	66	69	19,300	19,300	5,200
Neumann College; Aston, Pa. 19014-1298 (P)	1,117	89	72	19,590	19,590	6,300
Pennsylvania State University–Abington College; Abington, Pa. 19001-3918 (Pub)	3,187	84	52	5,482	8,534	4,640
Pennsylvania State University–Altoona College; Altoona, Pa. 16601-3760 (Pub)	3,721	92	47	5,482	8,534	4,640
Pennsylvania State University–Beaver College; Monaca, Pa. 15001-2799 (Pub)	802	91	37	5,454	8,478	4,640
Pennsylvania State University–Behrend College; Erie, Pa. 16563 (Pub)	3,174	86	36	5,632	11,774	4,640
Pennsylvania State University–Berks College; Reading, Pa. 19610-6009 (Pub)	1,808	89	42	5,482	8,534	4,640
Pennsylvania State University–Delaware County Campus; Media, Pa. 19063-5596 (Pub)	1,545	84	46	5,454	8,478	4,640
Pennsylvania State University–DuBois Campus; Dubois, Pa. 15801-3199 (Pub)	1,062	89	53	5,454	8,478	4,640
Pennsylvania State University–Fayette Campus; Uniontown, Pa. 15401-0519 (Pub)	871	93	56	5,454	8,478	4,640
Pennsylvania State University–Harrisburg; Middletown, Pa. 17057-4898 (Pub)	2,016		53	5,632	11,774	4,640
Pennsylvania State University–Hazleton Campus; Hazleton, Pa. 18201-1291 (Pub)	1,280	92	45	5,454	8,478	4,640
Pennsylvania State University–McKeesport Campus; McKeesport, Pa. 15132 (Pub)	836	89	40	5,454	8,478	4,640
Pennsylvania State University–Mont Alto Campus; Mont Alto, Pa. 17237-9703 (Pub)	1,099	89	53	5,454	8,478	4,640
Pennsylvania State University–New Kensington Campus; New Kensington, Pa. 15066-1798 (Pub)	841	89	42	5,454	8,478	4,640
Pennsylvania State University–Schuylkill Campus; Schuylkill Haven, Pa. 17972-2208 (Pub)	975	91	54	5,454	8,478	4,640
Pennsylvania State University–Shenango Campus; Sharon, Pa. 16146-1537 (Pub)	1,014	95	66	5,454	8,478	4,640
Pennsylvania State University–University Park; University Park, Pa. 16802-3000 (Pub)	34,264	38	46	5,454	12,306	4,338
Pennsylvania State University–Wilkes-Barre Campus; Lehman, Pa. 18627-0217 (Pub)	767	88	31	5,454	8,478	4,640
Pennsylvania State University–Worthington Scranton; Dunmore, Pa. 18512-1699 (Pub)	1,386	85	52	5,454	8,478	4,640
Pennsylvania State University–York Campus; York, Pa. 17403-3298 (Pub)	1,839	92	43	5,454	8,478	4,640
Philadelphia College of Bible; Langhorne, Pa. 19047 (P)	963	64	52	8,850	8,850	4,820
Philadelphia College of Textiles and Science; Philadelphia, Pa. 19144 (P)	2,706	81	61	14,140	14,140	6,300
Point Park College; Pittsburgh, Pa. 15222-1984 (P)	2,193	90	53	11,958	11,958	5,252
Robert Morris College; Moon Township, Pa. 15108-1189 (P)	3,947	91	50	7,650	7,650	4,744
Rosemont College; Rosemont, Pa. 19010-1699 (P)	795	67	85	12,960	12,960	6,500
Saint Charles Borromeo Seminary; Wynnewood, Pa. 19096 (P)	226		42	7,150	7,150	4,750
Saint Francis College (Pennsylvania); Loretto, Pa. 15940 (P)	1,475	80	58	13,312	13,312	6,290
Saint Joseph's University (Pennsylvania); Philadelphia, Pa. 19131 (P)	4,204	70	56	15,915	15,915	6,972
Saint Vincent College; Latrobe, Pa. 15650-2690 (P)	1,238	84	52	13,361	13,361	4,750
Seton Hill College; Greensburg, Pa. 15601 (P)	1,023	89	86	16,780	16,780	
Shippensburg University of Pennsylvania; Shippensburg, Pa. 17257-2299 (Pub)	5,673	74	55	3,468	8,824	3,722
Slippery Rock University of Pennsylvania; Slippery Rock, Pa. 16057 (Pub)	6,337	83	57	3,468	8,824	3,552
Susquehanna University; Selinsgrove, Pa. 17870 (P)	1,725	75	57	18,740	18,740	5,390
Swarthmore College; Swarthmore, Pa. 19081 (P)	1,370	23		23,020	23,020	7,500
Temple University; Philadelphia, Pa. 19122-6096 (Pub)	17,000	69	60	5,870	10,752	5,506
Thiel College; Greenville, Pa. 16125 (P)	1,012	88	52	13,676	13,676	5,374
University of Pennsylvania; Philadelphia, Pa. 19104 (P)	9,501	30	47	22,250	22,250	7,280
University of Pittsburgh-Bradford; Bradford, Pa. 16701 (Pub)	1,263	91	62	5,914	13,100	4,880

Institution name; city, state ZIP (control)	Students	Percent		Tuition		Room and board
		Accepted	Women	In-state	Out-of-state	
University of Pittsburgh-Greensburg; Greensburg, Pa. 15601 (Pub)	1,501	80%	53%	$ 5,658	$12,422	$4,130
University of Pittsburgh-Johnstown; Johnstown, Pa. 15904-1200 (Pub)	3,096	86	54	5,658	12,422	4,720
University of Pittsburgh-Pittsburgh; Pittsburgh, Pa. 15227 (Pub)	16,180	78	53	5,658	12,422	5,414
University of Scranton; Scranton, Pa. 18510-4699 (P)	4,111	67	58	16,620	16,620	7,346
University of the Arts; Philadelphia, Pa. 19102 (P)	1,488	58	49	15,300	15,300	6,050
University of the Sciences in Philadelphia; Philadelphia, Pa. 19104-4495 (P)	1,967	77	64	13,750	13,750	5,400
Ursinus College; Collegeville, Pa. 19426 (P)	1,194	81	53	21,890	21,890	
Villa Maria College; Erie, Pa. 16505 (P)				11,890	11,890	
Villanova University; Villanova, Pa. 19085 (P)	7,109	61	51	26,127	26,127	
Washington & Jefferson College; Washington, Pa. 15301 (P)	1,218	83	49	17,700	17,700	4,350
Waynesburg College; Waynesburg, Pa. 15370 (P)	1,226	78	48	10,290	10,290	4,260
West Chester University of Pennsylvania; West Chester, Pa. 19383 (Pub)	9,388	61	60	3,468	8,824	4,460
Westminster College (Pa.); New Wilmington, Pa. 16172 (P)	1,443	88	61	14,745	14,745	4,540
Widener University; Chester, Pa. 19013 (P)	3,621	87	56	19,560	19,560	
Wilkes University; Wilkes-Barre, Pa. 18766 (P)	1,963	78	51	15,050	15,050	6,830
Wilson College; Chambersburg, Pa. 17201 (P)	821	93	84	12,915	12,915	6,000
York College of Pennsylvania; York, Pa. 17405-7199 (P)	4,858	73		5,800	5,800	4,390
RHODE ISLAND						
Brown University; Providence, R.I. 02912 (P)	5,958	18	54	21,592	21,592	6,898
Bryant College; Smithfield, R.I. 02917 (P)	2,726	84	44	15,600	15,600	6,700
Johnson and Wales University-Providence; Providence, R.I. 02903-3703 (P)	7,612	80	47	12,330	12,330	5,550
Providence College; Providence, R.I. 02918 (P)	3,600	67	77	16,980	16,980	7,125
Rhode Island College; Providence, R.I. 02908 (Pub)	6,816	74	66	2,620	7,400	5,500
Rhode Island School of Design; Providence, R.I. 02903 (P)	8,505	43	56	6,645	6,645	6,390
Roger Williams University; Bristol, R.I. 02809-7144 (P)	2,100	92	46	15,960	15,960	7,340
Salve Regina University; Newport, R.I. 02840-4192 (P)	1,500	88	71	15,950	15,950	7,250
University of Rhode Island; Kingston, R.I. 02881 (Pub)	10,322	79	55	3,282	11,286	6,006
SOUTH CAROLINA						
Anderson College; Anderson, S.C. 29621 (P)	1,100		55	8,940	8,940	4,228
Benedict College; Columbia, S.C. 29204 (P)	2,208	79	53	7,284	7,284	4,182
Charleston Southern University; Charleston, S.C. 29423 (P)	2,226	68	59	9,820	9,820	3,776
Claflin College; Orangeburg, S.C. 29115 (P)	1,005	64	66	5,916	5,916	3,314
Clemson University; Clemson, S.C. 29634 (Pub)	12,710	74	46	3,062	8,676	3,888
Coastal Carolina University; Conway, S.C. 29528-6054 (Pub)	4,283	78	57	2,910	7,840	2,810
Coker College; Hartsville, S.C. 29550 (P)	970	70	65	13,900	13,900	4,516
College of Charleston; Charleston, S.C. 29424-0001 (Pub)	9,252	67	63	3,290	6,580	3,850
Columbia College (S.C.); Columbia, S.C. 29203 (P)	1,278	81	100	13,200	13,200	4,500
Columbia International University; Columbia, S.C. 29230 (P)	519	76		7,871	7,871	4,110
Converse College; Spartanburg, S.C. 29302 (P)	730	92	100	17,825	17,825	
Erskine College; Due West, S.C. 29639 (P)	479	86	58	13,944	13,944	4,697
Francis Marion University; Florence, S.C. 29501 (Pub)	3,294	75	55	3,180	6,360	3,310
Furman University; Greenville, S.C. 29613 (P)	2,571	80	55	17,056	17,056	4,608
Johnson and Wales University-Charleston; Charleston, S.C. 29403 (P)	1,325	87	36	11,139	11,139	3,738
Lander University; Greenwood, S.C. 29649 (Pub)	2,536	89	65	3,600	5,832	3,340
Limestone College; Gaffney, S.C. 29340 (P)		76		11,900	11,900	
Medical University of South Carolina; Charleston, S.C. 29425 (Pub)	1,048					
Morris College; Sumter, S.C. 29150 (P)	971	71	65	5,355	5,355	2,770
Newberry College; Newberry, S.C. 29108 (P)	716	82	47	12,712	12,712	3,700
Presbyterian College; Clinton, S.C. 29325 (P)	1,116	84	50	13,716	13,716	4,216
South Carolina State University; Orangeburg, S.C. 29117 (Pub)	4,911	59	57	2,400	4,880	4,100
Southern Wesleyan University; Central, S.C. 29630 (P)	5,424	42		12,796	12,796	
The Citadel; Charleston, S.C. 29409 (Pub)	1,936	86		6,860	10,854	3,950
University of South Carolina-Aiken; Aiken, S.C. 29801 (Pub)	2,955	73	66	2,848	6,910	3,410
University of South Carolina-Columbia; Columbia, S.C. 29208 (Pub)	15,828	77	54	3,380	8,575	3,690
University of South Carolina-Spartanburg; Spartanburg, S.C. 29303 (Pub)	3,285	71	63	2,874	7,184	3,200
Voorhees College; Denmark, S.C. 29042 (P)	924	80	63	8,034	8,034	
Winthrop University; Rock Hill, S.C. 29733 (Pub)	4,294	87	69	3,918	7,046	3,764
Wofford College; Spartanburg, S.C. 29303-3663 (P)	1,074	53	47	15,085	15,085	4,410
SOUTH DAKOTA						
Augustana College (S.D.); Sioux Falls, S.D. 57197 (P)	1,633	91	66	13,490	13,490	3,920
Black Hills State University; Spearfish, S.D. 57799-9502 (Pub)	3,323	90	59	1,728	5,496	2,614
Dakota State University; Madison, S.D. 57042 (Pub)	1,333	76	53	2,858	6,050	2,694
Dakota Wesleyan University; Mitchell, S.D. 57301-4398 (P)	661	83	60	9,355	9,355	3,540
Huron University; Huron, S.D. 57350 (P)	404	97	47	8,100	8,100	3,600

Institution name; city, state ZIP (control)	Students	Percent Accepted	Percent Women	Tuition In-state	Tuition Out-of-state	Room and board
Mount Marty College; Yankton, S.D. 57078 (P)	895	92%		$11,458	$11,458	
Northern State University; Aberdeen, S.D. 57401 (Pub)	2,871	97	57%	1,646	4,840	$2,407
Oglala Lakota College; Kyle, S.D. 57752 (P)				1,200	1,200	
Presentation College; Aberdeen, S.D. 57401 (P)	461		78	6,820	6,820	3,100
Sinte Gleska University; Rosebud, S.D. 57570 (P)	642	59%		1,660	1,660	
South Dakota School of Mines & Technology; Rapid City, S.D. 57701 (Pub)	2,225	75	26	1,797	5,717	2,900
South Dakota State University; Brookings, S.D. 57007 (Pub)	7,644		50	1,728	5,496	2,382
University of Sioux Falls; Sioux Falls, S.D. 57105 (P)	845	96	58	11,100	11,100	3,740
University of South Dakota; Vermillion, S.D. 57069 (Pub)	5,858	98	56	1,797	5,720	2,988
TENNESSEE						
Austin Peay State University; Clarksville, Tenn. 37040 (Pub)	7,201	56	55	2,280	6,876	2,930
Belmont University; Nashville, Tenn. 37212-3757 (P)	2,533	79	61	10,800	10,800	4,640
Bethel College (Tenn.); McKenzie, Tenn. 38201 (P)	504			6,990	6,990	
Bryan College; Dayton, Tenn. 37321 (P)	455	60		10,300	10,300	3,950
Carson-Newman College; Jefferson City, Tenn. 37760 (P)	2,063	89	59	10,000	10,000	3,830
Christian Brothers University; Memphis, Tenn. 38104 (P)	1,583	84	50	12,400	12,400	4,030
Cumberland University; Lebanon, Tenn. 37087-3554 (P)	966	72	52	8,000	8,000	5,200
East Tennessee State University; Johnson City, Tenn. 37614-0734 (Pub)	9,276	83	58	1,816	6,412	1,190
Fisk University; Nashville, Tenn. 37208-3051 (P)	700	76	71	8,000	8,000	4,650
Freed-Hardeman University; Henderson, Tenn. 38340 (P)	1,275	66	55	6,504	6,504	3,760
King College (Tenn.); Bristol, Tenn. 37620 (P)	537	70	58	13,004	13,004	
Knoxville College; Knoxville, Tenn. 37921 (P)	1,177	25	35	5,400	5,400	3,450
Lambuth University; Jackson, Tenn. 38301 (P)	1,036	65	55	9,874	9,874	
Lane College; Jackson, Tenn. 38301 (P)	768	58	50	8,400	8,400	
Lee University; Cleveland, Tenn. 37320-3450 (P)	2,827	63	56	5,826	5,826	3,760
LeMoyne-Owen College; Memphis, Tenn. 38126 (P)	1,121	87	60	10,300	10,300	
Lincoln Memorial University; Harrogate, Tenn. 37752 (P)	1,237	76	69	7,800	7,800	3,300
Lipscomb University; Nashville, Tenn. 37204-3951 (P)	2,447	89	55	10,795	10,795	
Maryville College; Maryville, Tenn. 37804-5907 (P)	955	82	52	14,200	14,200	4,500
Memphis College of Art; Memphis, Tenn. 38104 (P)	216	85	46	11,400	11,400	4,500
Middle Tennessee State University; Murfreesboro, Tenn. 37132 (Pub)	15,890	69	55	1,906	6,732	3,030
Milligan College; Milligan Coll, Tenn. 37682 (P)	765	81		10,420	10,420	3,800
Rhodes College; Memphis, Tenn. 38112 (P)	1,418	75	55	17,360	17,360	5,110
Southern College of Seventh-Day Adventists; Collegedale, Tenn. 37315 (P)		98		12,938	12,938	
Tennessee State University; Nashville, Tenn. 37209 (Pub)	6,929	50	62	2,118	6,714	2,980
Tennessee Technological University; Cookeville, Tenn. 38505 (Pub)	7,007	89	47	1,890	6,226	3,100
Tennessee Wesleyan College; Athens, Tenn. 37371-0040 (P)	2,090	84	61	10,000	10,000	
Trevecca Nazarene College; Nashville, Tenn. 37210 (P)	1,049	100	56	11,734	11,734	
Tusculum College; Greeneville, Tenn. 37743 (P)	1,137	76	54	11,800	11,800	3,900
Union University; Jackson, Tenn. 38305-3697 (P)	1,758	80	65	9,180	9,180	3,380
University of Memphis; Memphis, Tenn. 38152 (Pub)	15,485		57	2,112	6,448	3,995
University of Tennessee at Martin; Martin, Tenn. 38238 (Pub)	5,368	90	60	1,924	6,260	3,200
University of Tennessee-Chattanooga; Chattanooga, Tenn. 37403 (Pub)	7,240	55	57	2,170	6,766	1,900
University of Tennessee-Knoxville; Knoxville, Tenn. 37996 (Pub)	19,070	76	50	2,576	7,258	3,802
University of the South; Sewanee, Tenn. 37383 (P)	1,294	64	53	17,555	17,555	4,660
Vanderbilt University; Nashville, Tenn. 37203-1727 (P)	5,852	58	50	21,930	21,930	7,598
TEXAS						
Abilene Christian University; Abilene, Tex. 79699-9100 (P)	3,909	89	54	9,240	9,240	4,010
Angelo State University; San Angelo, Tex. 76909 (Pub)	5,828	71	55	1,904	8,324	4,152
Austin College; Sherman, Tex. 75090-4440 (P)	1,161	61	52	13,621	13,621	5,393
Baylor University; Waco, Tex. 76798-7056 (P)	10,597		57	9,240	9,240	4,566
Concordia Lutheran College; Austin, Tex. 78705 (P)	706	96	57	9,800	9,800	5,000
Dallas Baptist University; Dallas, Tex. 75211 (P)	2,695	88	60	7,800	7,800	3,510
East Texas Baptist University; Marshall, Tex. 75670 (P)	1,248	73	60	8,460	8,460	
East Texas State University; Commerce, Tex. 75429 (Pub)	5,347	67	57	1,854	1,854	3,600
Hardin-Simmons University; Abilene, Tex. 79698 (P)	1,973	88	52	11,680	11,680	
Houston Baptist University; Houston, Tex. 77074 (P)	1,610	76	63	11,289	11,289	
Howard Payne University; Brownwood, Tex. 76801 (P)	1,489	90	46	8,940	8,940	
Jarvis Christian College; Hawkins, Tex. 75765 (P)	533	90		10,179	10,179	
Lamar University; Beaumont, Tex. 77710 (Pub)	9,496	82	53	864	5,976	3,040
LeTourneau University; Longview, Tex. 75607 (P)	1,842	50	35	11,124	11,124	5,220
Lubbock Christian University; Lubbock, Tex. 79407 (P)	1,035	96	56	9,504	9,504	3,220
McMurry University; Abilene, Tex. 79697 (P)	1,410	76	45	7,560	7,560	3,767
Midwestern State University; Wichita Falls, Tex. 76308 (Pub)	5,093	77	57	768	5,904	3,534
Our Lady of the Lake University; San Antonio, Tex. 78207-4689 (P)	3,666	74	52	10,112	10,112	3,932
Paul Quinn College; Dallas, Tex. 75241 (P)	517			7,350	7,350	

Institution name; city, state ZIP (control)	Students	Percent		Tuition		Room and board
		Accepted	Women	In-state	Out-of-state	
Prairie View A&M University; Prairie View, Tex. 77446 (Pub)	4,778	93%	55%	$ 2,436	$ 7,470	$4,862
Rice University; Houston, Tex. 77005-1892 (P)	2,764	27	46	13,706	13,706	6,400
Saint Edward's University; Austin, Tex. 78704-6489 (P)	2,527	76	60	10,730	10,730	4,700
Saint Mary's University (Tex.); San Antonio, Tex. 78228-8572 (P)	2,620	87	59	10,380	10,380	4,768
Sam Houston State University; Huntsville, Tex. 77341 (Pub)	11,223	84	55	1,670	6,898	3,300
Schreiner College; Kerrville, Tex. 78028 (P)	647	74	57	10,490	10,490	6,480
Southern Methodist University; Dallas, Tex. 75275 (P)	5,449	88	54	15,640	15,640	6,579
Southwest Texas State University; San Marcos, Tex. 78666 (Pub)	17,533	75	54	816	5,952	3,901
Southwestern Adventist University; Keene, Tex. 76059 (P)	1,065	100	58	11,918	11,918	
Southwestern Christian College; Terrell, Tex. 75160 (P)				5,926	5,926	
Southwestern University; Georgetown, Tex. 78626 (P)	1,215	73	57	14,600	14,600	5,190
Stephen F. Austin State University; Nacogdoches, Tex. 75962 (Pub)	10,116	71	56	1,080	7,470	4,118
Sul Ross State University; Alpine, Tex. 79832 (Pub)	2,270	99	53	1,080	7,470	3,480
Tarleton State University; Stephenville, Tex. 76402 (Pub)	5,551	74	50	1,080	7,470	3,400
Texas Christian University; Fort Worth, Tex. 76129 (P)	5,893	79	57	10,350	10,350	4,000
Texas A&M University-College Station; College Station, Tex. 77843 (Pub)	33,945	73	47	2,100	8,490	3,800
Texas A&M University-Galveston; Galveston, Tex. 77553 (Pub)	1,111	90	47	2,164	8,614	3,652
Texas College; Tyler, Tex. 75702 (P)				7,430	7,430	
Texas Lutheran College; Seguin, Tex. 78155 (P)	1,324		60	10,800	10,800	3,830
Texas Southern University; Houston, Tex. 77004 (Pub)	8,832		70	2,058	7,180	4,000
Texas Tech University; Lubbock, Tex. 79409 (Pub)	20,420	81	46	1,080	7,470	4,496
Texas Wesleyan University; Fort Worth, Tex. 76105-1536 (P)	2,090	81	61	7,550	7,550	3,700
Texas Woman's University; Denton, Tex. 76204 (Pub)	5,752		95	2,084	7,196	3,578
The College of Saint Thomas More; Fort Worth, Tex. 76109 (P)	60		50	5,200	5,200	300
The Criswell College; Dallas, Tex. 75246 (P)	575			2,490	2,490	
Trinity University; San Antonio, Tex. 78212 (P)	2,244	77	52	14,580	14,580	5,970
University of Central Texas; Killeen, Tex. 76540-1416 (P)	747		57	3,144	3,144	3,449
University of Dallas; Irving, Tex. 75062 (P)	1,131	94	56	13,606	13,606	5,186
University of Houston; Houston, Tex. 77204-2161 (Pub)	23,572	70	53	864	5,952	4,405
University of Houston-Downtown; Houston, Tex. 77002 (Pub)	21,522	62		816	5,904	
University of Houston-Victoria Campus; Victoria, Tex. 77091-4450 (Pub)	711		74	816	5,952	
University of Mary Hardin-Baylor; Belton, Tex. 76513 (P)	2,010	71	69	6,500	6,500	4,000
University of North Texas; Denton, Tex. 76203 (Pub)	19,181	76	51	2,075	7,187	3,938
University of Saint Thomas (Tex.); Houston, Tex. 77006 (P)	1,539	83	66	8,880	8,880	4,730
University of Texas at Austin; Austin, Tex. 78712 (Pub)	36,861	78	50	2,040	8,460	
University of Texas at Tyler; Tyler, Tex. 75701-6699 (Pub)	2,378			2,492	8,912	
University of Texas–Arlington; Arlington, Tex. 76019-0088 (Pub)	15,441	95	51	816	5,952	1,350
University of Texas–Dallas; Richardson, Tex. 75083-0688 (Pub)	5,458	65	50	864	5,976	5,574
University of Texas–El Paso; El Paso, Tex. 79968 (Pub)	13,159	79	54	1,956	7,560	1,100
University of Texas–Pan American; Edinburg, Tex. 78539 (Pub)		100		991	3,486	1,241
University of Texas–Permian Basin; Odessa, Tex. 79762 (Pub)	1,219		64	1,776	8,166	3,934
University of Texas–San Antonio; San Antonio, Tex. 78249-0617 (Pub)	14,879	86	54	1,950	8,370	5,000
University of the Incarnate Word; San Antonio, Tex. 78209-6397 (P)	2,659	70	71	11,200	11,200	4,780
Wayland Baptist University; Plainview, Tex. 79072 (P)	3,794	99	43	6,120	6,120	3,314
West Texas A&M University; Canyon, Tex. 79016-0001 (Pub)	5,458	79	53	1,296	6,432	2,969
Wiley College; Marshall, Tex. 75670 (P)	463	97	50	4,080	4,080	3,230
UTAH						
Brigham Young University (Utah); Provo, Utah 84602 (P)	29,426	71	53	2,630	2,630	4,130
Southern Utah University; Cedar City, Utah 84720 (Pub)	5,636	93	56	1,440	5,439	
University of Utah; Salt Lake City, Utah 84112 (Pub)	21,275	95	45	2,601	7,998	4,620
Utah State University; Logan, Utah 84322 (Pub)	17,473	99	53	1,701	5,979	3,579
Weber State University; Ogden, Utah 84408-1103 (Pub)	14,465	100	54	1,518	5,313	
Westminster College of Salt Lake City; Salt Lake City, Utah 84105 (P)	1,608	93	64	14,558	14,558	
VERMONT						
Bennington College; Bennington, Vt. 05201 (P)	347	81	69	26,400	26,400	
Burlington College; Burlington, Vt. 05401 (P)	160	91	60	6,200	6,200	
Castleton State College; Castleton, Vt. 05735 (Pub)	1,867	87	54	3,924	9,192	5,206
Champlain College; Burlington, Vt. 05401 (P)	2,249	86	60	10,075	10,075	7,165
College of Saint Joseph in Vermont; Rutland, Vt. 05701 (P)		93		13,150	13,150	
Goddard College; Plainfield, Vt. 05667 (P)	315	81	59	15,218	15,218	5,288
Green Mountain College; Poultney, Vt. 05764-1199 (P)	608	83	47	16,035	16,035	3,320
Johnson State College; Johnson, Vt. 05656 (Pub)	1,569	78	47	4,753	9,553	5,240
Lyndon State College; Lyndonville, Vt. 05851 (Pub)	1,202	88	47	3,432	7,944	4,854
Marlboro College; Marlboro, Vt. 05344 (P)	289	74	54	20,300	20,300	6,750
Middlebury College; Middlebury, Vt. 05753 (P)	2,176	31	51	30,475	30,475	

Institution name; city, state ZIP (control)	Students	Percent Accepted	Percent Women	Tuition In-state	Tuition Out-of-state	Room and board
Norwich University; Northfield, Vt. 05663 (P)	2,062	87%	40%	$14,926	$14,926	$2,762
Saint Michael's College; Colchester, Vt. 05439 (P)	1,800	70	61	16,455	16,455	7,245
Southern Vermont College; Bennington, Vt. 05201 (P)	472	91	78	10,990	10,990	5,150
Trinity College of Vermont; Burlington, Vt. 05401-9892 (P)	829	92	88	13,620	13,620	6,566
University of Vermont; Burlington, Vt. 05405 (Pub)	8,777	85	54	7,320	18,288	5,306
VIRGINIA						
Averett College; Danville, Va. 24541 (P)	1,563	82	59	12,585	12,585	4,200
Bluefield College; Bluefield, Va. 24605 (P)	818	91	52	12,810	12,810	
Bridgewater College; Bridgewater, Va. 22812-1599 (P)	1,066	81	56	13,010	13,010	5,970
Christendom College; Front Royal, Va. 22630 (P)	223	91	52	10,850	10,850	3,850
Christopher Newport University; Newport News, Va. 23606 (Pub)	4,565	82	61	3,474	8,424	4,950
Clinch Valley College of the University of Virginia; Wise, Va. 24293 (Pub)	1,515	76	56	2,368	7,236	4,284
Eastern Mennonite University; Harrisonburg, Va. 22802-2462 (P)	1,013	91	61	12,600	12,600	4,500
Emory and Henry College; Emory, Va. 24327 (P)	893	85	50	11,978	11,978	4,970
Ferrum College; Ferrum, Va. 24088 (P)	908	79	44	10,750	10,750	4,850
George Mason University; Fairfax, Va. 22030-4444 (Pub)	13,933	68	56	4,296	12,240	5,120
Hampden–Sydney College; Hampden–Sydney, Va. 23943 (P)	962	85	0	14,909	14,909	5,557
Hampton University; Hampton, Va. 23668 (P)	5,711	52	60	12,076	12,076	
Hollins University; Roanoke, Va. 24020-1688 (P)	866	85	100	15,070	15,070	5,975
James Madison University; Harrisonburg, Va. 22807 (Pub)	12,943	55	55	4,104	8,580	4,546
Johnson and Wales University-Norfolk; Norfolk, Va. 23513 (P)	552	84	39	12,867	12,867	5,274
Liberty University; Lynchburg, Va. 24502 (P)	5,867	92	49	13,300	13,300	
Longwood College; Farmville, Va. 23909 (Pub)	2,960	76	67	4,416	9,888	4,360
Lynchburg College; Lynchburg, Va. 24501 (P)	1,413	86	64	19,200	19,200	
Mary Baldwin College; Staunton, Va. 24402 (P)	1,160	86	98	19,600	19,600	
Mary Washington College; Fredericksburg, Va. 22401 (Pub)	3,801	55	66	3,556	8,516	5,080
Marymount University; Arlington, Va. 22207 (P)	1,910	78	74	13,300	13,300	5,980
Norfolk State University; Norfolk, Va. 23504 (Pub)	6,734	96	62	3,000	6,802	4,166
Old Dominion University; Norfolk, Va. 23529 (P)	8,346	81	53	8,530	8,530	
Radford University; Radford, Va. 24142 (Pub)	7,334	80	59	2,016	6,978	4,636
Randolph-Macon College; Ashland, Va. 23005 (P)	1,093	81	49	16,710	16,710	6,910
Randolph-Macon Woman's College; Lynchburg, Va. 24503 (P)	674	89	100	16,710	16,710	6,910
Roanoke College; Salem, Va. 24153-3794 (P)	1,698	81	58	15,380	15,380	5,090
Saint Paul's College; Lawrenceville, Va. 23868 (P)		72		9,090	9,090	
Shenandoah University; Winchester, Va. 22601 (P)	1,320	81	61	18,700	18,700	
Sweet Briar College; Sweet Briar, Va. 24595 (P)	758	94	96	15,730	15,730	6,520
The College of William and Mary; Williamsburg, Va. 23187-8795 (Pub)	5,563	46	60	5,178	16,138	4,586
University of Richmond; Richmond, Va. 23173 (P)	3,637	45	52	18,595	18,595	2,955
University of Virginia; Charlottesville, Va. 22903 (Pub)	13,246	36	53	3,832	14,780	4,421
Virginia Commonwealth University; Richmond, Va. 23284-9005 (Pub)	15,009	80	59	3,125	11,382	
Virginia Intermont College; Bristol, Va. 24201-4298 (P)	848	79	76	10,775	10,775	4,800
Virginia Military Institute; Lexington, Va. 24450 (Pub)	1,282	76		3,655	10,680	3,695
Virginia State University; Petersburg, Va. 23806 (Pub)	3,288	86	58	1,951	6,430	4,910
Virginia Tech; Blacksburg, Va. 24061 (Pub)	21,013	73	40	3,500	10,464	3,420
Virginia Union University; Richmond, Va. 23220 (P)	1,307	94	57	8,980	8,980	3,950
Virginia Wesleyan College; Norfolk/Virginia Beach, Va. 23502 (P)	1,568	88	67	18,250	18,250	
Washington and Lee University; Lexington, Va. 24450-0303 (P)	1,685	31	43	16,470	16,470	5,398
WASHINGTON						
Central Washington University; Ellensburg, Wash. 98926 (Pub)	7,166	76	60	2,622	9,315	5,000
Cornish College of the Arts; Seattle, Wash. 98102 (P)	621	76	56	12,600	12,600	2,500
Eastern Washington University; Cheney, Wash. 99004 (Pub)	6,674	90	57	2,622	9,315	4,294
Gonzaga University; Spokane, Wash. 99258 (P)	2,900	90	55	15,960	15,960	5,170
Griffin College; Seattle, Wash. 98121 (P)				4,800	4,800	
Heritage College; Toppenish, Wash. 98948 (P)	664			6,450	6,450	
Lutheran Bible Institute of Seattle; Issaquah, Wash. 98029 (P)	158			7,950	7,950	
Northwest College; Kirkland, Wash. 98083-0579 (P)	858	97	58	8,850	8,850	4,530
Pacific Lutheran University; Tacoma, Wash. 98447 (P)	3,087	86	60	15,680	15,680	4,890
Saint Martin's College; Lacey, Wash. 98503-1297 (P)	1,000	92	74	13,510	13,510	4,590
Seattle Pacific University; Seattle, Wash. 98119-1997 (P)	2,610	92	67	14,130	14,130	5,418
Seattle University; Seattle, Wash. 98122-4340 (P)	3,500	66	52	15,255	15,255	5,637
The Evergreen State College; Olympia, Wash. 98505 (Pub)	3,812	88	58	2,346	8,295	4,806
University of Puget Sound; Tacoma, Wash. 98416 (P)	2,734	79	60	19,640	19,640	5,070
University of Washington; Seattle, Wash. 98195 (Pub)	25,740	69	51	3,356	10,656	4,671
Walla Walla College; College Place, Wash. 99324 (P)	1,482	46	49	12,570	12,570	3,380
Washington State University; Pullman, Wash. 99164-1009 (Pub)	16,690	44	50	3,396	10,554	4,540

Institution name; city, state ZIP (control)	Students	Percent Accepted	Percent Women	Tuition In-state	Tuition Out-of-state	Room and board
Western Washington University; Bellingham, Wash. 98225 (Pub)	10,184	83%	59%	$ 2,521	$ 8,956	$4,635
Whitman College; Walla Walla, Wash. 99362 (P)	1,300	51	59	20,120	20,120	5,720
Whitworth College; Spokane, Wash. 99251 (P)	1,577	85	59	15,370	15,370	5,300
WEST VIRGINIA						
Alderson-Broaddus College; Philippi, W. Va. 26416 (P)	709	61	58	15,516	15,516	
Bethany College (W.Va.); Bethany, W. Va. 26032 (P)	730		46	17,362	17,362	5,830
Bluefield State College; Bluefield, W. Va. 24701 (Pub)	2,700	64	55	2,110	5,126	
Concord College; Athens, W. Va. 24712 (P)	2,600	93		5,686	5,686	
Davis & Elkins College; Elkins, W. Va. 26241 (P)	683	84	61	11,500	11,500	5,080
Fairmont State College; Fairmont, W. Va. 26554 (Pub)	6,623	99	55	2,040	4,840	7,200
Glenville State College; Glenville, W. Va. 26351 (Pub)	2,179	100	56	1,956	4,560	3,480
Marshall University; Huntington, W. Va. 25755 (Pub)	9,041	91	55	1,798	5,680	4,420
Ohio Valley College; Parkersburg, W. Va. 26101 (P)	430	35	48	6,220	6,220	3,620
Salem–Teikyo University; Salem, W. Va. 26426-0500 (P)	730	99	41	12,428	12,428	4,208
Shepherd College; Shepherdstown, W. Va. 25443-3210 (Pub)	4,025	62	60	2,228	5,348	4,139
University of Charleston; Charleston, W. Va. 25304 (P)	1,424	79	70	12,350	12,350	4,098
West Liberty State College; West Liberty, W. Va. 26074 (Pub)	2,397	95	55	2,190	5,630	3,100
West Virginia Institute of Technology; Montgomery, W. Va. 25136 (Pub)	2,460	100	34	2,564	6,256	4,048
West Virginia State College; Institute, W. Va. 25112 (Pub)	4,530		55	1,127	2,726	3,550
West Virginia University; Morgantown, W. Va. 26506-6009 (Pub)	14,959	93	47	2,412	7,596	4,832
West Virginia Wesleyan College; Buckhannon, W. Va. 26201 (P)	1,569	86	55	15,750	15,750	4,100
Wheeling Jesuit University; Wheeling, W. Va. 26003 (P)	1,296	88	59	17,870	17,870	
WISCONSIN						
Alverno College; Milwaukee, Wis. 53234 (P)	2,107	69	95	10,104	10,104	4,250
Beloit College; Beloit, Wis. 53511 (P)	1,150	72	66	19,570	19,570	4,326
Cardinal Stritch College; Milwaukee, Wis. 53217-3985 (P)	2,609	78		5,040	5,040	3,880
Carroll College (Wis.); Waukesha, Wis. 53186 (P)	2,444		66	14,200	14,200	4,440
Carthage College; Kenosha, Wis. 53406 (P)	2,060	93	59	18,795	18,795	
Concordia University (Wis.); Mequon, Wis. 53097 (P)	4,022	73	59	1,190	1,190	3,600
Edgewood College; Madison, Wis. 53711 (P)	1,451	41	73	10,100	10,100	4,254
Lakeland College; Sheboygan, Wis. 53082 (P)	3,300	87	55	15,040	15,040	
Lawrence University; Appleton, Wis. 54912-0599 (P)	1,179	80	53	20,274	20,274	4,470
Marian College of Fond Du Lac; Fond du Lac, Wis. 54935 (P)	1,600	90	66	11,500	11,500	4,400
Marquette University; Milwaukee, Wis. 53201-1881 (P)	7,299	86	53	15,620	15,620	5,700
Milwaukee Institute of Art and Design; Milwaukee, Wis. 53202 (P)	503	83	42	14,500	14,500	6,000
Milwaukee School of Engineering; Milwaukee, Wis. 53202 (P)	2,543	91	16	16,920	16,920	
Mount Mary College; Milwaukee, Wis. 53222 (P)	1,174	83	99	11,380	11,380	3,970
Mount Senario College; Ladysmith, Wis. 54848 (P)	1,048	68	31	12,110	12,110	
Northland College; Ashland, Wis. 54806 (P)	875	94	57	15,440	15,440	
Ripon College; Ripon, Wis. 54971 (P)	669	89	52	17,350	17,350	4,400
Saint Norbert College; De Pere, Wis. 54115-2099 (P)	1,926	89	59	14,789	14,789	5,162
Silver Lake College; Manitowoc, Wis. 54220 (P)	822	57	70	13,454	13,454	
University of Wisconsin Oshkosh; Oshkosh, Wis. 54901 (Pub)	9,295	89	58	2,778	9,060	2,658
University of Wisconsin–Eau Claire; Eau Claire, Wis. 54701 (Pub)	9,990	82	60	2,891	9,173	3,133
University of Wisconsin–Green Bay; Green Bay, Wis. 54311-7001 (Pub)	5,282	88	63	2,916	9,196	2,896
University of Wisconsin–LaCrosse; LaCrosse, Wis. 54601-3742 (Pub)	8,471	78	57	2,879	9,161	3,260
University of Wisconsin–Madison; Madison, Wis. 53706 (Pub)	27,535	69	51	3,406	11,586	4,206
University of Wisconsin–Milwaukee; Milwaukee, Wis. 53201 (Pub)	17,032	84	54	3,479	11,370	3,594
University of Wisconsin–Parkside; Kenosha, Wis. 53141 (Pub)	4,486	93	60	2,838	9,120	3,730
University of Wisconsin–Platteville; Platteville, Wis. 53818 (Pub)	4,665	83	35	2,806	9,068	3,254
University of Wisconsin–River Falls; River Falls, Wis. 54022 (Pub)	5,037	80	59	2,797	9,079	3,274
University of Wisconsin–Stevens Point; Stevens Point, Wis. 54481 (Pub)	8,024	77	53	2,642	9,124	3,292
University of Wisconsin–Stout; Menomonie, Wis. 54751 (Pub)	6,749	94	48	2,836	9,118	3,156
University of Wisconsin–Superior; Superior, Wis. 54880 (Pub)	2,314	83	51	2,768	9,050	3,296
University of Wisconsin–Whitewater; Whitewater, Wis. 53190 (Pub)	9,537	84	53	2,831	9,113	2,800
Viterbo College; La Crosse, Wis. 54601 (P)	1,747	88	74	15,940	15,940	4,250
Wisconsin Lutheran College; Milwaukee, Wis. 53226 (P)	440	93	60	11,960	11,960	4,500
WYOMING						
University of Wyoming; Laramie, Wyo. 82071 (Pub)	8,567	94	51	2,326	7,414	4,244

The Olympic Games

1896	Athens
1900	Paris
1904	St. Louis
1906	Athens
1908	London
1912	Stockholm
1920	Antwerp
1924	Chamonix (W)
1924	Paris (S)
1928	St. Moritz (W)
1928	Amsterdam (S)
1932	Lake Placid (W)
1932	Los Angeles (S)
1936	Garmisch-Partenkirchen (W)
1936	Berlin (S)
1948	St. Moritz (W)
1948	London (S)
1952	Oslo (W)
1952	Helsinki (S)
1956	Cortina d'Ampezzo, Italy (W)
1956	Melbourne (S)
1960	Squaw Valley, Calif. (W)
1960	Rome (S)
1964	Innsbruck, Austria (W)
1964	Tokyo (S)
1968	Grenoble, France (W)
1968	Mexico City (S)
1972	Sapporo, Japan (W)
1972	Munich (S)
1976	Innsbruck, Austria (W)
1976	Montreal (S)
1980	Lake Placid (W)
1980	Moscow (S)
1984	Sarajevo, Yugoslavia (W)
1984	Los Angeles (S)
1988	Calgary, Alberta (W)
1988	Seoul, South Korea (S)
1992	Albertville, France (W)
1992	Barcelona, Spain (S)
1994	Lillehammer, Norway (W)
1996	Atlanta, Ga. (S)
1998	Nagano, Japan (W)
2000	Sydney, Australia (S)
2002	Salt Lake City (W)
2004	Athens (S)

(W)—Site of Winter Games. (S)—Site of Summer Games

The first Olympic Games of which there is record were held in 776 B.C.E., and consisted of one event, a great foot race of about 200 yards held on a plain by the River Alpheus (now the Ruphia) just outside the little town of Olympia in Greece. It was from that date the Greeks began to keep their calendar by "Olympiads," the four-year spans between the celebrations of the famous games.

The modern Olympic Games, which started in Athens in 1896, are the result of the devotion of a French educator, Baron Pierre de Coubertin, to the idea that, since young people and athletics have gone together through the ages, education and athletics might go hand-in-hand toward a better international understanding.

The principal organization responsible for the staging of the Games is the International Olympic Committee (IOC). Other important roles are played by the National Olympic Committees in each participating country, international sports federations, and the organizing committee of the host city.

Beginning in 1994, the IOC decided to change the format of having both the Summer and Winter Games in the same year. Summer and Winter Olympics now alternate every two years. In 1994, the Winter Games were staged in Lillehammer, Norway, just two years after they'd been held in Albertville, France. The Winter Games will next be held in Salt Lake City, Utah, in 2002. The next Summer Olympics will be 2000 in Sydney, Australia.

The headquarters of the 89-member International Olympic Committee are in Lausanne, Switzerland. The president of the IOC is Juan Antonio Samaranch of Spain.

The Olympic motto is "Citius, Altius, Fortius,"—"Faster, Higher, Stronger." The Olympic symbol is five interlocking circles colored blue, yellow, black, green, and red, on a white background, representing the five continents. At least one of those colors appears in the national flag of every country.

In February, 1998, IOC President Samaranch announced that if any new sports are added to future Olympics, they must include women's events.

Winter Games: Gold Medals

FIGURE SKATING–MEN

1908	Ulrich Salchow, Sweden
1920	Gillis Grafström, Sweden
1924	Gillis Grafström, Sweden
1928	Gillis Grafström, Sweden
1932	Karl Schäfer, Austria
1936	Karl Schäfer, Austria
1948	Dick Button, United States
1952	Dick Button, United States
1956	Hayes Alan Jenkins, United States
1960	David Jenkins, United States
1964	Manfred Schnelldorfer, Germany
1968	Wolfgang Schwarz, Austria
1972	Ondrej Nepela, Czechoslovakia
1976	John Curry, Great Britain
1980	Robin Cousins, Great Britain
1984	Scott Hamilton, United States
1988	Brian Boitano, United States
1992	Viktor Petrenko, Unified Team*
1994	Alexei Urmanov, Russia
1998	Ilia Kulik, Russia

*Former Soviet Union team.

FIGURE SKATING–WOMEN

1908	Madge Syers, Britain
1920	Magda Julin-Mauroy, Sweden
1924	Herma Planck-Szabö, Austria
1928	Sonja Henie, Norway
1932	Sonja Henie, Norway
1936	Sonja Henie, Norway
1948	Barbara Ann Scott, Canada
1952	Jeanette Altwegg, Great Britain
1956	Tenley Albright, United States
1960	Carol Heiss, United States
1964	Sjoukje Dijkstra, Netherlands
1968	Peggy Fleming, United States
1972	Beatrix Schuba, Austria
1976	Dorothy Hamill, United States
1980	Anett Pötzsch, East Germany
1984	Katarina Witt, East Germany
1988	Katarina Witt, East Germany
1992	Kristi Yamaguchi, United States
1994	Oksana Baiul, Ukraine
1998	Tara Lipinski, United States

SPEED SKATING–MEN

(U.S. winners only)

500 Meters

1924 Charles Jewtraw 44.00
1932 Jack Shea 43.40
1952 Ken Henry 43.20
1964 Terry McDermott 40.10
1980 Eric Heiden 38.03

1,000 Meters

1976 Peter Mueller 1:19.32
1980 Eric Heiden 1:15.18
1994 Dan Jansen 1:12.43[1]

1,500 Meters

1932 Jack Shea 2:57.50
1980 Eric Heiden 1:55.44

5,000 Meters

1932 Irving Jaffee 9:40.80
1980 Eric Heiden 7:02.29

10,000 Meters

1932 Irving Jaffee 19:13.60
1980 Eric Heiden 14:28.13

1. World record.

SPEED SKATING–WOMEN

(U.S. winners only)

500 Meters

1972 Anne Henning 43.33
1976 Sheila Young 42.76
1988 Bonnie Blair 39.10
1992 Bonnie Blair 40.33
1994 Bonnie Blair 39.25

1,000 Meters

1992 Bonnie Blair 1:21.90
1994 Bonnie Blair 1:18.74

1,500 Meters

1972 Dianne Holum 2:20.85

SKIING, ALPINE–MEN

Downhill

1948 Henri Oreiller, France 2:55.00
1952 Zeno Colò, Italy 2:30.80
1956 Toni Sailer, Austria 2:52.20
1960 Jean Vuarnet, France 2:06.00
1964 Egon Zimmermann, Austria 2:18.16
1968 Jean-Claude Killy, France 1:59.85
1972 Bernhard Russi, Switzerland 1:51.43
1976 Franz Klammer, Austria 1:45.73
1980 Leonhard Stock, Austria 1:45.50
1984 Bill Johnson, United States 1:45.59
1988 Pirmin Zurbriggen, Switzerland 1:59.63
1992 Patrick Ortlieb, Austria 1:50.37
1994 Tommy Moe, United States 1:45.75
1998 Jean-Luc Cretier, France 1:50.11

Slalom

1948 Edi Reinalter, Switzerland 2:10.30
1952 Othmar Schneider, Austria 2:00.00
1956 Toni Sailer, Austria 3:14.70
1960 Ernst Hinterseer, Austria 2:08.90
1964 Pepi Stiegler, Austria 2:11.13
1968 Jean-Claude Killy, France 1:39.73
1972 Francisco Ochoa, Spain 1:49.27
1976 Piero Gros, Italy 2:03.29
1980 Ingemar Stenmark, Sweden 1:44.26
1984 Phil Mahre, United States 1:39.41
1988 Alberto Tomba, Italy 1:39.47
1992 Finn Christian Jagge, Norway 1:44.39
1994 Thomas Stangassinger, Austria 2:02.02
1998 Hans-Petter Buraas, Norway 1:49.31

Giant Slalom

1952 Stein Eriksen, Norway 2:25.00
1956 Toni Sailer, Austria 3:00.10
1960 Roger Staub, Switzerland 1:48.30
1964 François Bonlieu, France 1:46.71
1968 Jean-Claude Killy, France 3:29.28
1972 Gustav Thöni, Italy 3:09.62
1976 Heini Hemmi, Switzerland 3:26.97
1980 Ingemar Stenmark, Sweden 2:40.74
1984 Max Julen, Switzerland 2:41.18
1988 Alberto Tomba, Italy 2:06.37
1992 Alberto Tomba, Italy 2:06.98
1994 Markus Wasmeier, Germany 2:52.46
1998 Hermann Maier, Austria 2:38.51

Super Giant Slalom

1988 Frank Piccard, France 1:39.66
1992 Kjetil Andre Aamadt, Norway 1:13.04
1994 Markus Wasmeier, Germany 1:32.53
1998 Hermann Maier, Austria 1:34.84

Men's Combined (Downhill and Slalom)

Points

1936 Franz Pfnür, Germany 99.25
1948 Henri Oreiller, France 3.27
1952–1984 Not held
1988 Hubert Strolz, Austria 36.55
1992 Josef Polig, Italy 14.58

Time

1994 Lasse Kjus, Norway 3:17.53
1998 Mario Reiter, Austria 3:08.06

SKIING, ALPINE–WOMEN

Downhill

1948 Hedy Schlunegger, Switzerland 2:28.30
1952 Trude Jochum-Beiser, Austria 1:47.10
1956 Madeleine Berthod, Switzerland 1:40.70
1960 Heidi Biebl, Germany 1:37.60
1964 Christl Haas, Austria 1:55.39
1968 Olga Pall, Austria 1:40.87
1972 Marie-Theres Nadig, Switzerland 1:36.68
1976 Rosi Mittermaier, West Germany 1:46.16
1980 Annemarie Moser-Pröll, Austria 1:37.52
1984 Michela Figini, Switzerland 1:13.36
1988 Marina Kiehl, West Germany 1:25.86
1992 Kerrin Lee-Gartner, Canada 1:52.55
1994 Katja Seizinger, Germany 1:35.93
1998 Katja Seizinger, Germany 1:28.89

Slalom

1948 Gretchen Fraser, United States 1:57.20
1952 Andrea Mead Lawrence, United States 2:10.60
1956 Renée Colliard, Switzerland 1:52.30
1960 Anne Heggtveit, Canada 1:49.60
1964 Christine Goitschel, France 1:29.86
1968 Marielle Goitschel, France 1:25.86
1972 Barbara Cochran, United States 1:31.24
1976 Rosi Mittermaier, West Germany 1:30.54
1980 Hanni Wenzel, Liechtenstein 1:25.09
1984 Paoletta Magoni, Italy 1:36.47
1988 Vreni Schneider, Switzerland 1:36.69
1992 Petra Kronberger, Austria 1:32.68
1994 Vreni Schneider, Switzerland 1:56.01
1998 Hilde Gerg, Germany 1:32.40

Giant Slalom

1952 Andrea Mead Lawrence, United States 2:06.80
1956 Ossi Reichert, Germany 1:56.50
1960 Yvonne Rügg, Switzerland 1:39.90
1964 Marielle Goitschel, France 1:52.24
1968 Nancy Greene, Canada 1:51.97
1972 Marie-Theres Nadig, Switzerland 1:29.90
1976 Kathy Kreiner, Canada 1:29.13
1980 Hanni Wenzel, Liechtenstein 2:41.66
1984 Debbie Armstrong, United States 2:20.98

1988	Vreni Schneider, Switzerland	2:06.49
1992	Pernilla Wiberg, Sweden	2:12.74
1994	Deborah Compagnoni, Italy	2:30.97
1998	Deborah Compagnoni, Italy	2:50.59

Super Giant Slalom

1988	Sigrid Wolf, Austria	1:19.03
1992	Deborah Compagnoni, Italy	1:21.22
1994	Diann Roffe-Steinrotter, United States	1:22.15
1998	Picabo Street, United States	1:18.02

Combined (Downhill and Slalom)

		Points
1936	Christl Cranz, Germany	97.06
1948	Trude Beiser, Austria	6.58
1952-84	Not held	
1988	Anita Wachter, Austria	29.25
1992	Petra Kronberger, Austria	2.55
		Time
1994	Pernilla Wiberg, Sweden	3:05.16
1998	Katja Seizinger, Germany	2:40.74

FREESTYLE SKIING—MEN

Moguls

1992 Edgar Grospiron, France
1994 Jean-Luc Brassard, Canada
1998 Jonny Moseley, United States

Aerials

1994 Andreas Schoenbaechler, Switzerland
1998 Eric Bergoust, United States

FREESTYLE SKIING—WOMEN

Moguls

1992 Donna Weinbrecht, United States
1994 Stine Lise Hattestad, Norway
1998 Tae Satoya, Japan

Aerials

1994 Lina Cherjazova, Uzbekistan
1998 Nikki Stone, United States

ICE HOCKEY

MEN

1920 Canada
1924 Canada
1928 Canada
1932 Canada
1936 Great Britain
1948 Canada
1952 Canada
1956 U.S.S.R.
1960 United States
1964 U.S.S.R.
1968 U.S.S.R.
1972 U.S.S.R.
1976 U.S.S.R.
1980 United States
1984 U.S.S.R.
1988 U.S.S.R.
1992 Unified Team*
1994 Sweden
1998 Czech Republic

WOMEN

1998 United States

*Former Soviet Union team.

1998 Men's Championship
Czech Republic 1, Russia 0
1998 Women's Championship
United States 3, Canada 1

DISTRIBUTION OF MEDALS 1998 WINTER OLYMPIC GAMES

(Nagano, Japan)

	Gold	Silver	Bronze	Total
Germany	12	9	8	29
Norway	10	10	5	25
Russia	9	6	3	18
Austria	3	5	9	17
Canada	6	5	4	15
United States	6	3	4	13
Finland	2	4	6	12
Netherlands	5	4	2	11
Japan	5	1	4	10
Italy	2	6	2	10
France	2	1	5	8
China	0	6	2	8
Switzerland	2	2	3	7
South Korea	3	1	2	6
Czech Republic	1	1	1	3
Sweden	0	2	1	3
Belarus	0	0	2	2
Kazakhstan	0	0	2	2
Bulgaria	1	0	0	1
Denmark	0	1	0	1
Ukraine	0	1	0	1
Australia	0	0	1	1
Belgium	0	0	1	1
Britain	0	0	1	1

1998 UNITED STATES MEDALISTS

Figure Skating

Women—GOLD—Tara Lipinski, Sugarland, Texas
Women—SILVER—Michelle Kwan, Torrance, Calif.

Alpine Skiing

Women's Super Giant Slalom—GOLD—Picabo Street, Sun Valley, Idaho

Freestyle Skiing

Men's Moguls—GOLD—Jonny Moseley, Tiburon, Calif.
Men's Aerials—GOLD—Eric Bergoust, Missoula, Mont.
Women's Aerials—GOLD—Nikki Stone, Westborough, Mass.

Hockey

Women—GOLD—Sara Decosta, Tara Mounsey, Elizabeth Brown, Angela Ruggiero, Colleen Coyne, Karyn Bye, Suzanne Merz, Laurie Baker, Sandra Whyte, Allison Mleczko, Jennifer Schmidgall, Victoria Movsessian, Shelley Looney, Alana Blahoski, Kathryn King, Catherine Granato, Gretchen Ulion, Christina Bailey, Patricia Dunn, Sarah Tueting

Luge

Men's Doubles—SILVER—Chris Thorpe, Marquette, Mich. and Gordy Sheer, Croton, N.Y.
Men's Doubles—BRONZE—Mark Grimmette, Muskegon, Mich. and Brian Martin, Palo Alto, Calif.

Snowboarding

Men's Halfpipe—BRONZE—Ross Powers, South Londonderry, Vt.
Women's Halfpipe—BRONZE—Shannon Dunn, Steamboat Springs, Colo.

Speedskating

Women's 1,000 Meters—SILVER—Chris Witty, West Allis, Wis.
Women's 1,500 Meters—BRONZE—Chris Witty, West Allis, Wis.

Other 1998 Winter Olympic Games Champions

Biathlon
Men's 10-kilometer—Ole Einar Bjoerndalen, Norway
Men's 20-kilometer—Halvard Hanevold, Norway
Men's 4 × 7.5-kilometer relay—Germany
Women's 7.5-kilometer—Galina Koukleva, Russia
Women's 15-kilometer—Ekaterina Dafovska, Bulgaria
Women's 4 × 7.5-kilometer relay—Germany

Bobsledding
2-man—Canada I and Italy I
4-man—Germany II

Curling
Men—Switzerland
Women—Canada

Figure Skating
Pairs—Oksana Kazakova and Artur Dmitriev, Russia
Ice dancing—Pasha Grishuk and Yevgeny Platov, Russia

Luge
Men's singles—Georg Hackl, Germany
Men's doubles—Stefan Krausse, Jan Behrendt, Germany
Women's singles—Silke Kraushaar, Germany

Skiing, Nordic—Men
Combined team—Norway
Combined—Bjarte Engen Vik, Norway
70-meter jump—Jani Soininen, Finland
90-meter jump—Kazuyoshi Funaki, Japan
Team 120-meter jump—Japan
10-km cross country classical—Bjorn Dählie, Norway
15-km cross country free pursuit—Thomas Alsgaard, Norway
30-km cross country classical—Mika Myllylae, Finland
50-km cross country freestyle—Bjorn Dählie, Norway
4 x 10 kilometer relay—Norway

Skiing, Nordic—Women
5-kilometer classical—Larissa Lazutina, Russia
10-kilometer free pursuit—Larissa Lazutina, Russia
15-kilometer classical—Olga Danilova, Russia
30-kilometer freestyle—Yulia Tchepalova, Russia
4 x 5 kilometer relay—Russia

Snowboarding—Men
Giant slalom—Ross Rebagliati, Canada
Halfpipe—Gian Simmen, Switzerland

Snowboarding—Women
Giant slalom—Karine Ruby, France
Halfpipe—Nicola Thost, Germany

Speed Skating—Men
500m—Hiroyashu Shimizu, Japan
1,000m—Ids Postma, Netherlands
1,500m—Aadne Sondral, Norway
5,000m—Gianni Romme, Netherlands
10,000m—Gianni Romme, Netherlands

Speed Skating—Women
500m—Catriona LeMay-Doan, Canada
1,000m—Marianne Timmer, Netherlands
1,500m—Marianne Timmer, Netherlands
3,000m—Gunda Niemann-Stirnemann, Germany
5,000m—Claudia Pechstein, Germany

Speed Skating, Short Track—Men
500m—Takafumi Nishitani, Japan
1,000m—Kim Dong-sung, South Korea
5,000m relay—Canada

Speed Skating, Short Track—Women
500m—Annie Perreault, Canada
1,000m—Chun Lee-kyung, South Korea
3,000m relay—South Korea

Summer Games: Gold Medals

TRACK AND FIELD–MEN

100-Meter Dash

Year	Winner	Time
1896	Thomas Burke, United States	12.00
1900	Francis W. Jarvis, United States	10.80
1904	Archie Hahn, United States	11.00
1906	Archie Hahn, United States	11.20
1908	Reginald Walker, South Africa	10.80
1912	Ralph Craig, United States	10.80
1920	Charles Paddock, United States	10.80
1924	Harold Abrahams, Great Britain	10.60
1928	Percy Williams, Canada	10.80
1932	Eddie Tolan, United States	10.30
1936	Jesse Owens, United States	10.30[1]
1948	Harrison Dillard, United States	10.30
1952	Lindy Remigino, United States	10.40
1956	Bobby Morrow, United States	10.50
1960	Armin Hary, Germany	10.20
1964	Robert Hayes, United States	10.00
1968	James Hines, United States	09.90
1972	Valery Borzow, U.S.S.R.	10.14
1976	Hasely Crawford, Trinidad and Tobago	10.06
1980	Allan Wells, Britain	10.25
1984	Carl Lewis, United States	09.99
1988	Carl Lewis, United States	09.92[2]
1992	Linford Christie, Great Britain	09.96
1996	Donovan Bailey, Canada	09.84[3]

1. Wind assisted. 2. Lewis was awarded the gold medal when Ben Johnson of Canada, the original winner in 09.79s, was stripped of the medal after testing positive for steroid use. 3. World record.

200-Meter Dash

Year	Winner	Time
1900	John Tewksbury, United States	22.20
1904	Archie Hahn, United States	21.60
1908	Robert Kerr, Canada	22.60
1912	Ralph Craig, United States	21.70
1920	Allan Woodring, United States	22.00
1924	Jackson Scholz, United States	21.60
1928	Percy Williams, Canada	21.80
1932	Eddie Tolan, United States	21.20
1936	Jesse Owens, United States	20.70
1948	Melvin E. Patton, United States	21.10
1952	Andrew Stanfield, United States	20.70
1956	Bobby Morrow, United States	20.60
1960	Livio Berruti, Italy	20.50
1964	Henry Carr, United States	20.30
1968	Tommie Smith, United States	19.80
1972	Vallery Borzov, U.S.S.R.	20.00
1976	Don Quarrie, Jamaica	20.23
1980	Pietro Mennea, Italy	20.19
1984	Carl Lewis, United States	19.80
1988	Joe DeLoach, United States	19.75
1992	Mike Marsh, United States	20.01
1996	Michael Johnson, United States	19.32[1]

1. World record.

400-Meter Dash

Year	Winner	Time
1896	Thomas Burke, United States	54.20
1900	Maxwell Long, United States	49.40
1904	Harry Hillman, United States	49.20
1906	Paul Pilgrim, United States	53.20
1908	Wyndham Halswelle, Great Britain (walkover)	50.00
1912	Charles Reidpath, United States	48.20

1920 Bevil Rudd, South Africa 49.60
1924 Eric Liddell, Great Britain 47.60
1928 Ray Barbuti, United States 47.80
1932 William Carr, United States 46.20
1936 Archie Williams, United States 46.50
1948 Arthur Wint, Jamaica, B.W.I. 46.20
1952 George Rhoden, Jamaica, B.W.I. 45.90
1956 Charles Jenkins, United States 46.70
1960 Otis Davis, United States 44.90
1964 Mike Larrabee, United States 45.10
1968 Lee Evans, United States 43.80
1972 Vincent Matthews, United States 44.66
1976 Alberto Juantorena, Cuba 44.26
1980 Viktor Markin, U.S.S.R. 44.60
1984 Alonzo Babers, United States 44.27
1988 Steve Lewis, United States 43.87
1992 Quincy Watts, United States 43.50
1996 Michael Johnson, United States 43.49

800-Meter Run

1896 Edwin Flack, Australia 2:11.00
1900 Alfred Tysoe, Great Britain 2:01.40
1904 James Lightbody, United States 1:56.00
1906 Paul Pilgrim, United States 2:01.20
1908 Mel Sheppard, United states 1:52.80
1912 Ted Meredith, United States 1:51.90
1920 Albert Hill, Great Britain 1:53.40
1924 Douglas Lowe, Great Britain 1:52.40
1928 Douglas Lowe, Great Britain 1:51.80
1932 Thomas Hampson, Great Britain 1:49.80
1936 John Woodruff, United States 1:52.90
1948 Malvin Whitfield, United States 1:49.20
1952 Malvin Whitfield, United States 1:49.20
1956 Tom Courtney, United States 1:47.70
1960 Peter Snell, New Zealand 1:46.30
1964 Peter Snell, New Zealand 1:45.10
1968 Ralph Doubell, Australia 1:44.30
1972 David Wottle, United States 1:45.90
1976 Alberto Juantorena, Cuba 1:43.50
1980 Steve Ovett, Britain 1:45.40
1984 Joaquin Cruz, Brazil 1:43.00
1988 Paul Ereng, Kenya 1:43.45
1992 William Tanui, Kenya 1:43.66
1996 Vebjoern Rodal, Norway 1:42.58

1,500-Meter Run

1896 Edwin Flack, Australia 4:33.20
1900 Charles Bennett, Great Britain 4:06.00
1904 James Lightbody, United States 4:05.40
1906 James Lightbody, United States 4:12.00
1908 Mel Sheppard, United States 4:03.40
1912 Arnold Jackson, Great Britain 3:56.80
1920 Albert Hill, Great Britain 4:01.80
1924 Paavo Nurmi, Finland 3:53.60
1928 Harry Larva, Finland 3:53.20
1932 Luigi Becali, Italy 3:51.20
1936 Jack Lovelock, New Zealand 3:47.80
1948 Henri Eriksson, Sweden 3:49.80
1952 Joseph Barthel, Luxembourg 3:45.20
1956 Ron Delany, Ireland 3:41.20
1960 Herb Elliott, Australia 3:35.60
1964 Peter Snell, New Zealand 3:38.10
1968 Kipchoge Keino, Kenya 3:34.90
1972 Pekka Vasala, Finland 3:36.30
1976 John Walker, New Zealand 3:39.17
1980 Sebastian Coe, Britain 3:38.40
1984 Sebastian Coe, Britain 3:32.53
1988 Peter Rono, Kenya 3:35.96
1992 Fermin Cacho Ruiz, Spain 3:40.12
1996 Noureddine Morceli, Algeria 3:35.78

5,000-Meter Run

1912 Hannes Kolehmainen, Finland 14:36.60
1920 Joseph Guillemot, France 14:55.60
1024 Paavo Nurmi, Finland 14:31.20
1928 Willie Ritola, Finland 14:38.00
1932 Lauri Lehtinen, Finland 14:30.00
1936 Gunnar Hockert, Finland 14:22.20
1948 Gaston Reiff, Belgium 14:17.60
1952 Emil Zatopek, Czechoslovakia 14:06.60
1956 Vladimir Kuts, U.S.S.R. 13:39.60
1960 Murray Halberg, New Zealand 13:43.40
1964 Bob Schul, United States 13:48.80
1968 Mohamed Gammoudi, Tunisia 14:05.00
1972 Lasse Viren, Finland 13:26.40
1976 Lasse Viren, Finland 13:24.76
1980 Miruts Yifter, Ethiopia 13:21.00
1984 Saud Aouita, Morocco 13:05.59
1988 John Ngugi, Kenya 13:11.70
1992 Dieter Baumann, Germany 13:12.52
1996 Venuste Niyongabo, Burundi 13:07.96

10,000-Meter Run

1912 Hannes Kolehmainen, Finland 31:20.80
1920 Paavo Nurmi, Finland 31:45.80
1924 Willie Ritola, Finland 30:23.20
1928 Paavo Nurmi, Finland 30:18.80
1932 Janusz Kusocinski, Poland 30:11.40
1936 Ilmari Salminen, Finland 30:15.40
1948 Emil Zatopek, Czechoslovakia 29:59.60
1952 Emil Zatopek, Czechoslovakia 29:17.00
1956 Vladimir Kuts, U.S.S.R. 28:45.60
1960 Peter Bolotnikov, U.S.S.R. 28:32.20
1964 Billy Mills, United States 28:24.40
1968 Nartali Temu, Kenya 29:27.40
1972 Lasse Viren, Finland 27:38.40
1976 Lasse Viren, Finland 27:40.38
1980 Miruts Yifter, Ethiopia 27:42.70
1984 Alberto Cova, Italy 27:47.50
1988 Mly Brahim Boutaib, Morocco 27:21.46
1992 Khalid Skah, Morocco 27:47.70
1996 Haile Gebrselassie, Ethiopia 27:07.34

Marathon

1896 Spiridon Loues, Greece 2:58:50.00
1900 Michel Teato, France 2:59:45.00
1904 Thomas Hicks, United States 3:28:53.00
1906 William J. Sherring, Canada 2:51:23.65
1908 John J. Hayes, United States 2:55:18.40
1912 Kenneth McArthur, South Africa 2:36:54.80
1920 Hannes Kolehmainen, Finland 2:32:35.80
1924 Albin Stenroos, Finland 2:41:22.60
1928 A.B. El Quafi, France 2:32:57.00
1932 Juan Zabala, Argentina 2:31:36.00
1936 Kitei Son, Japan 2:29:19.20
1948 Delfo Cabrera, Argentina 2:34:51.60
1952 Emil Zatopek, Czechoslovakia 2:23:30.20
1956 Alain Mimoun, France 2:25:00.00
1960 Abebe Bikila, Ethiopia 2:15:16.20
1964 Abebe Bikila, Ethiopia 2:12:11.20
1968 Mamo Wold, Ethiopia 2:20:26.40
1972 Frank Shorter, United States 2:12:19.80
1976 Walter Cierpinski, East Germany 2:09:55.00
1980 Walter Cierpinski, East Germany 2:11:30.00
1984 Carlos Lopes, Portugal 2:09:21.00
1988 Gelindo Bordin, Italy 2:10:47.00
1992 Hwang Young-Cho, South Korea 2:13:23.00
1996 Josia Thugwane, South Africa 2:12:36.00

110-Meter Hurdles

1896 Thomas Curtis, United States 17.60
1900 Alvin Kraenzlein, United States 15.40
1904 Frederick Schule, United States 16.00
1906 R.G. Leavitt, United States 16.20
1908 Forrest Smithson, United States 15.00
1912 Frederick Kelly, United States 15.10
1920 Earl Thomson, Canada 14.80
1924 Daniel Kinsey, United States 15.00

1928	Sydney Atkinson, South Africa	14.80
1932	George Saling, United States	14.60
1936	Forrest Towns, United States	14.20
1948	William Porter, United States	13.90
1952	Harrison Dillard, United States	13.70
1956	Lee Calhoun, United States	13.50
1960	Lee Calhoun, United States	13.80
1964	Hayes Jones, United States	13.60
1968	Willie Davenport, United States	13.30
1972	Rodney Milburn, United States	13.24
1976	Guy Drut, France	13.30
1980	Thomas Munkett, East Germany	13.20
1984	Roger Kingdom, United States	13.20
1988	Roger Kingdom, United States	12.98
1992	Mark McCoy, Canada	13.12
1996	Allen Johnson, United States	12.95

200-Meter Hurdles

1900	Alvin Kraenzlein, United States	25.40
1904	Harry Hillman, United States	24.60

400-Meter Hurdles

1900	John Tewksbury, United States	57.60
1904	Harry Hillman, United States	53.00
1908	Charles Bacon, United States	55.00
1920	Frank Loomis, United States	54.00
1924	F. Morgan Taylor, United States	52.60
1928	Lord David Burghley, Great Britain	53.40
1932	Robert Tisdall, Ireland	51.80[1]
1936	Glenn Hardin, United States	52.40
1948	Roy Cochran, United States	51.10
1952	Charles Moore, United States	50.80
1956	Glenn Davis, United States	50.10
1960	Glenn Davis, United States	49.30
1964	Rex Cawley, United States	49.60
1968	David Hemery, Great Britain	48.10
1972	John Akii-Bua, Uganda	47.80
1976	Edwin Moses, United States	47.64
1980	Volker Beck, East Germany	48.70
1984	Edwin Moses, United States	47.75
1988	Andre Phillips, United States	47.19
1992	Kevin Young, United States	46.78
1996	Derrick Adkins, United States	47.54

1. Record not allowed.

2,500-Meter Steeplechase

1900	George Orton, United States	7:34.00
1904	James Lightbody, United States	7:39.60

3,000-Meter Steeplechase

1920	Percy Hodge, Great Britain	10:00.40
1924	Willie Ritola, Finland	09:33.60
1928	Toivo Loukola, Finland	09:21.80
1932	Volmari Iso-Hollo, Finland	10:33.40[1]
1936	Volmari Iso-Hollo, Finland	09:03.80
1948	Thure Sjoestrand, Sweden	09:04.60
1952	Horace Ashenfelter, United States	08:45.40
1956	Chris Brasher, Great Britain	08:41.20
1960	Zdzislaw Krzyskowiak, Poland	08:34.20
1964	Gaston Roelants, Belgium	08:30.80
1968	Amos Biwott, Kenya	08:51.00
1972	Kipchoge Keino, Kenya	08:23.60
1976	Anders Gardervd, Sweden	08:08.02
1980	Bronislaw Malinowski, Poland	08:09.70
1984	Julius Korir, Kenya	08:11.80
1988	Julius Karluki, Kenya	08:05.51
1992	Matthew Birir, Kenya	08:08.84
1996	Joseph Keter, Kenya	08:07.12

1. About 3,450 meters-extra lap by error.

10,000-Meter Walk

1912	George Goulding, Canada	46:28.40
1920	Ugo Frigerio, Italy	48:06.20
1924	Ugo Frigerio, Italy	47:49.00
1948	John Mikaelsson, Sweden	45:13.20
1952	John Mikaelsson, Sweden	45:02.80

20,000-Meter Walk

1956	Leonid Spirin, U.S.S.R.	1:31:27.40
1960	Vladimir Golubnichy, U.S.S.R.	1:34:07.20
1964	Ken Mathews, Great Britain	1:29:34.00
1968	Vladimir Golubnichy, U.S.S.R.	1:33:58.40
1972	Peter Frenkel, East Germany	1:26:42.40
1976	Daniel Bautista, Mexico	1:24:40.60
1980	Maurizio Damiliano, Italy	1:23:35.50
1984	Ernesto Conto, Mexico	1:23.13.00
1988	Jozef Pribilinec, Czechoslovakia	1:19:57.00
1992	Daniel Plaza, Spain	1:21:45.00
1996	Jefferson Perez, Ecuador	1:20:07.00

50,000-Meter Walk

1932	Thomas W. Green, Great Britain	4:50:10.00
1936	Harold Whitlock, Great Britain	4:30:41.10
1948	John Ljunggren, Sweden	4:41:52.00
1952	Giuseppe Dordoni, Italy	4:28:07.80
1956	Norman Read, New Zealand	4:30:42.80
1960	Donald Thompson, Great Britain	4:25:30.00
1964	Abdon Pamich, Italy	4:11:12.40
1968	Christoph Hohne, East Germany	4:20:13.60
1972	Bern Kannernberg, West Germany	3:56:11.60
1980	Hartwig Guader, East Germany	3:49:24.00
1984	Raul Gonzalez, Mexico	3:37:26.00
1988	Viacheslau Ivanenko, U.S.S.R.	3:48:29.00
1992	Andrei Perlov, Unified Team[1]	3:50:13.00
1996	Robert Korzeniowski, Poland	3:43:30.00

1. Former Soviet Union team.

400-Meter Relay (4x100)

1912	Great Britain	42.40
1920	United States	42.20
1924	United States	41.00
1928	United States	41.00
1932	United States	40.00
1936	United States	39.80
1948	United States	40.60
1952	United States	40.10
1956	United States	39.50
1960	Germany	39.50
1964	United States	39.00
1968	United States	38.20
1972	United States	38.19
1976	United States	38.33
1980	U.S.S.R.	38.26
1984	United States	37.83
1988	U.S.S.R.	38.19
1992	United States	37.40[1]
1996	Canada	37.69

1. World record.

1,600-Meter Relay (4x400)

1912	United States	3:16.60
1920	Great Britain	3:22.20
1924	United States	3:16.00
1928	United States	3:14.20
1932	United States	3:08.20
1936	Great Britain	3:09.00
1948	United States	3:10.40
1952	Jamaica, B.W.I.	3:03.90
1956	United States	3:04.80
1960	United States	3:02.20
1964	United States	3:00.70
1968	United States	2:56.10
1972	Kenya	2:59.80
1976	United States	2:58.65
1980	U.S.S.R.	3:01.10
1984	United States	2:57.91
1988	United States	2:56.16
1992	United States	2:55.74[1]
1996	United States	2:55.99

1. World record.

Team Race

		Pts
1900	Great Britain (5,000 meters)	26
1904	United States (4 miles)	27
1908	Great Britain (3 miles)	6
1912	United States (3,000 meters)	9
1920	United States (3,000 meters)	10
1924	Finland (3,000 meters)	9

Standing High Jump

1900	Ray Ewry, United States	5 ft. 5 in.
1904	Ray Ewry, United States	4 ft. 11 in.
1906	Ray Ewry, United States	5 ft. 1⅝ in.
1908	Ray Ewry, United States	5 ft. 2 in.
1912	Platt Adams, United States	5 ft. 4⅛ in.

Running High Jump

1896	Ellery Clark, United States	5 ft. 11¼ in.
1900	Irving Baxter, United States	6 ft. 2¾ in.
1904	Samuel Jones, United States	5 ft. 11 in.
1906	Con Leahy, Ireland	5 ft. 9⅞ in.
1908	Harry Porter, United States	6 ft. 3 in.
1912	Alma Richards, United States	6 ft. 4 in.
1920	Richmond Landon, United States	6 ft. 4¼ in.
1924	Harold Osborn, United States	6 ft. 5¹⁵⁄₁₆ in.
1928	Robert W. King, United States	6 ft. 4⅜ in.
1932	Duncan McNaughton, Canada	6 ft. 5⅝ in.
1936	Cornelius Johnson, United States	6 ft. 7¹⁵⁄₁₆ in.
1948	John Winter, Australia	6 ft. 6 in.
1952	Walter David, United States	6 ft. 8¹⁵⁄₁₆ in.
1956	Charles Damas, United States	6 ft. 11¼ in.
1960	Robert Shavlakadze, U.S.S.R.	7 ft. 1 in.
1964	Valeri Brumel, U.S.S.R.	7 ft. 1¾ in.
1968	Dick Fosbury, United States	7 ft. 4¼ in.
1972	Yuri Tarmak, U.S.S.R.	7 ft. 3¾ in.
1976	Jacek Wszola, Poland	7 ft. 4½ in.
1980	Gerd Wessig, East Germany	7 ft. 8¾ in.
1984	Dietmar Mogenburg, West Germany	7 ft. 8½ in.
1988	Guennadi Avdeenko, U.S.S.R.	7 ft. ½ in.
1992	Javier Sotomayer, Cuba	7 ft. 8½ in.
1996	Charles Austin, United States	7 ft. 10 in.

Long Jump

1896	Ellery Clark, United States	20 ft. 9¾ in.
1900	Alvin Kraenzlein, United States	23 ft. 6⅞ in.
1904	Myer Prinstein, United States	24 ft. 1 in.
1906	Myer Prinstein, United States	23 ft. 7½ in.
1908	Frank Irons, United States	24 ft. 6½ in.
1912	Albert Gutterson, United States	24 ft. 11¼ in.
1920	William Petterssen, Sweden	23 ft. 5½ in.
1924	DeHart Hubbard, United States	24 ft. 5⅛ in.
1928	Edward B. Hamm, United States	25 ft. 4¾ in.
1932	Edward Gordon, United States	25 ft. ¾ in.
1936	Jesse Owens, United States	26 ft. 5⁵⁄₁₆ in.
1948	Willie Steele, United States	25 ft. 8 in.
1952	Jerome Biffle, United States	24 ft. 10 in.
1956	Gregory Bell, United States	25 ft. 8¼ in.
1960	Ralph Boston, United States	26 ft. 7¾ in.
1964	Lynn Davies, Great Britain	26 ft. 5¾ in.
1968	Bob Beamon, United States	29 ft. 2½ in.
1972	Randy Williams, United States	27 ft. ½ in.
1976	Arnie Robinson, United States	24 ft. 7¾ in.
1980	Lutz Dombrowski, E. Germany	28 ft. ¼ in.
1984	Carl Lewis, United States	28 ft. ¼ in.
1988	Carl Lewis, United States	28 ft. 7¼ in.
1992	Carl Lewis, United States	28 ft. 5½ in.
1996	Carl Lewis, United States	27 ft. 10¾ in.

Triple Jump

1896	James B. Connolly, United States	45 ft.
1900	Myer Prinstein, United States	47 ft. 4¼ in.
1904	Myer Prinstein, United States	47 ft.
1906	P.G. O'Connor, Ireland	46 ft. 2 in.
1908	Timothy Ahearne, Great Britain	48 ft. 1¼ in.
1912	Gustaf Lindblom, Sweden	48 ft. 5⅛ in.
1920	Vilho Tuulos, Finland	47 ft. 6⅞ in.
1924	Archie Winter, Australia	50 ft. 11⅛ in.
1928	Mikio Oda, Japan	49 ft. 10¹³⁄₁₆ in.
1932	Chuhei Nambu, Japan	51 ft. 7 in.
1936	Naoto Tajima, Japan	52 ft. 5⅞ in.
1948	Arne Ahman, Sweden	50 ft. 6¼ in.
1952	Adhemar da Silva, Brazil	53 ft. 2½ in.
1956	Adhemar da Silva, Brazil	53 ft. 7½ in.
1960	Jozef Schmidt, Poland	55 ft. 1¾ in.
1964	Jozef Schmidt, Poland	55 ft. 3¼ in.
1968	Viktor Saneyev, U.S.S.R.	57 ft. ¾ in.
1972	Viktor Saneyev, U.S.S.R.	56 ft. 11 in.
1976	Viktor Saneyev, U.S.S.R.	56 ft. 8¾ in.
1980	Jaak Uudmae, U.S.S.R.	56 ft. 11⅛ in.
1984	Al Joyner, United States	56 ft. 7½ in.
1988	Hristo Markov, Bulgaria	57 ft. 9¼ in.
1992	Mike Conley, United States	59 ft. 7½ in.
1996	Kenny Harrison, United States	59 ft. 4¼ in.

Pole Vault

1896	William Hoyt, United States	10 ft. 9¾ in.
1900	Irving Baxter, United States	10 ft. 9⅞ in.
1904	Charles Dvorak, United States	11 ft. 6 in.
1906	Fernand Gouder, France	11 ft. 6 in.
1908	Alfred Gilbert, United States, and Edward Cook, United States (tie)	12 ft. 2 in.
1912	Harry Babcock, United States	12 ft. 11½ in.
1920	Frank Foss, United States	13 ft. 5 ⁹⁄₁₆ in.
1924	Lee Barnes, United States	12 ft. 11½ in.
1928	Sabin W. Carr, United States	13 ft. 9⅜ in.
1932	William Miller, United States	14 ft. 1⅞ in.
1936	Earle Meadows, United States	14 ft. 3¼ in.
1948	Guinn Smith, United States	14 ft. ¼ in.
1952	Robert Richards, United States	14 ft. 11⅛ in.
1956	Robert Richards, United States	14 ft. 11½ in.
1960	Don Bragg, United States	15 ft. 5⅛ in.
1964	Fred Hansen, United States	16 ft. 8¾ in.
1968	Bob Seagren, United States	17 ft. 8½ in.
1972	Wolfgang Nordwig, East Germany	18 ft. ½ in.
1976	Tadeusz Slusarski, Poland	18 ft. ½ in.
1980	Wladyslaw Kozakiewics, Poland	18 ft. 11½ in.
1984	Pierre Quinon, France	18 ft. 10¼ in.
1988	Sergei Bubka, U.S.S.R.	18 ft. 4¼ in.
1992	Maxim Tarassov, Unified Team[1]	19 ft. 0¼ in.
1996	Jean Galfione, France	19 ft. 5¼ in.

1. Former Soviet Union team.

16-lb Shot-Put

1896	Robert Garrett, United States	36 ft. 9¾ in.
1900	Richard Sheldon, United States	46 ft. 3⅛ in.
1904	Ralph Rose, United States	48 ft. 7 in.
1906	Martin Sheridan, United States	40 ft. 4⅘ in.
1908	Ralph Rose, United States	46 ft. 7½ in.
1912	Pat McDonald, United States	50 ft. 4 in.
1920	Ville Porhola, Finland	48 ft. 7⅛ in.
1924	Clarence Houser, United States	49 ft. 2½ in.
1928	John Kuck, United States	52 ft. 11¹¹⁄₁₆ in.
1932	Leo Sexton, United States	52 ft. 6³⁄₁₆ in.
1936	Hans Woellke, Germany	53 ft. 1¾ in.
1948	Wilbur Thompson, United States	56 ft. 2 in.
1952	Parry O'Brien, United States	57 ft. 1½ in.
1956	Parry O'Brien, United States	60 ft. 11 in.
1960	Bill Nieder, United States	64 ft. 6¾ in.
1964	Dallas Long, United States	66 ft. 8¼ in.
1968	Randy Matson, United States	67 ft. 4¾ in.
1972	Wladyslaw Komar, Poland	69 ft. 6 in.
1976	Udo Beyer, East Germany	69 ft. ¾ in.
1980	Vladmir Klselyov, U.S.S.R.	70 ft. ½ in.
1984	Alessandro Andrei, Italy	69 ft. 9 in.
1988	Uhf Timmerman, East Germany	73 ft. 8¾ in.
1992	Michael Stulze, United States	71 ft. 2½ in.
1996	Randy Barnes, United States	70 ft. 11¼ in.

Discus Throw

1896	Robert Garrett, United States	95 ft. 7½ in.
1900	Rudolf Bauer, Hungary	118 ft. 2⅞ in.
1904	Martin Sheridan, United States	128 ft. 10½ in.
1906	Martin Sheridan, United States	136 ft. ⅓ in.
1908	Martin Sheridan, United States	134 ft. 2 in.
1912	Armas Taipale, Finland	145 ft. 9/16 in.
1920	Elmer Niklander, Finland	146 ft. 7 in.
1924	Clarence Houser, United States	151 ft. 5¼ in.
1928	Clarence Houser, United States	155 ft. 2⅘ in.
1932	John Anderson, United States	162 ft. 4⅞ in.
1936	Ken Carpenter, United States	165 ft. 7⅜ in.
1948	Adolfo Consolini, Italy	173 ft. 2 in.
1952	Simeon Iness, United States	180 ft. 6½ in.
1956	Al Oerter, United States	184 ft. 10½ in.
1960	Al Oerter, United States	194 ft. 2 in.
1964	Al Oerter, United States	200 ft. 1½ in.
1968	Al Oerter, United States	212 ft. 6 in.
1972	Ludvik Danek, Czechoslovakia	211 ft. 3 in.
1976	Mac Wilkins, United States	221 ft. 5 in.
1980	Viktor Rashchupkin, U.S.S.R.	218 ft. 8 in.
1984	Rolf Dannenberg, West Germany	218 ft. 6 in.
1988	Jurgen Schult, East Germany	225 ft. 9¼ in.
1992	Romas Ubartas, Lithuania	213 ft. 7¾ in.
1996	Lars Riedel, Germany	227 ft. 8 in.

Javelin Throw

1906	Eric Lemming, Sweden	175 ft. 6 in.
1908	Eric Lemming, Sweden	179 ft. 10½ in.
1912	Eric Lemming, Sweden	198 ft. 11¼ in.
1920	Jonni Myyra, Finland	215 ft. 9¾ in.
1924	Jonni Myyra, Finland	206 ft. 6¾ in.
1928	Eric Lundquist, Sweden	218 ft. 6⅛ in.
1932	Matti Jarvinen, Finland	238 ft. 7 in.
1936	Gerhard Stoeck, Germany	235 ft. 8 5/16 in.
1948	Kaj Rautavaara, Finland	228 ft. 10½ in.
1952	Cy Young, United States	242 ft. ¾ in.
1956	Egil Danielsen, Norway	281 ft. 2¼ in.
1960	Viktor Tsibuelnko, U.S.S.R.	277 ft. 8⅜ in.
1964	Pauli Nevala, Finland	271 ft. 2¼ in.
1968	Janis Lusis, U.S.S.R.	295 ft. 7 in.
1972	Klaus Wolfermann, West Germany	296 ft. 10 in.
1976	Miklos Nemeth, Hungary	310 ft. 4 in.
1980	Dainis Kula, U.S.S.R.	299 ft. 2⅜ in.
1984	Arto Haerkoenen, Finland	284 ft. 8 in.
1988	Tapio Korjus, Finland	276 ft. 6 in.
1992	Jan Zelezny, Czechoslovakia	294 ft. 2 in.
1996	Jan Zelezny, Czech Republic	289 ft. 3 in.

16-lb Hammer Throw

1900	John Flanagan, United States	167 ft. 4 in.
1904	John Flanagan, United States	168 ft. 1 in.
1908	John Flanagan, United States	170 ft. 4¼ in.
1912	Matt McGrath, United States	179 ft. 7⅛ in.
1920	Pat Ryan, United States	173 ft. 5⅝ in.
1924	Fred Tootell, United States	174 ft. 10¼ in.
1928	Patrick O'Callaghan, Ireland	168 ft. 7½ in.
1932	Patrick O'Callaghan, Ireland	176 ft. 11⅛ in.
1936	Karl Hein, Germany	185 ft. 4 in.
1948	Imre Nemeth, Hungary	183 ft. 11½ in.
1952	Jozsef Csermak, Hungary	197 ft. 11 9/16 in.
1956	Harold Connolly, United States	207 ft. 2¾ in.
1960	Vasily Rudenkov, U.S.S.R.	220 ft. 1⅝ in.
1964	Romuald Klim, U.S.S.R.	228 ft. 9½ in.
1968	Gyula Zsivotzky, Hungary	240 ft. 8 in.
1972	Anatoly Bondarchuk, U.S.S.R.	247 ft. 8½ in.
1976	Yuri Sedykh, U.S.S.R.	254 ft. 4 in.
1980	Yuri Sedykh, U.S.S.R.	(81.80m) 268 ft. 4½ in.
1984	Juha Tiainen, Finland	256 ft. 2 in.
1988	Sergei Litvinov, U.S.S.R.	278 ft. 2½ in.
1992	Andrey Abduvaliyev, Unified Team[1]	270 ft. 9½ in.
1996	Balasz Kiss, Hungary	266 ft. 6 in.

1. Former Soviet Union team.

Decathlon

1912	Jim Thorpe, United States	—
	Hugo Wieslander, Sweden	—
1920	Helge Lovland, Norway	6,804.35 pts.
1924	Harold Osborn, United States	7,710.775 pts.
1928	Paavo Yrjola, Finland	8,053.29 pts.
1932	James Bausch, United States	8,462.23 pts.
1936	Glenn Morris, United States	7,900 pts.[1]
1948	Robert B. Mathias, United States	7,139 pts.
1952	Robert B. Mathias, United States	7,887 pts.
1956	Milton Campbell, United States	7,937 pts.
1960	Rafer Johnson, United States	8,392 pts.
1964	Willi Holdorf, Germany	7,887 pts.[1]
1968	Bill Toomey, United States	8,193 pts.
1972	Nikolai Avilov, U.S.S.R.	8,454 pts.
1976	Bruce Jenner, United States	8,618 pts.
1980	Daley Thompson, Britain	8,495 pts.
1984	Daley Thompson, Britain	8,797 pts.
1988	Christian Schenk, East Germany	8,488 pts.
1992	Robert Zmelik, Czechoslovakia	8,611 pts.
1996	Dan O'Brien, United States	8,824 pts.

1. Point system revised.

TRACK AND FIELD–WOMEN

100-Meter Dash

1928	Elizabeth Robinson, United States	12.20
1932	Stella Walsh, Poland	11.90
1936	Helen Stephens, United States	11.50
1948	Fanny Blankers-Koen, Netherlands	11.90
1952	Marjorie Jackson, Australia	11.50
1956	Betty Cuthbert, Australia	11.50
1960	Wilma Rudolph, United States	11.00
1964	Wyomia Tyus, United States	11.40
1968	Wyomia Tyus, United States	11.00
1972	Renate Stecher, East Germany	11.07
1976	Annegret Richter, West Germany	11.08
1980	Lyudmila Kondratyeva, U.S.S.R.	11.06
1984	Evelyn Ashford, United States	10.97
1988	Florence Griffith-Joyner, United States	10.54
1992	Gail Devers, United States	10.82
1996	Gail Devers, United States	10.94

200-Meter Dash

1948	Fanny Blankers-Koen, Netherlands	24.40
1952	Marjorie Jackson, Australia	23.70
1956	Betty Cuthbert, Australia	23.40
1960	Wilma Rudolph, United States	24.00
1964	Edith McGuire, United States	23.00
1968	Irena Szewinska, Poland	22.50
1972	Renate Stecher, East Germany	22.40
1976	Baerbel Eckert, East Germany	22.37
1980	Barbara Wockel, East Germany	22.03
1984	Valerie Brisco-Hooks, United States	21.81
1988	Florence Griffith-Joyner, United States	21.34
1992	Gwen Torrence, United States	21.81
1996	Marie-Jose Perec, France	22.12

400-Meter Dash

1964	Betty Cuthbert, Australia	52.00
1968	Colette Besson, France	52.00
1972	Monika Zehrt, East Germany	51.08
1976	Irena Szewinska, Poland	49.29
1980	Marita Koch, East Germany	48.88
1984	Valerie Brisco-Hooks, United States	48.83
1988	Olga Bryzguina, U.S.S.R.	48.65
1992	Marie Jose-Perec, France	48.83
1996	Marie Jose-Perec, France	48.25

800-Meter Run

1928	Lina Radke, Germany	2:16.80
1960	Ljudmila Shevcova, U.S.S.R.	2:04.30
1964	Ann Packer, Great Britain	2:01.10
1968	Madeline Manning, United States	2:00.90
1972	Hildegard Falck, West Germany	1:58.60

1976	Tatiana Kazankina, U.S.S.R.	1:54.94
1980	Nadezhda Olizarenko, U.S.S.R.	1:53.50
1984	Doina Melinte, Romania	1:57.60
1988	Sigrun Wodars, East Germany	1:56.10
1992	Ellen Van Langen, Netherlands	1:55.54
1993	Svetlana Masterkova, Russia	1:57.73

1,500-Meter Run

1972	Ludmila Bragina, U.S.S.R.	4:01.40
1976	Tatiana Kazankina, U.S.S.R.	4:05.48
1980	Tatiana Kazankina, U.S.S.R.	3:56.60
1984	Gabriella Dorio, Italy	4:03.25
1988	Paula Ivan, Romania	3:53.96
1992	Hassiba Boulmerka, Algeria	3:55.30
1996	Svetlana Masterkova, Russia	4:00.83

5,000-Meter Run

1996	Wang, Jun-Xia, China	14:59.88

10,000-Meter Run

1992	Derartu Tulu, Ethiopia	31:60.02
1996	Fernanda Ribeiro, Portugal	31:01.63

80-Meter Hurdles

1932	Mildred Didrikson, United States	11.70
1936	Trebisonda Valla, Italy	11.70
1948	Fanny Blankers-Koen, Netherlands	11.20
1952	Shirley S. de la Hunty, Australia	10.90
1956	Shirley S. de la Hunty, Australia	10.70
1960	Irina Press, U.S.S.R.	10.80
1964	Karin Balzer, Germany	10.50[1]
1968	Maureen Caird, Australia	10.30

1. Wind assisted.

100-Meter Hurdles

1972	Annelie Ehrhardt, East Germany	12.59
1976	Johanna Schaller, East Germany	12.77
1980	Vera Komisova, U.S.S.R.	12.56
1984	Benita Fitzgerald-Brown, United States	12.84
1988	Jordanka Donkova, Bulgaria	12.38
1992	Paraskevi Patoulidou, Greece	12.64
1996	Ludmila Engquist, Sweden	12.58

400-Meter Hurdles

1984	Nawai El Moutawakel, Morocco	54.61
1988	Debra Flintoff-King, Australia	53.17
1992	Sally Gunnell, Great Britain	53.23
1996	Deon Hemmings, Jamaica	52.82

400-Meter Relay

1928	Canada	48.40
1932	United States	47.00
1936	United States	46.90
1948	Netherlands	47.50
1952	United States	45.90
1956	Australia	44.50
1960	United States	44.50
1964	Poland	43.60
1968	United States	42.80
1972	West Germany	42.81
1976	East Germany	42.50
1980	East Germany	41.60
1984	United States	41.65
1988	United States	41.98
1992	United States	42.11
1996	United States	41.95

1,600-Meter Relay

1972	East Germany	3:23.00
1976	East Germany	3:19.23
1980	U.S.S.R.	3:20.20
1984	United States	3:18.29
1988	U.S.S.R.	3:15.18
1992	Unified Team[1]	3:20.20
1996	United States	3:20.91

1. Former Soviet Union team.

10,000-Meter Walk

1992	ChenYue-Ling, China	44:32
1996	Yelena Nikolayeva, Russia	41:49

Marathon

1984	Joan Benoit, United States	2:24:52
1988	Rose Mota, Portugal	2:25.40
1992	Valentina Yegorova, Unified Team	2:32.41
1996	Fatuma Roba, Ethiopia	2:26.05

Running High Jump

1928	Ethel Catherwood, Canada	5 ft. 3 in.
1932	Jean Shiley, United States	5 ft. 5¼ in.
1936	Ibolya Csak, Hungary	5 ft. 3 in.
1948	Alice Coachman, United States	5 ft. 6⅛ in.
1952	Ester Brand, South Africa	5 ft. 5¾ in.
1956	Mildred McDaniel, United States	5 ft. 9¼ in.
1960	Iolanda Balas, Romania	6 ft. ¾ in.
1964	Iolanda Balas, Romania	6 ft. 2¾ in.
1968	Miloslava Rezkova, Czechoslovakia	5 ft. 11¾ in.
1972	Ulrike Meyfarth, West Germany	6 ft. 3⅝ in.
1976	Rosemarie Ackerman, E. Germany	6 ft. 4 in.
1980	Sara Simeoni, Italy	6 ft. 5½ in.
1984	Ulrike Meyfarth, West Germany	6 ft. 7½ in.
1988	Louise Ritter, United States	6 ft. 8 in.
1992	Heike Henkel, Germany	6 ft. 7½ in.
1996	Stefka Kostadinova, Bulgaria	6 ft. 8¾ in.

Long Jump

1948	Olga Gyarmati, Hungary	18 ft. 8¼ in.
1952	Yvette Williams, New Zealand	20 ft. 5¾ in.
1956	Elzbieta Krzesinska, Poland	20 ft. 9¾ in.
1960	Vera Krepkina, U.S.S.R.	20 ft. 10¾ in.
1964	Mary Rand, Great Britain	22 ft. 2 in.
1968	Viorica Ciscopoleanu, Romania	22 ft. 4½ in.
1972	Heidemarie Rosendahl, West Germany	22 ft. 3 in.
1976	Angela Voigt, East Germany	22 ft. ½ in.
1980	Tatiana Kolpakova, U.S.S.R.	23 ft. 2 in.
1984	Anisoara Stanciu, Romania	22 ft. 10 in.
1988	Jackie Joyner-Kersee, United States	24 ft. 3½ in.
1992	Heike Drechsler, Germany	23 ft. 5¼ in.
1996	Chioma Ajunwa, Nigeria	23 ft. 4½ in.

Triple Jump

1996	Inessa Kravets, Ukraine	50 ft. 3½ in.

Shot-Put

1948	Micheline Ostermeyer, France	45 ft. 1½ in.
1952	Galina Zybina, U.S.S.R.	50 ft. 1½ in.
1956	Tamara Tishkyevich, U.S.S.R.	54 ft. 5 in.
1960	Tamara Press, U.S.S.R.	56 ft. 9⅞ in.
1964	Tamara Press, U.S.S.R.	59 ft. 6 in.
1968	Margitta Gummel, East Germany	64 ft. 4 in.
1972	Nadezhda Chizhova, U.S.S.R.	69 ft.
1976	Ivanka Christova, Bulgaria	69 ft. 5 in.
1980	Ilona Sluplanek, East Germany	73 ft. 6 in.
1984	Claudia Losch, West Germany	67 ft. 2¼ in.
1988	Natalya Lisovskaya, U.S.S.R.	72 ft. 11½ in.
1992	Svetlana Kriveleva, Unified Team[1]	69 ft. 1¼ in.
1996	Astrid Kumbernuss, Germany	67 ft. 5½ in.

1. Former Soviet Union team.

Discus Throw

1928	Helena Konopacka, Poland	129 ft. 11⅞ in.
1932	Lillian Copeland, United States	133 ft. 2 in.
1936	Gisela Mauermayer, Germany	156 ft. 3³⁄₁₆ in.
1948	Micheline Ostermeyer, France	137 ft. 6½ in.
1956	Olga Fikotova, Czechoslovakia	176 ft. 1½ in.
1960	Nina Ponomareva, U.S.S.R.	180 ft. 8¼ in.
1964	Tamara Press, U.S.S.R.	187 ft. 10¾ in.
1968	Lia Manoliu, Romania	191 ft. 2½ in.
1972	Faina Melnik, U.S.S.R.	218 ft. 7 in.
1976	Evelin Schlaak, East Germany	226 ft. 4 in.
1980	Evelin Jahl, East Germany	229 ft. 6½ in.
1984	Ria Stalman, Netherlands	214 ft. 5 in.
1988	Martina Hellmann, East Germany	237 ft. 2¼ in.
1992	Maritza Marten, Cuba	229 ft. 10¼ in.
1996	Ilke Wyludda, Germany	228 ft. 6½ in.

Javelin Throw

1932	Mildred Didrikson, United States	143 ft. 4 in.
1936	Tilly Fleischer, Germany	148 ft. 2¾ in.
1948	Herma Bauma, Austria	149 ft. 6 in.
1952	Dana Zatopek, Czechoslovakia	165 ft. 7 in.
1956	Inessa Janzeme, U.S.S.R.	176 ft. 8 in.
1960	Elvira Ozolina, U.S.S.R.	183 ft. 8 in.
1964	Mihaela Penes, Romania	198 ft. 7½ in.
1968	Angela Nemeth, Hungary	198 ft.
1972	Ruth Fuchs, East Germany	209 ft. 7 in.
1976	Ruth Fuchs, East Germany	216 ft. 4 in.
1980	Maria Colon, Cuba	224 ft. 5 in.
1984	Tessa Sanderson, Britain	228 ft. 2 in.
1988	Petra Felke, East Germany	245 ft.
1992	Silke Renke, Germany	224 ft. 2½ in.
1996	Heli Rantanen, Finland	222 ft. 11 in.

Pentathlon

1964	Irina Press, U.S.S.R.	5,246 pts.
1968	Ingrid Becker, West Germany	5,098 pts.
1972	Mary Peters, Britain	4,801 pts.
1976	Siegrun Siegl, East Germany	4,745 pts.
1980	Nadyeszhda Tkachenko, U.S.S.R.	5,083 pts.
1984	Daniele Masala, Italy	5,469 pts.
1988	Jackie Joyner-Kersee, United States	7,291 pts.

Heptathlon

1992	Jackie Joyner-Kersee, United States	7,044 pts.
1996	Ghada Shouaa, Syria	6,780 pts.

SWIMMING–MEN

50-Meter Freestyle

1988	Matt Biondi, United States	22.14
1992	Alexander Popov, Unified Team[1]	21.91
1996	Alexander Popov, Russia	22.13

1. Former Soviet Union team.

100-Meter Freestyle

1896	Alfred Hajos, Hungary	1:22.20
1904	Zoltan de Halmay, Hungary	1:02.80[1]
1906	Charles Daniels, United States	1:13.00
1908	Charles Daniels, United States	1:05.60
1912	Duke P. Kahanamoku, United States	1:03.40
1920	Duke P. Kahanamoku, United States	1:01.40
1924	John Weissmuller, United States	0:59.00
1928	John Weissmuller, United States	0:58.60
1932	Yasuji Miyazaki, Japan	0:58.20
1936	Ferenc Csik, Hungary	0:57.60
1948	Walter Ris, United States	0:57.30
1952	Clarke Scholes, United States	0:57.40
1956	Jon Henricks, Australia	0:55.40
1960	John Devitt, Australia	0:55.20
1964	Don Schollander, United States	0:53.40
1968	Michael Wenden, Australia	0:52.20
1972	Mark Spitz, United States	0:51.22
1976	Jim Montgomery, United States	0:49.99
1980	Jorg Woithe, East Germany	0:50.40
1984	Rowdy Gaines, United States	0:49.80
1988	Matt Biondi, United States	0:48.63
1992	Alexander Popov, Unified Team[2]	0:49.02
1996	Alexander Popov, Russia	48.74s

1. 100 yards. 2. Former Soviet Union team.

200-Meter Freestyle

1900	Frederick Lane, Australia	2:25.20
1904	Charles Daniels, United States	2:44.20[1]
1968	Michael Wenden, Australia	1:55.20
1972	Mark Spitz, United States	1:52.78
1976	Bruce Furniss, United States	1:50.29
1980	Sergei Kopiliakov, U.S.S.R.	4:49.81
1984	Michael Gross, West Germany	1:47.44
1988	Duncan Armstrong, Australia	1:47.25
1992	Evgueni Sadovyi, Unified Team[2]	1:46.70
1996	Danyon Loader, New Zealand	1:47.63

1. 220 yards 2. Former Soviet Union team.

400-Meter Freestyle

1896	Paul Neumann, Austria	8:12.60[1]
1904	Charles Daniels, United States	6:16.20[2]
1906	Otto Sheff, Austria	6:23.80
1908	Henry Taylor, Great Britain	5:36.80
1912	George Hodgson, Canada	5:24.40
1920	Norman Ross, United States	5:26.80
1926	John Weissmuller, United States	5:04.20
1928	Albert Zorilla, Argentina	5:01.60
1932	Clarence Crabbe, United States	4:48.40
1936	Jack Medica, United States	4:44.50
1948	William Smith, United States	4:41.00
1952	Jean Boiteux, France	4:30.70
1956	Murray Rose, Australia	4:27.30
1960	Murray Rose, Australia	4:18.30
1964	Don Schollander, United States	4:12.20
1968	Mike Burton, United States	4:09.00
1972	Bradford Cooper, Australia	4:00.27[3]
1976	Brian Goodell, United States	3:51.93
1980	Vladimir Salnikov, U.S.S.R.	3:51.31
1984	George DiCarlo, United States	3:51.23
1988	Uwe Dassier, East Germany	3:46.95
1992	Evgueni Sadovyi, Unified Team	3:45.00[4]
1996	Danyon Loader, New Zealand	3:47.97

1. 500 meters. 2. 440 yards. 3. Rich DeMont, United States, won but was disqualified following day for medical reasons. 4. World record.

1,500-Meter Freestyle

1904	Emil Rausch, Germany	27:18.20[1]
1906	Henry Taylor, Great Britain	28:28.00[2]
1908	Henry Taylor, Great Britain	22:48.40
1912	George Hodgson, Canada	22:00.00
1920	Norman Ross, United States	22:23.20
1924	Andrew Charlton, Australia	20:06.60
1928	Arne Borg, Sweden	19:51.80
1932	Kusuo Kitamura, Japan	19:12.40
1936	Noboru Terada, Japan	19:13.70
1948	James McLane, United States	19:18.50
1952	Ford Konno, United States	18:30.00
1956	Murray Rose, Australia	17:58.90
1960	Jon Konrads, Australia	17:19.60
1964	Robert Windle, Australia	17:01.70
1968	Michael Burton, United States	16:38.90
1972	Michael Burton, United States	15:52.58
1976	Brian Goodell, United States	15:02.40
1980	Vladimir Salnikov, U.S.S.R.	14:58.27
1984	Michael O'Brien, United States	15:05.20
1988	Vladimir Salnikov, U.S.S.R.	15:00.40
1992	Kieren Perkins, Australia	14:43.48
1996	Kieren Perkins, Australia	14:56.40

1. One mile. 2. 1,600 meters

100-Meter Backstroke

1904	Walter Brack, Germany	1:16.80[1]
1908	Arno Bieberstein, Germany	1:24.60
1912	Harry Hebner, United States	1:21.20
1920	Warren Kealoha, United States	1:15.20
1924	Warren Kealoha, United States	1:13.20
1928	George Kojac, United States	1:08.20
1932	Masaji Kiyokawa, Japan	1:08.60
1936	Adolph Kiefer, United States	1:05.90
1948	Allen Stack, United States	1:06.40
1952	Yoshinobu Oyakawa, United States	1:05.40
1956	David Thiele, Australia	1:02.20
1960	David Thiele, Australia	1:01.90
1968	Roland Matthes, East Germany	0:58.70
1972	Roland Matthes, East Germany	0:56.58
1976	John Naber, United States	0:55.49
1980	Bengt Baron, Sweden	0:56.53
1984	Rick Carey, United States	0:55.79

1988 Daichi Suzuki, Japan 0:55.05
1992 Mark Tewksbury, Canada 0:53.98
1996 Jeff Rouse, United States 0:54.10
1. 100 yards

200-Meter Backstroke
1900 Ernst Hoppenberg, Germany 2:47.00
1964 Jed Graef, United States 2:10.30
1968 Roland Matthes, East Germany 2:09.60
1972 Roland Matthes, East Germany 2:02.82
1976 John Naber, United States 1:59.19
1980 Sandor Wladar, Hungary 2:01.93
1984 Rick Carey, United States 2:00.23
1988 Igor Polianski, U.S.S.R. 1:59.37
1992 Martin Lopez Zubero, Spain 1:58.47
1996 Brad Bridgewater, United States 1:58.54

100-Meter Breaststroke
1968 Donald McKenzie, United States 1:07.70
1972 Nobutaka Taguchi, Japan 1:04.94
1976 John Hencken, United States 1:03.11
1980 Duncan Goodhew, Britain 1:03.34
1984 Steve Lindquist, United States 1:01.65
1988 Adrian Moorhouse, Great Britain 1:02.04
1992 Nelson Diebel, United States 1:01.50
1996 Fred Deburghgraeve, Belgium 1:00.60[1]
1. World record.

200-Meter Breaststroke
1908 Frederick Holman, Great Britain 3:09.20
1912 Walter Bathe, Germany 3:01.80
1920 Haken Malmroth, Sweden 3:04.40
1924 Robert Skelton, United States 2:56.60
1928 Yoshiyuki Tsuruta, Japan 2:48.80
1932 Yoshiyuki Tsuruta, Japan 2:45.40
1936 Tetsuo Hamuro, Japan 2:41.50
1948 Joseph Verdeur, United States 2:39.30
1952 John Davies, Australia 2:34.40
1956 Masaura Furukawa, Japan 2:34.70
1960 Bill Muliken, United States 2:37.40
1964 Ian O'Brien, Australia 2:07.80
1968 Felipe Munoz, Mexico 2:28.70
1972 John Hencken, United States 2:21.55
1976 David Willkie, Britain 2:15.11
1980 Robertas Zulpa, U.S.S.R. 2:15.85
1984 Victor Davis, Canada 2:13.34
1988 Jozef Szabo, Hungary 2:13.52
1992 Mike Barrowman, United States 2:10.16
1996 Norbert Rozsa, Hungary 2:12.57

100-Meter Butterfly
1968 Douglas Russell, United States 55.90
1972 Mark Spitz, United States 54.27
1976 Matt Vogel, United States 54.35
1980 Par Arvidsson, Sweden 54.92
1984 Michael Gross, West Germany 53.08
1988 Anthony Nesty, Surinam 53.00
1992 Pablo Morales, United States 53.32
1996 Denis Pankratov, Russia 52.27[1]
1. World record.

200-Meter Butterfly
1956 Bill Yorzyk, United States 2:19.30
1960 Mike Troy, United States 2:12.80
1964 Kevin Berry, Australia 2:06.60
1968 Carl Robie, United States 2:08.70
1972 Mark Spitz, United States 2:00.70
1976 Mike Bruner, United States 1:59.23
1980 Sergei Fesenko, U.S.S.R. 1:59.76
1984 Jon Sieben, Australia 1:57.00
1988 Michael Gross, East Germany 1:56.94
1992 Mel Stewart, United States 1:56.26
1996 Denis Pankratov, Russia 1:56.51

200-Meter Individual Medley
1968 Charles Hickcox, United States 2:12.00
1972 Gunnar Larsson, Sweden 2:07.17
1988 Tamas Darnyi, Hungary 2:00.17
1992 Tamas Darnyi, Hungary 2:00.76
1996 Attila Czene, Hungary 1:59.91

400-Meter Individual Medley
1964 Dick Roth, United States 4:45.40
1968 Charles Hickox, United States 4:48.40
1972 Gunnar Larsson, Sweden 4:31.98
1976 Rod Strachan, United States 4:23.68
1980 Aleksandr Sidorenko, U.S.S.R. 4:22.80
1984 Alex Baumann, Canada 4:17.41
1988 Tamas Darnyi, Hungary 4:14.75
1992 Tamas Darnyi, Hungary 4:14.23
1996 Tom Dolan, United States 4:14.90

400-Meter Freestyle Relay
1964 United States 3:32.20
1968 United States 3:31.70
1972 United States 3:26.42
1988 United States 3:16.52
1992 United States 3:16.74
1996 United States 3:15.41

800-Meter Freestyle Relay
1908 Great Britain 10:55.60
1912 Australia 10:11.20
1920 United States 10:04.40
1924 United States 09:53.40
1928 United States 09:36.20
1932 Japan 08:58.40
1936 Japan 08:51.50
1948 United States 08:46.10
1952 United States 08:31.10
1956 Australia 08:23.60
1960 United States 08:10.20
1964 United States 07:52.10
1968 United States 07:52.30
1972 United States 07:35.78
1976 United States 07:23.22
1980 U.S.S.R. 07:23.50
1984 United States 07:16.59
1988 United States 07:12.51
1992 Unified Team[1] 07:11.95
1996 United States 07:14.84
1. Former Soviet Union team.

400-Meter Medley Relay
1960 United States 4:05.40
1964 United States 3:58.40
1968 United States 3:54.90
1972 United States 3:48.16
1976 United States 3:42.22
1980 Australia 3:45.70
1984 United States 3:39.30
1988 United States 3:36.93
1992 United States 3:36.93
1996 United States 3:34.84[1]
1. World record.

Springboard Dive **Points**
1908 Albert Zuerner, Germany 85.50
1912 Paul Guenther, Germany 79.23
1920 Louis Kuehn, United States 675.00
1924 Albert White, United States 696.40
1928 Pete Desjardins, United States 185.04
1932 Michael Galitzen, United States 161.38
1936 Richard Degener, United States 163.57
1948 Bruce Harlan, United States 163.64
1952 David Browning, United States 205.59
1956 Robert Clotworthy, United States 159.56
1960 Gary Tobian, United States 170.00
1964 Ken Sitzberger, United States 159.90
1968 Bernard Wrightson, United States 170.15
1972 Vladimir Vasin, U.S.S.R. 594.09
1976 Phil Boggs, United States 619.05
1980 Alexsandr Portnov, U.S.S.R. 905.02

1984	Greg Louganis, United States	754.41
1988	Greg Louganis, United States	730.80
1992	Mark Lenzi, United States	676.53
1996	Xiong Ni, China	701.46

Platform Dive **Points**

1904	G.E. Sheldon, United States	12.75
1906	Gottlob Walz, Germany	156.00
1908	Hialmar Johansson, Sweden	83.75
1912	Erik Adlerz, Sweden	73.94
1920	Clarence Pinkston, United States	100.67
1924	Albert White, United States	487.30
1928	Pete Desjardins, United States	98.74
1932	Harold Smith, United States	124.80
1936	Marshall Wayne, United States	113.58
1948	Samuel Lee, United States	130.05
1952	Samuel Lee, United States	156.28
1956	Joaquin Capilla, Mexico	152.44
1960	Bob Webster, United States	165.56
1964	Bob Webster, United States	148.58
1968	Klaus Dibiasi, Italy	164.18
1972	Klaus Dibiasi, Italy	504.12
1976	Klaus Dibiasi, Italy	600.51
1980	Falk Hoffman, E. Germany	835.65
1984	Greg Louganis, United States	710.91
1988	Greg Louganis, United States	638.61
1992	Sun, Shu-Wei, China	677.31
1996	Dmitri Saoutine, Russia	692.34

SWIMMING–WOMEN

50-Meter Freestyle

1988	Kristin Otto, East Germany	25.49
1992	Yang, Wen-Yi, China	24.79
1996	Amy Van Dyken, United States	24.87

100-Meter Freestyle

1912	Fanny Durack, Australia	1:22.20
1920	Ethelda Bleibtrey, United States	1:13.60
1924	Ethel Lackie, United States	1:12.40
1928	Albina Osipowich, United States	1:11.00
1932	Helene Madison, United States	1:06.80
1936	Hendrika Mastenbroek, Netherlands	1:05.90
1948	Greta Andersen, Denmark	1:06.30
1952	Katalin Szoke, Hungary	1:06.80
1956	Dawn Fraser, Australia	1:02.00
1960	Dawn Fraser, Australia	1:01.20
1964	Dawn Fraser, Australia	0:59.50
1968	Marge Jan Henne, United States	1:00.00
1972	Sandra Neilson, United States	0:58.59
1976	Kornelia Ender, East Germany	0:55.65
1980	Barbara Krause, East Germany	0:54.79
1984	Carrie Steinseifer, United States	0:55.92
1988	Kristin Otto, East Germany	0:54.93
1992	Zhuang Yong, China	0:54.64
1996	Le Jingyi, China	0:54.50

200-Meter Freestyle

1968	Debbie Meyer, United States	2:10.50
1972	Shane Gould, Australia	2:03.56
1976	Kornelia Ender, East Germany	1:59.26
1980	Barbara Krause, East Germany	1:58.33
1984	Mary Wayle, United States	1:59.23
1988	Heike Friedrich, East Germany	1:57.65
1992	Nicole Haislett, United States	1:57.90
1996	Claudia Poll, Costa Rica	1:58.16

400-Meter Freestyle

1920	Ethelda Bleibtrey, United States	4:34.00[1]
1924	Martha Norelius, United States	6:02.20
1928	Martha Norelius, United States	5:42.80
1932	Helene Madison, United States	5:28.50
1936	Hendrika Mastenbroek, Netherlands	5:26.40
1948	Ann Curtis, United States	5:17.80
1952	Valerie Gyenge, Hungary	5:12.10
1956	Lorraine Crapp, Australia	4:54.60
1960	Chris von Saltza, United States	4:50.60
1964	Ginny Duenkel, United States	4:43.30
1968	Debbie Meyer, United States	4:31.80
1972	Shane Gould, Australia	4:19.04
1976	Petra Thumer, East Germany	4:09.89
1980	Ines Diers, East Germany	4:08.76
1984	Tiffany Cohen, United States	4:07.10
1988	Janet Evans, United States	4:03.85
1992	Dagmar Hase, Germany	4:07.18
1996	Michelle Smith, Ireland	4:07.25

1. 300 meters.

800-Meter Freestyle

1968	Debbie Meyer, United States	9:24.00
1972	Keena Rothhammer, United States	8:53.68
1976	Petra Thumer, East Germany	8:37.14
1980	Michelle Ford, Australia	8:28.90
1984	Tiffany Cohen, United States	8:24.95
1988	Janet Evans, United States	8:20.20
1992	Janet Evans, Unites States	8:25.52
1996	Brooke Bennett, Unites States	8:27.89

100-Meter Backstroke

1924	Sybil Bauer, United States	1:23.20
1928	Marie Braun, Netherlands	1:22.00
1932	Eleanor Holm, United States	1:19.40
1936	Dina Senff, Netherlands	1:18.90
1948	Karen Harup, Denmark	1:14.40
1952	Joan Harrison, South Africa	1:14.30
1956	Judy Grinham, Great Britain	1:12.90
1960	Lynn Burke, United States	1:09.30
1964	Cathy Ferguson, United States	1:07.70
1968	Kaye Hall, United States	1:06.20
1972	Melissa Belote, United States	1:05.78
1976	Ulrike Richter, East Germany	1:01.83
1980	Rica Reinisch, East Germany	1:00.86
1084	Theresa Andrews, United States	1:02.55
1988	Kristin Otto, East Germany	1:00.89
1992	Krisztina Egerszegi, Hungary	1:00.68
1996	Beth Botsford, United States	1:01.19

200-Meter Backstroke

1968	Pokey Watson, United States	2:24.80
1972	Melissa Belote, United States	2:19.19
1976	Ulrike Richter, East Germany	2:13.43
1980	Rica Reinisch, East Germany	2:11.77
1984	Jolanda DeRover, Netherlands	2:12.38
1988	Krisztina Egerszegi, Hungary	2:09.29
1992	Krisztina Egerszegi, Hungary	2:07.06
1996	Krisztina Egerszegi, Hungary	2:07.83

100-Meter Breaststroke

1968	Djurdjica Bjedov, Yugoslavia	1:15.80
1972	Catherine Carr, United States	1:13.58
1976	Hannelore Anke, East Germany	1:11.16
1980	Ute Geweniger, East Germany	1:10.22
1984	Petra Van Staveren, Netherlands	1:09.88
1988	Tainia Dangalakova, Bulgaria	1:07.95
1992	Elena Roudkovskaia, Unified Team	1:08.00
1996	Penny Heyns, South Africa	1:07.73

200-Meter Breaststroke

1924	Lucy Morton, Great Britain	3:33.20
1928	Hilde Schrader, Germany	3:12.60
1932	Clare Dennis, Australia	3:06.30
1936	Hideko Maehata, Japan	3:03.60
1948	Nel van Vliet, Netherlands	2:57.20
1952	Eva Szekely, Hungary	2:51.70
1956	Ursala Happe, Germany	2:53.10
1960	Anita Lonsbrough, Great Britain	2:49.50
1964	Galina Prozumenschikova, U.S.S.R.	2:46.40
1968	Sharon Wichman, United States	2:44.40
1972	Beverly Whitfield, Australia	2:41.71
1976	Marina Koshevaia, U.S.S.R.	2:33.35
1980	Lina Kachushite, U.S.S.R.	2:29.54
1984	Anne Ottenbrite, Canada	2:30.38

1988 Silke Hoerner, East Germany 2:26.71
1992 Kyoko Iwasaki, Japan 2:26.65
1996 Penny Heyns, South Africa 2:25.41

100-Meter Butterfly
1956 Shelley Mann, United States 1:11.00
1960 Carolyn Schuler, United States 1:09.50
1964 Sharon Stouder, United States 1:04.70
1968 Lynn McClements, Australia 1:05.50
1972 Mayumi Aoki, Japan 1:03.34
1976 Kornelia Ender, East Germany 1:00.13
1980 Caren Metschuck, East Germany 1:00.42
1984 Mary Meagher, United States 0:59.26
1988 Kristin Otto, East Germany 0:59.00
1992 Qian Hong, China 0:58.62
1996 Amy Van Dyken, United States 0:59.13

200-Meter Butterfly
1968 Ada Kok, Netherlands 2:24.70
1972 Karen Moe, United States 2:15.57
1976 Andrea Pollack, East Germany 2:11.41
1980 Ines Geissler, East Germany 2:10.44
1984 Mary Meagher, United States 2:06.90
1988 Kathleen Nord, East Germany 2:09.51
1992 Summer Sanders, United States 2:06.67
1996 Susan O'Neill, Australia 2:07.76

200-Meter Individual Medley
1968 Claudia Kolb, United States 2:24.70
1972 Shane Gould, Australia 2:23.07
1984 Tracy Caulkins, United States 2:12.64
1988 Daniela Hunger, East Germany 2:12.59
1992 Lin Lee, China 2:11.55[1]
1996 Michelle Smith, Ireland 2:13.93

1. World record.

400-Meter Individual Medley
1964 Donna de Varona, United States 5:18.70
1968 Claudia Kolk, United States 5:08.50
1972 Gail Neall, Australia 5:02.97
1976 Ulrike Tauber, East Germany 4:42.77
1980 Petra Schneider, East Germany 4:36.29
1984 Tracy Caulkins, United States 4:39.21
1988 Janet Evans, United States 4:37.76
1992 Krisztina Egerszegi, Hungary 4:36.54
1996 Michelle Smith, Ireland 4:39.18

400-Meter Freestyle Relay
1912 Great Britain 5:52.80
1920 United States 5:11.60
1924 United States 4:58.80
1928 United States 4:47.60
1932 United States 4:38.00

DISTRIBUTION OF MEDALS—1996 SUMMER GAMES

Country	Gold	Silver	Bronze	Total
United States	44	32	25	101
Germany	20	18	27	65
Russia	26	21	16	63
China	16	22	12	50
Australia	9	9	23	41
France	15	7	15	37
Italy	13	10	12	35
South Korea	7	15	5	27
Cuba	9	8	8	25
Ukraine	9	2	12	23
Canada	3	11	8	22
Hungary	7	4	10	21
Romania	4	7	9	20
Netherlands	4	5	10	19
Poland	7	5	5	17
Spain	5	6	6	17
Britain	1	8	7	16
Bulgaria	3	7	5	15
Belarus	1	6	8	15
Brazil	3	2	10	15
Japan	3	6	5	14
Czech Republic	4	3	4	11
Kazakhstan	3	4	4	11
Greece	4	4	0	8
Sweden	2	4	2	8
Kenya	1	4	3	8
Switzerland	4	3	0	7
Norway	2	2	3	7
Denmark	4	1	1	6
Turkey	4	1	1	6
New Zealand	3	2	1	6
Belgium	2	2	2	6
Nigeria	2	1	3	6
Jamaica	1	3	2	6
South Africa	3	1	1	5
North Korea	2	1	2	5
Ireland	3	0	1	4
Finland	1	2	1	4
Indonesia	1	1	2	4
Yugoslavia	1	1	2	4
Ethiopia	2	0	1	3
Algeria	2	0	1	3
Iran	1	1	1	3
Slovakia	1	1	1	3
Argentina	0	2	1	3
Austria	0	1	2	3
Armenia	1	1	0	2
Croatia	1	1	0	2
Portugal	1	0	1	2
Thailand	1	0	1	2
Namibia	0	2	0	2
Slovenia	0	2	0	2
Malaysia	0	1	1	2
Moldova	0	1	1	2
Uzbekistan	0	1	1	2
Georgia	0	0	2	2
Morocco	0	0	2	2
Trinidad & Tobago	0	0	2	2
Burundi	1	0	0	1
Costa Rica	1	0	0	1
Ecuador	1	0	0	1
Hong Kong	1	0	0	1
Syria	1	0	0	1
Azerbaijan	0	1	0	1
Bahamas	0	1	0	1
Latvia	0	1	0	1
Philippines	0	1	0	1
Taiwan	0	1	0	1
Tonga	0	1	0	1
Zambia	0	1	0	1
India	0	0	1	1
Israel	0	0	1	1
Lithuania	0	0	1	1
Mexico	0	0	1	1
Mongolia	0	0	1	1
Mozambique	0	0	1	1
Puerto Rico	0	0	1	1
Tunisia	0	0	1	1
Uganda	0	0	1	1

1936	Netherlands	4:36.00
1948	United States	4:29.20
1952	Hungary	4:24.40
1956	Australia	4:17.10
1960	United States	4:08.90
1964	United States	4:03.80
1968	United States	4:02.50
1972	United States	3:55.19
1976	United States	3:44.82
1980	East Germany	3:42.71
1984	United States	3:44.43
1988	East Germany	3:40.63
1992	United States	3:39.46
1996	United States	3:39.29

800-Meter Freestyle Relay

1996	United States	7:59.87

400-Meter Medley Relay

1960	United States	4:41.10
1964	United States	4:33.90
1968	United States	4:28.30
1972	United States	4:20.75
1976	East Germany	4:07.95
1980	East Germany	4:06.67
1984	United States	4:08.34
1988	East Germany	4:03.74
1992	United States	4:02.54[1]
1996	United States	4:02.88

1. World record.

Springboard Dive		Points
1920	Aileen Riggin, United States	539.90
1924	Elizabeth Becker, United States	474.50
1928	Helen Meany, United States	78.62
1932	Georgia Coleman, United States	87.52
1936	Marjorie Gestring, United States	89.27
1948	Victoria M. Draves, United States	108.74
1952	Patricia McCormick, United States	147.30
1956	Patricia McCormick, United States	142.36
1960	Ingrid Kramer, Germany	155.81
1964	Ingrid Kramer Engel, Germany	145.00
1968	Sue Gossick, United States	150.77
1972	Micki King, United States	450.03
1976	Jennifer Chandler, United States	506.19
1980	Irina Kalinina, U.S.S.R.	725.91
1984	Sylvie Bernier, Canada	530.70
1988	Gao Min, China	580.23
1992	Gao Min, China	572.40
1996	Fu Ming-Xia, China	547.68

Platform Dive		Points
1912	Greta Johansson, Sweden	39.90
1920	Stefani Fryland, Denmark	34.60
1924	Caroline Smith, United States	166.00
1928	Elizabeth B. Pinkston, United States	31.60
1932	Dorothy Poynton, United States	40.26
1936	Dorothy Poynton Hill, United States	33.92
1948	Victoria M. Draves, United States	68.87
1952	Patricia McCormick, United States	79.37
1956	Patricia McCormick, United States	84.85
1960	Ingrid Kramer, Germany	91.28
1964	Lesley Bush, United States	99.80
1968	Milena Duchkova, Czechoslovakia	109.59
1972	Ulrika Knape, Sweden	390.00
1976	Elena Vaytsekhovskaia, U.S.S.R.	406.59
1980	Martina Jaschke, East Germany	596.25
1984	Zhou Ji-Hong, China	435.51
1988	Xu Yan-Mei, China	445.20
1992	Fu Ming-Xia, China	461.43
1996	Fu Ming-Xia, China	521.58

BASKETBALL–MEN

1904 United States
1936 United States
1948 United States
1952 United States
1956 United States
1960 United States
1964 United States
1968 United States
1972 U.S.S.R.
1976 United States
1980 Yugoslavia
1984 United States
1988 U.S.S.R.
1992 United States
1996 United States

BASKETBALL–WOMEN

1976 U.S.S.R.
1980 U.S.S.R.
1984 United States
1988 United States
1992 Unified Team[1]
1996 United States

1. Former Soviet Union team.

BOXING

(U.S. winners only)

(U.S. boycotted Olympics in 1980)

Flyweight-112 pounds (51 kilograms)

1904 George Finnegan
1920 Frank De Genaro
1924 Fidel La Barba
1952 Nate Brooks
1976 Leo Randolph
1984 Steve McCrory

Bantamweight-119 (54 kg)

1904 O.L. Kirk
1988 Kennedy McKinney

Featherweight-126 pounds (57 kg)

1904 O.L. Kirk
1924 Jackie Fields
1984 Meldrick Taylor

Lightweight-132 pounds (60 kg)

1904 H.J. Spanger
1920 Samuel Mosberg
1968 Ronnie Harris
1976 Howard Davis
1984 Pernell Whitaker
1992 Oscar De La Hoya

Light Welterweight-140 pounds (63.5 kg)

1952 Charles Adkins
1972 Ray Seales
1976 Ray Leonard
1984 Jerry Page

Welterweight-148 pounds (67 kg)

1904 Al Young
1932 Edward Flynn
1984 Mark Breland

Light Middleweight-157 pounds (71 kg)

1960 Wilbert McClure
1984 Frank Tate
1996 David Reid

Middleweight-165 pounds (75 kg)

1904 Charles Mayer
1932 Carmen Barth
1952 Floyd Patterson
1960 Eddie Cook
1976 Michael Spinks

Light Heavyweight-179 pounds (81 kg)

1920 Edward Eagan
1952 Norvel Lee
1956 James Boyd
1960 Cassius Clay
1976 Leon Spinks
1988 Andrew Maynard

Heavyweight-201 pounds

1904 Sam Berger
1952 Edward Sanders
1956 Pete Rademacher
1964 Joe Frazier
1968 George Foreman
1984 Henry Tilman
1988 Ray Mercer

Super Heavyweight (unlimited)

1984 Tyrell Biggs

Other 1996 Summer Olympic Games Champions

Archery
Women's individual—Kim Kyung Wook, South Korea
Women's team—South Korea
Men's individual—Justin Huish, United States
Men's team—United States

Badminton
Men's singles—Poul-Erik Hoyer-Larsen, Denmark
Men's doubles—Indonesia (Rexy Mainaky, Ricky Subagja)
Women's singles—Bang Soo-Hyun, South Korea
Women's doubles—China (Ge Fei, Gu Jun)
Mixed doubles—South Korea (Gil Young-Ahl, Kim Dong-Moon)

Baseball
Men—Cuba

Beach Volleyball
Women—Jackie Silva/Sandra Pires, Brazil
Men—Karch Kiraly/Kent Steffes, United States

Canoe-Kayak—Men
Canoe single slalom—Michal Martikan, Slovakia
Canoe slalom pairs—France
Kayak slalom singles—Oliver Fix, Germany
Canoe singles 500m—Martin Doktor, Czech Republic
Canoe singles 1,000m—Martin Doktor, Czech Republic
Canoe pairs 500m—Csaba Horvath/Gyorgy Kolonics, Hungary
Canoe pairs 1,000m—Andreas Dittmer/Gunar Kirchbach, Germany
Kayak singles 500m—Antonio Rossi, Italy
Kayak singles 1,000m—Knut Holmann, Norway
Kayak pairs 500m—Kay Bluhm/Torsten Gutsche, Germany
Kayak pairs 1,000m—Antonio Rossi/Daniele Scarpa, Italy
Kayak fours 1,000m—Germany

Kayak—Women
Single slalom—Stepnka Hilgertova, Czech Republic
500m singles—Rita Koban, Hungary
500m pairs—Agneta Andersson/Susanne Gunnarsson, Sweden
500m pairs—Germany

Cycling—Men
Individual road race—Pascal Richard, Switzerland
1 km time trial—Florian Rousseau, France
Individual pursuit—Andrea Collinelli, Italy
Individual spring—Jens Fiedler, Germany
Individual point race—Silvio Martinello, Italy
Team pursuit—France
Cross country—Bart Jan Brentjens, Netherlands
Individual time trial—Miguel Indurain, Spain

Cycling—Women
Individual road race—Jeannie Longo-Ciprelli, France
Track sprint—Felicia Ballanger, France
Individual pursuit—Antonella Bellutti, Italy
Point race—Nathalie Lancien, France
Cross country—Paola Pezzo, Italy
Individual time trial—Zulfiya Zabirova, Russia

Equestrian
Three-day team event—Australia
Individual three-day—Blyth Tait, New Zealand
Team dressage—Germany
Individual dressage—Isabell Werth, Germany
Team jumping—Germany
Show jumping—Ulrich Kirchhoff, Germany

Fencing—Men
Individual epee—Aleksandr Beketov, Russia
Individual sabre—Stanislav Pozdnakov, Russia
Individual foil—Alessandro Puccini, Italy
Team epee—Italy
Team sabre—Russia
Team foil—Russia

Fencing—Women
Individual epee—Laura Flessel, France
Individual foil—Laura Badea, Romania
Team epee—France
Team foil—Italy

Field Hockey
Women—Australia
Men—Netherlands

Gymnastics—Men
Team—Russia
All-around—Li Xiao-Shuang, China
Floor exercise—Ioannis Melissanidis, Greece
Vault—Alexei Nemov, Russia
Parallel bars—Rustram Sharipov, Ukraine
High bar—Andreas Wecker, Germany
Pommel horse—Li Dong-Hua, Switzerland
Rings—Yuri Chechi, Italy

Gymnastics—Women
Team—United States
All-around—Lilia Podkopayeva, Ukraine
Balance beam—Shannon Miller, United States
Floor exercise—Lilia Podkopayeva, Ukraine
Uneven bars—Svetlana Chorkina, Russia
Vault—Simona Amanar, Romania

Judo—Men
Extra-lightweight—Tadahiro Nomura, Japan
Half-lightweight—Udo Quellmalz, Germany
Lightweight—Kenzo Nakamura, Japan
Half-middleweight—Djamel Bouras, France
Middleweight—Jeon Ki Young, South Korea
Light-heavyweight—Pawel Nastula, Poland
Heavyweight—David Douillet, France

Judo—Women
Extra-lightweight—Sun Kye, North Korea
Half-lightweight—Marie-Claire Restoux, France
Lightweight—Driulis Gonzalez, Cuba
Half-middleweight—Yuko Emoto, Japan
Middleweight—Cho Min Sun, South Korea
Light-heavyweight—Ulla Werbrouck, Belgium
Heavyweight—Sun Fu-Ming, China

Modern Pentathlon
Individual—Aleksandr Parygin, Kazakhstan

Rhythmic Gymnastics
Team—Spain
Individual—Ekaterina Serebryanskaya, Ukraine

Rowing—Men
Coxless pairs—Great Britain
Coxless four—Australia
Single sculls—Xeno Müller, Switzerland
Double sculls—Italy
Lightweight double sculls—Switzerland
Eight—Netherlands
Quadruple sculls—Germany
Lightweight coxless four—Denmark

Rowing—Women
Coxless pairs—Australia
Single sculls—Yekaterina Khodotovich, Belarus
Double sculls—Canada
Eight—Romania
Quadruple sculls—Germany
Lightweight double sculls—Romania

Shooting—Women
10m air rifle—Renata Mauer, Poland
10m air pistol—Olga Klochneva, Russia
Double trap—Kim Rhode, United States
Rifle three position—Aleksandra Ivosev, Yugoslavia
24m sport pistol—Li Dui-Hong, China

Shooting—Men

10m air pistol—Roberto Di Donna, Italy
Trap—Michael Diamond, Australia
Air rifle—Artem Khadzhibekov, Russia
50m free pistol—Boris Kokorev, Russia
Double trap—Russell Mark, Australia
25m rapid fire pistol—Ralf Schumann, Germany
50m rifle prone—Christian Klees, Germany
Running game target—Yank Ling, China
50m free rifle 3-position—Jean-Pierre Amat, France
Skeet shooting—Ennio Falco, Italy

Soccer

Women—United States
Men—Nigeria

Softball

United States

Synchronized Swimming

Team—United States

Table Tennis

Women's singles—Deng Ya-Ping, China
Women's doubles—China (Deng Ya-Ping, Qiao Hong)
Men's singles—Liu Guo-Liang, China
Men's doubles—China (Kong Ling-Hui, Liu, Guo-Liang)

Team Handball

Women—Denmark
Men—Croatia

Tennis

Men's singles—Andre Agassi, United States
Men's doubles—Todd Woodbridge and Mark Woodforde, Australia
Women's singles—Lindsay Davenport, United States
Women's doubles—Gigi Fernandez and Mary Jo Fernandez, United States

Volleyball

Women—Cuba
Men—Netherlands

Water Polo

Spain

Weightlifting

119 lb—Halil Mutlu, Turkey
130 lb—Tang Ling-Shen, China
141 lb—Naim Suleymanoglu, Turkey
154 lb—Zhan Xu-Gang, China
161.5 lb—Pablo Lara, Cuba
183 lb—Pyrros Dias, Greece
200.5 lb—Aleksey Petrov, Russia
218 lb—Akakide Kakiashvilis, Greece
238 lb—Timur Taimazov, Ukraine
238+ lb—Andre Chemerkin, Russia

Wrestling—Greco-Roman

105.5 lb—Sim Kwon-Ho, South Korea
114.5 lb—Armen Nazaryan, Armenia
125.5 lb—Yuri Melnichenko, Kazakhstan
136.5 lb—Wlodzimierz Zwadzki, Poland
149.5 lb—Ryszard Wolny, Poland
163 lb—Feliberto Ascuy Aquilera, Cuba
180.5 lb—Hamza Yerlikiya, Turkey
198 lb—Vyacheslav Oleynyk, Ukraine
220 lb—Andrzej Wronski, Poland
286 lb—Aleksandr Karelin, Russia

Wrestling—Freestyle

105.5 lb—Kim Il, North Korea
114.5 lb—Valentin Jordanov, Bulgaria
125.5 lb—Kendall Cross, United States
136.5 lb—Tom Brands, United States
149.5 lb—Vadim Bogiev, Russia
163 lb—Bouvaisa Satiev, Russia
180.5 lb—Khadzhimurad Magomedov, Russia
198.5 lb—Rsaul Khadem, Iran
220 lb—Kurt Angle, United States
286 lb—Mahmut Demir, Turkey

Yachting

Men's Mistral—Nikolaos Kaklamanakis, Greece
Men's 470—Ukraine
Men's Finn—Mateusz Kusznierewicz, Poland
Women's Mistral—Lee Lai-Shan, Hong Kong
Women's Europe—Kristine Rough, Denmark
Women's 470—Spain
Open Laser—Robert Scheidt, Brazil
Open Tornado—Spain
Open Soling—Germany
Open Star- Brazil

Iditarod

26TH IDITAROD TRAIL SLED DOG RACE—1998

(Alaska, March 7–17, 1998)

The annual race stretches from Anchorage to Nome, Alaska. Begun in 1973, the course follows an old frozen river route and is named after a deserted mining town along the way. The Iditarod also commemorates a famous midwinter emergency mission to get medical supplies to Nome during a 1925 diphtheria epidemic. Men and women mushers compete together.

Course: Anchorage to Nome.

1998 Champion—

Jeff King of Denali Park, Alaska, 41 years old, won the 26th annual Iditarod Trail Sled Dog Race on March 17, 1998. King, who also won the race in 1993 and 1996, reached Nome and the finish line of the 1,151-mile course in 9 days, 5 hours, and 52 minutes. The Iditarod began March 7 in Anchorage. In even-numbered years, the trail follows the 1,151-mile long Northern Route, while odd-numbered years it takes the slightly different 1,161-mile Southern Route. One dog died during the 1998 race. King took home $51,000 and a new pickup. DeeDee Jonrowe, of Willow, Alaska, came in second with a time of 9 days, 8 hours, and 49 minutes.

Winning times since 1980:

1980, Joe May, 14 days-7 hours-11 minutes; 1981, Rick Swenson, 12-8-45; 1982, Rick Swenson, 16-4-40; 1983, Rick Mackey, 12-14-10; 1984, Dean Osmar, 12-15-7; 1985, Libby Riddles, 18-00-20; 1986, Susan Butcher, 11-15-6; 1987, Susan Butcher, 11-2-5; 1988, Susan Butcher, 11-11-41; 1989, Joe Runyan, 11-5-24; 1990, Susan Butcher, 11-1-34; 1991, Rick Swenson, 12-16-34; 1992, Martin Buser, 10-19-17; 1993, Jeff King, 10-15-38; 1994, Martin Buser, 10-13-2; 1995, Doug Swingly, 9-2-42; 1996, Jeff King, 9-5-43; 1997, Martin Buser, 9-8-31; 1998, Jeff King, 9-5-52.

Football

The pastime of kicking around a ball goes back beyond the limits of recorded history. Ancient savage tribes played football of a primitive kind. There was a ball-kicking game played by Athenians, Spartans, and Corinthians 2500 years ago, which the Greeks called *Episkuros*. The Romans had a somewhat similar game called *Harpastum* and are supposed to have carried the game with them when they invaded the British Isles in the First Century, B.C.

Undoubtedly the game known in the United States as Football traces directly to the English game of Rugby, though the modifications have been many. Informal football was played on college lawns well over a century ago, and an annual freshman-sophomore series of "scrimmages" began at Yale in 1840. The first formal intercollegiate football game was the Princeton-Rutgers contest at New Brunswick, N.J. on Nov. 6, 1869, with Rutgers winning by 6 goals to 4.

In those days, games were played with 25, 20, 15, or 11 men on a side. In 1880, there was a convention at which Walter Camp of Yale persuaded the delegates to agree to a rule calling for 11 players on a side.

The first professional game was played in 1895 at Latrobe, Pa. The National Football League was founded in 1921. The All-American Conference went into action in 1946. At the end of the 1949 season the two circuits merged, retaining the name of the older league. In 1960, the American Football League began operations. In 1970, the leagues merged. The United States Football League played its first season in 1983, from March to July. It suspended spring operations after the 1985 season, and planned a 1986 move to fall, but suspended operations again.

In 1991, another effort at spring football was launched, but this time it had the backing of the National Football League. The World League of American Football debuted in March 1991 with ten teams. Three of them were in Europe. The other seven were in North America, including the Montreal Machine in Canada. With television contracts signed with ABC and USA Cable Network, the league seemed to be on sound footing from the beginning. But after just two seasons, it was suspended. The league returned in 1995, but only with six teams in Europe.

College Football

NATIONAL COLLEGE FOOTBALL CHAMPIONS

The "National Collegiate Athletic Association Football Guide" recognizes as unofficial national champion the team selected each year by press association polls. The Associated Press poll (of writers) does not always agree with the United Press International poll (of coaches); the guide lists both teams selected.

1936	Minnesota
1937	Pittsburgh
1938	Texas Christian
1939	Texas A & M
1940	Minnesota
1941	Minnesota
1942	Ohio State
1943	Notre Dame
1944	Army
1945	Army
1946	Notre Dame
1947	Notre Dame
1948	Michigan
1949	Notre Dame
1950	Oklahoma
1951	Tennessee
1952	Mich. State
1953	Maryland
1954	Ohio State and UCLA
1955	Oklahoma
1956	Oklahoma
1957	Auburn and Ohio State
1958	Louisiana State
1959	Syracuse
1960	Minnesota
1961	Alabama
1962	So. Calif.
1963	Texas
1964	Alabama
1965	Alabama and Mich. State
1966	Notre Dame
1967	So. Calif.
1968	Ohio State
1969	Texas
1970	Texas and Nebraska
1971	Nebraska
1972	So. Calif.
1973	Notre Dame and U. of Ala.
1974	Oklahoma and So. Calif.
1975	Oklahoma
1976	Pittsburgh
1977	Notre Dame
1978	Alabama and So. Calif.
1979	Alabama
1980	Georgia
1981	Clemson
1982	Penn State
1983	Miami
1984	Brigham Young
1985	Oklahoma
1986	Penn State
1987	Miami
1988	Notre Dame
1989	Miami
1990	Colorado and Georgia Tech
1991	Miami and Washington
1992	Alabama
1993	Florida State
1994	Nebraska
1995	Nebraska
1996	Univ. of Florida
1997	Michigan and Nebraska

RECORD OF ANNUAL MAJOR COLLEGE FOOTBALL BOWL GAMES

Rose Bowl (At Pasadena, Calif.)

1902	Michigan 49, Stanford 0
1916	Washington State 14, Brown 0
1917	Oregon 14, Pennsylvania 0
1918	Mare Island Marines 19, Camp Lewis 7
1919	Great Lakes 17, Mare Island Marines 0
1920	Harvard 7, Oregon 6
1921	California 28, Ohio State 0
1922	Washington and Jefferson 0, California 0
1923	So. Calif. 14, Penn State 3
1924	Navy 14, Washington 14
1925	Notre Dame 27, Stanford 10
1926	Alabama 20, Washington 19
1927	Alabama 7, Stanford 7
1928	Stanford 7, Pittsburgh 6
1929	Georgia Tech 8, California 7
1930	So. Calif. 47, Pittsburgh 14
1931	Alabama 24, Wash. State 0
1932	So. Calif. 21, Tulane 12
1933	So. Calif. 35, Pittsburgh 0
1934	Columbia 7, Stanford 0
1935	Alabama 29, Stanford 13
1936	Stanford 7, So. Methodist 0
1937	Pittsburgh 21, Washington 0
1938	California 13, Alabama 0
1939	So. Calif. 7, Duke 3
1940	So. Calif. 14, Tennessee 0
1941	Stanford 21, Nebraska 13
1942	Oregon State 20, Duke 16[1]
1943	Georgia 9, UCLA 0
1944	So. Calif. 29, Washington 0
1945	So. Calif. 25, Tennessee 0
1946	Alabama 34, So. Calif. 14
1947	Illinois 45, UCLA 14
1948	Michigan 49, So. Calif. 0
1949	Northwestern 20, California 14
1950	Ohio State 17, California 14
1951	Michigan 14, California 6
1952	Illinois 40, Stanford 7
1953	So. Calif. 7, Wisconsin 0
1954	Michigan State 28, UCLA 20
1955	Ohio State 20, So. Calif. 7
1956	Michigan State 17, UCLA 14
1957	Iowa 35, Oregon State 19
1958	Ohio State 10, Oregon 7
1959	Iowa 38, California 12
1960	Washington 44, Wisconsin 8

1961 Washington 17, Minnesota 7
1962 Minnesota 21, UCLA 3
1963 So. Calif. 42, Wisconsin 37
1964 Illinois 17, Washington 7
1965 Michigan 34, Oregon State 7
1966 UCLA 14, Michigan State 12
1967 Purdue 14, So. Calif. 13
1968 So. Calif. 14, Indiana 3
1969 Ohio State 27, So. Calif. 16
1970 So. Calif. 10, Michigan 3
1971 Stanford 27, Ohio State 17
1972 Stanford 13, Michigan 12
1973 So. Calif. 42, Ohio State 17
1974 Ohio State 42, So. Calif. 21
1975 So. Calif. 18, Ohio State 17
1976 UCLA 23, Ohio State 10
1977 So. Calif. 14, Michigan 6
1978 Washington 27, Michigan 20
1979 So. Calif. 17, Michigan 10
1980 So. Calif. 17, Ohio State 16
1981 Michigan 23, Washington 6
1982 Washington 28, Iowa 0
1983 UCLA 24, Michigan 14
1984 UCLA 45, Illinois 9
1985 So. Calif. 20, Ohio St. 17
1986 UCLA 45, Iowa 28
1987 Arizona State 22, Michigan 15
1988 Michigan State 20, So. Calif. 17
1989 Michigan 22, So. Calif. 14
1990 So. Calif. 17, Michigan 10
1991 Washington 46, Iowa 34
1992 Washington 34, Michigan 14
1993 Michigan 38, Washington 31
1994 Wisconsin 21, UCLA 16
1995 Penn State 38, Oregon 20
1996 South Carolina 41, Northwestern 32
1997 Ohio State 20, Arizona State 17
1998 Michigan 21, Washington State 16

1. Played at Durham, N.C.

Orange Bowl (At Miami)

1933 Miami (Fla.) 7, Manhattan 0
1934 Duquesne 33, Miami (Fla.) 7
1935 Bucknell 26, Miami (Fla.) 0
1936 Catholic 20, Mississippi 19
1937 Duquesne 13, Mississippi State 12
1938 Auburn 6, Michigan State 0
1939 Tennessee 17, Oklahoma 0
1940 Georgia Tech 21, Missouri 7
1941 Mississippi State 14, Georgetown 7
1942 Georgia 40, Texas Christian 26
1943 Alabama 37, Boston College 21
1944 Louisiana State 19, Texas A & M 14
1945 Tulsa 26, Georgia Tech 12
1946 Miami (Fla.) 13, Holy Cross 6
1947 Rice 8, Tennessee 0
1948 Georgia Tech 20, Kansas 14
1949 Texas 41, Georgia 28
1950 Santa Clara 21, Kentucky 13
1951 Clemson 15, Miami (Fla.) 14
1952 Georgia Tech 17, Baylor 14
1953 Alabama 61, Syracuse 6
1954 Oklahoma 7, Maryland 0
1955 Duke 34, Nebraska 7
1956 Oklahoma 20, Maryland 6
1957 Colorado 27, Clemson 21
1958 Oklahoma 48, Duke 21
1959 Oklahoma 21, Syracuse 6
1960 Georgia 14, Missouri 0
1961 Missouri 21, Navy 14
1962 Louisiana State 25, Colorado 7
1963 Alabama 17, Oklahoma 0
1964 Nebraska 13, Auburn 7
1965 Texas 21, Alabama 17
1966 Alabama 39, Nebraska 28
1967 Florida 27, Georgia Tech 12
1968 Oklahoma 26, Tennessee 24
1969 Penn State 15, Kansas 14
1970 Penn State 10, Missouri 3
1971 Nebraska 17, Louisiana State 12
1972 Nebraska 38, Alabama 6
1973 Nebraska 40, Notre Dame 6
1974 Penn State 16, Louisiana State 9
1975 Notre Dame 13, Alabama 11
1976 Oklahoma 14, Michigan 6
1977 Ohio State 27, Colorado 10
1978 Arkansas 31, Oklahoma 6
1979 Oklahoma 31, Nebraska 24
1980 Oklahoma 24, Florida State 7
1981 Oklahoma 18, Florida State 17
1982 Clemson 22, Nebraska 15
1983 Nebraska 21, Louisiana State 20
1984 Miami (Fla.) 31, Nebraska 30
1985 Washington 28, Oklahoma 17
1986 Oklahoma 25, Penn St. 10
1987 Oklahoma 42, Arkansas 8
1988 Miami (Fla.) 20, Oklahoma 14
1989 Miami (Fla.) 23, Nebraska 3
1990 Notre Dame 21, Colorado 6
1991 Colorado 10, Notre Dame 9
1992 Miami (Fla.) 22, Nebraska 0
1993 Florida State 27, Nebraska 14
1994 Florida State 18, Nebraska 16
1995 Nebraska 24, Miami (Fla.) 17
1996 Florida State 31, Notre Dame 26
1997 Nebraska 41, Virginia Tech 21
1998 Nebraska 42, Tennessee 17

Sugar Bowl (At New Orleans)

1935 Tulane 20, Temple 14
1936 Texas Christian 3, Louisiana State 2
1937 Santa Clara 21, Louisiana State 14
1938 Santa Clara 6, Louisiana State 0
1939 Texas Christian 15, Carnegie Tech 7
1940 Texas A & M 14, Tulane 13
1941 Boston College 19, Tennessee 13
1942 Fordham 2, Missouri 0
1943 Tennessee 14, Tulsa 7
1944 Georgia Tech 20, Tulsa 18
1945 Duke 29, Alabama 26
1946 Oklahoma A & M 33, St. Mary's (Calif.) 13
1947 Georgia 20, North Carolina 10
1948 Texas 27, Alabama 7
1949 Oklahoma 14, North Carolina 6
1950 Oklahoma 35, Louisiana State 0
1951 Kentucky 13, Oklahoma 7
1952 Maryland 28, Tennessee 13
1953 Georgia Tech 24, Mississippi 7
1954 Georgia Tech 42, West Virginia 19
1955 Navy 21, Mississippi 0
1956 Georgia Tech 7, Pittsburgh 0
1957 Baylor 13, Tennessee 7
1958 Mississippi 39, Texas 7
1959 Louisiana State 7, Clemson 0
1960 Mississippi 21, Louisiana State 0
1961 Mississippi 14, Rice 6
1962 Alabama 10, Arkansas 3
1963 Mississippi 17, Arkansas 13
1964 Alabama 12, Mississippi 7
1965 Louisiana State 13, Syracuse 10
1966 Missouri 20, Florida 18
1967 Alabama 34, Nebraska 7
1968 Louisiana State 20, Wyoming 13
1969 Arkansas 16, Georgia 2
1970 Mississippi 27, Arkansas 22
1971 Tennessee 34, Air Force Academy 13
1972 Oklahoma 40, Auburn 22
1973 Oklahoma 14, Penn State 0
1974 Notre Dame 24, Alabama 23
1975 Nebraska 13, Florida 10
1976 Alabama 13, Penn State 6
1977 Pittsburgh 27, Georgia 3
1978 Alabama 35, Ohio State 6
1979 Alabama 14, Penn State 7
1980 Alabama 24, Arkansas 9
1981 Georgia 17, Notre Dame 10
1982 Pittsburgh 24, Georgia 20
1983 Penn State 27, Georgia 23
1984 Auburn 9, Michigan 7
1985 Nebraska 28, Louisiana State 10
1986 Tennessee 35, Miami (Fla.) 7
1987 Nebraska 30, Louisiana State 15
1988 Syracuse 16, Auburn 16 (tie)
1989 Florida State 13, Auburn 7
1990 Miami (Fla.) 33, Alabama 25
1991 Tennessee 23, Virginia 22
1992 Notre Dame 39, Florida 28
1993 Alabama 34, Miami (Fla.) 13
1994 Florida 41, West Virginia 7
1995 Florida State 23, Florida 17
1996 Virginia Tech 28, Texas 10
1997 Florida 52, Florida State 20
1998 Florida State 31, Ohio State 14

Cotton Bowl (At Dallas)

1937 Texas Christian 16, Marquette 6
1938 Rice 28, Colorado 14
1939 St. Mary's (Calif.) 20, Texas Tech. 13
1940 Clemson 6, Boston College 3
1941 Texas A & M 13, Fordham 12
1942 Alabama 29, Texas A & M 21
1943 Texas 14, Georgia Tech 7
1944 Randolph Field 7, Texas 7
1945 Oklahoma A & M 34, Texas Christian 0
1946 Texas 40, Missouri 27
1947 Louisiana State 0, Arkansas 0
1948 So. Methodist 13, Penn State 13
1949 So. Methodist 21, Oregon 13
1950 Rice 27, North Carolina 13
1951 Tennessee 20, Texas 14
1952 Kentucky 20, Texas Christian 7
1953 Texas 16, Tennessee 0
1954 Rice 28, Alabama 6
1955 Georgia Tech 14, Arkansas 6
1956 Mississippi 14, Texas Christian 13

1957 Texas Christian 28, Syracuse 27
1958 Navy 20, Rice 7
1959 Air Force 0, Texas Christian 0
1960 Syracuse 23, Texas 14
1961 Duke 7, Arkansas 6
1962 Texas 12, Mississippi 7
1963 Louisiana State 13, Texas 0
1964 Texas 28, Navy 6
1965 Arkansas 10, Nebraska 7
1966 Louisiana State 14, Arkansas 7
1967 Georgia 24, So. Methodist 9
1968 Texas A & M 20, Alabama 16
1969 Texas 36, Tennessee 13
1970 Texas 21, Notre Dame 17
1971 Notre Dame 24, Texas 11
1972 Penn State 30, Texas 6
1973 Texas 17, Alabama 13
1974 Nebraska 19, Texas 3
1975 Penn State 41, Baylor 20
1976 Arkansas 31, Georgia 10
1977 Houston 30, Maryland 21
1978 Notre Dame 38, Texas 10
1979 Notre Dame 35, Houston 34
1980 Houston 17, Nebraska 14
1981 Alabama 30, Baylor 2
1982 Texas 14, Alabama 12
1983 Southern Methodist 7, Pittsburgh 3
1984 Georgia 10, Texas 9
1985 Boston College 45, Houston 28
1986 Texas A & M 36, Auburn 16
1987 Ohio State 28, Texas A&M 12
1988 Texas A & M 35, Notre Dame 10
1989 UCLA 17, Arkansas 3
1990 Tennessee 31, Arkansas 27
1991 Miami (Fla.) 46, Texas 3
1992 Florida State 10, Texas A&M 2
1993 Notre Dame 28, Texas A&M 3
1994 Notre Dame 24, Texas A&M 21
1995 Southern California 55, Texas Tech 14
1996 Colorado 38, Oregon 6
1997 Brigham Young 19, Kansas State 15
1998 UCLA 29, Texas A & M 23

Gator Bowl (At Jacksonville, Fla.)

1953 Florida 14, Tulsa 13
1954 Texas Tech 35, Auburn 13
1955 Auburn 33, Baylor 13
1956 Vanderbilt 25, Auburn 13
1957 Georgia Tech 21, Pittsburgh 14
1958 Tennessee 3, Texas A & M 0
1959 Mississippi 7, Florida 3
1960 Arkansas 14, Georgia Tech 7
1961 Florida 13, Baylor 12
1962 Penn State 30, Georgia Tech 15
1963 Florida 17, Penn State 7
1964 No. Carolina 35, Air Force 0
1965 Florida State 36, Oklahoma 19
1966 Georgia Tech 31, Texas Tech 21
1967 Tennessee 18, Syracuse 12
1968 Penn State 17, Florida State 17 (tie)
1969 Missouri 35, Alabama 10
1970 Florida 14, Tennessee 13
1971 Auburn 35, Mississippi 28
1972 Georgia 7, North Carolina 3
1973 Auburn 24, Colorado 3
1974 Texas Tech 28, Tennessee 19
1975 Auburn 27, Texas 3
1976 Maryland 13, Florida 0
1977 Notre Dame 20, Penn State 9
1978 Pittsburgh 34, Clemson 3
1979 Clemson 17, Ohio State 15
1980 North Carolina 17, Michigan 15
1981 Pittsburgh 37, South Carolina 9
1982 North Carolina 31, Arkansas 27
1983 Florida State 31, West Virginia 12
1984 Florida 14, Iowa 6
1985 Oklahoma St. 21, South Carolina 14
1986 Florida State 34, Oklahoma State 23
1987 Clemson 27, Stanford 21
1988 Louisiana State 30, South Carolina 13
1989 Georgia 34, Michigan St. 27
1990 Clemson 27, West Virginia 7
1991 Michigan 35, Mississippi 3
1992 Oklahoma 38, Virginia 14
1993 Florida 27, No. Carolina St. 10
1994 Alabama 24, No. Carolina 10
1995 Tennessee 45, Virginia Tech 23
1996 Syracuse 41, Clemson 0
1997 North Carolina 20, West Virginia 13
1998 North Carolina 42, Virginia Tech 3

RESULTS OF OTHER 1997 SEASON BOWL GAMES

Alamo (San Antonio, Texas, Dec. 30, 1997)—Purdue 33, Oklahoma State 20
Aloha (Honolulu, Hawaii, Dec. 25, 1997)—Washington 51, Michigan State 23
Carquest (Miami, Fla., Dec. 29, 1997)—Georgia Tech 35, West Virginia 30
Citrus (Orlando, Fla., Jan. 1, 1998)—Florida 21, Penn State 6
Fiesta (Tempe, Ariz., Dec. 31, 1997)—Kansas State 35, Syracuse 18
Heritage (Atlanta, Ga., Dec. 27, 1997)—Southern 34, South Carolina State 28
Holiday (San Diego, Calif., Dec. 29, 1997)—Colorado State 35, Missouri 24
Independence (Shreveport, La., Dec. 28, 1997)—Louisiana State University 27, Notre Dame 9
Insight.com (Tucson, Ariz., Dec. 27, 1997)—Arizona 20, New Mexico 14
Las Vegas (Las Vegas, Nev., Dec. 20, 1997)—Oregon 41, Air Force 13
Liberty (Memphis, Tenn., Dec. 31, 1997)—Southern Mississippi 41, Pittsburgh 7
Motor City (Pontiac, Mich., Dec. 26, 1997)—Mississippi 34, Marshall 31
Outback (Tampa, Fla., Jan. 1, 1998)—Georgia 33, Wisconsin 6
Peach (Atlanta, Ga., Jan. 2, 1998)—Auburn 21, Clemson 17
Sports Humanitarian (Boise, Idaho, Dec. 29, 1997)—Cincinnati 35, Utah State 19
Sun (El Paso, Texas, Dec. 31, 1997)—Arizona State 17, Iowa 7

HEISMAN MEMORIAL TROPHY WINNERS

The Heisman Memorial Trophy is presented annually by the Downtown Athletic Club of New York City to the nation's outstanding college football player, as determined by a poll of sportswriters and sportscasters.

1935 Jay Berwanger, Chicago
1936 Larry Kelley, Yale
1937 Clinton Frank, Yale
1938 Davey O'Brien, Texas Christian
1939 Nile Kinnick, Iowa
1940 Tom Harmon, Michigan
1941 Bruce Smith, Minnesota
1942 Frank Sinkwich, Georgia
1943 Angelo Bertelli, Notre Dame
1944 Leslie Horvath, Ohio State
1945 Felix Blanchard, Army
1946 Glenn Davis, Army
1947 Johnny Lujack, Notre Dame
1948 Doak Walker, So. Methodist
1949 Leon Hart, Notre Dame
1950 Vic Janowicz, Ohio State
1951 Dick Kazmaier, Princeton
1952 Billy Vessels, Oklahoma
1953 Johnny Lattner, Notre Dame
1954 Alan Ameche, Wisconsin
1955 Howard Cassady, Ohio State
1956 Paul Hornung, Notre Dame
1957 John Crow, Texas A & M
1958 Pete Dawkins, Army
1959 Billy Cannon, Louisiana State
1960 Joe Bellino, Navy
1961 Ernie Davis, Syracuse
1962 Terry Baker, Oregon State
1963 Roger Staubach, Navy
1964 John Huarte, Notre Dame
1965 Mike Garrett, Southern California
1966 Steve Spurrier, Florida
1967 Gary Beban, UCLA
1968 O.J. Simpson, Southern California
1969 Steve Owens, Oklahoma
1970 Jim Plunkett, Stanford
1971 Pat Sullivan, Auburn
1972 Johnny Rodgers, Nebraska
1973 John Cappelletti, Penn State
1974-75 Archie Griffin, Ohio State
1976 Tony Dorsett, Pittsburgh
1977 Earl Campbell, Texas
1978 Billy Sims, Oklahoma

1979 Charles White, Southern California
1980 George Rogers, South Carolina
1981 Marcus Allen, Southern California
1982 Hershel Walker, Georgia
1983 Mike Rozier, Nebraska
1984 Doug Flutie, Boston College
1985 Bo Jackson, Auburn
1986 Vinnie Testeverde, Miami
1987 Tim Brown, Notre Dame
1988 Barry Sanders, Oklahoma State
1989 Andre Ware, Houston
1990 Ty Detmer, Brigham Young
1991 Desmond Howard, Michigan
1992 Gino Torretta, Miami
1993 Charlie Ward, Florida State
1994 Rashaan Salaam, Colorado
1995 Eddie George, Ohio State
1996 Danny Wuerffel, Florida
1997 Charles Woodson, Michigan

1997 N.C.A.A. CHAMPIONSHIP PLAYOFFS

DIVISION I-AA

Quarterfinals
(Dec. 9, 1997)
Youngstown State 37, Villanova 34
Eastern Washington 38, Western Kentucky 21
Delaware 16, Georgia Southern 7
McNeese State 14, Western Illinois 12

Semifinals
(Dec. 13, 1997)
Youngstown State 25, Eastern Washington 14
McNeese State 23, Delaware 21

Championship
(Dec. 20, 1997)
Youngstown State 10, McNeese State 9

DIVISION II

Quarterfinals
(Nov. 29, 1997)
UC Davis 50, Angelo State 33
New Haven 49, Slippery Rock 21
Northern Colorado 35, NW Missouri State 19
Carson-Newman 23, Albany State 22

Semifinals
(Dec. 6, 1997)
New Haven 27, UC Davis 25
Northern Colorado 30, Carson-Newman 29

Championship
(Dec. 13, 1997)
Northern Colorado 51, New Haven 0

DIVISION III

Quarterfinals
(Nov. 29, 1997)
Mount Union 59, John Carroll 7
Simpson 61, Augsburg 21
Lycoming 46, Trinity 26
Rowan 13, Coll. of New Jersey 7

Semifinals
(Dec. 6, 1997)
Mount Union 54, Simpson 7
Lycoming 28, Rowan 20

Championship
(Dec. 13, 1997)
Mount Union 61, Lycoming 12

1997 NATIONAL ASSOCIATION OF INTERCOLLEGIATE ATHLETICS CHAMPIONSHIPS

Quarterfinals
(Dec. 6, 1997)

University of Findlay, Ohio 28, Geneva College, Pa. 7
University of Sioux Falls, S.D. 29, Jamestown College, N.D. 6
Doane College, Neb. 59, Evangel College, Mo. 20
Willamette University, Ore. 50, Montana Tech 24

Semifinals
(Dec. 13, 1997)
University of Findlay, Ohio 26, Doane College, Neb. 25
Willamette University, Ore. 17, University of Sioux Falls, S.D. 7

Championship
(Dec. 20, 1997)
University of Findlay, Ohio 14, Willamette University, Ore. 7

COLLEGE FOOTBALL HALL OF FAME

(P.O. Box 11146, South Bend, Indiana)
(Date given is player's last year of competition)

Players

Abell, Earl—Colgate, 1915
Agase, Alex—Purdue/Illinois, 1946
Agganis, Harry—Boston Univ., 1952
Albert, Frank—Stanford, 1941
Aldrich, Chas. (Ki)—T.C.U., 1938
Aldrich, Malcolm—Yale, 1921
Alexander, Joseph—Syracuse, 1920
Alworth, Lance—Arkansas, 1961
Ameche, Alan (Horse)—Wisconsin, 1954
Amling, Warren—Ohio State, 1946
Anderson, Dick—Colorado, 1967
Anderson, Donny—Texas Tech, 1965
Anderson, H. (Hunk)—Notre Dame, 1921
Atkins, Doug—Tennessee, 1952
Babich, Bob—Miami-Ohio, 1968
Bacon, C. Everett—Wesleyan, 1912
Bagnell, Francis (Reds)—Penn, 1950
Baker, Hobart (Hobey)—Princeton, 1913
Baker, John—So. Calif., 1931
Baker, Terry—Oregon State, 1962
Ballin, Harold—Princeton, 1914
Banker, Bill—Tulane, 1929
Banonis, Vince—Detroit, 1941
Barnes, Stanley—So. Calif., 1921
Barrett, Charles—Cornell, 1915
Baston, Bert—Minnesota, 1916
Battles, Cliff—W. Va. Wesleyan, 1931
Baugh, Sammy—Texas Christian U., 1936
Baughan, Maxie—Georgia Tech, 1959
Bausch, James—Kansas, 1930
Beagle, Ron—Navy, 1955
Beban, Gary—UCLA, 1967
Bechtol, Hub—Texas Tech, 1946
Beck, Ray—Georgia Tech, 1951
Beckett, John—Oregon, 1913
Bednariok, Chuck—Pennsylvania 1948
Behm, Forrest—Nebraska, 1940
Bell, Bobby—Minnesota, 1962
Bellino, Joe—Navy, 1960
Below, Marty—Wisconsin, 1923
Benbrook, A.—Michigan, 1911
Bentrim, Jeff—North Dakota State, 1986
Bertelli, A.—Notre Dame, 1943
Berry, Charlie—Lafayette, 1924
Berwanger, John (Jay)—Chicago, 1935
Bettencourt, Larry—St. Mary's, 1927
Biletnikoff, Fred—Florida State, 1964
Blanchard, Felix (Doc)—Army, 1946
Bock, Ed—Iowa State, 1938
Bomar, Lynn—Vanderbilt, 1924
Bomeisler, Doug (Bo)—Yale, 1913
Booth, Albie—Yale, 1931
Borries, Fred—Navy, 1934
Bosely, Bruce—West Virginia, 1955
Bosseler, Don—Miami, Fla., 1956
Bottari, Vic—California, 1939
Boynton, Ben—Williams, 1920
Bozis, Al—Georgetown, 1941
Bradshaw, Terry—Louisiana Tech, 1969
Brewer, Charles—Harvard, 1895
Bright, John—Drake, 1951
Brodie, John—Stanford, 1956
Brooke, George—Pennsylvania, 1895
Brosky, Al—Illinois, 1952
Brown, Bob—Nebraska, 1963
Brown, George—Navy/San Diego St., 1947
Brown, Gordon—Yale, 1900
Brown, Jim—Syracuse, 1956
Brown, John, Jr.—Navy, 1913
Brown, Johnny Mack—Alabama, 1925
Brown, Raymond (Tay)—So. Calif., 1932
Buchanan, Buck—Grambling State, 1962
Budde, Brad—So. Calif., 1979
Bunker, Paul—Army, 1902
Burford, Chris—Stanford, 1959
Burton, Ron—Northwestern, 1956
Butkus, Dick—Illinois, 1964
Butler, Robert—Wisconsin, 1912
Cafego, George—Tennessee, 1939
Cagle, Chris—SW La./Army, 1929
Cain, John—Alabama, 1932
Cameron, Eddie—Wash. & Lee, 1924
Campbell, David C.—Harvard, 1901
Campbell, Earl—Texas, 1977
Cannon, Billy—Louisiana State, 1959
Cannon, Jack—Notre Dame, 1929
Cappelletti, John—Penn State, 1973
Carideo, Frank—Notre Dame, 1930
Caroline, J.C.—Illinois, 1954
Carney, Charles—Illinois, 1921
Carpenter, Bill—Army, 1959
Carpenter, C. Hunter—VPI, 1905
Carroll, Charles—Washington, 1928
Casanova, Tommy—Louisiana State, 1971
Casey, Edward L.—Harvard, 1919
Cassady, Howard—Ohio State, 1955
Chamberlain, Guy—Nebraska, 1915
Chapman, Sam—Cal.-Berkeley, 1938
Chappuis, Bob—Michigan, 1947

Christman, Paul—Missouri, 1940
Cichy, Joe—North Dakota State, 1970
Clark, Earl (Dutch)—Colo. College, 1929
Cleary, Paul—So. Calif., 1947
Clevenger, Zora—Indiana, 1903
Cloud, Jack—William & Mary, 1948
Cochran, Gary—Princeton, 1895
Cody, Josh—Vanderbilt, 1920
Coleman, Don—Mich. State, 1951
Conerly, Chuck—Mississippi, 1947
Connor, George—Notre Dame, 1947
Corbin, W.—Yale, 1888
Corbus, William—Stanford, 1933
Cowan, Hector—Princeton, 1889
Coy, Edward H. (Tad)—Yale, 1909
Crawford, Fred—Duke, 1933
Crow, John D.—Texas A&M, 1957
Crowley, James—Notre Dame, 1924
Csonka, Larry—Syracuse, 1967
Cutter, Slade—Navy, 1934
Czarobski, Ziggie—Notre Dame, 1947
Dale, Carroll—Virginia Tech, 1959
Dalrymple, Gerald—Tulane, 1931
Dalton, John—Navy, 1912
Daly, Charles—Harvard/Army, 1902
Daniell, Averell—Pittsburgh, 1936
Daniell, James—Ohio State, 1941
Davies, Tom—Pittsburgh, 1921
Davis, Ernest—Syracuse, 1961
Davis, Glenn—Army, 1946
Davis, Robert T.—Georgia Tech, 1947
Dawkins, Pete—Army, 1958
Delaney, Joe—Northwestern State, 1980
Deery, Tom—Widener, 1981
DeLong, Steve—Tennessee, 1964
Dement, Kenneth—SE Missouri, 1954
Den Herder, Vern—Central (Iowa), 1970
De Rogatis, Al—Duke, 1940
DesJardien, Paul—Chicago 1914
Devino, Aubrey—Iowa, 1921
DeWitt, John—Princeton, 1903
Dial, Buddy—Rice, 1958
Ditka, Mike—Pittsburgh, 1960
Dobbs, Glenn—Tulsa, 1942
Dodd, Bobby—Tennessee, 1930
Donan, Holland—Princeton, 1950
Donchess, Joseph—Pittsburgh, 1929
Dorsett, Tony—Pittsburgh, 1976
Dougherty, Nathan—Tennessee, 1909
Drahos, Nick—Cornell, 1940
Driscoll, Paddy—Northwestern, 1917
Drury, Morley—So. Calif., 1927
Dryer, Fred—San Diego State, 1968
Dudek, Joe—Plymouth State, 1985
Dudley, William (Bill)—Virginia, 1941
Duncan, Randy—Iowa, 1958
Easley, Ken—UCLA, 1980
Eckersall, Walter—Chicago, 1906
Edwards, Turk—Washington State, 1931
Edwards, William—Princeton, 1900
Eichenlaub, R.—Notre Dame, 1913
Eisenhauer, Steve—Navy, 1953
Elking, Larry—Baylor, 1964
Elliott, Chalmers—Purdue, 1944 & Mich., 1947
Elliott, Pete—Michigan, 1948
Elmendorf, Dave—Texas A&M, 1970
Evans, Ray—Kansas, 1947
Exendine, Albert—Carlisle, 1908
Falaschi, Nello—Santa Clara, 1937
Fears, Tom—Santa Clara/UCLA, 1947
Feathers, Beattie—Tennessee, 1933
Fenimore, Robert—Oklahoma State, 1947
Fenton, G.E. (Doc)—Louisiana State, 1910
Ferguson, Bob—Ohio State, 1961
Ferraro, John—So. Calif., 1944
Fesler, Wesley—Ohio State, 1930
Fincher, Bill—Georgia Tech, 1920
Fischer, Bill—Notre Dame, 1948
Fish, Hamilton—Harvard, 1909
Fisher, Robert—Harvard, 1911
Flowers, Abe—Georgia Tech, 1920
Flowers, Charlie—Mississippi, 1959
Fortmann, Daniel—Colgate, 1935
Fralic, Bill—Pittsburgh, 1984
Francis, Sam—Nebraska, 1936
Franco, Edmund (Ed)—Fordham, 1937
Frank, Clint—Yale, 1937
Franz, Rodney—California, 1949
Frederickson, Tucker—Auburn, 1964
Friedman, Benny—Michigan, 1926
Gabriel, Roman—North Carolina St., 1961
Gain, Bob—Kentucky, 1950
Galiffa, Arnold—Army, 1949
Gallarneau, Hugh—Stanford, 1941
Garbisch, Edgar—Army, 1924
Garrett, Mike—So. Calif., 1965
Gelbert, Charles—Pennsylvania, 1896
Geyer, Forest—Oklahoma, 1915
Gibbs, Jake—Mississippi, 1960
Giel, Paul—Minnesota, 1953
Gifford, Frank—So. Calif., 1951
Gilbert, Walter—Auburn, 1936
Gilmer, Harry—Alabama, 1947
Gipp, George—Notre Dame, 1920
Gladchuk, Chet—Boston College, 1940
Glass, Bill—Baylor, 1956
Glover, Rich—Nebraska, 1972
Goldberg, Marshall—Pittsburgh, 1938
Goodreault, Gene—Boston College, 1940
Gordon, Walter—California, 1918
Governale, Paul—Columbia, 1942
Grabowski, Jim—Illinois, 1965
Graham, Otto—Northwestern, 1943
Gradishar, Randy—Ohio State, 1973
Grange, Harold (Red)—Illinois, 1925
Grayson, Roberty—Stanford, 1935
Green, Hugh—Pittsburgh, 1980
Green, Joe—North Texas State, 1968
Griese, Bob—Purdue, 1966
Griffin, Archie—Ohio State, 1975
Grinnell, William—Tufts, 1934
Groom, Jerry—Notre Dame, 1950
Gulick, Merel—Hobart, 1929
Guyon, Joe—Georgia Tech, 1919
Hadl, John—Kansas, 1961
Hale, Edwin—Mississippi Col, 1921
Hall, Parker—Mississippi, 1938
Ham, Jack—Penn State, 1970
Hamilton, Robert (Bones)—Stanford, 1935
Hamilton, Tom—Navy, 1925
Hanson, Vic—Syracuse, 1926
Harder, Pat—Wisconsin, 1942
Hardwick, H. (Tack)—Harvard, 1914
Hare, T. Truxton—Pennsylvania, 1900
Harley, Chick—Ohio State, 1919
Harmon, Tom—Michigan, 1940
Harpster, Howard—Carnegie Tech, 1928
Hart, Edward J. Princeton, 1911
Hart, Leon—Notre Dame, 1949
Hartman, Bill—Georgia, 1937
Hawkins, Frank—Nevada, 1980
Hazel, Homer—Rutgers, 1924
Healey, Ed—Dartmouth, 1916
Heffelfiner, W. (Pudge)—Yale, 1891
Hein, Mel—Washington State, 1930
Heinrich, Don—Washington, 1952
Hendricks, Ted—Miami, 1968
Henry, Wilbur—Wash. & Jefferson, 1919
Herschberger, Clarence—Chicago, 1899
Herwig, Robert—California, 1937
Heston, Willie—Michigan, 1904
Hickman, Herman—Tennessee, 1931
Hickok, William—Yale, 1895
Hill, Dan—Duke, 1938
Hillebrand, A.R. (Doc)—Princeton, 1900
Hinkey, Frank—Yale, 1894
Hinkle, Carl—Vanderbilt, 1937
Hinkle, Clark—Bucknell, 1932
Hirsch, Elroy—Wis./Mich., 1943
Hitchcock, James—Auburn, 1932
Hoffman, Frank—Notre Dame, 1931
Hogan, James J.—Yale, 1904
Holland, Jerome (Brud)—Cornell, 1938
Holleder, Don—Army, 1955
Hollenbeck, William—Penn., 1908
Holovak, Michael—Boston College, 1942
Holt, Pierce—Angelo State, 1980
Holub, E.J.—Texas Tech, 1960
Hornung, Paul—Notre Dame, 1956
Horrell, Edwin—California, 1924
Horvath, Les—Ohio State, 1944
Howe Arthur—Yale, 1911
Howell, Millard (Dixie)—Alabama, 1934
Hubbard, Cal—Centenary, 1926
Hubbard, John—Amherst, 1906
Hubert, Allison—Alabama, 1925
Huff, Robert Lee (Sam)—W. Va., 1955
Humble, Weldon G.—Rice, 1946
Hunley, Ricky—Arizona, 1983
Hunt, Joel—Texas A&M, 1927
Huntington, Ellery—Colgate, 1914
Hutson, Don—Alabama, 1934
Ingram, James—Navy, 1906
Isbell, Cecil—Purdue, 1937
Jablonsky, Harvey—Wash. U./Army, 1933
Jackson, Bo—Auburn, 1985
Janowicz, Vic—Ohio State, 1951
Jenkins, Darold—Missouri, 1941
Jensen, Jack—Cal-Berkeley, 1948
Joesting, Herbert—Minnesota, 1927
Johnson, Billy—Widener, 1973
Johnson, Gary—Grambling State, 1974
Johnson, James—Carlisle, 1903
Johnson, Robert—Tennessee, 1967
Johnson, Ron—Michigan, 1968
Jones, Calvin—Iowa, 1955
Jones, Gormer—Ohio State, 1935
Jordan, Lee Roy—Alabama, 1962
Juhan, Frank—Univ. of South, 1910
Justice, Charlie—North Carolina, 1949
Kaer, Mort—So. Calif., 1926
Karras, Alex—Iowa, 1957
Kavanaugh, Kenneth—Louisiana State, 1939
Kaw, Edgar—Cornell, 1922
Kazmaier, Richard—Princeton, 1951
Keck, James—Princeton, 1921
Kelley, Larry—Yale, 1936
Kelly, William—Montana, 1926
Kenna, Ed—Syracuse, 1966
Kern, George—Boston College, 1941
Ketcham, Henry—Yale, 1913
Keyes, Leroy—Purdue, 1968
Killinger, William—Penn State, 1922
Kimbrough, John—Texas A&M, 1940
Kinard, Frank—Mississippi, 1937
King, Philip—Princeton, 1893
Kinnick, Nile—Iowa, 1939
Kipke, Harry—Michigan, 1923
Kirkpatrick, John Reed—Yale, 1910
Kitzmiller, John—Oregon, 1929
Koch, Barton—Baylor, 1931
Kitner, Malcolm—Texas, 1942
Kramer, Ron—Michigan, 1956
Kroll, Alex—Rutgers, 1961
Krueger, Charlie—Texas A&M, 1957
Kwalick, Ted—Penn State, 1968
Lach, Steve—Duke, 1941
Lane, Myles—Dartmouth, 1927
Lattner, Joseph J.—Notre Dame, 1953
Lauricella, Hank—Tennessee, 1952
Lautenschlaeger—Tulane, 1925
Layden, Elmer—Notre Dame, 1924
Layne, Bobby—Texas, 1947
Lea, Langdon—Princeton, 1895
LeBaron, Eddie—Univ. of Pacific, 1949
Leech, James—Va. Mil. Inst., 1920
Lester, Darrell—Texas Christian, 1935
Lilly, Bob—Texas Christian, 1960
Little, Floyd—Syracuse, 1966
Lio, Augie—Georgetown, 1940
Locke, Gordon—Iowa, 1922
Lomax, Neil—Portland (Ore.) State, 1980
Long, Mel—Toledo, 1971
Lourie, Don—Princeton, 1921
Lucas, Richard—Penn State, 1959
Luckman, Sid—Columbia, 1938
Lujack, John—Notre Dame, 1947
Lund, J.L. (Pug)—Minnesota, 1934
Lynch, Jim—Notre Dame, 1966
MacAfee, Ken—Notre Dame, 1977
Macomber, Bart—Illinois, 1915
MacLeod, Robert—Dartmouth, 1938
Maegle, Dick—Rice, 1954
Mahan, Edward W.—Harvard, 1915
Majors, John—Tennessee, 1956

Mallory, William—Yale, 1893
Mancha, Vaughn—Alabama, 1947
Mann, Gerald—So. Methodist, 1927
Manning, Archie—Mississippi, 1970
Manske, Edgar—Northwestern, 1933
Marinaro, Ed—Cornell, 1971
Markov, Vic—Washington, 1937
Marshall, Robert—Minnesota, 1907
Martin, Jim—Notre Dame, 1949
Matson, Ollie—San Fran. U., 1952
Matthews, Ray—Texas Christ. U., 1928
Maulbetsch, John—Michigan, 1914
Mauthe, J.L. (Pete)—Penn State, 1912
Maxwell, Robert—Chi./Swarthmore, 1906
McAfee, George—Duke, 1939
McClung, Thomas L.—Yale, 1891
McColl, William F.—Stanford, 1951
McCormick, James B.—Princeton, 1907
McDonald, Tom—Oklahoma, 1956
McDowall, Jack—No. Car. State, 1927
McElhenny, Hugh—Washington, 1951
McEver, Gene—Tennessee, 1931
McEwan, John—Minn./Army, 1916
McFadden, J.B.—Clemson, 1939
McFadin, Bud—Texas, 1950
McGee, Mike—Duke, 1959
McGinley, Edward—Pennsylvania, 1924
McGovern, J.—Minnesota, 1910
McGraw, Thurman—Colorado State, 1949
McGriff, Tyrone—Florida A&M, 1979
McKeever, Mike—So. Calif., 1960
McLaren, George—Pittsburgh, 1918
McMahon, Jim—Brigham Young, 1981
McMillan, Dan—So. Calif./California, 1922
McMillin, A.N. (Bo)—Centre, 1921
McWhorter, Robert—Georgia, 1913
Mercer, Leroy—Pennsylvania, 1912
Meredith, Don—Southern Methodist, 1959
Merritt, Frank—Army, 1943
Metzger, Bert—Notre Dame, 1930
Meyland, Wayne—Nebraska, 1967
Michaels, Lou—Kentucky, 1957
Michels, John—Tennessee, 1952
Mickal, Abe—Louisiana State, 1935
Miller, Creighton—Notre Dame, 1943
Miller, Don—Notre Dame, 1925
Miller, Edgar (Rip)—Notre Dame, 1924
Miller, Eugene—Penn State, 1913
Miller, Fred—Notre Dame, 1928
Millner, Wayne—Notre Dame, 1935
Milstead, Century—Wabash, Yale, 1923
Minds, John—Pennsylvania, 1897
Minisi, Anthony—Navy/Pennsylvania, 1947
Modzelewski, Dick—Maryland, 1952
Moffatt, Alex—Princeton, 1884
Molinski, Ed—Tennessee, 1940
Montgomery, Cliff—Columbia, 1933
Montgomery, Wilbert—Abilene Christian, 1976
Moomaw, Donn—UCLA, 1952
Morley, William—Columbia, 1903
Morris, George—Georgia Tech, 1952
Morris, Larry—Georgia Tech., 1954
Morton, Craig—California, 1964
Morton, William—Dartmouth, 1931
Moscrip, Monk—Stanford, 1935
Muller, Harold (Brick)—Calif., 1922
Nagurski, Bronko—Minnesota, 1929
Nevers, Ernie—Stanford, 1925
Newell, Marshall—Harvard, 1893
Newman, Harry—Michigan, 1932
Newsome, Ozzie—Alabama, 1977
Nielsen, Gifford—Brigham Young, 1976
Nobis, Tommy—Texas, 1965
Nomellini, Leo—Minnesota, 1949
Oberland, Andrew—Dartmouth, 1925
O'Brien, Davey—Texas Christ. U., 1938
O'Brien, Ken—UC-Davis, 1982
O'Dea, Pat—Wisconsin, 1899
Odell, Robert—Pennsylvania, 1943
O'Hearn, J.—Cornell, 1915
Olds, Robin—Army, 1942
Oliphant, Elmer—Purdue/Army, 1917
Olsen, Merlin—Utah State, 1961
Onkotz, Dennis—Penn State, 1969
Oosterbaan, Ben—Michigan, 1927

O'Rourke, Charles—Boston College, 1940
Orsi, John—Colgate, 1931
Osgood, W.D.—Cornell/Penn, 1895
Osmanski, William—Holy Cross, 1938
Owen, George—Harvard, 1922
Owens, Jim—Oklahoma, 1949
Owens, Steve—Oklahoma, 1969
Page, Alan—Notre Dame, 1966
Pardee, Jack—Texas A&M, 1956
Parilli, Vito (Babe)—Kentucky, 1951
Parker, Clarence (Ace)—Duke, 1936
Parker, Jackie—Miss. State, 1953
Parker, James—Ohio State, 1956
Payton, Walter—Jackson State, 1974
Pazzetti, V.J.—Wes./Lehigh, 1912
Peabody, Endicott—Harvard, 1941
Peck, Robert—Pittsburgh, 1916
Pellegrini, Bob—Maryland, 1955
Pennock, Stanley B.—Harvard, 1914
Pfann, George—Cornell, 1923
Phillips, H.D.—U. of South, 1904
Phillips, Loyd—Arkansas, 1966
Pingel, John—Michigan State, 1938
Pihos, Pete—Indiana, 1945
Pinckert, Ernie—So. Calif., 1931
Plunkett, Jim—Stanford, 1970
Poe, Arthur—Princeton, 1899
Pollard, Fritz—Brown, 1916
Poole, Barney—Miss./Army, 1947
Powell, Marvin—So. Calif., 1976
Pregulman, Merv—Michigan, 1943
Price, Eddie—Tulane, 1949
Pugh, Larry—Westminster, Pa., 1964
Pund, Henry—Georgia Tech, 1928
Ramsey, Gerrard—Wm. & Mary, 1942
Reasons, Gary—Northwestern State (La.), 1983
Redman, Rick—Washington, 1964
Reeds, Claude—Oklahoma, 1913
Reid, Mike—Penn St., 1970
Reid, Steve—Northwestern, 1936
Reid, William—Harvard, 1900
Reifsnyder, Bob—Navy, 1960
Renfro, Mel—Oregon, 1963
Rentner, Ernest—Northwestern, 1932
Reynolds, Robert—Nebraska, 1952
Reynolds, Robert—Stanford, 1935
Rhome, Jerry—Tulsa, 1964
Richter, Les—California, 1951
Richter, Pat—Wisconsin, 1962
Riley, John—Northwestern, 1931
Rimington, Dave—Nebraska, 1982
Rinehart, Charles—Lafayette, 1897
Ritchie, Richard—Texas A&M, 1977
Ritcher, Jim—North Carolina State, 1979
Roberts, J.D.—Oklahoma, 1953
Robeson, Paul—Rutgers, 1918
Robinson, Dave—Penn State, 1962
Robinson, Jerry—UCLA, 1978
Rodgers, Ira—West Virginia, 1919
Rogers, Edward L.—Minnesota, 1903
Rogers, George—South Carolina, 1980
Roland, Johnny—Missouri, 1965
Romig, Joe—Colorado, 1961
Rosenberg, Aaron—So. Calif., 1934
Rote, Kyle—So. Methodist, 1950
Routt, Joe—Texas A&M, 1937
Salmon, Louis—Notre Dame, 1904
Sarkisian, Alex—Northwestern, 1948
Sauer, George—Nebraska, 1933
Savitsky, George—Pennsylvania, 1947
Saxon, Jimmy—Texas, 1961
Sayers Gale—Kansas, 1964
Scarbath, Jack—Maryland, 1952
Scarlett, Hunter—Pennsylvania, 1909
Schloredt, Bob—Washington, 1960
Schoonover, Wear—Arkansas, 1929
Schreiner, Dave—Wisconsin, 1942
Schultz, Adolf (Germany)—Mich., 1908
Schwab, Frank—Lafayette, 1922
Schwartz, Marchmont—Notre Dame, 1931
Schwegler, Paul—Washington, 1931
Scott, Clyde—Arkansas, 1949
Scott, Richard—Navy, 1947
Scott, Tom—Virginia, 1953
Seibels, Henry—Sewanee, 1899

Sellers, Ron—Florida State, 1968
Selmon, Lee Roy—Oklahoma, 1975
Shakespeare, Bill—Notre Dame, 1935
Shell, Donnie—South carolina St., 1973
Shelton, Murray—Cornell, 1915
Shevlin, Tom—Yale, 1905
Shively, Bernie—Illinois, 1926
Simons, Claude—Tulane, 1934
Sims, Billy—Oklahoma, 1979
Simpson, O.J.—So. Calif., 1968
Singletary, Mike—Baylor, 1980
Sington, Fred—Alabama, 1930
Sinkwich, Frank—Georgia, 1942
Sitko, Emil—Notre Dame, 1949
Skladany, Joe—Pittsburgh, 1933
Slater, F.F. (Duke)—Iowa, 1921
Smith, Bruce—Minnesota, 1941
Smith, Bubba—Michigan State, 1966
Smith, Ernie—So. Calif., 1932
Smith, Harry—So. Calif., 1939
Smith, Jim Ray—Baylor, 1954
Smith, John (Clipper)—Notre Dame, 1927
Smith, Riley—Alabama, 1935
Smith, Vernon—Georgia, 1931
Snow, Neil—Michigan, 1901
Sparlis, Al—UCLA, 1945
Spears, Clarence W.—Dartmouth, 1915
Spears, W.D.—Vanderbilt, 1927
Sprackling, William—Brown, 1911
Sprague, M. (Bud)—Texas/Army, 1928
Spurrier, Steve—Florida, 1966
Stafford, Harrison—Texas, 1932
Stagg, Amos Alonzo—Yale, 1889
Stanfill, Bill—Georgia, 1968
Starcevich, Max—Washington, 1936
Staubach, Roger—Navy, 1963
Steffen, Walter—Chicago, 1908
Steffy, Joe—Army, 1947
Stein, Herbert—Pittsburgh, 1921
Steuber, Robert—Missouri, 1943
Stevens, Mal—Yale, 1923
Stevenson, Vincent—Pennsylvania, 1905
Stillwagon, Jim—Ohio State, 1970
Stinchcomb, Gaylord—Ohio State, 1920
Strom, Brock—Air Force, 1959
Strong, Ken—New York Univ., 1928
Strupper, George—Georgia Tech, 1917
Stuhldreher, Harry—Notre Dame, 1924
Stydahar, Joe—West Virginia, 1935
Suffridge, Robert—Tennessee, 1940
Suhey, Steve—Pennsylvania State, 1947
Sullivan, Pat—Auburn, 1971
Sundstrom, Frank—Cornell, 1923
Swann, Lynn—So. Calif., 1973
Swanson, Clarence—Nebraska, 1921
Swiacki, Bill—Holy Cross/Colombia, 1947
Swink, Jim—Texas Christian, 1956
Taliaferro, George—Indiana, 1948
Tarkenton, Fran—Georgia, 1960
Tavener, John—Indiana, 1944
Taylor, Bruce—Boston Univ., 1969
Taylor, Charles—Stanford, 1942
Thomas, Aurelius—Ohio St., 1957
Thompson, Joe—Pittsburgh, 1907
Thomsen, Lynn—Austana, 1986
Thorne, Samuel B.—Yale, 1906
Thorpe, Jim—Carlisle, 1912
Ticknor, Ben—Harvard, 1930
Tigert, John—Vanderbilt, 1904
Tinsley, Gaynell—Louisiana State, 1936
Tipton, Eric—Duke, 1938
Tonnemaker, Clayton—Minnesota, 1949
Torrey, Robert—Pennsylvania, 1906
Travis, Ed Tarkio—Missouri, 1920
Trippi, Charles—Georgia, 1946
Tryon, J. Edward—Colgate, 1925
Tubbs, Jerry—Oklahoma, 1956
Utay, Joe—Texas A&M, 1907
Van Brocklin, Norm—Oregon, 1948
Van Sickel, Dale—Florida, 1929
Van Surdam, Henderson—Wesleyan, 1905
Very, Dexter—Penn State, 1912
Vessels, Billy—Oklahoma, 1952
Vick, Ernie—Michigan, 1921
Wagner, Huber—Pittsburgh, 1913
Walker, Doak—So. Methodist, 1949

Wallace, Bill—Rice, 1935
Walsh, Adam—Notre Dame, 1924
Warburton, I. (Cotton)—So. Calif., 1934
Ward, Robert (Bob)—Maryland, 1951
Warner, William—Cornell, 1903
Washington, Ken—UCLA, 1939
Weatherall, Jim—Oklahoma, 1951
Webster, George—Michigan St., 1966
Wedemeyer, Herman J.—St. Mary's, 1947
Weekes, Harold—Columbia, 1902
Weiner, Art—North Carolina, 1949
Weir, Ed—Nebraska, 1925
Welch, Gus—Carlisle, 1914
Weller, John—Princeton, 1935
Wendell, Percy—Harvard, 1913
West, D. Belford—Colgate, 1919
Westfall, Bob—Michigan, 1941
Weyand, Alex—Army, 1915
Wharton, Charles—Pennsylvania, 1896
Wheeler, Arthur—Princeton, 1894
White, Byron (Whizzer)—Colorado, 1937
White, Charles—So. Calif., 1979
White, Danny—Arizona State, 1973
White, Randy—Maryland, 1974
Whitmire, Don—Alabama/Navy, 1944
Wickhorst, Frank—Navy, 1926
Widseth, Ed—Minnesota, 1936
Wildung, Richard—Minnesota, 1942
Williams, Bob—Notre Dame, 1950
Williams, James—Rice, 1949
Willis, William—Ohio State, 1945
Wilson, George—Washington, 1925
Wilson, George—Lafayette, 1928
Wilson, Harry—Penn State/Army, 1923
Wilson, Marc—BYU, 1979
Wistert, Albert A.—Michigan, 1942
Wistert, Al—Michigan, 1942
Wistert, Frank (Whitey)—Mich., 1933
Wood, Barry—Harvard, 1931
Wojciechowicz, Alex—Fordham, 1936
Wyant, Andrew—Bucknell/Chicago, 1894
Wyatt, Bowden—Tennessee, 1938
Wyckoff, Clint—Cornell, 1896
Yarr, Tom—Notre Dame, 1931
Yary, Ron—So. Calif., 1968
Yoder, Lloyd—Carnegie Tech, 1926
Young, Claude (Buddy)—Illinois, 1946
Young, Harry—Wash. & Lee, 1916
Young, Walter—Oklahoma, 1938
Youngblood, Jack—Florida, 1970
Youngblood, Jim—Tennessee, 1972
Zarnas, Gus—Ohio State, 1937

Coaches

Bill Alexander
Dr. Ed Anderson
Ike Armstrong
Earl Banks
Harry Baujan
Matty Bell
Hugo Bezdek
Dana X. Bible
Bernie Bierman
Bob Blackman
Earl (Red) Blaik
Frank Broyles
Paul "Bear" Bryant
Harold Burry
Jim Butterfield
James "Wally" Butts
Charles W. Caldwell
Walter Camp
Len Casanova
Frank Cavanaugh
Richard Colman
Fritz Crisler
Duffy Daugherty
Bob Devaney
Dan Devine
Gil Dobie
Bobby Dodd
Michael Donohue
Vince Dooley
Gus Dorais
Bill Edwards
Charles (Rip) Engle
Don Faurot
Jake Gaither
Sid Gillman
Ernest Godfrey
Ray Graves
Andy Gustafson
Jack Harding
Edward K. Hall
Richard Harlow
Jesse Harper
Percy Haughton
Woody Hayes
John W. Heisman
R.A. (Bob) Higgins
Paul Hoernemann
Orin E. Hollingberry
Frank Howard
William Ingram
Don James
Morley Jennings
Howard Jones
L. (Biff) Jones
Thomas (Tad) Jones
Ralph (Shug) Jordan
Bob Keade
Andy Kerr
Chuck Klausing
Frank Kush
Frank Leahy
George E. Little
Lou Little
El (Slip) Madigan
Dave Maurer
Charley McClendon
Herbert McCracken
Daniel McGugin
John McKay
Allyn McKeen
DeOrmond (Tuss) McLaughry
John Merritt
L.R. (Dutch) Meyer
Bernie Moore
Scrappy Moore
Jack Mollenkopf
Ray Morrison
George A. Munger
Clarence Munn
Frank Murray
William Murray
Ed (Hooks) Mylin
Earle (Greasy) Neale
Jess Neely
David Nelson
Robert Neyland
Homer Norton
Frank (Buck) O'Neill
Tom Osborne
Bennie Owen
Ara Parseghian
Doyt Perry
James Phalea
Tommy Prothro
John Ralston
E.N. Robinson
Knute Rockne
E.L. (Dick) Romney
William W. Roper
Darrell Royal
Ad Rutschman
Henry (Red) Sanders
George F. Sanford
Bo Schembechler
Francis A. Schmidt
Floyd (Ben) Schwartzwalder
Clark Shaughnessy
Buck Shaw
Edgar Sherman
Andrew L. Smith
Carl Snavely
Amos A. Stagg
Gilbert Steinke
Jock Sutherland
James Tatum
Frank W. Thomas
Lee Tressell
Thad Vann
John H. Vaught
Wallace Wade
Lynn Waldorf
Glenn (Pop) Warner
E.E. (Tad) Wieman
John W. Wilce
Bud Wilkinson
Henry L. Williams
George W. Woodruff
Warren Woodson
Bowden Wyatt
Fielding H. Yost
Robert Zuppke

Professional Football

NATIONAL FOOTBALL LEAGUE FINAL STANDINGS 1997

AMERICAN FOOTBALL CONFERENCE

	W	L	T	Pct	Pts	PA
Eastern Division						
New England Patriots[1]	10	6	0	.625	369	289
Miami Dolphins[2]	9	7	0	.563	339	327
New York Jets	9	7	0	.563	348	287
Buffalo Bills	6	10	0	.375	255	367
Indianapolis Colts	3	13	0	.188	313	401
Central Division						
Pittsburgh Steelers[1]	11	5	0	.688	372	307
Jacksonville Jaguars[2]	11	5	0	.688	394	318
Tennessee Oilers	8	8	0	.500	333	310
Cincinnati Bengals	7	9	0	.438	355	405
Baltimore Ravens	6	9	1	.406	326	345
Western Division						
Kansas City Chiefs [1]	13	3	0	.813	375	232
Denver Broncos [2]	12	4	0	.750	472	287
Seattle Seahawks	8	8	0	.500	327	353
Oakland Raiders	4	12	0	.250	324	419
San Diego Chargers	4	12	0	.250	266	425

1. Division champion. 2. Wild card qualifier for playoffs. **Wildcard:** Denver 42, Jacksonville 17; New England 17, Miami 3. **Division:** Pittsburgh 7, New England 6; Denver 14, Kansas City 10. **Conference:** Denver 24, Pittsburgh 21

NATIONAL FOOTBALL CONFERENCE

	W	L	T	Pct	Pts	PA
Eastern Division						
New York Giants[1]	10	5	1	.656	307	265
Washington Redskins	8	7	1	.531	327	289
Philadelphia Eagles	6	9	1	.406	317	372
Dallas Cowboys	6	10	0	.375	304	314
Arizona Cardinals	4	12	0	.250	283	379
Central Division						
Green Bay Packers[1]	13	3	0	.813	422	282
Tampa Bay Buccaneers[2]	10	6	0	.625	299	263
Detroit Lions[2]	9	7	0	.563	379	306
Minnesota Vikings[2]	9	7	0	.563	354	359
Chicago Bears	4	12	0	.250	263	421
Western Division						
San Francisco 49ers[1]	13	3	0	.813	366	227
Carolina Panthers	7	9	0	.438	265	314
Atlanta Falcons	7	9	0	.438	320	361
New Orleans Saints	6	10	0	.375	237	327
St. Louis Rams	5	11	0	.313	299	359

1. Division champion. 2. Wild card qualifier for playoffs. **Wildcard:** Minnesota 23, N.Y. Giants 22; Tampa Bay 20, Detroit 10. **Division:** San Francisco 38, Minnesota 22; Green Bay 21, Tampa Bay 7. **Conference:** Green Bay 23, San Francisco 10

LEAGUE CHAMPIONSHIP—SUPER BOWL XXXII

(January 25, 1998, Qualcomm Stadium, San Diego, Calif. Attendance: 68,912, no shows: 0. Time: 3:25)

Scoring

	1st Q	2nd Q	3rd Q	4th Q	Final
Green Bay Packers	7	7	3	7	24
Denver Broncos	13	4	7	7	31

First Quarter: Green Bay (10:58)—A. Freeman 22 yd. pass from B. Favre (R. Longwell, kick). Denver (5:39)—T. Davis 1 yd. run (J. Elam, kick).

Second Quarter: Denver (14:55)—J. Elway 1 yd. run (J. Elam, kick). Denver (12:21)—J. Elam 51 yd. field goal. Green Bay (0:12)—M. Chmura 6 yd. pass from B. Favre (R. Longwell, kick).

Third Quarter: Green Bay (11:59)—R. Longwell 27 yd. field goal. Denver (0:34)—T. Davis 1 yd. run (J. Elam, kick).

Fourth Quarter: Green Bay (13:32)—A. Freeman 13 yd. pass from B. Favre (R. Longwell, kick). Denver (1:45)—T. Davis 1 yd. run (J. Elam, kick).

Individual Statistics

Rushing: GREEN BAY: D. Levens 19–90, R. Brooks 1–5. DENVER: T. Davis 30–157, J. Elway 5–17, V. Hebron 3–3, H. Griffith 1–2.

Passing: GREEN BAY: B. Favre 25–42. DENVER: J. Elway 12–22.

Receiving: GREEN BAY: A. Freeman 9–126, D. Levens 6–56, M. Chmura 4–43, R. Brooks 3–16, W. Henderson 2–9, T. Mickens 1–6. DENVER: S. Sharpe 5–38, E. Mccaffrey 2–45, T. Davis 2–8, H. Griffith 1–23, V. Hebron 1–5, D. Carswell 1–4.

Statistics of the Game

	Green Bay	Denver
First downs	21	21
Rushing	4	14
Total net yards	350	302
Total plays	63	61
Average gain	5.6	5.0
Net yards rushing	95	179
Rushes	20	39
Net yards passing	255	123

	Green Bay	Denver
Completed-attempted	25–42	12–22
Punts–average	4–35.5	4–36.5
Return yardage	121	95
Kickoffs–returns	6–104	5–95
Interceptions–returns	1–17	1–0
Penalties–yards	9–59	7–65
Fumbles–lost	2–2	1–1
Time of possession	27:35	32:25

SUPER BOWLS I-XXXII

Game	Date	Winner	Loser	Site	Attendance
XXXII	Jan. 25, 1998	Denver (AFC) 31	Green Bay (NFC) 24	Qualcomm Stadium, San Diego, Calif.	68,912
XXXI	Jan. 26, 1997	Green Bay (NFC) 35	New England (AFC) 21	Superdome, New Orleans, La.	72,301
XXX	Jan. 28, 1996	Dallas (NFC) 27	Pittsburgh (AFC) 17	Sun Devil Stadium, Tempe, Ariz.	76,347
XXIX	Jan. 29, 1995	San Francisco (NFC) 49	San Diego (AFC) 26	Joe Robbie Stadium, Miami, Fla.	74,107
XXVIII	Jan. 30, 1994	Dallas (NFC) 30	Buffalo (AFC) 13	Georgia Dome, Atlanta, Ga.	72,817
XXVII	Jan. 31, 1993	Dallas (NFC) 52	Buffalo (AFC) 17	Rose Bowl, Pasadena, Calif.	98,374
XXVI	Jan. 26, 1992	Washington (NFC) 37	Buffalo (AFC) 24	Metrodome, Minneapolis, Minn.	63,130
XXV	Jan. 27, 1991	Giants (NFC) 20	Buffalo (AFC) 19	Tampa Stadium, Tampa, Fla.	73,813
XXIV	Jan. 28, 1990	San Francisco (NFC) 55	Denver (AFC) 10	Superdome, New Orleans	72,919
XXIII	Jan. 22, 1989	San Francisco (NFC) 20	Cincinnati (AFC) 16	Joe Robbie Stadium, Miami, Fla.	75,179
XXII	Jan. 31, 1988	Washington (NFC) 42	Denver (AFC) 10	Jack Murphy Stadium, San Diego, Calif.	73,302
XXI	Jan. 25, 1987	Giants (NFC) 39	Denver (AFC) 20	Rose Bowl, Pasadena, Calif.	101,063
XX	Jan. 26, 1986	Chicago (NFC) 46	New England (AFC) 10	Superdome, New Orleans	73,818
XIX	Jan. 20, 1985	San Francisco (NFC) 38	Miami (AFC) 16	Stanford Stadium, Palo Alto, Calif.	84,059
XVIII	Jan. 22, 1984	Los Angeles Raiders (AFC) 38	Washington (NFC) 9	Tampa Stadium, Tampa, Fla	72,920
XVII	Jan. 30, 1983	Washington (NFC) 27	Miami (AFC) 17	Rose Bowl, Pasadena, Calif.	103,667
XVI	Jan. 24, 1982	San Francisco (NFC) 26	Cincinnati (AFC) 21	Silverdome, Pontiac, Mich.	81,270
XV	Jan. 25, 1981	Oakland (AFC) 27	Philadelphia (NFC) 10	Superdome, New Orleans	75,500
XIV	Jan. 20, 1980	Pittsburgh (AFC) 31	Los Angeles (NFC) 19	Rose Bowl, Pasadena	103,985
XIII	Jan. 21, 1979	Pittsburgh (AFC) 35	Dallas (NFC) 31	Orange Bowl, Miami	79,484
XII	Jan. 15, 1978	Dallas (NFC) 27	Denver (AFC) 10	Superdome, New Orleans	75,583
XI	Jan. 9, 1977	Oakland (AFC) 32	Minnesota (NFC) 14	Rose Bowl, Pasadena	103,424
X	Jan. 18, 1976	Pittsburgh (AFC) 21	Dallas (NFC) 17	Orange Bowl, Miami	80,187
IX	Jan. 12, 1975	Pittsburgh (AFC) 16	Minnesota (NFC) 6	Tulane Stadium, New Orleans	80,997
VIII	Jan. 13, 1974	Miami (AFC) 24	Minnesota (NFC) 7	Rice Stadium, Houston	71,882
VII	Jan. 14, 1973	Miami (AFC) 14	Washington (NFC) 7	Memorial Coliseum, Los Angeles	90,182
VI	Jan. 16, 1972	Dallas (NFC) 24	Miami (AFC) 3	Tulane Stadium, New Orleans	81,591
V	Jan. 17, 1971	Baltimore (AFC) 16	Dallas (NFC) 13	Orange Bowl, Miami	79,204
IV	Jan. 11, 1970	Kansas City (AFL) 23	Minnesota (NFL) 7	Tulane Stadium, New Orleans	80,562
III	Jan. 12, 1969	New York (AFL) 16	Baltimore (NFL) 7	Orange Bowl, Miami	75,389
II	Jan. 14, 1968	Green Bay (NFL) 33	Oakland (AFL) 14	Orange Bowl, Miami	75,546
I	Jan. 15, 1967	Green Bay (NFL) 35	Kansas City (AFL) 10	Memorial Coliseum, Los Angeles	61,946

NOTE: Super Bowls I to IV were played before the American Football League and National Football League merged into the NFL, which was divided into two conferences, the NFC and AFC.

NATIONAL LEAGUE CHAMPIONS

Year	Champion	(W-L-T)	Year	Champion	(W-L-T)	Year	Champion	(W-L-T)
1921	Chicago Bears (Staley's)	(10-1-1)	1926	Frankford Yellow Jackets	(14-1-1)	1930	Green Bay Packers	(10-3-1)
1922	Canton Bulldogs	(10-0-2)	1927	New York Giants	(11-1-1)	1931	Green Bay Packers	(12-2-0)
1923	Canton Bulldogs	(11-0-1)	1928	Providence Steamrollers	(8-1-2)	1932	Chicago Bears	(7-1-6)
1924	Cleveland Indians	(7-1-1)	1929	Green Bay Packers	(12-0-1)			
1925	Chicago Cardinals	(11-2-1)						

Year	Eastern Conference winners (W-L-T)	Western Conference winners (W-L-T)	League champion playoff results
1933	New York Giants (11-3-0)	Chicago Bears (10-2-1)	Chicago Bears 23, New York 21
1934	New York Giants (8-5-0)	Chicago Bears (13-0-0)	New York 30, Chicago Bears 13
1935	New York Giants (9-3-0)	Detroit Lions (7-3-2)	Detroit 26, New York 7
1936	Boston Redskins (7-5-0)	Green Bay Packers (10-1-1)	Green Bay 21, Boston 6
1937	Washington Redskins (8-3-0)	Chicago Bears (9-1-1)	Washington 28, Chicago Bears 21
1938	New York Giants (8-2-1)	Green Bay Packers (8-3-0)	New York 23, Green Bay 17
1939	New York Giants (9-1-1)	Green Bay Packers (9-2-0)	Green Bay 27, New York 0
1940	Washington Redskins (9-2-0)	Chicago Bears (8-3-0)	Chicago Bears 73, Washington 0
1941	New York Giants (8-3-0)	Chicago Bears (10-1-1)[2]	Chicago Bears 37, New York 9
1942	Washington Redskins (10-1-1)	Chicago Bears (11-0-0)	Washington 14, Chicago Bears 6
1943	Washington Redskins (6-3-1)[2]	Chicago Bears (8-1-1)	Chicago Bears 41, Washington 21
1944	New York Giants (8-1-1)	Green Bay Packers (8-2-0)	Green Bay 14, New York 7
1945	Washington Redskins (8-2-0)	Cleveland Rams (9-1-0)	Cleveland 15, Washington 14
1946	New York Giants (7-3-1)	Chicago Bears (8-2-1)	Chicago Bears 24, New York 14
1947	Philadelphia Eagles (8-4-0)[2]	Chicago Cardinals (9-3-0)	Chicago Cardinals 28, Philadelphia 21
1948	Philadelphia Eagles (9-2-1)	Chicago Cardinals (11-1-0)	Philadelphia 7, Chicago Cardinals 0
1949	Philadelphia Eagles (11-1-0)	Los Angeles Rams (8-2-2)	Philadelphia 14, Los Angeles 0
1950[1]	Cleveland Browns (10-2-0)[2]	Los Angeles Rams (9-3-0)[2]	Cleveland 30, Los Angeles 28
1951[1]	Cleveland Browns (11-1-0)	Los Angeles Rams (8-4-0)	Los Angeles 24, Cleveland 17
1952[1]	Cleveland Browns (8-4-0)	Detroit Lions (9-3-0)[2]	Detroit 17, Cleveland 7
1953	Cleveland Browns (11-1-0)	Detroit Lions (10-2-0)	Detroit 17, Cleveland 16
1954	Cleveland Browns (9-3-0)	Detroit Lions (9-2-1)	Cleveland 56, Detroit 10
1955	Cleveland Browns (9-2-1)	Los Angeles Rams (8-3-1)	Cleveland 38, Los Angeles 14
1956	New York Giants (8-3-1)	Chicago Bears (9-2-1)	New York 47, Chicago Bears 7
1957	Cleveland Browns (9-2-1)	Detroit Lions (8-4-0)[2]	Detroit 59, Cleveland 14
1958	New York Giants (9-3-0)[2]	Baltimore Colts (9-3-0)	Baltimore 23, New York 17[3]
1959	New York Giants (10-2-0)	Baltimore Colts (9-3-0)	Baltimore 31, New York 16
1960	Philadelphia Eagles (10-2-0)	Green Bay Packers (8-4-0)	Philadelphia 17, Green Bay 13
1961	New York Giants (10-3-1)	Green Bay Packers (11-3-0)	Green Bay 37, New York 0
1962	New York Giants (12-2-0)	Green Bay Packers (13-1-0)	Green Bay 16, New York 7
1963	New York Giants (11-3-0)	Chicago Bears (11-1-2)	Chicago 14, New York 10
1964	Cleveland Browns (10-3-1)	Baltimore Colts (12-2-0)	Cleveland 27, Baltimore 0
1965	Cleveland Browns (11-3-0)	Green Bay Packers (11-3-1)[2]	Green Bay 23, Cleveland 12
1966	Dallas Cowboys (10-3-1)	Green Bay Packers (12-2-0)	Green Bay 34, Dallas 27
1967	Dallas Cowboys (9-5-0)[2]	Green Bay Packers (9-4-1)[2]	Green Bay 21, Dallas 17
1968	Cleveland Browns (10-4-0)[2]	Baltimore Colts (13-1-0)[2]	Baltimore 34, Cleveland 0
1969	Cleveland Browns (10-3-1)[2]	Minnesota Vikings (12-2-0)[2]	Minnesota 27, Cleveland 7

1. League was divided into American and National Conferences, 1950-52 and again in 1970, when leagues merged. 2. Won divisional playoff. 3. Won at 8:15 of sudden death overtime period.

NATIONAL CONFERENCE CHAMPIONS

Year	Eastern Division	Central Division	Western Division	Champion
1970	Dallas Cowboys (10-4-0)	Minnesota Vikings (12-2-0)	San Francisco 49ers (10-3-1)	Dallas
1971	Dallas Cowboys (11-3-0)	Minnesota Vikings (11-3-0)	San Francisco 49ers (9-5-0)	Dallas
1972	Washington Redskins (11-3-0)	Green Bay Packers (10-4-0)	San Francisco 49ers (8-5-1)	Washington
1973	Dallas Cowboys (10-4-0)	Minnesota Vikings (12-2-0)	Los Angeles Rams (12-2-0)	Minnesota
1974	St. Louis Cardinals (10-4-0)	Minnesota Vikings (10-4-0)	Los Angeles Rams (10-4-0)	Minnesota
1975	St. Louis Cardinals (11-3-0)	Minnesota Vikings (12-2-0)	Los Angeles Rams (10-4-0)	Dallas
1976	Dallas Cowboys (11-3-0)	Minnesota Vikings (11-2-1)	Los Angeles Rams (10-3-1)	Minnesota
1977	Dallas Cowboys (12-2-0)	Minnesota Vikings (9-5-0)	Los Angeles Rams (10-4-0)	Dallas
1978	Dallas Cowboys (12-4-0)	Minnesota Vikings (8-7-1)	Los Angeles Rams (12-4-0)	Dallas
1979	Dallas Cowboys (11-5-0)	Tampa Bay Buccaneers (10-6-0)	Los Angeles Rams (9-7-0)	Los Angeles
1980	Philadelphia Eagles (12-4-0)	Minnesota Vikings (9-7-0)	Atlanta Falcons (12-4-0)	Philadelphia
1981	Dallas Cowboys (12-4-0)	Tampa Bay Buccaneers (9-7-0)	San Francisco 49ers (13-3-0)	San Francisco
1982*				
1983	Washington Redskins (14-2-0)	Detroit Lions (8-8-0)	San Francisco 49ers (10-6-0)	Washington
1984	Washington Redskins (11-5-0)	Chicago Bears (10-6-0)	San Francisco 49ers (15-1-0)	San Francisco
1985	Dallas Cowboys (10-6-0)	Chicago Bears (15-1-0)	Los Angeles Rams (11-5-0)	Chicago
1986	New York Giants (14-2-0)	Chicago Bears (14-2-0)	San Francisco 49ers (10-5-1)	New York
1987	Washington Redskins (11-4-0)	Chicago Bears (11-4-0)	San Francisco 49ers (13-2-0)	Washington

Year	Eastern Division	Central Division	Western Division	Champion
1988	Philadelphia Eagles (10-6-0)	Chicago Bears (12-4-0)	San Francisco 49ers (10-6-0)	San Francisco
1989	New York Giants (12-4-0)	Minnesota Vikings (10-6-0)	San Francisco 49ers (14-2-0)	San Francisco
1990	New York Giants (13-3-0)	Chicago Bears (11-5-0)	San Francisco 49ers (14-2-0)	New York
1991	Washington (14-2-0)	Detroit Lions (12-4-0)	New Orleans Saints (11-5-0)	Washington
1992	Dallas Cowboys (13-3-0)	Minnesota Vikings (11-5-0)	San Francisco 49ers (14-2-0)	Dallas
1993	Dallas Cowboys (12-4-0)	Detroit Lions (10-6-0)	San Francisco 49ers (10-6-0)	Dallas
1994	Dallas Cowboys (12-4-0)	Minnesota Vikings (10-6-0)	San Francisco 49ers (13-3-0)	San Francisco
1995	Dallas Cowboys (12-4-0)	Green Bay Packers (11-5-0)	San Francisco 49ers (11-5-0)	Dallas
1996	Dallas Cowboys (10-6-0)	Green Bay Packers (13-3-0)	Carolina Panthers (12-4-0)	Green Bay
1997	New York Giants (10-5-1)	Green Bay Packers (13-3-0)	San Francisco 49ers (13-3-0)	Green Bay

*Schedule reduced to 9 games from usual 16, with no standings kept in Eastern, Central, and Western Divisions, because of 57-day player strike. Washington Redskins won conference title and also had best regular-season record (8-1-0).

AMERICAN LEAGUE CHAMPIONS

Year	Eastern Division (W-L-T)	Western Division (W-L-T)	League champion, playoff results
1960	Houston Oilers (10-4-0)	Los Angeles Chargers (10-4-0)	Houston 24, Los Angeles 16
1961	Houston Oilers (10-3-1)	San Diego Chargers (12-2-0)	Houston 10, San Diego 3
1962	Houston Oilers (11-3-0)	Dallas Texans (11-3-0)	Dallas 20, Houston 17[1]
1963	Boston Patriots (8-6-1)[2]	San Diego Chargers (11-3-0)	San Diego 51, Boston 10
1964	Buffalo Bills (12-2-0)	San Diego Chargers (8-5-1)	Buffalo 20, San Diego 7
1965	Buffalo Bills (10-3-1)	San Diego Chargers (9-2-3)	Buffalo 23, San Diego 0
1966	Buffalo Bills (9-4-1)	Kansas City Chiefs (11-2-1)	Kansas City 31, Buffalo 7
1967	Houston Oilers (9-4-1)	Oakland Raiders (13-1-0)	Oakland 40, Houston 7
1968	New York Jets (11-3-0)	Oakland Raiders (12-2-0)[2]	New York 27, Oakland 23
1969	New York Jets (10-4-0)	Oakland Raiders (12-1-1)	Kansas City 17, Oakland 7[3]

1. Won at 2:45 of second sudden death overtime period. 2. Won divisional playoff. 3. Kansas City defeated New York, 13-6, and Oakland defeated Houston, 56-7, in interdivisional playoffs.

AMERICAN CONFERENCE CHAMPIONS

Year	Eastern Division	Central Division	Western Division	Champion
1970	Baltimore Colts (11-2-1)	Cincinnati Bengals (8-6-0)	Oakland Raiders (8-4-2)	Baltimore
1971	Miami Dolphins (10-3-1)	Cleveland Browns (9-5-0)	Kansas City Chiefs (10-3-1)	Miami
1972	Miami Dolphins (14-0-0)	Pittsburgh Steelers (11-3-0)	Oakland Raiders (10-3-1)	Miami
1973	Miami Dolphins (12-2-0)	Cincinnati Bengals (10-4-0)	Oakland Raiders (9-4-1)	Miami
1974	Miami Dolphins (11-3-0)	Pittsburgh Steelers (10-3-1)	Oakland Raiders (12-2-0)	Pittsburgh
1975	Baltimore Colts (10-4-0)	Pittsburgh Steelers (12-2-0)	Oakland Raiders (12-2-0)	Pittsburgh
1976	Baltimore Colts (11-3-0)	Pittsburgh Steelers (10-4-0)	Oakland Raiders (13-1-0)	Oakland
1977	Baltimore Colts (10-4-0)	Pittsburgh Steelers (9-5-0)	Denver Broncos (12-2-0)	Denver
1978	New England Patriots (11-5-0)	Pittsburgh Steelers (14-2-0)	Denver Broncos (10-6-0)	Pittsburgh
1979	Miami Dolphins (10-6-0)	Pittsburgh Steelers (12-4-0)	San Diego Chargers (12-4-0)	Pittsburgh
1980	Buffalo Bills (11-5-0)	Cleveland Browns (11-5-0)	San Diego Chargers (11-5-0)	Oakland
1981	Miami Dolphins (11-4-1)	Cincinnati Bengals (12-4-0)	San Diego Chargers (10-6-0)	Cincinnati
1982*	Miami Dolphins won the conference title, but the Los Angeles Raiders had best regular-season record (8-1-0).			
1983	Miami Dolphins (12-4-0)	Pittsburgh Steelers (10-6-0)	Los Angeles Raiders (12-4-0)	Los Angeles
1984	Miami Dolphins (14-2-0)	Pittsburgh Steelers (9-7-0)	Denver Broncos (13-3-0)	Miami
1985	Miami Dolphins (12-4-0)	Cleveland Browns (8-8)	Los Angeles Raiders (12-4-0)	New England
1986	New England Patriots (11-5-0)	Cleveland Browns (12-4-0)	Denver Broncos (11-5-0)	Denver
1987	Indianapolis Colts (9-6-0)	Cleveland Browns (10-5-0)	Denver Broncos (10-4-1)	Denver
1988	Buffalo Bills (12-4-0)	Cincinnati Bengals (12-4-0)	Seattle Seahawks (9-7-0)	Cincinnati
1989	Buffalo Bills (9-7-0)	Cleveland Browns (9-6-1)	Denver Broncos (11-5-0)	Denver
1990	Buffalo Bills (13-3-0)	Cincinnati Bengals (9-7-0)	Los Angeles Raiders (12-4-0)	Buffalo
1991	Buffalo Bills (13-3-0)	Houston Oilers (11-5-0)	Denver Broncos (12-4-0)	Buffalo
1992	Miami Dolphins (11-5-0)	Pittsburgh Steelers (11-5-0)	San Diego Chargers (11-5-0)	Buffalo
1993	Buffalo Bills (12-4-0)	Houston Oilers (12-4-0)	Kansas City Chiefs (11-5-0)	Buffalo
1994	Miami Dolphins (10-6-0)	Pittsburgh Steelers (12-4-0)	San Diego Chargers (11-5-0)	San Diego
1995	Buffalo Bills (10-6-0)	Pittsburgh Steelers (11-5-0)	Kansas City Chiefs (13-3-0)	Pittsburgh
1996	New England Patriots (11-5-0)	Pittsburgh Steelers (10-6-0)	Denver Broncos (13-3-0)	New England
1997	New England Patriots (10-6-0)	Pittsburgh Steelers (11-5-0)	Kansas City Chiefs (13-3-0)	Denver

*Schedule reduced to 9 games from usual 16, with no standings kept in Eastern, Central, and Western Divisions, because of 57-day player strike.

PRO FOOTBALL HALL OF FAME

(National Football Museum, Canton, Ohio)

Teams named are those with which player is best dentified; figures in parentheses indicate number of laying seasons.

dderley, Herb, defensive back, Packers, Cowboys (12) 1961–72
lworth, Lance, wide receiver, Chargers, Cowboys (12) 1962–72
tkins, Doug, defensive end, Browns, Bears, Saints (17) 1953–69
adgro, Morris, end, N.Y. Yankees, Giants, Bklyn. Dodgers (8) 1927, 1930–36
arney, Lem, defensive back, Lions (11) 1967–78
attles, Cliff, back, Redskins (6) 1932–37
augh, Sammy, quarterback, Redskins (16) 1936–52
ednarik, Chuck, center-linebacker, Eagles (14) 1949–62
ell, Bert, NFL founder, Eagles and Steelers, NFL Commissioner 1946–59
ell, Bobby, linebacker, Chiefs (12) 1963–74
erry, Raymond, end, Colts (13) 1955–67
idwell, Charles W., owner, Chicago Cardinals 1933–47
iletnikoff, Fred, wide receiver, Raiders (14) 1965–78
landa, George, quarterback-kicker, Bears, Oilers, Raiders (27) 1949–75
lount, Mel, cornerback, Pittsburgh Steelers (14) 1970–83
radshaw, Terry, quarterback, Pittsburgh Steelers (14) 1970–83
rown, Jim, fullback, Browns (9) 1957–65
rown, Paul E., coach, Browns (1946–62), Bengals (1968–75) 1946–75
rown, Roosevelt, tackle, Giants (13) 1953–65
rown, Willie, cornerback, Broncos, Raiders (16) 1963–78
uchanan, Buck, tackle, Chiefs (11) 1963–73
utkus, Dick, linebacker, Bears (9) 1965–73
ampbell, Earl, running back, Oilers, Saints (8) 1978–85
anadeo, Tony, back, Packers (11) 1941–52
arr, Joe, NFL president (18) 1921–39
hamberlin, Guy, end, 4 teams (9) 1919–27
hristiansen, Jack, defensive back, Lions (8) 1951–58
lark, Earl (Dutch), quarterback, Spartans, Lions (7) 1931–38
onnor, George, tackle, linebacker, Bears (8) 1948–55
onzelman, Jimmy, quarterback, 5 teams (10), owner 1921–48
reekmur, Lou, offensive tackle/guard, Lions (10) 1950–59
sonka, Larry, back, Dolphins, Giants (11) 1968–79
avis, Al, owner, Raiders, coach, general manager 1963–
avis, Willie, defensive end, Packers (10) 1960–69
awson, Len, quarterback, Steelers, Browns, Texans, Chiefs (19) 1957–75
ierdorf, Dan, tackle/center, Cardinals (13) 1971–83
itka, Mike, tight end, Bears, Eagles, Cowboys (12) 1961–72
onovan, Art, defensive tackle, Colts (12) 1950–61
orsett, Tony, running back, Cowboys, Broncos (12) 1977–88
riscoll, John (Paddy), quarterback, Cards, Bears (11) 1919–29
udley, Bill, back, Steelers, Lions, Redskins (9) 1942–53
dwards, Albert Glen (Turk), tackle, Redskins (9) 1932–40
wbank, Weeb, coach, Colts, Jets (20) 1954–73
ears, Tom, end, Rams (9); coach, Saints 1948–56
inks, Jim, administrator/general manager, Vikings, Bears, Saints 1964–93
laherty, Ray, end, Yankees, Giants (9); coach, Redskins, Yankees (14) 1928–49
ord, Len, end, def. end, Browns, Packers (11) 1948–58
outs, Dan, quarterback, Chargers (15) 1973–87
ortmann, Daniel J., guard, Bears (8) 1936–43
atski, Frank, offensive lineman, Browns (12) 1946–57
eorge, Bill, linebacker, Bears, Rams (15) 1952–66
ibbs, Joe, coach, Redskins (11) 1981–92
ifford, Frank, back, Giants (12) 1952–64
illman, Sid, coach, Rams, Chargers, Oilers (18) 1955–70, 73–74
raham, Otto, quarterback, Browns (10) 1946–55
range, Harold (Red), back, Bears, Yankees (9) 1925–34
rant, Bud, coach, Vikings (18) 1967–85
reene, Joe, defensive tackle, Steelers (13) 1968–81
regg, Forrest, tackle, Packers (15) 1956–71
riese, Bob, quarterback, Dolphins (14) 1967–80
roza, Lou, place-kicker, tackle, Browns (21) 1946–67
uyon, Joe, back, 6 teams (8) 1919–27
lalas, George, NFL founder, owner and coach, Staleys and Bears, end (11) 1919–27
Ham, Jack, linebacker, Steelers (13) 1970–82
Hannah, John, guard, Patriots (13) 1973–85
Harris, Franco, running back, Steelers, Seahawks (13) 1972–84
Haynes, Mike, defensive back, Patriots, Raiders (10) 1976–85
Healey, Ed, tackle, Bears (8) 1920–27
Hein, Mel, center, Giants (15) 1931–45
Hendricks, Ted, linebacker, Colts, Packers, Raiders (15) 1969–83
Henry, Wilbur (Pete), tackle, Bulldogs, Giants (8) 1920–28
Herber, Arnie, quarterback, Packers, Giants (13) 1930–45
Hewitt, Bill, end, Bears, Eagles (9) 1932–43
Hinkle, Clarke, fullback, Packers (10) 1932–41
Hirsch, Elroy (Crazy Legs), back, end, Rams (12) 1946–57
Hornung, Paul, running back, Packers (9) 1957–62, 64–66
Houston, Ken, def. back, Oilers, Redskins (14) 1967–80
Hubbard, R. (Cal), tackle, Giants, Packers (9) 1927–36
Huff, Sam, linebacker, Giants, Redskins (13) 1956–67, 1969
Hunt, Lamar, founder A.F.L., owner Texans, Chiefs 1959–
Hutson, Don, end, Packers (11) 1935–45
Johnson, John Henry, back, 49ers, Lions, Steelers, Oilers (13) 1954–66
Johnson, Jimmy, cornerback, 49ers (16) 1961–76
Joiner, Charlie, receiver, Oilers, Bengals, Chargers (18) 1969–86
Jones, David (Deacon), defensive end, Rams, Chargers, Redskins (14) 1961–74
Jones, Stan, defensive tackle, Bears, Redskins (13) 1954–66
Jordan, Henry, defensive tackle, Browns, Packers 1957–69
Jurgensen, Sonny, quarterback, Eagles, Redskins (18) 1957–74
Kelly, Leroy, running back, Browns (10) 1964–73
Kiesling, Walt, guard, 6 teams (13) 1926–38
Kinard, Frank (Bruiser), tackle, Dodgers (9) 1938–47
Krause, Paul, safety, Redskins, Vikings 1964–79
Lambeau, Earl (Curly), NFL founder, coach, end, back, Packers (11) 1919–53
Lambert, Jack, linebacker, Steelers (11) 1974–84
Landry, Tom, coach, Cowboys (29) 1960–88
Lane, Richard (Night Train), defensive back, Rams, Cardinals, Lions (14) 1952–65
Langer, Jim, center, Dolphins, Vikings (12) 1970–81
Lanier, Willie, linebacker, Chiefs (11) 1967–77
Largent, Steve, receiver, Seahawks 1976–89
Lary, Yale, defensive back, punter, Lions (11) 1952–64
Laveill, Dante, end, Browns (11) 1946 56
Layne, Bobby, quarterback, Bears, Lions, Steelers (15) 1948–62
Leemans, Alphonse (Tuffy), back, Giants (8) 1936–43
Lilly, Bob, defensive tackle, Cowboys (14) 1961–74
Little, Larry, guard, Dolphins, Chargers (14) 1967–80
Lombardi, Vince, coach, Packers, Redskins (11) 1959–70
Luckman, Sid, quarterback, Bears (12) 1939–50
Lyman, Roy (Link), tackle, Bulldogs, Bears (11) 1922–34
Mackey, John, tight end, Colts, Chargers (10) 1963–72
Mara, Tim, NFL founder, owner, Giants 1925–59
Mara, Wellington, NFL executive, owner, Giants 1937–
Marchetti, Gino, defensive end, Colts (14) 1952–66
Marshall, George P., NFL founder, owner, Redskins 1932–65
Matson, Ollie, back, Cardinals, Rams, Lions, Eagles (14) 1952–66
Maynard, Don, receiver, Giants, Jets, Cardinals (15) 1958–73
McAfee, George, back, Bears (8) 1940–50
McCormack, Mike, tackle, N.Y. Yankees, Cleveland Browns (10) 1951–62
McDonald, Tommy, wide receiver, Eagles, Cowboys, Rams, Falcons, Browns 1957–68
McElhenny, Hugh, back, 49ers, Vikings, Giants (13) 1952–64
McNally, John (Blood), back, 7 teams (15) 1925–39
Michalske, August, guard, Yankees, Packers (11) 1926–37
Millner, Wayne, end, Redskins (7) 1936–45
Mitchell, Bobby, wide receiver, Browns, Redskins (11) 1958–68
Mix, Ron, tackle, Chargers (11) 1960–71
Moore, Lenny, back, Colts (12) 1956–67
Motley, Marion, fullback, Browns, Steelers (9) 1946–55
Munoz, Anthony, tackle, Bengals 1980–92
Musso, George, guard-tackle, Bears (12) 1933–44
Nagurski, Bronko, fullback, Bears (9) 1930–43
Namath, Joe, quarterback, Jets, Rams (13) 1965–77
Neale, Earle (Greasy), coach, Eagles 1941–50

Nevers, Ernie, fullback, Chicago Cardinals (5) 1926–31
Nitschke, Ray, linebackers, Packers (15) 1958–72
Noll, Chuck, coach, Steelers (23) 1969–81
Nomellini, Leo, defensive tackle, 49ers (14) 1950–63
Olsen, Merlin, defensive tackle, Rams (15) 1962–76
Otto, Jim, center, Raiders (15) 1960–74
Owen, Steve, tackle, Giants (9), coach, Giants (13) 1924–53
Page, Alan, defensive tackle, Vikings, Bears (15) 1967–81
Parker, Clarence (Ace), quarterback, Dodgers (7) 1937–46
Parker, Jim, guard, tackle, Colts (11) 1957–67
Payton, Walter, running back, Bears (13) 1977–89
Perry, Joe, fullback, 49ers, Colts (16) 1948–63
Pihos, Pete, end, Eagles (9) 1947–55
Ray, Hugh, Shorty, NFL advisor 1938–52
Reeves, Dan, owner, Rams 1941–71
Renfro, Mel, cornerback, safety, Cowboys (14) 1964–77
Riggins, John, running back, Jets, Redskins (14) 1971–84
Ringo, Jim, center, Packers (15) 1953–67
Robustelli, Andy, def. end, Rams, Giants (14) 1951–64
Rooney, Art, NFL founder, owner Steelers 1933–
Rozelle, Pete, commissioner, NFL 1960–89
St. Claire, Bob, tackle, 49ers (11) 1953–63
Sayers, Gale, back, Bears (7) 1965–71
Schmidt, Joe, linebacker, Lions (13) 1953–65
Schramm, Tex, administrator, Rams, Cowboys (42) 1947–89
Selmon, Lee Roy, defensive end, Buccaneers 1976–84
Shell, Art, tackle, Raiders (15) 1968–82
Shula, Don, coach, Colts, Dolphins (33) 1963–95
Simpson, O.J., back, Bills, 49ers (11) 1969–79
Singletary, Mike, linebacker, Bears 1981–92
Smith, Jackie, tight end, Cardinals, Cowboys (16) 1963–78
Starr, Bart, quarterback, coach, Packers (16) 1956–71
Staubach, Roger, quarterback, Cowboys (11) 1969–7
Stautner, Ernie, defensive tackle, Steelres (14) 1950–6
Stenerud, Jan, placekicker, Chiefs, Packers, Vikings (19) 1967–8
Stephenson, Dwight, center, Dolphins 1980–8
Strong, Ken, back, Giants, Yankees (14) 1929–4
Stydahar, Joe. tackle, Bears (9); coach, Rams, Cardinals (5) 1936–5
Tarkenton, Fran, quarterback, Vikings, Giants (18) 1961–7
Taylor, Charlie, wide receiver, Redskins (14) 1964–7
Taylor, Jim, fullback, Packers, Saints (10) 1958–6
Thorpe, Jim, back, 7 teams (12) 1915–2
Tittle, Y.A., quarterback, Colts, 49ers, Giants (17) 1948–6
Trafton, George, center, Bears (13) 1920–3
Trippi, Charley, back, Chicago Cardinals (9) 1947–5
Tunnell, Emlen, def. back, Giants, Packers (14) 1948–6
Turner, Clyde (Bulldog), center, Bears (13) 1940–5
Unitas, John, quarterback, Colts (18) 1956–7
Upshaw, Gene, guard, Raiders (15) 1967–8
Van Brocklin, Norm, quarterback, Rams, Eagles (12) 1949–6
Van Buren, Steve, back, Eagles (8) 1944–5
Walker, Doak, running back, def. back, kicker, Lions (6) 1950–5
Walsh, Bill, coach, 49ers (10) 1979–8
Warfield, Paul, wide receiver, Browns, Dolphins (13) 1964–74, 76–7
Waterfield, Bob, quarterback, Rams (8) 1945–5
Webster, Mike, center, Steelers, Chiefs (17) 1974–9
Weinmeister, Arnie, tackle, N.Y. Yankees, Giants (6) 1948–5
White, Randy, defensive tackle, Cowboys (14) 1975–8
Willis, Bill, guard, Browns (8) 1946–5
Wilson, Larry, defensive back, Cardinals (13) 1960–7
Winslow, Kellen, tight end, Chargers (9) 1979–8
Wood, Willie, safety, Packers (12) 1960–7
Wojciechowicz, Alex, center, Lions, Eagles (13) 1938–5

N.F.L. INDIVIDUAL LIFETIME, SEASON, AND GAME RECORDS

(American Football League records were incorporated into NFL records after merger of the leagues)

Players listed in boldface were active during the 1997 season. The All American Football Conference (AAFC) existed from 1946 to 1949. The 49ers Browns, and Colts merged with the NFL in 1949.

All-Time Leading Touchdown Scorers (Through 1997)

		Yrs	Rush	Rec	Ret	Total
1	**Jerry Rice**	13	10	155	1	166
2	**Marcus Allen**	16	123	21	1	145
3	Jim Brown	9	106	20	0	126
4	Walter Payton	13	110	15	0	125
5	**Emmitt Smith**	8	112	7	0	119
6	John Riggins	14	104	12	0	116
7	Lenny Moore	12	63	48	2	113
8	Don Hutson	11	3	99	3	105
	Barry Sanders	9	95	10	0	105
10	Steve Largent	14	1	100	0	101
11	Franco Harris	13	91	9	0	100
12	Eric Dickerson	11	90	6	0	96
13	Jim Taylor	10	83	10	0	93
14	Tony Dorsett	12	77	13	1	91
	Bobby Mitchell	11	18	65	8	91

All-Time Leading Receivers (Through 1997)

		Yrs	No	Yards	Avg	T
1	**Jerry Rice**	13	1,057	16,455	15.6	15
2	Art Monk	16	940	12,721	13.5	6
3	**Andre Reed**	13	826	11,764	14.2	8
4	Steve Largent	14	819	13,089	16.0	10
5	**Henry Ellard**	15	807	13,662	16.9	6
6	James Lofton	16	764	14,004	18.3	7
7	**Cris Carter**	11	756	9,436	12.5	8
8	Charlie Joiner	18	750	12,146	16.2	6
9	**Irving Fryar**	14	736	11,427	15.5	7
10	Gary Clark	11	699	10,856	15.5	6
11	**Michael Irvin**	10	666	10,680	16.0	6
12	Ozzie Newsome	13	662	7,980	12.1	4
13	Charley Taylor	13	649	9,110	14.0	7
14	**Andre Rison**	9	641	8,839	13.8	7
15	Drew Hill	15	634	9,831	15.5	6

All-Time Leading Passers

(Minimum 1,500 attempts. Through 1997)

		Yrs	Att	Cmp	Cmp%	Yards	Avg Gain	TD	TD%	Int	Rating
1	**Steve Young**	13	3,548	2,300	64.8	28,508	8.03	193	5.4	91	97.0
2	Joe Montana	15	5,391	3,409	63.2	40,551	7.52	273	5.1	139	92.3
3	**Brett Favre**	7	3,206	1,971	61.5	22,591	7.05	182	5.7	95	89.3
4	**Dan Marino**	15	7,452	4,453	59.8	55,416	7.44	385	5.2	220	87.8
5	Jim Kelly	11	4,779	2,874	60.1	35,467	7.42	237	5.0	175	84.4
6	Roger Staubach	11	2,958	1,685	57.0	22,700	7.67	153	5.2	109	83.4
7	Neil Lomax	8	3,153	1,817	57.6	22,771	7.22	136	4.3	90	82.7
8	Sonny Jurgensen	18	4,262	2,433	57.1	32,224	7.56	255	6.0	189	82.6
9	Len Dawson	19	3,741	2,136	57.1	28,711	7.67	239	6.4	183	82.6
10	**Troy Aikman**	9	3,696	2,292	62.0	26,016	7.04	129	3.5	110	82.3
11	Ken Anderson	16	4,475	2,654	59.3	32,838	7.34	197	4.4	160	81.9

		Yrs	Att	Cmp	Cmp%	Yards	Avg Gain	TD	TD%	Int	Rating
12	Bernie Kosar	12	3,365	1,994	59.3	23,301	6.92	124	3.7	87	81.8
13	Danny White	13	2,950	1,761	59.7	21,959	7.44	155	5.3	132	81.7
14	**Dave Krieg**	18	5,290	3,093	58.5	37,948	7.17	261	4.9	199	81.5
15	**Warren Moon**	14	6,528	3,827	58.6	47,465	7.27	279	4.3	224	81.2

Note: The NFL does not recognize records from the All-American Football Conference (1946-49). If it did, **Otto Graham** would rank 5th (after Marino) with the following stats: 10 Yrs; 2,626 Att; 1,464 Comp; 55.8 Comp Pct; 23,584 Yards; 8.98 Avg Gain; 174 TD; 6.6 TD Pct; 135 Int; 5.1 Int Pct; and 86.6 Rating Pts.

All-Time Leading Scorers (Through 1997)

		Yrs	TD	FG	PAT	Total
1	George Blanda	26	9	335	943	2,002
2	Nick Lowery	18	0	383	562	1,711
3	Jan Stenerud	19	0	373	580	1,699
4	**Gary Anderson**	16	0	385	526	1,681
5	**Morten Andersen**	16	0	378	507	1,641
6	**Norm Johnson**	16	0	322	592	1,558
7	**Eddie Murray**	17	0	337	521	1,532
8	Pat Leahy	18	0	304	558	1,470
9	Jim Turner	16	1	304	521	1,439
10	Matt Bahr	17	0	300	522	1,422
11	Mark Moseley	16	0	300	482	1,382
12	Jim Bakken	17	0	282	534	1,380
13	Fred Cox	15	0	282	519	1,365
14	Lou Groza	17	1	234	641	1,349
15	Jim Breech	14	0	243	517	1,246

All-Time Leading Rushers (Through 1997)

		Yrs	Car	Yards	Avg	TD
1	Walter Payton	13	3,838	16,726	4.4	110
2	**Barry Sanders**	9	2,719	13,778	5.1	95
3	Eric Dickerson	11	2,996	13,259	4.4	90
4	Tony Dorsett	12	2,936	12,739	4.3	77
5	Jim Brown	9	2,359	12,312	5.2	106
6	**Marcus Allen**	16	3,022	12,243	4.1	123
7	Franco Harris	13	2,949	12,120	4.1	91
8	**Thurman Thomas**	10	2,720	11,405	4.2	63
9	John Riggins	14	2,916	11,352	3.9	104
10	O.J. Simpson	11	2,404	11,236	4.7	61
11	**Emmitt Smith**	8	2,595	11,234	4.3	112
12	Ottis Anderson	14	2,562	10,273	4.0	81
13	Earl Campbell	8	2,187	9,407	4.3	74
14	Jim Taylor	10	1,941	8,597	4.4	83
15	Joe Perry	14	1,737	8,378	4.8	53

Scoring

Most points scored, lifetime—2,002, George Blanda, Chicago Bears, 1949-58; Baltimore, 1950; Houston, 1960–1966; Oakland, 1967–1975 (9 tds, 943 pat, 335 fgs).

Most points, season—176, Paul Hornung, Green Bay, 1960 (15 td, 41 pat, 15 fg).

Most points, game—40, Ernie Nevers, Chicago Cardinals, 1929 (6 td, 4 pat).

Most touchdowns, lifetime—165, Jerry Rice, San Francisco, 1985–1996.

Most touchdowns, season—25, Emmitt Smith, Dallas, 1995.

Most points after touchdown, lifetime—943, George Blanda, Chicago Bears, 1949–1958; Baltimore, 1950; Houston, 1960–1966; Oakland, 1967–1975.

Most points after touchdown, game—9, Pat Harder, Cardinals vs. N.Y. Giants, 1948; Bob Waterfield, Los Angeles vs. Baltimore, 1950; Charlie Gogolak, Washington vs. N.Y. Giants, 1966.

Most field goals, lifetime—383, Nick Lowery, New England, 1978; Kansas City Chiefs, 1980–1993; N.Y. Jets, 1994–1996.

Most field goals, season—37, John Kasay, Carolina, 1996.

Most field goals, game—7, Jim Bakken, St. Louis, 1967; Rick Karlis, Minnesota, 1989; and Chris Boniol, Dallas, 1996.

Longest field goal—63 yards, Tom Dempsey, New Orleans, 1970.

Rushing

Most yards gained, lifetime—16,726, Walter Payton, Chicago Bears, 1975–1987.

Most yards gained, season—2,105, Eric Dickerson, Los Angeles, 1984.

Most yards gained, game—275, Walter Payton, Chicago, 1977.

Most touchdowns, lifetime—110, Walter Payton, Chicago, 1975–1987.

Most touchdowns, season—25, Emmitt Smith, Dallas, 1995.

Most touchdowns, game—6, Ernie Nevers, Chicago Cardinals, 1929.

Longest run from scrimmage—99 yards, Tony Dorsett, Dallas, Jan. 3, 1983.

Receiving

Most pass receptions, lifetime—1,050, Jerry Rice, San Francisco, 1985–1996.

Most pass receptions, season—123, Herman Moore, Detroit, 1995.

Most pass receptions, game—18, Tom Fears, Los Angeles, 1950.

Most yards gained, pass receptions, lifetime—16,377, Jerry Rice, San Francisco, 1985–1996.

Most yards gained, receptions, season—1,848, Jerry Rice, San Francisco, 1995.

Most yards gained, receptions, game—336, Willie Anderson, Los Angeles Rams, Nov. 26, 1989 vs. New Orleans.

Most touchdown receptions, lifetime—154, Jerry Rice, San Francisco, 1985–1996.

Most touchdown pass receptions, season—22, Jerry Rice, San Francisco 49ers, 1987.

Most touchdown pass receptions, game—5, Bob Shaw, Chicago Cards, 1950; Kellen Winslow, San Diego Chargers, 1981; Jerry Rice, San Francisco 49ers, 1990.

Interceptions

Most pass interceptions, lifetime—277, George Blanda, 1949–1975.

Most pass interceptions, season—14, Richard (Night Train) Lane, Los Angeles, 1952.

Most pass interceptions, game—4, by 17 players.

Longest pass interception return—104 yards, James Willis, Philadelphia vs. Dallas, Nov. 3, 1996.

Kicking

Highest average punting, lifetime—45.16 yards, Sammy Baugh, Washington, 1937–52.

Longest punt return—103 yards, Robert Bailey, L.A. Rams, 1994.

Longest kick-off return—106 yards, Roy Green, St. Louis, 1979; Al Carmichael, Green Bay, 1956; Noland Smith, Kansas City, 1967.

Passing

Most touchdown passes, season—48, Dan Marino, Miami, 1984.

Most touchdown passes, game—7, Sid Luckman, Chicago Bears, 1943; Adrian Burk, Philadelphia, 1954; George Blanda, Houston, 1961; Y.A. Tittle, New York Giants, 1962; Joe Kapp, Minnesota, 1969.

Longest pass completion—99 yards, Frank Filchock (to Andy Farkas), Washington, 1939; George Izo (to Bob Mitchell), Washington, 1963; Karl Sweetan (to Pat Studstill), Detroit, 1966; Sonny Jurgensen (to Gerry Allen), Washington, 1968; Jim Plunkett (to Cliff Branch) L.A. Raiders, 1985; Ron Jaworksi (to Mike Quick), Philadelphia, 1985; Stan Humphries (to Tony Martin), San Diego, 1994; Brett Favre (to Robert Brooks), Green Bay, 1995.

Most passes completed, lifetime—4,134, Dan Marino Miami, 1983–96.

Most passes completed, season—404, Warren Moon, 1991

Most passes completed, game—45, Drew Bledsoe, New England, 1994.

Most touchdown passes, lifetime—369, Dan Marino, Miami, 1983–96.

Most yards gained, lifetime—51,636, Dan Marino, Miami, 1983–96.

Most yards gained, season—5,084, Dan Marino, Miami, 1984.

Most yards gained, game—554, Norm Van Brocklin, Los Angeles, 1951.

Sports Personalities

A name in parentheses is the original name or form of name. Localities are places of birth. Dates of birth appear as month/day/year. **Boldface** years in parentheses are dates of **(birth-death)**.

Information has been gathered from many sources, including the individuals themselves. However, the almanac cannot guarantee the accuracy of every individual item.

Aaron, Hank (Henry) (baseball); Mobile, Ala., 2/5/34
Abdul-Jabbar, Kareem (Lewis Ferdinand Alcindor, Jr.) (basketball); New York City, 4/16/47
Affleck, Francis (auto racing) **(1951–1985)**
Agassi, Andre (tennis); Las Vegas, Nev., 4/29/70
Aikman, Troy (football); Henryetta, Okla., 11/21/66
Ali, Muhammad (Cassius Clay) (boxing); Louisville, Ky., 1/18/42
Allen, Dick (Richard Anthony) (baseball); Wampum, Pa., 3/8/42
Allen, George (football) **(1918–1990)**
Allison, Bobby (Robert Arthur) (auto racing); Hueytown, Ala., 12/3/37
Allison, Davey (auto racing); Hueytown, Ala. **(1961–1993)**
Alston, Walter (baseball); Venice, Ohio **(1911–1984)**
Alworth, Lance (football); Houston, 8/3/40
Ameche, Alan (football); Houston, Tex. **(1933–1988)**
Anderson, Sparky (George) (baseball); Bridgewater, S.D., 2/22/34
Andretti, Mario (auto racing); Montona, Trieste, Italy, 2/28/40
Anthony, Earl (bowling); Kent, Wash., 4/27/38
Appling, Luke (baseball); High Point, N.C **(1907–1990)**
Arcaro, Eddie (George Edward) (jockey); Cincinnati **(1916–1997)**
Ashe, Arthur (tennis); Richmond, Va. **(1943–1993)**
Ashford, Evelyn (track & field); Shreveport, La., 4/15/57
Austin, Tracy (tennis); Rolling Hills, Calif., 12/2/62
Averill, Earl (baseball); Everett, Wash. **(1915–1983)**
Babashoff, Shirley (swimming); Whittier, Calif., 1/31/57
Baer, Max (boxing); Omaha, Neb. **(1909–1959)**
Bailey, Donovan (track); Canada, 12/16/67
Banks, Ernie (baseball); Dallas, 1/31/31
Bannister, Roger (runner); Harrow, England, 3/24/29
Barkley, Charles (basketball); Leeds, Ala., 2/20/63
Barry, Rick (Richard) (basketball); Elizabeth, N.J., 3/28/44
Bauer, Hank (Henry) (baseball); East St. Louis, Ill., 7/31/22
Baugh, Sammy (football); Temple, Tex., 3/17/14
Baylor, Elgin (basketball); Washington, D.C., 9/16/34
Beamon, Bob (long jumper); New York City, 8/2/46
Becker, Boris (tennis); Leiman, W. Germany, 11/22/67
Bee, Clair (basketball); Cleveland, Ohio **(1896–1983)**
Beliveau, Jean (hockey); Three Rivers, Quebec, Canada, 8/31/31
Belle, Albert (baseball); Shreveport, La., 8/25/66
Beman, Deane (golf); Washington, D.C., 4/22/38
Bench, Johnny (Johnny Lee) (baseball); Oklahoma City, 12/7/47
Berg, Patty (Patricia Jane) (golf); Minneapolis, 2/13/18
Berra, Yogi (Lawrence) (baseball); St. Louis, 5/12/25
Biletnikoff, Frederick (football); Erie, Pa., 2/23/43
Bing, Dave (basketball); Washington, D.C., 11/24/43
Bird, Larry (basketball); French Lick, Ind., 12/7/56
Blaik, Earl H. (football); Detroit **(1897–1989)**
Blanda, George Frederick (football); Youngwood, Pa., 9/17/27
Bledsoe, Drew (football); Walla Walla, Wash., 2/14/72
Blue, Vida (baseball); Mansfield, La., 7/28/49
Bodine, Brett (auto racing); Chemung, N.Y., 1/11/59
Bodine, Geoff (auto racing); Chemung, N.Y., 4/18/49
Boggs, Wade (baseball); Omaha, Neb., 6/15/58
Bonds, Barry (baseball); Riverside, Calif., 7/24/64
Borg, Björn (tennis); Stockholm, Sweden, 6/6/56
Boros, Julius (golf); Fairfield, Conn. **(1920–1994)**
Bossy, Mike (hockey); Montreal, 1/22/57
Boston, Ralph (long jumper); Laurel, Miss., 5/9/39
Bourque, Ray (hockey); Montreal, Que., 12/28/60
Bradley, Bill (William Warren) (basketball); Crystal City, Mo., 7/28/43
Bradley, Pat (golf); Westford, Mass., 3/24/51
Bradshaw, Terry (football); Shreveport, La., 9/2/48
Breedlove, Craig (Norman) (speed driving); Los Angeles, 3/23/38
Brett, George (baseball); Glendale, W. Va., 5/15/53
Brock, Louis Clark (baseball); El Dorado, Ark., 6/18/39
Brown, Jimmy (football); St. Simon Island, Ga., 2/17/36
Brumel, Valeri (high jumper); Tolbuzino, Siberia, 4/14/42
Bryant, Paul "Bear" (football); Tuscaloosa, Ala. **(1913–1983)**
Bryant, Rosalyn Evette (track); Chicago, 1/7/56
Burton, Michael (swimming); Des Moines, Iowa, 7/3/47
Butkus, Dick (Richard Marvin) (football); Chicago, 12/0/42
Calipari, John (basketball); Moon, Pa., 2/10/59
Campanella, Roy (baseball); Homestead, Pa. **(1921–1993)**
Campbell, Earl (football); Tyler, Tex., 3/29/55
Canseco, Jose (baseball); Havana, Cuba, 7/2/64
Caponi, Donna Maria (golf); Detroit, 1/29/45
Cappelletti, Gino (football); Keewatin, Minn., 3/26/34
Carew, Rod (Rodney Cline) (baseball); Gatun, Panama, 10/1/45
Carlos, John (sprinter); New York City, 6/5/45
Carlton, Steven Norman (baseball); Miami, Fla., 12/22/44
Carner, Joanne Gunderson, Mrs. Don (golf); Kirkland, Wash., 3/4/39
Casals, Rosemary (tennis); San Francisco, 9/16/48
Casper, Billy (golf); San Diego, Calif., 6/24/31
Caulkins, Tracy (swimming); Winona, Minn., 1/11/63
Cauthen, Steve (jockey); Covington, Ky., 5/1/60
Chamberlain, Wilt (Wilton) (basketball); Philadelphia, 8/21/36
Chandler, A.B. (Happy) (baseball); Louisville, Ky. **(1899–1991)**
Chandler, Spud (baseball); Commerce, Ga. **(1907–1990)**
Chang, Michael (tennis); Hoboken, N.J., 2/22/72
Chapot, Frank (equestrian); Camden, N.J., 2/24/34
Chinaglia, Giorgio (soccer); Carrara, Italy, 1/24/47
Clarke, Bobby (Robert Earle) (hockey); Flin Flon, Manitoba, Canada, 8/13/49
Clemens, Roger (baseball); Dayton, Ohio, 8/4/62
Clemente, Roberto Walker (baseball); Carolina, Puerto Rico **(1934–1972)**
Cobb, Ty (Tyrus Raymond) (baseball); Narrows, Ga. **(1886–1961)**
Cochran, Barbara Ann (skiing); Claremont, N.H., 1/14/51
Cochran, Marilyn (skiing); Burlington, Vt., 2/7/50
Cochran, Robert (skiing); Claremont, N.H., 12/11/51
Coe, Sebastian Newbold (track); London, England, 9/29/56
Coffey, Paul (hockey); Weston, Ont., 6/1/61
Colavito, Rocky (Rocco Domenico) (baseball); New York City, 8/10/33
Coleman, Derrick (basketball); Mobile, Ala., 6/21/67
Comaneci, Nadia (gymnast); Onesti, Romania, 11/12/61
Conigliaro, Tony (baseball); Revere, Mass. **(1945–1990)**
Connors, Jimmy (James Scott) (tennis); East St. Louis, Ill., 9/2/52
Cordero, Angel (jockey); Santurce, Puerto Rico, 5/8/42
Cosell, Howard (broadcaster); Winston-Salem, N.C. **(1918–1995)**
Courier, Jim (tennis); Sanford, Fla., 8/17/70
Cournoyer, Yvan Serge (hockey); Drummondville, Quebec, Canada, 11/22/43
Court, Margaret Smith (tennis); Albury, New South Wales, Australia, 7/16/42
Cousy, Bob (basketball); New York City, 8/9/28
Crabbe, Buster (swimming); Scottsdale, Ariz. **(1908–1983)**
Crenshaw, Ben (golf); Austin, Tex., 1/11/52

Cronin, Joe (baseball executive); San Francisco **(1906–1984)**
Cruyff, Johan (soccer); Amsterdam, Netherlands, 4/25/47
Csonka, Larry (Lawrence Richard) (football); Stow, Ohio, 12/25/46
Dancer, Stanley (harness racing); New Egypt, N.J., 7/25/27
Dark, Alvin (baseball); Comanche, Okla., 1/7/22
Davenport, Willie (track); Troy, Ala., 6/6/43
Dawson, Andre (baseball); Miami, Fla., 7/10/54
Dawson, Leonard Ray (football); Alliance, Ohio, 6/20/35
Dean, Dizzy (Jay Hanna) (baseball); Lucas, Ark. **(1911–1974)**
DeBusschere, Dave (basketball); Detroit, 10/16/40
Delvecchio, Alex Peter (hockey); Fort William, Ontario, Canada, 12/4/31
Demaret, Jim (golf); Houston **(1910–1983)**
Dempsey, Jack (William H.) (boxing); Manassa, Colo. **(1895–1983)**
DeVicenzo, Roberto (golf); Buenos Aires, 4/14/23
Dibbs, Edward George (tennis); Brooklyn, New York, 2/23/51
Dietz, James W. (rowing); New York, N.Y., 1/12/49
DiMaggio, Joe (baseball); Martinez, Calif., 11/25/14
Dionne, Marcel (hockey); Drummondville, Quebec, Canada, 8/3/51
Dorsett, Tony (football); Rochester, Pa., 4/7/54
Dryden, Kenneth (hockey); Hamilton, Ontario, Canada, 8/4/47
Drysdale, Don (baseball); Van Nuys, Calif. **(1936–1993)**
Duran, Roberto (boxing); Panama City, 6/16/51
Durocher, Leo (baseball); West Springfield, Mass. **(1906–1991)**
Durr, Francois (tennis); Algiers, Algeria, 12/25/42
Eckersley, Dennis (baseball); Oakland, Calif., 10/3/54
Elder, Lee (golf); Dallas, 7/14/34
Elway, John (football); Port Angeles, Wash., 6/28/60
Emerson, Roy (tennis); Kingsway, Australia, 11/3/36
Ender, Kornelia (swimming); Plauen, East Germany, 10/25/58
Erving, Julius ("Dr. J") (basketball); Roosevelt, N.Y., 2/22/50
Esposito, Phil (Philip Anthony) (hockey); Sault Ste. Marie, Ontario, Canada, 2/20/42
Evans, Lee (runner); Mandena, Calif., 2/25/47
Evert, Chris (Christine Marie) (tennis); Fort Lauderdale, Fla., 12/21/54
Ewbank, Weeb (football); Richmond, Ind., 5/6/07
Ewing, Patrick (basketball); Kingston, Jamaica, 8/5/62
Favre, Brett (football); Gulfport, Miss., 10/10/69
Feller, Robert (Bob) (baseball); Van Meter, Iowa, 11/3/18
Feuerbach, Allan Dean (track); Preston, Iowa, 1/12/48
Finley, Charles O. (sportsman); Ensley, Ala. **(1918–1996)**
Fischer, Bobby (chess); Chicago, 3/9/43
Fitzsimmons, Bob (Robert Prometheus) (boxing); Cornwall, England **(1862–1917)**
Fleming, Peggy Gale (ice skating); San Jose, Calif., 7/27/48
Ford, Whitey (Edward) (baseball); New York City, 10/21/28
Foreman, George (boxing); Marshall, Tex., 1/10/49
Fosbury, Richard (high jumper); Portland, Ore., 3/6/47
Fox, Nellie (Jacob Nelson) (baseball); St. Thomas, Pa. **(1927–1975)**
Foxx, James Emory (baseball); Sudlersville, Md. **(1907–1967)**
Foyt, A. J. (auto racing); Houston, 1/16/35
Frazier, Joe (boxing); Beauford, S.C., 1/17/44
Frazier, Walt (basketball); Atlanta, 3/29/45
Frick, Ford C. (baseball); Wawaka, Ind. **(1894–1978)**
Furniss, Bruce (swimming); Fresno, Calif., 5/27/57
Gable, Dan (wrestling); Waterloo, Iowa, 10/25/45
Gabriel, Roman (football); Wilmington, N.C., 8/5/40
Gallagher, Michael Donald (skiing); Yonkers, N.Y., 10/3/41
Garvey, Steve (baseball); Tampa, Fla., 12/22/48
Gehrig, Lou (Henry Louis) (baseball); New York City **(1903–1941)**
Gehringer, Charlie (baseball); Fowlerville, Mich. **(1903–1993)**
Geoffrion, "Boom Boom" (Bernie) (hockey); Montreal, 2/14/31
Gerulaitis, Vitas (tennis); Brooklyn, N.Y. **(1954–1994)**
Gervin, George (basketball); Long Beach, Calif., 4/27/52
Giacomin, Ed (hockey); Sudbury, Ontario, Canada, 6/6/39
Giamatti, A. Bartlett (baseball); South Hadley, Mass. **(1938–1989)**
Gibson, Bob (baseball); Omaha, Neb., 11/9/35
Gifford, Frank (football); Santa Monica, Calif., 8/16/30
Gilbert, Rod (Rodrique) (hockey); Montreal, 7/1/41
Gilmore, Artis (basketball); Chipley, Fla., 9/21/49
Glance, Harvey (track); Phenix City, Ala., 3/28/57
Gonzalez, Pancho (tennis); Los Angeles **(1928–1995)**
Goodell, Brian Stuart (swimming); Stockton, Calif., 4/2/59
Gooden, Dwight (baseball); Tampa, Fla., 11/16/64
Goodrich, Gail (basketball); Los Angeles, 4/23/43
Goolagong, Cawley, Evonne (tennis); Griffith, Australia, 7/31/51
Gordon, Jeff (auto racing); Vallejo, Calif., 8/4/71
Gossage, "Goose" (Rich) (baseball); Colorado Springs, Colo., 4/5/51
Graf, Steffi (tennis); Mannheim, W. Germany, 6/14/69
Graham, David (golf); Windson, Australia, 5/23/46
Graham, Otto Everett (football); Waukegan, Ill., 12/6/21
Grange, Red (Harold) (football); Forksville, Pa. **(1904–1991)**
Green, Hubert (golf); Birmingham, Ala., 12/28/46
Greene, Charles E. (sprinter); Pine Bluff, Ark., 3/21/45
Greene, "Mean" (Joe) (football); Temple, Tex., 9/24/46
Gretzky, Wayne (hockey); Brantford, Ont., 1/26/61
Griese, Bob (Robert Allen) (football); Evansville, Ind., 2/3/45
Griffey, Ken, Jr. (baseball); Donora, Pa., 11/21/69
Grove, Lefty (Robert Moses) (baseball); Lonaconing, Md. **(1900–1975)**
Groza, Lou (football); Martins Ferry Ohio, 1/25/24
Guidry, Ronald Ames (baseball); Lafayette, La., 8/28/50
Gwynn, Tony (baseball); Los Angeles, Calif., 5/9/60
Halas, George (football); Chicago **(1895–1983)**
Hall, Gary (swimming); Fayetteville, N.C., 8/7/51
Hamill, Dorothy (figure skating); Chicago, 1956(?)
Hamilton, Scott (figure skating); Bowling Green, Ohio, 8/28/58
Hamm, Mia (soccer); Selma, Ala., 3/17/72
Hammond, Kathy (runner); Sacramento, Calif., 11/2/51
Hardaway, Anfernee (basketball); Memphis, Tenn., 7/18/72
Harding, Tonya (figure skating); Portland, Ore., 11/12/70
Harris, Franco (football); Ft. Dix, N.J., 3/7/50
Hartack, William, Jr. (jockey); Colver, Pa., 12/9/32
Hasek, Dominik (hockey); Pardubice, Czechoslovakia, 1/29/65
Haughton, William (harness racing); Gloversville, N.Y. **(1923–1986)**
Havlicek, John (basketball); Martins Ferry, Ohio, 4/8/40
Hayes, Elvin (basketball); Rayville, La., 11/17/45
Hayes, Woody (football); Upper Arlington, Ohio **(1913–1987)**
Heiden, Eric (speed skating); Madison, Wis., 6/14/58
Hencken, John (swimming); Culver City, Calif., 5/29/54
Henderson, Rickey (baseball); Chicago, 12/25/58
Henie, Sonja (ice skater); Oslo **(1912–1969)**
Herman, Floyd Caves (Babe) (baseball); Buffalo, N.Y. **(1903–1987)**
Hernandez, Keith (baseball); San Francisco, 10/20/53
Hershiser, Orel (baseball); Buffalo, N.Y., 9/16/58
Hickcox, Charles (swimming); Phoenix, Ariz., 2/6/47
Hines, James (sprinter); Dumas, Ark., 9/10/46
Hingis, Martina (tennis); Kosice, Slovakia, 9/30/80
Hodges, Gil (baseball); Princeton, Ind. **(1924–1972)**
Hogan, Ben (golf); Dublin, Tex. **(1912–1997)**
Holmes, Larry (boxing); Cuthert, Ga., 11/3/49
Holyfield, Evander (boxing); Atlanta, Ga., 10/19/62
Hornsby, Rogers (baseball); Winters, Tex. **(1896–1963)**
Hornung, Paul (football); Louisville, Ky., 12/23/35
Houk, Ralph (baseball); Lawrence, Kan., 8/9/19
Howard, Elston (baseball); St. Louis **(1929–1980)**
Howe, Gordon (hockey); Floral, Sask., Canada, 3/31/28
Howell, Jim Lee (football); Lonoke, Ark. **(1914–1995)**
Howser, Dick (baseball); Miami, Fla. **(1937–1987)**
Hubbell, Carl (baseball); Carthage, Mo. **(1903–1988)**
Huff, Sam (Robert Lee) (football); Morgantown, W. Va., 10/4/34
Hull, Bobby (hockey); Point Anne, Ontario, Canada, 1/3/39
Hunter, "Catfish" (Jim) (baseball); Hertford, N.C., 4/8/46
Hutson, Donald (football); Pine Bluff, Ark. **(1913–1997)**
Irwin, Hale (golf); Joplin, Mo., 6/3/45
Jacobs, Helen Hull (tennis); Globe, Ariz. **(1908–1997)**
Jackson, Phil (basketball coach); Deer Lodge, Mont., 9/17/45
Jackson, Reggie (baseball); Wyncote, Pa., 5/18/46
Jagr, Jaromir (hockey); Kladno, Czechoslovakia, 2/15/72
Jeffries, James J. (boxing); Carroll, Ohio **(1875–1953)**
Jenkins, Ferguson Arthur (baseball); Chatham, Ontario, Canada, 12/13/43
Jenner, (W.) Bruce (track); Mt. Kisco, N.Y., 10/28/49
Jezek, Linda (swimming); Palo Alto, Calif., 3/10/60
Johnson, "Magic" (Earvin) (basketball); E. Lansing, Mich., 8/14/59
Johnson, Anthony (rowing); Washington, D.C., 11/16/40
Johnson, Jack (John Arthur) (boxing); Galveston, Tex. **(1876–1946)**
Johnson, Jimmy (football); Port Arthur, Tex., 8/14/43
Johnson, Michael (track); Dallas, Tex., 9/13/67
Johnson, Rafer (decathlon); Hillsboro, Tex., 8/18/35
Johnson, Randy (baseball); Walnut Creek, Calif., 9/10/63
Johnson, Wilham Julius (Judy) (baseball); Wilmington, Del. **(1899–1989)**
Jones, Cobi (soccer); Detroit, Mich., 6/16/70
Jones, Deacon (David) (football); Eatonville, Fla., 12/9/38
Jordan, Michael (basketball); Brooklyn, N.Y., 2/17/63
Joyner, Florence Griffith (sprinter); Mojave Desert, Calif. **(1959–1998)**
Joyner-Kersee, Jackie (track); East St. Louis, Ill., 3/3/62
Juantoreno, Alberto (track); Santiago, Cuba, 12/3/51
Jurgensen, Sonny (football); Wilmington, N.C., 8/23/34
Justice, Dave (baseball); Cincinnati, Ohio, 4/14/66
Kaat, Jim (baseball); Zeeland, Mich., 11/7/38
Kaline, Al (Albert) (baseball); Baltimore, 12/19/34
Keino, Kipchoge (runner); Kapchemoiymo, Kenya, 1/17/40
Kelly, Leroy (football); Philadelphia, 5/20/42
Kelly, Red (Leonard Patrick) (hockey); Simcoe, Ontario, Canada, 7/9/27
Kerrigan, Nancy (figure skating); Woburn, Mass., 10/13/69
Killebrew, Harmon (baseball); Payette, Idaho, 6/29/36
Killy, Jean-Claude (skiing); Saint-Cloud, France, 8/30/43
Kilmer, Bill (William Orland) (football); Topeka, Kan., 9/5/39
King, Bille Jean (Bille Jean Moffitt) (tennis); Long Beach, Calif., 11/22/43
Kinsella, John (swimming); Oak Park, Ill., 8/26/52

Kluszewski, Ted (baseball); Argo, Ill. **(1924–1988)**
Kodes, Jan (tennis); Prague, 3/1/46
Kolb, Claudia (swimming); Hayward, Calif., 12/19/49
Korbut, Olga (gymnast); Grodno, Byelorussia, U.S.S.R., 5/16/55
Koufax, Sandy (Sanford) (baseball); Brooklyn, N.Y., 12/30/35
Kramer, Jack (tennis); Las Vegas, Nev., 8/1/21
Kramer, Jerry (football); Jordan, Mont., 1/23/36
Kuenn, Harvey (baseball); West Allis, Wis. **(1930–1988)**
Kuhn, Bowie Kent (baseball); Takoma Park, Md., 10/28/26
Kwan, Michelle (figure skating); Torrance, Calif., 7/7/80
Lafleur, Guy Damien (hockey); Thurson, Quebec, Canada, 8/20/51
Laird, Ronald (walker); Louisville, Ky., 5/31/35
Lalas, Alexi (soccer); Birmingham, Mich., 6/1/70
Lamonica, Daryle (football); Fresno, Calif., 7/17/41
Landis, Kenesaw Mountain (1st baseball commissioner); Millville, Ohio **(1866–1944)**
Landry, Tom (football); Mission, Tex., 9/11/24
Landy, John (runner); Australia, 4/4/30
Larrieu, Francie (track); Palo Alto, Calif., 11/28/52
La Russa, Tony (baseball); Tampa, Fla., 10/4/44
Lasorda, Tom (baseball); Norristown, Pa., 9/22/27
Laver, Rod (tennis); Rockhampton, Australia, 8/9/38
Layne, Bobby (football); Lubbock, Texas **(1927–1986)**
Leetch, Brian (hockey); Corpus Christi, Tex., 3/3/68
Lemieux, Mario (hockey); Montreal, Quebec, Canada, 10/5/65
Lendl, Ivan (tennis); Prague, 3/7/60
Leonard, Benny (Benjamin Leiner) (boxing); New York City **(1896–1947)**
Leonard, Sugar Ray (boxing); Wilmington, N.C., 5/17/56
Lewis, Carl (track); Willingboro, N.J., 7/1/61
Lindros, Eric (hockey); London, Ont., 2/28/73
Lipinski, Tara (figure skating); Sugarland, Tex., 6/10/82
Liquori, Marty (runner); Montclair, N.J., 9/11/49
Little, Lou (football); Leominster, Mass. **(1893–1979)**
Littler, Gene (golf); La Jolla, Calif., 7/21/30
Lobo, Rebecca (basketball); Southwick, Mass., 10/6/73
Lombardi, Vince (football); Brooklyn, N.Y. **(1913–1970)**
Longden, Johnny (horse racing); Wakefield, England, 2/14/07
Lopat, Eddie (baseball); New York, N.Y. **(1918–1992)**
Lopez, Al (baseball); Tampa, Fla., 8/20/08
Lopez, Nancy (golf); Torrance, Calif., 1/6/57
Louis, Joe (Joe Louis Barrow) (boxing); Lafayette, Ala. **(1914–1981)**
Lukas, D. Wayne (horse racing); Antigo, Wis., 9/2/35
Lynn, Frederic Michael (baseball); Chicago, Ill., 2/3/52
Lynn, Janet (figure skating); Rockford, Ill., 4/6/53
Mack, Connie (Cornelius Alexander McGillicuddy) (baseball executive); East Brookfield, Mass. **(1862–1956)**
Mackey, John (football); New York City, 9/24/41
Maddux, Greg (baseball); San Angelo, Texas, 4/15/67
Mahovlich, Frank (Francis William) (hockey); Timmins, Ontario, Canada, 1/10/38
Mahre, Phil (skiing); White Pass, Wash., 5/10/57
Malone, Karl (basketball); Summerfield, La., 7/24/63
Malone, Moses (basketball); Petersburg, Va., 3/23/55
Mandlikova, Hana (tennis); Prague, Czechoslovakia, 2/62
Mann, Carol (golf); Buffalo, N.Y., 2/3/41
Manning, Madeline (runner); Cleveland, 1/11/48
Mantle, Mickey Charles (baseball); Spavinaw, Okla. **(1931–1995)**
Maravich, "Pistol Pete" (Peter) Aliquippa, Pa. **(1948–1988)**
Marble, Alice (tennis); Palm Springs, Calif. **(1913–1990)**
Marciano, Rocky (boxing); Brockton, Mass. **(1923–1969)**
Marichal, Juan (baseball); Laguna Verde, Montecristi, Dominican Republic, 10/20/37
Marino, Dan (football); Pittsburgh, Pa., 9/15/61
Maris, Roger (baseball); Hibbing, Minn. **(1934–1985)**
Martin, Billy (Alfred Manuel) (baseball); Berkeley, Calif. **(1928–1989)**
Martin, Christy (boxing); Mullers, W.Va.,
Martin, Rick (Richard Lionel) (hockey); Verdun, Quebec, Canada, 7/26/51
Mathews, Ed (Edwin) (baseball); Texarkana, Tex., 10/13/31
Mattingly, Don (baseball); Evansville, Ind., 4/20/61
Matson, Randy (shot putter); Kilgore, Tex., 3/5/45
Mays, Willie (baseball); Westfield, Ala., 5/6/31
McAdoo, Bob (basketball); Greensboro, N.C., 9/25/51
McCarthy, Joe (Joseph Vincent) (baseball); Philadelphia **(1887–1978)**
McCovey, Willie Lee (baseball); Mobile, Ala., 1/10/38
McDonald, Lanny (hockey); Hanna, Alberta, Canada, 2/16/53
McDowell, Jack (baseball); Van Nuys, Calif., 1/16/66
McEnroe, John Patrick, Jr. (tennis); Wiesbaden, Germany, 2/16/59
McGraw, John Joseph (baseball); Truxton, N.Y. **(1873–1934)**
McGwire, Mark (baseball); Pomona, Calif., 10/1/63
McLain, Dennis (baseball); Chicago, 3/24/44
McMillan, Kathy Laverne (track); Raeford, N.C., 11/7/57
Merrill, Janice (track); New London, Conn., 6/18/62
Messier, Mark (hockey); Edmonton, Alberta, Canada, 1/18/61
Meyer, Deborah (swimming); Haddonfield, N.J., 8/14/52
Meyers, Anne (basketball); San Diego, Calif., 3/26/55
Middlecoff, Cary (golf); Halls, Tenn., 1/6/21
Mikita, Stan (hockey); Sokolce, Czechoslovakia, 5/20/40
Milburn, Rodney, Jr. (hurdler); Opelousas, La., 5/18/50
Miller, Cheryl (basketball); Riverside, Calif., 1/3/64
Miller, Johnny (golf); San Francisco, 4/29/47
Miller, Reggie (basketball); Riverside, Calif., 8/24/65
Montana, Joe (football); New Eagle, Pa., 6/11/56
Montgomery, Jim (swimming); Madison, Wis., 1/24/55
Moody, Helen Willis (tennis); Centerville, Calif. **(1906–1998)**
Moore, Archie (boxing); Benoit, Miss., 12/13/16
Morgan, Joe Leonard (baseball); Bonham, Tex., 9/19/43
Morrall, Earl (football); Muskegon, Mich., 5/17/34
Morton, Craig L. (football); Flint, Mich., 2/5/43
Mosconi, Wilie (pocket billiards); Philadelphia **(1913–1993)**
Moses, Edwin Corley (track); Dayton, Ohio, 8/31/58
Mungo, Van Lingo (baseball); Pageland, S.C. **(1911–1985)**
Munson, Thurman (baseball); Akron, Ohio **(1947–1979)**
Murphy, Calvin (basketball); Norwalk, Conn., 5/9/48
Murray, Eddie (baseball); Los Angeles, Calif., 2/24/56
Musial, Stan (baseball); Donora, Pa., 11/21/20
Myers, Linda (archery); York, Pa., 6/19/47
Naber, John (swimming); Evanston, Ill., 1/20/56
Namath, Joe (Joseph William) (football); Beaver Falls, Pa., 5/31/43
Nastase, Ilie (tennis); Bucharest, 7/19/46
Navratilova, Martina (tennis); Prague, 10/18/56
Nehemiah, Renaldo (track); Newark, N.J., 3/24/59
Nelson, Cindy (skiing); Lutsen, Minn., 8/19/55
Newcombe, John (tennis); Sydney, Australia, 5/23/43
Niekro, Phil (baseball); Lansing, Ohio, 4/1/39
Nicklaus, Jack (golf); Columbus, Ohio, 1/21/40
Norman, Gregory (golf); Mount Isa, Australia, 2/10/55
Oerter, Al (discus thrower); New York City, 9/19/36
Olajuwon, Hakeem (basketball); Lagos, Nigeria, 1/21/63
Oldfield, Barney (racing driver); Fulton County, Ohio **(1878–1946)**
Oliva, Tony (Pedro) (baseball); Pinar Del Rio, Cuba, 7/20/40
Olsen, Merlin Jay (football); Logan, Utah, 9/15/40
O'Malley, Walter (baseball executive); New York City **(1903–1979)**
O'Neal, Shaquille (basketball); Newark, N.J., 3/6/72
Orantes, Manuel (tennis); Granada, Spain, 2/6/49
Orr, Bobby (hockey); Parry Sound, Ontario, Canada, 3/20/48
Ovett, Steve (track); Brighton, England, 10/9/55
Owens, Jesse (track); Decatur, Ala. **(1914–1980)**
Paige, Satchel (Leroy) (baseball); Mobile, Ala. **(1906–1982)**
Palmer, Arnold (golf); Latrobe, Pa., 9/10/29
Palmer, James Alvin (baseball); New York City, 10/15/45
Parcells, Bill (football coach); Englewood, N.J., 8/22/41
Parent, Bernard Marcel (hockey); Montreal, 4/3/45
Park, Brad (Douglas Bradford) (hockey); Toronto, Ontario, Canada 7/6/48
Parseghian, Ara (football); Akron, Ohio, 5/21/23
Pasarell, Charles (tennis); San Juan, Puerto Rico, 2/12/44
Patterson, Floyd (boxing); Waco, N.C., 1/4/35
Peete, Calvin (golf); Detroit, Mich., 7/18/43
Pelé (Edson Arantes do Nascimento) (soccer); Tres Coracoes, Brazil, 10/23/40
Perry, Gaylord (baseball); Williamston, N.C., 9/15/38
Perry, Jim (baseball); Williamston, N.C., 10/30/36
Pettit, Bob (basketball); Baton Rouge, La., 12/12/32
Petty, Richard Lee (auto racing); Randleman, N.C., 7/2/37
Pincay, Laffit, Jr. (jockey); Panama City, Panama, 12/29/46
Pippen, Scottie (basketball); Trenton, N.J., 9/25/65
Plager, Barclay (ice hockey); Kirkland Lake, Ontario **(1941–1988)**
Plante, Jacques (hockey); Sahwinigan Falls, Quebec, Canada, 1/17/29
Player, Gary (golf); Johannesburg, South Africa, 11/1/35
Plunkett, Jim (football); San Jose, Calif., 12/5/47
Potvin, Denis Charles (hockey); Hull, Quebec, Canada, 10/29/53
Powell, Boog (John) (baseball); Lakeland, Fla., 8/17/41
Powell, Mike (track); Philadelphia, 11/10/63
Prefontaine, Steve Roland (runner); Coos Bay, Ore. **(1951–1975)**
Prince, Bob (baseball announcer); Pittsburgh **(1917–1985)**
Proell, Annemarie Moser (Alpine skier); Kleinarl, Austria, 3/27/53
Rafter, Patrick (tennis); Brisbane, Australia, 12/28/72
Ralston, Dennis (tennis); Bakersfield, Calif., 7/27/42
Rankin, Judy Torluemke (golf); St. Louis, Mo., 2/18/45
Raschi, Vic (baseball); West Springfield, Mass. **(1919–1988)**
Ratelle, Jean (Joseph Gilbert Yvon Jean) (hockey); St. Jean, Quebec, Canada, 10/29/53
Rawls, Betsy (Elizabeth Earle) (golf); Spartanburg, S.C., 5/4/28
Reed, Willis (basketball); Hico, La., 6/25/42
Reese, Pee Wee (Harold) (baseball); Ekron, Ky., 7/23/19
Resch, Glenn "Chico" (hockey); Moose Jaw, Saskatchewan, Canada, 7/10/48
Rice, Jerry (football); Crawford, Miss., 10/13/62
Richard, Maurice (hockey); Montreal, 8/14/24
Riessen, Martin (tennis); Hinsdale, Ill., 12/4/41

Rigney, William (baseball); Alameda, Calif., 1/29/18
Rios, Marcelo (tennis); Santiago, Chile, 12/26/75
Ripken, Cal, Jr. (baseball); Havre de Grace, Md., 8/24/60
Rizzuto, Phil (baseball); New York City, 9/25/18
Robertson, Oscar (basketball); Charlotte, Tenn., 11/24/38
Robinson, Arnie (track); San Diego, Calif., 4/7/48
Robinson, Brooks (baseball); Little Rock, Ark., 5/18/37
Robinson, David (basketball); Key West, Fla., 8/6/65
Robinson, Frank (baseball); Beaumont, Tex., 8/31/35
Robinson, Jackie (baseball); Cairo, Ga. **(1919–1972)**
Robinson, Larry Clark (hockey); Marvelville, Ontario, Canada, 6/2/51
Robinson, "Sugar" Ray (boxing); Detroit **(1920–1989)**
Rockne, Knute Kenneth (football); Voss, Norway **(1888–1931)**
Rockwell, Martha (skiing); Providence, R.I., 4/26/44
Rodman, Dennis (basketball); Trenton, N.J., 5/13/61
Ronaldo (soccer); Bento Ribeiro, Brazil, 9/22/76
Rono, Harry (track); Kiptaragon, Kenya, 2/12/52
Rooney, Art (football); Pittsburgh, Pa. **(1901–1988)**
Rose, Pete (Peter Edward) (baseball); Cincinnati, 4/14/42
Rosenbloom, Maxie (boxing); New York City **(1904–1976)**
Rosewall, Ken (tennis); Sydney, Australia, 11/2/34
Rote, Kyle (football); San Antonio, 10/27/28
Roush, Edd (baseball); Oakland City, Ind. **(1893–1988)**
Rozelle, Pete (Alvin Ray) (commissioner of National Football League); South Gate, Calif. **(1926–1996)**
Rudolph, Wilma Glodean (sprinter); St. Bethlehem, Tenn. **(1940–1994)**
Russell, Bill (basketball); Monroe, La., 2/12/34
Ruth, Babe (George Herman Ruth) (baseball); Baltimore **(1895–1948)**
Rutherford, Johnny (auto racing); Fort Worth, 3/12/38
Ryan, Nolan (Lynn Nolan, Jr.) (baseball); Refugio, Tex., 1/31/47
Ryon, Luann (archery); Long Beach, Calif., 1/13/53
Ryun, Jim (runner); Wichita, Kan., 4/29/47
Salazar, Alberto (track); Havana, 8/7/58
Sampras, Pete (tennis); Washington, D.C., 8/12/71
Samuels, Howard (horse racing soccer); New York City **(1920–1984)**
Sanders, Barry (football); Wichita, Kan., 7/16/68
Sanders, Deion (baseball/football); Ft. Myers, Fla., 8/9/67
Santana, Manuel (Manuel Santana Martinez) (tennis); Chamartin, Spain, 5/10/38
Sayers, Gale (football); Wichita, Kan., 5/30/43
Schmidt, Mike (baseball); Dayton, Ohio, 9/27/49
Shoendienst, Red (Albert) (baseball); Germantown, Ill., 2/2/23
Schollander, Donald (swimming); Charlotte, N.C., 4/30/46
Seagren, Bob (Robert Lloyd) (pole vaulter); Pomona, Calif., 10/17/46
Seau, Junior (football); Oceanside, Calif., 1/19/69
Seaver, Tom (baseball); Fresno, Calif., 11/17/44
Seidler, Maren (track); Brooklyn, N.Y., 6/11/62
Seles, Monica (tennis); Novi Sad, Yugoslávia, 12/2/73
Selke, Frank (ice hockey); Canada **(1893–1985)**
Sewell, Joe (baseball); Titus, Ala. **(1898–1990)**
Shepherd, Lee (auto racing) **(1945–1985)**
Shero, Fred (hockey); Camden, N.J. **(1925–1990)**
Shoemaker, Willie (jockey); Fabens, Tex., 8/19/31
Shore, Eddie (ice hockey); Saskatchewan, Canada **(1902–1985)**
Shorter, Frank (runner); Munich, Germany, 10/31/47
Shriver, Pam (tennis); Baltimore, 7/4/62
Shula, Don (Donald Francis) (football); Grand River, Ohio, 1/4/30
Silvester, Jay (discus thrower); Tremonton, Utah, 2/27/37
Simpson, O.J. (Orenthal James) (football); San Francisco, 7/9/47
Sims, Billy (football); St. Louis, 9/18/55
Smith, Bubba (Charles Aaron) (football); Orange, Tex., 2/28/45
Smith, Emmitt (football); Escambia, Fla., 5/15/69
Smith, Ozzie (baseball); Mobile, Ala., 12/26/54
Smith, Ronnie Ray (sprinter); Los Angeles, 3/28/49
Smith, Stanley Roger (tennis); Pasadena, Calif., 12/14/46
Smith, Tommie (sprinter); Clarksville, Tex., 6/5/44
Smoke, Marcia Jones (canoeing); Oklahoma City, 7/18/41
Snead, Sam (golf); Hot Springs, Va., 5/27/12
Sneva, Tom (auto racing); Spokane, Wash., 6/1/48
Snider, Duke (Edwin) (baseball); Los Angeles, 9/19/26
Solomon, Harold (tennis); Washington, D.C., 9/17/52
Sosa, Sammy (Samuel) (baseball); San Pedro de Macoris, Dominican Republic, 11/12/68
Spahn, Warren (baseball); Buffalo, N.Y., 4/23/21
Speaker, Tristram (baseball); Hubbard City, Tex. **(1888–1958)**
Spencer, Brian (ice hockey); Fort St. James, British Columbia **(1949–1988)**
Spinks, Leon (boxing); St. Louis, 7/11/53
Spitz, Mark (swimming); Modesto, Calif., 2/10/50
Stabler, Kenneth (football); Foley, Ala., 12/25/45
Stagg, Amos Alonzo (football); West Orange, N.J. **(1862–1965)**
Stargell, Willie (Wilver Dornell) (baseball); Earlsboro, Okla., 3/6/41
Starr, Bart (football); Montgomery, Ala., 1/9/34
Staub, "Rusty" (Daniel) (baseball); New Orleans, 4/4/44
Staubach, Roger (football); Cincinnati, 2/5/42
Steinkraus, William C. (equestrian); Cleveland, 10/12/25
Stenerud, Jan (football); Fetsund, Norway, 11/26/42
Stengel, Casey (Charles Dillon) (baseball); Kansas City, Mo. **(1891–1975)**
Stenmark, Ingemar (Alpine skier); Tarnaby, Sweden, 3/18/56
Stevens, Scott (hockey); Completon, New Brunswick, 5/4/66
Stockton, Richard LaClede (tennis); New York City, 2/18/51
Stones, Dwight Edwin (track); Los Angeles, 12/6/53
Strawberry, Darryl (baseball); Los Angeles, 3/12/62
Street, Picabo (skiing); Triumph, Idaho, 4/3/71
Sullivan, John Lawrence (boxing); Boston **(1858–1918)**
Summitt, Pat (basketball); Henrietta, Tenn., 6/14/52
Sutton, Don (Donald Howard) (baseball); Clio, Ala., 4/2/45
Swann, Lynn (football); Alcoa, Tenn., 3/7/52
Swoopes, Sheryl (basketball); Brownfield, Tex., 3/25/71
Tanner, Leonard Roscoe III (tennis); Chattanooga, Tenn., 10/15/51
Tarkenton, Fran (Francis) (football); Richmond, Va., 2/3/40
Tebbetts, Birdie (George R.) (baseball); Nashua, N.H., 11/10/14
Theismann, Joe (football); New Brunswick, N.J., 9/9/46
Thomas, Frank (baseball); Columbus, Ga., 5/27/68
Thomas, Isiah (basketball); Chicago, Ill., 4/30/61
Thomas, Thurman (football); Houston, Texas, 5/16/66
Thompson, David (basketball); Shelby, N.C., 7/13/54
Thorpe, Jim (James Francis) (all-around athlete); nr. Prague, Okla. **(1888–1953)**
Tilden, William Tatem II (tennis); Philadelphia **(1893–1953)**
Tittle, Y. A. (Yelberton Abraham) (football); Marshall, Tex., 10/24/26
Toomey, William (decathlon); Philadelphia, 1/10/39
Trevino, Lee (golf); Dallas, 12/1/39
Trottier, Bryan (hockey); Val Marie, Sask., Canada, 7/17/56
Tunney, Gene (James J.) (boxing); New York City **(1898–1978)**
Tyson, Mike (boxing); Brooklyn, N.Y., 6/30/66
Tyus, Wyomia (runner); Griffin, Ga., 8/29/45
Ueberroth, Peter (baseball); Evanston, Ill., 9/2/37
Unitas, John (football); Pittsburgh, 5/7/33
Unser, Al (auto racing); Albuquerque, N. Mex., 5/29/39
Unser, Bobby (auto racing); Albuquerque, N. Mex., 2/20/34
Valenzuela, Fernando (baseball); Sonora, Mexico, 11/1/60
Valvano, Jim (basketball); New York, N.Y. **(1946–1993)**
Van Brocklin, Norm (football); Eagle Butte, S. Dak. **(1926–1983)**
Vaughn, Mo (baseball); Norwalk, Conn., 12/15/67
Vilas, Guillermo (tennis); Mar del Plata, Argentina, 8/17/52
Viola, Frank (baseball); Hempstead, N.Y., 4/19/60
Viren, Lasse (track); Myrskyla, Finland, 7/12/49
Vitale, Dick (basketball); E. Rutherford, N.J., 6/9/39
Wade, Virginia (tennis); Bournemouth, England, 7/10/45
Wagner, Honus (John Peter Honus) (baseball); Carnegie, Pa. **(1867–1955)**
Waitz, Grete (Andersen) (running); Oslo, Norway, 10/1/53
Walcott, Jersey Joe (Arnold Cream) (boxing); Merchantville, N.J. **(1914–1994)**
Wallace, Rusty (auto racing); St. Louis, Mo., 8/14/56
Walsh, Adam (football) **(1902–1985)**
Walton, Bill (basketball); La Mesa, Calif., 11/5/52
Waterfield, Bob (football); Burbank, Calif **(1921–1983)**
Watson, Martha Rae (track); Long Beach, Calif., 8/19/46
Watson, Tom (golf); Kansas City, Mo., 9/4/49
Weaver, Earl (baseball); St. Louis, 8/14/30
Weiskopf, Tom (golf); Massillon, Ohio, 11/9/42
Weiss, George (baseball executive); New Haven, Conn. **(1895–1972)**
Weissmuller, Johnny (swimmer and actor); Windber, Pa. **(1904–1984)**
West, Jerry (basketball); Cheylan, W. Va., 5/28/38
White, Reggie (football); Chattanooga, Tenn., 12/19/61
White, Willye B. (long jumper); Money, Miss., 1/1/36
Whitworth, Kathy (golf); Monahans, Tex., 9/27/39
Wilkens, Mac Maurice (track); Eugene, Ore., 11/15/50
Wilkins, Lennie (basketball) 11/25/37
Wilkinson, Bud (football); Minneapolis, 4/23/16
Williams, Dick (baseball); St. Louis, 5/7/29
Williams, Ted (baseball); San Diego, Calif., 8/30/18
Wills, Maury (baseball); Washington, D.C., 10/2/32
Winfield, Dave (baseball); St. Paul, Minn., 10/3/51
Wohlhuter, Richard C. (runner); Geneva, Ill., 12/23/45
Wood, "Smokey Joe" (Joseph) (baseball); Kansas City, Mo. **(1890–1985)**
Woods, Tiger (Eldrick) (golf); Long Beach, Calif.,, 12/30/75
Wottle, David James (runner); Canton, Ohio, 8/7/50
Wright, Mickey (Mary Kathryn) (golf); San Diego, Calif., 2/14/35
Yarborough, Cale (William Caleb) (auto racing); Timmonsville, S.C., 3/27/39
Yastrzemski, Carl (baseball); Southampton, N.Y., 8/22/39
Young, Cy (Denton True) (baseball); Gilmore, Ohio **(1867–1955)**
Young, Sheila (speed skater, bicycle racer); Detroit, 10/14/50
Young, Steve (football); Salt Lake City, Utah, 10/11/61
Zaharias, Babe Didrikson (golf); Port Arthur, Tex. **(1913–1956)**

Basketball

Basketball may be the one sport whose exact origin is definitely known. In the winter of 1891–92, Dr. James Naismith, an instructor in the Y.M.C.A. Training College (now Springfield College) at Springfield, Mass., deliberately invented the game of basketball in order to provide indoor exercise and competition for the students between the closing of the football season and the opening of the baseball season. He affixed peach baskets overhead on the walls at opposite ends of the gymnasium and organized teams to play his new game in which the purpose was to toss an association (soccer) ball into one basket and prevent the opponents from tossing the ball into the other basket. The game is fundamentally the same today, though there have been improvements in equipment and some changes in rules.

Because Dr. Naismith had eighteen available players when he invented the game, the first rule was: "There shall be nine players on each side." Later the number of players became optional, depending upon the size of the available court, but the five-player standard was adopted when the game spread over the country. United States soldiers brought basketball to Europe in World War I, and it soon became a world-wide sport.

College Basketball

NATIONAL COLLEGIATE A.A. CHAMPIONS

1938 Temple
1939 Oregon
1940 Indiana & USC
1941 Wisconsin
1942 Stanford
1943 Wyoming
1944 Utah
1945 Oklahoma A & M
1946 Oklahoma A & M
1947 Holy Cross
1948 Kentucky
1949 Kentucky
1950 C.C.N.Y.
1951 Kentucky
1952 Kansas
1953 Indiana
1954 La Salle
1955 San Francisco
1956 San Francisco
1957 North Carolina
1958 Kentucky
1959 California
1960 Ohio State
1961 Cincinnati
1962 Cincinnati
1963 Loyola (Chicago)
1964 UCLA
1965 UCLA
1966 Texas Western
1967–73 UCLA
1974 No. Carolina State
1975 UCLA
1976 Indiana
1977 Marquette
1978 Kentucky
1979 Michigan State
1980 Louisville
1981 Indiana
1982 North Carolina
1983 North Carolina State
1984 Georgetown
1985 Villanova
1986 Louisville
1987 Indiana
1988 Kansas
1989 Michigan
1990 Nevada-Las Vegas
1991 Duke
1992 Duke
1993 North Carolina
1994 Arkansas
1995 UCLA
1996 Kentucky
1997 Arizona
1998 Kentucky

NATIONAL INVITATION TOURNAMENT (NIT) CHAMPIONS

1939 Long Island U.
1940 Colorado
1941 Long Island U.
1942 West Virginia
1943–44 St. John's (N.Y.C.)
1945 DePaul
1946 Kentucky
1947 Utah
1948 St. Louis
1949 San Francisco
1950 C.C.N.Y.
1951 Brigham Young
1952 La Salle
1953 Seton Hall
1954 Holy Cross
1955 Duquesne
1956 Louisville
1957 Bradley
1958 Xavier (Cincinnati)
1959 St. John's (N.Y.C.)
1960 Bradley
1961 Providence
1962 Dayton
1963 Providence
1964 Bradley
1965 St. John's (N.Y.C.)
1966 Brigham Young
1967 So. Illinois
1968 Dayton
1969 Temple
1970 Marquette
1971 North Carolina
1972 Maryland
1973 Virginia Tech
1974 Purdue
1975 Princeton
1976 Kentucky
1977 St. Bonaventure
1978 Texas
1979 Indiana
1980 Virginia
1981 Tulsa
1982 Bradley
1983 Fresno State
1984 Michigan
1985 UCLA
1986 Ohio State
1987 So. Mississippi
1988 Connecticut
1989 St. John's
1990 Vanderbilt
1991 Stanford
1992 Virginia
1993 Minnesota
1994 Villanova
1995 Virginia Tech
1996 Nebraska
1997 Michigan
1998 Minnesota

N.C.A.A. DIVISION I INDIVIDUAL SCORING RECORDS

Points	Yrs	Last	Gm	Pts
Pete Maravich, LSU	3	1970	83	3,667
Freeman Williams, Port. St.	4	1978	106	3,249
Lionel Simmons, La Salle	4	1990	131	3,217
Alphonzo Ford, Miss. Val. St.	4	1993	109	3,165
Harry Kelly, Texas-Southern	4	1983	110	3,066
Hersey Hawkins, Bradley	4	1988	125	3,008
Oscar Robertson, Cincinnati	3	1960	88	2,973
Danny Manning, Kansas	4	1988	147	2,951
Alfredrick Hughes, Loyola-Ill.	4	1985	120	2,914
Elvin Hayes, Houston	3	1968	93	2,884

Average	Yrs	Last	Pts	Avg
Pete Maravich, LSU	3	1970	3,667	44.2
Austin Carr, Notre Dame	3	1971	2,560	34.6
Oscar Robertson, Cincinnati	3	1960	2,973	33.8
Calvin Murphy, Niagara	3	1970	2,548	33.1
Dwight Lamar, SW La.	2	1973	1,862	32.7
Frank Selvy, Furman	3	1954	2,538	32.5
Rick Mount, Purdue	3	1970	2,323	32.3
Darrell Floyd, Furman	3	1956	2,281	32.1
Nick Werkman, Seton Hall	3	1964	2,273	32.0
Willie Humes, Idaho St.	2	1971	1,510	31.5

N.C.A.A. DIVISION I INDIVIDUAL REBOUND RECORDS

Before 1973

Total	Yrs	Last	Gm	No
Tom Gola, La Salle	4	1955	118	2,201
Joe Holup, G. Washington	4	1956	104	2,030
Charlie Slack, Marshall	4	1956	88	1,916
Ed Conlin, Fordham	4	1955	102	1,884
Dickie Hemric, Wake Forest	4	1955	104	1,802
Paul Silas, Creighton	3	1964	81	1,751
Art Quimby, Connecticut	4	1955	80	1,716
Jerry Harper, Alabama	4	1956	93	1,688
Jeff Cohen, Wm. & Mary	4	1961	103	1,679
Steve Hamilton, Morehead St.	4	1958	102	1,675

Since 1973

Total	Yrs	Last	Gm	No
Tim Duncan, Wake Forest	4	1997	128	1,570
Derrick Coleman, Syracuse	4	1990	143	1,537
Ralph Sampson, Virginia	4	1983	132	1,511
Pete Padgett, Nevada-Reno	4	1976	104	1,464
Lionel Simmons, La Salle	4	1990	131	1,429
Anthony Bonner, St. Louis	4	1990	133	1,424
Tyrone Hill, Xavier (Ohio)	4	1990	126	1,380
Popeye Jones, Murray St.	4	1992	123	1,374
Michael Brooks, La Salle	4	1980	114	1,372
Xavier McDaniel, Wichita St.	4	1985	117	1,359

N.C.A.A. INDIVIDUAL ASSISTS RECORDS

Total	Yrs	Last	Gm	No
Bobby Hurley, Duke	4	1993	140	1,076
Chris Corchiani, N.C. State	4	1991	124	1,038
Keith Jennings, E. Tenn. St.	4	1991	127	983
Sherman Douglas, Syracuse	4	1989	138	960
Tony Miller, Marquette	4	1995	123	956
Greg Anthony, Portland/UNLV	4	1991	138	950
Gary Payton, Oregon St.	4	1990	120	938
Orlando Smart, San Fran	4	1994	116	902
Andre LaFleur, N'eastern	4	1987	128	894
Jim Les, Bradley	4	1986	118	884

Average	Yrs	Last	No	Avg
A. Johnson,Cameron/Southern	3	1988	838	8.91
Sam Crawford, N. Mexico St.	2	1993	592	8.84
Mark Wade, Okla/UNLV	3	1987	693	8.77
Chris Corchiani, N.C.State	4	1991	1,038	8.37
Taurence Chisholm, Delaware	4	1988	877	7.97
Van Usher, Tennessee Tech	3	1992	676	7.95
Anthony Manuel, Bradley	3	1989	855	7.92
Gary Payton, Oregon St.	4	1990	938	7.82
Orlando Smart, San Fran	4	1994	902	7.78
Tony Miller, Marquette	4	1995	956	7.77

Note: minimum 550 assists.

TOP SINGLE-GAME SCORING MARKS

Player, Team (Opponent)	Yr	Pts
Selvy, Furman (Newberry)	1954	100[1]
Arizin, Villanova (Phi. NAMC)	1949	85
Williams, Portland State (Rocky Mtn.)	1978	81
Mlkvy, Temple (Wilkes)	1951	73
Bradshaw, U.S. International (Loyola-CA)	1991	72
Williams, Portland State (So. Oregon)	1977	71
Maravich, LSU (Alabama)	1970	69
Murphy, Niagara (Syracuse)	1969	68
Floyd, Furman (Morehead)	1955	67
Maravich, LSU (Tulane)	1969	66
Handlan, W & L (Furman)	1951	66
Roberts, Oral Roberts (N.C. A&T)	1977	66

1. Record.

MEN'S N.C.A.A. BASKETBALL CHAMPIONSHIPS—1998

Division I

First Round—East

North Carolina 88, Navy 52
UNC–Charlotte 77, Illinois–Chicago 62
Princeton 69, UNLV 57
Michigan St. 83, Eastern Michigan 71
Washington 69, Xavier 68
Richmond 62, South Carolina 61
Indiana 94, Oklahoma 87 (OT)
Connecticut 93, Fairleigh Dickinson 85

First Round—West

Arizona 99, Nicholls St. 60
Illinois St. 82, Tennessee 81 (OT)
Illinois 64, South Alabama 51
Maryland 82, Utah State 68
Arkansas 74, Nebraska 65
Utah 85, San Francisco 68
West Virginia 82, Temple 52
Cincinnati 65, Northern Arizona 62

First Round—Midwest

Kansas 110, Prairie View A&M 52
Rhode Island 97, Murray State 74
Florida State 96, TCU 87
Valparaiso 70, Mississippi 69
Western Michigan 75, Clemson 72
Stanford 67, Charleston 57
Detroit 66, St. John's 64
Purdue 95, Delaware 56

First Round—South

Duke 99, Radford 63
Oklahoma St. 74, George Washington 59
Syracuse 63, Iona 61
New Mexico 79, Butler 62
UCLA 65, Miami (Fla.) 62
Michigan 80, Davidson 61
Saint Louis 51, Massachusetts 46
Kentucky 82, S. Carolina St. 67

Second Round—East

North Carolina 93, UNC–Charlotte 83 (OT)
Michigan State 63, Princeton 56
Washington 81, Richmond 66
Connecticut 78, Indiana 68

Second Round—West

Arizona 82, Illinois State 49
Maryland 67, Illinois 61
Utah 75, Arkansas 69
West Virginia 75, Cincinnati 74

Second Round—Midwest

Rhode Island 80, Kansas 75
Valparaiso 83, Florida State 77
Stanford 83, Western Michigan 65
Purdue 80, Detroit 65

Second Round—South

Duke 79, Oklahoma State 73
Syracuse 56, New Mexico 46
UCLA 85, Michigan 82
Kentucky 88, Saint Louis 61

Third Round—East

North Carolina 73, Michigan State 58
Connecticut 75, Washington 74

Third Round—West

Arizona 87, Maryland 79
Utah 65, West Virginia 62

Third Round—Midwest

Rhode Island 74, Valparaiso 67
Stanford 67, Purdue 59

Third Round—South

Duke 80, Syracuse 67
Kentucky 94, UCLA 68

Regional Finals

East—North Carolina 75, Connecticut 64
West—Utah 76, Arizona 51
Midwest—Stanford 79, Rhode Island 77
West—Kentucky 86, Duke 84

National Semifinals

March 28, 1998, San Antonio, Texas
Utah 65, North Carolina 59
Kentucky 86, Stanford 85 (OT)

National Final

March 30, 1998, San Antonio, Texas
Kentucky 78, Utah 69

Division II

Semifinals

UC Davis 88, St. Rose, N.Y. 76
Kentucky Wesleyan 80, Virginia Union 72

Championship

UC Davis 83, Kentucky Wesleyan 77

WOMEN'S N.C.A.A. CHAMPIONSHIPS—1998

Division I

First Round—East
Old Dominion 92, St. Francis (Pa.) 39
Nebraska 79, New Mexico 59
Youngstown St. 91, Memphis 80
NC State 89, Maine 64
Virginia 77, SMU 68
Arizona 75, Santa Clara 63
George Washington 74, Georgia 72
UConn 93, Fairfield 52

First Round—Mideast
Tennessee 102, Liberty 58
W. Kentucky 88, S.F. Austin 76
Rutgers 79, Oregon 76
Iowa St. 79, Kent 76
UC–Santa Barbara 76, Vanderbilt 71
Illinois 82, Wis.–Green Bay 58
Fla. International 59, Marquette 45
North Carolina 91, Howard 71

First Round—Midwest
Texas Tech 87, Grambling 75
Notre Dame 78, SW Missouri St. 64
Colorado St. 85, Drake 81
Purdue 88, Washington 71
Clemson 60, Miami, Fla. 49
Louisiana Tech 86, Holy Cross 85
UCLA 65, Michigan 58
Alabama 94, NC–Greensboro 46

First Round—West
Harvard 71, Stanford 67
Arkansas 76, Hawaii 70
Kansas 72, Tulane 68
Iowa 77, UMass 59
Virginia Tech 75, Wisconsin 64
Florida 85, Montana 64
Louisville 69, Utah 61
Duke 92, Middle Tenn. St. 67

Second Round—East
Old Dominion 75, Nebraska 60
NC State 88, Youngstown St. 61
Arizona 94, Virginia 77
UConn 75, George Washington 67

Second Round—Mideast
Tennessee 82, W. Kentucky 62
Rutgers 62, Iowa St. 61
Illinois 69, Santa Barbara 65
North Carolina 85, Fla. International 72

Second Round—Midwest
Notre Dame 74, Texas Tech 59
Purdue 77, Colorado St. 63
Louisiana Tech 74, Clemson 52
Alabama 75, UCLA 74

Second Round—West
Arkansas 82, Harvard 64
Kansas 62, Iowa 58
Florida 89, Virginia Tech 57
Duke 69, Louisville 53

Third Round—East
NC State 55, Old Dominion 54
UConn 74, Arizona 57

Third Round—Mideast
Tennessee 92, Rutgers 60
North Carolina 80, Illinois 74

Third Round—Midwest
Purdue 70, Notre Dame 65
Louisiana Tech 71, Alabama 57

Third Round—West
Arkansas 79, Kansas 63
Duke 71, Florida 58

Regional Finals
East—NC State 60, UConn 52
Mideast—Tennessee 76, North Carolina 70
Midwest—Louisiana Tech 72, Purdue 65
West—Arkansas 77, Duke 72

National Semifinals
March 27, 1998, Kansas City, Mo.
Louisiana Tech 84, NC State 65
Tennessee 86, Arkansas 58

National Championship
March 29, 1998, Kansas City, Mo.
Tennessee 93, Louisiana Tech 75

Division II

Semifinals
North Dakota 79, Northern Michigan 69
Emporia St. 90, Francis Marion 75

Championship
North Dakota 92, Emporia St. 76

LEADING N.C.A.A. DIVISION I MEN—1997–1998

Scoring

	Gm	Pts	Avg
Charles Jones, LIU Brooklyn	29	824	28.4
Earl Boykins, Eastern Mich.	28	728	26.0
Lee Nailon, TCU	31	764	24.7
Brett Eppehimer, Lehigh	27	665	24.6
Wally Szczerbiak, Miami (Ohio)	21	512	24.4
Bonzi Wells, Ball St.	28	653	23.3
Cory Carr, Texas Tech	27	628	23.3
Pat Garrity, Notre Dame	27	627	23.2
Mike Powell, Loyola (Md.)	28	647	23.1
Antawn Jamison, North Carolina	32	732	22.9

Rebounding

	Gm	No	Avg
Ryan Perryman, Dayton	31	373	12.0
Eric Taylor, St. Francis (Pa.)	27	321	11.9
Raef Lafrentz, Kansas	28	313	11.2
Tremaine Fowlkes, Fresno St.	27	301	11.2
TJ Lux, Northern Ill.	26	289	11.1
Michael Olowokandi, Pacific	32	352	11.0
Rashon Turner, Fairleigh Dickinson	28	308	11.0
Thad Burton, Wright St.	28	305	10.9
Allen Ledbetter, Maine	27	294	10.9
Kenyon Ross, Mississippi Valley St.	27	292	10.8

Assists

	Gm	No	Avg
Ahlon Lewis, Arizona St.	31	288	9.3
Chico Fletcher, Arkansas St.	29	240	8.3
Sean Colson, NC–Charlotte	27	205	7.6
Mateen Cleaves, Michigan St.	27	204	7.6
Ed Cota, North Carolina	32	239	7.5
Charles Jones, LIU Brooklyn	29	216	7.5
Rafer Alston, Fresno St.	28	207	7.4
Anthony Carter, Hawaii	26	192	7.4
Kenny Brunner, Georgetown	19	139	7.3
Craig Claxton, Hofstra	31	224	7.2

LEADING N.C.A.A. DIVISION I WOMEN—1997–1998

Scoring

	Gm	Pts	Avg
Allison Feaster, Harvard	26	734	28.2
Cindy Blodgett, Maine	25	685	27.4
Korie Hlede, Duquesne	28	758	27.1
Amy O'Brien, Holy Cross	29	763	26.3
Tamika Whitmore, Memphis	27	690	25.6
Karalyn Church, Vermont	29	712	24.6
Becky Hammon, Colorado St.	28	648	23.1
Chamique Holdsclaw, Tennessee	33	757	22.9
Marlene Stollings, Ohio	28	642	22.9
Alicia Thompson, Texas Tech	29	663	22.9

Rebounding

	Gm	No	Avg
Murriel Page, Florida	29	378	13.0
Alisha Hill, Howard	29	372	12.8
Jessica Zinobile, St. Francis (Pa.)	29	354	12.2
Leticia Oseguera, UC–Irvine	22	262	11.9
Nyree Roberts, Old Dominion	29	345	11.9
Mfon Udoka, DePaul	24	281	11.7
Amy O'Brien, Holy Cross	29	337	11.6
Elise James, Robert Morris	26	291	11.2
Felicia Tarver, Prairie View	27	300	11.1
Kristina Behnfeldt, Marshall	29	322	11.1

Assists

	Gm	No	Avg
Dalma Ivanyi, Florida Int'l	29	280	9.7
Alli Bills, Utah	26	205	7.9
Nicki Taggart, Marquette	28	213	7.6
Gina Graziani, Miami (Fla.)	28	207	7.4
Ticha Penicheiro, Old Dominion	29	211	7.3
Joyce Howard, Texas–San Antonio	28	201	7.2
Lisa Witherspoon, Virginia Tech	29	206	7.1
Keisha Cox, Drake	29	203	7.0
Tori Boudreaux, NE Ill.	26	181	7.0
Amber DeWall, Northwestern	30	205	6.8

OTHER TOURNAMENTS—1997–1998

MEN

NIT—Minnesota 79, Penn State 72

NAIA Div. I—Georgetown (Ky.) 83, Southern Nazarene (Okla.) 69

NAIA Div. II—Bethel College (Ind.) 89, Oregon Institute of Technology 87

WOMEN

NIT—Penn State 59, Baylor 56

NAIA Div. I—Union University (Tennessee) 73, Southern Nazarene (Okla.) 70

NAIA Div. II—Walsh University (Ohio) 73, University of Mary Hardin-Baylor (Texas) 66

Professional Basketball

NATIONAL BASKETBALL ASSOCIATION CHAMPIONS

The National Basketball Association was originally the Basketball Association of America. It took its current name in 1949 when it merged with the National Basketball League. The following table lists the teams with the most wins in the conference. Playoff champions may have been wild card teams.

Season	Eastern Conference (W-L)	Western Conference (W-L)	Playoff Champions[1]
1946–47	Washington Capitols (49-11)	Chicago Stags (39-22)	Philadelphia Warriors
1947–48	Philadelphia Warriors (27-21)	St. Louis Bombers (29-19)	Baltimore Bullets
1948–49	Washington Capitols (38-22)	Rochester Royals (45-15)	Minneapolis Lakers
1949–50	Syracuse Nationals (51-13)	Indianapolis Olympians (39-25)	Minneapolis Lakers
1950–51	Philadelphia Warriors (40-26)	Minneapolis Lakers (44-24)	Rochester Royals
1951–52	Syracuse Nationals (40-26)	Rochester Royals (41-25)	Minneapolis Lakers
1952–53	New York Knickerbockers (47-23)	Minneapolis Lakers (48-22)	Minneapolis Lakers
1953–54	New York Knickerbockers (44-28)	Minneapolis Lakers (46-26)	Minneapolis Lakers
1954–55	Syracuse Nationals (43-29)	Ft. Wayne Pistons (43-29)	Syracuse Nationals
1955–56	Philadelphia Warriors (45-27)	Ft. Wayne Pistons (37-35)	Philadelphia Warriors
1956–57	Boston Celtics (44-28)	St. Louis Hawks (38-34)	Boston Celtics
1957–58	Boston Celtics (48-23)	St. Louis Hawks (41-31)	St. Louis Hawks
1958–59	Boston Celtics (52-20)	St. Louis Hawks (49-23)	Boston Celtics
1959–60	Boston Celtics (59-16)	St. Louis Hawks (46-29)	Boston Celtics
1960–61	Boston Celtics (57-22)	St. Louis Hawks (51-28)	Boston Celtics
1961–62	Boston Celtics (60-20)	Los Angeles Lakers (54-26)	Boston Celtics
1962–63	Boston Celtics (58-22)	Los Angeles Lakers (53-27)	Boston Celtics
1963–64	Boston Celtics (59-21)	San Francisco Warriors (48-32)	Boston Celtics
1964–65	Boston Celtics (62-18)	Los Angeles Lakers (49-31)	Boston Celtics
1965–66	Philadelphia 76ers (55-25)	Los Angeles Lakers (45-35)	Boston Celtics
1966–67	Philadelphia 76ers (68-13)	San Francisco Warriors (44-37)	Philadelphia 76ers
1967–68	Philadelphia 76ers (62-20)	St. Louis Hawks (56-26)	Boston Celtics
1968–69	Baltimore Bullets (57-25)	Los Angeles Lakers (55-27)	Boston Celtics
1969–70	New York Knickerbockers (60-22)	Atlanta Hawks (48-34)	New York Knicks
1970–71	Baltimore Bullets (42-40)	Milwaukee Bucks (66-16)	Milwaukee Bucks
1971–72	New York Knickerbockers (48-34)	Los Angeles Lakers (69-13)	Los Angeles Lakers
1972–73	New York Knickerbockers (57-25)	Los Angeles Lakers (60-22)	New York Knicks
1973–74	Boston Celtics (56-26)	Milwaukee Bucks (59-23)	Boston Celtics
1974–75	Washington Bullets (60-22)	Golden State Warriors (48-34)	Golden State Warriors
1975–76	Boston Celtics (54-28)	Phoenix Suns (42-40)	Boston Celtics
1976–77	Philadelphia 76ers (50-32)	Portland Trail Blazers (49-33)	Portland Trail Blazers
1977–78	Washington Bullets (44-38)	Seattle Super Sonics (47-35)	Washington Bullets
1978–79	Washington Bullets (54-28)	Seattle Super Sonics (52-30)	Seattle Super Sonics
1979–80	Philadelphia 76ers (59-23)	Los Angeles Lakers (60-22)	Los Angeles Lakers
1980–81	Boston Celtics (62-20)	Houston Rockets (40-42)	Boston Celtics
1981–82	Philadelphia 76ers (58-24)	Los Angeles Lakers (57-25)	Los Angeles Lakers
1982–83	Philadelphia 76ers (65-17)	Los Angeles Lakers (58-24)	Philadelphia 76ers
1983–84	Boston Celtics (56-26)	Los Angeles Lakers (58-24)	Boston Celtics
1984–85	Boston Celtics (63-19)	Los Angeles Lakers (62-20)	Los Angeles Lakers
1985–86	Boston Celtics (67-15)	Houston Rockets (51-31)	Boston Celtics
1986–87	Boston Celtics (59-23)	Los Angeles Lakers (65-17)	Los Angeles Lakers
1987–88	Detroit Pistons (54-28)	Los Angeles Lakers (62-20)	Los Angeles Lakers
1988–89	Detroit Pistons (63-18)	Los Angeles Lakers (57-25)	Detroit Pistons
1989–90	Detroit Pistons (59-23)	Portland Trail Blazers (59-23)	Detroit Pistons
1990–91	Chicago Bulls (61-21)	Los Angeles Lakers (58-24)	Chicago Bulls
1991–92	Chicago Bulls (67-15)	Portland Trail Blazers (57-25)	Chicago Bulls

Season	Eastern Conference (W-L)	Western Conference (W-L)	Playoff Champions[1]
1992–93	Chicago Bulls (57-25)	Phoenix Suns (62-20)	Chicago Bulls
1993–94	New York Knicks (57-25)	Houston Rockets (58-24)	Houston Rockets
1994–95	Orlando Magic (57-25)	Houston Rockets (47-35)	Houston Rockets
1995–96	Chicago Bulls (72-10)	Seattle SuperSonics (64-18)	Chicago Bulls
1996–97	Chicago Bulls (69-13)	Utah Jazz (64-18)	Chicago Bulls
1997-98	Chicago Bulls (62-20)	Utah Jazz (62-20)	Chicago Bulls

1. Playoffs may involve teams other than conference winners.

INDIVIDUAL N.B.A. SCORING CHAMPIONS

Season	Player, Team	G	FG	FT	Pts	Avg
1953–54	Neil Johnston, Philadelphia Warriors	72	591	577	1,759	24.4
1954–55	Neil Johnston, Philadelphia Warriors	72	521	589	1,631	22.7
1955–56	Bob Pettit, St. Louis Hawks	72	646	557	1,849	25.7
1956–57	Paul Arizin, Philadelphia Warriors	71	613	591	1,817	25.6
1957–58	George Yardley, Detroit Pistons	72	673	655	2,001	27.8
1958–59	Bob Pettit, St. Louis Hawks	72	719	667	2,105	29.2
1959–60	Wilt Chamberlain, Philadelphia Warriors	72	1,065	577	2,707	37.6
1960–61	Wilt Chamberlain, Philadelphia Warriors	79	1,251	531	3,033	38.4
1961–62	Wilt Chamberlain, Philadelphia Warriors	80	1,597	835	4,029	50.4
1962–63	Wilt Chamberlain, San Francisco Warriors	80	1,463	660	3,586	44.8
1963–64	Wilt Chamberlain, San Francisco Warriors	80	1,204	540	2,948	36.9
1964–65	Wilt Chamberlain, San Francisco Warriors-Phila. 76ers	73	1,063	408	2,534	34.7
1965–66	Wilt Chamberlain, Philadelphia 76ers	79	1,074	501	2,649	33.5
1966–67	Rick Barry, San Francisco Warriors	78	1,011	753	2,775	35.6
1967–68	Dave Bing, Detroit Pistons	79	835	472	2,142	27.1
1968–69	Elvin Hayes, San Diego Rockets	82	930	467	2,327	28.4
1969–70	Jerry West, Los Angeles Lakers	74	831	647	2,309	31.2
1970–71	Lew Alcindor,[1] Milwaukee Bucks	82	1,063	470	2,596	31.7
1971–72	Kareem Abdul-Jabbar, Milwaukee Bucks	81	1,159	504	2,822	34.8
1972–73	Nate Archibald, Kansas City-Omaha Kings	80	1,028	663	2,719	34.0
1973–74	Bob McAdoo, Buffalo Braves	74	901	459	2,261	30.8
1974–75	Bob McAdoo, Buffalo Braves	82	1,095	641	2,831	34.5
1975–76	Bob McAdoo, Buffalo Braves	78	934	559	2,427	31.1
1976–77	Pete Maravich, New Orleans Jazz	73	886	501	2,273	31.1
1977–78	George Gervin, San Antonio Spurs	82	864	504	2,232	27.2
1978–79	George Gervin, San Antonio Spurs	80	947	471	2,365	29.6
1979–80	George Gervin, San Antonio Spurs	78	1,024	505	2,585	33.1
1980–81	Adrian Dantley, Utah Jazz	80	909	632	2,452	30.7
1981–82	George Gervin, San Antonio Spurs	79	993	555	2,551	32.3
1982–83	Alex English, Denver Nuggets	82	959	406	2,326	28.4
1983–84	Adrian Dantley, Utah Jazz	79	802	813	2,418	30.6
1984–85	Bernard King, New York Knicks	55	691	426	1,809	32.9
1985–86	Dominique Wilkins, Atlanta Hawks	78	888	527	2,366	30.3
1986–87	Michael Jordan, Chicago Bulls[2]	82	1,098	833	3,041	37.1
1987–88	Michael Jordan, Chicago Bulls[3]	82	1,069	723	2,868	35.0
1988–89	Michael Jordan, Chicago Bulls[4]	81	966	674	2,633	32.5
1989–90	Michael Jordan, Chicago Bulls[5]	82	1,034	593	2,753	33.6
1990–91	Michael Jordan, Chicago Bulls[6]	82	990	571	2,580	31.5
1991–92	Michael Jordan, Chicago Bulls[7]	80	943	491	2,404	30.1
1992–93	Michael Jordan, Chicago Bulls[8]	78	992	476	2,541	32.6
1993–94	David Robinson, San Antonio Spurs[9]	80	840	693	2,383	29.8
1994–95	Shaquille O'Neal, Orlando Magic[10]	79	930	455	2,315	29.3
1995–96	Michael Jordan, Chicago Bulls[11]	82	916	548	2,491	30.4
1996–97	Michael Jordan, Chicago Bulls[11]	82	920	480	2,431	29.6
1997-98	Michael Jordan, Chicago Bulls [12]	82	881	565	2,357	28.7

1. (Kareem Abdul-Jabbar). 2. Also had 12 3-point field goals. 3. Also had 7 3-point field goals. 4. Also had 27 3-point field goals. 5. Also had 92 3-point field goals. 6. Also had 29 3-point field goals. 7. Attempted 27 3-point field goals in 1991–1992. 8. Also had 81 3-point field goals. 9. Also had 10 3-point field goals. 10. O'Neal scored no 3-point field goals in 1994–1995. 11. Also had 111 3-point field goals in both 1995–96 and 1996–97 12. Also had 30 3-point field goals in 1997–98

N.B.A. MOST VALUABLE PLAYERS

1956 Bob Pettit, St. Louis
1957 Bob Cousy, Boston
1958 Bill Russell, Boston
1959 Bob Pettit, St. Louis
1960 Wilt Chamberlain, Philadelphia
1961–63 Bill Russell, Boston
1964 Oscar Robertson, Cincinnati
1965 Bill Russell, Boston
1966–68 Wilt Chamberlain, Philadelphia
1969 Wes Unseld, Baltimore
1970 Willis Reed, New York
1971–72 Lew Alcindor (Kareem Abdul-Jabbar), Milwaukee
1973 Dave Cowens, Boston
1974 Kareem Abdul-Jabbar, Milwaukee
1975 Bob McAdoo, Buffalo
1976–77 Kareem Abdul-Jabbar, Los Angeles
1978 Bill Walton, Portland
1979 Moses Malone, Houston
1980 Kareem Abdul-Jabbar, Los Angeles
1981 Julius Erving, Philadelphia
1982 Moses Malone, Houston

1983 Moses Malone, Philadelphia
1984 Larry Bird, Boston
1985 Larry Bird, Boston
1986 Larry Bird, Boston
1987 Earvin Johnson, Los Angeles
1988 Michael Jordan, Chicago
1989 Earvin Johnson, Los Angeles
1990 Earvin Johnson, Los Angeles
1991 Michael Jordan, Chicago
1992 Michael Jordan, Chicago
1993 Charles Barkley, Phoenix
1994 Hakeem Olajuwon, Houston
1995 David Robinson, San Antonio
1996 Michael Jordan, Chicago
1997 Karl Malone, Utah
1998 Michael Jordan, Chicago

N.B.A. LIFETIME LEADERS

(Through 1997–98 season)

NBA and ABA records combined

Most Games Played

Robert Parish	1,611	Paul Silas	1,254
Kareem Abdul-Jabbar	1,560	Alex English	1,193
Moses Malone	1,455	James Edwards	1,168
Buck Williams[1]	1,307	Tree Rollins	1,156
Elvin Hayes	1,303	Hal Greer	1,122
John Havlicek	1,270		

Free Throws

	FT	Att	Pct
Moses Malone	8,531	11,090	.769
Oscar Robertson	7,694	9,185	.838
Jerry West	7,160	8,801	.814
Karl Malone[1]	7,133	9,808	.727
Dolph Schayes	6,979	8,273	.844
Adrian Dantley	6,832	8,351	.818
Michael Jordan[1]	6,798	8,115	.838
Kareem Abdul-Jabbar	6,712	9,304	.721
Bob Pettit	6,182	8,119	.761
Charles Barkley[1]	6,086	8,266	.736

Blocked Shots

Hakeem Olajuwon[1]	3,458	Robert Parish	2,361
Kareem Abdul-Jabbar	3,189	David Robinson[1]	2,197
Mark Eaton	3,064	Manute Bol	2,086
Patrick Ewing[1]	2,574	George Johnson	2,082
Tree Rollins	2,543	Larry Nance	2,027

Field Goals

	FG	Att	Pct
Kareem Abdul-Jabbar	15,837	28,307	.559
Wilt Chamberlain	12,681	23,497	.540
Elvin Hayes	10,976	24,272	.452
Michael Jordan[1]	10,962	21,686	.505
Alex English	10,659	21,036	.507
John Havlicek	10,513	23,930	.439
Karl Malone[1]	10,290	19,504	.528
Dominique Wilkins	9,913	21,457	.462
Hakeem Olajuwon[1]	9,706	18,859	.515
Robert Parish	9,614	17,914	.537

1. Active going in 1997–98 season.

Scoring Average
Minimum of 400 games or 10,000 points.

	Gm	Pts	Avg
Michael Jordan[1]	930	29,277	31.5
Wilt Chamberlain	1,045	31,419	30.1
Elgin Baylor	846	23,149	27.4
Shaquille O'Neal[1]	406	11,054	27.2
Jerry West	932	25,192	27.0
Bob Pettit	792	20,880	26.4
Karl Malone[1]	1,061	27,782	26.2
George Gervin	791	20,708	26.2
Oscar Robertson	1,040	26,710	25.7
Dominique Wilkins	1,047	26,454	25.3

Steals

John Stockton[1]	2,620	Derek Harper[1]	1,914
Maurice Cheeks	2,310	Hakeem Olajuwon[1]	1,895
Michael Jordan[1]	2,304	Isiah Thomas	1,861
Clyde Drexler	2,203	Scottie Pippen[1]	1,771
Alvin Robertson	2,112	Earvin Johnson	1,724

Rebounds

Wilt Chamberlain	23,924	Robert Parish	14,715
Bill Russell	21,620	Nate Thurmond	14,464
Kareem Abdul-Jabbar	17,440	Walt Bellamy	14,241
Elvin Hayes	16,279	Wes Unseld	13,769
Moses Malone	16,212	Buck Williams[1]	13,023

Assists

John Stockton[1]	12,713	Maurice Cheeks	7,392
Earvin Johnson	10,141	Len Wilkens	7,215
Oscar Robertson	9,887	Bob Cousy	6,955
Isiah Thomas	9,061	Guy Rodgers	6,917
Mark Jackson[1]	7,534	Kevin Johnson[1]	6,687

Points

Kareem Abdul-Jabbar	38,387	Elvin Hayes	27,313
Wilt Chamberlain	31,419	Oscar Robertson	26,710
Michael Jordan[1]	29,277	Dominique Wilkins	26,534
Karl Malone[1]	27,782	John Havlicek	26,395
Moses Malone	27,409	Alex English	25,613

N.B.A. INDIVIDUAL RECORDS

(Through 1997–98 season)

Most points, game—100, Wilt Chamberlain, Philadelphia, 1962

Most points, quarter—33, George Gervin, San Antonio, 1978

Most points, half—59, Wilt Chamberlain, Philadelphia, 1962

Most free throws, game—28, Wilt Chamberlain, Philadelphia, 1962; 28, Adrian Dantley, Utah, 1984

Most free throws, quarter—14, Rick Barry, San Francisco, 1966; 14, Johnny Newman, Denver, 1998

Most free throws, half—20, Michael Jordan, Chicago, 1992

Most field goals, game—36, Wilt Chamberlain, Philadelphia, 1962

Most consecutive field goals, game—18, Wilt Chamberlain, San Francisco, 1963; Philadelphia, 1967

Most assists, game—30, Scott Skiles, Orlando vs. Denver, 1990

Most rebounds, game—55, Wilt Chamberlain, Philadelphia vs. Boston, 1960

Most 3-pt. field goals, game—11, Dennis Scott, Orlando vs. Atlanta, 1996

N.B.A. TEAM RECORDS

Most points, game—186, Detroit at Denver, 3 overtimes, 1983
Most points, quarter—58, Buffalo at. Boston, 1972
Most points, half—107, Phoenix vs. Denver, 1990
Most points, overtime period—22, Detroit vs. Cleveland, 1973
Most field goals, game—74, Detroit, 1983
Most field goals, quarter—24, Phoenix, 1990
Most field goals, half—43, Phoenix, 1990
Most assists, game—53, Milwaukee, 1978
Most rebounds, game—109, Boston, 1960
Most points, both teams, game—370 (Detroit 186, Denver 184) 3 overtimes, Denver, December 13, 1983
Most points, both teams, quarter—99 (San Antonio 53, Denver 46), 1984
Most points, both teams, half—174 (Phoenix 107, Denver 67), 1990
Longest winning streak—33, Los Angeles, 1971–72
Longest losing streak—24, Cleveland, Mar.–Nov. 1982
Longest winning streak at home—44, Chicago, Mar. 1995–April 1996
Most games won, season—72, Chicago, 1995–96
Most games lost, season—73, Philadelphia, 1972–73
Highest average points per game—126.5, Denver, 1981–82

NATIONAL BASKETBALL ASSOCIATION FINAL STANDINGS—1997–98

EASTERN CONFERENCE

Atlantic Division

	W	L	Pct	GB
*Miami	55	27	.671	—
xNew York	43	39	.524	12
xNew Jersey	43	39	.524	12
Washington	42	40	.512	13
Orlando	41	41	.500	14
Boston	36	46	.439	19
Philadelphia	31	51	.378	24

Central Division

	W	L	Pct	GB
*Chicago	62	20	.756	—
xIndiana	58	24	.707	4
xCharlotte	51	31	.622	11
xAtlanta	50	32	.610	12
xCleveland	47	35	.573	15
Detroit	37	45	.451	25
Milwaukee	36	46	.439	26
Toronto	16	66	.195	46

*Division champion. xPlayoff qualifier.

WESTERN CONFERENCE

Midwest Division

	W	L	Pct	GB
*Utah	62	20	.756	—
xSan Antonio	56	26	.683	6
xMinnesota	45	37	.549	17
xHouston	41	41	.500	21
Dallas	20	62	.244	42
Vancouver	19	63	.232	43
Denver	11	71	.134	51

Pacific Division

	W	L	Pct	GB
*Seattle	61	21	.744	—
xL.A. Lakers	61	21	.744	—
xPhoenix	56	26	.683	5
xPortland	46	36	.561	15
Sacramento	27	55	.329	34
Golden State	19	63	.232	42
L.A. Clippers	17	65	.207	44

N.B.A. PLAYOFFS—1998

(All caps denotes home team)

EASTERN CONFERENCE

First Round
(Best of 5)
Chicago defeated New Jersey, 3 games to 0
Indiana defeated Cleveland, 3 games to 1
New York defeated Miami, 3 games to 2
Charlotte defeated Atlanta, 3 games to 1

Second Round
(Best of 7)
Chicago defeated Charlotte, 4 games to 1
Indiana defeated New York, 4 games to 1

Conference Finals
(Best of 7)
Chicago defeated Indiana, 4 games to 3
May 17—CHICAGO 85, Indiana 79
May 19—CHICAGO 104, Indiana 98
May 23—INDIANA 107, Chicago 105
May 25—INDIANA 96, Chicago 94
May 27—CHICAGO 106, Indiana 87
May 29—INDIANA 92, Chicago 89
May 31—CHICAGO 88, Indiana 83

WESTERN CONFERENCE

First Round
(Best of 5)
Utah defeated Houston, 3 games to 2
Seattle defeated Minnesota, 3 games to 2
San Antonio defeated Phoenix, 3 games to 1
Los Angeles defeated Portland, 3 games to 1

Second Round
(Best of 7)
Utah defeated San Antonio, 4 games to 1
L.A. Lakers defeated Seattle, 4 games to 1

Conference Finals
(Best of 7)
Utah defeated L.A. Lakers, 4 games to 0
May 16—UTAH 112, L.A. Lakers 77
May 18—UTAH 99, L.A. Lakers 95
May 22—Utah 109, L.A. LAKERS 98
May 24—Utah 96, L.A. LAKERS 92

CHAMPIONSHIP

Chicago Bulls defeated Utah Jazz, 4 games to 2
Michael Jordan named Finals MVP

June 3—UTAH 88, Chicago 85
June 5—Chicago 93, UTAH 88
June 7—CHICAGO 96, Utah 54
June 10—CHICAGO 86, Utah 82
June 12—Utah 83, CHICAGO 81
June 14—Chicago 87, UTAH 86

LEADING SCORERS—1997–1998

Minimum of 49 games played or 1,344 points scored

	Gm	Pts	Avg
Michael Jordan, Chicago	82	2,357	28.7
Shaquille O'Neal, L.A. Lakers	60	1,699	28.3
Karl Malone, Utah	81	2,190	27.0
Mitch Richmond, Washington	70	1,623	23.2
Antoine Walker, Boston	82	1,840	22.4
Shareef Abdur-Rahim, Vancouver	82	1,829	22.3
Glen Rice, Charlotte	82	1,826	22.3
Allen Iverson, Philadelphia	80	1,758	22.0
Chris Webber, Sacramento	71	1,555	21.9
David Robinson, San Antonio	73	1,574	21.6
Michael Finley, Dallas	82	1,763	21.5
Tim Duncan, San Antonio	82	1,731	21.1
Grant Hill, Detroit	81	1,712	21.1
Steve Smith, Atlanta	73	1,464	20.1
Isaiah Rider, Portland	74	1,458	19.7

STEALS LEADERS—1997–1998

Minimum of 49 games played or 120 steals

	Gm	Stl	Avg
Mookie Blaylock, Atlanta	70	183	2.61
Brevin Knight, Cleveland	80	196	2.45
Doug Chritstie, Toronto	78	190	2.44
Gary Payton, Seattle	82	185	2.26
Allen Iverson, Philadelphia	80	176	2.20
Eddie Jones, L.A. Lakers	80	160	2.00
Jason Kidd, Phoenix	82	162	1.98
Kendall Gill, New Jersey	81	156	1.93
Clyde Drexler, Houston	70	126	1.80
Hersey Hawkins, Seattle	82	148	1.80

ASSISTS LEADERS—1997–1998

Minimum of 49 games played or 384 assists

	Gm	Ast	Avg
Rod Strickland, Washington	76	801	10.5
Jason Kidd, Phoenix	82	745	9.1
Mark Jackson, Indiana	82	713	8.7
Stephon Marbury, Minnesota	82	704	8.6
John Stockton, Utah	64	543	8.5
Tim Hardaway, Miami	81	672	8.3
Gary Payton, Seattle	82	679	8.3
Brevin Knight, Cleveland	80	656	8.2
Damon Stoudamire, Portland	71	580	8.2
Sam Cassell, New Jersey	75	603	8.0
Avery Johnson, San Antonio	75	591	7.9
Nick Van Exel, L.A. Lakers	64	442	6.9
Allen Iverson, Philadelphia	76	567	7.5
Grant Hill, Detroit	81	551	6.8
Mookie Blaylock, Atlanta	70	469	6.7

BLOCKED-SHOTS LEADERS—1997–1998

Minimum of 49 games played or 96 block shots

	Gm	Blk	Avg
Marcus Camby, Toronto	63	230	3.65
Dikembe Mutombo, Atlanta	82	277	3.38
Shawn Bradley, Dallas	64	214	3.34
Theo Ratliff, Philadelphia	82	258	3.15
David Robinson, San Antonio	73	192	2.63
Tim Duncan, San Antonio	82	206	2.51
Michael Stewart, Sacramento	81	195	2.41
Shaquille O'Neal, L.A. Lakers	60	144	2.40
Alonzo Mourning, Miami	58	130	2.24
Charles Outlaw, Orlando	82	181	2.21

FIELD GOAL PERCENTAGE LEADERS—1997–1998

Minimum of 288 field goals made

	Gm	FG	Att	Pct
Shaquille O'Neal, L.A. Lakers	60	670	1,147	.584
Charles Outlaw, Orlando	82	301	543	.554
Alonzo Mourning, Miami	58	403	732	.551
Tim Duncan, San Antonio	82	706	1,287	.549
Vin Baker, Seattle	82	631	1,164	.542
Dikembe Mutombo, Atlanta	82	399	743	.537
Antonio McDyess, Phoenix	81	497	927	.536
Rasheed Wallace, Portland	77	466	875	.533
Karl Malone, Utah	81	780	1,472	.530
Bryant Reeves, Vancouver	74	492	941	.523

FREE-THROW PERCENTAGE LEADERS—1997–1998

Minimum of 120 free throws made

	Gm	FT	Att	Pct
Cris Mullin, Indiana	82	154	164	.939
Jeff Hornacek, Utah	80	285	322	.885
Ray Allen, Milwaukee	82	342	391	.875
Derek Anderson, Cleveland	66	275	315	.873
Kevin Johnson, Phoenix	50	162	186	.871
Tracy Murray, Washington	82	182	209	.871
Hersey Hawkins, Seattle	82	177	204	.868
Reggie Miller, Indiana	81	382	440	.868
Christian Laettner, Atlanta	74	306	354	.864
Mitch Richmond, Washington	70	407	471	.864

REBOUND LEADERS—1997–1998

Minimum of 49 games played or 768 rebounds

	Gm	Reb	Avg
Dennis Rodman, Chicago	80	1201	15.0
Jayson Williams, New Jersey	65	883	13.6
Tim Duncan, San Antonio	82	977	11.9
Dikembe Mutombo, Atlanta	82	932	11.4
David Robinson, San Antonio	73	775	10.6
Karl Malone, Utah	81	834	10.3
Anthony Mason, Charlotte	81	826	10.2
Antoine Walker, Boston	82	836	10.2
Arvydas Sabonis, Portland	73	729	10.0
Kevin Garnett, Minnesota	82	786	9.6
Chris Webber, Sacramento	71	674	9.5
Shawn Kemp, Cleveland	80	745	9.3
Charles Oakley, New York	79	724	9.2
Brian Williams, Detroit	78	695	8.9
Zydrunas Ilgauskas, Cleveland	82	723	8.8

3-POINT FIELD GOAL PERCENT LEADERS—1997–1998

Minimum of 82 3-point field goals made

	Gm	3FG	Att	Pct
Dale Ellis, Seattle	79	127	274	.464
Chris Mullin, Indiana	82	107	243	.440
Hubert Davis, Dallas	81	101	230	.439
Glen Rice, Charlotte	82	130	300	.433
Wesley Person, Cleveland	82	192	447	.430
Reggie Miller, Indiana	81	164	382	.429
Kerry Kittles, New Jersey	77	110	263	.418
Matt Bullard, Houston	67	96	231	.416
Hersey Hawkins, Seattle	82	125	301	.415
Eric Piatkowski, L.A. Clippers	67	106	259	.409

Women's Professional Basketball

AMERICAN BASKETBALL LEAGUE—1997–1998 SEASON

Western Conference

	W	L	Pct	GB
*Portland	27	17	.614	—
†Long Beach	26	18	.591	1
†Colorado	21	23	.477	6
†San Jose	21	23	.477	6
Seattle	15	29	.341	12

Eastern Conference

	W	L	Pct	GB
*Columbus	36	8	.818	—
†New England	24	20	.545	12
Atlanta	15	29	.341	21
Philadelphia	13	31	.295	23

NOTE: Clinched conference title (*) and clinched playoff berth (†) are noted. GB refers to Games Behind leader.

ABL PLAYOFFS—1998

Semifinals (Best of 3)

Date	Result
Feb. 27	Long Beach 72, Portland 62
March 1	Long Beach 70, Portland 69
	Long Beach wins series, 2-0
Feb. 28	Columbus 94, San Jose 88
March 1	Columbus 74, San Jose 62
	Columbus wins series, 2-0

Finals (Best of 5)

Columbus wins series, 3 games to 2

Date	Result
Mar. 8	Long Beach 65, Columbus 62
Mar. 9	Long Beach 71, Columbus 61
Mar. 11	Columbus 70, Long Beach 61
Mar. 13	Columbus 68, Long Beach 53
Mar. 15	Columbus 86, Long Beach 81

ABL ANNUAL AWARDS—1997–1998

Most Valuable Player: Natalie Williams, Portland
Defensive Player of the Year: Yolanda Griffith, Long Beach

Rookie of the Year: Shalonda Enis, Seattle
Coach of the Year: Lin Dunn, Portland

WOMEN'S NATIONAL BASKETBALL ASSOCIATION—1998 SEASON

Eastern Conference

	W	L	Pct	GB
x-Cleveland	20	10	.667	—
x-Charlotte	18	12	.600	2
x New York	18	12	.600	2
Detroit	17	13	.567	3
Washington	3	27	.100	17

Western Conference

	W	L	Pct	GB
x-Houston	27	3	.900	—
x-Phoenix	19	11	.633	8
Los Angeles	12	18	.400	15
Sacramento	8	22	.267	19
Utah	8	22	.267	19

NOTE: x—clinched WNBA championship playoff spot. GB refers to Games Behind leader.

Semifinals (Best of 3)

Date	Result
Aug. 22	Houston 85, Charlotte 71
Aug. 24	Houston 77, Charlotte 61
	Houston wins series, 2–0
Aug. 22	Phoenix 78, Cleveland 68
Aug. 24	Cleveland 67, Phoenix 66
Aug. 25	Phoenix 71, Cleveland 60
	Phoenix wins series, 2–1

Championship Series (Best of 3)

Date	Result
Aug. 27	Phoenix 54, Houston 51
Aug. 29	Houston 74, Phoenix 69 (OT)
Sept. 1	Houston 80, Phoenix 71
	Houston wins series, 2–0

WNBA ANNUAL AWARDS—1998 SEASON

Most Valuable Player: Cynthia Cooper, Houston
Defensive Player of the Year: Teresa Weatherspoon, New York
Sportsmanship Award: Suzie McConnell Serio, Cleveland

Coach of the Year: Van Chancellor, Houston
Newcomer of the Year: Suzie McConnell Serio, Cleveland
Rookie of the Year: Tracy Reid, Charlotte

POINTS LEADERS—1998

	Gm	PPG	Pts
Cynthia Cooper, Houston	30	22.7	680
Jennifer Gillon, Phoenix	30	20.8	624
Lisa Leslie, Los Angeles	28	19.6	549
Nikki McCray, Washington	29	17.7	512
Sheryl Swoopes, Houston	29	15.6	453

STEALS LEADERS—1998

	Gm	Steals	SPG
Teresa Weatherspoon, New York	30	100	3.33
Kim Perrot, Houston	30	84	2.80
Sheryl Swoopes, Houston	29	72	2.48
Ticha Penicheiro, Sacramento	30	67	2.23
Vicky Bullett, Charlotte	30	66	2.20

Hockey

Ice hockey, by birth and upbringing a Canadian game, is an offshoot of field hockey. Some historians say that the first ice hockey game was played in Montreal in December 1879 between two teams composed almost exclusively of McGill University students, but others assert that earlier hockey games took place in Kingston, Ontario, or Halifax, Nova Scotia. In the Montreal game of 1879, there were fifteen players on a side, who used an assortment of crude sticks to keep the puck in motion. Early rules allowed nine men on a side, but the number was reduced to seven in 1886 and later to six.

The first governing body of the sport was the Amateur Hockey Association of Canada, organized in 1887. In the winter of 1894–95, a group of college students from the United States visited Canada and saw hockey played. They became enthused over the game and introduced it as a winter sport when they returned home. The first professional league was the International Hockey League, which operated in northern Michigan in 1904–06.

Until 1910, professionals and amateurs were allowed to play together on "mixed teams," but this arrangement ended with the formation of the first "big league," the National Hockey Association, in eastern Canada in 1910. The Pacific Coast League was organized in 1911 for western Canadian hockey. The league included Seattle and later other American cities. The National Hockey League replaced the National Hockey Association in 1917. Boston, in 1924, was the first American city to join that circuit. The league expanded to include western cities in 1967. The Stanley Cup was competed for by "mixed teams" from 1894 to 1910, thereafter by professionals. It was awarded to the winner of the NHL playoffs from 1926–67 and now to the league champion. The World Hockey Association was organized in October 1972 and was dissolved after the 1978–79 season when the NHL absorbed four of the teams.

Rule changes have been implemented to steer the league from its violent reputation in order to better showcase the world's most talented stars.

Hockey, once considered a cold-weather sport, has taken major strides in increasing its fan base to the southern and western part of the United States as well. In the 1995–96 season, Florida and Colorado battled in the Stanley Cup Finals, the San Jose Sharks sold out all 41 of their home games, and the second team in two years (Winnipeg) migrated from Canada to the Southwest region of the U.S. (Phoenix).

The league continues to expand as the Nashville Predators joins the league in the 1998–99 season. In 1999–2000, the Atlanta Thrashers will begin to play, and the 2000–2001 season will see the addition of the Columbus Blue Jackets and the Minnesota Wild.

STANLEY CUP WINNERS

Emblematic of World Professional Championship; N.H.L. Championship after 1967

1893 Montreal A.A.A.
1894 Montreal A.A.A.
1895 Montreal Victorias
1896 (Feb.) Winnipeg Victorias
1896 (Dec.) Montreal Victorias
1897–99 Montreal Victorias
1899–1900 Montreal Shamrocks
1901 Winnipeg Victorias
1902 Montreal A.A.A.
1903–05 Ottawa Silver Seven
1906 Montreal Wanderers
1907 Kenora Thistles[1]
1907 Montreal Wanderers[2]
1908 Montreal Wanderers
1909 Ottawa Senators
1910 Montreal Wanderers
1911 Ottawa Senators
1912–13 Quebec Bulldogs
1914 Toronto Blueshirts
1915 Vancouver Millionaries
1916 Montreal Canadiens
1917 Seattle Metropolitans
1918 Toronto Arenas
1919 No champion
1920–21 Ottawa Senators
1922 Toronto St. Patricks
1923 Ottawa Senators
1924 Montreal Canadiens
1925 Victoria Cougars
1926 Montreal Maroons
1927 Ottawa Senators
1928 N.Y. Rangers
1929 Boston Bruins
1930–31 Montreal Canadiens
1932 Toronto Maple Leafs
1933 N.Y. Rangers
1934 Chicago Black Hawks
1935 Montreal Maroons
1936–37 Detroit Red Wings
1938 Chicago Red Hawks
1939 Boston Bruins
1940 N.Y. Rangers
1941 Boston Bruins
1942 Toronto Maple Leafs
1943 Detroit Red Wings
1944 Montreal Canadiens
1945 Toronto Maple Leafs
1946 Montreal Canadiens
1947–49 Toronto Maple Leafs
1950 Detroit Red Wings
1951 Toronto Maple Leafs
1952 Detroit Red Wings
1953 Montreal Canadiens
1954–55 Detroit Red Wings
1956–60 Montreal Canadiens
1961 Chicago Black Hawks
1962–64 Toronto Maple Leafs
1965–66 Montreal Canadiens
1967 Toronto Maple Leafs
1968–69 Montreal Canadiens
1970 Boston Bruins
1971 Montreal Canadiens
1972 Boston Bruins
1973 Montreal Canadiens
1974–75 Philadelphia Flyers
1976–79 Montreal Canadiens
1980–83 New York Islanders
1984–85 Edmonton Oilers
1986 Montreal Canadiens
1987–88 Edmonton Oilers
1989 Calgary Flames
1990 Edmonton Oilers
1991–92 Pittsburgh Penguins
1993 Montreal Canadiens
1994 N.Y. Rangers
1995 N.J. Devils
1996 Colorado Avalanche
1997–98 Detroit Red Wings

1. January. 2. March.

N.H.L. CHAMPIONS

Wales Trophy

1939–41 Boston
1942 New York
1943 Detroit
1944–47 Montreal
1948 Toronto
1948–55 Detroit
1956 Montreal
1957 Detroit
1958–62 Montreal
1963 Toronto
1964 Montreal
1965 Detroit
1966 Montreal
1967 Chicago

Eastern Division

1968–69 Montreal
1970 Chicago
1971–72 Boston

1973 Montreal
1974 Boston

Eastern Conference[1]

1975 Buffalo
1976–79 Montreal
1980 Buffalo
1981 Montreal
1982–84 New York Islanders
1985 Philadelphia
1986 Montreal
1987 Philadelphia
1988 Boston
1989 Montreal
1990 Boston
1991–92 Pittsburgh
1993 Montreal
1994 N.Y. Rangers
1995 New Jersey
1996 Florida
1997 Philadelphia
1998 Washington

1. Prior to 1994 was the Wales Conference.

CAMPBELL BOWL

Western Division

1968–70 St. Louis
1971–73 Chicago
1974 Philadelphia

Western Conference[2]

1975–77 Philadelphia
1978–79 N.Y. Islanders
1980 Philadelphia
1981 New York Islanders
1982–85 Edmonton
1986 Calgary
1987–88 Edmonton
1989 Calgary
1990 Edmonton
1991 Minnesota
1992 Chicago
1993 Los Angeles
1994 Vancouver
1995 Detroit
1996 Colorado
1997–98 Detroit

2. Prior to 1994 was the Campbell Conference.

NATIONAL HOCKEY LEAGUE YEARLY TROPHY WINNERS

The Hart Trophy—Most Valuable Player

1924 Frank Nighbor, Ottawa
1925 Billy Burch, Hamilton
1926 Nels Stewart, Montreal Maroons
1927 Herb Gardiner, Montreal Canadiens
1928 Howie Morenz, Montreal Canadiens
1929 Roy Worters, N.Y. Americans
1930 Nels Stewart, Montreal Maroons
1931–32 Howie Morenz, Montreal Canadiens
1933 Eddie Shore, Boston
1934 Aurel Joliat, Montreal Canadiens
1935–36 Eddie Shore, Boston
1937 Babe Siebert, Montreal Canadiens
1938 Eddie Shore, Boston
1939 Toe Blake, Montreal Canadiens
1940 Ebbie Goodfellow, Detroit
1941 Bill Cowley, Boston
1942 Tommy Anderson, N.Y. Americans
1943 Bill Cowley, Boston
1944 Babe Pratt, Toronto
1945 Elmer Lach, Montreal Canadiens
1946 Max Bentley, Chicago
1947 Maurice Richard, Montreal Canadiens
1948 Buddy O'Connor, N.Y. Rangers
1949 Sid Abel, Detroit
1950 Chuck Rayner, N.Y. Rangers
1951 Milt Schmidt, Boston
1952–53 Gordie Howe, Detroit
1954 Al Rollins, Chicago
1955 Ted Kennedy, Toronto
1956 Jean Belveau, Montreal Canadiens
1957–58 Gordie Howe, Detroit
1959 Andy Bathgate, N.Y. Rangers
1960 Gordie Howe, Detroit
1961 Bernie Geoffrion, Montreal Canadiens
1962 Jacques Plante, Montreal Canadiens
1963 Gordon Howe, Detroit
1964 Jean Beliveau, Montreal Canadiens
1965–66 Bobby Hull, Chicago
1967–68 Stan Mikita, Chicago
1969 Phil Esposito, Boston
1970–72 Bobby Orr, Boston
1973 Bobby Clarke, Philadelphia
1974 Phil Esposito, Boston
1975–76 Bobby Clarke, Philadelphia
1977–78 Guy Lafleur, Montreal
1979 Bryan Trottier, N.Y. Islanders
1980–87 Wayne Gretzky, Edmonton
1988 Mario Lemieux, Pittsburgh
1989 Wayne Gretzky, Los Angeles
1990 Mark Messier, Edmonton
1991 Brett Hull, St. Louis
1992 Mark Messier, N.Y. Rangers
1993 Mario Lemieux, Pittsburgh
1994 Sergei Fedorov, Detroit
1995 Eric Lindros, Philadelphia
1996 Mario Lemieux, Pittsburgh
1997–98 Dominik Hasek, Buffalo

Vezina Trophy—Leading Goalkeeper

1956–60 Jacques Plante, Montreal
1961 Johnny Bower, Toronto
1962 Jacques Plante, Montreal
1963 Glenn Hall, Chicago
1964 Charlie Hodge, Montreal
1965 Terry Sawchuk—Johnny Bower, Toronto
1966 Gump Worsley—Charlie Hodge, Montreal
1967 Glen Hall—Denis Dejordy, Chicago
1968 Gump Worsley—Rogie Vachon, Montreal
1969 Glenn Hall—Jacques Plante, St. Louis
1970 Tony Esposito, Chicago
1971 Ed Giacomin—Gilles Villemure, N.Y. Rangers
1972 Tony Esposito—Gary Smith, Chicago
1973 Ken Dryden, Montreal
1974 Bernie Parent, Philadelphia and Tony Esposito, Chicago
1975 Bernie Parent, Philadelphia
1976 Ken Dryden, Montreal
1977–79 Ken Dryden—Bunny Larocque, Montreal
1980 Bob Sauve—Don Edwards, Buffalo
1981 Richard Sevigny—Denis Herron—Bunny Larocque, Montreal
1982 Billy Smith, N.Y. Islanders
1983 Pete Peeters, Boston
1984 Tom Barrasso, Buffalo
1985 Pelle Lindbergh, Philadelphia
1986 John Vanbiesbrouck, N.Y. Rangers
1987 Ron Hextall, Philadelphia
1988 Grant Fuhr, Edmonton
1989–90 Patrick Roy, Montreal
1991 Ed Belfour, Chicago
1992 Patrick Roy, Montreal
1993 Ed Belfour, Chicago
1994–95 Dominik Hasek, Buffalo
1996 Jim Carey, Washington
1997–98 Dominik Hasek, Buffalo

James Norris Trophy—Defenseman

1954 Red Kelly, Detroit
1955–58 Doug Harvey, Montreal
1959 Tom Johnson, Montreal
1960–62 Doug Harvey, Montreal, N.Y. Rangers (62)
1963–65 Pierre Pilote, Chicago
1966 Jacques Laperriere, Montreal
1967 Harry Howell, N.Y. Rangers
1968–75 Bobby Orr, Boston
1976 Denis Potvin, N.Y. Islanders
1977 Larry Robinson, Montreal
1978–79 Denis Potvin, N.Y. Islanders
1980 Larry Robinson, Montreal
1981 Randy Carlyle, Pittsburgh
1982 Doug Wilson, Chicago
1983–84 Rod Langway, Washington
1985–86 Paul Coffey, Edmonton
1987–88 Ray Bourque, Boston
1989 Chris Chelios, Montreal
1990–91 Ray Bourque, Boston
1992 Brian Leetch, N.Y. Rangers
1993 Chris Chelios, Chicago
1994 Ray Bourque, Boston
1995 Paul Coffey, Detroit
1996 Chris Chelios, Chicago
1997 Brian Leetch, N.Y. Rangers
1998 Rob Blake, Los Angeles

Lady Byng Trophy—Sportsmanship

1960 Don McKenney, Boston
1961 Red Kelly, Toronto
1962–63 Dave Keon, Toronto

1964 Ken Wharram, Chicago
1965 Bobby Hull, Chicago
1966 Alex Delvecchio, Detroit
1967–68 Stan Mikita, Chicago
1969 Alex Delvecchio, Detroit
1970 Phil Goyette, St. Louis
1971 Johnny Bucyk, Boston
1972 Jean Ratelle, N.Y. Rangers
1973 Gilbert Perreault, Buffalo
1974 Johnny Bucyk, Boston
1975 Marcel Dionne, Detroit
1976 Jean Ratelle, N.Y. Rangers, Boston
1977 Marcel Dionne, Los Angeles
1978 Butch Goring, Los Angeles
1979 Bob MacMillan, Atlanta
1980 Wayne Gretzky, Edmonton
1981 Rick Kehoe, Pittsburgh
1982 Rick Middleton, Boston
1983–84 Mike Bossy, N.Y. Islanders
1985 Jari Kurri, Edmonton
1986 Mike Bossy, N.Y. Islanders
1987 Joey Mullen, Calgary
1988 Mats Naslund, Montreal
1989 Joey Mullen, Calgary
1990 Brett Hull, St. Louis
1991–92 Wayne Gretzky, Los Angeles
1993 Pierre Turgeon, N.Y. Islanders
1994 Wayne Gretzky, Los Angeles
1995 Ron Francis, Pittsburgh
1996–97 Paul Kariya, Anaheim
1998 Ron Francis, Pittsburgh

Calder Trophy—Rookie

1962 Bobby Rousseau, Montreal
1963 Kent Douglas, Toronto
1964 Jacques Laperriere, Montreal
1965 Roger Crozier, Detroit
1966 Brit Selby, Toronto
1967 Bobby Orr, Boston
1968 Derek Sanderson, Boston
1969 Danny Grant, Minnesota
1970 Tony Esposito, Chicago
1971 Gilbert Perreault, Buffalo
1972 Ken Dryden, Montreal
1973 Steve Vickers, N.Y. Rangers
1974 Denis Potvin, N.Y. Islanders
1975 Eric Vail, Atlanta
1976 Bryan Trottier, N.Y. Islanders
1977 Willi Plett, Atlanta
1978 Mike Bossy, N.Y. Islanders
1979 Bobby Smith, Minnesota
1980 Ray Bourque, Boston
1981 Peter Stastny, Quebec
1982 Dale Hawerchuk, Winnipeg
1983 Steve Larmer, Chicago
1984 Tom Barrasso, Buffalo
1985 Mario Lemieux, Pittsburgh
1986 Gary Suter, Calgary
1987 Luc Robitaille, Los Angeles
1988 Joe Nieuwendyk, Calgary
1989 Brian Leetch, N.Y. Rangers
1990 Sergei Makarov, Calgary
1991 Ed Belfour, Chicago
1992 Pavel Bure, Vancouver
1993 Teemu Selanne, Winnipeg
1994 Martin Brodeur, New Jersey
1995 Peter Forsberg, Quebec
1996 Daniel Alfredsson, Ottawa
1997 Bryan Berard, N.Y. Islanders
1998 Sergei Samsonov, Boston

Art Ross Trophy—Leading Scorer

1955 Bernie Geoffrion, Montreal
1956 Jean Beliveau, Montreal
1957 Gordie Howe, Detroit
1958–59 Dickie Moore, Montreal
1960 Bobby Hull, Chicago
1961 Bernie Geoffrion, Montreal
1962 Bobby Hull, Chicago
1963 Gordie Howe, Detroit
1964–65 Stan Mikita, Chicago
1966 Bobby Hull, Chicago
1967–68 Stan Mikita, Chicago
1969 Phil Esposito, Boston
1970 Bobby Orr, Boston
1971–74 Phil Esposito, Boston
1975 Bobby Orr, Boston
1976–78 Guy Lafleur, Montreal
1979 Bryan Trottier, N.Y. Islanders
1980 Marcel Dionne, Los Angeles
1981–87 Wayne Gretzky, Edmonton
1988–89 Mario Lemieux, Pittsburgh
1990–91 Wayne Gretzky, Los Angeles
1992–93 Mario Lemieux, Pittsburgh
1994 Wayne Gretzky, Los Angeles
1995 Jaromir Jagr, Pittsburgh
1996–97 Mario Lemieux, Pittsburgh
1998 Jaromir Jagr, Pittsburgh

STANLEY CUP PLAYOFFS—1998

NOTE: Home teams are in capitals.

EASTERN CONFERENCE

Ottawa Senators defeated New Jersey Devils, 4 games to 2
Buffalo Sabres defeated Philadelphia Flyers, 4 games to 1
Montreal Canadians defeated Pittsburgh Penguins, 4 games to 2
Washington Capitals defeated Boston Bruins, 4 games to 2

Semifinals

Buffalo Sabres defeated Montreal Canadians, 4 games to 0
Washington Capitals defeated Ottawa Senators, 4 games to 1

Finals

Washington Capitals defeated Buffalo Sabres, 4 games to 2
May 23—Buffalo 2, WASHINGTON 0
May 25—WASHINGTON 3, Buffalo 2 OT
May 28—Washington 4, BUFFALO 3 OT
May 30—Washington 2, BUFFALO 0
June 2—Buffalo 2, WASHINGTON 1
June 4—Washington 3, BUFFALO 2 OT

WESTERN CONFERENCE

Quarterfinals

Edmonton Oilers defeated Colorado Avalanche, 4 games to 3
Dallas North Stars defeated San Jose Sharks, 4 games to 2
Detroit Red Wings defeated Phoenix Coyotes, 4 games to 2
St. Louis Blues defeated Los Angeles Kings, 4 games to 0

Semifinals

Dallas North Stars defeated Edmonton Oilers, 4 games to 1
Detroit Red Wings defeated St. Louis Blues, 4 games to 2

Finals

Detroit Red Wings defeated Dallas North Stars, 4 games to 2
May 24—Detroit 2, DALLAS 0
May 26—DALLAS 3, Detroit 1
May 29—DETROIT 5, Dallas 3
May 31—DETROIT 3, Dallas 2
June 3—DALLAS 3, Detroit 2 OT
June 5—DETROIT 2, Dallas 0

STANLEY CUP CHAMPIONSHIP FINALS

Detroit Red Wings defeated Washington Capitals, 4 games to 0

June 9—DETROIT 2, Washington 1
June 11—DETROIT 5, Washington 4 OT
June 13—Detroit 2, WASHINGTON 1
June 16—Detroit 4, WASHINGTON 1

Conn Smythe Award for most valuable player in the playoffs: Steve Yzerman

OTHER N.H.L. AWARDS—1998

Frank Selke Trophy (top defensive forward)—Jere Lehtinen, Dallas

King Clancy Trophy (Humanitarian community involvement)—Kelly Chase, St. Louis

Jack Adams Trophy (Coach of the Year)—Pat Burns, Boston

Bill Masterson Trophy (Perseverance, sportsmanship, and dedication to hockey)—Jamie McLennan, St. Louis

NATIONAL HOCKEY LEAGUE FINAL STANDINGS OF THE CLUBS—1997–1998

EASTERN CONFERENCE

Northeast Division

	W	L	T	Pts	GF	GA
[1]Pittsburgh	40	24	18	98	228	188
[2]Boston	39	30	13	91	221	194
[2]Buffalo	36	29	17	89	211	187
[2]Montreal	37	32	13	87	235	208
[2]Ottawa	34	33	15	83	193	200
Carolina	33	41	8	74	200	219

Atlantic Division

	W	L	T	Pts	GF	GA
[1]New Jersey	48	23	11	107	225	166
[2]Philadelphia	42	29	11	95	242	193
[2]Washington	40	30	12	92	219	202
N.Y. Islanders	30	41	11	71	212	225
N.Y. Rangers	25	39	18	68	197	231
Florida	24	43	15	63	203	256
Tampa Bay	17	55	10	44	151	269

WESTERN CONFERENCE

Central Division

	W	L	T	Pts	GF	GA
[1]Dallas	49	22	11	109	242	167
[2]Detroit	44	23	15	103	250	196
[2]St. Louis	45	29	8	98	256	204
[2]Phoenix	35	35	12	82	224	227
Chicago	30	39	13	73	192	199
Toronto	30	43	9	69	194	237

Pacific Division

	W	L	T	Pts	GF	GA
[1]Colorado	39	26	17	95	231	205
[2]Los Angeles	38	33	11	87	227	225
[2]Edmonton	35	37	10	80	215	224
[2]San Jose	34	38	10	78	210	216
Calgary	26	41	15	67	217	252
Anaheim	26	43	13	65	205	261
Vancouver	25	43	14	64	224	273

1. Division champion. 2. Playoff qualifier.

N.H.L. LEADING SCORERS—1998

	GP	G	A	Pts
Jaromir Jagr, Pittsburgh	77	35	67	102
Peter Forsberg, Colorado	72	25	66	91
Wayne Gretzky, N.Y. Rangers	82	23	67	90
Pavel Bure, Vancouver	82	51	39	90
Ron Francis, Pittsburgh	81	25	62	87
Zigmund Palffy, N.Y. Islanders	82	45	42	87
John LeClair, Philadelphia	82	51	36	87
Teemu Selanne, Anaheim	73	52	34	86
Jason Allison, Boston	81	33	50	83
Jozef Stumpel, Los Angeles	77	21	58	79

N.H.L. LEADING GOALTENDERS—1998

	Gm	Min	GAA	Record
Ed Belfour, Dallas	61	3,581	1.88	37–12–10
Martin Brodeur, New Jersey	70	4,128	1.89	43–17–8
Tom Barrasso, Pittsburgh	63	3,542	2.07	31–14–13
Dominik Hasek, Buffalo	72	4,220	2.09	33–23–13
Ron Hextal, Philadelphia	46	2,688	2.17	21–17–7
Trevor Kidd, Carolina	47	2,685	2.17	21–21–3
Jeff Hackett, Chicago	58	3,441	2.20	21–25–11
Olaf Kolzig, Washington	64	3,788	2.20	33–18–10
Chris Osgood, Detroit	64	3,807	2.21	33–20–11
Byron Dafoe, Boston	65	3,693	2.24	30–25–9

N.H.L. CAREER SCORING LEADERS

(Through 1997–1998 season)

		Yrs	Gm	G	A	Pts
1	**Wayne Gretzky**	19	1,417	885	1,910	2,795
2	Gordie Howe	26	1,767	801	1,049	1,850
3	Marcel Dionne	18	1,348	731	1,040	1,771
4	**Mark Messier**	19	1,354	597	1,014	1,611
5	Phil Esposito	18	1,282	717	873	1,590
6	Mario Lemieux	12	745	613	881	1,494
7	**Paul Coffey**	18	1,268	383	1,090	1,473
8	Stan Mikita	22	1,394	541	926	1,467
9	**Ron Francis**	17	1,247	428	1,006	1,434
10	Bryan Trottier	18	1,279	524	901	1,425
11	**Ray Bourque**	19	1,372	375	1,036	1,411
12	**Steve Yzerman**	15	1,098	563	846	1,409
13	Dale Hawerchuk	16	1,188	518	891	1,409
14	**Jari Kurri**	17	1,251	601	796	1,397
15	John Bucyk	23	1,540	556	813	1,369
16	Guy Lafleur	17	1,126	560	793	1,353
17	Denis Savard	17	1,196	473	865	1,338
18	**Mike Gartner**	19	1,432	708	627	1,335
19	Gilbert Perreault	17	1,191	512	814	1,326
20	Alex Delvecchio	24	1,549	456	825	1,281

Players active during 1997–98 season in **bold** type.

Chess

WORLD CHAMPIONS

1894–1921	Emanuel Lasker, Germany
1921–27	Jose R. Capablanca, Cuba
1927–35	Alexander A. Alekhine, U.S.S.R.
1935–37	Dr. Max Euwe, Netherlands
1937–46	Alexander A. Alekhine, U.S.S.R.[1]
1948–57	Mikhail Botvinnik, U.S.S.R.
1957–58	Vassily Smyslov, U.S.S.R.
1958–60	Mikhail Botvinnik, U.S.S.R.
1960–61	Mikhail Tal, U.S.S.R.
1961–63	Mikhail Botvinnik, U.S.S.R.
1963–68	Tigran Petrosian, U.S.S.R.
1969–71	Boris Spassky, U.S.S.R.
1972–74	Bobby Fischer, Los Angeles
1975	Bobby Fischer[2], Anatoly Karpov, U.S.S.R.
1976–85	Anatoly Karpov, U.S.S.R.[3]
1985–	Garry Kasparov, Russia[4]
1993–	Anatoly Karpov[5]

1. Alekhine, a French citizen, died while champion. 2. Relinquished title. 3. In 1978, Karpov defeated Viktor Korchnoi 6 games to 5. 4. PCA (Professional Chess Association) world champion after 1993. 5. FIDE (International Chess Federation) world champion.

UNITED STATES CHAMPIONS

1909–36	Frank J. Marshall, New York
1936–44	Samuel Reshevsky, New York[1]
1944–46	Arnold S. Denker, New York
1946	Samuel Reshevsky, Boston
1948	Herman Steiner, Los Angeles
1951–52	Larry Evans, New York
1954–57	Arthur Bisguier, New York
1958–61	Bobby Fischer, Brooklyn, N.Y.
1962	Larry Evans, New York
1963–67	Bobby Fischer, New York
1968	Larry Evans, New York
1969–71	Samuel Reshevsky, Spring Valley, N.Y.
1972	Robert Byrne, Ossining, N.Y.
1973	Lubomir Kavelek, Washington; John Grefe, San Francisco
1974–77	Walter Browne, Berkeley, Calif.
1978–79	Lubomir Kavalek, New York
1980	Tie, Walter Browne, Berkeley, Calif. Larry Christiansen, Modesto, Calif. Larry Evans, Reno, Nev.
1981–82[2]	Tie, Walter Browne, Berkeley, Calif. Yasser Seirawan, Seattle, Wash.
1983	Tie, Walter Browne, Berkeley, Calif. Larry Christiansen, Los Angeles, Calif., Roman Dzindzichashvili, Corona, N.Y.
1984–85	Lev Alburt, New York City
1986	Yasser Seirawan, Seattle, Wash.
1987	Tie, Nick Defirmian, San Francisco Joel Benjamin, Brooklyn, N.Y.
1988	Michael Wilder, Princeton, N.J.
1989	Tie, Stuart Rachels, Birmingham, Ala. Yasser Seirawan, Seattle, Wash. Roman Dzindzichashvili, New York, N.Y.
1990–91	Lev Alburt, New York, N.Y.
1992	Gata Kamsky, Brooklyn, N.Y. Patrick Wolff, Somerville, Mass.
1993	Tie, Alexander Shabalov, Pittsburgh, Pa. Alex Yermolinski, Edison, N.J.
1994	Boris Gulko, Fairlawn, N.J.
1995	Patrick Wolff, Somerville, Mass.
1996	Alex Yurmolinsky, Cleveland, Ohio
1997	Esther Epstein, Mass. (women) Joel Benjamin, N.Y. (men)

1998—Held after the almanac went to press

1. In 1942, Isaac I. Kashdan of New York was co-champion for a while because of a tie with Reshevsky in that year's tournament. Reshevsky won the play-off. 2. Championship not contested in 1982.

Bowling

The game of bowling in the United States is an indoor development of the more ancient outdoor game that survives as lawn bowling. The outdoor game is prehistoric in origin and probably goes back to Primitive Man and round stones that were rolled at some target. It is believed that a game something like nine-pins was popular among the Dutch, Swiss and Germans as long ago as A.D. 1200 at which time the game was played outdoors with an alley consisting of a single plank 12 to 18 inches wide along which was rolled a ball toward three rows of three pins each placed at the far end of the alley. When the first indoor alleys were built and how the game was modified from time to time are matters of dispute.

It is supposed that the early settlers of New Amsterdam (New York City), being Dutch, brought their two bowling games with them. About a century ago the game of nine-pins was flourishing in the United States but so corrupted by gambling on matches that it was barred by law in New York and Connecticut. Since the law specifically barred "nine-pins," it was eventually evaded by adding another pin and thus legally making it a new game.

Various organizations were formed to make rules for bowling and supervise competition in the United States but none was successful until the American Bowling Congress, organized Sept. 9, 1895, became the ruling body.

AMERICAN BOWLING CONGRESS CHAMPIONS

Year	Singles	All-events
1959	Ed Lubanski	Ed Lubanski
1960	Paul Kulbaga	Vince Lucci
1961	Lyle Spooner	Luke Karen
1962	Andy Renaldo	Billy Young
1963	Fred Delello	Bus Owalt
1964	Jim Stefanich	Les Zikes, Jr.
1965	Ken Roeth	Tom Hathaway
1966	Don Chapman	John Wilcox
1967	Frank Perry	Gary Lewis
1968	Wayne Kowalski	Vince Mazzanti
1969	Greg Campbell	Eddie Jackson
1970	Jake Yoder	Mike Berlin
1971	Al Cohn	Al Cohn
1972	Bill Pointer	Mac Lowry

Year	Singles	All-events	Year	Singles	All-events
1973	Ed Thompson	Ron Woolet	1987	Terry Taylor	Ryan Schafer
1974	Gene Krause	Bob Hart	1988	Steve Hutkowski	Rick Steelsmith
1975	Jim Setser	Bobby Meadows	1989	Paul Tetreault	George Hall
1976	Mike Putzer	Jim Lindquist	1990	Bob Hochrein	Mike Neumann
1977	Frank Gadaleto	Bud Debenham	1991	Ed Deines	Tom Howery
1978	Rich Mersek	Chris Cobus	1992	Bob Youker and Gary Blatchford (tie)	Mike Tucker
1979	Rick Peters	Bob Basacchi	1993	Dan Bock	Jeff Nimke
1980	Mike Eaton	Steve Fehr	1994	John Weltzien	Thomas Holt
1981	Rob Vital	Rod Toft	1995	Matt Surina	Jeff Kwiatkowsk
1982	Bruce Bohm	Rich Wonders	1996	Donald Scudder, Jr.	Scott Kurtz
1983	Rick Kendrick	Tony Cariello	1997	John Socha	Jeff Richgels
1984	Bob Antczak and Neal Young (tie)	Bob Goike	1998	John Gaines	Chris Barnes
1985	Glen Harbison	Barry Asher			
1986	Jess Mackey	Ed Marazka			

PROFESSIONAL BOWLERS ASSOCIATION

National Championship Tournament

1960 Don Carter
1961 Dave Soutar
1962 Carmen Salvino
1963 Billy Hardwick
1964 Bob Strampe
1965 Dave Davis
1966 Wayne Zahn
1967 Dave Davis
1968 Wayne Zahn
1969 Mike McGrath
1970 Mike McGrath
1971 Mike Lemongello
1972 Johnny Guenther
1973 Earl Anthony
1974 Earl Anthony
1975 Earl Anthony
1976 Paul Colwell
1977 Tommy Hudson
1978 Warren Nelson
1979 Mike Aulby
1980 Johnny Petraglia
1981 Earl Anthony
1982 Earl Anthony
1983 Earl Anthony
1984 Bob Chamberlain
1985 Mike Aulby
1986 Tom Crites
1987 Randy Pedersen
1988 Brian Voss
1989 Pete Weber
1990 Jim Pencak
1991 Mike Miller
1992 Eric Forkel
1993 Ron Palombi
1994 David Traber
1995 Scott Alexander
1996 Butch Soper
1997 Rich Steelsmith
1998 Pete Weber

BOWLING PROPRIETORS' ASSOCIATION OF AMERICA—MEN

United States Open[1]

1971 Mike Lemongello
1972 Don Johnson
1973 Mike McGrath
1974 Larry Laub
1975 Steve Neff
1976 Paul Moser
1977 Johnny Petraglia
1978 Nelson Burton, Jr.
1979 Joe Berardi
1980 Steve Martin
1981 Marshall Holman
1982 Dave Husted
1983 Gary Dickinson
1984 Mark Roth
1985 Marshall Holman
1986 Steve Cook
1987 Del Ballard
1988 Pete Weber
1989 Mike Aulby
1990 Ron Palumbi, Jr.
1991 Pete Weber
1992 Robert Lawrence
1993 Del Ballard, Jr.
1994 Justin Hromek
1995 Dave Husted
1996 Dave Husted
1997 Not held
1998 Walter Ray Williams, Jr.

1. Replaced All-Star tournament and is rolled as part of B.P.A. tour.

WOMEN'S INTERNATIONAL BOWLING CONGRESS CHAMPIONS

Year	Singles	All-events	Year	Singles	All-events
1959	Mae Bolt	Pat McBride	1981	Virginia Norton	Virginia Norton
1960	Marge McDaniels	Judy Roberts	1982	Gracie Freeman	Aleta Rzepecki
1961	Elaine Newton	Evelyn Teal	1983	Aleta Rzepecki	Virginia Norton
1962	Martha Hoffman	Flossie Argent	1984	Freida Gates	Shinobu Saitoh
1963	Dot Wilkinson	Helen Shablis	1985	Polly Schwarzel	Aleta Sill
1964	Jean Havlish	Jean Havlish	1986	Dana Stewart	Robin Romeo and Maria Lewis (tie)
1965	Doris Rudell	Donna Zimmerman	1987	Regi Junak	Leanne Barrette
1966	Gloria Bouvia	Kate Helbig	1988	Michelle Meyer-Welty	Lisa Wagner
1967	Gloria Paeth	Carol Miller	1989	Lorraine Anderson	Nancy Fehn
1968	Norma Parks	Susie Reichley	1990	Dana Miller-Mackie and Paula Carter (tie)	Carol Norman
1969	Joan Bender	Helen Duval	1991	Debbie Kuhn	Debbie Kuhn
1970	Dorothy Fothergill	Dorothy Fothergill	1992	Patty Ann	Mitsuko Tokimoto
1971	Mary Scruggs	Lorrie Nichols	1993	Karen Collurs and Kari Murph (tie)	Bertha Blackshur and Sharon Davis (tie)
1972	D. D. Jacobson	Mildred Martorella	1994	Vicki Fifield	Wendy Macpherson-Papanos
1973	Bobby Buffaloe	Toni Calvery	1995	Beth Owen	Beth Owen
1974	Shirley Garms	Judy C. Soutar	1996	Cindy Berlanga	Lorrie Nichols
1975	Barbara Leicht	Virginia Norton	1997	Jean Schmidt	Kendra Cameron
1976	Bev Shonk	Betty Morris	1998	Nellie Glandon	Liz Johnson
1977	Akiko Yamaga	Akiko Yamaga			
1978	Mae Bolt	Annese Kelly			
1979	Betty Morris	Betty Morris			
1980	Betty Morris	Cheryl Robinson			

BOWLING PROPRIETORS' ASSOCIATION OF AMERICA—WOMEN

United States Open

1971	Paula Carter	1978	Donna Adamek	1985	Pat Mercatanti	1992	Tish Johnson
1972	Lorrie Nichols	1979	Diana Silva	1986	Wendy Macpherson	1993	Dede Davidson
1973	Mildred Martorella	1980	Pat Costello (Calif.)	1987	Carol Nurman	1994	Aleta Sill
1974	Pat Costello (Calif.)	1981	Donna Adamek	1988	Lisa Wagner	1995	Tish Johnson
1975	Paula Carter	1982	Shinobu Saitoh	1989	Robin Romeo	1996	Liz Johnson
1976	Patty Costello (Pa.)	1983	Dana Miller	1990	Dana Miller-Mackie	1997	Not held
1977	Betty Morris	1984	Karen Ellingsworth	1991	Anne Marie Duggan	1998	Aleta Sill

WIBC QUEENS TOURNAMENT CHAMPIONS

1961	Janet Harman	1971	Mildred Martorella	1981	Katsuko Sugimoto	1991	Dede Davidson
1962	Dorothy Wilkinson	1972	Dorothy Fothergill	1982	Katsuko Sugimoto	1992	Cindy Coburn-Carroll
1963	Irene Monterosso	1973	Dorothy Fothergill	1983	Aleta Rzepecki	1993	Jan Schmidt
1964	D.D. Jacobson	1974	Judy Soutar	1984	Kazue Inahashi	1994	Anne Marie Duggan
1965	Betty Kuczynski	1975	Cindy Powell	1985	Aleta Sill	1995	Sandy Postma
1966	Judy Lee	1976	Pamela Buckner	1986	Cora Fiebig	1996	Lisa Wagner
1967	Mildred Martorella	1977	Dana Stewart	1987	Cathy Almeida	1997	Sandra-Jo Shiery-Odom
1968	Phyllis Massey	1978	Loa Boxberger	1988	Wendy Macpherson	1998	Lynda Norry
1969	Ann Feigel	1979	Donna Adamek	1989	Carol Gianotti		
1970	Mildred Martorella	1980	Donna Adamek	1990	Patty Ann		

PROFESSIONAL BOWLERS ASSOCIATION CHAMPIONSHIP—1998

(Toledo, Ohio, Feb. 17–22, 1998)

Winner—Pete Weber, St. Ann, Mo., defeated David Ozio, Vidor, Tex., 277–236 in title match.
3. Tom Baker, Buffalo, N.Y.
4. Mike Aulby, Indianapolis, Ind.
5. Jim Johnson, Jr., Tampa Fla.

AMERICAN BOWLING CONGRESS TOURNAMENT—1998

(Feb. 14–July 1, 1998, Reno, Nev.)

Regular Division

Singles— John Gaines, Davidsonville, Md.	814
Doubles— Keith Klenck, Chicago, and Rick Hara, Mt. Prospect, Ill.	1,455
All Events—Chris Barnes, Wichita, Kan.	2,151
Team—Drillings Amoco, Wis.	3,361

Booster Division

Team— Earth Service, Inc., Gowen, Mich.	2,814

WOMEN'S INTERNATIONAL BOWLING CONGRESS TOURNAMENT—1998

(Apr. 1–July 1, 1998, Quad Cities, Illinois/Iowa)

Singles— Nellie Glandon, London, Ohio	714
Doubles— Lynda Norry, Wichita, Kansas, and Kendra Cameron, Gambrills, Md.	1,305
All Events— Liz Johnson, Niagara Falls, N.Y.	1,989
Team— Bowlers Choice Pro Shop II, Skaneateles, N.Y.	3,044

B.P.A.A. U.S. OPEN—1998

(April 3–April 11, 1998, Milford, Conn.)

Men

Walter Ray Williams, Jr., Stockton, Calif., defeated Tim Criss, Bel Air, Md. 221–189 in final match.
3. Ryan Shafer, Elmira, N.Y., and Martin Letscher, Niles, Ohio (tie)

Women

Aleta Sill, Dearborn, Mich., defeated Tammy Turner, Stow, Ohio 276–151 in final match.
3. Marianne DiRupo, Succasunna, N.J., and Kim Adler, Las Vegas, Nev. (tie)

Skiing

HISTORY OF SKIING IN THE UNITED STATES

Skis were devised for utility, to aid those who had to travel over snow. The Norwegians, Swedes, Lapps, and other inhabitants of northern lands used skis for many centuries before skiing became a sport. Emigrants from these countries brought skis to the United States with them. The first skier of record in the United States was a mailman by the name of "Snowshoe" Thompson, born and raised in Telemarken, Norway, who came to the United States and, beginning in 1850, used skis through 20 successive winters in carrying mail from Northern California to Carson Valley, Idaho.

Ski clubs sprang up over 100 years ago where there were Norwegian and Swedish settlers in Wisconsin and Minnesota and ski contests were held in that territory in 1886. On Feb. 21, 1904, at Ishpening, Mich., a small group of skiers organized the National Ski Association. In 1961 it was renamed the United States Ski Association.

1998 UNITED STATES ALPINE CHAMPIONSHIPS

(March 21–25, 1998, Jackson Hole, Wyo.)

Women

Downhill—1. Kirsten Clark, Raymond, Maine; 2. Jonna Mendes, S. Lake Tahoe, Calif.; 3. Julie Parisien, Auburn, Maine

Giant Slalom—1. Sarah Schleper, Vail, Colo.; 2. Julie Parisien, Auburn, Maine; 3. Caroline Lalive, Steamboat Springs, Colo.

Slalom—1. Kristina Koznick, Burnsville, Minn.; 2. Tasha Nelson, Mound, Minn.; 3. Alex Krebs, Waitsfield, Vt.

Combined—1. Julie Parisien, Auburn, Maine; 2. Katie Monahan, Aspen, Colo.; 3. Alex Shaffer, Aspen, Colo.

Men

Downhill—1. Ed Podivinsky, Canada; 2. AJ Kitt, Boulder, Colo.; 3. Daron Rahlves, Truckee, Calif.

Giant Slalom—1. Bode Miller, Franconia, N.H.; 2. (tie) Dane Spencer, Boise, Idaho, and Thomas Grandi, Canada

Slalom—1. Sacha Gros, Vail, Colo.; 2. Andrezej Bachleda, Poland; 3. Andy LeRoy, Silverthorne, Colo.

Combined—1. Dane Spencer, Boise, Idaho; 2. Jakub Fiala, Breckenridge, Colo.; 3. Andy LeRoy, Silverthorne, Colo.

1998 ALPINE WORLD CUP CHAMPIONS

Women	Pts
Overall— Katja Seizinger, Germany	1,655
Downhill— Katja Seizinger, Germany	520
Super G— Katja Seizinger, Germany	445
Giant Slalom— Martina Ertl, Germany	591
Slalom— Ylva Nowen, Sweden	620

Men	Pts
Overall— Hermann Maier, Austria	1,685
Downhill— Andreas Schifferer, Austria	655
Super G— Hermann Maier, Austria	400
Giant Slalom— Hermann Maier, Austria	620
Slalom— Thomas Sykora, Austria	521

NORDIC SKIING/SKI JUMPING

1998 United States Ski Jumping Championships

(March 20–22, 1998, Steamboat Springs, Colo.)

Large Hill (K=112m)—Todd Lodwick, Steamboat Springs, Colo.

Normal Hill (K=88m)—Randy Weber, Steamboat Springs, Colo.

1998 Nordic Combined World Cup

	Pts
1. Bjarte Engen Vik, Norway	1,468
2. Mario Stecher, Austria	1,440
3. Felix Gottwald, Austria	854
4. Todd Lodwick, United States	848
5. Hannu Manninen, Finland	763

1998 Cross Country U.S. Nationals

March 29–April 2, Mt. Bachelor, Oregon

Women

5k Classic—Wendy Kay Wagner
5k Classic (Disabled)—Nancy Stevens
10k Freestyle—Laura Wilson
10k Freestyle (Disabled)—Nancy Stevens
15k Freestyle—Laura Wilson
15k Freestyle (Disabled)—Nancy Stevens
15k Relay—Jen Douglas, Jenny Fayette, Laura Wilson

Men

10k Classic—Marcus Nash
10k Classic (Disabled)—Mike Crenshaw
15k Freestyle—Marcus Nash
15k Freestyle (Disabled)—Willie Stewart
30k Freestyle—Patrick Weaver
30k Freestyle (Disabled)—Willie Stewart
30k Relay—Patrick Weaver, Ben Husaby, Justin Wadsworth
5k Sit Ski—Bob Balk
10k Sit Ski—Bob Balk

FREESTYLE SKIING

1998 Freestyle Skiing World Cup

Women

Acro—Elena Batalova, Russia
Moguls—Marja Elfman, Sweden
Aerials—Nikki Stone, United States
Dual Moguls—Kari Traa, Norway
Overall—Nikki Stone, United States

Men

Acro—Fabrice Becker, France
Moguls—Jonny Moseley, United States
Aerials—Nicolas Fontaine, Canada
Dual Moguls—Jesper Rönnbäck, Sweden
Overall—Fabrice Becker, France

1998 U.S. Freestyle Championships

March 23–29, 1998, Sugarloaf, Maine

Women

Acro—Maria Guarnieri, Mahopoc, N.Y.
Moguls—Liz McIntyre, Winter Park, Colo.
Aerials—Nikki Stone, Westborough, Mass.
Dual Moguls—Ann Battelle, Steamboat Springs, Colo.

Men

Acro—Steve Roxberg, Lakeville, Minn.
Moguls—Jonny Moseley, Tiburon, Calif.
Aerials—Matt Chojnacki, Aurora, Colo.
Dual Moguls—Garth Hager, Bothell, Wash.

SNOWBOARDING

1998 U.S. Snowboarding Championships

March 23–28, 1998, Sunday River, Maine

Men

Halfpipe—Ross Powers, South Londonderry, Vt.
Slalom—Mike Kildevaeld, San Diego, Calif.
Giant Slalom—Rob Berney, Whitefish, Mont.

Women

Halfpipe—Griselda Gonzalez, Saratoga, Calif.
Slalom—Sondra Van Ert, Ketchum, Idaho
Giant Slalom—Sondra Van Ert, Ketchum, Idaho

JAMES E. SULLIVAN MEMORIAL AWARD WINNERS
(Amateur Athlete of Year Chosen in Amateur Athletic Union Poll)

1930	Robert Tyre Jones, Jr.	Golf
1931	Bernard E. Berlinger	Track and field
1932	James A. Bausch	Track and field
1933	Glenn Cunningham	Track and field
1934	William R. Bonthron	Track and field
1935	W. Lawson Little, Jr.	Golf
1936	Glenn Morris	Track and field
1937	J. Donald Budge	Tennis
1938	Donald R. Lash	Track and field
1939	Joseph W. Burk	Rowing
1940	J. Gregory Rice	Track and field
1941	Leslie MacMitchell	Track and field
1942	Cornelius Warmerdam	Track and field
1943	Gilbert L. Dodds	Track and field
1944	Ann Curtis	Swimming
1945	Felix (Doc) Blanchard	Football
1946	Y. Arnold Tucker	Football
1947	John B. Kelly, Jr.	Rowing
1948	Robert B. Mathias	Track and field
1949	Richard T. Button	Figure skating
1950	Fred Wilt	Track and field
1951	Robert E. Richards	Track and field
1952	Horace Ashenfelter	Track and field
1953	Sammy Lee	Diving
1954	Malvin Whitfield	Track and field
1955	Harrison Dillard	Track and field
1956	Patricia McCormick	Diving
1957	Bobby Jo Morrow	Track and field
1958	Glenn Davis	Track and field
1959	Parry O'Brien	Track and field
1960	Rafer Johnson	Track and field
1961	Wilma Rudolph Ward	Track and field
1962	Jim Beatty	Track and field
1963	John Pennel	Track and field
1964	Don Schollander	Swimming
1965	Bill Bradley	Basketball
1966	Jim Ryun	Track and field
1967	Randy Matson	Track and field
1968	Debbie Meyer	Swimming
1969	Bill Toomey	Decathlon
1970	John Kinsella	Swimming
1971	Mark Spitz	Swimming
1972	Frank Shorter	Marathon
1973	Bill Walton	Basketball
1974	Rick Wohlhuter	Track and field
1975	Tim Shaw	Swimming
1976	Bruce Jenner	Track and field
1977	John Naber	Swimming
1978	Tracy Caulkins	Swimming
1979	Kurt Thomas	Gymnastics
1980	Eric Heiden	Speed skating
1981	Carl Lewis	Track and field
1982	Mary Decker Tabb	Track and field
1983	Edwin Moses	Track and field
1984	Greg Louganis	Diving
1985	Joan Benoit-Samuelson	Marathon
1986	Jackie Joyner-Kersee	Heptathlon
1987	Jim Abbott	Baseball
1988	Florence Griffith-Joyner	Track and field
1989	Janet Evans	Swimming
1990	John Smith	Wrestling
1991	Mike Powell	Track and field
1992	Bonnie Blair	Speed skating
1993	Charles Ward	Football/Basketball
1994	Dan Jansen	Speed skating
1995	Bruce Baumgartner	Wrestling
1996	Michael Johnson	Track and field
1997	Peyton Manning	Football

Speed Skating

WORLD SPEED SKATING RECORDS (LONG TRACK)

Distance	Time	Skater	Place	Year
Men				
500m	34.82	Hiroyasu Shimizu, Japan	Calgary, Canada	March 28, 1998
1,000m	1:09.60	Sylvain Bouchard, Canada	Calgary, Canada	March 29, 1998
1,500m	1:46.43	Ådne Søndrål, Norway	Calgary, Canada	March 28, 1998
3,000m	3:48.91	Bart Veldkamp, Belgium	Calgary, Canada	March 21, 1998
5,000m	6:21.49	Gianni Romme, Netherlands	Calgary, Canada	March 27, 1998
10,000m	13:08.71	Gianni Romme, Netherlands	Calgary, Canada	March 29, 1998
Women				
500m	37.55	Catriona LeMay-Doan, Canada	Calgary, Canada	Dec. 29, 1997
1,000m	1:14.96	Christine Witty, United States	Calgary, Canada	March 28, 1998
1,500m	1:56.95	Anna Friesinger, Germany	Calgary, Canada	March 29, 1998
3,000m	4:01.67	Gunda Niemann-Stirnemann, Germany	Calgary, Canada	March 27, 1998
5,000m	6:58.63	Gunda Niemann-Stirnemann, Germany	Calgary, Canada	March 28, 1998

WORLD SPRINT CHAMPIONSHIPS—1998
(Jan. 24–25, 1998, Berlin, Germany)

Men	Time
500m—Jeremy Wotherspoon, Canada	35.99
1,000m—Jan Bos, Netherlands	1:11.10
Overall standings:	**Points**
1. Jan Bos, Netherlands	143.735
2. Jeremy Wotherspoon, Canada	144.425
3. Erben Wennemars, Netherlands	145.235

Women	Time
500m—Catriona LeMay-Doan, Canada	38.65
1,000m—Franziska Schenk, Germany	1:17.49
Overall standings:	**Points**
1. Catriona LeMay-Doan, Canada	154.890
2. Sabine Völker, Germany	156.125
3. Chris Witty, United States	156.320

1997–98 WORLD CUP CHAMPIONS

Men

500m	Jeremy Wotherspoon, Canada
1,000m	Jeremy Wotherspoon, Canada
1,500m	Ids Postma, Netherlands
5,000m/10,000m	Gianni Romme, Netherlands

Women

500m	Catriona LeMay-Doan, Canada
1,000m	Catriona LeMay-Doan, Canada
1,500m	Gunda Niemann-Stirnemann, Germany
3,000m/5,000m	Gunda Niemann-Stirnemann, Germany

WORLD SHORT TRACK CHAMPIONSHIPS—1998

(March 20–22, 1998, Vienna, Austria)

Men	Time
500m—Kai Feng, China	42.458
1,000m—Marc Gagnon, Canada	1:34.117
1,500m—Marc Gagnon, Canada	2:16.929
3,000m—Dong-Sung Kim, South Korea	5:15.007
Relay—Canada	7:01.557

Women	Time
500m—Chunlu Wang, China	45.087
1,000m—Yang Yang, China	1:33.562
1,500m—Marinella Canclini, Italy	2:25.291
3,000m—Lee-Kyung Chun, South Korea	5:19.340
Relay—China	4:21.122

WORLD CHAMPIONSHIPS—1998

(March 13–15, 1998, Heerenveen, Netherlands)

Men

500 meters	Ids Postma, Netherlands
1,500 meters	Ids Postma, Netherlands
5,000 meters	Ids Postma, Netherlands
10,000 meters	Bart Veldkamp, Belgium
All-around	Ids Postma, Netherlands

Women

500 meters	Chris Witty, United States
1,500 meters	Gunda Niemann-Stirnemann, Germany
3,000 meters	Gunda Niemann-Stirnemann, Germany
5,000 meters	Gunda Niemann-Stirnemann, Germany
All-around	Gunda Niemann-Stirnemann, Germany

Figure Skating

WORLD CHAMPIONS

Men

1960	Alain Gilotti, France
1961	No competition
1962	Donald Jackson, Canada
1963	Don McPherson, Canada
1964	Manfred Schnelldorfer, West Germany
1965	Alain Calmat, France
1966–68	Emmerich Danzer, Austria
1969–70	Tim Wood, United States
1971–73	Ondrej Nepela, Czechoslovakia
1974	Jan Hoffman, East Germany
1975	Sergei Yolkov, U.S.S.R.
1976	John Curry, Britain
1977	Vladimir Kovalev, U.S.S.R.
1978	Charles Tickner, United States
1979	Vladimir Kovalev, U.S.S.R.
1980	Jan Hoffman, East Germany
1981–84	Scott Hamilton, United States
1985	Alexandr Fadeev, U.S.S.R.
1986	Brian Boitano, United States
1987	Brian Orser, Canada
1988	Brian Boitano, United States
1989–91	Kurt Browning, Canada
1992	Viktor Petrenko, Unified Team
1993	Kurt Browning, Canada
1994	Elvis Stojko, Canada
1995	Elvis Stojko, Canada
1996	Todd Eldredge, United States
1997	Elvis Stojko, Canada
1998	Alexei Yagudin, Russia

Women

1956–60	Carol Heiss, United States
1961	No competition
1962–64	Sjoukje Dijkstra, Netherlands
1965	Petra Burka, Canada
1966–68	Peggy Fleming, United States
1969–70	Gabriele Seyfert, East Germany
1971–72	Beatrix Schuba, Austria
1973	Karen Magnusson, Canada
1974	Christine Errath, East Germany
1975	Dianne de Leeuw, Netherlands
1976	Dorothy Hamill, United States
1977	Linda Fratianne, United States
1978	Anett Poetzsch, East Germany
1979	Linda Fratianne, United States
1980	Anett Poetzsch, East Germany
1981	Denise Beillmann, Switzerland
1982	Elaine Zayak, United States
1983	Rosalynn Sumners, United States
1984–85	Katarina Witt, East Germany
1986	Debi Thomas, United States
1987–88	Katarina Witt, East Germany
1989	Midori Ito, Japan
1990	Jill Trenary, United States
1991–92	Kristi Yamaguchi, United States
1993	Oksana Baiul, Ukraine
1994	Yuka Sato, Japan
1995	Chen Lu, China
1996	Michelle Kwan, United States
1997	Tara Lipinski, United States
1998	Michelle Kwan, United States

U.S. CHAMPIONS

Men

1946–52	Richard Button
1953–56	Hayes Jenkins
1957–60	David Jenkins
1961	Bradley Lord
1962	Monty Hoyt
1963	Tommy Liz
1964	Scott Allen
1965	Gary Visconti
1966	Scott Allen
1967	Gary Visconti
1968–70	Tim Wood
1971	John M. Petkevich
1972	Ken Shelley
1973–75	Gordon McKellen
1976	Terry Kubicka
1977–80	Charles Tickner
1981–84	Scott Hamilton

1985–88 Brian Boitano
1989 Christopher Bowman
1990–91 Todd Eldredge
1992 Christopher Bowman
1993–94 Scott Davis
1995 Todd Eldredge
1996 Rudy Galindo
1997–98 Todd Eldredge

Women

1943–48 Gretchen Merrill
1949–50 Yvonne Sherman
1951 Sonya Klopfer
1952–56 Tenley Albright
1957–60 Carol Heiss
1961 Laurence Owen
1962 Barbara Roles Pursley
1963 Lorraine Hanlon
1964–68 Peggy Fleming
1969–73 Janet Lynn
1974–76 Dorothy Hamill
1977–80 Linda Fratianne
1981 Elaine Zayak
1982–84 Rosalynn Sumners
1985 Tiffany Chin
1986 Debi Thomas
1987 Jill Trenary
1988 Debi Thomas
1989–90 Jill Trenary
1991 Tonya Harding
1992 Kristi Yamaguchi
1993 Nancy Kerrigan
1994 Tonya Harding
1995 Nicole Bobek
1996 Michelle Kwan
1997 Tara Lipinski
1998 Michelle Kwan

1998 UNITED STATES CHAMPIONSHIPS

Jan. 4–11, 1998, Philadelphia

Men's singles
1. Todd Eldredge, Chatham, Mass.
2. Michael G. Weiss, Fairfax, Va.
3. Scott Davis, Great Falls, Mont.

Women's singles
1. Michelle Kwan, Torrance, Calif.
2. Tara Lipinski, Sugar Land, Texas
3. Nicole Bobek, Chicago, Ill.

Pairs
1. Kyoko Ina, Guttenberg, N.J., and Jason Dungjen, Goshen, N.Y.
2. Shelby Lyons, Oswego, N.Y., and Brian Wells, St. Louis, Mo.
3. Danielle and Steve Hartsell, Westland, Mich.

Dance
1. Elizabeth Punsalan and Jerod Swallow, Pontiac, Mich.
2. Jessica Joseph, Bloomfield Hills, Mich., and Charles Butler, Kalamazoo, Mich.
3. Naomi Lang, Allegan, Mich., and Peter Tchernyshev, Lake Placid, N.Y.

1998 WORLD CHAMPIONSHIPS

March 29–April 3, 1998, Minneapolis

Men's singles
1. Alexei Yagudin, Russia
2. Todd Eldredge, United States
3. Evgeni Plushenko, Russia

Women's singles
1. Michelle Kwan, United States
2. Irina Slutskaya, Russia
3. Maria Butyrskaya, Russia

Pairs
1. Elena Berezhnaya and Anton Sikharulidze, Russia
2. Jenni Meno and Todd Sand, United States
3. Peggy Schwarz and Mirko Müller, Germany

Dance
1. Anjelika Krylova and Oleg Ovsyannikov, Russia
2. Marina Anissina and Gwendal Peizerat, France
3. Shae-Lynn Bourne and Victor Kraatz, Canada

Swimming

WORLD RECORDS—MEN

(Through Sept. 19, 1998)

Distance	Record	Holder	Country	Date
Freestyle				
50 meters	0:21.81	Tom Jager	United States	March 24, 1990
100 meters	0:48.21	Alexander Popov	Russia	June 18, 1994
200 meters	1:46.69	Georgio Lamberti	Italy	Aug. 15, 1989
400 meters	3:43.80	Kieren Perkins	Australia	Sept. 9, 1994
800 meters	7:46.00	Kieren Perkins	Australia	Aug. 24, 1994
1,500 meters	14:41.66	Kieren Perkins	Australia	Aug. 24, 1994
Backstroke				
100 meters	0:53.86	Jeff Rouse	United States	July 31, 1992
200 meters	1:56.57	Martin Zubero	Spain	Nov. 23, 1991
Breaststroke				
100 meters	1:00.60	Fred DeBurghgraeve	Belgium	July 20, 1996
200 meters	2:10.16	Mike Barrowman	United States	July 29, 1992
Butterfly				
100 meters	0:52.15	Michael Klim	Australia	Oct. 9, 1997
200 meters	1:55.22	Denis Pankratov	Russia	June 14, 1995
Individual medley				
200 meters	1:58.16	Jani Sievinen	Finland	Sept. 11, 1994
400 meters	4:12.30	Tom Dolan	United States	Sept. 6, 1994

Distance	Record	Holder	Country	Date
Medley relay				
400 meters	3:34.84	Olympic Team	United States	July 26, 1996
Freestyle relay				
400 meters	3:15.11	National Team	United States	Aug. 12, 1995
800 meters	7:11.95	Unified Team	Former Soviet Union	July 27, 1992

Approved by the International Swimming Federation (F.I.N.A.). (F.I.N.A. discontinued acceptance of records in yards in 1968). *Source:* United States Swim Team.

WORLD RECORDS—WOMEN

(Through Sept. 19, 1998)

Distance	Record	Holder	Country	Date
Freestyle				
50 meters	0:24.51	Jingyi Le	China	Sept. 11, 1994
100 meters	0:54.01	Jingyi Le	China	Sept. 5, 1994
200 meters	1:56.78	Franziska van Almsick	Germany	Sept. 6, 1994
400 meters	4:03.85	Janet Evans	United States	Sept. 22, 1988
800 meters	8:16.22	Janet Evans	United States	Aug. 20, 1989
1,500 meters	15:52.10	Janet Evans	United States	March 26, 1988
Backstroke				
100 meters	1:00.16	Cihong He	China	Sept. 10, 1994
200 meters	2:06.62	Krisztina Egerszegi	Hungary	Aug. 25, 1991
Breaststroke				
50 meters	0:30.95	Penny Heyns	South Africa	Aug. 1, 1998
100 meters	1:07.02	Penny Heyns	South Africa	July 21, 1996
200 meters	2:24.76	Rebecca Brown	Australia	March 16, 1994
Butterfly				
100 meters	0:57.93	Mary T. Meagher	United States	Aug. 16, 1981
200 meters	2:05.96	Mary T. Meagher	United States	Aug. 13, 1981
Individual medley				
200 meters	2:09.72	Yanyan Wu	China	Oct. 17, 1997
400 meters	4:34.79	Chon Yan	China	Oct. 13, 1997
Medley relay				
400 meters	4:01.67	National Team	China	Sept. 10, 1994
Freestyle relay				
400 meters	3:37.91	National Team	China	Sept. 7, 1994
800 meters	7:55.47	National Team	East Germany	Aug. 18, 1987

Approved by the International Swimming Federation (F.I.N.A.). (F.I.N.A. discontinued acceptance of records in yards in 1968). *Source:* United States Swim Team.

AMERICAN SWIMMING RECORDS

(Through Sept. 19, 1998)

Distance	Record	Holder	Date
MEN			
Freestyle			
50 meters	0:21.81	Tom Jager	March 24, 1990
100 meters	0:48.42	Matt Biondi	Aug. 10, 1988
200 meters	1:47.72	Matt Biondi	Aug. 8, 1988
400 meters	3:48.06	Matt Cetlinski	Aug. 11, 1988
800 meters	7:52.45	Sean Killion	July 27, 1987
1,500 meters	15:01.51	George DiCarlo	June 30, 1984
Backstroke			
100 meters	0:53.86	Jeff Rouse	July 31, 1992
200 meters	1:57.38	Lenny Krayzelburg	Aug. 12, 1998
Breaststroke			
100 meters	1:00.77	Jeremy Linn	July 20, 1996
200 meters	2:10.16	Mike Barrowman	July 29, 1992
Butterfly			
100 meters	0:52.76	Neil Walker	Aug. 12, 1997
200 meters	1:55.69	Mel Stewart	Jan. 12, 1991
Individual medley			
200 meters	2:00.11	David Wharton	Aug. 20, 1989
400 meters	4:12.30	Tom Dolan	Sept. 6, 1994

Distance	Record	Holder	Date
Medley relay			
400 meters	3:34.84	U.S. Olympic Team	July 26, 1996
Freestyle relay			
400 meters	3:15.11	U.S. National Team	Aug. 12, 1995
800 meters	7:12.51	U.S. National Team	Sept. 21, 1988

Distance	Record	Holder	Date
WOMEN			
Freestyle			
50 meters	0:24.87	Amy Van Dyken	July 26, 1996
100 meters	0:54.48	Jenny Thompson	March 1, 1992
200 meters	1:57.90	Nicole Haislett	July 27, 1992
400 meters	4:03.85	Janet Evans	Sept. 22, 1988
800 meters	8:16.22	Janet Evans	Aug. 20, 1989
1,500 meters	15:52.10	Janet Evans	March 26, 1988
Backstroke			
100 meters	1:00.77	Lea Maurer	Jan. 14, 1998
200 meters	2:08.60	Betsy Mitchell	June 27, 1986
Breaststroke			
100 meters	1:08.09	Amanda Beard	July 21, 1996
200 meters	2:25.35	Anita Nall	March 2, 1992
Butterfly			
100 meters	0:57.93	Mary T. Meagher	Aug. 16, 1981
200 meters	2:05.96	Mary T. Meagher	Aug. 13, 1981
Individual medley			
200 meters	2:11.91	Summer Sanders	July 30, 1992
400 meters	4:37.58	Summer Sanders	July 26, 1992
Medley relay			
400 meters	4:01.93	U.S. National Team	Jan. 16, 1998
Freestyle relay			
400 meters	3:39.29	U.S. Olympic Team	July 22, 1996
800 meters	7:59.87	U.S. National Team	July 25, 1996

Source: United States Swim Team.

N.C.A.A. SWIMMING AND DIVING CHAMPIONSHIPS—1998

Men

(March 26–28, 1998, Auburn, Ala.)

50-yard freestyle—Brendon Dedekind, Florida State	0:19.22
100-yard freestyle—Lars Frolander, Southern Methodist	0:42.12
200-yard freestyle—Ryk Neethling, Arizona	1:34.19
500-yard freestyle—Ryk Neethling, Arizona	4:13.42
1,650-yard freestyle—Ryk Neethling, Arizona	14:32.50
100-yard backstroke—Neil Walker, Texas	0:46.66
200-yard backstroke—Tate Blahnik, Stanford	1:41.21
100-yard breaststroke—Jeremy Linn, Tennessee	0:53.01
200-yard breaststroke—Tom Wilkens, Stanford	1:55.02
100-yard butterfly—Lars Frolander, Southern Methodist	0:45.59
200-yard butterfly—Matthew Pierce, Stanford	1:43.68
200-yard individual medley—Tom Wilkens, Stanford	1:45.16
400-yard individual medley—Tom Wilkens, Stanford	3:43.96
200-yard freestyle relay—Stanford	1:16.76
400-yard freestyle relay—Stanford	2:51.37
800-yard freestyle relay—Texas	6:23.78
200-yard medley relay—Auburn	1:25.24
400-yard medley relay—Stanford	3:07.73
1-meter springboard dive—Rio Ramirez, Miami	630.70 pts
3-meter springboard dive—Bryan Gillooly, Miami	631.40 pts
Platform dive—Brent Roberts, Alabama	834.45 pts
Team standings:	
1. Stanford	599.00 pts
2. Auburn	394.50 pts
3. Texas	362.50 pts

Women

(March 19–21, 1998, University of Minnesota, Minneapolis)

50-yard freestyle—Catherine Fox, Stanford	0:22.21
100-yard freestyle—Martina Moravcova, Southern Methodist	0:48.81
200-yard freestyle—Martina Moravcova, Southern Methodist	1:45.11
500-yard freestyle—Cristina Teuscher, Columbia	4:35.45
1650-yard freestyle—Trina Jackson, Arizona	15:49.25
100-yard backstroke—Catherine Fox, Stanford	0:52.71
200-yard backstroke—Misty Hyman, Stanford	1:53.12
100-yard breaststroke—Kristy Kowal, Georgia	0:59.05
200-yard breaststroke—Kristy Kowal, Georgia	2:09.14
100-yard butterfly—Misty Hyman, Stanford	0:51.34
200-yard butterfly—Misty Hyman, Stanford	1:55.70
200-yard individual medley—Martina Moravcova, Southern Methodist	1:57.37
400-yard individual medley—Cristina Teuscher, Columbia	4:05.62
200-yard freestyle relay—Arizona	1:29.16
400-yard freestyle relay—Arizona	3:15.77
800-yard freestyle relay—Arizona	7:10.79
200-yard medley relay—Stanford	1:37.80
400-yard medley relay—Stanford	3:33.61
1-meter springboard dive—Vera Ilyina, Texas	495.70 pts
3-meter springboard dive—Vera Ilyina, Texas	612.60 pts
Platform dive—Kathy Presek, Tennessee	659.65 pts
Team standings:	
1. Stanford	422.00 pts
2. Arizona	378.00 pts
3. Georgia	368.00 pts

1998 WORLD SWIMMING CHAMPIONSHIPS

(January 7–18, 1998, Perth, Australia)

Men

50-meter freestyle—Bill Pilczuk, United States	0:22.29
100-meter freestyle—Alexander Popov, Russia	0:48.93
200-meter freestyle—Michael Klim, Australia	1:47.41
400-meter freestyle—Ian Thorpe, Australia	3:46.29
1500-meter freestyle—Grant Hackett, Australia	14:51.70
100-meter backstroke—Lenny Krayzelburg, United States	0:55.00
200-meter backstroke—Lenny Krayzelburg, United States	1:58.84
100-meter breaststroke—Frederik Deburghgraeve, Belgium	1:01.34
200-meter breaststroke—Kurt Grote, United States	2:13.40
100-meter butterfly—Michael Klim, Australia	0:52.25
200-meter butterfly—Denys Sylantyev, Ukraine	1:56.61
200-meter individual medley—Marcel Wouda, Netherlands	2:01.18
400-meter individual medley—Tom Dolan, United States	4:14.95
800-meter freestyle relay—Australia	7:12.48
400-meter freestyle relay—United States (Scott Tucker, Neil Walker, Jon Olsen, Gary Hall, Jr.)	3:16.69
400-meter medley relay—Australia	3:37.98
5-kilometer open water—Alexei Akatiev, Russia	55:18.60
25-kilometer open water—Alexei Akatiev, Russia	5:05:42.10

Women

50-meter freestyle—Amy Van Dyken, United States	0:25.15
100-meter freestyle—Jenny Thompson, United States	0:54.95
200 meter freestyle—Claudia Poll, Costa Rica	1:58.90
400-meter freestyle—Chen Yan, China	4:06.72
800-meter freestyle—Brooke Bennett, United States	8:28.71
100-meter backstroke—Lea Maurer, United States	1:01.16
200-meter backstroke—Roxanna Maracineanu, France	2:11.26
100-meter breaststroke—Kristy Kowal, United States	1:08.42
200-meter breaststroke—Agnes Kovacs, Hungary	2:25.45
100-meter butterfly—Jenny Thompson, United States	0:58.46
200-meter butterfly—Susie O'Neill, Australia	2:07.93
200-meter individual medley—Wu Yanyan, China	2:10.88
400-meter individual medley—Chen Yan, China	4:36.66
400-meter freestyle relay—United States (Lindsey Farella, Amy Van Dyken, B.J. Bedford, Jenny Thompson)	3:42.11
800-meter freestyle relay—Germany	8:01.46
400-meter medley relay—United States (Lea Maurer, Kristy Kowal, Jenny Thompson, Amy Van Dyken)	4:01.93
5-kilometer open water—Erica Rose, United States	59:23.50
25-kilometer open water—Tobie Smith, United States	5:31:20.10

5-kilometer open water teams: 1. United States, 18 points; 2. Russia, 16; 3. Italy, 14

25–kilometer open water teams: 1. Italy, 18 points; 2. Australia, 16; 3. United States, 14

Boxing

Whether it be called pugilism, prize fighting, or boxing, there is no tracing "the Sweet Science" to any definite source. Tales of rivals exchanging blows for fun, fame, or money go back to earliest recorded history and classical legend. There was a mixture of boxing and wrestling called the "pancratium" in the ancient Olympic Games; in such contests rivals belabored one another with hands fortified by heavy leather wrappings that were sometimes studded with metal. More than one Olympic competitor lost his life in this brutal exercise.

There was little law or order in pugilism until Jack Broughton, one of the early champions of England, drew up a set of rules for the game in 1743. Broughton, called "the father of English boxing," also is credited with having invented boxing gloves. However, these gloves—or "mufflers" as they were called—were used only in teaching "the manly art of self-defense" or in training bouts. All professional championship fights were contested with bare knuckles until 1892, when John L. Sullivan lost the heavyweight championship of the world to James J. Corbett in New Orleans in a bout in which both contestants wore regulation gloves.

The Broughton Rules were superseded by the London Prize Ring Rules of 1838. In 1986 the eighth marquis of Queensberry, with the help of John G. Chambers, put forward the Queensberry Rules, a code that called for gloved contests. Amateurs took to the Queensberry Rules more quickly than the professionals did.

HISTORY OF WORLD HEAVYWEIGHT CHAMPIONSHIP FIGHTS

(Bouts in which a new champion was crowned)

Date	Where held	Winner, weight, age	Loser, weight, age	Rounds
Sept. 7, 1892	New Orleans, La.	James J. Corbett, 178 (26)	John L. Sullivan, 212 (33)	21
March 17, 1897	Carson City, Nev.	Bob Fitzsimmons, 167 (34)	James J. Corbett, 183 (30)	KO 14
June 9, 1899	Coney Island, N.Y.	James J. Jeffries, 206 (24)[1]	Bob Fitzsimmons, 167 (37)	KO 11
Feb. 23, 1906	Los Angeles	Tommy Burns, 180 (24)[2]	Marvin Hart, 188 (29)	20
Dec. 26, 1908	Sydney, N.S.W.	Jack Johnson, 196 (30)	Tommy Burns, 176 (27)	KO 14
April 5, 1915	Havana, Cuba	Jess Willard, 230 (33)	Jack Johnson, 205½ (37)	KO 26
July 4, 1919	Toledo, Ohio	Jack Dempsey, 187 (24)	Jess Willard, 245 (37)	KO 3
Sept. 23, 1926	Philadelphia	Gene Tunney, 189 (28)[3]	Jack Dempsey, 190 (31)	10
June 12, 1930	New York	Max Schmeling, 188 (24)	Jack Sharkey, 197 (27)	WF 4
June 21, 1932	Long Island City	Jack Sharkey, 205 (29)	Max Schmeling, 188 (26)	15
June 29, 1933	Long Island City	Primo Carnera, 260½ (26)	Jack Sharkey, 201 (30)	KO 6
June 14, 1934	Long Island City	Max Baer, 209½ (25)	Primo Carnera, 263¼ (27)	KO 11
June 13, 1935	Long Island City	Jim Braddock, 193¾ (29)	Max Baer, 209½ (26)	15
June 22, 1937	Chicago	Joe Louis, 197¼ (23)	Jim Braddock, 197 (31)	KO 8
June 22, 1949	Chicago	Ezzard Charles, 181¾ (27)[4]	Joe Walcott, 195½ (35)	15
Sept. 27, 1950	New York	Ezzard Charles, 184½ (29)[5]	Joe Louis, 218 (36)	15
July 18, 1951	Pittsburgh	Joe Walcott, 194 (37)	Ezzard Charles, 182 (30)	KO 7
Sept. 23, 1952	Philadelphia	Rocky Marciano, 184 (29)[6]	Joe Walcott, 196 (38)	KO13
Nov. 30, 1956	Chicago	Floyd Patterson, 182¼ (21)	Archie Moore, 187¾ (42)	KO 5
June 26, 1959	New York	Ingemar Johansson, 196 (26)	Floyd Patterson, 182 (24)	KO 3
June 20, 1960	New York	Floyd Patterson, 190 (25)	Ingemar Johansson, 194¾ (27)	KO 5
Sept. 25, 1962	Chicago	Sonny Liston, 214 (28)	Floyd Patterson, 189 (27)	KO 1
Feb. 25, 1964	Miami Beach, Fla.	Cassius Clay, 210 (22)[7]	Sonny Liston, 218 (30)	KO 7
March 4, 1968	New York	Joe Frazier, 204½ (24)[8]	Buster Mathis, 243½ (23)	KO 11
April 27, 1968	Oakland, Calif.	Jimmy Ellis, 197 (28)[9]	Jerry Quarry, 195 (22)	15
Feb. 16, 1970	New York	Joe Frazier, 205 (26)[10]	Jimmy Ellis, 201 (29)	KO 5
Jan. 22, 1973	Kingston, Jamaica	George Foreman, 217½ (24)	Joe Frazier, 214 (29)	KO 2
Oct. 30, 1974	Kinshasa, Zaire	Muhammad Ali, 216½ (32)	George Foreman, 220 (26)	KO 8
Feb. 15, 1978	Las Vegas, Nev.	Leon Spinks, 197 (25)	Muhammad Ali, 224½ (36)	15
June 9, 1978	Las Vegas, Nev.	Larry Holmes, 212 (28)[11]	Ken Norton, 220 (32)	15
Sept. 15, 1978	New Orleans	Muhammad Ali, 221 (36)[12]	Leon Spinks, 201 (25)	15
Oct. 20, 1979	Pretoria, S. Africa	John Tate, 240 (24)[13]	Gerrie Coetzee, 222 (24)	15
March 31, 1980	Knoxville, Tenn.	Mike Weaver, 207½ (27)	John Tate, 232 (25)	KO 15
Dec. 10, 1982	Las Vegas, Nev.	Michael Dokes, 216 (24)	Mike Weaver, 209½ (30)	KO 1
Sept. 23, 1983	Richfield, Ohio	Gerrie Coetzee, 215 (28)	Michael Dokes, 217 (25)	KO 10
March 9, 1984	Las Vegas, Nev.	Tim Witherspoon, 220½ (26)[14]	Greg Page, 239½ (25)	12
Aug. 31, 1984	Las Vegas, Nev.	Pinklon Thomas, 216 (26)	Tim Witherspoon, 217 (26)	12
Nov. 9, 1984	Las Vegas, Nev.	Larry Holmes, 221½ (35)[15]	James Smith, 227 (31)	KO 12
Dec. 1, 1984	Sun City, S. Africa	Greg Page, 236 (25)[16]	Gerry Coetzee, 217 (29)	KO 8
April 29, 1985	Buffalo, N.Y.	Tony Tubbs, 229 (26)[16]	Greg Page, 239½ (26)	15
Sept. 21,1985	Las Vegas, Nev.	Michael Spinks, 200 (29)	Larry Holmes, 221 (35)	15
Jan. 17, 1986	Atlanta, Ga.	Tim Witherspoon, 227 (28)	Tony Tubbs, 229 (27)	15
Nov. 23, 1986	Las Vegas, Nev.	Mike Tyson, 217 (20)[17]	Trevor Berbick, 220 (29)	KO 2
Dec. 12, 1986	New York, N.Y.	James Smith, 230 (33)[16]	Tim Witherspoon, 218 (29)	KO 1
March 7, 1987	Las Vegas, Nev.	Mike Tyson, 217 (20)[16]	James Smith, 230 (33)	12
Feb. 10, 1990	Tokyo	James "Buster" Douglas,[18] 231½ (29)	Mike Tyson, (220) (23)	KO 10

Date	Where held	Winner, weight, age	Loser, weight, age	Rounds
Oct. 25, 1990	Las Vegas, Nev.	Evander Holyfield, 208 (28)	James "Buster" Douglas, 246 (30)	KO 3
Nov. 13, 1992	Las Vegas, Nev.	Riddick Bowe,[19] 235 (25)	Evander Holyfield, 205 (30)	12
Nov. 6, 1993	Las Vegas, Nev.	Evander Holyfield, 217 (30)	Riddick Bowe, 246 (26)	12
April 22, 1994	Las Vegas, Nev.	Michael Moorer, 214 (26)	Evander Holyfield,[20] 214 (31)	12
Sept 24, 1994	London, England	Oliver McCall,[21] 228 (29)	Lennox Lewis, 238 (28)	2
Nov. 5, 1994	Las Vegas, Nev.	George Foreman,[22] 250 (45)	Michael Moorer, 222 (26)	10
April 8, 1995	Las Vegas, Nev.	Bruce Seldon,[23] 232 (28)	Tony Tucker, 238 (36)	7
Dec.9, 1995	Stuttgart, Ger.	Frans Botha,[24] 227 (28)	Axel Schulz, 222 (27)	12
March 16, 1996	Las Vegas, Nev.	Mike Tyson,[25] 220 (29)	Frank Bruno, 247 (34)	3
June 22, 1996	Dortmund, Ger.	Michael Moorer, 222 (28)	Axel Schulz, 222 (27)	12
Sept. 7, 1996	Las Vegas, Nev.	Mike Tyson, 219 (30)	Bruce Seldon, 229 (29)	1
Nov. 9, 1996	Las Vegas, Nev.	Evander Holyfield,[23] 215 (34)	Mike Tyson, 222 (30)	11
Feb. 7, 1997	Las Vegas, Nev.	Lennox Lewis,[25] 251 (31)	Oliver McCall, 237 (30)	5
Nov. 8, 1997	Las Vegas, Nev.	Evander Holyfield,[26] 214 (35)	Michael Moorer, 223 (30)	8

1. Jeffries retired as champion in March 1905. He named Marvin Hart and Jack Root as leading contenders and agreed to referee their fight in Reno, Nev., on July 3, 1905, with the stipulation that he would term the winner the champion. Hart, 190 (28), knocked out Root, 171 (29), in the 12th round. 2. Burns claimed the title after defeating Hart. 3. Tunney retired as champion after defeating Tom Heeney on July 26, 1928. 4. After Louis announced his retirement as champion on March 1, 1949, Charles won recognition from the National Boxing Association as champion by defeating Walcott. 5. Charles gained undisputed recognition as champion by defeating Louis, who came out of retirement. 6. Retired as champion April 27, 1956. 7. The World Boxing Association later withdrew its recognition of Clay as champion and declared the winner of a bout between Ernie Terrell and Eddie Machen would gain its version of the title. Terrell, 199 (25), won a 15-round decision from Machen, 192 (32), in Chicago on March 5, 1965. Clay, 212¼ (25). and Terrell, 212½ (27), met in Houston on Feb. 6, 1967, Clay winning a 15-round decision. 8. Winner recognized by New York, Massachusetts, Maine, Illinois, Texas and Pennsylvania to fill vacated title when Clay was stripped of championship for failing to accept U.S. Induction. 9. Bout was final of eight-man tournament to fill Clay's place and is recognized by World Boxing Association. 10. Bout settled controversy over title. 11. Holmes won World Boxing Council title after WBC had withdrawn recognition of Spinks, March 18, 1978, and awarded its title to Norton. WBC said Spinks had reneged on agreement to fight Norton. 12. Ali regained World Boxing Association championship. 13. Tate won WBA title after Ali retired and left it vacant. 14. Tim Witherspoon and Greg Page fought for the WBC heavyweight title vacated by Larry Holmes, who could not come to agreement on a deal to fight Page, the No. 1 contender. Holmes declared he would fight under the banner of the International Boxing Federation. Several dates were set and postponed for fights between Holmes and Gerry Coetzee, the WBA champ, the latest being Nov. 16, 1984. 15. First fight under banner of International Boxing Federation. 16. New WBA champion. 17. New WBC champion. 18. New undisputed champion. 19. The WBC stripped Bowe of its version of the title in December 1992 and named Lennox Lewis champion. 20. After the loss, Holyfield retired. 21. New WBC champion. Lennox Lewis had been named champion in 1992 and had won three title defenses before losing to McCall. 22. For combined WBA/IBF titles. Later WBA stripped Foreman of title for failing to fight no. 1 contender Tony Tucker. IBF also stripped Foreman on June 29, 1995. 23. New WBA champion. 24. Botha later tested positive for steroids and was stripped of the title. 25. New WBC champion. 26. New IBF champion.

OTHER WORLD BOXING TITLEHOLDERS

(Through Sept. 21, 1998)

Light Heavyweight

1903	Jack Root, George Gardner
1903–05	Bob Fitzsimmons
1905–12	Philadelphia Jack O'Brien[1]
1912–16	Jack Dillon
1916–20	Battling Levinsky
1920–22	Georges Carpentier
1923	Battling Siki
1923–25	Mike McTigue
1925–26	Paul Berlenbach
1926–27	Jack Delaney[2]
1927	Mike McTigue
1927–29	Tommy Loughran
1930	Jimmy Slattery
1930–34	Maxie Rosenbloom
1934–35	Bob Olin
1935–39	John Henry Lewis
1939	Melio Bettina
1939–41	Billy Conn[2]
1941	Anton Christoforidis (NBA)
1941–48	Gus Lesnevich
1948–50	Freddie Mills
1950–52	Joey Maxim
1952–61	Archie Moore[3]
1961–63	Harold Johnson
1963–65	Willie Pastrano
1965–66	José Torres
1966–67	Dick Tiger
1968	Dick Tiger, Bob Foster
1969–70	Bob Foster
1971	Vicente Rondon (WBA), Bob Foster (WBC)
1972–73	Bob Foster (WBA, WBC)
1974	John Conteh (WBA), Bob Foster (WBC)[1 4]
1975–76	Victor Galindez (WBA), John Conteh (WBC)
1977	Victor Galindez (WBA), John Conteh (WBC),[4] Miguel Cuello (WBC)
1978	Victor Galindez (WBA), Mike Rossman (WBA), Miguel Cuello (WBC), Mate Parlov (WBC), Marvin Johnson (WBC)
1979	Mike Rossman (WBA), Victor Galindez (WBA), Marvin Johnson (WBC), Matthew (Franklin) Saad Muhammad (WBC)
1980	Matthew Saad Muhammad (WBC), Marvin Johnson (WBA), Eddie (Gregory) Mustafa Muhammad (WBA)
1981	Matthew Saad Muhammad (WBC), Eddie Mustafa Muhammad (WBA), Michael Spinks (WBA), Dwight Braxton (WBC)
1982	Dwight Braxton (WBC), Michael Spinks (WBA)
1983	Michael Spinks (undisputed)
1984	Michael Spinks (undisputed)
1985	Michael Spinks (undisputed)[5]
1986	Marvin Johnson (WBA), Dennis Andries (WBC)
1987	Thomas Hearns (WBC), Virgil Hill (WBA), Bobby Czyz (IBF)
1988	Charles Williams (IBF), Virgil Hill (WBA), Donny LaLonde (WBC), Sugar Ray Leonard (WBC)
1989	Dennis Andries (WBC), Virgil Hill (WBA), Charles Williams (IBF), Jeff Harding (WBC)
1990	Virgil Hill (WBA), Charles Williams (IBF), Jeff Harding (WBC), Dennis Andries (WBC)
1991	Virgil Hill (WBA), Thomas Hearns (WBA), Dennis Andries (WBC), Charles Williams (IBF)

1992	Charles Williams (IBF), James Waring (IBF), Jeff Harding (WBC)
1993	Virgil Hill (WBA), Jeff Harding (WBC), Henry Maske (IBF)
1994	Virgil Hill (WBA), Mike McCallum (WBC), Henry Maske (IBF)
1995	Virgil Hill (WBA), Fabio Tiozzo (WBC), Henry Maske (IBF)
1996–97	Virgil Hill (WBA), Fabio Tiozzo (WBC), Henry Maske (IBF)
1998	Roy Jones (WBA, WBC), Reggie Johnson (IBF)

1. Retired. 2. Abandoned title. 3. NBA withdrew recognition in 1961, New York Commission in 1962; recognized thereafter only by California and Europe. 4. WBC withdrew recognition. 5. Spinks relinquished title in 1985 to fight for heavyweight title.

Middleweight

1867–72	Tom Chandler
1872–81	George Rooke
1881–82	Mike Donovan[1]
1884–91	Jack (Nonpareil) Dempsey
1891–97	Bob Fitzsimmons[2]
1908	Stanley Ketchel, Billy Papke
1908–10	Stanley Ketchel[3]
1913	Frank Klaus
1913–14	George Chip
1914–17	Al McCoy
1917–20	Mike O'Dowd
1920–23	Johnny Wilson
1923–26	Harry Greb
1926	Tiger Flowers
1926–31	Mickey Walker[2]
1931–41	Gorilla Jones, Ben Jeby, Marcel Thil, Lou Brouillard, Vince Dundee, Teddy Yarosz, Babe Risko, Freddy Steele, Al Hostak, Solly Kreiger, Fred Apostoli, Cerferino Garcia, Ken Overlin, Billy Soose, Tony Zale[4]
1941–47	Tony Zale
1947–48	Rocky Graziano
1948	Tony Zale
1948–49	Marcel Cerdan
1949–51	Jake LaMotta
1952	Ray Robinson, Randy Turpin
1951–52	Ray Robinson[1]
1953–55	Carl Olson
1955–57	Ray Robinson[5]
1957	Gene Fullmer, Ray Robinson
1957–58	Carmen Basilio
1958–60	Ray Robinson[6]
1960–61	Paul Pender[7]
1959–62	Gene Fullmer (NBA)
1961–62	Terry Downes[1]
1962	Paul Pender[1]
1962–63	Dick Tiger
1963–65	Joey Giardello
1965–66	Dick Tiger
1966	Emile Griffith
1967	Nino Benvenuti, Emile Griffith
1968	Emile Griffith, Nino Benvenuti
1969	Nino Benvenuti
1970	Nino Benvenuti, Carlos Monzon
1971–73	Carlos Monzon
1974–75	Carlos Monzon (WBA), Rodrigo Valdez (WBC)
1976	Carlos Monzon (WBA, WBC), Rodrigo Valdez (WBC)
1977	Carlos Monzon (WBA, WBC),[1] Rodrigo Valdez (WBA, WBC)
1978	Rodrigo Valdez, Hugo Corro
1979	Hugo Corro, Vito Antuofermo
1980	Vito Antuofermo, Alan Minter, Marvin Hagler
1981	Marvin Hagler
1982–86	Marvin Hagler (undisputed)
1987	Marvin Hagler (undisputed), Sugar Ray Leonard (undisputed)
1988	Sumbu Kalambay (WBA), Thomas Hearns (WBC), Iran Barkley (WBC), Frank Tate (IBF), Michael Nunn (IBF), James Kinchen (NABF)
1989	Michael Nunn (IBF), Mike McCallum (WBA), Iran Barkley (WBC), Roberto Duran (WBC)
1990	Michael McCallum (WBA), Michael Nunn (IBF), Iran Barkley (WBC)
1991	Michael Nunn (IBF), James Toney (IBF), Michael McCallum (WBA)
1992	James Toney (IBF), Julian Jackson (WBC), Reggie Johnson (WBA)
1993	Reggie Johnson (WBA), Gerald McClellan (WBA), Roy Jones (IBF)
1994	Julian Jackson (WBA), Gerald McClellan (WBA), Roy Jones (IBF)
1995	Jorge Castro (WBA), Julian Jackson (WBC), Bernard Hopkins (IBF)
1996	William Joppy (WBA), Keith Holmes (WBC), Bernard Hopkins (IBF)
1997	Shinji Takehara (WBA), Quincy Taylor (WBC), Bernard Hopkins (IBF)
1998	William Joppy (WBA), Hassine Cherifi (WBC), Bernard Hopkins (IBF)

1. Retired. 2. Abandoned title. 3. Died. 4. National Boxing Association and New York Commission disagreed on champions. Those listed were accepted by one or the other until Zale gained worldwide recognition. 5. Ended retirement in 1954. 6. NBA withdrew recognition. 7. Recognized by New York, Massachusetts, and Europe.

Welterweight

1892–94	Mysterious Billy Smith
1894–96	Tommy Ryan
1896	Kid McCoy[2]
1896–1900	Mysterious Billy Smith
1900	Rube Ferns
1900–01	Matty Matthews
1901	Ruby Ferns
1901–04	Joe Walcott
1904	Dixie Kid[2]
1904–06	Joe Walcott
1906–07	Honey Mellody
1907	Mike (Twin) Sullivan[2]
1915–19	Ted Lewis
1919–22	Jack Britton
1922–26	Mickey Walker
1926–27	Pete Latzo
1927–29	Joe Dundee
1929–30	Jackie Fields
1930	Young Jack Thompson
1930–31	Tommy Freeman
1931	Young Jack Thompson
1931–32	Lou Brouillard
1932–33	Jackie Fields
1933	Young Corbett 3rd
1933–34	Jimmy McLarnin, Barney Ross
1934–35	Jimmy McLarnin
1935–38	Barney Ross
1938–40	Henry Armstrong
1940–41	Fritzie Zivic
1941–46	Freddie Cochrane
1946	Marty Servo[1]
1946–51	Ray Robinson[2]
1951	Johnny Bratton (NBA)
1951–54	Kid Gavilan
1954–55	Johnny Saxton
1955	Tony DeMarco
1955–56	Carmen Basilio
1956	Johnny Saxton
1956–57	Carmen Basilio[2]
1958	Virgil Akins
1959–60	Don Jordan
1960–61	Benny (Kid) Paret
1961	Emile Griffith
1961–62	Benny (Kid) Paret
1962–63	Emile Griffith, Luis Rodriguez
1963–66	Emile Griffith[2]
1966–69	Curtis Cokes
1969	Curtis Cokes, José Napoles
1970	José Napoles, Billy Backus
1971	Billy Backus, José Napoles
1972–74	José Napoles
1975	José Napoles (WBA, WBC),[3] Angel Espada (WBA), John Stracey (WBC)
1976	Angel Espada (WBA), José Cuevas (WBA), John Stracey (WBC), Carlos Palomino
1977–78	José Cuevas (WBA), Carlos Palomino (WBC)
1979	José Cuevas (WBA), Carlos Palomino (WBC), Wilfredo Benitez (WBC)
1980	José Cuevas (WBA), Ray Leonard (WBC), Roberto Duran (WBC), Thomas Hearns (WBA)
1981	Ray Leonard (WBC), Thomas Hearns (WBA), Ray Leonard (WBC, WBA)
1982	Ray Leonard
1983–85	Donald Curry (WBA)
1983–85	Milton McCrory (WBC)
1985–86	Donald Curry (undisputed)
1987	Mark Breland (WBA), Marlon Starling (WBA), Lloyd Honeyghan (IBF)
1988	Marlon Starling (WBA), Tomas Molinares (WBA), Lloyd Honeyghan (WBC), Simon Brown (IBF)

1989	Mark Breland (WBA), Marlon Starling (WBC), Simon Brown (IBF)
1990	Mark Breland (WBA), Aaron Davis (WBA), Simon Brown (IBF), Marlon Starling (WBC), Maurice Blocker (WBC)
1991	Meldrick Taylor (WBA), Simon Brown (IBF, WBC)
1992	Meldrick Taylor (WBA), James "Buddy" McGirt (WBC), Maurice Blocker (IBF)
1993	Cristianto Espana (WBA), Pernell Whitaker (WBC), Felix Trinidad (IBF)
1994	Ike Quartey (WBA), Pernell Whitaker (WBC), Felix Trinidad (IBF)
1995	Ike Quartey (WBA), Pernell Whitaker (WBC), Felix Trinidad (IBF)
1996–97	Ike Quartey (WBA), Pernell Whitaker (WBC), Felix Trinidad (IBF)
1998	Ike Quartey (WBA), Oscar De La Hoya (WBC), Felix Trinidad (IBF)

1. Retired. 2. Abandoned title. 3. WBA withdrew recognition.

Lightweight

1869–99	Kid Lavigne
1899–1902	Frank Erne
1902–08	Joe Gans
1908–10	Battling Nelson
1910–12	Ad Wolgast
1912–14	Willie Ritchie
1914–17	Freddy Welsh
1917–25	Benny Leonard[1]
1925	Jimmy Goodrich
1925–26	Rocky Kansas
1926–30	Sammy Mandell
1930	Al Singer
1930–33	Tony Canzoneri
1933–35	Barney Ross[2]
1935–36	Tony Canzoneri
1936–38	Lou Ambers
1938–39	Henry Armstrong
1939–40	Lou Ambers
1940–41	Lew Jenkins
1941–42	Sammy Angott[1]
1943–47	Beau Jack (N.Y.), Bob Montgomery (N.Y.), Sammy Angott (NBA), Juan Zurita (NBA), Ike Williams (NBA)
1947–51	Ike Williams
1951–52	James Carter
1952	Lauro Salas
1952–54	James Carter
1954	Paddy DeMarco
1954–55	James Carter
1955–56	Wallace Smith
1956–62	Joe Brown
1962–65	Carlos Ortiz
1965	Ismael Laguna
1965–68	Carlos Ortiz
1968	Teo Cruz
1969	Teo Cruz, Mando Ramos
1970	Mando Ramos, Ismael Laguna, Ken Buchanan
1971	Ken Buchanan (WBA), Mando Ramos (WBC), Pedro Carrasco (WBC)
1972	Ken Buchanan (WBA), Roberto Duran (WBA), Pedro Carrasco (WBC), Mando Ramos (WBC), Chango Carmona (WBC), Rodolfo Gonzalez (WBC)
1973	Roberto Duran (WBA), Rodolfo Gonzalez (WBC)
1974	Roberto Duran (WBA), Rodolfo Gonzalez (WBC), Guts Ishimatsu (WBC)
1975	Roberto Duran (WBA), Guts Ishimatsu (WBC)
1976	Roberto Duran (WBA), Guts Ishimatsu (WBC), Esteban De Jesus (WBC)
1977	Roberto Duran (WBA), Esteban De Jesus (WBC)
1978	Roberto Duran (WBA, WBC)
1979	Roberto Duran,[2] Jim Watt (WBC), Ernesto Espana (WBA)
1980	Ernesto Espana (WBA), Hilmer Kenty (WBA), Jim Watt (WBC)
1981	Hilmer Kenty (WBA), Sean O'Grady (WBA), James Watt (WBC), Alexis Arguello (WBC), Arturo Frias (WBA)
1982	Arturo Frias (WBA), Ray Mancini (WBA), Alexis Arguello (WBC)
1983	Edwin Rosario (WBC), Ray Mancini (WBA)
1984	Edwin Rosario (WBC), Livingstone Bramble (WBA)
1985	Jose Luis Ramirez (WBC), Hector Camacho (WBC), Livingstone Bramble (WBA)
1986	Hector Camacho (WBC), Livingstone Bramble (WBA), Jim Paul (IBF)
1987	Edwin Rosario (WBA), Jose Luis Ramirez (WBC), Greg Haugen (IBF)
1988	Jose Luis Ramirez (WBC), Julio Cesar Chavez (WBA), Greg Haugen (IBF), Julius Cesar Chavez (WBC & WBA title unified)
1989	Pernell Whitaker (IBF, WBC), Edwin Rosario (WBA)
1990	Pernell Whitaker (IBF, WBC), Juan Nazario (WBA)
1991	Pernell Whitaker (IBF, WBA, WBC)
1992	Pernell Whitaker (IBF, WBA, WBC),[3] Joey Gamache (WBA).
1993	Dingaan Thobela (WBA), Angel Gonzalez (WBC), Freddie Pendleton (IBF)
1994	Orzubek Nazarov (WBA), Angel Gonzalez (WBC), Rafael Ruelas (IBF)
1995	Orzubek Nazarov (WBA), Angel Gonzalez (WBC), Oscar de la Hoya (IBF)
1996	Gusshie Nazarov (WBA), Jean Baptiste Mendy (WBC), Phillip Holiday (IBF)
1997	Orzubek Nazarov (WBA), Jean Baptiste Mendy (WBC), Philip Holiday (IBF)
1998	Jean Baptiste Mendy (WBA), Cesar Bazan (WBC), Shane Mosley (IBF)

1. Retired. 2. Abandoned title. 3. Moving up in weight class, so resigned titles.

Featherweight

1889	Dal Hawkins[1]
1890	Billy Murphy
1892–1900	George Dixon
1900–01	Terry McGovern
1901	Young Corbett[1]
1901–12	Abe Attell
1912–23	Johnny Kilbane
1923	Eugene Criqui
1923–25	Johnny Dundee[1]
1925–27	Louis (Kid) Kaplan[1]
1927–28	Benny Bass
1928	Tony Canzoneri
1928–29	Andre Routis
1929–32	Battling Battalino[1]
1932	Tommy Paul (NBA), Kid Chocolate (N.Y.)
1933–36	Freddie Miller
1936–37	Petey Sarron
1937–38	Henry Armstrong[1]
1938–40	Joey Archibald
1940–41	Harry Jefra, Joey Archibald
1941–42	Chalky Wright
1942–48	Willie Pep
1948–49	Sandy Saddler[2]
1949–50	Willie Pep
1950–57	Sandy Saddler
1957–59	Kid Bassey
1959–63	Davey Moore
1963–64	Sugar Ramos
1964–67	Vicente Saldivar[2]
1968	Howard Winstone, José Legra,[3] Paul Rojas (WBA), Sho Saijo (WBA)
1969	Sho Saijo (WBA), Johnny Famechon[3]
1970	Sho Saijo (WBA), Johnny Famechon,[3] Vicente Salvidar,[3] Kunlaki Shibata[3]
1971	Sho Saijo (WBA), Antonio Gomez (WBA), Kuniaki Shibata (WBC)
1972	Antonio Gomez (WBA), Ernesto Marcel (WBA), Kuniaki Shibata (WBC), Clemente Sanchez (WBC), José Legra (WBC)
1973	Ernesto Marcel (WBA), José Legra (WBC), Eder Jofre (WBC)
1974	Ernesto Marcel (WBA),[2] Ruben Olivares (WBA), Alexis Arguello (WBA), Eder Jofre (WBC), Bobby Chacon (WBC)
1975	Alexis Arguello (WBA), Bobby Chacon (WBC), Ruben Olivares (WBC), David Kotey (WBC)
1976	Alexis Arguello (WBA),[2] David Kotey (WBC), Danny Lopez (WBC)
1977	Rafael Ortega (WBA), Danny Lopez (WBC)

978 Rafael Ortega (WBA), Cecilio Lastra (WBA), Eusebio Pedroza (WBA), Danny Lopez (WBC)
979 Eusebio Pedroza (WBA), Danny Lopez (WBC)
980 Eusebio Pedroza (WBA), Danny Lopez (WBC), Salvador Sanchez (WBC)
981 Eusebio Pedroza (WBA), Salvador Sanchez (WBC)
982 Eusebio Pedroza (WBA), Salvador Sanchez (WBC)[4]
983 Juan Laporte (WBC), Eusebio Pedroza (WBA)
984 Wilfred Gomez (WBC), Eusebio Pedroza (WBA)
985 Eusebio Pedroza (WBA), Barry McGuigan (WBA), Azumah Nelson (WBC)
1986 Barry McGuigan (WBA), Stevie Cruz (WBA), Azumah Nelson (WBC)
1987 Azumah Nelson (WBC), Antonio Esparragoza (WBA)
1988 Calvin Grove (IBF), Jorge Paez (IBF), Antonio Esparragoza (WBA), Jeff Fenech (WBC)
1989 Jorge Paez (IBF), Antonio Esparragoza (WBA), Jeff Fenech (WBC)
1990 Marcos Villasana (WBC), Antonio Esparragoza (WBA), Jorge Paez (IBF)
1991 Yung-Kyun Park (WBA), Troy Dorsey (IBF), Marcos Villagana (WBC)
1992 Paul Hodkinson (WBC), Manuel Medina (IBF), Yung-Kyun Park (WBA)
1993 Yung-Kyun Park (WBA), Goyo Vargas (WBC), Tom Johnson (IBF)
1994 Eloy Rojas (WBA), Kevin Kelley (WBC), Tom Johnson (IBF)
1995 Eloy Rojas (WBA), Alejandro Gonzalez (WBC), Tom Johnson (IBF)
1996 Wilfredo Vázquez (WBA), Luisto Espinoza (WBC), Tom Johnson (IBF)
1997 Elroy Rojas (WBA), Luisito Espinoza (WBC), Tom Johnson (IBF)
1998 Vacant (WBA), Luisito Espinoza (WBC), Manuel Medina (IBF)

1. Abandoned title. 2. Retired. 3. Recognized in Europe, Mexico, and Orient. 4. Killed in auto accident.

Bantamweight

1890–92 George Dixon[1]
1894–99 Jimmy Barry[2]
1899–1900 Terry McGovern[1]
1901 Harry Harris[1]
1902–03 Harry Forbes
1903–04 Frankie Neil
1904 Joe Bowker[1]
1905–07 Jimmy Walsh[1]
1910–14 Johnny Coulon
1914–17 Kid Williams
1917–20 Pete Herman
1920 Joe Lynch
1920–21 Joe Lynch, Pete Herman, Johnny Buff
1922 Johnny Buff, Joe Lynch
1923 Joe Lynch
1924 Joe Lynch, Abe Goldstein
1924 Abe Goldstein, Eddie "Cannonball" Martin
1925 Eddie "Cannonball" Martin, Charlie "Phil "Rosenberg[3]
1927–28 Bud Taylor (NBA)[1]
1929–34 Al Brown
1935 Al Brown, Baltazar Sangchili
1936 Baltazar Sangchili, Tony Marino, Sixto Escobar
1937 Sixto Escobar, Harry Jeffra
1938 Harry Jeffra, Sixto Escobar
1939–40 Sixto Escobar[2]
1940–42 Lou Salica
1942–46 Manuel Ortiz
1947 Manuel Ortiz, Harold Dade
1948–50 Manuel Ortiz
1950–52 Vic Toweel
1952–54 Jimmy Carruthers[2]
1954–55 Robert Cohen
1956 Robert Cohen, Mario D'Agata, Raul Macias (NBA)
1957 Mario D'Agata, Alphonse Halimi
1958–59 Alphonse Halimi
1959–60 Jose Becerra[2]
1960–61 Alphonse Halimi[4]
1961–62 Johnny Caldwell[4]
1961–65 Eder Jofre
1965–68 Masahika "Fighting" Harada
1968 Masahika "Fighting" Harada, Lionel Rose
1969 Lionel Rose, Ruben Olivares
1970 Ruben Olivares, Chucho Castillo
1971 Chucho Castillo, Ruben Olivares
1972 Ruben Olivares, Rafael Herrera, Enrique Pinder
1973 Enrique Pinder (WBA), Romeo Anaya (WBA), Arnold Taylor (WBA), Rodolfo Martinez (WBC), Rafael Herrera
1974 Arnold Taylor (WBA), Soo Hwan Hong (WBA), Rafael Herrera (WBC), Rodolfo Martinez (WBC)
1975 Soo Hwan Hong (WBA), Alfonso Zamora (WBA), Rodolfo Martinez (WBC)
1976 Alfonso Zamora (WBA), Rodolfo Martinez (WBC), Carlos Zarate (WBC)
1977 Alfonso Zamora (WBA), Jorge Lujan (WBA), Carlos Zarate (WBC)
1978 Jorge Lujan (WBA), Carlos Zarate (WBC)
1979 Jorge Lujan (WBA), Carlos Zarate (WBC), Lupe Pintor (WBC)
1980 Jorge Lujan (WBA), Lupe Pintor (WBC), Julian Solis (WBA), Jeff Chandler (WBA)
1981 Lupe Pintor (WBC), Jeff Chandler (WBA)
1982 Lupe Pintor (WBC), Jeff Chandler (WBA)
1983 Jeff Chandler (WBA), Albert Dauila (WBC)
1984 Richie Sandqual (WBA), Albert Dauila (WBC)
1985 Richard Sandoval (WBA), Daniel Zaragoza (WBC), Miguel Lora (WBC)
1986 Richard Sandoval (WBA), Bernardo Pinango (WBA), Jeff Fenech (IBF)
1987 Bernardo Pinango (WBA), Takuya Muguruma (WBA), Miguel Lora (WBC)
1988 Wilfredo Vásquez (WBA), Jibaro Perez (WBC), Moon Sung-gil (WBA), Orlando Canizales (IBF)
1989 Jibaro Perez (WBC), Moon Sung-gil (WBA), Orlando Canizales (IBF), Kaokor Galaxy (WBA), Luis Espinosa (WBA)
1990 Orlando Canizales (IBF), Jibaro Perez (WBC), Luis Espinosa (WBA)
1991 Greg Richardson (WBC), Orlando Canizales (IBF), Luis Espinosa (WBA)
1992 Joichiro Tatsuyoshi (WBC), Victor Manuel Rabanales (WBC), Eddie Cook (WBA), Orlando Gonzales (IBF)
1993 Jorge Julio (WBA), Byun-Jong-il (WBC), Orlando Canizales (IBF)
1994 John Michael Johnson (WBA), Yasuei Yakushiji (WBC), Orlando Canizales (IBF)
1995 Daorun Chuwatang (WBA), Yasuei Yakushiji (WBC), Mbulelo Botile (IBF)
1996–97 Nana Konadu (WBA), Wayne McCullough (WBC), Mbulelo Botile (IBF)
1998 Nana Konadu (WBA), Joichiro Tatsuyoshi (WBC), Tim Austin (IBF)

1. Abandoned title. 2. Retired. 3. Deprived of title for failing to make weight. 4. Recognized in Europe.

Horse Racing

Ancient drawings on stone and bone prove that horse racing is at least 3,000 years old, but thoroughbred racing is a modern development. Practically every thoroughbred in training today traces its registered ancestry back to one or more of three sires that arrived in England about 1728 from the Near East and became known, from the names of their owners, as the Byerly Turk, the Darley Arabian, and the Godolphin Arabian. The Jockey Club (English) was founded at Newmarket in 1750 or 1751 and became the custodian of the Stud Book as well as the court of last resort in deciding turf affairs.

Horse racing took place in this country before the Revolution, but the great lift to the breeding industry came with the importation in 1798, by Col. John Hoomes of Virginia, of Diomed, winner of the Epsom Derby of 1780. Diomed's lineal descendants included such famous stars of the American turf a American Eclipse and Lexington. From 1800 to th time of the Civil War there were race courses an breeding establishments plentifully scattere through Virginia, North Carolina, South Carolina Tennessee, Kentucky, and Louisiana.

The oldest stake event in North America is th Queen's Plate, a Canadian fixture that was first ru in the Province of Quebec in 1836. The oldest stak event in the United States is the Travers, which wa first run at Saratoga in 1864. The gambling that goe with horse racing and trickery by jockeys, trainers owners, and track officials caused attacks on th sport by reformers and a demand among horse rac ing enthusiasts for an honest and effective control o some kind, but nothing of lasting value to racing came of this until the formation in 1894 of th Jockey Club.

"TRIPLE CROWN" WINNERS IN THE UNITED STATES

(Kentucky Derby, Preakness and Belmont Stakes)

Year	Horse	Owner
1919	Sir Barton	J. K. L. Ross
1930	Gallant Fox	William Woodward
1935	Omaha	William Woodward
1937	War Admiral	Samuel D. Riddle
1941	Whirlaway	Warren Wright
1943	Count Fleet	Mrs. John Hertz
1946	Assault	Robert J. Kleberg
1948	Citation	Warren Wright
1973	Secretariat	Meadow Stable
1977	Seattle Slew	Karen Taylor
1978	Affirmed	Louis Wolfson

KENTUCKY DERBY

Churchill Downs; 3-year-olds; 1¼ miles.

Year	Winner	Jockey	Wt.	Win val.
1919	Sir Barton	J. Loftus	112½	20,825
1920	Paul Jones	T. Rice	126	30,375
1921	Behave Yourself	C. Thompson	126	38,450
1922	Morvich	A. Johnson	126	46,775
1923	Zev	E. Sande	126	53,600
1924	Black Gold	J. D. Mooney	126	52,775
1925	Flying Ebony	E. Sande	126	52,950
1926	Bubbling Over	A. Johnson	126	50,075
1927	Whiskery	L. McAtee	126	51,000
1928	Reigh Count	C. Lang	126	55,375
1929	Clyde Van Dusen	L. McAtee	126	53,950
1930	Gallant Fox	E. Sande	126	50,725
1931	Twenty Grand	C. Kurtsinger	126	48,725
1932	Burgoo King	E. James	126	52,350
1933	Brokers Tip	D. Meade	126	48,925
1934	Cavalcade	M. Garner	126	28,175
1935	Omaha	W. Saunders	126	39,525
1936	Bold Venture	I. Hanford	126	37,725
1937	War Admiral	C. Kurtsinger	126	52,050
1938	Lawrin	E. Arcaro	126	47,050
1939	Johnstown	J. Stout	126	46,350
1940	Gallahadion	C. Bierman	126	60,150
1941	Whirlaway	E. Arcaro	126	61,275
1942	Shut Out	W. D. Wright	126	64,225
1943	Count Fleet	J. Longden	126	60,725
1944	Pensive	C. McCreary	126	64,675
1945	Hoop Jr.	E. Arcaro	126	64,850
1946	Assault	W. Mehrtens	126	96,400
1947	Jet Pilot	E. Guerin	126	92,160
1948	Citation	E. Arcaro	126	83,400
1949	Ponde	S. Brooks	126	91,600
1950	Middleground	W. Boland	126	92,650
1951	Count Turf	C. McCreary	126	98,050
1952	Hill Gail	E. Arcaro	126	96,300
1953	Dark Star	H. Moreno	126	90,050
1954	Determine	R. York	126	102,050
1955	Swaps	W. Shoemaker	126	108,400
1956	Needles	D. Erb	126	123,450
1957	Iron Liege	W. Hartack	126	107,950
1958	Tim Tam	I. Valenzuela	126	116,400
1959	Tomy Lee	W. Shoemaker	126	119,650
1960	Venetian Way	W. Hartack	126	114,850
1961	Carry Back	J. Sellers	126	120,500
1962	Decidedly	W. Hartack	126	119,650
1963	Chateauguay	B. Baeza	126	108,900
1964	Northern Dancer	W. Hartack	126	114,300
1965	Lucky Debonair	W. Shoemaker	126	112,000
1966	Kauai King	D. Brumfield	126	120,500
1967	Proud Clarion	R. Ussery	126	119,700
1968	Forward Pass[1]	I. Valenzuela	126	122,600
1969	Majestic Prince	W. Hartack	126	113,200
1970	Dust Commander	M. Manganello	126	127,800
1971	Canonero II	G. Avila	126	145,500
1972	Riva Ridge	R. Turcotte	126	140,300
1973	Secretariat	R. Turcotte	126	155,050
1974	Cannonade	A. Cordero, Jr.	126	274,000
1975	Foolish Pleasure	J. Vasquez	126	209,600
1976	Bold Forbes	A. Cordero, Jr.	126	165,200
1977	Seattle Slew	J. Cruguet	126	214,700
1978	Affirmed	S. Cauthen	126	186,900
1979	Spectacular Bid	R. Franklin	126	228,650
1980	Genuine Risk	J. Vasquez	121	250,550
1981	Pleasant Colony	J. Velasquez	126	317,200
1982	Gato del Sol	E. Delahoussaye	126	417,600
1983	Sunny's Halo	E. Delahoussaye	126	426,000
1984	Swale	L. Pincay, Jr.	126	537,400
1985	Spend a Buck	A. Cordero, Jr.	126	406,800
1986	Ferdinand	W. Shoemaker	126	609,400

Year	Winner	Jockey	Wt.	Win val.
1987	Alysheba	C. McCarron	126	618,600
1988	Winning Colors	Gary Stevens	121	611,200
1989	Sunday Silence	Patrick Valenzuela	126	574,200
1990	Unbridled	Craig Perret	126	581,000
1991	Strike the Gold	Chris Antley	126	655,800
1992	Lil E. Tee	P. Day	126	724,800
1993	Sea Hero	Jerry Bailey	126	735,900
1994	Go For Gin	Chris McCarron	126	628,800
1995	Thunder Gulch	Gary Stevens	126	707,400
1996	Grindstone	Jerry Bailey	126	869,800
1997	Silver Charm	Gary Stevens	126	700,000
1998	Real Quiet	Kent Desormeaux	126	738,800

1. Dancer's Image finished first but was disqualified after traces of drug were found in system.

PREAKNESS STAKES

Pimlico; 3-year-olds; 1 3/16 miles.

Year	Winner	Jockey	Wt.	Win val.
1919	Sir Barton	J. Loftus	126	$24,500
1920	Man o' War	C. Kummer	126	(1)
1921	Broomspun	F. Coltiletti	126	(1)
1922	Pillory	L. Morris	126	(1)
1923	Vigil	B. Marinelli	126	(1)
1924	Nellie Morse	J. Merimee	126	(1)
1925	Coventry	C. Kummer	126	(1)
1926	Display	J. Maiben	126	(1)
1927	Bostonian	W. Abel	126	(1)
1928	Victorian	S. Workman	126	(1)
1929	Dr. Freeland	L. Schaefer	126	(1)
1930	Gallant Fox	E. Sande	126	51,925
1931	Mate	G. Ellis	126	48,225
1932	Burgoo King	E. James	126	50,375
1933	Head Play	C. Kurtsinger	126	26,850
1934	High Quest	R. Jones	126	25,175
1935	Omaha	W. Saunders	126	25,325
1936	Bold Venture	G. Woolf	126	27,325
1937	War Admiral	C. Kurtsinger	126	45,600
1938	Dauber	M. Peters	126	51,875
1939	Challedon	G. Seabo	126	53,710
1940	Bimelech	F.A. Smith	126	53,230
1941	Whirlaway	E. Arcaro	126	49,365
1942	Alsab	B. James	126	58,175
1943	Count Fleet	J. Longden	126	43,190
1944	Pensive	C. McCreary	126	60,075
1945	Polynesian	W.D. Wright	126	66,170
1946	Assault	W. Mehrtens	126	96,620
1947	Faultless	D. Dodson	126	98,005
1948	Citation	E. Arcaro	126	91,870
1949	Capot	T. Atkinson	126	79,985
1950	Hill Prince	E. Arcaro	126	56,115
1951	Bold	E. Arcaro	126	83,110
1952	Blue Man	C. McCreary	126	86,135
1953	Native Dancer	E. Guerin	126	65,200
1954	Hasty Road	J. Adams	126	91,600
1955	Nashua	E. Arcaro	126	67,550
1956	Fabius	W. Hartack	126	84,250
1957	Bold Ruler	E. Arcaro	126	65,250
1958	Tim Tam	I. Valenzuela	126	97,900
1959	Royal Orbit	W. Harmatz	126	136,200
1960	Bally Ache	R. Ussery	126	121,000
1961	Carry Back	J. Sellers	126	126,200
1962	Greek Money	J. Rotz	126	135,800
1963	Candy Spots	W. Shoemaker	126	127,500
1964	Northern Dancer	W. Hartack	126	124,200
1965	Tom Rolfe	R. Turcotte	126	128,100
1966	Kauai King	D. Brumfield	126	129,000
1967	Damascus	W. Shoemaker	126	141,500
1968	Forward Pass	I. Valenzuela	126	142,700
1969	Majestic Prince	W. Hartack	126	129,500
1970	Personality	E. Belmonte	126	151,300
1971	Canonero II	G. Avila	126	137,400
1972	Bee Bee Bee	E. Nelson	126	135,300
1973	Secretariat	R. Turcotte	126	129,900
1974	Little Current	M. Rivera	126	156,000
1975	Master Derby	D. McHargue	126	158,100
1976	Elocutionist	J. Lively	126	129,700
1977	Seattle Slew	J. Cruguet	126	138,600
1978	Affirmed	S. Cauthen	126	136,200
1979	Spectacular Bid	R. Franklin	126	165,300
1980	Codex	A. Cordero	126	180,600
1981	Pleasant Colony	J. Velasquez	126	270,800
1982	Aloma's Ruler	J. Kaenel	126	209,900
1983	Deputed Testamony	D. Miller	126	251,200
1984	Gate Dancer	A. Cordero	126	243,600
1985	Tank's Prospect	Pat Day	126	423,200
1986	Snow Chief	A. Solis	126	411,900
1987	Alysheba	C. McCarron	126	421,100
1988	Risen Star	E. Delahoussaye	126	413,700
1989	Sunday Silence	P. Valenzuela	126	438,230
1990	Summer Squall	Pat Day	126	445,900
1991	Hansel	Jerry Bailey	126	432,770
1992	Pine Bluff	C. McCarron	126	484,120
1993	Prairie Bayou	Mike Smith	126	471,835
1994	Tabasco Cat	Pat Day	126	447,720
1995	Timber Country	Pat Day	126	446,810
1996	Louis Quatorze	Pat Day	126	458,120
1997	Silver Charm	Gary Stevens	126	488,150
1998	Real Quiet	Kent Desormeaux	126	650,000

1. Data not available.

BELMONT STAKES

Belmont Park; 3-year-olds; 1½ miles.

Run at Jerome Park 1867 to 1890; at Morris Park 1890–94; at Belmont Park 1905–62; at Aqueduct 1963–67. Distance 1⅝ miles prior to 1874; reduced to 1½ miles, 1874; reduced to 1¼ miles, 1890; reduced to 1⅛ miles, 1893; increased to 1¼ miles, 1895; increased to 1⅜ miles, 1896; reduced to 1¼ miles in 1904; increased to 1½ miles, 1926.

Year	Winner	Jockey	Wt.	Win val.
1919	Sir Barton	J. Loftus	126	$11,950
1920	Man o' War	C. Kummer	126	(1)
1921	Grey Lag	E. Sande	126	(1)
1922	Pillory	C.H. Miller	126	(1)
1923	Zev	E. Sande	126	(1)
1924	Mad Play	E. Sande	126	(1)
1925	American Flag	A. Johnson	126	(1)
1926	Crusader	A. Johnson	126	(1)

Year	Winner	Jockey	Wt.	Win val.
1927	Chance Shot	E. Sande	126	([1])
1928	Vito	C. Kummer	126	([1])
1929	Blue Larkspur	M. Garner	126	([1])
1930	Gallant Fox	E. Sande	126	66,040
1931	Twenty Grand	C. Kurtsinger	126	58,770
1932	Faireno	T. Malley	126	55,120
1933	Hurryoff	M. Garner	126	49,490
1934	Peace Chance	W.D. Wright	126	43,410
1935	Omaha	W. Saunders	126	35,480
1936	Granville	J. Stout	126	29,800
1937	War Admiral	C. Kurtsinger	126	38,020
1938	Pasteurized	J. Stout	126	34,530
1939	Johnstown	J. Stout	126	37,020
1940	Bimelech	F.A. Smith	126	35,030
1941	Whirlaway	E. Arcaro	126	39,770
1942	Shut Out	E. Arcaro	126	44,520
1943	Count Fleet	J. Longden	126	35,340
1944	Bounding Home	G.L. Smith	126	55,000
1945	Pavot	E. Arcaro	126	56,675
1946	Assault	W. Mehrtens	126	75,400
1947	Phalanx	R. Donoso	126	78,900
1948	Citation	E. Arcaro	126	77,700
1949	Capot	T. Atkinson	126	60,900
1950	Middleground	W. Boland	126	61,350
1951	Counterpoint	D. Gorman	126	82,000
1952	One Count	E. Arcaro	126	82,400
1953	Native Dancer	E. Guerin	126	82,500
1954	High Gun	E. Guerln	126	89,000
1955	Nashua	E. Arcaro	126	83,700
1956	Needles	D. Erb	126	83,600
1957	Gallant Man	W. Shoemaker	126	77,300
1958	Cavan	P. Anderson	126	73,440
1959	Sword Dancer	W. Shoemaker	126	93,525
1960	Celtic Ash	W. Hartack	126	96,785
1961	Sherluck	B. Baeza	126	104,900
1962	Jaipur	W. Shoemaker	126	109,550
1963	Chateauguay	B. Baeza	126	101,700
1964	Quadrangle	M. Ycaza	126	110,850
1965	Hail to All	J. Sellers	126	104,150
1966	Amberoid	W. Boland	126	117,700
1967	Damascus	W. Shoemaker	126	104,950
1968	Stage Door Johnny	H. Gustines	126	117,700
1969	Arts and Letters	B. Baeza	126	104,050
1970	High Echelon	J. Rotz	126	115,000
1971	Pass Catcher	R. Blum	126	97,710
1972	Riva Ridge	R. Turcotte	126	93,540
1973	Secretariat	R. Turcotte	126	90,120
1974	Little Current	M. Rivera	126	101,970
1975	Avatar	W. Shoemaker	126	116,160
1976	Bold Forbes	A. Cordero, Jr.	126	117,000
1977	Seattle Slew	J. Cruguet	126	109,080
1978	Affirmed	S. Cauthen	126	110,580
1979	Coastal	R. Hernandez	126	161,400
1980	Temperence Hill	E. Maple	126	176,220
1981	Summing	G. Martens	126	170,580
1982	Conquistador Cielo	L. Pincay, Jr.	126	159,720
1983	Caveat	L. Pincay, Jr.	126	215,100
1984	Swale	L. Pincay, Jr.	126	310,020
1985	Creme Fraiche	Eddie Maple	126	307,740
1986	Danzig Connection	C. McCarron	126	338,640
1987	Bet Twice	C. Perret	126	329,160
1988	Risen Star	E. Delahoussaye	126	303,720
1989	Easy Goer	P. Day	126	413,520
1990	Go And Go	Michael Kinane	126	411,600
1991	Hansel	Jerry Bailey	126	417,480
1992	A.P. Indy	E. Delahoussaye	126	458,880
1993	Colonial Affair	Julie Krone	126	444,450
1994	Tabasco Cat	Pat Day	126	392,280
1995	Thunder Gulch	Gary Stevens	126	415,440
1996	Editor's Note	R. Douglas	126	437,880
1997	Touch Gold	C. McCarron	126	432,600
1998	Victory Gallop	Gary Stevens	126	600,000

1. Data not available.

TRIPLE CROWN RACES—1998

Kentucky Derby (Churchill Downs, Louisville, Ky., May 2, 1998). Gross purse: $1,000,000. Distance: 1¼ miles. Order of finish: 1. Real Quiet (Desormeaux), mutuel returns: $18.80, $8.80, $5.80. 2. Victory Gallop (Solis), $13.00, $7.60. 3. Indian Charlie (Stevens), $4.20. 4. Halory Hunter (Nakatani). 5. Cape Town (Bailey). 6. Parade Ground (Sellers). 7. Hanuman Highway (Flores). 8. Favorite Trick (Day). 9. Nationalore (Almeida). 10. Old Trieste (Albarado). 11. Chilito (Boulanger).

12. Robinwould (Fires). 13. Artax (McCarron). 14. Rock and Roll (Torres). 15. Basic Trainee (Velazquez). Winner's purse: $738,800. Margin of victory: ½ length. Time of race: 2:02.38.

Preakness Stakes (Pimlico, Baltimore Md., May 16, 1998). Gross purse: $1,000,000. Distance: 1 3⁄16 miles. Order of finish: 1. Real Quiet (Desormeaux), mutuel returns: $7.00, $3.60, $3.00. 2. Victory Gallop (Stevens), $3.20, $2.80. 3. Classic Cat (Albarado), $4.80. 4. Hot Wells (Prado). 5. Black Cash (Sellers). 6. Spartan Cat (Wilson). 7. Baquero (Day). 8. Basic Trainee (Velazquez). 9. Cape Town (Bailey). 10. Silver's Prospect (Douglas). Winner's purse: $650,000. Margin of victory: 2¼ lengths. Time of race: 1:54.75.

Belmont Stakes (Belmont Park, Belmont N.Y., June 6, 1998). Gross purse: $1,000,000. Distance: 1½ miles. Order of finish: 1. Victory Gallop (Stevens), mutuel returns: $11.00, $3.60, $3.20. 2. Real Quiet (Desormeaux), $3.00, $2.60. 3. Thomas Jo (McCarron), $5.30. 4. Parade Ground (Day). 5. Raffie's Majesty (Chavez). 6. Chilito (Davis). 7. Grand Slam (Bailey). 8. Classic Cat (Velazquez). 9. Limit Out (Samyn). 10. Yarrow Brae (Smith). 11. Basic Trainee (Bravo). Winner's purse: $600,000. Margin of victory: Nose. Time of race: 2:29.16.

ECLIPSE AWARDS—1997

(Presented Feb. 10, 1998)

Horse of the Year	Favorite Trick
2-year-old colt or gelding	Favorite Trick
2-year-old filly	Countess Diana
3-year-old colt or gelding	Silver Charm
3-year-old filly	Ajina
4-year-old and up colt, horse, or gelding	Skip Away
4-year-old and up filly or mare	Hidden Lake
Male turf horse	Chief Bearheart
Female turf horse	Ryafan
Sprinter	Smoke Glacken
Steeplechaser	Lonesome Glory
Owner	Carolyn Hine
Breeders	John and Betty Mabee
Trainer	Bob Baffert
Jockey	Jerry Bailey
Apprentice jockeys	Roberto Rosado and Philip Teator
Award of Merit	Robert and Beverly Lewis

(Based on vote by the Thoroughbred Racing Associations, the *Daily Racing Form,* and the National Turf Writers Association.)

Track and Field

WORLD RECORDS—MEN

(Through Aug. 30, 1998)

Recognized by the International Athletic Federation. The I.A.A.F. decided late in 1976 not to recognize records in yards except for the one-mile run. The I.A.A.F. also requires automatic timing for all records for races of 400 meters or less.

Event	Record	Holder	Home country	Where made	Date
Running					
100 m	0:09.84	Donovan Bailey	Canada	Atlanta, Ga.	July 27, 1996
200 m	0:19.32	Michael Johnson	United States	Atlanta, Ga.	Aug. 1, 1996
400 m	0:43.29	Harry Reynolds	United States	Zurich, Switzerland	Aug. 17, 1988
800 m	1:41.11	Wilson Kipketer	Denmark	Köln, Germany	Aug. 24, 1997
1,000 m	2:12.18	Sebastian Coe	England	Oslo, Norway	July 11, 1981
1,500 m	3:26.00	Hicham El Guerouj	Morocco	Rome, Italy	July 14, 1998
1 mile	3:44.39	Noureddine Morceli	Algeria	Rieti, Italy	Sept. 5, 1993
2,000 m	4:47.88	Noureddine Morceli	Algeria	Paris, France	July 3, 1995
3,000 m	7:20.67	Daniel Komen	Kenya	Rieti, Italy	Sept. 1, 1996
3,000 m steeplechase	7:55.72	Bernard Barmasai	Kenya	Köln, Germany	Aug. 24, 1997
5,000 m	12:39.36	Haile Gebrselassie	Ethiopia	Helsinki, Finland	June 13, 1998
10,000 m	26:22.75	Haile Gebrselassie	Ethiopia	Hengelo, Netherlands	June 1, 1998
20,000 m	56:55.60	Arturo Barrios	Mexico	La Fleche, France	March 30, 1991
25,000 m	1:13:55.80	Toshihiko Seko	Japan	Christchurch, N.Z.	March 22, 1981
30,000 m	1:29:18.80	Toshihiko Seko	Japan	Christchurch, N.Z.	March 22, 1981
1 hour	21,101 m	Arturo Barrios	Mexico	La Fleche, France	March 30, 1991
Marathon	2:06.50	Belayneh Dinsamo	Ethiopia	Rotterdam, Netherlands	April 17, 1988
Walking					
20,000 m	1:17:25.60	Bernardo Segura	Mexico	Bergen, Norway	May 7, 1994
30,000 m	2:01:44.10	Maurizio Damilano	Italy	Cuneo, Italy	Oct. 3, 1992
50,000 m	3:40:57.90	Thierry Toutain	France	Héricourt, France	Sept. 29, 1996
2 hours	29,572 m	Maurizio Damilano	Italy	Cuneo, Italy	Oct. 3, 1992
Hurdles					
110 m	0:12.91	Colin Jackson	Great Britain	Stuttgart, Germany	Aug. 20, 1993
400 m	0:46.78	Kevin Young	United States	Barcelona, Spain	Aug. 6, 1992
Relay races					
400 m (4 × 100)	0:37.40	National Team	United States	Barcelona, Spain	Aug. 8, 1992
	0:37.40	National Team	United States	Stuttgart, Germany	Aug. 21, 1993
800 m (4 × 200)	1:18.68	Santa Monica T.C.	United States	Walnut, Calif.	April 17, 1994
1,600 m (4 × 400)	2:54.20	National Team	United States	New York, N.Y.	July 22, 1998
3,200 m (4 × 800)	7:03.89	National Team	Britain	London	Aug. 30, 1982
Field events					
High jump	2.45 m	Javier Sotomayor	Cuba	Salamanca, Spain	July 27, 1993
Long jump	8.95 m	Mike Powell	United States	Tokyo, Japan	Aug. 30, 1991
Triple jump	18.29 m	Jonathan Edwards	Great Britain	Goteborg, Sweden	Aug. 7, 1995
Pole vault	6.14 m	Sergey Bubka	Ukraine	Sestriere, Italy	July 31, 1994
Shot-put	23.12 m	Randy Barnes	United States	Los Angeles	May 20, 1990
Discus throw	74.08 m	Jürgen Schult	East Germany	Neubrandenburg, E. Germany	June 6, 1986
Hammer throw	86.74 m	Yuriy Sedykh	U.S.S.R.	Stuttgart, Germany	Aug. 30, 1986
Javelin throw	98.48 m	Jan Zelezny	Czech Republic	Jena, Germany	May 25, 1996
Decathlon	8,891 pts.	Dan O'Brien	United States	Talence, France	Sept. 4–5, 1992

WORLD RECORDS—WOMEN

(Through Aug. 30, 1998)

Event	Record	Holder	Home country	Where made	Date
Running					
100 m	0:10.49	Florence Griffith-Joyner	United States	Indianapolis, Ind.	July 16, 1988
200 m	0:21.34	Florence Griffith-Joyner	United States	Seoul, South Korea	Sept. 29, 1988
400 m	0:47.60	Martina Koch	East Germany	Canberra, Australia	Oct. 6, 1985
800 m	1:53.28	Jarmila Kratochvilova	Czechoslovakia	Munich, W. Germany	July 26, 1983
1000 m	2:28.98	Svetlana Masterkova	Russia	Brussels, Belgium	Aug. 23, 1996
1,500 m	3:50.46	Qu Yunxia	China	Beijing, China	Sept. 11, 1993
1 mile	4:12.56	Svetlana Masterkova	Russia	Zurich, Switzerland	Aug. 14, 1996
2,000 m	5:25.36	Sonia O'Sullivan	Ireland	Edinburgh, Scotland	July 8, 1994
3,000 m	8:06.11	Wang Junxia	China	Beijing, China	Sept. 13, 1993
5,000 m	14:28.09	Jiang Bo	China	Shanghai, China	Oct. 23, 1997
10,000 m	29:31.78	Wang Junxia	China	Beijing, China	Sept. 8, 1993
20,000 m	1:06:48.80	Izumi Maki	Japan	Amagasaki, Japan	Sept. 19, 1993
25,000 m	1:29:29.20	Karolina Szabo	Hungary	Budapest, Hungary	April 22, 1988

Event	Record	Holder	Home country	Where made	Date
30,000 m	1:47:05.60	Karolina Szabo	Hungary	Budapest, Hungary	April 22, 1988
Marathon	2:21:06.0	Ingrid Kristiansen	Norway	London, United Kingdom	April 21, 1985
Walking					
5,000 m	20:13.26	Kerry Saxby-Junna	Australia	Hobart, Australia	Feb. 25, 1996
10,000 m	41:56.23	Nadezhda Ryashkina	Russia	Seattle, Wash.	July 24, 1990
Hurdles					
100-m hurdles	0:12.21	Yordanka Donkova	Bulgaria	Stara Zagora, Bulgaria	Aug. 20, 1988
400 m	0:52.61	Kim Batten	United States	Goteborg, Sweden	Aug. 11, 1995
Relay races					
400 m (4 × 100)	0:41.37	East Germany	E. Germany	Canberra, Australia	Oct. 6, 1985
800 m (4 × 200)	1:28.15	East Germany	E. Germany	Jena, E. Germany	Aug. 9, 1980
1,600 m (4 × 400)	3:15.17	U.S.S.R	U.S.S.R.	Seoul, South Korea	Oct. 1, 1988
3,200 m (4 × 800)	7:50.17	U.S.S.R.	U.S.S.R.	Moscow, U.S.S.R.	Aug. 5, 1984
Field events					
High jump	2.09 m	Stefka Kostadinova	Bulgaria	Rome, Italy	Aug. 30, 1987
Pole vault	4.59 m	Emma George	Australia	Brisbane, Australia	March 21, 1998
Long jump	7.52 m	Galina Chistyakova	U.S.S.R.	Leningrad, Russia	June 11, 1988
Triple jump	15.50 m	Inessa Kravets	Ukraine	Goteborg, Sweden	Aug. 10, 1995
Shot-put	22.63 m	Natalya Lisovskaya	U.S.S.R.	Moscow, Russia	June 7, 1987
Discus throw	76.80 m	Gabriele Reinsch	East Germany	Neubrandenburg, E. Ger.	July 9, 1988
Hammer	73.14 m	Michaela Melinte	Romania	Poiana Brasov, Romania	July 16, 1998
Javelin throw	80.00 m	Petra Felke	East Germany	Potsdam, Germany	Sept. 9, 1988
Heptathlon	7,291 pts	Jackie Joyner-Kersee	United States	Seoul, South Korea	Sept. 24, 1988

AMERICAN RECORDS—MEN

(Through Aug. 30, 1998)

Event	Record	Holder	Where Made	Date
Running				
100 m	0:09.85	Leroy Burrell	Lausanne, Switzerland	July 6, 1994
200 m	0:19.32	Michael Johnson	Atlanta, Ga.	Aug. 1, 1996
400 m	0:43.29	Butch Reynolds	Indianapolis, Ind.	Aug. 17, 1988
800 m	1:42.60	Johnny Gray	Koblenz, W. Ger.	Aug. 29, 1985
1,000 m	2:13.90	Richard Wohlhuter	Oslo, Norway	July 30, 1974
1,500 m	3:29.77	Sydney Maree	Cologne, W. Ger.	Aug. 25, 1985
1 mile	3:47.69	Steve Scott	Oslo, Norway	July 7, 1982
2,000 m	4:54.71	Steve Scott	Ingelhelm, W. Ger.	Aug. 31, 1982
3,000 m	7:31.69	Bob Kennedy	Brussels, Belgium	Aug. 23, 1996
5,000 m	12:58.21	Bob Kennedy	Zurich, Switzerland	Aug. 14, 1996
10,000 m	27:20.56	Mark Nenow	Brussels	Sept. 5, 1986
20,000 m	58:15.00	Bill Rodgers	Boston, Mass.	Aug. 9, 1977
25,000 m	1:14:11.80	Bill Rodgers	Saratoga, Cal.	Feb. 21, 1979
30,000 m	1:31:49.00	Bill Rodgers	Saratoga, Cal.	Feb. 21, 1979
1 hour	12 mi., 1,351 yds	Bill Rodgers	Boston, Mass.	Aug. 9, 1977
3,000-m steeplechase	8:09.17	Henry Marsh	Koblenz, W. Ger.	Aug. 29, 1985
Hurdles				
110 m	0:12.92	Roger Kingdom	Berlin	Aug. 16, 1989
		Allen Johnson	Brussels, Belgium	Aug. 23, 1996
400 m	0:46.78	Kevin Young	Barcelona	Aug. 6, 1992
Relay races				
400 m (4 × 100)	0:37.40	USA National Team	Stuttgart, Germany	Aug. 21, 1993
800 m (4 × 200)	1:18.68	Santa Monica T.C.	Walnut, Calif.	April 17, 1994
1,600 m (4 × 400)	2:54.20	USA National Team	New York, N.Y.	July 22, 1998
3,200 m (4 × 800)	7:06.50	Santa Monica T.C.	Walnut, Calif.	Apr. 26, 1986
Field events				
High jump	7 ft. 10½ in.	Charles Austin	Zurich	Aug. 7, 1991
Long jump	29 ft. 4½ in.	Mike Powell	Tokyo, Japan	Aug. 30, 1991
Triple jump	59 ft. 4 in.	Kenny Harrison	Atlanta, Ga.	July 27, 1996
Pole vault	19 ft. 8¼ in.	Jeff Hartwig	St. Denis, France	June 4, 1998
Shot-put	75 ft. 10¼ in.	Randy Barnes	Los Angeles	May 20, 1990
Discus throw	237 ft. 4 in.	Ben Plucknett	Stockholm, Swe.	July 7, 1981
Javelin throw	285 ft. 10 in.	Tom Pukstys	Jena	May 25, 1997
Hammer throw	270 ft. 9 in.	Lance Deal	Milan, Italy	July 9, 1996
Decathlon	8,891 pts	Dan O'Brien	Talence, France	Sept. 4–5, 1992

AMERICAN RECORDS—WOMEN

(Through Aug. 30, 1998)

Event	Record	Holder	Where Made	Date
Running				
100 m	0:10.49	Florence Griffith-Joyner	Indianapolis, Ind.	July 16, 1988
200 m	0:21.56	Florence Griffith-Joyner	Seoul, South Korea	Oct. 1, 1988
400 m	0:48.83	Valerie Brisco-Hooks	Los Angeles, Cal.	Aug. 6, 1984
800 m	1:56.78	Jearl Miles-Clark	Brussels, Belgium	Aug. 22, 1997
1,500 m	3:57.12	Mary Decker Slaney	Stockholm, Swe.	July 26, 1983
1,000 m	2:34.8	Mary Decker Slaney	Eugene, Ore.	July 4, 1985
1 mile	4:16.71	Mary Decker Slaney	Zurich	Aug. 21, 1985
3,000 m	8:29.69	Mary Decker Slaney	Cologne	Aug. 25, 1985
5,000 m	14:52.49	Regina Jacobs	Brunswick, Maine	July 4, 1998
10,000 m	31:28.92	Francie L. Smith	Austin, Texas	April 4, 1991
Hurdles				
100 m hurdles	0:12.46	Gail Devers	Stuttgart, Germany	Aug. 20, 1993
400 m hurdles	0:52.61	Kim Batten	Gothenburg, Sweden	Aug. 11, 1995
Relay races				
400 m (4 × 100)	41.47	U.S.A. National Team	Athens, Greece	Aug. 9, 1997
800 m (4 × 200)	1:30.20	Nike International	Philadelphia, Pa.	Apr. 26, 1997
1,600 m (4 × 400)	3:15.51	U.S. Olympic Team	Seoul, South Korea	Oct. 1, 1988
Field events				
Pole vault	14 ft. 7¼ in.	Stacy Dragila	Modesto, Calif.	May 10, 1997
High jump	6 ft. 8 in.	Louise Ritter	Austin, Tex.	July 9, 1988
Long jump	24 ft. 7 in.	Jackie Joyner-Kersee	New York, N.Y.	May 22, 1994
Triple jump	47 ft. 3½ in.	Sheila Hudson	Stockholm, Sweden	July 8, 1996
Shot-put	66 ft. 2½ in.	Ramon Pagel	San Diego, Calif.	June 25, 1988
Discus throw	216 ft. 10 in.	Carol Cady	San Jose, Calif.	May 31, 1986
Hammer throw	210 ft. 8 in.	Dawn Ellerbe	Walnut, Calif.	April 19, 1997
Javelin throw	227 ft. 5 in.	Kate Schmidt	Furth, W. Ger.	Sept. 10, 1977
Heptathlon	7,291 pts	Jackie Joyner-Kersee	Seoul, South Korea	Sept. 23–24, 1988

HISTORY OF THE RECORD FOR THE MILE RUN

Source: USA Track & Field

Time	Athlete	Country	Year	Location
4:36.5	Richard Webster	England	1865	England
4:29.0	William Chinnery	England	1868	England
4:28.8	Walter Gibbs	England	1868	England
4:26.0	Walter Slade	England	1874	England
4:24.5	Walter Slade	England	1875	London
4:23.2	Walter George	England	1880	London
4:21.4	Walter George	England	1882	London
4:18.4	Walter George	England	1884	Birmingham, England
4:18.2	Fred Bacon	Scotland	1894	Edinburgh, Scotland
4:17.0	Fred Bacon	Scotland	1895	London
4:15.6	Thomas Conneff	United States	1895	Travers Island, N.Y.
4:15.4	John Paul Jones	United States	1911	Cambridge, Mass.
4:14.4	John Paul Jones	United States	1913	Cambridge, Mass:
4:12.6	Norman Taber	United States	1915	Cambridge, Mass.
4:10.4	Paavo Nurmi	Finland	1923	Stockholm
4:09.2	Jules Ladoumegue	France	1931	Paris
4:07.6	Jack Lovelock	New Zealand	1933	Princeton, N.J.
4:06.8	Glenn Cunningham	United States	1934	Princeton, N.J.
4:06.4	Sydney Wooderson	England	1937	London
4:06.2	Gundar Hägg	Sweden	1942	Goteborg, Sweden
4:06.2	Arne Andersson	Sweden	1942	Stockholm
4:04.6	Gunder Hägg	Sweden	1942	Stockholm
4:02.6	Arne Andersson	Sweden	1943	Goteborg, Sweden
4:01.6	Arne Andersson	Sweden	1944	Malmo, Sweden
4:01.4	Gunder Hägg	Sweden	1945	Malmo, Sweden
3:59.4	Roger Bannister	England	1954	Oxford, England
3:58.0	John Landy	Australia	1954	Turku, Finland
3:57.2	Derek Ibbotson	England	1957	London
3:54.5	Herb Elliott	Australia	1958	Dublin
3:54.4	Peter Snell	New Zealand	1962	Wanganui, N.Z.
3:54.1	Peter Snell	New Zealand	1964	Auckland, N.Z.
3:53.6	Michel Jazy	France	1965	Rennes, France
3:51.3	Jim Ryun	United States	1966	Berkeley, Calif.
3:51.1	Jim Ryun	United States	1967	Bakersfield, Calif.
3:51.0	Filbert Bayi	Tanzania	1975	Kingston, Jamaica
3:49.4	John Walker	New Zealand	1975	Goteborg, Sweden

Time	Athlete	Country	Year	Location
3:49.0	Sebastian Coe	England	1979	Oslo
3:48.8	Steve Ovett	England	1980	Oslo
3:48.53	Sebastian Coe	England	1981	Zurich, Switzerland
3:48.40	Steve Ovett	England	1981	Koblenz, W. Ger.
3:47.33	Sebastian Coe	England	1981	Brussels
3:46.31	Steve Cram	England	1985	Oslo
3:44.39	Noureddine Morceli	Algeria	1993	Rieti, Italy

TOP TEN WORLD'S FASTEST OUTDOOR MILES

Source: USA Track & Field

Time	Athlete	Country	Date	Location
3:44.39	Nouraddine Morceli	Algeria	Sept. 5, 1993	Rieti, Italy
3:46.31	Steve Cram	England	July 27, 1985	Oslo
3:47.33	Sebastian Coe	England	Aug. 28, 1981	Brussels
3:47.69	Steve Scott	United States	July 7, 1982	Oslo
3:47.79	Jose Gonzalez	Spain	July 27, 1985	Oslo
3:48.40	Steve Ovett	England	Aug. 26, 1981	Koblenz, W. Ger.
3:48.53	Sebastian Coe	England	Aug. 19, 1981	Zurich
3:48.53	Steve Scott	United States	June 26, 1982	Oslo
3:48.8	Steve Ovett	England	July 1, 1980	Oslo
3:48.83	Sydney Maree	United States	Sept. 9, 1981	Rieti, Italy

NOTE: Professional marks not included.

TOP TEN WORLD'S FASTEST INDOOR MILES

Source: USA Track & Field

Time	Athlete	Country	Date	Location
3:48.45	Hicham El Guerrouj	Morocco	Feb, 12, 1997	Gent, Netherlands
3:49.78	Eamonn Coghlan	Ireland	Feb. 27, 1983	East Rutherford, N.J.
3:50.6	Eamonn Coghlan	Ireland	Feb. 20, 1981	San Diego
3:50.7	Noureddine Morceli	Algeria	Feb. 20, 1993	Birmingham, England
3:50.94	Marcus O'Sullivan	Ireland	Feb. 13, 1988	East Rutherford, N.J.
3:51.2	Ray Flynn[1]	Ireland	Feb. 27, 1983	East Rutherford, N.J.
3:51.66	Marcus O'Sullivan	Ireland	Feb. 10, 1989	East Rutherford, N.J.
3:51.8	Steve Scott[1]	United States	Feb. 20, 1981	San Diego
3:52.28	Steve Scott[2]	United States	Feb. 27, 1983	East Rutherford, N.J.
3:52.30	Frank O'Mara	Ireland	Feb. 1986	New York

1. Finished second. 2. Finished third.

IAAF WORLD CUP IN ATHLETICS—1998

(Johannesburg, South Africa, Sept. 11–13, 1998)

Men's Events

100m—Obadele Thompson, Americas	09.87
200m—Frank Fredericks, Africa	19.97
400m—Iwan Thomas, Great Britain	45.33
800m—Nils Schumann, Germany	1:48.66
1,500m—Laban Rotich, Africa	3:40.87
3,000m—Dieter Baumann, Germany	7:56.24
5,000m—Daniel Komen, Africa	13:46.57
3,000m steeplechase—Damian Kallabis, Germany	8:31.25
110m hurdles—Falk Balzer, Germany	13.10
400m hurdles—Samuel Matete, Africa	48.08
High jump—Charles Austin, United States	2.31m
Pole vault—Maksim Tarasov, Europe	5.85m
Long jump—Ivan Pedroso, Americas	8.37m
Triple jump—Charles Friedek, Germany	17.42m
Shot put—John Godina, United States	21.48m
Discus throw—Virgilijus Alekna, Europe	69.66m
Hammer throw—Tibor Gecsek, Europe	82.68m
Javelin throw—Steve Backley, Great Britain	88.71m
4 x 100m—Great Britain & Northern Ireland	38.09
4 x 400m—United States	2:59.28

Women's Events

100m—Marion Jones, United States	10.65
200m—Marion Jones, United States	21.62
400m—Falilat Ogunkoya, Africa	49.52
800m—Maria Mutola, Africa	1:59.88
1,500m—Svetlana Masterkova, Russia	4:09.41
3,000m—Gabriela Szabo, Europe	9:00.54
5,000m—Sonia O'Sullivan, Europe	16:42.52
100m hurdles—Glory Alozie, Africa	12.58
400m hurdles—Nezha Bidouane, Africa	52.96
High jump—Monica Iagar-Dinescu, Europe	1.98m
Long jump—Heike Drechsler, Germany	7.07m
Triple jump—Olga Vasdeki, Europe	14.64m
Shot put—Vita Pavlysh, Europe	20.59m
Discus throw—Franka Dietzsch, Germany	67.07m
Javelin throw—Joanna Stone, Oceania	69.85m
4 x 100m—United States	42.00
4 x 400m—Germany	3:24.26

1998 USA OUTDOOR CHAMPIONSHIPS

(New Orleans, La., June 19–21, 1998)

MEN'S EVENTS

100m—Tim Harden, Mizuno	9.88
200m—Gentry Bradley, Nike	20.47
400m—Jerome Young, St. Augustine's College	44.09
800m—Mark Everett, Powerbar International	1:45.28
1,500m—Jamey Harris, Reebok	3:37.99
5,000m—MarcDavis, Nike	13:40.62
10,000m—Daniel Browne, U.S. Army	29:46.06
110m hurdles—Reggie Torian, Asics	13.03
400m hurdles—Bryan Bronson, Nike	47.03
3,000m steeplechase—Pascal Dobert, Nike	8:33.91
High jump—Charles Austin, Mizuno	2.30m
Pole vault—Jeff Hartwig, Bell Athletics	5.85m
Long jump—Roland McGhee	8.28m
Triple jump—LaMark Carter, Nike	17.44m
Shot put—John Godina, Reebok–Bruin Track Club	21.71m
Discus throw—John Godina, Reebok–Bruin Track Club	67.09m
Hammer throw—Lance Deal, N.Y. Athletic Club	78.19m
Javelin throw—Tom Pukstys, Adidas	82.37m
Decathlon—Chris Huffins, Mizuno	8,694 pts.
20,000m race walk—Tim Seaman, N.Y. Athletic Club	1:35:07.70

WOMEN'S EVENTS

100m—Marion Jones, Nike	10.72
200m—Marion Jones, Nike	22.24
400m—Kim Graham, Asics	50.69
800m—Jearl Miles-Clark, Reebok	1:58.78
1,500m—Suzy Hamilton (Favor), Nike	4:05.28
5,000m—Regina Jacobs, Mizuno	15:32.31
10,000m—Lynn Jennings, Nike	34:09.86
200m hurdles—Cheryl Dickey, Nike	12.82
400m hurdles—Kim Batten, Reebok	53.61
3,000m steeplechase—Courtney Meldrum, Brigham Young Univ.	10:21.00
High jump—Tisha Waller, Nat's Athletic Training	1.94m
Pole vault—Kellie Suttle, Bell Athletics	4.27m
Long jump—Marion Jones, Nike	7.21m
Triple jump—Sheila Hudson, Unattached	13.72m
Shot put—Connie Price-Smith, Adidas	18.67m
Discus throw—Seiala Sua, UCLA	62.24m
Hammer throw—Windy Dean, Southern Methodist Univ.	64.12m
Javelin throw—Nicole Carroll, Asics	56.58m
Hepathlon—Kelly Blair-Labounty, Reebok	6,402 pts.
10,000m race walk—Joanne Dow, Adidas	47:06.50

Tennis

Lawn tennis is a comparatively modern modification of the ancient game of court tennis. Major Walter Clopton Wingfield thought that something like court tennis might be played outdoors on lawns, and in December, 1873, at Nantclwyd, Wales, he introduced his new game under the name of *Sphairistike* at a lawn party. The game was a success and spread rapidly, but the name was a total failure and almost immediately disappeared when all the players and spectators began to refer to the new game as "lawn tennis." In the early part of 1874, a young lady named Mary Ewing Outerbridge returned from Bermuda to New York, bringing with her the implements and necessary equipment of the new game, which she had obtained from a British Army supply store in Bermuda. Miss Outerbridge and friends played the first game of lawn tennis in the United States on the grounds of the Staten Island Cricket and Baseball Club in the spring of 1874.

For a few years, the new game went along in haphazard fashion until about 1880, when standard measurements for the court and standard equipment within definite limits became the rule. In 1881, the U.S. Lawn Tennis Association (whose name was changed in 1975 to U.S. Tennis Association) was formed and conducted the first national championship at Newport, R.I. The international matches for the Davis Cup began with a series between the British and United States players on the courts of the Longwood Cricket Club, Chestnut Hill, Mass., in 1900, with the home players winning.

Professional tennis, which got its start in 1926 when the French star Suzanne Lenglen was paid $50,000 for a tour, received full recognition in 1968. Staid old Wimbledon, the London home of what are considered the world championships, let the pros compete. This decision ended a long controversy over open tennis and changed the format of the competition. The United States championships were also opened to the pros and the site of the event, long held at Forest Hills, N.Y., was shifted to the National Tennis Center in Flushing Meadows, N.Y., in 1978. Pro tours for men and women became worldwide in play that continued throughout the year.

DAVIS CUP CHAMPIONSHIPS

No matches in 1901, 1910, 1915–18, and 1940–45.

1900 United States 3, British Isles 0
1902 United States 3, British Isles 2
1903 British Isles 4, United States 1
1904 British Isles 5, Belgium 0
1905 British Isles 5, United States 0
1906 British Isles 5, United States 0
1907 Australasia 3, British Isles 2
1908 Australasia 3, United States 2
1909 Australasia 5, United States 0
1911 Australasia 5, United States 0
1912 British Isles 3, Australasia 2
1913 United States 3, British Isles 2
1914 Australasia 3, United States 2
1919 Australasia 4, British Isles 1
1920 United States 5, Australasia 0
1921 United States 5, Japan 0
1922 United States 4, Australasia 1
1923 United States 4, Australasia 1
1924 United States 5, Australasia 0
1925 United States 5, France 0
1926 United States 4, France 1
1927 France 3, United States 2
1928 France 4, United States 1
1929 France 3, United States 2

1930 France 4, United States 1
1931 France 3, Great Britain 2
1932 France 3, United States 2
1933 Great Britain 3, France 2
1934 Great Britain 4, United States 1
1935 Great Britain 5, United States 0
1936 Great Britain 3, Australia 2
1937 United States 4, Great Britain 1
1938 United States 3, Australia 2
1939 Australia 3, United States 2
1946 United States 5, Australia 0
1947 United States 4, Australia 1
1948 United States 5, Australia 0
1949 United States 4, Australia 1
1950 Australia 4, United States 1
1951 Australia 3, United States 2
1952 Australia 4, United States 1
1953 Australia 3, United States 2
1954 United States 3, Australia 2
1955 Australia 5, United States 0
1956 Australia 5, United States 0
1957 Australia 3, United States 2
1958 United States 3, Australia 2
1959 Australia 3, United States 2
1960 Australia 4, Italy 1
1961 Australia 5, Italy 0
1962 Australia 5, Mexico 0
1963 United States 3, Australia 2
1964 Australia 3, United States 2
1965 Australia 4, Spain 1
1966 Australia 4, India 1
1967 Australia 4, Spain 1
1968 United States 4, Australia 1
1969 United States 5, Romania 0
1970 United States 5, West Germany 0
1971 United States 3, Romania 2
1972 United States 3, Romania 2
1973 Australia 5, United States 0
1974 South Africa (Default by India)
1975 Sweden 3, Czechoslovakia 2
1976 Italy 4, Chile 1
1977 Australia 3, Italy 1
1978 United States 4, Britain 1
1979 United States 5, Italy 0
1980 Czechoslovakia 3, Italy 2
1981 United States 3, Argentina 1
1982 United States 3, France 0
1983 Australia 3, Sweden 2
1984 Sweden 4, United States 1
1985 Sweden 3, West Germany 2
1986 Australia 3, Sweden 2
1987 Sweden 5, Austria 0
1988 West Germany 4, Sweden 1
1989 West Germany 3, Sweden 2
1990 United States 3, Australia 2
1991 France 3, United States 1
1992 United States 3, Switzerland 1
1993 Germany 4, Australia 1
1994 Sweden 4, Russia 1
1995 United States 3, Russia 1
1996 France 3, Sweden 2
1997 Sweden 5, United States 0

FEDERATION CUP CHAMPIONSHIPS

World team competition for women conducted by International Lawn Tennis Federation.

1963 United States 2, Australia 1
1964 Australia 2, United States 1
1965 Australia 2, United States 1
1966 United States 3, West Germany 0
1967 United States 2, Britain 0
1968 Australia 3, Netherlands 0
1969 United States 2, Australia 1
1970 Australia 3, West Germany 0
1971 Australia 3, Britain 0
1072 South Africa 2, Britain 1
1973 Australia 3, South Africa 0
1974 Australia 2, United States 1
1975 Czechoslovakia 3, Australia 0
1976 United States 2, Australia 1
1977 United States 2, Australia 1
1978 United States 2, Australia 1
1979 United States 3, Australia 0
1980 United States 3, Australia 0
1981 United States 3, Britain 0
1982 United States 3, West Germany 0
1983 Czechoslovakia 2, West Germany 1
1984 Czechoslovakia 2, Australia 1
1985 Czechoslovakia 2, United States 1
1986 United States 3, Czechoslovakia 0
1987 West Germany 2, United States
1988 Czechoslovakia 2, Soviet Union
1989 United States 3, Spain 0
1990 United States 2, Soviet Union 1
1991 Spain 2, United States 1
1992 Germany 2, Spain 1
1993 Spain 3, Australia 0
1994 Spain 3, United States 0
1995 Spain 3, United States 2
1996 United States 5, Spain 0
1997 France 4, Netherlands 1
1998 Spain 3, Switzerland 2

U.S. NATIONAL AND OPEN CHAMPIONS

SINGLES—MEN

NATIONAL

1881–87 Richard D. Sears
1888–89 Henry Slocum, Jr.
1890–92 Oliver S. Campbell
1893–94 Robert D. Wrenn
1895 Fred H. Hovey
1896–97 Robert D. Wrenn
1898–1900 Malcolm Whitman
1901–02 William A. Larned
1903 Hugh L. Doherty
1904 Holcombe Ward
1905 Beals C. Wright
1906 William J. Clothier
1907–11 William A. Larned
1912–13 Maurice McLoughlin[1]
1914 R. N. Williams II
1915 William Johnston
1916 R. N. William II
1917–18 R. Lindley Murray[2]
1919 William Johnston
1920–25 Bill Tilden
1926–27 Jean Rene Lacoste
1928 Henri Cochet
1929 Bill Tilden
1930 John H. Doeg
1931–32 Ellsworth Vines
1933–34 Fred J. Perry
1935 Wilmer L. Allison
1936 Fred J. Perry
1937–38 Don Budge
1939 Robert L. Riggs
1940 Donald McNeill
1941 Robert L. Riggs
1942 Fred Schroeder
1943 Joseph Hunt
1944–45 Frank Parker
1946–47 Jack Kramer
1948–49 Richard Gonzales
1950 Arthur Larsen
1951–52 Frank Sedgman
1953 Tony Trabert
1954 Vic Seixas
1955 Tony Trabert
1956 Ken Rosewall
1957 Mal Anderson
1958 Ashley Cooper
1959–60 Neale Fraser
1961 Roy Emerson
1962 Rod Laver
1963 Rafael Osuna
1964 Roy Emerson
1965 Manuel Santana
1966 Fred Stolle
1967 John Newcombe
1968 Arthur Ashe
1969 Rod Laver

OPEN

1968 Arthur Ashe
1969 Rod Laver
1970 Ken Rosewall
1971 Stan Smith
1972 Ilie Nastase
1973 John Newcombe
1974 Jimmy Connors
1975 Manuel Orantes
1976 Jimmy Connors
1977 Guillermo Vilas
1978 Jimmy Connors
1979 John McEnroe
1980–81 John McEnroe
1982 Jimmy Connors
1983 Jimmy Connors
1984 John McEnroe
1985–87 Ivan Lendl
1988 Mats Wilander
1989 Boris Becker
1990 Pete Sampras
1991 Stefan Edberg
1992 Stefan Edberg
1993 Pete Sampras
1994 Andre Agassi
1995 Pete Sampras
1996 Pete Sampras
1997–98 Patrick Rafter

1. Challenge Round Abandoned in 1912. 2. Patriotic Tournament in 1917.

SINGLES—WOMEN

NATIONAL

1887	Ellen F. Hansel
1888–89	Bertha Townsend
1890	Ellen C. Roosevelt
1891–92	Mabel E. Cahill
1893	Aline M. Terry
1894	Helen R. Helwig
1895	Juliette P. Atkinson
1896	Elisabeth H. Moore
1897–98	Juliette P. Atkinson
1899	Marion Jones
1900	Myrtle McAteer
1901	Elisabeth H. Moore
1902	Marion Jones
1903	Elisabeth H. Moore
1904	May Sutton
1905	Elisabeth H. Moore
1906	Helen Homans
1907	Evelyn Sears
1908	Maud Bargar-Wallach
1909–11	Hazel V. Hotchkiss
1912–14	Mary K. Browne
1915–18	Molla Bjurstedt
1919	Hazel Hotchkiss Wightman
1920–22	Molla Bjurstedt Mallory
1923–25	Helen N. Wills
1926	Molla B. Mallory
1927–29	Helen N. Wills
1930	Betty Nuthall
1931	Helen Wills Moody
1932–35	Helen Jacobs
1936	Alice Marble
1937	Anita Lizana
1938–40	Alice Marble
1941	Sarah Palfrey Cooke
1942–44	Pauline Betz
1945	Sarah Cooke
1946	Pauline Betz
1947	Louise Brough
1948–50	Margaret Osborne duPont
1951–53	Maureen Connolly
1954–55	Doris Hart
1956	Shirley Fry
1957–58	Althea Gibson
1959	Maria Bueno
1960–61	Darlene Hard
1962	Margaret Smith
1963–64	Maria Bueno
1965	Margaret Smith
1966	Maria Bueno
1967	Billie Jean King
1968–69	Margaret Smith Court[1]

OPEN

1968	Virginia Wade
1969–70	Margaret Court
1971–72	Billie Jean King
1973	Margaret Court
1974	Billie Jean King
1975–78	Chris Evert
1979	Tracy Austin
1980	Chris Evert-Lloyd
1981	Tracy Austin
1982	Chris Evert-Lloyd
1983–84	Martina Navratilova
1985	Hana Mandlikova
1986–87	Martina Navratilova
1988	Steffi Graf
1989	Steffi Graf
1990	Grabriela Sabatini
1991	Monica Seles
1992	Monica Seles
1993	Steffi Graf
1994	Arantxa Sanchez Vicario
1995	Steffi Graf
1996	Steffi Graf
1997	Martina Hingis
1998	Lindsay Davenport

1. With the inaugural of the Open Tournament in 1968, the United States Lawn Tennis Association held a championship at Longwood, Chestnut Hill, Mass. which barred contract professionals in 1968 and 1969.

DOUBLES—MEN

NATIONAL

1920	Bill Johnston–C. J. Griffin
1921–22	Bill Tilden–Vincent Richards
1923	Bill Tilden–B. I. C. Norton
1924	H. O. Kinsey–R. G. Kinsey
1925–26	Vincent Richards–R. N. Williams II
1927	Bill Tilden–Frank Hunter
1928	G. M. Lott, Jr.–V. Hennessy
1929–30	G. M. Lott, Jr.–J. H. Doeg
1931	W. L. Allison–John Van Ryn
1932	E. H. Vines, Jr.–Keith Gledh
1933–34	G. M. Lott, Jr.–L. R. Stoefen
1935	W. L. Allison–John Van Ryn
1936	Don Budge–Gene Mako
1937	G. von Cramm–H. Henkel
1938	Don Budge–Gene Mako
1939	A. K. Quist–J. E. Bromwich
1940–41	Jack Kramer–F. R. Schroeder
1942	Gardnar Mulloy–Bill Talbert
1943	Jack Kramer–Frank Parker
1944	Don McNeill–Bob Falkenburg
1945	Gardnar Mulloy–Bill Talbert
1946	Gardnar Mulloy–Bill Talbert
1947	Jack Kramer–Fred Schroeder
1948	Gardnar Mulloy–Bill Talbert
1949	John Bromwich–William Sidwell
1950	John Bromwich–Frank Sedgman
1951	Frank Sedgman–Ken McGregor
1952	Vic Seixas–Mervyn Rose
1953	Mervyn Rose–Rex Hartwig
1954	Vic Seixas–Tony Trabert
1955	Kosei Kamo–Atsushi Miyagi
1956	Lewis Hoad–Ken Rosewall
1957	Ashley Cooper–Neale Fraser
1958	Ham Richardson–Alex Olmedo
1959–60	Neale Fraser–Roy Emerson
1961	Chuck McKinley–Dennis Ralston
1962	Rafael Osuna–Antonio Palafox
1963–64	Chuck McKinley–Dennis Ralston
1965–66	Fred Stolle–Roy Emerson
1967	John Newcombe–Tony Roche
1968	Stan Smith–Bob Lutz[1]
1969	Richard Crealy–Allan Stone[1]

OPEN

1968	Stan Smith–Bob Lutz
1969	Fred Stolle–Ken Rosewall
1970	Nikki Pilic–Fred Barthes
1971	John Newcombe–Roger Taylor
1972	Cliff Drysdale–Roger Taylor
1973	John Newcombe–Owen Davidson
1974	Bob Lutz–Stan Smith
1975	Jimmy Connors–Ilie Nastase
1976	Marty Riessen–Tom Okker
1977	Frew McMillan–Bob Hewitt
1978	Bob Lutz–Stan Smith
1979	John McEnroe–Peter Fleming
1980	Stan Smith–Bob Lutz
1981	John McEnroe–Peter Fleming
1982	Kevin Curren–Steve Denton
1983	John McEnroe–Peter Fleming
1984	John Fitzgerald–Tomas Smid
1985	Ken Flach–Robert Seguso
1986	Andres Gomez–Slobodan Zivojinovic
1987	Stefan Edberg–Anders Jarryd
1988	Sergio Casal–Emilio Sanchez
1989	John McEnroe–Mark Woodforde
1990	Pieter Aldrich–Danie Visser
1991	John Fitzgerald–Anders Jarryd
1992	Jim Grabb–Richey Reneberg
1993	Ken Flach–Rick Leach
1994	Jacco Hingh–Paul Haarhuis
1995–96	Todd Woodbridge–Mark Woodforde
1997	Yevgeny Kafelnikov–Daniel Vacek
1998	Sandon Stolle–Cyril Zuk

1. With the inaugural of the Open Tournament in 1968, the United States Lawn Tennis Association held a national championship at Longwood, Chestnut Hill, Mass. which barred contract professionals in 1968 and 1969.

DOUBLES—WOMEN

NATIONAL

1924 G. W. Wightman–Helen Wills
1925 Mary K. Browne–Helen Wills
1926 Elizabeth Ryan–Eleanor Goss
1927 L. A. Godfree–Ermyntrude Harvey
1928 Hazel Hotchkiss Wightman–Helen Wills
1929 Phoebe Watson–L. R. C. Michell
1930 Betty Nuthall–Sarah Palfrey
1931 Betty Nuthall–E. B. Witting-stall
1932 Helen Jacobs–Sarah Palfrey
1933 Betty Nuthall–Freda James
1934 Helen Jacobs–Sarah Palfrey
1935 Helen Jacobs–Sarah Palfrey Fabyan
1936 Marjorie G. Van Ryn–Carolin Babcock
1937–40 Sarah Palfrey Fabyan–Alice Marble
1941 Sarah Palfrey Cooke–Margaret Osborne
1942–47 A. Louise Brough–Margaret Osborne
1948–50 A. Louise Brough–Margaret O. duPont
1951–54 Doris Hart–Shirley Fry
1955–57 A. Louise Brough–Margaret O. duPont
1958–59 Darlene Hard–Jeanne Arth
1960 Darlene Hard–Maria Bueno
1961 Darlene Hard–Lesley Turner
1962 Darlene Hard–Maria Bueno
1963 Margaret Smith–Robyn Ebbern
1964 Karen Hantze Susman–Billie Jean Moffitt
1965 Nancy Richey–Carole Caldwell Graebner
1966 Nancy Richey–Maria Bueno
1967 Billie Jean King–Rosemary Casals
1968 Margaret Court–Maria Bueno[1]
1969 Margaret Court–Virginia Wade[1]

OPEN

1968 Maria Bueno–Margaret Court
1969 Darlene Hard–Francoise Durr
1970 Margaret Court–Judy Dalton
1971 Rosemary Casals–Judy Dalton
1972 Francoise Durr–Betty Stove
1973 Margaret Court–Virginia Wade
1974 Billie Jean King–Rosemary Casals
1975 Margaret Court–Virginia Wade
1976 Linky Boshoff–Ilana Kloss
1977 Martina Navratilova–Betty Stove
1978 Billie Jean King–Martina Navratilova
1979 Betty Stove–Wendy Turnbull
1980 Billie Jean King–Martina Navratilova
1981 Kathy Jordan–Anne Smith
1982 Rosemary Casals–Wendy Turnbull
1983–84 Martina Navratilova–Pam Shriver
1985 Claudia Khode-Kilsch–Helena Sukova
1986–87 Martina Navratilova–Pam Shriver
1988 Gigi Fernandez–Robin White
1989 Hana Mandlikova–Martina Navratilova
1990 Gigi Fernandez–Martina Navratilova
1991 Pam Shriver–Natalia Zvereva
1992 Gigi Fernandez–Natalia Zvereva
1993 Arantxa Sanchez Vicario–Helena Sukova
1994 Jana Novotna–Arantxa Sanchez Vicario
1995 Gigi Fernandez–Natasha Zvereva
1996 Gigi Fernandez–Natasha Zvereva
1997 Lindsay Davenport–Jana Novotna
1998 Martina Hingis–Jana Novotna

1. With the inaugural of the Open Tournament in 1968, the United States Lawn Tennis Association held a national championship at Longwood, Chestnut Hill, Mass. which barred contract professionals in 1968 and 1969.

U.S. OPEN CHAMPIONS—1998

United States Open

(Flushing Meadow, N.Y., Aug. 31–Sept. 13, 1998)

Men's singles—Patrick Rafter defeated Mark Philippoussis, 6–3, 3–6, 6–2, 6–0.

Women's singles—Lindsay Davenport defeated Martina Hingis, 6–3, 7–5.

Men's doubles—Sandon Stolle and Cyril Suk defeated Mark Knowles and Daniel Nestor, 4–6, 7–6 (10–8), 6–2.

Women's doubles—Martina Hingis and Jana Novotna defeated Lindsay Davenport and Natasha Zvereva, 6–3, 6–3.

Serena Williams and Max Mirnyi defeated Lisa Raymond and Patrick Galbraith, 6–2, 6–2.

BRITISH (WIMBLEDON) CHAMPIONS

(Amateur from inception in 1877 through 1967)

SINGLES—MEN

1908–09 Arthur Gore
1910–13 A. F. Wilding
1914 N. E. Brookes
1919 G. L. Patterson
1920–21 Bill Tilden
1922 G. L. Patterson
1923 William Johnston
1924 Jean Borotra
1925 Rene Lacoste
1926 Jean Borotra
1927 Henri Cochet
1928 Rene Lacoste
1929 Jean Cochet
1930 Bill Tilden
1931 S. B. Wood
1932 Ellsworth Vines
1933 J. H. Crawford
1934–36 Fred Perry
1937–38 Don Budge
1939 Robert L. Riggs
1946 Yvon Petra
1947 Jack Kramer
1948 R. Falkenburg
1949 Fred Schroeder
1950 Budge Patty
1951 Richard Savitt
1952 Frank Sedgman
1953 Vic Siexas
1954 Jaroslav Drobny
1955 Tony Trabert
1956–57 Lewis Hoad
1958 Ashley Cooper
1959 Alex Olmedo
1960 Neale Fraser
1961–62 Rod Laver
1963 Chuck McKinley
1964–65 Roy Emerson
1966 Manuel Santana
1967 John Newcombe
1968–69 Rod Laver
1970–71 John Newcombe
1972 Stan Smith
1973 Jan Kodes
1974 Jimmy Connors
1975 Arthur Ashe
1976–80 Bjorn Borg
1981 John McEnroe
1982 Jimmy Connors
1983–84 John McEnroe
1985–86 Boris Becker
1987 Pat Cash
1988 Stefan Edberg
1989 Boris Becker
1990 Stefan Edberg
1991 Michael Stich
1992 Andre Agassi
1993 Peter Sampras
1994 Pete Sampras
1995 Pete Sampras
1996 Richard Krajicek
1997–98 Pete Sampras

SINGLES—WOMEN

1919–23 Lenglen
1924 Kathleen McKane
1925 Lenglen
1926 Godfree
1927–29 Helen Wills
1930 Helen Wills Moody
1931 Frl. C. Aussen
1932–33 Helen Wills Moody
1934 D. E. Round
1935 Helen Wills Moody
1936 Helen Jacobs
1937 D. E. Round
1938 Helen Wills Moody
1939 Alice Marble
1946 Pauline M. Betz
1947 Margaret Osborne
1948–50 A. Louise Brough
1951 Doris Hart
1952–54 Maureen Connolly
1955 A. Louise Brough
1956 Shirley Fry
1957–58 Althea Gibson
1959–60 Maria Bueno
1961 Angela Mortimer
1962 Karen Susman
1963 Margaret Smith
1964 Maria Bueno
1965 Margaret Smith
1966–67 Billie Jean King
1968 Billie Jean King
1969 Ann Jones
1970 Margaret Court
1971 Evonne Goolagong
1972–73 Billie Jean King
1974 Chris Evert
1975 Billie Jean King
1976 Chris Evert
1977 Virginia Wade
1978–79 Martina Navratilova
1980 Evonne Goolagong Cawley
1981 Chris Evert-Lloyd
1982–87 Martina Navratilova
1988–89 Steffi Graf
1990 Martina Navratilova
1991 Steffi Graf
1992 Steffi Graf
1993 Steffi Graf
1994 Conchita Martinez
1995 Steffi Graf
1996 Steffi Graf
1997 Martina Hingis
1998 Jana Novotna

DOUBLES—MEN

1953 K. Rosewall–L. Hoad
1954 R. Hartwig–M. Rose
1955 R. Hartwig–L. Hoad
1956 L. Hoad–K. Rosewall
1957 Gardnar Mulloy–Budge Patty
1958 Sven Davidson–Ulf Schmidt
1959 Roy Emerson–Neale Fraser
1960 Dennis Ralston–Rafael Osuna
1961 Roy Emerson–Neale Fraser
1962 Fred Stolle–Bob Hewitt
1963 Rafael Osuna–Antonio Palafox
1964 Fred Stolle–Bob Hewitt
1965 John Newcombe–Tony Roche
1966 John Newcombe–Ken Fletcher
1967 Bob Hewitt–Frew McMillan
1968–70 John Newcombe–Tony Roche
1971 Rod Laver–Roy Emerson
1972 Bob Hewitt–Frew McMillan
1973 Jimmy Connors–Ilie Nastase
1974 John Newcombe–Tony Roche
1975 Vitas Gerulaitis–Sandy Mayer
1976 Brian Gottfried–Raul Ramirez
1977 Ross Case–Geoff Masters
1978 Fred McMillan–Bob Hewitt
1979 Peter Fleming–John McEnroe
1980 Peter McNamara–Paul McNamee
1981 John McEnroe–Peter Fleming
1982 Paul McNamee–Peter McNamara
1983–84 John McEnroe–Peter Fleming
1985 Heinz Gunthardt–Balazs Taroczy
1986 Joakim Nystrom–Mats Wilander
1987 Ken Flach–Robert Seguso
1988 Ken Flach–Robert Seguso
1989 John Fitzgerald–Anders Jarryd
1990 Rick Leach–Jim Pugh
1991 Anders Jarryd–John Fitzgerald
1992 John McEnroe–Michael Stich
1993–97 Todd Woodbridge–Mark Woodforde
1998 Jacco Eltingh–Paul Haarhuis

DOUBLES—WOMEN

1956 Althea Gibson–Angela Buxton
1957 Althea Gibson–Darlene Hard
1958 Althea Gibson–Maria Bueno
1959 Darlene Hard–Jeanne Arth
1960 Darlene Hard–Maria Bueno
1961 Karen Hantze–Billie Jean Moffitt
1962 Karen Hantze Susman–Billie Jean Moffitt
1963 Darlene Hard–Maria Bueno
1964 Margaret Smith–Les Turnerley
1965 Billie Jean Moffitt–Maria Bueno
1966 Nancy Richey–Maria Bueno
1967–68 Billie Jean King–Rosemary Casals
1969 Margaret Court–Judy Tegart
1970–71 Billie Jean King–Rosemary Casals
1972 Billie Jean King–Betty Stove
1973 Billie Jean King–Rosemary Casals
1974 Evonne Goolagong–Peggy Michel
1975 Ann Kiyomura–Kazuko Sawamatsu
1976 Chris Evert–Martina Navratilova
1977 Helen Cawley–JoAnne Russell
1978 Wendy Turnbull–Kerry Reid
1979 Billie Jean King–Martina Navratilova
1980 Kathy Jordan–Anne Smith
1981 Martina Navratilova–Pam Shriver
1982–84 Pam Shriver–Martina Navratilova
1985 Kathy Jordan–Elizabeth Smylie
1986 Pam Shriver–Martina Navratilova
1987 Claudia Khode-Kilsch–Helena Sukova
1988 Steffi Graf–Gabriela Sabatini
1989 Jana Novotna–Helena Sukova
1990 Jana Novotna–Helena Sukova
1991 Pam Shriver–Natalia Zvereva
1992 Gigi Fernandez–Natalia Zvereva
1993 Gigi Fernandez–Natalia Zvereva
1994 Gigi Fernandez–Natalia Zvereva
1995 Jana Novotna–Arantxa Sanchez Vicario
1996 Martina Hingis–Helena Sukova
1997 Gigi Fernandez–Natasha Zvereva
1998 Martina Hingis–Jana Novotna

OTHER 1998 CHAMPIONS

Wimbledon Open

(Wimbledon, England, June 30–July 5, 1998)

Men's singles—Pete Sampras defeated Goran Ivanisevic, 6–7 (2–7), 7–6 (11–9), 6–4, 3–6, 6–2.
Women's singles—Jana Novotna defeated Nathalie Tauziat, 6–4, 7–6 (7–2).
Men's doubles—Jacco Eltingh and Paul Haarhuis defeated Todd Woodbridge and Mark Woodforde, 2–6, 6–4, 7–6 (7–3), 5–7, 10–8.
Women's doubles—Martina Hingis and Jana Novotna defeated Lindsay Davenport and Natasha Zvereva, 6–3, 3–6, 8–6.
Mixed doubles—Max Mirnyi and Serena Williams defeated Mahesh Bhupathi and Mirjana Lucic, 6–4, 6–4.

French Open

(Paris, May 25–June 7, 1998)

Men's singles—Carlos Moya defeated Alex Corretja, 6–3, 7–5, 6–3.
Women's singles—Arantxa Sanchez Vicario defeated Monica Seles, 7–6 (7–5), 0–6, 6–2.
Men's doubles—Jacco Eltingh and Paul Haarhuis defeated Mark Knowles and Daniel Nestor, 6–3, 3–6, 6–3.
Women's doubles—Martina Hingis and Jana Novotna defeated Lindsay Davenport and Natasha Zvereva, 6–1, 7–6 (7–4).
Mixed doubles—Venus Williams and Justin Gimelstob defeated Serena Williams and Luis Lobo, 6–4, 6–4.

1998 Australian Open

(Melbourne, Australia, Jan. 19–Feb. 1, 1998)

Men's singles—Petr Korda, Czech Republic, defeated Marcelo Rios, Chile, 6–2, 6–2, 6–2.
Women's singles—Martina Hingis, Switzerland, defeated Conchita Martinez, Spain, 6–3, 6–3.
Men's doubles—Jonas Bjorkman, Sweden, and Jacco Eltingh, The Netherlands, defeated Todd Woodbridge and Mark Woodforde, Australia, 6–2, 5–7, 2–6, 6–4, 6–3.
Women's doubles—Martina Hingis, Switzerland, and Mirjana Lucic, Croatia, defeated Lindsay Davenport, United States, and Natasha Zvereva, Belarus, 6–4, 2–6, 6–3.
Mixed doubles—Justin Gimelstob and Venus Williams, United States, defeated Cyril Suk and Helena Sukova, Czech Republic, 6–2, 6–1.

MEN'S MONEY WINNERS—1998

(through Sept. 20, 1998)

1.	Patrick Rafter, Australia	$2,085,807
2.	Marcelo Rios, Chile	1,681,071
3.	Pete Sampras, United States	1,541,537
4.	Carlos Moya, Spain	1,536,423
5.	Alex Corretja, Spain	1,167,839
6.	Petr Korda, Czech Republic	1,027,213
7.	Yevgeny Kafelnikov, Russia	956,422
8.	Albert Costa, Spain	941,326
9.	Goran Ivanisevic, Croatia	882,922
10.	Mark Philippoussis, Australia	865,320
11.	Karol Kucera, Slovakia	857,277
12.	Andre Agassi, United States	840,018
13.	Jonas Bjorkman, Sweden	822,344
14.	Richard Krajicek, Netherlands	818,144
15.	Tim Henman, Britain	790,420
16.	Paul Haarhuis, Netherlands	661,377
17.	Cedric Pioline, France	656,738
18.	Gustavo Kuerten, Brazil	646,904
19.	Greg Rusedski, Britain	631,237
20.	Alberto Berasategui, Spain	620,760

WOMEN'S MONEY WINNERS—1998

(through Sept. 20, 1998)

1.	Martina Hingis, Switzerland	2,391,971
2.	Lindsay Davenport, United States	1,944,443
3.	Jana Novotna, Czech Republic	1,819,675
4.	Arantxa Sanchez Vicario, Spain	1,236,419
5.	Venus Williams, United States	913,346
6.	Monica Seles, United States	740,864
7.	Conchita Martinez, Spain	695,982
8.	Natasha Zvereva, Belarus	675,415
9.	Nathalie Tauziat, France	598,764
10.	Patty Schnyder, Switzerland	512,913
11.	Amanda Coetzer, South Africa	460,803
12.	Anna Kournikova, Russia	427,473
13.	Mary Pierce, France	359,162
14.	Irina Spirlea, Romania	324,643
15.	Sandrine Testud, France	317,685
16.	Lisa Raymond, United States	316,293
17.	Dominique van Roost, Belgium	312,574
18.	Ai Sugiyama, Japan	282,190
19.	Serena Williams, United States	273,261
20.	Iva Majoli, Croatia	271,141

Rowing

Rowing goes back so far in history that there is no possibility of tracing it to any particular aboriginal source. The oldest rowing race still on the calendar is the "Doggett's Coat and Badge" contest among professional watermen of the Thames (England) that began in 1715. The first Oxford-Cambridge race was held at Henley in 1829. Competitive rowing in the United States began with matches between boats rowed by professional oarsmen of the New York waterfront. They were oarsmen who rowed the small boats that plied as ferries from Manhattan Island to Brooklyn and return, or who rowed salesmen down the harbor to meet ships arriving from Europe. Since the first salesman to meet an incoming ship had some advantage over his rivals, there was keen competition in the bidding for fast boats and the best oarsmen. This gave rise to match races.

Amateur boat clubs sprang up in the United States between 1820 and 1830 and seven students of Yale joined together to purchase a four-oared lap-streak gig in 1843. The first Harvard-Yale race was held Aug. 3, 1852, on Lake Winnepesaukee, N.H. The first time an American college crew went abroad was in 1869 when Harvard challenged Oxford and was defeated on the Thames. There were early college rowing races on Lake Quinsigamond, near Worcester, Mass., and on Saratoga Lake, N.Y., but the Intercollegiate Rowing Association in 1895 settled on the Hudson, at Poughkeepsie, as the setting for the annual "Poughkeepsie Regatta." In 1950 the I.R.A. shifted its classic to Marietta, Ohio, and in 1952 it was moved to Syracuse, N.Y. The National Association of Amateur Oarsmen, organized in 1872, has conducted annual championship regattas since that time.

INTERCOLLEGIATE ROWING ASSOCIATION REGATTA

(Varsity Eight-Oared Shells)

Rowed at 4 miles, Poughkeepsie, N.Y., 1895–97, 899–1916, 1925–32, 1934–41. Rowed at 3 miles, aratoga, N.Y., 1898; Poughkeepsie, 1921–24, 947–49; Syracuse, N.Y., 1952–1963, 1965–67. owed at 2,000 meters, Syracuse, N.Y., 1964 and 1968–1994. Rowed at Camden, N.J., 1995–present. Rowed at 2 miles, Ithaca, N.Y., 1920; Marietta, Ohio, 1950–51. Suspended 1917–19, 1933, 1942–46.

ear	Time	First	Second
895	21:25	Columbia	Cornell
896	19:59	Cornell	Harvard
897	20:47 ⅘	Cornell	Columbia
898	15:51 ½	Pennsylvania	Cornell
899	20:04	Pennsylvania	Wisconsin
900	19:44 ⅗	Pennsylvania	Wisconsin
901	18:53 ⅕	Cornell	Columbia
902	19:03 ⅗	Cornell	Wisconsin
903	18:57	Cornell	Georgetown
904	20:22 ⅗	Syracuse	Cornell
905	20:29	Cornell	Syracuse
906	19:36 ⅘	Cornell	Pennsylvania
907	20:02 ⅖	Cornell	Columbia
908	19:24 ⅕	Syracuse	Columbia
909	19:02	Cornell	Columbia
910	20:42 ⅕	Cornell	Pennsylvania
911	20:10 ⅘	Cornell	Columbia
912	19:31 ⅖	Cornell	Wisconsin
913	19:28 ⅗	Syracuse	Cornell
914	19:37 ⅘	Columbia	Pennsylvania
915	19:36 ⅗	Cornell	Stanford
916	20:15 ⅖	Syracuse	Cornell
920	11:02 ⅗	Syracuse	Cornell
921	14:07	Navy	California
922	13:33 ⅗	Navy	Washington
923	14:03 ⅕	Washington	Navy
924	15:02	Washington	Wisconsin
925	19:24 ⅘	Navy	Washington
926	19:28 ⅗	Washington	Navy
927	20:57	Columbia	Washington
928	18:35 ⅘	California	Columbia
929	22:58	Columbia	Washington
930	21:42	Cornell	Syracuse
931	18:54 ⅕	Navy	Cornell
932	19:55	California	Cornell
934	19:44	California	Washington
935	18:52	California	Cornell
936	19:09 ⅗	Washington	California
937	18:33 ⅗	Washington	Navy
938	18:19	Navy	California
939	18:12 ⅗	California	Washington
940	22:42	Washington	Cornell
941	18:53 3/10	Washington	California
947	13:59 ⅕	Navy	Cornell
948	14:06 ⅖	Washington	California
949	14:42 ⅗	California	Washington
950	8:07.5	Washington	California
951	7:50.5	Wisconsin	Washington
1952	15:08.1	Navy	Princeton
1953	15:29.6	Navy	Cornell
1954	16:04.4	Navy[1]	Cornell
1955	15:49.9	Cornell	Pennsylvania
1956	16:22.4	Cornell	Navy
1957	15:26.6	Cornell	Pennsylvania
1958	17:12.1	Cornell	Navy
1959	18:01.7	Wisconsin	Syracuse
1960	15:57	California	Navy
1961	16:49.2	California	Cornell
1962	17:02.9	Cornell	Washington
1963	17:24	Cornell	Navy
1964	6:31.1	California	Washington
1965	16:51.3	Navy	Cornell
1966	16:03.4	Wisconsin	Navy
1967	16:13.9	Pennsylvania	Wisconsin
1968	6:15.6	Pennsylvania	Washington
1969	6:30.4	Pennsylvania	Dartmouth
1970	6:39.3	Washington	Wisconsin
1971	6:06	Cornell	Washington
1972	6:22.6	Pennsylvania	Brown
1973	6:21	Wisconsin	Brown
1974	6:33	Wisconsin	M.I.T.
1975	6:08.2	Wisconsin	M.I.T.
1976	6:31	California	Princeton
1977	6:32.4	Cornell	Pennsylvania
1978	6:39.5	Syracuse	Brown
1979	6:26.4	Brown	Wisconsin
1980	6:46	Navy	Northeastern
1981	5:57.3	Cornell	Navy
1982	5:57.5	Cornell	Princeton
1983	6:14.4	Brown	Navy
1984	5:54.7	Navy	Pennsylvania
1985	5:49.9	Princeton	Brown
1986	5:50.2	Brown	Pennsylvania
1987	6:02.9	Brown	Wisconsin
1988	6:14.0	Northeastern	Brown
1989	5:56.0	Penn	Wisconsin
1990	5:55.5	Wisconsin	Pennsylvania
1991	6:05.2	Northeastern	Pennsylvania
1992	6:10.5	Dartmouth	Harvard
1993	5:59.1	Brown	Pennsylvania
1994	5:54.4	Brown	Princeton
1995	5:31.3[2]	Brown	Navy
1996	5:29.6[2]	Princeton	Washington
1997	5:51.0	Washington	Brown
1998	5:31.48	Princeton	Washington

1. Disqualified. 2. New course record.

Harness Racing

Oliver Wendell Holmes, the famous Autocrat of he Breakfast Table, wrote that the running horse vas a gambling toy but the trotting horse was useul and, furthermore, "horse-racing is not a republiian institution; horse-trotting is." Oliver Wendell Iolmes was a born-and-bred New Englander, and New England was the nursery of the harness racing sport in America. Pacers and trotters were matters of local pride and prejudice in Colonial New England, and, shortly after the Revolution, the Messenger and Justin Morgan strains produced many winners in harness racing "matches" along the turnpikes of New York, Connecticut, Rhode Island, Massachusetts, Vermont, and New Hampshire.

There was English thoroughbred blood in Messenger and Justin Morgan, and, many years later, it was blended in Rysdyk's Hambletonian, foaled in 1849. Hambletonian was not particularly fast under harness but his descendants have had almost a monopoly of prizes, titles, and records in the harness racing game. Hambletonian was purchased as a foal with its dam for a total of $124 by William Rysdyk of Goshen, N.Y., and made a modest fortune for the purchaser.

Trotters and pacers often were raced under sadd in the old days, and, in fact, the custom still surviv in some places in Europe. Dexter, the great trott that lowered the mile record from 2:19 ¾ to 2:17 in 1867, was said to handle just as well under sadd as when pulling a sulky. But as sulkies were ligh ened in weight and improved in design, trottin under saddle became less common and finally fade out in this country.

WORLD RECORDS

Established in a race or against time at one mile.
(through Sept. 24, 1998)

Source: United States Trotting Association.

Pacing on Mile Track

Div.	Horse	Driver	Track	Date	Tim
2C	The Big Dog	Joe S. Anderson	Woodbine	8/17/96	1:51.
	Gothic Dream	John D. Campbell	Woodbine	8/31/96	1:51.
2F	Miss Easy	John D. Campbell	Lexington, Ky.	9/25/90	1:51.
2G	Hot Chilli Pepper	Andy Ray Miller	Springfield, Ill.	8/15/96	1:52.
	Wrestling Matt	John D. Campbell	Woodbine	8/30/96	1:52.
3C	Jenna's Beach Boy	William R. Fahy	Lexington, Ky.	9/30/95	1:48.
3F	Shady Daisy	Michel La Chance	Lexington, Ky.	10/4/91	1:51.
	Ellamony	Jack G. Moiseyev	Meadowlands	8/12/93	1:51.
	Immortality	John D. Campbell	Lexington, Ky.	10/7/93	1:51.
3G	Gee Gee Digger	Howard G. Parker	Meadowlands	8/10/96	1:49.
4H	Jenna's Beach Boy	William R. Fahy	Meadowlands	6/22/96	1:47.
4M	Sweetgeorgiabrown	Mark J. Kesmodel	Meadowlands	8/9/96	1:50.
4G	Staying Together	William A. O'Donnell	Meadowlands	6/19/93	1:48.
5+H	Riyadh	William Roy Gale	Woodbine	8/17/96	1:48.
5+M	Ellamony	Ronald W. Waples	Meadowlands	6/23/95	1:50.
5+G	Armbro Maestro	Mark J. Kermodel	Meadowlands	6/15/96	1:49.
	Darth Raider	James A. Morrill, Jr.	Meadowlands	7/6/96	1:49.

Trotting on a Mile Track

Div.	Horse	Driver	Track	Date	Tim
2C	Mack Lobell	John D. Campbell	Lexington, Ky.	10/3/86	1:55.
2F	CR Kay Suzie	Carl E. Allen	Meadowlands	8/3/94	1:55.
2G	I'm Impeccable	David A. Rankin	Lexington, Ky.	9/28/89	1:57.
	Harmony Oaks Royal	Andy Ray Miller	Springfield, Ill.	8/12/95	1:57.
3C	Mack Lobell	John D. Campbell	Springfield, Ill.	8/21/87	1:52.
3F	Continental Victory	Michel La Chance	Meadowlands	8/3/96	1:52.
3G	Champion On Ice	David R. Magee	Springfield, Ill.	8/12/94	1:53.
4H	Pine Chip	John D. Campbell	Meadowlands	8/6/94	1:52.
4M	Beat The Wheel	Catello R. Manzi	Meadowlands	7/8/94	1:51.
4G	Champion On Ice	David R. Magee	Springfield, Ill.	8/12/95	1:53.
5+H	Wesgate Crown	Catello R. Manzi	Meadowlands	7/27/96	1:52.
5+M	Beat The Wheel	Catello R. Manzi	Meadowlands	7/6/95	1:53.
5+G	Oaklea Count	Ronald W. Waples	Meadowlands	8/3/96	1:52.

HISTORY OF TRADITIONAL HARNESS RACING STAKES

THE HAMBLETONIAN

Year	Winner	Driver	Best time	Total purse
1967	Speedy Streak	Del Cameron	2:00	$122,650
1968	Nevele Pride	Stanley Dancer	1:59 ⅖	116,190
1969	Lindy's Pride	Howard Beissinger	1:57 ⅗	124,910
1970	Timothy T.	John Simpson, Jr.	1:58 ⅖[1]	143,630
1971	Speedy Crown	Howard Beissinger	1:57 ⅖	129,770
1972	Super Bowl	Stanley Dancer	1:56 ⅖	119,090
1973	Flirth	Ralph Baldwin	1:57 ⅕	144,710
1974	Christopher T	Billy Haughton	1:58 ⅗	160,150
1975	Bonefish	Stanley Dancer	1:59[2]	232,192
1976	Steve Lobell	Billy Haughton	1:56 ⅖	263,524
1977	Green Speed	Billy Haughton	1:55 ⅗	284,131
1978	Speedy Somolli	Howard Beissinger	1:55[3]	241,280
1979	Legend Hanover	George Sholty	1:56 ⅕	300,000
1980	Burgomeister	Billy Haughton	1:56 ⅗	293,570
1981	Shiaway St. Pat	Ray Remmen	2:01 ⅕[4]	838,000
1982	Speed Bowl	Tommy Haughton	1:56 ⅘	875,750

Year	Winner	Driver	Best time	Total purse
1983	Duenna	Stanley Dancer	1:57 ⅖	1,000,000
1984	Historic Free	Ben Webster	1:56 ⅖	1,219,000
1985	Prakas	Bill O'Donnell	1:54 ⅗	1,272,000
1986	Nuclear Kosmos	Ulf Thoresen	1:56	1,172,082
1987	Mack Lobell	John Campbell	1:53 ⅗	1,046,300
1988	Armbro Goal	John Campbell	1:54 ⅗	1,156,800
1989	Park Avenue Joe	Ron Waybles	1:55 ⅗	1,131,000
1990	Embassy Lobell	Michel Lachance	1:56 ⅕	1,346,000
1991	Giant Victory	Jack Moiseyev	1:54 ⅘	1,238,000
1992	Alf Palema	Mickey McNichol	1:56 ⅗	1,288,000
1993	American Winner	Ron Pierce	1:53 ⅕	1,200,000
1994	Victory Dream	Michel Lachance	1:53 ⅘	1,200,000
1995	Tagliabue	John Campbell	1:54 ⅗	1,200,000
1996	Continentalvictory	Michel La Chance	1:52 ⅘	1,200,000
1997	Malabar Man	Malvern Burroughs	1:55	1,000,000
1998	Muscles Yankee	John Campbell	1:52 ⅖	1,000,000

Three-year-old trotters. One mile. Guy McKinney won first race at Syracuse in 1926; held at Goshen, N.Y., 1930–1942, 1944–1956; at Yonkers, N.Y., 1943; at Du Quoin, Ill., 1957–1980. Since 1981, the race has been held at The Meadowlands in East Rutherford, N.J. 1. By Formal Notice. 2. By Yankee Bambino. 3. By Speedy Somolli and Florida Pro. 4. By Super Juan.

LITTLE BROWN JUG

Year	Winner	Driver	Best time	Total purse
1967	Best of All	Jim Hackett	1:59[1]	$84,778
1968	Rum Customer	Billy Haughton	1:59 ⅗	104,226
1969	Laverne Hanover	Billy Haughton	2:00 ⅖	109,731
1970	Most Happy Fella	Stanley Dancer	1:57 ⅕	100,110
1971	Nansemond	Herve Filion	1:57 ⅖	102,994
1972	Strike Out	Keith Waples	1:56 ⅗	104,916
1973	Melvin's Woe	Joe O'Brien	1:57 ⅗	120,000
1974	Ambro Omaha	Billy Haughton	1:57	132,630
1975	Seatrain	Ben Webster	1:57[2]	147,813
1976	Keystone Ore	Stanley Dancer	1:56 ⅘[3]	153,799
1977	Governor Skipper	John Chapman	1:56 ⅕	150,000
1978	Happy Escort	William Popfinger	1:55 ⅖[4]	186,760
1979	Hot Hitter	Herve Filion	1:55 ⅗	226,455
1980	Niatross	Clint Galbraith	1:54 ⅘	207,361
1981	Fan Hanover	Glen Garnsey	1:56[5]	243,799
1982	Merger	John Campbell	1:56 ⅗	328,900
1983	Ralph Hanover	Ron Waples	1:55 ⅗	358,800
1984	Colt 46	Norman Boring	1:53 ⅗	366,717
1985	Nihilator	Bill O'Donnell	1:52 ⅕	350,730
1986	Barberry Spur	Bill O'Donnell	1:52 ⅘	407,684
1987	Jaguar Spur	Richard Stillings	1:55 ⅗	412,330
1988	B.J. Scoot	Michel Lachance	1:52 ⅗	486,050
1989	Goalie Jeff	Michel Lachance	1:54 ⅕	500,200
1990	Beach Towel	Ray Remmen	1:53 ⅗	253,049
1991	Precious Bunny	Jack Moiseyev	1:54 ⅕	575,150
1992	Fake Left	Ron Waples	1:54 ⅖	556,210
1993	Life Sign	John Campbell	1:52	465,500
1994	Magical Mike	Michel LaChance	1:52 ⅗	512,830
1995	Nick's Fantasy	John Campbell	1:51 ⅖	543,670
1996	Armbro Operative	Michel La Chance	1:52 ⅗	542,220
1997	Western Dreamer	Michel La Chance	1:51 ⅕	605,210
1998	Shady Character	Ron Pierce	1:52 ⅗	566,630

Three-year-old pacers. One Mile. Raced at Delaware County Fair Grounds, Delaware, Ohio. 1. By Nardin's Byrd. 2. By Albert's Star. 3. By Armbro Ranger. 4. By Falcon Almahurst. 5. By Seahawk Hanover.

HARNESS HORSE OF THE YEAR

1959	Bye Bye Byrd, Pacer	1975	Savoir, Trotter	1987–88	Mack Lobell
1960–61	Adios Butler, Pacer	1976	Keystone Ore, Pacer	1989	Matt's Scooter
1962	Su Mac Lad, Trotter	1977	Green Speed, Trotter	1990	Beach Towell
1963	Speedy Scot, Trotter	1978	Abercrombie, Pacer	1991	Precious Bunny
1964–66	Bret Hanover, Pacer	1979–80	Niatross, Pacer	1992	Artsplace
1967–69	Nevele Pride, Trotter	1981	Fan Hanover, Pacer	1993	Staying Together
1970	Fresh Yankee, Trotter	1982–83	Cam Fella, Pacer	1994	Cam's Card Shark
1971–72	Albatross, Pacer	1984	Fancy Crown, Trotter	1995	CR Kay Suzie
1973	Sir Dalrae, Pacer	1985	Nihilator, Trotter	1996	Continentalvictory
1974	Delmonica Hanover, Trotter	1986	Forrest Skipper	1997	Malabar Man

Chosen in poll conducted by United States Trotting Association in conjunction with the U.S. Harness Writers Assn.

Golf

It may be that golf originated in Holland—historians believe it did—but certainly Scotland fostered the game and is famous for it. In fact, in 1457 the Scottish Parliament, disturbed because football and golf had lured young Scots from the more soldierly exercise of archery, passed an ordinance that "futeball and golf be utterly cryit doun and nocht usit." James I and Charles I of the royal line of Stuarts were golf enthusiasts, whereby the game came to be known as "the royal and ancient game of golf."

The golf balls used in the early games were leather-covered and stuffed with feathers. Clubs of all kinds were fashioned by hand to suit individual players. The great step in spreading the game came with the change from the feather ball to the gutta-percha ball about 1850. In 1860, formal competition began with the establishment of an annual tournament for the British Open championship. There are records of "golf clubs" in the United States as far back as colonial days but no proof of actual play before John Reid and some friends laid out six holes on the Reid lawn in Yonkers, N.Y., in 1888 and played there with golf balls and clubs brought over from Scotland by Robert Lockhart. This group then formed the St. Andrews Golf Club of Yonkers, and golf was established in this country.

However, it remained a rather sedate and almost aristocratic pastime until a 20-year-old ex-caddy, Francis Ouimet of Boston, defeated two great British professionals, Harry Vardon and Ted Ray, in the United States Open championship at Brookline, Mass., in 1913. This feat put the game and Francis Ouimet on the front pages of the newspapers and stirred a wave of enthusiasm for the sport. The greatest feat so far in golf history is that of Robert Tyre Jones, Jr., of Atlanta, who won the British Open, the British Amateur, the U.S. Open, and the U.S. Amateur titles in one year, 1930.

THE MASTERS TOURNAMENT WINNERS

Augusta National Golf Club, Augusta, Ga.

Year	Winner	Score	Year	Winner	Score	Year	Winner	Score
1934	Horton Smith	284	1957	Doug Ford	283	1978	Gary Player	277
1935	Gene Sarazen[1]	282	1958	Arnold Palmer	284	1979	Fuzzy Zoeller[1]	280
1936	Horton Smith	285	1959	Art Wall, Jr.	284	1980	Severiano Ballesteros	275
1937	Byron Nelson	283	1960	Arnold Palmer	282	1981	Tom Watson	280
1938	Henry Picard	285	1961	Gary Player	280	1982	Craig Stadler[1]	284
1939	Ralph Guldahl	279	1962	Arnold Palmer[1]	280	1983	Severiano Ballesteros	280
1940	Jimmy Demaret	280	1963	Jack Nicklaus	286	1984	Ben Crenshaw	277
1941	Craig Wood	280	1964	Arnold Palmer	276	1985	Bernhard Langer	282
1942	Byron Nelson[1]	280	1965	Jack Nicklaus	271	1986	Jack Nicklaus	279
1943–45	No Tournaments		1966	Jack Nicklaus[1]	288	1987	Larry Mize[1]	285
1946	Herman Keiser	282	1967	Gay Brewer, Jr.	280	1988	Sandy Lyle	281
1947	Jimmy Demaret	281	1968	Bob Goalby	277	1989	Nick Faldo[1]	283
1948	Claude Harmon	279	1969	George Archer	281	1990	Nick Faldo	278
1949	Sam Snead	282	1970	Billy Casper[1]	279	1991	Ian Woosnam	277
1950	Jimmy Demaret	283	1971	Charles Coody	279	1992	Fred Couples	275
1951	Ben Hogan	280	1972	Jack Nicklaus	286	1993	Bernard Langer	277
1952	Sam Snead	286	1973	Tommy Aaron	283	1994	Jose Maria Olazabal	279
1953	Ben Hogan	274	1974	Gary Player	278	1995	Ben Crenshaw	274
1954	Sam Snead[1]	289	1975	Jack Nicklaus	276	1996	Nick Faldo	276
1955	Cary Middlecoff	279	1976	Ray Floyd	271	1997	Tiger Woods	270
1956	Jack Burke	289	1977	Tom Watson	276	1998	Mark O'Meara	279

1. Winner in playoff.

U.S. OPEN CHAMPIONS

Year	Winner	Score	Where played	Year	Winner	Score	Where played
1895	Horace Rawlins	173	Newport	1912	John McDermott	294	Buffalo
1896	James Foulis	152	Shinnecock Hills	1913	Francis Ouimet[1,2]	304	Brookline
1897	Joe Lloyd	162	Chicago	1914	Walter Hagen	290	Midlothian
1898[3]	Fred Herd	328	Myopia	1915	Jerome D. Travers[2]	297	Baltusrol
1899	Willie Smith	315	Baltimore				
1900	Harry Vardon	313	Chicago	1916	Charles Evans, Jr.[2]	286	Minikahda
1901	Willie Anderson[1]	331	Myopia				
1902	Laurie Auchterlonie	307	Garden City	1917–18	No tournaments[4]		
1903	Willie Anderson[1]	307	Baltusrol	1919	Walter Hagen[2]	301	Brae Burn
1904	Willie Anderson	303	Glen View	1920	Edward Ray	295	Inverness
1905	Willie Anderson	314	Myopia	1921	Jim Barnes	289	Columbia
1906	Alex Smith	295	Onwentsia	1922	Gene Sarazen	288	Skokie
1907	Alex Ross	302	Philadelphia	1923	R. T. Jones, Jr.[1,2]	296	Inwood
1908	Fred McLeod[1]	322	Myopia	1924	Cyril Walker	297	Oakland Hills
1909	George Sargent	290	Englewood	1925	Willie Macfarlane[1]	291	Worcester
1910	Alex Smith[1]	298	Philadelphia	1926	R. T. Jones, Jr.[2]	293	Scioto
1911	John McDermott[1]	307	Chicago	1927	Tommy Armour[1]	301	Oakmont

ear	Winner	Score	Where played
928	Johnny Farrell[1]	294	Olympia Fields
929	R. T. Jones, Jr.[1 2]	294	Winged Foot
930	R. T. Jones, Jr.[2]	287	Interlachen
931	Billy Burke[1]	292	Inverness
932	Gene Sarazen	286	Fresh Meadow
933	John Goodman[2]	287	North Shore
934	Olin Dutra	293	Merion
935	Sam Parks, Jr.	299	Oakmont
936	Tony Manero	282	Baltusrol
937	Ralph Guldahl	281	Oakland Hills
938	Ralph Guldahl	284	Cherry Hills
939	Byron Nelson[1]	284	Philadelphia
940	Lawson Little[1]	287	Canterbury
941	Craig Wood	284	Colonial
942–45	No tournaments[5]		
946	Lloyd Mangrum[1]	284	Canterbury
947	Lew Worsham[1]	282	St. Louis
948	Ben Hogan	276	Riviera
949	Cary Middlecoff	286	Medinah
950	Ben Hogan[1]	287	Merion
951	Ben Hogan	287	Oakland Hills
952	Julius Boros	281	Northwood
953	Ben Hogan	283	Oakmont
954	Ed Furgol	284	Baltusrol
955	Jack Fleck[1]	287	Olympic
956	Cary Middlecoff	281	Oak Hill
957	Dick Mayer[1]	298	Inverness
958	Tommy Bolt	283	Southern Hills
959	Bill Casper, Jr.	282	Winged Foot
960	Arnold Palmer	280	Cherry Hills
961	Gene Littler	281	Oakland Hills
962	Jack Nicklaus[1]	283	Oakmont
963	Julius Boros[1]	293	Country Club
964	Ken Venturi	278	Congressional
965	Gary Player[1]	282	Bellerive
966	Bill Casper[1]	278	Olympic
967	Jack Nicklaus	275	Baltusrol
1968	Lee Trevino	275	Oak Hill
1969	Orville Moody	281	Champions G. C.
1970	Tony Jacklin	281	Hazeltine
1971	Lee Trevino[1]	280	Merion
1972	Jack Nicklaus	290	Pebble Beach
1973	Johnny Miller	279	Oakmont
1974	Hale Irwin	287	Winged Foot
1975	Lou Graham[1]	287	Medinah
1976	Jerry Pate	277	Atlanta A.C.
1977	Hubert Green	278	Southern Hills
1978	Andy North	285	Cherry Hills
1979	Hale Irwin	284	Inverness
1980	Jack Nicklaus	272	Baltusrol
1981	David Graham	273	Merion
1982	Tom Watson	282	Pebble Beach
1983	Larry Nelson	280	Oakmont
1984	Fuzzy Zoeller[1]	276	Winged Foot
1985	Andy North	279	Oakland Hills
1986	Ray Floyd	279	Shinnecock Hills
1987	Scott Simpson	277	Olympic Golf Club
1988	Curtis Strange[1]	278	The Country Club
1989	Curtis Strange	278	Oak Hill Country Club
1990	Hale Irwin[1]	280	Medinah C.C.
1991	Payne Stewart[1]	282	Hazeltine
1992	Tom Kite	285	Pebble Beach
1993	Lee Janzen	272	Baltusrol
1994	Ernie Els	279	Oakmont
1995	Corey Pavin	280	Shinnecock Hills
1996	Steve Jones	278	Oakland Hills
1997	Ernie Els	276	Congressional C.C.
1998	Lee Janzen	280	Olympic Country Club

. Winner in playoff. 2. Amateur. 3. In 1898, competition was extended to 72 holes. 4. In 1917, Jock Hutchison, with a 292, on an Open Patriotic Tournament for the benefit of the American Red Cross at Whitemarsh Valley Country Club. 5. In 1942, en Hogan, with a 271 won a Hale American National Open Tournament for the benefit of the Navy Relief Society and USO Ridgemoor Country Club.

U.S. AMATEUR CHAMPIONS

895	Charles B. Macdonald
896–97	H. J. Whigham
898	Findlay S. Douglas
899	H. M. Harriman
900–01	Walter J. Travis
902	Louis N. James
903	Walter J. Travis
904–05	H. Chandler Egan
906	Eben M. Byers
907–08	Jerome D. Travers
909	Robert A. Gardner
910	W. C. Fownes, Jr.
911	Harold H. Hilton
912–13	Jerome D. Travers
914	Francis Ouimet
915	Robert A. Gardner
916	Charles Evans, Jr.
919	S. D. Herron
920	Charles Evans, Jr.
921	Jesse P. Guilford
922	Jess W. Sweetser
923	Max R. Marston
1924–25	R. T. Jones, Jr.
1926	George Von Elm
1927–28	R. T. Jones, Jr.
1929	H. R. Johnston
1930	R. T. Jones, Jr.
1931	Francis Ouimet
1932	Ross Somerville
1933	G. T. Dunlap, Jr.
1934–35	Lawson Little
1936	John W. Fischer
1937	John Goodman
1938	Willie Turnesa
1939	Marvin H. Ward
1940	R. D. Chapman
1941	Marvin H. Ward
1946	Ted Bishop
1947	Robert Riegel
1948	Willie Turnesa
1949	Charles Coe
1950	Sam Urzetta
1951	Billy Maxwell
1952	Jack Westland
1953	Gene Littler
1954	Arnold Palmer
1955–56	Harvie Ward
1957	Hillman Robbins
1958	Charles Coe
1959	Jack Nicklaus
1960	Deane Beman
1961	Jack Nicklaus
1962	Labron Harris, Jr.
1963	Deane Beman
1964	Bill Campbell
1965[2]	Robert Murphy, Jr.
1966	Gary Cowan[1]
1967	Bob Dickson
1968	Bruce Fleisher
1969	Steven Melnyk
1970	Lanny Wadkins
1971	Gary Cowan
1972	Vinny Giles 3d
1973[3]	Craig Stadler
1974	Jerry Pate
1975	Fred Ridley
1976	Bill Sander
1977	John Fought
1978	John Cook
1979	Mark O'Meara
1980	Hal Sutton
1981	Nathaniel Crosby
1982	Jay Sigel
1983	Jay Sigel
1984	Scott Verplank
1985	Sam Randolph
1986	Buddy Alexander
1987	Bill Mayfair
1988	Eric Meeks
1989	Chris Patton
1990	Phil Mickelson
1991	Mitch Voges
1992	Justin Leonard
1993	John Harris
1994	Tiger Woods
1995	Tiger Woods
1996	Tiger Woods
1997	Matthew Kuchar
1998	Hank Kuehne

. Winner in playoff. 2. Tourney switched to medal play through 1972. 3. Return to match play.

U.S. P.G.A. CHAMPIONS

1916	Jim Barnes	1944	Bob Hamilton	1963	Jack Nicklaus	1982	Ray Floyd
1919	Jim Barnes	1945	Byron Nelson	1964	Bobby Nichols	1983	Hal Sutton
1920	Jock Hutchison	1946	Ben Hogan	1965	Dave Marr	1984	Lee Trevino
1921	Walter Hagen	1947	Jim Ferrier	1966	Al Geiberger	1985	Hubert Green
1922–23	Gene Sarazen	1948	Ben Hogan	1967	Don January[1]	1986	Bob Tway
1924–27	Walter Hagen	1949	Sam Snead	1968	Julius Boros	1987	Larry Nelson
1928–29	Leo Diegel	1950	Chandler Harper	1969	Ray Floyd	1988	Jeff Sluman
1930	Tommy Armour	1951	Sam Snead	1970	Dave Stockton	1989	Payne Stewart
1931	Tom Creavy	1952	Jim Turnesa	1971	Jack Nicklaus	1990	Mac Grady
1932	Olin Dutra	1953	Walter Burkemo	1972	Gary Player	1991	John Daly
1933	Gene Sarazen	1954	Chick Harbert	1973	Jack Nicklaus	1992	Nick Price
1934	Paul Runyan	1955	Doug Ford	1974	Lee Trevino	1993	Paul Azinger[1]
1935	Johnny Revolta	1956	Jack Burke, Jr.	1975	Jack Nicklaus	1994	Nick Price
1936–37	Denny Shute	1957	Lionel Hebert	1976	Dave Stockton	1995	Steve Elkington
1938	Paul Runyan	1958[2]	Dow Finsterwald	1977	Lanny Wadkins[1]	1996	Mark Brooks
1939	Henry Picard	1959	Bob Rosburg	1978	John Mahaffey	1997	Davis Love III
1940	Byron Nelson	1960	Jay Hebert	1979	David Graham[1]	1998	Vijay Singh
1941	Victor Ghezzi	1961	Jerry Barber[1]	1980	Jack Nicklaus		
1942	Sam Snead	1962	Gary Player	1981	Larry Nelson		

1. Winner in playoff. 2. Switched to medal play.

U.S. WOMEN'S AMATEUR CHAMPIONS

1916	Alexa Stirling	1941	Mrs. Frank Newell	1963	Anne Quast Welts	1981	Juli Inkster
1919–20	Alexa Stirling	1946	Mildred Zaharias	1964	Barbara McIntire	1982	Juli Inkster
1921	Marion Hollins	1947	Louise Suggs	1965	Jean Ashley	1983	Joanne Pacillo
1922	Glenna Collett	1948	Grace Lenczyk	1966	JoAnne Gunderson	1984	Deb Richard
1923	Edith Cummings	1949	Mrs. D. G. Porter	1967	Lou Dill	1985	Michiko Hattori
1924	Dorothy Campbell	1950	Beverly Hanson	1968	JoAnne G. Carner	1986	Kay Cockerill
	Hurd	1951	Dorothy Kirby	1969	Catherine LaCoste	1987	Kay Cockerill
1925	Glenna Collett	1952	Jacqueline Pung	1970	Martha Wilkinson	1988	Pearl Sinn
1926	Helen Stetson	1953	Mary Lena Faulk	1971	Laura Baugh	1989	Vicki Goetze
1927	Mrs. M. B. Horn	1954	Barbara Romack	1972	Mary Ann Budke	1990	Pat Hurst
1928–30	Glenna Collett	1955	Patricia Lesser	1973	Carol Semple	1991	Amy Fruhwirth
1931	Helen Hicks	1956	Marlene Stewart	1974	Cynthia Hill	1992	Vicki Goetze
1932–34	Virginia Van Wie	1957	JoAnne Gunderson	1975	Beth Daniel	1993	Jill McGill
1935	Glenna Collett Vare	1958	Anne Quast	1976	Donna Horton	1994	Wendy Ward
1936	Pamela Barton	1959	Barbara McIntire	1977	Beth Daniel	1995	Kelli Kuehne
1937	Mrs. J. A. Page, Jr.	1960	JoAnne Gunderson	1978	Cathy Sherk	1996	Kelli Kuehne
1938	Patty Berg	1961	Anne Quast Decker	1979	Carolyn Hill	1997	Silvia Cavalleri
1939–40	Betty Jameson	1962	JoAnne Gunderson	1980	Juli Inkster	1998	Grace Park

U.S. WOMEN'S OPEN CHAMPIONS

Year	Winner	Score	Year	Winner	Score	Year	Winner	Score
1946	Patty Berg (match	—	1963	Mary Mills	289	1981	Pat Bradley	279
	play)		1964	Mickey Wright[1]	290	1982	Janet Alex	283
1947	Betty Jameson	295	1965	Carol Mann	290	1983	Jan Stephenson	290
1948	Mildred D. Zaharias	300	1966	Sandra Spuzich	297	1984	Hollis Stacy	290
1949	Louise Suggs	291	1967	Catherine LaCoste[2]	294	1985	Kathy Baker	280
1950	Mildred D. Zaharias	291	1968	Susie Berning	289	1986	Jane Geddes[1]	287
1951	Betsy Rawls	293	1969	Donna Caponi	294	1987	Laura Davies[1]	285
1952	Louise Suggs	284	1970	Donna Caponi	287	1988	Liselotte Neumann	277
1953	Betsy Rawls[1]	302	1971	JoAnne Carner	288	1989	Betsy King	278
1954	Mildred D. Zaharias	291	1972	Susie Berning	299	1990	Betsy King	284
1955	Fay Crocker	299	1973	Susie Berning	290	1991	Meg Mallon	283
1956	Katherine Cornelius[1]	302	1974	Sandra Haynie	295	1992	Patty Sheehan	280
1957	Betsy Rawls	299	1975	Sandra Palmer	295	1993	Lauri Merten	280
1958	Mickey Wright	290	1976	JoAnne Carner[1]	292	1994	Patty Sheehan	277
1959	Mickey Wright	287	1977	Hollis Stacy	292	1995	Annika Sorenstam	278
1960	Betsy Rawls	291	1978	Hollis Stacy	289	1996	Annika Sorenstam	272
1961	Mickey Wright	293	1979	Jerilyn Britz	284	1997	Alison Nicholas	274
1962	Murle Lindstrom	301	1980	Amy Alcott	280	1998	Se Ri Pak	290

1. Winner in playoff. 2. Amateur.

BRITISH OPEN CHAMPIONS

(First tournament, held in 1860, was won by Willie Park, Sr.)

ear	Winner	Score	Year	Winner	Score	Year	Winner	Score
920	George Duncan	303	1951	Max Faulkner	285	1976	Johnny Miller	279
921	Jock Hutchison[1]	296	1952	Bobby Locke	287	1977	Tom Watson	268
922	Walter Hagen	300	1953	Ben Hogan	282	1978	Jack Nicklaus	281
923	A. G. Havers	295	1954	Peter Thomson	283	1979	Severiano Ballesteros	283
924	Walter Hagen	301	1955	Peter Thomson	281	1980	Tom Watson	271
925	Jim Barnes	300	1956	Peter Thomson	286	1981	Bill Rogers	276
926	R. T. Jones, Jr.	291	1957	Bobby Locke	279	1982	Tom Watson	284
927	R. T. Jones, Jr.	285	1958	Peter Thomson[1]	278	1983	Tom Watson	275
928	Walter Hagen	292	1959	Gary Player	284	1984	Severiano Ballesteros	276
929	Walter Hagen	292	1960	Kel Nagle	278	1985	Sandy Lyle	282
930	R. T. Jones, Jr.	291	1961	Arnold Palmer	284	1986	Greg Norman	280
931	Tommy Armour	296	1962	Arnold Palmer	276	1987	Nick Faldo	279
932	Gene Sarazen	283	1963	Bob Charles[1]	277	1988	Seve Ballesteros	273
933	Denny Shute1	292	1964	Tony Lema	279	1989	Mark Calcavecchia	275
934	Henry Cotton	283	1965	Peter Thomson	285	1990	Nick Faldo	270
935	A. Perry	283	1966	Jack Nicklaus	282	1991	Ian Baker-Finch	272
936	A. H. Padgham	287	1967	Roberto de Vicenzo	278	1992	Nick Faldo	272
937	Henry Cotton	290	1968	Gary Player	289	1993	Greg Norman	267
938	R. A. Whitcombe	295	1969	Tony Jacklin	280	1994	Nick Price	268
939	R. Burton	290	1970	Jack Nicklaus[1]	283	1995	John Daly	282
940	Sam Snead	290	1971	Lee Trevino	278	1996	Tom Lehman	271
947	Fred Daly	294	1972	Lee Trevino	278	1997	Justin Leonard	272
948	Henry Cotton	283	1973	Tom Weiskopf	276	1998	Mark O'Meara	280
949	Bobby Locke[1]	283	1974	Gary Player	282			
950	Bobby Locke	279	1975	Tom Watson[1]	279			

OTHER 1998 PGA TOUR WINNERS

(Through Sept. 21, 1998)

ercedes Championships—Phil Mickelson	$306,000
ob Hope Chrysler Classic—Fred Couples	414,000
hoenix Open—Jesper Parnevik	450,000
T&T Pebble Beach National Pro-Am—Phil Mickelson	450,000
uick Invitational—Scott Simpson	378,000
issan Open—Billy Mayfair	378,000
oral-Ryder Open—Michael Bradley	360,000
onda Classic—Mark Calcavecchia	324,000
he Players Championship—Justin Leonard	720,000
ICI Classic—Davis Love III	342,000
hell Houston Open—David Duval	360,000
ellSouth Classic—Tiger Woods	324,000
TE Byron Nelson Classic—John Cook	450,000
lasterCard Colonial—Tom Watson	414,000
emper Open—Stuart Appleby	360,000
uick Classic—J.P. Hayes	324,000
edEx St. Jude Classic—Nick Price	324,000
uick Open—Billy Mayfair	324,000
print International—Vijay Singh	360,000
IEC World Series of Golf—David Duval	405,000

OTHER 1998 LPGA TOUR WINNERS

(Through Sept. 21, 1998)

The Office Depot—Helen Alfredsson	$90,000
Cup Noodles Hawaiian Ladies Open—Wendy Ward	97,500
Australian Ladies Masters—Karrie Webb	105,000
Welch's Circle K Championship—Helen Alfredsson	75,000
Nabisco Dinah Shore—Pat Hurst	150,000
Chick-Fil-A Charity Championship—Liselotte Neumann	105,000
Titleholders Championship—Danielle Ammaccapane	150,000
Sara Lee Classic—Barb Mucha	112,500
McDonald's LPGA Championship—Se Ri Pak	104,666
Rochester International—Rosie Jones	105,000
Michelob Light Classic—Annika Sörenstam	90,000
Oldsmobile Classic—Lisa Walters	97,500
Friendly's Classic—Amy Fruhwirth	90,000
ShopRite LPGA Classic—Annika Sörenstam	150,000
U.S. Women's Open—Se Ri Pak	267,500
Jamie Farr Kroger Classic—Se Ri Pak	120,000
JAL Big Apple Classic—Annika Sörenstam	116,250
Giant Eagle LPGA Classic—Se Ri Pak	120,000
du Maurier Classic—Brandie Burton	180,000
Weetabix Women's British Open—Sherri Steinhauer	162,000
The Safeway LPGA Golf Championship—Danielle Ammaccapane	90,000

Auto Racing

INDIANAPOLIS 500

Year	Winner	Car	Time	mph	Second place
1911	Ray Harroun	Marmon	6:42:08.000	74.590	Ralph Mulford
1912	Joe Dawson	National	6:21:06.000	78.720	Teddy Tetzloff
1913	Jules Goux	Peugeot	6:35:05.000	75.930	Spencer Wishart
1914	René Thomas	Delage	6:03:45.000	82.470	Arthur Duray
1915	Ralph DePalma	Mercedes	5:33:55.510	89.840	Dario Resta
1916[1]	Dario Resta	Peugeot	3:34:17.000	84.000	Wilbur D'Alene
1919	Howard Wilcox	Peugeot	5:40:42.870	88.050	Eddie Hearne
1920	Gaston Chevrolet	Monroe	5:38:32.000	88.620	René Thomas
1921	Tommy Milton	Frontenac	5:34:44.650	89.620	Roscoe Sarles
1922	Jimmy Murphy	Murphy Special	5:17:30.790	94.480	Harry Hartz
1923	Tommy Milton	H. C. S. Special	5:29.50.170	90.950	Harry Hartz
1924	L. L. Corum-Joe Boyer	Dusenberg Special	5:05:23.510	98.230	Earl Cooper
1925	Peter DePaolo	Dusenberg Special	4:56:39.450	101.130	Dave Lewis
1926[2]	Frank Lockhart	Miller Special	4:10:14.950	95.904	Harry Hartz
1927	George Souders	Dusenberg Special	5:07:33.080	97.540	Earl DeVore
1928	Louis Meyer	Miller Special	5:01:33.750	99.480	Lou Moore
1929	Ray Keech	Simplex Special	5:07:25.420	97.580	Louis Meyer
1930	Billy Arnold	Miller-Hartz Special	4:58:39.720	100.448	Shorty Cantlon
1931	Louis Schneider	Bowes Special	5:10:27.930	96.629	Fred Frame
1932	Fred Frame	Miller-Hartz Special	4:48:03.790	104.144	Howard Wilcox
1933	Louis Meyer	Tydol Special	4:48:00.750	104.162	Wilbur Shaw
1934	Bill Cummings	Boyle Products Special	4:46:05.200	104.863	Mauri Rose
1935	Kelly Petillo	Gilmore Special	4:42:22.710	106.240	Wilbur Shaw
1936	Louis Meyer	Ring Free Special	4:35:03.390	109.069	Ted Horn
1937	Wilbur Shaw	Shaw-Gilmore Special	4:24:07.800	113.580	Ralph Hepburn
1938	Floyd Roberts	Burd Piston Ring Special	4:15:58.400	117.200	Wilbur Shaw
1939	Wilbur Shaw	Boyle Special	4:20:47.390	115.035	Jimmy Snyder
1940	Wilbur Shaw	Boyle Special	4:22:31.170	114.277	Rex Mays
1941	Floyd Davis-Mauri Rose	Noc-Out Hose Clamp Special	4:20:36.240	115.117	Rex Mays
1946	George Robson	Thorne Engineering Special	4:21:26.710	114.820	Jimmy Jackson
1947	Mauri Rose	Blue Crown Special	4:17:52.170	116.338	Bill Holland
1948	Mauri Rose	Blue Crown Special	4:10:23.330	119.814	Bill Holland
1949	Bill Holland	Blue Crown Special	4:07:15.970	121.327	Johnny Parsons
1950[3]	Johnnie Parsons	Wynn's Friction Proof Special	2:46:55.970	124.002	Bill Holland
1951	Lee Wallard	Belanger Special	3:57:38.050	126.244	Mike Nazaruk
1952	Troy Ruttman	Agajanian Special	3:52:41.880	128.922	Jim Rathmann
1953	Bill Vukovich	Fuel Injection Special	3:53:01.690	128.740	Art Cross
1954	Bill Vukovich	Fuel Injection Special	3:49:17.270	130.840	Jim Bryan
1955	Bob Sweikert	John Zink Special	3:53:59.13	128.209	Tony Bettenhausen
1956	Pat Flaherty	John Zink Special	3:53:28.840	128.490	Sam Hanks
1957	Sam Hanks	Belond Exhaust Special	3:41:14.250	135.601	Jim Rathmann
1958	Jimmy Bryan	Belond A-P Special	3:44:13.800	133.791	George Amick
1959	Rodger Ward	Leader Card 500 Roadster	3:40:49.200	135.857	Jim Rathmann
1960	Jim Rathmann	Ken-Paul Special	3:36:11.360	138.767	Rodger Ward
1961	A. J. Foyt	Bowes Special	3:35:37.490	139.130	Eddie Sachs
1962	Rodger Ward	Leader Card Special	3:33:50.330	140.293	Len Sutton
1963	Parnelli Jones	Agajanian Special	3:29:35.400	143.137	Jim Clark
1964	A. J. Foyt	Sheraton-Thompson Spl.	3:23:35.830	147.350	Rodger Ward
1965	Jim Clark	Lotus-Ford	3:19:05.340	150.686	Parnelli Jones
1966	Graham Hill	Red Ball Lola-Ford	3:27:52.530	144.317	Jim Clark
1967[4]	A. J. Foyt	Sheraton-Thompson Coyote-Ford	3:18:24.220	151.207	Al Unser
1968	Bobby Unser	Rislone Eagle-Offenhauser	3:16:13.760	152.882	Dan Gurney
1969	Mario Andretti	STP Hawk-Ford	3:11:14.710	156.867	Dan Gurney
1970	Al Unser	Johnny Lightning P. J. Colt-Ford	3:12:37.040	155.749	Mark Donohue
1971	Al Unser	Johnny Lightning P. J. Colt-Ford	3:10:11.560	157.735	Peter Revson
1972	Mark Donohue	Sunoco McLaren-Offenhauser	3:04:05.540	162.962	Al Unser
1973[5]	Gordon Johncock	STP Eagle-Offenhauser	2:05:26.590	159.036	Bill Vukovich, Jr.
1974	Johnny Rutherford	McLaren-Offenhauser	3:09:10.060	158.589	Bobby Unser
1975[6]	Bobby Unser	Jorgensen Eagle-Offenhauser	2:54:55.080	149.213	Johnny Rutherford
1976[7]	Johnny Rutherford	Hy-gain McLaren-Offenhauser	1:42:52.480	148.725	A. J. Foyt
1977	A. J. Foyt	Gilmore Coyote-Foyt	3:05:57.160	161.331	Tom Sneva
1978	Al Unser	1st Nat'l City Lola-Cosworth	3:05:54.990	161.363	Tom Sneva
1979	Rick Mears	Gould Penske-Cosworth	3:08:27.970	158.899	A. J. Foyt
1980	Johnny Rutherford	Pennzoil Chaparral-Cosworth	3:29:59.560	142.862	Tom Sneva
1981[8]	Bobby Unser	Norton Penske-Cosworth	3:35:41.780	139.029	Mario Andretti

Year	Winner	Car	Time	mph	Second place
1982	Gordon Johncock	STP Wildcat-Cosworth	3:05:09.140	162.029	Rick Mears
1983	Tom Sneva	Texaco Star March-Cosworth	3:05:03.060	162.117	Al Unser
1984	Rick Mears	Pennzoil March-Cosworth	3:03:21.000	162.962	Roberto Guerrero
1985	Danny Sullivan	Miller March-Cosworth	3:16:06.069	152.982	Mario Andretti
1986	Bobby Rahal	Budweiser March-Cosworth	2:55:43.480	170.722	Kevin Cogan
1987	Al Unser, Sr.	Cummins March-Cosworth	3:04:59.147	162.175	Roberto Guerrero
1988	Rick Mears	Pennzoil Penske P.C.17-Chevrolet	3:27:10.204	144.809	Emerson Fittipaldi
1989	Emerson Fittipaldi	Marlboro Penske-Cosworth	2:59:01.040	167.581	Al Unser, Jr.
1990	Arie Luyendyk	Domino's Pizza Lola-Cosworth	2:41:18.248	185.987	Bobby Rahal
1991	Rick Mears	Marlboro Penske-Cosworth	2:50:01.018	176.460	Michael Andretti
1992	Al Unser, Jr.	Valvoline-Chevrolet	3:43.05.148	134.477	Scott Goodyear
1993	Emerson Fittipaldi	Penske-Chevrolet	3:10:49.860	157.207	Arie Luyendyk
1994	Al Unser, Jr.	Penske-Mercedes	3:06:29.006	160.872	Jacques Villeneuve
1995	Jacques Villeneuve	Reynard-Ford	3:15:17.561	156.616	Christian Fittipaldi
1996	Buddy Lazier	Reynard-Ford	3:22:45.753	147.956	Davy Jones
1997	Arie Luyendyk	G Force-Aurora	3:25:43.388	145.827	Scott Goodyear
1998	Eddie Cheever	Dallara-Aurora	3:26:40.524	145.155	Buddy Lazier

1. 300 miles. 2. Race ended at 400 miles because of rain. 3. Race ended at 345 miles because of rain. 4. Race, postponed after 18 laps because of rain on May 30, was finished on May 31. 5. Race postponed May 28 and 29 was cut to 332.5 miles because of rain, May 30. 6. Race ended at 435 miles because of rain. 7. Race ended at 255 miles because of rain. 8. Andretti was awarded the victory the day after the race after Bobby Unser, whose car finished first, was penalized one lap and dropped from first place to second for passing other cars illegally under a yellow caution flag. Unser appealed the decision to the U.S. Auto Club and was upheld. A panel ruled the penalty was too severe and instead fined Unser $40,000, but restored the victory to him.

U.S. 500

The U.S. 500 was started in 1996 by IndyCar, after Indianapolis 500 race officials joined forced with IndyCar's upstart rivals the Indy Racing League. A disagreement over the number of automatic qualifiers that would be given to IRL drivers spurred IndyCar to stage a Memorial Day race of its own to go head-to-head with the Indy 500. In 1998 the race was held on July 26.

Year	Winner	Car	Time	mph	Second place
1996	Jimmy Vasser	Reynard-Honda	3:11:48.000	156.403	Mauricio Gugelmin
1997	Alex Zanardi	Reynard-Honda	2:59:35.580	167.044	Mark Blundell
1998	Greg Moore	Reynard-Mercedes	3:00:48.785	165.913	Jimmy Vasser

NATIONAL ASSOCIATION FOR STOCK CAR AUTO RACING WINSTON CUP CHAMPIONS

1949	Red Byron	1962–63	Joe Weatherly	1979	Richard Petty	1990	Dale Earnhardt
1950	Bill Rexford	1964	Richard Petty	1980	Dale Earnhardt	1991	Dale Earnhardt
1951	Herb Thomas	1965	Ned Jarrett	1981	Darrell Waltrip	1992	Alan Kulwicki
1952	Tim Flock	1966	David Pearson	1982	Darrell Waltrip	1993	Dale Earnhardt
1953	Herb Thomas	1967	Richard Petty	1983	Bobby Allison	1994	Dale Earnhardt
1954	Lee Petty	1968–69	David Pearson	1984	Terry Labonte	1995	Jeff Gordon
1955	Tim Flock	1970	Bobby Isaac	1985	Darrell Waltrip	1996	Terry Labonte
1956–57	Buck Baker	1971–72	Richard Petty	1986	Dale Earnhardt	1997	Jeff Gordon
1958–59	Lee Petty	1973	Benny Parsons	1987	Dale Earnhardt	1998[1]	Jeff Gordon
1960	Rex White	1974–75	Richard Petty	1988	Bill Elliott		
1961	Ned Jarrett	1976–78	Cale Yarborough	1989	Rusty Wallace		

1. As of Oct. 11, 1998.

INDYCAR NATIONAL CHAMPIONS

1910	Ray Harroun	1924	James Murphy	1939	Wilbur Shaw	1959	Rodger Ward
1911	Ralph Mulford	1925	Peter DePaolo	1940–41	Rex Mays	1960–61	A. J. Foyt
1912	Ralph DePalma	1926	Harry Hartz	1946–48	Ted Horn	1962	Rodger Ward
1913	Earl Cooper	1927	Peter DePaolo	1949	Johnnie Parsons	1963–64	A. J. Foyt
1914	Ralph DePalma	1928–29	Louis Meyer	1950	Henry Banks	1965–66	Mario Andretti
1915	Earl Cooper	1930	Billy Arnold	1951	Tony Bettenhausen	1967	A. J. Foyt
1916	Dario Resta	1931	Louis Schneider			1968	Bobby Unser
1917	Earl Cooper	1932	Bob Carey	1952	Chuck Stevenson	1969	Mario Andretti
1918	Ralph Mulford	1933	Louis Meyer	1953	Sam Hanks	1970	Al Unser
1919	Howard Wilcox	1934	Bill Cummings	1954	Jimmy Bryan	1971–72	Joe Leonard
1920	Gaston Chevrolet	1935	Kelly Petillo	1955	Bob Sweikert	1973	Roger McCluskey
1921	Tommy Milton	1936	Mauri Rose	1956–57	Jimmy Bryan	1974	Bobby Unser
1922	James Murphy	1937	Wilbur Shaw	1958	Tony Bettenhausen	1975	A. J. Foyt
1923	Eddie Hearne	1938	Floyd Roberts			1976	Gordon Johncock

1977–78	Tom Sneva	1983	Al Unser	1990	Al Unser, Jr.	1996	Jimmy Vasser
1979	Rick Mears (CART), A.J. Foyt (USAC)[1]	1984	Mario Andretti	1991	Michael Andretti	1997–98	Alessandro Zanardi
		1985	Al Unser	1992	Bobby Rahal		
		1986–87	Bobby Rahal	1993	Nigel Mansell		
1980	Johnny Rutherford	1988	Danny Sullivan	1994	Al Unser, Jr.		
1981–82	Rick Mears	1989	Emerson Fittipaldi	1995	Jacques Villeneuve		

1. Two separate series were held in 1979. NOTE: There have been three sanctioning bodies for the series: the Automobile Association of America (1909–1955), the U.S. Auto Club (1956–1979), and the Championship Auto Racing Team (CART) 1979–present.

1998 INDY RACING LEAGUE LEADING POINT WINNERS

Driver	Pts	Winnings	Driver	Pts	Winnings
1. Kenny Brack	332	$1,096,700	11. John Paul, Jr.	216	$ 693,900
2. Davey Hamilton	292	856,850	12. Stephan Gregoire	201	686,550
3. Tony Stewart	289	1,002,850	13. Billy Boat	194	1,004,150
4. Scott Sharp	272	808,900	14. Sam Schmidt	186	662,800
5. Buddy Lazier	262	984,850	15. Mark Dismore	180	595,450
6. Jeff Ward	252	811,650	16. Robby Unser	176	517,850
7. Scott Goodyear	244	761,750	17. Robbie Buhl	174	557,150
8. Arie Luyendyk	227	746,100	18. Brian Tyler	140	317,700
9. Eddie Cheever, Jr.	222	1,811,200	19. Buzz Calkins	134	484,300
10. Marco Greco	219	561,900	20. Raul Boesel	132	471,300

1998 NASCAR LEADING POINT WINNERS
(as of Oct. 11, 1998)

Driver	Pts	Winnings	Driver	Pts	Winnings
1. Jeff Gordon	4,632	$5,668,477	11. Bobby Hamilton	3,256	$1,596,895
2. Mark Martin	4,344	3,042,675	12. Ken Schrader	3,168	1,565,456
3. Dale Jarrett	4,098	2,095,070	13. Sterling Marlin	3,133	1,077,650
4. Rusty Wallace	3,883	1,902,095	14. Ernie Irvan	3,120	1,426,566
5. Jeff Burton	3,800	1,908,675	15. Michael Waltrip	3,076	1,259,730
6. Jeremy Mayfield	3,761	1,819,481	16. Jimmy Spencer	3,064	1,464,696
7. Bobby Labonte	3,759	2,441,325	17. Chad Little	3,039	1,211,311
8. Dale Earnhardt	3,357	2,416,125	18. Bill Elliott	2,921	1,322,725
9. Terry Labonte	3,323	1,651,260	19. Ward Burton	2,813	1,241,203
10. John Andretti	3,278	1,479,415	19. Johnny Benson	2,798	1,158,631

WORLD GRAND PRIX DRIVER CHAMPIONS

1950 Giuseppe Farina, Italy, Alfa Romeo
1951 Juan Fangio, Argentina, Alfa Romeo
1952 Alberto Ascari, Italy, Ferrari
1953 Alberto Ascari, Italy, Ferrari
1954 Juan Fangio, Argentina, Maserati, Mercedes-Benz
1955 Juan Fangio, Argentina, Mercedes-Benz
1956 Juan Fangio, Argentina, Lancia-Ferrari
1957 Juan Fangio, Argentina, Masserati
1958 Mike Hawthorn, England, Ferrari
1959 Jack Brabham, Australia, Cooper
1960 Jack Brabham, Australia, Cooper
1961 Phil Hill, United States, Ferrari
1962 Graham Hill, England, BRM
1963 Jim Clark, Scotland, Lotus-Ford
1964 John Surtees, England, Ferrari
1965 Jim Clark, Scotland, Lotus-Ford
1966 Jack Brabham, Australia, Brabham-Repco
1967 Denis Hulme, New Zealand, Brabham-Repco
1968 Graham Hill, England, Lotus-Ford
1969 Jackie Stewart, Scotland, Matra-Ford
1970 Jochen Rindt, Austria, Lotus-Ford
1971 Jackie Stewart, Scotland, Tyrrell-Ford
1972 Emerson Fittipaldi, Brazil, Lotus-Ford
1973 Jackie Stewart, Scotland, Tyrrell-Ford
1974 Emerson Fittipaldi, Brazil, McLaren-Ford
1975 Niki Lauda, Austria, Ferrari
1976 James Hunt, Britain, McLaren-Ford
1977 Niki Lauda, Austria, Ferrari
1978 Mario Andretti, United States, Lotus
1979 Jody Scheckter, South Africa, Ferrari
1980 Alan Jones, Australia, Williams-Ford
1981 Nelson Piquet, Brazil, Brabham-Ford
1982 Kiki Rosberg, Finland, Williams-Ford
1983 Nelson Piquet, Brazil. Brabham-BMW
1984 Nikki Lauda, Austria, McLaren-Porsche
1985 Alain Prost, France, McLaren-Porsche
1986 Alain Prost, France, McLaren-Porsche
1987 Nelson Piquet, Brazil, Williams-Honda
1988 Aryton Senna, Brazil, McLaren-Honda
1989 Alain Prost, France, McLaren-Honda
1990 Ayrton Senna, Brazil, McLaren-Honda
1991 Aryton Senna, Brazil, McLaren-Honda
1992 Nigel Mansell, Britain, Williams-Renault
1993 Alain Prost, France, Williams-Renault
1994 William Schumacher, Germany, Benetton
1995 William Schumacher, Germany, Benetton Renault
1996 Damon Hill, Britain, Williams
1997 Jacques Villeneuve, Canada, Williams-Renault
1998[1] Mika Hakkinen, Finland, McLaren-Mercedes

1. As of Oct. 12, 1998.

achting

AMERICA'S CUP RECORD

First race in 1851 around Isle of Wight, Cowes, ngland. First defense and all others through 1920 eld 30 miles off New York Bay. Races since 1930 eld 30 miles off Newport, R.I. Conducted as one ace only in 1851 and 1870; best four-of-seven basis, 1871; best two-of-three, 1876–1887; best three-of-five, 1893–1901; best four-of-seven, since 1930. Figures in parentheses indicate number of races won.

ear	Winner and owner	Loser and owner
351	AMERICA (1), John C. Stevens, U.S.	AURORA, T. Le Marchant, England[1]
370	MAGIC (1), Franklin Osgood, U.S.	CAMBRIA, James Ashbury, England[2]
371	COLUMBIA (2), Franklin Osgood, U.S.[3] SAPPHO (2), William P. Douglas, U.S.	LIVONIA (1), James Ashbury, England
376	MADELEINE (2), John S. Dickerson, U.S.	COUNTESS OF DUFFERIN, Chas. Gifford, Canada
381	MISCHIEF (2), J. R. Busk, U.S.	ATALANTA, Alexander Cuthbert, Canada
385	PURITAN (2), J. M. Forbes-Gen. Charles Paine, U.S.	GENESTA, Sir Richard Sutton, England
386	MAYFLOWER (2), Gen. Charles Paine, U.S.	GALATEA, Lt. William Henn, England
387	VOLUNTEER (2), Gen. Charles Paine, U.S.	THISTLE, James Bell et al., Scotland
393	VIGILANT (3), C. Oliver Iselin et al., U.S.	VALKYRIE II, Lord Dunraven, England
395	DEFENDER (3), C. O. Iselin–W. K. Vanderbilt–E. D. Morgan, U.S.	VALKYRIE III, Lord Dunraven–Lord Lonsdale–Lord Wolverton, England
399	COLUMBIA (3), J. P. Morgan–C. O. Iselin, U.S.	SHAMROCK I, Sir Thomas Lipton, Ireland
901	COLUMBIA (3), Edwin D. Morgan, U.S.	SHAMROCK II, Sir Thomas Lipton, Ireland
903	RELIANCE (3), Cornelius Vanderbilt et al., U.S.	SHAMROCK III, Sir Thomas Lipton, Ireland
920	RESOLUTE (3), Henry Walters et al., U.S.	SHAMROCK IV (2), Sir Thomas Lipton, Ireland
930	ENTERPRISE (4), Harold S. Vanderbilt et al., U.S.	SHAMROCK V, Sir Thomas Lipton, Ireland
934	RAINBOW (4), Harold S. Vanderbilt, U.S.	ENDEAVOUR (2), T. O. M. Sopwith, England
937	RANGER (4), Harold S. Vanderbilt, U.S.	ENDEAVOUR II, T. O. M. Sopwith, England
958	COLUMBIA (4), Henry Sears et al., U.S.	SCEPTRE, Hugh Goodson et al., England
962	WEATHERLY (4), Henry D. Mercer et al., U.S.	GRETEL (1), Sir Frank Packer et al., Australia
964	CONSTELLATION (4), New York Y.C. Syndicate, U.S.	SOVEREIGN (0), J. Anthony Bowden, England
967	INTREPID (4), New York Y.C. Syndicate, U.S.	DAME PATTIE (0), Sydney (Aust.) Syndicate
970	INTREPID (4), New York Y.C. Syndicate, U.S.	GRETEL II (1), Sydney (Aust.) Syndicate
974	COURAGEOUS (4), New York, N.Y. Syndicate, U.S.	SOUTHERN CROSS (0), Sydney (Aust.) Syndicate
977	COURAGEOUS (4), New York, N.Y. Syndicate, U.S.	AUSTRALIA (0), Sun City (Aust.) Syndicate
980	FREEDOM (4), New York, N.Y. Syndicate, U.S.	AUSTRALIA (1), Alan Bond et al, Australia
983	AUSTRALIA II (4), Alan Bond et al., Australia	LIBERTY, (3) New York, N.Y. Syndicate, U.S.
987	STARS & STRIPES (4), Dennis Conner et al., United States	KOOKABURRA III (0), Iain Murray et al., Australia
988[4]	STARS & STRIPES, Dennis Conner, et al., United States	NEW ZEALAND, Michael Fay, et al., New Zealand
992	AMERICA 3, Bill Koch, et al., United States	IL MORO DI VENEZIA, Paul Cayard, et al., Italy
995	BLACK MAGIC, Peter Blake, et al., New Zealand	YOUNG AMERICA, Dennis Conner, et al., United States

. Fourteen British yachts started against America; Aurora finished second. 2. Cambria sailed against 23 U.S. yachts and nished tenth. 3. Columbia was disabled in the third race, after winning the first two; Sappho substituted and won the fourth nd fifth. 4. Shortly after Dennis Conner and his 60-foot, twin-hulled catamaran easily defeated the challenge of the New ealand, a 133-foot, single-hulled yacht in the waters off San Diego in early September 1988, a New York State Supreme ourt judge ruled that the Americans did not live up to the America's Cup Deed of Gift, which means competing boats must e similar. The judge ruled that the Americans had an unfair advantage over the monohulled ship, and awarded the Cup to ew Zealand. However, an Appeal awarded the Cup to the United States.

Rodeo

PROFESSIONAL RODEO COWBOY ASSOCIATION, ALL AROUND COWBOY

953	Bill Linderman	1963–65	Dean Oliver	1976–79	Tom Ferguson	1988	Dave Appleton
954	Buck Rutherford	1966–70	Larry Mahan	1980	Paul Tierney	1989–94	Ty Murray
955	Casey Tibbs	1971–72	Phil Lyne	1981	Jimmie Cooper	1995–96	Joe Beaver
956–59	Jim Shoulders	1973	Larry Mahan	1982	Chris Lybbert	1997	Dan Mortensen
960	Harry Tompkins	1974	Tom Ferguson	1983	Roy Cooper	1998[1]	Ty Murray
961	Benny Reynolds	1975	Leo Camarillo and Tom Ferguson	1984	Dee Pickett		
962	Tom Nesmith			1985–87	Lewis Field		

. Unofficial standing as of Oct. 13, 1998.

Marathons

BOSTON MARATHON

(April 20, 1998)

Men	Time
1. Moses Tanui, Kenya	2:07:34
2. Joseph Chebet, Kenya	2:07:37
3. Gert Thys, South Africa	2:07:52
4. Andre Ramos, Brazil	2:08:26
5. John Kagwe, Kenya	2:08:51
Wheelchair—Franz Nietlispach, Switzerland	1:21:52

Women	Tim
1. Fatuma Roba, Ethiopia	2:23:2
2. Renata Paradowska, Poland	2:27:1
3. Anuta Catuna, Romania	2:27:3
4. Manuela Machado, Portugal	2:29:1
5. Colleen De Reuck, South Africa	2:29:4
Wheelchair—Louise Sauvage, Australia	1:41:1

OTHER 1997–98 MARATHONS

Los Angeles (March 29, 1998)

	Time
Men	
Zebedayo Bayo, Tanzania	2:11:20
Wheelchair—Saul Mendoza, Mexico	1:30:01
Women	
Lornah Kiplagat, Kenya	2:34:05
Wheelchair—Kazu Hatanaka, Japan	1:56:58

London (April 26, 1998)

Men	
Abel Anton, Spain	2:07:57
Wheelchair—Heinz Frei, Switzerland	1:35:18
Women	
Catherina McKiernan, Ireland	2:26:26
Wheelchair—Tanni Grey, Great Britain	2:02:01

Rotterdam (April 19, 1998)

Men	Fabian Roncero, Spain	2:07:2
Women	Tegla Loroupe, Kenya	2:20:4

New York City (Nov. 2, 1997)

	Tim
Men	
John Kagwe, Kenya	2:08:1
Wheelchair—Guido Muller, Switzerland	1:50:2
Women	
Franziska Rochat-Moser, Switzerland	2:28:4
Wheelchair—Tatyana Tarasova, Russia	3:42:5

Curling

UNITED STATES CHAMPIONSHIPS—1998

	Site	Winner's Home Club	Skip
Men's	Bismarck, N.D.	Wisconsin 1 (Stevens Pt., Wis.)	Paul Pustova
Women's	Bismarck, N.D.	Illinois (Wilmette, Ill.)	Kari Erickson
Junior Men's	Hartland, Wis.	Ak-Sar-Ben (Omaha, Neb.)	Andy Roza
Junior Women's	Hartland, Wis.	Minnesota II (Bemidji, Minn.)	Hope Schmit

WORLD CHAMPIONSHIPS—1998

	Site	Winner's Country	Skip
Men's	Kamloops, British Columbia, Canada	Canada	Wayne Middaugh
Women's	Kamloops, British Columbia, Canada	Sweden	Eilsabet Gustafso
Junior Men's	Thunder Bay, Ontario, Canada	Canada	John Morris
Junior Women's	Thunder Bay, Ontario, Canada	Canada	Melissa McClure

Little League

LITTLE LEAGUE WORLD SERIES CHAMPIONS

Year	Champion	Runner-up	Score
1947	Williamsport, Pa.	Lock Haven, Pa.	16–7
1948	Lock Haven, Pa.	St. Petersburg, Fla.	6–5
1949	Hammontown, N.J.	Pensacola, Fla.	5–0
1950	Houston, Tex.	Bridgeport, Conn.	2–1
1951	Stamford, Conn.	Austin, Tex.	3–0
1952	Norwalk, Conn.	Monongahela, Pa.	4–3
1953	Birmingham, Ala.	Schenectady, N.Y.	1–0
1954	Schenectady, N.Y.	Colton, Calif.	7–5
1955	Morrisville, Pa.	Merchantville, N.J.	4–3
1956	Roswell, N.M.	Merchantville, N.J.	3–1
1957	Monterrey, Mex.	LaMesa, Calif.	4–0
1958	Monterrey, Mex.	Kankakee, Ill.	10–1
1959	Hamtramck, Mich.	Auburn, Calif.	12–0
1960	Levittown, Pa.	Ft. Worth, Tex.	5–0
1961	El Cajon, Calif.	El Campo, Tex.	4–
1962	San Jose, Calif.	Kankakee, Ill.	3–
1963	Granada Hills, Calif.	Stratford, Conn.	2–
1964	Staten Island, N.Y.	Monterrey, Mex.	4–
1965	Windsor Locks, Conn.	Stoney Creek, Can.	3–
1966	Houston, Tex.	W. New York, N.J.	8–
1967	West Tokyo, Japan	Chicago, Ill.	4–
1968	Osaka, Japan	Richmond, Va.	1–
1969	Taipei, Taiwan	Santa Clara, Calif.	5–
1970	Wayne, N.J.	Campbell, Calif.	2–
1971	Tainan, Taiwan	Gary, Ind.	12-
1972	Taipei, Taiwan	Hammond, Ind.	6–
1973	Tainan City, Taiwan	Tucson, Ariz.	12-
1974	Kao Hsiung, Taiwan	El Cajon, Calif.	7–

Year	Champion	Runner-up	Score
1975	Lakewood, N.J.	Tampa, Fla.	4–3
1976	Tokyo, Japan	Campbell, Calif.	10–3
1977	Kao Hsiung, Taiwan	El Cajon, Calif.	7–2
1978	Pin-Tung, Taiwan	Danville, Calif.	11–1
1979	Hsien, Taiwan	Campbell, Calif.	2–1
1980	Hua Lian, Taiwan	Tampa, Fla.	4–3
1981	Tai-Chung, Taiwan	Tampa, Fla.	4–2
1982	Kirkland, Wash.	Hsien, Taiwan	6–0
1983	Marietta, Ga.	Barahona, D. Rep.	3–1
1984	Seoul, S. Korea	Altamonte Springs, Fla.	6–2
1985	Seoul, S. Korea	Mexicali, Mex.	7–1
1986	Tianan Park, Taiwan	Tucson, Ariz.	12–0
1987	Hua Lian, Taiwan	Irvine, Calif.	21–1
1988	Tai-Chung, Taiwan	Pearl City, Haw.	10–0
1989	Trumbull, Conn.	Kaohsiung, Taiwan	5–2
1990	Taipei, Taiwan	Shippensburg, Pa.	9–0
1991	Tai-Chung, Taiwan	San Ramon Valley, Calif.	11–0
1992*	Long Beach, Calif.	Zamboanga, Phil.	6–0
1993	Long Beach, Calif.	David Chiriqui, Pan.	3–2
1994	Maracaibo, Venezuela	Northridge, Calif.	4–3
1995	Tainan, Taiwan	Spring, Texas	17–3
1996	Kao-Hsuing City, Taipei	Cranston, R.I.	13–3
1997	Guadalupe, Mexico	South Mission Viejo, Calif.	5–4
1998	Toms River, N.J.	Kashima, Japan	12–9

* Long Beach declared a 6–0 winner after the international tournament committee determined that Zamboanga City had used players that were not within its city limits.

Baseball

The popular tradition that baseball was invented by Abner Doubleday at Cooperstown, N.Y., in 1839 has been enshrined in the Hall of Fame and National Museum of Baseball erected in that town, but research has proved that a game called "Base Ball" was played in this country and England before 1839. The first team baseball as we know it was played at the Elysian Fields, Hoboken, N.J., on June 19, 1846, between the Knickerbockers and the New York Nine. The next fifty years saw a gradual growth of baseball and an improvement of equipment and playing skill.

Historians have it that the first pitcher to throw a curve was William A. (Candy) Cummings in 1867. The Cincinnati Red Stockings were the first all-professional team, and in 1869 they played 64 games without a loss. The standard ball of the same size and weight, still the rule, was adopted in 1872. The first catcher's mask was worn in 1875. The National League was organized in 1876. The first chest protector was worn in 1885. The three-strike rule was put on the books in 1887, and the four-ball ticket to first base was instituted in 1889. The pitching distance was lengthened to 60 feet 6 inches in 1893, and the rules have been modified only slightly since that time.

The American League, under the vigorous leadership of B. B. Johnson, became a major league in 1901. Judge Kenesaw Mountain Landis, by action of the two major leagues, became Commissioner of Baseball in 1921.

MAJOR LEAGUE ALL-STAR GAME

Year	Date	Winning league and manager	Runs	Losing league and manager	Runs	Winning pitcher	Losing pitcher	Site	Paid attendance
1933	July 6	A.L. (Mack)	4	N.L. (McGraw)	2	Gomez	Hallahan	Chicago A.L.	47,595
1934	July 10	A.L. (Cronin)	9	N.L. (Terry)	7	Harder	Mungo	New York N.L.	48,363
1935	July 8	A.L. (Cochrane)	4	N.L. (Frisch)	1	Gomez	Walker	Cleveland A.L.	69,831
1936	July 7	N.L. (Grimm)	4	A.L. (McCarthy)	3	J. Dean	Grove	Boston N.L.	25,556
1937	July 7	A.L. (McCarthy)	8	N.L. (Terry)	3	Gomez	J. Dean	Washington A.L.	31,391
1938	July 6	N.L. (Terry)	4	A.L. (McCarthy)	1	Vander Meer	Gomez	Cincinnati N.L.	27,067
1939	July 11	A.L. (McCarthy)	3	N.L. (Hartnett)	1	Bridges	Lee	New York A.L.	62,892
1940	July 9	N.L. (McKechnie)	4	A.L. (Cronin)	0	Derringer	Ruffing	St. Louis N.L.	32,373
1941	July 8	A.L. (Baker)	7	N.L. (McKechnie)	5	E. Smith	Passeau	Detroit A.L.	54,674
1942	July 6	A.L. (McCarthy)	3	N.L. (Durocher)	1	Chandler	Cooper	New York N.L.	34,178
1943	July 13	A.L. (McCarthy)	5	N.L. (Southworth)	3	Leonard	Cooper	Philadelphia A.L.	31,938
1944	July 11	N.L. (Southworth)	7	A.L. (McCarthy)	1	Raffensberger	Hughson	Pittsburgh N.L.	29,589
1946	July 9	A.L. (O'Neill)	12	N.L. (Grimm)	0	Feller	Passeau	Boston A.L.	34,906
1947	July 8	A.L. (Cronin)	2	N.L. (Dyer)	1	Shea	Sain	Chicago N.L.	41,123
1948	July 13	A.L. (Harris)	5	N.L. (Durocher)	2	Raschi	Schmitz	St. Louis A.L.	34,009
1949	July 12	A.L. (Boudreau)	11	N.L. (Southworth)	7	Trucks	Newcombe	Brooklyn N.L.	32,577
1950	July 11	N.L. (Shotton)	4	A.L. (Stengel)	3[1]	Blackwell	Gray	Chicago A.L.	46,127
1951	July 10	N.L. (Sawyer)	8	A.L. (Stengel)	3	Maglie	Lopat	Detroit A.L.	52,075
1952	July 8	N.L. (Durocher)	3	A.L. (Stengel)	2[2]	Rush	Lemon	Philadelphia N.L.	32,785
1953	July 14	N.L. (Dressen)	5	A.L. (Stengel)	1	Spahn	Reynolds	Cincinnati N.L.	30,846
1954	July 13	A.L. (Stengel)	11	N.L. (Alston)	9	Stone	Conley	Cleveland A.L.	68,751
1955	July 12	N.L. (Durocher)	6	A.L. (Lopez)	5[3]	Conley	Sullivan	Milwaukee N.L.	45,643
1956	July 10	N.L. (Alston)	7	A.L. (Stengel)	3	Friend	Pierce	Washington A.L.	28,843
1957	July 9	A.L. (Stengel)	6	N.L. (Alston)	5	Bunning	Simmons	St. Louis N.L.	30,693
1958	July 8	A.L. (Stengel)	4	N.L. (Haney)	3	Wynn	Friend	Baltimore A.L.	48,829
1959[4]	July 7	N.L. (Haney)	5	A.L. (Stengel)	4	Antonelli	Ford	Pittsburgh N.L.	35,277
	Aug. 3	A.L. (Stengel)	5	N.L. (Haney)	3	Walker	Drysdale	Los Angeles N.L.	55,105
1960[4]	July 11	N.L. (Alston)	5	A.L. (Lopez)	3	Friend	Monbouquette	Kansas City A.L.	30,619
	July 13	N.L. (Alston)	6	A.L. (Lopez)	0	Law	Ford	New York A.L.	38,362

Year	Date	Winning league and manager	Runs	Losing league and manager	Runs	Winning pitcher	Losing pitcher	Site	Paid attendance
1961[4]	July 11	N.L. (Murtaugh)	5	A.L. (Richards)	4[5]	Miller	Wilhelm	San Francisco	44,115
	July 31	N.L (Murtaugh)	1	A.L. (Richards)	1[6]	—	—	N.L. Boston A.L.	31,851
1962[4]	July 10	N.L. (Hutchinson)	3	A.L. (Houk)	1	Marichal	Pascual	Washington A.L.	45,480
	July 30	A.L. (Houk)	9	N.L. (Hutchinson)	4	Herbert	Mahaffey	Chicago N.L.	38,359
1963	July 9	N.L. (Dark)	5	A.L. (Houk)	3	Jackson	Bunning	Cleveland A.L.	44,160
1964	July 7	N.L. (Alston)	7	A.L. (Lopez)	4	Marichal	Radatz	New York N.L.	50,850
1965	July 13	N.L. (March)	6	A.L. (Lopez)	5	Koufax	McDowell	Minnesota A.L.	46,706
1966	July 12	N.L. (Alston)	2	A.L. (Mele)	1[5]	Perry	Rickert	St. Louis N.L.	49,926
1967	July 11	N.L. (Alston)	2	A.L. (Bauer)	1[7]	Drysdale	Hunter	Anaheim A.L.	46,309
1968	July 9	N.L. (Schoendienst)	1	A.L. (Williams)	0	Drysdale	Tiant	Houston N.L.	48,321
1969	July 23	N.L. (Schoendienst)	9	A.L. (M. Smith)	3	Carlton	Stottlemyre	Washington A.L.	45,259
1970	July 14	N.L. (Hodges)	5	A.L. (Weaver)	4	Osteen	Wright	Cincinnati N.L.	51,838
1971	July 13	A.L. (Weaver)	6	N.L. (Anderson)	4	Blue	Ellis	Detroit A.L.	53,559
1972	July 25	N.L. (Murtaugh)	4	A.L. (Weaver)	3[5]	McGraw	McNally	Atlanta N.L.	53,107
1973	July 24	N.L. (Anderson)	7	A.L. (Williams)	1	Wise	Blyleven	Kansas City A.L.	40,849
1974	July 23	N.L. (Berra)	7	A.L. (Williams)	2	Brett	Tiant	Pittsburgh N.L.	50,706
1975	July 15	N.L. (Alston)	6	A.L. (Dark)	3	Matlack	Hunter	Milwaukee A.L.	51,540
1976	July 13	N.L. (Anderson)	7	A.L. (D. Johnson)	1	R. Jones	Fidrych	Philadelphia N.L.	63,974
1977	July 19	N.L. (Anderson)	7	A.L. (Martin)	5	Sutton	Palmer	New York A.L.	56,683
1978	July 11	N.L. (Lasorda)	7	A.L. (Martin)	3	Sutter	Gossage	San Diego N.L.	51,549
1979	July 17	N.L. (Lasorda)	7	A.L. (Lemon)	6	Sutter	Kern	Seattle A.L.	58,905
1980	July 8	N.L. (Tanner)	4	A.L. (Weaver)	2	Reuss	John	Los Angeles N.L.	56,088
1981[8]	Aug. 9	N.L. (Green)	5	A.L. (Frey)	4	Blue	Fingers	Cleveland A.L.	72,086
1982	July 13	N.L. (Lasorda)	4	A.L. (Martin)	1	Rogers	Eckersley	Montreal N.L.	59,057
1983	July 6	A.L. (Kuenn)	13	N.L. (Herzog)	3	Steib	Soto	Chicago A.L.	43,801
1984	July 11	N.L. (Owens)	3	A.L. (Altobelli)	1	Leg	Steib	San Francisco, N.L.	57,756
1985	July 16	N.L. (Williams)	6	A.L. (Anderson)	1	Hoyt	Morris	Minneapolis, A.L.	54,960
1986	July 15	A.L. (Howser)	3	N.L. (Herzog)	2	Clemens	Gooden	Houston, N.L.	45,774
1987	July 14	N.L. (Johnson)	2	A.L. (McNamara)	0	Smith	Howell	Oakland, A.L.	49,671
1988	July 12	A.L. (Kelly)	2	N.L. (Herzog)	1	Viola	Gooden	Cincinnati, N.L	55,837
1989	July 11	A.L. (LaRussa)	5	N.L. (Lasorda)	3	Ryan	Smoltz	California, A.L.	64,036
1990	July 10	A.L. (LaRussa)	2	N.L. (Craig)	0	Saberhagen	Brantley	Chicago, N.L.	39,071
1991	July 9	A.L. (LaRussa)	4	N.L. (Pinlella)	2	Key	Martinez	Toronto, A.L.	52,383
1992	July 14	A.L. (Kelly)	13	N.L. (Cox)	6	Brown	Glavine	San Diego, N.L.	59,372
1993	July 13	A.L. (Gaston)	9	N.L. (Cox)	3	McDowell	Burkett	Baltimore, A.L.	48,147
1994	July 12	N.L. (Fregosi)	8	A.L. (Gaston)	7	Jones	Bere	Pittsburgh, N.L.	59,568
1995	July 11	N.L. (Alou)	3	A.L. (Showalter)	2	Slocumb	Rogers	Texas, A.L.	50,920
1996	July 9	N.L. (Cox)	6	A.L. (Hargrove)	0	Smoltz	Nagy	Philadelphia, N.L.	62,670
1997	July 8	A.L. (Torre)	3	N.L. (Cox)	1	Johnson	Maddux	Cleveland, A.L.	44,916
1998	July 7	A.L. (Hargrove)	13	N.L. (Leyland)	3	Colon	Urbina	Denver, N.L.	51,267

1. Fourteen innings. 2. Five innings, rain. 3. Twelve innings. 4. Two games. 5. Ten innings. 6. Called because of rain after nine innings. 7. Fifteen innings. 8. Game was originally scheduled for July 14, but was put off because of players' strike. NOTE: No game in 1945.

NATIONAL BASEBALL HALL OF FAME

Cooperstown, N.Y.

Fielders

Member	Active years	Member	Active years	Member	Active years
Aaron, Henry (Hank)	1954–1976	Bresnahan, Roger	1897–1915	Comiskey, Charles	1882–1894
Anson, Adrian (Cap)	1876–1897	Brock, Lou	1961–1980	Combs, Earle	1924–1935
Aparicio, Luis	1956–1973	Brouthers, Dennis	1879–1896	Connor, Roger	1880–1897
Appling, Lucius (Luke)	1930–1950	Burkett, Jesse	1890–1905	Crawford, Samuel	1899–1917
Ashburh, Richie	1948–1962	Campanella, Roy	1948–1957	Cronin, Joseph	1926–1945
Averill, H. Earl	1929–1941	Carew, Rod	1967–1985	Cuyler, Hazen (Kiki)	1921–1938
Baker, J. Frank (Home Run)	1908–1922	Carey, Max	1910–1929	Dandridge, Ray[1]	1933–1953
		Chance, Frank	1898–1914	Davis, George	1890–1909
Bancroft, David	1915–1930	Charleston, Oscar[1]	1915–1954	Delahanty, Edward	1888–1903
Banks, Ernest	1953–1971	Clarke, Fred	1894–1915	Dickey, William	1928–1946
Beckley, Jacob	1888–1907	Clemente, Roberto	1955–1972	Dihigo, Martin[1]	1923–1945
Bell, James (Cool Papa)[1]	1920–1947	Cobb, Tyrus	1905–1928	DiMaggio, Joseph	1936–1951
Bench, John	1967–1983	Cochrane, Gordon (Mickey)	1925–1937	Doby, Larry	1947–1959
Berra, Lawrence (Yogi)	1946–1965			Doerr, Bobby	1937–1951
Bottomley, James	1922–1937	Collins, Edward	1906–1930	Duffy, Hugh	1888–1906
Boudreau, Louis	1938–1952	Collins, James	1895–1908	Ewing, William	1880–1897

Member	Active years
Eyers, John	1902–1919
Ferrell, Rick	1929–1947
Flick, Elmer	1898–1910
Fox, Nellie	1947–1965
Foxx, James	1925–1945
Frisch, Frank	1919–1937
Gehrig, H. Louis (Lou)	1923–1939
Gehringer, Charles	1924–1942
Gibson, Josh[1]	1929–1946
Goslin, Leon (Goose)	1921–1938
Greenberg, Henry (Hank)	1933–1947
Hafey, Charles (Chick)	1924–1937
Hamilton, William	1888–1901
Hartnett, Charles (Gabby)	1922–1941
Heilmann, Harry	1914–1932
Herman, William	1931–1947
Hooper, Harry	1909–1925
Hornsby, Rogers	1915–1937
Irvin, Monford (Monte)[1]	1939–1956
Jackson, Reggie	1967–1987
Jackson, Travis	1922–1936
Jennings, Hugh	1891–1918
Johnson, William (Judy)[1]	1921–1937
Kaline, Albert W.	1953–1974
Keeler, William (Wee Willie)	1892–1910
Kell, George	1943–1957
Kelley, Joseph	1891–1908
Kelly, George	1915–1932
Kelly, Michael (King)	1878–1893
Killebrew, Harmon	1954–1975
Kiner, Ralph	1946–1955
Klein, Charles H. (Chuck)	1928–1944
Lajoie, Napoleon	1896–1916
Lazzeri, Tony	1926–1939
Leonard, Walter (Buck)[1]	1933–1955
Lindstrom, Frederick	1924–1936
Lloyd, John Henry[1]	1905–1931
Lombardi, Ernie	1932–1947
Mantle, Mickey	1951–1968
Manush, Henry (Heinie)	1923–1939
Maranville, Walter (Rabbit)	1912–1935
Matthews, Edwin	1952–1968
Mays, Willie	1951–1973
McCarthy, Thomas	1884–1896
McGraw, John J.	1891–1906
McCovey, Willie	1959–1980
Medwick, Joseph (Ducky)	1932–1948
Mize, John (The Big Cat)	1936–1953
Morgan, Joe	1963–1984
Musial, Stanley	1941–1963
O'Rourke, James	1876–1894
Ott, Melvin	1926–1947
Reese, Harold (Pee Wee)	1940–1958
Rice, Edgar (Sam)	1915–1934
Rizzuto, Phil	1941–1956
Robinson, Brooks	1955–1977
Robinson, Frank	1956–1976
Robinson, Jack	1947–1956
Robinson, Wilbert	1886–1902
Roush, Edd	1913–1931
Ruth, Babe	1914–1935
Schalk, Raymond	1912–1929
Schoendienst, Red	1945–1963
Schmidt, Mike	1973–1989
Sewell, Joseph	1920–1933
Simmons, Al	1924–1944
Sisler, George	1915–1930
Slaughter, Enos	1938–1959
Snider, Edwin D. (Duke)	1947–1964
Speaker, Tristram	1907–1928
Stargell, Willie	1962–1982
Terry, William	1923–1936
Thompson, Samuel	1885–1906
Tinker, Joseph	1902–1916
Traynor, Harold (Pie)	1920–1937
Vaughan, Arky	1932–1948
Wagner, John (Honus)	1897–1917
Wallace, Roderick (Bobby)	1894–1918
Waner, Lloyd	1927–1945
Waner, Paul	1926–1945
Ward, John (Monte)	1878–1894
Wells, Willie	1924–1949
Wheat, Zachariah	1909–1927
Williams, Billy	1959–1976
Williams, Theodore	1939–1960
Wilson, Lewis R. (Hack)	1923–1934
Yastrzemski, Carl	1961–1983
Youngs, Ross (Pep)	1917–1926

1. Negro League player selected by special committee.

Pitchers

Member	Active years
Alexander, Grover	1911–1930
Bender, Charles (Chief)	1903–1925
Brown, Mordecai (3-Finger)	1903–1916
Bunning, Jim	1955–1971
Carlton, Steve	1965–1988
Chesbro, John	1899–1909
Clarkson, John	1882–1894
Coveleski, Stanley	1912–1928
Day, Leon[1]	1935–1955
Dean, Jerome (Dizzy)	1930–1947
Drysdale, Don	1956–1969
Faber, Urban (Red)	1914–1933
Feller, Robert	1936–1956
Fingers, Rollie	1968–1985
Ford, Edward (Whitey)	1950–1967
Foster, Andrew (Rube)	1897–1926
Foster, Bill	1923–1937
Galvin, James (Pud)	1876–1892
Gibson, Bob	1959–1975
Gomez, Vernon (Lefty)	1930–1943
Griffith, Clark	1891–1914
Grimes, Burleigh	1916–1934
Grove, Robert (Lefty)	1925–1941
Haines, Jesse	1918–1937
Hoyt, Waite	1918–1938
Hubbell, Carl	1928–1943
Hunter, Jim (Catfish)	1965–1979
Jenkins, Ferguson	1965–1983
Johnson, Walter	1907–1927
Joss, Adrian	1902–1910
Keefe, Timothy	1880–1893
Koufax, Sanford (Sandy)	1955–1966
Lemon, Robert	1946–1958
Lyons, Theodore	1923–1946
Marichal, Juan	1960–1975
Marquard, Richard (Rube)	1908–1924
Mathewson, Christopher	1900–1916
McGinnity, Joseph	1899–1908
Newhouser, Hal	1939–1955
Nichols, Charles (Kid)	1890–1906
Niekro, Phil	1959–1987
Paige, Leroy (Satchel)[1]	1926–1965
Palmer, Jim	1965–1984
Pennock, Herbert	1912–1934
Perry, Gaylord	1962–1983
Plank, Edward	1901–1917
Radbourn, Charles (Hoss)	1880–1891
Rixey, Eppa	1912–1933
Roberts, Robert (Robin)	1948–1966
Rogan, Wilber	1920–1938
Ruffing, Charles (Red)	1924–1947
Rusie, Amos	1889–1901
Seaver, Tom	1967–1986
Spahn, Warren	1942–1965
Sutton, Don	1966–1988
Vance, Arthur (Dazzy)	1915–1935
Waddell, Rube	1897–1910
Walsh, Edward	1904–1917
Welch, Michael (Mickey)	1880–1892
Wilhelm, Hoyt	1952–1972
Willis, Vic	1898–1910
Wynn, Early	1939–1963
Young, Denton (Cy)	1890–1911

1. Negro League player selected by special committee.

Officials and Others

Alston, Walter[1]
Barlick, Al[4]
Barrow, Edward[1 2]
Bulkeley, Morgan G.[2]
Cartwright, Alexander[2]
Chadwick, Henry[3]
Chandler, A.B.[6]
Comiskey, Charles[1]
Conlan, John[2]
Connolly, Thomas[4]
Cummings, William A.[5]
Durocher, Leo[1]
Evans, William G.[4 2]
Foster, Rube[2]
Frick, Ford C.[6 2]
Giles, Warren C.[2]
Hanlon, Ned[2]
Harridge, William[2]
Harris, Stanley R.[7]
Hubbard, R. Calvin[4]
Huggins, Miller J.[1]
Hulbert, William[2]
Johnson, B. Bancroft[2]
Klem, William[4]
Landis, Kenesaw M.[6]
Lasorda, Tommy[1]
Lopez, Alfonso R.[7]
Mack, Connie[1 2]
MacPhail, Jr., Lee[2]
MacPhail, Leland S.[2]
McCarthy, Joseph V.[1]
McGowan, Bill[4]
McKechnie, William B.[1]
Rickey, W. Branch[1 2]
Spalding, Albert G.[4]
Stengel, Charles D.[7]
Veeck, Bill[2]
Weaver, Earl[1]
Weiss, George M.[2]
Wright, George[5]
Wright, Harry[5 1]
Yawkey, Thomas[2]

1. Manager. 2. Executive. 3. Writer-statistician. 4. Umpire. 5. Early player. 6. Commissioner. 7. Player-manager.

BASEBALL'S PERFECTLY PITCHED GAMES[1]

(no opposing runner reached base)

Lee Richmond—Worcester vs. Cleveland (N.L.) June 12, 1880	(1–0)
John M. Ward—Providence vs. Buffalo (N.L.) June 17, 1880	(5–0)
Cy Young—Boston vs. Philadelphia (A.L.) May 5, 1904	(3–0)
Addie Joss—Cleveland vs. Chicago (A.L.) Oct. 2, 1908	(1–0)
Ernest Shore[2]—Boston vs. Washington (A.L.) June 23, 1917	(4–0)
Charles Robertson—Chicago vs. Detroit (A.L.) April 30, 1922	(2–0)
Don Larsen[3]—New York (A.L.) vs. Brooklyn (N.L.) Oct. 8, 1956	(2–0)
Jim Bunning—Philadelphia vs. New York (N.L.) June 21, 1964	(6–0)
Sandy Koufax—Los Angeles vs. Chicago (N.L.) Sept. 9, 1965	(1–0)
Jim Hunter—Oakland vs. Minnesota (A.L.) May 8, 1968	(4–0)
Len Barker—Cleveland vs. Toronto (A.L.) May 15, 1981	(3–0)
Mike Witt—California vs. Texas (A.L.) Sept. 30, 1984	(1–0)
Tom Browning—Cincinnati vs. Los Angeles (N.L.) Sept. 16, 1988	(1–0)
Dennis Martinez—Montreal vs. Los Angeles (N.L.) July 28, 1991	(2–0)
Kenny Rogers—Texas vs. California (A.L.) July 28, 1994	(4–0)
David Wells—New York vs. Minnesota (A.L.) May 17, 1998	(4–0)

1. Harvey Haddix, of Pittsburgh, pitched 12 perfect innings against Milwaukee (N.L.), May 26, 1959 but lost game in 13th on error and hit. 2. Shore, relief pitcher for Babe Ruth who walked first batter before being ejected by umpire, retired 26 batters who faced him and baserunner was out stealing. 3. World Series.

LIFETIME BATTING, PITCHING, AND BASE-RUNNING RECORDS

(Records Through 1998)

Hits (3,000+)

Pete Rose	4,256
Ty Cobb	4,191
Henry Aaron	3,771
Stan Musial	3,630
Tris Speaker	3,515
Honus Wagner	3,430
Carl Yastrzemski	3,419
Paul Molitor	3,319
Eddie Collins	3,313
Willie Mays	3,283
Eddie Murray	3,255
Nap Lajoie	3,251
George Brett	3,154
Paul Waner	3,152
Robin Yount	3,142
Dave Winfield	3,110
Rod Carew	3,053
Cap Anson	3,041
Lou Brock	3,023
Al Kaline	3,007
Roberto Clemente	3,000

Earned Run Average (Minimum 1,500 innings pitched)

Ed Walsh	1.82
Addie Joss	1.88
Mordecai Brown	2.06
John Ward	2.10
Christy Mathewson	2.13
Rube Waddell	2.16
Walter Johnson	2.17
Orval Overall	2.23
Tommy Bond	2.25
Ed Reulbach	2.28
Will White	2.28
Jim Scott	2.30
Ed Plank	2.35
Larry Corcoran	2.36
Ed Cicotte	2.38
Ed Killian	2.38
George McQuillan	2.38
Doc White	2.38
Nap Rucker	2.42
Terry Larkin	2.43
Jim McCormick	2.43
Jeff Tesreau	2.43

Runs Scored

Ty Cobb	2,246
Hank Aaron	2,174
Babe Ruth	2,174
Pete Rose	2,165
Willie Mays	2,062
Rickey Henderson	2,014
Cap Anson	1,996
Stan Musial	1,949
Lou Gehrig	1,888
Tris Speaker	1,882
Mel Ott	1,859
Frank Robinson	1,829
Eddie Collins	1,821
Carl Yastrzemski	1,816
Ted Williams	1,798
Paul Molitor	1,782
Charlie Gehringer	1,774
Jimmie Foxx	1,751
Honus Wagner	1,736
Jim O'Rourke	1,729
Jesse Burkett	1,720
Willie Keeler	1,719
Billy Hamilton	1,690
Bid McPhee	1,678
Mickey Mantle	1,677
Dave Winfield	1,669
Joe Morgan	1,650

Strikeouts, Pitching

Nolan Ryan	5,714
Steve Carlton	4,136
Bert Blyleven	3,701
Tom Seaver	3,640
Don Sutton	3,574
Gaylord Perry	3,534
Walter Johnson	3,509
Phil Niekro	3,342
Ferguson Jenkins	3,192
Roger Clemens	3,153
Bob Gibson	3,117
Jim Bunning	2,855
Mickey Lolich	2,832
Cy Young	2,803
Frank Tanana	2,773
Warren Spahn	2,583
Bob Feller	2,581
Tim Keefe	2,560
Jerry Koosman	2,556
Christy Mathewson	2,502

Home Runs (350+)

Hank Aaron	755
Babe Ruth	714
Willie Mays	660
Frank Robinson	586
Harmon Killebrew	573
Reggie Jackson	563
Mike Schmidt	548
Mickey Mantle	536
Jimmie Foxx	534
Willie McCovey	521
Ted Williams	521
Eddie Mathews	512
Ernie Banks	512
Mel Ott	511
Eddie Murray	504
Lou Gehrig	493
Stan Musial	475
Willie Stargell	475
Dave Winfield	465
Mark McGwire	457
Carl Yastrzemski	452
Dave Kingman	442
Andre Dawson	438
Billy Williams	426
Darrell Evans	414
Duke Snider	407
Al Kaline	399
Dale Murphy	398
Graig Nettles	390
Johnny Bench	389
Dwight Evans	385
Cal Ripken	384
Frank Howard	382
Jim Rice	382
Tony Perez	379
Orlando Cepeda	379
Norm Cash	377
Carlton Fisk	376
Rocky Colavito	374
Gil Hodges	370
Ralph Kiner	369
Joe DiMaggio	361
Johnny Mize	359
Yogi Berra	358
Joe Carter	357
Lee May	354

Shutouts

Walter Johnson	110
Grover Alexander	90
Christy Mathewson	79
Cy Young	76
Ed Plank	69
Warren Spahn	63
Nolan Ryan	61
Tom Seaver	61
Bert Blyleven	60
Don Sutton	58
Pud Galvin	57
Ed Walsh	57
Bob Gibson	56
Mordecai Brown	55
Steve Carlton	55
Jim Palmer	53
Gaylord Perry	53
Juan Marichal	52

trikeouts, Batting

eggie Jackson	2,597
Villie Stargell	1,936
Mike Schmidt	1,883
ony Perez	1,867
ave Kingman	1,816
obby Bonds	1,757
ale Murphy	1,748
ou Brock	1,730
ickey Mantle	1,710
armon Killebrew	1,699
wight Evans	1,697
Dave Winfield	1,686
Jose Canseco	1,630
Andres Galarraga	1,615
Chili Davis	1,598
Lee May	1,570
Dick Allen	1,556
Willie McCovey	1,550
Gary Gaetti	1,548
Dave Parker	1,537
Frank Robinson	1,532
Lance Parrish	1,527
Willie Mays	1,526

Walks

Babe Ruth	2,056
Ted Williams	2,019
Rickey Henderson	1,890
Joe Morgan	1,865
Carl Yastrzemski	1,845
Mickey Mantle	1,733
Mel Ott	1,708
Eddie Yost	1,614
Darrell Evans	1,605
Stan Musial	1,599
Pete Rose	1,566
Harmon Killebrew	1,559
Lou Gehrig	1,508
Mike Schmidt	1,507
Eddie Collins	1,499
Willie Mays	1,464
Jimmie Foxx	1,452
Eddie Mathews	1,444
Frank Robinson	1,420
Hank Aaron	1,402

RECORD OF WORLD SERIES GAMES
(Through 1997)

Figures in parentheses for winning pitchers (WP) nd losing pitchers (LP) indicate the game number n the series.

903—Boston A.L. 5 (Jimmy Collins); Pittsburgh N.L. 3 (Fred Clarke). WP—Bos.: Dinneen (2, 6, 8), Young (5, 7); Pitts.: Phillippe (1, 3, 4). LP—Bos.: Young (1), Hughes (3), Dinneen (4); Pitts.: Leever (2, 6), Kennedy (5), Phillippe (7, 8).

904—No series.

905—New York N.L. 4 (John J. McGraw); Philadelphia A.L. 1 (Connie Mack). WP—N.Y.: Mathewson (1, 3, 5); McGinnity (4); Phila.: Bender (2). LP—N.Y.: McGinnity (2); Phila.: Plank (1, 4), Coakley (3), Bender (5).

906—Chicago A.L. 4 (Fielder Jones); Chicago N.L. 2 (Frank Chance). WP—Chi.: A.L.: Altrock (1), Walsh (3, 5), White (6); Chi.: N.L.: Reulbach (2), Brown (4). LP—Chi. A.L.: White (2), Altrock. (4); Chi.: N.L.: Brown (1, 6), Pfeister (3, 5).

907—Chicago N.L. 4 (Frank Chance); Detroit A.L. 0 (Hugh Jennings). First game tied 3–3, 12 innings. WP—Pfeister (2), Reulbach (3), Overall (4), Brown (5). LP—Mullin (2, 5), Siever (3), Donovan (4).

908—Chicago N.L. 4 (Frank Chance); Detroit A.L. 1 (Hugh Jennings). WP—Chi.: Brown (1, 4), Overall (2, 5); Det.: Mullin (3). LP—Chi.: Pfeister (3); Det.: Summers (1, 4), Donovan (2, 5).

1909—Pittsburgh N.L. 4 (Fred Clarke); Detroit A.L. 3 (Hugh Jennings). WP—Pitts.: Adams (1, 5, 7), Maddox (3); Det.: Donovan (2), Mullin (4, 6). LP—Pitts.: Camnitz (2), Leifield (4), Willis (6); Det.: Mullin (1), Summers (3, 5), Donovan (7).

1910—Philadelphia A.L. 4 (Connie Mack); Chicago N.L. 1 (Frank Chance). WP—Phila.: Bender (1), Coombs (2, 3, 5); Chi.: Brown (4). LP—Phila.: Bender (4); Chi.: Overall (1), Brown (2, 5), McIntyre (3).

1911—Philadelphia A.L. 4 (Connie Mack); New York N.L. 2 (John J. McGraw). WP—Phila.: Plank (2), Coombs (3), Bender (4, 6); N.Y.: Mathewson (1), Crandall (5). LP—Phila.: Bender (1), Plank (5); N.Y.: Marquard (2), Mathewson (3, 4), Ames (6).

1912—Boston A.L. 4 (J. Garland Stahl); New York N.L. 3 (John J. McGraw). Second game tied, 6–6, 11 innings. WP—Bos.: Wood (1, 4, 8), Bedient (5); N.Y.: Marquard (3, 6), Tesreau (7). LP—Bos.: O'Brien (3, 6), Wood (7); N.Y.: Tesreau (1, 4), Mathewson (5, 8).

1913—Philadelphia A.L. 4 (Connie Mack); New York N.L. 1 (John J. McGraw). WP—Phila.: Bender (1, 4), Bush (3), Plank (5); N.Y.: Mathewson (2); LP—Phila.: Plank (2); N.Y.: Marquard (1), Tesreau (3), Demaree (4), Mathewson (5).

1914—Boston N.L. 4 (George Stallings); Philadelphia A.L. 0 (Connie Mack). WP—Rudolph (1, 4), James (2, 3). LP—Bender (1), Plank (2), Bush (3), Shawkey (4).

1915—Boston A.L. 4 (Bill Carrigan); Philadelphia N.L. 1 (Pat Moran). WP—Bos.: Foster (2, 5), Leonard (3), Shore (4); Phila.: Alexander (1). LP—Bos.: Shore (1); Phila.: Mayer (2), Alexander (3), Chalmers (4), Rixey (5).

1916—Boston A.L. 4 (Bill Carrigan); Brooklyn N.L. 1 (Wilbert Robinson). WP—Bos.: Shore (1, 5), Ruth (2), Leonard (4); Bklyn.: Coombs (3). LP—Bos.: Mays (3); Bklyn.: Marquard (1, 4), Smith (2), Pfeffer (5).

1917—Chicago A.L. 4 (Clarence Rowland); New York N.L. 2 (John J. McGraw). WP—Chi.: Cicotte (1), Faber (2, 5, 6); N.Y.: Benton (3), Schupp (4), LP—Chi.: Cicotte (3), Faber (4); N.Y.: Sallee (1, 5), Anderson (2), Benton (6).

1918—Boston A.L. 4 (Ed Barrow); Chicago N.L. 2 (Fred Mitchell). WP—Bos.: Ruth (1, 4), Mays (3, 6); Chi.: Tyler (2), Vaughn (5). LP—Bos.: Bush (2), Jones (5); Chi.: Vaughn (1, 3), Douglas (4), Tyler (6).

1919—Cincinnati N.L. 5 (Pat Moran); Chicago A.L. 3 (William Gleason). WP—Cin.: Ruether (1), Sallee (2), Ring (4), Eller (5, 8); Chi.: Kerr (3, 6), Cicotte (7). LP—Cin.: Fisher (3), Ring (6), Sallee (7); Chi.: Cicotte (1, 4), Williams (2, 5, 8).

1920—Cleveland A.L. 5 (Tris Speaker); Brooklyn N.L. 2 (Wilbert Robinson). WP—Cleve.: Coveleski (1, 4, 7), Bagby (5), Mails (6); Bklyn.: Grimes (2), Smith (3). LP—Cleve.: Bagby (2), Caldwell (3). Bklyn.: Marquard (1), Cadore (4), Grimes (5, 7), Smith (6).

1921—New York N.L. 5 (John J. McGraw); New York A.L. 3 (Miller Huggins). WP—N.Y. N.L.: Barnes (3, 6), Douglas (4, 7), Nehf (8); N.Y. A.L.: Mays (1), Hoyt (2, 5). LP—N.Y. N.L.: Nehf (2, 5), Douglas (1). N.Y. A.L.: Quinn (3), Mays (4, 7), Shawkey (6), Hoyt (8).

1922—New York N.L. 4 (John J. McGraw); New York A.L. 0 (Miller Huggins). Second game tied 3–3, 10 innings. WP—Ryan (1), Scott (3), McQuillan (4), Nehf (5); LP—Bush (1, 5), Hoyt (3), Mays (4).

1923—New York A.L. 4 (Miller Huggins); New York N.L. 2 (John J. McGraw). WP—N.Y. A.L.: Pennock (2, 6), Shawkey (4), Bush (5); N.Y. N.L.: Ryan (1), Nehf (3). LP—N.Y. A.L.: Bush (1), Jones (3); N.Y. N.L.: McQuillan (2), Scott (4), Bentley (5), Nehf (6).

1924—Washington A.L. 4 (Bucky Harris); New York N.L. 3 (John J. McGraw). WP—Wash.: Zachary (2, 6), Mogridge (4), Johnson (7); N.Y.: Nehf (1), McQuillan (3), Bentley (5). LP—Wash.: Johnson (1, 5), Marberry (3); N.Y.: Bentley (2, 7), Barnes (4), Nehf (6).

1925—Pittsburgh N.L. 4 (Bill McKechnie); Washington A.L. 3 (Bucky Harris). WP—Pitts.: Aldridge (2, 5), Kremer (6, 7); Wash.: Johnson (1, 4), Ferguson (3). LP—Pitts.: Meadows (1), Kremer (3), Yde (4); Wash.: Coveleski (2, 5), Ferguson (6), Johnson (7).

1926—St. Louis N.L. 4 (Rogers Hornsby); New York A.L. 3 (Miller Huggins). WP—St. L.: Alexander (2, 6), Haines (3, 7); N.Y.: Pennock (1, 5), Hoyt (4). LP—St. L.: Sherdel (1, 5), Reinhart (4); N.Y.: Shocker (2), Ruether (3), Shawkey (6), Hoyt (7).

1927—New York A.L. 4 (Miller Huggins); Pittsburgh N.L. 0 (Donie Bush). WP—Hoyt (1), Pipgras (2), Pennock (3), Moore (4). LP—Kremer (1), Aldridge (2), Meadows (3), Miljus (4).

1928—New York A.L. 4 (Miller Huggins); St. Louis N.L. 0 (Bill McKechnie). WP—Hoyt (1, 4), Pipgras (2), Zachary

(3). LP—Sherdel (1, 4), Alexander (2), Haines (3).

1929—Philadelphia A.L. 4 (Connie Mack); Chicago N.L. 1 (Joe McCarthy). WP—Phila.: Ehmke (1), Earnshaw (2), Rommel (4), Walberg (5); Chi.: Bush (3). LP—Phila.: Earnshaw (3) Chi.: Root (1), Malone (2, 5), Blake (4).

1930—Philadelphia A.L. 4 (Connie Mack); St. Louis N.L. 2 (Gabby Street). WP—Phila.: Grove (1, 5), Earnshaw (2, 6); St. L.: Hallahan (3), Haines (4). LP—Phila.: Walberg (3), Grove (4); St. L.: Grimes (1, 5), Rhem (2), Hallahan (6).

1931—St. Louis N.L. 4 (Gabby Street); Philadelphia A.L. 3 (Connie Mack). WP—St. L.: Hallahan (2, 5), Grimes (3, 7); Phila.: Grove (1, 6), Earnshaw (4). LP—St. L.: Derringer (1, 6), Johnson (4); Phila.: Earnshaw (2, 7), Grove (3), Hoyt (5).

1932—New York A.L. (Joe McCarthy); Chicago N.L. 0 (Charles Grimm). WP—Ruffing (1), Gomez (2), Pipgras (3), Moore (4). LP—Bush (1), Warneke (2), Root (3), May (4).

1933—New York N.L. 4 (Bill Terry); Washington A.L. 1 (Joe Cronin.). WP—N.Y.: Hubbell (1, 4), Schumacher (2), Luque (5); Wash.: Whitehill (3). LP—N.Y.: Fitzsimmons (3); Wash.: Stewart (1), Crowder (2), Weaver (4), Russell (5).

1934—St. Louis N.L. 4 (Frank Frisch); Detroit A.L. 3 (Mickey Cochrane). WP—St. L.: J. Dean (1, 7), P. Dean (3, 6); Det.: Rowe (2), Auker (4), Bridges (5). LP—St. L.: W. Walker (2, 4), J. Dean (5); Det.: Crowder (1), Bridges (3), Rowe (6), Auker (7).

1935—Detroit A.L. 4 (Mickey Cochrane); Chicago N.L. 2 (Charles Grimm). WP—Det.: Bridges (2, 6), Rowe (3), Crowder (4); Chi.: Warneke (1, 5); LP—Det.: Rowe (1, 5), Chi.: Root (2), French (3, 6), Carleton (4).

1936—New York A.L. 4 (Joe McCarthy); New York N.L. 2 (Bill Terry). WP—N.Y. A.L.: Gomez (2, 6), Hadley (3), Pearson (4); N.Y. N.L.: Hubbell (1), Schumacher (5); LP—N.Y. A.L.: Ruffing (1), Malone (5); N.Y. N.L.: Schumacher (2), Fitzsimmons (3, 6), Hubbell (4).

1937—New York A.L. 4 (Joe McCarthy); New York N.L. 1 (Bill Terry). WP—N.Y. A.L.: Gomez (1, 5), Ruffing (2), Pearson (3); N.Y. N.L.: Hubbell (4). LP—N.Y. A.L.: Hadley (4); N.Y. N.L.: Hubbell (1), Melton (2, 5), Schumacher (3).

1938—New York A.L. 4 (Joe McCarthy); Chicago N.L. 0 (Gabby Hartnett). WP—Ruffing (1, 4), Gomez (2), Pearson (3) LP—Lee (1, 4), Dean (2), Bryant (3).

1939—New York A.L. 4 (Joe McCarthy); Cincinnati N.L. 0 (Bill McKechnie). WP—Ruffing (1), Pearson (2), Hadley (3), Murphy (4). LP—Derringer (1), Walters (2, 4), Thompson (3).

1940—Cincinnati N.L. 4 (Bill McKechnie); Detroit A.L. 3 (Del Baker). WP—Cin.: Walters (2, 6), Derringer (4, 7); Det.: Newsom (1, 5), Bridges (3). LP—Cin.: Derringer (1), Turner (3), Thompson (5); Det.: Rowe (2, 6), Trout (4), Newsom (7).

1941—New York A.L. 4 (Joe McCarthy); Brooklyn N.L. 1 (Leo Durocher). WP—N.Y.: Ruffing (1), Russo (3), Murphy (4), Bonham (5); Bklyn: Wyatt (2). LP—N.Y.: Chandler (2); Bklyn: Davis (1), Casey (3, 4), Wyatt (5).

1942—St. Louis N.L. 4 (Billy Southworth); New York A.L. 1 (Joe McCarthy). WP—St. L.: Beazley (2, 5), White (3), Lanier (4); N.Y.: Ruffing (1). LP—St. L.: Cooper (1); N.Y.: Bonham (2), Chandler (3), Donald (4), Ruffing (5).

1943—New York A.L. 4 (Joe McCarthy); St. Louis N.L. 1 (Billy Southworth). WP—N.Y.: Chandler (1, 5), Borowy (3), Russo (4); St. L.: Cooper (2). LP—N.Y.: Bonham (2); St. L.: Lanier (1), Brazle (3), Brecheen (4), Cooper (5).

1944—St. Louis N.L. 4 (Billy Southworth); St. Louis A.L. 2 (Luke Sewell). WP—St. L. N.L.: Donnelly (2), Brecheen (4), Cooper (5), Lanier (6); St. L. A.L.: Galehouse (1), Kramer (3). LP—St. L. N.L.: Cooper (1), Wilks (3); St. L. A.L.: Muncrief (2), Jakucki (4), Galehouse (5), Potter (6).

1945—Detroit A.L. 4 (Steve O'Neill); Chicago N.L. 3 (Charles Grimm). WP—Det.: Trucks (2), Trout (4), Newhouser (5, 7); Chi.: Borowy (1, 6), Passeau (3). LP—Det.: Newhouser (1), Overmire (3), Trout (6); Chi.: Wyse (2 Prim (4), Borowy (5, 7).

1946—St. Louis N.L. 4 (Eddie Dyer); Boston A.L. 3 (Jo Cronin). WP—St. L.: Brecheen (2, 6, 7), Munger (4 Bos.: Johnson (1), Ferriss (3), Dobson (5). LP—St. L Pollet (1), Dickson (3), Brazle (5); Bos.: Harris (2, 6 Hughson (4), Klinger (7).

1947—New York A.L. 4 (Bucky Harris); Brooklyn N.L. (Burt Shotton). WP—N.Y.: Shea (1, 5), Reynolds (2 Page (7); Bklyn.: Casey (3, 4), Branca (6). LP—N.Y Newsom (3), Bevens (4), Page (6); Bklyn.: Branca (1 Lombardi (2), Barney (5), Gregg (7).

1948—Cleveland A.L. 4 (Lou Boudreau); Boston N.L. (Billy Southworth). WP—Cleve.: Lemon (2, 6), Bearde (3), Gromek (4); Bos.: Sain (1), Spahn (5). LP—Cleve Feller (1, 5); Bos.: Spahn (2), Bickford (3), Sain (4 Voiselle (6).

1949—New York A.L. 4 (Casey Stengel); Brooklyn N.L. (Burt Shotton). WP—N.Y.: Reynolds (1), Page (3), Lopa (4), Raschi (5); Bklyn.: Roe (2). LP—N.Y.: Raschi (2 Bklyn.: Newcombe (1, 4), Branca (3), Barney (5).

1950—New York A.L. 4 (Casey Stengel); Philadelphia N.L 0 (Eddie Sawyer). WP—Raschi (1), Reynolds (2), Ferric (3), Ford (4). LP—Konstanty (1), Roberts (2), Meyer (3 Miller (4).

1951—New York A.L. 4 (Casey Stengel); New York N.L. (Leo Durocher). WP—N.Y. A.L.: Lopat (2, 5), Reynold (4), Raschi (6); N.Y. N.L.: Koslo (1), Hearn (3). LP—N.Y A.L.: Reynolds (1), Raschi (3); N.Y. N.L.: Jansen (2, 5 Maglie (4), Koslo (6).

1952—New York A.L. 4 (Casey Stengel); Brooklyn N.L. (Chuck Dressen). WP—N.Y.: Raschi (2, 6), Reynolds (4 7); Bklyn.: Black (1), Roe (3), Erskine (5). LP—N.Y.: Reynolds (1), Lopat (3), Sain (5); Bklyn.: Erskine (2), Black (4, 7), Loes (6).

1953—New York A.L. 4 (Casey Stengel); Brooklyn N.L. (Chuck Dressen). WP—N.Y.: Sain (1), Lopat (2) McDonald (5), Reynolds (6); Bklyn.: Erskine (3), Loes (4) LP—N.Y.: Raschi (3), Ford (4); Bklyn.: Labine (1, 6), Roe (2), Podres (5).

1954—New York N.L. 4 (Leo Durocher); Cleveland A.L. (Al Lopez). WP—Grissom (1), Antonelli (2), Gomez (3) Liddie (4). LP—Lemon (1, 4), Wynn (2), Garcia (3).

1955—Brooklyn N.L. 4 (Walter Alston); New York A.L. 3 (Casey Stengel). WP—Bklyn.: Podres (3, 7), Labine (4) Craig (5); N.Y.: Ford (1, 6), Byrne (2). LP—Bklyn.: Newcombe (1), Loes (2), Spooner (6); N.Y.: Turley (3), Larsen (4), Grim (5), Byrne (7).

1956—New York A.L. 4 (Casey Stengel); Brooklyn N.L. 3 (Walter Alston). WP—N.Y.: Ford (3), Sturdivant (4), Larsen (5), Kucks (7); Bklyn.: Maglie (1), Bessent (2), Labine (6). LP—N.Y.: Ford (1), Morgan (2), Turley (6); Bklyn.: Craig (3), Erskine (4), Maglie (5), Newcombe (7).

1957—Milwaukee N.L. 4 (Fred Haney); New York A.L. 3 (Casey Stengel). WP—Mil.: Burdette (2, 5, 7), Spahn (4); N.Y.: Ford (1), Larsen (3), Turley (6). LP—Mil.: Spahn (1), Buhl (3), Johnson (6); N.Y.: Shantz (2), Grim (4), Ford (5), Larsen (7).

1958—New York A.L. 4 (Casey Stengel); Milwaukee N.L. 3 (Fred Haney). WP—N.Y.: Larsen (3), Turley (5, 7), Duren (6); Mil.: Spahn (1, 4), Burdette (2). LP—N.Y.: Duren (1), Turley (2), Ford (4); Mil.: Rush (3), Burdette (5, 7), Spahn (6).

1959—Los Angeles N.L. 4 (Walter Alston); Chicago A.L. 2 (Al Lopez). WP—L.A.: Podres (2), Drysdale (3), Sherry (4, 6); Chi.: Wynn (1), Shaw (5). LP—L.A.: Craig (1), Koufax (5); Chi.: Shaw (2), Donovan (3), Staley (4), Wynn (6).

1960—Pittsburgh N.L. 4 (Danny Murtaugh); New York A.L. 3 (Casey Stengel). WP—Pitts.: Law (1, 4), Haddix (5, 7); N.Y.: Turley (2), Ford (3, 6). LP—Pitts.: Friend (2, 6), Mizell (3); N.Y.: Ditmar (1, 5), Terry (4, 7).

1961—New York A.L. 4 (Ralph Houk); Cincinnati N.L. 1 (Fred Hutchinson). WP—N.Y.: Ford (1, 4), Arroyo (3),

Daley (5); Cin.: Jay (2). LP—N.Y.: Terry (2); Cin.: O'Toole (1, 4), Purkey (3), Jay (5).

1962—New York A.L. 4 (Ralph Houk); San Francisco N.L. 3 (Al Dark). WP—N.Y.: Ford (1), Stafford (3), Terry (5, 7); S.F. Sanford (2), Larsen (4), Pierce (6). LP—N.Y.: Terry (2), Coates (4), Ford (6); S.F.: O'Dell (1), Pierce (3), Sanford (5, 7).

1963—Los Angeles N.L. 4 (Walter Alston); New York A.L. 0 (Ralph Houk). WP—Koufax (1, 4), Podres (2), Drysdale (3). LP—Ford (1, 4), Downing (2), Bouton (3).

1964—St. Louis N.L. 4 (Johnny Keane); New York A.L. 3 (Yogi Berra). WP—St. L.: Sadecki (1), Craig (4), Gibson (5, 7); N.Y.: Stottlemyre (2), Bouton (3, 6). LP—St. L.: Gibson (2), Schultz (3), Simmons (6); N.Y.: Ford (1), Downing (4), Mikkelsen (5), Stottlemyre (7).

1965—Los Angeles N.L. 4 (Walter Alston); Minnesota A.L. 3 (Sam Mele). WP—L.A.: Osteen (3), Drysdale (4), Koufax (5, 7); Minn.: Grant (1, 6), Kaat (2). LP—L.A.: Drysdale (1), Koufax (2), Osteen (6); Minn.: Pascual (3), Grant (4), Kaat (5, 7).

1966—Baltimore A.L. 4 (Hank Bauer); Los Angeles N.L. 0 (Walter Alston). WP—Drabowsky (1), Palmer (2), Bunker (3), McNally (4). LP—Drysdale (1, 4), Koufax (2), Osteen (3).

1967—St. Louis N.L. 4 (Red Schoendienst); Boston A.L. 3 (Dick Williams). WP—St. L.: Gibson (1, 4, 7), Briles (3); Bos.: Lonborg (2, 5); Wyatt (6). LP—St. L.: Hughes (2), Carlton (5), Lamabe (6); Bos.: Santiago (1, 4), Bell (3), Lonborg (7).

1968—Detroit A.L. 4 (Mayo Smith); St. Louis N.L. 3 (Red Schoendienst). WP—Det.: Lolich (2, 5, 7), McLain (6); St. L.: Gibson (1, 4), Washburn (3), LP—Det.: McLain (1, 4), Wilson (3); St. L.: Briles (2), Hoerner (5), Washburn (6), Gibson (7).

1969—New York N.L. 4 (Gil Hodges); Baltimore A.L. 1 (Earl Weaver). WP—N.Y.: Koosman (2, 5), Gentry (3), Seaver (4); Balt.: Cuellar (1). LP—N.Y.: Seaver (1); Balt.: McNally (2), Palmer (3), Hall (4), Watt (5).

1970—Baltimore A.L. 4 (Earl Weaver); Cincinnati N.L. 1 (Sparky Anderson) 1. WP—Balt.: Palmer (1), Phoebus (2), McNally (3), Cuellar (5); Cin.: Carroll (4). LP—Cin.: Nolan (1), Wilcox (2), Cloninger (3), Merritt (5); Balt.: Watt (4).

1971—Pittsburgh N.L. 4 (Danny Murtaugh); Baltimore A.L. 3 (Earl Weaver). WP—Pitts.: Blass (3, 7), Kison (4), Briles (5); Balt.: McNally (1, 6), Palmer (2). LP—Pitts.: Ellis (1), R. Johnson (2), Miller (6); Balt.: Cuellar (3, 7), Watt (4) McNally (5).

1972—Oakland A.L. 4 (Dick Williams); Cincinnati N.L. (Sparky Anderson) 3. WP—Oakland: Holtzman (1), Hunter (2, 7), Fingers (4); Cincinnati: Billingham (3), Grimsley (5, 6). LP—Oakland: Odom (3), Fingers (5), Blue (6); Cincinnati: Nolan (1), Grimsley (2), Carroll (4), Borbon (7).

1973—Oakland A.L. 4 (Dick Williams): New York N.L. 3 (Yogi Berra). WP—Oakland: Holtzman (1, 7), Lindblad (3), Hunter (6). New York: McGraw (2), Matlack (4), Koosman (5). LP—Oakland: Fingers (2), Holtzman (4), Blue (5). New York: Matlack (1, 7) Parker (3), Seaver (6).

1974—Oakland A.L. 4 (Al Dark); Los Angeles N.L. 1 (Walter Alston). WP—Oakland: Fingers (1), Hunter (3), Holtzman (4), Odom (5). Los Angeles: Sutton (2). LP—Oakland: Blue (2), Los Angeles: Messersmith (1, 4), Downing (3), Marshall (5).

1975—Cincinnati N.L. 4 (Sparky Anderson); Boston A.L. 3 (Darrell Johnson). WP—Cincinnati: Eastwick (2, 3), Gullett (5), Carroll (7); Boston: Tiant (1, 4), Wise (6). LP—Cincinnati: Gullett (1), Norman (4), Darcy (6); Boston: Drago (2), Willoughby (3), Cleveland (5), Burton (7).

1976—Cincinnati N.L. 4 (Sparky Anderson); New York A.L. 0 (Billy Martin). WP—Gullett (1), Billingham (2), Zachry (3), Nolan (4). LP—Alexander (1), Hunter (2), Ellis (3), Figueroa (4).

1977—New York A.L. 4 (Billy Martin); Los Angeles N.L. 2 (Tom Lasorda). WP—New York: Lyle (1), Torrez (3, 6), Guidry (4); Los Angeles: Hooton (2), Sutton (5). LP—New York: Hunter (2), Gullett (5); Los Angeles: Rhoden (1), John (3), Rau (4), Hooton (6).

1978—New York A.L. 4 (Bob Lemon), Los Angeles N.L. 2 (Tom Lasorda); WP—New York: Guidry (3), Gossage (4); Beattie (5), Hunter (6); Los Angeles: John (1), Hooton (2). LP—New York: Figueroa (1), Hunter (2); Los Angeles: Sutton (3, 6), Welch (4), Hooton (5).

1979—Pittsburgh N.L. 4 (Chuck Tanner), Baltimore A.L. 3 (Earl Weaver); WP—Pittsburgh: D. Robinson (2), Blyleven (5), Candelaria (6), Jackson (7); Baltimore: Flanagan (1), McGregor (3), Stoddard (4). LP—Pittsburgh: Kison (1), Candelaria (3), Tekulve (4); Baltimore: Stanhouse (2), Flanagan (5), Palmer (6), McGregor (7).

1980—Philadelphia N.L. 4 (Dallas Green), Kansas City A.L. 2 (Jim Frey); WP—Philadelphia: Walk (1), Carlton (2), McGraw (5), Carlton (6); Kansas City: Quisenberry (3), Leonard (4). LP—Philadelphia: McGraw (3), Christenson (4); Kansas City: Leonard (1), Quisenberry (2), Quisenberry (5), Gale (6).

1981—Los Angeles N.L. 4 (Tom Lasorda), New York A.L. 2 (Bob Lemon); WP—Los Angeles: Valenzuela (3), Howe (4), Reuss (5), Hooton (6); New York: Guidry (1), John (2). LP—Los Angeles: Reuss (1), Hooton (2); New York: Frazier (3), Frazier (4), Guidry (5), Frazier (6).

1982—St. Louis N.L. 4 (Whitey Herzog), Milwaukee A.L. 3 (Harvey Kuenn); WP—St. Louis: Sutter (2), Andujar (3), Stuper (6), Andujar (7). Milwaukee: Caldwell (1), Slaton (4), Caldwell (5). LP—St. Louis: Forsch (1), Bair (4), Forsch (5). Milwaukee: McClure (2), Vuckovich (3), Sutton (6), McClure (7).

1983—Baltimore A.L. 4 (Joe Altobelli), Philadelphia N.L. 1 (Paul Owens); WP—Baltimore: Boddicker (2), Palmer (3), Davis (4), McGregor (5). Philadelphia: Denny (1).

1984—Detroit A.L. 4 (Sparky Anderson), San Diego N.L. 1 (Dick Williams); WP—Det.: Morris (1,4), Wilcox (3), Lopez (5), San Diego: Hawkins (2). LP—Det.: Petry (2), San Diego: Thurmond (1), Lollar (3), Show (4), Hawkins (5).

1985—Kansas City A.L. 4 (Dick Howser), St. Louis N.L. 3 (Whitey Herzog); WP—KC: Saberhagen (3,7) Quisenberry (6), Jackson (5). St. Louis: Tudor (1,4) Dayley (2). LP—KC: Jackson (1), Leibrandt (2), Black (4); St. Louis: Andujar (3), Forsch (5), Worrell (6), Tudor (7).

1986—New York N.L. 4 (Dave Johnson); Boston A.L. (John McNamara) 3 WP—N.Y.—Ojeda (3), Darling (4), Aguilera (6), McDowell (7), Bos: Hurst (1), (5), Crawford (2). LP—N.Y. Darling (1), Gooden (2, 5).

1987—Minnesota, A.L. 4 (Tom Kelly); St. Louis N.L. (Whitey Herzog) 3. WP—Minn. Viola (1, 7), Blyleven (2), Schatzeder (6), St. Louis: Tudor (3), Forsch (4), Cox (5). LP—Minn. Berenguer (3), Viola (4), Blyleven (5); St. Louis: Magrane (1), Cox (2, 7), Tudor (6).

1988—Los Angeles N.L. 4 (Tommy Lasorda); Oakland A.L. (Tony LaRussa) 1. WP—Los Angeles: Hershiser (2, 5), Pena (1), Belcher (4); Oakland: Honeycutt (3). LP—Los Angeles: Howell (3); Oakland: Davis (2, 5), Eckersley (1), Stewart (4).

1989—Oakland, A.L. 4 (Tony LaRussa); San Francisco N.L. 0 (Roger Craig). WP—Oakland: Dave Stewart (1, 3), Mike Moore (2, 4). LP—San Francisco: Scott Garrelts (1, 3), Don Robinson (4), Rick Reuschel (2).

1990—Cincinnati N.L. 4 (Lou Piniella); Oakland A.L. 0 (Tony LaRussa). WP—Cincinnati: Jose Rijo (1, 4), Rob Dibble (2), Tom Browning (3). LP—Oakland: Dave Stewart (1, 4), Dennis Eckersley (2), Mike Moore (3).

1991—Minnesota, A.L. 4 (Tom Kelly); Atlanta, N.L. 3 (Bobby Cox). WP—Minnesota: Morris (1,7), Tapani (2), Aguilera (6). Atlanta: Clancy (3), Stanton (4), Glavine (5). LP—Minnesota: Aguilera (3), Gurhtie (4), Tapani (5). Atlanta: Leibrandt (1, 6), Glavine (2), Pena (7).

1992—Toronto, A.L. 4 (Cito Gaston); Atlanta, N.L. 2 (Bobby

Cox). WP—Toronto: Ward (2, 3), Key (4, 6). Atlanta: Glavine (1), Smoltz (5). LP—Toronto: Morris (1, 5). Atlanta: Leibrandt (6), Reardon (2), Avery (3), Glavine (4).

1993—Toronto, A.L. 4 (Cito Gaston); Philadelphia, N.L. 2 (Jim Fregosi). WP—Toronto: Leiter (1), Hentgen (3), Castillo (4), Ward (6). Philadelphia: Mullholland (2), Schilling (5). LP—Toronto: Stewart (2), Guzman (5). Philadelphia: Schilling (1), Jackson (3), Williams (4, 6).

1994—World Series cancelled due to players' strike.

1995—Atlanta, N.L. 4 (Bobby Cox); Cleveland, A.L. 2 (Mike Hargrove). WP—Atlanta: Maddux (1), Glavine (2,6), Avery (4). Cleveland: Mesa (3), Hershiser (5). LP—Atlanta: Pena (3), Maddux (5). Cleveland: Hershis (1), Martinez (2), Hill (4), Poole (6).

1996—New York, A.L. 4 (Joe Torre); Atlanta, N.L. 2 (Bobb Cox). WP—New York: Cone (3), Lloyd (4), Pettitte (5 Key (6). Atlanta: Smoltz (1), Maddux (2). LP—New Yor Pettitte (1), Key (2). Atlanta: Glavine (3), Avery (4 Smoltz (5), Maddux (6).

1997—Florida, N.L. 4 (Jim Leyland); Cleveland, A.L. 3 (Mik Hargrove). WP—Florida: Hernandez (1, 5), Cook (3 Powell (7). Cleveland: Ogea (2, 6), Wright (4 LP—Florida: Brown (2, 6), Saunders (4). Cleveland: He shiser (1, 5), Plunk (3), Nagy (7).

WORLD SERIES CLUB STANDINGS

(Through 1997)

	Series	Won	Lost	Pct.
Toronto (A)	2	2	0	1.000
Florida (N)	1	1	0	1.000
Pittsburgh (N)	7	5	2	.714
New York (A)	34	23	11	.676
Oakland (A)	6	4	2	.667
Minnesota (A)	3	2	1	.667
New York (N-Mets)	3	2	1	.667
Philadelphia (A)	8	5	3	.625
St. Louis (N)	15	9	6	.600
Boston (A)	9	5	4	.556
Los Angeles (N)	9	5	4	.556
Cincinnati (N)	9	5	4	.556
Milwaukee (N)	2	1	1	.500
Boston (N)	2	1	1	.500
Chicago (A)	4	2	2	.500
Baltimore (A)	6	3	3	.500
Kansas City (A)	2	1	1	.500

	Series	Won	Lost	Pct.
Detroit (A)	9	4	5	.444
Cleveland (A)	5	2	3	.400
New York (N-Giants)	14	5	9	.357
Washington (A)	3	1	2	.333
Atlanta (N)	4	1	3	.250
Philadelphia (N)	5	1	4	.200
Chicago (N)	10	2	8	.200
Brooklyn (N)	9	1	8	.111
St. Louis (A)	1	0	1	.000
San Francisco (N)	2	0	2	.000
Milwaukee (A)	1	0	1	.000
San Diego (N)	1	0	1	.000

Recapitulation

	Wor
American League	53
National League	38

LIFETIME WORLD SERIES RECORDS

(Through 1997)

Most hits—71, Yogi Berra, New York A.L., 1947, 1949–53, 1955–58, 1960–63.

Most runs—42, Mickey Mantle, New York A.L., 1951–53, 1955–58, 1960–64.

Most runs batted in—40, Mickey Mantle, New York A.L., 1951–53, 1955–58, 1960–64.

Most home runs—18, Mickey Mantle, New York A.L., 1951–53, 1955–58, 1960–64.

Most bases on balls—43, Mickey Mantle, New York A.L., 1951–53, 1955–58, 1960–64.

Most strikeouts—54, Mickey Mantle, New York A.L., 1951–53, 1955–58, 1960–64.

Most stolen bases—14, Eddie Collins, Philadelphia A.L. 1910–11, 13–14; Chicago A.L., 1917, 1919. Lou Brock, St. Louis N.L., 1964, 67–68.

Most victories, pitcher—10, Whitey Ford, New York A.L. 1950, 1953, 1955–58, 1960–64.

Most times member of winning team—10, Yogi Berra, New York A.L., 1947, 1949–53, 1956, 1958, 1961–62.

Most victories, no defeats—6, Vernon Gomez, New York A.L., 1932, 1936(2), 1937(2), 1938.

Most shutouts—4, Christy Mathewson, New York N.L., 1905 (3), 1913.

Most innings pitched—146, Whitey Ford, New York A.L. 1950, 1953, 1955–58, 1960–1964

Most consecutive scoreless innings—33⅔, Whitey Ford, New York A.L., 1960 (18), 1961 (14), 1962 (1⅔).

Most strikeouts by pitcher—94, Whitey Ford, New York A.L., 1950, 1953, 1955–58, 1960–64.

SINGLE GAME AND SINGLE SERIES RECORDS

(Through 1997)

Most hits game—5, Paul Molitor, Milwaukee A.L., first game vs. St. Louis, N.L., 1982.

Most 4-hit games, series—2, Robin Yount, Milwaukee A.L., first and fifth games vs. St. Louis N.L., 1982.

Most hits inning—2, held by many players.

Most hits series—13 (7 games) Bobby Richardson, New York A.L., 1964; Lou Brock, St. Louis N.L., 1968; 12 (6 games) Billy Martin, New York A.L., 1953; 12 (8 games) Buck Herzog, New York N.L., 1912; Joe Jackson, Chicago A.L., 1919; 10 (4 games) Babe Ruth, New York A.L., 1928; 9 (5 games) held by 8 players.

Most home runs, series—5 (6 games) Reggie Jackson, New York A.L., 1977; 4 (7 games) Babe Ruth, New York A.L., 1926; Duke Snider, Brooklyn N.L., 1952, 1955; Hank Bauer, New York A.L., 1958; Gene Tenace, Oakland A.L., 1972; 4 (4 games) Lou Gehrig, New York A.L., 1928; 3 (6 games) Babe Ruth, New York A.L., 1923; Ted Kluszewski, Chicago A.L., 1959; 3 (5 games) Donn Clendenon, New York Mets N.L., 1969.

Most home runs, game—3, Babe Ruth, New York A.L., 1926 and 1928; Reggie Jackson, New York A.L., 1977.

Most strikeouts, series—12 (6 games) Willie Wilson, Kansas City A.L., 1980; 11 (7 games) Ed Mathews, Milwaukee N.L., 1958; Wayne Garrett, New York N.L., 1973: 10 (8 games) George Kelly, New York N.L., 1921; 9 (6 games) Jim Bottomley, St. Louis N.L., 1930; 9 (5 games)

Carmelo Martinez, San Diego, N.L., 1984; Duke Snider, Brooklyn N.L., 1949; 7 (4 games) Bob Muesel, New York A.L., 1927.

Most stolen bases, game—3, Honus Wagner, Pittsburgh N.L., 1909; Willie Davis, Los Angeles N.L., 1965; Lou Brock, St. Louis N.L., 1967 and 1968.

Most strikeouts by pitcher, game—17, Bob Gibson, St. Louis N.L. 1968.

Most strikeouts by pitcher in succession—6, Horace Eller, Cincinnati N.L., 1919; Moe Drabowsky, Baltimore A.L., 1966.

Most strikeouts by pitcher, series—35 (7 games) Bob Gibson, St. Louis N.L., 1968; 28 (8 games) Bill Dinneen, Boston A.L., 1903; 23 (4 games) Sandy Koufax, Los Angeles, 1963; 20 (6 games) Chief Bender, Philadelphia A.L., 1911; 18 (5 games) Christy Mathewson, New York N.L., 1905.

Most bases on balls, series—11 (7 games) Babe Ruth, New York A.L., 1926; Gene Tenace, Oakland A.L., 1973; 9 (6 games) Willie Randolph, New York A.L., 1981; 7 (5 games) James Sheckard, Chicago N.L., 1910; Mickey Cochrane, Philadelphia A.L., 1929; Joe Gordon, New York A.L., 1941; 7 (4 games) Hank Thompson, New York N.L., 1954.

Most consecutive scoreless innings one series—27, Christy Mathewson, New York N.L., 1905.

AMERICAN LEAGUE HOME RUN CHAMPIONS

Year	Player, team	No.
1901	Nap Lajoie, Phila.	13
1902	Ralph Seybold, Phila.	16
1903	Buck Freeman, Bost.	13
1904	Harry Davis, Phila.	10
1905	Harry Davis, Phila.	8
1906	Harry Davis, Phila.	12
1907	Harry Davis, Phila.	8
1908	Sam Crawford, Det.	7
1909	Ty Cobb, Det.	9
1910	J. Garland Stahl, Bost.	10
1911	Franklin Baker, Phila.	9
1912	Franklin Baker, Phila.	10
1913	Franklin Baker, Phila.	12
1914	Franklin Baker, Phila., and Sam Crawford, Det.	8
1915	Robert Roth, Chi.-Cleve.	7
1916	Wally Pipp, N.Y.	12
1917	Wally Pipp, N.Y.	9
1918	Babe Ruth, Bost., and Clarence Walker, Phila.	11
1919	Babe Ruth, Bost.	29
1920	Babe Ruth, N.Y.	54
1921	Babe Ruth, N.Y.	59
1922	Ken Williams, St. L.	39
1923	Babe Ruth, N.Y.	41
1924	Babe Ruth, N.Y.	46
1925	Bob Meusel, N.Y.	33
1926	Babe Ruth, N.Y.	47
1927	Babe Ruth, N.Y.	60
1928	Babe Ruth, N.Y.	54
1929	Babe Ruth, N.Y.	46
1930	Babe Ruth, N.Y.	49
1931	Lou Gehrig, N.Y., and Babe Ruth, N.Y.	46
1932	Jimmy Foxx, Phila.	58
1933	Jimmy Foxx, Phila.	48
1934	Lou Gehrig, N.Y.	49
1935	Jimmy Foxx, Phila., and Hank Greenberg, Det.	36
1936	Lou Gehrig, N.Y.	49
1937	Joe DiMaggio, N.Y.	46
1938	Hank Greenberg, Det.	58
1939	Jimmy Foxx, Bost.	35
1940	Hank Greenberg, Det.	41
1941	Ted Williams, Bost.	37
1942	Ted Williams, Bost.	36
1943	Rudy York, Det.	34
1944	Nick Etten, N.Y.	22
1945	Vern Stephens, St. L.	24
1946	Hank Greenberg, Det.	44
1947	Ted Williams, Bost.	32
1948	Joe DiMaggio, N.Y.	39
1949	Ted Williams, Bost.	43
1950	Al Rosen, Cleve.	37
1951	Gus Zernial, Chi.-Phila.	33
1952	Larry Doby, Cleve.	32
1953	Al Rosen, Cleve.	43
1954	Larry Doby, Cleve.	32
1955	Mickey Mantle, N.Y.	37
1956	Mickey Mantle, N.Y.	52
1957	Roy Sievers, Wash.	42
1958	Mickey Mantle, N.Y.	42
1959	Rocky Colavito, Cleve., and Harmon Killebrew, Wash.	42
1960	Mickey Mantle, N.Y.	40
1961	Roger Maris, N.Y.	61
1962	Harmon Killebrew, Minn.	48
1963	Harmon Killebrew, Minn.	45
1964	Harmon Killebrew, Minn.	49
1965	Tony Conigliaro, Bost.	32
1966	Frank Robinson, Balt.	49
1967	Carl Yastrzemski, Bost., and Harmon Killebrew, Minn.	44
1968	Frank Howard, Wash.	44
1969	Harmon Killebrew, Minn.	49
1970	Frank Howard, Wash.	44
1971	Bill Melton, Chicago	33
1972	Dick Allen, Chicago	37
1973	Reggie Jackson, Oak.	32
1974	Dick Allen, Chicago	32
1975	Reggie Jackson, Oak., and George Scott, Mil.	36
1976	Graig Nettles, N.Y.	32
1977	Jim Rice, Boston	39
1978	Jim Rice, Boston	46
1979	Gorman Thomas, Milwaukee	45
1980	Reggie Jackson, N.Y., and Ben Oglivie, Mil.	41
1981[1]	Tony Armas, Oak., Dwight Evans, Bost., Bobby Grich, Calif., and Eddie Murray, Balt. (tie)	22
1982	Gorman Thomas, Mil., and Reggie Jackson, Calif.	39
1983	Jim Rice, Boston	39
1984	Tony Armas, Boston	43
1985	Darrell Evans, Detroit	40
1986	Jesse Barfield, Toronto	40
1987	Mark McGwire, Oakland	49
1988	Jose Canseco, Oakland	42
1989	Fred McGriff, Toronto	36
1990	Cecil Fielder, Detroit	51
1991	Jose Canseco, Oakland and Cecil Fielder, Detroit (tie)	44
1992	Juan Gonzalez, Texas	43
1993	Juan Gonzalez, Texas	46
1994[2]	Ken Griffey, Jr., Seattle	40
1995	Albert Belle, Cleveland	50
1996	Mark McGwire, Oakland	52
1997	Ken Griffey, Jr., Seattle	56
1998	Ken Griffey, Jr., Seattle	56

1. Split season because of players' strike. 2. Season ended on August 12 because of a players' strike.

AMERICAN LEAGUE BATTING CHAMPIONS

Year	Player, team	Avg
1901	Nap Lajoie, Phila.	.422
1902	Ed Delahanty, Wash.	.376
1903	Nap Lajoie, Cleve.	.355
1904	Nap Lajoie, Cleve.	.381
1905	Elmer Flick, Cleve.	.306
1906	George Stone, St. L.	.358
1907	Ty Cobb, Det.	.350
1908	Ty Cobb, Det.	.324
1909	Ty Cobb, Det.	.377
1910	Ty Cobb, Det.	.385
1911	Ty Cobb, Det.	.420
1912	Ty Cobb, Det.	.410
1913	Ty Cobb, Det.	.390
1914	Ty Cobb, Det.	.368
1915	Ty Cobb, Det.	.369
1916	Tris Speaker, Cleve.	.386
1917	Ty Cobb, Det.	.383
1918	Ty Cobb, Det.	.382
1919	Ty Cobb, Det.	.384
1920	George Sisler, St. L.	.407
1921	Harry Heilmann, Det.	.394
1922	George Sisler, St. L.	.420
1923	Harry Heilmann, Det.	.403
1924	Babe Ruth, N.Y.	.378
1925	Harry Heilmann, Det.	.393
1926	Heinie Manush, Det.	.378
1927	Harry Heilmann, Det.	.398
1928	Goose Goslin, Wash.	.379
1929	Lew Fonseca, Cleve.	.369
1930	Al Simmons, Phila.	.381
1931	Al Simmons, Phila.	.390
1932	Dale Alexander, Det.-Bost.	.367
1933	Jimmy Foxx, Phila.	.356
1934	Lou Gehrig, N.Y.	.363
1935	Buddy Myer, Wash.	.349
1936	Luke Appling, Chi.	.388
1937	Charley Gehringer, Det.	.371
1938	Jimmy Foxx, Bost.	.349
1939	Joe DiMaggio, N.Y.	.381

Year	Player, team	Avg
1940	Joe DiMaggio, N.Y.	.352
1941	Ted Williams, Bost.	.406
1942	Ted Williams, Bost.	.356
1943	Luke Appling, Chi.	.328
1944	Lou Boudreau, Cleve.	.327
1945	George Sternweiss, N.Y.	.309
1946	Mickey Vernon, Wash.	.353
1947	Ted Williams, Bost.	.343
1948	Ted Williams, Bost.	.369
1949	George Kell, Det.	.343
1950	Billy Goodman, Bost.	.354
1951	Ferris Fain, Phila.	.344
1952	Ferris Fain, Phila.	.327
1953	Mickey Vernon, Wash.	.337
1954	Bobby Avila, Cleve.	.341
1955	Al Kaline, Det.	.340
1956	Mickey Mantle, N.Y.	.353
1957	Ted Williams, Bost.	.388
1958	Ted Williams, Bost.	.328
1959	Harvey Kuenn, Det.	.353

Year	Player, team	Avg
1960	Pete Runnels, Bost.	.320
1961	Norman Cash, Det.	.361
1962	Pete Runnels, Bost.	.326
1963	Carl Yastrzemski, Bost.	.321
1964	Tony Oliva, Minn.	.323
1965	Tony Oliva, Minn.	.321
1966	Frank Robinson, Balt.	.316
1967	Carl Yastrzemski, Bost.	.326
1968	Carl Yastrzemski, Bost.	.301
1969	Rod Carew, Minn.	.332
1970	Alex Johnson, Calif.	.329
1971	Tony Oliva, Minn.	.337
1972	Rod Carew, Minn.	.318
1973	Rod Carew, Minn.	.350
1974	Rod Carew, Minn.	.364
1975	Rod Carew, Minn.	.359
1976	George Brett, Kansas City	.333
1977	Rod Carew, Minn.	.388
1978	Rod Carew, Minn.	.333
1979	Fred Lynn, Boston	.333

Year	Player, team	Avg
1980	George Brett, Kansas City	.390
1981[1]	Carney Lansford, Bost.	.336
1982	Willie Wilson, Kansas City	.332
1983	Wade Boggs, Boston	.361
1984	Don Mattingly, New York	.343
1985	Wade Boggs, Boston	.368
1986	Wade Boggs, Boston	.357
1987	Wade Boggs, Boston	.363
1988	Wade Boggs, Boston	.366
1989	Kirby Puckett, Minnesota	.339
1990	George Brett, Kansas City	.328
1991	Julio Franco, Texas	.341
1992	Edgar Martinez, Seattle	.343
1993	John Olerud, Toronto	.363
1994[2]	Paul O'Neill, New York	.359
1995	Edgar Martinez, Seattle	.356
1996	Alex Rodriguez, Seattle	.358
1997	Frank Thomas, Chicago	.347
1998	Bernie Williams, New York	.339

1. Split season because of players' strike. 2. Season ended on August 12 because of a players' strike.

NATIONAL LEAGUE HOME RUN CHAMPIONS

Year	Player, team	No.
1876	George Hall, Phila. Athletics	5
1877	George Shaffer, Louisville	3
1878	Paul Hines, Providence	4
1879	Charles Jones, Bost.	9
1880	James O'Rourke, Bost., and Harry Stovey, Worcester	6
1881	Dan Brouthers, Buffalo	8
1882	George Wood, Det.	7
1883	William Ewing, N.Y.	10
1884	Ed Williamson, Chi.	27
1885	Abner Dalrymple, Chi.	11
1886	Arthur Richardson, Det.	11
1887	Roger Connor, N.Y., and Wm. O'Brien, Wash.	17
1888	Roger Connor, N.Y.	14
1889	Sam Thompson, Phila.	20
1890	Tom Burns, Bklyn, and Mike Tiernan, N.Y.	13
1891	Harry Stovey, Bost., and Mike Tiernan, N.Y.	16
1892	Jim Holliday, Cin.	13
1893	Ed Delahanty, Phila.	19
1894	Hugh Duffy, Bost., and Robert Lowe, Bost.	18
1895	Bill Joyce, Wash.	17
1896	Ed Delahanty, Phila., and Sam Thompson, Phila.	13
1897	Nap Lajoie, Phila.	10
1898	James Colins, Bost.	14
1899	John Freeman, Wash.	25
1900	Herman Long, Bost.	12
1901	Sam Crawford, Con.	16
1902	Tom Leach, Pitts.	6
1903	James Sheckard, Bklyn.	9
1904	Harry Lumley, Bklyn.	9
1905	Fred Odwell, Cin.	9
1906	Tim Jordan, Bklyn	12
1907	David Brain, Bost.	10
1908	Tim Jordan, Bklyn.	12
1909	John Murray, N.Y.	7
1910	Fred Beck, Bost., and Frank Schulte, Chi.	10
1911	Frank Schulte, Chi.	21
1912	Henry Zimmerman, Chi.	14
1913	Cliff Cravath, Phila.	19

Year	Player, team	No.
1914	Cliff Cravath, Phila.	19
1915	Cliff Cravath, Phila.	24
1916	Davis Robertson, N.Y., and Fred Williams, Chi.	12
1917	Davis Robertson, N.Y., and Cliff Cravath, Phila.	12
1918	Cliff Cravath, Phila.	8
1919	Cliff Cravath, Phila.	12
1920	Cy Williams, Phila.	15
1921	George Kelly, N.Y.	23
1922	Rogers Hornsby, St. L.	42
1923	Cy Williams, Phila.	41
1924	Jacques Fournier, Bklyn.	27
1925	Rogers Hornsby, St. L.	39
1926	Hack Wilson, Chi.	21
1927	Hack Wilson, Chi., and Cy Williams, Phila.	30
1928	Hack Wilson, Chi., and Jim Bottomley, St. L.	31
1929	Chuck Klein, Phila.	43
1930	Hack Wilson, Chi.	56
1931	Chuck Klein, Phila.	31
1932	Chuck Klein, Phila., and Mel Ott, N.Y.	38
1933	Chuck Klein, Phila.	28
1934	Mel Ott, N.Y., and Rip Collins, St. L.	35
1935	Wally Berger, Bost.	34
1936	Mel Ott, N.Y.	33
1937	Mel Ott, N.Y., and Joe Medwick, St. L.	31
1938	Mel Ott, N.Y.	36
1939	John Mize, St. L.	28
1940	John Mize, St. L.	43
1941	Dolph Camilli, Bklyn.	34
1942	Mel Ott, N.Y.	30
1943	Bill Nicholson, Chi.	29
1944	Bill Nicholson, Chi.	33
1945	Tommy Holmes, Bost.	28
1946	Ralph Kiner, Pitts.	23
1947	Ralph Kiner, Pitts., and John Mize, N.Y.	51
1948	Ralph Kiner, Pitts., and John Mize, N.Y.	40
1949	Ralph Kiner, Pitts.	54

Year	Player, team	No.
1950	Ralph Kiner, Pitts.	47
1951	Ralph Kiner, Pitts.	42
1952	Ralph Kiner, Pitts., and Hank Sauer, Chi.	37
1953	Ed Mathews, Mil.	47
1954	Ted Kluszewski, Cin.	49
1955	Willie Mays, N.Y.	51
1956	Duke Snider, Bklyn.	43
1957	Henry Aaron, Mil.	44
1958	Ernie Banks, Chi.	47
1959	Ed Mathews, Mil.	46
1960	Ernie Banks, Chi.	41
1961	Orlando Cepeda, San Fran.	46
1962	Willie Mays, San Fran.	49
1963	Henry Aaron, Mil., and Willie McCovey, San Fran.	44
1964	Willie Mays, San Fran.	47
1965	Willie Mays, San Fran.	52
1966	Henry Aaron, Atlanta	44
1967	Henry Aaron, Atlanta	39
1968	Willie McCovey, San Fran.	36
1969	Willie McCovey, San Fran.	45
1970	Johnny Bench, Cin.	45
1971	Willie Stargell, Pitts.	48
1972	Johnny Bench, Cin.	40
1973	Willie Stargell, Pitts.	44
1974	Mike Schmidt, Phila.	36
1975	Mike Schmidt, Phila.	38
1976	Mike Schmidt, Phila.	38
1977	George Foster, Cin.	52
1978	George Foster, Cin.	40
1979	Dave Kingman, Chicago	48
1980	Mike Schmidt, Phila.	48
1981[1]	Mike Schmidt, Phila.	31
1982	Dave Kingman, N.Y.	37
1983	Mike Schmidt, Phila.	40
1984	Mike Schmidt, Phila. and Dale Murphy, Atlanta	36
1985	Dale Murphy, Atlanta	37
1986	Mike Schmidt, Phila.	37
1987	Andre Dawson, Chicago	49
1988	Darryl Strawberry, N.Y.	39
1989	Kevin Mitchell, San Francisco	47
1990	Ryne Sandberg, Chicago	40

Year	Player, team	No.	Year	Player, team	No.	Year	Player, team	No.
1991	Howard Johnson, N.Y.	38	1994[2]	Matt Williams, San Francisco	43	1996	Andreas Galarraga, Colorado	40
1992	Fred McGriff, San Diego	35	1995	Dante Bichette, Colorado	40	1997	Larry Walker, Colorado	49
1993	Barry Bonds, San Francisco	46				1998	Mark McGwire, St. Louis	70

1. Split season because of players' strike. 2. Season ended on August 12 because of a players' strike.

NATIONAL LEAGUE BATTING CHAMPIONS

Year	Player, team	Avg	Year	Player, team	Avg	Year	Player, team	Avg
1876	Roscoe Barnes, Chicago	.404	1917	Edd Roush, Cincinnati	.341	1959	Henry Aaron, Mil.	.355
1877	Jim White, Boston	.385	1918	Zack Wheat, Brooklyn	.335	1960	Dick Groat, Pittsburgh	.325
1878	Abner Dalrymple, Mil.	.356	1919	Edd Roush, Cincinnati	.321	1961	Roberto Clemente, Pitts.	.351
1879	Cap Anson, Chicago	.407	1920	Rogers Hornsby, St. Louis	.370	1962	Tommy Davis, L. A.	.346
1880	George Gore, Chicago	.365	1921	Rogers Hornsby, St. Louis	.397	1963	Tommy Davis, L. A.	.326
1881	Cap Anson, Chicago	.399	1922	Rogers Hornsby, St. Louis	.401	1964	Roberto Clemente, Pitts.	.339
1882	Dan Brouthers, Buffalo	.367	1923	Rogers Hornsby, St. Louis	.384	1965	Roberto Clemente, Pitts.	.329
1883	Dan Brouthers, Buffalo	.371	1924	Rogers Hornsby, St. Louis	.424	1966	Matty Alou, Pittsburgh	.342
1884	James O'Rourke, Buffalo	.350	1925	Rogers Hornsby, St. Louis	.403	1967	Roberto Clemente, Pitts.	.357
1885	Roger Connor, N. Y.	.371	1926	Gene Hargrave, Cincinnati	.353	1968	Pete Rose, Cincinnati	.335
1886	King Kelly, Chicago	.388	1927	Paul Waner; Pittsburgh	.380	1969	Pete Rose, Cincinnati	.348
1887	Cap Anson, Chicago	.421	1928	Rogers Hornsby, Boston	.387	1970	Rico Carty, Atlanta	.366
1888	Cap Anson, Chicago	.343	1929	Lefty O'Doul, Phila.	.398	1971	Joe Torre, St. Louis	.363
1889	Dan Brouthers, Boston	.373	1930	Bill Terry, N.Y.	.401	1972	Billy Williams, Chicago	.333
1890	John Glasscock, N. Y.	.336	1931	Chick Hafey, St. Louis	.349	1973	Pete Rose, Cincinnati	.338
1891	William Hamilton, Phila.	.338	1932	Lefty O'Doul, Brooklyn	.368	1974	Ralph Garr, Atlanta	.353
1892	Dan Brouthers, Bklyn., and Clarence Childs, Cleve.	.335	1933	Chuck Klein, Phila.	.368	1975	Bill Madlock, Chicago	.354
			1934	Paul Waner, Pittsburgh	.362	1976	Bill Madlock, Chicago	.339
1893	Hugh Duffy, Boston	.378	1935	Arky Vaughan, Pittsburgh	.385	1977	Dave Parker, Pittsburgh	.338
1894	Hugh Duffy, Boston	.438	1936	Paul Waner, Pittsburgh	.373	1978	Dave Parker, Pittsburgh	.334
1895	Jesse Burkett, Cleveland	.423	1937	Joe Medwick, St. Louis	.374	1979	Keith Hernandez, St. Louis	.344
1896	Jesse Burkett, Cleveland	.410	1938	Ernie Lombardi, Cin.	.342	1980	Bill Buckner, Chicago	.324
1897	Willie Keeler, Baltimore	.432	1939	John Mize, St. Louis	.349	1981[1]	Bill Madlock, Pittsburgh	.341
1898	Willie Keeler, Baltimore	.379	1940	Debs Garms, Pittsburgh	.355	1982	Al Oliver, Montreal	.331
1899	Ed Delahanty, Phila.	.408	1941	Pete Reiser, Brooklyn	.343	1983	Bill Madlock, Pittsburgh	.323
1900	Honus Wagner, Pittsburgh	.381	1942	Ernie Lombardi, Boston	.330	1984	Tony Gwynn, San Diego	.351
1901	Jesse Burkett, St. Louis	.382	1943	Stan Musial, St. Louis	.357	1985	Willie McGee, St. Louis	.353
1902	Clarence Beaumont, Pitts.	.357	1944	Dixie Walker, Brooklyn	.357	1986	Tim Raines, Montreal	.334
1903	Honus Wagner, Pittsburgh	.355	1945	Phil Cavarretta, Chicago	.355	1987	Tony Gwynn, San Diego	.370
1904	Honus Wagner, Pittsburgh	.349	1946	Stan Musial, St. Louis	.365	1988	Tony Gwynn, San Diego	.313
1905	Cy Seymour, Cincinnati	.377	1947	Harry Walker, St. L.-Phila.	.363	1989	Tony Gwynn, San Diego	.336
1906	Honus Wagner, Pittsburgh	.339	1948	Stan Musial, St. Louis	.376	1990	Willie McGee, St. Louis	.335
1907	Honus Wagner, Pittsburgh	.350	1949	Jackie Robinson, Brooklyn	.342	1991	Terry Pendleton, Atlanta	.319
1908	Honus Wagner, Pittsburgh	.354	1950	Stan Musial, St. Louis	.346	1992	Gary Sheffield, San Diego	.330
1909	Honus Wagner, Pittsburgh	.339	1951	Stan Musial, St. Louis	.355	1993	Andres Galarraga, Colorado	.370
1910	Sherwood Magee, Phila.	.331	1952	Stan Musial, St. Louis	.336	1994[2]	Tony Gwynn, San Diego	.394
1911	Honus Wagner, Pittsburgh	.334	1953	Carl Furillo, Brooklyn	.344	1995	Tony Gwynn, San Diego	.368
1912	Henry Zimmerman, Chicago	.372	1954	Willie Mays, N. Y.	.345	1996	Ellis Burks, Colorado	.344
1913	Jake Daubert, Brooklyn	.350	1955	Richie Ashburn, Phila.	.338	1997	Tony Gwynn, San Diego	.372
1914	Jake Daubert, Brooklyn	.329	1956	Henry Aaron, Mil.	.328	1998	Larry Walker, Colorado	.363
1915	Larry Doyle, New York	.320	1957	Stan Musial, St. Louis	.351			
1916	Hal Chase, Cincinnati	.339	1958	Richie Ashburn, Phila.	.350			

1. Split season because of players' strike. 2. Season ended on August 12 because of a players' strike.

AMERICAN LEAGUE PENNANT WINNERS

Year	Club	Manager	Won	Lost	Pct	Year	Club	Manager	Won	Lost	Pct
1901	Chicago	Clark C. Griffith	83	53	.610	1914	Philadelphia	Connie Mack	99	53	.651
1902	Philadelphia	Connie Mack	83	53	.610	1915[1]	Boston	William F. Carrigan	101	50	.669
1903[1]	Boston	Jimmy Collins	91	47	.659	1916[1]	Boston	William F. Carrigan	91	63	.591
1904[2]	Boston	Jimmy Collins	95	59	.617	1917[1]	Chicago	Clarence H. Rowland	100	54	.649
1905	Philadelphia	Connie Mack	92	56	.622	1918[1]	Boston	Ed Barrow	75	51	.595
1906[1]	Chicago	Fielder A. Jones	93	58	.616	1919	Chicago	William Gleason	88	52	.629
1907	Detroit	Hugh A. Jennings	92	58	.613	1920[1]	Cleveland	Tris Speaker	98	56	.636
1908	Detroit	Hugh A. Jennings	90	63	.588	1921	New York	Miller J. Huggins	98	55	.641
1909	Detroit	Hugh A. Jennings	98	54	.645	1922	New York	Miller J. Huggins	94	60	.610
1910[1]	Philadelphia	Connie Mack	102	48	.680	1923[1]	New York	Miller J. Huggins	98	54	.645
1911[1]	Philadelphia	Connie Mack	101	50	.669	1924[1]	Washington	Stanley R. Harris	92	62	.597
1912[1]	Boston	J. Garland Stahl	105	47	.691	1925	Washington	Stanley R. Harris	96	55	.636
1913[1]	Philadelphia	Connie Mack	96	57	.627	1926	New York	Miller J. Huggins	91	63	.591

Year	Club	Manager	Won	Lost	Pct
1927[1]	New York	Miller J. Huggins	110	44	.714
1928[1]	New York	Miller J. Huggins	101	53	.656
1929[1]	Philadelphia	Connie Mack	104	46	.693
1930[1]	Philadelphia	Connie Mack	102	52	.662
1931	Philadelphia	Connie Mack	107	45	.704
1932[1]	New York	Joseph V. McCarthy	107	47	.695
1933	Washington	Joseph E. Cronin	99	53	.651
1934	Detroit	Gordon Cochrane	101	53	.656
1935[1]	Detroit	Gordon Cochrane	93	58	.616
1936[1]	New York	Joseph V. McCarthy	102	51	.667
1937[1]	New York	Joseph V. McCarthy	102	52	.662
1938[1]	New York	Joseph V. McCarthy	99	53	.651
1939[1]	New York	Joseph V. McCarthy	106	45	.702
1940	Detroit	Delmar D. Baker	90	64	.584
1941[1]	New York	Joseph V. McCarthy	101	53	.656
1942	New York	Joseph V. McCarthy	103	51	.669
1943[1]	New York	Joseph V. McCarthy	98	56	.636
1944	St. Louis	Luke Sewell	89	65	.578
1945[1]	Detroit	Steve O'Neill	88	65	.575
1946	Boston	Joseph E. Cronin	104	50	.675
1947[1]	New York	Stanley R. Harris	97	57	.630
1948[1]	Cleveland	Lou Boudreau	97	58	.626
1949[1]	New York	Casey Stengel	97	57	.630
1950[1]	New York	Casey Stengel	98	56	.636
1951[1]	New York	Casey Stengel	98	56	.636
1952[1]	New York	Casey Stengel	95	59	.617
1953[1]	New York	Casey Stengel	99	52	.656
1954	Cleveland	Al Lopez	111	43	.721
1955	New York	Casey Stengel	96	58	.623
1956[1]	New York	Casey Stengel	97	57	.630
1957	New York	Casey Stengel	98	56	.636
1958[1]	New York	Casey Stengel	92	62	.597
1959	Chicago	Al Lopez	94	60	.610
1960	New York	Casey Stengel	97	57	.630
1961[1]	New York	Ralph Houk	109	53	.673
1962[1]	New York	Ralph Houk	96	66	.593
1963	New York	Ralph Houk	104	57	.646
1964	New York	Yogi Berra	99	63	.611
1965	Minnesota	Sam Mele	102	60	.630
1966[1]	Baltimore	Hank Bauer	97	53	.606
1967	Boston	Dick Williams	92	70	.568
1968[1]	Detroit	Mayo Smith	103	59	.636
1969	Baltimore[3]	Earl Weaver	109	53	.673
1970[1]	Baltimore[3]	Earl Weaver	108	54	.667
1971	Baltimore[4]	Earl Weaver	101	57	.639
1972[1]	Oakland[5]	Dick Williams	93	62	.600
1973[1]	Oakland[6]	Dick Williams	94	68	.580
1974[1]	Oakland[6]	Alvin Dark	90	72	.556
1975	Boston[4]	Darrell Johnson	95	65	.594
1976	New York[7]	Billy Martin	97	62	.610
1977[1]	New York[7]	Billy Martin	100	62	.617
1978[1]	New York[7]	Billy Martin and Bob Lemon	100	63	.613
1979	Baltimore[8]	Earl Weaver	102	57	.642
1980	Kansas City[9]	Jim Frey	97	65	.599
1981	New York[10]	Gene Michael-Bob Lemon	59	48	.551*
1982	Milwaukee[11]	Harvey Kuenn	95	67	.586
1983[1]	Baltimore[12]	Joe Altobelli	98	64	.605
1984[1]	Detroit[13]	Sparky Anderson	104	58	.642
1985[1]	Kansas City[14]	Dick Howser	91	71	.562
1986	Boston[11]	John McNamara	95	66	.590
1987	Minnesota[15]	Tom Kelly	85	77	.525
1988	Oakland[16]	Tony LaRussa	104	58	.642
1989	Oakland[17]	Tony LaRussa	99	63	.611
1990	Oakland[18]	Tony LaRussa	103	59	.636
1991	Minnesota[19]	Tom Kelly	95	67	.586
1992	Toronto[10]	Cito Gaston	96	66	.593
1993	Toronto[12]	Cito Gaston	95	67	.586
1994	Strike ended season Aug. 11. No playoffs, no pennant winner.				
1995	Cleveland[20]	Mike Hargrove	100	44	.694
1996	New York[21]	Joe Torre	92	70	.568
1997	Cleveland[6]	Mike Hargrove	86	75	.534
1998	New York[22]	Joe Torre	114	48	.704

* Split season because of players' strike. 1. World Series winner. 2. No World Series. 3. Defeated Minnesota, Western Division winner, in playoff. 4. Defeated Oakland, Western Division Leader, in playoff. 5. Defeated Detroit, Eastern Division winner, inplayoff. 6. Defeated Baltimore, Eastern Division winner, in playoff. 7. Defeated Kansas City, Western Division winner, in playoff. 8. Defeated California, Western Division winner, in playoff. 9. Defeated New York, Eastern Division winner, in playoff. 10. Defeated Oakland, Western Division winner, in playoff. 11. Defeated California, Western Division winner, in playoff. 12. Defeated Chicago, Western Division winner, in playoff. 13. Defeated Kansas City, Western Division winner, in playoff. 14. Defeated Toronto, Eastern Division winner, in playoff. 15. Defeated Detroit, Eastern winner, in playoff. 16. Defeated Boston, Eastern division winner, in playoffs. 17. Defeated Toronto, Eastern Division winner, in playoffs. 18. Defeated Boston, Eastern Division winner, in playoffs. 19. Defeated Toronto, Eastern Division winner, in playoffs. 20. Defeated Seattle Mariners, Western Division winner, in playoffs. 21. Defeated Baltimore Orioles, Eastern Division wild-card team, in playoffs. 22. Defeated Cleveland Indians, Central Division winner, in playoffs.

NATIONAL LEAGUE PENNANT WINNERS

Year	Club	Manager	Won	Lost	Pct
1876	Chicago	Albert G. Spalding	52	14	.788
1877	Boston	Harry Wright	31	17	.646
1878	Boston	Harry Wright	41	19	.683
1879	Providence	George Wright	55	23	.705
1880	Chicago	Adrian C. Anson	67	17	.798
1881	Chicago	Adrian C. Anson	56	28	.667
1882	Chicago	Adrian C. Anson	55	29	.655
1883	Boston	John F. Morrill	63	35	.643
1884	Providence	Frank C. Bancroft	84	28	.750
1885	Chicago	Adrian C. Anson	87	25	.777
1886	Chicago	Adrian C. Anson	90	34	.726
1887	Detroit	W. H. Watkins	79	45	.637
1888	New York	James J. Mutrie	84	47	.641
1889	New York	James J. Mutrie	83	43	.659
1890	Brooklyn	Wm. H. McGunnigle	86	43	.667
1891	Boston	Frank G. Selee	87	51	.630
1892	Boston	Frank G. Selee	102	48	.680
1893	Boston	Frank G. Selee	86	44	.662
1894	Baltimore	Edward H. Hanlon	89	39	.695
1895	Baltimore	Edward H. Hanlon	87	43	.669
1896	Baltimore	Edward H. Hanlon	90	39	.698
1897	Boston	Frank G. Selee	93	39	.705
1898	Boston	Frank G. Selee	102	47	.685
1899	Brooklyn	Edward H. Hanlon	88	42	.677
1900	Brooklyn	Edward H. Hanlon	82	54	.603
1901	Pittsburgh	Fred C. Clarke	90	49	.647
1902	Pittsburgh	Fred C. Clarke	103	36	.741
1903	Pittsburgh	Fred C. Clarke	91	49	.650
1904	New York[2]	John J. McGraw	106	47	.693
1905	New York[1]	John J. McGraw	105	48	.686
1906	Chicago	Frank L. Chance	116	36	.763
1907	Chicago[1]	Frank L. Chance	107	45	.704
1908	Chicago[1]	Frank L. Chance	99	55	.643
1909	Pittsburgh[1]	Fred C. Clarke	110	42	.724

Year	Club	Manager	Won	Lost	Pct
1910	Chicago	Frank L. Chance	104	50	.675
1911	New York	John J. McGraw	99	54	.647
1912	New York	John J. McGraw	103	48	.682
1913	New York	John J. McGraw	101	51	.664
1914	Boston[1]	George T. Stallings	94	59	.614
1915	Philadelphia	Patrick J. Moran	90	62	.592
1916	Brooklyn	Wilbert Robinson	94	60	.610
1917	New York	John J. McGraw	98	56	.636
1918	Chicago	Fred L. Mitchell	84	45	.651
1919	Cincinnati[1]	Patrick J. Moran	96	44	.686
1920	Brooklyn	Wilbert Robinson	93	61	.604
1921	New York[1]	John J. McGraw	94	59	.614
1922	New York[1]	John J. McGraw	93	61	.604
1923	New York	John J. McGraw	95	58	.621
1924	New York	John J. McGraw	93	60	.608
1925	Pittsburgh[1]	Wm. B. McKechnie	95	58	.621
1926	St. Louis[1]	Rogers Hornsby	89	65	.578
1927	Pittsburgh	Donie Bush	94	60	.610
1928	St. Louis	Wm. B. McKechnie	95	59	.617
1929	Chicago	Joseph V. McCarthy	98	54	.645
1930	St. Louis	Gabby Street	92	62	.597
1931	St. Louis[1]	Gabby Street	101	53	.656
1932	Chicago	Charles J. Grimm	90	64	.584
1933	New York[1]	William H. Terry	91	61	.599
1934	St. Louis[1]	Frank F. Frisch	95	58	.621
1935	Chicago	Charles J. Grimm	100	54	.649
1936	New York	William H. Terry	92	62	.597
1937	New York	William H. Terry	95	57	.625
1938	Chicago	Gabby Hartnett	89	63	.586
1939	Cincinnati	Wm. B. McKechnie	97	57	.630
1940	Cincinnati[1]	Wm. B. McKechnie	100	53	.654
1941	Brooklyn	Leo E. Durocher	100	54	.649
1942	St. Louis[1]	Wm. H. Southworth	106	48	.688
1943	St. Louis	Wm. H. Southworth	105	49	.682
1944	St. Louis[1]	Wm. H. Southworth	105	49	.682
1945	Chicago	Charles J. Grimm	98	56	.636
1946	St. Louis[1]	Edwin H. Dyer	98	58	.628
1947	Brooklyn	Burton E. Shotton	94	60	.610
1948	Boston	Wm. H. Southworth	91	62	.595
1949	Brooklyn	Burton E. Shotton	97	57	.630
1950	Philadelphia	Edwin M. Sawyer	91	63	.591
1951	New York	Leo E. Durocher	98	59	.624
1952	Brooklyn	Charles W. Dressen	96	57	.630
1953	Brooklyn	Charles W. Dressen	105	49	.682
1954	New York[1]	Leo E. Durocher	97	57	.630
1955	Brooklyn[1]	Walter Alston	98	55	.641
1956	Brooklyn	Walter Alston	93	61	.604
1957	Milwaukee1	Fred Haney	95	59	.617
1958	Milwaukee	Fred Haney	92	62	.597
1959	Los Angeles[1]	Walter Alston	88	68	.564
1960	Pittsburgh[1]	Danny Murtaugh	95	59	.617
1961	Cincinnati	Fred Hutchinson	93	61	.604
1962	San Francisco	Alvin Dark	103	62	.624
1963	Los Angeles[1]	Walter Alston	99	63	.611
1964	St. Louis[1]	Johnny Keane	93	69	.574
1965	Los Angeles[1]	Walter Alston	97	65	.599
1966	Los Angeles	Walter Alston	95	67	.586
1967	St. Louis[1]	Red Schoendienst	101	60	.627
1968	St. Louis	Red Schoendienst	97	65	.599
1969	New York[1 3]	Gil Hodges	100	62	.617
1970	Cincinnati[4]	Sparky Anderson	102	60	.630
1971	Pittsburgh[1 5]	Danny Murtaugh	97	65	.599
1972	Cincinnati[4]	Sparky Anderson	95	59	.617
1973	New York[6]	Yogi Berra	82	79	.509
1974	Los Angeles[4]	Walter Alston	102	60	.630
1975	Cincinnati[1 4]	Sparky Anderson	108	54	.667
1976	Cincinnati[7 1]	Sparky Anderson	102	60	.630
1977	Los Angeles[7]	Tom Lasorda	98	64	.605
1978	Los Angeles[7]	Tom Lasorda	95	67	.586
1979[1]	Pittsburgh[6]	Chuck Tanner	98	64	.605
1980[1]	Philadelphia[8]	Dallas Green	91	71	.562
1981	Los Angeles[1 9]	Tom Lasorda	63	47	.573*
1982[1]	St. Louis[3]	Whitey Herzog	92	70	.568
1983	Philadelphia[11]	Paul Owens	90	72	.556
1984	San Diego[12]	Dick Williams	92	70	.568
1985	St. Louis[11]	Whitey Herzog	101	61	.623
1986	New York[8]	Dave Johnson	108	54	.667
1987	St. Louis[5]	Whitey Herzog	95	67	.586
1988	Los Angeles[10]	Tom Lasorda	94	67	.584
1989	San Francisco[12]	Roger Craig	92	70	.568
1990	Cincinnati[4]	Lou Piniella	91	71	.562
1991	Atlanta[4]	Bobby Cox	94	68	.580
1992	Atlanta[4]	Bobby Cox	98	64	.605
1993	Philadelphia[3]	Jim Fregosi	97	65	.599
1994	Strike ended season Aug. 11. No playoffs, no pennant winner.				
1995	Atlanta[13]	Bobby Cox	90	54	.625
1996	Atlanta[14]	Bobby Cox	96	66	.593
1997	Florida[15]	Jim Leyland	92	70	.568
1998	San Diego[16]	Bruce Bochy	98	64	.605

* Split season because of players' strike. 1. World Series winner. 2. No World Series. 3. Defeated Atlanta, Western Division winner, in playoff. 4. Defeated Pittsburgh, Eastern Division winner, in playoff. 5. Defeated San Francisco, Western Division winner, in playoff. 6. Defeated Cincinnati, Western Division winner, in playoff. 7. Defeated Philadelphia, Eastern Division winner, in playoff. 8. Defeated Houston, Western Division winner, in playoff. 9. Defeated Montreal, Eastern Division winner, in playoff. 10. Defeated New York, Eastern Division winner, in playoff. 11. Defeated Los Angeles, Western Division winner, in playoff. 12. Defeated Chicago, Eastern Division champion, in playoff. 13. Defeated Cincinnati, Central Division winner, in playoff. 14. Defeated St. Louis, Central Division winner, in playoff. 15. Eastern Division wildcard Florida defeated Atlanta, Eastern Division winner, in playoff. 16. Defeated Atlanta, Eastern Division winner, in playoff.

MOST VALUABLE PLAYERS

(Baseball Writers Association selections)

American League

1931	Lefty Grove, Philadelphia
1932–33	Jimmy Foxx, Philadelphia
1934	Mickey Cochrane, Detroit
1935	Hank Greenberg, Detroit
1936	Lou Gehrig, New York
1937	Charlie Gehringer, Detroit
1938	Jimmy Foxx, Boston
1939	Joe DiMaggio, New York
1940	Hank Greenberg, Detroit
1941	Joe DiMaggio, New York
1942	Joe Gordon, New York
1943	Spurgeon Chandler, New York
1944–45	Hal Newhouser, Detroit
1946	Ted Williams, Boston
1947	Joe DiMaggio, New York
1948	Lou Boudreau, Cleveland
1949	Ted Williams, Boston
1950	Phil Rizzuto, New York
1951	Yogi Berra, New York
1952	Bobby Shantz, Philadelphia
1953	Al Rosen, Cleveland
1954–55	Yogi Berra, New York
1956–57	Mickey Mantle, New York
1958	Jackie Jensen, Boston
1959	Nellie Fox, Chicago
1960–61	Roger Maris, New York
1962	Mickey Mantle, New York
1963	Elston Howard, New York
1964	Brooks Robinson, Baltimore

1965 Zoilo Versalles, Minnesota
1966 Frank Robinson, Baltimore
1967 Carl Yastrzemski, Boston
1968 Dennis McLain, Detroit
1969 Harmon Killebrew, Minnesota
1970 John (Boog) Powell, Baltimore
1971 Vida Blue, Oakland
1972 Dick Allen, Chicago
1973 Reggie Jackson, Oakland
1974 Jeff Burroughs, Texas
1975 Fred Lynn, Boston
1976 Thurman Munson, New York
1977 Rod Carew, Minnesota
1978 Jim Rice, Boston
1979 Don Baylor, California
1980 George Brett, Kansas City
1981 Rollie Fingers, Milwaukee
1982 Robin Yount, Milwaukee
1983 Cal Ripken, Jr., Baltimore
1984 Willie Hernandez, Detroit
1985 Don Mattingly, New York
1986 Roger Clemens, Boston
1987 George Bell, Toronto
1988 Jose Canseco, Oakland
1989 Robin Yount, Milwaukee
1990 Rickey Henderson, Oakland
1991 Cal Ripken, Jr., Baltimore
1992 Dennis Eckersley, Oakland
1993 Frank Thomas, Chicago
1994 Frank Thomas, Chicago
1995 Mo Vaughn, Boston
1996 Juan Gonzales, Texas
1997 Ken Griffey, Jr., Seattle

National League

1931 Frank Frisch, St. Louis
1932 Chuck Klein, Philadelphia
1933 Carl Hubbell, New York
1934 Dizzy Dean, St. Louis
1935 Gabby Hartnett, Chicago
1936 Carl Hubbell, New York
1937 Joe Medwick, St. Louis
1938 Ernie Lombardi, Cincinnati
1939 Bucky Walters, Cincinnati
1940 Frank McCormick, Cincinnati
1941 Dolph Camilli, Brooklyn
1942 Mort Cooper, St. Louis
1943 Stan Musial, St. Louis
1944 Marty Marion, St. Louis
1945 Phil Cavarretta, Chicago
1946 Stan Musial, St. Louis
1947 Bob Elliott, Boston
1948 Stan Musial, St. Louis
1949 Jackie Robinson, Brooklyn
1950 Jim Konstanty, Philadelphia
1951 Roy Campanella, Brooklyn
1952 Hank Sauer, Chicago
1953 Roy Campanella, Brooklyn
1954 Willie Mays, New York
1955 Roy Campanella, Brooklyn
1956 Don Newcombe, Brooklyn
1957 Henry Aaron, Milwaukee
1958–59 Ernie Banks, Chicago
1960 Dick Groat, Pittsburgh
1961 Frank Robinson, Cincinnati
1962 Maury Wills, Los Angeles
1963 Sandy Koufax, Los Angeles
1964 Ken Boyer, St. Louis
1965 Willie Mays, San Francisco
1966 Roberto Clemente, Pittsburgh
1967 Orlando Cepeda, St. Louis
1968 Bob Gibson, St. Louis
1969 Willie McCovey, San Francisco
1970 Johnny Bench, Cincinnati
1971 Joe Torre, St. Louis
1972 Johnny Bench, Cincinnati
1973 Pete Rose, Cincinnati
1974 Steve Garvey, Los Angeles
1975–76 Joe Morgan, Cincinnati
1977 George Foster, Cincinnati
1978 Dave Parker, Pittsburgh
1979 Willie Stargell, Pittsburgh
1979 Keith Hernandez, St. Louis
1980 Mike Schmidt, Philadelphia
1981 Mike Schmidt, Philadelphia
1982 Dale Murphy, Atlanta
1983 Dale Murphy, Atlanta
1984 Ryne Sandberg, Chicago
1985 Willie McGee, St. Louis
1986 Mike Schmidt, Philadelphia
1987 Andre Dawson, Chicago
1988 Kirk Gibson, Los Angeles
1989 Kevin Mitchell, San Francisco
1990 Barry Bonds, Pittsburgh
1991 Terry Pendleton, Atlanta
1992 Barry Bonds, Pittsburgh
1993 Barry Bonds, San Francisco
1994 Jeff Bagwell, Houston
1995 Barry Larkin, Cincinnati
1996 Ken Caminiti, San Diego
1997 Larry Walker, Colorado

CY YOUNG AWARD

1956 Don Newcombe, Brooklyn N.L.
1957 Warren Spahn, Milwaukee N.L.
1958 Bob Turley, New York A.L.
1959 Early Wynn, Chicago A.L.
1960 Vernon Law, Pittsburgh, N.L.
1961 Whitey Ford, New York A.L.
1962 Don Drysdale, Los Angeles N.L.
1963 Sandy Koufax, Los Angeles N.L.
1964 Dean Chance, Los Angeles A.L.
1965 Sandy Koufax, Los Angeles N.L.
1966 Sandy Koufax, Los Angeles N.L.
1967 Jim Lonborg, Boston A.L.; Mike McCormick, San Francisco N.L.
1968 Dennis McLain, Detroit A.L.; Bob Gibson, St. Louis N.L.
1969 Mike Cuellar, Baltimore A.L. and Dennis McLain, Detroit A.L. (tied); Tom Seaver, N.Y. N.L.
1970 Jim Perry, Minnesota A.L; Bob Gibson, St. Louis N.L.
1971 Vida Blue, Oakland A.L.; Ferguson Jenkins, Chicago N.L.
1972 Gaylord Perry, Cleveland A.L.; Steve Carlton, Phila. N.L.
1973 Jim Palmer, Baltimore A.L.; Tom Seaver, New York N.L.
1974 Catfish Hunter, Oakland A.L.; Mike Marshall, Los Angeles N.L.
1975 Jim Palmer, Baltimore A.L.; Tom Seaver, New York N.L.
1976 Jim Palmer, Baltimore A.L.; Randy Jones, San Diego N.L.
1977 Sparky Lyle, N.Y., A.L.; Steve Carlton, Philadelphia N.L.
1978 Ron Guidry, N.Y., A.L.; Gaylord Perry, San Diego N.L.
1979 Mike Flanagan, Baltimore, A.L.; Bruce Sutter, Chicago, N.L.
1980 Steve Stone, Baltimore, A.L.; Steve Carlton, Philadelphia, N.L.
1981 Rollie Fingers, Milwaukee, A.L.; Fernando Valenzuela, Los Angeles, N.L.
1982 Pete Vuckovich, Milwaukee, A.L.; Steve Carlton, Philadelphia, N.L.
1983 LaMarr Hoyt, Chicago, A.L.; John Denny, Philadelphia, N.L.
1984 Willie Hernandez, Detroit, A.L.; Rick Sutcliffe, Chicago, N.L.
1985 Bret Saberhagen, A.L.; Dwight Gooden, N.L.
1986 Roger Clemens, Boston, A.L.; Mike Scott, Houston, N.L.
1987 Roger Clemens, Boston, A.L.; Steve Bedrosian, Philadelphia, N.L.
1988 Frank Viola, Minnesota, A.L.; Orel Hershiser, Los Angeles, N.L.
1989 Bret Saberhagen, Kansas, A.L.; Mark Davis, San Diego, N.L.
1990 Bob Welch, Oakland, A.L.; Doug Drabek, Pittsburgh, N.L.
1991 Roger Clemens, Boston, A.L.; Tom Glavine, Atlanta, N.L.
1992 Dennis Eckersley, Oakland, A.L.; Greg Maddux, Atlant, N.L.
1993 Jack McDowell, Chicago, A.L.; Greg Maddux, Atalanta, N.L.
1994 David Cone, Kansas, A.L.; Greg Maddux, Atlanta, N.L.
1995 Randy Johnson, Seattle, A.L.; Greg Maddux, Atlanta, N.L.
1996 Pat Hentgen, Toronto, A.L.; John Smoltz, Atlanta, N.L.
1997 Roger Clemens, Toronto, A.L.; Pedro Martinez, Montreal, N.L.

MAJOR LEAGUE ALL-TIME PITCHING RECORDS

(Through 1998)

Most Games Won—511, Cy Young, Cleveland N.L., 1890–98, St. Louis N.L., 1899–1900, Boston A.L., 1901–08, Cleveland A.L., 1909–11, Boston N.L., 1911.

Most Games Won, Season—59, Hoss Radbourne, Providence N.L., 1884. (Since 1900—41, Jack Chesbro, New York A.L., 1904.)

Most Consecutive Games Won—24, Carl Hubbell, New York N.L., 1936 (16) and 1937 (8).

Most Consecutive Games Won, Season—19, Tim Keefe, New York N.L., 1888; Rube Marquard, New York N.L., 1912.

Most Years Won 20 or More Games—16, Cy Young, Cleveland N.L., 1891–98, St. Louis N.L., 1899–1900, Boston A.L., 1901–04, 1907–08.

Most Shutouts—113, Walter Johnson, Wash. A.L., 1907–27.

Most Shutouts, Season—16, Grover Alexander, Philadelphia N.L., 1916.

Most Consecutive Shutouts—6, Don Drysdale, Los Angeles, N.L., 1968.

Most Consecutive Scoreless Innings—59, Orel Hershiser, Los Angeles Dodgers, 1988.

Most Strikeouts—5,714, Nolan Ryan, New York N.L., California A.L., Houston N.L., 1968–1988 Texas, 1989–93.

Most Strikeouts, Season—513, Matthew Kilroy, Baltimore A.A., 1886. (Since 1900—383, Nolan Ryan, California, A.L., 1973.)

Most Strikeouts, Game—21, Tom Cheney, Washington A.L., 1962, 16 innings. Nine innings: 20, Roger Clemens, Boston, A.L., 1986; Kerry Wood, Chicago, N.L., 1998.

Most Consecutive Strikeouts—10, Tom Seaver, New York N.L. vs. San Diego, April 22, 1970.

Most Games, Season—106, Mike Marshall, Los Angeles, N.L., 1974.

Most Complete Games, Season—75, William White, Cincinnati N.L., 1879. (Since 1900—48, Jack Chesbro, New York A.L., 1904.)

MAJOR LEAGUE LIFETIME RECORDS

(Through 1998)

Wins

***Indicates left-handed pitcher.**

		Yrs	GS	W	L
1	Cy Young	22	815	**511**	316
2	Walter Johnson	21	666	**416**	279
3	Christy Mathewson	17	551	**373**	188
	Grover Alexander	20	598	**373**	208
5	Warren Spahn*	21	665	**363**	245
6	Kid Nichols	15	561	**361**	208
	Pud Galvin	14	682	**361**	308
8	Tim Keefe	14	594	**342**	225
9	Steve Carlton*	24	709	**329**	244
10	Eddie Plank*	17	527	**327**	193
11	John Clarkson	12	518	**326**	177
12	Don Sutton	23	756	**324**	256
13	Nolan Ryan	27	773	**324**	292
14	Phil Niekro	24	716	**318**	274
15	Gaylord Perry	22	690	**314**	265
16	Old Hoss Radbourn	12	503	**311**	194
	Tom Seaver	20	647	**311**	205
18	Mickey Welch	13	549	**308**	209
19	Lefty Grove*	17	456	**300**	141
	Early Wynn	23	612	**300**	244
21	Tommy John*	26	700	**288**	231
22	Bert Blyleven	22	685	**287**	250
23	Robin Roberts	19	609	**286**	245
24	Tony Mullane	13	505	**285**	220
25	Ferguson Jenkins	19	594	**284**	226

Pitchers Active in 1998

		Yrs	GS	W	L
1	Dennis Martinez	23	562	**245**	193
2	Roger Clemens	15	449	233	124
3	Greg Maddux	13	399	202	117
4	Dennis Eckersley	24	361	197	171
5	Orel Hershiser	16	428	190	133
6	Jimmy Key*	15	389	186	117
7	Dwight Gooden	14	374	183	103
8	Mark Langston*	15	423	178	156
9	Tom Glavine*	12	364	173	105
10	Danny Darwin	21	371	171	182

Leading Batters, by Batting Average

***Indicates left-handed hitter.**

Boldface indicates player active in 1998.

		Yrs	AB	H	Avg
1	Ty Cobb*	24	11,429	4191	.367
2	Rogers Hornsby	23	8,137	2930	.358
3	Joe Jackson*	13	4,981	1774	.356
4	Ed Delahanty	16	7,509	2597	.346
5	Tris Speaker*	22	10,197	3514	.345
6	Ted Williams*	19	7,706	2654	.344
7	Billy Hamilton*	14	6,284	2163	.344
8	Willie Keeler*	19	8,585	2947	.343
9	Dan Brouthers*	19	6,711	2296	.342
10	Babe Ruth*	22	8,399	2873	.342
11	Harry Heilmann	17	7,787	2660	.342
12	Pete Browning	13	4,820	1646	.341
13	Bill Terry*	14	6,428	2193	.341
14	George Sisler*	15	8,267	2812	.340
15	Lou Gehrig*	17	8,001	2721	.340
16	Jesse Burkett*	16	8,413	2853	.339
17	**Tony Gwynn***	17	8,648	2,928	.339
18	Nap Lajoie	21	9,592	3244	.338
19	Riggs Stephenson	14	4,508	1515	.336
20	Al Simmons	20	8,761	2927	.334
21	Paul Waner*	20	9,459	3152	.333
22	Eddie Collins*	25	9,951	3313	.333
23	**Mike Piazza**	7	3,119	1,038	.333
24	Stan Musial*	22	10,972	3630	.331
25	Sam Thompson*	14	6,005	1986	.331

Players Active in 1998

		Yrs	AB	H	Avg
1	Tony Gwynn*	17	8,648	2,928	.339
2	Mike Piazza	7	3,119	1,038	.333
3	Wade Boggs*	17	8,888	2,922	.329
4	Frank Thomas	9	4,406	1,416	.321
5	Edgar Martinez	12	4,374	1,389	.318
6	Kenny Lofton*	8	3,914	1,216	.311
7	Mark Grace	9	6,053	1,875	.310
8	Paul Molitor	21	10,835	3,319	.306
	Hal Morris*	11	3,727	1,140	.306
10	Larry Walker*	10	4,154	1,265	.305

MAJOR LEAGUE INDIVIDUAL ALL-TIME RECORDS
(Through 1998)

Highest Batting Average, Season—.442, James O'Neill, St. Louis, A.A., 1887; .438, Hugh Duffy, Boston, N.L., 1894 (Since 1900—.424, Rogers Hornsby, St. Louis, N.L., 1924; .422, Nap Lajoie, Phil., A.L., 1901)
Most Times at Bat—14,053, Pete Rose, Cincinnati, N.L., 1963–78; Philadelphia, N.L., 1979–83; Montreal, N.L., 1984; Cincinnati, N.L., 1984–86.
Most Years Batted .300 or Better—23, Ty Cobb, Detroit A.L., 1906–26, Philadelphia A.L., 1927–28.
Most Hits—4,256, Pete Rose, Cincinnati 1963–79, Philadelphia 1980–83, Montreal 1984, Cincinnati 1984–86.
Most Hits, Season—257, George Sisler, St. Louis A.L., 1920.
Most Hits, Game (9 innings)—7, Wilbert Robinson, Baltimore N.L., 6 singles, 1 double, 1892. Rennie Stennett, Pittsburgh N.L., 4 singles, 2 doubles, 1 triple, 1975.
Most Hits, Game (extra innings)—9, John Burnett, Cleveland A.L., 18 innings, 7 singles, 2 doubles, 1932.
Most Hits in Succession—12, Mike Higgins, Boston A.L., in four games, 1938; Walt Dropo, Detroit A.L., in three games, 1952.
Most Consecutive Games Batted Safely—56, Joe DiMaggio, New York A.L., 1941.
Most Runs—2,245, Ty Cobb, Detroit A.L., 1905–26, Philadelphia A.L., 1927–28.
Most Runs, Season—196, William Hamilton, Philadelphia N.L., 1894. (Since 1900—177, Babe Ruth, New York A.L., 1921.)
Most Runs, Game—7, Guy Hecker, Louisville A.A., 1886. (Since 1900—6, by Mel Ott, New York N.L., 1934, 1944; Johnny Pesky, Boston A.L., 1946; Frank Torre, Milwaukee N.L., 1957.)
Most Runs Batted in—2,297, Henry Aaron, Milwaukee N.L., 1954–1965; Atlanta N.L., 1966–74; Milwaukee A.L., 1975–76.
Most Runs Batted in, Season—190, Hack Wilson, Chicago N.L., 1930.
Most Runs Batted In, Game—12, Jim Bottomley, St. Louis N.L., 1924, and Mark Whiten, St. Louis N.L., 1993.
Most Home Runs—755, Henry Aaron, Milwaukee N.L., 1954–1965; Atlanta N.L., 1966–74; Milwaukee A.L., 1975–76.
Most Home Runs, Season—70, Mark McGwire, St. Louis N.L., 1998 (162-game season); 66, Sammy Sosa, Chicago N.L., 1998 (162-game season); 61, Roger Maris, New York A.L., 1961 (162-game season); 60, Babe Ruth, New York A.L., 1927 (154-game season)
Most Home Runs with Bases Filled—23, Lou Gehrig, New York A.L., 1927–39.
Most 2-Base Hits—793, Tris Speaker, Boston A.L., 1907–15, Cleveland A.L., 1916–26, Washington A.L., 1927, Philadelphia A.L., 1928.
Most 2-Base Hits, Season—67, Earl Webb, Boston A.L., 1931.
Most 2-base Hits, Game—4, by many.
Most 3-Base Hits—312, Sam Crawford, Cincinnati N.L., 1899–1902, Detroit A.L., 1903–17.
Most 3-Base Hits, Season—36, Owen Wilson, Pittsburgh N.L., 1912.
Most 3-Base Hits, Game—4, George Strief, Philadelphia A.A., 1885; William Joyce, New York N.L., 1897. (Since 1900—3, by many.)
Most Games Played—3,562, Pete Rose, Cincinnati N.L., Philadelphia N.L., Montreal N.L., 1964–86.
Most Consecutive Games Played—2,632, Cal Ripken, Jr., Baltimore Orioles, A.L., 1981–
Most Bases on Balls—2,056, Babe Ruth, Boston A.L., 1914–19; New York A.L., 1920–34, Boston N.L., 1935.
Most Bases on Balls, Season—170, Babe Ruth, New York A.L., 1923.
Most Bases on Balls, Game—6, Jimmy Foxx, Boston A.L., 1938.
Most Strikeouts, Season—189, Bobby Bonds, San Francisco N.L., 1970.
Most Strikeouts, Game (9 innings)—5, by many.
Most Strikeouts, Game (extra innings)—6, Carl Weilman, St. Louis A.L., 15 innings, 1913; Don Hoak, Chicago N.L., 17 innings, 1956; Fred Reichardt, California A.L., 17, innings, 1966; Billy Cowan, California A.L., 20, 1971; Cecil Cooper, Boston A.L., 15, 1974.
Most Pinch-hits, Lifetime—150, Manny Mota, S.F., 1962; Pitt., 1963–68; Montreal, 1969; L.A., 1969–80, N.L.
Most Pinch-hits, Season—25, Jose Morales, Montreal N.L., 1976.
Most Consecutive Pinch-hits—9, Dave Philley, Phil., N.L., 1958 (8), 1959 (1).
Most Pinch-hit Home Runs, Lifetime—20, Cliff Johnson, Houston N.L., 1972–77; New York A.L., 1977–79; Cleveland A.L., 1979–80; Chicago N.L., 1980; Oakland A.L., 1981–82; Toronto A.L., 1983–84, 1985–86; Texas A.L., 1985.
Most Pinch-hit Home Runs, Season—6, Johnny Frederick, Brooklyn, N.L., 1932.
Most Stolen Bases, Lifetime—1,297, Rickey Henderson, 1979–84 Oakland, 1985–89 New York (A.L.), 1989–93 Oakland, 1993 Toronto, 1994–95 Oakland, 1996 San Diego, 1997 Anaheim, 1998 Oakland.
Most Stolen Bases, Season—156, Harry Stovey, Phil., A.A., 1888. Since 1900: 130, Rickey Henderson, Oak., A.L., 1982; 118, Lou Brock, St. Louis, N.L., 1974.
Most Stolen Bases, Game—7, George Gore, Chicago N.L. 1881; William Hamilton, Philadelphia N.L. 1894. (Since 1900—6, Eddie Collins, Philadelphia A.L., 1912.) and Otis Nixon, Atlanta N.L., 1991.
Most Time Stealing Home, Lifetime—50, Ty Cobb, Detroit-Phil. A.L., 1905–28.

ROOKIE OF THE YEAR
(Baseball Writers Association selections)

American League

1949 Roy Sievers, St. Louis
1950 Walt Dropo, Boston
1951 Gil McDougald, New York
1952 Harry Byrd, Philadelphia
1953 Harvey Kuenn, Detroit
1954 Bob Grim, New York
1955 Herb Score, Cleveland
1956 Luis Aparicio, Chicago
1957 Tony Kubek, New York
1958 Albie Pearson, Washington
1959 Bob Allison, Washington
1960 Ron Hansen, Baltimore
1961 Don Schwall, Boston
1962 Tom Tresh, New York
1963 Gary Peters, Chicago
1964 Tony Oliva, Minnesota
1965 Curt Blefary, Baltimore
1966 Tommy Agee, Chicago
1967 Rod Carew, Minnesota
1968 Stan Bahnsen, New York
1969 Lou Piniella, Kansas City
1970 Thurman Munson, New York
1971 Chris Chambliss, Cleveland
1972 Carlton Fisk, Boston
1973 Alonzo Bumbry, Baltimore
1974 Mike Hargrove, Texas
1975 Fred Lynn, Boston
1976 Mark Fidrych, Detroit
1977 Eddie Murray, Baltimore
1978 Lou Whitaker, Detroit
1979 Alfredo Griffin, Toronto
1979 John Castino, Minnesota
1980 Joe Charboneau, Cleveland

1981 Dave Righetti, New York
1982 Cal Ripken, Jr., Baltimore
1983 Ron Kittle, Chicago
1984 Alvin Davis, Seattle
1985 Ozzie Guillen, Chicago
1986 Jose Canseco, Oakland
1987 Mark McGwire, Oakland
1988 Walter Weiss, Oakland
1989 Gregg Olson, Baltimore
1990 Sandy Alomar Jr., Cleveland
1991 Chuck Knoblauch, Minnesota
1992 Pat Listach, Milwaukee
1993 Tim Salmon, California
1994 Bob Hamelin, Kansas City
1995 Marty Cordova, Minnesota
1996 Derek Jeter, New York
1997 Nomar Garciaparra, Boston

National League

1949 Don Newcombe, Brooklyn
1950 Sam Jethroe, Boston
1951 Willie Mays, New York
1952 Joe Black, Brooklyn
1953 Jim Gilliam, Brooklyn
1954 Wally Moon, St. Louis
1955 Bill Virdon, St. Louis
1956 Frank Robinson, Cincinnati
1957 Jack Sanford, Philadelphia
1958 Orlando Cepeda, San Francisco
1959 Willie McCovey, San Francisco
1960 Frank Howard, Los Angeles
1961 Billy Williams, Chicago
1962 Ken Hubbs, Chicago
1963 Pete Rose, Cincinnati
1964 Richie Allen, Philadelphia
1965 Jim Lefebvre, Los Angeles
1966 Tommy Helms, Cincinnati
1967 Tom Seaver, New York
1968 Johnny Bench, Cincinnati
1969 Ted Sizemore, Los Angeles
1970 Carl Morton, Montreal
1971 Earl Williams, Atlanta
1972 Jon Matlack, New York
1973 Gary Matthews, San Francisco
1974 Bake McBride, St. Louis
1975 John Montefusco, San Francisco
1976 Pat Zachry, Cincinnati
1976 Bruce Metzger, San Diego
1977 Andre Dawson, Montreal
1978 Bob Horner, Atlanta
1979 Rick Sutcliffe, Los Angeles
1980 Steve Howe, Los Angeles
1981 Fernando Valenzuela, Los Angeles
1982 Steve Sax, Los Angeles
1983 Darryl Strawberry, New York
1984 Dwight Gooden, New York
1985 Vince Coleman, St. Louis
1986 Todd Worrell, St. Louis
1987 Benito Santiago, San Diego
1988 Chris Sabo, Cincinnati
1989 Jerome Walton, Chicago
1990 Dave Justice, Atlanta
1991 Jeff Baguell, Houston
1992 Eric Karros, Los Angeles
1993 Mike Piazza, Los Angeles
1994 Raul Mondesi, Los Angeles
1995 Hideo Nomo, Los Angeles
1996 Todd Hollandsworth, Los Angeles
1997 Scott Rolen, Philadelphia

MOST HOME RUNS IN ONE SEASON

(45 or More)

HR	Player/Team	Year
70	Mark McGwire, St. Louis (N.L.)	1998
66	Sammy Sosa, Chicago (N.L.)	1998
61	Roger Maris, New York (A.L.)	1961
60	Babe Ruth, New York (A.L.)	1927
59	Babe Ruth, New York (A.L.)	1921
58	Jimmy Foxx, Philadelphia (A.L.)	1932
58	Hank Greenberg, Detroit (A.L.)	1938
58	Mark McGwire, Oakland (A.L.), St. Louis (N.L.)	1997
56	Hack Wilson, Chicago (N.L.)	1930
56	Ken Griffey, Jr., Seattle (A.L.)	1997
56	Ken Griffey, Jr., Seattle (A.L.)	1998
54	Babe Ruth, New York (A.L.)	1920
54	Babe Ruth, New York (A.L.)	1928
54	Ralph Kiner, Pittsburgh (N.L.)	1949
54	Mickey Mantle, New York (A.L.)	1961
52	Mickey Mantle, New York (A.L.)	1956
52	Willie Mays, San Francisco (N.L.)	1965
52	George Foster, Cincinnati (N.L.)	1977
52	Mark McGwire, Oakland (A.L.)	1996
51	Ralph Kiner, Pittsburgh (N.L.)	1947
51	John Mize, New York (N.L.)	1947
51	Willie Mays, New York (N.L.)	1955
51	Cecil Fielder (A.L.)	1990
50	Jimmy Foxx, Boston (A.L.)	1938
50	Albert Belle, Cleveland (A.L.)	1995
50	Brady Anderson, Baltimore (A.L.)	1996
50	Greg Vaughn, San Diego (N.L.)	1998
49	Babe Ruth, New York (A.L.)	1930
49	Lou Gehrig, New York (A.L.)	1934
49	Lou Gehrig, New York (A.L.)	1936
49	Ted Kluszewski, Cincinnati (N.L.)	1954
49	Willie Mays, San Francisco (N.L.)	1962
49	Harmon Killebrew, Minnesota (A.L.)	1964
49	Frank Robinson, Baltimore (A.L.)	1966
49	Harmon Killebrew, Minnesota (A.L.)	1969
49	Mark McGwire, Oakland (A.L.)	1987
49	Andre Dawson, Chicago (N.L.)	1987
49	Ken Griffey, Jr., Seattle (A.L.)	1996
49	Larry Walker, Colorado (N.L.)	1997
49	Albert Belle, Chicago (A.L.)	1998
48	Jimmy Foxx, Philadelphia (A.L.)	1933
48	Harmon Killebrew, Minnesota (A.L.)	1962
48	Frank Howard, Washington (A.L.)	1969
48	Willie Stargell, Pittsburgh (N.L.)	1971
48	Dave Kingman, Chicago (N.L.)	1979
48	Mike Schmidt, Philadelphia (N.L.)	1980
48	Albert Belle, Cleveland (A.L.)	1996
47	Babe Ruth, New York (A.L.)	1926
47	Ralph Kiner, Pittsburgh (N.L.)	1950
47	Ed Mathews, Milwaukee (N.L.)	1953
47	Ernie Banks, Chicago (N.L.)	1958
47	Willie Mays, San Francisco (N.L.)	1964
47	Henry Aaron, Atlanta (N.L.)	1971
47	Reggie Jackson, Oakland (A.L.)	1969
47	George Bell, Toronto (A.L.)	1987
47	Kevin Mitchell, San Francisco (N.L.)	1989
47	Andres Galarraga, Colorado (N.L.)	1996
47	Juan Gonzalez, Texas (A.L.)	1996
46	Babe Ruth, New York (A.L.)	1924
46	Babe Ruth, New York, (A.L.)	1929
46	Babe Ruth, New York (A.L.)	1931
46	Lou Gehrig, New York (A.L.)	1931
46	Joe DiMaggio, New York (A.L.)	1937
46	Ed Mathews, Milwaukee (N.L.)	1959
46	Orlando Cepeda, San Francisco (N.L.)	1961
46	Jim Rice, Boston (A.L.)	1978
46	Juan Gonzalez, Texas (A.L.)	1993
46	Barry Bonds, San Francisco (N.L.)	1993
46	Jose Canseco, Toronto (A.L.)	1998
46	Vinnie Castilla, Colorado (N.L.)	1998
45	Harmon Killebrew, Minnesota (A.L.)	1963
45	Willie McCovey, San Francisco (N.L.)	1969
45	Johnny Bench, Cincinnati (N.L.)	1970
45	Gorman Thomas, Milwaukee (A.L.)	1979
45	Henry Aaron, Milwaukee (N.L.)	1962
45	Ken Griffey, Jr., Seattle (A.L.)	1993
45	Juan Gonzalez, Texas (A.L.)	1998
45	Manny Ramirez, Cleveland (A.L.)	1998

MAJOR LEAGUE BASEBALL—1998

AMERICAN LEAGUE FINAL STANDINGS—1998

EASTERN DIVISION

Team	W	L	Pct	GB
New York Yankees	114	48	.704	—
Boston Red Sox	92	70	.568	22
Toronto Blue Jays	88	74	.543	26
Baltimore Orioles	79	83	.488	35
Tampa Bay Devil Rays	63	99	.389	51

CENTRAL DIVISION

Team	W	L	Pct	GB
Cleveland Indians	89	73	.549	—
Chicago White Sox	80	82	.494	9
Kansas City Royals	72	89	.447	16½
Minnesota Twins	70	92	.432	19
Detroit Tigers	65	97	.401	24

WESTERN DIVISION

Team	W	L	Pct	GB
Texas Rangers	88	74	.543	—
Anaheim Angels	85	77	.525	3
Seattle Mariners	76	85	.472	11½
Oakland Athletics	74	88	.457	14

AMERICAN LEAGUE LEADERS—1998

Batting—Bernie Williams, New York	.339
Home runs—Ken Griffey, Jr., Seattle	56
Runs batted in—Juan Gonzalez, Texas	157
Stolen bases—Rickey Henderson, Oakland	66
Slugging percentage—Albert Belle, Chicago	.655
Runs scored—Derek Jeter, New York	127
Walks—Rickey Henderson, Oakland	118
Doubles—Juan Gonzalez, Texas	50
Triples—Jose Offerman, Kansas City	13
Total bases—Albert Belle, Chicago	399

A.L. Pitching

Wins—Roger Clemens, Toronto	20
Earned run average—Roger Clemens, Toronto	2.65
Saves—Tom Gordon, Boston	46
Innings pitched—Scott Erickson, Baltimore	251.1
Strikeouts—Roger Clemens, Toronto	271
Complete games—Scott Erickson, Baltimore	11
Shutouts—David Wells, New York	5

American League Division Series

Cleveland Indians defeat Boston Red Sox, 3 games to 1
- Sept. 29—Boston 11, CLEVELAND 3
- Sept. 30—CLEVELAND 9, Boston 5
- Oct. 2—Cleveland 4, BOSTON 3
- Oct. 3—Cleveland 2, BOSTON 1

New York Yankees defeat Texas Rangers, 3 games to 0
- Sept. 29—NEW YORK 2, Texas 0
- Sept. 30—NEW YORK 3, Texas 1
- Oct. 2—New York 4, TEXAS 0

(HOME TEAM IN CAPS.)

NATIONAL LEAGUE FINAL STANDINGS—1998

EASTERN DIVISION

Team	W	L	Pct	GB
Atlanta Braves	106	56	.654	—
New York Mets	88	74	.543	18
Philadelphia Phillies	75	87	.463	31
Montreal Expos	65	97	.401	41
Florida Marlins	54	108	.333	52

CENTRAL DIVISION

Team	W	L	Pct	GB
Houston Astros	102	60	.630	—
Chicago Cubs	90	73	.552	12½
St. Louis Cardinals	83	79	.512	19
Cincinnati Reds	77	85	.475	25
Milwaukee Brewers	74	88	.457	28
Pittsburgh Pirates	69	93	.426	33

WESTERN DIVISION

Team	W	L	Pct	GB
San Diego Padres	98	64	.605	—
San Francisco Giants	89	74	.546	9½
Los Angeles Dodgers	83	79	.512	15
Colorado Rockies	77	85	.475	21
Arizona Diamondbacks	65	97	.401	33

NATIONAL LEAGUE LEADERS—1998

Batting—Larry Walker, Colorado	.363
Home runs—Mark McGwire, St. Louis	70
Runs batted in—Sammy Sosa, Chicago	158
Stolen bases—Tony Womack, Pittsburgh	58
Slugging percentage—Mark McGwire, St. Louis	.752
Runs scored—Sammy Sosa, Chicago	134
Hits—Dante Bichette, Colorado	219
Walks—Mark McGwire, St. Louis	162
Doubles—Craig Biggio, Houston	51
Triples—Dave Dellucci, Arizona	12
Total bases—Sammy Sosa, Chicago	416

N.L. Pitching

Wins—Tom Glavine, Atlanta	20
Earned run average—Greg Maddux, Atlanta	2.22
Saves—Trevor Hoffman, San Diego	53
Innings pitched—Curt Schilling, Philadelphia	268.2
Strikeouts—Curt Schilling, Philadelphia	300
Complete games—Curt Schilling, Philadelphia	15
Shutouts—Greg Maddux, Atlanta	5

National League Division Series

Atlanta Braves defeat Chicago Cubs, 3 games to 0
- Sept. 30—ATLANTA 7, Chicago 1
- Oct. 1—ATLANTA 2, Chicago 1 (10 innings)
- Oct. 3—Atlanta 6, CHICAGO 2

San Diego Padres defeat Houston Astros, 3 games to 1
- Sept. 29—San Diego 2, HOUSTON 1
- Oct. 1—HOUSTON 5, San Diego 4
- Oct. 3—SAN DIEGO 2, Houston 1
- Oct.4—SAN DIEGO 6, Houston 1

(HOME TEAM IN CAPS.)

AMERICAN LEAGUE AVERAGES—1998

Team Batting

	Avg	AB	R	H	HR	RBI
Texas	.289	5,672	940	1,637	201	894
New York	.288	5,463	965	1,625	207	907
Boston	.280	5,601	876	1,568	205	827
Seattle	.276	5,628	859	1,553	234	822
Baltimore	.273	5,565	817	1,520	214	783
Anaheim	.272	5,630	787	1,530	147	739
Cleveland	.272	5,616	850	1,530	198	811
Chicago	.271	5,585	861	1,516	198	806
Minnesota	.266	5,641	734	1,499	115	691
Toronto	.266	5,580	816	1,482	221	776
Detroit	.264	5,664	722	1,494	165	691
Kansas City	.263	5,543	715	1,459	134	686
Tampa Bay	.261	5,559	620	1,450	111	579
Oakland	.257	5,490	803	1,413	149	755

Individual Batting
(Based on 300 plate appearances.)

	Avg	AB	R	H	HR	RBI
Bernie Williams, New York	.339	499	101	169	26	97
Mo Vaughn, Boston	.337	609	107	205	40	115
Albert Belle, Chicago	.328	609	113	200	49	152
Eric Davis, Baltimore	.327	452	81	148	28	89
Derek Jeter, New York	.324	626	127	203	19	84
Nomar Garciaparra, Boston	.323	604	111	195	35	122
Edgar Martinez, Seattle	.322	556	86	179	29	102
Ivan Rodriguez, Texas	.321	579	88	186	21	91
Tony Fernandez, Toronto	.321	486	71	156	9	72
Juan Gonzalez, Texas	.318	606	110	193	45	157
Paul O'Neill, New York	.317	602	95	191	24	116
Todd Walker, Minnesota	.316	528	85	167	12	62
Jose Offerman, Kansas City	.315	607	102	191	7	66
Alex Rodriguez, Seattle	.310	686	123	213	42	124
Hal Morris, Kansas City	.309	472	50	146	1	40
Jim Edmonds, Anaheim	.307	599	115	184	25	91
Rusty Greer, Texas	.306	598	107	183	16	108
Mike Caruso, Chicago	.306	523	81	160	5	55
David Segui, Seattle	.305	522	79	159	19	84
Will Clark, Texas	.305	554	98	169	23	102

Individual Pitching
(Based on 10 decisions.)

	W	L	ERA	IP	H	BB	SO
Roger Clemens, Toronto	20	6	2.65	234.2	169	88	271
Pedro Martinez, Boston	19	7	2.89	233.2	188	67	251
Kenny Rogers, Oakland	16	8	3.17	238.2	215	67	138
Chuck Finley, Anaheim	11	9	3.39	223.1	210	109	212
David Wells, New York	18	4	3.49	214.1	195	29	163
Mike Mussina, Baltimore	13	10	3.49	206.1	189	41	175
Jamie Moyer, Seattle	15	9	3.53	234.1	234	42	158
David Cone, New York	20	7	3.55	207.2	186	59	209
Rolando Arrojo, Tampa Bay	14	12	3.56	202.0	195	65	152
Bartolo Colon, Cleveland	14	9	3.71	204.0	205	79	158
Brian Moehler, Detroit	14	13	3.90	221.1	220	56	123
Bret Saberhagen, Boston	15	8	3.96	175.0	181	29	100
Jeff Fassero, Seattle	13	12	3.97	224.2	223	66	176
Scott Erickson, Baltimore	16	13	4.01	251.1	284	69	186
Omar Olivares, Anaheim	9	9	4.03	183.0	189	91	112
Justin Thompson, Detroit	11	15	4.05	222.0	227	79	149
Hideki Irabu, New York	13	9	4.06	173.0	148	76	126
Dave Burba, Cleveland	15	10	4.11	203.2	210	69	132
Tony Saunders, Tampa Bay	6	15	4.12	192.1	191	111	172
Aaron Sele, Texas	19	11	4.23	212.2	239	84	167

Team Pitching

	W	ERA	SHO	SV	IP	H	HR
New York	114	3.82	16	48	1,456.2	1,357	156
Boston	92	4.19	8	53	1,436.0	1,406	168
Toronto	88	4.29	11	47	1,465.0	1,443	169
Tampa Bay	63	4.35	8	28	1,443.0	1,425	171
Cleveland	89	4.45	4	47	1,460.0	1,552	171
Anaheim	85	4.49	5	52	1,444.0	1,481	164
Baltimore	79	4.73	10	37	1,431.1	1,505	169
Minnesota	70	4.76	9	42	1,447.2	1,622	180
Oakland	74	4.83	4	39	1,434.0	1,555	179
Detroit	65	4.93	4	32	1,446.1	1,551	185
Seattle	76	4.95	7	31	1,424.1	1,530	196
Texas	88	5.00	8	46	1,431.1	1,624	164
Kansas City	72	5.16	7	46	1,436.1	1,590	196
Chicago	80	5.24	4	42	1,438.2	1,569	211

NATIONAL LEAGUE AVERAGES—1998

Team Batting

	Avg	AB	R	H	HR	RBI
Colorado	.291	5,632	826	1,640	183	791
Houston	.280	5,641	874	1,578	166	818
San Francisco	.274	5,628	845	1,540	161	800
Atlanta	.272	5,484	826	1,489	215	794
Chicago	.264	5,649	831	1,494	212	788
Philadelphia	.264	5,617	713	1,482	126	672
Cincinnati	.262	5,496	750	1,441	138	723
Milwaukee	.260	5,541	707	1,439	152	673
New York	.259	5,510	706	1,425	136	671
St. Louis	.258	5,593	810	1,444	223	781
Pittsburgh	.254	5,493	650	1,395	107	613
San Diego	.253	5,490	749	1,390	167	715
Los Angeles	.252	5,461	669	1,374	159	630
Montreal	.249	5,417	644	1,348	147	602
Florida	.248	5,558	667	1,381	114	621
Arizona	.246	5,491	665	1,353	159	621

Individual Batting
(Based on 300 plate appearances.)

	Avg	AB	R	H	HR	RBI
Larry Walker, Colorado	.363	454	113	165	23	67
John Olerud, New York	.354	557	91	197	22	93
Dante Bichette, Colorado	.331	662	97	219	22	122
Mike Piazza, New York	.328	561	88	184	32	111
Jason Kendall, Pittsburgh	.327	535	95	175	12	75
Craig Biggio, Houston	.325	646	123	210	20	88
Vladimir Guerrero, Montreal	.324	623	108	202	38	109
Jeff Cirillo, Milwaukee	.321	604	97	194	14	68
Tony Gwynn, San Diego	.321	461	65	148	16	69
Vinny Castilla, Colorado	.319	645	108	206	46	144
Brian Jordan, St. Louis	.316	564	100	178	25	91
Todd Helton, Colorado	.315	530	78	167	25	97
Derek Bell, Houston	.314	630	111	198	22	108
Chipper Jones, Atlanta	.313	601	123	188	34	107
Bobby Abreu, Philadelphia	.312	497	68	155	17	74
Moises Alou, Houston	.312	584	104	182	38	124
Fernando Vina, Milwaukee	.311	637	101	198	7	45
Dmitri Young, Cincinnati	.310	536	81	166	14	83
Barry Larkin, Cincinnati	.409	538	93	166	17	72
Mark Grace, Chicago	.309	595	92	184	17	89

Individual Pitching
(Based on 10 decisions.)

	W	L	ERA	IP	H	BB	SO
Greg Maddux, Atlanta	18	9	2.22	251.0	201	45	204
Kevin Brown, San Diego	18	7	2.38	257.0	225	49	257
Tom Glavine, Atlanta	20	6	2.47	229.1	202	74	157
Al Leiter, New York	17	6	2.47	193.0	151	71	174
Omar Daal, Arizona	8	12	2.88	162.2	146	51	132
John Smoltz, Atlanta	17	3	2.90	167.2	145	44	173
Dustin Hermanson, Montreal	14	11	3.13	187.0	163	56	154
Pete Harnisch, Cincinnati	14	7	3.1	209.0	176	64	157
Curt Schilling, Philadelphia	15	14	3.25	268.2	236	61	300
Francisco Cordova, Pittsburgh	13	14	3.31	220.1	204	69	157
Andy Ashby, San Diego	17	9	3.34	226.2	223	58	151
Mike Hampton, Houston	11	7	3.36	211.2	227	81	137
Kerry Wood, Chicago	13	6	3.40	166.2	117	85	233
Rick Reed, New York	16	11	3.48	212.1	208	29	153
Shane Reynolds, Houston	19	8	3.51	233.1	257	53	209
Denny Neagle, Atlanta	16	11	3.55	210.1	196	60	165
Carlos Perez, Los Angeles	11	14	3.59	241.0	244	63	128
Jose Lima, Houston	16	8	3.70	233.1	229	32	169
Chan Ho Park, Los Angeles	15	9	3.71	220.2	199	97	191
Sean Bergman, Houston	12	9	3.72	172.0	183	42	100

Team Pitching

	W	ERA	SHO	SV	IP	H	HR
Atlanta	106	3.25	23	45	1,438.2	1,291	117
Houston	102	3.50	11	44	1,471.1	1,435	147
San Diego	98	3.63	11	59	1,454.2	1,384	139
New York	88	3.77	16	46	1,458.0	1,381	152
Los Angeles	83	3.81	10	47	1,447.1	1,332	135
Pittsburgh	69	3.91	10	41	1,449.0	1,433	147
San Francisco	89	4.19	6	44	1,477.0	1,457	171
St. Louis	83	4.32	10	44	1,469.2	1,513	151
Montreal	65	4.39	5	39	1,427.0	1,448	156
Cincinnati	77	4.44	8	42	1,441.1	1,400	170
Chicago	90	4.50	7	56	1,477.1	1,528	180
Milwaukee	74	4.63	2	39	1,451.0	1,538	188
Arizona	65	4.64	6	37	1,432.1	1,463	188
Philadelphia	75	4.64	11	32	1,463.0	1,476	188
Colorado	77	5.00	5	36	1,432.2	1,583	174
Florida	54	5.20	3	24	1,449.2	1,617	182

AMERICAN LEAGUE CHAMPIONSHIP SERIES—1998

New York Yankees win series, 4 games to 2

1st Game, at New York, Oct. 6, 1998

Cleveland	000	000	002	—	2	5	0
New York	500	001	10x	—	7	11	0

Pitchers—Cleveland: Wright, Ogea, Poole, Reed, Shuey. New York: Wells, Nelson. Winner: Wells. Loser: Wright. Attendance: 57,138.

2nd Game, at New York, Oct. 7, 1998

Cleveland	000	100	000	003	4	7	1
New York	000	000	100	000	1	7	1

Pitchers—Cleveland: Nagy, Reed, Poole, Shuey, Assenmacher, Burba, Jackson. New York: Cone, Rivera, Stanton, Nelson, Lloyd. Winner: Burba. Loser: Nelson. Attendance: 57,128.

3rd Game, at Cleveland, Oct. 9, 1998

New York	100	000	000	—	1	4	0
Cleveland	020	040	00x	—	6	12	0

Pitchers—New York: Pettitte, Mendoza, Stanton. Cleveland: Colon. Winner: Colon. Loser: Pettitte. Attendance: 44,904.

4th Game, at Cleveland, Oct. 10, 1998

New York	100	200	001	—	4	4	0
Cleveland	000	000	000	—	0	4	3

Pitchers—New York: Hernandez, Stanton, Rivera. Cleveland: Gooden, Poole, Burba, Shuey. Winner: Hernandez. Loser: Gooden. Attendance: 44,981.

5th Game, at Cleveland, Oct. 11, 1998

New York	310	100	000	—	5	6	0
Cleveland	200	001	000	—	3	8	0

Pitchers—New York: Wells, Nelson, Rivera. Cleveland: Ogea, Wright, Reed, Assenmacher, Shuey. Winner: Wells. Loser: Ogea. Attendance: 44,966.

6th Game, at New York, Oct. 13, 1998

Cleveland	000	050	000	—	5	8	3
New York	213	003	00x	—	9	11	1

Pitchers—Cleveland: Nagy, Burba, Poole, Shuey, Assenmacher. New York: Cone, Mendoza, Rivera. Winner: Cone. Loser: Nagy. Attendance: 57,142.

Series MVP—David Wells

NATIONAL LEAGUE CHAMPIONSHIP SERIES—1998

San Diego Padres win series, 4 games to 2

1st Game, at Atlanta, Oct. 7, 1998

San Diego	000	001	002	—	3	11	0
Atlanta	000	000	000	—	0	3	1

Pitchers—San Diego: Brown. Atlanta: Glavine, Rocker, Seanez, O. Perez, Ligtenberg. Winner: Brown. Loser: Glavine. Attendance: 43,083.

2nd Game, at Atlanta, Oct. 8, 1998

San Diego	000	010	010	1	3	7	0
Atlanta	001	000	001	0	2	8	3

Pitchers—San Diego: Ashby, R. Myers, Miceli, Hoffman, Wall. Atlanta: Smoltz, Rocker, Martinez, Ligtenberg. Winner: Hoffman. Loser: Ligtenberg. Attendance: 42,117.

3rd Game, at San Diego, Oct. 10, 1998

Atlanta	001	000	000	—	1	8	2
San Diego	000	020	02x	—	4	7	0

Pitchers—Atlanta: Maddux, Martinez, Rocker, Seanez. San Diego: Hitchcock, Wall, Miceli, R. Myers, Hoffman. Winner: Maddux. Loser: Hitchcock. Attendance: 62,799.

4th Game, at San Diego, Oct. 11, 1998

Atlanta	000	101	600	—	8	12	0
San Diego	002	001	000	—	3	8	0

Pitchers—Atlanta: Neagle, Martinez, Rocker, O. Perez, Seanez, Ligtenberg. San Diego: Hamilton, R. Myers, Miceli, Boehringer, Langston. Winner: Martinez. Loser: Hamilton. Attendance: 65,042.

5th Game, at San Diego, Oct. 12, 1998

Atlanta	000	101	050	—	7	14	1
San Diego	200	002	002	—	6	10	1

Pitchers—Atlanta: Smoltz, Rocker, Seanez, Ligtenberg, Maddux. San Diego: Ashby, Langston, Brown, Wall, Boehringer, R. Myers. Winner: Rocker. Loser: Brown. Attendance: 58,988.

6th Game, at Atlanta, Oct. 14, 1998

San Diego	000	005	000	—	5	10	0
Atlanta	000	000	000	—	0	2	1

Pitchers—San Diego: Hitchcock, Boehringer, Langston, Hamilton, Hoffman. Atlanta: Glavine, Rocker, Martinez, Neagle. Winner: Hitchcock. Loser: Glavine. Attendance: 50,988.

Series MVP—Sterling Hitchcock

WORLD SERIES—1998

New York Yankees win series, 4 games to 0

1st Game—New York, Oct. 17
New York 9, San Diego 6

SAN DIEGO (N.L.)	AB	R	H	RBI	NEW YORK (A.L.)	AB	R	H	RBI
Veras 2b	4	1	1	0	Knoblauch 2b	4	1	2	3
Gwynn rf	4	1	3	2	Jeter ss	4	1	1	0
Vaughn lf	4	3	2	3	O'Neill rf	5	0	0	0
Caminiti 3b	3	0	0	0	Williams cf	4	1	0	0
Leyritz dh	4	0	0	0	Davis dh	3	2	1	0
Joyner 1b	3	0	0	0	Martinez 1b	3	2	1	0
Finley cf	4	0	1	0	Brosius 3b	4	0	1	0
Hernandez c	3	0	0	0	Posada c	3	1	1	0
G. Myers ph	1	0	0	0	Ledee lf	3	1	2	2
Gomez ss	3	1	1	0					
Vander Wal ph	1	0	0	0					
Totals	**34**	**6**	**8**	**5**	**Totals**	**33**	**9**	**9**	**9**

San Diego	002	030	010	—	6	8	1
New York	020	000	70x	—	9	9	1

E—San Diego: Vaughn. New York: Knoblauch. LOB—San Diego 4, New York 7. 2B—San Diego: Finley. New York: Ledee. HR—San Diego: Vaughn 2 (3rd inning off Wells, 5th inning off Wells), Gwynn (5th inning off Wells). New York: Knoblauch (7th inning off Wall), Martinez (7th inning off Langston). RBI—Vaughn 3, Gwynn 2, Ledee 2, Knoblauch 3, Martinez 4. GIDP—San Diego: Vaughn. DP—2 New York (Knoblauch-Martinez, Martinez).

	IP	H	R	ER	BB	SO	HR	ERA
San Diego								
Brown	6⅓	6	4	4	3	5	0	5.68
Wall (L, 0-1)	0	2	2	2	0	0	1	0.00
Langston	⅔	1	3	3	2	0	1	40.50
Boehringer	⅓	0	0	0	1	1	0	0.00
R. Myers	⅔	0	0	0	0	2	0	0.00
New York								
Wells (W, 1-0)	7	7	5	5	2	4	3	6.43
Nelson	⅔	1	1	0	1	1	0	0.00
Rivera (S, 1)	1⅓	0	0	0	0	2	0	0.00

WP—Langston. Ibb—Williams (by Langston). HBP—Knoblauch (by Boehringer). Umpires—Home: Rich Garcia, 1B: Mark Hirschbeck, 2B: Dale Scott, 3B: Dana Demuth, LF: Tim Tschida, RF: Jerry Crawford. T—3:29. Att.—56,712.

2nd Game—New York, Oct. 18
New York 9, San Diego 3

SAN DIEGO (N.L.)	AB	R	H	RBI	NEW YORK (A.L.)	AB	R	H	RBI
Veras 2b	5	0	1	1	Knoblauch 2b	3	2	2	0
Gwynn rf	4	0	1	0	Jeter ss	5	1	2	1
Vaughn dh	4	0	0	0	O'Neill rf	5	1	1	0
Caminiti 3b	5	1	1	0	Williams cf	4	1	1	2
Joyner 1b	2	0	0	0	Davis dh	3	1	1	1
Leyritz ph-1b	1	0	0	0	Bush pr-dh	0	0	0	0
Finley cf	4	0	0	0	Martinez 1b	5	1	3	0
Vander Wal lf	3	0	2	0	Brosius 3b	5	1	3	1
R Rivera ph-lf	1	1	1	1	Posada c	4	1	1	2
G. Myers c	3	0	0	0	Ledee lf	3	0	2	1
Hernandez ph-c	1	0	1	0					
Gomez ss	3	1	2	0					
Sweeney ph	1	0	1	1					
Sheets ss	0	0	0	0					
Totals	**37**	**3**	**10**	**3**	**Totals**	**37**	**9**	**16**	**8**

San Diego	000	010	020	—	3	10	1
New York	331	020	00x	—	9	16	0

LOB—San Diego 10, New York 11. 2B—San Diego: Veras, Vander Wal, Caminiti, R. Rivera. New York: Ledee. 3B—San Diego: Gomez. HR—New York: Williams (2nd inning off Ashby), Posada (5th inning off Boehringer). RBI—San Diego: Veras, R. Rivera, Sweeney. New York: Davis, Brosius, Jeter, Williams 2, Ledee, Posada 2. SB—New York: Knoblauch. CS—New York: Ledee. GIDP—San Diego: Posada. New York: Brosius, Jeter. E—San Diego: Caminiti. DP—3 San Diego (Veras-Gomez-Joyner, Veras-Joyner, Wall-Gomez-Joyner).

	IP	H	R	ER	BB	SO	HR	ERA
San Diego								
Ashby (L, 0–1)	2⅔	10	7	4	1	1	1	13.50
Boehringer	1⅔	4	2	2	1	2	1	9.00
Wall	2⅔	1	0	0	3	1	0	6.75
Miceli	1	1	0	0	2	1	0	0.00
New York								
Hernandez (W, 1–0)	7	6	1	1	3	7	0	1.29
Stanton	⅔	3	2	2	0	1	0	27.00
Nelson	1⅓	1	0	0	0	2	0	0.00

Umpires—Home: Mark Hirschbeck. 1B: Dale Scott. 2B: Dana Demuth. 3B: Tim Tschida. LF: Jerry Crawford. RF: Rich Garcia. T—3:31. Att.—56,692.

3rd Game—San Diego, Oct. 20
New York 5, San Diego 4

NEW YORK (A.L.)	AB	R	H	RBI	SAN DIEGO (N.L.)	AB	R	H	RBI
Knoblauch 2b	4	0	1	0	Veras 2b	3	2	1	0
Jeter ss	4	0	1	0	Gwynn rf	4	1	2	1
O'Neill rf	4	1	1	0	R. Rivera pr-rf	0	0	0	0
Williams cf	4	0	0	0	Vaughn lf	3	0	0	1
Martinez 1b	3	1	0	0	Caminiti 3b	2	0	0	1
Brosius 3b	4	2	3	4	Joyner 1b	3	0	0	0
Spencer lf	3	1	1	0	Finley cf	4	0	0	0
Ledee ph-lf	1	0	0	0	Leyritz c	2	0	0	0
Girardi c	2	0	0	0	C. Hernandez c	2	0	1	0
Posada ph-c	2	0	1	0	Vander Wal pr	0	0	0	0
Cone p	2	0	1	0	Gomez ss	3	0	1	0
Davis ph	1	0	0	1	Hoffman p	0	0	0	0
Bush pr	0	0	0	0	Sweeney ph	1	0	1	0
Lloyd p	0	0	0	0	Hitchcock p	2	1	1	0
Mendoza p	1	0	0	0	Hamilton p	0	0	0	0
M. Rivera p	0	0	0	0	R. Myers p	0	0	0	0
					Sheets ss	2	0	0	0
Totals	**35**	**5**	**9**	**5**	**Totals**	**31**	**4**	**7**	**3**

New York	000	000	230	—	5	9	1
San Diego	000	003	010	—	4	7	1

E—New York: O'Neill. San Diego: Caminiti. LOB—New York: 7, San Diego: 5. 2B—New York: Spencer. San Diego: Veras. HR—New York: Brosius 2 (7th inning off Hitchcock, 8th inning off Hoffman). SF—San Diego: Caminiti, Vaughn. RBI: New York: Brosius 4, Davis. San Diego: Gwynn, Caminiti, Vaughn. GIDP—New York: O'Neill. PB: San Diego: Leyritz. DP—San Diego 2 (Gomez-Veras-Joyner, Gomez-Veras).

	IP	H	R	ER	BB	SO	HR	ERA
New York								
Cone	6	2	3	2	3	4	0	3.00
Lloyd	⅓	0	0	0	0	0	0	0.00
Mendoza (W, 1–0)	1	2	1	1	0	1	0	9.00
M. Rivera (S, 2)	1⅔	3	0	0	0	2	0	0.00
San Diego								
Hitchcock	6	7	2	1	1	7	1	1.50
Hamilton (H, 1)	1	0	0	0	1	1	0	0.00
R. Myers (H, 1)	0	0	1	1	1	0	0	13.50
Hoffman (L, 0–1)	2	2	2	2	1	0	1	9.00

Umpires—Home: Dale Scott. 1B: Dana Demuth. 2B: Tim Tschida. 3B: Jerry Crawford. LF: Rich Garcia. RF: Mark Hirschbeck. T—3:14. Att.—64,667.

4th Game—San Diego, Oct. 21
New York 3, San Diego 0

NEW YORK (A.L.)	AB	R	H	RBI	SAN DIEGO (N.L.)	AB	R	H	RBI
Knoblauch 2b	5	0	1	0	Veras 2b	3	0	0	0
Jeter ss	4	2	2	0	Gwynn rf	4	0	2	0
O'Neill rf	5	1	2	0	Vaughn lf	4	0	0	0
Williams cf	4	0	0	1	Caminiti 3b	4	0	1	0
Martinez 1b	2	0	1	0	Leyritz 1b	3	0	0	0
Brosius 3b	4	0	1	1	R. Rivera cf	4	0	3	0
Ledee lf	3	0	2	1	C. Hernandez c	4	0	0	0
Girardi c	4	0	0	0	Gomez ss	2	0	0	0
Pettitte p	2	0	0	0	Sweeney ph	1	0	0	0
Nelson p	0	0	0	0	Brown p	2	0	1	0
M. Rivera p	1	0	0	0	Vander Wal ph	1	0	0	0
					Miceli p	0	0	0	0
					R. Myers p	0	0	0	0
Totals	**34**	**3**	**9**	**3**	**Totals**	**32**	**0**	**7**	**0**

					R	H	E
New York	000	001	020	—	3	9	0
San Diego	000	000	000	—	0	7	0

LOB—New York 9. San Diego 8. 2B—New York: Ledee, O'Neill. San Diego: R. Rivera. S—New York: Pettitte. SF: New York: Ledee. RBI—New York: Williams, Brosius, Ledee. GIDP—San Diego: Caminiti, C. Hernandez. DP—New York: 2 (Knoblauch-Jeter-Martinez, Jeter-Knoblauch-Martinez).

	IP	H	R	ER	BB	SO	HR	ERA
New York								
Pettitte (W, 1–0)	7⅓	5	0	0	3	4	0	0.00
Nelson (H, 1)	⅓	0	0	0	0	1	0	0.00
M. Rivera (S, 3)	1⅓	2	0	0	0	0	0	0.00
San Diego								
Brown (L, 0–1)	8	8	3	3	3	8	0	4.40
Miceli	⅔	1	0	0	0	0	0	0.00
R. Myers	⅓	0	0	0	0	0	0	9.00

Ibb: Martinez 2 (by Brown 2). Umpires—Home: Dana Demuth. 1B: Tim Tschida. 2B: Jerry Crawford. 3B: Rich Garcia. LF: Mark Hirschbeck. RF: Dale Scott. T—2:58. Att—65,427.

Series MVP—Scott Brosius.

1998 GOLD GLOVE AWARDS

Pitchers
National League: Greg Maddux, Atlanta
American League: Mike Mussina, Baltimore

Catchers
National League: Charles Johnson, Los Angeles
American League: Ivan Rodriguez, Texas

First Basemen
National League: J. T. Snow, San Francisco
American League: Rafael Palmeiro, Baltimore

Second Basemen
National League: Bret Boone, Cincinnati
American League: Roberto Alomar, Baltimore

Third Basemen
National League: Scott Rolen, Philadelphia
American League: Robin Ventura, Chicago

Shortstop
National League: Rey Ordonez, New York
American League: Omar Vizquel, Cleveland

Outfielders
National League: Barry Bonds, San Francisco; Andruw Jones, Atlanta; Larry Walker, Colorado
American League: Ken Griffey, Jr., Seattle; Jim Edmonds, Anaheim; Bernie Williams; New York

Extreme Sports

1998 EXTREME GAMES

(San Diego, Calif., June 19–28, 1998)

MEN

Big-air snowboarding: Kevin Jones
Skateboarding: Andy Macdonald (vert), Tony Hawk and Andy Macdonald (vert doubles), Rodil de Araujo (street)
Aggressive in-line: Cesar Mora (vert), Jonathon Bergeron (street), Paul Malina, Sam Fogarty, and Viorel Popa (triples)
Downhill in-line: Patrick Naylor
Sportsclimbing: Vladimir Netsvetaev (speed), Christian Core (difficulty)
Bicycle stunt riding: Dave Mirra (vert), Dave Mirra (street), Trevor Meyer (flatland), Brian Foster (dirt jumping), Dave Mirra and Dennis McCoy (vert doubles)
Skysurfing: Valery Rozov and Cliff Burch
Street luge: Rat Sult (super mass), Rat Sult (mass), Biker Sherlock (dual)
Watersports: Darin Shapiro (wakeboard), Peter Fleck (barefoot jumping)

WOMEN

Big-air snowboarding: Janet Matthews
Aggressive in-line: Fabiola da Silva (vert), Jenny Curry (street)
Downhill in-line: Julie Brandt
Sportsclimbing: Elena Ovchinnikova (speed), Katie Brown (difficulty)
Watersports: Andrea Gaytan (wakeboard)

Bicycling

TOUR DE FRANCE–1998

(July 11–Aug. 2, 1998)

1. Marco Pantani, Italy—92 hours, 49 minutes, 46 seconds
2. Jan Ullrich, Germany—03:21 behind
3. Bobby Julich, United States—04:08 behind
4. Christophe Rinero, France—09:16 behind
5. Michaël Boogerd, Netherlands—11:26 behind
6. Jean-Cyril Robin, France—14:57 behind
7. Roland Meier, Switzerland—15:13 behind
8. Daniele Nardello, Italy—16:07 behind
9. Giuseppe Di Grande, Italy—17:35 behind
10. Axel Merckx, Belgium—17:39 behind

Soccer

The early history of the sport is uncertain. A form of the game in which a leather ball was dribbled was played in China as early as the 4th century B.C.E. The Romans played a variation of soccer which eventually spread throughout Europe. British schools and universities played soccer (known as football) during the 1800s, however, each school used different sets of rules and the number of players varied. This difficulty was corrected on Oct. 26, 1863, when the Football Association (FA) was formed in London for the purpose of unifying the rules of the game.

The Federation of International Football Associations (FIFA) was created in 1913 as a world governing body to coordinate all of the national associations in the world. The FIFA held the first World Cup Championship tournament in 1930 in Montevideo, Uruguay. Today, soccer is the world's most popular sport.

WORLD CUP

1930 Uruguay
1934 Italy
1938 Italy
1942 No competition
1946 No competition
1950 Uruguay
1954 West Germany
1958 Brazil
1962 Brazil
1966 England
1970 Brazil
1974 West Germany
1978 Argentina
1982 Italy
1986 Argentina
1990 West Germany
1994 Brazil
1998 France

WORLD CUP—1998

FINAL GROUP STANDINGS

	W	L	T	Pts	GF	GA
Group A						
x-Brazil	2	1	0	6	6	3
x-Norway	1	0	2	5	5	4
Morocco	1	1	1	4	5	5
Scotland	0	2	1	1	2	6
Group B						
x-Italy	2	0	1	7	7	3
x-Chile	0	0	3	3	4	4
Austria	0	1	2	2	3	4
Cameroon	0	1	2	2	2	5
Group C						
x-France	3	0	0	9	9	1
x-Denmark	1	1	1	4	3	3
South Africa	0	1	2	2	3	6
Saudi Arabia	0	2	1	1	2	7
Group D						
x-Nigeria	2	1	0	6	5	5
x-Paraguay	1	0	2	5	3	1
Spain	1	1	1	4	8	4
Bulgaria	0	2	1	1	1	7
Group E						
x-Netherlands	1	0	2	5	7	2
x-Mexico	1	0	2	5	7	5
Belgium	0	0	3	3	3	3
South Korea	0	2	1	1	2	9
Group F						
x-Germany	2	0	1	7	6	2
x-Yugoslavia	2	0	1	7	4	2
Iran	1	2	0	3	2	4
United States	0	3	0	0	1	5
Group G						
x-Romania	2	0	1	7	4	2
x-England	2	1	0	6	5	2
Colombia	1	2	0	3	1	3
Tunisia	0	2	1	1	1	4
Group H						
x-Argentina	3	0	0	9	7	0
x-Croatia	2	1	0	6	4	2
Jamaica	1	2	0	3	3	9
Japan	0	3	0	0	1	4

x-Advance to next round.

QUARTERFINALS
Denmark 2, Brazil 3
Argentina 1, Netherlands 2
France 0, Italy 0 (France won 4–3 in shootout)
Croatia 3, Germany 0

SEMIFINALS
Netherlands 1, Brazil 1 (Brazil won 4–2 in shootout)
Croatia 1, France 2

THIRD PLACE
Croatia 2, Netherlands 1

CHAMPIONSHIP
France 3, Brazil 0

WORLD CUP

All-Time Top 10

	Points	Matches	Record (W–T–L)	GF	GA
1. Brazil	120	80	53–14–13	173	78
2. West Germany	107	78	45–17–16	162	103
3. Italy	92	66	38–16–12	105	62
4. Argentina	68	57	29–10–18	100	69
5. England	53	45	20–13–12	62	42
6. France	48	41	21–6–14	86	58
7. Spain	42	40	16–10–14	61	48
8. Yugoslavia	40	37	16–8–13	60	46
9. Uruguay	38	37	15–8–14	61	52
10. U.S.S.R./ Russia	38	34	16–6–12	60	40

MAJOR LEAGUE SOCCER 1998 FINAL STANDINGS

Conference champions (*) and playoff qualifiers (+) are noted. SOW refers to shootout wins. Teams receive three points for a win but just one point for a shootout win. The GF and GA columns refer to Goals For and Goals Against in regulation play. All caps denotes home team.

EASTERN CONFERENCE

	W	L	Pts	GF	GA	SOW
*D.C. United	24	8	58	74	48	7
+Columbus Crew	15	17	45	67	56	0
+MetroStars	15	17	39	54	63	3
+Miami Fusion	15	17	35	46	68	5
Tampa Bay Mutiny	12	20	34	46	57	1
N.E. Revolution	11	21	29	53	66	2

*Conference champions. +Playoff qualifiers.

Eastern Conference Semifinals (Best of 3)

Columbus Crew defeats MetroStars, 2 games to 0
Sept. 30—Columbus Crew 5, MetroStars 3
Oct. 3—Columbus Crew 2, MetroStars 1 (SO)

D.C. United defeats Miami Fusion, 2 games to 0
Sept. 30—D.C. United 2, Miami Fusion 1
Oct. 4—D.C. United 1, Miami Fusion 0 (SO)

Eastern Conference Finals (Best of 3)

D.C. United wins series 2 games to 1, advances to MLS Cup

Oct. 11—D.C. United 2, Columbus Crew 0
Oct. 18—Columbus Crew 4, D.C. United 2
Oct. 21—D.C. United 3, Columbus Crew 0

WESTERN CONFERENCE

	W	L	Pts	GF	GA	SOW
*Los Angeles Galaxy	24	8	68	85	44	2
+Chicago Fire	20	12	56	62	45	2
+Colorado Rapids	16	16	44	62	69	2
+Dallas Burn	15	17	37	43	59	4
San Jose Clash	13	19	33	48	60	3
Kansas City Wizards	12	20	32	45	50	2

*Conference champions. +Playoff qualifiers.

Western Conference Semifinals (Best of 3)

L.A. Galaxy defeats Dallas Burn, 2 games to 0
Oct. 1—L.A. Galaxy 6, Dallas Burn 1
Oct. 4—L.A. Galaxy 3, Dallas Burn 2

Chicago Fire defeats Colorado Rapids, 2 games to 0
Oct. 1—Chicago Fire 2, Colorado Rapids 1 (SO)
Oct. 5—Chicago Fire 1, Colorado Rapids 0

Western Conference Finals (Best of 3)

Chicago Fire wins series 2 games to 0, advances to MLS Cup

Oct. 10—Chicago Fire 1, L.A. Galaxy 0
Oct. 16—Chicago Fire 2, L.A. Galaxy 1 (SO)

MLS CUP

Oct. 25, 1998, Rose Bowl, Pasadena, Calif.

Chicago Fire 2, D.C. United 0

	1st	2nd	Total
D.C. United	0	0	0
Chicago Fire	2	0	2

First half—Chicago Fire goal scored by Jerzy Podbrozny, assisted by Peter Nowak and Ante Razov, 29th minute. Second Chicago goal scored by Diego Gutierrez, assisted by Peter Nowak, 45th minute.

1998 REGULAR SEASON

LEADING SCORERS

	Gm	G	A	Pts
Stern John, Columbus	27	26	5	57
Cobi Jones, Los Angeles	24	19	13	51
Welton, Los Angeles	31	17	11	45
Roy Lassiter, D.C.	31	18	8	44
Raul Diaz Arce, New England	32	18	8	44
Jaime Moreno, D.C.	31	16	11	43
Mauricio Cienfuegos, Los Angeles	30	13	16	42
Marco Etcheverry, D.C.	29	10	19	39
Ronald Cerritos, San Jose	31	13	12	38
Eduardo Hurtado, MetroStars	29	11	15	37

LEADING GOALKEEPERS

	Gm	Min	Shots	Svs	W–L
Zach Thornton, Chicago	25	2,076	118	85	16–8
Kevin Hartman, Los Angeles	29	2,544	146	103	22–7
Scott Garlick, D.C.	25	2,205	129	88	19–5
Mike Ammann, Kansas City	27	2,430	134	85	11–16
David Kramer, San Jose	24	2,125	132	82	10–14
Thomas Ravelli, Tampa Bay	23	2,053	179	131	7–13
Juergen Sommer, Columbus	21	1,890	143	106	11–10
Mark Dodd, Dallas	25	2,205	182	134	11–13
Marcus Hahnemann, Colorado	28	2,520	200	138	16–12
Jeff Cassar, Miami	21	1,890	151	107	12–9

GOAL-SCORING

	Gm	Goals
Stern John, Columbus	27	26
Cobi Jones, Los Angeles	24	19
Roy Lassiter, D.C.	31	18
Raul Diaz Arce, New England	32	18
Welton, Los Angeles	31	17

SHOTS

	Gm	Shots
Stern John, Columbus	27	116
Eduardo Hurtado, MetroStars	29	101
Roy Lassiter, D.C.	31	101
Jason Kreis, Dallas	30	97
Paul Bravo, Colorado	30	90
Raul Diaz Arce, New England	32	90

ASSISTS

	Gm	Assists
Marco Etcheverry, D.C.	29	19
Mauricio Cienfuegos, Los Angeles	30	16
Joe-Max Moore, New England	21	15
Eduardo Hurtado, MetroStars	29	15
Jerzy Podbrozny, Chicago	26	14
Martin Machon, Los Angeles	31	14

SHOT ON GOALS

	Gm	Shots
Roy Lassiter, D.C.	31	52
Raul Diaz Arce, New England	32	51
Ronald Cerritos, San Jose	31	50
Eduardo Hurtado, MetroStars	29	48
Jaime Moreno, D.C.	31	48

History of the Income Tax in the United States

Source: Ernst & Young LLP

The nation had few taxes in its early history. From 1791 to 1802, the United States Government was supported by internal taxes on distilled spirits, carriages, refined sugar, tobacco and snuff, property sold at auction, corporate bonds, and slaves. The high cost of the War of 1812 brought about the nation's first sales taxes on gold, silverware, jewelry, and watches. In 1817, however, Congress did away with all internal taxes, relying on tariffs on imported goods to provide sufficient funds for running the Government.

In 1862, in order to support the Civil War effort, Congress enacted the nation's first income tax law. It was a forerunner of our modern income tax in that it was based on the principles of graduated, or progressive, taxation and of withholding income at the source. During the Civil War, a person earning from $600 to $10,000 per year paid tax at the rate of 3%. Those with incomes of more than $10,000 paid taxes at a higher rate. Additional sales and excise taxes were added, and an "inheritance" tax also made its debut. In 1866, internal revenue collections reached their highest point in the nation's 90-year history—more than $310 million, an amount not reached again until 1911.

The Act of 1862 established the office of Commissioner of Internal Revenue. The Commissioner was given the power to assess, levy, and collect taxes, and the right to enforce the tax laws through seizure of property and income and through prosecution. His powers and authority remain very much the same today.

In 1868, Congress again focused its taxation efforts on tobacco and distilled spirits and eliminated the income tax in 1872. It had a short-lived revival in 1894 and 1895. In the latter year, the U.S. Supreme Court decided that the income tax was unconstitutional because it was not apportioned among the states in conformity with the Constitution.

In 1913, the 16th Amendment to the Constitution made the income tax a permanent fixture in the U.S. tax system. The amendment gave Congress legal authority to tax income and resulted in a revenue law that taxed incomes of both individuals and corporations. In fiscal year 1918, annual internal revenue collections for the first time passed the billion-dollar mark, rising to $5.4 billion by 1920. With the advent of World War II, employment increased, as did tax collections—to $7.3 billion. The withholding tax on wages was introduced in 1943 and was instrumental in increasing the number of taxpayers to 60 million and tax collections to $43 billion by 1945.

In 1981, Congress enacted the largest tax cut in U.S. history, approximately $750 billion over six years. The tax reduction, however, was partially offset by two tax acts, in 1982 and 1984, which attempted to raise approximately $265 billion.

On Oct. 22, 1986, President Reagan signed into law The Tax Reform Act of 1986, one of the most far-reaching reforms of the United States tax system since the adoption of the income tax. In an attempt to remain revenue neutral, the Act called for a $120 billion increase in business taxation and a corresponding decrease in individual taxation over a five-year period.

Following what seemed to be a yearly tradition of new tax acts which began in 1986, the Revenue Reconciliation Act of 1990 was signed into law on November 5, 1990. As with the '87, '88, and '89 acts, the 1990 act, while providing a number of substantive provisions, was small in comparison with the 1986 act. The emphasis of the 1990 act was increased taxes on the wealthy.

On August 10, 1993, President Clinton signed the Revenue Reconciliation Act of 1993 into law. The Act's purpose was to reduce by approximately $496 billion the Federal deficit that would otherwise accumulate in fiscal years 1994 through 1998. Approximately $241 billion of the deficit reduction will be accomplished through tax increases.

On August 5, 1997, President Clinton signed the Taxpayer Relief Act of 1997. The Act included $152 billion in tax cuts. The bill includes a cut in capital gains tax for individuals, a $500 per child tax credit, estate tax relief, tax incentives for education and a host of revenue-raising and tax-simplification provisions.

Internal Revenue Service

The Internal Revenue Service (IRS), a bureau of the U.S. Treasury Department, is the federal agency charged with the administration of the tax laws passed by Congress. The IRS functions through a national office in Washington, 4 regional offices, 63 district offices, and 10 service centers.

Operations involving most taxpayers are carried out in the district offices and service centers. District offices are organized into Resources Management, Examination, Collection, Taxpayer Service, Employee Plans and Exempt Organizations, and Criminal Investigation. All tax returns are filed with the service centers, where the IRS computer operations are located.

IRS service centers are processing an ever increasing number of returns and documents. Prior to 1987, all tax return processing was performed by hand. This process was time consuming and costly. In an attempt to improve the speed and efficiency of the manual processing procedure, the IRS began testing an electronic return filing system beginning with the filing of 1985 returns.

Internal Revenue Service

	1996	1995	1994	1993	1992	1970
U.S. population (in thousands)	266,109	263,730	261,698	259,015	256,219	204,878
Number of IRS employees	102,082	112,023	110,665	113,352	116,673	68,683
Cost to govt. of collecting $100 in taxes	$0.49	$0.55	$0.58	$0.60	$0.58	$0.45
Tax per capita	$5,586.00	$5,216.44	$4,878.00	$4,543.33	$4,374.38	$955.31
Collections by principal sources (in thousands of dollars)						
Total IRS collections	$1,486,546,674	$1,375,731,835	$1,276,466,776	$1,176,685,625	$1,120,799,558	$195,722,096
Income and profits taxes						
Individual	$745,313,276	$675,779,337	$619,819,153	$585,774,159	$557,723,156	$103,651,585
Corporation	$189,054,791	$174,422,173	$154,204,684	$131,547,509	$117,950,796	$35,036,983
Employment taxes	$492,365,178	$465,405,305	$443,831,352	$411,510,516	$400,080,904	$37,449,188
Estate and gift taxes	$17,591,817	$15,144,394	$15,606,793	$12,890,965	$11,479,116	$3,680,076
Alcohol taxes	NOTE 2	NOTE 2	NOTE 2	NOTE 2	NOTE 2	$4,746,382
Tobacco taxes	NOTE 2	NOTE 2	NOTE 2	NOTE 2	NOTE 2	$2,094,212
Manufacturers' excise taxes	NOTE 1	NOTE 1	NOTE 1	NOTE 1	NOTE 1	6,683,061
All other taxes	$42,221,611	$44,980,627	$43,004,794	$34,962,476	$33,565,587	$2,380,609

NOTE: For fiscal year ending September 30th. NOTE 1: Manufacturers' excise taxes are included in the "All other taxes" amount. NOTE 2: Alcohol and tobacco tax collections are now collected and reported by the Bureau of Alcohol, Tobacco, and Firearms. *Source:* IRS 1996 Annual Report.

The two most significant results of the test were that refunds for the electronically-filed returns were issued more quickly and the tax processing error rate was significantly lower when compared to paper returns. Electronic filing of individual income tax returns with refunds became an operational program in selected areas for the 1987 processing year. In 1994 13,510,000 individual returns were filed electronically, compared to 11,143,000 in 1995, and 14,977,123 in 1996.

Auditing Tax Returns

Most taxpayers' contacts with the IRS arise through the auditing of their tax returns. The Service has been empowered by Congress to inquire about all persons who may be liable for any tax and to obtain for review the books and/or records pertinent to those taxpayers' returns. A wide-ranging audit operation is carried out in the 63 district offices by 16,078 revenue agents and 2,831 tax auditors.

The primary method used by the IRS in selecting returns for audits is a computer program that measures the probability of tax error in each return. The higher the score, the greater the tax change potential. Other returns are selected for examination on the basis of claims for refund, multi-year audits, related return audits, and other audits initiated by the IRS as a result of informants' information, special compliance programs, and the information document matching program. In 1996, the IRS recommended additional tax and penalties on 1,941,546 individual returns, totaling $7.6 billion.

The Appeals Process

The IRS attempts to resolve tax disputes through an administrative appeals system. Taxpayers who, after audit of their tax returns, disagree with a proposed change in their tax liabilities are entitled to an independent review of their cases. Taxpayers are able to seek an immediate, informal appeal with the Appeals Office. If, however, the dispute arises from a field audit and the amount in question exceeds $10,000, a taxpayer must submit a written protest. Alternatively, the taxpayer can wait for the examiner's report and then request consideration by the Appeals Office and file a protest if necessary. Taxpayers may represent themselves or be represented by an attorney, accountant, or any other advisor authorized to practice before the IRS. Taxpayers can forego their right to the above process and await receipt of a deficiency notice. At this juncture, taxpayers can either (1) not pay the deficiency and petition the Tax Court by a required deadline or (2) pay the deficiency and file a claim for refund with the District Director's office. If the claim is not allowed, a suit for refund may be brought either in the District Court or the Claims Court within a specified period.

Federal Income Tax Comparisons

Taxes at Selected Rate Brackets After Standard Deductions and Personal Exemptions[1]

Adjusted gross income	Single return listing no dependents					Joint return listing two dependents				
	1998	1997	1996	1995	1975	1998	1997	1996	1995	1975
$10,000	$ 457	$ 493	$ 518	$ 540	$ 1,506	$ –5,200	$ –3,500	$ –3,556	$–3,110[2]	$ 829
20,000	1,958	1,980	2,018	2,040	4,153	720	975	–1,324	–773	2,860
30,000	3,458	3,480	3,518	3,573	8,018	2,200	2,475	1,965	2,018	5,804
40,000	5,595	6,092	6,246	6,373	12,765	3,720	3,975	3,465	3,518	9,668
50,000	6,549	8,892	9,046	9,173	18,360	6,449	5,475	4,965	5,018	14,260

1. For comparison purposes, tax rate schedules were used. 2. Refund based on a basic earned income credit for families with dependent children.

Federal Individual Income Tax

Tax Brackets—1998 Taxable Income

Joint return	Single taxpayer	Rate
$0–$42,350	$0–$25,350	15.0%
42,350–102,300	25,350–61,400	28.0%
102,300–155,950	61,400–128,100	31.0%[2]
155,950–278,450	128,100–278,450	36.0%[2]
278,450 and up[1]	278,450 and up[1]	39.6%[2]

1. The deduction for personal exemptions is phased out as the taxpayer's gross income exceeds $186,800 for a joint return and $124,500 for single taxpayers. 2. The tax rate is effectively increased because total otherwise allowable itemized deductions are reduced by 3% of the taxpayer's adjusted gross income in excess of $124,500.

The Federal individual income tax is levied on the worldwide income of U.S. citizens and resident aliens and on certain types of U.S. source income of non-residents. For a non-itemizer, "tax table income" is adjusted gross income less $2,700 for each personal exemption and the standard deduction. If a taxpayer itemizes, tax table income is adjusted gross income minus total itemized deductions and personal exemptions. In addition, individuals may also be subject to the alternative minimum tax.

Who Must File a Return[1]

You must file a return if you are:	and your gross income is at least:
Single (legally separated, divorced, or married living apart from spouse with dependent child)	$6,950
Head of household	$8,950
Married, filing jointly, living together at end of year (or at date of death of spouse)	$12,500
Married, filing separate return, or married but not living together at end of year over age 65	$2,700

1. In 1997.

Adjusted Gross Income

Gross income consists of wages and salaries, unemployment compensation, tips and gratuities, interest, dividends, annuities, rents and royalties, up to 85% of Social Security benefits if the recipient's income exceeds a base amount, and certain other types of income. Among the items excluded from gross income, and thus not subject to tax, are public assistance benefits and interest on exempt securities (mostly state and local bonds).

Adjusted gross income is determined by subtracting from gross income: alimony paid, penalties on early withdrawal of savings, payments to an I.R.A. (reduced proportionately based upon adjusted gross income levels if taxpayer is an active participant in an employer maintained retirement plan), payments to a Keogh retirement plan, and self-employed health insurance payments and moving expenses.

Itemized Deductions

Taxpayers may itemize deductions or take the standard deduction. The standard deduction amounts for 1998 are as follows: Married filing jointly and surviving spouses, $7,100; Heads of household, $6,250; Single, $4,250; and Married filing separate returns, $3,550. Taxpayers who are age 65 or over or are blind are entitled to an additional standard deduction of $1,000 for single taxpayers and $800 for a married taxpayer.

In itemizing deductions, the following are major items that may be deducted in 1998: state and local income and property taxes, charitable contributions, employee moving expenses, medical expenses (exceeding 7.5% of adjusted gross income), casualty losses (only the amount over the $100 floor which exceeds 10% of adjusted gross income), mortgage interest, and miscellaneous deductions (deductible only to the extent by which cumulatively they exceed 2% of adjusted gross income).

Personal Exemptions

Personal exemptions are available to the taxpayer for himself, his spouse, and his dependents. The 1998 amount is $2,700 for each individual. No exemption is allowed to a taxpayer who can be claimed as a dependent on another taxpayer's return.

Credits

Taxpayers can reduce their income tax liability by claiming the benefit of certain tax credits. Each dollar of tax credit offsets a dollar of tax liability. The following are a few of the available tax credits:

Certain low-income households may claim an Earned Income Credit. The maximum Earned Income Credit is $341 for taxpayers with no qualifying children, $2,271 for taxpayers with one qualifying child and $3,756 for taxpayers with two or more qualifying children. This maximum credit will be reduced if earned income or adjusted gross income exceeds $12,260, or $5,570 for taxpayers with no qualifying children. For families with one qualifying child, the credit will be zero if earned income or adjusted gross income exceeds $26,473; for families with two or more qualifying children, the credit will be zero if income exceeds $30,095, and for families with no qualifying children, the credit will be zero if income exceeds $10,030. The earned income credit is a refundable credit.

A credit for Child and Dependent Care Expenses is available for amounts paid to care for a child or other dependent so that the taxpayer can work. The credit is between 20% and 30% (depending on adjusted gross income) of up to $2,400 of employment-related expenses for one qualifying child or dependent and up to $4,800 of expenses for two or more qualifying individuals.

The elderly and those under 65 who are retired under total disability may be entitled to a credit of up to $750 (if single) or $1,125 (if married and filing jointly). No credit is available if the taxpayer is single and has adjusted gross income of $17,500 or more. Similarly, the credit is unavailable to a married couple filing jointly if their adjusted gross income exceeds $25,000.

Effective for tax years beginning after December 1, 1997, taxpayers who have qualifying children for whom the taxpayer may claim a dependency exemption and who is less than 17 years old as of the close of the tax year are entitled to the child tax credit. The amount of the credit for 1998 is $400. The child credit begins to phase out when AGI reaches $110,000 for joint filers and $75,000 for singles. Taxpayers who have three or more qualifying children may also be entitled to an additional credit.

State Taxes on Individuals

State	Sales/use tax (percent)[1]	Income tax (percent)[2]
Alabama	4.0	2.0 – 5.0
Alaska	none	none
Arizona	5.0	2.9 – 5.7
Arkansas	4.625	1.0 – 7.0
California	7.25	1.0 – 9.3
Colorado	3.0	5.0
Connecticut	6.0	3.0 – 4.5
Delaware	none	3.1 – 6.9
Florida	6.0	none
Georgia	4.0	1.0 – 6.0
Hawaii	.05 – 4.0	2.0 – 10.0
Idaho	5.0	2.0 – 8.2
Illinois	6.25	3.0
Indiana	5.0	3.4
Iowa	5.0	0.4 – 9.98
Kansas	4.9	3.5 – 6.95
Kentucky	6.0	2.0 – 6.0
Louisiana	4.0	2.0 – 6.1
Maine	6.0	2.0 – 8.5
Maryland	5.0	2.0 – 5.0
Massachusetts	5.0	5.95 – 12.0 [3]
Michigan	6.0	4.4
Minnesota	6.5	6.0 – 8.5
Mississippi	7.0	3.0 – 5.0
Missouri	4.225	1.5 – 6.0
Montana	none	2.0 – 11.0
Nebraska	5.0	2.51 – 6.68
Nevada	2.0	none
New Hampshire	none	5.0[4]
New Jersey	6.0	1.4 – 6.37
New Mexico	5.0	1.7 – 8.5
New York	4.0	4.0 – 7.125
North Carolina	4.0	6.0 – 7.75
North Dakota	5.0	2.67 – 12.0
Ohio	5.0	.713 – 7.201
Oklahoma	4.5	0.5 – 7.0
Oregon	none	5.0 – 9.0
Pennsylvania	6.0	2.8
Rhode Island	7.0	27.5[5]
South Carolina	5.0	2.5 – 7.0
South Dakota	4.0	none
Tennessee	6.0	6.0[4]
Texas	6.25	none
Utah	4.75	2.3 – 7.0
Vermont	5.0	25[5]
Virginia	3.5	2.0 – 5.75
Washington	6.5	none
West Virginia	6.0	3.0 – 6.5
Wisconsin	5.0	4.9 – 6.93
Wyoming	4.0	none
Washington, D.C.	5.75	6.0 – 9.5

1. Local and county taxes, if any, are additional. 2. Tax rate for individuals; unless otherwise noted, range denotes progressive structure; higher income pays higher rate. 3. Higher rate applies to interest and dividend income. 4. Income tax limited to dividends and interest income only. 5. Percent of federal tax liability (e.g., if you owe the IRS $2,000 for the year, you owe the State of Vermont 25% of that, or $500). *Source:* The Federation of Tax Administrators, web:sso.org/fta/ind_inc.html, and *Information Please Almanac* questionnaires to the states.

Federal Corporation Taxes

Corporations are taxed under a graduated tax rate structure. If a corporation has taxable income in excess of $100,000, the amount of tax shall be increased by the lesser of five percent of such excess or $11,750. When a corporation has taxable income in excess of $15,000,000 the amount of tax shall be increased by an additional amount equal to the lesser of three percent of such excess or $100,000.

If the corporation qualifies, it may elect to be an S corporation. If it makes this election, the corporation will not (with certain exceptions) pay corporate tax on its income. Its income is instead passed through and taxed to its shareholders. There are several requirements a corporation must meet to qualify as an S corporation, including having 75 or fewer shareholders and having only one class of stock.

Tax Brackets—1998

Taxable income	Tax rate
$0–$50,000	15%
$50,001–$75,000	25%
$75,001–$100,000	34%
$100,001–$335,000	39%
$335,001–$10,000,000	34%
$10m–$15m	35%
$15m–$18.3m	38%
$18.3m and up	35%

State Corporation Income and Franchise Taxes

All states except Texas, Nevada, South Dakota, Washington, and Wyoming impose a tax on corporation net income. The majority of states impose the tax at flat rates ranging from 2.3% to approximately 10.75%. Several states have adopted a graduated basis of rates for corporations.

Nearly all states follow the federal law in defining net income. However, many states provide for varying exclusions and adjustments.

A state is empowered to tax all of the net income of its domestic corporations. With regard to nonresident corporations, however, it may only tax the net income on business carried on within its boundaries. Corporations are, therefore, required to apportion their incomes among the states where they do business, and pay a tax to each of these states. Nearly all states provide an apportionment to their domestic corporations, too, in order that they not be unduly burdened. Several states tax unincorporated businesses separately.

Federal Estate and Gift Taxes

A Federal Estate Tax Return must generally be filed for the estate of every U.S. citizen or resident whose gross estate, adjusted taxable gifts, and specific exemption exceed $625,000. An estate tax return must also generally be filed for the estate of a non-resident who died during 1998 if the value of his gross estate in the U.S. is more than $60,000 at the date of death. The estate tax return is due 9 months after the date of death of the decedent, but a 6-month extension of time to file may be obtained for good reason.

Under the unified federal estate and gift tax structure, individuals who made taxable gifts during the calendar year are required to file a gift tax return by April 15 of the following year.

A unified credit of $202,050 is available to offset both estate and gift taxes. Any part of the credit used to offset gift taxes is not available to offset estate taxes. As a result, although they are still taxable as gifts, lifetime taxable transfers no longer cushion the impact of progressive estate tax rates. Lifetime transfers and transfers made at death are combined for estate tax rate purposes.

Gift taxes are computed by applying the uniform rate schedule to lifetime taxable transfers (after deducting the unified credit) and subtracting the taxes payable for prior taxable periods. In general, estate taxes are computed by applying the uniform rate schedule to cumulative transfers and subtracting the gift taxes paid. An appropriate adjustment is made for taxes on lifetime transfers—such as certain gifts within three years of death—in a decedent's estate.

Among the deductions allowed in computing the amount of the estate subject to tax are funeral expenditures, administrative costs, claims and bequests to religious, charitable, and fraternal organizations or government welfare agencies, and state inheritance taxes. For transfers made after 1981 during life or death, there is an unlimited marital deduction.

An annual gift tax exclusion is provided that permits tax-free gifts to each donee of $10,000 for each year. A husband and wife who agree to treat gifts to third persons as joint gifts can exclude up to $20,000 a year to each donee. An unlimited exclusion for medical expenses and school tuition both paid directly to the institution for the benefit of any donee is also available in addition to the annual gift tax exclusion.

Federal Taxes Collected and Spent, by State

Federal Expenditures for Every Dollar of Taxes Sent to Washington
FY 1997

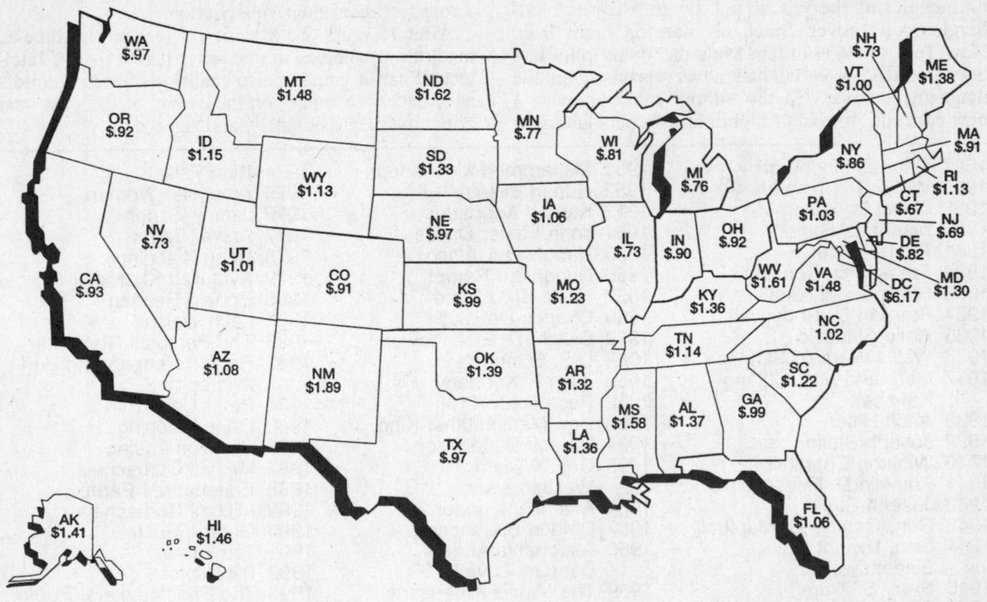

Source: Tax Foundation.

The Man of the Year

How "Lucky Lindy"—and a slow week for news—gave birth to a memorable annual tradition

The founders of TIME Magazine, Henry Luce and Briton Haddon, were strong believers in the idea that history is shaped by the deeds of extraordinary men and women. This thesis, most memorably advanced by the British writer Thomas Carlyle, was well-suited to the American vision of the two Yale graduates since it ran counter to the assertions of Karl Marx and others that history is the residue of impersonal economic and social forces.

TIME's insistence on the primacy of the individual found its most memorable form in the magazine's annual designation of a Man or Woman of the Year—the person whose actions had most affected the course of the news within the last twelve months. But the magazine's signature annual tribute was not the result of high-level philosophizing: rather, it was driven by something far more important to journalists—a deadline.

The year was 1927; it was the last week in December. During the holiday season, the normal flow of public events had temporarily ebbed to a trickle. Looking to 1928, the editors at TIME were having trouble finding a newsworthy cover subject for the first issue of the new year. At the same time, they realized that they had passed up several opportunities during the year to put aviator Charles Lindbergh on its cover. Since his nonstop flight from New York to Paris in late May, the young pilot had been idolized—yet he had never appeared on the magazine's cover. So the editors came up with a new concept: instead of highlighting a personality of the week, it was decided that the cover for January 2, 1928, would feature Lindbergh, and that beneath his likeness would be the words "Man of the Year."

A year later, the cover for TIME's first issue of 1929 revealed that its editors had named car magnate Walter P. Chrysler as Man of the Year for 1928—and it was obvious that an annual tradition had been born. By the mid-1930s, TIME readers were happily forwarding their suggestions for the Man of the Year to the editors as early as October.

The term "Man of the Year"—redolent of countless Chamber of Commerce dinners—suggests to many people that it is awarded as an accolade. It is not. Rather, it designates the person who, in the editors' opinion, has most affected the course of history in the past twelve months—for good or for ill.

In 1938, for instance, Adolf Hitler completed his Anschluss of Austria and brokered the tragic agreement at Munich that put Czechoslovakia into his hands. However reluctantly, the editors concluded that Hitler's actions had most affected history's course, and he became the 1938 Man of the Year. Similarly, in 1979, Ayatullah Khomeini was named Man of the Year, even while he held Americans hostage in Tehran. TIME received more than 14,000 letters complaining about the choice; many readers wrote to cancel their subscription.

After 75 years, the Man of the Year has become an institution: whereas in one sense it is a sort of intellectual parlor game, it also challenges TIME's editors and readers to reflect on the events of the past year critically, dispassionately, and rigorously. □

1927 Charles Lindbergh
1928 Walter P. Chrysler
1929 Owen D. Young
1930 Mahatma Gandhi
1931 Pierre Laval
1932 Franklin D. Roosevelt
1933 Hugh S. Johnson
1934 Franklin D. Roosevelt
1935 Haile Selassie
1936 Wallis Warfield Simpson
1937 Gen. and Mrs. Chiang Kai-shek
1938 Adolf Hitler
1939 Joseph Stalin
1940 Winston Churchill
1941 Franklin D. Roosevelt
1942 Joseph Stalin
1943 Gen. George C. Marshall
1944 Gen. Dwight D. Eisenhower
1945 Harry S. Truman
1946 James F. Byrnes
1947 Gen. George C. Marshall
1948 Harry S. Truman
1949 Winston Churchill
1950 G.I. Joe
1951 Mohammed Mossadegh
1952 Queen Elizabeth II
1953 Konrad Adenauer
1954 John Foster Dulles
1955 Harlow H. Curtice
1956 Hungarian Patriot
1957 Nikita Khrushchev
1958 Charles DeGaulle
1959 Dwight D. Eisenhower
1960 U.S. Scientists
1961 John F. Kennedy
1962 Pope John XXIII
1963 Rev. Martin Luther King, Jr.
1964 Lyndon B. Johnson
1965 Gen. William Westmoreland
1966 Americans under 25
1967 Lyndon B. Johnson
1968 Astronauts Anders, Borman, Lovell
1969 The Middle Americans
1970 Willy Brandt
1971 Richard M. Nixon
1972 Richard M. Nixon and Henry Kissinger
1973 Judge John J. Sirica
1974 King Faisal
1975 American Women
1976 Jimmy Carter
1977 Anwar Sadat
1978 Deng Xiaoping
1979 Ayatullah Khomeini
1980 Ronald Reagan
1981 Lech Walesa
1982 The Personal Computer
1983 Ronald Reagan and Yuri Andropov
1984 Peter Ueberroth
1985 Deng Xiaoping
1986 Corazon Aquino
1987 Mikhail Gorbachev
1988 Endangered Earth
1989 Mikhail Gorbachev
1990 George Bush
1991 Ted Turner
1992 Bill Clinton
1993 The Peacemakers: Rabin, Arafat, Mandela, De Klerk
1994 Pope John Paul II
1995 Newt Gingrich
1996 Dr. David Ho
1997 Andrew Grove

The Time 100

The mission: to identify the 100 most influential individuals of the last 100 years

As the 20th century ends, people seem gripped by an urge to review the last 100 years, to assess our century and try to see it whole. In the Time tradition of emphasizing the impact of individuals on history, Managing Editor Walter Isaacson launched an ambitious project to herald the century's end: to identify the 100 most influential men and women of the century, in every area of endeavor.

Over the course of two years, the magazine is designating 20 individuals as the "most influential" in five categories: Leaders and Revolutionaries, Artists and Entertainers, Builders and Titans, Scientists and Thinkers, and Heroes and Inspirations. The editors invited readers to nominate individuals for the list—and were surprised to find themselves on the receiving end of a well-orchestrated campaign by Turkish citizens to see their national hero, Kemal Ataturk, named as one of the "Time 100." The Time website (www.time.com) received nearly 7 million votes before the first 20 individuals chosen were even named—with several million of those e-mails nominating Ataturk. When the list of the Leaders and Revolutionaries appeared in Time's April 13, 1998, issue, there was no joy in Istanbul: Kemal Ataturk did not make the list.

To find out who did—and to learn Time's choice of the 20 most influential Artists and Entertainers of the century—see the list below. To share your thoughts on the magazine's upcoming selections of the 20 most influential Builders and Titans, Scientists and Thinkers, and Heroes and Inspirations, visit the website or write: Time 100, Time Letters Dept., 1271 Ave. of the Americas, New York, N.Y. 10020.

Leaders & Revolutionaries

Theodore Roosevelt
V. I. Lenin
Margaret Sanger
Franklin D. Roosevelt
Adolf Hitler
Winston Churchill
Eleanor Roosevelt
Mahatma Gandhi
David Ben-Gurion
Mao Zedong
Ho Chi Minh
Rev. Martin Luther King, Jr.
Pope John Paul II
Ayatullah Khomeini
Margaret Thatcher
Ronald Reagan
Lech Walesa
Mikhail Gorbachev
Nelson Mandela
The Unknown Rebel

Artists & Entertainers

Pablo Picasso
Le Corbusier
Martha Graham
Coco Chanel
James Joyce
T. S. Eliot
Charlie Chaplin
Steven Spielberg
Marlon Brando
Igor Stravinsky
Louis Armstrong
Frank Sinatra
Rodgers and Hammerstein
The Beatles
Bob Dylan
Aretha Franklin
Lucille Ball
Jim Henson
Oprah Winfrey
Bart Simpson

People in the News

Marv Albert, 55, penitent sportscaster, was hired by the Madison Square Garden Network in New York City to host a half-hour show and call radio play-by-play for the Knicks. Albert was forced to resign from the network in September 1997 following a lurid trial in which he pleaded guilty to a misdemeanor for biting a former lover.

Yasir Arafat, 69, Palestinian leader, and **Benjamin Netanyahu,** 49, Israeli Prime Minister, brokered a reluctant peace agreement in Maryland with the help of **President Clinton** and **King Hussein** of Jordan. The talks seemed to be stagnating early on and were in danger of closing without an agreement after a Palestinian terrorist injured 60 by bombing an Israeli bus station on the fifth day of the meeting. A compromise was ultimately hashed out. Israel agreed to withdraw from an additional 13% of the West Bank, while the Palestinians promised to remove anti-Israeli clauses in the Palestinian National Charter and to heighten their vigilance against terrorism.

Richard Ashby, 31, **Joseph Schweitzer,** 30, **William Raney II,** 26, and **Chandler Seagraves,** 28, were charged with negligent homicide and involuntary manslaughter after their jet severed a gondola cable in Italy on Feb. 3, killing 20 people. Seagraves's and Raney's charges were later dropped because they were not in direct control of the operation of the jet; Ashby and Schweitzer could face life in prison if found guilty in their trials.

Mike Barnicle, 54, longtime columnist for the *Boston Globe,* resigned in August while serving a two-month suspension following accusations that he had fabricated sources and facts and had stolen and altered material from other writers. The *Globe* was criticized for having double standards, after having two months earlier called for the resignation of a black woman who wrote a regular column. **Patricia Smith** had also admitted to basing some of her columns on information that she made up.

Marion Barry, 62, shameless mayor of the District of Columbia for four controversial terms (interrupted by a stint in prison) that left the city insolvent and under near total congressional rule, announced he will not seek reelection when his term expires in Jan. 1999.

Michael J. Blassie, 1st lieutenant shot down over Vietnam, was identified as the serviceman whose remains had been interred in the Tomb of the Unknown Soldier for 14 years. His identity was determined by the Pentagon, with the aid of DNA testing.

Julian Bond, 58, veteran civil rights activist, was elected by the NAACP board of directors in February as the organization's new chairman. The distinguished scholar replaced **Myrlie Evers-Williams,** widow of slain civil-rights leader Medgar Evers.

Martin Bormann, fanatical Nazi henchman and Adolf Hitler's right-hand man whose death had been disputed for 26 years, was confirmed dead in Frankfurt am Main. Sentenced in absentia by the Nuremberg courts after he vanished in 1945, Bormann was allegedly sighted over the years in locales as far afield as Paraguay and Russia. DNA tests linking a skeleton unearthed near Hitler's Berlin bunker to a Bormann descendant will quell the debate.

Sam Bowers, 73, former Ku Klux Klan Imperial Wizard and subject of a May 18 TIME special investigation, was convicted in the 1966 firebomb murder of civil rights leader Vernon Dahmer, Sr., in Hattiesburg, Miss. The conviction carried an automatic sentence of life in prison.

Chuck Burris, 46, was inaugurated as the first African-American mayor of Stone Mountain, Ga., longtime headquarters of the National Knights of the Ku Klux Klan.

James Cameron, 44, Hollywood director, proclaimed himself "king of the world" as his blockbuster *Titanic* picked up awards in 11 categories at the 70th annual Academy Awards ceremony. Captivating millions of fans with its real-life premise, its powerfully romantic storyline, and the enormous popularity of its young stars, **Leonardo DiCaprio** and **Kate Winslet,** the movie replaced *Star Wars* as the top-grossing film of all time.

Viktor Chernomyrdin, 60, on-again, off-again Prime Minister of Russia, was selected for reappointment by **Boris Yeltsin** in August, five months after the Russian president fired him. With the hope of turning around Russia's faltering economy in March, Yeltsin had replaced Chernomyrdin with young reformer **Sergei Kiriyenko.** When it became clear in August that the economy was still suffering, Yeltsin again fired his cabinet, including Kiriyenko. In another turn of events, Yeltsin was unable to find Parliamentary support for Chernomyrdin's nomination and Chernomyrdin asked that his name be withdrawn. Yeltsin then nominated Foreign Minister **Yevgeny Primakov,** who took office in September with Parliament's approval.

Lt. Col. Eileen Collins, 42, of the Air Force, was named commander of the *Columbia* space shuttle mission, scheduled to launch in early 1999. Collins, who already holds the distinction of being the first female space shuttle pilot, will also be the first American woman to command a shuttle mission.

Macaulay Culkin, 17, yesterday's Hollywood boy wonder, and **Rachel Miner,** 17, a television and Broadway actress, were married in Connecticut on June 21 with their parents' consent.

Betty Currie, 58, President Clinton's secretary of five years, was queried by **Ken Starr**'s team on her involvement in covering up the affair between **the President** and **Monica Lewinsky.** Currie asked **Vernon Jordan** to help Lewinsky find a job in New York in Dec. 1997, soon after lawyers for **Paula Jones** revealed they would like to question Lewinsky about a possible sexual relationship with the President.

Lindsay Davenport, 22, in her first appearance in the finals of a Grand Slam event, nabbed a victory over top-ranked Martina Hingis at the U.S. Open tennis tournament in New York City. Davenport is the first American-born player to win the U.S. competition since Chris Evert in 1982.

Ira Einhorn, 57, counterculture guru and peripatetic fugitive, was arrested in France for the 1977 murder of his girlfriend in Philadelphia. The former Harvard lecturer fled to Europe just before the start of his 1981 trial for killing Holly Maddux. He was convicted in absentia in 1993 and arrested last year. But a French court refused to allow his extradition, citing a lack of provisions in Pennsylvania state law—since added—that would grant him a new trial.

Calista Flockhart, 34, actress, found stardom in 1998 in the title role of television's quirky *Ally McBeal*. Her noticeable weight loss since the second season began landed her on the covers of tabloids and magazines, fueling suspicion that she suffers from an eating disorder. Despite Flockhart's denial of having a problem, parents worried about the consequences of the new trend toward paper-thin TV stars.

Frank Gifford, 67, co-host of ABC's *Monday Night Football* for the past 27 years, was demoted in January and replaced by **Boomer Esiason,** 36, the Cincinnati Bengals quarterback who quit the team the same week, to join the network.

John Glenn, 77, U.S. senator and legendary astronaut, was cleared to become the oldest person to fly in space, 36 years after he became the first American to orbit Earth. NASA decided to include Glenn in the October launch of the space shuttle *Discovery* as the subject of geriatric research.

Andrew Golden, 11, and **Mitchell Johnson,** 13, students at Westside Middle School in Jonesboro, Ark., shocked the nation by opening fire on their classmates on March 24. The rampage, possibly meant as revenge against Johnson's ex-girlfriends, left four students and one teacher dead and 10 others wounded. Johnson later pleaded guilty, while Golden pleaded not guilty due to mental incompetence. He was nonetheless convicted by a juvenile court judge.

John Gotti, Jr., 33, reputed successor of jailed Mob boss **John Gotti,** was indicted in January on charges that included racketeering and extortion. He was released on bail in September, pending a January 1999 trial. The senior Gotti, who is serving a life sentence for crimes including murder and racketeering, was diagnosed in September with throat cancer.

Alan Greenspan, 72, chairman of the Federal Reserve, was frequently in the news during a year marked by a heavily weakened global economy. The Fed lowered interest rates twice in October in a move to promote economic activity and protect the U.S. from financial disaster.

Amy Grossberg, 20, and **Brian Peterson,** also 20, were sentenced in Wilmington, Del., to 2½ and 2 years in prison, respectively. The college students and former high-school sweethearts

pleaded guilty to manslaughter in the death of their newborn son in a Newark, Del., motel in 1996.

Andrew Grove, 61, announced that he was stepping aside as CEO of Intel Corp. in Santa Clara, Calif. Under Grove, TIME's 1997 Man of the Year, Intel became the world's leading chipmaker. He remains chairman; **Craig Barrett,** 58, is his well-groomed successor.

Albert Hale, president of the Navajo Nation, resigned Feb. 19 with the possibility of indictment looming. He was under investigation regarding $52,000 in undocumented charges on the tribe's credit card. Hale denied wrongdoing, claiming that he had charged $5,000 in personal expenses, but that he had reimbursed the account.

Ryan Harris, 11, Chicago youth, was found dead in the yard of an abandoned house in her neighborhood. Police charged two young boys, ages 7 and 8, with killing Harris after they confessed that they hit her in the head with a brick so they could steal her bike. The charges were dropped a month later, when semen detected on the girl's clothing proved the boys' guilt unlikely.

Ryutaro Hashimoto, 61, Japanese prime minister, took the world by surprise when he stepped down, accepting responsibility for his party's humiliating defeat in the July national elections. He was quickly replaced by Foreign Minister **Keizo Obuchi,** who faces the daunting tasks of whipping the Japanese economy back into shape and overcoming his image as a party hack and lifeless bore.

Henry Hyde, 74, representative from Illinois, is the Republican chairman of the House Judiciary Committee. Hyde's committee has the responsibility of leading the impeachment inquiry on **President Clinton,** which was approved by the House on October 7 in an historic vote. Hyde himself became the subject of scandal when *Salon,* an online magazine, revealed his own adulterous affair.

Paula Jones, 31, former Arkansas state employee, filed an appeal after her sexual harassment lawsuit against **President Clinton** was dismissed by U.S. district judge **Susan Webber Wright** on April 1. The judge concluded that even if the allegations against Clinton were true, Jones's lawyers failed to prove any emotional, financial, or professional harm from the alleged incident.

Vernon Jordan, 62, close friend and adviser of **President Clinton,** was accused of aiding in a cover-up of the President's affair with **Monica Lewinsky.** Ultimately, the allegations that Jordan asked Lewinsky to lie to investigators and arranged a job for her in New York in exchange for her silence were not addressed in the report that **Ken Starr** delivered to Congress.

Jean Kambanda, former prime minister of Rwanda, was convicted of genocide and sentenced to life in prison after becoming the first person to plead guilty to genocide before an international tribunal. Kambanda promised to offer information on others who were involved in the more than 500,000 killings of minority Tutsis in 1994. Rwandan ex-mayor **Jean-Paul Akayesu** also made history when the U.N. tribunal hearing his case ruled him guilty of genocide in September—his was the first verdict by the tribunal since it was set up 1994, and the first international court verdict on charges of genocide.

Mir Aimal Kansi, 33, Pakistani terrorist who in 1993 ambushed CIA headquarters in Fairfax, Va., was sentenced to death for killing two CIA employees.

Theodore Kaczynski, 55, infamous Unabomber responsible for a 17-year series of explosions that killed three people, injured 23, and baffled the F.B.I., was given four life sentences plus 30 years in prison. The verdict, foreordained by a January plea bargain, spares the life of the former mathematician, who offered no apologies or explanations in his brief courtroom comments. According to the government, Kaczynski's motivations for the 16 bombings were hatred and revenge, rather than politics.

Joseph P. Kennedy II, 45, six-term Massachusetts Congressman and eldest son of Robert F. Kennedy, announced his retirement from politics in March. He plans to run the nonprofit Citizens Energy Corp. that his brother Michael oversaw until his death in Dec. 1997.

Martin Luther King III, 40, eldest son of the late civil rights leader, was sworn in as president of the Southern Christian Leadership Conference. The younger King, who replaced the **Rev. Joseph Lowery,** vowed to reinvigorate the group his father helped found in 1957. King's family raised controversy in 1998 by contending that a larger conspiracy was guilty of killing **Martin Luther King** rather than **James Earl Ray,** who was convicted in the crime. Ray died of liver failure in prison on April 23.

Kip Kinkel, 15, Eugene, Ore., high school student, was arrested on May 20 when it was discovered that he had a gun at school. After being released to this parents, Kinkel shot them to death in their home, then returned to school and opened fire in the cafeteria. Two classmates were killed and another 22 were wounded.

Osama bin Laden, Saudi millionaire and powerful leader of a terrorist network, was accused by the U.S. government of organizing the August 7 bombing of the U.S. embassies in Kenya and Tanzania. The U.S. responded to the attacks, which killed more than 250 people, with a cruise missile strike on bin Laden's suspected base in Afghanistan. Afghanistan's ruling Taliban government said in October that it would be willing to put the terrorist on trial if the U.S. could produce significant evidence of bin Laden's involvement in the bombings.

Mary Kaye LeTourneau, 36, Tacoma, Wash., schoolteacher, was ordered to serve her suspended 7½ year child-rape sentence after being found with the 14-year-old student with whom she has a nine-month-old daughter. In October, LeTourneau gave birth to a second baby fathered by the same boy. No new charges were brought against her.

Monica S. Lewinsky, 25, former White House intern, was granted immunity to testify about her relationship with **President Clinton.** Though she had denied having a sexual relationship with the President when allegations first arose, secretly recorded conversations with former friend **Linda Tripp** revealed otherwise. Lewinsky testified before the grand jury in August that she had fallen in love with Clinton in the course of their affair.

Tara Lipinski, 15, youngest U.S. and world figure skating champion and youngest individual athlete ever to win a gold medal at the Winter Olympics, announced her decision to turn professional. This was not the first time she surprised figure

skating fans; pre-Olympic hype had the public expecting **Michelle Kwan** to beat out Lipinski for the gold in Nagano. Kwan placed second.

Rev. Henry Lyons, 56, president-shepherd of the National Baptist Convention U.S.A. Inc., largest association of black churches, was indicted in St. Petersburg, Fla., in February. He was charged with racketeering and theft, for siphoning off church money to buy a luxury villa, a Mercedes, as well as a diamond ring for his mistress.

Casey Martin, 25, disabled pro golfer, was awarded the right to use a golf cart during tourney play. Golfers argued that their strolls between holes made golf an endurance sport and that Martin's use of a cart, compensation for a circulatory disorder, was an unfair advantage. Martin is the first professional athlete to sue successfully under the Americans with Disabilities Act.

Mike McCurry, 43, likable, verbally nimble presidential press secretary whose 3½-year tenure was marked by his artful and droll containment of a voracious White House press corps, announced his resignation. He will be replaced by deputy press secretary **Joseph Lockhart.**

Susan McDougal, 43, ever-incarcerated Whitewater figure, was charged with embezzlement and tax fraud in a case unrelated to the Arkansas land deal. The latest charges were brought by conductor **Zubin Mehta** and his wife, for whom McDougal was bookkeeper and personal assistant from 1989 to 1992. After serving 18 months in prison for refusing to answer questions about **President and Mrs. Clinton** before the Whitewater grand jury, McDougal immediately began a 90-day detention at home for fraud in the Whitewater dealings. Although some felt her imprisonment for sticking to her principles in the Clinton investigation gave her a saintly aura, the embezzlement charges knocked her off the pedestal. Ex-husband **Jim McDougal,** also a key Whitewater figure, made headlines in March when he died in prison due to heart failure.

Mark McGwire, 35, first-baseman for the St. Louis Cardinals, beat out Chicago Cub **Sammy Sosa** in a heated race to break **Roger Maris**'s season home-run record (61). Though the good-natured Sosa also topped Maris, hitting 66 by season's end, McGwire held on to the "home run king" title, finishing with 70. The pair brought renewed interest to their sport and provided Americans with a welcomed diversion from news about the presidential sex scandal.

Master Sergeant Gene McKinney, 47, the Army's former top-enlisted soldier, was acquitted of 18 counts of sexual misconduct and obstruction of justice in a court-martial brought about by six servicewomen. A demotion from the top rank of sergeant major was the punishment for his only guilty count, for attempting to coach one of the women on how to respond to military investigators.

Timothy McVeigh, 36, decorated sailor (no relation to the Oklahoma City bomber) who faced dismissal after the Navy discovered that he had identified himself as "gay" on America Online, was exonerated in February. A federal judge ruled that the Navy had violated its "don't ask, don't tell" policy.

George Michael, 34, "I Want Your Sex"-singing pop star, pleaded no contest to committing a "lewd act" in a public rest room; in Beverly Hills, Calif. A judge placed Michael on probation and ordered him to perform community service and undergo sexual counseling.

Slobodan Milosevic, 57, President of Yugoslavia was given stern warnings by NATO to withdraw Yugoslav troops and weapons from the ethnically Albanian province of Kosovo, which saw much bloodshed in 1998. U.S. special envoy **Richard Holbrooke** and NATO officials threatened air strikes as Milosevic dragged his heels until just before the NATO deadline in October.

George Mitchell, respected former U.S. senator helped Northern Ireland reach an historic peace agreement after serving as moderator in 22 months of talks. Although he was considered a bland politician, as a mediator he blossomed. Key figures in the talks in Northern Ireland included **David Trimble,** Protestant leader of the Ulster Unionists and a Nobel Peace Prize winner; **John Hume,** Trimble's co-Nobel winner and leader of the Social Democratic and Labor Party (the moderate Catholic party in Northern Ireland); **Gerry Adams,** leader of Sinn Fein, the political wing of the Irish Republican Army; as well as Irish and British political leaders. The Good Friday Accord, which won enough support to pass the people's vote on May 22, called for the creation of a new assembly in which Catholics and Protestants in Northern Ireland will share power. Ties to the Irish Republic are to be strengthened in a new north-south council, as well.

Dominique Moceanu, 17, gymnast on the 1996 gold-winning U.S. Olympic team, filed court papers to gain legal status as an adult and requested a restraining order against her parents. The diminutive athlete went into hiding claiming that her domineering parents had mismanaged her finances and were living solely off of her earnings. The case, which was reportedly settled out of court the following week, illustrated the excesses of modern-day gymnastics.

Maurice Papon, 87, high-ranking functionary in France's wartime Vichy regime, was convicted of complicity in crimes against humanity, in Bordeaux, France. After a grueling six-month trial that dredged up the darkest moments of the country's past, Papon was sentenced to ten years in prison.

Gen. Augusto Pinochet, 82, Chilean dictator from 1973 to 1990, was arrested in a London hospital in October while recovering from surgery on a herniated disk. He was charged by a Spanish magistrate on grounds of murder, kidnapping, and torturing political opponents while he was in office. Allegedly to blame for up to 4,000 murders in Chile and abroad, the autocrat disingenuously claimed to know little of the excesses that went on under his watch. Spain's warrants were quashed by British judges who ruled that Pinochet was entitled to immunity from prosecution but had to remain in custody pending appeal.

Cal Ripken, Jr., Baltimore Orioles third-baseman, ended his hallowed streak of consecutive games played, at 16 years and 2,632 games, a major league record. In 1995 Ripken surpassed **Lou Gehrig**'s mark of 2,130 consecutive games, which had stood for 56 years.

Scott Ritter, 37, a key arms inspector for the U.N., resigned from his post in Iraq. Chief weapons inspector **Richard Butler** denied Ritter's claims that the U.N. special commission, as well as U.N. and U.S. leaders, backed off in the investigation even as they were on the verge of uncovering Iraq's hidden arsenal of weapons of mass destruction.

Eric Robert Rudolph, 32, fugitive accused of the fatal bombing of a Birmingham, Ala., abortion clinic in January, was additionally charged with the 1996 bombing of the Olympic Park in Atlanta, which killed one person and caused injuries to hundreds more. Federal authorities began an intensive manhunt in the forests of North Carolina.

Ronaldo, 21, the world's top soccer player, was both powerful and popular as a forward on the Brazilian team at the 1998 World Cup in France. Many, however, questioned Brazil's decision to allow the celebrity to play in the World Cup final after he went into convulsions just hours before the game.

Sang Lan, 17, Chinese gymnast, was paralyzed after landing head-first during a practice vault at the Goodwill Games in New York. Doctors reported that it is unlikely she will regain the ability to walk.

Dr. David Satcher, 56, head of the Centers for Disease Control and Prevention, was confirmed as Surgeon General in February. Political wrangling had left the white coat of "America's family doctor" hanging empty for the past three years.

Gerhard Schröder, 54, unseated 16-year chancellor **Helmut Kohl** to become Germany's next leader. The Social Democrat triumphed on promises of modernization and reform.

Jerry Seinfeld, 44, beloved television comedian, brought a close to his popular sitcom, *Seinfeld.* Months of speculation and commercialized hype preceded the series finale, which ended with the show's four main characters locked away in a prison cell. Seinfeld was ranked the highest paid entertainer of the year.

Matthew Shepard, 21, student at the University of Wyoming, died on Oct. 12 after spending several days in critical condition at a Fort Collins, Colo., hospital. In what was labelled a hate crime, the gay student was allegedly beaten and tied to a fence by Arthur Henderson, 21, and Aaron James McKinney, 22, whose first-degree murder charges could carry the death penalty. The case served as a reminder of the still volatile animosity toward gays in the U.S.

Dr. Barnett Slepian, 51, Amherst, N.Y., doctor who performed abortions, was killed by a sniper in October while sitting in his home. Slepian had been receiving death threats from anti-abortion activists since the 1980s. N.Y. governor **George Pataki** labelled the murder an "act of terrorism" as the search for the killer began.

Latrell Sprewell, 28, guard for the Golden State Warriors, had a one year suspension from the N.B.A. reduced by five months and his contract reinstated after the Players' Association filed grievances on his behalf. Sprewell had been fired by the Warriors after choking coach P. J. Carlesimo during a Dec. 1997 practice.

Kenneth W. Starr, 51, independent counsel in the Whitewater investigation since Aug. 1994, delivered a 445-page report on President Clinton to the House Judiciary Committee on Sept. 9. The historic report, which was released to the American public, outlined 11 possible grounds for impeachment and contained explicit descriptions of Clinton's sexual encounters with Monica Lewinsky, but no mention of Whitewater. The fairness of conservative Starr's investigation became almost as hotly debated as the fate of Clinton's presidency.

Hugh Thompson, Lawrence Colburn, and Glenn Andreotta, who 30 years ago halted the My Lai massacre by turning their weapons on fellow U.S. soldiers, were honored at the Vietnam Veterans Memorial in Washington. Thompson and Colburn attended the ceremony, in which the three were awarded the prestigious Soldier's Medal. Andreotta was killed in battle three weeks after the My Lai incident.

Yah Lin ("Charlie") Trie, 49, former restaurateur and fund-raising friend of **President Clinton,** was indicted in Washington on federal charges that include election-law violations. Trie surrendered himself to federal officials in February, after having fled to China when Congress began investigating him the year before. He entered a plea of not guilty on the 15 counts with which he was charged.

Linda Tripp, 48, a former White House secretary who came to epitomize the self-righteous tattletale, threw herself into the middle of the Clinton investigation by secretly taping revealing conversations with one-time friend **Monica Lewinsky.** With school-girl breathiness, Lewinsky confided the details of her affair with **President Clinton,** providing Tripp with 20 hours of recorded evidence. The legality of and motives behind Tripp's actions became new material for investigation.

Karla Faye Tucker, 38, guilty of murdering a couple with a pick ax in 1983, was executed by lethal injection at a Huntsville, Texas, prison on Feb. 3. Americans debated the ethicality of the death penalty as they anxiously waited to hear if Tucker, who became a born-again Christian while in prison, would be spared at the last minute. The U.S. Supreme Court and Texas Governor **George Bush** denied her clemency.

Mordechai Vanunu, 43, Israeli nuclear technician jailed for treason when photos he provided a London newspaper in 1986 exposed his nation's nuclear capacity, was denied parole in the Israeli city of Ashkelon. The unrepentant Vanunu, whose decade in solitary confinement was a cause celebre for human rights advocates worldwide, has served two-thirds of his sentence. Israel has labeled him a "continuing threat" to national security.

Wang Dan, 29, Chinese dissident who helped lead the ill-fated 1989 democracy rallies in Beijing, was released on "medical parole" from an 11-year sentence for subversion. He flew to the U.S. for treatment of a possible brain tumor, but was found to be in good health, and began a life in exile in the U.S.

Russell Weston, Jr., 41, the Illinois man charged in the July 24 Capitol shooting that left guards **Jacob Chestnut** and **John Gibson** dead, was ordered by a federal judge to undergo a psychiatric evaluation. Weston, who is a diagnosed paranoid schizophrenic, may face the death penalty.

Kathleen Willey, 51, a former White House volunteer, testified in the **Paula Jones** sexual harassment case on March 10. She created a stir the following week when she went on *60 Minutes* to discuss the details of an alleged sexual advance made by **President Clinton** in 1993. The President denied under oath that he had groped Willey.

Diane Zamora, 20-year-old former Naval Academy midshipman, was found guilty of assisting in the 1995 murder of a 16-year-old girl who had slept with her boyfriend. Zamora was sentenced to life in prison with no chance of parole for 40 years.

Deaths

(January through October, 1998)

Abacha, Sani, 54: Nigerian dictator who wrested power in a 1993 coup and maintained his grip on Africa's most populous and oil-rich nation by canceling free elections and silencing critics through imprisonment or execution; from an apparent heart attack; in Abuja, Nigeria. Perhaps Abacha's most notorious act as president was hanging the playwright and environmentalist Ken Saro-Wiwa and eight associates accused of treason. June 8.

Abzug, Bella, 77: champion of women, labor, blacks, and any other underdog society could muster; in New York City. With the slogan "This woman's place is in the House—the House of Representatives," she won a seat in Congress in 1970 and bowled over Washington with her in-your-face manner, flamboyant hats, and raspy voice for reform. March 31.

Amory, Cleveland, 81: best-selling author and animal lover extraordinaire; in New York City. Amory chronicled his most famous rescue—of his pet cat Polar Bear—in *The Cat Who Came for Christmas.* But he was also well versed in the habits of two-legged creatures, penning a sardonic series on society's upper crust. Oct. 14.

Autry, Gene, 91: Hollywood's first singing cowboy; in Los Angeles. The Texas-born, Oklahoma-raised crooner planned to play baseball (he later settled for owning the California Angels). Instead he entered show business, heeding the advice of Will Rogers, who recommended a radio career after hearing Autry, on break from a job as a telegrapher at a train station, sing and play his guitar. His first hit, 1931's *That Silver-Haired Daddy of Mine,* was followed by TV and radio shows, almost 100 films, and 635 recordings—including his signature "Back in the Saddle Again." Oct. 1.

Barton, Derek H. R., 79: 1969 Nobel laureate in chemistry who added a new dimension (the third) to chemical analysis and sired the field known as conformational analysis; in College Station, Tex. March 16.

Belanger, Mark, 54: premier fielding shortstop of the 1970s who was a nimble barricade that no ball could pass; of lung cancer; in New York City. Nicknamed Blade, Belanger won eight Gold Gloves in 16 seasons with the Baltimore Orioles. Oct. 6.

Bono, Sonny, 62: recent politician and 1960s television performer who starred with his former wife in the *Sonny and Cher Show;* of head and neck injuries caused by a skiing accident; in South Lake Tahoe, Calif. Bono, a Republican, was elected by fellow Californians to serve in the U.S. House of Representatives in 1994 and 1996. Jan. 5.

Bradley, Owen, 82: country-music impresario and creator of the "Nashville sound," which helped push the genre into the mainstream; in Nashville, Tenn. In 1955 Bradley opened the first recording studio in Nashville, where he later crafted some of country music's most enduring tunes, including "I Fall to Pieces" with Patsy Cline and "Coal Miner's Daughter" with Loretta Lynn. Jan. 7.

Bradley, Tom, 80: quietly commanding five-term former mayor of the nation's second-largest city; in Los Angeles. First elected in 1973, Bradley, a former police officer, became Los Angeles' first black mayor, triumphing with such projects as the 1984 Olympic Games but faltering in the aftermath of the 1992 riots. Sept. 29.

Bridges, Lloyd, 85: protean actor and patriarch of an acting dynasty, whose myriad roles ranged from the dramatic *(High Noon)* to the slapstick *(Airplane!)* and, most famously, to the adventurous *(Sea Hunt)*; in Los Angeles. In later life he presided over the careers of sons Beau and Jeff, who got their start acting alongside Dad in *Sea Hunt.* March 10.

Burney, Leroy Edgar, 91: Surgeon General from 1956 to 1961 and the first in that office to implicate smoking as a cause of lung cancer; in Arlington Heights, Ill. Burney's pronouncements helped set the stage for the Surgeon General's landmark antismoking report in 1964. July 31.

Buscaglia, Leo, 74: avuncular, affectionate professor and author of numerous books on the permutations of love and self-acceptance; of a heart attack; near Lake Tahoe, Nev. Relentlessly upbeat, Buscaglia taught at U.S.C. for nearly 20 years, including a course in 1969 called Love 1A. He became known as Dr. Hug because of his habit of embracing the thousands of fans worldwide who turned out in droves to hear his aphorisms and elevated four of his books to the bestseller list at one time. June 12.

Campanis, Al, 81: behind-the-scenes Dodgers exec for four decades who became a household name—and killed his career—after remarking on national TV that black people lacked "some of the necessities" to be major league managers; in Fullerton, Calif. June 21.

Caray, Harry, 83: irrepressible baseball announcer who had much more to say than "Holy cow!"; in Rancho Mirage, Calif. He spent nearly 60 years behind the mike, the last 27 in Chicago. Feb. 18.

Carter, Betty, 69: boldly idiosyncratic jazz singer and nurturer of young jazz talent, who won a National Medal Of Arts Award in 1997; of cancer; in New York City. Sept. 26.

Cassilly, Richard, 70: American tenor and operatic star of the 1950s, '60s, and '70s; of a cerebral hemorrhage. A pure heldentenor, Cassilly possessed a booming, heroic voice that ideally suited grand Wagnerian roles. Debuting at New York City's Metropolitan Opera in 1970, he sang in more than 100 performances there. Jan. 30.

Castaneda, Carlos, believed to be 72: enigmatic personality who was either an unfairly vilified anthropologist or a wildly inventive novelist, depending on whether his mind-bending encounters with a Yaqui Indian sorcerer are taken as fact or fiction; of liver failure; in Los Angeles. As an anthropology grad student at UCLA, Castaneda published *The Teachings of Don Juan: A Yaqui Way of Knowledge* in 1968, the first of many accounts of his apprenticeship to Mexican shaman Don Juan. April 27.

Clifford, Clark, 91: consummate Washington insider; in Bethesda, Md. Tall, elegant, and impeccably attired, Clifford advised four Democratic presidents, using a knack for crystallizing issues to advocate causes from civil rights to environmental protection. An architect of Harry S. Truman's 1948 election victory, he later counseled winding down the Vietnam War as Lyndon

Johnson's Defense Secretary. Clifford's chairmanship of a bank embroiled in international scandal led to 1992 criminal charges that were dropped because of his age and frailty. Oct. 10.

Cleaver, Eldridge, 62: former Black Panther firebrand and prophet of black empowerment; of undisclosed causes; in Pomona, Calif. While serving a jail term for assault, Cleaver took up the idea of black power and penned *Soul on Ice,* his radical 1968 polemic on black rage. He joined the Black Panther Party on his release. Two years later, after a gunfight with police in Oakland, he fled to Algeria, Cuba, and Paris, living in exile for eight years. Addiction to crack and petty crimes followed his return to the U.S., as did an unsuccessful 1986 bid for a G.O.P. Senate nomination in California. May 1.

Commager, Henry Steele, 95: pre-eminent chronicler of American history and ardent defender of the Constitution upon which the country was founded; in Amherst, Mass. For close to 70 years, Commager's essays, books, and meditations probed the nation's politics and psyche. A teacher for 65 years, Commager wrote books that served as lucid primers for generations of students. An early and vocal opponent of Senator Joseph McCarthy, Commager embraced the Jeffersonian view that given adequate information, Americans would ultimately use common sense to make informed decisions. March 2.

Derek, John, 71: Pygmalion actor-director whose real talent lay not in his so-so acting (in *All the King's Men* and *The Ten Commandments*) but in marrying often and well (the four foxy actresses Patti Behrs, Ursula Andress, Linda Evans, and, most recently, Bo Derek); of heart complications; in Santa Maria, Calif. May 22.

Donegan, Dorothy, 76: exuberant jazz pianist; reportedly of colon cancer; in Los Angeles. A flamboyant performer, Donegan was known as much for her jokes and gyrations as for her music (a patchwork of swing, pop, ragtime, boogie-woogie, and classical). May 19.

Douglas, Marjory Stoneman, 108: ever vigilant empress of the Florida Everglades, who led a half-century crusade to preserve the fabled watery wilderness; in Miami. A Wellesley College educated New Englander, Douglas first came to Florida in 1915. She penned her classic book *The Everglades: River of Grass* in 1947, lyrically making the case for conserving the swath of swampland, long considered an impediment to real estate developers. She continued as the irrepressible mouthpiece for the marshes, in 1970 founding the Friends of the Everglades—dubbed "Marjory's army." May 14.

Estermann, Alois, 43: commander of the Pope's Swiss Guards; and his wife, Gladys Meza Romero, 49. Both were shot by disgruntled Swiss Guard Cedric Tornay, 23, who then shot himself, in the first murders on Vatican land in 150 years. May 4.

Faye, Alice, 86: one of Hollywood's biggest late '30s and early '40s movie box-office draws; in Rancho Mirage, Calif. Faye starred in Tinseltown's popular and lucrative cookie-cutter musicals and, with her distinctive contralto, introduced several songs that became pop standards, notably "You'll Never Know" in *Hello, Frisco, Hello* (1943). She was one of Irving Berlin's favorite singers. In 1945 she left her film career after Betty Grable supplanted her as Hollywood's favorite musical-comedy actress. May 9.

Flock, Tim, 73: legendary NASCAR racer; of lung and liver cancer; in Charlotte, N.C. Flock, who came from a family of racers, was selected early in 1998 as one of the top 50 drivers in the sport's first 50 years. March 31.

Frann, Mary, 55: known to television viewers as Bob Newhart's chirpy wife on the CBS series *Newhart;* of undetermined causes; in Beverly Hills, Calif. Sept. 23.

Friendly, Fred, 82: broadcasting pioneer and former president of CBS News whose early documentary work set the standard for journalistic integrity; in New York. Friendly quit CBS when the network ran a repeat of *I Love Lucy* while NBC broadcast a live Senate hearing on Vietnam. March 3.

Gellhorn, Martha, 89: war correspondent, novelist and, only incidentally, Ernest Hemingway's third wife; in London. Gellhorn's dispatches, first filed during the Spanish Civil War and continuing through World War II and Vietnam, focused on the ordinary and powerless. An avid traveler and prolific journalist, she also wrote novels and short stories. Gellhorn married Hemingway in 1940. She left him five years later, the only one of his four wives to do so. He reportedly remained bitter for the rest of his life, and she remained irritated for being best known as his former wife. Feb. 15.

Goldwater, Barry, 89: conservative former senator from Arizona and presidential candidate; of natural causes; in Paradise Valley, Ariz. A politician perhaps ironically known for his direct honesty, Goldwater was credited by many with remaking the Republican party despite his failure to attain the nation's highest office. May 29.

Griffith Joyner, Florence, 38: incandescent American sprinter and winner of three gold medals at the 1988 Seoul Summer Olympics; of an epileptic seizure; in Mission Viejo, Calif. Sept. 21.

Hartman, Phil, 49: Emmy award-winning actor; from gunshot wounds believed to have been inflicted by his wife, Brynn, who was also found dead at the scene; in Los Angeles. Hartman was best known for his spot-on comedic performances on the sketch comedy television show *Saturday Night Live* and for his role as the humorously overbearing Bill McNeal on *News Radio.* May 28.

Hayes, Peter Lind, 82: stage and screen performer; in Las Vegas. Hayes starred in the vaudevillian *Peter Lind Hayes Show* in the late 1950s and in the comedy *Peter Loves Mary* in the early '60s, along with wife Mary Healy. April 21.

Junger, Ernst, 102: militaristic German writer, in Wilflingen, Germany. Junger's controversial early novels extolled German nationalism and totalitarianism and attracted a following among the emerging Nazi Party. He rejected the party, however, and in 1939 wrote a novel critical of a thinly disguised Hitler. In later years he publicly repudiated the bellicosity of his youth. Feb. 17.

Karamanlis, Constantine, 91: patriarchal former President and Prime Minister of Greece, nicknamed "God" by his countrymen and credited with restoring the country's democracy in 1974 after seven years of military rule; in Athens. A pragmatic autocrat, Karamanlis inspired impassioned devotion; his 60 years in public office were marked by his efforts to align Greece with Europe, resulting in the country's acceptance into the European Union in 1981. April 23.

Kazin, Alfred, 83: one of his generation's most eloquent literary critics; in New York City. The Brooklyn-born Kazin collected his thoughtful critiques in *On Native Grounds,* his seminal 1942 appraisal of American writers, and in countless other essays, reviews and memoirs dwelling in depth on New York, Judaism, and above all literature, the three topics dearest to Kazin's heart. June 5.

Kellogg, Junius, 71: incorruptible cager who as a star collegiate center in 1951 exposed a point-shaving scheme that rocked the sport; in New York City. Kellogg, Manhattan College's first black basketball player, notified his coach after being asked to participate in what was revealed to be a widespread plot to fix games at seven colleges, a fateful decision that led to numerous players' arrests. Kellogg joined the Harlem Globetrotters after graduation, but a 1954 car accident left him paralyzed and confined to a wheelchair. He went on to popularize and coach wheelchair basketball. Sept. 16.

Kurosawa, Akira, 88: cinematic visionary whose visceral and visually compelling films integrated Japanese culture into the global movie idiom and inspired a generation of Western directors; in Tokyo. *Rashomon* (1950), the tale of a murder seen four ways, first brought him fame outside Japan, its title now a byword for the fragility of truth. Even as his samurai epics like *Throne of Blood* (1957) and *Ran* (1985) borrowed from the West, particularly Shakespeare, movies outside Japan borrowed from him: *The Seven Samurai* is at the heart of *The Magnificent Seven; The Hidden Fortress* is concealed in *Star Wars.* Sept. 5.

Lewis, Shari, 65: puppeteer who animated both her inquisitive sidekick Lamb Chop and the quest for quality children's programming; of pneumonia; in Los Angeles. Lewis and Lamb Chop, a woolly sock with exaggerated eyelashes, first appeared on morning television in 1957 on *The Captain Kangaroo Show.* Lewis's talent for ventriloquism and aptitude for engaging children without condescension led to four different series of her own. A talented musician, conductor, and dancer, Lewis wrote 60 children's books and won 12 Emmys during her 40-year career. Aug. 2.

Link, Arthur S., 77: former Princeton University historian and Woodrow Wilson scholar, who authored the meticulous five-volume biography of Wilson and amassed the comprehensive collection of his papers; in Advance, N.C. March 26.

Lord, Jack, 77: clean-cut actor who played his TV tough guys straight and a little bit square; of heart failure; in Honolulu. The West and its clichés suited Lord as the rodeo-going Stoney Burke, but he left the range for *Hawaii Five-O.* The locale changed, but his lawman soul didn't, as Detective ("Book 'Em, Danno") McGarrett on TV's longest-running crime drama. Jan. 21.

Luckman, Sid, 81: Chicago Bears Hall of Fame quarterback with a mind as potent as his arm; in North Miami Beach. After joining the Bears in 1939, Luckman perfected the T-formation offense, memorizing 350 plays in the team's repertoire and changing the way the game was played for the next decade. He led an All Star–packed lineup, dubbed the Monsters of the Midway, to four NFL championships in seven years, beginning with a 73–0 rout of the Washington Redskins in the 1940 title game. July 5.

Marshall, E. G., 84: Emmy-winning actor whose resonant voice and stoic demeanor led him to portray a succession of authoritative and trustworthy characters; in Mount Kisco, N.Y. Perhaps best known for roles on *The Defenders* (1961–1965) and *The New Doctors* (1969–1973), Marshall also starred in films and appeared in the 1956 Broadway premiere performance of *Waiting for Godot.* Aug. 24.

Martin, William McChesney, Jr., 91: even-keeled chairman of the Federal Reserve for 19 years; in Washington. Martin, who helped define the Federal Reserve as an independent entity, was known for his cautious, if not entirely dire, predictions; he described economic booms as "the party that leads to the hangover." His no-nonsense style—and occasionally unpopular stands—nevertheless managed to inspire the trust of presidents from Truman to Nixon. July 29.

McCartney, Linda Eastman, 56: fetching photographer of '60s rockers who trounced the hopes of teenyboppers when she wed one of her dreamiest subjects, Beatle Paul; after battling breast cancer; in Tucson, Ariz. The devoted couple spent just one voluntary night apart in their 29 years together. Linda became Paul's muse (the lovely, long-haired lady of his post-Beatles love ballads) and his sometime partner in the soft-rock group Wings. April 17.

McDougal, James, 57: eccentric Arkansas banker and former friend of Bill and Hillary's, who snitched on his business dealings with the Clintons and sparked the ongoing Whitewater investigation; of cardiac arrest; in Fort Worth, Tex., where he was in prison. March 8.

McDowell, Roddy, 70: child star who went on to become a Hollywood fixture and one of the industry's more versatile actors; of cancer; in Los Angeles. He survived a run of sensitive-boy roles in the '40s (including *Lassie Come Home* and *How Green Was My Valley*) to appear in adult parts ranging from Octavian in *Cleopatra* (with close friend Elizabeth Taylor) to the chimpanzee Cornelius in the *Planet of the Apes* film series. Oct. 3.

Merrill, Bob, 77: songwriting polymath whose hits ranged from "How Much Is That Doggie in the Window?" to Barbra Streisand's signature "People"; in Los Angeles. Merrill started his career writing such airy novelties for Tin Pan Alley as "If I Knew You Were Coming I'd've Baked a Cake" and "Mambo Italiano." He racked up 18 Top-10 hits between 1949 and 1956. His success continued on Broadway where he wrote the lyrics for *Funny Girl* and *Carnival,* among many others. Merrill also wrote screenplays, including one for *Mahogany,* starring Diana Ross. Feb. 17.

Middlecoff, Cary, 77: dentist who traded in his drill to become a top golfer and the leading money earner on the PGA Tour in the 1950s; in Memphis, Tenn. Middlecoff won 40 professional tournaments in his prime playing years, including two U.S. Opens and the Masters. Sept. 1.

Mifune, Toshiro, 77: rugged actor in epic Japanese films; in Mitaka, Japan. In his 16-film collaboration with director Akira Kurosawa, Mifune came to embody the heroic, archetypical loner with his rough features and angry intensity. America had cowboys; Japan had Mifune, wielding a sword and his trademark glare in the Oscar-winning *Rashomon, The Seven Samurai,* and *Yojimbo.* Dec. 24, 1997.

Moody (Roark), Helen Wills, 92: imperturbable tennis ace; in Carmel, Calif. Her trademark white eyeshade set an enduring fashion trend, but there was nothing frivolous about Little Miss Poker Face, as she was known. She stood her ground

like a tank, drilling out bullet serves and powerful baseline drives. Her casualties were legion: she won 31 major championships, including eight at Wimbledon, and her frequent rival Helen Jacobs was dubbed "Helen the Second." Jan. 1.

Morris, Wright, 88: writer-photographer of the middle-American gothic, who spun *Fargo*-like tales of small-town strangeness about his native Nebraska; in Mill Valley, Calif. His 33 books netted awards, but his plainspoken prose didn't sell well, dooming Morris to the dubious distinction of being one of America's most admired but least read men of letters. April 25.

Murray, Jim, 78: irrepressible *Los Angeles Times* sports columnist whose witty dispatches made him a most valuable player on the sports beat; of cardiac arrest; in Los Angeles. Murray spent 37 years at the *Times* giving sports junkies a morning fix of his laugh-a-line musings. One of four sports writers to score a Pulitzer Prize for commentary, Murray greeted his award with characteristic humor: "This is going to make it a little easier on the guy who writes my obit." Aug. 16.

O'Sullivan, Maureen, 87: demure silver-screen actress who originated Tarzan's sarong-clad jungle-gal Jane; in Scottsdale, Ariz. The convent-educated colleen scandalized '30s audiences with her tree-house trysts. Though she appeared in some 60 films (*Pride and Prejudice* among them), to her dismay, O'Sullivan remained best known as homemaker for Johnny Weissmuller and his simian sidekicks—and for mothering a real-life brood of seven that included actress Mia Farrow. June 22.

Nitschke, Ray, 61: rock-solid middle linebacker for the Green Bay Packers who anchored the defense of the Lombardi-era championship teams; of a heart attack; in Venice, Fla. March 3.

Paz, Octavio, 84: Mexico's prolific man of letters who plumbed the mythic depths of his country's psyche in more than 40 volumes of poems and essays; of undisclosed causes; in Mexico City. Using his hybrid heritage (part Spanish, part Indian) as his starting point, Paz wrote *The Labyrinth of Solitude,* considered the seminal book on the Mexican mind-set. His starkly haunting metaphors of apathy and isolation made enemies among his countrymen but moved readers and, eventually, won him the Nobel Prize. April 19.

Perkins, Carl, 65: Big Daddy of rockabilly; after a series of strokes; in Jackson, Tenn. "Blue Suede Shoes," his anthem to teenage vanity nearly became his requiem when, en route to a key national-TV performance in 1956, a car crash hobbled him and his career. Drinking binges followed, but so did songs—"Honey Don't," "Matchbox"—that helped teach the Beatles rock 'n' roll. Jan. 19.

Pilatus, Rob, 32: half of the famously seen-but-not-heard Europop duo Milli Vanilli, which had to relinquish its 1989 Grammy after it was revealed that the pretty boys had lip-synched their album; after reportedly overdosing on drugs and alcohol; near Frankfurt, Germany. Pilatus never really recovered from the humiliation: in 1990 he tried to commit suicide and later spent time in rehab after pleading no contest to assault charges. April 2.

Pol Pot, 73: Cambodian dictator; reportedly of heart failure; in Cambodia, near the Thai border. Pol Pot's Marxist reign of terror in the 1970s, backed by the notorious Khmer Rouge, resulted in the killing of an estimated 1–2 million Cambodians. April 15.

Powell, Lewis, 90: the Burger court's balanced conservative—appointed in 1971 by Richard Nixon—whose 1978 Bakke opinion barred racial quotas but opened the door for affirmative action; in Richmond, Va. Aug. 25.

Powers, Dave, 85: constant companion and amiable aide-de-camp of John F. Kennedy; in Arlington, Mass. Powers joined congressional candidate Kennedy in 1946 and stayed with him all the way to the White House and beyond. Powers was riding in the presidential motorcade the day Kennedy was shot, and he accompanied Jacqueline Kennedy on the flight of Air Force One back to Washington. He continued to serve the family, as a companion to the young Kennedy children and as curator of the John F. Kennedy Library and Museum. March 27, 1998

Rabbitt, Eddie, 56: rangy country singer who, despite all his down-homey hits—among them "I Love a Rainy Night" and "Drivin' My Life Away"—was the Brooklyn-born son of Irish immigrants; after battling lung cancer; in Nashville, Tenn. May 17.

Ray, James Earl, 70: criminal who confessed to killing Martin Luther King Jr.; of liver failure caused by chronic hepatitis; in Nashville, Tenn. After an international manhunt following the assassination, Ray was captured in England. Three days after pleading guilty to the killing, Ray performed one of criminology's most infamous about-faces, protesting his innocence for the remainder of his 99-year sentence. His prison term was marked by botched jailbreaks and his steady insistence that he had only been the fall guy in a larger conspiracy to slay King, a claim that received the unlikely backing of the King family, who joined his bid for a new trial. April 23.

Rebozo, Charles ("Bebe"), 85: Florida banker and controversial confidant of Richard Nixon; in Miami. Rebozo, who lent Nixon money to buy his San Clemente, Calif., home, also accepted $100,000 in cash in 1970 from Howard Hughes for a private campaign fund for Nixon. He said he returned the money, and no charges were filed. May 8.

Redding, Jheri, 91: shampoo guru who founded the eponymous beauty-products empire; in Santa Barbara, Calif. Unhappy with lackluster hair-care products, Redding experimented with ingredients from his own kitchen cabinet including vinegar and mayonnaise. His creative combos yielded such innovations as creme rinse, pH-balanced shampoo, and the perm product Jheri Curl. March 15.

Reines, Frederick, 80: Nobel-prizewinning scientist known as the father of neutrino physics; in Orange, Calif. Undeterred by skeptics who doubted the invisible neutrino's existence, Reines persevered, often locking himself for hours in his lab, where he could be heard indulging his other great passion: singing opera. Aug. 26.

Ribicoff, Abraham, 87: Connecticut statesman who helped guide a junior senator from Massachusetts to the White House, becoming a member of John Kennedy's first Cabinet; in New York City. In 1956, as governor of the Constitution State, Ribicoff suspended 10,346 driver's licenses—compared with 372 in the previous year—to curb speeding; as a senator, he combatted de facto desegregation in the North. Ribicoff prized civility, but his career was branded by a fiery, televised image of him on the podium at the 1968 Democratic Convention, railing against the "Gestapo tactics" of Chicago's police. Feb. 27.

Ridenhour, Ronald, 52: Vietnam vet turned investigative journalist whose dogged accusations as an ex-G.I. led to the exposure of the massacre at My Lai; of a heart attack while playing handball; in Metairie, La. Shocked by comrades' talk of the March 16, 1968, killings, Ridenhour investigated and sent a long letter to several congressmen and President Nixon when he returned to the U.S. His account that "something rather dark and bloody" had transpired seared the nation's conscience. May 10.

Robbins, Jerome, 79: legendary Broadway and New York City Ballet choreographer; from complications after suffering a stroke; in New York City. Robbins, whose long list of achievements includes two Oscars for his work on *West Side Story,* was celebrated for his ability to successfully combine pop-culture and high art. July 29.

Rogers, Roy, 86: iconic singing cowboy who wore a white hat in more than 90 westerns; of heart failure; in Apple Valley, Calif. Rogers was an uncomplicated hero and one of the most beloved public figures in the decades following World War II. A canny businessman, he also founded the chain of Roy Rogers fast-food outlets. July 6.

Rysanek, Leonie, 71: show-stopping Austrian soprano whose soaring arias so entranced fans she once kept them standing—and clapping—throughout the entire intermission of a Wagner opera; of bone cancer; in Vienna. March 7.

Sanford, Terry, 80: governor, senator and presidential candidate from North Carolina; of cancer; in Raleigh, N.C. Tagged one of the century's 10 best governors in a Harvard study, Sanford aided integration and overhauled public education in his state; he was also president of Duke University for 16 years. April 18.

Sayre, Anne, 74: chronicler of sexism in the sciences; of scleroderma; in Bridgewater, N.J. Sayre's 1975 book, *Rosalind Franklin and DNA,* accorded overdue and posthumous credit to the female British crystallographer for her crucial role in the discovery of the structure of DNA and positioned Franklin alongside her Nobel-winning male contemporaries, James Watson and Francis Crick. March 13.

Schiff, Steven, 51: Congressman from New Mexico; of skin cancer; in Albuquerque. Schiff, a Republican, was serving his fifth term in the U.S. House of Representatives. March 25.

Schnittke, Alfred, 63: iconoclastic Russian composer whose brooding, dissonant works reflected the private despair rather than the officially sanctioned glory of the Soviet Union; of a stroke; in Hamburg. Schnittke's works, termed "polystylistic," incorporated influences from diverse musical eras. Blacklisted by the Soviet Composer's Union for his nonconformity, Schnittke supported himself for years by writing movie scores. Despite his international reputation, he was barred from attending any performances of his work abroad until the mid-1980s. Aug. 3.

Shepard, Alan, 74: unflappable space hero who in 1961 became the first American in space and, in 1971, one of only 12 men to walk on the moon; in Monterey, Calif. July 21.

Sherer, Moshe, 77: well-known rabbi who gained political influence on the national level through his activism for Orthodox Jewish causes; after a brief illness; in New York. May 17.

Sinatra, Frank, 82: legendary heartthrob whose music and films were appreciated by fans of all generations; of a heart attack; in Los Angeles. Nicknamed "Ol' Blue Eyes" and "Chairman of the Board," the crooner had an influence on American culture that earned him the Kennedy Center honor in 1983 and the Presidential Medal of Freedom in 1985. May 14.

Smith, "Buffalo Bob", 80: revered TV icon and host of the medium's first smash hit, *The Howdy Doody Show;* in North Carolina. Starting in 1947 the avuncular would-be cowboy (along with his famous marionette) cheerfully presided over Doodyville U.S.A.—home to such goofy characters as Clarabell the Clown and Flubadub. *Howdy Doody* ran for 13 years, partly a result of Smith's respect for his fans ("You can't kid a kid"). Among the show's contributions to the pop lexicon: the "Peanut Gallery" (his studio audience) and—sorry, Bart Simpson fans—"Cowabunga!" July 30.

Smythe, Reg, 80: industrious British cartoonist who sketched the ne'er-do-well Andy Capp for more than 40 years; in Hartlepool, England. It was a comic strip sprung from the heart: Smythe patterned the beer-guzzling, bumptious bloke and his long-suffering wife Flo on his parents. Although Capp spoke in the vernacular of working-class northern England, his chatter had universal appeal, enlivening the funny pages in dozens of countries. June 13.

Spock, Benjamin, 94: world-famous pediatrician after a long illness; in San Diego. His book *Baby and Child Care,* the famous parenting guide first published on the brink of the baby boom in 1946 is one of the biggest-selling titles of all time. March 15.

Stans, Maurice, 90: the power behind Richard Nixon's 1972 re-election purse, who bagged the record $61 million in donations that would later help fund Watergate's dirty tricks; in Pasadena, Calif. An accountant by training and Nixon's Commerce Secretary, Stans had a knack for getting fat cats to show him the money, but he maintained that he was not behind its scandalous use. He eventually pleaded guilty to five campaign-finance violations, but the disgrace never eclipsed his fund-raising powers or his loyalty: he raised $30 million for the Nixon library. April 14.

Stickney, Dorothy, 101: legendary stage actress, in New York. Her long list of credits in theatrical smash hits included a role in the longest running non-musical play on Broadway, *Life With Father.* June 2.

Suzuki, Shinichi, 99: Japan's Pied Piper, whose methods of instruction have taught millions of toddlers worldwide a new mother tongue, classical music; in Tokyo. Putting his techniques into widespread practice in the 1950s, Suzuki coached his tiny pupils to memorize "Twinkle, Twinkle, Little Star" and, later, Mozart's concertos—without their necessarily being able to read a note. Jan. 27.

Taylor, Telford, 90: formidable Nuremberg prosecutor who held that "the laws of war are not a one-way street"; in New York City. An ardent New Dealer, Taylor joined the war effort in 1942 and worked on Nazi codes. Though at the hub of military intelligence, he learned of the Holocaust only as an assistant prosecutor at the first Nuremberg trial. He was chair of the next 12 trials, and his clarity and eloquence (he called Nazi Germany "an infernal combination of a lunatic asylum and a charnel house") led to 142 convictions. Later, as a lawyer and a professor, he scrutinized public officials, and spoke out against McCarthyism and the Vietnam War. May 23.

Thompson, Kay, in her 90s: entertainer and creator of the Plaza Hotel's most memorable guest, six-year-old Eloise; in New York City. Thompson was a successful nightclub performer who appeared as a Vreelandesque fashion editor in the movie *Funny Face,* but her most enduring character was Eloise, an irascible girl whose mischievous exploits while living in New York City's Plaza Hotel were first chronicled by Thompson in a 1955 book. Originally targeted for adults but beloved by children ever since, Eloise starred in three more best-selling books and a line of merchandise. July 2.

von Rezzori, Gregor, 83: accomplished Eastern European author; of a heart attack; near Florence, Italy. His novels and autobiographical works drew on the changing political and geographic landscapes of his homeland, which was part of the Austro-Hungarian Empire at the time of his birth. April 23.

Wallace, George, 79: four-term Alabama governor, four-time presidential hopeful, and political penitent nonpareil who in his 1963 inaugural address as governor promised, "Segregation now! Segregation tomorrow! Segregation forever!" He attempted to make good on his word in 1963, when he drew national attention by physically blocking two black students from entering the administration building at the University of Alabama. Wallace later renounced his divisive rhetoric and was able to convince many that he was not a racist; in Montgomery, Ala. Sept. 13.

Walsh, J. T., 54: character actor and specialist in obdurate personae; of a heart attack; outside San Diego. Walsh's sense of icy machismo made him perfect for David Mamet's anomic world; the playwright gave Walsh his first big break when he cast him in the 1984 Broadway production of *Glengarry Glen Ross.* Walsh did not start acting until he was 30, yet he brought his skill to nearly 60 film roles, including a turn as John Ehrlichman in *Nixon* and recently as a redneck kidnapper in the 1997 thriller *Breakdown.* Feb. 27.

Waters, Benny, 96: jazz's ebullient elder statesman who toured with and taught some of the genre's greats; in Columbia, Md. A saxophonist, clarinetist, and arranger, Waters was playing jazz before jazz was officially created. In the '20s and '30s he played nightclubs in New York City's Harlem with Benny Carter, among others, and was a member of the house band at the Apollo Theater; but partly because of his legendary carousing, he never achieved the fame enjoyed by many of his colleagues. Blind from failed cataract surgery since 1992, he continued his hectic international touring schedule until this past June. Aug. 11.

Weidman, Jerome, 85: novelist and playwright who depicted Big Apple archetypes from fast-talking garmentos to frenetic politicians; in New York City. His works include the musical *Fiorello!,* about Mayor Fiorello La Guardia, for which he won a Pulitzer Prize. Oct. 6.

Wells, Junior, 63: blues master of the harmonica; of cancer; in Chicago. Playing the blues came naturally to a youth angling for tips in the streets of West Memphis, Ark. But he hit his groove in the Windy City as one-third of the Little Chicago Devils and later on tour with Muddy Waters. *Hoodoo Man Blues,* his classic jam session with guitarist Buddy Guy, was Wells at his finest—fiery, raw, defiant. Jan. 15.

West, Dorothy, 91: sole surviving voice of the Harlem Renaissance; in Boston. West was just a teen when she tied with Zora Neale Hurston for second place in a short-story contest, winning swift admission into the gifted clique of black intellectuals. The daughter of an ex-slave, West settled in tony Martha's Vineyard, Mass., and in 1995, after years of literary silence, published *The Wedding,* a novel about the black bourgeoisie that she dedicated to her editor, Jacqueline Kennedy Onassis. Aug. 16.

Whitney, Betsey Cushing Roosevelt, 89: grande dame of society; in Manhasset, N.Y. The middle child of the three glamorous Cushing sisters (the oldest married Vincent Astor, the youngest was the legendary society figure Babe Paley), she wrote the book on marrying money. The first wife of F.D.R.'s oldest son, James Roosevelt (when mother-in-law Eleanor was away, Betsey played White House hostess), she was the widow of tycoon John Hay ("Jock") Whitney. March 25.

Williams, Wendy O., 48: radically raunchy star of the '80s punk band the Plasmatics, who shocked fans with her onstage shenanigans (chain-sawing guitars, sometimes clad in little more than strategically placed electrical tape); of a self-inflicted gunshot wound; in Storrs, Conn. April 4.

Wilson, Carl, 51: a founder of America's quintessential pop group, the Beach Boys; of complications from cancer; in Los Angeles. A gifted guitarist and the youngest of the band's Wilson brothers, Carl was seen as the relatively levelheaded and dependable sibling, while Brian, the eldest, brooded as the troubled genius and Dennis, who drowned in 1983, played the lovable rogue. However, Carl too went through bouts with drugs and alcohol. His sweet, smooth pitch is heard in lead vocals in a number of the Beach Boys' most beloved hits, including "Good Vibrations" and "God Only Knows." Feb. 6.

Wood, Beatrice, 105: ceramist and bon vivant, whose affairs with early 20th century artists and writers earned her the name "Mama of Dada"; near Ojai, Calif. Wood, who credited her longevity to "chocolate and young men," also inspired the character of Rose in the film *Titanic.* March 12.

Wynette, Tammy, 55: country music's down-home diva; of a blood clot; in Nashville, Tenn. A beautician turned songstress, she performed often plaintive ballads that imitated her life story: five marriages, bankruptcy, a painkiller addiction, and a kidnapping. Her iconic anthem, "Stand by Your Man," made feminists wince—Hillary Clinton among them—but Wynette stood by her twangy tunes through more than 50 albums and 20 No. 1 hits. April 6.

Young, Robert, 91: television's benevolent authority figure for two decades, first as the patriarch on *Father Knows Best* and later as Marcus Welby, M.D.; in Los Angeles. In 1954, after a solid but unspectacular movie career during the 1930s and '40s, he accepted the role of Jim Anderson on *Father Knows Best,* a highly glossed depiction of family life that was comforting and enormously popular. His controlled characters belied a troubled off-screen life, however, as over the years Young struggled with alcoholism and depression and in 1991 attempted suicide. July 22.

Youngman, Henny, 91: motormouth comic who was once clocked at 250 one-liners in 45 minutes; in New York City. One favorite standby: "Take my wife—please!" Feb. 24.

MILESTONES

SPORTS

BUSINESS, ECONOMY, AND PERSONAL FINANCE

U.S. CITIES, STATES, AND STATISTICS

[illegible]

PEOPLE

CROSSWORD PUZZLE GUIDE

ENVIRONMENT, WEATHER, AND CLIMATE

SCIENCE, INVENTIONS, AND COMPUTERS

THE YEAR IN PICTURES

See first page of book for additional tabs.